# RHS PLANT FINDER 2010-2011


DEVISED BY CHRIS PHILIP
AND REALISED BY TONY LORD

**EDITOR-IN-CHIEF**
JANET CUBEY

**RHS EDITORS**
JAMES ARMITAGE DAWN EDWARDS
NEIL LANCASTER CHRISTOPHER WHITEHOUSE

**COMPILER**
JUDITH MERRICK

**CONSULTANT EDITOR**
TONY LORD

A Dorling Kindersley Book

London, New York, Munich, Melbourne, Delhi

Published by
Dorling Kindersley Ltd
80 Strand, London WC2R 0RL
A Penguin company


First edition April 1987
Twenty-fourth edition April 2010



British Library Cataloguing Publication Data.
A Catalogue record for this book is available from the British Library.

ISBN 978-1-4053-5370-0

Compiled by
The Royal Horticultural Society
80 Vincent Square,
London SW1P 2PE
Registered charity no: 222879/SCO38262

**www.rhs.org.uk**

Illustrations by Sarah Young
Maps by Alan Cooper

Produced for Dorling Kindersley Ltd by
**COOLING BROWN**

Printed and bound in England by Clays Ltd, St Ives Plc

**The Compiler and the Editors of the *RHS Plant Finder* have taken every care, in the time available, to check all the information supplied to them by the nurseries concerned. Nevertheless, in a work of this kind, containing as it does hundreds of thousands of separate computer encodings, errors and omissions will, inevitably, occur. Neither the RHS, the Publisher nor the Editors can accept responsibility for any consequences that may arise from such errors.**

If you find mistakes we hope that you will let us know so that the matter can be corrected in the next edition.

**Back cover photographs from top to bottom:** Gaura *lindheimeri* 'Rosyjane', *Clematis* Diana's Delight, *Heuchera* 'Blackberry Jam', *Geranium pratense* var. *pratense* f. *albiflorum* 'Laura', *Sedum* 'Mr.Goodbud'
**Front cover and spine:** *Dahlia* 'Magic Sunrise' by GAP Photos: Visions

# Contents

# INTRODUCTION

The *RHS Plant Finder* exists to put enthusiastic gardeners in touch with suppliers of plants. The book is divided into two related sections – **PLANTS** and **NURSERIES. PLANTS** includes an A–Z Plant Directory of about 70,000 plant names, against which are listed a series of nursery codes. These codes point the reader to the full nursery details contained in the **NURSERIES** section towards the back of the book.

The *RHS Plant Finder* is comprehensively updated every year and provides the plant lover with the richest source of suppliers known to us.

As you will see from the entries in the **NURSERY DETAILS BY CODE** many nurseries do not now publish a printed catalogue but produce an online version only. This is a growing trend, fuelled by the cost of printing a full catalogue.

It is important to remember when ordering that many of the nurseries listed in the book are small, family-run, businesses that propagate their own material. They cannot therefore guarantee to hold large stocks of the plants they list. Some will, however, propagate to order.

## NEW IN THIS EDITION

In this edition's topical essay Dr John David, RHS Principal Scientist, summarises a major reclassification of plants, and flowering plants in particular, which the RHS has now adopted for use in the RHS Horticultural Database, from which the *RHS Plant Finder* is produced. As a result, you will notice that some of the family attributions in the book have changed. Please read the essay for the full story.

There are some changes to genera this year reflecting the deliberations of the RHS Advisory Committee on Nomenclature and Taxonomy (ACONAT). These include recognising *Lamprocapnos, Dactylicapnos, Adlumia, Ichthyoselmis* and *Ehrendorferia* as being distinct from *Dicentra*; *Sinopodophyllum* as being distinct from *Podophyllum*, while *Dysosma* is retained within *Podophyllum*; *Rigidella* is now included within *Tigridia*. *Plagiorhegma* was also discussed but is retained within *Jeffersonia*.

If there is a botanical issue that you wish to bring to the attention of the editors, or that you wish ACONAT to discuss, please contact us.

## AVAILABLE FROM THE COMPILER

### APPLICATION FOR ENTRY

Nurseries appearing in the *RHS Plant Finder* for the first time this year are printed in bold type in the *Nursery Index by Name* starting on p.936.

If you wish your nursery to be considered for inclusion in the next edition of the *RHS Plant Finder* (2011-2012), contact the Compiler at the address below.

### PLANTS LAST LISTED IN EARLIER EDITIONS

Plants cease to be listed for a variety of reasons. For more information turn to *How to Use the Plant Directory* on p.22. A listing of the 50,000 or so plants listed in earlier editions, but for which we currently have no known supplier, is available online at www.rhs.org.uk/rhsplantfinder/documents.asp.

### LISTS OF NURSERIES FOR PLANTS WITH MORE THAN 30 SUPPLIERS

To prevent the book from becoming too big, we do not print the nursery codes where more than 30 nurseries offer the same plant. The plant is then listed as being "Widely available". This is detailed more fully in *How to Use the Plant Directory* on p.22.

If any readers have difficulty in finding such a plant, we will be pleased to send a full list of all the nurseries that we have on file as stockists. All such enquiries must include the full name of the plant being sought, as shown in the *RHS Plant Finder*, together with an A5 size SAE.

The above may be obtained from:
**The Compiler, *RHS Plant Finder*, RHS Garden Wisley, Woking, Surrey GU23 6QB**
**Email: plantfinder@rhs.org.uk**

This information is also available online.

## THE RHS PLANT FINDER ONLINE

The *RHS Plant Finder* is available on the Internet. Visit the Royal Horticultural Society's website www.rhs.org.uk and search the *RHS Plant Finder Online*.

# ACKNOWLEDGMENTS

Judith Merrick, helped by June Skinner, compiled this edition. Richard Sanford managed the editing of the plant names on the database. Rupert Wilson and Julia Barclay administered the Horticultural Database, using the BG-Base™ Collection Management Software.

RHS Botanists James Armitage, Dawn Edwards, Neil Lancaster and Christopher Whitehouse have undertaken the task of editing the new plant names in this edition of the book.

As always, we are greatly indebted to Peter Cooling of Cooling Brown (Publishing), for his skill in enabling us to turn our mass of raw data into a published format.

We should also like to acknowledge the help of John David, RHS Chief Scientist, Tony Lord, Consultant Editor, Carol Sheppard, RHS Images Co-ordinator (Science and Advice), Louise Bowering, RHS Special Publications Manager, Simon Maughan, RHS Editor, Kerry Walter of BG-BASE (UK) Ltd., Max Phillips of Strange Software Ltd. and Alan Cooper.

Our colleagues on the RHS Advisory Committee on Nomenclature and Taxonomy, along with the RHS International Cultivar Registrars, have all provided valuable guidance and information. Many nurseries have supplied helpful information on plants, which has proved useful in verifying some of the more obscure names, and have suggested corrections to existing entries. Some of these remain to be checked and will be entered in the next edition, although those that contravene the Codes of Nomenclature may have to be rejected. We appreciate your patience while these checks are made. We are also grateful to all our regular correspondents and to the many readers who have made comments and suggestions.

| | |
|---|---|
| *Clematis* | D. Donald, Int. Cultivar Registrar, RHS |
| *Chrysanthemum* | J. Barker (2007–08) |
| Conifers | L. Springate, former Int. Cultivar Registrar, RHS |
| *Dahlia* | R. Hedge, S. McDonald, RHS Wisley |
| *Dianthus* | Dr A.C. Leslie, Int. Cultivar Registrar, RHS |
| *Geranium* | D.X. Victor (2003), Int. Cultivar Registrar |
| Heathers | Dr E.C. Nelson, Int. Cultivar Registrar |
| *Ilex* | S. Andrews (2006) |
| *Iris* | J. Hewitt (2005, 2007–08) |
| *Lavandula* | S. Andrews (2003 & 2005) |
| *Lilium* | K. Donald, former Int. Cultivar Registrar, RHS |
| *Meconopsis* | Dr E. Stevens (2003,'05 & 2007) |
| Narcissus | S. McDonald, Int. Cultivar Registrar, RHS |
| *Nerine* | Dr J.C. David (2009) |
| *Quercus* | P. Trehane, Int. Cultivar Registrar (2009) |
| *Rhododendron* | Dr A.C. Leslie, Int. Cultivar Registrar, RHS |
| *Sorbus* | Dr H. McAllister |
| *Thymus* | M. Easter (2003–09) |
| *Viburnum* | C. Sanders |

**Janet Cubey**, RHS Chief Horticultural Data Development Manager,
February 2010

# CONSERVATION AND THE ENVIRONMENT

As the *RHS Plant Finder* demonstrates, gardens in Britain have been greatly enriched by the diversity of plants introduced to cultivation from abroad. Whilst the vast majority of those introduced have enhanced our gardens, a few have proved to be highly invasive and to threaten native habitats. Once such plants are established it is very difficult, costly and potentially damaging to native ecosystems to eradicate or control the invasive "alien" species. Gardeners can help by choosing not to buy or distribute non-native invasive plants and by taking steps to prevent them escaping into the wild and by disposing of them in a responsible way.

The top eight invasive non-native species are no longer listed in the *RHS Plant Finder*. Any cultivars or varieties of them that are listed are believed to be less invasive than the species themselves. These 10 plants are:

*Azolla filiculoides* – fairy fern
*Crassula helmsii* – New Zealand pygmy weed
*Elodea nuttalli* – Nuttall's waterweed
*Fallopia japonica* – Japanese knotweed
*Heracleum mantegazzianum* – giant hogweed
*Hydrocotyle ranunculoides* – floating pennywort
*Impatiens glandulifera* – Himalayan balsam
*Lagarosiphon major* – curly waterweed
*Ludwigia grandiflora* – water primrose
*Myriophyllum aquaticum* – parrot's feather

**Bringing plants back from abroad**

Travelling can be a great source of inspiration for gardeners and often provides an introduction to new and interesting plants. Anyone thinking of bringing plants back into Britain from overseas must realise, however, that this is a complex matter. Various regulations are in force which apply to amateur gardeners as well as to commercial nurseries. The penalties for breaking these can be serious.

Some of the most important regulatory bodies are listed below.

**Plant Health regulations** are in place to control the spread of pests and diseases. Plants are divided into the categories of prohibited, controlled and unrestricted, but there are also limits that vary according to the part of the world you are travelling from. For full details contact the Plant Health division of DEFRA, or visit www.defra.gov.uk/planth/ph.htm

DEFRA has produced a leaflet that summarises the Horticultural Code of Practice. This is available online at www.defra.gov.uk or by phoning the helpline on 08459 335577.

**The Convention on International Trade in Endangered Species (CITES)** affects the transport of animal and plant material across international boundaries. Its aim is to prevent exploitative trade and thereby to prevent harm and the ultimate extinction of wild populations. Export and import licences are required for any plants listed on the CITES Appendices. A broad range of plants is covered in these Appendices, including *Cactaceae* and *Orchidaceae* and, although species are mentioned in the convention title, the restrictions cover all cultivars and hybrids too. Details of the plants listed in the Appendices can be found on the CITES website, www.ukcites.gov.uk/intro/cites_species.htm, or in the leaflets detailed below.

**The Convention on Biological Diversity** (CBD or the "Rio Convention") recognises the property rights of individual countries in relation to their own biodiversity. It exists to enable access to that biodiversity, but equally to ensure the sharing of any benefit derived from it. Export permits are required for plant material taken from the country of origin, with prior informed consent being gained for any uses that the material will be used for in the future. Further information on the Convention can be found on the CBD website, www.cbd.int.

If you would like to read more about these subjects, *Conservation and Environment Guidelines* leaflets are available on request from the RHS. Please write to the Compiler at the address given on page 4 enclosing an A4 SAE, or find them online at www.rhs.org.uk/Gardening/Sustainable-gardening. Leaflets are also available on a wider range of subjects, with topics including:

*Peat and the gardener*
*Potentially harmful garden plants*
*The use of limestone in horticulture*
*Trees and timber products*
*Wild and endangered plants in cultivation*
*Wildlife in gardens*

# Plants in their proper places – the new classification of flowering plants

**Introduction**
Most gardeners are familiar with the Latin names for plants, even if they do not like using them. What they may also notice on labels in public gardens, as well as in the *RHS Plant Finder*, are the family names, which end in -aceae. The family is the next main rank above that of genus and is the means to indicate that genera belonging to the same family are more similar to each other than to those that belong in another family. This is part of a botanical hierarchy used to organise plants into an overall system of relatedness, generally referred to as a classification. Man has been classifying plants since at least Theophrastus (*c.* 300BC) and our current system dates back to Linnaeus (1753), who introduced the concept of the binomial (genus and species name) as well as the arrangement of plants according to their flower structure. Both concepts have dominated our thinking about how we name and classify plants although, over time, we have been able to find different ways of collecting information about plants, and different kinds of data with which to test our classifications. The most recent of these techniques has been the analysis of genetic material (genome) and this has been applied to plants as much as it has to other kinds of organisms. The results of analysing many thousands of different plants have brought about a new understanding of plant relationships and, consequently, a major reclassification of plants, and flowering plants (angiosperms) in particular.

The new classification is known by the acronym APG (Angiosperm Phylogeny Group) which refers to the international team of scientists that have been carrying out the analysis of plant genetic material over the past 15 to 20 years. There have been three classifications published (APG, 1998, 2003 and 2009), generally known as APG, APG II and APG III. While the work has been known about for some time it is only really over the past five years that its impact has begun to be felt more widely, with major institutions such as the Royal Botanic Gardens, Kew and Edinburgh adopting the APG system for their herbaria and plant labelling. A recent Plant Network conference (www.plantnetwork.org/proceeds/wales2009/summary.htm) showed how the new system is being taken up in public gardens in the UK (Latta, 2008; *Horticulture Week*, 7 August 2009). In view of this, the RHS's Advisory Committee on Nomenclature and Taxonomy took the decision that it was appropriate for the RHS to adopt the classification as presented in the latest edition of Mabberley's *Plant-book* (2008) for use in the RHS horticultural database, from which the *RHS Plant Finder* is produced as well as the labels for plants in our gardens. This is broadly the same as the classification presented in the latest version of the APG classification (APG, 2009) and the differences are shown in the table with this article.

**The importance of classification**
A classification is, in the most abstract sense, a method of organising information. It has at least two functions: to enable communication, as such names are a shorthand to indicate relationships, and to predict, in that in associating entities you should be able to ascertain the properties of one entity from its position in the classification. It should also be possible to incorporate new information. For plants, as for any other living organisms, that element of predictiveness means that the basis for the classification must be genetic relatedness (or shared descent). Although Linnaeus's most famous classification, which is predictive, is not based on relatedness, only shared characters, even Linnaeus realised its artificiality and drew up a parallel system based on what he thought was a more natural arrangement. In the context of classification the word natural is normally used to mean that it is based on relatedness. Linnaeus, of course, classified organisms over 100 years before Darwin published his book *On the Origin of Species by Means of Natural Selection*, which revolutionised the theoretical basis of classification. It took a while for the first classifications based on his theory of evolution to be produced but ever since almost every classification published represents the classifier's concept of evolutionary relationships.

The consequence of this is that every scientific name we use conveys some information about the plant's relationships. The basic unit is the species, and these are clustered together in genera so that those that are most closely related belong in the same genus, those more distantly related will belong in other genera, which in turn are brought together in families and so on, in a hierarchy that ultimately reaches the level of Kingdom (such as *Plantae*, or Plants). It is this premise of a plant's relationships being revealed through its name and classification that is one source for name changes. As relationships are better understood, so it is necessary to change the position of the plant and this will generally lead to a change in name. While this is so, it is also widely accepted that such classifications are hypotheses and that the categories in which we arrange organisms are artificial constructs. In nature there are no genera or families or orders: some argue that species are real but as Linnaeus said, 'nature does not make leaps', or to put it another way, when you look at the individuals and populations that make up plants that you are studying, it is often hard to see where the divisions lie or whether those divisions are there at all.

This explanation attempts to show why classifications matter and, in particular, why the APG classification and the changes it is making to plant labels and information about plants matter to gardeners. By and large the new classification does not affect the genera – although these also are being changed by the application of molecular methods – but does make significant differences at the levels of family and above. While molecular data have confirmed many previously recognised relationships based on morphological characters, what has been fascinating is where families not previously thought to be close together have been found to be closely related. This has in many cases subsequently brought to light other features such as plant chemistry and microscopic characters, generally far less prone to rapid evolutionary change than those features we have traditionally relied on, like the flower, that support the new classification. Molecular data have also shown that our concepts of what are early evolving plants and which have a more recent origin need to change. This too affects the classification as early evolving plants are customarily placed at the beginning of a linear sequence of a classification, while those that appeared later are at the end.

**A survey of the new system**

A long-standing fundamental division of flowering plants is based on the number of seed leaves, and the groups thus distinguished are known as monocotyledons (one seed-leaf) and dicotyledons (two seed-leaves). While the molecular data show that the monocotyledons are a natural group, they are found to have arisen from an ancestor with two seed-leaves and so do not have a separate origin to the dicots. It also shows that the earliest diverging flowering plants are dicotyledonous in the traditional sense of the word. It is of interest that this relationship is borne out by the structure of the pollen: the monocots and those dicots that arose before the monocot-dicot divergence all have pollen grains with either a single pore or single groove; the later dicots (or eudicots) all have pollen grains based on the three-pore or three-groove pattern.

The living flowering plant which diverged first has been found to be a woody shrub (*Amborella*) which is endemic to New Caledonia. While it had always been regarded as being among the early arising dicots, it had not been thought to be as significant in flowering plant evolution as the molecular data now indicate. It may be something of a surprise that the water lilies are next in the sequence, given the apparent complexity and conspicuousness of their flowers. However, water lilies (*Nymphaeaceae*) are beetle-pollinated and it has been observed that many of the earliest flowering plants are beetle-pollinated; a reflection of the co-evolution of flowers and many insect groups. It turns out that beetles are amongst the earliest insect groups to evolve, and that flower pollination, and thus flower structure, has co-evolved with the insect pollinators, as insect diversity increased rapidly alongside flowering plant diversity. Also amongst the cluster of early diverging angiosperms is another group of woody plants and of these the best known to gardeners are *Illicium* (allspice) and *Schisandra* in the family *Schisandraceae*.

Next in the sequence and still before the divergence of the monocots is a group of predominantly woody, tropical plants characterised by *Magnolia*. Those familiar with previous classifications will be aware that *Magnolia* and its allies were thought to be the earliest flowering plants to arise due to their relatively unspecialised floral morphology. In addition to *Magnolia*, also included in this group are *Drimys* (*Winteraceae*), *Aristolochia* and *Asarum* (*Aristolochiaceae*), *Peperomia* (*Piperaceae*), *Chimonanthus* (*Calycanthaceae*), *Laurus* and *Persea* (*Lauraceae*) and the nutmeg (*Myristica*, *Myristacaceae*).

It is after this point that the monocots and dicots diverge and the remainder of the dicots are informally referred to as the eudicots. It is amongst this group that we start to see the differentiation of perianth segments into petals and sepals, although this is not universal and many eudicot flowers are much reduced or adapted and have lost this feature. The first eudicot group to arise is that which is represented by the paradigm of flower morphology, *Ranunculus*. Closely related are *Berberis* and *Mahonia* (*Berberidaceae*), and the poppies (*Papaveraceae*, which also includes *Corydalis* and *Dicentra*). It is the next group, however, which probably causes one of the biggest surprises. Associated together are three families of very different appearance: another group of water lilies (*Nelumbo*), the planes (*Platanaceae*) and the proteas (*Proteaceae*). While there are no obvious features that all three types of plant share, there are some characteristics that link the planes and the proteas particularly, most notably the stipules that surround the stem. Also among the early diverging eudicots is the box family, *Buxaceae*, which in previous classifications was thought to be closer to the *Euphorbiaceae*.

This brings us to the group referred to as the "core eudicots" amongst which the arrangement of flower parts in fives is the basic plan, although as with the differentiation of the perianth, there are many variations in form where this basic plan is not evident. At the bottom of the core eudicots, sister to all the rest is *Gunnera* (*Gunneraceae*), the flower parts of which are still in twos. Next to the gunneras comes a large group around the *Saxifragaceae* which brings together families which had never previously been associated, such as *Cercidophyllum* (*Cercidophyllaceae*); *Crassula* (*Crassulaceae*); *Ribes* (*Grossulariaceae*); *Hamamelis* and *Corylopsis* (*Hamamelidaceae*); *Itea* (*Iteaceae*) and *Paeonia* (*Paeoniaceae*). This highly diverse group appears to have evolved rapidly towards the middle of the Cretaceous and, as yet, no single uniting characteristic has been identified.

At this point the eudicots divide into two major lineages, the rosids and the asterids. Broadly this reflects the organisation of the perianth into those with separate petals and those where the petals are fused, at least partially, into a tube. Earlier botanists referred to these two groups as Polypetalae and Gamopetalae respectively so it is fascinating to see this reflected in the results from molecular analysis. Amongst the rosids there are some more surprises: the previously unsuspected relationship between the euphorbias (*Euphorbiaceae*), the passion flowers (*Passifloraceae*), the willows (*Salicaceae*), the violets (*Violaceae*) and the tropical parasite with the largest solitary flower, *Rafflesia*. Initially unexpected was the revelation that the families related to the roses (*Rosaceae*) are *Cannabis* (*Cannabaceae*), *Elaeagnus* (*Elaeagnaceae*), the elms (*Ulmaceae*) and the nettles (*Urticaceae*). The striking difference in appearance of the flowers is largely due to wind pollination, which favours reduced flowers with small petals or no petals at all, a feature not unknown in the *Rosaceae* (e.g. *Sanguisorba*, *Polylepis*).

While all these surprises might bring one to question whether the molecular data are reliable as a foundation for classification, or that errors may have crept into the analysis, it should be pointed out that this work has been carried out on many representatives of each family and for up to six different regions of the genome. Although there are some discrepancies, and these are still the subject of debate (leading to some plants still being "unplaced" in the classification), most of the results are consistent and therefore give confidence that these are giving a more accurate picture of relationships.

Another cluster is the group of families which all share the chemical feature of producing mustard oils, distinctive for the pungent smell plants in these families give off, especially if crushed. Although the presence of mustard oils has been known for some time, it was not until the molecular data showed that the plants that produce these oils are related that the significance of the oils for plant classification was fully appreciated. This grouping includes the cabbage family (*Brassicaceae*), the capers (*Capparaceae*), the paw paws (*Caricaceae*), *Cleome* (*Cleomaceae*) and the nasturtiums (*Tropaeolaceae*). Shared chemistry is also to be found in the group of families related to the pinks (*Caryophyllaceae*) which also includes the ice plants (*Aizoaceae*), the cacti (*Cactaceae*), pokeweeds (*Phytolaccaceae*) as well as spinach and beets (*Chenopodiaceae*); to these have been added, on molecular evidence, many of the families of carnivorous plants (e.g. *Droseraceae* and *Nepenthaceae*) as well as the sea heath (*Frankeniaceae*) and tamarisk (*Tamaricaceae*).

In the other main lineage, the asterids, there are two early diverging groups: one around the *Cornaceae* which, unexpectedly, proves to be closer to the *Hydrangeaceae* than indicated by floral morphology; the other, a large cluster around the *Ericaceae* which itself now includes the *Epacridaceae*, *Empetraceae* and *Pyrolaceae*. This cluster contains families long known to be related but also the phlox family (*Polemoniaceae*) and the pitcher plants (*Sarraceniaceae*). A contentious issue in APG I and II has been the boundary between the *Primulaceae* and the *Myrsinaceae*, the latter being largely tropical shrubs and trees; however, under the current classification these have been merged into one family, *Primulaceae*.

It is amongst the core asterids that some major families of horticulturally important plants are to be found and one of the most keenly debated questions has been the fate of the foxglove family (*Scrophulariaceae*). Whereas in many cases the molecular data have indicated that families might be merged together, it is quite the reverse in the *Scrophulariaceae* where some former members are, according to APG II and III, placed in new or different families, such as *Calceolariaceae* (*Calceolaria*), *Paulowniaceae* (*Paulownia*) or *Phrymaceae* (*Mimulus*). The greatest upheaval is, perhaps, the transfer of many genera, such *Antirrhinum*, *Digitalis* and *Hebe* to the *Plantaginaceae*, previously a small family of predominantly wind-pollinated plants. What remains in the *Scrophulariaceae* are a few of the original genera, such as *Verbascum* and *Phygelius*, together with others not originally thought to belong there including *Buddleja* and *Myoporum*. While at first this may seem an unlikely rearrangement, it should be remembered that the *Scrophulariaceae* were never well defined morphologically.

A similar situation arises with the systematics of the honeysuckle family (*Caprifoliaceae*), which in an earlier version was broken up into a number of different families. In the latest treatment (APG III), they have all been combined, together with the teasel family (*Dipsacaceae*) and the valerians (*Valerianaceae*), into one family, *Caprifoliaceae*, with the exception of *Sambucus* and *Viburnum*. These have been referred to the *Adoxaceae*, a family originally of small herbaceous woodland plants.

Some may be surprised by the appearance of the umbellifers (*Apiaceae* and the closely related family *Araliaceae*) among the asterids alongside *Pittosporum* and *Griselinia*. Also notable is *Escallonia*, traditionally considered to be closely related to the currants (*Grossulariaceae*) and broadly associated with the roses, which now comes out as a distinctive lineage among the asterids.

As mentioned above, the monocots have been recognised as being a natural group, as defined by the possession of one seed leaf, in the APG classification, but changes to relationships within the group have been proposed. The principal horticultural groups are the aroids, the palms, the grasses, bromeliads, gingers, orchids and the diverse cluster of bulbous, cormous or rhizomatous monocot plants. These latter have been treated in many different ways, from a broadly circumscribed *Liliaceae* to a large number of much smaller families (*Hyacinthaceae*, *Convallariaceae*, etc.). Molecular data have helped to resolve many of these uncertainties and, as with the dicots, have pointed out a number of more unexpected groupings.

The earliest diverging monocot lineage has been found to be that leading to *Acorus* (sweet flag), previously thought to be a member of the *Araceae* (*Arum* family) and it is perhaps interesting to observe that among the early diverging monocots, the majority are aquatic. Other distinctive groups of monocots such as the palms (*Arecaceae*) and the gingers (*Zingiberaceae*) are still recognised, although the pineapple family (*Bromeliaceae*) has been revealed to be much more closely related to the grasses (*Poaceae*) than previously thought.

Molecular data have helped greatly to improve our understanding of the bulbous petaloid monocotyledons and given greater significance to a character, the nature of the seed coat, which had not formerly been seen to be of importance. In this group of plants there are two types of seed coat; one type has a dark, non-cellular covering, the other has a pale, cellular covering. This distinction neatly fits with the molecular data, and consequently two main groups are recognised: the asparagoids (*Asparagales*) with dark-coated seeds, and the lilioids (*Liliales*) with pale-coated seeds. The *Liliaceae* is now circumscribed as a much smaller group of genera, including *Lilium*, *Tulipa*, *Fritillaria*, *Erythronium* and *Tricyrtis*; while *Disporum*, *Uvularia* and *Colchicum* are now in the *Colchicaceae*.

The other main cluster, the asparagoids, includes an unchanged *Iridaceae* and *Amaryllidaceae*, which may be expanded to include *Agapanthus* and the *Alliaceae* (onions). Many of the genera formerly included in *Liliaceae* are now placed in an enlarged *Asparagaceae*, such as *Convallaria*, *Ornithogalum*, *Scilla*, *Agave*, *Cordyline*, *Polygonatum* and *Ruscus*. *Phormium* and *Hemerocallis* come together in the *Hemerocallidaceae*. The orchids, however, long held to be an isolated group among the monocots, are now shown to belong among the asparagoids, reflecting the over-emphasis given in previous classifications to conspicuous floral features of this highly adapted group of plants.

**Further research**

As has been observed on a number of points in this piece, the more startling rearrangements revealed by molecular analysis often lack the shared characteristics that would enable recognition by more traditional means. The task now is to re-examine the many kinds of data available to characterise plants to see which one or ones fit the molecular data. These will vary from group to group as evolution is driven by different pressures over time. Further, there are still uncertainties in the position of some groups, such as the *Boraginaceae*, and these questions are still being worked on, so further changes can be expected, although these will be relatively minor. As this research continues and new information comes to light, these are incorporated in the Angiosperm Phylogeny Website (www.mobot.org/MOBOT/Research/APweb/welcome.html). This is an invaluable resource for anyone interested in finding out more. For those that prefer their information in print, the standard reference is the third edition of Mabberley's *Plant-book* but the updated edition of Heywood *et al.* (*Flowering Plants of the World*) is also based on APG, although it diverges significantly in the treatment of certain families.

**Dr John David**
RHS Chief Scientist

**References**

Angiosperm Phylogeny Group (1998). An Ordinal Classification for the Families of Flowering Plants. *Annals of the Missouri Botanical Garden* 85: 531–553.

Angiosperm Phylogeny Group (2003). An Update of the Angiosperm Phylogeny Group Classification for the Orders and Families of Flowering Plants: APG II. *Botanical Journal of the Linnean Society* 141: 399–436.

Angiosperm Phylogeny Group (2009). An Update of the Angiosperm Phylogeny Group Classification for the Orders and Families of Flowering Plants: APG III. *Botanical Journal of the Linnean Society* 161: 105–121.

Heywood, V.H., Brummitt, R.K., Culham, A. & Seberg, O. (2007). *Flowering Plant Families of the World*. Kew, RBG Kew.

Latta, J. (2008). Changing to APG II – Theory Put into Practice. *Sibbaldia* 6: 133–153.

Mabberley, D.J. (2008). *Mabberley's Plant-book*. Third Edition. Cambridge, CUP.

# CLASSIFICATION OF A SELECTION OF PLANTS FOUND IN UK HORTICULTURE ACCORDING TO THE ARRANGEMENT IN MABBERLEY'S PLANT-BOOK, ED. 3 (2008)

Only those families with one or more representative genera in cultivation are given. Groups in square brackets are ones for which there are no representatives in UK horticulture.

**Subclass MAGNOLIIDAE**
[Superorder AMBORELLANAE]

Superorder NYMPHAEANAE
  Order Nymphaeales
    Family Nymphaeaceae (Nymphaea)

Superorder AUSTROBAILEYANAE
  Order Austrobaileyales
    Family Schizandraceae (Schisandra, Illicium)
  Order Chloranthales
    Family Chloranthaceae (Chloranthus)

Superorder MAGNOLIANAE
  Order Canellales
    Family Winteraceae (Drimys, Pseudowintera)
  Order Piperales
    Family Aristolochiaceae (Aristolochia, Asarum)
    Family Saururaceae (Saururus)
  Order Magnoliales
    Family Annonaceae (Asimina)
    Family Magnoliaceae (Magnolia, Liriodendron)
  Order Laurales
    Family Atherospermataceae (Atherosperma, Laurelia)
    Family Calycanthaceae (Chimonanthus, Calycanthus)
    Family Lauraceae (Laurus, Lindera, Neolitsea, Sassafras)

## Monocots

Superorder LILIANAE
  Order Alismatales
    Family Acoraceae[1] (Acorus)
    Family Araceae (Arum, Dracunculus, Arisaema, Zantedeschia, Lysichiton)
  [Order Petrosaviales]
  Order Dioscoreales
    Family Dioscoreaceae (Dioscorea, Tacca)
  Order Pandanales
    Family Pandanaceae (Pandanus)
  Order Liliales
    Family Alstroemeriacae (Alstroemeria, Bomarea)
    Family Colchicaceae (Colchicum, Disporum, Uvularia, Gloriosa)
    Family Liliaceae (Lilium, Erythronium, Fritillaria, Tulipa)
    Family Melanthiaceae (Veratrum, Paris, Trillium)
    Family Philesiaceae (Philesia, Lapageria)
    Family Smilacaceae (Smilax)
  Order Asparagales
    Family Amaryllidaceae (Amaryllis, Narcissus, Galanthus, Sternbergia, Crinum)
    Family Alliaceae[2] (Allium, Tulbaghia, Nectaroscordum)
    Family Agapanthaceae[2] (Agapanthus)
    Family Asparagaceae (Agave, Hosta, Yucca, Cordyline, Convallaria, Polygonatum, Ruscus, Asparagus, Triteleia, Scilla, Hyacinthus, Ornithogalum, Eucomis, Dianella)
    Family Asteliaceae (Astelia)
    Family Hypoxidaceae (Rhodohypoxis)
    Family Iridaceae (Iris, Gladiolus, Moraea, Sisyrinchium, Crocus, Watsonia, Crocosmia, Dierama)
    Family Ixoliriaceae (Ixolirion)
    Family Orchidaceae (Bletilla, Cypripedium, Dactylorhiza, Pleione, Dendrobium)
    Family Tecophilaeaceae (Tecophilaea)
    Family Hemerocallidaceae[3] (Hemerocallis, Phormium)
    Family Asphodelaceae[3](Asphodeline, Kniphofia, Eremurus, Aloe, Gasteria)
    Family Xanthorrhoeaceae (Xanthorrhoea)
  [Order Dasypogonales]
  Order Arecales
    Family Arecaceae (Palmae) (Trachycarpus, Phoenix)
  Order Poales
    Family Bromeliaceae (Dyckia, Fascicularia, Puya)
    Family Cyperaceae (Cyperus)
    Family Restionaceae (Thamnochortus, Elegia)
    Family Poaceae (Poa, Miscanthus, Arundo, Phyllostachys, Cortaderia, Stipa, Zea)
  Order Commelinales
    Family Commelinaceae (Tradescantia, Commelina)
    Family Pontederiaceae (Pontederia)
    Family Haemadoraceae (Anigozanthus)
  Order Zingiberales
    Family Musaceae (Musa)
    Family Strelitziaceae (Strelitzia)

1 Treated as a separate order, Acorales in APG III

2 Both families are included in Amaryllidaceae in APG III
3 Both families are included in Xanthorrhoeaceae in APG III

Family Zingiberaceae (Cautleya, Hedychium, Roscoea)
Family Cannaceae (Canna)

## Eudicots

Superorder CERATOPHYLLANAE
Order Ceratophyllales
Family Ceratophyllaceae (Ceratophyllum)

Superorder RANUNCULANAE
Order Ranunculales
Family Eupteleaceae (Euptelea)
Family Lardizabalaceae (Akebia, Decaisnea, Holboellia)
Family Menispermaceae (Menispermum)
Family Berberidaceae (Berberis, Nandina, Podophyllum, Epimedium)
Family Ranunculaceae (Clematis, Anemone, Adonis, Delphinium, Aquilegia, Helleborus, Glaucidium)
Family Papaveraceae (Papaver, Corydalis, Romneya, Macleaya, Meconopsis, Dicentra)

Unplaced Order Sabiales[4]
Family Sabiaceae (Meliosma)

Superorder PROTEANAE
Order Proteales
Family Proteaceae (Protea, Banksia, Grevillea, Hakea, Telopea, Embothrium)
Family Platanaceae (Platanus)

Unplaced Order Trochodendrales[4]
Family Trochodendraceae (Trochodendron, Tetracentron)

Superorder BUXANAE
Order Buxales
Family Buxaceae (Buxus, Sarcococca, Pachysandra)

## Core Eudicots

Superorder MYROTHAMNANAE
Order Gunnerales
Family Gunneraceae (Gunnera)

Superorder BERBERIDOPSIDANAE
Order Berberidopsidales
Family Berberidopsidaceae (Berberidopsis, Aextoxicon)

Unplaced order Dilleniales[5]
Family Dilleniaceae (Hibbertia)

Superorder CARYOPHYLLANAE
Order Caryophyllales
Family Nepenthaceae (Nepenthes)
Family Droseraceae (Dionaea, Drosera)
Family Tamaricaceae (Tamarix)
Family Frankeniaceae (Frankenia)
Family Plumbaginaceae (Plumbago, Ceratostigma, Armeria, Limonium)
Family Polygonaceae (Polygonum, Persicaria, Rheum)
Family Caryophyllaceae (Dianthus, Lychnis, Gypsophila)
Family Amaranthaceae (Amaranthus, Beta, Chenopodium)
Family Portulacaceae (Portulaca, Lewisia, Calandrinia)
Family Cactaceae (Opuntia, Cereus)
Family Aizoaceae (Carpobrotus, Delosperma, Ruschia)
Family Phytolaccaceae (Phytolacca, Ercilla)
Family Nyctaginaceae (Mirabilis)

Superorder SANTALANAE
Order Santalales
Family Loranthaceae (Viscum)
Order Saxifragales[6]
Family Cercidophyllaceae (Cercidophyllum)
Family Crassulaceae (Crassula, Kalanchoe, Sedum, Sempervivum, Echeveria)
Family Daphniphyllaceae (Daphniphyllum)
Family Grossulariaceae (Ribes)
Family Haloragaceae (Haloragis)
Family Hamamelidaceae (Hamamelis, Parrotia, Corylopsis, Liquidambar[7])
Family Iteaceae (Itea)
Family Paeoniaceae (Paeonia)
Family Saxifragaceae (Saxifraga, Astilbe, Bergenia, Darmera, Heuchera, Rodgersia, Tiarella)

Superorder ROSANAE
Order Vitales
Family Vitaceae (Vitis, Parthenocissus)
Order Crossosomatales
Family Staphyleaceae (Staphylaea)
Family Stachyuraceae (Stachyurus)
Order Geraniales[8]
Family Melianthaceae (Melianthus, Greyia)
Family Francoaceae[9] (Francoa)
Family Geraniaceae (Geranium, Pelargonium, Erodium)
Order Myrtales[8]

---

4 The position of these two orders with respect to the Proteanae and Buxanae is still unresolved and hence they are treated as "unplaced"

5 Order Dilleniales not recognised in APG III; the family is left as "unplaced"

6 Treated as "unplaced" in APG III, i.e. not assigned to a Superorder

7 Recognised in APG III in the separate family Altingiaceae

8 APG III has these orders in the Malvids – Eurosids II

9 Included in Melianthaceae in APG III

Family Lythraceae (Lythrum, Punica, Lagerstroemia, Cuphea, Heimia)
Family Onagraceae (Fuchsia, Clarkia, Oenothera, Gaura)
Family Myrtaceae (Myrtus, Eucalyptus, Callistemon, Luma, Acca, Leptospermum)
Family Melastomataceae (Tibouchina, Osbeckia, Heterocentron)

### Fabids – Eurosids I

Order Zygophyllales
Family Zygophyllaceae (Peganum)
Order Celastrales
Family Celastraceae (Euonymus, Maytenus, Parnassia)
Order Malpighiales
Family Salicaceae[10] (Salix, Azara, Idesia, Poliothyrsis, Populus)
Family Violaceae (Viola, Melicytus)
Family Passifloraceae (Passiflora)
Family Euphorbiaceae (Euphorbia, Ricinus, Codiaeum, Acalypha, Croton, Mallotus)
Family Hypericaceae (Hypericum)
Family Linaceae (Linum)
Order Oxalidales
Family Oxalidaceae (Oxalis, Biophytum)
Family Cunoniaceae (Eucryphia, Weinmannia)
Family Elaeocarpaceae (Crinodendron, Aristotelia)
Order Fabales
Family Quillajaceae (Quillaja)
Family Fabaceae (Acacia, Cercis, Gleditsia, Caesalpinia, Sophora, Baptisia, Cytisus, Genista, Lupinus, Indigofera, Wisteria, Phaseolus, Robinia, Coronilla, Clianthus, Trifolium, Lathyrus, Pisum)
Family Polygalaceae (Polygala)
Order Rosales
Family Rosaceae (Rosa, Potentilla, Geum, Alchemilla, Acaena, Filipendula, Exochorda, Spiraea, Kerria, Dryas, Rubus, Prunus, Chaenomeles, Malus, Sorbus, Cotoneaster, Pyracantha)
Family Elaeagnaceae (Elaeagnus, Hippophae)
Family Rhamnaceae (Rhamnus, Ceanothus, Colletia)
Family Ulmaceae (Ulmus, Celtis, Zelkova)
Family Cannabaceae (Cannabis, Humulus)
Family Moraceae (Morus, Ficus, Broussonetia)
Family Urticaceae (Urtica, Boehmeria)
Order Cucurbitales
Family Corynocarpaceae (Corynocarpus)
Family Coriariaceae (Coriaria)
Family Cucurbitaceae (Cucumis, Cucurbita, Bryonia, Ecballium, Citrullus)
Family Datiscaceae (Datisca)

10 Includes a number of genera formerly assigned to the Flacourtiaceae

Family Begoniaceae (Begonia)
Order Fagales
Family Nothofagaceae[11] (Nothofagus)
Family Fagaceae (Fagus, Quercus, Castanea, Lithocarpus)
Family Myricaceae (Myrica, Morella, Comptonia)
Family Betulaceae (Corylus, Betula, Carpinus, Alnus)
Family Casuarinaceae (Allocasuarina)
Family Juglandaceae (Juglans, Carya, Pterocarya)

### Malvids – Eurosids II

[Order Huerteales]
[Order Picramniales]
Order Brassicales
Family Tropaeolaceae (Tropaeolum)
Family Limnanthaceae (Limnanthes)
Family Resedaceae (Reseda)
Family Capparaceae (Capparis)
Family Cleomaceae (Cleome)
Family Brassicaceae (Brassica, Erysimum, Aubrieta, Matthiola, Lunaria, Iberis, Raphanus, Crambe)
Order Malvales
Family Malvaceae (Tilia, Lavatera, Fremontodendron, Hoheria, Althaea, Alcea, Hibiscus, Abutilon)
Family Thymelaeaceae (Daphne, Edgeworthia, Wikstroemia)
Family Cistaceae (Cistus, Halimum, Helianthemum)
Order Sapindales
Family Sapindaceae (Acer, Aesculus, Dodonaea, Koelreuteria)
Family Simourabaceae (Ailanthus, Picrasma)
Family Anacardiaceae (Rhus, Cotinus, Schinus)
Family Rutaceae (Citrus, Choisya, Skimmia, Phellodendron, Dictamnus, Ruta, Cneorum)

Superorder ASTERANAE
Order Cornales
Family Cornaceae (Cornus, Alangium)
Family Nyssaceae (Nyssa, Davidia)
Family Hydrangeaceae (Hydrangea, Deutzia, Philadelphus, Carpenteria, Kirengashoma)
Family Loasaceae (Loasa, Mentzelia)
Order Ericales
Family Balsaminaceae (Impatiens)
Family Polemoniaceae (Phlox, Polemonium, Cantua, Cobaea, Gilia)
Family Theaceae (Camellia, Stewartia)
Family Pentaphylacaceae (Cleyera, Eurya)
Family Ebenaceae (Diospyros)
Family Primulaceae (Primula, Cyclamen, Dodecatheon, Lysimachia, Myrsine)

11 Previously included in the Fagaceae

Family Styracaceae (Styrax, Halesia, Pterostyrax)
Family Diapensiaceae (Diapensia, Galax, Shortia)
Family Actinidiaceae (Actinidia, Clematoclethra, Saurauia)
Family Sarraceniaceae (Sarracenia)
Family Clethraceae (Clethra)
Family Ericaceae[12] (Erica, Calluna, Cassiope, Kalmia, Rhododendron, Vaccinium, Pyrola, Empetrum, Cyathodes, Richea)

### Lamiids – Euasterids I

Family Boraginaceae[13] (Borago, Echium, Nemophila, Anchusa, Lithodora, Omphalodes, Pulmonaria, Phacelia)
Order Garryales
Family Eucommiaceae (Eucommia)
Family Garryaceae (Aucuba, Garrya)
Order Gentianales
Family Rubiaceae (Coprosma, Bouvardia, Luculia, Asperula, Phuopsis)
Family Gentianaceae (Gentiana, Eustoma, Exacum, Centaurium)
Family Apocynaceae[14] (Nerium, Trachelospermum, Vinca, Asclepias, Hoya, Dregea, Stapelia)
Order Solanales
Family Solanaceae (Solanum, Lycium, Cestrum, Nicotiana, Datura, Petunia, Salpiglossis)
Family Convolvulaceae (Convolvulus, Ipomoea)
Order Lamiales
Family Oleaceae (Fraxinus, Jasminum, Olea, Osmanthus, Syringa, Ligustrum)
Family Gesneriaceae (Haberlea, Ramonda, Mitraria, Achimenes, Streptocarpus)
Family Calceolariaceae (Calceolaria, Jovellana)
Family Scrophulariaceae (Verbascum, Phygelius, Diascia, Nemesia, Buddleja, Myoporum)
Family Acanthaceae (Acanthus, Justicia, Strobilanthes)
Family Verbenaceae (Aloysia, Verbena, Rhaphithamnus)
Family Bignoniaceae (Catalpa, Eccremocarpus, Campsis, Incarvillea)
Family Lamiaceae[15] (Lamium, Clerodendrum, Vitex, Callicarpa, Caryopteris, Phlomis, Salvia, Mentha, Thymus, Plectranthus, Stachys)
Family Phrymaceae (Mimulus)
Family Paulowniaceae (Paulownia)
Family Orobanchaceae (Castilleja, Lathraea)
Family Plantaginaceae[16] (Digitalis, Antirrhinum, Penstemon, Hebe, Rehmannia, Bacopa)

### Campanulids – Euasterids II

Desfontaniaceae[17] (Desfontania)
Escalloniaceae[18] (Escallonia)
Order Aquifoliales
Family Helwingiaceae (Helwingia)
Family Aquifoliaceae (Ilex)
Order Apiales
Family Griseliniaceae (Griselinia)
Family Araliaceae (Aralia, Schefflera, Pseudopanax, Hedera, Hydrocotyle)
Family Apiaceae (Astrantia, Eryngium, Daucus, Bupleurum, Angelica, Foeniculum)
Family Pittosporaceae (Billardieria, Pittosporum)
Order Dipsacales
Family Adoxaceae (Adoxa, Viburnum, Sambucus)
Family Caprifoliaceae[19] (Lonicera, Abelia, Diervilla, Linnaea, Knautia, Scabiosa, Valeriana, Centranthus, Morina)
Order Asterales
Family Rousseaceae (Carpodetus)
Family Campanulaceae[20] (Campanula, Platycodon, Adenophora, Codonopsis, Lobelia)
Family Argophyllaceae (Corokia)
Family Menyanthaceae (Menyanthes)
Family Goodeniaceae (Scaevola)
Family Asteraceae (Aster, Echinops, Eupatorium, Centaurea, Senecio, Dahlia, Helichrysum, Osteospermum, Bellis, Erigeron, Chrysanthemum, Helianthus, Mutisia, Olearia)

12 Including Empetraceae and Epacridaceae
13 Family is "unplaced" (unassigned to an order) in both Mabberley & APG III; also includes Hydrophyllaceae
14 Including Asclepiadaceae
15 Including some genera formerly in the Verbenaceae
16 Including Globulariaceae
17 Treated as "unplaced" family by Mabberley, but included in the Columelliaceae, in the order Bruniales (not recognised by Mabberley) in APG III
18 Treated as "unplaced" family by Mabberley, but placed in the order Escalloniales (not recognised by Mabberley) in APG III
19 Including Dipsaceae, Valerianaceae and Morinaceae
20 Including Lobeliaceae

# EXTENDED GLOSSARY

This glossary combines some of the helpful introductory sections from older editions in an alphabetical listing. A fuller, more discursive account of plant names, *Guide to Plant Names,* and a detailed guide to the typography of plant names, *Recommended Style for Printing Plant Names*, are both available as RHS Advisory Leaflets. To request a copy of either please send an A4 SAE to The Compiler at the contact address given on page 4.

## ADVISORY COMMITTEE ON NOMENCLATURE AND TAXONOMY

This Panel advises the RHS on individual problems of nomenclature regarding plants in cultivation and, in particular, use of names in the *RHS Horticultural Database*, reflected in the annual publication of the *RHS Plant Finder*.

The aim is always to make the plant names in the *RHS Plant Finder* as consistent, reliable and stable as possible and acceptable to gardeners and botanists alike, not only in the British Isles but around the world. Recent proposals to change or correct names are examined with the aim of creating a balance between the stability of well-known names and botanical and taxonomic correctness. In some cases the Panel feels that the conflicting views on the names of some groups of plants will not easily be resolved. The Panel's policy is then to wait and review the situation once a more obvious consensus is reached, rather than rush to rename plants only to have to change them again when opinions have shifted.

The Panel is chaired by Dr Alan Leslie (RHS) with Dr Janet Cubey (RHS) (Vice-Chair) and includes: Dr Crinan Alexander (RBGE), Susyn Andrews, Chris Brickell, Dr James Compton, Dr John David (RHS), Mike Grant (RHS Publications), John Grimshaw, Dr Stephen Jury (University of Reading), Dr Tony Lord, Dr Charles Nelson, Julian Shaw (RHS) & Adrian Whiteley, with Dr Christopher Whitehouse (RHS) as Secretary.

## AUTHORITIES

In order that plant names can be used with precision throughout the scientific world, the name of the person who coined the name of a plant species (its author, or authority) is added to the plant name. Usually this information is of little consequence to gardeners, except in cases where the same name has been given to two different plants or a name is commonly misapplied. Although only one usage is correct, both may be encountered in books, so indicating the author is the only way to be certain about which plant is being referred to. This can happen equally with cultivars. Authors' names, where it is appropriate to cite them, appear in a smaller typeface after the species or cultivar name to which they refer and are abbreviated following Brummitt and Powell's *Authors of Plant Names*.

## 🏆 AWARD OF GARDEN MERIT

The Award of Garden Merit (AGM) is intended to be of practical value to the ordinary gardener and is therefore awarded only after a period of assessment by the Society's Standing and Joint Committees. An AGM plant:

- must be available
- must be of outstanding excellence for garden decoration or use
- must be of good constitution
- must not require highly specialist growing conditions or care
- must not be particularly susceptible to any pest or disease
- must not be subject to an unreasonable degree of reversion

The AGM symbol is cited in conjunction with the **hardiness** rating. A full list of AGM plants may be found on the RHS website at www.rhs.org.uk/plants/plant-trials-and-awards/plant-awards.

## BOTANICAL NAMES

The aim of the botanical naming system is to provide each different plant with a single, unique, universal name. The basic unit of plant classification is the species. Species that share a number of significant characteristics are grouped together to form a genus (plural **genera**). The name of a species is made up of two elements; the name of the genus followed by the specific epithet, for example, *Narcissus romieuxii*.

Variation within a species can be recognised by division into subspecies (usually abbreviated to subsp.), varietas (or variety abbreviated to var.) and forma (or form abbreviated to f.). Whilst it is unusual for a plant to have all of these, it is possible, as in this example, *Narcissus romieuxii* subsp. *albidus* var. *zaianicus* f. *lutescens.*

The botanical elements are always given in italics, with only the genus taking an initial capital letter. The rank indications are never in italics. In instances where the rank is not known it is necessary to form an invalid construction by quoting a second epithet without a rank. This is an unsatisfactory situation, but requires considerable research to resolve.

In some genera, such as *Hosta*, we list the cultivar names alphabetically with the species or **hybrid** to which they are attributed afterwards in parentheses. For example, *Hosta* 'Reversed' (*sieboldiana*). In other situations where the aim is not to create a list alphabetically by cultivar name we would recommend styling this as *Hosta sieboldiana* 'Reversed'.

## Classification of Genera

Genera that include a large number of species or with many cultivars are often subdivided into informal horticultural classifications or more formal Cultivar Groups, each based on a particular characteristic or combination of characteristics. Colour of flower or fruit and shape of flower are common examples and, with fruit, whether a cultivar is grown for culinary or dessert purposes. How such groups are named differs from genus to genus.

To help users of the *RHS Plant Finder* find the plants they want, the classifications used within cultivated genera are listed using codes and plants are marked with the appropriate code in brackets after its name in the Plant Directory. To find the explanation of each code, simply look it up under the genus concerned in the **Classification of Genera** starting on p.32. The codes relating to edible fruits are also listed here, but these apply across several genera.

## Collectors' References

Abbreviations (usually with numbers) following a plant name refer to the collector(s) of the plant. These abbreviations are expanded, with a collector's name or expedition title, in the section **Collectors' References** starting on p.24.

A collector's reference may indicate a new, as yet unnamed range of variation within a species. The inclusion of collectors' references in the *RHS Plant Finder* supports the book's role in sourcing unusual plants.

The Convention on Biological Diversity calls for conservation of biodiversity, its sustainable use and the fair and equitable sharing of any derived benefits. Since its adoption in 1993, collectors are required to have prior informed consent from the country of origin for the acquisition and commercialisation of collected material.

## Common Names

In a work such as this, it is necessary to refer to plants by their botanical names for the sake of universal comprehension and clarity. However, at the same time we recognise that with fruit and vegetables most people are more familiar with their common names than their botanical ones. Cross-references are therefore given from common to botanical names for fruit, vegetables and the commoner culinary herbs throughout the Plant Directory.

## Cultivar

Literally meaning cultivated variety, cultivar names are given to denote variation within species and that generated by hybridisation, in cultivation. To make them easily distinguishable from botanical names, they are not printed in italics and are enclosed in single quotation marks. Cultivar names coined since 1959 should follow the rules of the International Code of Nomenclature for Cultivated Plants (**ICNCP**).

## Descriptive Terms

Terms that appear after the main part of the plant name are shown in a smaller font to distinguish them. These descriptive elements give extra information about the plant and may include the **collector's reference**, **authority**, or what colour it is. For example, *Fritillaria thessala* SBEL 443, *Penstemon* 'Sour Grapes' M. Fish, *Lobelia tupa* dark orange.

## Families

**Genera** are grouped into larger groups of related plants called families. Most family names, with the exception of eight familiar names, end with the same group of letters, *-aceae*. While it is still acceptable to use these eight exceptions, the modern trend adopted in the *RHS Plant Finder* is to use alternative names with *–aceae* endings. The families concerned are *Compositae* (*Asteraceae*), *Cruciferae* (*Brassicaceae*), *Gramineae* (*Poaceae*), *Guttiferae* (*Clusiaceae*), *Labiatae* (*Lamiaceae*), *Leguminosae* (split here into *Caesalpiniaceae*, *Mimosaceae* and *Papilionaceae*), *Palmae* (*Arecaceae*) and *Umbelliferae* (*Apiceae*).

Apart from these exceptions we now follow (from 2010) *Mabberley's Plant Book* (3rd edition).

## Genus (plural – genera)

Genera used in the *RHS Plant Finder* are almost always those given in Brummitt's *Vascular Plant*

*Families and Genera*. For spellings and genders of generic names, Greuter's *Names in Current Use for Extant Plant Genera* has also been consulted. See **Botanical Names**.

## GREX

Within orchids, hybrids of the same parentage, regardless of how alike they are, are given a grex name. Individuals can be selected, given cultivar names and propagated vegetatively. For example, *Pleione* Versailles gx 'Bucklebury', where Versailles is the grex name and 'Bucklebury' is a selected **cultivar**.

## GROUP

This is a collective name for a group of cultivars within a genus with similar characteristics. The word Group is always included and, where cited with a cultivar name, it is enclosed in brackets, for example, *Actaea simplex* (Atropurpurea Group) 'Brunette', where 'Brunette' is a distinct cultivar in a group of purple-leaved cultivars.

Another example of a Group is *Rhododendron polycladum* Scintillans Group. In this case *Rhododendron scintillans* was a species that is now botanically 'sunk' within *R. polycladum*, but it is still recognised horticulturally as a Group.

Group names are also used for swarms of hybrids with the same parentage, for example, *Rhododendron* Polar Bear Group. These were formerly treated as **grex** names, a term now used only for orchids. A single clone from the Group may be given the same cultivar name, for example, *Rhododendron* 'Polar Bear'.

## HARDINESS

Hardiness ratings are shown for **Award of Garden Merit** plants. The categories used are as follows:

H1 = plants requiring heated glass in the British Isles
H2 = plants requiring unheated glass in the British Isles
H3 = plants hardy outside in some regions of the British Isles or in particular situations, or which, while usually grown outside in summer, need frost-free protection in winter (eg. dahlias)
H4 = plants hardy throughout the British Isles
H1-2, H2-3, H3-4 = plants intermediate between the two ratings given
H1+3 = requiring heated glass; may be grown outside in summer

## HYBRIDS

Some species, when grown together, in the wild or in cultivation, are found to interbreed and form hybrids. In some instances a hybrid name is coined, for example hybrids between *Primula hirsuta* and *P. minima* are given the name *Primula* × *forsteri*, the multiplication sign indicating hybrid origin. Hybrid formulae that quote the parentage of the hybrid are used where a unique name has not been coined, for example *Rhododendron calophytum* × *R. praevernum*. In hybrid formulae you will find parents in alphabetical order, with the male (m) and female (f) parent indicated where known. Hybrids between different genera are also possible, for example × *Mahoberberis* is the name given to hybrids between *Mahonia* and *Berberis*.

There are also a few special-case hybrids called graft hybrids, where the tissues of two plants are physically rather than genetically mixed. These are indicated by an addition rather than a multiplication sign, so *Laburnum* + *Cytisus* becomes + *Laburnocytisus*.

## ICNCP

The ICNCP is the International Code of Nomenclature for Cultivated Plants. First published in 1959, the most recent (8th) edition was published in 2009.

**Cultivar** names that do not conform to this Code, and for which there is no valid alternative, are flagged I (for invalid). This code states that the minimum requirement is for a cultivar name to be given in conjunction with the name of the genus. However, in the *RHS Plant Finder* we choose to give as full a name as possible to give the gardener and botanist more information about the plant, following the Recommendation in the Code.

## NOTES ON NOMENCLATURE AND IDENTIFICATION

The **Notes on Nomenclature and Identification**, starting on p.27, give further information for names that are complex or may be confusing. See also **Advisory Committee on Nomenclature and Taxonomy**.

## PLANT BREEDERS' RIGHTS

Plants covered by an *active* grant of Plant Breeders' Rights (PBR) are indicated throughout the Plant Directory. Grants indicated are those awarded by both UK and EU Plant Variety Rights offices. Because grants can both come into force and lapse at any time, this book can only aim to represent the situation at one point in time, but it is hoped that this will act as a useful guide to growers and gardeners. UK grants represent the position as of the end of December 2009 and EU grants as of the end of October 2009. We do not give any indication where PBR grants may be pending.

To obtain PBR protection, a new plant must be registered and pass tests for distinctness, uniformity and stability under an approved name. This approved name, under the rules of the **ICNCP**, established by a legal process, has to be regarded as the cultivar name. Increasingly however, these approved names are a code or "nonsense" name and are therefore often unpronounceable and meaningless, so the plants are given other names designed to attract sales when they are released. These secondary names are often referred to as selling names but are officially termed **trade designations**.

For further information on UK PBR contact:
**Plant Variety Rights Office, White House Lane, Huntingdon Road, Cambridge CB3 0LF**
**Tel: (01223) 342396**
**Fax: (01223) 342386.**
**Website: www.defra.gov.uk/planth/pvs/default.htm**

For details of plants covered by EU Community Rights contact:
**Community Plant Variety Office (CPVO),**
**3 Boulevard Maréchal Foch, BP 10121**
**FR-49101 Angers, Cedex 02, France**
**Tel: 00 33 (02) 41 25 64 00**
**Fax: 00 33 (02) 41 25 64 10**
**Website: www.cpvo.europa.eu**

The *RHS Plant Finder* takes no responsibility for ensuring that nurseries selling plants with PBR are licensed to do so.

## Reverse Synonyms

It is likely that users of this book will come across names in certain genera that they did not expect to find. This may be because species have been transferred from another genus (or **genera**). In the list of **Reverse Synonyms** on p.37, the name on the left-hand side is that of an accepted genus to which species have been transferred from the genus on the right. Sometimes all species will have been transferred, but in many cases only a few will be affected. Consulting **Reverse Synonyms** enables users to find the genera from which species have been transferred. Where the right-hand genus is found in the Plant Directory, the movement of species becomes clear through the cross-references in the nursery code column.

## Selling Names

See **Trade Designations**

## Series

With seed-raised plants and some popular vegetatively-propagated plants, especially bedding plants and pot plants such as *Petunia* or *Impatiens*, Series have become increasingly popular. A Series contains a number of similar cultivars, but differs from a **Group** in that it is a marketing device, with cultivars added to create a range of flower colours in plants of similar habit. Individual colour elements within a series may be represented by slightly different cultivars over the years.

The word Series is always included and, where cited with a cultivar name it is enclosed in brackets, for example *Aquilegia* 'Robin' (Songbird Series). The Series name usually follows the rest of the plant name, but sometimes in this book we list it before the cultivar name in order to group members of a series together when they occur next to one another on the page.

## Species

See under **Botanical Names**

## Subspecies

See under **Botanical Names**

## Synonyms

Although the ideal is for each species or cultivar to have only one name, anyone dealing with plants soon comes across a situation where one plant has received two or more names, or two plants have received the same name. In each case, only one name and application, for reasons of precision and stability, can be regarded as correct. Additional names are known as synonyms. Further information on synonyms and why plants change names is available in *Guide to Plant Names*. See the introduction to this glossary for details of how to request a copy.

See also **Reverse Synonyms**.

## Trade Designations

A **trade designation** is the name used to market a plant when the cultivar name is considered unsuitable for selling purposes. It is styled in a different typeface and without single quotation marks.

In the case of **Plant Breeders' Rights** it is a legal requirement for the cultivar name to appear with the trade designation on a label at the point of sale. Most plants are sold under only one trade designation, but some, especially roses, are sold under a number of names, particularly when cultivars are introduced from other countries. Usually, the correct cultivar name is the only way to ensure that the same plant is not bought unwittingly under two or more different trade designations. The *RHS Plant Finder* follows the recommendations of the **ICNCP** when dealing with trade designations and PBR. These are always to quote the cultivar name and trade designation together and to style the trade designation in a different typeface, without single quotation marks.

## TRANSLATIONS

When a cultivar name is translated from the language of first publication, the translation is regarded as a **trade designation** and styled accordingly. We endeavour to recognise the original cultivar name in every case and to give an English translation where it is in general use.

## VARIEGATED PLANTS

Following a suggestion from the Variegated Plant Group of the Hardy Plant Society, a (v) is cited after those plants which are "variegated". The dividing line between variegation and less distinct colour marking is necessarily arbitrary and plants with light veins, pale, silver or dark zones, or leaves flushed in paler colours, are not shown as being variegated unless there is an absolutely sharp distinction between paler and darker zones.

For further details of the Variegated Plant Group, please write to:

**Jerry Webb, Esq.,**
**17 Heron Way, Minster Heights,**
**Ilminster TA19 0BX**

## VARIETY

See under **Botanical Names** and **Cultivar**

*'The question of nomenclature is always a vexed one. The only thing certain is, that it is impossible to please everyone.'*

W.J. BEAN – PREFACE TO FIRST EDITION OF *Trees & Shrubs Hardy in the British Isles*

**HORTAX**
The Horticultural Taxonomy Group

If you have an interest in the names of garden plants and wish to learn more or would like to make a comment about the International Code of Nomenclature for Cultivated Plants (ICNCP) visit the HORTAX website: www.hortax.org.uk

# Symbols and Abbreviations

## Symbols Appearing to the Left of the Name

| | |
|---|---|
| * | Name not validated. Not listed in the appropriate International Registration Authority checklist nor in works cited in the Bibliography. For fuller discussion see p.15 |
| I | Invalid name. See *International Code of Botanical Nomenclature 2000* and *International Code of Nomenclature for Cultivated Plants 2004*. For fuller discussion see p.15 |
| N | Refer to Notes on Nomenclature and Identification on p.27 |
| § | Plant listed elsewhere in the Plant Directory under a synonym |
| × | Hybrid genus |
| + | Graft hybrid genus |

## Symbols Appearing to the Right of the Name

| | |
|---|---|
| ✿ | Plant Heritage (NCCPG) National Plant Collection® exists for all or part of this genus. Provisional Collections appear in brackets. Full details of the Plant Heritage Collections are found in the *2010 National Plant Collections® Directory* available from: www.plantheritage.com or Plant Heritage, 12 Home Farm, Loseley Park, Guildford, Surrey GU3 1HS |
| ♀H4 | The Royal Horticultural Society's Award of Garden Merit, see p.15 |
| (d) | double-flowered |
| (F) | Fruit |
| (f) | female |
| (m) | male |
| (v) | variegated plant, see p.19 |
| PBR | Plant Breeders Rights see p.17 |
| **new** | New plant entry in this edition |

For abbreviations relating to individual genera see **Classification of Genera** p.32
For **Collectors' References** see p.24
For symbols used in the **Nurseries** section see p.833

## Symbols and Abbreviations used as Part of the Name

| | |
|---|---|
| × | hybrid species |
| aff. | affinis (akin to) |
| agg. | aggregate, a single name used to cover a group of very similar plants, regarded by some as separate species |
| ambig. | ambiguous, a name used by two authors for different plants and where it is unclear which is being offered |
| cf. | compare to |
| cl. | clone |
| f. | forma (botanical form) |
| gx | grex |
| sensu lato | in the broadest sense |
| sp. | species |
| subsp. | subspecies |
| subvar. | subvarietas (botanical subvariety) |
| var. | varietas (botanical variety) |

**It is not within the remit of this book to check that nurseries are applying the right names to the right plants or to ensure nurseries selling plants with Plant Breeders' Rights are licensed to do so.**

*Please, never use an old edition*

# Plants

Whatever plant you are looking for, maybe an old favourite or a more unusual cultivar, search here for a list of the suppliers that are closest to you.

# How to Use the Plant Directory

## Nursery Codes

Look up the plant you require in the alphabetical Plant Directory. Against each plant you will find one or more four-letter codes, for example WCru, each code represents one nursery offering that plant. The first letter of each code indicates the main area of the country in which the nursery is situated. For this geographical key, refer to the **Nursery Codes and Symbols** on p.832.

Turn to the **Nursery Details by Code** starting on p.836 where, in alphabetical order of codes, you will find details of each nursery which offers the plant in question. If you wish to visit any nursery, you may find its location on one of the maps (following p.945). Please note, however, that not all nurseries, especially mail order only nurseries, choose to be shown on the maps. For a fuller explanation of how to use the nursery listings please turn to p.833. **Always check that the nursery you select has the plant in stock before you set out.**

## Plants with more than 30 Suppliers

In some cases, against the plant name you will see the term 'Widely available' instead of a nursery code. If we were to include every plant listed by all nurseries, the *RHS Plant Finder* would become unmanageably bulky. We therefore ask nurseries to restrict their entries to those plants that are not already well represented. As a result, if more than 30 nurseries offer any plant the Directory gives no nursery codes and the plant is listed instead as being 'Widely available'.

You should have little difficulty in locating these in local nurseries or garden centres. However, if you are unable to find such plants, we will be pleased to send a full list of all the nurseries that we have on file as stockists. To obtain a list, please see the Introduction on p.4 or go to www.rhs.org.uk/rhsplantfinder/.

## Finding Fruit, Vegetables and Herbs

You will need to search for these by their botanical names. Common names are cross-referenced to their botanical names in the Plant Directory.

## If you have Difficulty Finding your Plant

If you cannot immediately find the plant you seek, look through the various species of the genus. You may be using an incomplete name. The problem is most likely to arise in very large genera such as *Phlox* where there are a number of possible species, each with a large number of cultivars. A search through the whole genus may well bring success. Please note that, for space reasons, the following are not listed in the Plant Directory: annuals, orchids, except hardy terrestrial orchids; cacti, except hardy cacti.

## Cross-references

It may be that the plant name you seek is a synonym. Our intention is to list nursery codes only against the correct botanical name. Where you find a synonym you will be cross-referred to the correct name. Occasionally you may find that the correct botanical name to which you have been referred is not listed. This is because it was last listed in an earlier edition as explained below.

## Plants Last Listed in Earlier Editions

It may be that the plant you are seeking has no known suppliers and is thus not listed.

The loss of a plant name from the Directory may arise for a number of reasons – the supplier may have gone out of business, or may not have responded to our latest questionnaire and has therefore been removed from the book. Such plants may well be still available but we have no current knowledge of their whereabouts. Alternatively, some plants may have been misnamed by nurseries in previous editions, but are now appearing under their correct name.

To obtain a listing of plants last listed in earlier editions please see the Introduction on p.4 or go to our website where it is available as a pdf.

*Please, never use an old edition*

# USING THE PLANT DIRECTORY

The main purpose of the Plant Directory is to help the reader correctly identify the plant they seek and find its stockist. Each nursery has a unique identification code which appears to the right of the plant name. Turn to **Nursery Details by Code** on p.836 for the address, opening times and other details of the nursery. The first letter of each nursery code denotes its geographical region. Turn to the map on p.832 to find your region code and then identify the nurseries in your area.

Another purpose of the Directory is to provide more information about the plant through the symbols and other information. For example, if it has an alternative names, is new to this edition or has received the RHS Award of Garden Merit.

## *Euonymus* (*Celastraceae*)

| | Plant name | Nursery codes |
|---|---|---|
| | B&L 12543 | EPla EWes |
| | B&SWJ 4457 | WPGP |
| | CC 4522 | CPLG |
| | ***alatus*** 🏆H4 | Widely available |
| | - B&SWJ 8794 | WCru |
| | - var. ***apterus*** | EPfP |
| | - Chicago Fire | see *E. alatus* 'Timber Creek' |
| | - 'Ciliodentatus' | see *E. alatus* 'Compactus' |
| § | - 'Compactus' 🏆H4 | Widely available |
| § | - 'Fire Ball' | EPfP |
| | - Little Moses = 'Odom' | MBlu |
| * | - 'Macrophyllus' | EPfP |
| | - 'Rudy Haag' | CPMA EPfP |
| | - 'Select' | see *E. alatus* 'Fire Ball' |
| | - 'Silver Cloud' **new** | EPfP |
| § | - 'Timber Creek' | CPMA EPfP MBlu MBri NLar |
| | ***americanus*** | EPfP GIBF MBlu NLar |
| | - 'Evergreen' **new** | EPfP |
| | - narrow-leaved | EPfP NLar |
| | ***atropurpureus*** | EPfP |
| | 'Benkomoki' **new** | MGos |
| | ***bungeanus*** | CMCN EPfP EPla NLar |
| | - 'Dart's Pride' | CPMA EPfP NLar |
| | - 'Fireflame' | EPfP NLar |
| * | - var. ***mongolicus*** | EPfP |
| | - 'Pendulus' | EPfP MBlu SIFN |
| | - var. ***semipersistens*** | CPMA EPla |
| | ***carnosus*** | EPfP NLar |
| | 'Copper Wire' | EMil SPoG |
| | ***cornutus*** var. ***quinquecornutus*** | CPMA EPfP LPan MBlu NBhm NLar SIFN SPoG WPGP WPat |
| | 'Den Haag' | EPfP MBri |
| | ***echinatus*** | EPfP EPla |
| | - BL&M 306 | SLon |
| | ***europaeus*** | Widely available |
| | - f. ***albus*** | CPMA CTho EPfP LTwo NLar |
| | - 'Atropurpureus' | CMCN CTho EPfP MBlu MBri NLar SIFN |
| | - 'Atrorubens' | CPMA |
| | - 'Aucubifolius' (v) | EPfP |
| * | - 'Aureus' | CNat |
| | - 'Brilliant' **new** | EPfP |
| * | - f. ***bulgaricus*** | EPfP |
| | - 'Chrysophyllus' | EPfP MBlu NLar |
| | - 'Howard' | EPfP |
| | - var. ***intermedius*** | ENot EPfP MAsh MBlu NLar |
| | - 'Miss Pinkie' | CEnd CMCN |
| | - 'Pumilis' **new** | EPfP |
| | - 'Red Cascade' 🏆H4 | Widely available |
| | - 'Scarlet Wonder' | CPMA EPfP MBri NLar |
| | - 'Thornhayes' | CTho EPfP |
| I | - 'Variegatus' **new** | EPfP |
| | ***farreri*** | see *E. nanus* |
| | ***fimbriatus*** | EPfP |
| | ***fortunei*** Blondy = 'Interbolwi' PBR (v) | Widely available |

*ABBREVIATIONS*
*To save space a dash indicates that the previous heading is repeated. If written out in full the name would be* Euonymus alatus *'Fire Ball'.*

*NEW*
*Plant new to this edition.*

*DESCRIPTIVE TERM*
*See p.16.*

*SYMBOLS TO THE LEFT OF THE NAME*
*Provides information about the name of the plant. See p.20 for the key.*

*SYMBOLS TO THE RIGHT OF THE NAME*
*Tells you more about the plant itself, e.g.* (v) *indicates that the plant is variegated,* (F) *= fruit. See p.20 for the key.*

*SELLING NAMES*
*See p.18.*

🏆H4
*This plant has received the RHS Award of Garden Merit. See p.15.*

*CROSS-REFERENCES*
*Directs you to the correct name of the plant and the nursery codes. See p.22.*

*NURSERY CODE*
*A unique code identifying each nursery. Turn to p.836 for details of the nurseries.*

*WIDELY AVAILABLE*
*Indicates that more than 30 Plant Finder nurseries supply the plant, and it may be available locally. See p.22.*

*PBR*
*Plant Breeders' Rights. See p.17.*

# Supplementary Keys to the Directory

## Collectors' References

Abbreviations following a plant name, refer to the collector(s) of the plant. These abbreviations are expanded below, with a collector's name or expedition title. For a fuller explanation, see p.16.

A&JW A. & J. Watson
A&L Ala, A.; Lancaster, Roy
AB&S Archibald, James; Blanchard, John W; Salmon, M.
AC Clark, Alan J.
AC&H Apold, J.; Cox, Peter; Hutchison, Peter
AC&W Albury; Cheese, M.; Watson, J.M.
ACE AGS Expedition to China (1994)
ACL Leslie, Alan C.
AER Robinson, Allan
AGS/ES AGS Expedition to Sikkim (1983)
AGSJ AGS Expedition to Japan (1988)
AH Hoog, A.
AIM Avent, Tony Mexico 1994
Airth Airth, Murray
Akagi Akagi Botanical Garden
AL&JS Sharman, Joseph L.; Leslie, Alan C.
ARG Argent, G.C.G.
ARJA Ruksans, J. & Siesums, A.
B Blanchard, John
B&F MA Brown, Robert & Fisher, Rif & Middle Atlas 2007
B L. Beer, Len
B&L Brickell, Christopher D.; Leslie, Alan C.
B&M & BM Brickell, Christopher D.; Mathew, Brian
B&S Bird P. & Salmon M.
B&SWJ Wynn-Jones, Bleddyn; Wynn-Jones, Susan
B&V Burras, K. & Vosa, C.G.
BB Bartholomew, B.
BC Chudziak, W.
BC&W Beckett; Cheese, M.; Watson, J.M.
Beavis Beavis, Derek S.
Berry Berry, P.
Berry & Brako Berry, P. & Brako, Lois
BKBlount Blount, B.K.
BL&M University of Bangor Expedition to NE Nepal
BM Mathew, Brian F.
BM&W Binns, David L.; Mason, M.; Wright, A.
BOA Boardman, P.
Breedlove Breedlove, D.
BR Rushbrooke, Ben
BS Smith, Basil
BSBE Bowles Scholarship Botanical Expedition (1963)
BSSS Crûg Expedition, Jordan (1991)
Bu Bubert, S.
Burtt Burtt, Brian L.
C Cole, Desmond T.
C&C Cox, P.A. & Cox, K.N.E.
C&Cu Cox, K.N.E. & Cubey, J.
C&H Cox, Peter; Hutchison, Peter
C&K Chamberlain & Knott
C&R Christian & Roderick
C&S Clark, Alan; Sinclair, Ian W.J.
C&V K.N.E. Cox & S. Vergera
C&W Cheese, M.; Watson, J.M.
CC Chadwell, Christopher
CC&H Chamberlain, David F.; Cox, Peter; Hutchison, P.
CC&McK Chadwell, Christopher; McKelvie, A.
CC&MR Chadwell, Christopher; Ramsay
CCH&H Chamberlain, D.F.; Cox, P.; Hutchison, P.; Hootman, S.
CCH&H Chamberlain, Cox, Hootman & Hutchison
CD&R Compton, J.; D'Arcy, J.; Rix, E.M.
CDB Brickell, Christopher D.
CDC Coode, Mark J.E.; Dockrill, Alexander
CDC&C Compton, D'Arcy, Christopher & Coke
CDPR Compton, D'Arcy, Pope & Rix
CE&H Christian, P.J.; Elliott; Hoog
CEE Chengdu Edinburgh Expedition China 1991
CGV Vosa, Canio
CGW Grey-Wilson, Christopher
CH Christian, P. & Hoog, A.
CH&M Cox, P.; Hutchison, P.; Maxwell-MacDonald, D.
CHP&W Kashmir Botanical Expedition
CL Lovell, Chris
CLD Chungtien, Lijiang & Dali Exped. China (1990)
CM&W Cheese M., Mitchel J. & Watson, J.
CN&W Clark; Neilson; Wilson

CNDS Nelson, C. & Sayers D.
Cooper Cooper, R.E.
Cox Cox, Peter A.
CPC Cobblewood Plant Collection
CPN Compton, James
CS Stapleton, Christopher
CSE Cyclamen Society Expedition (1990)
CT Teune, Carla
CWJ Colley, Finlay; Wynn-Jones, Bleddyn, Taiwan 2007
Dahl Dahl, Sally
DBG Denver Botanic Garden, Colorado
DC Cheshire, David
DF Fox, D.
DG Green, D.
DHTU Hinkley, D., Turkey 2000
DJH Hinkley, Dan
DJHC Hinkley China
DJHV Hinkley, Dan, Vietnam
DM Millais, David
Doleshy Doleshy, F.L.
DS&T Drake, Sharman J.; Thompson
DWD Rose, D.
DZ Zummell, D.
ECN Nelson, E. Charles
EDHCH Hammond, Eric D.
EGM Millais, T.
EKB Balls, Edward K.
EM East Malling Research Station
EMAK Edinburgh Makalu Expedition (1991)
EMR Rix, E.Martyn
EN Needham, Edward F.
ENF Fuller, E. Nigel
ETE Edinburgh Taiwan Expedition (1993)
ETOT Kirkham, T.S.; Flanagan, Mark
F Forrest, G.
F&M Fernandez & Mendoza, Mexico
F&W Watson, J.; Flores, A.
Farrer Farrer, Reginald
FK Kinmonth, Fergus W.
FMB Bailey, F.M.
G Gardner, Martin F.
G&K Gardner, Martin F.; Knees, Sabina G.
G&P Gardner, Martin F.; Page, Christopher N.
GDJ Dumont, Gerard
GG Gusman, G.
GS Sherriff, George
Green Green, D.
Guitt Guittoneau, G.G.
Guiz Guizhou Expedition (1985)
GWJ Goddard, Sally; Wynne-Jones, Bleddyn & Susan
G-W&P Grey-Wilson, Christopher; Phillips
H Huggins, Paul
H&B Hilliard, Olive M.; Burtt, Brian L.
H&D Howick, C.; Darby
H&M Howick, Charles; McNamara, William A.
H&W Hedge, Ian C.; Wendelbo, Per W.
Harry Smith Smith, K.A.Harry
Hartside Hartside Nursery
HCM Heronswood Expedition to Chile (1998)
HECC Hutchison, Evans, Cox, P., Cox, K.
Hird Hird
HH&K Hannay, S&S & Kingsbury, N
HLMS Springate, L.S.
HM&S Halliwell, B., Mason, D. & Smallcombe
HOA Hoog, Anton
Hummel Hummel, D.
HW&E Wendelbo, Per; Hedge, I.; Ekberg, L.
HWEL Hirst, J.Michael; Webster, D.
HWJ Crûg Heronswood Joint Expedition
HWJCM Crûg Heronswood Expedition
HWJK Crûg Heronswood Expedition, East Nepal (2002)
HZ Zetterlund, Henrik
ICE Instituto de Investigaciónes Ecológicas Chiloé & RBGE
IDS International Dendrological Society
ISI Int. Succulent Introductions
J&JA Archibald, James; Archibald, Jennifer
J. Jurasek Jurasek, J.
JCA Archibald, James
JE Jack Elliott
JJ Jackson, J.
JJ&JH Halda, J.; Halda, J.
JJH Halda, Joseph J.
JLS Sharman, J.L.
JM-MK Mahr, J.; Kammerlander, M.
JMT Mann Taylor, J.
JN Nielson, Jens
JR Russell, J.
JRM Marr, John
JW Watson, J.M.
K Kirkpatrick, George
K&LG Gillanders, Kenneth; Gillanders, L.
K&Mc Kirkpatrick, George; McBeath, Ronald J.D.
K&P Josef Kopec, Milan Prasil
K&T Kurashige, Y.; Tsukie, S.
KC Cox, Kenneth
KEKE Kew/Edinburgh Kanchenjunga Expedition (1989)
KGB Kunming/Gothenburg Botanical Expedition (1993)
KM Marsh, K.
KR Rushforth, K.D.
KRW Wooster, K.R. (distributed after his death by Kath Dryden)
KW Kingdon-Ward, F.
KWJ Crûg-World of Ferns Joint Expedition, Vietnam 2007
L Lancaster, C. Roy
L&S Ludlow, Francis; Sherriff, George
LA Long Ashton Research Station clonal selection scheme
LB Bird P., Salmon, M.
LEG Lesotho Edinburgh/Gothenburg Expedition (1997)
Lismore Lismore Nursery, Breeder's Number

| | |
|---|---|
| LM&S | Leslie, Mattern & Sharman |
| LP | Palmer, W.J.L. |
| LS&E | Ludlow, Frank; Sherriff, George; Elliott, E. E. |
| LS&H | Ludlow, Frank; Sherriff, George; Hicks, J. H. |
| LS&T | Ludlow, Frank; Sherriff, George; Taylor, George |
| M&PS | Mike & Polly Stone |
| M&T | Mathew; Tomlinson |
| Mac&W | McPhail & Watson |
| McB | McBeath, R.J.D. |
| McLaren | McLaren, H.D. |
| MDM | Myers, Michael D. |
| MECC | Scottish Rock Garden Club, Nepal (1997) |
| MESE | Alpine Garden Society Expedition, Greece 1999 |
| MF | Foster, Maurice |
| MH | Heasman, Matthew T. |
| MK | Kammerlander, Michael |
| MP | Pavelka, Mojmir |
| MPF | Frankis, M.P. |
| MS | Salmon, M. |
| MS&CL | Salmon, M.; Lovell, C. |
| MSF | Fillan, M.S. |
| NICE | North India Expedition 1997 |
| NJM | Macer, N.J. |
| NNS | Ratko, Ron |
| NS | Turland, Nick |
| NVFDE | Northern Vietnam First Darwin Expedition |
| Og | Ogisu, Mikinori |
| OS | Sonderhousen, O. |
| P. Bon | Bonavia, P. |
| P&C | Paterson, David S.; Clarke, Sidney |
| P&W | Polastri; Watson, J. M. |
| PB | Bird, Peter |
| PC&H | Pattison, G.; Catt, P.; Hickson, M. |
| PD | Davis, Peter H. |
| PF | Furse, Paul |
| PJC | Christian, Paul J. |
| PJC&AH | P.J. Christian & A. Hogg |
| PNMK | Nicholls, P.; Kammerlander, M. |
| Polunin | Polunin, Oleg |
| Pras | Prasil, M. |
| PS&W | Polunin, Oleg; Sykes, William; Williams, John |
| PW | Wharton, Peter |
| R | Rock, J.F.C. |
| RB | Brown, R. |
| RBS | Brown, Ray, Sakharin Island |
| RCB AM | Brown, Robert, Expedition to Armenia |
| RCB/Arg | Brown, Robert, Argentina, (2002) |
| RCB E | Brown, Robert, Expedition to Spain (Andalucia) |
| RCB/Eq | Brown, Robert, Ecuador, (1988) |
| RCB RA | Brown, Robert |
| RCB RL | Brown, Robert, Expedition to Lebanon |
| RCB/TQ | Brown, Robert, Turkey (2001) |
| RH | Hancock, R. |
| RKMP | Ruksans, J., Krumins, A., Kitts, M., Paivel, A. |
| RM | Ruksans, J. & Kitts, M. |
| RMRP | Rocky Mountain Rare Plants, Denver, Colorado |
| RS | Suckow, Reinhart |
| RSC | Richard Somer Cocks |
| RV | Richard Valder |
| RWJ | Crûg Farm-Rickards Ferns Expedition to Taiwan (2003) |
| S&B | Blanchard, J.W.; Salmon, M. |
| S&F | Salmon, M. & Fillan, M. |
| S&L | Sinclair, Ian W.J.; Long, David G. |
| S&SH | Sheilah and Spencer Hannay |
| Sandham | Sandham, John |
| SB&L | Salmon, Bird and Lovell |
| SBEC | Sino-British Expedition to Cangshan |
| SBEL | Sino-British Lijiang Expedition |
| SBQE | Sino-British Expedition to Quinghai |
| Sch | Schilling, Anthony D. |
| SD | Sashal Dayal |
| SDR | Rankin, Stella; Rankin, David |
| SEH | Hootman, Steve |
| SEP | Swedish Expedition to Pakistan |
| SF | Forde, P. |
| SG | Salmon, M. & Guy, P. |
| SH | Hannay, Spencer |
| Sich | Simmons, Erskine, Howick & Mcnamara |
| SJ | Johansson, Stellan |
| SLIZE | Swedish-Latvian-Iranian Zagros Expedition to Iran (May 1988) |
| SOJA | Kew / Quarryhill Expedition to Southern Japan |
| SS&W | Stainton, J.D.Adam; Sykes, William; Williams, John |
| SSNY | Sino-Scottish Expedition to NW Yunnan (1992) |
| T | Taylor, Nigel P. |
| T&K | Taylor, Nigel P.; Knees, Sabina |
| TH | Hudson, T. |
| TS&BC | Smythe, T and Cherry, B |
| TSS | Spring Smyth, T.L.M. |
| TW | Tony Weston |
| USDAPI | US Department of Agriculture Plant Index Number |
| USDAPQ | US Dept. of Agriculture Plant Quarantine Number |
| USNA | United States National Arboretum |
| VHH | Vernon H. Heywood |
| VV | Victor, David |
| W | Wilson, Ernest H. |
| WM | McLewin, William |
| Woods | Woods, Patrick J.B. |
| Wr | Wraight, David & Anke |
| WWJ | Wharton, Peter; Wynn-Jones, Bleddyn & Susan |
| Yu | Yu, Tse-tsun |

# NOTES ON NOMENCLATURE AND IDENTIFICATION

These notes refer to plants in the Plant Directory that are marked with a 'N' to the left of the name. 'Bean Supplement' refers to W.J. Bean *Trees & Shrubs Hardy in the British Isles* (Supplement to the 8th edition) edited by D L Clarke 1988.

***Acer davidii*** **'Ernest Wilson' and** ***A. davidii*** **'George Forrest'**
These cultivars should be grafted in order to retain the characteristics of the original clones. However, many plants offered under these names are seed-raised.

***Acer palmatum*** **'Sango-kaku' / 'Senkaki'**
Two or more clones are offered under these names. *A. palmatum* 'Eddisbury' is similar with brighter coral stems.

***Achillea ptarmica*** **The Pearl Group /** ***A. ptarmica*** **(The Pearl Group) 'Boule de Neige' /** ***A. ptarmica*** **(The Pearl Group) 'The Pearl'**
In the recent trial of achilleas at Wisley, only one of the several stocks submitted as 'The Pearl' matched the original appearance of this plant according to Graham Stuart Thomas, this being from Wisley's own stock. At rather less than 60cm (2ft), this needed little support, being the shortest of the plants bearing this name, with slightly grey, not glossy dark green, leaves and a non-invasive habit. This has been designated as the type for this cultivar and only this clone should bear the cultivar name 'The Pearl'. The Pearl Group covers all other double-flowered clones of this species, including seed-raised plants which are markedly inferior, sometimes scarcely double, often invasive and usually needing careful staking. It has been claimed that 'The Pearl' was a re-naming of Lemoine's 'Boule de Neige' but not all authorities agree: all plants submitted to the Wisley trial as 'Boule de Neige' were different from each other, not the same clone as Wisley's 'The Pearl' and referrable to The Pearl Group.

***Anemone nemorosa*** **'Alba Plena'**
This name is used for several double white forms including *A. nemorosa* 'Flore Pleno' and *A. nemorosa* 'Vestal'.

***Artemisia ludoviciana*** **subsp.** ***ludoviciana*** **var.** ***latiloba*** **/** ***A. ludoviciana*** **'Valerie Finnis'**
Leaves of the former are glabrous at maturity, those of the latter are not.

***Artemisia stelleriana*** **'Boughton Silver'**
This was thought to be the first validly published name for this plant, 'Silver Brocade' having been published earlier but invalidly in an undated publication. However, an earlier valid publication for the cultivar name 'Mori' has subsequently been found for the same plant. A proposal to conserve 'Boughton Silver' has been tabled because of its more widespread use.

***Aster amellus*** **Violet Queen**
It is probable that more than one cultivar is sold under this name.

***Aster dumosus***
Many of the asters listed under *A. novi-belgii* contain varying amounts of *A. dumosus* blood in their parentage. It is not possible to allocate these to one species or the other and they are therefore listed under *A. novi-belgii*.

***Aster × frikartii*** **'Mönch'**
The true plant is very rare in British gardens. Most plants are another form of *A. × frikartii*, usually 'Wunder von Stäfa'.

***Aster novi-belgii***
See note under *A. dumosus*. *A. laevis* is also involved in the parentage of most cultivars.

***Berberis buxifolia*** **'Nana' misapplied / 'Pygmaea'**
See explanation in Bean Supplement.

***Betula utilis*** **var.** ***jacquemontii***
Plants are often the clones *B. utilis* var. *jacquemontii* 'Inverleith' or *B. utilis* var. *jacquemontii* 'Doorenbos'

***Brachyscome***
Originally published as *Brachyscome* by Cassini who later revised his spelling to *Brachycome*. The original spelling has been internationally adopted.

***Calamagrostis × acutiflora*** **'Karl Foerster'**
*C. × acutiflora* 'Stricta' differs in being 15cm taller, 10–15 days earlier flowering with a less fluffy inflorescence.

***Calceolaria integrifolia sensu lato***
Christine Ehrhart (*Systematic Botany*. (2005. 30(2):383–411) has demonstrated that this is a complex involving nine distinct species (*C. andina, C. angustifolia, C. auriculata, C. georgiana, C. integrifolia sensu stricto, C. rubiginosa, C. talcana, C. verbascifolia* and *C. viscosissima*). However, it is not yet clear to which species plants in cultivation belong or whether they are hybrids.

***Caltha polypetala***
This name is often applied to a large-flowered variant of *C. palustris*. The true species has more (7–10) petals.

***Camassia leichtlinii*** **'Alba'**
The true cultivar has blueish-white, not cream flowers.

***Camassia leichtlinii*** **'Plena'**
This has starry, transparent green-white flowers; creamy-white 'Semiplena' is sometimes offered under this name.

***Campanula lactiflora* 'Alba'**
This refers to the pure white-flowered clone, not to blueish- or greyish-white flowered plants, nor to seed-raised plants.

***Canna***
Species names marked 'N' are among those sometimes included within *Canna indica* L. See *Blumea* 53:247–318 for a complete list.

***Carex morrowii* 'Variegata'**
*C. oshimensis* 'Evergold' is sometimes sold under this name.

***Carya illinoinensis***
The correct spelling of this name is discussed in *Baileya*, **10**(1) (1962).

***Cassinia retorta***
Now included within *C. leptophylla*. A valid infra-specific epithet has yet to be published.

***Ceanothus* 'Italian Skies'**
Many plants under this name are not true to name.

***Chamaecyparis lawsoniana* 'Columnaris Glauca'**
Plants under this name might be *C. lawsoniana* 'Columnaris' or a new invalidly named cultivar.

***Clematis chrysocoma***
The true *C. chrysocoma* is a non-climbing erect plant with dense yellow down on the young growth, still uncommon in cultivation.

***Clematis montana***
This name should be used for the typical white-flowered variety only. Pink-flowered variants are referable to *C. montana* var. *rubens*.

***Clematis* 'Victoria'**
Raised by Cripps (1867). There is also a Latvian cultivar of this name with petals with a central white bar in the collection of Janis Ruplēns which is probably, though not certainly, of his own raising.

***Colchicum* 'Autumn Queen'**
Entries here might refer to the slightly different *C.* 'Prinses Astrid'.

***Cornus* 'Norman Hadden'**
See note in Bean Supplement, p.184.

***Cotoneaster dammeri***
Plants sold under this name are usually *C. dammeri* 'Major'.

***Cotoneaster frigidus* 'Cornubia'**
According to Hylmø this cultivar, like all other variants of this species, is fully deciduous. Several evergreen cotoneasters are also grown under this name; most are clones of *C.* × *watereri* or *C. salicifolius*.

***Crataegus coccinea***
*C. intricata*, *C. pedicellata* and *C. biltmoreana* are occasionally supplied under this name.

***Crocus cartwrightianus* 'Albus'**
The plant offered is the true cultivar and not *C. hadriaticus*.

***Dianthus* fringed pink**
*D.* 'Old Fringed Pink' and *D.* 'Old Fringed White' are also sometimes sold under this name.

***Dianthus* 'Musgrave's Pink' (p)**
This is the registered name of this white-flowered cultivar.

***Epilobium glabellum* misapplied**
Plants under this name are not *E. glabellum* but are close to *E. wilsonii* Petrie or perhaps a hybrid of it.

***Erodium glandulosum***
Plants under this name are often hybrids.

***Erodium guttatum***
Doubtfully in commerce; plants under this name are usually *E. heteradenum, E. cheilanthifolium* or hybrids.

***Fagus sylvatica* Atropurpurea Group / Cuprea Group**
It is desirable to provide a name, Cuprea Group, for less richly coloured forms, used in historic landscapes before the purple clones appeared.

***Fagus sylvatica* 'Pendula'**
This name refers to the Knap Hill clone, the most common weeping form in English gardens. Other clones occur, particularly in Cornwall and Ireland.

***Fuchsia loxensis***
For a comparison of the true species with the hybrids 'Speciosa' and 'Loxensis' commonly grown under this name, see Boullemier's Check List (2nd ed.) p.268.

***Geum* 'Borisii'**
This name refers to cultivars of *G. coccineum* Sibthorp & Smith, especially *G.* 'Werner Arends' and not to *G.* × *borisii* Kelleper.

***Halimium halimifolium***
Plants under this name are sometimes *H.* × *pauanum* or *H.* × *santae*.

***Hebe* 'Carl Teschner'**
See note in Bean Supplement, p.264.

***Hedera helix* 'Caenwoodiana' / 'Pedata'**
Some authorities consider these to be distinct cultivars while others think them different morphological forms of the same unstable clone.

***Hedera helix* 'Oro di Bogliasco'**
Priority between this name and 'Jubiläum Goldherz' and 'Goldheart' has yet to be finally resolved.

***Helleborus* × *hybridus* / *H. orientalis* misapplied**
The name *H.* × *hybridus* for acaulescent hellebore hybrids does not seem to follow the *International Code of Botanical Nomenclature* Article H.3.2 requiring one of the parent species to be designated and does not seem to have been typified, contrary to Article 7 of the Code. However, the illustration accompanying the original description in Vilmorin's *Blumengärtnerei* 3(1): 27 (1894) shows that one parent of the cross must have been *H. guttatus*, now treated as part of *H. orientalis*. Taking this illustration as the type for this hybrid species makes it possible to retain *H.* × *hybridus* formally as a hybrid binomial (rather than *H. hybridus* as in a previous edition), as the Code's requirement to distinguish one parent is now met.

***Hemerocallis fulva* 'Kwanso', 'Kwanso Variegata', 'Flore Pleno' and 'Green Kwanso'**
For a discussion of these plants see *The Plantsman*, 7(2).

***Heuchera villosa* 'Palace Purple'**
This cultivar name refers only to plants with deep purple-red foliage. Seed-raised plants of inferior colouring should not be offered under this name.

***Hosta montana***
This name refers only to plants long grown in Europe, which differ from *H. elata.*

***Hydrangea macrophylla* Teller Series**
This is used both as a descriptive common name for Lacecap hydrangeas (German *teller* = plate, referring to the more or less flat inflorescence) and for the series of hybrids raised by Wädenswil in Switzerland bearing German names of birds. It is not generally possible to link a hydrangea described by the series name plus a colour description (e.g. Teller Blau, Teller Rosa, Teller Rot) to a single cultivar.

***Hypericum fragile***
The true *H. fragile* is probably not available from British nurseries.

***Hypericum* 'Gemo'**
Either a selection of *H. prolificum* or *H. prolificum* × *H. densiflorum.*

***Ilex* × *altaclerensis***
The argument for this spelling is given by Susyn Andrews, *The Plantsman*, 5(2) and is not superseded by the more recent comments in the Supplement to Bean's Trees and Shrubs.

***Iris***
Apart from those noted below, cultivar names marked 'N' are not registered. The majority of those marked 'I' have been previously used for a different cultivar.

***Iris histrioides* 'Major'**
Two clones are offered under this name, the true one pale blue with darker spotting on the falls, the incorrect one violet-blue with almost horizontal falls.

***Juniperus* × *media***
This name is illegitimate if applied to hybrids of *J. chinensis* × *J. sabina*, having been previously used for a different hybrid (P.A. Schmidt, *IDS Yearbook 1993*, 47–48). Because of its importance to gardeners, a proposal to conserve its present use was tabled but subsequently rejected.

***Lavandula spica***
This name is classed as a name to be rejected (*nomen rejiciendum*) by the *International Code of Botanical Nomenclature.*

***Lavatera olbia* and *L. thuringiaca***
Although *L. olbia* is usually shrubby and *L. thuringiaca* usually herbaceous, both species are very variable. Cultivars formerly ascribed to one species or the other have been shown to be hybrids and are referable to the recently-named hybrid species *L.* × *clementii.*

***Lobelia* 'Russian Princess'**
This name, originally for a pink-flowered, green-leaved cultivar, is now generally applied to a purple-flowered, dark-leaved cultivar that seems to lack a valid name.

***Lonicera periclymenum* 'Serotina'**
See note in Bean Supplement, p.315.

***Lonicera sempervirens* f. *sulphurea***
Plants in the British Isles usually a yellow-flowered form of *L. periclymenum.*

***Malus domestica* 'Dummellor's Seedling'**
The phonetic spelling 'Dumelow's Seedling' contravenes the ICBN ruling on orthography, i.e. that, except for intentional latinisations, commemorative names should be based on the original spelling of the person's name (Article 60.11). The spelling adopted here is that used on the gravestone of the raiser in Leicestershire.

***Meconopsis* Fertile Blue Group**
This Group comprises seed-raised and intrinsically perennial tall blue poppies of as yet indeterminate origin. The only cultivars so far established are 'Lingholm' (synonyms 'Blue Ice' and 'Correnie') and 'Kingsbarns'.

***Meconopsis napaulensis* misapplied**
In his revision of the evergreen monocarpic species, Dr C. Grey-Wilson has established that *M. napaulensis* DC., a dwarfish yellow-flowered species not usually more than 1.1m tall and endemic to C Nepal, is not currently in cultivation. The well-known plants of gardens which pass for *M. napaulensis* are hybrids, for the present to be known as *M. napaulensis* misapplied. The parents of the hybrids are *M. staintonii* (from W Nepal) and *M. paniculata* (a yellow-flowered species with a purple stigma) or *M. staintonii* and *M. regia* or a complex mixture of all three species. *M. staintonii*, newly described by C. Grey-Wilson (*Bot. Mag.* (2006) 23(2):176–209), is a tall (to 2.5m), robust species with red or pink flowers and a dark green stigma, near in appearance to *M. napaulensis* of gardens, but less so to true *M. napaulensis.* As *M. staintonii*, like its near relatives, readily hybridises in cultivation, it is rarely seen in an unadulterated form.

***Melissa officinalis* 'Variegata'**
The true cultivar of this name has leaves striped with white.

***Osmanthus heterophyllus* 'Gulftide'**
Probably correctly *O.* × *fortunei* 'Gulftide'.

***Pelargonium* 'Lass o' Gowrie'**
The American plant of this name has pointed, not rounded leaf lobes.

***Pelargonium quercifolium***
Plants under this name are mainly hybrids. The true species has pointed, not rounded leaf lobes.

***Penstemon* 'Taoensis'**
This name for a small-flowered cultivar or hybrid of *P. isophyllus* originally appeared as 'Taoense' but must be corrected to agree in gender with *Penstemon* (masculine). Presumably an invalid name (published in Latin form since 1958), it is not synonymous with *P. crandallii* subsp. *glabrescens* var. *taosensis*.

***Pernettya***
Botanists now consider that *Pernettya* (fruit a berry) is not separable from *Gaultheria* (fruit a capsule) because in some species the fruit is intermediate between a berry and a capsule. For a fuller explanation see D. Middleton, *The Plantsman*, **12(3)**.

***Pinus ayacahuite***
*P. ayacahuite* var. *veitchii* (syn. *P. veitchii)* is occasionally sold under this name.

***Pinus nigra* 'Cebennensis Nana'**
A doubtful name, possibly a synonym for *P. nigra* 'Nana'.

***Polemonium archibaldiae***
Usually sterile with lavender-blue flowers. A self-fertile white-flowered plant is sometimes sold under this name.

***Prunus laurocerasus* 'Castlewellan'**
We are grateful to Dr Charles Nelson for informing us that the name 'Marbled White' is not valid because although it has priority of publication it does not have the approval of the originator who asked for it to be called 'Castlewellan'.

***Prunus serrulata* var. *pubescens***
See note in Bean Supplement, p.398.

***Prunus × subhirtella* 'Rosea'**
Might be *P. pendula* var. *ascendens* 'Rosea', *P. pendula* 'Pendula Rosea', or *P.* × *subhirtella* 'Autumnalis Rosea'.

***Rheum × cultorum***
The name *R.* × *cultorum* was published without adequate description and must be abandoned in favour of the validly published *R.* × *hybridum*.

***Rhododendron* (azaleas)**
All names marked 'N', except for the following, refer to more than one cultivar.

***Rhododendron nuttallii* 'Hinomayo'**
This name is based on a faulty transliteration (should be 'Hinamoyo') but the spelling 'Hinomayo' is retained in the interests of stability.

***Rhus hirta and R. typhina***
Linnaeus published both *R. typhina* and *R. hirta* as names for the same species. Though *R. hirta* has priority, it has been proposed that the name *R. typhina* should be conserved.

***Rosa gentiliana***
Plants under this name are usually the cultivar 'Polyantha Grandiflora' but might otherwise be *R. multiflora* 'Wilsonii', *R. multiflora* var. *cathayensis, R. henryi* or another hybrid.

***Rosa* 'Jacques Cartier' misapplied**
For a discussion on the correct identity of this rose see *Heritage Rose Foundation News*, Oct. 1989 & Jan. 1990.

***Rosa* 'Kazanlik'**
For a discussion on the correct identity of this rose see *Heritage Roses,* Nov. 1991.

***Rosa* Sweetheart**
This is not the same as the Sweetheart Rose, a common name for *R.* 'Cécile Brünner'.

***Rosa wichurana***
This is the correct spelling according to the ICBN 1994 Article 60.11 (which enforces Recommendation 60C.1c) and not *wichuraiana* for this rose commemorating Max Wichura.

***Rubus fruticosus* L. agg.**
Though some cultivated blackberries do belong to *Rubus fruticosus* L. *sensu stricto,* others are more correctly ascribed to other species of *Rubus* section *Glandulosus* (including *R. armeniacus, R. laciniatus* or *R. ulmifolius)* or are hybrids of species within this section. Because it is almost impossible to ascribe every cultivar to a single species or hybrid, they are listed under *R. fruticosus* L. agg. (i.e. aggregate) for convenience.

***Salvia microphylla* var. *neurepia***
The type of this variety is referable to the typical variety, *S. microphylla* var. *microphylla*.

***Salvia officinalis* 'Aurea'**
*S. officinalis* var. *aurea* is a rare variant of the common sage with leaves entirely of gold. It is represented in cultivation by the cultivar 'Kew Gold'. The plant usually offered as *S. officinalis* 'Aurea' is the gold variegated sage *S. officinalis* 'Icterina'.

***Sambucus nigra* 'Aurea'**
Plants under this name are usually not *S. nigra.*

***Skimmia japonica* 'Foremanii'**
The true cultivar, which belongs to *S. japonica* Rogersii Group, is believed to be lost to cultivation. Plants offered under this name are usually *S. japonica* 'Veitchii'.

***Spiraea japonica* 'Shirobana'**
Shirobana-shimotsuke is the common name for *S. japonica* var. *albiflora*. Shirobana means white-flowered and does not apply to the two-coloured form.

***Staphylea holocarpa* var. *rosea***
This botanical variety has woolly leaves. The cultivar 'Rosea', with which it is often confused, does not.

***Thymus serpyllum* cultivars**
Many cultivars are probably correctly considered hybrids though they will remain listed under *T. serpyllum* pending further research.

***Tricyrtis* Hototogisu**
This is the common name applied generally to all Japanese *Tricyrtis* and specifically to *T. hirta.*

***Tricyrtis macropoda***
This name has been used for at least five different species.

***Uncinia rubra***
This name is also misapplied to *U. egmontiana* and *U. uncinata.*

***Viburnum opulus* 'Fructu Luteo'**
See note below.

***Viburnum opulus* 'Xanthocarpum'**
Some entries under this name might be the less compact *V. opulus* 'Fructu Luteo'.

***Viburnum plicatum***
Entries may include the 'snowball' form, *V. plicatum* f. *plicatum* (syn. *V. plicatum* 'Sterile'), as well as the 'lacecap' form, *V. plicatum* f. *tomentosum.*

***Viola labradorica***
See Note in *The Garden*, **110**(2): 96.

***Wisteria floribunda* 'Violacea Plena' and *W. floribunda* 'Yae-kokuryū'**
We are grateful to Yoko Otsuki, who has established through Engei Kyokai (the Horticultural Society of Japan) that there are two different double selections of *Wisteria floribunda*. 'Violacea Plena' has double lavender/lilac flowers, while 'Yae-kokuryū' has more ragged and tightly double flowers with purple/indigo centres. Each is distinctive but it is probable that both are confused in the British nursery trade. 'Yae-fuji' might be an earlier name for 'Violacea Plena' or a Group name covering a range of doubles but, as *fuji* is the Japanese common name for the species, it would not be a valid name under the ICNCP.

# CLASSIFICATION OF GENERA

Genera including a large number of species, or with many cultivars, are often subdivided into informal horticultural classifications, or formal cultivar groups in the case of *Clematis* and *Tulipa*. The breeding of new cultivars is sometimes limited to hybrids between closely-related species, thus for *Saxifraga* and *Primula*, the cultivars are allocated to the sections given in the infrageneric treatments cited. Please turn to p.16 for a fuller explanation.

## ACTINIDIA

(s-p) Self-pollinating

## BEGONIA

(C) Cane-like
(R) Rex Cultorum
(S) Semperflorens Cultorum
(T) × *tuberhybrida* (Tuberous)

## CHRYSANTHEMUM

(By the National Chrysanthemum Society)
(1) Indoor Large (Exhibition)
(2) Indoor Medium (Exhibition)
(3a) Indoor Incurved: Large-flowered
(3b) Indoor Incurved: Medium-flowered
(3c) Indoor Incurved: Small-flowered
(4a) Indoor Reflexed: Large-flowered
(4b) Indoor Reflexed: Medium-flowered
(4c) Indoor Reflexed: Small-flowered
(5a) Indoor Intermediate: Large-flowered
(5b) Indoor Intermediate: Medium-flowered
(5c) Indoor Intermediate: Small-flowered
(6a) Indoor Anemone: Large-flowered
(6b) Indoor Anemone: Medium-flowered
(6c) Indoor Anemone: Small-flowered
(7a) Indoor Single: Large-flowered
(7b) Indoor Single: Medium-flowered
(7c) Indoor Single: Small-flowered
(8a) Indoor True Pompon
(8b) Indoor Semi-pompon
(9a) Indoor Spray: Anemone
(9b) Indoor Spray: Pompon
(9c) Indoor Spray: Reflexed
(9d) Indoor Spray: Single
(9e) Indoor Spray: Intermediate
(9f) Indoor Spray: Spider, Quill, Spoon or Any Other Type
(10a) Indoor, Spider
(10b) Indoor, Quill
(10c) Indoor, Spoon
(11) Any Other Indoor Type
(12a) Indoor, Charm
(12b) Indoor, Cascade
(13a) October-flowering Incurved: Large-flowered
(13b) October-flowering Incurved: Medium-flowered
(13c) October-flowering Incurved: Small-flowered
(14a) October-flowering Reflexed: Large-flowered
(14b) October-flowering Reflexed: Medium-flowered
(14c) October-flowering Reflexed: Small-flowered
(15a) October-flowering Intermediate: Large-flowered
(15b) October-flowering Intermediate: Medium-flowered
(15c) October-flowered Intermediate: Small-flowered
(16) October-flowering Large
(17a) October-flowering Single: Large-flowered
(17b) October-flowering Single: Medium-flowered
(17c) October-flowering Single: Small-flowered
(18a) October-flowering Pompon: True Pompon
(18b) October-flowering Pompon: Semi-pompon
(19a) October-flowering Spray: Anemone
(19b) October-flowering Spray: Pompon
(19c) October-flowering Spray: Reflexed
(19d) October-flowering Spray: Single
(19e) October-flowering Spray: Intermediate
(19f) October-flowering Spray: Spider, Quill, Spoon or Any Other Type
(20) Any Other October-flowering Type
(21a) Korean: Anemone
(21b) Korean: Pompon
(21c) Korean: Reflexed
(21d) Korean: Single
(21e) Korean: Intermediate
(21f) Korean: Spider, Quill, Spoon, or any other type
(22a) Charm: Anemone
(22b) Charm: Pompon
(22c) Charm: Reflexed
(22d) Charm: Single
(22e) Charm: Intermediate
(22f) Charm: Spider, Quill, Spoon or Any Other Type
(23a) Early-flowering Outdoor Incurved: Large-flowered

(23b) Early-flowering Outdoor Incurved: Medium-flowered
(23c) Early-flowering Outdoor Incurved: Small-flowered
(24a) Early-flowering Outdoor Reflexed: Large-flowered
(24b) Early-flowering Outdoor Reflexed: Medium-flowered
(24c) Early-flowering Outdoor Reflexed: Small-flowered
(25a) Early-flowering Outdoor Intermediate: Large-flowered
(25b) Early-flowering Outdoor Intermediate: Medium-flowered
(25c) Early-flowering Outdoor Intermediate: Small-flowered
(26a) Early-flowering Outdoor Anemone: Large-flowered
(26b) Early-flowering Outdoor Anemone: Medium-flowered
(27a) Early-flowering Outdoor Single: Large-flowered
(27b) Early-flowering Outdoor Single:Medium-flowered
(28a) Early-flowering Outdoor Pompon: True Pompon
(28b) Early-flowering Outdoor Pompon: Semi-pompon
(29a) Early-flowering Outdoor Spray: Anemone
(29b) Early-flowering Outdoor Spray: Pompon
(29c) Early-flowering Outdoor Spray: Reflexed
(29d) Early-flowering Outdoor Spray: Single
(29e) Early-flowering Outdoor Spray: Intermediate
(29f) Early-flowering Outdoor Spray: Spider, Quill, Spoon or Any Other Type
(30) Any Other Early-flowering Outdoor Type

## CLEMATIS

(Cultivar Groups as per Matthews, V. (2002) *The International Clematis Register & Checklist 2002*, RHS, London.)

(A) Atragene Group
(Ar) Armandii Group
(C) Cirrhosa Group
(EL) Early Large-flowered Group
(F) Flammula Group
(Fo) Forsteri Group
(H) Heracleifolia Group
(I) Integrifolia Group
(LL) Late Large-flowered Group
(M) Montana Group
(T) Texensis Group
(Ta) Tangutica Group
(V) Viorna Group
(Vb) Vitalba Group
(Vt) Viticella Group

## DAHLIA

(Classification according to The International Dahlia Register (1969), 20th Supp. (2009) formed through consultation with national dahlia societies.)

(Sin) 1 Single
(Anem) 2 Anemone-flowered
(Col) 3 Collerette
(WL) 4 Waterlily (unassigned)
(LWL) 4B Waterlily, Large
(MWL) 4C Waterlily, Medium
(SWL) 4D Waterlily, Small
(MinWL) 4E Waterlily, Miniature
(D) 5 Decorative (unassigned)
(GD) 5A Decorative, Giant
(LD) 5B Decorative, Large
(MD) 5C Decorative, Medium
(SD) 5D Decorative, Small
(MinD) 5E Decorative, Miniature
(SBa) 6D Small Ball
(MinBa) 6E Miniature Ball
(Pom) 7 Pompon
(C) 8 Cactus (unassigned)
(GC) 8A Cactus, Giant
(LC) 8B Cactus, Large
(MC) 8C Cactus, Medium
(SC) 8D Cactus, Small
(MinC) 8E Cactus, Miniature
(S-c) 9 Semi-cactus (unassigned)
(GS-c) 9A Semi-cactus, Giant
(LS-c) 9B Semi-cactus, Large
(MS-c) 9C Semi-cactus, Medium
(SS-c) 9D Semi-cactus, Small
(MinS-c) 9E Semi-cactus, Miniature
(Misc) 10 Miscellaneous
(Fim) 11 Fimbriated
(SinO) 12 Single Orchid (Star)
(DblO) 13 Double Orchid
(B) Botanical
(DwB) Dwarf Bedding
(Lil) Lilliput (in combination)

## DIANTHUS

(By the RHS)

(b) Carnation, border
(M) Carnation, Malmaison
(pf) Carnation, perpetual-flowering
(p) Pink
(p,a) Pink, annual

## FRUIT

(B) Black (*Vitis*), Blackcurrant (*Ribes*)
(Ball) Ballerina (*Malus*)
(C) Culinary (*Malus, Prunus, Pyrus, Ribes*)
(Cider) Cider (*Malus*)

(D) Dessert (*Malus, Prunus, Pyrus, Ribes*)
(F) Fruit
(G) Glasshouse (*Vitis*)
(O) Outdoor (*Vitis*)
(P) Pinkcurrant (*Ribes*)
(Perry) Perry (*Pyrus*)
(R) Red (*Vitis*), Redcurrant (*Ribes*)
(S) Seedless (*Citrus, Vitis*)
(W) White (*Vitis*), Whitecurrant (*Ribes*)

## Fuchsia

(E) Encliandra
(T) Variants and hybrids of F. triphylla

## Gladiolus

(B) Butterfly
(E) Exotic
(G) Giant
(L) Large
(M) Medium
(Min) Miniature
(N) Nanus
(P) Primulinus
(S) Small
(Tub) Tubergenii

## Hepatica nobilis

(Adapted from the International Hepatica Society classification for *Hepatica nobilis*)
(1) Hyoujun (normal)
(2) (degenerated anther)
(3) Otome (degenerated stamen)
(4) Henka (petal deformity)
(5/d) Herashibe (semi-double, primitive)
(5A/d) Choji (semi-double, primitive)
(6/d) Nidan (semi-double, advanced)
(7/d) Sandan (double, primitive)
(8/d) Karako (double, advanced)
(9/d) Sene-e (double, completed)

## Hydrangea macrophylla

(H) Hortensia
(L) Lacecap

## Iris

(By the American Iris Society)
(AB) Arilbred
(BB) Border Bearded
(Cal-Sib) Series *Californicae* × Series *Sibiricae*
(CH) Californian Hybrid
(DB) Dwarf Bearded (not assigned)
(Dut) Dutch
(IB) Intermediate Bearded
(J) Juno (subgenus *Scorpiris*)
(La) Louisiana Hybrid
(MDB) Miniature Dwarf Bearded
(MTB) Miniature Tall Bearded
(Rc) Regeliocyclus (Section *Regelia* × Section *Oncocyclus*)
(SDB) Standard Dwarf Bearded
(Sino-Sib) Series *Sibiricae*, chromosome number 2n=40
(SpH) Species Hybrid
(Spuria) Spuria
(TB) Tall Bearded

## Lilium

(Classification according to *The International Lily Register* (ed. 4, 2007))
(I) Asiatic hybrids derived from *L. amabile, L. bulbiferum, L. callosum, L. cernuum, L. concolor, L. dauricum, L. davidii, L. × hollandicum, L. lancifolium, L. lankongense, L. leichtlinii, L. × maculatum* and *L. pumilum, L. × scottiae, L. wardii* and *L. wilsonii.*
(II) Martagon hybrids derived from *L. dalhansonii, L. hansonii, L. martagon, L. medeoloides and L. tsingtauense*
(III) Euro-Caucasian hybrids derived from *L. candidum, L. chalcedonicum, L. kesselringianum, L. monadelphum, L. pomponium, L. pyrenaicum* and *L. × testaceum.*
(IV) American hybrids derived from *L. bolanderi, L. × burbankii, L. canadense, L. columbianum, L. grayi, L. humboldtii, L. kelleyanum, L. kelloggii, L. maritimum, L. michauxii, L. michiganense, L. occidentale, L. × pardaboldtii, L. pardalinum, L. parryi, L. parvum, L. philadelphicum, L. pitkinense, L. superbum, L. vollmeri, L. washingtonianum* and *L. wigginsii.*
(V) Longiflorum lilies derived from *L. formosanum, L. longiflorum, L. philippinense and L. wallichianum.*
(VI) Trumpet and Aurelian hybrids derived from *L. × aurelianense, L. brownii, L. × centigale, L. henryi, L × imperiale, L. × kewense, L. leucantheum, L. regale, L. rosthornii, L. sargentiae, L. sulphureum* and *L. sulphurgale* (but excluding hybrids of *L. henryi* with all species listed in Division VII).
(VII) Oriental hybrids derived from *L. auratum, L. japonicum, L. nobilissimum, L. × parkmanii, L rubellum* and *L. speciosum* (but excl. all hybrids of these with *L. henryi*).
(VIII) Other hybrids not covered by any of the previous divisions (I-VII)
(IX) Species and cultivars of species

a/ upward-facing flowers
b/ outward-facing flowers
c/ downward-facing flowers
/a trumpet-shaped flowers
/b bowl-shaped flowers
/c flat flowers (or with only tepal tips recurved)
/d recurved flowers

## Malus *see* Fruit

## Narcissus

(By the RHS, revised 1998)

(1) Trumpet
(2) Large-cupped
(3) Small-cupped
(4) Double
(5) Triandrus
(6) Cyclamineus
(7) Jonquilla and Apodanthus
(8) Tazetta
(9) Poeticus
(10) Bulbocodium
(11a) Split-corona: Collar
(11b) Split-corona: Papillon
(12) Miscellaneous
(13) Species

## Nymphaea

(H) Hardy
(D) Day-blooming
(N) Night-blooming
(T) Tropical

## Papaver

(SPS) Super Poppy Series

## Paeonia

(S) Shrubby

## Pelargonium

(A) Angel
(C) Coloured Foliage (in combination)
(Ca) Cactus (in combination)
(d) Double (in combination)
(Dec) Decorative
(Dw) Dwarf
(DwI) Dwarf Ivy-leaved
(Fr) Frutetorum
(I) Ivy-leaved
(Min) Miniature
(MinI) Miniature Ivy-leaved
(R) Regal
(Sc) Scented-leaved
(St) Stellar (in combination)
(T) Tulip (in combination)
(U) Unique
(Z) Zonal

## Primula

(Classification by Section as per Richards. J. (2002) *Primula* (2nd edition). Batsford, London)

(Ag) *Auganthus*
(Al) *Aleuritia*
(Am) *Amethystinae*
(Ar) *Armerina*
(Au) *Auricula*
  (A) Alpine Auricula
  (B) Border Auricula
  (S) Show Auricula
  (St) Striped Auricula
(Bu) *Bullatae*
(Ca) *Capitatae*
(Cf) *Cordifoliae*
(Ch) *Chartaceae*
(Co) *Cortusoides*
(Cr) *Carolinella*
(Cu) *Cuneifoliae*
(Cy) *Crystallophlomis*
(Da) *Davidii*
(De) *Denticulatae*
(Dr) *Dryadifoliae*
(F) *Fedtschenkoanae*
(G) *Glabrae*
(Ma) *Malvaceae*
(Mi) *Minutissimae*
(Mo) *Monocarpicae*
(Mu) *Muscarioides*
(Ob) *Obconicolisteri*
(Or) *Oreophlomis*
(Pa) *Parryi*
(Pe) *Petiolares*
(Pf) *Proliferae*
(Pi) *Pinnatae*
(Pr) *Primula*
  (Poly) Polyanthus
  (Prim) Primrose
(Pu) *Pulchellae*
(Py) *Pycnoloba*
(R) *Reinii*
(Si) *Sikkimenses*
(So) *Soldanelloides*
(Sp) *Sphondylia*
(Sr) *Sredinskya*
(Su) *Suffrutescentes*
(Y) *Yunnanenses*

## Prunus *see* Fruit

## Pyrus *see* Fruit

## Rhododendron

(A) Azalea (deciduous, species or unclassified hybrid)
(Ad) Azaleodendron
(EA) Evergreen azalea
(G) Ghent azalea (deciduous)

(K) Knap Hill or Exbury azalea (deciduous)
(M) Mollis azalea (deciduous)
(O) Occidentalis azalea (deciduous)
(R) Rustica azalea (deciduous)
(V) Vireya rhododendron
(Vs) Viscosa azalea (deciduous)

## RIBES *SEE* FRUIT

## ROSA

(A) Alba
(Bb) Bourbon
(Bs) Boursault
(Ce) Centifolia
(Ch) China
(Cl) Climbing (in combination)
(D) Damask
(DPo) Damask Portland
(F) Floribunda or Cluster-flowered
(G) Gallica
(Ga) Garnette
(GC) Ground Cover
(HM) Hybrid Musk
(HP) Hybrid Perpetual
(HT) Hybrid Tea or Large-flowered
(Min) Miniature
(Mo) Moss (in combination)
(N) Noisette
(Patio) Patio, Miniature Floribunda or Dwarf Cluster-flowered
(Poly) Polyantha
(Ra) Rambler
(RH) Rubiginosa hybrid (Hybrid Sweet Briar)
(Ru) Rugosa
(S) Shrub
(SpH) Spinosissima Hybrid
(T) Tea

## SAXIFRAGA

(Classification by Section from Gornall, R.J. (1987). *Botanical Journal of the Linnean Society,* 95(4): 273-292)

(1) *Ciliatae*
(2) *Cymbalaria*
(3) *Merkianae*
(4) *Micranthes*
(5) *Irregulares*
(6) *Heterisia*
(7) *Porphyrion*
(8) *Ligulatae*
(9) *Xanthizoon*
(10) *Trachyphyllum*
(11) *Gymnopera*
(12) *Cotylea*
(13) *Odontophyllae*
(14) *Mesogyne*
(15) *Saxifraga*

## TULIPA

(Classification by Cultivar Group from *Classified List and International Register of Tulip Names* by Koninklijke Algemeene Vereening voor Bloembollenculture 1996)

(1) Single Early Group
(2) Double Early Group
(3) Triumph Group
(4) Darwin Hybrid Group
(5) Single Late Group (including Darwin Group and Cottage Group)
(6) Lily-flowered Group
(7) Fringed Group
(8) Viridiflora Group
(9) Rembrandt Group
(10) Parrot Group
(11) Double Late Group
(12) Kaufmanniana Group
(13) Fosteriana Group
(14) Greigii Group
(15) Miscellaneous

## VERBENA

(G) Species and hybrids considered by some botanists to belong to the separate genus *Glandularia*.

## VIOLA

(C) Cornuta Hybrid
(dVt) Double Violet
(ExVa) Exhibition Viola
(FP) Fancy Pansy
(PVt) Parma Violet
(SP) Show Pansy
(T) Tricolor
(Va) Viola
(Vt) Violet
(Vtta) Violetta

## VITIS *SEE* FRUIT

# REVERSE SYNONYMS

The following list of reverse synonyms is intended to help users find from which genus an unfamiliar plant name has been cross-referred. For a fuller explanation see p.18.

*Abelmoschus – Hibiscus*
*Abronia – Verbena*
*Abutilon – Corynabutilon*
*Acacia – Racosperma*
*Acca – Feijoa*
× *Achicodonia – Eucodonia*
*Achillea – Anthemis*
*Achillea – Tanacetum*
*Acinos – Calamintha*
*Acinos – Clinopodium*
*Acinos – Micromeria*
*Acis – Leucojum*
*Acmella – Spilanthes*
*Actaea – Cimicifuga*
*Actaea – Souliea*
*Adlumia – Dicentra*
*Aethionema – Eunomia*
*Agapetes – Pentapterygium*
*Agarista – Leucothoe*
*Agastache – Cedronella*
*Agathosma – Barosma*
*Agave – Manfreda*
*Agave –* × *Mangave*
*Ageratina – Eupatorium*
*Agrostis – Eragrostis*
*Aichryson – Aeonium*
*Ajania – Chrysanthemum*
*Ajania – Dendranthema*
*Ajania – Eupatorium*
*Albizia – Acacia*
*Alcea – Althaea*
*Allardia – Waldheimia*
*Allocasuarina – Casuarina*
*Aloysia – Lippia*
*Althaea – Malva*
*Alyogyne – Anisodontea*
*Alyogyne – Hibiscus*
*Alyssum – Ptilotrichum*
*Amana – Tulipa*
× *Amarygia – Amaryllis*
*Amaryllis – Brunsvigia*
*Amberhoa – Centaurea*
*Amomyrtus – Myrtus*
*Amsonia – Rhazya*
*Anacamptis – Orchis*
*Anaphalis – Gnaphalium*
*Anchusa – Lycopsis*
*Androsace – Douglasia*
*Androstoma – Cyathodes*
*Anemanthele – Oryzopsis*
*Anemanthele – Stipa*
*Anemone – Eriocapitella*
*Anisodontea – Malvastrum*
*Anisodus – Scopolia*
*Anomatheca – Freesia*
*Anomatheca – Lapeirousia*
*Anredera – Boussingaultia*
*Antirrhinum – Asarina*
*Aphanes – Alchemilla*
*Arctanthemum – Chrysanthemum*
*Arctostaphylos – Arbutus*
*Arctotis – Venidium*
*Arctotis –* × *Venidioarctotis*
*Arenga – Didymosperma*
*Argyranthemum – Anthemis*
*Argyranthemum – Chrysanthemum*
*Armoracia – Cochlearia*
*Arnoglossum – Cacalia*
*Arundinaria – Pseudosasa*
*Asarina – Antirrhinum*
*Asarum – Hexastylis*
*Asparagus – Myrsiphyllum*
*Asparagus – Smilax*
*Asperula – Galium*
*Asphodeline – Asphodelus*
*Asplenium – Camptosorus*
*Asplenium – Ceterach*
*Asplenium – Phyllitis*
*Asplenium – Scolopendrium*
*Aster – Crinitaria*
*Aster – Doellingeria*
*Aster – Erigeron*
*Aster – Microglossa*
*Aster – Symphyotrichum*
*Astilboides – Rodgersia*
*Asyneuma – Campanula*
*Athanasia – Hymenolepis*
*Atropanthe – Scopolia*
*Aurinia – Alyssum*
*Austrocedrus – Libocedrus*
*Austromyrtus – Myrtus*
*Azorella – Bolax*
*Azorina – Campanula*

*Bambusa – Arundinaria*
*Barnadesia- Mutisia*
*Bashania – Arundinaria*
*Bassia – Kochia*
*Beaucarnea – Nolina*
*Bellevalia – Muscari*
*Bellis – Erigeron*
*Bignonia – Campsis*
*Blechnum – Lomaria*
*Blechnum – Struthiopteris*
*Blepharocalyx – Temu*
*Bolax – Azorella*
*Bolboschoenus – Scirpus*
*Bonia – Indocalamus*
*Borago – Anchusa*
*Bothriochloa – Andropogon*
*Bouteloua – Chondrosum*
*Boykinia – Telesonix*
*Brachychiton – Sterculia*
*Brachyglottis – Senecio*
*Brimeura – Hyacinthus*
*Brodiaea – Triteleia*
*Brugmansia – Datura*
*Brunnera – Anchusa*
*Buglossoides – Lithospermum*
*Bulbine – Bulbinopsis*

*Cacalia – Adenostyles*
*Caladium – Xanthosoma*
*Calamagrostis – Stipa*
*Calamintha – Clinopodium*
*Calamintha – Thymus*
*Calibrachoa – Petunia*
*Callisia – Phyodina*
*Callisia – Tradescantia*
*Calocedrus – Libocedrus*
*Calomeria – Humea*
*Caloscordum – Nothoscordum*
*Calylophus – Oenothera*
*Calytrix Lhotzkya*
*Camellia – Thea*
*Campanula – Symphyandra*
*Cardamine – Dentaria*
*Carmichaelia –* × *Carmispartium*
*Carmichaelia – Chordospartium*
*Carmichaelia – Corallospartium*
*Carpobrotus – Lampranthus*
*Cedronella – Agastache*
*Centaurium – Erythraea*
*Centella – Hydrocotyle*
*Centranthus – Kentranthus*
*Centranthus – Valeriana*
*Cephalaria – Scabiosa*
*Ceratostigma – Plumbago*
*Chaenomeles – Cydonia*
*Chaenorhinum – Linaria*
*Chamaecytisus – Cytisus*
*Chamaedaphne – Cassandra*
*Chamaemelum – Anthemis*
*Chamerion – Chamaenerion*
*Chamerion – Epilobium*
*Chasmanthium – Uniola*
*Cheilanthes – Notholaena*
*Chiastophyllum – Cotyledon*
*Chimonobambusa – Arundinaria*
*Chimonobambusa – Qiongzhuea*
*Chionohebe – Parahebe*

*Chionohebe – Pygmea*
× *Chionoscilla – Scilla*
*Chlorophytum – Diuranthera*
*Chromolaena – Eupatorium*
*Chrysanthemum – Dendranthema*
*Chrysopsis – Heterotheca*
*Cicerbita – Lactuca*
*Cionura – Marsdenia*
*Cissus – Ampelopsis*
*Cissus – Parthenocissus*
× *Citrofortunella – Citrus*
*Clarkia – Eucharidium*
*Clarkia – Godetia*
*Clavinodum – Arundinaria*
*Claytonia – Calandrinia*
*Claytonia – Montia*
*Clematis – Atragene*
*Clematis – Clematopsis*
*Cleyera – Eurya*
*Clinopodium – Calamintha*
*Clytostoma – Bignonia*
*Clytostoma – Pandorea*
*Cnicus – Carduus*
*Conoclinium – Eupatorium*
*Codariocalyx – Desmodium*
*Codonopsis – Campanumoea*
*Collospermum – Astelia*
*Colobanthus – Arenaria*
*Consolida – Delphinium*
*Cordyline – Dracaena*
*Cornus – Chamaepericlymenum*
*Cornus – Dendrobenthamia*
*Coronilla – Securigera*
*Cortaderia – Gynerium*
*Corydalis – Capnoides*
*Corydalis – Fumaria*
*Corydalis – Pseudofumaria*
*Cosmos – Bidens*
*Cotinus – Rhus*
*Cotula – Leptinella*
*Crassula – Rochea*
*Crassula – Sedum*
*Crassula – Tillaea*
× *Crataegosorbus – Sorbus*
*Cremanthodium – Ligularia*
*Crinodendron – Tricuspidaria*
*Crocosmia – Antholyza*
*Crocosmia – Curtonus*
*Crocosmia – Montbretia*
*Cruciata – Galium*
*Ctenanthe – Calathea*
*Ctenanthe – Stromanthe*
*Cupressus – Chamaecyparis*
× *Cuprocyparis – Chamaecyparis*
× *Cuprocyparis – Cupressocyparis*
*Cyclosorus – Pneumatopteris*
*Cylindropuntia – Opuntia*
*Cymbalaria – Linaria*
*Cymophyllus – Carex*
*Cyperus – Mariscus*
*Cypripedium – Criogenes*
*Cyrtanthus – Anoiganthus*
*Cyrtanthus – Vallota*
*Cyrtomium – Phanerophlebia*
*Cyrtomium – Polystichum*
*Cytisophyllum – Cytisus*
*Cytisus – Argyrocytisus*
*Cytisus – Genista*
*Cytisus – Lembotropis*
*Cytisus – Spartocytisus*

*Daboecia – Menziesia*
*Dacrycarpus – Podocarpus*
*Dactylicapnos – Dicentra*
*Dactylorhiza – Orchis*
*Dalea – Petalostemon*
*Danae – Ruscus*
*Darmera – Peltiphyllum*
*Datura – Brugmansia*
*Davallia – Humata*
*Delairea – Senecio*
*Delosperma – Lampranthus*
*Delosperma – Mesembryanthemum*
*Dendrocalamus – Bambusa*
*Desmodium – Lespedeza*
*Deuterocohnia – Abromeitiella*
*Dicentra – Corydalis*
*Dichelostemma – Brodiaea*
*Dicliptera – Barleria*
*Dicliptera – Justicia*
*Diervilla – Weigela*
*Dietes – Moraea*
*Diplazium – Athyrium*
*Dipogon – Dolichos*
*Disporopsis – Polygonatum*
*Dolichothrix – Helichrysum*
*Dracaena – Pleomele*
*Dracunculus – Arum*
*Dregea – Wattakaka*
*Drepanostachyum – Bambusa*
*Drepanostachyum – Chimonobambusa*
*Drepanostachyum – Gelidocalamus*
*Drepanostachyum – Thamnocalamus*
*Drimys – Tasmannia*
*Duchesnea – Fragaria*
*Dypsis – Chrysalidocarpus*
*Dypsis – Neodypsis*

*Echeveria – Cotyledon*
*Echinacea – Rudbeckia*
*Echinospartum – Genista*
*Edraianthus – Wahlenbergia*
*Egeria – Elodea*
*Elatostema – Pellionia*
*Eleutherococcus – Acanthopanax*
*Elliottia – Botryostege*
*Elliottia – Cladothamnus*
*Elymus – Agropyron*
*Elymus – Leymus*
*Ensete – Musa*
*Epipremnum – Philodendron*
*Epipremnum – Scindapsus*
*Episcia – Alsobia*
*Eranthis – Aconitum*
*Eremophila – Myoporum*
*Erepsia – Semnanthe*
*Erigeron – Haplopappus*
*Erysimum – Cheiranthus*
*Eucalyptus – Corymbia*
*Eupatorium – Ageratina*
*Eupatorium – Ayapana*
*Eupatorium – Bartlettina*
*Euphorbia – Poinsettia*
*Euryops – Senecio*
*Eustachys – Chloris*
*Eustoma – Lisianthus*
*Euthamia – Solidago*

*Fallopia – Bilderdykia*
*Fallopia – Polygonum*
*Fallopia – Reynoutria*
*Farfugium – Ligularia*
*Fargesia – Arundinaria*
*Fargesia – Borinda*
*Fargesia – Semiarundinaria*
*Fargesia – Sinarundinaria*
*Fargesia – Thamnocalamus*
*Fatsia – Aralia*
*Felicia – Agathaea*
*Felicia – Aster*
*Fibigia – Farsetia*
*Filipendula – Spiraea*
*Ficinia – Isolepis*
*Foeniculum – Ferula*
*Fortunella – Citrus*
*Frangula – Rhamnus*

*Galium – Asperula*
*Gaultheria – Chiogenes*
*Gaultheria – Pernettya*
*Gaultheria –* × *Gaulnettya*
*Gelasine – Sisyrinchium*
*Genista – Chamaespartium*
*Genista – Cytisus*
*Genista – Echinospartum*
*Genista – Teline*
*Gethyum – Ancrumia*
*Geum – Sieversia*
*Gladiolus – Acidanthera*
*Gladiolus – Anomalesia*
*Gladiolus – Homoglossum*
*Gladiolus – Petamenes*
*Glebionis – Chrysanthemum*
*Glebionis – Xanthophthalmum*
*Glechoma – Nepeta*
*Gloxinia – Seemannia*
*Gloxinia – Sinningia*
*Gomphocarpus – Asclepias*
*Gomphocarpus – Asclepias*

*Goniolimon – Limonium*
*Goniophlebium – Polypodium*
*Graptopetalum – Sedum*
*Graptopetalum – Tacitus*
*Greenovia – Sempervivum*
*Gymnadenia – Nigritella*
*Gymnospermium – Leontice*

*Habranthus – Zephyranthes*
*Hacquetia – Dondia*
× *Halimiocistus – Cistus*
× *Halimiocistus – Halimium*
*Halimione – Atriplex*
*Halimium – Cistus*
*Halimium – Helianthemum*
*Halimium –* × *Halimiocistus*
*Halocarpus – Dacrydium*
*Hanabusaya – Symphyandra*
*Harrimanella – Cassiope*
*Hedychium – Brachychilum*
*Helianthella – Helianthus*
*Helianthemum – Cistus*
*Helianthus – Coreopsis*
*Helianthus – Heliopsis*
*Helichrysum – Gnaphalium*
*Helicodiceros – Dracunculus*
*Helictotrichon – Avena*
*Helictotrichon – Avenula*
*Hepatica – Anemone*
*Herbertia – Alophia*
*Hermodactylus – Iris*
*Heterocentron – Schizocentron*
*Heteromeles – Photinia*
*Heterotheca – Chrysopsis*
× *Heucherella – Heuchera*
× *Heucherella – Tiarella*
*Hibbertia – Candollea*
*Hieracium – Andryala*
*Himalayacalamus – Arundinaria*
*Himalayacalamus – Chimonobambusa*
*Himalayacalamus – Drepanostachyum*
*Himalayacalamus – Drepanostachyum*
*Himalayacalamus – Thamnocalamus*
*Hippocrepis – Coronilla*
*Hippolytia – Achillea*
*Hippolytia – Tanacetum*
*Hoheria – Plagianthus*
*Homalocladium – Muehlenbeckia*
*Howea – Kentia*
*Hyacinthoides – Endymion*
*Hyacinthoides – Scilla*
*Hydrangea – Schizophragma*
*Hylomecon – Chelidonium*
*Hymenocallis – Elisena*
*Hymenocallis – Ismene*
*Hymenoxys – Dugaldia*
*Hymenoxys – Helenium*
*Hyophorbe – Mascarena*
*Hypoxis – Rhodohypoxis*

*Ichthyoselmis – Dicentra*
*Incarvillea – Amphicome*
*Indocalamus – Sasa*
*Iochroma – Acnistus*
*Iochroma – Cestrum*
*Iochroma – Dunalia*
*Iostephane – Coreopsis*
*Ipheion – Tristagma*
*Ipheion – Triteleia*
*Ipomoea – Calonyction*
*Ipomoea – Mina*
*Ipomoea – Pharbitis*
*Ipomopsis – Gilia*
*Ischyrolepis – Restio*
*Isolepis – Scirpus*
*Isotoma – Laurentia*
*Isotoma – Solenopsis*

*Jamesbrittenia – Sutera*
*Jeffersonia – Plagiorhegma*
*Jovibarba – Sempervivum*
*Juncus – Scirpus*
*Junellia – Verbena*
*Jurinea – Jurinella*
*Justicia – Beloperone*
*Justicia – Duvernoia*
*Justicia – Jacobinia*
*Justicia – Libonia*

*Kadsura – Schisandra*
*Kalanchoe – Bryophyllum*
*Kalanchoe – Kitchingia*
*Kalimeris – Aster*
*Kalimeris – Asteromoea*
*Kalimeris – Boltonia*
*Kalopanax – Acanthopanax*
*Kalopanax – Eleutherococcus*
*Keckiella – Penstemon*
*Keckiella – Penstemon*
*Kitagawia – Peucedanum*
*Knautia – Scabiosa*
*Kniphofia – Tritoma*
*Kohleria – Isoloma*
*Krascheninnikovia – Ceratoides*
*Kunzea – Leptospermum*

*Lablab – Dolichos*
*Lagarosiphon – Elodea*
*Lagarostrobos – Dacrydium*
*Lamium – Galeobdolon*
*Lamium – Lamiastrum*
*Lampranthus – Mesembryanthemum*
*Lamprocapnos – Dicentra*
*Laserpitium – Siler*
*Lavatera – Malva*
*Ledebouria – Scilla*
× *Ledodendron – Rhododendron*
*Ledum – Rhododendron*
*Leontodon – Microseris*
*Lepechinia – Sphacele*
*Lepidothamnus – Dacrydium*
*Leptecophylla – Cyathodes*
*Leptinella – Cotula*
*Leptodactylon – Gilia*
*Leucanthemella – Chrysanthemum*
*Leucanthemella – Leucanthemum*
*Leucanthemopsis – Chrysanthemum*
*Leucanthemum – Chrysanthemum*
*Leucochrysum – Helipterum*
*Leucocoryne – Beauverdia*
*Leucophyta – Calocephalus*
*Leucopogon – Cyathodes*
*Leucopogon – Styphelia*
× *Leucoraoulia – Raoulia*
*Leymus – Elymus*
*Ligularia – Senecio*
*Ligustrum – Parasyringa*
*Lilium – Nomocharis*
*Limonium – Statice*
*Linanthus – Linanthastrum*
*Lindelofia – Adelocaryum*
*Ligularia – Cacalia*
*Lindera – Parabenzoin*
*Lindernia – Ilysanthes*
*Liriope – Ophiopogon*
*Lithodora – Lithospermum*
*Lobelia – Monopsis*
*Lophomyrtus – Myrtus*
*Lophospermum – Asarina*
*Lophospermum – Maurandya*
*Lophostemon – Tristania*
*Lotus – Dorycnium*
*Lotus – Tetragonolobus*
*Ludwigia – Jussiaea*
*Luma – Myrtus*
× *Lycene – Lychnis*
*Lychnis – Agrostemma*
*Lychnis – Silene*
*Lychnis – Viscaria*
*Lycianthes – Solanum*
*Lytocaryum – Cocos*
*Lytocaryum – Microcoelum*

*Macfadyena – Bignonia*
*Macfadyena – Doxantha*
*Machaeranthera – Xylorhiza*
*Machaerina – Baumea*
*Mackaya – Asystasia*
*Macleaya – Bocconia*
*Maclura – Cudrania*
*Macropiper – Piper*
*Magnolia – Manglietia*
*Magnolia – Michelia*
*Magnolia – Parakmeria*
*Mahonia – Berberis*

*Maianthemum – Smilacina*
*Mandevilla – Dipladenia*
*Mandragora – Atropa*
*Marrubium – Ballota*
*Matricaria – Tripleurospermum*
*Maurandella – Asarina*
*Maurandya – Asarina*
*Melanoselinum – Thapsia*
*Melicytus – Hymenanthera*
*Melinis – Rhynchelytrum*
*Mentha – Preslia*
*Merremia – Ipomoea*
*Merwilla – Scilla*
*Mimulus – Diplacus*
*Minuartia – Arabis*
*Minuartia – Arenaria*
*Moltkia – Lithodora*
*Moltkia – Lithospermum*
*Monochoria – Pontederia*
*Monopsis – Lobelia*
*Morina – Acanthocalyx*
*Morina – Acanthocalyx*
*Mukdenia – Aceriphyllum*
*Muscari – Hyacinthus*
*Muscari – Leopoldia*
*Muscari – Muscarimia*
*Muscari – Pseudomuscari*
*Myrteola – Myrtus*

*Naiocrene – Claytonia*
*Naiocrene – Montia*
*Nectaroscordum – Allium*
*Nematanthus – Hypocyrta*
*Nemesia – Diascia × Linaria*
*Neolitsea – Litsea*
*Neopanax – Pseudopanax*
*Neopaxia – Claytonia*
*Neopaxia – Montia*
*Neoregelia – Nidularium*
*Nepeta – Dracocephalum*
*× Niduregelia – Guzmania*
*Nipponanthemum – Chrysanthemum*
*Nipponanthemum – Leucanthemum*
*Nolina – Beaucarnea*
*Notospartium – Carmichaelia*
*Nymphoides – Villarsia*

*Ochagavia – Fascicularia*
*Oemleria – Osmaronia*
*Oenothera – Chamissonia*
*Olsynium – Sisyrinchium*
*Onixotis – Dipidax*
*Onoclea – Matteuccia*
*Ophiopogon – Convallaria*
*Orbea – Stapelia*
*Orchis – Anacamptis*
*Orchis – Dactylorhiza*
*Oreopteris – Thelypteris*
*Orostachys – Sedum*
*Oscularia – Lampranthus*
*Osmanthus – Phillyrea*
*Osmanthus – × Osmarea*
*Othonna – Hertia*
*Othonna – Othonnopsis*
*Oxygraphis – Ranunculus*
*Oziroë – Fortunatia*
*Ozothamhus – Helichrysum*

*Pachyphragma – Cardamine*
*Pachyphragma – Thlaspi*
*Pachystegia – Olearia*
*Packera – Senecio*
*Paederota – Veronica*
*Pallenis – Asteriscus*
*Papaver – Meconopsis*
*Parahebe – Derwentia*
*Parahebe – Hebe*
*Parahebe – Veronica*
*Parasenecio – Cacalia*
*Paraserianthes – Albizia*
*Paris – Daiswa*
*Parthenocissus – Ampelopsis*
*Parthenocissus – Vitis*
*Passiflora – Tetrapathaea*
*Paxistima – Pachystema*
*Pecteilis – Habenaria*
*Pelargonium – Geranium*
*Peltoboykinia – Boykinia*
*Penstemon – Chelone*
*Penstemon – Nothochelone*
*Penstemon – Pennellianthus*
*Pentaglottis – Anchusa*
*Pericallis – Cineraria*
*Pericallis – Senecio*
*Persea – Machilus*
*Persicaria – Aconogonon*
*Persicaria – Antenoron*
*Persicaria – Bistorta*
*Persicaria – Polygonum*
*Persicaria – Tovara*
*Petrocoptis – Lychnis*
*Petrophytum – Spiraea*
*Petrorhagia – Tunica*
*Petroselinum – Carum*
*Phalocallis – Cypella*
*Phegopteris – Thelypteris*
*Phlebodium – Polypodium*
*Phoenicaulis – Parrya*
*Photinia – Stransvaesia*
*Photinia – × Stravinia*
*Phuopsis – Crucianella*
*Phyla – Lippia*
*Phymatosorus – Microsorum*
*Phymosia – Sphaeralcea*
*Physoplexis – Phyteuma*
*Physostegia – Dracocephalum*
*Pieris – Arcterica*
*Pilosella – Hieracium*
*Platycladus – Thuja*
*Plecostachys – Helichrysum*
*Plectranthus – Coleus*
*Plectranthus – Solenostemon*
*Pleioblastus – Arundinaria*
*Pleioblastus – Sasa*
*Podophyllum – Dysosma*
*Podranea – Tecoma*
*Polianthes – Bravoa*
*Polygonum – Persicaria*
*Polypodium – Phlebodium*
*Polyscias – Nothopanax*
*Polyspora – Gordonia*
*Poncirus – Aegle*
*Potentilla – Comarum*
*Pratia – Lobelia*
*Prenanthes – Nabalus*
*Pritzelago – Hutchinsia*
*Prumnopitys – Podocarpus*
*Prunus – Amygdalus*
*Pseudocydonia – Chaenomeles*
*Pseudogynoxys – Senecio*
*Pseudopanax – Metapanax*
*Pseudopanax – Neopanax*
*Pseudosasa – Arundinaria*
*Pseudotsuga – Tsuga*
*Pseudowintera – Drimys*
*Pterocephalus – Scabiosa*
*Pteryxia – Cymopterus*
*Ptilostemon – Cirsium*
*Pulicaria – Inula*
*Pulsatilla – Anemone*
*Purshia – Cowania*
*Puschkinia – Scilla*
*Pycreus – Cyperus*
*Pyrrocoma – Aster*
*Pyrrocoma – Haplopappus*

*Reineckea – Liriope*
*Retama – Genista*
*Retama – Lygos*
*Rhapis – Chamaerops*
*Rhodanthe – Helipterum*
*Rhodanthemum – Argyranthemum*
*Rhodanthemum – Chrysanthemopsis*
*Rhodanthemum – Chrysanthemum*
*Rhodanthemum – Leucanthemopsis*
*Rhodanthemum – Leucanthemum*
*Rhodanthemum – Pyrethropsis*
*Rhodiola – Clementsia*
*Rhodiola – Rosularia*
*Rhodiola – Sedum*
*Rhododendron – Azalea*
*Rhododendron – Azaleodendron*
*Rhododendron – Rhodora*
*Rhododendron – Therorhodion*
*Rhododendron – Tsusiophyllum*
*Rhodophiala – Hippeastrum*
*× Rhodoxis – Rhodohypoxis*

*Rhus – Toxicodendron*
*Rhyncospora – Dichromena*
*Rosularia – Cotyledon*
*Rosularia – Sempervivella*
*Rothmannia – Gardenia*
*Ruellia – Dipteracanthus*

*Saccharum – Erianthus*
*Sagina – Minuartia*
*Sanguisorba – Dendriopoterium*
*Sanguisorba – Poterium*
*Sasa – Arundinaria*
*Sasaella – Arundinaria*
*Sasaella – Pleioblastus*
*Sasaella – Sasa*
*Sauromatum – Arum*
*Saussurea – Jurinea*
*Scadoxus – Haemanthus*
*Schefflera – Brassaia*
*Schefflera – Dizygotheca*
*Schefflera – Heptapleurum*
*Schizachyrium – Andropogon*
*Schizostachyum – Arundinaria*
*Schizostachyum – Thamnocalamus*
*Schizostylis – Hesperantha*
*Schoenoplectus – Scirpus*
*Scilla – Oncostema*
*Scirpoides – Scirpus*
*Securigera – Coronilla*
*Sedum – Cotyledon*
*Sedum – Hylotelephium*
*Sedum – Sedastrum*
*Semiaquilegia – Aquilegia*
*Semiaquilegia – Paraquilegia*
*Semiarundinaria – Arundinaria*
*Semiarundinaria – Oligostachyum*
*Senecio – Cineraria*
*Senecio – Kleinia*
*Senecio – Ligularia*
*Senna – Cassia*
*Seriphidium – Artemisia*
*Shortia – Schizocodon*
*Sibbaldiopsis – Potentilla*
*Sieversia – Geum*
*Silene – Lychnis*
*Silene – Melandrium*
*Silene – Saponaria*
*Sinacalia – Ligularia*
*Sinacalia – Senecio*
*Sinningia – Gesneria*
*Sinningia – Rechsteineria*
*Sinobambusa – Pleioblastus*
*Sinobambusa – Pseudosasa*
*Siphocranion – Chamaesphacos*
*Sisymbrium – Hesperis*
*Sisyrinchium – Phaiophleps*
*Smallanthus – Polymnia*
*Solanum – Syphomandra*
*Soleirolia – Helxine*
*Solenostemon – Coleus*
*Solidago – Aster*
*Solidago – × Solidaster*
*× Solidaster – Aster*
*× Solidaster – Solidago*
*Sophora – Styphnolobium*
*Sorbaria – Spiraea*
*Sparaxis – Synnotia*
*Sphaeralcea – Iliamna*
*Sphaeromeria – Tanacetum*
*Spirodela – Lemna*
*Spraguea – Calyptridium*
*Stachys – Betonica*
*Stemmacantha – Centaurea*
*Stemmacantha – Leuzea*
*Stenomesson – Urceolina*
*Stenotus – Haplopappus*
*Stewartia – Stuartia*
*Stipa – Achnatherum*
*Stipa – Agrostis*
*Stipa – Calamagrostis*
*Stipa – Lasiagrostis*
*Stipa – Nassella*
*Strobilanthes – Parachampionella*
*Strobilanthes – Pteracanthus*
*Styphnolobium – Sophora*
*Succisa – Scabiosa*
*Sutera – Bacopa*
*Syagrus – Arecastrum*
*Syagrus – Cocos*
*Syncarpha – Helipterum*
*Syzygium – Caryophyllus*

*Talbotia – Vellozia*
*Tanacetum – Achillea*
*Tanacetum – Balsamita*
*Tanacetum – Chrysanthemum*
*Tanacetum – Matricaria*
*Tanacetum – Pyrethrum*
*Tanacetum – Spathipappus*
*Tecoma – Tecomaria*
*Telanthophora – Senecio*
*Telekia – Buphthalmum*
*Tetradium – Euodia*
*Tetraneuris – Actinella*
*Tetraneuris – Actinella*
*Tetraneuris – Hymenoxys*
*Tetrapanax – Fatsia*
*Thamnocalamus – Arundinaria*
*Thlaspi – Hutchinsia*
*Thlaspi – Noccaea*
*Thlaspi – Vania*
*Thuja – Thujopsis*
*Thymus – Origanum*
*Tiarella – × Heucherella*
*Tigridia – Rigidella*
*Tonestus – Haplopappus*
*Toona – Cedrela*
*Trachelium – Diosphaera*
*Trachycarpus – Chamaerops*
*Tradescantia – Rhoeo*
*Tradescantia – Setcreasea*
*Tradescantia – Zebrina*
*Trichopetalum – Anthericum*
*Trichophorum – Scirpus*
*Tripetaleia – Elliottia*
*Tripleurospermum – Gentiana*
*Tripleurospermum – Matricaria*
*Tripogandra – Tradescantia*
*Tristaniopsis – Tristania*
*Triteleia – Brodiaea*
*Tritonia – Crocosmia*
*Tritonia – Montbretia*
*Trochiscanthes – Angelica*
*Tropaeolum – Nasturtium hort.*
*Tupistra – Campylandra*
*Tutcheria – Pyrenaria*
*Tweedia – Oxypetalum*

*Ugni – Myrtus*
*Utricularia – Polypompholyx*
*Uvularia – Oakesiella*

*Vaccaria – Melandrium*
*Vaccinium – Oxycoccus*
*Verbascum – Celsia*
*Verbascum – × Celsioverbascum*
*Verbena – Glandularia*
*Verbena – Lippia*
*Veronicastrum – Veronica*
*Vigna – Phaseolus*
*Viola – Erpetion*
*Vitaliana – Androsace*
*Vitaliana – Douglasia*

*Wedelia – Zexmenia*
*Weigela – Diervilla*
*Weigela – Macrodiervilla*

*Xanthocyparis – Cupressus*
*Xanthorhiza – Zanthorhiza*
*Xerochrysum – Bracteantha*
*Xerochrysum – Helichrysum*

*Yushania – Arundinaria*
*Yushania – Sinarundinaria*
*Yushania – Thamnocalamus*

*Zantedeschia – Calla*
*Zauschneria – Epilobium*
*Zephyranthes – × Cooperanthes*
*Zephyranthes – Cooperia*

# THE PLANT DIRECTORY

# A

## *Abelia* ✿ (*Caprifoliaceae*)

| | | |
|---|---|---|
| | ***chinensis*** misapplied | see *A.* × *grandiflora* |
| § | ***chinensis*** R.Br. | CBcs CMac CPLG EBee ELan EPfP LRHS MAsh MMuc SBfd SEND SKHP SPer SRms WFar WGrn WPat |
| | 'Edward Goucher' | CAlb CBar CDoC CDul CWSG CWib EBee ECrN ELan EPfP LBMP LRHS LSRN LTen MAsh MGos MRav MSwo NBir SBfd SEND SGol SPer SPlb SRGP SWvt WDin WFar WPat WSHC |
| | ***engleriana*** | CPLG EBee EPfP LRHS MAsh MBlu NLar SEND SLon WFar |
| | ***floribunda*** ♀H3 | CBcs CDul CMac CPLG CSBt CSam CWib EBee ECre ELan EPfP EWTr IDee LHop LRHS MRav NLar SEND SGol SKHP SPer SPoG SSpi WAbe WFar WGob WPat |
| § | × ***grandiflora*** ♀H4 | Widely available |
| | - 'Aurea' | see *A.* × *grandiflora* 'Gold Spot' |
| | - 'Compacta' | CBar LRHS WFar |
| | - Confetti = 'Conti'PBR (v) | CBcs CDoC CMac CSBt CSPN CWSG EBee ELan EPfP LAst LRHS LSRN LTen MAsh MGos MRav MSwo NEgg NLar SBfd SGol SLim SPer SPoG SWvt WDin WFar WGob |
| | - dwarf | CDoC |
| § | - 'Francis Mason' (v) | Widely available |
| § | - 'Gold Spot' (v) | CWSG EPfP LRHS MGos MWat NMun SGol SPoG WGob WPat |
| | - 'Gold Strike' | see *A.* × *grandiflora* 'Gold Spot' |
| | - Golden Panache = 'Minpan' | MRav |
| | - 'Goldsport' | see *A.* × *grandiflora* 'Gold Spot' |
| | - 'Hopleys'PBR (v) | CBcs CDoC CDul CMac CSBt CTri CWib EBtc ELan EPfP LHop LRHS MAsh MGos MRav NHol SBrd SEND SLim SLon SPoG SWvt WCot WFar WGob WGrn WHar |
| | - 'Kaleidoscope'PBR (v) | CAbP CDoC CMac EHoe ELan EPfP EShb LRHS LSRN MAsh MGos NCGa SBfd SGol SLim SPoG SPtl SSta SWvt WGob WGrn |
| | - 'Panache' (v) | CAlb CDoC LLHF LTen WCot |
| | - 'Prostrate White' | EBee LRHS NLar |
| | - 'Semperflorens' | EBee EMil LRHS SBfd |
| | - 'Sherwoodii' | EMil EPfP LRHS MAsh SLim WPat |
| | - 'Sunrise' (v) | ELan EPfP MGos NLar SLim |
| | - 'Variegata' | see *A.* × *grandiflora* 'Francis Mason' |
| | ***mosanensis*** | EPfP IVic LLHF LRHS MBlu MBri NLar SBrd SLon SPoG SSpi |
| | ***parvifolia*** 'Bumblebee' | SPoG |
| | ***rupestris*** misapplied | see *A.* × *grandiflora* |
| | ***rupestris*** Lindl. | see *A. chinensis* R.Br. |
| | ***schumannii*** ♀H4 | CAbP CBcs CBot CMHG CMac CPLG CSBt EBee ECrN ELan EPfP LHop LRHS LSRN MAsh MBri MMuc MRav NLar SBrd SEND SKHP SLim SLon SPer SWvt WFar WGrn WPat |
| | ***spathulata*** | WFar |
| | ***triflora*** | CAbP CBot CPLG CWib ECre EPfP LAst LHop LRHS MMuc NLar SEND SKHP WFar WGob WSHC |

## *Abeliophyllum* (*Oleaceae*)

| | | |
|---|---|---|
| | ***distichum*** | CBcs CBot CDoC CEnd CWib EBee ECrN ELan ELon EPfP EWTr IDee LAst LBMP LRHS LSou MAsh MBlu MBri MGos SBfd SGol SPer SSpi SWvt WCFE WDin WFar WSHC |
| | - Roseum Group | CBcs CDoC CPLG CPMA EBee ELan ELon EPfP LHop LRHS MAsh MGos MMuc MRav SKHP SLon SPoG WFar |

## *Abelmoschus* (*Malvaceae*)

| | | |
|---|---|---|
| | ***esculentus*** new | SVic |
| § | ***manihot*** | XDel |

## *Abies* (*Pinaceae*)

| | | |
|---|---|---|
| | ***alba*** | CDul NWea |
| | - 'Compacta' | CKen |
| | - 'Green Spiral' | NLar |
| | - 'King's Dwarf' | CKen |
| | - 'Microphylla' | CKen |
| | - 'Münsterland' | CKen NLar |
| | - 'Nana' misapplied | see *Picea glauca* 'Nana' |
| | - 'Nana' ambig. | CKen |
| | - 'Pendula' | CKen |
| | ***amabilis*** | GLin WEve |
| | ***arizonica*** | see *A. lasiocarpa* var. *arizonica* |
| | ***balsamea*** | CDul GKin NWea STre |
| | - 'Cook's Blue' | CKen |
| | - Hudsonia Group ♀H4 | CDoC CKen EHul EPot LRHS NHol NLar NMen NMun NWad SLim SPoG WEve |
| | - 'Jamie' | CKen MAsh NLar |
| | - 'Le Feber' | CKen |
| | - 'Nana' | CKen EHul EPla MAsh NPCo NWad WDin WFar |
| | - var. ***phanerolepis*** 'Bear Swamp' | CKen NLar |
| | - 'Piccolo' | CDoC CKen EHul LRHS NLar WEve WFar WGor |
| | - 'Prostrata' | EHul WEve |
| | - 'Renswoude' | CKen |
| | - 'Tyler Blue' | CKen |
| | - 'Verkade's Prostrate' | CKen |
| * | ***borisii-regis*** 'Pendula' | CKen |
| | ***brachyphylla*** dwarf | see *A. homolepis* 'Prostrata' |
| | ***cephalonica*** | CDul CKen CMCN NWea |
| | - 'Greg's Broom' | CKen |

| | | |
|---|---|---|
| § | – 'Meyer's Dwarf' | EHul LRHS NLar NPCo SCoo SLim SPoG WEve |
| | – 'Nana' | see *A. cephalonica* 'Meyer's Dwarf' |
| | ***cilicica*** 'Spring Grove' | CKen |
| | ***colimensis*** NJM 09.074 **new** | WPGP |
| | ***concolor*** ♀H4 | CBcs CDul CTho LMaj LTen MMuc NWea SEND WDin WEve |
| | – 'Archer's Dwarf' | CKen MGos NLar SLim |
| | – 'Argentea' Niemetz, 1903 | CKen |
| | – 'Aurea' | MGos NLar WEve |
| | – 'Birthday Broom' | CKen |
| | – 'Blue Sapphire' | CKen NLar |
| | – 'Blue Spreader' | CKen |
| § | – 'Compacta' ♀H4 | CDoC CKen LRHS MBri MGos NLar NWea SCoo SLim SPoG WEve WFar |
| | – 'Fagerhult' | CKen |
| | – 'Gable's Weeping' | CKen |
| | – 'Glauca' | see *A. concolor* Violacea Group |
| | – 'Glauca Compacta' | see *A. concolor* 'Compacta' |
| | – 'Hillier Broom' | see *A. concolor* 'Hillier's Dwarf' |
| § | – 'Hillier's Dwarf' | CKen |
| | – 'Husky Pup' | CKen |
| | – (Lowiana Group) 'Creamy' | CKen |
| | – 'Masonic Broom' | CKen |
| | – 'Mike Stearn' | CKen |
| | – 'Mora' | CKen |
| | – 'Ostrov nad Ohri' | CKen |
| | – 'Piggelmee' | CKen NLar |
| | – 'Pygmy' | CKen |
| | – 'Scooter' | CKen |
| * | – 'Swift's Silver' | WEve |
| § | – Violacea Group | CKen MAsh MGos SLim WEve WFar |
| | – – prostrate **new** | LRHS |
| | – 'Wattez Prostrate' | LRHS NLar SLim SPoG WFar |
| | – 'Wattezii' | CKen |
| | – 'Wintergold' | CKen MGos NLar NPCo SLim WEve |
| | ***delavayi*** | CDul MGos NWea |
| | – SDR 3269 | GKev |
| | – var. ***delavayi*** Fabri Group | see *A. fabri* |
| I | – 'Nana' | CKen |
| | – 'Nana Headfort' | see *A. fargesii* 'Headfort' |
| § | ***fabri*** | CDul CKen |
| | ***fargesii*** | CKen NLar |
| § | – 'Headfort' | NLar |
| | ***forrestii*** | CKen |
| | – var. ***georgei*** | NWea |
| | ***fraseri*** | CTho NWea WEve |
| | – 'Blue Bonnet' | CKen NLar |
| | – 'Piglet's' witches' broom | NLar |
| | – 'Raul's Dwarf' | CKen |
| | ***grandis*** | CBcs CDul NWea WDin |
| | – 'Compacta' | CKen |
| | – 'Van Dedem's Dwarf' | CKen NLar SLim WEve |
| | ***holophylla*** | NLar NWea |
| | ***homolepis*** | CKen NLar NWea |
| § | – 'Prostrata' | CKen |
| | ***kawakamii*** | CKen |
| | ***koreana*** | Widely available |
| | – 'Alpin Star' | CKen MAsh NLar |
| | – 'Aurea' | see *A. koreana* 'Flava' |
| | – 'Blaue Zwo' | CKen MAsh NLar |
| | – 'Blauer Eskimo' | CKen MAsh NLar SLim |
| | – 'Blauer Pfiff' | CKen NLar |
| | – 'Blinsham Gold' | CKen |
| | – 'Blue Emperor' | CKen NLar |
| | – 'Blue Magic' | CKen NLar |
| | – 'Blue 'n' Silver' | NLar WEve |
| | – 'Bonsai Blue' | IVic NLar |
| | – 'Cis' | CDoC CKen LRHS NHol NLar SCoo SLim SPoG |
| | – 'Compact Dwarf' | MGos NLar WEve |
| | – 'Crystal Globe' | CKen NLar |
| | – 'Dark Hill' | NLar |
| | – 'Doni Tajuso' | CKen |
| | – 'Eisregen' | CKen |
| | – 'Festival' | NLar |
| § | – 'Flava' | CKen MGos NPCo WEve |
| | – 'Fliegender Untertasse' **new** | IVic |
| | – 'Frosty' | SLim SPoG |
| | – 'Gait' | CKen NLar |
| | – 'Golden Dream' | CKen |
| | – 'Golden Glow' | NLar SLim WFar |
| | – 'Green Carpet' | CKen LRHS NLar SLim |
| | – 'Grübele' witches' broom | CKen |
| | – 'Horstmann' | CKen |
| | – 'Ice Breaker' **new** | MAsh NLar |
| | – 'Inverleith' | CKen |
| | – 'Kleiner Prinz' | NLar |
| | – 'Kohout' | CKen |
| | – 'Lippetal' | CKen |
| | – 'Luminetta' | CKen LRHS MGos NLar |
| | – 'Nadelkissen' | CKen |
| | – 'Nisbet' | LRHS NPCo SCoo SLim SPoG WEve WGor |
| | – 'Oberon' | CDoC CKen MAsh MBri NHol NLar NWad SLim |
| | – 'Piccolo' | CKen |
| | – 'Pinocchio' | CDoC CKen MGos |
| | – 'Prostrata' | see *A. koreana* 'Prostrate Beauty' |
| § | – 'Prostrate Beauty' | NPCo WEve WFar WGor |
| | – 'Scherenbach' | NLar |
| | – 'Schweden König' | NLar SLim |
| | – 'Sherwood Compact' | CKen |
| | – 'Silberkugel' | CKen CMen IVic NLar NWad SLim |
| | – 'Silberlocke' ♀H4 | CDoC CDul CKen EPla GKin LRHS MAsh MBlu MBri MGos NEgg NLar SCoo SLim SPer SPoG SSpi WEve WFar WHar |
| | – 'Silbermavers' | CKen |
| | – 'Silberperl' | CKen CMen LRHS NLar SPoG |
| | – 'Silberschmelze' | MGos NLar |
| | – 'Silver Show' | CDoC CKen |
| | – 'Taiga' | NLar |
| | – 'Threave' | CKen |
| | – 'Tundra' | NLar SLim |
| | – 'Vengels' | NLar |
| | – 'Verdener Dom' | NLar |
| | – 'Winter Goldtip' | WEve |
| | ***lasiocarpa*** | CDul NWea |
| | – 'Alpine Beauty' | CKen MAsh NLar |
| § | – var. ***arizonica*** | CDul |
| | – – 'Argentea' | WEve |
| | – – 'Compacta' Hornibr. ♀H4 | CDoC CKen CMac EHul ELan EPla LRHS MBri MGos SLim SPoG WFar WGor |
| | – – 'Kenwith Blue' | CKen MGos SLim WEve WFar |
| | – 'Compacta' Beissn. | LRHS MAsh MBri NHol WEve WFar |
| | – 'Day Creek' | CKen |
| | – 'Duflon' | CKen |
| | – 'Elaine' | CKen |
| | – 'Glauca' | see *A. lasiocarpa* var. *arizonica* 'Argentea' |
| | – 'Green Globe' | CKen LRHS NLar WEve |
| | – 'Joe's Alpine' | CKen |
| * | – 'King's Blue' | CKen |
| | – 'Logan Pass' | CKen NLar |
| | – 'Mulligan's Dwarf' | CKen |
| | – 'Prickly Pete' | CKen NLar |

| | |
|---|---|
| I - 'Prostrata' | CMac |
| - 'Stevens Blue' new | MAsh |
| - 'Toenisvorst' | CKen |
| - 'Utah' | CKen |
| I ***magnifica*** 'Nana' | CKen |
| - witches' broom | CKen |
| ***nebrodensis*** | CKen |
| ***nobilis*** | see *A. procera* |
| ***nordmanniana*** $\Upsilon^{H4}$ | CAlb CCVT CDul CMac CTri EHul |
| | EPfP EWTr LBuc LMaj LTen MGos |
| | MMuc NEgg NWea SEND SPer |
| | SPoG WDin WEve WMou |
| - 'Arne's Dwarf' | CKen |
| - 'Barabits' Compact' | EPla MGos NLar |
| - 'Barabits' Spreader' | CKen |
| - 'Dahlheim' new | MAsh |
| - subsp. ***equi-trojani*** | CDul NWea |
| - - 'Archer' | CKen NPCo |
| - 'Golden Spreader' $\Upsilon^{H4}$ | CDoC CKen CMac ECho EPla LRHS |
| | MAsh MBri MGos NLar NPCo SCoo |
| | SLim SPoG WEve WFar |
| - 'Hasselt' | CKen |
| - 'Jakobsen' | CKen |
| - 'Silberspitze' | CKen |
| ***numidica*** | CKen |
| - 'Glauca' | CKen |
| - 'Lawrenceville' | NPCo WFar |
| ***pinsapo*** | CDul SEND |
| - 'Atlas' | MAsh NLar |
| - 'Aurea' | CKen LRHS MGos MPkF NLar SLim |
| | SPoG WEve WFar |
| I - 'Aurea Nana' | CKen |
| - 'Fastigiata' | MPkF SGol |
| - 'Glauca' $\Upsilon^{H4}$ | CDoC CDul CKen CTho EHul ELan |
| | LMaj LRHS MBlu NLar SCoo SLim |
| | SPoG WDin WEve |
| - 'Hamondii' | CKen |
| I - 'Horstmann' | CKen NLar NPCo SLim WEve |
| - 'Kelleriis' | NLar |
| - 'Pendula' | CKen MGos MPkF NLar WEve |
| - 'Quicksilver' | CKen |
| § ***procera*** $\Upsilon^{H4}$ | CAlb CBcs CDul NWea WDin WEve |
| - 'Bizarro' | NLar WEve |
| - 'Blaue Hexe' | CKen IVic LRHS MAsh NLar SLim |
| | SPoG WFar |
| - Glauca Group | CDoC CDul CTho GKin LRHS LTen |
| | MAsh MBlu MBri MGos SLim WEve |
| | WFar |
| - - 'Glauca Prostrata' | EPla GKin MGos SCoo SLim WEve |
| | WFar |
| - 'La Graciosa' | NLar |
| - 'Noble's Dwarf' | SLim |
| - 'Obrighofen' | NLar |
| - 'Seattle Mount' | NLar |
| - 'Sherwoodii' | CKen SLim |
| ***recurvata*** | NLar |
| Rosemoor hybrid | CKen |
| ***sachalinensis*** | CKen |
| ***veitchii*** | CTho |
| - 'Heddergott' | CKen MGos NLar SLim |
| - 'Heine' | CKen |
| - 'Kramer' | CKen |
| I - 'Pendula' | CKen IVic |
| - 'Rumburg' | CKen MAsh NLar |
| - 'Syców' | CKen |

## *Abromeitiella* see *Deuterocohnia*

## *Abrotanella* (*Asteraceae*)

| | |
|---|---|
| sp. | ECho |

## *Abutilon* ✿ (*Malvaceae*)

| | |
|---|---|
| sp. | CArn |
| 'Amiti' | ELar |
| 'Apricot Belle' | SMDP WTcb |
| 'Ashford Red' | CBcs CCCN ELan IVic LRHS MAsh |
| | MOWG SAga SBfd SKHP SMDP |
| | SVen WKif WTcb |
| 'Boule de Neige' | CBot MOWG SMrm WTcb |
| 'Canary Bird' $\Upsilon^{H2}$ | CBcs CBot CCCN CHEx ELon |
| | SMDP SUsu SVen WKif WTcb |
| 'Cannington Carol' (v) $\Upsilon^{H2}$ | CCCN CHll ELan LSRN SEND SLim |
| | SMDP WTcb |
| 'Cannington Peter' (v) $\Upsilon^{H2}$ | CCCN LSRN SMDP |
| 'Cannington Sonia' (v) | SMDP |
| 'Cloth of Gold' | CMac WTcb |
| 'Cynthia Pike' (v) | LRHS |
| 'Eric Lilac' new | EShb |
| 'Flamenco' | CWGN LRHS NEgg SLim |
| 'Frances Elizabeth' | SMDP |
| 'Heather Bennington' | SMDP |
| 'Henry Makepeace' | ELar SMDP |
| 'Hinton Seedling' | CCCN CRHN WTcb |
| × ***hybridum*** | CHEx WTcb |
| apricot-flowered | |
| - red-flowered | CHEx |
| ***indicum*** | CCCN |
| 'Ines' new | WPGP |
| 'Isles of Scilly' | CCCN |
| 'Jacqueline Morris' | LRHS MAsh SMrm |
| 'John Thompson' | CCCN CWGN LSRN |
| 'Kentish Belle' $\Upsilon^{H2-3}$ | CBcs CCCN CDoC CHEx CMHG |
| | CMac CRHN CSBt CWGN EBee |
| | ELan ELon EPfP GKin LRHS LSRN |
| | NEgg NPal SBfd SCoo SEND SKHP |
| | SLPl SLim SPer SPlb WCot WFar |
| | WTcb XLum |
| 'Kentish Belle Variegatum' (v) | ELan |
| 'Kreutzberger' | ELar |
| 'Lemon Queen' | ELar |
| 'Linda Vista Peach' $\Upsilon^{H2}$ | ELar SMDP |
| 'Louis Marignac' | ELar |
| 'Marion' $\Upsilon^{H2}$ | CRHN ELar LRHS LSRN SMDP |
| | SMrm SPoG WCot |
| 'Master Michael' | CMac GKin SMDP |
| ***megapotamicum*** $\Upsilon^{H3}$ | Widely available |
| - 'Variegatum' (v) | CBcs CCCN CMac EBee ELan ELar |
| | EPfP LRHS MAsh MGos MOWG |
| | MSCN NEgg SBfd SKHP SLim SLon |
| | SPer SPoG SWvt WFar WTcb |
| | XLum |
| - 'Wisley Red' | CRHN CSBt GGar GKin LRHS SKHP |
| | SMDP |
| × ***milleri*** $\Upsilon^{H2}$ | CMac CRHN WCot WWlt |
| - 'Variegatum' (v) | CCCN CHEx CMac LRHS NEgg |
| | WCot |
| - 'Ventnor Gold' | SBfd SVen |
| 'Millie Houghton' new | WTcb |
| 'Nabob' $\Upsilon^{H2}$ | CCCN CDoC CHGN CPLG CRHN |
| | LRHS MOWG SBfd SMDP SMrm |
| | SPoG WTcb |
| 'Old Rose Belle' | SMDP |
| 'Orange Hot Lava' new | WPGP |
| 'Orange Vein' | EShb SMDP |
| 'Patrick Synge' | CCCN CHGN CMHG EBtc EShb |
| | MOWG SBfd SPhx SUsu WPGP |
| | WTcb |
| ***pictum*** 'Thompsonii' (v) | CHEx EShb SBfd SMDP SVen WDyG |
| | WTcb |

I – 'Variegatum' (v) — EShb
'Pink Lady' — SMDP
'Red Bells' — ELar SVen
'Red Queen' — ELar
'Russels Dwarf' — CCCN
'Satin Pink Belle' — SMDP
'Savitzii' (v) ♀H2 — MCot MOWG MSCN SBfd SBrd SMDP SVen
'Silver Belle' — SMDP
'Simcox White' — CCCN
'Snow Boy' — ELar
'Snowfall' — SMDP
'Sophia Jackson' new — WTcb
'Souvenir de Bonn' (v) ♀H2 — ELar EShb LSou SBfd SMDP SMrm WTcb
× ***suntense*** — CBcs CCCN CHll CMHG CSBt EBee ELan EPfP ESwi GGar LHop LRHS MOWG MSCN NPer SChF SEND
– 'Jermyns' ♀H3 — CAbP EBee ELan EPfP GCra LRHS LSRN MAsh MBri MGos SCoo SKHP SPoG SSpi SVen SWvt WFar
'Tango' — CWGN LRHS SEND SLim
variegated, salmon-flowered (v) — LAst SEND
'Victory' — CCCN CWGN SEND SKHP SLim
***vitifolium*** — CBcs CBot CCCN CDTJ CWib EPfP EQua EShb GGar NBid NEgg NLar SBrt SPad SPoG SVen WBor WHil WKif
– 'Album' — CBcs CDul CHll CPLG EBee ELan EQua GCal GQui LHop NChi SEND SPer SSpi WFar
– 'Buckland' — CGHE
– 'Ice Blue' — CBot
– 'Tennant's White' ♀H3 — CAbP CBot CCCN CPLG EBee EPfP GGal LRHS MBri SKHP WTcb
– 'Veronica Tennant' ♀H3 — CPLG GQui WKif
'Waltz' — CWGN LRHS SBfd SEND SLim
'Westfield Bronze' — CRHN SMDP

## *Acacia* (*Mimosaceae*)

sp. — LSRN NLar SEND
***acinacea*** — IDee SPlb
***adunca*** — SPad SPlb
***armata*** — see *A. paradoxa*
***axillaris*** — SPlb
***baileyana*** ♀H2 — Widely available
– var. ***aurea*** — SPlb
– 'Purpurea' ♀H2 — Widely available
***boormanii*** — SBrt WPGP
***brachybotrya*** — CDTJ
***cardiophylla*** — SEND
***caven*** NJM 08.0021 — WPGP
***covenyi*** new — CTrC
***cultriformis*** — CCCN CTrC CTsd ESwi SBfd SEND
***dealbata*** ♀H2 — Widely available
– 'Gaulois Astier' — CDoC CSBt ELon LRHS LSRN MBri MGos MREP SBfd SPoG SSpi SWvt WPGP
– subsp. ***subalpina*** — WPGP
'Exeter Hybrid' — CDoy CSBt
***fimbriata*** — CRHN
***julibrissin*** — see *Albizia julibrissin*
***juniperina*** — see *A. ulicifolia*
***karroo*** — CArn CCCN CDTJ CTrC SPlb
***kybeanensis*** — EBee WPGP
***longifolia*** — CBcs CCCN CDTJ EPfP EPri IDee LRHS SEND SPer SRms
– subsp. ***sophorae*** — CCCN
***macradenia*** — SPlb
***mearnsii*** — CCCN
***melanoxylon*** — CBcs CDTJ CTsd ELan ESwi IGor MTPN SEND SLim
***mucronata*** — CTrC EShb
§ ***paradoxa*** ♀H2 — CCCN ECou ELon ESwi IDee LRHS WPat
***pataczekii*** — CSBt EPfP EWes
***podalyriifolia*** — CAbb CCCN LTod SPlb
***pravissima*** ♀H2-3 — Widely available
– 'Bushwalk Baby' — MOWG
***retinodes*** ♀H2 — CBcs CCCN CDTJ CDoC CRHN CTsd EAmu EBee EPfP ESwi ETod IDee LRHS LSRN MTPN SBfd SEND SLim SPad SWvt WCFE
– blue-leaved — ESwi SEND
***riceana*** — CCCN CTsd SBrt SVen
***rubida*** — MGos SPlb
***sentis*** — see *A. victoriae*
***spectabilis*** — CCCN SPlb
***suaveolens*** — SPlb
§ ***ulicifolia*** — CSBt
***verticillata*** — CBcs CCCN CDTJ CHGN CHll CTsd MOWG MTPN
– riverine form — CPLG EPfP LRHS SEND
§ ***victoriae*** — ECre

## *Acaena* (*Rosaceae*)

***adscendens*** misapplied — see *A. affinis*, *A. magellanica* subsp. *magellanica*, *A. saccaticupula* 'Blue Haze'
***adscendens*** Vahl — see *A. magellanica* subsp. *laevigata*
***adscendens*** ambig. 'Glauca' — EHoe NBir
§ ***affinis*** — ECha SDix
***anserinifolia*** misapplied — see *A. novae-zelandiae*
***buchananii*** — CTri EBee ECho EHoe GAbr GGar MBrN MMuc NLar SRms STre WFar WPer
***caerulea*** hort. — see *A. caesiiglauca*
§ ***caesiiglauca*** — CTri GAbr GGar GQue MLHP NBid SGar
– 'Frikart' — EBee
***eupatoria*** — EBee
***inermis*** — SPlb
– 'Purpurea' — EBee ECha EHoe ETod GAbr GBin GGar GKev GQue LRHS NDov NLar SPlb WHoo WMoo WPtf
***magellanica*** — EBee GCal GGar GKev MSCN
§ – subsp. ***laevigata*** — GGar
***microphylla*** ♀H4 — CSam CTri EBee ECho LRHS MBrN MLLN NLar NMen SPlb SRms WFar WMoo
– 'Braune Feder' — EBee
– Copper Carpet — see *A. microphylla* 'Kupferteppich'
– 'Dichte Matte' — EBee
– 'Glauca' — see *A. caesiiglauca*
– 'Grüner Zwerg' — EBee
§ – 'Kupferteppich' — EBee ECho ECtt EHoe ETod GAbr GCal GGar GQue LHop MBri MMuc MRav NBir NBro NDov NLar WMoo WPat WPer WWEG
***myriophylla*** — EBee ECho EDAr
§ ***novae-zelandiae*** — CTri EBee GGar SDix WMoo
'Pewter' — see *A. saccaticupula* 'Blue Haze'
'Purple Carpet' — see *A. microphylla* 'Kupferteppich'
'Purple Haze' — CSpe
***saccaticupula*** — WFar
§ – 'Blue Haze' — EBee ECha ECho EDAr EHoe ETod GGar LHop LRHS MBrN MRav NChi SPer SPlb SRms WFar WHoo WMoo WPtf WWEG
***splendens*** — SPlb

## *Acalypha* (*Euphorbiaceae*)

| | | |
|---|---|---|
| | ***pendula*** | see *A. reptans* |
| § | ***reptans*** | CCCN EShb |

## *Acanthocalyx* see *Morina*

## *Acantholimon* (*Plumbaginaceae*)

| | | |
|---|---|---|
| | sp. | EDAr |
| | ***acerosum*** | XSen |
| | ***androsaceum*** | see *A. ulicinum* |
| § | ***ulicinum*** | WAbe XSen |

## *Acanthopanax* see *Eleutherococcus*

| | |
|---|---|
| ***ricinifolius*** | see *Kalopanax septemlobus* |

## *Acanthus* ✿ (*Acanthaceae*)

| | | |
|---|---|---|
| | ***balcanicus*** misapplied | see *A. hungaricus* |
| | ***caroli-alexandri*** | see *A. spinosus* |
| | ***dioscoridis*** | EBee GCal MAvo |
| | - var. ***perringii*** | CDes CRDP ECha GBin LRHS MAvo MNrw WCot WFar XLum |
| | - smooth-leaved | WCot |
| | ***eminens*** | WCot WHil |
| | ***hirsutus*** | EPri IFoB SBig WCot |
| | - f. ***roseus*** | WFar |
| | - subsp. ***syriacus*** | GCal NLar WCot WFar |
| | 'Hollande du Nort' | EBee GBin WHil |
| § | ***hungaricus*** | CArn CHid CMac EBee EBla ECtt ELan EShb EWTr GAbr GBBs LPla LRHS MLLN MMuc MRav MSCN NLar SDix SEND SPer SPhx SWat WCot WFar WMnd WWEG XLum |
| | - AL&JS 90097YU | WHil |
| | - MESE 561 | EPPr WHil |
| | ***longifolius*** Host | see *A. hungaricus* |
| | ***mollis*** | Widely available |
| | - from Turkey | GCal |
| | - 'Fielding Gold' | see *A. mollis* 'Hollard's Gold' |
| | - free-flowering | GCal XLum |
| § | - 'Hollard's Gold' | Widely available |
| | - 'Jefalba' | see *A. mollis* (Latifolius Group) 'Rue Ledan' |
| | - Latifolius Group | EBee EPfP MRav NHol SRms WHil WHoo WTin |
| § | - - 'Rue Ledan' | EBee ECtt EShb GBin IPot LHop MAvo MDKP NBPC NGdn NLar SPhx SUsu WCot WFar WHil WTin WWEG XLum |
| | - - 'Sjaak' | WHil |
| | - 'Long Spike' | EBee GCal WHil |
| | - 'Niger' | LRHS WHil |
| | - 'Tasmanian Angel' (v) | WCot |
| | ***montanus*** | WHil |
| | - 'Crocodile' **new** | WHil |
| | 'Morning's Candle' | CBct EBee ECtt MAvo MBri NGdn WHil |
| | ***sennii*** | CCse CDes EBee SMad SPhx WSHC XLum |
| | ***spinosus*** misapplied | see *A. spinosus* Spinosissimus Group |
| § | ***spinosus*** L. ♀H4 | Widely available |
| | - Ferguson's form | WCot WHil XLum |
| | - 'Lady Moore' (v) | MCCP NLar WHil XLum |
| | - 'Royal Haughty' | EWes GBin GCal MAvo WFar XLum |
| § | - Spinosissimus Group | CBct CFir CMHG EBee ECha ELan ELon GBin GCal GCra LEdu MCCP MRav SBfd SMad SWat WCot WFar WMnd WTin |
| | 'Summer Beauty' | EBee ECtt EWes GBin GCal LHop MAvo MBri NLar WCot WFar XLum |

## *Acca* (*Myrtaceae*)

| | |
|---|---|
| sp. | SWvt |
| ***sellowiana*** (F) | CBcs CDTJ CDul CMHG CMac CPLG EBee ECrN ELan EPfP ERom GQui LAst LHop LRHS MGos MNHC MOWG MREP SBfd SBrd SLPl SLim SPer SPlb SPoG SVic WFar WSHC XSen |
| - 'Apollo' (F) | LRHS |
| - 'Coolidge' (F) | CAgr ERea |
| - 'Gemini' (F) | LRHS |
| - 'Mammoth' (F) | CAgr CBcs CCCN |
| - 'Triumph' (F) | CAgr CBcs CCCN |
| - 'Unique' (F) | CAgr ERea |
| - 'Variegata' (F/v) | CCCN EBee ELan LAst SPoG |

## *Acer* ✿ (*Sapindaceae*)

| | | |
|---|---|---|
| | ***amoenum*** B&SWJ 10916 | WCru |
| | ***barbinerve*** | EPfP |
| | ***buergerianum*** | CLnd CMCN CMen CPMA LMaj MMuc MPkF NEgg NLar SEND SGol STre |
| | - var. ***formosanum*** B&SWJ 7032 | WCru |
| | - - CWJ 12477 | WCru |
| | - 'Himcode' | NLar |
| | - 'Mino-yatsubusa' | MPkF |
| | - 'Miyasama-yatsubusa' | MPkF |
| | - 'Naruto' | CMCN MPkF |
| | ***calcaratum*** | CMCN |
| | ***campbellii*** B&SWJ 7685 | WCru |
| | - subsp. ***campbellii*** var. ***serratifolium*** GWJ 9360 | WCru |
| | - 'Exuberance' **new** | CPMA |
| * | - var. ***fansipanense*** B&SWJ 8270 | WCru |
| | - - HWJ 569 | WCru |
| | - - HWJ 944 | WCru |
| | ***campestre*** ♀H4 | Widely available |
| | - 'Carnival' (v) | CCVT CDul CEnd CPMA EBee ECrN ELon EMil MAsh MBlu MBri MPkF NLar NPCo SMad SPer SPoG SPur SWvt WHar |
| | - 'Elsrijk' | CCVT CLnd EBee LMaj SCoo SGol |
| | - 'Evelyn' | see *A. campestre* 'Queen Elizabeth' |
| | - 'Pendulum' | CEnd ECrN |
| | - 'Postelense' | CMCN CPMA MBlu |
| | - 'Pulverulentum' (v) | CEnd CMCN CPMA NPCo SMad SSta |
| § | - 'Queen Elizabeth' | LMaj MGos |
| | - 'Royal Ruby' | CPMA CWSG MGos SKHP WFar |
| * | - 'Ruby Glow' | CEnd ECrN |
| | - 'Schwerinii' | CDul |
| I | - 'Silver Celebration' (v) | CPMA |
| | - 'William Caldwell' | CEnd CTho ECrN MBri |
| | ***capillipes*** ♀H4 | CAlb CBcs CDul CLnd CMCN CTho CWib EBee ECrN GKin LMaj MAsh MGos MMuc NWea SPer SPlb SPoG WDin WFar WHCr WHar WPGP |
| | - B&SWJ 11473 | WCru |
| | - 'Candy Stripe' | see *A. × conspicuum* 'Candy Stripe' |
| | - 'Gimborn' | WPGP |
| | - 'Honey Dew' | NLar |
| | ***cappadocicum*** | CCVT CDul CEnd CMCN ECrN LMaj MMuc MSnd NWea SEND WDin |

|  |  |
|---|---|
| - 'Aureum' ♀H4 | CBcs CCVT CDoC CDul CEnd CLnd CMCN CTho EBee ECrN ELan EPfP GBin GKin IArd MAsh MBlu MBri MGos MRav NLar SGol SLim SPer SPoG SSpi SWvt WDin WFar WHar |
| § - subsp. ***divergens*** | CMCN |
| - var. ***mono*** | see *A. pictum* |
| - 'Rubrum' ♀H4 | CBcs CDul CLnd CMCN EBee ECrN EPfP GKin LMaj MBlu MBri MGos MRav SGol SLim SPer WDin WFar WHar WHer |
| - var. ***sinicum*** | EPfP GBin WFar WPGP |
| - var. ***tricaudatum*** | CPLG |
| ***carpinifolium*** | IArd MBlu MPkF NLar SBir |
| - B&SWJ 10955 | WCru |
| - B&SWJ 11124 | WCru |
| § ***caudatifolium*** | CMCN EWTr |
| - CWJ 12403 | WCru |
| - RWJ 9843 | WCru |
| § ***caudatum*** CWJ 12403 | WCru |
| - GWJ 9279 | WCru |
| - GWJ 9317 | WCru |
| - HWJK 2240 | WCru |
| - HWJK 2338 | WCru |
| - subsp. ***ukurunduense*** | MPkF |
| - - B&SWJ 8658 | WCru |
| ***circinatum*** | CBcs CCVT CDoC CDul CLnd CMCN CPMA EBee ECrN EPfP GBin IVic MBlu MMuc MPkF MSnd NLar NWea SPlb SSta WDin WFar WMou |
| - B&SWJ 9565 | WCru |
| - 'Burgundy Jewel' new | CPMA |
| - 'Little Gem' | CPMA |
| - 'Little Joe' | CPMA |
| - 'Monroe' | CPMA |
| - 'Pacific Fire' | CPMA |
| - 'Sunglow' | CPMA NLar |
| ***circinatum* × *palmatum*** | SBig |
| ***cissifolium*** | CMCN EPfP EPla IArd NLar |
| - B&SWJ 10801 | WCru |
| § × ***conspicuum*** 'Candy Stripe' | CBcs CLnd CPMA NLar SLim SSpi SSta WPGP |
| - 'Elephant's Ear' | CPMA EPfP NLar |
| - 'Mozart' | CPMA MBlu MPkF SSta |
| - 'Phoenix' | CBcs CEnd CMCN CPMA EPfP GKin IVic MBlu MBri NLar SSta WDin WHar WPGP WPat |
| - 'Silver Ghost' | MPkF |
| § - 'Silver Vein' | CDoC CEnd CMCN CPMA EBee EPfP MWea NLar SSta WPGP |
| ***crataegifolium*** B&SWJ 11036 | WCru |
| - B&SWJ 11355 | WCru |
| - 'Ittai-san-nishiki' new | SSta |
| - 'Meuri-keade-no-fuiri' (v) | MPkF |
| - 'Meuri-no-ōfu' (v) | MPkF |
| - 'Veitchii' (v) | CMCN CPMA EBee EPfP MBri MPkF SBig SSpi SSta |
| ***creticum*** L., non F. Schmidt. | see *A. sempervirens* |
| ***dasycarpum*** | see *A. saccharinum* |
| ***davidii*** | CBcs CDoC CDul CLnd CMCN CPLG CSam ECrN EWTr GAuc GCal LMaj LTen MAsh MBlu MGos MRav SGol SLim SPer SSta WDin WFar WPat |
| § - 'Canton' | CPMA |
| - 'Cantonspark' | see *A. davidii* 'Canton' |
| - 'Cascade' | CPMA SSta |
| - 'Chinese Temple' | SBir |
| N - 'Ernest Wilson' | CBcs EBee NLar |
| N - 'George Forrest' ♀H4 | CCVT CDoC CDul CMCN CMac CPLG CPMA CTho CWSG EBee ECrN ELan EPfP GBin LAst LRHS MMuc NLar NWea SBfd SEND SLim SPer SPoG WDin WFar WHar |
| 'Hagelunie' | SBir |
| - 'Hansu-suru' (v) new | SSta |
| - 'Karmen' | CBcs CDul CGHE CPMA WPGP |
| - 'Madeline Spitta' | CMCN CPMA MBri |
| - 'Purple Bark' | CPLG CPMA NLar SBir |
| - 'Rosalie' | CBcs CPMA EPfP MBlu MBri SBir |
| - 'Serpentine' ♀H4 | CBcs CDoC CMCN CPMA ELan EPfP GBin IDee MBlu MBri NEgg NLar SBir SMad SSta WFar WPGP |
| - 'Silver Vein' | see *A.* × *conspicuum* 'Silver Vein' |
| ***discolor*** | CMCN |
| ***distylum*** | CMCN |
| ***divergens*** | see *A. cappadocicum* subsp. *divergens* |
| ***elegantulum*** | CDoC CPLG CPMA GBin IDee WPGP |
| ***erianthum*** | MSnd |
| ***erythranthum*** B&SWJ 11733 | WCru |
| - DJHV 06147 | WCru |
| ***fabri*** | CDul CPLG |
| - WWJ 11614 | WCru |
| ***flabellatum*** var. ***yunnanense*** | MBri MSnd |
| ***forrestii*** | CMCN CPLG EPfP |
| - BWJ 7515 | WCru |
| - 'Alice' | CBcs CEnd CPMA |
| - 'Sirene' | CPMA |
| - 'Sparkling' | CPMA |
| × ***freemanii*** | CMCN |
| - 'Armstrong' | CCVT SGol WFar |
| - Autumn Blaze = 'Jeffersred' | CBcs CCVT CDoC CDul CMCN EBee EPfP LMaj LRHS MBlu MGos MMuc SBir SCoo SMad SPoG WDin WFar WHar |
| - Celebration = 'Celzam' | CCVT CDul MGos WFar |
| - 'Indian Summer' | see *A.* × *freemanii* 'Morgan' |
| § - 'Morgan' | CPMA SBir |
| ***fulvescens*** | see *A. longipes* |
| ***ginnala*** | see *A. tataricum* subsp. *ginnala* |
| ***globosum*** | see *A. platanoides* 'Globosum' |
| ***grandidentatum*** | see *A. saccharum* subsp. *grandidentatum* |
| ***griseum*** ♀H4 | Widely available |
| ***grosseri*** | CDul CMCN CTri IGor SGol |
| - var. ***hersii*** ♀H4 | CBcs CCVT CDoC CDul CLnd CMac CWib EBee ECrN ELan EPfP LRHS MAsh MBri MMuc MRav NLar NWea SPer SPoG SWvt WDin WFar WHCr WHar |
| - 'Leiden' | EPfP |
| ***heldreichii*** | EGFP |
| ***henryi*** | CDul EPfP LMaj NEgg NLar |
| ***heptaphlebium*** B&SWJ 11695 | WCru |
| - B&SWJ 11713 | WCru |
| - DJHV 06063 | WCru |
| ***hyrcanum*** | LRHS |
| ***japonicum*** | CMCN MMuc SEND SEWo WHCr |
| - B&SWJ 8417 | WCru |
| § - 'Aconitifolium' ♀H4 | Widely available |
| - 'Ao-jutan' | CPMA |
| - 'Attaryi' | CMen LRHS MPkF |
| - 'Aureum' | see *A. shirasawanum* 'Aureum' |

| | |
|---|---|
| - 'Ezo-no-momiji' | see *A. shirasawanum* 'Ezo-no-momiji' |
| - 'Filicifolium' | see *A. japonicum* 'Aconitifolium' |
| - 'Green Cascade' | CEnd CMCN CMac CMen CPMA CWGN IVic LRHS MPkF NLar NPCo SBig WPGP WPat |
| - 'Kalmthout' | NLar |
| - 'King's Copse' | CPMA |
| - 'Laciniatum' | see *A. japonicum* 'Aconitifolium' |
| - f. ***microphyllum*** | see *A. shirasawanum* 'Microphyllum' |
| - 'Ogurayama' | see *A. shirasawanum* 'Ogurayama' |
| - 'Ō-isami' | EPfP MPkF NLar SBig |
| - 'Ō-taki' | CPMA |
| - 'Vitifolium' ♀H4 | CDoC CEnd CMCN CMac CPMA CSBt ELan EPfP GBin LRHS LTen MBlu MBri MGos MPkF NEgg NLar NPCo SBig SGol SPer SSta WCFE WDin WPGP |
| ***kawakamii*** | see *A. caudatifolium* |
| ***laevigatum*** | CMCN |
| - B&SWJ 11684 | WCru |
| § - var. ***reticulatum*** B&SWJ 11698 | WCru |
| ***laxiflorum*** HWJK 2249 | WCru |
| ***lobelii*** Bunge | see *A. turkestanicum* |
| § ***longipes*** | CMCN |
| ***macrophyllum*** | CMCN EPfP MBlu |
| ***mandschuricum*** | CDul EPfP MBlu MPkF WDin |
| § ***maximowiczianum*** | CBcs CMCN CTho ELan MMuc MPkF SGol WFar |
| ***maximowiczii*** | ECrN MPkF WHCr |
| ***metcalfii*** GWJ 9360 | WCru |
| ***micranthum*** | CDoC CDul CGHE CMCN EBee EPfP GKin MPkF NLar SSpi WHar WPGP |
| ***miyabei*** | MPkF |
| ***mono*** | see *A. pictum* |
| * - f. ***ambiguum*** B&SWJ 8806 | WCru |
| ***monspessulanum*** | CLnd CMCN SEND |
| ***morifolium*** | EBee MPkF |
| - B&SWJ 11473 | WCru |
| ***morrisonense*** | see *A. caudatifolium* |
| ***negundo*** | CDul CMCN CWib ECrN LMaj NWea |
| - 'Auratum' | CMCN SGol WDin |
| - 'Aureomarginatum' (v) | ECrN LMaj SGol |
| - 'Aureovariegatum' (v) | CBcs |
| § - 'Elegans' (v) | CDul CEnd CMCN ECrN SCoo WFar WHar |
| - 'Elegantissimum' | see *A. negundo* 'Elegans' |
| - 'Flamingo' (v) | CBcs CCVT CDoC CDul CEnd CMCN CMac CWSG CWib ECrN ELan EPfP LBMP LHop LRHS MAsh MBri NLar NWea SBfd SGol SLim SMad SPer SPoG SWvt WDin WFar WHar |
| - 'Kelly's Gold' | CBcs CCVT MAsh NLar NMun NWea SBfd SGol SLim SPoG WDin WFar WHar |
| - subsp. ***mexicanum*** F&M 48 | WPGP |
| - 'Variegatum' (v) | ECrN SGol WDin WFar |
| - var. ***violaceum*** | CEnd CMCN EPla SVen |
| - 'Winter Lightning' | CPMA |
| ***nikoense*** | see *A. maximowiczianum* |
| ***oblongum*** | CMCN |
| - KWJ 12232 | WCru |
| - var. ***concolor*** HWJ 869 | WCru |
| - - WWJ 11851 | WCru |
| ***oliverianum*** | CPLG EBee EPfP |
| - subsp. ***formosanum*** RWJ 9912 | WCru |
| ***opalus*** | CMCN SEND |
| ***orientale*** | see *A. sempervirens* |
| ***orizabense*** | EBee |
| Pacific Sunset = 'Warrenred' | EBee |
| ***palmatum*** | CBar CBcs CCVT CDoy CDul CMCN CMHG CMen CSBt CTri CWib EPfP EWTr GKin MBlu MGos NEgg NWea SEWo SGol SPlb STre SWvt WDin WFar WHar WPat |
| - 'Akane' | CMen MPkF |
| § - 'Aka-shigitatsu-sawa' | CBcs CMCN CMac CMen CPMA LRHS MGos MPkF NLar SGol WFar |
| - 'Akegarasu' | CMen NLar |
| - 'Akita-yatsubusa' | MPkF |
| - 'Alpenweiss' | CPMA |
| - 'Alpine Sunrise' | MPkF |
| - 'Amagi-shigure' | CPMA |
| - 'Amber Ghost' **new** | CPMA |
| - 'Aoba-jo' | CMen CPMA MPkF NLar NPCo |
| - 'Ao-kanzashi' (v) | MPkF |
| - 'Aoshime-no-uchi' | see *A. palmatum* 'Shinobuga-oka' |
| - 'Aoyagi' | CEnd CMCN CMen CPMA EPfP LRHS MGos MPkF NHol NLar NPCo SSta WFoF WPat |
| § - 'Arakawa' | CEnd CMCN CMac CMen MPkF NLar NPCo |
| - 'Arakawa-ukon' | CPMA NLar |
| - 'Aratama' | CBty CMen CPMA LRHS MGos MPkF NLar |
| - 'Ariake-nomura' | CMen MPkF |
| - 'Asahi-zuru' (v) | CBcs CDoC CMCN CMen CPMA EBee LRHS MBri MGos MPkF NLar NPCo SPer WDin WFar WFoF |
| - 'Ashurst Wood' | SBig |
| - 'Atrolineare' | CMen MPkF NLar WPat |
| - 'Atropurpureum' | Widely available |
| - 'Atropurpureum Novum' | MPkF NLar SGol |
| - 'Attraction' | CMCN CMen NPCo |
| - 'Aureum' | CMCN CMac CMen CWib ELan EPfP LAst LMil LRHS MAsh MGos MPkF NHol NLar NPCo SPoG SSpi WCFE WFar |
| - Autumn Glory Group | CEnd CMac CMen CPMA |
| - 'Autumn Red' | CMen NPCo |
| * - 'Autumn Showers' | CEnd CPMA |
| - 'Azuma-murasaki' | CMen CPMA MPkF NLar |
| - 'Beni-chidori' | CMen |
| - 'Beni-gasa' | CPMA MPkF |
| - 'Beni-hime' | MBri MPkF NLar |
| - 'Beni-hoshi' | MPkF |
| - 'Beni-kagami' | CEnd CMCN CPMA EPfP MPkF NLar SGol |
| - 'Beni-kawa' | CMen CPMA LRHS MPkF NPCo SBig WPat |
| - 'Beni-komachi' | CBcs CBty CEnd CMCN CMen CPMA EGxp ELon EPfP LRHS MBri MGos MPkF NLar SSta WPat |
| - 'Beni-maiko' | CEnd CMCN CMen CPMA CWib EPfP LBuc LRHS MBri MGos MPkF NLar NPCo SBig SCoo SWvt WDin WPGP WPat |
| - 'Beni-musume' | MPkF NLar |
| - 'Beni-otake' | CBcs CBty CLnd CMen CPMA ELan EPfP IVic LRHS MBri MGos MPkF NLar NPCo SBig SPer |
| - 'Beni-otome' | MPkF |

| | | | | | |
|---|---|---|---|---|---|
| | - 'Beni-schichihenge' (v) | CBcs CBty CEnd CMCN CMen CPMA CWCL CWGN GKin LRHS MAsh MBri MGos MPkF NBlu NHol NPCo SBig SCoo SSta WPGP WPat | | - - 'Beni-shidare Variegated' (v) | CMCN CPMA |
| | - 'Beni-shi-en' | CPMA MPkF NLar | | - - 'Berrima Bridge' | CPMA |
| | - 'Beni-shigitatsu-sawa' | see *A. palmatum* 'Aka-shigitatsu-sawa' | | - - 'Bewley's Red' | CPMA |
| | - 'Beni-tsukasa' (v) | CEnd CMen CPMA EPfP LMil LRHS MAsh MPkF NPCo SChF SSpi SSta WPGP | | - - 'Brocade' | IVic MPkF WPat |
| | - 'Beni-tsuru' **new** | MPkF | | - - 'Bronzewing' | CPMA |
| | - 'Beni-ubi-gohon' | CPMA MPkF NLar | | - - 'Chantilly Lace' | CPMA MPkF |
| | - 'Berry Broom' | MPkF NLar | | - - 'Crimson Princess' | CBcs LMil LRHS MPkF |
| | - 'Berry Dwarf' | CPMA MPkF | | - - 'Crimson Queen' ♀H4 | Widely available |
| | - 'Bi Hō' **new** | CPMA IVic NLar SGol | | - - Dissectum Atropurpureum Group | CBcs CCVT CMac CPMA CTri ELan EPfP LRHS MGos NLar NWea SBig SCoo SLim SRcu SSta WDin WFar |
| | - 'Bloodgood' ♀H4 | Widely available | | - - 'Dissectum Flavescens' | CEnd CMac CMen CPMA MBlu MPkF NPCo |
| | - 'Bonfire' misapplied | see *A. palmatum* 'Seigai' | § | - - 'Dissectum Nigrum' | CMac CMen CPMA LRHS MPkF NHol NLar NPCo WPat |
| | - 'Bonfire' ambig. | CPMA | | - - 'Dissectum Palmatifidum' | CDoC CLnd CMen EQua LRHS MPkF NPCo SCoo SPer WFar |
| | - 'Bonnie Bergman' | CPMA | | - - 'Dissectum Rubrifolium' | MPkF |
| | - 'Brandt's Dwarf' | MPkF WPat | § | - - 'Dissectum Variegatum' (v) | CPMA MPkF NPCo |
| | - 'Burgundy Lace' ♀H4 | CBty CDoC CEnd CMCN CMen CPMA CWib ELan ELon EPfP GKin LMil LRHS LSRN MAsh MBri MGos MPkF NBlu NPCo SBig SCoo SGol SPoG SSta WDin WFar WPGP WPat | | - - Dissectum Viride Group | CBcs CMCN CMac CMen CPMA CSBt CWSG ELan ELon EPfP LMil LRHS MAsh MBlu MGos MSwo NEgg NPCo NWea SBfd SLim SPer SSta WFar |
| | - 'Butterfly' (v) | Widely available | | - - 'Ellen' | CPMA MPkF WPat |
| | - 'Calico' | CPMA | | - - 'Emerald Lace' | CPMA GKin LRHS MBri MPkF NLar SSta WCFE |
| | - 'Caperci Dwarf' | MPkF | | - - 'Felice' | CPMA MPkF WPat |
| | - 'Carlis Corner' | CPMA MPkF | | - - 'Filigree' (v) | CMCN CMen CPMA EPfP MAsh MGos MPkF NLar NPCo SBig SSpi SSta WCFE WDin WPGP |
| | - 'Carminium' | see *A. palmatum* 'Corallinum' | | - - 'Garnet' ♀H4 | Widely available |
| | - 'Chikuma-no' | CMen MPkF | | - - 'Goshiki-shidare' (v) | CEnd CMen CPMA MPkF |
| | - 'Chirimen-nishiki' (v) | MPkF | | - - 'Green Globe' | CPMA LRHS NLar |
| | - 'Chitose-yama' ♀H4 | CBty CEnd CMCN CMac CMen CPMA CWCL EPfP GKin LMil LRHS MAsh MBri MGos MPkF MRav NHol NLar NPCo SBrd SLim SSpi SSta WFar WPat | | - - 'Green Hornet' | CPMA WPat |
| § | - 'Chiyo-hime' | ELan EPfP MGos NPCo | | - - 'Green Lace' | CMen MPkF |
| | - 'Coonara Pygmy' | CBty CCVT CMCN CMac CMen CPMA GKin LRHS MGos MPkF NLar NPCo SCoo WFar | | - - 'Green Mist' | CPMA SSta WPat |
| | - 'Coral Pink' | CMen CPMA MPkF SSta | | - - 'Hanzel' | WPat |
| § | - 'Corallinum' | CEnd CMCN CMen CPMA MPkF NLar NPCo SChF WCFE WDin WPGP WPat | | - - 'Inaba-shidare' ♀H4 | Widely available |
| | - var. ***coreanum*** B&SWJ 8606 | WCru | | - - 'Jeddeloh Orange' | MPkF |
| | - - 'Korean Gem' | CMen CPMA MPkF NPCo | I | - - 'Kawaii' | CPMA |
| | - 'Crimson Prince' | CPMA LTen MPkF SCoo | | - - 'Kiri-nishiki' | CMen CPMA LRHS MPkF NLar NPCo |
| | - 'Crippsii' | CBcs CBty CMac CMen GBin LRHS MGos MPkF SCoo WFar WPat | * | - - 'Lionheart' | CMen CPMA CWGN LRHS MGos MPkF NLar SCoo WFar |
| | - 'Curtis Strapleaf' | MPkF | | - - 'Nomura-nishiki' (v) | CMen |
| | - 'Deshojo' | CBty CMCN CMen CWSG CWib EGxp GKin LRHS MBlu MGos MPkF NLar SCoo SGol | | - - 'Octopus' | CPMA NLar |
| | - 'Diana' | CMen MPkF NLar SGol | | - - 'Orangeola' | CBcs CBty CMen CPMA CSBt IVic LRHS MAsh MBri MGos MPkF NHol NLar NPCo SBfd SBig SCoo SPer SSta WPat |
| | - 'Diane Verkade' | MPkF | | - - 'Ornatum' | CMCN CMen CWCL CWib EPfP GBin LRHS LSRN LTen MGos MPkF NBlu NEgg NPCo NPri SBfd SCoo WCFE WDin WFar |
| | - var. ***dissectum*** ♀H4 | Widely available | | - - 'Otto's Dissectum' | CPMA |
| | - - 'Ao-shidare' | CPMA LRHS | | - - 'Pendulum Julian' | CMCN LRHS MPkF NLar |
| | - - 'Ariadne' (v) | CBty CEnd CPMA CWib MBri MGos MPkF NLar SBig SCoo SPoG WPat | | - - 'Pink Ballerina' (v) | CPMA |
| | - - 'Autumn Fire' | CPMA | | - - 'Pink Filigree' | CMen MPkF |
| | - - 'Baby Lace' | CPMA CWGN IVic MPkF NLar SSta | | - - 'Raraflora' | CPMA |
| | - - 'Balcombe Green' | SBig | | - - 'Red Autumn Lace' | CPMA WPat |
| | - - 'Baldsmith' | CLnd CPMA LMil LRHS MPkF NLar WPat | | - - 'Red Dragon' | CDoC CMen CPMA CWGN EQua LMil LRHS MPkF NLar NPCo SBig WPat |
| | - - 'Barrie Bergman' | CPMA | | - - 'Red Feather' | CPMA |
| | - - 'Beni-fushigi' | MPkF WPat | | - - 'Red Filigree Lace' | CEnd CMCN CMen CPMA CWGN MGos MPkF NPCo SBig WPat |
| | - - 'Beni-shidare Tricolor' (v) | CMen MAsh MPkF NLar | | - - 'Red Select' | CBty LRHS MPkF |

| | | |
|---|---|---|
| | - - 'Seiryū' $\mathbb{Y}^{H4}$ | Widely available |
| § | - - 'Shōjō-shidare' | CDul CEnd CMen CPMA MPkF NLar |
| | - - 'Shu-shidare' **new** | CPMA |
| | - - 'Spring Delight' | CPMA MPkF NLar |
| | - - 'Suisei' (v) | MPkF |
| | - - 'Sunset' | CPMA MPkF WPat |
| | - - 'Tamukeyama' | CBcs CBty CLnd CMCN CMen CPMA EBee ELan LMil LRHS MBri MGos MPkF NLar NPCo SCoo SGol SLau WFar WHar WPat |
| | - - 'Toyama-nishiki' (v) | CMCN CMen CWGN LRHS MPkF NPCo |
| | - - 'Waterfall' | CMCN CPMA |
| | - - 'Watnong' | CPMA MPkF |
| | - - 'Zaaling' | CMen NPCo |
| | - 'Doctor Tilt' | MPkF |
| | - 'Donzuru-bo' **new** | CPMA |
| | - 'Dormansland' | SBig |
| | - 'Earthfire' | MPkF WPat |
| I | - 'Ebbingii' | CMac |
| | - 'Eddisbury' | CEnd CMen CPMA MPkF NLar SSta WPGP WPat |
| | - 'Edna Bergman' | CPMA |
| | - 'Effegi' | see *A. palmatum* 'Fireglow' |
| | - 'Eimini' | MPkF |
| | - 'Elegans' | CMen EPfP MPkF NPCo WDin |
| | - 'Elizabeth' | CPMA MPkF |
| | - Emperor 1 | see *A. palmatum* 'Wolff' |
| | - 'Englishtown' | MPkF WPat |
| | - 'Enkan' | CBty CEnd CMen CPMA CWGN MBri MGos MPkF NLar NPri SGol WPat |
| | - 'Eono-momiji' | CMen |
| | - 'Ever Red' | see *A. palmatum* var. *dissectum* 'Dissectum Nigrum' |
| | - 'Fairy Hair' **new** | CPMA |
| | - 'Fall's Fire' | CPMA |
| | - 'Fascination' | CPMA |
| | - 'Fior d'Arancio' | CPMA IVic MPkF NLar NPCo WPat |
| | - 'Fireball' **new** | CPMA |
| § | - 'Fireglow' | CBcs CBty CDoC CEnd CLnd CMCN CMen CPMA CSBt CWCL CWib LMaj LMil LRHS MBri MGos MPkF NEgg NLar NPCo SCoo SPer WFar WPGP WPat |
| | - 'First Ghost' | CPMA |
| | - 'Fjellheim' | CPMA MPkF |
| | - 'Frederici Guglielmi' | see *A. palmatum* var. *dissectum* 'Dissectum Variegatum' |
| | - 'Garyū' | MPkF |
| | - 'Geisha' | CPMA MPkF |
| | - 'Geisha Gone Wild' **new** | CPMA MPkF |
| | - 'Genshu-yama-momiji' **new** | NLar |
| | - 'Gentaku' **new** | CPMA |
| | - 'Germaine's Gyration' | CPMA |
| | - 'Ghost' **new** | CPMA |
| | - 'Gibbsii' | CMen NPCo |
| I | - 'Globosum' | MPkF |
| | - 'Glowing Embers' | CPMA MPkF WPat |
| | - 'Golden Pond' | CPMA |
| | - 'Goshiki-kotohime' (v) | CBty CMCN CPMA MPkF |
| | - 'Goten-nomura' | NLar |
| | - 'Grace' **new** | CPMA |
| | - 'Grandma Ghost' **new** | CPMA |
| | - 'Green Flag' **new** | CPMA |
| | - 'Green Trompenburg' | CMen CPMA MGos MPkF NEgg NLar NPCo |
| | - 'Groundcover' | MPkF |
| § | - 'Hagoromo' | CMac CMen MPkF NPCo SCoo WFar |
| | - 'Hamano-maru' **new** | MPkF |
| | - 'Hana-matoi'$^{PBR}$ (v) **new** | CMCN MPkF |
| | - 'Hanami-nishiki' | CMen MPkF NEgg WPat |
| | - 'Haru-iro' | CPMA |
| | - 'Harusame' (v) | MPkF NLar |
| | - 'Hazeroino' (v) | CMen MPkF |
| | - 'Heartbeat' | CPMA LRHS MPkF |
| | - 'Heffner's Red' **new** | CPMA |
| | - 'Helena' | see *A. shirasawanum* 'Helena' |
| | - var. ***heptalobum*** | CMCN |
| § | - 'Heptalobum Elegans' | LRHS |
| | - 'Heptalobum Elegans Purpureum' | see *A. palmatum* 'Hessei' |
| | - 'Heptalobum Rubrum' **new** | NLar |
| | - 'Herbstfeuer' | CPMA MPkF |
| § | - 'Hessei' | CEnd CMCN CMen MPkF NLar |
| | - 'Higasayama' (v) | CBcs CEnd CMCN CMen CPMA CWGN IVic LRHS MGos MPkF NHol NLar NPCo WPGP WPat |
| | - 'Hino-tori-nishiki' | CMen NLar SGol |
| | - 'Hōgyoku' | CMCN CMen CPMA MPkF WPat |
| | - 'Hondoshi' | NLar |
| | - 'Hono-ō' | MPkF NLar |
| | - 'Hoshi-kuzu' | MPkF NLar |
| | - 'Hupp's Dwarf' | CPMA MPkF |
| | - 'Ibo-nishiki' | CMen MPkF |
| | - 'Ichigyōji' | CEnd CMen CPMA IVic MAsh NLar NPCo SBig SChF WPGP WPat |
| | - 'Ightham Gold' **new** | SSta |
| | - 'Iijima-sunago' | CMen MPkF |
| | - 'Inazuma' | CBcs CDoC CMCN CMen CPMA EPfP LRHS MGos MPkF NBlu NLar SCoo SLau WFar WPat |
| | - 'Irish Lace' | CPMA MPkF |
| | - 'Iso-chidori' | MPkF |
| | - 'Issai-nishiki' | CMen MPkF NLar NPCo |
| * | - 'Issai-nishiki-kawazu' | MPkF |
| | - 'Jane' | MPkF NLar |
| | - 'Japanese Sunrise' | CPMA LRHS MPkF WPat |
| | - 'Jerre Schwartz' | MGos MPkF NLar WPat |
| | - 'Jirō-shidare' | CPMA EPfP MPkF NLar SBig |
| | - 'JJ' | CPMA |
| | - 'Julia D.' | CPMA NLar |
| | - 'Kaba' | CMen IVic MPkF |
| | - 'Kagero' (v) | MPkF WFar |
| § | - 'Kagiri-nishiki' (v) | CBcs CDul CMCN CMac CMen CPMA CWGN IVic LRHS LTen MPkF NEgg NHol NLar WFar |
| | - 'Kamagata' | CBty CEnd CMCN CMen CPMA CWSG EPfP IVic LMil LRHS MAsh MGos MPkF NHol NLar NPCo SCoo SPer WPGP WPat |
| | - 'Kandy Kitchen' | CMen CPMA MBri MPkF |
| | - 'Karaori-nishiki' (v) | CMen MPkF NLar |
| | - 'Karasugawa' (v) | CMen CPMA CWGN MGos MPkF NLar NPCo |
| | - 'Kasagiyama' | CEnd CMCN CMen CPMA MGos MPkF WPGP |
| | - 'Kasen-nishiki' | CMen MPkF |
| | - 'Kashima' | CEnd CMCN CMen CPMA LRHS MPkF NPCo WFar WPat |
| | - 'Kashima-yatsubusa' | LRHS MPkF |
| | - 'Katja' | CMen MPkF |
| | - 'Katsura' $\mathbb{Y}^{H4}$ | Widely available |
| | - 'Katsura-nishiki' **new** | MPkF |
| | - 'Kawahara Rose' **new** | MPkF |

|  |  |
|---|---|
| - 'Ki-hachijō' | CMCN CMen CPMA EPfP MPkF NLar WPat |
| - 'Killarney' **new** | CPMA |
| - 'Kingsville Variegated' (v) | MPkF |
| - 'Kinky Krinkle' | CPMA MPkF |
| - 'Kinran' | CMen LRHS MPkF NPCo WPat |
| - 'Kinshii' | CBty CEnd CMCN CMen CPMA EPfP IVic LRHS MPkF NHol NLar NPCo WHar WPGP WPat |
| - 'Kiyohime' | CDoC CMCN CMen MPkF WFar WPat |
| - 'Koba-shōjō' | MPkF |
| - 'Kogane-nishiki' | CMen NLar SGol |
| - 'Kogane-sakae' | CPMA MPkF |
| - 'Kokobunji-nishiki' (v) | MPkF |
| - 'Komache-hime' | CMen CPMA MPkF WPat |
| * - 'Komaru' | NLar |
| - 'Komon-nishiki' (v) | CMen CPMA MPkF |
| - 'Koriba' | CPMA MPkF NLar |
| - 'Koshibori-nishiki' | MPkF |
| § - 'Koshimino' | CPMA |
| - 'Kotohime' | CMCN CMen CPMA IVic MBri MGos MPkF NLar SBig SCoo SPoG SSta |
| - 'Koto-ito-komachi' | CMen CPMA ELon MPkF NLar NPCo WPat |
| - 'Koto-maru' | MPkF |
| - 'Koto-no-ito' | CMCN CWGN LRHS MGos MPkF NLar WPat |
| - 'Koya-san' | CMen MPkF |
| - 'Kurabu-yama' | CMen MPkF NLar |
| - 'Kurui-jishi' | MGos MPkF |
| - 'Kyōryū' | MPkF |
| - 'Kyra' | CMen MPkF |
| - 'Leather Leaf' | MPkF |
| § - 'Linearilobum' | CBcs CBty CDoC CMen EPfP GBin IVic LMil MGos MPkF NLar NPCo SCoo SLau WFar |
| - 'Little Princess' | see *A. palmatum* 'Chiyo-hime' |
| - 'Long Men' **new** | MPkF |
| - 'Lozita' | NLar WPat |
| - 'Lutescens' | CMen MPkF NPCo |
| - 'Lydia' | MPkF NLar |
| - 'Maiko' | CMen MPkF |
| - 'Mama' | CMen NPCo |
| - 'Mapi-no-machihime' | CEnd CMCN CMen CPMA ELan LRHS MAsh MBri MGos MPkF NHol WPGP WPat |
| - 'Marakumo' | MPkF |
| - 'Marasaki-yama' | MPkF |
| - 'Mardi Gras' | CPMA |
| - 'Margaret' | MPkF |
| - 'Margaret Bee' | CPMA MPkF |
| - 'Marjan' | MPkF NLar |
| - 'Marlo'[PBR] **new** | MRav |
| - 'Masamurasaki' | CMen MPkF |
| - 'Masukagami' (v) | CEnd CPMA MPkF NLar |
| - 'Matsuga-e' (v) | CMen MPkF NPCo |
| - 'Matsukaze' | CMCN CMen CPMA |
| - var. ***matsumurae*** B&SWJ 11100 | WCru |
| - 'Matsuyoi' | CPMA MPkF |
| - 'Meihō-nishiki' | CPMA |
| - 'Melanie' | CPMA SBig |
| - 'Meoto' | CPMA |
| - 'Midori-no-teiboku' | MPkF |
| - 'Mikawa-yatsubusa' | CMCN CMac CMen IVic LRHS MGos MPkF NLar NPCo |
| - 'Mikazuki' **new** | CPMA |
| - 'Mimaye' | CPMA |
| - 'Mini Mondo' | MPkF |
| - 'Mino-gasa' **new** | NLar |
| - 'Mirte' | CMen CPMA MPkF SBig WFar WPat |
| - 'Mizuho-beni' | CMen CPMA NLar NPCo |
| - 'Mizu-kuguri' | MPkF NLar |
| - 'Momoiro-koya-san' | CPMA MPkF NLar SGol WPat |
| - 'Mon Papa' | CMen CPMA NLar |
| - 'Monzukushi' | CPMA MPkF |
| - 'Moonfire' | CMCN CPMA EPfP LRHS MAsh MGos MPkF NLar WPat |
| - 'Mr Sun' | CPMA |
| * - 'Muncaster' | SBig |
| - 'Murasaki-hime' | MPkF |
| - 'Murasaki-kiyohime' | CBty CEnd CMCN CMen CPMA GBin LRHS MPkF NLar NPCo WPGP WPat |
| - 'Mure-hibari' | CMen CPMA MPkF |
| - 'Murogawa' | CMen CPMA NPCo |
| - 'Nakata' **new** | NLar |
| - 'Nanase-gawa' | MPkF |
| - 'Nicholsonii' | CMen CTri EPfP IVic MPkF NLar NPCo WFar WPat |
| - 'Nigrum' 🏆H4 | CMCN WPat |
| - 'Nishiki-gasane' (v) | CMen MPkF |
| § - 'Nishiki-gawa' | CEnd CMCN CMen CPMA MPkF NPCo WPGP |
| - 'Nishiki-momiji' | CMen |
| - 'Nishiki-yamato' **new** | NLar |
| - 'Nomura' | CMen CPMA |
| - 'Nomurishidare' misapplied | see *A. palmatum* var. *dissectum* 'Shojo-shidare' |
| - 'Nomurishidare' Wada | SSpi |
| - 'Nuresagi' | CEnd CPMA MPkF WPat |
| - 'Ōgi-nagashi' (v) | MPkF NLar |
| - 'Ōgi-no-sen' | MPkF |
| - 'Ōgon-sarasa' | CPMA MPkF |
| - 'Ojishi' | CMen MPkF |
| - 'Ō-kagami' | CBcs CBty CDoC CEnd CMac CMen CPMA CSBt ELon EPfP LMil LRHS MAsh MGos MPkF NLar NPCo SCoo WPGP |
| - 'Okukuji-nishiki' | CPMA |
| - 'Okushimo' | CEnd CMCN CMen CPMA IVic LRHS MPkF NHol NLar NPCo SSta WPGP |
| - 'Omato' | CPMA MPkF SBig WFar |
| - 'Omurayama' | CBcs CBty CDoC CEnd CMCN CMen CPMA EPfP LMil LRHS MGos MPkF NLar NPCo SBod SCoo SPer SSta WFar |
| - 'Orange Dream' | Widely available |
| - 'Oranges and Lemons' **new** | NLar |
| - 'Oregon Sunset' | CPMA MPkF NLar |
| - 'Oridono-nishiki' (v) | CBcs CDoC CDul CEnd CMCN CMac CMen CPMA CWCL CWGN ELan ELon EPfP LAst LMil LRHS LTen MAsh MBlu MGos MPkF NEgg NLar NPCo SBfd SLim SPer SPoG SSta WFar |
| - 'Ōsakazuki' 🏆H4 | Widely available |
| - 'Ōshio-beni' | CMen CPMA NPCo |
| - 'Ōshū-shidare' | CMen CPMA EPfP MPkF WFar |
| - 'Oto-hime' | CMen CPMA LRHS MPkF NPCo |
| - 'Otome-zakura' | CMen CPMA LRHS MPkF WPat |
| - 'Peaches and Cream' (v) | CBcs CMen CPMA LRHS MPkF NLar NPCo SPer SSta WPat |
| - 'Peve Chameleon' | MPkF NLar |
| - 'Peve Dave' | MPkF NLar |
| - 'Peve Multicolor' | CPMA MPkF NLar |

| | | |
|---|---|---|
| | - 'Peve Ollie'[PBR] | GKin MPkF NLar |
| | - 'Peve Stanley' | MPkF NLar |
| | - 'Phoenix' | MBri MPkF |
| | - 'Pine Bark Maple' | see *A. palmatum* 'Nishiki-gawa' |
| | - 'Pixie' | CBty CMen CPMA IVic LRHS MGos MPkF NLar WPat |
| | - 'Pung-kil' | IVic MPkF |
| | - 'Purple Ghost' | CPMA NLar SLim |
| | - 'Red Baron' | CPMA |
| | - 'Red Blush' **new** | CPMA |
| | - 'Red Cloud' | CPMA MPkF NLar |
| | - 'Red Crusader' | NLar |
| | - 'Red Elf' | MPkF |
| | - 'Red Embers' | CWib |
| | - 'Red Emperor' | CWGN ELan GBin MPkF NLar SPer WPat |
| | - 'Red Flame' | NLar |
| | - 'Red Flash' | CMen CPMA MPkF |
| | - 'Red Jonas' | MPkF NLar |
| | - 'Red Pygmy' ♀H4 | Widely available |
| | - 'Red Spider' | CPMA |
| | - 'Red Wood' | CBcs CCVT CDoC CPMA GBin MPkF SGol SLau SPer |
| | - 'Renjaku-maru' | MPkF |
| | - 'Reticulatum' | see *A. palmatum* 'Shigitatsu-sawa' |
| | - 'Ribesifolium' | see *A. palmatum* 'Shishigashira' |
| * | - 'Rigassii' | LMaj |
| | - 'Rising Sun' | CPMA NLar |
| | - 'Rokugatsu-en-nishiki' | WPat |
| | - 'Roseomarginatum' | see *A. palmatum* 'Kagiri-nishiki' |
| | - 'Rough Bark Maple' | see *A. palmatum* 'Arakawa' |
| | - 'Royle' | CPMA |
| | - 'Rubrum' | CMen |
| | - 'Rubrum Kaiser' | CPMA |
| | - 'Ruby Ridge' | CPMA |
| | - 'Ruby Star' | CPMA MPkF NLar |
| | - 'Rufescens' | MPkF |
| | - 'Ryokū-ryū' | CMen MPkF |
| | - 'Ryusen' **new** | CPMA |
| | - 'Ryuzu' | CPMA LRHS MPkF WPat |
| | - 'Sagara-nishiki' (v) | CEnd CMen CPMA LRHS MPkF NPCo |
| | - 'Sai-ho' | MPkF |
| | - 'Saint Jean' | MPkF |
| | - 'Samidare' | CPMA EPfP MPkF NLar |
| | - 'Sandra' | CMen MPkF |
| N | - 'Sango-kaku' ♀H4 | Widely available |
| | - 'Saoshika' | CMen CPMA MPkF |
| | - 'Sa-otome' | CMen MPkF |
| | - 'Satsuki-beni' | CMen CPMA MPkF NPCo |
| | - 'Sazanami' | CDoC CEnd CMen CPMA CWCL MPkF NLar WPGP WPat |
| | - 'Scolopendriifolium' | see *A. palmatum* 'Linearilobum' |
| § | - 'Seigai' | CPMA MPkF WCFE |
| | - 'Seigen' | CEnd CMCN CMen CPMA MPkF NPCo WPGP |
| I | - 'Seigen Aureum' | CPMA |
| | - 'Seiun-kaku' | CMen CPMA MPkF WPat |
| | - 'Sekimori' | CPMA NLar SBig |
| | - 'Sekka-yatsubusa' | CMCN CMen MPkF NLar |
| | - 'Semi-no-hane' **new** | NLar |
| N | - 'Senkaki' | see *A. palmatum* 'Sango-kaku' |
| | - 'Septemlobum Elegans' | see *A. palmatum* 'Heptalobum Elegans' |
| | - 'Septemlobum Purpureum' | see *A. palmatum* 'Hessei' |
| | - 'Sessilifolium' dwarf | see *A. palmatum* 'Hagoromo' |
| | - 'Sessilifolium' tall | see *A. palmatum* 'Koshimino' |
| | - 'Shaina' | CBcs CDoC CEnd CMen CPMA CSBt CWGN CWib EPfP IVic LRHS LTen MBlu MBri MGos MPkF NLar NPCo SCoo SGol SLim WFar WHar |
| | - 'Sharp's Pygmy' | CBty CMen CPMA GBin LRHS MPkF NPCo WPat |
| | - 'Sherwood Flame' | CDoC CMCN CMen CPMA CWib LRHS MAsh MGos MPkF NLar NPCo SCoo WFar WPat |
| | - 'Shichigosan' | CMen LRHS |
| | - 'Shidava Gold' | CPMA MPkF |
| | - 'Shi-en' | MPkF |
| | - 'Shigarami' | CMen CPMA MPkF |
| § | - 'Shigitatsu-sawa' (v) | CBcs CBty CEnd CMCN CMac CMen CPMA MGos MPkF NLar NPCo SBig |
| | - 'Shigure-bato' | CPMA MPkF |
| | - 'Shigurezome' | MPkF NLar |
| | - 'Shikageori-nishiki' | CMen CPMA MPkF |
| | - 'Shime-no-uchi' | CPMA MPkF SBig |
| | - 'Shimofuri-nishiki' **new** | MPkF |
| | - 'Shindeshōjō' | Widely available |
| § | - 'Shinobuga-oka' | CBcs CMCN CMen CPMA MPkF SLau |
| | - 'Shinonome' | CMen CPMA MPkF |
| | - 'Shirazz' (v) | CBty CDoC CWGN LMil LRHS MBri MGos MPkF |
| § | - 'Shishigashira' | CDoC CMCN CMac CMen CPMA CWGN EBee EPfP GKin IArd IVic LRHS MBlu MBri MGos MPkF NLar NPCo SBfd SCoo SGol SPoG WDin WFar WPat |
| | - 'Shishio' | CBcs CBty CMCN CMen LAst LMil LRHS MPkF NPCo SBig SSpi WPat |
| | - 'Shishio Improved' | CEnd CMCN CMac CMen CPMA CWSG ELon EPfP LRHS MAsh MGos MPkF NHol NLar NPCo SBig SChF SWvt |
| | - 'Shishio-hime' | MPkF |
| | - 'Shishi-yatsubusa' | CPMA MPkF |
| | - 'Shōjō' | CMCN CPMA WFar |
| | - 'Shōjō-no-mai' | CPMA |
| | - 'Shōjō-nomura' | CEnd CMen MGos MPkF NLar WPGP WPat |
| | - 'Sister Ghost' | CPMA |
| | - 'Skeeter's Broom' | CBcs CBty CMen CPMA ELan LBuc LMil LRHS MBri MGos MPkF NPCo SBig SChF SCoo WPGP WPat |
| * | - 'Sode-nishiki' | CPMA MPkF NLar |
| | - 'Stella Rossa' | CEnd CPMA MPkF NLar WPat |
| | - 'Sumi-nagashi' | CBcs CBty CDoC CMen CWCL GBin LMil MGos MPkF NBlu NLar NPCo SChF SCoo SGol SLau WHar WPat |
| I | - 'Summer Gold' | MBri MPkF SWvt |
| * | - 'Sunago' | NLar |
| | - 'Sunshine' **new** | MPkF |
| | - 'Susan' | MPkF |
| | - 'Taiyō-nishiki' | CPMA MPkF |
| | - 'Takao' | CMen |
| | - 'Tama-hime' | CMen CPMA MPkF NPCo |
| | - 'Tana' | CMCN CMen CPMA EPfP MPkF WFar WPat |
| | - 'Tarō-yama' | CPMA MPkF WPat |
| | - 'Tatsuta' | CMen MPkF WHar |
| | - 'Taylor'[PBR] (v) | CEnd CWGN EGxp IVic LRHS MGos MPkF NLar NPri SCoo SPoG WPat |
| | - 'Tennyo-no-hoshi' | CMen MPkF NLar NPCo |
| | - 'Tiger Rose' | CPMA NLar |
| | - 'Tiny Tim' | CPMA MPkF |

| | |
|---|---|
| - 'Tobiosho' **new** | CPMA |
| - 'Trompenburg' ♀H4 | Widely available |
| - 'Tsuchigumo' | CMen CPMA MPkF NLar |
| - 'Tsukasa Silhouette' **new** | CPMA |
| - 'Tsukuma-no' | MPkF |
| - 'Tsukushigata' | MPkF WPat |
| - 'Tsuma-beni' | CMCN CMen EPfP LRHS MPkF NPCo |
| - 'Tsuma-gaki' | CDoC CMen CPMA EGxp EPfP MBri MGos MPkF NLar NPCo WPat |
| - 'Tsuri-nishiki' | CMen CPMA MPkF NLar |
| - 'Twombly's Red Sentinel' | MBlu MPkF |
| - 'Ueno-homare' | CMen MPkF WPat |
| - 'Ueno-yama' | CBcs CPMA GBin MGos MPkF WPat |
| - 'Ukigumo' (v) | CBcs CEnd CLnd CMCN CMac CMen CPMA CSBt CWib ELan GKin LMil LRHS MBri MGos MPkF NHol NLar NPCo SBfd SBig SCoo SPer SPoG SSta WDin WFar WPat |
| - 'Ukon' | CCVT CMen CPMA GBin LMil LRHS MPkF NBlu NPCo SCoo |
| - 'Umegae' | CPMA |
| - 'Uncle Ghost' | CPMA |
| - 'Usu-midori' | CPMA |
| - 'Utsu-semi' | CPMA MPkF |
| - 'Van der Akker' | CPMA |
| - 'Versicolor' (v) | CMCN CPMA MPkF |
| - 'Vic Pink' | CPMA |
| - 'Victoria' | MPkF |
| - 'Villa Taranto' | CBty CDoC CEnd CMCN CMen CPMA ELon EPfP IVic LMil LRHS MBri MGos MPkF NHol NLar NPCo SChF SCoo SSpi SSta WPGP WPat |
| - 'Volubile' | CMCN CMen EPfP MPkF NPCo |
| - 'Wabito' | CMen CPMA MPkF |
| - 'Waka-midori' | CMen |
| - 'Waka-momiji' (v) | CPMA |
| - 'Wakehurst Pink' (v) | CMCN MPkF WPat |
| - 'Wendy' | CMen CPMA IVic MPkF NLar SGol WPat |
| - 'Wetumpka Red' | CPMA |
| - 'Whitney Red' | CMen |
| - 'Wildgoose' | MPkF |
| - 'Will D' | CPMA |
| - 'Wilson's Pink Dwarf' | CBty CEnd CMen CPMA CWib GKin IVic LRHS MGos MPkF NLar NPCo NPri SChF SCoo SLim SPoG WPGP |
| - 'Winter Flame' | CPMA GBin LMil LRHS MPkF NHol NLar WPat |
| § - 'Wolff' | MPkF |
| - 'Wolff's Broom' | MPkF WPat |
| - 'Wou-nishiki' | CMCN CMen MPkF NPCo |
| - 'Yana-gawa' | CMen |
| - 'Yasemin' | CMen CPMA CWGN IVic LRHS MPkF NLar NPCo SBig |
| - 'Yatsubusa' | MPkF NLar |
| - 'Yezo-nishiki' | CMen LRHS MPkF WFar |
| - 'Yūba-e' | MPkF WFar WPat |
| - 'Yūgure' | IVic MPkF NLar WFar |
| - 'Yuri-hime' | MPkF |
| ***papilio*** | see *A. caudatum* |
| ***pectinatum*** GWJ 9354 | WCru |
| ***pensylvanicum*** ♀H4 | CBcs CDul CLnd CMCN CTho EBee ECrN ELan EPfP LMaj MGos MMuc MRav NWea SEND SLim SPer SSpi SSta WDin WFar WHCr |
| - 'Erythrocladum' | CEnd CMCN CPMA EPfP MBri NEgg NHol NLar SBig SLim SPur SSta WFar WPGP |
| ***pentaphyllum*** | CDul SBig SBir |

| | |
|---|---|
| * ***phlebanthum*** B&SWJ 9751 | WCru |
| § ***pictum*** | CMCN |
| - subsp. ***okamotoanum*** | CMCN |
| - - B&SWJ 8516 | WCru |
| - 'Shufu-nishiki' | CMCN |
| - 'Usugomo' | WPat |
| ***platanoides*** ♀H4 | CBcs CCVT CDoC CDul CLnd CMCN CSBt CTri CWib EBee ECrN ELan EPfP MGos MMuc MSwo NWea SBfd SEND SEWo SGol SPer STre WDin WFar WHar WMou |
| - 'Charles Joly' | LMaj |
| - 'Cleveland' | CBcs CCVT |
| - 'Columnare' | CCVT CDul CLnd CMCN CWib SCoo |
| - 'Crimson King' ♀H4 | Widely available |
| - 'Crimson Sentry' | CCVT CDoC CDul CEnd CLnd CMCN ECrN ELan EPfP IArd IVic LAst LRHS LTen MAsh MGos MRav SBfd SEWo SGol SPoG WDin WFar WHar |
| - 'Deborah' | CBcs CDul CTho LMaj SGol |
| - 'Drummondii' (v) | Widely available |
| - 'Emerald Queen' | CCVT ECrN LMaj WDin |
| - 'Faassen's Black' | CPMA |
| § - 'Globosum' | CLnd CMCN EBee ECrN LBuc LMaj NLar SWvt |
| - 'Goldsworth Purple' | CLnd NEgg |
| - 'Laciniatum' | CMCN |
| - 'Marit' | WPat |
| - Princeton Gold = 'Prigo'[PBR] | CBcs CDoC CDul EBee ECrN ELan EMil LRHS MAsh MBri MGos SBfd SCoo SEWo SGol SLim SPer SPoG WHar |
| - 'Reitenbachii' | CDul LMaj |
| - 'Royal Red' | CDul CWib ECrN LMaj MRav NLar SCoo SEWo |
| - 'Schwedleri' ♀H4 | CDul CMCN EPfP SGol WDin |
| ***pseudoplatanus*** | CBcs CCVT CDul CLnd CMCN CSBt CTri ECrN ELan LBuc MGos NWea SBfd SGol SPer WDin WFar WHar WMou |
| § - 'Atropurpureum' | CDoC CDul CLnd ECrN NWea SEWo WDin WHar |
| - 'Brilliantissimum' ♀H4 | Widely available |
| - 'Erectum' | WFar |
| - 'Erythrocarpum' | CMac |
| - 'Gadsby' | CDul |
| - 'Leopoldii' misapplied | see *A. pseudoplatanus* f. *variegatum* |
| - 'Prinz Handjéry' | CBcs CDul CEnd CMCN CTri CWib EBee MGos NHol NLar NWea SGol SPer SPoG WHar |
| - f. ***purpureum*** | SEND |
| - 'Spaethii' misapplied | see *A. pseudoplatanus* 'Atropurpureum' |
| § - f. ***variegatum*** (v) | NEgg |
| - - 'Esk Sunset' (v) | CBcs EBee LRHS MGos MPkF NLar WHar |
| - - 'Leopoldii' ambig. (v) | CBcs CDul CLnd CMCN ECrN ELan LAst SEND SPer SWvt WDin WFar |
| - - 'Leopoldii' Vervaene (v) | SCrf |
| - - 'Simon-Louis Frères' (v) | CBcs CCVT CDul CLnd CMCN CWSG CWib EBee ECrN LAst MAsh MGos NEgg NLar SBfd SBod SCrf SGol SPer SPoG SWvt WFar WFoF WHar |
| - 'Worley' | CBcs CDul CLnd CMCN CMac ECrN MRav NWea SBfd SEND SGol SLim SPer WDin |

| | | |
|---|---|---|
| | ***pseudosieboldianum*** | CMCN CPMA IArd MBlu MPkF |
| | - B&SWJ 8468 | WCru |
| | - B&SWJ 8746 | WCru |
| | - B&SWJ 8769 | WCru |
| | - var. ***microsieboldianum*** B&SWJ 8766 | WCru |
| | ***pycnanthum*** | EPfP |
| | 'Red Flamingo' (v) | CPMA LRHS MBri MGos MPkF SGol SSta |
| | ***reticulatum*** | see *A. laevigatum* var. *reticulatum* |
| | ***rubescens*** | CPMA WPGP |
| | - B&SWJ 6735 | WCru |
| | - CWJ 12438 | WCru |
| | - RWJ 9840 | WCru |
| | - variegated (v) | CPMA WPGP |
| | ***rubrum*** | Widely available |
| | - Autumn Flame | see *A. rubrum* 'Pete's Red' |
| | - 'Autumn Spire' | CPMA |
| | - 'Bowhall' | SBir |
| | - 'Brandywine' | CDul CPMA CTho EBee LRHS MAsh MBlu MBri NWea SBir SCoo SPoG WHar |
| | - 'Candy Ice' (v) | CPMA |
| | - 'Columnare' | CMCN EPfP |
| | - 'Embers' | CPMA |
| | - Fireball = 'Firzam' | CPMA |
| | - 'Firedance' | CPMA |
| | - 'New World' | NLar SCoo |
| | - 'Northwind' | CPMA |
| | - 'Northwood' | CPMA |
| | - 'October Glory' ♀H4 | Widely available |
| § | - 'Pete's Red' | CLnd EBee MPkF |
| | - 'Red King' | CPMA |
| | - 'Red Rocket' | SPoG |
| | - Red Sunset = 'Franksred' | CCVT CDul CEnd CLnd CMCN CPMA CTho EBee EPfP LMaj LTen NLar SBir SCoo SGol SLim SSta |
| | - 'Scanlon' | CBcs CDul CEnd CMCN CPMA CTho EBee ELan EPfP LAst LMaj MBlu SPer |
| | - 'Schlesingeri' | CEnd CMCN CMac CPMA EPfP |
| | - 'Somerset' | CDul CPMA CTho CTri EBee LRHS SCoo WHar |
| | - Summer Red = 'Hosr' | CPMA SCoo SPoG |
| | - 'Sun Valley' | CPMA MAsh SCoo WHar |
| | - 'Tilford' | CPMA SCoo SSta |
| § | ***rufinerve*** ♀H4 | CAlb CBcs CCVT CDoC CDul CLnd CMCN CTho CTri EBee ECrN ELan EPfP EPla EWTr LMaj LRHS MBri MMuc NEgg NLar NWea SCoo SGol SPer WDin WHar WMou |
| | - B&SWJ 10845 | GKin WCru |
| | - B&SWJ 10924 | WCru |
| | - B&SWJ 10959 | WCru |
| | - B&SWJ 11571 | WCru |
| | - 'Albolimbatum' | see *A. rufinerve* 'Hatsuyuki' |
| | - 'Erythrocladum' | CPMA EBee SKHP |
| § | - 'Hatsuyuki' (v) | CEnd CMCN CPMA SBig SSta |
| | - 'Ko-fuji-nishiki' **new** | SSta |
| | - 'Winter Gold' | CPMA EPfP NLar SSta |
| | - 'Yakushima-nishiki' **new** | SSta |
| § | ***saccharinum*** | CBcs CCVT CDoC CDul CLnd CMCN CMac CTri CWib EBee ECrN ELan EPfP LRHS MGos MMuc MSnd NWea SCoo SGol SPer STre WDin WFar WHar |
| | - 'Born's Gracious' | CPMA |
| | - 'Fastigiatum' | see *A. saccharinum* f. *pyramidale* |
| | - f. ***laciniatum*** | CCVT EBee MBlu MGos MMuc SGol SPer WDin |
| | - 'Laciniatum Wieri' | CDul CMCN ECrN SGol WDin |
| | - f. ***lutescens*** | CDul CMCN |
| § | - f. ***pyramidale*** | CDoC CLnd EBee ECrN LMaj SPer WDin |
| | ***saccharum*** | CAgr CBcs CDoC CDul CLnd CMCN CTho ECrN EPfP MBlu NWea SPer |
| | - 'Brocade' | CPMA |
| | - 'Fiddlers Creek' | CPMA |
| § | - subsp. ***grandidentatum*** | EPfP NLar |
| § | ***sempervirens*** | CPMA EBee LEdu SChF WPGP |
| | 'Sensu' | CPMA |
| | ***serrulatum*** CWJ 12437 | WCru |
| | - RWJ 9912 | WCru |
| | ***shirasawanum*** | CMCN |
| § | - 'Aureum' ♀H4 | Widely available |
| | - 'Autumn Moon' | CBcs CBty CEnd CMCN CMen CPMA CWGN EPfP IArd LRHS MBri MPkF NLar NPCo NPri SBfd SCoo SGol SLim WPat |
| § | - 'Ezo-no-momiji' | CMen CPMA MPkF NLar NPCo |
| | - 'Gloria' | LRHS MPkF |
| § | - 'Helena' | MPkF NLar |
| | - 'Johin' | CPMA |
| | - 'Jordan'PBR | CEnd CWGN EBee MBri MGos NLar |
| | - 'Lovett' | CPMA |
| § | - 'Microphyllum' | MPkF |
| § | - 'Ogurayama' | CMen CPMA NPCo |
| | - 'Palmatifolium' | CPMA |
| | - 'Red Dawn' **new** | CPMA |
| | - 'Susanne' | CPMA MPkF |
| | - var. ***tenuifolium*** B&SWJ 11073 | WCru |
| | ***sieboldianum*** | CDul CMen CTho CTri ECrN MMuc SGol WHCr WHar WMou WPat |
| | - B&SWJ 10849 | WCru |
| | - B&SWJ 11049 | WCru |
| | - B&SWJ 11090 | WCru |
| | - 'Sode-no-uchi' | CMen MPkF NPCo |
| | - var. ***tsushimense*** B&SWJ 10962 | WCru |
| | ***sikkimense*** B&SWJ 11613 | WCru |
| | - B&SWJ 11689 | WCru |
| | - B&SWJ 11703 | WCru |
| | - DJHV 06152 | WCru |
| | - WWJ 11601 | WCru |
| | - WWJ 11613 | WCru |
| | - WWJ 11853 | WCru |
| | 'Silver Cardinal' (v) | CBcs CEnd CMCN CPMA EBee EPfP MGos MPkF NLar WHar |
| | 'Silver Vein' | see *A.* × *conspicuum* 'Silver Vein' |
| | ***spicatum*** | EPfP NLar |
| § | ***stachyophyllum*** | GAuc GQui |
| | - BWJ 8101 | WCru |
| § | ***sterculiaceum*** | CMCN WPGP |
| | - subsp. ***franchetii*** | NLar |
| | - subsp. ***sterculiaceum*** GWJ 9317 | WCru |
| | ***takesimense*** B&SWJ 8500 | WCru |
| | - B&SWJ 8540 | WCru |
| | ***tataricum*** | CCVT CMCN |
| | - subsp. ***aidzuense*** B&SWJ 10958 | WCru |
| § | - subsp. ***ginnala*** | CBcs CCVT CDul CLnd CMCN CTri ECrN EWTr GKin LMaj MBlu MGos NLar NPal NWea SEND SPer WDin |
| | - - 'Flame' | CDul CPMA EBee ECrN ELan EPfP MGos MMuc MSnd NLar NWea |
| | - - 'Red Wing' | CPMA EBee |

| | | |
|---|---|---|
| | ***tegmentosum*** | CBcs CMCN CPMA EPfP MBlu |
| | - B&SWJ 8421 | WCru |
| | - subsp. ***glaucorufinerve*** | see *A. rufinerve* |
| | ***tetramerum*** | see *A. stachyophyllum* |
| | ***tonkinense*** subsp. ***liquidambarifolium*** DJHV 06173 new | WCru |
| | ***trautvetteri*** | CMCN EPfP |
| | ***triflorum*** ♀H4 | CBcs CDul CMCN CPMA EPfP LMaj MBlu NLar SSpi WDin WFar |
| | ***truncatum*** | MBlu MPkF |
| | - 'Akikaze' new | WCru |
| | - 'Akikaze-nishiki' (v) | CPMA MPkF |
| | ***tschonoskii*** | GQui |
| | - subsp. ***koreanum*** | MPkF |
| § | ***turkestanicum*** | SSta WFar |
| | ***velutinum*** | CMCN |
| | ***villosum*** | see *A. sterculiaceum* |
| | 'White Tigress' | CDoC CPMA CTho NLar WPGP |
| | × ***zoeschense*** | CMCN |
| | - 'Annae' | SGol |

# *Aceriphyllum* see *Mukdenia*

# × *Achicodonia* (*Gesneriaceae*)

| | |
|---|---|
| 'Dark Velvet' | WDib |

# *Achillea* (*Asteraceae*)

| | | |
|---|---|---|
| | ***ageratifolia*** ♀H4 | EBla ECho ECtt EDAr LBee LRHS NBre NGdn SRms WFar WHil |
| § | ***ageratum*** | CArn CHby CPrp ECho EGHP ELau EOHP GPoy LEdu MHer MNHC SIde SRms WGwG WHer WJek WPer XLum |
| | 'Alabaster' | EBee NDov SAga SPhx |
| | ***aleppica*** new | WCot |
| | Anthea = 'Anblo'PBR | CKno CWCL EBee EBla ECtt GBBs LBMP LRHS LSRN MRav NChi NLar SRGP SRms SWvt WFar |
| § | 'Apfelblüte' (Galaxy Series) | CWCL EBee EBla ECha ECtt ELan EPfP EWTr GKin LRHS LSRN MLLN MMuc MRav NDov NGdn NHol NSti NWad SEND SPer SPoG WCAu WFar WMnd WPer WPtf WWEG |
| | Appleblossom | see *A.* 'Apfelblüte' (Galaxy Series) |
| | 'Apricot Beauty' | EBee ECtt GBBs GMaP GQue LSRN |
| | 'Apricot Delight' (Tutti Frutti Series) new | MAsh NCGa |
| | ***argentea*** misapplied | see *A. clavennae, A. umbellata* |
| | ***argentea*** Lamarck | see *Tanacetum argenteum* |
| | ***argentea*** ambig. | NMen |
| I | ***argentifolia*** hort. | WKif |
| | ***aurea*** | see *A. chrysocoma* |
| | 'Bahama' | GBin GQue NBre NBro |
| | 'Belle Epoque' ♀H4 | WWEG |
| | ***biebersteinii*** new | XLum |
| | ***brachyphylla*** | EHoe |
| | 'Breckland Bouquet' | ECtt EWes |
| | 'Breckland Ruby' | EWes |
| | 'Carmina Burana' | CMea |
| | ***cartilaginea*** | see *A. salicifolia* |
| | 'Christine's Pink' ♀H4 | MSpe MTis |
| § | ***chrysocoma*** | ECho EDAr MMuc MWat WMoo |
| | - 'Grandiflora' | ECha LPla NGdn |
| § | ***clavennae*** | CMea ECho EDAr MWat SMrm SRms WAbe WFar WPat |
| | - SDR 5452 | GKev |
| | ***clypeolata*** Sibth. & Sm. | EBee EPPr LRHS NBre NLar SMad SPlb SRms |
| | ***coarctata*** | NBir WPer XSen |
| | Colorado Group | CWCL LRHS NChi SPav WFar |
| | 'Coronation Gold' ♀H4 | CDoC CPrp CWCL EBee EBla ECtt ELan EPfP LAst LRHS MNFA MRav MWat NChi NDov SAga SWvt WCAu WCot WFar WWEG XLum |
| | 'Credo' ♀H4 | CPrp EBee EBla ECha ECtt ELon EPPr EPfP EWTr LPla LRHS MCot MLLN MNFA MRav MSpe NGdn NHol NLar NSti NWad SMad SMrm SPer SPhx SUsu SWat WMnd WPtf WWEG |
| | ***crithmifolia*** | XLum |
| | ***decolorans*** | see *A. ageratum* |
| | ***erba-rotta*** | WPer |
| | - subsp. ***moschata*** | NBro |
| § | 'Fanal' | Widely available |
| | 'Faust' | CHar EBla ELon MNrw SMrm STes SUsu |
| | 'Federsee' | MArl |
| | 'Feuerland' | CMac CSam EBee EBla ECha ECtt ELon EPPr EPfP GKin LRHS MLLN MRav MTis NBir NDov NGdn NSti SMad SMrm SPer SPoG SWat WCot WFar WPer WWEG |
| | ***filipendulina*** | MLLN WHrl |
| | - 'Cloth of Gold' ♀H4 | Widely available |
| | - 'Gold Plate' ♀H4 | Widely available |
| | - 'Parker's Variety' ♀H4 | EBee GQue NBre WFar WMoo |
| | 'Fleur van Zonneveld' | NDov |
| | Flowers of Sulphur | see *A.* 'Schwefelblüte' |
| | (Forncett Series) 'Forncett Beauty' | SWvt WPtf |
| | - 'Forncett Bride' | NBre WHil |
| | - 'Forncett Candy' | WWEG |
| | - 'Forncett Citrus' | MAvo NBre |
| | - 'Forncett Fletton' | CFir CWCL EBee ECtt ELon EPPr EPfP EShb GBin GKin LHop LRHS MAsh MLLN MNFA MNrw MRav MSpe MTis NCGa NGdn NHol NWad WFar WPtf WWEG WWlt |
| | - 'Forncett Ivory' | EPPr NBre WPtf |
| | ***fraasii*** | MCot MDKP XSen |
| | ***glaberrima*** hybrid | WPtf |
| | 'Gloria Jean' | SHar SPhx SUsu |
| | 'Gold and Grey' | SMrm WWEG |
| | 'Goldstar' | EBee NBPC WFar |
| | ***grandifolia*** misapplied | see *Tanacetum macrophyllum* (Waldst. & Kit.) Sch.Bip. |
| § | ***grandifolia*** Friv. | CElw COIW CSam EBee LPla MRav NBro SSvw WAul WBor WFar WHer WMnd WMoo WOut |
| | 'Gravat' | MArl |
| | 'Great Expectations' | see *A.* 'Hoffnung' |
| | 'Hannelore Pahl' | NDov |
| | 'Heidi' ♀H4 | CCVN WPtf WWEG |
| | 'Heinrich Vogeler' | EBee |
| | 'Hella Glashoff' ♀H4 | CMea CWCL CWan EBee ECtt ELon GBin LRHS SAga WCot WFar |
| § | 'Hoffnung' | CPrp CWCL EBee EBla ECtt MRav MSpe SPer WMnd WPer WWEG |
| | × ***huteri*** | ECho ECtt EDAr EPfP LBee LRHS MRav NGdn WAbe WFar WNew WPer |
| | 'Inca Gold' | CWCL EBee EBla ECGP ECha ECtt EPPr EShb GQue LRHS MRav MTis NGdn NHol NSti NWad SAga WCFE WWEG |
| | 'Jacqueline' | EWll MSpe MTis |
| | × ***kellereri*** | XSen |
| | 'King Alfred' | CMea EPfP |

| | Name | Suppliers |
|---|---|---|
| | × ***kolbiana*** | MWat NMen SRms WPat |
| § | 'Lachsschönheit' (Galaxy Series) 🏆H4 | Widely available |
| | × ***lewisii*** | NMen |
| | - 'King Edward' 🏆H4 | ECho EDAr EPfP GMaP NBir SPoG WFar |
| | ***ligustica*** | WCot |
| | 'Lucky Break' 🏆H4 | EBla MSpe SDix SUsu |
| | ***macrophylla*** | MBNS NBre |
| | 'Marie Ann' | CWCL EBee ECtt EKen GQue LSRN MNrw NBPC NLar NPnk NSti SPhx SRGP |
| | 'Marmalade' | MSpe NDov SMrm WMnd WPGP WWEG |
| | 'Martina' 🏆H4 | CDoC CMMP CPrp EBee ECtt EPPr GKin IPot LAst LBMP LHop MAsh MBNS MCot MLLN MRav MSCN NCGa NDov NGdn NHol NOrc NWad SRGP WWEG |
| | 'McVities' | CWCL ECtt EPPr LEdu MSpe MTis STes WMnd WPtf WWEG |
| | ***millefolium*** | CArn CHab CWan ELau EWil GPoy MNHC NLan NMir SPlb WHer WJek WSFF XLum |
| | - 'Bloodstone' | EBee ECtt EWes MRav WPtf |
| | - 'Bright Cerise' | WFar |
| | - 'Carla Hussey' | WFar |
| | - 'Cassis' | CCVN CSpe ETod GQue LRHS MNHC NGBl NLar SGar SPav SPet SWal WBrk WFar |
| § | - 'Cerise Queen' | Widely available |
| | - 'Cherry King' | NBir |
| | - 'Christel' | CCVN EWes GBin SUsu |
| | - 'Christine' | GBin |
| | - 'Circus' **new** | XLum |
| | - 'Dark Lilac Beauty' | EWTr |
| | - 'Harlekin' | EBee |
| | - 'Kelwayi' 🏆H4 | WPtf |
| | - Kirschkönigin | see *A. millefolium* 'Cerise Queen' |
| | - 'Lansdorferglut' 🏆H4 | LPla LRHS SPhx WWEG |
| | - 'Laura' **new** | CSam LSou MAsh MBri WHil |
| | - 'Lavender Beauty' | see *A. millefolium* 'Lilac Beauty' |
| § | - 'Lilac Beauty' | CAby CBar CHar COIW CPrp EBee ECha EGHP ELon EPfP GBin IPot LBMP LRHS LSRN MAsh MRav MSpe NBir NEgg NSti NWad SBfd WFar WHoo WPer WWEG XLum |
| * | - 'Lilac Queen' | MArl |
| | - 'Little Suzie' **new** | MAsh MBri |
| | - 'Oertels Rose' | WFar |
| | - 'Old Brocade' | EShb MTis WPtf WWEG |
| | - Pastel Shades | IFoB |
| | - 'Peggy Sue' **new** | MAsh MBri |
| | - 'Pretty Woman' **new** | CSam MAsh MBri |
| | - 'Raspberry Ripple' | GBin |
| | - 'Red Beauty' | CWCL EPfP MAsh MBNS MSpe MWea SMad SMrm SRms SWat WCFE WWEG XLum |
| | - 'Red Salmon' | EWes |
| | - 'Red Velvet' | Widely available |
| | - 'Rose Madder' | CPrp CWCL EBee EBla ECtt EGHP EHoe EPPr GKin GMaP LPla LRHS MBri MNrw MSCN MSpe NBir NCGa NGdn NHol NLar NSti SMrm SPav SWvt WCot WGwG XLum |
| | - 'Ruby Port' | WFar |
| | - 'Salmon Pink' | ITim WFar |
| | - 'Salmon Queen' | EGHP NHol |

| | Name | Suppliers |
|---|---|---|
| | - 'Sammetriese' | CWan LRHS MNrw NCGa SMad SPhx WFar WWEG |
| | - 'Schneetaler' | EBee GBin |
| | - 'Serenade' | EBee EBla ECtt MSpe WFar |
| | - 'Sue's Pink' | CSam MSpe |
| | - 'Summertime' | LAst |
| | - 'Tickled Pink' | WPer |
| | - 'White Queen' | EBee |
| | 'Mondpagode' 🏆H4 | CHar CPrp EBee EPPr EWTr LPla LRHS LSRN MAvo MBNS MCot MNFA MRav MWea NGdn SPhx SSvw WFar WKif |
| * | 'Moonbeam' | GKin SEND |
| | 'Moonshine' 🏆H3 | Widely available |
| | 'Moonwalker' | CAbP EBee NBre NGBl SIde SPav WBrk WCot WFar WPer |
| | ***nana*** | GEdr |
| | ***nobilis*** | SEND |
| | - subsp. ***neilreichii*** | EBee EBla ECGP EHoe EWTr IKil LRHS MMHG MNrw NSti SWvt WHal WPtf WTin WWEG |
| | 'Nostalgia' | LAst |
| * | ***odilis*** | LRHS |
| | 'Paprika' (Galaxy Series) | Widely available |
| | 'Peardrop' | NBre |
| | ***pindicola*** subsp. ***integrifolia*** | EWes |
| | pink-flowered from Santa Cruz Island | CKno CWCL |
| | 'Pink Grapefruit' (Tutti Frutti Series) **new** | MAsh NCGa |
| | 'Pink Lady' | EBee EBla GBBs |
| | 'Pomegranate' (Tutti Frutti Series) **new** | CWGN MAsh NCGa |
| | 'Pretty Belinda' | EBee ECtt EPfP GMac LRHS LSRN LSou MAsh MBNS MSpe NBPC NCGa NLar NPri NSti SKHP SPoG STes WWlt |
| | 'Prospero' | WCot WWEG |
| | ***ptarmica*** | CArn CBre ELau EWil MHer NMir NPri SIde XLum |
| * | - 'Ballerina' | MBNS MWhi NBre NDov NGdn NLar |
| | - Innocence | see *A. ptarmica* 'Unschuld' |
| | - 'Major' | NBre |
| | - 'Nana Compacta' | CSpe EBee EBla ECha EPPr GBin LRHS NBir NCGa SPlb SUsu WCFE WFar WHil WWEG |
| | - 'Perry's White' | CBcs CBre EBee ECha IPot MNrw NDov NGdn SRGP WCot |
| | - 'Stephanie Cohen' | see *A. sibirica* 'Stephanie Cohen' |
| N | - The Pearl Group seed-raised (d) | CTri ELan MMuc NVic SPlb SWat WFar WMoo WPer WTin |
| N | - - 'Boule de Neige' (clonal) (d) | GKin MRav MSpe NBre NPer NSti SPer SPet WFar XLum |
| N | - - 'The Pearl' (clonal) (d) 🏆H4 | Widely available |
| § | - 'Unschuld' | NBir |
| | ***pyrenaica*** **new** | XLum |
| | 'Rougham Salmon' | WPtf |
| § | ***salicifolia*** | WFar |
| | - 'Silver Spray' | EBee GQue NLar SPav WOut |
| | 'Sally' | EPPr MSpe |
| | Salmon Beauty | see *A.* 'Lachsschönheit' |
| | 'Sandstone' | see *A.* 'Wesersandstein' |
| | 'Saucy Seduction' (Tutti Frutti Series) **new** | MAsh NCGa |
| § | 'Schwefelblüte' | MRav NBir SBch SMrm |
| | 'Schwellenburg' | CDes CHar NBre WCot WPGP |
| | ***sibirica*** | SRGP |

- subsp. ***camschatica*** WPtf
- - 'Love Parade' EAEE EBee EPfP ITim LRHS MBNS MMuc MNFA MNrw MRav NBPC NGdn NLar SAga SPer SRGP SSvw WFar WMoo WWEG XLum
§ - 'Stephanie Cohen' CPrp EBee GBee GBin NGdn WFar WWEG
'Stephanie' ECtt EPPr EWes LSRN MSpe
Summer Berries Group CSpe LRHS
Summer Pastels Group EPfP IFro LRHS NBir NBlu NLar NOrc SBfd SPav SPoG SRms SWal WFar WHil
'Summerwine' ♀H4 Widely available
'Sunbeam' SHar
I 'Taygetea' CSam EBee EBla ECtt ELan EPPr EPfP EShb LRHS MBNS NPnk SDix SPer SPet WCAu WCot WFar WPer WSHC WWEG
'Terracotta' Widely available
'The Beacon' see *A.* 'Fanal'
'Tissington Old Rose' MAvo MNrw MSpe MTis
***tomentosa*** ♀H4 CTri ECha ECho ECtt MAsh WCot
§ - 'Aurea' EBla ECho LRHS NBlu NBre NBro
- 'Goldie' **new** EDAr
- 'Maynard's Gold' see *A. tomentosa* 'Aurea'
'Tri-colour' NGdn NWad WHlf
§ ***umbellata*** WBrk XSen
'W.B. Childs' ECha ELan MCot MNrw NDov SHar
'Walther Funcke' Widely available
§ 'Wesersandstein' CHar CWCL EBee ECtt EPPr ETod GBin GMaP LPla LRHS MAvo MLLN MNrw NBir NPro STes WCot WFar WPer WWEG
'Wilczekii' NBre SRms
'Yellowstone' EWes

## × *Achimenantha* (*Gesneriaceae*)

'Aries' EABi WDib
'Himalayan Sunrise' LAma
'Inferno' ♀H1 EABi WDib
'Tyche' EABi

## *Achimenes* (*Gesneriaceae*)

'Addano' WDib
'Ambroise Verschaffelt' ♀H1 EABi LAma WDib
'Ami Van Houtte' WDib
'Apricot Glow' EABi
'Aquamarine' WDib
'Ballerina' WDib
'Blue David' EABi
'Boy David' EABi
'Camille Brozzoni' EABi
'Cascade Fashionable Pink' WDib
'Cascade Rose Red' **new** WDib
'Cascade Violet Night' WDib
'Cattleya' LAma
'Charity' WDib
'Claret' **new** WDib
'Clouded Yellow' EABi
'Coral Cameo Mix' EABi
'Cornell Favourite' EABi
'Crackerjack' **new** WDib
'Crummock Water' EABi WDib
'Derwentwater' EABi
'Donna' EABi
'Dot' EABi
'Double Pink Rose' (d) **new** WDib
'Electra' **new** EABi
'English Waltz' EABi
***erecta*** EABi WDib
'Erlkönig' WDib
'Extravaganza' WDib
'Flamenco' WDib
'Glory' WDib
***grandiflora*** 'Robert Dressler' EABi
'Grape Wine' EABi
'Hard to Get' **new** EABi
'Harry Williams' LAma WDib
'Hilda Michelssen' ♀H1 EABi WDib
'Jay Dee Coral' **new** WDib
'Jay Dee Large White' **new** WDib
'Jay Dee Pink' WDib
'Jay Dee Purple' **new** WDib
'Jennifer Goode' EABi WDib
'Johanna Michelssen' WDib
'Jubilee Gem' EABi
'Just Divine' EABi WDib
'Kim Blue' WDib
'Light Lilac' WDib
'Little Beauty' WDib
***longiflora*** EABi
- 'Major' WDib
'Luneberg' EABi
'Maxima' LAma
'Menuett' WDib
'Mozelle' EABi
'Opal' **new** WDib
'Orange Delight' WDib
'Orange Queen' EABi
(Palette Series) 'Palette Lilac' EABi
- 'Palette Red Dwarf' EABi
- 'Palette Red' EABi
- 'Palette Salmon' EABi
- 'Palette White' EABi
'Pally' WDib
'Patens Major' WDib
'Peach Blossom' LAma WDib
'Peach Glow' EABi WDib
'Pearly Queen' EABi
'Petite Fadette' **new** EABi
'Pink Beauty' EABi
'Pink Rose' (d) EABi
'Platinum' EABi
'Primadonna' **new** WDib
I 'Purple Hybrid' EABi
'Purple Queen' WDib
'Purple Triumph' **new** WDib
'Queen of Queens' **new** WDib
'Rainbow' EABi WDib
'Red Elfe' **new** EABi
'Red Giant' EABi
'Red Hilda Michelssen' **new** WDib
'Rosa Charm' **new** EABi
'Rose Dream' EABi
'Sergé Saliba' **new** EABi
'Show-off' WDib
'Stan's Delight' (d) ♀H1 EABi WDib
'Sterntaler' **new** WDib
'Summer Sunset' EABi
'Sweet & Sour' **new** EABi
'Tarantella' EABi WDib
'Teresa' EABi
(Tetra Series) 'Tetra Verschaffelt' EABi
- 'Tetra Wine Red Charm' EABi
'Tiger Eye' WDib

| | |
|---|---|
| 'Trailing Yellow' | EABi |
| 'Vie-en-Rose' new | EABi |
| 'Violacea Semiplena' | WDib |
| 'Vivid' | EABi WDib |
| 'Weinrot Elfe' | WDib |
| 'Wetterflow's Triumph' | EABi WDib |
| 'Yellow Beauty' | WDib |

## *Achlys* (*Berberidaceae*)

| | |
|---|---|
| ***japonica*** | GEdr WCru |
| ***triphylla*** | GGar WCru |

## *Achnatherum* see *Stipa*

## *Achyranthes* (*Amaranthaceae*)

| | |
|---|---|
| ***bidentata*** | CArn |

## *Acidanthera* see *Gladiolus*

## *Acinos* (*Lamiaceae*)

| | |
|---|---|
| § ***alpinus*** | CPBP EDAr GJos LLHF MHer MMuc SPhx WJek XLum |
| § ***corsicus*** | NMen NWCA WHoo |

## *Aciphylla* (*Apiaceae*)

| | |
|---|---|
| ***aurea*** | GAbr GBin GCal NWCA SMad SPlb |
| ***dieffenbachii*** | CBrP CHid GBin GKev |
| ***ferox*** | GBin |
| ***glaucescens*** | ECou GBin SPlb |
| ***kirkii*** | GBin |
| 'Lomond' | GBin |
| ***monroi*** | LLHF |
| ***montana*** | GLin |
| ***pinnatifida*** | GKev SMad |
| ***scott-thomsonii*** | CHid GBin |
| ***squarrosa*** | GBin |

## *Acis* ✿ (*Amaryllidaceae*)

| | |
|---|---|
| § ***autumnalis*** ♀H4 | CAvo CBro CDes CElw CFee CPBP CTca CTri EBee ECha ECho EPot EWes GEdr GKev ITim LAma LEdu LRHS NBir NMen SMrm SPhx SRms SRot WAbe WHil WHoo WPGP WSHC |
| - 'Cobb's Variety' | EBee ECho WCot |
| - var. ***oporantha*** | CWCL EPri LWst |
| - - from Morocco | ECho |
| * - - f. ***dispathaceous*** new | LWst |
| - var. ***pulchella*** | ECho GKev |
| - 'September Snow' new | GKev LWst |
| § ***longifolia*** | ECho |
| ***nicaeensis*** ♀H2-3 | CPBP ECho EPot GCal GKev LLHF LRHS SCnR WAbe WCot |
| - PJC 277 | LWst |
| § ***rosea*** | ECho MAvo NMen NWCA SCnR WAbe WThu |
| § ***tingitana*** | CBro ECho WCot |
| - SB&L 203 | WCot |
| § ***trichophylla*** | ECho LLHF SCnR WCot |
| - f. ***purpurascens*** | ECho WCot |
| * - var. ***rosea*** | ECho |
| § ***valentina*** | CBro CPBP ECho EPot SCnR SRot WCot |

## *Acmella* (*Asteraceae*)

| | |
|---|---|
| § ***oleracea*** | CArn EOHP |

## *Acmena* (*Myrtaceae*)

| | |
|---|---|
| ***smithii*** | EShb |

## *Acnistus* (*Solanaceae*)

| | |
|---|---|
| ***australis*** | see *Iochroma australe* |

## *Acoelorrhaphe* (*Arecaceae*)

| | |
|---|---|
| ***wrightii*** | EAmu |

## *Aconitum* (*Ranunculaceae*)

| | |
|---|---|
| B&SWJ 2954 from Nepal | WCru |
| CNDS 036 from Burma | WCru |
| KR 7589 | CDes WPGP |
| GWJ 9393 from northern India | WCru |
| GWJ 9417 from northern India | WCru |
| ***alboviolaceum*** | WCot |
| - var. ***alboviolaceum*** f. ***albiflorum*** B&SWJ 4105 | WCru |
| - - - B&SWJ 8444 | WCru |
| - var. ***purpurascens*** B&SWJ 8477 new | WCru |
| ***altissimum*** | see *A. lycoctonum* subsp. *vulparia* |
| ***anglicum*** | see *A. napellus* subsp. *napellus* Anglicum Group |
| § ***anthora*** | CArn EBee EPfP IKil LRHS SBfd |
| ***arcuatum*** | see *A. fischeri* var. *arcuatum* |
| ***austroyunnanense*** | WSHC |
| - BWJ 7902 | WCru |
| ***autumnale*** misapplied | see *A. carmichaelii* Wilsonii Group |
| ***autumnale*** Rchb. | see *A. fischeri* Rchb. |
| × ***bicolor*** | see *A.* × *cammarum* 'Bicolor' |
| 'Blue Lagoon'PBR new | CWGN |
| 'Blue Opal' | CDes EBee ECtt EWes SSvw WPGP |
| 'Blue Sceptre' | LRHS |
| 'Bressingham Spire' ♀H4 | EBee ECtt ELan EPfP GCra GKin GMaP IKil LAst LPla LRHS MAvo MBri MCot MLLN MWhi NBPC NCGa NDov NGdn NOrc NPer SPer SRms WCAu WMoo WWEG |
| ***bulbilliferum*** HWJK 2120 new | WCru |
| § × ***cammarum*** 'Bicolor' ♀H4 | Widely available |
| - 'Eleanora' | CFir EBee ECtt EGHP EPPr EWes GCra LHop LRHS LSou MLLN MSCN NBPC NGdn NLar SPer WCot WWEG |
| - 'Grandiflorum Album' | CAby LPla MNrw |
| - 'Pink Sensation'PBR | CAby CFir EBee EKen EPfP GQue LLHF MBNS MLLN NBPC NBre NDov NLar NPnk NSti |
| § ***carmichaelii*** | CArn CBot CMea CSam ELan EPfP GCra GKin IFoB IFro LAst LRHS LSou MBri MMuc MNrw NBro NChi NEgg NGdn NOrc SMrm SRms WCot WFar WHoo WHrl WTin |
| - HWJ 732 | EBee |
| - Arendsii Group | ECtt LAst LRHS SPhx SRot |
| - - 'Arendsii' ♀H4 | Widely available |
| - 'Blue Bishop' | LSou |
| - 'Redleaf'PBR | see *A. carmichaelii* 'Royal Flush' |
| - 'River Arrow' | WCot |
| - 'River Avon' | WCot |
| - 'River Dee' new | WCot |
| - 'River Devon' new | WCot |
| - 'River Finn' new | WCot |
| - 'River Lugg' | WCot |
| - 'River Lune' | WCot |
| - 'River Medway' new | WCot |

| Name | Suppliers |
|---|---|
| - 'River Nene' | WCot |
| - 'River Ouse' | WCot |
| - 'River Severn' new | WCot |
| - 'River Spey' new | WCot |
| - 'River Tees' | WCot |
| - 'River Teifi' | WCot |
| - 'River Trent' | WCot |
| - 'River Welland' | WCot |
| § - 'Royal Flush'PBR | CWGN MAvo MLLN MNrw NGdn NLar WCot WHil |
| - var. ***truppelianum*** | EBee |
| - - HWJ 732 | WCru |
| § - Wilsonii Group | CPrp EBee ECGP GGar GMaP LEdu LPla LRHS MCot MRav MWat NCGa NDov NEgg SPhx WFar WPGP WPer |
| - - 'Barker's Variety' | CFir CKno EBee ECtt ELon EPfP GCal GQue LRHS NGdn NHol NLar NSti SSvw |
| - - 'Kelmscott' ♀H4 | EBee ECtt EWes MCot MRav SAga SDix SMrm SSvw WFar WRHF |
| - - 'Spätlese' | CAbP CWGN EBee ECtt ELon EPfP GCal LEdu MCot MNFA NBir NDov NGdn SMrm SPer SUsu WCot WWEG |
| ***chiisanense*** B&SWJ 4446 | WCru |
| ***cilicicum*** | see *Eranthis hyemalis* Cilicica Group |
| 'Cloudy' | CPrp EBee ECtt NBPC NGdn SPer WCot |
| ***compactum*** | see *A. napellus* subsp. *vulgare* |
| ***confertiflorum*** | see *A. anthora* |
| ***delphiniifolium*** | CPLG |
| ***elwesii*** | EBee NBre |
| ***episcopale*** | NDov WCru WFar |
| aff. ***episcopale*** CLD 1426 | WFar |
| ***excelsum*** | see *A. lycoctonum* subsp. *lycoctonum* |
| ***ferox*** | EBee ELon EWes LLHF |
| - CC 5492 | GKev |
| - HWJK 2217 | WCru |
| ***fischeri*** misapplied | see *A. carmichaelii* |
| § ***fischeri*** Rchb. | CWib EBee MMuc NCGa WCot |
| - B&SWJ 8809 | WCru |
| § - var. ***arcuatum*** B&SWJ 774 | WCru |
| ***formosanum*** | LEdu |
| - B&SWJ 3057 | WCru |
| ***fukutomei*** | NBre |
| - B&SWJ 337 | MRav WCru |
| ***gammiei*** GWJ 9418 | WCru |
| ***gmelinii*** | see *A. lycoctonum* subsp. *lycoctonum* |
| § ***hemsleyanum*** | CBot CPLG CRHN CWGN ECtt EPfP GCra GGar GKev GQue NBid NHol SPhx WCru WFar |
| - 'Red Wine' new | CFir WWEG |
| ***hyemale*** | see *Eranthis hyemalis* |
| ***incisofidum*** | WCot |
| 'Ivorine' | CBot CMac CRow CTri EBee ECha ELan EPfP GCra GMaP LAst LRHS LSRN MAvo MCot NCGa NGdn NPri SMad SPer WCAu WFar WPnP WTin |
| ***jaluense*** B&SWJ 8741 | WCru |
| ***japonicum*** | EBee GCal WFar |
| - var. ***hakonense*** | CPLG |
| - var. ***montanum*** B&SWJ 5507 | WCru |
| § - subsp. ***napiforme*** | EWes SAga |
| - - B&SWJ 943 | CDes EBee ELon WCru WPGP |
| § - subsp. ***subcuneatum*** B&SWJ 6228 | WCru |
| ***krylovii*** | WCot |
| ***laciniatum*** GWJ 9254 | WCru |
| - GWJ 9324 | WCru |
| ***lamarckii*** | see *A. lycoctonum* subsp. *neapolitanum* |
| ***lasianthum*** | see *A. lycoctonum* subsp. *vulparia* |
| ***loczyanum*** B&SWJ 11529 new | WCru |
| ***longecassidatum*** B&SWJ 4277 | WCru |
| - B&SWJ 8486 | WCru |
| - B&SWJ 8488 | WCru |
| ***lycoctonum*** | NLar SBfd SRms |
| - 'Darkeyes' | CAbP LRHS LSou NGdn WCot |
| - 'Graupe' | WCot |
| - 'Langhuso' | WCot |
| § - subsp. ***lycoctonum*** | SRms WCot |
| - - var. ***rubicundum*** new | LRHS |
| § - subsp. ***moldavicum*** | LRHS WCot |
| § - subsp. ***neapolitanum*** | ECtt ELan GCal GMaP MLLN MMuc NBPC NLar WFar WWEG |
| - 'Russian Yellow' | EWld GCal |
| § - subsp. ***vulparia*** | CArn CFir CMac CPrp EBee GMac GPoy MNFA MNrw MRav NEgg NGdn WAul WCot WPer |
| ***mairei*** | see *A. vilmorinianum* |
| ***moldavicum*** | see *A. lycoctonum* subsp. *moldavicum* |
| ***napellus*** | Widely available |
| - 'Bergfürst' | CAby CMea LPla MBri SPhx |
| - 'Blue Valley' | EBee EPfP EWes NPro SBfd WFar |
| - subsp. ***fissurae*** new | LRHS |
| - subsp. ***napellus*** | LEdu |
| § - - Anglicum Group | CSev CWan MCot NLar WCot |
| - 'Rubellum' | EBee ECtt ELan LRHS MMuc NBir NBro NEgg NPri SMrm SPoG SPur WMnd |
| - 'Schneewittchen' | EBee EWes IPot SSvw |
| - 'Sphere's Variety' | NOrc |
| § - subsp. ***vulgare*** | WFar |
| - - 'Albidum' | CPrp EBee EGHP ELan ELon EPfP EWTr GAbr GKev GMaP LEdu NBid NHol NLar NPri SPer SPet SUsu WAul WBor WFar WPer |
| - - 'Carneum' | GCra WFar WHer WKif |
| ***napiforme*** | see *A. japonicum* subsp. *napiforme* |
| ***neapolitanum*** | see *A. lycoctonum* subsp. *neapolitanum* |
| 'Newry Blue' | EBee ELan LRHS NBir NHol NLar SBfd SRms WFar WPer WWEG |
| ***orientale*** misapplied | see *A. lycoctonum* subsp. *vulparia* |
| ***orientale*** ambig. | NPro |
| ***paniculatum*** misapplied | see *A. variegatum* subsp. *paniculatum* |
| ***piepunense*** | GKev |
| ***proliferum*** B&SWJ 4107 | WCru |
| ***pseudohuiliense*** | CPLG WCot |
| ***pseudolaeve*** | EWld WCot |
| - B&SWJ 8663 | WCru |
| - var. ***erectum*** B&SWJ 8466 | WCru |
| ***pubiceps*** white-flowered | GCal WCot |
| ***pyramidale*** | see *A. napellus* subsp. *vulgare* |
| ***pyrenaicum*** misapplied | see *A. lycoctonum* subsp. *neapolitanum* |
| ***ranunculifolius*** | see *A. lycoctonum* subsp. *neapolitanum* |
| ***seoulense*** B&SWJ 694 | WCru |

| | |
|---|---|
| - B&SWJ 864 | WCru |
| ***septentrionale*** | see *A. lycoctonum* subsp. *lycoctonum* |
| 'Spark's Variety' 🏆H4 | Widely available |
| ***spicatum*** GWJ 9393 | WCru |
| - GWJ 9394 | WCru |
| - GWJ 9418 | WCru |
| 'Stainless Steel' | Widely available |
| ***subcuneatum*** | see *A. japonicum* subsp. *subcuneatum* |
| × ***tubergenii*** | see *Eranthis hyemalis* Tubergenii Group |
| ***uchiyamae*** B&SWJ 1005 | WCru |
| - B&SWJ 1216 | ELon EPPr WCru |
| - B&SWJ 4446 | NLar |
| § ***variegatum*** subsp. ***paniculatum*** | MBri NBre WCot |
| - - 'Roseum' | WFar |
| § ***vilmorinianum*** BWJ 8055 | WCru |
| ***volubile*** misapplied | see *A. hemsleyanum* |
| ***volubile*** Pall. | CFir GCal |
| ***vulparia*** | see *A. lycoctonum* subsp. *vulparia* |
| ***yamazakii*** | WCru |
| ***yezoense*** | GCal WCot |
| ***zigzag*** var. ***ryohakuense*** B&SWJ 8906 new | WCru |

## *Aconogonon* see *Persicaria*

## *Acorus* ✿ (*Acoraceae*)

| | |
|---|---|
| ***calamus*** | CArn CBen CKno CWat EHon ELau EWil GPoy LPBA MSKA NPer SWat WHer |
| - subsp. ***angustatus*** | GPoy |
| - 'Argenteostriatus' (v) | CBen CRow CWat EBee ECha ECtt EHon LPBA MCot MMuc MWts NOrc SEND SWat WMAq WWEG |
| * ***christophii*** | EBee ELon EPPr EWes SApp WMoo |
| ***gramineus*** | ELau GPoy LPBA MSKA NPer SWat WHer WMoo |
| - 'Golden Edge' (v) | EBee EWes NHol |
| - 'Hakuro-nishiki' (v) | EBee ECtt EHoe EHul EPPr EShb LPBA MCCP MGos MMoz NBid NHol SBfd SRms SWvt WMoo XLum |
| - 'Kinchinjunga' (v) | IFro |
| - 'Licorice' | EBee EPPr GCal MBNS MDKP NHol NWad SPoG WGrn WMoo |
| - 'Masamune' (v) | EBee EPla EWes GBin GCal SApp WMoo WPat WTin |
| - 'Minimus Aureus' | CBre GCal |
| - 'Oborozuki' misapplied | see *A. gramineus* 'Ogon' |
| - 'Oborozuki' (v) | EBee EHoe SMrm |
| § - 'Ōgon' (v) | Widely available |
| - var. ***pusillus*** | EBee EPla NBro WWEG |
| - 'Variegatus' (v) | Widely available |
| - 'Yodo-no-yuki' (v) | EPla |
| 'Intermedius' | NPer |

## *Acradenia* (*Rutaceae*)

| | |
|---|---|
| ***frankliniae*** | CBcs CCCN CMHG CMac CTrC CTsd EWTr GGar IDee MBlu SKHP WFar WPGP WSHC |

## *Actaea* (*Ranunculaceae*)

| | |
|---|---|
| ***alba*** misapplied | see *A. pachypoda*, *A. rubra* f. *neglecta* |
| ***arizonica*** | CLAP EBee GCal LPla WCru |
| ***asiatica*** | CLAP WPGP |
| - B&SWJ 616 | WCru |
| - B&SWJ 6351 from Japan | WCru |
| - B&SWJ 8694 from Korea | WCru |
| - BWJ 8174 from China | WCru |
| ***biternata*** | CLAP |
| - B&SWJ 5591 | WCru |
| - B&SWJ 8917 | WCru |
| - B&SWJ 11190 | WCru |
| 'Chocoholic' new | NCGa |
| § ***cimicifuga*** | CLAP EBee GCal GPoy LRHS |
| - B&SWJ 2657 | WCru |
| § ***cordifolia*** | EBee GBin GMaP LPBA LRHS NBPC NGdn SMrm WBor WCot |
| - 'Blickfang' | CLAP |
| - variegated (v) new | LRHS |
| ***dahurica*** | EBee NLar SWat WCot |
| - B&SWJ 8426 | WCru |
| - B&SWJ 8573 | WCru |
| - tall | GCal |
| ***erythrocarpa*** | see *A. rubra* |
| ***frigida*** B&SWJ 2966 | WCru |
| ***heracleifolia*** B&SWJ 8843 | WCru |
| - DJHC 970139 | CDes |
| § ***japonica*** | CLAP GAbr GCal WFar |
| - B&SWJ 5828 | WCru |
| - B&SWJ 11136 | WCru |
| - var. ***acutiloba*** B&SWJ 6257 | WCru |
| - compact | GBin |
| - - B&SWJ 8758A | WCot WCru |
| ***mairei*** | GCal |
| - BWJ 7635 | WCru |
| - BWJ 7939 | WCru |
| § ***matsumurae*** | CPLG |
| - B&SWJ 11187 | WCru |
| - B&SWJ 11528 | WCru |
| - 'Elstead Variety' 🏆H4 | CPLG GCal MBri MRav NBre |
| - 'Frau Herms' | CLAP |
| - 'White Pearl' | CBcs CPLG CRow EBee ECha ELan EPfP GAbr GGar GKev GMaP LHop LPla LRHS MMuc MRav NBPC NBid NCGa NSti SMad SPer SPoG WCAu WCot WFar WMnd WPGP WWEG WWlt |
| § ***pachypoda*** 🏆H4 | CBro CPLG EBee ECGP ECha EPfP GCal GPoy IGor LRHS NBid NLar SMad WCru |
| - f. ***rubrocarpa*** | GCal |
| § ***podocarpa*** | CAby SPlb SRms WCru |
| ***racemosa*** 🏆H4 | CArn CMac CRow EBee ELan EPfP GCal GPoy LRHS NBid NGdn NSti SPer SWvt WFar WMnd |
| - 'Washfield' | WCot |
| § ***rubra*** 🏆H4 | CBro CHid CMHG EBee ECha ELan GCal GGar LRHS MCot MMHG NBid SMad WCru WFar |
| - B&SWJ 9555 | WCru |
| - ***alba*** | see *A. pachypoda*, *A. rubra* f. *neglecta* |
| § - f. ***neglecta*** | GAbr GCal GKev GQue SKHP WCot WCru |
| ***simplex*** | CBot EBee ECha GCra LRHS NEgg NPri SEND SWat |
| - B&SWJ 8653 | WCru |
| - B&SWJ 8664 | WCru |
| - B&SWJ 10957 | WCru |
| - B&SWJ 11133 | WCru |
| § - Atropurpurea Group | Widely available |
| - - 'Bernard Mitchell' | CFir |
| - - 'Black Negligee' | CLAP CPLG CWGN EBee ECtt GQue LLHF LSou MAvo MLLN MTis |

NCGa NDov NMyG SBfd SPad SPoG WCot WCra WWEG
- - 'Brunette' ♀H4 — Widely available
- - 'Carbonella' **new** — CSpe CWGN
- - 'Hillside Black Beauty' — CCVN CLAP EBee GMaP MNrw NBir NLar NPnk WBor WCot
- - 'James Compton' — Widely available
- - 'Mountain Wave' — CLAP EBee ECtt IPot WCot WFar WPGP
- 'Hugo' **new** — CSpe
- 'Pink Spike' — Widely available
§ - 'Prichard's Giant' — CLAP ECha EWTr GBin GKev MBri MRav MSpe NDov WFar
- ***ramosa*** — see *A. simplex* 'Prichard's Giant'
- 'Silver Axe' — GCal NBre NGdn
- variegated (v) — CDes WCot
***spicata*** — EBee GBin GCra GPoy LRHS NLar WCru
- from England — GCal WCru
***taiwanensis*** — CLAP WBox
- B&SWJ 343 — CLAP
- B&SWJ 3413 — WCru
- RWJ 9996 — WCru
***yesoensis*** B&SWJ 6355 — WCru
- B&SWJ 10860 — WCru
***yunnanensis*** — GCal

## *Actinella* see *Tetraneuris*

## *Actinidia* (*Actinidiaceae*)

BWJ 8161 from China — WCru
***arguta*** (f/F) — CAgr NLar
- 74-32 (m) — CAgr
- B&SWJ 569 — WCru
- B&SWJ 4455 from Jejudo, South Korea **new** — WCru
- B&SWJ 4823 from Japan **new** — WCru
- B&SWJ 8529 from Ulleungdo, South Korea **new** — WCru
- 'Ananasnaya' (f/F) — CAgr
- var. ***cordifolia*** (f/F) — CAgr
- 'Geneva 2' (f/F) — CAgr
- 'Issai' (s-p/F) — CAgr CBcs CCCN EPfP ERea LBuc LRHS LSRN MGos NLar
- 'Ken's Red' (F) — CAgr
- 'Kiwai Vert' (f/F) — CAgr
- LL#1 (m) — CAgr
- LL#2 (f/F) — CAgr
- LL#3 (m) — CAgr
- 'Meader' (m) — CAgr
- 'MSU' (F) — CAgr
- 'Shoko' (F) — WCru
- 'Unchae' (m) — WCru
***chinensis*** misapplied — see *A. deliciosa*
***chinensis*** ambig. — CDoy
§ ***deliciosa*** — ERom MGos MRav SBfd WFar WSHC
- 'Atlas' (m) — CAgr ERea NLar SDea
* - 'Boskoop' — ELan MCoo MGos MWat
- 'Buitenpost' — IArd
- 'Hayward' (f/F) — CAgr CBcs CCCN CDoC CHEx CMac EBee EPfP ERea LHop LRHS LSRN MCoo MREP NLar NPal SDea SPer SWvt WFar
- hermaphrodite (F) — ELan SBfd
- 'Jenny' (s-p/F) — CAgr CHEx CMac CSut CTri EPfP EPom ERea LAst LBuc LRHS MBri MGos SBfd SDea SLim SPoG SVic
- 'Solo' — CCCN CDoC CMac CSBt EPfP LBuc LRHS LSRN MCoo NLar SBfd SPer SPoG SWvt WPGP
- 'Tomuri' (m) — CBcs CCCN CDoC CHEx CMac EBee EPfP ERea LRHS LSRN MCoo NLar NPal SPer SWvt
***hypoleuca*** B&SWJ 5942 — WCru
***kolomikta*** ♀H4 — Widely available
- (m) — MBlu NPla
- B&SWJ 4243 — LSRN WCru
- 'Red Beauty' (F) — CAgr
- 'Tomoko' (f/F) — WCru
- 'Yazuaki' (m) — WCru
***latifolia*** B&SWJ 3563 — WCru
***melanandra*** — SPlb
***petelotii*** HWJ 628 — WCru
***pilosula*** — CBcs CCCN CPLG CSPN CWGN EBee ELon EPfP GCal GGal LHop LRHS LSRN LTen MBri MGos SBfd SBrt SCoo SKHP SPoG WCru WPGP WSHC
***polygama*** (F) — GCal
- B&SWJ 5444 — WCru
- B&SWJ 8525 from Korea — WCru
- B&SWJ 8923 from Japan — WCru
***rufa*** B&SWJ 3525 — WCru
aff. ***strigosa*** HWJK 2367 — WCru
***tetramera*** B&SWJ 3564 — WCru

## *Adansonia* (*Malvaceae*)

***grandidieri*** — SPlb
***gregorii*** — SPlb
***rubrostipa*** **new** — SPlb

## *Adelocaryum* see *Lindelofia*

## *Adenia* (*Passifloraceae*)

***glauca*** — LToo
***spinosa*** — LToo

## *Adenium* (*Apocynaceae*)

***obesum*** ♀H1 — LToo
- subsp. ***boehmianum*** — LToo
- subsp. ***oleifolium*** — LToo
- subsp. ***swazicum*** — LToo

## *Adenocarpus* (*Papilionaceae*)

***decorticans*** — SPlb

## *Adenophora* (*Campanulaceae*)

BWJ 7696 from China — WCru
'Afterglow' — see *Campanula rapunculoides* 'Afterglow'
***asiatica*** — see *Hanabusaya asiatica*
***aurita*** — CFir CRDP EWTr WCot
***bulleyana*** — CFir ELan GCra GJos IKil LRHS MSCN NBid NGdn SPav SPlb WCot WFar
***capillaris*** — WCru
subsp. ***leptosepala*** BWJ 7986
***coelestis*** — CPLG NBid NBre
- B&SWJ 7998 — WCru
***confusa*** — LHop MDKP NBre SAga WFar WHer WSHC
* ***cymerae*** — LEdu WTcb
***divaricata*** — WFoF
***forrestii*** — NBre WFar
***grandiflora*** B&SWJ 8555 — WCru
***jasionifolia*** BWJ 7946 — WCru

| | |
|---|---|
| ***khasiana*** | CPLG LLHF LRHS MDKP NLar |
| ***koreana*** | NBre |
| ***lamarkii*** B&SWJ 8738 | WCru |
| ***latifolia*** misapplied | see *A. pereskiifolia* |
| ***latifolia*** ambig. white-flowered | MMuc |
| ***latifolia*** Fischer | WFar |
| ***liliifolia*** | EBee ELan EPfP GCal GGar MMuc NPer WFar WPtf XLum |
| ***morrisonensis*** RWJ 10008 | WCru |
| § ***nikoensis*** | ECtt GAuc NBid |
| § - var. ***stenophylla*** | NBre |
| ***nipponica*** | see *A. nikoensis* var. *stenophylla* |
| § ***pereskiifolia*** | EWes NBre SHar SPlb WCot WTcb |
| ***polyantha*** | LRHS NLar SRms WFar |
| ***polymorpha*** | see *A. nikoensis* |
| ***potaninii*** | CFir ELan MMuc SEND WFar WHal |
| - pale-flowered | MMuc SEND WHal |
| ***remotiflora*** B&SWJ 8562 | WCru |
| - B&SWJ 8714 | WCru |
| - B&SWJ 11016 | WCru |
| ***stricta*** subsp. ***sessilifolia*** | NBre |
| ***takedae*** | NGdn |
| - B&SWJ 11424 | WCru |
| - var. ***howozana*** | LRHS MLHP |
| ***taquetii*** | EBee GKev |
| ***tashiroi*** | CPrp EPfP XLum |
| ***triphylla*** | NBir SPav |
| - B&SWJ 10916 | WCru |
| - var. ***hakusanensis*** | LLHF NBre |
| - var. ***japonica*** B&SWJ 8835 | WCru |
| - - B&SWJ 10933 | WCru |
| ***uehatae*** | GEdr |
| - B&SWJ 126 | WCru |

## *Adiantum* ✿ (*Pteridaceae*)

| | |
|---|---|
| ***aethiopicum*** | CHVG WRic |
| § ***aleuticum*** ♀H4 | CLAP ELan NBid NBro NLar WFib WPGP WRic |
| - 'Imbricatum' | CBty CElw CLAP ELon GBin IKil LRHS MGos MRav NBid NLar NMyG SBfd SDix SRms WCot WFar WFib WRic |
| § - 'Japonicum' | EBee ELan LRHS NBir SRms WFar WHal WPGP |
| - 'Laciniatum' | SRms |
| - 'Miss Sharples' | CDTJ CLAP ELan LRHS MGos NLar SRms WFar WRic |
| § - 'Subpumilum' ♀H4 | CLAP LRHS MRav NBid NMyG SRms WAbe WFib WRic |
| ***bonatianum*** | CPLG |
| ***capillus-veneris*** | CBty ISha WFib WRic |
| - 'Mairisii' | see *A.* × *mairisii* |
| ***chilense*** | EFtx GBin WCot WRic |
| ***cuneatum*** | see *A. raddianum* |
| ***fulvum*** | WRic |
| ***hispidulum*** | CBty CCCN ISha LRHS SRms WRic |
| - 'Bronze Venus' | CCCN EBee LRHS |
| § × ***mairisii*** ♀H3 | CBty EFtx ISha WRic |
| ***pedatum*** misapplied | see *A. aleuticum* |
| ***pedatum*** ambig. | CBty EBee ISha |
| ***pedatum*** L. ♀H4 | CBcs CHEx CLAP ECha EFer ELan ELon EPfP GEdr GMaP LAst LPBA LRHS MBri MMoz NVic SApp SPer SSpi SWat WFar WPGP |
| - from Japan **new** | LWst |
| - Asiatic form | see *A. aleuticum* 'Japonicum' |
| - 'Japonicum' | see *A. aleuticum* 'Japonicum' |
| - 'Roseum' | see *A. aleuticum* 'Japonicum' |
| - var. ***subpumilum*** | see *A. aleuticum* 'Subpumilum' |
| ***pubescens*** | WRic |
| § ***raddianum*** ♀H2 | EFtx |
| - 'Fragrans' | see *A. raddianum* 'Fragrantissimum' |
| § - 'Fragrantissimum' | EShb LRHS WRic |
| - 'Micropinnulum' | EFtx WRic |
| - 'Monocolor' | WRic |
| ***sulphureum*** | WRic |
| ***venustum*** ♀H4 | CBty CGHE CHEx CLAP EFer EFtx ISha MCot MWat SChr SDix SKHP SRms SSpi SWat WAbe WCot WFar WFib WHal WIvy WPGP WRic |

## *Adina* (*Rubiaceae*)

| | |
|---|---|
| ***rubella*** | NLar |

## *Adlumia* (*Papaveraceae*)

| | |
|---|---|
| ***fungosa*** | CSpe LBMP LRHS |

## *Adonis* (*Ranunculaceae*)

| | |
|---|---|
| ***amurensis*** misapplied | see *A.* 'Fukujukai', *A. multiflora* |
| ***amurensis*** ambig. | CMea EPot GEdr LAma LEdu LLHF LRHS SCnR WCot WFar |
| - 'Pleniflora' | see *A. multiflora* 'Sandanzaki' |
| ***cyllenea*** **new** | GLam |
| § 'Fukujukai' | ECha GEdr LWst WFar |
| § ***multiflora*** | CAby LRHS SRot |
| § - 'Sandanzaki' (d) | EPot EWes GEdr LRHS MMHG WCot |
| ***vernalis*** | GPoy LRHS NLar |

## *Adoxa* (*Adoxaceae*)

| | |
|---|---|
| ***moschatellina*** | CRWN NMen NRya WAbe WHer WSFF WShi |

## *Adromischus* (*Crassulaceae*)

| | |
|---|---|
| ***cooperi*** | STre |

## *Aechmea* (*Bromeliaceae*)

| | |
|---|---|
| sp. | XBlo |
| ***caudata*** var. ***variegata*** | CHEx |
| ***fasciata*** ♀H1 | XBlo |
| ***ramosa*** | XBlo |
| ***victoriana*** | XBlo |

## *Aegle* (*Rutaceae*)

| | |
|---|---|
| ***sepiaria*** | see *Poncirus trifoliata* |

## *Aegopodium* (*Apiaceae*)

| | |
|---|---|
| ***podagraria*** 'Dangerous' (v) | CHid |
| - gold-margined (v) | EPPr |
| - 'Variegatum' (v) | CDoC COIW CRow ECha EHoe EPPr EPla EShb GMaP LHop LRHS MLLN MMuc MRav MWhi NBid NSti SBfd SEND SPer SPoG WCFE WCot WMoo WSHC WWEG XLum |

## *Aeonium* (*Crassulaceae*)

| | |
|---|---|
| sp. | CArn |
| ***arboreum*** ♀H1 | CAbb CDTJ CHEx EShb GCal NPal SBfd SEND SMrm STre WNew |
| - 'Albovariegatum' (v) | MSCN |
| - 'Atropurpureum' ♀H1 | CAbb CHEx COIW EAmu EPfP EShb IDee MRav NEgg NPer SBfd SEND SPer SPoG SWal WNew |
| I - 'Magnificum' | ETod GBin SArc |
| - 'Variegatum' (v) | NPer |
| ***balsamiferum*** | CCCN CDTJ CHEx COIW IDee SBfd SChr |

'Black Cap' CCCN
'Blushing Beauty' CAbb SBst SPoG WCot
***canariense*** CCCN CDTJ CHEx ETod
***castello-paivae*** EShb SChr
***ciliatum*** SPlb
'Cristata Sunburst' WCot
***cuneatum*** SEND
***decorum*** SEND
* - 'Variegatum' (v) WCot
'Dinner Plate' CHEx
'Dinner Plate' × ***haworthii*** CHEx
***gomerense*** STre
***haworthii*** ♀H1 CHEx EOHP MSCN SBHP SEND
- 'Variegatum' (v) EOHP EShb SChr
***hierrense*** new SPlb
***holochrysum*** Webb & Berth. CAbb
***lindleyi*** SChr
***nobile*** CBrP IDee
***percarneum*** EShb
***simsii*** variegated (v) EShb
***tabuliforme*** ♀H1 CCCN CDTJ CSpe STre WCot
- 'Cristatum' WCot
***urbicum*** CHEx EShb
'Voodoo' new EAmu ETod
'Zwartkop' ♀H1 Widely available

## *Aeschynanthus* (*Gesneriaceae*)

'Big Apple' WDib
Black Pagoda Group WDib
***buxifolius*** KR 7798 WAbe
'Fire Wheel' WDib
***hildebrandii*** WDib
'Hot Flash' WDib
***longicalyx*** WDib
§ ***longicaulis*** ♀H1 WDib
***marmoratus*** see *A. longicaulis*
'Mona Lisa' EShb
***radicans*** ♀H1 WDib
'Scooby Doo' WDib
***speciosus*** ♀H1 WDib

## *Aesculus* ✿ (*Sapindaceae*)

***arguta*** see *A. glabra* var. *arguta*
× ***arnoldiana*** CDul CMCN
- 'Autumn Splendor' EPfP
***assamica*** WWJ 11886 WCru
§ × ***bushii*** CMCN MGos NLar
***californica*** CDul CMCN CMac EPfP SKHP WPGP
× ***carnea*** CDul CTri SGol WHar
- 'Aureomarginata' (v) LLHF WHar WPat
- 'Briotii' ♀H4 Widely available
- 'Plantierensis' CDul ECrN
* - 'Variegata' (v) CDul CMCN MGos
***chinensis*** CMCN MBri
***flava*** ♀H4 CCVT CDul CLnd CMCN CTho EBee ECrN EPfP EWTr LMaj MBri MMuc SEND SLim SSpi WFar
- f. ***vestita*** CDul MBlu
***georgiana*** see *A. sylvatica*
***glabra*** CDul CMCN CTho
- 'April Fire' MBlu
§ - var. ***arguta*** CMCN
- 'Autumn Blaze' EPfP MBlu
- 'October Red' EPfP MBlu MBri
***glaucescens*** see *A.* × *neglecta*
***hippocastanum*** ♀H4 Widely available
- 'Aureomarginata' (v) CMac
§ - 'Baumannii' (d) ♀H4 CDoC CDul CLnd CMCN EBee ECrN ELan EPfP LMaj MGos MSwo NWea SPer WDin WFar
- 'Digitata' CDul CMCN WPat
- 'Flore Pleno' see *A. hippocastanum* 'Baumannii'
- 'Hampton Court Gold' CBcs CMCN CMac
f. ***laciniata*** CDul CMCN IArd MAsh MBlu NLar SMad WPat
- 'Wisselink' CDul CMCN ECrN MBlu SMad
***indica*** CDul CHEx CLnd CMCN CTho EBee ECrN ELan EPfP IArd IDee LMaj SEND SGol SPer WDin
- 'Sydney Pearce' ♀H4 CBcs CDul CEnd CMCN EBee EPfP EWTr GKin MBlu MBri MGos NLar SBrt SSpi WDin WPat
× ***marylandica*** CDul
× ***mississippiensis*** see *A.* × *bushii*
× ***mutabilis*** 'Harbisonii' NLar WPat
- 'Induta' CDul CLnd CMCN EBee EPfP IArd MBri NLar NSti SKHP SMad WFar
§ - 'Penduliflora' CDul
§ × ***neglecta*** CMCN
- 'Autumn Fire' MBlu
- 'Erythroblastos' ♀H4 CBcs CDul CEnd CMCN CPMA EBee EPfP MAsh MBlu MBri MRav NLar SCoo SMad SSpi SSta WCot WDin WPat
***parviflora*** ♀H4 CBcs CDul CLnd CMCN CMac CTri EBee ELan EPfP EWTr GKin IDee LMaj MBlu MGos MMuc MPkF MRav NEgg SEND SGol SLPl SLim SMad SPer SSpi SWvt WDin WFar WHar
§ ***pavia*** ♀H4 CBcs CDul CLnd CMCN CTho EPfP SSpi WDin
- 'Atrosanguinea' CEnd CLnd CMCN EPfP MBlu MBri SDix SKHP SMad
I - 'Biltmore Buckeye' MPkF
- var. ***discolor*** 'Koehnei' CDul CMCN EPfP MBlu MBri NLar
- 'Penduliflora' see *A.* × *mutabilis* 'Penduliflora'
- 'Rosea Nana' CMCN LLHF WPat
***splendens*** see *A. pavia*
§ ***sylvatica*** CMCN
***turbinata*** CDul
***wilsonii*** CDul CPLG

## *Aethionema* (*Brassicaceae*)

***armenum*** EDAr
- 'Mavis Holmes' EDAr
***capitatum*** EDAr
§ ***grandiflorum*** ♀H4 EDAr LRHS NBro SGar SRms WFar
- Pulchellum Group ♀H4 CSpe
***iberideum*** MDKP MWat SRms
* ***kotschyi*** hort. WAbe
***membranaceum*** CPBP EDAr WFar
***oppositifolium*** MWat
***pulchellum*** see *A. grandiflorum*
***schistosum*** EDAr LLHF
***spicatum*** WFar
'Warley Rose' ♀H4 ECho ELan GJos GMaP LHop LRHS MAsh MSCN MWat NBir NMen NWCA SBch SRms WFar WThu
'Warley Ruber' CMea NBir NMen WAbe WFar

## *Aethusa* (*Apiaceae*)

***cynapium*** new CSpe

## *Aextoxicon* (*Aextoxicaceae*)

***punctatum*** CBcs

## *Afrocarpus* (*Podocarpaceae*)

| | Name | Suppliers |
|---|---|---|
| | ***falcatus*** | ECou |

## *Agapanthus* ✿ (*Agapanthaceae*)

| | Name | Suppliers |
|---|---|---|
| | from Johannesburg | ECha |
| | 'Adonis' | IBlr |
| | 'African Moon' | CPen CPne CPrp MAvo |
| | ***africanus*** misapplied | CElw COlW CWCL CWib EBee ECho ELan EPfP GAbr GBBs LEdu LRHS MNHC MWat SArc SChr SPav SPer SRot SWat SVic WFar WPer WWEG XLum |
| | – 'Albus' misapplied | CBcs CDoC CWCL EBee ECho ELan EPfP GBBs IFoB ITim LSRN LTen MGos SEND SPav SPer WFar WGwG WHil WPer WWEG XLum |
| | 'Aimee' **new** | CBro |
| | 'Albatross' | CPne ECha GCra |
| | 'Albus' ambig. | GKev GMaP LRHS MGos MHer MWat SAga SPad |
| I | 'Albus Nanus' | LRHS |
| | 'Amsterdam' | CPen EBee NHoy |
| | 'Angela' | CPen CPne CYeo ELon IBal MAvo NHoy |
| | 'Aphrodite' | IBlr |
| | 'Aquamarine' | CAvo CFFs NHoy SBch |
| | 'Arctic Star' | CKno CPLG CPar CPen CPne CPou CPrp CTca CWCL CYeo EBee ELon IBal LRHS LSou NHoy SDys SFai STes |
| | Ardernei hybrid | CAby CDes CPrp EBee ECha ECtt EWes GAbr GCal GQue IBal IBlr LSou MAvo NEgg SAga SMrm WCot WGwG WPGP |
| § | 'Argenteus Vittatus' (v) ♀H1 | CPen CPrp ELan NHoy WPGP |
| | 'Atlas' | IBlr |
| | 'Aureovittatus' (v) | IBal NHoy |
| | 'Baby Blue' | see *A.* 'Blue Baby' Rom. |
| | 'Baby Pete' **new** | SFai |
| | Back in Black = 'B in B'PBR | CPLG CSpe CWCL CWGN ELan EPfP EWes MAsh MAvo MBNS NBPC NBid NHoy NOrc SPtl |
| | 'Ballerina' **new** | CPne |
| | 'Ballyrogan' | IBlr |
| | 'Balmoral' | CPne |
| | 'Bangor Blue' | IBal IBlr |
| | 'Barnfield Blue' **new** | CPne |
| | 'Barnsley' | NHoy |
| | 'Basutoland' | EBla |
| | 'Beatrice' | CPne |
| | 'Beeches Dwarf' | ELan NHoy |
| | 'Beloved' | NHoy |
| | 'Ben Hope' | CBro IBal IBlr NHoy WCot |
| | 'Beth Chatto' | see *A. campanulatus* 'Albovittatus' |
| | 'Bethlehem Star' | CPne |
| | 'Bicton Bell' | CPne IBal IBlr |
| * | 'Bicton Hybrid' | CPrp |
| | 'Big Blue' | CChe CMac CPrp EBee EPfP GKev LSRN LSou SBfd SEND SRkn |
| | Birr hybrids | WCot |
| | 'Black Buddhist' | CPMA CPrp EBee ECtt EPri EWll GKev LSou MAvo MGos NGdn NHoy SPer WHil |
| | 'Black Magic' | CPne |
| | 'Black Pantha'PBR | Widely available |
| § | 'Blue Baby' Rom. | CCCN CChe CPen EBee ELan ELon IBlr LRHS NHoy WFar |
| | 'Blue Bird' | LRHS |

| | Name | Suppliers |
|---|---|---|
| | 'Blue Brush' | CPen CPrp CSBt EBee EPfP IBal LRHS LSou NHoy SCoo SEND SFai SPoG |
| | 'Blue Cascade' | IBlr |
| | 'Blue Companion' | CPne CPrp IBal IBlr NHoy WMnd |
| | 'Blue Crane' | EBla |
| | 'Blue Diamond' ambig. | CMac NHoy |
| | 'Blue Dot' | CPrp EBee ECtt LLHF LRHS LSou NGdn SDys |
| | 'Blue Dragon' | NHoy |
| | 'Blue Formality' | IBal IBlr |
| | 'Blue Fortune' | WWEG |
| | 'Blue Giant' | CBcs CBro CKno CPen CPrp EBee EPfP IBal IBlr LRHS MBri MGos NHoy SAga SWat WCFE WCot WFar WPGP WWEG |
| | 'Blue Globe' | CHid CMMP CPen EBee EPri GMaP LAst LRHS MSCN WWEG |
| | 'Blue Gown' | CPne CSam IBal |
| | 'Blue Heaven'PBR | CPne EBee MBri NHoy NPnk |
| | 'Blue Ice' | CAvo CPen CPne |
| | 'Blue Imp' | CBro EBee GBin IBlr SApp |
| | 'Blue Jay' | CPen |
| | 'Blue Moon' | CAbP CBro COlW CPen CPrp CSev CYeo EBee ECha IBal IBlr LRHS LSou MNrw NHoy SAga SMrm SPer WCot |
| | 'Blue Nile' | CPen CPne |
| | 'Blue Peter' | CSpr |
| | 'Blue Prince' | CPen EBee LRHS NHoy |
| | 'Blue Skies' ambig. | NCGa NHoy |
| I | 'Blue Skies' Dunlop | IBlr |
| | 'Blue Sparkler' | CPne |
| | 'Blue Spear' | CPen |
| | 'Blue Triumphator' | CTca EBee EPfP EWTr EWll GMaP IBlr LRHS MHer NHoy NPla SMrm WWEG |
| | 'Blue Umbrella' | EBee NHoy |
| | 'Blue Velvet' | CPne |
| | blue-flowered | WCFE |
| | Bluestorm = 'Atiblu'PBR | EPfP NHoy |
| | 'Bluety'PBR | CPen NHoy |
| | 'Bressingham Blue' | CBro CPne CPrp CTri EWes GCal IBal IBlr IFoB LRHS MRav NHoy NVic SWat WCot |
| | 'Bressingham Bounty' | LRHS |
| | 'Bressingham White' | EBee ECGP LEdu LRHS MBri MRav NCGa NHoy SWat |
| | 'Brody' | CPne |
| | 'Buckingham Palace' | CBro CDes CPrp EBee EWes GAbr IBlr NHoy WCot WPGP |
| | 'Cally Blue' | GAbr GCal IBal NHoy |
| | 'Cally Longstem' | GCal |
| | 'Cally Pale Blue' | GCal IBal |
| | 'Cambridge' | CPne |
| | ***campanulatus*** | CMac CPMA CPrp EBee EBla ECho ELan EPfP EWTr GKin IBal IBlr IGor ITim LRHS MMuc MRav NEgg NHoy NSti SEND SWat WCot WFar WPGP |
| | – var. ***albidus*** | CPMA CYeo EBee ECha ECho ELan EPfP EShb GKev GKin IBlr LHop LRHS MMuc NBid NGdn NHol NHoy NMRc NSti NVic SBrd SEND SPer WFar WGwG WHoo WPGP |
| § | – 'Albovittatus' | CPrp CSam ECho IBal LRHS NHoy |
| | – 'Beth Chatto' (v) | CPrp EBla IBal LSou |
| | – bright blue-flowered | GCal |
| | – 'Buckland' | IBlr |
| | – 'Cobalt Blue' | CPrp GKin LRHS NGdn NHoy |

- 'Oxford Blue' CPrp IBal IBlr NHoy WPGP
- subsp. ***patens*** ♀H3 CPrp EBla EPfP GKev IBal LRHS SWat WPGP
- - deep blue-flowered CFir CPrp IBlr NHoy WWEG
- 'Profusion' CBro CPne ECha IBal IBlr NHoy WFar
- variegated (v) EBla ECha NPer
- 'Wedgwood Blue' CPrp EBee IBal IBlr NHoy WHil
- 'Wendy' CPne IBal IBlr NHoy
- 'White Hope' IBal IBlr

'Carefree' CPrp IBal
'Castle of Mey' CBro CPen GAbr IBal IBlr LPla NHoy WPGP
'Catharina' CPne
§ ***caulescens*** ♀H1 IBal IBlr WCot WPGP
- subsp. ***angustifolius*** EBee IBlr SPer WCot WPGP
- subsp. ***caulescens*** IBlr SWat
- 'Nigel Marshall' GCal

'Cedric Morris' CPen IBlr NHoy
'Celebration' CPne
'Chandra' IBlr
'Charlotte'[PBR] CMac CPen EBee EPfP LRHS NHoy SPoG
'Cherry Holley' ELon
'Chika's Blue' MAvo
'Clarence House' CBro CPen
'Cloudy Days' **new** CPne
***coddii*** CPLG CPne EWes IBlr SMrm WCot
'Colin Edward' NHoy
'Columba' CPen CTca CYeo EBee ELon IBal LAma NBid NHoy
***comptonii*** see *A. praecox* subsp. ***minimus***
'Congratulations' NHoy
'Cool Blue' CPne
'Corina' EBee
'Cornish Sky' CPne
'Crystal' **new** GCal
'Crystal Drop' CPen CPne CPou EPri SWat
'Dainty Lady' NHoy
Danube see *A.* 'Donau'
'Dark Star' WFar
'Dartmoor' CPne
'Dawn Star' CPne
'Delft' CPrp IBal IBlr
'Density' IBlr
'Dokter Brouwer' CCVN CPen CYeo EBee ECtt IBal IKil LRHS LSRN MCot MDKP NBid NHoy
§ 'Donau' CBro CDoC CPen CYeo EBee EPri EShb IBal LAst LSou NBid NBir NHoy NOrc SWat WFar WHil
'Dorothy Kate' CPne
Double Diamond = 'Rfdd' CPen CPne CSev CWCL CWGN EBee EPri IBal LBMP LSRN LSou NBid NHoy SFai SPoG SUsu
'Dream' NHoy
'Dublin' CPne
'Duivenbrugge Blue' CPne
'Duivenbrugge White' CPne
***dyeri*** see *A. inapertus* subsp. ***intermedius***
'Ed Carman' (v) LSou WCot
'Eggesford Sky' CPne
'Elaine Anne' **new** NHoy
'Elisabeth' CPne
'Elizabeth Salisbury' CPne
'Enigma' CAbb CBro CCCN CPLG CPar CPen CPne CWCL CWGN CYeo EBee ECha EKen EPri EShb GBin IBal LRHS LSRN LSou MWea NHoy SBfd SFai SLon SRkn SUsu SWat
'Essence of Summer' WCot
'Ethel's Joy' CPen
'Eve' IBlr
'Evening Star' CPne ECha
'Exmoor' CPne
'Fast Track' WCot
'Findlay's Blue' MAvo WHil WPGP
'Finnline' (v) CPne CPrp
'Flore Pleno' (d) Widely available
'Forget-me-not' NHoy
'Gayle's Lilac' CBcs CElw CPen CPne CPrp CSam CWGN CYeo EBee ECtt ELan ELon GKin IBal LRHS LSRN LSou MRav NBPC NGdn NHoy NSti SApp SBfd SEND SMrm WCAu WWEG
'Gem' CPne ELon
'Getty White' GBin
I 'Giganteus Albus' CPne
'Glacier Stream' CBro CPen EBee ECtt EPri IKil NHoy
'Glen Avon' CAbb CBro CFir CPen CPne CPrp CYeo EBee IBal LRHS LSRN NBPC NHoy NLar SApp SCoo SEND SFai SLon SPoG
Gold Strike = 'Geagold' **new** SFai
'Golden Rule' (v) CPrp EBee EHoe IBal IBlr
'Goldfinger' (v) CPne
'Goliath' CPne
'Grey Ruler' LSou WCot
'Hanneke' CPen
'Happy Birthday' NHoy
§ Headbourne hybrids Widely available
'Headbourne White' **new** EPri
'Heather Gail' NHoy
'Heavenly Blue' CCCN CPne
'Helen' IBlr
'Holbeach' CPen
'Holbrook' CSam
'Holly Ann' NHoy
'Hoyland' NHoy
'Hyacinth' NHoy
'Ice Blue Star' CPne
'Ice Lolly' CBro CPen EBee EWTr IKil
***inapertus*** CAvo CBro CPrp CSpe EWes GGal SAga SMrm SWat WCot WPGP
- dwarf IBlr
- subsp. ***hollandii*** CPne CPom EBee GCal IBal IBlr MAvo NHoy SWat WCot
- - 'Zealot' IBlr
- 'Ice Cascade' **new** CPen IBal NHoy SBfd
- 'Icicle' GCal
- subsp. ***inapertus*** IBlr SWat
I - - 'Albus' EPPr IBlr LRHS
- - 'Cyan' IBlr
- - 'White' CPMA CPne
§ - subsp. ***intermedius*** CBro CPrp EBee IBal IBlr NHoy SWat
- - 'Long Tom' **new** CYeo EPri
- - white-flowered CPen CPou
- large IBal
- 'Little Black Number' **new** CPen
- 'Margaret' **new** EBee
- 'Midnight Cascade' CPar CPen CPne EBee IBal IPot NBid NHoy SBfd SUsu SWat
I - 'Nigrescens' CPen
- subsp. ***parviflorus*** IBlr
- subsp. ***pendulus*** CDes CFir CPne GCal IBlr WPGP
- - 'Graskop' CAbb CBro CCCN CFir CHVG CPLG CPen CPne CPrp CSpe CWGN CYeo EBee ELon EPri GBin

| | | |
|---|---|---|
| | | IBal IBlr LRHS LSou NHoy NSti SBfd SFai SKHP SPoG |
| | - - 'Violet Dusk' | IBlr |
| | - 'Sapphire Cascade' | CPen CYeo IBal NHoy SBfd SWat |
| | 'Inkspots' | CAbb CCCN CMac CPen CWCL EBee IBal LRHS LSou SBfd SFai SPoG |
| | 'Innocence' | IBlr |
| | 'Intermedius' Leichtlin | IBal |
| I | 'Intermedius' van Tubergen | EBee NBid |
| | 'Isis' | CAvo CBro CFir CPne CPrp CSam CTri EBla ECha IBal IBlr MAvo NHoy |
| | 'Jack's Blue' | Widely available |
| | 'Jersey Giant' | IBal NHoy |
| | 'Jodie' | CPne |
| | 'Johanna' | CPen CPne EBee |
| | 'Jolanda' | CPne CPrp ELon |
| | 'K. Wiley' | SUsu WSHC |
| | 'Kalmthout Blue' | CSpe |
| | 'Kingston Blue' | EBee ECha IBal IBlr IGor NBid NHoy WFar WSHC WWEG |
| | 'Kobaltglocke' | EBee |
| | 'Kobold' | EBee NHoy WFar |
| | 'Lady Edith' | IBlr |
| § | 'Lady Grey' | IBlr |
| | 'Lady Moore' | CBro CSpe IBlr IGor |
| | 'Lapis' **new** | CPne |
| | 'Latent Blue' | CPrp IBlr |
| | 'Lavender Haze' | CPen CPne EBee EPfP IBal LRHS LSou NHoy SFai |
| | 'Leicester' | CPen CPne |
| | 'Liam's Lilac' | CPLG CPar CPen CPne CPou CPrp ELon IBal SFai |
| | 'Lilac Bells' | CPne |
| | 'Lilac Flash' | CPen CPne |
| | 'Lilac Time' | CPLG CPne CPrp IBlr SAga SFai |
| | 'Lilliput' | CBcs CBro CMac CMea CSpe EBee ECha ECho ECtt ELan EPfP GGar GKev GMaP IBal LBMP LHop LRHS MAvo MRav NGdn SApp SEND SMrm SUsu WCFE WFar |
| | 'Little Beauty' | NHoy |
| | 'Little White' | CPen |
| | 'Littlecourt' | CBro |
| | 'Loch Hope' ♀H3 | CBro CCtw CDoC CPMA CPne CSam EBee ELon EPfP GAbr GGar LRHS LSou MRav NHoy SApp SFai WCot WHoo |
| | 'Luly' | CPen CPrp IBal LRHS NHoy SWat |
| | 'Lydenburg' | CPen CPrp EPri IBal IBlr NHoy |
| | 'Lyn Valley' | CPne |
| | 'Mabel Grey' | see *A.* 'Lady Grey' |
| | 'Magnifico' | IBal IBlr |
| | 'Margaret' | NHoy |
| | 'Mariètte' | CPen EBee |
| | 'Marjorie' | CPne SApp |
| | 'Martine' | CPen EBee |
| | 'Maureen' **new** | CPne |
| | 'May Snow' (v) | WCot |
| | 'Megan's Mauve' | CPne ELon EPri |
| | 'Meibont' (v) | CPne IBal WCot |
| | 'Mercury' | IBlr |
| | 'Metalica' | NHoy |
| | Midknight Blue = 'Monmid' | LRHS NHoy |
| | 'Midnight' | CPen EWes MAvo SAga WSHC |
| | 'Midnight Blue' ambig. | CAby CMea CPen ELan IBal IGor MGos MHer SFai SPav WFar |
| | 'Midnight Blue' P. Wood | GCal IBlr |
| § | 'Midnight Star' | Widely available |
| | 'Miniature Blue' | SWat WHil |
| | 'Misty Dawn' (v) **new** | WCot |

| | | |
|---|---|---|
| | mixed seedlings | EPfP IBal MGos NHoy NOrc WHil |
| | mixed whites | WCFE |
| | 'Mood Indigo' | CPne |
| | 'Moonshine' | CPen |
| I | 'Mooreanus' misapplied | EBee EPfP IBal IBlr IGor NBid WPGP |
| | 'Morning Star' | CPne |
| | 'Mount Stewart' | IBal IBlr |
| | 'My Love' | NHoy |
| | 'Navy Blue' | see *A.* 'Midnight Star' |
| | 'New Love' | EBee |
| | 'Night Sky' | CPne |
| | 'Nikki' | CPne |
| | 'Norman Hadden' | IBlr |
| | 'Northern Light' | CPen EBee LLHF |
| | 'Northern Star' | CAbb CPLG CPen CPne CPrp CYeo ELon LBMP LRHS LSou SBfd SFai SLon SPoG |
| | ***nutans*** | see *A. caulescens* |
| | 'Nyx' | IBlr |
| | 'Oslo' | CPne NHoy |
| | 'Oxbridge' | IBlr |
| | Palmer's hybrids | see *A.* Headbourne hybrids |
| | 'Paris' | CPen |
| | 'Patent Blue' | IBlr |
| | 'Patriot' | CYeo LRHS |
| | 'Pauline' | NHoy |
| | 'Penelope Palmer' | IBal IBlr |
| | 'Penny Slade' | SAga |
| | 'Peter Pan' ambig. | Widely available |
| | 'Phantom' | CDes CPne CPrp GCal IBal IBlr |
| | Pine Cottage hybrids **new** | CPne |
| | 'Pinocchio' | CPen CWib EBee ECho NHol NHoy |
| | 'Plas Merdyn Blue' | CPrp IBal IBlr |
| | 'Plas Merdyn White' | CFir CPne CPrp IBal IBlr NHoy |
| | 'Podge Mill' | IBlr |
| | 'Polar Ice' | CFir CPen CYeo EBee ECtt ELon EPri GAbr GBin IBal IBlr LRHS WCAu WFar |
| | 'Polar White' | NHoy |
| | 'Porcelain' | IBal IBlr |
| | ***praecox*** | CPrp EShb GAbr IBal IBlr NHoy |
| | - 'Albiflorus' | CBro CPne CPou CTri EPri IBal LRHS NEgg NHoy SEND |
| | - 'Floribundus' | SWat |
| | - 'Maximus Albus' | CPou IBal IBlr |
| § | - subsp. ***minimus*** | CElw CPne CPou EWTr GAbr IBal IBlr NHoy SWat WCot WHil |
| | - - 'Adelaide' | CPrp EBee |
| | - - blue-flowered | SWat |
| | - - white-flowered | CPne SWat |
| | - 'Neptune' | IBlr |
| § | - subsp. ***orientalis*** | CBro CCCN CPne CSut IBlr SAga SBfd SWat |
| | - - 'Cape Blue' | CPrp |
| | - - 'Silver Star' (v) **new** | CPen |
| | - subsp. ***praecox*** | IBlr |
| | - - azure-flowered | CPrp SWat |
| | - - 'Variegatus' | see *A.* 'Argenteus Vittatus' |
| | - 'Saturn' | IBlr |
| | - Slieve Donard form | IBlr |
| | - 'Uranus' | IBlr |
| | - 'Venus' | IBlr |
| | - 'Vittatus' (v) | NHoy WCot WFar |
| | 'Premier' | CPrp EBee IBal IBlr NHoy |
| | 'Pride of Bicton' | CPne |
| § | 'Purple Cloud' | Widely available |
| | 'Purple Delight' **new** | CPne |
| | 'Purple Haze' | CPen |
| | 'Purple Star' | CCCN CKno |

| | |
|---|---|
| 'Queen Anne' | NHoy |
| 'Queen Mother' | CPrp LRHS |
| 'Queen Mum' **new** | CPne |
| 'Radiant Star' **new** | NHoy |
| 'Regal Beauty' | CPar CPen CPne CSBt CWGN EBee EShb IBal LRHS LSRN LSou MBri NBid NHoy SBfd SFai SRkn |
| 'Remembrance' | NHoy |
| 'Rhone' | IBlr |
| 'Rosemary' | CPne SAga |
| 'Rosewarne' | CCCN CKno CMac CPLG CPrp EBee EPfP GBin IBal IBlr LRHS NHoy SFai |
| 'Rotterdam' | CPen CPne EBee NHoy |
| 'Royal Blue' | CBro CHar GBin GMaP NHol NHoy SBfd |
| 'Sally Anne' | CPne |
| 'San Gabriel' (v) | CPne |
| 'Sandringham' | CDes CPen CPne CPrp EBee EWes IBlr WPGP |
| 'Sapphire' | IBlr |
| 'Sarah'PBR | LSou NHoy |
| 'Sea Coral' | CCCN CFir CMac CPne EBee EWTr GAbr GGar LRHS MAvo NHoy NSti SHom |
| 'Sea Foam' | CMac CPen CPne EBee IBal NLar SBfd |
| 'Sea Mist' | CCCN CPne EBee IBal |
| 'Sea Spray' | CCCN CKno EBee IBal LRHS LSRN NHoy |
| 'Selma Bock' | CPen CPne |
| 'Senna' | CPLG CWGN EBee IBal LRHS LSou NHoy |
| 'Septemberhemel' | CPen |
| 'Silver Anniversary' **new** | NHoy |
| 'Silver Baby' | CKno CPMA CPen CPne CWGN CYeo ELon EPfP LRHS MAvo MNrw NHoy WHil |
| 'Silver Lining' **new** | EBee NHoy |
| 'Silver Mist' | CPMA CPen CPne EBee IBlr LRHS SWat |
| Silver Moon = 'Notfred'PBR (v) | CBro CPne CWGN EBee ELan EPfP IBal LSou MGos NHoy SFai SPer |
| 'Silver Sceptre' | IBlr |
| 'Silver Stream' | NHoy |
| 'Sky' | CAbb CPar CSBt CWGN CYeo EBee GBin IBal IBlr LBuc LRHS LSRN LSou NBid SBfd SFai SHar SKHP SPoG SRkn SWat |
| 'Sky Rocket' | IBal IBlr |
| 'Sky Star' | IBal |
| 'Slieve Donard' | IBlr WFar |
| 'Snow Cloud' | CAbb CBro CPMA CPen CPne CSBt EBee ELon EPfP IBal LRHS NEgg NHoy SBfd SFai SLon |
| 'Snow Pixie' | CBro CSpe CWGN EBee IBal LSRN LSou NHoy SFai SPoG |
| 'Snow Princess' | CPen IBal LRHS |
| 'Snow Shadows' **new** | CBro |
| 'Snow White' | CSpr |
| 'Snowball' | CBcs CDoC COIW CPLG CPen CPne CYeo EBee EWTr GAbr GKev LRHS LSou NBPC NHoy NPnk SBfd WWEG |
| 'Snowdrops' | CCCN EBee GAbr IBal LHop LSRN MNrw SApp SKHP SMrm WCFE WFar |
| 'Sofie' **new** | NHoy |
| 'Southern Star' | CPne |
| 'Spokes' | IBlr |
| 'Starburst' | IBlr |
| 'Stars and Stripes' **new** | SFai |
| 'Stéphanie Charm' | CPen |
| 'Storm Cloud' Reads | see *A.* 'Purple Cloud' |
| 'Storm Cloud' (d) | CBro CFir |
| 'Streamline' | Widely available |
| 'Summer Clouds' | CPne ELan NHoy |
| 'Summer Skies' | CPne IBal NHoy |
| 'Sunfield' | CKno CPen CPrp EBee EPfP GBin IBal LAma LRHS LSRN NHoy NLar NPer |
| 'Super Star' | CPne |
| I 'Supreme' | IBal IBlr |
| 'Sylvia'PBR | NHoy |
| 'Sylvine' | CPen CPne |
| 'Tall Boy' | IBal IBlr |
| 'Tarka' | CPen CPne CPrp CWCL CYeo EBee ELon IBal SDys SFai |
| 'Taw Valley' | CHVG CPen CPne CPrp ELon SLon |
| 'Thumbelina' | CBro CKno CPne CSev CWCL EBee IBal LSou NHoy SFai |
| 'Timaru' | Widely available |
| 'Tinkerbell' (v) | Widely available |
| 'Tiny Tim' | EBee |
| 'Titan' | IBlr |
| 'Tom Thumb' | CAvo CPLG ECtt EPfP IBal LRHS LSou NHoy SFai SRot WGor |
| 'Torbay' | CPne CPrp CYeo EAEE EBee ECtt ELon EShb GKin IBlr LLWG LRHS NCGa NEgg WWEG |
| 'Tornado' | CPen EBee ECtt LRHS MNrw NGdn NHoy |
| 'Tranquil' | NHoy |
| Tresco hybrid | CHEx |
| 'Tresco Select' | NHoy |
| 'Triangle' | CPen CPne |
| 'Twilight' | IBlr |
| ***umbellatus*** L'Hérit. | see *A. africanus* |
| ***umbellatus*** Redouté | see *A. praecox* subsp. *orientalis* |
| 'Underway' | EWes GCal GKev IBal IBlr SMrm |
| 'Velvet Night' | CPen |
| 'Violetta' | CPne |
| 'Wavy Navy' | CPen |
| 'Wedding Day' | CPne |
| 'Wembworthy' | CPne |
| 'White Dragon' | NHoy |
| 'White Dwarf' | see *A.* white dwarf hybrids |
| § white dwarf hybrids | CBro CPen ECha ECtt EPfP EShb GGar IBal LRHS NBir NGdn WFar |
| 'White Heaven'PBR | CAby CKno CPen CPne CSpe EBee ECtt ELon GAbr IBal LPla LRHS LSou MAvo MBri MLLN MNrw NHoy NPnk SFai SMrm SUsu SWat WCot WWEG |
| 'White Ice' | CBcs CPen EBee LRHS SApp |
| 'White Orb' | IBal MBri NHoy |
| 'White Smile' **new** | EPri |
| 'White Star' | COIW |
| 'White Starlet' | NHoy |
| 'White Superior' | CMMP CPen CSpe GMaP LAst MSCN SPet WCAu WHil |
| 'White Triumphator' | WCot |
| 'White Umbrella' | NHoy |
| white-flowered | CHEx GGar |
| 'Whitestorm' | NHoy |
| 'Whitney'PBR | CPen IBlr |
| 'Wholesome' | IBal |
| 'Windlebrooke' | CCCN CPne ECha EPri |
| 'Windsor Castle' | CPen CPrp IBal IBlr |
| 'Windsor Grey' | Widely available |

'Winsome' IBlr
'Wolga' CPMA EWll
'Wolkberg' Kirstenbosch CPne IBlr
'Woodcote Paleface' SRms
'Yellow Tips' CPne
'Yolande' LAma
'Yves Klein' CPrp IBlr
'Zachary' CPen CPne CPou CYeo ELon IBal LRHS
'Zebra' NHoy
'Zella Thomas' EBee
'Zomba' CPne

## *Agapetes* (*Ericaceae*)

'Ludgvan Cross' ♀H1-2 CCCN CDoC CTsd SSpi
***serpens*** ♀H1 CCCN CHEx CWib EShb SBrd SLon
- 'Scarlet Elf' CCCN WCot

## *Agarista* (*Ericaceae*)

§ ***populifolia*** WFar

## *Agastache* (*Lamiaceae*)

'After Eight' EBee NDov
***anethiodora*** see *A. foeniculum* (Pursh) Kuntze
***anisata*** see *A. foeniculum* (Pursh) Kuntze
***aurantiaca*** CMea GCal NLar SPhx WFar
- 'Apricot Sprite' EBee EPfP LRHS MBri MHer MNHC MSCN NEgg NGdn SBch SGar SPoG SRkn WFar
- 'Lilac Sprite' **new** LRHS
'Black Adder' Widely available
'Blue Delight' SBch
'Blue Fortune' ♀H3-4 CBcs EBee EPfP LRHS MBri MCot MSCN NBro NDov SMrm SPer SPhx SWvt WFar WWEG
§ ***cana*** WFar
- 'Cinnabar Rose' WFar
- 'Purple Pygmy' CCVN CSpe EBee EPfP LHop LRHS MWea SMrm SPer SRot SUsu
'Cotton Candy' **new** EBee
'Firebird' CBot EAEE EBee ECtt ELan GKin LHop LRHS MBri MLLN NBPC NBir NGdn SMrm SPer SWat SWvt WAul WFar WWEG
'Fleur' EBee
***foeniculum*** misapplied see *A. rugosa*
§ ***foeniculum*** (Pursh) Kuntze CArn CMea EBee ECha EGHP ELan GMaP GPoy LRHS MCot MHer MNHC SPav SPhx SRms WFar WJek WPer WWEG
- 'Alabaster' CBcs EBee LRHS NLar SPhx
- 'Alba' EGHP NBre SBfd SHDw SPav WFar
'Giant' SUsu
'Glowing Embers' ECtt EPfP
'Heatwave' **new** WCot
'Kolibri' EBee
'Linda' NDov
§ ***mexicana*** SMrm SPav
- 'Red Fortune'PBR CWGN EAEE EBee ECtt EPPr LHop LRHS LSou MBri MLLN NDov NEgg SMrm SPad WCot
- 'Rosea' see *A. cana*
- 'Sangria' EBee EDif NDov NGdn SBch SBfd SPad
***nepetoides*** EPPr SPav
'Painted Lady' CSpe ECtt MWea SAga WTcb
***pallidiflora*** EBee EPfP MRav
var. ***neomexicana*** 'Lavender Haze'
'Pink Beauty' ECtt
'Pink Pop' EBee EPfP LRHS
'Purple Candle' EWes
'Purple Haze' NDov
'Raspberry Summer' ECtt NCGa NDov SBfd
'Rose Mint' **new** CSpe
§ ***rugosa*** CArn ELau GKev GPoy LHop MNHC NEgg SPav SPhx SWat WCAu WHfH WJek WMoo WPer
- B&SWJ 4187 from Korea WCru
- f. ***albiflora*** NBre NEgg
- - 'Liquorice White' EBee EPfP GQue LRHS MLLN NBre NLar SMrm SPer SPlb
- 'Golden Jubilee'PBR CSam CSpe EAEE EBee ECha ECtt ELan EPfP LHop LRHS MCCP MHer MNHC MSCN MSpe NLar NOrc NSti SBfd SPoG WFar WHil WJek WMoo WWEG XLum
- 'Honey Bee Blue' LRHS
- 'Korean Zest' WCru
- 'Liquorice Blue' EBee EPfP LRHS MLLN NEgg NGBl NGdn NLar NOrc SBfd SPer SPoG SWvt WBox WFar WMoo WPer
- pink-flowered CEnt
***rupestris*** CSpe EDif EWTr NLar SBch SPhx
- 'Apache Sunset' MBri SBch SPlb
***scrophulariifolia*** WBox
'Serpentine' EBee NDov SPhx
'Summer Glow' **new** EBee ECtt NCGa
'Summer Love' EBee
'Tangerine Dreams' ♀H3 CDoC EBee ECtt EDif EPfP LHop LRHS LSou MWea NCGa NEgg NGdn SCoo SMrm SPoG SUsu WGwG
'Tutti-frutti' CWGN ECtt NCGa SPhx
***urticifolia*** CSpe NBre
- 'Alba' CSpe NBre WPer

## *Agathaea* see *Felicia*

## *Agathis* (*Araucariaceae*)

***australis*** CBrP CDoC

## *Agathosma* (*Rutaceae*)

***ovata*** CCCN

## *Agave* ✿ (*Asparagaceae*)

***acicularis*** MAga
***aktites*** MAga
***albescens*** MAga
***albomarginata*** CDTJ MAga
***amaniensis*** MAga
***americana*** ♀H1 CAbb CBcs CBen CDoC CHEx CSpe CTrC EAmu EPfP EShb IBlr LPal MAga MCCP MSCN SArc SBfd SBst SChr SEND SMad SPer SPlb SPoG STrG SWvt WFoF
- var. ***expansa*** MAga
I - - 'Mediopicta Pallida' MAga
- 'Marginata' (v) ♀H3-4 CBrP CChe CDTJ CHll IBlr MAga MAvo MREP SEND STre WCot
- 'Mediopicta' misapplied see *A. americana* 'Mediopicta Alba'
- 'Mediopicta' (v) ♀H1 CDTJ CHEx ETod SArc SBig
§ - 'Mediopicta Alba' (v) ♀H1 CBrP CDTJ EAmu EShb ESwi MAga SChr SEND WCot
- 'Mediopicta Aurea' (v) MAga WCot
- var. ***oaxacensis*** MAga
- subsp. ***protamericana*** MAga WPGP
- subsp. ***protamericana*** × ***scabra*** F&M 310 WPGP

| | | |
|---|---|---|
| | - - - NJM 05.057 | WPGP |
| | - 'Striata' (v) | EShb MAga MCot WCot |
| | - 'Variegata' (v) ♀H1 | Widely available |
| | ***angustiarum*** | MAga |
| | ***angustifolia*** | see *A. vivipara* var. *vivipara* |
| | - var. ***marginata*** hort. | SBig WCot |
| | ***applanata*** | MAga WPGP |
| | ***asperrima*** | CDTJ MREP |
| § | - subsp. ***maderensis*** | MAga SPlb |
| | - subsp. ***potosiensis*** | MAga |
| § | - subsp. ***zarcensis*** | MAga |
| | ***atrovirens*** var. ***mirabilis*** F&M 245 new | WPGP |
| | ***attenuata*** | CAbb CBrP EAmu MAga SArc SBig SPlb WPGP |
| | ***attenuata* × *shawii*** | MAga |
| | ***aurea*** | MAga |
| | ***avellanidens*** | MAga |
| | ***beauleriana*** | EAmu MAga SBig |
| | ***boldinghiana*** | MAga WCot |
| | ***bovicornuta*** | MAga WCot |
| | ***bracteosa*** | CCCN MAga SChr |
| | ***brittoniana*** | MAga |
| | ***cantala*** | MAga |
| | ***capensis*** | MAga |
| | ***celsii*** | see *A. mitis* var. *mitis* |
| | ***cerulata*** subsp. ***nelsonii*** | MAga |
| | ***chazaroi*** | MAga |
| | ***chiapensis*** | MAga |
| | ***chrysantha*** | CCCN CTrC EAmu EBee ETod MAga WCot WGrn WPGP |
| | - 'Black Canyon' | WCot |
| | ***chrysoglossa*** | MAga WPGP |
| | ***cocui*** from Venezuela | MAga |
| | ***colimana*** | see *A. ortgiesiana* |
| | ***colorata*** | CCCN CDTJ WCot |
| | - dwarf | MAga |
| | ***congesta*** | MAga |
| | 'Cornelius' | WCot |
| | ***cundinmarcensis*** from Columbia | MAga |
| | ***cupreata*** | ETod MAga |
| | ***dasylirioides*** | MAga |
| | ***datylio*** | MAga |
| | ***decipiens*** | MAga |
| | - dwarf | MAga |
| | ***delamateri*** | MAga |
| | ***de-meesteriana*** | EAmu MAga |
| | - var. ***marginata*** (v) | EAmu MAga |
| | ***deserti*** | CBrP CDoC LRHS WCot |
| | - var. ***simplex*** variegated (v) | MAga |
| | ***difformis*** | ETod MAga |
| | - NJM 05.034 | WPGP |
| | ***durangensis*** | MAga SPlb |
| | ***eggersiana*** | MAga |
| | ***ellemeetiana*** | MAga |
| | ***elongata*** | see *A. vivipara* var. *vivipara* |
| | ***ensifera*** | MAga |
| | - var. ***marginata*** | MAga |
| | - variegated (v) | MAga |
| | ***evadens*** | MAga |
| | ***felgeri*** | CDTJ MAga |
| | ***ferdinandi-regis*** | see *A. victoriae-reginae* |
| | ***ferox*** | see *A. salmiana* var. *ferox* |
| | ***filifera*** ♀H1 | CCCN CDTJ CHEx EAmu ETod MAga SBst SChr SEND SPlb WCot |
| | - 'Compacta' | MAga |
| | - subsp. ***microceps*** ISI 1184 | MAga |
| I | - 'Variegata' (v) | MAga |
| | ***flexispina*** | ETod MAga SPlb |
| | ***fortiflora*** | MAga |
| | ***fourcroydes*** | MAga MREP |
| | ***funkiana*** | MAga |
| | - blue-leaved | MAga |
| | ***garciae-mendozae*** | CDTJ |
| | - NJM 05.073 | WPGP |
| | ***geminiflora*** | CCCN CDTJ EAmu EShb MAga WCot |
| | ***gentryi*** | CDTJ ETod MAga |
| | - F&M 213A | WPGP |
| | ***ghiesbreghtii*** | EAmu MAga MREP |
| | ***gigantea*** | see *Furcraea foetida* |
| | ***gigantensis*** | MAga |
| | × ***glomeruliflora*** | MAga |
| | ***goldmaniana*** | see *A. shawii* subsp. *goldmaniana* |
| | × ***gracilipes*** | MAga WPGP |
| | ***guadalajarana*** | CDTJ MAga WCot WPGP |
| | - dwarf | MAga |
| | ***guiengola*** | MAga |
| | ***gypsophila*** | MAga |
| | ***havardiana*** | CTrC EAmu MAga WCot WPGP XSen |
| | - DJH 1326 | WCot |
| | - dwarf | MAga |
| | ***hiemiflora*** | MAga |
| | ***hookeri*** | MAga |
| | ***horrida*** | ETod MAga SBig |
| | - subsp. ***horrida*** | SPlb |
| | - 'Perotensis' | EShb |
| | ***hurteri*** | CDTJ MAga |
| | ***impressa*** | WCot |
| | ***inaequidens*** | MAga |
| | ***karwinskii*** | MAga |
| | ***kerchovei*** | MAga WCot |
| | ***lechuguilla*** | CDTJ MAga SChr WPGP XSen |
| | ***lechuguilla* × *univittata*** | MAga |
| | ***lechuguilla* × *victoriae-reginae*** | MAga |
| | ***lophantha*** | see *A. univittata* |
| | - var. ***caerulescens*** | see *A. univittata* |
| | ***lurida*** Aiton | see *A. vera-cruz* |
| § | 'Macha Mocha' | WCot |
| | ***macroacantha*** | CDTJ MAga |
| | ***maculosa*** | WCot WPGP |
| | ***maculosa* × *obscura*** | MAga |
| | ***mapisaga*** | MAga |
| | - NJM 05.036 | WPGP |
| | - var. ***lisa*** | MAga |
| | ***marmorata*** | MAga WCot |
| | ***maximilliana*** | MAga SPlb |
| | - 'Katharinae' | MAga |
| | ***missionum*** from The Virgin Islands | MAga |
| | ***mitis*** var. ***albidior*** | MAga |
| § | - var. ***mitis*** | CDoC EAmu MAga SArc SChr |
| | ***mitis*** var. ***mitis* × *variegata*** | WCot |
| | ***montana*** | CDTJ CGHE EAmu ETod MAga SBst SPlb |
| | - F&M 221 | WPGP |
| | - F&M 289 | WPGP |
| | ***moranii*** | MAga |
| | ***multifilifera*** | MAga |
| | ***nayaritensis*** | MAga |
| | ***neglecta*** | MAga |
| | ***neomexicana*** | CCCN EAmu ETod MAga WPGP |
| | - S&B 948 | WCot |
| | × ***nigra*** hort. | EAmu |
| | ***nizandensis*** | CHEx MAga |

| | | |
|---|---|---|
| § | ***obscura*** | CDTJ ETod MAga |
| | ***ocahui*** | ETod MAga |
| | - var. ***longifolia*** | MAga |
| | ***ornithobroma*** | MAga |
| | ***oroensis*** | MAga WCot |
| § | ***ortgiesiana*** | MAga |
| | ***ovatifolia*** | MAga SKHP SPlb |
| | ***pachycentra*** | MAga |
| | ***palmeri*** | CCCN CTrC MAga WPGP |
| | ***panamana*** | see *A. vivipara* var. *vivipara* |
| | ***parrasana*** | EAmu MAga WCot WPGP |
| | - dwarf | MAga |
| | ***parryi*** | CBcs CDTJ CDoC CSpe EAmu ETod GKev MAga MDev SBst SChr SPlb WPGP XSen |
| | - var. ***couesii*** | SKHP XSen |
| | - 'Cream Spike' (v) | WCot |
| | - var. ***huachucensis*** | CDTJ WCot |
| | - 'Ohi Kissho ten Nishiki' (v) | WCot |
| | - subsp. ***parryi*** | CBrP CDTJ MAga MREP WPGP |
| | - - JCA 1.035.000 | WPGP |
| | - var. ***truncata*** | EAmu |
| I | - 'Variegata' (v) | MAga |
| | ***parvidentata*** | MAga |
| | - blue-leaved | MAga |
| | ***parviflora*** ♀H1 | MAga WCot |
| | - subsp. ***flexiflora*** | MAga |
| | - - dwarf | MAga |
| | × ***peacockii*** | MAga |
| | ***pedunculifera*** | MAga |
| | ***pelona*** | MAga |
| | ***pendula*** | MAga |
| | ***petiolata*** | MAga |
| | ***polianthiflora*** | MAga |
| | ***polyacantha*** | MAga |
| | - F&M 120 | WPGP |
| | - var. ***xalapensis*** | see *A. obscura* |
| | ***potatorum*** ♀H1 | ETod |
| | - var. ***potatorum*** | MAga |
| | - var. ***verschaffeltii*** | EAmu MREP |
| | - - dwarf | MAga |
| | ***potreriana*** new | MAga |
| | ***promontorii*** | MAga |
| | ***pumila*** | MAga |
| | ***pygmaea*** | see *A. seemanniana* |
| | ***rhodacantha*** | MAga |
| | × ***romani*** | MAga |
| | ***salmiana*** | CDTJ EAmu MAga SBig SPlb |
| | - F&M 290 | WPGP |
| | - var. ***angustifolia*** | MAga |
| | - subsp. ***crassispina*** | MAga SPlb |
| § | - var. ***ferox*** | CDTJ CDoC CTrC EAmu ETod MAga MDev MREP SArc SBig SChr WCot |
| | - - 'Marginata' (v) | MAga |
| | - subsp. ***salmiana*** variegated (v) | MAga |
| | ***scabra*** | CCCN CDoC EBee MAga |
| | - subsp. ***maderensis*** | see *A. asperrima* subsp. *maderensis* |
| | - subsp. ***zarcensis*** | see *A. asperrima* subsp. *zarcensis* |
| | ***scabra*** × ***univittata*** | MAga |
| | ***scaposa*** | MAga |
| | ***schidigera*** | CBrP ETod MAga WCot |
| | - 'Shira-ito-no-ohi' (v) | WCot |
| | ***schottii*** | CDTJ MAga |
| | - var. ***treleasei*** | MAga |
| § | ***seemanniana*** | MAga |
| | 'Sharkskin' | WCot |
| | ***shawii*** | MAga |
| § | - subsp. ***goldmaniana*** | MAga |
| | ***shrevei*** | ETod |
| | - subsp. ***magna*** | SPlb |
| | - subsp. ***matapensis*** | MAga |
| | ***sileri*** | WCot |
| | ***sisalana*** | EAmu ETod MAga |
| I | - f. ***armata*** | MAga |
| | - 'Mediopicta' | MAga |
| | - 'Variegata' (v) new | EAmu |
| | ***sobria*** | MAga |
| | - subsp. ***frailensis*** | MAga |
| | - subsp. ***sobria*** | MAga |
| § | ***spicata*** | MAga |
| | ***stictata*** | WCot |
| | ***striata*** | EAmu ETod |
| | - subsp. ***falcata*** | MAga |
| * | - ***rubra*** | CDTJ SPlb |
| | ***stricta*** ♀H1 | CCCN CDTJ EAmu ETod MAga MREP WCot |
| | - blue-leaved new | ETod |
| | - dwarf | CBrP MAga |
| | - 'Nana' | CDTJ |
| | - 'Nana' blue-leaved | MAga |
| | ***stringens*** | MAga |
| | ***subsimplex*** | MAga |
| | ***tecta*** | MAga |
| | ***tenuifolia*** | MAga |
| | ***tequilana*** blue-leaved | MAga |
| | - green-leaved | MAga |
| | - variegated (v) | MAga WCot |
| | ***thomasiae*** | MAga |
| | ***titanota*** | EAmu MAga |
| | ***toumeyana*** | MAga WCot |
| | - var. ***bella*** | CDTJ MAga |
| | ***triangularis*** | CDTJ ETod MAga |
| | ***underwoodii*** | MAga |
| § | ***univittata*** | CDTJ MAga WCot |
| | - 'Quadricolor' (v) | WCot |
| | ***utahensis*** ♀H1 | ETod MAga SEND XSen |
| | - var. ***discreta*** | MAga |
| | - dwarf | MAga |
| | - var. ***eborispina*** | MAga |
| | - var. ***nevadensis*** | MAga |
| | ***valenciana*** | MAga |
| | ***variegata*** | WCot |
| § | ***vera-cruz*** | MAga |
| § | ***victoriae-reginae*** ♀H1 | CBrP CCCN CDTJ EAmu EShb MAga SWal |
| | - dwarf | MAga |
| I | - 'Marginata Pallida' | MAga |
| | - f. ***ornata*** | MAga |
| | ***vilmoriniana*** | MAga |
| | ***virginica*** | WCot |
| | ***vivipara*** | MAga |
| | - var. ***letonae*** | MAga |
| | - 'Marginata' | MAga |
| | - var. ***nivea*** | MAga |
| | - var. ***sargentii*** | MAga |
| § | - var. ***vivipara*** | MAga SBig |
| | ***vizcainoensis*** | MAga |
| | ***warelliana*** | MAga |
| | ***weberi*** | EAmu MAga |
| | ***wendtii*** | MAga |
| | ***wercklei*** | MAga |
| | × ***winteriana*** | MAga |
| | ***wocomahi*** | MAga |
| | ***xylonacantha*** | ETod MAga SChr SPlb |
| | ***yuccifolia*** | see *A. spicata* |
| | ***zebra*** | MAga |

## *Ageratina* (*Asteraceae*)

§ ***altissima*** CHid CMac EBee ELan EPfP MCot WFar WHfH WTin
- 'Braunlaub' CPrp EBee ECtt LPla LRHS MMuc NBir NBre SEND SWat WCAu WHrl WMoul WPtf
- 'Chocolate' ♀H4 Widely available

§ ***aromatica*** EBee EDAr MRav NBre NBro SWat WSFF
§ ***glechonophylla*** WHil
§ ***ligustrina*** ♀H3 Widely available
§ ***occidentalis*** NNS 94-53 WCot

## *Ageratum* (*Asteraceae*)

***corymbosum*** CHll CSpe EShb MWea

## *Aglaomorpha* (*Polypodiaceae*)

***coronans*** WRic

## *Agonis* (*Myrtaceae*)

***flexuosa*** CCCN CTrC

## *Agrimonia* (*Rosaceae*)

***eupatoria*** CArn CHab CRWN EBee EWil GPoy MHer MNHC NMir SIde SWat WHer WHfH
* - var. ***alba*** NLar
***grandiflora*** EBee
***odorata*** misapplied see *A. procera*
***odorata*** (L.) Mill. see *A. repens*
***pilosa*** CArn EBee
§ ***procera*** EBee
§ ***repens*** WMoo

## *Agropyron* (*Poaceae*)

***glaucum*** see *Elymus hispidus*
***magellanicum*** see *Elymus magellanicus*
***pubiflorum*** see *Elymus magellanicus*

## *Agrostemma* (*Caryophyllaceae*)

***coronaria*** see *Lychnis coronaria*
***githago*** CArn CHab MNHC SBch
- 'Ocean Pearl' CSpe

## *Agrostis* (*Poaceae*)

***calamagrostis*** see *Stipa calamagrostis*
§ ***canina*** 'Silver Needles' (v) EWes LRHS NBir WFar WWEG
***capillaris*** new CHab
§ ***montevidensis*** NWsh SMad
***nebulosa*** CKno SPhx
- 'Fibre Optics' CSpe MCot
***stolonifera*** 'Julia Ann' (v) WCot

## *Aichryson* (*Crassulaceae*)

× ***aizoides*** EBak WCot
var. ***domesticum*** 'Variegatum' (v) ♀H1
***tortuosum*** CFee
***villosum*** ESem

## *Ailanthus* (*Simaroubaceae*)

§ ***altissima*** CBcs CCVT CDul CHEx CLnd CMac CPLG CTho EBee EPfP EWTr LAst MBlu NWea SEND SPer SPlb SWvt WDin
- var. ***tanakae*** RWJ 9906 WCru
***glandulosa*** see *A. altissima*

## *Ainsliaea* (*Asteraceae*)

***acerifolia*** B&SWJ 4795 WCru
- B&SWJ 6059 WCru
***apiculata*** B&SWJ 11397 WCru
***chapaensis*** B&SWJ 11720 new WCru
aff. ***elegans*** WWJ 11720 WCru
***nervosa*** B&SWJ 11344 new WCru
***petelotii*** B&SWJ 11732 WCru
***tonkinensis*** B&SWJ 11819 WCru
***uniflora*** B&SWJ 11336 WCru

## *Ajania* (*Asteraceae*)

§ ***pacifica*** CSpr WCot
- 'Silver Edge' EBee XLum

## *Ajuga* (*Lamiaceae*)

***ciliata*** var. ***villosior*** CFir GBin
***genevensis*** CArn LRHS MHer NMun SPhx
***incisa*** EBee GCal
- 'Bikun' (v) CLAP EBee EPPr LRHS SRGP
- 'Blue Enigma' CLAP CPLG EBee EWes NCGa

'Little Court Pink' see *A. reptans* 'Purple Torch'
***metallica*** hort. see *A. pyramidalis*
'Pink Spires' NCot
§ ***pyramidalis*** CFee LRHS
- 'Metallica Crispa' CBct EBee ECho ECtt ELan EPPr EPfP EPri EWes GKin LBMP LRHS MBNS NBPC NLar SPoG SRms SWvt WCot WFar

***reptans*** CArn CHab CRWN CTri CWan EBee ECtt GKev GPoy LPBA LRHS MCot MHer MNHC NMir SGar WFar WJek
- f. ***albiflora*** WHfH
- - 'Alba' CArn EBee ECtt EPfP LRHS MRav MSCN NBro SBfd SRms WCAu WFar WMoo
- - 'Sanne' EBee
- - 'Silver Shadow' WHil
- 'Arctic Fox' (v) EBee ECho MRav MSCN NRya SWvt WCot WFar WHer
- 'Argentea' see *A. reptans* 'Variegata'

§ - 'Atropurpurea' CBar CWan EBee ECha ECho ELan EPfP GAbr LPBA LRHS MAvo MGos MLHP MSCN MSpe NHol NVic SGol SPer SPlb SRms SWvt WBrk WFar WJek WWEG
- Black Scallop = 'Binblasca'PBR Widely available
- 'Braunherz' Widely available
- 'Burgundy Glow' (v) CBcs CWCL EBee ECha ECho ELan EPfP EShb GMaP LAst LBuc LRHS MAsh MGos MHer MLLN MSCN NPri SBfd SEND SGol SPer SPlb SPoG SRms SWvt WFar WGwG WMoo WWEG

§ - 'Catlin's Giant' ♀H4 Widely available
- 'Chocolate Chip' see *A. reptans* 'Valfredda'
- 'Delight' (v) EBee ECho
- 'Dixie Chip' EPfP MLLN
- 'Ebony' LSRN
- 'Evening Glow' GGar WMoo
- 'Flisteridge' CNat
- 'Golden Beauty' EBee ECho ECtt LAst WNew
- 'Harlequin' (v) SWvt
- 'Jumbo' see *A. reptans* 'Jungle Beauty'

§ - 'Jungle Beauty' EAEE EBee EPfP GKin LRHS MRav WFar

| | | |
|---|---|---|
| | - 'Macrophylla' | see *A. reptans* 'Catlin's Giant' |
| § | - 'Multicolor' (v) | CBcs EBee ECho ELan LRHS MAsh MAvo MRav SPer SPlb SPoG SRms SWvt WFar WMoo WNew WWEG |
| | - 'Palisander' | EBee LRHS NEgg NLar |
| | - 'Party Colours' | CLAP |
| | - 'Pink Elf' | CMHG ECho GCra MRav NBro SWat WBrk WFar WWEG |
| | - 'Pink Splendour' | NBre NChi |
| | - 'Pink Surprise' | EBee ECtt EHoe EPri MHer MLHP NRya WFar WGwG WMoo WWEG |
| | - 'Purple Brocade' | EHoe LRHS |
| § | - 'Purple Torch' | EBee NLar WWFP |
| | - 'Purpurea' | see *A. reptans* 'Atropurpurea' |
| | - 'Rainbow' | see *A. reptans* 'Multicolor' |
| | - 'Rosea' | EAEE EBee LRHS NPnk WCAu WFar WMoo |
| | - 'Rowden Amethyst' | CRow |
| | - 'Rowden Royal Purple' | CRow |
| | - 'Silver Carpet' | EBee |
| | - 'Silver Queen' | EBee ECtt |
| | - 'Stölzle' | EBee |
| | - 'Sugar Plum' | ECtt ELon EPPr EShb |
| | - 'Toffee Chip' (v) | SGol |
| | - 'Tricolor' | see *A. reptans* 'Multicolor' |
| § | - 'Valfredda' | CEnt EBee ECho ECtt EPfP GKev LAst LRHS NEgg NLar SHar WCot WFar WGwG WMoo WWEG |
| | - 'Vanilla Chip' (v) | EBee |
| § | - 'Variegata' (v) | EBee ECho ECtt EPfP NPri SPer SPoG SRms SWat WFar |

## Akebia ✿ (*Lardizabalaceae*)

| | | |
|---|---|---|
| | sp. new | GGal |
| | ***longeracemosa*** | NLar |
| | - B&SWJ 3606 | CPLG LEdu WCot WCru WPGP |
| | × ***pentaphylla*** | ELan EPfP LRHS MAsh MRav NLar SPer |
| | - B&SWJ 2829 | WCru |
| | ***quinata*** | Widely available |
| | - B&SWJ 4425 | WCru |
| | - 'Alba' | CBcs CHII CSPN CSpe CWGN NLar WPat |
| | - 'Amethyst' | EBee SKHP |
| | - 'Amethyst Glow' | EPfP LRHS NLar SPer SPoG |
| | - cream-flowered | EBee EPfP EWld LRHS LSRN MRav MWea SBfd SKHP SPer SPoG SSta SWvt WCru WPGP |
| | - variegated (v) | CBcs LLHF SMad WCot WCru WPat |
| | - 'White Chocolate' | ESwi NLar WCru WSHC |
| | ***trifoliata*** | CAlb CBcs EBee ELan EPfP LRHS MBlu SEND SLim SLon WOld |
| | - B&SWJ 2829 | WCru |
| | - B&SWJ 5063 | WCru |

## Alangium (*Cornaceae*)

| | | |
|---|---|---|
| | ***chinense*** | EPla |
| | ***platanifolium*** | CAbP CBcs CPLG NLar WPGP |
| | - var. ***macrophyllum*** | EPfP SEND SPoG WBor |
| | - var. ***platanifolium*** | NLar |

## Albizia (*Mimosaceae*)

| | | |
|---|---|---|
| | ***chinensis*** | EBee LRHS |
| | ***distachya*** | see *Paraserianthes lophantha* |
| § | ***julibrissin*** | CArn CChe CDTJ CTrC CWib EAmu EPfP LMaj NEgg NMun WDin |
| | - 'Ernest Wilson' | MTPN WGrn |
| | - Ombrella = 'Boubri'PBR | CTho EBee ELan EMil LRHS MBri SCoo SPoG WHar |
| | - f. ***rosea*** ♀H2-3 | Widely available |
| | - 'Rouge d'Été' | EBee |
| I | - 'Rouge Selection' | LRHS SLim WPGP |
| | - 'Summer Chocolate' | CBcs CWGN ELan EPfP LRHS MPkF SBrd SCoo SMad SPoG WHar |
| | ***kalkora*** new | SBrt SPlb |
| | ***lophantha*** | see *Paraserianthes lophantha* |

## Albuca ✿ (*Asparagaceae*)

| | | |
|---|---|---|
| | sp. | WCot |
| | JCA 15856 | CTca NWCA WHil |
| | from Lesotho | GCal |
| | ***angolensis*** | CPou |
| | ***aurea*** | CTca EBee WCot |
| * | ***batliana*** | ECho |
| | ***batteniana*** | CFir CPrp EBee ECho |
| | ***canadensis*** (L.) F.M. Leight. | CPou MAvo |
| | ***cooperi*** | ECho |
| | 'Dirk Wallace' | CPLG |
| | ***fastigiata*** | ECho |
| | - f. ***floribunda*** | WCot |
| | ***flaccida*** | WHil |
| | ***fragrans*** | EBee WHil |
| | ***glauca*** | CPrp EBee ECho |
| | ***humilis*** | CDes CPLG CPrp EBee ECho LLHF NMen NRya WCot WHil WPat |
| | ***juncifolia*** | WHil |
| | ***longifolia*** | ECho |
| | ***nelsonii*** | CAvo CPne CPrp CTca EBee ECho |
| | ***setosa*** | CTca EBee ECho |
| | ***shawii*** | CBro CPne CPou CPrp CTca EAEE EBee EBla ECho EPri GKin LAst LRHS MHer NCGa NWCA SAga SEND SGar SPet SPoG SUsu WHil |
| | ***trichophylla*** | ECho |

## × Alcalthaea (*Malvaceae*)

| | | |
|---|---|---|
| | ***suffrutescens*** 'Parkallee' (d) | CAbP CDes EBee ECtt ELon EPPr GMac LPla LRHS LSou MAvo MNrw NGdn NLar NSti SPhx WBrk WCot WHil WHoo WOut |
| | - 'Parkfrieden' (d) | CSpe EBee ECtt ELon EPPr MAvo SPhx WCot |
| | - 'Parkrondell' (d) | EBee ECha ECtt ELon EPPr GMac LPla MAvo MNrw NDov WCot WHil WOut |
| | - white-flowered | IFro |

## Alcea (*Malvaceae*)

| | | |
|---|---|---|
| | 'Apple Blossom' (d) | EPfP GMac |
| | 'Arabian Nights' | SPav |
| | 'Blackcurrant Whirl' | SPav |
| | ***ficifolia*** | MCCP NChi SPav SWal WFar WHil WMoo |
| | 'Happy Lights' | CWib |
| | 'Peaches 'n' Dreams' | CWib EBee EPfP NGBl |
| § | ***rosea*** | SVic WFar |
| | - Chater's Double Group (d) | CWib ECtt EPfP MBri NBlu SPoG SRms WRHF |
| | - - chamois (d) | EPfP |
| | - - chestnut brown-flowered (d) | EPfP |
| | - - pink-flowered (d) | ELan EPfP NPri |
| | - - purple-flowered (d) | EGxp EPfP LAst SBrd SPoG |
| | - - red-flowered (d) | ELan EPfP NPri SPoG |
| | - - salmon pink-flowered (d) | ELan EPfP |
| | - - scarlet-flowered (d) | EPfP SPoG |
| | - - violet-flowered (d) | EPfP |
| | - - white-flowered (d) | ELan EPfP NPri SBrd SPoG |
| | - - yellow-flowered (d) | EPfP NPri SBrd SPoG |
| | - Cottage Mixed | GKev |

- 'Crème de Cassis' EPfP NBPC NGBl SPav WHil
- double pink-flowered (d) MHer
- double red-flowered (d) MHer
- double rose-flowered (d) EBee
- double white-flowered (d) MHer
- double yellow-flowered (d) EBee MHer
- 'Nigra' CSpe EBee ECtt ELan EPfP GMac LHop LSRN MHer MNHC MSpe NGBl NGdn NPri SBfd SPer WCAu WFar WWEG
- Summer Carnival Group CWib LAst SRms

§ ***rugosa*** MSpe SHar SPav SWal XSen

## *Alchemilla* ✿ (*Rosaceae*)

***abyssinica*** EBee WHrl
***alpina*** misapplied see *A. conjuncta*, *A. plicatula*
***alpina*** ambig. MCot
***alpina*** L. CEnt CFee CMea EBla ECho EHoe ELan EPfP LHop LRHS MMuc MRav MWat NChi SBch SRms SWat WFar WKif WMoo WNew WPer WSHC
***aroanica*** EBee EBla
§ ***conjuncta*** Widely available
***ellenbeckii*** CDes EBee ECho EDAr EPfP GAbr GGar NChi WFar WMoo WPGP WWEG WWFP
***epipsila*** EBee ELan EShb EWTr LRHS NBPC NLar SPhx WPer
***erythropoda*** $\mathbb{Y}^{H4}$ Widely available
- 'Alba' **new** LAst
***faeroensis*** LRHS WMoo WPer WPtf
- var. ***pumila*** GEdr NMen WAbe
***glaucescens*** CNat EBla
***iniquiformis*** EBee WPGP
***lapeyrousei*** EBee NChi
***mollis*** $\mathbb{Y}^{H4}$ Widely available
* - 'Robusta' MMuc SEND SPlb SWat WFar WMoo WPnP
- 'Thriller' LRHS
***monticola*** WPer
'Mr Poland's Variety' see *A. venosa*
***pedata*** NChi
***pentaphylla*** EBee
***psilomischa*** LRHS
***pumila*** NBre
***saxatilis*** IFoB
***sericata*** 'Gold Strike' **new** MWhi
***speciosa*** LRHS
***straminea*** MRav NBre
§ ***venosa*** LRHS
***vetteri*** EBee WHrl
***vulgaris*** misapplied see *A. xanthochlora*
§ ***xanthochlora*** CArn EBee GPoy NBre NLar SRms WFar WHer

## *Aldrovanda* (*Droseraceae*)

***vesiculosa*** EFEx

## alecost see *Tanacetum balsamita*

## *Alectryon* (*Sapindaceae*)

***excelsus*** ECou

## *Aletris* (*Nartheciaceae*)

***farinosa*** CArn

## *Alisma* (*Alismataceae*)

***plantago-aquatica*** CBen CHab CRow CSpe EHon EWil LPBA MSKA NPer SWat WMAq WPnP XBlo
- var. ***parviflorum*** CBen LPBA MSKA MWts SPlb SWat WMAq

## *Alkanna* (*Boraginaceae*)

***tinctoria*** CArn CHab

## *Allamanda* (*Apocynaceae*)

***cathartica*** CCCN
- 'Silver Dwarf' **new** LRHS
***neriifolia*** see *A. schottii*
§ ***schottii*** $\mathbb{Y}^{H1}$ CCCN

## *Alliaria* (*Brassicaceae*)

***petiolata*** CArn CHab GPoy NLan WHer WSFF

## *Allium* (*Alliaceae*)

SSSE 250 GEdr
§ ***acuminatum*** CPom EBee ECho GBin NBir NMen
I - 'Album' ECho LRHS
***acutiflorum*** LAma
***aflatunense*** misapplied see *A. hollandicum*
***aflatunense*** ambig. ECho IBal LRHS LSRN SDeJ SEND WCot WFar WWEG
***aflatunense*** B. Fedtsch. SApp
I - 'Alba' ECho
'Akbulak' EBee ECho LAma
***albopilosum*** see *A. cristophii*
***altaicum*** ECho
***altissimum*** LAma
- 'Goliath' CTca EBee GKev WCot
***amabile*** see *A. mairei* var. *amabile*
'Ambassador' CBro CMea CTca EBee ERCP LAma MNrw SPhx WCot
***ampeloprasum*** CPrp EBee ECha ECho EGHP LAma SEND SVic WHer WShi
- var. ***babingtonii*** CAgr CArn CPom CPrp CTca GPoy ILis LEdu WHer WHil WShi
§ - 'Elephant' CArn
***amphibolum*** ECho LAma
***amplectens*** EBee ECho LAma
§ ***angulosum*** CAvo CMea CTca EBee ECho LAma LPla WCot
***aschersonianum*** **new** ERCP
***atropurpureum*** EBee ECha ELan EPfP ERCP LAma LEdu MWat SDeJ SEND SPer SPhx
***atropurpureum* × *schubertii*** LSRN
***atroviolaceum*** EBee ECho
***azureum*** see *A. caeruleum*
***backhousianum*** LAma
***balansae*** ECho
***barszczewskii*** ECho
'Beau Regard' $\mathbb{Y}^{H4}$ CTca CWCL EBee ERCP LAma NLar
***beesianum*** misapplied see *A. cyaneum*
***beesianum*** W.W. Smith CDes CPne CPom EPot GEdr NBir NRya
- 'Album' ECho
***blandum*** see *A. carolinianum*
***bodeanum*** see *A. cristophii*
***bolanderi*** ECho
***brevicaule*** ECho
***bucharicum*** ECho
***bulgaricum*** see *Nectaroscordum siculum* subsp. *bulgaricum*
§ ***caeruleum*** $\mathbb{Y}^{H4}$ Widely available
- ***azureum*** see *A. caeruleum*
***caesium*** $\mathbb{Y}^{H4}$ ECho SMad
- tall LWst
***caespitosum*** ECho
***callimischon*** CBro

| |  |  |
|---|---|---|
| | - subsp. ***callimischon*** | ECho SPhx |
| | - subsp. ***haemostictum*** | CDes CPom ECho NMen WAbe WCot |
| | ***canadense*** | CArn EBee ECho |
| § | ***carinatum*** | ECho |
| § | - subsp. ***pulchellum*** ♀H4 | CArn CAvo CBro CMea EBee ECha ECho ELon EPot LAma LHop LLWP LRHS MHer MNrw MWat NMen SPhx WHil WPer |
| | - - f. ***album*** ♀H4 | CArn CAvo CBro CMea EBee ECha ECho ELon LEdu LLWP MNrw NMen SBch SMrm SPhx |
| | - - 'Tubergen' | ECho |
| | 'Carlito' | LAma |
| § | ***carolinianum*** | ECho LAma |
| | ***cepa*** | SVic |
| | - Aggregatum Group | ELau GPoy |
| | - 'Kew White' | WCot |
| | - 'Perutile' | CArn CHby GPoy ILis LEdu MHer SBfd SHDw |
| | - Proliferum Group | CArn CHab CHby CPrp CSev CWan EGHP EOHP EWhm GPoy ILis LEdu MHer MNHC SBfd SIde WGwG WHer WJek |
| | - var. ***viviparum*** | ECho LAma |
| | - 'White Lisbon' ♀H4 | SVic |
| | ***cernuum*** | CAby CArn CAvo CBro CFFs CMea CTca CWCL CYeo EBee ECha ECho EPfP EPot ERCP GAuc IFoB LAma LEdu LHop LRHS MLHP MLLN MNrw NBPC NMen SHom SKHP SPhx SRms |
| § | - 'Hidcote' ♀H4 | CSam WKif |
| | - 'Major' | see *A. cernuum* 'Hidcote' |
| | - var. ***obtusum*** | ECho |
| | - pink-flowered | NBir |
| | - 'White Dwarf' | EBee ECho SPhx |
| | ***chinense*** | GPoy |
| | ***cirrhosum*** | see *A. carinatum* subsp. *pulchellum* |
| | ***colchicifolium*** | CPom |
| | ***commutatum*** | ECho |
| | ***cowanii*** | see *A. neapolitanum* Cowanii Group |
| | ***crenulatum*** | ECho LAma |
| § | ***cristophii*** ♀H4 | Widely available |
| | ***cupanii*** | EBee ECho |
| | ***cupuliferum*** | CPom ECho |
| | ***curtum*** RCB RL 13 | WCot |
| § | ***cyaneum*** ♀H4 | CPBP CPom EBee ECho GEdr LAma LBee LRHS MHer NMen NRya SPhx WCot |
| * | - ***album*** | ECho |
| | - 'Cobalt Blue' | ECho |
| | ***cyathophorum*** | CYeo ECho EWld LRHS NWCA |
| § | - var. ***farreri*** | CArn CAvo CBre CBro EBee ECho EPot GAuc GEdr LEdu LLWP LRHS MLHP MRav NChi NRya SBch SSvw WCot |
| | ***darwasicum*** | ECho |
| | - RM 8274 | ECho |
| | ***decipiens*** | ECho LAma |
| | ***dichlamydeum*** | ECho LWst |
| § | ***drummondii*** | CPom ECho LRHS |
| | 'Early Emperor' | CWCL EBee ERCP LAma |
| | ***elatum*** | see *A. macleanii* |
| | 'Emir' | CAvo EBee |
| | ***ericetorum*** | EBee ECho WCot |
| | ***falcifolium*** | EBee ECho EPot LAma NMen NMin WCot |
| | ***farreri*** | see *A. cyathophorum* var. *farreri* |
| | ***fasciculatum*** | LAma |
| | ***fimbriatum*** | ECho |
| | - var. ***abramsii*** | ECho |
| | - var. ***purdyi*** | ECho |
| | 'Firmament' | CAvo CBro EBee ECGP ECha ECho ERCP LAma NLar SDeJ SPhx |
| | ***fistulosum*** | CArn CHby CWan EBee ECho EGHP ELau GPoy ILis LAma LEdu MHer MMuc MNHC NPri SIde SVic WGwG WJek WPer |
| | - 'Red Welsh' | CPrp ILis WJek |
| | - red-flowered | CHby |
| | ***flavum*** ♀H4 | CAby CArn CBro CTca ECha ECho EPot ERCP GKev IFoB LAma MRav SDeJ SMad WGwG WThu WWEG |
| § | - 'Blue Leaf' | ECho LEdu NBir SMrm |
| | - subsp. ***flavum*** | EBee ECho MMHG |
| | - - var. ***minus*** | EBee ECho |
| | - 'Glaucum' | see *A. flavum* 'Blue Leaf' |
| | - var. ***nanum*** | CYeo EPot GEdr |
| | - subsp. ***tauricum*** | CSpe EBee ECho SPhx |
| | 'Forelock' | CAvo CHid CTca EBee ERCP LAma LRHS MNrw SPhx WCot |
| | ***forrestii*** | EBee ECho GBin GKev MDKP WCot |
| | ***geyeri*** | EBee ECho WCot |
| | ***giganteum*** ♀H4 | Widely available |
| | 'Gladiator' ♀H4 | CFir CTca CWCL EBee ECtt ERCP GMaP LAma LRHS LSRN MNrw MRav MWat NOrc SBfd SDeJ SMrm SPad WWEG |
| | ***glaucum*** | see *A. senescens* subsp. *glaucum* |
| | 'Globemaster' ♀H4 | Widely available |
| | ***globosum*** | ECho |
| | 'Globus' | CTca IBal LAma |
| | ***goodingii*** | EBee ECho |
| | ***guttatum*** | ECho |
| | subsp. ***dalmaticum*** | |
| | - - HOA 9114 | ECho |
| | - subsp. ***sardoum*** | ECho |
| | - - CH 859 | ECho |
| | ***haemanthoides*** new | WCot |
| | ***haematochiton*** | ECho WCot |
| | - NNS 95-23 | EBee |
| | 'Hair' | see *A. vineale* 'Hair' |
| | ***heldreichii*** | EBee ECho |
| * | ***hirtifolium*** var. ***album*** | EBee ECho LAma |
| | 'His Excellency' | CFir EBee ERCP IBal LAma |
| § | ***hollandicum*** ♀H4 | CAvo CBro CFFs CTca CWCL EBee ECha ECtt EPfP GKev LAma MWat NEgg NOrc SPer SPlb WFar |
| | - 'Purple Sensation' ♀H4 | Widely available |
| | ***hookeri*** ACE 2430 | EBee WCot |
| | - var. ***muliense*** | GEdr |
| | - - CLD 1205 | GLam |
| | ***humile*** | ECho GEdr |
| | - CC 1818 | WCot |
| | ***hyalinum*** pink-flowered | EBee WCot |
| | ***hymenorrhizum*** | ECho |
| | ***inconspicuum*** | LAma |
| § | ***insubricum*** ♀H4 | ECho GEdr GLam LWst NBir NMen |
| | ***jajlae*** | see *A. rotundum* subsp. *jajlae* |
| | ***jesdianum*** | CBro |
| | - 'Michael Hoog' | see *A. rosenorum* 'Michael H. Hoog' |
| | - 'Purple King' | EBee LAma MNrw |
| | - 'White Empress'PBR new | CAvo SPhx |
| | ***kansuense*** | see *A. sikkimense* |
| | ***karataviense*** ♀H3 | CAby CArn CAvo CBro CElw CMea CTca EBee ECha ECtt ELan EPfP |

| | | |
|---|---|---|
| | | EPot GAbr GKev IBal LAma LRHS MBri MCot NBir NLar SBfd SDeJ SGar SMrm SWvt WFar |
| | - 'Ivory Queen' | CAby CAvo CBro CFFs CMea CTca EBee ECha ECtt EPfP ERCP GKev IBal LAma LRHS LSRN NLar SBfd SDeJ SMrm SPad SPlb WFar |
| | ***komarovianum*** | see *A. thunbergii* |
| | ***komarovii*** | CPom |
| | ***ledebourianum*** | EBee ECho LAma |
| | ***lenkoranicum*** | CAvo EBee ECho LAma WCot |
| | ***libani*** | WPer |
| § | ***lineare*** | ECho |
| | ***litvinovii*** | ECho LAma LWst |
| | ***longicuspis*** | ECho |
| | ***loratum*** | LAma |
| | 'Lucy Ball' | EBee ERCP LAma LRHS NBir NLar SDeJ |
| § | ***lusitanicum*** | CBro CTca EBla ECha ECho ERCP LAma NBre NMen SDix WAbe WCot WHlf |
| § | ***macleanii*** | CArn EBee ECho LAma |
| | ***macranthum*** | CPom EBee ECho GEdr GLam LAma LRHS WCot |
| | ***macrochaetum*** | ECho |
| | ***macropetalum*** | ECho |
| | ***mairei*** | CYeo ECho LHop LLWP LRHS NMen NRya WTin |
| § | - var. ***amabile*** | CYeo ECho GEdr NChi NRya NSla WThu |
| | - - pink-flowered | ECho |
| | - - red-flowered | ECho |
| | ***maximowiczii*** | EBee ECho |
| | - white-flowered | LAma NMen |
| | 'Mercurius'PBR | EBee ERCP LAma MNrw SPhx WCot |
| | ***meteoricum*** | EBee |
| | ***moly*** | CArn CWCL EBee ECho IFoB LAma LRHS MBri MMuc MRav NBPC NRya SBfd SDeJ SEND SMrm SRms SWal WCot WTin XLum |
| | - 'Jeannine' ♀H4 | CBro CTca EBee ECho EPot GAbr LAma LRHS MMHG WShi |
| | 'Mont Blanc' | CMea EBee ELan ERCP GBin GQue LAma MNrw NLar |
| | ***multibulbosum*** | see *A. nigrum* |
| | ***murrayanum*** misapplied | see *A. unifolium* |
| | ***murrayanum*** Reg. | see *A. acuminatum* |
| | ***myrianthum*** | ECho LAma |
| | ***narcissiflorum*** misapplied | see *A. insubricum* |
| § | ***narcissiflorum*** Villars | CRDP ECho LWst MNrw |
| | ***neapolitanum*** | EBee ECho EPot LAma MBri MCot SEND SPer SRms WGwG |
| § | - Cowanii Group | CBro EBee ECho LHop LRHS MWat SDeJ WCot |
| | - 'Grandiflorum' | EBee ECho |
| | ***nevskianum*** | CYeo EBee ECho LAma |
| § | ***nigrum*** | CArn CAvo CBro CFFs EBee ECho EPfP EPot ERCP LAma LRHS MCot MRav MWat NBir SDeJ SPhx WCot |
| | ***nutans*** | CBod CPrp EBee ECho EGHP LAma LEdu MHer SHDw WHal WHil |
| | ***nuttallii*** | see *A. drummondii* |
| § | ***obliquum*** | CArn CAvo CPom EBee ECha ECho ERCP SPhx WCot WTin |
| | ***ochotense*** | WCot |
| | ***odorum*** L. | see *A. ramosum* L. |
| | ***oleraceum*** | EBee ECho WHer |
| | ***olympicum*** | CDes ECho LWst |

| | | |
|---|---|---|
| § | ***oreophilum*** | CArn CBro CSam CYeo EBee ECha ECho ECtt EPfP LAma LRHS MLHP NRya SMrm SPer SRms WCot WHoo WWEG |
| | - 'Agalik' | ECho |
| | - 'Zwanenburg' ♀H4 | ECho EPot |
| | ***orvotrasum*** | ECho |
| | ***oschaninii*** | LAma |
| | ***ostrowskianum*** | see *A. oreophilum* |
| | ***ovalifolium*** var. ***leuconeurum*** | WCot |
| | ***palentinum*** | LAma |
| | ***pallasii*** | ECho |
| | ***pallens*** | CBre ECho NBir |
| § | ***paniculatum*** | CAvo EBee SCnR |
| * | - var. ***minor*** | LAma |
| | ***paradoxum*** | ECho LEdu NBir |
| | - var. ***normale*** | CBro CDes CPom CRDP EBee ECho EPot ERCP MMHG MRav NBir NMen WCot |
| | ***pedemontanum*** | see *A. narcissiflorum* Villars |
| | ***pendulinum*** | ECho |
| | ***peninsulare*** | LWst |
| | 'Pinball Wizard' | CBro CTca EBee ERCP LAma LRHS |
| | ***platycaule*** | ECho LAma WCot |
| | ***platyspathum*** | ECho |
| | ***plummerae*** | EBee ECho SKHP |
| | ***plurifoliatum*** | ECho LAma |
| | ***polyastrum*** | CPom |
| | ***polyphyllum*** | see *A. carolinianum* |
| | ***polyrrhizum*** | ECho |
| | ***przewalskianum*** | LAma |
| | ***pskemense*** | EBee ECho LAma WCot |
| | ***pulchellum*** | see *A. carinatum* subsp. *pulchellum* |
| | 'Purple Rain' | LAma |
| | ***pyrenaicum*** misapplied | see *A. angulosum* |
| | ***pyrenaicum*** Costa & Vayreda | SEND |
| | ***ramosum*** Jacquin | see *A. obliquum* |
| § | ***ramosum*** L. | EBee ECho EGHP LAma LEdu WPer |
| | 'Rien Poortvliet' | ECho LAma |
| | ***robustum*** | ECho |
| | ***rosenbachianum*** misapplied | see *A. stipitatum* |
| | ***rosenbachianum*** Regel | CBro EBee |
| | - 'Album' | EBee ERCP LAma WCot |
| | - 'Michael Hoog' | see *A. rosenorum* 'Michael H. Hoog' |
| | - 'Shing' | EBee IBal LAma MNrw |
| § | ***rosenorum*** 'Michael H. Hoog' | EBee ECho EPot LAma |
| | ***roseum*** | CArn CMea CPBP EBee ECho ECtt EPfP EPot LAma MDKP SMrm |
| | - ***album*** | ECho |
| § | - var. ***bulbiferum*** | ECho |
| | - 'Grandiflorum' | see *A. roseum* var. *bulbiferum* |
| | ***rotundum*** | ECho |
| § | - subsp. ***jajlae*** | EBee ECho LLWP |
| | - subsp. ***rotundum*** | ECho |
| | 'Round and Purple' | EBee ERCP LAma |
| | ***sanbornii*** var. ***sanbornii*** | ECho |
| | ***sarawschanicum*** | ECho |
| | - 'Bright Boy' | EBee |
| | ***sativum*** | CArn ECho MHer NPri SIde SPoG |
| | - 'Albigensian Wight' | EGHP |
| | - 'Elephant' | see *A. ampeloprasum* 'Elephant' |
| | - 'Iberian Wight' | EGHP |
| | - 'Lautrec' | EGHP |
| | - 'Mediterranean Wight' | EGHP |
| | - var. ***ophioscorodon*** | EBee ECho GPoy ILis LAma |

| | |
|---|---|
| - - 'Early Wight' ♀$^{H4}$ | EGHP |
| - - 'Purple Wight' | EGHP |
| - 'Purple Heritage Moldovan' | EGHP |
| - 'Solent White' ♀$^{H4}$ | EGHP |
| ***saxatile*** | EBee ECho |
| ***schmitzii*** | ECho SSvw |
| ***schoenoprasum*** | Widely available |
| - f. ***albiflorum*** | CArn CPbn CPrp ECha ECho LEdu MHer NBir NCGa SIde WHer |
| - 'Black Isle Blush' | CPbn CTca GPoy LEdu LPla MHer |
| - 'Corsican White' | LEdu |
| - fine-leaved | ELau |
| - 'Forescate' | CPrp CTca EBee EBla ECha EWes LAma LAst LHop LRHS MRav NBir NGdn NWad SIde SPet SSvw XLum |
| - medium-leaved | ELau |
| - 'Netherbyres Dwarf' | CArn |
| - 'Pink Perfection' | GPoy LEdu LPla MHer |
| - 'Polyphant' | CBre |
| - var. ***sibiricum*** | GGar SDix WShi |
| - 'Silver Chimes' | CAvo CDes CWan EBee EWhm MRav SBfd SHDw |
| - thick-leaved | ELau NPri |
| - 'Wilau' | ELau |
| ***schubertii*** | CAby CAvo CBro CElw CFFs CMea CSpe CTca CWCL EBee ECtt ELan EPfP EPot ERCP GBin GKev IBal LAma LRHS MBri MNrw MWat SDeJ SPer SPhx WCot WFar |
| ***scorodoprasum*** | EBee ECho SIde |
| - subsp. ***jajlae*** | see *A. rotundum* subsp. *jajlae* |
| - subsp. ***scorodoprasum*** | ECho LAma LEdu |
| ***semenowii*** | ECho |
| ***senescens*** | CArn CBro CTca CTri CYeo EBee ECGP EPot LAma LEdu LRHS MRav NChi SApp SBch SEND SMrm SRms SSvw WTin XLum XSen |
| § - subsp. ***glaucum*** | CArn CMea CPBP CPom CPrp CSpe EAEE EBee EBla ECha ECho EPla GEdr LEdu LRHS NGdn NRya SAga SBrt SPet SUsu SWat WBox WCot WPer WTin |
| - subsp. ***senescens*** | CAvo EBee ECho LEdu NMRc SAga |
| ***serra*** | WCot |
| ***sessiliflorum*** | ECho |
| ***setifolium*** | ECho |
| ***sewerzowii*** | ECho |
| ***sibthorpianum*** | see *A. paniculatum* |
| ***siculum*** | see *Nectaroscordum siculum* |
| § ***sikkimense*** | CFir CPom CWCL CYeo EBee EBla ECho EPot LEdu LRHS MDKP NMen NSla SPet SPoG SSvw WCot WPer |
| 'Silver Spring' | CAvo CTca EBee ECho EPot ERCP LAma MNrw MWat SPhx WCot |
| ***siskiyouense*** | ECho |
| ***sordidiflorum*** | CPom |
| ***sphaerocephalon*** | Widely available |
| ***splendens*** | ECho |
| ***stellatum*** | LRHS WGwG |
| ***stellerianum*** | WPer |
| - var. ***kurilense*** | CPBP WThu |
| § ***stipitatum*** | ECho ERCP IFro LAma LRHS SPhx WCot |
| - 'Album' | CArn CBro EBee ECho |
| - 'Mars' | CFir EBee EPfP ERCP LAma LRHS MWat NLar |
| - 'Mount Everest' | CAvo CBro CFFs CFir CHid CTca EBee EPfP EPot ERCP GKev GMaP LAma MNrw MWat NBPC NChi NLar SDeJ SMrm SPer SPhx WCot WShi |
| - 'Violet Beauty' | CCse CWCL EBee LAma SBfd WCot |
| - 'White Giant' | CTca EBee ERCP LAma MNrw |
| ***stracheyi*** | WCot |
| 'Stratos' | EBee ERCP LAma LRHS |
| ***strictum*** Ledeb. | see *A. szovitsii* |
| ***strictum*** Schrad. | see *A. lineare* |
| ***subhirsutum*** | CPom EBee XLum |
| ***subvillosum*** | LWst WCot |
| 'Summer Beauty' | see *A. lusitanicum* |
| 'Summer Drummer' | CTca EBee ERCP |
| 'Sweet Discovery' | EBee LAma |
| § ***szovitsii*** | ECho |
| ***tanguticum*** | LRHS |
| ***taquetii*** | see *A. thunbergii* |
| ***texanum*** | LAma SPhx |
| § ***thunbergii*** ♀$^{H4}$ | CAvo EBee ECho EPot LAma NBir NRya SCnR SPhx WAbe WWEG |
| - 'Album' | WAbe |
| - 'Ozawa' | CDes EBee ECho NMen WAbe WCot |
| ***tibeticum*** | see *A. sikkimense* |
| ***togashii*** | ECho |
| * ***tournefortii*** | EBee ECho |
| ***triquetrum*** | CTca EBee ECho ELan ELau EPfP EPot GGar IBlr LAma LEdu NBir NLar NSti SEND WCot WHer WMoo XLum |
| ***tschimganicum*** | LAma |
| ***tuberosum*** | Widely available |
| - B&SWJ 8881 | WCru |
| - purple/mauve-flowered | CHby ECho ELau |
| ***tubiflorum*** | ECho |
| ***turkestanicum*** | ECho |
| § ***unifolium*** ♀$^{H4}$ | CArn CAvo CBro CFFs CPom CSam EBee ECho EPfP EPot ERCP GAbr GKev LAma MNrw MRav NBir NLBP SDeJ SEND WFar WPer |
| ***ursinum*** | CArn CHab CHby CWan EBee ECho EOHP EWil GGar GPoy LAma LRHS MWat NMir STre WFar WJek WSFF WShi |
| 'Valerie Finnis' | CPBP |
| ***validum*** | WCot |
| - NNS 06-41 | WCot |
| ***victorialis*** | ECho |
| - 'Cantabria' | EBee |
| ***vineale*** | CArn NMir WHer |
| § - 'Hair' | CTca EBee EPfP ERCP GKev ITim LAma LRHS MCot MWat NBir SGar WHoo |
| ***violaceum*** | see *A. carinatum* |
| ***virgunculae*** | CMea CPBP NRya WAbe |
| ***wallichii*** | ECho GAuc GMaP MBNS NBir NChi SKHP WCot WTin XLum |
| - ACE 2458 | EBee WCot |
| - dark-flowered | CPne CPom ECho GKev WCot |
| - - CLD 1029 | GLam |
| - purple-flowered | GEdr |
| ***zaprjagajevii*** | WCot |
| ***zebdanense*** | EBee ECho LAma SPhx |

## *Allocasuarina* (*Casuarinaceae*)

| | |
|---|---|
| ***monilifera*** | ECou |

## almond see *Prunus dulcis*

## *Alnus* ✿ (*Betulaceae*)

| | |
|---|---|
| NJM 09.070 | WPGP |

| | |
|---|---|
| ***cordata*** ♀H4 | Widely available |
| ***cremastogyne*** | EGFP NLar |
| ***crispa*** | see *A. viridis* subsp. *crispa* |
| ***fauriei*** from Niigata, Japan | CSto |
| ***firma*** | CDul CMCN CSto |
| ***glutinosa*** | CBcs CCVT CDoC CDul CHab CLnd CMac CRWN CSBt CTho CTri EBee ECrN EPfP LBuc LMaj MGos NWea SEWo SGol SPer STre WDin WHar WMou WSFF |
| - 'Aurea' | CDul CEnd CTho CWib MBlu MGos |
| - var. ***barbata*** | CSto |
| - 'Imperialis' ♀H4 | CCVT CDoC CDul CEnd CLnd CPMA CTho EBee ECrN ELan EPfP EWTr LHop LRHS MAsh MBlu MBri MDun MMuc NBro NLar NWea SBfd SEND SEWo SGol SPer WDin WHar |
| - 'Laciniata' | CDoC CDul CMac CTho ECrN MBlu MGos WFar |
| ***hirsuta*** | CSto NWea |
| ***incana*** | CCVT CDoC CDul CLnd CMCN CTho CWib ECrN LBuc MGos MSnd NLar NWea SGol SPer WDin WHar WMou |
| - 'Aurea' | Widely available |
| - 'Laciniata' | CTho MGos NLar SCoo WDin WFar |
| - 'Pendula' | CTho |
| § - subsp. ***rugosa*** | CMCN |
| ***japonica*** | CSto NLar |
| ***maximowiczii*** | CSto NLar |
| ***nitida*** | CMCN CSto |
| ***oregana*** | see *A. rubra* |
| ***pendula*** | CSto |
| - B&SWJ 10895 | WCru |
| § ***rubra*** | CCVT CDoC CDul CLnd CMCN CTho ECrN ELan NWea WDin |
| - f. ***pinnatisecta*** | CMCN CTho MBlu |
| ***serrulata*** | see *A. incana* subsp. *rugosa* |
| × ***spaethii*** | MBlu MMuc |
| ***subcordata*** | CSto |
| ***viridis*** | CAgr CSto NWea |
| § - subsp. ***crispa*** | CSto |
| - subsp. ***sinuata*** | CAgr CSto GAuc |

## *Alocasia* ✿ (*Araceae*)

| | |
|---|---|
| sp. | SArc |
| × ***amazonica*** ♀H1 | XBlo |
| 'Aurora' | EAmu |
| 'Calidora' | CDTJ SBrd SBst SPlb |
| ***cucullata*** | XBlo |
| ***gageana*** | CDTJ |
| ***lauterbachiana*** | EAmu |
| ***macrorrhiza*** | CDTJ CFir EAmu SBig SBst |
| ***odora*** | CDTJ EAmu SPlb XBlo |
| ***plumbea*** | XBlo |
| 'Portodora' | EAmu WCot |
| ***sanderiana*** new | SPlb |
| 'Stingray' new | EAmu |
| ***wentii*** | CDTJ EAmu WCot |
| - 'Aline'PBR (v) | EAmu |
| - 'Victory' (v) new | EAmu |

## *Aloe* ✿ (*Asphodelaceae*)

| | |
|---|---|
| ***aculeata*** | CAbb EShb |
| ***africana*** | CAbb |
| ***arborescens*** | CAbb CBrP CDTJ CDoC CHEx EAmu EShb SBst SChr SEND |
| ***aristata*** ♀H1 | CAbb CHEx ETod SArc SBfd SChr SEND SWvt WPGP |
| ***barbadensis*** | see *A. vera* |
| ***barberae*** | CAbb CCCN |
| ***brevifolia*** ♀H1 | CAbb CBrP EAmu EShb SBst |
| ***broomii*** | CAbb CCCN CDoC EPfP SChr SPlb |
| ***camperi*** 'Maculata' | SChr SEND |
| ***castanea*** | CAbb |
| ***ciliaris*** | CHll EShb SChr |
| ***comptonii*** | CAbb EShb |
| ***cooperi*** | CCCN CDTJ CDoC EShb |
| ***dawei*** | EShb |
| ***dichotoma*** | CAbb |
| ***distans*** | SEND |
| ***ecklonis*** | CCCN CTrC SPlb |
| ***ferox*** | CAbb CBod CBrP CCCN CDTJ CDoC CTrC EAmu GPoy MDev SBfd SBig SChr SEND |
| ***fosteri*** | CDTJ |
| ***greatheadii*** | CTrC |
| - var. ***davyana*** | SChr |
| ***humilis*** | CBrP CTrC SChr SEND |
| ***juvenna*** | EShb |
| ***kedongensis*** | SEND |
| ***krapohliana*** | CAbb |
| ***littoralis*** | CAbb |
| ***maculata*** | CDTJ MDev |
| ***marlothii*** | CAbb CCCN EShb |
| ***melanacantha*** ♀H1 | STre |
| ***microstigma*** | CCCN MDev |
| ***mitriformis*** | CBrP EPfP SChr SEND |
| ***mutabilis*** | CHEx SChr SEND |
| ***peglerae*** | CAbb |
| ***plicatilis*** | CCCN CDTJ EShb |
| ***polyphylla*** | CAbb EAmu WPGP |
| ***pratensis*** | CCCN CDTJ SChr |
| ***reitzii*** | CAbb CTrC SPlb |
| ***speciosa*** | CAbb EShb |
| ***spicata*** | CAbb |
| × ***spinosissima*** | CDoC SChr STre |
| ***striata*** | CAbb CCCN EShb GGal |
| ***striatula*** | CAbb CBrP CDTJ CDoC CGHE CHEx CSam CTca CTrC EAmu EBee EShb IBlr LPJP LTen SArc SBHP SBig SChr SEND SKHP SPlb SVen WCot WPGP |
| - var. ***caesia*** | IBlr |
| ***succotrina*** | CAbb |
| ***thraskii*** | CAbb |
| ***variegata*** (v) ♀H1 | EShb STre SWal SWvt |
| § ***vera*** ♀H1 | CArn CCCN CDoC CHab CHby CTca EOHP ERea EShb GPoy ILis MNHC NPer NPla NPri SBch SBfd SEND SIde SPlb SVic SWal WJek |
| ***wickensii*** | CAbb |

## *Alonsoa* (*Scrophulariaceae*)

| | |
|---|---|
| 'Bright Spark' | CSpe |
| ***incisifolia*** | CCCN CSpe |
| ***meridionalis*** | CCCN WAle |
| - 'Rebel' | LAst LSou SBfd SRkn WBor |
| * - 'Salmon Beauty' | LRHS |
| 'Pink Beauty' | CSpe |
| ***warscewiczii*** | CCCN ELan |
| - 'Peachy-keen' | CSpe |

## *Alopecurus* (*Poaceae*)

| | |
|---|---|
| ***alpinus*** | see *A. borealis* |
| § ***borealis*** | LRHS |
| - subsp. ***glaucus*** | EBee ELan EPPr GBin SPer |
| ***geniculatus*** | CRWN |
| ***pratensis*** | CHab NOrc |

| | |
|---|---|
| - 'Aureovariegatus' (v) | CWan EBee EHoe EPPr EPla GMaP LBMP MMoz NBid SApp SLim SPer WFar WMoo XLum |
| - 'Aureus' | ECha GBin LRHS MRav NBro SPlb WWEG |
| - 'No Overtaking' (v) | EPPr |

## *Alophia* (*Iridaceae*)

| | |
|---|---|
| ***lahue*** | see *Herbertia lahue* |

## *Aloysia* (*Verbenaceae*)

| | |
|---|---|
| ***citriodora*** | see *A. citrodora* |
| § ***citrodora*** ♀H2 | Widely available |
| ***gratissima*** | EOHP WJek |
| ***triphylla*** | see *A. citrodora* |

## *Alpinia* (*Zingiberaceae*)

| | |
|---|---|
| ***formosana*** | LEdu |
| ***galanga*** | CArn |
| ***japonica*** | CPLG LEdu |
| - B&SWJ 8889 | WCru |
| ***nutans*** misapplied | see *A. zerumbet* |
| ***officinarum*** | CArn CDTJ |
| ***speciosa*** | see *A. zerumbet* |
| § ***zerumbet*** | EAmu |
| - 'Variegata' (v) | CDTJ XBlo |

## *Alsobia* see *Episcia*

## *Alstroemeria* (*Alstroemeriaceae*)

| | |
|---|---|
| 'Adonis'PBR | LRHS WViv |
| 'Aimi' | CFir ELan LRHS SPer SWvt WFar WViv |
| 'Alexis'PBR | LRHS WViv |
| 'Angelina' | LRHS SWvt |
| 'Apollo' ♀H4 | CBcs CTsd MBNS MNrw NBre SPer SWvt WViv |
| 'Athena' | LRHS WViv |
| ***aurantiaca*** | see *A. aurea* |
| § ***aurea*** | GGar MRav NBPC NLar SRms |
| - 'Apricot' | GCal |
| - 'Dover Orange' | IGor |
| - 'Lutea' | SPlb |
| - 'Orange King' | CTsd EGxp ELan EPfP NLar SMrm |
| 'Avanti' | LRHS |
| 'Blushing Bride' | CFir ELon LRHS MBNS SWvt |
| 'Bolero' | WViv |
| 'Bonanza' | SLon SPer WViv |
| ***brasiliensis*** | CTsd GCal MNrw NChi WCot WSHC WViv |
| 'Cahors' | LBuc LRHS |
| 'Candy Floss' | EBee EPfP |
| 'Celine' **new** | WViv |
| 'Charm' | LRHS WFar WViv |
| 'Chi Chi' **new** | WCot |
| § 'Christina'PBR | LRHS MBNS NPri SLon SWvt WHlf WViv |
| 'Coronet' ♀H4 | MBNS WViv |
| 'Dandy Candy' | CAbP CWGN ELon EWll ITim MNrw NBPC NGdn NLar SPad SPoG SUsu WCot |
| 'Dayspring Delight' (v) | CRDP |
| § Diana, Princess of Wales = 'Stablaco' | LRHS NLar |
| ***diluta*** subsp. ***chrysantha*** F&W 8700 | WCot |
| Doctor Salter's hybrids | LLHF SRms |
| 'Douceur d'Automne' | LBuc LRHS |
| 'Elvira' | LRHS SPer WViv |
| 'Evening Song' | CFir EKen LRHS MBNS SLon SPer SWal SWvt WViv |
| 'Flaming Star' | CBcs LRHS WViv |
| 'Freedom' | CWGN EBee ECtt ELon GBin LAst LSou NBPC NEgg NGdn NLar SMad SPoG SUsu WCot |
| 'Friendship' ♀H4 | CBcs CTsd ELan LRHS NBre SWvt WViv |
| 'Gloria' | MBNS SWvt WViv |
| 'Glory of the Andes' (v) | CWGN NGdn NLar WWEG |
| 'Golden Delight' | LRHS SPer WViv |
| 'Golden Queen' | WFar |
| ***haemantha*** | MDKP |
| I 'Hatch Hybrid' | GCal |
| 'Hawera' | GCal SMrm |
| ***hookeri*** | ECho GBin GCal GGar NLar SCnR |
| - subsp. ***cummingiana*** | LLHF WCot |
| Inca Adore = 'Koadore'PBR | LHop MBri NBPC SPoG |
| Inca Avanti = 'Koncavanti' **new** | WViv |
| Inca Azure = 'Konazur' | WViv |
| Inca Birdy = 'Konirdy' | WViv |
| Inca Classic = 'Konclassic' | WViv |
| Inca Coral = 'Konocoral' **new** | WViv |
| Inca Desert = 'Konesert' | WViv |
| Inca Devotion = 'Konevotio'PBR | MBri NMir |
| Inca Exotica = 'Koexotica'PBR | LRHS MBri MGos NBPC NMir SPoG WViv |
| Inca Ginger **new** | WViv |
| Inca Glow = 'Koglow'PBR | MGos WViv |
| Inca Ice = 'Koice' | LHop LRHS MGos NLar SPoG WViv |
| Inca Joli = 'Koncajoli' **new** | WViv |
| Inca Lake = 'Koncalake' **new** | WViv |
| Inca Moonlight = 'Komolight' | WViv |
| Inca Obsession = 'Koobsion' | LRHS SPoG WViv |
| Inca Pride = 'Kopride' | WViv |
| Inca Pulse = 'Konpulse'PBR | LRHS MBri WViv |
| Inca Rocky = 'Konyrock' | WViv |
| Inca Serin = 'Koserin'PBR | LRHS SPoG WViv |
| Inca Tropic = 'Kotrop' | LHop LRHS MBri MGos SPoG WViv |
| Inticancha Creamy Dark Pink = 'Tescreda' **new** | WViv |
| Inticancha Dark Purple = 'Tesdarklin' **new** | WViv |
| Inticancha Purple = 'Tespurplin' | WViv |
| Inticancha Red = 'Tesrobiri' | EGxp WViv |
| Inticancha Sunday = 'Tessunday' **new** | WViv |
| Inticancha Sunlight = 'Tessunlight' **new** | WViv |
| Inticancha White Pink Blush = 'Tesblushin' **new** | WViv |
| Inticancha White Pink Heart = 'Tesheartin' **new** | WViv |
| Inticancha White = 'Teswhitin' **new** | WViv |
| Isabella = 'Stalis' | LSRN |
| ***kingii*** | see *A. versicolor* |
| 'Laguna' | LRHS WViv |
| ***ligtu*** hybrids | CAvo CBcs CFFs ECha ELan EPfP IFoB LAst LHop MNrw NLar NPer NVic SRms SWvt WFar WHoo WWEG |

|  |  |
|---|---|
| - var. ***ligtu*** | WCot |
| 'Little Eleanor' | GBin WFar WViv |
| 'Little Miss Charlotte' | WFar |
| 'Little Miss Christina'$^{PBR}$ | see *A.* 'Christina' |
| 'Little Miss Davina' | NPri WViv |
| 'Little Miss Gina' **new** | NPri WViv |
| 'Little Miss Isabel' | LRHS WViv |
| 'Little Miss Lucy' | NPri WViv |
| 'Little Miss Matilda' | WViv |
| 'Little Miss Natalie'$^{PBR}$ | see *A.* 'Natalie' |
| 'Little Miss Rosanna' | WViv |
| 'Little Miss Roselind' | see *A.* 'Roselind' |
| 'Little Miss Sophie'$^{PBR}$ | see *A.* 'Sophie' |
| 'Little Miss Tara'$^{PBR}$ | see *A.* 'Tara' |
| 'Little Miss Veronica' | MBNS WViv |
| 'Louise' **new** | LSRN |
| 'Lucinda' | CBcs SWvt |
| 'Maestro'$^{PBR}$ **new** | WViv |
| ***magnifica*** | WCot |
| - subsp. ***maxima*** | WCot |
| 'Marina' | MBNS |
| 'Marissa' | GMaP |
| 'Mars' | LRHS SWal |
| 'Mauve Majesty' | ECtt ELon LSou MNrw SPoG SUsu WCot |
| 'Moulin Rouge' | ELan LRHS MBNS SLon WViv |
| § 'Natalie'$^{PBR}$ | LRHS NPri WViv |
| 'Neptune' | LBuc LRHS |
| 'Orange Gem' ♀$^{H4}$ | MBNS WFar |
| 'Orange Glory' ♀$^{H4}$ | ELon GMaP MBNS SWvt WFar WViv WWlt |
| 'Orange Supreme' | LRHS WViv |
| 'Oriana' | LRHS SWvt WViv |
| ***patagonica*** | WAbe |
| § ***paupercula*** | WCot |
| - F&W 10560 | WCot |
| ***pelegrina*** | ECho |
| 'Perfect Blue' | WViv |
| 'Perfect Love' | MNrw |
| ***philippii*** | WCot |
| 'Phoenix' (v) | CFir LRHS SLon SWvt WViv |
| 'Pink Perfection' | NLar |
| 'Pink Sensation' | WViv |
| 'Polka' | MBNS SWal WViv |
| ***presliana*** RB 94103 | WCot |
| - subsp. ***australis*** | SMrm |
| Princess Aiko = 'Zapriko' | LRHS |
| Princess Angela = 'Staprilan' | CBcs ELan LRHS MBNS NLar |
| Princess Anouska = 'Zaprinous'$^{PBR}$ | LRHS MNrw NLar SLon SPer WViv |
| Princess Ariane = 'Zapriari' | WViv |
| Princess Camilla = 'Stapricamil'$^{PBR}$ | CBcs LRHS SLon SPer SPoG |
| § Princess Charlotte = 'Staprizsa'$^{PBR}$ | LRHS |
| Princess Daniela = 'Stapridani'$^{PBR}$ | SCoo SPoG |
| Princess Diana | see *A.* Diana, Princess of Wales = 'Stablaco', *A.* Princess Diana = 'Zapridapal' |
| § Princess Diana = 'Zapridapal'$^{PBR}$ | WViv |
| Princess Ella = 'Staprirange' | NLar |
| Princess Emma = 'Zaprimma' | WViv |
| Princess Fabiana = 'Zaprifabi'$^{PBR}$ | ELan LRHS MGos SPoG WViv |

|  |  |
|---|---|
| Princess Felicia = 'Zapricia'$^{PBR}$ | LBuc LRHS SPer |
| Princess Isabella = 'Zapribel'$^{PBR}$ | LRHS LSRN NLar WViv |
| Princess Ivana = 'Staprivane'$^{PBR}$ | LRHS NLar SPoG |
| Princess Juliana = 'Staterpa' | SPoG |
| Princess Julieta = 'Zaprijul'$^{PBR}$ | LRHS NLar SPoG WViv |
| Princess Letizia = 'Zaprilet'$^{PBR}$ | LRHS MNrw |
| Princess Leyla = 'Stapriley'$^{PBR}$ | CBcs LRHS MBNS MNrw SLon SPer SPoG |
| Princess Lilian = 'Zaprilian' **new** | WViv |
| Princess Louise = 'Zaprilou' | LRHS LSRN WViv |
| Princess Margaret | NLar |
| Princess Marilene = 'Staprilene'$^{PBR}$ | LRHS MBNS |
| Princess Mary = 'Zaprimary'$^{PBR}$ | LRHS MNrw NLar |
| Princess Mathilde = 'Zaprimat' | WViv |
| Princess Monica = 'Staprimon'$^{PBR}$ | MBNS SPoG |
| Princess Oxana = 'Staprioxa'$^{PBR}$ | MNrw NLar |
| Princess Paola = 'Stapripal'$^{PBR}$ | MBNS MNrw SCoo WViv |
| Princess Ragna | see *A.* Princess Stephanie |
| Princess Sara = 'Staprisara'$^{PBR}$ | MNrw SPoG |
| Princess Sarah = 'Stalicamp' | MBNS |
| Princess Sissi = 'Staprisis' | LRHS MNrw SPoG |
| § Princess Sophia = 'Stajello' | SPoG |
| § Princess Stephanie = 'Stapirag' | NLar |
| Princess Susana = 'Staprisusa'$^{PBR}$ | LRHS NLar SCoo SPoG |
| Princess Theresa = 'Zapriteres'$^{PBR}$ | LRHS NLar |
| Princess Zavina = 'Staprivina'$^{PBR}$ | CBcs CFir LRHS MBNS MNrw NLar SPer |
| Princess Zsa Zsa$^{PBR}$ | see *A.* Princess Charlotte |
| § ***psittacina*** | CAvo CBro CGHE CHll CMea CSam EBee EBla ECha ELan EPfP EPla GBin GCal GCra GGar IFoB LHop MCot MHer NChi WFar WSHC WViv |
| - 'Mona Lisa' | EWll LLHF LSou NLar WCot |
| - 'Royal Star' (v) | CBod CBro CPLG CWCL EBee EBla ELan ELon EPPr EPfP EPla GCal GGar LHop LRHS LSou MAvo NGdn NLar SHar SMrm SPoG SUsu WCot WFar WHil WHoo WSHC WWEG XLum |
| ***pulchella*** Sims | see *A. psittacina* |
| ***pulchra*** | LLHF |
| 'Purple Rain' | ELan LRHS MNrw SLon SWvt WViv |
| 'Red Beauty' (v) | see *A.* 'Spitfire' |
| 'Red Beauty' | ELan GMaP LRHS MBNS NBir SPer SPlb SWvt WCot |
| 'Red Elf' | MBNS SUsu SWvt WFar WViv |
| 'Rhubarb and Custard' | EBee EPfP |
| § 'Roselind' | CFir ELan LRHS MBNS NPri SWvt WViv |
| 'Saturne' | EPfP LBuc LRHS |

| | | |
|---|---|---|
| | 'Selina' | MBNS NBre SWal WFar WViv |
| | 'Serenade' | CBcs CFir LRHS WViv |
| | 'Short Purple' | LSou WCot |
| | 'Solent Wings' | WFar |
| | 'Sonata' | WViv |
| § | 'Sophie' PBR | ELan LRHS MBNS NPri SLon SWvt WViv |
| § | 'Spitfire' (v) | CRDP EPfP LRHS SLon SWvt WViv |
| | 'Spring Delight' (v) | CRDP WCot |
| | 'Strawberry Lace' | EBee EPfP |
| | 'Sunrise' | WWlt |
| | 'Sunstar' | GMaP |
| | 'Sweet Laura' PBR | CAbP ECtt ELon LLHF LSRN NBPC NEgg NGdn NLar SMad SPoG WCot WCra |
| | 'Tanya' | WViv |
| § | 'Tara' PBR | MBNS NPri SWvt WViv |
| | 'Tessa' | LRHS MBNS NBre SLon WViv |
| | 'Turkish Delight' | EBee EPfP |
| | 'Uranus' | LBuc LRHS |
| | 'Ventura' | LRHS WViv |
| § | ***versicolor*** | WCot |
| | ***violacea*** | see *A. paupercula* |
| | 'White Apollo' | WCot |
| | 'Yellow Friendship' ♀H4 | MBNS NLar SPlb SWvt WFar WViv |
| | Yellow King | see *A.* Princess Sophia |

## *Alternanthera* (*Amaranthaceae*)

| | | |
|---|---|---|
| | ***dentata*** 'Purple Knight' | EShb SBst |
| | - 'Royal Tapestry' new | EShb |

## *Althaea* (*Malvaceae*)

| | | |
|---|---|---|
| | ***armeniaca*** | EBee LPla NLar WCot WOut |
| | ***cannabina*** | CAby CFir CSpe EBee ELan GCal GMac GQui MHer MNrw MWea NGBl SUsu WBor WHal WHoo WOld WSHC WTcb |
| | ***officinalis*** | CArn CHab CPrp CSev CWan EBee ELan EWil GPoy ILis MHer MNHC SIde WHfH WJek XLum |
| | - ***alba*** | LSou NLar WHer |
| § | - 'Romney Marsh' | EBee EWll GCal MRav SEND WFar WKif WSHC |
| | ***rosea*** | see *Alcea rosea* |
| | ***rugosostellulata*** | see *Alcea rugosa* |

## *Altingia* (*Hamamelidaceae*)

| | | |
|---|---|---|
| | ***poilanei*** B&SWJ 11756 | WCru |

## × *Alworthia* (*Asphodelaceae*)

| | | |
|---|---|---|
| | 'Black Gem' | EBee EPfP EShb |

## *Alyogyne* (*Malvaceae*)

| | | |
|---|---|---|
| | 'Attraction' | ECou |
| | ***hakeifolia*** | CSpe ECou |
| | - 'Elle Maree' | ECou MOWG |
| | - 'Melissa Anne' | ECou MOWG |
| § | ***huegelii*** | CBod CCCN CSpe ECou EShb SRkn WDyG |
| | - 'Lavender Lass' | ECou |
| | - 'Santa Cruz' | CCCN CCse CHll CSpe EBee ECou LHop MOWG SEND SLon SUsu WPGP |
| | 'Joy' new | ECou |
| | Magic Moments = 'Hutwow' new | LBuc SBrd SPoG |
| | 'Shepherds Delight' new | ECou |

## *Alyssoides* (*Brassicaceae*)

| | | |
|---|---|---|
| | ***utriculata*** | NBre WHil XSen |

## *Alyssum* (*Brassicaceae*)

| | | |
|---|---|---|
| | ***argenteum*** | NBre |
| | ***montanum*** | ECha ECho MAsh NBlu SPlb SRms |
| § | - 'Berggold' | EPfP LRHS MMuc |
| | - Mountain Gold | see *A. montanum* 'Berggold' |
| | ***obovatum*** new | EDAr |
| | ***ovirense*** | GKev |
| | ***oxycarpum*** | EPot |
| | ***repens*** | NBre |
| | ***saxatile*** | see *Aurinia saxatilis* |
| | - 'Summit' new | EDAr |
| | ***scardicum*** | LLHF |
| | ***spinosum*** | EPot |
| § | - 'Roseum' ♀H4 | CMea CTri ECha ELan GMaP LBee MLHP MWat NMen SBch WAbe WFar |
| * | - 'Roseum Variegatum' | EPot |
| | - 'Strawberries and Cream' | WAbe WFar |
| | ***tortuosum*** | SEND WAbe |
| | ***wulfenianum*** | EDAr IFoB LLHF NBre SEND |

## *Amaranthus* (*Amaranthaceae*)

| | | |
|---|---|---|
| | ***caudatus*** | WTou |
| | ***hypochondriacus*** | CSpe |
| | 'Pygmy Torch' ♀H3 | |

## × *Amarcrinum* (*Amaryllidaceae*)

| | | |
|---|---|---|
| | 'Dorothy Hannibal' | GCal WCot |
| | ***memoria-corsii*** | CPrp ECho |
| | - 'Howardii' | CFir EBee ECho EShb LEdu WCot |

## × *Amarine* (*Amaryllidaceae*)

| | | |
|---|---|---|
| | ***tubergenii*** | CAvo |
| | - 'Zwanenburg' | EBee WCot |

## × *Amarygia* (*Amaryllidaceae*)

| | | |
|---|---|---|
| | ***parkeri*** | ECho |
| § | - 'Alba' | CAvo CBro EBee ECho WCot |

## *Amaryllis* (*Amaryllidaceae*)

| | | |
|---|---|---|
| § | ***belladonna*** ♀H2-3 | CAby CBcs CBro CHEx CPne CPrp CTca EBee ECho EPfP ERCP EShb GBin LAma LEdu NBPC NCGa SChr SDeJ SEND SMrm SPav SPer WCot |
| | - 'Bloemfontein' | CAvo |
| | - 'Johannesburg' | CAvo WCot |
| | - 'Kimberley' | CPne |
| | - 'Major' | CAvo |
| | - 'Parkeri Alba' | see × *Amarygia parkeri* 'Alba' |
| | - 'Purpurea' | WCot |
| | - white-flowered | ECho SDeJ WCot |

## *Amberboa* (*Asteraceae*)

| | | |
|---|---|---|
| § | ***moschata*** | WCot |

## *Ambrosina* (*Araceae*)

| | | |
|---|---|---|
| | ***bassii*** from Tunisia | ECho |

## *Amelanchier* ✿ (*Rosaceae*)

| | | |
|---|---|---|
| | ***alnifolia*** | CTho |
| | - 'Forestburg' | NLar |
| | - 'Obelisk' PBR | CDoC EBee GKin LBuc LHop LLHF LRHS MAsh MBri MGos NCGa NSti SCoo SSta WHar |
| | - pink-fruited | NLar |
| § | - var. ***pumila*** | CPMA LHop MMHG WTin |
| | - 'Regent' (F) | NLar |

- var. ***semi-integrifolia*** NLar
- 'Smokey' CDul

§ ***arborea*** CTho SRms
***asiatica*** LSRN
- var. ***sinica*** NLar
***bartramiana*** CTho SSta
- 'Eskimo' NLar
***canadensis*** K. Koch see *A. lamarckii*
***canadensis*** Sieb. & Zucc. see *A. arborea*
***canadensis*** ambig. GAuc NPri SEWo SGol SPoG WHar
***canadensis*** (L.) Medik. CAgr CDoC CDul CLnd CMac CPMA CSBt CSam CTho CTri CWSG CWib EBee ECrN ELan EPfP LAst LEdu LHop LRHS MGos MRav MSwo NCGa NWea SPer WDin WFar WMoo WPat
- 'Prince William' CAgr SSta
- Rainbow Pillar = 'Glenn Form' EBee LRHS MAsh MBlu MBri MGos SGol SSta WHar
× ***grandiflora*** 'Autumn Brilliance' CEnd CPMA NHol NLar SGol
- 'Ballerina' ♀H4 Widely available
- 'Cole's Select' EBee LRHS
- 'Princess Diana' MBlu NLar SCoo
- 'Robin Hill' CBcs CCVT CDul CMac EBee ECrN LAst LBuc LRHS MAsh MBlu MGos MRav NEgg NLar NWea SCoo SEWo SLim SMad SPoG WFar WHar
- 'Rubescens' CDul CEnd CPMA EBee EPfP NLar SLon
***humilis*** GAuc
'La Paloma' EBee EPfP LRHS MAsh MBri NLar SCoo WHar
***laevis*** CBcs CDul CTri EPfP MGos MSwo NLar STre
- 'Cumulus' NLar
- 'Prince Charles' NLar
- 'R.J. Hilton' MBri SCoo WHar
- 'Snow Cloud' CDoC
- 'Snowflakes' CEnd CPMA EBee LRHS MAsh MGos NHol NLar SEWo SLim SPer SPoG SPur WHar

§ ***lamarckii*** ♀H4 Widely available
***ovalis*** misapplied see *A. spicata* (Lam.) K. Koch.
***ovalis*** Medik. SPlb
- 'Edelweiss' CPMA IArd MBlu NEgg NLar SCoo
- 'Helvetia' NLar
***pumila*** see *A. alnifolia* var. *pumila*
***rotundifolia*** ambig. MCoo

§ ***spicata*** (Lam.) K. Koch. ECrN MCoo SSta

## × *Amelasorbus* (*Rosaceae*)

***raciborskiana*** MBlu MBri

## *Amicia* (*Papilionaceae*)

***zygomeris*** CBot CCse CHEx CHGN CHll CPom CSpe ELon EWes EWld GBin GCal LHop MCot SAga SDix SEND SMad SMrm SUsu WCot WSHC

## *Amitostigma* (*Orchidaceae*)

Enomotoe gx 'Kou Itten' LWSt NLAp

## *Ammi* (*Apiaceae*)

***majus*** CArn CSpe SDix SMrm SPhx
***visnaga*** CArn CBre CHby CSpe ELau MNHC SPhx WHal

## *Ammobium* (*Asteraceae*)

***calyceroides*** ECou

## *Ammocharis* (*Amaryllidaceae*)

***coranica*** ECho WCot

## *Ammophila* (*Poaceae*)

***arenaria*** CBod CKno CRWN SMea XLum
***breviligulata*** SPhx

## *Amomyrtus* (*Myrtaceae*)

§ ***luma*** CAgr CDoC CDul CHEx CTri EBee ELan GGal GQui IDee SArc WAle WCot WJek

## *Amorpha* (*Papilionaceae*)

***canescens*** EBee LRHS SPlb
***fruticosa*** CBcs EBtc EShb EWTr LEdu MBlu MMuc NLar SEND SPlb
***herbacea*** NLar
***ouachitensis*** NLar
***paniculata*** NLar

## *Amorphophallus* ✿ (*Araceae*)

Chen Yi A-102 WCot
***albus*** CDTJ LEdu SChr WCot
***bulbifer*** CDTJ EAmu LAma SBig SBrd
***dunnii*** CDTJ
***kerrii*** CPLG WCot
***kiusianus*** WCot
- B&SWJ 4845 WCru
***konjac*** CDTJ CDes CFir CGHE CHEx CPLG CSpe EAmu LEdu SChF WCot WPGP
***nepalensis*** CDTJ
***rivieri*** GCal LRHS WCot
***stipitatus*** CAby WCot

## *Ampelocalamus* (*Poaceae*)

***scandens*** EPla WPGP

## *Ampelocissus* (*Vitaceae*)

***sikkimensis*** HWJK 2066 WCru

## *Ampelodesmos* (*Poaceae*)

***mauritanica*** CHar CHid CKno COIW CSam CSpe EBee ECha EHoe EShb EWes LRHS MNrw MWhi SEND SPlb WBox WCot WPGP WWEG XLum

## *Ampelopsis* (*Vitaceae*)

***aconitifolia*** MGos NLar
- 'Chinese Lace' EBee LRHS MRav NLar WPGP
***arborea*** WCru
***brevipedunculata*** ELan MMHG SCoo SGar SKHP SLim SPer SPoG WDin WFar
- var. ***maximowiczii*** 'Elegans' (v) CBcs CHEx CMac CWib EBee ELan EPfP EShb LAst LBMP LHop LRHS MGos MRav NBro SAga SPer SPoG SWvt WCot WDin WPat WSHC
***delavayana*** MMuc
***henryana*** see *Parthenocissus henryana*
***megalophylla*** CBot CHEx EBee ELan EShb GCal IArd IDee NCGa NLar SKHP SPer WCru WFar
***sempervirens*** hort. ex Veitch see *Cissus striata*
***tricuspidata*** 'Veitchii' see *Parthenocissus tricuspidata* 'Veitchii'

## *Amphicome* see *Incarvillea*

## *Amsonia* (*Apocynaceae*)

**ciliata** CHid CPom EBee ELan IKil SKHP SPoG SUsu XLum
§ **elliptica** EBee LRHS
**hubrichtii** CAby CCse CEnt CFir CSpe EBee ECha ELon EPPr LEdu LHop NLar SMad SMrm SPad SPhx WCAu WHoo WPer WPnP WPtf WSHC
**illustris** CAbP CEnt CPom EBee EPPr GCal LRHS NLar SHar WHoo WHrl WPer WSHC WTin
§ **orientalis** CFir CHar CHll CMea CTri EBee ECha GBBs GCal LEdu LHop LRHS MLHP MMuc MRav NDov NLar SAga SEND SGar SMrm SPoG SUsu WAul WBor WCAu WFar WPtf WTin
**palmeri** SPhx
**sinensis** see *A. elliptica*
**tabernaemontana** Widely available
- var. **salicifolia** CEnt CSpe EBee NBPC NDov WCAu WTin
- 'Stella Azul' new EBee

## *Amygdalus* see *Prunus*

## *Anacamptis* (*Orchidaceae*)

**coriophora** NLAp
§ **laxiflora** NLAp
§ **morio** NLAp
**morio** × **papilionacea** NLAp
**pyramidalis** EFEx NLAp WHer
**sancta** NLAp

## *Anacyclus* (*Asteraceae*)

**pyrethrum** GPoy
- var. **depressus** CTri EBee ECho ELan EPfP EPot GGar GMaP LRHS MAsh NBlu NVic NWCA SPlb SRot WCFE WFar WHoo WPer
- - 'Garden Gnome' CTri ECho SRms WFar WHil
- - 'Silberkissen' EDAr NSla

## *Anagallis* (*Primulaceae*)

**arvensis** var. **caerulea** EDif
**monellii** ♀H4 MNrw
- Blue Compact = 'Wesanacomp' LSou
- subsp. **linifolia** 'Blue Light' CSpe
- 'Skylover' CCCN LAst SAga
- 'Sunrise' SUsu
**tenella** LLWG
- 'Studland' CEnt EPot GAbr NWCA WAbe

## *Ananas* (*Bromeliaceae*)

**comosus** (F) CCCN
- 'Champaca' (F) CCCN
**lucidus** new LRHS

## *Anaphalioides* (*Asteraceae*)

§ **bellidioides** CTri ECha ECou GGar

## *Anaphalis* (*Asteraceae*)

**alpicola** EBee EPot NBre NMen
**margaritacea** CBcs EBee ECha ECtt GMaP NBid NMun SBfd SRms WCAu WFar WMoo WPtf
§ - 'Neuschnee' CTri EBee EPfP NBPC NBre NGdn WFar WPer WWEG XLum
- New Snow see *A. margaritacea* 'Neuschnee'
- var. **yedoensis** ♀H4 CTri EBee MCot MLHP NBre SDix SGar SPer
§ **nepalensis** var. **monocephala** ELan MCot NBre NSti
**nubigena** see *A. nepalensis* var. *monocephala*
**subumbellata** LRHS
**transnokoensis** EWes
§ **trinervis** CPLG XLum
**triplinervis** ♀H4 EHoe ELan EPfP GMaP IFoB LRHS MCot MRav NBid NLar NVic SPer SRms WCAu WCot WFar WHoo WMoo WWEG
- CC 1620 EBee EPPr NBir
§ - 'Sommerschnee' ♀H4 CMac EBee ECha ECtt EHoe EPfP LBMP LRHS MCot MRav NEgg NLar SPer WMnd WPer
- Summer Snow see *A. triplinervis* 'Sommerschnee'

## *Anchusa* (*Boraginaceae*)

sp. CHab
**angustissima** see *A. leptophylla* subsp. *incana*
§ **azurea** EGxp MLLN NLar
- 'Dropmore' CTri EBee ELan EPfP LAst MNHC NBPC NEgg NLar NOrc SBfd SPav SRms WPer WWEG
- 'Feltham Pride' EBee LRHS SPav SRms SWvt WFar WHoo WPer WTcb
- 'Little John' SRms
- 'Loddon Royalist' ♀H4 Widely available
- 'Opal' EBee ECtt EPfP GCal LRHS MMHG
**caespitosa** misapplied see *A. leptophylla* subsp. *incana*
**capensis** 'Blue Angel' LRHS MNHC SWvt WFar
**cespitosa** Lam. ECho ELan EWes LLHF WAbe
**italica** see *A. azurea*
**laxiflora** see *Borago pygmaea*
§ **leptophylla** subsp. **incana** F&W 9550 MDKP
**myosotidiflora** see *Brunnera macrophylla*
**officinalis** CArn MNHC SPav
**sempervirens** see *Pentaglottis sempervirens*

## *Ancylostemon* (*Gesneriaceae*)

**convexus** B&SWJ 6624 WCru

## *Andrachne* (*Phyllanthaceae*)

**colchica** EBee WCot

## *Androcymbium* (*Colchicaceae*)

**cuspidatum** 'Karoopoort' ECho
**dregei** 'Loeriesfontein' ECho
**eucomoides** 'Varsputs' ECho
**gramineum** ECho
- from Morocco ECho
**melanthioides** ECho
**volutare** 'Tanqua' ECho

## *Andromeda* (*Ericaceae*)

**glaucophylla** f. **latifolia** IVic
**polifolia** ECho GAuc MAsh NWCA WDin WFar
- 'Alba' ECho EPot GLam LRHS MAsh NBlu NRya SPer SPlb SWvt WFar WThu
- 'Blue Ice' EBee ELan EPfP GAbr LRHS MAsh MNHC NHar NLar NMen SLim SPoG SSpi WAbe WFar WPat WThu
- 'Compacta' ♀H4 CDoC CMac EBee ECho EPfP GEdr GGar LSRN LTen MAsh NMen

NWad SBfd SPoG SRms SWvt WGwG WSHC
- 'Compacta Alba' ♀H4 — ECho
- 'Grandiflora' — ECho GEdr GLam
- 'Kirigamine' — LRHS MAsh NHar
- 'Macrophylla' ♀H4 — ECho EPot GEdr GLam NHar WAbe WPat WThu
- 'Nana' — CSBt ELan EPfP LRHS MAsh NMen
- 'Nikko' — CMac
- 'Shibutsu' — NHar NMen

## *Andropogon* (*Poaceae*)

***gerardii*** — CKno CRWN EBee EHoe EHul EPPr LEdu MWhi NWsh SApp SPhx WWEG
***scoparius*** — see *Schizachyrium scoparium*
***ternarius*** new — EPPr

## *Androsace* (*Primulaceae*)

***albana*** — GKev GLam
***alpina*** — WAbe
***armeniaca*** var. ***macrantha*** — EDAr
***bisulca*** var. ***aurata*** — EPot GKev
***bulleyana*** — WAbe
***caduca*** — WAbe
***carnea*** — ECho
- SDR 6357 — GKev
- subsp. ***brigantiaca*** — GLam NRya NSla WAbe WHoo
- var. ***halleri*** — see *A. carnea* subsp. *rosea*
- subsp. ***laggeri*** ♀H4 — ECho LLHF NSla WAbe WFar
- - 'Andorra' — NHar
- subsp. ***laggeri*** × ***carnea*** subsp. ***rosea*** — NWCA
§ - subsp. ***rosea*** ♀H4 — ECho WAbe
***carnea*** × ***pyrenaica*** — CYeo ECho EPot GLam NMen
***chamaejasme*** — ECho EPot
***ciliata*** — WAbe
***cylindrica*** — ECho LRHS NMen WFar
***cylindrica*** × ***hirtella*** — ECho LRHS WAbe
***delavayi*** — WAbe
- ACE 1786 — WAbe
***geraniifolia*** — ECha EWld SRms WAbe
***globifera*** — EPot WAbe
***gracilis*** PB 99/20 — EPot
***halleri*** — see *A. carnea* subsp. *rosea*
***hedraeantha*** — NRya WAbe
***himalaica*** — CPBP EPot GEdr NMen WAbe
***hirtella*** — ITim WAbe
***idahoensis*** — WAbe
***idahoensis*** × ***laevigata*** — WAbe
***incana*** — WAbe
***jacquemontii*** — see *A. villosa* var. *jacquemontii*
***kosopoljanskii*** — GJos NWCA WAbe
***lactea*** — WAbe
***laevigata*** — ITim NMen WAbe
- 'Gothenburg' — WAbe WPat
- 'Saddle Mount' — WAbe
***lanuginosa*** ♀H4 — CMea CPBP CSpe ECho ECtt EHoe EPot GEdr GGar MSCN MWat NHar NMen NWCA SMrm SRms SRot WAbe WFar WNew
- 'Leichtlinii' — GKev
***lehmanniana*** — WAbe
- 'Gotëborg Yellow' new — WAbe
***lehmannii*** — GKev
***limprichtii*** — see *A. sarmentosa* var. *watkinsii*
***mariae*** — GKev WAbe
- SDR 4768 — GKev
× ***marpensis*** — EPot NMen NWCA WAbe
***microphylla*** — see *A. mucronifolia* G.Watt
***minor*** — EPot WAbe
§ ***mollis*** — CPBP
***montana*** — WAbe
***mucronifolia*** misapplied — see *A. sempervivoides*
§ ***mucronifolia*** G.Watt — WAbe
***mucronifolia*** × ***sempervivoides*** — EPot GLam ITim
***muscoidea*** — WAbe
- SEP 132 — CPBP WAbe
- 'Breviscapa' — EPot
- f. ***longiscapa*** — CPBP WAbe
- Schacht's form — WAbe
***nivalis*** 'Chumstick Form' — LLHF
***ochotensis*** — WAbe
***primuloides*** — see *A. studiosorum*
***pubescens*** — ECho LLHF LRHS NMen WAbe
***pyrenaica*** — ECho EPot ITim LRHS NMen WAbe
***rigida*** — EPot GKev WAbe
***robusta*** subsp. ***purpurea*** — WAbe
- - 'Dolpo Dwarf' new — WAbe
***rotundifolia*** — GEdr GKev
- stoloniferous — GEdr
***sarmentosa*** misapplied — see *A. studiosorum*
***sarmentosa*** ambig. — EDAr GJos GKev MWat
***sarmentosa*** Wall. — SRms WHoo
- from Namche, Nepal — EWld WAbe
- Galmont's form — see *A. studiosorum* 'Salmon's Variety'
- 'Sherriffii' — ECho EPot SRms WHoo
§ - var. ***watkinsii*** — EPot GKev NMen
- var. ***yunnanensis*** misapplied — see *A. studiosorum*
- var. ***yunnanensis*** Knuth — see *A. mollis*
***selago*** — WAbe
- 'Red Eye' — WAbe
§ ***sempervivoides*** ♀H4 — CYeo ECho EDAr EPot GEdr GJos GKev GMaP LHop LRHS NMen NWCA SPlb SRms WAbe WPat
- CC 4622 — GKev
- CC 4631 — GKev
- CC 5299 — GKev
- 'Susan Joan' — EPot GEdr GKev WAbe
***sericea*** — WAbe
***spinulifera*** — GKev
- SDR 5948 — GKev
***strigillosa*** — GKev GLam WAbe
§ ***studiosorum*** ♀H4 — EPot GAbr GEdr GKev WAbe WPat
- 'Chumbyi' — GEdr LLHF SRms WPat WThu
- 'Doksa' — CPBP EPot GEdr NMen WAbe WPat
§ - 'Salmon's Variety' — CMea CTri WAbe
***tangulashanensis*** — WAbe
***tapete*** — EPot
- ACE 1725 — WAbe
***vandellii*** — ITim WAbe
§ ***villosa*** var. ***jacquemontii*** — EDAr GEdr NHar
- - lilac-flowered — EPot WAbe
- - pink-flowered — EPot WAbe
- subsp. ***taurica*** — WAbe
***vitaliana*** — see *Vitaliana primuliflora*
***wardii*** — WAbe
***watkinsii*** — see *A. sarmentosa* var. *watkinsii*
***yargongensis*** — WAbe
***zambalensis*** — WAbe

## *Androstoma* (*Ericaceae*)

§ ***empetrifolia*** — WThu

## *Andryala* (*Asteraceae*)

***agardhii*** — WPat

| | |
|---|---|
| ***lanata*** | see *Hieracium lanatum* |

## *Anemanthele* (*Poaceae*)

| | |
|---|---|
| § ***lessoniana*** ♀H4 | Widely available |
| - 'Gold Hue' | CKno |

## *Anemarrhena* (*Asparagaceae*)

| | |
|---|---|
| ***asphodeloides*** | CArn WCot |

## *Anemone* ✿ (*Ranunculaceae*)

| | |
|---|---|
| Chen Yi T49 | WCot |
| ***aconitifolia*** Michx. | see *A. narcissiflora* |
| ***altaica*** | LWst NLar SRms |
| ***amurensis*** | CPLG |
| ***apennina*** ♀H4 | CAvo CLAP EBla ECGP ECha ECho LWst WShi WTin |
| - var. ***albiflora*** | CDes CLAP ECho EPPr EPot MAvo WPnP |
| - double, white-flowered (d) new | LRHS |
| - double-flowered (d) | CDes CPBP EBla ECho EPPr WCru |
| - 'Petrovac' | CLAP EPot LLHF LWst SPhx |
| ***baldensis*** | ECho EDAr GKev IGor SRms |
| - SDR 5418 | GKev |
| ***barbulata*** | CPLG EWes GAuc GEdr GKev GMac NLar WSHC |
| ***blanda*** ♀H4 | ECho LAma LRHS MAsh MAvo MBri MLHP MNHC MWat NLar SBfd SEND SGar SWal WBor WFar WShi |
| I - 'Alba' | LRHS |
| - 'Blue Star' | ECho |
| - blue-flowered | CAvo CBro CFFs CMea CSam CTri ECGP ECho ELan EPfP EPot ERCP GAbr GKev GMaP IGor LAma LRHS MBri MNFA NBlu SDeJ SMrm SPer SPhx SPoG SRms WFar WHoo WRHF |
| - 'Charmer' | ECho EPot ERCP NMen SMrm |
| - 'Ingramii' | LWst WCot |
| - var. ***rosea*** ♀H4 | ECho ELan EPfP GKev LAma LRHS SBch SPer SPoG WFar |
| - - 'Pink Charmer' | ECho NLar |
| - - 'Pink Star' | ECho ERCP GKev LAma NBir |
| - - 'Radar' ♀H4 | CMea ECho EPot ERCP LAma LRHS MNrw NBir SDeJ WAbe |
| - 'Violet Star' | ECho ERCP GKev NLar SDeJ SPhx |
| - 'White Charmer' | ECho |
| - 'White Splendour' ♀H4 | CAvo CBro CFFs CMea CSam CTri ECho ELan EPfP EPot ERCP GAbr GKev LAma LEdu LRHS NBir NLar NMen SDeJ SMrm SPer SPhx SPoG SRms WCot WFar |
| blue-flowered from China | CDes |
| ***caerulea*** new | LWst |
| ***canadensis*** | CSpe EBee ELon EPPr LRHS WCot |
| ***caroliniana*** | ECho LRHS |
| ***caucasica*** | ECho LWst SCnR |
| ***chapaensis*** HWJ 631 | WCru |
| ***coronaria*** | SVic |
| - 'Bicolor' | GKev |
| - De Caen Group | EPfP GKev LAma LRHS SPoG SWal WFar |
| § - - 'Die Braut' | ERCP NBir SDeJ WFar |
| - - 'His Excellency' | see *A. coronaria* (De Caen Group) 'Hollandia' |
| § - - 'Hollandia' | LRHS |
| - - 'Mister Fokker' | CTca ERCP LAma LRHS WFar |
| - - The Bride | see *A. coronaria* (De Caen Group) 'Die Braut' |
| - - 'The Governor' | CTca GKev SDeJ WFar |
| - Jerusalem hybrids | WFar |
| - Saint Bridgid Group (d) | EPfP GKev LAma WFar |
| - - 'Lord Lieutenant' (d) | CMea EPfP ERCP GKev NBir WFar |
| - - 'Mount Everest' (d) | ERCP GKev NBir SDeJ |
| - - 'Saint Bridgid' (d) | LRHS |
| - - 'The Admiral' (d) | EPfP GKev LRHS NBir SDeJ WFar |
| - 'Sylphide' (Mona Lisa Series) | ERCP NBir SDeJ WFar |
| ***crinita*** | GLam |
| ***cylindrica*** | EBee MDKP NBre NLar |
| ***decapetala*** | MHer |
| ***demissa*** SDR 3307 | EBee |
| - SDR 4306 | GKev |
| ***dichotoma*** | SSvw |
| ***drummondii*** | GAbr GKev NChi WHrl |
| ***eranthoides*** | ECho LWst |
| ***fanninii*** | GCal |
| ***fasciculata*** | see *A. narcissiflora* |
| ***flaccida*** | CAby CLAP EBee ECho EPPr GEdr GMac LRHS MAvo MMHG MNrw SBch WCot WCru WFar WHal WSHC |
| × ***fulgens*** | ECha |
| ***globosa*** | see *A. multifida* Poir. |
| 'Guernica' | ECho EWes |
| 'Hatakeyama Double' (d) | GCal |
| 'Hatakeyama Single' | WCot |
| ***hepatica*** L. | see *Hepatica nobilis* |
| § ***hortensis*** | ECho |
| § ***hupehensis*** | CBot CPLG EBee GMaP NOrc WFar WPer |
| - BWJ 8190 | WCru |
| - f. ***alba*** | CLAP CSpe EBla IFro WPGP |
| § - 'Bowles's Pink' ♀H4 | CElw CPLG EBee ECho MWat SPet WCru WPGP WTin |
| - 'Crispa' | see *A.* × *hybrida* 'Lady Gilmour' Wolley-Dod |
| - 'Eugenie' | ECtt LRHS NBir NHol SBrd |
| - 'Hadspen Abundance' ♀H4 | Widely available |
| - 'Hadspen Red' | WFar |
| § - var. ***japonica*** | CPou MLLN NBPC XLum |
| - - B&SWJ 4886 | WCru |
| - - 'Bodnant Burgundy' | CDes EBee LRHS WPGP |
| § - - 'Bressingham Glow' | CMHG CMac CPLG CSam EAEE EBee ECtt ELan EPfP EPot GKin LRHS MBri MRav NBir NHol NOrc NVic SPet WAbb WBrk WCAu WFar WWEG |
| § - - 'Pamina' ♀H4 | Widely available |
| - - Prince Henry | see *A. hupehensis* var. *japonica* 'Prinz Heinrich' |
| § - - 'Prinz Heinrich' ♀H4 | Widely available |
| § - - 'Rotkäppchen' | EBee EBla ECtt GAbr GBin GKin GQue ITim IVic LSou MAvo NGdn NHol NLar SMrm SWvt WCot WHoo WSHC |
| - - 'Splendens' | CMHG COIW EBee EPfP GBBs LAst LHop LRHS MAsh MCot MMuc NEgg NGdn SBrd SPer SPur SUsu SWvt WAbb WFar WHal WWEG XLum |
| - 'Little Princess' | CHid EBee ECtt |
| - 'Ouvertüre' | EBee ECtt MAvo WCot WPGP |
| - 'Praecox' | CKno CMea EAEE EBee EBla EPfP GBBs LRHS LSou MBNS NBPC NBir NCGa NGdn NHol NSti SBfd SBrd SWvt WAbb WFar WHal WMnd WWEG |
| - 'September Charm' | see *A.* × *hybrida* 'September Charm' |
| - 'Superba' | EPfP WKif |

| | | |
|---|---|---|
| § | × ***hybrida*** | ECho LRHS MWat NChi NEgg SEND SGar WFar WMoo |
| | - 'Alba' misapplied (UK) | see *A.* × *hybrida* 'Honorine Jobert' |
| | - 'Alba Dura' | see *A. tomentosa* 'Albadura' |
| | - 'Albert Schweitzer' | see *A.* × *hybrida* 'Elegans' |
| | - 'Alice' **new** | LRHS |
| | - 'Andrea Atkinson' | Widely available |
| | - 'Bowles's Pink' | see *A. hupehensis* 'Bowles's Pink' |
| | - 'Bressingham Glow' | see *A. hupehensis* var. *japonica* 'Bressingham Glow' |
| | - 'Coupe d'Argent' | EBee IKil NBre WCot |
| § | - 'Elegans' ♀H4 | CSam EBee ECtt GMaP LHop LRHS MMuc MRav NBPC NBir NGdn SEND SWat SWvt WFar WHil |
| § | - 'Géante des Blanches' | EBee LPla |
| § | - 'Honorine Jobert' ♀H4 | Widely available |
| § | - 'Königin Charlotte' ♀H4 | Widely available |
| | - 'Kriemhilde' | EBee GBin |
| | - 'Lady Gilmour' misapplied | see *A.* × *hybrida* 'Montrose' |
| | - 'Lady Gilmour' ambig. | GMaP MLLN MSCN NBPC SPad |
| § | - 'Lady Gilmour' Wolley-Dod | CSam CSpe EBee ECtt EPfP GAbr GCra GMac LEdu LRHS LSou MBri MRav NBPC NBir NEgg NGdn SAga SBrd WCot WCru WFar WWEG XLum |
| | - 'Loreley' | CMea CPrp EBee EPfP LRHS NLar SBfd SWvt WWEG |
| | - 'Luise Uhink' | CPou NBir |
| | - 'Märchenfee' | EBee |
| | - 'Margarete' Kayser & Seibert | CPLG CPar EBee ECtt ELan EPPr EPfP LAst LHop LRHS MBri MGos NGdn SBfd WCru |
| | - 'Max Vogel' | see *A.* × *hybrida* 'Elegans' |
| | - 'Monterosa' | see *A.* × *hybrida* 'Montrose' |
| § | - 'Montrose' | CPou EBee ECha EWes GCal GMaP LSou MLLN NBir NLar SRms SWat WCAu |
| | - 'Pamina' | see *A. hupehensis* var. *japonica* 'Pamina' |
| | - Prince Henry | see *A. hupehensis* var. *japonica* 'Prinz Heinrich' |
| | - 'Profusion' | CTri LBuc LRHS WHal |
| | - Queen Charlotte | see *A.* × *hybrida* 'Königin Charlotte' |
| | - 'Richard Ahrens' | EBee ECtt EPfP EShb GCal GMaP GMac LAst LHop LRHS MGos MLHP MSCN NBPC NEgg NGdn NHol NLar NOrc SBfd SBrd SPad SWat WCru WFar WMnd WWEG |
| § | - 'Robustissima' | EBee ECtt EPfP GBBs GMaP GMac LLWP LRHS LSRN MCot MGos MRav NBir NDov NGdn NSti SBrd SEND SPer SWat SWvt WAbb WFar WMnd WMoo WWEG |
| | - 'Rosenschale' | EBee GMac WCru |
| | - 'Rotkäppchen' | see *A. hupehensis* var. *japonica* 'Rotkäppchen' |
| § | - 'September Charm' ♀H4 | Widely available |
| | - 'Serenade' | CChe CPar CSam EBee ECtt EPfP GBBs GMac IVic LRHS LSRN MAsh MRav NBir NCGa NLar SBrd SPoG SRkn WCAu WFar WHoo WMoo WWEG |
| | - Tourbillon | see *A.* × *hybrida* 'Whirlwind' |
| § | - 'Whirlwind' | Widely available |
| | - 'White Queen' | see *A.* × *hybrida* 'Géante des Blanches' |
| | - Wirbelwind | see *A.* × *hybrida* 'Whirlwind' |
| | ***japonica*** | see *A.* × *hybrida*, *A. hupehensis*, *A. hupehensis* var. *japonica* |
| | ***keiskeana*** | GEdr WCru |
| § | × ***lesseri*** | CBro CFir CSpe EBee ECha ECho ECtt EDAr ELan GKev LHop MHer SPhx SRms WFar |
| | ***leveillei*** | CAby CElw CLAP CSpe EBee EDAr EPPr EWTr GBBs GKev GMac IFoB LAst LPla LRHS LSou MNFA NBPC NBir NGdn NLar NPnk NSti SPoG WAbe WCru WHoo WKif WPnP WSHC |
| | - BWJ 7919 | WCru |
| § | × ***lipsiensis*** | CAby CAvo CBro CDes CPBP EBee EBla ECho EPfP EPot EShb GBBs GEdr GMaP MAvo MCot MNrw NDov NLar NMen NRya NWCA SMrm WCot WCru WFar WHal WPGP WSHC |
| | - 'Pallida' ♀H4 | CPMA CSam CSpe EBee ECho ELon GEdr GKev IGor LLWP LWSt MAvo NLar NWCA SKHP SSvw WCot WShi |
| | - 'Vindobonensis' | WCot |
| | ***magellanica*** hort. ex Wehrh. | see *A. multifida* Poir. |
| | ***matsudae*** B&SWJ 1452 | WCru |
| | ***multifida*** misapplied, red-flowered | see *A.* × ***lesseri*** |
| § | ***multifida*** Poir. | EBee ECha ECho EPfP GJos IFoB LHop LRHS NBir NSti NSum SPoG SRms WFar WHoo WTin |
| | - Annabella Series | EPfP GAbr GKev |
| | - - 'Annabella Deep Rose' **new** | WHrl |
| | - 'Major' | CFir CHar CMea CPrp CSpe EPfP NPro NWCA SMrm WFar |
| | - f. ***polysepala*** | NEgg |
| | - 'Rubra' | CMea CPrp EAEE EBee EDAr EPfP EWll GAbr GEdr GGar GKev LRHS NBPC NBir NEgg NLar SMrm SPoG STes WHoo WPtf |
| | - white-flowered | LRHS WGwG |
| | - yellow-flowered | GBBs GGar MCot NSum |
| § | ***narcissiflora*** | CSpe ECho GKev LRHS NBir NChi NPnk WFar |
| | - var. ***citrina*** | LRHS |
| | ***nemorosa*** ♀H4 | Widely available |
| N | - 'Alba Plena' (d) | CPMA CSam EBee EBla ECha ECho EPPr GEdr GGar GMac MAvo NGdn NPnk WAbb WCru WFar WPnP WSHC |
| | - 'Allenii' ♀H4 | CAby CBro EBee EBla ECha ECho ELon EPot GEdr GMaP ITim LRHS MAvo MRav NMen NRya NWCA WCru WFar WShi |
| | - 'Amy Doncaster' | CLAP ECho |
| | - 'Atley' | EBee |
| | - 'Atrocaerulea' | CLAP EBla IBlr NLar WCru WFar |
| | - 'Atrorosca' | EBcc EBla |
| | - 'Ballyrogan Blue' | MNrw |
| | - 'Bill Baker's Pink' | CDes CLAP LEdu |
| | - 'Blue Beauty' | CLAP CPMA EBee EBla ELon GMaP IBlr LWSt MAvo NMen SBch WCru |
| | - 'Blue Bonnet' | CAby CElw CPMA EBla ECho IGor ITim MAvo MNrw |
| | - 'Blue Eyes' (d) | CDes CElw CLAP EBee EBla GEdr GKev GMaP IBlr IGor ITim LWSt MAvo NBir NWCA WCot WCru WFar WSHC |
| | - 'Blue Queen' | GAbr |
| | - 'Bowles's Purple' | CAby CPMA CPom EBla ECho ELon GBBs GMaP IBlr LRHS MAvo MNrw |

| | | |
|---|---|---|
| | | NBid NHar NMyG NRya SKHP WBor WCot WCru WFar WPnP WTin |
| | – 'Bracteata' | CAby CBro ECho GEdr MMHG NMen |
| | – 'Bracteata Pleniflora' (d) | CLAP CPMA EBee EBla ECho ELon GMaP IBlr IGor LHop MAvo MNrw NBir NMen NPnk WCot WCru WFar WHal |
| | – 'Buckland' | CAby CDes CFwr CLAP EBee EBla EPfP IBlr LWst SKHP SMad WCru WFar |
| | – 'Caerulea' | ITim |
| | – 'Cedric's Pink' | CLAP CPMA EBla EPPr IBlr LLHF MMHG MNrw WCru WFar |
| | – 'Celestial' | EBee EBla ECho EPPr MAvo |
| | – 'Dee Day' | CLAP EBee EBla MAvo MNrw SCnR WCru WFar |
| | – 'Dell Garden' | EPPr |
| | – 'Evelyn Meadows' ♀$^{H4}$ | CLAP EBla |
| | – 'Flore Pleno' (d) | CAby CDes EBla ECho GAbr MMoz NBir NMen WBor WCru |
| | – 'Frühlingsfee' | CPMA EBee NLar |
| | – 'Gerda Ramusen' | CBro CLAP EBla ECho ELon LLHF |
| I | – 'Gigantea Rubra' **new** | WCot |
| | – 'Green Fingers' | CAby CLAP CPMA EBla ECho EPPr EPot GEdr GMaP ITim MAvo MMHG MNrw SCnR WCot WCru WSHC |
| | – 'Hakumane Senjuizaki' **new** | WCot |
| | – 'Hannah Gubbay' | CLAP IBlr MAvo MNrw |
| | – 'Hilda' | EBla ECho EPot GEdr MAvo MNrw NBir NMen NPnk NRya |
| | – 'Ice and Fire' | SSvw |
| | – 'Jack Brownless' | CLAP ITim |
| | – 'Kassari Kirju' **new** | LWst |
| | – 'Kentish Pink' | GBBs GMaP NPnk |
| | – 'Knightshayes Vestal' (d) | CLAP CPLG EBee EBla MRav NHol WCot WCru |
| | – 'Lady Doneraile' | CAvo CDes CLAP EBla EPot ITim MDKP NBir NLar SSvw WCru WFar |
| | – 'Latvian Pink' | EBee ECho EPot LWst |
| | – 'Leeds' Variety' | CLAP CSam EPot GAbr GMaP ITim LWst MAvo MNrw NMen NPnk |
| | – 'Lionel Bacon' | LWst |
| | – 'Lismore Blue' | EBee ECho EPPr EPot |
| | – 'Lismore Pink' | GEdr |
| | – 'Lucia' | EPot LWst |
| | – 'Lychette' | CAby CHid CPMA EBee EBla ECho EPPr EPot GAbr IBlr ITim MAvo MNrw NWCA SHar WCru WFar |
| | – 'Marie Rose' | EPot |
| | – 'Miss Eunice' | CLAP |
| | – 'Monstrosa' | EBee EBla ECho SSvw |
| | – 'New Pink' | CAby CLAP CPom IBlr |
| | – 'Parlez Vous' | CPLG EBee ECho EPPr GEdr MAvo MNrw NMen NPnk SCnR SSvw WCru WFar |
| | – 'Pat's Pink' | WShi |
| | – 'Pentre Pink' | EBla EPot IBlr MAvo MCot MNrw MSSP WCru WFar |
| | – 'Picos Pink' | LWst SCnR |
| | – 'Pink Carpet' | EBla GEdr |
| | – pink-flowered | CLAP EBla ECho WCru |
| | – 'Polar Star' | CLAP |
| | – 'Robinsoniana' ♀$^{H4}$ | Widely available |
| | – 'Rosea' | CLAP EBla ECho GEdr MNrw SMrm WCru |
| | – 'Royal Blue' | CAby CBro CDes CLAP CPMA EBee ECho EPPr GAbr GEdr GMaP LAma LWst MAvo NHol NMen NPnk WCot WCru WFar WHil WPnP WTin |
| | – 'Rubra' | EPot MNrw |
| | – 'Salt and Pepper' | MAvo |
| | – 'Stammheim' (d) | CLAP EBla |
| | – 'Super Allenii' | EBee |
| | – 'Tinney's Blush' | CLAP |
| | – 'Tomas' | CLAP EBee ECho ELon EPot GBin GEdr ITim NHar NWCA |
| | – 'Vestal' (d) ♀$^{H4}$ | Widely available |
| | – 'Virescens' ♀$^{H4}$ | CAby CAvo CFFs CLAP CWCL EBee ECho ELon EPPr EPot GAbr GEdr GKev GMaP MAvo NBir NHar NWCA WPtf WShi |
| | – 'Viridiflora' | CFwr CLAP CPLG EBla ECho EPfP GAbr LHop MNrw NBir NSti SSvw WCot WCru WFar WSHC |
| | – 'Westwell Pink' | CAby CLAP CPMA EBee ECho EPPr LLHF MAvo MNrw MSSP SPhx WCot WShi |
| | – 'Wilks' Giant' | EBla ITim MAvo WCru WFar |
| | – 'Wilks' White' | EBla ELon EPPr GEdr WCru WFar |
| | – 'Wisley Pink' | EPot |
| | – 'Wyatt's Pink' | CLAP CPMA EBla ELon MAvo NCGa WCru WFar WPnP WTin |
| | – 'Yerda Ramusem' | EBee ECho EPPr MAvo |
| | ***nemorosa* × *ranunculoides*** | see *A.* × *lipsiensis* |
| | ***nikoensis*** | ECho LWst |
| | ***obtusiloba*** | CLAP GEdr GMac SRms WAbe |
| | – CLD 1549 | GEdr GLam |
| | – 'Alba' | GMac WAbe |
| I | – 'Sulphurea' | CDes GEdr NMen WCot |
| | – yellow-flowered | WAbe |
| | ***palmata*** | EDAr EPot LEdu MDKP MWea NBre NPnk SMad WCru WFar |
| | ***parviflora*** | EBee ECho GKev |
| | ***patens*** | see *Pulsatilla patens* |
| | ***pavonina*** | CAby CPMA CSpe ECha LRHS MAsh MSSP NBir SLon SPoG SUsu WAbe WCot WCru |
| | – 'Grecian Sunset' | MAsh |
| | – lilac-flowered | MAsh NBir SUsu |
| | – pink-flowered | MAsh NBir SUsu |
| | ***polyanthes*** | CSpe LRHS |
| | ***prattii*** | CLAP CPLG EPPr GEdr WCot WHal |
| | ***pseudoaltaica*** | GEdr LWst WCru |
| | – blue-flowered **new** | LWst |
| | – pale blue-flowered | CAby CLAP |
| | – 'Yuki-no-sei' (d) | GEdr |
| | ***pulsatilla*** | see *Pulsatilla vulgaris* |
| | ***quinquefolia*** | CLAP WCot |
| | ***raddeana*** | ECho LWst |
| | ***ranunculoides*** ♀$^{H4}$ | Widely available |
| | – 'Frank Waley' | WCot |
| * | – ***laciniata*** | CLAP NMen WCot |
| | – 'Pleniflora' (d) | CAvo CLAP EBla ECha ECho EPot GBBs LEdu LWst NLar NMen WCot WFar |
| | – subsp. ***ranunculoides*** | ECho GKev WHil |
| | – 'Semi Plena' | CAby EBee ECho |
| | – subsp. ***wockeana*** | CDes CSam EBee ECho MAvo |
| | ***reflexa*** | GKev LLHF |
| | ***riparia*** | see *A. virginiana* var. *alba* |
| | ***rivularis*** | CAvo CBro CLAP CMea CPar EBee ECha GAbr GGar GKev GMac GPoy ITim LEdu LHop NBir NChi NHar NHol NLar NPnk SBrt WCru WFar WHoo WKif WMoo WTin |
| | – BWJ 7611 | WCru |

| | |
|---|---|
| - CC 4587 | GKev |
| - CC 4588 | CPLG |
| - GWJ 9391 | WCru |
| - 'Blue Back' | GCal |
| - 'Glacier' | NEgg WPer |
| aff. ***rivularis*** | WPtf |
| ***rupicola*** | CAby IGor NDir |
| × ***seemannii*** | see *A.* × *lipsiensis* |
| ***stellata*** Lam. | see *A. hortensis* |
| ***stolonifera*** new | LWst |
| - double-flowered (d) | CElw LWst WCot WSHC |
| ***sulphurea*** misapplied | see *Pulsatilla alpina* subsp. *apiifolia* |
| ***sumatrana*** | WCru |
| B&SWJ 11265 new | |
| ***sylvestris*** | Widely available |
| - 'Elise Fellmann' (d) | CSpe EBee EPfP GMac WHal |
| - 'Flore Pleno' (d) | NMen |
| - 'Macrantha' | EBee EPfP GAbr NGdn SMrm WCot |
| ***tetrasepala*** | WCot |
| § ***tomentosa*** | EBee ECha GGar LBMP LRHS NBre SDix SRms SWat WFar |
| § - 'Albadura' | EBee |
| - 'Robustissima' | see *A.* × *hybrida* 'Robustissima' |
| ***trifolia*** L. | CAby EBee EPPr NBid SCnR SRms WCot WPat |
| - pink-flowered | CLAP WFar |
| ***trullifolia*** | GBin GCra GEdr GKev GMac ITim NSla WAbe |
| - ***alba*** | GMac |
| ***vernalis*** | see *Pulsatilla vernalis* |
| ***virginiana*** | EBee GAbr LEdu MDKP NBid NPnk SPhx WFar WHrl WWEG |
| § - var. ***alba*** | EKen NSti WPtf |
| ***vitifolia*** misapplied | see *A. tomentosa* |
| ***vitifolia*** DC. B&SWJ 8202 from Vietnam | WCru |
| - HWJK 2044 | WCru |
| - GWJ 9434 | WCru |

## *Anemonella* (*Ranunculaceae*)

| | |
|---|---|
| ***thalictroides*** | CBct CElw CFir CLAP CWCL EBee ECho EFEx ELon GAbr GEdr GKev ITim LAma MAvo MMoz NHar NHol NMen NPnk NRya NWCA WAbe WAul WCru WFar WSHC XLum |
| - 'Alba Plena' (d) | ECho |
| - 'Amelia' | CLAP EPPr GEdr NHar SCnR WAbe |
| - 'Babe' | LWst |
| - 'Betty Blake' (d) | CDes GEdr WCot |
| - 'Big' | LWst |
| - 'Cameo' | CLAP EFEx EPPr GEdr LWst NHar SCnR WCot WCru WFar |
| - 'Charlotte' | LWst |
| - 'Diamante' | LWst WCot |
| - 'Double Green' (d) | CLAP EFEx GEdr LWst |
| - 'Full Double White' (d) | EFEx GEdr LWst |
| - 'Green Hurricane' (d) | EFEx GEdr LWst |
| - 'Jade Feather' | CElw |
| - f. ***rosea*** | CAby CElw CLAP CRDP ECho IPot WAbe WCru WFar |
| - - 'Oscar Schoaf' (d) | CBcs CLAP GEdr LWst WAbe |
| - - semi-double, pink-flowered (d) | CElw CLAP CRDP LWst MAvo NLar |
| - semi-double, white-flowered (d) | CElw CLAP CRDP EPPr NMen WAbe WCot |
| - 'Tairin' | GEdr LWst |

## *Anemonopsis* (*Ranunculaceae*)

| | |
|---|---|
| ***macrophylla*** | CAby CElw CLAP CPBP CRDP ECha ECho GCal GEdr GMac LRHS MNrw SMad SPhx WCru WFar WSHC |
| - 'White Swan' | WCru WSHC |

## *Anemopsis* (*Saururaceae*)

| | |
|---|---|
| ***californica*** | CDes EBee IFoB LLWG MSKA MWts NLar WCot WPGP |

## *Anethum* (*Apiaceae*)

| | |
|---|---|
| ***graveolens*** | CArn GPoy MHer MNHC SBfd SIde SVic SWal |
| - 'Dukat' | CSev EGHP ELau |

## angelica see *Angelica archangelica*

## *Angelica* (*Apiaceae*)

| | |
|---|---|
| sp. | CHab |
| ***acutiloba*** | CSpe MMHG NLar WFar |
| - var. ***iwatensis*** B&SWJ 11197 | WCru |
| ***anomala*** B&SWJ 10886 | WCru |
| ***archangelica*** | Widely available |
| - subsp. ***archangelica*** | GAuc |
| - 'Corinne Tremaine' (v) | MDKP WCot |
| ***arguta*** | MHer |
| ***atropurpurea*** | CArn EBee ECtt EPfP GKev LRHS MHer MNHC MNrw MRav NCGa SWat WFar WJek WMnd WWEG |
| ***dahurica*** | XLum |
| - B&SWJ 8603 | WCru |
| ***decursiva*** | CArn |
| - B&SWJ 5746 | WCru |
| 'Ebony' | CBod CMea CSpe GKev LEdu MDKP MHer NExo SBfd SPad SPoG WCot |
| ***edulis*** | LEdu WCru |
| ***gigas*** | Widely available |
| - B&SWJ 4170 | WCru |
| ***hispanica*** | see *A. pachycarpa* |
| ***japonica*** B&SWJ 11480 | WCru |
| - B&SWJ 8816a | WCru |
| ***montana*** | see *A. sylvestris* |
| ***morii*** RWJ 9802 | WCru |
| § ***pachycarpa*** | CArn CSpe EBee EGHP ELan EOHP EPri EPyc GMaP LHop LRHS MCCP MHer NBir NPnk SBfd SGar SIde SPhx SPoG WFar WJek WOut WWEG XLum |
| ***pubescens*** | SPhx |
| - B&SWJ 5593 | WCru |
| - B&SWJ 11129 | WCru |
| - var. ***matsumurae*** B&SWJ 6387 | WCru |
| ***sinensis*** | CArn GPoy |
| 'Summer Delight' | see *Ligusticum scoticum* |
| § ***sylvestris*** | CArn CHab CRWN EGHP LLWG |
| * - 'Purpurea' | CKno CSpe EWes WPGP |
| - 'Vicar's Mead' | CDes EBee LEdu LPla LRHS LSRN MDKP MLLN NBPC NCGa NChi NLar NPnk NSti SPhx WCot WJek |
| ***taiwaniana*** | CArn CDTJ ELan MDKP MLLN SGar WTcb |
| ***ursina*** | GAuc |
| - B&SWJ 10829 | WCru |

## *Angelonia* (*Plantaginaceae*)

| | |
|---|---|
| Angelface Wedgwood Blue = 'Anwedg' (Angelface Series) | NPri |
| ***angustifolia*** 'Zebra' new | NPri |

## *Anigozanthos* (*Haemodoraceae*)

sp. WHil
'Big Red' MOWG
'Bush Ranger' (Bush Gems Series) CCCN
***flavidus*** EAmu ECre EOHP MOWG SPlb
- 'Ember' CCCN
- 'Illusion' CCCN
- 'Opal' CCCN
- 'Pearl' CCCN
- 'Splendour' CCCN
- 'Yellow Gem' CCCN
***humilis*** Lindl. ♀H1 MOWG
***manglesii*** ♀H1 MOWG SPlb

## *Anisacanthus* (*Acanthaceae*)

***quadrifidus*** var. ***wrightii*** WCot

## *Anisodontea* (*Malvaceae*)

§ ***capensis*** CCCN CHGN CHll EBee ELan EPri EShb GBee LAst MCot MOWG NBir SBfd SChF SLim SMrm SPad SPlb SRkn SRms SVen SWvt WDyG
- 'Pink Pearl' **new** LRHS
- 'Tara's Pink' CSpe EWes IFoB SAga SMrm SPhx
'El Royo' WCot
***elegans*** SAga
'Elegant Lady' CSpe GFai SUsu
***huegelii*** see *Alyogyne huegelii*
× ***hypomadara*** misapplied see *A. capensis*
§ × ***hypomadara*** (Sprague) D.M.Bates SEND
***julii*** SPlb
Lady in Pink = 'Nuanilaninp' LHop
'Large Magenta' **new** LSou
***malvastroides*** WWlt
'Orchard Pink' SEND
***scabrosa*** CChe CSev

## *Anisodus* (*Solanaceae*)

§ ***luridus*** EWld GCal

## *Anisotome* (*Apiaceae*)

***lyallii*** GBin GKev ITim

## *Annona* (*Annonaceae*)

***cherimola*** (F) CCCN XBlo

## *Anoiganthus* see *Cyrtanthus*

## *Anomalesia* see *Gladiolus*

## *Anomatheca* (*Iridaceae*)

***cruenta*** see *A. laxa*
§ ***grandiflora*** CHll CPLG ECho WCot
***grandiflora*** × ***laxa*** **new** CDes
§ ***laxa*** ♀H2-3 CAvo CPLG CRHN CSev CSpe CTri EBee ECha ECho ELan EPfP EPot EPri IFoB LEdu LRHS MAvo MCot NMen NWCA SHom SRms WAbe WBrk WPat WPer
- var. ***alba*** ♀H2-3 CPLG CPom CRHN CSev CSpe ECho EDif ELan EPri ITim MCot MWea NMen WAbe WBrk
- blue-flowered ECho WAbe WBrk
- 'Joan Evans' CRHN CSpe ECho ELan LLHF NMen NWCA SBch SHom SRms WAbe WBrk
- red-spotted CPLG ECho EDif
- ***viridiflora*** ECho
***viridis*** CDes CPLG CPou EBee ECho

## *Anopterus* (*Escalloniaceae*)

***glandulosus*** IBlr WSHC

## *Anredera* (*Basellaceae*)

§ ***cordifolia*** CRHN ECho EShb LEdu

## *Antennaria* (*Asteraceae*)

***aprica*** see *A. parvifolia*
***aromatica*** EDAr
***dioica*** CArn CTri ECtt EDAr GAbr GJos GPoy NSla SPlb SRms WFar
- 'Alba' EHoe
- 'Alex Duguid' EPot GEdr GLam LBee LRHS
- 'Aprica' see *A. parvifolia*
- 'Minima' ECho EPot MWat NBro NHar NMen WAbe
- 'Nyewoods Variety' EPot
- red-flowered ECho
- var. ***rosea*** see *A. rosea*
- 'Rotes Wunder' CMea EPot SBch
* - 'Rubra' ECha ECho ECtt EDAr GBin LRHS MHer NMen WAbe
'Joy' EPot WAbe
***macrophylla*** hort. see *A. microphylla*
§ ***microphylla*** SRms
§ ***parvifolia*** CTri ECho NPri SRms SRot
- var. ***rosea*** see *A. microphylla*
***plantaginifolia*** EBee LRHS
§ ***rosea*** ♀H4 ECho GMaP LRHS MAsh NMen SPlb SRms WFar WHoo WPer

## *Antenoron* see *Persicaria*

## *Anthemis* ✿ (*Asteraceae*)

from Turkey ECtt EWes LLWP
***arvensis*** CHab
§ 'Beauty of Grallagh' GMac MDKP SDix
'Cally Cream' GCal NCGa SMrm
'Cally White' GCal
***carpatica*** LRHS NBro
- compact **new** NSla
- 'Karpatenschnee' EBee GGar LBMP LRHS NBre WWEG
***caucasica*** **new** GLam
§ ***cretica*** subsp. ***cretica*** NWCA
'Daisy Bee' EBee MAvo
***frutescens*** see *Argyranthemum frutescens*
'Grallagh Gold' misapplied, orange-yellow see *A.* 'Beauty of Grallagh'
'Grallagh Gold' ECtt EWes MWat NPer WFar
§ ***marschalliana*** CMea CPBP EBee ECha ECho ECtt EDAr EPot LBee LRHS SAga SMrm SPlb WCot
***montana*** see *A. cretica* subsp. *cretica*
***nobilis*** see *Chamaemelum nobile*
***punctata*** WNew
- subsp. ***cupaniana*** ♀H3-4 Widely available
- - 'Nana' NPer SHar
***rudolphiana*** see *A. marschalliana*
***sancti-johannis*** CWib EAEE EBee EPPr EPfP LRHS LSou NDov NPer NWad SBfd SMrm SPer SRms WMoo WRHF
'Sauce Béarnaise' WMnd
Susanna Mitchell = 'Blomit' CHar EBee ECtt ELon EPfP EShb EWll GMaP GMac LRHS LSRN MAvo MLHP MNrw NBir NDov

| | |
|---|---|
| | NPnk SMrm SRGP SUsu SWvt WMnd WPer WSHC WTin WWEG XLum |
| 'Tetworth' | CElw EBee ECha ECtt ELan EPfP LSRN MBNS SMad SUsu WFar WWEG |
| ***tinctoria*** | CArn CHby CMac EBee GPoy LRHS MHer NPer SWvt WHfH WJek WSFF |
| - 'Alba' | EBee GGar NBre NLar WFar WWEG |
| - 'Charme'PBR | EBee LAst LHop LRHS SPoG SWvt WCot |
| - 'Compacta' | EWes GCal NBre NGdn XLum |
| - dwarf | EBee SBri SUsu WFar |
| - 'E.C. Buxton' | Widely available |
| - 'Eva' | NBre NDov NLar WWEG |
| I - 'Golden Rays' | MDKP SBfd SDix WWEG |
| - 'Kelwayi' | CPrp CSBt CTri EBee EPfP LRHS NBPC NBro NLar NPer SBfd SGar SPer SPoG SRms SWat WFar WMoo WWEG |
| - 'Lemon Ice' | GMaP |
| - 'Lemon Maid' | CFir ELon EPfP GBin LRHS NBre SMrm |
| - 'Sauce Hollandaise' | Widely available |
| - subsp. ***tinctoria*** | SMrm |
| - 'Wargrave Variety' | Widely available |
| 'Tinpenny Sparkle' | CSam EBee ECtt EWll GMaP LSou MAvo NDov NLar NSti WBrk WCot WHoo WTin |
| ***triumfettii*** | EBee NPer NPnk |
| ***tuberculata*** | NChi SAga SBch |
| 'White Water' | WAbe WFar |

## *Anthericum* (*Asparagaceae*)

| | |
|---|---|
| ***algeriense*** | see *A. liliago* |
| * ***bovei*** | CBro |
| § ***liliago*** | EBee ECho ELan GCal GKev GMaP IFoB LHop MAvo MCot MLLN MRav NCGa NLar WAul WHrl WPer WWEG |
| - 'Major' ♀H4 | CAvo CBro ECGP ECha ECho IGor MLHP NBre WPGP |
| ***plumosum*** | see *Trichopetalum plumosum* |
| ***ramosum*** | CAby CDes CSpe EBee ECha ECho ELan EPot EWTr EWes GCal GMac MBrN MLLN NBid NBir NCGa NLar NWCA SMrm SPhx WPGP WPer |

## *Antholyza* (*Iridaceae*)

| | |
|---|---|
| ***coccinea*** | see *Crocosmia paniculata* |
| × ***crocosmioides*** | see *Crocosmia* × *crocosmioides* |
| ***paniculata*** | see *Crocosmia paniculata* |

## *Anthoxanthum* (*Poaceae*)

| | |
|---|---|
| ***odoratum*** | CArn CHab CRWN ELau GPoy XLum |

## *Anthriscus* (*Apiaceae*)

| | |
|---|---|
| ***cerefolium*** | CArn CHby ELau EPfP GPoy ILis MHer MNHC SBfd WJek |
| ***sylvestris*** | CHab NMir SPhx WSFF |
| - 'Broadleas Blush' | CNat |
| - 'Moonlit Night' | EHoe |
| - 'Ravenswing' | Widely available |

## *Anthurium* (*Araceae*)

| | |
|---|---|
| ***andraeanum*** 'Glowing Pink' | XBlo |
| - 'Red Heart' | XBlo |
| - 'Tivolo' | XBlo |
| 'Aztec' | XBlo |
| Baleno = 'Anthauf4'PBR | XBlo |
| 'Caribo' | XBlo |
| ***crenatum*** | XBlo |
| 'Crimson' | XBlo |
| 'Magenta' | XBlo |
| 'Mikra' | XBlo |
| 'Octavia' | XBlo |
| 'Pico Bello' | XBlo |
| 'Pink Champion' | XBlo |
| 'Porcelaine White' | XBlo |
| Red Champion = 'Anthbnena'PBR | XBlo |
| 'Vitara' | XBlo |
| White Champion = 'Anthefaqyr'PBR | XBlo |

## *Anthyllis* (*Papilionaceae*)

| | |
|---|---|
| ***barba-jovis*** | CSpe |
| ***hermanniae*** | WPat |
| - 'Compacta' | see *A. hermanniae* 'Minor' |
| § - 'Minor' | NLar NMen |
| ***montana*** | LRHS |
| subsp. ***atropurpurea*** | |
| - 'Rubra' ♀H4 | ECho EDAr EPot EWes LHop LLHF NLar NMen |
| - 'Rubra Compacta' | WAbe |
| ***vulneraria*** | CFee CHab EWil NMir NRya SEND WSFF |
| - var. ***coccinea*** | CMea CSpe EDAr ELan GAbr GBin GGar GKev ITim MCCP MLLN MSCN MWea NLar NSla NWCA WCFE WFar WHal WHil |

## *Antigonon* (*Polygonaceae*)

| | |
|---|---|
| ***leptopus*** | MOWG |

## *Antirrhinum* (*Plantaginaceae*)

| | |
|---|---|
| ***asarina*** | see *Asarina procumbens* |
| ***barrelieri*** | SEND |
| ***braun-blanquetii*** | CSpr SEND WCAu WCot WMoo XLum |
| 'Carambola Yellow' (Fruit Salad Series) | LSou |
| § ***hispanicum*** | CPBP |
| - 'Avalanche' | ECtt |
| - subsp. ***hispanicum*** 'Roseum' | CMea CSpe |
| ***majus*** | WCot |
| - 'Black Prince' | CSpe ECtt LHop SPhx |
| - 'Bronze Dragon' new | EWTr NPri |
| - 'Night and Day' | CSpe |
| ***molle*** | CSpe ECtt MCot NBir NPer NSla NWCA SChF WAbe |
| - pink-flowered | WAbe |
| ***pulverulentum*** | SAga WAbe |
| ***sempervirens*** | SAga WAbe XLum |

**añu** see *Tropaeolum tuberosum*

## *Aphelandra* (*Acanthaceae*)

| | |
|---|---|
| ***squarrosa*** 'Citrina' | XBlo |

## *Aphyllanthes* (*Asparagaceae*)

| | |
|---|---|
| ***monspeliensis*** | CFee ECho XLum |

## *Apios* (*Papilionaceae*)

| | |
|---|---|
| § ***americana*** | CAgr CPom EBee ECho GBin LEdu NBir NLar NSti WCot WCru WSHC |

| | |
|---|---|
| ***tuberosa*** | see *A. americana* |

## *Apium* (*Apiaceae*)

| | |
|---|---|
| ***graveolens*** | CArn CHab CPrp ELau GPoy MHer MNHC SBfd SIde WJek |
| - (Secalinum Group) 'Par-cel' | EGHP MHer |

## *Apium* × *Petroselinum* (*Apiaceae*)

| | |
|---|---|
| hybrid, misapplied | see *Apium graveolens* Secalinum Group |

## *Apocynum* (*Apocynaceae*)

| | |
|---|---|
| ***cannabinum*** | CArn GPoy |

## *Apodolirion* (*Amaryllidaceae*)

| | |
|---|---|
| ***macowanii*** | ECho |

## *Aponogeton* (*Aponogetonaceae*)

| | |
|---|---|
| ***distachyos*** | CBen CRow CWat EHon LPBA MSKA MWts NPer SCoo SVic SWat WFar WMAq WPnP XLum |

## apple see *Malus domestica*

## apricot see *Prunus armeniaca*

## *Aptenia* (*Aizoaceae*)

| | |
|---|---|
| ***cordifolia*** ♀H1-2 | CCCN NPer SChr SEND SPet |
| - 'Variegata' (v) | CCCN |

## *Aquilegia* ✿ (*Ranunculaceae*)

| | | |
|---|---|---|
| | sp. | SVic |
| | ***akitensis*** misapplied | see *A. flabellata* var. *pumila* |
| * | ***alba variegata*** (v) | ECho |
| | ***alpina*** | CBot CMea CPrp EBee ECho ECtt EPfP MAsh MNHC MRav NGdn SBfd SPer SRms WCAu WFar WMoo WPer WTou XLum |
| | ***amaliae*** | see *A. ottonis* subsp. *amaliae* |
| | ***amurensis*** | CLAP |
| | 'Apple Blossom' | LRHS NBir |
| | ***aragonensis*** | see *A. pyrenaica* |
| § | ***atrata*** | CLAP CPou EBee ECho MDKP MWea NBre WTou |
| | ***atrovinosa*** | MWea |
| | ***aurea*** misapplied | see *A. vulgaris* golden-leaved |
| | ***bernardii*** | NMun |
| | ***bertolonii*** ♀H4 | CMea ECho EPot GKev LHop LRHS MAsh NMen NRya SRms WHoo |
| | - ***alba*** | NWCA |
| | Biedermeier Group | EBee ECho EPfP GAbr LRHS NGdn NNor NOrc SBfd SPoG SRot WFar WPer WTou |
| | 'Blue Jay' (Songbird Series) | LRHS MHer SWvt |
| | 'Blue Star' (Star Series) | EAEE EBee ELan EPfP LRHS NEgg NPnk WPer |
| | 'Bluebird' (Songbird Series) ♀H2 | LBuc LRHS NBir NPer |
| | ***brevistyla*** | NNor |
| | ***buergeriana*** | GEdr MDKP WTou |
| | - 'Calimero' | EBee LRHS MBNS MDKP NLar WFar |
| | - f. ***flavescens*** | WTou |
| | - var. ***oxysepala*** | see *A. oxysepala* |
| | 'Bunting' (Songbird Series) ♀H2 | NLar SCoo SWal WFar |
| | ***canadensis*** ♀H4 | CLAP CSpe EBee EHoe ELan GKev LRHS NBir NBro NWCA SBfd SGar SRms SUsu SWal WTcb WTou XLum |
| | - SDR 1068 | GKev |
| | - 'Corbett' | GEdr MDKP WHil |
| | - 'Little Lanterns' | ECtt EPPr GKev LHop LRHS MDKP MPnt NLar NSum WFar |
| | - 'Nana' | GEdr GKev WThu |
| | - 'Pink Lanterns' | LRHS SMrm |
| | 'Cardinal' (Songbird Series) | LRHS MHer NLar NPri WFar |
| | ***chaplinei*** | CBot NBir SBch |
| | ***chrysantha*** | EWTr GKev NBre SRms WKif WPer WTou |
| | - 'Denver Gold' | WRHF |
| | - var. ***hinckleyana*** **new** | WTou |
| | - 'Yellow Queen' | CPLG CPrp CWCL EBee EPPr EPfP GAbr GMaP LBMP LHop LRHS MBri MDKP NBre NGdn NLar SMrm SPad SPur SSvw STes WCFE WHil WTou XLum |
| | ***clematiflora*** | see *A. vulgaris* var. *stellata* |
| | Clementine Series | EPfP LRHS |
| | ***coerulea*** ♀H4 | EBee GKev MDKP NNor SRms |
| | - var. ***alpina*** **new** | GKev |
| | - var. ***coerulea*** | GKev |
| | - 'Himmelblau' | NBre |
| | 'Colorado' (State Series) | MBri |
| | 'Crimson Star' | EBee EPfP GJos LRHS MDKP SPer SPoG SPur WMoo WTou WWEG |
| | 'Debutante' | EBee MDKP MWea |
| | ***desertorum*** | MDKP |
| | ***discolor*** | GKev LLHF WThu WTou |
| | 'Double Rubies' (d) | LSRN WMoo |
| | 'Dove' (Songbird Series) ♀H2 | EWll LRHS MHer NLar NPri SMrm SWal WFar |
| I | 'Dragonfly' | CBcs CWib EPfP LRHS MAvo NBlu NBre NGdn SBfd SPer SPet SPoG WFar WTou WWEG |
| | ***ecalcarata*** | see *Semiaquilegia ecalcarata* |
| | ***einseleana*** | EBee LLHF |
| | 'Elegance' | WTou |
| | ***elegantula*** | MWea |
| | ***flabellata*** ♀H4 | GCra GGar WTou |
| | - f. ***alba*** | CTri ECho ELan WTou |
| | - 'Blackcurrant Ice' | LRHS |
| | - Cameo Series | GKev GMaP LRHS WFar WGor |
| | - - 'Cameo Blue and White' | CWib NCGa SRot WFar |
| | - - 'Cameo Blush' | WFar |
| | - - 'Cameo Pink and White' | MHer NCGa SRot WFar |
| | - - 'Cameo White' | SRot |
| | - 'Georgia' (State Series) ♀H3-4 | MBri SMrm |
| | - Jewel Series | ECho |
| | - 'Ministar' | ECho EPfP NBlu NVic WFar WHil |
| | - 'Nana Alba' | see *A. flabellata* var. *pumila* f. *alba* |
| § | - var. ***pumila*** ♀H4 | CFir CWCL ECha ECho EPfP GGar GKev LHop LRHS MAsh MDKP NGdn WAbe WFar WTou |
| § | - - f. ***alba*** ♀H4 | CBot ECha ECho GKev LHop LRHS SRms WTou |
| | - - 'Atlantis' | EPPr GAbr LRHS |
| | - - 'Flore Pleno' | ECho |
| I | - - f. ***kurilensis*** 'Rosea' | CFir GKev NWCA |
| | 'Flamboyant' | WTou |
| | 'Florida' (State Series) ♀H2 | GAbr |
| | ***formosa*** | CBot CMea EBee GKev LBMP MDKP NChi NPri WKif WTou |
| | - NNS 07-39 | GKev |
| | - var. ***truncata*** | EBee |
| § | ***fragrans*** | CLAP CTsd EBee EPfP GEdr GJos GKev LRHS NWCA SMrm WGwG WHoo WKif WTou |
| | 'Fruit and Nut Chocolate' | WCot |

| | |
|---|---|
| ***glandulosa*** | LLHF NLar WTou |
| – var. ***jacunda*** **new** | WTou |
| ***glauca*** | see *A. fragrans* |
| 'Golden Guiness' | WPnP WTou |
| 'Goldfinch' (Songbird Series) | LBuc LRHS MHer NBir NPri SCoo SWal |
| ***grata*** | MDKP |
| 'Heavenly Blue' | CChe LRHS SMrm SPhx WTou |
| 'Hensol Harebell' ♀H4 | SRms WPtf |
| 'Honeydew' **new** | WTou |
| 'Iceberg' (fragrans hybrid) | WTou |
| ***japonica*** | see *A. flabellata* var. *pumila* |
| ***jonesii*** | GKev |
| ***jonesii* × *saximontana*** | GKev |
| 'Kansas' (State Series) | MBri |
| 'Koralle' | MDKP NBre WFar WHil |
| 'Kristall' | EShb LSRN MDKP NBre SPhx SSvw STes XLum |
| ***laramiensis*** | CPBP WAbe |
| 'Leprechaun Gold' (v) | EPfP NGdn SMrm |
| 'Lime Sorbet' **new** | NCGa |
| ***longissima*** ♀H4 | CMea GKev MDKP MHer MWea NPnk SBrt SHar STes WHoo WTou |
| 'Louisiana' (State Series) ♀H2 | MBri SMrm |
| 'Magpie' | see *A. vulgaris* 'William Guiness' |
| 'Maxi' | MDKP NBre WHil WTou |
| McKana Group | CTri EAEE ELan ELon EPfP GAbr GJos GMaP LAst LBMP LHop LRHS MGos MLHP MLLN NEgg NGdn NVic SBfd SPer SPlb SPoG SRms SWal WMnd WMoo WTou WWEG WWlt XLum |
| 'Milk and Honey' | WTou |
| 'Montana' (State Series) | MBri |
| Mrs Scott-Elliot hybrids | CSBt EPfP GAbr SGar SPet WFar WHil |
| Music Series ♀H4 | SRms |
| 'Nightingale' (Songbird Series) | SWal |
| ***nigricans*** | see *A. atrata* |
| ***nivalis*** | LLHF MAsh |
| ***olympica*** | EBee EWes |
| 'Oranges and Lemons' | WTou |
| Origami Series | WFar |
| § ***ottonis*** subsp. ***amaliae*** | CPBP GEdr |
| § ***oxysepala*** | CPLG EBee GCal WTou |
| – B&SWJ 4775 | WCru |
| Perfumed Garden Group | LRHS WTou |
| pleated burgundy-flowered | LRHS |
| 'Purple Emperor' PBR | EPfP LRHS |
| § ***pyrenaica*** | GKev WTou |
| * – f. ***alba*** **new** | WTou |
| 'Red Hobbit' | CBct CChe CSBt CSpe EAEE EBee EPfP GGar GKev LHop LRHS LSou MDKP MHer NBre NEgg NGdn SUsu WFar WGwG WHil WHoo |
| 'Red Star' (Star Series) | CPrp EAEE EBee EPfP LRHS NEgg WFar WHil WPer |
| 'Robin' (Songbird Series) | MHer NPri SCoo SWal WFar |
| ***rockii*** | CFir CLAP EBee EWes GCal GJos GKev MDKP SBrt SSvw WAbe |
| – B&SWJ 7965 | WCru |
| – SDR 1680 | GKev |
| 'Roman Bronze' | see *Aquilegia* × *Semiaquilegia* 'Roman Bronze' |
| 'Rose Queen' | EBee EPfP MDKP NBre NNor WHoo |
| ***saximontana*** | GEdr GKev NLar WTou |
| § 'Schneekönigin' | CWCL GMaP LRHS WCFE |
| ***scopulorum*** | GKev GLam LLHF WAbe |
| ***shockleyi*** | CDes WTou |
| ***sibirica*** | CFir LLHF |
| 'Silver Queen' | EBee ELan MDKP |
| ***skinneri*** | CPLG CSpe EBee EShb IFro LRHS WMnd |
| – 'Tequila Sunrise' | CWCL CWib EBee LSRN LSou MHer NNor |
| Snow Queen | see *A.* 'Schneekönigin' |
| Songbird Series | WFar |
| 'Spitfire' | LRHS NCGa |
| Spring Magic Series **new** | LRHS |
| – 'Spring Magic Blue and White' | LRHS NGdn WTou |
| – 'Spring Magic Pink and White' | WTou |
| – 'Spring Magic Rose and Ivory' | WTou |
| ***stellata*** | see *A. vulgaris* var. *stellata* |
| 'Sunburst Ruby' | LRHS MDKP WMoo WTou |
| ***triternata*** | NNor |
| 'Virginia' (State Series) | MBri |
| ***viridiflora*** | CBot CLAP EBee ELan EPfP GAbr GCal GLam MLLN NCGa SGar SUsu WCot WFar WHil WMnd WPer WPtf |
| – 'Chocolate Soldier' | CSpe CWCL EDif MWat |
| ***vulgaris*** | CArn CHab CMHG CRWN EPfP EWil GPoy LLWP LRHS MHer MMuc MNHC NBro NGdn NMir SGar SPlb WCAu WMoo WShi WTin WWEG |
| – SDR 5436 | GKev |
| – 'Adelaide Addison' | ECha LRHS SUsu WFar WHoo WTou |
| – var. ***alba*** | CMea EBee EPPr LBMP LLWP LRHS WTou |
| – 'Altrosa' | NBre |
| – 'Aureovariegata' | see *A. vulgaris* Vervaeneana Group |
| – 'Burnished Rose' | WHil |
| – ***clematiflora*** | see *A. vulgaris* var. *stellata* |
| – (Clementine Series) 'Clementine Dark Purple' (d) | EPfP SPoG |
| – – 'Clementine Red' (d) | EPfP SPoG |
| – – 'Clementine Salmon Rose' (d) | EPfP SPoG |
| – – 'Clementine White' (d) | EPfP SPoG |
| – 'Crystal Star' | LRHS |
| – var. ***flore-pleno*** (d) | LLWP WTou |
| – – bicolour | WTou |
| – – black-flowered (d) | LRHS LSou MLLN WCot WTou |
| – – blue-flowered (d) | WTou |
| – – 'Dorothy Rose' (Dorothy Series) (d) | LSRN |
| – – 'Double Pleat' blue/white-flowered (d) | CPrp WPer |
| – – 'Double Pleat' pink/white-flowered (d) | CPrp |
| – – 'Jane Hollow' (d) | CPou |
| – – pale blue-flowered (d) | WCot WTou |
| – – 'Pink Bonnet' (d) | WFar |
| – – pink-flowered (d) | WTou |
| – – purple-flowered (d) | WTou |
| – – red-flowered (d) | WTou |
| – – 'Strawberry Ice Cream' (d) | NBro NNor |
| – – 'Tower Light Blue' (Tower Series) (d) | CSpr |
| – – white-flowered (d) | WTou |
| – 'Foggy Bottom Blues' | LRHS |
| § – golden-leaved | ECho WTou |

| | |
|---|---|
| - 'Heidi' | CBot NBre |
| - 'Mellow Yellow' | CTsd GKev LRHS MDKP SDix WMoo WTou |
| - 'Miss M. J. Huish' **new** | WTou |
| - Munstead White | see *A. vulgaris* 'Nivea' |
| - subsp. ***nevadensis*** | EBee |
| § - 'Nivea' ♀H4 | CBot CPou CSpe EBee ECha EPfP MBri NChi SPoG |
| - 'Pink Spurless' | see *A. vulgaris* var. *stellata* pink-flowered |
| - 'Pom Pom Crimson' (Pom Pom Series) | MTis NBro WCot |
| - scented | WTou |
| - 'Sorcery' **new** | WTou |
| § - var. ***stellata*** | ELan GKev LEdu LRHS LSou MWhi NBir NBro NNor WMoo WTou |
| - - Barlow Series (d) | WFar WTou WWEG |
| - - - 'Black Barlow' (d) | Widely available |
| - - black-flowered **new** | WTou |
| - - 'Blue Barlow' (Barlow Series) (d) | CSpe EBee ECtt EPfP GMaP IBal LRHS LSRN NBre SPer WMnd WPer WTou WWEG |
| - - 'Blue Fountain' | WTou |
| - - blue-flowered | LRHS WTou |
| - - 'Bordeaux Barlow' (Barlow Series) | LRHS WTou |
| - - 'Christa Barlow' (Barlow Series) (d) | EBee EPfP LRHS NBre NGdn SPer WTou |
| - - double-flowered (d) | WTou |
| - - 'Firewheel' | LRHS WMoo WTou |
| - - 'Greenapples' (d) | CAbP CBre CPrp CWCL EBee GKev GQue LRHS MLLN MTis MWat NDov NGdn NPri SMrm WCot WHlf WTou WWEG |
| * - - 'Iceberg' | LRHS |
| - - 'Nora Barlow' (Barlow Series) (d) ♀H4 | Widely available |
| § - - pink-flowered | WTou |
| - - red-flowered | ELan WTou |
| - - 'Rose Barlow' (Barlow Series) (d) | EPfP IBal LRHS LSRN WMnd WTou |
| - - 'Royal Purple' (d) | LRHS NBro NNor WMoo WTou |
| - - 'Ruby Port' (d) | CBcs CWCL EAEE EBee ECha EPfP EShb EWTr GCal GGar GMaP IBal LAst LHop LRHS LSRN MLHP MLLN MNrw MWat NBPC NChi NGdn NPri SPad SPer SSvw SUsu WFar WTou |
| - - 'Ruby Port' crimped (d) | WPnP |
| - - (Vervaeneana Group) 'Sweet Dreams' (v/d) | WTou |
| - - 'White Barlow' (Barlow Series) (d) | LRHS SPer WTou |
| - - white-flowered | CSpe GCra LRHS NBro WFar WTou |
| - variegated foliage | see *A. vulgaris* Vervaeneana Group |
| § - Vervaeneana Group (v) | CMHG CWCL ECtt EPfP LRHS MNrw NBir NBre NPer SBfd SPer SPlb SRms SWat WFar WHoo WMoo WTou |
| - - 'Woodside Blue' (v) | LRHS WTou WWEG |
| - - 'Woodside White' (v) | NBir WBrk WTou |
| - - 'Lime Frost' (v) **new** | WTou |
| § - 'William Guiness' | Widely available |
| - 'William Guiness Doubles' (d) | WMoo WTou |
| 'White Star' (Star Series) | CPrp EBee ELan EPfP LAst LRHS MRav NEgg WHil WPer WTou WWEG |
| white-flowered | WTou |
| Winky Series | NCGa NNor WRHF |
| - 'Winky Blue-White' | LRHS NLar NPri SMrm WCFE WFar |
| - 'Winky Double White-White' (d) | NPri |
| - 'Winky Purple-White' | NLar NPri WFar |
| - 'Winky Red-White' | LRHS NLar NPri SRot SWvt WFar |
| - 'Winky Rose-Rose' | LRHS |
| ***yabeana*** | EBee EWld GKev MWhi WCot WMoo |
| 'Yellow Star' (Star Series) ♀H3-4 | WWEG |

## *Aquilegia* × *Semiaquilegia* (*Ranunculaceae*)

| | |
|---|---|
| hybrid, blue-flowered | NGdn WCru |
| § 'Roman Bronze' | LRHS WMoo WTou |

## *Arabis* (*Brassicaceae*)

| | |
|---|---|
| ***albida*** | see *A. alpina* subsp. *caucasica* |
| ***alpina*** | MAsh SPlb |
| § - subsp. ***caucasica*** | ECho WFar |
| - - 'Corfe Castle' | ECtt |
| - - 'Douler Angevine' (v) | ECtt ELon MPnt NBlu NPri SPoG WFar |
| - - 'Flore Pleno' (d) ♀H4 | CElw CSpe CTri CWCL ECho ECtt ELan GAbr GJos GMaP SBch SRms WFar WHoo WNew |
| - - 'Pink Pearl' | NBlu |
| - - 'Pinkie' | ECho ELon SGar |
| - - 'Pixie Cream' | LBMP NGdn |
| - - 'Rosea' | GJos LRHS NBir SRms WFar |
| § - - 'Schneehaube' ♀H4 | CTri CWib ECho ECtt EPfP GMaP LRHS MAsh NBir NBlu NGdn SPoG SRms SWal |
| - - Snowcap | see *A. alpina* subsp. *caucasica* 'Schneehaube' |
| - - 'Snowdrop' | WFar |
| - - 'Variegata' (v) | ECho ECtt ELan ELon GMaP LAst LBee LRHS SPoG SRms WFar |
| ***androsacea*** | GLam SRms WFar |
| × ***arendsii*** 'Compinkie' | GJos LBMP SPlb SRms |
| ***blepharophylla*** | EPfP WFar |
| § - 'Frühlingszauber' ♀H4 | CTri EPfP GJos LRHS MAsh NBir NBlu NGdn NPri SPoG SRms WCot WFar |
| - 'Rose Delight' | LRHS |
| - 'Rote Sensation' | NGdn |
| - Spring Charm | see *A. blepharophylla* 'Frühlingszauber' |
| ***bryoides*** | NMen |
| ***carduchorum*** | XLum |
| ***caucasica*** | see *A. alpina* subsp. *caucasica* |
| double white-flowered (d) | CFee |
| ***ferdinandi-coburgi*** | ECho MWat WNew XLum |
| - 'Aureovariegata' (v) | CMea CTri ECho ECtt EDAr SPet SWvt |
| - 'Old Gold' | ECho EDAr EHoe EPfP GGar LBee LRHS MAsh MHer SPoG SRms SRot SWvt WCFE WFar WHoo |
| - 'Variegata' | see *A. procurrens* 'Variegata' |
| § ***procurrens*** 'Variegata' (v) ♀H4 | CTri ECha ECho ECtt EHoe ELan EPfP EWes GEdr GKev LBee LEdu LRHS MAsh MBrN MHer SPlb SRms SRot WFar WNew |
| § ***scabra*** | CNat |
| Snow Cap | see *A. alpina* subsp. *caucasica* 'Schneehaube' |
| ***stelleri*** | NBre |
| ***stricta*** | see *A. scabra* |

× **wilczekii** EPot

## Arachniodes (Dryopteridaceae)

**davalliaeformis** ISha LRHS WRic
**simplicior** (v) CBty CCCN CKel ISha LRHS WCot WPat WRic
**standishii** CBty WRic

## Araiostegia (Davalliaceae)

**faberiana** CPLG
**hymenophylloides** SKHP WCot
**parvipinnata** see *A. perdurans*
§ **perdurans** WCot WPGP WRic
- B&SWJ 1608 EBla WCru

## Aralia ✿ (Araliaceae)

**apioides** EDHCH 9720 WCru
**armata** B&SWJ 6719 WCru
- RWJ 10060 WCru
**cachemirica** CDTJ CLAP EWes EWld GAbr GCal NBid NLar SDix SMad SPlb WCru WHal
**californica** GCal GPoy IGor LEdu NLar SDix SKHP WCru
**chapaensis** B&SWJ 11812 WCru
- HWJ 723 WCru
**chinensis** misapplied see *A. elata*, *A. stipulata*
**chinensis** L. BWJ 8102 WCru
**continentalis** CLAP IGor NLar
- B&SWJ 4152 WCru
- B&SWJ 8524 WCru
**cordata** EBee EWes GCal GKev LEdu NLar
- B&SWJ 5511 WCru
- B&SWJ 5596 WCru
**decaisneana** B&SWJ 6828 WCru
- RWJ 9910 WCru
§ **elata** ♀H4 CBcs CCVT CDoC CDul CHEx CHll CMac CPLG EBee ELan EPfP GKev LRHS LSRN MBlu MGos MMuc NBid SArc SCoo SGol SLim SPer SPoG SWvt WDin WFar
- B&SWJ 5480 WCru
- 'Albomarginata' see *A. elata* 'Variegata'
- 'Aureo-marginata' (v) CMac
- 'Aureovariegata' (v) CBcs CDoC ELan EWes MBlu NLar NPal SCoo WDin
- 'Golden Umbrella' (v) LSRN NLar WDin
- 'Silver Umbrella' (v) CDoC NLar
§ - 'Variegata' (v) ♀H4 CBcs CBot CDoC ELan EPfP MBlu MGos NLar NPal SCoo WDin
**foliolosa** B&SWJ 8360 WCru
**kansuensis** BWJ 7650 WCru
- CD&R 2289 WCru
**leschenaultii** B&SWJ 9515 WCru
- B&SWJ 11789 WCru
**montana** RWJ 10101 WCru
**papyrifera** see *Tetrapanax papyrifer*
**racemosa** CArn EBee GPoy GQue LEdu LPla MNrw NLar SRms WFar
- B&SWJ 9570 WCru
**searelliana** B&SWJ 11736 WCru
**sieboldii** de Vriese see *Fatsia japonica*
**spinifolia** B&SWJ 11745 WCru
**spinosa** L. MBlu NLar SPlb
§ **stipulata** NLar
**subcordata** HWJK 2385 WCru
**verticillata** B&SWJ 11797 WCru
**vietnamensis** B&SWJ 12349E WCru

## Araucaria (Araucariaceae)

**angustifolia** WPGP
§ **araucana** Widely available
**bidwillii** CTrC
**cunninghamii** ECou
**excelsa** misapplied see *A. heterophylla*
§ **heterophylla** ♀H1 CCCN CDoC EShb MBri SArc SEND
**imbricata** see *A. araucana*

## Araujia (Apocynaceae)

**sericifera** CHll CMac CPne CRHN CSam CSpe EBee GEdr GQui SGar SPav SVen WCot WFoF WSHC

## Arbutus ✿ (Ericaceae)

**andrachne** EPfP IDee
- from Cyprus SKHP
× **andrachnoides** ♀H4 CAbP CHGN CPMA CTri ELan EPfP GGal LRHS LSRN MAsh MRav SArc SMad SPer SPoG WPGP WPat
**glandulosa** see *Arctostaphylos glandulosa*
'Marina' CAbP CDoC CPMA CTrC EBee ELan EPfP IVic LHop LRHS MAsh MBlu NLar SBfd SEND SLPl SMad SPer SPoG SReu SSpi SSta SWvt WFar WPGP WPat
**menziesii** ♀H3 CDoC CMCN CTho ECrN EPfP IGor LRHS LSRN MGos MMuc NLar SMad SPer WDin WFar
**unedo** ♀H4 Widely available
- 'Atlantic' CAlb CCCN CPMA GGar IVic LRHS LSRN MAsh MGos SBfd SBig SLim SPtl SWvt WPGP WPat
- 'Compacta' CBcs CCCN CDoC IArd LRHS MAsh MGos NLar SGol SLon SPoG SWvt WCFE WDin
- 'Elfin King' ELan EPfP LRHS MAsh NLar SBrd SLon SPoG
- 'Quercifolia' CPMA EBee ELan LLHF MMHG NLar WFar WPat
- Roselily = 'Minlily'PBR SBig
- f. **rubra** ♀H4 Widely available
**xalapensis** NJM 09.026 WPGP

## Archontophoenix (Arecaceae)

**alexandrae** EAmu LPal SChr
**cunninghamiana** ♀H1 CBrP EAmu LPal XBlo

## Arctanthemum (Asteraceae)

§ **arcticum** CKno ECha LBMP NBre NLar WPer
- 'Roseum' EBee GBin
- 'Schwefelglanz' NCGa

## Arcterica see *Pieris*

## Arctium (Asteraceae)

**lappa** CArn GPoy MHer NMir SIde SVic
- 'Takinogawa Long' MNHC

## Arctostaphylos (Ericaceae)

§ **glandulosa** SArc
**uva-ursi** GPoy NLar NMen SPlb WDin
- 'Massachusetts' NLar
- 'Snowcap' MAsh
- 'Vancouver Jade' CDoC EBee GKin LRHS LSRN MAsh SBfd SCoo SLon SPer SPoG SReu SRms SSta SWvt

## *Arctotis* (*Asteraceae*)

Hannah = 'Archnah'[PBR] CSpe ECtt MBNS WHil
Hayley = 'Archley'[PBR] CCCN ECtt MBNS WHil
'Hello' **new** SMrm
× ***hybrida*** 'Apricot' CCCN CHEx ECtt LAst SAga SMrm SVen WHil
- 'China Rose' SMrm
- cream-flowered CHEx SAga
- 'Flame' ♀H1+3 CAby CCCN ECtt LAst MBNS SAga SCoo SMrm SVen WHlf
- 'Midday Sun' ECtt
- 'Red Devil' CCCN LAst LSou MBNS SAga SCoo SMrm SUsu SVen
- 'Wine' CCCN CHEx LAst LSou MBNS SCoo SMrm SRkn SUsu WHil
'Prostrate Raspberry' SAga

## *Ardisia* (*Primulaceae*)

***japonica*** B&SWJ 1032 **new** WCru
- var. ***angusta*** WCot
- var. ***minor*** B&SWJ 1841 WCru
- - B&SWJ 3809 WCru
- 'Miyo-nishiki' (v) WCot
***pusilla*** GBin

## *Areca* (*Arecaceae*)

***triandra*** XBlo

## *Arecastrum* see *Syagrus*

## *Arenaria* (*Caryophyllaceae*)

***aggregata*** subsp. ***erinacea*** GKev
***alfacarensis*** see *A. lithops*
***balearica*** CWCL CYeo ECho EWes LLWG MAsh NSla SPlb SRms
***capillaris*** CTri
***grandiflora*** GKev XLum
***ledebouriana*** EDAr MWat NLar
§ ***lithops*** EPot
***montana*** ♀H4 CMea ECha ECho ECtt EDAr EPfP GGar GMaP LHop LRHS MAsh MDun MGos MLHP NBlu NMen NPri NVic SPet SPlb SRms WAbe WFar WWFP
- 'Avalanche' ECtt
- 'Blizzard' EPfP
***pinifolia*** see *Minuartia circassica*
***pseudacantholimon*** WAbe
***pulvinata*** see *A. lithops*
***purpurascens*** CMea CYeo ECho EPot EWes LLHF MAsh NLar NMen NWCA SRms SRot WFar
- 'Elliott's Variety' NMen WPat
***serpyllifolia*** EDAr
***tetraquetra*** subsp. ***amabilis*** NMen NSla WAbe
***tmolea*** NMen
***verna*** see *Minuartia verna*

## *Arenga* (*Arecaceae*)

***engleri*** EAmu LPal

## *Argania* (*Sapotaceae*)

***spinosa*** WPGP

## *Argemone* (*Papaveraceae*)

***grandiflora*** CSpe SBch SPav
***mexicana*** ELan

## *Argyranthemum* ✿ (*Asteraceae*)

'Anastasia' MAJR
'Beth' GBee MAJR
'Blanche' (Courtyard Series) MAJR
Blazer Rose = 'Supaglow' (Daisy Crazy Series) MAJR
§ 'Blizzard' (d) MAJR
Blushing Rose = 'Supaellie' (Daisy Crazy Series) MAJR
'Bofinger' MAJR
'Bon Bon' MAJR
'Bridesmaid' CCCN MAJR
Bright Carmine = 'Supalight'[PBR] (Daisy Crazy Series) LSou MAJR
***broussonetii*** MAJR
Butterfly = 'Ulyssis' ♀H1+3 LAst MAJR WGor
'Camilla Ponticelli' MAJR
***canariense*** hort. see *A. frutescens* subsp. *canariae*
'Champagne' MAJR
Cherry Harmony = 'Supa532' (Daisy Crazy Series) (d) MAJR
Cherry Love = 'Supacher'[PBR] (Daisy Crazy Series) CCCN EPfP MAJR
'Christy Bell' MAJR
'Citronelle' MAJR
* ***compactum*** MAJR
'Comtesse de Chambord' MAJR
'Cornish Gold' ♀H1+3 CBcs CCCN CWCL MAJR SBfd
***coronopifolium*** MAJR
'Donington Hero' ♀H1+3 MAJR MHom
double pink-flowered **new** SVen
double white-flowered (d) MAJR
'Edelweiss' (d) MAJR
'Ella' MAJR
'Flamingo' see *Rhodanthemum gayanum*
§ ***foeniculaceum*** misapplied CTri ELan WKif
- pink-flowered see *A.* 'Petite Pink'
§ ***foeniculaceum*** (Willd.) Webb & Sch.Bip. MAJR MCot
- 'Royal Haze' ♀H1+3 CCCN CHll MAJR NPer
'Frosty' MAJR
§ ***frutescens*** CHEx MAJR
§ - subsp. ***canariae*** ♀H1+3 CCCN MAJR
- subsp. ***succulentum*** MAJR
- - 'Margaret Lynch' MAJR
'Fuji Sundance' MAJR
'George' MAJR
'Gill's Pink' CCCN MAJR MHom WPnn
'Golden Treasure' GBee MAJR
***gracile*** CHll
- 'Chelsea Girl' ♀H1+3 CCCN CHEx MAJR MCot MHom WKif
'Gretel' MAJR
'Guernsey Pink' MAJR MHom
Gypsy Rose = 'M9/18d' CCCN MAJR
'Icknield Jubilee' MAJR
'Icknield Lemon Ice' MAJR
'Icknield Pink' MAJR
'Icknield Surprise' MAJR
'Icknield Sylvia' MAJR
'Icknield Yellow' MAJR
'Jamaica Primrose' ♀H1+3 CBot CHEx CSpe CTri ECtt MAJR MAsh MCot MHom SAga SDix
'Jamaica Snowstorm' see *A.* 'Snow Storm'
'Julieanne' CBcs CWCL MAJR MBNS SMrm
'Lemon Delight' MAJR

***lemsii*** MAJR
'Levada Cream' ♀H1+3 MAJR MHom
'Libby Brett' MAJR
'Lilliput' MAJR
Machio Double Pink = 'Ohar01245' (Madeira Series) MAJR
§ ***maderense*** ♀H1+3 CHll GBee GCal MAJR SVen
- pale-flowered MAJR
'Mary Cheek' (d) ♀H1+3 CCCN MAJR SRGP
'Mary Wootton' (d) ECtt MAJR MHom
***mawii*** see *Rhodanthemum gayanum*
'Mike's Pink' MAJR
'Millennium Star' MAJR
'Mini-snowflake' see *A.* 'Blizzard'
§ Molimba Duplo Pearl = 'Argydupea' (d) MAJR
Molimba First Blush see *A.* Molimba Duplo Pearl
Monte = 'Ohar01241'PBR (Madeira Series) MAJR
§ 'Mrs F. Sander' (d) MAJR MCot MHom
***ochroleucum*** see *A. maderense*
Pacific Gold = 'Pacargone'PBR (d) CBcs MAJR
§ 'Petite Pink' ♀H1+3 CCCN ECtt MAJR
Ping-Pong = 'Innping'PBR (d) CCCN MAJR
'Pink Australian' (d) CCCN MAJR MHom
'Pink Delight' see *A.* 'Petite Pink'
'Pink Pixie' MAJR
Pink Wonder = 'Supalily' (Daisy Crazy Series) MAJR
***pinnatifidium*** subsp. ***succulentum*** MAJR
Polly = 'Innpolly'PBR MAJR SBfd
Pomponette Pink = 'Supa392'PBR (d) CBcs
'Porto Moritz' MAJR
'Powder Puff' (d) ECtt MAJR
'Primrose Petite' (Courtyard Series) MAJR
prostrate double pink-flowered (d) MAJR
'Reflection Pink' **new** NPri
'Rising Sun' MAJR
'Saimi' MAJR
Santana = 'Ohmadsant' (Madeira Series) MAJR
São Martinho = 'Ohmadsaom' (Madeira Series) MAJR
São Vicente = 'Ohmadsavi'PBR (Madeira Series) MAJR
'Silver Leaf' MAJR
'Silver Queen' see *A. foeniculaceum* misapplied
§ 'Snow Storm' ♀H1+3 LAst MAJR MHom WPnn
'Snowball' MAJR
'Snowflake' misapplied see *A.* 'Mrs F. Sander'
Sole Mio = 'Supa3047' CWCL MAJR
'Starlight' MAJR
'Starlight Red' (Daisy Crazy Series) **new** MAJR
Strawberry Pink = 'Suparosa' (Daisy Crazy Series) EPfP
'Sugar and Ice' (d) CCCN MAJR
'Sugar Baby'PBR (d) CCCN
Sugar Cheer = 'Cobeer' (d) MAJR
'Sugar Lace' MAJR
Sultan's Dream = 'Supadream' (Daisy Crazy Series) EPfP
Sultan's Lemon = 'Supalem'PBR (Daisy Crazy Series) EPfP MAJR
Sultan's Pride = 'Cosupri' (Daisy Crazy Series) MAJR
'Summer Angel' (d) MAJR
'Summer Cloud' MCot
'Summer Eyes' (d) GBee
'Summer Melody'PBR (d) CBcs CCCN MAJR
'Summer Pink' CCCN MAJR
'Summer Stars' (Daisy Crazy Series) (d) MAJR
Summersong Lemon = 'Supa601' (Daisy Crazy Series) LSou MAJR
Summersong White = 'Supa594' (Daisy Crazy Series) LSou MAJR
'Summertime' MAJR
Summit Pink = 'Cobsing'PBR (Daisy Crazy Series) EPfP MAJR
'Sweety' MAJR
'Tweeny' MAJR
'Tweety' MAJR
'Vancouver' (d) ♀H1+3 CBot CCCN CHll CWCL ECtt EShb LAst MAJR SBHP
Vanilla Ripple = 'Supabright' (Daisy Crazy Series) MAJR
* 'Vera' CCCN
'Wellwood Park' CCCN
'Weymouth Pink' MAJR
'Weymouth Surprise' MAJR
White Blush = 'Supamorni' (Daisy Crazy Series) MAJR
White Crystal = 'Supagem' (Daisy Crazy Series) MAJR
'White Spider' CCCN ELan GBee MAJR MHom
'White Star' (d) MAJR
'Whiteknights' ♀H1+3 GBee MAJR
'Yellow Australian' (d) CCCN MAJR

## *Argyrocytisus* see *Cytisus*

## *Arisaema* ✿ (Araceae)

ACE 2130 NWCA
C&H 7026 LWSt NMen
CC 4904 CPLG
CC 5511 CPLG
Chen Yi 14 WCot
Chen Yi 97 WCot
***amurense*** CElw CLAP EBee ECho GAuc GCal LAma MMoz WFar
§ - subsp. ***robustum*** ECho LWSt NMen WCot
* ***angustatum*** var. ***amurense*** GEdr LAma
- var. ***peninsulae*** LWSt
***asperatum*** LAma WCot
***biauriculatum*** see *A. wattii*
***brachyspathum*** see *A. heterophyllum*
***brevipes*** CPLG GEdr
***candidissimum*** ♀H4 Widely available
- from Yunnan **new** WCot
- pink-flowered NWCA
- white-flowered GEdr LAma LEdu WCot

| | |
|---|---|
| ***ciliatum*** | CDes CWCL EBee EBla ELon GEdr LAma LEdu MMoz MNrw NHar NLar SRot WCot |
| - var. ***liubaense*** | CAby CFwr CGHE CMea CWCL EPot EWld MMoz WIvy |
| - - CT 369 | CLAP CPLG CSpr EBee EPfP LWst SCnR SDys SKHP WCot WPGP WSHC |
| - variegated (v) | WCot |
| aff. ***ciliatum*** new | WCot |
| ***concinnum*** | CFir EAmu EBee EPot EWld GAuc GBin GEdr GGar LAma NHol NLar XLum |
| ***consanguineum*** | CAby CDes CFwr CGHE CHEx CLAP CPLG EPfP GBin GCal GEdr GGar GKev LAma LWst MLLN MMoz NHar NHol NLar NSla WCot WFar WPGP XLum |
| - B&SWJ 071 | WCru |
| - CLD 1519 | ECho EBee NMen WCot |
| - GG 84193 | WCot |
| - PJ 277 | WCot |
| - dark-flowered | WCot |
| - 'J. Balis' | WCot |
| - subsp. ***kelung-insulare*** B&SWJ 256 | WCru |
| - 'Qinling' | WCot |
| - variegated (v) | WCot |
| ***costatum*** | CCCN CHEx CLAP EAmu EBee ECho EPfP EPot GBin GEdr GKev LAma LEdu MMoz NHol NMen WPGP XLum |
| ***dilatatum*** | LAma |
| ***dracontium*** | CLAP EBee ECho LAma NLar NMen XLum |
| ***ehimense*** | LWst |
| ***elephas*** | EBee ECho LAma LWst |
| ***erubescens*** | NLar |
| - marbled-leaved | GEdr |
| aff. ***erubescens*** | WCot |
| ***exappendiculatum*** | CDes EBee MMoz WPGP |
| ***fargesii*** | CLAP CPLG ECho GEdr LAma LWst MMoz SChF SKHP WCot |
| ***flavum*** | CDes CGHE CLAP CWCL EBee ECho ELon EPfP EWld GCal LAma LWst MMoz NHar NHol NLar NMen NWCA SPlb WCot WPGP |
| - CC 6303 | ITim |
| - subsp. ***abbreviatum*** CC 6300 | ITim |
| * - ***minus*** | NWCA |
| - tall | ECho |
| - subsp. ***tibeticum*** | EBee |
| ***formosanum*** B&SWJ 280 | WCru |
| - var. ***bicolorifolium*** B&SWJ 3528 | WCru |
| - f. ***stenophyllum*** B&SWJ 1477 | WCru |
| § ***franchetianum*** | CPLG GEdr LAma WCot |
| ***fraternum*** | LWst WCot |
| ***galeatum*** | EBee ECho EPot LAma NHol WCot XLum |
| ***grapsospadix*** B&SWJ 7000 | WCru |
| § ***griffithii*** | CBro EBee ECho GAuc GEdr GGar LAma LRHS NHol SBrd XLum |
| - 'Numbuq' | GCra |
| - var. ***pradhanii*** | EBee GAuc LWst XLum |
| ***helleborifolium*** | see *A. tortuosum* |
| § ***heterophyllum*** | GEdr LWst |

| | |
|---|---|
| ***intermedium*** | EBee ECho GEdr GGar LAma MNrw NHol NMen |
| ***iyoanum*** | GEdr LWst |
| subsp. ***nakaianum*** | |
| ***jacquemontii*** | CAby CLAP EBee EBla ECho EWld GCra GEdr NLar NMen WCot WPGP |
| - CC 5184 | ITim |
| aff. ***jacquemontii*** MECC 29 | NMen |
| - MECC 76 | NMen |
| ***japonicum*** Blume | see *A. serratum* var. *mayebarae* |
| ***japonicum*** Komarov | see *A. serratum* |
| ***jinshajiangense*** | CPLG |
| ***kishidae*** | GEdr LWst |
| ***kiushianum*** | EBee EFEx GEdr LAma LWst MMoz WCot |
| ***leschenaultii*** | LAma LWst |
| ***lichiangense*** | LAma WCot |
| § ***lobatum*** | CPLG EBee LAma |
| ***maximowiczii*** | EBee GEdr LWst |
| ***meleagris*** | LAma |
| ***negishii*** | LWst |
| § ***nepenthoides*** | CBcs CBro EAmu EBee ECho EPot GBin GEdr GGar GKev ITim LAma LRHS MMoz MNrw NHol NLar SBrd XLum |
| ***ochraceum*** | see *A. nepenthoides* |
| ***omeiense*** | WCot |
| ***onoticum*** | see *A. lobatum* |
| ***petelotii*** B&SWJ 9706 | WCru |
| ***polyphyllum*** B&SWJ 3904 | WCru |
| ***propinquum*** | CLAP ECho GBin LAma NMen WCot |
| ***purpureogaleatum*** | see *A. franchetianum* |
| ***rhizomatum*** | LAma |
| ***rhombiforme*** | LAma LWst |
| ***ringens*** misapplied | see *A. amurense* subsp. *robustum* |
| ***ringens*** ambig. | SKHP |
| ***ringens*** (Thunberg) Schott | CDes EFEx GEdr LAma LEdu LWst |
| - f. ***praecox*** B&SWJ 1515 | WCru |
| - f. ***sieboldii*** B&SWJ 551 | WCru |
| ***robustum*** | see *A. amurense* subsp. *robustum* |
| ***saxatile*** | LAma LWst WCot |
| ***sazensoo*** | GEdr LAma LRHS LWst |
| § ***serratum*** | ECho LAma MMoz MNrw |
| § - var. ***mayebarae*** | LWst |
| ***sikokianum*** | CBcs CBro EBee ECho EFEx EPPr GEdr LAma LRHS SKHP |
| - green-flowered | LRHS |
| - var. ***serratum*** | CFir |
| - variegated (v) | GEdr LRHS LWst |
| ***speciosum*** | CHEx CPLG EAmu EBee ECho EPot EWld GAbr GEdr GGar LAma LRHS NHol NLar NMen SBrd SPlb WCot WFar XLum |
| - CC 3100 | WCot |
| * - var. ***magnificum*** | EBee EWld GEdr GKev NHol WCot |
| - var. ***mirabile*** | EBee GEdr |
| * - var. ***sikkimense*** | LAma |
| ***taiwanense*** | CLAP SKHP WCot |
| - B&SWJ 269 | WCru |
| - B&SWJ 356 | WCot |
| - var. ***brevipedunculatum*** B&SWJ 1859 | WCru |
| - f. ***cinereum*** B&SWJ 19121 | WCru |
| - silver-leaved | WCot |
| ***tashiroi*** | GEdr LWst |
| ***ternatipartitum*** | GEdr LWst |

***thunbergii*** EFEx EPPr LRHS WCot
- subsp. ***autumnale*** B&SWJ 1425 WCru
- subsp. ***urashima*** CLAP EBee EFEx GEdr LAma LWst WCot

§ ***tortuosum*** CBro CLAP CPLG EAmu EBee ECha ECho EWld GBin GEdr GGar LAma LEdu LWst MNrw NEgg NHol NLar NWCA SBrd SChF WCot WPGP XLum
- CC 1452 CPou
- CC 1760 WCot
- from high altitude NMen

***tosaense*** LWst
***triphyllum*** CElw CLAP CPLG EBee ECho EPot GGar LAma LEdu MMoz NHol NLar NWCA SPlb WCot WFar WPnP
- subsp. ***stewardsonii*** EBee LWst NMen
- subsp. ***triphyllum*** var. ***atrorubens*** CLAP

§ ***utile*** EAmu ECho EPot GAuc GBin GEdr LAma XLum
- CC 3101 WCot

***verrucosum*** see *A. griffithii*
- var. ***utile*** see *A. utile*

§ ***wattii*** LAma
***yamatense*** LWst
- subsp. ***sugimotoi*** LAma

***yunnanense*** CLAP LAma

## *Arisarum* (*Araceae*)

***proboscideum*** Widely available
***vulgare*** ECho WCot
- from Crete ECho
- * - f. ***maculatum*** ECho
- subsp. ***simorrhinum*** ECho
- subsp. ***vulgare*** ECho

## *Aristea* (*Iridaceae*)

sp. GGal
***africana*** 'Worcester' ECho
***angolensis*** EBee
***ecklonii*** CDes CHEx CPLG CPou CPrp CTca CTrC CTsd EBee EPri EShb IGor MSCN SGar SHom WBor WCot WDyG WHil
- GWJ 9469 WCru

***ensifolia*** ELan MWea SAga WSHC
***grandis*** CFir WCot
§ ***major*** CCtw CHll CPrp CSpe CTrC SGar
- pink-flowered CPrp EPri

***spiralis*** 'Paarl' ECho
***thyrsiflora*** see *A. major*
***woodii*** 'Clarens' ECho

## *Aristolochia* (*Aristolochiaceae*)

***baetica*** CArn CPLG SKHP
***californica*** LEdu SKHP
***chilensis*** CCCN
***clematitis*** CArn ECho GPoy LEdu LPla
***cucurbitifolia*** B&SWJ 7043 WCru
***delavayi*** CHEx SVen
***durior*** see *A. macrophylla*
***gigantea*** CCCN CHll
***grandiflora*** CCCN CHll
***griffithii*** B&SWJ 2118 WCru
***heterophylla*** see *A. kaempferi* f. *heterophylla*
***kaempferi*** CCCN
- B&SWJ 293 WCru
- § - f. ***heterophylla*** B&SWJ 3109 WCru

× ***kewensis*** CCCN
***liukiuensis*** B&SWJ 4960 WCru
§ ***macrophylla*** CArn CBcs CBot CCCN CHEx CMac EBee EPfP MRav NEgg NPal SLim WDin
***manshuriensis*** B&SWJ 962 WCru
***moupinensis*** BWJ 8181 WCru
***onoei*** B&SWJ 4960 WCru
***pearcei*** CCCN
***rotunda*** SKHP
***sempervirens*** SKHP WDin WSHC
***sipho*** see *A. macrophylla*
***tomentosa*** SKHP

## *Aristotelia* (*Elaeocarpaceae*)

§ ***chilensis*** LEdu WAle
- 'Variegata' (v) CCCN CMac CWib EBee GQui MAsh SEND SPlb

***fruticosa*** IGor
- (f) ECou
- (m) ECou
- black-fruited (f) ECou
- white-fruited (f) ECou

***macqui*** see *A. chilensis*
***peduncularis*** CPLG
***serrata*** ECou SVen
- (f) ECou
- (m) ECou

## *Armeria* (*Plumbaginaceae*)

§ ***alliacea*** (Cav.) Hoffsgg. & Link. CSpe ECha LRHS
- f. ***leucantha*** SRms WMoo

***alpina*** GAuc MWat
Bees' hybrids WMoo
'Bloodgood' ECho ECtt
'Brutus' EDAr MAvo SUsu
***caespitosa*** see *A. juniperifolia*
- 'Bevan's Variety' see *A. juniperifolia* 'Bevan's Variety'

***euscadiensis*** CSpe
Joystick Series GJos NVic
- 'Joystick Lilac Shades' EBee EDAr EPfP EShb LRHS NLar
- 'Joystick Pink' EDAr SWal
- 'Joystick Red' EBee EDAr EPfP EShb LRHS WHil
- 'Joystick White' EPfP LRHS NLar

§ ***juniperifolia*** ♀H4 CMea ECho ELan EPfP EPot GMaP LBee LRHS MAsh MHer MWat NMen NSla NWCA SPoG SRms XLum
- 'Alba' CMea CYeo ECho ELan EPfP GBin GKev GMaP LRHS MAsh MHer NMen NWCA SBch SPoG SRms WAbe WFar WHoo WThu
- § - 'Bevan's Variety' ♀H4 CYeo ECha ECho ECtt ELan EPfP GGar GMaP LEdu MMuc MWat NLar NMen NRya SPoG SRms SRot WAbe WFar WHoo WNew WPat
- 'Brookside' EPot GJos
- dark-flowered WAbe
- 'New Zealand Form' see *A. juniperifolia* 'Sugar Baby'
- rose-flowered ITim
- § - 'Sugar Baby' **new** CSpe

***juniperifolia*** × ***maritima*** SBch
§ ***maritima*** CArn CHab ECho EPfP EWil GJos LAst LRHS MNHC MSCN NEgg SPet WCFE WFar WHfH WJek WMoo WNew

| | | |
|---|---|---|
| | - from Andes new | GLam |
| | - 'Alba' | CArn CBcs CTri ECha ECho ELan EPfP GJos GKev GMaP LEdu LRHS MCot MLHP MMuc NBlu NRya SBfd SEND SPet SPlb SPoG SWal WCFE WFar WMoo WNew |
| | - 'Armada Rose' | LRHS |
| | - 'Bloodstone' | CTri ECho ECtt ELan MAsh MWat |
| | - 'Corsica' | CTri ECha NBir SBch WFar |
| | - Düsseldorf Pride | see *A. maritima* 'Düsseldorfer Stolz' |
| § | - 'Düsseldorfer Stolz' | CElw COIW ECha ECho ECtt EDAr ELan EPfP GGar GKev GMaP LHop LRHS MCot MLHP NDov NMen NPri NWad SPoG WNew XLum |
| | - 'Laucheana' | SBch WHoo WMoo |
| | - 'Nifty Thrifty' (v) | CBod CMea CTri EBee ECho ECtt EHoe EWes LRHS MHer SCoo SIde SPoG SRot WFar WPat |
| * | - 'Pink Lusitanica' | LBMP LRHS |
| | - 'Rosa Stolz' | NDov |
| | - 'Rossi' | NWad |
| I | - 'Rubrifolia' | Widely available |
| I | - 'Rubrifolia Compacta' new | GLam |
| | - 'Ruby Glow' | CTri SBch |
| | - 'Schöne von Fellbach' new | XLum |
| | - 'Splendens' | CBcs COIW CTri ECho EDAr EPfP GGar GMaP LAst MAsh MGos MMuc NBlu NMir NRya NVic SBch SBfd SBrd SEND SPoG SWal WFar WMoo WPer XLum |
| | - 'Splendens Alba' | XLum |
| | - 'Varretu' new | GLam |
| | - 'Vindictive' ♀H4 | CMea CTri EPfP |
| | ***morisii*** | SBch |
| | 'Ornament' | SBfd |
| | ***plantaginea*** | see *A. alliacea* (Cav.) Hoffsgg. & Link. |
| | ***pseudarmeria*** | ECho ELan EPfP GCal MWhi NBlu XLum |
| | - 'Alba' new | SSvw |
| | - 'Drumstick White' | WPer |
| | - hybrids | CTri ELan GGar |
| | 'Vesuvius' | NDov WCot XLum |
| | ***vulgaris*** | see *A. maritima* |
| | ***welwitschii*** | IFoB SRms |
| | 'Westacre Beauty' | EWes |

## *Armoracia* (*Brassicaceae*)

| | | |
|---|---|---|
| § | ***rusticana*** | CArn CBod CHby CPrp CSev CTri ELau EPfP GAbr GGar GPoy ILis MHer MMuc MNHC NPer NPri SBfd SIde SVic WHer WJek |
| | - 'Variegata' (v) | ELau EWhm GCal IFoB LHop MAvo NSti SMad WHer WJek WMoo |

## *Arnica* (*Asteraceae*)

| | | |
|---|---|---|
| | ***angustifolia*** subsp. ***alpina*** | SRms |
| | - subsp. ***iljinii*** | NBir |
| | ***chamissonis*** Schmidt | see *A. sachalinensis* |
| | ***chamissonis*** Less. | CHby EBee MNHC NLar WJek XLum |
| | ***montana*** | CArn EOHP GPoy MHer MNHC NMun SRms SWat |
| § | ***sachalinensis*** RBS 0206 | EPPr |

## *Aronia* (*Rosaceae*)

| | | |
|---|---|---|
| | ***arbutifolia*** | CBcs CDul CTri EPfP LSRN MBlu SGol SLon SPlb WDin |
| | - 'Erecta' | CDul EBee ELan EPfP GBin LHop LRHS MBlu MBri MMuc NLar SBfd SLPl SRms SSpi |
| | ***melanocarpa*** | CDul CMCN CSpe CTsd CWib EBee ELan EPfP EWTr GKin IGor LEdu LRHS MAsh WDin WFar |
| | - 'Autumn Magic' | CBcs CDoC CPMA EBee ELan EPfP GBin IVic LAst LHop LRHS MAsh MMuc NMyG SCoo SLPl SLon SPer |
| | - var. ***grandifolia*** | CPMA |
| | - 'Hugin' | CAgr CPMA NLar |
| * | - 'Red Viking' | GGar |
| | × ***prunifolia*** | CDoC GAbr LEdu |
| | - 'Aron' (F) | CPMA |
| | - 'Brilliant' | CDoC CTri EBee EMil EPfP LRHS NEgg NLar SCoo SPer SPur |
| | - 'Nero' (F) | CAgr GBin NLar |
| | - 'Serina' (F) | CPMA NLar |
| | - 'Viking' (F) | CAgr CAlb CPMA EBee EBtc ECrN EPfP LBuc LHop LRHS MBlu NBro NLar SLim WDin |

## *Aronia* × *Sorbus* (*Rosaceae*)

| | | |
|---|---|---|
| § | 'Burka' | WPat |

## *Arracacia* (*Apiaceae*)

| | | |
|---|---|---|
| | B&SWJ 9023 from Guatemala | WCru |

## *Arrhenatherum* (*Poaceae*)

| | | |
|---|---|---|
| | ***elatius*** new | CHab |
| | - var. ***bulbosum*** | WFar |
| | - - 'Variegatum' (v) | EBee EHoe ELan EPPr GBin GKev GMaP LBMP LEdu MMoz MMuc MWhi NBid NOak NOrc SEND SWal WFar WMoo WPtf WWEG |

## *Artemisia* ✿ (*Asteraceae*)

| | | |
|---|---|---|
| | RBS 0207 | CPLG |
| | from Taiwan | WHer |
| § | ***abrotanum*** ♀H4 | Widely available |
| | ***absinthium*** | CArn CEls CHab CPbn CSev CWan ELan GPoy MHer MNHC NSti SIde SVic SWat WJek XSen |
| | - 'Lambrook Giant' | CEls |
| | - 'Lambrook Mist' ♀H3-4 | CEls CMac CPrp CSev EBee ECtt ELan EPfP GCal GMac GQue LRHS MRav SWat WMnd WWEG XLum |
| | - 'Lambrook Silver' ♀H4 | CArn CEls CPLG CSam EBee ECha ELan EPfP EWTr GMaP LHop LRHS LSRN MHer MMuc MRav NBro SEND SLim SPer SWat SWvt WDin WFar WMnd WPer WWEG |
| | - 'Silver Ghost' | CEls |
| | ***afra*** | CArn CEls EBee IFro |
| § | ***alba*** | CEls EOHP GPoy MHer SIde WJek WPer XSen |
| § | - 'Canescens' ♀H4 | CArn CEls CSam CTri EBee ECha ECtt ELan EPfP GMaP LAst LBMP MAsh MHer MRav SDix SEND SPer WAul WCFE WCot WFar WMnd WPer |
| | ***annua*** | CEls SIde |
| | ***anomala*** | CArn CEls |
| | ***arborescens*** ♀H3 | CArn CEls CMHG NEgg SDix SPer WDin WKif |
| | - 'Brass Band' | see *A.* 'Powis Castle' |
| | - 'Faith Raven' | CEls EBee EPfP GBin MBNS WFar |
| | - 'Little Mice' | CEls EBee SSvw WWEG |
| | - 'Porquerolles' | CEls |

| | | |
|---|---|---|
| | ***argyi*** | CEls |
| § | ***armeniaca*** | CEls ECho LRHS XSen |
| | ***assoana*** | see *A. caucasica* |
| | ***atrata*** | CEls |
| | ***barrelieri*** | CEls |
| | ***caerulescens*** | see *Seriphidium caerulescens* |
| | ***californica*** | CEls |
| | - 'Canyon Gray' | CEls |
| | ***campestris*** | XLum XSen |
| | - subsp. ***borealis*** | CEls |
| | - subsp. ***campestris*** | CEls |
| | - subsp. ***maritima*** | CEls |
| | - - from Wales | CEls |
| | ***camphorata*** | see *A. alba* |
| | ***cana*** | see *Seriphidium canum* |
| | ***canariensis*** | see *A. thuscula* |
| | ***canescens*** misapplied | see *A. alba* 'Canescens' |
| | ***canescens*** Willd. | see *A. armeniaca* |
| | ***capillaris*** | CArn CEls XLum |
| § | ***caucasica*** ♀H3-4 | CEls ECho EPot EWes MBrN MHer SChF SPhx SRms SRot WPer XSen |
| | - ***caucasica*** | CEls WFar |
| | ***chamaemelifolia*** | CEls MHer NBre WJek XSen |
| | ***cretacea*** | see *Seriphidium nutans* |
| | ***discolor*** Dougl. ex Besser | see *A. michauxiana* |
| | ***douglasiana*** | CEls XLum |
| | - 'Valerie Finnis' | see *A. ludoviciana* 'Valerie Finnis' |
| | ***dracunculus*** | ECha MCot MNHC MRav NVic SBfd SPlb SWal WBrk WFar WHfH WPer |
| | - French | CArn CBod CEls CHby CSev CWan EGHP ELau EWhm GPoy LEdu MHer NPri SBfd SEND SIde WGwG WJek XLum |
| | - Russian | CEls SVic |
| | ***ferganensis*** | see *Seriphidium ferganense* |
| | ***filifolia*** | CEls XSen |
| | ***fragrans*** Willd. | see *Seriphidium fragrans* |
| | ***frigida*** ♀H3-4 | CEls |
| | ***genipi*** | CEls |
| | ***glacialis*** | CEls |
| | ***gmelinii*** | CEls |
| | ***gnaphalodes*** | see *A. ludoviciana* |
| | ***gorgonum*** | CEls CSpr EWes SEND |
| | 'Hausserman' **new** | XLum |
| | ***herba-alba*** | CEls XSen |
| | 'Huntington' | CEls WFar |
| | ***japonica*** | CEls |
| | ***kawakamii*** B&SWJ 088 | WCru |
| | ***kitadakensis*** | CEls |
| | - 'Guizhou' | see *A. lactiflora* Guizhou Group |
| | ***laciniata*** | CEls |
| | ***lactiflora*** ♀H4 | CDoy CEls CPrp EBee ECha ECtt ELan GAbr GBee GMaP MRav NGdn NOrc SDix SMrm SPer SRms WFar WHfH WMoo WTin XLum |
| | - 'Elfenbein' | EBee GBin GCal LHop LPla |
| § | - Guizhou Group | Widely available |
| | - - 'Dark Delight' | CAby ECtt EWes GBin NBPC SPoG |
| | - 'Jim Russell' | CDes CElw ECtt EWes MAvo NBre NDov WWFP |
| | - ***purpurea*** | see *A. lactiflora* Guizhou Group |
| | - 'Stonyford' | MSCN |
| | - 'Weisses Wunder' | EBee |
| | ***lagocephala*** | CEls |
| | ***lanata*** Willd. non Lam. | see *A. caucasica* |
| | ***laxa*** | see *A. umbelliformis* |
| § | ***ludoviciana*** | CEls ELan ETod GBee IFoB NLar NOrc NPer SBch SRms WCFE XLum |
| | - var. ***latifolia*** | see *A. ludoviciana* subsp. *ludoviciana* var. *latiloba* |

| | | |
|---|---|---|
| | - subsp. ***ludoviciana*** var. ***incompta*** | CEls LAst |
| N | - - var. ***latiloba*** | CEls EHoe LHop NBro NPnk SWvt WCot WHoo WPer |
| | - subsp. ***mexicana*** var. ***albula*** | CEls SMrm WFar |
| | - 'Silver Queen' ♀H4 | Widely available |
| N | - 'Valerie Finnis' ♀H4 | Widely available |
| | ***maritima*** | see *Seriphidium maritimum* |
| | ***mauiensis*** | CEls |
| § | ***michauxiana*** | CEls EBee NSti XSen |
| | ***molinieri*** | CEls XSen |
| | ***mutellina*** | see *A. umbelliformis* |
| | ***niitakayamensis*** | CEls |
| | ***nitida*** | CEls |
| | ***nutans*** | see *Seriphidium nutans* |
| | ***palmeri*** hort. | see *A. ludoviciana* |
| | ***pamirica*** | CEls |
| | aff. ***parviflora*** CLD 1531 | CEls |
| | ***pedemontana*** | see *A. caucasica* |
| | ***pontica*** | CArn CEls CWan EBee ECha ECrN EHoe ELan GMaP GPoy MBNS MHer MNHC MRav NBro NSti SPer SSvw WCAu WFar WHfH WHoo WJek WPer WWEG XSen |
| § | 'Powis Castle' ♀H3 | Widely available |
| | ***princeps*** | CArn CEls ELau SIde WTou |
| | ***procera*** | see *A. abrotanum* |
| | ***purshiana*** | see *A. ludoviciana* |
| | ***pycnocephala*** | CEls |
| | - 'David's Choice' | CEls SMad |
| | ***ramosa*** | CEls |
| | 'Rosenschleier' | EWes LPla MAvo NBre WFar WPGP WTin WWEG |
| | ***schmidtiana*** ♀H4 | CEls ECha MWat NOrc SRms WKif |
| | - 'Nana' ♀H4 | Widely available |
| | - 'Nana Attraction' | LRHS |
| | 'Sea Foam' | LRHS |
| | ***selengensis*** | CEls |
| | ***splendens*** misapplied | see *A. alba* 'Canescens' |
| | ***splendens*** Willd. | ELan SPhx |
| | - var. ***brachyphylla*** | MAsh |
| | ***stelleriana*** | CArn CEls CTri ECha GBee GKev IFoB LBMP LHop MAvo MCot MHer NBro NPri SPer SRms WCAu |
| | - RBS 0207 | CEls NLar |
| N | - 'Boughton Silver' | CEls EBee ECtt EHoe ELan EPfP GBBs GMaP GMac IKil LRHS MCot MRav NSti NWad SBfd SMrm SPer SRms SWvt WFar WMnd WWEG |
| N | - 'Mori' | see *A. stelleriana* 'Boughton Silver' |
| | - 'Nana' | CEls SWvt |
| | - 'Prostrata' | see *A. stelleriana* 'Boughton Silver' |
| | - 'Silver Brocade' | see *A. stelleriana* 'Boughton Silver' |
| | ***taurica*** | CEls |
| § | ***thuscula*** | CEls |
| | ***tridentata*** | see *Seriphidium tridentatum* |
| § | ***umbelliformis*** | CEls |
| | ***vallesiaca*** | see *Seriphidium vallesiacum* |
| | ***verlotiorum*** | CEls |
| | ***vulgaris*** L. | CArn CEls ELau GPoy MHer MNHC WHer |
| | - 'Cragg-Barber Eye' (v) | EBee NBid SAga |
| | - Oriental Limelight = 'Janlim' (v) | CEls COIW EBee ECtt EHoe EPfP GAbr LBMP LEdu LHop LRHS MCCP MWhi NBir NEgg SBfd SWvt WFar WHer WJek |
| | - 'Variegata' (v) | CEls CEnt EBee EPfP NBir WFar WHer WMoo XLum |
| | × ***wurzellii*** | CEls |

## *Arthropodium* (*Asparagaceae*)

| | |
|---|---|
| ***candidum*** | CBot ECGP ECho ECou EHoe MMuc MSCN NWCA |
| - 'Cappucino' | CBcs |
| - 'Maculatum' | ECho GEdr LEdu SBrt SPlb WWEG |
| - ***purpureum*** | ECho GGar IKil NWCA |
| ***cirratum*** | CHEx CSpe ECho ECou GGar IKil LEdu MHer SBch SWal |
| - 'Matapouri Bay' | CAbb CBcs CDes CHEx ECre MAvo WPGP |
| ***milleflorum*** | SBrt |
| ***minus*** | CPLG ECou |

## *Arthrostylidium* (*Poaceae*)

| | |
|---|---|
| ***naibuense*** | CDTJ |

## artichoke, globe see *Cynara cardunculus* Scolymus Group

## artichoke, Jerusalem see *Helianthus tuberosus*

## *Arum* (*Araceae*)

| | |
|---|---|
| ***alpinum*** | see *A. cylindraceum* |
| ***besserianum*** | ECho LWst |
| ***byzantinum*** | ECho LWst |
| 'Chameleon' | ELon EPPr MAvo MNrw NBir NLar SKHP SMad SPer WCot WCru WFar WHil WHoo WPGP WTin WWEG |
| § ***concinnatum*** | EBee ECho NLar SChr SKHP |
| - black-spotted | ECho |
| - 'Mount Ida' | ECho EWld SKHP |
| - purple | ECho |
| - variegated (v) | WCot |
| ***concinnatum* × *cyrenaicum*** | ECho |
| - - from Crete | LWst |
| ***cornutum*** | see *Sauromatum venosum* |
| ***creticum*** | CArn CBro CFir CMea CSpe EBee ECha ECho EPot GCal MNrw MRav NLar SCnR SKHP SRot SUsu WBor WFar |
| - MS 696 | MNrw |
| - FCC form | see *A. creticum* 'Karpathos' |
| - 'Karpathos' | CPLG ECho GKev LAma LWst MMoz SKHP WAbe WCot WPGP |
| - 'Marmaris White' | SCnR WCot |
| - yellow-spotted | NBir WFar WIvy |
| ***creticum* × *italicum*** | WFar |
| § ***cylindraceum*** | ECho |
| ***cyrenaicum*** | EBee ECho EWld LEdu LWst WCot |
| - from Crete | ECho |
| - MS 696 from Crete | WCot |
| ***dioscoridis*** | CPom ECho EWes EWld GCra GKev MMoz NLar SKHP WCot |
| - JCA 195.197 | WCot |
| - var. ***cyprium*** | EBee ECho GKev LWst |
| § - var. ***dioscoridis*** | LWst WCot |
| - - JCA | LWst |
| - var. ***liepoldtii*** | see *A. dioscoridis* var. *dioscoridis* |
| - var. ***philistaeum*** | LWst |
| - var. ***smithii*** | see *A. dioscoridis* var. *dioscoridis* |
| - var. ***syriacum*** new | LWst |
| ***dracunculus*** | see *Dracunculus vulgaris* |
| ***elongatum*** | CPom |
| - RS 274/87 | EBee LWst |
| ***euxinum*** | ECho |
| ***hygrophilum*** | CPom LWst |
| ***italicum*** | CArn CEnt CLAP CTri ECho GAbr LAma LBMP NBPC NLar SDeJ SWat WCot WFar WSHC WShi |
| - subsp. ***albispathum*** | CHid CPom EBee ECho GLam MMoz WCot WFar WPGP |
| - 'Black Spot' | EPPr |
| - black-spotted | ECho SCnR WFar |
| - 'Edward Dougal' new | WCot |
| - giant | ECho WHil |
| - 'Green Marble' | CBct SEND WFar WWEG |
| - subsp. ***italicum*** | CBct EBee ECho EPla EShb NWCA WBrk |
| - - 'Bill Baker' | WFar |
| - - 'Cyclops' | CHid WWEG |
| § - - 'Marmoratum' ♀H4 | Widely available |
| - - 'Sparkler' | WCot |
| - - 'Spotted Jack' | EBee MNrw WCot WCru WWEG |
| - - 'Tiny' | CFir CPLG GCal SCnR SWvt WFar WWEG |
| § - - 'White Winter' | CElw ECGP WBrk WCot |
| - 'Nancy Lindsay' | MMoz |
| - subsp. ***neglectum*** | SChr WFar |
| - - 'Miss Janay Hall' (v) | EBee EWes LLHF MDKP MMoz WCot |
| - 'Pictum' | see *A. italicum* subsp. *italicum* 'Marmoratum' |
| - 'Splish Splash' | CAvo |
| ***jacquemontii*** | ECho |
| ***korolkowii*** | GAuc |
| from Kazakhstan new | |
| ***maculatum*** | CArn CRWN EBee ECho EPot GKev GPoy LAma MHer MRav NLar NMir WHer WShi |
| - 'Painted Lady' (v) | WCot |
| - 'Pleddel' | MRav |
| ***nickelii*** | see *A. concinnatum* |
| § ***nigrum*** | CPom ECho EWes LLHF WGwG |
| - CE&H 524 | LWst |
| ***orientale*** | EPot |
| - VV RR.55 | LWst |
| ***palaestinum*** | EBee LWst |
| ***petteri*** misapplied | see *A. nigrum* |
| ***pictum*** | CLAP CMac CPLG EBee ECho EWes LEdu LLHF LWst WCot |
| - from Majorca | WCot |
| - 'Taff's Form' | see *A. italicum* subsp. *italicum* 'White Winter' |
| ***purpureospathum*** | CPom EBee ECho EPPr EWld GKev WCot |
| - VV CR.543 | LWst |
| ***rupicola* var. *rupicola*** | ECho LWst |
| - var. ***virescens*** | ECho LWst |

## *Aruncus* ✿ (*Rosaceae*)

| | |
|---|---|
| ***aethusifolius*** ♀H4 | Widely available |
| - 'Little Gem' | ECho WCru |
| ***asiaticus*** B&SWJ 8624 | WCru |
| ***dioicus*** | Widely available |
| § - (m) ♀H4 | CDoC CRow ECha ELan EPla MBNS MRav MWts NBro NSti SBfd SMad SPer SRms SWat WMoo WPer |
| - var. ***acuminatus*** | EBee |
| - Child of Two Worlds | see *A. dioicus* 'Zweiweltenkind' |
| - 'Glasnevin' | CSev ECtt GBee MRav WFar |
| - var. ***kamtschaticus*** | EBee EWes LRHS MCCP MGos NBre NHol NLar WHrl |
| - - RBS 0208 | NGdn |
| - 'Kneiffii' | Widely available |
| § - 'Zweiweltenkind' | CEnt EBee LRHS NBre NLar SMad WCot |

| | | |
|---|---|---|
| | 'Guinea Fowl' | EBee GQue LSou MAvo NCGa NHar WHoo |
| | 'Horatio' | EBee GBin IPot ITim LPla MMuc NDov SAga SPhx SUsu WCot |
| | 'Johannifest' | CDes EBee ECtt GBin IPot NDov WCot |
| | 'Misty Lace' | EBee MAvo NGdn NHar NLar SMrm SPoG |
| | 'Noble Spirit' | CEnt NGdn NLar NMRc SPoG SWat |
| | 'Perlehuhn' | CDes |
| | ***plumosus*** | see *A. dioicus* |
| | ***sinensis*** | NBre WFar |
| | ***sylvestris*** | see *A. dioicus* |
| | 'Woldemar Meier' | EBee GBin NDov WCot |

## *Arundinaria* (*Poaceae*)

| | | |
|---|---|---|
| | ***amabilis*** | see *Pseudosasa amabilis* (McClure) Keng f. |
| | ***anceps*** | see *Yushania anceps* |
| | ***angustifolia*** | see *Pleioblastus chino* 'Murakamianus' |
| | ***auricoma*** | see *Pleioblastus viridistriatus* |
| | ***chino*** | see *Pleioblastus chino* |
| | ***disticha*** | see *Pleioblastus pygmaeus* 'Distichus' |
| | ***falconeri*** | see *Himalayacalamus falconeri* |
| | ***fargesii*** | see *Bashania fargesii* |
| | ***fastuosa*** | see *Semiarundinaria fastuosa* |
| | ***fortunei*** | see *Pleioblastus variegatus* |
| | ***funghomii*** | see *Schizostachyum funghomii* |
| § | ***gigantea*** | CDTJ MWht WJun |
| | - subsp. ***tecta*** | CBcs |
| | ***hindsii*** | see *Pleioblastus hindsii* |
| | ***hookeriana*** misapplied | see *Himalayacalamus falconeri* 'Damarapa' |
| | ***hookeriana*** Munro | see *Himalayacalamus hookerianus* |
| | ***humilis*** | see *Pleioblastus humilis* |
| | ***japonica*** | see *Pseudosasa japonica* |
| | ***jaunsarensis*** | see *Yushania anceps* |
| | ***maling*** | see *Yushania maling* |
| | ***marmorea*** | see *Chimonobambusa marmorea* |
| | ***murielae*** | see *Fargesia murielae* |
| | ***nitida*** | see *Fargesia nitida* |
| | ***oedogonata*** | see *Clavinodum oedogonatum* |
| | ***palmata*** | see *Sasa palmata* |
| | ***pumila*** | see *Pleioblastus argenteostriatus* f. *pumilus* |
| | ***pygmaea*** | see *Pleioblastus pygmaeus* |
| | ***quadrangularis*** | see *Chimonobambusa quadrangularis* |
| | ***simonii*** | see *Pleioblastus simonii* |
| | ***spathiflora*** | see *Thamnocalamus spathiflorus* |
| | ***tessellata*** | see *Thamnocalamus tessellatus* |
| | ***vagans*** | see *Sasaella ramosa* |
| | ***variegata*** | see *Pleioblastus variegatus* |
| | ***veitchii*** | see *Sasa veitchii* |
| | ***viridistriata*** | see *Pleioblastus viridistriatus* |
| | 'Wang Tsai' | see *Bambusa multiplex* 'Floribunda' |

## *Arundo* (*Poaceae*)

| | | |
|---|---|---|
| | ***donax*** | Widely available |
| | - 'Golden Chain' (v) | CEnt CKno EBee ELan EPPr EShb EWes LHop LRHS SBfd SMad |
| | - 'Macrophylla' | CGHE CHGN CKno ETod LEdu LPJP SApp WPGP |
| | - 'Variegata' | see *A. donax* var. *versicolor* |
| § | - var. ***versicolor*** (v) | Widely available |
| I | - - 'Aureovariegata' (v) | CDTJ MDKP |
| | ***formosana*** | CKno EPPr |
| | - 'Golden Showers' | EBee ESwi SBfd SEND |

## *Asarina* (*Plantaginaceae*)

| | | |
|---|---|---|
| | ***antirrhiniflora*** | see *Maurandella antirrhiniflora* |
| | ***barclayana*** | see *Maurandya barclayana* |
| | ***erubescens*** | see *Lophospermum erubescens* |
| | ***hispanica*** | see *Antirrhinum hispanicum* |
| | ***lophantha*** | see *Lophospermum scandens* |
| | ***lophospermum*** | see *Lophospermum scandens* |
| § | ***procumbens*** | CEnt CSpr CTri ECho EPfP GKev LBMP NRya SGar SPhx SRms WBrk WFar WKif |
| | - 'Alba' | IFro |

## *Asarum* (*Aristolochiaceae*)

| | | |
|---|---|---|
| | Chen Yi 5 | WCot |
| | ***albomaculatum*** | ECho |
| | - B&SWJ 1726 | WCru |
| | ***arifolium*** | EPPr GBBs |
| | ***asaroides*** | LWst |
| | ***campaniflorum*** | ECho LAma LWst WCot WCru |
| | ***canadense*** | CArn EBee ECho EPfP GBBs GEdr GPoy LEdu MMoz NLar WCru WWEG |
| | ***caudatum*** | CDes CHEx CLAP CRow EBee ECha ECho EPfP GEdr LEdu NBro NHol NLar NWCA SRms WCot WCru WFar WPGP |
| | - HWJ 641 from Vietnam **new** | WCru |
| | - deciduous **new** | WCru |
| | - white-flowered | CLAP SKHP WCru |
| | ***caudigerum*** | WCot |
| | - B&SWJ 1517 | WCru |
| | ***caulescens*** | EBee ECho EPPr LAma LWst WCru |
| | - B&SWJ 5886 | WCru |
| | ***delavayi*** | EBee ECho LAma LWst WCot WCru |
| | ***epigynum*** B&SWJ 3443 | WCru |
| | - 'Kikko' | GEdr |
| | - 'Silver Web' | WCru |
| | ***europaeum*** ♀H4 | Widely available |
| | ***fauriei*** | WCru |
| | ***forbesii*** | ECho LWst MMoz NLar |
| | ***geophilum*** | MMoz |
| | ***hartwegii*** | CLAP IGor LWst NLar WCot WCru WPtf WThu |
| | ***hatsushimae*** | GEdr |
| | ***himalaicum*** GWJ 9341 | WCru |
| | ***hypogynum*** B&SWJ 3628 | WCru |
| | ***infrapurpureum*** B&SWJ 1994 | LEdu WCru |
| | - 'Taroko Web' **new** | WCru |
| | ***kumageanum*** | WCot |
| | ***lemmonii*** | LRHS |
| | ***leptophyllum*** B&SWJ 1983 | WCru |
| | ***longirhizomatosum*** | WCru |
| | ***macranthum*** | WCot |
| | - B&SWJ 1691 | WCru |
| | ***maculatum*** B&SWJ 1114 | WCru |
| | ***magnificum*** | LAma LWst MMoz WCru |
| | ***maximum*** | CFir CLAP ECho LAma MMoz NMen WCot WCru |
| | - 'Silver Panda' | CBct CMil CPLG CWGN EBee ECtt GEdr LRHS LSou MLLN NLar NPnk SKHP SMad SPoG WCot |
| | ***megacalyx*** | GEdr |
| | ***naniflorum*** 'Eco Decor' | CLAP EBla GEdr LAst LRHS LSou MCot NPnk WCot |
| | ***nipponicum*** | GEdr |
| | - B&SWJ 2839 | WCru |

| | |
|---|---|
| ***petelotii*** HWJ 1043 | WCru |
| ***pulchellum*** | CAby LWst WCot WCru |
| ***satsumense*** | GEdr |
| ***sieboldii*** | GEdr WCru WFar |
| ***simile*** | GEdr |
| ***splendens*** | Widely available |
| ***taipingshanianum*** B&SWJ 1688 | WCot WCru |
| - 'Elfin Yellow' | WCru |
| ***taitonense*** | LWst |
| ***unzen*** | GEdr |
| ***viridiflorum*** | GEdr LWst |
| ***wulingense*** | CPLG WCru |

## *Asclepias* (*Apocynaceae*)

| | |
|---|---|
| 'Cinderella' | EBee LSou NBPC NGdn |
| ***curassavica*** | CCCN EShb LLWG SRkn XLum |
| - 'Red Butterfly' | SLon |
| - 'Silky Red' **new** | EShb |
| - 'Silky Yellow' **new** | EShb |
| § ***fascicularis*** | SBrt |
| ***fasciculata*** | see *A. fascicularis* |
| ***incarnata*** | ELan EPau IFoB LRHS MRav NBre SBrt SMrm SPlb WPer XLum |
| - 'Alba' | CPom ELan |
| - 'Ice Ballet' | CAbP CPrp EBee ELan IFoB LHop LLWG LRHS LSou NBPC NBre NGdn NLar SAga SBrt SPer SPoG WPer |
| - 'Soulmate' | ELan EPfP MMHG MMuc NBPC NBre NGdn |
| - 'White Superior' | EBee |
| ***physocarpa*** | see *Gomphocarpus physocarpus* |
| ***purpurascens*** | CArn CPom |
| ***speciosa*** | EBee NBre |
| ***sullivantii*** | EBee NBre |
| ***syriaca*** | CArn CPom EBee LRHS MLLN NBre XLum |
| ***tuberosa*** | CArn CBcs CPom CPrp CWib EBee GPoy GQue LRHS LSou MHer MNHC NEgg SMad SPoG XLum XSen |
| - Gay Butterflies Group | NBre |
| - 'Hello Yellow' | EBee |

## *Asimina* (*Annonaceae*)

| | |
|---|---|
| ***triloba*** (F) | CDTJ MBlu MBri NLar SGol SPlb |
| - 'Davis' (F) | CAgr |
| - 'Nc-1' (F) **new** | CAgr |
| - 'Pennsylvania Golden' (F) **new** | CAgr |
| - 'Prolific' (F) **new** | CAgr |
| - 'Sunflowers' | CCCN |

## *Asparagus* (*Asparagaceae*)

| | |
|---|---|
| B&SWJ 8309 from northern Vietnam | WCru |
| RCB AM 23 | WCot |
| from Malawi, hardy | SKHP |
| ***asparagoides*** ♀H1 | EShb |
| ***cochinchinensis*** | WPGP |
| ***crassicladus*** | EShb |
| ***densiflorus*** 'Mazeppa' | EShb |
| - 'Myersii' ♀H1 | EShb SEND |
| - Sprengeri Group ♀H1 | SEND |
| - - 'Variegatus' (v) | EShb |
| ***denudatus*** | EShb |
| ***falcatus*** | EShb SEND |
| ***filicinus*** var. ***giraldii*** | WCot |
| ***officinalis*** | WFar |
| - 'Argenteuil' **new** | LEdu |
| - 'Backlim' ♀H4 | ECrN EMil EPom ERea |
| - 'Cito' (m) | NPri |
| - 'Connover's Colossal' ♀H4 | CSBt CWan ERea LSRN MNHC SEND SVic |
| - 'Crimson Pacific' **new** | SVic |
| - 'Dariana' | EMil ERea SDea |
| - 'Franklim' | WFar |
| - 'Gijnlim' ♀H4 | ECrN EMil EPom ERea SDea WFar |
| - 'Guelph Millennium' | EPom |
| - 'Jersey Knight' | SVic |
| - 'Pacific 2000' | EPom LSRN |
| - 'Pacific Purple' | EPom |
| - var. ***prostratus*** from Britain | GCal |
| - 'Stewart's Purple' | EPom |
| ***plumosus*** | see *A. setaceus* |
| ***pseudoscaber*** 'Spitzenschleier' | EShb MAvo SDix SMad WCot |
| ***racemosus*** | EShb |
| ***retrofractus*** | EShb |
| ***scandens*** | EShb |
| ***schoberioides*** | LEdu |
| - B&SWJ 8814 | WCru |
| § ***setaceus*** ♀H1 | EShb |
| ***suaveolens*** | EShb |
| ***virgatus*** | EShb WCot WPGP |

## *Asperula* (*Rubiaceae*)

| | |
|---|---|
| § ***arcadiensis*** ♀H3 | ECho WAbe WPat WThu |
| ***aristata*** subsp. ***scabra*** | CSpe EBee ECha ELan WCot |
| - subsp. ***thessala*** | see *A. sintenisii* |
| ***boissieri*** | ECho |
| ***daphneola*** | ECho EWes WAbe |
| ***gussonei*** | CMea ECho EPot MWat NMen NWCA WAbe |
| ***lilaciflora*** | ECho |
| - var. ***caespitosa*** | see *A. lilaciflora* subsp. *lilaciflora* |
| § - subsp. ***lilaciflora*** | ECho NMen |
| ***nitida*** | CPBP ECho |
| - subsp. ***puberula*** | see *A. sintenisii* |
| ***odorata*** | see *Galium odoratum* |
| § ***sintenisii*** ♀H2-3 | CMea ECho EPot NMen NWCA WAbe WHoo WPat WThu |
| ***suberosa*** misapplied | see *A. arcadiensis* |
| ***taurina*** subsp. ***caucasica*** | NLar WBor |
| ***tinctoria*** | CArn GPoy MHer SRms |

## *Asphodeline* (*Asphodelaceae*)

| | |
|---|---|
| § ***brevicaulis*** | GAuc WCot |
| ***liburnica*** | CAvo CBro CSam EBee ECha ELan GAbr MRav SEND SSvw WCAu WCot WFar WHoo WPer XLum XSen |
| § ***lutea*** | Widely available |
| § - 'Gelbkerze' | EPfP LRHS |
| - Yellow Candle | see *A. lutea* 'Gelbkerze' |
| ***taurica*** | ECho GAuc LBMP LRHS MBNS NBre WPer |

## *Asphodelus* (*Asphodelaceae*)

| | |
|---|---|
| ***acaulis*** | ECho LLHF SCnR WAbe WCot |
| - SF 37 | WCot |
| § ***aestivus*** | EWes GCal MLLN SPhx SSvw WPer |
| - Cally Spear strain | GCal NCGa |
| ***albus*** | CArn CAvo CBot CSpe ECha EPPr GAuc GBin IFoB MCot NBid NCGa SPlb SRms WAul WPer WWEG XLum |

| | |
|---|---|
| ***brevicaulis*** | see *Asphodeline brevicaulis* |
| ***cerasiferus*** | see *A. ramosus* |
| ***fistulosus*** | LEdu NBir SAga SPhx |
| ***lusitanicus*** | see *A. ramosus* |
| ***luteus*** | see *Asphodeline lutea* |
| ***microcarpus*** | see *A. aestivus* |
| § ***ramosus*** | CPar ECho GAuc GCal MNrw NCGa WPer |

## *Aspidistra* (*Asparagaceae*)

| | |
|---|---|
| Chen Yi 135 | WCot |
| from China | WCot |
| ***attenuata*** | IBlr |
| - B&SWJ 377 | WCru |
| ***caespitosa*** 'Jade Ribbons' | EShb IBlr WCot |
| 'China Star' | CHEx IBlr WCot |
| ***daibuensis*** | IBlr |
| - B&SWJ 312b | WCru |
| ***elatior*** ♀H1 | CBct CHEx CTsd EBak EBee EShb IBlr LEdu NLar NPal NPla SArc SEND SMad STre WCot WWFP |
| - 'Akebono' (v) | WCot |
| - 'Asahi' (v) | IBlr WCot |
| - 'Goldfeather' | IBlr |
| - 'Hoshi-zora' (v) | IBlr WCot |
| - 'Lennon's Song' (v) | WCot |
| - 'Milky Way' (v) | CBct CHid EShb IBlr MMoz SEND WCot |
| - 'Morning Frost' | IBlr |
| - 'Okame' (v) | IBlr WCot |
| - 'Variegata' (v) ♀H1 | CBct CHEx EShb IBlr IFoB NBir SEND WCot |
| - 'Variegata Exotica' (v) | XBlo |
| ***leshanensis*** (v) | IBlr |
| ***linearifolia*** 'Leopard' | IBlr WCot |
| ***lurida*** | CBct EShb |
| - 'Irish Mist' (v) | IBlr |
| marbled-leaved (v) | WCot |
| ***minutiflora*** | WCot |
| ***mushaensis*** B&SWJ 1953 | WCru |
| aff. ***mushaensis*** 'Spotty Dotty' (v) | WCru |
| ***omeiensis*** aff. | WCot |
| ***patentiloba*** aff. | WCot |
| ***saxicola*** 'Uan Fat Lady' | see *A. zongbayi* 'Uan Fat Lady' |
| ***sutepensis*** B&SWJ 5216 | WCru |
| ***typica*** | IBlr |
| - 'China Sun' | IBlr WCot |
| - 'Old Glory' | WCot |
| ***zongbayi*** | WCot |
| § - 'Uan Fat Lady' | WCot WCru |

## *Asplenium* ✿ (*Aspleniaceae*)

| | |
|---|---|
| ***adiantum-nigrum*** | CBty SRms WAbe |
| ***antiquum*** | CBty |
| ***australasicum*** | EShb |
| ***boltonii*** | WRic |
| ***bulbiferum*** misapplied | see *A.* × *lucrosum* |
| ***bulbiferum*** ambig. × ***oblongifolium*** | WRic |
| ***bulbiferum*** Forst.f. | ESwi |
| § ***ceterach*** | CBty EFer WAbe WHer WRic |
| ***daucifolium*** | EOHP |
| ***difforme*** × ***dimorphum*** new | CBty |
| × ***ebenoides*** | CBty WCot WRic |
| ***flaccidum*** | WRic |
| ***fontanum*** | WRic |
| ***incisum*** | WRic |
| § × ***lucrosum*** ♀H1-2 | CBty CDTJ CKel EFtx ESwi |
| ***lyallii*** | WRic |
| 'Maori Princess' | CBcs GBin WFib |
| ***nidus*** ♀H1 | WRic XBlo |
| ***oblongifolium*** | GBin WRic |
| ***obovatum*** subsp. ***lanceolatum*** | WRic |
| ***oligosorum*** | WRic |
| ***onopteris*** | WRic |
| * ***plicatum*** new | WRic |
| ***polyodon*** | WRic |
| ***protensum*** new | WRic |
| ***ruprechtii*** | WRic |
| ***ruta-muraria*** | EFer |
| § ***scolopendrium*** ♀H4 | Widely available |
| - 'Angustatum' | Widely available |
| - 'Conglomeratum' | SRms |
| - Crispum Group | CLAP EFer ELan GBin MRav NBid NHol SApp SRms SRot WFib WPGP |
| - - 'Crispum Bolton's Nobile' ♀H4 | WCot WFib |
| - - 'Golden Queen' | CLAP |
| - Crispum Cristatum Group | CLAP LTen MMuc NVic SEND |
| - Crispum Fimbriatum Group | CLAP GQui |
| - Cristatum Group | Widely available |
| - Fimbriatum Group | CLAP WRic |
| - 'Furcatum' | CBty CDTJ CLAP EBee GEdr LRHS NHol NLar WRic |
| - 'Kaye's Lacerated' ♀H4 | CLAP EFer WFib WRic |
| - Laceratum Group | CLAP SRms |
| - Marginatum Group | EFer SWat |
| - - 'Irregulare' | SRms |
| - 'Muricatum' | CLAP ELan GBin MRav MWhi NBid NHol SRms WFib WTin |
| - 'Ramocristatum' | CLAP |
| - Ramomarginatum Group | CLAP ELan SRms WFar WRic |
| - 'Sagittatocristatum' | SRms |
| - 'Sagittatoprojectum Sclater' | WFib |
| * - 'Sagittatum' | SRms |
| - 'Stagshorn' | SRms |
| - Undulatum Group | CBty CDTJ CLAP EAEE EBee ECha EFtx EPfP GBin LRHS MMoz MMuc NBir NEgg NHol NLar SBfd SEND SRms SWat WIvy WPnP WRic |
| - Undulatum Cristatum Group | CLAP |
| ***splendens*** new | WRic |
| ***trichomanes*** ♀H4 | Widely available |
| - Cristatum Group | SRms WFar |
| - Incisum Group | CLAP EFer NOrc SRms WAbe WRic |

## *Astelia* (*Asteliaceae*)

| | |
|---|---|
| ***alpina*** | IBlr |
| ***banksii*** | CBcs CDoC CHEx CHll CSpe CTrC EBee ECou GCal GGar IBal LRHS LSRN LTen MGos SBfd SLim WCot |
| 'Bronze Spear' new | EBee |
| § ***chathamica*** ♀H3 | Widely available |
| - 'Silver Spear' | see *A. chathamica* |
| ***chathamica*** × ***fragrans*** | ECou |
| ***cunninghamii*** | see *A. solandri* |
| ***fragrans*** | CBcs CSpe ECou GGar IBlr LEdu |
| ***graminea*** | GCal IBlr |
| ***grandis*** | CBcs IBlr LEdu |
| ***nervosa*** | CTsd ECou IBlr LEdu LSRN SArc WPat |
| - 'Alpine Ruby' PBR | IBlr |
| - 'Bronze Giant' | IBlr |
| - 'Silver Sabre' | IBlr |

| | | |
|---|---|---|
| | – 'Westland' | CBcs CDoC CKno CSBt CTrC CTsd EBee EShb GBin GCal GGar IBlr LEdu LRHS LSRN MBri MGos MRav SBfd SEND SLim SMrm SPad SPlb SPoG WCot |
| | ***nivicola*** 'Golden Gem' | IBlr |
| | – 'Red Gem' | GCal LEdu |
| | ***petriei*** | IBlr |
| | 'Red Devil' | CBcs CHid EShb WHer |
| | 'Silver Mound' | EPfP |
| § | ***solandri*** | ECou IBlr |
| | ***trinervia*** | IBlr |

## *Aster* ✿ (*Asteraceae*)

| | | |
|---|---|---|
| | ***acris*** | see *A. sedifolius* |
| | ***ageratoides*** | CPou CPrp LRHS SEND WOld |
| | – 'Ashvi' | WCot |
| | – 'Asran' | CWan EBee ECtt EHoe EPPr EWes LSou MMuc SSvw WCot WOld XLum |
| | – 'Harry Smith' | EBee NDov |
| | – 'Starshine'PBR | EPPr NSti WCot |
| § | ***albescens*** | LRHS |
| | ***alpinus*** ♀H4 | CSpr ECho EPfP GJos GKev MAsh MWat NBlu SRms WFar XSen |
| | – var. ***albus*** | EBee EDAr EPfP LRHS NBre NBro NLar SPoG SRGP |
| | – Dark Beauty | see *A. alpinus* 'Dunkle Schöne' |
| § | – 'Dunkle Schöne' | EBee EDAr GGar NBre NVic SPoG SRGP SRms |
| | – 'Goliath' | EBee EPfP LRHS NBre NBro NLar SPlb WFar |
| | – 'Happy End' | CMMP ECho NBre NLar SPoG SRGP SRms WFar |
| | – 'Pinkie' | EBee EDAr EPfP LRHS NLar |
| | – 'Trimix' | ECho NBir SRms WFar |
| | – 'White Beauty' | SRms |
| * | – 'Wolfii' | SRms |
| | ***amelloides*** | see *Felicia amelloides* |
| | ***amellus*** | CArn LRHS LSou WMoo |
| | – 'Blue King' | EBee SMrm SWvt |
| | – 'Breslau' | EBee LRHS |
| | – 'Brilliant' | CPrp EBee EBla ECtt EPPr LAst LEdu LRHS LSou MAvo MBNS MNFA MRav MWat SMrm SMrs SPer SRGP WHoo WOld |
| | – 'Forncett Flourish' | WCot WOld |
| | – 'Framfieldii' ♀H4 | NDov WCot WOld |
| | – 'Gründer' | ECtt LRHS MAvo WHil WOld |
| | – 'Jacqueline Genebrier' ♀H4 | CHar ELon WSHC |
| | – 'Jubilee' **new** | LRHS |
| | – 'King George' ♀H4 | Widely available |
| | – 'Lac de Genève' | WOld |
| | – 'Lady Hindlip' | CSam EBee WFar |
| | – 'Louise' | LRHS MBrN SBch SUsu |
| | – 'Nocturne' | WCot WOld |
| | – 'Peach Blossom' | EBee NBPC |
| | – Pink Zenith | see *A. amellus* 'Rosa Erfüllung' |
| § | – 'Rosa Erfüllung' | CMac EBee EBla ECtt ELon EPPr EPfP GBin GMaP GMac LAst LHop LRHS MAvo MCot MRav NDov SAga SRGP SWvt WCot WMnd WOld |
| | – 'Rotfeuer' | ELon GQue WCot |
| | – 'Rudolph Goethe' | EBee ECtt EMil EPPr EPfP LAst LRHS MRav SBHP SRGP WFar WMoo WOld WWEG |
| | – 'Silbersee' | CSam NDov |
| | – 'Sonia' | MNFA MRav SUsu |
| | – 'Sonora' | ECGP LPla SAga SMrm SPhx SRGP SUsu WOld |
| | – 'Sternkugel' | WOld |
| | – 'Vanity' | WOld |
| § | – 'Veilchenkönigin' ♀H4 | Widely available |
| N | – Violet Queen | see *A. amellus* 'Veilchenkönigin' |
| | – 'Weltfriede' | WOld |
| | 'Anita Pfeiffer' | LRHS |
| | 'Anja's Choice' | EBee LHop NBre WOld |
| | ***asper*** | see *A. bakerianus* |
| | ***asperulus*** misapplied | see *A. peduncularis* |
| § | ***bakerianus*** | WFar |
| | 'Blue Autumn' **new** | NCGa |
| | ***capensis*** 'Variegatus' | see *Felicia amelloides* variegated |
| § | ***carolinianus*** | EShb WFar |
| | 'Cassandra' | WOld |
| | 'Cheavers' | LRHS |
| | 'Chesters Star' **new** | WOld |
| | ***ciliolatus*** | LRHS |
| | 'Climax' misapplied | see *A. laevis* 'Arcturus', *A. laevis* 'Calliope' |
| | 'Climax' ambig. | CElw GCal GQue MMuc MRav NBid NSti SAga SMrm XLum |
| | 'Climax' Vicary Gibbs | WOld |
| | ***coelestis*** | see *Felicia amelloides* |
| | ***coloradoensis*** | CPBP LLHF NSla XSen |
| | 'Connecticut Snow Flurry' | see *A. ericoides* f. *prostratus* 'Snow Flurry' |
| | ***conspicuus*** | GCal |
| | 'Coombe Fishacre' ♀H4 | CAby COlW CSam EBee ELan GCal LPla MCot MNFA MRav NBre NCGa NLar SBfd SMrm SMrs SSvw SUsu WCAu WFar WHoo WOld WTin |
| | ***cordifolius*** | LRHS WFar |
| | – 'Blutenregen' | EBee |
| | – 'Chieftain' ♀H4 | MNrw SAga SPhx WOld |
| | – 'Elegans' | CSam EBee LRHS MWea WMnd WMoo WOld |
| | – 'Ideal' | EBee NLar WOld XLum |
| | – 'Silver Queen' | WOld |
| | – 'Silver Spray' | CPrp EBee ECtt GMaP GMac GQue MHom MWat NBre SRGP WOld WPer XLum |
| | – 'Sweet Lavender' ♀H4 | SBfd WOld |
| | – 'White Chief' | WOld |
| | ***corymbosus*** | see *A. divaricatus* |
| | 'Cotswold Gem' | WCot WOld |
| | 'Dark Pink Star' | WOld |
| | ***delavayi*** | SUsu |
| | ***diffusus*** | see *A. lateriflorus* |
| | ***diplostephioides*** | EBee EDAr EPPr EPfP EWTr GBin GCal GGar GQue IKil LBMP LRHS MBNS MMHG NBPC NBre NLar SPlb WAul WPer WPtf |
| § | ***divaricatus*** | Widely available |
| § | – 'Eastern Star' | NCGa WCot WFar WOld |
| | – Raiche form | see *A. divaricatus* 'Eastern Star' |
| N | ***dumosus*** | CPLG WFar WPer |
| | – 'Biteliness' | NBre NLar |
| | – Sapphire = 'Kiesapphire'PBR | CPrp LHop LRHS LSRN MBri NEgg SPoG SRGP SWvt |
| | 'Dwarf Barbados' | EPfP LRHS |
| | ***ericoides*** | CKno MCot NBre NOrc WWEG |
| | – 'Blue Star' ♀H4 | CPrp CSam EBee LRHS NBPC NLar SPer WMnd WOld |
| | – 'Blue Wonder' | XLum |
| | – 'Brimstone' ♀H4 | MRav NBre WOld |
| | – 'Cinderella' | COlW CPrp GBee GMac LRHS NSti WOld WWEG |

| | | |
|---|---|---|
| | - 'Constance' | WOld |
| | - 'Erlkönig' | EBee ECGP EPri EShb GCal GQue LAst LRHS MRav MWea NGdn NLar NPnk SWat WCAu WCot WMnd WOld WPer XLum |
| | - 'Esther' | CPrp EBee ECha ELan NCGa SMrm WOld |
| | - 'Golden Spray' ♀H4 | EBee EPfP GMaP GQue NLar SPer WFar WMnd WOld |
| | - 'Herbstmyrte' | CSam LRHS |
| | - 'Hon. Edith Gibbs' | WOld |
| | - 'Monte Cassino' | see *A. pilosus* var. *pringlei* 'Monte Cassino' |
| | - 'Pink Cloud' ♀H4 | CHVG COIW CPrp EBee ECtt EPfP EPri EShb GCal GGar GMac LAst LRHS MNFA MRav NCGa NLar NOrc SBrd SPer SRGP SWat WCAu WFar WMnd WOld WPer WWEG |
| | - f. ***prostratus*** | EPot GQue WFar XSen |
| § | - - 'Snow Flurry' ♀H4 | CAby CMea EBee ECha ECtt GMac LEdu LPla MAvo MNFA MNrw MSCN NLar SAga SMrm WCot WMnd WOld WOut XLum |
| | - 'Rosy Veil' | GMac MHom NBir NGdn WCot |
| | - 'Schneegitter' | EBee LRHS WCot WFar WOld |
| | - 'Schneetanne' | NBre |
| | - 'Star Shower' **new** | LRHS |
| | - 'Sulphurea' | MWat |
| | - 'Vimmer's Delight' | WCot |
| | - 'White Heather' | CPrp NLar WMnd WOld WPer WRHF |
| | - 'Yvette Richardson' | MHom WOld WWEG |
| | ***falcatus*** | WCot |
| | - var. ***commutatus*** | WCot |
| | 'Fanny's Fall' | see *A. oblongifolius* 'Fanny's' |
| § | ***flaccidus*** | LRHS |
| | ***foliaceus*** from Montana | EPPr |
| | - var. ***parryi*** | EBee |
| | × ***frikartii*** | CMac EBee ELan EPfP EShb LRHS MRav SAga SMrm SRms SWvt WOld WSHC |
| | - 'Eiger' | WOld |
| | - 'Flora's Delight' | GCal NDov WOld WWEG |
| | - 'Jungfrau' | CWGN EBee EPPr GMaP GQue MRav NLar SPhx WOld WWEG |
| N | - 'Mönch' ♀H4 | Widely available |
| | - Wonder of Stafa | see *A.* × *frikartii* 'Wunder von Stäfa' |
| § | - 'Wunder von Stäfa' ♀H4 | CEnd CKno CPLG EBee ECtt ELan ELon EPfP GMaP LHop LRHS LSRN LSou MBNS MCot MRav NBir NLar NVic SWvt WCot WMnd WOld WWEG XLum |
| | ***furcatus*** **new** | XLum |
| | ***glehnii*** 'Aglenii' | EBee |
| | 'Glow in the Dark' **new** | MAvo WCot |
| | ***greatae*** | EBee |
| | ***hayatae*** B&SWJ 8790 | WCru |
| | 'Herfstweelde' | CPrp EBee MAvo SMad SUsu WFar WOld |
| § | × ***herveyi*** | CFir CSam EBee EBla ECtt ELan EPfP GCal LLWP LRHS MMuc MNFA MSpe NDov NLar NSti SAga SDix SPer SPhx SPoG SRGP WBor WCAu WCot WFar WKif WMnd WMoo WOld |
| | ***himalaicus*** | SRms |
| | 'Hon. Vicary Gibbs' (*ericoides* hybrid) | MNFA WOld WOut |
| | ***hybridus luteus*** | see *Solidago* × *luteus* |
| | 'Ivy House' | ECtt |

| | | |
|---|---|---|
| | 'Kylie' ♀H4 | CAby CDes CHVG CPrp ECtt GMac LRHS LSRN MHom NCGa NDov SRGP SUsu WBor WBrk WCot WFar WHil WOld WTin |
| | ***laevis*** | LEdu NBre NLar WPer WTin |
| | - 'Anneke Van der Jeugd' | EBee |
| § | - 'Arcturus' | CFir LRHS MHom MNrw NBir NBre NCGa NSti SSvw WCot WFar WWlt XLum |
| | - 'Blauhügel' | LPla |
| | - 'Blue Bird' | LRHS SUsu |
| § | - 'Calliope' | Widely available |
| | - 'Cally Compact' | GQue NLar |
| | - var. ***geyeri*** | MNrw |
| | - 'Nightshade' | MNrw WOld |
| | - 'Vesta' **new** | WOld |
| | - white-flowered | WOld |
| | ***lanceolatus*** Willd. | CSam EPPr NCGa |
| | - 'Edwin Beckett' | CBre MHom MNrw WOld |
| § | ***lateriflorus*** | EBee MAvo WOld WPer |
| | - 'Bleke Bet' | WCot WOld |
| | - 'Buck's Fizz' | NDov NLar SBfd WOld |
| | - 'Chloe' | CSam EBee NCGa SPhx |
| | - 'Datschi' | NDov WFar XLum |
| | - var. ***horizontalis*** ♀H4 | Widely available |
| | - 'Jan' | WOld |
| | - 'Lady in Black' | Widely available |
| | - 'Lovely' | CSam EBee LRHS NBre SRGP WCot |
| | - 'Prince' | Widely available |
| | ***laterifolius*** 'Snow Flurry' | see *A. ericoides* f. *prostratus* 'Snow Flurry' |
| | 'Les Moutiers' **new** | MHom MNrw WOld |
| § | ***linosyris*** | EBee EPfP EWes GBin GQue LRHS NBre NLar SMrm WHer WOld XLum |
| | - 'Goldilocks' | see *A. linosyris* |
| | 'Little Carlow' (*cordifolius* hybrid) ♀H4 | Widely available |
| | 'Little Dorrit' (*cordifolius* hybrid) | WOld |
| | ***maackii*** | SMrm |
| | ***macrophyllus*** | ELan LRHS NLar WOld |
| | - 'Albus' | EBee EPPr GBin WFar WOld |
| | - 'Twilight' | see *A.* × *herveyi* |
| | ***mongolicus*** | see *Kalimeris mongolica* |
| | 'Mrs Dean' | ECtt |
| | ***natalensis*** | see *Felicia rosulata* |
| | 'Natasha' | LSRN |
| | 'Noreen' | MAvo |
| | ***novae-angliae*** | CArn NBPC NBre WOld |
| | - 'Alex Deamon' | WOld |
| | - 'Andenken an Alma Pötschke' | Widely available |
| | - 'Andenken an Paul Gerber' | EBee ECtt MAvo MHom MNrw NDov WBrk WOld |
| | - 'Annabelle de Chazal' | ECtt MAvo SMrs WOld |
| | - 'Augusta' | WOld |
| | - Autumn Snow | see *A. novae-angliae* 'Herbstschnee' |
| | - 'Barr's Blue' | CMac EBee EPfP GCra MAvo MHom MMuc MWat NLar SEND SPer SRms WBrk WMoo WOld |
| | - 'Barr's Pink' | CBre CMac EBee ECtt EPfP MCot MHer MHom MLHP MMuc MRav MWat NLar SEND WBrk WFar WOld WPer WSFF WWEG |
| * | - 'Barr's Purple' | ECtt WBrk WCFE WOld |
| | - 'Barr's Violet' | CHVG ECtt MAvo MHom SRms WBrk WCot WHal WHoo WHrl WMoo WOld WPer WTin WWEG |
| | - 'Brockamin' | MNrw WBrk |

- 'Christopher Harbutt' LEdu SRGP WOld
- 'Colwall Constellation' WOld
- 'Colwall Galaxy' MAvo WHrl WOld
- 'Colwall Orbit' MAvo WOld
- 'Crimson Beauty' EPPr GMac MAvo MHom MNrw MWat WBrk WOld WWEG
- 'Dapper Tapper' **new** WCot
- 'Evensong' ECtt WOld
- 'Festival' WBrk
- 'Foxy Emily' MAvo WOld
- 'Harrington's Pink' ♀H4 Widely available
- 'Helen Picton' CSam ECtt MAvo MBrN MHom MWat WBrk WOld
- § - 'Herbstschnee' Widely available
- 'James Ritchie' EWes LLHF WHoo WOld
- 'John Davies' MAvo MNrw WHil WOld
- 'Lachsglut' GMac MAvo SMrm WCot
- 'Ladies Day' **new** WOld
- 'Lou Williams' ECtt MAvo MNrw MWat SMrs WHil WOld
- I - 'Lucida' MAvo WHal WOld
- 'Lye End Beauty' CKno ECtt EPyc LLWP MAvo MHom MNFA MNrw MRav MWat SMrs WBrk WCot WHoo WMoo WOld WTin
- 'Marina Wolkonsky' CAby EBee ECtt EWes GMac LHop MAvo MNrw MWat SMrs SPhx SUsu WBrk WCot WOld WWFP
- 'Millennium Star' MAvo WOld
- 'Miss K.E. Mash' MAvo MHom SRGP WBrk WOld WWEG
- 'Mrs S.T. Wright' CAby CPrp CTri ECtt EWes MAvo MBrN MHom MNrw MWea SMrs SRGP WFar WOld WWEG
- 'Mrs S.W. Stern' WOld
- 'Naomi' **new** WOld
- 'Pink Parfait' CSam ECtt GMac LRHS NBre NGdn SMrs SRms WBrk WCot WOld
- 'Pink Victor' CTri EPPr SRms WMoo
- 'Pride of Rougham' **new** EWes
- 'Primrose Upward' CAby MNrw WCot WOld
- 'Purple Cloud' CAby GMac LHop MHer MHom MWat NBre NGdn WBrk WHal WOld WWEG
- I - 'Purple Dome' Widely available
- 'Quinton Menzies' CSam WBrk WOld WWEG
- 'Red Cloud' NBre WBrk WOld
- 'Rosa Sieger' ♀H4 CAby CBre CPrp CSam EBee ECtt GQue MAvo MHom MNrw NGdn SUsu WBor WBrk WHil WOld WWEG XLum
- 'Rose Williams' MAvo WOld WOut
- 'Roter Stern' ECtt WBrk
- 'Rougham Purple' **new** EWes
- 'Rubinschatz' CAby EBee LRHS MAvo MHom MWat NBre SRms WOld XLum
- 'Rudelsburg' MAvo NDov
- 'Saint Michael's' WOld
- 'Sayer's Croft' LRHS MHom MWat NBre WCot WHil WHoo WOld WOut WTin
- September Ruby see *A. novae-angliae* 'Septemberrubin'
- § - 'Septemberrubin' CAby CMea EBee ECtt ELon EPfP EWTr GMac IFoB LEdu LHop MNFA MRav SMrs SPhx SRGP SUsu WFar WOld XLum
- 'Treasure' CBre ECtt EWes LRHS MAvo NBre SMrm SMrs WBrk WMoo WOld
- 'Vibrant Dome' **new** NLar
- 'Violet Haze' CMea
- 'Violetta' EBee ECtt ELon LRHS LSou MAvo MHom MNFA MWea NMRc SMrs WBrk WFar WHil WHoo WOld WTin
- 'W. Bowman' WOld
- 'Wow' SMrm

N ***novi-belgii*** NBlu WHer

- 'Ada Ballard' CMac EBee LRHS LSRN NBre NEgg SBfd SMrm SMrs SPer SPoG SRGP WMoo WOld WWEG
- 'Albanian' WOld
- 'Alderman Vokes' WOld
- 'Alex Norman' WOld
- 'Algar's Pride' ECtt WOld WWEG
- 'Alice Haslam' CAby CMac EBee ECtt LRHS MCCP NEgg NLar NOrc NPri SBfd SRGP SRms WCAu WOld WPer WWEG
- 'Alpenglow' WOld
- 'Angela Peel' LRHS
- 'Anita Ballard' WOld
- 'Anita Webb' NBir WOld
- 'Anneke' EBee LRHS NLar SRGP SRkn WOld
- 'Apollo' LRHS MWat NEgg NLar WFar WOld
- 'Apple Blossom' WOld
- 'Arctic' WOld
- 'Audrey' CEnt CMac EBee ECtt GMaP LRHS LSRN MBNS NEgg NGdn NOrc SRGP STes WFar WOld
- 'Autumn Beauty' CHVG WOld
- 'Autumn Days' WOld
- 'Autumn Glory' WOld
- 'Autumn Rose' SMrs WOld
- 'Baby Climax' WOld
- 'Bahamas' (Island Series) EWll LRHS LSou NLar SBfd SGar SWvt WCot WHil
- 'Barbados' (Island Series) EPfP LRHS LSou MBri NLar SWvt
- 'Beauty of Colwall' WOld
- 'Beechwood Challenger' WOld
- 'Beechwood Charm' WOld
- 'Beechwood Rival' CTri EBee LRHS MBri
- 'Beechwood Supreme' WOld
- 'Bewunderung' WOld
- 'Blandie' CTri EBee EPfP SRGP WOld
- 'Blauglut' WOld
- 'Blue Baby' CMac WPer
- 'Blue Bouquet' CTri SRms WOld
- 'Blue Boy' WOld WWEG
- 'Blue Danube' SMrs WOld
- 'Blue Eyes' SMrs SUsu WOld
- 'Blue Gown' CCse GCal GQue SMrs WOld
- 'Blue Lagoon' CMea ELan MBri SMrs SRGP WBrk WOld
- 'Blue Patrol' WOld
- 'Blue Radiance' WOld
- 'Blue Spire' WOld
- 'Bonanza' WOld
- 'Boningale Blue' WOld
- 'Boningale White' NDov WOld
- 'Bridesmaid' WOld
- 'Bridgette' NBPC NPnk
- 'Bright Eyes' SRGP
- 'Brightest and Best' WOld
- 'Brigitte' **new** NLar
- 'Cameo' WOld
- 'Cantab' WOld
- 'Carlingcott' WOld
- 'Carnival' CMMP EBee ECtt MMHG MWea NEgg NOrc SMrs SPer SRGP WOld
- 'Cecily' WOld WWEG
- 'Charles Wilson' WOld

| | |
|---|---|
| – 'Chatterbox' | CPrp EPfP LRHS MRav MWat NEgg NLar SRms WOld |
| – 'Chelwood' | WOld |
| – 'Chequers' | CMMP EBee MBNS MWea NEgg SMrs SRGP WOld |
| – 'Christina' | see *A. novi-belgii* 'Kristina' |
| – 'Christine Soanes' | WOld |
| – 'Cliff Lewis' | WOld |
| – 'Climax Albus' | see *A.* 'White Climax' |
| – 'Cloudy Blue' | WOld |
| – 'Coombe Gladys' | WOld |
| – 'Coombe Joy' | WOld |
| – 'Coombe Margaret' | WOld |
| – 'Coombe Queen' | WOld |
| – 'Coombe Radiance' | WOld |
| – 'Coombe Ronald' | MWat WOld |
| – 'Coombe Rosemary' | ECtt LRHS NLar WBor WOld |
| – 'Coombe Violet' | MWat WOld |
| – 'Countess of Dudley' | WOld WPer |
| – 'Court Herald' | WOld |
| – 'Crimson Brocade' | CFir EBee ECtt ELan EPfP LRHS MRav MWea NDov NLar SBfd SPoG SRGP WOld |
| – 'Dandy' | CMac EBee ELan LRHS NBir NEgg NGdn SRGP WFar WOld |
| – 'Daniela' | SRms WBrk WOld |
| – 'Daphne Anne' | WOld |
| – 'Dauerblau' | GBin WOld |
| – 'Davey's True Blue' | CTri SMrs WOld XLum |
| – 'David Murray' | WOld |
| – 'Dazzler' | WOld WWEG |
| – 'Destiny' | WOld |
| – 'Diana' | WOld |
| – 'Diana Watts' | WOld |
| – 'Dietgard' | MWat WOld WWEG |
| – 'Dolly' | NBir SRms WOld WWEG |
| – 'Dora Chiswell' | WOld |
| – 'Dusky Maid' | WOld |
| – 'Dwarf Ibiza' | LRHS |
| – 'Elizabeth' | CAby CElw WOld |
| – 'Elizabeth Bright' | WOld |
| – 'Elizabeth Hutton' | WOld |
| – 'Elsie Dale' | WOld |
| – 'Elta' | WOld |
| – 'Erica' | CElw MWat WOld |
| – 'Ernest Ballard' | WOld |
| – 'Eva' | SRms WOld |
| – 'Eventide' | CElw CTri EBee LSRN WOld WRHF |
| – 'Fair Lady' | CHVG LRHS MWat WOld |
| – 'Faith' | WOld |
| – 'Farncombe Lilac' | LRHS |
| – 'Farrington' | WOld |
| – 'Fellowship' ♀H4 | CDes CFir COlW EBee ECtt LEdu MAvo MBri MMuc NCGa NDov SHar SMrs SPer SRGP SRms SUsu WBrk WCot WOld WWEG |
| – 'Flamingo' | LRHS WOld |
| – 'Fontaine' | WOld |
| – 'Freda Ballard' | ECtt GMaP LRHS LSRN MWat SMrs SRGP WCAu WNew WOld WWEG |
| – 'Freya' | LSRN WOld WSHC |
| – 'Fuldatal' | WOld |
| – 'Gayborder Blue' | WOld |
| – 'Gayborder Royal' | CFir WOld |
| – 'Glory of Colwall' | WOld |
| – 'Goliath' | WOld |
| – 'Grey Lady' | WOld WWEG |
| – 'Guardsman' | WOld |
| – 'Gulliver' | WOld WWEG |
| – 'Gurney Slade' | WOld |
| – 'Harrison's Blue' | MWat SMrs WOld WPer |
| – 'Heinz Richard' | CMMP COlW EBee ECha LRHS MHer NBir NBre NGdn SBch SMrs SRGP SRms WOld WWEG |
| – 'Helen' | WOld |
| – 'Helen Ballard' | SRms WBrk WOld |
| – 'Herbstgruss vom Bresserhof' | NBre NLar WBox |
| – 'Herbstpurzel' | WOld |
| – 'Hilda Ballard' | WOld |
| – 'Ibiza' | LRHS WCot |
| – 'Ilse Brensell' | WOld WWEG |
| – 'Irene' | WOld |
| – 'Isabel Allen' | WOld |
| – 'Janet Watts' | WOld |
| – 'Jean' | MWat SBfd SRms WOld |
| – 'Jean Gyte' | WOld |
| – 'Jeanette' | SRms WOld |
| – 'Jenny' | COlW CSBt EBee ECtt EPPr EPfP GBin GKev GMaP LHop LRHS LSRN MBri MRav MWat NBir NDov NEgg NGdn SBfd SPer SPoG SRGP SRkn SRms WFar WMnd WOld WWEG |
| – 'Jollity' | WOld |
| – 'Julia' | WOld |
| – 'Karminkuppel' | NBre WOld |
| – 'Kassel' | SRms WOld |
| – 'King of the Belgians' | WOld |
| – 'King's College' | WOld |
| § – 'Kristina' | COlW CWan EBee ECha EPPr LRHS MRav NBir WCot WOld WWEG |
| – 'Lady Evelyn Drummond' | WOld |
| – 'Lady Frances' | EBee SRms WOld |
| – 'Lady in Blue' | Widely available |
| – 'Lady Paget' | WOld |
| – 'Lassie' | CElw MWat WOld |
| – 'Lavender Dream' | WOld |
| – 'Lawrence Chiswell' | WOld |
| – 'Lederstrumpf' | NDov |
| – 'Lilac Time' | WOld |
| – 'Lisa Dawn' | CSpr ECtt SMrs WOld |
| – 'Little Boy Blue' | LRHS NBre SRms WOld XLum |
| – 'Little Man in Blue' | WOld WWEG |
| – 'Little Pink Beauty' | CEnt COlW EBee ECtt ELan EPfP EWTr LAst LHop LRHS MBNS NEgg NGdn NVic NWad SBrd SPer SRGP SRms WFar WOld WWEG |
| – 'Little Pink Lady' | LRHS SRms WOld |
| – 'Little Pink Pyramid' | SRms WWEG |
| – 'Little Red Boy' | WOld |
| – 'Little Treasure' | WOld |
| – 'Lucy' | WOld |
| – 'Madge Cato' | MAvo WOld |
| – 'Mammoth' | WOld |
| – 'Margaret Rose' | WOld |
| – 'Margery Bennett' | WOld |
| – 'Marie Ballard' | Widely available |
| – 'Marie's Pretty Please' | WOld |
| – 'Marjorie' | LSRN SBfd SPoG WOld XLum |
| – 'Marjory Ballard' | WOld |
| – 'Martonie' | WOld WPer |
| – 'Mary Ann Neil' | SMrs WOld |
| – 'Mary Deane' | WOld WPer |
| – 'Mauve Magic' | MWat SRms WOld WWEG |
| – 'Melbourne Belle' | WOld |
| – 'Melbourne Magnet' | WOld |
| – 'Michael Watts' | WOld |
| – 'Midget' | WOld |
| – 'Milka' **new** | NCGa |
| – 'Mistress Quickly' | MCot SMrs WOld WWEG |

- 'Mittelmeer' XLum
- 'Mount Everest' LHop NCGa SPhx WOld WPer WWEG
- 'Mrs J. Sangster' WOld
- 'Mrs Leo Hunter' WOld
- (Mystery Lady Series) Debbie = 'Dasdebi' (d) new LRHS
- - Demi = 'Dasdem' (d) new LRHS
- - Ingrid = 'Dasing' (d) new LRHS
- - Jessica = 'Dasjes' (d) new LRHS
- - Katharine = 'Daskat' (d) new LRHS
- 'Neron' NDov
- 'Nesthäkchen' WOld
- 'Niobe' CMac WOld
- 'Nobilis' WOld
- 'Norman's Jubilee' EBee EPfP LRHS NBir NEgg SMrs WOld WWEG
- 'Nursteed Charm' WOld
- 'Oktoberschneekuppel' WOld
- 'Orlando' WOld
- 'Pamela' WOld
- 'Patricia Ballard' CBcs CFir CHab CMac CPrp CSBt GCra GMaP LRHS MWat MWhi NBir NLar NPer NWad SBfd SMrs SPer SRGP WCAu WFar WNew WOld WPer WWEG
- 'Peace' WOld
- 'Percy Thrower' ECtt SMrs WOld
- 'Peter Chiswell' SRms WOld
- 'Peter Harrison' GMaP GMac NBir WMnd WOld WPer XLum
- 'Peter Pan' GBee LRHS NLar SHar WOld
- 'Picture' NBre WOld
- 'Pink Gown' WOld
- 'Pink Lace' MBNS WOld WPer
- 'Pink Pyramid' WOld
- 'Plenty' WOld
- 'Porzellan' CAby CElw CMMP COIW EBee ECGP ECtt MAvo MBNS NDov NGdn SMrs SRGP WCot
- 'Priory Blush' CAby WOld
- 'Professor Anton Kippenberg' CEnt CWan EBee EPfP GMaP LLWP LRHS MRav NBre NLar SPer SRGP SWvt WMnd WOld XLum
- 'Prosperity' NBre WOld
* - 'Prunella' GAbr WOld
- 'Purple Dome' ECha LEdu LSRN MCCP MHer MWat SHar SRkn WOld
- 'Queen Mary' WOld
- 'Queen of Colwall' WOld
- 'Ralph Picton' WOld
- 'Raspberry Ripple' WOld
- 'Rector' see *A. novi-belgii* 'The Rector'
- 'Red Robin' MWat
- 'Red Sunset' SRms WOld
* - 'Reitlinstal' EBee
- 'Rembrandt' ECtt NEgg NGdn SHar SMrs SRGP
- 'Remembrance' MWat SRms WBrk WOld WWEG
- 'Reverend Vincent Dale' WOld
- 'Richness' MAvo SAga WOld
- 'Robin Adair' WOld
- 'Roland Smith' WOld
- 'Rose Bonnet' CSBt SPlb
- 'Rose Bouquet' WOld
- 'Roseanne' WOld
- 'Rosebud' ambig. WOld WWEG
- 'Rosebud' Ballard ECtt
- 'Rosenquartz' new NLar
- 'Rosenschein' NDov
- 'Rosenwichtel' LRHS NLar WOld WWEG
- 'Royal Ruby' EBee ECtt LRHS NLar WOld WWEG
- 'Royal Velvet' WOld
- 'Rozika' WOld
- 'Rufus' WOld
- 'Sailor Boy' NCGa WOld
- 'Saint Egwyn' WOld
- 'Sam Banham' WOld
- 'Samoa' (Island Series) EPfP EWll LRHS LSou MBri NBPC NLar SBfd WCot
- 'Sandford White Swan' MHom WBrk WWEG
- 'Sarah Ballard' SRGP WOld
§ - 'Schneekissen' CPrp EBee ECtt EPfP EWTr GMaP LRHS MBNS MHer MMuc SBfd SBrd SPer SRGP SWvt WFar WOld WWEG XLum
- 'Schöne von Dietlikon' MAvo MWat WBox WOld XLum
- 'Schoolgirl' WOld WWEG
- 'Sheena' SRGP WOld
- 'Silberblaukissen' GBin WOld
- Snow Cushion see *A. novi-belgii* 'Schneekissen'
- 'Snowdrift' WOld
- 'Snowsprite' CBcs CSBt ELan LRHS MWat NEgg NLar NOrc NPro SMrs SRGP SRms SWat WOld
- 'Sonata' GMaP WOld
- 'Sophia' MWat SMrs WOld
- 'Starlight' EBee NLar WFar WOld WRHF
- 'Steinebrück' WOld
- 'Sterling Silver' WOld
- 'Sunset' WOld
- 'Susan' WOld
- 'Sweet Briar' CElw WOld
- 'Tapestry' WOld
- 'Terry's Pride' EBee SRGP WOld WWEG
- 'The Archbishop' ECtt WOld
- 'The Bishop' WOld
- 'The Cardinal' WOld
- 'The Choristers' WOld
- 'The Dean' WOld
§ - 'The Rector' WOld
- 'The Sexton' WOld
- 'Thundercloud' CAby MWat WOld
- 'Timsbury' SRms WBrk WOld WWEG
- 'Tony' WOld
- 'Tovarich' WOld
- 'Trudi Ann' NBir WOld
- 'Twinkle' WOld
- 'Victor' WOld
- 'Vignem' NSti
- 'Violet Lady' WOld
- 'Violetta' SMrs
- 'Waterperry' MWat WOld
- 'Weisses Wunder' WOld
- 'White Ladies' CBcs CHab ECtt GCra GMaP LRHS MMuc MWat NLar NOrc SBfd SPer SRGP XLum
- 'White Swan' CAby ECtt WOld
- 'White Wings' MWat WOld
- 'Winston S. Churchill' CEnt CMMP COIW CTri EBee ELan EPfP GMaP LRHS MWat SBfd SPlb SPoG SRGP WOld

***oblongifolius*** GCal SAga WOld WPer XSen
§ - 'Fanny's' CPrp EBee EBla ECtt GCal GQue MMuc MNFA SPoG SRGP WCot WFar WOld

| | | |
|---|---|---|
| | 'Ochtendgloren' (*pringlei* hybrid) 🏆H4 | CDes CPrp CSam EBee ECtt EPPr EWes MAvo MHom MNrw NCGa SMrm WCot WFar WHal WOld WOut |
| | Octoberlight | see *A.* 'Oktoberlicht' |
| § | 'Oktoberlicht' | LRHS NCGa SMrm WOld |
| | ***oolentangiensis*** | LRHS WPer |
| | 'Orchidee' | EPri EWes |
| | 'Orpheus' | MNrw |
| | ***pappei*** | see *Felicia amoena* |
| | 'Pearl Star' | WOld |
| § | ***peduncularis*** | EPPr LPla MBri NDov SPhx SUsu WCot |
| | ***petiolatus*** | see *Felicia petiolata* |
| | 'Photograph' 🏆H4 | CHVG CSam EBee GMac LRHS MAvo MHom SMrm WFar WMnd WOld |
| § | ***pilosus*** var. ***demotus*** 🏆H4 | ECha EWes MRav WFar WOld WTin |
| § | - var. ***pringlei*** 'Monte Cassino' 🏆H4 | CHid CSBt EBee ECtt EPfP GQue LEdu LHop LRHS MBNS MRav MWat NBPC SMrm SPer SPhx SRGP WFar WOld WWEG XLum |
| | - - 'October Glory' | CCse NDov WFar |
| | - - 'Phoebe' | WOld |
| | - - 'Pink Cushion' | CMHG WCot |
| | 'Pink Star' | CMea EBee ECtt GMaP GMac LRHS MNFA MRav MWat NDov NSti SBch SBfd WFar WHoo WOld WOut WTin XLum |
| | 'Pixie Dark Eye' (*ericoides* hybrid) | CDes EBee WCot |
| | 'Pixie Red Eye' (*ericoides* hybrid) | WCot |
| | 'Plowden's Pink' | WOld |
| | 'Prairie Lavender' | WOld |
| | 'Prairie Pink' | WOld |
| | 'Prairie Purple' **new** | WOld |
| | 'Prairie Violet' | WOld |
| | 'Primrose Path' | EBee MNrw WCot |
| | ***ptarmicoides*** | see *Solidago ptarmicoides* |
| | ***puniceus*** | EBee NBre XLum |
| | ***purdomii*** | see *A. flaccidus* |
| | ***pyrenaeus*** 'Lutetia' | CAby CPrp CSam EBee ECha GAbr GCal GMaP MAvo MHom MMuc MNFA MWat NCGa NDov NLar SBrd SEND SPoG SRGP WCAu WCot WFar WOld WWEG XLum |
| | ***radula*** | CSam EBee EPPr EWes LPla MAvo MNrw NBre NLar WOld WSHC |
| | 'Ringdove' (*ericoides* hybrid) 🏆H4 | CAby CKno CPrp EBee EBla GMac MCot MHom MNFA NCGa NSti SRGP WCot WOld WOut |
| | 'Rosa Star' | WOld |
| | 'Rose Queen' | MAvo |
| | ***rotundifolius*** 'Variegatus' | see *Felicia amelloides* variegated |
| | ***rugulosus*** 'Asrugo' | EBee |
| | ***sagittifolius*** Wed. **new** | XLum |
| | × ***salignus*** | WOld |
| | - Scottish form | WOld |
| * | ***sativus atrocaeruleus*** | LRHS |
| § | ***scaber*** | EBee WCot |
| | ***scandens*** | see *A. carolinianus* |
| | ***schreberi*** | CFir EBee EPPr EWes MAvo NBre NCGa WBor WCot WOld |
| § | ***sedifolius*** | EBee ECtt ELan GQue LEdu MDKP MWat NBid SDix SEND SPoG SUsu WCot WFar WMnd WOld WPer |
| | - RCBAM -5 | WCot |
| | - 'Nanus' | CAby CPLG ELan GCal LRHS MHom MNFA MRav NBir NLar SPer WCot WFar WMnd WOld WTin XLum |
| | - 'Roseus' | LRHS |
| § | ***sibiricus*** | NBre NLar WOld |
| | 'Snow Flurry' | see *A. ericoides* f. *prostratus* 'Snow Flurry' |
| | 'Snow Star' | WOld |
| | ***souliei*** | GLam |
| | ***spathulifolius*** | XLum |
| | ***spectabilis*** | LRHS WOld |
| | ***stracheyi*** | EDAr |
| | ***subcaeruleus*** | see *A. tongolensis* |
| | 'Sunhelene' | CDes WCot |
| | 'Sunqueen' | WCot |
| | ***tataricus*** | LPla |
| | - 'Jindai' | EBee WFar |
| | ***thomsonii*** | WFar WOld |
| | - 'Nanus' | CAby CCse GMaP GQue LRHS MCot SAga SBch WCot WOld WSHC |
| | ***tibeticus*** | see *A. flaccidus* |
| | 'Tina' **new** | NDov |
| | Tonga = 'Dasfour' | CWGN EPfP EWTr LRHS LSou NBir NLar SWvt WCot WHil |
| § | ***tongolensis*** | GKev SBHP SRms |
| | - 'Berggarten' | CHar EBee LRHS |
| | - 'Dunkleviolette' | NBro SRms |
| | - 'Napsbury' | EBee LRHS |
| | - 'Wartburgstern' | CFir EBee EPfP NGdn STes WWEG |
| | ***tradescantii*** misapplied | see *A. pilosus* var. *demotus* |
| | ***tradescantii*** L. | EBee ELan MBNS MMuc MRav NBre NSti SMad WBrk WCot WOld WTin |
| | ***trinervius*** var. ***harae*** | SSvw WOld |
| | ***tripolium*** | WHer |
| | 'Triumph' | WCot |
| | ***turbinellus*** misapplied 🏆H4 | CAby CKno EPfP GCal IKil LPla NGdn SPhx SRkn SUsu WBox WCot WHoo WOld WPtf WTin |
| | ***turbinellus*** Lindl. | CSam EPfP EWTr GBee LRHS MWat NCGa NLar |
| | - hybrid | SMrm SSvw WFar |
| | ***umbellatus*** | CBre CKno EBee GBin GQue NBir NBre NCGa NDov NLar SMrm SRms WCot WOld WTin |
| | 'Vasterival' | EBee MAvo NCGa NDov SSvw WBrk |
| | ***vimineus*** Lam. | see *A. lateriflorus* |
| | - 'Ptarmicoides' | see *Solidago ptarmicoides* |
| § | 'White Climax' | CAby EBee MHom WBox WBrk WCot |
| | 'Wood's Pink' | EBee |
| | 'Yvonne' | CBre |

## *Asteranthera* (*Gesneriaceae*)

| | |
|---|---|
| ***ovata*** | CGHE EPfP GGar LRHS LSou MAsh MOWG SBrd SLon SPoG WAbe WPGP WSHC |

## *Asteriscus* (*Asteraceae*)

| | |
|---|---|
| 'Gold Coin' | see *Pallenis maritima* |
| ***maritimus*** | see *Pallenis maritima* |

## *Asteromoea* (*Asteraceae*)

| | |
|---|---|
| ***mongolica*** | see *Kalimeris mongolica* |
| ***pinnatifida*** | see *Kalimeris pinnatifida* |

## *Asteropyrum* (*Ranunculaceae*)

| | |
|---|---|
| ***cavaleriei*** | GEdr WCot WCru |

## *Asterotrichion* (*Malvaceae*)

| | |
|---|---|
| ***discolor*** | ECou GGar SVen |

## *Astilbe* ✿ (*Saxifragaceae*)

| | |
|---|---|
| CC 5201 | CPLG |
| 'Alive and Kicking' | MBri |
| 'Amerika' (× *arendsii*) | CMHG CSBt ECtt |
| 'Amethyst' (× *arendsii*) | CMHG CMac ELon EPfP GBin LLWG MRav NBir NBre SApp SPer SPoG WFar WHoo WMoo WWEG |
| 'Angel Wings' (× *arendsii*) | NPro |
| 'Anita Pfeifer' (× *arendsii*) | CMHG ELon GBin LPBA NLar WFar |
| 'Aphrodite' (*simplicifolia* hybrid) | CBcs CWCL GCal MDKP MLHP MSCN NBre NPro WGor WWEG |
| × ***arendsii*** | IFoB NBre WMoo WPer |
| ***astilboides*** | CMHG SWvt |
| 'Atrorosea' (*simplicifolia* hybrid) | LRHS NCot SRms |
| 'Avalanche' | GAbr GBin NHol SPad WMnd WWEG |
| § 'Beauty of Ernst' (× *arendsii*) | LPBA LRHS SPoG WMoo |
| § 'Beauty of Lisse' (× *arendsii*) | LRHS |
| Bella Group (× *arendsii*) | NBre SPet WMnd |
| 'Bergkristall' (× *arendsii*) | CMHG |
| 'Betsy Cuperus' (*thunbergii* hybrid) | CMHG EBee GBin MRav NBre SApp WCAu |
| 'Bonn' (*japonica* hybrid) | CWCL CWat LRHS NLBP SCoo SRms |
| 'Boogie Woogie'[PBR] (× *arendsii*) **new** | MAsh |
| § 'Brautschleier' (× *arendsii*) ♀H4 | CMHG CMMP CMac CPrp CTri ECtt EPfP GBin GCra GKev LRHS LSRN MDun MSCN NGdn NLBP NLar WPnP WPtf XLum |
| 'Bremen' (*japonica* hybrid) | CMHG GBin LPBA LRHS |
| 'Bressingham Beauty' (× *arendsii*) | CMHG CPrp CSam CWCL ECtt ELan EPfP EPla GBin GKev GMaP LAst LHop LLWG LPBA LRHS MCot MDun MRav MWhi NHol NPro SPer SWvt WBor WFar WMoo WWEG |
| Bridal Veil (× *arendsii*) | see *A.* 'Brautschleier' |
| § 'Bronce Elegans' (*simplicifolia* hybrid) ♀H4 | CFir CMHG CPrp EBee ECha EPfP GBin GMaP LRHS MRav NHol NOrc NPro NWad WFar WMoo WOut WWEG |
| 'Bronzelaub' (× *arendsii*) | GBin |
| * ***bumalda*** 'Bronze Pygmy' | MMoz NHol STes |
| 'Bumalda' (× *arendsii*) | CFir CSBt CWCL GBin GMaP LRHS MWts NChi NGdn NMyG NOrc NPro SPlb WFar WMoo |
| 'Burgunderrot' (× *arendsii*) | CWCL EPfP GAbr MAsh MBri MLLN MNrw NCGa NLar SMrm |
| 'Carnea' (*simplicifolia* hybrid) | CMHG |
| 'Catherine Deneuve' | see *A.* 'Federsee' |
| 'Cattleya Dunkel' (× *arendsii*) | CMHG WFar |
| 'Cattleya' (× *arendsii*) | CMHG CSam LRHS NBPC NLar WFar WMoo |
| 'Ceres' (× *arendsii*) | CMHG |
| 'Cherry Ripe' | see *A.* 'Feuer' |
| ***chinensis*** | CMHG ECho LRHS NBre WFar WSHC |
| - B&SWJ 8178 | WCru |
| - from Russia | GCal |
| - 'Brokat' | GBin |
| - 'Christian' | GBin |
| - var. ***davidii*** | CMHG |
| - - B&SWJ 8583 | WCru |
| - - B&SWJ 8645 | WCru |
| - 'Diamonds and Pearls'[PBR] | CWGN GAbr LSou MAvo MBri |
| - 'Finale' | CHar COlW NHol NPro SPer WFar WOut |
| - 'Frankentroll' | CMHG |
| - 'Intermezzo' | GCal GMaP LRHS NLar |
| - 'Little Vision in Pink' **new** | WHil |
| - 'Love and Pride' | LSou MBri |
| - 'Milk and Honey'[PBR] | ECtt LSou MBNS |
| § - var. ***pumila*** ♀H4 | Widely available |
| - - 'Serenade' | CMac NGdn WFar |
| - 'Purple Glory' | CMHG EWll IKil MDun |
| - 'Spätsommer' | CMHG |
| - var. ***taquetii*** | CMac EBee LRHS NBre NSti SRms |
| - - Purple Lance | see *A. chinensis* var. *taquetii* 'Purpurlanze' |
| § - - 'Purpurlanze' | Widely available |
| § - - 'Superba' ♀H4 | CMHG CMac CRow CTri ECha GBin LRHS MCCP MLHP NBro SDix SPer SRms STes WFar WMoo |
| - 'Troll' | GBin |
| - 'Veronika Klose' | CMHG EBee GBin NLar NPro WWEG |
| - 'Vision in Pink'[PBR] | CMil CWCL LSou MAsh MBNS NPri SBfd WHil |
| - 'Vision in Red'[PBR] | CMil CWCL CWat ECtt EKen EWll GBin GGar LRHS LSou MBNS MBri MNrw NLar NPri SBfd SMad SPoG WCAu WFar WHil |
| - 'Vision in White' **new** | NPri SBfd SPoG WHil |
| - 'Visions' | CMHG CMac CMil CWCL EBee GBin GQue LRHS LSou MBNS MBri NBro NGdn NMyG NPro SBfd STes WFar |
| Cologne | see *A.* 'Köln' |
| Color Flash | see *A.* 'Beauty of Ernst' |
| Color Flash Lime | see *A.* 'Beauty of Lisse' |
| 'Country and Western'[PBR] (× *arendsii*) **new** | LSou |
| 'Crimson Feather' | see *A.* 'Gloria Purpurea' |
| × ***crispa*** | ECho WCFE WFar |
| - 'Gnom' | NHar SAga |
| - 'Lilliput' | ECtt GBee GBin GGar NBir NHar NLar NPro NRya |
| § - 'Perkeo' ♀H4 | CBcs CFir ECha ECho ECtt ELan EPfP GBin GGar GMaP LRHS NBir NHar NLar NMen NMyG NPri NPro SRms WAul WCot WFar WMoo WWEG |
| - 'Peter Pan' | see *A.* × *crispa* 'Perkeo' |
| - 'Snow Queen' | NBir NHar NMen NPro WFar |
| 'Darwin's Dream' | NLar NPri WFar |
| 'Darwin's Favourite' (× *arendsii*) | CWCL |
| 'Deutschland' (*japonica* hybrid) | Widely available |
| § 'Diamant' (× *arendsii*) | CMHG EShb LRHS LSRN MMuc NGdn NHol WFar |
| Diamond | see *A.* 'Diamant' |
| 'Drayton Glory' (× *arendsii*) | see *A.* × *rosea* 'Peach Blossom' |
| 'Drum and Bass'[PBR] | LSou NLar |
| 'Dunkelachs' (*simplicifolia* hybrid) | LRHS LTen MSCN NBPC NMyG WFar |
| 'Dusseldorf' (*japonica* hybrid) | CMHG CSam CWCL GKev LRHS NHol |
| 'Eden's Odysseus' | GBin NHol |
| 'Elegans' (*simplicifolia* hybrid) | CMHG CMac WFar |
| Elizabeth Bloom = 'Eliblo'[PBR] (× *arendsii*) | CHVG EBee ELon EPla LLWG LRHS MRav NDov NEgg NGdn NHol WFar |

| |  |  |
|---|---|---|
| | 'Elizabeth' (*japonica* hybrid) | CMHG EBee |
| | 'Ellie' (× *arendsii*) | CMHG CMac CWCL GBin GQue LSRN LSou MAsh MBNS MBri NBPC NGdn NHol NLar SAga SMrm WPtf |
| | 'Else Schluck' (× *arendsii*) | ECha |
| | 'Erica' (× *arendsii*) | CMHG CTri EWll GKev MRav NLar NPnk NPro WCAu WFar WMnd WMoo WWEG |
| | 'Etna' (*japonica* hybrid) | CBcs CMHG CSam EBee LRHS MMuc NEgg NGdn NHol NLar SMrm SRms WPnP |
| | 'Europa' (*japonica* hybrid) | CMHG CMac ECtt GBin LRHS MGos MRav NGdn SBfd SPoG WFar WMoo |
| | 'Fanal' (× *arendsii*) ♀H4 | Widely available |
| | 'Fata Morgana' (× *arendsii* hybrid) | CMHG |
| § | 'Federsee' (× *arendsii*) | CBcs CMHG ECha ECtt ELan LRHS MBNS NBPC NBre NBro NDov NGdn NPro SMrm SPer WFar XLum |
| § | 'Feuer' (× *arendsii*) | CMHG CMMP CMac CPrp ECtt ELan EPfP LBMP LRHS NEgg NGdn NHol NLar NOrc NPro NVic WBor WMoo |
| | Fire | see *A*. 'Feuer' |
| | 'Fireberry' (Short 'n' Sweet Series) new | NLar |
| | 'Flamingo'PBR (× *arendsii*) | GAbr GBin MBNS SMrm |
| § | ***formosa*** B&SWJ 10946 new | WCru |
| | 'Gertrud Brix' (× *arendsii*) | CBcs CWat GKev MMuc NBir NGdn NPro XLum |
| § | ***glaberrima*** | NBid NMen |
| § | - var. ***saxatilis*** ♀H4 | CRow EPfP GBin GLam IFro NHar NSla WAbe WHal WThu |
| | - ***saxosa*** | see *A. glaberrima* var. *saxatilis* |
| | 'Gladstone' (× *arendsii*) | see *A*. 'W.E. Gladstone' |
| § | 'Gloria Purpurea' (× *arendsii*) | CMHG NLBP NMyG WMoo |
| | 'Gloria' (× *arendsii*) | CMHG CMac CTri ECtt LPBA MRav WFar |
| | Glow | see *A*. 'Glut' |
| § | 'Glut' (× *arendsii*) | CFir CMHG CWCL ECtt GBin LLWG LRHS MMuc NGdn NHol SRms WFar WHil |
| | 'Granat' (× *arendsii*) | CMHG CMMP CMac NBir NBre NEgg NGdn NHol WFar WMoo |
| * | Grande Group (× *arendsii*) | NBre |
| | ***grandis*** | CMHG GBee LRHS WHer |
| | 'Grete Püngel' (× *arendsii*) | ECha GBin WFar WWEG |
| | 'Harmony' (× *arendsii*) | CMHG |
| | 'Heart and Soul'PBR | EPfP LSou MAvo MBri |
| | 'Hennie Graafland' (*simplicifolia* hybrid) | CBcs CMHG CWCL GAbr GBin GQue LRHS LSou NCGa NLar SHar |
| | 'Henry Noblett' | GBin |
| | 'Holden Clough' (*japonica* hybrid) | NHol NWad |
| | Hyacinth | see *A*. 'Hyazinth' |
| § | 'Hyazinth' (× *arendsii*) | CMHG CPLG CPrp GBin GMaP LBMP LLWG LSou WFar |
| | 'Inshriach Pink' (*simplicifolia* hybrid) | CBcs CCVN CMHG CPrp CYeo EHoe ELan GBin LRHS MBri NBir NHar NHol SAga SBch WFar WHal WOut |
| | 'Irrlicht' (× *arendsii*) | CMHG CMac ELan EPfP EPla EShb GGar LHop LPBA NWad SMrm SPer SWat WAul WWEG |
| | ***japonica*** | CPLG |
| * | - 'Pumila' | NBir NGdn |
| | - var. ***terrestris*** | see *A. glaberrima* |
| | 'Jo Ophorst' (*davidii* hybrid) | CMHG ECtt GBin LRHS MRav NEgg NGdn NHol NLar WFar |
| | 'Jump and Jive'PBR | LSou MAsh |
| | 'Koblenz' (*japonica* hybrid) | CMHG CWCL MDKP |
| § | 'Köln' (*japonica* hybrid) | CMHG CWat GBin LPBA LRHS NMyG WFar |
| | ***koreana*** | GGar WCot WPGP |
| | - B&SWJ 8611 | WCru |
| | - B&SWJ 8680 | WCru |
| | 'Kriemhilde' | CMHG MSCN |
| | 'Kvële' (× *arendsii*) | CMHG WFar WMoo |
| § | 'Lachskönigin' (× *arendsii*) | CMHG |
| | 'Lilli Goos' (× *arendsii*) | CMHG GBin GCal |
| | 'Lollipop' | GBin MAsh MBNS NPro SRms |
| | ***longicarpa*** B&SWJ 6711 | WCru |
| | ***macroflora*** | GCal |
| | 'Maggie Daley' | CMMP EBee NBro NPro WMoo |
| | 'Mainz' (*japonica* hybrid) | CHVG CMHG ECtt ELan LPBA |
| | 'Mars' (× *arendsii*) | CMHG |
| | ***microphylla*** | CMHG |
| | - B&SWJ 11085 | WCru |
| | - pink-flowered | CMHG NWad |
| | 'Moerheim Glory' (× *arendsii*) | CMMP GBin MSCN NBre NGdn NLar |
| | 'Moerheimii' (*thunbergii* hybrid) | CMHG |
| | 'Mont Blanc' (× *arendsii*) | CMHG |
| | 'Montgomery' (*japonica* hybrid) | CMHG CWCL CWGN EShb EWTr GAbr GBin IKil LBMP LRHS LSRN MAvo MBNS MBri MCot MMuc MRav NBro NCGa NEgg NGdn NHol SAga SBfd SMrm WFar |
| | 'Nikki' | NCGa NLar NPro |
| | 'Obergärtner Jürgens' (× *arendsii*) | CMMP GBin |
| § | ***okuyamae*** B&SWJ 10975 new | WCru |
| | Ostrich Plume | see *A*. 'Straussenfeder' |
| | 'Paul Gaärder' (× *arendsii*) | CMHG |
| | 'Peaches and Cream' | EBee MMHG NBro NLar NPnk |
| | 'Peter Barrow' (*glaberrima* hybrid) | GBin SRms |
| | 'Pink Fanal' | LRHS |
| | 'Pink Lightening'PBR (*simplicifolia* hybrid) | CWCL EBee EShb MAvo MBNS MBri NBPC NLar NOrc SMrm |
| | Pink Pearl (× *arendsii*) | see *A*. 'Rosa Perle' |
| | 'Poschka' | CFir |
| | 'Poschka Alba' | CFir NPro |
| | 'Professor van der Wielen' (*thunbergii* hybrid) | CFir CMHG EBee GGar GQue MDun NHol NLar SDix SPer SRms WCAu WFar WWEG |
| | ***pumila*** | see *A. chinensis* var. *pumila* |
| * | 'Queen' | LPBA |
| | 'Radius' | CMMP GBin LPBA MSCN NGdn NLar WHil WPnP |
| | 'Red Baron' new | SPad |
| | Red Light | see *A*. 'Rotlicht' |
| | 'Red Sentinel' (*japonica* hybrid) | CBcs CMMP CWCL CWat EPfP GBin GMaP LRHS MBri MSCN NBro NGdn NHol NPro SBfd WFar WHrl |
| | 'Rheinland' (*japonica* hybrid) ♀H4 | CBcs CMHG CMMP CWCL CYeo GBin GKev LPBA LRHS MLLN MMuc NGdn SBrd SRot STes WFar WHoo WPnP |
| | 'Rhythm and Blues'PBR | ECtt NLar |
| | ***rivularis*** | CMHG GBin WCot |
| | - CC 4547 | EBee |
| | - CC 5201 | GKev |
| | - GWJ 9366 | WCru |
| § | - var. ***myriantha*** | NBre |

| | |
|---|---|
| - - BWJ 8076a | WCru |
| - - SICH 757 | CPLG |
| 'Robinson's Pink' **new** | NGdn |
| 'Rock and Roll'[PBR] | CMil LPBA LSRN NBPC WHil |
| § 'Rosa Perle' (× *arendsii*) | CHVG CMHG CSam NHol |
| § × ***rosea*** 'Peach Blossom' | CBcs CHVG CMHG CMMP ELon GCra LPBA LRHS NBir NGdn NPro SBfd SPoG WFar WHoo WMoo |
| - 'Queen Alexandra' | WFar |
| 'Rosea' (*simplicifolia* hybrid) | GBin NHol WFar |
| 'Rot Straussenfeder' (× *arendsii*) | GBin MSCN |
| § 'Rotlicht' (× *arendsii*) | CMHG CMac LRHS NGdn NHol NPro SBfd WFar WGor |
| 'Salland' | GCal LRHS |
| Salmon Queen | see *A.* 'Lachskönigin' |
| 'Salmonea' (*simplicifolia* hybrid) | CMHG |
| 'Saxosa' | see *A. glaberrima* var. *saxatilis* |
| Showstar Group (× *arendsii*) | LRHS MSnd WHil |
| ***simplicifolia*** 🏆[H4] | CAby CRow SKHP WFar |
| - 'Alba' | CMHG NPro |
| - Bronze Elegance | see *A.* 'Bronce Elegans' |
| - 'Darwin's Snow Sprite' | CMac GBin NHol NLar NMyG NPri WFar |
| - 'Jacqueline' | EBee LSou NHol WFar |
| * - 'Nana Alba' | NPro |
| - 'Praecox Alba' | EBee GBin NEgg WWEG |
| - 'Rose of Cimarron' | NPro |
| - 'Sheila Haxton' | LRHS NHar |
| - 'White Sensation'[PBR] | LRHS NBPC NLar |
| 'Snowdrift' (× *arendsii*) | CHid CMHG CWat EPla EWTr GMaP IKil LBMP LLWG LRHS MBNS MDKP MLLN MMuc MWat NBir NEgg NOrc NPro SPer SWat WFar WWEG |
| 'Solferino' (× *arendsii*) | CMHG |
| 'Spartan' (× *arendsii*) | see *A.* 'Rotlicht' |
| 'Spinell' (× *arendsii*) | CWCL LRHS MDun NBre NCGa NMRc WFar WPnP WWEG |
| 'Sprite' (*simplicifolia* hybrid) 🏆[H4] | Widely available |
| 'Stand and Deliver'[PBR] | ECtt MBri |
| § 'Straussenfeder' (*thunbergii* hybrid) 🏆[H4] | CMHG CMac CTri ECtt EPfP EPla GBin GMaP LBMP LHop LRHS NBid NBir NBro NGdn NHol NLar NOrc NWad SPer SPoG WAul WCAu WFar WMoo WPtf WWEG |
| 'Sugar Plum' (*simplicifolia* hybrid) | NGdn |
| 'Sugarberry' (Short 'n' Sweet Series) **new** | NLar |
| 'Superba' | see *A. chinensis* var. *taquetii* 'Superba' |
| ***thunbergii*** | CEnt CPLG LRHS |
| - var. ***congesta*** B&SWJ 10961 | WCru |
| - var. ***formosa*** | see *A. formosa* |
| - var. ***hachijoensis*** | EBee |
| - - B&SWJ 5622 | WCru |
| - var. ***okuyamae*** | see *A. okuyamae* |
| - var. ***sikokumontanum*** B&SWJ 11164 | WCru |
| - var. ***terrestris*** B&SWJ 6125 | WCru |
| 'To Have and To Hold' | LSou |
| 'Venus' (× *arendsii*) | CSam ECha ECtt GBin GGar GMaP LPBA LRHS MBNS MCot NGdn NHol NOrc NVic SPer SWat WCAu WFar WMoo |
| 'Vesuvius' (*japonica* hybrid) | CBcs EWTr LRHS MDKP NBro NLar |
| ***virescens*** | see *A. rivularis* var. *myriantha* |
| § 'W.E. Gladstone' (*japonica* hybrid) | CWat WGor |
| 'Walküre' (× *arendsii*) | CMHG |
| 'Walter Bitner' | GBin LLWG LRHS MBNS NBre NHol SRGP |
| 'Washington' (*japonica* hybrid) | EBee LAst MDKP NBre NGdn SHar |
| § 'Weisse Gloria' (× *arendsii*) | CMHG CMac CPrp ECha GBin LLWG LPBA LRHS NBPC NBro NDov NEgg NHol NMyG NOrc SBfd SCoo SMrm WBor WMoo WTin |
| White Gloria | see *A.* 'Weisse Gloria' |
| 'White Wings'[PBR] (*simplicifolia* hybrid) | NLar |
| 'William Reeves' (× *arendsii*) | CMHG NHol |
| 'Willie Buchanan' (*simplicifolia* hybrid) | CBcs CHid CMHG CPrp CYeo EHoe GAbr GBin GGar GKev GLam GMaP LBMP LRHS NEgg NGdn NHar NHol NMen SApp SPer SRms WAbe WFar WMoo WNew WWEG |
| Younique Carmine = 'Verscarmine'[PBR] | LSou WHil |
| Younique Pink = 'Verspink'[PBR] **new** | WHil |
| Younique Silvery Pink = 'Versilverypink'[PBR] | WHil |
| 'Zuster Theresa' (× *arendsii*) | CMHG EBee LPBA LRHS MBNS MNrw MSCN NBPC NBro WFar |

## *Astilboides* (*Saxifragaceae*)

| | |
|---|---|
| § ***tabularis*** | Widely available |

## *Astragalus* (*Papilionaceae*)

| | |
|---|---|
| ***canadensis*** | LRHS SPhx |
| ***glycyphyllos*** | CArn SPhx |
| ***membranaceus*** | CArn MNHC |
| ***purshii*** | ECho |

## *Astrantia* ✿ (*Apiaceae*)

| | |
|---|---|
| 'Atomic Sunburst' | GQue |
| ***bavarica*** | GCal MDKP MFie WFar |
| 'Berendien Stam' | EBee MAvo MFie |
| 'Bloody Mary' | CBct EBee ELan LSRN MBNS MFie NBPC NGdn NLar |
| 'Buckland' | Widely available |
| 'Bury Court' **new** | NDov |
| ***carniolica*** | EPyc NEgg WCAu |
| - ***major*** | see *A. major* |
| - 'Rubra' | CBcs EBee GMaP LRHS MFie MPkF NBre WHal |
| - 'Variegata' | see *A. major* 'Sunningdale Variegated' |
| 'Clear Pink' **new** | NDov |
| 'Dark Shiny Eyes' | CBct CLAP CPLG CWCL EBee ECtt LLHF MAvo MBNS NCGa NGBo NGdn NLar NSti SPoG SWvt |
| 'Hadspen Blood' | Widely available |
| Harptree hybrid | CHar |
| 'Helen' | NLar |
| ***helleborifolia*** misapplied | see *A. maxima* |
| 'Larch Cottage Clear Pink' **new** | NLar |
| 'Larch Cottage Magic' | MAvo NLar |
| 'Madeleine' | see *A. major* 'Madeleine van Bennekom' |

| | | |
|---|---|---|
| § | ***major*** | Widely available |
| | - 'Abbey Road'[PBR] | CBct CKno CLAP CPLG CWCL EBee EBla ECtt EWTr LHop LLWG LSou MFie NBPC NEgg NLar SMrm WCAu |
| I | - 'Alba' | CBcs CMHG CWCL EBee EBla ECha IBal IKil LRHS MCot MFie MRav NBir NGdn NPer SPer STes WMnd WMoo |
| | - 'Ann Cann' | CBct |
| | - subsp. ***biebersteinii*** | MFie NBir NBre |
| | - 'Bo-Ann' | CWCL MFie NLar WAul WFar |
| | - 'Celtic Star' | CSpe EBee LRHS MFie SWvt |
| | - 'Claret' | Widely available |
| | - Cliff's form | MFie |
| | - 'Cottage Herbery' | MAvo |
| | - dwarf | WFar |
| | - 'Elmblut' | MAvo MFie WHil |
| | - 'Florence'[PBR] | LBuc LRHS NCGa NDov SBrd SPoG STes |
| | - 'Gill Richardson' | CKno CLAP CPLG EAEE EBee EBla ECha EPri EShb GCal IPot LHop LLWG LRHS LSRN MFie MNFA MRav NDov NGdn NOrc SUsu WMoo |
| | - 'Gracilis' | EBee |
| | - 'Greenfingers' | EWes |
| | - 'Gwaun Valley' | WFar |
| | - 'Hillview Red' | EBee |
| | - subsp. ***involucrata*** | EBee EBla MFie MLLN SWat WFar |
| | - - 'Barrister' | CSam CWCL MAvo MFie NLar WFar |
| | - - 'Canneman' | EBee EBla EWes LPla MFie NLar WCot WFar |
| | - - 'Jumble Hole' | NDov |
| | - - 'Margery Fish' | see *A. major* subsp. *involucrata* 'Shaggy' |
| | - - 'Moira Reid' | CBct CKno CLAP CMil CPLG CSam EBee EBla ECtt ELan EShb GCal GMaP IPot LAst LRHS LSRN LSou MAvo MCot MFie MRav MWhi NDov NPnk SUsu WFar |
| | - - 'Orlando' | CLAP EBee MFie |
| § | - - 'Shaggy' ♀H4 | Widely available |
| | - 'Jade Lady' | WFar |
| | - 'Jitse' | EBee MAvo |
| | - 'Lars' | Widely available |
| | - 'Little Snowstar' | IBal |
| | - 'Lola' | CBcs EBee LLWG MAvo NCGa |
| § | - 'Madeleine van Bennekom' | CLAP |
| | - 'Paper Moon' | WFar |
| | - 'Penny's Pink' | MFie |
| | - 'Percy Picton' | MAvo |
| | - 'Pink Pride' | EBee LSou NCGa |
| | - 'Primadonna' | EBee EBla EPri GMaP MFie NHol NLar SPlb WFar WPer WWEG |
| | - 'Princesse Sturdza' | EBee NCGa |
| | - 'Reverse Sunningdale Variegated' (v) | LSou MAvo MFie |
| | - 'Rosa Lee' | EBee MFie NPnk WAul |
| | - var. ***rosea*** | CBre CWCL EBee EBla EPfP LHop LRHS LSRN MFie MRav MWat MWhi NGdn SAga SMrm SPer WCAu WFar WMoo WWEG |
| | - - George's form | CBct CKno CLAP CPrp CSam CWCL EAEE EBee EBla ECtt LHop LRHS LSRN LSou MFie NCGa NDov NEgg NHol NPnk SMrm SPoG SPur |
| | - 'Rosensinfonie' | EBee EBla GMaP MFie NBro NGdn NPnk NPro WFar WMnd |
| § | - 'Rubra' | Widely available |
| | - 'Ruby Cloud' | CHid CPrp EBee EBla EPri IBal LLWG LRHS MFie MNrw NBro NGdn NSti SRot WFar WFoF WMnd WWEG |
| | - 'Ruby Glow' | MFie |
| | - 'Ruby Star' | CLAP ECGP ECtt ELon MAvo MFie MLLN MTis NDov NLar SUsu SWvt WCot WCra |
| | - 'Ruby Wedding' | Widely available |
| | - 'Silver Glow' | CSpr ECtt IBal NBPC NMyG WFar |
| | - 'Star of Billion'[PBR] **new** | LSou |
| | - 'Star of Summer' | EBee EKen |
| | - 'Starburst' | CDes MFie WFar |
| | - 'Sue Barnes' (v) | EBee GCal MAvo MFie |
| § | - 'Sunningdale Variegated' (v) ♀H4 | Widely available |
| | - 'Titoki Point' | MFie WCot |
| | - 'Venice'[PBR] | CWCL CWGN IPot LRHS LSou MLLN NCGa NDov NLar NSti SBrd SPoG STes |
| § | ***maxima*** ♀H4 | Widely available |
| | - 'Mark Fenwick' | MFie NBir |
| * | - ***rosea*** | ECtt MDKP MNrw MWhi NBir NGdn WWEG |
| | ***minor*** | EBee WCru WFar |
| | 'Moulin Rouge'[PBR] | Widely available |
| | 'Pink Crush' **new** | LRHS |
| | 'Queen's Children' | EBee |
| | 'Rainbow' | MFie NLar |
| | 'Roma'[PBR] | Widely available |
| | ***rubra*** | see *A. major* 'Rubra' |
| | 'Sheila's Red' | LRHS LSRN NCGa NDov |
| | 'Snow Star'[PBR] | CWCL CWib EBee GBin LRHS MBNS MFie NLar NPnk SBrd SPoG |
| | 'Star of Beauty'[PBR] | CWCL ECtt LSou MFie MMHG MSCN NGdn NLar NSti SMrm |
| | 'Star of Fire' **new** | LSou MLLN NCGa |
| | 'Star of Heaven' | NLar |
| | 'Star of Royals'[PBR] | ECtt LSou SBfd |
| | 'Superstar' | ECtt LRHS MLLN MTis NDov NLar SWvt WCot |
| | 'Warren Hills' | CCVN CLAP EBla GMaP MFie NLar NPnk |
| | 'Washfield' | CYeo NDov |

## *Astrodaucus* (*Apiaceae*)

| | | |
|---|---|---|
| | ***orientalis*** | SPhx |

## *Asyneuma* (*Campanulaceae*)

| | | |
|---|---|---|
| | ***canescens*** | CEnt LRHS LSou NBre SGar |
| § | ***prenanthoides*** | SMrm |
| | - 'Cambell Blue' **new** | LRHS |
| | ***pulvinatum*** | CPBP ITim WAbe |

## *Asystasia* (*Acanthaceae*)

| | | |
|---|---|---|
| | ***bella*** | see *Mackaya bella* |
| § | ***gangetica*** | CSev WHil |
| | ***violacea*** | see *A. gangetica* |

## *Athamanta* (*Apiaceae*)

| | | |
|---|---|---|
| | ***turbith*** | CSpe |
| | ***vestina*** | SPhx |

## *Athanasia* (*Asteraceae*)

| | | |
|---|---|---|
| § | ***parviflora*** | SPlb |

## *Atherosperma* (*Atherospermataceae*)

| | | |
|---|---|---|
| | ***moschatum*** | CBcs CHII IRar SKHP WSHC |

## *Athrotaxis* (*Cupressaceae*)

| | |
|---|---|
| ***cupressoides*** | CDoC CDul CKen WThu |
| ***laxifolia*** | CDoC CKen MGos WThu |
| ***selaginoides*** | CDoC IGor |

## *Athyrium* ✿ (*Woodsiaceae*)

| | | |
|---|---|---|
| | 'Branford Beauty' | CBty CCCN CDes CLAP EFtx ISha LRHS NLar WPGP WRic |
| | 'Branford Rambler' | CLAP ISha WRic |
| | ***filix-femina*** ♀H4 | Widely available |
| § | - subsp. ***angustum*** | CBty CLAP ELan GBin MMoz NGdn SRms WMoo WRic |
| | - - f. ***rubellum*** 'Lady in Red' | CCCN CDes CElw CKel CLAP EBee EFtx ELon ESwi ISha LLHF LRHS LSRN LTen MGos NBid NLar SPoG WMoo WRic WWEG |
| | - 'Corymbiferum' | SRms |
| | - 'Crispum Grandiceps Kaye' | NGdn SRms |
| | - Cristatum Group | CLAP EBee EFer EFtx ELan LSRN MMoz NGdn SWat WFib |
| | - 'Dre's Dagger' | EFtx NLar SPoG WFar WWEG |
| | - 'Encourage' | WFar |
| | - 'Fieldii' | CLAP SRms |
| | - 'Frizelliae' ♀H4 | Widely available |
| | - 'Frizelliae Capitatum' | CLAP WFib WPGP |
| | - 'Frizelliae Cristatum' | EFtx SRms |
| | - 'Grandiceps' | CLAP EBee SRms |
| | - 'Lady-in-Lace' **new** | CBty |
| | - 'Minutissimum' | CBty CDes CGHE CLAP EBee ECha ELan ISha MMoz SUsu |
| * | - 'Nudicaule' | SRms |
| | - Plumosum Group | CLAP WFib |
| | - 'Plumosum Axminster' | CBty CLAP EFer NLar NMyG WFar |
| | - 'Plumosum Divaricatum' | SRms |
| | - 'Plumosum Druery' | CLAP |
| | - Red Stem | see *A. filix-femina* 'Rotstiel' |
| § | - 'Rotstiel' | CDTJ CLAP EBee MMoz MMuc SBfd WFar WMoo WPnP WRic WWEG |
| | - 'Vernoniae' ♀H4 | CBty CDTJ CLAP ELan LPBA MMoz NLar WRic |
| | - 'Vernoniae Cristatum' | CLAP WFib |
| | - 'Victoriae' | CBty CCCN CDTJ CDes CPrp CWCL EBee EFer EKen GEdr GMaP ISha LPBA LRHS LTen MMuc NBPC NBid NGdn NLar NMyG SEND WMoo WPat WWEG XLum |
| | - Victoriae Group | see *A. filix-femina* subsp. *angustum* |
| | - 'Victoriae' seedling | MBri WPtf |
| | 'Ghost' | CBty CCCN CDes CKel CLAP EFtx ISha LRHS LSou LTen MAvo MGos NLar NMyG NSti WPat WPtf WRic |
| | ***goeringianum*** 'Pictum' | see *A. niponicum* var. *pictum* |
| | ***niponicum*** | WHal |
| | - f. ***metallicum*** | see *A. niponicum* var. *pictum* |
| § | - var. ***pictum*** ♀H3 | Widely available |
| | - - 'Apple Court' | CBty CCCN EFtx ISha LRHS NLar WRic |
| | - - 'Burgundy Lace' PBR | CBty CLAP EFtx MNrw NLar NMyG NPri SHeu SMrm WPat WPtf |
| * | - - 'Cristatoflabellatum' | CLAP |
| | - - 'Pewter Lace' PBR | CBty EFtx NLar |
| | - - 'Red Beauty' | CBty CDTJ CEnt CLAP EBee ECha EPfP GAbr GBin GCal LRHS LSRN LTen NHol NLar SBfd SGol SPad SPoG WCot WPat WPnP WWEG |
| | - - 'Regal Red' | CBty ISha LRHS |
| | - - 'Silver Falls' | CBty CLAP CMil EAmu EShb GBin GKev NMyG WCot WHal WPGP |
| | - - 'Soul Mate' | CLAP |
| | - - 'Ursula's Red' | CBcs CBty CCVN CElw CLAP CTrC EFtx EShb GBin IBal LHop LRHS LSRN LSou MAvo NBid NBir NEgg NLar NPnk SMrm SPer WCot WFar WPGP |
| | - - 'Wildwood Twist' | CBty CLAP EFtx |
| | 'Ocean's Fury' | CBty EFtx |
| | ***oppositipinnum*** | WRic |
| | ***otophorum*** ♀H4 | ISha NBid SRms WIvy WPGP WRic |
| | - var. ***okanum*** | Widely available |
| | ***reflexipinnum*** | WRic |
| | ***vidalii*** | CDTJ CLAP EBee ISha LRHS LSou MAvo MMoz NEgg NLar NMyG SMrm WFib WRic WWEG |
| | ***wardii*** | WRic |

## *Atractylodes* (*Asteraceae*)

| | |
|---|---|
| ***japonica*** | EFEx |
| ***macrocephala*** | CArn EFEx |

## *Atragene* see *Clematis*

## *Atriplex* (*Amaranthaceae*)

| | |
|---|---|
| ***canescens*** | NLar WDin |
| ***cinerea*** | ECou |
| ***halimus*** | CArn CBcs CBot ECha ECre EHoe ELau EPPr LTen MBri MRav NLar SDix SEND SLon SPer SPlb WCot WDin WKif |
| ***hortensis*** var. ***rubra*** | CArn CEnt CSpe EGHP ELan LSou MHer MNHC SIde SMrm WCot WJek |

## *Atropa* (*Solanaceae*)

| | |
|---|---|
| ***acuminata*** | CArn |
| ***bella-donna*** | CArn GPoy SBrt SEND |
| ***mandragora*** | see *Mandragora officinarum* |

## *Aubrieta* (*Brassicaceae*)

| | | |
|---|---|---|
| | 'Alba' | see *A.* 'Fiona' |
| | ***albomarginata*** | see *A.* 'Argenteovariegata' |
| | 'Alix Brett' | CMea LRHS |
| | 'Ann Kendall' | ECtt |
| § | 'Argenteovariegata' (v) ♀H4 | ECho ELan LRHS WFar |
| | 'Astolat' (v) | ECho SRms |
| § | 'Aureovariegata' (v) ♀H4 | CMea ECho ELan NPer WAbe WFar XLum |
| | (Axcent Series) 'Axcent Antique Magenta' | WGor |
| | - 'Axcent Antique Rose' | WGor |
| | bicolour **new** | CMea |
| | Blaue Schönheit | see *A.* 'Blue Beauty' |
| | 'Blaumeise' | LRHS |
| § | 'Blue Beauty' | CMea ECtt EPfP GAbr MAsh NBlu WHil WHoo WNew |
| | 'Blue Chip' | ECtt |
| | 'Blue Whale' | ECtt LHop SRot SWvt |
| § | 'Bob Saunders' (d) | CMea ECho LRHS NCGa |
| | 'Bressingham Pink' (d) ♀H4 | CMea ECtt ELan EPfP SPoG WFar |
| | 'Bressingham Red' | ECho ECtt EPfP SPoG |
| | 'Bubble Purple' | EPfP |
| | ***canescens*** | XSen |
| | - subsp. ***cilicica*** | EPot |
| | Cascade Series | GJos MAsh SPoG |
| | - 'Blue Cascade' | EPfP MBNS MWat SPlb SPoG WGor WRHF |
| | - 'Lilac Cascade' | SPoG |

| | |
|---|---|
| - 'Purple Cascade' | CTri CWib EPfP LSRN MBNS MWat SPhx SPlb SPoG SRms WFar WGor |
| - 'Red Cascade' ♀H4 | CTri CWib ECtt EPfP LSRN MBNS SPhx SPlb SPoG STre SWal |
| ***deltoidea*** | SVic XSen |
| * - 'Gloria' | CMea CWCL SRot |
| - 'Nana Variegata' (v) | CPBP WGor |
| - Variegata Group (v) | ECtt NSla WFar |
| 'Doctor Mules' ♀H4 | ECtt LRHS MAsh SRms WAbe |
| 'Doctor Mules Variegata' (v) | CTri ECho ECtt EPfP LAst MHer NBlu SPoG SWvt WFar WHoo |
| 'Downers Variegata' (v) | EPot |
| 'Eila' (d) | STre |
| 'Elsa Lancaster' | CPBP NMen WAbe WPat |
| § 'Fiona' | ECtt |
| § 'Frühlingszauber' | SRms |
| ***glabrescens*** | WAbe |
| 'Gloria' **new** | EPot |
| 'Gloriosa' | GAbr MAsh |
| 'Golden King' | see *A.* 'Aureovariegata' |
| ***gracilis*** | EPot GEdr NMen WAbe |
| - 'Kitte Rose' | ECtt |
| * 'Graeca' | LRHS |
| 'Greencourt Purple' ♀H4 | CMea ECho ELan MHer MWat |
| 'Gurgedyke' | SRms |
| 'Hamburger Stadtpark' | ECho ECtt EPfP NBlu SRot |
| 'Hemswell Purity' PBR | see *A.* 'Snow Maiden' |
| 'Hendersonii' | SRms |
| 'J.S. Baker' | SRms |
| 'Joy' (d) | ECtt |
| 'Kati' | NCGa |
| 'Kitte' | ECho ECtt EPfP LRHS NBlu NLar NPri SPoG |
| 'Kitte Blue' **new** | LRHS |
| 'Kitte Purple' **new** | LRHS |
| 'Leichtlinii' | LRHS XLum |
| ***macedonica*** | WAbe |
| 'Maurice Prichard' | LRHS |
| 'Moerheim' | GQue MAsh |
| 'Mrs Rodewald' ♀H4 | SRms |
| 'Novalis Blue' | SRms |
| ***pinardii*** | WAbe XSen |
| 'Pink Beauty' | ECtt |
| 'Purple Charm' | SRms |
| 'Red Carpet' | ECho ECtt ELan EPot MAsh MHer SPoG SRms |
| 'Red Carpet Variegated' (v) | CMea |
| 'Rose Queen' | CMea CPBP SMrm |
| Royal Series ♀H4 | COIW |
| - 'Royal Blue' | EPfP LRHS NEgg WFar WMoo WRHF XLum |
| - 'Royal Lavender' | LRHS WFar |
| - 'Royal Lilac' | WFar |
| - 'Royal Red' | EPfP LRHS SBch SRms WFar WGor WMoo |
| - 'Royal Rose' | LRHS NBre WFar |
| - 'Royal Violet' | CTri EPfP LRHS SBch WFar WMoo XLum |
| 'Schloss Eckberg' | GQue |
| 'Schofield's Double' | see *A.* 'Bob Saunders' |
| 'Silberrand' | ECha |
| § 'Snow Maiden' PBR | ECtt WFar |
| 'Somerfield Silver' | EPfP NPri |
| 'Somerford Lime' (v) | ECtt EPfP |
| Spring Charm | see *A.* 'Frühlingszauber' |
| 'Swan Red' (v) | ECtt GKev LIMB LRHS MHer NEgg NSla SPoG WFar WHil WHoo |
| ***thessala*** | CPBP |
| 'Triumphante' | ECtt LRHS |
| 'Valerie' (v) **new** | EPot |
| 'Whitewell Gem' | SRms WMoo |

## *Aucuba* ✿ (*Garryaceae*)

| | |
|---|---|
| ***japonica*** | CAlb CCVT MSCN SEWo WCru |
| - (f) | CDul WDin |
| - 'Crassifolia' (m) | EBtc EQua SArc |
| - 'Crotonifolia' (f/v) ♀H4 | Widely available |
| - 'Crotonifolia' (m/v) | CMac MAsh SGol SRms WRHF |
| - 'Dentata' | CHEx WCru |
| - 'February Star' (f/v) | SDix |
| - 'Golden King' (m/v) ♀H4 | CAlb CDoC CMac CWib EBee ELan ELon EPfP LRHS LSRN MAsh MGos MWat NLar SGol SLim SPer SPoG |
| - 'Golden Spangles' (f/v) | CAlb CBcs CDoC EBee IVic NLar NMun SLim SWvt |
| - 'Goldstrike' (v) | EBee LRHS LSRN MAsh NEgg SMad |
| - 'Hillieri' (f) | EBtc EQua |
| - f. ***longifolia*** ♀H4 | CMac NLar SArc SDix WCot WCru |
| - - 'Lance Leaf' (m) | EPla EQua |
| - - 'Salicifolia' (f) | CHEx LAst MRav NLar WCru WDin WFar WPGP |
| - 'Maculata' hort. | see *A. japonica* 'Variegata' |
| - 'Marmorata' | LRHS |
| - 'Mr Goldstrike' (m/v) | EPfP LRHS SBfd |
| - 'Nana Rotundifolia' (f) | EPla |
| - Pepper Pot = 'Shilpot' (m/v) | CHEx EPfP LRHS MAsh SLon SPoG |
| - 'Picturata' (m/v) | CDul CHEx CMac CSBt EBee ELan LRHS MAsh MGos MRav NHol NLar SEND SLim SPer WFar |
| - 'Rozannie' (f/m) ♀H4 | CBar CBcs CDoC CDul CEnd CMac CSBt EBee ECrN ELan ELon EPfP EPla IVic LRHS LSRN MAsh MBlu MGos MRav NLar NPri SBfd SLim SPer SPoG SWvt WDin WFar |
| - 'Sulphurea Marginata' (f/v) | CBcs CMac CTri EBee ECrN ESwi LRHS NLar SPer |
| § - 'Variegata' (f/v) | Widely available |
| - Windsor form (f) | EQua |
| ***omeiensis*** | WPGP |
| - BWJ 8048 | WCru |

## *Aulax* (*Proteaceae*)

| | |
|---|---|
| ***cancellata*** | SPlb |

## *Aurinia* (*Brassicaceae*)

| | |
|---|---|
| § ***saxatilis*** ♀H4 | ECho EPfP MAsh MMuc NPri SPlb STre WFar WNew |
| - 'Argentea' | ECho |
| - 'Citrina' ♀H4 | ECha ECtt MWat SRms |
| - 'Compacta' | CTri ECtt GJos |
| - 'Dudley Nevill Variegated' (v) | ECha ECho ECtt ELon EWes MHer NBir NSla WFar |
| - Gold Ball | see *A. saxatilis* 'Goldkugel' |
| - 'Gold Dust' | ECho ECtt SRms |
| - 'Golden Queen' | ECtt MHer |
| § - 'Goldkugel' | ECho EPfP IFoB NBlu SPoG WFar |
| - 'Variegata' (v) | NPri SPoG |

## *Austrocedrus* (*Cupressaceae*)

| | |
|---|---|
| § ***chilensis*** | CBcs CKen CMen GBin IGor SBig WAle |
| - 'Thornhayes Ghost' | CTho |

## *Austromyrtus* (*Myrtaceae*)

| | |
|---|---|
| § ***dulcis*** | ECou |

## *Avena* (*Poaceae*)

| | |
|---|---|
| ***candida*** | see *Helictotrichon sempervirens* |
| ***sativa*** 'French Black' | CSpe |

## *Avenula* see *Helictotrichon*

## *Averrhoa* (*Oxalidaceae*)

***carambola*** (F) CCCN

## avocado see *Persea americana*

## *Azalea* see *Rhododendron*

## *Azara* ✿ (*Salicaceae*)

sp. NEgg
***celastrina*** IArd
***dentata*** CBcs CHll CMac GGal LAst WDin WFar
- 'Variegata' see *A. integrifolia* 'Variegata'
* ***integerrima*** GQui
***integrifolia*** CBcs CCCN
- 'Uarie' CCCN
§ - 'Variegata' (v) CWib EBee IRar LRHS NEgg
***lanceolata*** CDul CMCN CPLG CTri GGal LEdu NSti WFar WGrn
***microphylla*** ♀H3 CBcs CDoy CDul CLnd CMCN CMac CPLG CTri EBee EPfP GGal IVic LAst LRHS MAsh NSti SArc SBfd SDix SEND SLim SPer SPlb SSpi WFar WPGP WSHC
- 'Gold Edge' (v) LRHS WFar
- 'Variegata' (v) CBcs CDoC CMac CPLG CPMA CWGN CWib EBee EBtc EHoe EPfP GQui LAst LBMP LRHS MAsh MRav MSCN NLar NSti SEND SLon SPoG SSpi SSta STre WFar WPat WSHC
* ***patagonica*** MBlu
***petiolaris*** EPfP
***serrata*** ♀H3 CBcs CDul CEnd CEnt CMCN CWib EBee EPfP GBin GGar LRHS MSCN NCGa NLar NMun SDix SEND SGar SGol SPer SPoG SRms SVen WBor WDin WFar WHar WSHC
- 'Maurice Mason' CDoC GGar SPlb WFar
***uruguayensis*** CCCN CPLG EBtc GBin

## *Azorella* (*Apiaceae*)

***filamentosa*** ECou WAbe
***glebaria*** misapplied see *A. trifurcata*
***glebaria*** A. Gray see *Bolax gummifer*
***gummifer*** see *Bolax gummifer*
***lycopodioides*** GEdr GLam WAbe
***patagonica*** new GLam
* ***speciosa*** EPot
§ ***trifurcata*** CPar CTri ECho ECtt EPot GAbr GEdr MMuc NBir NWCA SPlb WPer
- 'Nana' ECho GGar MWat WPat WThu XLum

## *Azorina* (*Campanulaceae*)

§ ***vidalii*** CBot CSpe SGar

# B

## *Babiana* (*Iridaceae*)

***angustifolia*** CDes CPLG ECho GGar
'Blue Gem' ECho
***fragrans*** 'Porterville' ECho
- 'Rawsonville' ECho
***framesii*** var. ***kamiesbergensis*** CPLG
***nana*** CPBP
***pygmaea*** WCot
***ringens*** CPLG
***stricta*** ♀H1-2 CCCN CPLG ECho
- 'Purple Star' CPLG ECho
- 'Tubergen's Blue' ECho
***vanzyliae*** WCot
***villosa*** ECho WCot
- 'Tulbagh' ECho
'Zwanenburg's Glory' ECho SAga

## *Baccharis* (*Asteraceae*)

***halimifolia*** CTrC GLin GQui LRHS SEND XLum
***patagonica*** EBee GGar LRHS MMuc SArc SEND SPhx SVen
***salicifolia*** WCot
***sphaerocephala*** IDee

## *Backhousia* (*Myrtaceae*)

***citriodora*** CArn

## *Bacopa* (*Plantaginaceae*)

***monnieri*** LLWG
'Snowflake' see *Sutera cordata* 'Snowflake'

## *Baeckea* (*Myrtaceae*)

***densifolia*** ECou
***gunniana*** CPLG
***linifolia*** SPlb
***virgata*** CTrC ECou SPlb

## *Baeometra* (*Colchicaceae*)

***uniflora*** 'Malmesbury' ECho

## *Balbisia* (*Ledocarpaceae*)

***peduncularis*** CCCN SEND

## *Baldellia* (*Alismataceae*)

***ranunculoides*** CRow WMAq
- f. ***repens*** LLWG

## *Ballota* ✿ (*Lamiaceae*)

***acetabulosa*** ♀H3-4 CMHG ECha EWes WCot XSen
'All Hallow's Green' see *Marrubium bourgaei* var. *bourgaei* 'All Hallow's Green'
***hirsuta*** XSen
***nigra*** CArn GPoy MHer MNHC NMir WMoo
***pseudodictamnus*** ♀H3-4 Widely available
- B&M 8119 WCot
- from Crete ECha SEND
***rupestris*** 'Frogswell Carolyn' (v) IFro

## *Balsamita* see *Tanacetum*

## *Balsamorhiza* (*Asteraceae*)

***sagittata*** ECho

## *Bambusa* (*Poaceae*)

***glaucescens*** see *B. multiplex*
§ ***multiplex*** XBlo
- 'Alphonso-Karrii' CEnt EPla SBig
- 'Elegans' see *B. multiplex* 'Floribunda'
- 'Fernleaf' see *B. multiplex* 'Floribunda'
§ - 'Floribunda' CHEx EShb XBlo
- 'Golden Goddess' XBlo
- 'Silverstripe' see *B. multiplex* 'Variegata'

| | | |
|---|---|---|
| § | - 'Variegata' (v) | XBlo |
| | - 'Wang Tsai' | see *B. multiplex* 'Floribunda' |
| | ***pubescens*** | see *Dendrocalamus strictus* |
| | ***textilis*** | WJun |
| | ***ventricosa*** | SBig XBlo |
| | ***vulgaris*** | XBlo |
| | - 'Vittata' | XBlo |

## banana see *Ensete, Musa*

## *Banksia* (*Proteaceae*)

| | |
|---|---|
| ***aemula*** | MOWG |
| ***canei*** | SPlb |
| ***coccinea*** | MOWG |
| ***ericifolia*** | CDTJ |
| - var. ***ericifolia*** | CCCN CTrC MOWG |
| - var. ***macrantha*** | SPlb |
| ***grandis*** | CBcs CCCN LTen MOWG |
| ***integrifolia*** | CBcs CCCN CDTJ CTrC EAmu MOWG SPlb WCot WPGP |
| ***marginata*** | CTrC CTsd ECou SPlb |
| ***media*** | SPlb |
| ***oblongifolia*** | SPlb WCot |
| ***paludosa*** | CTrC SPlb |
| ***robur*** | CBcs CCCN SPlb |
| ***serrata*** | LEdu MOWG SPlb |
| ***speciosa*** | SPlb |
| ***spinulosa*** | CTrC |
| - var. ***collina*** | CTrC MOWG SPlb |
| - var. ***spinulosa*** | CBcs CCCN |
| ***violacea*** | SPlb |

## *Baptisia* (*Papilionaceae*)

| | | |
|---|---|---|
| § | ***alba*** | EPfP GBBs GMac NLar |
| § | - var. ***macrophylla*** | CCse EPPr EWes LPla NBir SDix SPhx WCot |
| | ***australis*** ♀H4 | Widely available |
| | - 'Caspian Blue' | CWCL LEdu WFar WSHC |
| | - 'Exaltata' | ELan LHop LRHS |
| | - var. ***minor*** | EBee NLar SPhx WPGP |
| | - 'Nelson's Navy' | LRHS MMHG |
| | × ***bicolor*** 'Starlite' (Prairieblues Series) | EBee SKHP |
| | ***bracteata*** new | LRHS |
| | - var. ***leucophaea*** | EBee LSou SPhx WFar |
| | 'Carolina Moonlight' | EBee SKHP |
| | ***lactea*** | see *B. alba* var. *macrophylla* |
| | ***leucantha*** | see *B. alba* var. *macrophylla* |
| | ***megacarpa*** | LRHS SKHP |
| | ***pendula*** | see *B. alba* |
| | 'Purple Smoke' | CAbP CSpe EBee EPPr LEdu LRHS MAvo MMuc MNrw NBre SEND SPhx SUsu WCot WCra WKif |
| | ***sphaerocarpa*** 'Screamin' Yellow' | LRHS |
| | ***tinctoria*** | CArn |
| | × ***varicolor*** 'Twilite' (Prairieblues Series) | EBee SKHP |

## *Barbarea* (*Brassicaceae*)

| | | |
|---|---|---|
| | ***praecox*** | see *B. verna* |
| | ***rupicola*** 'Sunnyola' | EDAr |
| § | ***verna*** | EGHP GPoy MHer SVic |
| | ***vulgaris*** 'Variegata' (v) | NBro WMoo |
| | - 'Variegated Winter Cream' (v) | CSpr WFar |

## *Barleria* (*Acanthaceae*)

| | |
|---|---|
| ***micans*** | CCCN |
| ***obtusa*** | WHil |
| ***suberecta*** | see *Dicliptera sericea* |

## *Barosma* see *Agathosma*

## *Bartlettina* (*Asteraceae*)

| | | |
|---|---|---|
| § | ***sordida*** | CCCN IRar SPoG |

## *Basella* (*Basellaceae*)

| | |
|---|---|
| ***rubra*** | SVic |

## *Bashania* (*Poaceae*)

| | | |
|---|---|---|
| | ***faberi*** Og 94053 | EPla |
| § | ***fargesii*** | CDoC ENBC EPla MRav MWht SEND WJun |
| I | ***qingchengshanensis*** | EPla MWht WJun |

## basil see *Ocimum basilicum*

## *Bauera* (*Cunoniaceae*)

| | |
|---|---|
| ***rubioides*** | WAbe |
| - var. ***alba*** | ECou |
| - pink-flowered | ECou |
| - 'Trial Harbour' new | ECou |

## *Bauhinia* (*Caesalpiniaceae*)

| | | |
|---|---|---|
| | ***galpinii*** | SPlb |
| * | ***lutea*** | CCCN |
| | ***natalensis*** | SPlb |
| | ***purpurea*** L. | CCCN SPlb |
| | ***tomentosa*** | CCCN EShb |
| | ***variegata*** 'Candida' new | CSpe |
| | 'White Lady' | CCCN |
| | ***yunnanensis*** | EDif MOWG SBrt |

## *Baumea* see *Machaerina*

## bay see *Laurus nobilis*

## *Beaucarnea* (*Asparagaceae*)

| | |
|---|---|
| ***recurvata*** ♀H1 | CTrC LPal LRHS SEND WFar |
| ***stricta*** | SPlb |

## *Beaufortia* (*Myrtaceae*)

| | |
|---|---|
| ***sparsa*** | MOWG |
| ***squarrosa*** | SPlb |

## *Beaumontia* (*Apocynaceae*)

| | |
|---|---|
| ***grandiflora*** | MOWG |

## *Beauverdia* see *Leucocoryne*

## *Beckmannia* (*Poaceae*)

| | |
|---|---|
| ***eruciformis*** | XLum |

## *Bedfordia* (*Asteraceae*)

| | |
|---|---|
| ***linearis*** | GGar SVen |

## *Beesia* (*Ranunculaceae*)

| | |
|---|---|
| ***calthifolia*** | CFir CLAP EPfP EShb IGor LLHF WCru WPGP WSHC |
| - DJHC 98447 | CDes CLAP CPLG |
| ***deltophylla*** | EWld WCot |

## *Begonia* ✿ (*Begoniaceae*)

| | |
|---|---|
| sp. | WWlt |
| B&SWJ 2692 from Sikkim, India | WCot |
| B&SWJ 10279 from Mexico | CHEx WCru |
| B&SWJ 10442 from Guatemala | WCru |

| | | |
|---|---|---|
| | BWJ 7840 from China | WCru |
| | Chen Yi 5 | WCot |
| | Chen Yi 7 | WCot |
| | DJHC 580 | WCot |
| | from Argentina | CSpe |
| | from Argentina, hardy | CSpe EShb ETod SKHP WCot |
| | from Vietnam | ERhR |
| | 'Abel Carrière' (R) | ERhR WDib |
| | ***acida*** | ERhR |
| | ***aconitifolia*** (C) | ERhR EShb |
| | ***acutifolia*** Jacq. | ERhR |
| | 'Aladdin' | ERhR |
| | 'Alamo III' | ERhR |
| | ***albopicta*** (C) | EBak ERhR |
| | - 'Rosea' (C) | CDoC EShb WDib |
| | ***alice-clarkiae*** | ERhR |
| | 'Alleryi' | ERhR |
| | ***alnifolia*** | ERhR |
| | 'Alto Scharff' ♀H1 | ERhR |
| | 'Alzasco' (C) | ERhR |
| | 'Amigo Pink' (C) | ERhR |
| | 'Anita Roseanna' (C) | ERhR |
| | 'Ann Anderson' (C) | ERhR |
| | 'Anna Christine' (C) | ERhR |
| § | ***annulata*** | ERhR |
| | - HWJK 2424 | WCru |
| | 'Aquarius' | ERhR |
| | 'Arabian Sunset' (C) | ERhR |
| | ***arborescens*** var. ***arborescens*** | ERhR |
| | 'Argentea' (R) | EBak |
| | 'Argenteo-guttata' | ERhR EShb |
| | 'Aries' | ERhR |
| | 'Arthur Mallet' (Mallet Series) (C) | ERhR |
| | 'Aruba' | ERhR |
| | 'Autumn Glow' (T) | ERhR |
| | 'Avalanche' (T) | ERhR |
| | 'Aya' (C) | WDib |
| | 'Bahamas' | ERhR |
| | 'Bantam Delight' | ERhR |
| | 'Barbara Ann' (C) | ERhR |
| | 'Barbara Hamilton' (C) | ERhR |
| | 'Barbara Parker' (C) | ERhR |
| | 'Barclay Griffiths' | ERhR |
| | 'Beatrice Haddrell' | ERhR WDib |
| | 'Benitochiba' (R) | ELon ERhR EShb LSou MNrw WCot WDib |
| | 'Bertinii Compacta' **new** | EPot |
| | 'Bess' | ERhR |
| | 'Bessie Buxton' | ERhR |
| | 'Bethlehem Star' | ERhR WDib |
| § | 'Bettina Rothschild' (R) | ERhR EShb WDib |
| | 'Beverly Jean' | ERhR |
| | 'Big Mac' | ERhR |
| | 'Bill's Beauty' | ERhR |
| | 'Black Jack' (C) | ERhR |
| | 'Black Raspberry' | ERhR |
| | 'Blackberry Swirl' (R) | WDib |
| | 'Blanc de Neige' | ERhR |
| | 'Blue Vein' | ERhR |
| | 'Bokit' | ERhR WDib |
| | 'Bokit' × ***imperialis*** | WDib |
| | ***boliviensis*** (T) | CDes CDoC CWGN ETod GCal WCot WCru |
| | - 'Firecracker' | WDib |
| | - pale pink-flowered **new** | CSpe |
| | Bonfire = 'Nzcone'PBR | EPfP ERhR LBuc SPoG |
| | 'Boomer' (C) | ERhR |
| | ***bowerae*** | ERhR |
| § | - var. ***nigramarga*** | ERhR |
| | 'Boy Friend' | ERhR |
| | ***bracteosa*** | ERhR |
| | ***bradei*** | ERhR |
| | ***brevirimosa*** | ERhR |
| | - subsp. ***exotica*** | ERhR |
| | 'Brown Twist' | WDib |
| | 'Bunchii' | ERhR |
| | 'Burgundy Velvet' | ERhR WDib |
| | 'Burle Marx' ♀H1 | ERhR EShb SDix WDib |
| | 'Calico Kew' | ERhR |
| | 'Calla Queen' (S) | ERhR |
| | 'Can-can' | see *B.* 'Herzog von Sagan' |
| | 'Candy Floss' | CDes WCru |
| | 'Captain Nemo' (R) | ERhR |
| | ***cardiocarpa*** | ERhR |
| | 'Carol Mac' | ERhR |
| | 'Carolina Moon' (R) ♀H1 | ERhR |
| | ***carolineifolia*** | WDib |
| | ***carrieae*** | ERhR |
| | 'Casey Corwin' (R) | WDib |
| | 'Cathedral' | CDoC ERhR WDib |
| | 'Chantilly Lace' | ERhR |
| I | ***chapaensis*** HWJ 642 | WCru |
| | 'Charles Chevalier' | ERhR |
| | 'Charles Jaros' | ERhR |
| | 'Charm' (S) | ERhR |
| | 'Cherry Sundae' (S) | ERhR |
| | 'Chesson' | ERhR |
| | 'China Curl' (R) ♀H1 | ERhR WDib |
| | ***chitoensis*** B&SWJ 1954 | WCru |
| | ***chloroneura*** | ERhR WDib |
| | 'Chocolate Box' | ERhR |
| | 'Chocolate Chip' | ERhR |
| | 'Christmas Candy' | ERhR |
| | 'Chumash' | ERhR |
| | 'Cistine' | ERhR |
| | 'Cleopatra' ♀H1 | ERhR WDib |
| | 'Clifton' | ERhR |
| | ***coccinea*** (C) | ERhR WDib |
| | 'Coconut Ice' | EShb |
| | ***conchifolia*** f. ***rubrimacula*** | ERhR |
| | 'Concord' | ERhR |
| | 'Connee Boswell' | ERhR WDib |
| | ***convolvulacea*** | ERhR |
| | ***cooperi*** | ERhR |
| | 'Cora Anne' | ERhR |
| | 'Cora Miller' (R) | ERhR |
| § | ***corallina*** (C) | EBak |
| | - 'Lucerna Amazon' (C) | ERhR |
| | 'Corbeille de Feu' | ERhR |
| | 'Cowardly Lion' (R) | ERhR |
| | 'Cracklin' Rosie' (C) | ERhR |
| | ***crassicaulis*** | ERhR |
| | 'Crestabruchii' | ERhR |
| | 'Crystal Brook' | ERhR |
| § | ***cubensis*** | ERhR |
| | ***cucullata*** (S) | ERhR |
| | 'Curly Fireflush' (R) | ERhR MSCN WDib |
| | 'Dales' Delight' (C) | ERhR |
| | 'Dancin' Fred' | ERhR |
| | 'Dancing Girl' | ERhR |
| | 'D'Artagnan' | ERhR |
| | 'David Blais' (R) ♀H1 | WDib |
| | 'Dawnal Meyer' (C) | ERhR WDib |
| I | 'de Elegans' | ERhR WDib |
| | 'Decker's Select' | ERhR |
| | 'Deco Diamond Dust' | ERhR |
| | ***decora*** | ERhR |

***deliciosa*** ERhR
(Devil Series) 'Devil Red' (S) LAst
- 'Devil Rose' (S) LAst
- 'Devil White' (S) LAst
'Dewdrop' (R) ♀H1 ERhR WDib
***diadema*** ERhR
'Di-anna' (C) ERhR
'Dibleys Pink Showers'PBR WDib
***dichotoma*** ERhR
***dichroa*** (C) ERhR
'Dielytra' ERhR
'Di-erna' (C) ERhR
***dietrichiana*** ERhR
'Digswelliana' ERhR
***dipetala*** ERhR
***discolor*** see *B. grandis* subsp. *evansiana*
***domingensis*** ambig. ERhR
'Don Miller' (C) ERhR WDib
(Doublet Series) 'Doublet Pink' (S/d) ERhR
- 'Doublet Red' (S/d) ERhR
- 'Doublet White' (S/d) ERhR
'Douglas Nisbet' (C) ERhR
Dragon Wing Red = 'Bepared'PBR ♀H1+3 LAst
§ ***dregei*** (T) ♀H1 ERhR GCal
- 'Bonsai' (T) STre
- var. ***dregei*** (T) ERhR
- 'Glasgow' (T) ERhR
'Druryi' ERhR
'Dwarf Houghtonii' ERhR
'Earl of Pearl' ERhR
'Ebony' (C) ERhR
***echinosepala*** ERhR
***edmundoi*** (C) ERhR
***egregia*** ERhR
'Elaine' ERhR
'Elaine Ayres' (C) ERhR
§ 'Elaine Wilkerson' ERhR
'Elaine's Baby' see *B.* 'Elaine Wilkerson'
'Elda' ERhR
'Elda Haring' (R) ERhR
'Elizabeth Hayden' ERhR
'Elsie M. Frey' ERhR
***emeiensis*** CSpe ERhR SKHP
'Emerald Beauty' (R) ♀H1 ERhR
'Emerald Giant' (R) ERhR WDib
'Emma Watson' ERhR
'Enchantment' ERhR
'Enech' ERhR
'English Knight' ERhR
'English Lace' ERhR
***epipsila*** ERhR
'Erythrophylla' EShb
'Erythrophylla Bunchii' ERhR
§ 'Erythrophylla Helix' ERhR
'Escargot' (R) ♀H1 WDib
'Essie Hunt' ERhR
'Esther Albertine' (C) ♀H1 ERhR
'Evening Star' ERhR
'Fairy' ERhR
***feastii*** 'Helix' see *B.* 'Erythrophylla Helix'
***fernando-costae*** ERhR
***ferruginea*** B&SWJ 10479 from Costa Rica WCru
§ 'Feuerkönigin' (S) ERhR
'Fiji Islands' WJun
'Filigree' (R) ERhR
'Fire Flush' see *B.* 'Bettina Rothschild'
'Fireworks' (R) ♀H1 ERhR WDib
'Five and Dime' ERhR
'Flamboyant' (T) ERhR WGor
Flaming Queen see *B.* 'Feuerkönigin'
'Flamingo' (C) ERhR
'Flamingo Queen' (C) ERhR
'Flo 'Belle Moseley' (C) ERhR WDib
'Florence Carrell' ERhR
'Florence Rita' (C) ERhR
'Flutterbye Salmon' LAst
'Flying High' ERhR
***foliosa*** ERhR
- var. ***amplifolia*** see *B. holtonis* var. *holtonis*
§ - var. ***miniata*** ♀H1 CDoC CHII EBak ERhR EShb IDee MArl SDix WDib
- - pink-flowered CCCN CDTJ
- - red-flowered CCCN CDTJ
- - 'Rosea' CDoC
'Frances Lyons' (C) ERhR
'Frau Helene Harms' (T) **new** ERhR
'Freckles' (R) ERhR
'Fred Bedson' ERhR
***friburgensis*** ERhR
'Friendship' ERhR
'Frosty Fairyland' ERhR
'Frosty Knight' ERhR
'Fuchsifoliosa' ERhR
***fuchsioides*** see *B. foliosa* var. *miniata*
***fusca*** ERhR
'Fuscomaculata' ERhR
***gehrtii*** ERhR
***geranioides*** (T) ERhR
***glabra*** ERhR
***glandulosa*** misapplied see *B. multinervia*
***glandulosa*** ambig. ERhR
***glaucophylla*** see *B. radicans* Vell.
'Gloire de Sceaux' ERhR
'Glowing Embers' **new** LBuc
***goegoensis*** ERhR
'Good 'n' Plenty' ERhR
***gracilis*** (T) F&M 266 WPGP
- F&M 337 WPGP
'Granada' ERhR
***grandis*** (T) XLum
§ - subsp. ***evansiana*** ♀H3-4 CHEx CSam CSpe CTsd EBee ERhR EShb ETod GCal LEdu LPla NMRc SBch SDix SKHP SPlb SUsu WCot WCru WFar WMoo
- - B&SWJ 11188 WCru
- - var. ***alba*** hort. CSam CSpe ERhR EShb ESwi EWld EWll GCal LEdu LPla LRHS SBch SKHP SPoG SSpi WCot WMoo WPGP XLum
- - 'Claret Jug' EBee ELon EShb ESwi ETod WCot WGrn WPGP WWEG
- - 'Pink Parasol' EBee ESwi WCru
- - 'Simsii' WFar
- 'Maria' EBee
- 'Sapporo' EBee EPPr ESwi GCal WCru
§ - subsp. ***sinensis*** ERhR WCot
- - BWJ 8011 EBee WCru
I - - 'Red Undies' **new** ESwi
aff. ***grandis*** subsp. ***sinensis*** (T) SKHP
- - BWJ 8133 WCru
* 'Great Beverly' ERhR
'Green Acres' ERhR
'Green Gold' (R) WDib
'Green Lace' ERhR
'Grey Feather' ERhR

| | | |
|---|---|---|
| | ***griffithii*** | see *B. annulata* |
| | 'Gum Drop Cherry Blossom' (S/d) new | LSou |
| | 'Gustav Lind' (S) | ERhR |
| | ***haageana*** hort. ex W. Watson | see *B. scharffii* |
| | ***handelii*** | ERhR |
| * | 'Happy Heart' | ERhR |
| * | 'Harry's Beard' | ERhR |
| | 'Hastor' | ERhR |
| | ***hatacoa*** | ERhR |
| | - silver-leaved | ERhR EShb WDib |
| | - spotted-leaved | ERhR |
| | 'Hazel's Front Porch' (C) | ERhR |
| | 'Helen Lewis' ♀H1 | ERhR |
| | 'Helen Teupel' (R) | ERhR WDib |
| | 'Helene Jaros' | ERhR |
| | 'Her Majesty' (R) | ERhR |
| § | ***heracleifolia*** | ERhR |
| | - var. ***longipila*** | see *B. heracleifolia* |
| | - var. ***nigricans*** | see *B. heracleifolia* |
| § | 'Herzog von Sagan' (R) | ERhR |
| | 'Hilo Holiday' (R) ♀H1 | WDib |
| | ***hispida*** var. ***cucullifera*** | ERhR |
| | 'Holmes Chapel' | ERhR |
| § | ***holtonis*** var. ***holtonis*** | ERhR |
| | ***homonyma*** | see *B. dregei* |
| | 'Honeysuckle' (C) | ERhR |
| | 'Hot Tamale' | ERhR |
| | ***hydrocotylifolia*** | ERhR |
| | ***hypolipara*** | see *B. sericoneura* |
| | (Illumination Series) | SCoo WGor |
| | 'Illumination Apricot' (T/d) | |
| | - 'Illumination Orange' (T/d) ♀H2-3 | WGor |
| | - 'Illumination Rose' (T/d) | SCoo WGor |
| | - 'Illumination Salmon Pink' (T/d) ♀H2-3 | SCoo |
| | - 'Illumination Scarlet' (T/d) | WGor |
| | - 'Illumination White' (T/d) | SCoo WGor |
| | ***imperialis*** | ERhR |
| | ***incarnata*** | ERhR |
| | - 'Metallica' | see *B. metallica* |
| | 'Ingramii' | ERhR |
| | 'Interlaken' (C) | ERhR |
| | 'Ivy Ever' | ERhR |
| | 'Jelly Roll Morton' | ERhR |
| | 'Joe Hayden' | ERhR |
| | 'John Tonkin' (C) | ERhR |
| | ***johnstonii*** | ERhR |
| | 'Jubilee Mine' | ERhR |
| | ***juliana*** | ERhR |
| | 'Jumbo Jeans' | ERhR |
| | 'Jumbo Jet' (C) | ERhR |
| | 'Kagaribi' (C) | ERhR |
| | ***kellermanii*** | ERhR |
| | ***keniensis*** | GCal |
| | 'Kentwood' (C) | ERhR |
| | ***kenworthyae*** | ERhR |
| | 'Kit Jeans' | ERhR |
| | 'Kit Jeans Mounger' | ERhR |
| | 'La Paloma' (C) | WDib |
| | 'Lacewing' | ERhR |
| | 'Lady Clare' | ERhR |
| * | 'Lady France' | ERhR |
| | 'Laurie's Love' (C) | ERhR |
| | 'Lawrence H. Fewkes' | ERhR |
| | ***leathermaniae*** (C) | ERhR |
| | 'Legia' | ERhR |
| | 'Lenore Olivier' (C) | ERhR |
| | 'Leopard' | ERhR |
| | 'Lexington' | ERhR |
| | 'Libor' (C) | ERhR |
| | 'Lime Swirl' | ERhR WDib |
| | 'Limeade' | WDib |
| | ***limmingheana*** | see *B. radicans* Vell. |
| | 'Linda Dawn' (C) | ERhR |
| | 'Linda Harley' | ERhR |
| | 'Linda Myatt' | ERhR |
| | ***lindeniana*** | ERhR |
| | ***listada*** ♀H1 | ERhR WDib |
| | 'Lithuania' | ERhR |
| | 'Little Brother Montgomery' ♀H1 | ERhR EShb GGar SDix WDib |
| | 'Little Darling' | ERhR |
| | 'Lois Burks' (C) | ERhR WDib |
| | 'Loma Alta' | ERhR |
| | 'Looking Glass' (C) | ERhR WDib |
| | 'Lospe-tu' | ERhR |
| | 'Lubbergei' (C) | ERhR |
| | 'Lucerna' (C) | EBak ERhR |
| | 'Lulu Bower' (C) | ERhR |
| | ***luxurians*** ♀H1 | CHEx CHll CSpe ERhR WCot |
| | - 'Ziesenhenne' | ERhR |
| | ***lyman-smithii*** | ERhR |
| | 'Mabel Corwin' | ERhR |
| | ***macduffieana*** | see *B. corallina* |
| | 'Mac's Gold' | ERhR |
| | ***maculata*** (C) ♀H1 | ERhR |
| | - 'Wightii' (C) | CSpe ERhR WDib |
| | 'Mad Hatter' | ERhR |
| | 'Madame Butterfly' (C) | ERhR |
| | 'Magic Carpet' | ERhR |
| | 'Magic Lace' | ERhR |
| | 'Manacris' | ERhR |
| | ***manicata*** | ERhR |
| | 'Margaritae' | ERhR |
| | 'Marmaduke' ♀H1 | WDib |
| | 'Martha Floro' (C) | ERhR |
| | 'Martin Johnson' (R) ♀H1 | ERhR WDib |
| | 'Martin's Mystery' | ERhR |
| | ***masoniana*** ♀H1 | CTsd ERhR WDib WSFF |
| | 'Maurice Amey' | ERhR |
| | 'Maverick' | ERhR |
| | ***mazae*** | ERhR |
| | 'Medora' (C) | ERhR |
| | 'Merry Christmas' (R) ♀H1 | ERhR WDib |
| | ***metachroa*** | ERhR |
| | 'Metallic Mist'PBR | WCot |
| § | ***metallica*** ♀H1 | ERhR EShb |
| | ***meyeri-johannis*** | CFir |
| | 'Michaele' | ERhR |
| | 'Midnight Sun' | ERhR |
| | 'Midnight Twister' | ERhR |
| | 'Mikado' (R) ♀H1 | ERhR |
| § | Million Kisses Series new | ERhR |
| | - Elegance = 'Yagance'PBR | LSou SPoG |
| | - Passion = 'Yabos'PBR | LBuc LSou SPoG WBor |
| | ***minor*** | ERhR |
| | 'Mirage' ♀H1 | ERhR |
| | 'Mishmi Silver' new | GCal |
| | ***mollicaulis*** | ERhR |
| | 'Moon Maid' | ERhR |
| | 'Mrs Hashimoto' (C) | ERhR |
| | 'Mrs Hatcher' (R) | ERhR |
| § | ***multinervia*** | ERhR |
| | 'Munchkin' ♀H1 | ERhR WDib |
| | 'My Best Friend' | WDib |

| | | |
|---|---|---|
| * | 'Mystic' | ERhR |
| | 'Mystique' | ERhR |
| | 'Namur' (R) ♀H1 | WDib |
| | 'Nancy Cummings' | ERhR |
| | ***natalensis*** | see *B. dregei* |
| | 'Nelly Bly' | ERhR |
| | ***nelumbiifolia*** | ERhR |
| | ***nigramarga*** | see *B. bowerae* var. *nigramarga* |
| | ***nigritarum*** | ERhR |
| | 'Nokomis' (C) | ERhR |
| | 'Norah Bedson' | ERhR |
| | 'Northern Lights' (S) | ERhR |
| § | ***obliqua*** L. | ERhR |
| | ***obscura*** | ERhR |
| | 'Obsession' (C) | ERhR |
| | ***odorata*** | see *B. obliqua* L. |
| | 'Odorata Alba' | ERhR |
| | ***olbia*** | ERhR |
| | 'Old Gold' (T) | ERhR |
| | 'Oliver Twist' | ERhR |
| | 'Orange Dainty' | ERhR |
| | 'Orange Pinafore (C)' | ERhR |
| | 'Orange Rubra' (C) ♀H1 | ERhR |
| | 'Orient' (R) | ERhR |
| | 'Orpha C. Fox' (C) | ERhR |
| | 'Orrell' (C) | ERhR |
| | 'Othello' | ERhR |
| | ***paleata*** | ERhR |
| | ***palmata*** | CDTJ CHEx EBee EBla EShb GCal SKHP WCot WPGP |
| | - B&SWJ 2692 from Sikkim | WCot |
| | - from China | EBla |
| | 'Palomar Prince' | ERhR |
| | 'Panasoffkee' | ERhR |
| | 'Panther' | ERhR |
| | 'Papillon' (T) | ERhR |
| | ***paranaënsis*** | ERhR |
| | ***parilis*** | ERhR |
| | ***partita*** | see *B. dregei* |
| | 'Passing Storm' | ERhR |
| | 'Patricia Ogdon' | ERhR |
| | 'Paul Bee' | ERhR |
| | 'Paul Harley' | ERhR |
| | ***paulensis*** | ERhR |
| | 'Peach Parfait' (C) | ERhR |
| | ***pearcei*** (T) | ERhR |
| | 'Peardrop' | SPoG |
| | 'Pearl Ripple' | ERhR |
| | 'Pearls' (C) | ERhR |
| | ***pedatifida*** | SKHP |
| | - DJHC 98473 | WCru |
| | 'Peggy Stevens' (C) | ERhR |
| | ***peltata*** | ERhR |
| * | 'Penelope Jane' | ERhR |
| | 'Persian Brocade' | ERhR |
| | 'Petite Marie' (C) | ERhR |
| | 'Piccolo' | ERhR |
| | 'Pickobeth' (C) | ERhR |
| | 'Picotee' (T) | CSut |
| | 'Pinafore' (C) ♀H1 | ERhR |
| | 'Pink Champagne' (R) ♀H1 | WDib |
| I | 'Pink Lady' | WCru |
| | 'Pink Nacre' | ERhR |
| | 'Pink Parade' (C) | ERhR |
| | 'Pink Spot Lucerne' (C) | ERhR |
| | 'Pink Taffeta' | ERhR |
| | ***plagioneura*** | see *B. cubensis* |
| | 'Plum Rose' | ERhR |
| | ***plumieri*** | ERhR |
| | 'Pollux' | WDib |
| | ***polyantha*** | ERhR |
| | ***polygonoides*** | ERhR |
| | ***popenoei*** | ERhR |
| | 'Potpourri' | ERhR |
| | 'Président Carnot' (C) | ERhR |
| | 'Pretty Rose' | ERhR |
| | 'Preussen' | ERhR |
| | 'Princess of Hanover' (R) ♀H1 | ERhR WDib |
| * | 'Princessa Rio de Plata' | ERhR |
| | ***prismatocarpa*** | ERhR |
| | ***procumbens*** | see *B. radicans* Vell. |
| | ***pustulata*** 'Argentea' | ERhR |
| | ***putii*** B&SWJ 7245 | WCru |
| | 'Queen Mother' (R) | ERhR |
| | 'Queen Olympus' | ERhR WDib |
| | 'Quinebaug' | ERhR |
| § | ***radicans*** Vell. ♀H1 | ERhR |
| | 'Raquel Wood' | ERhR |
| | 'Raspberry Swirl' (R) ♀H1 | ERhR WDib |
| | ***ravenii*** (T) | CHEx GCal SKHP |
| | - B&SWJ 1954 | GCal WCot |
| | 'Raymond George Nelson' ♀H1 | ERhR |
| | 'Razzmatazz' (R) | WDib |
| | 'Red Berry' (R) | ERhR |
| | 'Red Dragon' (R) | WDib |
| | 'Red Planet' | ERhR |
| | 'Red Reign' | ERhR |
| | 'Red Robin' (R) | WDib |
| | 'Red Spider' | ERhR |
| | 'Red Undies' (C) | WCru |
| | 'Red Undies' (*grandis*) | see *B. grandis* subsp. ***sinensis*** 'Red Undies' |
| | 'Regal Minuet' (R) | WDib |
| | ***reniformis*** | ERhR |
| | 'Richard Galle' | LAst |
| | 'Richmondensis' (S) | ERhR EShb |
| | 'Ricinifolia' | ERhR EShb GCal |
| | 'Ricky Minter' ♀H1 | ERhR |
| | 'Rip van Winkle' | ERhR |
| | 'Robin' (R) | ERhR |
| | 'Robin's Red' (C) | ERhR |
| | 'Rocheart' (R) ♀H1 | WDib |
| | 'Roi de Roses' (R) ♀H1 | ERhR |
| | 'Rose With Bronze Leaf' (Big Series) **new** | LSou |
| | ***roxburghii*** | ERhR |
| | 'Royal Lustre' | ERhR |
| | 'Rubacon' | ERhR |
| | ***rubro-setulosa*** | ERhR |
| | 'Sabre Dance' (R) | ERhR |
| | 'Sachsen' | ERhR |
| | 'Sal's Comet' (R) ♀H1 | WDib |
| | 'Sal's Moondust' | WDib |
| | ***sanguinea*** | ERhR |
| | 'Scarlett O'Hara' (R) | ERhR |
| § | ***scharffii*** | EBak ERhR SDix |
| | 'Scherzo' | ERhR WDib |
| | 'Secpuoc' | ERhR |
| § | ***sericoneura*** | ERhR |
| | 'Serlis' | ERhR |
| | ***serratipetala*** | EBak ERhR WDib |
| | 'Shamus' | ERhR |
| * | ***sheperdii*** | WDib |
| | 'Sherbet Bon Bon' **new** | LBuc |
| | 'Shiloh' (R) | ERhR |
| * | 'Shinihart' | ERhR |
| | 'Sierra Mist' (C) | ERhR |
| | ***sikkimensis*** | GCal |

| | |
|---|---|
| - B&SWJ 2692 | WCru |
| ***silletensis*** | GCal |
| subsp. ***mengyangensis*** | |
| 'Silver Cloud' (R) ♀H1 | ERhR WDib |
| 'Silver Dawn' (R) | ERhR |
| 'Silver Giant' (R) | ERhR |
| 'Silver Jewell' | WDib |
| 'Silver Lace' | WDib |
| 'Silver Mist' (C) | ERhR |
| 'Silver Points' | ERhR |
| 'Silver Sweet' (R) | ERhR |
| 'Silver Wings' | ERhR |
| 'Sinbad' (C) | ERhR |
| ***sinensis*** | see *B. grandis* subsp. *sinensis* |
| * 'Sir Charles' | ERhR |
| 'Sir John Falstaff' | ERhR |
| ***sizemoreae*** | WDib |
| Skeezar Group | ERhR |
| - 'Brown Lake' | ERhR |
| 'Snow Storm' | WDib |
| * 'Snowcap' (C) ♀H1 | ERhR EShb WDib |
| ***socotrana*** (T) | ERhR |
| ***solananthera*** A. DC. ♀H1 | ERhR EShb GGar WDib |
| ***soli-mutata*** | WDib |
| ***sonderiana*** (T) | GCal |
| 'Speculata' (R) | ERhR |
| 'Spellbound' | ERhR |
| 'Spindrift' | ERhR |
| 'Splotches' | ERhR |
| 'Stained Glass' | WDib |
| 'Stichael Maeae' | ERhR |
| ***stipulacea*** ambig. | ERhR |
| ***subvillosa*** | ERhR |
| 'Sugar Plum' | ERhR |
| (Super Olympia Series) | LAst |
| 'Super Olympia Red' (S) | |
| - 'Super Olympia Rose' (S) | LAst |
| - 'Super Olympia White' (S) | LAst |
| (Superba Group) | ERhR |
| 'Irene Nuss' (C) ♀H1 | |
| - 'Lana' (C) | ERhR |
| - 'Sophie Cecile' (C) ♀H1 | ERhR |
| ***sutherlandii*** (T) ♀H1 | CAvo CCCN CFFs EABi EBak EOHP ERhR EWld GGar IGor MDev NBir NPer SAdn SBch SDix WCot WDib WFar WHer |
| - 'Papaya' (T) | CSpe |
| 'Swan Song' | ERhR |
| 'Sweet Magic' | ERhR |
| 'Swirly Top' (C) | ERhR |
| 'Sylvan Triumph' (C) | ERhR |
| ***taliensis*** | SKHP |
| - EDHCH 042 | WCru |
| - 'White-boned Demon' | SKHP |
| 'Tapestry' | ERhR |
| 'Tar Baby' (T) | ERhR |
| 'Tea Rose' | ERhR |
| ***teuscheri*** | ERhR |
| 'Texastar' | ERhR WDib |
| 'The Wiz' | ERhR |
| ***thelmae*** | ERhR |
| 'Thumotec' | ERhR |
| 'Thunderclap' | ERhR |
| 'Thurstonii' ♀H1 | ERhR EShb |
| 'Tiger Paws' ♀H1 | ERhR EShb |
| 'Tingley Mallet' | ERhR |
| (Mallet Series) (C) | |
| 'Tiny Bright' (R) | ERhR |
| 'Tiny Gem' | ERhR |
| 'Tom Ment' (C) | ERhR |
| 'Tom Ment II' (C) | ERhR |
| 'Tomoshiba' | ERhR |
| 'Tondelayo' | ERhR |
| 'Tribute' | ERhR |
| 'Trinidad' | ERhR |
| * ***tripartita*** (T) | ERhR WDib |
| 'Twilight' | ERhR |
| 'Two Face' | ERhR WDib |
| ***ulmifolia*** | ERhR |
| ***undulata*** (C) | ERhR |
| 'Universe' | ERhR |
| 'Venetian Red' (R) | ERhR |
| ***venosa*** | ERhR |
| 'Venus' | ERhR |
| 'Verschaffeltii' | ERhR |
| ***versicolor*** | ERhR |
| 'Vesuvius' (R) | WDib |
| 'Viaudii' | ERhR |
| 'Viau-Scharff' | ERhR |
| 'Weltonensis' | ERhR |
| 'Weltoniensis Alba' (T) | ERhR |
| 'White Cascade' | ERhR |
| 'Wild Swan' | WCru |
| ***williamsii*** Rusby & Nash | see *B. wollnyi* |
| 'Witchcraft' (R) | ERhR |
| 'Withlacoochee' | ERhR |
| § ***wollnyi*** | ERhR |
| 'Wood Nymph' (R) | ERhR |
| 'Zuensis' | ERhR |

## Beilschmiedia (*Lauraceae*)

| | |
|---|---|
| ***berteroana*** | IDee |

## Belamcanda (*Iridaceae*)

| | |
|---|---|
| ***chinensis*** | CArn CBro CHll EBee ELan EPfP GKev GPoy MAvo MHer SBfd SGar SMrm SPav SPlb SRms WGwG WOut WPer WPtf WSHC |
| - B&SWJ 8692B | WCru |
| - 'Crûg Colossal' | WCru |
| - 'Freckle Face' | CMac EBee EKen LSou NBPC SPad WHil |
| - 'Hello Yellow' | EShb MAvo |

## Bellevalia (*Asparagaceae*)

| | |
|---|---|
| ***atroviolacea*** | ECho |
| ***brevipedicellata*** | ECho |
| ***ciliata*** | ECho GLam |
| 'Cream Pearl' | ECho WCot |
| ***desertorum*** JCA 0.227.690 | WCot |
| ***dubia*** | CDes CPom ECho WCot |
| - subsp. ***hackelii*** | ECho |
| ***forniculata*** | ECho |
| ***hyacinthoides*** | ECho WCot |
| ***longipes*** | ECho |
| * ***maura*** | ECho |
| § ***paradoxa*** | CAby CHid CMea CTca EBee ECho ERCP LLHF MNrw WCot |
| - white-flowered | ECho |
| ***pycnantha*** misapplied | see *B. paradoxa* |
| ***romana*** | CPom CTca EBee ECho ERCP GKev WCot WHil |
| ***sarmatica*** | ECho |
| ***sessiliflora*** | ECho |
| ***tabriziana*** | ECho WCot |
| ***trifoliata*** | ECho |
| ***webbiana*** | ECho |

## Bellis (*Asteraceae*)

| | |
|---|---|
| § ***caerulescens*** | GAbr |

***perennis*** CArn EWil
- 'Alice' GAbr WCot
- 'Dresden China' EWes GAbr
- 'Galaxy White' (Galaxy Series) EPfP
- Hen and Chickens see *B. perennis* 'Prolifera' single-flowered
- 'Parkinson's Great White' GAbr
- 'Pomponette Red' new NBlu
§ - 'Prolifera' single-flowered LRHS WHer
- 'Red Buttons' NBlu
- 'Robert' GAbr
- Roggli Series new NBlu
- 'Rusher Rose' EPfP
- 'Single Blue' see *B. caerulescens*
- 'The Pearl' GAbr WCot
- 'White Pearl' new LRHS
***rotundifolia*** 'Caerulescens' see *B. caerulescens*
***sylvestris*** CArn

## *Bellium* (*Asteraceae*)

* ***crassifolium canescens*** WPer

## *Beloperone* see *Justicia*

***guttata*** see *Justicia brandegeeana*

## *Bensoniella* (*Saxifragaceae*)

***oregona*** CPLG

## *Benthamiella* (*Solanaceae*)

***nordenskjoldii*** WAbe
***patagonica*** WAbe
- F&W 9345 WAbe

## *Berberidopsis* (*Berberidopsidaceae*)

sp. GGal
***beckleri*** SSpi
***corallina*** Widely available

## *Berberis* ✿ (*Berberidaceae*)

CC 4730 CPLG
SDR 4219 GKev
***actinacantha*** new WAle
***aetnensis*** GAuc
***aggregata*** NBir SPer SRms
***amurensis*** var. ***latifolia*** B&SWJ 8539 WCru
***angulosa*** GCal
***aquifolium*** see *Mahonia aquifolium*
- 'Fascicularis' see *Mahonia* × *wagneri* 'Pinnacle'
***aristata*** misapplied see *B. glaucocarpa*
***aristata*** ambig. CArn
***asiatica*** CPLG GPoy
'Baby Bear' CPMA
***bealei*** see *Mahonia japonica* Bealei Group
'Blenheim' WFar
***brevipaniculata*** Schneider GAuc
***brevipedunculata*** Bean see *B. prattii*
× ***bristolensis*** SRms
N ***buxifolia*** 'Nana' misapplied see *B. microphylla* 'Pygmaea'
***calliantha*** WFar
***candidula*** C.K. Schneid. CDul EPfP LRHS MMuc MSwo NLar SLon SPer WDin
- 'Jytte' see *B.* 'Jytte'
× ***carminea*** 'Barbarossa' WDin
- 'Pirate King' CSBt LRHS MAsh SPoG SWvt WFar WPat
***chilensis*** var. ***chilensis*** new WAle
***chrysosphaera*** WFar
***coxii*** GBin GGar
***darwinii*** ΨH4 Widely available
I - 'Compacta' CChe CDoC CMac EBee EPfP LBuc LHop LRHS LTen MAsh NBlu NEgg NLar SLim SPoG
***dictyophylla*** ΨH4 CPMA EPfP LHop LRHS MGos MMuc NLar SKHP SPer SPoG SSpi WDin WKif WPat WSHC
***dulcis*** 'Nana' see *B. microphylla* 'Pygmaea'
***dumicola*** MSnd
'Fireball' LRHS
× ***frikartii*** CDoC EBee ELan EPfP LAst LRHS
'Amstelveen' ΨH4 MBNS MRav NLar SBfd SEND WDin WFar WMoo
- 'Telstar' EBtc EWTr LBuc MRav NLar NPro SLim WMoo
***gagnepainii*** misapplied see *B. gagnepainii* var. *lanceifolia*
***gagnepainii*** C.K. Schneid. CDul CMac EBee NHol SLPl
§ - var. ***lanceifolia*** CTri EBee EPla MGos MMuc NWea SEND SGol SLim WDin WFar
- - 'Fernspray' EPfP EPla MRav SRms
- 'Purpurea' see *B.* × *interposita* 'Wallich's Purple'
'Georgei' ΨH4 CMHG CWib EPfP GQui LRHS
§ ***glaucocarpa*** EPla
'Goldilocks' CPMA EPfP LAst LSRN MBlu SBrd SSpi
***goudotii*** B&SWJ 10769 WCru
× ***hybridogagnepainii*** 'Chenaultii' ELan
***hypokerina*** CMac
***insignis*** GCal IDee WFar
- subsp. ***insignis*** var. ***insignis*** WPat
- - B&SWJ 2432 WCru WFar
§ × ***interposita*** 'Wallich's Purple' CCVT EPfP MRav MSwo SPer WDin WMoo
***jamesiana*** WPat
***julianae*** ΨH4 CBar CBcs CDul CHab CMac CTri EBee ECrN ELan EPfP LAst MGos MMuc MRav MSwo NHol NPla NWea SBfd SEND SGol SLPl SPer SRms SWvt WDin WFar WHar WSHC
§ 'Jytte' EBee EMil WDin
***kawakamii*** SLPl
***koreana*** EBee EPfP NLar WFar
- 'Rubin' CAgr
***linearifolia*** 'Orange King' CBcs CMac CTri EBee ELan EPfP LRHS MAsh MBlu MGos NEgg NLar SCoo SPer SPoG WDin WFar WHar WPat
'Little Favourite' see *B. thunbergii* f. *atropurpurea* 'Atropurpurea Nana'
× ***lologensis*** WDin
- 'Apricot Queen' ΨH4 CBcs CMac EBee EPfP LRHS MAsh MGos MRav NLar SBrd SCoo SPer SPoG WDin WPat
- 'Mystery Fire' EBee MAsh MBri MGos NHol NLar SGol SPoG SWvt WDin WFar WHar WMoo
- 'Stapehill' CMac ELan EPfP LRHS MAsh SPoG
× ***media*** Park Jewel see *B.* × *media* 'Parkjuweel'
§ - 'Parkjuweel' CBcs CMac EBee IArd MRav WDin WFar WMoo
- 'Red Jewel' ΨH4 CDoC CMac EBee ECrN EPfP EPla LRHS MGos MMuc MRav SCoo

| | |
|---|---|
| | SEND SPer SPoG WCFE WDin WFar WMoo |
| ***microphylla*** | CAlb EPfP LEdu WCFE |
| § - 'Pygmaea' | CAbP CAlb CBcs CSBt EPfP EWTr GGar LRHS MAsh MGos MRav NLar SLim SPer SPoG WDin WFar |
| ***mitifolia*** | NLar |
| ***montana*** | WPGP WPat |
| ***morrisonensis*** | GBin |
| ***morrisonicola*** | GAuc |
| × ***ottawensis*** 'Auricoma' | LTen SEND SGol SWvt |
| - f. ***purpurea*** | CCVT CMac CWib LRHS MGos WDin WFar WHar |
| § - - 'Superba' ♀H4 | Widely available |
| § - 'Silver Miles' (v) | EHoe MRav NLar WFar WPat |
| ***panlanensis*** 'Cally Rose' | GCal |
| ***poiretii*** | CPLG NLar |
| ***polyantha*** misapplied | see *B. prattii* |
| § ***prattii*** | GAuc |
| ***pruinosa*** | SBrd |
| 'Red Tears' | CPMA MRav NLar SPer WMoo |
| 'Rubrostilla' | EBee |
| × ***rubrostilla*** 'Cherry Ripe' | CMac |
| - 'Wisley' | LRHS |
| ***sargentiana*** | SLPl |
| ***sieboldii*** | LLHF MAsh MRav WPat |
| § ***soulieana*** | EPfP LRHS |
| ***stenophylla*** Hance | see *B. soulieana* |
| ***stenophylla*** Lindl. ♀H4 | CDoC CDul CSBt CTri EBee EPfP LBuc LTen MBri MRav NWea SBfd SBrd SEND SGol SPer WDin WFar WHar WMoo |
| - 'Claret Cascade' | EBee MGos MMuc MRav NLar SPer WFar |
| - 'Corallina Compacta' ♀H4 | CMac CMea ECho ELan EPfP EPot LHop LRHS MAsh NRya NSla SPer SPoG SRms WAbe WPat |
| - 'Crawley Gem' | GBin NLar WFar |
| - 'Etna' | ELan LRHS MAsh SCoo SPoG |
| - 'Irwinii' | CMac LAst LRHS MGos SPer WFar |
| - 'Nana' | LRHS SRms |
| - 'Pink Pearl' (v) | CMHG |
| ***taliensis*** | CPLG |
| ***temolaica*** ♀H4 | CGHE CPMA CSam EBtc EPfP MAsh MDun MGos MRav MSnd NEgg NLar NWea SPer SSta WCot WDin WPGP WPat |
| - SF 95186 | NLar NSti |
| ***thunbergii*** ♀H4 | CBar CBcs CDoC CDul CMac ECrN EPfP GBin LBuc MRav NLar NWea SPer SPlb SPoG SWvt WDin WFar WMou |
| - f. ***atropurpurea*** | CBar CBcs CCVT CDul CMac CSBt CTri EBee EPfP GGar LAst LBuc LTen MAsh MGos MSwo NEgg NLar NWea SCoo SGol SPer WDin WFar WMoo WMou |
| - - 'Admiration'PBR | CAbP CBcs CDoC CSBt ELan EPfP LBMP LBuc LLHF LRHS LSRN LSqu MAsh MBri MGos MMHG NEgg NLar SBfd SCoo SLim SLon SPer SPoG SPtl SWvt WPat |
| § - - 'Atropurpurea Nana' ♀H4 | Widely available |
| - - 'Aurea' | CBcs CBot CDoC CDul CMac EBee EHoe ELan EPfP EWTr LRHS LSRN MAsh MBlu MGos MRav MWat NBlu NHol NPri SBod SLim SPlb SSpi SWvt WDin WFar WMoo WSHC |
| - - 'Bagatelle' ♀H4 | CDoC EBee ELan EPfP EPot IArd IVic LAst LBMP LHop LRHS LSRN MAsh MBri MGos MLHP MRav NEgg NLar SLim SPer SPoG SWvt WCFE WDin WFar WMoo WPat |
| - - 'Concorde' **new** | MBlu |
| - - 'Dart's Purple' | WFar |
| - - 'Dart's Red Lady' | CPLG CPMA CSBt CWib EBee EHoe ELan EPfP LRHS LSRN MAsh MRav NLar NPro SLim SPer SPoG SWvt WDin WFar WPat |
| - - 'Erecta' | CMac EPfP MRav SPer SPoG WCFE WDin |
| - - 'Golden Ring' ♀H4 | CBcs CChe CDoC CDul CMac EBee EHoe ELan EPfP LBMP LHop LRHS LSRN MAsh MGos MMuc MRav NEgg NHol SBfd SLim SPer SPoG SWvt WDin WFar WMoo WPat |
| - - 'Harlequin' (v) | CBcs CChe CDoC EBee ELan EPfP LRHS LSRN MAsh MBri MGos MRav NEgg SBfd SGol SLim SPer SPoG SWvt WDin WFar WHar WPat |
| - - 'Helmond Pillar' | Widely available |
| - - 'Pink Queen' (v) | CDul EBee ELan EPfP LHop LRHS MAsh NLar SPur WDin WFar WPat |
| - - 'Red Chief' ♀H4 | CBcs CMHG CMac EBee EHoe ELan EPfP LRHS LSRN MAsh MGos MMuc MRav MSwo NEgg SBfd SGol SLim SLon SPer SPoG SWvt WDin WFar WHar WMoo WPat |
| - - 'Red King' | MRav WDin |
| - - 'Red Pillar' | CAlb CChe CDoC CMac EBee EHoe ELan EPfP IVic LAst LRHS MAsh MGos MWat NEgg SLim SWvt WDin WFar WPat |
| - - 'Red Rocket' | EPfP LBuc LRHS NLar WMoo |
| - - 'Rose Glow' (v) ♀H4 | Widely available |
| - - 'Rosy Rocket'PBR (v) | LBuc LRHS MBri SPoG |
| - 'Atropurpurea Superba' | see *B.* × *ottawensis* f. *purpurea* 'Superba' |
| - Bonanza Gold = 'Bogozam'PBR | CBcs CDoC EBee ELan EPfP LBMP LRHS MAsh MRav NLar SLim SPer SPoG WDin WFar WPat |
| - 'Boum' | EHoe |
| - 'Carpetbagger' | WHar |
| - 'Crimson Pygmy' | see *B. thunbergii* f. *atropurpurea* 'Atropurpurea Nana' |
| - 'Diabolic' | LRHS SPer SPoG |
| - 'Fireball' **new** | SPoG |
| - 'Golden Rocket'PBR | EPfP LBuc LLHF LRHS MAsh MGos SBfd SPer |
| - 'Golden Torch' | CAlb CSBt EBee ELan EMil EPfP LRHS LSRN MAsh MBri MRav MSCN NEgg SBfd SLim SWvt WPat |
| - 'Green Carpet' | CDul CMac EBee LHop LRHS MBlu NLar SGol SPoG WFar |
| - 'Green Mantle' | see *B. thunbergii* 'Kelleriis' |
| - 'Green Marble' | see *B. thunbergii* 'Kelleriis' |
| - 'Green Ornament' | NHol |
| - 'Green Ring' | EQua |
| § - 'Kelleriis' (v) | LHop LRHS MGos MMuc MRav NHol NLar SLon WDin WFar |
| - 'Kobold' | CMac EBee EPfP LHop LRHS MAsh MGos NEgg NLar SLim SPer SPoG WFar WMoo |
| - 'Maria'PBR | ELon EMil GGar LLHF LRHS LSou MGos NCGa NEgg NHol NLar SLim SPoG WHar WMoo |
| - 'Moia' | EKen |
| - 'Orange Rocket' | EPfP LRHS MAsh MBri SPoG WCot |

| | | |
|---|---|---|
| | - 'Pow-wow' | CDoC EBee IVic LRHS MAsh MBri MGos NEgg NLar SCoo SLim SPoG SWvt WDin WPat |
| | - 'Silver Beauty' (v) | CBcs CMHG EBee ELan MGos MSwo WDin |
| | - 'Silver Mile' | see *B.* × *ottawensis* 'Silver Miles' |
| | - 'Somerset' | CMac |
| | - 'Starburst'PBR (v) | CBcs CDoC CDul CSBt EPfP LRHS LSRN MAsh MBri MGos NEgg NPri SBfd SCoo SLim SLon SWvt |
| | - Sunsation = 'Monry' | IVic |
| | - 'Tiny Gold'PBR | GBin LBuc LRHS LSRN MAsh MGos NPro SLim SLon SPoG SWvt |
| * | - 'Tricolor' (v) | CMac MRav WFar WPat |
| | ***valdiviana*** | CBcs CDul CGHE CMHG CPLG CPMA EBee EPfP EPla SBrd SKHP SMad SSpi WPGP WPat |
| | ***verruculosa*** ♀H4 | CBcs CDoy CDul EBee EPfP EWTr LAst LHop LRHS MGos NLar NWea SCoo SPer SRms SWvt WDin WFar |
| | - 'Hard's Rob' | NLar |
| | aff. ***verticillata*** B&SWJ 10672 | WCru |
| | ***virescens*** B&SWJ 2646D | WCru |
| | ***vulgaris*** | CArn CHab CNat EPfP GPoy MCoo |
| | - 'Wiltshire Wonder' (v) | CNat |
| | ***wilsoniae*** | CBcs CDoy CDul CMac CTri EBee ELan EPfP LHop MAsh MMuc NHol NLar NWea SCoo SPer WCFE WDin WFar |
| | - L 650 | CGHE MMuc |
| | - blue-leaved | WFar WPat |
| | - var. ***guhtzunica*** | EWes |

## *Berchemia* (*Rhamnaceae*)

| | |
|---|---|
| ***racemosa*** | CMen NLar WSHC |

## bergamot see *Citrus bergamia*

## *Bergenia* ✿ (*Saxifragaceae*)

| | | |
|---|---|---|
| | 'Abendglocken' | CMac EBee ECGP ECha ECtt EPfP GQue LRHS NGdn NSti WCot WFar |
| § | 'Abendglut' | Widely available |
| | 'Admiral' | CBct ECha MLHP MNFA WCot |
| | ***afghanica*** | XLum |
| * | ***agavifolia*** | CBct XLum |
| | 'Andrea' | WCot |
| | 'Autumn Magic' | CBct COlW GQue LAst LHop LRHS LSou NEgg NPri SPoG WFar |
| | 'Baby Doll' | Widely available |
| | 'Bach' | WCot |
| § | 'Ballawley' clonal ♀H4 | ECha GCal IBlr IGor LRHS MLHP MRav NEgg WCot WFar WMnd WWEG XLum |
| § | Ballawley hybrids | GBin SDix |
| | 'Ballawley Red' | GBin NEgg |
| | 'Ballawley' seed-raised | see *B.* Ballawley hybrids |
| | 'Bartók' | WCot |
| | ***beesiana*** | see *B. purpurascens* |
| | 'Beethoven' | CBct CDes EBee ECha GCra IGor MRav NBir NBre SUsu WCot WPGP |
| | Bell Tower | see *B.* 'Glockenturm' |
| | 'Biedermeier' | ECha |
| | 'Bizet' | CBct XLum |
| | 'Borodin' | CBct |
| | 'Brahms' | CBct EBee WCot |
| | 'Bressingham Bountiful' | CBct |
| | 'Bressingham Ruby'PBR | CBcs CBct CLAP EBee ECha ECtt IPot LBMP LRHS LSRN MGos MRav NBir NEgg WCot WPGP |
| | 'Bressingham Salmon' | EBee ELan ELon GMaP LRHS LSRN MRav NLar WCot WMnd |
| | 'Bressingham White' ♀H4 | Widely available |
| | 'Britten' | WCot |
| | ***ciliata*** | CBct CDes CHEx CLAP CMac CTca EBee EBla EShb GCra LEdu LRHS MLHP MRav NBir NHol NLar SDix SUsu WKif WPGP WSHC WTin XLum |
| | - f. ***ligulata*** | see *B. pacumbis* |
| | - 'Patricia Furness' | CLAP |
| | - 'Wilton' | CBct CDes CLAP WCot |
| | ***ciliata* × *crassifolia*** | see *B.* × *schmidtii* |
| | 'Claire Maxine' | GCal WCot |
| | ***cordifolia*** | Widely available |
| | - 'Flore Pleno' | LAst |
| | - 'Jelle' | GBin |
| | - 'Lunar Glow' **new** | EBee |
| | - 'Purpurea' ♀H4 | CBcs CDoC EAEE EBee ECha ELan EPfP LBuc LRHS MLHP MRav NBir NBlu NEgg SMrm SPer SRms WFar WPnP XLum |
| | - 'Rosa Schwester' | ECha |
| | - 'Rosa Zeiten' | EBee GBin |
| | - 'Rose' **new** | LRHS |
| | - 'Tubby Andrews' (v) | CBct EBla EShb GEdr LEdu LRHS MAvo MBrN MBri MCCP MDKP MLLN NEgg NLar NPro SBfd WHrl WWEG |
| | - 'Vinterglöd' | EBee ELan ELon GMaP GQue IFoB LRHS MWat NBre NGdn NLar SWvt WFar WHil XLum |
| | ***crassifolia*** | EBee EPfP GKev ITim NBre SRms WWEG XLum |
| | - 'Autumn Red' | CBct ECha |
| | - 'Orbicularis' | see *B.* × *schmidtii* |
| I | - var. ***pacifica*** | XLum |
| | - - 'Cally Gem' | GCal |
| * | ***cyanea*** | CLAP WCot |
| | 'David' | ECha EWes GBin WWEG |
| | 'Delbees' | see *B.* 'Ballawley' clonal |
| | 'Doppelgänger' | EBee |
| | 'Eden's Dark Margin' | CBct EBee LAst MSCN NCGa NPro WCot |
| | 'Eden's Magic Giant' | CBct CFir EBee EWll GBin MBNS NCGa |
| | ***emeiensis*** | CDes CLAP IGor SUsu WCot WPGP |
| | - hybrid | CBct |
| | 'Eric Smith' | CBct EBee ECha GBin GCal GCra MBri WCAu WCot WMnd |
| | 'Eroica' | CBct COlW CSpe EBee ECha ECtt ELan EPfP GBBs GBin GEdr LHop LRHS LSou MBri MMuc MRav NBre NSti SPer SPoG WCAu WHoo WMnd WPtf |
| | 'Evening Glow' | see *B.* 'Abendglut' |
| | 'Frau Holle' | EBee MBri |
| § | 'Glockenturm' | CBct NEgg |
| | 'Goldfisch' **new** | EBee |
| | 'Harzkristall' | CBct COlW GQue LHop LRHS SPoG |
| | 'Hellen Dillon' | see *B. purpurascens* 'Irish Crimson' |
| | 'Herbstblute' | EBee |
| | 'Jo Watanabe' | CBct MRav |
| | 'Kashmir' **new** | XLum |
| | 'Lambrook' | see *B.* 'Margery Fish' |
| § | 'Margery Fish' | CBct ECha SPer |
| | ***milesii*** | see *B. stracheyi* |
| § | 'Morgenröte' ♀H4 | CBcs CBct EBee ECha ELon EPfP GEdr GMaP LAst LRHS LSRN MGos |

| | |
|---|---|
| | MRav NHol NLar NSti SBfd SPer SRms SWvt WCAu WCFE WCot WWEG |
| 'Morning Light' | ECtt NPro |
| Morning Red | see *B.* 'Morgenröte' |
| 'Mrs Crawford' | CBct ECha |
| 'Oeschberg' | CBct GBin GCal |
| 'Opal' | CBct EBee |
| 'Overture' | CAby CBct CDes CSpe EBee ECtt ELan ELon GBin GEdr ITim LHop LRHS LSRN MAvo MBri MGos MNFA MWhi NGdn NLar SUsu WCAu WCot WFar WWEG |
| § ***pacumbis*** | CHEx CLAP EBtc GBin GCal NBid NBre NSti |
| - B&SWJ 2693 | WCru |
| - CC 1793 | SBch WCot |
| - CC 3616 | CBct CDes GEdr WCot WPGP |
| 'Perfect' | WMnd |
| 'Pink Dragonfly' | CDes CMac CMil EBee ECtt GBin LBMP LRHS MBri SPoG WCot |
| 'Pinneberg' | GBin |
| 'Pugsley's Pink' | CBct |
| § ***purpurascens*** ♀H4 | CMac EBee EPfP GMaP IFoB IGor LRHS MBrN SBfd SPer WCot WTin WWEG |
| - SDR 4548 | GKev |
| - var. ***delavayi*** ♀H4 | LRHS MBri NBre NLar SRms |
| § - 'Irish Crimson' | CGHE WCot |
| aff. ***purpurascens*** | NGdn |
| - ACE 2175 | WCot |
| 'Purpurglocken' | EBee ECtt LRHS WAul |
| 'Red Beauty' | CSpe EHoe ITim LRHS MSnd SBfd WPnP |
| 'Reitheim' | EBee |
| 'Rosi Klose' | CDes CFee CLAP EBee ECha ECtt EHoe EWes GBin GCra GEdr GQue LHop LRHS MBri MNFA MRav MWat NBre NGdn SUsu WCot WFar WGwG WHoo WWEG |
| 'Rosi Ruffles' | EBee MBNS |
| 'Rotblum' | CBct EBee ECtt EHoe ELon EPfP EShb GMaP MSCN NBir NGdn NOrc NVic WFar WWEG |
| § × ***schmidtii*** ♀H4 | CBct CMac MRav NBir NBre NLar WCot WWEG |
| 'Schneekissen' | CBct CMac CPrp EBee ECGP ECtt LRHS MRav WCAu |
| § 'Schneekoenigin' | CBct ECha GBin GCal MRav |
| § 'Silberlicht' ♀H4 | Widely available |
| Silverlight | see *B.* 'Silberlicht' |
| 'Simply Sweet' | WCot |
| Snow Queen | see *B.*'Schneekoenigin' |
| § ***stracheyi*** | CBct CFir CPLG ECha GCal MLHP MRav NBid NLar SApp SDix WCot |
| - CC 4609 | EBee |
| - CC 5225 | GKev |
| - Alba Group | EBee ECha GCal SUsu WPGP |
| - 'Ice Queen' | WCot |
| 'Sunningdale' | CBcs CMac EBee ECha ELan EPfP GCra GMaP LHop LRHS MRav NBir NGdn SPer SWvt WMnd WWEG |
| ***tianquanensis*** | CDes EBee WPGP |
| 'Walter Kienli' | EBee GBin |
| Winter Fairy Tales | see *B.*'Wintermärchen' |
| § 'Wintermärchen' | CBct CChe EBee ECha ECtt ELan ELon EPfP GBin GCra LAst LRHS MGos MLHP MMuc MRav NHol NPro SBfd WCot WMnd WWEG |
| 'Winterzauber' | EBee |

## *Bergeranthus* (*Aizoaceae*)

| | |
|---|---|
| ***multiceps*** | SChr |
| ***scapiger*** | WCot |
| ***vespertinus*** **new** | XLum |

## *Berkheya* (*Asteraceae*)

| | |
|---|---|
| ***multijuga*** | GMac LRHS NBre SBHP WSHC |
| - 'Golden Spike' | EBee EWll LRHS LSou WHil |
| ***purpurea*** | CBcs CCVN CPom CSpe EBee ELon EPfP GCal GKev GMac LEdu LRHS MCCP MDKP MWea NEgg SBch SGar SMrm SPet SPlb WCot WHil WKif WSHC |
| - 'Pink Sensation' **new** | WCot |
| - 'Silver Spike' | EAEE EPfP EWll LHop LRHS LSRN NGdn |
| - 'Zulu Warrior' | CMac EDif EKen GBin NGBl SBHP SRkn |

## *Berlandiera* (*Asteraceae*)

| | |
|---|---|
| ***lyrata*** | CArn |
| - 'Chocolate Drop' | LRHS |

## *Berneuxia* (*Diapensiaceae*)

| | |
|---|---|
| ***thibetica*** | IBlr |

## *Berula* (*Apiaceae*)

| | |
|---|---|
| ***erecta*** | NPer |

## *Berzelia* (*Bruniaceae*)

| | |
|---|---|
| ***galpinii*** | SPlb |

## *Beschorneria* (*Asparagaceae*)

| | |
|---|---|
| ***albiflora*** | CSpe WPGP |
| ***rigida*** | WPGP |
| ***septentrionalis*** | CAbP CDTJ CFir CGHE CSpe CTrC EBee ESwi GAbr LRHS LSou MAvo MBNS MLLN MSCN SBfd SEND SMrm SPad WCot WGrn WPGP |
| ***septentrionalis*** × ***yuccoides*** | CHll WPGP |
| ***tubiflora*** | CDTJ CHEx |
| ***yuccoides*** ♀H3 | CAbb CBcs CHEx CPne CTrC EAmu EBee ESwi GGal IBlr IDee LEdu NVic SArc SEND |
| - 'Quicksilver' | CBcs CCCN CChe CDoC CEnd CKno CMHG CSBt CTrC EBee EPfP IVic LHop LRHS MBri MGos MPkF SBfd SLim SSpi WGrn WPGP |

## *Bessera* (*Asparagaceae*)

| | |
|---|---|
| ***elegans*** | CAvo CFFs CFir EBee ECho EPot LAma MNrw WCot |

## *Beta* (*Amaranthaceae*)

| | |
|---|---|
| ***trigyna*** | WCot |
| ***vulgaris*** | SVic WHer |
| - 'Bull's Blood' | CSpe WJek |
| - subsp. ***cicla*** | SVic |
| var. ***flavescens*** Bright Lights ♀H3 | |
| - - - 'Rhubarb Chard' ♀H3 | WJek |
| - subsp. ***maritima*** | CAgr |

## *Betonica* see *Stachys*

## *Betula* ✿ (*Betulaceae*)

| | |
|---|---|
| ***alba*** L. | see *B. pendula*, *B. pubescens* |
| ***albosinensis*** misapplied | see *B. utilis* |

| |  |  |
|---|---|---|
| | ***albosinensis*** Burkill ♀H4 | CDul CLnd CMCN EBee EPfP EWTr NWea WDin WFar WMou |
| | - W 4106 | CSto |
| | - from Gansu, China | CSto |
| | - 'Bowling Green' | CPMA MBlu WPGP |
| | - 'China Ruby' | CPMA CSto SSpi SSta WPGP |
| | - 'Chinese Garden' | CPMA |
| | - clone F | see *B. albosinensis* 'Ness' |
| | - 'Fascination' | CCVT CMCN EBee IDee LMaj LTen MGos WHar |
| | - 'Hergest' | CPMA EBee EPfP MAsh MBri MGos NPal SCoo SLau WHar WPGP |
| | - 'K.Ashburner' | CPMA CTho |
| § | - 'Ness' | CPMA CTho |
| | - 'Pink Champagne' | CPMA CSto WPGP |
| | - 'Rhinegold' | MBlu |
| | - 'Sable' | SLim |
| | - var. ***septentrionalis*** ♀H4 | Widely available |
| | - - 'Kansu' | CEnd CPMA EBee LRHS MBri SBig SCoo SMad SSpi SSta WHar |
| | - - 'Purdom' | CPMA SBig |
| § | ***alleghaniensis*** | CCVT CDul CMCN CSto EBee ECrN EPfP MMuc NLar NWea SEND SGol WDin |
| | ***apoiensis*** 'Mount Apoi' | CPMA SBig |
| § | × ***caerulea*** | CSto |
| | ***caerulea-grandis*** | see *B.* × *caerulea* |
| | ***chichibuensis*** | CSto WHer |
| | 'Conyngham' | CPMA CTho MBlu SLau |
| | ***cordifolia*** | see *B. papyrifera* var. *cordifolia* |
| | ***costata*** misapplied | see *B. ermanii* 'Grayswood Hill' |
| | ***costata*** ambig. | CMCN ECrN MMuc SEND SGol |
| | ***costata*** Trautv. | CLnd EBee ELan MSwo WDin |
| * | - 'Fincham Cream' | CPMA SBig WHCr |
| I | × ***cruithnei*** | GAuc |
| | ***cylindrostachya*** | EBee |
| | ***dahurica*** Pall. | CDul CSto GAuc |
| | - 'Maurice Foster' | CPMA CTho SBir WPGP |
| | - 'Stone Farm' | CPMA |
| | ***delavayi*** | EBee |
| | ***divaricata*** | CPMA |
| | ***ermanii*** | Widely available |
| | - B&SWJ 8801 from South Korea | WCru |
| | - from Hokkaido, Japan | CSto |
| | - 'Blush' | CPMA MBlu SBig SCoo WHCr |
| | - var. ***ermanii*** | LSRN |
| | - - MSF 825 | EBee |
| | - - MSF 865 | WPGP |
| § | - 'Grayswood Hill' ♀H4 | CDul CEnd CMCN CPMA CSBt CTho CTri EBee EPfP GQui MBlu MGos NLar SCoo SLim SMad SPer WHCr WPGP |
| | - 'Hakkoda Orange' | CPMA CTho MBri SCoo WHar WPGP |
| | - 'Holland' | LMaj NLar |
| | - 'Moonbeam' | WHar |
| | - 'Mount Zao' | CPMA CSto WPGP |
| * | - 'Pendula' | CPMA EBee LLHF MBlu NPal SBig SBir SCoo |
| | - 'Polar Bear' | CPMA EBee MBlu MBri NLar NPal SCoo SMad SSta WHCr |
| | - 'Zao Purple' | CDul |
| | 'Fetisowii' | CDul CEnd CPMA CTho ECrN LRHS MBlu SBig SSta WHar |
| | ***fruticosa*** | see *B. humilis* |
| | ***globispica*** | CPMA |
| § | ***humilis*** | GQui WDin |
| | ***insignis*** | CSto |
| | - B&SWJ 11751 | WCru |
| | 'Inverleith' | see *B. utilis* var. *jacquemontii* 'Inverleith' |
| | ***jacquemontii*** | see *B. utilis* var. *jacquemontii* |
| | ***kamtschatica*** | see *B. humilis* |
| § | ***kenaica*** | SSta |
| | ***lenta*** | CDul CMCN CSto EPfP IArd MBlu MMuc NLar NWea SEND WDin |
| § | - f. ***uber*** | SBir |
| | ***luminifera*** | CPMA EBee EBtc NLar SBir |
| | ***lutea*** | see *B. alleghaniensis* |
| § | ***mandshurica*** | CSto GQui NEgg WHCr |
| § | - var. ***japonica*** | ECrN GAuc MMuc MSnd NWea |
| | - - 'Whitespire Senior' | CDul |
| | ***maximowicziana*** | CDoC CDul CMCN CWib EPfP IDee LHop NMun SGol WDin |
| | ***medwedewii*** | CDul CMCN CPMA CSto EBee EPfP NWea |
| | - 'Gold Bark' | CMCN CPMA MBlu |
| | ***michauxii*** | NLar |
| | ***nana*** | GAuc MGos MRav NHar NHol NWea SRms SSta STre WDin |
| | - 'Glengarry' | EPot GEdr NLar |
| | ***nigra*** | CBcs CCVT CDoC CDul CEnd CLnd CMCN CSBt CTho CTri EBee ECrN LMaj MAsh MBri SEWo SGol SSta WDin WFar WMou |
| | - Dura-Heat = 'Bnmtf' | MGos NLar |
| | - Heritage = 'Cully' ♀H4 | CDul CLnd CPMA CTho EBee LHop LRHS LTen MGos NWea SBfd SBig SBir SCoo SGol SSta WDin WFar WMou |
| | - 'Little King' | CPMA MGos MPkF NLar SKHP |
| | - 'Peter Collinson' new | CPMA |
| | - 'Summer Cascade' | LRHS SBfd SKHP SLon SPoG |
| | - Tecumseh Compact = 'Studetec' | MBlu MPkF SGol |
| | - Wakehurst form | EPfP SPer SPoG |
| | ***papyrifera*** | Widely available |
| | - var. ***commutata*** | WDin |
| § | - var. ***cordifolia*** | CSto |
| | - - 'Clarenville' | CPMA WPGP |
| | - var. ***kenaica*** | see *B. kenaica* |
| | - 'Saint George' | CPMA CTho |
| | - 'Vancouver' | CPMA CTho MBlu |
| § | ***pendula*** ♀H4 | Widely available |
| | - 'Bangor' | CLnd CPMA SSta |
| | - f. ***crispa*** | see *B. pendula* 'Laciniata' |
| | - 'Dalecarlica' misapplied | see *B. pendula* 'Laciniata' |
| | - 'Dalecarlica' ambig. | CBcs CCVT CSBt ECrN LRHS MRav SCrf SLim WFar |
| | - 'Dark Prince' | CPMA |
| | - 'Fastigiata' | CCVT CDul CEnd CLnd CSBt CTho EBee ECrN ELan LMaj MGos NEgg SCoo SGol SPer WDin WFar |
| * | - 'Golden Beauty' | CCVT CDoC CMac EBee MAsh MGos NLar NPal SBfd SCoo SLim SPer SPoG SSpi WDin WFar WHar |
| | - 'Golden Cloud' | CMac GKin LAst |
| § | - 'Laciniata' ♀H4 | CDul CMCN CMac CTho CWib EBee ECrN ELan EPfP LAst LMaj MBlu MGos MRav MSwo NWea SBfd SCoo SGol SPer WCFE WDin WHar WPat |
| | - 'Long Trunk' | CDul EBee ECrN LLHF LSRN MBlu SGol SLim WHar |
| | - 'Purpurea' | CCVT CDul CLnd CMCN CMac CSBt CWib EBee ECrN ELan ELon EPfP EWTr GKin LAst LSRN MGos MSwo NLar SBfd SCoo SGol SPer SPoG WDin WFar |

| | | |
|---|---|---|
| | - 'Silver Grace' | CPMA EBee ECrN LSRN SSpi |
| | - 'Swiss Glory' | LMaj |
| | - 'Tristis' ♀H4 | Widely available |
| | - 'Youngii' | Widely available |
| | - 'Zwisters Gloire' **new** | SKHP |
| § | ***pendulata*** 'Spider Alley'PBR **new** | LRHS |
| | ***platyphylla*** misapplied | see *B. mandshurica* |
| | ***platyphylla*** subsp. ***kamtschatica*** | see *B. mandshurica* var. *japonica* |
| | ***platyphylla*** Sukaczev | CMCN |
| | - Dakota Pinnacle = 'Fargo' | EBee SCoo WHar |
| | ***populifolia*** | CSto |
| | ***pseudomiddendorffii*** | GKev |
| § | ***pubescens*** | CCVT CDul CHab CLnd CSto CTri ECrN GQue NWea SLPl WDin WFar WMou |
| * | - var. ***scotica*** **new** | GAuc |
| I | ***refugia*** | GAuc |
| | 'Royal Frost' | CDul CPMA EBee IArd IDee MAsh MBlu NLar NPal SLim SPoG WHar |
| | 'Silver Trestles'PBR | see *B. pendulata* 'Spider Alley' |
| | ***szechuanica*** | GQui NEgg NPCo WDin WPGP |
| | - W 983 | WPGP |
| | - 'Liuba White' | CPMA CTho |
| | - 'Moonlight' | SLau |
| | 'Trost Dwarf' | WDin WFoF |
| | ***uber*** | see *B. lenta* f. *uber* |
| § | ***utilis*** | CDul CMCN CSBt CSto ECrN EMil LMaj MAsh MMuc NWea SEND SSta WDin WFar |
| | - BL&M 100 from central Nepal | CSto WPGP |
| | - F 19505 | WPGP |
| | - GWJ 9259 | WCru |
| | - H&M 1480 from Sichuan, China | CSto WPGP |
| | - HWJK 2250 | WCru |
| | - HWJK 2345 | WCru |
| | - SCH 2168 | EBee |
| | - SICH 667 from Sichuan, China | CSto |
| | - Yu 10163 from Yunnan, China | CSto |
| | - from eastern Nepal | CSto |
| | - from Nepal S&L | CDul |
| | - from Uttar Pradesh, India | GAuc |
| | - 'Buckland' | ECrN |
| | - 'Darkness' | SLon |
| | - 'Fascination' | CDul CEnd CPMA EPfP IArd MBri MGos NWea SBir SCoo SLim SSpi SSta WHCr |
| * | - 'Fastigiata' | CLnd CPMA SBig SSta |
| | - 'Forrest's Blush' | CDul CEnd CPMA CSto EBee LSRN MBri SBig SBir WHar |
| N | - var. ***jacquemontii*** | Widely available |
| | - - Polunin | WPGP |
| | - - 'Doorenbos' ♀H4 | Widely available |
| | - - 'Grayswood Ghost' ♀H4 | CDul CEnd CMCN CPMA CTho CTri EBee ECrN EPfP LRHS MAsh MBlu MBri MDun NWea SBig SBir SLau SLim SMad SPer SPoG SSta WHar WPGP |
| § | - - 'Inverleith' | CDul CEnd CLnd CPMA EBee MAsh SBig SBir SCoo SLim WFar WPGP |
| | - - 'Jermyns' ♀H4 | CDul CEnd CLnd CMac CPMA CTri EBee EPfP LMaj LSRN MAsh MBlu MBri SCoo SLau SMad SPer SSta WHCr WHar |
| | - - 'McBeath' | SLau |
| | - - 'Silver Shadow' ♀H4 | CDul CEnd CPMA CTho EBee EPfP LRHS LSRN MBlu NLar NWea SBig SBir SCoo SKHP SLau SLim SMad SPer SPoG SSta |
| | - - 'Trinity College' | CDul CPMA CTri EBee MBri SBig SBir SSpi SSta WHCr WHar |
| | - 'Khumbii' **new** | SSta |
| | - 'Knightshayes' | CTho |
| | - 'Moonbeam' | CDul CLnd CPMA EBee LRHS MBri SBig SBir SCoo SPoG SPur WHar |
| | - var. ***occidentalis*** 'Kyelang' | CPMA CTho |
| | - 'Polar Bear' | LRHS |
| | - var. ***prattii*** | CEnd CPMA |
| | - - Parkwood 1123 | CSto EBee WPGP |
| | - 'Ramdana River' | CLnd WPGP |
| | - 'Schilling' | CPMA |
| | - 'Wakehurst Place Chocolate' | CDul CPMA CSBt MBlu MBri NPal SBig SCoo SLim SSpi SSta WHCr WHar |
| | cf. ***utilis*** | CTri SGol |
| | ***verrucosa*** | see *B. pendula* |

## *Biarum* (*Araceae*)

| | | |
|---|---|---|
| | S&L 604 | WCot |
| | SB&L 597 | WCot |
| | ***bovei*** | ECho LWst WCot |
| | - LB 351 | WCot |
| | ***carduchorum*** | LWst |
| | ***carratracense*** | WCot |
| | - from Spain | WCot |
| | ***davisii*** | ECho EPot WCot |
| | ***dispar*** | WCot |
| | - S&L 290/2 | WCot |
| | - SB&L 294 | WCot |
| | - SB&L 564 | WCot |
| | ***ditschianum*** | WCot |
| | - from Turkey | WCot |
| | ***marmarisense*** | ECho LWst WCot |
| | ***ochridense*** hort. | see *B. tenuifolium* subsp. *abbreviatum* autumn-flowering |
| | ***tenuifolium*** | EBee ECho WCot |
| | - LB 223 | WCot |
| | - LB 295 | WCot |
| | - PB 357 | WCot |
| | - SL 174 | WCot |
| | - subsp. ***abbreviatum*** | LWst |
| | - - MS 974 | WCot |
| | - - from Greece | ECho |
| § | - - autumn-flowering | WCot |
| | - subsp. ***arundanum*** | WCot |
| | - subsp. ***galianii*** PB 435 | WCot |
| | - subsp. ***idomenaeum*** MS 738 | WCot |
| | - subsp. ***zelebori*** | ECho WCot |
| | - - CRL 502 | WCot |
| | - - LB 300 | WCot |
| | - - PB 224 | WCot |
| | - - PB 334 | WCot |

## *Bidens* (*Asteraceae*)

| | | |
|---|---|---|
| | B&SWJ 10276 from Mexico | WCru |
| | ***atrosanguinea*** | see *Cosmos atrosanguineus* |
| § | ***aurea*** | CEnt EBee EBla ECtt EPPr EWes GCal GGar LAst LEdu MDKP MNrw MSpe NBlu NCGa NPer SAga SGar SPet WBor WFar WOld |
| | - B&SWJ 9049 from Guatemala | WCru |
| | - 'Blacksmith's Flame' | EBla |

- 'Cream Streaked Yellow' GCal GQue
- cream-flowered MNrw
- 'Golden Drop' EBee EWes LSou
- 'Hannay's Lemon Drop' CAby CBod CCVN CEnt CKno CSev EBee EBla ECtt ELon EPPr EPfP EShb GCal LHop LPla LSou MDKP MNrw MSpe SAga SPoG SSvW SUsu WBor WHil WHrl WMoo WPGP
- 'Rising Sun' EBee EWes
- white-flowered GCal

***ferulifolia*** ♀H1+3 ECtt MLLN NPer
- Golden Flame = 'Samsawae' NBlu
- Peter's Gold Rush = 'Topteppich'PBR LSou
- Solaire = 'Bidtis 1'PBR WGor
- Sun Kiss = 'Balbidsuki'PBR new NPri
- 'Yellow Charm' new LAst LSou

***heterophylla*** Ortega see *B. aurea*
***heterophylla*** misapplied CAby CEnt CKno CPrp ECtt MCot MRav MSCN MWat WFar WHal WHrl WMoo XLum
- CD&R 1515 LPla

***humilis*** see *B. triplinervia* var. *macrantha*
***integrifolia*** SMad
***pilosa*** EBee
'Southon Star' SUsu
***triplinervia*** B&SWJ 10413 WCru
- B&SWJ 10696 WCru
§ - var. ***macrantha*** ELon LHop

## *Bignonia* (*Bignoniaceae*)

***capreolata*** CCCN EBee WCot WSHC
- 'Dragon Lady' SKHP WCot

***lindleyana*** see *Clytostoma calystegioides*
***tweedieana*** see *Macfadyena unguis-cati*
***unguis-cati*** see *Macfadyena unguis-cati*

## *Bilderdykia* see *Fallopia*

## *Billardiera* (*Pittosporaceae*)

***cymosa*** MOWG WSHC
***longiflora*** ♀H3 Widely available
- 'Cherry Berry' CBcs CMac EBee ELan EPfP LRHS LSRN MAsh NLar SLim SPer SPoG SRms SWvt WSHC
- ***fructu-albo*** CBcs EBee ELan EWes GKev LRHS SLon SPer SWvt
- red-berried GGar

## *Billbergia* (*Bromeliaceae*)

***nutans*** CBen CHEx CHll EBak EOHP EShb ESwi IBlr LEdu MRav NPal SChr SEND SRms WGwG WSFF
- var. ***schimperiana*** EShb
* - 'Variegata' (v) CFir CHll EShb NPal SChr WCot

***pyramidalis*** ♀H1 XBlo
I - 'Variegata' (v) IBlr

× ***windii*** ♀H1 CFir CHEx EBak SRms

## *Bismarckia* (*Arecaceae*)

***nobilis*** CCCN EAmu LPal WCot

## *Bistorta* see *Persicaria*

## *Bituminaria* (*Papilionaceae*)

***bituminosa*** WTcb
–HH&K 174 WSHC

## blackberry see *Rubus fruticosus*

## blackcurrant see *Ribes nigrum*

## *Blackstonia* (*Gentianaceae*)

***perfoliata*** new CRDP

## *Blechnum* (*Blechnaceae*)

***alpinum*** see *B. penna-marina* subsp. *alpinum*
***arcuatum*** WRic
***auriculatum*** IDee WRic
***brasiliense*** ♀H1 WRic
***chambersii*** WRic
§ ***chilense*** ♀H3 CBty CDTJ CDes CGHE CHEx CLAP EAmu EBee EFtx EPfP GCal GCra GGar IArd IBlr IDee LEdu LRHS MMoz NVic SArc SBig SDix SKHP WCot WCru WMoo WPGP WRic
***colensoi*** CKel WRic
***discolor*** CBcs CKel CLAP CTrC EFtx GBin LPal WRic
***fluviatile*** CBcs CDTJ CKel CLAP CTrC EFtx GBin MMoz WRic
***fraseri*** WRic
***gibbum*** CBty EFtx
- 'Silver Lady' WRic

***magellanicum*** misapplied see *B. chilense*
***magellanicum*** (Desv.) Mett. CKel EFtx SBig SKHP WPGP WRic
***minus*** CBty WRic
§ ***niponicum*** GBin
***novae-zelandiae*** CBcs CDTJ CKel CTrC EFtx GBin WRic
***nudum*** CBty CDTJ CKel EAmu EFtx EQua ESwi LTen WRic
***penna-marina*** ♀H4 CBty CCCN CElw CKel CLAP CPLG EFer EFtx GAbr GCal GGar GMaP LEdu LRHS NBir NRya NVic NWCA SRms WFib WMoo WOut WRic WWEG XLum
§ - subsp. ***alpinum*** CLAP EBee ECha GGar SKHP WMoo
- 'Cristatum' CLAP GAbr GGar SRms WPGP

***punctulatum*** WRic
***spicant*** ♀H4 Widely available
***tabulare*** misapplied see *B. chilense*
***tabulare*** (Thunb.) Kuhn ♀H1 CBcs CDTJ CKel EFtx EPfP GGal NMun WPGP WRic
***vulcanicum*** WRic
***wattsii*** CDes

## *Blepharocalyx* (*Myrtaceae*)

***cruckshanksii*** CPLG IDee
- 'Heaven Scent' CCCN EBee GGar LAst MCCP NLar WBor

## *Blephilia* (*Lamiaceae*)

***ciliata*** SPhx

## *Bletilla* ✿ (*Orchidaceae*)

sp. NDav
**Brigantes gx** CDes EBee
***formosana*** NLAp
***hyacinthina*** see *B. striata*
***ochracea*** CPLG NLAp WCot
**Penway Bouquet gx** NLAp
**Penway Classic gx** NLAp
**Penway Coral gx** NLAp

| | |
|---|---|
| **Penway Fancy gx** | NLAp |
| **Penway Fantasy gx** | NLAp |
| **Penway Harlequin gx** | NLAp |
| **Penway Majestic gx** | NLAp |
| **Penway Paris gx** | NLAp |
| **Penway Pixie gx** | NLAp |
| **Penway Prelude gx** | NLAp |
| - Penway Dancer Group new | NLAp |
| **Penway Pride gx** | NLAp |
| **Penway Rainbow gx** | NLAp |
| **Penway Rose gx** | NLAp |
| **Penway Sunset gx** | NLAp WCot |
| ***sinensis*** | CPLG |
| § ***striata*** | CAby CBct CDes CPLG CPom CTri EBee ECho EPot GBBs LAma LEdu LRHS MNrw NLAp NMen NWCA SAga SPer WCot WFar WPGP |
| - ***alba*** | see *B. striata* f. *gebina* |
| - 'Albostriata' | CBct EBee ECho ELan LAma LRHS NLAp NWCA WCot |
| § - f. ***gebina*** | CCse CDes CTri EBee ECho EPot LAma LEdu LRHS NLAp NLar WCot WFar WPGP |
| - - variegated (v) | EPot LEdu NMen WCot WHal |
| - var. ***japonica*** | IGor |
| - 'Junpaku' new | LWst |
| - 'Lips' | LWst |
| - 'Murasaki Shikibu' new | LWst |
| - 'Soryu' | LWst |

## *Bloomeria* (*Asparagaceae*)

| | |
|---|---|
| ***crocea*** | ECho |
| - var. ***aurea*** | ECho GKev GLin |
| - var. ***montana*** | ECho |

## blueberry see *Vaccinium corymbosum*

## *Blumea* (*Asteraceae*)

| | |
|---|---|
| ***balsamifera*** new | CHab |

## *Bocconia* (*Papaveraceae*)

| | |
|---|---|
| ***cordata*** | see *Macleaya cordata* (Willd.) R. Br. |
| ***frutescens*** F&M 358 | WPGP |
| ***microcarpa*** | see *Macleaya microcarpa* |

## *Boehmeria* (*Urticaceae*)

| | |
|---|---|
| ***nipononivea*** 'Kogane-mushi' (v) | WCot |
| ***nivea*** | WCot |
| ***sylvatica*** | NLar |

## *Boenninghausenia* (*Rutaceae*)

| | |
|---|---|
| ***albiflora*** | CRDP CSpe |
| - B&SWJ 1479 | WCru |
| - B&SWJ 3112 pink-flowered | WCru |
| - BWJ 8141 from China | WCru |
| ***japonica*** | GKev |
| - B&SWJ 11186 | WCru |

## *Bolax* (*Apiaceae*)

| | |
|---|---|
| ***glebaria*** | see *B. gummifer* |
| § ***gummifer*** | ECho EPot WAbe |

## *Bolboschoenus* (*Cyperaceae*)

| | |
|---|---|
| § ***maritimus*** | CRWN LPBA SMea WFar |

## *Boltonia* (*Asteraceae*)

| | |
|---|---|
| ***asteroides*** | CFee CSam CSpe ECtt GCra LRHS MMuc SMrm SPer SWat WRHF XLum |
| - var. ***latisquama*** | EBee GMaP GQue LSou MAvo MRav MWat NCGa NLar SHar SSvw WBor WFar WHal WHil |
| - - 'Nana' | EWTr MRav NBre WFar |
| - - 'Snowbank' | EBee EBla ELan GCal LHop LRHS NDov |
| - 'Pink Beauty' | LEdu LHop MSpe |
| ***decurrens*** | EBee MAvo NBre |
| ***incisa*** | see *Kalimeris incisa* |

## *Bolusanthus* (*Papilionaceae*)

| | |
|---|---|
| ***speciosus*** | SPlb |

## *Bomarea* (*Alstroemeriaceae*)

| | |
|---|---|
| F&M 130 | WPGP |
| ***acutifolia*** | SKHP |
| - B&SWJ 9094 | WCru |
| - B&SWJ 9130 | WCru |
| - B&SWJ 10388 | WCru |
| aff. ***andreana*** B&SWJ 10617 | WCru |
| ***boliviensis*** | WCru |
| ***caldasii*** | see *B. multiflora* |
| ***costaricensis*** | ERea |
| - B&SWJ 10467 | WCru |
| ***distichifolia*** | WCot |
| § ***edulis*** | CDes CGHE CRHN CWGN EBee EWld WCot WHer WKif WPGP WThu |
| - B&SWJ 9017 | LEdu WCru |
| - F&M 104 | WPGP |
| ***frondea*** | see *B. multiflora* |
| aff. ***frondea*** B&SWJ 10681 | WCru |
| ***hirsuta*** B&SWJ 10774 new | WCru |
| ***hirtella*** | see *B. edulis* |
| § ***multiflora*** ♀H1 | CBcs CCCN CFir CHEx EBee ERea EShb GCal IKil SKHP SMad WBor WCot WCru WFoF WPGP WSHC |
| ***patacocensis*** | WCot |
| ***salsilla*** | CAvo CCCN SKHP WCot WHil WPGP WSHC |

## *Bombax* (*Malvaceae*)

| | |
|---|---|
| ***ceiba*** new | SPlb |

## *Bongardia* (*Berberidaceae*)

| | |
|---|---|
| ***chrysogonum*** | CAvo CFFs ECho LLHF LRHS WCot WHal |

## *Bonia* (*Poaceae*)

| | |
|---|---|
| § ***solida*** | CHEx MMoz MMuc MWht SEND WDyG WJun |

## borage see *Borago officinalis*

## *Borago* (*Boraginaceae*)

| | |
|---|---|
| ***alba*** | MNHC |
| ***laxiflora*** | see *B. pygmaea* |
| ***officinalis*** | CArn CHby CSev CWan EGHP ELau EPfP GPoy MHer MNHC NBir NVic SBch SBfd SVic WJek |
| - 'Alba' | CBre CSev EGHP ELau SBch SBfd SIde WJek |
| - 'Bill Archer' (v) | CNat |
| § ***pygmaea*** | CArn CHid CPLG CSpe EGHP ELan MHer MNrw NSti SWat WGwG WHer WJek WMoo |

## *Borinda* (*Poaceae*)

| | |
|---|---|
| KR 5950 | WPGP |
| ***albocerea*** | EPla MWht WDyG WJun |

| | |
|---|---|
| – Yunnan 1 | EPla WJun WPGP |
| – Yunnan 2 | CDTJ CEnt EPla MMoz WJun WPGP |
| – Yunnan 3a | CDTJ CEnt EPla WJun WPGP |
| – Yunnan 3b | WJun |
| – Yunnan 4 | CDTJ CEnt EPla WPGP |
| ***boliana*** | EPla SBig WJun |
| ***edulis*** | EPla WJun |
| ***frigida*** | CDTJ CEnt EPla WJun WPGP |
| – KR 4059 | MWht |
| ***grossa*** | EPla |
| – KR 5931 | MWht |
| ***lushuiensis*** | EPla WJun |
| ***macclureana*** KR 5050 | WJun |
| – KR 5177 from Gyala, Nepal | EPla ESwi MWht WJun WPGP |
| – KR 6236 | ESwi |
| – KR 6243 | WJun |
| – KR 6400 from Show La | ESwi |
| – KR 6438 from Pasm Tso | ESwi |
| * ***muliensis*** | WJun |
| ***papyrifera*** | CEnt EPla WJun WPGP |
| – CS 1046 | WJun |
| – KR 3968 | WJun |
| – KR 7613 | EPla MWht WJun |
| ***scabrida*** | CDTJ CEnt EPla ETod MMoz MWht WJun WPGP |
| – 'Asian Wonder' | EPla LRHS MBlu MGos NLar SPoG |

## *Boronia* (*Rutaceae*)

| | |
|---|---|
| ***citriodora*** | MOWG |
| ***heterophylla*** | CBcs CCCN CTsd IDee MOWG WAbe |
| – 'Ice Charlotte' | CBcs CCCN IDee |
| ***mollis*** | MOWG |
| ***pinnata*** | MOWG |

## *Bossiaea* (*Papilionaceae*)

| | |
|---|---|
| ***riparia*** | SPlb |

## *Bothriochloa* (*Poaceae*)

| | |
|---|---|
| § ***bladhii*** | CKno EPPr |
| ***caucasica*** | see *B. bladhii* |

## *Bougainvillea* (*Nyctaginaceae*)

| | |
|---|---|
| 'Ailsa Lambe' | see *B.* (Spectoperuviana Group) 'Mary Palmer' |
| 'Alexandra' | LRHS |
| 'Aussie Gold' | see *B.* 'Carson's Gold' |
| 'Begum Sikander' | ERea |
| 'Brilliant' misapplied | see *B.* × *buttiana* 'Raspberry Ice' |
| × ***buttiana*** 'Asia' | ERea |
| – 'Killie Campbell' ♀H1 | ERea |
| – 'Lady Mary Baring' | ERea |
| § – 'Mahara' (d) | ERea |
| § – 'Mrs Butt' ♀H1 | ERea |
| § – 'Poultonii' | ERea |
| § – 'Poulton's Special' ♀H1 | ERea |
| § – 'Raspberry Ice' (v) | ERea EShb |
| – 'Ratana Red' (v) | ERea |
| – 'Tiggy' | ERea |
| § Camarillo Fiesta = 'Monle' (*spectabilis* hybrid) | ERea |
| § 'Carson's Gold' (d) | ERea |
| § 'Chiang Mai Beauty' | ERea |
| 'Crimson Lake' misapplied | see *B.* × *buttiana* 'Mrs Butt' |
| 'Donya' | ERea |
| 'Double Yellow' | see *B.* 'Carson's Gold' |
| 'Flamingo Pink' | see *B.* 'Chiang Mai Beauty' |
| 'Floribunda' | ERea |
| ***glabra*** ♀H1 | CMen ERea LRHS |
| § – 'Harrissii' (v) | ERea |
| § – 'Sanderiana' | ERea LRHS |
| 'Glowing Flame' (v) | ERea |
| 'Golden Tango' | ERea |
| 'Harrissii' | see *B. glabra* 'Harrissii' |
| 'Hawaiian Scarlet' | see *B.* 'San Diego Red' |
| 'James Walker' | ERea |
| 'Jennifer Fernie' | ERea |
| 'Juanita Hatten' | ERea |
| 'Klong Fire' | see *B.* × *buttiana* 'Mahara' |
| 'Little Caroline' | MOWG |
| 'Lord Willingdon' misapplied | see *B.* 'Torch Glow' |
| § 'Louis Wathen' | ERea |
| 'Mahara Double Red' | see *B.* × *buttiana* 'Mahara' |
| 'Manila Magic Red' | see *B.* × *buttiana* 'Mahara' |
| 'Mini-Thai' | see *B.* 'Torch Glow' |
| 'Mrs Butt' | see *B.* × *buttiana* 'Mrs Butt' |
| 'Orange Glow' | see *B.* Camarillo Fiesta |
| 'Orange King' | see *B.* 'Louis Wathen' |
| 'Orange Stripe' (v) | ERea |
| 'Pixie' | see *B.* 'Torch Glow' |
| 'Poultonii' | see *B.* × *buttiana* 'Poultonii' |
| 'Poultonii Special' | see *B.* × *buttiana* 'Poulton's Special' |
| 'Princess Mahara' | see *B.* × *buttiana* 'Mahara' |
| 'Purple Robe' | ERea MREP |
| 'Ratana Orange' (v) | ERea |
| 'Red Fantasy' (v) | ERea |
| 'Reggae Gold' (v) | ERea |
| 'Rubyana' | ERea |
| § 'San Diego Red' ♀H1 | ERea EShb |
| 'Sanderiana' | see *B. glabra* 'Sanderiana' |
| Scarlett O'Hara | see *B.* 'San Diego Red' |
| 'Smartipants' | see *B.* 'Torch Glow' |
| 'Snow Cap' | see *B.* (Spectoperuviana Group) 'Mary Palmer' |
| ***spectabilis*** 'Vera Deep Purple'PBR **new** | LRHS |
| § (Spectoperuviana Group) 'Mary Palmer' | ERea |
| – 'Mrs H.C. Buck' | ERea |
| Surprise | see *B.* (Spectoperuviana Group) 'Mary Palmer' |
| § 'Torch Glow' | EAmu |
| 'Tropical Rainbow' | see *B.* × *buttiana* 'Raspberry Ice' |
| 'Variegata' | see *B. glabra* 'Harrissii' |

## *Boussingaultia* (*Basellaceae*)

| | |
|---|---|
| ***baselloides*** | see *Anredera cordifolia* |

## *Bouteloua* (*Poaceae*)

| | |
|---|---|
| ***curtipendula*** | CRWN EBee LRHS |
| § ***gracilis*** | EBee EHoe LEdu MWhi NWsh SMea SMrm SUsu SWal WPGP WWEG XLum |

## *Bouvardia* (*Rubiaceae*)

| | |
|---|---|
| × ***domestica*** | EShb |
| ***longiflora*** | ERea MOWG |
| ***ternifolia*** | CWGN LSou SPoG WCot |

## *Bowiea* (*Asparagaceae*)

| | |
|---|---|
| ***volubilis*** | EBee EShb |

## *Bowkeria* (*Stilbaceae*)

| | |
|---|---|
| sp. **new** | CCCN |
| ***cymosa*** | SPlb |
| ***verticillata*** | CHII WBor |

## *Boykinia* (*Saxifragaceae*)

| | |
|---|---|
| ***aconitifolia*** | CMac EBla EWld GGar LRHS MRav NLar NRya SMad WCru WMoo |

| | | |
|---|---|---|
| | ***elata*** | see *B. occidentalis* |
| | ***heucheriformis*** | see *B. jamesii* |
| § | ***jamesii*** | GEdr LRHS NWCA |
| | ***lycoctonifolia*** | EBee GLam NLar |
| | ***major*** | EBee GAuc |
| § | ***occidentalis*** | EBee EPot GGar MMHG WCru WMoo WPtf XLum |
| | ***rotundifolia*** | EBee EWld GJos GKev NBir WCru WMoo |
| | ***tellimoides*** | see *Peltoboykinia tellimoides* |

## boysenberry see *Rubus* 'Boysenberry'

## *Brachychilum* see *Hedychium*

## *Brachychiton* (*Malvaceae*)

| | | |
|---|---|---|
| | ***acerifolius*** | CHEx EShb SPlb |
| | ***discolor*** | EShb |
| | ***populneus*** | SPlb |
| § | ***rupestris*** | EShb |

## *Brachyelytrum* (*Poaceae*)

| | | |
|---|---|---|
| | ***japonicum*** | EPPr NLar |

## *Brachyglottis* ✿ (*Asteraceae*)

| | | |
|---|---|---|
| § | ***bidwillii*** | CBcs GGar IRar |
| | - 'Basil Fox' | WAbe |
| § | ***buchananii*** | WSHC |
| | - 'Silver Shadow' | GGar |
| § | ***compacta*** | ECou ELan EPfP LRHS MAsh SLon SPer SPoG |
| | ***compacta*** × ***monroi*** | ECou |
| | 'County Park' | ECou |
| | (Dunedin Group) 'Drysdale' | ELan EPfP GGar LRHS MAsh SBfd SKHP SLon SRGP SWvt |
| § | - 'Moira Reid' (v) | CPLG CTsd GGar |
| § | - 'Sunshine' ♀H4 | CBar CDoC CDul CSBt CTri CWib ELan EPfP GGar IVic LRHS MGos MMuc MRav MSwo MWat NPer NPri NWea SBfd SEND SLim SPer SPlb SPoG SRGP SRms SWvt WDin WFar |
| | 'Frosty' | ECou |
| | ***greyi*** misapplied | see *B.* (Dunedin Group) 'Sunshine' |
| § | ***greyi*** (Hook. f.) B. Nord. | CMac EBee EPfP MWhi SBrd SGol |
| | ***greyi*** × ***repanda*** | CDoC EShb GGar |
| | ***huntii*** | SVen |
| | ***huntii*** × ***stewartii*** | GGar SEND |
| | ***laxifolia*** misapplied | see *B.* (Dunedin Group) 'Sunshine' |
| | 'Leith's Gold' | CBcs CTrC |
| § | ***monroi*** ♀H4 | CBcs CMac CSBt CWib EBee ECou EHoe ELan EPfP GGar IVic LRHS MMuc MRav SEND SGol SKHP SLon SPoG SVen WDin |
| | - 'Clarence' | ECou |
| | ***repanda*** | CBcs WCot |
| | - 'Purpurea' | CBcs |
| | - var. ***rangiora*** | CTsd |
| § | ***rotundifolia*** | CCCN CDoC GGar NLar SEND |
| | 'Silver Waves' | ECou |
| § | ***spedenii*** | GGar |
| I | 'Sunshine Improved' | CBcs EHoe NBir STre SWvt |
| | 'Sunshine Variegated' | see *B.* (Dunedin Group) 'Moira Reid' |
| | Walberton's Silver Dormouse = 'Walbrach'PBR | LBuc LRHS MAsh SPoG |

## *Brachypodium* (*Poaceae*)

| | | |
|---|---|---|
| | ***pinnatum*** | EHoe EPPr |
| | ***sylvaticum*** | CHab GCal MMuc SEND |

## *Brachyscome* (*Asteraceae*)

| | | |
|---|---|---|
| | 'Blue Mist' | SPet |
| | ***formosa*** | ECou |
| | ***iberidifolia*** | LAst |
| | Mauve Mystique = 'Pacimamy'PBR | LHop |
| | 'Metallic Blue' | NPri |
| | ***nivalis*** var. ***alpina*** | see *B. tadgellii* |
| | 'Pink Mist' | SPet |
| | ***rigidula*** | CPBP ECou |
| | 'Strawberry Mousse' | LAst SPet |
| | 'Strawberry Pink' new | LAst NPri |
| § | ***tadgellii*** | ECou |

## *Brachystachyum* (*Poaceae*)

| | | |
|---|---|---|
| | ***densiflorum*** | EPla NLar |

## *Brachystelma* (*Apocynaceae*)

| | | |
|---|---|---|
| | ***barberiae*** new | LToo |
| | ***bracteolatum*** | LToo |
| | ***caffrum*** | LToo |
| | ***circinatum*** | LToo |
| | ***filifolium*** | LToo |
| | ***foetidum*** | LToo |
| | ***longifolium*** | LToo |
| | ***meyerianum*** | LToo |
| | ***pygmaeum*** new | LToo |
| | ***tuberosum*** | LToo |
| | ***vahrmeijeri*** | LToo |

## *Bracteantha* see *Xerochrysum*

## *Brahea* (*Arecaceae*)

| | | |
|---|---|---|
| | ***armata*** | CAbb CBrP CDTJ CPHo EAmu EPfP EShb ESwi ETod LPal MGos MREP SBst SChr SPlb STrG WCot |
| | ***edulis*** | CBrP EAmu LPal SChr |
| | 'Super Silver' | WCot |

## *Brainea* (*Blechnaceae*)

| | | |
|---|---|---|
| | ***insignis*** | WRic |

## *Brassaia* see *Schefflera*

## *Brassica* (*Brassicaceae*)

| | | |
|---|---|---|
| | ***japonica*** | see *B. juncea* var. *crispifolia* |
| § | ***juncea*** var. ***crispifolia*** | MNHC |
| | ***nigra*** | CArn |
| | ***oleracea*** | SVic WHer |
| | - 'Nine Star Perennial' | CAgr SVic |

## *Bravoa* (*Agavaceae*)

| | | |
|---|---|---|
| | ***geminiflora*** | see *Polianthes geminiflora* |

## *Brighamia* (*Campanulaceae*)

| | | |
|---|---|---|
| | ***insignis*** new | CCCN |

## *Brillantaisia* (*Acanthaceae*)

| | | |
|---|---|---|
| | ***kirungae*** | CCCN ECre EShb WHil |

## *Brimeura* (*Asparagaceae*)

| | | |
|---|---|---|
| § | ***amethystina*** ♀H4 | CPLG CPom ECho GBin GKev GMac LEdu LRHS NMRc NWCA SDeJ SPhx WCot |
| | - 'Alba' | ECho GKev SDeJ SMrm SPhx WCot |

## *Briza* (*Poaceae*)

| | | |
|---|---|---|
| | ***maxima*** | CEnt CKno CTri EHoe EPla LEdu LHop NGdn NSti WHal WHer WHil WTou |

| | | |
|---|---|---|
| | ***media*** | Widely available |
| | – 'Golden Bee' | CBod CKno EHoe ELon EPPr MMHG NLar |
| | – 'Limouzi' | CElw CFir CKno EBee EHoe ELon EPPr EPfP GCal LEdu MAvo NSti SMad SMea XLum |
| | – 'Russells'[PBR] | CBod CHid CKno EBee EHoe EPPr GBin LEdu LHop LRHS NBPC NCGa SBfd SMea SPer SPoG SWvt WGrn WPtf |
| | ***subaristata*** | EBee EPPr GCal LRHS MWhi WHrl |
| | ***triloba*** | EWes MMHG NWsh SMea |

## *Brodiaea* (*Asparagaceae*)

| | | |
|---|---|---|
| § | ***californica*** | EBee ECho GKev NMen WCot |
| | – NNS 00-108 | WCot |
| | – NNS 06-102 | WCot |
| | ***coronaria*** | CPBP WCot |
| | 'Corrina' | see *Triteleia* 'Corrina' |
| | ***elegans*** | EBee ECho |
| | ***ida-maia*** | see *Dichelostemma ida-maia* |
| | ***laxa*** | see *Triteleia laxa* |
| | ***pallida*** | WCot |
| | ***peduncularis*** | see *Triteleia peduncularis* |
| | ***stellaris*** | ECho |

## *Bromus* (*Poaceae*)

| | | |
|---|---|---|
| | ***erectus*** | CHab |
| | ***inermis*** 'Skinner's Gold' (v) | EBee EHoe EPPr EWes NLar NMRc SMea SMrm WCot WWEG |
| | ***sterilis*** 'Chinese Brushstrokes' | CSpe |

## *Broussonetia* (*Moraceae*)

| | | |
|---|---|---|
| | ***kazinoki*** | CArn NLar WDin |
| | ***papyrifera*** | CAbP CBcs CDul EGFP ELan GBin IVic LMaj WDin WPGP |
| | – 'Billardii' **new** | NLar |
| | – 'Laciniata' | NLar SMad |

## *Browallia* (*Solanaceae*)

| | | |
|---|---|---|
| | from Sikkim | CSpe |

## *Bruckenthalia* see *Erica*

## *Brugmansia* ✿ (*Solanaceae*)

| | | |
|---|---|---|
| § | ***arborea*** | CDTJ SEND SRms |
| § | – 'Knightii' (d) 🏆H1 | CDTJ ELan |
| | ***aurea*** | CCCN CHEx SAdn |
| | × ***candida*** | CCCN CHEx |
| § | – 'Grand Marnier' 🏆H1 | CBot CDTJ CHEx CHll ELan MOWG |
| | – 'Plena' | see *B. arborea* 'Knightii' |
| § | – 'Variegata' (v) | CCCN CDTJ CHll CSam |
| § | ***chlorantha*** | CBcs |
| | × ***cubensis*** 'Charles Grimaldi' | CSam |
| | 'Flowerdream' (d) | ERea |
| | 'Herzenbrucke' | ERea |
| § | × ***insignis*** | CHll |
| § | – pink-flowered | CHEx SEND |
| | 'Mobishu' | EShb |
| | ***rosei*** | see *B. sanguinea* subsp. *sanguinea* var. *flava* |
| § | ***sanguinea*** | CBcs CCCN CHEx CHll EGxp EShb IDee IRar MOWG SEND |
| | – red-flowered | CHEx |
| | – 'Rosea' | see *B.* × *insignis* pink-flowered |
| § | – subsp. ***sanguinea*** var. ***flava*** | CHEx |
| § | ***suaveolens*** 🏆H1 | CHEx CHll EGxp ELan SPlb |
| | – 'Flore Pleno' (d) | EGxp |
| | – pink-flowered | EShb |
| | – ***rosea*** | see *B.* × *insignis* pink-flowered |
| | – 'Variegata' (v) | EShb |
| | – yellow-flowered | EShb |
| | ***suaveolens*** × ***versicolor*** | see *B.* × *insignis* |
| | 'Variegata Sunset' | see *B.* × *candida* 'Variegata' |
| | ***versicolor*** misapplied | see *B. arborea* |
| § | ***versicolor*** Lagerh. | CCCN MOWG |
| | yellow-flowered | LRHS |

## *Brunfelsia* (*Solanaceae*)

| | | |
|---|---|---|
| | ***americana*** | CCCN MOWG |
| | ***calycina*** | see *B. pauciflora* |
| | ***jamaicensis*** | MOWG |
| | ***lactea*** | CCCN |
| | ***nitida*** | ERea |
| § | ***pauciflora*** 🏆H1 | CCCN ELan ERea |
| | – 'Floribunda' | ERea MOWG |

## *Brunia* (*Bruniaceae*)

| | | |
|---|---|---|
| | ***albiflora*** | SPlb |

## *Brunnera* ✿ (*Boraginaceae*)

| | | |
|---|---|---|
| § | ***macrophylla*** 🏆H4 | Widely available |
| | – 'Agnes Amez' | CLAP EBla |
| | – 'Alba' | see *B. macrophylla* 'Betty Bowring' |
| § | – 'Betty Bowring' | Widely available |
| | – 'Blaukuppel' | CLAP EBee EBla EWes GBin LRHS NBir WFar |
| | – 'Blue Louise' | EBla |
| | – 'Dawson's White' (v) | Widely available |
| | – 'Emerald Mist' (v) **new** | EBee ECtt MAsh NLar NSti SHeu |
| | – 'Gordano Gold' (v) | EBla EHoe EPPr NBir WCot |
| | – 'Green Gold' (v) **new** | EBee NLar SHeu |
| | – 'Hadspen Cream' (v) 🏆H4 | Widely available |
| | – 'Jack Frost'[PBR] 🏆H4 | Widely available |
| | – 'King's Ransom' (v) **new** | EBee ECtt MAsh NLar NSti SHeu |
| | – 'Langford Hewitt' (v) | MNrw |
| | – 'Langtrees' | CBct CMac EBee EBla ECha ECtt EHoe EPla GCal GCra IBal LHop LRHS MCot MMuc MRav MWhi NBir NGdn NOrc NVic SEND SPer SWat WFar WKif WPtf WWEG |
| | – 'Looking Glass'[PBR] | Widely available |
| | – 'Marley's White' | CAbP CLAP EBee LLHF MCot NDov NEgg NLar SUsu WCot |
| | – 'Mister Morse'[PBR] (v) | Widely available |
| | – 'Silver Wings' | CBct CElw EAEE EBee ECtt EPfP EWll GEdr LRHS MBri NBir NGdn NLar NSti SHar SHeu SPoG SWat |
| | – 'Spring Yellow' | CBcs EBla ECtt NLar SHeu |
| | ***sibirica*** | CDes CLAP EBee EBla EPPr EWes NBid |

## *Brunsvigia* (*Amaryllidaceae*)

| | | |
|---|---|---|
| | ***bosmaniae*** | ECho WCot |
| | ***marginata*** | ECho WCot |
| | ***pulchra*** | ECho WCot |
| | ***radula*** 'Vanrhynsdorp' | ECho |
| | ***radulosa*** | ECho |
| | ***rosea*** 'Minor' | see *Amaryllis belladonna* |
| | ***striata*** | ECho |

## *Bryonia* (*Cucurbitaceae*)

| | | |
|---|---|---|
| | ***dioica*** | CArn GPoy NMir |

## *Bryophyllum* see *Kalanchoe*

## *Buchloe* (*Poaceae*)

|  |  |
|---|---|
| ***dactyloides*** | CRWN |

## *Buddleja* ✿ (*Scrophulariaceae*)

|  |  |
|---|---|
| HCM 98.017 from Chile | WPGP |
| ***agathosma*** | CBot CPLG MOWG SLon WKif WLav WPGP WSHC |
| ***albiflora*** | SLon WLav |
| ***alternifolia*** ♀H4 | Widely available |
| - 'Argentea' | CBcs CBot CDoC EBee ELan EPfP GBin LRHS MBNS MRav NLar SKHP SPoG SRGP WCot WLav WPat WSHC XSen |
| ***asiatica*** ♀H2 | CBot EShb IDee MOWG SLon WLav |
| - B&SWJ 11278 | WCru |
| ***auriculata*** | CBcs CBot CDul CHid CPLG CTca CWib ECre ELan EPfP EShb LRHS MOWG MRav NSti SDix SKHP SLon SPlb SPoG SVen WCru WLav WPat |
| 'Autumn Surprise' **new** | SLon |
| 'Blue Chip' **new** | LBuc LRHS SLon |
| * 'Blue Trerice' | CPLG |
| ***caryopteridifolia*** | GQui SEND SLon |
| ***colvilei*** | CBcs CDoC CDul ELan EPfP GCal GGal GKin IDee SLon WBor WPat |
| - B&SWJ 2121 | WCru |
| - GWJ 9399 | WCru |
| - 'Kewensis' | CBot CHGN CHid CPLG CRHN EBee EWes GCal GGal NLar SLon SVen WCFE WCru WLav WPat WSHC |
| ***cordata*** | MOWG SLon |
| - B&SWJ 10433 | WCru |
| - F&M 220 | WPGP |
| ***coriacea*** | SLon |
| § ***crispa*** | CBot CPLG CSpe CTca ECha ELan EPfP LRHS MOWG SEND SLon SPer SRkn WFar WKif WPGP WSHC XSen |
| - var. ***farreri*** | CHGN CHid SLon |
| ***crotonoides*** subsp. ***amplexicaulis*** | SLon |
| ***curviflora*** f. ***venenifera*** | SLon |
| - - B&SWJ 6036 | WCru |
| ***davidii*** | CArn CCVT NWea SGar STre WDin |
| - B&SWJ 8083 | WCru |
| - Adonis Blue = 'Adokeep'PBR | CBcs LBuc LRHS NPri SBrd SLon |
| - 'African Queen' | CAni SLon SRGP WLav |
| - var. ***alba*** | CWib |
| § - 'Autumn Beauty' | CAni SLon WLav |
| - 'Bath Beauty' | CAni |
| - 'Beijing' | see *B. davidii* 'Autumn Beauty' |
| - 'Bishop's Velvet' | CAni CTsd |
| - 'Black Knight' ♀H4 | Widely available |
| - 'Blue Horizon' | CAni CSam MMuc NLar SLon SRGP WCot WLav WMoo WRHF |
| - 'Border Beauty' | CAni SLon WLav |
| - 'Boskoop Beauty' | CAni |
| - 'Brown's Beauty' | CAni |
| - Camberwell Beauty = 'Camkeep' (English Butterfly Series) | CSBt LBuc NHol SBrd SLon |
| - 'Car Wash' | CAni |
| - 'Castle Blue' | SLon |
| - 'Castle School' | CAni CSam |
| § - 'Charming' | CDul WMoo WSHC WWlt |
| - 'Clive Farrell' | see *B. davidii* 'Autumn Beauty' |
| - 'Corinne Tremaine' **new** | WHer |
| - 'Croyde' | CSam |
| - 'Dartmoor' ♀H4 | CAni CDul CEnd CFee CMHG CMac CPLG CTri EBee ECre ECtt ELan EPfP GCal LRHS MAsh MGos MRav NLar NPer SDix SIde SLim SPer SPlb SPoG WFar WSHC |
| - 'Dart's Ornamental White' | MRav SLon WLav |
| - 'Dart's Papillon Blue' | CAni SLon WLav |
| - 'Dart's Purple Rain' | CAni SLon WLav |
| - 'Dubonnet' | CAni SLon WLav |
| - 'Dudley's Compact Lavender' | CAni |
| - 'Ecolonia' | CAni SLon WLav |
| - 'Empire Blue' ♀H4 | CAni CBar CBcs CDoC CDul CHab CSBt EBee ECtt EPfP GKin LRHS LSRN MGos MRav NBir NPer NWea SBfd SEND SPer SPlb SPoG SRGP SRms SWat SWvt WDin WFar WWlt |
| - 'Fascinating' | CAni GCal MRav NBir SLon WLav |
| - 'Flaming Violet' | CAni SLon WLav |
| - 'Florence' | EBee LLHF LRHS LSRN LSou NEgg NLar SLon SRGP WFar WHar WMoo |
| - 'Fortune' | CAni |
| - 'Glasnevin Hybrid' | CAni NSti SDix SLon WLav |
| - 'Gonglepod' | CAni SLon WLav |
| - 'Greenway's River Dart' | CAni SLon |
| - 'Grey Dawn' **new** | WLav |
| - 'Harlequin' (v) | Widely available |
| - 'Heath' **new** | SPhx |
| - 'Ile de France' | CAni CBcs CWib EBee NBlu NWea SLon SRms WLav |
| - 'Leela Kapila' | MGos SLon |
| - 'Les Kneale' | CAni SLon WLav |
| - 'Lyme Bay' | CAni |
| - Marbled White = 'Markeep'PBR | CSBt LBuc SBrd SLon |
| - Masquerade = 'Notbud'PBR (v) | MRav SLon WGor |
| § - Nanho Blue = 'Mongo' ♀H4 | Widely available |
| - 'Nanho Petite Indigo' | see *B. davidii* Nanho Blue |
| - 'Nanho Petite Plum' | see *B. davidii* Nanho Purple |
| - 'Nanho Petite Purple' | see *B. davidii* Nanho Purple |
| § - Nanho Purple = 'Monum' ♀H4 | CAni CDoC CMHG CTri CWib EBee ELan EPPr EPfP LRHS LSRN MGos MRav NLar SGol SLim SLon SPer SPlb SPoG SRGP WHar |
| - Nanho White = 'Monite' | EHoe ELan EPfP LRHS SGol SLon SPer SPoG SRms WFar |
| - var. ***nanhoensis*** | CAni CDul EBee MAsh SEND SGol SIde WLav |
| - - blue-flowered | NHol NWad SLon SPer |
| - 'Orchid Beauty' | CAni SLon WLav |
| - 'Orpheus' | CAni SLon WLav |
| - 'Panache' | EPfP SLon |
| - 'Peace' | CMac CTri EBee EPfP LSRN MRav NLar SLon SPoG WLav |
| - Peacock = 'Peakeep'PBR (English Butterfly Series) | CBcs LBuc SBrd |
| - 'Persephone' | SLon WLav |
| - 'Petite Indigo' | see *B. davidii* Nanho Blue |
| - 'Pink Beauty' | LSRN SRGP |
| - 'Pink Charming' | see *B. davidii* 'Charming' |
| - 'Pink Pearl' | CAni SEND SLon WLav |
| - 'Pink Spreader' | CAni SLon WLav |
| - 'Pixie Blue' | CAni LBMP LBuc LRHS MAsh NBlu SLon SRGP WLav |
| - 'Pixie Red' | CAni LBMP LBuc LRHS MAsh MMuc NEgg NLar SEND WLav |
| - 'Pixie White' | LBuc LRHS MAsh MMuc NLar SEND SRGP WLav |

| |  |  |
|---|---|---|
| | - Purple Emperor = 'Pyrkeep' (English Butterfly Series) | CBcs LBuc NBir SBrd SLon |
| | - 'Purple Friend' | CAni SLon WLav |
| | - 'Purple Prince' | CAni |
| | - 'Red Admiral' | CAni LLHF LRHS MAsh SLon SPoG SRGP |
| | - Rêve de Papillon = 'Minpap' | EMil |
| | - Rêve de Papillon White **new** | EMil |
| | - 'Royal Purple' | CAni SLim SWvt |
| | - 'Royal Red' ♀H4 | Widely available |
| | - 'Saith Ffynnon Early' | WSFF |
| | - 'Santana' (v) | CAni CDul CMac EBee EHoe ELon EPfP EWes LRHS LSou MRav NEgg NHol NLar SAga SBfd SWvt WCot WHar WMoo WPat |
| | - 'Shapcott Blue' | CAni |
| | - 'Shire Blue' | WLav |
| | - 'Southcombe Splendour' | CAni |
| | - 'Summer Beauty' | CAni CWib EBee LRHS MGos MRav SLon WLav |
| | - 'Summer House Blue' | SLon WLav |
| | - 'Twotones' | WLav |
| | - 'Variegata' (v) | CAni LRHS MAsh SLon SWvt WLav |
| | - var. ***veitchiana*** | CTca |
| | - 'White Ball' | EBee EHoe ELan EPfP SLon WLav |
| | - 'White Bouquet' | CAlb CAni CCVT CDul CSBt EBee EPfP EWTr GKin LAst LRHS MHer MMuc MSwo MWat NWea SEND SPer SRGP SWvt WLav |
| | - 'White Cloud' | CAni ECrN GQui MGos SGar SRms WGwG |
| | - 'White Harlequin' (v) | SLon WCFE |
| | - 'White Profusion' ♀H4 | CAlb CAni CBar CBcs CDul CHab CSam EBee ECtt ELan EPfP LRHS MGos MRav NBir NEgg NLar NPri NWea SBfd SGol SLim SWat SWvt WCFE WDin WFar WHar |
| | - 'White Wings' | SLon WLav |
| | - 'Widecombe' | CAni |
| § | ***delavayi*** | CPLG ECre SEND WCru |
| | ***fallowiana*** misapplied | see *B.* 'West Hill' |
| | ***fallowiana*** Balf.f. & W.W.Sm | ELan GQui LRHS WLav |
| | - ACE 2481 | LRHS |
| | - BWJ 7803 | WCru |
| | - var. ***alba*** ♀H3 | CBot CDoC CHGN CHid CMac EBee ECrN ELan EPfP GBin LRHS MAsh MRav NChi NLar NSti SBrd SLon SPer WFar WPGP WSHC |
| | 'Flower Power' | see *B.* × *weyeriana* 'Bicolor' |
| | ***forrestii*** | CBot CRHN WCru |
| | ***globosa*** ♀H4 | Widely available |
| | - RCB/Arg C-11 | WCot |
| | - 'Cally Orange' | GCal GGar |
| | - 'Lemon Ball' | MBlu NPer SLon WLav |
| | ***glomerata*** | EShb SLon WPGP |
| | - 'Silver Service' | CMHG ELan LRHS SKHP |
| | 'Gulliver' | NLar SGol SLon |
| | ***heliophila*** | see *B. delavayi* |
| | ***indica*** | SLon WBor |
| | ***japonica*** | SLon |
| | - B&SWJ 8912 | WCru |
| | × ***lewisiana*** 'Margaret Pike' | CBot MOWG SLon |
| | ***limitanea*** | SLon |
| | ***lindleyana*** | Widely available |
| | aff. ***lindleyana*** B&SWJ 11478 | WCru |
| | 'Lochinch' ♀H3-4 | Widely available |
| | ***longifolia*** | SLon XSen |
| | 'Longstock' **new** | SLon |
| | 'Longstock Silver' **new** | SLon |
| | ***loricata*** | CBot CFee CHGN CPLG CTca CTsd CWib GBin GQui IDee LRHS MMuc MOWG SEND SGar SKHP SLon SPlb WCFE WLav WPGP |
| | ***macrostachya*** | GBin GLin |
| | - HWJ 602 | WCru |
| | - WWJ 12016 | WCru |
| § | ***madagascariensis*** ♀H1 | CBcs CRHN MOWG NLar SGar SLon SPlb SVen WHar |
| * | 'Malvern Blue' (English Butterfly Series) | CAni |
| | ***megalocephala*** B&SWJ 9106 | WCru |
| § | 'Morning Mist'[PBR] | CDoC CMHG CPLG CWGN EBee EGxp EHoe ELan EPfP GBin LLHF LRHS LSRN LSou MOWG NBir NEgg NHol NLar NPri SBfd SLon SPoG WCot WHar WPGP |
| | ***myriantha*** | CPLG SLon XSen |
| * | - f. ***fragrans*** | WCot |
| | ***nappii*** | NMun SLon |
| | ***nicodemia*** | see *B. madagascariensis* |
| | ***nivea*** | CBot CMHG CPLG MOWG SLon WLav |
| | - B&SWJ 2679 | WCru |
| | - pink-flowered | SLon |
| | ***officinalis*** ♀H2 | CBot CPLG CTca MOWG SLon |
| | ***paniculata*** | SLon |
| | ***parvifolia*** | SLon |
| | - MPF 148 | WLav |
| | × ***pikei*** 'Hever' | GCal XSen |
| | 'Pink Delight' ♀H4 | Widely available |
| | 'Pink Perfection' | CAni WFar |
| | 'Pride of Hever' | MOWG |
| | 'Pride of Longstock' | LRHS SLon |
| | 'Purple Splendour' | GGal |
| | ***saligna*** | SLon |
| | 'Salmon Spheres' | SLon |
| | ***salviifolia*** | CBcs CBot CDul CHid CPLG CRHN CTca CTsd ELan GGal GGar GQui IDee LRHS MBlu NSti SEND SPlb SWal WGwG WHer WLav WPGP |
| | - white-flowered | SLon WPGP |
| | Silver Anniversary[PBR] | see *B.* 'Morning Mist' |
| | 'Silver Surprise' **new** | EMil |
| | ***stachyoides*** | MOWG |
| | ***stenostachya*** | CPLG SLon |
| | ***sterniana*** | see *B. crispa* |
| | 'Sugar Plum' **new** | SLon |
| | ***tibetica*** | see *B. crispa* |
| | ***tubiflora*** | CBot MOWG SLon WLav |
| | ***venenifera*** B&SWJ 895 | WCru |
| § | 'West Hill' | SLon SRGP WLav |
| | × ***weyeriana*** | CDul CRHN EBee ECtt EPfP GGal GQui MMuc MNrw MSwo NBir SBfd SGar SPad SPlb SWvt WDin WFar |
| § | - 'Bicolor' | MCCP MNrw |
| | - 'Golden Glow' (v) | CEnt CTri ECrN EPfP GBin LSRN NLar SLon WLav WSFF |
| | - 'Honeycomb' | NLar |
| | - 'Lady de Ramsey' | SEND |
| | - 'Moonlight' | CBcs CPLG ELan IFro SBfd SLon WCot WLav |
| | - 'Pink Pagoda' **new** | SLon |
| | - 'Sungold' ♀H4 | Widely available |
| | 'Winter Sun' | SLon |
| | ***yunnanensis*** | GCal GGar SLon |

| | |
|---|---|
| - B&SWJ 8146 | WCru |

## *Buglossoides* (*Boraginaceae*)

| | |
|---|---|
| § ***purpurocaerulea*** | CEnt CHll CMHG CPom CSpe CWGN EBee ECha ELan LHop MLHP MWhi NBid NBir NChi WAle WCot WSHC XLum |

## *Bukiniczia* (*Plumbaginaceae*)

| | |
|---|---|
| ***cabulica*** | WAbe |

## *Bulbine* (*Asphodelaceae*)

| | |
|---|---|
| SH 74 | CCse |
| ***abyssinica*** | ECho |
| ***alooides*** | ECho |
| ***annua*** misapplied | see *B. semibarbata* |
| ***bulbosa*** misapplied | see *B. semibarbata* |
| ***capitata*** 'Bloemfontein' | ECho |
| ***caulescens*** | see *B. frutescens* |
| § ***frutescens*** | CDoC CHll CTca EShb GGar MBNS SVen WBrk WJek |
| - 'Hallmark' | CCCN |
| ***latifolia*** | CCCN EShb |
| ***narcissifolia*** 'Ladybrand' | ECho |
| § ***semibarbata*** | CCCN |

## *Bulbinella* (*Asphodelaceae*)

| | |
|---|---|
| ***angustifolia*** | ECho |
| ***cauda-felis*** | WCot |
| - 'Tulbagh' | ECho |
| ***eburnifolia*** | ECho WCot |
| ***elata*** | WCot |
| ***gibbsii*** var. ***balanifera*** | ECho |
| ***graminifolia*** 'Clanwilliam' | ECho |
| ***hookeri*** | CPom ECho ECou EWld GBee GEdr GGar GKev ITim NWCA SRms WHal |
| ***latifolia*** | ECho |
| - subsp. ***doleritica*** | ECho |
| - subsp ***latifolia*** | IBlr |
| ***nutans*** | ECho WPGP |
| ***punctulata*** 'Piketberg' | ECho |

## *Bulbinopsis* see *Bulbine*

## *Bulbocodium* (*Colchicaceae*)

| | |
|---|---|
| ***vernum*** | ECho EPot GKev LAma LLHF LRHS NMin SDeJ |

## bullace see *Prunus insititia*

## *Bunias* (*Brassicaceae*)

| | |
|---|---|
| ***orientalis*** | CAgr ELau |

## *Bunium* (*Apiaceae*)

| | |
|---|---|
| ***bulbocastanum*** | CSpe LEdu SBfd SHDw XLum |

## *Buphthalmum* (*Asteraceae*)

| | |
|---|---|
| ***salicifolium*** | CSam EBee ELan EPfP MMuc MNFA NBPC NBlu NBro NGdn SEND SPer SRms SWat WCAu WCot WFar WPer WWEG XLum |
| - 'Alpengold' | ECha GMaP NBre NLar |
| - 'Dora' | CSam ECtt LRHS WCot |
| - 'Sunwheel' | LRHS SRms |
| ***speciosum*** | see *Telekia speciosa* |

## *Bupleurum* (*Apiaceae*)

| | |
|---|---|
| ***angulosum*** | CSpe NBir WFar WTcb |
| - copper-leaved | see *B. longifolium* |
| ***candollei*** GWJ 9405 | WCru |
| ***falcatum*** | CArn CSpe ECGP ECha NDov SPur WCot WFar |
| ***fruticosum*** | CAbb CBcs CBot CSpe ECtt EPfP LPla LRHS MAsh SDix SEND SKHP SLon SPer SSpi SSta WCot WDin WPGP WPat XSen |
| § ***longifolium*** | CAby CElw CFee CPom CSpe EBee EWes GBBs GBin LEdu LRHS MDKP MLLN MNrw NChi SKHP |
| - subsp. ***aureum*** | SPhx WFar |
| - bronze-leaved | MAvo |
| ***ranunculoides*** | XLum |
| ***rotundifolium*** 'Copper' | WCot |
| ***spinosum*** | SMad WHil XSen |
| ***tenue*** | CArn |

## *Burchellia* (*Rubiaceae*)

| | |
|---|---|
| ***capensis*** new | SPlb |

## *Bursaria* (*Pittosporaceae*)

| | |
|---|---|
| ***spinosa*** | CCCN ECou EShb NLar |

## *Butia* (*Arecaceae*)

| | |
|---|---|
| ***capitata*** | CAbb CBcs CBrP CCCN CDTJ CHEx CPHo CTrC EAmu EPla ESwi ETod LMaj LPJP LPal LTen MGos MREP NPal SArc SBst SChr |
| § - var. ***odorata*** | EAmu LPal SPlb |
| ***eriospatha*** | CDTJ EAmu LPal SChr |
| ***odorata*** | see *B. capitata* var. *odorata* |
| ***yatay*** | CDTJ EAmu LPal SBig |

## *Butomus* (*Butomaceae*)

| | |
|---|---|
| ***umbellatus*** ♀H4 | CBen CRow CWat ECha EHon EPfP EWil GQue LPBA MCCP MNrw MRav MSKA MWts NPer SWat WMAq WPnP WTin XLum |
| - f. ***albiflorus*** | MSKA |
| - 'Rosenrot' | CRow LLWG |
| - 'Schneeweisschen' | CRow LLWG MNrw MWts NLar |

## butternut see *Juglans cinerea*

## × *Butyagrus* (*Arecaceae*)

| | |
|---|---|
| ***nabonnandii*** | EAmu |

## *Buxus* ✿ (*Buxaceae*)

| | |
|---|---|
| ***aurea*** 'Marginata' | see *B. sempervirens* 'Marginata' |
| ***balearica*** ♀H4 | EPla EQua MBlu |
| ***bodinieri*** | EPla EQua |
| 'Green Gem' | NHol NWad |
| 'Green Velvet' | EPfP |
| ***harlandii*** hort. | CMen EPla SRiv |
| - 'Richard' | STre |
| ***japonica*** 'Nana' | see *B. microphylla* |
| § ***microphylla*** | MHer NWad SGol STre |
| - 'Asiatic Winter' | see *B. microphylla* var. *japonica* 'Winter Gem' |
| § - 'Compacta' | CMen LLHF MHer NMen SRiv WCot WPat WThu |
| - 'Curly Locks' | EPla MHer NWad |
| - 'Faulkner' | CCVT ELan EPfP EQua LBuc LHop LRHS LSRN MAsh MBNS MGos MREP SEWo SGol SPer SPoG SRiv WDin WMoo |
| - Golden Dream = 'Peergold'PBR | NLar |
| - 'Golden Triumph'PBR | EPfP MWat |
| - 'Green Pillow' | EPfP MHer SRiv |

| | | |
|---|---|---|
| | - var. ***insularis*** | see *B. sinica* var. *insularis* |
| | - var. ***japonica*** 'Morris Midget' | IArd NWad |
| § | - - 'Winter Gem' | MHer MRav NLar SLPl |
| | - 'John Baldwin' | SRiv |
| | ***riparia*** | EPla |
| | ***sempervirens*** ♀H4 | Widely available |
| § | - 'Angustifolia' | EPla MGos MHer MRav NWad SMad |
| | - 'Arborescens' | EQua |
| | - 'Argentea' | see *B. sempervirens* 'Argenteo-variegata' |
| § | - 'Argenteo-variegata' (v) | EPfP IFoB NEgg SGol WFar |
| | - 'Aurea' | see *B. sempervirens* 'Aureovariegata' |
| | - 'Aurea Maculata' | see *B. sempervirens* 'Aureovariegata' |
| | - 'Aurea Marginata' | see *B. sempervirens* 'Marginata' |
| | - 'Aurea Pendula' (v) | CPMA EPla WDin |
| § | - 'Aureovariegata' (v) | EPfP EShb LRHS MGos MHer MRav NSti SPer SRiv WDin WFar WMoo |
| | - 'Bentley Blue' | NHol NWea |
| | - 'Blauer Heinz' | ELan IVic MHer MRav SRiv |
| § | - 'Blue Cone' | NHol |
| | - 'Blue Spire' | see *B. sempervirens* 'Blue Cone' |
| | - 'Bowles's Blue' | EQua |
| I | - 'Brilliantissima' | WMoo |
| | - clipped ball | CWib EPfP LSRN MGos NBlu NLar SGol SLim SRiv WFar |
| | - clipped bird | SRiv |
| | - clipped cone | LSRN SGol SRiv |
| | - clipped pyramid | CWib EPfP LSRN MGos NLar SGol SLim SRiv |
| | - clipped spiral | LSRN SGol SLim SRiv |
| | - 'Elegans' | IFoB LRHS |
| § | - 'Elegantissima' (v) ♀H4 | Widely available |
| | - 'Gold Tip' | see *B. sempervirens* 'Notata' |
| | - 'Golden Frimley' (v) | LHop |
| § | - 'Graham Blandy' | MHer SGol SRiv |
| | - 'Green Balloon' | EPfP LBuc |
| | - 'Greenpeace' | see *B. sempervirens* 'Graham Blandy' |
| | - 'Handsworthiensis' | CLnd NHol NLar SEND SPer WMoo |
| | - 'Handsworthii' | CTri NWea SRms |
| | - 'Japonica Aurea' | see *B. sempervirens* 'Latifolia Maculata' |
| | - 'King Midas' | IVic |
| | - 'Kingsville' | see *B. microphylla* 'Compacta' |
| | - 'Kingsville Dwarf' | see *B. microphylla* 'Compacta' |
| | - 'Krakow' | NLar |
| | - 'Lace' | NSti |
| | - 'Latifolia Macrophylla' | SLon |
| § | - 'Latifolia Maculata' (v) ♀H4 | CAbP CDoC CWib EBee EPfP EPla LRHS NHol NPer SEND SPoG SRiv STre WJek |
| | - 'Longifolia' | see *B. sempervirens* 'Angustifolia' |
| § | - 'Marginata' (v) | CTca EPla IFoB LHop LRHS LTen SGol SLon WHar |
| | - 'Memorial' | MHer NHol NWad SRiv |
| | - 'Myosotidifolia' | CMHG NPro SRiv |
| | - 'Myrtifolia' | CBot EPla MHer NHol |
| § | - 'Notata' (v) | IFoB MAsh SBfd WDin WMoo |
| | - 'Parasol' | MHer |
| | - 'Prostrata' | NHol NWad NWea |
| * | - 'Pygmaea' | WAbe |
| | - 'Pyramidalis' | SEND WFar |
| | - 'Rosmarinifolia' | MHer MRav |
| | - 'Rotundifolia' | ELan SEND SIde WDin WMoo |
| | - 'Silver Beauty' (v) | NEgg |
| | - 'Silver Variegated' | see *B. sempervirens* 'Elegantissima' |
| | - 'Suffruticosa' ♀H4 | Widely available |
| | - 'Suffruticosa Blue' | NHol |
| | - 'Suffruticosa Variegata' (v) | EOHP SRms SWvt |
| | - 'Sunningdale Silver' | EQua |
| | - 'Twisty' | WFar |
| | - 'Vardar Valley' | NPro SRiv |
| * | - 'Varicgata' (v) | ELan WRHF |
| | - 'Waterfall' | MHer |
| § | ***sinica*** var. ***insularis*** | MAsh |
| | - - 'Justin Brouwers' | MHer SRiv |
| | - - 'Tide Hill' | MHer SRiv WFar |
| | ***wallichiana*** | EPla |

# C

## *Cachrys* (*Apiaceae*)

| | | |
|---|---|---|
| | ***alpina*** new | SPhx |

## *Caesalpinia* (*Caesalpiniaceae*)

| | | |
|---|---|---|
| | ***gilliesii*** | CBcs CSpe EBee LSRN MOWG SBrt SPlb |
| | - RCB/Arg N-1 | SEND XSen |
| | ***mexicana*** | WPGP |
| | ***pulcherrima*** | CCCN MOWG SPlb |
| | ***spinosa*** | CBcs SPlb WAle WSHC |

## *Caiophora* (*Loasaceae*)

| | | |
|---|---|---|
| | ***coronata*** | SPlb |

## *Calamagrostis* (*Poaceae*)

| | | |
|---|---|---|
| | from Korea | NDov |
| | × ***acutiflora*** | XLum |
| | - 'Avalanche' | CKno EBee EHoe EPPr LRHS MWhi |
| | - 'Eldorado' (v) | WCot |
| N | - 'Karl Foerster' | Widely available |
| | - 'Overdam' (v) | Widely available |
| | - 'Stricta' | EBee EPPr NWsh |
| | - 'Waldenbuch' | CKno EBee GBin |
| | ***argentea*** | see *Stipa calamagrostis* |
| | ***arundinacea*** | CElw COIW CPLG CSpe ECou EPla LEdu NBid NHol NVic SDix SGar SPlb WFar WMoo WPGP XLum |
| | 'Avalanche' | CKno GBin GQue |
| § | ***brachytricha*** ♀H4 | Widely available |
| | ***canadensis*** new | EPPr |
| | ***emodensis*** | CEnt CKno CWCL EBee ECha EHoe EPla LEdu MAvo MMoz NOak NWsh SMad WGrn WMoo WPGP |
| | ***epigejos*** | EBee LEdu WHrl |
| | ***nutkaensis*** | EPPr |
| | ***splendens*** misapplied | see *Stipa calamagrostis* |
| | ***splendens*** Trin. | LPla NDov |
| | ***varia*** | CKno EHoe NDov WHrl |

## *Calamintha* (*Lamiaceae*)

| | | |
|---|---|---|
| | ***alpina*** | see *Acinos alpinus* |
| § | ***ascendens*** | CArn EBee SGar SPhx WMoo |
| | ***clinopodium*** | see *Clinopodium vulgare* |
| | ***cretica*** | EBee WPer |
| * | 'Fritz Kuhn' | WWEG |
| § | ***grandiflora*** | CArn EBee ECha EDAr ELan GGar GJos GPoy LEdu LRHS MHer MMuc MNHC MRav MWhi NBir NPer SEND SMrm SPer SPlb SSvw SWat WCAu WFar WJek WMoo WTin XLum |

- 'Elfin Purple' EBee EPfP SBfd
- 'Variegata' (v) CPrp EBee ECtt ELan EPPr EPfP LAst NPri SPoG WCAu WFar
§ ***menthifolia*** NBre NLar WJek XLum
§ ***nepeta*** Widely available
- subsp. ***glandulosa*** CEnt ECGP WMoo
- - ACL 1050/90 EBee WHoo
- - 'White Cloud' CSpe EBee ELan LLWP MRav NBir WCAu WMoo
- 'Gottfried Kuehn' EBee LPla MRav
§ - subsp. ***nepeta*** CPrp ELan ELon EPfP MHer MLHP MRav MWat NDov NSti SPer SUsu WFar WHal WTin XLum
- - 'Blue Cloud' CSam CSpe EBee ECha EPfP LRHS MMuc NBir NCGa NDov SPhx SPoG SWat WCAu WFar WMoo
- 'Weisse Riese' SPhx
***nepetoides*** see *C. nepeta* subsp. *nepeta*
***officinalis*** misapplied see *C. ascendens*
***sylvatica*** see *C. menthifolia*
I - 'Menthe' EBee
***vulgaris*** see *Clinopodium vulgare*

## calamondin see × *Citrofortunella microcarpa*

## *Calandrinia* (*Portulacaceae*)

***grandiflora*** LLHF
* ***ranunculina*** CPBP
***sericea*** CPBP
***sibirica*** see *Claytonia sibirica*
***umbellata*** EDAr LBMP MAsh WPer
- 'Ruby Tuesday' NPri

## *Calanthe* (*Orchidaceae*)

***alismifolia*** EFEx
***arcuata*** EFEx
***arisanenesis*** EFEx
***aristulifera*** EFEx GEdr LWst NLAp
***bicolor*** see *C. striata*
***discolor*** EFEx EPot GEdr LAma LWst NLAp WCot
- subsp. ***amamiana*** EFEx
- var. ***flava*** see *C. striata*
- subsp. ***tokunoshimensis*** EFEx
***fargesii*** LWst WCot
***graciliflora*** EFEx
**Hizen gx** GEdr LWst NLAp
**Kozu gx** GEdr LEdu LWst
- red-flowered GEdr
***mannii*** EFEx
***nipponica*** CBct EFEx GEdr LAma LWst NLAp
***reflexa*** EFEx EPot GEdr LAma LWst NLAp
***sieboldii*** see *C. striata*
§ ***striata*** CBct EBee EFEx EPot GEdr LAma LWst NLAp WCot
**Takane gx** GEdr LWst NLAp
***tricarinata*** CBct EFEx GEdr LAma LWst NLAp

## *Calathea* (*Marantaceae*)

***argyrophylla*** 'Exotica' XBlo
***louisae*** 'Maui Queen' XBlo
§ ***majestica*** ♀H1 XBlo
***makoyana*** ♀H1 XBlo
***oppenheimiana*** see *Ctenanthe oppenheimiana*
***ornata*** see *C. majestica*
***picturata*** 'Argentea' ♀H1 XBlo
***roseopicta*** ♀H1 XBlo
***rufibarba*** XBlo
* ***stromata*** XBlo
***zebrina*** ♀H1 XBlo
'Zoizia' XBlo

## *Calceolaria* (*Calceolariaceae*)

***acutifolia*** see *C. polyrhiza* Cav.
***arachnoidea*** GKev SKHP SPlb
§ ***biflora*** ECho EPfP GGar GKev MAsh NLar WPer
- 'Goldcap' ECho
- 'Goldcrest Amber' SPlb
'Camden Hero' GCal MAJR
***cavanillesii*** new WAle
***chelidonioides*** GGar
***corymbosa*** GKev
***falklandica*** ECho GKev SRms
***fothergillii*** GKev WAbe
'Goldcrest' ECho LRHS SRms
'Hall's Spotted' NWCA
N ***integrifolia*** ♀H3 CAbb CDTJ CPLG CSpe CTri ECtt ELan EPfP GKev MSCN SEND SGar SPer SPoG SRms WAbe WAle WWlt
- bronze MSCN SPer
- 'Gaines' Yellow' EBee GCal
'John Innes' ECho
'Kentish Hero' CSpe GCal MAJR WAbe
***morisii*** new WAle
aff. ***pavonii*** CRHN
***perfoliata*** B&SWJ 10638 WCru
***plantaginea*** see *C. biflora*
§ ***polyrhiza*** Cav. ECho
***rugosa*** see *C. integrifolia*
Sunset Series EPfP NBlu
***tenella*** NSla WAbe
***uniflora*** var. ***darwinii*** ECho GKev NSla WAbe
'Walter Shrimpton' ECho EPot EWes WAbe

## *Calendula* (*Asteraceae*)

***arvensis*** CCCN
***meuselii*** CFee
***officinalis*** CArn ELau GPoy MHer MNHC SBfd SIde SPav SWvt WJek
- Fiesta Gitana Group ♀H4 CPrp WJek
- 'Touch of Red' (Touch of Red Series) CSpe
'Tarifa' new SEND

## *Calibanus* (*Asparagaceae*)

***hookeri*** EShb

## *Calibrachoa* (*Solanaceae*)

(Cabaret Series) Cabaret Apricot = 'Balcabapt' LAst NPri
- Cabaret Blue new NPri
- Cabaret Hot Pink = 'Balcabhopi'PBR NPri
- Cabaret Red Improved = 'Balcabimred' new NPri
- Cabaret Rose = 'Balcabrose'PBR new LAst
- Cabaret Scarlet = 'Balcabscar'PBR LAst
- Cabaret White Improved = 'Balcabwitim' NPri
- Cabaret Yellow = 'Balcabyelow'PBR NPri
- Cabaret Yellow Improved LAst
(Can-can Series) Can-can Mocha = 'Balcanoa' new LAst
- Can-can Strawberry = 'Balcanerry' new LAst

(Million Bells Series) Million Bells Cherry = 'Sunbelchipi'PBR LSou WGor
- Million Bells Crackling Fire = 'Sunbelfire'PBR LAst LSou
- Million Bells Orange Glow = 'Sunbelore' LSou
- Million Bells Pink Terracotta = 'Sunbelrkist' new LAst
- Million Bells Trailing Blue = 'Sunbelkubu'PBR LAst
- Million Bells Trailing Fuchsia = 'Sunbelrkup' ♀H3 WGor
- Million Bells Trailing Ice = 'Sunbelkuriho'PBR LAst LSou
- Million Bells Trailing Pink Morn = 'Sunbelkupapi'PBR LAst
Minifamous Double Blue = 'Kleca07162'PBR (MiniFamous Series) (d) new WGor
(Noa Series) Noa Mega Pink = 'Danoa38' WGor
- Noa Orange Eye LSou
- Noa Ultra Purple LSou
- Noa Yellow WGor
(Superbells Series) Superbells Candy White = 'Uscali48'PBR LSou
- Superbells Imperial Purple = 'Uscali100'PBR WGor
- Superbells Indigo = 'Uscali51'PBR LSou
- Superbells Magenta = 'Uscali17'PBR LSou
- Superbells Red = 'Uscali28'PBR WGor

## *Calibrachoa* × *Petunia* see × *Petchoa*

## *Calla* (*Araceae*)

***aethiopica*** see *Zantedeschia aethiopica*
***palustris*** CRow CWat EHon LPBA MCCP MSKA MWts NPer SWat WFar WMAq WPnP

## *Calliandra* (*Mimosaceae*)

'Dixie Pink' CCCN
***eriophylla*** new SPlb
***haematocephala*** MOWG
***portoricensis*** CCCN
***surinamensis*** CCCN
***tweediei*** CCCN MOWG

## *Callianthemum* (*Ranunculaceae*)

***anemonoides*** WAbe
***kernerianum*** WAbe
***miyabeanum*** LWst

## *Callicarpa* (*Lamiaceae*)

***americana*** CPLG NLar
- var. ***lactea*** CMCN
***bodinieri*** NBir WFar
- var. ***giraldii*** GBin MRav NLar SGol WDin
- - 'Profusion' ♀H4 Widely available
***cathayana*** CMCN NLar
***dichotoma*** CBcs CPLG EBee ELan NLar WFar WPat
- 'Issai' LLHF NLar SBfd SPur WPat
- 'Shirobana' NLar
***japonica*** CMen CPLG NLar
- f. ***albibacca*** NLar
- 'Koshima-no-homate' NLar
- 'Leucocarpa' CBcs CMac CPLG EBee ELan EPfP MRav NLar SPer SPoG SPur WFar
- var. ***luxurians*** B&SWJ 8521 WCru
***kwangtungensis*** CBcs CMCN EPfP MBri NLar
***mollis*** CPLG NLar
***shikokiana*** NLar
× ***shirasawana*** NLar
aff. ***tikusikensis*** B&SWJ 7127 new WCru
***yunnanensis*** NLar

## *Callirhoe* (*Malvaceae*)

***involucrata*** ELon GGar MWea NWCA SBrt SMad WHrl
***triangulata*** LRHS

## *Callisia* (*Commelinaceae*)

***fragrans*** new EShb
***rosea*** new LRHS

## *Callistemon* (*Myrtaceae*)

***acuminatus*** CCCN
'Awanga Dam' ECou
***brachyandrus*** SVen
'Burgundy' MOWG
* 'Burning Bush' MOWG
'Candy Pink' MOWG
***chisholmii*** MOWG
***citrinus*** CHll CTri CWSG EBee ECou EPfP EPri ERom EShb GAbr GGar MOWG MREP MSCN SEND SGar SPlb WDin WHar
- 'Albus' see *C. citrinus* 'White Anzac'
- 'Angela' MOWG
- 'Canberra' MOWG
- 'Firebrand' CDoC LRHS MOWG
- 'Splendens' ♀H3 Widely available
§ - 'White Anzac' CDoC CMac ELan EPfP MOWG SEND SSta
***comboynensis*** CCCN GBin MOWG
'Coochy Coochy Station' MOWG
'Dawson River Weeper' MOWG
'Eureka' MOWG
***flavescens*** MOWG
***flavovirens*** MOWG
***formosus*** MOWG
***glaucus*** see *C. speciosus*
'Hannah's Child' MOWG
'Happy Valley' MOWG
'Harkness' MOWG
'Havering Gold' new ECou
'Havering Pink' new ECou
'Havering Red' new ECou
'Horse Paddock' MOWG
'Inferno' new LRHS
'Injune' MOWG
'Kings Park Special' MOWG
***laevis*** hort. see *C. rugulosus*
***linearifolius*** LSRN
***linearis*** ♀H3 CBcs CMac CTrC CTri ECou ECrN ELan EPfP LRHS LSRN MAsh MHer MMuc MOWG SCoo SEND SLim SLon SPlb SRms SWal SWvt WSHC
***macropunctatus*** MOWG SPlb SVen

'Masotti'[PBR] new — LRHS
'Mauve Mist' — CCCN CDoC ELan ELon EPfP EPri GBin LRHS MOWG SPoG WGrn
***pachyphyllus*** — ECou MOWG
- var. ***viridis*** — MOWG
***pallidus*** — CCCN CHEx CMHG CMac CTrC CWib EBee ECou ELan EPfP GGar LRHS MAsh MHer MOWG MRav SBrd SBrt SEND SPer SPlb SPoG SSta
- 'Candle Glow' — MOWG
- 'Father Christmas' — MOWG
***paludosus*** — see *C. sieberi* DC.
***pearsonii*** — MOWG
- prostrate — MOWG
- 'Rocky Rambler' — MOWG
'Perth Pink' — CBcs CCCN CDoC ELan EPfP IVic LRHS MOWG SAga SLim
'Phil May' — MOWG
***phoeniceus*** — ECou MOWG
- 'Pink Ice' — MOWG
***pinifolius*** — CTsd MOWG SPlb SVen
- green-flowered — MOWG
- red-flowered — MOWG
- 'Sockeye' — MOWG
'Pink Champagne' — MOWG
§ ***pityoides*** — CPLG ECou IRar MOWG
- from Brown's Swamp, Australia — ECou
***polandii*** — MOWG
- dwarf — MOWG
'Purple Splendour' — MOWG
***recurvus*** — MOWG
'Red Clusters' — CDoC CMac CTsd EBee ELan EPfP IArd LRHS MAsh MOWG NEgg NPri SBfd SChF SPoG SWvt
'Reeve's Pink' — MOWG
***rigidus*** — CBcs CChe CDoC CEnt CHEx CMHG CTri CWib ELan EPfP EPri GGar IArd LRHS LSRN LTen MGos MMuc MOWG MRav NLar SBfd SPer SVen SWvt WDin
'Rose Opal' — CTrC
§ ***rugulosus*** — CBcs CCCN EQua IDee MOWG SWvt
'Running River' — MOWG
***salignus*** ♀H3 — CBcs CCCN CDoC CEnt CHEx CMac CTrC CTri EPfP GLin MHer MOWG MRav NEgg NLar SEND SLim SPer SVen WDin
- Flaming Fire = 'Flaipp' — NLar
***sieberi*** misapplied — see *C. pityoides*
§ ***sieberi*** DC. — CDoC CMHG CTrC ECou ELan EPfP GGar IVic LRHS MMuc MOWG NBir NLar NPal SAga SBrd SEND SLim SPlb WFar
- purple-flowered — MOWG
§ ***speciosus*** — CDul CTrC EBee MOWG NLar SEND SPlb
***subulatus*** — CDoC CHEx CTrC EBee ECou GGal MCCP MOWG NLar SArc SPlb WMoo
- 'Crimson Tail' — EBee GBin MMuc NLar SBfd SEND
I - 'Packer's Selection' — ECou MOWG
'Taree Pink' — MOWG
***teretifolius*** — MOWG
***viminalis*** — CBcs CCCN MOWG SPlb
- 'Captain Cook' — CAlb CMac ECou LBuc LRHS LSRN MAsh MGos MOWG NLar SBfd SRms SVen SWvt
- 'Endeavor' — CCCN
- 'Hannah Ray' — MOWG
- Hot Pink = 'Kkho1'[PBR] new — LRHS
- 'Little John' — CAlb CSBt CWSG LRHS LSRN MAsh MOWG SBfd SEND SPad SWvt
- 'Malawi Giant' — MOWG
- 'Wilderness White' — MOWG
'Violaceus' — IRar SVen
***viridiflorus*** — CTrC ECou GGal GQui LRHS MCCP MOWG SEND SPlb WGwG
- 'County Park Dwarf' — ECou
'White Anzac' — see *C. citrinus* 'White Anzac'
'Wildfire' — CTrC

## *Callitriche* (*Plantaginaceae*)

sp. new — WSFF
§ ***palustris*** — MSKA MWts
***verna*** — see *C. palustris*

## *Callitris* (*Cupressaceae*)

***rhomboidea*** — CTrC IGor

## *Calluna* ✿ (*Ericaceae*)

***vulgaris*** — SWhi
- 'Aberdeen' — SHeS
- 'Adrie' — SHeS SWhi
- 'Alba Argentea' — SHeS
- 'Alba Aurea' — SHeS
- 'Alba Carlton' — SHeS
- 'Alba Dumosa' — SHeS
- 'Alba Elata' — SHeS
- 'Alba Elegans' — SHeS
- 'Alba Elongata' — see *C. vulgaris* 'Mair's Variety'
- 'Alba Erecta' — SHeS
- 'Alba Jae' — SHeS
- 'Alba Minor' — SHeS
- 'Alba Multiflora' — SHeS
- 'Alba Pilosa' — SHeS
§ - 'Alba Plena' (d) — SHeS
- 'Alba Praecox' — SHeS
- 'Alba Pumila' — SHeS
§ - 'Alba Rigida' — MAsh SHeS SRms
- 'Alec Martin' (d) — SHeS
- 'Alex Warwick' — SHeS
- 'Alexandra'[PBR] (Garden Girls Series) ♀H4 — IVic NHol SCoo SHeS SPoG SRms
- 'Alice Knight' — SHeS
- 'Alicia'[PBR] (Garden Girls Series) ♀H4 — CBcs CHab NHol SCoo SHeS SPoG SWhi
- 'Alieke' — SHeS
- 'Alina' — SHeS
- 'Alison Yates' — SHeS
- 'Allegretto' — SHeS
- 'Allegro' ♀H4 — EPfP MMuc SCoo SHeS SRms SWhi
- 'Alportii' — SHeS
- 'Alportii Praecox' — SHeS
- 'Alys Sutcliffe' — SHeS
- 'Amanda Wain' — SHeS
- 'Amethyst'[PBR] (Garden Girls Series) — MMuc NHol SHeS SPoG SWhi
- 'Amilto' — SHeS SRms
- 'Andrew Proudley' — SHeS
- 'Anette'[PBR] (Garden Girls Series) ♀H4 — SCoo SHeS SWhi
- 'Angela Wain' — MAsh SHeS
- 'Anna' — SHeS
- 'Annabel' (d) — SHeS
- 'Anne Dobbin' — SHeS
- 'Annegret' — see *C. vulgaris* 'Marlies'

| |  |  |
|---|---|---|
| | - 'Anneke' | SHeS |
| | - 'Annemarie' (d) ♀H4 | CSBt EPfP IVic MAsh NHol SCoo SHeS SPlb SRms SWhi |
| | - 'Anne's Zwerg' | SHeS SRms |
| | - 'Anthony Davis' ♀H4 | NHol SHeS |
| | - 'Anthony Wain' | SHeS |
| | - 'Anton' | SHeS |
| | - 'Antrujo Gold' | SHeS |
| | - 'Aphrodite'PBR (Garden Girls Series) | CBcs CHab SHeS SWhi |
| | - 'Apollo' | SHeS |
| | - 'Applecross' (d) | SHeS |
| | - 'Arabella'PBR | SHeS SRms |
| | - 'Argentea' | SHeS |
| | - 'Ariadne' | SHeS |
| | - 'Arina' | MAsh SCoo SHeS |
| | - 'Arran Gold' | SHeS |
| | - 'Ashgarth Amber' | SHeS |
| | - 'Ashgarth Amethyst' | SHeS |
| | - 'Ashgarth Shell Pink' | SHeS |
| | - 'Asterix' | SHeS |
| | - 'Atalanta' | SHeS |
| | - 'Atholl Gold' | SHeS |
| | - 'August Beauty' | SHeS |
| | - 'Aurea' | SHeS |
| | - 'Aurora' | SHeS |
| | - 'Autumn Glow' | SHeS |
| | - 'Babette' | SHeS |
| | - 'Baby Ben' | SHeS |
| | - 'Baby Wicklow' | SHeS |
| | - 'Barbara' | SHeS |
| | - 'Barbara Fleur' | SHeS |
| | - 'Barja' | SHeS |
| | - 'Barnett Anley' | SHeS |
| | - 'Battle of Arnhem' | SHeS |
| | - 'Bayport' | SHeS |
| | - 'Beechwood Crimson' | SHeS |
| I | - 'Bella Rosa' | SHeS |
| | - 'Ben Nevis' | SHeS |
| | - 'Bennachie Bronze' | SHeS |
| | - 'Bennachie Prostrate' | SHeS |
| | - 'Beoley Crimson' | MAsh SCoo SHeS |
| | - 'Beoley Crimson Variegated' (v) | SHeS |
| | - 'Beoley Gold' ♀H4 | CSBt CTri EPfP NHol SCoo SHeS SPer SRms SWhi |
| | - 'Beoley Silver' | SCoo SHeS SWhi |
| | - 'Bernadette' | SHeS |
| | - 'Betty Baum' | SHeS |
| | - 'Bispingen' | SHeS |
| | - 'Blazeaway' | CTri EPfP MAsh NHol SCoo SHeS SPer SRms SWhi |
| | - 'Blueness' | SHeS |
| | - 'Bognie' | SHeS |
| | - 'Bonfire Brilliance' | CSBt NHol SHeS |
| | - 'Bonita'PBR (Garden Girls Series) | SHeS SWhi |
| | - 'Bonne's Darkness' | SHeS |
| | - 'Bonsaï' | SHeS |
| | - 'Boreray' | SHeS |
| | - 'Boskoop' | MAsh NHol SHeS SWhi |
| | - 'Bradford' | SHeS |
| | - 'Braemar' | SHeS |
| | - 'Braeriach' | SHeS |
| | - 'Branchy Anne' | SHeS |
| | - 'Bray Head' | SHeS |
| | - 'Brita Elisabeth' (d) | SHeS |
| | - 'Bronze Beauty' | SHeS |
| | - 'Bud Lyle' | SHeS |
| | - 'Bunsall' | SHeS |
| | - 'Buxton Snowdrift' | SHeS |
| | - 'C.W. Nix' | CSBt SHeS |
| | - 'Caerketton White' | SHeS |
| | - 'Caleb Threlkeld' | SHeS |
| | - 'Calf of Man' | SHeS |
| | - 'Californian Midge' | NHol SHeS |
| | - 'Camla Variety' | SHeS |
| | - 'Carl Röders' (d) | SHeS |
| | - 'Carmen' | SHeS |
| | - 'Carngold' | SHeS |
| | - 'Carole Chapman' | SHeS |
| | - 'Carolyn' | SHeS |
| | - 'Cassa' | SHeS |
| | - 'Catherine' | SHeS |
| | - 'Catherine Anne' | SHeS |
| | - 'Celtic Gold' | SHeS |
| | - 'Charles Chapman' | SHeS |
| § | - 'Chernobyl' (d) | MAsh NHol SHeS |
| | - 'Chindit' | SHeS |
| I | - 'Christin' | SHeS |
| | - 'Christina' | SHeS |
| | - 'Cilcennin Common' | SHeS |
| | - 'Clare Carpet' | SHeS |
| | - 'Coby' | SHeS |
| | - 'Coccinea' | SHeS |
| | - 'Colette' | SHeS |
| | - 'Con Brio' | SCoo SHeS SRms SWhi |
| | - 'Copper Glow' | SHeS |
| | - 'Coral Island' | SHeS |
| | - 'Corbett's Red' | SHeS |
| | - 'Corrie's White' | SHeS |
| | - 'Cottswood Gold' | NHol SCoo SHeS SRms |
| | - 'County Wicklow' (d) ♀H4 | CBcs CTri EPfP GGar MAsh MMuc NBlu NHol SCoo SHeS SPer SRms SWhi |
| | - 'Craig Rossie' | SHeS |
| | - 'Crail Orange' | SHeS |
| | - 'Cramond' (d) | SHeS |
| | - 'Cream Steving' | SHeS |
| | - 'Crimson Glory' | MAsh SHeS |
| | - 'Crimson Sunset' | SHeS |
| | - 'Crinkly Tuft' | SHeS |
| | - 'Crowborough Beacon' | SHeS |
| | - 'Cuprea' | EPfP MAsh NHol SCoo SHeS SWhi |
| | - 'Dainty Bess' | SHeS |
| | - 'Dapiali' | SHeS |
| | - 'Dark Alicia' | SHeS |
| | - 'Dark Beauty'PBR (d) ♀H4 | CBcs EPfP IVic MAsh NHol SCoo SHeS SWhi |
| | - 'Dark Star' (d) ♀H4 | CBcs EPfP MAsh MMuc NHol SCoo SHeS SRms SWhi |
| | - 'Darkness' ♀H4 | CTri EPfP MAsh NHol SCoo SHeS SRms SWhi |
| | - 'Darleyensis' | SHeS |
| | - 'Dart's Amethyst' | SHeS |
| | - 'Dart's Beauty' | SHeS |
| | - 'Dart's Brilliant' | SHeS |
| | - 'Dart's Flamboyant' | SHeS |
| | - 'Dart's Gold' | MAsh NHol SHeS |
| | - 'Dart's Hedgehog' | SHeS |
| | - 'Dart's Parakeet' | SHeS |
| | - 'Dart's Parrot' | SHeS |
| | - 'Dart's Silver Rocket' | SHeS |
| | - 'Dart's Squirrel' | SHeS |
| | - 'David Eason' | SHeS |
| | - 'David Hagenaars' | SHeS SWhi |
| | - 'David Hutton' | SHeS |
| | - 'David Platt' (d) | SHeS |
| | - 'Denkewitz' | SHeS |
| | - 'Denny Pratt' | SHeS |

- 'Desiree' SHeS
- 'Devon' (d) SHeS
- 'Diana' SHeS
- 'Dickson's Blazes' SHeS
- 'Dirry' NHol SHeS
- 'Doctor Murray's White' see *C. vulgaris* 'Mullardoch'
- 'Doris Rushworth' SHeS
- 'Drum-ra' SHeS SRms
- 'Dunnet Lime' SHeS SPlb
- 'Dunnydeer' SHeS
- 'Dunwood' SHeS
§ - 'Durford Wood' SHeS
- 'Dwingeloo Delight' SHeS
- 'E.F. Brown' SHeS
- 'E. Hoare' SHeS
- 'Easter-bonfire' NHol SCoo SHeS SWhi
- 'Eckart Miessner' SHeS
- 'Edith Godbolt' SHeS
- 'Elaine' SHeS
- 'Elegant Pearl' SHeS
- 'Elegantissima' MAsh MMuc SHeS
- 'Eleonore' (d) SHeS
- 'Elkstone White' SHeS
- 'Ellen' SHeS
- 'Ellie Barbour' SHeS
- 'Elly' SHeS
- 'Else Frye' (d) SHeS
- 'Elsie Purnell' (d) ♀H4 EPfP MAsh NHol SCoo SHeS SPlb SRms
- 'Emerald Jock' SHeS
- 'Emma Louise Tuke' SHeS
- 'Eric Easton' SHeS
- 'Eskdale Gold' SHeS
- 'Eurosa' SHeS
- 'Fairy' SHeS
- 'Falling Star' SHeS
- 'Feuerwerk' SCoo SHeS
§ - 'Finale' SHeS
- 'Findling' SHeS
- 'Fire King' SHeS
- 'Fire Star' SHeS
- 'Firebreak' NHol SHeS
- 'Firefly' ♀H4 CBcs CSBt EPfP MAsh MMuc NHol SCoo SHeS SRms SWhi
- 'Flamingo' MAsh MMuc NHol SCoo SHeS SPer SRms SWhi
- 'Flatling' SHeS
- 'Flore Pleno' (d) SHeS
- 'Floriferous' SHeS
- 'Florrie Spicer' SHeS
- 'Fokko' (d) SHeS
- 'Fort Bragg' SHeS
- 'Fortyniner Gold' SHeS
- 'Foxhollow Wanderer' SHeS
- 'Foxii' SHeS
- 'Foxii Floribunda' SHeS
- 'Foxii Lett's Form' see *C. vulgaris* 'Velvet Dome', 'Mousehole'
- 'Foxii Nana' NHol SHeS SRms SWhi
- 'Foya' SHeS
- 'Fraser's Old Gold' SHeS
- 'Fred J. Chapple' MAsh NBlu SHeS SWhi
- 'Fréjus' SHeS
- 'French Grey' SHeS
- 'Fritz Kircher'[PBR] SHeS
- 'Gaia' SHeS
- Garden Girls Series MMuc
- 'Gerda' SHeS
- 'Ginkel's Glorie' SHeS
- 'Glasa' SHeS
- 'Glen Mashie' SHeS
- 'Glencoe' (d) SHeS
- 'Glendoick Silver' SHeS
- 'Glenfiddich' CSBt MAsh NHol SHeS
- 'Glenlivet' SHeS
- 'Glenmorangie' SHeS
- 'Gloucester Boy' SHeS
- 'Gnome' SHeS
- 'Gold Charm' SHeS
- 'Gold Finch' SHeS
- 'Gold Flame' SHeS
- Gold Hamilton see *C. vulgaris* 'Chernobyl'
- 'Gold Haze' ♀H4 CTri MAsh NHol SCoo SHeS SRms SWhi
- 'Gold Knight' EPfP MAsh SCoo SHeS
- 'Gold Kup' SHeS
- 'Gold Mist' NBlu SHeS
- 'Gold Spronk' SHeS
- 'Goldcarmen' SHeS
- 'Golden Blazeaway' SHeS
- 'Golden Carpet' CSBt MAsh NHol SHeS SRms
- 'Golden Dew' SHeS
- 'Golden Dream' (d) SHeS
- 'Golden Feather' SHeS
- 'Golden Fleece' SHeS SRms
- 'Golden Max' SHeS
- 'Golden Rivulet' SHeS
- 'Golden Turret' MAsh NHol SHeS
- 'Golden Wonder' (d) SHeS
- 'Goldsworth Crimson' SHeS
- 'Goldsworth Crimson Variegated' (v) SHeS
- 'Goscote Wine' SHeS
- 'Grasmeriensis' SHeS
- 'Green Cardinal' SHeS
- 'Grey Carpet' SHeS SRms
- 'Grijsje' SHeS
- 'Grizabella' SHeS
- 'Grizzly' SHeS
- 'Grönsinka' SHeS
- 'Guinea Gold' MAsh SHeS
§ - 'H.E. Beale' (d) CTri EPfP NHol SCoo SHeS
- 'Hamlet Green' SHeS
- 'Hammondii' SHeS
- 'Hammondii Aureifolia' MAsh SHeS SPlb SWhi
- 'Hammondii Rubrifolia' SHeS SRms SWhi
- 'Harlekin' SHeS
- 'Harry Gibbon' (d) SHeS
- 'Harten's Findling' SHeS
- 'Hatje's Herbstfeuer' (d) SHeS
- 'Hayesensis' SHeS
- 'Heidberg' SHeS
- 'Heidepracht' SHeS
- 'Heidesinfonie' SHeS
- 'Heideteppich' SHeS
- 'Heidezwerg' SHeS
- 'Heike' (d) SHeS
- 'Herbert Mitchell' SHeS
- 'Hester' SHeS
- 'Hetty' SHeS
- 'Hibernica' SHeS
- 'Hiemalis' SHeS
- 'Hiemalis Southcote' see *C. vulgaris* 'Durford Wood'
- Highland Cream see *C. vulgaris* 'Punch's Dessert'
- 'Highland Rose' SHeS SPlb SRms
- 'Highland Spring' SHeS
- 'Hilda Turberfield' SHeS
- 'Hillbrook Limelight' SHeS
- 'Hillbrook Orange' SHeS
- 'Hillbrook Sparkler' SHeS

- 'Hinton White' SHeS
- 'Hirsuta Albiflora' SHeS
- 'Hirsuta Typica' SHeS
- 'Hollandia' SHeS
- 'Holstein' SHeS
- 'Hookstone' SHeS
- 'Hoyerhagen' SHeS
§ - 'Hugh Nicholson' SHeS
- 'Humpty Dumpty' NHol SHeS
- 'Hypnoides' SHeS
- 'Ide's Double' (d) SHeS
- 'Inchcolm' SHeS
- 'Inchkeith' SHeS
- 'Ineke' SHeS
- 'Inge' SHeS
- 'Ingrid Bouter' (d) SHeS
- 'Inshriach Bronze' SHeS
- 'Iris van Leyen' SHeS
- 'Islay Mist' SHeS
- 'Isle of Hirta' SHeS
- 'Isobel Frye' SHeS
- 'Isobel Hughes' (d) SHeS
- 'J.H. Hamilton' (d) ♀H4 CTri MAsh NHol SCoo SHeS SRms SWhi
- 'Jan' SHeS
- 'Jan Dekker' MAsh NHol SHeS SPer SWhi
- 'Janice Chapman' SHeS
- 'Japanese White' SHeS
- 'Jenny' SHeS
- 'Jill' SHeS
- 'Jimmy Dyce' (d) SHeS
- 'Joan Sparkes' (d) SHeS
- 'Jochen' SHeS
- 'Johan Slegers' SHeS
- John Denver see *C. vulgaris* 'Marleen Select'
- 'John F. Letts' NHol SHeS SRms
- 'Johnson's Variety' SCoo SHeS
- 'Jos' Lemon' SHeS
- 'Jos' Whitie' SHeS
- 'Josefine' SHeS SWhi
- 'Joseph's Coat' SHeS
- 'Joy Vanstone' ♀H4 EPfP MAsh NHol SHeS SRms
- 'Julia' SHeS
- 'Julie Ann Platt' SHeS
- 'Juno' SHeS
- 'Kaiser' SHeS
- 'Karin Blum' SHeS
- 'Kermit' SHeS
- 'Kerstin' ♀H4 MMuc NBlu NHol SCoo SHeS SPlb SRms SWhi
- 'Kerstin Jacke' NHol
- 'Kinlochruel' (d) ♀H4 CBcs CSBt CTri EPfP GGar MAsh MMuc NBlu NHol SHeS SPer SPlb SRms SWhi
- 'Kir Royal' SHeS
- 'Kirby White' MAsh NBlu NHol SHeS SPlb SWhi
- 'Kirsty Anderson' SHeS
- 'Kit Hill' SHeS
- 'Knaphill' SHeS
I - 'Kontrast' SHeS
- 'Kuphaldtii' SHeS
- 'Kuppendorf' SHeS
- 'Kynance' SHeS
- 'Lady Maithe' SHeS
- 'Lambstails' SHeS
- 'L'Ancresse' SHeS
- 'Larissa'PBR (Garden Girls Series) SHeS
- 'Lemon Gem' SHeS
- 'Lemon Queen' SHeS
- 'Leprechaun' NHol SWhi
- 'Leslie Slinger' NHol SCoo SHeS SWhi
- 'Lewis Lilac' SHeS
- 'Liebestraum' SHeS
- 'Lilac Elegance' SHeS
- 'Lime Glade' SHeS
- 'Lime Gold' SHeS
- 'Little John' LSRN SHeS
- 'Llanbedrog Pride' (d) SHeS
- 'Loch Turret' SHeS SPer
- 'Loch-na-Seil' SHeS
- 'Long White' SHeS SWhi
- 'Loni' SHeS
- 'Lüneberg Heath' SHeS
- 'Lyle's Late White' SHeS
- 'Lyle's Surprise' SHeS
- 'Lyndon Proudley' SHeS
- 'Macdonald of Glencoe' SHeS
§ - 'Mair's Variety' ♀H4 SCoo SHeS
- 'Mallard' SHeS
- 'Manitoba' SHeS
- 'Manuel' SHeS
- 'Marianne' SHeS
- 'Marie' SHeS
- 'Marion Blum' SHeS
- 'Marleen' MAsh NHol SHeS SWhi
§ - 'Marleen Select' SHeS
§ - 'Marlies' SHeS SWhi
- 'Martha Hermann' SHeS
- 'Martine Langenberg' SHeS
- 'Masquerade' SHeS
- 'Matita' SHeS
- 'Mauvelyn' SHeS
- 'Mazurka' SHeS
- 'Melanie' (Garden Girls Series) MAsh NHol SCoo SHeS
- 'Mick Jamieson' (d) SHeS
- 'Mies' SHeS
- 'Minima' SHeS
- 'Minima Smith's Variety' SHeS
- 'Miniöxabäck' SHeS
- 'Minty' SHeS
- 'Mirato' IVic SHeS
- 'Mirelle' SHeS
- 'Miss Muffet' NHol SHeS
- 'Molecule' SHeS
- 'Monika' (d) SHeS
- 'Moon Glow' SHeS
- 'Mountain Snow' SHeS
§ - 'Mousehole' NHol SHeS
- 'Mrs Alf' SHeS
- 'Mrs E. Wilson' (d) SHeS
- 'Mrs Pat' MAsh NHol SHeS
- 'Mrs Pinxteren' SHeS
- 'Mrs Ronald Gray' SHeS
- 'Mullach Mor' SHeS
§ - 'Mullardoch' SHeS
- 'Mullion' ♀H4 SHeS
- 'Multicolor' MAsh NHol SHeS SRms
- 'Murielle Dobson' SHeS
§ - 'My Dream' (d) ♀H4 CSBt EPfP NHol SCoo SHeS
- 'Nana' SHeS
- 'Nana Compacta' SHeS
- 'Natasja' SHeS
- 'Naturpark' SHeS
- 'Nele' (d) SHeS
- 'Nico' SHeS
- 'Nofretete' SHeS
- Nordlicht see *C. vulgaris* 'Skone'
- 'October White' SHeS

| | | | | |
|---|---|---|---|---|
| | - 'Odette' | SHeS | | - 'Redbud' | SHeS |
| | - 'Oiseval' | SHeS | | - 'Redgauntlet' | SHeS |
| | - 'Old Rose' | SHeS | | - 'Reini' | SHeS SWhi |
| | - 'Olive Turner' | SHeS | | - 'Rica' | SHeS |
| | - 'Olympic Gold' | SHeS | | - 'Richard Cooper' | SHeS |
| | - 'Orange and Gold' | SHeS | | - 'Rieanne' | SHeS |
| | - 'Orange Carpet' | SHeS | | - 'Rigida Prostrata' | see *C. vulgaris* 'Alba Rigida' |
| | - 'Orange Max' | NHol SHeS | | - 'Rivington' | SHeS |
| | - 'Orange Queen' | CSBt SHeS | | - 'Robber Knight' | SHeS |
| | - 'Öxabäck' | SHeS | | - 'Robert Chapman' ♀H4 | CSBt CTri MAsh NHol SHeS SRms SWhi |
| | - 'Oxshott Common' | SHeS | I | - 'Rock Spray' | SHeS |
| | - 'Pallida' | SHeS | | - 'Röding' | SHeS |
| | - 'Parsons' Gold' | SHeS | | - 'Rokoko' | SHeS |
| | - 'Parsons' Grey Selected' | SHeS | | - 'Roland Haagen' ♀H4 | SHeS |
| | - 'Pastell' (d) | SHeS | | - 'Roma' | SHeS |
| | - 'Pat's Gold' | SHeS | | - 'Romina' | NHol SHeS |
| | - 'Peace' | SHeS | | - 'Ronas Hill' | SHeS |
| | - 'Pearl Drop' | SHeS | | - 'Roodkapje' | SHeS |
| | - 'Peggy' | SHeS | | - 'Rosalind' ambig. | EPfP |
| | - 'Penhale' | SHeS | | - 'Rosalind, Crastock Heath' | SHeS |
| | - 'Penny Bun' | SHeS | | - 'Rosalind, Underwood's' | EPfP NHol SHeS |
| | - 'Pennyacre Gold' | SHeS | | - 'Rosita'PBR | IVic |
| | - 'Pennyacre Lemon' | SHeS | | - 'Ross Hutton' | SHeS |
| | - 'Pepper and Salt' | see *C. vulgaris* 'Hugh Nicholson' | | - 'Roswitha' | SHeS |
| | - 'Perestrojka' | SHeS | | - 'Roter Oktober' | SHeS SWhi |
| | - 'Peter Sparkes' (d) ♀H4 | CBcs CHab CSBt EPfP MAsh MMuc NHol SCoo SHeS SRms SWhi | | - 'Rotfuchs' | SHeS |
| | - 'Petra' | SHeS | | - 'Ruby Slinger' | NHol SHeS SWhi |
| | - 'Pewter Plate' | SHeS | | - 'Rusty Triumph' | SHeS |
| | - 'Pink Alicia'PBR (Garden Girls Series) | SHeS | | - 'Ruth Sparkes' (d) | NHol SHeS |
| | - 'Pink Beale' | see *C. vulgaris* 'H.E. Beale' | | - 'Sabrina' (d) | SHeS |
| | - 'Pink Dream' (d) | SHeS | | - 'Saima' | SHeS |
| | - 'Pink Gown' | SHeS | | - 'Saint Nick' | SHeS |
| | - 'Pink Spreader' | SHeS | | - 'Salland' | SHeS |
| | - 'Pink Tips' | SHeS | | - 'Sally Anne Proudley' | SHeS |
| | - 'Plantarium' | SHeS | | - 'Salmon Leap' | NHol SHeS |
| | - 'Platt's Surprise' (d) | SHeS | | - 'Sam Hewitt' | SHeS |
| | - 'Polly' | SHeS | | - 'Sampford Sunset' | SHeS |
| | - 'Poolster' | SHeS | | - 'Sandhammaren' | SHeS |
| | - 'Porth Wen White' | SHeS | | - 'Sandwood Bay' | SHeS |
| | - 'Prizewinner' | SHeS | | - 'Sandy'PBR (Garden Girls Series) | NHol SHeS SPoG SWhi |
| * | - 'Procumbens' | SHeS | | - 'Sarah Platt' (d) | SHeS |
| | - 'Prostrata Flagelliformis' | SHeS | | - 'Saskia' | SHeS |
| | - 'Prostrate Orange' | MAsh SHeS | | - 'Schneewolke' | SHeS |
| § | - 'Punch's Dessert' | SHeS | | - 'Scholje's Jimmy' | SHeS |
| | - 'Purple Passion' | EPfP SCoo | | - 'Scholje's Rubin' (d) | SHeS |
| | - 'Pygmaea' | SHeS | | - 'Scholje's Super Star' (d) | SHeS |
| | - 'Pyramidalis' | SHeS | | - 'Schurig's Sensation' (d) | IVic SHeS |
| | - 'Pyrenaica' | SHeS | | - 'Schurig's Wonder' (d) | SHeS |
| | - 'R.A. McEwan' | SHeS | | - 'Scotch Mist' | SHeS |
| | - 'Radnor' (d) ♀H4 | CSBt MAsh SHeS | | - 'Sedloňov' | SHeS |
| | - 'Radnor Gold' (d) | SHeS | | - 'Sellingsloh' | SHeS |
| | - 'Raket' | SHeS | | - 'September Pink' | SHeS |
| | - 'Ralph Purnell' | SCoo SHeS | | - 'Serlei' | SHeS |
| | - 'Ralph Purnell Select' | SHeS | | - 'Serlei Aurea' ♀H4 | CSBt EPfP MAsh NHol SHeS SRms |
| | - 'Ralph's Pearl' | SHeS | | - 'Serlei Grandiflora' | SHeS |
| | - 'Ralph's Red' | SHeS | | - 'Serlei Purpurea' | SHeS |
| | - 'Randall's Crimson' | SHeS | | - 'Serlei Rubra' | SHeS |
| | - 'Rannoch' | SHeS | | - 'Sesam' | SHeS |
| | - 'Rebecca's Red' | SHeS SRms | | - 'Sesse' | SHeS |
| | - 'Red Carpet' | SHeS | | - 'Shirley' | MAsh SHeS |
| | - 'Red Favorit' (d) | CBcs SHeS SRms | | - 'Silberspargel' | SHeS |
| | - 'Red Fred' | NHol SCoo SHeS | | - 'Silver Cloud' | SHeS |
| | - 'Red Haze' | EPfP NHol SCoo SHeS | | - 'Silver Fox' | SHeS |
| | - 'Red Max' | SHeS | | - 'Silver King' | SHeS |
| | - 'Red Pimpernel' | EPfP IVic NHol SCoo SHeS SWhi | | - 'Silver Knight' | CSBt EPfP MAsh NHol SCoo SHeS SPer SPlb SRms SWhi |
| | - 'Red Rug' | SHeS | | - 'Silver Pearl' | SHeS |
| | - 'Red Star' (d) | MAsh NHol SHeS | | - 'Silver Queen' ♀H4 | MAsh NHol SHeS SRms SWhi |
| | - 'Red Wings' | SHeS | | | |

| | | |
|---|---|---|
| | – 'Silver Rose' ♀H4 | SHeS |
| | – 'Silver Sandra' | SHeS |
| | – 'Silver Spire' | SHeS |
| | – 'Silver Stream' | SHeS |
| | – 'Silvie' | SHeS |
| | – 'Simone' | SHeS |
| | – 'Sir Anthony Hopkins' | SHeS |
| | – 'Sir John Charrington' ♀H4 | CSBt EPfP MAsh NHol SHeS SWhi |
| | – 'Sirsson' | SHeS |
| | – 'Sister Anne' ♀H4 | CSBt EPfP MAsh MMuc NBlu NHol SCoo SHeS SRms SWhi |
| | – 'Skipper' | NHol SHeS |
| § | – 'Skone' (v) | SHeS |
| | – 'Snowball' | see *C. vulgaris* 'My Dream' |
| | – 'Snowflake' | SHeS |
| | – 'Soay' | SHeS |
| | – 'Sonja' (d) | IVic SHeS |
| | – 'Sonning' (d) | SHeS |
| | – 'Sonny Boy' | SHeS |
| | – 'Sophia' (d) | SHeS |
| | – 'Sparkling Stars' | NHol SHeS |
| | – 'Sphinx' | SHeS |
| | – 'Spicata' | SHeS |
| | – 'Spicata Aurea' | SHeS |
| | – 'Spicata Nana' | SHeS |
| | – 'Spider' | SHeS |
| | – 'Spitfire' | MAsh NHol SHeS |
| | – 'Spook' | SHeS |
| | – 'Spring Cream' ♀H4 | MAsh MMuc NHol SCoo SHeS SPer SPoG SWhi |
| | – 'Spring Glow' | SHeS |
| | – 'Spring Torch' | CSBt MAsh NBlu NHol SCoo SHeS SPoG SRms SWhi |
| | – 'Springbank' | SHeS |
| | – 'Stag's Horn' | SHeS |
| I | – 'Startler' | SHeS |
| | – 'Stefanie' | IVic NHol SHeS SRms SWhi |
| | – 'Stranger' | SHeS |
| | – 'Strawberry Delight' (d) | EPfP SCoo SHeS |
| | – 'Summer Elegance' | SHeS |
| | – 'Summer Gold' | SRms |
| | – 'Summer Orange' | NHol SHeS |
| | – 'Summer White' (d) | SHeS |
| | – 'Sunningdale' | see *C. vulgaris* 'Finale' |
| | – 'Sunrise' | EPfP SHeS |
| | – 'Sunset' ♀H4 | MAsh SHeS SRms SWhi |
| | – 'Sunset Glow' | SHeS |
| | – 'Talisker' | SHeS |
| | – 'Tenella' | SHeS |
| | – 'Tenuis' | SHeS |
| | – 'Terrick's Orange' | SHeS |
| | – 'The Pygmy' | SHeS |
| | – 'Theresa' (Garden Girls Series) | SHeS |
| | – 'Tib' (d) ♀H4 | CSBt MAsh NBlu NHol SHeS SPer SRms SWhi |
| | – 'Tijdens Copper' | SHeS |
| | – 'Tino' | SHeS |
| | – 'Tom Thumb' | SHeS |
| | – 'Tomentosa Alba' | SHeS |
| | – 'Torogay' | SHeS |
| | – 'Torulosa' | SHeS |
| | – 'Tremans' | SHeS |
| | – 'Tricolorifolia' | EPfP MAsh NHol SCoo SHeS SPer SWhi |
| | – 'Underwoodii' | SHeS |
| | – 'Unity' | SHeS |
| | – 'Valorian' | SHeS |
| | – 'Van Beek' | SHeS |
| § | – 'Velvet Dome' | SHeS |
| | – 'Velvet Fascination' ♀H4 | EPfP NHol SCoo SHeS SWhi |
| | – 'Violet Bamford' | SHeS |
| | – 'Visser's Fancy' | SHeS |
| | – 'Walter Ingwersen' | SHeS |
| | – 'Waquoit Brightness' | SHeS |
| | – 'Westerlee Gold' | SHeS |
| | – 'Westerlee Green' | SHeS |
| | – 'Westphalia' | SHeS |
| | – 'White Bouquet' | see *C. vulgaris* 'Alba Plena' |
| | – 'White Carpet' | SHeS |
| | – 'White Coral' (d) | EPfP IVic SCoo SHeS |
| | – 'White Gold' | SHeS |
| | – 'White Gown' | SHeS |
| | – 'White Lawn' ♀H4 | MAsh MMuc NHol SHeS SRms SWhi |
| | – 'White Mite' | SHeS |
| | – 'White Pearl' (d) | SHeS |
| | – 'White Princess' | see *C. vulgaris* 'White Queen' |
| § | – 'White Queen' | SHeS |
| | – 'White Star' (d) | SHeS |
| | – 'Whiteness' | SHeS |
| | – 'Wickwar Flame' ♀H4 | CBcs CHab CSBt EPfP MMuc NBlu NHol SCoo SHeS SPer SPlb SRms SWhi |
| | – 'Wilma' | SHeS |
| | – 'Wingates Gem' | SHeS |
| | – 'Wingates Gold' | SHeS |
| | – 'Winter Chocolate' | CSBt EPfP MAsh NHol SCoo SHeS SWhi |
| | – 'Winter Fire' | SHeS |
| | – 'Winter Red' | SHeS |
| | – 'Wollmer's Weisse' (d) | SHeS |
| | – 'Wood Close' | SHeS |
| | – 'Yellow Basket' | SHeS |
| | – 'Yellow Beauty'PBR | SHeS |
| | – 'Yellow Globe' | SHeS |
| | – 'Yellow One' | SHeS |
| | – 'Yvette's Gold' | SHeS |
| | – 'Yvette's Silver' | SHeS |
| | – 'Yvonne Clare' | SHeS |

## *Calocedrus* (*Cupressaceae*)

| | | |
|---|---|---|
| § | ***decurrens*** ♀H4 | CBcs CDoC CDul CLnd CMac CMen CTho CTri EHul EPfP LRHS MBlu MGos MMuc NPCo NWea SBfd SLim SPer SPoG WEve WFar |
| | – 'Aureovariegata' (v) | CBcs CWib EHul EPla LRHS MBlu MBri NLar SCoo SLim SPoG WEve WFar |
| | – 'Berrima Gold' | CDoC CKen LRHS MGos NLar SLim SPoG WEve |
| | – 'Columnaris' | LMaj |
| § | – 'Depressa' | CKen |
| | – 'Intricata' | CKen NLar SLim |
| | – 'Maupin Glow' (v) | NLar SLim |
| | – 'Nana' | see *C. decurrens* 'Depressa' |
| | – 'Pillar' | CKen MBri NLar |
| | ***formosana*** | WFar |
| | ***macrolepis*** | NMun |

## *Calocephalus* (*Asteraceae*)

| | |
|---|---|
| ***brownii*** | see *Leucophyta brownii* |
| 'Silver Sand' | LAst LSou |

## *Calochortus* (*Liliaceae*)

| | |
|---|---|
| 'Cupido'PBR | ECho GKev LAma |
| ***invenustus*** | ECho |
| ***luteus*** Douglas ex Lindl. | EPot |
| – 'Golden Orb'PBR | CGrW ECho GKev LAma SDeJ |

| | | |
|---|---|---|
| | ***splendens*** | LAma |
| | – 'Violet Queen' | CGrW ECho GKev LAma |
| | ***superbus*** | ECho EPot GKev SDeJ |
| | 'Symphony'PBR | ECho EPot GKev LAma |
| | ***venustus*** | CGrW ECho EPot GKev LAma SDeJ |

## *Calomeria* (*Asteraceae*)

| | | |
|---|---|---|
| § | ***amaranthoides*** | WJek |

## *Calonyction* see *Ipomoea*

## *Calopogon* (*Orchidaceae*)

| | | |
|---|---|---|
| | ***tuberosus*** | NLAp |

## *Calopsis* (*Restionaceae*)

| | | |
|---|---|---|
| | ***paniculata*** | CCCN CCtw CDTJ CHEx CHVG CTsd |

## *Caloscordum* (*Alliaceae*)

| | | |
|---|---|---|
| § | ***neriniflorum*** | WAbe |

## *Calothamnus* (*Myrtaceae*)

| | | |
|---|---|---|
| | ***blepharospermus*** | MOWG |
| | ***gilesii*** | MOWG |
| | ***homolophyllus*** | MOWG |
| | ***quadrifidus*** | ECou MOWG |
| | – yellow-flowered | MOWG |
| | ***rupestris*** | MOWG |
| | ***sanguineus*** | MOWG |
| | ***validus*** | MOWG SPlb |

## *Calpurnia* (*Papilionaceae*)

| | | |
|---|---|---|
| | ***aurea*** | SPlb |

## *Caltha* ✿ (*Ranunculaceae*)

| | | |
|---|---|---|
| | ***appendiculata*** | WAbe |
| | ***introloba*** | SWat |
| | ***laeta*** | see *C. palustris* var. *palustris* |
| | ***leptosepala*** | CLAP CRow EBee EWTr LLHF LRHS NLar |
| | ***palustris*** ♀H4 | Widely available |
| | – var. ***alba*** | Widely available |
| | – 'Auenwald' | CLAP CRow |
| | – var. ***barthei*** | CFir GEdr |
| | – – f. ***atrorubra*** | GEdr |
| | – 'Flore Pleno' (d) ♀H4 | Widely available |
| | – 'Honeydew' | CLAP CRow |
| | – 'Marilyn' | CLAP |
| | – 'Multiplex' (d) | EBee GKev SRot |
| | – Newlake hybrid | LLWG |
| § | – var. ***palustris*** | CBen CBre CRow ECha EHon ELan GGar LPBA SWat WFar |
| | – – 'Plena' (d) | CRow CWat EPfP GGar LRHS MCot MSKA NBPC WFar |
| | – var. ***radicans*** | CRow GEdr |
| | – – 'Flore Pleno' (d) | CRow |
| | – 'Stagnalis' | CRow MSKA MWts |
| | – 'Tyermannii' | CRow |
| N | ***polypetala*** misapplied | see *C. palustris* var. *palustris* |
| N | ***polypetala*** Hochst. ex Lorent | CFir CWat EWll GCal MSCN MSKA NPer SWat WBor WMAq |
| | ***sagittata*** | WSHC |

## *Calycanthus* (*Calycanthaceae*)

| | | |
|---|---|---|
| | ***fertilis*** | see *C. floridus* var. *glaucus* |
| | ***floridus*** | CAgr CArn CBcs CDul CMCN CPMA CTri CWib EBee ELan EPfP EWTr IDee LAst LEdu LRHS MBNS MBlu MBri MMuc NLar SEND SPer SPlb SPoG SSpi WCFE WDin WSHC |
| | – 'Athens' | CBcs CPMA NLar |
| § | – var. ***glaucus*** | EPfP LRHS MAsh MGos NLar WSHC |
| | – – 'Purpureus' | CBcs CPMA MBlu MBri NLar |
| | – var. ***laevigatus*** | see *C. floridus* var. *glaucus* |
| | – 'Michael Lindsay' | CPMA MBri NLar |
| | ***occidentalis*** | CAgr CArn CBcs CDul CMCN CSpe CWib EPPr MBlu MMuc SEND SGar SSpi WCFE |

## *Calystegia* (*Convolvulaceae*)

| | | |
|---|---|---|
| | 'Angel's Trumpets' | SKHP |
| § | ***hederacea*** 'Flore Pleno' (d) | SMad WCot |
| | ***japonica*** 'Flore Pleno' | see *C. hederacea* 'Flore Pleno' |
| | ***soldanella*** NNS 99-85 | WCot |

## *Calytrix* (*Myrtaceae*)

| | | |
|---|---|---|
| | ***tetragona*** | SPlb |
| | – compact, pink-flowered | MOWG |

## *Camassia* ✿ (*Asparagaceae*)

| | | |
|---|---|---|
| | ***biflora*** F&W 8669 | EBee |
| | ***cusickii*** | Widely available |
| | – white-flowered | IFoB |
| | – 'Zwanenburg' | CTca EBee ERCP GKev WCot |
| | ***esculenta*** Lindl. | see *C. quamash* |
| | ***leichtlinii*** misapplied | see *C. leichtlinii* subsp. *suksdorfii* |
| N | – 'Alba' hort. | see *C. leichtlinii* subsp. *leichtlinii* |
| * | – 'Alba Plena' | MNrw MWat NBPC NBir |
| | – 'Blue Wave' | NHol NWad SBch |
| § | – subsp. ***leichtlinii*** ♀H4 | Widely available |
| | – 'Magdalen' | CAvo |
| N | – 'Plena' (d) | ECha |
| | – 'Sacajawea' | CMea CTca ERCP GGar LRHS SBch |
| | – 'Semiplena' (d) | CAvo CBro CFFs CMea CMil CRDP CTca EBee ERCP GGar LRHS MLLN MNrw NSti SDix SPhx WAul WCot WHoo |
| | – 'Sky Blue' | CMea GAbr LRHS |
| § | – subsp. ***suksdorfii*** | CSam GCra WCot |
| | – – 'Alba' **new** | LRHS |
| | – – Caerulea Group | Widely available |
| | – – 'Electra' | CAvo ECha SUsu |
| § | ***quamash*** | CArn CAvo CBro CFFs CTca CWCL EBee ECha EGHP EPfP EPot ERCP GKev LAma LEdu LRHS MBri MCot NBir NCGa NMen SDeJ SGar SRms WFar WShi XLum |
| | – 'Blue Melody' (v) | CAvo CBro CSam CTca EBee EPot ERCP GKev GMaP GMac LEdu MCCP NMRc NMen SDeJ WRHF |
| | – 'Orion' | CBro EBee NSti WAul WCot |

## *Camellia* ✿ (*Theaceae*)

| | | |
|---|---|---|
| | 'Adorable' (*pitardii* hybrid) | LRHS LSRN SCam |
| | 'Alpen Glo' | MPkF SCam |
| | 'Annette Carol' | CDoC |
| | 'April Blush' **new** | SCog |
| | 'Ariel's Song' | CDoC |
| | 'Auburn White' | see *C. japonica* 'Mrs Bertha A. Harms' |
| | 'Baby Bear' | CDoC MPkF SCam |
| | 'Barbara Clark' | CDoC LRHS LSRN MGos SCog |
| | (*saluenensis* × *reticulata*) | SCoo |
| | 'Bertha Harms Blush' | see *C. japonica* 'Mrs Bertha A. Harms' |
| | 'Bett's Supreme' | CDoC |
| | 'Black Lace' ♀H4 | CAlb CBcs CDul CTrh CTri EPfP LBuc LRHS LSRN MBri MMuc NLar NPri SCam SCog SCoo SEND WGob |

| |  |  |
|---|---|---|
| | 'Bonnie Marie' | CBcs CDoC MGos SCog |
| | 'Canterbury' | CDoC |
| | 'Champêtres Spring Awakening' **new** | MPkF |
| * | 'Chatsworth Belle' | CTrh SCam |
| | 'China Lady' (*granthamiana* × *reticulata*) | MBri SCam |
| | 'Christmas Daffodil' (*japonica* hybrid) | LRHS |
| | 'Cinnamon Cindy' | CDoC LRHS SCam SCog |
| | 'Cinnamon Sensation' | SCog |
| | Classique = 'Kerguelen'PBR | LRHS MPkF |
| | 'Confucius' (*reticulata* hybrid) **new** | SCam |
| | 'Congratulations' | CSBt LSRN |
| | 'Contessa Lavinia Maggi' | see *C. japonica* 'Lavinia Maggi' |
| | 'Cornish Cream' (*cuspidata* × *saluenensis*) **new** | MAsh |
| | 'Cornish Snow' (*cuspidata* × *saluenensis*) ♀H4 | CAlb CBcs CDoC CSBt CSam CTri EPfP GGal MGos SCam SCog SPer SSpi WFar |
| | 'Cornish Spring' (*cuspidata* × *japonica*) ♀H4 | CAlb CCCN CDoC CSBt CTrh CTsd EPfP LRHS MGos SCam SCog SPoG |
| | 'Crimson Candles' | LRHS MPkF SCam |
| | 'Czar' | see *C. japonica* 'The Czar' |
| | 'Dainty Dale' | CDoC LRHS SCam |
| | 'Delia Williams' | see *C.* × *williamsii* 'Citation' |
| | 'Den Burton' **new** | SCam |
| | 'Diamond Head' (*japonica* × *reticulata*) | CBcs |
| | 'Diana's Charm' | CDoC LSRN |
| | 'Doctor Clifford Parks' (*japonica* × *reticulata*) ♀H2 | CDoC LRHS SCam SCog |
| | 'Donckelaeri' | see *C. japonica* 'Masayoshi' |
| | ***edithae*** | LRHS |
| | 'El Dorado' (*pitardii* × *japonica*) | CDoC |
| | 'Elizabeth Bolitho' | SCam |
| | 'Extravaganza' (*japonica* hybrid) | CBcs CTrh IArd MBri SCam SCog |
| | 'Fairy Blush' | CDoC LRHS MPkF SCam |
| | 'Fairy Wand' | CDoC LRHS MPkF |
| | 'Faustina Lechi' | see *C. japonica* 'Faustina' |
| | 'Felice Harris' (*reticulata* × *sasanqua*) | CDoC MBri SCam SCog |
| | 'Fiesta Grande' | LRHS SCam |
| | 'Fire 'n' Ice' | CDoC SCam |
| | ***forrestii*** | NLar |
| | 'Forty-niner' (*reticulata* × *japonica*) | CBcs |
| | 'Fox's Fancy' | CDoC |
| | 'Fragrant Pink' (*japonica* subsp. *rusticana* × *lutchuensis*) | CTrh SCam |
| | 'Francie L' (*reticulata* × *saluenensis*) ♀H3-4 | CDoC EPfP LRHS SCam SCog SSta |
| | 'Freedom Bell' ♀H4 | CDoC CMHG CTrh ELon EPfP GGal GGar GKin LRHS MPkF SCam SCog SCoo |
| | 'Gael's Dream' (*reticulata* hybrid) **new** | SCam |
| | 'Gay Baby' | CDoC |
| | 'Golden Anniversary' | see *C. japonica* 'Dahlohnega' |
| | ***grijsii*** | CPLG CTrh SCam |
| | ***handelii*** | CPLG |
| | 'Happy Anniversary' | CSBt LSRN |
| § | ***hiemalis*** 'Bonanza' | CTrh SCam |
| | - 'Chansonette' | CDoC ELon SCam SCog |
| § | - 'Dazzler' | CSBt SCam SCog |
| | - 'Kanjirō' | CDoC SCam |
| | - 'Shōwa-no-sakae' | CDoC LRHS SCam SCog |
| § | - 'Sparkling Burgundy' ♀H3 | CBcs CDoC ELon EPfP LRHS MGos SCam SCog |
| | 'Hierathlyn' | GGal |
| | 'High Fragrance' | LRHS MPkF |
| | 'Hooker' | CDoC |
| | 'Ice Follies' | SCam |
| | 'Imbricata Rubra' | see *C. japonica* 'Imbricata' |
| | 'Inspiration' (*reticulata* × *saluenensis*) ♀H4 | CDoC CMHG CMac CSBt CTrh CWSG EPfP GGar GKin LRHS LSRN MBri MGos NLar SCam SCog SPer SSpi WGob |
| | 'Invitation' **new** | NHim |
| | ***japonica*** | CBcs SArc SEWo |
| | - 'Aaron's Ruby' | CBcs CDoC ELon LRHS MAsh SCog |
| | - 'Ace of Hearts' | MBri |
| | - 'Ada Pieper' | CTrh |
| | - 'Adelina Patti' ♀H4 | CBcs CDoC CMHG CTrh ELon SCam SCog |
| | - 'Adelina Patti' carmine sport | SCam |
| | - 'Adolphe Audusson' ♀H4 | Widely available |
| | - 'Adolphe Audusson Special' | LSRN |
| § | - 'Akashigata' ♀H4 | CBcs CDoC CMac ELon EPfP LRHS LSRN MGos SCog SLim SPer SPoG SSta |
| | - 'Alba Plena' ♀H4 | CTrh CWSG MGos SCog SPer WFar |
| | - 'Alba Simplex' | CAlb CDoC CMac CTrh ELan EPfP LRHS MGos SCam SCog SPer SSta |
| | - 'Alexander Hunter' ♀H4 | CDoC LRHS SCog |
| | - 'Alison Leigh Woodroof' | CDoC |
| § | - 'Althaeiflora' | CBcs CDoC ELon LRHS MGos SCog |
| | - 'Amazing Graces' | CDoC |
| | - 'Anemoniflora' | CBcs CDoC ELan LRHS SCam SCog WFar |
| | - 'Angel' | CBcs LSRN SCam SCog WBor |
| | - 'Angello' | WGob |
| | - 'Ann Sothern' | CBcs |
| | - 'Annette Gehry' | CBcs |
| | - 'Annie Wylam' ♀H4 | CTrh SCog |
| | - 'Apollo' ambig. | CBcs CDoC LRHS MAsh MGos WGob |
| | - 'Apollo' Paul, 1911 | CSam MGos MSwo SCam SCog |
| § | - 'Apple Blossom' ♀H4 | CBcs CTsd ELan |
| | - 'Arajishi' misapplied | see *C. japonica* subsp. *rusticana* |
| * | - 'Augustine Supreme' | CMac |
| | - 'Augusto Leal de Gouveia Pinto' | CBcs |
| | - 'Australis' ♀H4 | MAsh SCam |
| | - 'Ave Maria' ♀H4 | CDoC CTrh SCam |
| | - 'Baby Pearl' | LSRN SCam |
| | - 'Baby Sis' | CDoC LRHS MAsh |
| | - 'Ballet Dancer' ♀H4 | CDoC ELon LSRN MGos SCam SCog |
| | - 'Bambino' | CDoC |
| | - 'Barbara Woodroof' | CBcs |
| | - 'Baron Gomer' | see *C. japonica* 'Comte de Gomer' |
| | - 'Baronne Leguay' | SCam |
| | - 'Beau Harp' | CDoC LRHS SCam |
| | - 'Bella Lambertii' | NMun |
| | - 'Bella Romana' | SCam |
| | - 'Benten' (v) | SMad |
| | - 'Benten-kagura' (v) **new** | CDoC |
| | - 'Berenice Boddy' ♀H4 | CDoC CTrh LRHS |
| | - 'Berenice Perfection' | CDoC SCog WFar |
| | - 'Betty Foy Sanders' | CTrh |
| | - 'Betty Robinson' | CDoC LRHS |
| | - 'Betty Sheffield' | CDoC MAsh MGos SCog WFar |
| | - 'Betty Sheffield Pink' | LRHS SCam |
| | - 'Betty Sheffield Supreme' | CBcs |

- 'Betty's Beauty' **new** LRHS
- 'Billie McCaskill' SCam
- 'Black Magic' **new** CTrh
- 'Black Tie' CDoC ELon LRHS MAsh MGos SCam SCog SPur
- 'Blackburnia' see *C. japonica* 'Althaeiflora'
- 'Blaze of Glory' SCog

§ - 'Blood of China' CBcs CDoC CSBt LBuc LRHS LSRN MGos MMuc SCog SCoo SEND SPer WFar WGob WMoo
- 'Bob Hope' ♀H4 CBcs CDoC CTrh CTri LRHS MAsh MGos
- 'Bob's Tinsie' ♀H4 CBcs CDoC CMHG CSBt CTrh EPfP GBin LRHS LSRN MAsh MPkF NLar SCog WGob

§ - 'Bokuhan' ♀H4 CDoC LRHS MPkF SCam
- 'Bright Buoy' CDoC
- 'Brushfield's Yellow' ♀H4 CBcs CDoC CMHG CSBt CWSG ELan ELon EPfP IArd LMil LRHS LSRN MAsh MBri MDun MGos NEgg NHim NLar SBfd SCam SCog SCoo SPer SSta WFar WGob WGwG
- 'Bush Hill Beauty' see *C. japonica* 'Lady de Saumarez'

§ - 'C.M. Hovey' ♀H4 CMHG CMac LRHS MAsh
- 'C.M. Wilson' CDoC CMac SCog
- 'Campsii Alba' CDoC CTsd
- 'Can Can' CBcs CDoC ELon SCog
- 'Candy Apple' CTrh
- 'Candy Stripe' CDoC SCam
- 'Captain Blood' **new** CDoC
- 'Cara Mia' CBcs CDoC CTsd SCam
- 'Carolina Beauty' LRHS
- 'Carter's Sunburst' ♀H4 CBcs CDoC ELan EPfP SCog WGob
- 'Cassandra' LRHS
- 'Chandleri Elegans' see *C. japonica* 'Elegans'
- 'Charlotte de Rothschild' CTrh CTri EPfP SCam
- 'Cheryll Lynn' CDoC
- 'Christmas Beauty' SCam
- 'Cinderella' CDoC SCog SSta
- 'Clarise Carleton' MBri
- 'Clarke Hubbs' **new** CDoC
- 'Colonel Firey' see *C. japonica* 'C.M. Hovey'
- 'Commander Mulroy' ♀H4 CDoC CTrh MBri SCam

§ - 'Comte de Gomer' CDoC ELan ELon EPfP LRHS SCog
- 'Conspicua' CBcs
- 'Contessa Samailoff' CDoC

§ - 'Coquettii' ♀H4 CBcs CDul LRHS MAsh SCam SCog
- 'Coral Beauty' WFar
- 'Coral Pink Lotus' CDoC
- 'Coral Queen' CDoC SCam
- 'Cornish Excellence' CDoC SCam
- 'Curly Lady' PBR MMuc MPkF NPri WMoo

§ - 'Dahlohnega' CDoC CSBt CTrh ELon LRHS LSRN MAsh MPkF SPoG
- 'Daikagura' CBcs CDoC
- 'Dainty' CBcs
- 'Daitairin' see *C. japonica* 'Dewatairin'
- 'Dark of the Moon' CDoC
- 'Dear Jenny' CBcs
- 'Debutante' CBcs CDoC CMac ELon SCam SCog
- 'Deep Secret' ♀H4 CDoC SCog
- 'Desire' ♀H4 CBcs CDoC CMHG CSBt CTrh CTsd CWSG EPfP GEdr LRHS LSRN MAsh MDun MPkF NMun SBfd SCam SCog SCoo SPoG WGob
- 'Devonia' CBcs SCog

§ - 'Dewatairin' (Higo) CBcs CDoC MGos SCam SCog
- 'Dixie Knight' CBcs CDoC LRHS MGos SCam SCog
- 'Dobreei' CMac
- 'Doctor Burnside' CBcs CDoC CTrh LRHS SCam SCog
- 'Doctor King' CWSG GEdr LRHS
- 'Doctor Tinsley' ♀H4 CDoC LRHS MAsh NPri SCoo
- 'Dolly Dyer' CDoC LRHS
- 'Dona Herzilia de Freitas Magalhaes' CDoC ELon SCam SCog
- 'Dona Jane Andresson' SCam
- 'Donckelaeri' see *C. japonica* 'Masayoshi'
- 'Donnan's Dream' CTrh
- 'Drama Girl' ♀H2 CBcs CDoC CTsd EPfP MGos SCam SCog
- 'Dream Time' CBcs
- 'Duc de Bretagne' SCog
- 'Duchesse Decazes' CBcs MBri
- 'Ed Combatalade' CDoC
- 'Edelweiss' CDoC MGos SCam SCog
- 'Effendee' see *C. sasanqua* 'Rosea Plena'
- 'Eleanor Hagood' CBcs

§ - 'Elegans' ♀H4 CBcs CDoC ELon EPfP LMil LRHS NEgg SBfd SCam SCog SCoo SLim SPer SPoG SSta WFar
- 'Elegans Champagne' EPfP NPri
- 'Elegans Splendor' CDoC
- 'Elisabeth' CDoC WFar
- 'Elizabeth Cooper' **new** CTrh LSRN
- 'Elizabeth Dowd' CBcs SCog
- 'Elizabeth Hawkins' CTrh LRHS MMuc NCGa SEND
- 'Emily Wilson' CDoC
- 'Emmett Barnes' SCam
- 'Emmett Pfingstl' SCam
- 'Emperor of Russia' CBcs CDoC
- 'Eric Baker' CDoC SCam
- 'Erin Farmer' CBcs
- 'Eugène Lizé' SCam
- 'Eximia' EPfP LRHS MAsh NPri SCam SCog
- 'Faith' CBcs
- 'Fashionata' CDoC

§ - 'Faustina' MAsh
- 'Feast Perfection' CDoC
- 'Finlandia Variegated' CDoC SCam SCog
- 'Fire Dance' CDoC
- 'Fire Falls' ♀H4 CDoC CMHG
- 'Firebird' CBcs
- 'Flame' CBcs NBlu
- 'Flamingo' CDoC
- 'Flashlight' CDoC EPfP

§ - 'Fleur Dipater' SCam WGob
- 'Flowerwood' SCog WFar
- 'Forest Green' CDoC ELan MAsh
- 'Fortune Teller' CBcs
- 'Frans van Damme' CBcs
- 'Fred Sander' CDoC ELon MGos NMun SCam SCog
- 'Frizzle White' SApp
- 'Frosty Morn' CBcs CDoC ELan
- 'Furo-an' CBcs MAsh
- 'Geisha Girl' SCog
- 'Général Lamoricière' LRHS

§ - 'Gigantea' LRHS SCam
- 'Giuditta Rosani' CDoC
- 'Gladys Wannamaker' SCog
- 'Glen 40' see *C. japonica* 'Coquettii'
- 'Gloire de Nantes' ♀H4 CTrh NMun SCam SCog
- 'Gold Tone' CDoC MGos SCam
- 'Goshozakura' CDoC
- 'Grace Bunton' CBcs CDoC ELon MGos SCam SCog
- 'Granada' SCog
- 'Grand Prix' ♀H4 CDoC ELon LSRN MGos SCam SCog

- 'Grand Slam' ♀H2 CBcs CDoC CDul MAsh SCam
- 'Grand Sultan' CDoC
- 'Guest of Honor' CBcs CDoC
- 'Guilio Nuccio' ♀H4 CBcs CDoC CTri EPfP IArd LMil LRHS LSRN MGos NEgg SBfd SCam SCog SCoo SLim SPer
- 'Gus Menard' SCam
- 'Gwenneth Morey' CBcs CDoC ELan
- 'H.A. Downing' CDoC SCam
- § - 'Hagoromo' ♀H4 CBcs CDoC CTrh ELan MAsh SBfd SCam SCog SPer WFar
- 'Hakugan' EMil EPfP NLar
- § - 'Hakurakuten' ♀H4 CDoC CMHG CTri IArd NHim SCog
- 'Hanafūki' CDoC MAsh MGos SCam SCog
- 'Happy Birthday' LSRN
- 'Haru-no-utena' **new** CTrh
- 'Hatsuzakura' see *C. japonica* 'Dewatairin'
- 'Hawaii' CBcs CDoC CMac CTrh MGos SCog
- 'Her Majesty Queen Elizabeth II' CDoC
- Herme see *C. japonica* 'Hikarugenji'
- 'High Hat' CBcs SCog
- 'High, Wide 'n' Handsome' CDoC
- § - 'Hikarugenji' CDoC MGos SCog
- 'Hinomaru' CDoC CMac
- 'Holly Bright' CTrh SCam
- 'Honeyglow' CDoC
- 'Ichisetsu' SCog
- § - 'Imbricata' CAlb LBuc LRHS MAsh MMuc SCog SEND
- 'Incarnata' SCam
- 'Italiana Vera' LBuc LRHS MAsh
- 'J.J. Whitfield' CMac SCam
- 'Jack Jones Scented' CMHG
- 'Janet Waterhouse' CBcs SCam WFar
- § - 'Japonica Variegata' (v) CDoC LRHS SCam
- 'Jean Clere' CDoC MGos MWea SCog
- 'Jean Renaud' NBlu
- 'Jennifer Turnbull' CDoC
- 'Jessie Katz' CDoC
- 'Jingle Bells' CBcs
- 'Jitsugetsusei' CDoC
- 'Joseph Pfingstl' ♀H4 CDoC CTri EPfP LRHS MMuc NPri SCam SCog SEND
- 'Joshua E. Youtz' SCog
- 'Jovey Carlyon' CBcs LRHS MAsh
- 'Joy Sander' see *C. japonica* 'Apple Blossom'
- 'Julia France' SCog
- 'June McCaskill' CDoC
- 'Juno' CBcs LRHS SCam SCoo
- 'Jupiter' Paul, 1904 ♀H4 CBcs CDoC CMac CTri EPfP LMil LRHS LSRN MGos SCog SPer
- 'Kellingtoniana' see *C. japonica* 'Gigantea'
- 'Kentucky' LRHS SCam
- 'Kick-off' CBcs CTrh SCog
- 'Kimberley' CBcs CDoC LSRN NMun SCog
- 'King Size' CDoC MGos
- 'King's Ransom' CDoC CMac CTsd LRHS MAsh
- 'Kingyoba-shiro-wabisuke' CDoC CHll
- 'Kingyo-tsubaki' CDoC SCam SSta
- 'Kitty Berry' CTrh
- 'Kokinran' CDoC SCam
- § - 'Konronkoku' ♀H4 CBcs CDoC LRHS MAsh SCog
- 'Kouron-jura' see *C. japonica* 'Konronkoku'
- 'Kramer's Beauty' LRHS
- 'Kramer's Supreme' CBcs CCCN CDoC ELon LBuc LRHS LSRN MGos NHim NLar SCog SCoo SPer WFar
- § - 'Kumasaka' CTri
- 'La Pace Rubra' SCam
- 'Lady Campbell' CTri CWSG GEdr GGar GKev LRHS NBlu NLar NMun SCam SPad
- 'Lady Clare' see *C. japonica* 'Akashigata'
- § - 'Lady de Saumarez' CBcs CDoC CMac
- 'Lady Loch' CTrh MAsh MBri MGos SCam
- 'Lady Mackinnon' MAsh
- 'Lady Marion' see *C. japonica* 'Kumasaka'
- 'Lady McCulloch' LRHS NPri
- 'Lady Saint Clair' CDoC
- 'Lady Vansittart' CAlb CChe CDoC CDul CTrh ELan EPfP LRHS LSRN MAsh MGos MPkF NPri SBfd SCam SCog SCoo SLim SPer SPoG SSta WGob
- § - 'Lady Vansittart Pink' CMac SBfd
- 'Lady Vansittart Red' see *C. japonica* 'Lady Vansittart Pink'
- 'Lady Vansittart Shell' see *C. japonica* 'Yours Truly'
- 'Lady Vere de Vere' (d) CDoC
- 'Lanarth' CBcs
- 'Latifolia' SCam
- 'Laura's Red' **new** CTsd
- 'Laurie Bray' SCog WFar
- § - 'Lavinia Maggi' ♀H4 CAlb CBcs CDoC CTrh CTri ELan ELon EPfP LBuc LMil LRHS LSRN MAsh MGos NPri SCam SCog SCoo SPoG SReu SRms SSta WGob
- 'L'Avvenire' SCog
- § - 'Le Lys' SCam
- 'Lemon Drop' CTrh
- 'Leonora Novick' CDoC SCog
- 'Lillian Rickets' CDoC
- 'Lily Pons' ♀H4 CDoC CTrh
- 'Little Bit' CBcs CDoC CMHG CTrh ELon MGos SCam SCog SSta
- 'Little Red Riding Hood' CDoC
- 'Little Slam' CDoC
- 'Lovelight' ♀H4 CTrh LRHS
- 'Lucy Hester' CDoC
- 'Ludgvan Red' LRHS SCam
- 'Lulu Belle' SCog
- 'Mabel Blackwell' SCam
- 'Madame de Strekaloff' CMac CSBt SCam
- 'Madame Hahn' CDoC
- 'Madame Lebois' CBcs CDoC SCam
- 'Madame Martin Cachet' SCog
- 'Magic Moments' SCog
- 'Magnoliiflora' see *C. japonica* 'Hagoromo'
- 'Maiden's Blush' CMac
- 'Man Size' CDoC
- 'Manuroa Road' **new** LRHS MPkF
- 'Margaret Davis' CCCN CDoC CSBt ELan ELon EPfP LBuc LRHS LSRN MAsh MDun MGos MPkF MWea NEgg SBfd SBrd SCam SCoo SLim SPoG WGob
- 'Margaret Davis Picotee' ♀H4 CBcs CMHG CTrh SCog SPer
- 'Margaret Rose' SCam
- 'Margaret Short' CDoC
- 'Marguérite Gouillon' CBcs CDoC LRHS SSta
- 'Marian Mitchell' SCam
- 'Mariana' CDoC SCog
- I - 'Marie Antoinette' NBlu
- 'Marie Bracey' CBcs
- 'Marinka' CBcs
- 'Marjorie Magnificent' LBuc LRHS MAsh SCoo
- 'Mark Alan' CDoC LRHS LSRN MPkF
- 'Maroon and Gold' CDoC LRHS LSRN SCog
- 'Marquis of Exeter' NMun
- 'Mars' ♀H4 CBcs LMil MGos SCam SCog SPer WFar

| | | |
|---|---|---|
| | – 'Mary Alice Cox' | CDoC |
| | – 'Mary Costa' | CDoC CTrh WFar |
| | – 'Mary J. Wheeler' | LSRN |
| § | – 'Masayoshi' ♀H4 | CBcs CSBt LRHS MAsh SCam SCog |
| | – 'Mathotiana Alba' ♀H4 | CDoC CMac CTri CTsd ELan EPfP LSRN MGos MMuc SCam SCog SPer |
| § | – 'Mathotiana Rosea' ♀H4 | CMac SCam |
| | – 'Mathotiana Supreme' | CDoC SCam SCog |
| | – 'Matterhorn' | CTrh MAsh |
| | – 'Mattie Cole' | CDoC SCam |
| | – 'Maui' | CDoC |
| | – 'Mercury' ♀H4 | CBcs CMac CWSG LRHS SCog |
| | – 'Mercury Variegated' | CMHG |
| | – 'Mermaid' | CDoC |
| | – 'Midnight' | CBcs CDoC CMHG LBuc LRHS MAsh SCoo WFar |
| | – 'Midnight Magic' | CTrh CTri |
| | – 'Midnight Serenade' | CDoC LRHS |
| | – 'Midsummer's Day' | CBcs |
| § | – 'Mikenjaku' | CBcs CDoC EPfP LBuc LRHS MAsh NMun SCog WGob |
| | – 'Miriam Stevenson' | SCam |
| | – 'Miss Charleston' | CBcs SCog |
| | – 'Miss Lyla' | MMuc NLar |
| | – 'Modern Art' | MPkF |
| | – 'Momiji-gari' | CDoC SCam |
| | – 'Monstruosa Rubra' | see *C. japonica* 'Gigantea' |
| | – 'Monte Carlo' | CDoC SCam SCog |
| | – 'Moonlight' | CDoC |
| | – 'Moonlight Bay' | CTrh SCog |
| | – 'Moshe Dayan' | CAlb CDoC CWSG LBuc LRHS MAsh SCog SCoo WGob |
| | – 'Moshio' | CDoC |
| § | – 'Mrs Bertha A. Harms' | CDoC LRHS MGos SCam SCog |
| | – 'Mrs Charles Cobb' | LRHS |
| | – 'Mrs D.W. Davis' | CBcs CDoC EPfP SCam |
| | – 'Mrs Lyman Clarke' | CDoC |
| | – 'Mrs William Thompson' | SCam |
| § | – 'Mystic' | CDoC |
| | – 'Nagasaki' | see *C. japonica* 'Mikenjaku' |
| | – 'Nigra' | see *C. japonica* 'Konronkoku' |
| | – 'Nina Avery' | CDoC |
| | – 'Nioi-fubuki' (Higo) | CDoC |
| | – 'Nobilissima' | CDoC CMac CTrh CTri EPfP GKev LRHS MBlu MMuc NBlu NLar NPri SCam SCog SCoo SPer SPoG WFar |
| | – 'Nokogiriba-tsubaki' **new** | MPkF SCam |
| | – 'Nuccio's Amigo' | MAsh |
| | – 'Nuccio's Cameo' | CDoC CTrh LRHS MAsh SCoo |
| | – 'Nuccio's Carousel' | MPkF |
| | – 'Nuccio's Gem' ♀H4 | CDoC CMHG ELan EPfP LRHS MGos SCog SCoo SSta |
| | – 'Nuccio's Jewel' ♀H4 | CDoC CSBt CTrh CWSG ELon EPfP GEdr LBuc LRHS LSRN MAsh MPkF SCam SCog SPer WGob WMoo |
| | – 'Nuccio's Pearl' | CDoC EPfP LRHS LSRN MMuc NEgg NPri SCam SCog SCoo SEND WGob |
| | – 'Nuccio's Pink Lace' | CDoC CTri |
| | – 'Olga Anderson' | CDoC MGos |
| | – 'Onetia Holland' | CDoC EPfP LSRN MGos SBfd SCam SCog SLim |
| | – 'Oo-La-La' | CTrh LRHS MPkF |
| | – 'Optima' | CDoC LRHS MAsh SCam SCog SCoo |
| | – 'Optima Rosea' | SPoG |
| | – 'Orandakō' | LRHS |
| | – 'Paeoniiflora Alba' | SCam |
| | – 'Patricia Ann' | LSRN |
| | – 'Paul Jones Supreme' | CDoC |
| | – 'Paulette Goddard' | SCam |
| | – 'Paul's Apollo' | see *C. japonica* 'Apollo' Paul, 1911 |
| | – 'Peachblossom' | see *C. japonica* 'Fleur Dipater' |
| | – 'Pearl Harbor' | SCam |
| | – 'Pensacola Red' | CDoC |
| | – 'Pink Clouds' | CBcs |
| | – 'Preston Rose' | CBcs CDoC NMun |
| | – 'Primavera' | CTrh SCam SCog |
| | – 'Prince Murat' | CDoC LRHS |
| | – 'Princess Baciocchi' | CBcs SCam |
| | – 'Princess du Mahe' | CMac |
| | – 'R.L. Wheeler' ♀H4 | CBcs CDoC CSBt CTri EPfP LRHS LSRN MWea NBlu NPri SBfd SCog SCoo SLim |
| | – 'Red Dandy' | CDoC MGos SCam SCog |
| | – 'Red Red Rose' | CDoC LRHS |
| | – 'Reg Ragland' | CDoC CMHG MGos SCam SCog |
| | – 'Roger Hall' | CBcs CDoC CTrh LRHS LSRN MAsh MPkF SCog SCoo SPoG WGob |
| | – 'Roman Soldier' | CBcs |
| | – 'Rosa Baroveira Nella' **new** | NBlu |
| | – 'Rosa Mundi' | LRHS |
| | – 'Rosularis' | CDoC SCam SCog |
| | – 'Royal Velvet' | CDoC CTrh |
| | – 'Rubescens Major' ♀H4 | CBcs |
| | – 'Ruddigore' | CTrh |
| § | – subsp. ***rusticana*** | CBcs CDoC SCog WFar |
| | – – 'Arajishi' misapplied | see *C. japonica* subsp. *rusticana* |
| | – – 'Arajishi' Ko'emon | SCam |
| | – – 'Botanyuki' **new** | LRHS |
| | – – 'Reigyoku' (v) | CBcs CDoC |
| | – 'Sabiniana' | LRHS |
| | – 'Sacco Nova' | NBlu |
| | – 'Saint André' | CMac LRHS MAsh SCoo |
| | – 'Sally Harrell' | SCam |
| | – 'San Dimas' ♀H4 | CDoC CTrh SCam SCog |
| | – 'Saturnia' | CDoC ELon LBuc LRHS MAsh MMuc WBor |
| | – 'Sawada's Dream' | CDoC SCog |
| | – 'Scented Red' | CDoC SCog |
| | – 'Scentsation' ♀H4 | CDoC CMHG CTri NPri SCog |
| | – 'Sea Foam' | LRHS MAsh SSta |
| | – 'Sea Gull' | CTrh |
| | – 'Senator Duncan U. Fletcher' | CDoC |
| | – 'Shikibu' | CTrh |
| | – 'Shiragiku' | CBcs CDoC LRHS SCog |
| | – 'Shiro Chan' | CDoC ELon MGos SCog |
| | – 'Shirobotan' | CDoC ELon LRHS MAsh MGos SCam SCog SCoo SPur |
| | – 'Silver Anniversary' | CAlb CBcs CDoC CMHG CSBt CTrh CTri ELan ELon EPfP LMil LRHS LSRN MAsh MGos NEgg NPri SBfd SBrd SCam SCog SCoo SLim SPer SPoG SReu SSta WGob |
| | – 'Silver Ruffles' | CDoC |
| | – 'Something Beautiful' | CDoC |
| | – 'Souvenir de Bahuaud-Litou' ♀H4 | CDoC SCam SCog |
| | – 'Spencer's Pink' | CBcs CDoC |
| | – 'Splendens Carlyon' | LRHS MAsh SCoo |
| | – 'Spring Fever' | SCam |
| | – 'Spring Fling' | CTrh |
| | – 'Spring Formal' | CTrh |
| | – 'Spring Frill' | SCam SCog |
| | – 'Spring Sonnet' | NBlu |
| | – 'Stardust' | SCam |
| | – 'Strawberry Blonde' | SCog |
| | – 'Strawberry Parfait' | CDoC CTrh LRHS SCog |
| | – 'Strawberry Swirl' | CBcs SCog |

| | | |
|---|---|---|
| | – 'Sugar Babe' | CDoC CTrh LRHS MAsh SCam SCog SCoo |
| | – 'Sunset Glory' | SCam |
| | – 'Sweetheart' | SCog |
| | – 'Sylva' 🏆$^{H4}$ | GGal SSpi |
| | – 'Sylvia' | CMac |
| | – 'Takanini' | CDoC CTrh |
| | – 'Tama-no-ura' | CDoC |
| | – 'Tammia' | CDoC LRHS MAsh |
| | – 'Tarō'an' | CDoC GGal |
| | – 'Teresa Ragland' | CDoC SCam |
| | – 'Teringa' | CDoC |
| § | – 'The Czar' | CBcs |
| | – 'The Mikado' | CDoC LRHS SCog |
| | – 'Tickled Pink' | CDoC |
| | – 'Tiffany' | CBcs CDoC LRHS MGos SCam SCog SCoo |
| | – 'Tiki' | MBri WFar |
| | – 'Tinker Bell' | CDoC MAsh MBri SCog |
| | – 'Tom Pouce' **new** | MPkF |
| | – 'Tom Thumb' 🏆$^{H4}$ | CDoC CTrh LRHS MAsh SRms SSta |
| | – 'Tomorrow' | CDoC CTsd CWSG LRHS MAsh MMuc NEgg SCam SCog |
| | – 'Tomorrow Park Hill' | CBcs SCog |
| § | – 'Tomorrow Variegated' | MGos SCam |
| | – 'Tomorrow's Dawn' | CDoC |
| | – 'Touchdown' | SCam |
| | – 'Trewithen White' | CDoC CSam |
| § | – 'Tricolor' 🏆$^{H4}$ | CBcs CDoC CMHG CMac CSBt CTrh ELon LRHS MAsh MGos MMuc NBlu SBfd SCam SCog SCoo SPer WFar |
| | – 'Tricolor Red' | see *C. japonica* 'Lady de Saumarez' |
| | – 'Trinkett' | CDoC |
| | – 'Valtevareda' | CDoC |
| | – variegated (v) | SCog |
| | – 'Victor de Bisschop' | see *C. japonica* 'Le Lys' |
| | – 'Victor Emmanuel' | see *C. japonica* 'Blood of China' |
| | – 'Ville de Nantes' | LRHS MGos |
| | – 'Virginia Carlyon' | CBcs CDoC |
| | – 'Virginia Robinson' | SCam |
| | – 'Virgin's Blush' | SCam |
| | – 'Vittorio Emanuele II' | CDoC CTrh LBuc LRHS MAsh MGos SCoo |
| | – 'Volcano' | CDoC MPkF |
| | – 'Vosper's Rose' | CDoC |
| | – 'Warrior' | CDoC SCog |
| | – 'White Nun' | CBcs CTsd SCog |
| | – 'White Swan' | CSBt LRHS MAsh SCoo |
| | – 'Wilamina' 🏆$^{H4}$ | CDoC CMHG LRHS |
| | – 'Wildfire' | LRHS SCam |
| | – 'William Bartlett' | CTrh CWSG LRHS |
| | – 'William Honey' | CTrh |
| | – 'Wisley White' | see *C. japonica* 'Hakurakuten' |
| | – 'Witman Yellow' **new** | CTrh |
| § | – 'Yours Truly' | CBcs CDoC CMac CTrh CTsd LRHS LSRN MAsh MDun SCog |
| | – 'Yukimi-guruma' | CDoC |
| | 'John Tooby' | CDoC |
| | 'Jury's Yellow' | see *C.* × *williamsii* 'Jury's Yellow' |
| | 'Larry Piet' (*reticulata* hybrid) **new** | SCam |
| | 'Lasca Beauty' (*japonica* × *reticulata*) | CBcs SCam |
| | 'Lavender Queen' | see *C. sasanqua* 'Lavender Queen' |
| | 'Leonard Messel' (*reticulata* × *williamsii*) 🏆$^{H4}$ | CBcs CDoC CDul CMHG CMac CTrh CTri CTsd EPfP GGal LRHS MAsh MDun MGos MPkF SCam SCog SCoo SPer SPoG SReu WGwG |
| | 'Liz Henslowe' | CDoC |
| | 'Madame Victor de Bisschop' | see *C. japonica* 'Le Lys' |
| | 'Magic Mum' **new** | LSRN |
| | 'Mandalay Queen' (*reticulata* hybrid) **new** | SCam |
| | 'Maud Messel' (× *williamsii* × *reticulata*) | SCam |
| | 'Milo Rowell' | CDoC |
| | 'Mimosa Jury' | CDoC |
| | 'Monticello' | CDoC |
| | 'Mystique' | see *C. japonica* 'Mystic', *C. reticulata* 'Mystique' |
| | 'Nicky Crisp' (*japonica* × *pitardii*) | CDoC |
| | 'Nijinski' (*reticulata* hybrid) | CDoC |
| | 'Nikisi Kerin' **new** | NBlu |
| | 'Nonie Haydon' (*pitardii* hybrid) | CDoC |
| | ***oleifera*** | CPLG NLar SCog WFar |
| | 'Phyl Doak' (*reticulata* × *saluenensis*) | CDoC |
| | 'Pink Spangles' | see *C. japonica* 'Mathotiana Rosea' |
| | ***pitardii*** | CDoC |
| | – 'Snippet' | CDoC |
| | 'Polar Ice' (*oleifera* hybrid) | CBcs CDoC SCog |
| | 'Polyanna' | CDoC SCog |
| | 'Portuense' | see *C. japonica* 'Japonica Variegata' |
| | 'Quintessence' (*japonica* × *lutchuensis*) | CDoC CTrh LRHS SCam SCog |
| | ***reticulata*** 'Arch of Triumph' | SCam |
| | – 'Captain Rawes' | SCam |
| | – 'Jean Morel' **new** | SCam |
| | – 'Les Jury' | LMil |
| | – 'Mary Williams' | CDul GKev LMil NBlu NLar SCoo |
| | – 'Miss Tulare' | CDoC |
| § | – 'Mystique' | CDoC |
| | – 'Simpatica' **new** | SCam |
| | – 'Songzilin' **new** | SCam |
| | 'Rosa Betanzas' **new** | NBlu |
| | 'Rose de Steir' **new** | MPkF SCam |
| | ***rosiflora*** 'Roseaflora Cascade' | CDoC |
| | 'Royalty' (*japonica* × *reticulata*) 🏆$^{H3}$ | CBcs |
| | ***rusticana*** | see *C. japonica* subsp. *rusticana* |
| | 'Salutation' (*reticulata* × *saluenensis*) | SCam |
| | ***sasanqua*** Thunb. | CDul |
| I | – 'Alba' | CTri |
| I | – 'Apple Blossom' | MAsh |
| | – 'Baronesa de Soutelinho' | ELon SCam SCog |
| | – 'Bettie Patricia' | SCog |
| | – 'Bonanza' | see *C. hiemalis* 'Bonanza' |
| | – Borde Hill form | SCam |
| | – 'Cleopatra' | EPfP MAsh |
| | – 'Cotton Candy' | CDoC |
| | – 'Crimson King' 🏆$^{H3}$ | CDoC NMun SCam |
| | – 'Dazzler' | see *C. hiemalis* 'Dazzler' |
| | – 'Early Pearly' | CDoC SCam |
| I | – 'Exquisite' | CDoC |
| | – 'Flamingo' | see *C. sasanqua* 'Fukuzutsumi' |
| | – 'Fragrans' | ELon SCog |
| | – 'Fuji-no-mine' | ELon SCog |
| § | – 'Fukuzutsumi' | CSBt SCam |
| | – 'Gay Sue' | CDoC CTrh SCam |
| | – 'Hiryū' | SCam |
| | – 'Hugh Evans' 🏆$^{H3}$ | CAbP CBcs CDoC CTrh ELon LRHS SCam SCog SCoo SRkn SSta |
| | – 'Jean May' 🏆$^{H3}$ | CDoC ELon EPfP LRHS SCam SCog SCoo SSta |

| | |
|---|---|
| - 'Kenkyō' | ELon SCam SCog SSta |
| § - 'Lavender Queen' | SCam |
| - 'Maiden's Blush' | LRHS SCam SCog WFar |
| - 'Narumigata' | CAbP CBcs CDoC CHll CMac CSBt CTrh ELon EPfP LRHS MBlu SCam SPoG SSta |
| - 'New Dawn' | SCam SCog |
| - 'Nyewoods' | CMac |
| - 'Papaver' | SCam SCog |
| - 'Paradise Audrey' **new** | LRHS |
| - 'Paradise Belinda' PBR | CDoC LRHS |
| - 'Paradise Blush' | CBcs CDoC LRHS SCog |
| - 'Paradise Glow' | CBcs CDoC LRHS SCam SCog SPoG |
| - 'Paradise Helen' | LRHS SCam |
| - 'Paradise Hilda' | CBcs CDoC LRHS SCam SCog SPoG |
| - 'Paradise Joan' | CDoC |
| - 'Paradise Little Liane' PBR | CBcs CDoC SCam SCog |
| - 'Paradise Pearl' | CBcs CDoC LRHS SCam SCog |
| - 'Paradise Petite' PBR | SCog |
| - 'Paradise Sayaka' | CDoC |
| - 'Paradise Venessa' PBR | CBcs CDoC EPfP LRHS SCam SCog |
| - 'Peach Blossom' | CBcs |
| - 'Plantation Pink' | CSBt CWSG EPfP LRHS SCam SCog SLim SPoG SRkn |
| - 'Rainbow' | CAbP CDoC CTrh CWSG ELon EPfP GGal LRHS MPkF NMun SCam SCoo SRkn SSta WFar |
| - 'Rosea' | ELon SCam SCog |
| § - 'Rosea Plena' | CBcs CMac SCam |
| - 'Sasanqua Rubra' | CMac ELon SCam SCog |
| - 'Sasanqua Variegata' (v) | MPkF SCam SCog SSta |
| - 'Setsugekka' | CDoC SCog |
| - 'Silver Dollar' | CDoC |
| - 'Snowflake' | SCam SCog SSta |
| - 'Souvenir de Claude Brivet' **new** | CDoC |
| - 'Sparkling Burgundy' | see *C. hiemalis* 'Sparkling Burgundy' |
| - 'Tanya' | CDoC |
| - 'Versicolor' | MPkF |
| - 'Winter's Joy' | CBcs |
| - 'Winter's Snowman' | CDoC LRHS SCam SCog |
| 'Satan's Robe' (*reticulata* hybrid) | CDoC MGos SCog WFar |
| 'Scented Gem' | MPkF SCam |
| 'Scented Sun' | CTrh |
| 'Scentuous' (*japonica* × *lutchuensis*) | CDoC CTrh |
| 'Show Girl' (*reticulata* × *sasanqua*) | SCam SCog |
| § ***sinensis*** | CBcs CCCN CTrh GPoy LRHS SCam SPlb WCot |
| 'Sir Victor Davis' | CDoC |
| 'Snow Flurry' (*oleifera* hybrid) | CBcs LRHS SCam SCog |
| 'Spring Festival' (*cuspidata* hybrid) ♀H4 | CDoC CMHG CTrh LRHS MMuc MPkF NLar SCog SPoG WMoo |
| 'Spring Mist' (*japonica* × *lutchuensis*) | CDoC CMHG CTrh |
| 'Sugar Dream' | CDoC CTrh SCam |
| 'Superscent' | CTrh |
| 'Survivor' | MPkF SCam |
| 'Swan Lake' | SCog |
| 'Sweet Emily Kate' (*japonica* × *lutchuensis*) | CDoC |
| 'Sweet Jane' | LRHS MPkF SBfd SCam SCog |
| 'Tarōkaja' (wabisuke) | SCam |
| ***thea*** | see *C. sinensis* |
| 'Tinsie' | see *C. japonica* 'Bokuhan' |

| | |
|---|---|
| 'Tiny Princess' (*fraterna* × *japonica*) | CMac |
| 'Tom Knudsen' (*japonica* × *reticulata*) ♀H3 | CDoC CTrh SCam |
| 'Tomorrow Supreme' | see *C. japonica* 'Tomorrow Variegated' |
| ***transnokoensis*** | CMac CPLG SCam |
| 'Tricolor Sieboldii' | see *C. japonica* 'Tricolor' |
| 'Tristrem Carlyon' (*reticulata* hybrid) ♀H4 | CBcs CDoC CTri EPfP SCam WGob |
| ***tsaii*** | CDoC CHEx |
| 'Valley Knudsen' (*reticulata* × *saluenensis*) | SCog |
| × ***vernalis*** 'Star Above Star' | CMHG |
| - 'Yuletide' | CDoC CTrh LRHS LSRN MAsh MPkF SCam SCog |
| 'Volcano' | CDoC |
| 'White Retic' (*japonica* × *reticulata*) **new** | SCam |
| × ***williamsii*** 'Angel Wings' | LRHS |
| - 'Anticipation' ♀H4 | CBcs CDoC CDul CMHG CMac CSBt CSam CTrh EPfP GGal GKin LMil LRHS MAsh MBri MDun MGos MSwo NBlu NEgg NPri SBfd SCam SCog SLim SPer SPoG SSpi WFar WGob |
| - 'Ballet Queen' | CBcs CDoC CSBt LRHS MGos SCam WFar |
| - 'Ballet Queen Variegated' | CDoC MGos SCog |
| - 'Bartley Number Five' | CMac |
| - 'Beatrice Michael' | CMac |
| - 'Blue Danube' | CBcs |
| - 'Bow Bells' | CDoC CTri SCam SSta |
| - 'Bowen Bryant' ♀H4 | SCog |
| - 'Brigadoon' ♀H4 | CBcs CDoC CMHG CTrh CTri EPfP GGal GKin MBri MGos SCam SCog |
| - 'Burncoose' | CBcs |
| - 'Burncoose Apple Blossom' | CBcs CDoC |
| - 'Buttons 'n' Bows' | CDoC LRHS SCog |
| - 'C.F. Coates' | CDoC SCam SCog |
| - 'Caerhays' | CBcs SCam |
| - 'Carnation' | MAsh |
| - 'Carolyn Williams' | CBcs SCam |
| - 'Celebration' | CBcs CSBt LSRN |
| - 'Charlean' | CDoC SCam |
| - 'Charles Colbert' | CDoC LRHS |
| - 'China Clay' ♀H4 | CBcs CDoC EPfP |
| § - 'Citation' | CBcs CMac SCog |
| - 'Clarrie Fawcett' ♀H4 | CDoC |
| - 'Contribution' | CTrh |
| - 'Coral Delight' **new** | MPkF |
| - 'Crinkles' | CDoC CDul NPri SCam |
| - 'Daintiness' ♀H4 | CDoC SCog |
| - 'Dark Nite' | CMHG |
| - 'Debbie' ♀H4 | Widely available |
| - 'Debbie's Carnation' | CDoC CMHG |
| - 'Donation' ♀H4 | Widely available |
| - 'Dream Boat' | CBcs CDoC LRHS |
| - 'E.G. Waterhouse' | CBcs CDoC CMHG CTrh CTri ELon EPfP GKin LRHS MAsh MGos MMuc SCam SCog SEND SPoG SSta WGob |
| - 'E.T.R. Carlyon' ♀H4 | CBcs CDoC CTrh CTri ELon EPfP LBuc LRHS MAsh MPkF NLar SBrd SCog SCoo SLim |
| - 'Elegant Beauty' ♀H4 | CBcs CDoC CSBt ELon SCam SCog SPer |
| - 'Elizabeth Anderson' ♀H4 | CTrh CTsd SCam |
| - 'Ellamine' | CBcs |

| | |
|---|---|
| – 'Elsie Jury' 🏆H3 | CBcs CDoC CMac CTri GKin GQui MGos SCam SCog SPer |
| – 'Exaltation' | CDoC SCam SCog |
| – 'Fiona Colville' | CDoC |
| – 'Francis Hanger' | CDoC CTrh SCam SCog SPer |
| – 'Galaxie' 🏆H4 | CBcs CDoC SCog |
| – 'Gay Time' | SCog |
| – 'George Blandford' 🏆H4 | CBcs CMac GGal |
| – 'Glenn's Orbit' 🏆H4 | CDoC SCam SCog |
| – 'Golden Spangles' (v) | CBcs CDoC CMac CTrh ELan EPfP GKin LRHS MDun MGos MMuc NLar SBfd SCam SCog SLim |
| – 'Grand Jury' | LRHS |
| – 'Gwavas' | CBcs CCCN CDoC LRHS MAsh SCam SCog SCoo |
| – 'Hilo' | CDoC SCam |
| – 'Hiraethlyn' | CBcs |
| – 'Holland Orchid' | SCog |
| – 'J.C. Williams' 🏆H4 | CBcs CMac CSam CTri EPfP MMuc SCog SEND |
| – 'Jamie' | CDoC |
| – 'Jean Claris' | CDoC SCog |
| – 'Jenefer Carlyon' | CBcs CDoC |
| – 'Jill Totty' | CTrh SCog |
| – 'Joan Trehane' 🏆H4 | NPri SCam |
| – 'Julia Hamiter' 🏆H4 | CBcs CDoC |
| § – 'Jury's Yellow' 🏆H4 | Widely available |
| – 'Laura Boscawen' | CDoC SCam |
| – 'Les Jury' 🏆H4 | CDoC CGHE CMHG CSBt CTrh LMil LSRN MWea NEgg SBfd SCog SLim SPoG |
| – 'Little Lavender' | CDoC |
| – 'Margaret Waterhouse' | CBcs CDoC SCam SCog |
| – 'Marjorie Waldegrave' | LRHS |
| – 'Mary Christian' 🏆H4 | CBcs GGal SCam SSta |
| – 'Mary Larcom' | CBcs |
| – 'Mary Phoebe Taylor' 🏆H4 | CBcs CDoC GGal LRHS MPkF NLar SCam SCog SCoo SLim |
| – 'Mildred Veitch' | CDoy CSBt |
| – 'Mirage' | CDoC SCam |
| – 'Moira Reid' | CDoC |
| – 'Monica Dance' | CBcs CDoC SCam |
| – 'Muskoka' 🏆H4 | CBcs |
| – 'New Venture' | CBcs |
| – 'Night Rider' | CDoC MPkF SCam |
| – 'Palaxie' | SCam |
| – 'Phillippa Forward' | CBcs CMac |
| – 'Pink Dahlia' **new** | SCam |
| – 'Rendezvous' | CDoC MGos SCam SCog |
| – 'Rose Bouquet' | CDoC |
| – 'Rosemary Williams' | CBcs |
| – 'Ruby Bells' | CMHG |
| – 'Ruby Wedding' (d) | CDoC CMHG CSBt CTrh CWSG EPfP GQui LMil LRHS LSRN MAsh MWea NEgg NPri SBfd SBrd SCog SCoo SLim SPoG |
| – 'Saint Ewe' 🏆H4 | CBcs CDoC CSBt CTrh CTri EPfP GGal LBuc LRHS MBri MGos NHim NLar NPri SCam SCog SCoo SPer WGob |
| – 'Saint Michael' | CBcs CDoC |
| – 'Sayonara' | CBcs SCam SCog |
| – 'Senorita' 🏆H4 | CDoC CTrh ELon GKin SCam SCog |
| – 'Simon Bolitho' | SCog |
| – 'Sun Song' | SCog |
| – 'Taylor's Perfection' | SCam |
| – 'The Duchess of Cornwall' | CDoC SCam |
| – 'Tiptoe' | CDoC GKin MBri |
| – 'Tulip Time' **new** | MPkF |
| – 'Waltz Time' | CDoC SCam |
| – 'Water Lily' 🏆H4 | CBcs CDoC CTri ELon EPfP MGos SCam SPur |
| – 'Wilber Foss' 🏆H4 | CBcs CDoC ELon GKin LRHS MGos MMuc SCog SEND |
| – 'Winter Gem' **new** | LRHS |
| – 'Winton' (*cuspidata* × *saluenensis*) | CBcs CDoC SCam WFar |
| – 'Wynne Rayner' | CDoC SCam |
| – 'Yesterday' | MMuc |
| 'Winter's Charm' (*oleifera* × *sasanqua*) | SCog |
| 'Winter's Dream' (*hiemalis* × *oleifera*) | SCog |
| 'Winter's Interlude' (*oleifera* × *sinensis*) | CDoC SCam SCog |
| 'Winter's Joy' | SCog |
| 'Winter's Toughie' (*sasanqua* hybrid) | CDoC SCam SCog |
| 'Wirlinga Belle' | SCog |
| 'Yoimachi' (*fraterna* × *sasanqua*) | CDoC CTrh |
| ***yunnanensis*** **new** | IDee |

## *Camissonia* (Onagraceae)

| | |
|---|---|
| § ***bistorta*** **new** | CSpe |

## *Campanula* ✿ (Campanulaceae)

| | |
|---|---|
| sp. | WCot |
| RCB AM 13 | WCot |
| RCB UA 13 | WCot |
| ***abietina*** | see *C. patula* subsp. *abietina* |
| ***alaskana*** | see *C. rotundifolia* var. *alaskana* |
| § ***alliariifolia*** | Widely available |
| – DHTU 0126 | WCru |
| – 'Ivory Bells' | see *C. alliariifolia* |
| ***alpina*** | GLam MDKP |
| ***americana*** | XLum |
| ***ardonensis*** | GKev |
| ***argaea*** | GKev |
| ***armena*** | ELan |
| ***arvatica*** | EACa ECho EDAr GMaP LRHS MDKP NHar NMen |
| – 'Alba' | GMaP |
| ***aucheri*** | see *C. bellidifolia* subsp. *aucheri* |
| ***autraniana*** | EACa |
| ***barbata*** | CFir EACa EBee ECho EDAr GLam MWat NWCA WAbe WMoo |
| – SDR 6365 | GKev |
| ***bayerniana*** | GKev |
| 'Belinda' | CMea CPBP |
| ***bellidifolia*** | NBir NBre |
| § – subsp. ***aucheri*** | EDAr EPot ITim NWCA WFar |
| – subsp. ***saxifraga*** | EPot GKev GLam ITim NMen |
| ***besenginica*** | EPot |
| § ***betulifolia*** 🏆H4 | CSam NSla WFar |
| ***biebersteiniana*** | EDAr |
| 'Birch Hybrid' 🏆H4 | EACa EBee ECho ECtt EDAr ELan EPfP LRHS MMuc WFar XLum |
| ***bononiensis*** | EACa LLHF NBre SRms XLum |
| 'Bumblebee' | WAbe |
| 'Burghaltii' 🏆H4 | CHar CPom ELan GCal GMac NLar SHar WFar WMnd WOut WPer |
| 'Cantata' | EPot WAbe |
| § ***carnica*** | ECho WTcb |
| ***carpatica*** 🏆H4 | ECho EPfP MLHP MLLN NBre NBro NGdn SPlb SRms SWat XLum |
| – f. ***alba*** | ECho LRHS MLLN NBre NGdn SPlb SWat XLum |
| § – – 'Weisse Clips' | CBar EAEE EBee ECho ECtt ELan EPfP GGar GKin GMaP LAst LHop |

| | | |
|---|---|---|
| | | LRHS MAsh NBlu NDov NEgg NGdn NPri NWCA SBfd SBrd SPer SPoG SRms STes SWvt WFar |
| § | - 'Blaue Clips' | CBar CBcs EBee ECho ECtt ELan EPfP GGar GKin GMaP IFoB LAst LHop LRHS MAsh MGos NBlu NDov NEgg NGdn NPri NWCA SBfd SBrd SPer SPoG SRms STes SWvt WFar |
| | - Blue Clips | see *C. carpatica* 'Blaue Clips' |
| | - 'Blue Moonlight' | EACa ECho LHop LRHS |
| | - 'Chewton Joy' | CTri EACa ECho LLHF LRHS |
| | - dwarf | EACa |
| | - 'Karpatenkrone' | EACa EBee NBre NDov |
| | - 'Kathy' | EPot |
| | - 'Silberschale' | NBre |
| | - 'Suzie' | CSpr IPot |
| | - var. ***turbinata*** | ECho SRms WAbe |
| | - - 'Foerster' | EACa ECho IPot LRHS XLum |
| | - - 'Isabel' | EACa ECho LLHF LRHS |
| | - - 'Jewel' | EACa ECho LHop LRHS |
| | - White Clips | see *C. carpatica* f. *alba* 'Weisse Clips' |
| § | ***cashmeriana*** | NWCA |
| | - 'Blue Cloud' | CWib |
| | ***cenisia*** | WFar |
| | ***cephallenica*** | see *C. garganica* subsp. *cephallenica* |
| | ***cervicaria*** | WAbe |
| | ***cespitosa*** | WAbe |
| § | ***chamissonis*** | ECho GEdr LLHF WPat |
| | - 'Alba' | GEdr |
| | - 'Major' | CYeo EWes GKev LBee |
| | - 'Oyobeni' | EACa |
| § | - 'Superba' ♀[H4] | ECho ELan GLam NMen NRya WAbe |
| | ***choruhensis*** | EPot |
| § | ***cochlearifolia*** ♀[H4] | CEnt CSpe CTri EBee ECho EDAr EPfP GJos GMaP LRHS MAsh MMuc SBch SBfd SPoG STre SVic WFar WHoo XLum |
| | - var. ***alba*** | CSpe CTri EDAr GLam GMaP MHer MMuc NBlu NMen NRya NWCA SBch SRms WHoo WPer XLum |
| | - - 'Bavaria White' | ECho WFar |
| | - - double white-flowered (d) | WPat |
| | - - 'White Baby' (Baby Series) | CYeo ECho ECtt ELon EPfP GAbr GGar GJos LRHS NHol NWCA SPet SPoG |
| | - 'Annie Hall' | ECho |
| | - 'Bavaria Blue' | ECho ELon GJos NHol NWCA SPet |
| | - 'Blue Baby' (Baby Series) | CSpr ECho ECtt EPfP GGar GJos LRHS MHer SPoG SRms SRot |
| | - 'Blue Wonder' | ITim |
| | - 'Cambridge Blue' | EACa WFar |
| | - 'Elizabeth Oliver' (d) | CFir CTri ECho ECtt EDAr EPot GCal GMaP LHop LRHS MAsh MHer NWCA SPlb SRms WAbe WFar WHil WHoo WPat |
| | - 'Miss Willmott' | NBir |
| | - 'Oakington Blue' | LLHF WAbe |
| | - var. ***pallida*** 'Silver Chimes' | ECho |
| | - 'R.B. Loder' (d) | LRHS |
| | - 'Tubby' | ECho EPot GJos LLHF MHer SRms |
| | - 'Warleyensis' | see *C.* × *haylodgensis* W. Brockbank 'Warley White' |
| | ***collina*** | CTri EACa LLHF |
| | 'Covadonga' | CMea EACa ECho LHop LLHF LRHS SBch WAbe |
| | ***cretica*** | NBPC |
| | 'Crystal' | ECtt MAvo MNrw MSpe SUsu |
| | ***dasyantha*** | see *C. chamissonis* |
| | ***dolomitica*** | EACa GKev LLHF NMen |
| | 'E.K. Toogood' | CElw CFir CPBP EACa ECho ECtt GJos NVic SRms XLum |
| | ***elatines*** | LRHS |
| | ***ephesia*** | GKev |
| | - SDR 1111 | GKev |
| | ***eriocarpa*** | see *C. latifolia* 'Eriocarpa' |
| | 'Faichem Lilac' | GCra LLHF LRHS NPro STes WCot |
| | ***fenestrellata*** | EACa NMen SRms WAbe WFar |
| | ***finitima*** | see *C. betulifolia* |
| | ***foliosa*** | EACa WPer |
| | ***formanekiana*** ♀[H2-3] | GLam |
| | ***fragilis*** | ECho IFoB WPat |
| | - 'Hirsuta' | ECho |
| | ***garganica*** ♀[H4] | EACa ECho EPfP GGar GKev GMaP LAst LRHS MAsh MDKP MMuc MRav NBlu NEgg SBfd SEND SPet SWvt WFar WMoo XLum |
| | - 'Aurea' | see *C. garganica* 'Dickson's Gold' |
| | - 'Backhouse' **new** | LRHS |
| | - 'Blue Diamond' | ECho IVic LHop MAsh WAbe WFar |
| § | - subsp. ***cephallenica*** | CElw EACa NBro |
| § | - 'Dickson's Gold' | Widely available |
| | - 'Erinus Major' | EACa IVic XLum |
| | - 'Hirsuta' | ECho |
| | - 'Major' | ECho LAst SPoG WFar |
| | - 'Mrs Resholt' | ECtt ESwi EWll LAst NBlu SDix SWvt WFar WGor |
| | - 'W.H. Paine' ♀[H4] | ECho ECtt EPot IFoB IGor MDKP NMen WAbe WFar WHoo |
| | 'Glandore' | XLum |
| | ***glomerata*** | CBot CElw CEnt CPLG CRWN EWil GJos LSRN MNHC NBro NLan NMir SPet WBrk WFar XSen |
| | - var. ***acaulis*** | EACa EBee EPfP NLar NWCA SBfd SPet WFar WPer XLum |
| * | - - f. ***alba*** **new** | GLam |
| | - var. ***alba*** | CBcs CFir EACa EAEE EBee ECtt ELan EPfP EShb GJos GMaP LBMP LRHS MLHP MRav NBPC SBfd SMrm SPer SPlb SPoG STes SWat WCAu WFar WMnd WPer WWEG XLum |
| § | - - 'Schneekrone' | ECha NBre SMrm WFar |
| | - 'Caroline' | Widely available |
| | - Crown of Snow | see *C. glomerata* var. *alba* 'Schneekrone' |
| | - var. ***dahurica*** | CFir ELon LRHS NBre NLar SMrm SPet WPer WRHF |
| | - 'Emerald' | EBee ECtt LRHS MHer WHlf |
| | - 'Joan Elliott' | CMac EBee ECGP ECha ECtt EShb LEdu LSRN MNFA MRav MWat WAul WCra |
| | - 'Purple Pixie' | LRHS |
| | - 'Superba' ♀[H4] | Widely available |
| | ***grossekii*** | CFir LLHF LRHS WHrl WTcb |
| | ***hakkiarica*** | WCot |
| | 'Hannah' | EACa ECho LHop LRHS |
| | × ***haylodgensis*** misapplied | see *C.* × *haylodgensis* 'Plena' |
| § | × ***haylodgensis*** W. Brockbank 'Marion Fisher' (d) | ECtt EDAr EPot WAbe WCot WHoo |
| § | - 'Plena' (d) | ECho ECtt ELan EPot LBee LHop LRHS NMen NPri SRms WAbe WCot WFar WHoo WKif |

| |  |  |
|---|---|---|
| § | – 'Warley White' (d) | EACa ECho ELan XLum |
| | – 'Yvonne' | CMea ECtt GMaP LHop WFar WNew |
| | 'Hemswell Starlight' | WAbe |
| | ***hercegovina*** 'Nana' | EACa LLHF NMen WAbe |
| | 'Hilltop Snow' | CPBP NMen WAbe |
| | ***hofmannii*** | EBee EDAr ELan GGar GKev MBNS NLar WFar |
| § | ***incurva*** | CSpe EACa ELan EWld GJos GKev WMoo |
| | – 'Alba' | GKev |
| | ***isophylla*** ♀H2 | ECho |
| | – 'Alba' ♀H2 | ECho |
| | – Starina Bicolor Star = 'Camp Bulewhit'PBR **new** | LRHS |
| | Jenny = 'Harjen' | CWGN EPPr SHar |
| | 'Joe Elliott' ♀H2-3 | ECho WAbe |
| | ***kemulariae*** | LLHF |
| | – 'Alba' | ITim |
| | 'Kent Belle' ♀H4 | Widely available |
| | ***khasiana*** | GKev |
| | ***lactiflora*** | CAby CElw CMac EBee ECha EPfP GAbr GCra GMaP IFoB LRHS MCot MLHP MSCN MWhi NEgg NVic SPer WFar WHoo WMoo WPer WWEG XLum |
| | – ***alba*** | see *C. lactiflora* white-flowered |
| N | – 'Alba' ♀H4 | EBee EPfP EWTr GMaP IVic MDKP MLHP STes WFar WMnd |
| | – 'Avalanche' | EACa ECtt NCGa WCot |
| | – 'Blue Cross' | EBee GMac LEdu LRHS NLar |
| | – 'Blue Lady' | WFar |
| | – 'Dixter Presence' | IPot NDov SUsu |
| | – dwarf pink-flowered | EACa EBee EPfP MBNS NBre |
| | – 'Favourite' | CFir CSpe EBee ECtt MNrw NBPC NCGa NGdn NLar WFar |
| | – 'Loddon Anna' ♀H4 | Widely available |
| | – 'Moorland Rose' | WMoo |
| | – hybrids | GJos |
| | – 'Pouffe' | CHid CPrp EACa EAEE EBee EBla ECtt ELan ELon EPfP GMaP IVic LRHS MDKP MRav NBro NGdn NLar SPer SWat SWvt WFar |
| | – 'Prichard's Variety' ♀H4 | Widely available |
| | – 'Superba' ♀H4 | ECtt IVic |
| | – 'Violet' | SWat WPer |
| | – 'White Pouffe' | CPrp EACa EAEE EBee ECtt ELan ELon EPfP GMaP IVic LRHS LSRN MDKP NBPC NLar SPer SPoG STes SWat WFar |
| § | – white-flowered | CBot ECha MBNS NBir SPer SWat WFar WPer |
| | ***lasiocarpa*** | CPBP |
| | ***latifolia*** | ECha GJos MCot MLLN NBid NOrc NVic SPer SRms WCot WFar WMoo |
| | – var. ***alba*** | EBee ELan EPfP GCra GJos LRHS MMuc MWea NGdn SEND SPav SPer SRms WFar WHal WPer WWEG |
| * | – 'Amethyst' | CPrp |
| | – 'Brantwood' | GAbr LRHS MRav MWhi SPav SRms SWat WCot WMnd |
| § | – 'Eriocarpa' | LRHS |
| | – 'Gloaming' | ECtt LRHS MCot NPnk |
| | – var. ***macrantha*** | EBee ELan ELon EPfP GMaP IPot LHop MBri MCot MWat NGdn NSti SBfd SPav SPer SWat SWvt WMoo WPer WWEG |
| | – – 'Alba' | CMMP EBee ECha ECtt GMaP LHop MCot MRav SBfd WCot WMoo WPer WWEG |
| | – 'Misty Dawn' | WCot WFar |
| | ***latiloba*** | CElw CMHG MWhi SBch SGar SSvw WBrk WCot WFar WKif |
| § | – 'Alba' ♀H4 | CElw EBee ELan EPPr GCal GCra MCot MDKP NEgg NGdn NLar SBch SGar WBrk |
| | – 'Hidcote Amethyst' ♀H4 | COIW CSpe CWGN EBee ECtt ELan ELon EPfP EWII GAbr GCal LRHS MCot MRav MSpe MWhi NBid NBir NCGa NDov NGdn NLar SGar WCot WFar WKif WMnd WWEG |
| | – 'Highcliffe Variety' ♀H4 | CPrp EBee ECtt ELan EPfP EShb GCra LRHS MDKP MRav NCGa NDov NLar SMrm SPoG WCot WKif WMnd WWEG |
| * | – 'Highdown' | WFar |
| | – 'Percy Piper' ♀H4 | EACa ECtt ELan LRHS MRav NBre NBro NLar WFar |
| | – 'Splash' | MAvo |
| | 'Linda' **new** | LSRN |
| | ***linifolia*** | see *C. carnica* |
| | 'Lynchmere' | CPBP WAbe |
| | ***makaschvilii*** | CEnt CSpe EACa EBee GKev GMac MHer MWhi SMad SMrm STes WCot WHrl WPer WSHC |
| | 'Marion Fisher' | see *C.* × *baylodgensis* W. Brockbank 'Marion Fisher' |
| | ***medium*** | LAst NBlu SBrd |
| § | – var. ***calycanthema*** hort. | EPfP |
| | – 'Cup and Saucer' | see *C. medium* var. *calycanthema* hort. |
| | 'Mevr. V. Vollenhove' **new** | WCot |
| | ***mirabilis*** 'Mist Maiden' | WFar |
| | ***moesiaca*** | LRHS |
| | 'Monic' | EPfP NBlu |
| | ***muralis*** | see *C. portenschlagiana* |
| | ***nitida*** | see *C. persicifolia* var. *planiflora* |
| | 'Norman Grove' | EPot |
| | ***ochroleuca*** | CMea CPom CSpe EBee SWat WCAu WCFE WCot WHrl |
| | – 'White Beauty' | CWib |
| | – 'White Bells' | MWhi |
| | ***odontosepala*** | EBee |
| | – from Iran | EPPr NLar |
| | 'Oliver's Choice' | WHrl |
| | ***olympica*** misapplied | see *C. rotundifolia* 'Olympica' |
| | ***orphanidea*** | WAbe |
| | ***ossetica*** | EBee ECtt MLHP |
| | ***pallida*** subsp. ***tibetica*** | see *C. cashmeriana* |
| | ***patula*** | GJos NLar WKif XLum |
| § | – subsp. ***abietina*** | NBre NLar |
| | 'Paul Furse' | EBee ECtt MDKP NBre NCGa NPro NSti WTin WWEG |
| | ***pelviformis*** | MNrw |
| | ***pendula*** | EPfP EWes MBNS NBlu NLar WCAu |
| | ***persicifolia*** | Widely available |
| | – var. ***alba*** | Widely available |
| § | – 'Alba Coronata' (d) | GAbr NBir WFar |
| | – 'Alba Plena' | see *C. persicifolia* 'Alba Coronata' |
| | – Ashfield double ice blue (d) | NBre |
| | – 'Azure Beauty' | CSpe EBee ECtt ELan EPPr EWTr NCGa WCot |
| | – 'Beau Belle' | EBee EPfP LSou NBPC NLar |
| § | – 'Bennett's Blue' (d) | EBla ELan EPfP MRav SPer SRms SWat WFar |
| | – 'Best China' (d) | MAvo |
| | – 'Blue Bloomers' (d) | CElw CHar CLAP EBee ECtt EPri EWes GGar GMac IKil LRHS MAvo MLLN MNFA MRav SMrm WBrk WCot WHal WPer XLum |

- blue cup-in-cup (d) — EBla ELon MDKP MTis WFar WPtf
- 'Blue-eyed Blonde' (v) — ECtt
- blue-flowered — IFoB LAst MRav SPlb WFar
- 'Boule de Neige' (d) — CMMP ECtt WCFE WWEG
- 'Caerulea Coronata' — see *C. persicifolia* 'Coronata'

§ - 'Chettle Charm' PBR 𝕐H4 — Widely available
- 'Cornish Mist' — CDes CFir CPLG EBee ECtt ELan EPfP LSou MAvo MCot MTis WCot

§ - 'Coronata' (d) — GCra LRHS
- cup and saucer blue (d) — GCra

§ - cup and saucer white (d) — ELan WFar
- double blue-flowered (d) — NBro
- double white-flowered (d) — ELan
- 'Fleur de Neige' (d) 𝕐H4 — ECtt NBre WCot WHoo WWEG
- 'Frances' (d) — CLAP WCot
- 'Gawen' — EBee ECtt GBee GMaP MAvo MTis NBre NDov SMrm WCot
- 'George Chiswell' PBR — see *C. persicifolia* 'Chettle Charm'
- 'Grandiflora' — NBre SMrm
- 'Grandiflora Alba' — NBre NLar XLum
- 'Grandiflora Caerulea' — NLar

§ - 'Hampstead White' (d) — EWhm GCal NBro WHil WMnd WWEG
- 'Hetty' — see *C. persicifolia* 'Hampstead White'
- 'Kelly's Gold' — CFir ELon EPfP LAst LRHS MCCP MTis NBir NLar NPri WBor WWEG
- 'La Belle' — CWGN EBee ECtt EPyc LSou NLar
- 'La Bello' PBR — CWGN EBee ECtt
- 'La Bonne Amie' — CDes ECtt IKil IPot NLar
- 'Moerheimii' (d) — EPfP EShb NBir
- 'Perry's Boy Blue' — NPer

§ - var. ***planiflora*** — CPBP WThu
- - f. ***alba*** — GLam MWat
- 'Powder Puff' (d) — EBee GBin ITim LSou MLLN NEgg SMrm WCot
- 'Pride of Exmouth' (d) — CHar CMMP ECtt ELan EShb MCCP MHer MWea WCFE WMnd WPer WWEG
- subsp. ***sessiliflora*** 'Alba' — see *C. latiloba* 'Alba'
- 'Snowdrift' — ELan SRms
- Takion Series — CSpe
- - 'Takion Blue' — LRHS MSCN
- - 'Takion White' — LRHS
- 'Telham Beauty' ambig. — EAEE LAst LRHS MCot MSCN NEgg NGBl SBfd SWvt WWEG XLum
- 'Telham Beauty' misapplied — CSBt CWCL EBee ECtt ELan EPfP EShb LRHS MRav SMrm SPer SRms SWvt WFar WMnd WPer
- 'Telham Beauty' D.Thurston — NLar
- 'Tinpenny Blue' — WTin
- 'White Cup and Saucer' — see *C. persicifolia* cup and saucer white
- 'White Queen' (d) — WMnd
- 'Wortham Belle' misapplied — see *C. persicifolia* 'Bennett's Blue'
- 'Wortham Belle' ambig. — CWGN
- 'Wortham Belle' Bloom — ECtt LRHS MBNS MCot NDov NEgg WFar WGwG

***petrophila*** — WAbe
***pilosa*** — see *C. chamissonis*
- 'Superba' — see *C. chamissonis* 'Superba'

'Pink Octopus' PBR — CSev CWGN EBee ECtt IPot LLHF LRHS MBNS MCot MLLN MTis NBPC NCGa NGdn NLar NPnk WCot WCra

***planiflora*** — see *C. persicifolia* var. *planiflora*

§ ***portenschlagiana*** 𝕐H4 — Widely available
- 'Biokovo' **new** — XLum
- 'Catharina' — ECtt
- 'Lieselotte' — CElw CPBP LIMB LLHF
- 'Major' — LAst WFar WMoo
- 'Resholdt's Variety' — CBar CMea CSam EBee ECho ECtt EDAr EPfP EPot GMaP LHop LRHS MMuc MRav NPri SMrm WMoo WPer XLum

***poscharskyana*** — Widely available
- 'Blauranke' — EACa EBee EWes
- 'Blue Gown' — EACa GMaP GMac IPot MNFA
- 'Blue Rivulet' PBR **new** — LRHS
- 'Blue Waterfall' — CWCL CWGN EACa LRHS MBNS NCGa NDov SPoG WCot WFar
- 'E.H. Frost' — CBre CElw EACa EBee ECho ECtt EDAr EPPr EPfP GMaP LHop MAsh MBri MCot MMuc MWat NBro NRya SAga SEND SRGP SRms SWvt WBrk WFar WMoo WPer XLum
- 'Freya' **new** — XLum
- 'Lilacina' — EPPr
- 'Lisduggan Variety' — CElw EACa EBee ECtt EDAr EPPr EWes GMaP LHop LIMB MAsh MBri MHer MNFA NBro SBch WCot WFar WMoo WPer XLum
- 'Nana Alba' — EACa EPPr
- 'Pinkins' **new** — EACa
- 'Stella' 𝕐H4 — EBee ECha ECho ECtt EPPr EPfP LRHS LSRN MAsh MAvo MRav NBro NDov SDix SPer SRGP SWvt WFar WMoo WRHF XLum
- 'Trollkind' — EPPr
- variegated (v) — EHoe
- white-flowered — CTri ECho ELan MDKP WFar

***prenanthoides*** — see *Asyneuma prenanthoides*
***primulifolia*** — ELan GAbr LRHS MNrw SRms SWat WMoo XLum
- 'Blue Oasis' — LSRN

× ***pseudoraineri*** — EACa EWes LRHS NMen
***pulla*** — CMea CPBP CSpe CWCL EACa ECho ECtt EDAr GGar GMaP IFro LRHS MAsh NSla NWCA SPoG SRot WAbe WFar WHoo
- 'Alba' — EACa ECho ECtt EDAr EPot GLam LRHS MAsh WAbe

× ***pulloides*** — EACa EBee ECho ECtt EPot SRkn
- 'G.F. Wilson' 𝕐H4 — WFar
- 'Jelly Bells' **new** — IPot

***punctata*** — CBot CMHG CSpe EBee GJos GKev LEdu LRHS MCot NBPC NBro NSti SBfd SPer SWat WFar WGwG WMoo WPer
- f. ***albiflora*** — GKev MNrw WFar WMnd
- - 'Alba' — CCVN
- 'Alina's Double' (d) — GBee GMac MLLN MNrw MSpe WCot WWEG
- 'Cherry Pie' — EPfP LRHS MMuc
- dwarf — CPBP
- 'Einhorn JP' — IVic
- 'Golddrache JP' — IVic
- 'Hexe JP' — IVic
- var. ***hondoensis*** — GKev LRHS MLHP SAga
- - 'Bossy Boots' — SMrm
- hose-in-hose (d) — MMHG NLar WFar WGwG
- 'Hot Lips' — CChe CMMP EBee EBla ELan EPPr EPfP EShb LRHS LSRN NBPC NPnk NPro SAga SBfd SPet SPoG SRGP WWEG

* - var. ***howozana*** — GKev
- var. ***microdonta*** B&SWJ 5553 — WCru

| |  |  |
|---|---|---|
| | - 'Milky Way' | EPPr |
| | - 'Millennium' | WFar |
| | - 'Milly' | IVic LLHF |
| | - 'Moorgeist JP' | IVic |
| * | - 'Nana' | CCVN |
| | - 'Nasachtal' | IVic |
| | - 'Pantaloons' (d) | CMac EBee EBla ECtt EDif EWTr LRHS LSRN MDKP SMrm |
| | - 'Pink Chimes'[PBR] | GKev IVic LSou MBNS MTis |
| | - 'Plum Wine' | MSpe |
| | - 'Pumpernickel JP' | IVic |
| | - 'Reifrock' | IVic SMrm |
| | - 'Rosea' | SRms WFar |
| | - f. ***rubriflora*** | CCVN ECtt ELan EPfP EPla GAbr GCra GJos LBMP LHop LRHS MCot MNrw MWat MWhi NEgg NOrc SBfd SGar SMrm SPer WFar WMnd WPat WPer WTcb WWEG XLum |
| | - - 'Beetroot' | ECtt IKil ITim IVic LAst MHer MTis NLar WHrl WPer |
| | - - 'Bowl of Cherries'[PBR] | EACa ECtt EPPr EPfP ESwi IVic LLHF LRHS LSRN LSou MMHG MTis NBPC NLar NPnk SRkn SRot |
| | - - 'Cherry Bells' | EBla ECtt EPfP GMac IVic LSRN MNrw NLar SPet SPoG |
| | - - 'Vienna Festival' | CSBt GKev LEdu LSou NLar WCot |
| | - - 'Wine 'n' Rubies' | ECtt GMac LSRN LSou MDKP MNrw MSCN WCot |
| | - 'Seejungfrau JP' | IVic |
| | - 'Troll JP' | IVic |
| | - 'Twilight Bells' | NBre |
| | - 'Wedding Bells' | CMMP ECtt ELan EPri GKev IVic LAst LRHS LSRN MHer MSCN MTis NBPC NCGa NLar NSti SPet SPoG SRkn WCAu WFar WHil WWEG |
| | - 'Weisser Schwan JP' | IVic |
| | - 'Weisser Turm JP' | IVic |
| I | - 'White Bells' | ELan EPPr MDKP |
| | - white hose-in-hose (d) | MNrw WBrk |
| | 'Purple Sensation'[PBR] | EACa EBee ECtt EPfP GMac ITim LSou MDev MLLN MNrw NCGa NPnk NSti WCot |
| | ***pusilla*** | see *C. cochlearifolia* |
| | ***pyramidalis*** | CBot CSpe EBee ELan EPfP GJos LRHS MCCP NGBl NOrc SBfd SPav SPlb WTcb WTou WWEG XLum |
| | - 'Alba' | CSpe CWib EBee ELan EPfP GJos LRHS NLar SBfd SPav SPlb WWEG XLum |
| | - lavender blue-flowered | CWib |
| | ***raddeana*** | EACa MDKP WBrk |
| | ***raineri*** ♀[H4] | ECho EPot NMen NSla WAbe |
| * | - 'Alba' | ECho NMen WAbe |
| | - 'Nettleton Gold' | ECho EPot LRHS |
| § | ***rapunculoides*** | EBee GJos GKev NBre SWat WCFE WFar XLum |
| § | - 'Afterglow' | EBee MAvo WCot WDyG |
| | - 'Alba' | EACa MAvo XLum |
| | ***rapunculus*** | CArn ILis WCot XLum |
| | ***recurva*** | see *C. incurva* |
| | ***rhomboidalis*** Gorter | see *C. rapunculoides* |
| | ***rhomboidalis*** L. | XLum |
| | ***rigidipila*** | WHer |
| | ***rotundifolia*** | CArn CRWN EACa ECho EPfP EWil GJos MCot MHer MNHC NBre NGBl NLan SIde SPlb SWat WAbe WBrk WPer XLum |
| | - SDR 5476 | GKev |
| § | - var. ***alaskana*** | LRHS |
| | - var. ***alba*** | EWes WAbe |
| § | - 'Olympica' | IGor MMuc NLar STre WFar WHoo |
| | - 'Superba' | ECho |
| | - 'White Gem' | EBee EPfP GJos LBMP LRHS NBre WPtf |
| | 'Royal Wave' | ECtt IPot WCot |
| | ***rupestris*** | LLHF WPat |
| | ***rupicola*** | WAbe |
| | 'Samantha' | CSpe ECtt GMac LHop LRHS LSRN SMrm SRGP |
| | ***samarkandensis*** | GKev |
| | 'Sarastro' | Widely available |
| | ***sarmatica*** | ECGP EPfP EWTr GAbr GKev GLam LRHS MNFA MWhi NBid SMrm SRms WKif |
| | - 'Hemelstraling' | EBee NLar |
| | ***scabrella*** | GKev |
| | 'Senior' | EPPr IVic SHar |
| | 'Serafinental' | IVic |
| | ***speciosa*** | MWhi NBre |
| | 'Stansfieldii' | CPBP ECho LLHF LRHS NMen WPat |
| | 'Summer Pearl' | CPBP ECtt EWll GKev SBfd SMrm |
| | 'Summertime Blues' **new** | NLar |
| | 'Swannables' | CPou EBee ECtt LLHF MNFA MRav NCGa NChi WOut |
| | ***takesimana*** | Widely available |
| | - B&SWJ 8499 | WCru |
| I | - 'Alba' | CSpr LBMP MDKP NBre WMoo |
| | - 'Beautiful Trust' | CCVN CFir CLAP EBee GBee GMac LHop MCot NBPC NPnk SRkn SUsu WCru |
| | - 'Elizabeth' | Widely available |
| | - 'Elizabeth II' (d) | ECtt MDKP WCot |
| | ***teucrioides*** | NWCA |
| | ***thyrsoides*** | ELan SPav WAbe |
| | 'Timsbury Perfection' | EPot NHar WAbe |
| | 'Tiny Bells' | LLHF |
| | ***tommasiniana*** ♀[H4] | WAbe |
| | ***trachelium*** | CEnt CMHG CMea EBee ELon EWil GJos LRHS MRav NBPC NLan NMir SGar SWat WCot WFar WHer WMoo WOut WPer WWEG |
| | - var. ***alba*** | CLAP GKev LRHS MNrw MWhi NLar STes SWat WCot WFar WMoo WPer |
| | - - 'Alba Flore Pleno' (d) | CHar CLAP LEdu STes WFar |
| | - 'Bernice' (d) | Widely available |
| | - lilac-blue-flowered | SWat |
| | - 'Snowball' | EShb LSRN |
| | 'Tymonsii' | CPBP ECho LLHF NBir NMen WAbe WFar |
| | 'Van-Houttei' | CDes CHar EWes GMac SAga WCot WFar WPer |
| | ***versicolor*** | NBre WAbe |
| | ***vidalii*** | see *Azorina vidalii* |
| | 'Viking' **new** | WHil |
| | ***waldsteiniana*** | CPBP WAbe |
| | ***wanneri*** | EBee EPfP NLar |
| | 'Warley White' | see *C.* × *haylodgensis* W. Brockbank 'Warley White' |
| | 'Warleyensis' | see *C.* × *haylodgensis* W. Brockbank 'Warley White' |
| | × ***wockei*** 'Puck' | EACa ECho ECtt EPot LHop LLHF LRHS WAbe |
| | ***zangezura*** | EBee EDAr EPfP GKev IKil NGdn SBfd STes |
| | ***zoysii*** | NMen |

## *Campanula* × *Symphyandra* see *Campanula*

## *Campanumoea* see *Codonopsis*

## *Campsis* (*Bignoniaceae*)

| | | |
|---|---|---|
| | ***grandiflora*** | CArn CBcs CSBt CSPN CWGN EBee ELan EPfP LRHS LSRN SPer SRms SWvt WCFE |
| | ***radicans*** | CArn CBcs CDul CMac CRHN CWib EBee ECrN ELan EPfP LRHS LSRN MCot MSwo NBlu SBfd SLon SPer SPlb STre WDin |
| | - 'Flamenco' | CDoC CMac EBee ELan LRHS LSRN MAsh NLar SAdn SBfd SBrd SCoo SLim SVen SWvt WFar WGwG |
| § | - f. ***flava*** ♀H4 | CBcs CDoC CHEx CMac CTri EBee ELan ELon EPfP LHop LRHS MAsh MBlu MCCP MGos NLar NPal NPla NSti SBfd SBrd SLim SPer SPoG SWvt WSHC |
| | - 'Indian Summer' | CBcs CSBt CWGN EBee EPfP LRHS LSRN LSou MBlu MBri MGos MREP NLar SBfd SCoo SLim SPoG WHar |
| | - 'Stromboli' | EPfP |
| | - 'Yellow Trumpet' | see *C. radicans* f. *flava* |
| | × ***tagliabuana*** Dancing Flame = 'Huidan'PBR | CWGN EBee LRHS SGol |
| | - 'Madame Galen' ♀H4 | Widely available |

## *Camptosema* (*Papilionaceae*)

| | | |
|---|---|---|
| | ***praeandinum*** | WPGP |

## *Camptosorus* see *Asplenium*

## *Camptotheca* (*Nyssaceae*)

| | | |
|---|---|---|
| | ***acuminata*** | WPGP |

## *Campylandra* see *Tupistra*

## *Campylotropis* (*Papilionaceae*)

| | | |
|---|---|---|
| | ***macrocarpa*** | EPfP NLar WCot |

## *Canarina* (*Campanulaceae*)

| | | |
|---|---|---|
| | ***canariensis*** ♀H1 | CCCN ECho MOWG WPGP |

## *Candollea* see *Hibbertia*

## *Canna* ✿ (*Cannaceae*)

| | | |
|---|---|---|
| | 'Adam's Orange' | CDTJ CHEx XBlo |
| | 'Alaska' ♀H3 | EAmu |
| N | ***altensteinii*** | CDTJ SPlb XBlo |
| | 'Ambassador' | LAma |
| | 'Ambassadour' | SBfd |
| | 'Annaeei' ♀H3 | EAmu |
| | 'Annaeei-Rubra' **new** | SBfd |
| | 'Argentina' | SBfd |
| | 'Assaut' | SBfd |
| | 'Atlantis' | XBlo |
| | 'Australia' | CDTJ EAmu EPfP SBfd WCot XBlo |
| | 'Austria' | SBfd |
| | 'Bethany' **new** | SBfd |
| | 'Black Knight' | CFir ECGP LAma LRHS LSRN SBfd SEND SPad XBlo |
| | 'Bonfire' | CDTJ CHEx |
| | ***brasiliensis*** | CFee CFir CHll CRHN SBfd WTcb XBlo |
| | 'Brillant' | LAma SBfd SBst WDyG |
| | 'Canary' | XBlo |
| | 'Centurion' | LAma |
| | 'Chinese Coral' Schmid | CHEx LAma |
| I | 'Citrina' | XBlo |
| § | 'City of Portland' | LAma |
| § | 'Cleopatra' | CCCN EAmu LAma SBfd XBlo |
| * | 'Cléopâtre' | NGdn |
| § | 'Colibri' | LAma |
| | 'Confetti' | see *C.* 'Colibri' |
| | 'Corsica' (Island Series) | SBfd |
| | 'Creamy White' | CHEx XBlo |
| | 'Crimson Beauty' | LAma |
| | 'Délibáb' | LAma WDyG |
| | 'Di Bartolo' | XBlo |
| | 'Durban' ambig. | CChe CWGN EBee ECtt EPfP LAma LAst LSRN MAvo MCCP |
| | 'Durban' Hiley, orange-flowered | see *C.* 'Phasion' |
| N | ***edulis*** | CDTJ CHEx SBfd |
| | - purple-leaved | SBfd |
| § | × ***ehemanii*** ♀H3 | CAvo CDTJ CRHN ETod LPJP SBfd SDix WPGP |
| | 'En Avant' | CHEx LAma SPlb |
| | 'Endeavour' | CHEx LPJP MSKA |
| | 'Erebus' ♀H3 | CHVG MSKA SBfd SDix |
| | 'Ermine' | WCot |
| | 'Espresso Festival' | NGdn |
| | 'Étoile du Feu' | XBlo |
| | 'Eureka' | SBfd |
| | 'Evening Star' | LAma |
| | 'Fatamorgana' | LAma |
| | 'Felix Ragout' | LAma |
| | Firebird | see *C.* 'Oiseau de Feu' |
| | 'Flame' | XBlo |
| § | 'Florence Vaughan' | SBfd |
| | 'General Eisenhower' ♀H3 | EAmu SBfd |
| | ***glauca*** | SDix |
| | 'Gnom' | SBfd |
| * | 'Gold Ader' | LAma |
| | 'Gold Dream' | LAma |
| | 'Golden Girl' | SBfd |
| | 'Golden Lucifer' | ELan LAma |
| | 'Gran Canaria' | SBfd |
| | 'Grande' | CFir MAJR SBfd |
| | 'Heinrich Seidel' | CHEx CHll SBfd |
| | Henlade hybrids | CDTJ SBfd |
| | 'Hercule' | CHEx |
| | hybrids | ELan |
| | 'Ibis' | EAmu EPfP |
| | ***indica*** | CAbb CDTJ EShb LTen SArc SBfd SGar SPlb |
| | - 'Kreta' (Island Series) | SBfd |
| | - 'Purpurea' | CDTJ CHEx EAmu SBfd SChr SDix SMrm SPlb WDyG WPGP |
| | - 'Red King Rupert' | CCCN |
| | - Tropicanna Gold = 'Mactro'PBR | CCCN EPfP SBfd SPoG |
| | 'Ingeborg' ♀H3 | LAma |
| | 'Intrigue' | SBfd |
| | ***iridiflora*** misapplied | see *C.* × ***ehemanii*** |
| | ***iridiflora*** Ruiz & Pav. | CDTJ CHEx CSpe SArc |
| | 'Italia' | SBfd |
| | ***jacobiniflora*** | SBfd |
| | 'Kalimpong' | CDTJ SBfd |
| I | 'King Humbert' (blood-red) | CBcs CDTJ CHEx EPfP LAma SBfd XBlo |
| | King Humbert (orange-red) | see *C.* 'Roi Humbert' |
| | 'King Midas' | see *C.* 'Richard Wallace' |
| | 'Königin Charlotte' | SBfd |
| | 'La Bohème' (Grand Opera Series) | LAma |
| | 'La France' | SBfd |
| | 'Lesotho Lil' | CHll SBfd |
| | 'Liberté' | see *C.* 'Wyoming' |
| | 'Louis Cayeux' ♀H3 | SBrd SDix |

| | | |
|---|---|---|
| | 'Louis Cottin' | CBcs CCCN CDTJ CHEx EPfP LAma LAst |
| | 'Lucifer' | CCCN CHEx LAma LAst NEgg NPer SPad SPlb |
| N | ***lutea*** | CHEx XBlo |
| | 'Madame Angèle Martin' | XBlo |
| | 'Madeira' (Island Series) | SBfd |
| | 'Malawiensis Variegata' | see *C.* 'Striata' |
| | 'Marabout' | SBfd SBst |
| | 'Marvel' | LAma |
| | 'Maudie Malcolm' | EPfP |
| | 'Moonshine' **new** | CCCN |
| | 'Mrs Oklahoma' | LAma SBfd |
| | 'Musifolia' ♀H3 | CDTJ CHEx EAmu ETod EWes LPJP SBfd SDix WDyG XBlo |
| | 'Mystique' ♀H3 | EWes SBfd SDix |
| | 'Ointment Pink' | XBlo |
| § | 'Oiseau de Feu' | LAma |
| | 'Orange Beauty' | SBfd |
| | 'Orange Perfection' | CFir CSam LAma SBfd SMrm |
| | 'Orange Punch' | EAmu WCot |
| | 'Orchid' | see *C.* 'City of Portland' |
| | 'Osric' | CSpe |
| | 'Panache' | CDTJ CHEx CRHN SBfd WCot WDyG |
| | 'Peach Pink' | XBlo |
| | 'Pearlescent Pink' | XBlo |
| | 'Perkeo' | LAma |
| § | 'Phasion' (v) ♀H3 | CCCN CHEx CHll CSpe ELan EPfP EWes LSRN MSCN NPer NPla NVic SBfd SBst SDix SEND SPoG WCot XBlo |
| | 'Picasso' ♀H3 | CBcs CCCN CDTJ CHEx CPLG LAma SBrd SEND XBlo |
| | 'Pink Champagne' | XBlo |
| | 'Pink Futurity' (Futurity Series) | CCCN SBfd |
| | 'Pink Sunburst' (v) | CDTJ NGdn SBfd SPlb |
| | 'Plaster Pink' | XBlo |
| | 'President' | LAma SBfd XBlo |
| | 'Pretoria' | see *C.* 'Striata' |
| | 'Prince Charmant' | SBfd |
| | 'Pringle Bay' (v) | SBfd |
| | 'Professor Lorentz' | see *C.* 'Wyoming' |
| | 'Ra' ♀H3 | MSKA |
| | 'Red Futurity' (Futurity Series) | SBfd |
| § | 'Richard Wallace' | CPLG LAma SBfd SPlb XBlo |
| § | 'Roi Humbert' | LAst SBfd |
| | 'Roi Soleil' ♀H3 | LAma |
| | 'Roitelet' | CHEx |
| | 'Roma' | SBfd |
| | 'Rose Futurity' (Futurity Series) | SBfd |
| | 'Rosemond Coles' | CHEx CSam LAma SBfd XBlo |
| | 'Sémaphore' | CSpe EAmu ECtt NGdn SBfd WCot XBlo |
| | 'Shenandoah' ♀H3 | SBfd |
| | 'Singapore Girl' | SBfd |
| | 'Snow-white' | XBlo |
| | 'Soudan' | CDTJ SBfd |
| N | ***speciosa*** | CDTJ XBlo |
| | 'Strasbourg' | CSam LAma NPer SBfd |
| | 'Strawberry Pink' | XBlo |
| | 'Striata' misapplied | see *C.* 'Stuttgart' |
| § | 'Striata' (v) ♀H3 | CCCN CDTJ CHEx CSpe CWGN EBee ECtt EPfP LPJP LSRN MCCP MREP NPla SBfd SEND SMad SPad WCot WDyG XBlo |
| | 'Striped Beauty' (v) | CCCN CDTJ CHVG SBfd |
| § | 'Stuttgart' (v) | CDTJ CSpe EAmu EWes SBfd WCot |
| | 'Südfunk' | SBfd |
| | 'Summer Gold' | XBlo |
| | 'Sunset' | CWGN NGdn WCot |
| | 'Talisman' | LAma SBrd XBlo |
| | 'Taney' | MSKA |
| | 'Tenerife' **new** | LAst |
| | 'Tirol' | SBfd |
| | 'Tricarinata' | CHEx |
| | (Tropical Series) 'Tropical Red' | SBfd |
| | - 'Tropical Rose' | SBfd SBrd SRms |
| | - 'Tropical Salmon' | SBfd |
| | - 'Tropical White' | SBfd |
| | - 'Tropical Yellow' | SBfd SBrd |
| | Tropicanna | see *C.* 'Phasion' |
| | ***tuerckheimii*** | SBfd |
| | 'Valentine' | WCot |
| | 'Vanilla Pink' | XBlo |
| * | 'Variegata' (v) | LAma LSou |
| | 'Verdi' ♀H3 | CSpe LAma SBfd |
| N | ***warscewiczii*** | CDTJ CPLG CRHN SBfd SBst |
| | 'Weymouth' | CDTJ |
| | 'Whithelm Pride' ♀H3 | SBfd |
| | 'Wintzer's Colossal' | SBfd |
| | 'Woodbridge Pink' | XBlo |
| § | 'Wyoming' ♀H3 | CBcs CCCN CDTJ CHEx CHVG ECGP ETod LAma MCCP NVic SBfd SBrd SBst SEND XBlo |
| | 'Yara' | SBfd |
| | 'Yellow Humbert' misapplied | see *C.* 'Richard Wallace', *C.* 'Cleopatra', *C.* 'Florence Vaughan' |
| | 'Yellow Humbert' | LAma |

## *Cannomois* (*Restionaceae*)

| | |
|---|---|
| ***virgata*** | CCtw |

## *Cantua* (*Polemoniaceae*)

| | |
|---|---|
| ***buxifolia*** ♀H2-3 | CAbb CBcs CCCN CFee CPLG EBee ECre LRHS MOWG WPGP |
| - 'Alba' | CCCN EShb |
| - 'Dancing Oaks' | WCot |

## Cape gooseberry see *Physalis peruviana*

## *Capnoides* see *Corydalis*

## *Capparis* (*Capparaceae*)

| | |
|---|---|
| ***spinosa*** | CCCN |
| - subsp. ***rupestris*** | SPlb |

## *Capsicum* (*Solanaceae*)

| | |
|---|---|
| ***annuum*** | CCCN |
| - var. ***annuum*** (Longham Group) cayenne | CCCN |
| - - (Longum Group) jalapeno | SVic |
| - - 'Prairie Fire' ♀H2 | CCCN |
| - 'Apache' ♀H2 | CCCN SEND |
| ***chinense*** Habanero Group ♀H2 | SVic |

## *Caragana* (*Papilionaceae*)

| | |
|---|---|
| CC 3945 | CPLG |
| ***arborescens*** | CAgr CMCN EBee EPfP NWea SEND SPer SPlb WDin |
| - 'Lorbergii' | CEnd MBlu SPer WFoF |
| - 'Pendula' | CMac CWib ELan ESwi LAst NEgg NLar SCoo SLim SPer WDin |
| - 'Walker' | CDul CEnd CMac CWib ELan EPfP MBlu MBri MGos NHol NLar NWea SCoo SLim SPer SPoG |

| | |
|---|---|
| ***franchetiana*** | EGFP |
| ***pygmaea*** | NLar |

## carambola see *Averrhoa carambola*

## caraway see *Carum carvi*

## *Cardamine* ✿ (*Brassicaceae*)

| | |
|---|---|
| ***angustata*** | WCru |
| ***asarifolia*** misapplied | see *Pachyphragma macrophyllum* |
| ***asarifolia*** L. | LRHS |
| ***bulbifera*** | CLAP EBee ELon EPPr GBin GEdr LEdu NRya WCru WSHC |
| ***californica*** | EBee EPPr NRya WCru WMoo |
| ***concatenata*** | WCru |
| ***digitata*** | EBee NCGa |
| ***diphylla*** | CDes CLAP LEdu NLar SKHP WCot WCru WFar |
| - 'American Sweetheart' | CPLG WCot |
| - 'Eco Cut Leaf' | CDes CPLG EBee WCot WCru WPGP |
| - 'Eco Moonlight' | WCru |
| ***enneaphylla*** | CLAP GMaP NDov NLar |
| ***glanduligera*** | EBee ECha ELon EPPr GEdr LEdu MMoz MNrw NSla WCot WCru WPGP WSHC |
| § ***heptaphylla*** | CAby CAvo CLAP ECha ELon IGor LRHS |
| - 'Big White' | GCal NCGa |
| - Guincho form | CLAP EPPr GBin WCot WPGP |
| - white-flowered | CLAP GMaP |
| § ***kitaibelii*** | CLAP GBin LEdu WCru |
| ***latifolia*** Vahl | see *C. raphanifolia* |
| ***macrophylla*** | CLAP EBee LEdu SWat WCot |
| - CD&R 561 | NCGa |
| - 'Bright and Bronzy' | CPLG GEdr WCru |
| ***maxima*** | LEdu WCru |
| ***microphylla*** | EBee WAbe |
| ***pentaphylla*** ♀H4 | CBro CSpe EBee ECho ELan ELon EPPr GEdr GGar IFro IGor LPla LRHS MCot NBir NLar WBor WCot |
| - bright pink-flowered | CLAP WCot |
| ***pratensis*** | CArn CRWN CWat EBee EHon EWil LRHS MCot MHer MNHC MSKA MWts NLan NMir NPri SIde SWat WFar WHer WMoo WSFF WShi |
| - 'Diane's Petticoat' | MHer MNrw WHoo |
| - 'Edith' (d) | CLAP GBin LRHS MMoz MNrw |
| - 'Flore Pleno' (d) | CAby CBre CFee CHVG CSpe EBee ECha ELan EPfP GMaP IFro MHer MNrw NBid NBir NBro NLar NPnk NPri NSla SBch SWat WCot WFar WSFF WSHC |
| - 'William' (d) | MNrw WMoo |
| ***quinquefolia*** | CDes CElw CLAP CMea CPom CSpe EBee ECha ELon LEdu MCot MMoz NCGa NDov NLar NMyG SDys SMrm SSvw WBrk WCot WCru WOut WPGP |
| § ***raphanifolia*** | CBre CDes CPLG CRow EBee ECha EPPr GAbr GBin GCal GGar IFro LEdu LLWG LRHS NBid NBro NLar NSti SKHP SWat WMoo WOut WPGP WTin |
| ***trifolia*** | CMac CSpe EBee ECha ELon EPPr GBin GCal GEdr GGar GMaP IFro LRHS MRav NBir NBro NLar NRya NVic SWat WCot WCru WFar WMoo |
| ***waldsteinii*** | CAby CDes CLAP CPLG CSpe EBee ECho GEdr LEdu NCGa SBch SCnR SUsu WCru WSHC WTcb |
| ***yezoensis*** B&SWJ 4659 | WCru |

## cardamon see *Elettaria cardamomum*

## *Cardiandra* (*Hydrangeaceae*)

| | |
|---|---|
| ***alternifolia*** | CLAP LLHF |
| - B&SWJ 5719 | WCru |
| - B&SWJ 5845 | WCru |
| - B&SWJ 6177 | WCru |
| - B&SWJ 6354 | WCru |
| - subsp. ***moellendorffii*** **new** | WPGP |
| - 'Pink Geisha' | WCru |
| ***amamiohshimensis*** | WCru |
| ***formosana*** | CGHE CPLG WPGP |
| - B&SWJ 2005 | WCru |
| - 'Crûg's Abundant' | WCru |
| - 'Hsitou' | WCru |
| - 'Hsitou Splendour' | WCru |

## *Cardiocrinum* (*Liliaceae*)

| | |
|---|---|
| ***cathayanum*** | CBct GEdr LWst WCot WPGP |
| ***cordatum*** | ECho WAul |
| - B&SWJ 2812 | WCru |
| - B&SWJ 4841 | WCru |
| - B&SWJ 5427 | WCru |
| - B&SWJ 6336 | WCru |
| - var. ***glehnii*** | CCCN ECho GEdr LWst |
| - - B&SWJ 4722 | WCru |
| - - B&SWJ 4758 | WCru |
| - red-veined | GEdr MNrw |
| ***giganteum*** | Widely available |
| - B&SWJ 2419 | WCru |
| - GWJ 9219 from Sikkim **new** | WCru |
| - HWJK 2158 from Nepal | WCru |
| - var. ***yunnanense*** | CAby CMil CPom ECho EPfP GAbr GAuc GEdr GLin GMaP LWst NBid WCru WPGP |
| aff. ***giganteum*** from Nagaland **new** | GAuc |

## cardoon see *Cynara cardunculus*

## *Carduus* (*Asteraceae*)

| | |
|---|---|
| ***benedictus*** | see *Cnicus benedictus* |

## *Carex* (*Cyperaceae*)

| | |
|---|---|
| from Uganda | SApp |
| ***acuta*** | MSKA |
| - 'Variegata' (v) | CBen CRow EHoe EHon EPla EShb GMaP IFro LLWG LPBA MMoz MMuc MWts NBro NOak SApp SBfd SEND WCot WFar WHal WMoo WWEG |
| ***acutiformis*** | CRWN NMir |
| ***alba*** | EPPr WCot |
| 'Amazon Mist' | EPPr WNew |
| ***appalachica*** | EPPr |
| ***appressa*** | SApp |
| ***arenaria*** | GBin |
| ***atrata*** | EBee EHoe EPla WHrl |
| § - subsp. ***pullata*** | GCal |
| ***aurea*** | EPPr GLam IFoB NHol |
| ***baccans*** | CPLG GCal |
| ***bebbii*** | EPPr |
| ***berggrenii*** | EBee ECou EHoe ELan EPPr LPBA LRHS NLar NWCA SPlb SWat WTin WWEG |
| ***binervis*** | CRWN |

| |  |  |
|---|---|---|
| | ***boottiana*** | EWes |
| | ***brunnea*** | EWes SBfd SHDw |
| | – 'Jenneke' (v) | CChe CKno EBee EPPr EPfP EPla LRHS MBri SBfd SHDw SLim SMrm SWvt WCot |
| | – 'Variegata' (v) | CChe CEnt EHoe SApp SBfd SHDw |
| | ***buchananii*** $\Upsilon^{H4}$ | Widely available |
| | – 'Green Twist' new | CKno |
| | – 'Viridis' | ELan EPPr GBin XLum |
| | ***buxbaumii*** | SRms |
| § | ***canescens*** subsp. ***canescens*** | CRWN |
| | ***chathamica*** | EBee LRHS SApp SGar WPtf |
| | 'China Blue' | MMoz SApp |
| | ***ciliatomarginata*** 'Treasure Island' (v) | EPPr |
| | ***comans*** | EPPr EPfP NBro NWsh |
| | – from Dunedin, New Zealand | EPPr |
| | – 'Bronze Perfection' | SMea SWal WFar XLum |
| | – bronze-leaved | Widely available |
| | – 'Bronzita' | EPPr LRHS |
| | – 'Copper Green' | SMea |
| | – 'Dancing Flame' | CPrp CSpr CWCL EBee ELon MBri NWsh |
| | – 'Feebers Dwarf' | WWEG |
| | – 'Frosted Curls' | Widely available |
| | – 'Kupferflamme' | EPPr |
| | – red-leaved | CWCL LAst NLar SRms |
| | – 'Small Red' | see *C. comans* 'Taranaki' |
| § | – 'Taranaki' | EPPr EPfP MBNS MMoz SCoo |
| | ***conica*** | MWat |
| | – 'Hime-kan-suge' | see *C. conica* 'Snowline' |
| | – 'Kiku-sakura' (v) | EPPr NHol |
| § | – 'Snowline' (v) | EBee ECha EHoe ELan EPfP EPla GKev GMaP LEdu LLWP LPBA LRHS LTen MMoz NBro NHol NLar NWsh SBfd SBrd SGol SWal SWvt WMoo WPer WTin XLum |
| | ***crinita*** | EPPr |
| | ***cristatella*** | EPPr |
| § | ***cuprina*** | CHab CRWN |
| | 'Curly Whirly' | SPad |
| | ***curta*** | see *C. canescens* subsp. *canescens* |
| | ***dallii*** | EKen EWes WHrl |
| | ***davisii*** | EPPr |
| | ***demissa*** | see *C. viridula* subsp. *oedocarpa* |
| | ***depauperata*** | CRWN EHoe |
| | ***digitata*** | CRWN |
| | ***dioica*** | CRWN |
| | ***dipsacea*** | CKno CWCL EBee EHoe EHul EPPr EShb GMaP MMoz MNrw NWsh SBch SBfd WDin WHal WMoo WPer WTin WWEG |
| | – 'Dark Horse' | CKno EBee EHoe EPPr ETod GCal LLHF LRHS SBfd SMea WPtf |
| | ***divulsa*** | CKno |
| | – subsp. ***divulsa*** | CRWN |
| | – subsp. ***leersii*** | EPPr |
| § | ***dolichostachya*** 'Kaga-nishiki' (v) | CSBt EBee EPPr LEdu LHop LRHS SLim WPnP WWEG |
| | ***duthiei*** | see *C. atrata* subsp. *pullata* |
| | ***ebenea*** new | LRHS |
| | ***echinata*** | CRWN |
| § | ***elata*** 'Aurea' (v) $\Upsilon^{H4}$ | Widely available |
| | – 'Bowles's Golden' | see *C. elata* 'Aurea' |
| | – 'Knightshayes' $\Upsilon^{H4}$ | CKno EWes GBin MWhi NLar WCot |
| | 'Evergold' | see *C. oshimensis* 'Evergold' |
| | ***firma*** 'Variegata' (v) | GEdr MWat NMen WThu |
| | ***flacca*** | CHab CKno CRWN EHoe EPPr GBin XLum |

| |  |  |
|---|---|---|
| | – 'Bias' (v) | EPla MMoz |
| | – 'Blue Zinger' | CKno WWEG |
| § | – subsp. ***flacca*** | EBee EWes MMoz NSti SMea |
| | ***flagellifera*** | CBcs CHEx CMea CSpe CTri CWCL EBee EHoe EPPr EPfP EPla EShb GCal GMaP LRHS LSRN MBrN MLHP MMuc MWhi NBir NWCA NWad SEND SMrm SPlb WFar WWEG XLum |
| | – 'Auburn Cascade' | EBee LHop LRHS NBPC NHol NWad SApp SBfd |
| | – 'Coca-Cola' | NOak |
| | – 'Rapunzel' | EBee EPPr |
| | ***flava*** | CKno EHoe EPPr |
| | ***fortunei*** | see *C. morrowii* Boott |
| | ***fraseri*** | see *Cymophyllus fraserianus* |
| | ***fraserianus*** | see *Cymophyllus fraserianus* |
| | ***glauca*** Bosc. ex Boott | see *C. glaucescens* |
| | ***glauca*** Scop. | see *C. flacca* subsp. *flacca* |
| § | ***glaucescens*** | CWCL EPPr EPla SBfd |
| | 'Gold Fountains' | see *C. dolichostachya* 'Kaga-nishiki' |
| | ***granularis*** | EPPr |
| I | 'Grayassina' | CKno EPPr |
| | ***grayi*** | CDes EBee EHoe LEdu LLWG LRHS MBlu MSCN MSKA NCGa NLar NOak NPnk WPtf XLum |
| § | ***hachijoensis*** | WFar |
| | 'Happy Wanderer' | SLPl |
| | ***hirta*** | CRWN |
| | ***hostiana*** | CRWN |
| | ***hystricina*** | LRHS |
| | 'Ice Dance' (v) | CKno EBee EHon EPPr EPfP EPla GGar GKev GQue LEdu LRHS MMoz NHol NOak NOrc SBch SBfd SGol SWvt WCot WPtf WWEG |
| | ***kaloides*** | EBee EHoe EPPr LRHS XLum |
| | 'Kan-suge' | see *C. morrowii* Boott |
| * | ***leformeri*** new | XLum |
| § | ***leporina*** | CRWN |
| | ***lupulina*** | NOak |
| | ***lurida*** | EPfP MBNS |
| | – 'Silver' | EPPr MBNS |
| | ***maorica*** | EPPr |
| | ***maritima*** Gunnerus | CRWN |
| | ***mertensii*** NNS 07-98 | EPPr |
| | Milk Chocolate = 'Milchoc'$^{PBR}$ (v) | EBee EPfP NMun SApp |
| | ***morrowii*** misapplied | see *C. oshimensis*, *C. hachijoensis* |
| § | ***morrowii*** Boott | CWCL EPPr NWad |
| I | – 'Fisher's Form' (v) | CKno CTri EBee EPPr EPla LHop MMoz MRav NGdn NHol NLar NWsh SApp SBfd SEND SWvt WFar WPer WWEG |
| | – 'Gilt' (v) | EAEE EBee EHoe EPPr EPla LRHS MBNS NHol |
| | – 'Nana Variegata' (v) | CTri NBir |
| | – 'Pinkie' new | WPtf |
| | – var. ***temnolepis*** 'Silk Tassel' (v) | EPPr |
| N | – 'Variegata' (v) | EHoe ELan EPPr EPla GCal GKev GMaP LAst LPBA MMoz MMuc MRav NBir NBlu NHol NSti SGol SLPl SRms WCot WFar WPnP XLum |
| | ***muehlenbergii*** | EPPr |
| | ***muricata*** | EPPr |
| | ***muskingumensis*** | Widely available |
| | – 'Ice Fountains' (v) | EPPr WWEG |
| | – 'Little Midge' | CKno EBee EPPr EShb GCal LEdu WCot WWEG |

- 'Oehme' (v) CKno CWCL EBee EPPr EPla EShb GBin GCal LEdu LLWG NBid NHol NWad WPtf WTin WWEG
- 'Silberstreif' (v) CKno EBee EPPr GBin GGar LEdu MMuc NLar SApp XLum
***nigra*** (L.) Reichard CRWN EHon EPPr XLum
§ - 'On-line' (v) CKno EPPr MBNS MMoz NWsh SApp
- 'Variegata' see *C. nigra* 'On-line'
No 1, Nanking (Greg's broad leaf) MMoz
No 4, Nanking (Greg's thin leaf) EPPr MMoz SApp
***normalis*** EPPr
***obnupta*** CKno EPPr
***ornithopoda*** 'Aurea' see *C. ornithopoda* 'Variegata'
§ - 'Variegata' (v) EBee ECtt EPPr NBro NGdn NHol NOak NWsh SBch WMoo WWEG
§ ***oshimensis*** EPPr MMoz
- Everest = 'Fiwhite' (v) **new** LRHS SBfd
§ - 'Evergold' (v) ♀H4 Widely available
- 'Variegata' (v) NBir
***otrubae*** see *C. cuprina*
***ovalis*** see *C. leporina*
***panicea*** CKno CRWN CSBt CWCL EBee EHoe EPPr EPla LLWG MMoz MSKA SApp WGrn WMoo
***paniculata*** CRWN XLum
***parviflora*** SMea
***pendula*** Widely available
- 'Cool Jazz' (v) EPPr MAvo MSKA
- 'Moonraker' (v) CBot CWCL EHoe EPPr EPla ESwi MAvo MBNS MLLN MSKA NOak SApp SLPl WCot WWEG
***petriei*** CWCL ECha ELon ETod EWes LLWP MBNS NVic WCot WFar WTin
***phyllocephala*** EShb
- 'Sparkler' (v) CKno EBee ECtt EHoe ELon EPfP EPla EShb LAst LEdu LRHS NSti SBfd SPad SRms SWvt WCot WFar XLum
***plantaginea*** EBee EHoe EPPr EPla GBin LEdu SApp WCot WMoo WWEG
***praegracilis*** CKno EPPr
Pritchard's selection (v) IFro
***projecta*** EPPr
***pseudocyperus*** CPom CRWN EHoe EHon GBin LPBA MMoz MSKA NPer NWsh SWat WMoo WPnP
***pulicaris*** CRWN
***punctata*** **new** XLum
'Red Rooster' WNew
***remota*** CKno CRWN EHoe EPPr SMea
***riparia*** CRWN LPBA MMoz MMuc MSKA NHol NPer SEND SMea SWat WFar WShi
- 'Bowles's Golden' see *C. elata* 'Aurea'
***rosea*** **new** EPPr
***rostrata*** CRWN MMuc SEND
***sabynensis*** see *C. umbrosa* subsp. *sabynensis*
***secta*** CKno ECou EPPr GGar GMaP MNrw SHDw WDyG WMoo WPer
- from Dunedin, New Zealand EPPr
***siderosticha*** EPla SLPl
- 'Banana Boat' see *C. siderosticha* 'Golden Falls'
- 'Echigo-nishiki' (v) EPPr
§ - 'Golden Falls' (v) LEdu LRHS NOrc SMad
- 'Golden Fountains' WCot
- 'Kisokaido' (v) EPPr LEdu WCot
- 'Old Barn' EBee
- 'Shima-nishiki' (v) CPMA EBee ECtt EPPr EPfP LAst LRHS MBNS NOak NPro SAga WFar WWEG
- 'Variegata' (v) Widely available
'Silver Sceptre' (v) CChe EBee ECtt EHoe EPPr EPla EShb LBMP LRHS LTen MBNS MGos NHol NPro NSti NWsh SBfd SLim SPlb SPoG SWal SWvt WBrk WFar WMoo
'Silver Sparkler' NBir
'Silver Streams' WWEG
***solandri*** CKno LEdu NWsh SApp SBfd SHDw
***spissa*** CKno MNrw
***stricta*** 'Bowles's Golden' see *C. elata* 'Aurea'
***sylvatica*** CRWN EHoe
***tenuiculmis*** CKno CWCL EBee EPPr EShb LBMP LHop MAvo NBPC NHol NOak NSti NWad NWsh SBfd SRms WCot WTin WWEG
- 'Cappucino' CKno
***tereticaulis*** LRHS
***testacea*** Widely available
- 'Autumn Gold' **new** CSpe
- dark-leaved EPfP
- 'Old Gold' ELan EPPr EWes LRHS MMuc NOak SBfd SMad SPlb WFar WGrn WMoo
- 'Prairie Fire' EPPr LRHS
***texensis*** EPPr
'The Beatles' EHoe EPPr NBir NHol
'Triffid' **new** WPtf
***trifida*** CHEx CKno EHoe EKen GGar MNrw NWsh WFar
- 'Chatham Blue' CHid EPPr GBin LRHS MMoz MMuc SEND
- 'Rekohu Sunrise' (v) CKno EBee EPPr ESwi LRHS SBfd
***umbrosa*** CKno EPPr EShb
subsp. ***sabynensis*** 'Thinny Thin' (v)
***uncifolia*** ECou
§ ***viridula*** subsp. ***oedocarpa*** CRWN
- subsp. ***viridula*** CRWN
***vulpina*** EPPr LRHS
***vulpinoidea*** EPPr LRHS

## *Carica* (*Caricaceae*)

***papaya*** (F) XBlo
- 'Babaco' CCCN

## *Carissa* (*Apocynaceae*)

***grandiflora*** see *C. macrocarpa*
§ ***macrocarpa*** (F) CCCN EShb

## *Carlina* (*Asteraceae*)

***acaulis*** CArn ECho ELan EPfP GEdr GKev NWCA SPav SPlb WFar
- SDR 3566 GKev
- subsp. ***acaulis*** GPoy
- bronze-leaved MCCP NBPC
- var. ***caulescens*** see *C. acaulis* subsp. *simplex*
§ - subsp. ***simplex*** EBee ECha GGar GMaP LRHS NPri WFar
- - bronze-leaved EBee SMad SPhx
***vulgaris*** 'Silver Star' LRHS SPhx

## *Carmichaelia* (*Papilionaceae*)

'Abundance' ECou
'Angie' ECou

| | |
|---|---|
| ***angustata*** 'Buller' | ECou |
| ***appressa*** | ECou |
| - 'Ellesmere' | ECou |
| ***astonii*** | ECou |
| - 'Ben More' | ECou |
| - 'Chalk Ridge' | ECou |
| ***australis*** | WSHC |
| 'Charm' | ECou |
| 'Clifford Bay' | ECou |
| ***corrugata*** | ECou |
| ***curta*** | ECou |
| ***enysii*** | CCCN LLHF |
| ***fieldii*** 'Westhaven' | ECou |
| ***flagelliformis*** 'Roro' | ECou |
| ***glabrata*** | WCot |
| 'Hay and Honey' | ECou |
| × ***hutchinsii*** 'County Park' | GGar |
| ***kirkii*** | ECou WThu |
| 'Lilac Haze' | ECou |
| ***monroi*** | ECou |
| - 'Rangitata' | ECou |
| - 'Tekapo' | ECou |
| ***odorata*** | CPLG ECou |
| - 'Lakeside' | ECou |
| - 'Riverside' | ECou |
| ***ovata*** 'Calf Creek' | ECou |
| 'Parson's Tiny' | ECou |
| ***petriei*** | ECou SMad |
| - 'Aviemore' | ECou |
| - 'Lindis' | ECou |
| - 'Pukaki' | ECou |
| 'Porter's Pass' | ECou |
| 'Spangle' | ECou |
| ***stevensonii*** | EPfP WSHC |
| 'Tangle' | ECou |
| ***uniflora*** | ECou |
| - 'Bealey' | ECou |
| ***williamsii*** | ECou |

## × *Carmispartium* see *Carmichaelia*

## *Carpenteria* (*Hydrangeaceae*)

| | |
|---|---|
| ***californica*** ♀H3 | CBot CPMA CSBt CTri EBee ELan EPfP EPla EWTr LAst LRHS MBri MGos MWat NLar NPal NPri SBrd SEND SGar SSpi SWvt WDin WPat |
| - 'Bodnant' | CDul CWGN EBee ELan LRHS MBri MGos MWea SWvt WPGP |
| - 'Elizabeth' | CAbP CBcs CPMA CSBt ELan EPfP LRHS LSRN MAsh SPoG SSpi SSta WDin WPGP WPat |
| - 'Ladhams' Variety' | CBcs CPMA CSBt EBee EPfP LRHS MGos MRav NLar SRkn SWvt WCFE |

## *Carpinus* ✿ (*Betulaceae*)

| | |
|---|---|
| sp. | CMen LSRN |
| ***betulus*** ♀H4 | Widely available |
| - 'Columnaris' | CDul CLnd CTho EBee |
| * - 'Columnaris Nana' | CMCN MPkF |
| § - 'Fastigiata' ♀H4 | Widely available |
| - 'Frans Fontaine' | CCVT CDoC CDul CEnd CMCN CTho EBee EPfP IArd LMaj MBlu MBri MGos NLar NWea SCoo SLim SPer SPoG WHar |
| - 'Globus' | MBlu |
| - 'Incisa' | WMou |
| - 'Monument' **new** | MPkF |
| I - 'Monumentalis' | LMaj |
| - 'Pendula' | CDul CEnd CLnd CTho EBee MBlu SPoG WDin |
| - 'Purpurea' | CEnd LMaj MBlu MGos NLar |
| - 'Pyramidalis' | see *C. betulus* 'Fastigiata' |
| - 'Quercifolia' | CDul |
| ***caroliniana*** | CLnd CMCN EPfP SBir SMad WMou |
| - 'Sentinel Dries' | MBlu MBri |
| ***cordula*** | MBlu SBir WDin |
| ***coreana*** | EGFP IArd SBir |
| ***fangiana*** | CBcs CDul CEnd CGHE CPLG CTho EPfP SKHP SMad WPGP |
| ***fargesiana*** | EGFP |
| ***fargesii*** | see *C. viminea* |
| ***henryana*** | CMen CPLG SBir |
| ***japonica*** ♀H4 | CDul CEnd CMCN CMen EGFP EPfP LLHF MBlu MBri NLar SBir SCoo SEWo SMad WDin |
| - B&SWJ 10803 | WCru |
| - B&SWJ 11072 | WCru |
| ***kawakamii*** CWJ 12412 | WCru |
| - CWJ 12449 | WCru |
| ***laxiflora*** | CMen CPLG MPkF WFar WPGP |
| - B&SWJ 10809 | WCru |
| - B&SWJ 11035 | WCru |
| - var. ***longispica*** B&SWJ 8772 | WCru |
| - var. ***macrostachya*** | see *C. viminea* |
| ***orientalis*** | CMCN SBir |
| ***polyneura*** | SBir |
| ***pubescens*** | WPGP |
| ***rankanensis*** RWJ 9839 | WCru |
| × ***schuschaensis*** | EBtc SBir |
| ***shensiensis*** | CDul |
| ***tschonoskii*** B&SWJ 10800 | WCru |
| ***turczaninowii*** ♀H4 | CDul CMen EGFP IDee NLar SBir STre WDin WPGP |
| § ***viminea*** | CEnd CPLG SBir |

## *Carpobrotus* (*Aizoaceae*)

| | |
|---|---|
| § ***edulis*** | CCCN CDTJ CDoC EShb SArc SEND SVen WHer XLum |
| - var. ***edulis*** | CHEx |
| - var. ***rubescens*** | CCCN CHEx |
| ***muirii*** | CCCN EShb SVen |
| ***sauerae*** | CCCN |

## *Carpodetus* (*Rousseaceae*)

| | |
|---|---|
| ***serratus*** | CBcs |

## *Carrierea* (*Salicaceae*)

| | |
|---|---|
| ***calycina*** | WPGP |

## carrot see *Daucus carota*

## *Carthamus* (*Asteraceae*)

| | |
|---|---|
| ***tinctorius*** | CArn MNHC SPav |

## *Carum* (*Apiaceae*)

| | |
|---|---|
| ***carvi*** | CArn CWan ELau GPoy MHer MNHC SIde SVic WJek |
| ***petroselinum*** | see *Petroselinum crispum* |

## *Carya* ✿ (*Juglandaceae*)

| | |
|---|---|
| ***aquatica*** | CMCN |
| ***cordiformis*** | CTho EPfP MBlu |
| N ***illinoinensis*** (F) | CAgr CBcs MBri |
| - 'Carlson No 3' seedling (F) | CAgr |
| - 'Colby' seedling (F) | CAgr |
| - 'Cornfield' (F) | CAgr |
| - 'Lucas' (F) | CAgr |
| ***laciniosa*** (F) | CTho EPfP |

| | |
|---|---|
| - 'Henry' (F) | CAgr |
| - 'Keystone' seedling (F) | CAgr |
| ***ovata*** (F) | CAgr CMCN CTho EPfP MBlu SSpi WDin |
| - 'Grainger' seedling (F) | CAgr |
| - 'Neilson' seedling (F) | CAgr |
| - 'Weschcke' seedling (F) | CAgr |
| - 'Yoder no 1' seedling (F) | CAgr |
| ***tomentosa*** | EGFP EPfP |

## *Caryophyllus* see *Syzygium*

## *Caryopteris* ✿ (*Lamiaceae*)

| | |
|---|---|
| × ***clandonensis*** | CMac ECtt MLHP MWat NBir WDin WFar |
| - 'Arthur Simmonds' ♀H4 | CTri ECha EPfP LHop LSRN SPer WGor |
| - 'Dark Knight' | CMea CSpe EBee ECtt ELan EPfP LAst LBuc MAsh MBri MWat NPnk SBfd SPoG SPtl SPur SWvt WHoo |
| - 'Ferndown' | CDoC CWib EBee ELon EPfP NLar SEND SPoG SRms |
| - 'First Choice' ♀H3-4 | CAbP CDul CMac CSpe EBee ECtt ELan EPPr EPfP EShb LAst LHop LRHS LSRN LSqu MAsh MGos SBrd SLim SPer SPoG SRkn SWvt |
| - 'Gold Giant' | LRHS MAsh SPer |
| - Grand Bleu = 'Inoveris'PBR | CAlb CMac CSBt EBee ELan EPfP EQua EShb EWTr LRHS LSRN MGos MSwo NLar SGol STes SWvt WPat WRHF |
| - 'Heavenly Baby' ♀H3-4 | EPfP LRHS MAsh SKHP SLon SPoG |
| - 'Heavenly Blue' | Widely available |
| - Hint of Gold = 'Lisaura'PBR ♀H3-4 | EPfP LRHS MAsh SBfd |
| - 'Kew Blue' | Widely available |
| - 'Longwood Blue' | CCse ELan EPfP LRHS MAsh |
| - Petit Bleu = 'Minbleu'PBR **new** | CAlb |
| - Sterling Silver = 'Lissilv' | LRHS MAsh SPoG |
| - 'Summer Gold' | ELan MRav |
| - 'Summer Sorbet'PBR (v) ♀H3-4 | CDoC EBee EHoe ELan EPfP EWes LHop LRHS MAsh MGos MTPN NEgg NHol NPnk SBfd SCoo SEND SLim SPad SPer SPoG SWvt WHar |
| - 'White Surprise'PBR **new** | CWGN EMil LRHS SPoG |
| - 'Worcester Gold' ♀H3-4 | Widely available |
| ***divaricata*** | SBrt |
| - 'Electrum' | LSou |
| - 'Jade Shades' | LSou |
| § ***incana*** | EBee EPfP SPer |
| - 'Autumn Pink'PBR | EBee ECrN ELan EPfP LSRN SEND |
| - 'Blue Cascade' | EBee EBtc ELan GQue MRav NLar WGrn WPat |
| § - 'Jason'PBR | EPPr EPfP NEgg SPoG |
| - Sunshine BluePBR | see *C. incana* 'Jason' |
| ***mastacanthus*** | see *C. incana* |

## *Caryota* (*Arecaceae*)

| | |
|---|---|
| ***mitis*** ♀H1 | CCCN EAmu LPal |
| - 'Himalaya' | EAmu LPal |
| ***obtusa*** | EAmu |
| ***urens*** | LPal |

## *Cassandra* see *Chamaedaphne*

## *Cassia* (*Caesalpiniaceae*)

| | |
|---|---|
| ***corymbosa*** | see *Senna corymbosa* |
| ***marilandica*** | see *Senna marilandica* |

## *Cassinia* (*Asteraceae*)

| | |
|---|---|
| ***aculeata*** | GGar |
| ***leptophylla*** | CBcs GGar SPer |
| - 'Avalanche Creek' | ECou |
| - subsp. ***fulvida*** | CBcs ECou EHoe GGar SVen |
| - subsp. ***vauvilliersii*** | GGar SEND SPer SVen |
| - - BR 55 | GGar |
| - - var. ***albida*** | SPer |
| - - 'Silberschmelze' | MOWG |
| N ***retorta*** | ECou |
| 'Ward Silver' | CBot CTrC ECou EHoe EWes SEND |

## *Cassinia* × *Helichrysum* (*Asteraceae*)

| | |
|---|---|
| hybrid | WKif |

## *Cassiope* ✿ (*Ericaceae*)

| | |
|---|---|
| 'Askival Arctic Fox' | ITim |
| 'Askival Freebird' | see *C.* Freebird Group |
| 'Askival Snowbird' | ITim NHar |
| 'Askival Snow-wreath' | see *C.* Snow-wreath Group |
| 'Badenoch' | ECho EPot GEdr GGar GLam |
| 'Edinburgh' ♀H4 | ECho EPot GBin GEdr GLam IVic NHar NWad WThu |
| § Freebird Group | NHar |
| ***lycopodioides*** | ECho GEdr GGar NHar SRms WThu |
| 'Beatrice Lilley' | |
| - 'Jim Lever' | NHar WAbe |
| - 'Rokujō' | ITim |
| ***mertensiana*** | ECho EPot GEdr GLam SRms |
| - 'California Pink' | NHar |
| - var. ***californica*** | NWad WThu |
| - var. ***gracilis*** | ITim IVic NHar NWad WThu |
| 'Muirhead' ♀H4 | ECho NHar SRms WThu |
| 'Randle Cooke' ♀H4 | ECho EPot GEdr GLam NHar SRms WThu |
| ***selaginoides*** LS&E 13284 | ITim WAbe WThu |
| § Snow-wreath Group | ITim |
| ***tetragona*** | ITim SRms WAbe |

## *Castanea* ✿ (*Fagaceae*)

| | |
|---|---|
| 'Bouche de Bétizac' (F) | CAgr |
| ***crenata*** | CAgr CDul |
| 'Ferosacre' (F) | MCoo |
| ***henryi*** | CMCN EGFP |
| 'Maraval' (F) | CAgr CTho LRHS MBlu MBri MCoo NWea SGol WHar |
| 'Maridonne' (F) | CAgr |
| 'Marigoule' (F) | CAgr EPom MCoo NWea WHar |
| 'Marlhac' (F) | CAgr |
| 'Marsol' (F) | CAgr MCoo SGol |
| ***mollissima*** | EGFP |
| 'Précoce Migoule' (F) | CAgr ECrN |
| ***sativa*** ♀H4 | Widely available |
| § - 'Albomarginata' (v) ♀H4 | CDoC CDul CEnd EBee EPfP LHop LMaj MAsh MBlu MBri MGos SPoG WDin WFar WPat |
| - 'Anny's Red' | MBlu |
| - 'Anny's Summer Red' | CDul |
| - 'Argenteovariegata' | see *C. sativa* 'Albomarginata' |
| - 'Aspleniifolia' | CDul |
| - 'Aureomarginata' | see *C. sativa* 'Variegata' |
| - 'Belle Epine' (F) | CAgr |
| - 'Bournette' (F) | CAgr |
| * - 'Doré de Lyon' | CAgr |
| - 'Marron Comballe' (F) | CAgr |
| - 'Marron de Goujounac' (F) | CAgr |
| - 'Marron de Lyon' (F) | CAgr CDul CEnd EPfP MBri SVic |
| - 'Pyramidalis' | WDin |
| § - 'Variegata' (v) | CBcs CLnd CMCN ELan LMaj MGos |

## *Castanopsis* (*Fagaceae*)

| | |
|---|---|
| ***eyrei*** | CMCN |
| ***sclerophylla*** | CBcs WPGP |

## *Castanospermum* (*Papilionaceae*)

| | |
|---|---|
| ***australe*** | CArn |

## *Castilleja* (*Orobanchaceae*)

| | |
|---|---|
| ***miniata*** | WAbe |

## *Casuarina* (*Casuarinaceae*)

| | |
|---|---|
| ***cunninghamiana*** | ECou |

## *Catalpa* (*Bignoniaceae*)

| | |
|---|---|
| ***bignonioides*** ♀H4 | Widely available |
| - 'Aurea' ♀H4 | Widely available |
| * - 'Aurea Nana' | CEnd MBri |
| - 'Nana' | EBee LMaj LRHS MBri WDin WHar WPat |
| - 'Purpurea' | see *C.* × *erubescens* 'Purpurea' |
| - 'Variegata' (v) | EPfP LRHS MAsh MGos NWea WPat |
| ***bungei*** | EGFP MBlu SArc SGol |
| - 'Purpurea' | LAst |
| § × ***erubescens*** 'Purpurea' ♀H4 | CBcs CBot CDoC CDul CEnd CLnd CMac CTho EAmu EBee ELan EPfP EWTr LRHS LTen MAsh MBlu MBri MGos MRav NLar SBfd SPer SPoG WDin WFar WHar WPGP WPat |
| ***fargesii*** f. ***duclouxii*** | CDul CEnd EPfP MBlu MBri NLar WPGP |
| ***ovata*** | CMCN CTho EGFP |
| - 'Slender Silhouette' | NLar |
| ***speciosa*** | CDul CTho EWTr SEND |
| - 'Frederik' | NLar |
| - 'Pulverulenta' (v) | CDoC CDul CEnd CMCN MGos SBig |
| * ***szechuanica*** new | NLar |

## *Catananche* (*Asteraceae*)

| | |
|---|---|
| ***caerulea*** | Widely available |
| - 'Alba' | CMea EBee EBla ECha EPfP IFoB LBMP LRHS NBir NPri SBfd SMrm SPer SPoG SWvt WGwG WMoo WPer |
| - 'Amor Blue' | LRHS |
| - 'Amor White' | WOut |
| - 'Bicolor' | CMMP MHer MSpe WHoo WMoo |
| - 'Major' ♀H4 | LRHS SRms WHlf |

## *Catha* (*Celastraceae*)

| | |
|---|---|
| ***edulis*** | CArn GPoy WHfH WJek |

## *Catharanthus* (*Apocynaceae*)

| | |
|---|---|
| ***roseus*** ♀H1 | GPoy |

## *Caulokaempferia* (*Zingiberaceae*)

| | |
|---|---|
| ***petelotii*** B&SWJ 11818 new | WCru |

## *Caulophyllum* (*Berberidaceae*)

| | |
|---|---|
| ***thalictroides*** | EBee EPPr GEdr LEdu SRot WCru WFar WMoo WPnP WSHC |
| - subsp. ***robustum*** | WCru |

## *Cautleya* ✿ (*Zingiberaceae*)

| | |
|---|---|
| ***cathcartii*** | CPLG LEdu |
| - 'Tenzing's Gold' | LWst WCru |
| § ***gracilis*** | CDTJ CPLG EBee EPfP ETod GCal IBlr MNrw NMyG SBig SBrd WHal XLum |
| - B&SWJ 7186 | LEdu WCru WDyG |
| - 'Edinburgh Lemon' | IBlr |
| ***lutea*** | see *C. gracilis* |
| ***spicata*** | CBct CCCN CDTJ CDoC CHEx CSpe CTsd EBee ECho GGar IBlr NPal SBHP SBig XLum |
| - CC 3676 | CPLG EPPr |
| - 'Arun Flame' | LEdu WCru |
| - 'Crûg Canary' | LEdu WCru |
| * - var. ***lutea*** | CBct CHEx ETod LEdu WBor |
| - 'Robusta' | CAvo CGHE CHEx CPLG CPrp EAmu EBee GCal GCra IBlr LEdu LRHS MNrw NPal SChF SMad WBor WCru WPGP WSHC |

## *Cayratia* (*Vitaceae*)

| | |
|---|---|
| ***japonica*** B&SWJ 6636 | WCru |
| § ***thomsonii*** BWJ 8123 | WCru |

## *Ceanothus* ✿ (*Rhamnaceae*)

| | |
|---|---|
| 'A.T. Johnson' | ECrN SGol SLim SPer SRms |
| ***americanus*** | CArn |
| ***arboreus*** | SArc |
| - 'Trewithen Blue' ♀H3 | CBcs CDul CMac CSBt CWSG CWib EBee ELan EPfP LHop LRHS LSRN MAsh MBri MGos MRav MSwo SBfd SCoo SEND SLim SPer SPlb SPoG SWvt WDin WFar WFoF WSHC |
| 'Autumnal Blue' ♀H3 | Widely available |
| 'Blue Cushion' | CAlb CBcs CDoC CPMA CTri EBee LRHS MAsh MGos MRav NHol NLar SLim SLon SWvt WFar |
| 'Blue Diamond'PBR | LSRN NLar |
| 'Blue Dreams' | WFar |
| 'Blue Jeans' | EBee ELan IArd LRHS MAsh MMuc NLar SBrd SPoG |
| 'Blue Mound' ♀H3 | Widely available |
| 'Blue Sapphire'PBR | CAlb CBcs CDoC CMac CWGN EBee ELan ELon EPfP GBin LAst LRHS LSRN MAsh MGos MRav NEgg NLar NPri SBrd SPer SPoG SWvt |
| 'Burkwoodii' ♀H3 | CAlb CBcs CDoC CDul CHab CSBt EPfP LAst LRHS LSRN MAsh MGos MRav NEgg SBfd SLim SPer SPoG SWvt WFar |
| 'Cascade' ♀H3 | CBcs CHab CWSG EBee LRHS LSRN MAsh MGos MWat SBrd SLim SLon SPer SPlb |
| 'Centennial' | MRav |
| 'Concha' ♀H3 | Widely available |
| § ***cuneatus*** var. ***rigidus*** | SRms |
| 'Cynthia Postan' | EBee EPfP LRHS MAsh MBlu MWat NLar SCoo |
| 'Dark Star' ♀H3 | CAlb CBcs CChe CDoC CMHG CSPN CTri CWGN EBee EPfP GGal LBMP LRHS LSRN MAsh MGos MOWG NHol SCoo SEND SLim SPoG SPtl SSta SWvt |
| 'Delight' | CBcs EBee ELan EPfP WDin WFar |
| × ***delileanus*** 'Gloire de Versailles' ♀H4 | CBcs CBot CDoC CDul CTri CWib EBee ELan ELon EPfP EWTr LAst LHop LRHS MGos MRav MSwo MWhi NLar SGol SPer SWvt WDin WFar WSHC |
| - 'Henri Desfossé' | ELan EPfP LRHS LSRN MOWG MRav NLar SPer SPoG WDin WKif |
| - 'Indigo' | EPfP |
| - 'Topaze' ♀H4 | ELan EPfP LRHS MOWG NLar SGol SLon WDin WHar |

| | | |
|---|---|---|
| | ***dentatus*** misapplied | see *C.* × *lobbianus* |
| | ***dentatus*** Torr. & A.Gray | SPlb |
| | - var. ***floribundus*** | SDix |
| | - 'Prostratus' | SBfd |
| * | - 'Superbus' | EBee |
| | 'Diamond Heights' | see *C. griseus* var. *horizontalis* 'Diamond Heights' |
| | 'Edinburgh' ♀H3 | CWSG EPfP MAsh WFar |
| | El Dorado = 'Perado' (v) | LRHS MAsh NLar |
| | ***gloriosus*** | EBee EWes |
| | - 'Anchor Bay' | ELan EPfP LRHS MAsh MOWG |
| | - 'Emily Brown' | CAlb CBcs CDoC CSPN CTrC ELan LAst LRHS LSRN MRav NLar SBfd |
| | ***griseus*** | MAsh |
| § | - var. ***horizontalis*** 'Diamond Heights' (v) | CMac EPfP LSRN MBri SPer WFar |
| | - - 'Silver Surprise'PBR (v) | CSPN EBee ELan EPfP LBuc LRHS LSRN MAsh MGos NEgg NLar SLim SPoG |
| | - - 'Yankee Point' | CAlb CBcs CDoC CMac CSBt CWib EBee ECrN EPfP GGar LRHS LSRN LTen MAsh MGos MNHC MRav MSwo NBlu NLar SBfd SCoo SEND SLim SPlb SPoG SWvt WDin |
| | - 'Kurt Zadnik' | LRHS MAsh SPoG |
| | ***impressus*** | CMHG CTri EBee EPfP MAsh MBlu SEND SLPl SPer SWvt WCFE WFar |
| | - 'Victoria' | CWSG LSRN MGos MNHC NLar SBfd SRGP |
| N | 'Italian Skies' ♀H3 | CAlb CBcs CDoC CHab CSBt CWSG CWib EBee ELan EPfP LAst LBMP LHop LRHS LSRN MAsh MGos MSwo NEgg NLar SCoo SGol SLim SLon SPer SPlb SPoG SWvt WDin WFar |
| | 'Julia Phelps' | CMHG |
| | 'Lemon and Lime' **new** | LBuc LRHS |
| § | × ***lobbianus*** | CDul CTri WDin |
| | 'Madagascar' | ELon EPfP LRHS SCoo SPoG |
| | × ***pallidus*** 'Georges Simon' | EPfP |
| | - 'Marie Simon' | CBcs CBot CWib EBee ELan EPfP LAst LBMP LRHS LSRN MAsh MGos SPer SPoG SRms SWvt WCFE WDin WHar WKif |
| | - 'Perle Rose' | CBcs CDul EPfP LLHF LRHS MGos MOWG NLar SPer SPoG WKif WSHC |
| § | 'Pershore Zanzibar'PBR (v) | CBcs CChe CMac CSBt CSPN CWSG EBee EHoe ELan EPfP LAst LBuc LRHS LSRN MGos MRav MSwo MWat NEgg NLar NPri SCoo SEND SGol SLim SPer SPoG SWvt |
| | 'Pin Cushion' | CWSG CWib EPfP LRHS MAsh NHol |
| | 'Point Millerton' | see *C. thyrsiflorus* 'Millerton Point' |
| | 'Popcorn' | LRHS MGos |
| | ***prostratus*** | MAsh |
| | 'Puget Blue' ♀H4 | Widely available |
| | 'Ray Hartman' | NLar |
| | ***repens*** | see *C. thyrsiflorus* var. *repens* |
| | ***rigidus*** | see *C. cuneatus* var. *rigidus* |
| | 'Snow Flurries' | see *C. thyrsiflorus* 'Snow Flurry' |
| | 'Southmead' ♀H3 | CDoC CTri EBee ELan EPfP LRHS MAsh MGos MSwo MWat NBlu WDin WMoo |
| | ***thyrsiflorus*** | CTri CWib MAsh SPer SRms SWvt WDin WHar |
| § | - 'Millerton Point' | EPfP LAst LRHS MAsh MGos NBlu NLar SBfd SBrd SCoo SLim SPoG |
| § | - var. ***repens*** ♀H3 | Widely available |
| | - 'Skylark' ♀H3 | Widely available |
| § | - 'Snow Flurry' | CBcs CWSG CWib EGxp EPfP MSwo NBlu WFar |
| | 'Tilden Park' | LRHS |
| | 'Tuxedo' | EMil LBuc LRHS MSCN WCot |
| | × ***veitchianus*** | CDoy CSBt EBee ELan LRHS MAsh SEND SPer |
| | 'Zanzibar'PBR | see *C.* 'Pershore Zanzibar' |

## *Cedrela* (Meliaceae)

| | | |
|---|---|---|
| | ***sinensis*** | see *Toona sinensis* |

## *Cedronella* (Lamiaceae)

| | | |
|---|---|---|
| § | ***canariensis*** | CArn CBod CHby CPrp EGHP EShb GPoy ILis MHer MNHC MOWG SIde SWat WJek |
| | ***mexicana*** | see *Agastache mexicana* |
| | ***triphylla*** | see *C. canariensis* |

## *Cedrus* (Pinaceae)

| | | |
|---|---|---|
| | ***atlantica*** | CDul CLnd CMac CMen CPMA EHul NWea SEND SGol WEve WMou |
| | - 'Aurea' | CDul MBri MGos NLar NPCo SSta WDin WHar |
| | - 'Fastigiata' | EHul LRHS MAsh MGos NLar SCoo SLim WEve |
| | - Glauca Group ♀H4 | Widely available |
| | - - 'Glauca Fastigiata' | CKen CMen WEve |
| | - - 'Glauca Pendula' | CDoC CDul CMen ECrN EHul EPfP LMaj LRHS MBlu MBri MGos NEgg NPCo SCoo SGol SLim SPoG SSta WDin WEve WFar WHar |
| | - - 'Silberspitz' | CKen |
| | - 'Pendula' | ECho MAsh |
| | - 'Sahara Frost' | NLar |
| | - 'Saphir Nymph' | MAsh SLim |
| | ***brevifolia*** | CAlb LTen MGos NLar SBfd STre WEve |
| | - 'Epstein' | MGos NLar |
| | - 'Hillier Compact' | CKen MGos NLar |
| | - 'Kenwith' | CKen NLar |
| | ***deodara*** ♀H4 | Widely available |
| | - 'Albospica' (v) | MAsh SWvt |
| | - 'Aurea' ♀H4 | CDoC CDul CKen CSBt CTho ECho EHul EPfP GBin LMaj LRHS MAsh MBri MGos NEgg NLar NWea SGol SLim WDin WEve WFar WHar |
| I | - 'Aurea Pendula' | ECho |
| | - 'Blue Dwarf' | CKen WEve |
| * | - 'Blue Mountain Broom' | CKen |
| | - 'Blue Snake' | CKen IVic NLar |
| | - 'Blue Surprise' | SLim |
| | - 'Bush's Electra' | CPMA NLar |
| | - 'Cream Puff' | ECho MGos |
| | - 'Deep Cove' **new** | SLim |
| | - 'Devinely Blue' | CKen LRHS SLim SPoG |
| | - 'Feelin' Blue' | CDoC CDul CKen EHul EPla LRHS MAsh MBri MGos NEgg NLar NPCo SCoo SLim SWvt WEve WFar |
| | - 'Gold Cascade' | SLim |
| | - 'Gold Cone' | MGos |
| | - 'Gold Mound' | CKen WEve |
| | - 'Golden Horizon' | CDoC CKen CMac CMen CSBt EHul EPla LBee LRHS MAsh MBri MGos NEgg NPCo SCoo SLim SPoG WDin WEve WFar |
| | - 'Karl Fuchs' | EWTr LTen NLar WGor |
| | - 'Kelly Gold' | WEve |
| | - 'Klondyke' | MAsh |

| | |
|---|---|
| - 'Lime Glow' | SLim |
| - 'Miles High' | CPMA |
| - 'Mountain Beauty' | CKen |
| - 'Nana' | CKen |
| - 'Nivea' | CKen |
| - 'Pendula' | CKen ECho EHul LMaj MGos SLim WEve WGor |
| - 'Pygmy' | CKen |
| - 'Raywood's Prostrate' | CKen |
| - 'Robusta' | WEve |
| - 'Roman Candle' | CSBt ECho NPCo WEve WFar |
| - 'Scott' | CKen |
| - 'Silver Mist' | CKen MGos |
| - 'Silver Spring' | EPla NLar |
| ***libani*** 🏆H4 | Widely available |
| - 'Blue Angel' | NLar SLim |
| - 'Comte de Dijon' | EHul NLar |
| - 'Fontaine' | NLar |
| - 'Gold Tip' | NLar |
| - 'Green Prince' | NLar |
| - 'Hedgehog' | NLar |
| - 'Home Park' | CKen NLar |
| - 'May' | NLar |
| - Nana Group | CKen NPCo |
| - 'Pampisford' | NLar |
| - 'Sargentii' | CKen EHul MGos NLar NPCo WEve |
| - 'Taurus' | NLar |

## *Celastrus* (*Celastraceae*)

| | |
|---|---|
| ***dependens*** CWJ 12478 new | WCru |
| ***flagellaris*** B&SWJ 8572 | WCru |
| ***hookeri*** B&SWJ 11667 | WCru |
| ***kusanoi*** CWJ 12445 new | WCru |
| ***orbiculatus*** | CBcs CDoC CMac ELan IGor LHop LRHS MRav NSti SLon SPer WBor |
| - 'Diana' (f) | CMac |
| - 'Hercules' (m) | CMac |
| - Hermaphrodite Group 🏆H4 | EBee SDix SEND SKHP WSHC |
| - var. ***papillosus*** B&SWJ 591 | WCru |
| - var. ***punctatus*** CWJ 12439 | WCru |
| ***scandens*** | CMac EBee SPhx SPlb WDin |
| ***stephanotiifolius*** B&SWJ 4727 | WCru |

## *Celmisia* (*Asteraceae*)

| | |
|---|---|
| ***allanii*** | IBlr WAbe |
| ***angustifolia*** | IBlr |
| - silver-leaved | GKev |
| ***argentea*** | GLam WAbe |
| Ballyrogan hybrids | IBlr |
| ***bellidioides*** | EPot EWes MDKP NHar NSla WAbe |
| ***bonplandii*** | GKev IBlr |
| ***brevifolia*** | IBlr |
| ***coriacea*** misapplied | see *C. semicordata* |
| ***coriacea*** Raoul | see *C. mackaui* |
| 'David Shackleton' | IBlr |
| ***densiflora*** | GKev IBlr |
| - silver-leaved | IBlr |
| ***discolor*** | IBlr |
| 'Eggleston Silver' | GKev NEgg |
| ***glandulosa*** | IBlr |
| ***gracilenta*** | ITim NSla WAbe |
| ***haastii*** | IBlr |
| 'Harry Bryce' | IBlr |
| ***hectorii*** | GLam IBlr WAbe |
| ***hectorii*** × ***ramulosa*** | WAbe |
| ***hookeri*** | IBlr |
| Inshriach hybrids | IBlr |
| ***latifolia*** | IBlr |
| - large-leaved | IBlr |
| ***longifolia*** large-leaved | IBlr |
| - small-leaved | IBlr |
| § ***mackaui*** | GGar IBlr |
| ***munroi*** | IBlr |
| ***prorepens*** | IBlr |
| ***ramulosa*** | IBlr NSla |
| var. ***tuberculata*** | |
| § ***semicordata*** | GCra IBlr ITim NSla WAbe |
| - subsp. ***aurigans*** | IBlr |
| - subsp. ***stricta*** | IBlr |
| ***spectabilis*** | GGar |
| ***verbascifolia*** | IBlr |
| § ***walkeri*** | IBlr |
| ***webbiana*** | see *C. walkeri* |

## *Celsia* see *Verbascum*

## × *Celsioverbascum* see *Verbascum*

## *Celtica* see *Stipa*

## *Celtis* (*Cannabaceae*)

| | |
|---|---|
| ***australis*** | CBcs EBtc MGos MMuc SEND |
| ***biondii*** | EGFP |
| ***bungeana*** | NLar |
| ***caucasica*** | GAuc NLar |
| ***julianae*** | NLar |
| ***occidentalis*** | CDul ELan SGol |
| ***reticulata*** | EGFP |
| ***sinensis*** | CMen |
| ***tenuifolia*** | EGFP |

## *Cenolophium* (*Apiaceae*)

| | |
|---|---|
| ***denudatum*** | CDes EBee ECha EPPr NChi WPGP |

## *Centaurea* ✿ (*Asteraceae*)

| | |
|---|---|
| HH&K 271 | NBid |
| RCB AM -6 | WCot |
| RCB EA-1 | ECtt WCot |
| ***alpestris*** | MSpe NBre NLar SPhx WPGP WPer |
| 'Amethyst on Ice' new | LRHS |
| ***argentea*** | CBot |
| § ***atropurpurea*** | CDes CMea CSpe EBee EPPr EPfP EWes GMac GQue LRHS MRav MSpe NBPC NLar SHar SMrm SPhx SUsu WHil WHrl WPGP |
| ***bagadensis*** | GKev |
| ***bella*** | Widely available |
| - 'Katherine' (v) | MAvo |
| ***benoistii*** misapplied | see *C. atropurpurea* |
| ***benoistii*** × ***orientalis*** ambig. | SPhx |
| 'Blewit' | CDes EBee MAvo MSpe SHar WPGP |
| ***cana*** | see *C. triumfettii* subsp. *cana* |
| ***candidissima*** misapplied | see *C. cineraria* |
| 'Caramia' | MAvo |
| ***carniolica*** SDR 5443 | GKev MSpe |
| ***cheiranthifolia*** | CDes EPPr MSpe NBir NLBP WFar WPGP XSen |
| § ***cineraria*** | ECre ELon SRms |
| - subsp. ***cineraria*** 🏆H3 | CSpe EBee SEND WCot |
| ***clementei*** | CSpe |
| ***cyanoides*** new | LRHS |
| ***cyanus*** | CArn CHab MHer MNHC NPri SVic WJek |
| - 'Black Ball' | CSpe MNHC |
| - 'Blue Ball' new | CSpe |

| | |
|---|---|
| ***cynaroides*** | see *Stemmacantha centaureoides* |
| ***dealbata*** | Widely available |
| - 'Steenbergii' | CMac EBee EBla ELan GCal GGar LEdu MSpe NBid NBir NGdn NPer NSti SPer SPoG WAbb WCAu WCot WFar WMnd |
| ***debeauxii*** subsp. ***nemoralis*** | NLar |
| ***fischeri*** | CDes EBee MSpe WPGP |
| ***glastifolia*** | EBee GCal LRHS MSpe NBre WPGP |
| ***gymnocarpa*** | see *C. cineraria* |
| ***hypoleuca*** | NBid |
| ***jacea*** | CSam EShb GAbr GMac GQue MSpe NBid NLar WCot WPer |
| 'John Coutts' | Widely available |
| 'Jordy' | EBee ECtt IPot MAvo MSpe SPhx SSvw WCAu WKif |
| ***karabaghensis*** | WPGP |
| ***kotschyana*** | CDes EBee NBre WPGP |
| ***macrocephala*** | Widely available |
| ***mollis*** | NBid |
| ***montana*** | Widely available |
| - 'Alba' | Widely available |
| - 'Amethyst in Snow' | CSpr GBin IPot MAvo NLar SBfd |
| § - 'Carnea' | CAby CCVN CDes CElw CPom CSam CTca EBee EBla GCra GMaP GMac MAvo MSpe NBir NChi NLar SAga SPhx STes WCAu WMoo WWEG |
| - 'Gold Bullion' | CPrp CSpe EBla ECtt ELan ELon EPfP EWes EWll GMaP LRHS MAvo MCCP MRav MSpe NBid NBir NLar NPro NSti SAga SMad SMrm WCAu WSHC WWEG |
| - 'Grandiflora' | EBee MBri MSpe |
| - 'Joyce' | CElw CPom EBee EBla MAvo MSpe NBid NLar |
| - 'Lady Flora Hastings' | CBre CCse CDes CElw CKno CPom CSam CSpe CTca EBee EBla LEdu MAvo MSpe NBid WPGP WWEG |
| - lilac-flowered | NBid |
| - 'Ochroleuca' | CDes MSpe NBid NBre WPGP |
| - 'Parham' | CPrp CSev EBee EBla ECtt ELan EPPr GCal LBMP LLWP LRHS LSRN MBri MCot MLLN MNrw MRav MSpe MWat NEgg NSti SPer SPlb SPoG WFar WMnd WSHC WWEG |
| - 'Purple Heart' | EBee EBla EKen ELon GMac IPot LSou MAvo MLLN MNrw MSpe NBPC NLar NPri SMrm SRot |
| - 'Purple Prose' | MAvo WWEG |
| - 'Purpurea' | CAby CDes CPom EBee MSpe SUsu |
| - 'Rosea' | see *C. montana* 'Carnea' |
| * - ***violacea*** | NBid |
| - 'Violetta' | EBee IPot NBir WFar WMoo |
| ***moschata*** | see *Amberboa moschata* |
| ***nervosa*** | see *C. uniflora* subsp. *nervosa* |
| ***nigra*** | CArn CHab CRWN EBla EWil GJos GMac MNHC MSpe NBre NLan NMir SMrm WMoo WSFF XLum |
| - var. ***alba*** | CArn CBre NBid |
| - 'Elstead' **new** | MSpe |
| - subsp. ***rivularis*** | ECha MMuc NBid NBre SEND |
| ***nogmovii*** | EBee |
| ***orientalis*** | CMea CSpe EBee ECGP EWes GCal MSpe NBre NLar SPhx SPoG WHoo |
| ***pannonica*** | NBid WSHC |
| subsp. ***pannonica*** HH&K 259 | |
| ***phrygia*** | COlW GMac MSpe NBre WPer |
| ***pulcherrima*** | EBee GMac LRHS NBre |
| 'Pulchra Major' | see *Stemmacantha centaureoides* |
| ***rupestris*** | EBee EPfP MSpe NBre SGar SPhx WPer |
| ***ruthenica*** | EBee GMac MAvo NBre NLar SKHP SMad SPer SPhx SPlb WCot |
| ***salicifolia*** | MSpe NBir |
| ***salonitana*** RCBAM 1 | WCot |
| ***scabiosa*** | CArn CHab CRWN CWib EWil MHer MNHC MSpe NBid NBir NBre NLan NLar NMir SGar SPhx WPer |
| - f. ***albiflora*** | EBee GQue MSpe |
| ***simplicicaulis*** | CDes CSam GAbr LRHS MAsh MSpe SBch SMrm SRms WHoo WSHC XSen |
| ***thracica*** | CDes SAga WCot |
| 'Totnes Fat Lemon' | CDes |
| ***triumfettii*** | CPBP |
| - 'Blue Dreams' | CDes MSpe |
| § - subsp. ***cana*** **new** | XSen |
| I - - 'Rosea' | WBrk |
| - 'Hoar Frost' | CDes EBee MSpe NDov WPGP |
| - subsp. ***stricta*** | CPrp CSpr EBee MSpe WFar |
| ***uniflora*** | CDes XSen |
| § - subsp. ***nervosa*** | MSpe NBid NBre NBro NLar WPer |
| ***woronowii*** | MSpe |

## *Centaurium* (*Gentianaceae*)

| | |
|---|---|
| ***erythraea*** | CArn GPoy MHer MNHC |
| ***scilloides*** | CPBP NMen NSla NWCA WAbe |

## *Centella* (*Apiaceae*)

| | |
|---|---|
| § ***asiatica*** | CArn EOHP GPoy LEdu WJek |

## *Centradenia* (*Melastomataceae*)

| | |
|---|---|
| ***floribunda*** | LAst |
| ***inaequilateralis*** | CCCN |
| - 'Cascade' | LAst MBri SPet |

## *Centranthus* (*Caprifoliaceae*)

| | |
|---|---|
| § ***lecoqii*** | ECtt EWes LPla SPhx WCot |
| § ***ruber*** | Widely available |
| * - 'Alba Pura' | NBPC |
| § - 'Albus' | Widely available |
| - 'Atrococcineus' | ECha MAvo MMuc WPer |
| - 'Clair' | CNat |
| - var. ***coccineus*** | CBcs CHab EBee ELan EPfP GAbr GBin GKin GMaP LBMP LRHS MCot MNHC MRav MWat NPri NVic SBfd SBrd SEND SPer SPhx SRot SWat WCAu WCot WFar WWEG |
| - mauve-flowered misapplied | see *C. lecoqii* |
| - mauve-flowered | NBir |
| - 'Pink Sensation' **new** | NBPC |
| - 'Roseus' | WMoo |
| - 'Rosy Red' | GMac SBfd |
| - 'Snowcloud' | CSev ECtt EPfP MNHC WHil |
| 'White Cloud' | WJek |

## *Centropogon* (*Campanulaceae*)

| | |
|---|---|
| § ***ayavacensis*** | WCru |
| subsp. ***ayavacensis*** B&SWJ 10663 | |
| ***cordifolius*** B&SWJ 10282 | WCru |
| ***costaricae*** B&SWJ 10455 | WCru |
| ***ferrugineus*** B&SWJ 10665 | WCru |
| ***hirsutus*** B&SWJ 10657 | WCru |
| aff. ***valerii*** B&SWJ 10341 | WCru |

| | |
|---|---|
| ***willdenowianus*** | see *C. ayavacensis* subsp. *ayavacensis* |

## *Cephalanthera* (*Orchidaceae*)

| | |
|---|---|
| ***falcata*** | EFEx LWSt NLAp |
| ***longibracteata*** | EFEx NLAp |

## *Cephalanthus* (*Rubiaceae*)

| | |
|---|---|
| ***occidentalis*** | CWib EBee ELon GBin LRHS LSou MAsh MBNS MBlu MBri MGos NLar SLim SPoG SRms WFar WGob |

## *Cephalaria* (*Caprifoliaceae*)

| | |
|---|---|
| § ***alpina*** | COIW EBee EBla EPPr EPfP LBMP MHer MNrw MRav NLar SPhx SRms SWat WCot WFar WPer XLum |
| - 'Nana' | NWCA |
| ***ambrosioides*** | MLLN |
| - MESE 503 | EBee |
| ***anatolica*** KMT-04-72 | EBee |
| ***caucasica*** | see *C. gigantea* |
| ***dipsacoides*** | CEnt CFee EBee EBla ECha LPla MSpe NLar SKHP SPhx WMoo WTcb |
| § ***flava*** | EBee LRHS NBre |
| ***galpiniana*** | SPlb |
| - subsp. ***simplicior*** | EBee |
| § ***gigantea*** | Widely available |
| ***graeca*** | see *C. flava* |
| ***leucantha*** | CArn EBee MLLN NBid NBre SPhx WFar WMoo |
| ***litvinovii*** | CElw SPhx |
| ***radiata*** | EBee GBin |
| ***tatarica*** hort. | see *C. gigantea* |
| ***tchihatchewii*** | EBee MLLN |

## *Cephalotaxus* (*Taxaceae*)

| | |
|---|---|
| ***fortunei*** | CDul |
| - 'Prostrate Spreader' | SLim WEve |
| ***harringtonii*** | ERom LEdu |
| - var. ***drupacea*** | CDoC NWea |
| - 'Fastigiata' | CBcs CDoC CDul EHul IArd IDee LRHS MAsh MBri MDev MGos NLar NPal SCoo SLim SPoG WDin WFar |
| - 'Korean Gold' | CKen LRHS MBri MDev NLar SLim SPoG |
| - 'Prostrata' | LRHS SPoG |
| ***sinensis*** | CMCN |

## *Cephalotus* (*Cephalotaceae*)

| | |
|---|---|
| ***follicularis*** | SHmp |

## *Cerastium* (*Caryophyllaceae*)

| | |
|---|---|
| ***alpinum*** | ECho IFoB SRms |
| - var. ***lanatum*** | ECho EDAr EWes |
| ***arvense*** | XLum |
| ***candidissimum*** | EWes |
| ***fontanum*** **new** | CHab |
| ***tomentosum*** | CBar ECho EPfP LAst MMuc NBlu NPri SEND SPer SPet SPlb SPoG WFar |
| - var. ***columnae*** | ECha ECho EHoe EWes XLum |
| - 'Silberteppich' | LBMP |
| - 'Yo Yo' | WFar |

## *Ceratonia* (*Caesalpiniaceae*)

| | |
|---|---|
| ***siliqua*** | CBcs |

## *Ceratophyllum* (*Ceratophyllaceae*)

| | |
|---|---|
| ***demersum*** | CBen CWat EHon EWil MSKA MWts SWat WMAq WSFF |

## *Ceratostigma* ✿ (*Plumbaginaceae*)

| | |
|---|---|
| ***abyssinicum*** | ELan |
| ***asperrimum*** B&SWJ 7260 | WCru |
| 'Autumn Blue' | EPfP LRHS |
| ***capensis*** | CMac |
| ***griffithii*** | Widely available |
| - wild-collected | GCal |
| § ***plumbaginoides*** ♀H3-4 | Widely available |
| ***willmottianum*** ♀H3-4 | Widely available |
| - BWJ 8140 | WCru |
| - Desert Skies = 'Palmgold'PBR | CBcs EBee ELan EPfP LAst MBlu MGos NLar SGol SLim SPer SWvt |
| - Forest Blue = 'Lice'PBR | CDoC CMac CSBt CSev CSpe CWSG EBee ELan EPPr EPfP LAst LRHS LSRN MBri MGos NLar NPri SBfd SCoo SLim SPer SPoG SPtl SReu SWvt WDin WPat |

## *Cercidiphyllum* ✿ (*Cercidiphyllaceae*)

| | |
|---|---|
| ***japonicum*** ♀H4 | Widely available |
| - 'Boyd's Dwarf' | CPMA LLHF LRHS MAsh NLar SPoG WAbe WCot |
| - 'Herkenrode Dwarf' | NLar |
| - 'Heronswood Globe' | CPMA EPfP MBlu NLar SSta |
| - 'Kreukenberg Dwarf' | CPMA |
| - 'Morioka Weeping' | CPMA CTho MPkF SChF SMad SSta WPGP |
| - 'Peach' | CPMA NLar |
| § - f. ***pendulum*** ♀H4 | CBcs CDul CEnd CLnd CMCN CMac CPLG CPMA CTri EBee ELan EPfP GBin GKin LRHS MAsh MBlu MGos NEgg NLar SCoo SLim SPoG SSpi WDin WHar |
| - - 'Amazing Grace' | CTho MBlu NLar SSta |
| - 'Raspberry' | CPMA MBri NLar |
| - Red Fox | see *C. japonicum* 'Rotfuchs' |
| § - 'Rotfuchs' | Widely available |
| - 'Ruby' | CPMA MBlu MBri NLar SChF WPGP |
| - 'Strawberry' | CBcs CPMA EBee MBlu NLar |
| - 'Tidal Wave' | CPMA NLar |
| ***magnificum*** | CDoC CDul CEnd CMCN CPLG EPfP IDee MBlu NEgg NLar WPGP |
| - f. ***pendulum*** | see *C. japonicum* f. *pendulum* |

## *Cercis* (*Caesalpiniaceae*)

| | |
|---|---|
| sp. | WFoF |
| ***canadensis*** | CBcs CDul CLnd CMCN CWGN EPfP MGos MMuc NEgg NLar NWea SCoo SLim SPer WPat WRHF |
| - 'Ace of Hearts'PBR **new** | MPkF |
| - f. ***alba*** | CBcs ESwi LSRN |
| - - 'Royal White' | CPMA EPfP IArd LRHS MBlu |
| - 'Appalachian Red' | CPMA LSRN MAsh MBlu MGos NLar SGol SKHP |
| - 'Cascading Hearts' | CBcs ESwi MBri NLar |
| - 'Flame' | CPMA LRHS SKHP SSta WPGP WPat |
| - 'Forest Pansy' ♀H4 | Widely available |
| - 'Hearts of Gold'PBR | CTho CWGN EBee EWTr LRHS MAsh MBlu MBri MGos MPkF NLar SBfd SKHP SLim SPoG WHar |
| - Lavender Twist = 'Covey' | CBcs EBee ESwi LAst LRHS LSRN MBlu MBri MGos NLar SBfd SGol SKHP SLim SPoG WHar |
| - Little Woody = 'Litwo'PBR **new** | MPkF SGol |
| - var. ***mexicana*** NJM 09.024 | WPGP |
| - - 'Sanderson' **new** | SSta |

| | |
|---|---|
| § - var. ***occidentalis*** | LEdu MOWG NLar NMun SSta |
| - 'Pauline Lily' | NLar |
| - 'Pink Heartbreaker' **new** | SGol |
| - 'Rubye Atkinson' | CPMA NLar SSpi |
| - 'Tennessee Pink' | CPMA NLar |
| - 'Texan White' | SGol |
| - var. ***texensis*** 'Traveller' | SGol |
| - 'Wither's Pink Charm' | SSta |
| ***chinensis*** | CBcs NLar SPer WDin |
| - f. ***alba*** | CTho |
| - 'Avondale' | Widely available |
| - 'Don Egolf' | CPMA LRHS LSRN MGos MPkF NLar SGol SKHP SSta |
| ***chingii*** | CPLG |
| ***gigantea*** | NLar |
| ***griffithii*** | LLHF NLar NMun SSta |
| ***occidentalis*** | see *C. canadensis* var. *occidentalis* |
| ***racemosa*** | CPLG IDee NLar WPGP |
| ***reniformis*** 'Oklahoma' | CPMA EBee ESwi LSRN MGos MPkF NLar NPCo SKHP WHar |
| - 'Texas White' | CBcs CPMA EBee MAsh MBri MPkF NLar SGol SKHP SLim SPoG WHar WPat |
| ***siliquastrum*** 🏆H4 | Widely available |
| - f. ***albida*** | CBot CTho ECrN ELan EPfP EPri LRHS SKHP SSpi WCFE |
| - 'Bodnant' | CTho EBee EPfP EWes LAst LLHF LRHS LSRN MAsh MBlu MBri MGos NLar SSta WHar |
| - 'White Swan' | CPMA CTho EWes |
| ***yunnanensis*** | NLar |

## *Cerinthe* (*Boraginaceae*)

| | |
|---|---|
| ***glabra*** | LBMP NBre SPlb |
| ***major*** | MLLN SWvt |
| - 'Kiwi Blue' | CHll MDKP |
| - 'Purpurascens' | CMea CSpe ELan EPfP EWTr IFoB LBMP LRHS MNHC NLar SDix SEND SGar SMrm SPer SPoG SWal WKif WWEG |
| - 'Yellow Gem' | ELan NLar |

## *Ceropegia* (*Apocynaceae*)

| | |
|---|---|
| ***barklyi*** | LToo |
| ***conrathii*** | LToo |
| ***floribunda*** | LToo |
| ***fusca*** | EShb |
| § ***linearis*** | EShb SRms STre |
| subsp. ***woodii*** 🏆H1 | |
| § - - 'Lady Heart' (v) | EShb |
| - - 'Variegata' | see *C. linearis* subsp. *woodii* 'Lady Heart' |
| ***multiflora*** | LToo |
| ***pubescens*** GWJ 9441 | WCru |
| ***woodii*** | see *C. linearis* subsp. *woodii* |

## *Ceroxylon* (*Arecaceae*)

| | |
|---|---|
| ***alpinum*** | LPal |
| ***ventricosum*** | LPal |

## *Cestrum* (*Solanaceae*)

| | |
|---|---|
| ***aurantiacum*** | EShb |
| ***auriculatum*** | MOWG |
| × ***cultum*** | CHll EShb |
| - 'Cretan Pink' | MOWG |
| - 'Cretan Purple' | CBcs CHGN CHid CHll CRHN EBee ELan ELon EPfP EShb EWTr LHop LRHS MOWG SEND SMad SPoG WKif WSHC |
| ***diurnum*** × ***nocturnum*** | EShb |
| § ***elegans*** | CDoC CHEx CHll CPLG CRHN CTsd ELon EPfP EWTr LRHS MOWG NEgg SBrd SEND SLon SPad WDin |
| ***fasciculatum*** | EShb MOWG |
| 'Newellii' 🏆H2 | CBcs CMHG CPLG CSev CWGN CWib EBak ELan ELon EPfP EShb LRHS MOWG SEND SGar WBor WKif WSHC |
| ***nocturnum*** | CCCN CDoC CHll EBak EOHP ERea EShb IDee MOWG NExo |
| ***parqui*** 🏆H3 | CAbb CBcs CHll CMHG CTsd CWib EBee ELan EPfP ERea EShb EWTr LHop LRHS MOWG SDix SEND SGar SLon SMad SMrm SUsu WJek WKif WSHC WWlt |
| ***psittacinum*** | CPLG |
| ***purpureum*** (Lindl.) Standl. | see *C. elegans* |
| ***roseum*** | CPLG |
| * ***splendens*** | MOWG |

## *Ceterach* (*Aspleniaceae*)

| | |
|---|---|
| ***officinarum*** | see *Asplenium ceterach* |

## *Chaenomeles* (*Rosaceae*)

| | |
|---|---|
| ***cathayensis*** | CAgr CTho LEdu NLar |
| § ***japonica*** | MMuc SEND WDin WFar |
| - 'Chojubai' | CMen |
| - 'Cido' | CAgr LBuc MCoo |
| - 'Orange Beauty' | LRHS SPer WFar |
| - 'Sargentii' | CMac EPfP MGos NBro SGol |
| 'John Pilger' | NHol |
| ***lagenaria*** | see *C. speciosa* |
| Madame Butterfly = 'Whitice' | CAlb CDoC EBee EPfP LAst LRHS LSRN MAsh MBri MMuc MRav NEgg SBfd SBod SEND SLim SPer SPoG WGrn |
| ***maulei*** | see *C. japonica* |
| 'Orange Star' | CEnd EBee LRHS NLar |
| ***sinensis*** | see *Pseudocydonia sinensis* |
| § ***speciosa*** | NWea SMrm |
| - 'Apple Blossom' | see *C. speciosa* 'Moerloosei' |
| - 'Brilliant' | EPfP |
| - 'Contorta' | LBMP LRHS MAsh |
| - 'Eximia' | CAlb LRHS LTen |
| - 'Falconnet Charlet' (d) | LRHS MRav SBfd |
| - 'Flocon Rose' **new** | LRHS |
| - 'Friesdorfer' | LRHS |
| - 'Geisha Girl' (d) 🏆H4 | Widely available |
| - 'Grayshott Salmon' | NHol NPro WFar |
| - Hot Fire = 'Minvesu' **new** | EPfP |
| - 'Kinshiden' | EPfP LRHS |
| - 'Knap Hill Radiance' | SLim |
| § - 'Moerloosei' 🏆H4 | Widely available |
| - 'Nivalis' | Widely available |
| - 'Rubra Grandiflora' | LRHS WBor |
| - 'Simonii' (d) | CBcs EBee EPfP MGos MRav NWea SPer WFar |
| - 'Snow' | LBMP MAsh MSwo |
| - 'Umbilicata' | MBlu NLar SPer SRms |
| - 'Yukigotan' | CDoC EBee LRHS MMuc NLar SBfd SEND SGol WPat |
| × ***superba*** | STre |
| - 'Boule de Feu' | CTri CWib ECtt MCoo |
| - 'Cameo' (d) | CBot CChe CEnd EBee ELon EPfP LHop LRHS MBNS MBri MRav NCGa NLar SGol SLPl |
| - 'Clementine' | CWib EBee |
| - 'Coquelicot' **new** | LRHS |
| - 'Crimson and Gold' 🏆H4 | Widely available |

- 'Elly Mossel' CMac CWib NLar WFar
- 'Etna' CAlb
- 'Fascination' NLar
- 'Fire Dance' CDul CHll CWib EBee ECtt LRHS MAsh MSwo NHol NLar SGol SPer WRHF
- 'Fusion' CAgr
- 'Hever Castle' CPMA
- 'Issai White' MRav
- 'Jet Trail' CAlb CBcs CSBt EBee ECtt ELan EPfP LAst LRHS LSRN MAsh MGos MRav MSwo NLar SGol SLPl SLim SPoG SWvt WFar
- 'Knap Hill Scarlet' ♀H4 CAlb CDoC CDul EBee ECtt EPfP GGal LRHS MAsh MGos MMuc NHol SEND SLim SPer SPoG SRms SWvt WDin WFar
- 'Lemon and Lime' ELan EPfP EWTr MAsh MGos MRav SLon
- 'Nicoline' ♀H4 CBcs CDoC CDul EBee EPfP EWTr MBri MGos NEgg SLim WDin WFar
- 'Pink Lady' ♀H4 Widely available
- 'Red Joy' LRHS NLar WGrn
- 'Red Trail' MRav
- 'Rowallane' ♀H4 CHll EBee ELan EPfP MRav SPer
- 'Salmon Horizon' EPfP EWTr MGos NLar
- 'Tortuosa' EBee LHop WGrn

'Toyo-nishiki' MBlu NLar

## *Chaenorhinum* (*Plantaginaceae*)

§ ***origanifolium*** ECho NRya SBch SPlb
- 'Blue Dream' CSpe ECho EPfP GKev IPot MAsh NVic NWCA SPoG SWvt WFar WMoo WPer WRHF
- 'Dreamcatcher' EPfP
- 'Summer Skies' NPri SPet WFar

## *Chaerophyllum* (*Apiaceae*)

***hirsutum*** CRow
- 'Roseum' Widely available

## *Chamaecyparis* ✿ (*Cupressaceae*)

'Erecta Viridis' CSBt MGos

***formosensis*** CKen

***funebris*** see *Cupressus funebris*

***lawsoniana*** CDul EHul NWea WDin WMou
- SIN 1820 GLin
- 'Albospica' (v) WFar
- 'Allumii Aurea' see *C. lawsoniana* 'Alumigold'
- 'Allumii Magnificent' CDul NLar
- 'Allumii White Spot' **new** ECho

§ - 'Alumigold' MAsh MGos SCoo WDin
- 'Alumii' EHul MAsh MGos NWea
- 'Aurea' CDul
- 'Aurea Densa' ♀H4 CKen CMac CSBt CTri EHul EPfP MAsh MGos NEgg WEve WGor
- 'Barry's Silver' WEve
- 'Bleu Nantais' CKen CMac ECho EHul LBee LRHS MAsh MGos NBlu SCoo SLim SPoG WCFE WEve WFar WGor
- 'Blom' CKen EHul

§ - 'Blue Gown' EHul SRms
- 'Blue Surprise' CKen EHul WFar
- 'Brégéon' CKen NLar
- 'Broomhill Gold' CDoC CSBt ECho EHul LRHS MAsh MGos NPri SCoo SLim SPer SPoG WBor WDin WEve
- 'Caudata' CKen NLar
- 'Chantry Gold' EHul WEve

§ - 'Chilworth Silver' ♀H4 CSBt EHul LBee LRHS MAsh NBlu SCoo SLim SPer SPoG SRms WDin WFar
- 'Columnaris' CBcs CDoC ECho EPfP LAst LBee LMaj LRHS MBri MGos NEgg NWea SCoo SPoG WFar
- 'Columnaris Aurea' see *C. lawsoniana* 'Golden Spire'

N - 'Columnaris Glauca' CMac CWib EHul MAsh MGos NEgg NWea SBrd SCoo SPer WDin WFar
- 'Crawford's Compact' CMac
- 'Cream Crackers' ECho EHul
- 'Cream Glow' CKen CSBt LRHS MAsh MGos NLar SCoo SLim SPoG WFar WGor
- 'Croftway' EHul
- 'Dik's Weeping' CDoC NLar NWea SLim WEve
- 'Duncanii' ECho EHul
- 'Dutch Gold' EHul MAsh
- 'Dwarf Blue' see *C. lawsoniana* 'Pick's Dwarf Blue'
- 'Eclipse' CKen
- 'Elegantissima' ambig. CKen MGos
- 'Ellwoodii' ♀H4 CDul CMac CSBt CTri CWib ECho EHul EPfP LAst LRHS MGos NBlu NPri NWea SBrd SCoo SLim SPer SPoG WDin WFar WMoo

I - 'Ellwoodii Glauca' SPlb
- 'Ellwood's Empire' EHul
- 'Ellwood's Gold' ♀H4 CBcs CDoC CSBt CWib ECho EHul ELan EPfP LBee LRHS MAsh MBri MGos NBlu NHol NPri NWea SBrd SPer SPlb SPoG STre WDin WEve WFar WMoo
- 'Ellwood's Gold Pillar' ECho EHul LBee LRHS MAsh MGos NHol SCoo SLim SPoG WBor WFar WGor

§ - 'Ellwood's Nymph' CKen ECho LRHS MAsh SCoo SLim WFar WGor
- Ellwood's Pillar = 'Flolar' CDoC CMac ECho EHul LAst LBee LRHS MBri MGos NHol NLar SCoo SLim WCFE WDin WFar
- 'Ellwood's Pygmy' CMac
- 'Ellwood's Silver' MAsh WFar
- 'Ellwood's Silver Threads' CMac
- 'Ellwood's Variegata' see *C. lawsoniana* 'Ellwood's White'

§ - 'Ellwood's White' (v) CKen CSBt ECho EHul EPfP SPoG WFar

I - 'Emerald' CKen
- 'Emerald Spire' MAsh
- 'Empire' WFar
- 'Erecta Aurea' EHul MGos
- 'Erecta Viridis' CBcs NEgg NWea WDin WFar
- 'Ericoides' EHul
- 'Filiformis Compacta' EHul
- 'Filip's Golden Tears' MAsh SLim
- 'Fleckellwood' CWib EHul MAsh NBlu
- 'Fletcheri' ♀H4 CMac EHul NWea WDin WFar
- 'Fletcheri Aurea' see *C. lawsoniana* 'Yellow Transparent'
- 'Fletcher's White' EHul
- 'Forsteckensis' CKen EHul NLar NWea SRms WFar

I - 'Forsteckensis Aurea' CDoC NLar
- 'Fraseri' NWea
- 'Gimbornii' ♀H4 EHul LBee NBlu SCoo SLim SRms WFar
- 'Glauca' CDul
- 'Gnome' CDoC CMac ECho EHul GEdr LAst LRHS MGos SCoo SLim SPoG WEve WGor WThu

§ - 'Golden Pot' CDoC CMac CSBt CWib EHul LBee LRHS MGos NBlu SCoo WDin WFar

| | | |
|---|---|---|
| § | – 'Golden Queen' | EHul |
| | – 'Golden Showers' | EHul |
| § | – 'Golden Spire' | MAsh NLar WFar |
| | – 'Golden Triumph' | EHul |
| | – 'Golden Wonder' | ECho EHul MAsh MGos NEgg NLar NWea SCoo SRms WDin WEve WFar |
| | – 'Goldfinger' | NLar |
| | – 'Grayswood Feather' | CDoC CSBt EHul LBee LRHS MAsh MGos SCoo SPlb WEve |
| | – 'Grayswood Gold' | EHul WEve |
| | – 'Grayswood Pillar' 𝕐H4 | CDul EHul MGos |
| | – 'Green Globe' | CDoC CKen CMen CSBt EHul LBee MAsh MGos NLar SCoo SLim WDin WEve WThu |
| § | – 'Green Hedger' 𝕐H4 | CDul CSBt NWea SCoo SRms WFar |
| § | – 'Green Pillar' | CWib ECho LAst LBee NEgg SCoo |
| | – 'Green Spire' | see *C. lawsoniana* 'Green Pillar' |
| | – 'Hogger's Blue Gown' | see *C. lawsoniana* 'Blue Gown' |
| | – 'Imbricata Pendula' | CDoC CKen IDee LRHS NLar SLim SMad |
| | – 'Intertexta' 𝕐H4 | WEve |
| | – 'Ivonne' | EHul MGos WEve |
| | – 'Jackman's Green Hedger' | see *C. lawsoniana* 'Green Hedger' |
| | – 'Jackman's Variety' | see *C. lawsoniana* 'Green Pillar' |
| | – 'Kelleriis Gold' | EHul |
| | – 'Killarny Salmon' | CMac |
| | – 'Kilmacurragh' 𝕐H4 | CMac MAsh MGos NWea |
| | – 'Kilworth Column' | CDoC MGos NLar NWea |
| | – 'Kingswood' | CDoC |
| | – 'Knowefieldensis' | CMac ECho |
| | – 'Lane' misapplied | see *C. lawsoniana* 'Lanei Aurea' |
| | – 'Lane' den Ouden | CWib ECho MGos MRav NEgg SCoo WDin WFar |
| § | – 'Lanei Aurea' 𝕐H4 | EHul MGos SPoG WFar |
| | – 'Lemon Pillar' | WDin WEve |
| | – 'Lemon Queen' | CDul EHul LBee WEve |
| | – 'Little Spire' 𝕐H4 | CDoC ECho EPla LRHS MBri MGos NHol NLar SBfd SCoo SLim SPoG WEve WGor |
| | – 'Lombartsii' | WFar |
| | – 'Lutea' 𝕐H4 | CMac EHul MGos |
| § | – 'Lutea Nana' 𝕐H4 | CMac EHul EPla MAsh MGos NLar |
| § | – 'Lutea Smithii' | NWea |
| | – 'Luteocompacta' | LBee |
| * | – 'MacPenny's Gold' | CMac |
| § | – 'Minima' | SRms |
| | – 'Minima Argentea' | see *C. lawsoniana* 'Nana Argentea' |
| | – 'Minima Aurea' 𝕐H4 | CDoC CDul CKen CMac CWib ECho EHul EPfP EPla LAst LBee LRHS MAsh MBri MGos NBlu NEgg SLim SPer SPoG WBor WCFE WDin WEve WFar WMoo |
| | – 'Minima Densa' | see *C. lawsoniana* 'Minima' |
| | – 'Minima Glauca' 𝕐H4 | CMac CSBt ECho EHul EPfP GEdr LAst LRHS MGos NEgg NWea SCoo SLim SPer WDin WEve WFar |
| * | – 'Moonsprite' | ECho EHul LAst LRHS NLar SCoo SLim SPoG WGor |
| | – 'Nana' | CMac |
| | – 'Nana Albospica' (v) | ECho EHul LBee SCoo SPoG WFar WGor |
| § | – 'Nana Argentea' | CKen CMac ECho EHul EPfP SCoo SPoG WFar WGor |
| | – 'Nana Lutea' | see *C. lawsoniana* 'Lutea Nana' |
| | – 'Nicole' | ECho EHul MAsh SCoo WGor |
| | – 'Nidiformis' | EHul SRms |
| | – 'Nyewoods' | see *C. lawsoniana* 'Chilworth Silver' |
| | – 'Nymph' | see *C. lawsoniana* 'Ellwood's Nymph' |
| | – 'Pagoda' | MAsh |
| § | – 'Pelt's Blue' 𝕐H4 | CBcs CDoC CDul CKen CSBt EHul LBee LRHS MGos NLar SBfd SCoo SLim SPoG WDin WFar |
| | – 'Pembury Blue' 𝕐H4 | CDoC CSBt CWib ECho EHul EPfP LBee LRHS MAsh MGos NEgg NLar NWea SBrd SCoo SLim SPer SPoG WDin WFar |
| § | – 'Pick's Dwarf Blue' | LRHS MGos SCoo WEve |
| | – Pot of Gold | see *C. lawsoniana* 'Golden Pot' |
| | – 'Pottenii' | CMac CSBt ECho EHul LBee MAsh MGos NWea WDin WFar |
| | – 'Pygmaea Argentea' (v) 𝕐H4 | CKen CMac CSBt CWib ECho EHul ELan EPfP EPla LBee MAsh MBri MGos NBlu NEgg NHol SLim SPer SPoG SRms WBor WCFE WDin WFar |
| | – 'Pygmy' | EHul LRHS NHol NLar NWea SCoo SLim WEve |
| | – 'Rijnhof' | EHul LBee |
| | – 'Rimpelaar' | CDoC MGos |
| | – 'Rock Gold' | WEve |
| | – 'Rogersii' | SRms WFar |
| | – 'Royal Gold' | EHul NBlu |
| | – 'Silver Queen' (v) | CKen |
| | – 'Silver Threads' (v) | ECho EHul EPla LBee LRHS MAsh SPoG WFar |
| | – 'Silver Tip' (v) | ECho EHul LRHS SCoo SLim |
| | – 'Smithii' | see *C. lawsoniana* 'Lutea Smithii' |
| | – 'Snow Flurry' (v) | CKen ECho EHul SPoG WFar |
| | – 'Snow White'[PBR] (v) | ECho EHul LBee LRHS MAsh MBri MGos NHol SCoo SLim SPoG WFar WGor |
| | – 'Springtime'[PBR] | CSBt EHul LBee LRHS MAsh SCoo SLim SPoG WGor |
| | – 'Stardust' 𝕐H4 | CBcs CDoC CDul CSBt CTri CWib EHul ELan LRHS MAsh NEgg NPri SCoo SLim SPoG WDin |
| | – 'Stewartii' | CDul CTri NEgg NWea SCoo |
| * | – 'Summer Cream' | EHul |
| | – 'Summer Snow' (v) | CDoC ECho EHul EPfP LBee LRHS MGos NBlu NHol NPri SCoo SLim SRms WFar |
| | – 'Sunkist' | LRHS SCoo SLim WFar |
| | – 'Tamariscifolia' | CDoC EHul WCFE WDin WFar |
| | – 'Tharandtensis Caesia' | WFar |
| | – 'Tilford' | EHul |
| | – 'Treasure' (v) | CSBt EHul EPfP EPla LRHS MAsh NBlu SCoo SLim SPoG WFar |
| | – 'Van Pelt' | see *C. lawsoniana* 'Pelt's Blue' |
| | – 'Westermannii' (v) | CMac |
| | – 'White Edge' | WFar |
| | – 'White Spot' (v) | EHul NPri WFar |
| | – 'Winston Churchill' | MGos NWea |
| | – 'Wisselii' 𝕐H4 | CDoC CKen CMac ECho EHul NLar NWea SCoo SRms WCFE WDin WFar WMoo |
| | – 'Wisselii Nana' | CKen EHul |
| | – 'Wissel's Saguaro' | CDoC CKen IVic MGos NLar SLim |
| | – 'Witzeliana' | CDul CSBt MGos NLar |
| | – 'Yellow Queen' | see *C. lawsoniana* 'Golden Queen' |
| | – 'Yellow Success' | see *C. lawsoniana* 'Golden Queen' |
| § | – 'Yellow Transparent' | CMac SBrd |
| | – 'Yvonne' | CDoC CDul ECho LRHS MAsh MGos NEgg NLar SCoo SLim SPoG WEve |
| | ***leylandii*** | see × *Cuprocyparis leylandii* |
| | ***obtusa*** 'Albovariegata' (v) | CKen |
| | – 'Arneson's Compact' | CKen |

– 'Aurea' CDoC SCoo WEve
– 'Aurora' CKen ECho ELan MAsh MGos SLim WEve
– 'Bambi' CDoC CKen MGos NLar WEve WThu
– 'Barkenny' CKen
– 'Bartley' CKen
– 'Bassett' CKen
– 'Bess' CKen
– 'Brigitt' CKen
– 'Buttonball' CKen
– 'Chabo-yadori' CDoC EHul LRHS MGos SCoo SLim WFar
– 'Chilworth' CDoC CKen MGos NLar
– 'Chima-anihiba' CKen
– 'Chirimen' CDoC CKen MGos NHol NLar NWad SLim
– 'Clarke's Seedling' CDoC NLar
– 'Confucius' CDoC EHul MGos
§ – 'Crippsii' ♀H4 CBcs CDoC CDul CMac LRHS MGos SCoo SLim
– 'Crippsii Aurea' see *C. obtusa* 'Crippsii'
– 'Dainty Doll' CDoC CKen MGos NLar
– 'Densa' see *C. obtusa* 'Nana Densa'
– 'Draht' CDoC MGos NLar
– 'Draht Hexe' CKen
– 'Elf' CKen
– 'Ellie B' CKen
– 'Ericoides' CKen
– 'Fernspray Gold' CDoC CDul CKen CTri ECho EHul LRHS MAsh NEgg SBfd SCoo SLim SPer SPoG WFar
– 'Flabelliformis' CKen
– 'Gnome' CKen CMen
– 'Gold Fern' CKen MGos WFar
– 'Golden Fairy' CDoC CKen MGos WEve
– 'Golden Filament' (v) CKen
– 'Golden Nymph' CDoC CKen MGos NLar
– 'Golden Sprite' CDoC CKen MGos NLar WEve WThu
– 'Goldilocks' EHul
– 'Gracilis Aurea' CKen CMac
– 'Green Diamond' CKen
– 'Hage' CKen
– 'Hannah' **new** NLar
– 'Hypnoides Nana' CKen
– 'Intermedia' CDoC CKen MGos
– 'Ivan's Column' CKen
– 'Junior' CKen
– 'Juniperoides' CKen WThu
– 'Kamarachiba' CDoC CKen CSBt ECho EHul EPla LAst LBee LRHS MAsh NLar SCoo SLim SPoG WEve WFar WGor
– 'Kerdalo' LRHS NLar SLim SPoG
– 'Konijn' ECho EHul
– 'Kosteri' CDoC CKen CMac ECho EHul ELan EPot GLam LBee MAsh NBlu NEgg NHol SCoo WEve
– 'Kyoto Creeper' CKen
– 'Leprechaun' NLar
– 'Limerick' CKen
– 'Little Markey' CKen
– 'Lucas' CDoC NLar SLim
– 'Marian' CKen MGos NLar
§ – 'Mariesii' (v) CKen SCoo
– 'Melody' CKen NLar
– 'Meroke' NLar
– 'Minima' CKen MGos
– 'Nana' ♀H4 CDoC CKen CMac CMen LBee MGos NHol NWad WEve
– 'Nana Aurea' ♀H4 CDoC CMac CMea CSBt ECho EHul EPfP MAsh MGos NHol SBrd WEve WFar
§ – 'Nana Densa' CDoC CKen CMac NLar
– 'Nana Gracilis' ♀H4 CDoC CDul CKen CMen CSBt ECho EHul ELan EPfP EPla EPot GEdr IVic LAst LRHS MAsh MBri MGos NBlu NEgg NWad NWea SCoo SLim SPoG STre WDin WEve WFar
I – 'Nana Gracilis Aurea' CMen EHul WEve
I – 'Nana Lutea' CDoC CKen ECho EHul EPfP LBee LRHS MAsh MGos NBlu SCoo SLim SPoG
– 'Nana Rigida' see *C. obtusa* 'Rigid Dwarf'
– 'Nana Variegata' see *C. obtusa* 'Mariesii'
– 'Pygmaea' CSBt ECho EHul LRHS MGos SCoo SLim WEve
– 'Rashahiba' SLim
§ – 'Rigid Dwarf' CDoC CKen ECho EHul LBee NLar SCoo SPoG WEve
– 'Saffron Spray' LRHS SLim
– 'Snowflake' (v) CDoC CKen NWad SBfd WEve WFar
– 'Snowkist' (v) CKen
– 'Spiralis' CKen
– 'Stoneham' CKen
– 'Suirova-hiba' SLim
– 'Tempelhof' CKen ECho EHul LRHS MAsh MGos NEgg NLar SCoo SLim WEve
– 'Tetragona Aurea' CBcs CMac EHul LRHS MGos NLar SCoo SLim WEve
– 'Timothy' CMac
– 'Tonia' (v) CKen EHul EPla LRHS NHol NLar SLim WEve WGor
– 'Topsie' CKen NLar
– 'Tsatsumi' CDoC EMil
– 'Tsatsumi Gold' CDoC CKen EHul LRHS MPkF NLar SCoo SLim SPoG
– 'Verdon' CKen
– 'Winter Gold' WEve
– 'Wissel' CKen
– 'Wyckoff' CKen
– 'Yellowtip' (v) CKen ECho MAsh MGos WEve
***pisifera*** 'Aurea Nana' misapplied see *C. pisifera* 'Strathmore'
– 'Avenue' EHul
– 'Baby Blue' ECho EHul ELan EPfP LRHS MGos SCoo SLim WGor
– 'Blue Globe' CKen
– 'Boulevard' ♀H4 CBcs CDoC CDul CMac CPMA CSBt CWib ECho EHul ELan EPfP LAst LBee LRHS MAsh MGos NBlu NEgg NWea SBfd SBrd SLim SPer SRms STre WDin WEve WFar WMoo
– 'Compacta Variegata' (v) ECho MAsh NEgg
– 'Curly Tops' CSBt ECho EHul LRHS MGos SCoo SLim WEve
– 'Devon Cream' ECho MGos NEgg SCoo WFar
– 'Filifera' CMac CSBt LRHS SCoo WFar
– 'Filifera Aurea' ♀H4 CKen CMac CWib ECho EHul EPfP EPla LBee MAsh MGos NEgg NHol NWea SCoo SPer SRms WCFE WDin WEve WFar
– 'Filifera Aureovariegata' (v) EHul LRHS SCoo
– 'Filifera Nana' ECho EHul ELan LRHS SLim SPoG STre WDin WFar
– 'Filifera Nana Aurea' see *C. pisifera* 'Golden Mop'
– 'Filifera Sungold' see *C. pisifera* 'Sungold'

- 'Fuiri-tsukomo' CKen
- 'Gold Cushion' CKen
- 'Gold Dust' see *C. pisifera* 'Plumosa Aurea'
- 'Gold Spangle' CKen ECho EHul WFar
§ - 'Golden Mop' ♀H4 CKen EHul NLar
- 'Green Pincushion' CKen CMen
- 'Hime-himuro' CKen
- 'Hime-sawara' CKen CMen
- 'Margaret' CKen
- 'Nana' CKen CMen ECho EHul EPfP MAsh MGos NHol WFar
I - 'Nana Albovariegata' (v) CDoC MAsh SPoG WFar WThu
- 'Nana Aureovariegata' (v) CDoC CSBt ECho EHul LBee LRHS NBlu SCoo SLim SPer WEve WFar
I - 'Nana Compacta' CMac SRms
- 'Nana Variegata' (v) CMac LBee NWad SLim WFar
I - 'Parslorii' CKen
- 'Pici' CKen
§ - 'Plumosa Aurea' CKen EHul MAsh SBrd WDin WFar
- 'Plumosa Aurea Compacta' CKen
- 'Plumosa Aurea Nana' MAsh MGos WFar
I - 'Plumosa Aurea Nana Compacta' CMac
- 'Plumosa Aurescens' CDoC CMac
§ - 'Plumosa Compressa' CDoC CKen EHul NWad SCoo SLim WFar WGor WThu
- 'Plumosa Densa' see *C. pisifera* 'Plumosa Compressa'
- 'Plumosa Flavescens' EHul
I - 'Plumosa Juniperoides' CKen ECho EHul SCoo SLim WFar WGor
I - 'Plumosa Pygmaea' WGor
§ - 'Plumosa Rogersii' EHul NHol WGor
- 'Pygmaea Tsukumo' NLar
- 'Rogersii' see *C. pisifera* 'Plumosa Rogersii'
- 'Silver and Gold' (v) EHul
- 'Silver Lode' (v) CKen
- 'Snow' (v) CKen
- 'Snowflake' CKen EHul MGos
- 'Spaan's Cannon Ball' CKen
§ - 'Squarrosa' WDin WFar
- 'Squarrosa Dumosa' CKen EHul
- 'Squarrosa Lombarts' CSBt EHul
- 'Squarrosa Lutea' CKen
- 'Squarrosa Sulphurea' CSBt ECho EHul EPfP LRHS SLim WDin WFar
- 'Squarrosa Veitchii' see *C. pisifera* 'Squarrosa'
§ - 'Strathmore' CKen EHul NWad WDin
§ - 'Sungold' CDoC CKen CSBt ECho EHul EPla LAst LRHS MAsh NBlu SCoo SLim SPoG WEve
- 'Tama-himuro' CKen
- 'Teddy Bear' MBri NLar
- 'True Blue' ECho EHul MGos NLar
- 'Winter Beauty' LRHS

***thyoides*** 'Andelyensis' CMac CSBt ECho EHul LAst NBlu NEgg SCoo WFar
- 'Andelyensis Nana' CKen
- 'Aurea' EHul
- 'Conica' CKen MAsh
- 'Ericoides' ♀H4 CKen CTri ECho EHul LBee SBrd SPlb WDin WFar
- 'Little Jamie' CKen
- 'Red Star' see *C. thyoides* 'Rubicon'
§ - 'Rubicon' CMac CSBt ECho EHul EPfP EPla LBee LRHS MGos NEgg SBfd SLim SPoG WFar
- 'Top Point' ECho LBee LRHS MAsh MGos SCoo SLim SPoG
- 'Variegata' (v) EHul

## *Chamaecytisus* (*Papilionaceae*)

§ ***albus*** (Hacq.) Rothm. GQui WDin
§ ***hirsutus*** WPGP
***prolifer*** CPLG
§ ***purpureus*** CSBt CWCL EBee ELan EPfP LHop MRav NWea SPer WDin WFar WPat
- f. ***albus*** EPfP
§ - 'Atropurpureus' ♀H4 NWea
- 'Incarnatus' see *C. purpureus* 'Atropurpureus'
- 'Lilac Lady' LRHS
§ ***supinus*** CPLG IRar SRms

## *Chamaedaphne* (*Ericaceae*)

***calyculata*** CBcs
- 'Nana' NHar

## *Chamaedorea* (*Arecaceae*)

***elegans*** ♀H1 LPal
***erumpens*** see *C. seifrizii*
***metallica*** misapplied see *C. microspadix*
***metallica*** O.F. Cook ex H.E. Moore ♀H1 LPal
§ ***microspadix*** CPHo EAmu LPal SChr
***radicalis*** CBrP CPHo EAmu LPJP LPal SChr
§ ***seifrizii*** ♀H1 LPal

## *Chamaemelum* (*Asteraceae*)

§ ***nobile*** CArn CHby CPrp CSev CTri CWan EGHP ELau EPfP EWil GMac GPoy MBri MHer MMuc MNHC NGdn NPri SBfd SEND SPlb SRms SVic WJek WPer
- dwarf LMor SVic
- dwarf, double-flowered (d) LEdu
- 'Flore Pleno' (d) Widely available
- 'Treneague' Widely available

## *Chamaenerion* see *Chamerion*

## *Chamaepericlymenum* see *Cornus*

## *Chamaerops* (*Arecaceae*)

***excelsa*** misapplied see *Trachycarpus fortunei*
***excelsa*** Thunb. see *Rhapis excelsa*
***humilis*** ♀H3 CAbb CBcs CBrP CHEx CTrC CWSG EPfP ESwi LPJP LPal LRHS MGos MMuc MREP NBlu NPal NPla SArc SBfd SChr SEND SPlb SPoG STrG WCot WPGP
§ - var. ***argentea*** CBrP CDTJ CPHo CTrC EAmu EGxp ETod LPJP LRHS MGos NPal SBfd SPlb WCot
- var. ***cerifera*** see *C. humilis* var. *argentea*
- 'Vulcano' CDTJ EAmu MBri MGos SChr

## *Chamaespartium* see *Genista*

## *Chamaesphacos* (*Lamiaceae*)

***ilicifolius*** misapplied see *Siphocranion macranthum*

## *Chambeyronia* (*Arecaceae*)

***macrocarpa*** EAmu LPal

## *Chamelaucium* (*Myrtaceae*)

***axillare*** MOWG
***floriferum*** CFee
***uncinatum*** CCCN EShb MOWG
- 'Snowflake' **new** LRHS

## Chamerion (Onagraceae)

§ **angustifolium** EWil SWat WSFF XLum
§ – 'Album' CBot CElw CEnt CMea CSpe EBee ECha ELan EPfP LRHS MMuc MNrw MRav NBid NBir NSti SPer SPhx SPoG SWat WCAu WCot WFar WHal WMoo WPGP WPer WSFF WSHC
– 'Isobel' CSpe MRav WCot
– 'Stahl Rose' CBot CElw CHid CMea EBee EPfP EWes LPla NSti SMrm SPhx SPoG SSvw STes SWat WCAu WCot WOut WPGP WSHC
§ **dodonaei** ELan EWes MMuc SPhx WCot WFar

## Chasmanthe (Iridaceae)

**aethiopica** CPou GGar
**bicolor** CDes CPLG CPou CPrp CTca EBee IDee
**floribunda** CAbb CHEx CPrp CTca EBee LRHS
– var. **duckittii** CFir CPrp ECho EPfP WPGP
– 'Saturnes' EBee

## Chasmanthium (Poaceae)

§ **latifolium** CBod CHar CKno EBee ECha EHoe ELan ELon EPPr EPfP EPla EShb LRHS MAvo MBrN MMoz MSCN NBPC SGol SMrm SPad SPoG WAul WBor WCot WFar WWEG WWFP XLum
– 'Variegatum' (v) new WCot
**laxum** new CKno EPPr SMea

## Cheilanthes (Pteridaceae)

**albomarginata** WAbe
**argentea** WAbe WRic
**cucullans** WAbe
**distans** SRms WAbe WRic
**eatonii** WAbe
**grisea** WAbe
**lanosa** CBty CCCN CHid CLAP EBee EFer EWes GCal ISha LRHS SRms WCot
**sinuata** ISha
**tomentosa** CBty CCCN CLAP ISha LRHS SRms WRic
**wootonii** WAbe

## Cheiranthus see *Erysimum*

## Cheirolophus (Asteraceae)

**benoistii** misapplied see *Centaurea atropurpurea*
**benoistii** (Humb.) Holub CSpe EBee SKHP
**teydis** SPlb

## Chelidonium (Papaveraceae)

**japonicum** see *Hylomecon japonica*
**majus** CArn CRWN GPoy GQui MHer MNHC NMir WHer WSFF
– 'Flore Pleno' (d) CBre MMHG NBid NBro WCFE WHer WTou
– var. **laciniatum** NBir WCot

## Chelone (Plantaginaceae)

**barbata** see *Penstemon barbatus*
§ **glabra** Widely available
**lyonii** EBee ELan MDKP NBre NLar SPad SPet SPhx WMoo WPer WPnP WShi
– 'Hot Lips' WCAu
– 'Pink Temptation' EBee EWTr SPet
**obliqua** Widely available
– var. **alba** see *C. glabra*
– 'Forncett Foremost' GQui
– 'Forncett Poppet' NBre
– 'Pink Sensation' EBee NBre WFar
* – **rosea** EBee MLLN MMHG NBPC WGwG

## Chelonopsis (Lamiaceae)

**moschata** CLAP CPom LEdu MMoz WMoo WPGP
**yagiharana** CAby EBee MCCP MDKP MWea NBPC NBid NPnk SHar WMoo WPer

## Chengiopanax (Araliaceae)

**sciadophylloides** B&SWJ 4728 WCru

## Chenopodium (Amaranthaceae)

**bonus-henricus** CAgr CArn CHab CHby CWan GPoy ILis MCoo MHer MNHC SBfd SIde WHer WJek
**giganteum** ILis MNHC WJek

## cherimoya see *Annona cherimola*

## cherry, Duke see *Prunus × gondouinii*

## cherry, sour or morello see *Prunus cerasus*

## cherry, sweet see *Prunus avium*

## chervil see *Anthriscus cerefolium*

## chestnut, sweet see *Castanea sativa*

## Chiastophyllum (Crassulaceae)

§ **oppositifolium** ♀H4 CBcs CSam CTri EBee ECha ECho EDAr ELan EPfP GAbr GEdr GGar GJos GKev LAst LRHS MAsh MLHP MRav MSCN NBid NMen NWCA SPlb SRms WAbe WKif WMoo WSHC XLum
– 'Frosted Jade' see *C. oppositifolium* 'Jim's Pride'
– 'Jane's Reverse' (v) WCot
§ – 'Jim's Pride' (v) EBee ECha ECho EHoe EWes GEdr GGar GKev GMaP LAst LRHS MHer MRav NHar NMen NPer NPri SPlb SPoG SRGP SRms SRot WAbe WFar WMoo WSHC WWEG
**simplicifolium** see *C. oppositifolium*

## Chiliotrichum (Asteraceae)

**diffusum** (G.Forst.) Kuntze CWib GGar
– dark-leaved GGar
– 'Siska' CBcs GBin SMad

## Chilopsis (Bignoniaceae)

**linearis** (Cav.) Sweet CArn

## Chimonanthus ✿ (Calycanthaceae)

**fragrans** see *C. praecox*
**nitens** CBcs CMCN IArd NLar
§ **praecox** Widely available
– 'Brockhill Goldleaf' NLar
– 'Grandiflorus' ♀H4 CEnd CPMA EPfP LRHS MAsh SPoG SSta WPGP WPat
– 'Luteus' ♀H4 CEnd CPMA ECrN ELan EPfP LRHS LSRN MAsh MGos MRav SPoG SSpi SSta WPGP WPat

| | |
|---|---|
| - 'Sunburst' | CPMA |
| - 'Trenython' | CEnd CPMA WPGP WPat |
| ***yunnanensis*** | CPne NLar |

## *Chimonobambusa* (*Poaceae*)

| | |
|---|---|
| KR 7592 | MWht |
| ***hejiangensis*** | EPla |
| ***hookeriana*** misapplied | see *Himalayacalamus falconeri* 'Damarapa' |
| ***macrophylla*** f. ***intermedia*** | EPla |
| § ***marmorea*** | CDTJ CEnt EAmu EPla LPal MMoz MMuc MWht NPal SBig SEND WDyG WJun |
| - 'Variegata' (v) | CDTJ EPla MMoz SLPl WDyG WJun |
| § ***quadrangularis*** | CBcs CDTJ CDoC CEnt CHEx EPfP EPla ESwi MMoz MWht NPal SBig WDyG WJun WPGP |
| - 'Nagaminei' (v) | EPla WJun |
| - 'Suow' (v) | CDTJ EPla WPGP |
| - 'Tatejima' | EPla WJun |
| ***tumidissinoda*** | CDTJ CEnt EPfP EPla ESwi MMoz MMuc MWhi MWht NPal SBig SGol WDyG WJun WPGP |

## Chinese chives see *Allium tuberosum*

## *Chiogenes* see *Gaultheria*

## *Chionanthus* (*Oleaceae*)

| | |
|---|---|
| ***retusus*** | CBcs CDul CMCN EBee EPfP LRHS MBri MPkF NLar SKHP SPer SSpi WDin |
| ***virginicus*** | CBcs CDoC CDul CEnd CMCN CPMA EBee ECrN ELan EPfP EWTr GBin GKin IArd IDee LHop LRHS MBlu MBri MMuc MRav NEgg SKHP SPer SPlb SSpi WDin WPGP |

## *Chionochloa* (*Poaceae*)

| | |
|---|---|
| ***beddiei*** | GBin |
| ***conspicua*** | CAby CGHE CKno EBee EKen GBin GCal MAvo MMuc NBid NBir SMea WPGP WWEG |
| - subsp. ***conspicua*** | GGar |
| - 'Rubra' | see *C. rubra* |
| ***flavescens*** | EHoe GBin LRHS MAvo WPtf |
| ***flavicans*** | CKno GBin LRHS SMea |
| § ***rubra*** | CBcs CElw CGHE CKno CSpe EBee EHoe ELan EPla EWes GAbr GCal GMaP LEdu LHop LRHS MAvo MMoz MRav NChi SApp SGar SMad SMrm WCot WMoo WPGP WTin WWEG |
| - subsp. ***cuprea*** | CAby EBee GBin GGar NDov SMad |

## *Chionodoxa* ✿ (*Asparagaceae*)

| | |
|---|---|
| ***cretica*** | see *C. nana* |
| § ***forbesii*** | CBro CWCL ECGP ECho EPfP EPot GKev NBir SDeJ SMrm SPer SRms WFar WShi |
| - 'Alba' | ECho LAma |
| - 'Blue Giant' | ECho EPot ERCP |
| - 'Rosea' | ECho LAma |
| - Siehei Group | see *C. siehei* |
| - 'Tmoli' | ECho |
| - 'Violet Beauty' | ECho GKev |
| - 'Zwanenburg' | ECho |
| ***gigantea*** | see *C. luciliae* Gigantea Group |
| ***lochiae*** | LWst |
| ***luciliae*** misapplied | see *C. forbesii* |
| ***luciliae*** ambig. | CAvo ECho SEND |
| ***luciliae*** Boiss. 🏆H4 | CAby CAvo CBro EPfP GGar LAma LRHS MBri MMuc SPer |
| - 'Alba' | ECho GGar LRHS MCot SDeJ SMrm SPer |
| § - Gigantea Group | ECho ELan GKev LAma |
| - - 'Alba' | EPot GKev |
| § ***nana*** | ECho |
| 'Pink Giant' | CAvo CBro ECho ELan EPfP EPot ERCP GGar GKev LAma MCot SDeJ SMrm WCot XLum |
| ***sardensis*** 🏆H4 | CBro CPrp ECho EPot ERCP GKev LAma LRHS SDeJ SPhx WCot WShi |
| § ***siehei*** 🏆H4 | CBro |

## *Chionographis* (*Melanthiaceae*)

| | |
|---|---|
| ***japonica*** | EFEx WCru |

## *Chionohebe* (*Plantaginaceae*)

| | |
|---|---|
| ***pulvinaris*** | NSla |

## × *Chionoscilla* (*Asparagaceae*)

| | |
|---|---|
| § ***allenii*** | CAvo ECho SPhx WCot |

## *Chirita* (*Gesneriaceae*)

| | |
|---|---|
| 'Aiko' | WDib |
| 'Candy' | WDib |
| 'Chastity' | WDib |
| 'Diane Marie' | WDib |
| 'Erika' | WDib |
| ***flavimaculata*** | WDib |
| ***heterotricha*** | WDib |
| 'Keiko' | WDib |
| * ***latifolia*** × ***linearifolia*** | WDib |
| ***linearifolia*** | WDib |
| ***linearifolia*** × ***sinensis*** | WDib |
| ***longgangensis*** | WDib |
| 'New York' | CSpe WDib |
| ***sinensis*** 🏆H1 | WDib |
| - 'Hisako' | CSpe WDib |
| ***speciosa*** 'Crûg Cornetto' | WCru |
| 'Stardust' | WDib |
| 'Sweet Dreams' new | WDib |
| ***tamiana*** | CSpe WDib |

## *Chironia* (*Gentianaceae*)

| | |
|---|---|
| ***baccifera*** | SPlb |

## × *Chitalpa* (*Bignoniaceae*)

| | |
|---|---|
| ***tashkentensis*** | CBcs CEnd EBee EPfP WPGP WPat |
| - 'Morning Cloud' | MBlu |
| - 'Pink Dawn' | ESwi LRHS MBlu MBri NLar SPad |
| - Summer Bells = 'Minsum' | CDoC EBee LHop MAsh MGos MMuc NPri SBig WCot |

## chives see *Allium schoenoprasum*

## *Chlidanthus* (*Amaryllidaceae*)

| | |
|---|---|
| ***fragrans*** | CCCN ECho EShb GGar SEND XLum |

## *Chloranthus* (*Chloranthaceae*)

| | |
|---|---|
| ***fortunei*** | CDes CLAP WPGP |
| - 'Domino' | WCot |
| ***japonicus*** | CLAP WCru |
| ***oldhamii*** | GEdr |
| - B&SWJ 2019 | LEdu WCru |
| ***serratus*** | WCru |

## *Chloris* (*Poaceae*)

***distichophylla*** see *Eustachys distichophylla*

## *Chlorophytum* (*Asparagaceae*)

***comosum*** EShb SEND SVic
'Aureomarginata' SEND
- 'Variegatum' (v) $\mathbb{Y}^{H1+3}$ CDTJ EShb SEND SRms
- 'Vittatum' (v) $\mathbb{Y}^{H1+3}$ EShb SRms
***krookianum*** CFir EBee WCot
***macrophyllum*** EShb
***majus*** WCot
***nepalense*** WCot
- B&SWJ 2393 WCru
- B&SWJ 2528 WCru
***saundersiae*** CPLG

## *Choisya* (*Rutaceae*)

× ***dewitteana*** Widely available
'Aztec Pearl' $\mathbb{Y}^{H4}$
- White Dazzler = 'Londaz'$^{PBR}$ CWGN LBuc LRHS LSRN MAsh NPri SBfd SLon SRkn WCot WGrn
***dumosa*** LHop
- var. ***arizonica*** WCot
'Golden Gift' LRHS LSqu MAsh SBrd SSpi
Goldfingers = 'Limo'$^{PBR}$ CBcs CDul CWGN CWSG EBee ELan ELon EPfP LAst LHop LRHS LSRN MAsh MBri MGos MRav MSwo NEgg NHol NLar SBfd SCoo SLim SLon SPad SPer SPoG SWvt WCot
***ternata*** $\mathbb{Y}^{H4}$ Widely available
- Moonshine = 'Walcho'$^{PBR}$ EBee GBin NHol NLar WCot
- Moonsleeper$^{PBR}$ see *C. ternata* Sundance
- Snow Flurries = 'Lisflurry' LRHS LSqu MAsh
§ - Sundance = 'Lich'$^{PBR}$ $\mathbb{Y}^{H3}$ Widely available

## *Chondropetalum* (*Restionaceae*)

* ***elephantinum*** CCtw CFir LTen
***hookerianum*** NEgg
***mucronatum*** CTrC WPGP
***tectorum*** CAbb CBct CCtw CDoC CFir CHEx CKno CPrp CSpe CTrC EAmu EBee EPfP GBin LRHS LSRN MGos NOak NPla SApp SBfd SHDw SPer SPlb SPoG WCot WHal WPGP
- dwarf CDes CTrC WPGP

## *Chondrosum* (*Poaceae*)

***gracile*** see *Bouteloua gracilis*

## *Chordospartium* see *Carmichaelia*

## *Chorisia* (*Malvaceae*)

***speciosa*** CCCN EAmu EShb

## *Chorizema* (*Papilionaceae*)

***cordatum*** $\mathbb{Y}^{H1}$ ECou
***ilicifolium*** CCCN CSPN

## *Chromolaena* (*Asteraceae*)

***arnottiana*** RCB/Arg L2 CDes
- 'Salsipuede' WCot

## *Chronanthus* see *Cytisus*

## *Chrysalidocarpus* see *Dypsis*

## *Chrysanthemopsis* see *Rhodanthemum*

## *Chrysanthemum* ✿ (*Asteraceae*)

'Action Bronze' EPfP LAst
'Action Yellow' (22) $\mathbb{Y}^{H3}$ LAst
'Agnes Ann' (21d) MNrw
'Alec Bedser' (25a) NHal
'Alehmer Rote' (21) MNrw WWEG
'Alexandra' NHal
'Aline' (21) MNrw SPhx
'Alison' (29c) MNrw
'Alison's Dad' MNrw
'Allouise' (25b) $\mathbb{Y}^{H3}$ NHal
'Allyson Peace' (14a) MCms NHal
***alpinum*** see *Leucanthemopsis alpina*
'Amber Matlock' (24b) MCms
'American Beauty Lemon' MCms
'American Beauty White' MCms
'Anastasia' (21c) CHid EBee ECtt ELon LRHS MNrw MRav NSti SPhx WFar WHoo WWEG
'Angela Blundell' WCot
'Anja's Bouquet' see *C.* 'Mei-Kyō'
'Anne Ratsey' (21) CSam MNrw
'Anne, Lady Brocket' (21d) ECtt MNrw SSvw
'Anthony Peace' (25b) **new** NHal
'Antigua'$^{PBR}$ MCms
'Apollo' LLHF MNrw WCot WTin
'Apollo' (21) EBee EWll NCGa SMrs SPhx SSvw WHoo
'Apricot' (21) see *C.* 'Cottage Apricot'
'Apricot Chessington' (25a) NHal
'Apricot Courtier' (24a) NHal
'Apricot Enbee Wedding' see *C.* 'Bronze Enbee Wedding'
***arcticum*** L. see *Arctanthemum arcticum*
***argenteum*** see *Tanacetum argenteum*
'Astro' NHal
'Aunt Millicent' (21d) LLHF MNrw NHal SPhx
'Balcombe Perfection' (5a) NHal
***balsamita*** see *Tanacetum balsamita*
Barbara = 'Yobarbara' (22) EPfP NHal
'Beacon' (5a) $\mathbb{Y}^{H2}$ NHal
'Belle' (21d) MNrw SSvw
'Beppie Bronze' (29) MCms
'Beppie Purple' (29) MCms
'Beppie Red' (29) MCms
'Beppie Rose' MCms
'Beppie Yellow' (29) MCms
'Bernadette Wade' (23a) NHal
'Bestman' (25c) **new** MCms
'Bill Holden' (14a) **new** NHal
'Bill Wade' (25a) NHal
'Billy Bell' (25a) MCms NHal
'Blanche Poitevene' (5b) EMal
'Bobby Swinburn' (13b) NHal
Bravo = 'Yobra' (22c) $\mathbb{Y}^{H3}$ EPfP NHal
'Breezers'$^{PBR}$ **new** MCms
* 'Breitner's Supreme' MNrw WWEG
'Brennpunkt' SMrs
'Brierton Violet' (17b) NHal
'Bright Eye' (21b) LRHS MNrw WMnd
'Brightness' (21) SSvw SUsu
'Bronze Beauty' (25b) WFar
'Bronze Cassandra' (5b) $\mathbb{Y}^{H2}$ NHal
'Bronze Dee Gem' (29c) NHal
§ 'Bronze Elegance' (28b) CTri LRHS MNrw NBir NGdn NSti SMrs SRms SSvw WBor WMnd WPer
§ 'Bronze Enbee Wedding' (29d) $\mathbb{Y}^{H3}$ NHal
'Bronze Matlock' (24b) NHal

| Name | Suppliers |
|---|---|
| 'Bronze Max Riley' (23b) 🏆H3 | NHal |
| 'Bronze Mayford Perfection' (5a) 🏆H2 | NHal |
| 'Bronze Mei-kyō' | see *C.* 'Bronze Elegance' |
| 'Bronze William Florentine' (15a) | MCms |
| 'Browney' **new** | MCms |
| 'Bullfinch' (12a) | MWea |
| burnt orange-flowered | CAby CPrp MNrw |
| 'Burnwood Belle' (3b) | NHal |
| 'Candy Floss' (7a) | NHal |
| 'Capel Manor' | CAby EBee MNrw WCot |
| 'Carmine Blush' (21) | EBee MNrw SMrs SPhx SSvw WCot |
| 'Cassandra' (5b) 🏆H2 | NHal |
| 'Caukeel Cadet' (29c) | NHal |
| 'Caukeel Copper' (29c) | NHal |
| 'Chelsea Physic Garden' | CAby EBee IGor LLHF MNrw SPhx SSvw SUsu WCot |
| 'Cherry Chessington' (25a) | NHal |
| 'Cherry Riley's Dynasty' (14a) **new** | MCms |
| Chesapeake = 'Yochesapeake'PBR | NHal |
| 'Chestnut Talbot Maid' **new** | MCms |
| 'Christopher Lawson' (24b) | NHal |
| 'Cinderella' | WMnd |
| ***cinerariifolium*** | see *Tanacetum cinerariifolium* |
| 'Clapham Delight' (23a) | NHal |
| 'Clara Curtis' (21d) | Widely available |
| 'Clive Skinner' (25b) | NHal |
| ***coccineum*** | see *Tanacetum coccineum* |
| 'Conjuror'PBR | LAst |
| 'Coral Reef' | NHal |
| 'Cornetto' (25b) | NHal |
| ***corymbosum*** | see *Tanacetum corymbosum* |
| § 'Cottage Apricot' | CPrp EBee ECGP EWoo LRHS MBNS MLHP MNrw MRav SSvw |
| 'Cottage Bronze' | MNrw |
| 'Cottage Lemon' | MNrw |
| 'Cottage Pink' | see *C.* 'Emperor of China' |
| 'Cottage Yellow' | SSvw WHoo |
| 'Coup de Soleil' **new** | WCot |
| 'Courtier' (24a) | NHal |
| 'Cousin Joan' | EBee LLHF MNrw NCGa WCot |
| 'Cream Elegance' (9c) | NHal |
| 'Cream Patricia Millar' (14b) | NHal |
| 'Cream Talbot Maid' **new** | MCms |
| 'Cream West Bromwich' (14a) | MCms |
| Dana = 'Yodana' (25b) 🏆H3 | NHal |
| Dance = 'Fidance'PBR | MCms |
| Dance Salmon = 'Fidancesal'PBR | MCms |
| 'Dance Sunny' **new** | MCms |
| 'Dance White' **new** | MCms |
| 'Daniel Cooper' (21) | MNrw |
| 'Darren Pugh' (3b) | NHal |
| Debonair = 'Yodebo'PBR (22c) 🏆H3 | EPfP |
| 'Dee Gem' (29c) 🏆H3 | NHal |
| 'Delta' (5b) | NHal |
| 'Delta Copper Bronze' | NHal |
| 'Delta Crimson' (29d) | NHal |
| 'Delta Yellow' (29) | NHal |
| 'Dezianne' | MCms |
| 'Dezianne Yellow' | MCms |
| § 'Doctor Tom Parr' (21c) | CPLG ELan GCal LAst LHop MNrw SUsu |

| Name | Suppliers |
|---|---|
| 'Doreen Statham' (4b) | NHal |
| 'Doris Ozols' (25a) | NHal |
| 'Dorothy Stone' (25b) | NHal |
| 'Dorridge Crystal' (24a) | MCms NHal |
| 'Dublin' **new** | MCms |
| 'Duchess of Edinburgh' (21d) | CPrp EBee ECtt ELan EPfP EShb GBin LRHS MNrw SBfd SDys SMrs SPhx SPoG SSvw WMnd XLum |
| 'Duke of Kent' (1) | NHal |
| 'Dutchy'PBR | MCms |
| 'Early Yellow' | MNrw |
| 'Edelweiss' (21) | CAby |
| 'Egret' (23b) | MCms NHal |
| 'Elaine Johnson' (3b) | NHal |
| 'Elegance' (9c) | NHal |
| 'Elizabeth Lawson' (5b) | NHal |
| 'Elizabeth Shoesmith' (1) | NHal |
| 'Ellen' (29c) | NHal |
| § 'Emperor of China' (21) | CAby CElw CSam EBee ECtt GCal IGor MNrw MRav NHal SMrs SPhx SSvw SUsu WBor WCot WFar WMnd WWEG XLum |
| 'Enbee Wedding' (29d) 🏆H3 | MCms NHal |
| 'Energy'PBR | MCms |
| 'Esther' (21d) | EWTr MNrw NCGa SMrs |
| 'Ethel Edwards' (25b) **new** | NHal |
| 'Feeling Green Dark' | MCms |
| 'Fleur de Lis' (10a) **new** | SMrs |
| ***foeniculaceum*** | see *Argyranthemum foeniculaceum* |
| 'Fondant' | NHal |
| 'Froggy'PBR | MCms |
| ***frutescens*** | see *Argyranthemum frutescens* |
| 'Gala Burgundy' | EPfP |
| 'Gambit' (24a) | NHal |
| 'Geof Brady' (5a) | NHal |
| 'Geoff Amos' (3b) | NHal |
| 'Geoff Bradey' (15a) **new** | MCms |
| 'Geoff Sylvester' (25a) | NHal |
| 'George Griffiths' (24b) 🏆H3 | NHal |
| 'Gigantic' (1) | NHal |
| 'Gladys Emerson' (3b) | NHal |
| 'Golden Cassandra' (5b) 🏆H2 | NHal |
| 'Golden Chalice' (12a) | NHal |
| 'Golden Courtier' (24a) | NHal |
| 'Golden Gigantic' (1) | NHal |
| 'Golden Mayford Perfection' (5a) 🏆H2 | NHal |
| 'Golden Plover' (22) | NHal |
| 'Golden Rain' (10a) 🏆H2 | NHal |
| 'Golden Wedding' (21) | MNrw |
| 'Golden William Florentine' (15a) | NHal |
| 'Golden Woolman's Glory' (7a) | NHal |
| 'Goldengreenheart' (21) | EShb LLHF MNrw WHoo |
| 'Goldmarianne' (21) | GBin |
| 'Grace Wade' (25b) | NHal |
| 'Grandchild' (21c) | LLHF MNrw NHal SPhx |
| § × ***grandiflorum*** | SRms |
| – 'Corinna' | GBin |
| 'Hanenburg' | NHal |
| ***haradjanii*** | see *Tanacetum haradjanii* |
| 'Harold Lawson' (5a) | NHal |
| 'Harry Gee' (1) | NHal |
| 'Harry Tolley' (4b) **new** | MCms |
| 'Heather James' (3b) | NHal |
| 'Hebe' (21d) | EBee |
| 'Heide' (29c) 🏆H3 | NHal |
| 'Herbstbrokat' | GBin XLum |

| | |
|---|---|
| 'Hesketh Knight' (5b) ♀H2 | NHal |
| Holly = 'Yoholly' (22b) ♀H3 | NHal |
| 'Honey Enbee Wedding' (29d) | NHal |
| 'Horningsea Pink' (19d) | ECGP WBor |
| 'Innocence' (21) | CSam EBee ECtt ELan IGor MNrw MRav NGdn NSti SAga SSvw WHoo |
| 'Janet South' | MNrw |
| 'Jante Wells' (21b) | MNrw WBor WWEG |
| 'Jenny Wren' (12a) | NHal |
| 'Jessie Cooper' misapplied | see *C.* 'Mrs Jessie Cooper' (21) |
| 'Jimmy Tranter' (14b) **new** | NHal |
| 'John Harrison' (25b) | NHal |
| 'John Hughes' (3b) | NHal |
| 'John Lowery' **new** | MCms |
| 'John Riley' (14a) | NHal |
| 'John Wingfield' (14b) | MCms NHal |
| 'Joyce Fountain' (24a) | MCms NHal |
| 'Joyce Frieda' (23b) | MCms NHal |
| 'Julia' (28) | EPfP SRGP |
| 'Julia Peterson' | WCot WHoo WTin |
| Julia = 'Yojulia' | EBee |
| 'Julie Lagravère' (28) | MNrw WPtf XLum |
| 'Juweeltja' | NHal |
| 'Karen Taylor' (29c) ♀H3 | NHal |
| 'Kath Stephenson' (7b) | NHal |
| 'Kath Stephenson Rose' (7b) | NHal |
| 'Katie Jane' (7b) | NHal |
| 'Kay Woolman' (13b) | MCms NHal |
| 'Kenny Buglass' (25b) **new** | NHal |
| 'Kimberley Marie' (15b) | NHal |
| 'Kindly Salmon' **new** | MCms |
| 'Kiyominomeisui' | NHal |
| 'Kleiner Bernstein' | WCot |
| × ***koreanum*** | see *C.* × *grandiflorum* |
| § 'Lady in Pink' (21) | LRHS MNrw NBir |
| 'Lakelanders' (3b) | NHal |
| 'Le Bonheur Red' | NHal |
| ***leucanthemum*** | see *Leucanthemum vulgare* |
| 'Lexy' PBR **new** | MCms |
| 'Lexy Red' PBR | MCms |
| 'Lilac Chessington' (25a) | NHal |
| Linda = 'Lindayo' PBR (22c) ♀H3 | NHal |
| 'Lindie' (28) | WHil |
| 'L'Innocence' (21) | CAby |
| 'Lollipop' PBR | MCms |
| 'Lorna Wood' (13b) | NHal |
| 'Louise' (25b) | MNrw |
| 'Lucy' (29a) ♀H3 | NHal |
| 'Lucy Simpson' (21d) | SBch |
| 'Lundy' (2) | NHal |
| 'Luv Purple' | NHal |
| 'Lynn Johnson' (15a) | NHal |
| Lynn = 'Yolynn' (22c) ♀H3 | NHal |
| ***macrophyllum*** | see *Tanacetum macrophyllum* (Waldst. & Kit.) Sch.Bip. |
| 'Malcolm Perkins' (25a) | NHal |
| 'Mancetta Comet' (29a) | NHal |
| 'Mancetta Symbol' (5a) | MCms |
| ***maresii*** | see *Rhodanthemum hosmariense* |
| 'Margaret' (29c) ♀H3 | NHal WCot |
| 'Marion' (25a) | CAby MNrw SPhx WCot |
| 'Mark Woolman' (1) | NHal |
| 'Mary' (21f) | MNrw NHal |
| 'Mary Stoker' (21d) | CAby CPrp CSam EBee ECtt ELan EPfP LRHS MNrw MRav NCGa NHal NLar NSti SPoG SRGP SSvw SUsu WAul WCAu WFar WMnd WWEG |

| | |
|---|---|
| 'Matador' (14a) | NHal |
| 'Matlock' (24b) | NHal |
| 'Mauve Gem' (21f) | MNrw NHal |
| ***mawii*** | see *Rhodanthemum gayanum* |
| 'Max Riley' (23b) ♀H3 | NHal |
| ***maximum*** misapplied | see *Leucanthemum* × *superbum* |
| ***maximum*** Ramond | see *Leucanthemum maximum* (Ramond) DC. |
| 'Maxine Johnson' (25b) | NHal |
| 'May Shoesmith' (5a) ♀H2 | NHal |
| 'Mayford Perfection' (5a) ♀H2 | NHal |
| § 'Mei-Kyō' (28b) | CMea CTri EBee ECtt IGor MNrw SMrs SPhx SRms SSvw WBor WCAu WFar WHil WPer WWEG |
| 'Membury' (24b) | NHal |
| 'Michelle Preston' (13b) | NHal |
| 'Millennium' (25b) ♀H3 | MCms NHal |
| 'Minty' PBR **new** | MCms |
| 'Misty Cream' | MCms |
| 'Misty Golden' | MCms |
| 'Misty Lemon' | MCms |
| 'Moonlight' (29d/K) | MRav |
| 'Morning Star' (12a) | NHal |
| § 'Mrs Jessie Cooper' (21) | CAby CHGN ELan GQue MNrw NBir NLar SDys SSvw WCot WHil WHoo WPtf WTin |
| 'Mrs Jessie Cooper No 1' | NCGa WBrk |
| 'Mrs Jessie Cooper No 2' | MNrw |
| 'Muriel Odell' (7b) | NHal |
| 'Music' (23b) | NHal |
| 'Muxton Sable' (10a) | NHal |
| 'Myss Carol' (29c) | NHal |
| 'Myss Debbie' (29e) | NHal |
| 'Myss Goldie' (29c) | MCms |
| 'Myss Jem' (29e) | NHal |
| 'Myss Jem Red' (29e) | NHal |
| 'Myss Marion' (29c) ♀H3 | NHal |
| 'Myss Saffron' (29c) ♀H3 | NHal |
| 'Nancy Perry' (21d) | CSam MNrw MRav SSvw XLum |
| ***nankingense*** | WFar |
| 'Nantyderry Sunshine' (28b) ♀H4 | CPrp CSam EBee LLHF MNrw SPhx SSvw WBor WMnd WPer WWEG |
| 'Naru' (9c) | NHal |
| 'Nell Gwynn' (21d) | MNrw NHal |
| 'Netherhall Moonlight' | MNrw SSvw |
| Nicole = 'Yonicole' (22c) ♀H3 | NHal |
| ***nipponicum*** | see *Nipponanthemum nipponicum* |
| 'Norton Vic' (5b) | NHal |
| 'Olga Patterson' (5b) **new** | SMrs |
| 'Olwyn' (4b) | NHal |
| 'Orange Allouise' (25b) | MCms NHal |
| 'Orange Enbee Wedding' (29d) | NHal |
| ***pacificum*** | see *Ajania pacifica* |
| 'Parrot' **new** | MCms |
| ***parthenium*** | see *Tanacetum parthenium* |
| 'Patricia Millar' (14b) | NHal |
| 'Paul Boissier' (30Rub) | CAby ECtt MNrw NSti SPhx SSvw WCot WMnd |
| 'Peach Courtier' (24a) | NHal |
| 'Peach Enbee Wedding' (29d) ♀H3 | NHal |
| 'Peach John Wingfield' (14b) | NHal |
| 'Peach Patricia Millar' (14b) **new** | MCms |
| 'Pennine Bullion' | NHal |
| 'Pennine Gift' (29c) | NHal |
| 'Pennine Marie' (29a) ♀H3 | NHal |
| 'Pennine Oriel' (29a) ♀H3 | MCms NHal |

| Name | Suppliers |
|---|---|
| 'Pennine Point' (19c) | NHal |
| 'Pennine Polo' (29d) ♀H3 | NHal |
| 'Pennine Ranger' (29d) | NHal |
| 'Pennine Swan' (29c) | NHal |
| 'Pennine Toy' (19d) | NHal |
| 'Penny's Yellow' | LLHF |
| 'Perry's Peach' (21a) | LLHF MNrw NCGa NHal NPer SPhx SSvw |
| 'Peter Rowe' (23b) | NHal |
| 'Peterkin' | CMac CPrp ECtt ELon LRHS WWEG |
| 'Pink Allouise' | MCms |
| 'Pink John Wingfield' (14b) | NHal |
| 'Pink Progression' | see *C.* 'Lady in Pink' |
| 'Pink Splendour' (10a) ♀H2 | SMrs |
| 'Polar Gem' (3a) | NHal |
| 'President Osaka' **new** | MNrw |
| 'Primrose Allouise' (24b) ♀H3 | NHal |
| 'Primrose Courtier' | see *C.* 'Yellow Courtier' |
| 'Primrose Dorothy Stone' (25b) | NHal |
| 'Primrose Enbee Wedding' (29d) ♀H3 | MCms NHal |
| 'Primrose John Hughes' (3b) | NHal |
| 'Primrose Mayford Perfection' (5a) ♀H2 | NHal |
| 'Primrose West Bromwich' (14a) | MCms NHal |
| 'Princess' (21d) | LLHF |
| 'Promise' (25a) | NHal |
| ***ptarmiciflorum*** | see *Tanacetum ptarmiciflorum* |
| 'Purleigh White' (28b) | ECtt MNrw NSti SSvw WCot WWEG |
| 'Purple Chempak Rose' (14b) | NHal |
| 'Ralph Lambert' (1) | NHal |
| 'Raquel' (21) | EPfP MNrw |
| 'Red Balcombe Perfection' (5a) | NHal |
| 'Red Chempak Rose' (14b) | MCms |
| 'Red Mayford Perfection' (5a) | NHal |
| 'Red Pennine Gift' (29c) | NHal |
| 'Red Regal Mist' (25b) | MCms |
| 'Red Shirley Model' (3a) | NHal |
| 'Redbreast' | NHal |
| 'Regal Mist Purple' (25b) | MCms NHal |
| 'Richmond' (3b) | NHal |
| 'Riley's Dynasty' (14a) | MCms |
| 'Ringdove' (12a) | NHal |
| 'Rita McMahon' (29d) ♀H3 | NHal |
| 'Robeam' (9c) ♀H2 | NHal |
| Robin = 'Yorobi' (22c) | NHal |
| 'Roen Sarah' (29c) | NHal |
| 'Romany' (2) | CElw |
| 'Rose Enbee Wedding' (29d) | NHal |
| 'Rose Madder' | MNrw WCot |
| 'Rose Mayford Perfection' (5a) ♀H2 | NHal |
| 'Rose Patricia Millar' (14b) | NHal |
| 'Rosetta' | WCot |
| ***roseum*** | see *Tanacetum coccineum* |
| 'Royal Command' (21) | MNrw NGBo SMrs WCot |
| ***rubellum*** | see *C. zawadskii* |
| 'Ruby Enbee Wedding' (29d) ♀H3 | NHal WPtf |
| 'Ruby Mound' (21c) ♀H3 | CAby LLHF MNrw NHal SDys SMrs SPhx SSvw SUsu |
| 'Ruby Raynor' (21) ♀H4 | MNrw NHal SDys SPhx SSvw SUsu |
| 'Rumpelstilzchen' (21d) | CElw CMea ECtt MNrw SMrs WPer |
| 'Salhouse Joy' (10a) | NHal |
| 'Salmon Allouise' (25b) | NHal |
| 'Salmon Enbee Wedding' (29d) ♀H3 | NHal |
| 'Salmon John Wingfield' (24b) **new** | MCms |
| 'Salmon Talbot Maid' **new** | MCms |
| 'Sam Vinter' (5a) | NHal |
| 'Sarah Louise' (25b) | NHal |
| 'Sea Urchin' (21f) ♀H3 | MNrw NHal SDys SPhx SSvw |
| 'Seaton's Galaxy' (10a) **new** | SMrs |
| 'Sheena' (9f/10) | NHal |
| 'Sheila Coles' (7b) | NHal |
| 'Shining Light' (21f) | LLHF MNrw |
| 'Shirley Primrose' (1) | NHal |
| ***sinense*** | see *C.* × *grandiflorum* |
| 'Sonnenschein' | LHop |
| 'Sophie Elizabeth' (24a) | NHal |
| 'Sound' **new** | MCms |
| 'Southway Sheba' (29d) | NHal |
| 'Southway Shimmer' (29d) | NHal |
| 'Southway Shiraz' (29d) | NHal |
| 'Southway Ski' (29d) **new** | MCms |
| 'Southway Snoopy' (29d) | NHal |
| 'Southway Strontium' (29d) | NHal |
| 'Southway Sunkissed' (29d) | NHal |
| 'Spartan Canary' | SWal |
| 'Spartan Display' | SWal |
| 'Spartan Fire' | SWal |
| 'Spartan Glory' (25b) | SWal |
| 'Spartan Linnet' | SWal |
| 'Spartan Raspberry' (21d) | SWal |
| 'Spartan Seagull' (21d) | MNrw SSvw SWal |
| 'Spartan Star' (29d) | SWal |
| 'Stallion' PBR **new** | MCms |
| 'Starlet' (21f) | LLHF NHal |
| 'Stockton' (3b) ♀H2 | NHal |
| 'Suffolk Pink' **new** | EShb MNrw |
| 'Sunbeam' (28) | EBee |
| 'Sundae' PBR (22c) | EPfP |
| Sundoro = 'Yosun' (22d) | NHal |
| Swan = 'Fiswan' PBR | MCms |
| 'Syllabub' ♀H3 | ECtt |
| 'Symphony' (10a) | NHal |
| 'Talbot Maid' (29c) **new** | MCms |
| 'Talbot Parade' (29c) ♀H3 | MCms |
| 'Tapestry Rose' (21d) | CMea MNrw NCGa SMrs SPhx SSvw WBor |
| 'Thoroughbred' (24a) | NHal |
| 'Tom Parr' | see *C.* 'Doctor Tom Parr' |
| 'Tom Snowball' (3b) | NHal |
| 'Tracy Waller' (24b) | NHal |
| Triumph = 'Yotri' (22) | NHal |
| ***uliginosum*** | see *Leucanthemella serotina* |
| 'Uri' | CAby SAga SPhx |
| 'Vagabond Prince' | MNrw NCGa SPhx WBor WHoo |
| 'Venice' (24b) | NHal |
| 'Venus' (21) | NCGa WCot |
| 'Venus One' | MNrw NHal SPhx |
| 'Vibrant' (9c) ♀H2 | NHal |
| 'Virginia' (21) | NHal |
| 'Vulcano Dark' **new** | MCms |
| 'Wedding Day' (29k) | EBee MNrw WTin |
| 'Wedding Sunshine' (21) | MNrw |
| ***welwitschii*** | see *Glebionis segetum* |
| 'Wembley' (24b) | NHal |
| 'Wendy Tench' (21d) | ECtt |
| 'West Bromwich' (14a) | NHal |
| ***weyrichii*** | EBee ECho LEdu MWea NLar NRya NWCA SRms WWEG |

'White Allouise' (25b) ♀H3 MCms NHal
'White Beppie' (29e) MCms
'White Cassandra' (5b) NHal
'White Enbee Wedding' (29d) NHal
'White Gem' (21f) NHal
'White Gloss' (21e) LLHF MNrw SSvw
'White Skylark' (22) NHal
'White Tower' MNrw
'Wilder Charms' WHil
'William Florentine' (15a) MCms NHal
'Win' (9c) NHal
'Winning's Red' (21) LHop NCGa SSvw
'Wizard'PBR EPfP
'Woolman's Glory' (7a) NHal
'Woolman's Star' (3a) NHal
'Woolman's Venture' (4b) MCms NHal
'Yellow Allouise' (25b) MCms
'Yellow American Beauty' (5b) ♀H2 MCms
'Yellow Billy Bell' (15a) NHal
'Yellow Clapham Delight' (23a) NHal
§ 'Yellow Courtier' (24a) MCms NHal
'Yellow Egret' (23b) NHal
'Yellow Ellen' (29c) NHal
'Yellow Enbee Wedding' (29d) NHal
'Yellow Harold Lawson' (5a) NHal
'Yellow Heide' (29c) ♀H3 NHal
'Yellow John Hughes' (3b) ♀H2 NHal
'Yellow John Wingfield' (14b) MCms NHal
'Yellow May Shoesmith' (5a) NHal
'Yellow Mayford Perfection' (5a) ♀H2 NHal
'Yellow Pennine Oriel' (29a) ♀H3 MCms NHal
'Yellow Starlet' (21f) LLHF MNrw
***yezoense*** ♀H4 CSam ELan LRHS MNrw SSvw WPer
- B&SWJ 10872 WCru
- 'Roseum' CSam ECtt NSti
§ ***zawadskii*** CMac WFar

## *Chrysocoma* (*Asteraceae*)

***ciliata*** JJH 9401633 NWCA

## *Chrysogonum* (*Asteraceae*)

***australe*** EBee LRHS
***virginianum*** CMea CPrp ECha EWes LRHS MRav SBch SPer WFar WWEG

## *Chrysopogon* (*Poaceae*)

***gryllus*** EBee SApp WPGP

## *Chrysopsis* (*Asteraceae*)

§ ***mariana*** WOld
***villosa*** see *Heterotheca villosa*

## *Chrysosplenium* (*Saxifragaceae*)

***davidianum*** CBre CSam EBee ECha EPot EWld GEdr GGar GJos GKev LRHS NBir NLar NSla WBor WCot WCru WFar WMoo WPtf
- SBEC 233 CPLG
***flagelliferum*** B&SWJ 8902 WCru
***hebetatum*** B&SWJ 9835 new WCru
***lanuginosum*** var. ***formosanum*** B&SWJ 6979 WCru
***macrophyllum*** CDes CPLG EWld GCal GMaP IGor MAvo MMHG MTPN NLar SHar WBor WCot WCru
***macrostemon*** var. ***shiobarense*** B&SWJ 6173 WCru
***oppositifolium*** EBee WSFF WShi

## *Chusquea* (*Poaceae*)

***breviglumis*** misapplied see *C. culeou* 'Tenuis'
***culeou*** ♀H4 CAbb CBcs CDoC CEnd CEnt CHEx CHid ENBC EPfP EPla GBin LAst LEdu LPal MAvo MGos MMoz MWht SBig SSta WDyG WJun WPGP
- 'Breviglumis' see *C. culeou* 'Tenuis'
- 'Purple Splendour' EPla WJun WPGP
§ - 'Tenuis' EPla WJun
- weeping CDTJ WPGP
***cumingii*** CBcs GBin WJun WPGP
***delicatula*** from Machu Picchu, Peru WPGP
***gigantea*** CDTJ CEnt CPLG EPfP EPla ESwi MMoz MWht SBig WDyG WJun WPGP
***macrostachya*** WPGP
***montana*** CDTJ EPla GBin
***mulleri*** F&M 104A from Mexico WPGP
***quila*** EPla MMoz WPGP
***valdiviensis*** WJun WPGP

## *Cibotium* (*Cibotiaceae*)

***glaucum*** WRic
***schiedei*** WRic

## *Cicerbita* (*Asteraceae*)

BWJ 7891 from China WCru
§ ***alpina*** EBee NBid SPlb
***bourgaei*** LRHS
***plumieri*** EWes IFro WCot WFar WMoo
- 'Blott' (v) WCot

## *Cichorium* (*Asteraceae*)

***intybus*** Widely available
- f. ***album*** CPrp EBee EBla ECha ECtt GKin LHop MCot MLLN MRav NBir NCGa NGdn SPer SWat WCAu
- var. ***foliosum*** EBee
- 'Roseum' CPrp EBee EBla ECha ECtt ELan GKin GMac LHop MCot MLLN MRav NBir NCGa NGdn SPer SPoG SWat WHrl

## *Cicuta* (*Apiaceae*)

***virosa*** LLWG MMuc

## *Cimicifuga* see *Actaea*

***acerina*** see *Actaea japonica*
***americana*** see *Actaea podocarpa*
***cordifolia*** (DC.) Torrey & A.Gray see *Actaea cordifolia*
***cordifolia*** Pursh see *Actaea podocarpa*
***foetida*** see *Actaea cimicifuga*
***racemosa*** var. ***cordifolia*** see *Actaea cordifolia*
- 'Purpurea' see *Actaea simplex* Atropurpurea Group

| | | |
|---|---|---|
| | ***ramosa*** | see *Actaea simplex* 'Prichard's Giant' |
| | ***rubifolia*** | see *Actaea cordifolia* |
| | ***simplex*** var. ***matsumurae*** | see *Actaea matsumurae* |

## *Cineraria* (*Asteraceae*)

| | | |
|---|---|---|
| | ***maritima*** | see *Senecio cineraria* |
| | ***saxifraga*** | EShb |

## *Cinnamomum* (*Lauraceae*)

| | | |
|---|---|---|
| | ***camphora*** | CBcs CHEx CPLG IGor IRar LRHS |
| | ***micranthum*** | WPGP |
| | ***parthenoxylon*** new | EGFP |

## *Cionura* (*Apocynaceae*)

| | | |
|---|---|---|
| | ***oreophila*** | CRHN EBee ELan SKHP WPGP WSHC |

## *Circaea* (*Onagraceae*)

| | | |
|---|---|---|
| | ***alpina*** | EBee MMuc |
| | ***lutetiana*** | EWil WHer |
| | - 'Caveat Emptor' (v) | CHid EBee NBid WCot WHer |

## *Cirsium* (*Asteraceae*)

| | | |
|---|---|---|
| | ***acaule*** | NLar |
| | ***anartiolepis*** F&M 252 | WPGP |
| | ***arvense*** | WSFF |
| * | ***atroroseum*** | SWat |
| | ***diacantha*** | see *Ptilostemon diacantha* |
| | ***helenioides*** | see *C. heterophyllum* |
| § | ***heterophyllum*** | CHid CPom CSam EWld LEdu NBre NChi NLar SHar WPGP |
| | ***japonicum*** 'Pink Beauty' | WWEG |
| | - 'Rose Beauty' | IPot |
| | 'Mount Etna' | CDes CPrp EBee EBla EWhm GKin LHop LRHS MBNS MMuc MSpe NGdn SEND SPoG WPGP |
| | ***oleraceum*** | LEdu LRHS NBid NBre NLar |
| | ***purpuratum*** | WPGP |
| | ***rivulare*** 'Atropurpureum' | Widely available |
| | ***tuberosum*** | NDov SKHP SPhx |
| | ***vulgare*** | WSFF |

## *Cissus* (*Vitaceae*)

| | | |
|---|---|---|
| | ***antarctica*** ♀H1 | CCCN EShb SEND |
| | ***pedata*** B&SWJ 2371 | WCru |
| | ***quadrangularis*** | SBfd |
| | ***rhombifolia*** ♀H1 | EOHP SEND |
| § | ***striata*** | CBcs CDoC CHEx CMac CRHN CTrC CWCL EBee ELon EShb LRHS MRav SBfd SEND SLim SWvt WSHC |

## *Cistus* ✿ (*Cistaceae*)

| | | |
|---|---|---|
| | ***acutifolius*** misapplied | see *C. inflatus*, *C.* × *pulverulentus* |
| | × ***aguilarii*** | CBcs CHEx CSBt CTri LAst MRav WSHC |
| | - 'Maculatus' ♀H3 | CBot CDoC CDul CPLG CSam CTrC EBee ELan EPfP GBin LRHS LSRN MAsh MMuc NCGa NLar SBfd SCoo SLPl SPer SPoG SWvt WKif WPGP |
| | ***albidus*** | CArn WKif XSen |
| | ***algarvensis*** | see *Halimium ocymoides* |
| | 'Ann Baker' | SLPl |
| | 'Anne Palmer' | see *C.* × *fernandesiae* 'Anne Palmer' |
| | × ***argenteus*** 'Blushing Peggy Sammons' | CDoC NLar SVen XSen |
| | - Golden Treasure = 'Nepond' (v) | MSCN SWvt |
| | - 'Paper Moon' | LSRN SVen |
| § | - 'Peggy Sammons' ♀H3 | CBot CDoC EBee ECha ELan EPfP EWTr GGar LAst LBMP LRHS LSRN MAsh MGos NLar SBrd SCoo SEND SLim SPer SWvt WFar WHar WSHC |
| | - 'Silver Ghost' | LRHS SLim SVen |
| | - 'Silver Pink' ambig. | Widely available |
| | 'Blanche' | see *C. ladanifer* 'Blanche' |
| | × ***bornetianus*** 'Jester' | CSBt EBee LRHS MAsh NMun SBrd SVen |
| | × ***canescens*** f. ***albus*** | CWib EQua MSCN WKif XSen |
| § | ***clusii*** | NLar |
| | - subsp. ***multiflorus*** | XSen |
| | × ***corbariensis*** | see *C.* × *hybridus* |
| | ***creticus*** | CDoC CPLG CSam ELau EQua LAst MAsh MBri MGos MLHP MSpe NMun SBfd SBrd SLon SPoG SVen WKif WPGP |
| | - subsp. ***corsicus*** | XSen |
| § | - subsp. ***creticus*** | EBee ELan ELon EPfP LRHS MRav SCoo SPer |
| | - subsp. ***eriocephalus*** | MSpe |
| | × ***crispatus*** | XSen |
| § | - 'Warley Rose' | EWTr GMaP SBrd WKif |
| | ***crispus*** misapplied | see *C.* × *pulverulentus*, *C.* × *purpureus* |
| § | ***crispus*** L. | EBee ELan LRHS SEND SGol |
| | - 'Prostratus' | see *C. crispus* L. |
| | - 'Sunset' | see *C.* × *pulverulentus* 'Sunset' |
| § | × ***cyprius*** ♀H4 | CArn EBee ELan EPfP GBin MGos MNHC MRav MWat SBrd SDix SEND SPer SRms WDin WFar |
| | - var. ***ellipticus*** f. ***bicolor*** | NMun |
| § | - - 'Elma' ♀H3 | ELan EPfP LRHS MAsh SPer |
| § | × ***dansereaui*** | CMHG CSBt CWib EBee LRHS MGos MRav SVen SWvt WFar |
| | - 'Albiflorus' | see *C.* × *dansereaui* 'Portmeirion' |
| | - 'Decumbens' ♀H4 | CBod CChe CDul CMHG CTri EBee ELan EPfP EWTr LHop LRHS MAsh MBNS MRav MSwo NCGa SArc SBfd SCoo SPer SPoG SWvt WDin WPGP |
| | - 'Jenkyn Place' | CBod CDoC GMaP IVic LSRN MBNS MGos SBrd SLPl SPer SPoG SUsu WKif |
| § | - 'Portmeirion' | NMun WFar |
| | 'Elma' | see *C.* × *cyprius* var. *ellipticus* 'Elma' |
| | 'Enigma' | CDoC |
| § | × ***fernandesiae*** 'Anne Palmer' | EPfP GBin LHop LLHF LRHS LSRN MAsh SEND SPoG SRGP WFar |
| | × ***florentinus*** misapplied | see × *Halimiocistus* 'Ingwersenii' |
| § | × ***florentinus*** Lam. | CAbP EBee GMaP XSen |
| | - 'Fontfroide' | MMuc NMun SBrd SEND SVen |
| | 'Gordon Cooper' | LSRN MMuc NMun SBrd SPoG |
| | × ***heterocalyx*** 'Chelsea Bonnet' | CBod EPfP GMaP LRHS MBNS NMun SCoo SEND SLim SPoG |
| | ***heterophyllus*** | SVen |
| § | × ***hybridus*** | Widely available |
| | - 'Gold Prize' (v) | CAlb CMHG CWGN CWSG EBee ELan MBri MGos NEgg NLar SBfd SWvt WFar WGrn WHar WPat |
| | - Little Miss Sunshine = 'Dunnecis' (v) new | SPer SPoG |
| | - Rospico = 'Rencis' (v) | EMil LBuc LRHS |
| | ***ingwerseniana*** | see × *Halimiocistus* 'Ingwersenii' |
| | 'Jessamy Beauty' | NMun SLPl |
| | 'Jessamy Bride' | SLPl SVen |
| | ***ladanifer*** misapplied | see *C.* × *cyprius* |
| | ***ladanifer*** ambig. | CMac SArc WKif |
| | ***ladanifer*** L. ♀H3 | CDoC CDul CSBt CTri ECha ELan EPfP EWTr GCra GPoy MRav MSwo SBfd SPer SWvt WFar WHar |

| | | |
|---|---|---|
| | – var. ***albiflorus*** | EQua |
| § | – 'Blanche' | LLHF LSRN SEND SSpi WKif |
| § | – 'Paladin' | SBfd |
| | – Palhinhae Group | see *C. ladanifer* var. *sulcatus* |
| | – 'Pat' | ELan EPfP LRHS LSRN MAsh NBir SPoG SSpi |
| § | – var. ***sulcatus*** | CDoC ELan EPfP LHop LRHS WFar |
| | – – SDR 5620 | GKev |
| | ***lasianthus*** | see *Halimium lasianthum* |
| | ***laurifolius*** ♀H4 | CDoC CDul EBee EPfP GGar MGos NBir NEgg NLar SEND SKHP SLPl SPer SPoG XLum XSen |
| | × ***laxus*** | NMun |
| | – 'Snow White' | CAbP CDoC EBee EPfP GGar LAst LRHS MGos NPer NPro SLPl SLim SLon SRms SUsu WGrn |
| | × ***ledon*** | NMun SLPl |
| § | × ***lenis*** 'Grayswood Pink' ♀H4 | CAlb CDoC CMHG CPLG CTri CWSG EBee ECrN ELan EPfP EQua LHop LRHS LSRN MAsh MCot MGos MMuc MSwo NLar SEND SLim SPer SPlb SVen SWvt WFar WKif XLum |
| | ***libanotis*** | MSpe |
| | × ***longifolius*** | see *C.* × *nigricans* |
| | × ***loretii*** misapplied | see *C.* × *dansereaui* |
| | × ***loretii*** Rouy & Foucaud | see *C.* × *stenophyllus* |
| | × ***lucasii*** | XSen |
| | × ***lusitanicus*** Maund | see *C.* × *dansereaui* |
| | 'Merrist Wood Cream' | see × *Halimiocistus wintonensis* 'Merrist Wood Cream' |
| | ***monspeliensis*** | CAbP CMac EPfP EQua LRHS MAsh MBNS MMuc SEND SLon SPer WFar XSen |
| | – 'Vicar's Mead' | CCCN CDoC ELan EPfP LRHS MBNS MMuc SEND SRms |
| § | × ***nigricans*** | CTrC XSen |
| | × ***obtusifolius*** misapplied | see *C.* × *nigricans* |
| | × ***obtusifolius*** ambig. | LRHS SKHP WNew |
| | × ***obtusifolius*** Sweet | EPfP EWes SLPl |
| § | – 'Thrive' | LRHS MBri MGos SCoo |
| | ***ocymoides*** | see *Halimium ocymoides* |
| | × ***pagei*** new | NMun |
| | 'Paladin' | see *C. ladanifer* 'Paladin' |
| | ***palhinhae*** | see *C. ladanifer* var. *sulcatus* |
| | ***parviflorus*** misapplied | see *C.* × *lenis* 'Grayswood Pink' |
| | ***parviflorus*** Lam. | CBot WSHC |
| | 'Peggy Sammons' | see *C.* × *argenteus* 'Peggy Sammons' |
| | × ***platysepalus*** | SLPl |
| | ***populifolius*** | CMHG CMac ECha LLHF LRHS SGol SPer |
| | – var. ***lasiocalyx*** | see *C. populifolius* subsp. *major* |
| § | – subsp. ***major*** ♀H3 | EPfP LRHS LSRN SKHP WPGP |
| § | × ***pulverulentus*** | CPLG CTri EBee ECha EPfP MMHG SWal WDin WSHC XSen |
| § | – 'Sunset' ♀H3 | Widely available |
| | – 'Warley Rose' | see *C.* × *crispatus* 'Warley Rose' |
| § | × ***purpureus*** ♀H3 | Widely available |
| | – 'Alan Fradd' | Widely available |
| | – var. ***argenteus*** f. ***stictus*** | EBee LRHS LSRN XSen |
| | – 'Betty Taudevin' | see *C.* × *purpureus* |
| | × ***rodiaei*** 'Jessabel' | EPfP LRHS MAsh SCoo SEND SPoG |
| | – 'Jessica' | NLar |
| | ***rosmarinifolius*** | see *C. clusii* |
| | 'Ruby Cluster' | CBod CCCN LRHS LSRN MMuc SRms |
| | ***sahucii*** | see × *Halimiocistus sahucii* |
| | ***salviifolius*** | CAbP CArn CCCN WFar XSen |
| | – 'Avalanche' | LRHS MRav WAbe |
| | – 'Gold Star' | EBee LRHS |
| | – 'May Snow' | LRHS |
| | – 'Prostratus' | ELan EPfP IRar LRHS MMuc WPGP |
| | ***salviifolius*** × ***monspeliensis*** | see *C.* × *florentinus* Lam. |
| | 'Silver Pink' misapplied | see *C.* × *lenis* 'Grayswood Pink' |
| | 'Silver Pink' ambig. | CWSG WKif |
| | × ***skanbergii*** ♀H3 | CBcs CHEx CMac CSBt CTri CWib EBee ELan EPfP LHop LIMB LRHS MGos MLHP MMuc MRav MWat NBir SBrd SCoo SDix SEND SMrm SPer SPoG WFar XLum XSen |
| | 'Snow Fire' ♀H4 | CCCN CDoC EBee EPfP LRHS LSRN MAsh MGos MMuc NMun NPro SBfd SBrd SCoo SLPl SPoG WGrn |
| § | × ***stenophyllus*** | CWib MMuc SPer |
| | 'Stripey' | SVen |
| | 'Summer Snow' | LRHS |
| | 'Thornfield White' | LRHS |
| | 'Thrive' | see *C.* × *obtusifolius* 'Thrive' |
| | ***tomentosus*** | see *Helianthemum nummularium* subsp. *tomentosum* |
| | × ***verguinii*** | LHop SDix |
| | – f. ***albiflorus*** | NMun |
| | – var. ***albiflorus*** misapplied | see *C.* × *dansereaui* 'Portmeirion' |
| | ***villosus*** | see *C. creticus* subsp. *creticus* |
| | ***wintonensis*** | see × *Halimiocistus wintonensis* |

## *Citharexylum* (*Verbenaceae*)

| | | |
|---|---|---|
| | ***spicatum*** | CPLG WAle WBor WPGP |

## × *Citrofortunella* (*Rutaceae*)

| | | |
|---|---|---|
| | sp. | CCCN |
| § | ***microcarpa*** (F) ♀H1 | CBcs CCCN CDoC EPfP ERea LRHS NLar |
| | ***mitis*** | see × *C. microcarpa* |

## citron see *Citrus medica*

## *Citronella* (*Icacinaceae*)

| | | |
|---|---|---|
| § | ***gongonha*** | SVen |
| | ***mucronata*** | see *C. gongonha* |

## *Citrus* ✿ (*Rutaceae*)

| | | |
|---|---|---|
| | ***amblycarpa*** djeruk lime (F) | ERea |
| I | ***aurantiata*** 'Chinese Citron' (F) | ERea |
| | ***aurantiifolia*** (F) | CCCN EPfP ERea SVic |
| | – key lime (F) | ERea |
| | – 'Paduk' (F) | ERea |
| | ***aurantium*** | ERea SPlb |
| | – 'Bouquet de Fleurs' (F) | CCCN ERea |
| | – var. ***myrtifolia*** 'Chinotto' (F) | ERea |
| | – 'Seville' (F) | ERea LSRN |
| | ***bergamia*** bergamot | ERea |
| | calamondin | see × *Citrofortunella microcarpa* |
| | 'Fukushu' (F) | CCCN ERea |
| | ***hystrix*** | CCCN CDoC ERea LSRN NPla |
| | ***jambhiri*** 'Otaheite' (F) | CCCN |
| | ***japonica*** | see *Fortunella japonica* |
| | 'Kulci' (F) | CCCN |
| | kumquat | see *Fortunella margarita* |
| | 'La Valette' (F) | CCCN ERea LSRN SEND |
| | × ***latifolia*** (F/S) | CCCN CDoC EPfP LRHS MREP |
| | ***limetta*** | CCCN LRHS |
| | ***limettoides*** (F) | CArn ERea |
| | ***limon*** (F) | CHEx EPfP LRHS LSRN MREP STrG SVic |
| | – 'Amalfitanum' (F) | ERea |
| | – 'Eureka' (F) | CCCN |

| | |
|---|---|
| - 'Fino' (F) | CCCN |
| - 'Four Seasons' (F) | CCCN ERea LSRN NLar |
| § - 'Garey's Eureka' (F) | CDoC EPfP ERea |
| - 'Genova' (F) | ERea |
| - 'Imperial' (F) | ERea |
| - 'Lemonade' (F) | ERea |
| - 'Mosquito' (v) | CHll ERea |
| - 'Quatre Saisons' | see *C. limon* 'Garey's Eureka' |
| - 'Toscana' (F) | ERea |
| - 'Variegata' (F/v) 🏆$^{H1}$ | CCCN ERea |
| - 'Verna' (F) | CCCN |
| - 'Villa Franca' (F) | ERea SVic |
| - 'Yen Ben' (F) | ERea |
| × ***limonia*** 'Rangpur' (F) | ERea |
| 'Lipo' | CCCN NLar |
| ***macrophylla*** | ERea |
| ***madurensis*** | see *Fortunella japonica* |
| ***maxima*** (F) | ERea |
| ***medica*** (F) | CHll ERea |
| - 'Cidro Digitado' | see *C. medica* var. *digitata* |
| § - var. ***digitata*** (F) | CHll ERea |
| - 'Ethrog' (F) | ERea |
| - var. ***sarcodactylis*** | see *C. medica* var. *digitata* |
| × ***meyeri*** | CHEx |
| - 'Improved Meyer' (F) | ERea |
| - 'Meyer' (F) 🏆$^{H1}$ | CBcs CCCN CHll CTri EPfP ERea LRHS LSRN NLar SPer |
| ***microcarpa*** Philippine lime | see × *Citrofortunella microcarpa* |
| ***mitis*** | see × *Citrofortunella microcarpa* |
| × ***nobilis*** Ortanique Group (F) | CCCN |
| - 'Silver Hill Owari' (F) | ERea |
| - Tangor Group (F) | ERea |
| × ***paradisi*** (F) | CCCN MREP SVic |
| - 'Foster' (F) | ERea |
| - 'Golden Special' (F) | ERea SVic |
| - 'Marsh' (F) | ERea |
| - 'Red Blush' (F/S) | ERea |
| - 'Star Ruby' (F/S) | CCCN ERea |
| 'Ponderosa' (F) | ERea |
| 'Pursta' (F) | CCCN ERea |
| ***reticulata*** (F) | CCCN LRHS MREP |
| - 'Hernandina' (F) | CCCN |
| - Mandarin Group (F) | CDoC EPfP |
| - - 'Clementine' (F) | CDoC ERea LRHS |
| - - 'Esbal' (F) | CCCN |
| - - 'Nules' (F/S) | CCCN ERea |
| - 'Nova' | see *C.* × *tangelo* 'Nova' |
| - 'Orogrande' | ERea |
| - 'Suntina' | see *C.* × *tangelo* 'Nova' |
| ***sinensis*** (F) | CCCN LRHS SVic |
| - 'Egg' (F) | ERea |
| - 'Fukumoto' (F) | CCCN |
| - 'Harwood Late' (F) | ERea |
| - 'Jaffa' | see *C. sinensis* 'Shamouti' |
| - 'Lane Late' (F) | CCCN ERea |
| - 'Malta Blood' (F) | ERea |
| - 'Moro Blood' (F) | ERea |
| - 'Navelate' (F) | ERea |
| - 'Navelina' (F/S) | CCCN CDoC |
| - 'Newhall' (F) | ERea |
| - 'Saint Michael' (F) | ERea |
| - 'Sanguinelli' (F) | CCCN ERea |
| § - 'Shamouti' (F) | ERea |
| - 'Tarocco' (F) | ERea |
| - 'Trovita' (F) | ERea |
| - 'Valencia' (F) | CCCN |
| - 'Valencia Late' (F) | ERea |
| - 'Washington' (F/S) | ERea |
| × ***tangelo*** 'Minneola' (F) | ERea |
| § - 'Nova' (F/S) | CCCN |
| - 'Seminole' (F) | ERea |
| - 'Ugli' (F) | ERea |
| ***unshiu*** 'Miyagawa' | CCCN ERea |
| - 'Okitsu' (F/S) | CCCN |

## *Cladium* (*Cyperaceae*)

| | |
|---|---|
| ***mariscus*** | XLum |

## *Cladothamnus* see *Elliottia*

## *Cladrastis* (*Papilionaceae*)

| | |
|---|---|
| § ***kentukea*** | CBcs CDul CLnd CMCN ELan EPfP EWTr LRHS MBlu MBri MRav NLar SSpi WDin WHar |
| § - 'Perkins Pink' | MBlu MBri SSpi |
| - 'Rosea' | see *C. kentukea* 'Perkins Pink' |
| ***lutea*** | see *C. kentukea* |
| ***sinensis*** | CBcs CGHE CPLG EBee EPfP EPla IDee MBlu SKHP SSpi WPGP |

## *Clarkia* (*Onagraceae*)

| | |
|---|---|
| * ***repens*** | CSpe |

## *Clavinodum* (*Poaceae*)

| | |
|---|---|
| § ***oedogonatum*** | EPla MWht |

## *Claytonia* (*Portulacaceae*)

| | |
|---|---|
| ***alsinoides*** | see *C. sibirica* |
| § ***perfoliata*** | CArn GPoy ILis WHer |
| § ***sibirica*** | CAgr CArn CElw LSou WPtf XLum |
| - f. ***albiflora*** | CElw WCot WMoo |
| ***virginica*** | LAma LRHS MMoz WFar WMoo |

## *Clematis* ✿ (*Ranunculaceae*)

| | |
|---|---|
| BWJ 7630 from China | WCru |
| BWJ 8169 from China | WCru |
| CC 711 | CPLG |
| CC 4710 | CPLG |
| CC 5904 | GKev |
| SDR 6151 | GKev |
| 'Abundance' (Vt) 🏆$^{H4}$ | CDoC CRHN CSPN CWCL EBee EPfP ETho LRHS LSRN MAsh MBri MRav NHol NTay SBfd SDix SPer SPet |
| ***acuminata*** var. ***sikkimensis*** B&SWJ 7202 | WCru |
| ***addisonii*** | CBcs CSPN NHaw |
| ***aethusifolia*** | CSPN |
| ***afoliata*** | CSPN ECou WThu |
| ***afoliata*** × ***forsteri*** | ECou |
| 'Ai-Nor' (EL) | ETho |
| 'Akaishi' (EL) | ETho NTay |
| ***akebioides*** | NHaw |
| - SDR 5966 | GKev |
| - SDR 6110 | GKev |
| Alabast = 'Poulala'$^{PBR}$ (EL) 🏆$^{H4}$ | CSPN EBee ETho LRHS NHaw NTay SCoo SPoG SWCr |
| 'Alba Luxurians' (Vt) 🏆$^{H4}$ | Widely available |
| 'Albatross' (EL) | LSRN |
| 'Albert' (A) **new** | NTay |
| 'Albiflora' (A) | CSPN NSti NTay |
| 'Albina Plena' (A/d) | ETho MGos |
| 'Aleksandrit' (EL) | NHaw |
| 'Alice Fisk' (EL) | CAlb CSPN EBee EPfP ETho LSRN MSwo NHaw SLim WGor |
| 'Alionushka' (I) 🏆$^{H4}$ | CRHN EBee ELan ELon EPfP ETho LRHS LSRN MAsh MBri MGos NLar NPri SLim SPer SPet SPoG SWCr |

| | | |
|---|---|---|
| | 'Allanah' (LL) | CAlb EBee ETho LRHS LSRN MAsh MGos NHaw SCoo SLim SPoG WFar |
| | ***alpina*** ♀H4 | CBot EPfP GGal GKev GKin LSRN MAsh MRav MWhi NHaw NPer SPlb WFar |
| | BDR 3011 | [illegible] |
| | - 'Albiflora' | see *C. sibirica* |
| | - 'Columbine White' | see *C.* 'White Columbine' |
| I | - 'Odorata' | CSPN MGos NHaw |
| § | - 'Pamela Jackman' ♀H4 | CChe CDoC CMac CSPN CWSG EBee ELan IBal LRHS LSRN MAsh MGos MMuc NEgg NSti NTay SCoo SDix SEND SLim SPer SPet SPoG SWCr SWvt WFar |
| | - pink-flowered | GKev |
| | - 'Stolwijk Gold' (A) | ETho MBlu MGos NHaw NTay |
| | ***alternata*** | CWGN ETho |
| | 'Amelia Joan' (Ta) | MWat |
| | 'Ameshisuto' (EL) | ETho |
| | 'Amethyst Beauty' (A) | LRHS SBrd SPoG SWCr |
| | Amethyst Beauty = 'Evipo043' **new** | ETho LSqu SLon |
| | 'Andromeda' (EL) | CAlb CSPN EBee ETho LRHS NHaw NPri NTay WFar |
| | Angelique = 'Evipo017' (EL) | EPfP ETho LBuc LRHS LSqu NTay SBrd SCoo SLon SPer SPoG SWCr |
| | 'Anita' (Ta) | EPfP ETho LSRN NHaw NTay SLim SMDP |
| | Anna Louise = 'Evithree'[PBR] (EL) ♀H4 | CLng CSPN CWCL EBee EPfP ETho IBal LBuc LRHS LSRN LSqu MBri NTay SBrd SCoo SLim SPer SPoG SWCr |
| | 'Annabel' (EL) | CSPN LSRN MAsh |
| | Anniversary = 'Pynot' (EL) | LSRN SCoo |
| | 'Aotearoa' (LL) | NHaw |
| | 'Aphrodite Elegafumina' | CFir CRHN CWGN LRHS NHaw SWCr |
| | ***apiifolia*** B&SWJ 4838 | WCru |
| | 'Apple Blossom' (Ar) ♀H4 | Widely available |
| | 'Arabella' (I) ♀H4 | CRHN CSPN CSam CWCL EBee ELan ELon EPfP EShb ETho LRHS LSRN MAsh MBri NPri NTay SEND SLim SPer SWCr SWvt WFar WSHC |
| § | Arctic Queen = 'Evitwo'[PBR] (EL) ♀H4 | CLng CSPN CWCL EBee EPfP ETho LBuc LRHS LSRN LSqu MAsh NPri NTay SBrd SCoo SPer SPoG SWCr WFar |
| | ***armandii*** | Widely available |
| | - 'Enham Star' | LRHS MBri MGos |
| § | - 'Little White Charm' | CBcs CSPN EWTr LRHS SBfd SKHP SPoG |
| | - 'Meyeniana' | see *C. armandii* 'Little White Charm' |
| I | - 'Snowdrift' | CBcs CSBt CSPN CSam CWSG ELan EPfP ETho LRHS LSRN LTen MAsh MGos MSwo NEgg NLar NSti NTay SBfd SKHP SPer SPoG SRms SWCr |
| | × ***aromatica*** | CBcs CFir CPrp CSPN CWGN EAEE EBee ELan ELon EPfP ETho LRHS MAsh MRav NTay SCoo SPoG |
| § | 'Asagasumi' (EL) | ETho |
| | 'Asao' (EL) | EBee ELan EPfP ETho LRHS MAsh MGos MRav NTay SCoo SEND SPer SPoG SWCr |
| | 'Ascotiensis' (LL) | CBcs CLng CRHN CSPN EBee EPfP ETho LRHS MAsh NHaw NTay SCoo SPoG SWCr WFar |
| | 'Ashva' (LL) | CWGN MGos |
| | 'Aureolin' (Ta) | CSPN EBee |
| | Avant-garde = 'Evipo033'[PBR] (Vt) | CWGN EPfP ETho LRHS LSqu SBrd SLon SPoG SWCr |
| § | 'Bagatelle' (LL) | CLng CSPN LRHS LSRN NHaw NPri SGol SMDP WFar |
| | 'Bal Maiden' (Vt) | CRHN NHaw |
| § | 'Ballerina in Blue' (A/d) | NHaw |
| | 'Ballet Skirt' (A/d) ♀H4 | NHaw |
| | 'Bałtyk' (EL) | CSPN |
| | 'Barbara' (LL) | ETho LSRN MRav NHaw |
| | 'Barbara Dibley' (EL) | CLng CTri CWSG LRHS MAsh NHaw SCoo SDix SLim SPet |
| | 'Barbara Harrington'[PBR] (LL) | CLng LRHS LSRN MAsh NHaw SWCr |
| | 'Barbara Jackman' (EL) | CMac EBee ETho LRHS LSRN MAsh MGos MRav MSwo NTay SCoo SLim SPer SWCr WFoF |
| | 'Basil Bartlett' (Fo) | ECou |
| | 'Beata' (LL) | CAlb MGos NHaw |
| | 'Beauty of Worcester' (EL) | CFir CMac CSPN CWSG ELan ELon EPfP ETho LRHS LSRN MAsh MSwo NHaw NTay SCoo SDix SGol SLim SPer SPet WFar |
| | 'Bees' Jubilee' (EL) | CBcs CChe CMac CRHN CWSG EBee ELan ETho LRHS LSRN MAsh MGos MRav MSwo NBir NTay SDix SLim SPer SPet SPoG SWCr SWvt WFar |
| | 'Bella' (EL) | LSRN NHaw |
| | 'Belle Nantaise' (EL) | EBee SCoo SPet SRms |
| | 'Belle of Woking' (EL) | CAlb CRHN CSPN CWSG EBee ELan ELon ETho LRHS LSRN MAsh MRav NPri NTay SCoo SGol SLim SPoG SWCr |
| | 'Bells of Emei Shan' | ETho WCru |
| | 'Berry Red' (A) | CWGN |
| § | 'Beth Currie' (EL) | CLng CSPN EPfP LRHS SWCr |
| | 'Betina' | see *C.* 'Red Beetroot Beauty' |
| | 'Betty Corning' (Vt) ♀H4 | CRHN CSPN CWGN EBee ELan ELon EPfP ETho LRHS LSRN MBri MGos MLLN NTay SCoo SLim SLon SWCr WFar |
| | 'Betty Risdon' (EL) | ETho MAsh |
| | Bijou[PBR] | see *C.* Thumbelina |
| | 'Bill MacKenzie' (Ta) ♀H4 | CMHG CMac CSam CTri CWSG CWib EBee ELan EPfP ETho GGar LHop LRHS LSRN MAsh MBlu MBri MGos MRav MWat MWhi NTay SDix SLim SPer SPoG SWCr SWvt WFar WSHC |
| | 'Black Prince' (Vt) | CRHN CWGN EBee ELan ETho LRHS LSRN MGos NHaw NLar SLim SLon SMDP SRms |
| | 'Black Tea' (LL) | LRHS LSRN NHaw NTay SLim |
| § | 'Błękitny Anioł' (LL) ♀H4 | CAlb CLng CMac CRHN CSPN ELon ETho LRHS MAsh MGos NLar NTay SCoo SLim SPer SPet SPoG SWCr WFar |
| | Blue Angel | see *C.* 'Błękitny Anioł' |
| | 'Blue Belle' (Vt) | CRHN ELan NSti SLon SPoG WFar |
| | 'Blue Bird' (A/d) | CBcs CWCL EBee LRHS MBlu NTay SMDP SPer SPoG SRms |
| | Blue Blood | see *C.* 'Königskind' |
| | 'Blue Boy' (I) | see *C.* × *diversifolia* 'Blue Boy' (I) |
| | 'Blue Boy' (EL) | see *C.* 'Elsa Späth' |
| | 'Blue Dancer' (A) | CBcs CLng EBee EPfP EShb ETho LRHS MAsh MGos NLar NTay SWCr |
| | 'Blue Eclipse' (A) | CSPN CTri CWGN MBri MGos NHaw SBch |
| | 'Blue Eyes' (EL) | CSPN EBee ELon ETho LSRN NHaw NTay SLim |

§ 'Blue Light'[PBR] (EL/d) — CSPN ELan LRHS MGos NLar NTay WFar
Blue Moon = 'Evirin'[PBR] (EL) — CLng EPfP ETho LRHS LSRN NLar NTay SCoo SLim SPoG SWCr WFar
Blue Pirouette = 'Zobluepi'[PBR] (I) — CWGN LRHS NLar SMDP SWCr
Blue Rain — see *C.* 'Sinii Dozhd'
'Blue Ravine' (EL) — EPfP LRHS MGos NLar NTay SCoo
Blue River = 'Zoblueriver' — CWGN
'Blue Tapers' (A) — NHaw
Bonanza = 'Evipo031'[PBR] — CLng EPfP ETho LRHS LSqu NLar NTay SBrd SCoo SPer SPoG SWCr
§ × ***bonstedtii*** 'Campanile' (H) — NBir
- 'Crépuscule' (H) — MCot SMDP SRms
'Boskoop Beauty' (EL) — NHaw
Bourbon = 'Evipo018'[PBR] — EPfP ETho LBuc LRHS LSqu SBrd SCoo SPer SPoG SWCr
***brachyura*** B&SWJ 8854 — WCru
'Brocade' (Vt) — CRHN CSPN NHaw
'Broughton Bride' (A) — CSPN CTri CWGN ETho MAsh MBri NHol NTay SMDP
'Broughton Star' (M/d) ♀H4 — CAlb CMac CRHN CSBt CSPN CWib EBee ELan EPfP ETho GGar LRHS LSRN LTen MAsh MBlu MBri MGos MRav MSwo NBir NHol NSti NTay SLim SPet SPoG WFar
'Brunette' (A) — CSPN EBee ELan EPfP ETho LRHS MAsh MGos NHaw NLar NTay SPoG SWCr
***buchananiana*** Finet & Gagnep. — see *C. rehderiana*
***buchananiana*** DC. B&SWJ 8333a — WCru
'Buckland Beauty' (V) — CWGN GMac NTay SMDP
'Buckland Cascade' — SMDP
'Buckland Longshanks' (H) — SMDP
'Burford Bell' (V) — NHaw
'Burford Princess' (Vt) — CRHN NHaw
'Burford White' (A) — CSPN EBee NLar
'Burma Star' (EL) — CWGN ETho LRHS NHaw NTay
Caddick's Cascade = 'Semu' — CSPN CWGN ETho NHaw
***calycina*** — see *C. cirrhosa* var. *balearica*
***campaniflora*** — see *C. viticella* subsp. *campaniflora*
'Campanile' — see *C.* × *bonstedtii* 'Campanile'
'Candleglow' (A) — CSPN MBri NHaw
'Candy Stripe' — CLng EBee LRHS SCoo SLim SPoG SWCr
'Capitaine Thuilleaux' — see *C.* 'Souvenir du Capitaine Thuilleaux'
'Cardinal Wyszynski' — see *C.* 'Kardynał Wyszyński'
'Carmencita' (Vt) — CRHN CSPN EBee LRHS LSRN NHaw SCoo SLon SPet WFar
'Carnaby' (EL) — CBcs CSPN CWCL EBee ELan ELon EPfP ETho LRHS LSRN MAsh MBri MGos NTay SCoo SLim SPoG SWCr
'Carnival Queen' — CSPN MAsh
'Carol Leeds' (Vt) — NHaw
'Caroline' (LL) — CSPN CWGN ETho LSRN NHaw NTay SMDP
× ***cartmanii*** 'Avalanche'[PBR] (Fo/m) ♀H3 — CSPN ELan ETho GBin LBuc LRHS MGos NLar NPri NTay SBfd SCoo SLim SPoG
- 'Joe' (Fo/m) — CBcs EBee ELan EPfP EPot ETho EWes ITim LRHS LSRN MAsh MGos NTay SBfd SCoo SMrm SPer SPoG SWCr
- 'Joe' × ***marmoraria*** (Fo) — ECho MGos
- 'Joe' × 'Sharon' — LSRN
- 'White Abundance'[PBR] (Fo/f) — ETho LBuc LRHS NLar SPoG
× ***cartmanii*** × ***petriei*** (Fo) — ECho
Cassis = 'Evipo020'[PBR] — CWGN EPfP ETho LBuc LRHS LSRN LSqu NTay SBrd SCoo SLon SPer SPoG SWCr
Cezanne = 'Evipo023'[PBR] (EL) — EPfP ETho LBuc LRHS LSqu NTay SBrd SCoo SLon SPer SPoG SWCr
'Chacewater' (Vt) — CRHN
'Chalcedony' (EL) — CSPN CWGN ETho MGos NTay
Chantilly = 'Evipo021'[PBR] — EPfP ETho LBuc LRHS LSqu SBrd SCoo SPer SPoG SWCr
'Charissima' (EL) — CSPN CWGN EPfP LRHS MAsh MGos NLar SCoo SPet SWCr WFar
'Charlie Brown' (LL) — CRHN
'Chatsworth' (Vt) — CRHN EPfP LRHS SWCr
Chevalier = 'Evipo040' — EPfP ETho LRHS SBrd SLon SPer SPoG SWCr
***chiisanensis*** — CSPN WSHC
- B&SWJ 4560 — WCru
- B&SWJ 8706 — WCru
- B&SWJ 8800 — WCru
- 'Lemon Bells' (A) — ELan EPfP ETho LRHS MAsh SCoo SPoG SWCr
- 'Love Child' (A) — CSPN ELan NTay SLim
***chinensis*** misapplied — see *C. terniflora*
***chinensis*** Osbeck RWJ 10042 — WCru
Chinook = 'Evipo013'[PBR] — CLng LRHS NTay SLim SWCr
'Christian Steven' (LL) — CSPN
***chrysantha*** — see *C. tangutica*
***chrysocoma*** misapplied — see *C. spooneri*, *C.* × *vedrariensis*
N ***chrysocoma*** Franch. — SMDP
'Cicciolina' (Vt) — CRHN ETho NHaw
***cirrhosa*** — CBot CTri ELan LRHS MAsh MGos MWhi SWCr
§ - var. ***balearica*** — Widely available
- 'Jingle Bells' — CLng CMac CRHN EBee EGxp EPfP ETho LRHS LSRN MAsh NPri NTay SCoo SLim SPoG SWCr WFar
- 'Ourika Valley' — EBee EPfP ETho LRHS MAsh NLar NTay SWCr WFar
- var. ***purpurascens*** 'Freckles' ♀H3 — Widely available
- - 'Lansdowne Gem' — CMac CSPN CWGN CWib NTay SKHP SMDP SPoG
- 'Wisley Cream' ♀H3 — CBcs CDul CMac CSPN CWCL CWib EBee ELan EPfP ETho LRHS LSRN MAsh MGos MSwo NSti NTay SCoo SEND SKHP SLim SPer SPoG SRms SWCr SWvt WFar
***clarkeana*** misapplied — see *C. urophylla* 'Winter Beauty'
***columbiana*** var. ***tenuiloba*** 'Ylva' (A) — WAbe
'Columbine' (A) — CWSG EBee ETho LRHS MAsh MSwo NTay SDix SPer SPoG
'Columella' (A) — ETho MGos NHaw NLar
'Comtesse de Bouchaud' (LL) ♀H4 — CAlb CDoC CMac CSPN CTri CWCL CWSG EBee ELan EPfP EShb ETho LRHS LSRN MAsh MBri MGos MRav NPri NTay SBrd SDix SEND SLim SPer SPet SPoG SWCr WFar
Confetti = 'Evipo036'[PBR] — CLng EPfP ETho LRHS LSRN NTay SLim SPoG SWCr
***confusa*** HWJK 2200 — WCru
'Congratulations' (EL) — ELon LSRN NTay SLim
***connata*** — GQui
- GWJ 9386 — WCru
- HWJCM 132 — WCru

| | |
|---|---|
| aff. ***connata*** HWJK 2176 from Nepal | WCru |
| – GWJ 9431 from West Bengal | WCru |
| 'Constance' (A) ♀H4 | CMac CSPN CWCL EBee EPfP ETho LRHS LSRN NHaw NSti NTay SAga SCoo SPer SRms SWCr |
| 'Continuity' (M) | CWGN |
| 'Cora' (I) | CWGN |
| 'Cornish Spirit' (Vt) | CRHN |
| 'Corona' (EL) | CLng CSPN EPfP MAsh NHaw SCoo WFar |
| 'Corry' (Ta) | NLar |
| 'Côte d'Azur' (H) | CAlb CBcs CCse CPLG GCal LRHS MCCP NTay |
| 'Countess of Lovelace' (EL) | CBcs CSPN CWSG EBee ELan EPfP ETho LRHS LSRN MAsh MBri MGos MRav NTay SCoo SLim SPet WFar |
| County Park hybrids (Fo) | ECou |
| 'Cragside' (A) | EBee ETho MMuc |
| § 'Crimson King' (LL) | MAsh NHaw WGor |
| 'Crinkle'PBR (M) | CCCN CLng |
| § ***crispa*** | CElw CSPN GAuc NHaw |
| § Crystal Fountain = 'Evipo038'PBR (EL) | CLng CWCL CWGN EPfP ETho LBuc LRHS LSRN LSqu NTay SBrd SCoo SPer SPoG SWCr |
| × ***cylindrica*** | CSPN |
| 'Danae' (Vt) | CRHN NHaw |
| Dancing Queen = 'Zodaque'PBR (EL) | ETho NTay |
| 'Daniel Deronda' (EL) ♀H4 | CDoC CSPN CWCL CWSG ELan ELon ETho LRHS LSRN MAsh MGos MRav NBir NTay SCoo SDix SEND SLim SPoG SWCr WFar |
| 'Dark Eyes' (Vt) | CWGN ETho |
| 'Dark Secret' (A) | CSPN MBri NHaw |
| 'Dawn' (EL) | CCCN CLng CSPN ELon ETho LRHS LSRN MAsh NTay SCoo SLim SPer SPoG SWCr |
| 'Débutante' (EL) | NHaw |
| 'Denny's Double' (EL/d) | CSPN CWGN CWSG ETho MAsh NTay |
| Diamantina = 'Evipo039'PBR | ETho LRHS LSqu SBrd SLon SPer SPoG SWCr |
| 'Diana' (LL) | ETho LSRN NTay |
| Diana's Delight = 'Evipo026' | EPfP ETho LRHS LSqu NTay SBrd SLon SPer SPoG SWCr |
| ***dioscoreifolia*** | see *C. terniflora* |
| § × ***diversifolia*** | CRHN EBee MAsh MGos NHaw SDix |
| § – 'Blue Boy' (I) | CElw CRHN CSPN EBee MGos NHaw |
| – 'Heather Herschell' (I) | CRHN CSPN EBee ELon NHaw SMDP WSHC |
| § – 'Hendersonii' (I) | EAEE EBee ELan ELon EPfP ETho LHop LRHS LSRN MAsh MCot MRav MSwo NBir NTay SDix SPer SWat WKif |
| § – 'Olgae' (I) | CPLG CSPN NHaw SMDP WGwG |
| 'Doctor Ruppel' (EL) | CMac CSPN CWCL CWSG ELon EPfP ETho LRHS LSRN MAsh MBri MGos MRav MSwo NBir NBlu NPri NTay SDix SGol SLim SPer SWCr WFar |
| 'Dominika' (LL) | CSPN CWGN NHaw |
| 'Dorath' | CAlb ELon NHaw NTay |
| 'Dorothy Tolver' (EL) | ETho |
| 'Dorothy Walton' | see *C.* 'Bagatelle' |
| 'Double Cross' | ECou |
| ***douglasii*** | see *C. hirsutissima* var. *hirsutissima* |
| 'Duchess of Albany' (1897) (T) | CAlb CSPN CTri CWSG CWib EBee ELan EPfP ETho IBal LRHS LSRN MAsh MGos NEgg NHol NSti SGol SLim SPer SWCr WFar |
| 'Duchess of Edinburgh' (EL) | CBcs CMac CRHN CWSG EBee ELan EPfP GMac LAst LRHS LSRN MAsh MGos MMuc MSwo NEgg NTay SDix SEND SGol SLim SPet SPoG SWCr WFar |
| 'Duchess of Sutherland' (EL) | MAsh MGos NHaw SDix |
| 'Dulcie' | NHaw |
| × ***durandii*** ♀H4 | CBcs CBot CRHN CSPN CWCL EBee ELan EPfP ETho LRHS LSRN MAsh MBri MRav NPri NTay SCoo SLim SPer SPoG SWCr WFar |
| 'Dusky Star' (M) | EBee |
| 'Dutch Sky' (LL) | ETho MBri |
| 'Early Sensation' (Fo/f) | CAlb CBcs CSPN CTri CWCL CWSG CWib EBee ELan ELon EPfP ETho LRHS LSRN MAsh MBlu MGos MRav NSti NTay SBfd SCoo SLim SPer SPoG SWCr SWvt WFar WFoF |
| 'East Malling' (M) | NHaw |
| 'Eclipse' (H) | NHaw SMDP |
| 'Edith' (EL) ♀H4 | ETho LSRN MAsh NHaw NTay WGor |
| 'Edouard Desfossé' (EL) | CLng |
| 'Edward Prichard' | CSPN ELon EPfP MAsh MGos MWea NHaw NTay SDix SMDP |
| 'Eetika' (LL) | CRHN ETho |
| 'Eleanor' (Fo/f) | ECou GEdr |
| 'Elf' (Vt) | SMDP |
| 'Elfin' (Fo/v) | ECou |
| 'Elizabeth' (M) ♀H4 | Widely available |
| § 'Elsa Späth' (EL) | CElw CMac CPLG CSPN CTri EBee ELan EPfP ETho LRHS LSRN MAsh MBri MGos MRav NTay SDix SLim SPer SPoG SWCr WFar |
| 'Elten' (M) | CSPN SMDP |
| 'Elvan' (Vt) | CRHN NHaw NLar SPet |
| 'Emilia Plater' (Vt) | CRHN CSPN ETho LRHS MGos NHaw SLon |
| Empress = 'Evipo011'PBR (EL) | EPfP ETho LBuc LRHS LSqu NTay SBrd SLon SWCr |
| 'Entel' (Vt) | CRHN NHaw |
| × ***eriostemon*** | see *C.* × *diversifolia* |
| 'Ernest Markham' (LL) ♀H4 | CBcs CDoC CMac CSPN CWCL EBee ELan EPfP ETho LRHS LSRN LTen MAsh MBlu MBri MGos MSwo NEgg NPri NTay SDix SGol SLim SPer SPoG SWCr SWvt WFar |
| 'Esperanto' (LL) | MGos SMDP |
| 'Essex Star' (Fo) | ECou |
| 'Étoile de Malicorne' (EL) | MAsh WGor |
| 'Étoile Rose' (Vt) | CMac CRHN CSPN CTri CWCL ELan EPfP ETho LRHS LSRN MAsh MGos MRav NHol NTay SCoo SDix SLim SPer SWCr WBor WFar |
| 'Étoile Violette' (Vt) ♀H4 | Widely available |
| Evening Star = 'Evista' | EPfP WFar |
| 'Eximia' | see *C.* 'Ballerina in Blue' |
| 'Fair Rosamond' (EL) | EPfP MAsh MGos NHaw NLar NTay SPet |
| 'Fairy' (Fo/f) | ECou |
| Fairy BluePBR | see *C.* Crystal Fountain |
| × ***fargesioides*** | see *C.* 'Paul Farges' |
| ***fasciculiflora*** | CBot CMHG CRHN CSPN |
| – KWJ 2160 | WCru |
| – L 657 | WCru WPGP |
| 'Fascination'PBR (I) | CWGN EBee NHaw SMDP |

| | |
|---|---|
| ***fauriei*** | WSHC |
| Filigree = 'Evipo029'PBR | LBuc LRHS NTay SWCr |
| ***finetiana*** misapplied | see *C. paniculata* J.G. Gmel. |
| 'Firefly' (EL) | MGos |
| 'Fireworks' (EL) | CAlb CSPN CWGN EBee ELon EPfP ETho LRHS LSRN MAsh MBri MGos MRav NEgg NLar NTay SLim SPer SPoG SWCr WFar WFoF WGor |
| 'Flamingo' (EL) | CWCL CWSG |
| ***flammula*** | CMac CRHN CSPN CTri CWib EBee ELan EPfP EWil LRHS LSRN MAsh MBlu MRav MWhi NTay SDix SLim SPer SPoG SWCr SWvt WFar WGwG WSHC XLum |
| - 'Rubra Marginata' | see *C.* × *triternata* 'Rubromarginata' |
| Fleuri = 'Evipo042' | EPfP ETho LBuc LRHS NTay SBrd SCoo SPoG SWCr |
| § 'Floral Feast' (A/d) | CSPN |
| 'Floralia' | see *C.* 'Floral Feast' |
| ***florida*** | CSPN CWGN |
| - 'Bicolor' | see *C. florida* var. *florida* 'Sieboldiana' |
| - var. ***flore-pleno*** (d) | CCCN CSPN CWCL EBee ELan EPfP ETho LAst LRHS LSRN MAsh NEgg NTay SPoG SWCr WFar |
| § - var. ***florida*** 'Sieboldiana' (d) | CBcs CSPN CWCL CWSG EBee ELan EPfP ETho GMac IBal LAst LRHS LSRN MAsh MBri MGos NTay SLim SPer SPoG SRkn SWCr WFar WPGP |
| - var. ***normalis*** 'Thorncroft' (LL) | ETho |
| - Pistachio = 'Evirida' (LL) | CCCN CLng CSPN CWCL CWGN EBee EPfP ETho LRHS LSRN LSqu MAsh NLar NTay SBrd SLim SPoG SWCr WFar |
| 'Floris V' (I) | IPot NHaw NLar |
| 'Flutter' (M) | LRHS |
| ***foetida*** | CSPN |
| ***foetida*** × 'Lunar Lass' (Fo) | ECho ECou |
| ***foetida*** × ***petriei*** | ECho ECou |
| 'Fond Memories' (EL) | EPfP ETho LSRN NLar NTay |
| Forever Friends = 'Zofofri' **new** | ETho |
| I 'Forget-me-not' | LSRN NLar |
| ***forrestii*** | see *C. napaulensis* |
| § ***forsteri*** | CBcs CSPN ETho WSHC |
| 'Foxtrot' (Vt) | CRHN NHaw |
| 'Foxy' (A) ♀H4 | CLng EBee LRHS NHaw NTay SLon WGob |
| 'Fragrant Joy' (Fo/m) | ECou |
| 'Fragrant Oberon' (Fo) | WHlf |
| 'Fragrant Spring' (M) | CAlb CSPN CWGN ELon ETho LRHS MGos MMuc NBlu NHaw NLar SEND SLim SMDP WFar |
| 'Frances Rivis' (A) ♀H4 | CMac CSPN CSam CWCL EBee ELan EPfP ETho LRHS LSRN MAsh MBlu MBri MGos MMuc MRav MSwo NSla NTay NWea SAga SDix SEND SGol SPer SPoG SRms SWCr |
| 'Francesca' (A) | LSRN MGos |
| 'Frankie' (A) ♀H4 | CLng CSPN EBee ELan EPfP ETho LRHS LSRN MAsh NTay SCoo SWCr |
| Franziska Maria = 'Evipo008' (EL) | CLng EPfP ETho LBuc LRHS LSqu MAsh NTay SBrd SCoo SLon SPoG SWCr |
| 'Frau Mikiko' (EL) | ETho MGos |
| 'Frau Susanne' (EL) | ETho |
| 'Freda' (M) ♀H4 | CRHN CTri CWSG EBee ELan EPfP ETho LRHS LSRN MBlu MBri MGos MMuc MRav NHol NSti NTay SDix SLim SPer SPoG SWCr |
| 'Fryderyk Chopin' (EL) | CSPN EBee NHaw NLar |
| 'Fujimusume' (EL) ♀H4 | CSPN CWGN EBee ETho LRHS MAsh NHaw NTay SLim SPoG SWCr WFar |
| ***fujisanensis*** B&SWJ 11370 **new** | WCru |
| 'Fukuzono' | ETho LRHS LSRN NHaw NTay SWCr |
| ***fusca*** misapplied | see *C. japonica* |
| ***fusca*** Turcz. | MAsh WIvy WSHC |
| - dwarf | CWGN NHaw |
| § - var. ***fusca*** | ETho WSHC |
| - var. ***kamtschatica*** | see *C. fusca* Turcz. var. *fusca* |
| 'Fuyu-no-tabi' (EL) | ETho |
| 'Gabrielle' (EL) | CSPN LSRN NHaw |
| GalorePBR | see *C.* Vesuvius |
| Gazelle = 'Evipo014'PBR | CLng LRHS NTay SKHP SWCr |
| 'Gemini' (EL) | MGos |
| 'Generał Sikorski' (EL) | CBcs CMac CRHN CSPN CWSG ELan EPfP ETho LRHS LSRN MAsh MBri MGos NTay SCoo SLim SPer SWCr |
| ***gentianoides*** | ETho LSRN WAbe WCot |
| 'Geoffrey Tolver' (LL) | ETho |
| 'Georg' (A/d) | MGos NHaw |
| Giant Star = 'Gistar'PBR (M) | CLng LRHS MGos NEgg NLar NPer SLim SPoG |
| 'Gillian Blades' (EL) ♀H4 | CLng CRHN CSPN EBee ELan EPfP ETho LRHS LSRN MAsh NHaw SCoo SPer SPoG SWCr |
| § 'Gipsy Queen' (LL) ♀H4 | CAlb CBcs CMac CSPN CWCL CWSG EBee ELan EPfP ETho LRHS LSRN LTen MAsh MRav NTay SDix SGol SLim SPer SPoG SWCr WFar |
| 'Gladys Picard' (EL) | NHaw WFar |
| ***glauca*** Turcz. | see *C. intricata* |
| ***glauca*** ambig. | GAuc |
| ***glaucophylla*** | WCru |
| 'Gojōgawa' (EL) | ETho |
| 'Golden Harvest' (Ta) | NLar WFar |
| Golden Tiara = 'Kugotia'PBR (Ta) ♀H4 | CSPN CWGN ETho LSRN MAsh MGos NLar NTay SRms |
| 'Gothenburg' (M) | NHaw WFar |
| 'Grace' (Ta) | CRHN CSPN NHaw NLar SMDP |
| I 'Grandiflora' (F) | LRHS WFar |
| 'Grandiflora Sanguinea' Johnson | see *C.* 'Södertälje' |
| ***grata*** misapplied | see *C.* × *jouiniana* |
| ***grata*** Wall. B&SWJ 6774 | WCru |
| 'Gravetye Beauty' (T) | CMac CRHN CSPN EBee ELan EPfP ETho GMac LAst LRHS LSRN MAsh MBri MGos MRav NHol NSti NTay SDix SLim SPer SRkn SRms SWCr WCot |
| § 'Grażyna' | NTay |
| 'Green Velvet' (Fo/m) | ECou |
| ***grewiiflora*** B&SWJ 2956 | WCru |
| 'Guernsey Cream' (EL) | CFir CSPN CWCL CWSG EBee ETho LRHS LSRN MAsh MBri MGos NLar NTay SCoo SDix SLim SWCr WFar |
| Guiding Promise = 'Evipo053' **new** | LRHS |
| 'Guiding Star' (EL) | NHaw |
| 'H.F. Young' (EL) | CSPN CWSG EBee ELan EPfP ETho GMac LRHS LSRN MAsh MBri MGos MMuc NTay SCoo SDix SLim SPer SPoG SWCr |

| |  |  |
|---|---|---|
| | ***haenkeana*** | NHaw |
| | 'Hagley Hybrid' (LL) | Widely available |
| | 'Hakuōkan' (EL) | CAlb CSPN EBee EPfP ETho LRHS LSRN MAsh NLar SCoo SLim |
| | 'Hakuree' ambig. | LRHS |
| | 'Hakuree' (I) | ETho LRHS SMDP |
| | 'Hanaguruma' (EL) | CSPN EBee ETho LRHS LSRN NHaw SLim WFar |
| | 'Hanajima' (I) | ETho SMDP WAbe |
| | 'Hania' (EL) | ETho |
| | 'Happy Anniversary' (EL) | LBuc LSRN NLar NTay |
| | Harlow Carr = 'Evipo004'PBR | CLng CMac CWGN EBee EPfP LRHS NTay SCoo SLim SWCr |
| | 'Haru Ichiban' (EL) | ETho |
| | Havering Hybrids (Fo) | ECou |
| | 'Helen Cropper' (EL) | ETho MAsh |
| | 'Helios' (Ta) | CSPN ETho LRHS MGos NTay SCoo |
| | 'Helsingborg' (A) ♀H4 | CLng CSPN EBee ELan EPfP ETho LRHS MAsh NPri NSti NTay SCoo SLim SPoG SRms SWCr |
| I | 'Hendersonii' (I) | LSRN MNFA SRkn |
| | ***hendersonii*** Koch | see *C.* × *diversifolia* 'Hendersonii' |
| | ***hendersonii*** Stand. | see *C.* × *diversifolia* |
| I | 'Hendersonii Rubra' (Ar) | CSPN NLar SPoG |
| | 'Hendryetta'PBR (I) | CWGN EPfP LRHS SMDP SRkn SWCr |
| | ***henryi*** | EShb LSRN MAsh NTay |
| | - B&SWJ 3402 | WCru |
| | - var. ***morii*** B&SWJ 1668 | WCru |
| | 'Henryi' (EL) ♀H4 | CElw CMac CRHN CSPN CTri CWCL CWSG EBee ELan EPfP ETho LRHS LSRN MBri MGos MRav MSwo NEgg SDix SPer SPet SPoG SWCr WFar |
| | ***heracleifolia*** | CBot CFir CMac CPou ECtt GAuc MAsh MWhi NLar SBfd WWEG |
| | - Alan BloomPBR | see *C. tubulosa* Alan Bloom |
| | - 'Blue Dwarf' | ETho MGos SMDP |
| | - 'Campanile' | see *C.* × *bonstedtii* 'Campanile' |
| | - 'Cassandra' | CSam CWGN EAEE ECGP ECtt EPfP EShb ETho GCal LHop LRHS LSRN MAvo MCot MGos NBro NCGa NHol NLar NOrc SAga SChF SMDP SPoG WGwG WWlt |
| | - 'China Purple' | CPLG LRHS LSou MSCN NLar SMDP WHil WHoo |
| | - var. ***davidiana*** | see *C. tubulosa* |
| | - 'Pink Dwarf' (H) | CWGN ETho NLar NTay SMDP |
| | - 'Roundway Blue Bird' (H) | CBot LHop NHaw SMDP |
| | 'Herbert Johnson' (EL) | MAsh |
| | ***hexapetala*** misapplied | see *C. recta* subsp. *recta* var. *lasiosepala* |
| | ***hexapetala*** Forster | see *C. forsteri* |
| | ***hexasepala*** | see *C. forsteri* |
| | 'Hikarugenji' (EL) | CSPN NHaw |
| § | ***hirsutissima*** var. ***hirsutissima*** | GLam |
| | 'Honora' (LL) | CSPN CWGN EGxp LRHS MAsh NTay SCoo SPoG |
| | 'Horn of Plenty' (EL) | LRHS NHaw |
| | 'Huldine' (LL) ♀H4 | CBcs CRHN CSPN EBee ELan EPfP ETho LRHS LSRN MAsh MRav NSti NTay SDix SPet SPoG SWCr |
| | 'Huvi' (LL) | CWGN ETho NHaw |
| | 'Hybrida Sieboldii' (EL) | CRHN EBee SCoo |
| | Hyde Hall = 'Evipo009'PBR | CLng CMac CWGN EBee EPfP IBal LRHS LSqu MAsh SBrd SCoo SLim SLon SPer SWCr |
| | 'Hythe Egret' (Fo) | ECho ITim LLHF |

| |  |  |
|---|---|---|
| | I Am a Little Beauty = 'Zolibe' (Vt) | CRHN CWGN NHaw |
| | I Am Lady Q = 'Zoiamladyq'PBR (Vt) | CRHN CWGN |
| | I Am Red Robin = 'Zorero'PBR (A) | NTay |
| | I am Stanislaus = 'Stanislaus' | SMDP |
| | ***ianthina*** var. ***kuripoensis*** B&SWJ 700 | WCru |
| | 'Ibi' (EL) | CWGN |
| | Ice Blue = 'Evipo003'PBR (Prairie Series) (EL) | CLng EPfP ETho LBuc LRHS LSqu NTay SBrd SCoo SLim SLon SPer SPoG SWCr |
| | 'Ice Crystal' **new** | NLar |
| | 'Ice Maiden' (EL) | NTay |
| | 'Ice Queen' (EL) | MAsh |
| | 'Imperial' (EL) | NHaw |
| | ***indivisa*** Willd. | see *C. paniculata* J.G.Gmel. |
| | Inspiration = 'Zoin'PBR (I) | CSPN ELan EPfP ETho MGos NLar SCoo |
| | ***integrifolia*** | CElw CPLG CPou EBee EPfP GMac IFoB LHop MAsh MBri MGos MHer MLLN MWat MWhi NBPC NLar NPer SGar SMrm SPer SRms WCot WHoo WPer WWEG |
| | - RCB UA 10 | WCot |
| I | - 'Alba' | CBcs CBot CElw CSPN EBee ECtt ELon LHop LRHS LSRN MBNS MCot MDKP NBir NHaw NSti NTay SCoo WWlt |
| | - blue-flowered | ITim |
| | - 'Budapest' (I) | NHaw |
| | - 'Hendersonii' Koch | see *C.* × *diversifolia* 'Hendersonii' |
| | - var. ***latifolia*** | CElw |
| | - mid-blue-flowered | MGos |
| | - 'Olgae' | see *C.* × *diversifolia* 'Olgae' |
| | - 'Ozawa's Blue' (I) | CWGN EAEE ETho LRHS MBNS MCot |
| | - white-flowered | see *C. integrifolia* 'Alba' |
| § | ***intricata*** | CBcs CPLG CSPN MGos SLim |
| | 'Iola Fair' (EL) | CSPN NHaw |
| | ***ispahanica*** | SGar |
| | 'Ivan Olsson' (EL) | CSPN ETho MGos |
| | 'Jackmanii' (LL) ♀H4 | CBcs CMac CTri EBee EPfP ETho LRHS LSRN MAsh MGos NWea SCoo SEND SLim SPer SPet SPoG SWCr WFar |
| | 'Jackmanii Alba' (EL) | ELan ELon EPfP ETho LRHS LSRN MAsh SCoo SLim SPet SPoG SWCr |
| | Jackmanii Purpurea = 'Zojapur'PBR | ETho |
| | 'Jackmanii Rubra' (EL) | ETho |
| | 'Jackmanii Superba' misapplied | see *C.* 'Gipsy Queen' |
| | 'Jackmanii Superba' ambig. (LL) | CAlb CChe CMac CSPN CWCL CWSG ELan EPfP ETho LAst LRHS MAsh MBri MGos MMuc MRav MSwo NEgg NPer NPri NTay SDix SLim SPer SPoG SWCr WFar |
| | 'Jacqueline du Pré' (A) ♀H4 | CAlb CBcs CMac CSPN EBee ELan EPfP ETho LRHS MGos NHaw NLar NTay SLim SMDP |
| | 'Jacqui' (M/d) | ETho MGos NHaw NLar |
| | 'James Mason' (EL) | CSPN ETho LSRN NHaw NTay |
| | 'Jan Fopma'PBR (I) | CWGN ETho SMDP |
| | 'Jan Lindmark' (A/d) | CLng EPfP ETho LRHS MAsh MGos NLar NSti NTay SCoo SWCr WFar |
| § | 'Jan Paweł II' (EL) | EBee EGxp ELan ETho LRHS MAsh NTay SCoo SPer |

| |  |  |
|---|---|---|
| | 'Janina' | CWGN |
| § | ***japonica*** | CSPN NHaw SMDP |
| | - B&SWJ 11204 | WCru |
| § | - var. ***obvallata*** B&SWJ 8900 | WCru |
| | 'Jenny' (M/d) | CWGN ETho LRHS MGos NHaw NLar SMDP SWCr |
| | 'Jenny Caddick' (Vt) | CSPN ETho NHaw SMDP |
| | 'Jerzy Popiełuszko' (EL) | ETho |
| | 'Jim Hollis' (EL) | MAsh |
| | 'Joan Baker' (Vt) | CRHN |
| | 'Joan Picton' (EL) | LRHS MAsh |
| | John Howells = 'Zojohnhowells' (Vt) | ETho LSRN NTay SLon |
| | 'John Huxtable' (LL) ♀H4 | CLng CRHN EPfP ETho LRHS MAsh NHaw NPri NTay SWCr WGor |
| | John Paul II | see *C.* 'Jan Paweł II' |
| | 'John Treasure' (Vt) | CRHN EBee LRHS NHaw NLar |
| | 'John Warren' (EL) | CWSG EBee LRHS MAsh NHaw NTay SCoo SLim SWCr WFar |
| | Jolly Good = 'Zojogo'[PBR] (LL) | ETho NTay |
| | Josephine = 'Evijohill'[PBR] (EL) ♀H4 | CLng CSPN CWCL EBee EPfP ETho LRHS LSRN LSqu MAsh NLar NPri NTay SBrd SCoo SPer SPoG SWCr WFar |
| § | × ***jouiniana*** | MAsh MMuc MRav SEND SWCr WSHC |
| | - 'Chance' (H) | NHaw NTay |
| | 'Julka' (EL) | CAlb ETho NHaw NTay |
| | 'June Pyne' (EL) | ETho |
| | 'Justa' (Vt) | CWGN NHaw |
| | 'Juuli' (I) | LRHS LSRN |
| | 'Kaaru' (LL) | CAlb CRHN CSPN |
| | 'Kacper' (EL) | CSPN ETho MGos NHaw |
| | 'Kaen' (EL) | CWGN ETho NTay |
| | 'Kaiu' (V) | CWGN LRHS NHaw SLim SMDP |
| § | 'Kakio' (EL) | CLng ETho LRHS LSRN MAsh MGos NLar NTay SDix SLim SPer SPoG SWCr WFar |
| | 'Kalina' (EL) | ETho NHaw |
| I | 'Kamilla' (EL) | CWGN NTay |
| § | 'Kardynał Wyszyński' (EL) | EBee ETho MAsh MGos SMDP |
| § | 'Kasmu' (Vt) | NHaw |
| | 'Kathleen Dunford' (EL) | LSRN MAsh NHaw SCoo SMDP |
| | 'Kathleen Wheeler' (EL) | MAsh |
| | 'Kathryn Chapman' (Vt) | CRHN NHaw |
| | 'Keith Richardson' (EL) | MAsh |
| | 'Ken Donson' (EL) ♀H4 | EBee MGos SCoo |
| | 'Kermesina' (Vt) ♀H4 | CElw CFir CRHN CWCL EBee ELan EPfP ETho LRHS MAsh MBri MGos MHer MRav NSti SCoo SDix SLim SPoG SRms SWCr |
| | 'Kiev' (Vt) | NHaw |
| | 'Killifreth' (Vt) | CRHN NHaw |
| | 'King Edward VII' (EL) | EBee NTay WGor |
| | Kingfisher = 'Evipo037'[PBR] | EPfP ETho LBuc LRHS LSqu NTay SBrd SCoo SLon SPer SPoG SWCr |
| | 'Kinju Atarashi' (LL) **new** | ETho |
| | 'Kiri Te Kanawa' (EL) | CSPN EBee ELon ETho LRHS LSRN MAsh MGos NHaw NTay SMDP |
| | 'Kirsten Creed' | LRHS |
| | 'Kommerei' (LL) | ETho NHaw |
| § | 'Königskind' (EL) | CSPN ETho MGos |
| | ***koreana*** | MAsh WCru |
| | 'Kosmicheskaia Melodiia' (LL) | CSPN |
| | 'Küllus' (LL) | CWGN |
| | ***ladakhiana*** | CElw CSPN GQui MWhi NHaw SMDP WPGP |
| | 'Lady Betty Balfour' (LL) | CLng CMac CSPN CWSG ETho LRHS LTen MAsh NTay SCoo SDix SPet SPoG WFar |
| | 'Lady Bird Johnson' (T) | EBee ELon EPfP LRHS LSRN NTay SCoo SLim SWCr |
| | 'Lady Caroline Nevill' (EL) | CRHN MAsh |
| | 'Lady Londesborough' (EL) | EBee EPfP MAsh NHaw NTay SCoo SDix SEND |
| | 'Lady Northcliffe' (EL) | CLng CSPN CTri CWSG EPfP ETho LRHS MAsh NPri NTay SDix SPet |
| | 'Lambton Park' (Ta) ♀H4 | CFir CRHN EPfP ETho LRHS LSRN NHaw NLar SMDP |
| | 'Lantern Light' (A) | LRHS |
| | ***lasiandra*** | NHaw |
| | - B&SWJ 4888 | WCru |
| | - RWJ 9908 | WCru |
| | 'Last Dance' (Ta) | CRHN |
| | Lasting Love | see *C.* 'Grażyna' |
| | 'Lasurstern' (EL) ♀H4 | CBcs CElw CMac CPLG CRHN CSPN CTri EBee ELan EPfP ETho LRHS LSRN MAsh MBri MMuc MRav NTay SDix SPoG SWCr WFar |
| | 'Laura' (LL) | NHaw |
| | 'Laura Denny' (EL) | ETho MAsh |
| | 'Lavender Lace' (EL) | MAsh |
| | 'Lawsoniana' (EL) | CElw CMac CRHN MAsh |
| | 'Lech Wałęsa' | ETho |
| | 'Lemon Chiffon' (EL) | CLng CSPN EBee ETho LRHS NHaw NTay SWCr |
| | Liberation = 'Evifive'[PBR] (EL) | CLng EBee LRHS MAsh SCoo SPoG SWCr |
| § | ***ligusticifolia*** | GLam NHaw |
| | 'Lilacina Floribunda' (EL) | NHaw |
| | 'Lilactime' (EL) | NHaw |
| | 'Lincoln Star' (EL) | CLng CMac ELon LRHS MAsh MGos SDix SLim SPer SPet SPoG |
| | 'Little Bas' (Vt) | CRHN CSPN MBri NHaw NLar SLon |
| | 'Little Butterfly' (Vt) | CRHN MGos NHaw |
| | 'Little Mermaid' (EL) | CWGN |
| | 'Little Nell' (Vt) | CCCN CElw CRHN CSPN ELan EPfP ETho LRHS LSRN MAsh MRav NTay SCoo SDix SPer SPet WFar |
| | 'Lord Herschell' | CWGN ETho LRHS SMDP |
| | 'Lord Nevill' (EL) | CRHN CWSG EPfP LRHS MAsh SPer WFar |
| | 'Louise Pummell' (Fo) | ECou |
| | 'Louise Rowe' (EL) | CElw CLng EBee ELan ETho LRHS LSRN MAsh MGos NHaw NTay SWCr |
| | ***loureiroana*** HWJ 663 | WCru |
| | 'Love Jewelry' (EL) | ETho NHaw NTay |
| | 'Loving Memory' | ETho |
| I | 'Lucey' (LL) | NTay |
| | 'Lunar Lass' (Fo/f) | ECho ETho ITim LRHS SBfd WAbe |
| | 'Lunar Lass Variegata' (Fo/v) | ECho LLHF |
| | 'Luxuriant Blue' (Vt) | CRHN NHaw NTay |
| | 'M. Koster' (Vt) | CDoC CRHN EBee EPfP ETho LRHS MAsh NHaw SRms |
| | ***macropetala*** (d) | CBcs CDoy CElw CSBt EBee ELan EPfP ETho LAst LRHS MAsh MGos MRav MWhi SDix SPer SWCr WFar |
| | - 'Blue Lagoon' | see *C. macropetala* 'Lagoon' Jackman 1959 |
| | - 'Lagoon' Jackman 1956 | see *C. macropetala* 'Maidwell Hall' Jackman |
| | - 'Lagoon' ambig. | LSRN SLim SWCr |
| § | - 'Lagoon' Jackman 1959 (A/d) ♀H4 | CSPN EBee ETho LRHS LSRN MAsh MSwo NSti NTay SCoo SLim SPoG |
| § | - 'Maidwell Hall' Jackman (A/d) | CSPN CTri CWSG EBee EPfP ETho LSRN MGos |

| | | |
|---|---|---|
| | - 'Maidwell Hall' O.E.P.Wyatt (A) | MRav SCoo SPer |
| | - 'Wesselton' (A/d) ♀H4 | CSPN CTri EPfP ETho LRHS MAsh MBri MGos NHaw NTay SWCr WFar |
| | - 'White Moth' | see *C.* 'White Moth' |
| | 'Madame Baron-Veillard' (LL) | CLng LRHS MAsh NEgg SCoo SDix WFar |
| | 'Madame Edouard André' (LL) | CLng CSPN EPfP LRHS MAsh NTay SCoo SLim SPet SPoG SWCr WFar |
| | 'Madame Grangé' (LL) ♀H4 | CSPN EPfP LRHS MAsh NHaw NTay SCoo SPoG SWCr |
| | 'Madame Julia Correvon' (Vt) ♀H4 | Widely available |
| | 'Madame le Coultre' | see *C.* 'Mevrouw Le Coultre' |
| | 'Majojo' (Fo) | GEdr LLHF |
| | ***mandschurica*** | ETho GCal NHaw XLum |
| | - B&SWJ 1060 | WCru |
| | ***marata*** | WThu |
| | 'Margaret Hunt' (LL) | CSPN EGxp ELan ETho LSRN MAsh NHaw SGol |
| | 'Margaret Jones' (M/d) | NHaw |
| | 'Maria Cornelia' PBR (Vt) | CRHN CWGN ETho |
| | 'Marie Boisselot' (EL) ♀H4 | CBcs CMac CRHN CSPN CTri CWCL CWSG EBee ELan EPfP ETho LRHS LSRN MAsh MBri MGos MRav MSwo NTay SDix SEND SLim SPer SPet SPoG SWCr |
| | 'Marjorie' (M/d) | CBcs CDoC CSPN CTri CWSG ELan EPfP ETho GKin LRHS LSRN MAsh MGos MRav NBlu NEgg NHol NTay SLim SPer SPet SPoG SRms SWCr WFar WSHC |
| | 'Markham's Pink' (A/d) ♀H4 | Widely available |
| | ***marmoraria*** ♀H2-3 | ECho LHop LRHS WFar |
| | - hybrid (Fo) | ITim NSla |
| | ***marmoraria* × *petriei*** | ECho |
| | 'Marmori' (LL) | CWGN EBee ETho LRHS NHaw SLim SWCr |
| | 'Mary Rose' | see *C. viticella* 'Flore Pleno' |
| | 'Mary Whistler' (A) | MGos |
| § | 'Maskarad' (Vt) | CSPN |
| | Masquerade (Vt) | see *C.* 'Maskarad' |
| I | 'Masquerade' (EL) | MBri |
| | 'Matka Siedliska' (EL) | CSPN MAsh |
| | 'Maureen' (LL) | CSPN CWGN CWSG MAsh |
| | ***maximowicziana*** | see *C. terniflora* |
| | 'Mayleen' (M) ♀H4 | CPou CSBt CTri CWSG EBee EPfP ETho LRHS MAsh MBri MGos MMuc MRav NEgg NTay SBfd SCoo SLim SPer SPoG SRms SWCr WFar |
| | 'Mazury' (LL) **new** | ETho |
| | Medley = 'Evipo012' PBR | CLng LRHS SWCr |
| § | 'Mevrouw Le Coultre' (EL) | MBlu MGos SGol |
| | ***meyeniana*** var. ***insularis*** B&SWJ 6700 | WCru |
| | ***microphylla*** | ECou |
| | Mienie Belle = 'Zomibel' PBR (T) | CWGN ETho |
| | 'Mikelite' (Vt) | EBee NHaw |
| | 'Miniseelik' (LL) | NTay |
| | 'Minister' (EL) | EBee |
| | 'Minuet' (Vt) ♀H4 | CRHN CSPN EBee ELon EPfP ETho LRHS MAsh MSwo NTay SCoo SDix SPer |
| | 'Miriam Markham' (EL) | NHaw |
| | 'Miss Bateman' (EL) ♀H4 | CAlb CDoC CMac CRHN CSPN CTri CWCL CWSG EBee ELan EPfP ETho LRHS LSRN MAsh MBri MMuc NBlu NTay SDix SEND SGol SLim SPer SPet SPoG SWCr |
| | 'Miss Christine' (M) | ETho LSRN NTay SMDP WFar |
| | 'Miss Crawshay' (EL) | NHaw |
| | 'Moniuszko' (EL) | CWGN |
| N | ***montana*** | CPLG CSBt EBee GGal MAsh MGos SBfd SDix SEWo SPet WFar |
| | - B&SWJ 6724 from Taiwan | WCru |
| | - B&SWJ 6930 | WCru |
| | - BWJ 8189b from China | WCru |
| | - HWJK 2156 from Nepal | WCru |
| | - var. ***alba*** | see *C. montana* var. *montana* |
| | - 'Alexander' (M) | CPou CWSG EPfP LRHS MGos SWCr |
| | - var. ***grandiflora*** (M) ♀H4 | Widely available |
| I | - 'Lilacina' (M) | LRHS |
| § | - var. ***montana*** | CBar CDoy CDul |
| I | - 'Peveril' | CSPN |
| | - var. ***rubens*** misapplied | see *C. montana* var. *montana* |
| | - var. ***rubens*** E.H.Wilson | CDoC CSBt CTri ELan EPfP ETho GGal GGar LRHS LTen MBri MSwo NBlu NHol NWea SDix SPlb WFar |
| I | - - 'Odorata' (M) | EBee ETho GKin LRHS MGos MRav SCoo SLim SPoG WGor WGwG |
| | - - 'Pink Perfection' (M) | CAlb CDoC CMac CWSG EBee ELan EPfP GKin LAst LRHS LSRN MAsh NEgg NTay SCoo SPer SPoG SWCr WFar |
| | - - 'Tetrarose' (M) ♀H4 | Widely available |
| | - - 'Veitch' (M) | CBot |
| I | - 'Rubens Superba' (M) | CMHG CTri CWSG GKin NPri SGol SRms SWCr WFar |
| | - var. ***sericea*** | see *C. spooneri* |
| § | - var. ***wilsonii*** | CSPN CSam EBee ELan EPfP ETho GGar GKin LRHS LSRN MAsh MGos MNHC MRav MSwo NTay SDix SMDP SPer SRms SWCr WFar |
| | 'Monte Cassino' (EL) | CRHN CSPN CWGN EBee LRHS MAsh NTay SMDP |
| | 'Moonbeam' (Fo) | CMHG EAEE EBee ECou ELan EPot GEdr ITim LRHS MAvo MGos MRav NOrc WCot |
| § | 'Moonlight' (EL) | CElw CSPN MAsh |
| | 'Moonman' (Fo) | LLHF |
| | Morning Cloud | see *C.* 'Yukikomachi' |
| | Morning Star = 'Zoklako' PBR | CWGN ETho |
| | Morning Yellow = 'Cadmy' PBR (M) | CCCN CLng LRHS NEgg |
| | 'Mrs Cholmondeley' (EL) ♀H4 | CMac CRHN CSPN CWSG EBee ELan ELon EPfP ETho LRHS LSRN MAsh MBri MGos MSwo NPri NTay SDix SLim SPer SPoG SRms SWCr WFar |
| | 'Mrs George Jackman' (EL) ♀H4 | CLng CSPN ETho LRHS LTen MAsh MGos NLar NTay SCoo |
| | 'Mrs Hope' (EL) | MAsh |
| | 'Mrs James Mason' (EL) | NHaw SMDP |
| | 'Mrs N.Thompson' (EL) | CMac CSPN CTri CWCL EBee ELan ETho LRHS LSRN MAsh MBri MGos NBir NEgg NPer NTay SDix SGol SLim SPer SPet SPoG SWCr WFar |
| | 'Mrs P.B.Truax' (EL) | LRHS MAsh SMDP |
| | 'Mrs Robert Brydon' (H) | ECtt LRHS LSRN MBNS MSCN NBPC NLar SHar SRms WCot WFar |
| | 'Mrs Spencer Castle' (EL) | CSPN ETho MAsh |
| | 'Mrs T. Lundell' (Vt) | CRHN CSPN MGos NHaw |
| | 'Multi Blue' (EL) | CBcs CRHN CWSG EBee ELan ELon EPfP ETho LAst LRHS LSRN MAsh MBri MGos MRav NTay SGol SLim SPer SPoG SRms SWCr WFar |
| | 'My Angel' PBR (Ta) | CSPN ELan MGos NHaw NLar NTay |

| | | |
|---|---|---|
| | 'Myōjō' (EL) | CSPN |
| | 'Nadezhda' (LL) | SMDP |
| § | ***napaulensis*** | CSPN CTri CWCL EPfP ETho MNrw NTay SMDP WCru WFar WSHC |
| I | 'Natacha' (EL) | EBee NHaw NTay SCoo SWCr |
| | 'Natascha' (EL) | CLng LRHS LSRN NPri |
| | 'Negritianka' (LL) | CSPN EBee EPfP LRHS LSRN NHaw |
| | 'Negus' (LL) | MGos |
| | 'Nelly Moser' (EL) ℽ[H4] | CBcs CChe CDoC CMac CSPN CTri CWCL EBee ELan EPfP ETho GGar LRHS LSRN MAsh MBri MGos MRav MSwo NBir NBlu NEgg NPri SDix SEND SLim SPer SPoG SWCr WFar |
| | 'Nelly Moser Neu' (EL) | NTay |
| | 'New Dawn' (M) | CSPN NHaw |
| | 'New Love'[PBR] (H) | CSPN ETho LSRN MGos NHaw NLar NTay |
| | New Zealand hybrids (Fo) | ECou |
| | 'Night Veil' (Vt) | ETho |
| | 'Nikolai Rubtsov' (LL) | CSPN SMDP |
| | 'Niobe' (EL) ℽ[H4] | CBcs CMac CSPN CWCL CWSG EBee ELan EPfP EShb ETho GMac LRHS LSRN MAsh MBri MGos MMuc MSwo NBlu NPri NSti NTay SDix SLim SPer SPet SPoG SRms SWCr WFar |
| | North Star (LL) | see *C.* 'Põhjanael' |
| | 'North Star' (EL) | LRHS MAsh NTay |
| | 'Nunn's Gift' (Fo) | ETho |
| | ***nutans*** var. ***thyrsoidea*** | see *C. rehderiana*, *C. veitchiana* |
| | ***obvallata*** | see *C. japonica* var. *obvallata* |
| | 'Ocean Pearl' (A) | ETho LSRN NLar NTay |
| | ***ochotensis*** | CSPN SDys |
| | Octopus = 'Zooct' (A) | NTay |
| | 'Odoriba' (V) | CRHN CWGN ETho NHaw NLar SMDP |
| | 'Omoshiro' (EL) | CWGN ETho MGos NHaw NTay |
| | Ooh La La = 'Evipo041' | EPfP ETho LBuc LRHS NTay SBrd SCoo SPoG SWCr |
| | 'Oonagare Ichigoo' (Vt) | MGos |
| | Opaline | see *C.* 'Asagasumi' |
| | ***orientalis*** misapplied | see *C. tibetana* subsp. *vernayi* |
| | ***orientalis*** L. | CElw GCra SCoo WFar |
| | - 'Orange Peel' | see *C. tibetana* subsp. *vernayi* var. *vernayi* 'Orange Peel' |
| | 'Otto Fröbel' (EL) | CSPN |
| | 'Paddington' (EL) | ETho |
| | 'Pagoda' (Vt) ℽ[H4] | CBcs CDoC CRHN EBee EPfP MAsh MBri MRav NSti SCoo SRms |
| | Palette = 'Evipo034'[PBR] | CLng LRHS MBri SWCr |
| | 'Pamela' (F) | CSPN ETho NHaw NTay |
| | 'Pamela Jackman' | see *C. alpina* 'Pamela Jackman', *C.* 'Pamela Jackman' (Vt) |
| | 'Pamiat Serdtsa' (I) | EBee ETho NHaw |
| | 'Pamina' (EL) | ETho |
| | 'Pangbourne Pink' (I) ℽ[H4] | CSPN CWCL EBee EPfP ETho LRHS MAsh NHaw NTay SCoo SWCr |
| | ***paniculata*** Thunb. | see *C. terniflora* |
| § | ***paniculata*** J.G. Gmel. | CSPN |
| | ***paniculata*** (f) | ETho |
| | 'Paradise Queen' (EL) | LBuc NLar WFar |
| | 'Parasol' (EL) | CSPN MAsh |
| | Parisienne = 'Evipo019'[PBR] | EPfP ETho LBuc LRHS LSqu NTay SBrd SCoo SLon SPer SWCr |
| | ***parviflora*** DC. | see *C. viticella* subsp. *campaniflora* |
| | ***parviloba*** | WCru |
| | var. ***bartlettii*** B&SWJ 6788 | |
| | 'Pastel Blue' (I) | ETho SMDP |
| | 'Pastel Pink' (I) | SMDP |
| | 'Pastel Princess' (EL) | NHaw NTay |
| | 'Pat Coleman' (EL) | ETho |
| | ***patens*** | CElw |
| | - 'Korean Moon' (EL) | WCru |
| § | - 'Manshuu Ki' (EL) | CAlb CRHN CSPN EBee ELon EPfP ETho LRHS MAsh MMuc NTay SLim SPer SRms |
| | - 'Yukiokoshi' (EL) | ETho |
| | Patricia Ann Fretwell = 'Pafar' (EL) | CSPN |
| § | 'Paul Farges' (Vb) ℽ[H4] | CSPN CWGN EBee ETho MAsh NHaw NTay SMDP |
| | 'Pauline' (A/d) ℽ[H4] | CBcs CLng CWSG LRHS LSRN MGos NTay SCoo SLim SPoG SWCr |
| | 'Pearl Rose' (A/d) | CWSG |
| | 'Pendragon' (Vt) | CRHN NHaw |
| | 'Pennell's Purity' (LL) | NHaw |
| | Peppermint = 'Evipo005'[PBR] | EPfP LBuc LRHS LSqu NTay SBrd SCoo SPoG SWCr |
| | 'Percy Picton' (EL) | MAsh |
| | 'Perle d'Azur' (LL) | Widely available |
| | 'Perrin's Pride' (Vt) | CLng LRHS MGos NLar NTay SCoo SWCr |
| | Petit Faucon = 'Evisix'[PBR] (I) ℽ[H4] | CLng EBee EPfP ETho LAst LRHS LSRN LSqu MAsh MBri NPri SBrd SCoo SLim SPer SPoG SWCr |
| | ***petriei*** | ECou GBBs WThu |
| | - 'Princess' (Fo/f) | ECou |
| | - 'Steepdown' (Fo/f) | ECou |
| | 'Peveril Pearl' (EL) | ETho NTay |
| | 'Peveril Pristine' (Vt) **new** | SMDP |
| | 'Peveril Profusion' (T) | SMDP |
| | Picardy = 'Evipo024'[PBR] (EL) | EPfP ETho LBuc LRHS LSqu NTay SBrd SCoo SPer SWCr |
| I | 'Picton's Variety' (M) | CTri NHaw WFar |
| | ***pierotii*** B&SWJ 6281 | WCru |
| | 'Piilu' (EL) | CSPN CWGN EBee ELan ETho LBuc LRHS LSRN MAsh MBNS MBri MGos MWea NHaw NLar NTay SCoo SGol SLim SMDP SPoG SWCr |
| | 'Pink Celebration' (EL) | ETho |
| | Pink Champagne | see *C.* 'Kakio' |
| | 'Pink Delight'[PBR] | CWGN |
| | 'Pink Fantasy' (LL) | CLng CRHN CSPN CTri ETho LRHS MAsh MGos NBlu NLar NTay SCoo SLim SRkn SWCr |
| | 'Pink Flamingo' (A) ℽ[H4] | CLng CSPN CWCL EBee EGxp ELan EPfP ETho LRHS MAsh NTay SCoo SLim SPoG SRkn SWCr |
| | 'Pink Ice' (I) | LRHS NHaw |
| | 'Pirko' (Vt) | NHaw |
| § | ***pitcheri*** | NHaw SMDP |
| | 'Pixie' (Fo/m) | CSPN ECou ELan EPfP ETho GGar ITim LRHS MGos NHaw NLar NTay SCoo SLim SPoG SRms |
| I | 'Pleniflora' (M/d) | MGos NHaw |
| § | 'Plum Beauty' (A) | CSPN MGos NHaw |
| § | 'Põhjanael' (LL) | CSPN MGos NLar |
| | Polar Bear[PBR] | see *C.* Arctic Queen |
| | 'Poldice' (Vt) | CRHN |
| | 'Polish Spirit' (LL) ℽ[H4] | Widely available |
| | ***potaninii*** | CFir CSPN GCra NChi WPtf WSHC |
| | - 'Summer Snow' | see *C.* 'Paul Farges' |
| | 'Praecox' (H) ℽ[H4] | CRHN CWCL EAEE EBee ELan EPfP ETho LHop LRHS MAsh MBri MWhi NBir NSti SDix SPer SPoG |
| | 'Prairie River' (A) | ETho |
| | 'Primrose Star'[PBR] | see *C.* 'Star' |
| | 'Prince Charles' (LL) ℽ[H4] | CPou CRHN CSPN CTri EBee ELan EPfP ETho GMac LRHS LSRN MAsh |

MGos MMuc NLar NTay SCoo SDix SEND SGol SLim SPer SPet SPoG SWCr WFar WGwG
'Prince Philip' (EL) WFar
§ 'Princess Diana' (T) ♀H4 CRHN CSPN CWCL CWGN CWSG EBee ELan ETho GMac LBuc LRHS LSRN MAsh MBlu MGos MLLN MRav MSwo NHol NTay SCoo SEND SGol SLim SPer SPoG SRkn
§ 'Princess of Wales' (1875) (EL) LSRN NLar NSti SWCr WFar
'Prins Hendrik' (EL) WGor
'Prinsesse Alexandra'PBR (EL) ETho NTay
'Propertius' (A) CWGN ETho LRHS MGos NHaw SMDP
'Prosperity' ETho
'Proteus' (EL) CLng CSPN ELan ELon EPfP ETho LRHS MAsh MGos NTay SCoo SDix SLim SWCr
'Pruinina' see *C.* 'Plum Beauty'
***psilandra*** CWJ 12377 WCru
'Purple Haze' (Vt) CRHN NHaw
'Purple Princess' (H) NTay
'Purple Rain' (A) CTri LRHS
'Purple Spider' (A/d) CMac CSPN EBee ETho MAsh MBlu NHaw NHol NLar NTay SCoo
'Purpurea Plena Elegans' (Vt/d) ♀H4 CBcs CElw CMac CRHN CTri CWCL CWSG EBee ELan ELon EPfP ETho GMac LAst LRHS LSRN MAsh MBri MRav MSwo NEgg NSti NTay SDix SLim SPer SPoG SWCr WBor WFar
'Queen of Holland'PBR (I) CWGN
'Radar Love' (Ta) NLar
'Ragamuffin' (EL/d) MGos
'Rahvarinne' (LL) ETho
'Ramona' (LL) CLng LRHS LSRN MAsh NHaw SWCr
Rebecca = 'Evipo016' EPfP LBuc LRHS LSqu NTay SBrd SCoo SLon SPer SPoG SWCr
***recta*** CSPN ECtt MNrw MWhi NLar WHil WTin
- 'Lime Close' seedlings CAby
I - 'Peveril' (F) LRHS
- 'Purpurea' (F) CBcs CBot CMac CSpe EBee EHoe ELan EPfP LHop LRHS MAsh MMuc MSCN MWhi NBPC NBir NSti SDix SEND SPad SPer SWCr WHoo WTin XLum
§ - subsp. ***recta*** var. ***lasiosepala*** CSPN
- 'Velvet Night' (F) CSpe EAEE ECtt ETho MAvo MGos MLLN NEgg NLar SMDP SPoG WAul WCot
'Red Ballon' (Ta) SMDP
§ 'Red Beetroot Beauty' (A) CSPN MAsh
'Red Cooler' see *C.* 'Crimson King'
'Red Pearl' (EL) ETho LSRN MGos NTay SLim
Reflections = 'Evipo046' **new** ETho LRHS LSqu SBrd SLon SPoG SWCr
§ ***rehderiana*** ♀H4 CBot CFir CRHN CSPN CSam CTri EBee ELan EPfP ETho GAuc LRHS MAsh MBlu MRav MWhi NBir NTay SDix SPer WGwG WPGP WSHC
- BWJ 7700 WCru
'Remembrance' (LL) ETho LSRN
***repens*** Finet & Gagn. see *C. montana* var. *wilsonii*
'Rhapsody' ambig. CLng EPfP ETho LRHS MAsh MGos NTay SCoo SLim SPoG SWCr WFar
'Rhapsody' B. Fretwell (EL) CSPN LSRN NHaw
'Richard Pennell' (EL) ♀H4 EBee LRHS MAsh SDix SLim SWCr
'Rising Star' LRHS NHaw
'Robud'PBR (M/d) CLng NPer
'Roko-Kolla' (LL) CSPN ETho
'Romantika' (LL) CSPN EBee ELan ELon ETho LRHS LSRN MAsh NHaw NTay SCoo SGol SLim SPoG
'Rooguchi' (I) CWGN ETho GMac LRHS NHaw SMDP SPoG SWCr
'Rosa Königskind' (EL) ETho
'Rose Supreme' (EL) ETho
I 'Rosea' (I) ♀H4 CPrp CSPN EAEE EBee EPfP ETho LBMP LHop LRHS LSRN MCot NSti
Rosemoor = 'Evipo002'PBR CLng CWCL CWGN EPfP ETho IBal LBuc LRHS LSqu MAsh MBri NTay SBrd SCoo SLim SWCr
'Rosy O'Grady' (A) ♀H4 CWCL EBee ELan MAsh MBri MGos NLar NSti NTay
'Rosy Pagoda' (A) EBee ELan LRHS MBri NBir NHaw NLar SLim
'Rouge Cardinal' (LL) CChe CMac CSPN CWSG EBee ELan EPfP ETho LRHS LSRN MAsh MBri MGos NEgg NTay SDix SGol SLim SPer SPet SPoG SRms SWCr WFar
'Royal Velours' (Vt) ♀H4 CDoC CElw CRHN CSPN CTri EBee ELan EPfP ETho LRHS LSRN MAsh MGos MMuc NHol NSti SCoo SDix SEND SLim SPer SPoG SWCr
Royal Velvet = 'Evifour'PBR (EL) CLng CSPN CWCL EPfP IBal LRHS LSRN MBri NTay SCoo SLim SWCr
'Royalty' (EL) ♀H4 CBcs CLng CSPN ELan EPfP IBal LRHS LSRN MAsh NBir NTay SCoo SLim SPer SPoG SWCr
'Rubens Superba' see *C. montana* 'Rubens Superba'
'Rubra' (Vt) MBlu
'Ruby' (A) CSPN CWSG EBee EPfP ETho LRHS LSRN MAsh MGos NTay SCoo SLim SPer SRms
'Ruby Glow' (EL) CLng EPfP LRHS LSRN NTay SCoo SWCr
'Ruby Wedding' (T) **new** LBuc LSRN
'Rüütel' (EL) ETho LRHS MAsh MGos NHaw NTay SCoo SLim SMDP SPoG
'Sally Cadge' (EL) NHaw
'Samantha Denny' (EL) CSPN MAsh NHaw
'Sander' (H) CSPN ETho SMDP
Saphyra Indigo = 'Cleminov 51'PBR CLng
'Satsukibare' (EL) MGos
Savannah = 'Evipo015'PBR (Vt) CLng LRHS SLim SWCr
'Scartho Gem' (EL) CLng LRHS NTay SCoo SWCr
'Sealand Gem' (EL) MAsh NHaw
***serratifolia*** ETho GLog MDKP MWhi SDix SPlb SWal WFar
- B&SWJ 8458 from Korea WCru
'Sheila Thacker' (EL) ETho
Shimmer = 'Evipo028' **new** ETho LRHS LSqu SBrd SLon SPoG SWCr
'Shin-shigyoku' (EL) CWGN MGos NTay
'Shirayukihime' (EL) CSPN
§ 'Shiva' (A) MBri
'Shooun' (EL) EBee
§ ***sibirica*** EPfP
'Signe' (Vt) see *C.* 'Kasmu'
'Silver Lady' SPoG
'Silver Moon' (EL) CLng CSPN ETho LRHS MAsh NLar NTay SCoo
'Simplicity' (A) CSPN MBri

| | | |
|---|---|---|
| | ***simsii*** Small | see *C. pitcheri* |
| | ***simsii*** Sweet | see *C. crispa* |
| | 'Sinee Plamia' (LL) | NHaw |
| § | 'Sinii Dozhd' (I) | CSPN NHaw |
| | 'Sir Eric Savill' (M) | ETho |
| | 'Sir Garnet Wolseley' (EL) | LRHS MAsh SDix |
| | 'Sir Trevor Lawrence' (T) | CSPN EBee ETho LRHS MAsh NHaw NSti WFar |
| | 'Sizaia Ptitsa' (I) | ETho |
| | 'Snow Bells'^PBR | EGxp LRHS |
| | 'Snow Queen' (EL) | CFir CLng CSPN EBee ELon EPfP ETho LRHS MBri MGos NTay SLim SPet SPoG SRms SWCr |
| | 'Snowbird' (A/d) | CSPN EPfP LRHS MAsh NHaw NTay SPoG SWCr |
| | 'Snowdrift' | see *C. armandii* 'Snowdrift' |
| § | 'Södertälje' (Vt) | CRHN ETho LRHS MAsh SCoo WFar |
| | 'Solidarność' (EL) | ETho |
| | ***songarica*** | MAsh |
| | 'Sonnette' (V) | CWGN |
| | 'Southern Cross' (Fo) | ECou |
| § | 'Souvenir du Capitaine Thuilleaux' (EL) | MAsh MGos NTay |
| | 'Special Occasion' (EL) | CLng CSPN CWGN EBee ETho LRHS LSRN NHaw NLar NPri NTay SCoo SPoG SWCr WFar |
| § | ***spooneri*** | CTri GQui MAsh SCoo SLim SRms WFoF |
| | 'Sputnik' (I) | CSPN CWGN MAsh NHaw |
| | ***stans*** | CElw CPLG CPou EPfP IFro LRHS NLar NWCA SMDP SPoG SWCr |
| | - B&SWJ 5073 | WCru |
| | - B&SWJ 6345 | WCru |
| § | 'Star'^PBR (M/d) | CSPN CWGN EPfP ETho LRHS MGos MRav MSwo NLar NTay SLim SPer SRms SWCr WFar |
| | 'Star of India' (LL) | CElw CLng CRHN EBee EPfP ETho LRHS MAsh MGos MRav NTay SCoo SPoG SWCr WFar |
| | Star River = 'Zostarri' | CWGN |
| I | 'Starfish' (EL) | MGos NHaw |
| | 'Starlight' (M) | ELon LRHS NTay SLim |
| | 'Stasik' (LL) | NHaw |
| | Still Waters = 'Zostiwa'^PBR | CWGN ETho NTay |
| | Sugar Candy = 'Evione'^PBR (EL) | CLng IBal LRHS MAsh MBri NTay SCoo SLim SWCr |
| | Summer Dream = 'Zosumdre' | CWGN |
| | Summer Snow | see *C.* 'Paul Farges' |
| | 'Sundance' (Ta) | CSPN SMDP |
| | 'Sunrise'^PBR (M/d) | CSPN CWGN EBee ETho LRHS MSwo NHaw NLar NTay SLim WFar |
| | 'Sunset' (EL) ♀H4 | CLng ELon LRHS LSRN MAsh MBri NLar NTay SCoo SLim SWCr WFar |
| | 'Swedish Bells' (I) | ETho |
| | 'Sweet Scentsation' (F) **new** | EPfP |
| | 'Sylvia Denny' (EL) | CWSG EBee ELan ETho MRav NTay SPet |
| | 'Sympatia' (LL) | NHaw |
| | 'Syrena' (LL) | NHaw |
| | ***szuyuanensis*** B&SWJ 6791 | WCru |
| | - CWJ 12455 | WCru |
| | 'Tae' (EL) | ETho |
| | 'Tage Lundell' (A) | CLng CSPN EBee EPfP LRHS MGos NLar NTay SMDP |
| | 'Tango' (Vt) | CRHN NHaw |
| § | ***tangutica*** | Widely available |
| | 'Tapestry' (I) | NHaw SMDP |
| | 'Tartu' (EL) | CSPN ETho |
| | ***tashiroi*** purple-flowered B&SWJ 7005 | WCru |
| | - 'Yellow Peril' | WCru |
| | Temptation = 'Zotemp' (EL) **new** | ETho NTay |
| § | ***terniflora*** | CBcs EBee EPfP ETho NHaw SKHP |
| | - B&SWJ 5751 | WCru |
| | 'Teshio' (EL) | CSPN NHaw |
| | ***texensis*** | CElw WSHC |
| | - 'The Princess of Wales' | see *C.* 'Princess Diana' |
| | 'The Bride' (EL) | CSPN CWGN ETho LRHS LSRN MGos NHaw NTay |
| | 'The First Lady' (EL) | CSPN ETho MAsh NTay |
| | 'The President' (EL) ♀H4 | Widely available |
| | 'The Princess of Wales' (EL) | see *C.* 'Princess of Wales' (1875) (EL) |
| | 'The Princess of Wales' (T) | see *C.* 'Princess Diana' (T) |
| | 'The Vagabond' (EL) | CSPN ELan ELon ETho LRHS LSRN MAsh MGos NHaw NLar NTay SCoo SLim SPet |
| | 'The Velvet' (EL) | CAlb |
| § | Thumbelina = 'Evipo030'^PBR | LBuc LRHS NTay SWCr |
| | ***thunbergii*** misapplied | see *C. terniflora* |
| | 'Thyrislund' (EL) | CSPN |
| | 'Tibetan Mix' (Ta) | CSPN MAsh SMDP |
| | ***tibetana*** | MAsh NHaw |
| | - 'Black Tibet' (Ta) | SMDP |
| § | - subsp. ***vernayi*** | CMHG |
| § | - - var. ***vernayi*** 'Orange Peel' LS&E 13342 (Ta) | CBcs CDoC ETho MRav SEND SGar SLim WFar |
| | 'Tie Dye' (LL) **new** | ETho |
| | Timpany NZ hybrids (Fo) | ITim |
| | 'Tinkerbell' | see *C.* 'Shiva' |
| | 'Toki' (EL) | CWGN |
| | ***tongluensis*** GWJ 9358 | WCru |
| | - HWJK 2368 | WCru |
| | 'Treasure Trove' (Ta) | CSPN MAsh SMDP |
| | × ***triternata*** | LSRN |
| § | - 'Rubromarginata' ♀H4 | CDoC CFir CMac CRHN CSPN CSam CWGN EBee ELan ELon EPfP ETho GMac LRHS LSRN MBri MGos MRav NTay SDix SLim SPer SPoG SRkn SWCr |
| | 'Tsuzuki' (EL) | CSPN |
| § | ***tubulosa*** | CSPN ETho MGos SMDP |
| § | - Alan Bloom = 'Alblo'^PBR (H) | LRHS |
| | - 'Wyevale' (H) ♀H4 | CMac CPrp CSPN EAEE ELan EPfP GGar LHop LRHS MAsh MAvo MCot MRav NSti NTay SAga SCoo SDix SMDP SPoG WCot |
| | 'Twilight' (EL) | CLng CSPN EPfP LRHS MAsh NTay SWCr WFar |
| | ***uncinata*** | SDix |
| | - B&SWJ 11368 | WCru |
| | - CWJ 12373 | WCru |
| § | ***urophylla*** 'Winter Beauty' | CDoC CSam ETho LSRN MGos MRav SMDP SPoG |
| | ***urticifolia*** | GMac |
| | - B&SWJ 8651 | WCru |
| | - B&SWJ 8852 | WCru |
| | 'Valge Daam' (LL) | CWGN ETho NHaw |
| | 'Vanessa' (LL) | CRHN MAsh |
| | 'Vanilla Cream' (Fo) | ECou |
| | 'Vanso'^PBR | see *C.* 'Blue Light' |
| | × ***vedrariensis*** 'Hidcote' (M) | NHaw SMDP |
| § | ***veitchiana*** | NHaw |
| | 'Venosa Violacea' (Vt) ♀H4 | CElw CMac CRHN CSPN CSam EBee ELan ELon EPfP EShb ETho |

| | | |
|---|---|---|
| | | LRHS LSRN MAsh MRav NHol NSti NTay SCoo SDix SPer SPoG SRms SWCr WFar |
| | 'Vera' (M) | CSPN LRHS LSRN MLLN NTay SCoo SLim WFar |
| | ***vernayi*** | see *C. tibetana* subsp. *vernayi* |
| | 'Veronica's Choice' (EL) | CRHN CSPN ELan LRHS MGos MRav NHaw NTay SPet |
| | Versailles = 'Evipo025'PBR (EL) | LRHS NTay SWCr |
| § | Vesuvius = 'Evipo032'PBR | CLng EPfP LRHS LSqu NTay SBrd SCoo SLon SWCr |
| | Victor Hugo = 'Evipo007'PBR | CLng EPfP IBal LBuc LRHS NLar NPri SCoo SWCr |
| N | 'Victoria' (LL) ♀H4 | CRHN CSPN ETho LRHS LSRN MAsh MGos MRav NHaw NTay SCoo SDix SPoG SWCr |
| | Viennetta = 'Evipo006'PBR | EPfP ETho LBuc LRHS LSqu SBrd SCoo SLon SPer SPoG SWCr |
| | 'Vilhelmīne' | CWGN NTay |
| | 'Ville de Lyon' (LL) | CBcs CMac CRHN CSPN CWCL EBee ELan EPfP GGal LRHS LSRN MAsh MBri MGos NEgg SDix SEND SGol SLim SPer SPet SPoG SWCr WFar |
| | 'Vince Denny' (Ta) | NHaw SMDP |
| | Vino = 'Poulvo'PBR (EL) | CLng IBal LRHS NHaw NTay SCoo SLim SWCr |
| I | 'Viola' (LL) | CSPN CWGN EBee ELon ETho LRHS LSRN MAsh MBri MGos NHaw NTay SLim WFar |
| | 'Violet Charm' (EL) | MAsh |
| | 'Violet Elizabeth' (EL) | MRav NTay |
| I | 'Violet Purple' (A) | MGos NHaw |
| | ***viorna*** | NHaw WCru |
| | ***virginiana*** misapplied | see *C. vitalba* |
| | ***virginiana*** Hook. | see *C. ligusticifolia* |
| | ***virginiana*** L. | CElw MAsh |
| § | ***vitalba*** | CArn CRWN ECrN ETho NHaw NWea WHer WSFF |
| | ***viticella*** ♀H4 | CElw CRHN CWib ETho GKev MBri NHaw SDix WSHC |
| § | - subsp. ***campaniflora*** | CBot CSPN EPla EShb ETho GCal NHaw NWCA WCru |
| § | - 'Flore Pleno' | CRHN ELon EPfP ETho LRHS LSRN NHaw NTay SWCr WCot |
| | - 'Hågelby Pink' | CRHN CWGN |
| | - 'Hågelby White' | CWGN NHaw |
| | - 'Hanna' (Vt) | CRHN LSRN NHaw |
| | - 'Mary Rose' | see *C. viticella* 'Flore Pleno' |
| | 'Vivienne' | see *C.* 'Beth Currie' |
| | 'Vivienne Lawson' (LL) | MAsh |
| | 'Voluceau' (Vt) | CLng CPou CRHN ELan LRHS LSRN MAsh MGos MRav SRms SWCr |
| | 'Vostok' (LL) | MGos |
| | 'Vyvyan Pennell' (EL) | CAlb CBcs CMac CSPN CTri EBee ELan EPfP ETho LRHS LSRN MAsh MBri MGos MSwo NEgg NLar NTay SGol SLim SPer SPet SPoG SWCr WFar |
| | 'W.E. Gladstone' (EL) | CRHN ETho LRHS MAsh SDix SPer |
| | Wada's Primrose | see *C. patens* 'Manshuu Ki' |
| | 'Walenburg' (Vt) | CRHN CWGN ETho NHaw SLon |
| | 'Walter Pennell' (EL) | CBcs CLng CWSG EBee IBal LRHS MAsh SCoo SLim SWCr WGor |
| | 'Warsaw' (Ta) | NLar SWCr |
| | 'Warszawska Nike' (EL) ♀H4 | CLng CMac CRHN EBee ELan EPfP ETho LRHS MAsh MBri MGos NBlu NTay SCoo SGol SPer SPet SPoG |
| | 'Warszawska Olga' (EL) | ETho |
| | 'Warwickshire Rose' (M) | CLng CRHN CSPN CTri CWGN CWSG ETho LRHS LSRN MAsh MGos MWat NHaw NHol NTay SLim SPoG SWCr WFar |
| | 'Waterperry Star' (Ta) | MWat |
| | 'Wedding Day' (EL) | ETho LSRN NLar NTay |
| | 'Wee Willie Winkie' (M) | LRHS SCoo |
| | 'Westerplatte' (EL) | CLng CRHN CSPN CWGN EPfP ETho LRHS MAsh MGos NBlu NHaw NTay SMDP SPoG SWCr WFar |
| | 'Whirligig' (A) | CSPN |
| § | 'White Columbine' (A) ♀H4 | EBee ETho LRHS MGos NSti NTay SDix SGol SLim SPet |
| | 'White Fantasy' (EL) **new** | LRHS |
| | 'White Lady' (A/d) | NHaw NTay |
| | 'White Magic'PBR (Vt) | CRHN CWGN ETho MGos |
| § | 'White Moth' (A/d) | CSPN ELan ETho LSRN MAsh MGos MMuc MRav NHaw NTay SPer SPoG SRms |
| | 'White Satin' | LRHS SWCr |
| | 'White Swan' (A/d) | CSPN MAsh MBri MGos NHol NLar NPri NSti SCoo WFoF |
| | 'White Wings' (A/d) | EBee LSRN SPet |
| | 'Wilhelmina Tull' (EL) | CSPN |
| | 'Will Goodwin' (EL) ♀H4 | CBcs CLng CMac CWCL EBee ELan EPfP LRHS MAsh MBri SLim SRms SWCr |
| | 'William Kennett' (EL) | CElw CWSG EBee ELan EPfP ETho LTen MAsh MBri MGos SDix |
| | 'Willy' (A) | CBcs CSPN EBee ELan EPfP ETho GQui LRHS MAsh MBri MGos MSwo NLar NSti NTay SBrd SDix SLim SPer SPet SPoG SWCr |
| | Wisley = 'Evipo001'PBR | CBcs CLng EPfP IBal LRHS MAsh MBri NLar NTay SLim SLon SWCr |
| | 'Xerxes' misapplied | see *C.* 'Elsa Späth' |
| | 'Yatsuhashi' | CFir |
| | 'Yellow Queen' Holland | see *C. patens* 'Manshuu Ki' |
| | 'Yellow Queen' Lundell/Treasures | see *C.* 'Moonlight' |
| § | 'Yukikomachi' (EL) | CSPN ETho NHaw NTay |
| | 'Yvette Houry' (EL) | NHaw NLar |
| | 'Yvonne Hay' | SMDP |
| | 'Zephyr' (Vt) **new** | SMDP |

## *Clematopsis* see *Clematis*

## *Clementsia* see *Rhodiola*

## *Cleome* (*Cleomaceae*)

| | | |
|---|---|---|
| | ***hassleriana*** 'Helen Campbell' ♀H3 | CSpe SPhx |
| | Senorita Rosalita = 'Inncleosr'PBR | GBin |

## *Clerodendrum* (*Lamiaceae*)

| | | |
|---|---|---|
| | ***bungei*** | Widely available |
| | - 'Pink Diamond' (v) | CCCN CDoC CDul CWGN EBee ELan ELon EPfP EWes LBuc LHop LRHS LSRN MGos MPkF NLar NPri SBfd SEND SKHP SLim SPer SPoG SPtl WFar |
| § | ***chinense*** var. ***chinense*** (d) ♀H1 | CCCN CHII ERea |
| | - 'Pleniflorum' | see *C. chinense* var. *chinense* |
| | ***fragrans*** var. ***pleniflorum*** | see *C. chinense* var. *chinense* |
| * | ***mutabile*** B&SWJ 6651 | WCru |

| | |
|---|---|
| ***myricoides*** 'Ugandense' ♀H1 | CCCN CHll CRHN CSpe ELan MOWG SAga SMrm WSFF |
| ***philippinum*** | see *C. chinense* var. *chinense* |
| ***quadriloculare*** | CCCN |
| × ***speciosum*** | MOWG |
| ***splendens*** ♀H1 | MOWG |
| aff. ***subscaposum*** WWJ 11735 | WCru |
| ***thomsoniae*** ♀H1 | ELan MBri MOWG WSFF |
| ***trichotomum*** | CBcs CCVT CDul CElw CEnd CLnd CMCN CPLG CSam CSpe CTho CTri CWib EBee EPfP ERom EWTr IArd IVic LRHS MGos SLPl SLim SLon SPer SSta WBor WDin WHar |
| - 'Carnival' (v) | CAbP CBcs CCCN CDul CLnd CMac CPLG CPMA EBee ELan EPfP EWes IArd LRHS MAsh MBri MCCP NLar SBfd SKHP SLim SMad SPer SPoG WPat |
| - var. ***fargesii*** ♀H4 | Widely available |
| - 'Purple Blaze' | EPfP |
| - 'Purple Haze' | CPMA MBri NLar |
| - 'Shiro' | WCru |
| ***wallichii*** | CSpe EShb MOWG |

## *Clethra* ✿ (*Clethraceae*)

| | |
|---|---|
| ***acuminata*** | EPfP GKin |
| ***alnifolia*** | CBcs CMCN CMHG CPLG CTrC EBee MPkF SRms WCFE WCot WDin WFar |
| - 'Anne Bidwell' | MBlu NLar |
| - 'Creel's Calico' (v) | NLar |
| - 'Fern Valley Pink' | CCCN CMac CSBt EBee ELon GKin LLHF LRHS MDun NLar |
| - 'Hokie Pink' | GKin NLar |
| - 'Hummingbird' | CCCN CDoC CEnd CMac CPLG CWib EBee ELan EPfP GKin IDee LRHS MAsh MBlu MGos MWat NLar NPCo SLim SPoG SSpi SWvt WFar WSHC |
| - 'Paniculata' ♀H4 | CDoC EPfP LRHS MMuc SAga SPur WBor WFar |
| - 'Pink Spire' | CDoC CPLG EBee ECrN EPfP EWTr GKin MMHG MMuc MRav NEgg NLar NPal SCoo WDin WFar |
| - 'Rosea' | CBot CTri GKin GQui MGos MMHG MPkF SPer WFar |
| - 'Ruby Spice' | Widely available |
| - 'September Beauty' | MBri NLar |
| - 'Sixteen Candles' | GKin NLar |
| ***arborea*** | CBcs CHEx CMHG CTrC NLar |
| ***barbinervis*** ♀H4 | CBcs CDoC CMCN CPLG EBee EPfP GAuc GKin IDee IVic LRHS MBlu NLar SPer SSpi WFar WSHC |
| - B&SWJ 11562 | WCru |
| ***delavayi*** Franch. | CBcs CCCN CDoC EBee EPfP EWes GQui IDee NLar SKHP SSpi |
| - SBEC 1513 | CPLG |
| - Stone's hardy strain | SKHP |
| ***fargesii*** | CPLG EPfP GKin MGos NLar |
| ***monostachya*** | CPLG NLar |
| ***pringlei*** | NLar WSHC |
| ***tomentosa*** 'Cottondale' | NLar |

## *Cleyera* (*Pentaphylaceae*)

| | |
|---|---|
| ***fortunei*** | see *C. japonica* 'Fortunei' |
| - 'Variegata' | see *C. japonica* 'Fortunei' |
| § ***japonica*** 'Fortunei' (v) | CCCN CMHG CMac CWib IArd LRHS SSta WFar |
| - var. ***japonica*** | CGHE WPGP |
| - 'Tricolor' (v) | CBcs MPkF |
| - var. ***wallichii*** | WPGP |

## *Clianthus* ✿ (*Papilionaceae*)

| | |
|---|---|
| ***maximus*** | GDun IDee SVen |
| § ***puniceus*** ♀H2 | CAbb CDoy CHEx CHll CMHG CPLG CPne CPom CSBt CSpe CTsd CWib EBee EPfP GDun IDee LRHS MOWG MSCN SChF SEND SPer SPlb SPoG SVen WCot WPGP WSHC |
| § - 'Albus' ♀H2 | CBcs CBot CHEx CHGN CHll CPLG CSpe CWib EBee EPfP GDun IDee LRHS MOWG NExo SGar SPer SPoG SVen WCot WPGP |
| - 'Flamingo' | see *C. puniceus* 'Roseus' |
| - 'Kaka King' | CBcs EWes MREP |
| - 'Red Admiral' | see *C. puniceus* |
| - 'Red Cardinal' | see *C. puniceus* |
| - 'Red Kakatoo' | EGxp |
| § - 'Roseus' | CBcs CPLG CSpe EPfP GDun IVic LRHS NExo SPer SPoG WCot WPGP |
| - 'White Heron' | see *C. puniceus* 'Albus' |

## *Clinopodium* (*Lamiaceae*)

| | |
|---|---|
| ***ascendens*** | see *Calamintha ascendens* |
| ***calamintha*** | see *Calamintha nepeta* |
| ***grandiflorum*** | see *Calamintha grandiflora* |
| § ***vulgare*** | CArn CHab CRWN EBee EGHP EWil MHer MNHC NMir SGar SIde WDyG WFoF WMoo WOut WPtf |

## *Clintonia* (*Liliaceae*)

| | |
|---|---|
| ***andrewsiana*** | CLAP EBee ECho EWes GGar LWst WCru |
| ***udensis*** | LWst WCru |
| - HWJK 2339 from Nepal | WCru |
| ***umbellulata*** | CLAP GCal LRHS WCru |
| ***uniflora*** | CLAP ECho EWes LWst |

## *Clitoria* (*Papilionaceae*)

| | |
|---|---|
| ***ternatea*** | WCot |
| double-flowered (d) **new** | |

## *Clivia* ✿ (*Amaryllidaceae*)

| | |
|---|---|
| ***caulescens*** | ERea WCot |
| × ***cyrtanthiflora*** | ERea |
| ***gardenii*** | ERea WCot |
| ***gardenii*** × ***miniata*** | WCot |
| ***miniata*** ♀H1 | CBcs CTca CTsd ECho ERea SMrm SRms WCot |
| - 'Aurea' ♀H1 | CSpe |
| - 'Beverley's Delight' **new** | WCot |
| - var. ***citrina*** ♀H1 | CTca ECho LAma WCot |
| - - 'Butterball' | ERea |
| - - 'New Dawn' | ERea |
| - 'Citrina Spider' | CFwr |
| - Daruma Group | WCot |
| - green-centred **new** | WCot |
| - hybrids | NPal SEND |
| - 'Orange Spider' | CFwr |
| - pastel shades | CFwr WCot |
| - 'Striata' (v) | ERea |
| - 'Vico Yellow' | ERea |
| - 'Viscy Yellow' | CTsd |
| - 'Wide Leaf Monk' | WCot |
| ***nobilis*** ♀H1 | ERea WCot |
| 'San Marcus Yellow' × 'Solomone Yellow' | WCot |
| 'Solomone Yellow' | ERea |

## *Clusia* (*Clusiaceae*)

***rosea*** CCCN

## *Clypeola* (*Brassicaceae*)

***jonthlaspi*** WCot

## *Clytostoma* (*Bignoniaceae*)

§ ***calystegioides*** CCCN CHll CRHN EShb

## *Cneorum* (*Rutaceae*)

***tricoccon*** SKHP WPat WSHC

## *Cnicus* (*Asteraceae*)

§ ***benedictus*** CArn SIde

## *Cnidium* (*Apiaceae*)

***officinale*** GPoy

## *Coaxana* (*Apiaceae*)

***purpurea*** B&SWJ 9028 WCru

## *Cobaea* (*Polemoniaceae*)

***lutea*** B&SWJ 9142A WCru
***pringlei*** WPGP WSHC
***scandens*** ♀H3 CCCN CDTJ CSpe ELan EShb IFoB SBfd SGar SPer
- f. ***alba*** ♀H3 CSpe SPer

## cobnut see *Corylus avellana*

## *Cocculus* (*Menispermaceae*)

§ ***orbiculatus*** CPLG
- B&SWJ 535 WCru
***trilobus*** see *C. orbiculatus*

## *Cochlearia* (*Brassicaceae*)

***armoracia*** see *Armoracia rusticana*
***officinalis*** CArn ELau MHer WHer

## *Cocos* (*Arecaceae*)

***plumosa*** see *Syagrus romanzoffiana*
***weddelliana*** see *Lytocaryum weddellianum*

## *Codonanthe* (*Gesneriaceae*)

***gracilis*** WDib
'Paula' WDib

## × *Codonatanthus* (*Gesneriaceae*)

'Golden Tambourine' WDib
'Sunset' WDib
'Tambourine' WDib

## *Codonopsis* (*Campanulaceae*)

HWJK 2105 from Nepal WCru
SDR 6034 GKev
***affinis*** HWJCM 70 WCru
- HWJK 2151 WCru
***benthamii*** GWJ 9352 WCru
***bhutanica*** NEgg
***cardiophylla*** EWld GCal
***celebica*** HWJ 665 WCru
***clematidea*** CSpe EBee ECha ECho EPfP EWld GCal GKev LRHS MCCP NEgg NLar NSum SAga SPhx SPlb SRms SWvt WWEG
- 'Lilac Eyes' MCCP
***convolvulacea*** misapplied see *C. grey-wilsonii*
***convolvulacea*** Kurz NSla
- J&JA 4.220.705 NWCA
- 'Alba' see *C. grey-wilsonii* 'Himal Snow'
- Forrest's form see *C. forrestii* Diels
- var. ***hirsuta*** B&SWJ 7812 WCru
'Dangshen' see *C. pilosula*
***dicentrifolia*** HWJCM 267 WCru
***forrestii*** misapplied see *C. grey-wilsonii*
§ ***forrestii*** Diels ECho NHar WTcb
- BWJ 7776 WCru
- BWJ 7847 WCru
§ ***grey-wilsonii*** ♀H4 CAby CBro ECho EWld GEdr GLam WIvy
- B&SWJ 7532 WCru WFar
§ - 'Himal Snow' CAby ECho EWld GEdr GKev MDKP NCGa
***handeliana*** see *C. tubulosa*
***inflata*** GWJ 9442 WCru
***javanica*** B&SWJ 8145 WCru
***kawakamii*** B&SWJ 1592 WCru
- RWJ 10007 WCru
§ ***lanceolata*** CAby EWld
- B&SWJ 562 WCru
***lancifolia*** B&SWJ 3835 WCru
***mollis*** ECho NLar NSum WFar WWEG
***nepalensis*** Grey-Wilson see *C. grey-wilsonii*
***obtusa*** EWld
***ovata*** CBot GLam NBro SPhx SRms
§ ***pilosula*** EWld GKev GLam GPoy SPhx
- BWJ 7910 WCru
§ ***rotundifolia*** var. ***angustifolia*** EWld GKev MDKP WCru
- var. ***grandiflora*** EWld GKev
***silvestris*** see *C. pilosula*
***subsimplex*** BWJ 7502 WCru
***tangshen*** misapplied see *C. rotundifolia* var. *angustifolia*
***tangshen*** Oliv. CArn GKev
***thalictrifolia*** MECC 93 WCru
§ ***tubulosa*** LRHS
***ussuriensis*** see *C. lanceolata*
***vinciflora*** CPBP CPne ECho GEdr WIvy
***viridiflora*** WCru
***viridis*** HWJK 2435 WCru

## *Coffea* (*Rubiaceae*)

***arabica*** CCCN

## coffee see *Coffea*

## *Coincya* (*Brassicaceae*)

***wrightii*** PJL 20098 **new** CHid

## *Colchicum* ✿ (*Colchicaceae*)

***agrippinum*** ♀H4 CAvo CBro CFee CTca EBla ECha ECho EPot GGar GKev LWst MRav NBir NMen NRya NSla WHoo WTin
'Antares' ECha NBir
***asteranthum*** **new** LWst
***atropurpureum*** ECho LAma
- Drake's form ECho
'Attlee' LAma
'Autumn Herald' ECho GKev LAma
N 'Autumn Queen' CTca ECho GKev LAma
§ ***autumnale*** CArn CAvo CBro CFee CHab ECho EPot EWil GAuc GKev GPoy LAma NMen NRya SDeJ WFar WShi
- CH 871 LWst
* - 'Albopilosum' NBir
- 'Alboplenum' CBro CTca ECho EPot ERCP GKev LAma LWst WTin

| |  |  |
|---|---|---|
| | - 'Album' | CAvo CBro CTca ECho EPot ERCP GAbr GKev LAma NBir SPer WHoo WShi WTin |
| | - 'Atropurpureum' | ECho |
| | - 'Karin Persson' new | LWst |
| | - var. ***major*** | see *C. byzantinum* Ker Gawl. |
| | - var. ***minor*** | see *C. autumnale* |
| § | - 'Nancy Lindsay' ♀H4 | CBro EBla ECho EPot SCnR WCot WShi |
| | - 'Pannonicum' | see *C. autumnale* 'Nancy Lindsay' |
| § | - 'Pleniflorum' (d) | ECho EPot GAbr GKev LAma MMHG |
| * | - ***roseum*** | ECho |
| | - 'Roseum Plenum' | see *C. autumnale* 'Pleniflorum' |
| | ***baytopiorum*** | ECho GAuc |
| | - from Turkey | ECho |
| § | ***bivonae*** | ECho EPot |
| | - HOA 9139 | LWst |
| | - 'Apollo' | ECho GKev LWst |
| | - 'Petrovac' new | LWst |
| | - 'Vesta' new | LWst |
| | Blom's hybrid | WTin |
| § | ***boissieri*** | ECho EPot LWst |
| | ***bornmuelleri*** misapplied | see *C. speciosum* var. *bornmuelleri* hort. |
| | ***bornmuelleri*** Freyn | CBro ECho EPot GAuc GKev LAma |
| | ***bowlesianum*** | see *C. bivonae* |
| | ***brachyphyllum*** | LWst |
| | OS 1030 new | |
| § | ***byzantinum*** Ker Gawl. ♀H4 | CBro EPot GKev LAma NBir SDeJ WTin |
| | - ***album*** | see *C. byzantinum* 'Innocence' |
| § | - 'Innocence' | CBro EBla ECho EPot GKev |
| | ***chalcedonicum*** | LWst |
| | subsp. ***punctatum*** new | |
| | ***cilicicum*** | ECho EPot LAma WHoo |
| | - Bowles's form | ECho |
| | - 'Purpureum' | CTca ECho GKev LAma |
| | 'Conquest' | see *C.* 'Glory of Heemstede' |
| | ***corsicum*** | ECho LWst NMen WThu |
| | ***cupanii*** | ECho |
| | - HOA 9707 new | LWst |
| | - var. ***pulverulentum*** | ECho |
| | ***davisii*** | ECho LWst |
| | 'Dick Trotter' | ECho EPot GKev |
| | 'Disraeli' | CTca ECho GKev |
| | ***falcifolium*** | ECho LWst |
| § | ***giganteum*** | ECho LAma |
| § | 'Glory of Heemstede' | ECho GKev |
| | ***graecum*** | ECho |
| | - HOA 9141 new | LWst |
| | 'Harlekijn' | CTca ECho ERCP |
| | ***hierosolymitanum*** | LWst |
| | ***hungaricum*** | CFee ECho EPot LWst |
| | - f. ***albiflorum*** | ECho EPot GKev LWst |
| | - 'Valentine' | LWst |
| | - 'Velebit Star' | ECho GKev LWst |
| | ***illyricum*** | see *C. giganteum* |
| | 'Janis' new | LWst |
| | 'Jeanne' new | LWst |
| | 'Jochem Hof' | ECho GKev LEdu |
| | 'Jolanthe' | LWst |
| | ***kesselringii*** | ECho GKev LWst |
| | ***kotschyi*** | LWst |
| | ***laetum*** misapplied | see *C. parnassicum* |
| | 'Lilac Bedder' | ECho |
| | 'Lilac Wonder' | ECho EPfP GKev LAma MRav SDeJ SEND SPer WCot WFar |
| | ***longifolium*** | see *C. neapolitanum* |
| | ***lusitanum*** | LAma |
| | ***luteum*** | ECho |
| | ***macrophyllum*** | ECho LAma |
| | - HOA 9806 new | LWst |
| | ***micranthum*** | ECho |
| | ***minutum*** | ECho LWst |
| | ***munzurense*** | LWst |
| § | ***neapolitanum*** | LWst |
| | ***parlatoris*** | ECho LWst |
| § | ***parnassicum*** | ECha ECho LWst |
| | - CH 835 | LWst |
| | - HOA 8942 | LWst |
| | ***peloponnesiacum*** | LWst |
| | 'Pink Goblet' ♀H4 | CBro LAma |
| | 'Poseidon' | ECho |
| | ***procurrens*** | see *C. boissieri* |
| | ***psaridis*** | LWst |
| | ***pusillum*** | LWst |
| | - VV CR.441 | LWst |
| | 'Rosy Dawn' ♀H4 | CBro CTca ECha ECho GGar GKev NRya |
| | ***sfikasianum*** | ECho LWst |
| | ***sibthorpii*** | see *C. bivonae* |
| | ***speciosum*** ♀H4 | CAvo CBro ECho EPot GKev LAma NBir |
| | - 'Album' ♀H4 | CAvo CBro CFee EBla ECha ECho EPfP EPot GKev LAma MBri NBir SDeJ |
| | - 'Atrorubens' | ECha ECho MBri |
| I | - var. ***bornmuelleri*** hort. | ECho LWst |
| | - var. ***illyricum*** hort. | see *C. giganteum* |
| | - 'Ordu' | ECho |
| | - 'Rubrum' | ECho |
| | ***szovitsii*** Fisch. & B. Mey. | ECho |
| | - pink-flowered new | LWst |
| | - 'Snow White' | LWst |
| | - 'Tivi' | ECho LWst |
| | - white-flowered | ECho LWst |
| | ***tenorei*** ♀H4 | ECho EPot GKev LAma LLHF NBir |
| | 'The Giant' | CBro CTca ECho EPot GKev LAma SDeJ WCot |
| | ***triphyllum*** | ECho LWst |
| | ***troodi*** ambig. | ECho LWst |
| | ***variegatum*** | ECho LAma LWst |
| | 'Violet Queen' | ECho GKev LAma |
| | 'Waterlily' (d) ♀H4 | CAvo CBro CTca EBla ECho ELan EPfP EPot ERCP GGar GKev ITim LAma NBir SDeJ SPhx WHoo |
| | 'William Dykes' | EBla ECho |
| | 'Zephyr' | ECho LAma |

## *Coleonema* (*Rutaceae*)

| |  |  |
|---|---|---|
| | ***album*** | CSpe |
| | 'Mellow Yellow' new | SPtl |
| § | ***pulchellum*** | CCCN CHEx CSpe SVen |
| | ***pulchrum*** misapplied | see *C. pulchellum* |
| | 'Sunset Gold' | CSpe CTrC SAga SPlb |

## *Coleus* see *Solenostemon*

## *Colignonia* (*Nyctaginaceae*)

| |  |  |
|---|---|---|
| | ***ovalifolia*** B&SWJ 10644 | WCru |

## *Colletia* (*Rhamnaceae*)

| |  |  |
|---|---|---|
| | ***armata*** | see *C. hystrix* |
| | ***cruciata*** | see *C. paradoxa* |
| § | ***hystrix*** | CBcs CMac CTri CTsd GGar MOWG NLar SArc SMad WSHC |
| | - RCB RA S-3 | WCot |
| | - 'Rosea' | CMac CTrC GCal MBlu SKHP |

§ ***paradoxa*** CBcs CCCN CTrC CWib ELan EPfP GCal LAst LPJP NLar SBrd SKHP SMad SPoG WHil
***paradoxa* × *spinosissima*** SMad
***ulicina*** **new** SVen

## *Collinsonia* (*Lamiaceae*)

***canadensis*** CArn ELan

## *Collomia* (*Polemoniaceae*)

***grandiflora*** WCot

## *Colocasia* (*Araceae*)

***affinis*** var. ***jeningsii*** CDTJ CFir EAmu
***antiquorum*** see *C. esculenta*
§ ***esculenta*** ♀H1 CBct CDTJ CFir CHEx EAmu EGxp EShb MSKA SPlb XBlo
- 'Black Beauty' EAmu
- 'Black Magic' CAbb CBct CDTJ CHEx CHll EAmu EBee ECtt IKil LSou MLLN MSKA NBPC SArc SBfd SBig SBrd SBst SDix SEND SMad SPad WCot XBlo
- 'Black Ruffles' CDTJ
- 'Blue Hawaii' **new** CBct
- burgundy-stemmed CDTJ SBig
- 'Chicago Harlequin' CDTJ EAmu
- 'Diamond Head' **new** CBct
- 'Fontanesii' CDTJ CHEx EAmu WCot
- 'Hawaiian Eye' **new** CBct
- 'Hilo Bay' **new** CBct
- 'Hilo Beauty' EAmu XBlo
- 'Illustris' CDTJ LRHS SBst WCot
- 'Jack's Giant' **new** EAmu
- 'Mojito' (v) **new** EAmu
- 'Nancy's Revenge' EAmu
- 'Nigrescens' EAmu
- 'Pineapple Princess' **new** CBct
- 'Pink China' EAmu
- 'Tea Cup' EAmu
***fallax*** CFir CHEx EAmu
***formosana*** B&SWJ 6909 WCru
***gaoligongensis*** CFir
***gigantea*** CDTJ EAmu MSKA SBst
'Himalayan Dragon' SKHP

## *Colquhounia* (*Lamiaceae*)

***coccinea*** CArn CHll CMHG CSam CTrC EShb MBlu MRav NLar SBrt SGar SLon SSpi WSHC WTcb
- Sch 2458 WPGP
§ - var. ***mollis*** B&SWJ 7222 WCru
- var. ***vestita*** misapplied see *C. coccinea* var. *mollis*
- var. ***vestita*** ambig. CBcs CTsd EBee EPfP GGar LRHS SEND WAle XLum

## *Columnea* (*Gesneriaceae*)

'Aladdin's Lamp' WDib
'Apollo' WDib
× ***banksii*** ♀H1 EOHP WDib
'Bold Venture' WDib
§ 'Broget Stavanger' (v) WDib
'Chanticleer' ♀H1 WDib
I 'Firedragon' WDib
'Gavin Brown' EOHP WDib
***gloriosa*** EBak
***hirta*** ♀H1 WDib
- 'Variegata' see *C.* 'Light Prince'
'Inferno' WDib
'Katsura' WDib
§ 'Light Prince' (v) WDib
'Merkur' WDib
I 'Midnight Lantern' WDib
'Rising Sun' WDib
'Robin' WDib
***schiedeana*** EOHP WDib
'Sherbert' **new** WDib
'Stavanger' ♀H1 WDib
'Stavanger Variegated' see *C.* 'Broget Stavanger'

## *Colutea* (*Papilionaceae*)

***arborescens*** CBcs CMac CPLG CWib EBee ELan LRHS MBlu MGos MMuc NMun NWea SEND SPer SPlb SPoG WDin
§ ***buhsei*** MOWG
× ***media*** CPom MBlu SGar
- 'Copper Beauty' CBcs EPPr LRHS MGos NLar SPer
***orientalis*** CCCN
***persica*** misapplied see *C. buhsei*

## *Comarum* see *Potentilla*

## *Combretum* (*Combretaceae*)

***fruticosum*** CCCN

## *Commelina* (*Commelinaceae*)

***coelestis*** see *C. tuberosa* Coelestis Group
***dianthifolia*** GCal NWCA SRms WPer WPtf
- 'Electric Blue' EPfP LRHS SVic
***robusta*** EBee WCot
***tuberosa*** ELan EPfP NWad XLum
- B&SWJ 10353 WCru
- 'Alba' ELan GCal WPer
- 'Axminster Lilac' WPer
§ - Coelestis Group CAby CSpe EBee ECha ELon EPfP IGor LHop LRHS MCot SGar SRms WKif WPer WSHC
- - 'Sleeping Beauty' MSpe

## *Comptonia* (*Myricaceae*)

***peregrina*** IVic WCru

## *Conandron* (*Gesneriaceae*)

***ramondoides*** B&SWJ 8929 WCru
- 'Akabana' GEdr

## *Conanthera* (*Tecophilaeaceae*)

***campanulata*** GKev

## *Coniogramme* (*Pteridaceae*)

***intermedia*** WRic
***japonica*** WFib

## *Conium* (*Apiaceae*)

***maculatum*** CArn

## *Conoclinium* (*Asteraceae*)

§ ***coelestinum*** EBee EWes LHop LRHS MDKP SBrt WCAu WSFF XLum
***dissectum*** WSFF

## *Conopodium* (*Apiaceae*)

***majus*** CRWN WShi

## *Conostylis* (*Haemodoraceae*)

***candicans*** ECou

## *Conradina* (*Lamiaceae*)

***verticillata*** WPat

## *Consolida* (*Ranunculaceae*)

| | | |
|---|---|---|
| § | ***ajacis*** | MNHC |
| | ***ambigua*** | see *C. ajacis* |

## *Convallaria* ✿ (*Asparagaceae*)

| | | |
|---|---|---|
| | ***japonica*** | see *Ophiopogon jaburan* |
| | ***keiskei*** | EBla EPPr GAuc MAvo WHil WWEG |
| | ***majalis*** ♀H4 | Widely available |
| | - 'Albostriata' (v) | CBct CFwr CLAP CRDP CRow EBee EBla ECho EHoe ELan EPPr EPfP GAbr LRHS LWst MAvo MCot MNrw MRav NBir NPnk NSti WCot WFar WHer WPnP WSHC |
| | - 'Berlin Giant' | MAvo NBre NRya |
| | - 'Blush' | CAvo |
| | - 'Bordeaux' | CHid CPLG EBee EWhm |
| | - 'Bridal Choice' | EBee NLar WCAu |
| | - 'Dorien' | CBct CBre EBee EPPr |
| | - 'Flore Pleno' (d) | EBee WWEG |
| | - 'Géant de Fortin' | CAvo CBct CBro CFir CLAP CPLG CRow EBla ECho EPot GCal GEdr MMoz MRav NBir NBre NLar SBch WCAu WCot WFar |
| | - 'Gerard Debureaux' | see *C. majalis* 'Green Tapestry' |
| § | - 'Green Tapestry' (v) | CBct CLAP CRow MAvo WHil |
| | - 'Haldon Grange' (v) | CLAP EPPr |
| | - 'Hardwick Hall' (v) | CAvo CBct CCse CLAP CPLG CRow EBla ECha ECho EHoe EPla EPot MAvo NBre WAul WCot WFar WTin WWEG |
| | - 'Hofheim' (v) | CLAP CRow MAvo WWEG |
| | - 'Marcel' (v) | CLAP |
| | - 'Prolificans' | CAvo CBct CCse CFir CLAP CRDP EBee ECho EPPr EPfP GAbr LSou MAvo MRav NBir NLar NPnk NSti SSvw WCAu WCot WFar WHil WPnP |
| | - var. ***rosea*** | Widely available |
| | - 'Variegata' (v) | CAvo CHar EBee EBla EPla EPot LHop LRHS NMen NMyG SBch SMad SSvw WHil WWEG |
| | - 'Vic Pawlowski's Gold' (v) | CAby CBct CDes CLAP CMac CPLG CRow ELon EPPr LWst NSla |

## *Convolvulus* (*Convolvulaceae*)

| | | |
|---|---|---|
| | ***althaeoides*** | CBot CMea ECho ELan EPri NBir SEND SMrm SPhx WAbb WPat |
| § | - subsp. ***tenuissimus*** | CSpe ECtt EWes WCFE WSHC |
| § | ***boissieri*** | WAbe |
| | ***cantabricus*** | CHll LRHS MDKP WSHC XLum XSen |
| | ***chilensis*** | CCCN |
| | ***cneorum*** ♀H3 | Widely available |
| | - 'Snow Angel' | GBin GGar LBuc LRHS LSou MNHC SWvt WCot |
| | ***elegantissimus*** | see *C. althaeoides* subsp. *tenuissimus* |
| | ***humilis*** | ECho |
| | ***lineatus*** | ECho EWes NMen NWCA |
| | ***mauritanicus*** | see *C. sabatius* |
| | ***nitidus*** | see *C. boissieri* |
| § | ***sabatius*** ♀H3 | CCCN CHEx CSam CTri EBee ECho ECtt ELan EPfP EShb LAst LHop LRHS MCot MSCN NBlu NMen NWCA SBfd SEND SGar SLim SPer SPlb SPoG SVen WCFE WFar WKif XLum |
| | - dark-flowered | CCCN CSpe ECho ELan GCal SMrm SUsu |

## × *Cooperanthes* see *Zephyranthes*

## *Cooperia* see *Zephyranthes*

## *Copernicia* (*Arecaceae*)

| | | |
|---|---|---|
| | ***alba*** | EAmu LPal |

## *Coprosma* (*Rubiaceae*)

| | | |
|---|---|---|
| | ***acerosa*** | CTrC |
| | - 'Hawera' | CBcs |
| | - 'Live Wire' (f) | ECou |
| | - 'Red Rocks' | CBcs CTrC |
| | ***atropurpurea*** (f) | ECou |
| | - (m) | ECou |
| | 'Autumn Orange' (f) | ECou |
| | 'Autumn Prince' (m) | ECou |
| | ***baueri*** misapplied | see *C. repens* |
| | 'Beatson's Gold' (f/v) | CBcs CBot CDTJ CFee CHGN CHll CPLG CTrC CTsd EBee ELan EPfP GGar IVic LRHS MSCN SLim STre SWvt WDin WGrn WSHC |
| | 'Black Cloud' | CTrC LRHS SVen |
| | 'Blue Pearls' (f) | ECou |
| | 'Blue Skies' | NHar WThu |
| | ***brunnea*** | ECou WThu |
| | - 'Blue Beauty' (f) | ECou |
| | - 'Violet Fleck' (f) | ECou |
| | 'Bruno' (m) | ECou |
| | 'Cappuccino' | CBcs EBee GBin LSou |
| | ***cheesemanii*** (f) | ECou |
| | - (m) | ECou |
| | - 'Hanmer Red' (f) | ECou |
| | - 'Mack' (m) | ECou |
| | - 'Red Mack' (f) | ECou |
| | 'Clearwater Gold' | CTrC |
| | 'Coppershine' | CPLG CTrC |
| | ***crassifolia*** × ***repens*** (m) | ECou |
| | × ***cunninghamii*** (f) | ECou |
| | × ***cunninghamii*** × ***macrocarpa*** (m) | ECou |
| | 'Cutie' (f) | CTrC ECou |
| | 'Dark Spire' | CTrC |
| | ***depressa*** | ECou WThu |
| | - 'Orange Spread' (f) | ECou |
| | 'Evening Glow'PBR (f/v) | CCCN CDTJ CDoC CSBt EBee ELan EPfP EShb IVic LSRN LSou MAsh SLim |
| | 'Fire Burst'PBR | CBcs CCCN CDoC ELan EPfP EShb GGar LSou MRav SLim SPtl WCFE |
| | ***grandifolia*** | ECou |
| | 'Green Girl' (f) | ECou |
| | 'Green Globe' | CHll |
| | 'Hinerua' (f) | ECou |
| | 'Indigo Lustre' (f) | ECou |
| | 'Jewel' (f) | ECou |
| | 'Karo Red'PBR (v) | CBcs CDoC CTrC ELan ELon EPfP SLim |
| | × ***kirkii*** 'Gold Edge' | ECou |
| I | - 'Kirkii' (f) | CHll ECou |
| I | - 'Kirkii Variegata' (f/v) | CBcs CBot CDoC CTrC CTsd EBee ECou EPfP GGar LRHS MOWG SEND SLim STre |
| | 'Kiwi' (m) | ECou |
| | 'Kiwi-gold' (m/v) | ECou |
| | 'Lemon and Lime'PBR (v) | EPfP SPoG |
| | 'Lemon Drops' (f) | ECou |
| | ***linariifolia*** (m) | ECou |
| | ***macrocarpa*** (f) | ECou |
| | - (m) | CTrC ECou |
| | ***nitida*** (f) | ECou |

| | |
|---|---|
| ***parviflora*** (m) | ECou |
| – red-fruited (f) | ECou |
| – white-fruited (f) | ECou |
| 'Pearl Drops' (f) | ECou |
| 'Pearl's Sister' (f) | ECou |
| 'Pearly Queen' (f) | ECou |
| ***petriei*** | ECou WThu |
| – 'Don' (m) | ECou |
| – 'Lyn' (f) | ECou |
| – 'White Pearls' **new** | WThu |
| 'Pride' | CDoC |
| ***propinqua*** (f) | ECou |
| – (m) | ECou |
| – var. ***latiuscula*** (f) | ECou |
| – – (m) | ECou |
| 'Prostrata' (m) | ECou |
| ***pseudocuneata*** (m) | ECou |
| ***quadrifida*** | ECou |
| 'Rainbow Surprise'PBR (v) | CCCN CDoC CPLG CSBt EBee ELan LSou MRav SLim |
| § ***repens*** | CBcs CPLG EShb SPlb SVen |
| – (f) | ECou |
| – (m) | ECou |
| – 'County Park Plum' (v) | CBcs ECou ELon |
| – 'County Park Purple' (f) | ECou ELon |
| – 'County Park Red' | ECou ELon |
| – 'Exotica' (f/v) | ECou |
| – 'Marble King' (m/v) | ECou |
| – 'Marble Queen' (m/v) ♀H1-2 | CBcs ECou |
| – 'Orangeade' (f) | ECou |
| – 'Pacific Lady' **new** | ECou |
| – Pacific Night = 'Hutpac'PBR | CDoC CSBt CTrC ECou ELan EPfP IVic LBuc LRHS MDKP MGos MWea SPoG |
| – Pacific Sunset = 'Jwncopps' (v) **new** | LBuc SBrd SPoG |
| – 'Painter's Palette' (m) | CBcs ECou EShb SVen WDin |
| – 'Picturata' (m/v) ♀H1-2 | EBee ECou EShb |
| – 'Pina Colada' **new** | CBcs |
| – 'Pink Splendour' (m/v) | CBcs CDoC ECou |
| – 'Rangatiri' (f) | ECou |
| – 'Silver Queen' (m/v) | ECou |
| – 'Variegata' (m/v) | ECou MSCN |
| ***rigida*** | ECou |
| – 'Ann' (f) | ECou |
| – 'Tan' (m) | ECou |
| ***robusta*** | CBcs ECou |
| – 'Sally Blunt' (f) | ECou |
| – 'Steepdown' (f) | ECou |
| – 'Tim Blunt' (m) | ECou |
| – 'Variegata' (m/v) | ECou |
| – 'William' (m) | ECou |
| – 'Woodside' (f) | ECou |
| 'Roy's Red' (m) | CDoC EShb GGar LRHS LSRN SPoG |
| ***rugosa*** | CPLG |
| – (f) | ECou |
| 'Snowberry' (f) | ECou |
| 'Taiko' | CTrC |
| 'Translucent Gold' (f) | ECou |
| 'Violet Drops' (f) | ECou |
| ***virescens*** (f) | ECou |
| 'Walter Brockie' | CHGN CHll |
| 'White Lady' (f) | ECou |
| 'Winter Bronze' (f) | ECou |

## Coptis (*Ranunculaceae*)

| | |
|---|---|
| ***japonica*** | WCru |
| – var. ***dissecta*** | WCru |
| – var. ***major*** | CDes WCru WSHC |
| ***omeiensis*** | WCru |
| ***quinquefolia*** B&SWJ 1677 | WCru |
| ***ramosa*** B&SWJ 6000 | WCru |
| – B&SWJ 6030 | WCru |
| ***trifolia*** | WCru |

## Corallospartium see *Carmichaelia*

## Cordyline ✿ (*Asparagaceae*)

| | |
|---|---|
| ***australis*** ♀H3 | Widely available |
| – 'Albertii' (v) ♀H3 | CCCN CTrC MBri SArc SEND |
| – 'Atropurpurea' | CCCN CDoC IFoB SEND WDin WFar |
| – 'Black Night' | CCCN CTrC ESwi LRHS |
| – 'Black Tower' | CDoC |
| – Burgundy Spire = 'Jel01'PBR **new** | LBuc LRHS SPoG |
| – 'Claret' | CBcs CTrC |
| – 'Coffee Cream' | CCCN ELan EPfP SBfd SPer WDin WFar |
| – 'Olive Fountain' | CCCN |
| – 'Peko'PBR | CCCN |
| – 'Pink Champagne' | CCCN ELon LBuc LRHS LSRN MGos NEgg SBfd SLim SPoG |
| – Pink Passion = 'Seipin'PBR | EPfP LRHS NPri SBfd |
| – 'Pink Stripe' (v) | CCCN CDoC EBee ELan EPfP ESwi LRHS LSRN MBri MCCP NBlu NPla SEND SLim SWvt |
| – 'Purple Heart' | CCCN MSwo |
| – Purpurea Group | CBcs CBot CDTJ CMHG CTrC CWSG EBee ELan ELon EPfP LRHS MGos NBlu SEND SPer SPlb SWal WFar |
| – 'Red Sensation' | CCCN CHEx CTrC CTsd SWvt |
| – 'Sparkler' | CBcs CCCN CChe EPfP ESwi LRHS MGos |
| – 'Sundance' ♀H3 | CBcs CDoC CEnd CMac CTrC CWSG CWib EBee EPfP LRHS MAsh MBri MCCP MGos MSwo NPer SBfd SEND SLim SPoG SRms SWvt WFar |
| – 'Torbay Dazzler' (v) ♀H3 | Widely available |
| – 'Torbay Red' ♀H3 | CBcs CCCN CDoC CMac CWSG EBee ELan ELon EPfP LRHS LSRN MAsh MBri NPri SBfd SPer SWvt WFar |
| – 'Torbay Sunset' | CCCN CDoC CTrC |
| – 'Variegata' (v) | CBot |
| 'Autumn' | CCCN |
| ***banksii*** | CPne CTsd GCal GGar |
| 'Candy Cane' | EAmu ESwi |
| 'Cardinal'PBR | CBcs |
| ***congesta*** | SPlb |
| 'Dark Star' | CBcs CCCN CDTJ CDoC CMac SLim |
| 'Eurostar' | CTrC |
| Festival Grass = 'Jurred' | LBuc LRHS |
| 'Firecracker' | LRHS |
| ***fruticosa*** 'Red Edge' ♀H1 | XBlo |
| 'Green Goddess' | SBfd SLim |
| § ***indivisa*** | CBcs CDTJ CTsd EAmu EBak GCal GGar IDee LMaj SArc SPlb WPGP |
| 'Jurassic Jade' | CBcs CTrC |
| 'Jurassic Jasper' | CTrC |
| ***kaspar*** | CCCN CHEx CTsd SArc |
| ***obtecta*** | CCCN CTsd |
| – bronze-leaved | CTsd |
| 'Pacific Dawn' (v) | EGxp |
| ***pumilio*** | LRHS |
| 'Purple Sensation' | CBcs CCCN CMHG CTrC LRHS NPri |

| | |
|---|---|
| 'Purple Tower' ♀[H3] | CDoC CHEx MGos SLim |
| 'Red Bush' | XBlo |
| 'Red Fountain'[PBR] | ESwi |
| 'Red Star' | CAbb CBar CBcs CCCN CChe CDoC CSBt CTrC CWSG CWib EBee ELan EPfP GGar IVic LRHS LTen MCCP MSwo NPer SPoG SWvt WFar |
| Renegade = 'Tana' **new** | LBuc LRHS |
| 'Southern Splendour' | CBod CCCN ELan ELon ESwi LBuc LRHS |
| § ***stricta*** | CHEx |
| 'Sunrise' (v) | EAmu LRHS |
| ***terminalis*** | see *C. fruticosa* |

## *Coreopsis* (*Asteraceae*)

| | |
|---|---|
| 'Astolat' | EAEE EBee LSou MNFA MWea SPer |
| ***auriculata*** Cutting Gold | see *C.* 'Schnittgold' |
| - 'Elfin Gold' | EBee EDAr LBMP WFar |
| - 'Nana' | EBee MNrw NBre WFar |
| - 'Superba' | LRHS |
| - 'Zamphir' | EBee ECtt EPfP MNrw NBre |
| 'Autumn Blush' | EBee LRHS LSou MAsh MLLN MWea NBre NLar SBfd SPoG |
| 'Baby Gold' | see *C. lanceolata* 'Sonnenkind' (unblotched) |
| Baby Sun | see *C.* 'Sonnenkind' (red-blotched) |
| 'Calypso' (v) | ECtt EWes LBuc LRHS SMad |
| 'Cutting Edge' | CEnt |
| 'Dream' **new** | SRkn |
| 'Full Moon' (Big Bang Series) | EBee NDov |
| 'Gold Nugget' | SBfd |
| 'Golden Pompom'[PBR] (d) | EBee LRHS LSou MWat |
| ***grandiflora*** | NEgg |
| - 'Badengold' | EBee |
| - 'Bernwode' (v) | CMac EBee EShb LSou NLar SPoG SWvt |
| - 'Domino' | EBee MAvo NBre SMrm |
| - 'Early Sunrise' ♀[H4] | CSBt EBee ECtt EPfP LBMP LRHS MAsh MBri NBir NGBl NPer SAga SGar SPet SPhx SPoG STes SWal SWvt WFar WWEG XLum |
| - Flying Saucers = 'Walcoreop'[PBR] | EBee LBuc LRHS MAsh SBrd SCoo SPoG |
| - 'Heliot' | SAga |
| - 'Mayfield Giant' | CSBt EBee EShb LHop MNrw MWea NPri SPer SRms SWvt WHrl WWEG |
| - 'Presto' (d) | LBuc SBfd WHil |
| - 'Rising Sun' | EBee MBri NPri SPet SPhx WPer |
| - 'Sunburst' | EBee EPfP LTen NBre WPer XLum |
| - 'Sunfire' | MAsh MHer SPhx |
| - 'Sunray' | CBcs CDoC CSBt CWib EBee ECtt ELon EPfP EShb LRHS LSRN MAvo MBri MGos NBlu NGdn NPri SBfd SPad SPlb SPoG SRms SWvt WMoo XLum |
| - 'Tetra Riesen' | NBre |
| ***integrifolia*** | LRHS |
| 'Jethro Tull' | EBee |
| 'Jive' (Coloropsis Series) **new** | CSpe |
| ***lanceolata*** | NBre NSti |
| - 'Goldfink' | LRHS MRav SRms |
| - 'Goldteppich' | LRHS |
| - 'Little Sundial' | EBee LSou |
| § - 'Sonnenkind' (unblotched) | EBee EPfP XLum |
| - 'Walter' | EAEE EBee ECtt GGar LRHS LSou MWea NDov NEgg SBrd SPoG WWEG XLum |
| 'Limerock Passion'[PBR] | EBee LSou MWea NDov SBfd SRkn SUsu |
| 'Limerock Ruby'[PBR] | CBar CCVN EBee ECtt EKen GMaP LBMP LRHS LSou MAvo MLLN MWea NBPC NDov NEgg SBfd SMrm SPer SPoG SPur SRkn SWvt WCot WFar WGrn |
| ***major*** | CSam EBee |
| ***maximiliani*** | see *Helianthus maximiliani* |
| ***palmata*** | EBee MDKP |
| 'Pink Lady' **new** | CBar WHil |
| 'Pinwheel' | EBee LSou |
| ***pubescens*** | LSou |
| - 'Sunshine Superman' | EBee LSou |
| ***pulchra*** | LRHS |
| 'Redshift' **new** | NDov |
| ***rosea*** | WFar WPer |
| - 'American Dream' | CSBt EBee ELan EPfP GGar LAst LRHS LSRN NBir NGdn NPri SBfd SGar SPer SPlb SRms SWal SWvt WFar XLum |
| - 'Heaven's Gate'[PBR] | EBee ELan EPfP MAvo NBPC |
| - 'Nana' | XLum |
| - 'Sweet Dreams'[PBR] | EBee LHop LRHS LSRN MWea NCGa SPer SRkn SUsu WFar |
| 'Rum Punch'[PBR] | CWGN LHop MWea NLar SUsu WHil |
| 'Sangria' | LHop MWea SPoG WHil |
| § 'Schnittgold' | CWan EBee LSou NBre WPer |
| 'Snowberry' | CBod CWGN EBee ECtt LRHS LSou MAsh MWea NLar SBfd |
| I 'Sonnenkind' (red-blotched) | EBee ECtt LBMP LRHS NBre WPer |
| 'Sterntaler' | CFir CMea EBee ECtt EPPr EPau EPfP EShb LRHS MAsh MBri MWat NCGa NPri SBfd SMrm SPad SPet SWvt WPer XLum |
| Sun Child | see *C.* 'Sonnenkind' (red-blotched) |
| 'Tequila Sunrise' (v) | EBee ELan NLar |
| ***tripteris*** | CAby CSam EPfP LPla LRHS MDKP MMuc NBre SAga SEND SMad SPhx WMoo |
| - 'Mostenveld' | EBee |
| ***verticillata*** | CMac EBee ECha GCal MBrN MGos MHer MWat NPer SBfd SDix SRms WFar WHal |
| - Crème Brûlée = 'Crembru'[PBR] | EBee ECtt EWes LRHS MAvo MWea NBPC NEgg NPnk SCoo SMrm SPer SRkn SUsu WCot WCra WWEG |
| I - 'Golden Gain' | EBee ECtt LHop LRHS MArl NGdn SBfd WFar WMnd WWEG |
| - 'Golden Shower' | see *C. verticillata* 'Grandiflora' |
| § - 'Grandiflora' ♀[H4] | CAby CBcs COIW CPrp CTca EAEE EBee ELan EPfP GMaP LRHS MRav NCGa NGdn NHol NVic SPer WFar WMnd XLum |
| - 'Limerock Dream'[PBR] | EBee ECtt LRHS LSou NDov SBfd SMrm |
| - 'Moonbeam' ♀[H4] | Widely available |
| - 'Old Timer' ♀[H4] | SDix SUsu |
| - 'Ruby Red' | CAbP EBee LRHS SMad SUsu |
| - 'Zagreb' ♀[H4] | Widely available |

## coriander see *Coriandrum sativum*

## *Coriandrum* (*Apiaceae*)

| | |
|---|---|
| * ***citratus*** | ELau |
| ***sativum*** | CArn GPoy ILis MHer MNHC NVic SBfd SIde SPoG |
| - 'Leisure' | NPri SVic |
| - 'Santo' | EGHP ELau |
| - 'Slobolt' | EGHP ELau |

## *Coriaria* ✿ (*Coriariaceae*)

| | |
|---|---|
| ***arborea*** | WCru |
| ***intermedia*** B&SWJ 019 | WCru |
| ***japonica*** | NLar WCru |
| - B&SWJ 2833 | WCru |
| - subsp. ***intermedia*** B&SWJ 3877 | WCru |
| ***kingiana*** | EBee WCru WPGP |
| § ***microphylla*** | WCru |
| - B&SWJ 8999 | WCru |
| ***myrtifolia*** | EWld NLar WCru WFar |
| ***nepalensis*** | GGar NLar WCru |
| - BWJ 7755 | WCru |
| ***pteridoides*** | WCru |
| ***ruscifolia*** | WCru |
| - HCM 98178 | WCru |
| ***sarmentosa*** | WCru |
| ***terminalis*** f. ***fructu-rubro*** | GCal |
| - var. ***xanthocarpa*** | EPfP GCal GGar WCot WCru |
| - - GWJ 9204 | WCru |
| - - HWJK 2112c | WCru |
| ***thymifolia*** | see *C. microphylla* |

## *Cornus* ✿ (*Cornaceae*)

| | |
|---|---|
| ***alba*** L. | CBar CCVT CDoC CDul CLnd ECrN MHer MRav NWea SEWo SRms WDin WMou |
| - 'Alleman's Compact' | CPMA |
| - 'Argenteovariegata' | see *C. alba* 'Variegata' |
| - 'Aurea' ♀H4 | Widely available |
| - Baton Rouge = 'Minbat' | CAlb EMil EPfP LRHS SBfd |
| - Chief Bloodgood = 'Chblzam' | CPMA |
| - 'Cream Cracker'PBR (v) | EBee |
| - 'Elegantissima' (v) ♀H4 | Widely available |
| - 'Gouchaultii' (v) | CAlb CBcs CPMA GKin LBMP LRHS LTen MAsh MRav MWat NLar SBfd SGol SLim SPer SRms WDin WFar WMoo |
| - 'Hessei' misapplied | see *C. sanguinea* 'Compressa' |
| - 'Hessei' Hesse | CPMA WPat |
| - Ivory Halo = 'Bailhalo'PBR | EBee EMil EPfP LSRN MAsh MGos MRav NLar NWea SLim SPer SPoG SRms |
| - 'Kesselringii' | Widely available |
| - Red Gnome = 'Regnzam' | CPMA LLHF MAsh WPat |
| - 'Ruby' | CPMA |
| - 'Siberian Pearls' | CBcs CPMA ELan GKin MBlu NLar SSta |
| § - 'Sibirica' ♀H4 | Widely available |
| - 'Sibirica Variegata' (v) | CAlb CDoC CMac CPMA EBee EPfP EPla GCra GKin LRHS LSRN MAsh MBlu MGos NCGa NEgg SBfd SLim SPer SPoG SSpi SSta SWvt WCFE WFar WHar WMoo |
| - 'Snow Pearls' | CPMA |
| - 'Spaethii' (v) ♀H4 | Widely available |
| § - 'Variegata' (v) | CBcs ECho EQua LAst MGos SEND |
| - 'Westonbirt' | see *C. alba* 'Sibirica' |
| ***alternifolia*** | CBcs CCVT CMCN CTho ELan EWTr LAst |
| § - 'Argentea' (v) ♀H4 | Widely available |
| - 'Brunette' | CPMA NLar |
| - 'Golden Surprise' | CPMA |
| - 'Silver Giant' (v) | CPMA |
| - 'Variegata' | see *C. alternifolia* 'Argentea' |
| - 'Yellow Spring' | CPMA NLar |
| ***amomum*** | CAbP EBtc NLar WFar |
| - 'Blue Cloud' | CPMA |
| - 'Lady Jane' | NLar |
| ***angustata*** | CMCN SKHP SSpi |
| - 'Full Moon' **new** | CPMA |
| 'Ascona' | CBcs CEnd CPMA ELan EPfP IArd NLar SSpi SSta WPat |
| Aurora = 'Rutban' (Stellar Series) | CPMA MBlu NLar SGol SSpi |
| ***australis*** | GAuc |
| ***canadensis*** ♀H4 | Widely available |
| ***candidissima*** Marshall | see *C. racemosa* |
| ***capitata*** | CBcs CDoC CDul CEnd CMac CPMA CPne CTsd EBee EPfP EWTr GGar GKev IDee ITim LHop LRHS MGos SEND SGar SKHP SPoG SSpi WCru WFar WPGP WPat |
| - ACE 2033 | SSpi |
| - subsp. ***emeiensis*** | CPMA |
| § Celestial = 'Rutdan' (Stellar Series) | CPMA LRHS NLar SGol SKHP |
| 'Celestial Shadow' | MGos MPkF SGol |
| 'Centennial' | LRHS SSpi |
| ***chinensis*** | LMil SSta SWvt |
| 'Constellation' (Stellar Series) | CPMA LRHS MAsh SGol SSpi |
| ***controversa*** | CBcs CCVT CDul CLnd CMCN CTri ECho ECrN ELan EPfP EWTr MBlu MMuc NLar SEND SEWo SGol SLPl SLim SSpi SSta SWvt WDin WFar WHar |
| - 'Candlelight' | MBlu MBri NLar |
| § - 'Frans Type' (v) | CBcs CBot CPMA ECho ERom LSRN SReu SSta WDin |
| I - 'Marginata Nord' | NLar NPal |
| - 'Pagoda' | EPfP MBlu MBri NLar |
| - 'Troya Dwarf' | CPMA NLar |
| - 'Variegata' (v) ♀H4 | Widely available |
| - 'Variegata' Frans type | see *C. controversa* 'Frans Type' |
| - 'Winter Orange' | CPMA EPla NLar |
| 'Dorothy' | CPMA NLar |
| 'Eddie's White Wonder' ♀H4 | Widely available |
| ***florida*** | CDul CLnd CMCN CTho EBee LAst LRHS MMuc MSnd NWea SEND SPer WDin WHCr WHar |
| - 'Alba Plena' (d) | CPMA NLar |
| - 'Andrea Hart' | CPMA |
| - 'Appalachian Spring' | LRHS MGos |
| - 'Apple Blossom' | CMac CMen CPMA ECho NPCo WGob |
| - 'Aurea' × ***kousa*** | MPkF |
| - 'Autumn Gold' | CPMA SSta |
| - Cherokee Brave = 'Comco No 1' | CBcs CMen CPMA ECho ESwi LMil LRHS MAsh MGos NPCo SBfd SGol SPoG SSpi SSta WGob |
| - 'Cherokee Chief' ♀H4 | CBcs CDul CEnd CMen CPMA CTri ECho GKin IVic LSRN MGos MPkF NPCo SBfd SLim WDin WFar WGob WHar |
| - 'Cherokee Daybreak' | see *C. florida* 'Daybreak' |
| - 'Cherokee Princess' | CPMA ECho LRHS MAsh SGol SPoG SSta |
| - 'Cherokee Sunset' | see *C. florida* 'Sunset' |
| - 'Cloud Nine' | CBcs CDoC CMen CPMA CWGN ECho LRHS MGos MPkF NLar NPCo WGob WHar |
| - 'Daniela' (v) | NLar |
| § - 'Daybreak' (v) | CBcs CEnd CPMA ECho ESwi LRHS LSRN MAsh MBri MGos MPkF SBfd SPoG SSta WHar |
| - 'Eternal Dogwood' (d) | CBcs ESwi LRHS LSRN MGos SGol |

| | |
|---|---|
| - 'Firebird' | LRHS |
| - 'First Lady' (v) | CBcs CMac CMen CPMA ECho NPCo WGob |
| - 'Fragrant Cloud' | ECho |
| - 'G.H. Ford' (v) | CPMA NLar |
| - 'Golden Nugget' (v) | CPMA ECho |
| - 'Granary Gold' **new** | SSta |
| - 'Junior Miss' | CEnd |
| - 'Moonglow' | CPMA LMaj |
| - 'Pendula' | CBcs CPMA |
| - 'Pink Flame' (v) | NLar SSta |
| - f. ***pluribracteata*** (d) | NLar |
| - var. ***pringlei*** | CPMA |
| - 'Purple Glory' | CBcs CPMA ECho LRHS MPkF NLar |
| - 'Pygmaea' | NLar |
| - 'Rainbow' (v) | CAbP CBcs CPMA CWib EBee GKin LAst LRHS MAsh MBri MGos MPkF SBfd SLim SPoG SSpi WDin WHar |
| - 'Red Giant' | CAbP CBcs CPMA NLar |
| - f. ***rubra*** | CAlb CBcs CDul CTri CWib ECho ELan EWTr GKin LAst LMaj LRHS MGos MMuc MWea NPCo SEND SPer WDin WFar |
| - 'Spring Day' | CMen ECho NPCo WGob |
| - 'Spring Song' | CMac CMen CPMA ECho NPCo WGob |
| - 'Springtime' | CPMA ECho NLar |
| - 'Stoke's Pink' | CEnd CMen CPMA ECho NPCo |
| § - 'Sunset' (v) | CEnd CMen CPMA CWib ECho LRHS MAsh MGos NLar NPCo SBfd SPer SSta SWvt WHar |
| - 'Sweetwater' | CEnd CPMA |
| - 'Tricolor' | see *C. florida* 'Welchii' |
| - 'Weaver's White' | ECho |
| § - 'Welchii' (v) | CPMA |
| - 'White Cloud' | CPMA ELan |
| 'Gloria Birkett' | CAbP CPMA ECho EPfP LMil LRHS MAsh NPCo SSpi WGob |
| ***hemsleyi*** | EPla SKHP |
| ***hessei*** misapplied | see *C. sanguinea* 'Compressa' |
| ***hongkongensis*** B&SWJ 11700 | WCru |
| - subsp. ***melanotricha*** **new** | WPGP |
| -aff. subsp. ***gigantea*** KWJ 12225 **new** | WCru |
| -aff. subsp. ***tonkinensis*** B&SWJ 11791 | Wcru |
| 'Kelsey Dwarf' | see *C. sericea* 'Kelseyi' |
| 'Kenwyn Clapp' | CPMA SSpi |
| ***kousa*** | CCVT CDoC CDul CMCN CMac CTho ECho ECtt ELan EPfP ERom GKin LMaj MSnd NEgg NLar SBfd SLim SPer SPlb WDin WFar WHar |
| - 'Aget' | CPMA |
| - 'Akabana' | CPMA |
| - 'Akatsuki' | MPkF SSta |
| - 'All Summer' | CPMA |
| - 'Angyo Issai' | NLar |
| - 'Autumn Rose' | CPMA EPfP NLar |
| - 'Beni-fuji' | CPMA IVic NLar |
| - 'Big Apple' | CPMA LRHS MAsh NLar SSpi |
| - 'Blue Shadow' | CPMA MBri NLar SSta |
| - 'Boldre Beauty' | SSpi |
| - 'Bonfire' (v) | CPMA |
| - 'Bultinck's Beauty' | NLar |
| - 'Bultinck's Giant' | NLar |
| - 'Bush's Pink' | CPMA |
| - 'Cherokee' | CPMA |
| - 'China Dawn' (v) | CPMA SSta |
| - var. ***chinensis*** ♀H4 | Widely available |
| - - 'Bodnant Form' | CEnd CPMA ECho NLar NPCo |
| - - 'China Girl' | CAbP CDul CEnd CPMA EBee ELan EPfP EWTr GKin IArd LAst LBuc LMil LRHS LSRN MAsh MBlu MBri MGos MSwo NLar SLim SPoG SSpi SSta WDin WPat |
| - - 'Claudia' | IVic NLar SSta |
| - - 'Great Star' | MAsh SSta |
| - - 'Greta's Gold' (v) | CPMA |
| - - 'Ikone' | IVic |
| - - 'Milky Way' | CMCN CPMA EBee ECho LBuc LSRN MBlu MGos MPkF NLar NPCo SGol SSpi WPat |
| - - 'Snowflake' | CPMA |
| - - 'Spinners' | CPMA |
| - - 'Summer Stars' | CPMA NLar WPat |
| - - 'White Dusted' (v) | CPMA EPfP NLar |
| - - 'White Fountain' | CWSG LRHS MBri MPkF MPnt NLar WHar |
| - - 'Wieting's Select' | CPMA IVic MPkF NLar |
| - - 'Wisley Queen' | CAbP CPMA LRHS SSpi SSta |
| - 'Claudine' | CPMA |
| - 'Doctor Bump' | CPMA |
| - 'Doubloon' | CPMA ECho LRHS WPat |
| - 'Dwarf Pink' | CPMA |
| - 'Ed Mezitt' | CPMA NLar SSpi |
| - 'Elizabeth Lustgarten' | CPMA MBlu MPkF SSta |
| - 'Eurostar' | IVic NLar |
| - 'Fanfare' | CPMA NLar |
| - 'Fernie's Favourite' | CPMA |
| - Galilean = 'Galzam' | CPMA |
| - 'Gay Head' | CPMA |
| - 'Girard's Nana' | CPMA |
| - 'Gold Cup' (v) | CPMA MPkF |
| - 'Gold Star' (v) | CAbP CBcs CEnd CMac CPMA CWGN EBee ECho ELan EPfP IArd LMil LRHS MAsh MGos MPkF NLar NPCo SPoG SSta WGob |
| - 'Greensleeves' | CPMA SSta |
| - 'Heart Throb' | CBcs CPMA LRHS MGos NLar SGol |
| - 'Highland' | CPMA |
| - 'John Slocock' | NLar |
| - 'Kim' | NLar |
| - 'Kreutzdame' | CPMA NLar |
| - 'Little Beauty' | CPMA |
| - 'Lustgarten Weeping' | CPMA NLar |
| - 'Madame Butterfly' | CEnd CPMA IArd LRHS MBlu NLar NPCo |
| - 'Marwood Dawn' **new** | SSta |
| - 'Milky Way' | ESwi GBin SGol |
| - 'Milky Way Select' | CBcs CPMA ECho LMaj MGos |
| - 'Minuma' | NLar |
| - 'Miss Petty' | CPMA MPkF NLar |
| - 'Miss Satomi' ♀H4 | Widely available |
| - 'Moonbeam' | CPMA MBri NLar WPat |
| - 'Mount Fuji' | CPMA MBlu MBri NLar |
| - 'National' | CPMA ECho EPfP LMil LRHS MAsh MGos MPkF NLar SPoG SSpi SSta WPat |
| - 'Nicole' | CAlb CDoC LRHS NLar WDin WGob WPat |
| - 'Ohkan' **new** | CPMA |
| - 'Pevé Limbo' (v) | CPMA NLar |
| - 'Pevé Satomi Compact' | NLar |
| - 'Polywood' | CPMA NLar |
| - 'Radiant Rose' | CPMA LRHS MBri MPkF NLar SSpi SSta |
| - 'Rasen' | CPMA NLar |
| - 'Rel Whirlwind' | CPMA NLar |
| - 'Rosea' | CPMA |

| | |
|---|---|
| – Samaratin = 'Samzam' (v) | CBcs CEnd CPMA ESwi LRHS LSRN MBri MGos MPkF SGol SKHP SSta |
| – 'Schmetterling' | CPMA NLar WPat |
| – 'Silver Pheasant' (v) | NLar |
| – 'Snowbird' | CPMA |
| – 'Snowboy' (v) | CBcs CEnd CPMA NPCo SMad |
| – 'Snowflurries' | CPMA |
| – 'Southern Cross' | CPMA GBin |
| – 'Square Dance' | CPMA |
| – 'Steeple' | CPMA |
| – 'Summer Fun' | CPMA LRHS SSpi SSta |
| – 'Summer Gold' **new** | MPkF |
| – 'Summer Majesty' | CPMA |
| – 'Sunsplash' (v) | CPMA NLar |
| – 'Temple Jewel' (v) | CPMA |
| – 'Teutonia' | CPMA IArd IDee IVic MBri MGos NLar |
| – 'Tinknor's Choice' | CPMA |
| – 'Trinity Star' | CPMA SSpi |
| – 'Triple Crown' | CPMA |
| – 'Tsukubanomine' | CPMA NLar |
| – 'U.S.A.' | MPkF |
| – 'Vale Milky Way' (v) | NLar |
| – 'Weaver's Weeping' | CPMA MPkF NLar |
| – 'Weisse Fontäne' | CPMA NLar |
| – 'White Dream' | CPMA NLar |
| – 'White Giant' | CPMA |
| – 'Wolf Eyes' (v) | CPMA LRHS MAsh MBlu MPkF NLar SGol SPoG SSpi SSta |
| ***macrophylla*** Wall. | CMCN EPfP NLar WPGP |
| – MSF 821 | WPGP |
| ***mas*** | Widely available |
| – 'Aurea' (v) | CAbP CBcs CDul CPMA EBee ELan EPfP EPla LRHS MAsh MBlu MBri MGos MRav NEgg NLar NPCo SGol SLim SPer SPoG SSpi SSta WDin WPat |
| § – 'Aureoelegantissima' (v) | CEnd CGHE CMac CPMA EPla LRHS MAsh MBri NEgg NLar SPer SPoG SSpi WFar WPat WSHC |
| – 'Devin' | NLar |
| – 'Elegant' **new** | CAgr |
| – 'Elegantissima' | see *C. mas* 'Aureoelegantissima' |
| – 'Golden Glory' ♀H4 | CPMA EPfP MBri NLar |
| – 'Gourmet' | CAgr |
| – 'Happy Face' | NLar |
| – 'Hillier's Upright' | CPMA |
| – 'Jolico' | CPMA MBlu NLar |
| – 'Kasanlaker' | NLar |
| – 'Pioneer' | CPMA |
| – 'Redstone' | CPMA |
| – 'Spring Glow' | CPMA NLar |
| – 'Titus' | NLar |
| – 'Variegata' (v) ♀H4 | CAbP CBcs CBot CMCN CPMA EBee EPfP LRHS MAsh MBlu MBri MGos NLar NPCo NPal SKHP SPer SPoG SSpi WDin WFar |
| – 'Xanthocarpa' | CPMA NLar |
| – 'Yellow' **new** | CAgr |
| N 'Norman Hadden' ♀H4 | Widely available |
| ***nuttallii*** | CDul CTho CTri CWib ECho ELan EPfP GAuc GLin MGos MMuc SEND SPer SWvt WDin WFar |
| – 'Colrigo Giant' | CPMA |
| – 'Gold Spot' (v) | CMac CPMA ECho MGos NPCo NWea |
| – 'Monarch' | CPMA CTho NLar SKHP SSpi |
| – 'North Star' | CPMA ECho NLar |
| – 'Osmunda' | ECho |
| – 'Pink Blush' | NLar |
| – 'Portlemouth' | CEnd CPMA WGob |
| – 'Zurico' | CPMA MPkF NLar |
| ***officinalis*** | CAgr CAlb CDul CMCN CMac EBee EMil EPfP LRHS MWea NLar SKHP SPur WDin |
| – 'Ellen' | NLar |
| – 'Kintoki' | SKHP |
| 'Ormonde' | CPMA CWGN ECho NLar NPCo SSpi SSta WGob |
| 'Pink Blush' | CPMA |
| 'Porlock' ♀H4 | CDul CMCN CPMA EPfP ITim LRHS LSRN MAsh MBri NLar WDin WPat |
| ***pumila*** | CPMA NLar |
| § ***racemosa*** | NLar WFar |
| ***rugosa*** | EBtc NLar |
| × ***rutgersiensis*** Galaxy | see *C.* Celestial |
| Ruth Ellen = 'Rutlan' (Stellar Series) | CPMA NLar |
| ***sanguinea*** | CBcs CCVT CDul CHab CLnd CRWN CTri ECrN EPfP LBuc LMaj LRHS MMuc MRav MSwo NWea SEWo SGol SPer SVic WDin WHar WMou |
| – 'Anny' | CPMA MAsh MBlu WPat |
| – 'Anny's Winter Orange' | CPMA |
| § – 'Compressa' | EBee EPfP MRav NLar WFar |
| – 'Magic Flame' | CPMA EPfP NLar |
| – 'Midwinter Fire' | Widely available |
| – 'Winter Beauty' | CPMA CSBt CWib EBee EPfP MAsh MBlu NEgg NLar SBrd SLon SWvt WCFE WFar WHar WPat |
| § ***sericea*** | CArn EPla SRms WMoo |
| – 'Budd's Yellow' | LRHS MAsh MBlu MBri |
| – 'Cardinal' | CHGN EPfP LRHS MAsh MBri NLar SBrd |
| – 'Coral Red' | CPMA |
| – 'Flaviramea' ♀H4 | Widely available |
| – 'Hedgerows Gold' (v) | CPMA CSBt EBee ELan EMil EPfP LHop LRHS MAsh SBfd SPoG SPur WPat |
| – 'Isanti' | CPMA |
| § – 'Kelseyi' | CAlb CMac CPMA EBee EPla LTen MRav NLar SLPl SPer WDin WMoo |
| – Kelsey's Gold = 'Rosco' | MAsh |
| – subsp. ***occidentalis*** 'Sunshine' | CPMA NLar NPro |
| § – 'White Gold' (v) ♀H4 | CDoC CPMA EBee EHoe ELon EPfP MBri MRav MSwo NLar NPro SLon SPer SPoG WDin WFar WMoo |
| – 'White Spot' | see *C. sericea* 'White Gold' |
| Stardust = 'Rutfan' (Stellar Series) | CPMA |
| Stellar Pink = 'Rutgan' (Stellar Series) | CBcs CPMA IVic LRHS MAsh MBri MGos NLar SGol SKHP WGob |
| ***stolonifera*** | see *C. sericea* |
| × ***unalaschkensis*** | LLHF |
| – NNS 08-101 | GKev NWCA |
| Venus = 'Kn30 8'PBR | CPMA LBuc LRHS MBlu MBri MPkF SPoG SSta |
| ***walteri*** | CMCN WFar |
| – B&SWJ 8776 | WCru |

# *Corokia* (*Argyrophyllaceae*)

| | |
|---|---|
| ***buddlejoides*** | CBcs CDoC CHGN CMHG CTrC CTsd EBee ECou GGar MOWG SEND WFar |
| 'Coppershine' | CMHG |
| ***cotoneaster*** | CAbP CDul CMac CTrC CTri EBee ECho ECou ELan EPfP IDee LRHS MGos MPkF NLar SBfd SMad SPer |

SPoG SPtl SWvt WCot WFar WGrn WHar WPat WSHC
- 'Boundary Hill' ECou
- 'Brown's Stream' ECou
- 'Geenty's Ghost' CTrC
- 'Hodder River' ECou
- 'Little Prince' GGar
- 'Ohau Scarlet' ECou
- 'Ohau Yellow' ECou
- 'Swale Stream' ECou
- 'Wanaka' ECou

* ***daphnoides*** new NPnk
***macrocarpa*** CDoC ECou
* ***parviflora*** CTrC
× ***virgata*** CAbP CBcs CDoC CMHG CMac CTrC CTri ECou ELan EPfP GBin GGal LRHS MCCP NLar SArc SPer SWvt WHar WSHC
- 'Bronze King' CDoC EBee EPfP LRHS MOWG MPkF SPer SVen
- 'Bronze Lady' ECou
- 'Cheesemanii' ECou
- 'County Park Lemon' ECou MOWG
- 'County Park Orange' ECou
- 'County Park Purple' ECou
- 'County Park Red' ECou
- 'Frosted Chocolate' CAlb CBcs CDoC CMHG CTrC CTsd EBee ECou ELan EPfP ETod IVic LBMP LHop LLHF LRHS MAsh MGos MOWG MPkF SKHP SLim SPoG SWvt WCot WDin WFar WGrn WHar
- 'Geenty's Green' CTrC ECou LRHS
- 'Havering' ECou
- 'Mangatangi' CTrC MGos
- 'Pink Delight' CDoC EBee ECou EPfP ESwi MAsh MRav
- 'Red Wonder' CAlb CDoC CMHG CMac CTrC EBee ELan EPfP GGar IVic LRHS MMHG MOWG MPkF SEND SLim SPoG SVen WDin WFar WGrn WHar
- 'Sandrine' ECou
- 'Silver Ghost' CDoC ECou
- 'Sunsplash' (v) CAlb CBcs CDoC CMac CTrC CTsd EBee ECou EPfP ESwi LBMP LHop LLHF LRHS MAsh MGos MPkF NLar SBfd SEND SPoG SWvt WFar WGrn WHar

I - 'Virgata' ECou MGos
- 'Wingletye' ECou
- 'Yellow Wonder' CBcs CDoC CMHG CTrC EBee ESwi GGar LRHS MGos NLar SEND SLim SPoG SWvt WDin

## *Coronilla* (*Papilionaceae*)

***comosa*** see *Hippocrepis comosa*
***emerus*** see *Hippocrepis emerus*
***glauca*** see *C. valentina* subsp. *glauca*
***valentina*** CDoC CRHN CSPN EBee LHop SDix WSHC XLum
- 'Creamed Corn' CWGN WCot

§ - subsp. ***glauca*** ♀H3 Widely available
- - 'Brockhill Blue' IVic LRHS WCot
- - 'Citrina' ♀H3 Widely available

* - - 'Pygmaea' LRHS WCot WWFP
- - 'Variegata' (v) CBcs CBot CDoC CMac CSPN CTri CWib EBee EHoe ELan ELon EPfP LRHS MAsh MCot SBfd SEND SLim SLon SMad SMrm SPer SPoG SVen WCot WFar

***varia*** see *Securigera varia*

## *Correa* (*Rutaceae*)

***alba*** CCCN CDoC CPLG CTrC ECou EPfP LBMP WGwG WHar
- 'Pinkie' ♀H2 CBcs CPLG ECou LBMP MOWG SAga WCot

***alba* × *backhouseana*** MOWG
***backhouseana*** ♀H2 CAbb CBcs CDoC CHll CMac CPLG CTrC CTri EBee ECou ELan EPfP EWld GGar IDee IVic LHop LRHS MMuc MOWG NLar SAga SEND SGar SMrm SVen WGwG WHar WSHC
- 'Peaches and Cream' CSBt IVic SRkn

***baeuerlenii*** MOWG
***decumbens*** CAbb CTrC ECou IDee MOWG
'Dusky Bells' ♀H2 CBcs CCCN CDoC CHll CTri EBee ECou EPfP GGar IVic LBMP LHop LRHS MAsh MMuc MOWG SAga SEND SLim SMrm SPlb SPoG SPtl SRkn SVen
'Dusky Maid' CCCN CPLG
'Federation Belle' CDoC ECou MOWG
***glabra*** MOWG
'Gwen' CDoC ECou MOWG
'Harrisii' see *C.* 'Mannii'
'Inglewood Gold' ECou
'Ivory Bells' ECou EPfP
***lawrenceana*** CDoC CTrC ECou IRar SEND SVen WAbe
§ 'Mannii' ♀H2 CBcs CDoC CPLG CPom CTsd EBee ELan EPfP IVic LRHS MOWG SEND SPoG WSHC
'Marian's Marvel' ♀H2 CCCN CDoC CPLG CTrC ECou EWld LBMP MAsh MMuc MOWG SEND SGar SPoG SRkn SVen WAbe
'Peachy Cream' CDoC EBee EPfP LRHS
'Pink Mist' CDoC ECou
'Poorinda Mary' ECou MOWG
***pulchella*** ♀H2 CDoC CPLG CTri IRar LBMP MOWG
- orange-flowered ECou MOWG
- 'Pink Mist' MOWG

***reflexa*** ♀H2 CDoC CPLG ECou MOWG
- var. ***nummulariifolia*** ECou IRar LBMP MAsh MOWG WAbe WCot
- var. ***reflexa*** CPLG
- - 'Mary's Choice' CDoC
- var. ***scabridula*** 'Yanakie' MOWG

* - ***virens*** CPLG
***schlechtendalii*** ECou WAle

## *Cortaderia* ✿ (*Poaceae*)

***argentea*** see *C. selloana*
***fulvida*** misapplied see *C. richardii* (Endl.) Zotov
§ ***fulvida*** (Buchanan) Zotov CBcs CKno EBee EWes GBin IArd IDee MNrw WDin
***jubata*** 'Candy Floss' CKno
'Point du Raz' CKno
***richardii*** misapplied see *C. fulvida* (Buchanan) Zotov
***richardii*** ambig. CFir CPLG CTrC EHoe EPau GBin MMuc NLar WHrl WWEG
§ ***richardii*** (Endl.) Zotov ♀H3-4 CAby CBcs CKno EPPr ESwi EWes GGar GMaP IBlr MAvo NVic SArc WCot WCru WMnd WPGP
- BR 26 GGar

§ ***selloana*** CBcs CDul CHEx CTri CWib EHul EPfP MGos MRav NBir NBlu NGBl SBfd SGol SPlb WFar WMoo

| | | |
|---|---|---|
| § | – 'Albolineata' (v) | CBcs CBct EHoe ELon EWes MMuc MSCN MWht NOak SBfd SEND SLim SPer SPoG SWvt WFar WPat |
| § | – 'Aureolineata' (v) ♀H3 | CBcs CBct CDoC CMac EHoe ELan EPfP IVic LRHS MGos MMuc NBid NLar NOak NWsh SBfd SEND SLim SPer SPoG SWvt WFar WPat |
| | – 'Evita'PBR | CKno EPPr SMad SPer WCot |
| | – 'Gold Band' | see *C. selloana* 'Aureolineata' |
| | – 'Icalma' | EPPr |
| | – 'Monstrosa' | MMuc SEND SMad |
| | – 'Patagonia' | EHoe EPPr |
| | – 'Petite Plumes' (v) **new** | SBfd |
| | – 'Pink Feather' | EPfP LTen MMuc SApp SEND |
| | – 'Pumila' ♀H4 | Widely available |
| | – 'Rendatleri' | CBcs CDoC ELan EPfP LSRN SCoo SLim SPer SPoG WDin |
| | – 'Rosea' | EBee EGxp EPfP MGos NBPC NBlu NGdn NLar SBfd SGol WFar WWEG |
| | – 'Silver Comet' | EWes |
| | – Silver Feather = 'Notcort' (v) | MGos SLim |
| | – 'Silver Fountain' (v) | ELan EPfP LRHS |
| | – 'Silver Stripe' | see *C. selloana* 'Albolineata' |
| | – 'Splendid Star'PBR (v) | CBcs CDoC CKno EBee EGxp EHoe GBin LBuc LHop LRHS LTen MBri MGos MREP NLar NOak SAdn SBfd SLim SMad SPoG SRms SWvt WCot |
| | – 'Sunningdale Silver' ♀H3 | CDoC CDul CMac EBee ECha ECtt EHoe EHul ELan ELon EPfP LRHS LSRN MBri MGos MMuc SBfd SEND SLim SMad SPer SPoG SWvt WDin WFar |
| * | – 'White Feather' | CChe NGdn SApp SLim WFar WMoo WWEG |
| | Toe Toe | see *C. richardii* (Endl.) Zotov |

## *Cortia* (*Apiaceae*)

| | |
|---|---|
| ***depressa*** **new** | GKev |

## *Cortiella* (*Apiaceae*)

| | |
|---|---|
| aff. ***hookeri*** HWJK 2291 | WCru |

## *Cortusa* (*Primulaceae*)

| | | |
|---|---|---|
| | ***brotheri*** | ECho |
| * | ***caucasica*** 'Alba' **new** | GKev |
| | ***matthioli*** | EBee ECho EPfP GBBs GKev NMen SRms WFar |
| | – 'Alba' | CFir EBee ECho GEdr NMen NWCA SRms WCot |
| | – subsp. ***pekinensis*** | CFir ECho EDAr GEdr GGar GKev MLHP NLar NMen NWCA SPet SRms WFar WSHC XLum |
| | ***turkestanica*** | ECho GAuc LLHF |

## *Corydalis* ✿ (*Papaveraceae*)

| | | |
|---|---|---|
| | from Sichuan, China | MDKP |
| | × ***allenii*** 'Enno' | LWst |
| | ***ambigua*** misapplied | see *C. fumariifolia* |
| | ***ambigua*** Cham. & Schldlt. | LWst |
| | ***angustifolia*** | LWst |
| | – white-flowered | LWst |
| | ***anthriscifolia*** | CLAP MDKP SSvw WCot |
| | 'Blackberry Wine' | CPLG EBee ECtt EPfP IPot MDKP MPnt NLar SPoG WFar |
| | 'Blue Panda' | see *C. flexuosa* 'Blue Panda' |
| | 'Bronze Beauty' | WMoo |
| | ***bulbosa*** misapplied | see *C. cava* |
| | ***bulbosa*** (L.) DC. | see *C. solida* |
| | ***buschii*** | CAby CLAP CPBP EBee ECho GBin GEdr IFro NHar NRya SCnR |
| | 'Canary Feathers'PBR | CBct EBee ECtt GAbr LLHF MPnt NLar NPri SPoG WCot |
| | ***cashmeriana*** | GEdr LRHS NBid NHar NMen WAbe WHal |
| | – 'Kailash' | LRHS |
| | ***cashmeriana*** × ***flexuosa*** | CBro CLAP ECho LRHS WAbe |
| | ***caucasica*** | ECho NMen |
| | – var. ***alba*** misapplied | see *C. malkensis* |
| § | ***cava*** | CLAP EBee ECho EPot LAma SPhx WShi |
| | – 'Albiflora' | CLAP ECho SPhx |
| | – subsp. ***cava*** | ECho |
| | ***chaerophylla*** | IBlr |
| | ***cheilanthifolia*** | CDoy CPLG CRow CSpe EBee ECha EDAr EPfP LEdu LPla MDun MSCN SGar SMrm SPhx SRms WFar WTin XLum |
| | – 'Manchu' **new** | SPtl |
| | ***chionophila*** | LWst |
| | 'Craigton Blue' | GEdr GLam NHar WAbe |
| | ***curviflora*** | CPLG EWes SSvw |
| | subsp. ***rosthornii*** | |
| | – – 'Blue Heron' | NLar |
| | ***darwasica*** | LWst |
| | ***davidii*** | CPLG |
| | ***decipiens*** Schott, Nyman & Kotschy | see *C. solida* subsp. *incisa* |
| I | ***decipiens*** misapplied ♀H4 | CPom ECho EPot |
| I | – purple-flowered | EBee ECho LWst |
| | ***densiflora*** | LWst |
| | 'Early Bird' | ECtt EWes |
| | ***elata*** | CLAP CMil CSpe CYeo EBee EWes GEdr GKev GMaP IBlr IFro LHop LRHS LSou MArl MCot MNrw NBid SPhx SPoG WCru WFar WHal WMnd WPtf WSHC |
| | – 'Blue Summit' | CLAP ECtt EPPr |
| | ***elata*** × ***flexuosa*** clone 1 | CCse CLAP CPLG GEdr |
| | ***erdelii*** | LWst |
| | ***flexuosa*** ♀H4 | CFee CSpe EBee ECho EPfP MArl MLHP MNrw NSla SGar WAbe WBor WFar WSHC XLum |
| | – CD&R 528 | IFro NRya |
| | – 'Balang Mist' | CLAP CPLG NHar |
| | – 'Blue Dragon' | see *C. flexuosa* 'Purple Leaf' |
| § | – 'Blue Panda' | CPLG EBee EPPr EWes GMaP NHar NSla WFar |
| | – 'China Blue' | Widely available |
| | – 'Golden Panda'PBR (v) | CBct EBee ECtt ITim MBNS MPnt WCot |
| | – 'Hale Cat' | EBee ECtt EPPr |
| | – 'Hidden Purple' | CHid |
| | – 'Nightshade' | CPLG CYeo ECtt LLHF NBid WCot WFar WHoo |
| I | – 'Norman's Seedling' | EPPr IVic WPGP |
| | – 'Père David' | CMac CSBt CSam CSpe EBee ECha ECho ELan EPPr EPfP GGar GMaP LRHS MHer MSpe NBPC NBir NCGa NVic SBfd SPer SPlb SRGP SWvt WCru WFar WSHC WWEG XLum |
| § | – 'Purple Leaf' | Widely available |
| | 'Foundling' **new** | LWst |
| § | ***fumariifolia*** | ECho GKev |
| | ***glaucescens*** | LWst |
| | – 'Early Beauty' | LWst |
| | 'Golden Spinners' | IVic |
| | ***gracilis*** | LWst |

***haussknechtii*** LWst
'Heavenly Blue' **new** GKev
***henrikii*** LWst NMen
***incisa*** ECho ERCP LAma NMen
- B&SWJ 4417 WCru
***integra*** LWst
'Kingfisher' CDes CHid CLAP EWes GEdr LRHS NHar NLar NSla SBch WAbe WFar
***kusnetzovii*** LWst
***ledebouriana*** EPot LWst
***leucanthema*** DJHC 752 CDes CLAP CPLG
- 'Silver Spectre' (v) CPLG EBee ECtt LLHF LRHS MNrw NLar NSti WFar
***linstowiana*** LRHS
- CD&R 605 CLAP CPLG
§ ***lutea*** CBcs CRWN EBee EPfP IBlr IFoB IFro MMuc MSCN NBir NPer NVic NWad SEND SRms WCot WMoo
***magadanica*** LLHF LRHS MMoz
§ ***malkensis*** ♀H4 CAvo CWCL EBee ECho EPot GBin GKev LLHF LRHS LWst NBir NMen NRya SCnR WFar WThu
***maracandica*** LWst
'Maya' (v) **new** XLum
***moorcroftiana*** CPLG
***nariniana*** LWst
'New Contender' LWst
***nobilis*** CPom CSpe ECho IFoB IFro LWst SPhx WFar
***nudicaulis*** LWst
§ ***ochroleuca*** CElw CPom CRow CSpe GCal LPla LRHS MSCN NMRc WFar WMoo
***ophiocarpa*** CSpe CSpr EHoe ELan GCal IBlr SWal WMoo
***oppositifolia*** LWst
- subsp. ***kurdica*** LWst
***ornata*** LWst
***pachycentra*** CPLG WAbe
***paczoskii*** ECho GGar GKev LRHS LWst MNrw NMen
- RS 12180 EBee
***paschei*** LWst
***popovii*** LWst SCnR
***pseudofumaria alba*** see *C. ochroleuca*
***pumila*** EBee ECho
***quantmeyeriana*** 'Chocolate Stars' CWGN EBee ECtt LHop LLHF LPla LRHS LSou MBNS WCot WFar
'Rainier Blue' IVic
***repens*** LWst
***rosea*** 'American Dream' CWCL
***scandens*** see *Dactylicapnos scandens*
***schanginii*** LWst
subsp. ***ainii*** ♀H2
- subsp. ***schanginii*** LWst
***scouleri*** NBir
***seisumsiana*** LWst
***sempervirens*** 'Alba' WFoF
***sewerzowii*** LWst
***shimienensis*** CPom
- 'Berry Exciting'PBR CBct CHid CWCL CWGN ECtt ELon EPPr EPfP LSou MBNS MTis NPri SPoG WBor WHil
***siamensis*** IFoB
- B&SWJ 7200 WCru
***smithiana*** WFar
§ ***solida*** CAby CAvo CBro CPom EBee ECho ECtt ELan EPfP EPot GAbr IBlr ITim LAma LEdu LRHS MRav NLar NMen NPnk NRya SDeJ SMrm SPhx WCot WFar WShi WTin
- 'Firecracker' CBro ECho LLHF LRHS SPhx
- 'First Kiss' LWst
- 'Frodo' LAma
- 'Harkov' LWst WFar
- 'Ice Pink' NMen
§ - subsp. ***incisa*** ♀H4 EBee ECho GKev MNrw SPhx WCot WShi
- - CH 850 LWst
- - HOA 8943 LWst
- - white-flowered LWst
- lilac-flowered IFoB
- 'Linnet' **new** LWst
- 'Margaret' LWst
- 'Maxima' NMen
- 'Merlin' LWst
- 'Moonlight Shade' ECho
- Nettleton seedlings EPot
- 'Night Heron' **new** LWst
- 'Pink Discovery' LWst
- 'Purple Beauty' EBee ECho EPot LWst MNrw SPhx
- 'Purple Bird' **new** GKev LWst
- 'Quiet Elegance' LAma
- 'Redwing' **new** LWst
- 'Snowlark' LWst
§ - subsp. ***solida*** CLAP CMil ECho EPot GGar GKev NBir NRya SPhx
- - from Penza, Russia LAma LLHF LWst NCot NMen
- - 'Alba' GKev
- - 'Beth Evans' CAvo CBro EBee ECha ECho ECtt ELon EPPr EPot ERCP GBin GEdr GKev IPot LAma LEdu LLHF LRHS MCot NHar NLar NMen NWad SCnR SDeJ SPhx WCot WFar WWEG
- - 'Blue Dream' GEdr
- - 'Blushing Girl' ECho LAma
- - dark pink-flowered NDov
- - 'Dieter Schacht' ♀H4 EBee EPot GBin GKev ITim LAma LLHF NLar NMen WCot
- - 'Evening Shade' ECho LAma
- - 'George Baker' ♀H4 CAvo CBro CPom ECho ECtt ELon EPot ERCP GEdr GGar GKev IPot LAma LEdu LLHF LRHS LWst NDov NHol NLar NMen NWad SDeJ SMad SMrm SPhx SUsu WBor WCot WFar
- - 'Lahovice' WFar
- - pale pink-flowered NDov
- - Prasil Group EPot GKev LWst SPhx WBor
- - 'White Knight' LAma LWst
- 'Spoonbill' **new** LWst
- f. ***transsylvanica*** see *C. solida* subsp. *solida*
- 'White King' LWst
- 'White Swallow' GKev LLHF LWst NMen
- 'Zwanenberg' LWst
aff. ***solida*** subsp. ***incisa*** LAma
'Spinners' CDes CElw CLAP EBee ECha ECtt EPPr GCal GKev IVic MDKP SBch SSvw SUsu WSHC XLum
***stipulata*** B&SWJ 2951 WCru
***taliensis*** CPLG GLog SBfd
***tauricola*** EPot GEdr LWst NMen
***tomentella*** GEdr
'Tory MP' CBct CDes CEnt CHid CLAP CPLG CPne CPom CSam CSpe EPPr GAbr GEdr IFro LRHS MDKP MNrw MSpe NBid NCGa NHar WHoo WMnd WPGP
***transsylvanica*** see *C. solida* subsp. *solida*
***turtschaninovii*** LWst SKHP

- 'Gorin' **new** LWst
*vittae* IFoB LWst
- 'Goliath' **new** LWst
*wendelboi* GKev IFoB
- LS&T 05-73 LWst
- subsp. *congesta* LWst
Janis form NMen
- subsp. *wendelboi* LWst
'Wildside Blue' CLAP
*wilsonii* CPLG GEdr IFoB IGor
*zetterlundii* LWst

## *Corylopsis* ✿ (*Hamamelidaceae*)

*glabrescens* CHGN CPMA LRHS
- var. *gotoana* CPMA EPfP MAsh NLar SSpi SSta WPat
- - 'Chollipo' CAbP CBcs LRHS NLar SSta
- 'Lemon Drop' **new** NLar
*glandulifera* NLar SSpi
*himalayana* NLar
*multiflora* SSpi
*pauciflora* ♀H4 Widely available
*platypetala* see *C. sinensis* var. *calvescens*
- var. *laevis* see *C. sinensis* var. *calvescens*
*sinensis* WPGP
§ - var. *calvescens* CBcs CPMA NLar SSpi WPGP
§ - - f. *veitchiana* ♀H4 CDoy CPMA CSam ELan EPfP NLar SSpi WDin
§ - var. *sinensis* ♀H4 CBcs CDoC CPMA EBee ELon EPfP IDee IVic LAst LRHS MAsh NLar SLon SPoG SReu WAbe WDin WFar
- - 'Spring Purple' CAbP CBcs CEnd CGHE CMac CPMA EPfP IVic LRHS NCGa NLar SChF SKHP SSpi SSta WDin WFar WPGP
- 'Veitch's Purple' **new** CPMA NLar
*spicata* CBcs CDoy CDul CPMA EBee IDee IGor LRHS LTen MGos MRav NEgg NLar SGol SLim SSpi WPat
- 'Golden Spring' EPfP IArd NCGa NLar
- 'Red Eye' IVic NLar
*veitchiana* see *C. sinensis* var. *calvescens* f. *veitchiana*
*willmottiae* see *C. sinensis* var. *sinensis*

## *Corylus* ✿ (*Betulaceae*)

*avellana* (F) CBcs CCVT CDoC CDul CHab CLnd CMac CRWN CTho CTri ECrN EPfP EWTr GAbr LAst LBuc LRHS MAsh MBri MGos NEgg NLar NWea SBfd SEWo SPer SVic WDin WHar WMou
- 'Aurea' CBcs CDul CEnd CSBt CTho CTri ECrN ELan EPfP EWTr GBin LBuc LRHS MAsh MBlu MBri MGos MRav NLar NWea SLim SPer SSta SWvt WDin WFar
- 'Bollwylle' see *C. maxima* 'Halle'sche Riesennuss'
- 'Casina' (F) CAgr CTho
- 'Contorta' Widely available
- 'Corabel' (F) CAgr MBri MCoo
- 'Cosford Cob' (F) CAgr CCVT CDul CMac CSBt CTho CTri ECrN EPom ERea GTwe LBuc LRHS MBlu MBri MGos SDea SEWo SKee SPer WHar
- Emoa Series MCoo
- 'Fortin' (F) ECrN
§ - 'Fuscorubra' (F) CPMA EPom MRav MWat NLar
- 'Gustav's Zeller' (F) CAgr LRHS MCoo
§ - 'Heterophylla' CDul CEnd EBee EPfP MBri NLar SSta WHar
- 'Laciniata' see *C. avellana* 'Heterophylla'
§ - 'Lang Tidlig Zeller' (F) CAgr LRHS MCoo
- 'Merveille de Bollwyller' see *C. maxima* 'Halle'sche Riesennuss'
- 'Nottingham Prolific' see *C. avellana* 'Pearson's Prolific'
- 'Pauetet' (F) CAgr
§ - 'Pearson's Prolific' (F) CAgr CSBt GTwe LBuc MMuc SDea SEND SKee
- 'Pendula' EBee MBlu SCoo SLim WHar WPat
- 'Purpurea' see *C. avellana* 'Fuscorubra'
- 'Red Majestic' PBR Widely available
- 'Tonda di Giffoni' (F) CAgr MCoo
- 'Webb's Prize Cob' (F) CAgr CDul ECrN ERea GTwe MBlu MMuc NLar SDea SEND SKee SVic WMou
*colurna* ♀H4 CCVT CDul CLnd CMCN CMac CTho EBee ECrN EPfP EWTr LRHS MBlu MGos MWat NLar NWea SCoo SGol SPer WDin WHar WMou
- 'Te-Terra Red' CMCN CPMA EBee MAsh MBlu MBri NLar SLon SMad SSpi WHar WMou
× *colurnoides* 'Chinoka' (F) MCoo WHar
- 'Freeoka' (F) MCoo WHar
- 'Laroka' (F) ECrN
Early Long Zeller see *C. avellana* 'Lang Tidlig Zeller'
*ferox* GWJ 9293 WCru
*maxima* (F) CMac CTri EPom ERea GTwe MSwo NWea SDea WDin
- 'Butler' (F) CAgr CMac CTho CTri ECrN ERea GTwe MBri SDea SKee WHar
- 'Ennis' (F) CAgr ECrN ERea GTwe LRHS MBri SDea SKee WHar
- 'Fertile de Coutard' see *C. maxima* 'White Filbert'
- 'Frizzled Filbert' (F) ECrN
- 'Frühe van Frauendorf' see *C. maxima* 'Red Filbert'
- 'Garibaldi' (F) NLar
- 'Grote Lambertsnoot' see *C. maxima* 'Kentish Cob'
- 'Gunslebert' (F) CAgr CCVT CMac CSBt CTho CTri ECrN ERea GTwe MBri SDea SKee SPoG WHar
- Halle Giant see *C. maxima* 'Halle'sche Riesennuss'
§ - 'Halle'sche Riesennuss' (F) CAgr ECrN EPfP GTwe MMuc NLar SEND SKee WHar
§ - 'Kentish Cob' (F) CAgr CBcs CDul CMac CSBt CTho CWSG ECrN ELan EPfP EPom ERea GTwe LBuc MBlu MBri MGos SDea SEWo SKee SLim SPer SPoG SRms WHar
- 'Lambert's Filbert' see *C. maxima* 'Kentish Cob'
- 'Longue d'Espagne' see *C. maxima* 'Kentish Cob'
- 'Monsieur de Bouweller' see *C. maxima* 'Halle'sche Riesennuss'
- 'Purple Filbert' see *C. maxima* 'Purpurea'
§ - 'Purpurea' (F) ♀H4 Widely available
§ - 'Red Filbert' (F) CEnd CTho CWSG EPom ERea GTwe LRHS MAsh MBlu MBri NLar SCoo SGol SKee SLim SSta WHar WPat
- 'Red Zellernut' see *C. maxima* 'Red Filbert'
- 'Spanish White' see *C. maxima* 'White Filbert'
§ - 'White Filbert' (F) ERea GTwe SKee WHar
- 'White Spanish Filbert' see *C. maxima* 'White Filbert'
- 'Witpit Lambertsnoot' see *C. maxima* 'White Filbert'
'Nottingham Early' (F) NLar

## ***Corymbia*** see *Eucalyptus*

## ***Corynabutilon*** see *Abutilon*

## ***Corynephorus*** (*Poaceae*)

***canescens*** EBee NBir WWEG

## ***Corynocarpus*** (*Corynocarpaceae*)

***laevigatus*** CBcs CHEx ECou MBri

## ***Cosmos*** (*Asteraceae*)

§ ***atrosanguineus*** Widely available
- Chocamocha = 'Thomocha'PBR CAvo CBcs CCCN CChe CHar CHid CSpe CWCL CWGN EBee ECtt EPfP GBin LHop LSRN LSou MTis NLar NPri SBfd SBrd SMrm SPer SRot SUsu WHil

***bipinnatus*** CSpe
Bright Lights mixed (d)
- 'Purity' CSpe
- 'Sonata Carmine' LSou NPri
- 'Sonata Pink' LSou NBlu NPri SPoG
- 'Sonata White' CSpe LAst LSou NBlu NPri SPoG

***peucedanifolius*** CSpe MCot
- 'Flamingo' CSpe EBee EPfP ERCP LSou SPer WHil

## ***Cosmos × Dahlia*** (*Asteraceae*)

'Mexican Black' EBee ERCP GMac MLLN WCot

## **costmary** see *Tanacetum balsamita*

## ***Cotinus*** ✿ (*Anacardiaceae*)

***americanus*** see *C. obovatus*
§ ***coggygria*** ♀H4 CArn CBcs CDoC CMCN CMac CSBt CTri CWSG EBee ECrN ELan EPfP LHop MBri MMuc MRav MSwo MWat NWea SBfd SEND SGol SPer SWvt WDin WFar WHar
- Golden Spirit = 'Ancot'PBR Widely available
- 'Kanari' CPMA EBee NLar WPat
- 'Nordine' NLar WPat
- 'Notcutt's Variety' ELan EPfP MRav NSti
- 'Old Fashioned' MBri MGos MPkF
- 'Pink Champagne' CBcs CPMA EPfP MBri NLar SSpi SSta WPat
- Purpureus Group SGol
- 'Red Beauty' CPMA NLar
- Red Spirit = 'Firstpur' NLar
- 'Royal Purple' ♀H4 Widely available
- Rubrifolius Group CBcs EBee EPfP SGol SPer SWvt WDin WFar
- Smokey Joe = 'Lisjo'PBR EPfP LRHS MAsh NCGa SBrd SLon SPoG SPtl SSta SWvt WHar
- 'Smokey Joe Purple' LSou
- 'Velvet Cloak' CAbP CPMA EBee ELan EPfP GKin LRHS MBri MGos MPkF MRav NLar SGol SLon SWvt WHar
- 'Young Lady'PBR Widely available

Dusky Maiden = 'Londus' EPfP LRHS MAsh NLar SLon WPat
'Flame' ♀H4 CDul CPMA EBee ELan EPfP EWTr LRHS MBri MGos MRav NLar SKHP SLim SPer SWvt WPat
'Grace' Widely available
§ ***obovatus*** ♀H4 CPMA EBtc EPfP IArd LRHS MBlu MPkF MRav NLar SSpi SSta WPat

## ***Cotoneaster*** ✿ (*Rosaceae*)

***acuminatus*** SRms
***adpressus*** ♀H4 MSwo
§ - 'Little Gem' EBee ECho NHar NLar
- var. ***praecox*** see *C. nanshan*
- 'Tom Thumb' see *C. adpressus* 'Little Gem'

***affinis*** SRms
***albokermesinus*** SRms
***amoenus*** SLPl SRms
- 'Fire Mountain' NPro

§ ***apiculatus*** SRms
§ ***ascendens*** SRms
***assamensis*** SRms
§ ***astrophoros*** CMac MBlu NHar
***atropurpureus*** SRms
§ - 'Variegatus' (v) ♀H4 Widely available

***boisianus*** SRms
***bradyi*** SRms
§ ***bullatus*** ♀H4 CDul CTri ECrN EPfP IGor MGos MMuc NLar SPer SRms
- 'Firebird' see *C. ignescens*
- f. ***floribundus*** see *C. bullatus*
- var. ***macrophyllus*** see *C. rehderi*
- 'McLaren' SRms

***bumthangensis*** SRms
***buxifolius*** blue-leaved see *C. lidjiangensis*
- 'Brno' see *C. marginatus* 'Brno'
- f. ***vellaeus*** see *C. astrophoros*

***camilli-schneideri*** SRms
***canescens*** SRms
§ ***cashmiriensis*** ♀H4 MGos
***cavei*** MBlu SRms
***cinnabarinus*** SRms
§ ***cochleatus*** CDul EBee LAst MGos NMen SRms WRHF
§ ***congestus*** CSBt CWib EBee MGos MSwo NHol SPlb SRms WDin WHar XLum
- 'Nanus' CMea ELan GEdr MGos NHol WPat

***conspicuus*** CBcs LAst SRms
- 'Decorus' ♀H4 CAlb CDoC CDul CSBt CWSG EBee EPfP LHop LRHS MGos MMuc MSwo NEgg NLar NWea SBfd SGol SLim SPer SPlb SPoG SWvt WDin WHar WMoo
- 'Leicester Gem' SRms
- 'Red Glory' CMac WWau

***cooperi*** SRms
***cornifolius*** SRms
***cuspidatus*** MBlu
N ***dammeri*** ♀H4 Widely available
§ - 'Major' CBar LBuc SPoG
§ - 'Mooncreeper' MBri MMuc
- 'Oakwood' see *C. radicans* 'Eichholz'
- var. ***radicans*** misapplied see *C. dammeri* 'Major'
- var. ***radicans*** C.K.Schneid. see *C. radicans*

***dielsianus*** NLar NWea SRms
***distichus*** var. ***tongolensis*** see *C. splendens*
***divaricatus*** EPfP NLar NWea SPer SRms WFar
***duthieanus*** 'Boer' see *C. apiculatus*
***elatus*** SRms
***elegans*** SRms
***emeiensis*** SRms
'Erlinda' see *C. × suecicus* 'Erlinda'
'Exburiensis' CBcs CCVT CDoC CDul EPfP LAst MAsh MBri MGos MMuc MRav NLar SGol WDin WFar WHar
***falconeri*** SRms
***fastigiatus*** SRms
***flinckii*** SRms
***floccosus*** IVic NWea

| | | |
|---|---|---|
| | ***floridus*** | SRms |
| | ***forrestii*** | SRms |
| | ***franchetii*** | Widely available |
| | - var. ***cinerascens*** | SRms |
| | ***frigidus*** | SRms WDin |
| N | - 'Cornubia' ♀H4 | Widely available |
| | - 'Notcutt's Variety' | EPfP |
| | - 'Saint Monica' | MBlu |
| | ***gamblei*** | SRms |
| | ***ganghobaensis*** | SRms |
| | ***glabratus*** | SLPl SRms |
| | ***glacialis*** | SRms |
| | ***glaucophyllus*** | IArd SEND SRms |
| § | ***glomerulatus*** | SRms |
| | ***gracilis*** | SRms |
| | ***granatensis*** | SRms |
| | ***harrovianus*** | NLar SLPl SRms |
| I | ***hedegaardii*** 'Fructu Luteo' | SRms |
| | ***henryanus*** | SRms |
| | 'Herbstfeuer' | see *C. salicifolius* 'Herbstfeuer' |
| | 'Highlight' | see *C. pluriflorus* |
| § | ***hjelmqvistii*** | LBuc SRms |
| | - 'Robustus' | see *C. hjelmqvistii* |
| | - 'Rotundifolius' | see *C. hjelmqvistii* |
| | ***hodjingensis*** | SRms |
| | ***horizontalis*** ♀H4 | Widely available |
| | - 'Tangstedt' | SGol |
| | - 'Variegatus' | see *C. atropurpureus* 'Variegatus' |
| | - var. ***wilsonii*** | see *C. ascendens* |
| | ***hualiensis*** | SRms |
| | ***humifusus*** | see *C. dammeri* |
| | ***hummelii*** | SRms |
| | ***hunanensis*** B&SWJ 3143 | WCru |
| § | 'Hybridus Pendulus' | Widely available |
| § | ***hylmoei*** | SLPl SRms |
| | ***hypocarpus*** | SRms |
| | ***ignavus*** | SLPl SRms |
| § | ***ignescens*** | NWea SRms |
| | ***ignotus*** | SRms |
| | ***induratus*** | SLPl SRms |
| | ***insculptus*** | SRms |
| | ***integerrimus*** | SRms |
| § | ***integrifolius*** ♀H4 | EBee MAsh NMen SCoo SPoG SRms STre WMoo |
| | - 'Silver Shadow' | NLar |
| | ***kangdingensis*** | SRms |
| | ***lacteus*** ♀H4 | Widely available |
| | ***lancasteri*** | SRms |
| | ***langei*** | SRms |
| | ***laxiflorus*** | SRms |
| § | ***lidjiangensis*** | SRms WWau |
| § | ***linearifolius*** | GCra |
| | ***lucidus*** | NLar SRms |
| | - 'Mini' new | SLPl |
| | ***ludlowii*** | SRms |
| | ***magnificus*** | SRms |
| § | ***mairei*** | NWea SRms |
| | ***marginatus*** | SRms |
| § | - 'Blazovice' | SRms |
| § | - 'Brno' | SRms |
| | ***marquandii*** | SRms |
| § | ***meiophyllus*** | MBlu |
| | ***meuselii*** | SRms |
| | ***microphyllus*** misapplied | see *C. purpurascens* |
| | ***microphyllus*** Wall. ex Lindl. | CDul CTri EBee LRHS MGos NBlu NPla NWea SDix SPer SPoG STre WDin WMoo |
| | - NICE 004 | WCFE |
| | - var. ***cochleatus*** misapplied | see *C. cashmiriensis* |
| | - var. ***cochleatus*** (Franch.) Rehd. & Wils. | see *C. cochleatus* |
| | - var. ***cochleatus*** ambig. | NSla |
| | - 'Donard Gem' | see *C. astrophoros* |
| | - 'Ruby' | SRms |
| | - 'Teulon Porter' | see *C. astrophoros* |
| | - var. ***thymifolius*** misapplied | see *C. linearifolius* |
| | - var. ***thymifolius*** (Lindl.) Koehne | see *C. integrifolius* |
| | - var. ***thymifolius*** ambig. | LRHS |
| | ***milkedandai*** | SRms |
| | ***miniatus*** | SRms |
| | ***mirabilis*** | SRms |
| | ***monopyrenus*** | SRms |
| | 'Mooncreeper' | see *C. dammeri* 'Mooncreeper' |
| | ***morrisonensis*** | SRms |
| | ***moupinensis*** | SRms |
| | ***mucronatus*** | SRms |
| | ***multiflorus*** Bunge | NLar SRms |
| § | ***nanshan*** | CAbP NLar NWea SRms |
| | - 'Boer' | see *C. apiculatus* |
| | 'Naoujanensis' | LRHS MBri |
| | ***newryensis*** | SRms |
| | ***nitens*** | SRms |
| | ***nitidifolius*** | see *C. glomerulatus* |
| | ***nohelii*** | SRms |
| | ***notabilis*** | SRms |
| | ***nummularioides*** | SRms |
| | ***nummularius*** | SRms |
| | ***obscurus*** | SRms |
| | ***obtusus*** | SRms |
| | ***pangiensis*** | SRms |
| | ***pannosus*** | NLar SLPl SRms WFar |
| | - 'Speckles' | SRms |
| | ***paradoxus*** | SRms |
| | ***parkeri*** | SRms |
| | ***pekinensis*** | SRms |
| | ***permutatus*** | see *C. pluriflorus* |
| | ***perpusillus*** | SRms WFar |
| § | ***pluriflorus*** | CDul SRms |
| | ***poluninii*** | SRms |
| | ***polycarpus*** | SRms |
| | ***praecox*** 'Boer' | see *C. apiculatus* |
| | ***procumbens*** | SRms WDin |
| | - 'Queen of Carpets' | CDoC CDul EBee ELan EPfP EQua LRHS LSRN MAsh MGos MRav MWhi SBfd SCoo SLim SPoG SRms SWvt WMoo |
| | - 'Streib's Findling' | see *C.* 'Streib's Findling' |
| | ***prostratus*** | SRms |
| | ***przewalskii*** | SRms |
| | ***pseudo-obscurus*** | SRms |
| § | ***purpurascens*** | CSBt WFar |
| | ***pyrenaicus*** | see *C. congestus* |
| | ***qungbixiensis*** | SRms |
| | ***racemiflorus*** | SRms |
| § | ***radicans*** | MWat SBfd |
| § | - 'Eichholz' | EBee MGos NHol NWad SBfd SPoG WDin |
| § | ***rehderi*** | CMHG NLar SRms |
| | ***roseus*** | SRms |
| | 'Rothschildianus' ♀H4 | Widely available |
| | ***rugosus*** | SRms |
| | ***salicifolius*** | EBee MSwo NLar SRms WDin WFar |
| | - Autumn Fire | see *C. salicifolius* 'Herbstfeuer' |
| § | - 'Avonbank' | CDoC CEnd LTen MAsh NLar WHar |
| | - 'Bruno Orangeade' | SRms |
| | - 'Gnom' | CAlb CChe CDul CMac EBee ELan EPfP EQua LRHS MAsh MBlu MGos |

| | |
|---|---|
| | MRav NBir NEgg SPer SPoG SRms WDin WFar WHar WMoo |
| § - 'Herbstfeuer' | MRav MSwo SRms WFar |
| - 'Pendulus' | see *C.* 'Hybridus Pendulus' |
| - 'Repens' | CDoC CWib EPfP MWhi NHol NPla NPri NWea SGol SLim SPer SPoG SRms WDin WFar WHar |
| - var. ***rugosus*** hort. | see *C. hylmoei* |
| - 'Scarlet Leader' | CMac |
| ***salwinensis*** | SLPl SRms |
| ***sandakphuensis*** | SRms |
| ***scandinavicus*** | SRms |
| ***schantungensis*** | SRms |
| ***schlechtendalii*** 'Blazovice' | see *C. marginatus* 'Blazovice' |
| - 'Brno' | see *C. marginatus* 'Brno' |
| ***schubertii*** | SRms |
| ***serotinus*** misapplied | see *C. meiophyllus* |
| ***serotinus*** Hutchinson | NLar SLPl SRms |
| ***shannanensis*** | SRms |
| ***shansiensis*** | SRms |
| ***sherriffii*** | SRms |
| aff. ***sichuanensis*** | GAuc |
| ***sikangensis*** | SRms |
| ***simonsii*** ♀H4 | CBcs CCVT CDoC CDul CLnd CMac CTri EBee ECrN ELan EPfP LBuc LRHS MGos MMuc NHol NLar NPla NWad NWea SCoo SGol SPer SPoG SRms WDin WFar WHar WWau |
| § ***splendens*** | SRms WFar |
| - 'Sabrina' | see *C. splendens* |
| ***spongbergii*** | SRms |
| ***staintonii*** | SRms |
| ***sternianus*** ♀H4 | EBee EPfP SLPl SRms |
| - ACE 2200 | EPot |
| § 'Streib's Findling' | MAsh NLar SGol |
| ***suavis*** | SRms |
| ***subacutus*** | SRms |
| ***subadpressus*** | SRms |
| × ***suecicus*** 'Coral Beauty' | Widely available |
| § - 'Erlinda' (v) | NLar SRms |
| - 'Ifor' | SLPl SRms |
| - 'Juliette' (v) | EHoe GGar LRHS LSRN MAsh NLar SCoo SLim WFar WHar WRHF |
| - 'Skogholm' | CBcs CDul CWib EBee EPfP LRHS MAsh MGos NWea SPer SRms WDin WFar WHar |
| ***taoensis*** | SRms |
| ***tardiflorus*** | SRms |
| ***tauricus*** | SRms |
| ***teijiashanensis*** | SRms |
| ***tengyuehensis*** | SRms |
| ***thimphuensis*** | SRms |
| ***tomentellus*** | WCFE |
| ***tomentosus*** | SRms |
| ***turbinatus*** | SLPl SRms |
| 'Valkenburg' | SRms |
| ***vandelaarii*** | SLPl SRms |
| ***veitchii*** | MBri NLar SRms |
| ***verruculosus*** | SRms |
| ***villosulus*** | SRms |
| ***vilmorinianus*** | SRms |
| ***wardii*** misapplied | see *C. mairei* |
| ***wardii*** W.W.Sm. | GGal SRms |
| × ***watereri*** | CCVT CWib MMuc MSwo NWea SBfd SEND WDin WJas |
| - 'Avonbank' | see *C. salicifolius* 'Avonbank' |
| - 'Corina' | SRms |
| - 'Cornubia' | see *C. frigidus* 'Cornubia' |
| - 'John Waterer' ♀H4 | EPfP MGos SPoG WFar |
| - 'Pendulus' | see *C.* 'Hybridus Pendulus' |
| - 'Pink Champagne' | CMac EQua MRav |
| ***wilsonii*** | SRms |
| ***yallungensis*** | SRms |
| ***yinchangensis*** | SRms |
| ***zabelii*** | SRms |

## *Cotula* (*Asteraceae*)

| | |
|---|---|
| C&H 452 | NWCA |
| ***coronopifolia*** | CWat EHon LPBA NPer SWat WPtf |
| § ***hispida*** (DC.) Harv. | CMea CTri ECho EDAr EHoe EPot GKev GMaP ITim MAsh MHer MSCN MWat NPer NRya NWCA SPoG SRms WFar WJek WPat WPer XLum |
| ***lineariloba*** (DC.) Hilliard | ECha ECho EWes LBee LRHS |
| ***minor*** | see *Leptinella minor* |
| 'Platt's Black' | see *Leptinella squalida* 'Platt's Black' |
| ***potentilloides*** | see *Leptinella potentillina* |
| ***pyrethrifolia*** | see *Leptinella pyrethrifolia* |
| ***rotundata*** | see *Leptinella rotundata* |
| ***serrulata*** | see *Leptinella serrulata* |
| ***squalida*** | see *Leptinella squalida* |

## *Cotyledon* (*Crassulaceae*)

| | |
|---|---|
| ***chrysantha*** | see *Rosularia chrysantha* |
| ***gibbiflora*** var. ***metallica*** | see *Echeveria gibbiflora* var. *metallica* |
| ***oppositifolia*** | see *Chiastophyllum oppositifolium* |
| ***orbiculata*** | CHEx ETod SDix |
| - var. ***oblonga*** | EShb |
| - var. ***orbiculata*** | EShb |
| - 'Silver Waves' | MCot |
| ***simplicifolia*** | see *Chiastophyllum oppositifolium* |
| ***tomentosa*** | EShb |
| subsp. ***ladismithensis*** | |

## cranberry see *Vaccinium macrocarpon, V. oxycoccos*

## *Crambe* (*Brassicaceae*)

| | |
|---|---|
| ***cordifolia*** ♀H4 | Widely available |
| ***maritima*** ♀H4 | CArn CSev CSpe EBee ECha EPfP GMaP GPoy LRHS MCoo MCot MRav NEgg NLar NPnk NSti SEND SPer SWat WCot WFar WJek WMnd WPGP WPer WWEG XLum |
| - 'Lilywhite' | CAgr EBee ILis SVic |
| ***tatarica*** | NLar WPer XLum |

## *Crassula* (*Crassulaceae*)

| | |
|---|---|
| ***anomala*** | see *C. atropurpurea* var. *anomala* |
| ***arborescens*** | EShb SRms STre |
| ***argentea*** | see *C. ovata* |
| § ***atropurpurea*** var. ***anomala*** | SChr |
| - subsp. ***arborescens*** 'Blue Mist' | SEND |
| ***coccinea*** | EShb |
| § ***exilis*** subsp. ***cooperi*** | STre |
| ***lactea*** | STre |
| ***multicava*** | CHEx |
| ***muscosa*** | EShb SChr SRot STre |
| ***obtusa*** | SRot |
| ***orbicularis*** | WCot |
| § ***ovata*** ♀H1 | CDoC CHEx EBak EOHP EPfP NPer NPla SEND STre SWal WThu |
| - 'Gollum' | STre SWal |
| - 'Hummel's Sunset' (v) ♀H1 | CFee STre SWal |
| * - ***nana*** | STre |

- 'Obliqua' STre
- 'Variegata' (v) EBak STre WCot
* ***pellucida*** STre
subsp. ***marginalis*** 'Variegata' (v)
***perfoliata*** EShb NWCA SRot STre WCot
var. ***falcata*** ♀H1
***perforata*** NWCA SPlb
- 'Variegata' (v) SRot
***picturata*** see *C. exilis* subsp. *cooperi*
***portulacea*** see *C. ovata*
***rupestris*** ♀H1 STre
- subsp. ***marnieriana*** STre
§ ***sarcocaulis*** CBcs CHEx CTri ECho ELan ELon GEdr GMaP MAsh MSCN NMen NVic NWCA SEND SGar SPlb SPoG SRms SRot STre SWal WAbe WFar WPat WSHC XSen
I - 'Alba' GEdr GLam STre
- 'Ken Aslet' STre
***sedifolia*** see *C. setulosa* 'Milfordiae'
***sediformis*** see *C. setulosa* 'Milfordiae'
***setulosa*** SPlb
§ - 'Milfordiae' CTri ECho GLam NBir
***socialis*** EPot STre WAbe
- 'Major' SChr
***tetragona*** SEND STre
* ***tomentosa*** 'Variegata' (v) EShb

## + *Crataegomespilus* (*Rosaceae*)

'Jules d'Asnières' NLar

## × *Crataegosorbus* (*Rosaceae*)

***miczurinii*** 'Ivan's Belle' CAgr

## *Crataegus* (*Rosaceae*)

F&M 196 WPGP
***aestivalis*** new EGFP
***arnoldiana*** CAgr CDul CEnd CLnd CTri EBee ECrN EPfP MCoo MMuc NWea SCoo SEND SLPl SPer
'Autumn Glory' CEnd CLnd EBee ECrN WFar
***azarolus*** EPfP
***brachyacantha*** new EGFP
***calpodendron*** new EGFP
***champlainensis*** CLnd
***chrysocarpa*** EPfP
***chungtienensis*** SSpi
- SDR 5104 GKev
N ***coccinea*** misapplied see *C. intricata*, *C. biltmoreana*
N ***coccinea*** ambig. NWea
§ ***coccinea*** L. CAgr CTho EBee MAsh MCoo SCoo
***coccinioides*** EPfP
***cordata*** see *C. phaenopyrum*
***crus-galli*** misapplied see *C. persimilis* 'Prunifolia'
***crus-galli*** L. CCVT CDoC CDul CLnd CTho EBee ECrN EPfP IGor LAst NWea SPer WDin WFar WJas
***dahurica*** EPfP
× ***dippeliana*** EPfP
***douglasii*** GAuc
***dsungarica*** EPfP
× ***durobrivensis*** CAgr CDul CLnd EPfP MCoo NLar
***ellwangeriana*** CAgr ECrN EPfP SDix
- 'Fire Ball' MBlu
***eriocarpa*** CLnd
***gemmosa*** CEnd MCoo NLar NWea SSpi
***greggiana*** EPfP IGor
× ***grignonensis*** CBcs CDul CLnd CTho ECrN LMaj MAsh SPer WJas
§ ***intricata*** EPfP NWea
***irrasa*** EPfP
***jonesiae*** EPfP
***korolkowii*** new IGor
***laciniata*** Ucria see *C. orientalis*
§ ***laevigata*** CCVT CDul NWea
- 'Coccinea Plena' see *C. laevigata* 'Paul's Scarlet'
- 'Crimson Cloud' Widely available
- 'Gireoudii' CBcs CDul CPMA CWib EBee LAst MGos NLar NSti WPat
- 'Mutabilis' CLnd CTri SGol
§ - 'Paul's Scarlet' (d) ♀H4 Widely available
- 'Pink Corkscrew' EPfP LLHF MBlu SMad WPat
- 'Plena' (d) CBcs CDoC CDul CLnd CMac CSBt CTri CWib EBee ECrN EPfP LAst MGos MSwo MWat NWea SBfd SCrf SEWo SGol SLim SPer SPoG WDin WFar WHar
- 'Rosea' GKin SEND
- 'Rosea Flore Pleno' (d) ♀H4 Widely available
× ***lavalleei*** CCVT CDul CLnd CTri EBee ECrN ELan EPfP LAst LMaj MAsh MMuc MSwo NWea SCoo SEND SPer WDin
- 'Carrierei' ♀H4 CDoC CDul CMac CTho EPfP EWTr IVic LHop LMaj MAsh MBri NWea SCoo SEWo WCot WMou
***lobulata*** EPfP
***mexicana*** see *C. pubescens* f. *stipulacea*
***mollis*** CAgr CTho ECrN EPfP
***monogyna*** Widely available
§ - 'Biflora' CEnd CLnd CTho CTri EBee ECrN MAsh MCoo MGos NPal NWea SLim
- 'Compacta' MBlu WPat
- 'Flexuosa' WCot
- 'Praecox' see *C. monogyna* 'Biflora'
- 'Stricta' CCVT CDul CLnd CSBt EBee ECrN EPfP LMaj MMuc SEND SGol
- 'Variegata' (v) ECrN
× ***mordenensis*** 'Toba' (d) CDul CLnd EPfP SGol
***nigra*** EPfP IGor
§ ***orientalis*** CCVT CDul CEnd CLnd CMCN CTho CTri EBee ECrN EPfP IArd MAsh MBlu MBri MCoo MGos NWea SCoo SLim SMad SSpi WHar WJas WMou
***oxyacantha*** see *C. laevigata*
***pedicellata*** see *C. coccinea* L.
***pentagyna*** EPfP
§ ***persimilis*** 'Prunifolia' ♀H4 Widely available
- 'Prunifolia Splendens' CCVT EBee EWTr GBin LBuc LRHS MBri MCoo SCoo WPat
§ ***phaenopyrum*** CDul CLnd CTho EBee EPfP IDee MBri MGos SLPl SMad
***pinnatifida*** EPfP
- var. ***major*** CDul CEnd EPfP MBri MCoo NWea
- - 'Big Golden Star' CAgr CLnd CTho ECrN MAsh MBlu MCoo NLar SCoo
'Praecox' see *C. monogyna* 'Biflora'
***prunifolia*** see *C. persimilis* 'Prunifolia'
***pseudoheterophylla*** EPfP
§ ***pubescens*** f. ***stipulacea*** CDul CTho ECrN EPfP
***punctata*** CTho SLPl
- f. ***aurea*** EPfP
***saligna*** new EGFP
***sanguinea*** EPfP
***schraderiana*** CAgr CDul CLnd CTho EBtc EPfP MBri NLar NWea SCoo WHar

| | |
|---|---|
| ***songarica*** | GAuc |
| ***sorbifolia*** | EPfP |
| ***submollis*** new | IGor |
| ***succulenta*** | EPfP |
| - var. ***macracantha*** | EPfP |
| ***suksdorfii*** | EPfP |
| ***tanacetifolia*** | CAgr CDul CPMA CTho EPfP LLHF MBlu MBri SPer |
| ***tracyi*** new | MBri |
| ***turkestanica*** | EPfP |
| ***viridis*** 'Winter King' | CPMA EPfP MBlu MCoo SLim |
| ***wattiana*** | ELan EPfP |

## × *Crataemespilus* (*Rosaceae*)

| | |
|---|---|
| ***grandiflora*** | CBcs CDul CLnd |

## *Crawfurdia* (*Gentianaceae*)

| | |
|---|---|
| ***pasquieri*** B&SWJ 8264 | WCru |
| ***speciosa*** B&SWJ 2138 | WCru |

## *Cremanthodium* (*Asteraceae*)

| | |
|---|---|
| ***angustifolium*** SDR 1831 | GKev |
| ***arnicoides*** | EBee |

## *Cremastra* (*Orchidaceae*)

| | |
|---|---|
| ***variabilis*** | LWSt NLAp |

## × *Cremnosedum* (*Crassulaceae*)

| | |
|---|---|
| § 'Little Gem' | EPot NMen WAbe |

## *Crenularia* see *Aethionema*

## *Crepis* (*Asteraceae*)

| | |
|---|---|
| ***aurea*** | CSpr ECho |
| ***incana*** ♀H4 | CMea EBee ECho ECtt GLam MAsh MAvo NChi NMen NSla NWCA SPhx SRms WPat |
| - 'Pink Mist' | GBin NLar |

## *Crinitaria* see *Aster*

## *Crinodendron* (*Elaeocarpaceae*)

| | |
|---|---|
| ***hookerianum*** ♀H3 | Widely available |
| - 'Ada Hoffmann' | CAlb CBcs CDoC CEnd CMac CSam EBee ELan ELon EPfP GAbr GCal GGar GKin IVic LRHS LSRN MBlu MBri MGos MPkF MREP NLar NMun SBfd SChF SKHP SLim SPoG WPat |
| ***patagua*** | CBcs CCCN CDoy CSam CTri CWib EBee EPri EQua ESwi GGar IArd IDee IVic LRHS MMuc NEgg NLar SPoG SVen WAle WFar WSHC |

## *Crinum* (*Amaryllidaceae*)

| | |
|---|---|
| ***amoenum*** | CCCN EBee ECho WCot |
| ***asiaticum*** | WCot |
| - DJHC 970606 | WCot |
| - var. ***sinicum*** | WCot |
| § ***bulbispermum*** | CFir CPrp EBee ELan GCal LRHS MMHG WCot |
| ***campanulatum*** | WCot |
| ***capense*** | see *C. bulbispermum* |
| 'Carolina Beauty' | WCot |
| 'Elizabeth Traub' | WCot |
| 'Ellen Bosanquet' | CCCN CDes CFir CPrp CTca EBee ELan WCot |
| 'Emma Jones' | WCot |
| 'Hanibal's Dwarf' | EBee WCot WPGP |
| ***moorei*** | CAvo CBro CDes CFir CRHN CTca EBee ECho IVic LEdu SChr WPGP |
| - f. ***album*** | CCCN CTca EBee WCot |
| 'Ollene' | WCot |
| § × ***powellii*** ♀H3 | Widely available |
| - 'Album' ♀H3 | CAvo CBro CDes CHEx CPrp CTca CTri EBee ECha ECho ELan ELon EPfP EWes GCra LAma LEdu LRHS MNrw MRav SEND SPer SRms SSpi WCot WFar WHil WPGP |
| - 'Longifolium' | see *C. bulbispermum* |
| - 'Roseum' | see *C.* × *powellii* |
| 'Regina's Disco Lounge' | WCot |
| 'Sangria' | WCot |
| 'Summer Nocturne' | WCot |
| ***variabile*** | EBee WCot |
| 'White Queen' | WCot |
| ***yemense*** misapplied | WCot |

## *Criogenes* see *Cypripedium*

## *Crithmum* (*Apiaceae*)

| | |
|---|---|
| ***maritimum*** | CArn GPoy MNHC SPlb WJek XLum |

## *Crocosmia* ✿ (*Iridaceae*)

| | |
|---|---|
| 'Alistair' | ECtt |
| 'Anniversary' | IBlr |
| 'Apricot' | CTca IBal |
| ***aurea*** misapplied | see *C.* × *crocosmiiflora* 'George Davison' Davison |
| ***aurea*** ambig. | EShb GCal |
| ***aurea*** (Pappe ex Hook.f.) Planch. | CPne CPou ECtt IBlr NHol |
| - subsp. ***aurea*** | CTca IBlr |
| - - 'Maculata' | IBlr |
| - subsp. ***pauciflora*** | IBlr |
| 'Auricorn' | IBlr NCot NHol |
| 'Auriol' | IBlr NCot |
| 'Aurora' | CHVG NGdn |
| 'Beth Chatto' | CTca CYeo IBal MAvo |
| Bressingham Beacon = 'Blos' | CHVG CPrp IBlr WRHF |
| 'Bressingham Blaze' | CBre CMHG CTca EBee EBla ECtt IBlr LRHS NGdn NHol WCot WHil |
| Bridgemere hybrid | NHol |
| Bright Eyes = 'Walbreyes'PBR | LRHS MAvo |
| 'Cadenza' | IBal IBlr NHol |
| 'Carnival' | ECtt IBlr |
| 'Cascade' | IBal IBlr |
| 'Chinatown' | IBal IBlr MAvo NCot NHol WHil |
| 'Citronella' misapplied | see *C.* × *crocosmiiflora* 'Honey Angels' |
| 'Comet' Knutty | CTca GCal IBlr MAvo NCot NHol WMoo |
| × ***crocosmiiflora*** | CHEx CTca CTri EBee IBlr MCot NBPC NHol SEND SPlb SRms WBrk WCot WFar WMoo WShi |
| - 'A.E.Amos' | CTca ECtt |
| - 'A.J. Hogan' | CTca CYeo GBin IBal IBlr NHol |
| - 'African Glow' | CTca IBal |
| - 'Amber Sun' | IBlr |
| - 'Amberglow' | CBgR CElw CPLG IBal IBlr MAvo NBre NHol NPer WFar |
| - 'Apricot Queen' | CTca IBlr NHol |
| - 'Autumn Gold' | IBlr |
| - 'Baby Barnaby' | CBre CDes CTca EBee ECtt IBlr NHol WPGP |
| - 'Babylon' | Widely available |
| - 'Best of British' | CHVG |

| | | |
|---|---|---|
| | - 'Bicolor' | CTca IBal IBlr NHol WHil |
| | - 'Burford Bronze' | CTca IBal IBlr MAvo NHol |
| | - 'Buttercup' | CSam CTca EBee EPfP ERCP EWll IBal IBlr IKil MAvo MCot NBre NHol SBfd SRkn SRot STes WFar WMoo WWEG |
| | - 'Canary Bird' | CBro CPne CRow CSam CYeo EBee ECtt GAbr IBal IBlr NBPC NGdn NHol WBrk WRHF |
| | 'Cardinale' | IBlr |
| § | - 'Carmin Brillant' ♀H3-4 | Widely available |
| | - 'Carminea' | STes |
| | - 'Challa' | CTca |
| | - 'Citrina' | CTca |
| | - 'Citronella' J.E. Fitt | CBgR CBro CPLG CPrp CSam CTri EBee EBla ECha EPfP GMaP GQue LRHS MLLN MRav NGdn NHol SPer WCot |
| § | - 'Coleton Fishacre' | Widely available |
| § | - 'Columbus' | CAvo CPar CPrp CSam CTca EBee EPPr EPfP EPri GBin IBal IBlr LHop LSou MAvo MSCN NHol SGar SPer WFar WMnd WWEG |
| | - 'Colwall' | IBal IBlr MAvo NCot WHil |
| | - 'Constance' | CBgR CBro CSam CTca EBee GGar IBal IBlr LRHS MAvo MBri NBid NGdn NHol SRGP WBrk WFar WHil |
| | - 'Corona' | CTca IBal IBlr MAvo NHol |
| | - 'Corten' | IBlr |
| § | - 'Croesus' | CTca IBal IBlr MAvo MRav |
| | - 'Custard Cream' | CHVG CPrp CSpe CTca ECtt IBlr MAvo NHol WFar |
| | - 'D.H. Houghton' | IBlr |
| | - 'Debutante' | CDes CTca CYeo EBee ECtt EPri IBal IBlr NHol SHar SUsu WHoo WPGP WSHC |
| § | - 'Diadème' | CSam CTca CWCL LEdu NHol |
| | - 'Dusky Maiden' | Widely available |
| | - 'Dwarf Gold' | IBal |
| § | - 'E.A. Bowles' | CPou CTca EBee IBlr LRHS WCot |
| | - 'Eastern Promise' | CBre CPrp CTca ELon IBal IBlr MAvo WHil |
| | - 'Eclatant' | IBlr |
| | - 'Elegans' | CBre ECtt IBal IBlr |
| § | - 'Emily McKenzie' | Widely available |
| | - 'Etoile de Feu' | IBlr |
| | - 'Fantasie' | CBgR IBal |
| | - 'Festival Orange' | IBlr |
| | - 'Fire Jumper' | CDes CTca EBee MAvo WPGP |
| | - 'Firebrand' | IBlr NCot |
| | - 'Fireglow' | CTca ECtt IBal IBlr NCot WFar WPer |
| | - 'Flamethrower' | IBlr MAvo |
| | - 'George Davison' misapplied | see *C.* × *crocosmiiflora* 'Golden Glory' ambig., 'Sulphurea' |
| § | - 'George Davison' Davison | Widely available |
| | - 'Gloria' | CTca IBal IBlr MAvo WHil |
| | - 'Golden Glory' misapplied | see *C.* × *crocosmiiflora* 'Diadème' |
| § | - 'Golden Glory' ambig. | CPLG CWCL ELan IBal IBlr MSwo MWat NBir NHol SEND SPlb WCot WFar |
| | - 'Goldfinch' | CTca IBlr NCot NHol WHil WWEG |
| | - 'Goldie' | CTca MAvo |
| | - 'Hades' | CTca IBlr MAvo |
| | - 'Harvest Sun' | IBlr |
| | - 'Heligan' | EPfP |
| | - 'His Majesty' | CBro CPne CSam CSpe CTca CYeo ECtt IBal IBlr LRHS NHol WFar WHil WPer |
| | - 'Hoey Joey' | GMac NGdn |
| § | - 'Honey Angels' | Widely available |
| | - 'Honey Bells' | LRHS WBrk |
| | - 'Irish Dawn' | IBal IBlr NBre NCot NHol |
| § | - 'Jackanapes' | CPne CPrp CRow CTca CWCL EBee ECtt ELan ELon GCal GGar IBal IBlr LRHS MBri MGos MLHP NHol SBfd SLsu WFar WPGP |
| | - 'Jackanapes VI' | IBal |
| | - 'James Coey' misapplied | see *C.* × *crocosmiiflora* 'Carmin Brillant' |
| | - 'James Coey' J.E. Fitt | CHar COIW CRow EAEE EBee EBla ECha EHoe EPfP EPla GKin IFoB MLHP NDov NGdn NHol NLar SRGP WFar WMoo |
| | - 'Jesse van Dyke' | IBlr |
| § | - 'Jessie' | CElw CTca IBlr MAvo SMrm WPer |
| | - 'Judith' | CTca IBlr NCot |
| | - 'Kapoor' | IBlr |
| | - 'Kiautschou' | CHVG CTca CWCL EBee ECtt GMac IBal IBlr MAvo NBre NGdn NHol |
| | - 'Lady Hamilton' | CBro CElw CFir CHar CMHG CPLG CPne CSam CTca EBla ECtt GCal GCra GGar IBal IBlr ITim LRHS MAvo MBri MRav NCGa NHol SBfd WCot WFar WHil WHoo WMoo WWEG |
| | - 'Lady McKenzie' | see *C.* × *crocosmiiflora* 'Emily McKenzie' |
| | - 'Lady Oxford' | CTca CYeo IBlr MAvo NHol WHil |
| | - 'Lambrook Gold' | CAvo IBlr SUsu |
| | - 'Lord Nelson' | CTca IBal NHol |
| | - 'Loweswater' | CYeo MAvo SUsu |
| | - 'Lutea' | ECtt IBal IBlr NHol |
| | - 'Mars' | CElw EBla EWes EWll GAbr GGar GMac IBal IBlr IFoB LRHS MAvo NGdn NHol SBfd SPlb SRGP SRkn WFar WPGP WPer WWEG |
| | - 'Mephistopheles' | CTca IBlr MAvo NHol |
| | - 'Merryman' | CTca GAbr GMac IBal MAvo |
| | - 'Météore' | CBgR EPPr EPot GAbr GGar IBal LRHS MBNS NBre NHol NPri SBfd WWEG |
| | - 'Morgenlicht' | CTca ECtt IBal IBlr NHol WBrk WCot |
| | - 'Moses' | CTca |
| | - 'Mount Usher' | CCse CFir CPrp CTca GCal IBal IBlr MAvo NHol NLar SGar WFar |
| | - 'Mrs David Howard' | SApp |
| § | - 'Mrs Geoffrey Howard' | CDes CSam CTca CWCL ECtt GGar IBal IBlr LEdu NHol SHar SUsu WBrk WCru WPGP |
| | - 'Mrs Morrison' | see *C.* × *crocosmiiflora* 'Mrs Geoffrey Howard' |
| | - 'Newry Seedling' | see *C.* × *crocosmiiflora* 'Prometheus' |
| | - 'Nimbus' | CHVG CTca EBee IBal IBlr WHil |
| § | - 'Norwich Canary' | CBgR CBro CMHG COIW CTca EBee EBla ECha EPPr EPfP EPri GCra IBal IBlr LEdu LRHS MRav NBir NGdn NHol NLar NSti WBrk WCot WHil WMoo WOut WWEG |
| | - 'Olympic Fire' | CTca IBlr MAvo NCot NHol |
| | - 'Olympic Sunrise' | CTca |
| | - 'Pepper' | IBlr MAvo |
| | - 'Ping Pong' | CTca |
| | - 'Plaisir' | CTca IBal IBlr MAvo NBid NHol WFar WWEG |
| | - 'Polo' | CBgR CSam CTca CWCL |
| | - 'Princess' | see *C. pottsii* 'Princess' |

| | |
|---|---|
| § - 'Princess Alexandra' | IBlr |
| - 'Prolificans' | IBlr |
| § - 'Prometheus' | CTca IBal IBlr NHol |
| - 'Queen Alexandra' misapplied | see *C.* × *crocosmiiflora* 'Princess Alexandra' |
| § - 'Queen Alexandra' J.E. Fitt | CTca ECha IBlr LEdu NHol SPer WHal WMoo WPer |
| - 'Queen Charlotte' | CTca IBal IBlr MAvo |
| - 'Queen Mary II' | see *C.* × *crocosmiiflora* 'Columbus' |
| - 'Queen of Spain' | CTca IBal IBlr LRHS MDKP NHol WHil |
| - 'Rayon d'Or' | CDes IBlr MAvo WPGP |
| - 'Red King' | EBee EBla EPfP IBal IBlr LHop LRHS MPnt MWea NLar SBfd WFar WHil WMoo WRHF WWEG |
| - 'Red Knight' | CBgR CHVG CMMP GAbr IBlr NHol |
| - 'Rheingold' misapplied | see *C.* × *crocosmiiflora* 'Diadème' |
| - 'Rose Queen' | IBlr |
| - 'Saint Clements' | CTca IBlr NCot NHol |
| - 'Saracen' | Widely available |
| - 'Sir Mathew Wilson' | CDes EBee IBal IBlr WCot WPGP |
| - 'Solfatare' ♀H3 | Widely available |
| - 'Solfatare Coleton Fishacre' | see *C.* × *crocosmiiflora* 'Coleton Fishacre' |
| - 'Star of the East' ♀H3 | Widely available |
| - 'Starbright' | IBlr |
| - 'Starfire' | ECtt |
| - 'Sultan' | CDes CPLG CYeo IBlr WFar WMoo WPGP |
| - 'Tiger's Eye' **new** | CTca |
| - 'Venus' | CBgR CBre CPou CTca EBee ECtt EPPr EShb EWll IBal IBlr LRHS MAvo MCot MPnt NBre NHol NLar NPla SRGP WFar WHil WMoo |
| - 'Vesuvius' | GCal IBlr LRHS NCGa WFar WSHC |
| - 'Vic's Yellow' | SGar |
| - 'Voyager' | EBee ECtt ELon EPot ERCP GAbr IBal IBlr LHop LRHS MBri NHol NLar WHil WPer |
| - 'Zeal Tan' | CElw CMHG COlW CPLG CPar CSam CTca CWCL EBee ECGP ECtt ELan ELon GCal IBal IBlr LEdu MAvo MBNS MCot MNFA NBPC NEgg NLar SBfd SMrm SUsu WBrk WCot |
| § × ***crocosmioides*** | CTca IBlr WHil |
| - 'Castle Ward Late' | CBgR CHVG CPou CTca EAEE ECha GAbr GCal GCra GGar IBal IBlr LHop MAvo NCGa NDov NHol SUsu WMoo |
| - 'Mount Stewart Late' | IBlr |
| § - 'Vulcan' Leichtlin | CTca IBlr LRHS NHol WHil |
| 'Darkleaf Apricot' | see *C.* × *crocosmiiflora* 'Coleton Fishacre' |
| 'Devil's Advocate' | CTca |
| 'Doctor Marion Wood' | CYeo EBee |
| 'Eldorado' | see *C.* × *crocosmiiflora* 'E.A. Bowles' |
| 'Elegance' | IBlr |
| 'Elizabeth' | NHol |
| 'Ellenbank Canary' | CBgR CTca GMac MAvo |
| 'Ellenbank Firecrest' | CBgR CDes CTca EBee MAvo NCGa WOut WPGP |
| 'Ellenbank Goldcrest' **new** | GMac |
| 'Ellenbank Skylark' | CBgR GMac MAvo |
| 'Emberglow' | Widely available |
| 'Fandango' | IBal IBlr NCot NHol |
| 'Fernhill' | IBlr |
| * 'Feuerser' | ECtt |
| 'Fire King' misapplied | see *C.* × *crocosmiiflora* 'Jackanapes' |
| 'Fire King' ambig. | CBgR EBee ERCP GAbr IBal LRHS NBPC NLar NSti SWvt WHil |
| 'Fire Sprite' | IBlr |
| 'Firefly' | IBlr NHol |
| 'Fireworks' | NCot |
| 'Flaire' | IBlr |
| 'Fleuve Jaune' | CPne CTca ECtt |
| 'Forest Fire' **new** | LLHF LSou |
| ***fucata*** | IBlr |
| - 'Jupiter' | see *C.* 'Jupiter' |
| ***fucata* × *paniculata*** | CTca IBal NHol |
| 'Fugue' | IBlr |
| 'Fusilade' | IBlr |
| 'Gold Sprite' | IBlr NCot |
| 'Golden Ballerina' PBR | CPrp EBee ECtt EWes IBal LRHS LSou MWea NCGa SPoG SRkn |
| 'Golden Dew' | CBcs CBre CTca EBee ECtt EPfP GAbr GQue IBal MBNS NCGa NEgg SBfd SKHP WCot WGor |
| Golden Fleece *sensu* Lemoine | see *C.* × *crocosmiiflora* 'Coleton Fishacre' |
| 'Harlequin' | CElw CTca CYeo MAvo |
| 'Harmonia' | CDes CTca |
| 'Hellfire' | CBgR CDes CSam CSpe CTca ECtt ELon EWhm GAbr IBal LLHF LRHS MAvo MBNS MLLN MNrw MTis NCGa NDov NGdn SMad SPer WCot WCra WWlt |
| 'Highlight' | IBal IBlr MAvo NHol |
| 'Hill House' | MAvo |
| 'Irish Flame' | NHol |
| 'Irish Sunset' | NHol |
| 'Jennine' | EBee IBal NHol SRGP WHil |
| 'Jenny' | MAvo |
| Jenny Bloom = 'Blacro' PBR | COlW NBir NChi NLar SMrs |
| 'John Boots' | EBee ECtt GAbr IBal IBlr LRHS MCot MDev NBid NHol NLar SRGP WFar WHil |
| § 'Jupiter' | CBre CPou CPrp CSam CTca CWCL GCal GMac IBal IBlr MAvo MRav NCGa NHol SApp WFar WHil |
| 'King George' **new** | CTca |
| 'Krakatoa' | CHll CPrp CTca EBee IBal LLHF MWea SKHP SRkn SWvt WMoo |
| 'Lady Wilson' misapplied | see *C.* × *crocosmiiflora* 'Norwich Canary' |
| 'Lana de Savary' | CPrp CTca EBee EWes GBin GCal IBal IBlr LRHS NBid NHol |
| 'Late Cornish' | see *C.* × *crocosmiiflora* 'Queen Alexandra' J.E. Fitt |
| 'Late Lucifer' | CHEx CTca CTri GCal IBlr LSRN SDix |
| × ***latifolia*** | see *C.* × *crocosmioides* |
| 'Limpopo' | CBgR CMac CTca CYeo EBee ECha ECtt ELon EPri GAbr GMac GQue LRHS MAvo MBNS MNrw MSCN NEgg NLar NPnk SDix SMrm SPer WCot WCra |
| 'Lucifer' ♀H4 | Widely available |
| 'Malahide Castle Red' | CTca |
| 'Mandarin' | IBlr |
| 'Marcotijn' | CTca GGar IBal IBlr IGor LRHS NHol |
| ***masoniorum*** ♀H3 | Widely available |
| - from Satan's Nek | CTca |
| - 'African Dawn' | CTca ECtt GQue MAvo |
| - 'Amber' | IBlr |
| - 'Dixter Flame' | ECtt IBlr IFoB SDix WOut |
| - 'Firebird' | CTca GCra IBlr IGor MAvo NBre NHol |

| | |
|---|---|
| - 'Flamenco' | IBlr |
| - 'Golden Swan' | ECtt |
| - Holehird strain | ECtt |
| - 'Kiaora' | IBlr |
| - 'Moira Reid' | IBlr NHol |
| - red-flowered | IBlr |
| - 'Rowallane Apricot' | IBlr |
| - 'Rowallane Orange' | CPrp CTca GAbr IBlr NHol |
| - 'Rowallane Yellow' ♀H3-4 | CDes CPrp CTca ECtt GAbr GCal GMac IBlr IGor LRHS MBri MMuc NCGa NHol SUsu WCot |
| - Slieve Donard selection | CTca IBal |
| - 'Tropicana' | IBlr |
| ***mathewsiana*** | IBlr |
| ***mathewsiana* × *paniculata*** | CTca |
| 'Mex' | MAvo WCot |
| 'Minotaur' | IBlr |
| 'Miss Scarlet' **new** | LRHS |
| 'Mistral' | CBgR CCCN CMea CTca EBee ECtt EPPr EPfP EPot GKev GMac IBal IBlr LAst LRHS MSpe NBre NHol NLar SBfd WFar WMoo |
| 'Moorland Blaze' | WMoo |
| 'Mount Stewart' | see *C.* × *crocosmiiflora* 'Jessie' |
| 'Mr Bedford' | see *C.* × *crocosmiiflora* 'Croesus' |
| 'Mullard Pink' | CTca |
| 'Okavango'[PBR] | CBgR CBre CBro CMac CTca CYeo EBee ECGP ECtt ELon EPri GAbr GQue IBal MAvo MBNS MCot MNrw NBPC NGdn NLar SKHP SMrm WCot WCra WHil |
| Old Hat | see *C.* 'Walberton Red' |
| 'Orange Devil' | CBre ECtt GKin IBal IBlr MAvo MBNS MBri MNFA MWea NCGa SMrm |
| 'Orange Lucifer' | NBre |
| 'Orange River' | WCot |
| 'Orange Spirit' | WFar |
| 'Orangeade' | CTca ECtt GBin IBal IBlr NHol |
| § ***paniculata*** | CMac CPne CPou CTca EBla ECtt GAbr GGar MNFA NBid NHol NOrc SBfd SPet WBrk WCot WMoo WOut WShi WTin |
| - from Howick | CTca |
| - from Kologha | CTca |
| - brown/orange-flowered | IBlr |
| - 'Cally Greyleaf' | EWld GCal |
| - 'Cally Sword' | GCal |
| - 'Major' | CTri IBlr |
| - 'Natal' | CPrp CTca ECtt IBal NHol WFar |
| - red-flowered | CTca IBlr SWvt |
| - triploid | IBlr |
| aff. ***paniculata*** | ECtt IBlr |
| 'Paul's Best Yellow' | CDes CEnd CSam CTca ECGP ECtt EWes GAbr IBal LLHF LLWG MAvo MBNS MTis NSti SDix SHar SMad SPer SUsu SWvt WCot WWlt |
| ***pearsei*** | CTca IBlr |
| 'Phillipa Browne' | CTca EBee ECtt IBal LSou NCGa NEgg SRGP WCot WMoo |
| ***pottsii*** | CBgR CRow CTca ECtt EPla GBin IBal IBlr NHol NLar WFar WPtf WWEG |
| - CD&R 109 | CPou |
| - 'Culzean Pink' | CBgR CHVG COIW CPLG CPrp CTca EBee GAbr GBin GCal GMac IBal IBlr MLHP MRav MSpe NBir NHol NLar SMrm WCot WHil WOut WPGP WPtf WWEG |
| - deep pink-flowered | IBlr IGor WMoo |
| - 'Grandiflora' | IBlr |
| § - 'Princess' | IBal MAvo |
| - tall | CTca |
| 'Quantreau' | IBlr |
| 'R.W. Wallace' | CTca IBal NHol |
| 'Red Devils' | NHol |
| 'Red Star' | IBal |
| 'Roman Gold' | IBlr |
| ***rosea*** | see *Tritonia disticha* subsp. *rubrolucens* |
| 'Rowden Bronze' | see *C.* × *crocosmiiflora* 'Coleton Fishacre' |
| 'Rowden Chrome' | see *C.* × *crocosmiiflora* 'George Davison' Davison |
| 'Ruby Velvet' | IBlr |
| 'Rubygold' | CPrp IBlr |
| 'Sabena' | MAvo |
| 'Saffron Queen' | IBlr |
| 'Salsa' | WCot |
| 'Saturn' | see *C.* 'Jupiter' |
| 'Scarlatti' | CTca GAbr IBal IBlr NHol |
| 'Severn Sunrise' ♀H3-4 | Widely available |
| 'Shocking' | IBlr NHol |
| 'Son of Lucifer' | WFar |
| 'Sonate' | CTca NHol SPlb |
| 'Spitfire' | CBot CHVG CPLG CPne CPrp CSam CTca EBee EBla ECha ECtt ELan GAbr GGar GMac IBal IBlr LHop LRHS MArl MAvo MRav NHol NLar SRkn SWvt WFar |
| § 'Sulphurea' | CPLG CPou CPrp CSam ECtt EPfP IBal IBlr MSpe NHol SDix WBrk WCot WHal WPer |
| 'Sunzest' | CTca MAvo WFar |
| 'Tamar Glow' | CTca |
| 'Tamar New Dawn' **new** | CTca |
| 'Tamar Peace' **new** | CTca |
| 'Tangerine Queen' | CTca CYeo ECtt IBal IBlr LRHS NCot NHol WHil WMoo |
| 'Tiger' | CElw CTca IBlr MAvo |
| I 'Vulcan' A. Bloom | CTca CYeo ECtt GAbr GGar IBal IBlr MAvo NHol SAga WCot WFar |
| 'Vulcan' Leichtlin | see *C.* × *crocosmioides* 'Vulcan' Leichtlin |
| § 'Walberton Red' | CBgR CTca EWes IBal IBlr MAvo MBri SAga SApp SKHP SMad SUsu WCot |
| Walberton Yellow = 'Walcroy'[PBR] | LRHS SApp SUsu WCot |
| 'Zambesi'[PBR] | CBro CDes CKno CTca CYeo EBee ECtt ELon GAbr GBin GQue IBal LHop MAvo MBNS MCot MNrw MSCN MTis NBPC NCGa NLar SBfd SKHP SPer WCot WPGP |
| 'Zeal Giant' | CRow CTca ECtt IBlr MAvo NHol |
| 'Zeal Remembrance' | CTca |
| 'Zeal Unnamed' | CPrp CTca EBee GMac IBal IBlr NHol WFar WOut |

## *Crocus* ✿ (*Iridaceae*)

| | |
|---|---|
| ***abantensis*** | ECho |
| - VVVA.315 | LWst |
| - 'Sky Blue' | LWst |
| ***adanensis*** KPPZ 90-93 | LWst |
| 'Advance' | CBro ECho EPot ERCP LAma MBri SPer |
| ***alatavicus*** | ECho LWst |
| ***albiflorus*** | see *C. vernus* subsp. *albiflorus* |
| 'Alionka' | LWst |

|  |  |
|---|---|
| ***ancyrensis*** | ECho EPot GKev LAma |
| – 'Golden Bunch' | ECho SDeJ WShi |
| § ***angustifolius*** 🏆H4 | ECho EPot GKev SDeJ |
| – 'Berlin Gold' | ECho |
| – bronze-tinged | NMin |
| – 'Minor' | ECho EPot |
| – 'Oreanda' **new** | LWst |
| ***antalyensis*** | ECho LWst |
| – white-flowered **new** | LWst |
| – yellow-flowered **new** | LWst |
| 'Ard Schenk' | ECho GKev LAma LRHS |
| ***asturicus*** | see *C. serotinus* subsp. *salzmannii* |
| ***asumaniae*** | ECho |
| – JP 88-45 | LWst |
| 'Aubade' | ECho EPot GKev |
| ***aureus*** | see *C. flavus* subsp. *flavus* |
| ***banaticus*** 🏆H4 | ECho EPot GKev LLHF LWst MSSP NHar NMen |
| ***baytopiorum*** | ECho NMen |
| ***biflorus*** | ECho |
| – subsp. ***biflorus*** | ECho |
| – subsp. ***crewei*** | ECho |
| – subsp. ***isauricus*** | ECho |
| – subsp. ***melantherus*** | ECho GKev LWst |
| – 'Miss Vain' | ECho EPot ERCP GKev LAma MBri |
| – subsp. ***pulchricolor*** | LWst |
| – 'Serevan' | LWst NMin |
| – subsp. ***stridii*** **new** | LWst |
| – subsp. ***tauri*** | ECho LWst |
| – subsp. ***weldenii*** | ECho |
| – – 'Albus' | ECho EPot LAma |
| – – 'Fairy' | ECho LAma |
| 'Blue Bird' | CBro ECho EPot LAma |
| 'Blue Pearl' 🏆H4 | CAvo CBro CFFs ECho EPfP EPot GKev LRHS MBri NBir SDeJ SPer SPhx WShi |
| ***boryi*** | ECho LLHF WCot |
| – VV GR.1410 | LWst |
| ***cambessedesii*** | ECho SCnR |
| § ***cancellatus*** subsp. ***cancellatus*** | ECho EPot GKev LAma |
| – var. ***cilicicus*** | see *C. cancellatus* subsp. *cancellatus* |
| – subsp. ***lycius*** | ECho EPot |
| – subsp. ***mazziaricus*** | EPot |
| – – large-flowered | LWst |
| – – 'Menalo' **new** | LWst |
| – – 'Parnassus' **new** | LWst |
| – – 'Pilion' **new** | LWst |
| – – 'Rendina' | LWst |
| – subsp. ***pamphylicus*** | ECho |
| ***candidus*** | ECho LWst |
| – 'Lune' **new** | LWst |
| – var. ***subflavus*** | see *C. olivieri* subsp. *olivieri* |
| ***cartwrightianus*** 🏆H4 | ECho GKev LRHS SPhx |
| – CE&H 613 | LWst |
| – 'Albus' misapplied | see *C. hadriaticus* |
| N – 'Albus' Tubergen 🏆H4 | ECho EPot GKev SDeJ |
| – 'Halloween' | LWst |
| – white-flowered clone | LWst |
| ***chrysanthus*** 🏆H4 **new** | CHab |
| – 'Afyon' **new** | LWst |
| – 'Blue Peter' | ECho LWst |
| – 'Cream Beauty' 🏆H4 | CAvo CBro CFFs CMea ECho EPfP EPot GKev LAma MBri NBir SDeJ SPhx |
| – 'E.A. Bowles' 🏆H4 | ECho |
| – 'E.P. Bowles' | LAma MBri |
| – 'Early Gold' | ECho LWst |
| – var. ***fuscotinctus*** | ECho EPfP EPot LAma MBri SDeJ |
| – late-flowering **new** | LWst |
| – 'Milea' | LWst |
| – 'Moonlight' | LAma |
| – 'Prespa Gold' **new** | LWst |
| – 'Uschak Orange' | LWst |
| – 'Zwanenburg Bronze' 🏆H4 | ECho EPfP GKev LAma SGar |
| 'Cloth of Gold' | see *C. angustifolius* |
| ***clusii*** | see *C. serotinus* subsp. *clusii* |
| ***corsicus*** 🏆H4 | ECho EPot LWst |
| ***cvijicii*** | GKev |
| ***dalmaticus*** | EPot |
| – 'Petrovac' | LWst |
| 'Dorothy' | ECho EPot GKev LAma |
| 'Dutch Yellow' | see *C.* × *luteus* 'Golden Yellow' |
| 'Ego' | ECho LWst |
| ***etruscus*** 🏆H4 | GKev LWst |
| – 'Rosalind' | ECho GKev |
| – 'Zwanenburg' | ECho EPot GKev LAma LRHS SDeJ |
| ***flavus*** | ECho LWst |
| § – subsp. ***flavus*** 🏆H4 | ECho EPot LAma WShi |
| ***fleischeri*** | ECho EPot LAma |
| ***gargaricus*** | LWst |
| – subsp. ***herbertii*** | GKev LWst |
| ***gilanicus*** **new** | LWst |
| 'Golden Mammoth' | see *C.* × *luteus* 'Golden Yellow' |
| 'Goldilocks' | ECho GKev LAma SDeJ |
| ***goulimyi*** 🏆H4 | CBro ECho EPot GKev LAma LLHF LWst SDeJ WCot |
| – 'Albus' | see *C. goulimyi* subsp. *goulimyi* 'Mani White' |
| § – subsp. ***goulimyi*** 'Mani White' 🏆H4 | CAvo SCnR |
| – subsp. ***leucanthus*** | GKev |
| – – HOA 0183 | LWst |
| 'Gypsy Girl' | CAvo ECho EPot ERCP LAma LRHS MBri SPhx |
| § ***hadriaticus*** 🏆H4 | ECho EPot GKev LAma |
| – 'Alepohori' **new** | LWst |
| – var. ***chrysobelonicus*** | see *C. hadriaticus* |
| – 'Crystal' | LWst |
| – 'Elysean Pearl' | LWst |
| – subsp. ***hadriaticus*** f. ***lilacinus*** | EPot LWst |
| – 'Indian Summer' | LWst |
| – 'Jumbo' **new** | LWst |
| 'Herald' | CAvo LAma SPhx |
| ***imperati*** subsp. ***suaveolens*** | EPot |
| – – 'De Jager' | ERCP LAma |
| 'Janis Ruksans' | CAvo LWst |
| 'Jeanne d'Arc' | CAvo CBro CFFs ECho EPfP EPot GKev LAma MBri NBir SDeJ WShi |
| 'Jeannine' | ECho EPot |
| × ***jessoppiae*** | ECho LWst |
| ***karduchorum*** | ECho LAma |
| ***korolkowii*** | CGrW ECho GKev LAma |
| – 'Golden Nugget' | EPot |
| – 'Kiss of Spring' | EPot |
| ***kosaninii*** | EPot GKev NMin |
| – CH 801 | LWst |
| – 'April View' **new** | EPot |
| ***kotschyanus*** 🏆H4 | ECho NRya SPer |
| – HKEP 9205 | LWst |
| – 'Albus' | ECho SDeJ |
| § – subsp. ***kotschyanus*** | CBro ECho EPot LAma SDeJ |
| – 'Reliance' | ECho LWst |
| – stoloniferous HKEP 9317 | LWst |
| ***kotschyanus*** × ***ochroleucus*** | ECho LWst |

|  |  |
|---|---|
| 'Ladykiller' ♀H4 | CAvo CBro CFFs ECho EPot ERCP GKev LAma MBri NMin SPhx WShi |
| ***laevigatus*** ♀H4 | ECho GKev WCot |
| – CE&H 612 | LWst |
| – HOA 0138 | LWst |
| – HOA 0153 **new** | LWst |
| – 'Fontenayi' | CBro ECho EPot ERCP GKev |
| – white-flowered | ECho |
| 'Large Yellow' | see *C.* × *luteus* 'Golden Yellow' |
| ***ligusticus*** | ECho |
| 'Little Amber' | LWst |
| ***longiflorus*** ♀H4 | CBro ECho GEdr LLHF LWst |
| – HOA 9703 | LWst |
| § × ***luteus*** 'Golden Yellow' ♀H4 | CAvo CFFs EPfP EPot GKev LAma LRHS WShi |
| § – 'Stellaris' | ECho |
| ***malyi*** ♀H2-4 | ECho NMin |
| – 'Ballerina' | ECho LWst |
| – 'Sveti Roc' | EPot LWst |
| ***mathewii*** | ECho EPot WCot |
| – HKEP 9291 | LWst |
| – 'Dream Dancer' **new** | LWst |
| ***medius*** ♀H4 | CBro EPot LAma |
| ***michelsonii*** | LWst |
| ***minimus*** | ECho EPot ERCP LAma LLHF SBch |
| ***niveus*** | CBro ECho EPot GKev LAma LLHF |
| – late-flowering **new** | LWst |
| – pale blue-flowered | LWst |
| – white-flowered **new** | GKev |
| – – HOA 0164 **new** | LWst |
| ***nudiflorus*** | CBro ECho EPot GKev LAma NMen |
| ***ochroleucus*** ♀H4 | ECho EPot GKev SDeJ |
| ***olivieri*** | ECho |
| – subsp. ***balansae*** | ECho |
| – – 'Zwanenburg' | ECho EPot |
| – subsp. ***istanbulensis*** | LWst |
| § – subsp. ***olivieri*** | ECho LWst |
| – – 'Little Tiger' | ECho LWst |
| ***oreocreticus*** | ECho |
| – VV CR.114 | LWst |
| ***pallasii*** | ECho |
| – VV KR.75 | LWst |
| – subsp. ***pallasii*** | ECho |
| – subsp. ***turcicus*** VV TW.855 **new** | LWst |
| – white-flowered **new** | LWst |
| ***paschei*** HKEP 9034 **new** | LWst |
| ***pestalozzae*** | ECho LWst |
| – var. ***caeruleus*** | ECho SCnR |
| – – CRO 401 | LWst |
| 'Prins Claus' | ECho EPfP EPot LAma LRHS MBri SBch SDeJ |
| 'Prinses Beatrix' | ECho |
| ***pulchellus*** ♀H4 | ECho EPot ERCP GKev ITim LAma LRHS NWCA WCot |
| – 'Albus' | ECho EPot |
| – 'Inspiration' | ECho |
| – 'Michael Hoog' | ECho |
| 'Purple Heart' **new** | LWst |
| 'Purpureus' | see *C. vernus* 'Purpureus Grandiflorus' |
| ***reticulatus*** | ECho |
| – VV YY.306 | LWst |
| – subsp. ***reticulatus*** | ECho EPot |
| ***robertianus*** HOA 9856 **new** | LWst |
| 'Romance' | CAvo CFFs EPot GKev LAma MBri SDeJ SPer |
| 'Ruby Giant' | CAvo CBro ECho EPfP EPot GKev LAma LRHS MBri NBir SDeJ SPer SPhx WShi |
| ***rujanensis*** | ECho LWst |
| ***salzmannii*** | see *C. serotinus* subsp. *salzmannii* |
| ***sativus*** | CArn CAvo CBod CBro CPrp CTca ECho EGHP ELan EOHP EPot ERCP GKev GPoy LAma MMHG NBir SDeJ SPer |
| 'Saturnus' | EPot LAma |
| ***scardicus*** | LWst |
| ***scepusiensis*** | see *C. vernus* subsp. *vernus* |
| § ***serotinus*** subsp. ***clusii*** | ECho LAma |
| – – 'Poseidon' | LWst |
| § – subsp. ***salzmannii*** | ECho LAma |
| – – HOA 9911 | LWst |
| – – KPW 9425 | LWst |
| – – KPW 9432 | LWst |
| – – 'Atropurpureus' | WCot |
| ***sibiricus*** | see *C. sieberi* |
| § ***sieberi*** ♀H4 | EPot |
| § – 'Albus' ♀H4 | CAvo CBro CFFs ECho EPot GKev SDeJ |
| – subsp. ***atticus*** | ECho LAma |
| – – 'Firefly' | ECho EPot GKev LAma SDeJ SPhx |
| – – 'Stunner' **new** | LWst |
| – 'Bowles' White' | see *C. sieberi* 'Albus' |
| – 'Hubert Edelsten' ♀H4 | ECho LAma |
| – 'Ronald Ginns' | EPot |
| – subsp. ***sublimis*** 'Tricolor' ♀H4 | CAvo CBro CTca ECho EPfP EPot GKev LAma LRHS MBri NBir SDeJ SGar SPer |
| – 'Vardousia' **new** | LWst |
| – 'Violet Queen' | ECho LAma |
| 'Snow Bunting' ♀H4 | CAvo CBro CFFs CTca ECho EPfP EPot GKev LAma NBir SDeJ SPer SPhx WShi |
| ***speciosus*** ♀H4 | CAvo CBro CTca ITim LAma MLHP NBir SDeJ SPer WCot WShi |
| – 'Aino' | ECho LWst |
| – 'Aitchisonii' | ECho EPot GKev LAma LRHS SPhx |
| – 'Albus' ♀H4 | CAvo CBro ECho EPot GKev |
| – 'Artabir' | ECho EPot GKev LRHS SDeJ |
| – 'Cassiope' | ECho EPot GKev LAma LRHS SDeJ |
| – 'Conqueror' | CBro ECho EPot GKev LAma LRHS SDeJ WBor |
| – 'Lithuanian Autumn' | LWst |
| – 'Oxonian' | ECho EPot GKev LAma LWst SPhx |
| – subsp. ***speciosus*** | ECho EPot |
| – subsp. ***xantholaimos*** | LWst |
| × ***stellaris*** | see *C.* × *luteus* 'Stellaris' |
| ***susianus*** | see *C. angustifolius* |
| ***suterianus*** | see *C. olivieri* subsp. *olivieri* |
| ***thomasii*** BM 7589 | LWst |
| ***tommasinianus*** ♀H4 | CAvo CBro CFFs CGrW CHab CMea CTca ECho EPot LAma LLWP MBri MRav NBir SDeJ SPhx SRms WShi |
| – 'Albus' | EPot LAma WShi |
| – 'Barr's Purple' | ECho EPot GKev LAma SDeJ |
| – 'Claret' | ECho |
| – 'Lilac Beauty' | ECho EPfP EPot LAma SPer |
| – 'Pictus' | ECho EPot LAma LLHF WShi |
| – 'Roseus' | CAvo CMea ECho EPot ERCP GKev LAma NMin SPhx WCot |
| – 'Whitewell Purple' | CAvo CBro CFFs ECho EPot ERCP GKev LAma MBri NBir SDeJ SPhx WShi |
| ***tournefortii*** ♀H2-4 | CBro ECho EPot SCnR |
| * – 'Albus' | ECho |
| ***vallicola*** | LWst |

'Vanguard' ♀H4 CAvo CBro CFFs EPfP EPot LAma SBch SDeJ
***veluchensis*** ECho LWst
***veneris*** ECho
§ ***vernus*** subsp. ***albiflorus*** ECho EPot
- 'Fantasy' ECho
- 'Flower Record' GKev LAma NBir
- 'Graecus' ECho EPot LWst
- 'Grand Maître' CAvo CFFs LAma LRHS MBri SDeJ
- 'Haarlem Gem' ECho EPot
- 'King of the Striped' ECho LAma LRHS SPer
- 'Krasno Polje' **new** LWst
- 'Michael's Purple' ECho
- 'Negro Boy' EPot GKev LAma LRHS
- 'Pickwick' CAvo CFFs EPfP EPot LAma MBri NBir SDeJ WShi
§ - 'Purpureus Grandiflorus' CBro EPot SDeJ
- 'Queen of the Blues' CAvo CBro EPot WShi
- 'Remembrance' CBro EPfP EPot GKev LAma LRHS NBir SDeJ WShi
- 'Twilight' **new** EPot
- Uklin strain ECho
§ - subsp. ***vernus*** ECho
- - 'Grandiflorus' see *C. vernus* 'Purpureus Grandiflorus'
- - Heuffelianus Group EPot LWst
- - - 'Dark Eyes' LWst
- - 'Oradea' LWst
***versicolor*** ECho
- 'Picturatus' ECho EPot ERCP LAma LLHF NMin SDeJ
***vitellinus*** ECho EPot LWst
'White Triumphator' LAma
'Yalta' ECho ERCP GKev SPhx
'Yellow Mammoth' see *C.* × *luteus* 'Golden Yellow'
'Zenith' ECho EPot
'Zephyr' ♀H4 CBro ECho EPot LAma
***zonatus*** see *C. kotschyanus* subsp. *kotschyanus*

## *Croomia* (*Stemonaceae*)
***heterosepala*** WCru

## *Crotalaria* (*Papilionaceae*)
***laburnifolia*** CCCN

## *Croton* (*Euphorbiaceae*)
***yunnanensis*** **new** GKev

## *Crowea* (*Rutaceae*)
***exalata* × *saligna*** CPLG

## *Crucianella* (*Rubiaceae*)
***stylosa*** see *Phuopsis stylosa*

## *Cruciata* (*Rubiaceae*)
§ ***laevipes*** NMir

## *Crusea* (*Rubiaceae*)
***coccinea*** GEdr
- B&SWJ 10254 WCru

## *Cryptocarya* (*Lauraceae*)
***alba*** CBcs SVen

## *Cryptogramma* (*Pteridaceae*)
***crispa*** WHer WRic

## *Cryptomeria* (*Cupressaceae*)
***fortunei*** see *C. japonica* var. *sinensis*
***japonica*** ♀H4 CDul CMen CSpr CTho ELau MBlu MMuc SEND STre WEve
- Araucarioides Group EHul NLar
- 'Atawai' NLar
- 'Bandai' LBuc
- 'Bandai-sugi' ♀H4 CKen CMac CMen EHul EPfP EPot GKin LRHS MGos NHol SCoo SLim WGor
- 'Barabits Gold' MGos WEve
- 'Birodo' CKen
- 'Black Dragon' SLim
- 'Compressa' CDoC CKen ECho EHul EPfP LBee MGos SCoo SLim WGor WThu
§ - 'Cristata' CBcs CDoC CMac ECho ELan LRHS MGos MPkF NPal SCoo SLim SPoG
- 'Dacrydioides' CDoC GKin SLim
- Elegans Group CBcs CDoy CDul CMac CSBt ECho ECrN EHul ELan EPfP LAst LRHS MBri MGos MMuc NEgg NWea SBfd SCoo SEND SLim SPer SPoG WDin WFar
- 'Elegans Aurea' CBcs ECho EHul WDin WEve
- 'Elegans Compacta' ♀H4 CDoC CMac CSBt CWib ECho EHul ELan GBin LBee LRHS MAsh MBri MMuc NWea SBrd SCoo SEND SLim SPoG WEve
- 'Elegans Nana' LBee LRHS NEgg SRms WBor
- 'Elegans Viridis' ELan LRHS NEgg SCoo SLim SPer SPoG
- 'Globosa Nana' ♀H4 ECho EHul EPfP ERom LAst LBee LRHS MGos NEgg SArc SCoo SLim SPoG WFar WGor
- 'Golden Promise' LRHS MAsh NWad SCoo SLim SPer SPoG WEve WGor
- Gracilis Group CDoC
- 'Jindai-sugi' GKin NLar
- 'Karl Fuchs' SLim
- 'Kilmacurragh' CKen EHul NWea SLim
- 'Knaptonensis' (v) CDoC WEve
- 'Kohui-yatsubusa' CKen
* - 'Konijn-yatsubusa' CKen
- 'Koshyi' CKen
- 'Little Champion' CDoC CKen LRHS NLar SCoo SLim
- 'Little Diamond' CKen
- 'Littleworth Dwarf' see *C. japonica* 'Littleworth Gnom'
§ - 'Littleworth Gnom' NLar
- 'Lobbii Nana' hort. see *C. japonica* 'Nana'
§ - 'Mankichi-sugi' NHol WEve
- 'Monstrosa Nana' see *C. japonica* 'Mankichi-sugi'
- 'Mushroom' WFar
§ - 'Nana' CDoC CMac EHul EPfP WFar
- 'Osaka-tama' CKen
- 'Pipo' CKen NLar
- 'Pygmaea' MGos NHol NWad SRms
- 'Rasen' ELan
- 'Rasen-sugi' GKin IVic LBuc LRHS MGos NLar SCoo SLim SMad SPoG
- 'Rein's Dense Jade' SLim
- 'Sekkan-sugi' CBcs CCVN CDoC CDul CMac ECho EHul EPfP ESwi GBin GKin IArd LAst LBee LRHS MAsh MGos NLar SBfd SCoo SLim SPoG WBor WEve WFar
- 'Sekka-sugi' see *C. japonica* 'Cristata'
§ - var. ***sinensis*** CMCN
* - - 'Vilmoriniana Compacta' MAsh
§ - 'Spiralis' CDoC CKen CMac ECho EHul ELan EPfP GKin LAst LBee LRHS MAsh

MGos NEgg NHol NPal NWad SCoo SLim SPer SPoG WEve WFar
§ - 'Spiraliter Falcata' CDoC NLar
§ - 'Tansu' CDoC CKen MGos NHol
- 'Tenzan-sugi' CDoC CKen MGos NWad SLim WThu
- 'Tilford Cream' MAsh
- 'Tilford Gold' ECho EHul EPot MGos NBlu NEgg NHol WEve WFar WGor
- 'Toda' CKen
- 'Top Gold' (v) **new** NLar
- 'Vilmorin Gold' CKen MGos NHol WFar
- 'Vilmoriniana' ♀H4 CDoC CKen CMen CTri ECho EHul EPfP EPla GKin LBee MGos NBlu NEgg NHol SBrd SCoo SLim SPer SPoG WDin WEve WFar WMoo
- 'Winter Bronze' CKen
- 'Yatsubusa' see *C. japonica* 'Tansu'
- 'Yore-sugi' see *C. japonica* 'Spiralis', 'Spiraliter Falcata'
- 'Yoshino' CKen LRHS SLim
***sinensis*** see *C. japonica* var. *sinensis*

## *Cryptostegia* (*Apocynaceae*)

***grandiflora*** CCCN

## *Cryptotaenia* (*Apiaceae*)

***japonica*** CHby CPou MHer MNHC WHer WJek
- f. ***atropurpurea*** CSpe CSpr EBee EHoe EWTr GGar LEdu LRHS MLLN MNrw SDix SPhx WFar WPtf

## *Ctenanthe* (*Marantaceae*)

***lubbersiana*** ♀H1 XBlo
§ ***oppenheimiana*** XBlo

## *Ctenitis* (*Dryopteridaceae*)

***subglandulosa*** WRic

## *Cucubalus* (*Caryophyllaceae*)

***baccifer*** EWld NLar WPer

## *Cudrania* see *Maclura*

## cumin see *Cuminum cyminum*

## *Cuminum* (*Apiaceae*)

***cyminum*** CArn ELau MNHC SIde SVic

## *Cunninghamia* (*Cupressaceae*)

***konishii*** CPLG
- 'Coolyns Compact' **new** WThu
§ ***lanceolata*** CBcs CDTJ CDoC CDul CGHE CKen CMCN CMac CTho EPfP EPla GKin IArd LRHS MBlu NMun SBfd SCoo SLim SMad SSpi SSta STre WBor WEve WPGP
- 'Glauca' CPLG CTho IVic WPGP
- 'Grounded' STre
- 'Little Leo' CKen LRHS
***sinensis*** see *C. lanceolata*
***unicaniculata*** see *C. lanceolata*

## *Cunonia* (*Cunoniaceae*)

***capensis*** CPLG

## *Cuphea* (*Lythraceae*)

***caeciliae*** SGar WWlt
* ***compacta*** LAst
***cyanea*** CMHG SDix SUsu WWlt
'Firecracker' NPri
***hyssopifolia*** ♀H1 CHll EShb SBfd SWvt
- 'Alba' CCCN SBfd SWvt
- pink-flowered CCCN SBfd
- red-flowered CCCN
- 'Rosea' SEND SWvt
§ ***ignea*** ♀H1 EShb EWld MOWG SVen SVic WWlt
§ ***llavea*** 'Georgia Scarlet' CCCN LSou WWlt
- 'Tiny Mice' see *C. llavea* 'Georgia Scarlet'
I ***macrophylla*** hort. CHll WWlt
***maculata*** **new** CCCN
***platycentra*** see *C. ignea*
'Torpedo' LAst LSou
'Vienco Lavender' LAst LSou
***viscosissima*** CSpe MCot

## × *Cupressocyparis* see × *Cuprocyparis*

## *Cupressus* (*Cupressaceae*)

***arizonica*** var. ***arizonica*** MREP
- - 'Arctic' CDoC SLim
- var. ***glabra*** 'Angaston' SLim
- - 'Aurea' CMac ECho EHul LRHS MAsh MGos NPCo SGol SLim WBor WFar
- - 'Blue Ice' ♀H3 CBcs CDoC CDul CMac CTho ECho EHul LRHS MAsh MGos NPCo SCoo SLim SPer SPoG SWvt WFar
- - 'Compacta' CKen
- - 'Conica' CKen
I - - 'Fastigiata' CCVT CDoC ECrN EHul EPfP LMaj SBfd
- - 'Glauca' ECho EPfP MBlu
* - - 'Lutea' ECho SPoG
- var. ***nevadensis*** GAuc
- 'Pyramidalis' ♀H3 ECrN EPfP MMuc SEND SGol
***atlantica*** LRHS SLim
***cashmeriana*** ♀H2 CBcs CDTJ CDoC CTho ELan IGor LRHS NPCo SLim WFar
§ ***funebris*** IDee
***lusitanica*** 'Brice's Weeping' CKen LRHS SLim
- 'Glauca Pendula' CDoC CKen
- 'Pygmy' CKen
***macrocarpa*** CBcs CCVT CDoC CDul CTho EHul SEND
- 'Compacta' CKen
- 'Conybearii Aurea' NPCo
- 'Gold Spread' EHul LRHS SCoo SLim WFar
- 'Goldcrest' ♀H3 CBcs CCVT CDoC CDul CMac ECrN EHul ELan LBee LRHS MBri MGos NBir NBlu NPri SBfd SBrd SEWo SGol SLim SPer SPoG STre SWvt WCFE WDin WEve WFar
- 'Golden Cone' CKen NPCo
- 'Golden Pillar' ♀H3 CDoC CMac EHul SWvt WDin WFar
- 'Golden Spire' WFar
- 'Greenstead Magnificent' LRHS SCoo SLim
- 'Horizontalis Aurea' EHul
- 'Lohbrunner' CKen
- 'Lutea' CDoC NPCo WFar
I - 'Pendula' SLim
- 'Pygmaea' CKen
- 'Sulphur Cushion' CKen
- 'Wilma' CSBt ECho EHul LAst LBee LRHS MAsh MGos NBlu NEgg SBfd SCoo SGol SLim SPoG SWvt
- 'Woking' CKen

| | |
|---|---|
| ***sempervirens*** | CDul CMCN EAmu EHul ELan ERom LRHS MAsh NPri SBfd SPlb STrG WEve WFar |
| - 'Agrimed' | LMaj |
| - 'Bolgheri' | SBig |
| - 'Garda' | CDoC |
| - 'Green Pencil' | CKen |
| - 'Pyramidalis' | see *C. sempervirens* Stricta Group |
| - var. ***sempervirens*** | see *C. sempervirens* Stricta Group |
| § - Stricta Group ♀H3 | CBcs CCVT CDul CKen CMCN CTho EHul EPfP EWTr MREP NLar SArc SBfd SEND SEWo SGol WCFE WEve |
| - 'Swane's Gold' | CBcs CDoC CDul CKen ECho EHul EPfP LRHS NPCo SCoo SLim SPoG WCFE WEve WFar |
| - 'Totem Pole' | CCVT CKen CSBt CTri ECho EHul EPfP LBee LRHS MGos NEgg SCoo SEND SLim SPer SPoG SWvt WEve |

## × *Cuprocyparis* (*Cupressaceae*)

| | |
|---|---|
| § ***leylandii*** ♀H4 | CBcs CCVT CChe CDoC CDul CMac CTri EHul EPfP LBuc LSRN MAsh MBri MGos MMuc NEgg NWea SBfd SBrd SGol SLim SPer SPoG SWvt WDin WEve WHar WMou |
| I - '2001' | CCVT CDoC SGol SLim WMou |
| § - 'Castlewellan' | Widely available |
| - Excalibur Gold = 'Drabb'PBR new | CDoC |
| - 'Ferngold' new | MAsh |
| - 'Galway Gold' | see × *C. leylandii* 'Castlewellan' |
| - 'Gold Rider' ♀H4 | CBod CDoC EHul LBuc LTen MAsh MGos MMuc NEgg NWea SCoo SEND SPer SPoG SWvt WDin WEve WHar |
| § - 'Harlequin' (v) | CMac SEND SWvt |
| - 'Herculea' | CDoC |
| - 'Leighton Green' | WMou |
| - 'Naylor's Blue' | CMac |
| - 'Olive's Green' | EHul SWvt |
| - 'Robinson's Gold' ♀H4 | CMac EHul GQui LRHS MMuc NWea SLim WFar WMou |
| - 'Silver Dust' (v) | WFar |
| - 'Variegata' | see × *C. leylandii* 'Harlequin' |
| - 'Winter Sun' | WCFE |
| ***ovensii*** | EHul |

## *Curculigo* (*Hypoxidaceae*)

| | |
|---|---|
| ***capitulata*** | XBlo |
| ***crassifolia*** B&SWJ 2318 | WCru |

## *Curcuma* ✿ (*Zingiberaceae*)

| | |
|---|---|
| ***alismatifolia*** | EPfP |
| ***longa*** | CArn |
| ***roscoeana*** | LAma |
| ***zedoaria*** | LAma |
| - 'Bicolor Wonder' | CCCN |
| - 'Pink Wonder' | CCCN |
| - 'White Wonder' | CCCN |

## *Curtonus* see *Crocosmia*

## *Cussonia* (*Araliaceae*)

| | |
|---|---|
| ***paniculata*** | CDTJ CWGN EAmu EShb SPad WCot |
| ***spicata*** | CDTJ |

## custard apple see *Annona cherimola*

## *Cyananthus* (*Campanulaceae*)

| | |
|---|---|
| SDR 5914 | GKev |
| ***integer*** misapplied | see *C. microphyllus* |
| ***lobatus*** ♀H4 | GMaP |
| - 'Albus' | EPot EWes GLam WAbe |
| - dark | WAbe |
| - giant | EPot GEdr GLam NHar |
| - 'Midnight' | GEdr |
| ***lobatus × microphyllus*** | EPot NWCA WAbe |
| § ***microphyllus*** ♀H4 | EPot GEdr GJos GLam GMaP IFoB NSla WAbe |
| ***sherriffii*** | EPot GJos GLam IFoB WAbe WFar |
| ***spathulifolius*** | WAbe |

## *Cyanotis* (*Commelinaceae*)

| | |
|---|---|
| ***somaliensis*** ♀H1 | EShb |

## *Cyathea* (*Cyatheaceae*)

| | |
|---|---|
| ***australis*** | CBty CDTJ CKel EAmu ESwi ETod IDee LPal LRHS MGos NPal WPGP WRic |
| ***brownii*** | WRic |
| ***cooperi*** | CDTJ CKel EAmu EFtx ESwi GBin LRHS WFib WRic |
| * - 'Brentwood' | WRic |
| ***cunninghamii*** | EAmu EFtx |
| ***dealbata*** | CBcs CDTJ CKel CTrC EAmu LPal MGos WRic |
| ***dregei*** | SPlb WRic |
| ***incisoserrata*** | WRic |
| ***medullaris*** | CKel CTrC EAmu EFtx GBin LRHS MGos WRic |
| ***milnei*** | CDTJ WRic |
| ***robusta*** | WRic |
| ***smithii*** | CBcs CDTJ CKel CTrC EAmu WRic |
| ***tomentosissima*** | CDTJ CKel EFtx WRic |

## *Cyathodes* (*Ericaceae*)

| | |
|---|---|
| ***colensoi*** | see *Leucopogon colensoi* |
| ***empetrifolia*** | see *Androstoma empetrifolia* |
| ***fraseri*** | see *Leucopogon fraseri* |
| ***juniperina*** | see *Leptecophylla juniperina* |
| ***parviflora*** | see *Leucopogon parviflorus* |
| ***parvifolia*** | see *Leptecophylla juniperina* subsp. *parvifolia* |

## *Cybistetes* (*Amaryllidaceae*)

| | |
|---|---|
| ***longifolia*** | WCot |

## *Cycas* (*Cycadaceae*)

| | |
|---|---|
| ***circinalis*** | EAmu LPal |
| ***media*** | LPal SBst |
| ***panzhihuaensis*** | CBrP LPal SPlb |
| ***revoluta*** ♀H1 | CAbb CBrP CCCN CDoC CHEx CTrC EAmu EPfP LPal MBri MREP NLar SArc SBfd SBst SChr SEND SMad STrG WCot XBlo |
| ***revoluta × taitungensis*** | CBrP |
| § ***rumphii*** | CBrP LPal |
| ***taitungensis*** | CBrP |
| ***thouarsii*** | see *C. rumphii* |

## *Cyclamen* ✿ (*Primulaceae*)

| | |
|---|---|
| ***africanum*** | CBro ECho EJWh GKev ITim LAma LRHS LWst MAsh NWCA STil WCot |
| ***africanum × hederifolium*** | CWCL ECho |
| § ***alpinum*** | CBro ECho EJWh EPot GKev LAma LLHF LRHS LWst MAsh SDeJ STil |

| | |
|---|---|
| - 'Nettleton White' **new** | MAsh |
| ***balearicum*** | CBro ECho EJWh LAma LRHS LWst MAsh NMen STil |
| ***cilicium*** ♀H2-4 | CBro ECho EJWh EPot ERCP ITim LAma LRHS LWst MAsh MHer NMen STil WFar WHoo WIvy WPat WShi |
| - f. ***album*** | CBro ECho EJWh LAma LRHS LWst MAsh NMen STil WCot |
| - patterned-leaved | ECho NBir |
| ***colchicum*** | ECho MAsh STil |
| § ***coum*** ♀H4 | Widely available |
| - var. ***abchasicum*** | see *C. coum* subsp. *caucasicum* |
| § - subsp. ***caucasicum*** | GKev LWst MAsh STil |
| - subsp. ***coum*** | CBro ECho MAsh |
| - - f. ***albissimum*** 'George Bisson' | MAsh |
| - - - 'Golan Heights' | MAsh STil WIvy |
| - - f. ***coum*** Nymans Group | MAsh WFar |
| - - - Pewter Group ♀H2-4 | CPMA ECGP ECho GKev MAsh WFar WIvy |
| - - - - bicoloured | EJWh |
| - - - - 'Blush' | CPMA STil |
| - - - - 'Maurice Dryden' | CBro CLAP CPMA ECGP ECho LAma LRHS LWst MAsh STil WHoo |
| - - - - red-flowered | LAma WPat |
| - - - - 'Tilebarn Elizabeth' | GEdr MAsh NBir STil WHoo |
| - - - - white-flowered | MAsh |
| - - - plain-leaved, red-flowered | STil |
| - - - 'Roseum' | CAvo STil |
| - - - Silver Group | CBro CPMA ECho GEdr LHop LRHS LWst NPnk NRya WCot WFar WHoo |
| - - - - red-flowered | CAvo EPot STil WHoo |
| - - magenta-flowered | CWCL WHoo |
| - - f. ***pallidum*** 'Album' | CAvo CPMA ECho EPot GKev LAma LWst MAsh NMen SDeJ SMrm SPer STil WHoo WPat |
| - - - 'Marbled Moon' | STil |
| - dark pink-flowered | CAvo CLAP ECho WHoo |
| - hybrid | ERCP |
| - marble-leaved | ECho LHop WHoo |
| - plain-leaved | CLAP |
| - red-flowered | CLAP ECho NWad |
| I - 'Rubrum' | GKev LWst |
| - 'Tilebarn Graham' | MAsh |
| ***creticum*** | ECho EJWh MAsh STil |
| ***cyprium*** | CBro ECho EJWh LRHS LWst MAsh STil |
| - 'E.S.' | ECho MAsh STil WFar |
| - 'Galaxy' **new** | MAsh |
| × ***drydeniae*** | CPMA |
| ***elegans*** | EJWh STil |
| ***europaeum*** | see *C. purpurascens* |
| ***fatrense*** | see *C. purpurascens* subsp. *purpurascens* from Fatra, Slovakia |
| ***graecum*** | CBro ECho EJWh LLHF LRHS MAsh NMen STil WCot WIvy WThu |
| - subsp. ***anatolicum*** | MAsh STil |
| - subsp. ***candicum*** | EPot MAsh STil |
| - subsp. ***graecum*** f. ***album*** | CBro ECho EJWh LRHS LWst MAsh STil |
| - - f. ***graecum*** 'Glyfada' | MAsh STil |
| § ***hederifolium*** ♀H4 | Widely available |
| - SL 175/1 | WCot XLum |
| - arrow-head | CLAP ECho |
| - var. ***confusum*** | MAsh STil WCot |
| - var. ***hederifolium*** f. ***albiflorum*** | CAvo CBro CSam CTri ECho EPot GKev LAma LRHS NMen NMyG NPnk NWad SDeJ SPhx STil WCot WHoo WPat WPnP XLum |
| - - - 'Album' | CWCL MAsh |
| § - - - (Bowles's Apollo Group) 'Artemis' | MAsh STil |
| - - - - 'White Bowles's Apollo' | see *C. hederifolium* var. *hederifolium* f. *albiflorum* (Bowles's Apollo Group) 'Artemis' |
| - - - 'Daley Thompson' | WCot |
| - - - 'Linnett Stargazer' | WCot |
| - - - 'Nettleton Silver' | see *C. hederifolium* var. *hederifolium* f. *albiflorum* 'White Cloud' |
| - - - 'Perlenteppich' | GMaP |
| - - - 'Tilebarn Helena' | STil |
| § - - - 'White Cloud' | CLAP EBla ECho MAsh STil WCot WHoo WIvy |
| - - f. ***hederifolium*** Bowles's Apollo Group | CHid CLAP ECGP MAsh STil |
| - - - 'Fairy Rings' | MAsh |
| - - - 'Ruby Glow' | LRHS MAsh NBir WCot WPat WThu |
| - - - 'Silver Cloud' | CBro CHid CLAP MAsh NBir STil WCot WHoo WIvy WPat |
| - - - 'Silver Shield' | MAsh |
| - - - 'Stargazer' | MAsh WCot |
| - - 'Tilebarn Silver Arrow' | CPMA MAsh STil |
| - long-leaved | CPMA |
| - 'Pewter Mist' | LAma |
| - 'Red Sky' **new** | NWad |
| - 'Rose Pearls' | SRot |
| - 'San Marino Silver' | GEdr |
| - scented | STil |
| - Silver-leaved Group | CAvo CPMA EBla ECho EPot ITim LHop MAsh SRot STil WFar |
| - - 'Silver Leaf Pink' **new** | NWad |
| - - 'Silver Leaf White' **new** | NWad |
| - 'Turkish Delight' | EDAr |
| ***ibericum*** | see *C. coum* subsp. *caucasicum* |
| ***intaminatum*** | CBro ECho EJWh LAma LRHS LWst MAsh NMen STil WIvy |
| - patterned-leaved | EJWh MAsh STil |
| - pink-flowered | MAsh NMen STil |
| - plain-leaved | MAsh STil WThu |
| ***latifolium*** | see *C. persicum* |
| ***libanoticum*** | CBro ECho EJWh LAma LRHS LWst MAsh NMen STil WFar |
| ***mirabile*** ♀H2-3 | CBro ECho EJWh EPot GKev LAma LLHF LRHS LWst MAsh NMen SDeJ STil WIvy WThu |
| - f. ***mirabile*** 'Tilebarn Anne' | MAsh STil |
| - - 'Tilebarn Nicholas' | ECho MAsh STil |
| - f. ***niveum*** | EJWh |
| - - 'Tilebarn Jan' | CPMA ECho MAsh STil |
| ***neapolitanum*** | see *C. hederifolium* |
| ***orbiculatum*** | see *C. coum* |
| ***parviflorum*** | EJWh MAsh STil |
| § ***persicum*** | CBro CWCL ECho EJWh LRHS MAsh STil |
| - CSE 90560 | STil |
| - var. ***persicum*** f. ***puniceum*** from Lebanon | STil |
| - - - 'Tilebarn Karpathos' | STil |
| - white-flowered | ECho MAsh |
| ***pseudibericum*** ♀H2-3 | CBro ECho EJWh EPot GKev LAma LHop LLHF LRHS LWst MAsh NMen SDeJ STil WThu |
| - AC&W 664 | ITim |
| - f. ***roseum*** | MAsh NMen STil |

| | | |
|---|---|---|
| § | ***purpurascens*** ♀H4 | CBro ECho EJWh LLHF MAsh NMen NWCA STil WHoo WIvy WPat |
| | - var. ***fatrense*** | see *C. purpurascens* subsp. *purpurascens* from Fatra, Slovakia |
| | - 'Lake Garda' | MAsh WPGP |
| § | - subsp. ***purpurascens*** from Fatra, Slovakia | STil |
| | - silver-leaved | STil |
| | ***repandum*** | CAvo CBro ECho EJWh LAma LRHS LWst MAsh NMen STil WHer |
| | - 'Pelops' misapplied | see *C. rhodium* subsp. *peloponnesiacum* |
| | - subsp. ***repandum*** f. ***album*** | CLAP EJWh MAsh STil |
| | ***rhodium*** ♀H2-3 | EJWh GKev LWst MAsh WCot |
| § | - subsp. ***peloponnesiacum*** | ECGP STil |
| | - - white-flowered | STil |
| | - subsp. ***rhodium*** | MAsh STil |
| | - subsp. ***vividum*** | MAsh STil |
| | ***rohlfsianum*** | CBro ECho EJWh LRHS MAsh STil WThu |
| | × ***saundersiae*** | EJWh MAsh STil |
| | × ***schwarzii*** new | MAsh |
| | ***trochopteranthum*** | see *C. alpinum* |
| | × ***wellensiekii*** | MAsh STil |

## *Cyclea* (*Menispermaceae*)

| | | |
|---|---|---|
| | ***polypetala*** KWJ 12157 | WCru |

## *Cyclosorus* (*Thelypteridaceae*)

| | | |
|---|---|---|
| | ***esquirolii*** | WRic |
| | ***tottoides*** | WRic |

## *Cydonia* ✿ (*Rosaceae*)

| | | |
|---|---|---|
| | ***japonica*** | see *Chaenomeles speciosa* |
| | ***oblonga*** (F) | ECrN GKev LMaj |
| | - 'Agvambari' (F) | SKee |
| | - 'Aromatnaya' (F) | ERea |
| | - 'Champion' (F) | CAgr CBcs ECrN ERea GTwe LBuc MCoo NEgg NLar SKee SVic WHar |
| | - 'Early Prolific' (F) | ECrN LAst MMuc SEND |
| | - 'Ekmek' (F) | SKee |
| | - 'Isfahan' (F) | SKee |
| | - 'Krymsk' (F) | CAgr |
| | - 'Leskovac' (F) | CAgr ERea NLar |
| § | - 'Lusitanica' (F) | CAgr ECrN ERea GTwe MCoo NLar SKee SPer WHar |
| | - 'Meech's Prolific' (F) | CAgr CDul CLnd CTho CTri ECrN EMil EPom ERea GTwe LAst MAsh MBlu MBri MGos MRav MWat NLar SBfd SDea SEWo SFam SKee SLim SPer SPoG WHar WWct |
| | - pear-shaped (F) | ECrN MCoo NEgg SPer |
| | - Portugal | see *C. oblonga* 'Lusitanica' |
| | - 'Rea's Mammoth' (F) | NLar |
| | - 'Serbian Gold' (F) | CTho GTwe LRHS MBri WHar |
| | - 'Shams' (F) | SKee |
| | - 'Sobu' (F) | SKee |
| | - 'Vranja' (F) ♀H4 | Widely available |

## *Cymbalaria* (*Plantaginaceae*)

| | | |
|---|---|---|
| | ***aequitriloba*** 'Alba' | GAbr GGar |
| § | ***hepaticifolia*** | WPer |
| § | ***muralis*** | ECho ECtt LBMP MHer MSCN NPri WGor XLum |
| | - 'Albiflora' | see *C. muralis* 'Pallidior' |
| | - 'Kenilworth White' | WMoo |
| | - 'Nana Alba' | NPri SPhx WPer |
| § | - 'Pallidior' | ECho MAsh |
| § | ***pallida*** | CMea CPBP MMuc NSla SBch SEND SPlb WMoo WPer |
| | - 'Alba' | EWTr SEND |
| § | ***pilosa*** | ECtt MAsh NLar |

## *Cymbopogon* (*Poaceae*)

| | | |
|---|---|---|
| | ***citratus*** | CArn CBod CCCN EGHP ERea GPoy MNHC SBfd SHDw SIde SVic WJek |
| | ***flexuosus*** | CCCN ELau MHer WJek |
| | ***martini*** | CArn GPoy |
| | ***nardus*** | CArn GPoy |

## *Cymophyllus* (*Cyperaceae*)

| | | |
|---|---|---|
| § | ***fraserianus*** | CDes CHEx GBin |

## *Cynanchum* (*Apocynaceae*)

| | | |
|---|---|---|
| | ***acuminatifolium*** | GCal |
| | ***ascyrifolium*** | EBee |

## *Cynara* (*Asteraceae*)

| | | |
|---|---|---|
| § | ***baetica*** subsp. ***maroccana*** | WHil |
| | ***cardunculus*** ♀H3-4 | Widely available |
| | - ACL 380/78 | SWat |
| I | - 'Cardy' | CBot EBee LRHS NCGa SWat |
| I | - 'Florist Cardy' | IGor NLar |
| | - 'Gobbo di Nizza' | ELau ERea WHer |
| | - 'Porto Spineless' new | LEdu |
| § | - Scolymus Group | CBcs CHEx CWan EBee EHoe ERea EWes GPoy IGor ILis LEdu LRHS LSRN MBri MMuc MNHC MRav NPri SBfd SEND SMrm SPav SPer SPhx SPoG WFar WHer WHoo WWEG |
| | - - 'Carciofo Violetto Precoce' | WHer |
| | - - 'Gigante di Romagna' | WHer |
| | - - 'Gros Camus de Bretagne' | MAvo WCot |
| | - - 'Gros Vert de Lâon' | CBcs ECha ELan ELau ERea WCot |
| | - - 'Imperial Star' | ELau ERea LEdu |
| | - - 'Large Green' | NLar |
| | - - 'Monica Lynden-Bell' | WCot |
| | - - 'Purple Globe' | CArn CPrp ELau SMrm |
| | - - 'Romanesco' | ELau ERea SVic |
| | - - 'Vert Globe' | CBod CBot CHar CSBt CSev ELau ERea IFoB LEdu MWat NPer SMrm SVic SWal |
| | - - 'Violet de Provence' | CSBt ELau ERea SWal |
| | - - 'Violetto di Chioggia' | CSev ELau ERea LEdu WHer |
| | ***hystrix*** misapplied | see *C. baetica* subsp. *maroccana* |
| | ***scolymus*** | see *C. cardunculus* Scolymus Group |

## *Cynodon* (*Poaceae*)

| | | |
|---|---|---|
| | ***aethiopicus*** | EBee EHoe GBin LEdu SBfd SGar SHDw SWal WCot |

## *Cynoglossum* (*Boraginaceae*)

| | | |
|---|---|---|
| | ***dioscoridis*** | CBot SPhx |
| | ***nervosum*** | CBot EBee ELan EPfP LAst LHop LRHS MLHP MMuc MRav NChi NEgg SEND SPer SPhx SWat WCot WFar WWEG |
| | ***officinale*** | CArn MHer WHer WSFF |

## *Cynosurus* (*Poaceae*)

| | | |
|---|---|---|
| | ***cristatus*** | CHab NMir |
| | - viviparous | CNat |

## *Cypella* (Iridaceae)

***aquatilis*** LLWG
***herbertii*** CDes CPom EDif
***plumbea*** see *Phalocallis coelestis*

## *Cyperus* (Cyperaceae)

§ ***albostriatus*** CCCN CHEx EShb
***alternifolius*** misapplied see *C. involucratus*
***alternifolius*** L. CBen EAmu LPBA MSKA WMAq
- 'Compactus' see *C. involucratus* 'Nanus'
'Chira' EKen MBNS NWsh WGwG
***diffusus*** misapplied see *C. albostriatus*
§ ***eragrostis*** CArn CPom EHoe GCal MCCP MWts NSti SDix SPlb SWat WAbb WGrn WMAq WMoo WTcb
***esculentus*** CArn
***fuscus*** EKen MDKP WFar WHal WMoo WTcb
***glaber*** MBNS MMuc
***haspan*** misapplied see *C. papyrus* 'Nanus'
***haspan*** L. MSKA
§ ***involucratus*** ♀H1 CHEx EBak EHon EShb LPBA MSKA MWts SArc SEND SMad SWat WFar WMnd WMoo
- 'Gracilis' EBak
§ - 'Nanus' EShb LPBA
***longus*** CBen CWat EHoe EHon EPPr EWil GCal LPBA MMuc MWts NPer NSti NWsh SEND SWal SWat WFar WHal WMAq WPnP XLum
***papyrus*** ♀H1 CDTJ CHEx CKno EAmu ERea MSKA SArc SBig SEND XBlo
§ - 'Nanus' ♀H1 CHEx LPal XBlo
***prolifer*** LLWG
***rotundus*** MCCP
***ustulatus*** CKno MDKP
***vegetus*** see *C. eragrostis*
'Zumila' EShb

## *Cyphanthera* (Solanaceae)

***tasmanica*** new ECou

## *Cyphomandra* see *Solanum*

## *Cypripedium* (Orchidaceae)

***acaule*** LWst
**Aki gx** GEdr LWst NLAp XFro
- 'Pastel' GEdr LWst NLAp XFro
× ***alaskanum*** new NLAp
× ***andrewsii*** LWst
**Axel gx** NLAp
× ***barbeyi*** see *C.* × *ventricosum*
***calceolus*** CFir LWst NLAp
- from Kurilen Island NLAp
- from Lake Baikal NLAp
***calceolus*** × ***macranthos*** f. ***albiflorum*** NLAp
***californicum*** GEdr NLAp
× ***columbianum*** LWst NLAp
***corrugatum*** see *C. tibeticum*
***debile*** GEdr LWst
**Dietrich gx** GEdr LWst NLAp
**Emil gx** GEdr LWst NLAp XFro
***fargesii*** GEdr
***fasciolatum*** GEdr LWst NLAp
***fasciolatum*** × ***flavum*** NLAp
***flavum*** GBin GEdr NLAp
- white-flowered GEdr
- white-flowered × ***reginae*** GEdr
- yellow-flowered GEdr
**Florence gx** new NLAp
***formosanum*** GEdr LAma LWst NLAp SKHP
***franchetii*** GEdr
***franchetii*** × ***macranthos*** LWst
***franchetii*** × ***parviflorum*** LWst
**Gisela gx** GEdr LAma LWst NLAp XFro
- 'Pastel' GEdr LWst NLAp
- 'Yellow' LAma
***guttatum*** GEdr LWst
- var. ***yatabeanum*** see *C. yatabeanum*
**Hank Small gx** GEdr LWst NLAp XFro
**Hans Erni gx** NLAp
***henryi*** GEdr LAma NLAp
***himalaicum*** NLAp
**Inge gx** GEdr LWst NLAp XFro
**Ingrid gx** GEdr LWst XFro
**Irene gx** new LWst
***japonicum*** GBin GEdr LWst NLAp
***kentuckiense*** CCCN CFir GEdr LWst NLAp
**Kristi Lyn gx** GEdr LWst XFro
***lichiangense*** GEdr
***lichiangense*** × ***reginae*** GEdr
***macranthos*** GEdr LWst NLAp
- from Lake Baikal NLAp
- f. ***albiflorum*** NLAp
- var. ***hotei-atsumorianum*** × ***tibeticum*** NLAp
**Maria gx** GEdr LWst NLAp XFro
**Michael gx** GEdr LWst XFro
**Michael Pastel gx** new NLAp
***montanum*** LWst
***parviflorum*** NLAp
- var. ***makasin*** NLAp
§ - var. ***pubescens*** GBin GEdr LAma LWst NLAp
- var. ***pubescens*** × ***reginae*** GEdr
**Paul gx** new LWst XFro
**Philipp gx** GEdr LWst XFro
***plectrochilum*** GEdr
**Princess gx** NLAp
***pubescens*** see *C. parviflorum* var. *pubescens*
**Rascal gx** GEdr LWst
***reginae*** CCCN EBee EWes GEdr GKev LAma LRHS NLAp SKHP
- f. ***album*** GEdr LWst
- 'Red Pouch' GEdr
***reginae*** × **Tilman gx** GEdr
**Renate gx** pastel-flowered new LWst XFro
**Sabine gx** GEdr LWst NLAp XFro
- pastel-flowered GEdr LWst XFro
**Sebastian gx** GEdr LWst NLAp XFro
***segawae*** LAma
'Sunny' new NLAp
§ ***tibeticum*** NLAp
**Ulla Silkens gx** GEdr LAma LWst NLAp XFro
**Ursel gx** GEdr LWst XFro
§ × ***ventricosum*** GEdr LWst NLAp XFro
- dark-flowered LWst
- 'Pastel' LWst NLAp XFro
- red-flowered NLAp
- white-flowered GEdr LWst
**Victoria gx** GEdr LWst NLAp XFro
§ ***yatabeanum*** GEdr
***yunnanense*** GEdr

## *Cyrilla* (Cyrillaceae)

***racemiflora*** CMac

## *Cyrtanthus* (Amaryllidaceae)

sp. WHil

| | |
|---|---|
| from high altitude | WCot |
| 'Alaska' | ECho |
| § ***brachyscyphus*** | ECho EShb GGar |
| ***breviflorus*** | EBee ECho NMen WHil WPGP |
| 'Edwina' | CCCN ECho |
| § ***elatus*** ♀H1 | CPne ECho EWll LAma LEdu MCCP SEND SMrm WCot |
| - 'Cream Beauty' | ECho |
| - 'Pink Diamond' | ECho WCot |
| 'Elizabeth' | CCCN ECho |
| ***falcatus*** ♀H1 | CLak |
| ***mackenii*** | CPne ECho EShb WPGP |
| - var. ***cooperi*** | CAby CPne |
| - cream-white-flowered | CCCN |
| - 'Himalayan Pink' | CCCN |
| - red-flowered | CCCN |
| ***montanus*** | EBee ECho WCot |
| ***obliquus*** | WCot |
| ***parviflorus*** | see *C. brachyscyphus* |
| ***purpureus*** | see *C. elatus* |
| ***rhodesianus*** | GCal |
| ***sanguineus*** | ECho WCot |
| ***smithiae*** | ECho |
| ***speciosus*** | see *C. elatus* |

## Cyrtomium (*Dryopteridaceae*)

| | |
|---|---|
| § ***caryotideum*** | CBty CLAP ISha WRic WWEG |
| § ***falcatum*** ♀H3 | CBty CFir CHEx CHVG CLAP CMHG CTrC EBee ELan EPfP EWTr GCal GMaP IBal IVic LRHS NOrc SBfd SEND SPoG SRms SRot WCot WFar WMoo WRic XLum |
| - 'Rochfordianum' | CBcs CBty CCCN ISha LRHS LTen WFib WRic |
| § ***fortunei*** ♀H4 | CAby CHid CLAP EBee EFer ELan ELon EPfP IDee LRHS LTen MGos MRav NBid NGdn SBfd SPad SPer SPoG SRms WFib WMoo WPat WPnP WRic WWEG |
| - var. ***clivicola*** | CBty CEnt CKel CPrp CWCL EBee EPfP EShb GCal ISha LRHS LTen MGos MRav NLar SBfd SPad WPat WRic |
| ***hookerianum*** | WRic |
| ***macrophyllum*** | CLAP GLin |

## Cystopteris ✿ (*Woodsiaceae*)

| | |
|---|---|
| ***bulbifera*** | CLAP MNFA |
| ***diaphana*** | WRic |
| ***dickieana*** | CLAP GBin SRms WCot WFib WRic |
| ***fragilis*** | EBee ECha EFer SRms WFib |
| - from Chile | WRic |
| ***moupinensis*** | WRic |
| - B&SWJ 6767 | WCru |
| ***tennesseensis*** | WRic |

## Cytisus (*Papilionaceae*)

| | |
|---|---|
| ***albus*** misapplied | see *C. multiflorus* |
| ***albus*** Hacq. | see *Chamaecytisus albus* (Hacq.) Rothm. |
| 'Amber Elf'[PBR] | MBri SRms |
| 'Andreanus' | see *C. scoparius* f. *andreanus* |
| 'Apricot Gem' | LRHS NLar WFar |
| ***battandieri*** ♀H4 | Widely available |
| - 'Yellow Tail' ♀H4 | CDul CEnd EBee EPfP LRHS MBri SKHP |
| × ***beanii*** ♀H4 | CDul EBee ELan EPfP LRHS MAsh SLon SRms WDin WFar |
| 'Boskoop Glory' | NLar |
| 'Boskoop Ruby' ♀H4 | CDoC CSBt EPfP GGar LBMP LRHS LSRN MAsh MNHC NEgg NPri SBfd SPer SWvt WBor WFar WHar |
| 'Burkwoodii' ♀H4 | CBcs CDoC CDul EBee ELan EPfP EWTr LAst LRHS LSRN MRav MSwo MWat NEgg NHol SBfd SPoG WFar |
| ***canariensis*** | see *Genista canariensis* |
| 'Compact Crimson' | CDoC LRHS SBfd |
| § ***decumbens*** | MAsh |
| 'Donard Gem' | CDoC LRHS SBfd |
| 'Dorothy Walpole' | WFar |
| 'Firefly' | CBcs CMac NBro |
| 'Golden Cascade' | CBcs CDoC CWCL EBee ELan LBMP LRHS NEgg SBfd SLim |
| 'Golden Sunlight' | CSBt EBee EPfP MSwo |
| 'Golden Tears' **new** | NPri |
| 'Goldfinch' | CChe CDoC CSBt CWCL EBee ELan LRHS MBri MSwo NLar SPad SWal |
| ***hirsutus*** | see *Chamaecytisus hirsutus* |
| 'Hollandia' ♀H4 | CBcs CDoC CSBt CWCL EBee EPfP EWTr GAbr LBMP MAsh MGos MMuc MRav NBro NHol SEND SGol SPer WDin WFar |
| × ***kewensis*** ♀H4 | CDul CMac EBee ELan EPfP LRHS MAsh MGos MRav NHol NWea SPer SRms WDin |
| - 'Niki' | EPfP LRHS MAsh MMuc SEND SPer SPoG WRHF |
| 'Killiney Red' | ELan MBri |
| 'Killiney Salmon' | GGar LSRN MMuc MRav WFar |
| 'La Coquette' | CDoC EBee EPfP LRHS MAsh SBfd SPlb |
| 'Lena' ♀H4 | CDoC CHar CMac CSBt EPfP GGar LRHS LSRN LTen MAsh MBri MGos MMuc MWat NBir NEgg NHol NLar NPri SEND SGol SLim SPoG WBor WFar WHar |
| ***leucanthus*** | see *Chamaecytisus albus* (Hacq.) Rothm. |
| 'Luna' | WFar |
| ***maderensis*** | see *Genista maderensis* |
| 'Maria Burkwood' | NLar |
| 'Minstead' | CDoC ELan EPfP GGar LBuc NEgg SLim SPer |
| 'Moonlight' | EWTr NBro |
| 'Moyclare Pink' | CMHG |
| 'Mrs Norman Henry' | NLar |
| § ***multiflorus*** ♀H4 | SRms |
| ***nigricans*** 'Cyni' | ELan ELon IArd LAst LRHS MAsh MMuc SEND SPer SPoG SSpi |
| 'Palette' | MMuc |
| 'Porlock' | see *Genista* 'Porlock' |
| × ***praecox*** | CMac EWTr LAst LRHS MAsh NBlu NEgg SGol SPlb SPoG WFar WHar |
| - 'Albus' | CBcs CDoC CDul CHar CMac EBee ECrN ELan EPfP GAbr GGar LAst LRHS LSRN MAsh MGos MRav NBlu NHol SBfd SPer WFar WHar |
| - 'Allgold' ♀H4 | Widely available |
| - 'Canary Bird' | see *C.* × *praecox* 'Goldspeer' |
| - 'Frisia' | NBro WFar |
| § - 'Goldspeer' | MNHC |
| - 'Warminster' ♀H4 | EBee EPfP MBri MMuc MRav MWat NBlu NWea SBfd SEND SPer SRms |
| ***purpureus*** | see *Chamaecytisus purpureus* |
| - 'Atropurpureus' | see *Chamaecytisus purpureus* 'Atropurpureus' |
| ***racemosus*** | see *Genista* × *spachiana* |
| Red Favourite | see *C.* 'Roter Favorit' |
| 'Red Wings' | EWTr MMuc NHol SPer |

| | | |
|---|---|---|
| § | 'Roter Favorit' | EPfP LTen WGor |
| | ***scoparius*** | CArn CDul CRWN NWea SRms WDin |
| § | - f. ***andreanus*** ♀H4 | CDoC CTri EPfP NWea SPer WFar |
| | - 'Cornish Cream' | CDoC CDul CSBt EPfP LRHS SPer WFar |
| | - 'Fulgens' | CMac EPfP |
| § | - subsp. ***maritimus*** | MCoo SLPl |
| | - Monarch strain | GJos SWal |
| | - var. ***prostratus*** | see *C. scoparius* subsp. *maritimus* |
| | × ***spachianus*** | see *Genista* × *spachiana* |
| | ***supinus*** | see *Chamaecytisus supinus* |
| | 'Windlesham Ruby' | CDoC CPLG ELan EPfP LRHS LSRN NLar SBfd SLim SPad SPer WDin WFar |
| | 'Zeelandia' ♀H4 | CMac EBee ELon EPfP LRHS LTen MRav MWat NEgg NHol SPer WFar |

# D

## *Daboecia* ✿ (*Ericaceae*)

| | | |
|---|---|---|
| § | ***cantabrica*** | MMuc |
| § | - f. ***alba*** | CSBt MBri NWad SHeS SPer SRms SWhi |
| | - - 'Alba Globosa' | CCCN SHeS |
| | - - 'Bellita' | IVic SHeS |
| | - - 'Creeping White' | SHeS |
| | - - 'David Moss' ♀H4 | MMuc SHeS |
| I | - - 'Early Bride' | SHeS |
| | - - 'Snowdrift' | SHeS |
| | - - 'White Carpet' | SHeS |
| | - 'Amelie'PBR **new** | IVic SWhi |
| | - 'Arielle' ♀H4 | IVic SHeS |
| | - 'Atropurpurea' | CCCN CSBt MAsh NWad SHeS SPer SWhi |
| | - 'Barbara Phillips' ♀H4 | SHeS |
| | - 'Bicolor' ♀H4 | SHeS |
| | - 'Blueless' | SHeS |
| | - f. ***blumii*** 'Pink Blum' | SHeS |
| | - - 'Purple Blum' | SHeS |
| | - - 'White Blum' | SHeS SWhi |
| | - 'Bubbles' | SHeS |
| | - 'Celtic Star' | SHeS |
| | - 'Chaldon' | SHeS |
| | - 'Charles Nelson' (d) | SHeS |
| | - 'Cherub' | SHeS |
| | - 'Cinderella' | SHeS |
| | - 'Cleggan' | SHeS |
| | - 'Clifden' | SHeS |
| | - 'Covadonga' | SHeS |
| | - 'Cupido' | CTsd SHeS |
| § | - 'Donard Pink' | SHeS |
| | - 'Eskdale Baron' | SHeS |
| | - 'Eskdale Blea' | SHeS |
| | - 'Eskdale Blonde' | SHeS |
| | - 'Glamour' | SHeS |
| | - 'Globosa Pink' | SHeS |
| | - 'Harlequin' | SHeS |
| | - 'Heather Yates' | MAsh SHeS |
| | - 'Heraut' | SHeS |
| | - 'Hookstone Purple' | CCCN NHol NWad SHeS |
| | - 'Irish Shine' | SHeS |
| | - 'Johnny Boy' | SHeS |
| | - 'Lilac Osmond' | SHeS |
| | - 'Pink' | see *D. cantabrica* 'Donard Pink' |
| | - 'Pink Lady' | SHeS |
| | - 'Polifolia' | SHeS SRms |
| | - 'Porter's Variety' | SHeS |
| | - 'Praegerae' | CCCN CTri SHeS SWhi |
| | - 'Purpurea' | SHeS |
| | - 'Rainbow' (v) | SHeS SWhi |
| | - 'Rodeo' ♀H4 | SHeS |
| | - 'Rosea' | SHeS |
| | - 'Rubra' | SHeS |
| | - subsp. ***scotica*** 'Bearsden' | SHeS |
| | - - 'Ben' | SHeS |
| | - - 'Cora' | SHeS |
| | - - 'Golden Imp' | SHeS |
| | - - 'Goscote' | MGos SHeS |
| | - - 'Jack Drake' ♀H4 | GGar MBri SHeS SWhi |
| | - - 'Katherine's Choice' | CBcs SHeS |
| | - - 'Red Imp' | SHeS |
| | - - 'Robin' | SHeS |
| | - - 'Silverwells' ♀H4 | CBcs MAsh MBri SHeS SWhi |
| | - - 'Tabramhill' | SHeS |
| | - - 'William Buchanan' ♀H4 | GGar GJos IVic MAsh MBri NHol NWad SCoo SHeS SWhi |
| | - - 'William Buchanan Gold' (v) | CCCN MBri SHeS |
| | - 'Tinkerbell' | GJos |
| | - 'Tom Pearce' | CCCN |
| | - 'Waley's Red' ♀H4 | NHol NWad SHeS SWhi |
| | - 'Wijnie' | SHeS |

## *Dacrycarpus* (*Podocarpaceae*)

| | | |
|---|---|---|
| § | ***dacrydioides*** | CBrP ECou LEdu |
| | - 'Dark Delight' | ECou |

## *Dacrydium* (*Podocarpaceae*)

| | | |
|---|---|---|
| | ***bidwillii*** | see *Halocarpus bidwillii* |
| | ***cupressinum*** | CBcs CDoC CTrC SMad SPlb |
| | ***franklinii*** | see *Lagarostrobos franklinii* |
| | ***laxifolium*** | see *Lepidothamnus laxifolius* |

## *Dactylicapnos* (*Papaveraceae*)

| | | |
|---|---|---|
| § | ***lichiangensis*** | GKev WCru WSHC |
| | ***macrocapnos*** | CFir EPfP GCal GQui IFoB IFro MDKP WCru WTou |
| § | ***scandens*** | CRHN CRow EPfP GCal MNrw MSCN NLar SBrt SHar |
| | - GWJ 9438 | WCru |
| | - 'Shirley Clemo' | CPLG |
| | ***torulosa*** | WTou |
| | - B&SWJ 7814 | WCru |
| § | ***ventii*** | WTou |
| | - GWJ 9376 | WCru |

## *Dactylis* (*Poaceae*)

| | | |
|---|---|---|
| | ***glomerata*** | CHab WSFF |
| | - 'Variegata' (v) | EBee EPPr LTen MCCP MMuc NBid SBfd SEND SHDw WCot WFar |

## *Dactylorhiza* (*Orchidaceae*)

| | | |
|---|---|---|
| | sp. | NDav |
| | ***alpestris*** | CFir EBee MDun NLAp SKHP WCot |
| | ***aristata*** | EFEx LWst NLAp |
| | - f. ***alba*** | LWst |
| | × ***braunii*** | ECha |
| § | ***elata*** ♀H4 | GAbr IBlr LAma LWst NLAp SUsu |
| | - Duguid's **new** | WThu |
| | - 'Lydia' | GCra |
| | **Estella gx** | NLAp |
| § | ***foliosa*** ♀H4 | CAby CCCN CTsd EBee GCra GKev IBlr LWst MDun MNrw NLAp NWCA WFar WOld |
| | ***foliosa*** × ***incarnata*** subsp. ***coccinea*** | NLAp |

| | | |
|---|---|---|
| § | ***fuchsii*** | CCCN CMil CPrp EBee EPot GKev ITim LEdu LRHS MDun MNrw NLAp NMen NRya NSla SKHP SUsu WCot WFar WHer |
| | - 'Bressingham Bonus' | GKev LRHS NLAp |
| | - pink-flowered | CFir |
| | - white-flowered | CFir |
| | × ***grandis*** | IBlr SCnR SUsu |
| | - Blackthorn hybrid **new** | LWst |
| | ***incarnata*** | CPrp EBee LWst MDun NBid NLAp |
| | - subsp. ***coccinea*** | NLAp |
| | - subsp. ***incarnata*** **new** | NLAp |
| | ***insularis*** | NLAp |
| | ***lapponica*** | NLAp |
| § | ***maculata*** | CFir CHid EBee ELan EPfP GAbr LAma LWst MDun NLAp NMen WBor WCot WFar WHer |
| | - subsp. ***ericetorum*** | LWst NLAp |
| | - 'Madam Butterfly' | LRHS |
| | ***maderensis*** | see *D. foliosa* |
| § | ***majalis*** | CLAP CPrp EPot GKev LAma LRHS LWst MDun NLAp WFar WSFF |
| | - subsp. ***sphagnicola*** | LWst MDun NLAp |
| | ***mascula*** | see *Orchis mascula* |
| | × ***mixta*** **new** | NLAp |
| | ***pardalina*** | see *D. praetermissa* subsp. *praetermissa* |
| | ***praetermissa*** | CCCN CFir CLAP CPrp EBee LWst MDun NLAp NMen SKHP WCot WFar |
| § | - subsp. ***praetermissa*** **new** | LWst |
| | - - hybrid | LWst SKHP |
| | ***purpurella*** | CLAP CPrp GJos LWst MDun NLAp NMen NRya WFar |
| | - 'Palmengarten' | NLAp |
| | ***sambucina*** | NLAp |
| | 'Valerie Finnis' **new** | GKev |

# *Dahlia* ✿ (*Asteraceae*)

| | | |
|---|---|---|
| | NJM 05.008 | WPGP |
| | NJM 05.085 | WPGP |
| | 'Abba' (SD) | ECtt |
| | 'Abbie' (SD) | NHal |
| I | 'Acapulco' (S-c) **new** | ERCP |
| | 'Admiral Rawlings' (SD) | MWea WHal WWlt |
| | 'Aitara Caress' (MinC) | NHal |
| | 'Aitara Cloud' (MinC) | NHal |
| | 'Akita' (Misc) | CSut EPfP |
| | 'Alauna Clair-Obscur' (MC/Fim) | ERCP |
| | 'Alfred Grille' (MS-c) | SMrm SPer |
| | 'Allan Snowfire' (MS-c) | LAyl NHal |
| | 'Alloway Candy' | ERCP |
| | 'Alloway Cottage' (MD) | NHal |
| | 'Alstergruss' (Col) | CBgR |
| | 'Alva's Doris' (SS-c) ♀H3 | LAyl |
| | 'Alva's Regalia' (MD) | LRHS |
| | 'Alva's Supreme' (GD) ♀H3 | LAyl NHal |
| | 'Amber Festival' (SD) | NHal |
| | 'Amberglow' (MinBa) | LAyl |
| | 'Ambition' (SS-c) | ERCP |
| | American Pie = 'Vdtg26' PBR (Dark Angel Series) (Sin) **new** | LRHS |
| | 'Amira' (SBa) | NHal |
| | 'Amy Cave' (SBa) | NHal |
| | 'Andrea Clark' (MD) | NHal |
| | 'Andrea Lawson' | NHal |
| | 'Andrew Mitchell' (MS-c) | NHal |
| | 'Andries' Orange' (MinS-c) | LRHS LYaf |
| | 'Ann Breckenfelder' (Col) ♀H3 | CBgR ECtt ERCP LRHS NCGa NEgg NHal SDix SMrm WCot |
| | 'Anniversary Ball' (MinBa) | LAyl |
| | 'Apache' (MS-c/Fim) | ERCP SPer |
| | 'Apache Blauw' | ERCP |
| | 'April Heather' (Col) | NHal |
| | 'Arabian Night' (SD) | CAvo CBcs CBgR CFFs CHVG CSpe CSut EBee ECtt ELan ERCP EShb GBin LAst LAyl LRHS LSRN MBri MNrw MWat NHal SBfd SMrm SPer SWal WCot WWEG |
| | 'Aspen' (Dwf) | NBPC |
| | 'Audacity' (MD) | LAyl |
| | 'Aurora's Kiss' (MinBa) | NHal |
| | 'Aurwen's Violet' (Pom) | LAyl NHal |
| | ***australis*** | EBee WPGP |
| | - B&SWJ 10208 | WCru |
| | - B&SWJ 10358 | WCru |
| | - B&SWJ 10389 | WCru |
| | 'Autumn Choice' (MD) | LAyl |
| | 'Autumn Fairy' (D) | ERCP |
| | 'Avoca Comanche' (SS-c) | NHal |
| | 'Avoca Salmon' (MD) | NHal |
| | 'B.J. Beauty' (MD) | LAyl NHal |
| | 'Babette' (S-c) | LYaf SMrm |
| | 'Babylon Bronze' | CSut LSou |
| | 'Babylon Paars' (MD) **new** | LRHS |
| | 'Babylon Rose' (GD) **new** | LRHS |
| | 'Bantling' (MinBa) | ECtt ERCP |
| | 'Barbarry Banker' (MinD) | LAyl |
| | 'Barbarry Bluebird' (MinD) | NHal |
| | 'Barberry Maverick' | GBin |
| | 'Baret Joy' (LS-c) | NHal |
| | 'Bargaly Blush' (MD) | NHal |
| | 'Barton Memory' (S-c) | LAyl NHal |
| | 'Bednall Beauty' (Misc/DwB) ♀H3 | CBgR CHll COIW CSpe EBee ECtt ELan EShb EWes GBin LHop LRHS LSRN MBri MRav NEgg SBfd SDys SMrm SUsu WCot WHil WWEG |
| | 'Bell Boy' (MinBa) | ECtt |
| | 'Berger's Rekord' (S-c) | ERCP |
| | 'Berliner Orange' (MD) | ERCP |
| | 'Berwick Wood' (MD) | NHal |
| | 'Beth's Chaplet' | WCot |
| | 'Bishop of Auckland' PBR (Misc) | CBgR CSpe CWGN EBee ECtt ERCP LRHS NCGa NEgg SMrm WCot WWEG WWlt |
| | 'Bishop of Canterbury' PBR (Misc) | CPrp EBee ECtt EPfP LRHS LSou MBri MTis NGdn NHal SBrd |
| | 'Bishop of Dover' | EBee |
| | 'Bishop of Lancaster' (Misc) | EBee |
| | 'Bishop of Leicester' (Misc) | CSpe ECtt EPfP EPot LRHS LSou MBri MNrw SBrd SPet |
| | 'Bishop of Llandaff' (Misc) ♀H3 | Widely available |
| | 'Bishop of Oxford' (Misc) | CPrp CSpe EBee ELan EPfP LRHS LSou MBri MTis NBPC NGdn SBrd SMrm SPer SPet |
| | 'Bishop of York' (Misc) | CAvo CFFs CPrp CSpe EBee ECtt EPfP EPot LRHS LSou MBri MTis NBPC NGdn SBrd SPet |
| | 'Bishop Peter Price' (Sin) | CHar |
| | 'Black Barbara' (D) | ERCP |
| | 'Black Beauty' **new** | CSpe |
| | 'Black Fire' (SD) | LAyl |
| | 'Black Monarch' (GD) | NHal |
| | 'Black Narcissus' (MC) | CHVG EPfP SMrm SPer WWlt |
| | 'Black Star' (Sin) **new** | EPfP |
| | 'Black Touch' | ERCP |
| | 'Black Wizard' (MS-c) | EPfP |

|  |  |
|---|---|
| 'Blackberry Ripple' (S-c) | ERCP |
| 'Bloommaster' (MinD) | NHal |
| 'Blue Boy' (SD) **new** | SMrm SPer |
| 'Blue Record' | LAst |
| 'Blyton Lady in Red' (MinD) | NHal |
| 'Blyton Softer Gleam' (MinD) | NHal |
| 'Bonaventura' (C) **new** | LRHS |
| 'Bonaventure' (GD) | NHal |
| 'Boy Scout' (MinBa) | ERCP |
| 'Brackenridge Ballerina' (SWL) | CSam GBin LAyl NHal |
| 'Brantwood' (Sin) | CSam |
| Braveheart = 'Vdtg67'PBR (Dark Angel Series) (Sin) | LRHS |
| 'Brian's Dream' (MinD) | LAyl NHal |
| 'Bride's Bouquet' (Col) | ERCP |
| 'Bridge View Aloha' (MS-c) ♀H3 | SMrm |
| 'Broadheath Down' (SS-c) **new** | WWEG |
| 'Bryn Terfel' (GD) | NHal |
| 'Café au Lait' (GD) | IPot SEND SPer |
| 'Cameo' (WL) | CSam LAyl NHal |
| * 'Canary Fubuki' (MD) | ERCP |
| I 'Candlelight' (GD) | NHal |
| Candy Eyes = 'Zone Ten'PBR (Sin/DwB) | CWGN EBee EKen EPfP GBin LRHS LSRN LSou MGos SBrd SHar SPoG |
| 'Candy Keene' (LS-c) | NHal |
| 'Caribbean Fantasy' | NGdn |
| 'Carolina Moon' (SD) | LAyl NHal |
| 'Carstone Ruby' (SD) | NHal |
| 'Carstone Suntan' (MinC) | NHal |
| 'Carstone Valliant' (MinBa) | NHal |
| 'Catherine Deneuve' (Misc) | CWGN ECtt |
| 'Charlie Briggs' (SBa) | NHal |
| 'Charlie Dimmock' (SWL) ♀H3 | LAyl NHal |
| 'Charlie Two' (MD) | NHal |
| 'Chat Noir' (MS-c) | CAvo CFFs ERCP WHlf |
| 'Cheerio' (SS-c) | LRHS |
| 'Cherwell Goldcrest' (SS-c) | NHal |
| 'Cherwell Skylark' (SS-c) ♀H3 | NHal |
| 'Chic' (MinBa) | EBee ECtt LSou |
| 'Chic en Rouge' | LSou NBPC |
| 'Chimborazo' (Col) | LAyl SDix |
| 'Chocolate and Candy' (D) **new** | SMrm |
| 'Christine' (SD) | SMrm SPer |
| 'Christmas Carol' (Col) | ECtt |
| 'Christopher Taylor' (SWL) | NHal |
| 'Clair de Lune' (Col) ♀H3 | CBgR CWCL EBee ECtt ERCP LRHS MCot MWea NCGa NHal SMrm WCot WHrl |
| 'Clarion' (MS-c) | CSpe LRHS |
| 'Clarion 79' (DwB) | SUsu |
| 'Classic Rosamunde'PBR (Misc) | CBgR NHal |
| 'Classic Summertime' (Misc) | CBgR |
| 'Classic Swanlake'PBR (Misc) | ERCP SWal |
| 'Classic Thaïs'PBR (Misc) | CBgR |
| 'Clearview Irene' (MS-c) | NHal |
| 'Clearwater David' (SD) | GBin |
| ***coccinea*** (B) | CBgR CGHE CHll CSpe EPfP GBin GCal MCot SDix WCot WPGP |
| – B&SWJ 9126 | WCru |
| – NJM 05.072 | WPGP |
| – hybrids | WHil |
| – var. ***palmeri*** | CAvo SUsu WPGP |
| ***coccinea* × *merckii*** (B) | EWes |
| 'Confection' (MinD) | NHal |
| 'Cornel' (SBa) | ERCP LAyl LYaf NHal |
| 'Cornel Brons' (MinBa) | ERCP |
| 'Cornish Ruby' | CFir EPfP |
| 'Craigowan' (MS-c) | NHal |
| 'Czardas' | GCal |
| 'Daleko Jupiter' (GS-c) | NHal |
| Dalina Maxi Series **new** | LRHS |
| 'Dark Desire'PBR (Sin/DwB) | CAvo CBgR CFir CSpe CWCL ECtt GBin LAst LHop MCot MWea WCot WHil |
| 'David Digweed' (SD) | NHal |
| 'David Howard' (MinD) ♀H3 | Widely available |
| 'Dawn Sky' (SD) | LAyl |
| 'Deborah's Kiwi' (SC) | NHal |
| 'Debra Anne Craven' (GS-c) | NHal |
| 'Dikara Jodie' (MD) **new** | NHal |
| 'Dikara Moon' (MD) **new** | NHal |
| ***dissecta*** | WPGP |
| – F&M 191 | WPGP |
| 'Doctor John Grainger' (MinD) | CHVG LRHS |
| 'Don Hill' (Col) ♀H3 | NHal |
| 'Dora' **new** | LAst |
| 'Doris Day' (SC) | LYaf NHal |
| 'Doris Knight' (SC) | LYaf |
| 'Double Dream Fantasy' (Misc) **new** | LRHS |
| 'Dovegrove' (Sin) | CSam |
| 'Downham Royal' (MinBa) | ERCP |
| Dracula (Dark Angel Series) (Sin) **new** | LRHS |
| Dragon Ball (Dark Angel Series) (Sin) **new** | LRHS |
| 'Dream Fantasy' (Misc) **new** | MWea |
| 'Duddon Grace' (WL) **new** | NHal |
| 'Duet' (MD) | ECtt |
| 'Eastwood Moonlight' (MS-c) | NHal |
| 'Edge of Joy' | SPer |
| 'Edinburgh' (SD) | ERCP SWal |
| 'Elga' | ERCP |
| 'Ella Britton' (MinD) | LRHS |
| 'Ellen Huston' (Misc/DwB) ♀H3 | CBgR EBee ECtt ERCP LRHS NHal SBfd WCot |
| 'Elma E' (LD) | LAyl NHal |
| 'Embrace' (SC) | LAyl NHal |
| 'Engelhardt's Matador' (MD) | CBgR CHll ECtt LAst LRHS SBfd SMrm WCot WHrl |
| 'Eveline' (SD) | CBgR ERCP MBri |
| ***excelsa*** (B) | CHll WPGP |
| – B&SWJ 10233 | WCru |
| – B&SWJ 10238 | WCru |
| 'Excentrique' (Misc) | ECtt MBri |
| 'Exotic Dwarf' (Sin/Lil) | CWGN EBee ECtt LRHS NGdn NHal WCot |
| 'Eye Candy' | LRHS |
| 'Fabula' (Col) | LRHS |
| 'Fairfield Frost' (Col) | NHal |
| 'Fairway Spur' (GD) | NHal |
| 'Famoso' (Col) | ERCP |
| 'Fantastico' (Col) | ERCP |
| 'Fascination' ambig. | ERCP |
| 'Fascination' (SWL/DwB) ♀H3 | CBcs CHVG CHar COIW CSam EBee ECtt EPfP EWll LAyl LSou MCot MSCN MWea NEgg NGdn SBfd SMrm WHoo WWEG |
| I 'Fascination' (Misc) | SPer SPet |

| |  |  |
|---|---|---|
| | 'Fashion Monger' (Col) | ECtt ERCP NEgg NGdn NHal WCot |
| | 'Ferncliffe Illusion' (LD) | ERCP LRHS |
| | 'Festivo' (Col) | LRHS |
| | 'Fidalgo Supreme' (MD) | LAyl |
| | 'Finchcocks' (SWL) ♀H3 | LAyl |
| | 'Fire Mountain' (MinD) | NHal WCot |
| | 'Firebird' (MS-c) | see *D.* 'Vuurvogel' |
| | 'Firebird' (Sin) | LRHS |
| | 'Fleur' (MinD/Fim) | SMrm SPer |
| | 'Fleurel'PBR **new** | ERCP LRHS |
| | 'Florence Li Tim-Oi' (Sin) | CHar |
| | 'Forncett Furnace' (B) | GCal |
| | 'Fortuna' (Col) | ERCP |
| | 'Franz Kafka' (Pom) | ECtt ERCP |
| § | 'Freya's Paso Doble' (Anem) ♀H3 | LAyl |
| * | 'Friquolet' | CSut ERCP |
| | 'Fusion' (MD) ♀H3 | SHar WCot |
| | 'Fuzzy Wuzzy' (MD) | CSut |
| | 'G.F. Hemerik' (Sin) | LRHS |
| | 'Gainesville' (MinD) | EPfP |
| | (Gallery Series) 'Gallery Art Deco'PBR (SD) ♀H3 | ERCP LRHS NHal SBfd |
| | - 'Gallery Art Fair'PBR (MinD) ♀H3 | LRHS NHal |
| | - 'Gallery Art Nouveau'PBR (MinD) ♀H3 | ERCP LRHS NHal SBfd WCot |
| | - 'Gallery Cézanne'PBR (MinD) | LRHS |
| | - 'Gallery Matisse'PBR (SD) | LRHS |
| | - 'Gallery Renoir'PBR SD) ♀H3 | LRHS NHal |
| | - 'Gallery Rivera'PBR **new** | LRHS |
| | - 'Gallery Salvador'PBR (SD) | ERCP |
| | 'Garden Party' (MC/DwB) ♀H3 | LAyl |
| | 'Garden Wonder' (SD) | SBfd SMrm |
| | Gateshead Festival | see *D.* 'Peach Melba' (SD) |
| | 'Gay Princess' (SWL) | LAyl |
| | 'Geoffrey Kent' (MinD) ♀H3 | NHal |
| | 'Gerrie Hoek' (SWL) | CSam ERCP IPot LRHS LYaf MWea |
| | 'Gina Lombaert' (MS-c) | SEND |
| | 'Gipsy Night' **new** | ERCP SWal |
| | 'Giraffe' (DblO) | ERCP LRHS |
| | 'Giselle' | SPet |
| | 'Glorie van Heemstede' (SWL) ♀H3 | CSam ERCP LAyl LYaf NHal SEND WHrl |
| | 'Glorie van Naardwijk' (SD) | SWal |
| | 'Glorie van Noordwijk' (MinS-c) | ERCP |
| | 'Go American' (GD) | NHal |
| | 'Golden Emblem' (MD) | ECtt |
| | 'Good Earth' (MC) | SMrm |
| | 'Gracie S' (MinC) | NHal |
| | 'Grenadier' (Misc) ♀H3 | CBgR EBee ECtt LRHS SDix SDys WCot WWEG |
| | 'Grenidor Pastelle' (MS-c) | NHal |
| | 'Gurtla Twilight' (Pom) | NHal |
| | 'Gypsy Boy' (LD) | LAyl |
| | 'Hamari Accord' (LS-c) ♀H3 | LAyl |
| | 'Hamari Bride' (MS-c) ♀H3 | LAyl |
| | 'Hamari Girl' (GD) | NHal |
| | 'Hamari Gold' (GD) ♀H3 | NHal |
| | 'Hamari Rosé' (MinBa) ♀H3 | NHal |
| | 'Hamari Sunshine' (LD) ♀H3 | NHal |
| | (Happy Single Series) Happy Single First Love = 'HS First Love'PBR (Sin) | ERCP LSou WHil |
| | - Happy Single Flame = 'HS Flame'PBR (Sin) **new** | NPri |
| | - Happy Single Juliet = 'HS Juliet'PBR (Sin) | ERCP SPoG |
| | - Happy Single Party = 'HS Party'PBR (Sin) | ERCP LSou NPri WHil |
| | - Happy Single Princess = 'HS Princess' (Sin) **new** | ERCP NPri WHil |
| | - Happy Single Romeo = 'HS Romeo'PBR (Sin) | NPri WHil |
| | - Happy Single White = 'HS White' (Sin) | MWea |
| | - Happy Single Wink = 'HS Wink'PBR (Sin) | EPfP LRHS LSou |
| | 'Haresbrook' (Sin) | EShb NGdn |
| § | 'Harvest Samantha' (Sin/Lil) ♀H3 | NHal |
| | 'Hawai'PBR **new** | CSut |
| | 'Hayley Jayne' (S-Sc) | ERCP |
| | 'Helga' (MS-c) | ECtt |
| | 'Herbert Smith' (D) | SEND |
| | 'Hillcrest Delight' (MD) | NHal |
| | 'Hillcrest Desire' (SC) ♀H3 | LAyl |
| | 'Hillcrest Hannah' (MinD) | NHal |
| | 'Hillcrest Kismet' (MD) | LAyl NHal |
| | 'Hillcrest Royal' (MC) ♀H3 | LAyl NHal SDix |
| | 'Holland Festival' (GD) | LRHS |
| | 'Honka' (SinO) ♀H3 | CBgR ERCP LAyl LRHS MCot NHal WCot WWlt |
| | 'Honka Red' (Misc) | ERCP NHal |
| | 'Honka Surprise' (Misc) | EPfP ERCP NHal WCot |
| | 'Honka White' (Misc) | ERCP |
| | 'Honor Francis' **new** | WCot |
| | 'Hot Chocolate' (MinD) | WCot WHoo |
| | 'Hugs and Kisses' | EPfP SMrm SPer |
| | 'Imagion' **new** | EPfP |
| | ***imperialis*** (B) | CDTJ CFir CHEx CHll EWes LRHS SBig SDix WBox WHal |
| | - B&SWJ 8997 | WCru |
| | - 'Alba' (B) | CFir WBox WPGP |
| | - pink double-flowered (B) | WPGP |
| I | - 'Tasmania' (B) | GCal |
| | 'Impression Famosa' | LRHS |
| | 'Impression Fantastico' | LRHS |
| | 'Inca Dambuster' (GS-c) | NHal |
| | 'Indian Summer' (SC) | NHal |
| | 'Ivanetti' (MinBa) | EPfP NHal |
| | 'Jan van Schaffelaar' ambig. | ERCP |
| | 'Janal Amy' (GS-c) | NHal |
| | 'Jean Fairs' (MinWL) ♀H3 | LYaf |
| | 'Jean Marie'PBR (MD) | ERCP |
| | 'Jeanne d'Arc' (GC) | EPfP |
| | 'Jescot Jess' (MinD) | LYaf |
| | 'Jescot Julie' (DblO) | ERCP GBin LAyl |
| | 'Jessica Willows' (SWL) | NHal |
| | 'Jill Day' (SC) | LYaf |
| | 'Jim Branigan' (LS-c) | NHal |
| | 'Jocondo' (GD) | NHal |
| | 'Johann' (Pom) | NHal |
| | 'Jomanda' (MinBa) ♀H3 | GBin LYaf NHal |
| | 'Jo's Choice' (MinD) | LYaf |
| | 'Jules Dyson' (Misc) | SDys |
| | 'Jura' (SS-c) | EPfP ERCP |
| | 'Karenglen' (MinD) ♀H3 | GBin LYaf NHal |
| | 'Karma Amanda' (SD) | LRHS |
| | 'Karma Choc'PBR (SD) | EPfP ERCP LRHS MSCN MWea NHal SMrm SPer SWal |
| | 'Karma Fuchsiana' (SD) | ERCP SBfd |
| | 'Karma Irene'PBR (SD) **new** | ERCP |

| |  |  |
|---|---|---|
| | 'Karma Lagoon'PBR (SD) | ERCP LRHS SBfd |
| | 'Karma Naomi'PBR (SD) | ERCP LRHS |
| | 'Karma Prospero'PBR (SD) | ERCP LRHS MSCN SBfd |
| | 'Karma Royal Sea'PBR (SD) | ERCP |
| | 'Karma Sangria'PBR (SC) | LRHS |
| | 'Katie Dahl' (MinD) | NHal |
| | 'Kea Magic' (GD) | NHal |
| | 'Keith's Choice' (MD) | NHal |
| | 'Kelvin Floodlight' (GD) | SMrm SPer |
| | 'Kenn Emerland' (MS-c) | EPfP |
| | 'Kenora Challenger' (LS-c) | NHal |
| | 'Kenora Jubilee' (LS-c) | NHal |
| | 'Kenora Macop-B' (MC/Fim) | CSut LRHS |
| | 'Kenora Sunset' (MS-c) ♀H3 | LAyl LYaf NHal |
| | 'Kenora Superb' (LS-c) | NHal |
| | 'Kenora Valentine' (LD) ♀H3 | LAyl |
| | 'Kenora Wildfire' (LD) | NHal |
| | 'Ken's Choice' (SBa) | NHal |
| | 'Kidd's Climax' (GD) ♀H3 | ERCP |
| | 'Kilmorie' (SS-c) | NHal |
| | 'Kiss Me' (SD) | EPfP |
| | 'Kiwi Gloria' (SC) | NHal |
| | 'Klondike' (MS-c) | ERCP |
| | 'Knock Out' (MS-c) | SPoG |
| I | 'Knockout' (Sin) | EPfP GBin LRHS LSRN LSou MGos SBrd SHar |
| | 'L.A.T.E.' (MinBa) | GBin NHal |
| | 'La Recoleta' (D) **new** | ERCP WCot |
| | 'La Rouvre' (SS-c) | GBin |
| | 'Lady Linda' (SD) | LYaf NHal |
| | 'L'Ancresse' (MinBa) | GBin LAyl NHal |
| | 'Lauren's Moonlight' | see *D.* 'Pim's Moonlight' |
| | 'Lavender Line' (SS-c) | NHal |
| | 'Le Baron' (SD) | ERCP |
| | 'Lemon Elegans' (SS-c) ♀H3 | LYaf NHal |
| | 'Lemon Zing' (MinBa) | LAyl NHal |
| | 'Life Style' (Anem) **new** | SMrm SPer |
| | 'Lilac Bull' (MinD) **new** | LRHS |
| | 'Lilac Marston' (MinD) ♀H3 | GBin NHal |
| | 'Lilac Taratahi' (SC) ♀H3 | CSam LAyl |
| | 'Lilac Time' (MD) | ERCP |
| | 'Lilian Alice' (Col) | NHal |
| | 'Linda's Chester' (SC) | LYaf |
| | 'Lismore Carol' (Pom) | GBin NHal |
| | 'Lismore Moonlight' (Pom) | LAyl NHal |
| | 'Lismore Robin' (MinD) | NHal |
| | 'Lismore Willie' (SWL) ♀H3 | LYaf |
| | 'Little Robert' (MinD) | EPfP |
| | 'Little Treasure' | EPfP |
| | 'Loretta' (SBa) | GBin |
| | 'Lorona Dawn' (SinO) | ERCP NHal |
| | 'Lucky Number' (MD) | ERCP |
| | 'Ludwig Helfert' (S-c) | ERCP SEND |
| | 'Mabel Ann' (GD) | LAyl NHal |
| | 'Madame de Rosa' (LS-c) | NHal |
| | 'Madame Simone Stappers' (WL) | ETod LRHS MMHG |
| | 'Madame Vera' (SD) | LYaf |
| | 'Magenta Magic' (Sin/DwB) | NHal |
| | 'Magenta Star' (Sin) | CSam GBin |
| | 'Maggie C' (MS-c) | NHal |
| I | 'Mambo' **new** | ERCP |
| | 'Marble Ball' (MinD) | ERCP |
| | 'Margaret Haggo' (SWL) | CSam NHal |
| | 'Martina' (SD) | NHal |
| | 'Martin's Yellow' (Pom) | NHal |
| | 'Mary Eveline' (Col) | ECtt LAyl NHal |
| | 'Mary's Jomanda' (SBa) ♀H3 | GBin NHal |
| | 'Matador' (D) **new** | EPfP |
| | 'Matilda Huston' (SS-c) | NHal |
| | 'Maxine Bailey' (MinBa) | GBin |
| | 'Maya' (SD) | IPot |
| | 'Megan Dean' (MinBa) | NHal |
| | 'Melody Harmony'PBR (SD) | EPfP |
| | ***merckii*** (B) | CBgR CFir CGHE CSpe EWes LRHS MCot MNrw MRav SUsu WHil WPGP WSHC |
| | - F&M 222 | WPGP |
| | - ***alba*** (B) | CSpe SUsu WCru |
| | - compact (B) | WPGP |
| | 'Mermaid of Zennor' (Sin) | CFir |
| | 'Mevrouw Clement Andries' (MS-c/Fim) | ERCP |
| | 'Mingus Randy' (LS-c) | SPer |
| | 'Minley Carol' (Pom) ♀H3 | LAyl NHal |
| | 'Mistral' (MS-c/Fim) | ECtt |
| | 'Molly Trotter' (Sin) | CHar |
| | 'Mom's Special' (LD) | LRHS |
| | 'Moonfire' (Misc/DwB) ♀H3 | CBgR CHVG CMMP CSam CWCL CWGN EBee ECtt ELan EPfP ERCP EShb LAst LAyl LRHS MBri NEgg NGdn NHal NPri NVic SBfd SDix SMrm SPer WCot WHil WHoo WWEG |
| | 'Moonglow' (LS-c) | ERCP |
| | 'Moor Place' (Pom) | ERCP NHal |
| | 'Mrs Eileen' (GD) **new** | ERCP |
| | 'München' (MinD) | NGdn |
| | 'Murdoch' | CBgR ECtt LRHS SDys WCot WHrl WWlt |
| | 'Murillo' | LAyl WCot |
| | 'Musette' (MinD) | ECtt |
| | 'My Beverley' (MS-c/Fim) | LAyl NHal |
| | 'My Love' (SS-c) | CSut EPfP ERCP LAst SEND SMrm |
| | 'Myama Fubuki' (MS-c) | ERCP |
| | 'Mystery Day' (MD) | ECtt EPfP ERCP NBPC NGdn SBfd |
| | Mystic Desire | see *D.* 'Scarlet Fern' |
| | Mystic Mars | see *D.* 'Scarlet Fern' |
| | 'Nargold' (MS-c/Fim) | LAyl |
| | 'Narrow's Tricia' (MS-c) | NHal |
| | 'Natal' (MinBa) | ECtt EPfP ERCP |
| | 'Nathalie's Wedding' (SWL) **new** | ERCP |
| | 'Nepos' (SWL) | GBin |
| | 'Nescio' (Pom) | ERCP |
| | 'New Baby' (MinBa) | ERCP |
| | 'New Dimension' (SS-c) | ERCP |
| I | 'Night Queen' (Pom) | EPfP ERCP |
| | 'Nippon' (Sin) | EBee LRHS |
| | 'Nonette' (SWL) | CBgR CWGN EBee ECtt LRHS NEgg WCot |
| | 'Noreen' (Pom) | NHal |
| * | 'Nuit d'Eté' (MS-c) | CAvo CSpe EBee EPfP ERCP LAst LRHS MNrw MWea SEND SPad SWal |
| | 'Onesta' (SD) | ERCP |
| | 'Orchid Princess' (MS-c) **new** | ERCP |
| | 'Oreti Bliss' (SC) | NHal |
| | 'Oreti Classic' (MD) | NHal |
| | 'Orfeo' (MC) | ECtt ERCP MNrw |
| | 'Oriental Dream' (D) **new** | LRHS |
| | 'Osirium' (SD) | SPer |
| | 'Pablo' | LRHS |
| | 'Pacific Argyle' (SD) | NHal |
| | 'Painted Girl' (D) | ERCP |

| | | | | | |
|---|---|---|---|---|---|
| | 'Pam Howden' (SWL) | NHal | | 'Rossendale Natasha' (MinBa) | NHal |
| | 'Park Princess' (SC/DwB) | NGdn NHal | | 'Rothesay Robin' (SD) | GBin |
| | 'Party' | SPoG | I | 'Roxy' (Sin/DwB) | CBcs CBgR CMMP CSam EBee ECtt ELan EPfP ERCP LAst LAyl LRHS LSRN MAvo MNrw MSCN NEgg NGdn NHal NVic SBfd SMrm WCot WHoo WWEG |
| | 'Paso Doble' misapplied | see *D.* 'Freya's Paso Doble' | | 'Ruskin Andrea' (SS-c) | NHal |
| | 'Pat Mark' (LS-c) | LAyl | | 'Ruskin Bride' (MS-c) **new** | NHal |
| | 'Patricia' (Col) | NHal | | 'Ruskin Charlotte' (LS-c) | LAyl NHal |
| | 'Peach Brandy' (MinWL) | SMrm | | 'Ruskin Diana' (SD) | NHal |
| § | 'Peach Melba' (SD) | NHal | | 'Ruskin Marigold' (SS-c) | LAyl LYaf NHal |
| | 'Peaches and Cream'[PBR] (MinD) | SBfd | | 'Ruskin Michelle' (MS-c) | GBin |
| | 'Pearl of Heemstede' (SD) ♀H3 | LAyl NHal | | 'Ruskin Myra' (SS-c) | LAyl NHal |
| | 'Pembroke Levenna' (MinBa) | NHal | | 'Ruskin Penelope' (SS-c) | CAvo |
| | 'Pembroke Pattie' (Pom) | NHal | | 'Ruskin Splendour' (MS-c) | NHal |
| | 'Penelope' (MS-c) | IPot | * | 'Ruskin Tangerine' (SBa) | NHal |
| | 'Peter' (MinD) | ECtt | | 'Ryecroft Brenda T' (SD) **new** | NHal |
| § | 'Pim's Moonlight' (MS-c) | NHal | | 'Ryecroft Claire' (MinD) | NHal |
| | 'Pinelands Pixie' (MinC/Fim) | NHal | | 'Ryecroft Delight' (MinBa) | NHal |
| | 'Pink Giraffe' (O) ♀H3 | ERCP LRHS | | 'Ryecroft Gem' (MinBa) | NHal |
| | 'Pink Jupiter' (GS-c) | NHal | | 'Ryecroft Jan' (MinBa) ♀H3 | NHal |
| | 'Pink Pastelle' (MS-c) ♀H3 | NHal | | 'Ryecroft Jim' (Anem) | NHal |
| | 'Pink Shirley Alliance' (SC) | LAyl | | 'Ryecroft Laura' (MinBa) | NHal |
| | 'Pink Skin' (MD) | ERCP LRHS | | 'Ryecroft Magnum' (MD) | NHal |
| | ***pinnata*** B&SWJ 10240 | WCru | | 'Ryecroft Rebel' **new** | NHal |
| | 'Piper's Pink' (SS-c/DwB) | ERCP LAyl LRHS | | 'Ryecroft Sparkler' (MinC) **new** | NHal |
| | 'Poème' | MWea | | 'Ryecroft Zoe' (SS-c) | NHal |
| | 'Pontiac' (SC) | LAyl | | 'Sabrina' (SD) | IPot |
| | 'Pooh' (Col) | ERCP LAyl NHal | | 'Saint-Saëns' (S-c) | ERCP SEND |
| | 'Potgeiter' (MinBa) | ERCP | | 'Sakura Fubuki' | ERCP |
| | 'Preference' (SS-c) | ERCP | | 'Sam Hopkins' (SD) | NHal |
| | 'Preston Park' (Sin/DwB) ♀H3 | LAyl NHal | | 'Samantha' | see *D.* 'Harvest Samantha' |
| | Pretty Woman = 'Vdtg43'[PBR] (Dark Angel Series) (Sin) | LRHS | | 'Sandra' ambig. | ERCP |
| | Pride of Berlin | see *D.* 'Stolz von Berlin' | | 'Santa Claus' (MD) | SPer |
| | 'Primrose Pastelle' (MS-c) | NHal | | 'Sarah' (MinS-c) | LRHS |
| | 'Princesse Elisabeth' (MinD) **new** | ERCP | | 'Sascha' (SWL) ♀H3 | LAyl NHal |
| | 'Princesse Gracia' (MinD) **new** | ERCP | | 'Scarborough Fair' (MS-c) | NHal |
| | 'Princesse Laetitia' (MinD) **new** | ERCP | § | 'Scarlet Fern' (Sin) | EBee LSRN SBrd SPoG |
| | 'Procyon' (SD) | EPfP | | 'Scaur Swinton' (MD) | LAyl NHal |
| | 'Promise' (MS-c/Fim) | ECtt ERCP | | 'Scura' (DwSin) | ERCP |
| | aff. ***pteropoda*** F&M 312 **new** | WPGP | | 'Sean C' (Col) | NHal |
| | 'Pumpkin Pie' | CBgR WCot | | 'Seattle' (SD) | CSut |
| | 'Purple Gem' (SS-c) | ERCP SMrm | | 'Seduction' (MinD) | ERCP |
| | aff. ***purpusii*** B&SWJ 10321 | WCru | | 'Shandy' (SS-c) | LAyl NHal |
| | 'Radiance' (MC) | ERCP | | ***sherffii*** | MWea |
| | 'Raffles' (SD) | LAyl | | 'Shooting Star' (LS-c) | CSut |
| | 'Ragged Robin' (Misc) | CBgR CSpe CWGN EBee ECtt ERCP ETod LRHS MCot MNrw WCot WWlt | | 'Siberia'[PBR] (MinD) | ERCP |
| | 'Raiser's Pride' (MC) | NHal | | 'Silver City' (LD) | NHal |
| | 'Raymond Guernsey' **new** | LRHS | | 'Sir Alf Ramsey' (GD) | LAyl NHal |
| | 'Red Carol' (Pom) | NHal | | 'Small World' (Pom) ♀H3 | LAyl NHal |
| | 'Red Diamond' (MD) | NHal | | 'Smokey' | SEND |
| | 'Red Majorette' (SS-c) | SWal | | 'Sneezy' (Sin) | ELan LRHS |
| | 'Red Pygmy' (SS-c) | LAst | | 'Snowflake' (SWL) | ERCP |
| | 'Reginald Keene' (LS-c) | NHal | | 'Snowstorm' (MD) | SBfd |
| | 'Requiem' (SD) | ERCP | | 'So Dainty' (MinS-c) ♀H3 | LAyl |
| | 'Rhonda' (Pom) | NHal | | 'Sorbet' (DwB) | LRHS |
| | 'Richard S' (LS-c) | NHal | | 'Sorbet' (MS-c) | LAyl NHal |
| | 'Rip City' (SS-c) | CSpe ERCP MCot | | 'Soulman' (Anem) | CSpe |
| | 'Rocco' (MinBa) | ERCP | | 'Spartacus' (LD) | IPot LAyl NHal |
| | 'Romeo' | LRHS SPoG | | 'Staleen Condesa' (MS-c) ♀H3 | NHal |
| | 'Rose Jupiter' (GS-c) | NHal | | Star Wars (Dark Angel Series) **new** | LRHS |
| | | | | 'Starburst' | LRHS |
| | | | | 'Stars and Stripes' (MinD) **new** | SMrm |

| | | |
|---|---|---|
| | 'Star's Favourite' (MC) | ERCP |
| § | 'Stolz von Berlin' (MinBa) | ECtt ERCP |
| | 'Stoneleigh Cherry' (Pom) | LAyl |
| | 'Suffolk Punch' (MD) | LAyl |
| I | 'Summer Night' (SC) | CHVG ECGP LAyl MCot NHal |
| I | 'Sunshine' (Sin) | ECtt LAyl LRHS |
| | 'Susan Gilliott' (MS-c) | NHal |
| | 'Swan Lake' (SD) | EShb SPet |
| I | 'Sylvia' (SBa) | EPfP SMrm |
| | 'Tahoma Tom Tom' (MS-c) **new** | NHal |
| | 'Tally Ho' (Misc) ♀H3 | CBgR CMMP CSam EBee ECGP ECtt EPfP LRHS MRav SDys WCot WWEG |
| | 'Tam Tam' | EPfP SPer |
| | 'Taratahi Ruby' (SWL) ♀H3 | GBin LAyl LYaf NHal |
| | 'Taxi Driver' | LRHS SPoG |
| | 'Teesbrooke Audrey' (Col) | ECtt LAyl NHal |
| | 'Teesbrooke Red Eye' (Col) ♀H3 | ERCP NHal |
| | ***tenuicaulis*** | CDTJ CFir EBee SBig |
| | - F&M 99 | WPGP |
| | - F&M 257 | WPGP |
| | - F&M 355 | WPGP |
| | - F&M 369 | WPGP |
| | 'Terracotta' (DwB) | NHal |
| | 'The Phantom' (Anem) | ERCP |
| | 'Thomas A. Edison' (MD) | ERCP |
| | 'Tioga Spice' (MS-c/Fim) | NHal |
| | 'Tiptoe' (MinD) | LAyl NHal |
| | 'Tomo' (SD) | LAyl NHal |
| | 'Top Totty' (MinD) | NHal |
| | 'Toto' (Anem) | ERCP |
| | 'Treby Dainty' (MinBa) **new** | NHal |
| | 'Trelyn Kiwi' (SS-c) ♀H3 | NHal |
| | 'Trengrove Millennium' (MD) | NHal |
| | 'Troy Dyson' (Misc) | SDys |
| | 'Tsuki-ytori-no-shisha' (MC) | IPot |
| | 'Tudor 1' (DwB) | NHal |
| | 'Twyning's After Eight' (Sin) ♀H3 | CAvo CPLG CSam CSpe CWGN EBee ECtt ELan EPfP ERCP ETod LRHS MAvo MCot MMHG NCGa NEgg NHal SDix SMrm SPer SPoG SUsu WBor WCot WCra WHoo |
| | 'Twyning's Aniseed' (Sin) | EPfP ETod |
| | 'Twyning's Pink Fish' (Col) ♀H3 | ETod |
| | 'Twyning's Smartie' (Sin) ♀H3 | SMrm |
| | 'Tyrell' | EPfP SMrm |
| | 'Vancouver' (Misc) | CSut ERCP NBPC SWal |
| | 'Vulkan' (MS-c) **new** | ERCP |
| § | 'Vuurvogel' (MS-c) | ERCP |
| | 'Waltzing Mathilda' (Misc) **new** | ERCP |
| | 'Wanda's Aurora' (GD) | NHal |
| | 'War of the Roses' | SGar SWal WHer |
| | 'Weston Pirate' (MinC) ♀H3 | NHal |
| | 'Weston Spanish Dancer' (MinC) ♀H3 | LAyl LYaf NHal |
| | 'White Alva's' (GD) ♀H3 | LAyl NHal |
| | 'White Ballerina' (SWL) | CSam LAyl NHal |
| | 'White Ballet' (SD) ♀H3 | LAyl |
| | 'White Charlie Two' (MD) | NHal |
| | 'White Knight' (MinD) | NHal |
| | 'White Linda' (SD) | NHal |
| | 'White Moonlight' (MS-c) | LAyl NHal |
| | 'White Perfection' (LD) | ECtt EPfP ERCP |
| | 'White Star' (MS-c) | ERCP |
| | 'White Swallow' (SS-c) | NHal |
| | 'Willo's Borealis' (Pom) | NHal |
| | 'Willo's Surprise' (Pom) | NHal |
| | 'Willo's Violet' (Pom) | NHal |
| | 'Willowfield Matthew' (MinD) | NHal |
| | 'Windmill' (C) **new** | ERCP |
| | 'Winholme Diane' (SD) | NHal |
| | 'Winston Churchill' (MinD) | LYaf |
| | 'Winter Springs' (S-Sc) | ERCP |
| | 'Witteman's Best' (LS-c) **new** | ERCP |
| | 'Witteman's Superba' (SS-c) ♀H3 | NHal SDix |
| | 'Woodbridge' (Sin) **new** | CSpe |
| | 'Woodside Finale' (MinD) | NHal |
| | 'Wootton Impact' (MS-c) ♀H3 | NHal |
| | 'Worton Blue Streak' (SS-c) | ERCP |
| | 'Yellow Hammer' (Sin/DwB) ♀H3 | LAyl NHal |
| | 'Yellow Sneezy' (Sin/Lil) **new** | LRHS |
| | 'Yellow Star' (MS-c) | ERCP SMrm |
| | 'Yelno Enchantment' (SWL) | LAyl |
| | 'York and Lancaster' (MD) | CBgR |
| I | 'Yvonne' (MWL) | GBin |
| | 'Zorro' (GD) ♀H3 | ERCP NHal |

## *Daiswa* see *Paris*

## *Dalea* (*Papilionaceae*)

| | | |
|---|---|---|
| | ***candida*** | EBee |
| | ***purpurea*** | EBee EWll LRHS SPhx |
| | - 'Stephanie' **new** | EBee SMad |

## *Dalechampia* (*Euphorbiaceae*)

| | | |
|---|---|---|
| | ***dioscoreifolia*** | CCCN |
| | ***spathulata*** | CCCN |

## damson see *Prunus insititia*

## *Danae* (*Asparagaceae*)

| | | |
|---|---|---|
| § | ***racemosa*** | CBcs CTri EBee ELan EPfP EPla MGos MRav SArc SEND SPer SRms SSpi SWvt WCFE WCot WCru WDin WPat |

## *Daphne* ✿ (*Thymelaeaceae*)

| | | |
|---|---|---|
| | DJHC 98164 from China | WCru |
| | ***acutiloba*** | CPMA GKev |
| | - 'Fragrant Cloud' | CPLG CPMA EWes SChF |
| | ***albowiana*** | CPMA EWes LLHF LRHS SAga |
| | ***alpina*** | CPMA NEgg WAbe |
| | ***altaica*** | CPMA |
| | ***arbuscula*** ♀H4 | CPMA LLHF MWat NMen WThu |
| | - subsp. ***arbuscula*** f. ***albiflora*** | CPMA |
| | - 'Diva' | CPMA |
| | - 'Muran Pride' | CPMA |
| | - f. ***radicans*** | CPMA |
| | ***arbuscula*** × ***cneorum*** var. ***verlotii*** | CPMA |
| | ***arbuscula*** × 'Leila Haines' | see *D.* × *schlyteri* |
| | ***arisanensis*** B&SWJ 6983 | WCru |
| | ***bholua*** | CAbP CHll CPMA EPfP GGal LRHS MGos SReu SSpi WAbe |
| I | - 'Alba' | CBcs CLAP CMac CPMA ELan EPfP LRHS MGos WPGP |

|  |  |
|---|---|
| - 'Darjeeling' | CBcs CHll CLAP CPLG CPMA CWSG EPfP LRHS NLar SChF SKHP SLim SPer WGob WPGP |
| - var. ***glacialis*** 'Gurkha' | CGHE CPLG CPMA ELan EPfP IRar SChF SKHP SSpi WPGP |
| - 'Jacqueline Postill' ♀H3 | Widely available |
| - 'John Darly' new | SChF |
| - 'Limpsfield' | CPMA LRHS SCoo SSta |
| - 'Peter Smithers' | CLAP CPLG CPMA LRHS LSRN SReu SSta WPGP |
| - 'Wisley Purple' new | CPMA |
| ***blagayana*** | CPMA ECho NBir SRms WPat WThu |
| - 'Brenda Anderson' | CPMA GLam NMen WAbe |
| 'Bramdean' | see *D.* × *napolitana* 'Bramdean' |
| × ***burkwoodii*** ♀H4 | LSRN WDin |
| - 'Albert Burkwood' | CPMA |
| - 'Astrid' (v) | CBcs CPMA CWSG LRHS MGos NLar SLon WDin |
| - 'Briggs Moonlight' (v) | MAsh |
| § - 'Carol Mackie' (v) | CPMA MAsh NLar |
| - 'G.K.Argles' (v) ♀H4 | CPMA MAsh |
| I - 'Gold Sport' | CPMA SChF |
| - 'Gold Strike' (v) | CPMA |
| - 'Golden Treasure' | CPMA MAsh SChF |
| - 'Jan Dekker' new | NLar |
| - 'Lavenirei' | CPMA |
| - 'Somerset' | CBcs CPMA CWSG ELan MRav MSwo NLar NWea SLim WDin WThu |
| § - 'Somerset Gold Edge' (v) | CPMA |
| § - 'Somerset Variegated' (v) | WThu |
| - 'Variegata' broad cream edge | see *D.* × *burkwoodii* 'Somerset Variegated' |
| - 'Variegata' broad gold edge | see *D.* × *burkwoodii* 'Somerset Gold Edge' |
| - 'Variegata' narrow gold edge | see *D.* × *burkwoodii* 'Carol Mackie' |
| ***calcicola*** 'Gang-ho-ba' | CPMA WAbe |
| - 'Sichuan Gold' | CPMA |
| ***caucasica*** | CPMA |
| ***circassica*** | CPMA SChF |
| ***cneorum*** | CBcs CPMA GEdr IVic MGos NMen WDin |
| - f. ***alba*** | CPMA |
| - 'Benaco' | CPMA |
| - 'Blackthorn Triumph' | CPMA WAbe |
| - compact new | NLar |
| - 'Eximia' ♀H4 | CPMA SRms WAbe |
| - 'Klaus Patzner' | CPMA |
| - 'Lac des Gloriettes' | CPMA |
| - 'Puszta' | CPMA MAsh WAbe |
| - var. ***pygmaea*** | CPMA WAbe |
| - - 'Alba' | CPMA |
| - 'Ruby Glow' | CPMA |
| - 'Variegata' (v) | CPMA GEdr |
| - 'Velký Kosir' | CPMA SChF WAbe |
| ***collina*** | see *D. sericea* Collina Group |
| ***domini*** new | EPot |
| × ***eschmannii*** 'Jacob Eschmann' | CPMA |
| 'Forarch' | CPMA |
| ***genkwa*** | CPMA SKHP WCru |
| ***giraldii*** | CPMA WSHC |
| ***gnidioides*** | CPMA |
| 'Guardsman' | CPMA SChF |
| × ***hendersonii*** | CPMA |
| - 'Appleblossom' | CPMA SChF WAbe |
| - 'Aymon Correvon' | CPMA |
| - 'Blackthorn Rose' | CPMA |
| - 'Ernst Hauser' | CPMA MAsh WAbe WThu |
| - 'Fritz Kummert' | CPMA WAbe WThu |
| - 'Jeanette Brickell' | CPMA WAbe |
| - 'Kath Dryden' | CPMA SChF WAbe |
| - 'Marion White' | CPMA SChF |
| - 'Rosebud' | CPMA WThu |
| - 'Solferino' | CPMA |
| 'Hinton' | CPMA |
| × ***houtteana*** | CPMA NBir |
| × ***hybrida*** | CPMA |
| ***japonica*** 'Striata' | see *D. odora* 'Aureomarginata' |
| ***jasminea*** | CPMA ECho NMen WAbe |
| ***jezoensis*** | CPMA LRHS SSta |
| × ***jintyae*** 'Pink Cascade' | CPMA |
| ***juliae*** | CPMA |
| ***kamtschatica*** | CPMA |
| 'Kilmeston Beauty' | CPMA |
| ***kosaninii*** | CPMA |
| × ***latymeri*** 'Spring Sonnet' | CPMA SChF |
| ***laureola*** | CBcs CPMA EPfP GBin GKev GPoy MMHG NBir NPer WCFE |
| - 'Kingsley Green' | CPMA |
| - 'Margaret Mathew' | CPMA EPfP SChF |
| - subsp. ***philippi*** | CMac CPMA ELan EPfP LHop LRHS MAsh MBlu NLar NMen SKHP WPat |
| 'Leila Haines' | CPMA |
| × ***mantensiana*** 'Audrey Vockins' | CPMA SChF |
| - 'Manten' | CPMA MAsh |
| × ***mauerbachii*** 'Perfume of Spring' | CPMA ECho SChF |
| 'Meon' | see *D.* × *napolitana* 'Meon' |
| ***mezereum*** | CBot CMea CTri ECho GAbr GKev IFoB ITim MBri MGos NChi NPri NWea SGol SLim SWvt WCFE WDin WFar WHar WPGP |
| - f. ***alba*** | CLAP CPMA ECho GKev MGos NChi SRms SWvt WAbe WCFE |
| - - 'Bowles's Variety' | CBot CPMA EPot GLam |
| - 'Rosea' | ECho SRms |
| - var. ***rubra*** | CBcs CMac CPMA CWSG CWib ELan GKin LRHS MGos MRav MSwo NBlu SPer WAbe WDin WFar |
| × ***napolitana*** ♀H4 | CBcs CPMA EPfP SChF |
| § - 'Bramdean' | CPMA MAsh WThu |
| § - 'Meon' | CPMA MAsh WAbe WThu |
| ***odora*** | CBcs CPMA CWSG EBee EPfP LRHS LSRN MSwo NMen SLim WDin |
| § - f. ***alba*** | CCCN CMac CPMA |
| - - 'Sakiwaka' | CCCN CLAP CPLG CPMA EWes SKHP |
| § - 'Aureomarginata' (v) ♀H3-4 | Widely available |
| - 'Clotted Cream' (v) | CPMA |
| - 'Geisha Girl' (v) | CPMA MAsh MGos |
| - var. ***leucantha*** | see *D. odora* f. *alba* |
| - 'Limelight' | CPMA |
| - 'Mae-jima' (v) | CPLG CPMA ELan EPfP LLHF LRHS MAsh NLar SBrd SCoo SLon SMad SPoG WCot |
| - 'Marginata' | see *D. odora* 'Aureomarginata' |
| - 'Rebecca' (v) | LRHS SPoG |
| - var. ***rubra*** (v) | CCCN CFir CLAP CPMA LLHF |
| - 'Walberton' (v) | EPfP LRHS |
| ***oleoides*** | CPMA NLar |
| ***papyracea*** | CPLG |
| ***petraea*** | CPMA |
| - 'Cima Tombea' | CPMA |
| - 'Corna Blacca' | CPMA |
| - 'Garnet' | CPMA WAbe |
| - 'Grandiflora' | CPMA SChF WAbe |
| - 'Lydora' | CPMA |

- 'Michele' CPMA
- 'Persebee' CPMA
- 'Punchinello' CPMA
- 'Tuflungo' CPMA
'Pink Star' CPMA
***pontica*** ♀H4 CBcs CGHE CPMA CWSG EOHP EPfP GKev LRHS MAsh MBri NLar NWCA SBrd SDix SKHP SPer SSpi WPGP
***pseudomezereum*** WCru
***retusa*** see *D. tangutica* Retusa Group
'Richard's Choice' CPMA
× ***rollsdorfii*** 'Arnold Cihlarz' CPMA EPot MAsh WAbe
- 'Wilhelm Schacht' CAbP CPMA EPot IVic SChF WAbe WThu
'Rossetii' CPMA
'Rosy Wave' CPMA SChF
§ × ***schlyteri*** CPMA MAsh
- 'Lovisa Maria' CPMA WAbe
***sericea*** CPMA NLar
§ - Collina Group CAbP CPMA EPfP IRar MAsh SRms WThu
'Spring Beauty' CPMA
'Spring Herald' CPMA
'Stasek' (v) CPMA
× ***suendermannii*** 'Franz Suendermann' MAsh
× ***susannae*** 'Anton Fahndrich' CPMA NLar WAbe
- 'Cheriton' CPMA EPfP EPot LRHS NMen SChF WAbe
- 'Tage Lundell' CPMA IVic
- 'Tichborne' CAbP CPMA EPot MAsh NMen SChF WAbe WThu
***tangutica*** ♀H4 Widely available
§ - Retusa Group ♀H4 CPLG CPMA ECho ELan ELon EPot GAbr GBin GEdr GMaP LHop LRHS MAsh NMen NRya NSla NWCA SPer SRms
× ***thauma*** WAbe
× ***transatlantica*** 'Beulah Cross' (v) CAbP CPMA ELan LLHF LRHS MAsh SBrd SChF SCoo SLon SPoG
- Eternal Fragrance = 'Blafra'PBR CAbP CCCN CEnd CLAP CPLG CWGN ELan EPfP EPot GAbr GEdr LBuc LLHF LRHS LSqu MAsh MBri MGos NLar SBrd SKHP SLim SLon SPer SPoG SSpi WPGP
- 'Jim's Pride' SChF
'Valerie Hillier' CPMA IRar LRHS SChF
***velenovskyi*** CPMA
× ***whiteorum*** 'Beauworth' CPMA WAbe
- 'Kilmeston' CPMA NMen WAbe
- 'Warnford' CPMA
***wolongensis*** 'Kevock Star' CPLG GKev

## *Daphniphyllum* (*Daphniphyllaceae*)

aff. ***angustifolium*** B&SWJ 8225 WCru
- B&SWJ 11804 WCru
- WWJ 12020 WCru
***calycinum*** B&SWJ 4058 WCru
***glaucescens*** WCru
subsp. ***oldhamii*** var. ***kengii*** B&SWJ 6872
- - - B&SWJ 7119 WCru
- - var. ***oldhamii*** B&SWJ 7056 WCru
- - - CWJ 12351 WCru
***humile*** see *D. macropodum* var. *humile*
aff. ***longeracemosum*** B&SWJ 11788 WCru
***macropodum*** CBcs CCCN CGHE CHEx CWib EPfP LRHS NLar SArc SDix SKHP SSpi WCru WFar WPGP
- B&SWJ 581 WCru
- B&SWJ 2898 WCru
- B&SWJ 6809 from Taiwan WCru
- B&SWJ 8507 from Ulleungdo, South Korea WCru
- B&SWJ 8763 from Cheju-do, Korea WCru
- B&SWJ 11489 from Yakushima **new** WCru
- dwarf WCru
§ - var. ***humile*** B&SWJ 11232 WCru
***majus*** B&SWJ 11744 **new** WCru
***paxianum*** B&SWJ 9755 WCru
***pentandrum*** B&SWJ 6888 WCru
- B&SWJ 7056 WCru
- CWJ 12393 WCru
- RWJ 9836 WCru
***teijsmannii*** B&SWJ 11110 from Japan WCru
- B&SWJ 11112 WCru
- B&SWJ 11358 from Japan WCru
aff. ***teijsmannii*** CWJ 12350 from Taiwan **new** WCru

## *Darlingtonia* (*Sarraceniaceae*)

***californica*** ♀H1 CSWC EFEx NChu SHmp WSSs

## *Darmera* (*Saxifragaceae*)

***peltata*** ♀H4 Widely available
- 'Nana' CHEx EBee ECha LRHS LSou NBid NHol NLar SLPl SWat WFar WMoo

## *Dasylirion* (*Asparagaceae*)

§ ***acrotrichum*** CDTJ EShb SArc
***berlandieri*** NJM 05.048 WPGP
***cedrosanum*** CDTJ
***glaucophyllum*** EAmu MREP
***gracile*** Planchon see *D. acrotrichum*
***leiophyllum*** WPGP
***longissimum*** CAbb CBrP CTrC EAmu EShb ETod SChr
***miquihuanense*** F&M 301A WPGP
- F&M 321 WPGP
- NJM 05.062 WPGP
***quadrangulatum*** SPlb
- NJM 05.064 WPGP
***serratifolium*** EAmu ERom SChr
***texanum*** CTrC LEdu
***wheeleri*** ♀H1 CBrP CTrC EAmu LRHS SPlb

## *Dasyphyllum* (*Asteraceae*)

***diacanthoides*** WPGP

## date see *Phoenix dactylifera*

## *Datisca* (*Datiscaceae*)

***cannabina*** CArn CDTJ CFir EBee ECha EPPr GBin GCal LPla NChi NLar SBrt SDix SMrm SPhx SUsu WMoo WPGP

## *Datura* (*Solanaceae*)

***arborea*** see *Brugmansia arborea*
***chlorantha*** see *Brugmansia chlorantha*

***cornigera*** see *Brugmansia arborea*
***ferox*** new CArn
***rosea*** see *Brugmansia* × *insignis* pink-flowered
***rosei*** see *Brugmansia sanguinea*
***sanguinea*** see *Brugmansia sanguinea*
***stramonium*** CArn MNHC
***suaveolens*** see *Brugmansia suaveolens*
***versicolor*** see *Brugmansia versicolor* Lagerh.
- 'Grand Marnier' see *Brugmansia* × *candida* 'Grand Marnier'

## *Daubenya* (*Asparagaceae*)

***alba*** ECho
***aurea*** ECho
- var. ***coccinea*** ECho
***marginata*** ECho
***namaquensis*** ECho

## *Daucus* (*Apiaceae*)

***carota*** CArn CHab CRWN EWil NMir SVic WSFF

## *Davallia* (*Davalliaceae*)

***canariensis*** ♀H1 CMen ISha SEND
***mariesii*** ♀H3 CMen CTsd ISha WAbe WCot
- var. ***stenolepis*** CMen WRic
***tasmanii*** CMen WRic
***trichomanoides*** CBty CMen
- f. ***barbata*** CMen

## *Davidia* (*Nyssaceae*)

***involucrata*** ♀H4 Widely available
- 'Sonoma' MBlu
- var. ***vilmoriniana*** ♀H4 CBcs CDoC CWCL EBee ELan EPfP LRHS MAsh MBlu MCCP MGos SBfd SLim SPer

## *Daviesia* (*Papilionaceae*)

***cordata*** SPlb
* ***ovalifolia*** SPlb
***pectinata*** SPlb

## *Debregeasia* (*Urticaceae*)

***longifolia*** SVen
- WWJ 11686 WCru

## *Decaisnea* (*Lardizabalaceae*)

***fargesii*** Widely available
- B&SWJ 8070 WCru
***insignis*** WPGP

## *Decodon* (*Lythraceae*)

***verticillatus*** LLWG

## *Decumaria* (*Hydrangeaceae*)

***barbara*** CBcs CMac EBee MMuc NLar NSti SLim SSta WCru WFar WSHC
- 'Vicki' EBee NLar
***sinensis*** EBee EPfP LRHS MMuc SBrt SKHP SLon SPoG SSpi WCru WSHC

## *Deinanthe* (*Hydrangeaceae*)

***bifida*** CDes CLAP CMil EPfP EWes LRHS WCru WPGP
- B&SWJ 5436 EWld GEdr SBig WCru
- B&SWJ 5551 WCru
- B&SWJ 5655 LEdu NLar GEdr WCru
- 'Pink-Kii' WCru
- 'Pink-Shi' EWld WCru
***bifida*** × ***caerulea*** CLAP GEdr WCru
'Blue Blush' WCru
***caerulea*** CLAP CMil EBee GEdr IGor LEdu LRHS NLar NPnk SKHP WCru WPGP
- 'Blue Wonder' CLAP CPLG EBee EPPr

## *Delairea* (*Asteraceae*)

§ ***odorata*** CFee

## *Delonix* (*Caesalpiniaceae*)

***decaryi*** new SPlb
***regia*** MOWG SPlb

## *Delosperma* (*Aizoaceae*)

from Graaf Reinet, South Africa EPot NSla
from Sani Pass, South Africa EPot GLam WAbe
§ ***aberdeenense*** ♀H1 CHEx XLum
***ashtonii*** CCCN GEdr
***basuticum*** GLam NSla
'Basutoland' see *D. nubigenum*
***congestum*** CCCN CMea ECho EDAr EPot EWll GEdr GGar NWCA SAga WAbe
- 'Gold Nugget' ECho LRHS
***cooperi*** CCCN CTri ECho ECtt EDAr EPfP EPot EWll ITim LRHS MSCN SBfd SEND SPlb WFar WNew WPer WPnn XLum XSen
* ***deschampsii*** GEdr
***floribundum*** EDAr
'Starburst' new
aff. ***floribundum*** new GLam
***harazianum*** CPBP
***karrooicum*** NWCA
***kofleri*** × ***nubigenum*** new XLum
***lavisiae*** new SPlb
***lineare*** XLum
Mesa Verde = 'Kelaidis' new ECtt
§ ***nubigenum*** CTri ECho ECtt ELan EPfP EPot GAbr GEdr GGar GKev ITim MAsh MSCN SEND SPlb SPoG SWal WFar WNew WPer
'Ruby Coral' EPot
***sphalmanthoides*** CPBP EPot GEdr NWCA
***sutherlandii*** ECho EDAr NWCA SBfd SEND XLum
- 'Peach Star' CCCN EDAr LRHS NWCA SBfd
Table Mountain = 'John Proffitt' CCCN GGar GKev XLum

## *Delphinium* ✿ (*Ranunculaceae*)

sp. SVic
HWJK 2179 from Nepal WCru
HWJK 2263 from Nepal WCru
'Alice Artindale' (d) EWes EWld IFoB SAga SMrm WCot WPGP
***ambiguum*** see *Consolida ajacis*
'Ariel' ambig. LRHS
Astolat Group CBcs CBot CSBt CTri CWCL CWib EBee ELan EPfP GMaP LBMP LRHS MBri MGos MLHP MWat NBPC NBir NLar NPri SBfd SMrm SPer SPoG SWvt WCAu WFar WHoo XLum
'Atholl' ♀H4 ELar
(Aurora Series) 'Aurora Dark Blue' LRHS
- 'Aurora Deep Purple' LRHS

|  |  |
|---|---|
| – 'Aurora Lavender' | LRHS |
| 'Basil Clitheroe' | LRHS |
| Belladonna Group | ELan IFoB |
| – 'Atlantis' ♀H4 | EBee ECha ELar LRHS NLar SMrm WCot |
| – 'Balaton' | ELar |
| – 'Blue Bees' **new** | LRHS |
| – 'Capri' | EBee |
| – 'Casa Blanca' | EBee ELar EPfP GMaP LRHS NLar SBfd SMrm XLum |
| – 'Cliveden Beauty' | EBee EPfP GMaP LHop LRHS NLar SBfd SMrm XLum |
| – 'Delft Blue'PBR | EBee |
| § – 'Janny Arrow'PBR | LRHS |
| – 'Moerheimii' | LRHS |
| – 'Peace' | LRHS |
| – 'Piccolo' | ECha LRHS MAvo NCGa NLar |
| – 'Pink Sensation' | see *D.* × *ruysii* 'Pink Sensation' |
| – 'Völkerfrieden' ♀H4 | ELar LRHS MAvo MCot MRav NCGa WCot |
| × ***bellamosum*** | CBot EPfP GMaP LRHS MAvo NLar SBfd XLum |
| Black Knight Group | CBcs CSBt CTri CWCL CWib ECtt ELan EPfP GMaP IFoB LHop LRHS LSRN MBri MGos MRav MWat NGdn NLar NMir NVic SBfd SPer SPlb SPoG SWvt WCAu WFar WHoo XLum |
| 'Black Velvet' | CBcs |
| 'Blauwal' | GBin |
| 'Blue Arrow' | see *D.* 'Blue Max Arrow', *D.* (Belladonna Group) 'Janny Arrow', *D.* 'Kings Blue Arrow' |
| Blue Bird Group | CBcs CSBt CTri CWCL EBee ELan EPfP GMaP LRHS MGos MRav MWat NBPC NLar NMir NPri SBfd SBrd SPer SPoG WCAu WFar WHoo XLum |
| 'Blue Butterfly' | see *D. grandiflorum* 'Blue Butterfly' |
| 'Blue Dawn' ♀H4 | ELar |
| Blue Fountains Group | CSBt EPfP LRHS LSRN NBlu SPer SPet SPoG SRms |
| 'Blue Hex' | WCot |
| 'Blue Jay' | CBcs CTri EBee ECtt EPfP LRHS LSRN MWat NBir NLar NPri SBfd SMrm SPer XLum |
| 'Blue Lace' | STes |
| § 'Blue Max Arrow' | LRHS |
| 'Blue Mirror' | SRms |
| Blue River | CBcs |
| 'Blue Skies' | ECtt NLar |
| Blue Springs Group | NGdn NLar |
| 'Bruce' ♀H4 | ELar WCFE |
| ***brunonianum*** | WThu |
| ***bulleyanum*** | GAuc |
| 'Butterball' | ELar |
| Cameliard Group | CBcs CSBt EBee ECtt ELan EPfP LHop LRHS MWat NBPC NLar NPri SPer SPoG WCAu WRHF |
| 'Can-Can' ♀H4 | ELar |
| ***cardinale*** | SPlb |
| 'Centurion Sky Blue' (Centurion Series) ♀H4 | LRHS |
| ***ceratophorum*** | WCru |
| var. ***ceratophorum*** BWJ 7799 | |
| 'Cherry Blossom' | EPfP NLar |
| 'Cherub' ♀H4 | ELar |
| ***chinense*** | see *D. grandiflorum* |
| 'Christel' | LRHS LSRN |
| 'Christine Harbutt' | ELar |
| 'Claire' ♀H4 | ELar |
| 'Clear Springs Blue' (Clear Springs Series) | GAbr |
| 'Clifford Sky' ♀H4 | ELar LRHS |
| Connecticut Yankees Group | SMrm |
| 'Conspicuous' ♀H4 | ELar |
| 'Constance Rivett' ♀H4 | ELar |
| 'Coral Sunset'PBR (d) | MBri |
| 'Crown Jewel' | ELar WCFE |
| 'Cupid' | ELar |
| 'Darwin's Blue Indulgence'PBR | EPfP MBri |
| 'Darwin's Pink Indulgence'PBR | MBri |
| ***delavayi*** | LRHS |
| 'Desante Blue' **new** | LRHS |
| 'Diamant'PBR | EWTr EWll LRHS |
| 'Dreaming Spires' | SRms SWal |
| ***drepanocentrum*** HWJK 2263 | WCru |
| Dusky Maidens Group | IFoB MBNS STes WWEG |
| dwarf, dark blue-flowered | LRHS |
| ***elatum*** | GCal SRms SSth |
| – 'Double Innocence' (New Millennium Series) (d) | SMrm |
| 'Elisabeth Sahin' ♀H4 | ELar |
| 'Elizabeth Cook' ♀H4 | ELar |
| 'Elmfreude' | LRHS |
| 'Etonian' **new** | LRHS |
| 'Fanfare' | ELar |
| 'Faust' ♀H4 | ELar EWTr EWll |
| 'Fenella' ♀H4 | ELar LRHS WCFE |
| 'Finsteraarhorn' | GBin LRHS MAvo MCot |
| ***forrestii*** | GKev |
| 'Foxhill Nina' ♀H4 | ELar |
| 'Franjo Sahin' | ELar |
| Galahad Group | Widely available |
| 'Galahad' (Pacific Hybrids Series) | MGos XLum |
| 'Gillian Dallas' ♀H4 | ELar |
| ***glaciale*** HWJK 2299 | WCru |
| 'Gossamer' | IKil |
| § ***grandiflorum*** | GKev |
| § – 'Blauer Zwerg' | SPoG |
| § – 'Blue Butterfly' | CBot CSpe EPfP LRHS SPlb SPoG WSHC |
| – Blue Dwarf | see *D. grandiflorum* 'Blauer Zwerg' |
| – 'Delfix' | LRHS |
| – (Summer Series) 'Summer Blues' | LRHS SRot |
| – – 'Summer Nights' | LRHS |
| – – 'Summer Stars' | LRHS |
| 'Green Twist' (New Millennium Series) | EWll STes WWEG |
| (Guardian Series) 'Guardian Blue' | NPri |
| – 'Guardian Lavender' | LRHS NPri |
| – 'Guardian White' | LRHS NPri |
| Guinevere Group | CBcs CSBt CWib EBee ECtt EPfP LRHS MBri MWat NBPC NBir NLar NPri SBfd SPer SPoG WFar XLum |
| ***hansenii*** | LLHF |
| 'Harlekijn' | NLar |
| 'Heavenly Blue' | NLar |
| I 'Independence' | LRHS |
| Ivory Towers Group | ECtt |
| 'Jill Curley' ♀H4 | ELar LRHS |

| | |
|---|---|
| 'Kestrel' ♀H4 | ELar |
| King Arthur Group | CBcs CSBt EBee ECtt ELan EPfP LBMP LHop LRHS LSRN MGos MRav MWat NBPC NHol NLar NPri SBfd SBrd SMrm SPer SPoG WCAu WFar XLum |
| § 'Kings Blue Arrow'[PBR] | LRHS |
| 'La Bohème' | CWCL WCot |
| § 'Langdon's Royal Flush' ♀H4 | ELar LRHS |
| 'Lanzenträger' | LRHS |
| 'Leonora' | ELar |
| 'Lily Radley' | ELar |
| 'Loch Leven' ♀H4 | GBin |
| 'Lord Butler' ♀H4 | ELar LRHS |
| ***maackianum*** | CPom EWld GAuc GCal WCot |
| Magic Fountains Series | CSam IFoB LRHS MRav SGar SPlb SPoG WFar WGor |
| - 'Magic Fountains Cherry Blossom' | SBfd SPoG WFar |
| - 'Magic Fountains Dark Blue' | EPfP GMaP LSRN NEgg NLar SBfd SPoG WFar |
| - 'Magic Fountains Deep Blue' | NLar SBfd |
| - 'Magic Fountains Lavender' | EPfP SBfd |
| - 'Magic Fountains Lilac Pink' | SBfd SPoG |
| - 'Magic Fountains Lilac Rose' | NLar NVic WFar WGor |
| - 'Magic Fountains Pure White' | EPfP NEgg NLar SBfd WFar |
| - 'Magic Fountains Sky Blue' | EPfP NVic SBfd SPoG WFar |
| 'Margaret' | ELar |
| 'Merlin' ambig. | LRHS LSRN |
| 'Michael Ayres' ♀H4 | ELar |
| ***micropetalum*** CNDS 031 | WCru |
| 'Mighty Atom' | EWll |
| 'Min' ♀H4 | ELar |
| 'Misty Mauves' (New Millennium Series) (d) | SMrm |
| 'Moonbeam' | ELar |
| 'Morgentau' | LRHS |
| 'Mrs Newton Lees' | EWll IKil LRHS |
| 'Ned Wit' | IKil |
| New Century hybrids | CBcs |
| 'Nobility' | ELar |
| ***nudicaule*** | CBot |
| - 'Laurin' | LRHS WFar |
| 'Olive Poppleton' ♀H4 | SAga |
| 'Oliver' ♀H4 | ELar |
| 'Our Deb' ♀H4 | ELar |
| ***oxysepalum*** | LLHF |
| Pacific hybrids | CWCL EPfP LHop LSRN MHer MLHP NBlu NLar SBfd SPet SRms SWal SWvt WFar |
| 'Pagan Purples' (d) | IFoB |
| 'Patricia Johnson' | ELar |
| Percival Group | LRHS NLar |
| 'Pericles' | LRHS |
| Pink River = 'Barfourtythree'[PBR] | CBcs |
| 'Pink Ruffles' | ELar |
| 'Plagu Blue'[PBR] | WCot |
| Princess Caroline = 'Odabar'[PBR] | CBcs |
| 'Purple Passion' (New Millennium Series) | EWll WWEG |
| 'Purple Ruffles' | EPfP |
| 'Purple Velvet' ♀H4 | ELar |
| 'Red Caroline' | CBcs |
| ***requienii*** | CBot CSpe EWld NSti |
| 'Rosemary Brock' ♀H4 | ELar |
| Round Table Mixture | CTri |
| 'Royal Flush' | see *D.* 'Langdon's Royal Flush' |
| § × ***ruysii*** 'Pink Sensation' | CBot CWCL EWTr LRHS NGBo NLar WPGP |
| 'Sarita' | SUsu |
| 'Schönbuch' | LRHS |
| 'Secret'[PBR] | LRHS |
| § ***semibarbatum*** | CBot |
| 'Silver Jubilee' | ELar |
| 'Sky Sensation' | NLar |
| 'Snow Queen Arrow' | LRHS |
| 'Sommerabend' | LRHS |
| 'Spindrift' ♀H4 | ELar |
| ***stapeliosmum*** B&SWJ 2954 | WCru |
| - HWJK 2179 | WCru |
| ***staphisagria*** | CArn EOHP |
| 'Starmaker' | EPfP |
| Summer Skies Group | CBcs CSBt CTri EBee ECtt ELan EPfP LHop LRHS MBri MWat NBir NLar SBfd SMrm SPer SPoG WCAu WFar WHoo XLum |
| 'Summer Wine' | ELar |
| 'Summerfield Oberon' | ELar WCot |
| 'Sungleam' ♀H4 | EBee ELar EWTr IKil NLar |
| 'Sunkissed' ♀H4 | ELar |
| ***sutchuenense*** | CPom EWld WWlt |
| - BWJ 7867 | WCru |
| ***tatsienense*** | IFoB SRms |
| ***tenii*** BWJ 7693 | WCru |
| 'Tiddles' ♀H4 | ELar |
| 'Tiger Eye' | ELar |
| ***vestitum*** | EWld |
| 'Walton Gemstone' ♀H4 | ELar |
| White River = 'Barfourtyfive'[PBR] | CBcs |
| 'White Swan' | EPfP |
| 'Wishful Thinking'[PBR] | MBri |
| Woodfield strain | WHrl |
| 'Yvonne' | LRHS LSRN NLar |
| ***zalil*** | see *D. semibarbatum* |
| 'Zauberflöte' | LRHS |

## *Dendranthema* see *Chrysanthemum*

| | |
|---|---|
| ***pacificum*** | see *Ajania pacifica* |

## *Dendriopoterium* see *Sanguisorba*

## *Dendrobenthamia* see *Cornus*

## *Dendrocalamus* (*Poaceae*)

| | |
|---|---|
| ***asper*** | XBlo |
| ***calostachys*** | SPlb |
| ***giganteus*** | XBlo |
| § ***strictus*** | XBlo |

## *Dendromecon* (*Papaveraceae*)

| | |
|---|---|
| ***rigida*** | CBcs EPfP LRHS NLar SAga SKHP SMad WPGP WSHC |

## *Dendropanax* (*Araliaceae*)

| | |
|---|---|
| ***trifidus*** B&SWJ 11230 | WCru |

## *Dennstaedtia* (*Dennstaedtiaceae*)

| | |
|---|---|
| ***punctilobula*** | CLAP WCot WRic |

## *Dentaria* see *Cardamine*

**pinnata** see *Cardamine heptaphylla*
**polyphylla** see *Cardamine kitaibelii*

## *Dermatobotrys* (*Scrophulariaceae*)

**saundersii** ECre

## *Derwentia* see *Parahebe*

## *Deschampsia* (*Poaceae*)

**cespitosa** CKno COlW CRWN CWib EPPr EPfP EWTr LBMP LRHS MLLN MWat SMrm SPlb WCFE WCot WDin WGwG WMnd WMoo WPnP WTin WWEG XLum
- subsp. **alpina** LEdu
- Bronze Veil see *D. cespitosa* 'Bronzeschleier'
§ - 'Bronzeschleier' CKno CMea CPrp CSam CWCL EAEE EBee EHoe ELan EPPr EPfP EPla GMaP LEdu LRHS MAvo MBrN NGdn NOak NWsh SApp SPer SPhx SRms SSvw WMoo WPtf WTin WWEG XLum
- brown-leaved SApp
- 'Coral Cloud' new GQue
- 'Fairy's Joke' see *D. cespitosa* var. *vivipara*
- 'Fose' SApp
- Gold Dust see *D. cespitosa* 'Goldstaub'
- Golden Dew see *D. cespitosa* 'Goldtau'
- Golden Pendant see *D. cespitosa* 'Goldgehänge'
- Golden Shower see *D. cespitosa* 'Goldgehänge'
- Golden Veil see *D. cespitosa* 'Goldschleier'
§ - 'Goldgehänge' CSam EHoe EHul EPla MMHG NBir NPro WWEG
§ - 'Goldschleier' CPrp CSam CSpe EBee ECha EPPr EPla GCal GGar GMaP GQue LEdu LRHS NGdn NWsh SApp SBfd SPhx WMoo WPGP XLum
§ - 'Goldstaub' EPPr
§ - 'Goldtau' Widely available
- 'Morning Dew' WFar
- 'Northern Lights' (v) CWCL EBee ELan EPfP LBMP LEdu LRHS MBri MMuc NBro SApp SBfd SEND SLim SPer SPoG SRms SWvt WPGP WWEG
- 'Pixie Fountain' new EDAr EPPr
- 'Schottland' CKno EBee EPPr GBin
- 'Tardiflora' EBee
- 'Tauträger' EBee
§ - var. **vivipara** EHoe EPPr EPla LRHS NBro
- 'Waldschatt' EBee
- 'Willow Green' GCal MRav SCoo
**flexuosa** COlW EHoe NBir NWsh SMrm
- 'Tatra Gold' Widely available
**media** EHoe

## *Desfontainia* (*Desfontainiaceae*)

§ **spinosa** ♀H3 Widely available
- 'Harold Comber' CMac GKin WCru
- f. **hookeri** see *D. spinosa*

## *Desmodium* (*Papilionaceae*)

**callianthum** CMac LRHS SBrt WSHC
**canadense** CPom EBee LRHS NLar
§ **elegans** ♀H4 CBcs CHEx CPLG EBee ELan EPfP MBri NLar SBrt SKHP WHer WKif WPGP WSHC
- f. **albiflorum** new SBrt
**paniculatum** CPom
**praestans** see *D. yunnanense*
**tiliifolium** see *D. elegans*
§ **yunnanense** CHEx CPLG WSHC

## *Deuterocohnia* (*Bromeliaceae*)

**brevifolia** ♀H1 WPGP
**longipetala** RCB/Arg L-5 WCot

## *Deutzia* ✿ (*Hydrangeaceae*)

CC 4548 CPLG
CC 4550 CPLG
**calycosa** GQui
- B&SWJ 7442 WPat
- BWJ 8007 WCru
- 'Dali' CDoC CPLG SDys
aff. **calycosa** SIN 1878 GLin
**chunii** see *D. ningpoensis*
**compacta** CMCN SLon WFar WPGP
- GWJ 9202 WCru
- GWJ 9203 WCru
- GWJ 9339 WCru
- 'Lavender Time' CDoC CMac CPLG EBee NLar WCFE WPat
**cordatula** B&SWJ 3720 WCru
- B&SWJ 6917 WCru
**corymbosa** CDoC
**crenata** B&SWJ 8886 WCru
- B&SWJ 8896 WCru
- B&SWJ 8924 WCru
- 'Flore Pleno' see *D. scabra* 'Plena'
- var. **heterotricha** B&SWJ 8879 new WCru
- aff. var. **heterotricha** B&SWJ 5805 WCru
- var. **nakaiana** WPat
- - B&SWJ 11184 WCru
- - 'Nikko' see *D. gracilis* 'Nikko'
§ - 'Pride of Rochester' (d) CBcs CMCN CWib EBee ECrN GKin LRHS LSou LTen MGos MMuc MRav NLar SBod SEND SGol SLim SPoG SWvt WDin WGrn
**discolor** 'Major' CPLG WPat
× **elegantissima** SRms
- 'Fasciculata' EPfP LRHS SPer
- 'Rosealind' ♀H4 CBar CBcs CDul CPLG CTri EBee EPfP EWTr GKin LHop LRHS LSRN MGos MMuc MRav NCGa SEND SLim SPoG SRms SWvt WCFE WKif WPat WSHC
**glabrata** B&SWJ 617 GQui WCru
- B&SWJ 8427 WCru
**glomeruliflora** BWJ 7742 WCru
**gracilis** CDoC CDoy CSBt EBee ELan EPfP EWTr GGal GKin GQui LTen MAsh MGos MRav MSwo SPad SPer SPoG WDin WFar
- B&SWJ 8927 WCru
- 'Aurea' CBcs EPfP
- 'Carminea' see *D.* × *rosea* 'Carminea'
§ - 'Marmorata' (v) CPMA SLon
§ - 'Nikko' CBcs CMCN CMac CPBP CPLG CTri EBee ECho EShb EWes GKin LRHS MGos MHer MWhi NBlu NHol NLar NPro SGol SPlb SPoG WDin WKif WSHC
- var. **ogatae** B&SWJ 8911 WCru
- 'Rosea' see *D.* × *rosea*
- 'Variegata' see *D. gracilis* 'Marmorata'
**grandiflora** NChi WPGP
**hookeriana** LLHF WFar

| | |
|---|---|
| × ***hybrida*** 'Contraste' | CMac SPer |
| - 'Joconde' | CPLG WFar WKif |
| - 'Magicien' | CDoC CDul CMHG CMac CPLG CSBt CSam CWib EBee ECrN ELan EPfP EShb GQui LHop LRHS MAsh MBri MRav MSwo NBir SKHP SLon SMrm SPer SPoG SWvt WFar WPat |
| - 'Mont Rose' ♀H4 | CBar CDoC CDul CPLG EBee ELan EPfP GKin LBMP LBuc LRHS MAsh MBri MGos MMuc MRav MSwo MWhi NCGa NLar NPri SEND SGol SLim SPer SWvt WDin WFar WKif |
| § - 'Strawberry Fields' ♀H4 | CBcs CGHE CMCN CPLG CWCL EBee ELan ELon EPfP EPla EWTr GKin IArd LAst LBMP LBuc LRHS LSRN LSou MBlu MGos NEgg NLar SLon SPad SPoG WBor WFar WKif WPGP |
| 'Iris Alford' | CGHE LRHS SLon WPGP |
| × ***kalmiiflora*** | CMac CPLG CPMA CSBt CTri EBee GKin GQui LRHS MAsh MMuc NLar SLPl SPer SRms |
| × ***lemoinei*** | CBot |
| ***longifolia*** | WPGP |
| - 'Veitchii' ♀H4 | CDoy CSBt GQui MRav WCFE |
| - 'Vilmoriniae' | MRav |
| × ***magnifica*** | CBcs EBee ELan GQui SRms WDin |
| - 'Nancy' | GKin |
| - 'Rubra' | see *D.* × *hybrida* 'Strawberry Fields' |
| ***maximowicziana*** B&SWJ 11567 | WCru |
| ***monbeigii*** | CDoC CPLG WKif |
| - BWJ 7728 | WCru |
| ***multiradiata*** | WPGP |
| § ***ningpoensis*** ♀H4 | CAbP CPLG EBee EPfP GBin GQui SLPl SMrm SPer WPGP |
| ***paniculata*** B&SWJ 8592 **new** | WCru |
| ***parviflora*** var. ***barbinervis*** B&SWJ 8478 | WCru |
| 'Pink Pompon' | see *D.* 'Rosea Plena' |
| ***prunifolia*** B&SWJ 8588 **new** | WCru |
| ***pulchra*** | CAbP CDoC CMCN CPom EBee EPfP LRHS MRav NPro SBrd SLon SMrm SPer SSpi WFar WPGP WPat |
| - B&SWJ 3870 | WCru |
| - B&SWJ 6908 | GMac WCru |
| ***purpurascens*** BWJ 7859 | WCru |
| § × ***rosea*** | CDul CWib EBee EPfP LAst LRHS SRms WFar WKif |
| - 'Campanulata' | CPLG EPfP MAsh MSwo |
| § - 'Carminea' | SPlb SRms WDin WFar WPat |
| § 'Rosea Plena' (d) | CDoC CMac CPLG CSBt CWib EBee ECrN EPfP EWTr GKin LRHS MAsh MGos MMuc NBlu NEgg NLar SLim WFar WPat |
| ***rubens*** | WPat |
| ***scabra*** | CDul CTri |
| - B&SWJ 11127 | WCru |
| - B&SWJ 11168 | WCru |
| - B&SWJ 11178 | WCru |
| § - 'Candidissima' (d) | CDul CMac GQui MRav NLar SPer WPat |
| - 'Codsall Pink' | MRav |
| § - 'Plena' (d) | CPLG EBee ECrN ECtt ELan EPfP GKin SPer WCFE |
| - 'Pride of Rochester' | see *D. crenata* 'Pride of Rochester' |
| - 'Punctata' (v) | EBee EHoe MMuc SEND SRms WFar |
| - 'Robert Fortune' | SPlb |
| - 'Variegata' (v) | CDul CMac |
| ***setchuenensis*** | CMac GQui SSpi WPat WSHC |
| - var. ***corymbiflora*** ♀H4 | CBot CDoC CDul CGHE CPLG CSam CTri EBee EPfP IArd IDee LHop LRHS MBri MSwo SPoG WFar WKif WPGP |
| ***staminea*** HWJK 2180 | WCru |
| ***taiwanensis*** | SGol WPat |
| - B&SWJ 6858 | EBee WCru |
| - CWJ 12443 | WCru |
| - CWJ 12459 | WCru |
| 'Tourbillon Rouge' | EBee EQua LRHS LSRN NLar SBfd WDin |
| * ***vidalii*** | GGal |
| × ***wellsii*** | see *D. scabra* 'Candidissima' |
| × ***wilsonii*** | SRms |

## *Dianella* ✿ (*Hemerocallidaceae*)

| | |
|---|---|
| ***brevicaulis*** | ECou LEdu |
| ***caerulea*** | CHid CMac ECha ECou ELan EPri IFoB IGor LEdu MNrw MOWG NBir SBrd SMrm |
| - Breeze = 'Dcnco'[PBR] | ELan LTen MSCN NOak |
| - Cassa Blue = 'Dbb03'[PBR] | EBee ELan EPPr EPfP EWes GEdr GGar LAst LHop LRHS LTen MMHG NOak SPer SPoG |
| - 'Kulnura' | ECou |
| - Little Jess = 'Dcmp01'[PBR] | CPLG EBee GEdr GGar LRHS LTen MMHG NOak SPoG |
| - 'Variegata' | see *D. tasmanica* 'Variegata' |
| ***ensifolia*** | LEdu |
| ***intermedia*** | CTrC EWld IBlr |
| - 'Variegata' (v) | IBlr |
| ***nigra*** | CBcs CHid CPLG CPou CTrC EBee ECou IFro LEdu WFar |
| - 'Margaret Pringle' (v) | CBcs CPLG CTrC GGar NOak |
| ***prunina*** Utopia = 'Dp303'[PBR] | ESwi |
| ***revoluta*** | CFir ECou |
| - Baby Bliss = 'Dtn03'[PBR] | CKno EBee ECou NOak |
| - 'Hartz Mountain' | ECou |
| - Little Rev = 'Dr5000'[PBR] | EBee ELan EPfP ESwi GEdr GGar MMHG MSCN NOak SMrm WCot |
| 'Silver Streak' (v) | ESwi SPoG |
| ***tasmanica*** | Widely available |
| - from Logan | GCal |
| - 'Emerald Arch' | ELan ESwi NOak SPer |
| - 'Prosser' | ECou |
| - Tasred = 'Tr20'[PBR] | CPLG EBee ELan EPPr EPfP ESwi GBin GEdr LHop LTen MCot MMHG NOak SPer SPoG |
| § - 'Variegata' (v) | CBct CBod CCCN CDTJ CFir CPLG CSpe EAmu EBee ECou ELan EPfP LHop WCot |

## *Dianthus* ✿ (*Caryophyllaceae*)

| | |
|---|---|
| sp. | SVic WCot |
| AC&W 2116 | ECtt GEdr |
| RCB UA 7 | WCot |
| 'Alan Titchmarsh' (p) | EAEE EBee ECtt EPfP EWll LRHS LSRN LSou MGos MMHG MTis NCGa NEgg SPoG SWvt |
| 'Albert Hill' (p) **new** | SAll |
| 'Aldridge Yellow' (b) | SAll |
| 'Alfriston' (b) ♀H4 | SAll |
| 'Alice' (p) | LSRN SAll |
| 'Alice Lever' (p) | WAbe |

| | | |
|---|---|---|
| § | 'Allen's Maria' (p) | SAll |
| | 'Allspice' (p) | MRav WHoo |
| | Allwoodii Group (p) **new** | NNor |
| | Allwoodii Alpinus Group (p) | NGdn SRms WFar XLum |
| | 'Allwood's Celebration' (p) **new** | SAll |
| | 'Allwood's Crimson' (pf) | SAll |
| | 'Allwood's Delight' (p) **new** | SAll |
| | ***alpinus*** ♀H4 | GJos NBlu NMen NWCA SRms WFar WNew |
| | - 'Albus' | GLam NWad |
| | - 'Joan's Blood' ♀H4 | ELon EPot LSRN NMen SMad WAbe WFar |
| | 'Alyson' (p) | SAll |
| | ***amurensis*** | ECho EDAr GCal GKev MLHP NDov NNor SPhx SSvw |
| | - 'Andrey' (p) | NNor WHrl |
| | ***anatolicus*** | CTri ECho MHer NGdn NWCA WPer XLum |
| | 'Andrew Morton' (b) | SAll |
| | 'Angelo' (b) | SAll |
| | 'Anne Jones' (b) | EPfP |
| | 'Annette' (p) | EBee ECho GKev LRHS LSRN MAsh NGdn SWvt |
| | 'Antique' | SAll |
| | 'Apple Tea' (pf) **new** | SAll |
| | 'Arctic Star' (p) | CMea CTri EBee GMaP NEgg SPoG SRot SWvt WFar |
| | ***arenarius*** | EDAr GKev LEdu NGdn SPlb XLum |
| | - 'Little Maiden' | EDif NCGa NDov NGdn SBch SPhx |
| | - 'Snow Flurries' | ITim |
| | 'Argus' | IGor |
| | ***armeria*** | WHer WOut WTou |
| | ***arpadianus*** | GEdr GLam NGdn |
| | 'Arthur Leslie' (b) | SAll |
| | 'Artu' (pf) **new** | SAll |
| § | × ***arvernensis*** (p) ♀H4 | ECha ECho EPot GLam |
| | - 'Albus' | ECho |
| | 'Aurora' (b) | SAll |
| | 'Auvergne' | see *D.* × *arvernensis* |
| | 'Averiensis' | see *D.* 'Berlin Snow' |
| | 'Baby Treasure' (p) | ECtt SRot |
| | 'Badenia' (p) | ECha |
| | 'Bailey's Celebration' (p) | EAEE ECGP ECtt EPfP LRHS LSou MTis NCGa NDov SRGP |
| § | 'Bailey's Daily Mail' (p) ♀H4 | CBcs |
| | 'Barbara Norton' (p) | ECtt |
| | ***barbatus*** | GAuc MNrw SVic |
| | - SDR 6406 | GKev |
| | - Barbarini Series | WGor |
| | - 'Black Adder' | CSpe |
| | - 'Darkest of All' **new** | CSpe |
| | - Nigrescens Group (p,a) ♀H4 | CBre CMea CSpe MNHC SAga SPhx WHil |
| I | - 'Sooty' (p,a) | EDAr ELan EWld WCFE WFar |
| | - 'Super Parfait Strawberry' (Super Parfait Series) ♀H3 | LRHS |
| | - 'Tuxedo Black' | MWea |
| | 'Bath's Pink' (p) | GMac |
| § | 'Bat's Double Red' (p/d) | SAll SSvw |
| | 'Becky Robinson' (p) ♀H4 | SAll |
| § | 'Berlin Snow' (p) | CPBP ELan EWes ITim LRHS WPat |
| | 'Betty Miller' (b) | SAll |
| | 'Betty Morton' (p) ♀H4 | ECtt IFoB SSvw WFar WKif |
| | Black and White Minstrels Group | SAga |
| | 'Black Baccara' (pf) **new** | SAll |
| | 'Blue Hedgehog' | ECtt |
| | 'Blue Hills' (p) | ECho |
| | 'Blue Ice' (b) | SAll |
| | 'Blush' | see *D.* 'Souvenir de la Malmaison' |
| | 'Bobby' (p) | SAll |
| | 'Bombardier' (p) | ECtt |
| | 'Bookham Gleam' (b) | SAll |
| | 'Bookham Grand' (b) | SAll |
| | 'Bookham Heroine' (b) | SAll |
| | 'Bookham Lad' (b) | SAll |
| | 'Border Special' (b) | SAll |
| | 'Bouquet Purple' (p) | CSpe |
| | 'Bovey Belle' (p) ♀H4 | CBcs SAll |
| | 'Bressingham Pink' (p) | ECtt |
| | ***brevicaulis*** | WAbe |
| | 'Brian Tumbler' (b) ♀H4 | SAll |
| | 'Bridal Veil' (p) | SAll SBch SSvw WHer |
| | 'Brigadier' (p) | ECtt |
| | 'Brilliance' (p) | MSCN WMoo |
| | 'Brilliant' | see *D. deltoides* 'Brilliant' |
| | 'Brilliant Star' (p) ♀H4 | ECho ECtt LRHS MWat SEND SPet SWvt WWFP |
| | 'Brympton Red' (p) | ECha MRav SAll |
| | 'Bryony Lisa' (b) ♀H4 | SAll |
| | ***caesius*** | see *D. gratianopolitanus* |
| | ***callizonus*** | LLHF NMen |
| | 'Calypso' (pf) | CTri |
| | 'Calypso Star' (p) ♀H4 | EBee ECho ECtt GMaP NGdn SPet SPoG |
| | 'Cameron' (pf) **new** | SAll |
| | 'Can-can' (pf) | ECho ECtt |
| | 'Candy Clove' (b) | SAll |
| | Candy Floss = 'Devon Flavia'PBR (Scent First Series) (p) ♀H4 | ECtt EWTr LAst LBMP LRHS MTis NEgg SBfd SEND SMrm SPoG |
| | 'Candy Spice' (p) | MRav |
| § | 'Carmine Letitia Wyatt'PBR (p) ♀H4 | EAEE EBee ECtt LRHS MSpe NCGa SPoG |
| | ***carthusianorum*** | CArn CKno LPla MCot NDov NGdn SAga SAll SGar SPhx SPlb SSvw SWat WKif WPGP WPer WSHC WWFP |
| | - 'Rupert's Pink' | NGdn SBch |
| | ***caryophyllus*** | CArn ELau NBlu |
| | - Amelie = 'Jinsamelie' (pf) **new** | SAll |
| | - 'Birba' (pf) **new** | SAll |
| | - 'Coquette' (pf) **new** | SAll |
| | - 'Corsa'PBR **new** | SAll |
| | - Lion King = 'Hillik'PBR (pf) **new** | SAll |
| | - 'Milky Way' (pf) **new** | SAll |
| | - Splash = 'Barsplash' (pf) **new** | SAll |
| | - 'Wish' (p,a) **new** | SAll |
| | 'Casser's Pink' (p) | SBch |
| | 'Charles' (p) | SAll |
| | 'Charles Edward' (p) | SAll |
| | 'Charles Musgrave' | see *D.* 'Musgrave's Pink' |
| | Charlie = 'Hilcharly' (pf) **new** | SAll |
| | 'Chastity' (p) | WHoo |
| | Cheddar pink | see *D. gratianopolitanus* |
| | 'Cherly' | LSRN |
| | 'Cherry Clove' (b) | SAll |
| | 'Cherry Pie' (p) | ECtt LRHS SPoG WMnd |
| | 'Cheryl' | see *D.* 'Houndspool Cheryl' |
| | 'Chianti' (pf) | NGdn |
| | 'Chianti Double' (p) | SAll |
| | ***chinensis*** 'Black and White' | CSpe |
| | 'Chris Crew' (b) ♀H4 | SAll |
| | 'Clare' (p) | SAll |

| | | |
|---|---|---|
| | 'Claret Joy' (p) ♀H4 | CBcs ECtt EPfP LRHS MMuc NEgg SAll SEND |
| § | 'Cockenzie Pink' (p) | SAll SBch SSvw |
| | 'Coconut Sundae' (p) | ECtt ELon EWTr EWll LAst LRHS LSRN MSCN MTis NCGa NNor SBfd SMrm SRot WBor |
| | 'Constance' (p) | SAll |
| | 'Constance Finnis' | see *D.* 'Fair Folly' |
| | 'Consul' (b) | SAll |
| | 'Conwy Silver' | WAbe |
| | 'Conwy Star' | NMen WAbe |
| | 'Coral Reef' PBR (p) | ECtt MWat NNor SPoG WHil |
| | 'Coronation Ruby' (p) ♀H4 | SAll |
| | 'Cosmic Swirl Red' (p) | WHil |
| | 'Coste Budde' (p) | WSHC |
| | 'Cover Story' | NWCA |
| | 'Cracker' (p) **new** | GAbr |
| | 'Cranmere Pool' (p) ♀H4 | CBcs CMea EBee ECtt ELan EPfP GAbr LRHS NGdn NNor SBfd SPoG SWvt WFar WMnd WRHF WWEG |
| | 'Crimson Chance' (p) | EPot NSla |
| | 'Crock of Gold' (b) | SAll |
| | ***cruentus*** | NDov SPhx SSvw WPer WWEG |
| | 'D.D.R.' | see *D.* 'Berlin Snow' |
| | 'Dad's Favourite' (p) | CEnt SAll SRms SSvw |
| | 'Daily Mail' | see *D.* 'Bailey's Daily Mail' |
| | 'Dainty Dame' (p) ♀H4 | CPBP CSpe CTri EBee ECho EPfP LRHS MNHC MWea SAll SBch SPoG SRot WFar |
| | 'Dancing Queen' PBR (p) | MTis MWat NNor |
| | 'Daphne' (p) | SAll |
| | 'Dark Star' (p) | ECho |
| | 'Dartington Double' (p) | ECho SEND |
| | 'David' (p) | EPfP LSRN SAll SBch |
| | 'David Russell' (b) ♀H4 | SAll |
| | 'David Saunders' (b) ♀H4 | SAll |
| | 'Dawlish Joy' (p) | EBee SPoG SRGP |
| | 'Dawn' (b) | SAll |
| | 'Dawn' (pf) | ECho |
| | 'Dedham Beauty' | WCot WWEG |
| | ***deltoides*** ♀H4 | CArn CEnt CSev ECha ECho EPfP LEdu MAsh MMuc SPlb SRms WFar WJek WNew WPtf |
| | - 'Albus' | ECha EPfP EWTr MNHC NBlu NGdn NWCA WMoo |
| | - 'Arctic Fire' | CWib ECho EPfP NBlu NGdn WFar WMoo |
| | - 'Bright Eyes' (p) | ECho LRHS MTis MWat |
| § | - 'Brilliant' | CChe CTri ECho EPau GJos LAst MBNS MDun MNHC NGdn NSla NVic SAll SRms WFar WGor WRHF WWEG |
| | - 'Dark Eyes' (p) | EWes |
| | - 'Erectus' | EPfP |
| | - Flashing Light | see *D. deltoides* 'Leuchtfunk' |
| § | - 'Leuchtfunk' | CMea ECho ECtt EPfP GGar LAst LRHS MWat NBPC NChi NNor SPoG SWal WFar WMoo WWEG |
| I | - 'Luneburg Heath Maiden Pink' | NGdn SSvw |
| | - 'Microchip' | WFar WMoo |
| | - 'Nelli' (p) | ECho NGdn SSvw |
| | - red-flowered | NBlu SVic |
| | - 'Shrimp' | NGdn |
| | - 'Vampir' | GAbr |
| | 'Denis' (p) | LSRN SAll |
| | 'Desert Song' (b) | SAll |
| | 'Desmond' | EPfP |
| | 'Devon Blush' (p) | ECtt |
| | 'Devon Cream' PBR (p) | EAEE EBee ECtt LAst LRHS LSou MWat NEgg WMnd |
| | 'Devon Dove' PBR (p) ♀H4 | CMea CSBt CTri EAEE EBee ECtt EPfP LRHS LSou MRav MSpe MWat NCGa NDov NEgg SBfd |
| | 'Devon General' PBR (p) | CTri EBee ECtt SBfd |
| | 'Devon Glow' (p) ♀H4 | EBee EPfP |
| | 'Devon Magic' PBR (p) | EBee ECtt ELan WFar |
| | 'Devon Pearl' PBR (p) | WMnd |
| | 'Devon Wizard' PBR (p) ♀H4 | CSBt EAEE EBee ECtt EPfP LRHS MMuc MRav MSpe NCGa NDov NEgg NNor SBfd SEND WFar |
| | 'Dewdrop' (p) | CMea CTri EBee ECho ECtt EPfP MAsh MHer MMuc NBir NGdn NPro SAga SAll SEND WFar |
| | 'Diamond Scarlet' (Diamond Series) **new** | LRHS |
| | 'Diana' | see *D.* Dona |
| | 'Diane' (p) ♀H4 | EBee ELan EPfP LRHS NEgg SAll SPoG SWvt WMnd |
| * | 'Diane Cape' | SAll |
| | 'Diplomat' (b) | SAll |
| § | Dona = 'Brecas' (pf) | LSRN SRGP |
| | 'Dora' (p) | ECho LRHS |
| | 'Doris' (p) ♀H4 | Widely available |
| | 'Doris Allwood' (pf) | CSBt EMal SAll |
| | 'Doris Elite' (p) | SAll |
| | 'Doris Galbally' (b) | SAll |
| | 'Doris Majestic' (p) | SAll WFar |
| | 'Doris Ruby' | see *D.* 'Houndspool Ruby' |
| | 'Doris Supreme' (p) | SAll |
| | 'Double North' | ELon NWCA |
| | 'Dubarry' (p) | CTri CWan ECtt WPat WPer |
| | 'Duchess of Fife' (p) | ECtt EPfP |
| | 'Duchess of Roxburghe' (pf) | SAll |
| | 'Duchess of Westminster' (M) | EMal SAll |
| | 'Duke of Norfolk' (pf) | EMal SAll |
| | 'Earl of Essex' (p) | SAll |
| | 'Edenside Scarlet' (b) | SAll |
| | 'Edenside White' (b) | SAll |
| | 'Edna' (p) | SAll |
| | 'Edward Allwood' (pf) | SAll |
| | 'Edwin Cross' (b) **new** | SAll |
| | 'Eileen' (p) | SAll |
| | 'Eileen Lever' (p) | CPBP IFoB WAbe WFar |
| | 'Eileen Neal' (b) ♀H4 | SAll |
| | 'Eileen O'Connor' (b) ♀H4 | SAll |
| | 'Eleanor Parker' (p) | WAbe |
| | 'Eleanor's Old Irish' (p) | ELon LRHS MWhi WCot WHoo WTin WWEG |
| | 'Elfin Star' (p) | ECho SPet |
| | 'Elizabeth' (p) | CEnt |
| | 'Elizabethan' (p) | CFee GMac MCot |
| * | 'Elizabethan Pink' (p) | SAll |
| | 'Emperor' | see *D.* 'Bat's Double Red' |
| * | ***erectaceaus*** | GAuc |
| | ***erinaceus*** | ECho GJos WAbe WPat |
| | - var. ***alpinus*** | EPot ITim |
| | - Duguid's **new** | WThu |
| | 'Erycina' (b) | SAll |
| | 'Ethel Hurford' (p) | WHoo |
| | 'Eva Humphries' (b) | SAll |
| | 'Evening Star' (p) ♀H4 | CHVG CTri ECho MAsh NEgg SPet SPoG SWvt |
| | 'Excelsior' (p) | SSvw |
| | 'Exquisite' (b) | SAll |
| § | 'Fair Folly' (p) | IGor SAll SBch SSvw |
| | 'Fanal' (p) | NBir |

| |  |  |
|---|---|---|
| | 'Farnham Rose' (p) | SAll SSvw |
| | 'Fenbow Nutmeg Clove' (b) | SDix WMnd |
| | 'Fettes Mount' (p) | LPla MWhi WCot |
| | 'Feuerhexe' (p) | EPot |
| | 'Fimbriatus' (p) | WHoo |
| | 'Fiona' (p) | SAll |
| | 'Firestar' (p) | CTri EPot LRHS MAsh MWat SPet SRot SWvt |
| | 'First Lady' (b) | SAll |
| | Fizzy = 'Wp08 Ver03' (Early Bird Series) (p/d) | CMea LBMP SBfd |
| | 'Flanders' (b) ♀H4 | SAll |
| | 'Fleur' (p) | SAll |
| | 'Floristan Mix" (p, a) **new** | NNor |
| | 'Forest Princess' (b) | SAll |
| | 'Forest Sprite' (b) | SAll |
| | 'Forest Treasure' (b) | SAll |
| | 'Forest Violet' (b) | SAll |
| | 'Fortuna' (p) | SAll |
| | 'Fountain's Abbey' (p) | IGor |
| | 'Frances Isabel' (p) | SAll |
| | 'Freda' (p) | SAll |
| | 'Freda Woodliffe' (p) | NMen WAbe |
| | ***freynii*** | ECho EPot EWes GKev WAbe |
| * | - var. ***nana*** | GKev |
| * | 'Frilly' | LBMP |
| N | fringed pink | see *D. superbus* |
| | 'Fusilier' (p) | CElw CMea CTri ECho ECtt EDAr EPfP GMaP LHop LRHS MAsh NWCA SAll SEND SRot SWvt WFar |
| | 'Gail Graham' (b) | SAll |
| | 'Gail Tilsley' (b) | SAll |
| | 'Garland' (p) | CMea CTri SAga |
| | 'Gaydena' (b) | SAll |
| | ***giganteus*** | CSpe MWea WSHC |
| | 'Gingham Gown' (p) | ECtt EPot NBir SAll |
| | ***glacialis*** subsp. ***gelidus*** | EPot |
| | 'Gold Dust' | SAll |
| | 'Gold Flake' (p) | SBch |
| | 'Gold Fleck' | ECtt GLam |
| | 'Golden Cross' (b) ♀H4 | SAll |
| | 'Grandma Calvert' (p) | SAll SBch |
| | ***graniticus*** | EPot |
| | 'Gran's Favourite' (p) ♀H4 | Widely available |
| § | ***gratianopolitanus*** ♀H4 | CArn CBod CTri EPfP EPot GJos GKev GLam LEdu MHer MNHC MRav NBid SEND SRms WAbe WGwG |
| | - 'Albus' | MHer NWCA |
| | - dwarf | NWCA WAbe |
| | - 'Grandiflorus' | WFar |
| * | - 'Karlik' (p) | GJos |
| § | - 'Tiny Rubies' (p) | GLam NGdn WAbe |
| | 'Gravetye Gem' (b) | SRms |
| | 'Green Lane' (p) | CHll |
| | 'Greensides' (p) | SAll |
| | 'Grey Dove' (b) ♀H4 | SAll |
| | 'Greytown' (b) | GCal |
| | 'Gypsy Star' (p) | EBee ECho GMaP SPoG |
| | ***haematocalyx*** | EPot NMen WFar |
| | - 'Alpinus' | see *D. haematocalyx* subsp. *pindicola* |
| § | - subsp. ***pindicola*** | EPot GAuc GKev LLHF NMen |
| | 'Hannah Gertsen' (p/d) | SAll |
| | 'Harkell Special' (b) | SAll |
| | 'Harlequin' (p) | WPer |
| | 'Haytor Rock' (p) ♀H4 | EBee EPfP LRHS NCGa NNor |
| | 'Haytor White' (p) ♀H4 | CBcs CTri CWib EPfP MRav MWhi SAll SRms WCot WWEG |
| | 'Hazel Ruth' (b) ♀H4 | SAll |

| |  |  |
|---|---|---|
| | 'Heath' (b) | SAll |
| | 'Helen' (p) | ELon LSRN SAll |
| | 'Helena Hitchcock' (p) | SAll |
| | 'Hereford Butter Market' (p) | EBee SSvw |
| | 'Hidcote' (p) | CPBP CTri LRHS MAsh MWat WFar |
| | 'Hidcote Red' | ECho GLam MWat |
| | 'Highland Fraser' (p) | SRms WKif |
| | 'Hope' (p) | SAll SBch |
| | 'Hot Spice' (p) ♀H4 | SPoG |
| § | 'Houndspool Cheryl' (p) ♀H4 | CTri EBee EPfP SAll SBfd SRGP SRms WFar |
| § | 'Houndspool Ruby' (p) ♀H4 | CBcs EPfP LBMP LSRN SAll SBfd |
| | ***hyssopifolius*** | GJos WAbe WMoo |
| | 'Ian' (p) | LSRN SAll SBch WWEG |
| | Iced Gem = 'Wp06 Fatima' PBR (Scent First Series) (p/d) | LBMP LRHS LSRN MTis MWat NNor SBfd SPoG SRot |
| | 'Icomb' (p) | SRms WHoo WPer |
| | 'Ina' (p) | SRms |
| | 'Inchmery' (p) | SAll SBch SSvw WHoo |
| | 'India Star' PBR (p) ♀H4 | CTri EBee ECho EPfP EWTr LBMP LRHS MWat NEgg SEND WPat |
| | 'Inglestone' (p) | CTri WPer |
| | Inka = 'Barinka' PBR (pf) **new** | SAll |
| | 'Inshriach Dazzler' (p) ♀H4 | CPBP ECho ECtt EPot GGar GMaP LRHS MAsh MHer NEgg NGdn NHar NHol NRya SRot WAbe |
| | 'Inshriach Startler' (p) | CMea WNew |
| | 'Ipswich Pink' (p) | MNHC SRms |
| | × ***isensis*** **new** | CSpe |
| | 'James Portman' (p) | ELon WMnd |
| | 'Jane Austen' (p) | WPer |
| | 'Janet Walker' (p) | GMaP |
| | 'Jess Hewins' (pf) | SAll |
| * | 'Jewel' | ECtt |
| | 'Joan Schofield' (p) | SBch |
| | 'Joy' (p) ♀H4 | EBee ECtt EPfP LAst SAll SPoG WWEG |
| | 'Julian' (p) | SAll |
| | 'Julie Ann Davis' (b) | SAll |
| | 'Katherine Ingwersen' (p) **new** | NWCA |
| | 'Kathleen Hitchcock' (b) ♀H4 | SAll |
| | 'Kessock Charm' | MNrw |
| | 'Kesteven Chamonix' (p) | WPer |
| | 'Kesteven Kirkstead' (p) ♀H4 | MNrw |
| | 'Kim' (p) **new** | NDov |
| | ***kitaibelii*** | see *D. petraeus* subsp. *petraeus* |
| | ***knappii*** | SRms SSvw WMoo WPer |
| | - 'Yellow Harmony' (p, a) | GJos |
| | 'Kristina' (pf) ♀H1 | SAll |
| | ***kusnezovii*** | LLHF |
| | 'La Bourboule' (p) ♀H4 | CMea CTri ECho EDAr EPot GAbr LRHS MAsh MWat NMen NPri NWCA SBch SRms WFar WPat |
| | 'La Bourboule Alba' (p) | CTri ECho ECtt EDAr EPot GLam WFar WGor |
| | 'Laced Joy' (p) | SAll |
| | 'Laced Monarch' (p) | CBcs EAEE EBee ECtt EPfP EWTr GCra LHop LRHS MMuc NCGa NEgg NNor SAll SEND SMrm SPlb SPoG WWEG |
| | 'Laced Mrs Sinkins' (p) | SAll |
| | 'Laced Prudence' | see *D.* 'Prudence' |
| | 'Laced Romeo' (p) | SAll |

| |  |  |
|---|---|---|
| | 'Laced Treasure' (p) | SAll |
| | 'Lady Granville' (p) | IGor SAll SBch SSvw |
| | Lady in Red = 'Wp04 Xanthe'PBR (p) | CSBt EAEE EBee ECtt LRHS LSou MTis NNor |
| | 'Lady Madonna' (p) | MTis SSvw |
| | 'Lady Wharncliffe' (p) | SBch |
| | 'Lady Windermere' (M) | EMal |
| | 'Lancing Monarch' (b) | SAll |
| | 'Lancing Supreme' (p/d) | SAll |
| | ***langeanus*** NS 255 | NWCA |
| | 'Laura' (p) | SAll |
| | 'Lemsii' (p) ♀H4 | ECtt NGdn NMen WPer |
| | 'Leslie Rennison' (b) | SAll |
| | 'Letitia Wyatt' (p) ♀H4 | CMea EBee EPfP LRHS MRav MWat SBch SBfd SPoG SRGP |
| | 'Leuchtkugel' | ECho LLHF NMen |
| | 'Lily Lesurf' (b) | SAll |
| | Lily the Pink = 'WP05 Idare'PBR (p) | LRHS MTis |
| | 'Linfield Doreen Ashmore' (p) | SAll |
| | 'Linfield Dorothy Perry' (p) ♀H4 | SAll |
| | 'Linfield Isobel Croft' (p) | SAll |
| | 'Linfield Julie' (p) | SAll |
| | 'Linfield Kathy Booker' (p) ♀H4 | SAll |
| | 'Little Ben' (p) | SAll |
| | 'Little Jock' (p/d) | ECho ECtt EDAr GLam LRHS MAsh MHer MWat SAll SPlb SPoG SRms WFar |
| | 'Little Miss Muffet' (p) | CHll |
| | 'Liz Rigby' (b) | SAll |
| | 'London Brocade' (p) | SAll |
| | 'London Glow' (p) | SAll SBch |
| | 'London Lovely' (p) | SAll SSvw |
| | 'London Poppet' (p) | SAll |
| | 'Lord Nuffield' (b) **new** | SAll |
| | 'Loris' (pf) **new** | SAll |
| | 'Lowan' (p) **new** | NWCA |
| | ***lumnitzeri*** | GLam LLHF NGdn NMen WPer |
| | 'Lustre' (b) | SAll |
| | 'Madonna' (pf) | EPfP SSvw |
| | 'Maggie' (p) | LSRN |
| | 'Maisie Neal' (b) ♀H4 | SAll |
| | 'Mambo' (pf) ♀H4 | SAll |
| | 'Mandy' (p) | SAll |
| | 'Maria' | see *D.* 'Allen's Maria' |
| | 'Marjery Breeze' | SAll |
| | 'Marmion' (M) | EMal SAll |
| | 'Mars' (p) | ECho ECtt |
| | 'Matthew' (p) | WHoo |
| | 'Maudie Hinds' (b) | SAll |
| | 'Maybole' (b) | SAll |
| | 'Maythorne' (p) | SRms |
| | 'Mendip Hills' (b) | SAll |
| | Mendlesham Minx = 'Russmin'PBR (p) | EBee ECho EDAr EWTr GGar LRHS MWat MWea SAll SBfd SWvt |
| | 'Merlin' ♀H4 | NEgg |
| | 'Messines Pink' (p) | SAll |
| | 'Michael Saunders' (b) ♀H4 | SAll |
| | ***microlepis*** | ECho NGdn WAbe |
| | - f. ***albus*** | NSla |
| | - ED 791562 | NGdn |
| | - 'Leuchtkugel' | ECho WAbe |
| | - var. ***musalae*** | ECho EPot LLHF NMen |
| | 'Mike Briggs' (b) | SAll |
| | Minerva = 'Kormirva' (pf) **new** | SAll |
| | 'Miss Sinkins' (p) | CTri IFoB SPet |
| | ***monadelphus*** subsp. ***pallens*** | GAuc |
| | 'Monica Wyatt' (p) ♀H4 | CBcs EBee ECtt EPfP LRHS MTis NCGa NEgg SPoG WWEG WWFP |
| | 'Montrose Pink' | see *D.* 'Cockenzie Pink' |
| | 'Monty Allwood' (p) **new** | SAll |
| | Morning Star = 'Devon Winnie'PBR (p) | ECtt MAsh |
| | 'Mother of Pearl' (Perfume Pinks Series) **new** | MTis MWat SBfd |
| | 'Moulin Rouge' (p) ♀H4 | CMea CTri EAEE EBee ECGP ECtt EPfP GCra IPot LRHS LSou MSpe MTis MWat NDov SPhx SPoG WWEG |
| | 'Mrs Clark' | see *D.* 'Nellie Clark' |
| | 'Mrs Macbride' (p) | SAll |
| | 'Mrs Roxburgh' (p) | CSam |
| | 'Mrs Sinkins' (p) | Widely available |
| | 'Murray Douglas' (p) | SSvw |
| | 'Murray's Laced Pink' (p) | MWhi WHrl |
| N | 'Musgrave's Pink' (p) | CHid ECha MRav SAll SBch SSvw |
| | 'Musgrave's White' | see *D.* 'Musgrave's Pink' |
| | ***myrtinervius*** | ECho EPot GKev MHer NDov NGdn SRms WHoo |
| | 'Mystic Star' | CMea ELan EWTr GAbr IPot SBfd |
| | 'Napoleon III' (p) | SAll SSvw |
| | ***nardiformis*** | SPhx |
| | 'Natalie Saunders' (b) ♀H4 | SAll |
| | 'Nautilus' (b) | SAll |
| | ***neglectus*** misapplied | see *D. pavonius* |
| § | 'Nellie Clark' (p) | MWat |
| | 'Neon Star'PBR (p) ♀H4 | CTri EBee ECho EDAr ELan GKev LRHS MAsh MWat SPoG WFar |
| | 'Night Star' (p) ♀H4 | EBee ECho ELan EPfP GMaP LHop LRHS MAsh NEgg SBch SEND SPet SRot WFar WHil WPtf |
| | 'Nika' (pf) **new** | SAll |
| | ***nitidus*** | NBir NWCA |
| | ***nivalis*** | GLam |
| | ***noeanus*** | see *D. petraeus* subsp. *noeanus* |
| | 'Northland' (pf) | EMal SAll |
| | 'Nyewoods Cream' (p) | CMea CTri ECho EPot MHer NGdn NMen NPri WPer |
| § | 'Oakington' (p) | CTri MRav NWCA |
| | 'Oakington Rose' | see *D.* 'Oakington' |
| | 'Old Blush' | see *D.* 'Souvenir de la Malmaison' |
| | 'Old Crimson Clove' (b) | SBch |
| | 'Old Mother Hubbard' (p) | CFee CHll |
| | 'Old Red Clove' (p) | CFee WCot |
| § | 'Old Square Eyes' (p) | MNrw SAll SSvw WFar |
| | 'Old Velvet' (p) | GCal MNrw SAll |
| | 'Oliver' (p) | SAll |
| | 'Orange Maid' (b) | SAll |
| | ***oschtenicus*** | GKev |
| | 'Oxford Magic' (p) **new** | SAll |
| | 'Painted Lady' (p) | SAll |
| | 'Paisley Gem' (p) | SAll SSvw |
| | Passion = 'Wp Passion'PBR (Scent First Series) (p) | CWGN ECtt GAbr LBMP LRHS LSou MTis NNor SBfd SPoG WCot |
| § | ***pavonius*** ♀H4 | EWes MAsh NGdn NMen NWCA WPer |
| | 'Pax' (pf) | SAll |
| | 'Peach' (p) | SEND |
| § | ***petraeus*** | EWes NGdn SSvw WThu XLum |
| § | - subsp. ***noeanus*** | EPot LHop LLHF WHal WPer |
| § | - subsp. ***petraeus*** | WPer |
| | 'Petticoat Lace' (p) | SAll |
| | 'Pheasant's Eye' (p) | SAll SSvw WHer |

| | | |
|---|---|---|
| | 'Pike's Pink' (p) ♀H4 | CSpe CTri EBee ECho ECtt EDAr ELan EPfP LHop LRHS MAsh MHer MMuc MRav MWat NBir NGdn NMen SAga SAll SEND SPet SRms WAbe |
| | ***pindicola*** | see *D. haematocalyx* subsp. *pindicola* |
| | ***pinifolius*** | IFro |
| | 'Pink Dover' (pf) | SAll |
| | 'Pink Fantasy' (b) | SAll |
| | 'Pink Fizz' **new** | LRHS |
| | 'Pink Jewel' (p) | CMea CPBP ECtt EPot MAsh NMen SAll SBch |
| | 'Pink Mrs Sinkins' (p) | ECha MHer MLHP SAll |
| | 'Pink Pearl' (b) **new** | SAll |
| | 'Pixie' (b) | EPot NGdn |
| | 'Pixie Star'PBR (p) ♀H4 | ECho EPfP EWTr LBMP MAsh SPoG SRot |
| | ***plumarius*** | CArn MLHP SAll SRms SSvw WHer WMoo |
| | - 'Ipswich Pinks' | GJos |
| | - 'Sonata' | GJos |
| | Popstar = 'Wp04 Esther' (p) | EWll |
| | 'Prado' (pf) ♀H4 | SAll |
| | Pretty FlamingoPBR | see *D.* 'Carmine Letitia Wyatt' |
| | Primero Mango = 'Koprimang'PBR (pf) **new** | SAll |
| | 'Prince Charming' (p) | ECho ECtt MAsh SRms |
| | 'Princess of Wales' (M) | EMal SAll |
| | 'Priory Pink' (p) | SAll |
| § | 'Prudence' (p) | SAll |
| | 'Pudsey Prize' (p) | CPBP EPot WAbe |
| | 'Purple Jenny' (p) | SAll |
| | 'Queen of Hearts' (p) | CTri ECho GLam MMuc NWCA SEND |
| § | 'Queen of Henri' (p) | ECho ECtt LRHS MHer WFar |
| | 'Queen of Sheba' (p) | IGor SAll SBch SSvw WKif |
| | 'Rachel' (p) | ECtt |
| | 'Rainbow Loveliness' (p,a) | SAll SRms WHil |
| | 'Ralph Gould' (p) | ECho |
| | 'Raspberry Parfait' | LRHS |
| | 'Raspberry Sundae' (p) | ECtt EWTr LBMP LRHS LSRN MTis NCGa SBfd SEND SPoG WBor WHil |
| | 'Rebekah' | CPBP LBMP |
| | 'Red Star'PBR (p) ♀H4 | ECho ELan GGar GJos LRHS SRot |
| | Reina = 'Lonreina'PBR (pf) **new** | SAll |
| | 'Reine de Henri' | see *D.* 'Queen of Henri' |
| | 'Richard Pollak' (b) | SAll |
| | 'Rivendell' (p) | ECho NMen WAbe |
| | 'Robert Allwood' (pf) | SAll |
| | 'Robin Ritchie' (p) | WHoo |
| | 'Romance' (p) | LBMP LRHS MTis SBfd |
| | 'Rose de Mai' (p) | CSam SAll SBch SSvw WHoo |
| | 'Rose Devon Pearl'PBR | EPfP |
| | 'Rose Joy' (p) ♀H4 | EBee EPfP MWat |
| § | 'Rose Monica Wyatt'PBR (p) ♀H4 | EAEE LRHS NCGa |
| | 'Roysii' (p) | WPer |
| | 'Ruby' | see *D.* 'Houndspool Ruby' |
| | 'Ruby Doris' | see *D.* 'Houndspool Ruby' |
| | 'Ruby Wedding' (p) | LSRN |
| | 'Sam Barlow' (p) | SAll SSvw |
| | ***sanguineus*** | NDov |
| | 'Santa Claus' (b) | SAll |
| | Scarlet Beauty = 'Hilbeau' | NBlu |
| | ***seguieri*** | WHrl |
| | ***serotinus*** | EPot WCot |
| | Shooting Star = 'Wp04 Flores'PBR (p) | LRHS MAsh |
| | 'Shot Silk' (pf) | SAll |
| | 'Show Aristocrat' (p) | SAll |
| | 'Show Beauty' (p) | ECtt SAll |
| | Show Girl = 'Hilshow' (pf) | LRHS MTis SBfd |
| | 'Show Glory' (p) | SAll |
| | 'Show Harlequin' (p) | SAll |
| | 'Show Satin' (p) | ECtt SAll |
| | 'Shrimp' (b) | CWib |
| | 'Singapore Girl' (Kiwi Series) **new** | SGar |
| * | 'Six Hills' | WPat |
| | Slap 'n' Tickle = 'Wp05 Pp22'PBR (Scent First Series) (p) | ECtt GAbr LHop LRHS LSRN MTis NCGa SBfd SPoG SRot |
| | 'Snowshill Manor' (p) | WPer |
| | 'Solomon' (p) | IGor SAll SSvw |
| | Sonya = 'Avnya' | SBch |
| | 'Sops-in-wine' (p) | CSam ECha ECtt MSCN SAll |
| § | 'Souvenir de la Malmaison' (M) | EMal SAll |
| | 'Spangle' (b) | SAll |
| | 'Spencer' (pf) **new** | SAll |
| | 'Spencer Bickham' (p) | MNrw |
| | ***spiculifolius*** | EDAr EPot GAuc NWCA SBch SPhx WFar |
| | 'Spirit' (pf) | SAll |
| | 'Spring Star' (p) | ECtt MSCN SRot WJek |
| | 'Square Eyes' | see *D.* 'Old Square Eyes' |
| | ***squarrosus*** | ECho EPot GEdr NWCA WAbe |
| * | - ***alpinus*** | ECho |
| | - 'Nanus' | see *D.* 'Berlin Snow' |
| | 'Starburst'PBR (p) | CMea CPBP LRHS NCGa SBfd |
| | Starlight = 'Hilstar' | CMea EWTr LRHS NCGa |
| | 'Starry Eyes' (p) ♀H4 | CSam ECho ELan EWTr GBin GMaP LRHS MWea NEgg NPri SBch SRot SWvt WAbe WFar |
| | 'Storm' (pf) | EMal SAll |
| | 'Strawberries and Cream' (p) | CBcs EBee ECtt LRHS NEgg NOrc SPoG WMnd |
| * | ***strictus*** subsp. ***pulchellus*** | CPBP |
| | ***subacaulis*** | EDAr NGdn NWCA |
| | - subsp. ***brachyanthus*** | EPot GJos NMen WAbe |
| | - - 'Murray Lyon' | NMen WThu |
| | ***suendermannii*** | see *D. petraeus* |
| | Sugar Plum = 'Wp08 Ian04' (Scent First Series) (p) | EWTr MTis SBfd |
| | 'Summerfield Adam' (p) | SAll |
| | 'Summerfield Amy Francesca' (p) | SAll |
| | 'Summerfield Blaze' (p) | SAll |
| | 'Summerfield Daniel' (b) **new** | SAll |
| | 'Summerfield Debbie' (p) | SAll |
| | 'Summerfield Emma Louise' (p) | SAll |
| | 'Summerfield Rebecca' (p) | SAll |
| | SummertimePBR (p) | see *D.* 'Rose Monica Wyatt' |
| | (Sunflor Series) 'Sunflor Althea' | NBlu |
| | - 'Sunflor Campari' | NBlu |
| | - 'Sunflor Odessa Red' **new** | SGar |
| | - 'Sunflor Pink Campari' | NBlu |
| | 'Sunray' (b) | SAll |
| | 'Sunstar' (b) | SAll |
| § | ***superbus*** | CMHG GBBs LHop MNrw NNor SBch SPhx SSvw WHer WMoo WRHF |
| | - 'Crimsonia' | MBrN SBch |
| I | - 'Primadonna' | GQue |

| | | |
|---|---|---|
| | 'Susan' (p) | SAll |
| | 'Susannah' (p) | SAll |
| * | 'Susan's Seedling' (p) | SAll |
| | 'Swanlake' (p) | SAll |
| | 'Sweet Sue' (b) | SAll |
| | 'Sweetheart Abbey' (p) | IGor SSvw |
| I | 'Sweetness Mix' (p) | GJos |
| | ***sylvestris*** | CMea GEdr |
| | - dwarf | EPot |
| | 'Tamsin Fifield' (b) 𝕐H4 | SAll |
| | 'Tatra Blush' (p) | GCal |
| | 'Tatra Fragrance' (p) | CCse GCal SAll |
| | 'Tatra Ghost' (p) | GMac SAll SBch |
| | 'Tayside Red' (M) | EMal SAll |
| | 'Thomas' (p) | SBch |
| | 'Thora' (M) | EMal SAll |
| | Tickled Pink = 'Devon PP 11' (Scent First Series) (p) | EBee ECtt ELan EWTr LBMP LRHS LSRN MTis MWat SBfd SPoG |
| | 'Tiny Rubies' | see *D. gratianopolitanus* 'Tiny Rubies' |
| | 'Treasure' (p) | SAll |
| | 'Trevor' (p) | SAll |
| | 'Tudor' **new** | MNrw |
| | ***turkestanicus*** | NBir NNor WPtf |
| | Tyrolean trailing carnations | SAll |
| | 'Uncle Teddy' (b) 𝕐H4 | SAll |
| | 'Unique' (p) | IGor SAll SBch SSvw |
| | 'Ursula Le Grove' (p) | SSvw |
| | 'Valda Wyatt' (p) 𝕐H4 | CBcs EAEE EBee ELan EPfP GAbr LAst LRHS NCGa NEgg NNor SAll SBch SBfd SEND SPoG SRGP SWvt WMnd |
| | 'Vic Masters' | SPhx |
| | 'Violet Clove' (b) | SAll |
| | 'W.A. Musgrave' | see *D.* 'Musgrave's Pink' |
| | 'Waithman Beauty' (p) | CTri ECtt GEdr GMaP SAll WHoo WPer WTin |
| | 'Waithman's Jubilee' (p) | MWhi SAll SRms |
| | 'Warden Hybrid' (p) | CMea CTri ECho ECtt EPfP GAbr GMaP LAst LRHS MWea NGdn SBch SPoG SWvt WAbe WFar |
| | 'Waterloo Sunset'PBR (p) | CMea CSBt LRHS MTis SAga SBfd |
| | 'Weetwood Double' (p) | CFee MWhi SBch |
| | ***weyrichii*** | ECho EPot |
| | 'Whatfield Anona' (p) | SAll |
| | 'Whatfield Beauty' (p) | ECho ECtt ELan NWCA |
| | 'Whatfield Brilliant' (p) | ECho |
| | 'Whatfield Cancan' (p) 𝕐H4 | CMea ECho ECtt GMaP LHop LRHS MAsh MNHC NEgg NGdn NPri SAll SBch SMrm SPoG SWvt WJek WNew WWFP |
| | 'Whatfield Cream Lace' (p) | NWCA |
| | 'Whatfield Cyclops' (p) | ECho SAll |
| | 'Whatfield Dawn' (p) | ECho |
| | 'Whatfield Dorothy Mann' (p) | ECho SAll SBch |
| | 'Whatfield Fuchsia Floss' (p) | SAll |
| | 'Whatfield Gem' (p) | CPBP ECho ECtt ELan EPfP GEdr LRHS MWat NGdn NMen NPri SAll SPoG SWvt WFar WHoo WNew WPer |
| | 'Whatfield Joy' (p) | ECho ECtt ELan EPfP LRHS MAsh MHer NGdn NMen SAll WFar WHoo |
| | 'Whatfield Magenta' (p) 𝕐H4 | CSam ECho ELan EPfP EPot LRHS MAsh NMen SAll SPoG WAbe |
| | 'Whatfield Mini' (p) | SAll SRms WPer |
| | 'Whatfield Miss' (p) | SAll |
| | 'Whatfield Misty Morn' (p) | ECho SAll |
| | 'Whatfield Peach' (p) | SAll SBch |
| | 'Whatfield Polly Anne' (p) | EWld |
| | 'Whatfield Pretty Lady' (p) | ECho SAll |
| | 'Whatfield Rose' (p) | ECho EPot |
| | 'Whatfield Ruby' (p) | ECho ELan GJos NWCA SAll WFar |
| | 'Whatfield Supergem' (p) | ECho ECtt EPot |
| | 'Whatfield White' (p) | ECho ECtt SAll SRms |
| | 'Whatfield White Moon' (p) | ECho |
| | 'Whatfield Wisp' (p) | CTri ECho EPfP EPot GEdr MRav NBir NMen NWCA WNew |
| | 'White and Crimson' (p) | SAll |
| | 'White Joy'PBR (p) 𝕐H4 | MRav |
| | 'White Ladies' (p) | ELan MRav SAll |
| | 'White Liberty'PBR (pf) | SAll |
| | 'Whitehill' (p) 𝕐H4 | ECho ITim MHer NMen |
| | 'Whitesmith' (b) 𝕐H4 | SAll |
| | 'Widecombe Fair' (p) 𝕐H4 | CTri EBee ECtt ELan EWTr SAll SBfd SPoG SRms |
| | 'Yellow Viana' (pf) **new** | SAll |
| | 'Zebra' (b) | SAll |
| | ***zederbaueri*** | NWCA |
| | ***zonatus*** | NWCA |

## *Diapensia* (*Diapensiaceae*)

| | | |
|---|---|---|
| | ***lapponica*** var. ***obovata*** | NHar WAbe |

## *Diarrhena* (*Poaceae*)

| | | |
|---|---|---|
| | ***americana*** | EPPr |
| | ***japonica*** | EPPr MMoz |
| * | ***mandschurica*** | EPPr |
| | ***obovata*** | EPPr |

## *Diascia* ✿ (*Scrophulariaceae*)

| | | |
|---|---|---|
| | 'Alice Cap' | SBch |
| | 'Andrew' | SBch |
| | 'Appleby Appleblossom' | SBch |
| | 'Appleby Apricot' | NDov |
| | 'Apricot' | see *D. barberae* 'Hopleys Apricot' |
| | Apricot Delight = 'Codicot' (Sun Chimes Series) | WFar |
| | ***barberae*** 'Belmore Beauty' (v) | ECtt EWes LIMB WPer |
| | - 'Blackthorn Apricot' 𝕐H3-4 | CBar CBot EAEE ECha ECtt ELan EPfP GMaP LRHS LSRN MRav NDov SMrm SPer SPlb SPoG SWvt WFar WWEG |
| § | - 'Fisher's Flora' 𝕐H3-4 | EPyc NDov WFar |
| | - 'Fisher's Flora' × 'Lilac Belle' | ECtt |
| § | - 'Hopleys Apricot' | MSCN |
| § | - 'Ruby Field' 𝕐H3-4 | CBar CMea ECha ECtt ELan EPfP LHop LRHS LSRN MRav NEgg SPer SPoG SWvt WFar WHil WWEG |
| | Blue Bonnet = 'Hecbon' | ECtt GBee SBch SWvt WFar |
| | 'Blush' | see *D. integerrima* 'Blush' |
| | Blush Delight = 'Codiush' (Sun Chimes Series) | WFar |
| | Breezee Apricot = 'Diaspritwo'PBR **new** | SMrm |
| | Breezee Snow = 'Inndiabzsno' **new** | SMrm |
| | 'Candy Floss' | SBch |
| | Coral Belle = 'Hecbel'PBR 𝕐H3-4 | ECtt EPfP EWes LHop LRHS LSou SBfd WFar |
| | ***cordata*** misapplied | see *D. barberae* 'Fisher's Flora' |
| | ***cordifolia*** | see *D. barberae* 'Fisher's Flora' |
| | 'Denim Blue' | LAst NLar SPoG WHil |
| | Eclat = 'Heclat' | ECtt WFar |
| | ***elegans*** misapplied | see *D. fetcaniensis*, *D. vigilis* |
| | 'Elizabeth' 𝕐H3-4 | MWea WHrl |

| |  |  |
|---|---|---|
| | 'Emma' | SWvt |
| | ***felthamii*** | see *D. fetcaniensis* |
| § | ***fetcaniensis*** | CMHG CMea EShb GMaP LRHS MHer MWea NEgg SAga WBrk WCFE WHal WKif |
| | - 'Daydream' | LBuc SBch WHrl |
| | ***flanaganii*** misapplied | see *D. vigilis* |
| | (Flying Colours Series) Flying Colours Appleblossom = 'Diastara' | EPfP NBlu SPoG |
| | - Flying Colours Apricot = 'Diastina' | EPfP |
| | - Flying Colours Red = 'Diastonia'PBR | EPfP SPoG |
| | 'Frilly' ♀H3-4 | ECtt |
| | 'Hector Harrison' | see *D.* 'Salmon Supreme' |
| | Ice Cracker = 'Hecrack' | CMea ECtt ELan LHop LRHS SBch |
| | Ice Cream = 'Icepol' | SCoo |
| | Iceberg = 'Hecice'PBR | SWvt |
| § | ***integerrima*** ♀H3-4 | CSam ECha ELon LLWP NDov |
| | - from Lesotho | SAga SMrm |
| | - 'Alba' | see *D. integerrima* 'Blush' |
| § | - 'Blush' | CSpe NDov |
| | - 'Ivory Angel' | see *D. integerrima* 'Blush' |
| | ***integrifolia*** | see *D. integerrima* |
| | 'Jacqueline's Joy' | CMea NPer WFar |
| | 'Joyce's Choice' ♀H3-4 | EWes LRHS WFar |
| | 'Katherine Sharman' (v) | EWes SAga |
| | 'Lady Valerie' ♀H3-4 | EWes WPer |
| | 'Lilac Belle' ♀H3-4 | CMea ECtt ELan EPfP LHop LRHS NBir NDov NEgg SPlb SPoG WFar |
| | 'Lilac Gem' | SBch |
| | 'Lilac Mist' ♀H3-4 | NPer |
| | ***lilacina* × *rigescens*** | GBee |
| | Little Dancer = 'Pendan'PBR | LSou MSCN NLar SBfd SCoo SLon SMrm |
| | 'Little Dazzler' | WRHF |
| | Little Dreamer = 'Pender'PBR | NLar SBfd |
| | Little Drifter = 'Pendrif' | LSou NLar WRHF |
| | Little Maiden = 'Penmaid'PBR | NLar WGor |
| | Little Tango = 'Pentang' | LAst LHop LSou NLar SBfd SVen |
| | 'Marilyn' **new** | NDov SBch |
| | (Miracle Series) 'Miracle Carmine' | LSou |
| | - 'Miracle Orange' | LSou |
| | - 'Miracle Rose-Pink' | LSou |
| | - 'Miracle White' | LSou |
| | ***patens*** | CHll |
| | ***personata*** | CHVG CHll CPrp CSpe CTri ECtt ELon LLHF LPla LSou MCot SAga SDys SPer SUsu WCot |
| | - 'Hopleys' | EWes LHop MAvo NCGa SHar |
| | 'Peter' **new** | NDov |
| | Pink Delight = 'Codlink' | WFar |
| | Pink Panther = 'Penther' | ECtt NLar SCoo SWvt |
| | 'Pink Queen' | ECtt |
| | Red Ace = 'Hecrace'PBR | EPfP LHop NPer SWvt |
| | Redstart = 'Hecstart' | ECtt EPfP NGdn SWvt WFar |
| | ***rigescens*** ♀H3 | CBot CHEx COIW CPrp CSpe CWCL ECtt ELan EPfP EPot GEdr GGar MHer MRav NPer SAga SPlb SPoG SWvt WBor WCFE WFar WHlf WPGP WSHC |
| § | - 'Anne Rennie' | LRHS SWvt |
| | - pale-flowered | see *D. rigescens* 'Anne Rennie' |
| | 'Ruby Field' | see *D. barberae* 'Ruby Field' |
| | 'Rupert Lambert' ♀H3-4 | EWes NDov SBri WPer |
| § | 'Salmon Supreme' | ECtt ELan EPfP GBee LRHS NGdn NPer SPoG WFar WMoo WPer |
| | Susan = 'Winsue'PBR | WFar |
| | ***tugelensis*** | WFar |
| | 'Twinkle' ♀H3-4 | CBar ECtt EPfP LRHS NBir NPer WFar |
| * | 'Twins Gully' | EWes GCal SMrm |
| § | ***vigilis*** ♀H3 | CBot CMHG CMea CPLG ECha EPfP EPot GBee LHop LRHS NBro SAga SBch WHal |
| | - McB 2903 | GLam |
| | - 'Jack Elliott' | MRav |
| | (Whisper Series) Whisper Apricot Improved = 'Balwhisaptim'PBR | LAst NBlu NPri SCoo |
| | - Whisper Cranberry Red = 'Balwhiscran'PBR | SCoo |
| | - Whisper Pumpkin = 'Balwhispum' | SGar |
| | - Whisper Tangerine = 'Balwhistang' | LSou |
| | - Whisper White = 'Balwhiswhit'PBR | LAst |
| | White Belle = 'Penbel' | LSou |
| | (Wink Series) Wink Garnet = 'Balwingarn'PBR | LAst |
| | - Wink Pink Improved = 'Balwinlapi' | LAst |

## *Dicentra* ✿ (*Papaveraceae*)

| |  |  |
|---|---|---|
| | CC 4452 | CPLG |
| | 'Adrian Bloom' | CPLG EBee ECtt EPfP GBin LRHS LSRN MLLN NBPC NPri SMrm SWvt WFar WMoo |
| | 'Aurora' | EBee ECtt ELon EPfP GBin LAst LRHS LSou MRav NBPC NGdn NSti SBfd SPer SPoG SWvt WCAu WFar WMoo WPnP |
| | 'Boothman's Variety' | see *D.* 'Stuart Boothman' |
| | 'Bountiful' | CMac EBee LSou MRav NGdn SWvt |
| | 'Burning Hearts' | CWGN EBee IPot LLHF LSou MAsh MBri NCGa NGBo WHil |
| | ***canadensis*** | CAby CLAP EBee MAvo NLar WAbe WCot WCru WHal |
| | 'Candy Hearts'PBR | EBee ECtt ELan EPfP LHop MAsh MBri NBPC NBro NGdn NLar WFar WHil |
| | ***cucullaria*** | CElw CLAP CMea CRow CTca CWCL EBee ECho ELon EPot GGar GLam LRHS MRav NLar NMen NWCA WAbe WCru WFar |
| | - 'Pittsburg' | CRDP EBee EPPr MNrw SCnR |
| | ***eximia*** misapplied | see *D. formosa* |
| | ***eximia*** ambig. | CChe LRHS |
| | ***eximia*** (Ker Gawl.) Torr. | EBee |
| | - 'Alba' | see *D. eximia* 'Snowdrift' |
| § | - 'Snowdrift' | CLAP EBee ECtt ELan EPfP MCot SMrm SRms WFar WMoo |
| | 'Fire Island' **new** | NLar |
| | 'Firecracker' **new** | NLar |
| § | ***formosa*** | CBcs CTri EBee ECha ELan EPfP IFro LAma LAst LBMP LRHS MLHP NBPC NBro NGdn NMen NOrc SPlb SRms WFar WMoo WWEG |
| | - f. ***alba*** | ECha GCra GMaP NBir NCGa SRms WCru WFar WKif |
| | - 'Bacchanal' ♀H4 | Widely available |
| | - 'Coldham' | ELon WSHC |
| | - 'Cox's Dark Red' | CLAP CPLG EBee EWes GBin LLHF LWSt NMen SKHP WOut |

- 'Langtrees' 🏆H4 CMac CMil CRow CSam CSev EBee ECha EPau EPfP LHop MLHP MRav NBro SGar SMad SRms SWvt WCru WFar WMoo WOut WPtf WSHC
- subsp. ***oregana*** CLAP EBee EPPr GGar IGor LWSt NBre NChi NMen SKHP WHal
- - NNS 00-233 CLAP
- - 'Rosea' EPPr
- Snowflakes = 'Fusd' EWes MRav
- 'Spring Gold' ECha ELon LBuc LRHS NLar WMoo
- 'Spring Magic' **new** LBuc LRHS NCGa NLar
'Ivory Hearts'[PBR] CWGN EBee ECtt ELan EPfP LHop LSRN MAsh MAvo MCot NBPC NBro NCGa NGdn NLar NPnk NSti SMrm SPer SPtl WHil
§ 'Katie' EPPr
'Katy' see *D.* 'Katie'
'King of Hearts' Widely available
***lichiangensis*** see *Dactylicapnos lichiangensis*
'Luxuriant' 🏆H4 CBcs CSBt EBee ECtt ELan EPfP GBBs LAst LRHS MCot MGos MRav NBPC NPri SAga SBfd SMrm SPad SPer SPoG SRms SRot SWvt WFar WMoo WPnP WWEG
***macrantha*** see *Ichthyoselmis macrantha*
'Paramount' GBin
'Pearl Drops' CRow ELan GGar GMaP LRHS MCot MMoz MRav NBid NGdn NMen SRms WAbb WMoo
***peregrina*** GEdr LWSt WAbe
- ***alba*** GEdr LWSt
'Red Fountain' IPot LLHF LRHS MAsh NCGa NGBo NPnk WHil
***scandens*** see *Dactylicapnos scandens*
'Silver Beads' ELon
***spectabilis*** see *Lamprocapnos spectabilis*
'Spring Morning' CBod CElw CMHG CSam EAEE ECtt EPPr LBMP LRHS LSou WRHF
§ 'Stuart Boothman' 🏆H4 Widely available
***thalictrifolia*** see *D. scandens*
'Valentine' **new** NLar
***ventii*** see *Dactylicapnos ventii*

## *Dichelachne* (*Poaceae*)

***crinita*** SMea

## *Dichelostemma* (*Asparagaceae*)

***congestum*** CAvo CFFs EBee ECho GAuc LRHS
§ ***ida-maia*** CAvo CFFs CGrW CTca ECho EPot GAuc LRHS MCot MWea SDeJ
- 'Pink Diamond' CGrW EBee ECho SDeJ
***volubile*** CTca ECho WCot

## *Dichocarpum* (*Ranunculaceae*)

§ ***dicarpon*** B&SWJ 11555 **new** WCru

## *Dichondra* (*Convolvulaceae*)

***argentea*** 'Silver Falls' CSpe EShb LAst LSou NPri SCoo SPoG
§ ***micrantha*** EShb
***repens*** misapplied see *D. micrantha*

## *Dichopogon* (*Anthericaceae*)

***strictus*** ECou

## *Dichorisandra* (*Commelinaceae*)

***thyrsiflora*** Blue Bamboo = 'Bodine' **new** LRHS

## *Dichroa* (*Hydrangeaceae*)

***febrifuga*** CAbb CBcs CDoC CHEx CHGN CHll CMil CPLG CTsd CWGN CWib EBee ELan EWes LRHS MOWG WCru WPGP
- B&SWJ 2367 WCru
- HWJK 2430 WCru
- pink-flowered CHEx
***hirsuta*** B&SWJ 8207 from Vietnam WCru
aff. ***hirsuta*** B&SWJ 8371 from Lao WCru
***versicolor*** B&SWJ 6565 WCru
- B&SWJ 6605 from Thailand WCru
aff. ***versicolor*** Guiz 48 WPGP
aff. ***yunnanensis*** B&SWJ 9734 WCru

## *Dichromena* see *Rhynchospora*

## *Dicksonia* ✿ (*Dicksoniaceae*)

***antarctica*** 🏆H3 Widely available
***berteriana*** WRic
***fibrosa*** 🏆H3 CBcs CDTJ CKel CTrC EAmu EExo EFtx GBin GLin LTen MDev SPoG WRic
***sellowiana*** CDTJ CKel WRic
***squarrosa*** 🏆H2 CBcs CBty CCCN CDTJ CKel CTrC EAmu MGos SPoG WRic

## *Dicliptera* (*Acanthaceae*)

§ ***sericea*** CHll EBee EShb GCal IKil LHop MSCN MWea SEND SGar SMrm SRkn WCot WFar WHil WPGP WSHC WTcb
***suberecta*** see *D. sericea*

## *Dicoma* (*Asteraceae*)

***anomala*** SPlb

## *Dicranostigma* (*Papaveraceae*)

***leptopodum*** CSpe

## *Dictamnus* ✿ (*Rutaceae*)

***albus*** Widely available
- var. ***albus*** 🏆H4 MAvo NPnk
§ - var. ***purpureus*** 🏆H4 Widely available
* - var. ***roseus*** NBPC
* - ***turkestanicus*** GCal
***fraxinella*** see *D. albus* var. *purpureus*

## *Didymochlaena* (*Dryopteridaceae*)

***lunulata*** see *D. truncatula*
§ ***truncatula*** WRic XBlo

## *Dierama* ✿ (*Iridaceae*)

sp. MLLN WHil
***adelphicum*** EBee GAbr
***ambiguum*** EBee EWld GAbr IGor SBfd XLum
'Aphrodite' NFir
***argyreum*** CAlb CCCN CElw CMac CTsd CWCL EBee EPri GAbr GEdr NExo NFir SBfd SPoG SRot SUsu SWal WHil XLum
'Ariel' IBlr
'Ballyrogan Red' IBlr
'Black Knight' CPLG IBlr
'Blue Belle' CMac CPen CWCL CWGN EBee IBal LBMP LBuc LRHS LSou SPoG SPtl SUsu

'Blush' IBlr
'Buckland White' WPGP
'Candy Stripe' EBee
'Cherry Chimes' EPfP
***cooperi*** CElw CPou CTca CYeo EBee GAbr IBlr NBir WWEG
'Coral Bells' CDes EBee GCal WPGP
'Cosmos' CPLG EDAr EOHP EPri MHer MWhi NExo SBfd WHil WSHC
'Dark Angel' new NCGa
'Delicacy' IBlr
'Desire' IBlr
***dissimile*** IGor NFir
'Donard Legacy' IBlr NLar
§ ***dracomontanum*** Widely available
- JCA 3.141.100 WPGP
- dwarf, pale pink-flowered LRHS
- Wisley Princess Group MBri
***dracomontanum × pulcherrimum*** SMad
***dubium*** EBee IBlr
***ensifolium*** see *D. pendulum*
***erectum*** CBcs CCCN CHid CMac CWCL EBee EPri GAbr GEdr GKev IBlr ITim LRHS NLar SBfd SRot SUsu
'Fairy Bells' CPen EBee
'Fireworks' EBee
***floriferum*** IBlr
***formosum*** CFir CGHE EBee WPGP
***galpinii*** CCCN CGHE CYeo EBee ELan EPri GAbr GBin GEdr IGor LLHF LRHS NFir WPGP
***grandiflorum*** CPou CYeo IBlr IGor
'Guinevere' Widely available
***igneum*** Widely available
- CD&R 278 CPLG CPou
***insigne*** CCCN CHid
'Iris' IBlr
***jucundum*** EBee
'Knee-high Lavender' CDes EPla SAga WPGP
'Lancelot' Widely available
***latifolium*** CGHE CHid GAbr IBlr MNrw NFir
***luteoalbidum*** EBee EWld GAbr WPGP WThu
'Mandarin' IBlr WPGP
***medium*** CGHE CPen EBee ELon SUsu SWat WCot WPGP WWEG
* ***microphylla*** new NLar
'Milkmaid' CPLG IBlr NCot
'Miranda' CAbP CPen CYeo EBee ECtt GEdr GQue IBal LRHS MBNS MNrw NEgg NGdn NLar NPnk NSti SDix SPad WCot WCra
***mossii*** CBcs CCCN CDul CFir CHid CMHG CMac CPLG CWCL CYeo EBee ELan EPri GBin GEdr IBlr IGor LHop LRHS NExo NLar SBfd SPlb SRot WPGP XLum
***nixonianum*** EBee IBlr
'Oberon' MRav
'Painted Lady' CPen EBee LBuc LRHS SBfd SBrd SKHP SLon
pale pink frilly-flowered new WHil
***pallidum*** new SGar
'Pamina' CPLG CPrp IBlr
'Papagena' IBlr
'Papageno' IBlr
***pauciflorum*** CCCN CFir CGHE CHid CPLG CPrp CWCL CWib CYeo EBee EDAr EPri GEdr MHer NBir NFir NLar SMrm SRot SWat WPGP WSHC WWEG
- CD&R 197 CPBP MDKP
§ ***pendulum*** CBot CBro CFee EBee ELan EPfP GAbr GBBs GEdr IBlr LRHS LSRN MCCP MGos MNrw MRav SWvt WCot WFar WHil WWEG
'Petite Fairy' CPen
***pictum*** EBee IBlr
'Pink Rocket' new WHer
Plant World hybrids ELon GGar
Plant World Jewels CWCL
'Pretty Flamingo' CPLG CPrp IBlr
'Puck' CDes EBee GCal IBlr IGor MRav WHil WPGP
***pulcherrimum*** Widely available
- var. ***album*** CBcs CCCN CGHE CLAP CWCL CYeo EBee ELan GEdr GKev IBlr ITim LRHS MHer MNrw MWhi NExo WPGP WWEG
- 'Blackbird' Widely available
- dwarf ELon
- 'Falcon' IBlr
- 'Flamingo' IBlr
- lilac-flowered LHop
- 'Merlin' Widely available
- pale-flowered ECha
- 'Pearly Queen' CRow EBee
- 'Peregrine' WPGP
- purple-flowered new LRHS
- 'Redwing' IBlr
- Slieve Donard hybrids CLAP CWCL EBee ECtt EDAr ITim LAst LHop LRHS MCot MWat NEgg SBfd SMad SPet WFar WHil WHrl WMnd WWEG
***pumilum*** misapplied see *D. dracomontanum*
'Purple Passion' CPen NCGa
'Queen of the Night' IBlr
***reynoldsii*** Widely available
***robustum*** CDes CGHE CPLG CPou GAbr IBlr MNrw NFir SBfd WHer WPGP
'Sarastro' CPLG IBlr
'September Charm' IBlr
'Spring Dancer' CWCL EBee EHoe GKev NHol WHer
'Tamino' IBlr
'Tiny Bells' CDes EBee ECha EDAr GCal WPGP
'Titania' IBlr
***trichorhizum*** CCCN CFir CGHE CPBP CPLG CPrp CWCL CYeo EBee EKen ELan EPri GAbr IBlr LHop MCot NFir SBfd WWEG
'Tubular Bells' IBlr
***tyrium*** EBee NFir
'Violet Ice' IBlr
'Westminster Chimes' IBlr WPGP
'Zulu Bells' ELon

# *Diervilla* ✿ (*Caprifoliaceae*)

***lonicera*** CHar
***middendorffiana*** see *Weigela middendorffiana*
***rivularis*** 'Troja Black' NLar
§ ***sessilifolia*** CBcs CHGN CHar CMac EBee GAuc LAst MAsh MRav NLar NMRc SGar SLon STre WCot WFar WMoo
- 'Butterfly' CMac EPPr NLar WMoo
- Cool Splash = 'Lpdc Podaras' (v) new EMil EPfP LBuc NPri SBrd SPoG
× ***splendens*** CAbP CMHG CPLG CWib EBee EHoe ELan EPPr EPfP LHop LRHS MBNS MBlu MGos MRav MSwo SEND SGar SLPl SPer SPoG SPtl WDin

## *Dietes* (*Iridaceae*)

| |  |  |
|---|---|---|
| | ***bicolor*** | CAbb CBod CDes CHEx CPLG CPrp CTca EShb LEdu LSou SChr SHom |
| | ***butcheriana*** | CDes |
| | ***grandiflora*** | CAbb CArn CCse CFee CPLG CPne CTca EBee ECho EShb GBin SBch SHom WBor WCot WSHC |
| § | ***iridioides*** | CDes CPne CTca EBee ECho EShb GBin WCot WPGP |
| | ***robinsoniana*** | CSpe |

## *Digitalis* ✿ (*Plantaginaceae*)

| |  |  |
|---|---|---|
| | sp. | SVic |
| | RCB/TQ 059 from İkizdere | WCru |
| | 'Albino' **new** | EPfP LRHS |
| | ***ambigua*** | see *D. grandiflora* |
| | apricot hybrids | see *D. purpurea* 'Sutton's Apricot' |
| | ***cariensis*** | GAbr SPav |
| | ***ciliata*** | EBee ELan GCal SPav |
| | ***davisiana*** | CBot CPLG GAbr MNHC SPav SPhx WMoo |
| | ***dubia*** | CBot EPfP NBir NBre SPav |
| | 'Elsie Kelsey' | CEnt ECtt EShb NBir SWvt WHil |
| | ***eriostachya*** | see *D. lutea* |
| | ***ferruginea*** ♀H4 | Widely available |
| | - 'Gelber Herold' | CBot EBee GMaP NBre NLar SMrm SPhx |
| | - 'Gigantea' | EBee ETod GQue LRHS MBNS NBPC NChi NDov SWat WAul WBox WCot WWEG |
| | - subsp. ***schischkinii*** | SPav |
| * | ***floribunda*** | NBir SPav |
| | ***fontanesii*** | CEnt GKev NBir |
| | 'Foxley Primrose' | NPri |
| | 'Foxtrot' | LBuc LRHS |
| | × ***fulva*** | GKev NBir |
| | 'Glory of Roundway' | CBot CDes EBee ECtt LSou MAvo MHer MTis NDov NLar SPer WCot |
| § | 'Goldcrest' **new** | LBuc LRHS SBrd SPoG |
| § | ***grandiflora*** ♀H4 | Widely available |
| | - 'Carillon' | EBee EPau EPfP IFoB LBMP LRHS NBir NLar SRot WGor |
| | - 'Cream Bell' | EPfP LRHS |
| | - 'Dwarf Carillon' | ECtt EWld |
| | ***heywoodii*** | see *D. purpurea* subsp. *heywoodii* |
| | 'Illumination' **new** | LRHS |
| | 'John Innes Tetra' | EBee EShb WPGP |
| | ***kishinskyi*** | see *D. parviflora* |
| | ***laevigata*** | CBot CFir CSam EBee EGHP EPfP GKev LRHS MCot MWea NBro SEND SPav SPet WBox WMnd WMoo WPer |
| | ***lamarckii*** misapplied | see *D. lanata* |
| | ***lamarckii*** Ivanina | NBPC |
| § | ***lanata*** | CArn CBot EBee ECtt EGHP ELan EPfP LAst LRHS MBNS MNHC MWat NGdn NOrc SBfd SPav SPer SPhx SPlb SRms WFar WMnd WPer WWEG |
| | - 'Café Crème' | CSpr NBPC |
| § | ***lutea*** | Widely available |
| | - SDR 6377 | GKev |
| | - SDR 6413 | GKev |
| § | - subsp. ***australis*** | GLam WBox |
| | × ***mertonensis*** ♀H4 | Widely available |
| | - 'Summer King' | ECtt LSRN NBre SBrd |
| | ***micrantha*** | see *D. lutea* subsp. *australis* |
| | ***nervosa*** | SPav |
| | ***obscura*** | CBot ECho GKev IFoB LRHS MCot NBir SBrt SGar SIde SPav SPet WMnd |
| * | - 'Dusky Maid' | LRHS |
| | ***orientalis*** | see *D. grandiflora* |
| § | ***parviflora*** | Widely available |
| | - 'Milk Chocolate' | CBcs CMHG CSpe ECtt EPfP GJos GQue LHop LRHS LSRN LSou MCot MNHC NBPC NBre NEgg SBHP SIde SKHP SMrm SPet SSvw WFar |
| | 'Pink Chapel' **new** | WCot |
| | ***purpurea*** | CArn CHab EBee EPfP EWil GPoy LRHS MHer MLHP MMuc MNHC NLan NMir NPri SBfd SEND SIde SPlb SPoG WBrk WJek WMoo WWFP |
| | - 'Alba' | see *D. purpurea* f. *albiflora* |
| § | - f. ***albiflora*** | Widely available |
| | - - 'Anne Redetzky'^PBR^ | ELan IFoB LRHS WMnd |
| | - - unspotted | CWan |
| | - Camelot Series | WRHF |
| | - - 'Camelot Cream' | EAEE EPfP LRHS NLar NPri SWvt |
| | - - 'Camelot Lavender' | EPfP LRHS NEgg NLar NPri SWvt |
| | - - 'Camelot Rose' | EPfP LRHS NEgg NLar NPri SWvt |
| | - - 'Camelot White' | EPfP LRHS NEgg NLar |
| * | - 'Campanulata Alba' | MLLN |
| | - 'Candy Mountain' | MAvo |
| | - 'Dalmatian Purple' **new** | LRHS WGor |
| | - 'Dalmatian White' **new** | LRHS WGor |
| | - Excelsior Group | CBcs CBot CSBt CTri EAEE ECtt EPfP GJos GMaP LAst LRHS MBri MWat NBlu NMir NVic SBfd SBod SPer SPoG SRms SWvt WFar WGor WWEG XLum |
| | - - (Suttons; Unwins) ♀H4 | ECtt MRav |
| | - Foxy Group | CBot CWib ECtt EPfP LRHS SBfd SPet SPoG WFar WWEG |
| | - - 'Foxy Apricot' | SWvt |
| | - Giant Spotted Group | CBot ECtt EPfP LRHS SPoG |
| | - Glittering Prizes Group | SWat |
| | - Gloxinioides Group | ELan WFar |
| | - - 'Isabellina' | CBot |
| | - - 'The Shirley' ♀H4 | SGar WGor WMoo |
| § | - subsp. ***heywoodii*** | CBot EBee ELan SPav SPhx SSvw WMoo WTou WWEG |
| | - - 'Silver Fox' | ECtt EPri LRHS LSRN |
| | - subsp. ***nevadensis*** | CBot |
| | - 'Pam's Choice' | Widely available |
| | - 'Pam's Split' **new** | CHid |
| | - 'Primrose Carousel' | NEgg NLar |
| | - 'Snow Thimble' | EBee LBMP LRHS MAvo MBri MTis NLar NPnk NVic WWEG |
| § | - 'Sutton's Apricot' ♀H4 | Widely available |
| * | - 'Sutton's Giant Primrose' | CBot |
| | - 'Virtuosa' | WGor |
| | - white cen-type mutant | NChi |
| | ***purpurea*** × ***thapsi*** | CBot WWEG |
| | 'Red Skin' | CPom WMoo WTou |
| | 'Saltwood Summer' | LRHS |
| | 'Serendipity' **new** | LBuc LRHS |
| | 'Spice Island'^PBR^ | EBee ECGP ECtt ELon LRHS LSou MAvo MLLN MTis NCGa NDov NLar SPer SPoG WCot WCra WWlt |
| * | ***stewartii*** | ECtt ELan EWes GAbr GCra NBPC SPav WHil WMoo |
| | 'Strawberry Fayre' **new** | GJos |
| | ***thapsi*** | ECtt EDif EPfP GAbr LRHS MCot NBPC SBrt SIde SPav SPhx WBrk WMoo WPer WWFP XLum |
| | - JCA 410.000 | EBee |
| | - 'Spanish Peaks' | CHid LRHS LSou |

| | |
|---|---|
| ***trojana*** | CSpr EBee ECtt GKev IFoB SGar SPhx |
| - 'Helen of Troy' | ECtt NBPC SKHP |
| ***viridiflora*** | CPLG ECtt MCot NBro SGar SPav WFar |
| 'Walberton's Goldcrest' | see *D.*'Goldcrest' |

## dill see *Anethum graveolens*

## *Dimorphotheca* (*Asteraceae*)

| | |
|---|---|
| ***cuneata*** white-flowered | WCot |

## *Diocirea* (*Scrophulariaceae*)

| | |
|---|---|
| ***violacea*** new | ECou |

## *Dionaea* ✿ (*Droseraceae*)

| | |
|---|---|
| ***muscipula*** | CHew CSWC EECP MCCP NChu SHmp SKHP SPlb WSSs |
| - 'Akai Ryu' | CSWC EECP NChu SHmp WSSs |
| - 'B52' new | CSWC EECP |
| - 'Big Mouth' new | CSWC |
| - 'Red Piranha' | NChu |
| - 'Royal Red' | CHew CSWC NChu WSSs |
| - 'Sawtooth' new | EECP |
| - shark-toothed | CSWC EECP NChu |
| - 'Spider' | CSWC EECP NChu |

## *Dionysia* (*Primulaceae*)

| | |
|---|---|
| 'Annielle' | WAbe |
| ***archibaldii*** | WAbe |
| - 'Tora' new | WAbe |
| ***aretioides*** ♀H2 | WAbe |
| - 'Bevere' | WAbe |
| ***bryoides*** | WAbe |
| 'Charleson Thomas' | WAbe |
| 'Charlson Gem' | WAbe |
| 'Charlson Jake' | WAbe |
| 'Charlson Petite' | WAbe |
| 'Charlson Pip' new | WAbe |
| 'Charlson Primrose' | WAbe |
| ***curviflora*** | WAbe |
| 'Emmely' | WAbe |
| 'Eric Watson' | WAbe |
| 'Ewesley Iota' | WAbe |
| 'Ewesley Kappa' | WAbe |
| 'Ewesley Theta' | WAbe |
| ***janthina*** | WAbe |
| 'Judith Bramley' | WAbe |
| 'Manuela' new | WAbe |
| 'Monika' | WAbe |
| 'Pascal' | WAbe |
| 'Schneeball' | WAbe |
| ***tapetodes*** | WAbe |
| - 'Brimstone' | WAbe |
| - 'Peter Edwards' | WAbe |
| 'Tess' new | WAbe |

## *Dioon* (*Zamiaceae*)

| | |
|---|---|
| ***califanoi*** | CBrP |
| ***caputoi*** | CBrP |
| ***edule*** ♀H1 | CBrP LPal SBst SChr |
| - var. ***angustifolium*** | CBrP |
| ***mejiae*** | CBrP LPal |
| ***merolae*** | CBrP |
| ***rzedowskii*** | CBrP LPal |
| ***spinulosum*** | CBrP LPal SBig |

## *Dioscorea* (*Dioscoreaceae*)

| | |
|---|---|
| CC 5622 | EWld |
| ***araucana*** | LSou |
| ***batatas*** | CAgr LEdu |
| ***deltoidea*** | CPLG |
| ***japonica*** | CAgr EShb LEdu |
| ***villosa*** | CArn |

## *Diosma* (*Rutaceae*)

| | |
|---|---|
| ***ericoides*** | SEND SWvt |
| - 'Pink Fountain' | CAbb LBuc LRHS SPoG |
| - 'Sunset Gold' | CBod CWGN EBee LBuc LRHS MAsh SCoo SPoG |
| ***hirsuta*** 'Silver Flame' | SPoG |

## *Diosphaera* (*Campanulaceae*)

| | |
|---|---|
| ***asperuloides*** | see *Trachelium asperuloides* |

## *Diospyros* (*Ebenaceae*)

| | |
|---|---|
| ***austroafricana*** | SPlb |
| * ***hyrcanum*** | EGFP NLar |
| ***kaki*** (F) | CBcs CMCN EBee EPfP ERom MREP WDin WPGP |
| - 'Fuyu' | CAgr |
| - 'Kostata' | CAgr |
| - 'Mazelii' | CAgr WPGP |
| ***lotus*** | CAgr CBcs CMCN CMac LEdu NLar SPlb |
| - (f) | CAgr |
| - (m) | CAgr |
| ***lycioides*** | SPlb |
| 'Nikita's Gift' | CAgr |
| 'Russian Beauty' | CAgr |
| ***virginiana*** (F) | CAgr CBcs CMCN NLar SPlb SSpi |
| - 'Early Golden' new | CAgr |
| - 'Meader' new | CAgr |

## *Dipcadi* (*Asparagaceae*)

| | |
|---|---|
| ***ciliare*** | CLak |
| ***marlothii*** 'Bloemfontein' | ECho |
| ***serotinum*** | ECho ITim |
| - subsp. ***lividum*** | WPGP |
| ***viride*** | CLak |
| white-flowered | CLak |

## *Dipelta* (*Caprifoliaceae*)

| | |
|---|---|
| ***floribunda*** ♀H4 | CBcs CBot CDoy CMCN CMac CPLG CPMA ELan EPfP LRHS MBlu MBri NLar SAga WCFE WPGP WPat |
| ***ventricosa*** | CAbP CBcs CGHE CPLG CPMA ELan EPfP LRHS MAsh MBlu NLar SSpi WPGP WPat |
| ***yunnanensis*** | CBcs CPLG CPMA EBee ELan EPfP LRHS NLar SSpi WPGP WPat |

## *Diphylleia* (*Berberidaceae*)

| | |
|---|---|
| ***cymosa*** | CAby CLAP ECha GCal GEdr MRav SPhx WCot WCru WTin |
| - red-marked | CDes |
| ***grayi*** | CLAP GEdr LWst WCru |
| ***sinensis*** | CPLG GEdr WCru |

## *Dipidax* see *Onixotis*

## *Diplacus* see *Mimulus*

## *Dipladenia* see *Mandevilla*

## *Diplarrhena* (*Iridaceae*)

| | |
|---|---|
| § ***latifolia*** | CFir GBBs GCal GGar GMac IBlr IGor LRHS |
| - Helen Dillon's form | IBlr |

| | |
|---|---|
| ***moraea*** | CAbP CAbb CMac CMea CPen CWCL EBee ECho EDif GAbr GBBs GBin GCal IBlr IFoB IKil ITim MCot MSCN NCGa NLBP WAbe WPGP WSHC |
| - ***minor*** | IBlr |
| - 'Slieve Donard' | IBlr |
| - West Coast form | see *D. latifolia* |

## *Diplazium* (*Woodsiaceae*)

| | |
|---|---|
| ***australe*** new | WCot |
| ***caudatum*** | WRic |

## *Diplotaxis* (*Brassicaceae*)

| | |
|---|---|
| ***muralis*** | CArn ELau WJek |
| ***tenuifolia*** | EGHP ELau MNHC |

## *Dipsacus* (*Caprifoliaceae*)

| | |
|---|---|
| § ***fullonum*** | CArn CHab CMac CWan EPfP EWil GAbr MBri MHer MMuc MNHC NMir NPri SBch SEND SIde WHer WJek WSFF |
| ***inermis*** | CSam ECha NBid NLar WFar |
| ***japonicus*** HWJ 695 | SPhx WCru |
| ***pilosus*** | CPom WHil |
| ***sativus*** | NLar |
| ***strigosus*** | SPhx |
| ***sylvestris*** | see *D. fullonum* |

## *Dipteracanthus* see *Ruellia*

## *Dipteronia* (*Sapindaceae*)

| | |
|---|---|
| ***sinensis*** | CMCN EPla MBri NLar WPGP |

## *Disanthus* (*Hamamelidaceae*)

| | |
|---|---|
| ***cercidifolius*** ♀H4 | CAbP CBcs CMCN CMac CPMA EPfP GKin IArd LRHS MAsh MBlu MBri MPkF NLar SPer SSpi WPGP |
| - 'Ena-nishiki' (v) | NLar |

## *Discaria* (*Rhamnaceae*)

| | |
|---|---|
| ***chacaye*** | LEdu WPGP |
| ***toumatou*** | SVen |

## *Diselma* (*Cupressaceae*)

| | |
|---|---|
| ***archeri*** | CDoC CKen SCoo SLim |
| - 'Read Dwarf' | CKen |

## *Disphyma* (*Aizoaceae*)

| | |
|---|---|
| ***crassifolium*** | SChr |

## *Disporopsis* (*Asparagaceae*)

| | |
|---|---|
| B&SWJ 229 from Taiwan | WCru |
| B&SWJ 1864 from Taiwan | WCru |
| ***aspersa*** | CLAP CSpe EBee ECho EPPr EWld LEdu MAvo NBir WCru WPGP |
| - tall | CBct CPLG WCru |
| ***fuscopicta*** | CBct CLAP EBee EPPr MAvo WCru WTin WWEG |
| ***longifolia*** | CLAP |
| - B&SWJ 5284 | WCru |
| * ***luzoniensis*** B&SWJ 3891 | CBct CPLG GEdr LEdu WCru |
| 'Min Shan' | CPLG ELon |
| * ***nova*** | EPPr |
| § ***pernyi*** | Widely available |
| - B&SWJ 1864 | CBct EPPr |
| - 'Bill Baker' | LEdu MAvo |
| ***taiwanensis*** B&SWJ 3388 | CBct WCru |
| ***undulata*** | LEdu NBid WCru |

## *Disporum* (*Colchicaceae*)

| | |
|---|---|
| ***austrosinense*** B&SWJ 9777 | LEdu WCru |
| ***bodinieri*** | CDes CPLG LEdu WPnP |
| - BWJ 8128 | WCru |
| - DJHC 765 | WCru |
| aff. ***bodinieri*** | WPGP |
| ***cantoniense*** | CFir CPom EPPr EPri GEdr IFoB LEdu LWst WCru WFar |
| - B&L 12512 | CDes CLAP CPLG WPGP |
| - B&SWJ 1424 | WCru |
| - B&SWJ 9715 | WCru |
| - DJHC 98485 | CDes CLAP EBee MMoz SKHP WPGP |
| I - 'Aureovariegata' | CBct CDes EBee LEdu WCot WPGP |
| - var. ***cantoniense*** f. ***brunneum*** B&SWJ 5290 | WCru |
| - 'Green Giant' | CDes CLAP CPLG EBee IFoB IPot LEdu MAvo SSvw WFar WPGP WPnP |
| - var. ***kawakamii*** B&SWJ 350 | WCru |
| - - RWJ 10103 | WCru |
| - var. ***multiflorum*** B&SWJ 11252 | WCru |
| - - B&SWJ 11291 | WCru |
| - 'Night Heron' | CDes CLAP CPLG EBee IFoB MAvo WCot WFar WPnP |
| - var. ***sikkimense*** B&SWJ 2337 | WCru |
| - - B&SWJ 2358 | WCru |
| * ***flavum*** | CAby CAvo ECho MMHG SUsu |
| ***hookeri*** | CLAP CPom EBee ECho GGar LWst MAvo MNrw NMen WCru |
| - var. ***oreganum*** | EPPr IBlr IFoB LRHS WCru |
| ***lanuginosum*** | CBct EBee EPPr GEdr LEdu LRHS MAvo WCot WCru |
| ***leschenaultianum*** B&SWJ 9484 | WCru |
| - B&SWJ 9505 | WCru |
| ***leucanthum*** | WCru WFar |
| - B&SWJ 2389 | WCru |
| ***longistylum*** | LEdu |
| - B&SWJ 2859 | WCru |
| - L 1564 | WCru |
| ***lutescens*** | EPot WCru |
| ***maculatum*** | CAby CBct CLAP IFoB LEdu MNrw WCru |
| ***megalanthum*** | CLAP CPLG IFoB MMoz WCru |
| - CD&R 2412B | CLAP CPLG EBee EPPr |
| ***nantouense*** | IFoB LEdu WCot WPGP |
| - B&SWJ 359 | CBct WCru WFar |
| - B&SWJ 6812 | WCru |
| ***sessile*** | EBee ECho LEdu WCru |
| - AGSJ 146 | GGar NMen |
| - B&SWJ 2824 | WCru |
| I - 'Aureovariegatum' (v) | ECho MAvo WCru |
| - 'Cricket' | GEdr WFar |
| - 'Kinga' (v) | EBee GEdr MAvo |
| - f. ***macrophyllum*** B&SWJ 4316 | WCru |
| I - 'Robustum Variegatum' | EBee MAvo |
| - variegated (v) | CBct |
| - 'Variegatum' (v) | Widely available |
| - var. ***yakushimense*** | ECho LEdu |
| ***shimadae*** B&SWJ 399 | WCru |
| ***smilacinum*** | LWst NLar WCru WFar |
| - B&SWJ 713 | WCru |

| | | |
|---|---|---|
| * | – 'Aureovariegatum' (v) | LEdu MAvo WCru |
| | – pink-flowered | WCru |
| | ***smithii*** | CBct CPom EBee ECho EPfP GAbr GEdr GGar GKev LEdu NBir NMen WCru WFar WPGP |
| | ***taiwanense*** B&SWJ 1513 | WCru |
| | – B&SWJ 2018 | WCru |
| | ***tonkinense*** B&SWJ 11672 | WCru |
| | – B&SWJ 11814 | WCru |
| | – HWJ 882 | WCru |
| | ***trabeculatum*** | WCru |
| | – 'Nakafu' | LEdu WCru |
| | ***trachycarpum*** | CLAP |
| | ***uniflorum*** | CBct CGHE CLAP CPom ECho EPfP EPla IFoB LEdu MNrw NBid WFar WPGP WSHC WTin |
| | – B&SWJ 651 | CBct LEdu WCot WCru |
| | – B&SWJ 872 | WCru |
| | – B&SWJ 4100 | WCru |
| | ***viridescens*** | CBct EBee LEdu SKHP WCru |
| | – B&SWJ 4598 | WCru |

## *Distictis* (*Bignoniaceae*)

| | |
|---|---|
| ***buccinatoria*** | MOWG |
| 'Mrs Rivers' | MOWG |

## *Distylium* (*Hamamelidaceae*)

| | |
|---|---|
| ***myricoides*** | CMCN NLar WFar |
| ***racemosum*** | CBcs CMac EPfP GKin IGor MBlu NLar SLPl SSta WSHC |

## *Diuranthera* see *Chlorophytum*

## *Dizygotheca* see *Schefflera*

## *Dobinea* (*Anacardiaceae*)

| | |
|---|---|
| ***vulgaris*** B&SWJ 2532 | WCru |

## *Dodecatheon* (*Primulaceae*)

| | | |
|---|---|---|
| | ***alpinum*** | NHar SRms |
| | – subsp. ***majus*** | EBee |
| | ***amethystinum*** | see *D. pulchellum* |
| | 'Aphrodite' PBR | EBee EKen NBPC NLar |
| | ***austrofrigidum*** | GKev NCGa NHar |
| | ***clevelandii*** | MDKP |
| | – subsp. ***insulare*** | LLHF NWCA |
| | – subsp. ***patulum*** | ECho LRHS |
| | ***conjugens*** | LLHF |
| | ***cusickii*** | see *D. pulchellum* subsp. *cusickii* |
| | ***dentatum*** ♀H4 | CElw EBee GEdr GKev LEdu MDKP NHar NWCA WAbe WFar |
| | ***frigidum*** | WAbe |
| § | ***hendersonii*** ♀H4 | EPot GAuc NMen SRms |
| | ***integrifolium*** | see *D. hendersonii* |
| § | ***jeffreyi*** | EBee ECho EPPr GEdr GKev LEdu LRHS MDev MNFA MNrw NBPC NCGa NLar NMen NPnk WAbe WBor WFar |
| | – NNS 05-250 | NWCA |
| | – subsp. ***pygmaeum*** new | GKev |
| | – 'Rotlicht' | SRms WTcb |
| * | × ***lemoinei*** | WAbe |
| § | ***meadia*** ♀H4 | Widely available |
| | – from Cedar County, USA | WAbe |
| | – f. ***album*** ♀H4 | CBro EBee ECho ELan EPfP EPot GAuc GEdr GGar GKev LAma LEdu LHop LRHS MLLN MMoz MNrw NCGa NHol NLar NMen NMyG NPnk SKHP SPer SRms SWvt WPnP |
| | – 'Aphrodite' | EPfP GEdr LSou WBor |
| * | – 'Goliath' | EBee |
| | – membranaceous | WAbe |
| | – 'Queen Victoria' | EBee ECho GEdr LEdu NLar NPnk SKHP SRGP WCot WFar WPnP |
| | – red shades | SMrm |
| | ***pauciflorum*** misapplied | see *D. pulchellum* |
| | ***pauciflorum*** (Dur.) E. Greene | see *D. meadia* |
| | ***poeticum*** B&SWJ 197 | EBee NCGa |
| § | ***pulchellum*** ♀H4 | CBro EBee ECho EDAr GEdr GKev LHop LLWG LRHS MNrw NMen NWCA SBfd WTcb |
| § | – subsp. ***cusickii*** | LEdu SRms |
| | – subsp. ***pulchellum*** 'Red Wings' | EBee EBla ECho EPot LLHF LRHS MDKP NBir NLar NMen NMyG NPnk NWCA SKHP SPoG WFar WHoo WPnP |
| | – ***radicatum*** | see *D. pulchellum* |
| | – 'Sooke Variety' | WAbe |
| | ***radicatum*** | see *D. pulchellum* |
| | ***redolens*** | EBee WAbe |
| | ***tetrandrum*** | see *D. jeffreyi* |

## *Dodonaea* (*Sapindaceae*)

| | |
|---|---|
| ***viscosa*** | CArn CBcs CTrC ECou SPlb |
| – (f) | ECou |
| – (m) | ECou |
| – 'Purpurea' | CAbb CBcs CDoC CHGN CPLG CTrC CTsd EAmu EBee ECre EHoe ELon EShb EWTr GBin GGar IVic LRHS LTen MAsh SLim SVen |

## *Doellingeria* (*Asteraceae*)

| | |
|---|---|
| ***scabra*** | see *Aster scaber* |

## *Dolichandra* (*Bignoniaceae*)

| | |
|---|---|
| ***cynanchoides*** RCB RA Q-4 | WCot |

## *Dolichos* (*Papilionaceae*)

| | |
|---|---|
| ***purpureus*** | see *Lablab purpureus* |

## *Dombeya* (*Malvaceae*)

| | |
|---|---|
| ***burgessiae*** | IDee MOWG |
| ***calantha*** | CCCN |
| × ***cayeuxii*** | CCCN |
| ***wallichii*** | CCCN |

## *Dondia* see *Hacquetia*

## *Doodia* (*Blechnaceae*)

| | | |
|---|---|---|
| | ***aspera*** | WRic |
| § | ***caudata*** | WAbe WRic |
| | ***media*** | CBty CDes GBin ISha LLHF LRHS WAbe WRic |
| | ***squarrosa*** | see *D. caudata* |

## *Doronicum* (*Asteraceae*)

| | | |
|---|---|---|
| | ***austriacum*** | NBid |
| | ***caucasicum*** | see *D. orientale* |
| § | ***columnae*** | CBcs |
| | ***cordatum*** | see *D. columnae* |
| § | × ***excelsum*** | CPrp EBee LEdu LRHS MRav NPer |
| | 'Harpur Crewe' | NVic |
| | 'Finesse' | GCal LRHS SPoG SRms SRot |
| § | 'Frühlingspracht' (d) | LRHS |
| | 'Little Leo' | EBee ELan ELon EPfP GJos LRHS LSRN MBrN NBPC NLar NPri NVic SBfd SPet SPoG SRGP WWEG |
| § | ***orientale*** | CWan EBee EPfP GJos LRHS MMuc NBlu SEND SPer SPoG SWat WTou |

| | |
|---|---|
| - 'Leonardo Compact' new | LBuc |
| - 'Magnificum' | CSBt EPfP GMaP LRHS MBNS MBri NBPC NEgg NGBl NMir SMrm SPoG SRms WCot WFar |
| ***pardalianches*** | CMea ECha MMuc WRHF |
| ***plantagineum*** 'Excelsum' | see *D.* × *excelsum* 'Harpur Crewe' |
| Spring Beauty | see *D.* 'Frühlingspracht' |

## *Dorotheanthus* (*Aizoaceae*)

| | |
|---|---|
| ***bellidiformis*** ♀H3 new | EDAr |

## *Doryanthes* (*Doryanthaceae*)

| | |
|---|---|
| ***excelsa*** | CHEx CTrC |
| ***palmeri*** | CBrP CHEx |

## *Dorycnium* see *Lotus*

## *Douglasia* see *Androsace*

| | |
|---|---|
| ***vitaliana*** | see *Vitaliana primuliflora* |

## *Dovea* (*Restionaceae*)

| | |
|---|---|
| ***macrocarpa*** | CCCN SPlb |

## *Dovyalis* (*Salicaceae*)

| | |
|---|---|
| ***caffra*** (F) | XBlo |

## *Doxantha* see *Macfadyena*

## *Draba* (*Brassicaceae*)

| | |
|---|---|
| ***acaulis*** | WAbe |
| ***aizoides*** | ECho GKev LRHS MAsh MWat SGar SPlb SRms WFar WRHF XLum |
| ***aizoon*** | see *D. lasiocarpa* |
| ***athoa*** | EDAr |
| ***borealis*** new | XLum |
| ***bruniifolia*** | EWes XLum |
| - subsp. ***olympica*** | WFar |
| ***bryoides*** | see *D. rigida* var. *bryoides* |
| ***cappadocica*** | ITim |
| ***compacta*** | see *D. lasiocarpa* Compacta Group |
| ***cretica*** | NMen |
| ***cusickii*** | GKev |
| ***cuspidata*** | ITim |
| ***dedeana*** | EWes |
| ***dubia*** | EDAr |
| ***glacialis*** | EDAr |
| ***hispanica*** | EDAr NWCA |
| ***hoppeana*** | EDAr |
| ***imbricata*** | see *D. rigida* var. *imbricata* |
| § ***lasiocarpa*** | XLum |
| § - Compacta Group | NWCA |
| ***longisiliqua*** ♀H2 | ITim WAbe |
| - EMR 2551 | EPot |
| ***mollissima*** | EPot NWCA WAbe |
| - 'Göteborg' new | GLam |
| ***oligosperma*** subsp. ***subsessilis*** | NWCA |
| ***ossetica*** | WAbe |
| ***parnassica*** | EDAr |
| ***polytricha*** | GLam WAbe |
| § ***rigida*** var. ***bryoides*** | WThu |
| § - var. ***imbricata*** | NSla |
| - - f. ***compacta*** | EPot |
| ***rosularis*** | EPot |
| × ***salomonii*** | EPot |
| ***scardica*** | see *D. lasiocarpa* |
| ***ventosa*** | WAbe |

## *Dracaena* ✿ (*Asparagaceae*)

| | |
|---|---|
| ***cochinchinensis*** new | SPlb |
| ***congesta*** | see *Cordyline stricta* |
| ***draco*** ♀H1 | CTrC EShb XBlo |
| ***fragrans*** Deremensis Group | XBlo |
| ***indivisa*** | see *Cordyline indivisa* |
| 'Lemon Lime Tips' | XBlo |
| ***marginata*** (v) ♀H1 | XBlo |
| - 'Tricolor' (v) ♀H1 | XBlo |
| ***stricta*** | see *Cordyline stricta* |

## *Dracocephalum* (*Lamiaceae*)

| | |
|---|---|
| sp. | LLHF |
| ***argunense*** | GKev SBch SPhx SRms WPat |
| - 'Blue Carpet' | NLar |
| - 'Fuji Blue' | CEnt CPLG EBee EPfP EWes LRHS LSRN NBre SPoG |
| - 'Fuji White' | CEnt CPLG EBee GKev LSRN SPhx |
| ***botryoides*** | CPBP LLHF SPhx |
| aff. ***forrestii*** | LLHF |
| ***grandiflorum*** | CEnt GJos LLHF MMHG SBHP SBch SPhx WFar XLum |
| - 'Altai Blue' | LRHS |
| ***hemsleyanum*** | LLHF WPat |
| ***mairei*** | see *D. renatii* |
| ***moldavica*** | SIde |
| ***peregrinum*** 'Blue Dragon' | SPhx |
| ***prattii*** | see *Nepeta prattii* |
| § ***renatii*** | LLHF SPhx |
| ***rupestre*** | EBee NBre WCAu |
| ***ruyschiana*** | ELan EWes GEdr GLam LRHS MRav NWCA SPhx |
| - 'Blue Moon' | NBPC NBre NLar |
| ***sibiricum*** | see *Nepeta sibirica* |
| * ***tataricum*** | LRHS |
| ***virginicum*** | see *Physostegia virginiana* |
| ***wendelboi*** | NBir |

## *Dracunculus* (*Araceae*)

| | |
|---|---|
| ***canariensis*** | WCot |
| ***muscivorus*** | see *Helicodiceros muscivorus* |
| § ***vulgaris*** | CAby CHid CPom EBee ECho EPfP EPot ERCP LEdu MCCP MRav SDix SEND SMad SPlb WCot WFar |

## *Dregea* (*Apocynaceae*)

| | |
|---|---|
| ***sinensis*** | CBot CCCN CHll CRHN CWGN EBee ELan EPfP ERea EShb EWes LRHS MAsh MAvo MOWG MRav SEND SKHP SPer SPoG WCot WPGP WPat WSHC |
| - 'Brockhill Silver' | SKHP |
| - 'Variegata' (v) | CCCN EWes WCot |

## *Drepanostachyum* (*Poaceae*)

| | |
|---|---|
| ***falconeri*** J.J.N. Campbell. ex D. McClintock | see *Himalayacalamus falconeri*, *Himalayacalamus falconeri* 'Damarapa' |
| ***hookerianum*** | see *Himalayacalamus hookerianus* |
| § ***khasianum*** | CDTJ CPLG WPGP |
| § ***microphyllum*** | WJun WPGP |

## *Drimia* (*Asparagaceae*)

| | |
|---|---|
| ***angustifolia*** ambig. | ECho |
| ***anomala*** | CLak |
| ***elata*** | CLak |
| ***involuta*** | CLak |
| ***mzimvubuensis*** | CLak |
| ***sphaerocephala*** | CLak |
| ***uniflora*** | CLak |

## *Drimiopsis* (*Asparagaceae*)

**maculata** LToo WCot

## *Drimys* (*Winteraceae*)

**andina** CPLG EPfP WPGP
**aromatica** see *D. lanceolata*
**colorata** see *Pseudowintera colorata*
**granadensis** WCru
var. **grandiflora** B&SWJ 10777
**granatensis** WPGP
§ **lanceolata** Widely available
- (f) CTrC ECou GGar NCGa SPer
- (m) CDoC CTrC ECou GGar SPer
- 'Inverewe Prolific' (f) GGar
- 'Mount Wellington' GCal GGar
- 'Suzette' (v) LRHS MBlu
* **latifolia** CBcs CHEx IDee
**winteri** ♀H4 Widely available
§ - var. **chilensis** CPLG EPfP GGar LRHS SSpi WCru WPGP
- Latifolia Group see *D. winteri* var. *chilensis*

## *Drosanthemum* (*Aizoaceae*)

**hispidum** ECho ELan EPfP EPot GLam ITim LRHS MAsh NMen NWCA SBHP SPlb SPoG WAbe WNew
**speciosum** ECho
* **sutherlandii** ECho

## *Drosera* ✿ (*Droseraceae*)

**admirabilis** CHew CSWC
**aliciae** CHew CSWC EECP NChu SHmp
**andersoniana** EFEx
**androsacea** CHew
**anglica** CSWC NChu
**ascendens** CHew
**binata** CHew EECP SHmp
- var. **binata** CSWC
§ - subsp. **dichotoma** CHew CSWC SHmp
- 'Extrema' CHew
- 'Multifida' CHew MCCP
**browniana** EFEx
**bulbigena** EFEx
**bulbosa** subsp. **bulbosa** EFEx
- subsp. **major** EFEx
**callistos** CHew
**capensis** CHew CSWC MCCP NChu SHmp SPlb SWal
- 'Albino' CHew EECP MCCP SHmp SWal
- red CSWC NChu SWal
**cuneifolia** CHew
**dichotoma** see *D. binata* subsp. *dichotoma*
**dichrosepala** CHew EECP
**echinoblastus** CHew
**enodes** CHew
**ericksoniae** CHew
**erythrorhiza** EFEx
- subsp. **collina** EFEx
- subsp. **erythrorhiza** CHew EFEx
- subsp. **magna** EFEx
- subsp. **squamosa** EFEx
**filiformis** NChu
- var. **filiformis** CHew CSWC EECP SHmp
**gigantea** EFEx
**graniticola** EFEx
**helodes** CHew
**heterophylla** EFEx
× **hybrida** CSWC
**intermedia** CSWC
**lasiantha** CHew
**leioblastus** CHew
**loureiroi** EFEx
**macrantha** EFEx
- subsp. **macrantha** EFEx
**macrophylla** subsp. **macrophylla** EFEx
**madagascariensis** SHmp
**mannii** CHew
**marchantii** subsp. **prophylla** EFEx
**menziesii** subsp. **basifolia** EFEx
- subsp. **menziesii** EFEx
- subsp. **thysanosepala** EFEx
**modesta** EFEx
**nidiformis** CHew
**orbiculata** EFEx
**paleacea** subsp. **trichocaulis** CHew
**peltata** EFEx
**platypoda** EFEx
**pulchella** CHew
**pycnoblasta** CHew
**pygmaea** CHew
**ramellosa** EFEx
**roseana** CHew
**rosulata** EFEx
**rotundifolia** CSWC SHmp WHer
**salina** EFEx
**sargentii** CHew
**scorpioides** CHew CSWC EECP SHmp
**slackii** CHew CSWC NChu
**spatulata** CSWC SHmp
**stelliflora** CHew
**stolonifera** subsp. **compacta** EFEx
- subsp. **humilis** EFEx
- subsp. **porrecta** EFEx
- subsp. **rupicola** EFEx
- subsp. **stolonifera** EFEx
**tubaestylus** EFEx
**zonaria** EFEx

## *Drosophyllum* (*Drosophyllaceae*)

**lusitanicum** CHew

## *Dryandra* (*Proteaceae*)

**formosa** LTen SPlb WCot

## *Dryas* (*Rosaceae*)

**drummondii** ECho LLHF WAbe WFar
**grandis** GKev
§ **integrifolia** CMea NMen
- 'Greenland Green' WAbe
**octopetala** ♀H4 CMea ECho GAbr GJos LHop LRHS MAsh MWat NChi SPoG SRms WAbe
§ - dwarf EPot
- subsp. **hookeriana** LLHF
- 'Minor' ♀H4 NMen WAbe
**oxyodonta** new GKev
× **suendermannii** ♀H4 CYeo EPfP EPot GEdr GMaP NHar NMen WAbe
**tenella** misapplied see *D. octopetala* dwarf
**tenella** Pursh see *D. integrifolia*

## *Dryopteris* ✿ (*Dryopteridaceae*)

from Emei Shan, China WPGP

| |  |  |
|---|---|---|
| | ***aemula*** | EFer SRms WRic |
| § | ***affinis*** ♀H4 | CBty CLAP EBee ECha EPfP GMaP LBuc LPBA LRHS LTen MCot MGos MMoz MRav NHol NPri SPer SPoG SRms WFib WRic WShi WWEG |
| § | - subsp. ***borreri*** | SRms |
| | - subsp. ***cambrensis*** 'Crispa Barnes' | WPGP |
| | - - 'Insubrica' | EFer |
| | - 'Congesta' | CLAP EBee WWEG |
| | - 'Congesta Cristata' | CFee CLAP CWCL EFer GMaP LPBA SRot |
| | - Crispa Group | CLAP EHon GBBs LAst MMoz WWEG |
| § | - 'Crispa Gracilis' ♀H4 | CKel CLAP EFtx ELan GBin ISha LTen MCCP MMoz NBir NEgg NMyG WRic WWEG |
| * | - 'Crispa Gracilis Congesta' | CBty GEdr NGdn NWad SBfd WFib WPat |
| § | - 'Cristata' ♀H4 | Widely available |
| | - 'Cristata Angustata' ♀H4 | CBty CLAP EFer ELan EPfP ETod GBin LTen MMoz NBid NGdn NHol SRms WBor WFib WMoo WPGP WRic |
| | - 'Cristata The King' | see *D. affinis* 'Cristata' |
| | - 'Grandiceps Askew' | EFer SRms WFib |
| | - 'Pinderi' | CBty CLAP EBee ELan GBin MMuc NMyG SRms WRic WWEG |
| | - Polydactyla Group | CLAP WFar |
| | - - 'Polydactyla Dadds' | CBty CLAP EFtx EQua LLHF NLar NMyG SEND WWEG |
| | - - 'Polydactyla Mapplebeck' ♀H4 | CLAP GBin LPBA NBid SRms WFib WRic |
| | - 'Revolvens' | CLAP EFer SRms |
| | ***aitoniana*** | WRic |
| | ***atrata*** misapplied | see *D. cycadina* |
| | ***atrata*** (Wall. ex Kunze) Ching | CDTJ CKel CWCL EWTr SBfd SPoG XLum |
| | × ***australis*** | CLAP ISha LTen WRic |
| | ***austriaca*** | see *D. dilatata* |
| | ***bissetiana*** | ISha WRic |
| | ***blanfordii*** | WPGP WRic |
| | ***borreri*** | see *D. affinis* subsp. *borreri* |
| | ***buschiana*** | CBty CDTJ CLAP EBee EFtx MRav NLar WWEG |
| | ***carthusiana*** | CLAP EBee EFer GBin NLar SRms STre WPtf WRic |
| | - 'Cristata' | EFer |
| | ***celsa*** | ISha WRic |
| | ***championii*** | CCCN CLAP ISha LRHS WRic |
| | ***clintoniana*** | CLAP EFer GBin LRHS MMoz NMyG WPGP WRic |
| | × ***complexa*** | CBty ISha |
| | - 'Stablerae' | CLAP EFer EFtx GBin MWhi WFib WPGP WRic |
| | - 'Stablerae' crisped | NMyG WFib |
| | ***coreanomontana*** | NMyG |
| | ***costalisora*** | WRic |
| | ***crassirhizoma*** | CCCN CKel CLAP EBee GBin LRHS LWst MMoz NMyG WRic |
| | ***cristata*** | CLAP CWCL EBee EPfP WMoo WRic XLum |
| § | ***cycadina*** ♀H4 | CHEx CLAP EBee EFer EFtx ELan EPfP EShb GBin LPBA LRHS LTen MBri MCCP MGos MMoz MWat NBid NBir WFib WMoo WPnP WRic |
| | ***dickinsii*** | GLin |
| § | ***dilatata*** ♀H4 | CRWN ECha EFer EFtx ELan EPfP LRHS MRav SRms WFib WHal WRic WShi |
| | - 'Crispa Whiteside' ♀H4 | CBty CLAP CWCL EBee EFer EFtx EPfP LRHS LTen MBri MWhi NLar SBfd SMrm SPlb SRms WFib WMoo WPGP WRic WWEG |
| | - 'Grandiceps' | CLAP EFer WFib |
| | - 'Jimmy Dyce' | CLAP ISha |
| | - 'Lepidota Crispa Cristata' | CLAP EBee |
| | - 'Lepidota Cristata' ♀H4 | CBty CLAP CMHG CWCL EFtx ELan GBin LTen NGdn NMyG NVic SEND SRms WFar WFib WMoo WRic |
| | - 'Lepidota Grandiceps' | CLAP |
| * | - 'Recurvata' | CBty CLAP ISha LLHF NLar WRic |
| | ***erythrosora*** ♀H4 | Widely available |
| | - 'Brilliance' | CCCN CLAP GQue ISha LRHS LSou NLar WRic |
| | - var. ***prolifica*** ♀H4 | CBty CKel CLAP EBee EFtx GMaP LRHS LTen MGos MMoz NBir NEgg NLar NPri WFib WRic WWEG |
| | ***filix-mas*** ♀H4 | Widely available |
| | - 'Barnesii' | CLAP CWCL EBee EFer GBin ISha LTen MMuc NLar SEND SGol SPlb SPoG WRic WWEG |
| | - 'Crispa' | CBty CLAP EBee EHon LRHS LTen NHol SGol SRms WFib |
| | - 'Crispa Congesta' | see *D. affinis* 'Crispa Gracilis' |
| | - 'Crispa Cristata' | CBty CLAP CWCL EBee EFer EFtx ELan EPfP GMaP IKil LHop LRHS LTen MBri MMuc MWhi NBid NBir SEND SPoG SRms SWat WFib WGor WRic WWEG |
| | - 'Cristata' ♀H4 | CLAP EBee EFer ELan EPfP LTen MMoz NMyG NOrc SRms SWat WMoo |
| | - Cristata Group | EFer WRic |
| * | - - 'Cristata Grandiceps' | EFer |
| | - - 'Cristata Jackson' | CLAP SPlb |
| | - - 'Cristata Martindale' | CLAP NBid SRms WFib |
| | - - 'Fred Jackson' | CLAP WFib |
| | - 'Depauperata' | CLAP WPGP |
| | - 'Euxinensis' | CLAP |
| | - 'Furcans' | CLAP WRic |
| | - 'Grandiceps Wills' ♀H4 | NBid WFib |
| | - 'Linearis' | CMHG EBee EFer EHon ELan ISha LAst LPBA MCot MGos SRms WFib |
| | - 'Linearis Congesta' | WPGP |
| | - 'Linearis Cristata' | WRic |
| | - 'Linearis Polydactyla' | CBty CDes CLAP CWCL EBee EFer EFtx EPfP GBin LRHS LTen MMoz MMuc NGdn NMyG SEND SPoG WFar WIvy WMoo WPnP WPtf XLum |
| | - 'Parsley' | CLAP ISha |
| * | - Polydactyla Group | MGos MRav MWat NEgg |
| I | - 'Revolvens' | WFib |
| | - 'Rich Beauty' | LTen |
| | ***formosana*** | WRic |
| | ***fuscipes*** | WRic |
| | ***goldieana*** | CDTJ CLAP CMHG EBee EFer EFtx EWTr GBin GMaP LRHS NBid NBir NGdn NLar NMyG WCot WFar WFib WMoo WPnP WRic WWEG |
| | ***hirtipes*** misapplied | see *D. cycadina* |
| | ***hondoensis*** | EFtx WRic |
| | ***intermedia*** | ISha WRic |
| | ***labordei*** | CBty ISha LRHS |
| | ***lacera*** | ISha WRic |
| | ***lepidopoda*** | CBty EFtx GLin WRic |
| | ***ludoviciana*** | CBty EFtx ISha WRic |

| | |
|---|---|
| ***marginalis*** | CDTJ CKel CLAP EBee EKen GBin LRHS MMoz NHol NLar NMyG SBfd SEND WMoo WRic |
| ***oreades*** | SRms |
| ***pacifica*** | CLAP |
| ***paleacea*** | CLAP |
| ***pseudofilix-mus*** | ISha WRic |
| ***pseudomas*** | see *D. affinis* |
| ***pycnopteroides*** | EFtx WRic |
| × ***remota*** | ISha SRms WRic |
| ***scottii*** | WRic |
| × ***separabilis*** | ISha |
| ***sieboldii*** | CBty CEnt CFir CHEx CLAP CPrp CWCL EBee EFer ELan EShb GEdr LRHS LTen MAvo NBid NBir NGdn NLar NMyG SBfd SRms WMoo WPGP WRic WWEG |
| ***sordidipes*** | WRic |
| ***stewartii*** | CLAP GBin LLHF LTen NLar NMyG WRic WWEG |
| ***sublacera*** | EFtx |
| ***tokyoensis*** | CDTJ CDes CKel CLAP EBee EFtx GBin ISha LRHS LWst MMoz NLar NMyG WPGP WRic |
| ***uniformis*** | CLAP |
| ***wallichiana*** ♀H4 | Widely available |
| - F&M 107 | WPGP |

## *Duchesnea* (*Rosaceae*)

| | |
|---|---|
| ***chrysantha*** | see *D. indica* |
| § ***indica*** | GAbr LEdu MRav SEND WMoo WOut XLum |
| § - 'Harlequin' (v) | CPLG MCCP |
| * - 'Snowflake' (v) | EBee WMoo |
| - 'Variegata' | see *D. indica* 'Harlequin' |

## *Dugaldia* (*Asteraceae*)

| | |
|---|---|
| ***hoopesii*** | see *Hymenoxys hoopesii* |

## *Dulichium* (*Cyperaceae*)

| | |
|---|---|
| ***arundinaceum*** | LLWG LSRN |
| - 'Tigress' | LLWG |

## *Dunalia* (*Solanaceae*)

| | |
|---|---|
| ***australis*** | see *Iochroma australe* |
| - blue-flowered | see *Iochroma australe* 'Bill Evans' |
| - white-flowered | see *Iochroma australe* 'Andean Snow' |

## *Duranta* (*Verbenaceae*)

| | |
|---|---|
| § ***erecta*** | CCCN CHll EShb |
| § - 'Geisha Girl' | CCCN EShb |
| - 'Sapphire Swirl' | see *D. erecta* 'Geisha Girl' |
| - 'Variegata' (v) | CCCN EShb |
| ***plumieri*** | see *D. erecta* |
| ***repens*** | see *D. erecta* |
| ***serratifolia*** | CCCN |

## *Duvernoia* see *Justicia*

## *Dyckia* (*Bromeliaceae*)

| | |
|---|---|
| ***frigida*** | WCot WGrn |
| ***leptostachya*** | WCot WGrn |
| ***marnier-lapostollei*** | WCot |
| 'Morris Hobbs' | WCot |
| ***remotiflora*** | CBrP SChr |
| ***velascana*** | CHEx |

## *Dymondia* (*Asteraceae*)

| | |
|---|---|
| ***margaretae*** | CFee CPBP WAbe |

## *Dypsis* (*Arecaceae*)

| | |
|---|---|
| § ***decaryi*** | CCCN EAmu LPal XBlo |
| ***decipiens*** | CBrP |
| ***lutescens*** ♀H1 | LPal MBri XBlo |

## *Dysosma* see *Podophyllum*

# E

## *Ecballium* (*Cucurbitaceae*)

| | |
|---|---|
| ***elaterium*** | CArn CDTJ LEdu SGar SIde WPGP |

## *Eccremocarpus* (*Bignoniaceae*)

| | |
|---|---|
| ***scaber*** | CBcs CRHN ELan EPfP LBMP LRHS MBri MNrw NPer SBfd SEND SGar SLim |
| - 'Aureus' | EPfP MAsh |
| - 'Carmineus' | EPfP EWld GGar SGar |
| - coral-red-flowered | MAsh |
| - orange-flowered | MAsh SPoG |
| I - 'Roseus' | NLar |
| - 'Tresco Cream' | CSpe |

## *Echeandia* (*Asparagaceae*)

| | |
|---|---|
| ***formosa*** B&SWJ 9147 | WCru |

## *Echeveria* ✿ (*Crassulaceae*)

| | |
|---|---|
| ***affinis*** | SRot |
| ***agavoides*** ♀H1 | MRav |
| * 'Black Prince' | CAbb CDes CDoC MSCN NPer SPlb SRot WCot WDyG WFar WPGP |
| 'Blue Waves' | WCot |
| * ***cana*** | CDoC EWll SRot |
| ***coccinea*** | ELan |
| ***colorata*** new | WCot |
| 'Corymbosa' new | WCot |
| 'Crûg Ice' | WCru |
| 'Curly Locks' new | WCot |
| ***derenbergii*** ♀H1 | STre |
| × ***derosa*** | EPfP |
| - 'Worfield Wonder' ♀H1 | STre |
| 'Doris Taylor' | MSCN |
| 'Duchess of Nuremberg' | CDoC CHVG SMrm SPlb SRot WFar WNew |
| ***elegans*** ♀H1 | CDoC CHEx EPfP GAbr LSou SPlb WCot WDyG WGwG WNew |
| § ***gibbiflora*** var. ***metallica*** ♀H1 | EPfP |
| * × ***gilva*** 'Red' ♀H1 | WCot |
| ***glauca*** Baker | see *E. secunda* var. *glauca* |
| ***harmsii*** ♀H1 | CDoC STre WGwG |
| 'Hens and Chicks' | CHEx |
| ***lilacina*** | CDoC SMrm SPlb SRot |
| 'Mahogany' | CDoC SUsu WCot WGrn |
| 'Mauna Loa' | MCot WCot WGrn |
| ***maxonii*** B&SWJ 10396 | WCru |
| 'Meridian' | CHEx |
| 'Mexico City' new | CDoC |
| ***montana*** B&SWJ 10277 | WCru |
| ***multicaulis*** | MSCN |
| ***nodulosa*** | WCot |
| ***peacockii*** | EOHP MSCN NBlu SMrm SPet SPlb WNew |
| 'Perle d'Azur' | CHEx WCot |
| 'Perle von Nürnberg' ♀H1 | CAbb MSCN SMad SPet |

| | | |
|---|---|---|
| | ***prolifica*** | STre |
| | ***pulidonis*** ♀[H1] | EPfP WCot |
| I | ***pulvinata*** 'Rubra' | MSCN |
| | ***rosea*** | WCot |
| | ***runyonii*** 'Topsy Turvy' | CDoC CHEx EOHP EPfP MSCN SPet SRot |
| | ***secunda*** | CAbb STre SWal |
| § | - var. ***glauca*** ♀[H1] | CDTJ CDes CDoC CHEx EAmu EBee ELan EShb ETod GAbr LPJP NBir SArc STre WCot WPGP |
| * | - - 'Gigantea' | NDov NPer WPGP |
| | ***setosa*** ♀[H1] | EPfP MSCN |
| | - var. ***ciliata*** | EShb |
| | - var. ***deminuta*** | SPlb |
| | ***shaviana*** | SRot WCot |

## *Echinacea* ✿ (*Asteraceae*)

| | | |
|---|---|---|
| § | 'After Midnight' (Big Sky Series) | CHab CPar EBee EGHP NLar |
| | ***angustifolia*** | CArn CBod EBee EBla EGHP EPfP GMac GPoy LRHS MHer SPhx WCAu WJek |
| § | 'Art's Pride'[PBR] | CAby CBcs CBod CHab CHar CWGN EBee EBla ECtt ELan EPfP GMaP LRHS LSRN LSou MAvo MGos MRav NBir NEgg NGdn NPnk SBfd SMrm SPer SPoG SUsu WCot WFar |
| | 'Coral Reef' **new** | SBfd |
| | 'Dreamcoat' **new** | MSCN |
| | 'Emily Saul' | see *E.* 'After Midnight' (Big Sky Series) |
| | 'Evan Saul'[PBR] | see *E.* 'Sundown' |
| | 'Firebird' **new** | LRHS SBfd |
| | 'Flame Thrower' **new** | EBee LRHS NLar SBfd SHeu |
| | 'Green Envy'[PBR] | CBcs CPar CWGN EBee ECtt EKen ELan EPfP GQue LRHS LSou MBNS MLLN NEgg NGdn NLar NPnk NSti SBfd SKHP SMrm SPer SPoG SUsu WAul WCot WWEG |
| | 'Green Jewel' | LRHS NDov SHeu |
| § | 'Harvest Moon'[PBR] (Big Sky Series) | Widely available |
| | 'Hot Lava' **new** | EBee NDov SHeu |
| | 'Hot Papaya' (d) | EBee ECtt LRHS LSou MTis WCot |
| | 'Hot Summer' **new** | EBee ECtt GMac IPot NCGa SHeu WHlf |
| | 'Irresistible' (d) **new** | CWGN |
| | 'Katie Saul' | see *E.* 'Summer Sky' |
| | 'Mac 'n' Cheese' **new** | EBee LRHS |
| | Mango Meadowbrite = 'CBG Cone3' | EBee EPfP LRHS SPoG |
| | 'Matthew Saul'[PBR] | see *E.* 'Harvest Moon' |
| | 'Maui Sunshine' **new** | NDov SBfd |
| | 'Minstrel' | LRHS |
| | Orange Meadowbrite[PBR] | see *E.* 'Art's Pride' |
| | ***pallida*** | Widely available |
| | - 'Hula Dancer' | CMea CSam EBee EPfP GMac NGdn NPri SPhx SSvw WWEG |
| | ***paradoxa*** | CArn CHar CPou CSam EBee EBla ECtt EGHP ELan EPfP GMac GPoy LAst LRHS LSRN MCot MHer NGdn NPri SMrm SPav SPer SPhx SPlb SWvt WFar WWEG |
| | - 'Yellow Mellow' | EPfP LSRN |
| | Pixie Meadowbrite = 'CBG Cone 2' | CAbP CDes CWGN EBee ECtt IKil MTis NDov NSti WCot WCra WPGP |
| § | ***purpurea*** | Widely available |
| | - 'After Midnight' | CBcs ECtt LSou |
| | - 'Alaska'[PBR] | EBee MSCN NGdn NLar |
| | - 'Alba' | ECtt EPfP LBMP LRHS MNHC NVic XLum |
| | - 'Augustkönigin' | EBee NBir |
| | - 'Avalanche'[PBR] | EBee MWea SBfd |
| | - 'Baby Swan White' | CSam ELon LRHS MWea NLar STes WCot WWEG |
| | - Bressingham hybrids | EBla LRHS MRav SPer SPhx WFar WGwG |
| | - 'Coconut Lime'[PBR] | CWGN EBee ECtt EGHP EPfP LRHS LSou MTis MWea NPnk SPer SRkn SUsu WCot WHlf |
| | - Doppelganger | see *E. purpurea* 'Doubledecker' |
| § | - 'Doubledecker' | EBee ECtt EGHP EPfP LBMP LLHF LRHS MDKP NGdn NPri SBfd SMrm STes SWat WFar WWEG XLum |
| | - Elton Knight = 'Elbrook'[PBR] ♀[H3] | EBee ECtt EKen IPot LRHS LSRN MWea SDix SKHP SRkn SWvt WCra |
| | - 'Fancy Frills' | EBee ECtt LSou |
| | - 'Fatal Attraction'[PBR] | Widely available |
| | - 'Fragrant Angel'[PBR] | CHid CKno CMac CWGN EBee EBla ECtt EPfP GMac IPot LRHS LSRN LSou MCot MLLN MTis MWea NLar SKHP SMrm SPoG SUsu SWat SWvt WCot |
| | - 'Green Eyes'[PBR] | NLar |
| | - 'Green Jewel' **new** | CSpr LRHS |
| | - 'Hope'[PBR] | EBee NLar |
| | - 'Jade' | CAbP CAby CKno CMea CWGN EBee ECtt EPfP GQue LRHS LSRN LSou MBNS MCot NDov NEgg NGdn NLar NPnk SHeu SUsu SWat WCAu WCot |
| | - 'Kim's Knee High'[PBR] | Widely available |
| | - 'Kim's Mop Head' | CKno CMac EBee EBla ECtt ELon EPfP EWes LRHS LSou MAsh MCot MRav NGdn NLar NOrc NPnk WCot WFar WWEG |
| § | - 'Leuchtstern' | CKno EBee EGHP LRHS NBir NBre NGdn SSth SWat WMnd WWEG XLum |
| | - 'Lilliput' | NLar |
| | - 'Little Giant' | EBee |
| | - 'Little Magnus'[PBR] | EBee |
| | - 'Lucky Star' **new** | NCGa NDov WCFE WHoo |
| | - 'Magnus' ♀[H4] | Widely available |
| | - 'Mars' | IPot |
| | - 'Maxima' | CAbP EBee ECtt LRHS MTis NDov WCot WWEG |
| | - 'Merlot' | SHeu |
| | - 'Mistral' **new** | LRHS |
| | - 'Pica Bella' | CWGN EBee ECtt EPfP LAst LRHS MWea NDov NLar WWEG |
| | - 'Pink Double Delight'[PBR] | EGHP LHop LRHS MRav NGdn SWat WHlf WWEG |
| | - 'Pink Glow' | NDov |
| | - 'Pink Poodle' | EBee EPri LSou SBfd SHeu SPoG |
| | - 'Prairie Frost' (v) | EGHP |
| | - 'Prairie Splendor' | EPfP SPoG |
| | - 'Primadonna Deep Rose' | EBee LEdu NBre NGBl SRot |
| | - 'Primadonna White' | CChe GMac LEdu LRHS SRot |
| | - 'Purity' **new** | LRHS WWEG |
| | - 'Razzmatazz'[PBR] (d) | CAbP CWGN EBee ECtt EGHP ELan EPfP EWes GMaP LHop LRHS LSRN MGos MNrw MWea NEgg NGdn NPnk NSti SPer SUsu SWat SWvt WCot WWEG |
| | - 'Red Knee High' **new** | LRHS |
| | - 'Robert Bloom' | CAbP EBee EBla ECtt GQue LHop MCot NBir SMrm SWvt WCot WWEG |

| | | |
|---|---|---|
| | - 'Rubinglow' | CDes CElw CHar EBee EBla ECtt EGHP LSou MDKP MSCN NBir NDov NLar SBfd SPer SWvt WCot |
| | - 'Rubinstern' ♀H4 | Widely available |
| | - 'Ruby Giant' ♀H4 | Widely available |
| | - 'Sparkler' (v) | CWGN ECtt NLar |
| | - 'The King' | EBee ECtt EGHP NCGa NGdn |
| | - 'Verbesserter Leuchtstern' | EGHP NBre NLar |
| | - 'Vintage Wine' PBR | CKno CMac CWGN EBee ECtt EGHP ELan ELon GQue IKil LPla LRHS LSou MAsh MNrw MTis NEgg NLar NPnk NSti SPer SPoG SWvt WCot WWEG |
| | - 'Virgin' PBR | IPot MAsh NDov |
| | - 'White Lustre' | EBee ECha EPfP NBre SRms WFar |
| | - 'White Swan' | Widely available |
| | 'Raspberry Tart' | EBee LRHS SHeu |
| | ***ritro*** 'Blue Cloud' new | LRHS |
| | ***simulata*** | EBee SPhx SUsu |
| | 'Starlight' | see *E. purpurea* 'Leuchtstern' |
| § | 'Summer Sky' (Big Sky Series) | CPar CWCL CWGN ECtt EGHP GMac IPot LSou MBNS MTis NDov NLar NPnk STes SUsu WCot |
| § | 'Sundown' PBR (Big Sky Series) | CBcs CCVN CHab CMac CPar CSev CWCL CWGN ECtt EGHP EPfP ETod GMac IPot LBMP LRHS LSou MBNS MWea MWhi NLar NOrc NPnk SBfd SBrd SMrm SPoG SRkn WCAu |
| | 'Sunrise' PBR (Big Sky Series) | Widely available |
| | 'Sunset' PBR (Big Sky Series) | CAbP CBcs CWCL CWGN EBee EBla ECtt EGHP ELan EPfP EWes LAst LLHF LRHS LSRN LSou MBNS MGos NEgg NGdn NPnk SBfd SMrm SPer SPoG SUsu SWat SWvt |
| | 'Tangerine Dream' new | EBee NLar SHeu |
| | ***tennesseensis*** | CArn SPhx WPGP |
| | - 'Rocky Top' | CMea EBee ECtt EGHP EPfP GMac LRHS LSRN MNFA NBre SBfd SKHP SPhx SUsu WCot |
| | 'Tiki Torch' | CPar CWGN ECtt EWes GMaP LSou MCot MTis NDov NLar NSti SBfd SHeu SMad SPer SPoG WCot WWEG WWlt |
| | 'Tomato Soup' | CWGN EBee ECtt LLHF LRHS LSou MCot MTis NDov NLar NSti SBfd SHeu SPoG WCot |
| | 'Twilight' PBR (Big Sky Series) | CPar CWGN EBee ECtt EGHP EPfP LBMP LRHS LSou MNrw MWea NDov NOrc NPnk SHeu SRkn WCot |

## *Echinops* (*Asteraceae*)

| | | |
|---|---|---|
| | RCB AM -14 | WCot |
| | ***albus*** | see *E.* 'Nivalis' |
| § | ***bannaticus*** | CBcs CHab CSBt EBee NBid WCAu WFar WWEG |
| * | - 'Albus' | LAst MMuc NGdn |
| | - 'Blue Globe' | CMHG CSev EBee EHoe ELon EPfP EShb GCal GMaP LAst LRHS LSRN MCot MGos NBPC NChi NGdn SBfd SCoo SMrm SPhx SPoG STes WCAu WFar WMnd WWEG |
| | - 'Star Frost' | GQue NLar SBfd SPhx |
| | - 'Taplow Blue' ♀H4 | Widely available |
| | ***commutatus*** | see *E. exaltatus* |
| § | ***exaltatus*** | LPla NBir |
| | ***maracandicus*** | GCal |
| § | 'Nivalis' | CBre EBee SEND |
| * | ***perringii*** | GCal |
| | 'Real Stone' new | EBee LSou |
| | ***ritro*** misapplied | see *E. bannaticus* |
| § | ***ritro*** L. ♀H4 | Widely available |
| | - SDR 6415 | GKev |
| | - subsp. ***ruthenicus*** ♀H4 | ELan MRav |
| | - - 'Platinum Blue' | EBee ECtt GQue LRHS NBPC NEgg NLar SBfd SPad SPet WMnd WPer |
| | - 'Sea Stone' | EBee |
| | - 'Veitch's Blue' misapplied | see *E. ritro* L. |
| | - 'Veitch's Blue' | Widely available |
| | ***sphaerocephalus*** | NBir SMrm SPlb |
| | - 'Arctic Glow' | CMac CPou EBee ECha ECtt EHoe ELan EPfP LAst LRHS MAvo MCot MLLN MWhi NGdn NLar NVic SBfd SPer SPlb SPoG SWvt WCAu WFar WMnd WWEG |
| | ***strigosus*** | EBee |
| | ***terscheckii*** | EAmu |
| | ***tjanschanicus*** | CMea LRHS NBPC WWEG |
| | ***tournefortii*** | GBin |

## *Echinospartum* (*Papilionaceae*)

| | | |
|---|---|---|
| | sp. new | CArn |

## *Echium* (*Boraginaceae*)

| | | |
|---|---|---|
| | ***amoenum*** | NWCA |
| | ***boissieri*** | CCCN ELan |
| § | ***candicans*** ♀H2-3 | CAbb CBcs CCCN CFir CHEx CTrC CTsd ECre EShb IDee SArc SVen WFar |
| | ***fastuosum*** | see *E. candicans* |
| | ***giganteum*** | CHll |
| | ***italicum*** | CCCN NLar SIde |
| | ***lusitanicum*** | CCCN |
| | ***onosmifolium*** | CHll |
| | ***pininana*** ♀H2-3 | CAbb CBcs CDoC CHEx CTrC CTsd EAmu ECre ELan EWll GAuc IDee NVic SArc SBfd SBst SChr SEND SGar SIde SPav SSth SVen WSFF |
| | - 'Snow Tower' | CCCN CDTJ CTrC CTsd EAmu ELan SBst SVen |
| | 'Pink Fountain' | CCCN CDTJ CTrC ECre ELan MCot NLar SBst |
| | ***plantagineum*** | CCCN |
| | ***rosulatum*** | CCCN |
| | ***russicum*** | CAby CCCN CSpe EBee GAuc LHop NBPC NLar SGar SIde SPad SPav SPhx SPlb WCot WPer |
| | ***simplex*** | CCCN |
| | ***strictum*** | CCCN |
| | ***tuberculatum*** | CCCN SPhx WMoo |
| | ***vulgare*** | CArn CCCN CHab ELan EOHP EWil MHer MNHC NLar NMir SBch SIde WHer WHfH WJek WSFF |
| | - 'Blue Bedder' | WSFF |
| | - Drake's form | SGar SPhx |
| | ***webbii*** | MMHG |
| | ***wildpretii*** ♀H2-3 | CCCN CDTJ CTsd ELan SVen |
| | - subsp. ***wildpretii*** | SPav |

## *Edgeworthia* (*Thymelaeaceae*)

| | | |
|---|---|---|
| § | ***chrysantha*** | CBcs CHGN CHll CPLG CPMA CWib EBee ELan EPfP GBin GKin IDee LRHS MGos NLar NPal SBig SPer SPoG WCot WSHC |
| I | - 'Grandiflora' | CPMA GBin MBri MGos NLar NPal |
| § | - 'Red Dragon' | CPMA NLar |
| | - f. ***rubra*** hort. | see *E. chrysantha* 'Red Dragon' |

| | |
|---|---|
| ***papyrifera*** | see *E. chrysantha* |

## *Edraianthus* (*Campanulaceae*)

| | |
|---|---|
| ***croaticus*** | see *E. graminifolius* |
| ***dalmaticus*** | EPot |
| ***dinaricus*** | EPot NMen |
| § ***graminifolius*** | CPBP NMen WFar WPat XLum |
| ***owerinianus*** | GKev WAbe |
| § ***pumilio*** ♀H4 | EPot NMen SRms WAbe |
| § ***serpyllifolius*** | EPot NMen WPat |
| - 'Major' | NMen WAbe |
| ***tenuifolius*** | EPot |
| ***wettsteinii*** | EPot |

## *Egeria* (*Hydrocharitaceae*)

| | |
|---|---|
| § ***densa*** | CBen |

## *Ehretia* (*Boraginaceae*)

| | |
|---|---|
| ***dicksonii*** | CHEx IArd WPGP |

## *Ehrharta* (*Poaceae*)

| | |
|---|---|
| ***thunbergii*** | EPPr |

## *Eichhornia* (*Pontederiaceae*)

| | |
|---|---|
| ***crassipes*** | CBen CWat LPBA MSKA MWts SCoo |
| - 'Major' | NPer |

## *Elaeagnus* ✿ (*Elaeagnaceae*)

| | |
|---|---|
| ***angustifolia*** | CAgr CBcs CBot CDul EBee EPfP LMaj MBlu MCoo MGos NLar NWea SPer SRms WDin WFar |
| - Caspica Group | see *E.* 'Quicksilver' |
| ***argentea*** | see *E. commutata* |
| § ***commutata*** | CBcs CBot CMac EBee ECrN EHoe EPfP LHop MBlu MMuc MWhi NLar SPer WDin |
| § × ***ebbingei*** | Widely available |
| - 'Coastal Gold' (v) | CAbP CBcs CDoC CDul CTrC EBee EQua IVic LBMP LRHS LSRN MAsh MGos SGol SLim SRms |
| - 'Gilt Edge' (v) ♀H4 | Widely available |
| * - 'Gold Flash' | LAst |
| - Gold Splash = 'Lannou' (v) | CDoC CMac CTrC CWSG EBee EPfP EQua LRHS SPoG SWvt |
| - 'Lemon Ice' (v) | NLar |
| - 'Limelight' (v) | Widely available |
| - 'Moonlight' | LRHS |
| - 'Salcombe Seedling' | CCCN NLar |
| ***glabra*** | GGal |
| - 'Reflexa' | see *E.* × *reflexa* |
| ***macrophylla*** | CMac WMoo |
| ***multiflora*** | CDul NLar SPer |
| ***parvifolia*** | CCCN |
| ***pungens*** | ERom NBir |
| - 'Argenteovariegata' | see *E. pungens* 'Variegata' |
| - 'Aureovariegata' | see *E. pungens* 'Maculata' |
| - 'Dicksonii' (v) | CWib EBee LRHS NLar SBrd SLon SPer SRms WFar |
| - 'Forest Gold' (v) | ELan EPfP LRHS MAsh |
| - 'Frederici' (v) | CBcs CDoC CMHG CMac CTrC EBee ECrN EHoe ELan EPfP EPla LAst LBMP LHop LRHS MAsh MRav NLar SPer SPoG SWvt WAbe WDin WPat |
| - 'Goldrim' (v) ♀H4 | EPfP SLim WDin WMoo |
| - 'Hosuba-fukurin' (v) | GKin LLHF LRHS SLon SPoG |
| § - 'Maculata' (v) | Widely available |
| § - 'Variegata' (v) | CBcs CMac EPla EQua NBir SPer |
| § 'Quicksilver' ♀H4 | Widely available |
| § × ***reflexa*** | CBcs EPla WPGP |
| × ***submacrophylla*** | see *E.* × *ebbingei* |
| ***umbellata*** | CBcs CPLG EBee EPfP EWTr MAsh MBlu NLar SPer WPat WSHC |
| - 'Big Red' (F) | CAgr |
| - var. ***borealis*** 'Polar Lights' | NLar |
| - 'Brilliant Rose' (F) | CAgr |
| - 'Garnet' **new** | CAgr |
| - 'Hidden Springs' (F) | CAgr |
| - 'Jewel' (F) | CAgr |
| - 'Newgate' (F) | CAgr |
| - 'Red Cascade' (F) | CAgr |
| - 'Ruby' **new** | CAgr |
| - 'Sweet 'n' Tart' (F) | CAgr |

## *Elatostema* (*Urticaceae*)

| | |
|---|---|
| ***rugosum*** | CHEx |

## elderberry see *Sambucus nigra*

## *Elegia* (*Restionaceae*)

| | |
|---|---|
| ***capensis*** | CAbb CCCN CCtw CDTJ CDoC CFir CHEx CPLG CTrC EAmu ESwi ETod GBin GCal LTen SPlb WDyG WPGP |
| ***cuspidata*** | CCtw IDee |
| ***equisetacea*** | CCtw |
| ***fistulosa*** | CCtw |
| ***racemosa*** | CCtw |
| ***spathacea*** | CFir |
| ***stipularis*** **new** | CCtw |

## *Eleocharis* (*Cyperaceae*)

| | |
|---|---|
| ***acicularis*** | CWat EWil MSKA WPnP |
| ***palustris*** | CRWN |

## *Eleorchis* (*Orchidaceae*)

| | |
|---|---|
| ***japonica*** | LWst NLAp |
| * - f. ***alba*** | LWst |

## *Elettaria* (*Zingiberaceae*)

| | |
|---|---|
| ***cardamomum*** | CArn EOHP EShb GPoy LEdu SBfd SHDw WJek |

## *Eleutherococcus* (*Araliaceae*)

| | |
|---|---|
| aff. ***cissifolius*** BWJ 7713 | WCru |
| ***hypoleucus*** B&SWJ 5532 | WCru |
| ***nakaianus*** B&SWJ 5027 | WCru |
| ***pictus*** | see *Kalopanax septemlobus* |
| ***senticosus*** | GPoy |
| - B&SWJ 4568 | WCru |
| ***septemlobus*** | see *Kalopanax septemlobus* |
| ***sessiliflorus*** B&SWJ 4528 | WCru |
| - B&SWJ 8457 | WCru |
| ***sieboldianus*** | CBcs MRav SEND WDin WFar |
| - 'Variegatus' (v) | CBcs CBot EBee EHoe ELan ELon EPfP EQua GBin LAst MRav NEgg NLar NMun WHer WSHC |
| ***trifoliatus*** RWJ 10108 | WCru |

## *Elingamita* (*Primulaceae*)

| | |
|---|---|
| ***johnsonii*** | ECou |

## *Elisena* (*Amaryllidaceae*)

| | |
|---|---|
| ***longipetala*** | see *Hymenocallis longipetala* |

## *Elliottia* (*Ericaceae*)

| | |
|---|---|
| * ***paniculata latifolia*** | IVic |

## *Ellisiophyllum* (*Plantaginaceae*)

| | |
|---|---|
| ***pinnatum*** B&SWJ 197 | CDes EBee EWld WCot WCru WPGP |

## *Elmera* (*Saxifragaceae*)

| | | |
|---|---|---|
| | ***racemosa*** | EDif |

## *Elodea* (*Hydrocharitaceae*)

| | | |
|---|---|---|
| | ***canadensis*** | MSKA NBir WMAq |
| | ***densa*** | see *Egeria densa* |

## *Elsholtzia* (*Lamiaceae*)

| | | |
|---|---|---|
| | ***fruticosa*** | CArn |
| | ***stauntonii*** | CArn CBcs CBot CMHG EBee ECha GBin IDee IVic LRHS MHer MMuc NLar SBch SEND SPer SPoG WBor WSHC XLum |
| | - 'Alba' | CBot |

## *Elymus* (*Poaceae*)

| | | |
|---|---|---|
| | ***arenarius*** | see *Leymus arenarius* |
| | ***canadensis*** | CRWN EHoe EPPr WBox |
| | - f. ***glaucifolius*** | CFir GCal |
| | ***cinereus*** from Washington State, USA | WPGP |
| | ***elongatus*** | SApp |
| | ***glaucus*** misapplied | see *E. hispidus* |
| § | ***hispidus*** | EHoe EPPr EPau MBlu MBri MLHP SPer WCFE WCot |
| § | ***magellanicus*** | Widely available |
| | - 'Blue Sword' | LRHS MGos NBPC SRms WPtf |
| | ***riparius*** | EPPr |
| | ***sibiricus*** | EPPr |
| | ***solandri*** | EHoe EWes |
| | - JCA 5.345.500 | WPGP |
| | ***tenuis*** | LRHS |
| | ***villosus*** | EPPr MAvo |
| | - var. ***arkansanus*** | EPPr |
| | ***virginicus*** | EBee EPPr |

## *Embothrium* ✿ (*Proteaceae*)

| | | |
|---|---|---|
| | ***coccineum*** | CBcs CDoy CGHE CPne EPfP GKin IDee MGos MPhe SPlb WGwG WPGP WPat |
| | - Lanceolatum Group | CAby CDoC CDul CEnd CHid CTsd ELan ELon EPfP GKin LRHS MBlu MDun MMuc SArc SBfd SBrd SLim SMad SPer SSpi SSta WAbe WBor WDin |
| | - - 'Inca Flame' | CBcs CCCN CDoC CPMA ELan EPfP MAsh MGos NLar SBfd SPoG SWvt |
| | - - 'Ñorquinco' 🏆$^{H3}$ | CBcs CDoC GGal |
| | - Longifolium Group | CCCN GGal IBlr MMHG WPGP |

## *Emmenopterys* (*Rubiaceae*)

| | | |
|---|---|---|
| | ***henryi*** | CBcs CCCN CGHE EPfP EWTr IArd MBlu NLar SMad WPGP |

## *Empetrum* (*Ericaceae*)

| | | |
|---|---|---|
| | ***nigrum*** | GAuc GPoy |
| | ***rubrum*** | WAle |

## *Enantiophylla* (*Apiaceae*)

| | | |
|---|---|---|
| | B&SWJ 10318 from Guatemala | WCru |
| | ***heydeana*** B&SWJ 9114 | WCru |

## *Encephalartos* ✿ (*Zamiaceae*)

| | | |
|---|---|---|
| | ***altensteinii*** | CBrP |
| | ***caffer*** | CBrP |
| | ***cycadifolius*** | CBrP LPal |
| | ***ferox*** | CBrP |
| | ***friderici-guilielmi*** | CBrP |
| | ***ghellinckii*** | LPal |
| | ***horridus*** | CBrP |
| | ***kisambo*** | LPal |
| | ***lanatus*** | CBrP |
| | ***lebomboensis*** | CBrP |
| | ***lehmannii*** | CBrP LPal |
| | ***natalensis*** | CBrP LPal |
| | ***senticosus*** | LPal |
| | ***umbeluziensis*** | CBrP |
| | ***villosus*** | CBrP LPal |

## *Endymion* see *Hyacinthoides*

## *Enkianthus* ✿ (*Ericaceae*)

| | | |
|---|---|---|
| | ***campanulatus*** 🏆$^{H4}$ | Widely available |
| | - var. ***campanulatus*** f. ***albiflorus*** | CBcs GKin IVic LTen NLar |
| I | - 'Hollandia' | CBcs GKin |
| | - var. ***palibinii*** | EPfP GKin LRHS MAsh NLar SSpi SSta |
| | - 'Red Bells' | CDoC CMac EPfP GBin GKin LRHS MAsh MGos MMHG NLar SSpi SSta SWvt WFar |
| | - 'Red Velvet' | CBcs GKin NLar |
| | - 'Ruby Glow' | CBcs IVic NLar |
| | - var. ***sikokianus*** | EPfP GKin NLar |
| | - 'Tokyo Masquerade' | CPMA GKin NLar |
| * | - 'Variegatus' (v) | LRHS MAsh SPoG |
| | - 'Venus' | CBcs GKin NLar |
| | - 'Victoria' | CBcs NLar |
| | - 'Wallaby' | CBcs LRHS NLar WAbe |
| | ***cernuus*** f. ***rubens*** 🏆$^{H4}$ | CMac EPfP GBin GKin NLar WDin |
| | ***chinensis*** | CPne EPfP LRHS MAsh |
| | ***deflexus*** | CMCN MAsh SSpi WPGP |
| | ***perulatus*** 🏆$^{H4}$ | CDul CMac GBin GKin LRHS MGos MRav NLar SSpi WFar |

## *Ensete* (*Musaceae*)

| | | |
|---|---|---|
| | ***gilletii*** | XBlo |
| | - from Malawi **new** | XBlo |
| | - from Mozambique **new** | XBlo |
| | ***glaucum*** | CDTJ EAmu GCal SBst WCot |
| § | ***ventricosum*** 🏆$^{H1+3}$ | CBot CCCN CDTJ CDoC CHll EAmu LPal LSou SArc SBst SEND XBlo |
| | - from Uganda | GCal |
| § | - 'Maurelii' | CBct CBrP CCCN CDTJ CDoC CHEx CHll CSpe EAmu ESwi LRHS NPla SArc SDix SMad SPer SPoG WCot WPGP |
| | - 'Montbeliardii' | EAmu |
| | - 'Rubrum' | see *E. ventricosum* 'Maurelii' |
| | - 'Tandarra Red' | CAbb CBct CDoC LSou |

## *Entelea* (*Malvaceae*)

| | | |
|---|---|---|
| | ***arborescens*** | CHEx ECou EShb |

## *Eomecon* (*Papaveraceae*)

| | | |
|---|---|---|
| | ***chionantha*** | CDes CFir CHEx CMac CPLG CSam CSpe CWCL CYeo EBee ECho GAbr GCal GCra LEdu MLHP MRav NBid WFar WHer WMoo WPGP WWEG XLum |

## *Epacris* (*Ericaceae*)

| | | |
|---|---|---|
| | ***serpyllifolia*** | WThu |

## *Ephedra* (*Ephedraceae*)

| | | |
|---|---|---|
| | sp. | SArc |

***chilensis*** new — XLum
- 'Mellow Yellow' — EBee
- 'Quite White' — EBee
***distachya*** — GPoy
***equisetina*** — IFro
***fedtschenkoi*** — XSen
***gerardiana*** — CCCN GEdr IFro LRHS
- var. ***sikkimensis*** — WOld XLum
***intermedia*** RCB/TQ K-1 — WCot
***minima*** — GEdr NWCA WThu XLum
***minuta*** — CKen MSCN
***nevadensis*** — CArn GPoy
***sinica*** — CArn GEdr GPoy
***viridis*** — CArn

## *Epilobium* (*Onagraceae*)

***angustifolium*** — see *Chamerion angustifolium*
- f. ***leucanthum*** — see *Chamerion angustifolium* 'Album'
***californicum*** misapplied — see *Zauschneria californica*
***canum*** — see *Zauschneria californica* subsp. *cana*
***dodonaei*** — see *Chamerion dodonaei*
***garrettii*** — see *Zauschneria californica* subsp. *garrettii*
N ***glabellum*** misapplied — CSpe MSCN NSla SPhx SUsu WCFE WWlt
***microphyllum*** — see *Zauschneria californica* subsp. *cana*
***rosmarinifolium*** — see *Chamerion dodonaei*
***septentrionale*** — see *Zauschneria septentrionalis*
***villosum*** — see *Zauschneria californica* subsp. *mexicana*

## *Epimedium* ✿ (*Berberidaceae*)

from Yunnan, China — CDes CLAP CPom
***acuminatum*** — CDes CElw CFir CGHE CLAP EFEx GEdr LEdu MNrw SUsu WMoo WPGP WSHC
- L 575 — CPLG EBee
- 'Galaxy' — CDes CLAP CMil CPLG CPMA EBee WPGP
'Akakage' — CLAP
'Akebono' — CAby CDes CLAP CMil CPMA EBee EPPr GEdr IFoB NLar NMyG WCot
***alpinum*** — CMac EBee EBla EPPr GEdr LEdu NHol WMoo XLum
'Amanogawa' — CDes CLAP CMil CPMA CPom IFoB LEdu MAvo WPGP
'Amber Queen'PBR — CLAP EBee EPPr EWTr GEdr LLHF NCGa NHar NLar NPnk SPhx WCAu WCot
'Anju' — GEdr
'Arctic Wings'PBR — CLAP EBee EWTr GEdr MAvo NCGa NGdn WCot
'Asiatic Hybrid' — CLAP CPMA WHal
'Autumn Raspberry' new — CPMA
'Beni-kujaku' — CDes CLAP CPMA EBee GEdr
'Beni-yushima' — GEdr
'Black Sea' — CLAP CPMA CSpe EBee EPPr LHop MNrw NCGa NLar SMrm WCAu
***brachyrrhizum*** — CDes CLAP CMil CPLG CPMA CPom EBee GEdr LLHF WPGP
***brevicornu*** — CAby CLAP CPom WPGP
- Og 82.010 — CLAP CPMA EBee
- Og 88.010 — CLAP CPMA GEdr
'Buckland Spider' — CDes CLAP EBee EPPr MNrw WPGP
***campanulatum*** — CGHE LLHF
- Og 93087 — CPMA
× ***cantabrigiense*** — CBro CMac ECtt EPla GEdr GMaP MRav NBre SPur WWEG
***chlorandrum*** — CLAP IFoB LEdu SUsu WPGP
- Og 94.003 — CDes EBee
creeping yellow — LSou MBri MSCN WHil
***cremeum*** — see *E. grandiflorum* subsp. *koreanum*
***davidii*** — CDes CGHE CMil GEdr LEdu MNFA MNrw NLar SKHP WFar WHal WPGP WSHC
- CPC 960079 — CPLG EBee
- EMR 4125 — CElw CLAP CPLG CPMA NCGa
- dwarf — CPLG
***diphyllum*** — CAby CDes CGHE CPLG CPom EBee ELan WHal WPGP
- 'White Splash' — GEdr
***dolichostemon*** — CElw CLAP
- Og 81.010 — CPMA
***ecalcaratum*** — CAby CDes CLAP CPom EBee LEdu MNrw WPGP
- Og 93.082 — CPLG CPMA
***elongatum*** — CLAP
'Emperor' — see *E.*'Phoenix'
'Enchantress' — CLAP CMil CPMA CPom ECha EWTr EWld IFoB MNrw NCGa SAga WHal
***epsteinii*** — CAby CDes CLAP CMil CPLG CPMA CPom EBee EPPr GEdr LEdu LLHF MNrw WCot WPGP
- CPC 940347 — CPLG CPMA
***fangii*** — CPLG
***fargesii*** — CDes CMil CPLG EBee LEdu MAvo MNrw NCGa WCot WPGP
- 'Pink Constellation' — CDes CLAP CPMA CPom GEdr LEdu SBch WPGP
'Fire Dragon'PBR — CLAP CWCL EPfP GEdr LLHF MAvo MBNS NCGa NHar WHil
***flavum*** — Bee SKHP WPGP
- Og 92.036 — CDes CLAP CPMA
'Flowers of Sulphur'PBR new — CLAP EWTr GEdr
***franchetii*** — CFir CGHE CPLG SKHP
- 'Brimstone Butterfly' — CDes CLAP CMil CPLG CPMA EBee EPPr GEdr WCot WHoo WPGP
'Fukujuji' — CLAP GEdr
'Golden Eagle' — CDes CLAP CPLG CPMA CPom EWes EWld MNrw
§ ***grandiflorum*** ♀H4 — CBcs CElw CTri CYeo EBee ELan ELon EPfP EPot EWTr GEdr LBMP NBir NLar NMen NPnk SPer WFar WPnP WPtf WWEG
- 'Album' — CLAP
- 'Beni-chidori' — CLAP CPMA EBee GEdr
- 'Crimson Beauty' — CLAP CPMA MRav WHal WHoo WSHC
- 'Crimson Queen' — CDes IFoB LEdu WPGP
- 'Freya' — CDes WSHC
§ - var. ***higoense*** — CDes CPMA EBee GEdr WHal WPGP
- 'Jennie Maillard' — SUsu
- 'Koji' — CLAP NLar WSHC
§ - subsp. ***koreanum*** — CLAP ECha EFEx
- 'La Rocaille' — CLAP EBee
- lilac-flowered — CLAP WFar WHal
- 'Lilafee' — Widely available
- 'Mount Kitadake' — CLAP WAbe
- 'Nanum' ♀H4 — CDes CMil CPMA CPom EBee ECho EPot EWld GEdr MNrw NMen NMyG SKHP WAbe WPGP WThu

| | |
|---|---|
| - 'Purple Prince' | CDes CLAP CPLG WPGP |
| - 'Queen Esta' | CDes CLAP CMil CPMA LEdu MNrw SBch WPGP WSHC |
| - 'Red Beauty' | CLAP EBee GEdr NLar SBfd WGrn |
| - 'Rose Queen' ♀H4 | CAby CMMP CSam EBee ECha ELan EPfP GEdr GGar GMaP MAvo MBri MRav NBir NMyG NSti SUsu SWvt WMoo WWEG |
| - 'Roseum' | CLAP CMac CMil CSpr NMen SWvt |
| - 'Rubinkrone' | EBee GEdr GMaP MNrw |
| - 'Sirius' | CLAP CPMA EBee MAvo MNrw |
| - f. ***violaceum*** | CLAP CPMA LRHS WCFE WSHC |
| - 'White Beauty' | WSHC |
| - 'White Queen' ♀H4 | CElw CFir CPMA EBee EPPr MRav WCot WHal |
| - 'Wildside Red' | CPMA |
| - 'Yellow Princess' | CDes CElw CLAP CPMA |
| - 'Yubae' | GEdr IFoB LWSt |
| 'Hagoromo' | GEdr |
| 'Hakubai' | GEdr |
| 'Harugasumi' | GEdr |
| 'Heavenly Purple' **new** | CPMA |
| ***higoense*** | see *E. grandiflorum* var. *higoense* |
| ***ilicifolium*** | CDes CMil CPMA EBee LEdu WPGP |
| 'Jean O'Neill' | CDes CLAP EBee LEdu WCot WPGP |
| 'Jenny Pym' | EBee |
| 'Kaguyahime' | CLAP CMil CPMA EPPr IFoB WSHC |
| 'Koki' | GEdr |
| 'Kotobuki' **new** | GEdr |
| ***latisepalum*** | CAby CDes CLAP CMil CPom EBee LEdu MNrw NCGa NLar WCot WPGP |
| - Og. 91.002 | CPMA |
| 'Lemon Meringue Pie' **new** | CPMA |
| ***leptorrhizum*** | CAby CDes CElw CGHE CLAP CPLG CPMA EBee EPPr EWTr LEdu MNFA MNrw NCGa NHar NMyG SBch SKHP SUsu WCot WHal |
| - Og Y44 | WSHC |
| - 'Mariko' | CDes CLAP CPLG CPMA CPom WPGP |
| ***lishihchenii*** | CDes CLAP CPMA WPGP |
| - Og 96024 | GEdr |
| 'Little Shrimp' | CPMA CTri EBee LLHF MNFA MNrw NLar SUsu WPat |
| ***macranthum*** | see *E. grandiflorum* |
| 'Madame Butterfly' PBR | GEdr |
| 'Mandarin Star' **new** | WCot |
| ***membranaceum*** | CFir CGHE CLAP CMil EBee LEdu LLHF SUsu WHal WPGP |
| - Og. 93.047 | CPMA EPPr GEdr |
| ***mikinorii*** | CPom GEdr |
| ***myrianthum*** | CDes CPMA LEdu WPGP |
| ***ogisui*** | CAby CDes CLAP CMil CPom WPGP WThu |
| - Og 91.001 | CPLG CPMA EBee MNrw SKHP |
| § × ***omeiense*** 'Akame' | CAby CDes CGHE CLAP CMil CPLG CPMA EBee EPPr WPGP |
| - 'Emei Shan' | see *E.* × *omeiense* 'Akame' |
| - 'Myriad Years' | CLAP |
| - 'Pale Fire' | EWld |
| - 'Pale Fire Sibling' | CDes CPMA CPom |
| - 'Stormcloud' | CDes CGHE CLAP CMil CPLG CPMA CPom EBee EPPr MNrw WPGP |
| ***pauciflorum*** | CHid EPPr GEdr LEdu NHar NMyG WPGP |
| - Og 92.123 | CLAP CPMA |
| × ***perralchicum*** ♀H4 | CBro CMac CPMA CTri ECha GKev MLHP NLar SGar SLPl WPnP WSHC |

| | |
|---|---|
| - 'Fröhnleiten' | Widely available |
| - 'Lichtenberg' | CDes SUsu |
| - 'Wisley' | CElw CPMA CSam EWes |
| ***perralderianum*** | CHEx CMac CSam EBee ELan GEdr GMaP MCot MLLN MNrw SMrm SRms WHal WHoo WPnP XLum |
| - 'Weihenstephan' | MMoz WPnP |
| § 'Phoenix' | CDes WPGP |
| 'Pink Champagne' **new** | MBri SMrm WHil |
| 'Pink Elf' PBR | CLAP EBee EPfP EWTr GEdr LLHF NBPC NCGa NLar NOrc NPnk NSti WCAu WCot |
| ***pinnatum*** | ECho GMaP WHal |
| § - subsp. ***colchicum*** ♀H4 | CLAP CMac CPMA CPom CWCL EBee ELan EPfP EWTr GAbr GBBs GEdr LEdu LRHS MCot MRav NGdn NLar SBfd SDix SPoG WCAu WCot WFar WHoo WPnP WTin WWEG |
| - - L 321 | CDes WPGP |
| - ***elegans*** | see *E. pinnatum* subsp. *colchicum* |
| ***platypetalum*** | CLAP WCot WPGP |
| - Og 93.085 | CPMA |
| ***pubescens*** | CPMA EBee IFoB SAga |
| - Og 91.003 | WPGP |
| ***pubigerum*** | CAby CPMA CSam EBee ECha EWTr GAbr GEdr LEdu NLar NMRc NMyG NPri SBfd SWvt WCAu WHal WPtf WTcb WWEG |
| ***rhizomatosum*** | CAby CLAP EPPr GEdr LLHF WPGP WSHC |
| - Og 92.114 | CPMA EBee WCot |
| × ***rubrum*** ♀H4 | Widely available |
| ***sagittatum*** | CLAP EFEx |
| 'Sakura-maru' | GEdr |
| 'Sasaki' | CLAP EBee EPot EWTr GEdr MBri NHar NLar NMyG |
| ***sempervirens*** | CLAP CPMA EBee WHal |
| - 'Cream Sickle' | GEdr |
| - 'Okuda's White' | CDes WPGP |
| - var. ***sempervirens*** | CLAP |
| × ***setosum*** | CPMA CPom EBee ECha NLar WHal |
| 'Shiho' | GEdr |
| ***stellulatum*** 'Wudang Star' | CDes CGHE CLAP CMil CPLG CPMA CPom EWes GEdr IFoB WPGP |
| ***sutchuenense*** | CLAP |
| 'Suzuka' | GEdr LEdu |
| 'Tama-no-genpei' | CDes CPMA CPom |
| 'Tanima-no-yuki' | GEdr |
| 'Tokiwa-gozen' **new** | GEdr |
| × ***versicolor*** | CPLG |
| - 'Cherry Tart' | CLAP |
| - 'Cupreum' | CLAP CPMA CPom EBee SBfd WCAu |
| § - 'Discolor' | CDes CElw CLAP CPom EBla ECha EPPr EWld NBir |
| - 'Neosulphureum' | CBro CDes CLAP CMMP EBee EPPr SLPl WPGP WThu |
| - 'Sulphureum' ♀H4 | Widely available |
| - 'Versicolor' | see *E.* × *versicolor* 'Discolor' |
| × ***warleyense*** | Widely available |
| - 'Orangekönigin' | Widely available |
| 'William Stearn' | CLAP CPLG CPMA |
| ***wushanense*** | CLAP CMil EPPr LEdu |
| - Og 93.019 | CPMA |
| - 'Caramel' | CAby CDes CLAP CMil CPLG CPMA CPom EBee GEdr LEdu MAvo NMyG SKHP WPGP WSHC |
| × ***youngianum*** | CMac NEgg |

| | |
|---|---|
| - 'Merlin' | CLAP CMil CPMA EBee ECha EPfP EPot GEdr IFoB MBri NHar NLar NMyG NSti WHal WSHC |
| - 'Niveum' ♀H4 | Widely available |
| - 'Roseum' | Widely available |
| - 'Shikinomai' | CLAP CPLG CPMA EPot |
| - 'Tamabotan' | CAby CDes CLAP GEdr MAvo MNrw MRav |
| § - 'Typicum' | CLAP EWTr LRHS WSHC |
| - white-flowered | NMen |
| - 'Yenomoto' | CLAP CPMA |
| - 'Youngianum' | see *E.* × *youngianum* 'Typicum' |
| ***zhushanense*** | GEdr LEdu |

## *Epipactis* (*Orchidaceae*)

| | |
|---|---|
| **Barbarossa gx** new | LWst |
| **Catalina gx** new | LWst |
| ***gigantea*** | CAvo CBro CFir EBla ECha ECho ELan EPot GBin GEdr GKev LWst MAvo MNrw MRav NCGa NChi NDav NLAp NMen NMyG NWCA WFar WPGP |
| ***gigantea* × *mairei*** new | LWst |
| ***helleborine*** | WHer |
| **Lizzy Lou gx** new | LWst |
| **Lowland Legacy gx** 'Irène' | LWst |
| ***mairei*** | LWst |
| ***palustris*** | CPrp EBee EBla ECho GEdr NDav NLAp NLar NPnk NWCA WHer WPnP |
| **Renate gx** | LWst |
| ***royleana*** | LWst |
| **Sabine gx** | CAby GEdr LWst WFar |
| - 'Frankfurt' | CDes NMen |
| ***thunbergii*** | EFEx GEdr LWst NLAp |
| - yellow-flowered | GEdr LWst |
| ***veratrifolia*** | LWst |

## *Epipremnum* (*Araceae*)

| | |
|---|---|
| ***pinnatum*** | XBlo |
| 'Marble Queen' (v) | |

## *Episcia* (*Gesneriaceae*)

| | |
|---|---|
| ***dianthiflora*** | SRms WDib |
| 'San Miguel' | WDib |

## *Equisetum* ✿ (*Equisetaceae*)

| | |
|---|---|
| ***arvense*** | CArn |
| 'Bandit' (v) | CNat SMad WMoo |
| × ***bowmanii*** | CNat |
| * ***camtschatcense*** | CDes EBee EPPr ETod SBig SMad SPlb XLum |
| × ***dycei*** | CNat |
| ***fluviatile*** | CNat MSKA NLar |
| ***hyemale*** | CBen CChe CKno CTrC EHoe EPfP EPla MSCN MSKA MWts NOak NPer NSti SArc SPlb WDyG WFar WMoo WPnP XLum |
| § - var. ***affine*** | CNat CRow EBee ELan EPla EWll LEdu LSou MBlu MSKA MWts NPnk NVic WMAq WOld |
| - var. ***robustum*** | see *E. hyemale* var. *affine* |
| ***pratense*** | CNat |
| ***ramosissimum*** | CNat |
| - var. ***japonicum*** | LEdu LPBA MCCP NPla SWat WPnP |
| ***robustum*** | CTrC |
| ***scirpoides*** | CTrC EBee EFer EHoe LPBA MCCP MSKA MWts NLar NPer NWad SPlb SWat WMAq WMoo WPnP XLum |
| ***telmateia*** | CNat SMad |
| ***variegatum*** | EBee EFer EWll |

## *Eragrostis* (*Poaceae*)

| | |
|---|---|
| RCB/Arg S-7 | EBee WCot |
| ***airoides*** misapplied | see *Agrostis montevidensis* |
| ***airoides*** ambig. | CHar EKen GAbr WMnd WMoo |
| ***chloromelas*** | EPPr WPGP |
| ***curvula*** | CBod CElw CHar CMea CWCL EBee ECha EHoe GCal LEdu LRHS MCCP MMuc MRav MWat MWhi NBir NChi NGdn NOak NWsh SEND SPhx WMoo XLum |
| - S&SH 10 | CDes CKno EPPr WPGP |
| - 'Totnes Burgundy' | CAby CDes CKno CPLG CWCL EBee ECha EHoe EPPr MAvo MNrw NOak NWsh SMea SPhx SRms SUsu WHal WHrl WMoo WPGP |
| ***elliottii*** | CBod CKno EBee ECha EPPr LBMP LHop LRHS MAvo MMuc MWea NBPC NWsh SBfd SEND SHDw SMea WFar WWEG |
| - 'Wind Dancer' | EPPr LRHS |
| 'Silver Needles' | see *Agrostis canina* 'Silver Needles' |
| ***spectabilis*** | CFir CKno CSBt EBee EPfP LRHS MDKP MMHG MMuc MWea MWhi NBPC NGdn NLar NWsh SBfd SEND SMea SMrm SPur WFar WMoo WWEG |
| ***trichodes*** | CFir CKno EBee EHoe LEdu NBPC NWsh SMad SMea SUsu WHrl WPer |

## *Eranthemum* (*Acanthaceae*)

| | |
|---|---|
| ***pulchellum*** ♀H1 | ECre |

## *Eranthis* (*Ranunculaceae*)

| | |
|---|---|
| ***cilicica*** | see *E. hyemalis* Cilicica Group |
| § ***hyemalis*** ♀H4 | CBro CMea CSpe CTca CWCL ECho ELan ELon EPfP EWil GKev LAma LRHS MAvo MCot MRav MWat NLar SDeJ SMrm SPer SPhx WCot WFar WGwG WShi |
| § - Cilicica Group | CBro ECho ELan ELon EPot GKev GMaP LAma LRHS NLar SDeJ SPhx WCot WRHF |
| - 'Flore Pleno' (d) | ECho LWst WCot |
| - 'Grünling' | WCot |
| - 'Schwefelglanz' | CBro EPot GKev WCot |
| § - Tubergenii Group | ECho EPot LWst |
| - - 'Guinea Gold' ♀H4 | CBro CTca ECho |
| ***pinnatifida*** | EFEx GEdr LWst WCru |
| × ***tubergenii*** | see *E. hyemalis* Tubergenii Group |

## *Ercilla* (*Phytolaccaceae*)

| | |
|---|---|
| ***volubilis*** | CPLG CRHN CWGN EBee EWes LHop LRHS NSti SEND WCru WSHC |

## *Eremophila* (*Scrophulariaceae*)

| | |
|---|---|
| ***bignoniiflora*** | MOWG |
| § ***debilis*** | ECou |
| ***glabra*** new | SVen |
| - 'Burgundy' | MOWG |
| 'Kilbara Carpet' | ECou MOWG |
| ***longifolia*** | SPlb |
| ***maculata*** | ECou |
| - var. ***brevifolia*** | MOWG |
| - pale pink-flowered | MOWG |
| - 'Peaches and Cream' | MOWG |

| | |
|---|---|
| * 'Summer Blue' | MOWG |
| 'Yellow Trumpet' | ECou |

## *Eremostachys* (*Lamiaceae*)

| | |
|---|---|
| ***laciniata*** new | XSen |

## *Eremurus* (*Asphodelaceae*)

| | |
|---|---|
| ***altaicus*** JCA 0.443.809 | WCot |
| 'Brutus' | EBee LAma |
| ***bungei*** | see *E. stenophyllus* subsp. *stenophyllus* |
| ***cristatus*** JCA 0.444.029 | WCot |
| 'Disco' | EBee |
| 'Emmy Ro' | EBee LAma WCot |
| ***fuscus*** JCA 0.444.043 | WCot |
| 'Grace' | LAma |
| 'Helena' | EBee LAma MLLN MNrw |
| ***himalaicus*** | CAvo CBot CBro CTca EBee ELan EPot ERCP EWTr LAma LRHS MHer NLar SDeJ SPer SPhx WWEG |
| 'Image' | EBee |
| × ***isabellinus*** 'Cleopatra' | CAvo CWGN EBee ELon EPot ERCP GMaP LAma LRHS MBNS MGos MHer SDeJ SPad SPhx SPoG WWEG |
| - 'Obelisk' | EBee ELan LAma |
| - 'Pinokkio' | CAvo EBee EPot LAma MHer SDeJ |
| - Ruiter hybrids | CMea EBee ELan EPfP GKev GMaP LAma LAst LRHS MGos MLLN MNrw SEND SPer SPet SPhx SPoG WFar |
| - Shelford hybrids | CAvo CBcs EBee ELan GKev LAma MNrw SDeJ SPhx |
| - 'Tropical Dream' | EBee |
| 'Jeanne-Claire' | EBee LAma NLar |
| 'Joanna' | EBee LAma LSRN NLar |
| ***lactiflorus*** | EBee |
| - from Kazakhstan new | GAuc |
| 'Line Dance' | EBee ELon LAma |
| 'Luca Ro' | EBee NLar |
| 'Moneymaker' | EBee LAma |
| 'Oase' | EBee ELan LAma |
| 'Paradiso' | EBee |
| ***regelii*** JCA 444.083 | WCot |
| - from Kazakhstan new | GAuc |
| 'Rexona' | EBee LAma MBNS SDeJ |
| ***robustus*** ♀H4 | CAvo CBcs CBot CBro CMea EBee ELan EPot ERCP EWTr LAma MAvo MCot MHer MNrw NLar SDeJ SPhx SPlb WFar WWEG |
| 'Roford' | EBee LAma MNrw |
| 'Romance' | CAvo EBee ELon EPot ERCP LAma MBNS MNrw NLar NMRc SPhx WWEG |
| 'Rumba' | EBee LAma NLar |
| 'Samba' | EBee LAma |
| ***sogdianus*** | EBee |
| ***spectabilis*** | EBee |
| ***stenophyllus*** ♀H4 | CBro CTri CWib EPot ERCP LHop MLLN MPkF MWat NLar SDeJ SMrm SPhx SPoG WCot WFar WWEG |
| § - subsp. ***stenophyllus*** | CAvo CBcs EBee EPfP GMaP LAma MHer MNrw NBPC NLBP NPer NPri SPer WFar |
| 'Tap Dance' | EBee LAma |
| ***tianschanicus*** from Kazakhstan new | GAuc |
| 'White Beauty Favourite'PBR new | ERCP SPhx |
| 'Yellow Giant' | EBee |
| ***zenaidae*** | WCot |

## *Erepsia* (*Aizoaceae*)

| | |
|---|---|
| ***lacera*** | SPlb |

## *Erianthus* see *Saccharum*

## *Erica* ✿ (*Ericaceae*)

| | |
|---|---|
| ***abietina*** subsp. ***aurantiaca*** | CDes |
| ***aestiva*** | SPlb |
| 'African Fanfare' | SHeS |
| × ***afroeuropaea*** | SHeS |
| ***alopecurus*** | SPlb |
| ***arborea*** | GAbr IRar SPlb |
| - var. ***alpina*** ♀H4 | CDoC CTri EPfP GGal LRHS SBrd SHeS SPoG SRms SSpi SWhi |
| § - - f. ***aureifolia*** 'Albert's Gold' ♀H4 | CBcs CSBt CTri ELan EPfP LRHS MAsh MBri NHol SCoo SHeS SPer SPoG SRms SWhi WFar |
| - 'Arbora Gold' | see *E. arborea* var. *alpina* f. *aureifolia* 'Albert's Gold' |
| - 'Arnold's Gold' | see *E. arborea* var. *alpina* f. *aureifolia* 'Albert's Gold' |
| - 'Estrella Gold' ♀H4 | CBcs CDoC CSBt CTri ELan EPfP IVic MAsh SBrd SCoo SHeS SPer SPoG SRms SWhi |
| - 'Great Star' | SBfd |
| - 'Picos Pygmy' | SHeS |
| - 'Spanish Lime' | SHeS |
| - 'Spring Smile' | SHeS |
| ***australis*** f. ***albiflora*** 'Mr Robert' ♀H3 | SHeS |
| - 'Castellar Blush' | SHeS |
| - 'Holehird' | SHeS |
| - 'Riverslea' ♀H4 | CTri GCal GGar LRHS MAsh SBrd SHeS SPoG SWhi |
| ***caffra*** | SHeS SPlb |
| ***canaliculata*** ♀H3 | CBcs SHeS |
| ***carnea*** 'Accent' | SHeS |
| - 'Adrienne Duncan' ♀H4 | MAsh NHol SCoo SHeS |
| - 'Alan Coates' | SHeS |
| I - 'Alba' | SHeS |
| - f. ***alba*** 'C.J. Backhouse' | SHeS |
| - - 'Cecilia M. Beale' | SHeS |
| - - 'Golden Starlet' ♀H4 | CHab CSBt CTri EPfP MAsh NHol SCoo SHeS SPer SRms SWhi |
| - - 'Ice Princess' ♀H4 | EPfP MAsh NHol NPri SCoo SHeS SRms SWhi |
| - - 'Isabell' ♀H4 | CBcs EPfP IVic MAsh NPri SCoo SHeS SRms SWhi |
| - - Madame Seedling | see *E. carnea* f. *alba* 'Weisse March Seedling' |
| - - 'Romance' | SHeS |
| - - 'Rosalinde Schorn' | SHeS |
| - - 'Schneekuppe' | SHeS SWhi |
| - - 'Schneesturm' | SHeS SRms |
| - - 'Snow Prince' | SHeS |
| - - 'Snow Queen' | MAsh SHeS |
| - - 'Springwood White' ♀H4 | CSBt CTri ELan EPfP MAsh NBlu NHol SEND SHeS SLon SRms SWhi |
| § - - 'Weisse March Seedling' | SHeS |
| - - 'Whitehall' | MAsh NHol SCoo SHeS SRms SWhi |
| - - 'Winter Snow' | CSBt ELan MAsh SCoo SHeS SRms |
| - 'Amy Doncaster' | see *E. carnea* 'Treasure Trove' |
| - 'Ann Sparkes' ♀H4 | CSBt CTri ELan EPfP MAsh NHol SCoo SHeS SRms SWhi |
| - 'Atrorubra' | SHeS |
| - f. ***aureifolia*** 'Altadena' | SHeS |
| - - 'Aurea' | NHol SCoo SHeS SRms |
| - - 'Barry Sellers' | MAsh SHeS |

| | | |
|---|---|---|
| § | - - 'Bell's Extra Special' | EPfP SHeS |
| | - - 'Foxhollow' ♀H4 | CBcs CTri EPfP IArd MAsh NBlu NHol SCoo SHeS SRms SWhi |
| | - - 'Gelber Findling' | SHeS |
| | - - 'Gelderingen Gold' | SHeS |
| | - - 'Hilletje' | SHeS SRms |
| | - - 'January Sun' | SHeS |
| | - - 'Moonlight' | SHeS |
| | - - 'Netherfield Orange' | SHeS |
| | - - 'Sunshine Rambler' ♀H4 | SHeS |
| | - - 'Tybesta Gold' | SHeS |
| | - - 'Westwood Yellow' ♀H4 | CSBt MAsh NHol SHeS SPer SRms SWhi |
| | - - 'Winter Gold' | SHeS |
| | - 'Beoley Pink' | SHeS |
| I | - 'Carnea' | SHeS |
| | - 'Catherine Kolster' | SHeS |
| | - 'Challenger' ♀H4 | EPfP MAsh NHol SCoo SHeS SLon SRms SWhi |
| | - 'Christine Fletcher' | SHeS |
| | - 'Clare Wilkinson' | SHeS |
| | - 'David's Seedling' | SHeS |
| | - 'December Red' | ELan EPfP MAsh MMuc NHol SCoo SEND SHeS SRms SWhi |
| | - 'Diana Young' | SCoo SWhi |
| | - 'Dømmesmoen' | SHeS |
| | - 'Dwingeloo Pride' | SHeS |
| | - 'Early Red' | SHeS |
| | - 'Eileen Porter' | MAsh NHol SEND SHeS |
| | - 'Eva' | CBcs CHab IVic SHeS |
| | - 'Foxhollow Fairy' | CHab SHeS SRms |
| | - 'Gracilis' | SHeS |
| | - 'Hamburg' | SHeS |
| | - 'Heathwood' | MAsh NHol SCoo SHeS SRms |
| | - 'Jack Stitt' | SHeS |
| | - 'James Backhouse' | CTri SHeS |
| | - 'Jason Attwater' | SHeS |
| | - 'Jean' | SHeS |
| | - 'Jennifer Anne' | SHeS |
| | - 'John Kampa' | NHol SHeS |
| | - 'John Pook' | SCoo SHeS |
| | - 'King George' | CTri MAsh NHol SHeS SWhi |
| § | - 'Kramer's Rubin' | ELan SHeS |
| | - 'Lake Garda' | SHeS |
| | - 'Late Pink' | SHeS |
| | - 'Lena' | see *E.* × *darleyensis* 'Lena' |
| | - 'Lesley Sparkes' | SHeS |
| | - 'Little Peter' | SHeS |
| | - 'Lohse's Rubin' | IVic NHol SHeS |
| | - 'Lohse's Rubinfeuer' | SHeS |
| | - 'Lohse's Rubinschimmer' | SHeS |
| | - 'Loughrigg' ♀H4 | CSBt CTri MAsh NHol SCoo SHeS SRms |
| | - 'March Seedling' | EPfP MAsh NHol SCoo SHeS SLon SRms SWhi |
| | - 'Margery Frearson' | SHeS |
| I | - 'Martin' | SHeS |
| | - 'Mrs Sam Doncaster' | SHeS |
| | - 'Myretoun Ruby' ♀H4 | CBcs CSBt CTri EPfP MAsh NBlu NHol NPri SCoo SHeS SRms SWhi |
| | - 'Nathalie' ♀H4 | CSBt IVic MAsh NHol SCoo SHeS SRms SWhi |
| | - 'Oriënt' | MAsh SHeS SRms |
| | - 'Pallida' | SHeS |
| | - 'Pink Beauty' | see *E. carnea* 'Pink Pearl' |
| | - 'Pink Cloud' | SHeS |
| | - 'Pink Mist' | MAsh SHeS SRms SWhi |
| § | - 'Pink Pearl' | SHeS |
| | - 'Pink Spangles' ♀H4 | CBcs CHab CSBt CTri MAsh NHol SCoo SHeS SRms SWhi |

| | | |
|---|---|---|
| | - 'Pirbright Rose' | SHeS SRms |
| | - 'Polden Pride' | SHeS |
| | - 'Porter's Red' | SHeS |
| | - 'Praecox Rubra' ♀H4 | EPfP NHol SCoo SHeS |
| | - 'Prince of Wales' | SHeS |
| | - 'Queen Mary' | SHeS |
| | - 'Queen of Spain' | MAsh SHeS |
| | - 'R.B. Cooke' ♀H4 | EPfP MAsh SCoo SHeS SRms |
| | - 'Red Rover' | SHeS |
| | - 'Robert Jan' | SHeS |
| | - 'Rosalie' ♀H4 | CBcs EPfP IArd MAsh MMuc SCoo SHeS SRms SWhi |
| | - 'Rosantha' | CHab SHeS SRms |
| | - 'Rosea' | SPlb |
| | - 'Rosy Gem' | SHeS |
| | - 'Rosy Morn' | SHeS |
| | - 'Rotes Juwel' | SHeS |
| | - 'Rubinteppich' | SHeS SRms |
| | - 'Ruby Glow' | NHol SHeS |
| | - 'Scatterley' | SHeS |
| | - 'Schatzalp' | SHeS |
| | - 'Sherwood Creeping' | SHeS |
| | - 'Smart's Heath' | SHeS |
| | - 'Sneznik' | SHeS |
| | - 'Snow White' | ELan |
| | - 'Spring Cottage Crimson' | SHeS |
| | - 'Spring Day' | SHeS |
| | - 'Springwood Pink' | CSBt CTri MAsh NHol NPri SHeS SRms SWhi |
| I | - 'Startler' | MAsh NHol SHeS |
| | - 'Tanja' **new** | SWhi |
| | - 'Thomas Kingscote' | SHeS |
| § | - 'Treasure Trove' | NBlu SHeS |
| | - 'Viking' | MAsh NHol SHeS |
| | - 'Vivellii' ♀H4 | CTri MAsh NHol SCoo SHeS SRms SWhi |
| | - 'Vivellii Aurea' | SHeS |
| | - 'Walter Reisert' | SHeS |
| | - 'Wanda' | SHeS |
| | - 'Wentwood Red' | SHeS |
| | - Whisky | see *E. carnea* f. *aureifolia* 'Bell's Extra Special' |
| | - 'Winter Beauty' | MAsh NHol SHeS |
| | - 'Winter Melody' | SHeS |
| | - Winter Rubin | see *E. carnea* 'Kramer's Rubin' |
| | - 'Winter Sport' | SHeS |
| | - 'Winterfreude' | SHeS |
| | - 'Wintersonne' | CBcs CHab EPfP MMuc SHeS SRms SWhi |
| | ***ciliaris*** f. ***alba*** 'White Wings' | SHeS |
| | - f. ***albiflora*** 'Stoborough' ♀H4 | SHeS |
| | - f. ***aureifolia*** 'Aurea' | SHeS SRms |
| | - 'Bretagne' | SHeS SWhi |
| | - 'Camla' | SHeS |
| | - 'Corfe Castle' | SHeS |
| | - 'David McClintock' | SHeS SWhi |
| | - 'Fada das Serras' | SHeS |
| | - 'Globosa' | SHeS SWhi |
| | - 'Mawiana' | SHeS |
| | - 'Mrs C.H. Gill' ♀H4 | SHeS |
| | - 'Ram' | SHeS |
| | - 'Rotundiflora' | SHeS |
| | - 'Stapehill' | SHeS |
| | - 'Wych' | SHeS |
| | ***cinerea*** **new** | SWhi |
| | - f. ***alba*** 'Alba Major' | SHeS |
| | - - 'Alba Minor' ♀H4 | IVic MAsh NHol SHeS SWhi |
| | - - 'Celebration' | NBlu NHol SHeS SWhi |

| | | |
|---|---|---|
| | - - 'Doctor Small's Seedling' | SHeS |
| | - - 'Domino' | MAsh SHeS |
| | - - 'Geke' | SHeS |
| | - - 'Godrevy' | SHeS |
| | - - 'Honeymoon' | SHeS |
| | - - 'Hookstone White' ♀H4 | SHeS SWhi |
| | - - 'Jos' Honeymoon' | SHeS |
| | - - 'Marina' | SHeS |
| | - - 'Nell' | SHeS |
| | - - 'Snow Cream' | SHeS |
| | - - 'White Dale' | SHeS |
| | - 'Alette' | SHeS |
| | - 'Alfred Bowerman' | SHeS |
| | - 'Angarrack' | SHeS |
| | - 'Anja Bakker' | SHeS |
| | - 'Anja Blum' | SHeS |
| | - 'Anja Slegers' | SHeS |
| | - 'Apple Blossom' | SHeS |
| | - 'Aquarel' | SHeS |
| | - 'Ashdown Forest' | SHeS |
| | - 'Ashgarth Garnet' | SHeS |
| | - 'Atropurpurea' | MAsh SHeS |
| | - 'Atrorubens' | SHeS SRms |
| | - 'Atrorubens, Daisy Hill' | SHeS |
| | - 'Atrosanguinea Reuthe's Variety' | SHeS |
| | - 'Atrosanguinea Smith's Variety' | SHeS |
| I | - 'Aurea' | MMuc |
| | - f. ***aureifolia*** 'Alice Ann Davies' | SHeS |
| | - - 'Ann Berry' | SHeS |
| | - - 'Apricot Charm' | CSBt SHeS |
| | - - 'Constance' | SHeS |
| | - - 'Fiddler's Gold' ♀H4 | MAsh NHol SHeS |
| | - - 'Golden Charm' | NHol SHeS SWhi |
| | - - 'Golden Drop' | CSBt MAsh NBlu NHol SHeS |
| | - - 'Golden Hue' ♀H4 | MAsh NHol SHeS |
| | - - 'Golden Sport' | SHeS |
| | - - 'Golden Striker' | SHeS |
| | - - 'Golden Tee' | SHeS |
| | - - 'Goldilocks' | SHeS |
| | - - 'Jack London' | SHeS |
| | - - 'John Eason' | SHeS |
| | - - 'Jos' Golden' | SHeS |
| | - - 'Robert Michael' | SHeS |
| | - - 'Rock Pool' | NHol SHeS |
| | - - 'Screel' | SHeS |
| | - - 'Summer Gold' | SHeS SWhi |
| | - - 'Windlebrooke' ♀H4 | NHol SHeS |
| | - 'Baylay's Variety' | SHeS |
| | - 'Bemmel' | SHeS |
| | - 'Blossom Time' | SHeS |
| | - 'Bucklebury Red' | SHeS |
| | - 'C.D. Eason' ♀H4 | CBcs CSBt CTri EPfP IVic MAsh NBlu NHol SCoo SHeS SRms SWhi |
| § | - 'C.G. Best' ♀H4 | SHeS |
| | - 'Cairn Valley' | SHeS |
| | - 'Caldy Island' | SHeS |
| | - 'Cevennes' | GJos SHeS SWhi |
| | - 'Champs Hill' ♀H4 | SHeS |
| | - 'Cindy' ♀H4 | MAsh NHol SHeS |
| | - 'Coccinea' | SHeS |
| | - 'Colligan Bridge' | SHeS |
| | - 'Contrast' | SHeS |
| | - 'Crimson Glow' | SHeS |
| | - 'Discovery' | SHeS |
| | - 'Duncan Fraser' | SHeS |
| | - 'Eden Valley' ♀H4 | MAsh NHol SCoo SHeS SRms |
| | - 'Eline' | SHeS |
| | - 'England' | SHeS |
| | - 'Felthorpe' | SHeS |
| | - 'Flamingo' | SHeS |
| | - 'Foxhollow Mahogany' | SHeS |
| | - 'Frances' | SHeS |
| | - 'Frankrijk' | SHeS |
| | - 'Fred Corston' | SHeS |
| | - 'G. Osmond' | SHeS |
| | - 'Glasnevin Red' | IVic SHeS |
| | - 'Glencairn' | MMuc NHol SHeS SWhi |
| | - 'Graham Thomas' | see *E. cinerea* 'C.G. Best' |
| | - 'Grandiflora' | SHeS |
| | - 'Guernsey Lime' | SHeS |
| | - 'Guernsey Pink' | SHeS |
| | - 'Guernsey Plum' | SHeS |
| | - 'Guernsey Purple' | SHeS |
| | - 'Hardwick's Rose' | SHeS |
| | - 'Harry Fulcher' | SHeS |
| | - 'Heatherbank' | SHeS |
| | - 'Heathfield' | SHeS |
| | - 'Heidebrand' | SHeS |
| | - 'Hermann Dijkhuizen' | SHeS |
| | - 'Hookstone Lavender' | SHeS |
| | - 'Hutton's Seedling' | SHeS |
| | - 'Iberian Beauty' | SHeS |
| | - 'Janet' | SHeS |
| | - 'Jersey Wonder' | SHeS |
| | - 'Jiri' | SHeS |
| | - 'John Ardron' | SHeS |
| | - 'Joseph Murphy' | SHeS |
| | - 'Josephine Ross' | SHeS |
| | - 'Joyce Burfitt' | SHeS |
| | - 'Katinka' | CBcs GJos IVic NHol SHeS SWhi |
| | - 'Kerry Cherry' | SHeS |
| | - 'Knap Hill Pink' ♀H4 | SHeS |
| | - 'Lady Skelton' | SHeS |
| | - 'Lavender Lady' | SHeS |
| | - 'Lilac Time' | SHeS |
| | - 'Lilacina' | SHeS |
| | - 'Lime Soda' ♀H4 | SHeS |
| | - 'Lorna Anne Hutton' | SHeS |
| | - 'Michael Hugo' | SHeS |
| | - 'Miss Waters' | SHeS |
| | - 'Mrs Dill' | SHeS |
| | - 'Mrs E.A. Mitchell' | NHol SHeS SPlb |
| | - 'Mrs Ford' | SHeS |
| | - 'My Love' | SHeS SWhi |
| | - 'Neptune' | SHeS |
| | - 'Newick Lilac' | SHeS |
| | - 'Next Best' | SHeS |
| | - 'Novar' | SHeS |
| | - 'Old Rose' | SHeS |
| | - 'P.S. Patrick' ♀H4 | SHeS SWhi |
| | - 'Pallas' | SHeS |
| | - 'Pallida' | SHeS |
| | - 'Paul's Purple' | SHeS |
| | - 'Peñaz' | SHeS |
| | - 'Pentreath' ♀H4 | MMuc SHeS |
| | - 'Pink Foam' | SHeS |
| | - 'Pink Ice' ♀H4 | CTri EPfP MAsh NHol SHeS SWhi |
| | - 'Plummer's Seedling' | SHeS |
| | - 'Promenade' | SHeS |
| | - 'Prostrate Lavender' | SHeS |
| | - 'Providence' | SHeS |
| | - 'Purple Beauty' | MAsh SHeS SWhi |
| | - 'Purple Robe' | SHeS |
| | - 'Purple Spreader' | SHeS |
| | - 'Purpurea' | SHeS |
| | - 'Pygmaea' | SHeS |
| | - 'Red Pentreath' | SHeS |

| |  |  |
|---|---|---|
| | - 'Rock Ruth' | SHeS |
| | - 'Romiley' | MAsh SHeS |
| | - 'Rose Queen' | SHeS |
| | - 'Rosea' | SHeS |
| I | - 'Rosea Splendens' | SHeS |
| | - 'Rosy Chimes' | SHeS |
| | - 'Roter Kobold' **new** | SWhi |
| | - 'Rozanne Waterer' | SHeS |
| | - 'Ruby' | SHeS |
| | - 'Sandpit Hill' | SHeS |
| | - 'Schizopetala' | SHeS |
| | - 'Sea Foam' | SHeS |
| | - 'Sherry' | NBlu NHol SHeS SWhi |
| | - 'Smith's Lawn' | SHeS |
| | - 'Spicata' | SHeS |
| | - 'Splendens' | SHeS |
| | - 'Startler' | MAsh SHeS |
| | - 'Stephen Davis' ♀H4 | MAsh NHol SCoo SHeS SWhi |
| | - 'Strawberry Bells' | SHeS |
| | - 'Sue Lloyd' | SHeS |
| | - 'Tilford' | SHeS |
| | - 'Tom Waterer' | SHeS |
| | - 'Underwood Pink' | SHeS |
| | - 'Uschie Ziehmann' | SHeS |
| | - 'Velvet Night' ♀H4 | CSBt MAsh MMuc NHol SHeS SRms SWhi |
| | - 'Victoria' | SHeS |
| | - 'Violacea' | SHeS |
| | - 'Violetta' | SHeS |
| | - 'Vivienne Patricia' | SHeS SWhi |
| | - 'W.G. Notley' | SHeS |
| | - 'West End' | SHeS |
| | - 'Wine' | SHeS |
| | - 'Yvonne' | SHeS |
| | ***cooperi*** | SPlb |
| | ***curviflora*** | SHeS SPlb |
| | × ***darleyensis*** | GGal |
| | - 'Alba' | see *E.* × *darleyensis* f. *albiflora* 'Silberschmelze' |
| | - f. ***albiflora*** 'Ada S. Collings' | MAsh SHeS |
| | - - 'Dunreggan' | SHeS |
| | - - 'N.R. Webster' | MAsh SHeS |
| § | - - 'Silberschmelze' | CSBt CTri EPfP MAsh MMuc NBlu NHol NPri SCoo SEND SHeS SRms SWhi |
| | - - 'White Glow' | CTri MAsh SHeS |
| | - - 'White Perfection' ♀H4 | CBcs CSBt EPfP IArd IVic MAsh NHol NPri SBfd SCoo SHeS SPoG SRms SWhi |
| | - 'Archie Graham' | SHeS |
| | - 'Arthur Johnson' ♀H4 | CSBt CTri MAsh NHol SHeS SRms SWhi |
| § | - f. ***aureifolia*** 'Eva Gold'PBR | NHol SHeS SRms SWhi |
| | - - 'Jack H. Brummage' | CSBt CTri IArd MAsh NHol SHeS SRms SWhi |
| | - - 'Mary Helen' | CSBt EPfP MAsh NHol SCoo SHeS SRms SWhi |
| | - - 'Moonshine' | NHol SWhi |
| | - - 'Tweety' | CBcs SHeS |
| | - 'Aurélie Brégeon' | SHeS SRms |
| | - 'Bert' **new** | SCoo |
| | - 'Bing' **new** | SCoo |
| | - 'Cherry Stevens' | see *E.* × *darleyensis* 'Furzey' |
| § | - 'Darley Dale' | CSBt ELan EPfP MAsh MMuc NBlu NHol NPri SBfd SCoo SEND SHeS SLon SPer SPoG SRms SWhi |
| | - 'Epe' | SHeS |
| | - 'Erecta' | SHeS |
| | - 'Eva'PBR | see *E.* × *darleyensis* f. *aureifolia* 'Eva Gold' |
| § | - 'Furzey' ♀H4 | CSBt EPfP MAsh NBlu NHol SCoo SHeS SPer SRms SWhi |
| | - 'George Rendall' | CSBt CTri EPfP MAsh NHol SCoo SHeS |
| | - 'Ghost Hills' ♀H4 | CSBt EPfP MAsh NHol NPri SBfd SCoo SHeS SPoG SRms SWhi |
| | - 'J.W. Porter' ♀H4 | EPfP MMuc NBlu SCoo SEND SHeS SLon SRms SWhi |
| | - 'James Smith' | SHeS |
| | - 'Jenny Porter' ♀H4 | CSBt ELan EPfP MAsh SCoo SHeS SLon SWhi |
| | - 'Kramer's Rote' ♀H4 | CBcs CSBt CTri ELan EPfP IVic MAsh MMuc NBlu NHol NPri SBfd SCoo SHeS SPoG SRms SWhi |
| § | - 'Lena' | SHeS |
| | - 'Margaret Porter' | EPfP MAsh SCoo SHeS SPer SWhi |
| | - Molten Silver | see *E.* × *darleyensis* f. *albiflora* 'Silberschmelze' |
| | - 'Mrs Parris' Red' | SHeS |
| | - 'Pink Perfection' | see *E.* × *darleyensis* 'Darley Dale' |
| | - 'Spring Surprise'PBR | EPfP SCoo SHeS |
| | - 'W.G. Pine' | SHeS |
| | - 'White Fairy' | SHeS |
| | - 'Winter Surprise' **new** | SWhi |
| | ***discolor*** | SHeS |
| | ***erigena*** f. ***alba*** 'Alba' | SHeS |
| | - - 'Brian Proudley' | SHeS |
| | - - 'Ivory' | SHeS |
| | - - 'Mrs Parris' White' | SHeS |
| | - - 'Nana Alba' | SHeS |
| | - - 'Nana Compacta' | SHeS |
| | - - 'W.T. Rackliff' ♀H4 | CBcs CSBt EPfP MAsh NHol SCoo SHeS SRms SWhi |
| | - - 'W.T. Rackliff Variegated' (v) | SHeS |
| | - f. ***aureifolia*** 'Golden Lady' ♀H4 | CSBt MAsh NHol SCoo SHeS SWhi |
| | - - 'Thing Nee' | SHeS SWhi |
| | - 'Brightness' | CSBt EPfP MAsh NHol SCoo SHeS |
| | - 'Coccinea' | SHeS |
| | - 'Ewan Jones' | SHeS |
| | - 'Glauca' | SHeS |
| | - 'Hibernica' | SHeS |
| | - 'Hibernica Alba' | SHeS |
| | - 'Irish Dusk' ♀H4 | CBcs CSBt CTri EPfP MAsh MMuc NHol SCoo SEND SHeS SRms SWhi |
| | - 'Irish Salmon' | SHeS |
| | - 'Irish Silver' | SHeS |
| | - 'Maxima' | SHeS |
| | - 'Mrs Parris' Lavender' | SHeS |
| | - 'Nana' | SHeS |
| | - 'Rosea' | SHeS |
| | - 'Rosslare' | SHeS |
| | - 'Rubra' | SHeS |
| | - 'Superba' | MAsh SHeS SRms SWhi |
| | × ***garforthensis*** 'Tracy Wilson' | SHeS |
| | 'Ghislaine' | SHeS |
| | ***glauca*** var. ***elegans*** | CDes |
| | - var. ***glauca*** | SPlb |
| | ***gracilis*** | SPoG |
| | × ***griffithsii*** 'Ashlea Gold' | SHeS |
| | - 'Elegant Spike' | SHeS |
| § | - 'Heaven Scent' | SHeS SWhi |
| | - 'Jacqueline' | NHol SHeS SRms SWhi |
| | - 'Valerie Griffiths' | MAsh NHol SCoo SHeS SRms SWhi |
| | 'Heaven Scent' | see *E.* × *griffithsii* 'Heaven Scent' |
| | 'Hélène' | SHeS |

| | |
|---|---|
| ***holosericea*** | CDes |
| × ***krameri*** 'Otto' | SHeS |
| - 'Rudi' | IVic SHeS |
| ***lusitanica*** ♀H3 | SHeS SPoG |
| - f. ***aureifolia*** | ELan EPfP MAsh NHol SHeS SLon |
| 'George Hunt' | SPer SPoG |
| - 'Sheffield Park' | ELan EPfP MAsh SHeS SPer SPoG |
| ***mackayana*** | SHeS |
| subsp. ***andevalensis*** | |
| - - f. ***albiflora*** | SHeS |
| - 'Donegal' | SHeS |
| - f. ***eburnea*** | SHeS |
| 'Doctor Ronald Gray' | |
| - - 'Shining Light' | SDys SHeS |
| - 'Errigal Dusk' | SHeS |
| - 'Galicia' | SHeS |
| - 'Lawsoniana' | SHeS |
| - f. ***multiplicata*** | SHeS |
| 'Ann D. Frearson' (d) | |
| - - 'Maura' (d) | SHeS |
| - - 'Plena' (d) | IVic SHeS |
| - 'William M'Calla' | SHeS |
| ***mammosa*** | SPlb |
| ***manipuliflora*** 'Aldeburgh' | SHeS |
| § - 'Cascades' | SHeS |
| - 'Corfu' | SHeS |
| - 'Don Richards' | SHeS |
| - 'Ian Cooper' | SHeS |
| - 'Korçula' | SHeS |
| - 'Toothill Mustard' | SHeS |
| - 'Waterfall' | see *E. manipuliflora* 'Cascades' |
| ***mediterranea*** | see *E. erigena* |
| ***multiflora*** f. ***alba*** | SHeS |
| 'Formentor' | |
| × ***oldenburgensis*** | SCoo SHeS |
| 'Ammerland' | |
| - 'Oldenburg' | SHeS |
| ***patersonii*** | SPlb |
| ***perspicua*** new | CDes |
| ***plukenetii*** | CDes |
| ***racemosa*** | SHeS |
| ***scoparia*** subsp. ***azorica*** | SHeS |
| - subsp. ***maderincola*** | SHeS |
| f. ***aureifolia*** | |
| 'Madeira Gold' | |
| § - 'Minima' | SHeS |
| - subsp. ***platycodon*** | SHeS |
| - 'Pumila' | see *E. scoparia* 'Minima' |
| ***sphaerocephala*** | CDes |
| ***spiculifolia*** | WPat WThu |
| - f. ***albiflora*** | SHeS |
| - 'Balkan Rose' | GCal SHeS |
| - 'Typ Rot' new | IVic |
| 'Spring Field White' | MMuc |
| ***straussiana*** | SPlb |
| I × ***stuartii*** 'Charles Stuart' | SHeS |
| - 'Connemara' | SHeS |
| - 'Irish Lemon' ♀H4 | CSBt EPfP GGar MAsh NHol SHeS SWhi |
| - 'Irish Orange' | CSBt MAsh NHol SHeS SWhi |
| - 'Irish Rose' | SHeS |
| - 'Nacung' | SHeS |
| - 'Pat Turpin' | SHeS |
| ***subdivaricata*** | SHeS |
| ***taxifolia*** | CDes |
| ***terminalis*** ♀H4 | SHeS SRms |
| - 'Golden Oriole' | SHeS |
| - 'Thelma Woolner' | SHeS |
| ***tetralix*** | SRms |
| - f. ***alba*** 'Bartinney' | SHeS |
| - - 'Dee' | SHeS |
| - - 'Hailstones' | SHeS |
| - - 'Melbury White' | SHeS |
| § - - 'Ruby's Variety' | SHeS |
| - 'Alba' | SHeS |
| - 'Alba Mollis' ♀H4 | CSBt GGar MAsh NHol SHeS SWhi |
| - 'Ally Pearcey' | SHeS |
| - 'Allendale Pink' | SHeS |
| - 'Ardy' | SHeS |
| - f. ***aureifolia*** 'Renate' | SHeS |
| - - 'Ruth's Gold' | MAsh NHol SHeS |
| - - 'Swedish Yellow' | SHeS |
| - 'Bala' | SHeS |
| - 'Con Underwood' ♀H4 | CSBt MAsh NHol SHeS SRms SWhi |
| - 'Curled Roundstone' | SHeS |
| - 'Dänemark' | SHeS |
| - 'Daphne Underwood' | SHeS |
| - 'Darleyensis' | SHeS |
| - 'Delta' | SHeS |
| - 'Foxhome' | SHeS |
| - 'George Fraser' | SHeS |
| - 'Gratis' | SHeS |
| - 'Hookstone Pink' | SHeS |
| - 'Humoresque' | SHeS |
| - 'Jos' Creeping' | SHeS |
| - 'Ken Underwood' | SHeS |
| - 'L.E. Underwood' | NHol SHeS |
| - 'Mary Grace' | SHeS |
| - 'Morning Glow' | see *E.* × *watsonii* 'F. White' |
| - 'Pink Glow' | SHeS |
| - 'Pink Pepper' (v) | SHeS |
| - f. ***racemosa*** | SHeS |
| 'Terschelling' | |
| - 'Riko' | SHeS SRms |
| - 'Rosea' | SHeS |
| - 'Rubra' | SHeS |
| - 'Ruby's Velvet' | see *E. tetralix* f. *alba* 'Ruby's Variety' |
| - 'Salmon Seedling' | SHeS |
| - 'Samtpfötchen' | IVic SHeS |
| - 'Silver Bells' | CSBt SHeS |
| - f. ***stellata*** 'Helma' | SHeS |
| - - 'Helma Variegated' (v) | SHeS |
| - - 'Pink Star' ♀H4 | MAsh NHol SHeS SRms SWhi |
| - 'Stikker' | SHeS |
| - 'Tina' | SHeS |
| - 'Trixie' | SHeS |
| - 'White House' | SHeS |
| ***umbellata*** | SHeS |
| - f. ***albiflora*** 'Anne Small' | SHeS |
| - 'David Small' | SHeS |
| ***vagans*** f. ***alba*** | MMuc |
| - - 'Bianca' | SHeS |
| - - 'Cornish Cream' ♀H4 | EPfP NHol SHeS SWhi |
| - - 'Cream' | MAsh SHeS |
| - - 'Diana's Gold' | SHeS |
| - - 'French White' | SHeS |
| - - 'Golden Triumph' | SHeS SWhi |
| - - 'Kevernensis Alba' ♀H4 | NWad SHeS |
| - - 'Leucantha' | SHeS |
| § - - 'Nana' | SHeS |
| - - 'White Lady' | GGar SHeS |
| - - 'White Rocket' | SHeS |
| - - 'White Spire' | SHeS |
| - 'Alba Nana' | see *E. vagans* f. *alba* 'Nana' |
| - f. ***aureifolia*** 'Valerie Proudley' ♀H4 | CSBt MAsh NHol SHeS SRms |
| - - 'Yellow John' | SHeS SWhi |
| - 'Birch Glow' ♀H4 | EPfP MAsh SHeS SWhi |
| - 'Carnea' | SHeS |

| | | |
|---|---|---|
| | - 'Charm' | SHeS |
| | - 'Chittendenii' | SHeS |
| | - 'Diana Hornibrook' | SHeS |
| | - 'Fiddlestone' | SHeS |
| | - 'George Underwood' | SHeS |
| | - 'Grandiflora' | SHeS |
| | - 'Holden Pink' | MAsh SHeS |
| | - 'Hookstone Rose' | SHeS |
| | - 'Ida M. Britten' | SHeS |
| | - 'J.C. Fletcher' | SHeS |
| | - 'Keira' **new** | SWhi |
| | - 'Lilacina' | SHeS |
| | - 'Lyonesse' ♀H4 | CTri MAsh MMuc NBlu NHol SHeS SRms SWhi |
| | - 'Miss Waterer' | SHeS |
| | - 'Mrs D.F. Maxwell' ♀H4 | CSBt CTri MAsh NHol SHeS SRms SWhi |
| | - 'Mrs Donaldson' | SHeS |
| | - 'Pallida' | SHeS |
| | - 'Peach Blossom' | SHeS |
| | - 'Pyrenees Pink' | MAsh SHeS |
| | - 'Rosea' | SHeS |
| | - 'Rubra' | SHeS |
| | - 'Saint Keverne' | CSBt CTri IArd IVic MAsh NHol SHeS SWhi |
| | - 'Summertime' | SHeS |
| | - 'Valerie Smith' | SHeS |
| | - 'Viridiflora' | SHeS |
| | × ***veitchii*** | MMuc |
| | - 'Brockhill' | SHeS |
| | - 'Exeter' ♀H3 | CDoy CSBt ELan EPfP LRHS MAsh NHol SBrd SHeS SWhi WFar |
| | - 'Gold Tips' ♀H4 | CSBt EPfP LRHS NHol SHeS SWhi |
| | - 'Pink Joy' | SHeS |
| | ***versicolor*** | SPlb |
| | ***verticillata*** | SHeS |
| | ***vestita*** **new** | CDes |
| | ***viridescens*** | SHeS |
| | × ***watsonii*** 'Cherry Turpin' | SHeS |
| | - 'Dawn' ♀H4 | SHeS |
| | - 'Dorothy Metheny' | SHeS |
| | - 'Dorset Beauty' | SHeS |
| § | - 'F. White' | SHeS |
| | - 'Gwen' | SHeS |
| | - 'H. Maxwell' | SHeS |
| | - 'Mary' | IVic SHeS SWhi |
| | - 'Pink Pacific' | SHeS |
| | - 'Rachel' | SHeS |
| | - 'Truro' | SHeS |
| | × ***williamsii*** 'Cow-y-Jack' | SHeS |
| | - 'Croft Pascoe' | SHeS |
| | - 'David Coombe' | SHeS |
| | - 'Gew Graze' | SHeS |
| | - 'Gold Button' | SHeS |
| | - 'Gwavas' | SHeS |
| | - 'Jean Julian' | SHeS |
| | - 'Ken Wilson' | SHeS |
| | - 'Lizard Downs' | SHeS |
| | - 'Marion Hughes' | SHeS |
| | - 'P.D. Williams' ♀H4 | SHeS |
| I | 'Winter Fire' (*oatesii* hybrid) | SHeS |
| | ***woodii*** | SPlb |

## Ericameria (*Asteraceae*)

| | |
|---|---|
| ***discoidea*** NNS 06-209 | WCot |

## Erigeron ✿ (*Asteraceae*)

| | | |
|---|---|---|
| | from Big Horn, USA | NMen |
| | 'Adria' | EBla ECtt LLHF LRHS MBNS SPer WBrk WFar WMnd WWEG |
| | ***annuus*** | NDov |
| | ***aurantiacus*** | EPfP MBNS NBre NBro NPri |
| § | ***aureus*** | NWCA |
| | - 'Canary Bird' ♀H4 | EPfP NBir NMen NSla WAbe |
| | - 'The Giant' | CPBP WAbe |
| | 'Azure Beauty' | EBee EPfP SBfd |
| | Azure Fairy | see *E.* 'Azurfee' |
| § | 'Azurfee' | CSBt EBee ELan EPfP GMaP LSqH MBNS MMuc MWat NBir NLar NPri SGar SPer SPhx SPoG SWvt WMoo WPer WWEG |
| | Black Sea | see *E.* 'Schwarzes Meer' |
| | 'Blue Beauty' | CMac EPfP LRHS |
| | 'Charity' | MRav WBrk |
| | ***chrysopsidis*** var. ***brevifolius*** | CPBP |
| | - 'Grand Ridge' | ECho LHop LLHF LRHS NWCA WAbe |
| | ***compositus*** | CPBP CTri SRms |
| § | - var. ***discoideus*** | EDAr NBre NMen NSla SPlb |
| | - 'Rocky' | ECho GEdr |
| | Darkest of All | see *E.* 'Dunkelste Aller' |
| | deep pink-flowered | CHEx |
| | 'Dignity' | EBee EBla EKen ELan LLHF MBrN MRav MWat SMrm SPet SPoG SUsu WBrk WCot WFar WWEG |
| | 'Dimity' | CMea ECha NBir NBre SAga WAbe WBrk WFar WHal WSFF |
| | 'Dominator' | EBee GBin WCot |
| I | 'Dunkelste Aller' ♀H3 | CMea CSam EBee EBla ELan EPfP GMaP LBMP LHop LSou MAvo MRav MSpe NMRc SPoG SRms SWvt WCAu WFar WWEG |
| | ***eatonii*** var. ***villosus*** **new** | GKev |
| | ***elegantulus*** | CMea |
| * | ***ereganus*** | NBre WBrk |
| | 'Felicity' | EBee |
| | ***flettii*** | EDAr WPat |
| | 'Foersters Liebling' ♀H4 | EBee EBla GBin MNrw WCot WWEG |
| | ***formosissimus*** | GBin |
| | 'Four Winds' | CAbP ECtt ELan EWes MRav NGdn NMen WPer WWEG |
| | 'Gaiety' | LRHS NBre WBrk |
| | ***glaucus*** | CCCN CSBt EBee EWll GBee GGar GJos LRHS MAsh MBNS MRav NBre NGdn NVic SEND SMad WBrk WFar WHoo |
| | - 'Albus' | LHop MBNS SAga WFar WPer |
| | - 'Elstead Pink' | CTri EBee ECtt ELan LRHS SAga WFar WSHC |
| | - 'Roger Raiche' | MRav SMrm |
| | - 'Roseus' | CBcs SEND |
| | - 'Sea Breeze' | CCCN COIW CPrp ELon GGar GJos GMaP LAst LHop LRHS MBNS MBri NBre NCGa NPri SBfd SPoG WNew |
| | - 'Viewpoint Blue' **new** | LRHS |
| | ***howellii*** | NBre |
| | ***humilis*** | EDAr |
| § | ***karvinskianus*** ♀H3 | Widely available |
| | ***leiomerus*** | EPot GKev LBee LLHF |
| | ***linearis*** | LLHF NMen NWCA |
| | 'Mrs F.H. Beale' | EBee EBla ECtt LSou SRGP |
| | ***mucronatus*** | see *E. karvinskianus* |
| | ***multiradiatus*** | GCal |
| | 'Nachthimmel' | EBla ECtt NBre NGdn |
| | ***ochroleucus*** var. ***scribneri*** | LLHF |
| | 'Offenham Excellence' | WCot |

***oreganus*** LRHS
***philadelphicus*** CElw IGor NBir NBro
'Pink Beauty' SKHP
Pink Jewel see *E.* 'Rosa Juwel'
***pinnatisectus*** CPBP GKev
'Profusion' see *E. karvinskianus*
***pumilus*** CDes
***pygmaeus*** LLHF
***pyrenaicus*** Rouy see *Aster pyrenaeus*
'Quakeress' CElw CPrp EBee EBla ECtt EPfP EShb GMaP IKil LBMP LEdu LHop LRHS MNrw MRav MSpe NGdn SBfd SMrm SUsu WBrk WFar WWEG
§ 'Rosa Juwel' CSBt CTri EBee ECtt ELan EPfP GMaP LRHS LSqH MBNS MMuc MRav NBir NPri SPer SPoG SRms SWvt WMnd WMoo WPer
'Rosenballett' LRHS WCot
'Rotes Meer' CMac EBee EBla ELan MRav MSpe WFar
***rotundifolius*** 'Caerulescens' see *Bellis caerulescens*
***salsuginosus*** misapplied see *Aster sibiricus*, *E. peregrinus* subsp. *callianthemus*
§ 'Schneewittchen' EBee EBla ELan EPfP GMac MBNS MRav MSpe MWat NCGa NVic SBfd SHar SPet SPoG SWvt WWEG
§ 'Schwarzes Meer' EBee MNrw SPoG WCot WFar WRHF
***scopulinus*** CMea CPBP ITim LLHF WPat
'Serenity' LRHS
***simplex*** ECho LRHS
'Sincerity' SAga WBrk WFar
'Snow Queen' WFar
Snow White see *E.* 'Schneewittchen'
'Sommerabend' EBee
'Sommerneuschnee' EBee ECha GBin LPla NDov WCot WMnd
***speciosus*** 'Grandiflora' NBre
'Strahlenmeer' EBee MSpe NBre WFar
***trifidus*** see *E. compositus* var. *discoideus*
***uniflorus*** LLHF MAsh SRms
'Unity' LRHS
'Wayne Roderick' EBee LRHS SRGP
'White Quakeress' CMea EBee MRav WBrk WCot
'Wuppertal' EBee MRav NGdn

## *Erinacea* (*Papilionaceae*)

§ ***anthyllis*** ♀H4 WThu
***pungens*** see *E. anthyllis*

## *Erinus* (*Plantaginaceae*)

***alpinus*** ♀H4 CTri ECho ECtt EDAr EPfP GAbr GJos GKev MAsh MLHP MMuc MWat NBir NBlu NHol NSla NWCA SRms WFar WPer XLum
- var. ***albus*** ECho GJos NMen SRms WHoo WPer XLum
- 'Doktor Hähnle' ECho EDAr GMaP NMen SRms WFar WHoo XLum
- 'Mrs Charles Boyle' NMen

## *Eriobotrya* (*Rosaceae*)

'Coppertone' see × *Rhaphiobotrya* 'Coppertone'
***deflexa*** CBcs CHEx
***japonica*** (F) ♀H3 CAbb CBcs CBot CCCN CDul CHEx CWGN EAmu EBee ELan EPfP ERom ETod LEdu LMaj LRHS MGos MREP SArc SBfd SBrd SBst SCoo SEND SPer SPlb SVic WHer WPGP WSHC
- 'Baffico' (F) CAgr
- 'BB' (F) CAgr
- 'Gold Nugget' (F) XBlo
- 'Ottaviana' (F) CAgr

## *Eriocapitella* see *Anemone*

## *Eriocephalus* (*Asteraceae*)

***africanus*** SPlb WJek

## *Eriogonum* (*Polygonaceae*)

***cespitosum*** LLHF WAbe
- NNS 03-254 GKev
- NNS 08-159 GKev
***flavum*** GEdr
***jamesii*** WPat
***umbellatum*** ECho EPot GKev
- var. ***humistratum*** WPat
- var. ***porteri*** NNS 06-230 NWCA
- var. ***torreyanum*** CMea GEdr

## *Eriophorum* (*Cyperaceae*)

***angustifolium*** CBen CRWN CWat EHoe EHon ELon EWil LPBA MCCP MSKA MWts SPlb SWat WAbe WMAq WMoo WPer WPnP WSFF XLum
***latifolium*** LLWG LPBA MSKA MWts
***rousseauianum*** MSKA
***vaginatum*** CRow EHoe LLWG MSKA WSFF XLum

## *Eriophyllum* (*Asteraceae*)

***lanatum*** EBee ECha EPfP MDKP MWat NBid NBre NGBl SAga WWEG XLum

## *Erodium* (*Geraniaceae*)

***absinthoides*** LRHS NSla XSen
- var. ***amanum*** see *E. amanum*
§ ***acaule*** LLHF WFar
'Almodovar' GLam
§ ***amanum*** EWes
'Ardwick Redeye' GCal SUsu
***balearicum*** see *E.* × *variabile* 'Album'
'Bidderi' GJos NChi NWCA XSen
'Candy Store' **new** LRHS
'Caroline' CMea WHoo
***carvifolium*** GLam NWCA WFar
§ ***castellanum*** EBee LLHF NBro NMen SMrm
- 'Dujardin' SPhx
- 'La Féline' GLam
- 'Logroños Real' GLam
'Catherine Buñuel' NMen
***celtibericum*** EPot GLam XSen
- 'Peñagolosa' XSen
'Cézembre' GLam XSen
***chamaedryoides*** see *E. reichardii*
- 'Roseum' see *E.* × *variabile* 'Roseum'
***cheilanthifolium*** 'David Crocker' EPot IGor NMen
***chrysanthum*** Widely available
- pink-flowered CSpe EPot LHop NMen SMrm SRot XLum
***corsicum*** ECho NMen NWCA WAbe
- 'Album' ECho LLHF NMen WAbe
'County Park' CMea EBee ECha MLHP SRms
***daucoides*** misapplied see *E. castellanum*
'Florida' MAga

| |  |  |
|---|---|---|
| | ***foetidum*** | NMen |
| | - 'Couvé' | NMen |
| | 'Fran's Delight' | CMea ECtt EPot GJos GMaP MLHP NMen SBch WHoo |
| | 'Fripetta' | WAbe |
| | 'Gini's Choice' **new** | WCot |
| N | ***glandulosum*** ♀H4 | CMea EBee ECho EPfP MMuc SBch SEND SRms SRot WFar WKif WPat WSHC |
| | - 'Marie Poligné' | XSen |
| | 'Grey Blush' | WKif |
| | ***gruinum*** | EBee SPhx SWal |
| | ***guicciardii*** | XSen |
| | ***guttatum*** misapplied | see *E.* 'Katherine Joy' |
| N | ***guttatum*** (Desf.) Willd. | EPot EWTr LHop MWat NMen SRms WNew |
| | ***hymenodes*** L'Hér. | see *E. trifolium* |
| | 'Julie Ritchie' | CMea WHoo |
| § | 'Katherine Joy' | EBee EPot EWes MHer SRGP SRot WAbe |
| | × ***kolbianum*** | WAbe WCot WFar WHoo XSen |
| | - 'Natasha' | CMHG EBee ECtt EHoe EPot EWes GGar GLam GMaP LBee MHer NMen NSla SPoG SRGP WAbe WFar WKif XSen |
| | 'Las Meninas' | CRDP SUsu WCot XSen |
| | × ***lindavicum*** | ECha NChi XSen |
| | ***macradenum*** | see *E. glandulosum* |
| | ***manescavii*** | Widely available |
| | 'Marchants Mikado' | WKif |
| | 'Maryla' | NMen |
| | 'Merstham Pink' | CMHG GMaP SMrm SRms XLum XSen |
| | 'Mesquita' | CMea |
| | 'Norse Pink' **new** | GJos |
| | 'Nunwood Pink' | NWCA |
| | 'Pallidum' | CSam |
| | ***pelargoniiflorum*** | CBot CHid CSpe EBee ELan EPfP EWTr GGar ILis LRHS MCot NBro SEND SMrm SRms WFar WKif WPer WPtf WWFP |
| | 'Peter Vernon' | NWCA |
| | ***petraeum*** | EPot MSpe |
| | subsp. ***petraeum*** | |
| | 'Pickering Pink' | GLam LIMB NMen SEND |
| | 'Pippa Mills' | CElw CMea |
| | 'Princesse Marion' | GLam MLHP XSen |
| * | 'Purple Haze' | EBee MSCN SMrm SRms SRot WFar |
| § | ***reichardii*** | CTri ECho ECtt LRHS MBrN MHer NWCA SPet SPoG SRms WCFE |
| | - 'Album' | CEnt ECho GEdr MAsh NMen SGar SMrm SPet SPoG WFar WHoo |
| | - 'Pipsqueak' | NWCA |
| * | - 'Rubrum' | CElw ECho |
| | 'Robertino' | NMen WAbe |
| | 'Robespierre' | SPhx |
| | ***rodiei*** | EWes MAsh WKif |
| | ***romanum*** | see *E. acaule* |
| § | ***rupestre*** | CBot EBee ECho ECtt GMaP MAsh MWea NWCA SRms SRot WPat |
| | 'Sarck' | XSen |
| | ***sebaceum*** 'Polly' | NWCA |
| | ***sibthorpianum*** | XSen |
| | 'Spanish Eyes' | NEgg NPri SMrm SRot WCot WFar WKif |
| | 'Stephanie' | CMHG EBee ECho ELan EPot EWes GMaP LBee LRHS LSRN NMen SWal WAbe XSen |
| | ***supracanum*** | see *E. rupestre* |
| | 'Tiny Kyni' | WFar XSen |
| | ***trichomanifolium*** L'Hér. | EWes LBee LRHS |
| § | ***trifolium*** | ECho ELan EPfP EPot LRHS MHer NSla SGar SPhx |
| | × ***variabile*** | ECtt |
| § | - 'Album' | CMea CYeo EBee ECho EPfP EPot GKev LRHS MHer MMuc NEgg NPri NSla NWCA SPoG SRms SRot WAbe WBrk WFar WNew WPer |
| I | - 'Bishop's Form' | Widely available |
| | - 'Candy' | ELon GEdr GJos MHer |
| | - 'Derek' | ECho |
| | - 'Flore Pleno' (d) | CYeo ECho ELan EPfP EWes ITim LRHS NMen SPoG SRms WBrk WFar WPer |
| | - 'Red Rock' | CTri |
| § | - 'Roseum' ♀H4 | CBot ECho ECtt ELan ELon EPfP MMuc MSCN NSla NWCA SPlb SRms WBrk WFar WPer |
| I | 'Westacre Seedling' | EWes |
| | 'Whitwell Superb' | CDes CElw MSpe NWCA WPGP |
| | × ***willkommianum*** | NWCA |

## *Erpetion* see *Viola*

## *Eruca* (*Brassicaceae*)

| |  |  |
|---|---|---|
| | ***vesicaria*** | CWan NBlu |
| | - subsp. ***sativa*** | CSpe EGHP ELau GPoy MHer MNHC SIde |

## *Eryngium* ✿ (*Apiaceae*)

| |  |  |
|---|---|---|
| | F&M 208 | WPGP |
| | NJM 09.072 | WPGP |
| | PC&H 268 | EKen |
| § | ***agavifolium*** | Widely available |
| | ***alpinum*** ♀H4 | CBcs CHab CSpe EBee ECha ECho ECtt ELan ELon GKev GMaP LAst LHop MGos MLLN MRav MSCN NBir SKHP SPer SPet SRms SRot WFar |
| | - 'Amethyst' | IPot LRHS LSRN NBro SMrm |
| | - 'Blue Jacket' | NSti |
| | - 'Blue Star' | CBot CHar CPLG CSpe EBee EBla ECtt ELan ELon EPfP GAbr LRHS NGBl NLar SMrm SPtl WCot WPer WWEG |
| | - 'Holden Blue' | MAvo |
| | - 'Slieve Donard' | see *E.* × *zabelii* 'Donard Variety' |
| | - 'Superbum' | CBot CSpe ECtt GJos GLog LRHS MNrw SRms SWat |
| | ***amethystinum*** | CBot CCse CMac EBee EPfP EPri LRHS MCot SPoG WHoo WPer WWEG XLum |
| | ***biebersteinianum*** | see *E. caeruleum* |
| | 'Big Blue' **new** | LRHS NCGa WCot |
| | 'Blue Jackpot' | EBee EWes NPri |
| | 'Blue Steel' | LLHF MDKP NChi SBfd SHar SPoG |
| | ***bourgatii*** | Widely available |
| | - Graham Stuart Thomas's selection | Widely available |
| | - 'Oxford Blue' ♀H4 | CRDP EBee GMaP GMac LAst MHer NLar SAga SGar SKHP SWvt |
| | - 'Picos Amethyst' | CBcs CKno CMac CWCL CWGN EBee EKen LHop LSRN LSou MGos NLar NSti SCoo SKHP |
| | - 'Picos Blue' PBR | Widely available |
| | - 'Silver Blue' **new** | LRHS |
| | ***bromeliifolium*** misapplied | see *E. agavifolium*, *E. eburneum* |
| § | ***caeruleum*** | MNrw |
| | ***campestre*** | CArn CBot EWll MDKP NLar WFar WPer WWEG |

***caucasicum*** see *E. caeruleum*
'Cobalt Star' GMac MDKP
***creticum*** NBro SDix
***cymosum*** B&SWJ 10267 WCru
***decaisneanum*** misapplied see *E. pandanifolium*
***deppeanum*** CGHE SSvw
- F&M 54 WPGP
- NJM 05.031 LEdu WPGP
Dove Cottage hybrid NDov
***ebracteatum*** MAvo
- var. ***poterioides*** LPla SMad SPhx
§ ***eburneum*** CBot CFir CGHE EBee ECha EPfP EWes GCal GMaP LRHS MAvo MSpe NBPC NBro NChi NSti SBfd SKHP SMad WFar
aff. ***eburneum*** CMac WPGP
'Electric Haze' ECtt IPot LRHS LSou MWhi
***elegans*** var. ***elegans*** CGHE
- - CDPR 3076 WPGP
***foetidum*** CArn
§ ***giganteum*** ♀H4 Widely available
- 'Silver Ghost' ♀H4 CHar CMea CPLG CSam CSpe EBee ECtt EWll LHop LRHS MAvo NChi NDov NGdn NSti SBfd SGar SKHP SMad SMrm SWat SWvt WCot WFar WWEG
***gracile*** B&SWJ 10205 WCru
- B&SWJ 10441 WCru
'Green Jade' LRHS
***guatemalense*** CGHE WPGP
- B&SWJ 8989 WCru
- B&SWJ 10322 WCru
- B&SWJ 10420 WCru
***horridum*** misapplied see *E. eburneum*
***horridum*** ambig. EWes GGar LEdu MNrw NChi SArc WFar WMnd
***horridum*** Malme CCVN WCot
- HCM 98048 WPGP
***humile*** B&SWJ 10464 WCru
'Indigo Star' **new** GMac
'Lapis Blue' GMac
***leavenworthii*** LRHS
***maritimum*** CArn CBot CPou GKev GPoy MDKP MHer NLar SPhx SPlb WAbe WFar
Miss Willmott's ghost see *E. giganteum*
***monocephalum*** WPGP
× ***oliverianum*** ♀H4 CHar CMea EBee EBla ECha ECtt ELan EPfP GAbr GCal GMac LAst LHop LRHS MAvo MLHP MNFA MRav NBir NChi NLar SDix SUsu SWat WCot WHoo
***palmatum*** NChi
§ ***pandanifolium*** ♀H4 CFir CHEx CMHG EBee EBla ELan EPfP EWes GBin GCal LEdu MNrw NBPC SArc SBrd SEND SGar SKHP SMad SMrm SPlb SPoG SWvt WCot WCru WMnd WPGP WWEG
- 'Physic Purple' WCot
***paniculatum*** WPGP
***planum*** Widely available
- 'Bethlehem' ♀H4 EBee IPot MAvo NLar SWat
§ - 'Blauer Zwerg' CKno EBee GQue WFar
- 'Blaukappe' CBot CHar CMea COIW CPLG EBee ELon EPfP LRHS NLar SEND SKHP SMrm SPet SPhx WAul WTcb WWEG
* - 'Blue Candle' EBee NLar WFar
- Blue Dwarf see *E. planum* 'Blauer Zwerg'
- 'Blue Glitter' LRHS SPhx
- 'Blue Hobbit' CMea CPLG EAEE EPfP IPot LBuc LRHS MHer NGdn NLBP NLar SBrd SPet SPoG
- 'Blue Ribbon' EBee EBla LAst LRHS LSou MRav NGdn
- 'Flüela' EBee EBla EPfP EWes LRHS LSRN MLLN NBro NEgg SCoo SWat WCAu
- 'Jade Frost' PBR (v) CAbP CDes CPLG CWGN EBee ECtt ELon EPfP EWes LHop LLHF LRHS LSou MAvo MBNS MLLN MNrw MPnt MTis NCGa NLar NSti SKHP SPad SPoG WCAu WCot WCra
- 'Paradise Jackpot' PBR EBee MNrw NGdn SPer WHil
- 'Seven Seas' CFir EBee EBla ECtt LRHS MBNS MBri MLLN NEgg WPer
- 'Silver Stone' EBee EBla ECtt GMaP LRHS MDKP NGdn NLar WHil
- 'Sunny Jackpot' PBR NSti
- 'Tetra Petra' LRHS MAvo NEgg WPer
- 'Violet Blue' GCal
***proteiflorum*** EBee EPfP GBin GCal IGor LRHS MAvo MDKP NBPC SKHP SPlb WHil
- F&M 224 WPGP
'Sapphire Blue' CKno CWGN LSRN MSCN SPoG SRkn WHil
***serbicum*** GCal WCot
***serra*** EWes LRHS SEND
- RB 90454 EBee MAvo MDKP
***spinalba*** CBot
***strotheri*** B&SWJ 9109 WCru
- B&SWJ 10392 WCru
***tricuspidatum*** ECtt LRHS WPer WWEG
× ***tripartitum*** ♀H4 Widely available
* ***umbelliferum*** GBin GCal LAst MBNS MDKP NBPC NPri SKHP WFar
***variifolium*** Widely available
- 'Miss Marbel' **new** EPfP
***venustum*** CDes CPom EBee MCot SBfd SMrm WFar
***yuccifolium*** CKno EBee EBla EPfP EWes GCal LEdu NLar SBfd SDix SPhx SPlb SWvt WFar WHoo XLum
× ***zabelii*** CAby COIW CRDP ECha GMac NBir NChi WPGP
- 'Blaue Ritter' SKHP SWat
§ - 'Donard Variety' EBla ECtt GCal IPot ITim LRHS MAvo MDKP NLar SWat
- 'Forncett Ultra' GCal GMac WPGP
- 'Jewel' MAvo SApp SWat
- 'Jos Eijking' PBR CSpe CWCL ECtt EKen ELon IPot LBMP LRHS LSRN LSou MAvo MCot MMuc MRav MTis NCGa NDov NHol NLar NWad SEND SMad SPer SPoG SRot SUsu WBor WCot
- 'Violetta' ELan GMac IGor MBri NLar SWat WFar WHoo

## *Erysimum* ✿ (*Brassicaceae*)

***alpinum*** misapplied see *E. hieraciifolium*
***amoenum*** LLHF WAbe
'Anne Marie' EPfP
'Anthony Hicks' CHll
'Apricot Delight' see *E.* 'Apricot Twist'
§ 'Apricot Twist' Widely available
***arkansanum*** see *E. helveticum*

| | |
|---|---|
| ***asperum*** | GJos IFro |
| ***bicolor*** | GGar WCot |
| 'Bowles's Mauve' ♀H3 | Widely available |
| 'Bowles's Purple' | SRms SWvt |
| 'Bowles's Yellow' | WCot WHil |
| 'Bredon' ♀H3 | EPfP NPer WHoo |
| 'Butterscotch' | CSpe MMHG WHoo WTin |
| ***cheiri*** | CArn MHer |
| - 'Bloody Warrior' (d) | CBot CElw ECtt |
| - 'Deben' | CBot |
| - 'Harpur Crewe' (d) | CBot CFee CHll CTri ECtt ELan ELon EPfP GMaP MMuc NPer SRms SUsu WCot |
| - 'Orange Bedder' (Bedder Series) | NBir |
| - Rysi Gold = 'Innrysigol'PBR | WCot |
| 'Chelsea Jacket' | EPfP |
| 'Constant Cheer' | CBar CMea CPrp CSBt CSpe CWCL ECtt ELan ELon EPfP EShb EWTr GGar GMaP IFoB MCot NPer SAga SBfd SEND SPer SRGP SUsu SWal SWvt WCAu WHil WKif WWEG XLum |
| 'Cotswold Gem' (v) | EBee ECtt EHoe ELan ELon EPfP EShb LSou MAsh MHer NBPC NPer SAga SBfd SBri SEND SLim SWvt |
| 'Dawn Breaker' | ECtt EWes LRHS LSou MAsh NBPC SUsu WCot |
| 'Devon Sunset' | SAga |
| 'Dorothy Elmhirst' | see *E.* 'Mrs L.K. Elmhirst' |
| dwarf, lemon-flowered | WHoo |
| 'Ellen Willmott' | CEnt GBin |
| 'Emm's Variety' | GJos |
| 'Gold Rush' | GJos |
| 'Gold Shot' | GJos |
| 'Golden Gem' | EPfP NBlu |
| 'Golden Jubilee' | ECho ECtt ELon GGar LIMB WFar |
| ***grandiflorum*** | GAuc |
| 'Hector's Gatepost' | CWCL EBee LSRN NBPC SRGP SRkn |
| § ***helveticum*** | CSpr ECho GKev IFro LRHS MMuc SAga SRms XLum |
| - var. ***drenowskyi*** | GKev |
| § ***hieraciifolium*** | GKev |
| 'Jacob's Jacket' | ECha ECtt MBNS MHer NPer |
| 'Jenny Brook'PBR | LRHS WHlf |
| 'Joan Adams' | SAga |
| 'John Codrington' | LHop NPer SAga SUsu WKif |
| 'Joseph's Coat' | LIMB |
| 'Jubilee Gold' | WWEG |
| 'Julian Orchard' | CHll SAga SSth |
| ***kotschyanum*** | CPBP ECho ECtt EPot GEdr LBee LRHS NMen SRms WAbe WPat |
| ***linifolium*** | SRms WFar WGor |
| - 'Little Kiss Lilac' | GJos |
| - 'Rose Apricot' **new** | NLar |
| § - 'Variegatum' (v) | CCCN CSBt CWan EBee ECtt ELan ELon EPfP GBee GGar LRHS NEgg NLar NPer NPri SGar SPer SPoG SRot WPGP XLum |
| - 'Variegatum' peach-flowered (v) | MBNS NLBP |
| 'Moonlight' | ECtt EPot GMaP MHer NBir SRms WHoo |
| § 'Mrs L.K. Elmhirst' | ECtt ELon MMHG NPer WHoo |
| ***mutabile*** | CTri EBee EPfP MAsh MRav SIde SPhx WHal |
| 'My Old Mum' | CWGN EAEE EBee ECtt LRHS LSRN LSou MAsh MBNS MRav MWea |
| 'Orange Flame' | CMea ECha ECho ELon EPot LHop MHer NBlu NPer NWCA SEND WNew WPer |
| 'Parish's' | CCse CElw CSpe MRav SAga WWFP |
| 'Parkwood Gold' | CYeo EDAr GJos |
| 'Pastel Patchwork' | CSpe EBee LRHS LSou NBPC SAga SBfd SUsu SWal |
| Perry's hybrid | NPer |
| 'Perry's Peculiar' | NPer |
| 'Perry's Surprise' | NPer |
| 'Perry's Variegated' (v) | NPer |
| 'Plant World Lemon' | CBar CHGN ELon MTis NLar NPri |
| 'Poppet' | CSpe SAga |
| 'Poppet Heaton' **new** | CHll |
| § ***pulchellum*** | ECha GKev ITim SMrm |
| ***pumilum*** DC. | see *E. helveticum* |
| ***pusillum*** | WAbe |
| 'Roddy's Own' | EDif |
| ***rupestre*** | see *E. pulchellum* |
| 'Ruston Royal' | ECha |
| 'Rysi Bronze' | LHop LSou NLar |
| ***scoparium*** | ECha EDif |
| 'Sissinghurst Variegated' | see *E. linifolium* 'Variegatum' |
| 'Sprite' | CMea CTri EPot MMuc NPer SEND |
| 'Starbright' | CWCL LRHS LSou SPoG SUsu |
| 'Stars and Stripes' (v) | CWGN EBee EPfP LBuc LRHS LSou SBfd SPoG SRkn |
| Sunburst = 'Listrace' **new** | CWGN LSou MTis WHil |
| 'Sweet Sorbet' | CWCL EBee EPfP GMaP MBri MTis NBPC NDov NEgg NLar SPav SRkn SWal SWvt WHil |
| 'Walberton's Fragrant Star' (v) **new** | LRHS SPoG |
| Walberton's Fragrant Sunshine = 'Walfrasun' | CHll EPfP LRHS SBfd SCoo SPoG WWlt |
| 'Wenlock Beauty' | GBin SRms |
| 'Winter Joy' | ELon LLHF LSou MBNS NLar SUsu WCot WHil |
| 'Winter Sorbet' | ELon LBMP MTis MWea NPri |
| ***witmannii*** | SSth |
| 'Yellow Flame' | WPer |

## *Erythraea* see *Centaurium*

## *Erythrina* (*Papilionaceae*)

| | |
|---|---|
| ***abyssinica*** **new** | SPlb |
| ***amazonica*** **new** | SPlb |
| ***arborescens*** | SPlb |
| ***berteroana*** **new** | SPlb |
| × ***bidwillii*** | CCCN WPGP |
| ***crista-galli*** | CBcs CBot CCCN CDTJ CHll CSpe EAmu EBee ELan EPfP ESwi GQui LRHS MOWG MWea SPlb WPGP WPat |
| - 'Compacta' | SMad |
| ***guatemalensis*** **new** | SPlb |
| § ***humeana*** | CDTJ SPlb |
| ***latissima*** | CDTJ SPlb |
| ***lysistemon*** | SPlb |
| ***princeps*** | see *E. humeana* |
| ***smithiana*** **new** | SPlb |
| ***subumbrans*** **new** | SPlb |

## *Erythronium* ✿ (*Liliaceae*)

| | |
|---|---|
| ***albidum*** | CLAP EBee ECho EWTr GGar GKev IBlr LAma LWst MMoz NMen |
| ***americanum*** | CArn CLAP EBee ECho EPot EWTr IBlr LAma LWst MMoz MNrw MSSP NMen |

| | |
|---|---|
| 'Apple Blossom' | ECho LWst |
| 'Beechpark' | IBlr |
| 'Blush' | ECho IBlr LWst |
| 'Bronze Beauty' **new** | IBlr |
| 'Californian Star' | IBlr |
| ***californicum*** ♀H4 | CAby CFir CLAP ECho IBlr LWst SCnR |
| - J&JA 13216 | CLAP |
| - JCA 1.350.200 | LWst |
| - 'Brimstone' | IBlr LWst |
| - 'Bronze Edge' **new** | IBlr |
| - 'Dark Delight' **new** | IBlr |
| - 'Harvington Snowgoose' | CAvo CLAP EBee LLHF LRHS LWst MBri SKHP WCra |
| - Plas Merdyn form | IBlr |
| - 'White Beauty' ♀H4 | Widely available |
| ***californicum* × *hendersonii*** | IBlr |
| ***caucasicum*** | CLAP LWst |
| ***citrinum*** | LLHF MSSP NMen |
| - J&JA 13462 | CLAP LWst |
| ***citrinum* × *hendersonii*** | CAvo IBlr |
| 'Citronella' | CBro CFir CLAP EPot GEdr GKev IBlr LWst MSSP NMen WAbe |
| ***cliftonii*** hort. | see *E. multiscapideum* Cliftonii Group |
| 'Craigton Cream' **new** | LWst |
| 'Craigton Cover Girl' **new** | IBlr |
| 'Delicacy' **new** | IBlr |
| ***dens-canis*** ♀H4 | Widely available |
| - JCA 470.001 | CLAP |
| - from Slovenia | CLAP |
| - 'Charmer' | CMil ECho GEdr LWst MNrw |
| - 'Frans Hals' | CLAP EBee ECho EPot GCra GEdr GGar GKev IPot MNrw SKHP WHal |
| - 'Lilac Wonder' | EBee ECho EPot GEdr GKev GMaP IPot LAma LEdu LWst MAvo MNrw SDeJ |
| * - 'Moerheimii' (d) | CMil EBee ECho EPot GKev IBlr LWst |
| - var. ***niveum*** | IBlr LWst NEgg |
| - 'Old Aberdeen' | CLAP EBee IBlr LWst MNrw |
| - 'Pink Perfection' | EBee ECho EPot GEdr GGar GKev LEdu MNrw SDeJ |
| - 'Purple King' | EBee ECGP ECho EPot GEdr GKev GMaP IPot LAma LWst MMoz MNrw NHol NWad SDeJ |
| - 'Rose Queen' | CAvo CFir CMil EBee ECho EPot GGar GKev GMaP IPot LAma MAvo NMin NWad SDeJ SPhx WHal |
| * - 'Semi-plenum' (d) | IBlr |
| - 'Snowflake' | CAvo CLAP CTca EBee ECha ECho EPot GEdr GGar GKev IPot LAma MMoz MNrw NBir NMen NMin NWad SDeJ SPhx |
| - 'White Splendour' | ECho IBlr LWst MNrw |
| - white-flowered, from Serbia | ECho |
| ***elegans*** | ECho LLHF |
| 'Flash' | IBlr |
| § ***grandiflorum*** | CLAP ECho MSSP NMen |
| - M&PS 007 | CLAP NMen |
| - M&PS 96/024 | NMen |
| - subsp. ***chrysandrum*** | see *E. grandiflorum* |
| ***helenae*** | CLAP ECho IBlr |
| ***hendersonii*** | CLAP ECho EPot GAuc LWst MSSP SKHP WAbe |
| - J&JA 12945 | CLAP |
| ***howellii*** | CLAP |
| - J&JA 13441 | CLAP |
| 'Janice' | LWst |
| ***japonicum*** | CBcs EBee ECho EFEx EPot GEdr LAma MNrw NMen WCru WFar |
| 'Jeanette Brickell' | CLAP IBlr LWst |
| 'Jeannine' | GEdr IBlr LWst |
| 'Joan Wiley' | LWst |
| 'Joanna' | IBlr LWst MNrw NMen |
| 'John Brookes' **new** | LWst |
| 'Keith' **new** | LWst |
| ***klamathense*** | EPot |
| 'Kondo' | CFir CTri EBee ECho EPfP EPot GAbr GEdr GGar GKev GMaP IBlr LAma LEdu LWst NBir NHol NLar NMen NWad SMrm SPer WAbe WCot WHil |
| 'Margaret Mathew' | CLAP IBlr LWst WAbe |
| 'Minnehaha' | LWst |
| 'Miss Jessopp' **new** | LWst |
| ***montanum*** | ECho |
| § ***multiscapideum*** | CLAP ECho WCot |
| - JCA 1.352.100 | LWst |
| - NNS 99-163 | LWst |
| § - Cliftonii Group | CLAP LWst SKHP |
| 'Oregon Encore' | IBlr |
| ***oregonum*** | CLAP EBee ECha ECho EPot GGar IBlr LRHS MNrw MSSP SKHP |
| - subsp. ***leucandrum*** | CLAP LWst |
| - - JCA 4.352.400 | LWst |
| - subsp. ***oregonum*** | WCot |
| I - 'Sulphur Form' | CLAP |
| 'Pagoda' ♀H4 | Widely available |
| ***purdyi*** | see *E. multiscapideum* |
| ***revolutum*** ♀H4 | CAby CBro CLAP CPom EBee ECho EPot GEdr GGar GKev GMaP IBlr LAma LRHS LWst MNrw MSSP NMen SCnR SKHP SRot WCru |
| - from God's Valley | LWst MNrw |
| - 'Dark Dapple' **new** | IBlr |
| - 'Guincho Splendour' | IBlr |
| I - 'Inshriach Form' **new** | IBlr |
| - Johnsonii Group | EBee ECho LWst WCru |
| - 'Kinfauns' | LWst |
| - 'Knightshayes' | CAvo EBee LRHS MBri SKHP SPtl WCra |
| - 'Knightshayes Pink' | CLAP IBlr LWst NBir WShi |
| - 'Pink Beauty' | EBee GKev LWst |
| - Plas Merdyn form | IBlr |
| - 'Rose Beauty' | ECho NMen |
| - 'Wild Salmon' | CLAP LLHF LRHS LWst MBri |
| 'Rippling Waters' | IBlr |
| 'Rosalind' | IBlr LWst SCnR |
| ***sibiricum*** | ECho LWst NMen |
| - subsp. ***altaicum*** | LWst |
| 'Sundisc' | ECha ECho GEdr IBlr LWst MSSP NMen WAbe |
| 'Susannah' | IBlr LWst |
| ***taylorii*** | LWst |
| ***tuolumnense*** ♀H4 | CBro CFir CLAP CTca CWCL EBee ECho EPot GEdr GGar GKev GMaP IBlr LAma MCot MNrw NMen SDeJ |
| - EBA clone 2 | IBlr LWst |
| - EBA clone 3 | IBlr |
| - 'Edgar Klein' | LWst |
| - Plas Merdyn form | IBlr |
| - 'Spindlestone' | GEdr IBlr LRHS LWst |
| ***umbilicatum*** | GKev IBlr LWst MSSP |

## *Escallonia* ✿ (*Escalloniaceae*)

| | |
|---|---|
| 'Alice' | SLPl SPer |
| 'Apple Blossom' ♀H4 | Widely available |

| | |
|---|---|
| § ***bifida*** ♀H3 | CAlb CDoC CDul CHGN EQua LRHS SDix WFar WPat WSFF WSHC |
| 'C.F. Ball' | CBcs CSBt CTri EBee ELan GKin LBMP LBuc LRHS MAsh MMuc MSwo NEgg NPla NWea SEND SGol SRms WDin WFar WMoo |
| 'Compacta Coccinea' | LRHS |
| 'Dart's Rosy Red' | LBMP SLPl WMoo |
| 'Donard Beauty' | NEgg SRms |
| 'Donard Brilliance' | SGol |
| 'Donard Radiance' ♀H4 | CBcs CBod CDoC CDul CMac CSBt CWib ELan EPfP EShb LHop LRHS LSRN NWad NWea SGol SLim SPer SPoG SRms SWvt WDin WFar WMoo |
| 'Donard Red' | GGal |
| 'Donard Seedling' | CBcs CBod CCVT CDoC CDul CHab CSBt ECrN ELan EPfP GKin LAst LBuc LRHS MAsh MGos MSwo NPer NWea SBfd SGol SLPl SLim SPer SRms SWvt WFar WMoo |
| 'Donard Star' | CWib EPfP NLar NWad NWea SLPl WCFE |
| 'Donard White' | SPoG |
| 'Edinensis' | EBee EPfP GGar MGos NLar SLim WDin WFar WMoo |
| 'Everest' | EPfP LAst LBuc LRHS MAsh NEgg SLon SPoG |
| × ***exoniensis*** | SRms |
| 'Gwendolyn Anley' | SLPl WFar |
| 'Hopleys Gold'PBR | see *E. laevis* 'Gold Brian' |
| ***illinita*** | GQui LLHF NLar |
| 'Iveyi' ♀H3 | Widely available |
| 'Jamie'PBR | EShb LSRN STes WMoo |
| § ***laevis*** | LRHS WFar |
| § - 'Gold Brian'PBR | CDul CMHG CMac EHoe ELan EPau EPfP GGar LRHS LSRN MAsh MGos MWat SCoo SGol SPer SWal WFar WHar |
| - 'Gold Ellen' (v) | Widely available |
| 'Langleyensis' ♀H4 | CDoy CHab CMac CTri CWib GGal NWea SGol WDin WFar WHar |
| ***mexicana*** | CBot WFar |
| ***montevidensis*** | see *E. bifida* |
| ***organensis*** | see *E. laevis* |
| 'Peach Blossom' ♀H4 | CAlb CBar CBcs CBod CDoC CDul CWib EBee ELan ELon EPfP GGar GKin LHop LRHS MAsh MLHP MMuc MSwo NBir SBfd SCoo SEND SGol SLPl SLim SPer SPoG SRms WFar |
| 'Pink Elf' | MSwo |
| 'Pink Pyramid' | LRHS |
| 'Pride of Donard' ♀H4 | CBcs CDoC CHab CSBt EBee EPfP GKin LRHS LTen MGos SRms |
| ***punctata*** | see *E. rubra* |
| Red Carpet = 'Loncar'PBR | CSBt ELon LAst NHol SLon WHar |
| 'Red Dream' | CWSG EBee EPfP LBMP LRHS MAsh MBlu MBri MGos MSwo NLar NWad SAga SBfd SCoo SPoG SRms SWvt WFar |
| 'Red Elf' | CMac EBee ELan EPfP GGar GKin LAst LRHS MBri MGos MSCN MWat NEgg SCoo SGar SLPl SPer SPlb SPoG SRms SWvt WFar |
| 'Red Hedger' | CBod CDoC CHab CSBt CTsd CWib ELan GGal MRav SBfd SCoo SRms WMoo |
| 'Red Robin' | GGar SPoG |
| ***resinosa*** | CPLG SArc SPlb SVen WJek |
| ***revoluta*** | CTri |
| § ***rubra*** | MLHP |
| - 'Crimson Spire' ♀H4 | Widely available |
| - 'Ingramii' | CWib MMuc NWea SEND |
| - var. ***macrantha*** | Widely available |
| * - - ***aurea*** | NPla |
| - 'Pygmaea' | see *E. rubra* 'Woodside' |
| § - 'Woodside' | ECho EPfP LLHF MLHP NWad SGol SRms |
| 'Silver Anniversary' | MSwo |
| 'Slieve Donard' | CMac EBee EPfP MRav NEgg NWad NWea SLPl SLim SLon SRms WFar |
| ***tucumanensis*** | SPlb SVen |
| 'Ventnor' **new** | SVen WPGP |
| ***virgata*** | WAle |

## *Eschscholzia* (*Papaveraceae*)

| | |
|---|---|
| ***californica*** ♀H4 | MLLN |
| - 'Gini's Cream' **new** | CSpe |
| - 'Ivory Castle' | SPhx |
| - 'Jersey Cream' | CSpe |
| ***lobbii*** | CSpe |

## *Espeletia* (*Asteraceae*)

| | |
|---|---|
| aff. ***summapacis*** B&SWJ 10766 | WCru |

## *Esterhuysenia* (*Aizoaceae*)

| | |
|---|---|
| ***alpina*** | CPBP |

## *Eucalyptus* ✿ (*Myrtaceae*)

| | |
|---|---|
| ***aggregata*** | SArc |
| ***alpina*** | SPlb |
| ***amygdalina*** | SPlb |
| ***archeri*** | CCVT CDTJ CDoC CDul CTrC ECrN EPfP GQui LRHS MGos MMuc MWhi NLar SBfd SEND |
| ***botryoides*** | GLin |
| § ***bridgesiana*** | CCVT MGos |
| ***caesia*** | SPlb |
| ***camaldulensis*** | SPlb |
| ***camphora*** | CCCN CTho CTsd ESwi |
| ***cinerea*** | GQui SBig SPlb |
| ***citriodora*** | CArn EOHP GQui MHer MNHC SPlb |
| ***coccifera*** | CBcs CCVT CDoC CSBt CTho CTsd ELan EPfP GGar LMaj LRHS LTen MMuc NEgg NPer SBig SEND SPlb WDin WWau |
| ***cordata*** | CCVT CDul WWau |
| ***crenulata*** | CTrC GLin GQui |
| ***crucis*** subsp. ***crucis*** | SPlb |
| ***curtisii*** | SPlb |
| ***cypellocarpa*** | SPlb |
| ***dalrympleana*** ♀H3 | CBcs CDoC CDul CMHG CMac ELan EPfP EWes LRHS LSRN MGos MSwo NLar NPer SBig SEND SLim SPer SPlb SRms WCot WDin WWau |
| ***debeuzevillei*** | see *E. pauciflora* subsp. *debeuzevillei* |
| ***delegatensis*** | CMHG GLin NPer |
| - subsp. ***tasmaniensis*** | GGar |
| ***divaricata*** | see *E. gunnii* subsp. *divaricata* |
| ***erythrocorys*** | SPlb |
| ***eximia*** | SPlb |
| * - 'Nana' | SPlb |
| ***ficifolia*** | CDTJ EShb |
| ***fraxinoides*** | SPlb |

| | | |
|---|---|---|
| | ***gamophylla*** | SPlb |
| | ***glaucescens*** | CBod CMHG CTho CWCL ELan EPfP ETod EWes GQui LRHS SArc SBfd SPer WPtf |
| | ***globulus*** | CArn GGar MNHC SPlb WFar |
| | ***goniocalyx*** | EPfP |
| § | ***gregsoniana*** | CDoC CTho CTrC EPfP GGal SPlb |
| | ***gunnii*** 🏆H3 | Widely available |
| | - Azura = 'Cagire'[PBR] | LRHS LSRN SBfd SLon |
| | - 'Blue Ice' | CTho |
| § | - subsp. ***divaricata*** | CCVT EPfP GQui MBri |
| | ***johnstonii*** | CCVT CDul CTrC NLar SPer WWau |
| | ***kitsoniana*** | CBcs |
| | ***kruseana*** | SPlb |
| | ***kybeanensis*** | GQui |
| | ***lehmannii*** | MOWG |
| | ***leucoxylon*** subsp. ***megalocarpa*** | SPlb |
| | 'Little Boy Blue' | CWib LSRN |
| | ***macrocarpa*** | SPlb |
| * | ***moorei nana*** | CDTJ |
| | ***neglecta*** | GLin |
| | ***nicholii*** | CBcs CCVT CDul EHoe EPfP EWes GQui LRHS MGos NLar SCoo SEND SLim SPoG WCot WWau |
| | ***niphophila*** | see *E. pauciflora* subsp. *niphophila* |
| | ***nitens*** | CDTJ CDul CTsd EGFP SBig SEND SPlb |
| | ***parvifolia*** 🏆H4 | CCCN CCVT CDoC CDul CLnd CMac EPfP LRHS LTen MWhi SCoo SEND |
| | ***pauciflora*** | CCCN CDoC CSBt CTsd ELan MGos MMuc NLar SPer |
| § | - subsp. ***debeuzevillei*** | CDoC EPfP EWes GQui LMaj MGos SArc SBig |
| | - var. ***nana*** | see *E. gregsoniana* |
| § | - subsp. ***niphophila*** 🏆H4 | Widely available |
| | ***perriniana*** | CBcs CCCN CCVT CDul CMHG CSBt CWCL EBee ELan EPfP LRHS MAsh MGos MWhi NEgg SBfd SBig SBrd SCoo SLim SPer SPlb SPoG SWvt WDin WFar WPGP |
| | ***phoenicea*** | MOWG |
| | ***pulverulenta*** | CMac ETod SPlb |
| | - 'Baby Blue' | SPer SPoG SWvt |
| | ***risdonii*** | GGar |
| | ***rodwayi*** | GGar WWau |
| | ***rossii*** | SPlb |
| | ***rubida*** | CCCN CMHG |
| | ***sideroxylon*** | SPlb |
| | - 'Rosea' | SPlb |
| | ***stuartiana*** | see *E. bridgesiana* |
| | ***subcrenulata*** | CTrC EPfP GLin GQui |
| | ***tetraptera*** | SPlb |
| | ***torquata*** | SPlb |
| | ***urnigera*** | CDoC LHop WDin |
| | ***viminalis*** | CArn LRHS MGos WDin WWau |

## *Eucharidium* see *Clarkia*

## *Eucharis* (*Amaryllidaceae*)

| | | |
|---|---|---|
| § | ***amazonica*** 🏆H1 | CCCN ECho EShb LAma LRHS SPav |
| | ***grandiflora*** misapplied | see *E. amazonica* |

## *Eucodonia* (*Gesneriaceae*)

| | |
|---|---|
| 'Adele' | EABi |

## *Eucomis* ✿ (*Asparagaceae*)

| | | |
|---|---|---|
| | sp. | WHil |
| | 'African Bride' | CTca |
| | Aloha = 'Leia' **new** | CTca |
| | ***autumnalis*** misapplied | see *E. zambesiaca* |
| § | ***autumnalis*** (Mill.) Chitt. 🏆H2-3 | CAvo CBro CDes CFFs CHEx CPou CPrp CTsd EBee ECho EPot ERCP GKev LAma LRHS MCCP SPav SPer SPlb SWal WHil WPGP WTin |
| | - subsp. ***amaryllidifolia*** | WPGP |
| | - subsp. ***autumnalis*** | WPGP |
| | - - 'Peace Candles' | CTca |
| | - subsp. ***clavata*** | CTca |
| | ***bicolor*** 🏆H2-3 | Widely available |
| | - 'Alba' | CAvo CPLG CTca EAmu EBee ECho EPot LAma WHil |
| | - 'Stars and Stripes' | WCru |
| | 'Cabernet Candles' | CTca |
| § | ***comosa*** | CAvo CBro CFFs CHEx CHll CPrp CSam CTca EBee ERCP EShb GAbr LAma LEdu LRHS SMad SPav WHil WTin WWEG |
| | - 'Cornwood' | CAvo CFFs CTca WHil |
| | - 'First Red' | CDes CPou WPGP |
| | - green-leaved | CTca |
| | - 'Kilimanjaro' | CTca EBee |
| | - 'Lotte' **new** | CTca |
| | - 'Oakhurst' | ECtt LBuc MBri |
| | - purple-leaved | CTca EShb |
| | - 'Sparkling Burgundy' | Widely available |
| | - var. ***striata*** | CAby CDes |
| | 'Frank Lawley' | CDes |
| | ***humilis*** | CTca |
| | - 'Twinkle Stars' | EBee |
| | hybrid | SDix |
| | 'John Treasure' | WHil |
| | 'Joy's Purple' | CBro CPar CTca LRHS |
| | ***montana*** | CBro CPrp CTca EBee LAma WPGP |
| | - hybrids **new** | CTca |
| | ***pallidiflora*** 🏆H4 | CAvo CDes CGHE CHEx LEdu WHil WPGP |
| | ***pole-evansii*** | CBro CDes CFir CPLG CPne CTca CTrC EAEE EAmu EBee ECGP ELan EPri ERCP IGor IVic LAma LHop LRHS MMHG MRav SMrm WCru WPGP WTin WWEG |
| I | - 'Purpurea' | CPLG EBee GCal |
| | ***punctata*** | see *E. comosa* |
| | ***regia*** | CTca WCot |
| * | ***reichenbachii*** | CDTJ WHil |
| | 'Swazi Pride' | CTca |
| | ***undulata*** | see *E. autumnalis* (Mill.) Chitt. |
| | ***vandermerwei*** | CAvo CBro CDes CFwr CTca EBee EPot ERCP LAma LWst SKHP WHil WPGP WTin |
| | - 'Octopus' | CCCN CKno CPLG CPMA CPrp CSpr CTca CWGN EAmu EBee ELan ELon EPfP EShb ESwi LRHS LSou MAvo MGos SBfd SMad SPer SPoG SUsu WCot WHil WWEG |
| § | ***zambesiaca*** | CPrp CTca GCal SPad WCot WHil WWEG |
| | - 'White Dwarf' | ECho EShb SPer |
| | 'Zeal Bronze' | CGHE CMHG CMil CTca ELan EPfP GCal GCra LRHS NSti WHrl WPGP |

## *Eucommia* (*Eucommiaceae*)

| | |
|---|---|
| ***ulmoides*** | CCCN CMCN EBtc EPfP IDee IVic NLar WPGP |

## *Eucrosia* (*Amaryllidaceae*)

| | |
|---|---|
| ***bicolor*** | LAma |

## *Eucryphia* ✿ (*Cunoniaceae*)

| |  |  |
|---|---|---|
| | ***cordifolia*** | CAbP CBcs CDul CGHE CMac CWib GKin MBlu NMun WAle WDin |
| § | ***cordifolia* × *lucida*** | CBcs CCCN ELan GGal MSnd SLdr SPer WDin |
| | ***glutinosa*** 𝕐H4 | CBcs CCCN CDul CHab CTho EPfP GKev GKin LRHS MAsh SPer SSpi WAle WDin WFar |
| | - 'Miniature' | EPfP SChF WPGP |
| | × ***hillieri*** 'Winton' | CMHG GQui |
| | × ***intermedia*** | CMac CPLG CTrC CWSG EBee ELan EPfP GKin LRHS NLar NPal SLdr SRms SSpi WDin WFar |
| | - 'Rostrevor' 𝕐H3 | CBcs CMHG CMac CPLG CPMA CTho EBee ELan EPfP GAbr GBin GGal GQui IVic LRHS LSRN MAsh MBlu MDun MGos NHim NLar SReu SSta WFar WSHC |
| | 'Leatherwood Cream' | GKin |
| | ***lucida*** | CCCN CDoC CTho CTrC CTsd EBee ELan GGar IArd NHim NLar WFar |
| | - 'Ballerina' | CMHG CMac CPMA CTho ELon GKin LRHS MGos SCoo SPoG SSpi SSta WFar WPGP |
| | - 'Dumpling' | CGHE CPLG WPGP |
| | - 'Gilt Edge' (v) | CBcs CTrC CWGN GKin LLHF LRHS MMHG |
| | - 'Pink Cloud' | CBcs CDoC CDul CEnd CGHE CMac CPLG CPMA CTho CTrC EBee ELan EPfP GKin GQui IVic LHop LRHS LSRN MBlu SLdr SLim SMad SPer SSpi SSta SWvt WBor WFar WPGP |
| | - 'Pink Whisper' | see *E. milliganii* subsp. *pubescens* 'Pink Whisper' |
| | - 'Spring Glow' (v) | CTrC CWGN LLHF LRHS MAsh NHim SPoG SSta |
| | ***milliganii*** | CAbP CBcs CDoC CMac CTrC EBee ELan EPfP GGar GQui LHop LRHS MBlu MRav NPal SRms SSpi WPGP |
| § | - subsp. ***pubescens*** 'Pink Whisper' | NHim WPGP |
| | ***moorei*** | CBcs CCCN CMac CPLG GQui MMuc NHim NMun SSpi |
| | × ***nymansensis*** | CWib LSRN SArc SReu SRms SSpi |
| | - 'Nymans Silver' (v) | ELan LLHF LRHS MAsh NHim SPoG SSpi |
| | - 'Nymansay' 𝕐H3 | Widely available |
| | - 'Nymansay Variegated' (v) | CPMA |
| | 'Penwith' misapplied | see *E. cordifolia* × *lucida* |
| | 'Penwith' ambig. | CDoC CTsd GKin GQui MMuc SEND SPer WDin WFar |

## *Eugenia* (*Myrtaceae*)

| |  |  |
|---|---|---|
| | ***uniflora*** | CCCN |

## *Eunomia* see *Aethionema*

## *Euodia* (*Rutaceae*)

| |  |  |
|---|---|---|
| | ***daniellii*** | see *Tetradium daniellii* |
| | ***hupehensis*** | see *Tetradium daniellii* Hupehense Group |

## *Euonymus* ✿ (*Celastraceae*)

| |  |  |
|---|---|---|
| | B&L 12543 | EPla EWes |
| | CC 4522 | CPLG |
| | ***alatus*** 𝕐H4 | Widely available |
| | - B&SWJ 8794 | WCru |
| | - var. ***apterus*** | EPfP SPoG WGrn |
| | - Chicago Fire | see *E. alatus* 'Timber Creek' |
| | - 'Compactus' 𝕐H4 | Widely available |
| § | - 'Fire Ball' | CPMA EPfP |
| | - Little Moses = 'Odom' | NLar |
| * | - 'Macrophyllus' | CPMA EPfP |
| | - 'Rudy Haag' | CPMA EPfP NLar |
| | - 'Select' | see *E. alatus* 'Fire Ball' |
| | - 'Silver Cloud' | CPMA EPfP |
| § | - 'Timber Creek' | CPMA EPfP MBlu NLar WPat |
| | ***americanus*** | EPfP MBlu NLar |
| | - 'Evergreen' | EPfP |
| | - narrow-leaved | EPfP |
| | ***atropurpureus*** | EPfP |
| | 'Benkomoki' | EMil |
| | ***bungeanus*** | EPfP WPat |
| | - 'Dart's Pride' | CPMA EPfP NLar |
| | - 'Fireflame' | CPMA EPfP |
| * | - var. ***mongolicus*** | EPfP |
| | - 'Pendulus' | CPMA EPfP MBlu SCoo |
| | - var. ***semipersistens*** | CPMA |
| | ***carnosus*** | CPMA EPfP |
| | ***chibae*** B&SWJ 11159 | WCru |
| | 'Copper Wire' | EHoe |
| | ***cornutus*** var. ***quinquecornutus*** | CPMA ELan EPfP IDee IGor MBlu MMHG NLar SBrt WPGP WPat |
| | 'Den Haag' | CPMA EPfP NLar |
| | ***echinatus*** | EPfP |
| | - BL&M 306 | EPla |
| | ***europaeus*** | Widely available |
| | - f. ***albus*** | CBot CPMA CTho EPfP EQua NLar |
| | - 'Atropurpureus' | CMCN CTho EPfP |
| | - 'Atrorubens' | CPMA |
| | - 'Aucubifolius' (v) | CMac |
| * | - 'Aureus' | CNat |
| | - 'Brilliant' | CPMA EPfP NLar |
| * | - f. ***bulgaricus*** | EPfP |
| | - 'Chrysophyllus' | EPfP MBlu |
| | - 'Howard' | EPfP |
| | - var. ***intermedius*** | CPMA EPfP MBlu MBri NLar |
| | - 'Miss Pinkie' | CEnd |
| | - 'Red Cascade' 𝕐H4 | Widely available |
| | - 'Scarlet Wonder' | CPMA EPfP |
| | - 'Thornhayes' | CTho EPfP NLar |
| I | - 'Variegatus' | EPfP |
| | ***europeaus*** 'Pumilis' | EPfP |
| | ***farreri*** | see *E. nanus* |
| | ***fimbriatus*** | CPMA EPfP |
| | ***fortunei*** | LEdu NWad |
| | - Blondy = 'Interbolwi'PBR (v) | Widely available |
| | - 'Canadale Gold' (v) | EBee EPfP EPla EQua LRHS MAsh NHol NPri SLon SPoG WDin |
| | - 'Coloratus' | CMac EPfP MBlu MSwo SEND SPer WDin |
| | - 'Dart's Blanket' | CDul ELan EPPr MMuc MRav SEND WDin WFar |
| | - 'Emerald Cushion' | CDul |
| | - 'Emerald Gaiety' (v) 𝕐H4 | Widely available |
| | - 'Emerald 'n' Gold' (v) 𝕐H4 | Widely available |
| | - 'Emerald Surprise' (v) 𝕐H4 | EBee EPfP SRGP |
| | - 'Gold Spot' | see *E. fortunei* 'Sunspot' |
| | - 'Gold Tip' | see *E. fortunei* Golden Prince |
| | - 'Golden Harlequin' (v) | CSBt EGxp LRHS MAsh NWad SPoG |
| § | - 'Golden Pillar' (v) | EHoe EPla WFar |
| § | - Golden Prince (v) | CMac EHoe EPfP EPla MRav MSwo SLim SRms WGor |
| | - Goldy = 'Waldbolwi'PBR | NLar SGol |

| | | |
|---|---|---|
| | - 'Harlequin' (v) | Widely available |
| | - 'Hort's Blaze' | EPPr |
| | - 'Kewensis' | CDoC CMac CWib EPfP GCal GEdr LRHS MWhi SArc SPoG WCru |
| | - 'Minimus' | CDul CTri EPPr EPla NPro WFar XLum |
| * | - 'Minimus Variegatus' (v) | ECho EPPr EShb SPlb |
| § | - var. ***radicans*** | EWld |
| | - 'Sheridan Gold' | CMac CTri EPla MRav NWad SBod |
| | - 'Silver Gem' | see *E. fortunei* 'Variegatus' |
| | - 'Silver Pillar' (v) | EBee EHoe WFar |
| | - 'Silver Queen' (v) | Widely available |
| | - 'Silverstone'[PBR] (v) | EPfP LRHS MGos NPro SPoG |
| | - 'Sunshine' (v) | CAbP ELan EPfP LRHS MAsh SLon SPoG |
| § | - 'Sunspot' (v) | CBcs CMac EBee ELan MGos MMuc MSwo SBrd SEND SLim SRms WDin WFar WHar |
| | - 'Tustin' ♀H4 | EPPr LTen |
| § | - 'Variegatus' (v) | SRms STre WDin |
| | - var. ***vegetus*** | EPla |
| | - 'Wolong Ghost' | CDoC GKin IArd IDee MBlu MGos SGol SKHP WCot |
| | ***frigidus*** | EPfP WPGP |
| | ***grandiflorus*** | CPMA EPfP NLar SCoo SPur WFar |
| | - 'Red Wine' | CPMA CTho EMil EPfP LHop LRHS NLar SKHP WPGP WPat |
| | - f. ***salicifolius*** | CPMA EPfP |
| | ***hamiltonianus*** | CMCN EBtc ECrN EPfP SSpi |
| I | - 'Calocarpus' | CPMA SCoo |
| | - 'Fiesta' | CPMA EPfP NLar |
| | - subsp. ***hians*** | see *E. hamiltonianus* subsp. *sieboldianus* |
| | - 'Indian Summer' | CDul CPMA EBee EPfP LRHS MAsh MBri MMHG NLar SCoo SKHP SPoG SPur SSpi WPGP WPat |
| | - 'Koi Boy' | CPMA MAsh SPur |
| | - 'Miss Pinkie' | CDul CPMA EPfP MAsh MGos NLar SCoo SPur WPat |
| | - 'Pink Delight' | CPMA EPfP |
| | - 'Poort Bulten' | CPMA EPfP NLar |
| | - 'Popcorn' | CPMA EPfP WPat |
| | - 'Rainbow' | CPMA EPfP |
| | - 'Red Chief' | CPMA EPfP NLar |
| | - 'Red Elf' | CPMA EPfP NLar |
| | - 'Rising Sun' | CPMA EPfP MBri NLar |
| § | - subsp. ***sieboldianus*** | CMen CPLG CPMA CTho EPfP GAuc MAsh MRav NPCo SLPl WFar WPat |
| | - - B&SWJ 10941 | WCru |
| | - - 'Calocarpus' | EPfP |
| | - - 'Coral Charm' | CPMA EPfP NLar |
| | - - Semiexsertus Group | EPfP |
| * | - - var. ***yedoensis*** f. ***koehneanus*** | EPfP |
| | - 'Snow' | CPMA EPfP NLar WPat |
| | - 'Winter Glory' | CPMA EPfP MMHG NLar WPat |
| | - var. ***yedoensis*** | see *E. hamiltonianus* subsp. *sieboldianus* |
| | ***japonicus*** | CAlb CBcs CCVT CDoC CDul CMac CTri ECrN EPfP MMuc SArc SBfd SBod SEND SEWo SPer WDin |
| | - 'Albomarginatus' | CAlb CBcs CDul CTri EPfP MMuc SEND SRms |
| | - 'Aureopictus' | see *E. japonicus* 'Aureus' |
| | - 'Aureovariegatus' | see *E. japonicus* 'Ovatus Aureus' |
| § | - 'Aureus' (v) | CBcs CDoC CFee CSBt CWib EBee LAst LTen NPri SCoo SLon SPer WDin WHar |
| | - 'Benkomasaki' | EMil EPfP |
| | - 'Bravo' | CDoC CDul EBee EHoe EPfP IVic LRHS LTen MAsh MGos MWea NLar SBfd SCoo SEWo SLim SPer SPoG SWvt WDin WFar |
| | - 'Chollipo' ♀H4 | ELan EPfP EPla LRHS MAsh MMuc SBfd SEND SPoG |
| | - 'Compactus' | SArc SCoo |
| | - 'Duc d'Anjou' misapplied | see *E. japonicus* 'Viridivariegatus' |
| | - 'Duc d'Anjou' Carrière (v) | CBcs EBee EHoe ELan EPfP EPla EWes MRav SBfd SEND SPoG |
| | - 'Edward King' new | LRHS |
| | - Exstase = 'Goldbolwi'[PBR] (v) | SPoG |
| | - 'Extase' (v) | MAsh WCot |
| | - 'Gold Queen'[PBR] | LRHS |
| | - 'Golden Maiden' | ELan EPfP LRHS MAsh SLim SLon SPoG SWvt |
| | - 'Golden Pillar' | see *E. fortunei* 'Golden Pillar' |
| | - 'Green Rocket' | EPfP EShb LRHS SBfd SGol SPoG |
| | - 'Green Spider' | SPoG |
| | - 'Grey Beauty' | ELon EShb NLar |
| | - 'Hibarimisake' | EPfP |
| | - 'Kathy'[PBR] | EPfP LRHS NLar SPoG SRGP |
| § | - 'Latifolius Albomarginatus' | ELan EPfP MRav MSwo SBfd SPer WDin |
| | - 'Luna' | see *E. japonicus* 'Aureus' |
| | - 'Macrophyllus Albus' | see *E. japonicus* 'Latifolius Albomarginatus' |
| | - 'Maiden's Gold' | CSBt EBee |
| | - 'Marieke' | see *E. japonicus* 'Ovatus Aureus' |
| | - 'Microphyllus' | CDoC MRav SBfd STre WFar |
| § | - 'Microphyllus Albovariegatus' (v) | CBcs CDoC CDul CMac CMea CSBt CTri CWSG ELan EPfP EPla LAst LRHS MGos SBfd SBrd SLim SPoG SRms SWvt WDin WFar |
| § | - 'Microphyllus Aureovariegatus' (v) | CDoC CMea ELan EPfP LRHS MAsh NLar SBfd |
| | - 'Microphyllus Aureus' | see *E. japonicus* 'Microphyllus Pulchellus' |
| § | - 'Microphyllus Pulchellus' (v) | CBcs CDoC CMac CSBt EBee ECrN EPfP EPla LRHS LTen MAsh MGos SBfd SEND SWvt WDin |
| | - 'Microphyllus Variegatus' | see *E. japonicus* 'Microphyllus Albovariegatus' |
| § | - 'Ovatus Aureus' (v) ♀H4 | CAlb CBar CChe CDoC CDul CMac CPLG CSBt CTri CWSG EBee ELon EPfP LAst LRHS MAsh MGos MRav NLar SBfd SEND SGol SLim SPer SPlb SPoG SRms SWvt WDin WFar |
| | - 'Président Gauthier' (v) | CBar CDoC EBee EQua EShb LTen MGos MWea SBfd SCoo SLim SPer SWvt WCFE WDin |
| | - 'Pulchellus Aureovariegatus' | see *E. japonicus* 'Microphyllus Aureovariegatus' |
| I | - 'Pyramidatus' | EPfP |
| | - 'Robustus' | EPfP EPla |
| | - 'Rokujo' new | GEdr |
| | - 'Silver King' | CMac |
| | - 'Silver Krista' (v) | NLar SPoG |
| | - 'Susan' (v) | CDoC EPla EQua EShb MAsh SRGP |
| § | - 'Viridivariegatus' (v) | LRHS |
| | ***kachinensis*** B&SWJ 11668 | WCru |
| | ***kiautschovicus*** | EPfP |
| | - 'Berry Hill' | EPfP NLar |
| | - 'Manhattan' | EPfP NLar |
| | ***latifolius*** | CMCN CPMA EPfP WPat |
| | ***lucidus*** | CHll CPLG CPMA IRar SSpi WFar |
| | ***maackii*** | GKin MMHG |
| | ***macropterus*** | CPMA EPfP |
| | ***maximowiczianus*** | EPfP WPat |

| | | |
|---|---|---|
| | ***morrisonensis*** | EPfP |
| | - B&SWJ 3700 | WCru |
| | ***myrianthus*** | CPMA EPfP EWes MAsh MBlu NLar |
| § | ***nanus*** | CWib EPfP NLar WRHF WThu |
| | - var. ***turkestanicus*** | EBee EPfP GKin LHop LRHS SLon SRms WFar |
| | ***obovatus*** | EPfP NLar |
| | ***occidentalis*** | EPfP |
| | ***oresbius*** | CPMA EPfP |
| | ***oxyphyllus*** | CDul CMCN CPMA CTho EPfP IArd NLar SCoo WCru WDin |
| | - 'Angyo Elegant' (v) | EPfP |
| | - 'Waasland' | CPMA EPfP |
| | ***pauciflorus*** | EPfP |
| | ***phellomanus*** Y$^{H4}$ | CEnd CTho EBee EPfP EWTr GKin IDee LHop LRHS MAsh MBlu MGos MPkF MRav NLar SCoo SEND SKHP WDin WFar WPGP WPat |
| | - 'Silver Surprise' (v) | CPMA EPfP WPat |
| | Pierrolino = 'Heespierrolino'$^{PBR}$ | EGxp LRHS NWad SCoo SPoG |
| § | ***planipes*** Y$^{H4}$ | Widely available |
| | - 'Dart's August Flame' | CPMA EPfP |
| | - 'Gold Ore' | EPfP |
| | - 'Sancho' | CPMA EPfP IArd WPat |
| | ***quelpaertensis*** | EPfP |
| | ***radicans*** | see *E. fortunei* var. *radicans* |
| | 'Rokojō' | LLHF NWCA WPat |
| | 'Rokojō Variegated' (v) | LLHF |
| | ***rongchuensis*** | CPMA EPfP |
| | ***rosmarinifolius*** | see *E. nanus* |
| | ***sachalinensis*** misapplied | see *E. planipes* |
| | ***sacrosanctus*** | CPMA EPfP NLar |
| | ***sanguineus*** | CPMA EPfP NLar SSpi |
| | ***sieboldianus*** | WCru |
| | var. ***sanguineus*** B&SWJ 11140 | |
| | - - B&SWJ 11386 | WCru |
| | ***spraguei*** | CFee EPfP |
| | - CWJ 12446 | WCru |
| | ***theifolius*** GWJ 9377 new | WCru |
| | ***tingens*** | CPMA EPfP MSCN NLar |
| | ***trapococcus*** | EPfP |
| | ***vagans*** | EPfP |
| | - L 551 | EPla |
| | ***verrucosus*** | CPMA EPla MAsh NLar |
| | ***vidalii*** | EPfP |
| | ***yedoensis*** | see *E. hamiltonianus* subsp. *sieboldianus* |

## *Eupatoriadelphus* see *Eupatorium*

## *Eupatorium* ✿ (*Asteraceae*)

| | | |
|---|---|---|
| | B&SWJ 9052 from Guatemala | WCru |
| | ***album*** misapplied | see *Ageratina altissima* |
| | ***album*** L. | NBid SWat |
| | ***altissimum*** | CBot SRms |
| | ***aromaticum*** | see *Ageratina aromatica* |
| | ***atrorubens*** | see *Bartlettina sordida* |
| | ***cannabinum*** | CArn CHab CWan EBee EGHP EHon ELan EShb EWil GGar GPoy IFoB LPBA MBNS MHer MLLN MMuc MNHC MRav NBir NMir NPer SEND SPav SWat WHfH WPer WSFF |
| § | - f. ***albiflorum*** | SPhx |
| | - 'Album' | see *E. cannabinum* f. *albiflorum* |
| | - f. ***cannabinum*** 'Flore Pleno' (d) | Widely available |
| | - - 'Spraypaint' (v) | WSFF |
| | ***capillifolium*** Y$^{H3}$ | EBee ECtt EShb ESwi EWes GBin LEdu LHop LSou MDKP SAga SDix SHar SMad SMrm SPhx SUsu WCot WPGP WSFF WWEG |
| | ***coelestinum*** | see *Conoclinium coelestinum* |
| | ***dubium*** 'Baby Joe' | CWGN |
| | - 'Little Joe' | EBee |
| | ***fistulosum*** f. ***albidum*** 'Bartered Bride' | CKno ECtt EPPr EWes GCal WHil |
| | - - 'Joe White' | WSFF |
| | - - 'Massive White' Y$^{H4}$ | CFir GCal NBir NDov NSti |
| | - 'Berggarten' | EBee GCal |
| | - 'Carin' | WSFF |
| | ***fortunei*** | CArn |
| | - 'Fine Line' (v) | CKno EPPr LSou MHer WCot WPGP WSFF |
| | - 'Pink Elegance' (v) new | LRHS MAsh |
| | - 'Pink Frost' (v) new | NLar |
| | ***glechonophyllum*** | see *Ageratina glechonophylla* |
| | ***hyssopifolium*** | LRHS |
| | ***japonicum*** | GPoy |
| | ***ligustrinum*** | see *Ageratina ligustrina* |
| | ***lindleyanum*** | CKno |
| | ***maculatum*** | MDKP NGdn NLar NPnk SEND WHrl |
| | - Atropurpureum Group Y$^{H4}$ | Widely available |
| | - - 'Ankum's August' | NDov |
| | - - 'Gateway' | CRow EBee GCal MBri NBPC NBre NCGa NLar SPhx WHil WHoo WPtf WSFF WTin |
| | - - 'Glutball' | CHVG CKno EBee ELon GCal LBMP LPla MNrw NChi SMad |
| | - - 'Little Red' | WSFF |
| | - - 'Orchard Dene' Y$^{H4}$ | SPur |
| | - - 'Phantom'$^{PBR}$ | EBee ECtt GQue IPot LRHS MAsh MBri NCGa NLar SPoG SSvw |
| | - - 'Purple Bush' Y$^{H4}$ | CKno CSam EBee ECha ECtt ELon EPPr GCal GGar GQue LRHS MDKP NBre NCGa NDov NEgg SPhx SSvw WCAu WSFF WWEG |
| | - - 'Riesenschirm' Y$^{H4}$ | Widely available |
| | ***makinoi*** | WCru |
| | var. ***oppositifolium*** B&SWJ 8449 | |
| | ***micranthum*** | see *Ageratina ligustrina* |
| | ***occidentale*** | see *Ageratina occidentalis* |
| | ***perfoliatum*** | CArn CKno EBee GPoy LRHS MNrw NBre NLar SPav SPhx |
| | ***purpureum*** | Widely available |
| | - 'Album' | CTri MLLN SPhx |
| | ***rugosum*** | see *Ageratina altissima* |
| | - ***album*** | see *Ageratina altissima* |
| | ***variabile*** 'Golders Green' (v) | EWes WWEG |
| | ***weinmannianum*** | see *Ageratina ligustrina* |

## *Euphorbia* ✿ (*Euphorbiaceae*)

| | | |
|---|---|---|
| | 'Abbey Dore' | MAvo WCot |
| | ***ambovombensis*** | LToo |
| | ***amygdaloides*** | EBla ECtt SWat SWvt |
| | - 'Bob's Choice' | EWes |
| | - 'Craigieburn' | CDes EBla EWes GCal GCra LRHS MAsh MGos MRav NDov SUsu WPGP WWEG |
| § | - 'Purpurea' | Widely available |
| § | - var. ***robbiae*** Y$^{H4}$ | Widely available |
| | - - dwarf | EWes |
| | - - 'Pom Pom' | EBee ELon LSou WPGP |
| | - - 'Redbud' | EBee EPla EWes LSou SLPl |

| | |
|---|---|
| - 'Rubra' | see *E. amygdaloides* 'Purpurea' |
| - 'Winter Glow' | CSpe |
| - yellow-leaved | WCot |
| ***baselicis*** | CPom EBee WPer |
| ***biglandulosa*** Desf. | see *E. rigida* |
| Blackbird = 'Nothowlee'PBR | Widely available |
| 'Blue Dome' | CSpe |
| 'Blue Haze' | CDes CPom MAvo NWit WCot WPGP |
| Breathless Blush = 'Balbreblus' **new** | NPri |
| ***bupleurifolia*** | LToo |
| ***caerulescens*** **new** | LToo |
| ***canariensis*** | EPfP |
| ***capitulata*** | EWes |
| ***cashmeriana*** | NWit |
| - CC&McK 607 | EWes |
| - CC&McK 724 | GBin |
| ***ceratocarpa*** | CGHE CSpe EBee ECtt EWes GMaP LPla LRHS LSou MAvo NCGa NEgg NWit SEND SMad WCot WPGP WSHC |
| ***characias*** | CBcs CBot CHEx CMac EBee EBla ECtt EPfP LRHS MCot MLHP MRav NPer NVic SBfd SMrm SPer SRms SWvt WBrk WCot WMnd WPer WWEG XLum XSen |
| - 'Black Pearl' | CBcs CTca CWCL EBee ECtt EPfP LAst LRHS LSou MAvo MGos MNHC NBPC NEgg NPnk SBfd SMrm SPer SPoG SPtl SWvt WFar WWEG |
| - 'Blue Wonder' | CAby CMac CPLG EBee ECtt ELan EPfP GAbr GMaP LRHS LSou MAvo MCot MGos MTis NCGa NEgg NGdn NLar NSti NWit SPad WCot WHoo WWEG |
| - subsp. ***characias*** | GMaP SEND |
| - - 'Blue Hills' | ECtt WWEG |
| - - 'Burrow Silver' (v) | CFir EBee LSRN MRav NEgg SMrm SPer SWvt WFar |
| - - 'Humpty Dumpty' | CBar CPLG CSev EBee ECtt ELan ELon EPfP GMaP LRHS LSRN MCCP MGos NDov NGdn NLar NPer NPri SBfd SMrm SPer SRms SWvt WAul WCot WFar WWEG |
| - 'Dwarf Black Pearl' | ECtt WWEG |
| - 'Forescate' | CSev CTca EBee EPfP LHop LRHS LSRN NBPC SBfd WWEG |
| - 'Glacier Blue' **new** | LRHS |
| - 'Goldbrook' | EBla ECtt EHoe LRHS MRav NCGa NGdn |
| - 'Kestrel' (v) | WCot |
| - 'Portuguese Velvet' ♀H4 | Widely available |
| - Silver Swan = 'Wilcott'PBR (v) | Widely available |
| - 'Spring Splendour' | EWes |
| - 'Starbright' | EBee GBin |
| - 'Tasmanian Tiger'PBR (v) | CMac CSpe CWGN EWes LRHS LSou NBir NCGa NWit SBfd SKHP SPoG SRkn SWvt WCot |
| - 'Variegata' (v) | MAvo |
| - subsp. ***wulfenii*** ♀H3-4 | Widely available |
| - - 'Bosahan' (v) | CBcs CPLG |
| - - 'Emmer Green' (v) | CPLG EBee ELon EPfP EWTr EWes GAbr GCal GMaP LRHS MLLN MMHG MTis NPnk NSti NWit SMrm WCot WFoF WWEG |
| - - 'Jimmy Platt' | SRms WCot |
| § - - 'John Tomlinson' ♀H3-4 | EWes GBin LSRN MRav SUsu |

| | |
|---|---|
| - - Kew form | see *E. characias* subsp. *wulfenii* 'John Tomlinson' |
| - - 'Lambrook Gold' ♀H3-4 | CSam CWCL EPfP GCra GMaP MRav MWat NLar NPer SMad WCot WFar WMnd WWEG |
| - - 'Lambrook Gold' seed-raised | see *E. characias* subsp. *wulfenii* Margery Fish Group |
| - - 'Lambrook Yellow' | EBee GCal |
| § - - Margery Fish Group | CMac CSev EBee LRHS NBir NCGa SPer |
| - - 'Minuet' | ECtt |
| - - 'Perry's Tangerine' | EWes NPer NWit |
| § - - 'Purple and Gold' | EWes GMaP MAvo NLar NWit SWvt WWEG |
| - - 'Purpurea' | see *E. characias* subsp. *wulfenii* 'Purple and Gold' |
| - - 'Thelma's Giant' | MAvo NWit |
| - - 'Westacre Giant' **new** | EWes |
| ***clavarioides*** var. ***truncata*** | WCot |
| 'Copton Ash' | CSpe EBee EPPr EWes MAvo SKHP XSen |
| ***corallioides*** | EBee ECha IFro LRHS NPer NSti SPav WHer |
| § ***cornigera*** ♀H4 | ECha EPfP GBin GMac LRHS MAvo MCot MMuc MRav MSpe NBid NGdn NSti NWit SEND SPhx SWat WCru WPGP |
| - 'Goldener Turm' | EAEE EBee ECGP ECtt GBin GCal LSou MBNS MNrw NDov NWit SPer WCot WCra |
| ***corollata*** | EBee |
| ***croizatii*** | LToo |
| ***cylindrifolia*** var. ***tubifera*** | LToo |
| ***cyparissias*** | CBcs EBee ECha ELan LRHS MLHP MRav NBir NGdn NLar NMen SBfd SPav SRms WBrk WFar WFoF WPer XLum XSen |
| - 'Baby' | WFar |
| - 'Betten' | see *E.* × *gayeri* 'Betten' |
| - 'Clarice Howard' | see *E. cyparissias* 'Fens Ruby' |
| § - 'Fens Ruby' | Widely available |
| - 'Orange Man' | CTca EBee EBla ECtt EPfP EPla EWes GBin LRHS LSou NBro NEgg NGdn NLar SPoG SWat SWvt WBrk WFar WOut WWEG |
| - 'Purpurea' | see *E. cyparissias* 'Fens Ruby' |
| - 'Red Devil' | NWit SMrm WWEG |
| - 'Tall Boy' | EWes |
| ***decaryi*** var. ***cap-saintemariensis*** | LToo |
| - var. ***spirosticha*** | LToo |
| ***deflexa*** | EBee EWes MAvo |
| ***dendroides*** | WCot |
| § ***donii*** | EBee EWes MAvo NDov NWit SDix WCot |
| - HWJK 2405 | WCru |
| - 'Amjillasa' | SAga SDix |
| ***dulcis*** | CBre ECtt NBro NWit |
| - 'Chameleon' | Widely available |
| 'Efanthia'PBR | CEnd CPrp CSev EBee EPfP EWes LHop LRHS LSou NLar NPri SMrm SRot STes |
| ***enopla*** | EPfP |
| ***enormis*** **new** | LToo |
| ***epithymoides*** | see *E. polychroma* |
| ***esculenta*** | LToo |
| ***esula*** Baker's form | NWit |
| Excalibur = 'Froeup'PBR ♀H4 | CMac CPLG CWCL EBee ELan ELon EPPr GBin LHop LRHS MBNS MBri |

| | |
|---|---|
| | MCCP MMuc MRav NBir NEgg NSti SBfd SEND SPer SPoG WFar |
| ***flavicoma*** | GCal |
| ***fragifera*** | EBee NWit SUsu |
| 'Garblesham Enchanter' | EPPr |
| § × ***gayeri*** 'Betten' | EBee LPla |
| ***glauca*** | CFir ECou MAvo NWit SKHP |
| 'Golden Foam' | see *E. stricta* |
| ***griffithii*** | CAby CHll GGal IFoB NBro SPav SWat WFar WMoo |
| - 'Dixter' ♀H4 | Widely available |
| - 'Dixter Flame' | IFoB NWit |
| - 'Fern Cottage' | CElw CWCL EBee EWes MSpe WMnd WWEG |
| - 'Fireglow' | Widely available |
| - 'King's Caple' | EBee ELon EWes GBin SPoG WCru |
| - 'Wickstead' | COlW EBee GAbr GBin MLHP NLar |
| ***groenewaldii*** **new** | LToo |
| 'Helena'PBR (v) | CHVG CPLG EBee EPPr EPfP LHop LSRN MAsh NLar NPnk NPri SHeu SRot SWvt WHil WWEG |
| ***horrida*** ♀H1 | SPlb |
| ***hyberna*** | NMen SWat |
| ***hypericifolia*** | CCVN CSpe EPfP ESwi LHop LSou |
| Diamond Frost = 'Inneuphe'PBR | MWea SRkn WCot |
| ***jacquemontii*** | EBee IFoB MRav NChi NDov NLar NWit |
| 'Jade Dragon' | SBfd SWvt WWEG |
| 'Jessie' | MAvo NCGa |
| Kalipso = 'Innkalff' | EPfP NLar SHeu SRot |
| ***knobelii*** **new** | LToo |
| ***knuthii*** | LToo |
| 'Lambrook Silver' | SRkn |
| ***lathyris*** | CArn CBre CTca LRHS MHer MLHP NLar NPer NWit SRms SVic |
| ***longifolia*** misapplied | see *E. cornigera* |
| ***longifolia*** D. Don | see *E. donii* |
| ***longifolia*** Lam. | see *E. mellifera* |
| ***margalidiana*** | EWes MAvo NWit |
| × ***martini*** ♀H3 | Widely available |
| - 'Aperitif'PBR | EPfP |
| - 'Ascot Rainbow' **new** | LBuc LRHS MBri |
| - 'Baby Charm' | CWCL EAEE EBee EPPr GBBs GKin IPot LRHS LSRN MAvo NDov NGdn SMrm WCot |
| - 'Cherokee' | WCot |
| - dwarf | CFir CSpr |
| - 'Helen Robinson' | MAvo WCot WPGP |
| - Helena's Blush = 'Inneuphhel' (v) | EPfP MAvo |
| - 'Kolibri' | EBee EPfP LSou NLar SPoG SWvt |
| - 'Little John' **new** | LBuc LRHS |
| - Rudolph = 'Waleuphrud' | LBuc LRHS |
| - 'Tiny Tim' | EPPr EPfP LRHS LSRN MAsh SBfd SPoG SWvt |
| - 'Walberton's Rudolf' | SPoG |
| § ***mellifera*** ♀H3 | Widely available |
| ***milii*** ♀H1 | EBak |
| ***moratii*** | LToo |
| ***myrsinites*** ♀H4 | Widely available |
| ***nereidum*** | EWes NWit |
| ***nicaeensis*** | CPom GCal LRHS MSpe SEND SPer WPGP WSHC XSen |
| - subsp. ***glareosa*** | NWit |
| ***oblongata*** | EWes LRHS NWit SEND |
| ***palustris*** ♀H4 | Widely available |
| - 'Walenburg's Glorie' | CMHG CWCL EBee EBla ECha ELan GBin GQue MBri MNrw MRav NMRc NSti NWit SMad SWat WKif |
| - 'Zauberflöte' | SRms WFar |
| × ***paradoxa*** | NWit |
| ***paralias*** | WCot WHer |
| × ***pasteurii*** | CDTJ CFir EWes LSou MAvo MSpe NBir NWit SDix SMad SPhx WPGP |
| - 'Devil's Honey' | CHid WCot |
| - 'John Phillips' | CGHE CMHG CPLG CPom EPfP LRHS SBfd SChF WPGP |
| - 'Phrampton Phatty' **new** | WPGP |
| ***pekinensis*** | SKHP |
| ***pentagona*** **new** | SVen |
| ***perangusta*** **new** | LToo |
| ***persistens*** **new** | LToo |
| ***pilosa*** 'Major' | see *E. polychroma* 'Major' |
| ***piscatoria*** | WPGP |
| ***pithyusa*** | CBot CSpe EBee ECha ELan EPfP MAvo MRav SEND WCot |
| ***platyclada*** | LToo |
| § ***polychroma*** ♀H4 | Widely available |
| - 'Bonfire' | ECtt LRHS NCGa NDov NLar |
| § - 'Candy' | CBot EBee ECha ECtt ELan EPfP WFar WMnd |
| - compact | NWit |
| - 'Emerald Jade' | WPGP |
| - 'First Blush' (v) | CWGN EWes NBre NWit |
| - 'Golden Fusion' | LBuc LRHS MAsh MAvo WFar |
| § - 'Lacy' (v) | CDoC EBee ECtt EWes GCal LAst LRHS MCCP MRav NBir NGdn NWit SKHP WFar |
| § - 'Major' ♀H4 | CPLG LRHS SAga WCot WKif |
| - 'Midas' | CWCL GBin NWit SDix SMrm |
| - 'Purpurea' | see *E. polychroma* 'Candy' |
| * - 'Senior' | LRHS NWit |
| - 'Sonnengold' | EWes LRHS |
| - 'Variegata' | see *E. polychroma* 'Lacy' |
| ***portlandica*** | NWit SVen WHer |
| § × ***pseudovirgata*** | NWit |
| ***pulvinata*** **new** | LToo |
| 'Purple Preference' | EPPr |
| 'Red Flush' **new** | LRHS |
| Redwing = 'Charam'PBR ♀H4 | CBcs CMac EBee ELan EPfP IKil LBuc LRHS LSou MAsh MBri MGos MRav MWea NDov NLar NWit SCoo SLim SPer SPoG SRkn SWvt |
| ***reflexa*** | see *E. seguieriana* subsp. *niciciana* |
| § ***rigida*** ♀H4 | CAby CBot CBro CDes EBee EHoe ELan EPfP EPyc EWes MAvo MSpe NSti SPhx WFar WPGP WWEG XSen |
| - 'Sardis' | NWit |
| ***robbiae*** | see *E. amygdaloides* var. *robbiae* |
| ***rothiana*** GWJ 9479a | WCru |
| 'Roundway Titan' | SSpi WSHC |
| ***sarawschanica*** | ECha GBBs GBin GQue LPla LRHS NWit SMad SPhx |
| ***schillingii*** ♀H4 | CAbb CSam EBee EHoe ELan EPfP GCra GMaP LHop LRHS MRav MSCN SBod SBrd SDix SMrm SPer SPhx SPoG SUsu SWvt WCru WFar WHoo WPGP WWEG |
| ***seguieriana*** | ECha NLar WPer |
| § - subsp. ***niciciana*** | CBot GBin WHoo |
| ***serrulata*** Thuill. | see *E. stricta* |
| ***sikkimensis*** ♀H4 | CBot CMHG CPLG CPom CSam CWCL ECha ELan GCal GKev LRHS MAvo NEgg NLar NPer SRms WCot WCru WFar WHoo |
| - 'Crûg Contrast' | WCru |
| ***soongarica*** | NWit |
| ***spinosa*** | NWit SPlb |
| ***stellispina*** **new** | LToo |

| | | |
|---|---|---|
| § | ***stricta*** | LRHS WTin |
| | ***stygiana*** | CFir CMil CPLG CSam CSpe CWCL ELon EShb EWes GBin GCal MAvo MTis SAga SMrm SPlb WCot WCru WPGP |
| | - subsp. ***stygiana*** new | CGHE |
| | ***symmetrica*** | LToo |
| | Thalia = 'Innthal' | EPfP LTen |
| | ***tirucalli*** | EShb |
| | ***tortirama*** | LToo |
| | ***triangularis*** | SPlb |
| | ***umfoloziensis*** | LToo |
| | ***urulensis*** | see *E.* × *pseudovirgata* |
| | ***valdevillosocarpa*** | CPom CTca SPhx WCot WPer |
| | 'Velvet Ruby' | CSev CSpe EWes LSRN LSou MAvo NWit SPoG SWvt WCot |
| | ***verrucosa*** | WFar |
| | ***viguieri*** ♀H1 | LToo |
| | ***villosa*** Waldst. & Kit. ex Willd. | NWit |
| § | ***virgata*** | EWes NWit SPav |
| | × ***waldsteinii*** | see *E. virgata* |
| | ***wallichii*** misapplied | see *E. donii* |
| | ***wallichii*** Kohli | see *E. cornigera* |
| | ***wallichii*** ambig. | CSam NPnk |
| | ***wallichii*** Hook. f. | CPLG EBee EPfP GCal NOrc SKHP WPGP |
| | - 'Lemon and Lime' | CWib LSou WFar |
| | 'Whistleberry Garnet' | CWCL EBee EPfP LLHF LRHS LSou MWea NGdn NSti NWit SDix SKHP SPoG |

## *Euptelea* (*Eupteleaceae*)

| | | |
|---|---|---|
| | ***franchetii*** | see *E. pleiosperma* |
| § | ***pleiosperma*** | IDee NLar SSpi |
| | ***polyandra*** | EPfP NLar |

## *Eurya* (*Pentaphylacaceae*)

| | |
|---|---|
| ***japonica*** | WPGP |
| - 'Variegata' misapplied | see *Cleyera japonica* 'Fortunei' |

## *Euryops* (*Asteraceae*)

| | | |
|---|---|---|
| | ***abrotanifolius*** | CCCN SVen |
| § | ***acraeus*** ♀H4 | CMea CSBt ECho EPfP EPot EWes GEdr LRHS MAsh MWat NMen NWCA SAga WAbe WFar |
| § | ***chrysanthemoides*** | CCCN CHEx CTrC EShb MREP SEND SVen |
| | - 'Sonnenschein' | SPet |
| | ***evansii*** | see *E. acraeus* |
| | ***lateriflorus*** | SPlb |
| | ***linearis*** | SEND |
| | ***pectinatus*** ♀H2 | CBcs CBod CCCN CDTJ CDoC CHEx CPLG CSam CTca CTrC CTri EBee EPfP EShb GBin GGal GGar IVic LAst LRHS MNrw MOWG MRav NPri SEND SVen SWvt WCFE WHer |
| | ***tysonii*** | CTca CTrC EBee EWes GCal GEdr SPlb SVen WCot |
| | ***virgineus*** | CCCN CHVG CPLG CTrC GGar SVen |

## *Eustachys* (*Poaceae*)

| | | |
|---|---|---|
| § | ***distichophylla*** | NWsh WTcb |

## *Eustrephus* (*Philesiaceae*)

| | |
|---|---|
| ***latifolius*** | ECou |

## *Eutaxia* (*Papilionaceae*)

| | |
|---|---|
| ***obovata*** | ECou |

## *Euterpe* (*Arecaceae*)

| | |
|---|---|
| ***edulis*** | EAmu |

## *Euthamia* (*Asteraceae*)

| | |
|---|---|
| ***gymnospermoides*** | EWes |

## *Eutrochium* see *Eupatorium*

## *Ewartia* (*Asteraceae*)

| | |
|---|---|
| ***planchonii*** | NSla WAbe |

## *Exochorda* (*Rosaceae*)

| | | |
|---|---|---|
| | ***alberti*** | see *E. korolkowii* |
| | ***giraldii*** var. ***wilsonii*** | CMac CPLG EBee EPfP GBin LHop LRHS MBlu NLar SLim SSta SWvt |
| § | ***korolkowii*** | LRHS MAsh NLar |
| | × ***macrantha*** | EBee LRHS |
| | - 'Irish Pearl' | CPLG |
| | - 'The Bride' ♀H4 | Widely available |
| | ***racemosa*** | EPfP MMuc NLar SPer WDin |
| | ***serratifolia*** | CBcs EPfP EWTr GAuc LRHS |
| | - 'Snow White' | CMHG CPMA EBee EWes GKin IArd LRHS MBlu NLar SBfd SLon |

# F

## *Fabiana* (*Solanaceae*)

| | |
|---|---|
| ***imbricata*** | CAbP ELon EPfP LLHF LRHS SAga SLon SPer SPlb |
| - 'Prostrata' | EBee EPfP LRHS SSpi |
| - f. ***violacea*** ♀H3 | CSBt CTri EBee EPfP LLHF LRHS MMuc SEND SPer WKif |
| ***nana*** | WAbe |

## *Fagopyrum* (*Polygonaceae*)

| | | |
|---|---|---|
| | ***cymosum*** | see *F. dibotrys* |
| § | ***dibotrys*** | CArn EBee ECha ELan EWld LEdu |

## *Fagus* ✿ (*Fagaceae*)

| | | |
|---|---|---|
| § | ***crenata*** | CMen WDin |
| | - 'Mount Fuji' | CMen SBir |
| | ***engleriana*** | CMCN SBir |
| | ***grandifolia*** | SBir |
| | subsp. ***mexicana*** | |
| | ***japonica*** | SBir |
| | - var. ***multinervis*** | SBir |
| | ***orientalis*** | CMCN SBir |
| | - 'Iskander' | MBlu |
| | ***sieboldii*** | see *F. crenata* |
| | ***sylvatica*** ♀H4 | Widely available |
| § | - 'Albomarginata' (v) | CMCN |
| | - 'Albovariegata' | see *F. sylvatica* 'Albomarginata' |
| | - 'Ansorgei' | CEnd MBlu NLar |
| | - 'Arcuata' | SBir |
| N | - Atropurpurea Group | Widely available |
| | - - 'Swat Magret' | CAlb CDul |
| | - 'Aurea Pendula' | CEnd CMCN ECrN MBlu SBir |
| | - 'Bicolor Sartini' | MBlu |
| | - 'Birr Zebra' | CEnd |
| | - 'Black Swan' | CDul CMCN CPMA ECrN IArd MAsh MBlu MGos NEgg NLar NPCo SBir SLon |
| | - 'Cochleata' | CMCN |
| | - 'Cockleshell' | MBlu MBri SBir |
| | - 'Comptoniifolia' | see *F. sylvatica* var. *heterophylla* 'Comptoniifolia' |

| | | |
|---|---|---|
| | - 'Cristata' | MBlu |
| N | - Cuprea Group | NWea |
| § | - 'Dawyck' ♀H4 | CBcs CDoC CDul CLnd CMCN CMac CSBt CTho EBee ECrN ELan EPfP LAst LMaj MAsh MBri MGos NEgg NLar NPCo NWea SBir SGol SLau SLim SPer WDin |
| | - 'Dawyck Gold' ♀H4 | CAlb CBcs CDoC CDul CEnd CLnd CMCN CMac CTho CTri EBee GKin IVic LMaj MAsh MBlu MBri MGos MSwo NEgg NPCo NWea SBir SGol SLau SLim SPer WDin WFar |
| | - 'Dawyck Purple' ♀H4 | Widely available |
| | - 'Eugen' | SBir |
| | - 'Fastigiata' misapplied | see *F. sylvatica* 'Dawyck' |
| | - 'Felderbach' | MBlu SBir |
| | - 'Franken' (v) | MBlu SBir |
| | - 'Greenwood' | MBlu |
| | - var. ***heterophylla*** | CLnd CSBt CTho NWea |
| | - - 'Aspleniifolia' ♀H4 | CAlb CBcs CDoC CDul CEnd CMCN CMac EBee ECrN ELan EPfP EWTr GKin LRHS MAsh MBlu MBri MGos NPCo SBir SCoo SLau SPer SPoG WDin WFar WMou |
| § | - - 'Comptoniifolia' | SBir |
| | - - f. ***laciniata*** | MBlu |
| | - 'Horizontalis' | MBlu |
| | - 'Incisa' | MBlu |
| | - 'Luteovariegata' (v) | CEnd CMCN CPMA |
| | - 'Mercedes' | CDoC CMCN MBlu NPCo WPat |
| N | - 'Pendula' ♀H4 | CAlb CBcs CDoC CDul CEnd CMCN CSBt CTho EBee ECrN ELan EPfP LMaj MGos MSwo NEgg NPCo NWea SGol SLau SPer WDin WHar WMou |
| | - 'Prince George of Crete' | CDul CMCN SBir |
| | - 'Purple Fountain' ♀H4 | CDoC CDul CEnd CMCN CPMA EBee ELan LAst LHop LTen MAsh MBlu MBri MGos NLar SBir SLau SLim WFar WPat |
| | - Purple-leaved Group | see *F. sylvatica* Atropurpurea Group |
| | - 'Purpurea Latifolia' | LMaj |
| | - 'Purpurea Pendula' | Widely available |
| § | - 'Purpurea Tricolor' (v) | CDul CEnd CMCN CPMA ECrN MAsh MBlu MGos NWea SBir SCoo WDin |
| | - 'Quercifolia' | MBlu |
| I | - 'Quercina' | SBir |
| | - 'Red Obelisk' | see *F. sylvatica* 'Rohan Obelisk' |
| | - 'Riversii' ♀H4 | CBcs CDoC CDul CEnd CLnd CMCN CSBt CTho CTri CWib EBee ECrN ELan EPfP GKin LAst LRHS MAsh MBri MGos NEgg NWea SLim SPer SPoG WDin WFar WHar |
| | - 'Rohan Gold' | CDul CEnd CMCN EBee MBlu |
| § | - 'Rohan Obelisk' | CDul CEnd CMCN CTho EBee ELan EWTr IArd MBlu NLar SBir |
| | - 'Rohan Pyramidalis' | CEnd |
| | - 'Rohan Trompenburg' | CMCN MBlu |
| | - 'Rohan Weeping' | MBlu SBir |
| | - 'Rohanii' | CBcs CDoC CDul CEnd CLnd CMCN CTri EBee ELan EPfP GKin LHop MGos NPCo SBir SLau SPer WDin WFar WHar WMou |
| | - 'Roseomarginata' | see *F. sylvatica* 'Purpurea Tricolor' |
| | - 'Rotundifolia' | CDoC CDul MBlu SBir |
| | - 'Spaethiana' | EWTr GKin |
| | - 'Striata' | LLHF NPCo SBir |
| | - 'Sychrov' | SBir |
| | - 'Tortuosa Purpurea' | CDul MBlu |
| | - 'Tricolor' misapplied | see *F. sylvatica* 'Purpurea Tricolor' |
| | - 'Tricolor' ambig. (v) | SLau WFoF |
| | - 'Tricolor' (v) | CBcs CLnd CMac CSBt CWib EBee ELan NEgg WDin |
| | - 'Viridivariegata' (v) | CMCN |
| | - 'Zlatia' | CBcs CDul CLnd CMCN CSBt CWib ELan EPfP MBlu MGos MSwo NWea SBir SGol SLau SPer WDin WMou |
| | × ***taurica*** | SBir |

## *Fallopia* (*Polygonaceae*)

| | | |
|---|---|---|
| | ***aubertii*** | see *F. baldschuanica* |
| § | ***baldschuanica*** | Widely available |
| | - Summer Sunshine = 'Acofal'PBR | CBcs ELan |
| | × ***bohemica*** 'Spectabilis' (v) | CRow |
| § | ***japonica*** var. ***compacta*** | CRow NLar WFar WMoo |
| | - - 'Fuji Snow' | see *F. japonica* var. *compacta* 'Milk Boy' |
| § | - - 'Milk Boy' (v) | EShb LRHS NGBo |
| | - - f. ***rosea*** hort. | LRHS |
| | - - 'Variegata' misapplied | see *F. japonica* var. *compacta* 'Milk Boy' |
| | - 'Crimson Beauty' | CRow |
| § | ***multiflora*** | CArn EOHP |
| | - var. ***hypoleuca*** | MCCP SCoo SLim SPoG |
| | - - B&SWJ 120 | EBee WCru |
| | ***sachalinensis*** | NLar |

## *Farfugium* (*Asteraceae*)

| | | |
|---|---|---|
| § | ***japonicum*** | CHEx LRHS |
| | - B&SWJ 884 | WCru |
| | - 'Argenteum' (v) | CFir SMad WCot WFar |
| § | - 'Aureomaculatum' (v) ♀H1 | CFir CHEx CHII LEdu LRHS MCCP WFar |
| | - 'Bumpy Ride' **new** | WCot |
| | - 'Crispatum' | CAbP CFir ECtt ELan EPfP LAst LEdu MCCP NSti SMad WCot WFar WWEG |
| | - double-flowered (d) | WCru |
| | - var. ***formosanum*** B&SWJ 7125 | WCru |
| | - - CWJ 12356 | WCru |
| | - var. ***giganteum*** | CHEx |
| | - 'Kagami-jishi' (v) | WCot |
| | - 'Kaimon Dake' | WCot |
| I | - 'Nanum' | CHEx |
| | - 'Ryuto' | WCot |
| I | - 'Tsuwa-buki' | WCot |
| | ***tussilagineum*** | see *F. japonicum* |

## *Fargesia* (*Poaceae*)

| | | |
|---|---|---|
| | from Jiuzhaigou, China | CDTJ CEnt EPfP EPla ETod GBin MBri MMoz MMuc MWht NLar NWsh SBig WDyG WJun WPGP |
| | ***adpressa*** | EPla WJun |
| | ***angustissima*** | CDTJ CEnt ENBC MMuc MWht SBig WJun |
| | ***confusa*** | CDTJ |
| | ***denudata*** | CDTJ CEnt ENBC EPla SBig WJun |
| | - L 1575 | EPla MMoz MWht WPGP |
| | - Xian 1 | CDTJ EPla MMoz WPGP |
| | - Xian 2 | EPla |
| | ***dracocephala*** | CAbb CDoC CEnt EPfP EPla ESwi GBin LEdu LRHS MAvo MBrN MDev MMoz MMuc MWht NGdn SBig SLPl WDyG WJun WMoo WPGP |

| | |
|---|---|
| ***ferax*** | EPla WJun |
| ***fungosa*** | EPla ESwi WJun WPGP |
| § ***murielae*** ♀H4 | CDoC CEnt CHEx EBee EHul ELan ENBC EPau EPfP EPla GGar MCCP MGos MMoz MMuc MWhi MWht NGdn SArc SBfd SPlb SPoG WDin WFar WJun WMoo WPGP |
| - 'Amy' | NLar |
| - 'Bimbo' | CEnt EBee EPfP EPla ESwi ETod GBin LAst LRHS MWht NLar NPal NWsh STre WJun WMoo WPGP |
| - 'Dana Jumbo' | LRHS |
| - 'Grüne Hecke' | MWht SBig |
| - 'Harewood' | GBin MMoz MWht SWvt WFar WPGP |
| - 'Joy' | GBin NLar WMoo WPnP |
| - 'Jumbo' | CEnt CHEx CSBt EAmu ELan ELon ENBC EPfP EPla ESwi GBin LPal LRHS MAvo MBri MDev MGos MMoz MWht NGdn NWsh SBig SPoG SRms SWvt WFar WJun |
| - 'Kranich' | NLar |
| - 'Lava' | MBri |
| - 'Mae' | CDTJ MWht |
| - 'Pinocchio' | MBri |
| - 'Simba' ♀H4 | Widely available |
| - 'Vampire' | LRHS MBri SBig |
| - 'Willow' | MBri |
| * ***nepalensis*** | EPla ESwi |
| § ***nitida*** | Widely available |
| - 'Chennevières' | EPla |
| - 'Eisenach' | MMoz WFar WMoo |
| - 'Great Wall' | GBin MBlu MBri MGos MWhi MWht |
| - Jiuzhaigou 1 | see *F.* Red Panda |
| - 'Jiuzhaigou 2' | EPla WJun |
| - 'Jiuzhaigou 4' | EPla WPGP |
| - 'Jiuzhaigou 8' **new** | WPGP |
| - 'Jiuzhaigou Genf' | WPGP |
| - 'Nymphenburg' ♀H4 | CEnd CPMA MBri MMoz NLar SBig WFar WMoo |
| - 'Wakehurst' | NLar |
| ***nujiangensis*** | EPla |
| ***perlonga*** | EPla WJun |
| - Yunnan 95/6 | MMoz WPGP |
| § Red Panda = 'Jiu' | EPla LRHS WJun |
| ***robusta*** | CAbb CDTJ CEnd CEnt ENBC EPfP EPla ETod GCal LPal MAvo MBrN MBri MMoz MMuc MWht NGdn NLar SBig SEND SLPl WDyG WJun |
| - 'Ming Yunnan' | LEdu WJun |
| - 'Pingwu' | CDTJ CEnt ETod GBin MGos MWht NLar SBig WJun |
| - 'Red Sheath' | CEnt EPla MMoz MWht NPal NPla WJun WPGP |
| - 'Wolong' | CDoC EPla ETod GBin MMoz MWht WJun WPGP |
| ***rufa*** | CAbb CEnt ENBC EPPr EPfP EPla GCal LMaj LRHS LSRN MAvo MBrN MCCP MDev MGos MMoz MMuc MWhi MWht NLar NPal SBig WDyG WJun WPGP |
| - variegated (v) | EPla |
| ***spathacea*** misapplied | see *F. murielae* |
| ***utilis*** | CEnt EPla ETod LEdu MMoz MMuc MWht NLar SEND WDyG WJun |
| ***yulongshanensis*** | EPla MWht WJun |
| aff. ***yulongshanensis*** | EPla |

## *Fascicularia* (*Bromeliaceae*)

| | |
|---|---|
| ***andina*** | see *F. bicolor* |
| § ***bicolor*** | Widely available |
| § - subsp. ***bicolor*** | CPne SArc |
| § - subsp. ***canaliculata*** | CHEx EBee EPla IBlr LEdu SBfd SChr SKHP SPad WCot WPGP |
| ***kirchhoffiana*** | see *F. bicolor* subsp. *canaliculata* |
| ***litoralis*** | see *Ochagavia litoralis* |
| ***pitcairniifolia*** misapplied | see *F. bicolor* subsp. *bicolor* |
| ***pitcairniifolia*** (Verlot) Mez | see *Ochagavia litoralis* |

## × *Fatshedera* (*Araliaceae*)

| | |
|---|---|
| ***lizei*** ♀H3 | CAlb CBcs CDoC CDul CHEx CMac CTri EBee ECrN ELon EPfP EPla LRHS MAsh MMuc MRav NEgg SArc SBfd SDix SEND SPer SPlb SPoG SWvt WDin |
| § - 'Annemieke' (v) ♀H3 | CAlb CBcs CDoC CHEx CMac EBee ELan EPfP LHop LRHS MAsh MMuc MRav NEgg SBfd SEND SMad SPer SPoG WBor |
| § - 'Aurea' (v) | SEND |
| - 'Aureopicta' | see × *F. lizei* 'Aurea' |
| - 'Lemon and Lime' | see × *F. lizei* 'Annemieke' |
| - 'Maculata' | see × *F. lizei* 'Annemieke' |
| - 'Variegata' (v) ♀H3 | CHEx CMac EBee EBtc ELan EPfP LAst LRHS LTen MAsh MGos MLLN MMuc NEgg SBfd SBrd SEND SPer SPoG SWvt WCFE WDin |

## *Fatsia* (*Araliaceae*)

| | |
|---|---|
| § ***japonica*** ♀H4 | Widely available |
| - 'Annelise' (v) | EGxp |
| - 'Moseri' | COlW CPLG CSam CTrC ECtt ESwi LHop NGdn NLar SWvt WCot |
| 'Spider's Web' (v) | CPLG CWGN ECtt ELon ESwi LSou MAvo NGBo SPer SPoG WCot WGrn |
| - 'Variegata' (v) ♀H3 | CBcs CMac EAmu EGxp EPfP LRHS MBri MGos MRav SEND SLim |
| ***oligocarpella*** **new** | CHEx |
| ***papyrifera*** | see *Tetrapanax papyrifer* |
| ***polycarpa*** | CDTJ CPLG EAmu WPGP |
| - B&SWJ 7144 | CPLG WCru |
| - RWJ 10133 | WCru |

## *Faucaria* (*Aizoaceae*)

| | |
|---|---|
| ***felina*** | SWal |
| ***tigrina*** ♀H1 | EPfP |

## *Fauria* see *Nephrophyllidium*

## *Fedia* (*Valerianaceae*)

| | |
|---|---|
| ***cornucopiae*** **new** | CArn |

## *Feijoa* see *Acca*

## *Felicia* (*Asteraceae*)

| | |
|---|---|
| ***aethiopica*** | GFai |
| § ***amelloides*** | CCCN CHEx EShb LAst MCot SBfd SEND SGar SPlb |
| - 'Astrid Thomas' | see *F. amelloides* 'Read's Blue' |
| - 'Blue Eyes' | LAst |
| § - 'Read's Blue' | SGar |
| - 'Read's White' | SEND |
| - 'Santa Anita' ♀H3 | CTri SVen |
| § - variegated (v) | CCCN ECtt LAst MBri MCot NPer SBfd SPet |

| | | |
|---|---|---|
| § | ***amoena*** | CTri SRms |
| | - 'Variegata' (v) | CCCN CTri |
| | ***capensis*** | see *F. amelloides* |
| | ***coelestis*** | see *F. amelloides* |
| | ***echinata*** | CCCN |
| | ***erigeroides*** | GFai |
| | ***filifolia*** | SPlb |
| | - blue-flowered | SVen |
| | ***fruticosa*** | CHll |
| | ***natalensis*** | see *F. rosulata* |
| | ***pappei*** | see *F. amoena* |
| § | ***petiolata*** | CHVG CMea CTri NSti WWFP |
| § | ***rosulata*** | CMea CPBP ECho GGar MBrN MHer NBro NLar SFgr SRms SRot |
| | ***uliginosa*** | EWes GEdr WAbe |

## fennel see *Foeniculum vulgare*

## fenugreek see *Trigonella foenum-graecum*

## *Ferraria* (*Iridaceae*)

| | | |
|---|---|---|
| | LP 18095 new | WCot |
| § | ***crispa*** | ECho |
| | - var. ***nortieri*** | WCot |
| | ***schaeferi*** new | WCot |
| | ***undulata*** | see *F. crispa* |

## *Ferula* (*Apiaceae*)

| | | |
|---|---|---|
| | ***assa-foetida*** | CArn EOHP |
| | ***chiliantha*** | see *F. communis* subsp. *glauca* |
| § | ***communis*** | CArn CMea CSpe EBee ECGP ECha ELan EPfP GCra NBPC NLar SDix SEND SMad SPav SPhx SPlb WCAu WCot WFar WJek |
| | - 'Gigantea' | see *F. communis* |
| § | - subsp. ***glauca*** | EWes SDix SGar WCot WPGP |
| | 'Giant Bronze' | see *Foeniculum vulgare* 'Giant Bronze' |
| | ***tingitana*** 'Cedric Morris' | ECha GCra SDix |

## *Festuca* (*Poaceae*)

| | | |
|---|---|---|
| | NJM 09.071 | WPGP |
| | ***actae*** | XLum |
| | ***amethystina*** | CKno CWCL CWib EHoe LEdu LRHS MMuc NGdn SEND SMea SRot WMoo WTin WWEG XLum |
| | - 'Aprilgrün' | EPPr XLum |
| | ***arundinacea*** | CHab CRWN MMoz MMuc SEND |
| | ***californica*** | CKno EPPr |
| | ***coxii*** | CHid GBin MAvo WCot |
| | ***curvula*** subsp. ***crassifolia*** | EPla EShb |
| | 'Eisvogel' | EBee |
| | ***elegans*** | EPPr XLum |
| | ***eskia*** | EAEE EBee EHoe EHul EPPr LRHS WDyG XLum |
| | ***filiformis*** | CHab |
| | 'Fromefield Blue' | EHul |
| § | ***gautieri*** | EBee EGxp EPPr GBin NGdn SMea XLum |
| | - 'Pic Carlit' | GBin |
| | ***gigantea*** | CHab EBee SEND XLum |
| | ***glacialis*** | XLum |
| | ***glauca*** Vill. | CBar CBcs CFee CWib EBee ELan EPfP EShb GMaP LRHS MBNS MGos MRav MWat NGdn NOak SBfd SLim SPer SPlb SRms SWal WDin WFar WTin WWEG |
| I | - 'Auslese' | CPLG CSpr EPPr NGdn |
| | - 'Azurit' | EBee EHoe EPPr EWes NWad NWsh SPad SPoG |
| § | - 'Blaufuchs' ♀H4 | EAEE EBee EHon EPPr EPfP EWes GMaP LRHS MAvo MBlu MGos MMoz MRav NWad SBfd SBrd SLim SPer SPlb SPoG SWvt WFar WWEG XLum |
| § | - 'Blauglut' | EBee EHul EPPr EPfP LRHS MBri MRav SRms WFar |
| | - Blue Fox | see *F. glauca* 'Blaufuchs' |
| | - Blue Glow | see *F. glauca* 'Blauglut' |
| | - 'Elijah Blue' | Widely available |
| | - 'Euchre' | LSRN |
| | - 'Golden Toupee' | EBee ECha EHoe ELan EPfP EWes LAst LRHS MBlu MGos MRav NBir NBlu NEgg NSti SLim SPer SPlb SWvt WDin WFar WWEG |
| | - 'Harz' | EHoe EHul SApp |
| | - 'Intense Blue' new | SMad |
| * | - ***minima*** | CCCN SPoG WGrn WWEG |
| | - 'Pallens' | see *F. longifolia* |
| | - Sea Urchin | see *F. glauca* 'Seeigel' |
| § | - 'Seeigel' | EHoe EPPr LRHS NLar NWad |
| | - Select | see *F. glauca* 'Auslese' |
| | - 'Seven Seas' | see *F. valesiaca* 'Silbersee' |
| | - 'Silberreiher' | EPPr WWEG |
| | - 'Solling' new | XLum |
| | - 'Uchte' | CWCL EPPr WPtf |
| | - 'Zwergenkönig' new | EPPr |
| | 'Hogar' | EPPr |
| | ***idahoensis*** | EShb |
| | - 'Tomales Bay' | CKno |
| § | ***longifolia*** | EPPr |
| | ***mairei*** | CKno ECha EHoe EPPr GQue NWsh SPhx XLum |
| | ***novae-zelandiae*** | CWCL |
| | ***ovina*** | CHab CWan EPfP WSFF |
| | - var. ***gallica*** | NWsh |
| | - 'Söhrewald' | EHoe EPPr |
| * | - 'Tetra Gold' | SWvt |
| | ***paniculata*** | CKno EHoe EPPr NWsh XLum |
| | ***pratensis*** new | CHab |
| | ***punctoria*** | MMuc SEND SMea |
| | ***rubra*** | CHab CRWN WSFF XLum |
| | - subsp. ***rubra*** | CRWN |
| | ***scoparia*** | see *F. gautieri* |
| | 'Siskiyou Blue' | CKno EBee EPPr |
| | ***tatrae*** | WCot |
| | ***valesiaca*** | SMea |
| | - var. ***glaucantha*** | CWib EPPr NGdn NLar WWEG XLum |
| § | - 'Silbersee' | EAEE EBee EHoe EPPr LRHS NWsh SRms WFar |
| | - Silver Sea | see *F. valesiaca* 'Silbersee' |
| | ***violacea*** | CSpr EPPr SWal |
| | ***vivipara*** | CPrp EHoe LEdu NBid |
| * | 'Willow Green' | SLim SPlb |

## *Fibigia* (*Brassicaceae*)

| | | |
|---|---|---|
| I | ***clypeata*** 'Select' | CSpe |

## *Ficus* ✿ (*Moraceae*)

| | | |
|---|---|---|
| | ***afghanistanica*** | ERea |
| | ***benjamina*** ♀H1 | SRms |
| | - 'Alij' new | WCot |
| | ***carica*** (F) | CCCN ETod LMaj MBri MNHC MREP SArc SEWo SLon SPad |
| | - 'Abicou' (F) | ERea |
| | - 'Adam' (F) | CCCN ERea |
| | - 'Alma' (F) | ERea |
| | - 'Angélique' (F) | ERea |
| | - 'Archipel' (F) | ERea |

| | | |
|---|---|---|
| | - Bayernfeige Violetta | see *F. carica* 'Violetta' |
| | - 'Beall' (F) | ERea |
| | - 'Black Ischia' (F) | ERea |
| | - 'Black Jack' (F) | ERea |
| | - 'Black Neck Lady' (F) | LRHS |
| | - 'Bornholm' (F) **new** | NLar |
| | - 'Boule d'Or' (F) | ERea |
| | - 'Bourjassotte Grise' (F) | CAgr ERea SDea |
| | - 'Brogiotto' (F) | CCCN |
| | - 'Brown Turkey' (F) ♀H3 | Widely available |
| | - 'Brunswick' (F) | CAgr CCCN CHll EGHP ELan ELon EPfP ERea GTwe LRHS MCoo NLar SEND SLim WCot WHar |
| | - 'Castle Kennedy' (F) | ERea GTwe |
| | - 'Celeste' (F) **new** | SPer |
| | - 'Colummaro Black Apulia' (F) | CCCN |
| | - 'Colummaro White Apulia' (F) | CCCN |
| | - 'Conandria' (F) | ERea |
| | - 'Continental' (F) | LRHS |
| | - 'Dalmatie' (F) | CAgr CCCN ELan EPfP ERea LRHS MGos SEND |
| § | - 'Desert King' (F) | ERea |
| I | - 'Digitata' (F) | MBlu |
| | - 'Drap d'Or' (F) | ERea |
| | - 'Excel' (F) **new** | ERea |
| | - 'Figue d'Or' (F) | ERea |
| | - 'Filacciano' (F) | CCCN |
| | - 'Goutte d'Or' (F) | CAgr EPfP ERea SDea |
| | - 'Grise de Saint Jean' (F) | ERea |
| | - 'Ice Crystal' (F) | LRHS MBlu WHar |
| | - 'Kadota' (F) | CCCN ERea SBfd |
| | - 'King' | see *F. carica* 'Desert King' |
| * | - 'Laciniata' (F) | MBri |
| | - 'Lisa' (F) | ERea |
| | - 'Little Yellow Wonder' (F) | ERea |
| | - 'LSU Purple' (F) | ERea |
| | - 'Malcolm's Giant' (F) | ERea |
| | - 'Malta' (F) | GTwe |
| | - 'Marseillaise' (F) | GTwe SDea |
| | - 'Melanzana' (F) | CCCN |
| | - 'Nazaret' (F) | LRHS |
| | - 'Neck Lady White' (F) **new** | LRHS |
| | - 'Negro Largo' (F) | ERea |
| | - 'Nero' (F) | ELon SGol |
| | - 'Newlyn Harbour' (F) | ELon |
| | - 'Noir de Provence' | see *F. carica* 'Reculver' |
| | - 'Noire de Carombe' (F) | CAgr EPfP ERea LRHS |
| | - 'Osborn's Prolific' (F) | ECrN EMil EPfP ERea MAsh SEND SGol SWvt WPGP |
| | - 'Panachée' (F) | ERea |
| | - 'Pastilière' (F) | ERea |
| | - 'Peter's Honey' (F) | ERea |
| | - 'Petite Nigra' (F) | ERea |
| | - 'Pinet' (F) | LRHS |
| | - 'Pittaluse' (F) | ERea |
| | - 'Porthminster' (F) | CHEx |
| | - 'Précoce de Dalmatie' (F) | ERea NLar WPGP |
| | - 'Précoce Ronde de Bordeaux' (F) | ERea SEND |
| § | - 'Reculver' (F) | ERea SEND |
| | - 'Rouge de Bordeaux' (F) | CCCN ERea MAsh SDea SPlb |
| | - 'Saint Johns' (F) | ERea |
| | - 'San Pedro Miro' (F) | ERea |
| | - 'Sollies Pont' (F) | ERea |
| | - 'Sugar 12' (F) | ERea |
| | - 'Sultane' (F) | CAgr ERea |
| | - 'Tena' (F) | ERea |
| | - 'Texas Everbearing' (F) | ERea |
| § | - 'Violetta' PBR | LRHS MBri NLar WHar |
| | - 'Violette Dauphine' (F) | EPfP ERea |
| | - 'Violette de Sollies' (F) | ERea |
| | - 'Violette Normande' (F) | MAsh SEND |
| | - 'Violette Sepor' (F) | ERea |
| | - 'White Genoa' | see *F. carica* 'White Marseilles' |
| | - 'White Ischia' (F) | ERea |
| § | - 'White Marseilles' (F) | CAgr CCCN CWib ECrN EGHP ERea LRHS MBri MCoo SDea SEND WPGP |
| | ***pubigera*** | CPLG |
| | ***pumila*** ♀H1 | CHEx |
| | - 'Minima' | CFee |
| | - 'Variegata' (v) | CHEx EShb |
| | ***retusa*** (F) | STre |

## fig see *Ficus carica*

## filbert see *Corylus maxima*

## *Filipendula* ✿ (*Rosaceae*)

| | | |
|---|---|---|
| | ***alnifolia*** 'Variegata' | see *F. ulmaria* 'Variegata' |
| | ***camtschatica*** | CFir CRow EBee ECha ELan LEdu LRHS MCot NBid NLar WFar WPGP |
| | - B&SWJ 10828 | SMrm WCru |
| | - 'Rosea' | LHop MRav SMad |
| | ***digitata*** 'Nana' | see *F. multijuga* |
| | ***formosa*** B&SWJ 8707 | WCru |
| | ***hexapetala*** | see *F. vulgaris* |
| | - 'Flore Pleno' | see *F. vulgaris* 'Multiplex' |
| | 'Kahome' | CPrp CRow EBee ELon EPPr EPla EShb GMaP IFoB LLWG LRHS NBPC NBir NGdn NLar NMir NOrc SPer SPet SPhx SWat WFar WHoo WMoo WPnP WWEG |
| | ***kiraishiensis*** B&SWJ 1571 | EBee WCru |
| § | ***multijuga*** | CRow EBee EWTr EWhm GCal GGar IFoB LRHS NHol WFar WMoo |
| | ***palmata*** | ECha LLWG MLHP NBre SWat WMoo |
| | - 'Digitata Nana' | see *F. multijuga* |
| | - dwarf | CLAP MLHP |
| | - 'Elegantissima' | see *F. purpurea* 'Elegans' |
| | - 'Göteborg' **new** | EBee |
| | - 'Nana' | see *F. multijuga* |
| | - 'Rosea' | CMac LLWG NBir |
| | - 'Rubra' | CTri GCra MRav NGdn |
| | ***purpurea*** ♀H4 | CKno CRow CSBt ECha ELon EPfP EWTr GGar IBlr LPBA MBri MMuc SEND WCru WFar WMoo WPnP |
| | - f. ***albiflora*** | EBee EWTr LLWG MBri NPri WMoo |
| § | - 'Elegans' | CRow EBee ECha ELon GGar LLWG MLHP NBPC NBid NHol NSti SPer SPet SWat WMoo WPnP |
| | - 'Nephele' | EBee |
| | - 'Pink Dreamland' | EBee SPhx |
| * | - 'Plena' (d) | NLar |
| | 'Queen of the Prairies' | see *F. rubra* |
| § | ***rubra*** | CRow IFro LSRN MCot WSFF |
| § | - 'Venusta' ♀H4 | Widely available |
| | - 'Venusta Magnifica' | see *F. rubra* 'Venusta' |
| | ***rufinervis*** B&SWJ 8611 | WCru |
| § | ***ulmaria*** | CArn CBen CHab CHby CRWN CWan EBee EHon ELau EWil GMaP GPoy MCot MHer MNHC NLan NMir SIde SWat WHfH WJek WMoo WSFF WShi XLum |
| | - 'Aurea' | CArn CMac CRow EBee ECha ECtt EHoe ELan GAbr GMaP MLHP MRav NBid NLar SMad SPer SRms |

| | |
|---|---|
| | WCot WFar WMoo WSHC WTin WWEG |
| - 'Flore Pleno' (d) | CBre EBee LHop LLWG LRHS MRav NBPC NBid NBre SIde SPer SWat WCot WFar |
| - 'Rosea' | CDes EBee IBlr MHer MLLN |
| § - 'Variegata' (v) | CArn CBen CFee CPrp EBee ECtt EHoe ELan IFoB LBMP NBPC NBid NGdn NLar NMRc SPer WFar WHfH WHoo WMoo WOut WPGP WPnP WTin WWEG WWFP |
| § ***vulgaris*** | CArn CFee CHab CRWN CTri CWan MLHP MLLN MMuc MNHC NBlu NBro NMir SBfd SWat WHfH WJek WPer WWEG |
| - 'Alba' | EBee |
| - 'Flore Pleno' | see *F. vulgaris* 'Multiplex' |
| - 'Grandiflora' | CBre |
| § - 'Multiplex' (d) | CMac EBee ECha ELan GGar GMaP LLWG MHer MLLN MMuc MRav NBid NBir NPri NRya SEND SRms WAul WFar WMoo WTin XLum |
| - 'Plena' | see *F. vulgaris* 'Multiplex' |
| - 'Rosea' | NBre |

## *Firmiana* (*Malvaceae*)

| | |
|---|---|
| ***simplex*** | CHEx EShb IDee WPGP |

## *Fitzroya* (*Cupressaceae*)

| | |
|---|---|
| ***cupressoides*** | CBcs CDoC CMac CTho GBin IArd IDee LRHS NMun SCoo SLim WAle WThu |

## *Foeniculum* (*Apiaceae*)

| | |
|---|---|
| ***vulgare*** | CArn CHEx CHby CPrp CWan ECha EGHP ELan ELau EPfP EWil GPoy MGos MHer MNHC NBlu NPri SBfd SEND SIde SPer SPhx SPlb SPoG SVic SWvt WHfH WJek |
| - 'Bronze' | see *F. vulgare* 'Purpureum' |
| - var. ***dulce*** | CSev SIde |
| § - 'Giant Bronze' | EBee ELan SPhx WGrn |
| § - 'Purpureum' | Widely available |
| - 'Smokey' | ECha MRav |

## *Fontanesia* (*Oleaceae*)

| | |
|---|---|
| ***phillyreoides*** | CBcs |

## *Fontinalis* (*Fontinalaceae*)

| | |
|---|---|
| sp. | LPBA |

## *Forsythia* (*Oleaceae*)

| | |
|---|---|
| 'Arnold Dwarf' | NBir NLar SRms |
| 'Beatrix Farrand' ambig. | CTri EBee MWat SEND SRms |
| 'Beatrix Farrand' K. Sax | MMuc NLar |
| 'Fiesta' (v) | CPMA EPfP LAst LRHS MAsh MGos MRav MSwo NWea SBfd SLim SPer SPoG WCot WDin WFar |
| ***giraldiana*** | MSwo SLon SRms |
| Gold Tide[PBR] | see *F.* Marée d'Or |
| 'Golden Bells' | WHar |
| 'Golden Nugget' | CMac ELan EPfP LBuc LRHS MAsh SCoo SLon SPoG WCFE |
| 'Golden Times' (v) | CMac EWes LBuc LSRN MGos NLar NWea SCoo SPoG SWvt WDin WFar |
| × ***intermedia*** 'Arnold Giant' | MBlu |
| - 'Ashmount' **new** | IArd |
| - 'Casque D'Or' | see *F.* × *intermedia* 'Courdijau' |
| § - 'Courdijau' | EMil |
| - 'Goldrausch' | LRHS MAsh MGos NLar |
| - 'Goldzauber' | NWea |
| - 'Josefa' (v) | WPat |
| - 'Lynwood Variety' ♀H4 | Widely available |
| - 'Lynwood Variety' variegated (v) | CWib |
| - Minigold = 'Flojor' | CSBt MSwo MWat NLar SRms |
| - 'Spectabilis' | CDul EBee EPfP LBuc NWea SCoo SGol SLim WDin WFar |
| - 'Spectabilis Variegated' (v) | CMHG MBNS NPro |
| - 'Spring Glory' | MHer |
| - 'Variegata' (v) | WGwG |
| - Week-End = 'Courtalyn'[PBR] ♀H4 | CWSG EBee EPfP LBuc LRHS LSou MAsh MBri MMuc NLar SEND SGol SLPl SLim SLon SPlb WDin WFar |
| § Marée d'Or = 'Courtasol'[PBR] ♀H4 | IVic LRHS MGos MRav NLar NWea SLon SPoG WDin |
| Mêlée d'Or = 'Courtaneur' | SBrd SCoo SGol |
| Melissa = 'Courtadic' | NLar NWea |
| ***ovata*** 'Tetragold' | EBee NWea |
| 'Paulina' | NLar WAbe |
| ***suspensa*** | CDul CMac CTri CWib EOHP EPfP NWea SPlb SRms |
| - f. ***atrocaulis*** | NWea |
| - 'Nymans' | MBri MRav NSti SEND |
| § - 'Taff's Arnold' (v) | CPLG CPMA EBee |
| - 'Variegata' | see *F. suspensa* 'Taff's Arnold' |
| 'Tremonia' | NEgg NLar WGwG |
| ***viridissima*** | NWea |
| - 'Bronxensis' | CMac ECho GEdr LLHF NBir NLar WCot WPat |
| - 'Weber's Bronx' | NLar |

## *Fortunella* (*Rutaceae*)

| | |
|---|---|
| 'Fukushu' (F) ♀H1 | ERea |
| § ***japonica*** (F) | EPfP |
| § ***margarita*** (F) | CDoC LRHS LSRN |

## *Fothergilla* (*Hamamelidaceae*)

| | |
|---|---|
| ***gardenii*** | CBcs CPMA ELan EPfP EWTr LRHS MBlu MGos MRav NLar SPer SWvt WDin |
| - 'Blue Mist' | CAbP CDoC CEnd CPLG CPMA ELan ELon EPfP GKin GQue IVic LRHS MAsh MPkF NLar SBfd SKHP SPer SReu SSta WDin WFar WPat |
| - 'Harold Epstein' | NLar |
| - 'Suzanne' | NLar |
| - 'Zundert' | NLar |
| 'Huntsman' | CCCN EBee MMHG WFar |
| × ***intermedia*** Beaver Creek = 'Klmtwo' | NLar |
| - 'Blue Shadow' | CBcs CPMA EWTr LSRN MGos MPkF NLar SGol SKHP |
| - 'Mount Airy' | CMCN CPMA EBee EPfP GBin LRHS NLar SKHP SPoG SPtl SSpi SSta |
| - 'Red Licorice' | CPMA NLar |
| - 'Sea Spray' | CPMA |
| - 'Windy City' | CPMA NLar |
| ***major*** ♀H4 | CBcs CDul CPMA CWib EBee ELan EPfP GKev GKin LRHS LSRN MAsh MBlu MGos NEgg NLar NPri SPer SPoG SReu SWvt WDin WFar WPat |
| - Monticola Group | CDoC CDul CEnd CPMA ELan EPfP LRHS MAsh MGos NPal SBfd SBrd SEND SLim SPer SSpi SSta WFar |

## *Fouquieria* (*Fouquieriaceae*)

| | |
|---|---|
| ***diguetii*** | SPlb |

## Fragaria (Rosaceae)

| | |
|---|---|
| from Taiwan | WHer |
| ***alpina*** | see *F. vesca* 'Semperflorens' |
| - 'Alba' | see *F. vesca* 'Semperflorens Alba' |
| × ***ananassa*** 'Albion'PBR (F) | CSut LSRN MCoo SPer |
| - 'Alice'PBR (F) ♀H4 | CMac EPom ERea LBuc LRHS MCoo WWFS |
| - 'Aromel' (F) ♀H4 | CAgr EPfP GTwe LBuc LRHS |
| - 'Bogota' (F) | LRHS |
| - 'Bolero' (F) | LRHS MBri |
| - 'Calypso'PBR (F) | CAgr CSBt LBuc LRHS SDea SEND |
| - 'Cambridge Favourite' (F) ♀H4 | CAgr CMac CSBt CTri CWCL EGHP EMil EPfP EPom ERea GPri GTwe LBuc LRHS MBri MCoo MGos NBlu NEgg NPri SDea SEND SPlb WWFS |
| - 'Cambridge Vigour' (F) | CWCL LRHS |
| - 'Christine' (F) | CSut EMil EPom GPri LRHS WWFS |
| - 'Elegance' (F) new | EPom |
| - 'Elsanta' (F) | CSBt CTri CWCL EMil EPfP EPom GPri GTwe IArd LBuc LEdu LRHS NEgg NPri SBfd SDea SEND SPer |
| - 'Elvira' (F) | EPfP LRHS |
| * - 'Emily' (F) | CAgr GPri |
| - 'Eros'PBR (F) | GTwe LBuc |
| - 'Flamenco'PBR (F) | EGHP EPom ERea LRHS |
| - 'Florence'PBR (F) | CSBt CTri EMil EPfP EPom ERea GTwe LBuc LRHS MBri SPer WWFS |
| - Fraise des Bois | see *F. vesca* |
| - 'Fruitful Summer' (F) | LRHS |
| - 'Hapil' (F) ♀H4 | CTri EGHP EMil EPfP EPom ERea GPri GTwe LBuc LEdu LRHS NBlu WWFS |
| - 'Honeoye' (F) ♀H4 | CAgr CSBt CWCL EGHP EMil EPfP EPom GAbr GPri GTwe LBuc LEdu LRHS MBri MCoo NBlu SBfd SEND SPer WWFS |
| - 'Judibell'PBR (F) | LRHS WWFS |
| - 'Korona'PBR (F) | CMac EPom |
| - 'Loran' (F) | LAst LRHS |
| - 'Lucy' (F) new | CSut |
| - 'Malling Opal'PBR (F) | EPom GTwe |
| - 'Malling Pearl' (F) | EMil GTwe |
| - 'Pandora' (F) | LEdu LRHS |
| - 'Pegasus'PBR (F) ♀H4 | CSBt EGHP EPfP EPom GPri GTwe LBuc LRHS NPri WWFS |
| - Pink Panda = 'Frel'PBR (F) | CMac CTri EAEE EBee ELan LHop LRHS MGos MRav NEgg NHol NLar SPer SPoG WJek WWFP |
| - pink-flowered (F) | CFee MLLN |
| - 'Rabunda' (F) | LRHS |
| - Red Ruby = 'Samba'PBR (F) | CMac EAEE EBee GGar LHop LRHS MNrw NEgg NGdn NLar SPer SPoG |
| - 'Redgauntlet' (F) | EPfP GPri GTwe LRHS NBlu |
| - 'Rhapsody' (F) ♀H4 | GTwe LBuc LRHS LSRN |
| - 'Rosie'PBR (F) | SDea |
| - 'Royal Sovereign' (F) | CMac CTri GTwe LRHS NBir SVic |
| - 'Sasha' (F) new | GPri |
| - 'Senga Sengana' (F) | SVic |
| - 'Sonata'PBR (F) | CSut EPom |
| - 'Sophie'PBR (F) | EMil LEdu LRHS WWFS |
| - 'Symphony'PBR (F) ♀H4 | CAgr CSBt EPfP EPom LBuc LRHS LSRN MBri WWFS |
| - 'Totem' (F) | GTwe LRHS |
| § - 'Variegata' (v) | CArn CTri EAEE EBee EPla LHop LRHS MRav SPer SPoG WMoo XLum |
| 'Bowles's Double' | see *F. vesca* 'Multiplex' |
| ***chiloensis*** (F) | ILis LEdu |
| - 'Chaval' (F) | CHid ECha EPPr MRav NChi WMoo |
| - 'Variegata' misapplied | see *F.* × *ananassa* 'Variegata' |
| ***daltoniana*** | GCra |
| ***indica*** | see *Duchesnea indica* |
| 'Lipstick' | NLar |
| ***moschata*** | CAgr |
| ***nubicola*** | CAgr GPoy |
| 'Roman' | LAst LRHS |
| 'Tarpan' new | LAst |
| 'Variegata' | see *F.* × *ananassa* 'Variegata' |
| § ***vesca*** (F) | CAgr CArn CBcs CRWN CWan EGHP EPfP EWil GPoy MHer MNHC NBlu NMir NPri SEND SIde SPlb SVic WGwG WJek WSFF WShi |
| - 'Alexandra' (F) | CArn CBod CPrp ELau ERea GAbr NVic SBfd SIde |
| - 'Baron Solemacher' (F) | SBfd SHDw WHer |
| - 'Flore Pleno' | see *F. vesca* 'Multiplex' |
| - 'Fructu Albo' (F) | CAgr CArn CBre CRow CWan GLin NLar WMoo |
| - 'Golden Alexandra' | ECha EHoe ELau ERea EWes MHer NPro WHer WMoo |
| - 'Golden Surprise' | SBfd SHDw |
| - 'Mignonette' new | NDov |
| - 'Monophylla' (F) | CRow SIde WHer |
| § - 'Multiplex' (d) | CRow EGHP ILis MRav NChi NLar WBor WHer WOut |
| § - 'Muricata' | CBre CRow ILis LEdu WHer |
| - 'Pineapple Crush' (F) | WHer |
| - 'Plymouth Strawberry' | see *F. vesca* 'Muricata' |
| § - 'Semperflorens' (F) | ILis |
| § - 'Semperflorens Alba' (F) | CAgr ERea |
| - 'Variegata' misapplied | see *F.* × *ananassa* 'Variegata' |
| * - 'Variegata' ambig. (v) | EGHP EHoe LRHS NEgg WFar WHrl WWEG |
| ***virginiana*** | CAgr |
| - subsp. ***glauca*** | EPPr |
| ***viridis*** | CAgr |

## Francoa (Francoaceae)

| | |
|---|---|
| ***appendiculata*** | CAbP EBla GAbr GQui MDKP MMuc NBir SGar WAle WFar WHer WMoo WPnP |
| - red-flowered | CDes |
| Ballyrogan strain | IBlr |
| 'Confetti' | CAbP CAby CKno CPLG ELan LRHS MAvo WCot WFar |
| 'Purple Spike' | see *F. sonchifolia* Rogerson's form |
| ***ramosa*** | CCVN CTri EWld IBlr LRHS MNrw NBro SDix SPav WFar WKif WMoo |
| * - 'Alba' | CSpe EDif |
| ***sonchifolia*** | Widely available |
| - 'Alba' | MDKP SUsu WFar WMoo |
| - 'Culm View Lilac' | CCVN |
| - 'Doctor Tom Smith' | WCot |
| - 'Lynda Windsor' | CRDP MAvo |
| - 'Molly Anderson' | MAvo SUsu |
| - 'Pink Bouquet' new | SHar |
| - 'Pink Giant' | CHVG GBin GGar GKev MHer SMrm WCot WHil WMoo |
| § - Rogerson's form | CAby CCVN CElw CEnt CKno CRDP CSam EBee ELon GGar IVic LBMP LHop LRHS MAvo MBri MDKP MNHC MSCN NBir NChi SAga SDix SGar SUsu WCot WHil WMoo WWEG |

## *Frangula* (*Rhamnaceae*)

§ ***alnus*** CArn CCVT CDul CHab CRWN CTri ECrN EShb LBuc MBlu NWea SEWo STre WDin WFar WMou WSFF
- 'Aspleniifolia' CWSG EPfP LRHS MBlu MMuc MPkF NLar WDin WFar WPat
- 'Columnaris' SLPl
- 'Ron Williams' **new** MBlu

## *Frankenia* (*Frankeniaceae*)

***laevis*** SRms
***thymifolia*** CTri CYeo ECho MAsh MHer MWat NPri SEND SPlb WFar WTin XLum

## *Franklinia* (*Theaceae*)

***alatamaha*** CBcs MBlu MBri SEND WFar WPGP

## *Fraxinus* ✿ (*Oleaceae*)

***americana*** CDul CMCN EPfP EWTr NEgg WDin
- 'Autumn Purple' CDul CEnd CMCN CTho EBee ECrN EPfP MAsh MBlu WMou
***angustifolia*** CMCN
§ - subsp. ***oxycarpa*** SEND
- 'Raywood' ♀H4 Widely available
***bungeana*** EGFP
***caroliniana*** EGFP
***chinensis*** CLnd CMCN EGFP
***elonza*** CLnd
***excelsior*** CBcs CCVT CDoC CDul CHab CLnd CMac CRWN CSBt CTho CTri CWib EBee ECrN EPfP LAst LBuc MAsh MBri MGos MMuc NWea SBfd SEND SEWo SGol SLim STre WDin WMou
- 'Aurea Pendula' CCVT CDul CEnd CMac CWib EBee MBlu MGos NPal SPoG
- 'Crispa' MBlu NLar
- f. ***diversifolia*** CDul CLnd
- 'Jaspidea' ♀H4 Widely available
- 'Nana' LMaj WPat
- 'Pendula' ♀H4 CCVT CDoC CDul CEnd CLnd CMac EBee ECrN ELan LAst LMaj MBlu NEgg NPal NWea SGol SLim SPer SPoG WDin WMou
- 'R.E. Davey' CDul CNat
- variegated (v) CMac ECrN
- 'Westhof's Glorie' ♀H4 CCVT CDoC CDul CLnd EBee ECrN LMaj SBfd WDin WFar
***hopeiensis*** MBlu
***insularis*** var. ***henryana*** CDul
***latifolia*** CLnd CMCN MBlu
***mariesii*** see *F. sieboldiana*
***nigra*** CMCN
- 'Fallgold' CEnd
***ornus*** ♀H4 CArn CCVT CDul CLnd CMCN CMac CTri EBee ECrN ELan EPfP EWTr LAst LMaj MMuc MSnd MSwo NPal NWea SEND SPer WDin WFar WMoo
- 'Arie Peters' CDul
- 'Mecsek' MBlu
- 'Obelisk' EBee EBtc LMaj MAsh MBlu NLar SPoG
- 'Rotterdam' EBee
***oxycarpa*** see *F. angustifolia* subsp. *oxycarpa*
***paxiana*** EGFP
***pennsylvanica*** CDul CLnd CMCN
- Cimmaron = 'Cimmzam' CDul MAsh
- 'Variegata' (v) CLnd EBee WPat
***quadrangulata*** EGFP WDin
***richardi*** CDul
§ ***sieboldiana*** CDoC CDul CLnd CMCN CPMA EPfP MBlu MBri SSpi WPat
***velutina*** CDul CLnd SLPl
***xanthoxyloides*** MBlu NEgg
- var. ***dumosa*** EBee WPGP

## *Freesia* (*Iridaceae*)

sp. CWCL
***alba*** Foster see *F. lactea*
***alba*** (G.L. Mey.) Gumbl. CYeo
double mixed (d) CWCL SWal
***fucata*** ECho
***grandiflora*** see *Anomatheca grandiflora*
§ ***lactea*** CDes ECho
***laxa*** see *Anomatheca laxa*
Rainbow mixture SWal
***refracta*** 'Worcester' ECho
***xanthospila*** EBee WCot

## *Fremontodendron* (*Malvaceae*)

'California Glory' ♀H3 Widely available
***californicum*** CDoy CTri CWib EBee ELan MBri MOWG NLar SEND SLim SPlb WDin WFar
'Dara's Gold' **new** LRHS
'Pacific Sunset' EPfP LSRN MGos MRav NEgg SGol WFar
'Tequila Sunrise' CBcs CDoC CWGN EBee GBin LLHF NLar SBfd WPGP

## *Freylinia* (*Scrophulariaceae*)

***cestroides*** see *F. lanceolata*
§ ***lanceolata*** CBcs CCCN CTrC CWib SPlb SVen
***tropica*** CHII GFai
***visseri*** GFai MOWG

## *Fritillaria* ✿ (*Liliaceae*)

***acmopetala*** ♀H4 CAvo CBro CFFs CHid CWCL ECho EPot ERCP GKev ITim LAma LRHS MNrw MSSP NMen NMin SDeJ SPhx WCot
- 'Brunette' EPot LWst
- subsp. ***wendelboi*** ECho EPot GKev LAma WCot
- - 'Zwanenburg' LWst
***affinis*** CWCL ECho EPot GBin ITim LAma LWst MSSP NMen
§ - var. ***gracilis*** LWst
- 'Sunray' EPot GEdr LWst
§ - var. ***tristulis*** ITim NMen NWCA
- 'Vancouver Island' ECho
***alfredae*** subsp. ***glaucoviridis*** WCot
***amabilis*** **new** LWst
***amana*** CTca CWCL ECho EPot ERCP GKev ITim LAma LLHF MSSP NMen NMin WCot
- 'Cambridge' ♀H4 WCot
- 'Goksan Gold' **new** GKev
- yellow-flowered EPot
***arabica*** see *F. persica*
***armena*** MP 8146 LWst
***assyriaca*** EPfP EPot MWea
- subsp. ***melanthera*** LWst
***aurea*** NMen
- 'Golden Flag' ECho EPot GKev LLHF SPhx
***ayakoana*** **new** LWst
***biflora*** ECho EPot GEdr

| | | |
|---|---|---|
| | – 'Martha Roderick' | ECho GKev ITim LAma MSSP NMen SDeJ |
| § | ***bithynica*** | ECho EPot GEdr GKev ITim LAma LWst MSSP |
| | – from Turkey | WCot |
| | ***brandegeei*** | LWst |
| | ***bucharica*** | ECho EPot GKev LWst NMin |
| | – 'Nurek Giant' | ECho LWst |
| | ***camschatcensis*** | CAvo CBro CPom CWCL ECha ECho EFEx EPfP EPot ERCP GAuc GEdr GGar GKev GMaP LAma LRHS MSSP NBir NHar NLar NMen NSla NWCA SDeJ SPhx WAbe WCru |
| | – from Alaska | NHar |
| | – 'Aurea' | ECho LWst NMen SPhx |
| | – black-flowered | ECho NHar |
| | – double-flowered (d) | CFir ECho GEdr LAma NMen |
| | – f. ***flavescens*** | EFEx GEdr LAma |
| | – green-flowered | CAby MSSP NMen |
| | ***carduchorum*** | see *F. minuta* |
| | ***carica*** | ECho EPot GEdr NMen |
| | – brown-flowered | ECho |
| | – tall clone | LWst |
| | ***caucasica*** | ECho GAuc NMen |
| | ***cirrhosa*** | GEdr LWst |
| | – brown-flowered | GEdr LWst NMen |
| | – green-flowered | GEdr LWst NMen |
| | ***citrina*** | see *F. bithynica* |
| | ***conica*** | LWst NMen WCot |
| | ***crassifolia*** | LAma |
| § | – subsp. ***kurdica*** | GKev ITim NMen WCot |
| | ***davidii*** | SCnR |
| | ***davisii*** | ECho EPot GAuc GEdr GKev GLam LAma NMen NWCA WCot |
| | ***delphinensis*** | see *F. tubiformis* |
| | ***eduardii*** | ECho EPot GKev LWst WCot |
| | ***elwesii*** | ECho EPot ERCP GEdr ITim LRHS LWst NMen SPhx WCot |
| | ***ferganensis*** | see *F. walujewii* |
| | ***frankiorum*** | WCot |
| | ***gentneri*** | WCot |
| | ***glauca*** | LAma MSSP |
| * | – 'Golden Flag' | ECho |
| | – 'Goldilocks' | ECho NMen SDeJ |
| | ***graeca*** | ECho EPot GKev NMen NMin SDeJ WCot |
| | – subsp. ***ionica*** | see *F. graeca* subsp. *thessala* |
| § | – subsp. ***thessala*** | MSSP NMen WCot |
| | ***gussichiae*** | NMen SPhx |
| | ***hermonis*** | LWst |
| | ***hispanica*** | see *F. lusitanica* |
| | ***imperialis*** | ECGP MBri |
| | – 'April Flame' | LAma |
| | – 'Aureomarginata' (v) | EBee ELon LAma |
| | – 'Aurora' | EBee EPot ERCP GKev LAma LRHS NLar NPer SDeJ SPer WFar |
| | – 'Garland Star' | EBee GKev LAma LRHS NLar |
| | – 'Grenadier' | LAma |
| | – var. ***inodora*** | EBee LAma LRHS |
| | – 'Inodora Purpurea' | EBee |
| | – 'Lutea' | CAvo CTca EBee ELan EPfP ERCP GKev LRHS NBPC SPhx SPoG WFar |
| | – 'Maxima' | see *F. imperialis* 'Rubra Maxima' |
| | – 'Maxima Lutea' ♀H4 | CBro ELan EPfP EPot ERCP GAbr LAma NLar SDeJ SPer |
| | – 'Orange Brilliant' | EBee LAma |
| | – 'Prolifera' | EBee GKev LAma NLar |
| | – 'Rubra' | CTca EBee ERCP GAbr GKev LAma NLar SPer WFar |
| § | – 'Rubra Maxima' | CBro CTca EBee ELan EPfP EPot ERCP GKev LAma LRHS SDeJ SPhx |
| | – 'Slagzwaard' | EBee GKev |
| | – 'Striped Beauty' | CTca GKev LAma |
| | – 'Sulpherino' | EBee LAma |
| | – 'The Premier' | EBee GKev LAma SDeJ |
| | – 'William Rex' | CAvo CFFs EBee EPot ERCP GKev LAma LRHS SDeJ SPhx SPoG |
| | – yellow-flowered | CFFs |
| | ***involucrata*** | WCot |
| | ***ionica*** | see *F. graeca* subsp. *thessala* |
| | ***japonica*** new | LWst |
| | – var. ***koidzumiana*** | EFEx GEdr LWst |
| | ***karadaghensis*** | see *F. crassifolia* subsp. *kurdica* |
| | ***kotschyana*** | ECho EPot GEdr GLam LWst NMen WCot |
| | – subsp. ***grandiflora*** | WCot |
| | ***lanceolata*** | see *F. affinis* var. *tristulis* |
| | ***latakiensis*** | ECho EPot GEdr GKev LWst WCot |
| § | ***latifolia*** | GAuc GEdr NMen |
| | – var. ***nobilis*** | see *F. latifolia* |
| § | ***lusitanica*** | ITim MSSP NMen |
| | ***meleagris*** | Widely available |
| | – var. ***unicolor*** subvar. ***alba*** ♀H4 | CBro CSam ECho ERCP GKev LAma MBri MMHG MSSP MWat SDeJ SMrm SPer SPhx WAul WPnP WShi |
| | – – – 'Aphrodite' | EPot NBir |
| § | ***messanensis*** | MSSP |
| | – subsp. ***gracilis*** | MSSP |
| | ***michailovskyi*** ♀H2 | CAvo CFFs CHid CTri CWCL ECho EPfP EPot ERCP GEdr GKev LAma LRHS MNrw NMen SDeJ SRms WFar |
| | ***minima*** | ECho |
| § | ***minuta*** | ECho EPot ERCP GAuc LAma NMen NMin |
| | ***montana*** | NMen WCot |
| | ***muraiana*** new | LWst |
| | ***nigra*** misapplied | see *F. montana* |
| | ***nigra*** Mill. | see *F. pyrenaica* |
| | ***obliqua*** | WCot |
| | ***olivieri*** GBK 82 | LWst |
| § | ***orientalis*** | MSSP WCot |
| | ***pallidiflora*** ♀H4 | CAvo CBro CLAP CTca CWCL ECho EPot ERCP GKev LAma MLLN MSSP NBir NMen SPhx |
| § | ***persica*** | CAvo EBee ECha ECho ECtt ELon EPfP EPot ERCP GKev LAma LHop LRHS MBri MNrw NBPC NMen SPhx WFar |
| | – 'Adiyaman' ♀H4 | CAvo CBro ELan LRHS SDeJ |
| | – 'Chocolate' | CWCL |
| | – 'Ivory Bells' | CAvo EPot ERCP LAma NLar SDeJ SPhx |
| | – 'Ivory Queen' | CBro |
| * | – 'Senkoy' | LRHS |
| | ***phaeanthera*** | see *F. affinis* var. *gracilis* |
| | ***pinardii*** | ECho EPot NMen |
| | ***pontica*** ♀H4 | CAvo CBro CLAP CWCL ECho EPot ERCP GAuc GEdr GKev ITim LAma MNrw MSSP NMen SDeJ SPhx WCot WCru |
| | ***pudica*** | ECho GEdr GKev GLam ITim LAma MSSP NMen SPhx WCot |
| * | – 'Fragrant' | ECho NMen |
| | – 'Giant' | ECho EPot GKev NMin |
| | – 'Richard Britten' | NMen |
| | ***purdyi*** | ECho |

| | | |
|---|---|---|
| § | ***pyrenaica*** ♀H4 | CLAP CTca CWCL ECho EPot GCra GEdr LAma LWst MSSP NMen SPhx WCot WCru WTin |
| | – 'Cedric Morris' | MSSP WCot |
| | ***raddeana*** | CAvo ECho EPot ERCP GKev LAma LWst NLar SPhx WCot |
| | ***recurva*** HZ 95-037 | LWst |
| | ***rhodocanakis*** | GKev LRHS NMen NMin WCot |
| | – subsp. ***argolica*** | NMen |
| | ***rubra major*** | see *F. imperialis* 'Rubra Maxima' |
| | ***ruthenica*** | ECho NMen |
| | ***sewerzowii*** | ECho EPot LAma WCot |
| | – from Kazakhstan **new** | GAuc |
| | – from Uzbekhistan **new** | GAuc |
| | – 'Black Bear' **new** | LWst |
| | – 'Brown Eyes' | LWst |
| | – 'Gulliver' **new** | LWst |
| | – pale yellow-flowered **new** | GKev |
| | ***shikokiana*** **new** | LWst |
| | ***sinica*** | WCot |
| | ***sphaciotica*** | see *F. messanensis* |
| | ***stenanthera*** | ECho EPot LAma NMen |
| | ***tachengensis*** | see *F. yuminensis* |
| | ***tenella*** | see *F. orientalis* |
| | ***theophrasti*** | WCot |
| | ***thunbergii*** | ECho GEdr GKev NMen WCot |
| | ***tortifolia*** | NMen |
| § | ***tubiformis*** | GAuc GEdr MSSP |
| | ***tuntasia*** subsp. ***tuntasia*** | WCot |
| | ***uva-vulpis*** | CAby CMea CTca ECtt ELon EPfP EPot ERCP GEdr GGar GKev LAma LHop LRHS MNrw NBir NMen SDeJ SPhx SWal WCru WFar WHil |
| | ***verticillata*** | CBro ECha EPot GEdr GKev LAma LWst NMen SPhx WCru |
| | ***wabuensis*** | WCot |
| § | ***walujewii*** | MSSP WCot |
| | ***whittallii*** | ECho EPot GKev MSSP NMen |
| | – PW 72-64B | LWst |
| | – 'Green Light' | NMin |
| § | ***yuminensis*** | WCot |
| | ***yuzhongensis*** **new** | WCot |

## *Fuchsia* ✿ (*Onagraceae*)

| | | |
|---|---|---|
| | 'A.M. Larwick' | CSil EBak SRiF |
| | 'A.W. Taylor' | EBak |
| | 'Aalt Groothuis' (d) | SRiF |
| | 'Abbé Farges' (d) | CDoC CLoc CSil CWVF EBak EPts SPet SRiF SVic WRou |
| | 'Abbigayle Reine' (v) | SRiF |
| | 'Abigail' ambig. | CWVF SRiF WRou |
| | 'Abigail Storey' | CSil |
| | 'Abundance' | CSil |
| | 'Achievement' ♀H4 | CDoC CLoc CSil LCla MJac SPet SRiF SVic |
| | 'Adagio' (d) | CLoc |
| | 'Adalbert Bogner' (d) | CDoC |
| | 'Adelaide Hoodless' | WRou |
| | 'Adinda' (T) | CDoC EPts LCla SRiF WRou |
| | 'Admiration' | CSil |
| | 'Adrienne' (d) | SRiF |
| | 'Ailsa Garnett' (d) | EBak |
| | 'Aintree' | CTsd CWVF |
| | 'Airedale' | CWVF |
| | 'Aisen' | WRou |
| | 'Ajax' (d) | SRiF |
| | 'Aladna's Sander' (d) | CWVF SRiF |
| | 'Alan Ayckbourn' | CWVF SRiF |
| | 'Alan Titchmarsh' | CDoC EPts LCla SLBF SRiF |
| | 'Alaska' (d) | CLoc EBak SRiF SVic |
| | 'Albertina' | SRiF SVic WRou |
| | 'Albertus Schwab' | LCla |
| | 'Alde' | CWVF SRiF |
| | 'Alderford' | SLBF |
| | 'Alf Thornley' (d) | CTsd CWVF SRiF |
| | 'Alfie' (d) | SRiF |
| | 'Alfred Rambaud' (d) | CDoC CSil SRiF |
| | 'Alice Ashton' (d) | EBak |
| | 'Alice Blue Gown' (d) | CWVF |
| | 'Alice Doran' | CDoC CSil LCla SRiF |
| | 'Alice Hoffman' (d) ♀H3-4 | Widely available |
| | 'Alice Mary' (d) | EBak |
| | 'Alice Sweetapple' (d) | CWVF SRiF |
| | 'Alice Travis' (d) | EBak |
| | 'Alipat' | EBak |
| | 'Alisha Jade' | SRiF |
| | 'Alison Ewart' | CLoc CWVF EBak MJac SPet SRiF SVic |
| | 'Alison Patricia' ♀H3 | CWVF EBak LAst MJac SLBF SRiF SVic WRou |
| | 'Alison Reynolds' (d) | CWVF SRiF |
| | 'Alison Ruth Griffin' (d) | MJac |
| | 'Alison Ryle' (d) | EBak |
| | 'Alison Sweetman' ♀H1+3 | CSil CWVF MJac |
| | 'Allure' (d) | CWVF |
| | 'Alma Hulscher' (d) | SRiF |
| | Aloha = 'Sanicomf'PBR (Sunangels Series) | SLBF SRiF |
| | ***alpestris*** | CDoC CSil EBak LCla SRiF SVic |
| | 'Alsa Garnet' (d) | SRiF |
| | 'Alton Waters' (d/v) | SRiF |
| | 'Alwin' (d) | CWVF SRiF |
| | 'Alyce Larson' (d) | CWVF EBak MJac SRiF SVic |
| | 'Amanda Bridgland' (d) | SRiF |
| | 'Amanda Jones' | SRiF |
| | 'Amazing Grace' (d) | MJac |
| | 'Amazing Maisie' (d) | SLBF SRiF |
| | 'Ambassador' | CTsd EBak SRiF SVic |
| | 'Amelie Aubin' | CLoc CWVF EBak SVic |
| | 'America' | CWVF |
| | 'Amethyst Fire' (d) | CSil SRiF |
| | 'Amigo' ambig. | EBak SRiF |
| § | ***ampliata*** | CDoC LCla |
| | 'Amy' | MJac |
| | 'Amy Lye' | CLoc CSil EBak SVic |
| | 'Amy Ruth' | CWVF |
| § | 'Andenken an Heinrich Henkel' (T) | CDoC CLoc CWVF EBak SRiF WRou |
| | 'André Le Nostre' (d) | CWVF EBak SRiF SVic |
| | 'Andreas Schwab' | LCla |
| | ***andrei*** | CDoC LCla SRiF |
| | 'Andrew' | EBak SRiF |
| | 'Andrew Carnegie' (d) | CLoc |
| | 'Andrew George' | MJac |
| | 'Andrew Hadfield' | CWVF SRiF SVic WRou |
| | 'Andrew Ryle' | SRiF |
| | 'Andromeda' De Groot | CSil |
| | 'Angela Dawn' | WRou |
| | 'Angela Leslie' (d) | CLoc CWVF EBak SRiF SVic |
| | 'Angela Rippon' | CWVF MJac |
| | 'Angel's Flight' (d) | EBak SRiF |
| | 'Angel's Kiss' (E) | CDoC LCla |
| | 'Anita' (d) | CCCN CLoc CWVF EPts LAst MJac SLBF SRiF SVic WGor WRou |
| | 'Anjo' (v) | CWVF SRiF |
| | 'Ann Howard Tripp' | CDoC CLoc CWVF MJac SRiF SVic WRou |
| | 'Ann Lee' (d) | EBak SRiF |
| | 'Ann Marie McManus' **new** | CSil |

| | Name | Suppliers |
|---|---|---|
| | 'Anna of Longleat' (d) | CCCN CWVF EBak LAst MJac SPet SRiF |
| | 'Anna Silvena' | LSou |
| | 'Annabel' (d) 🏆$^{H3}$ | CCCN CDoC CLoc CTri CWVF EBak EPts LAst MJac SLBF SPet SRiF SVic WRou |
| | 'Annabelle Stubbs' (d) | SRiF |
| | 'Anne Strudwick' (d) | SRiF |
| | 'Anneke de Keijzer' | CDoC LCla |
| | 'Annie Earle' | SRiF |
| | 'Annie Geurts' | CDoC |
| | 'Annie M.G. Schmidt' | EPts |
| | 'Another Little Cracker' | WRou |
| | 'Another Storey' | CSil SRiF |
| | 'Ant and Dec' (d/v) | MJac |
| | 'Anthea Day' (d) | CLoc |
| | 'Anthony Heavens' | SRiF |
| | 'Antigone' | SLBF SRiF |
| | 'Aphrodite' (d) | CLoc CWVF EBak SRiF |
| | 'Applause' (d) | CLoc CWVF EBak EPts SPet SRiF SVic |
| | ***aprica*** misapplied | see *F.* × *bacillaris* |
| | ***aprica*** Lundell | see *F. microphylla* subsp. *aprica* |
| | 'Apricot Ice' | CLoc SVic |
| | 'Aquarius' | SRiF |
| | 'Arabella' | CWVF |
| | 'Arabella Improved' | CWVF SRiF SVic |
| | ***arborea*** | see *F. arborescens* |
| § | ***arborescens*** | CBcs CDoC CHEx CHll CLoc CSil CWVF EBak EWld LCla MCot SBrd SDys SRiF SVic WRou WWlt |
| | - B&SWJ 10475 | WCru |
| | 'Arcadia Gold' (d) | CWVF SRiF SVic |
| | 'Arcady' | CLoc CWVF |
| | 'Archie Owen' (d) | SRiF |
| | 'Ariel' (E) | CDoC CSil LRHS SVic WRou |
| | 'Arkie' | MJac |
| | 'Arlendon' (d) | CWVF |
| | 'Army Nurse' (d) 🏆$^{H4}$ | CDoC CLoc CSil CWVF ELan EPfP EPts LAst LRHS MGos NBir SEND SLBF SPet SRiF SVic |
| | 'Art Deco' (d) | SRiF |
| | 'Arthur Baxter' | EBak |
| | 'Ashley' | CDoC LCla |
| | 'Ashley and Isobel' | CWVF SRiF |
| | 'Ashtede' | SLBF |
| | 'Atahualpa' (T) | CDoC |
| | 'Athela' | EBak SRiF |
| | 'Athene' | SRiF |
| | 'Atlantic Star' | CWVF MJac SRiF |
| | 'Atlantis' (d) | CWVF MJac |
| | 'Atlas' | SRiF |
| | 'Atomic Glow' (d) | EBak SRiF SVic |
| | 'Aubergine' | see *F.* 'Gerharda's Aubergine' |
| | 'Aubrey Harris' (d) | SRiF |
| | 'Audray' | SRiF |
| | 'Audrey Booth' (d) | SRiF |
| | 'Audrey Dahms' | SRiF |
| | 'Audrey Hepburn' | CWVF |
| | 'Auenland' **new** | MJac |
| | 'Aunt Hilda' **new** | CSil |
| | 'Aunt Juliana' (d) | EBak SRiF |
| | 'Auntie Jinks' | CCCN CDoC CWVF EBak LAst MJac SLBF SPet SRiF SVic WRou |
| | 'Auntie Kit' | SRiF |
| | 'Aurora Superba' | CLoc CWVF EBak SLBF SRiF WRou |
| | 'Australia Fair' (d) | CWVF EBak SRiF |
| § | ***austromontana*** | EBak SRiF |
| | 'Autumnale' 🏆$^{H1+3}$ | CCCN CDoC CHEx CLoc CWVF EBak EPts LAst NVic SBfd SLBF SMrm SPet SPoG SVic WHil WRou |

| | Name | Suppliers |
|---|---|---|
| | 'Avalanche' ambig. (d) | CDoC CLoc EBak SLBF |
| | 'Avocet' | CLoc EBak SRiF |
| | 'Avon Celebration' (d) | CLoc |
| | 'Avon Gem' | CLoc CSil SRiF |
| | 'Avon Glow' (d) | CLoc |
| | 'Avon Gold' | CLoc |
| | ***ayavacensis*** | CDoC LCla |
| | 'Azure Sky' (d) | MJac |
| | 'Babette' (d) | SRiF |
| | 'Baby Blue Eyes' 🏆$^{H3-4}$ | CDoC CSil CWVF ELon EPfP LRHS LSRN MAsh MBri WRou |
| | 'Baby Blush' | CSil |
| | 'Baby Bright' | CWVF LCla SRiF WRou |
| | 'Baby Chang' | SRiF |
| | 'Baby Face' ambig. | SRiF |
| | 'Baby Love' | SRiF |
| | 'Baby Pink' (d) | CWVF |
| | 'Baby Thumb' (v) | EPts SRiF |
| | 'Babyface' Tolley (d) | SVic |
| § | × ***bacillaris*** (E) | CAbb CChe CDoC CDul CEnt CHGN CSil EBak EWes GCal ITim NLar NMun SBfd SEND SLBF SPoG SRms |
| § | - 'Cottinghamii' (E) | CDoC CSil EWld IDee IRar SPlb WSHC |
| | - 'Oosje' | see *F.* 'Oosje' |
| § | - 'Reflexa' (E) | CAbP CCCN CTrC GQui LSou |
| | 'Baden Powell' (E) | SRiF SVic |
| | 'Bagworthy Water' | CLoc |
| | 'Baker's Tri' (T) | EBak |
| | 'Balkonkönigin' | CLoc CWVF EBak SRiF |
| | 'Ballerina' | CDoC |
| | 'Ballerina Girl' (E) | SLBF |
| | 'Ballet Girl' (d) 🏆$^{H1+3}$ | CDoC CLoc CWVF EBak SLBF SRiF |
| | 'Balmoral' (d) | SRiF |
| | 'Bambini' | CWVF EPts SRiF |
| | 'Banks Peninsula' | GBin GQui |
| | 'Barbara' | CLoc CSil CTsd CWVF EBak EPts MJac SPet SRiF SVic WRou |
| | 'Barbara Evans' | SLBF SRiF |
| | 'Barbara Pountain' (d) | CWVF |
| | 'Barbara Windsor' | CWVF MJac SRiF |
| | 'Baron de Ketteler' (d) | SRiF |
| | 'Barry's Queen' | see *F.* 'Golden Border Queen' |
| | 'Bartje' | SLBF |
| | 'Bashful' (d) | CDoC CSil EPts LCla SPet SRiF SVic |
| | 'Basketfull' (d) | SRiF |
| | 'Beacon' | CDoC CLoc CSil CWVF EBak EPfP EPts LAst LCla LRHS MBri MJac MWat SEND SLBF SPet SPoG SRiF SVic WRou |
| | 'Beacon Rosa' | CCCN CDoC CLoc CSil CWVF ELon EPts LAst LCla LRHS MBri MJac NBlu SEND SLBF SPet SPoG SRiF SVic WRou |
| | 'Beacon Superior' | CSil |
| | 'Bealings' (d) | CLoc CWVF MBri SRiF SVic |
| | 'Beau Nash' | CLoc |
| | 'Beauty of Bath' (d) | CLoc EBak |
| | 'Beauty of Bexley' (d) | SRiF |
| | 'Beauty of Clyffe Hall' | CSil EBak |
| | 'Beauty of Exeter' (d) | CWVF EBak SRiF |
| | 'Beauty of Meise' (d) | CDoC |
| | 'Beauty of Prussia' (d) | CLoc CSil CWVF |
| | 'Beauty of Swanley' | EBak SRiF |
| | 'Beauty of Trowbridge' | CWVF LCla |
| | 'Beckey' (d) | SRiF |
| | 'Becky Jane' | CSil |
| | 'Becky Reynolds' | SRiF |
| | 'Bella Forbes' (d) 🏆$^{H1+3}$ | CSil EBak |

| | | |
|---|---|---|
| | 'Bella Harris' (d) | SRiF |
| | 'Bella Rosella' (California Dreamers Series) (d) | CCCN EPts LAst LBMP MJac SCoo SLBF SRiF |
| | 'Bellbottoms' | SRiF |
| | 'Belle de Spa' | SRiF |
| | 'Belsay Beauty' (d) | CWVF MJac SRiF SVic |
| | 'Belvoir Beauty' (d) | CLoc |
| | 'Ben de Jong' | CDoC LCla SLBF SRiF WRou |
| | 'Ben Jammin' | CDoC CLoc CSil CWVF EPfP EPts LAst LRHS MJac SEND SPoG SRiF SVic WRou |
| | 'Ben Jiggins' (d) | SRiF |
| | 'Béranger' Lemoine, 1897 (d) | CSil EBak |
| | 'Berba's Happiness' (d) | CWVF |
| | 'Berba's Trio' | SRiF |
| | 'Bergnimf' | SRiF |
| | 'Berliner Kind' (d) | CSil CWVF EBak SRiF |
| | 'Bermuda' (d) | CWVF SRiF |
| | 'Bernadette' (d) | CWVF |
| | 'Bernie's Big-un' (d) | MJac |
| | 'Bernisser Hardy' ♀H3-4 | CDoC CSil EPts LCla LRHS SEND SLBF SRiF |
| | 'Beryl Clarke' (v) **new** | EPts SLBF |
| | 'Beryl's Choice' (d) | SRiF |
| | 'Berys Elizabeth' | SRiF |
| | 'Bessie Kimberley' (T) | CDoC LCla |
| | 'Beth Robley' (d) | CWVF SRiF |
| | 'Betsy Ross' (d) | EBak |
| | 'Bette Sibley' (d) | SRiF |
| | Betty = 'Shabetty'[PBR] (Shadowdancer Series) | LAst |
| | 'Beverley' | CWVF EBak EPts SRiF |
| | 'Beverley Sisters' (d) | MJac |
| | 'Bewitched' (d) | EBak |
| | 'Bianca' (d) | CWVF SRiF SVic |
| | 'Bicentennial' (d) | CCCN CLoc CWVF EBak EPts LAst MJac SPet SRiF SVic |
| | 'Big Slim' | SLBF SRiF |
| | 'Bill Gilbert' | SRiF |
| | 'Bill Stevens' (d) | CTsd |
| | 'Billy'[PBR] | CDoC |
| | 'Billy Green' (T) ♀H1+3 | CDoC CLoc CWVF EBak EPts LCla MHer MJac SLBF SRiF SVic WRou |
| | 'Billy P' | LAst |
| | 'Bilton' **new** | CSil |
| | 'Bishop's Bells' (d) | CWVF SVic |
| | 'Bits' (d) | CTsd |
| | 'Bittersweet' (d) | SVic |
| | 'Black Beauty' (d) | CWVF |
| | 'Black Country 21' | SLBF |
| | 'Black Prince' | CDoC CWVF SRiF SVic |
| | 'Blackmore Vale' (d) | CWVF |
| | 'Blacky' (d) | CCCN EBak LAst LSou MSCN SBfd SEND SGar SMrm SPet SRiF SVic |
| I | 'Blanche Regina' (d) | CWVF MJac |
| | 'Bland's New Striped' | CDoC EBak EPts LAst SLBF SRiF |
| | 'Blaze Away' (d) | LAst MBri MJac SRiF WGor |
| | 'Blood Donor' (d) | MJac SRiF |
| | 'Blowick' | CDoC CWVF MBri MJac SPet SRiF |
| | 'Blue Beauty' (d) | CSil EBak SRiF |
| | 'Blue Bush' | CSil CWVF EPts MJac SRiF SVic |
| | 'Blue Butterfly' (d) | CWVF EBak SRiF SVic |
| | 'Blue Eyes' (d) | CDoC NBlu SPet SRiF |
| | 'Blue Gown' (d) | CDoC CLoc CSil CWVF EBak MGos SPet SRiF SVic WRou |
| | 'Blue Lace' (d) | CSil |
| | 'Blue Lagoon' ambig. (d) | CWVF |
| | 'Blue Lake' (d) | CWVF |
| | 'Blue Mink' | EBak SRiF |
| | 'Blue Mirage' (d) | CLoc CWVF LAst SRiF SVic |
| | 'Blue Mist' (d) | EBak |
| | 'Blue Pearl' (d) | CWVF EBak SRiF |
| | 'Blue Pinwheel' | CWVF EBak |
| | 'Blue Sails' | SRiF |
| | 'Blue Satin' (d) | LAst |
| | 'Blue Tit' | CSil LCla SRiF |
| | 'Blue Veil' (d) | CCCN CLoc CWVF MJac SCoo SRiF SVic |
| | 'Blue Waves' (d) | CLoc CSBt CWVF EBak MJac SPet SRiF SVic |
| | 'Blueberry Fizz' (d) | SRiF |
| | 'Blush o' Dawn' (d) | CLoc CTsd CWVF EBak EPts SPet SRiF SVic |
| | 'Blythe' (d) | SRiF |
| | 'Bob Bartrum' | EPts SLBF |
| | 'Bob Pacey' | CWVF |
| | 'Bob Paisley' (d) | SRiF |
| | 'Bobby Boy' (d) | EBak |
| | 'Bobby Dazzler' (d) | CWVF SRiF |
| | 'Bobby Shaftoe' (d) | EBak SRiF |
| | 'Bobby Wingrove' | EBak |
| | 'Bobby's Girl' | EPts |
| | 'Bobolink' (d) | EBak SRiF |
| | 'Bob's Best' (d) | CWVF EPts MJac SRiF |
| | 'Boerhaave' | EBak SRiF |
| | ***boliviana*** Britton | see *F. sanctae-rosae* |
| | ***boliviana*** ambig. | CBcs CTsd IDee |
| § | ***boliviana*** Carrière | CDoC CHEx CHll CLoc CWVF EBak LCla SRiF WRou |
| § | - var. ***alba*** ♀H1+3 | CDoC CHll CLoc EBak EPts LCla SRiF SVic WRou |
| | - var. ***boliviana*** | CRHN SVic |
| | - var. ***luxurians*** 'Alba' | see *F. boliviana* Carrière var. *alba* |
| | - f. ***puberulenta*** | see *F. boliviana* Carrière |
| | 'Bon Accorde' | CLoc CWVF EBak EPts SLBF SRiF SVic |
| | 'Bon Bon' (d) | CWVF EBak SRiF SVic |
| | 'Bonita' (d) | CWVF SVic |
| | 'Bonnie Bambini' | SRiF |
| | 'Bonnie Lass' (d) | EBak |
| | 'Bora Bora' (d) | CWVF EBak SRiF SVic |
| | 'Borde Hill' (d) | EPts |
| | 'Border Princess' | EBak SRiF |
| | 'Border Queen' ♀H3-4 | CDoC CLoc CSil CWVF EBak EPts EWes MJac MSCN SLBF SPet SRiF SVic |
| | 'Border Reiver' | CWVF EBak SVic |
| | 'Börnemann's Beste' | see *F.* 'Georg Börnemann' |
| | 'Bosom Pals' | SRiF |
| | 'Boson's Norah' | SRiF |
| | 'Bouffant' | CLoc SVic |
| | 'Bountiful' Lye | SRiF |
| | 'Bountiful' Munkner (d) | CLoc CWVF |
| | 'Bouquet' (d) | CDoC CSil SRiF |
| | 'Bow Bells' | CDoC CLoc CWVF MJac SPet SRiF SVic |
| | 'Boy Marc' (T) | LCla SRiF |
| | 'Braamt's Glorie' | CDoC |
| | ***bracelinae*** | CDoC CSil |
| | 'Brancaster' | SRiF |
| | 'Brandt's 500 Club' | CLoc EBak SRiF |
| | 'Brann's Blossom' | SRiF |
| | 'Breakaway' | SRiF |
| | 'Breckland' | EBak SRiF |
| | 'Breeders' Delight' | CSil CWVF MBri SRiF |
| | 'Breeder's Dream' (d) | EBak |
| | 'Breevis Minimus' | SLBF |
| | 'Brenda' (d) | CLoc CWVF EBak |
| | 'Brenda Megan Hill' | SRiF |
| | 'Brenda Pritchard' (d) | SRiF |

| | |
|---|---|
| 'Brenda White' | CDoC CLoc CWVF EBak SRiF SVic WRou |
| 'Brentwood' (d) | EBak |
| ***brevilobis*** | CSil |
| 'Brian C. Morrison' (T) | LCla SRiF |
| 'Brian G. Soanes' | EBak SRiF |
| 'Brian Kimberley' (T) | LCla |
| 'Bridal Pink' (d) | SRiF |
| 'Bridal Veil' (d) | EBak SRiF |
| 'Bridesmaid' (d) | CWVF EBak SPet SRiF SVic |
| 'Brigadoon' (d) | EBak |
| 'Brighton Belle' (T) | CDoC CWVF SRiF |
| 'Brilliant' ambig. | CWVF MBri |
| 'Brilliant' Bull, 1865 | CDoC CLoc CSil EBak LCla |
| 'Briony Caunt' | CSil |
| 'British Jubilee' (d) | CWVF SVic |
| 'British Sterling' (d) | SRiF |
| 'Brixham Orpheus' | CWVF |
| 'Broadbent' (d) | SRiF |
| 'Brodsworth' | CSil |
| 'Bronze Banks Peninsula' | CDoC CSil |
| 'Brookwood Belle' (d) | CTsd CWVF EPts LCla MJac SLBF SRiF |
| 'Brookwood Joy' (d) | CWVF SRiF |
| 'Brutus' 🏆H4 | CDoC CLoc CSil CWVF EBak EPfP EPts LRHS MAsh MBri MSCN MWat SCoo SLBF SPet SPoG SRiF SVic |
| 'Bryan Breary' (E) | LCla SRiF |
| 'Bubble Hanger' | SRiF |
| 'Buddha' (d) | EBak |
| 'Bugle Boy' | LCla SRiF |
| 'Bunny' (d) | CWVF EBak SLBF SRiF SVic |
| 'Burstwick' | CSil |
| 'Burton Brew' | MJac |
| 'Buster' (d) | LCla SRiF |
| 'Buttercup' | CLoc CWVF EBak SVic |
| 'C.J. Howlett' | CSil EBak SRiF |
| 'Caballero' (d) | EBak |
| 'Cabaret' (d) | SRiF |
| 'Cable Car' (d) | SRiF |
| 'Caesar' (d) | CWVF EBak SRiF |
| 'Caledonia' | CSil EBak SRiF |
| 'Callaly Pink' | CWVF |
| 'Cambridge Louie' | CWVF EBak MBri SPet SRiF |
| 'Camelot' | SRiF |
| ***campos-portoi*** | CDoC CSil CTsd LCla WHil WPGP |
| 'Candlelight' (d) | EBak |
| 'Candy Bells' (d) | CSBt |
| 'Candy Kisses' (d) | SRiF |
| ***canescens*** misapplied | see *F. ampliata* |
| 'Cannell's Gem' | SRiF |
| 'Cannenburgh Floriant' (d) | SRiF |
| 'Canny Bob' | MJac |
| 'Canopy' (d) | CWVF |
| 'Capri' (d) | CWVF EBak SRiF |
| 'Captivating Kelly' | SRiF |
| 'Cara Mia' (d) | CLoc CTsd SPet SRiF |
| 'Caradela' (d) | CLoc MJac |
| 'Cardinal' | CLoc |
| 'Cardinal Farges' (d) | CLoc CWVF SLBF SPet SRiF SVic |
| 'Careless Whisper' | CDoC LCla SLBF |
| 'Carioca' | EBak |
| 'Carisbrooke Castle' (d) | SRiF |
| 'Carl Drude' (d) | CSil CTsd SRiF SVic |
| 'Carl Wallace' (d) | SRiF |
| 'Carla Johnston' 🏆H1+3 | CDoC CLoc CWVF EPts MBri MJac SVic WRou |
| 'Carl's Brummagem Beauty' | MJac |
| 'Carmel Blue' | CCCN CDoC CLoc LAst MSCN SBfd SPet SRiF SVic WGor |

| | |
|---|---|
| 'Carmen' Lemoine (d) | CDoC CSil |
| 'Carmine Bell' | CSil |
| 'Carnea' | CSil CWib |
| 'Carnival' (d) | SRiF |
| 'Carnoustie' (d) | EBak |
| 'Carol Grace' (d) | CLoc |
| 'Carol Lynn Whittemore' (d) | SRiF |
| 'Carol Nash' (d) | CLoc |
| 'Caroline' | CLoc CWVF EBak EPts SLBF SRiF SVic WRou |
| 'Caroline's Joy' | LAst MJac SBfd SCoo SPet SRiF |
| 'Cascade' | CCCN CDoC CLoc CWVF EPts LBMP MBri MJac SLBF SPet SRiF |
| 'Caspar Hauser' (d) | CWVF SLBF SRiF SVic |
| 'Catharina' (T) | CDoC SRiF |
| 'Catherine Bartlett' | CWVF |
| 'Cathie MacDougall' (d) | EBak |
| 'Cecil Glass' | SRiF |
| 'Cecile' (d) | CCCN CDoC CWVF EPts LAst MJac SLBF SRiF SVic WRou |
| 'Celadore' (d) | CWVF SRiF SVic |
| 'Celebration' (d) | CLoc CWVF SRiF |
| 'Celia Smedley' 🏆H3 | CCCN CDoC CLoc CWVF EBak EPts LCla MBri MJac SLBF SPet SRiF SVic WRou |
| 'Centenary' (d) | SRiF |
| 'Centerpiece' (d) | EBak |
| 'Ceri' | CLoc |
| 'Cerrig' | SVic |
| 'Chameleon' | SRiF |
| 'Champagne Celebration' | CLoc |
| 'Champagne Gold' | SRiF |
| 'Champion' | SRiF |
| 'Chancellor' (d) | CWVF |
| 'Chandleri' | CWVF SLBF SRiF SVic |
| 'Chang' 🏆H1+3 | CDoC CLoc CWVF EBak LCla SLBF SRiF SVic |
| 'Chantelle Garcia' (d) new | SLBF |
| 'Chantry Park' (T) | LCla SRiF |
| 'Charisma' | SVic |
| § 'Charles de Gaulle' | SRiF |
| 'Charles Edward' (d) | CSil SRiF |
| 'Charles Lester' | SRiF |
| 'Charles Welch' | EPts |
| Charlie Dimmock = 'Foncha'$^{PBR}$ (d) | CLoc LAst SRiF |
| 'Charlie Gardiner' | CWVF EBak |
| 'Charlie Girl' (d) | EBak SRiF SVic |
| 'Charlie Pridmore' (d) | SRiF |
| 'Charlotte' | SRiF |
| 'Charlotte Clyne' | SRiF |
| 'Charming' | CDoC CLoc CSil CWVF EBak LRHS MAsh MJac SPet SVic WRou |
| 'Chase Delight' (v) | CDoC SLBF |
| 'Chatt's Delight' | SLBF |
| 'Checkerboard' 🏆H3 | CCCN CLoc CWVF EBak EPts LAst LCla MJac MSCN SLBF SPet SVic |
| 'Cheers' (d) | CWVF |
| 'Chelsea Louise' | EPts |
| 'Cherry'$^{PBR}$ Götz | LAst |
| 'Chessboard' | CLoc |
| 'Chillerton Beauty' 🏆H3 | CLoc CSil CTri CWVF ELan ELon EPts LAst LCla LRHS MJac SEND SLBF SPet SVic WMnd |
| 'China Doll' (d) | CWVF EBak SRiF SVic |
| 'China Lantern' | CLoc CSil CWVF EBak SRiF SVic |
| 'Chomal' (d) | SRiF |
| 'Chor Echo' | CDoC |
| 'Chris Coleman' | SRiF |
| 'Chris Nicholls' (d) | CSil |

| | Name | Suppliers |
|---|---|---|
| | 'Chris Tarrant' (d) | EPts |
| | 'Christina Becker' | SRiF SVic |
| | 'Christine Bamford' | CDoC CSil CTsd CWVF SRiF |
| | 'Christine Rogers' | CDoC |
| | 'Christine Truman' (d) | SRiF |
| | 'Churchtown' | CWVF SRiF |
| | 'Cicely Ann' | SRiF |
| | ***cinerea*** | CDoC LCla |
| | 'Cinnabarina' (E) | CLoc SRiF |
| | 'Cinnamon' (d) | SRiF |
| | 'Cinque Port Liberty' (d) | SLBF SRiF |
| | 'Cinvenu' | LCla |
| | 'Cinvulca' | LCla |
| | 'Circe' (d) | CWVF EBak SVic |
| | 'Circus' | EBak |
| | 'Circus Spangles' (d) | CLoc LAst |
| | 'Citation' | CLoc CWVF EBak SVic |
| | 'City Lights' | SLBF |
| | 'City of Adelaide' (d) | CLoc SRiF |
| | 'City of Leicester' | CWVF MHer SPet |
| | 'Clair de Lune' | CDoC CWVF EBak SRiF SVic WRou |
| | 'Claire Evans' (d) | CWVF |
| | 'Claire Oram' | CLoc |
| | 'Claudia' (d) | CDoC LAst LCla MJac SLBF WRou |
| | 'Cliantha' (d) | CDoC SRiF WRou |
| | 'Clifford Gadsby' (d) | EBak SRiF |
| | 'Cliff's Hardy' | CDoC CSil LCla SRiF |
| | 'Cliff's Own' | SVic |
| | 'Cliff's Unique' (d) | CWVF EPts |
| | 'Clifton Beauty' (d) | CWVF MJac SRiF |
| | 'Clifton Belle' (d) | CWVF |
| | 'Clifton Charm' | CSil EPts LCla MJac SVic |
| | 'Clipper' | CSil CWVF |
| | 'Cloth of Gold' | CLoc CWVF EBak MHer MJac SPet SRiF SVic |
| | 'Cloverdale Jewel' (d) | CDoC CWVF EBak SPet SRiF SVic |
| | 'Cloverdale Joy' | EBak SRiF |
| | 'Cloverdale Pearl' | CWVF EBak EPfP SPet SPoG SVic |
| | 'Coachman' ♀H4 | CLoc CWVF EBak EPts LAst LCla SLBF SPet SRiF SVic WRou |
| | ***coccinea*** | CDoC CSil CTsd |
| | 'Codringtonii' | CSil |
| | × ***colensoi*** | CDoC CSil ECou LCla |
| | 'Colibri' | SRiF |
| | 'Colin Chambers' (d) | SRiF |
| | 'Collingwood' (d) | CLoc CWVF EBak SRiF |
| | 'Colne Fantasy' (v) | CDoC SRiF |
| | 'Come Dancing' (d) | CDoC CWVF SPet SRiF SVic |
| | 'Comet' ambig. | SRiF |
| | 'Comet' Banks | CWVF |
| I | 'Comet' Tiret (d) | CDoC CLoc EBak SPet |
| | 'Comperen Lutea' (d) | CDoC |
| | 'Conchilla' (d) | EBak SRiF |
| | 'Connie' (d) | EBak SRiF SVic |
| | 'Connor's Cascade' **new** | SLBF |
| | 'Conspicua' ♀H3-4 | CSil CWVF EBak SLBF SRiF SVic |
| | 'Constable Country' (d) | CWVF SRiF |
| | 'Constance' (d) | CDoC CLoc CSil CWVF LCla MJac SLBF SPet SRiF SVic WRou |
| | 'Constance Comer' | MJac SRiF WRou |
| | 'Constellation' ambig. | CWVF |
| | 'Constellation' Schnabel, 1957 (d) | CLoc EBak |
| | 'Continental' (d) | SRiF |
| | 'Contraste' (d) | SBfd |
| | 'Coombe Park' | MJac |
| | 'Copycat' | CSil |
| | 'Coquet Bell' | CWVF EBak SRiF |
| | 'Coquet Dale' (d) | CWVF EBak SRiF |
| | 'Coquet Gold' (d/v) | SRiF |
| | 'Coral Baby' (E) | LCla |
| | 'Coral Rose' (d) | SVic |
| | 'Coral Seas' | EBak |
| | 'Coralle' (T) | CCCN CDoC CLoc CWVF EBak EPts LCla MHer MJac MSCN SLBF SRiF SVic WRou |
| | 'Corallina' ♀H3-4 | CDoC CLoc CSil CTsd EBak ELon SBfd SPet SRiF SVic WFar WPnn |
| I | 'Corallina Variegata' (v) | CSil |
| * | ***cordata*** B&SWJ 9095 | WCru |
| | - B&SWJ 10325 | WCru |
| | ***cordifolia*** misapplied | see *F. splendens* |
| | 'Core'ngrato' (d) | CLoc CWVF EBak SRiF |
| | 'Cornelia Smith' (T) | CDoC LCla |
| | 'Cornwall Calls' (d) | EBak |
| | 'Corsage' (d) | CWVF SVic |
| | 'Corsair' (d) | EBak SRiF SVic |
| | ***corymbiflora*** misapplied | see *F. boliviana* Carrière |
| | ***corymbiflora*** Ruíz & Pav. | CDoC EBak SVic |
| | 'Cosmopolitan' (d) | EBak SRiF |
| | 'Costa Brava' | CLoc EBak |
| | 'Cotta Bright Star' | CDoC CWVF LCla |
| | 'Cotta Carousel' | LCla WRou |
| | 'Cotta Christmas Tree' | CDoC LCla SLBF SRiF |
| | 'Cotta Fairy' | CWVF |
| | 'Cotta Vino' | SRiF SVic |
| | 'Cottinghamii' | see *F.* × *bacillaris* 'Cottinghamii' |
| | 'Cotton Candy' (d) | CLoc CWVF SRiF SVic |
| | 'Countdown Carol' (d) | EPts |
| | 'Countess of Aberdeen' | CWVF EBak SLBF SRiF |
| | 'Countess of Maritza' (d) | CLoc CWVF |
| | 'County Park' | ECou |
| | 'Court Jester' (d) | CLoc EBak SRiF |
| | 'Cover Girl' (d) | EBak EPts SPet SRiF |
| | 'Coxeen' | EBak |
| I | 'Cracker' (d) | SRiF |
| | 'Crackerjack' | CLoc EBak SRiF |
| | 'Creampuff' (d) | CDoC CTsd SRiF |
| | 'Crescendo' (d) | CLoc CWVF |
| | 'Crinkley Bottom' (d) | EPts MJac SLBF SRiF |
| | 'Crinoline' (d) | EBak SRiF |
| | 'Crosby Serendipity' | CLoc |
| | 'Crosby Soroptimist' | CWVF MJac SRiF WRou |
| | 'Cross Check' | CWVF MBri |
| | 'Crusader' (d) | CWVF SRiF |
| | 'Crystal Aniversary' (d) | SRiF |
| | 'Crystal Blue' | EBak SRiF SVic |
| | 'Crystal Stars' (d) | SVic |
| | 'Cupid' | CSil EBak |
| | 'Curly Q' | EBak SPet SRiF SVic |
| | 'Curtain Call' (d) | CWVF EBak SRiF SVic |
| | ***cylindracea*** misapplied | see *F.* × *bacillaris* |
| | ***cylindracea*** Lindl. (E) | CSil LCla SRiF |
| | - B&SWJ 10294 (E/f) | WCru |
| | 'Cymon' (d) | CWVF SRiF |
| | 'Cymru' (d) | SVic |
| | 'Cyndy Robyn' (d) | SRiF |
| | 'Cyril Holmes' | SRiF |
| | ***cyrtandroides*** | CSil |
| | 'Dainty' | EBak |
| | 'Dainty Lady' (d) | EBak |
| | 'Daisy Bell' | CDoC CLoc CTsd CWVF EBak LCla MJac SPet SRiF SVic WRou |
| | 'Dalton' | EBak |
| | 'Dana Samantha' | EPts |
| | 'Dancing Bloom' | EPts SRiF |
| | 'Dancing Flame' (d) ♀H1+3 | CCCN CLoc CWVF EBak EPts LAst LBMP MBri MJac SLBF SPet SRiF SVic |

| Name | Suppliers |
|---|---|
| 'Daniel Pfaller' (d) **new** | MJac |
| 'Danielle' | SRiF WRou |
| 'Danish Pastry' | CWVF SPet SRiF |
| 'Danny Boy' (d) | CLoc CWVF EBak SRiF SVic |
| 'Danson Belle' (d) | SRiF |
| 'Dark Eyes' (d) ♀H4 | CCCN CLoc CSil CWVF EBak LAst LBMP MBri MJac SBai SLBF SPet SRiF SVic |
| 'Dark Mystery' (d) | SRiF |
| 'Dark Night' (d) | CSil |
| 'Dark Secret' (d) | EBak |
| 'Dark Treasure' (d) | CDoC CTsd SRiF |
| 'Daryn John Woods' | CDoC LCla SRiF |
| 'David' ♀H3-4 | CDoC CLoc CSil CWVF ELon EOHP EPfP EPts LAst LCla LSRN SLBF SLPl SRiF WGor WHil WRou |
| 'David Alston' (d) | CLoc CWVF EBak |
| 'David Lockyer' (d) | CLoc CWVF SVic |
| 'David Savage' (d) | LCla |
| 'David Ward' (d) | NEgg |
| 'Dawn' | EBak SRiF |
| 'Dawn Carless' (d) | SRiF |
| 'Dawn Fantasia' (v) | CLoc EPts SRiF |
| 'Dawn Redfern' (d) | CWVF |
| 'Dawn Sky' (d) | EBak |
| 'Dawn Star' (d) | CLoc CWVF MJac SVic |
| 'Dawn Thunder' (d) | SVic |
| 'Day by Day' | CSil |
| 'Day Star' | EBak |
| 'Daytime Live' | SRiF |
| 'De Berckt' | SRiF |
| 'De Groot's Floriant' | LCla |
| 'De Groot's Moonlight' | SRiF |
| 'De Groot's Tricolore' | SRiF |
| 'De Mijnlamp' (d) | CDoC |
| 'Deal Marine' (d) | SRiF |
| 'Debby' (d) | EBak SRiF |
| 'Deben Petite' (E) | LCla |
| 'Deben Rose' | SRiF |
| 'Deborah Jane' | SLBF |
| 'Deborah Louise' | SRiF |
| 'Deborah Street' (d) | CLoc |
| § ***decussata*** Ruíz & Pav. | EBak |
| 'Dee Copley' (d) | EBak |
| 'Dee Star' (d) | SVic |
| 'Deep Purple' (d) | CCCN CDoC CLoc CWVF LAst LBMP MJac SCoo SLBF SRiF |
| 'Delia Smith' (d) | EPts |
| 'Delilah' (d) | CWVF |
| 'Delta's Bride' | SLBF |
| 'Delta's Dream' | CTsd CWVF SRiF |
| 'Delta's Drop' | SLBF SRiF SVic |
| 'Delta's Groom' | LCla SLBF SRiF WRou |
| 'Delta's Ko' (d) | SRiF SVic |
| 'Delta's Paljas' | SRiF |
| 'Delta's Parade' (d) | CDoC SRiF |
| 'Delta's Pim' | SRiF |
| 'Delta's Prelude' | SRiF |
| 'Delta's Rien' | SRiF SVic |
| 'Delta's Sara' | CDoC CSil LAst LRHS MBri MCCP MJac SPoG SRiF |
| 'Delta's Song' | SRiF WRou |
| 'Delta's Sprinkler' | SRiF |
| 'Delta's Symphonie' (d) | CWVF |
| 'Delta's Trick' | SRiF |
| 'Delta's Wonder' | CSil SRiF SVic |
| § ***denticulata*** | CDoC CLoc CWVF EBak EPts LAst LCla MHer SEND SLBF SRiF SVic WRou |
| 'Derby Imp' | CWVF SRiF |

| Name | Suppliers |
|---|---|
| 'Desperate Daniel' | EPts |
| 'Devonshire Dumpling' (d) | CCCN CDoC CLoc CTsd CWVF EBak EPts LAst MBri MJac SLBF SPet SRiF SVic |
| 'Diablo' (d) | EBak SRiF |
| 'Diament' | SRiF |
| 'Diamond Celebration' (d) | SRiF |
| 'Diamond Wedding' | SRiF SVic |
| 'Diana' (d) | EBak SRiF |
| 'Diana Simpson' | SRiF |
| 'Diana Wills' (d) | CWVF |
| 'Diana Wright' | CDoC CSil LPla SRiF |
| Diana, Princess of Wales = 'Fucdpw'PBR | LAst LBMP MJac SBfd |
| 'Diane Brown' | CWVF |
| 'Diane Stephens' | SLBF |
| 'Dick Swinbank' (d) | SRiF |
| § 'Die Schöne Wilhelmine' | SLBF SVic |
| 'Dilly-Dilly' (d) | CWVF SRiF |
| 'Dimples' (d) | CSil MBri SRiF |
| 'Dipton Dainty' (d) | CLoc EBak SRiF SVic |
| 'Display' ♀H4 | CCCN CDoC CDul CLoc CSil CWVF EBak EPfP EPts LAst LBMP LCla LRHS MBri MJac NPer SLBF SPet SPoG SRiF SVic WFar WRou |
| 'Doc' | CDoC CSil EPts SPet SRiF SVic |
| 'Docteur Topinard' | CLoc EBak |
| 'Doctor' | see *F.* 'The Doctor' |
| 'Doctor Foster' ♀H4 | CDoC CLoc CSil CTri EBak EPfP SRiF SVic |
| 'Doctor Mason' | CWVF |
| 'Doctor Olson' (d) | CLoc EBak SRiF |
| 'Doctor Robert' | CWVF EPts MBri MJac SRiF SVic |
| 'Dodo' | LCla SLBF |
| § 'Dollar Prinzessin' (d) ♀H4 | CCCN CDoC CLoc CMac CSil CTsd CWVF EBak EPfP EPts LAst LCla LRHS MAsh MBri MJac MWat NPer SGar SLBF SPet SPlb SRiF SVic WFar |
| 'Dolly Harris' | SRiF |
| 'Dominyana' | EBak LCla |
| 'Don Peralta' | EBak |
| 'Dopy' (d) | CDoC EPts SPet SRiF SVic |
| 'Doreen Redfern' | CLoc CWVF MJac SPet SRiF SVic WRou |
| 'Doreen Stroud' (d) | CWVF |
| 'Dorian Brogdale' | SRiF |
| 'Doris Coleman' (d) | SRiF |
| 'Doris Deaves' | SLBF |
| 'Doris Joan' | SLBF SRiF |
| 'Doris Yvonne' (d) | SRiF |
| 'Dorking Blue' (d) | SRiF |
| 'Dorking Delight' | SRiF |
| 'Dorothea Flower' | CLoc CWVF EBak SRiF |
| 'Dorothy' | LCla SLBF SPet SRiF |
| 'Dorothy Ann' | LCla SLBF |
| 'Dorothy Cheal' | CWVF |
| 'Dorothy Day' (d) | CLoc |
| 'Dorothy Hanley' (d) | CAlb CCCN CLoc CSil EPts LAst LRHS LSRN LSou MAsh MBri MJac SEND SLBF SPet SPoG SRiF SVic WRou |
| 'Dorothy Oosting' (d) | CDoC |
| 'Dorothy Shields' (d) | CWVF MJac SRiF |
| 'Dorrian Brogdale' (T) | LCla |
| 'Dorset Abigail' | CWVF |
| 'Dorset Delight' (d) | CWVF SRiF |
| 'Dot Woodage' | SRiF |
| 'Dovercourt Pride' | SRiF |
| 'Drake 400' (d) | CLoc |
| 'Drama Girl' (d) | CWVF SRiF |

| | |
|---|---|
| 'Drame' (d) | CDoC CSil CWVF EBak LCla SPet SRiF SVic WRou |
| 'Drum Major' (d) | EBak |
| 'Du Barry' (d) | EBak |
| 'Duchess of Albany' | CLoc EBak SRiF |
| 'Duchess of Cornwall' (d) | EPts SRiF |
| 'Duet' (d) | SRiF SVic |
| 'Duke of Wellington' Haag, 1956 (d) | CLoc |
| 'Dulcie Elizabeth' (d) | CWVF EBak MJac SPet SRiF |
| 'Dunrobin Bedder' | CSil |
| 'Dusky Beauty' | CWVF SRiF SVic |
| 'Dusky Blue' | SRiF |
| 'Dusky Rose' (d) | CLoc CWVF EBak MJac SVic |
| 'Dusted Pink' (d) | SRiF |
| 'Dutch Flamingo' | SRiF |
| 'Dutch Mill' | CLoc CWVF EBak SRiF |
| 'Dutch Shoes' (d) **new** | SRiF |
| 'Duyfken' | CWVF SRiF |
| 'Dying Embers' | CLoc MSCN WRou |
| 'Dymph Werker van Groenland' (E) | LCla |
| 'Earre Barré' | SRiF |
| 'East Anglian' | CLoc EBak SRiF |
| 'Easter Belle' | LRHS |
| 'Easter Bonnet' (d) | CLoc CWVF |
| 'Ebb 'n' Flow' | EBak SRiF |
| 'Ebbtide' (d) | CLoc EBak |
| 'Echo' | CWVF SRiF |
| 'Ed Largarde' (d) | EBak SRiF |
| 'Eden' | SRiF |
| 'Eden Lady' | CDoC CLoc SPet SRiF |
| 'Eden Princess' | CWVF MJac SRiF |
| 'Eden Rock' (d) | WGor |
| 'Edie Lester' | SRiF |
| 'Edith' ambig. | EPts WRou |
| 'Edith' Banks | SRiF |
| 'Edith' Brown (d) | CSil LCla SLBF |
| 'Edith Emery' (d) | SPet SRiF |
| 'Edna May' | CWVF |
| 'Edna W. Smith' | CWVF |
| 'Eileen Drew' | SLBF |
| 'Eileen Raffill' | EBak |
| 'Eileen Saunders' | CSil EBak |
| 'Eisleban' | SRiF |
| 'El Camino' (d) | CWVF SRiF |
| 'El Cid' | CLoc CSil EBak SRiF SVic |
| 'Elaine Ann' | EPts MJac |
| 'Elaine Taylor' (d) | MJac |
| 'Eleanor Leytham' | CWVF EBak SRiF SVic WRou |
| 'Eleanor Rawlins' | CSil EBak SRiF |
| 'Elf' | CSil |
| 'Elfin Glade' | CLoc CSil CWVF EBak SRiF |
| 'Elfrida' (d) | CSil |
| 'Elfriede Ott' (T) | CLoc EBak LCla SRiF |
| 'Elisabeth Schnedl' (d) | WRou |
| 'Elizabeth' ambig. | CTsd SRiF |
| 'Elizabeth' Whiteman, 1941 | EBak |
| 'Elizabeth Honnorine' | SVic |
| 'Elizabeth Travis' (d) | EBak |
| 'Ellen Morgan' (d) | CWVF EBak SRiF |
| 'Ellen White' (d) | SRiF |
| 'Elma' | LCla |
| 'Elsa' (d) | CWVF SPet SRiF SVic |
| 'Elsie Maude' (d) | CWVF SRiF |
| 'Elsie Mitchell' (d) | CTsd CWVF SPet SRiF WRou |
| 'Elsie Vert' (d) | SRiF |
| 'Elsstar' (d) | SRiF |
| 'Elysée' | CSil SRiF |
| § 'Emile de Wildeman' (d) | CWVF EBak SPet SRiF |
| 'Emile Zola' | CSil SRiF |
| 'Emily Austen' | CWVF SRiF |
| 'Emily Bright' | SRiF |
| 'Emma Alice' (d) | CWVF |
| 'Emma Louise' (d) | SRiF |
| 'Emma Margaret' | SLBF SRiF |
| 'Emma Massey' | SRiF |
| 'Empress of Prussia' ♀H4 | CDoC CLoc CSil CWVF EBak EPts SLBF SPet SRiF SVic WMnd WRou |
| 'Enchanted' (d) | CWVF EBak |
| ***encliandra*** (E) | IFoB |
| – subsp. ***encliandra*** (E) | CDoC WRou |
| * – var. ***gris*** (E) | CSil |
| § 'Enfant Prodigue' (d) | CDoC CLoc CSil SDix SLBF SMrm SRiF SVic WMnd |
| 'English Rose' (d) | CWVF |
| 'Enstone' | see *F. magellanica* var. *molinae* 'Enstone' |
| 'Erica Julie' (d) | SRiF |
| 'Eric's Hardy' (d) | CDoC |
| 'Eric's Majestic' (d) | MJac SRiF |
| 'Erika Köth' (T) | LCla SRiF |
| 'Ernest Rankin' | CSil SRiF SVic |
| 'Ernie'[PBR] | LAst SLBF |
| 'Ernie Bromley' | CSil CWVF SRiF |
| 'Ernie Wise' (d) | MJac SCoo SRiF |
| 'Eroica' | SVic |
| 'Eruption' | CDoC LAst |
| 'Esmerelda' | MJac |
| 'Estafette' (d) | SRiF |
| 'Estelle Marie' | CLoc CWVF EBak MBri SPet SRiF SVic |
| 'Eternal Flame' (d) | CWVF EBak EPts MBri SRiF SVic |
| 'Ethel May' (d) | MJac |
| 'Ethel May Lester' (d) | SRiF |
| 'Ethel Wilson' | CSil |
| 'Eureka Red' (Californian Dreamers Series) (d) | SRiF |
| 'Eusebia' (d) | CTsd SRiF SVic |
| 'Eva Boerg' | CCCN CLoc CSil CTri CWVF EBak LAst MBri MNHC SPet SRiF SVic WKif |
| 'Evelyn Stanley' (d) | CWVF |
| § 'Evelyn Steele Little' | EBak SRiF |
| 'Evening Sky' (d) | EBak SRiF |
| 'Evensong' | CLoc CWVF EBak SRiF SVic |
| ***excorticata*** | CAbb CBcs CDoC CPLG CSil CTsd MCot SPlb |
| 'Exmoor Paths' **new** | CSil |
| 'Exmoor Pearl' **new** | CSil |
| 'Exmoor Rose' **new** | CSil |
| 'Exmoor Silver' **new** | CSil |
| 'Exmoor Woods' | CSil SRiF |
| 'Expo '86' (d) | SRiF |
| 'Eynsford' (d) | SRiF |
| 'Fabian Franck' (T) | CDoC LCla SRiF |
| 'Falklands' (d) | CSil SLBF SRiF |
| 'Falling Stars' | CLoc CWVF EBak SRiF SVic |
| 'Fan Dancer' (d) | EBak |
| 'Fancy Free' (d) | MBri |
| 'Fancy Pants' (d) | CLoc CWVF EBak SRiF SVic |
| 'Fanfare' | CDoC EBak LCla SVic WRou |
| 'Farningham' | SRiF |
| 'Fascination' | see *F.* 'Emile de Wildeman' |
| 'Fashion' (d) | EBak |
| 'Favourite' | EBak SRiF |
| 'Felicity Kendal' (d) | MJac SCoo |
| 'Feltham's Pride' | CWVF |
| 'Fenman' | CWVF SRiF SVic |
| 'Fergie' (d) | SRiF |

'Festival Lights' (E) SLBF
'Festoon' EBak
'Fey' (d) CWVF SRiF
'Ffion' CDoC EPts SRiF
'Fiery Spider' EBak SRiF SVic
'Finn' CWVF EPts
'Fiona' CDoC CLoc CWVF EBak SPet SRiF SVic
'Fire Mountain' (d) CLoc SRiF SVic
'Firecracker'PBR see *F.* 'John Ridding'
'Firefly' SRiF SVic
'Firelite' (d) EBak SRiF
'Firenza' (d) CWVF SRiF
'First Kiss' (d) CWVF
'First Lady' (d) CWVF SRiF
'First Lord' CWVF SRiF
'First of the Day' SRiF
'First Success' (E) CDoC CWVF LCla SRiF SVic WRou
'Flair' (d) CLoc CWVF SRiF
'Flame' EBak
'Flamenco Dancer' (California Dreamers Series) (d) CLoc
'Flamingo' (d) SVic
'Flash' ♀H3-4 CLoc CSil CTri CWVF EBak EPfP EPts LCla MJac SLBF SPet SPoG SRiF SVic WRou
'Flashlight' CDoC CSil CWVF EPfP EWld LAst LCla MJac SCoo SRiF
'Flashlight Amélioré' CSil
'Flat Jack o' Lancashire' (d) CSil SLBF SRiF
'Flavia' (d) EBak
'Fleur de Picardie' SLBF
'Flirtation Waltz' (d) CLoc CWVF EBak MJac SRiF SVic
'Flocon de Neige' CSil EBak
'Flogman' LCla
'Floral City' (d) CLoc EBak
'Florence Taylor' (d) CWVF
'Florence Turner' CSil EBak SRiF
'Florentina' (d) CLoc CWVF EBak SRiF SVic
'Florrie Lester' (d) SRiF
'Florrie's Gem' (d) SLBF
'Flowerdream' (d) CWVF
'Flyaway' (d) EBak SRiF
'Fly-by-night' (d) CWVF
'Flying Cloud' (d) CDoC CLoc CSil CWVF EBak MBri SRiF SVic
'Flying Scotsman' (d) CCCN CDoC CLoc CWVF EBak EPts MJac SCoo SRiF SVic WRou
'Folies Bergères' (d) EBak
'Foline' SVic
'Foolke' CSil EBak SRiF
'Forfar's Pride' (d) CSil SRiF
'Forget-me-not' CLoc CSil CWVF EBak SVic
'Fort Bragg' (d) CWVF EBak SRiF
'Forward Look' SRiF
'Fountains Abbey' (d) CWVF
'Four Farthings' (d) EPts
'Foxgrove Wood' ♀H3-4 CSil CWVF EBak EPts SLBF SRiF
'Foxtrot' (d) CWVF
'Foxy Lady' (d) CWVF SRiF
'Frances Haskins' CSil SRiF WRou
'Frank Sanford' (d) SRiF
'Frank Saunders' CWVF LCla SLBF
'Frank Unsworth' (d) CWVF EPts MJac SPet SRiF
'Frankfurt 2006' MJac
'Frankie's Magnificent Seven' (d) EPts
'Franz von Zon' LCla SLBF
'Frau Hilde Rademacher' (d) CDoC CSil CWVF EBak EPts SLBF SRiF SVic
'Frauke' SVic
'Fred Hansford' CDoC CSil CWVF SRiF
'Fred Shepherd' SRiF
'Fred's First' (d) CDoC CSil SRiF
'Freefall' EBak
'Friendly Fire' (d) CLoc SRiF
'Friendship' (d) SRiF
'Frosted Flame' CCCN CLoc CTsd CWVF EBak LAst LCla MJac SLBF SPet SRiF
'Frozen Tears' SRiF
'Frühling' (d) CSil EBak
'Fuchsiade' WRou
'Fuchsiade '88' CLoc CSil CWVF EBak SLBF SRiF
'Fuchsiarama '91' (T) CWVF WRou
'Fuji-san' CDoC ELon EPts SRiF
'Fuksie Foetsie' (E) CDoC CSil SRiF
***fulgens*** (T) ♀H1+3 CDoC GCal LCla LRHS MRav WRou
* – 'Variegata' (T/v) CDoC CLoc EPts LCla SRiF WRou
'Fulpila' LCla SLBF SRiF
'Für Elise' (d) EBak
'Gala' (d) EBak SRiF
'Galadriel' WMoo
'Garden News' (d) ♀H3-4 CDoC CLoc COlW CSil CWVF EPfP EPts LAst LCla LRHS MAsh MBri MJac MSCN NPer SLBF SPet SRiF SVic WFar WMnd WRou
'Garden Week' (d) CDoC CWVF SRiF SVic
'Gartenmeister Bonstedt' (T) ♀H1+3 CCCN CDoC CLoc CWVF EBak EWld LCla SRiF SVic
'Gary Rhodes' (d) EBak MJac SBfd SCoo SRiF
'Gay Fandango' (d) CLoc CTsd CWVF EBak SPet SRiF
'Gay Parasol' (d) CLoc LAst MJac SRiF SVic WRou
'Gay Paree' (d) EBak
'Gay Senorita' EBak
'Gay Spinner' (d) CLoc
'Geeskie Guskie' SRiF
***gehrigeri*** EBak
'Gemma Fisher' (d) EPts
Gene = 'Goetzgene'PBR (Shadowdancer Series) LAst LSou SCoo
'Général Charles de Gaulle' see *F.* 'Charles de Gaulle'
'Général Monk' (d) CDoC CSil CWVF EBak EPts LAst MBri SRiF SVic
'Général Voyron' CSil
'General Wavell' (d) SRiF SVic
'Genii' ♀H4 Widely available
'Geoff Oke' CDoC SLBF
'Geoffrey Smith' (d) CSil EPts SRiF
§ 'Georg Börnemann' (T) CLoc EBak SRiF
'Georgana' (d) SRiF
'George Allen White' (d) CDoC CWVF
'George Barr' SRiF
'George Johnson' CDoC SRiF
'George Travis' (d) EBak SRiF
'Gerald Drewitt' CSil
§ 'Gerharda's Aubergine' CLoc CSil CWVF SRiF
'Gesneriana' CDoC CLoc EBak SRiF
'Ghislaine' (d) CDoC SRiF
'Giant Pink Enchanted' (d) CLoc EBak
'Gilda' (d) CWVF MJac SVic
'Gillian Althea' (d) CWVF SRiF
'Gilt Edge' (v) CLoc
'Gina Bowman' (E) CDoC LCla SLBF
Ginger = 'Goetzginger'PBR (Shadowdancer Series) LAst LSou SCoo
'Gingham Girl' (d) SRiF
'Giovanna and Wesley' (d) SRiF
'Gipsy Princess' (d) CLoc

| | | | |
|---|---|---|---|
| 'Girls' Brigade' | CWVF SRiF | 'Greta' (T) | SRiF |
| 'Gladiator' (d) | CMac EBak SRiF SVic | 'Gretna Chase' | MBri SRiF |
| 'Gladys Godfrey' | EBak | 'Grey Lady' (d) | CSil SRiF SVic |
| 'Gladys Lorimer' | CDoC CWVF EPts LRHS | 'Gris' | SRiF |
| 'Gladys Miller' | CLoc | 'Groene Kan's Glorie' | CTsd SVic |
| ***glazioviana*** | CDoC CSil CWVF EPts LCla MHer SLBF SRiF WGwG WRou | 'Grumpy' | CWVF EPts SPet SRiF SVic |
| | | 'Gruss aus dem Bodethal' | CLoc CWVF EBak EPts SLBF SRiF |
| 'Glenby' (d) | CWVF SRiF | 'Guinevere' | CWVF EBak |
| 'Glendale' | CWVF | 'Gustave Doré' (d) | CSil EBak SRiF |
| 'Glitters' | CWVF EBak | 'Guy Dauphine' (d) | EBak |
| § 'Globosa' | CAgr CSil EBak SRiF | 'Gwen Dodge' | SRiF SVic |
| 'Gloria Golding' **new** | SRiF | 'Gwend-a-ling' | SRiF |
| 'Glow' | CSil EBak SRiF | 'Gypsy Girl' (d) | CWVF SRiF |
| 'Glowing Embers' | EBak SRiF | 'H.G. Brown' | CSil EBak SRiF |
| 'Glowing Lilac' (d) | EPts | 'Halsall Beauty' (d) | MBri |
| 'Gold Brocade' | ELon EPfP SPet SRiF | 'Halsall Belle' (d) | MBri SRiF |
| 'Gold Crest' | EBak SRiF | 'Halsall Pride' (d) | MBri |
| 'Gold Leaf' | CWVF SRiF | 'Hampshire Blue' | CDoC CWVF SRiF SVic |
| 'Golden Amethyst' (d) | SRiF | 'Hanna Improved' | SRiF |
| 'Golden Anniversary' (d) | CLoc CWVF EBak MJac SRiF SVic | 'Hannah Louise' (d) | EPts |
| 'Golden Arrow' (T) | CDoC LCla SRiF SVic | 'Hannah Rogers' | SLBF SRiF |
| § 'Golden Border Queen' | CLoc EBak SPet | 'Hans Callaars' | LCla |
| 'Golden Dawn' | CLoc CWVF EBak SPet SRiF SVic | 'Happiness' (d) | SVic |
| 'Golden Girl' | SLBF | 'Happy' | CDoC CSil CTsd CWVF EPts LCla MSCN SPet SRiF SVic |
| 'Golden Herald' | CSil SLBF | | |
| 'Golden la Campanella' (d/v) | CLoc MBri | 'Happy Anniversary' | CLoc SVic |
| | | 'Happy Fellow' | CDoC CLoc CSil EBak SRiF |
| 'Golden Lena' (d/v) | CSil CWVF | 'Happy Wedding Day' (d) | CLoc CWVF EPts LAst MJac SCoo SLBF SPet SRiF SVic |
| 'Golden Marinka' (v) ♀H3 | CCCN CLoc EBak LSou MBri SPet SRiF SVic | | |
| | | 'Hapsburgh' | EBak SRiF |
| 'Golden Melody' (d) | SRiF | 'Harbour Lites' | SLBF WRou |
| 'Golden Peppermint Stick' (d) | SRiF | 'Harlow Car' | CDoC CWVF EPts SRiF |
| | | 'Harlow Perfection' | CDoC |
| 'Golden Swingtime' (d) | MBri MJac SPet SRiF SVic | 'Harmony' Niederholzer, 1946 | EBak |
| 'Golden Treasure' (v) | CLoc CSil CWVF MBri SRiF | 'Harnser's Flight' | SRiF |
| 'Golden Vergeer' (v) | SLBF | 'Harold Smith' | SRiF |
| 'Golden Wedding' | SRiF SVic | 'Harriet Lye' | SRiF |
| 'Goldsworth Beauty' | CSil SRiF | 'Harriett' (d) | SRiF |
| 'Golondrina' | CSil CWVF EBak | 'Harry Dunnett' (T) | EBak |
| 'Goody Goody' | EBak SRiF SVic | 'Harry Gray' (d) | CCCN CLoc CWVF EBak EPts LAst MBri MJac SLBF SPet SRiF SVic |
| 'Gooseberry Hill' | SRiF | | |
| 'Goosebery Belle' | SRiF WRou | 'Harry Pullen' | EBak |
| 'Gordon Boy' (d) | CSil | 'Harry Taylor' (d) | EPts SRiF |
| 'Gordon Thorley' | CSil | 'Harry's Sunshine' | SLBF |
| 'Gordon's China Rose' | LCla | 'Harti's Olivia' | CDoC |
| 'Gota' | CDoC SLBF | ***hartwegii*** | CDoC CSil LCla MHer |
| 'Göttingen' (T) | EBak SRiF | 'Harvey's Reward' | SLBF |
| 'Governor Pat Brown' (d) | EBak SRiF | 'Hathersage' (d) | EBak |
| 'Grace Darling' | CWVF EBak SRiF | ***hatschbachii*** | CDoC CSil CTsd ECre ELon EWes GCal LCla LRHS MCot MHer SDix SEND SPlb SPoG SRiF SVen WPnn |
| ***gracilis*** | see *F. magellanica* var. *gracilis* | | |
| 'Graf Witte' | CDoC CSil CWVF SPet SRiF SVic | | |
| 'Granada' (d) | SRiF | 'Haute Cuisine' (d) | CLoc SVic |
| 'Grand Duke' (T/d) | CWVF | 'Hawaiian Sunset' (d) | CLoc CWVF EPts SLBF SRiF |
| 'Grand Prix' (d) | SVic | 'Hawkshead' ♀H3-4 | Widely available |
| 'Grand Slam' (d) | SVic | 'Hayley Jay' (d) **new** | SLBF |
| 'Grandad Fred' (d) | SRiF | 'Hazel' (d) | CWVF SRiF SVic |
| 'Grandad Hobbs' (d) | LCla SLBF | 'Heart Throb' (d) | EBak |
| 'Grandma Sinton' (d) | CLoc CWVF MBri SRiF | 'Heather Rose' (d) | SRiF |
| 'Grandpa George' (d) | SRiF | 'Heavenly Hayley' (d) | SLBF SRiF |
| 'Grandpa Jack' (d) | SLBF | 'Hebe' | EBak SRiF |
| 'Granny Charlton' | WCFE | 'Heidi Ann' (d) ♀H3 | CCCN CDoC CLoc CSil CWVF EBak EPts LAst LRHS MAsh MBri MSCN NBlu SLBF SPet SRiF SVic |
| 'Grasmere' | SRiF | | |
| 'Grayrigg' | CDoC CSil CTsd ELon EPts LCla LSRN SEND SLBF SRiF | | |
| | | 'Heidi Blue' (d) | SLBF |
| 'Great Ouse' (d) | EPts SRiF | 'Heidi Joy' | CSil |
| 'Great Scott' (d) | CLoc | § 'Heidi Weiss' (d) | CDoC CLoc CSil CWVF MBri SPet |
| 'Green 'n' Gold' | EBak | 'Heinrich Henkel' | see *F.* 'Andenken an Heinrich Henkel' |
| 'Greenpeace' | CDoC SRiF SVic | | |
| 'Greg Walker' (d) | SRiF | 'Helen Clare' (d) | CLoc CWVF EBak |
| 'Gregory Wallis' **new** | SRiF | 'Helen Gair' (d) | CWVF SRiF |

| | |
|---|---|
| 'Helen Lang' | EPts |
| 'Hellen Devine' | CWVF |
| 'Hello Moideer' | SRiF |
| 'Hemsleyana' | see *F. microphylla* subsp. *hemsleyana* |
| 'Henning Becker' ♀H3 | CWVF ELan ELon |
| 'Henri Poincaré' | EBak SRiF |
| 'Henrieke Dimi' (d) | CDoC |
| 'Henriette Ernst' | SRiF |
| 'Herald' ♀H4 | CDoC CSil CWVF EBak EPfP LRHS LSou MAsh SLBF SRiF SVic |
| 'Herbé de Jacques' | see *F.* 'Mr West' |
| 'Heri Shusui' (d) | CDoC |
| 'Heritage' (d) | CLoc CSil EBak SRiF |
| 'Herman de Graaff' (d) | SLBF |
| 'Hermiena' | CLoc CWVF EPts SLBF SRiF SVic |
| 'Hermienne' | WRou |
| 'Heron' | CSil EBak SRiF |
| 'Herps Pierement' | SLBF |
| 'Hessett Festival' (d) | CWVF EBak SRiF |
| 'Heston Blue' (d) | CWVF SRiF |
| 'Heydon' | CWVF SRiF |
| 'Hi Jinks' (d) | EBak SRiF SVic |
| ***hidalgensis*** | see *F. microphylla* subsp. *hidalgensis* |
| 'Hidcote Beauty' | CLoc CWVF EBak LCla SLBF SPet SRiF SVic |
| 'Hidden Treasure' | WRou |
| 'Highland Pipes' | LCla SVic |
| 'Hilda May Salmon' | CWVF |
| 'Hindu Belle' | EBak SRiF |
| 'Hinnerike' (E) | CSil CWVF LCla SVic |
| 'Hiroshige' (T) | LCla SRiF |
| 'His Excellency' (d) | EBak SRiF |
| 'Hobo' (d) | CSil SRiF |
| 'Hobson's Choice' (d) | CWVF SLBF SRiF |
| 'Holly's Beauty' (d) | CDoC CLoc EPts LAst SRiF |
| 'Hollywood' (d) | SRiF |
| 'Hollywood Park' (d) | EBak |
| 'Hot Coals' | CWVF EPts MCot MJac SRiF SVic WRou |
| 'Howard's Own' | SRiF |
| 'Howerd Hebden' | CDoC |
| 'Howlett's Hardy' ♀H3-4 | CDoC CLoc CSil CWVF EBak NLar SRiF SVic WMnd |
| 'Huet's Kwarts' | CDoC |
| 'Huet's Turkoois' | CDoC |
| 'Hugh Morgan' (d) | SRiF |
| 'Hula Girl' (d) | CDoC CWVF EBak MJac SPet SRiF |
| 'Humboldt Holiday' (d) | SRiF |
| 'Huntsman' (d) | CCCN CDoC SRiF |
| 'Ian Leedham' (d) | EBak SRiF |
| 'Ian Storey' | CDoC CSil |
| 'Ice Cream Soda' (d) | EBak SRiF |
| 'Iceberg' | CWVF EBak SRiF SVic |
| 'Icecap' | CWVF MBri SVic |
| 'Iced Champagne' | CLoc CWVF EBak MJac |
| 'Ichiban' (d) | CLoc SRiF |
| 'Ida' (d) | EBak SRiF |
| 'Igloo Maid' (d) | CLoc CWVF EBak SPet SRiF SVic |
| 'Impala' (d) | CWVF SRiF |
| 'Imperial Fantasy' (d) | CWVF SRiF |
| 'Impudence' | CLoc CWVF EBak SPet SRiF |
| 'Impulse' (d) | CLoc |
| 'Independence' (d) | SRiF SVic |
| 'Indian Maid' (d) | CDoC CWVF EBak SRiF |
| 'Insulinde' (T) | CDoC CWVF EPts LCla MHer MJac SLBF SRiF |
| 'Interlude' (d) | EBak |
| 'Iolanthe' (T) | CWVF |
| 'Irene L. Peartree' (d) | CWVF LCla |
| 'Irene Sinton' (d) | MJac |
| 'Iris Amer' (d) | CLoc CWVF EBak |
| 'Irving Alexander' (d) | CDoC |
| 'Isabel Ryan' | CSil |
| 'Isis' Lemoine | CSil |
| 'Isle of Mull' | CSil SPet |
| 'Isle of Purbeck' | SRiF SVic |
| 'Italiano' (d) | CWVF MJac SVic |
| 'Ivy Grace' | CSil |
| 'Ixion' | SRiF |
| 'Jack Acland' | CWVF SRiF |
| 'Jack Coast' | SRiF |
| 'Jack King' | SRiF |
| 'Jack Rowlands' (d) | SRiF |
| 'Jack Shahan' ♀H3 | CCCN CDoC CLoc CSil CWVF EBak LAst LCla MBri MJac SLBF SPet SRiF |
| 'Jack Stanway' (v) | CDoC CWVF SRiF |
| 'Jack Wilson' | CSil |
| 'Jackie Bull' (d) | CWVF EBak |
| 'Jackpot' (d) | EBak |
| 'Jackqueline' (T) | CWVF SRiF |
| 'Jacky' | SRiF |
| 'Jamboree' (d) | EBak SRiF |
| 'James Eve' (d) | SRiF |
| 'James Hammond' | SRiF |
| 'James Lye' (d) | CWVF EBak SRiF |
| 'James Travis' (E/d) | CDoC CSil EBak LCla SLBF SRiF |
| 'Jan Bremer' | SVic |
| 'Jan Murray' | SRiF |
| 'Jandel' | CWVF SRiF |
| 'Jane Amanda' (d) | SRiF |
| 'Jane Humber' (d) | CWVF SRiF |
| 'Jane Lye' | EBak SRiF |
| 'Janice Ann' | LCla |
| 'Janice Perry's Gold' (v) | CLoc MJac SLBF SRiF |
| 'Janie' (d) | EPfP MAsh SRiF |
| 'Janneke Brinkman-Salentijn' | SRiF |
| 'Jap Vantveer' (T) | LCla |
| 'Jaunty Jack' | SLBF |
| 'Javelin' | CDoC |
| 'Jayess Helen' (d) | SRiF |
| 'Jean Baker' | CDoC |
| 'Jean Campbell' | EBak |
| 'Jean Frisby' | CLoc |
| 'Jean Taylor' | EPts |
| 'Jean Webb' (v) | WCot |
| 'Jennie Rachael' (d) | SRiF |
| 'Jennifer' | EBak MJac SRiF |
| 'Jennifer Ann' | SLBF |
| 'Jennifer Lister' (d) | CSil |
| 'Jenny May' | CLoc EPts |
| 'Jenny Sorensen' | CWVF SRiF |
| 'Jess' | LCla SLBF SRiF |
| 'Jessica Reynolds' | SRiF |
| 'Jessie Pearson' | CWVF |
| 'Jessimae' | CWVF SPet SRiF |
| 'Jester' Holmes (d) | CLoc CSil |
| 'Jet Fire' (d) | EBak |
| 'Jezebel' (d) | SRiF SVic |
| 'Jiddles' (E) | LCla SRiF WRou |
| 'Jill Holloway' (T) | SLBF |
| 'Jill Whitworth' | CDoC WPnn |
| 'Jim Coleman' | CWVF SRiF SVic |
| 'Jim Dodge' (d) | EPts |
| 'Jim Hawkins' | EBak SRiF |
| 'Jim Missin' (d/v) | SRiF |
| 'Jim Muncaster' | CWVF |
| 'Jim Todd' | SRiF |

| | | |
|---|---|---|
| | 'Jim Watts' | CDoC CTsd |
| | ***jimenezii*** | CDoC LCla |
| | 'Jimmy Cricket' (E) | CDoC SLBF |
| | 'Jingle Bells' | SRiF |
| | 'Joan Barnes' (d) | CWVF SRiF |
| | 'Joan Cooper' | CLoc CSil CWVF EBak SLBF SRiF SVic |
| | 'Joan Gilbert' (d) | SRiF |
| | 'Joan Goy' | CWVF MJac SRiF SVic |
| | 'Joan Knight' | CLoc |
| | 'Joan Margaret' (d) | MJac |
| | 'Joan Morris' | SLBF |
| | 'Joan Pacey' | CDoC CWVF EBak SRiF |
| | 'Joan Pawley' | SRiF |
| | 'Joan Smith' | EBak SRiF |
| | 'Joan Waters' (d) | CWVF |
| | 'Joanna Lumley' (d) | EPts MJac SRiF |
| | 'Jo-Anne Fisher' (d) | EPts |
| | 'Joe Kusber' (d) | CWVF EBak SRiF |
| | 'Johannes Nowinski' | SRiF |
| | 'John Bartlett' | CLoc |
| | 'John Grooms' (d) | CLoc SRiF SVic WRou |
| | 'John Lockyer' | CLoc CWVF EBak SRiF |
| | 'John Maynard Scales' (T) | CDoC CWVF LCla MJac SRiF WRou |
| § | 'John Ridding'[PBR] (T/v) | CLoc EPts LAst SPoG |
| | 'John Suckley' (d) | EBak |
| | 'John Wright' | LCla |
| | 'Jomam' ♀[H3] | CWVF SRiF |
| | 'Jon Oram' | CLoc CWVF |
| | 'Jonny Wilkinson' | MJac |
| | 'Jose's Joan' (d) | CWVF SRiF SVic |
| | 'Joy Patmore' | CLoc CTsd CWVF EBak MBri SLBF SPet SRiF |
| | 'Joyce Adey' (d) | CWVF SRiF |
| | 'Joyce Forward' | SRiF |
| | 'Joyce Sinton' | CLoc CWVF MBri SRiF |
| | 'Joyce Wilson' (d) | EPts |
| | 'Judith Coupland' | CWVF |
| | 'Juella' | SRiF |
| | 'Jülchen' | CWVF |
| | 'Jules Daloges' (d) | EBak SRiF |
| | 'Julie' | SRiF |
| | 'Julie Ann' | SRiF |
| | 'Julie Marie' (d) | CWVF MJac |
| | 'June Gardner' | CWVF SRiF |
| | 'Jungle' | LCla SLBF SRiF |
| I | 'Juno' Kennett | EBak |
| | ***juntasensis*** | SRiF |
| | 'Jupiter Seventy' | EBak SRiF |
| | 'Jus' For You' | MJac |
| | 'Just Pink' (E) | CDoC SLBF |
| | 'Just William' | SRiF |
| | 'Justin's Pride' | CDoC CSil SRiF |
| | 'Kalang Talinga' (d) | SRiF |
| | 'Kaleidoscope' (d) | EBak SRiF |
| | 'Kaley Jackson' **new** | SLBF |
| | 'Karen Isles' (E) | CDoC LCla SLBF WRou |
| | 'Karen Louise' (d) | CLoc |
| | 'Karin de Groot' | SVic |
| | 'Karl Hartness' | SRiF |
| | 'Kate Harriet' (d) | SRiF |
| | 'Kate Taylor' (d) | SLBF |
| | 'Kath van Hanegem' | SLBF SRiF WRou |
| | 'Kathleen Galea' | SRiF |
| | 'Kathleen van Hanegan' | CLoc |
| | 'Kathryn Maidment' | SVic |
| | 'Kathy Louise' (d) | SRiF |
| | 'Kathy's Sparkler' (d) | SRiF |
| | 'Katie Coast' | SRiF |
| | 'Katie James' | SRiF |

| | | |
|---|---|---|
| | 'Katie Reynolds' (d) | SRiF |
| | 'Katie Rogers' | EPts |
| | 'Katie Susan' | SLBF |
| | 'Katinka' (E) | CDoC CWVF LCla SLBF |
| | 'Katjan' | CSil LCla SLBF SRiF |
| | 'Katrien Michiels' | SRiF |
| | 'Katrina' (d) | CLoc EBak SRiF |
| | 'Katrina Thompsen' | CLoc CWVF EPts SLBF SRiF |
| | 'Katy Flynn' | CLoc SLBF |
| | 'Keepsake' (d) | CLoc EBak |
| | 'Kegworth Carnival' (d) | CWVF SRiF |
| | 'Kelly Jo' | SRiF |
| | 'Ken Goldsmith' (T) | CWVF |
| | 'Ken Jennings' | CWVF |
| | 'Ken Shelton' | SRiF |
| | 'Kenny Dalglish' (d) | CSil SRiF |
| | 'Kenny Holmes' | CWVF |
| | 'Kenny Walkling' | LCla SLBF |
| | 'Kentish Maid' | SRiF |
| | 'Kernan Robson' (d) | CLoc CWVF EBak SRiF |
| | 'Keystone' | EBak SRiF |
| | 'Kim Wright' (d) | SRiF |
| | 'Kimberly' (d) | EBak SRiF |
| | 'King George V' | SRiF |
| | 'King of Bath' (d) | EBak |
| | 'King of Hearts' (d) | EBak SRiF |
| | 'King's Ransom' (d) | CLoc CWVF EBak SPet SRiF SVic |
| | 'Kiss 'n' Tell' | CWVF MJac SRiF |
| | 'Kit Oxtoby' (d) | CDoC CWVF LCla MJac SRiF |
| | 'Kiwi' (d) | EBak SRiF |
| | 'Knockout' (d) | CWVF SVic |
| | 'Kobold' | SLBF |
| | 'Kolding Perle' | CWVF SLBF SPet SRiF |
| | 'Komeet' | CDoC SBfd |
| | 'Kon-Tiki' (d) | SPet |
| | 'Kuniko Atarashi' (d) | EPts |
| | 'Kwintet' | CWVF EBak MJac SPet SRiF |
| | 'La Bianca' | EBak |
| | 'La Campanella' (d) ♀[H3] | CCCN CDoC CLoc CWVF EBak EPts LAst MBri MJac MSCN NVic SBfd SLBF SPet SRiF SVic |
| | 'La Fiesta' (d) | EBak |
| | 'La France' (d) | EBak SRiF |
| | 'La Neige' ambig. | CTsd CWVF |
| | 'La Neige' Lemoine (d) | EBak |
| | 'La Porte' (d) | CLoc CWVF |
| | 'La Rosita' (d) | EBak SRiF |
| I | 'La Traviata' Blackwell (d) | EBak SRiF |
| | 'Lace Petticoats' (d) | EBak SRiF SVic |
| | 'Lady Bartle Frere' (d) | SRiF |
| | 'Lady Beth' (d) | SRiF SVic |
| | 'Lady Boothby' | Widely available |
| | 'Lady Edwards' (d) | SRiF |
| | 'Lady Framlingham' (d) | EPts |
| | 'Lady Heytesbury' | SRiF |
| | 'Lady in Grey' (d) | MJac SRiF SVic |
| | 'Lady Isobel Barnett' | CLoc CWVF EBak MBri MJac SPet SRiF SVic |
| | 'Lady Kathleen Spence' | CWVF EBak SPet SVic |
| | 'Lady Lupus' | EPts SRiF |
| | 'Lady Patricia Mountbatten' | CWVF SRiF SVic WRou |
| | 'Lady Ramsey' | EBak SRiF |
| | 'Lady Rebecca' (d) | CLoc |
| | 'Lady Thumb' (d) ♀[H3] | Widely available |
| | 'Laing's Hybrid' | CWVF EBak SRiF |
| | 'Lakeland Princess' | EBak |
| | 'Lakeside' | EBak SRiF |
| | 'Lambada' | LAst SLBF SRiF WRou |
| | 'Lancambe' | CSil |
| | 'Lancashire Lass' | CWVF MBri SRiF |

| | | |
|---|---|---|
| | 'Lancelot' | EBak SRiF |
| | 'Langsford' | SRiF |
| | 'Lapshead White' | CPLG |
| | 'Lark' (T) | CWVF SRiF |
| | 'Lassie' (d) | CDoC CLoc CWVF EBak SRiF |
| | 'Last Chance' (E) | SLBF |
| | 'Laura' ambig. | CWVF SVic WRou |
| I | 'Laura' (Dutch) | CLoc EPts LCla SLBF SRiF |
| | 'Laura Cross' (E) | CDoC SLBF |
| | 'Lauren' | CDoC |
| | 'Lavender Beauty' (d) | SRiF |
| | 'Lavender Kate' (d) | CWVF EBak |
| | 'Lazy Lady' (d) | CWVF EBak SRiF |
| | 'Lechlade Apache' | CDoC LCla SRiF |
| | 'Lechlade Bullet' | LCla SRiF |
| | 'Lechlade Chinaman' | CDoC SRiF SVic |
| | 'Lechlade Debutante' | CDoC LCla SRiF |
| | 'Lechlade Fire-eater' (T) | CDoC SRiF |
| | 'Lechlade Gorgon' | CDoC CWVF LCla SLBF |
| | 'Lechlade Magician' | CDoC CSil EPts LCla SPet SRiF SVic |
| | 'Lechlade Maiden' | CDoC CWVF LCla SRiF |
| | 'Lechlade Martianess' | LCla SRiF SVic |
| | 'Lechlade Potentate' | LCla |
| | 'Lechlade Tinkerbell' (E) | CDoC LCla SRiF |
| | 'Lechlade Violet' (T) | CSil LCla SRiF SVic |
| | ***lehmanii*** | LCla |
| | 'Len Bielby' (T) | CDoC CWVF LCla SRiF |
| | 'Lena' (d) 🏆$^{H3}$ | CDoC CLoc CMac CSil CTri CWVF EBak EPts MBri MJac SLBF SPer SPet SPlb SRiF SVic |
| | 'Lena Dalton' (d) | CLoc CWVF EBak SRiF SVic |
| | 'Leonora' | CDoC CLoc CWVF EBak MBri SLBF SPet SRiF SVic WRou |
| | 'Lesley' (T) | CWVF LCla SRiF |
| | 'Lesley's Wonder' **new** | MJac |
| | 'Leslie Bowman' **new** | LCla |
| | 'Lett's Delight' (d) | CWVF EPts SRiF |
| | 'Letty Lye' | EBak SRiF |
| | 'Leverhulme' | see *F.* 'Leverkusen' |
| § | 'Leverkusen' (T) | CDoC CLoc EBak LCla MJac SRiF |
| | 'Li Kai Lin' | SRiF |
| I | 'Liebesträume' Blackwell (d) | EBak |
| | 'Liebriez' (d) 🏆$^{H3-4}$ | CSil EBak SPet SRiF SVic |
| | 'Liemers Lantaern' | CWVF |
| | 'Likalin' | CWVF |
| | 'Lilac' | EBak |
| | 'Lilac Dainty' (d) | CSil |
| | 'Lilac Lustre' (d) | CLoc CWVF EBak SPet SRiF SVic |
| | 'Lilac Princess' | SRiF |
| | 'Lilac Queen' (d) | EBak |
| | 'Lilian' | SRiF |
| | 'Lillian Annetts' (d) | CCCN CDoC CWVF LCla MJac SLBF SRiF WRou |
| | 'Lillibet' (d) | CLoc CWVF EBak SRiF |
| | 'Lillydale' (d) | SRiF |
| | 'Lilo Vogt' (T) | SRiF |
| | 'Lime Lite' (d) | MJac |
| I | 'Limelight' Weston | SLBF |
| | 'Linda Goulding' | CTsd CWVF EBak SVic |
| | 'Linda Grace' | MJac |
| | 'Linda Rosling' (d) | CDoC |
| | 'Lindisfarne' (d) | CLoc CWVF EBak MJac SPet |
| | 'Lindsey Victoria' (d) | SVic |
| | 'Lionel' | CSil SRiF |
| | 'Lipstick' **new** | SLBF |
| | 'Lisa' (d) | EPts SPet SRiF |
| | 'Lisa Ashton' | SRiF |
| | 'Little Baby' | SRiF |
| | 'Little Beauty' | CDoC CSil CWVF SVic |
| | 'Little Boy Blue' | EPts SRiF |
| | 'Little Brook Gem' | SLBF |
| | 'Little Gene' | EBak |
| | 'Little Jewel' | SPet SRiF |
| | 'Little Nan' | SLBF |
| | 'Little Orphan Annie' | SRiF |
| | 'Little Ouse' (d) | CWVF |
| | 'Little Ronnie' (d) | SRiF |
| | 'Little Scamp' | SLBF WRou |
| | 'Little Witch' | SRiF |
| | 'Liz' (d) | CSil EBak SRiF |
| | Liza = 'Goetzliza'$^{PBR}$ (Shadowdancer Series) | LAst LSou |
| | 'Liza Todman' (d) | SRiF |
| | 'Lochinver' (d) | CWVF |
| | 'Loeky' | CDoC CLoc CWVF EBak SPet SRiF SVic |
| | 'Logan Garden' | see *F. magellanica* 'Logan Woods' |
| | 'Lolita' (d) | CWVF EBak SRiF |
| | 'London 2000' | CDoC LCla MJac SLBF SRiF WRou |
| | 'London in Bloom' | SLBF |
| | 'Lonely Ballerina' (d) | CLoc CWVF SRiF |
| | 'Long Distance' (T) | CDoC LCla |
| | 'Long Wings' | LCla SRiF SVic |
| | 'Lord Byron' | CLoc EBak SRiF |
| | 'Lord Derby' | CSil |
| | 'Lord Jim' | CDoC LCla |
| | 'Lord Lonsdale' | CWVF EBak EPts LCla MSCN SRiF SVic WRou |
| | 'Lord Roberts' | CLoc CWVF SLBF SRiF |
| | 'Lore Ritscka' (d) **new** | MJac |
| | 'Lorelei' | CDoC |
| | 'Lorna Fairclough' | MJac |
| | 'Lorna Florence' | SLBF |
| | 'Lorna Swinbank' | CLoc CWVF SRiF SVic |
| | 'Lorraine's Delight' (d) | SRiF SVic |
| | 'Lottie Hobby' (E) 🏆$^{H1+3}$ | CDoC CLoc CMac CSil CTrC CTsd CWVF EPfP EPts LCla MLHP SPet SRiF SVic WRou |
| | 'Louise Emershaw' (d) | CWVF EBak MJac SRiF SVic |
| | 'Louise Nicholls' | MJac SRiF |
| | 'Loulabel' | SVic |
| | 'Lovable' (d) | EBak |
| | 'Loveliness' | CLoc CWVF EBak SRiF SVic |
| | 'Lovely Les' (d) | SRiF |
| | 'Lovely Linda' | SLBF SRiF |
| | 'Love's Reward' 🏆$^{H1+3}$ | CLoc CWVF MJac SLBF SRiF SVic WRou |
| | 'Lower Raydon' | EBak SRiF |
| I | 'Loxensis' | CDoC CWVF EBak SVic |
| N | ***loxensis*** misapplied | see *F.* 'Speciosa', *F.* 'Loxensis' |
| | ***loxensis*** Kunth | SRiF |
| | 'Loxhore Herald' | CSil |
| | 'Loxhore Lullaby' (E) | CSil LCla |
| | 'Loxhore Mazurka' (T) | SRiF |
| | 'Loxhore Minuet' (T) | CDoC LCla SRiF WRou |
| | 'Loxhore Posthorn' (T) | CDoC LCla |
| | 'Lucinda' | CWVF SRiF |
| | 'Lucky Strike' (d) | EBak SRiF |
| | Lucy = 'Goetzlucy' (Shadowdancer Series) | EBak SRiF |
| | 'Lucy Locket' | MJac |
| | 'Lunter's Trots' (d) | SRiF |
| | 'Luscious' (d) | SRiF |
| | 'Lustre' | CWVF EBak SVic |
| | 'Lutz Bogemann' | SRiF |
| I | 'Lycioides' | LCla |
| | ***lycioides*** misapplied | see *F.* 'Lycioides' |
| § | ***lycioides*** Andrews | EBak |
| | 'Lye's Elegance' | SRiF |
| | 'Lye's Excelsior' | EBak SRiF |

| | | |
|---|---|---|
| | 'Lye's Own' | EBak SLBF SPet SRiF |
| | 'Lye's Unique' ♀H1+3 | CDoC CLoc CWVF EBak EPts LCla MJac SLBF SPet SRiF SVic |
| | 'Lynette' (d) | CLoc |
| | 'Lynn Cunningham' | CDoC |
| | 'Lynn Ellen' (d) | CDoC CWVF EBak |
| | 'Lynne Patricia' (d) | EPts SLBF |
| | 'Maartje' | SRiF |
| | 'Mabel Greaves' (d) | CWVF |
| | 'Mac Wagg' | WRou |
| | 'Machu Picchu' | CLoc CWVF EPts LCla SRiF SVic WRou |
| | ***macrophylla*** | CDoC WMoo |
| | 'Madame Aubin' | CSil |
| | 'Madame Butterfly' (d) | CLoc |
| | 'Madame Cornélissen' (d) ♀H3 | CDoC CLoc CMac CSBt CSil CTri CWVF EBak EBee EPfP EPts LAst LRHS MAsh MBri MRav SCoo SLBF SLim SPer SPet SPoG SRiF SVic WFar WHil WRou |
| | 'Madame Eva Boye' | EBak SRiF |
| | 'Madeleine Sweeney' (d) | MBri |
| | 'Maes-y-Groes' | CSil |
| | ***magellanica*** | CDoC CSil CTsd CWib GGar GKev MLHP MSCN NPer NWea SEND SPer SVic WFar WMoo WPnn |
| | - 'Alba' | see *F. magellanica* var. *molinae* |
| I | - 'Alba Aureovariegata' (v) | CDoC CMac CTrC EPfP SPer SVic WFar |
| | - 'Alba Variegata' (v) | CSil |
| | - 'Americana Elegans' | CDoC CSil |
| | - 'Angel's Teardrop' | CDoC |
| | - 'Comber' | CSil |
| | - var. ***conica*** | CDoC CSil |
| | - var. ***discolor*** | CSil |
| | - 'Duchy of Cornwall' | CDoC |
| | - 'Exmoor Gold' (v) | CSil |
| § | - var. ***gracilis*** ♀H3 | CAgr CDoC CHEx CLoc CSil CTri CWVF EPfP MLHP NBro SCoo SVic WGwG WMoo WPnn |
| | - - 'Aurea' ♀H3-4 | CBcs CBot CDoC CMac CSil CTsd CWVF EBee ELan EPfP GGar GQui LCla LRHS MHer MRav SAga SCoo SDix SLBF SPer SPet SPoG WFar WMoo WRou |
| | - - 'Purple Mountain' | EPfP LRHS |
| § | - - 'Tricolor' (v) ♀H3 | CDoC CSil CTsd EPfP EPts EWes LBMP LCla LRHS NLar SEND SLBF SRiF SRms WCFE WPnn WRou |
| | - - 'Variegata' (v) ♀H3 | CDoC CSil CTsd EBak EPfP GGar LCla LRHS MGos MRav SBfd SDix SPet SRiF WPnn |
| | - 'Guiding Star' | CDoC |
| | - 'Lady Bacon' | CDoC CSil ELon EPts EWes GCal GGar MCot SDys SEND SHom SLBF SRiF WSHC |
| § | - 'Logan Woods' | CDoC CSil ELon EQua GKin SLBF SMrm |
| | - 'Longipedunculata' | CDoC CSil SLPl |
| | - 'Lyonesse Lady' | CDoC |
| | - var. ***macrostema*** | CSil |
| § | - var. ***molinae*** | Widely available |
| § | - - 'Enstone' (v) | EHoe ELon LAst SRiF |
| | - - 'Golden Sharpitor' (v) | CCCN LAst MDKP SBfd |
| | - - 'Mr Knight's Blush' | GAbr |
| § | - - 'Sharpitor' (v) | CDoC CSil CTsd EBak EHoe ELan EPfP GQue IFro LRHS MAsh NPer SAga SBch SBfd SRiF SVic WFar WKif WMoo WRou WSHC |
| | - var. ***myrtifolia*** | CDoC CSil CTsd |

| | | |
|---|---|---|
| * | - var. ***prostrata*** | CSil |
| | - 'Pumila' | CDoC CEnt CSil EWes GCal GGar ITim LRHS MHer MLHP SAga SCoo SRot SVic WAbe |
| | - ***purpurea*** | LRHS |
| | - 'Red Mountain' | EWes |
| | - 'Sea King' | CDoC |
| | - 'Sea Spray' | CDoC |
| | - 'Seahorse' | CDoC |
| § | - 'Thompsonii' ♀H3-4 | CDoC CSil ECGP SBch SRiF |
| § | - 'Versicolor' (v) | Widely available |
| | 'Magenta Flush' | CDoC CWVF |
| | 'Maggie Rose' | SLBF |
| | 'Magic Flute' | CLoc CWVF MJac SVic |
| | 'Maharaja' (d) | EBak SRiF |
| | 'Majebo' (d) | SRiF |
| | 'Majestica' **new** | SRiF |
| | 'Major Heaphy' | CWVF EBak SRiF |
| | 'Making Waves' | WRou |
| | 'Malibu Mist' (d) | CWVF SRiF |
| | 'Mama Bleuss' (d) | EBak SRiF |
| | 'Mancunian' (d) | CWVF SRiF |
| I | 'Mandarin' Schnabel | EBak SRiF |
| | 'Mandi Oxtoby' (T) | LCla SRiF |
| | 'Mantilla' (T) | CDoC CLoc CWVF EBak MJac SRiF SVic |
| | 'Maori Maid' | SRiF |
| | 'Maori Pipes' (T) | SRiF |
| | 'Marbled Sky' | SVic |
| | 'Marcia'PBR (Shadowdancer Series) | CLoc LAst LSou |
| | 'Marcus Graham' (d) | CLoc CTsd CWVF EBak MSCN SCoo SRiF SVic WRou |
| | 'Marcus Hanton' (d) | CWVF SRiF |
| | 'Mardi Gras' (d) | EBak SRiF |
| | 'Margaret' (d) ♀H4 | CDoC CLoc CSil CTri CTsd CWVF EBak EPts SEND SLBF SPet SRiF SVic |
| | 'Margaret Berger' (d) | SRiF |
| | 'Margaret Bird' | LCla |
| | 'Margaret Brown' ♀H4 | CDoC CLoc CSil CTri CWVF EBak LCla LRHS SLBF SPet SRiF SVic WRou |
| | 'Margaret Davidson' (d) | CLoc |
| | 'Margaret Hazelwood' | SRiF |
| | 'Margaret Pilkington' | CTsd CWVF SRiF SVic |
| | 'Margaret Roe' | CDoC CSil CWVF EBak MJac SPet SRiF |
| | 'Margaret Rose' | SRiF |
| | 'Margaret Susan' | EBak |
| | 'Margarite Dawson' (d) | CSil SRiF |
| | 'Margery Blake' | CSil EBak SRiF |
| | 'Margharita' (d) | SRiF |
| | 'Maria Landy' | CWVF LCla MJac SRiF WRou |
| | 'Maria Mathilde' (d) | SLBF |
| | 'Maria Merrills' (d) | SRiF |
| | 'Mariah' (Diva Series) | SRiF |
| | 'Marietta' (d) | SRiF |
| | 'Marilyn Olsen' | CWVF SRiF |
| | 'Marin Belle' | EBak SRiF |
| | 'Marin Glow' ♀H3 | CLoc CWVF EBak SLBF SPet SRiF SVic |
| | 'Marina Kelly' | WRou |
| | 'Marinka' ♀H3 | CCCN CLoc CWVF EBak EPts LAst LBMP LCla MBri MJac NBlu SLBF SPet SRiF SVic WHil |
| | 'Marja' | SRiF |
| | 'Mark Kirby' (d) | CWVF EBak SRiF |
| | 'Marlies de Keijzer' (E) | CDoC LCla SLBF |
| | 'Marry Perry' | WRou |

| |  |  |
|---|---|---|
| | Martha = 'Goetzmart' (Shadowdancer Series) | LAst LHop |
| | 'Martina' | SLBF |
| | 'Martin's Inspiration' | CDoC LCla |
| | 'Martin's Little Beauty' | CDoC |
| | 'Martin's Yellow Surprise' (T) | LCla SLBF SRiF SVic |
| | 'Marty' (d) | EBak SRiF |
| | 'Mary' (T) ♀H1+3 | CDoC CLoc CWVF EPts LCla SLBF SRiF SVic |
| | 'Mary Lockyer' (d) | CLoc EBak SRiF |
| | 'Mary Poppins' | CWVF SRiF SVic |
| | 'Mary Reynolds' (d) | CWVF |
| | 'Mary Sturman' (E) | SRiF |
| | 'Mary Thorne' | CSil EBak SRiF |
| | 'Mary's Millennium' | CWVF |
| | 'Masquerade' (d) | EBak SVic |
| | 'Maurice Barber' **new** | SRiF |
| | 'Mauve Beauty' (d) | CSil CWVF SLBF |
| | 'Mauve Lace' (d) | CSil SRiF |
| | 'Mauve Wisp' (d) | SVic |
| | 'Max Jaffa' | CWVF SRiF |
| I | 'Maxima' | EPts LCla SLBF SRiF |
| | 'Maybe Baby' | SRiF |
| | 'Mayblossom' (d) | CWVF SPet |
| | 'Mayfayre' (d) | CLoc |
| | 'Mayfield' | CWVF |
| | 'Maytime' (d) | SRiF |
| | 'Mazda' | CWVF SRiF |
| | 'Meadowlark' (d) | CWVF EBak SRiF |
| | 'Mechtildis de Lechy' | SRiF |
| | 'Medard's Botsaert' (d) | CDoC |
| | 'Meditation' (d) | CLoc CSil |
| | 'Melanie' | CTsd SRiF SVic |
| | 'Melissa Heavens' | CWVF |
| | 'Melody' | EBak SPet SRiF SVic |
| | 'Melody Ann' (d) | EBak SRiF |
| | 'Melting Moments' (d) | SCoo SRiF |
| | 'Mendocino Rose' | SVic |
| | 'Mephisto' | CSil CWVF |
| | 'Mercurius' | CSil |
| | 'Merlin' | CDoC CSil LCla SRiF |
| | 'Merry Mary' (d) | CWVF EBak SRiF |
| | 'Meteor Storm' | SRiF |
| I | 'Mexicali Rose' Machado | CLoc |
| | 'Michael' (d) | CWVF EPts SRiF |
| | 'Michael Wallis' (T) | CDoC LCla SLBF SRiF |
| | 'Michelle Wallace' | SLBF SVic |
| | ***michoacanensis*** misapplied | see *F. microphylla* subsp. *aprica* |
| | ***michoacanensis*** Sessé & Moç. (E) B&SWJ 9027 | WCru |
| | - B&SWJ 9148 | WCru |
| | 'Micky Goult' ♀H1+3 | CLoc CWVF EPts MJac SLBF SPet SRiF SVic WRou |
| | 'Microchip' (E) | CSil LCla |
| | ***microphylla*** (E) | CBcs CDoC CElw CHid CLoc CPLG CSil CWVF EBak ELon GCal GGar MSCN NBro NLar STre SVic WBor |
| | - B&SWJ 10331 | WCru |
| § | - subsp. ***aprica*** (E) | CDoC LCla |
| | - - B&SWJ 9101 | WCru |
| | - - 'Dolly's Dress' | WCru |
| | - 'Cornish Pixie' | CDoC |
| § | - subsp. ***hemsleyana*** (E) | CDoC CPLG CSil LCla SRiF |
| | - - B&SWJ 10478 | WCru |
| | - - 'Silver Lining' | LHop WCru WSHC |
| § | - subsp. ***hidalgensis*** (E) | CDoC CSil LCla |
| | - subsp. ***microphylla*** (E) | CSil |
| § | - subsp. ***minimiflora*** (E) | SVic |
| | - subsp. ***quercetorum*** (E) | CDoC CSil CTsd LCla |

| |  |  |
|---|---|---|
| | - 'Variegata' (E/v) | EWes MCCP |
| | 'Midas' | CWVF MBri |
| | 'Midnight Sun' (d) | CWVF EBak SRiF |
| | 'Midwinter' | CWVF SRiF SVic |
| | 'Mieke Meursing' ♀H1+3 | CDoC CLoc CWVF EBak MJac SPet SRiF |
| | 'Miep Aalhuizen' | CDoC LCla SRiF SVic |
| | 'Mike Oxtoby' (T) | CWVF |
| | 'Millennium' | CLoc EBak EPts MJac SCoo SRiF |
| | 'Millie' | SRiF |
| | 'Millie Butler' | CWVF |
| | 'Ming' | CLoc SRiF |
| | 'Mini Skirt' (d) | SRiF |
| | 'Miniature Jewels' (E) | SLBF |
| | ***minimiflora*** misapplied | see *F.* × *bacillaris* |
| | ***minimiflora*** Hemsl. | see *F. microphylla* subsp. *minimiflora* |
| | 'Minirose' | CDoC CWVF EPts SLBF SRiF WRou |
| | 'Minnesota' (d) | EBak |
| | 'Miramere' | EPts |
| | 'Mirjana' | SRiF |
| | 'Mischief' | SVic |
| | 'Miss California' (d) | CDoC CLoc CWVF EBak LAst MBri SRiF |
| | 'Miss Debbie' (d) | SRiF |
| | 'Miss Grace' (d) | SRiF |
| | 'Miss Great Britain' | CWVF SRiF |
| | 'Miss Lye' | CSil SRiF |
| | 'Miss Marilyn' | SRiF |
| | 'Miss Muffett' (d) | CSil EPts SRiF |
| | 'Miss Vallejo' (d) | EBak SRiF |
| | 'Mission Bells' | CDoC CLoc CWVF EBak EPts SPet SRiF |
| | 'Mistoque' | SRiF |
| | 'Misty Blue' (d) | SVic |
| | 'Misty Haze' (d) | CWVF SRiF SVic |
| | Mojo Series **new** | SRiF |
| | 'Molesworth' (d) | CWVF EBak MJac SPet SRiF |
| | 'Mollie Beaulah' (d) | SRiF |
| | 'Molly Bellamy' | SRiF |
| | 'Monarch Mammoth' | SRiF |
| | 'Money Spinner' | CLoc EBak SRiF |
| | 'Monica' (d) | SRiF |
| | 'Monica Dare' (T) | SRiF |
| | 'Monsieur Thibaut' ♀H4 | CSil SPer SRiF |
| | 'Monte Rosa' (d) | CWVF SRiF |
| | 'Monterey' | SRiF |
| | 'Montevideo' (d) | CWVF SRiF |
| | 'Montrose' | SRiF |
| | 'Monument' (d) | CSil SRiF |
| | 'Mood Indigo' (d) | CWVF SLBF SRiF SVic |
| | 'Moody Blues' | SLBF SRiF |
| | 'Moonbeam' (d) | CLoc SRiF |
| | 'Moonglow' | CTsd MJac SRiF |
| | 'Moonlight' | CCCN |
| | 'Moonlight Sonata' | CLoc CWVF EBak SPet |
| | 'Moonraker' (d) | CWVF SRiF SVic |
| | 'More Applause' (d) | CLoc SRiF |
| | 'Morning Cloud' (d) | SRiF |
| | 'Morning Light' (d) | CLoc EBak SPet SRiF SVic |
| | 'Morning Mist' | EBak SRiF |
| | 'Morning Star' | MBri |
| | 'Morrells' (d) | EBak SRiF |
| | 'Moth Blue' (d) | CWVF EBak SPet SRiF |
| | 'Mother's Day' | SVic |
| | 'Mountain Mist' (d) | CWVF SVic |
| | 'Moyra' (d) | CWVF |
| | 'Mr A. Huggett' | CLoc CSil CWVF EPts SLBF SRiF |
| | 'Mr W. Rundle' | EBak SRiF SVic |
| § | 'Mr West' (v) | LRHS LSou MCot SPet WMoo WRou |

| | | |
|---|---|---|
| | 'Mrs Churchill' | CLoc |
| | 'Mrs Hobhouse' (d) | SRiF |
| | 'Mrs John D. Fredericks' | CSil |
| | 'Mrs Lawrence Lyon' (d) | EBak |
| | 'Mrs Lee Belton' (E) | CDoC LCla SLBF |
| | 'Mrs Lovell Swisher' ♀H4 | CWVF EBak LCla SPet SRiF SVic |
| | 'Mrs Marshall' | CWVF EBak SLBF SPet SRiF |
| | 'Mrs Minnie Pugh' new | CMac |
| | 'Mrs Popple' ♀H3 | Widely available |
| | 'Mrs Susan Brookfield' (d) | SRiF |
| | 'Mrs W. Castle' | CDoC CSil SVic |
| | 'Mrs W.P. Wood' ♀H3 | CDoC CLoc CSil CWVF ELon LRHS MSCN SRiF SVic WRou |
| | 'Mrs W. Rundle' | CLoc CWVF EBak SLBF SPet |
| | 'Multa' | SRiF |
| | 'Muriel' (d) | CLoc CWVF EBak SRiF |
| | 'Murru's Pierre Marie' (d) | SLBF |
| | 'My Delight' | CWVF |
| | 'My Fair Lady' (d) | CLoc CWVF EBak SPet SRiF |
| | 'My Little Cracker' | CDoC |
| | 'My Little Sparkler' new | SLBF |
| | 'My Mum' | LCla SLBF SRiF |
| | 'My Pat' | SLBF SRiF |
| | 'My Reward' (d) | CWVF |
| | 'Nananice' | SRiF |
| | 'Nancy Lou' (d) | CDoC CLoc CWVF LAst MJac SLBF SPet SRiF SVic WRou |
| | 'Nanny Ed' (d) | CWVF MBri |
| | 'Natal Bronze' | SRiF |
| | 'Natalie Jones' | SRiF |
| | 'Natasha Sinton' (d) | CCCN CLoc CWVF LAst MBri MJac NBlu SPet SRiF WRou |
| | 'Native Dancer' (d) | CWVF EBak |
| | 'Naughty Nicole' (d) | SRiF |
| | 'Nautilus' (d) | EBak |
| | 'Navy Blue' | CSil SRiF |
| | 'Neapolitan' (d) | CDoC SLBF |
| | 'Nell Gwyn' | CLoc CWVF EBak SRiF SVic |
| | 'Nellie Nuttall' ♀H3 | CLoc CWVF EBak EPts SPet SRiF SVic |
| | 'Neopolitan' (E) | CLoc CSil EPts SVic |
| | 'Nettala' | CDoC SRiF SVic |
| | 'Neue Welt' | CSil CWVF EBak SRiF |
| | 'New Fascination' (d) | EBak |
| | 'New Millennium' | CDoC |
| | 'Nice 'n' Easy' (d) | MBri MJac SRiF |
| | 'Nicki Fenwick-Raven' (E) | LCla |
| | 'Nicki's Findling' | CDoC CTsd CWVF EPts LCla MJac SRiF WRou |
| | 'Nicola' | EBak |
| | 'Nicola Jane' (d) | CDoC CSil CWVF EBak EPts LCla MBri MJac SHar SLBF SPet SRiF SVic WRou |
| | 'Nicolette' | CWVF MJac |
| | 'Nightingale' (d) | CLoc EBak |
| § | ***nigricans*** | CDoC |
| | 'Nikki' | SRiF |
| | 'Nimue' | SRiF |
| | 'Nina Wills' | EBak |
| | 'Niobe' (d) | EBak |
| | 'Niula' | CDoC LCla SRiF |
| | 'No Name' (d) | EBak |
| | 'Noel Freeman' | SRiF |
| | 'Nonchalance' (T) | LCla |
| | 'Norfolk Belle' (d) | SRiF |
| | 'Norfolk Ivor' (d) | SRiF |
| | 'Norman Greenhill' | SRiF |
| | 'Norman Welton' new | SLBF |
| | 'Normandy Bell' | EBak SVic |
| | 'Northilda' | SVic |
| | 'Northumbrian Belle' | EBak SRiF |
| | 'Northumbrian Pipes' | LCla |
| | 'Northway' | CLoc CWVF MJac SPet SRiF SVic |
| | 'Norvell Gillespie' (d) | EBak SRiF |
| | 'Novato' | EBak SRiF |
| | 'Novella' (d) | CWVF EBak SRiF |
| | 'Noyo Star' (d) | SRiF |
| | 'Nuance' | LCla |
| | 'Nunthorpe Gem' (d) | CDoC CSil SRiF |
| | 'O Sole Mio' | SVic |
| | ***obconica*** (E) | CDoC CSil LCla |
| | 'Obcylin' (E) | CDoC LCla SLBF SRiF WRou |
| | 'Obergärtner Koch' (T) | CDoC SRiF |
| | 'Ocean Beach' | CDoC EPts SRiF |
| | 'Oddfellow' (d) | SRiF |
| | 'Oetnang' (d) | CTri SCoo |
| | 'Oklahoma' (d) | SRiF |
| | 'Old Lottie Hobby' | SRiF |
| | 'Old Rose' | SRiF |
| | 'Old Somerset' (v) | CCCN CDoC SRiF SVic |
| | 'Oldbury' | SRiF |
| | 'Oldbury Gem' | SRiF |
| | 'Oldbury Pearl' | SRiF |
| | 'Olga Storey' | CDoC |
| | 'Olive Smith' | CWVF EPts LCla MJac SRiF WRou |
| | 'Olympic Lass' (d) | EBak |
| | 'Olympic Sunset' | SVic |
| | 'Omeomy' | SRiF |
| | 'Onward' | CSil |
| | 'Onward Dingle' | SRiF |
| § | 'Oosje' (E) | CDoC CSil LCla SLBF SRiF SVic WRou |
| | 'Opalescent' (d) | CLoc CWVF SVic |
| | 'Orange Crush' | CCCN CLoc CWVF EBak LAst MJac SPet |
| | 'Orange Crystal' | CCCN CWVF EBak MJac SLBF SVic |
| | 'Orange Drops' | CLoc CWVF EBak EPts SRiF SVic |
| | 'Orange Flare' | CLoc CWVF EBak SLBF SRiF SVic WRou |
| | 'Orange Heart' | LCla |
| | 'Orange King' (d) | CLoc CWVF |
| | 'Orange Mirage' | CLoc CWVF EBak LAst SLBF SPet SVic WRou |
| | 'Orange Queen' | SRiF |
| | 'Orange Star' (E) | CDoC |
| | 'Orangeblossom' | SLBF SRiF |
| | 'Oranje van Os' | CWVF |
| | 'Orient Express' (T) | CDoC CLoc CWVF MJac SRiF SVic |
| | 'Oriental Lace' | SRiF |
| | 'Oriental Sunrise' | CWVF |
| | 'Ornamental Pearl' (v) | CLoc CWVF EBak SRiF |
| | 'Orwell' (d) | CWVF |
| | 'Oso Sweet' | CWVF SRiF |
| | 'Other Fellow' | CWVF EBak EPts LCla MJac SLBF SPet SRiF SVic |
| | 'Oulton Empress' (E) | LCla SLBF |
| | 'Oulton Fairy' (E) | SLBF |
| | 'Oulton Painted Lady' | WRou |
| | 'Oulton Red Imp' (E) | LCla SLBF |
| | 'Oulton Travellers Rest' (E) | SLBF |
| | 'Our Darling' | CWVF SRiF |
| | 'Our Dereck' new | SRiF |
| | 'Our Hilary' | SLBF |
| | 'Our Joy' (d) new | SLBF |
| | 'Our Joyce' | SRiF |
| | 'Our Nan' (d) | MJac |
| | 'Our Nell' | SRiF |
| | 'Our Pamela' | MJac |
| | 'Our Spencer' | SLBF |
| | 'Our Ted' (T) | EBak EPts SRiF |

|  |  |
|---|---|
| 'Our Topsy' **new** | SRiF |
| 'Our William' | SLBF |
| 'Overbecks' | see *F. magellanica* var. *molinae* 'Sharpitor' |
| 'P.E. King' (d) **new** | SLBF |
| 'Pabbe's Wikwief' | CDoC |
| 'Pacemaker' | MGos |
| 'Pacific Grove' Greene | see *F.* 'Evelyn Steele Little' |
| 'Pacific Grove' Niederholzer (d) | EBak |
| 'Pacific Queen' (d) | EBak |
| 'Pacquesa' (d) | CWVF EBak SPet SRiF SVic |
| 'Padre Pio' (d) | CWVF EBak MJac |
| 'Pale Flame' (d) | SRiF |
| 'Pallas' | CSil |
| 'Palm Springs' (d) | SRiF |
| 'Pam Plack' | CDoC CSil LCla SLBF SRiF |
| 'Pamela Hutchinson' | SRiF |
| 'Pamela Knights' (d) | EBak |
| 'Pamela Wallace' | SLBF |
| 'Pam's People' | LCla |
| 'Pan' (T) | SRiF |
| 'Pan America' (d) | EBak |
| 'Panache' (d) | LCla |
| 'Pangea' (T) | LCla |
| ***paniculata*** (T) $\Upsilon^{H1+3}$ | CBot CCCN CDoC CFee CRHN CWVF EBak EPts IDee LCla MCot MHer MREP SLBF SRiF WCru |
| 'Panique' | CDoC LCla |
| 'Pantaloons' (d) | EBak |
| 'Pantomine Dame' (d) | CWVF SRiF |
| 'Panylla Prince' | CDoC LCla SLBF SRiF WRou |
| 'Papa Bleuss' (d) | CWVF EBak SRiF |
| 'Papoose' (d) | CDoC CSil EBak LCla SEND SRiF SVic |
| 'Paramour' | SRiF |
| 'Parkstone Centenary' (d) | CWVF |
| 'Party Frock' | CDoC CLoc CWVF EBak |
| 'Party Time' (d) | CWVF |
| ***parviflora*** misapplied | see *F.* × ***bacillaris*** |
| ***parviflora*** Lindl. | see *F. lycioides* Andrews |
| 'Pastel' | EBak SRiF |
| 'Pat Meara' | CLoc EBak SRiF |
| 'Pathétique' (d) | CLoc |
| 'Patience' (d) | CDoC CWVF EBak SLBF SRiF |
| 'Patio King' | EBak |
| 'Patio Princess' (d) | CCCN CLoc CWVF EPts LAst MBri |
| 'Patricia' Wood | EBak SRiF |
| 'Patricia Hodge' | WRou |
| 'Pat's Smile' | SLBF |
| 'Patty Evans' (d) | CWVF EBak SRiF |
| 'Patty Sue' (d) | MBri SRiF WRou |
| 'Paul Berry' (T) | LCla |
| 'Paul Cambon' (d) | EBak SRiF |
| 'Paul Fisher' | CDoC |
| 'Paul Meredith' | SRiF |
| 'Paul Pini' (d) | SRiF |
| 'Paul Roe' (d) | MJac |
| 'Paul Storey' | CDoC CSil SRiF |
| 'Paula Jane' (d) | CCCN CDoC CTsd CWVF LAst LCla MBri MJac SLBF SRiF SVic WGor WRou |
| 'Pauline Rawlins' (d) | CLoc EBak SRiF |
| 'Peace' (d) | EBak SRiF |
| 'Peachy' (California Dreamers Series) (d) | CCCN CDoC CLoc LAst SCoo SRiF |
| 'Peachy Keen' (d) | EBak SRiF |
| 'Peacock' (d) | CLoc |
| 'Pearly Gates' | SRiF |
| 'Pee Wee Rose' | CSil EBak SRiF SVic |
| 'Peggy Burford' (T) | LCla |
| Peggy = 'Goetzpeg'$^{PBR}$ (Shadowdancer Series) | LAst LHop LSou SCoo SRiF |
| 'Peggy King' | CDoC CSil EBak SPet SRiF SVic |
| 'Peloria' (d) | CLoc EBak |
| 'Pennine' | MBri |
| 'People's Princess' | MJac SRiF |
| 'Peper Harow' | EBak SRiF |
| 'Pepi' (d) | CWVF EBak SPet SRiF |
| 'Peppermint Candy' (d) | CDoC CWVF MJac |
| 'Peppermint Stick' (d) | CDoC CLoc CWVF EBak MBri SPet SVic |
| 'Percy Thorpe' | SRiF |
| 'Periwinkle' | SRiF |
| 'Perky Pink' (d) | CWVF EBak EPts SPet SRiF |
| 'Perry Park' | CWVF EBak MBri MJac SRiF SVic |
| 'Perry's Jumbo' | NPer |
| ***perscandens*** | CBcs CPLG CSil LCla WGwG |
| 'Personality' (d) | EBak SRiF |
| 'Peter Bielby' (d) | CWVF SRiF |
| 'Peter Crookes' (T) | CWVF SRiF |
| 'Peter Grange' | EBak |
| 'Peter Hornby' | SRiF |
| 'Peter James' (d) | CSil SRiF |
| 'Peter Pan' | CSil CWVF SRiF |
| ***petiolaris*** | CDoC LCla |
| 'Petit Four' | CWVF SRiF |
| 'Petit Point' | SRiF |
| 'Petite' (d) | EBak |
| 'Petronella' (d) | SRiF |
| 'Phaidra' | CDoC LCla |
| 'Pharaoh' | CLoc |
| 'Phénoménal' (d) | CSil CWVF EBak SRiF |
| 'Phillip Taylor' | MJac |
| 'Phil's Pill' **new** | SLBF |
| 'Phryne' (d) | CSil EBak SRiF SVic |
| 'Phyllis' (d) $\Upsilon^{H4}$ | CAgr CDoC CLoc CSil CWVF EBak ELon EPts LCla LRHS MJac SEND SLBF SPet SRiF SVic WFar WRou |
| 'Piet van der Sande' | CDoC LCla |
| 'Piggelmee' | CDoC |
| 'Pinch Me' (d) | CWVF EBak SPet SRiF SVic |
| 'Pink Aurora' | CLoc SRiF |
| 'Pink Ballet Girl' (d) | CLoc EBak SVic |
| 'Pink Bon Accord' | CLoc CTsd CWVF SRiF SVic |
| 'Pink Cloud' | CLoc EBak SRiF |
| 'Pink Cornet' | LCla SRiF |
| 'Pink Darling' | CLoc EBak SRiF |
| 'Pink Dessert' | EBak |
| 'Pink Domino' (d) | CSil |
| 'Pink Fairy' (d) | EBak SPet SRiF |
| 'Pink Fandango' (d) | CLoc |
| 'Pink Fantasia' | CDoC CLoc CWVF EBak EPts LAst LCla MJac SLBF SRiF SVic |
| 'Pink Flamingo' (d) | EBak SRiF |
| 'Pink Frills' | SRiF |
| 'Pink Galore' (d) | CCCN CLoc CWVF EBak LAst MBri MJac SLBF SPet SRiF SVic |
| 'Pink Goon' (d) | CDoC CSil LCla SLBF SRiF SVic |
| 'Pink Haze' | CSil SRiF SVic |
| 'Pink Jade' | CWVF EBak |
| 'Pink la Campanella' | CWVF EBak MBri SLBF SRiF WGor |
| 'Pink Lace' (d) | SPet |
| 'Pink Marshmallow' (d) $\Upsilon^{H1+3}$ | CCCN CDoC CLoc CWVF EBak MJac SLBF SPet SRiF SVic |
| 'Pink Panther' (d) | SRiF SVic |
| 'Pink Pearl' ambig. | SRiF |
| 'Pink Pearl' Bright (d) | CSil EBak |
| 'Pink Princess' | SRiF |
| 'Pink Profusion' | EBak SRiF |

| |  |  |
|---|---|---|
| | 'Pink Quartet' (d) | CLoc CWVF EBak SPet SRiF |
| | 'Pink Rain' | CWVF MJac SRiF WRou |
| | 'Pink Slippers' | CLoc |
| | 'Pink Spangles' | CCCN CWVF MBri SRiF SVic |
| | 'Pink Surprise' (d) | CTsd |
| | 'Pink Temptation' | CLoc CWVF EBak LAst SVic |
| | 'Pinto de Blue' (d) | SRiF |
| | 'Pinwheel' (d) | CLoc EBak SRiF |
| | 'Piper' (d) | CDoC CWVF SRiF |
| | 'Piper's Vale' (T) | CDoC MJac SLBF SRiF |
| | 'Pippa Rolt' | SRiF |
| | 'Pirbright' | CWVF |
| | 'Pixie' | CDoC CLoc CSil CWVF EBak MJac SLBF SPet SRiF SVic |
| | 'Playboy' (d) | SVic |
| | 'Playford' | CWVF EBak SRiF |
| | 'Plenty' | EBak SVic |
| | 'Plumb Bob' (d) | CWVF |
| | 'Pol Jannie' (d) | SRiF |
| | 'Pole Star' | CSil SRiF |
| | 'Polskie Fuksji' | CDoC |
| | 'Pop Whitlock' (v) | CWVF MCot SPet SRiF SVic |
| | 'Poppet' | CWVF |
| | 'Popsie Girl' | CDoC SLBF SRiF WRou |
| | 'Port Arthur' (d) | CSil EBak SRiF |
| | 'Postiljon' | CWVF EBak SRiF |
| | 'Postman' | CDoC SRiF |
| | 'Powder Puff' ambig. | CWVF MBri |
| | 'Powder Puff' Hodges (d) | CLoc SRiF SVic |
| I | 'Powder Puff' Tabraham (d) | CSil |
| | 'Prelude' ambig. | SVic |
| | 'Prelude' Blackwell | CLoc CSil |
| I | 'Prelude' Kennett (d) | EBak |
| | 'President' | CDoC CSil EBak LRHS SRiF |
| | 'President B.W. Rawlins' | EBak SRiF |
| | 'President Barrie Nash' **new** | CLoc |
| § | 'President Elliot' | CSil SRiF |
| | 'President George Bartlett' (d) | CDoC CLoc CSil EPts MJac SLBF SRiF WRou |
| | 'President Jim Muil' | SLBF |
| | 'President Joan Morris' (d) | SLBF |
| | 'President John Porter' **new** | SLBF |
| | 'President Leo Boullemier' | CWVF EBak MJac SPet SRiF SVic |
| | 'President Margaret Slater' | CLoc CWVF EBak SPet SRiF SVic |
| | 'President Moir' (d) | SLBF SRiF |
| | 'President Norman Hobbs' | CWVF |
| | 'President Roosevelt' (d) | CDoC |
| | 'President Stanley Wilson' (d) | CWVF EBak EPts SRiF |
| | 'President Wilf Sharp' (d) | SRiF SVic |
| | 'Preston Guild' ♀H1+3 | CDoC CLoc CSil CWVF EBak NPer SDys SLBF SPet SRiF SVic WRou |
| | 'Pride of Ipswich' | SRiF |
| | 'Pride of Roualeyn' | WRou |
| | 'Pride of the West' | EBak SRiF |
| | 'Prince of Orange' | CLoc CWVF EBak SRiF SVic |
| | 'Prince of Peace' (d) | SRiF |
| | 'Prince Syray' | SRiF |
| | 'Princess Dollar' | see *F.* 'Dollar Prinzessin' |
| | 'Princess Pamela' (d) | SLBF |
| | 'Princessita' | CWVF EBak SPet |
| | ***procumbens*** | CBcs CCCN CDoC CLoc CPLG CSil CTrC CWVF EBak ECou EPfP EPts GCal GGar IDee ITim LCla MCot MHer NWCA SLBF SRiF SWal WRou |
| | - 'Argentea' | see *F. procumbens* 'Wirral' |
| | - 'Variegata' | see *F. procumbens* 'Wirral' |
| § | - 'Wirral' (v) | CBcs CDoC CLoc CSil CTrC CTsd EQua SRiF WBor |
| | 'Prodigy' | see *F.* 'Enfant Prodigue' |

| |  |  |
|---|---|---|
| | 'Profusion' ambig. | SVic |
| | 'Profusion' Wood | SRiF |
| | 'Prosperity' (d) ♀H3 | CDoC CLoc CSil CWVF EBak EPfP EPts LCla LRHS MJac MRav SLBF SPet SRiF SVic WRou |
| | 'Pumila' | CMac CPLG CWib ELan EPfP EPts SDix SLBF SPet SRiF SVic WRou |
| | 'Purbeck Mist' (d) | CWVF |
| | 'Purperklokje' | CSil CWVF EBak SRiF SVic |
| | 'Purple Emperor' (d) | CLoc |
| | 'Purple Heart' (d) | CLoc EBak SRiF |
| | 'Purple Lace' | CSil SRiF SVic |
| | 'Purple Patch' | MBri |
| | 'Purple Pride' | MBri |
| | 'Purple Rain' | EPts WRou |
| | 'Purple Showers' | SRiF |
| | 'Purple Splendour' (d) | CDoC CSil SRiF |
| | 'Pussy Cat' (T) | CLoc CWVF EBak SRiF SVic |
| | 'Putney Pride' | EPts |
| | 'Put's Folly' | CWVF EBak MJac SPet SRiF |
| | ***putumayensis*** | CSil EBak SRiF |
| | 'Quasar' (d) | CCCN CDoC CLoc CWVF EPts LAst MJac SLBF SPet SRiF SVic WRou |
| | 'Queen Esther' | SRiF |
| | 'Queen Mabs' | EBak SRiF |
| | 'Queen Mary' | CLoc CSil EBak SRiF |
| | 'Queen of Bath' (d) | EBak SVic |
| | 'Queen of Derby' (d) | CSil CWVF SRiF |
| | 'Queen of Hearts' Kennett (d) | SVic |
| | 'Queen Victoria' Smith (d) | SRiF |
| | 'Queen's Park' (d) | EBak |
| | 'Query' | CSil EBak SRiF SVic |
| | 'R.A.F.' (d) | CCCN CLoc CWVF EBak EPts SLBF SPet SRiF SVic |
| | 'Rachel Sinton' (d) | MBri SRiF WRou |
| | 'Radcliffe Bedder' (d) | CSil |
| | 'Radings Gerda' (E) | LCla SLBF |
| | 'Radings Inge' (E) | CDoC LCla |
| | 'Radings Karin' | CDoC |
| | 'Radings Michelle' | CSil CWVF |
| | 'Rahnee' | CWVF SRiF |
| | 'Rainbow' | CWVF |
| | 'Raintree Legend' (d) | SRiF |
| | 'Ralph's Delight' (d) | CWVF SRiF |
| | 'Rambling Rose' (d) | CLoc CWVF EBak MJac SRiF |
| | 'Rambo' (d) | SRiF |
| | 'Rams Royal' (d) | CDoC CWVF SRiF |
| | 'Raspberry' (d) | CLoc CWVF EBak SRiF SVic |
| | 'Raspberry Red' | SRiF |
| | 'Raspberry Sweet' (d) | CWVF SRiF |
| | 'Ratae Beauty' | CWVF |
| | 'Ratatouille' (d) | SRiF SVic |
| | ***ravenii*** | CSil |
| | 'Ravensbarrow' | CSil |
| | 'Ravenslaw' | CSil |
| | 'Ray Redfern' | CWVF |
| | 'Razzle Dazzle' (d) | EBak SRiF |
| | 'Reading Show' (d) | CSil CWVF EPts SLBF SRiF |
| | 'Rebecca Williamson' (d) | CWVF MJac SRiF |
| | 'Rebeka Sinton' (v) | CLoc EBak MBri SRiF |
| | 'Red Ace' (d) | CSil |
| | 'Red Imp' (d) | CSil |
| | 'Red Jacket' (d) | CWVF EBak SRiF |
| | 'Red Petticoat' | CWVF SRiF |
| | 'Red Rain' | CWVF SRiF WRou |
| | 'Red Ribbons' (d) | EBak |
| | 'Red Rover' | SRiF WRou |
| | 'Red Rum' (d) | SPet |

| | |
|---|---|
| 'Red Shadows' (d) | CLoc CWVF EBak SRiF |
| 'Red Spider' | CCCN CLoc CWVF EBak LAst SCoo SPet SRiF SVic |
| 'Red Wing' | CLoc |
| 'Reflexa' | see *F.* × *bacillaris* 'Reflexa' |
| 'Reg Gubler' | SLBF |
| 'Regal' | CLoc |
| 'Regal Robe' (d) | CDoC SRiF |
| ***regia*** | CSil |
| - var. ***radicans*** | CSil |
| - subsp. ***regia*** | CDoC CSil CTsd LCla SRiF |
| - subsp. ***reitzii*** | CDul CSil EQua EWes LCla |
| - subsp. ***serrae*** | CDoC CSil |
| 'Remember Eric' | CDoC CSil SRiF WRou |
| 'Remembrance' (d) | CSil EPts LCla SLBF SRiF |
| 'Remus' (d) | SRiF SVic |
| 'Remy Kind' (d) | SRiF |
| 'Rene Schwab' | LCla |
| 'Requiem' | CLoc |
| 'Reverend Doctor Brown' (d) | EBak |
| 'Reverend Elliott' | see *F.* 'President Elliot' |
| 'Revival' | SRiF |
| 'Rhapsody' ambig. | SVic |
| I 'Rhapsody' Blackwell (d) | CLoc |
| 'Rhombifolia' | CSil |
| 'Rianne Foks' | SRiF |
| 'Riant' (d) | SRiF |
| 'Riccartonii' ♀$^{H3}$ | Widely available |
| 'Richard John' (v) | SRiF SVic |
| 'Richard John Carrington' | CSil |
| 'Ridestar' (d) | CLoc CWVF EBak SRiF |
| 'Rigoletto' | SVic |
| 'Rijs 2001' (E) | CDoC SLBF SRiF |
| 'Rina Felix' | CDoC |
| 'Ringwood Gold' | SVic |
| 'Ringwood Market' (d) | CSil CWVF EPts MJac SCoo SLBF SPet SRiF SVic |
| 'Rita Mary' | SRiF |
| 'Rivendell' | EPts |
| 'Riverdancer Claire' **new** | CDoC |
| 'Riverside' (d) | SRiF |
| 'Robbie' | SRiF |
| 'Robert Lutters' | SVic |
| 'Robin Hood' (d) | CSil SRiF |
| 'Rocket Fire' (California Dreamers Series) (d) | MJac SRiF |
| 'Roesse Blacky' | CDoC SBfd |
| 'Roesse Callisto' | CDoC |
| 'Roesse Juliet' | CDoC |
| 'Roesse Peacock' (d) | CDoC |
| 'Roger de Cooker' (T) | CLoc EPts LCla SRiF |
| 'Rohees Izar' | SRiF |
| 'Rohees Lava' | SLBF |
| 'Rohees Leada' (d) | SLBF SRiF |
| 'Rohees Merope' | SRiF |
| 'Rohees Naos' (d) | SRiF |
| 'Rohees New Millennium' (d) | SLBF SRiF |
| 'Rohees Reda' (d) | SRiF |
| 'Rohees Tethys' (d) | SLBF |
| 'Rolla' (d) | CWVF EBak SRiF |
| 'Rolt's Bride' (d) | SRiF |
| 'Rolt's Ruby' (d) | CSil CWVF SRiF SVic |
| 'Roman City' (d) | CLoc SRiF SVic |
| 'Romance' (d) | CWVF SRiF |
| 'Romany Rose' | CLoc SRiF |
| 'Ron Ewart' | WRou |
| 'Ron Holmes' | SRiF |
| 'Ronald L. Lockerbie' (d) | CLoc CWVF SRiF SVic |
| 'Rondo' | MJac |
| 'Ronnie Barker' (d) | MJac |
| 'Ron's Ruby' | CSil SRiF |
| 'Roos Breytenbach' (T) | CCCN CDoC LAst LCla MJac SRiF WRou |
| 'Rosamunda' (d) | CLoc |
| 'Rose Aylett' (d) | EBak |
| 'Rose Bradwardine' (d) | EBak SRiF |
| 'Rose Churchill' (d) | MBri MJac |
| 'Rose Fantasia' | CCCN CDoC CLoc CWVF EPts LAst MJac SLBF SRiF |
| 'Rose of Castile' | CDoC CLoc CSil EBak LCla MJac SLBF SVic WRou WWlt |
| 'Rose of Castile Improved' ♀$^{H4}$ | CSil CWVF EBak LCla MJac SPet SRiF |
| 'Rose of Denmark' | CCCN CLoc CSil CWVF EBak MBri MJac SCoo SLBF SPet SRiF WGor |
| 'Rose Reverie' (d) | EBak |
| 'Rose van der Bergh' | SRiF |
| 'Rose Winston' (d) | LAst SCoo |
| ***rosea*** misapplied | see *F.* 'Globosa' |
| ***rosea*** Ruíz & Pav. | see *F. lycioides* Andrews |
| 'Rosebud' (d) | EBak SRiF |
| 'Rosecroft Beauty' (d) | CSil CWVF EBak SRiF SVic |
| Rosella = 'Goetzrose'$^{PBR}$ (Shadowdancer Series) | LAst |
| 'Rosemarie Higham' | LAst MJac SCoo |
| 'Rosemary Day' | CLoc |
| 'Rosemoor' (T) | SRiF |
| 'Roslyn Lowe' (d) | CDoC |
| 'Ross Lea' (d) | CSil |
| 'Roswitha' | SLBF SRiF |
| 'Rosy Bows' | CWVF SRiF |
| 'Rosy Frills' (d) | CWVF MJac SRiF SVic |
| 'Rosy Morn' (d) | CLoc EBak |
| 'Rothbury Beauty' | SRiF |
| 'Rough Silk' | CLoc CWVF EBak SRiF |
| 'Roy Castle' (d) | CWVF |
| 'Roy Walker' (d) | CLoc CWVF SRiF |
| 'Royal Academy' (d) | EPts WRou |
| 'Royal and Ancient' | CWVF |
| 'Royal Mosaic' (California Dreamers Series) (d) | CCCN CDoC MJac SRiF |
| 'Royal Orchid' | EBak |
| 'Royal Purple' (d) | CSil EBak MBri SPet SRiF |
| 'Royal Ruby' | SRiF |
| 'Royal Serenade' (d) | CWVF |
| 'Royal Touch' (d) | EBak |
| 'Royal Velvet' (d) ♀$^{H3}$ | CCCN CLoc CWVF EBak EPts MAsh MJac SLBF SPet SRiF SVic WRou |
| 'Royal Wedding' | SRiF |
| 'Royal Welsh' | WRou |
| 'Rozientje' | SRiF |
| 'Rubra Grandiflora' | CWVF EBak LCla SDys SLBF SRiF WRou |
| 'Ruby' (d) | SRiF |
| 'Ruby Wedding' (d) | CWVF SLBF SRiF |
| 'Ruddigore' | CWVF SRiF |
| 'Ruffles' (d) | CWVF EBak SRiF |
| 'Rufus' ♀$^{H3-4}$ | CDoC CLoc CSil CWVF EBak ELan EPfP EPts LCla MJac MSCN SLBF SPet SRiF SVic WFar WRou |
| 'Ruth' | CSil SRiF SVic |
| 'Ruth Brazewell' (d) | CLoc |
| 'Ruth King' (d) | CWVF EBak SRiF |
| 'Rutland Water' | CDoC SRiF |
| 'S'Wonderful' (d) | CLoc EBak SRiF |
| 'Sabrina' | WRou |
| 'Sailor' | EPts SVic |
| 'Sally Ann' (d) | SRiF |
| 'Sally Bell' | CSil |

'Salmon Cascade' CWVF EBak EPts LCla MJac SLBF WRou
'Salmon Glow' CWVF MJac SVic
'Sam Sheppard' SLBF
'Samantha Reynolds' SRiF
'Samba' (d) LAst
'Sammy Girl' SRiF
'Sam's Song' (d) SRiF
'Samson' (d/v) EBak SRiF
'San Diego' (d) CWVF
'San Francisco' EBak
'San Leandro' (d) EBak
'San Mateo' (d) EBak
§ ***sanctae-rosae*** CDoC EBak LCla SRiF
'Sandboy' CWVF EBak
'Sanguinea' CSil
'Sanrina' CDoC
'Santa Cruz' (d) CSil CWVF EBak SLBF SRiF SVic
'Santa Lucia' (d) CLoc EBak
'Santa Monica' (d) EBak SRiF
'Sapphire' (d) EBak SRiF
'Sara Helen' (d) CLoc EBak
'Sarah Brightman' (d) MJac
'Sarah Eliza' (d) SCoo
'Sarah Jane' (d) CSil EBak SVic
'Sarah Louise' CWVF
'Sarina' SRiF
'Sarong' (d) EBak
'Satellite' CLoc CWVF EBak SRiF
'Saturnus' CSil CWVF EBak ELon LRHS MAsh SLBF SPet SPoG SRiF WRou
'Saxondale Sue' SRiF SVic
'Scabieuse' CSil
***scabriuscula*** CDoC LCla SRiF
***scandens*** see *F. decussata* Ruíz & Pav.
'Scarborough Rosette' (d) SRiF
'Scarcity' CDoC CSil CWVF EBak SRiF SVic
'Schneeball' (d) CDoC CSil EBak SRiF SVic
'Schneekoppen' (d) SRiF
'Schneewitcher' CDoC EPts SRiF
'Schneewittchen' Hoech CSil
'Schneewittchen' Klein CSil EBak
'Schönbrunner Schuljubiläum' (T) EBak
'Schone Hanaurin' SLBF
'Schöne Wilhelmine' see *F.* 'Die Schöne Wilhelmine'
'Scion of Longleat' SRiF
'Scotch Heather' (d) CWVF SRiF
'Sea Shell' (d) CWVF EBak SRiF
'Seaforth' EBak SRiF
'Sealand Prince' CDoC CSil CTsd CWVF LCla SRiF SVic
'Sebastopol' (d) CLoc
'Selma Lavrijsen' CDoC
***serratifolia*** Hook. see *F. austromontana*
***serratifolia*** Ruíz & Pav. see *F. denticulata*
'Seventh Heaven' (d) CCCN CLoc CTsd CWVF LAst MJac SCoo SRiF SVic
'Shady Blue' CWVF
'Shangri-La' (d) EBak
'Shania' (Diva Series) SRiF
'Shanley' CWVF SVic
'Sharon Allsop' (d) CWVF SRiF
'Sharon Caunt' (d) CSil
'Sharon Leslie' WRou
'Sharpitor' see *F. magellanica* var. *molinae* 'Sharpitor'
'Shawna Ree' (E) CDoC
'Sheila Crooks' (d) CDoC CWVF EBak SRiF
'Sheila Kirby' CWVF
'Sheila Purdy' SRiF
'Sheila Steele' (d) CWVF SRiF
'Sheila's Love' MJac
'Sheila's Surprise' (d) SRiF
'Shelford' CDoC CLoc CWVF EBak EPts MJac SLBF SRiF SVic WRou
'Shell Pink' SVic
'Shelley Lyn' (d) SRiF
'She's a Beauty' **new** MJac
'Shirley Halladay' (d) LCla SRiF
'Shirley'PBR (Shadowdancer Series) GKev LAst LSou SCoo SRiF
'Shooting Star' (d) EBak SRiF
'Showfire' EBak
'Showtime' (d) CWVF
'Shrimp Cocktail' CLoc MBri MSCN SRiF
'Shuna Lindsay' LCla
'Shy Lady' (d) SRiF
'Siberoet' (E) CDoC LCla SLBF
'Sierra Blue' (d) CDoC CLoc CWVF EBak SRiF
'Silver Anniversary' (d) SRiF SVic
'Silver Dawn' (d) SRiF
'Silver Dollar' SVic
'Silver Pink' CSil
'Silver Wedding' (d) SRiF
'Silverbell' **new** SRiF
'Silverdale' CDoC CSil EPts SRiF
'Simon J. Rowell' LCla SRiF
'Simple Simon' SRiF
***simplicicaulis*** CDoC EBak LCla
– pale-flowered GCal
'Sincerity' (d) CLoc
'Sinton's Standard' MBri
'Siobhan' CWVF
'Siobhan Evans' (d) SLBF
'Sipke Arjen' WRou
'Sir Alfred Ramsey' CWVF EBak
'Sir David Attenborough' (d) MJac
'Sir David Jason' MJac
'Sir Ian Botham' (d) MJac SRiF
'Sir Matt Busby' (d) EPts LAst MJac SRiF WRou
'Sir Steve Redgrave' (d) MJac
'Sir Thomas Allen' SLBF
'Siren' Baker (d) EBak
'Sister Ann Haley' EPts SRiF
'Sister Sister' (d) SLBF
'Sleepy' CDoC CSil CTsd EPts SPet SRiF SVic
'Sleigh Bells' CLoc CWVF EBak SPet SRiF SVic
'Small Pipes' CWVF SRiF
'Smokey Mountain' (d) SRiF SVic
'Sneezy' EPts SRiF SVic
'Snow Burner' (California Dreamers Series) (d) CCCN CDoC CLoc LAst SRiF
'Snow White' (d) SRiF SVic
'Snowbird' (d) SLBF
§ 'Snowcap' (d) ♀H3-4 CCCN CDoC CLoc CSil CWVF EBak EPts GKin LAst LCla LRHS MAsh MBri MGos MJac MWat NPer SBfd SCoo SLBF SPet SPoG SRiF SVic WFar WRou
'Snowdon' (d) CWVF SRiF
'Snowdrift' ambig. SRiF
'Snowdrift' Colville (d) CLoc
'Snowdrift' Kennett (d) EBak
'Snowfall' CWVF
'Snowfire' (d) CLoc CWVF SCoo SRiF SVic
'Snowflake' (E) CDoC EPts LCla SLBF WBor WRou
'Snowstorm' (d) SRiF
'So Big' (d) SRiF
'Software' (d) SRiF

| |  |  |
|---|---|---|
| | 'Sombrero' (d) | SRiF |
| | 'Son of Thumb' ♀H4 | CDoC CLoc CSil CWVF EPfP EPts LAst LBMP LRHS MAsh MGos MJac SLBF SLim SPer SPet SRiF SVic WFar WRou |
| | 'Sonata' (d) | CLoc CWVF EBak SRiF SVic |
| | 'Sophie Louise' | CWVF EPts SLBF SRiF WRou |
| | 'Sophie's Silver Lining' (d) | MJac SRiF |
| | 'Sophisticated Lady' (d) | CLoc CWVF EBak EPts SPet SRiF SVic |
| | 'Soroptimist International' | SRiF |
| | 'South Gate' (d) | CLoc CWVF EBak EPts LAst LBMP MBri MSCN SPet SRiF SVic |
| | 'South Lakeland' | CSil SRiF |
| | 'South Seas' (d) | EBak SVic |
| | 'South Today' (d) | SRiF |
| | 'Southern Pride' | SLBF |
| | 'Southlanders' | EBak |
| | 'Southwell Minster' | SRiF |
| | 'Space Shuttle' | CLoc LCla SLBF SRiF |
| | 'Sparky' (T) | CLoc CWVF EPts LCla SRiF WRou |
| § | 'Speciosa' | CDoC EBak LCla SRiF WRou |
| | 'Spice of Life' (d) | SRiF |
| | 'Spion Kop' (d) | CCCN CDoC CWVF EBak LAst SPet SRiF WGor |
| § | ***splendens*** ♀H1+3 | CCCN CDoC CLoc CSil EBak IDee LCla MCot MHer NPer SLBF SMrm SRiF WRou |
| | – B&SWJ 10469 | WCru |
| | – 'Karl Hartweg' | CDoC MAvo |
| | 'Spotlight' | SRiF |
| | 'Spring Bells' (d) | SRiF |
| | 'Spring Classic' (d) | SRiF |
| | 'Squadron Leader' (d) | CWVF EBak EPts SRiF |
| | 'Square Peg' (d) | SRiF |
| | 'Stanley Cash' (d) | CLoc CWVF SPet SRiF SVic |
| | 'Star Wars' | CDoC CLoc EPts MBri MJac SRiF WRou |
| | 'Stardust' | CDoC CWVF EBak MJac |
| | 'Steeley' (d) | SVic |
| | 'Steirerblut' (T) | SRiF |
| | 'Stella Ann' (T) | CWVF EBak EPts LCla SRiF |
| | 'Stella Didden' (d) | SRiF |
| | 'Stella Marina' (d) | EBak |
| | 'Stewart Taylor' | MJac |
| | 'Stolze von Berlin' (d) | SRiF |
| | 'Stoney Creek' (d) | SRiF |
| | 'Straat Cook' | LCla |
| | 'Straat Cumberland' | LCla |
| | 'Straat Fiji' | LCla |
| | 'Straat Fuknoka' | CDoC LCla |
| | 'Straat Futami' (e) | CDoC EPts LCla |
| | 'Straat Kobe' (T) | CDoC LCla SRiF |
| | 'Straat La Plata' | LCla |
| | 'Straat Magelhaen' | LCla |
| | 'Straat Malakka' | SRiF |
| | 'Straat Messina' | LCla |
| | 'Straat of Plenty' | CDoC LCla |
| | 'Strawberry Delight' (d) | CLoc CWVF EBak MJac SPet SVic |
| | 'Strawberry Fizz' (d) | SRiF |
| | 'Strawberry Sundae' (d) | CLoc CWVF EBak SRiF |
| | 'Strawberry Supreme' (d) | CSil |
| | 'String of Pearls' | CLoc CWVF MJac SLBF SPet SRiF SVic |
| | 'Stuart Joe' | CWVF |
| | 'Stuart Martin' | SRiF |
| | 'Sue' | SLBF SRiF |
| | 'Suffolk Punch' | SRiF |
| | 'Suffolk Splendour' (d) | EPts |
| | 'Sugar Almond' (d) | CWVF |
| | 'Sugar Blues' (d) | EBak SRiF |
| | 'Summerdaffodil' | SRiF |
| | 'Summerwood' (d) | SRiF |
| | 'Sundance' **new** | SRiF |
| | 'Sunkissed' (d) | EBak |
| | 'Sunningdale' (T) | CWVF |
| | 'Sunny' | SRiF |
| | 'Sunny Jim' | SVic |
| | 'Sunny Smiles' | CSil CWVF SPet SRiF |
| | 'Sunray' (v) | CChe CDoC CLoc COIW CWVF EBak ELon LBuc LRHS MAsh MGos MWat NEgg SBfd SCoo SEND SLim SMrm SPoG SRiF WCot |
| | 'Sunset' | CLoc CWVF EBak SPer SRiF |
| | 'Sunset Boulevard' (d) | SRiF |
| | 'Supersport' (d) | SVic |
| | 'Superstar' | CWVF EPts SRiF SVic |
| | 'Susan' (d) | SRiF |
| | 'Susan Ford' (d) | CWVF SPet SRiF |
| | 'Susan Green' | CSil CWVF EBak MJac SRiF |
| | 'Susan McMaster' | CLoc |
| | 'Susan Olcese' (d) | CWVF EBak SRiF |
| | 'Susan Skeen' | WRou |
| | 'Susan Travis' | CLoc CSil CWVF EBak SRiF SVic |
| | 'Swanley Gem' ♀H3 | CLoc CWVF EBak SLBF SPet SRiF SVic |
| | 'Swanley Pendula' | CLoc |
| | 'Swanley Yellow' | CWVF EBak SRiF SVic |
| | 'Sweet Lavender' (d) | SRiF |
| | 'Sweet Leilani' (d) | EBak SRiF |
| | 'Sweet Sarah' (E) | EPts |
| | 'Sweet Sixteen' (d) | CLoc |
| | 'Sweetheart' ambig. | SRiF |
| I | 'Sweetheart' van Wieringen | EBak |
| | 'Swingtime' (d) ♀H3 | CCCN CLoc CWVF EBak EPts LAst LBMP LCla MGos MJac NBlu SLBF SPet SRiF SVic |
| | ***sylvatica*** misapplied | see *F. nigricans* |
| | ***sylvatica*** Benth. | CDoC |
| | 'Sylvia' Veitch (d) | SRiF |
| | 'Sylvia Barker' | CWVF LCla SLBF SRiF WRou |
| | 'Sylvia Gale' | SRiF |
| | 'Sylvia Rose' (d) | CWVF SRiF |
| | 'Sylvia's Choice' | EBak |
| | 'Sylvy' | SRiF |
| | 'Symphony' | CLoc CWVF EBak |
| | 'T.S.J.' (E) | CDoC LCla |
| | 'T'Vöske' (d/v) | SRiF |
| | 'Taatje' | SRiF |
| | 'Taco' | CDoC LCla SRiF |
| | 'Taddle' | CWVF SLBF |
| | 'Taffeta Bow' (d) | CLoc SRiF SVic |
| | 'Taffy' (d) | EBak |
| | 'Tam O'Shanter' (d) | SRiF |
| | 'Tammy' | SRiF |
| | 'Tamworth' | CLoc CWVF EBak MJac SRiF SVic |
| | 'Tangerine' | CLoc CWVF EBak SRiF SVic WCot WRou |
| | 'Tania Leanne' | SRiF |
| | 'Tanya Bridger' (d) | EBak SRiF |
| | 'Tarra Valley' | LCla SRiF SVic |
| | 'Task Force' | CWVF SRiF SVic |
| | 'Tausendschön' (d) | CLoc |
| | 'Ted Perry' (d) | CWVF |
| | 'Ted Stiff' (d) | SRiF |
| | 'Ted's Tribute' | SRiF |
| | 'Television' (d) | SRiF |
| | 'Temptation' ambig. | CWVF SPet |
| | 'Temptation' Peterson | CLoc EBak SRiF |
| | 'Tennessee Maiden' (d) | SRiF |

| | |
|---|---|
| 'Tennessee Waltz' (d) ♀H3 | CDoC CLoc CSil CWVF EBak EPts SLBF SPet SRiF SVic WRou |
| 'Tequila Sunrise' | SRiF |
| 'Teresa' (d) | SRiF |
| 'Tessa Jane' | CSil |
| ***tetradactyla*** misapplied | see *F.* × *bacillaris* |
| 'Texas Longhorn' (d) | CLoc CWVF EBak SRiF SVic |
| 'Thalia' (T) ♀H1+3 | CCCN CDoC CDul CHEx CLoc CWVF EBak EPfP EPts LAst LCla LSRN MBri MCot MHer MJac NEgg NPri NVic SGar SLBF SMrm SPer SPlb SPoG SRiF SVic WPtf WRou WWlt |
| 'Thamar' | CDoC CLoc CWVF EPts SRiF SVic WRou |
| 'That's It' (d) | EBak SVic |
| 'The Aristocrat' (d) | CLoc EBak SRiF |
| 'The Cannons' (d) | SRiF |
| § 'The Doctor' | CLoc CSil CWVF EBak SRiF |
| 'The Jester' (d) | EBak |
| 'The Madame' (d) | CWVF EBak SRiF |
| 'The Marvel' | SRiF |
| 'The Speedbird' | SRiF |
| 'The Tarns' | CSil CWVF EBak SRiF SVic |
| 'Thelma Vint' | CDoC |
| 'Therese Dupois' | CSil SRiF |
| 'Théroigne de Méricourt' | EBak SRiF |
| 'Thilco' | CDoC CSil |
| 'This England' (d) | SRiF |
| 'Thistle Hill' (d) | CDoC CSil |
| 'Thomas' (d) | EPts |
| 'Thomas Ritchie' | SRiF |
| 'Thompsonii' | see *F. magellanica* 'Thompsonii' |
| 'Thornley's Hardy' | CSil MRav SPet SRiF SVic |
| 'Three Cheers' | CLoc EBak SRiF |
| 'Three Counties' | EBak SRiF |
| 'Thunderbird' (d) | CLoc CWVF EBak SRiF |
| ***thymifolia*** (E) | CWVF GCra GQui LRHS MHer WKif |
| - subsp. ***minimiflora*** (E) | CSil LCla |
| - subsp. ***thymifolia*** (E) | CDoC CSil CTsd LCla |
| 'Tiara' (d) | EBak |
| 'Tickled Pink' | WRou |
| 'Tiffany' ambig. | SRiF |
| 'Tiffany' Reedstrom (d) | EBak |
| 'Tillingbourne' (d) | CSil SLBF |
| 'Time After Time' | CLoc SRiF WRou |
| 'Timlin Brened' (T) | CWVF EBak SRiF |
| 'Timothy Titus' (T) | LCla SLBF SRiF |
| 'Ting-a-ling' | CLoc CWVF EBak SPet SRiF SVic |
| 'Tinker Bell' ambig. | SRiF |
| 'Tinker Bell' Hodges | EBak SVic |
| 'Tintern Abbey' | CWVF |
| 'Tjinegara' | CDoC LCla SRiF |
| 'Toby Bridger' (d) | CLoc EBak SRiF |
| 'Toby Foreman' | SLBF |
| 'Tolling Bell' | CWVF EBak SPet |
| 'Tom Boy' | SRiF |
| 'Tom Goedeman' | LCla |
| 'Tom H. Oliver' (d) | EBak SRiF |
| 'Tom Knights' | EBak SPet SRiF |
| 'Tom Thorne' | EBak |
| 'Tom Thumb' ♀H3 | Widely available |
| 'Tom West' misapplied | see *F.* 'Mr West' |
| 'Tom West' Meillez (v) | CDoC CHEx CLoc CMHG CSBt CSil CTsd CWVF CWib EBak EHoe EPts LAst LCla LHop LSRN MAsh MHer MJac MSCN NVic SAga SBfd SDix SLBF SLim SRiF WFar WHil |
| 'Tom Woods' | CWVF SRiF |
| 'Tommy Tucker' | SRiF |
| 'Ton Ten Hove' | CDoC LCla SRiF |
| 'Tony Galea' | SRiF |
| 'Tony Porter' (d) | SRiF |
| 'Tony's Treat' (d) | EPts |
| 'Toos' | SVic |
| 'Topaz' (d) | CLoc EBak |
| 'Topper' (d) | CWVF SRiF |
| 'Torch' (d) | CLoc CWVF EBak SRiF SVic |
| 'Torchlight' | CWVF EPts LCla |
| 'Torvill and Dean' (d) | CCCN CLoc CWVF EPts LAst MJac SLBF SPet WGor WRou |
| 'Tosca' | CWVF SRiF |
| 'Town Crier' | SLBF |
| 'Tracid' (d) | CSil |
| 'Tracie Ann' (d) | SRiF |
| 'Trail Blazer' (d) | CLoc CWVF EBak MJac SPet SRiF |
| 'Trailing Queen' | EBak MJac SRiF |
| 'Trase' (d) | CDoC CSil CWVF CWib EBak SRiF SVic |
| 'Traudchen Bonstedt' (T) | CDoC CLoc CWVF EBak LCla SRiF SVic |
| 'Traviata' | see *F.* 'La Traviata' Blackwell |
| 'Treasure' (d) | EBak |
| 'Tresco' | CSil SRiF |
| 'Tricolor' | see *F. magellanica* var. *gracilis* 'Tricolor' |
| 'Trident' | SRiF |
| 'Trientje' | LCla SLBF |
| 'Trimley Bells' | EBak SRiF |
| 'Trio' (d) | CLoc |
| ***triphylla*** (T) | EBak MHer |
| 'Trish's Triumph' | EPts SRiF |
| 'Tristesse' (d) | CLoc CWVF EBak SRiF |
| 'Troika' (d) | EBak SRiF |
| 'Troon' | CWVF SRiF |
| 'Tropic Sunset' (d) | MBri SRiF |
| 'Tropicana' (d) | CLoc CWVF EBak SRiF SVic |
| 'Troubador' Waltz (d) | CLoc |
| 'Troubadour' Bland (d) | SRiF |
| 'Troutbeck' | CSil |
| 'Trudi Davro' | LAst MJac SCoo SRiF |
| 'Trudy' | CDoC CSil CWVF EBak SRiF SVic |
| 'Truly Treena' (d) | SLBF SRiF |
| 'Trumpeter' ambig. | CDoC CWVF SRiF |
| 'Trumpeter' Fry | SRiF SVic |
| 'Trumpeter' Reiter (T) | CLoc EBak EPts LCla MJac |
| 'Tsjiep' | SRiF |
| 'Tubular Bells' (T) | LCla SRiF |
| 'Tuonela' (d) | CLoc CWVF EBak |
| 'Turkish Delight' | SRiF WRou |
| 'Tutone' (d) | SRiF |
| 'Tutti-frutti' (d) | CLoc |
| 'Twiggy' | SRiF |
| 'Twinkling Stars' | CWVF MJac SVic |
| 'Twinny' | CWVF EPts SRiF |
| 'Twister' | SRiF |
| 'Two Tiers' (d) | CSil CWVF SRiF |
| 'Twydale' | SRiF |
| 'U.B.' (d) | SRiF |
| 'U.F.O.' | CTsd CWVF SVic |
| 'Ullswater' (d) | CWVF EBak SRiF |
| 'Ultramar' (d) | EBak SRiF |
| 'Uncle Charley' (d) | CDoC CSil EBak SRiF SVic |
| 'Uncle Jinks' | SPet SRiF |
| 'Uncle Steve' (d) | EBak SRiF SVic |
| 'University of Liverpool' | CLoc MJac SRiF |
| 'Upward Look' | EBak SRiF |
| 'Valda May' (d) | CWVF |
| 'Vale of Belvoir' | SRiF |

| | |
|---|---|
| 'Valentine' (d) | EBak |
| 'Valerie Ann' (d) | EBak SPet SVic |
| 'Valerie Bradley' | EPts |
| 'Valiant' | EBak SRiF |
| 'Vanessa Jackson' | CLoc CWVF MJac SRiF SVic |
| 'Vanity Fair' (d) | CLoc EBak SRiF |
| 'Variegated Lottie Hobby' (E/v) | CSil SRiF |
| 'Variegated Pixie' (v) | CSil SRiF |
| 'Variegated Procumbens' | see *F. procumbens* 'Wirral' |
| 'Variegated Superstar' (v) | MBri |
| 'Variegated Swingtime' (v) | EBak LAst SLBF SRiF |
| 'Variegated Triphylla' (T/v) | SRiF |
| 'Variegated Vivienne Thompson' (d/v) | MBri |
| 'Variegated Waveney Sunrise' (v) | MBri |
| 'Veenlust' | EBak SRiF WRou |
| 'Velvet Crush' **new** | LAst |
| 'Vendeta' | CDoC LCla |
| 'Venus Victrix' | CSil EBak SRiF |
| ***venusta*** | CDoC EBak LCla |
| 'Verity Edwards' **new** | SRiF |
| 'Versicolor' | see *F. magellanica* 'Versicolor' |
| 'Vespa' | SRiF |
| 'Vicky' | SRiF |
| 'Victorian' (d) | SRiF SVic |
| 'Victory' Reiter (d) | EBak |
| 'Vielliebchen' | CDoC CSil |
| 'Vincent van Gogh' (T) | SRiF |
| 'Vintage Dovercourt' | LCla |
| 'Violet Bassett-Burr' (d) | CLoc EBak SRiF |
| 'Violet Gem' (d) | CLoc |
| 'Violet Lace' (d) | CSil |
| 'Violet Rosette' (d) | CWVF EBak SRiF SVic |
| Violetta = 'Goetzviol' (Shadowdancer Series) | CDoC LAst LSou SCoo |
| 'Violette Szabo' | SRiF |
| 'Viva Ireland' | EBak SRiF |
| 'Vivien Colville' | CLoc |
| 'Vobeglo' | CWVF |
| 'Vogue' (d) | EBak SRiF |
| 'Voltaire' | CSil EBak SRiF |
| 'Voodoo' (d) | CCCN CDoC CLoc CTsd CWVF EBak EPts LAst SBfd SCoo SLBF SRiF SVic WRou |
| ***vulcanica*** | CDoC LCla SRiF |
| 'Vuurwerk' | SRiF |
| 'Vyvian Miller' | CWVF |
| 'W.P. Wood' | CDoC CSil |
| 'Wagtails White Pixie' | CSil EBak EPfP |
| 'Waldfee' (E) | CCVN CDoC CSil LCla |
| 'Waldis Alina' | SLBF WRou |
| 'Waldis Geisha' (d) | SRiF |
| 'Waldis Junella' (d) | SLBF |
| 'Waldis Ovambo' | SLBF |
| 'Waldis Spezi' | CDoC LCla SRiF |
| 'Waldis Speziella' | SLBF |
| 'Wally Yendell' (v) | SRiF |
| 'Walsingham' (d) | CWVF EBak SRiF |
| 'Walton Jewel' | EBak SRiF |
| 'Waltzing Matilda' (d) | SRiF |
| 'Walz Bella' | LCla SRiF |
| 'Walz Blauwkous' (d) | CDoC CWVF SRiF |
| 'Walz Bombardon' | SRiF |
| 'Walz Cimbaal' | SRiF |
| 'Walz Doedelzak' | SRiF |
| 'Walz Duimelot' | SRiF |
| 'Walz Fagot' | SRiF |
| 'Walz Fanclub' | SRiF |
| 'Walz Fluit' | MJac WRou |
| 'Walz Fonola' | SRiF |
| 'Walz Freule' | CWVF MJac |
| 'Walz Harp' | CWVF SRiF SVic |
| 'Walz Jubelteen' | CAlb CDoC CLoc CWVF ELon EPts LCla MJac MSCN SLBF SRiF SVic WRou |
| 'Walz Klarinet' | SRiF |
| 'Walz Lucifer' | CWVF LCla SLBF SRiF |
| 'Walz Luit' | SRiF |
| 'Walz Mandoline' (d) | CWVF SRiF SVic |
| 'Walz Nugget' | SRiF |
| 'Walz Panfluit' | LCla |
| 'Walz Polka' | CDoC LCla SLBF SRiF |
| 'Walz Rail' | SRiF |
| 'Walz Sprietje' | CDoC |
| 'Walz Triangel' (d) | SRiF SVic |
| 'Walz Tuba' | CDoC SRiF |
| 'Wapenveld 150' | LCla |
| 'Wapenveld's Bloei' | CDoC LCla SLBF SRiF |
| 'War Paint' (d) | CLoc EBak SRiF |
| 'Warton Crag' | CWVF SRiF SVic |
| 'Water Nymph' | CLoc SLBF SRiF SVic |
| 'Wattenpost' | SLBF |
| 'Wave of Life' | CWVF SRiF |
| 'Waveney Gem' | CDoC CLoc CWVF EBak LCla MJac SLBF SPet SRiF |
| 'Waveney Queen' | CWVF SVic |
| 'Waveney Sunrise' | CWVF MJac SPet SRiF SVic |
| 'Waveney Unique' | CWVF |
| 'Waveney Valley' | CWVF EBak SRiF |
| 'Waveney Waltz' | CWVF EBak SRiF |
| 'Wedding Bells' ambig. | SRiF SVic |
| 'Welsh Dragon' (d) | CLoc CWVF EBak SRiF |
| 'Wendy' Catt | see *F.* 'Snowcap' |
| 'Wendy's Beauty' (d) | CCCN CLoc EBak EPts MJac SRiF WRou |
| 'Wentworth' | CWVF SRiF SVic |
| 'Wessex Belle' (d/v) | CWVF SRiF |
| 'Wessex Hardy' | CSil |
| 'Westham' | LCla SRiF |
| 'Westminster Chimes' (d) | CLoc CWVF SPet SRiF SVic |
| 'Wharfedale' ♀H3 | CSil ELon MJac SLBF SRiF SVic |
| 'Whickham Blue' | CWVF |
| 'Whirlaway' (d) | CLoc CWVF EBak SRiF SVic |
| 'White Ann' | see *F.* 'Heidi Weiss' |
| 'White Clove' | CDoC CSil SRiF SVic |
| 'White Fairy' (d) | SRiF |
| 'White Galore' (d) | CWVF EBak SRiF SVic |
| 'White Général Monk' (d) | CDoC CSil |
| 'White Gold' (v) | EBak SRiF |
| 'White Haven' | SVic |
| 'White Heidi Ann' (d) | CSil SRiF |
| 'White Joy' | EBak SRiF |
| 'White King' (d) | CLoc CWVF EBak SPet SRiF SVic WRou |
| 'White Lace' | CSil SRiF |
| 'White Pixie' ♀H3-4 | CDoC CSil EPts MJac SLBF SPer SPet SRiF SVic |
| 'White Princess' | SRiF |
| 'White Queen' ambig. | CWVF EPfP |
| 'White Queen' Doyle | EBak |
| 'White Sincerity' (d) **new** | SRiF |
| 'White Spider' | CLoc CWVF EBak SRiF SVic |
| 'White Veil' (d) | CWVF |
| 'White Water' (d) | SRiF |
| 'Whiteknights Amethyst' | CDoC CSil |
| 'Whiteknights Blush' | CChe CCse CDoC CPLG CSil EPfP EWes GCal GGar GQui LRHS NCGa NLar SMrm SRiF |

| | |
|---|---|
| 'Whiteknights Cheeky' (T) | CWVF EBak EPts LCla SRiF SVic |
| 'Whiteknights Green Glister' | CSil EPfP SRiF |
| 'Whiteknights Pearl' ♀$^{H1+3}$ | CSil CTsd CWVF ECha EPfP EPts LCla LRHS SEND SLBF SPet SRiF SVic |
| 'Whiteknights Ruby' (T) | SRiF |
| 'Whitney' (Diva Series) | SRiF |
| 'Whitton Starburst' | CDoC LCla |
| 'Wicked Queen' (d) | CSil SVic |
| 'Widow Twanky' (d) | CWVF |
| 'Wiebke Becker' | SRiF |
| 'Wigan Pier' (d) | EPts MJac SLBF SRiF WRou |
| 'Wight Magic' (d) | MJac SRiF |
| 'Wild and Beautiful' (d) | CTsd CWVF SRiF SVic |
| 'Wilf Langton' | SLBF WRou |
| 'Wilhelmina Schwab' | CDoC LCla |
| 'Willie Tamerus' | SRiF |
| 'Willow Tinsdale' **new** | LAst LSou |
| 'Willy Winky' | SRiF |
| 'Wilma van Druten' | CDoC LCla |
| 'Wilma Versloot' | SRiF |
| 'Wilson's Colours' | EPts |
| 'Wilson's Joy' | MJac |
| 'Wilson's Pearls' (d) | CTsd CWVF SLBF SPet SRiF |
| 'Wilson's Sugar Pink' | EPts LCla MJac SRiF |
| 'Win Oxtoby' (d) | CWVF |
| 'Windhapper' | LCla SLBF |
| 'Windmill' | CWVF |
| 'Wine and Roses' (d) | EBak SRiF |
| 'Wingrove's Mammoth' (d) | SRiF SVic |
| 'Wings of Song' (d) | CWVF EBak SRiF |
| 'Winifred' | SRiF |
| 'Winston Churchill' (d) ♀$^{H3}$ | CCCN CLoc CWVF EBak LAst MBri MJac NBlu SBfd SCoo SPet SPlb SRiF SVic |
| 'Winter's Touch' | SRiF |
| 'Witchipoo' | SLBF |
| 'Woodnook' (d) | CWVF SRiF |
| 'Woodside' (d) | CSil SVic |
| 'Wrotham' (d) | SRiF |
| 'Y Me' | SRiF |
| 'Ymkje' | EBak |
| 'Yolanda Franck' | CDoC LAst WRou |
| 'York Manor' | CDoC WRou |
| 'Yours' | SRiF |
| 'Yuletide' (d) | SRiF |
| 'Yvonne Priest' | SRiF |
| 'Yvonne Schwab' | CDoC LCla SRiF |
| 'Zara' | SRiF |
| 'Zeebrook' | SRiF SVic |
| 'Zellertal' | CDoC |
| 'Zets Alpha' | SRiF |
| 'Zets Bravo' | CDoC SRiF |
| 'Ziegfield Girl' (d) | EBak SRiF SVic |
| 'Zifi' | SLBF |
| 'Zulu King' | CDoC CSil SRiF SVic |
| 'Zulu Queen' | SVic |
| 'Zwarte Snor' (d) | CWVF |
| 'Zyzy' | SRiF |

## *Fumaria* (*Papaveraceae*)

| | |
|---|---|
| ***lutea*** | see *Corydalis lutea* |
| ***officinalis*** | CArn |

## *Furcraea* (*Asparagaceae*)

| | |
|---|---|
| ***bedinghausii*** | see *F. parmentieri* |
| § ***foetida*** | CCCN SBig |
| § - var. ***mediopicta*** (v) | SBig |
| - 'Variegata' | see *F. foetida* var. *mediopicta* |
| ***gigantea*** | see *F. foetida* |
| ***guatemalensis*** | MAga |
| ***longaeva*** misapplied | see *F. parmentieri* |
| ***longaeva*** ambig. | CAbb CBcs CDTJ CFir CHEx CHGN CPne CTrC CTsd EAmu GBin LEdu SArc SBst SPlb WCot WPGP |
| ***macdougalii*** | MAga SPlb |
| § ***parmentieri*** | CCCN CHll EAmu LEdu MAga WPGP |
| - NJM 05.081 | WPGP |
| ***selloa*** | MAga |
| - var. ***marginata*** (v) | CDoC CHEx EAmu MAga |

# G

## *Gahnia* (*Cyperaceae*)

| | |
|---|---|
| ***sieberiana*** | SPlb |

## *Gaillardia* (*Asteraceae*)

| | |
|---|---|
| ***aristata*** 'Maxima Aurea' | EBee EPfP MSpe NBre NPri NVic SPhx WCAu |
| - 'Primavera' | SMrm |
| 'Arizona Sun' | CChe EBee ECtt MHer NPri SVic |
| 'Bijou' | CMea EBee NBre NLar NVic SWvt |
| 'Dwarf Goblin' | NGBl SPet |
| § 'Fackelschein' | MSpe NBre SRms XLum |
| 'Fanfare'$^{PBR}$ | CMac CWGN EBee ECtt ELon LBuc LHop LRHS LSou MGos MSCN MWea NDov SCoo SPer SPoG |
| Goblin | see *G. × grandiflora* 'Kobold' |
| 'Golden Queen' **new** | XLum |
| × ***grandiflora*** 'Amber Wheels' | CSam EBee GMac LLHF NDov NGdn NPri SBfd WWEG |
| - 'Bremen' | EBee MSpe XLum |
| - 'Burgunder' | Widely available |
| - 'Dazzler' ♀$^{H4}$ | CMac CSBt EAEE EBee ECtt ELan EPfP LAst LRHS NBPC NLar NVic SMrm SPer SPoG WCAu WMoo WWEG XLum |
| § - 'Goldkobold' | NBlu XLum |
| § - 'Kobold' | CBcs CMac COlW CSBt EBee ECtt ELon EPfP GGar GMaP LAst LHop LRHS MBri NBre NEgg NLar NPri SMrm SPad SPer SPlb SPoG SRms SWvt WWEG XLum |
| - 'Summer's Kiss' | EBee |
| - 'Tokajer' | EBee EPfP LRHS NBre NDov NLar SMrm SPhx XLum |
| 'Mandarin' | SRms |
| 'Merriments Fanfare' **new** | SMrm |
| * giant hybrids | WFar |
| § 'Oranges and Lemons'$^{PBR}$ | EBee ECtt EGxp LHop LRHS LSou MWea NLar NPri SHar SPoG SUsu WCAu |
| 'Red Ribbons' | CSpe |
| Saint Clements$^{PBR}$ | see *G.* 'Oranges and Lemons' |
| Torchlight | see *G.* 'Fackelschein' |
| Yellow Goblin | see *G. × grandiflora* 'Goldkobold' |

## *Galactites* (*Asteraceae*)

| | |
|---|---|
| ***tomentosa*** | CSpe EHoe ELan EPfP EPyc EWTr MWea SGar SPav |

## *Galanthus* ✿ (*Amaryllidaceae*)

| | |
|---|---|
| × ***allenii*** | CBro WIvy |
| ***alpinus*** | CLAP |
| § - var. ***alpinus*** | NMen |

|  |  |
|---|---|
| ***angustifolius*** | LWst WCot |
| 'Anne of Geierstein' | WCot |
| 'Annette' | CElw LAma LWst NMyG |
| 'Armine' | CAvo CElw IFoB |
| 'Atkinsii' ♀H4 | CAvo CBgR CBro CElw CFFs CLAP ECha ECho EPot EWoo GAbr GEdr GKev IFoB IGor LAma LRHS MAsh MHom MRav NBir NMyG WCot WHoo WShi WTin |
| 'Autumn Beauty' **new** | CBro LRHS |
| 'Ballard's No Notch' **new** | WCot |
| 'Barbara's Double' (d) | CBgR CLAP |
| 'Benhall Beauty' | CAvo WTin |
| 'Bertram Anderson' | MAsh NCot WCot |
| 'Bess' | CElw CSna IFoB |
| 'Bill Bishop' | CAvo CDes ECha EWoo IPot LRHS MAsh |
| 'Brenda Troyle' | CBro CElw CLAP ECha ELon EPot GAbr GEdr GKev IGor IPot LRHS MAsh MHom NCot NMyG WCot WFar WIvy WPnP |
| ***byzantinus*** | see *G. plicatus* subsp. *byzantinus* |
| 'Castlegar' | IFoB |
| ***caucasicus*** misapplied | see *G. elwesii* var. *monostictus* |
| ***caucasicus*** (Bak.) Grossh. | see *G. alpinus* var. *alpinus* |
| ***caucasicus*** ambig. | GAbr IFoB |
| - 'Comet' | see *G. elwesii* 'Comet' |
| - var. ***hiemalis*** Stern | see *G. elwesii* var. *monostictus* Hiemalis Group |
| ***cilicicus*** | WCot |
| 'Clare Blakeway-Phillips' | CLAP |
| ***corcyrensis*** spring-flowering | see *G. reginae-olgae* subsp. *vernalis* |
| - winter-flowering | see *G. reginae-olgae* subsp. *reginae-olgae* Winter-flowering Group |
| 'Cordelia' (d) | CLAP IFoB IPot LRHS |
| 'Cornwood Gem' **new** | NCot |
| 'Curly' | CDes EWoo |
| 'Daglingworth' **new** | CElw |
| 'Desdemona' (d) | CBgR CBro CLAP EPot LRHS NMyG WCot WIvy |
| 'Ding Dong' | CAvo |
| 'Dionysus' (d) | CBgR CBro CLAP CPLG EBla ECha GEdr IGor LLHF LRHS LWst MHom NBir NMyG WBrk WTin |
| 'Double Scharlokii' (d) | EBla |
| 'Drummond's Giant' | IFoB |
| § ***elwesii*** ♀H4 | CBro CTri CWCL ECho ELan ELon EPfP EPot ERCP GKev IFoB IGor ITim LAma LRHS MAsh MWat NBir SDeJ SPoG SRms WCot WHoo WPnP WShi |
| - 'Abington Green' | CSna |
| - 'Broadleigh Gardens' **new** | LRHS |
| - 'Cedric's Prolific' | ECha EWoo IFoB IGor LRHS |
| § - 'Comet' | CElw ELon IFoB |
| - 'Daphne's Scissors' | CBgR CSna NCot |
| - 'David Shackleton' | IFoB LRHS |
| - Edward Whittall Group | CLAP |
| - var. ***elwesii*** 'Fenstead End' | CAvo |
| - - 'Magnus' | CLAP NBir |
| - - 'Maidwell L' | CAvo CBro CSna LRHS MAsh |
| - - 'Sibbertoft Magnet' | IFoB |
| - (Hiemalis Group) 'Barnes' | NCot WCot |
| - 'J. Haydn' | ECho LAma LWst NMyG |
| - 'Long 'drop' | IFoB |
| - 'Marielle' **new** | EPPr |
| - 'Marjorie Brown' **new** | LRHS |
| - 'Milkwood' | see *G. elwesii* 'Mrs Macnamara' |

|  |  |
|---|---|
| § - var. ***monostictus*** ♀H4 | CAvo ECho IFoB LRHS MAsh WBrk WFar WIvy |
| - - 'G. Handel' | ECho LAma LRHS LWst NMyG |
| - - 'H. Purcell' | ECho LAma LRHS LWst |
| § - - Hiemalis Group | CBgR CBro CDes ECha EPot LWst MHom WCot |
| - - late-flowering | LWst |
| - - 'Roger's Rough' **new** | SDys |
| - - 'Warwickshire Gemini' | CDes |
| § - 'Mrs Macnamara' | CDes EWoo IFoB LRHS |
| - 'Penelope Ann' | LRHS |
| - 'Sickle' | CDes CSna |
| - 'Sir Edward Elgar' | LAma LRHS LWst |
| 'Erway' **new** | MHom |
| 'F63' | IFoB |
| 'Faringdon Double' (d) | LRHS |
| ***fosteri*** | CBro ECho LRHS SCnR |
| 'G71' (d) | IFoB |
| 'Galatea' | CBro CLAP CSna ECha LRHS MAsh MHom SDys WIvy |
| 'Ginns' | CDes CLAP ELon EWoo IFoB LRHS |
| § ***gracilis*** | CAvo CBro CLAP CPLG LRHS |
| - 'Highdown' | CElw CLAP IFoB LWst MHom |
| - 'Vic Horton' | WThu |
| ***graecus*** misapplied | see *G. gracilis* |
| ***graecus*** Orph. ex Boiss. | see *G. elwesii* |
| 'Grande Juge' | IFoB |
| 'Grayling' | see *G. plicatus* 'Percy Picton' |
| Greatorex double (d) | CLAP |
| 'Greenfields' | CBgR CSna IFoB IGor |
| 'Heffalump' (d) | NCot |
| 'Hill Poë' (d) | CBro CDes CElw CLAP EPot IFoB IPot MHom NMyG |
| 'Hippolyta' (d) | CAvo CBro CElw CLAP ECha ELon EPot GAbr GEdr IFoB IGor LAma LRHS MAsh MHom NMyG SKHP WCot WFar WIvy WPnP |
| 'Hobson's Choice' **new** | LRHS |
| × ***hybridus*** 'Merlin' | CBro CElw IFoB IGor LRHS MAsh MHom WCot WIvy WTin |
| - 'Robin Hood' | CDes CFee CLAP IFoB LRHS WFar |
| 'Icicle' | CAvo |
| § ***ikariae*** Bak. | CBgR CElw EPfP GKev WFar |
| - 'Georgia' **new** | LRHS |
| - Latifolius Group | see *G. platyphyllus* |
| - subsp. ***snogerupii*** | see *G. ikariae* Bak. |
| 'Imbolc' | CAvo |
| 'Jacquenetta' (d) | CBro CDes CElw CFee CLAP CSna IFoB IGor ITim LRHS MAsh MHom WTin |
| 'James Backhouse' | CElw ECha LRHS WHoo |
| 'John Gray' | CBro CSna IFoB MAsh |
| 'Ketton' | CBro CElw CSna EWoo MAsh NRya WIvy |
| 'Kildare' **new** | CDes |
| 'Kingston Double' (d) | CBgR CLAP |
| 'Lady Beatrix Stanley' (d) | CAvo CBro CElw CLAP ECha EPot GAbr GEdr IFoB LLWP LRHS MAsh MHom NDov NMyG WCot WFar WTin |
| ***lagodechianus*** | MPhe |
| 'Lapwing' | MAsh |
| ***latifolius*** Rupr. | see *G. platyphyllus* |
| 'Lavinia' (d) | CAvo CElw CFee CLAP LRHS MHom WFar |
| 'Lerinda' | IFoB |
| 'Limetree' | CBgR CElw CLAP EPri LRHS MHom NCot |
| 'Little John' | LRHS WBrk |

| |  |  |
|---|---|---|
| | ***lutescens*** | see *G. nivalis* Sandersii Group |
| | 'Lyn' | CBro LRHS NBir |
| | 'Magnet' 𝕐H4 | Widely available |
| | 'Maidwell' | IFoB |
| | 'Mighty Atom' | CDes CFee CLAP WBrk |
| | 'Moccas' | CBgR CElw CSna |
| | 'Modern Art' | IFoB |
| | 'Mrs Backhouse No 12' | LRHS |
| | 'Mrs Thompson' | CAvo CDes CElw ECha WIvy |
| | 'Neill Fraser' | LRHS |
| | ***nivalis*** 𝕐H4 | Widely available |
| | - 'Anglesey Abbey' | CAvo IFoB MHom |
| | - 'April Fool' | MHom WTin |
| | - 'Bitton' | CLAP |
| | - 'Blonde Inge' | IFoB MAsh |
| | - 'Chedworth' | CElw WBrk |
| | - 'Christmas Wish' **new** | LWst |
| | - 'Dreycott Greentip' | IFoB |
| | - dwarf | GAbr |
| | - 'Elfin' **new** | CElw |
| | - 'Greenish' | CAvo CDes EWoo LRHS |
| | - subsp. ***imperati*** | CPLG |
| | - 'Lutescens' | see *G. nivalis* Sandersii Group |
| | - 'Major Pam' | IFoB |
| | - 'Maximus' | LRHS WShi |
| | - f. ***pleniflorus*** (d) | CTca ECha GKev MAsh NDov SPoG |
| | - - 'Bagpuize Virginia' (d) | CAvo |
| | - - 'Blewbury Tart' (d) | CAvo CBro CElw CLAP CSna IFoB LRHS WBrk |
| | - - 'Flore Pleno' (d) 𝕐H4 | CBro CPLG CWCL EPfP EPla EPot ERCP EWil IFoB ITim LAma LHop LLWP LRHS MMuc NCot NRya SDeJ SEND SMrm SPer SRms WBrk WCot WFar WHoo WPnP WShi |
| | - - 'Hambutt's Orchard' (d) | CFee |
| | - - 'Lady Elphinstone' (d) | CAvo CBgR CBro CDes CFee CLAP CRow CSna IFoB LRHS MAsh MHom NRya WIvy |
| | - - 'Pusey Green Tip' (d) | CBgR CBro CElw CLAP EPot GEdr IFoB IPot LRHS MHom NMyG WCot WTin |
| § | - - 'Wonston Double' (d) | CAvo IFoB |
| | - Poculiformis Group | CLAP |
| § | - Sandersii Group | CDes CRDP IFoB |
| § | - Scharlockii Group | CAvo CBgR CElw IGor LRHS WBrk |
| | - 'Tiny' | MHom NBir |
| | - 'Tiny Tim' | ITim LRHS NRya |
| | - 'Virescens' | CLAP IFoB |
| | - 'Viridapice' | CAvo CBgR CBro CElw CPLG ECha ECho EPot GEdr GKev IFoB IGor LAma LRHS MAsh NBir NMen SDeJ SKHP WCot WFar WHoo WPnP WShi WTin |
| | 'Ophelia' (d) | CAvo CBro EPot GAbr IGor LRHS MHom NDov SKHP WBrk WFar WHoo |
| | 'Orion' | CDes |
| | 'Peardrop' | NCot |
| | 'Peg Sharples' | IFoB MHom NCot |
| | ***peshmenii*** | EPot SCnR |
| | - HOA 0201 | LWst |
| § | ***platyphyllus*** | CPLG LRHS |
| | ***plicatus*** 𝕐H4 | CAvo CBro CElw CFee EPot GAbr GEdr LRHS MCot MHom NMen NMyG WBrk WCot WFar WHoo WShi WTin |
| | - from Coton Manor | MCot |
| | - 'Augustus' | CAvo CBro CDes CElw CFee ELon IFoB IGor ITim MAsh MHom WBrk WFar WIvy WTin |
| | - 'Baxendale's Late' | CAvo CLAP MAsh |
| | - 'Bolu Shades' | LWst |
| | - 'Bowles's Large' | CElw |
| § | - subsp. ***byzantinus*** | CBro LRHS MHom WThu |
| | - 'Colossus' | CBgR CBro IFoB |
| | - 'Gerard Parker' | IFoB |
| | - 'Greenpeace' **new** | CSna |
| | - late flowering | LWst |
| | - - 'Oreanda' | IPot |
| § | - 'Percy Picton' | CAvo |
| | - 'Sally Pasmore' | CAvo |
| | - 'Sophie North' | CElw CLAP IFoB |
| | - 'The Pearl' | IFoB |
| | - 'Three Ships' | CAvo EWoo |
| | - 'Trym' | CLAP WFar |
| | - 'Warham' | CBro EPot GAbr GEdr IFoB IGor LRHS MHom NMyG |
| | - 'Warham Rectory' **new** | LRHS |
| | - 'Wendy's Gold' | CBro CDes CSna EWld IFoB NCot WFar |
| | 'Primrose Warburg' | IFoB |
| | ***reginae-olgae*** | CAvo CBro EBla GKev LRHS MAsh WThu |
| | - HOA 0165 | LWst |
| | - HOA 0169 | LWst |
| § | - subsp. ***reginae-olgae*** Winter-flowering Group | CBro |
| § | - subsp. ***vernalis*** | EPot IFoB WCot |
| | 'Reverend Hailstone' **new** | LRHS |
| | 'Richard Ayres' (d) | IFoB LRHS |
| | ***rizehensis*** | CAvo CLAP IFoB LRHS LWst MHom |
| | - Baytop 34474 | IFoB LRHS |
| | 'S. Arnott' 𝕐H4 | CAvo CBro CElw CFFs CLAP CPLG ECha ECho ELon EPot EWoo GAbr GCal GEdr IFoB IGor LAma LRHS MAsh NBir NMen NRya WBrk WCot WFar WHoo WTin |
| | 'Saint Anne's' | CBgR CDes CElw CSna IFoB MAsh WIvy |
| | 'Scharlockii' | see *G. nivalis* Scharlockii Group |
| | 'Shaggy' | LRHS |
| | 'Silverwells' | CSna GEdr IFoB LRHS |
| | 'Spindlestone Surprise' **new** | EWoo NCot |
| § | 'Straffan' | CAvo CBro CElw EPot GEdr IFoB IGor LRHS MHom NMyG WBrk WCot WFar |
| | 'Sutton Courtenay' | CDes CSna |
| | 'The O'Mahoney' | see *G.* 'Straffan' |
| | 'Titania' (d) | CBro ELon IFoB IGor LRHS MHom WFar |
| | 'Tubby Merlin' | CAvo CDes CElw CLAP EWoo IFoB LRHS MAsh MCot WIvy |
| | × ***valentinei*** 'Compton Court' | CBro |
| * | 'Warley Duo' | CBgR |
| § | 'Washfield Colesbourne' | EWoo |
| | 'Washfield Warham' | ECha EWoo ITim LRHS MAsh |
| | 'White Admiral' | SKHP |
| | 'White Dreams' | LRHS WFar |
| | 'White Swan' Ballard (d) **new** | CElw LRHS |
| | 'William Thomson' | CSna |
| | 'Winifrede Mathias' | CElw CLAP |
| | 'Wisley Magnet' | LRHS |
| | 'Wonston Double' | see *G. nivalis* f. *pleniflorus* 'Wonston Double' |
| | ***woronowii*** 𝕐H4 | CBro CElw CHid CLAP CTca CTri ECho EPot GKev IFoB ITim LAma LRHS MAsh MBri MHom MWat NBir NMyG SDeJ WBrk WCot WFar |

## *Galax* (*Diapensiaceae*)

| | |
|---|---|
| ***aphylla*** | see *G. urceolata* |
| § ***urceolata*** | IBlr MNrw |

## *Galega* (*Papilionaceae*)

| | |
|---|---|
| ***bicolor*** | NBir NBre NChi SRms SWat WFar |
| 'Duchess of Bedford' | EBee GBin |
| × ***hartlandii*** | CPLG LRHS |
| – 'Alba' ♀H4 | EBee ELon EWes IBlr MArl MCot MRav SPhx SWat WBox WCot WHoo WSHC WTcb |
| – 'Candida' | NBir |
| – 'Lady Wilson' ♀H4 | CPom EBee ECtt ELon EWes EWld MArl MLHP WAul WCot WFoF WHoo WOut WTcb |
| – 'Spring Light' (v) | EWes LSou |
| 'Her Majesty' | see *G.* 'His Majesty' |
| § 'His Majesty' | CDes CKno ECtt IFro MArl MCot MDKP MLHP MRav NBre SMrm WBox WCot WFar WHoo WHrl WPGP |
| ***officinalis*** | Widely available |
| – 'Alba' ♀H4 | CPom CPrp ECtt ELan EPfP LEdu MBrN MHer MNHC NPnk SMrm SPer WFar WHer WHrl WMoo WOut |
| – Coconut Ice = 'Kelgal' (v) | CAbP WHer |
| – 'Lincoln Gold' | MTPN |
| ***orientalis*** | CDes ECha ECtt EWes LEdu MArl MCot SPhx WAbb WCot WMoo WPGP WSHC |

## *Galeobdolon* see *Lamium*

## *Galeopsis* (*Lamiaceae*)

| | |
|---|---|
| ***tetrahit*** | WSFF |

## *Galium* (*Rubiaceae*)

| | |
|---|---|
| ***cruciata*** | see *Cruciata laevipes* |
| ***mollugo*** | CArn CHab CRWN SIde |
| § ***odoratum*** | Widely available |
| ***palustre*** | EWil |
| ***verum*** | CArn CHab CRWN EWil GJos GPoy MCoo MHer NLan NMir NMun SIde WFar WHer |

## *Galtonia* (*Asparagaceae*)

| | |
|---|---|
| ***candicans*** ♀H4 | Widely available |
| – 'Moonbeam' (d) | CRDP EBee |
| ***princeps*** | CBro CDes CSam CTca ECha GCra GLam SGar WHil WPGP |
| ***regalis*** | CPLG CTca WPGP |
| ***viridiflora*** | CAvo CBot CBro CHar CTca EBee ECha ELan EPPr EPot ERCP GBin GCal GGal LEdu LRHS MNrw NChi NWCA WFar WHil XLum |
| – McB 2975 | GLam |

## *Gamblea* (*Araliaceae*)

| | |
|---|---|
| ***pseudoevodiifolia*** B&SWJ 11707 new | WCru |

## *Garcinia* (*Clusiaceae*)

| | |
|---|---|
| ***mangostana*** | CCCN |

## *Gardenia* (*Rubiaceae*)

| | |
|---|---|
| ***augusta*** | see *G. jasminoides* |
| ***florida*** L. | see *G. jasminoides* |
| ***grandiflora*** | see *G. jasminoides* |
| § ***jasminoides*** ♀H1 | CBcs CCCN EBak MBri |
| – 'Kleim's Hardy' | Widely available |
| – 'Star' | MOWG |
| ***magnifica*** | MOWG |
| ***thunbergia*** | EShb SPlb |

## garlic see *Allium sativum*

## garlic, elephant see *Allium ampeloprasum* 'Elephant'

## *Garrya* ✿ (*Garryaceae*)

| | |
|---|---|
| ***congdonii*** | NLar |
| ***elliptica*** | CBcs CDul CMac EBee ECrN EPfP GGal LSRN MBri MGos NPri NWea SBfd SEND SPlb WFar WHar WPat |
| – (f) | MSwo SWvt |
| – (m) | CDoC CTri LAst MAsh MBlu NLar SGol SLim |
| – 'James Roof' (m) ♀H4 | Widely available |
| ***fremontii*** | NLar |
| × ***issaquahensis*** 'Glasnevin Wine' | CAbP CDul CHGN CPMA ELan EPfP IArd LRHS MAsh MBri MGos NLar SCoo SLim SPer SPoG WFar |
| – 'Pat Ballard' (m) | EPfP NLar |
| × ***thuretii*** | CBcs CDul MBri MGos NLar WDin WFar |

## *Gasteria* ✿ (*Asphodelaceae*)

| | |
|---|---|
| ***bicolor*** var. ***bicolor*** new | GGar |
| – var. ***liliputana*** | SPlb |
| ***brachyphylla*** | STre |
| ***carinata*** var. ***verrucosa*** | EShb MSCN |
| ***nitida*** var. ***nitida*** variegated (v) | WCot |
| 'Smokey' new | EShb |

## × *Gaulnettya* see *Gaultheria*

## *Gaultheria* ✿ (*Ericaceae*)

| | |
|---|---|
| sp. | LSRN |
| ***adenothrix*** | NMen WThu |
| ***antarctica*** | WThu |
| ***antipoda*** 'Adpressa' | WThu |
| ***cardiosepala*** | GEdr |
| – CLD 1351 | GEdr GLam |
| ***cuneata*** ♀H4 | ECho GGar GLam LRHS NHar WThu |
| – 'Pinkie' | ECho |
| ***depressa*** var. ***novae-zelandiae*** | NWad |
| ***forrestii*** | CPLG |
| ***furiens*** | see *G. insana* |
| ***hispidula*** | ECho |
| § ***insana*** | WAle |
| ***itoana*** | ECho GEdr GJos GKev GLam NHar |
| ***miqueliana*** | WThu |
| § ***mucronata*** | CDul EPfP MAsh NWea WDin WFar |
| – (m) | CBcs CDoC CMac CSBt CTri CWSG EPfP LRHS MGos NEgg NHol SPer SRms |
| – 'Bell's Seedling' (f/m) ♀H4 | CBcs CDoC CDul CTri CWSG EPfP LRHS MMuc NBir NEgg SPer SPoG |
| – 'Cherry Ripe' (f) | CMac MMuc |
| – 'Crimsonia' (f) ♀H4 | CBcs CMac EPfP SPer SRms |
| – 'Indian Lake' | NWad |
| – 'Lilacina' (f) | CBcs CMac |
| – 'Lilian' (f) | CSBt NWad |
| – Mother of Pearl | see *G. mucronata* 'Parelmoer' |
| – 'Mulberry Wine' (f) ♀H4 | CSBt CTri NEgg NHol SPer |
| § – 'Parelmoer' (f) | CSBt NEgg SPer |

| | |
|---|---|
| - 'Pink Pearl' (f) ♀H4 | SRms |
| § - 'Signaal' (f) | CBcs EPfP MAsh NEgg NWad SPer |
| - Signal | see *G. mucronata* 'Signaal' |
| § - 'Sneeuwwitje' (f) | CBcs EPfP MAsh NBir SPer |
| - Snow White | see *G. mucronata* 'Sneeuwwitje' |
| - 'Thymifolia' (m) | EPfP |
| - white-berried (f) | MMuc |
| - 'Wintertime' (f) ♀H4 | CMac SRms |
| * ***mucronifolia*** dwarf | NWCA |
| § ***myrsinoides*** | WThu |
| ***nana*** Colenso | see *G. parvula* |
| ***nummularioides*** | GEdr NHar NLar |
| § ***parvula*** | WThu |
| 'Pearls' | NHar WThu |
| 'Pilgrim' **new** | LSRN |
| 'Pink Champagne' | ITim |
| ***procumbens*** ♀H4 | CAgr CBcs CDoC CMac CWSG EBee ECho EPfP GJos GMaP GPoy LRHS MAsh MBlu MBri MGos NEgg NWea SLim SPer SPlb SPoG SReu SRms SWvt WDin WFar |
| - 'Very Berry' | EShb NHol NWad |
| ***prostrata*** | see *G. myrsinoides* |
| ***pumila*** | GAbr LEdu NHar WAle |
| ***schultesii*** | WThu |
| ***shallon*** | CAgr CBcs CDul CSBt EPfP MGos SPer SRms SWvt WDin WFar |
| ***sinensis*** | NHar |
| - lilac-berried | NHar WThu |
| ***tasmanica*** | ECou GAbr |
| ***tetramera*** | CPLG |
| ***trichophylla*** | GAbr NHar |
| × ***wisleyensis*** | LRHS SLon SRms SSta |
| - 'Pink Pixie' | CBcs LRHS MAsh NLar SSta |
| - 'Ruby' | CMac |
| - 'Wisley Pearl' | CBcs GGar IBlr IRar NLar SCoo WFar |
| ***yunnanensis*** | CPLG |

## *Gaura* (Onagraceae)

| | |
|---|---|
| Karalee Petite Improved[PBR] | see *G. lindheimeri* Lillipop Pink |
| ***lindheimeri*** ♀H4 | Widely available |
| - 'Ballerina Blush' | LAst |
| - 'Ballerina Rose' | LAst SGar SPet |
| - Belleza Series | MWea WHil |
| - Cherry Brandy = 'Gauchebra'[PBR] | CBar EBee ECtt EPfP EWes LRHS SPur SWvt WFar |
| - compact pink-flowered | SPad |
| - 'Corrie's Gold' (v) | EAEE EBee ECha ECtt EHoe ELan EPfP EShb LRHS MHer SBfd SGar SPer SPet WCFE WMnd WWEG |
| - 'Crimson Butterflies'[PBR] | EBee ECtt EPfP LRHS WCot |
| § - 'Heather's Delight' | MRav |
| - 'Heaven's Harmony' | LBuc |
| - In the Pink | see *G. lindheimeri* 'Heather's Delight' |
| - 'Jo Adela' (v) | ELan EPfP |
| - Karalee Petite = 'Gauka' | CWCL EPfP |
| - Karalee Pink | LSRN MBri |
| - Karalee White = 'Nugauwhite'[PBR] | CSpe CWCL EPfP LAst LHop LRHS LSRN LSou MBri NLar SBfd SCoo SPoG |
| § - Lillipop Pink = 'Redgapi'[PBR] | CWCL EPfP EWll LAst LBMP LHop LRHS LSou MBrN MBri MWea NEgg NLar SBfd SMrm SPoG STes |
| - 'My Melody'[PBR] (v) | CWCL EBee SBfd WHil |
| - 'Occitania' (v) **new** | XLum |
| - Papillon = 'Nugaupapil' **new** | CWGN SMrm |
| - 'Passionate Blush'[PBR] | CBcs CChe CMac CWCL EBee EPfP LRHS LSRN LSou NDov SBrd SPoG |
| - 'Passionate Pink'[PBR] | LBuc |
| - 'Passionate Rainbow'[PBR] (v) | CWCL EBee EHoe EPfP LSou SPoG |
| - 'Pink Dwarf' | CMac EPfP LRHS |
| - 'Rosyjane' | CKno CSpe CWCL CWGN EBee EHoe EPPr LAst LRHS LSRN LSou MBri MWea SHar SLon SPer SPoG |
| - short | LSou SGar |
| - 'Siskiyou Pink' | CBcs CSBt CWCL EBee ECha ECtt EHoe ELan ELon EPfP EShb LBMP LRHS LSRN MAvo SBfd SMad SMrm SPer SWat SWvt WCFE WFar WMnd WWEG XLum |
| - Snow Fountain = 'Walsnofou' **new** | LRHS |
| - 'Summer Breeze' | COlW EDif SBfd SPhx WHil |
| - 'Sunset Dreams' | EPPr |
| - 'The Bride' | CEnt CTri EBee ECtt EPfP GCal LRHS LSRN LSou MAvo MMuc MRav MWat NDov SEND SPav SPet SRGP STes SWal SWvt WHil WMnd |
| - 'Tutti Frutti'[PBR] | CChe LBuc LRHS LSou SPoG |
| - 'Vanilla'[PBR] | CWCL LBuc LRHS LSou SPoG |
| - 'Whirling Butterflies' | CKno CSpe CWCL EBee ECtt ELan ELon EPfP GMaP LBMP LRHS MWat NBPC SMad SMrm SPav SPer SWat SWvt WMnd WWEG |
| - 'White Dove' | EPfP |
| - 'White Heron' | MNrw |
| ***sinuata*** | SHar |
| I 'Variegata' (v) | CWCL LRHS |

## *Gaylussacia* (Ericaceae)

| | |
|---|---|
| ***baccata*** (F) | NLar |

## *Gazania* (Asteraceae)

| | |
|---|---|
| 'Aztec' ♀H1+3 | CCCN SUsu |
| 'Bicton Orange' | CCCN COlW MAJR SCoo SVen |
| 'Big Kiss White Flame' (Kiss Series) **new** | SVen |
| 'Big Kiss Yellow Flame' (Kiss Series) **new** | SVen |
| 'Blackberry Ripple' | CCCN COlW GGar LAst MAJR SAga SCoo SVen |
| 'Blackcurrant Ice' | MCot |
| 'Caledon Giants' | SGar |
| 'Christopher' | SCoo |
| 'Christopher Lloyd' | CCCN COlW LAst MAJR SMrm SVen |
| 'Cookei' ♀H1+3 | CSpe |
| 'Cornish Pixie' | CCCN |
| 'Cream Beauty' | MCot |
| Daybreak Series | WFar |
| - 'Daybreak Red Stripe' | NGBl |
| - 'Daybreak Rose Stripe' | NGBl |
| Gazoo Series | SPoG |
| 'Jamaica Ginger' | SMrm |
| 'Kiss Bronze Star' (Kiss Series) | SVen |
| ***krebsiana*** | CCCN |
| ***linearis*** | COlW |
| 'Magic' | CCCN MAJR NPri SCoo SMrm |
| Nahui = 'Suga119' (Sunbathers Series) | CCCN |
| 'Northbourne' ♀H1+3 | GGar |
| 'Orange Beauty' | CHEx ELan |
| 'Red Velvet' | CHEx SAga |

| | | |
|---|---|---|
| | ***rigens*** var. ***uniflora*** 'Variegata' (v) | CBot |
| | - 'Variegata' (v) ♀H1+3 | CCCN COIW ELan |
| | Rumi = 'Suga116' (Sunbathers Series) | CCCN |
| | 'Silver Beauty' | CBot |
| | Sunset Jane Lemon Spot = 'Sugajale' (Sunbathers Series) **new** | CCCN |
| | Sunset Jane = 'Sugaja'PBR (Sunbathers Series) | CCCN |
| | 'Talent' | SEND |
| | Tiger Eye = 'Gazte'PBR (v) | CCCN LAst LSou |
| | Toptokai = 'Suga407' (Sunbathers Series) **new** | CCCN |
| | 'Torbay Silver' | CHEx |
| | Totonaca = 'Suga212' (Sunbathers Series) | CCCN |

## *Geissorhiza* (*Iridaceae*)

| | | |
|---|---|---|
| | ***aspera*** | ECho |
| | ***bracteata*** | ECho |
| | ***brehmii*** 'Rawsonville' | ECho |
| | ***darlingensis*** | ECho |
| | ***imbricata*** | ECho |
| | - subsp. ***bicolor*** | ECho |
| | ***inequalis*** | ECho |
| | ***inflexa*** | ECho |
| | ***monanthos*** | ECho |
| | ***ornithogaloides*** | ECho |
| | - subsp. ***marlothii*** | ECho |
| | ***radians*** | ECho |
| | ***rosea*** | ECho |
| | ***splendidissima*** | ECho |

## *Gelasine* (*Iridaceae*)

| | | |
|---|---|---|
| | ***azurea*** | see *G. coerulea* |
| § | ***coerulea*** | WSHC |

## *Gelidocalamus* (*Poaceae*)

| | | |
|---|---|---|
| | ***fangianus*** | see *Drepanostachyum microphyllum* |

## *Gelsemium* (*Gelsemiaceae*)

| | | |
|---|---|---|
| | ***rankinii*** | EBee |
| | ***sempervirens*** ♀H1-2 | CArn CCCN CHll CRHN EBee EShb LRHS LSRN MOWG SBrd SBrt SLim SPoG |

## *Genista* (*Papilionaceae*)

| | | |
|---|---|---|
| | ***aetnensis*** ♀H4 | CDul ELan EPfP EWTr NLar SArc SEND SPer SRms WDin WPat |
| § | ***canariensis*** | CPLG CWib |
| | ***cinerea*** | WCFE |
| | ***decumbens*** | see *Cytisus decumbens* |
| | ***delphinensis*** | see *G. sagittalis* subsp. *delphinensis* |
| | 'Emerald Spreader' | see *G. pilosa* 'Yellow Spreader' |
| | ***fragrans*** | see *G. canariensis* |
| | ***hispanica*** | CBcs CDul CSBt CTri EBee ELan EPfP GGal MGos SEND SLim SPer SRms SWvt WCFE WDin WFar WHar |
| | ***humifusa*** | see *G. pulchella* |
| | ***lydia*** ♀H4 | CBcs CChe CDul CSBt CWSG CWib EBee ECho ELan EPfP LAst LRHS MAsh MGos MMuc MRav MSwo NPri SBfd SBod SEND SLim SPer SPoG SRms SSta SWvt WDin WFar WHar |
| § | ***maderensis*** | EWes LRHS |
| | ***pilosa*** | EPot MAsh NMen |
| | - 'Goldilocks' | LRHS MMuc |
| | - 'Lemon Spreader' | see *G. pilosa* 'Yellow Spreader' |
| | - var. ***minor*** | GLam NLar NMen WAbe |
| | - 'Procumbens' | CMea MDKP MHer WPat |
| | - 'Vancouver Gold' | CBcs ELan EPfP GGar MGos MRav SMad SPer SRms WDin WFar WGor |
| § | - 'Yellow Spreader' | CBcs CMHG MMuc MSwo |
| § | 'Porlock' ♀H3 | CAlb CBod CDoC CDul CMac CPLG CSBt CSPN CTri CWSG CWib ELon GGal GGar LRHS MAsh MBri MMuc MNHC MRav NCGa SBfd SEND SLim WDin |
| § | ***pulchella*** | CTri |
| | ***sagittalis*** | CTri EBee LRHS MMuc NBir SPer WWFP |
| § | - subsp. ***delphinensis*** ♀H4 | NMen |
| | - ***minor*** | see *G. sagittalis* subsp. *delphinensis* |
| § | × ***spachiana*** ♀H1 | CTri LRHS SBfd SPoG |
| | ***tenera*** 'Golden Shower' | SLPl |
| | ***tinctoria*** | CArn CHab EOHP GPoy ILis MHer SIde WHer |
| § | - 'Flore Pleno' (d) ♀H4 | ECho GEdr NMen NPro |
| | - 'Humifusa' | EPot GEdr NWCA |
| | - 'Moesiaca' | WAbe |
| | - 'Plena' | see *G. tinctoria* 'Flore Pleno' |
| | - 'Royal Gold' ♀H4 | CWib EPfP MRav NWad SPer SPlb |
| | ***villarsii*** | see *G. pulchella* |

## *Gentiana* ✿ (*Gentianaceae*)

| | | |
|---|---|---|
| | sp. | LLWG |
| § | ***acaulis*** ♀H4 | CWCL ECho ELan EPfP EPot GEdr GKev GMaP LHop LRHS MAsh MWat NGdn NHar NMen NSla SPlb SRms SRot WAbe WCFE WFar WPat |
| | - f. ***alba*** | WThu |
| | - - 'Snowstorm' | GKev |
| | - 'Belvedere' | EPot NMen WAbe |
| | - 'Coelestina' | WThu |
| | - 'Dinarica' | see *G. dinarica* |
| | - 'Holzmannii' | IVic NMen WAbe |
| | - 'Krumrey' | EPot GEdr GKev |
| | - 'Max Frei' | NHar |
| | - 'Maxima Enzian' | EPot |
| | - 'Rannoch' | EPot GEdr GKev NMen |
| | - 'Stumpy' | EPot GEdr |
| | - 'Trotter's Variety' | EPot WAbe |
| | - 'Undulatifolia' | EPot |
| | - 'Velkokvensis' | EPot IVic |
| | ***affinis*** | GKev LHop |
| | 'Alex Duguid' | GEdr IVic NHar |
| | 'Amethyst' | EPot GEdr GMaP LRHS WAbe |
| | ***andrewsii*** | SPhx |
| | ***angulosa*** misapplied | see *G. verna* 'Angulosa' hort. |
| | ***angustifolia*** | WAbe |
| I | - 'Alba' | EPot GKev |
| | - 'Frei' **new** | GLam |
| | - Frei hybrid | GKev |
| | 'Ann's Special' | GEdr |
| | ***asclepiadea*** ♀H4 | Widely available |
| | - 'Alba' | CBot CLAP EBee GBee GCal GEdr GGar GKev IGor LEdu MDKP MNrw NBid SPer SRms WCFE WHoo WTin |
| | - 'Knightshayes' | CLAP EBee GKev LLHF |
| I | - 'Nana' | EBee |
| | - 'Phyllis' | EBee |
| | - 'Pink Cascade' | GEdr GKev |
| | - 'Pink Swallow' | CLAP GAbr GBBs GEdr GKev GMac NLar WHoo WWEG |

| | | |
|---|---|---|
| | - 'Rosea' | GKev GMaP MDKP MNrw |
| | 'Balmoral'[PBR] | GMaP |
| | 'Barbara Lyle' | WAbe |
| | ***bavarica*** var. ***subacaulis*** | SPlb |
| | × ***bernardii*** | see *G.* × *stevenagensis* 'Bernardii' |
| | 'Berrybank Dome' | CSam GEdr GMaP NHol |
| | 'Berrybank Sky' | GEdr GMaP NCGa NHol |
| | 'Berrybank Star' | GEdr GMaP |
| | ***bisetaea*** | GKev SRms |
| | 'Blauer Stern' | IVic |
| | 'Blue Heaven' | GEdr |
| | 'Blue Sea' | LRHS |
| | 'Blue Silk' | EPot EWes GEdr GKev IVic LRHS NHar NHol WAbe |
| | ***boissieri*** | GKev |
| | ***brachyphylla*** | WAbe |
| | - subsp. ***favratii*** | WAbe |
| | 'Braemar'[PBR] | GMaP |
| | 'Cairngorm' | GAbr GEdr LRHS NHar |
| | 'Carmen' | GEdr NHar |
| | × ***caroli*** | WAbe |
| | ***clusii*** | NMen WAbe |
| | - purple-flowered | WAbe |
| | ***coelestis*** | NHar |
| | 'Compact Gem' | EPot GEdr GLam NHar NHol WAbe |
| § | ***cruciata*** | ITim LHop MMHG NLar |
| | - SDR 6359 | GKev |
| | - SDR 6406 | GKev |
| § | ***dahurica*** | ECho GEdr GKev NGdn NHol |
| | 'Dark Hedgehog' | GEdr |
| | ***decumbens*** | EPot |
| | ***depressa*** | EPot WAbe |
| | 'Devonhall' | GEdr IVic NHar NHol NWad |
| | 'Diana'[PBR] | LRHS |
| § | ***dinarica*** | ECho EPot NHar NMen |
| | - 'Colonel Stitt' | GEdr WThu |
| | 'Dumpy' | GEdr |
| | 'Elehn' | NHar |
| | 'Elizabeth' | CSam GEdr |
| | 'Ettrick' | GEdr IVic NHar NHol |
| | 'Eugen's Allerbester' (d) | CCVN GEdr GKev GMaP IVic LRHS NHar NHol NWad SPer WAbe |
| | 'Eugen's Bester' | GLam NHar |
| | ***farreri*** | GGar |
| | - 'Duguid' | GEdr |
| | ***fetissowii*** | see *G. macrophylla* var. *fetissowii* |
| | 'Gellerhard' | GEdr NHar |
| | ***georgei*** new | EPot |
| | 'Gewahn' | GEdr IVic NHar |
| I | 'Glamis Strain' | GEdr LRHS NHar |
| | 'Glen Isla' | EWes |
| | 'Glen Moy' | GEdr |
| | 'Glendevon' | GEdr WAbe |
| § | ***gracilipes*** | GEdr GKev MWat SPlb SRms |
| | - 'Yuatensis' | see *G. macrophylla* var. *fetissowii* |
| | 'Henry' | GEdr WAbe |
| | Inshriach hybrids | LRHS SPer |
| | 'Inverleith' ♀H4 | EWes GEdr LRHS NHol SPlb |
| | 'Iona'[PBR] | GMaP |
| | 'Joan Ward' | LRHS SPer |
| | 'John Aitken' | GEdr |
| | 'Juwel' | GEdr |
| | 'Kirriemuir' | EWes |
| | ***kochiana*** | see *G. acaulis* |
| | ***kurroo*** | LHop |
| | - var. ***brevidens*** | see *G. dahurica* |
| | ***lagodechiana*** | see *G. septemfida* var. *lagodechiana* |
| | cf. ***lawrencei*** SSSE 237 | NHar |
| | 'Little Diamond'[PBR] | LRHS NLar |
| | 'Lucerna' | EPfP GEdr GKev LRHS NHol |
| | ***lutea*** | EBee GAbr GKev GPoy LRHS NBid NChi SMad SRms WPer WTou |
| | - SDR 3522 | GKev |
| | × ***macaulayi*** ♀H4 | SRms |
| | - 'Blue Bonnets' | GEdr |
| | - 'Elata' | GLam IVic NHol NWad |
| | - 'Kidbrooke Seedling' | CTri EWes GEdr GKev GMaP LRHS NHol WAbe |
| | - 'Kingfisher' | CTri GKev IVic LRHS NBir WAbe |
| § | - 'Praecox' | GEdr |
| § | - 'Wells's Variety' | GLam LRHS |
| § | ***macrophylla*** var. ***fetissowii*** | GKev LLHF |
| | ***makinoi*** 'Marsha'[PBR] | CHll EBee LRHS SPoG WCot |
| | - 'Royal Blue' | GCal LRHS |
| | 'Margaret' | GEdr WAbe |
| | 'Maryfield' | GEdr |
| | 'Melanie' | GEdr NHol |
| | ***microdonta*** | GEdr |
| | 'Multiflora' | LRHS |
| * | ***nepaulensis*** | GAuc |
| | ***occidentalis*** | EPot |
| | ***olgae*** | LHop |
| | ***olivieri*** | LLHF |
| | ***paradoxa*** | GKev LLHF NSla WAbe WPat |
| | - 'Blauer Herold' | LRHS MWat |
| | ***phlogifolia*** | see *G. cruciata* |
| | ***pneumonanthe*** | LRHS SPlb |
| | ***prolata*** | NHar |
| | ***pumila*** subsp. ***delphinensis*** | WAbe WPat |
| | ***purdomii*** | see *G. gracilipes* |
| | 'Saphir Select' | GEdr NHol |
| | ***saxosa*** | EPot GKev GLam LRHS NBir NSla |
| | ***scabra*** | LRHS |
| | - 'Zuikorindo' | NLar |
| | 'Selektra' | IVic |
| | 'Sensation' | GEdr NHar |
| | ***septemfida*** ♀H4 | GAbr GEdr GKev LBee LHop LRHS MAsh MBri NBir SPlb SRms WGwG WHoo WKif |
| | - 'Alba' | NBir |
| § | - var. ***lagodechiana*** ♀H4 | GLam LRHS NMen SRms WFar XLum |
| | 'Serenity' | EPot GEdr IVic LRHS NHol NWad WAbe |
| | 'Shot Silk' | CSam CTri EPot EWes GEdr GGar GJos GLam GMaP LRHS MGos NBir NCGa NHar NHol SPoG WAbe |
| | 'Silken Giant' | GEdr WAbe |
| | 'Silken Night' | GEdr WAbe |
| | 'Silken Seas' | GEdr NHar NHol WAbe |
| | 'Silken Skies' | GEdr NHar WAbe |
| | 'Silken Surprise' | WAbe |
| | ***sino-ornata*** ♀H4 | CTri ECho GAbr GGar GKev GMaP LSRN MAsh MBri MWat NCGa NMen SRms WAbe WFar |
| | - CLD 476B | GEdr |
| | - SDR 5127 | GAbr LRHS MGos |
| | - 'Alba' | NHol WFar |
| | - 'Angel's Wings' | GEdr LRHS NHol |
| | - 'Bellatrix' | GEdr IVic NHar NHol |
| | - 'Blautopf' | IVic |
| | - 'Brin Form' | SRms |
| | - 'Downfield' | GKev LRHS NHol |
| | - 'Edith Sarah' | GEdr GLam IVic SRms |
| | - 'Mary Lyle' | GEdr |
| | - 'Oha' | IVic |
| | - 'Praecox' | see *G.* × *macaulayi* 'Praecox' |

|  |  |
|---|---|
| - 'Purity' | GEdr LRHS WAbe |
| - 'Starlight' | NHar |
| I - 'Trotter's Form' | EWes |
| - 'Weisser Traum' | GEdr IVic LRHS NHol NLar |
| - 'White Wings' | EWes |
| 'Sir Rupert' | IVic NHar |
| 'Soutra' | GEdr |
| × ***stevenagensis*** ♀H4 | CTri LRHS |
| § - 'Bernardii' | GEdr GLam NHar |
| - dark-flowered | WAbe |
| ***straminea*** | GKev GLam LLHF MDKP |
| 'Strathmore' ♀H4 | CSam CSpr CTri EWes GAbr GEdr GGar GKev GMaP LRHS NBir NCGa NHar NHol NSla SPlb WAbe |
| 'Suendermannii' | GKev LLHF |
| ***syringea*** | WAbe |
| ***ternifolia*** 'Cangshan' | GEdr WAbe |
| - 'Dali' | GEdr GKev NBir NHar NHol |
| ***tianschanica*** | LHop |
| ***tibetica*** | CArn EBee GAuc GEdr GPoy LEdu LRHS NMun WAul WPer XLum |
| ***triflora*** | GKev LHop WFar |
| - 'Alba' | GKev |
| - f. ***horomuiensis*** | GCal |
| - var. ***japonica*** | WWEG |
| - 'Royal Blue' | EBee LRHS |
| ***veitchiorum*** | GKev |
| ***verna*** | CWCL ECho EPfP EPot EWes GKev LHop LRHS LSRN NMen NSla SPoG WAbe WFar WPat |
| - 'Alba' | NSla WAbe WPat |
| § - 'Angulosa' hort. ♀H4 | MAsh |
| - subsp. ***balcanica*** | SRms WPat |
| - subsp. ***oschtenica*** | WAbe |
| - subsp. ***tergestina*** | WAbe |
| ***villosa*** | LHop |
| 'Violette' | GEdr GLam LRHS NHar NHol SPer |
| ***waltonii*** | EWes |
| ***wellsii*** | see *G.* × *macaulayi* 'Wells's Variety' |
| ***wutaiensis*** | see *G. macrophylla* var. *fetissowii* |
| ***zekuensis*** new | GKev |

## *Geranium* ✿ (*Geraniaceae*)

|  |  |
|---|---|
| from Bambashata Altai Mountains | NCot |
| ***aconitifolium*** misapplied | see *G. palmatum* |
| ***aconitifolium*** L'Hér. | see *G. rivulare* |
| 'Alan Mayes' | CElw CSev EBee EBla ECtt EPPr GKin LRHS LSou MWea NGdn SRGP WCAu |
| 'Alan's Blue' | EBee NChi |
| ***albanum*** | CElw EPPr GAbr LLWP MMuc MNrw SDix SEND SRGP WMoo WPtf |
| ***albiflorum*** | WMoo |
| ***anemonifolium*** | see *G. palmatum* |
| 'Ann Folkard' ♀H4 | Widely available |
| 'Ann Folkard' × ***psilostemon*** | LSRN |
| 'Anne Thomson' ♀H4 | Widely available |
| × ***antipodeum*** 'Black Ice' | SBch |
| - 'Chocolate Candy' PBR | EPfP LBuc LRHS |
| § - Crûg strain | NBPC |
| - 'Elizabeth Wood' | SMrm |
| - (*G. sessiliflorum* subsp. *novae-zelandiae* 'Nigricans' × *G. traversii* var. *elegans*) | SRms |
| - 'Kahlua' | EPfP |
| - 'Pink Spice' PBR | EBla GKin LBuc LRHS MGos |
| - 'Sea Spray' | CMHG ECtt GCra MCot NBro WMnd |
| - 'Stanhoe' | ECtt |
| ***antrorsum*** | ECou |
| ***aristatum*** | CDes EBla EPPr EWes GCal GGar MNFA MNrw MRav NBir SRGP WCru WMoo WPtf |
| ***armenum*** | see *G. psilostemon* |
| 'Arnoldshof' | EPPr |
| ***asphodeloides*** | CBre CElw CHid IFro LLWP MBNS MNrw MWhi NBid NBir NCot SPav SRGP WBrk WFar WMnd WMoo WPnP WTin |
| - subsp. ***asphodeloides*** 'Prince Regent' | EBee WCra WPnP |
| - - white-flowered | CSpr EBla SRGP WFar WMoo |
| - 'Starlight' | NBid |
| ***atlanticum*** Hook. f. | see *G. malviflorum* |
| 'Aussie Gem' | EBee |
| 'Baby Blue' | see *G. himalayense* 'Baby Blue' |
| 'Benjamin Browne' | CSev |
| 'Bertie Crûg' | EBee ECtt EPPr LLHF NBir SBfd SMrm SPoG SRms SRot SWat SWvt WCru WFar |
| ***biuncinatum*** | IFro |
| 'Blue Boy' | NLar |
| 'Blue Cloud' ♀H4 | Widely available |
| 'Blue Pearl' | EBee EPPr NBir NSti SRGP WMoo WPnP |
| § Blue Sunrise = 'Blogold' PBR ♀H4 | CBod CMHG CWGN EBee EBla ECtt ELan ELon EPPr EPfP LAst LRHS LSRN MAvo MCCP MNrw NBPC NCGa NEgg NLar NMyG NSti SPoG SRms SRot WCot WCra WFar WPGP WWEG |
| 'Bob's Blunder' | CYeo EBee ECtt EPfP LRHS LSRN MBNS MLLN MNrw NBPC NLar SMrm SPoG SRGP SWvt WCot WFar WHoo WWlt |
| ***bohemicum*** | SRGP WHer |
| - 'Orchid Blue' | EPfP SBch SWvt WFar |
| 'Brookside' ♀H4 | Widely available |
| 'Buckland Beauty' | CDes CElw CPLG CSpr CYeo SBch WBor |
| 'Buxton's Blue' | see *G. wallichianum* 'Buxton's Variety' |
| ***caeruleatum*** | EBla EPPr GCal |
| ***caespitosum*** | LLHF |
| ***caffrum*** | SPlb SRGP |
| 'Cally Cooper' new | EPPr |
| ***canariense*** | see *G. reuteri* |
| ***candicans*** misapplied | see *G. lambertii* |
| § × ***cantabrigiense*** | CMac CSBt ECtt IFro LRHS MHer MNrw NBir NBro NPer NSti SGar SMrm SRms WBrk WCru WFar WMoo |
| - 'Berggarten' | CDes CElw EBee EPPr GBin SBch SRGP WPtf |
| - 'Biokovo' | Widely available |
| - 'Cambridge' | Widely available |
| - 'Harz' | EPPr |
| - 'Karmina' | CElw EBee EBla EPPr EPfP EPla LRHS MNFA MWhi SWat WBrk WHoo WMoo WPnP WWEG XLum |
| - 'Rosalina' | EPPr |
| - 'St Ola' | Widely available |
| - 'Vorjura' | EPPr |
| - 'Westray' PBR | CHVG CMac COIW EBee EPPr EShb GAbr GQue LAst LBMP LRHS LSou MCCP MMuc NGdn NLar SBfd |

| | |
|---|---|
| | SEND SMrm SPoG SRkn SRms STes SWvt WBrk WCra |
| 'Chantilly' | EBee EBla ECGP ECtt EPPr LRHS MAvo MNrw NBir NCGa NChi SBch WCra WCru WMoo WPtf |
| 'Chipchase Sapphire' **new** | NChi |
| ***christensenianum*** B&SWJ 8022 | WCru |
| ***cinereum*** | ECho |
| - 'Album' | NChi |
| - 'Apple Blossom' | see *G.* × *lindavicum* 'Apple Blossom' |
| - 'Elizabeth' | ECtt LSRN |
| (Cinereum Group) 'Alice'PBR | EBee EPPr GMaP IPot LLHF LSRN MBNS NDov NGdn NHar NLar NSti SRot WCra |
| § - 'Ballerina' ♀H4 | Widely available |
| - 'Carol' | CWGN EAEE EBee EBla EPPr EWes GKin LRHS LSRN LSou MAsh MBNS MBri NCGa NDov NHar NLar NSti SRkn SWvt WCra WFar |
| I - 'Heather' | EPPr |
| - 'Lambrook Helen' | CPLG |
| - 'Laurence Flatman' | Widely available |
| - 'Lizabeth'PBR | EPPr LSou NHar |
| - 'Penny Lane'PBR | EPPr |
| - 'Prima Ballerina' | NLar |
| - 'Purple Pillow' | Widely available |
| - René Macé = 'Progera' | LRHS SRkn |
| - Rothbury Gem = 'Gerfos'PBR ♀H4 | CMac CWGN EBee EBla EKen EPPr LLHF LRHS NBPC NChi NLar NSti SKHP SUsu SWvt |
| - 'Sateene'PBR | EBee EPPr GMaP LRHS MDev NBPC NCGa NDov SPoG SRot WCra |
| - 'Signal' | EBee EBla EPPr EPot GEdr MAsh NHar NLar |
| - 'Souvenir de René Macé' | EPPr |
| - 'Thumbling Hearts' **new** | EPPr |
| - Thumping Heart | see *G.* (Cinereum Group) 'Thumbling Hearts' |
| 'Claridge Druce' | see *G.* × *oxonianum* 'Claridge Druce' |
| ***clarkei*** 'Kashmir Pink' | Widely available |
| § - 'Kashmir White' ♀H4 | Widely available |
| - 'Mount Stewart' | CPLG EBee GCal WCru WPGP |
| - (Purple-flowered Group) 'Kashmir Purple' | Widely available |
| ***clarum*** B&SWJ 10246 | WCru |
| ***collinum*** | CSpr EPPr MNrw NBir NCot SRGP WCru WOut |
| 'Colour Carousel' | IPot |
| 'Coombland White' | CDes CFir CPLG CSam EBee EBla ECtt EPPr GMaP LAst LSou MAvo MCot MNrw NBPC NDov NGdn NLar NSti SBfd SKHP SMrm SRGP WCot WMoo |
| 'Criss Canning' | EPPr |
| Crûg strain | see *G.* × *antipodeum* Crûg strain |
| 'Cyril's Blue' | EBee NChi |
| 'Cyril's Fancy' | EBee EBla EPPr MAvo WPtf |
| ***dahuricum*** | WCru |
| ***dalmaticum*** ♀H4 | Widely available |
| - 'Album' | CYeo EBee EBla ECho ECtt ELan EPPr EPot LRHS MRav NMen NRya SBch SRGP SRms SWat WAbe WCru WFar |
| - 'Bressingham Pink' | EPPr |
| - 'Bridal Bouquet' | EBee LLHF NChi NMen NSla WAbe |
| - 'Stades Hellrosa' | EPPr |
| ***dalmaticum*** × ***macrorrhizum*** | see *G.* × *cantabrigiense* |
| ***delavayi*** misapplied | see *G. sinense* |
| 'Devon Pride' | CElw EBee |
| 'Dilys' ♀H4 | CElw CPrp EBee ELan EPPr MAvo MCot MLHP MNrw NBir NChi NDov NGdn NLar SBfd SRGP SUsu WCru WFar WHal WMoo WPnP |
| ***dissectum*** | CHll |
| 'Distant Hills' | EBee EPPr MAvo SRGP SUsu |
| 'Diva' | CSam EBee EBla EPPr EPfP LLHF SRGP WCru WPnP |
| 'Double Jewel' (d) | see *G. pratense* 'Double Jewel' |
| Dragon Heart = 'Bremdra'PBR | CMac CSev EBee ECtt EPPr LSRN MBri NSti SKHP SPoG SUsu WCra |
| 'Dusky Crûg' | CChe CDes CElw CLAP CSBt CSam EBee ECtt EHoe EPPr EPfP EShb ETod EWTr GKin LAst LRHS MCot MNrw NBPC NEgg NOrc SPoG SPtl SWvt WCot WCru WFar WHoo WMnd |
| 'Dusky Rose' | CBod CLAP CPrp CSpe EBee ELan EPfP LAst MBri MGos NCGa NLar SRGP SRot WFar |
| 'Edith May' | GSec |
| 'Elizabeth Ross' | MAvo WCru |
| 'Elke' | Widely available |
| 'Ella' | CWGN |
| 'Elworthy Dusky' | CElw |
| 'Elworthy Eyecatcher' | CDes CElw EPPr MAvo SBch SRGP SUsu WPGP |
| 'Elworthy Tiger' | CElw MAvo |
| 'Emily' | SRGP |
| ***endressii*** ♀H4 | CBre CElw CSev EBee EBla ECha ECho EPfP GAbr GLog GMaP MBNS MCot MHer MMuc NBro NPer SBrd SEND SGar SPlb SRGP SRms SWvt WFar WMoo WWEG XLum |
| - 'Album' | see *G.* 'Mary Mottram' |
| - 'Castle Drogo' ♀H4 | EBee EPPr SRGP |
| - 'Prestbury White' | see *G.* × *oxonianum* 'Prestbury Blush' |
| - 'Rose' | MAvo WPer |
| - 'Wargrave Pink' | see *G.* × *oxonianum* 'Wargrave Pink' |
| ***erianthum*** | GMaP MLHP NBre NCGa NLar SRGP STes WCru WMoo WPnP |
| - 'Axeltree' | SUsu |
| - 'Cally Pearl' | GCal |
| - 'Calm Sea' | SUsu WCru WMoo WPnP |
| - f. ***leucanthum*** 'Undine' | SUsu WCot |
| - 'Neptune' | MNFA WCru WPnP WWEG |
| ***eriostemon*** Fischer | see *G. platyanthum* |
| 'Eva' | EBee WPnP |
| 'Expression'PBR | see *G.* 'Tanya Rendall' |
| 'Extravaganza' **new** | EPPr |
| 'Farncombe Cerise Star' | CElw EPPr GCal |
| § ***farreri*** | CPLG ECho LHop LLHF LRHS NBir |
| 'Foundling' | MAvo NDov |
| ***fremontii*** | EWld |
| ***goldmannii*** | SKHP |
| ***gracile*** | EBee GMaP LRHS LSou MLLN MNrw NBir NBre SRGP WBrk WCru WMoo WPnP WPtf |
| - 'Blanche' | EPPr |
| - 'Blush' | CElw EPPr LPla MNFA |
| ***grandiflorum*** | see *G. himalayense* |
| 'Grasmere' | ECtt |
| 'Gwen Thompson' | WOut |

| | | |
|---|---|---|
| | ***gymnocaulon*** | CMac EBee EBla EPPr GKin LRHS MAvo NLar SRGP WCru |
| | ***gymnocaulon* × *platypetalum*** | NCot |
| | 'Harmony' | EBee EPPr |
| | ***harveyi*** | CMea EWes GCal LRHS NChi SPlb SRGP WCru WKif WPGP WPat |
| | ***hayatanum*** B&SWJ 164 | WCru WMoo |
| § | ***himalayense*** | Widely available |
| | - CC 1957 from Tibetan border | CPLG EPPr |
| | - ***alpinum*** | see *G. himalayense* 'Gravetye' |
| § | - 'Baby Blue' | CElw EBee EBla EPPr GCal GCra IFro LRHS MAvo MNFA MNrw NCot NGdn NLar NSti SBch SRGP WBrk WCAu WCra WCru WMoo WPnP WPtf |
| | - 'Birch Double' | see *G. himalayense* 'Plenum' |
| | - 'Derrick Cook' | CDes CElw EBee EPPr MAvo MNFA MWhi NCot SUsu WBrk WPtf |
| | - 'Devil's Blue' | EBee EPPr SRGP WPtf |
| § | - 'Gravetye' ♀H4 | Widely available |
| | - 'Irish Blue' | CElw EBee EBla ECtt EPPr GCal GCra IGor MSpe NCot NLar NSti SRGP WCra WCru WMoo WPnP WPtf WTin |
| | - ***meeboldii*** | see *G. himalayense* |
| | - 'Pale Irish Blue' | EBee GCal |
| § | - 'Plenum' (d) | Widely available |
| | ***hispidissimum*** | CFee |
| | ***ibericum*** misapplied | see *G.* × *magnificum* |
| | ***ibericum*** Cav. | CSBt CTri NBre NLar SPav SRGP STes WFar |
| | - 'Blue Springs' | ECtt |
| | - subsp. ***ibericum*** | CMac EBee EPPr |
| | - subsp. ***jubatum*** | EPPr LRHS MNFA MNrw SRms WCru |
| | - - 'White Zigana' | CPrp EAEE EBee ECGP ECtt EPPr EPfP GCal GGar LRHS MWea SBch SBfd SPoG WCra WPnP WPtf |
| | - subsp. ***jubatum* × *renardii*** | SWvt |
| | - var. ***platypetalum*** misapplied | see *G.* × *magnificum* |
| | - var. ***platypetalum*** Boiss. | see *G. platypetalum* Fisch. & C.A. Mey. |
| § | - 'Ushguli Grijs' | EBee NChi NLar WCot |
| | ***ibericum* × *libani*** | CDes |
| | ***incanum*** | CAbP CHII CMHG EBee EShb EWes MNrw NBir SGar SMrm SRGP WNew |
| | - white-flowered | SRGP |
| | 'Ivan' ♀H4 | CElw CEnt CLAP EBee EBla ECtt EPPr GMac LRHS MNFA NChi NCot NLar SRGP WCra WCru WHlf WMoo |
| | 'Jean Armour' | CDes EAEE EBee ECtt EPPr GGar LRHS MWea NGdn SPoG SRGP WPGP |
| | 'Johnson's Blue' ♀H4 | Widely available |
| | 'Jolly Bee'[PBR] ♀H4 | Widely available |
| | 'Joy' | EBee EBla ECtt ELon EPPr LSou LSqH MAvo MCot MMuc MNrw MRav NBPC NBir NCGa NEgg NLar NSti NWad SBfd SEND SRGP WCra WMoo WPnP |
| § | 'Kanahitobanawa' | CDes MAvo |
| | 'Karen Wouters' | EBee |
| | 'Kashmir Blue' | CPLG EBee ECtt EPPr EPfP GMaP LRHS MAvo NGdn NLar NPnk SBch SMrs SWat WCAu WFar WKif WMoo WPnP WPtf WWEG |
| | 'Kashmir Green' | EAEE EBee ECtt EPPr GBin LAst MAvo WMoo WPnP |
| § | 'Kate' | WCru |
| | 'Kate Folkard' | see *G.* 'Kate' |
| § | 'Khan' | EBee EBla EPPr IFro IPot MAvo NCot NPro SDys SRGP SUsu WBrk WCru |
| | 'Kirsty' | EBee EPPr |
| | ***kishtvariense*** | EBee EBla GCal MNrw MRav NCot NSti WCru |
| | ***koraiense*** | CDes EBla NBre WMoo |
| | - B&SWJ 797 | EBla WCru |
| | - B&SWJ 878 | CPLG WCru |
| | ***koreanum*** ambig. | EBee NLar WFar WMoo |
| | - B&SWJ 602 | CPLG EBla WCru |
| § | ***kotschyi*** var. ***charlesii*** | EBla EPPr |
| | ***krameri*** | NLar |
| | - B&SWJ 1142 | CPLG EBla WCru |
| | 'Lakwijk Star' | MAsh |
| § | ***lambertii*** | CSpr EWes GCal LRHS NBir |
| | - 'Swansdown' | GMac WCru WPtf WSHC |
| | ***lanuginosum*** | LRHS |
| I | ***libani*** | EBee ELon EPPr LLWP LRHS MCot NBid NChi NSti WBrk WCot WSHC WTin |
| | - RCB RL B-2 | WCot |
| | ***libani* × *peloponnesiacum*** | CDes EBee WPGP |
| | 'Libretto' | WCru |
| | 'Light Dilys' **new** | NDov |
| § | × ***lindavicum*** 'Apple Blossom' | CMea EPPr NMen |
| | - 'Lissadell' | EPot |
| | ***linearilobum*** subsp. ***transversale*** | EPPr NCot SRot WCru WPnP |
| I | - - 'Laciniatum' | LWst NCot |
| | - - 'Rose Foundling' | LWst |
| § | 'Little David' | EBee NLar SUsu |
| | 'Little Devil' | see *G.* 'Little David' |
| | 'Little Gem' | CMea EBla EPPr LRHS MAvo NChi NLar WFar WMoo |
| | ***lucidum*** | WPtf WSFF |
| | 'Luscious Linda' | EBee MAvo NLar WFar WPnP |
| | 'Lydia' | SRGP |
| § | ***macrorrhizum*** | CArn CFee CSBt CTca EBee ECrN ELon EPfP GKev GKin IFro LEdu MBNS MCot MRav MWat MWhi NBro NCGa NPnk SRms SWat WCAu WFar WGor WHil WWEG XLum |
| | - AL & JS 90179YU | CHid EPPr |
| | - 'Album' ♀H4 | Widely available |
| | - 'Bevan's Variety' ♀H4 | Widely available |
| | - 'Bulgaria' | EPPr |
| | - 'Cham-ce' | EPPr WBrk |
| | - 'Czakor' | Widely available |
| I | - 'De Bilt' | EBee EWes |
| | - 'Freundorf' | EBee EPPr EWes GCal |
| | - 'Ingwersen's Variety' ♀H4 | Widely available |
| | - 'Lohfelden' | CDes EBee EPPr EWes GCal SRGP WCru WPGP |
| | - 'Mount Olympus' | see *G. macrorrhizum* 'White-Ness' |
| | - 'Mytikas' ♀H4 | EBee EPPr |
| | - 'Pindus' | CBod CPrp CYeo EBee EBla EPPr GAbr LRHS MBNS NBre NSti SRGP WCru WFar WPtf |
| | - 'Prionia' | EPPr NCot |
| | - 'Purpurrot' | WWEG |

| |  |  |
|---|---|---|
| | – 'Ridsko' | CFee CSpr EPPr GCal LPla LRHS NBro SRGP WCru |
| | ***– roseum*** | see *G. macrorrhizum* |
| | – 'Rotblut' | EPPr SRGP WBrk |
| | – 'Sandwijck' | EPPr NCot |
| | – 'Snow Sprite' | CBod CEnt CMea CSpr EPPr EPyc MCCP NPro WHrl |
| | – 'Spessart' | CBar EBee EBla ELan ELon EPPr EPfP GMaP LAst MBri MGos MMuc NLar SBfd SEND SPer WBrk WFar WPnP WRHF WWEG XLum |
| | – 'Variegatum' (v) | EBee EBla ELan GMaP LEdu MHer NBPC NBir SPer SRGP SRms WBrk WCot WFar WHil WMnd WWEG |
| | – 'Velebit' | NCot SRGP WCru |
| § | – 'White-Ness' ♀[H4] | Widely available |
| | – 'Witoscha' | EBee LRHS |
| | ***macrostylum*** | GLam WCot WCru WPer |
| I | – 'Caeruleum' | WPtf |
| | – 'Leonidas' | EPPr NCot WCot WPnP |
| | – 'Talish' | EPPr NCot |
| | – 'Uln Oag Triag' | EPPr |
| | ***maculatum*** | CArn CElw CSev EPfP LLWP LRHS MMHG MNrw MRav NSti NWCA SRGP SWat WCra WCru WHal WPnP |
| | – from Kath Dryden | EBee EPPr |
| | – f. ***albiflorum*** | CLAP EBee EBla EPPr EPfP EWTr LRHS MNrw MWhi NChi NLar NSti SRGP STes WBrk WCru WMoo WPnP |
| | – 'Beth Chatto' | Widely available |
| | – 'Elizabeth Ann'[PBR] ♀[H4] | Widely available |
| | – 'Espresso' | Widely available |
| | – 'Shameface' | EBee EPPr SBch SDys SGar WMoo |
| | – 'Silver Buttons' | CDes EBee |
| | – 'Smoky Mountain' | EBee EPPr |
| | – 'Spring Purple' | CElw EBee EPPr MAvo NChi NCot NLar |
| | – 'Sweetwater' | EPPr |
| | – 'Vickie Lynn' | CLAP EBee EPPr MAvo NChi |
| | ***maderense*** ♀[H2] | CAbb CArn CBcs CFir CHEx CPrp CSpe CTrC CTsd EBee ELan EShb EWes LRHS NBir NPer SArc SChr SDix SMrm SPav SPhx SRGP SRkn SVen WCru |
| | – 'Guernsey White' | CFir COIW CTrC GCal NGBo SMrm SPhx SVen WCot WSHC |
| | – white-flowered | CSpe |
| | ***maderense × palmatum*** | CHII WCru |
| § | × ***magnificum*** ♀[H4] | Widely available |
| | – 'Blue Blood' | CElw CLAP CSev EBee ECtt EKen EPPr GAbr IPot LRHS LSou MBNS MCot MTis NBPC NDov NGdn NPnk NSti SBch SMrm SRGP WCot WCra WFar WPtf WWEG |
| | – 'Hylander' | EPPr |
| | – 'Peter Yeo' | EPPr SRGP |
| | – 'Rosemoor' | CElw CHid EBee EBla ELan EPPr EPfP GCal GGar IKil LHop MWhi NPro SBfd WCot WCra WMnd WPtf XLum |
| | ***magniflorum*** | EWes MRav NBid NGdn |
| | 'Maître Hugo' | EBee |
| § | ***malviflorum*** | CMHG ECha ELan EPPr GLam LRHS MNrw NCot SBch SPhx WAul WCot WCru WFar WPnP |
| | – from Spain | EWes WSHC |
| | – pink-flowered | EPPr |
| § | 'Mary Mottram' | CElw EPPr NBir WCot |
| | 'Mavis Simpson' ♀[H4] | Widely available |
| | ***maximowiczii*** | SBch WPtf |
| | 'Melinda'[PBR] | EBee EPPr MBri NMir WCot WCra |
| | 'Mellow Yellow' | SUsu |
| | 'Memories'[PBR] | CPar EBee ECtt EPPr LRHS LSRN MBNS NDov WFar |
| | 'Menna Bach' | MAvo |
| | 'Meryl Anne' | SRGP WPtf |
| | ***microphyllum*** | see *G. potentilloides* |
| | 'Midnight Star' **new** | EWes |
| | ***molle*** | NBir WSFF |
| | – white-flowered | NBir |
| | × ***monacense*** | CPrp EBee EBla ELan EPla IFoB LEdu LRHS MBNS SRGP SWat WCru WMoo WPnP |
| | – var. ***anglicum*** | CFir EBla ECtt EPPr GMaP LRHS MRav MTis MWhi WCAu WMoo WPnP |
| | – 'Anne Stevens' | EBee NCot WPtf |
| | – 'Claudine Dupont' | CAby CElw EBee EPPr IFro MAvo NChi NCot WCot WCra WPtf |
| | – dark-flowered | WMoo |
| | – 'Emma White' **new** | NChi |
| | – var. ***monacense*** | NEgg WFar |
| | – – 'Breckland Fever' | EBee EPPr NChi SRGP |
| § | – – 'Muldoon' | EBee EBla EPPr LRHS MLLN MTis NBir SRGP STes WFar WMoo WPnP |
| | 'Mourning Widow' | see *G. phaeum* 'Lady in Mourning' |
| | 'Mrs Jean Moss' | EBee EPPr EWes |
| | 'Mrs Judith Bradshaw' **new** | NChi |
| | ***napuligerum*** misapplied | see *G. farreri* |
| | ***napuligerum*** Franch. | NSla |
| | 'Natalie' | CSpr EBee EPPr LRHS LSRN MAvo NChi SUsu |
| | ***nepalense*** | SRGP SRms |
| | 'Nicola' | CElw EBee EPPr IFro MAvo MNFA NHaw NLar SAga SBch SRGP |
| | 'Nimbus' ♀[H4] | Widely available |
| | ***nodosum*** | Widely available |
| | – 'Blueberry Ice' **new** | CElw MAvo |
| | – 'Clos du Coudray' **new** | NLar |
| | – dark-flowered | see *G. nodosum* 'Swish Purple' |
| | – 'Darkleaf' | MAvo |
| | – 'Hexham Big Eyes' | CElw EWes |
| | – 'Hexham Lace' **new** | SBch |
| | – 'Julie's Velvet' | CDes LEdu MAvo WBor WHoo WPGP WTin |
| | – pale-flowered | see *G. nodosum* 'Svelte Lilac' |
| | – 'Pascal' | EPPr |
| | – 'Saucy Charlie' | SBch |
| | – 'Silverwood' | CElw EBee EPPr MAvo MNFA SBch SUsu |
| | – 'Simon' | EBee MAvo SRGP |
| § | – 'Svelte Lilac' | CElw EAEE EBee EBla EPPr EPfP LBMP LRHS LSou MNFA NBro NHol SPoG SRGP SWat WCra WCru WFar WMoo WPnP |
| § | – 'Swish Purple' | CElw EBee EBla EPPr MAvo NLar SRGP WCru WFar WMoo WPGP WPnP |
| | – 'Whiteleaf' | CElw CMac EBee EBla EPPr MAvo MNFA NChi NDov NPro SBch SMrs SRGP WCru WFar WHal WMoo WPGP WPnP |
| | – 'Whiteleaf' seedling | EBla |
| | 'Nora Bremner' | GMac SUsu |
| | 'Nunnykirk Pink' | EWes SUsu |
| | 'Nunwood Purple' | EBee EPPr MAvo WPtf |
| | 'Old Rose' | LAst SRGP WCru |

| | | |
|---|---|---|
| § | ***orientalitibeticum*** | CFir CMHG CPLG CSpe EBee EBla ECtt EPPr GAbr GGar GMac IFro LEdu MCot MHer MMuc NBid NBre NLar SEND SKHP SMad WFar WMoo WPGP WPnP WWEG |
| | 'Orion' ♈H4 | Widely available |
| | 'Orkney Blue' | CElw EPPr WCru WPnP |
| | 'Orkney Cherry' | CMac CWGN EBee EPPr EPfP GMaP LLHF MAvo MWea NLar NSti SPoG SRkn WMoo |
| | 'Orkney Dawn' | NHaw WCru WPnP |
| | 'Orkney Pink' | CMac EBee ECtt EPPr EPfP LAst LHop LSRN MLHP NSti NWCA SBfd SPer SPoG SRGP SRkn SWat WFar |
| | 'Out of the Blue' | WOut |
| | × ***oxonianum*** | LRHS NCot WMoo |
| | - 'A.T. Johnson' ♈H4 | CBcs EBee EBla ECtt ELan EPfP GKin LAst LBMP LRHS MRav MWat MWhi NBir NEgg NGdn NSti SBfd SBrd SPer SRGP SRms SWat WBrk WCAu WCru WMnd WMoo WWEG |
| | - 'Andy's Star' | NCot |
| | - 'Ankum's White' | NDov |
| | - 'Anmore' | EPPr SRGP |
| | - 'Annie' **new** | NCot |
| | - 'Beholder's Eye' ♈H4 | CHid CPrp EBee EBla EPPr GAbr NBre NLar SBch SRGP WPnP WPtf WWEG |
| | - 'Breckland Sunset' | EPPr MAvo SBch SRGP |
| | - 'Bregover Pearl' | CBre CElw EBee EBla EPPr SRGP WMoo |
| | - 'Bressingham's Delight' | EBla ECtt SRGP |
| | - 'Buttercup' | EBee EPPr SRGP |
| I | - 'Cally Seedling' | EBee EBla EWes GCal |
| | - 'Chocolate Strawberry' | EPPr EWes |
| § | - 'Claridge Druce' | Widely available |
| | - 'Coronet' | CFir GCal SRGP WMoo |
| | - 'David Rowlinson' | EPPr |
| | - 'Diane's Treasure' | NCot NHaw SBch |
| | - 'Dirk Gunst' | CElw |
| | - 'Elworthy Misty' | CElw EBla EPPr SBch SRGP |
| | - 'Frank Lawley' | EBla GMac LLWP NBid NChi SBch SRGP WBrk WMoo |
| § | - 'Fran's Star' (d) | EBla SRGP WBrk WCru |
| | - 'Frilly Gilly' | EBee EPPr |
| | - 'Hexham Pink' | EPPr EWes NChi SBch SRGP |
| | - 'Hollywood' | EBee EBla ELan EPPr EPfP NLar NPer SRGP SRms WBrk WCra WFar WMoo WWEG |
| | - 'JS Anne-Marie' **new** | EBee |
| | - 'Julie Brennan' | CHVG GAbr SMrs |
| | - 'Kate Moss' | EBee EBla EPPr EWes NSti SRGP WCra |
| | - 'Katherine Adele' | CBod EBee EBla ECtt EPPr EPfP EWes GCal LPla LSou MAvo MSpe MWea NCGa NCot NLar NSti SBfd SRGP SRms WCra WFar |
| § | - 'Kingston' | CElw EPPr |
| | - 'Klaus Schult' | EPPr |
| | - 'Königshof' | EPPr EWes |
| | - 'Kurt's Variegated' | see *G.* × *oxonianum* 'Spring Fling' |
| | - 'Lace Time' | CBod CBre CFir CPrp CSev EBee EBla ECtt EPPr GKin LBMP LRHS LSRN MBri MSpe NCot NEgg NGdn NHol SBch SBfd SBrd SPer SRGP SRms WCAu WMnd WMoo |
| | - 'Lady Moore' | EBla EPla LRHS MNrw NBro NCot SRGP WHoo WMoo |
| | - 'Lambrook Gillian' | EBee EPPr SBch SRGP WBrk |
| | - 'Lasting Impression' | EPPr SRGP |
| | - 'Laura Skelton' | CElw NCot NHaw |
| | - 'Little John' | EWes |
| | - 'Maid Marion' | EWes |
| | - 'Miriam Rundle' | CElw EPPr LRHS SRGP WCru WMoo WWEG |
| | - 'Moorland Jenny' | CElw WMoo |
| | - 'Moorland Star' | WMoo |
| | - 'Music from Big Pink' | EPPr EWes |
| | - 'Pale Walter's Gift' | GCal |
| | - 'Pat Smallacombe' | EBla NCot WMoo |
| | - 'Patricia Josephine' | WCAu |
| | - 'Pearl Boland' | EBee EPPr SRGP |
| | - 'Phantom' | EBee EPPr |
| | - 'Phoebe Noble' | CBre CElw CPrp EBla EPPr MNrw NCot NLar SRGP WMoo |
| | - 'Phoebe's Blush' | EBla EPPr GCal GQue SRGP |
| | - 'Pink Cluster' | CLAP |
| | - 'Pink Lace' | CSpr LSou |
| § | - 'Prestbury Blush' | CBre CElw EPPr SRGP |
| | - 'Prestbury White' | see *G.* × *oxonianum* 'Prestbury Blush' |
| | - 'Raspberry Ice' | EBee EBla EWes |
| | - 'Rebecca Moss' | CPrp EBee EBla ECtt EPPr GAbr GCra GMac LRHS LSRN NCot NSti SBch SRGP WCra WCru WFar WOut WPtf WWEG |
| | - 'Robin's Ginger Nut' | EBee EWes |
| | - 'Rodbylund' | EBee |
| | - 'Rose Clair' | CFir CTca EBee EBla EPPr EPfP LRHS MLLN MWhi NBir NLar SBfd SGar SRGP WCru WMnd WMoo WWEG |
| | - 'Rosemary' | SBch |
| | - 'Rosemary Verey' | SBch |
| | - 'Rosenlicht' | CPrp EBla ECGP EPPr GKin LRHS MNFA MRav NGdn NLar SRGP WCAu WCra WCru WMnd WMoo |
| | - 'Rothbury Sarah' **new** | NChi |
| | - 'Sandy' | EWes |
| § | - 'Spring Fling' (v) | EBee EBla ECtt EPPr EWes LPla NSti SRGP WFar |
| | - 'Stillingfleet Keira' | EBee NSti SRGP |
| | - 'Summer Surprise' | EPPr EWes WCru |
| | - 'Susan' | EBla EPPr EWes |
| | - 'Susie White' | EPPr SRGP WCru |
| § | - f. ***thurstonianum*** | Widely available |
| | - - 'Armitageae' | EPPr NCot SRGP |
| | - - 'Breckland Brownie' | CElw EBee EBla EPPr EWes MAvo MSpe SRGP |
| | - - 'Crûg Star' | WCru |
| | - - 'David McClintock' | SBch SRGP WFar WMoo |
| | - - 'Peter Hale' | CMea |
| | - - 'Red Sputnik' | EPPr SRGP |
| | - - 'Sherwood' | EBee EBla ECtt EPPr GCal GQue MLLN MSpe NBro NEgg NSti NVic SApp SGar SMrm SRGP WCAu WFar WMoo |
| | - - 'Southcombe Double' (d) | CElw CSev EBla ECtt EPPr EPfP GCra LAst LRHS LSou MBri NBPC SMrm SPer SPoG SRGP SRms WCru WFar WMoo WWEG |
| § | - - 'Southcombe Star' | EBee EBla EPPr GAbr GCal LRHS MTis NBro NGdn SRGP WCru WFar WMoo WPer WWEG |
| | - - 'Sue Cox' | EPPr |
| | - 'Trevor's White' | CLAP EBla EPPr LLWP MNFA SBch SRGP WCru |
| | - 'Wageningen' ♈H4 | CBre EBee EPPr GCal GMac LPla LRHS LSou MBri MMuc MNFA NGdn SBfd SEND SMrm SRGP |

| | | |
|---|---|---|
| | | SRms WCot WCra WCru WHer WMoo WPtf |
| | - 'Walter's Gift' | CYeo EBee EBla ECtt EPPr EPla EPri EShb LBMP LLWP LRHS LSou MAvo MLLN MRav MTis MWhi NBir NBro NLar NPer SGar WBrk WCru WFar WHoo WMoo |
| § | - 'Wargrave Pink' ♀H4 | Widely available |
| | - 'Waystrode' | EBla EPPr SRGP |
| | - 'Westacre White' | EWes |
| | - 'Whitehaven' | SRGP |
| | - 'Whiter Shade of Pale' | EPPr |
| | - 'Winscombe' | EBee EPfP GCal LLWP MRav SRGP WFar WMnd WMoo WWEG |
| § | ***palmatum*** ♀H3 | CAbb CBcs CBot CHEx CMac COlW CPLG CSpe CTrC EBee EHoe EPau GAbr GGar GKev IFro IKil LRHS NBro NPer SGar SMad SPhx SRkn WCru WKif WMoo WPGP |
| | ***palustre*** | CElw CSpr EBee EBla EPPr LRHS MMuc MNrw SEND SRGP WFar WMoo WPtf |
| | 'Pastel Clouds' | LRHS |
| | Patricia = 'Brempat' ♀H4 | Widely available |
| | ***peloponnesiacum*** | EAEE EBee EPPr EWes GQue LRHS MAsh MAvo NOrc SBch WFar WMoo WPtf |
| | 'Perfect Storm' | CWGN EBee ECtt EPPr LLHF MBri NDov NLar |
| | ***phaeum*** | Widely available |
| | - 'Album' | Widely available |
| | - 'Alec's Pink' | EBla EPPr LLWP SBch SHar WOut WPtf |
| | - 'All Saints' | EBee EPPr LEdu SRGP |
| | - 'Angelina' | EPPr NCot |
| | - 'Aureum' | see *G. phaeum* 'Golden Spring' |
| | - 'Blauwvoet' | EBee EPPr MAvo NChi NCot |
| | - 'Blue Shadow' | CAby CDes CElw EBee EBla EPPr LEdu LLWP MAvo NCot SRGP |
| | - 'Caborn Lilac' | LLWP |
| | - 'Calligrapher' | CElw EBla EPPr LLHF MAvo NChi NCot SBch SMrs SRGP SUsu WMoo WPtf |
| | - 'Chocolate Chip' | EBla |
| | - 'Conny Broe' (v) | CLAP NCot SBch |
| | - 'Countess of Grey' | SMrs |
| | - 'David Bromley' | EBla NCot WCru WPtf |
| | - 'David Martin' | NCot |
| | - 'Enid' | EPPr |
| | - 'George Stone' | EBee EBla EPPr LLHF |
| | - 'Golden Samobor' | CElw EBla EPPr |
| § | - 'Golden Spring' | EBee EBla EPPr MAvo NCot NPro SRGP |
| | - 'Hannah Perry' | CAby EBla EPPr LLWP MTis WPtf |
| | - 'Hector's Lavender' | EBee SRGP |
| | - var. ***hungaricum*** | EBee EPPr LLWP SRGP WPtf |
| | - 'James Haunch' | EBla EPPr |
| | - 'Judith's Blue' **new** | NChi |
| | - 'Klepper' | EBee EPPr GBin |
| | - 'Lady in Black' | NCot |
| § | - 'Lady in Mourning' | CPLG EPPr EShb GCal MCot MNFA NChi NCot SRGP SRms SWat WCru WMoo |
| | - 'Lavender Pinwheel' | EPfP MBri WHil |
| | - 'Lily Lovell' | Widely available |
| | - 'Lisa' (v) | EBee EPPr MNrw NCot WCot |
| | - 'Little Boy' | EBee EBla EPPr NGdn |
| | - var. ***lividum*** | CBre CFee CPrp GMaP LLWP MAvo MRav NCot SRGP SRms STes WFar WPnP XLum |
| | - - 'Joan Baker' | CBre CSam EBee EPPr LPla MAvo MNFA NChi NCot NGdn NSti SBch SRGP WCra WCru WFar WMoo WPnP WWEG |
| | - - 'Majus' | EBee ECtt EPPr EPfP EPyc LLWP LPla LRHS SBch WFar WMoo |
| | - 'Maggie's Delight' (v) | SRGP |
| | - 'Marchant's Ghost' | IFro MAvo NGdn |
| | - 'Margaret Hunt' | NLar |
| | - 'Margaret Wilson' (v) | Widely available |
| | - 'Mierhausen' | EBee EBla EPPr EShb MAvo NCot WPtf |
| | - 'Moorland Dylan' | EBla EPPr WMoo WOut |
| | - 'Mottisfont Rose' **new** | SBch |
| | - 'Mourning Widow' | see *G. phaeum* 'Lady in Mourning' |
| | - 'Mrs Charles Perrin' | CElw CSpr EBee EBla EPPr MAvo STes |
| | - 'Mrs Withey Price' | EPPr |
| | - 'Night Time' | EBee EPPr SBch WPtf |
| | - 'Nightshade' | EBla |
| | - 'Our Pat' ♀H4 | CDes EBee EPPr NChi NCot WCot WPtf |
| | - var. ***phaeum*** | MMuc NMRc SGar WPtf |
| | - - 'Langthorns Blue' | CSev CWCL EBee ELan EPPr EWes LEdu LRHS MAvo MNrw NBre SRGP SWvt WPtf |
| | - - 'Samobor' | Widely available |
| I | - 'Ploeger de Bilt' | EPPr |
| | - purple-flowered | NPnk |
| | - 'Rachel's Rhapsody' | CElw EBee EBla EPPr MAvo NCot WPtf |
| | - 'Raven' | EBee EPPr NChi SUsu WHlf WPtf |
| | - red-flowered | MRav |
| | - 'Rise Top Lilac' | EBee NCot WPGP WPtf |
| | - 'Rose' | LRHS |
| | - 'Rose Air' | EBee EPPr MAvo SRGP WMoo WPnP |
| | - 'Rose Madder' | CAby CElw CFir EBee EBla EPPr EPyc GCal LEdu LLWP LPla MNrw NChi NCot NMRc SBch SRGP SUsu WCru WMoo WPnP |
| | - 'Saturn' | EPPr |
| | - 'Séricourt' | CDes WCot WCra |
| | - 'Slatina' | EBla EPPr |
| | - 'Small Grey' | EBla EPPr |
| | - 'Springtime'PBR | CBod EBee EPPr EPfP LLHF MBNS NChi NCot NGdn WCAu WCra |
| | - 'Stillingfleet Ghost' | CAby EBee EBla EPPr LEdu LRHS MNrw NChi NCot NSti |
| | - 'Taff's Jester' (v) | CElw EBee EWes LPla NHol SApp SRGP WCot |
| § | - 'Variegatum' (v) | CBre CMac EBee EHoe ELan EPPr GMaP IFro LBMP LRHS MCot MLLN MNrw MRav NBir NBro NCot NEgg NPro SRGP WAbb WCru WFar WHer WMoo WTin |
| | - 'Vintage Dave' **new** | WOut |
| | - 'Walküre' | EBee EPPr EWes MAvo NLar WPtf |
| | 'Phantom of the Opera' (v) **new** | EPPr NChi |
| | 'Philippe Vapelle' | Widely available |
| | 'Pink Carpet' | SBfd |
| | 'Pink Delight' | CElw CMea EBla MAvo MNrw SBch |
| | 'Pink Ghost' | CSpr |
| | 'Pink Penny' | EBee EPPr EPfP IPot LRHS MWea NGBo SPoG SRGP WCra WMoo |
| | 'Pink Splash' | CSpr LSou WPtf |
| § | ***platyanthum*** | EPPr MNrw MWhi NBre SRGP WCru WPtf |

| | | |
|---|---|---|
| | - var. ***reinii*** | WCru |
| | - 'Russian Giant' | EPPr |
| | ***platypetalum*** misapplied | see *G.* × *magnificum* |
| | ***platypetalum*** Franch. | see *G. sinense* |
| § | ***platypetalum*** Fisch. & C.A. Mey. | EPPr LRHS NBid NBir NBre SRGP WCru XLum |
| | - 'Genyell' | EBee |
| | - 'Georgia Blue' | WCru WFar |
| | - 'Turco' | EPPr |
| § | ***pogonanthum*** | GLog IFro NBir NChi |
| | ***polyanthes*** | NChi WPtf |
| § | ***potentilloides*** | GCal NBir SRGP WMoo |
| | ***pratense*** | Widely available |
| | - 'Algera Double' **new** | EBee |
| | - 'Bittersweet' | EBee EPPr |
| | - Black Beauty = 'Nodbeauty'PBR | Widely available |
| | - 'Blue Lagoon' | EPPr |
| * | - 'Blue Skies' | LSou |
| | - 'Cluden Sapphire' | CSev EBla EPPr MWhi NChi NGdn NHol NPro WCru |
| § | - 'Double Jewel' | CSpr CWGN EPfP IPot LLHF LRHS MAsh MBNS MBri NLar NMRc WBor WCra |
| | - 'Else Lacey' (d) | EBee |
| | - 'Feebers Double' (d) | CFee |
| | - 'Flore Pleno' | see *G. pratense* 'Plenum Violaceum' |
| | - 'Ford' **new** | NChi |
| I | - 'Himalayanum' | NLar |
| | - 'Hocus Pocus' | EBee ECtt ELan EPfP LRHS MAvo MBNS MBri MDev MWea NBro NLar NSti SBfd |
| | - 'Ilja' | EBee |
| | - 'Janet's Special' | CBod WHoo |
| | - 'Lichtenstein' | NCot |
| | - 'Midnight Blues' **new** | MAsh |
| | - Midnight Reiter strain | CBcs CBct CHVG CHar CPLG CSev CSpe CWGN EBee EPfP GGar IFoB LRHS LSqH MAvo NBro NChi NGdn NLar NPnk SPhx SWat SWvt WCru WFar WPnP |
| | - 'Mrs Kendall Clark' ♀H4 | Widely available |
| | - 'New Dimension' | CBcs EBee ELan EPfP MWea NBre NSti |
| | - 'Okey Dokey' | EBee |
| | - pale-flowered | WPnP |
| | - 'Picotee' | EBee |
| | - 'Plenum Album' | CAby CBod CBre CLAP CSev ECtt ELan EPPr EWes LLHF MAvo MNrw NBPC NEgg NGdn NLar SPer WGwG WPtf WWEG |
| | - 'Plenum Caeruleum' (d) | CHar CMHG ECtt EPPr GAbr GCra MRav NBid NEgg NGdn NLar SWat WFar WSHC |
| § | - 'Plenum Violaceum' (d) ♀H4 | Widely available |
| | - var. ***pratense*** f. ***albiflorum*** | CBot CElw CSam EPPr GCra GMaP IFro LRHS MLLN MNrw NBid NCot NOrc SBfd WCAu WMnd WMoo |
| | - - - 'Galactic' | EBee ECGP EPPr LRHS MLLN MTis NBPC NBir NBre NCGa NLar SMrm SPhx WCot WCra WCru WMoo WPnP |
| | - - - 'Laura'PBR (d) | CPLG CSpr EPPr EWes LRHS LSRN LSou MWea NSti SKHP SPoG |
| | - - - 'Plenum Album' (d) | CDes EBee EPPr MTis NSti STes WCot WPnP |
| | - - - 'Silver Queen' | EBee EBla ECtt EPPr LRHS LSou MLLN MNrw NBir NBre SRGP WFar WMoo WPGP |
| | - 'Purple Heron' | CDes EBee LSRN MCCP MNrw MTPN WFar |
| * | - 'Purple-haze' | CSpr CTca MCCP MCot NLar WHrl WMoo WOut WTou |
| | - 'Rectum Album' | see *G. clarkei* 'Kashmir White' |
| § | - 'Rose Queen' | EBee EBla EPPr MNrw MRav NBir NHol NLar SRGP WCru |
| | - 'Roseum' | see *G. pratense* 'Rose Queen' |
| | - 'Splish-splash' | see *G. pratense* 'Striatum' |
| | - 'Stanton Mill' | NBid |
| | - var. ***stewartianum*** | MRav |
| | - - 'Elizabeth Yeo' | EBee EBla ECtt EPPr LRHS MWea NLar NWad WCra WCru |
| | - - 'Purple Silk' | EPPr |
| § | - 'Striatum' | Widely available |
| | - - dwarf | WCru |
| | - - pale-flowered | CBre |
| | - variegated, white-flowered (v) | WCot |
| § | - Victor Reiter Junior strain | CElw CPrp CSev CSpe EBee ELan EShb GMac LEdu MLHP MMHG MNFA MWhi NBPC NBir NGdn SMrm SPoG SRot WCot WCru WFar WPnP WPtf |
| | - 'Wisley Blue' | EBee EBla EPPr SBch SRGP WHal |
| | - 'Yorkshire Queen' | EBee EPPr NGdn NSti WCru |
| | 'Prelude' | CBre CDes CElw EBee ELon EPPr NBir NCot NLar NPro SRGP SUsu WPtf |
| | ***procurrens*** | CBre CElw COIW CSev CTri EPPr EShb GAbr GCal GCra GGar LLWP WBor WBrk WCru WFar WMoo |
| § | ***psilostemon*** ♀H4 | Widely available |
| | - 'Bressingham Flair' | CFir CPrp EBee EBla EPfP GAbr GCra LRHS MRav NBid NHol SPer SRms WCAu WCru WFar WMoo |
| | - 'Coton Goliath' | EPPr EWes NChi NCot WCot |
| | - 'Madelon' | CElw EBee MAvo NCot |
| | - 'Moorland Jack' | WMoo |
| | ***pulchrum*** | CHid CSpe CSpr EWes EWld LRHS NChi SRGP WCot WPGP WPer |
| | ***punctatum*** hort. | see *G.* × *monacense* var. *monacense* 'Muldoon' |
| | - 'Variegatum' | see *G. phaeum* 'Variegatum' |
| | 'Purple Rain' **new** | NChi |
| | ***pylzowianum*** | GGar MRav NBid NRya SBch WFar WMoo |
| | ***pyrenaicum*** | CRWN EWil GAbr NBre NSti WTou |
| | - f. ***albiflorum*** | EBla GAbr IFro MNrw NBir SAga SRGP WBrk WCot WPer WPnP WTou |
| | - 'Barney Brighteye' | SRGP |
| | - 'Bill Wallis' | CDes CFir CMea CSpe EBee EPPr EPfP EWTr LBMP LLWP LSRN MBrN MLHP MRav NBir NDov NPer SAga SGar SMrm SPhx SRGP WCFE WCot WFar WFoF WHoo WPGP WPnP XLum |
| | - 'Bright Eyes' | LLWP NCot |
| | - 'Isparta' | EPPr IFro NCot SBch SPhx SRGP WBrk WTou |
| | - 'Summer Sky' | GBin SPav SRGP |
| | - 'Summer Snow' | CFir NLar |
| | 'Rainbow'PBR | EPPr MBNS WCra |
| | Rambling Robin Group | ECre EHoe EPPr EPri EWes MCCP NLBP WHil |
| | ***rectum*** | EPPr NBre WCru |
| | - 'Album' | see *G. clarkei* 'Kashmir White' |
| | 'Red Admiral' | CBod EAEE EBee ECtt EPPr GCal GGar LAst LRHS LSou MAvo NCot |

| | |
|---|---|
| | NDov NLar NSti SRGP SUsu WCra WFar |
| 'Red Propellers' | CSpr |
| ***reflexum*** | CPrp EBla EPPr WCru WFar |
| - 'Katara Pass' **new** | EPPr NChi |
| ***refractum*** | CPLG |
| ***regelii*** | CSam EPPr GAuc GLam LEdu LRHS NCot WCru WMoo WPnP |
| ***renardii*** ♀H4 | Widely available |
| - 'Beldo' | MAvo |
| - blue-flowered | see *G. renardii* 'Whiteknights' |
| - 'Tcschelda' | CMHG EAEE EBee EBla ECha ECtt EPPr EShb GAbr GMac LRHS NBir SBfd SMrm SRms SUsu WCra WFar WMoo WPnP XLum |
| § - 'Whiteknights' | EBee NBir WCru |
| - 'Zetterlund' | CPrp EAEE EBee EBla ECGP EPPr EPfP EPri EWTr LHop LRHS MWat NEgg SBfd WBrk WFar WMnd WMoo |
| § ***reuteri*** | CBcs CTsd NChi SChr SGar SRGP WCru WOut |
| 'Richard Nutt' | EBee |
| ***richardsonii*** | CSpe EBee EBla EPPr EPfP GCal LRHS MAvo MCot MNrw NBir NBre NChi NWad SMrs SRGP WCru WPtf |
| - pink-flowered | MAvo |
| × ***riversleaianum*** 'Russell Prichard' ♀H4 | Widely available |
| § ***rivulare*** | EBla NBre NLar WMnd WPtf |
| - 'Album' | CSpr |
| ***robertianum*** | CArn EPPr EWil LLHF MHer SRms WSFF |
| § - 'Album' | EPPr SHar SRGP SRms |
| - f. ***bernettii*** | see *G. robertianum* 'Album' |
| - 'Celtic White' | CBre EPPr GCal IFro MHer SPav SRGP WOut |
| ***robustum*** | ECre EPPr EPri LRHS MGos MNrw NBir NBro SKHP SPav SPlb SRGP WCot WFar WKif WOut WPGP WSHC |
| - Hannays' form | WPGP |
| 'Rosetta'PBR | EBee NCGa |
| 'Rosie Crûg' | SWvt |
| ***rosthornii*** | WCru |
| 'Rothbury Red' | LLHF NChi |
| Rozanne = 'Gerwat'PBR ♀H4 | Widely available |
| ***rubescens*** | see *G. yeoi* |
| ***rubifolium*** | WCru |
| § 'Ruprecht' | LRHS WWEG |
| ***ruprechtii*** misapplied | see *G.* 'Ruprecht' |
| ***ruprechtii*** (Grossh.) Woronow | EPPr GAuc MNrw NBre SRGP WPer WPtf |
| Sabani Blue = 'Bremigo'PBR | CAbP CAby CMac CSev CSpe EBee EPPr EWes LBMP LPla MTis NChi NDov NLar NSti SPer SPoG SRkn WCot WCra WHil WPtf |
| 'Salome' | Widely available |
| 'Sandrine'PBR | CAby CBcs CMea CSev CSpe CWGN EBee ELon EPPr EPfP GAbr GBin GQue LLHF LRHS LSou MLLN MNrw MTis MWea NBPC SMrm SPoG WCot WPnP |
| ***sanguineum*** | Widely available |
| - Alan Bloom = 'Bloger'PBR | EPPr LRHS WCra |
| - 'Album' ♀H4 | Widely available |
| - 'Alpenglow' | EPPr SBch SRGP WBrk |
| - 'Ankum's Pride' ♀H4 | CElw CMMP EAEE EBee EBla EPPr GMac LSou MNFA MTis NCGa NDov NGdn NHar NLar NSti SBch SMrs SRGP SUsu SWat WBrk WCra WCru WFar WMoo WPnP WPtf |
| - 'Apfelblüte' | EBee EPPr GJos IPot MAsh MSCN NLar SSvw WFar |
| - 'Aviemore' ♀H4 | CElw EBee EPPr GBin GCal SBch |
| - 'Barnsley' | CElw CPrp EPPr NBro NPro WHrl |
| - 'Belle of Herterton' | EPPr MAvo NBid NPro SUsu WBrk WCru |
| - 'Bloody Graham' | EBee EPPr MAvo NHaw SBch WMoo |
| - 'Candy Pink' | EPPr |
| - 'Canon Miles' | CElw EBee EPPr LRHS SRGP |
| - 'Catforth Carnival' | EPPr |
| - 'Cedric Morris' | CElw CYeo EBla ECha ELon EPPr GCra LRHS MAvo NBid SMrs SRGP WBrk WCru WPnP |
| - 'Compactum' | EBee WMoo XLum |
| § - 'Droplet' | SRGP |
| - 'Elsbeth' | CElw CHVG CPrp EBee EBla ECha ECtt EPPr EWes GCal NGdn NLar NSti SBfd SPoG SRGP WBrk WCra WCru WFar WHal WMoo WPnP WWEG |
| - 'Feu d'Automne' | EBee EPPr |
| - 'Fran's Star' | see *G.* × *oxonianum* 'Fran's Star' |
| - 'Glenluce' | CElw CMea CPrp EBee EBla ECtt EPPr EPfP GGar LHop LRHS MNFA MRav NDov NOrc SGar SRGP SRms SWat WBrk WCra WFar WHal WMnd WPer WPnP WTin |
| - 'Hampshire Purple' | see *G. sanguineum* 'New Hampshire Purple' |
| - 'Holden' | CElw EPPr WBrk |
| - 'Inverness' | EBee EPPr |
| - 'Joanna' | MAvo |
| - 'John Elsley' | CPrp EAEE EBee EBla ECtt EHoe EPPr LAst LLWP LRHS LSou MAsh MSCN MSpe NBro NGdn SRGP SWat WMnd WPer WWEG |
| - 'John Innes' | EPPr |
| - 'Jubilee Pink' | EBla GCal WCru |
| - 'Kristin Jacob' | EPPr |
| - var. ***lancastrense*** | see *G. sanguineum* var. *striatum* |
| - 'Leeds Variety' | see *G. sanguineum* 'Rod Leeds' |
| § - 'Little Bead' ♀H4 | EBla ECho NWad WBrk XLum |
| - 'Max Frei' | Widely available |
| - 'Minutum' | see *G. sanguineum* 'Droplet' |
| - 'Nanum' | see *G. sanguineum* 'Little Bead' |
| § - 'New Hampshire Purple' | CLAP CPrp EBee ECtt EPPr GGar MNFA NBro NGdn NLar NSti SSvw WCra |
| - 'Nyewood' | CPrp EAEE EBee ECGP ECtt EPPr GGar LRHS MLLN SEND SRGP WBrk WCra WCru |
| I - 'Plenum' (d) | EPPr |
| - 'Pride of Coombland' | SMrs |
| - var. ***prostratum*** (Cav.) Pers. | see *G. sanguineum* var. *striatum* |
| - 'Purple Flame' | see *G. sanguineum* 'New Hampshire Purple' |
| § - 'Rod Leeds' | CLAP EBee MWea NPro SRGP WFar |
| - 'Sara' | MAvo WPnP |
| - 'Shepherd's Warning' ♀H4 | CMea CTri EBee EBla ECtt EPPr GCal MMuc NBir NLar SEND SRGP SUsu SWat WCra WCru WFar WHoo WTin |
| - 'Shooting Star' | NCot |
| - 'South Nutfield' | CElw MAvo NCot |
| § - var. ***striatum*** ♀H4 | Widely available |

| | |
|---|---|
| - - deep pink-flowered | CSBt MSwo SWvt |
| - - 'Mottisfont' | SBch |
| - - 'Reginald Farrer' | WCru |
| - - 'Splendens' ♀H4 | CElw CSev CWib EBla ELan EPPr LBee LHop LRHS NBid NChi NCot WCra WCru WTin |
| - 'Vision Light Pink' | WWEG |
| - 'Vision Violet' | CElw COlW EBee IFoB MAvo SGar SWvt WBrk WFar WPer |
| - 'Westacre Poppet' | CHVG EPPr EWes |
| 'Sanne' **new** | EBee MAvo WCot |
| ***saxatile*** | EPPr |
| 'Scapa Flow' **new** | GCal |
| ***schlechteri*** | CSpr ECre |
| 'Sea Pink' | EDAr |
| ***sessiliflorum*** | ECou |
| I - subsp. ***novae-zelandiae*** 'Nigricans' | ECha ECho ELan GAbr GGar GKev MCot MHer NLar NWCA SBch SRGP WFar |
| § - - 'Porters Pass' | EBee ECho EHoe EWes MCCP MNrw NBir SBch SPlb WHoo |
| - - red-leaved | see *G. sessiliflorum* subsp. *novae-zelandiae* 'Porters Pass' |
| 'Sheilah Hannay' | CSpe |
| ***shikokianum*** | CLAP CSpr MCCP NLar SAga SGar SRGP WHrl |
| - var. ***kaimontanum*** | WCru |
| - var. ***quelpaertense*** | MAvo WPtf |
| - - B&SWJ 1234 | EBla WCru |
| - var. ***yoshiianum*** B&SWJ 6147 | WCru |
| 'Shocking Blue' | EBee NSti WCra |
| 'Shouting Star' | see *G.* 'Kanahitobanawa' |
| 'Silva' | CElw EBee ECtt EPPr MNrw MRav SWat WCru |
| * 'Silver Shadow' | MCot SPhx |
| § ***sinense*** | CFir CPLG EBee EBla ECtt EPfP GCal GGar MCot MNrw NGdn NLar NMyG SMrs SRGP WCra WMnd XLum |
| 'Sirak' ♀H4 | Widely available |
| ***soboliferum*** | EBla ELan EPPr LRHS NBir NWCA SBch SMad SRGP WCru WMoo WPtf |
| - Cally strain | CDes GCal MAvo |
| - var. ***kiusianum*** | CElw MWea |
| - 'Starman' | CPar CWGN EBee EPPr LRHS LSou MBri MDev MWea NGBo NLar SKHP SPoG SUsu WCra WMoo |
| 'Solitaire' **new** | CDes CGHE |
| 'Southcombe Star' | see *G.* × *oxonianum* f. *thurstonianum* 'Southcombe Star' |
| 'Southease Celestial' | SSth |
| 'Spinners' | Widely available |
| ***stapfianum*** var. ***roseum*** | see *G. orientalitibeticum* |
| 'Stephanie' | CDes CElw EBee EPPr EPfP EWes LRHS MAsh MBNS MNFA MSpe MWea NGdn NLar NSti WCra WPnP |
| 'Storm Chaser' | CMac CSpe EPPr LRHS MWea NSti SPoG SUsu WCra |
| 'Strawberry Frost' | LLHF |
| ***subcaulescens*** ♀H4 | Widely available |
| - 'Giuseppii' ♀H4 | CPLG CYeo EAEE EBee ECtt GEdr GGar LRHS LSou MAsh MHer MLLN MRav NDov NLar NPnk NPri SBfd SRGP SRot SWvt WCra WFar WPnP |
| - 'Splendens' ♀H4 | CSpe CTri EAEE EBee ECtt EPPr LHop LRHS LSou MCot MHer NEgg NPri NSla SRms SWat WFar WGwG WPat |
| 'Sue Crûg' | EBee ECtt ELan EPfP EShb GCra GGar LAst LLWP LRHS LSou MNFA MSCN MWhi NEgg NGdn NLar NSti SDys SPer SPoG SRGP WAul WCru WFar WMoo WTin |
| 'Sue's Sister' | WCru |
| 'Summer Cloud' | EBla EPPr MNFA SRGP WOut |
| Summer Skies = 'Gernic'PBR (d) | CAby CMac CPLG CSev CWCL CWGN EBee ECtt EPPr EPfP GAbr GMaP LRHS LSou MSCN NBPC NBro NEgg NLar SBfd SMrs SPer SPoG SWvt WCAu WCot WCra WFar WPnP WSHC |
| ***suzukii*** | WPtf |
| - B&SWJ 016 | CPLG WCru |
| 'Sweet Heidy'PBR | EBee ECtt EKen EPPr LBMP LLHF LRHS MSwo NCGa NLar NSti SPoG WBor WCra |
| ***sylvaticum*** | CMMP CRWN EBee EBla EWil NBid NGdn NMir WMoo WShi |
| - 'Afrodite' | EPPr |
| - f. ***albiflorum*** | CBot CBre CElw EBee ELan NSti WCru |
| - 'Album' ♀H4 | Widely available |
| - 'Amanda' | EPPr |
| - 'Amy Doncaster' | CDes CElw CPLG EBee EBla ECtt ELan EPPr EPfP GAbr IFro MAvo MLHP MRav NBPC NBir NEgg SPer SPoG SRGP WBor WCot WCra WCru WFar WMnd WMoo WPnP |
| - 'Angulatum' | CElw EBee EPPr MNFA WMoo |
| - 'Birch Lilac' | CElw CSam EBee EBla EPPr EPri GCal LRHS MAvo NPnk SMrm WFar WMoo WPnP |
| - 'Birgit Lion' | EBee WCAu |
| - 'Coquetdale Lilac' **new** | NChi |
| - 'Ice Blue' | EBla EPPr GBin MNFA NChi |
| - 'Immaculée' | EPPr MRav |
| - 'Kanzlersgrund' | CElw EPPr |
| - 'Lilac Time' | EBla EPPr |
| - 'Mayflower' ♀H4 | Widely available |
| - 'Meran' | EPPr LRHS |
| - 'Nikita' | EPPr |
| - f. ***roseum*** | EPPr GGar NBre NLar WPtf |
| - - 'Baker's Pink' | CElw EBee EBla EPPr GCra MNFA MNrw MRav NBir SBch SRGP WCru WFar WMoo WPnP |
| - subsp. ***sylvaticum*** var. ***wanneri*** | EBee EPPr WCru |
| 'Sylvia's Surprise' **new** | LRHS |
| § 'Tanya Rendall'PBR | CAby CMHG CMea CSam EBee ECtt ELon EPPr GAbr GBin GQue ITim LRHS MBNS MBri MWea NBPC NDov SPer SPoG WCot WFar WPnP WWEG |
| 'Terre Franche' | EBee EPPr NLar SBch SMrs SSvw WFar WWEG XLum |
| § ***thunbergii*** | CFir CHid EBla EWes LSou SRGP WMoo WPnP |
| - 'Jester's Jacket' (v) | EBee EKen LRHS MCCP MGos MNrw SGar SRGP WBox WFar WHrl WPtf |
| - pink-flowered | SRGP |
| - white-flowered | EPPr SRGP |
| ***thurstonianum*** | see *G.* × *oxonianum* f. *thurstonianum* |
| 'Tinpenny Mauve' | WHoo WTin |
| 'Tiny Monster' | CDes EBee EBla EPPr EWes GBin IKil LSou MAvo MNFA MNrw MWhi |

| | |
|---|---|
| | NGdn NSti SBfd SPhx WBrk WCra WFar |
| ***transbaicalicum*** | EBee EPPr GBin NHaw |
| ***traversii*** | CWib GGar |
| - var. ***elegans*** | CFee CSpe CWib ECtt LRHS |
| ***tuberosum*** | CElw CHid EBla ECha ECho ELan EShb LRHS MRav NBir NBro NCot NGdn NLBP SBch SGar SKHP SPhx WFar WPnP |
| - var. ***charlesii*** | see *G. kotschyi* var. *charlesii* |
| - subsp. ***linearifolium*** | WCru |
| 'Ushguli Grijs' | see *G. ibericum* Cav. 'Ushguli Grijs' |
| 'Vera May' | SUsu |
| 'Verguld Saffier'[PBR] | see *G.* Blue Sunrise |
| ***versicolor*** | CMac CMea COIW CRWN EBee EBla EPPr EPfP GAbr GGar LRHS MAsh MBri MHer MLLN MMuc MNrw SRms WCAu WFar WMoo |
| - 'Kingston' | see *G.* × *oxonianum* 'Kingston' |
| § - 'Snow White' | ECtt EPPr MNrw SRGP WCru WMoo |
| - 'The Bride' | CMea ECtt |
| - 'White Lady' | see *G. versicolor* 'Snow White' |
| 'Victor Reiter' | see *G. pratense* Victor Reiter Junior strain |
| ***violareum*** | see *Pelargonium* 'Splendide' |
| ***viscosissimum*** | SRGP WMnd |
| - var. ***incisum*** | MCCP NBre |
| - rose pink-flowered | NBir |
| ***wallichianum*** | CMac CPou EBee IFro NBir NSti WMoo |
| § - 'Buxton's Variety' ♀H4 | Widely available |
| - 'Chris' | EWes SRGP SUsu |
| - 'Crystal Lake'[PBR] | CBcs CWGN EBee EKen EPfP EWTr IPot LAst LSou MBNS MBri MLLN NBir NLar NSti SMrm WCot WCra |
| - pale blue-flowered | CElw |
| - 'Pink Buxton' | EBee EWes GMac NLar |
| - pink-flowered | CSpr GCal GKev WCru |
| - 'Rosie' | SRGP |
| - 'Syabru' | EBla LRHS MNrw NLar WFar WMoo |
| 'Wednesday's Child' | WFar |
| ***wilfordii*** misapplied | see *G. thunbergii* |
| Wisley hybrid | see *G.* 'Khan' |
| ***wlassovianum*** | Widely available |
| - 'Blue Star' | IPot MRav NPro SRGP WCra WFar |
| § ***yeoi*** | CSpe EPPr NBir NBro NSti SRGP WCru WOut |
| ***yesoense*** | EBla EPPr NBir NSti SRGP |
| - var. ***nipponicum*** | WCru |
| ***yoshinoi*** misapplied | see *G. thunbergii* |
| ***yoshinoi*** Makino | MWhi WPtf |
| ***yunnanense*** misapplied | see *G. pogonanthum* |
| ***yunnanense*** ambig. | CFir |

## *Gerbera* (*Asteraceae*)

| | |
|---|---|
| 'Brandy' **new** | WHlf |
| (Everlast Series) Everlast Carmine = 'Amgerbcar' | LBuc LHop LRHS LSou MBNS NGBo SBfd SMrm SPoG WHil WHlf |
| - Everlast Orange = 'Amgerbora' **new** | LRHS |
| - Everlast Pink = 'Amgerbpink' | LBuc LRHS LSou MBNS NGBo SBfd SHar SPoG STes WHil WHlf |
| - Everlast White = 'Amgerbwhi' | LBuc LHop LRHS NGBo SBfd SHar SMrm SPoG STes WHil WHlf |
| - Everlast Yellow **new** | LSou MBNS SBfd WHil |
| 'Jilly' **new** | WHlf |
| 'Orangina' **new** | WCot |
| 'Pam' **new** | WCot |
| 'Rachel' **new** | WCot WHlf |
| 'Sunny' **new** | WCot |

## *Gesneria* (*Gesneriaceae*)

| | |
|---|---|
| ***cardinalis*** | see *Sinningia cardinalis* |
| * ***macrantha*** 'Compacta' | EShb |

## *Gethyllis* (*Amaryllidaceae*)

| | |
|---|---|
| ***afra*** 'Paarl' | ECho |
| ***barkerae*** | ECho |
| - 'Nardouwsberg' | ECho |
| - subsp. ***paucifolius*** | ECho |
| ***britteniana*** 'Rietputs' | ECho |
| ***ciliaris*** | ECho |
| - 'Porterville' | ECho |
| ***grandiflora*** | ECho |
| ***gregoriana*** | ECho |
| ***hallii*** 'Komiesberg' | ECho |
| ***linearis*** 'Piketburg' | ECho |
| ***oligophylla*** 'Moedverloor' | ECho |
| ***transkarooica*** 'Waboomsberg' | ECho |
| ***verticillata*** | ECho |
| - 'Pikenierskloof' | ECho |
| ***villosa*** | ECho |

## *Gethyum* (*Alliaceae*)

| | |
|---|---|
| ***atropurpureum*** | WCot |

## *Geum* ✿ (*Rosaceae*)

| | |
|---|---|
| from India | GCal |
| 'Abendsonne' | CDes CElw MAvo MSpe SBri SUsu WWEG |
| ***aleppicum*** | CFee NBre XLum |
| ***alpinum*** | see *G. montanum* |
| ***andicola*** | NBre |
| 'Apricot Beauty' | CWCL |
| 'Baby Tangerine' **new** | NMen |
| 'Beech House Apricot' | CAby CBre CElw CLAP EBee EBla ECtt EPri GCra LRHS MAvo MNFA MNrw MRav NCGa NChi NHol NLar NPro SApp SBri SPoG WMoo WPnP WTin WWEG XLum |
| 'Bell Bank' | Widely available |
| 'Birkhead's Creamy Lemon' | CElw MAvo NBir SBri |
| 'Blazing Sunset' (d) | Widely available |
| 'Blood Orange' **new** | NPro |
| N 'Borisii' | Widely available |
| 'Bremner's Gold' **new** | SBri |
| 'Bremner's Nectarine' | CElw MAvo MSpe NChi WWEG |
| ***bulgaricum*** | CElw EBee MRav NBir NLar NPro NRya WTin XLum |
| 'Butterscotch' | EBee MAvo |
| ***calthifolium*** | EPPr LRHS MCCP MRav NBre NBro |
| ***capense*** | NBre NPro SPlb |
| - JJ&JH 9401271 | EBee |
| § ***chiloense*** | EBla LEdu |
| - 'Farncombe' | NCot |
| - 'Red Dragon' | CWCL EBee LLHF LSRN MAvo NBPC NBre SWvt |
| 'Chipchase' | GJos MAvo NCGa NChi SHar WHoo WWEG |
| ***coccineum*** misapplied | see *G. chiloense* |
| ***coccineum*** ambig. | NCGa |
| - 'Ann' | EPPr EPri MSpe |
| - 'Cooky' | CElw CSam EBla EPfP GJos LRHS MSCN NGBl NLar NPri SPad SPoG SRms SWal SWvt WFar WOut WPer WWEG |
| - 'Eos' | CDes CElw CSpe CWCL EBee EBla ECtt EWes LEdu MAsh MAvo MBri |

| | |
|---|---|
| | NGdn NLar NPro SPoG WCot WWEG |
| – 'Queen of Orange' | CEnt CSpr WRHF |
| – 'Werner Arends' | CMHG EBee EBla GAbr GCal MAvo MBri MNrw MRav NDov SBri WCot WFar WMoo WWEG |
| 'Coppertone' | CElw CLAP EBee EBla ECtt ELan EPri LRHS MRav MSpe NBir NBro NCGa NChi NRya SBri WAul WHoo WMoo WTin |
| 'Cream Crackers' **new** | NPro |
| 'Custard Pie' **new** | NPro |
| 'Diana' | EBla MNrw NCot NPro SBri WWEG |
| 'Dingle Apricot' | CElw ECtt GAbr GBin MNrw MRav MSpe NBir WWEG |
| 'Dolly North' (d) | CCVN EBee EBla EPyc GAbr GMac MArl MAvo MNrw MRav MSpe NBro NGdn WCAu WHal WWEG |
| ***elatum*** | EBee EBla |
| 'Fancy Frills' | MDKP |
| 'Farmer John Cross' | CAby CBre CDes CElw CLAP EBee EBla ECtt EPri GBin GJos LPla MAvo MNrw MSpe NCGa NCot NLar SBri WHal WMoo WWEG |
| ***fauriei* × *kamtschatica*** | EBla |
| 'Feuermeer' | EBee EBla MAvo MSpe NLar NPro SBri |
| 'Fire Opal' (d) ♀H4 | CElw EBee EWes LPla MAvo NBir NBre SBri WMoo WWEG |
| 'Fireball' | MAvo NBre |
| 'Flame' | CElw MAvo SBri |
| 'Flames of Passion' PBR | CCVN CHar CWCL CWGN EBee EBla ECtt GMac GQue LLWG LSou MBNS MLLN NBPC NBir NDov NLar SPad SRGP WCAu WCot WCra WHil WWEG |
| 'Georgenberg' | Widely available |
| 'Hannay's' | MAvo MSpe SBri SUsu |
| 'Herterton Primrose' | CDes CElw CFir CWCL EBla ECtt EPPr GCal LLHF LLWG MAvo MSpe MTis NCGa NSti SBri SUsu WHal WHoo WWEG |
| 'Hilltop Beacon' (d) | CElw SBri WHoo |
| ***hispidum*** | SGar |
| 'Honeydew' **new** | MAvo |
| * ***hybridum luteum*** | NSti SBri |
| × ***intermedium*** | CBre EBla EPPr MAvo NGdn NLar NPro SBri WFar WMoo WWEG |
| – 'Diane' | CDes GJos MAvo MSpe NBre NChi SUsu WHoo |
| 'Jolly Roger' **new** | NPro |
| 'Karlskaer' | CElw CWCL EBee EBla ECtt EPri EWTr EWes GBin GQue LHop LRHS MAsh MAvo MBri MNrw MSpe MTis NGdn NLar SAga SBri SMrm WCot WFar WMoo WNew WPnP WPtf WWEG |
| 'Kashmir' | SBri |
| 'Kath Inman' | SBri WWEG |
| 'Lady Stratheden' (d) ♀H4 | Widely available |
| 'Lemon Delight' **new** | CElw |
| 'Lemon Drops' | Widely available |
| 'Lionel Cox' | Widely available |
| 'Lisanne' | CElw CSam EBee MAvo MSpe NCGa NCot NDov SBri SUsu |
| 'Little Twister' **new** | NPro |
| ***macrophyllum*** | EBee |
| ***magellanicum*** | EBla EWes NBre NLar |
| 'Mandarin' (d) | CDes CElw CFir EBla GAbr GCal MAvo SBri |
| 'Mango Lassi' | MAvo WCAu |
| 'Marmalade' | EBee EBla ECtt ELon EPri EWTr GAbr GJos LLWG MNrw MSpe MTis NBre NCGa NLar NMRc NPnk NPro SSvw SUsu WHrl WKif WMoo WOut WWEG |
| § ***montanum*** ♀H4 | CEnt EBla ECho EDAr GAuc GCra GGar GKev LRHS MAsh MMuc NBir NBro NPri NRya SEND SPet SRms WMoo WWEG |
| 'Moonlight Serenade' **new** | NPro |
| 'Moorland Sorbet' | NCot SBri WFar WMoo WPtf WWEG |
| 'Mrs J. Bradshaw' (d) ♀H4 | Widely available |
| 'Mrs W. Moore' | CBre CDes CElw CLAP CWCL CWGN EBee EBla ECtt EPPr EShb GAbr GJos MAvo MHer MNrw MTis NBir NCGa NChi NLBP NLar NPnk NPro SBri SRGP WHoo WMoo WWEG |
| 'Nordek' | EAEE EBee ECtt GAbr GCal GJos MNFA MRav NDov NEgg NGdn SBri WWEG |
| 'Octavie' **new** | SBri |
| 'Orangeman' | MAvo MNrw |
| ***parviflorum*** | NBre NBro |
| 'Paso Doble' | CElw |
| ***pentapetalum*** | see *Sieversia pentapetala* |
| – 'Flore Pleno' (d) | WAbe |
| 'Pink Frills' | CAby CElw CWCL EBee EBla ECtt EPPr EPri EWes GAbr GQue LLWG LPla MAvo MRav MSpe NCGa NLar SBri SMrm STes WCAu WWEG |
| 'Poco' | NPro SBri |
| 'Pomelos' **new** | SBri |
| ***ponticum*** | GAuc |
| 'Present' | CElw EBee EBla ECtt MAvo NBre NCGa NChi NPro SBri WWEG |
| 'Primrose' | GAbr GJos GQue NGdn NLar NPro SBri |
| 'Prince of Orange' (d) | CElw EBla GAbr MAvo MNrw MRav NBre WFar WHrl WWEG |
| 'Prinses Juliana' | Widely available |
| ***pyrenaicum*** | EBla NBre NCGa |
| ***quellyon*** | see *G. chiloense* |
| I 'Rearsby Hybrid' | MAvo MRav MSpe SPlb SUsu WHoo WWEG |
| 'Red Wings' (d) | EBee EBla EPPr GCal MAvo MRav NBir NCGa NPro SBri SHar SUsu WWEG |
| § ***reptans*** | GBin |
| × ***rhaeticum*** | NWCA |
| ***rhodopeum*** | LLHF |
| 'Rijnstroom' | EBee EBla ELan MAvo MSpe NBPC WCAu WPtf |
| ***rivale*** | CArn CBen CHab COlW EBee EBla EHon EPfP EWil MCot MHer MNHC NBro NLan NMir NPer SPet SPlb SRms SWat WFar WMAq WMoo WPer WWEG |
| – 'Album' | Widely available |
| – 'Apricot' | SBri |
| – 'Barbra Lawton' | EBla MAvo MDKP MSpe SBri WWEG |
| – 'Cream Drop' | EBla LLWG MSpe NCGa NChi NPnk NPro SBri SMrm WWEG |
| – cream-flowered, from Tien Shan, China | CFee |
| – 'Leonard's Double' (d) | CPrp CSev WFar WNew WWEG |
| – 'Leonard's Variety' | Widely available |

| | |
|---|---|
| – 'Marika' | CAby CCVN CHid CRow EBee EBla EPri GMac LRHS MSpe NBre NCGa NCot SBri SMrm SRGP WMoo WWEG |
| – 'Marmalade' | CBre CElw CWCL EBla NBPC NChi SApp SBri SUsu |
| – 'Snowflake' | MAvo MSpe NPro |
| 'Rubin' | CElw EBla ECtt EPPr EPyc GCra NBre NBro NDov SBri SUsu WCAu |
| 'Rusty Young' new | NPro |
| 'Savanna Sunset' new | NPro |
| 'Sigiswang' | CDes CElw EBee EWes GAbr GJos GMac MNrw MRav NBre NPro SBri SMrm WCAu WWEG |
| 'Stacey's Sunrise' | NPro |
| 'Starker's Magnificum' | MAvo WCot |
| 'Strawberries and Cream' new | NPro |
| 'Sunrise' (d) new | WHil |
| 'Tangerine' | EBla EPri LSou MRav MSpe NPro SBri WWEG |
| 'Terracotta' new | MAvo MTis |
| 'Tinpenny Orange' | CElw SBri WTin WWEG |
| × ***tirolense*** | EBee EBla NBre NCGa NPro |
| 'Totally Tangerine' | LRHS |
| ***triflorum*** | CElw EBee EBla EShb MCCP MNrw NLar NPnk SPhx STes WFar WTin |
| – var. ***campanulatum*** | CFir NPro WWEG |
| ***urbanum*** | CArn CHab EWil GJos NLan SWat WHer WHfH WMoo |
| – from Patagonia | EBla MDKP |
| 'Wallace's Peach' | SBri SWal |

## *Gevuina* (*Proteaceae*)

| | |
|---|---|
| ***avellana*** | CBcs CHEx WPGP |

## *Gilia* ✿ (*Polemoniaceae*)

| | |
|---|---|
| ***achilleifolia*** | SPhx |
| ***aggregata*** | see *Ipomopsis aggregata* |
| ***californica*** | see *Leptodactylon californicum* |

## *Gillenia* (*Rosaceae*)

| | |
|---|---|
| ***stipulata*** | CLAP EBee LEdu NLar SPhx SUsu |
| ***trifoliata*** ♀H4 | Widely available |

## *Ginkgo* (*Ginkgoaceae*)

| | |
|---|---|
| ***biloba*** ♀H4 | Widely available |
| – B&SWJ 8753 | WCru |
| – 'Autumn Gold' (m) | CBcs CEnd CMCN EBee ECrN LRHS MBlu MGos MPkF NLar SBig SLim |
| – 'Barabits Nana' | SBig |
| – 'Beijing Gold' | MBlu MPkF NLar SMad |
| – 'California Sunset' | NLar SMad |
| – 'Chase Manhattan' | MPkF |
| – 'Chi-chi' | MPkF SBig SLim |
| – 'Chotek' | SBig |
| – 'Chris' Dwarf' | NLar |
| – 'Doctor Causton' (f) | CAgr |
| – 'Doctor Causton' (m) | CAgr |
| – 'Eastern Star' (f) new | CAgr |
| – 'Elmwood' | NLar |
| – 'Elsie' | SBig |
| – 'Fairmount' (m) | CMCN MBlu SBig |
| – 'Fastigiata' (m) | CMCN EPfP ESwi MBlu MGos |
| – 'Gnome' | ESwi LSRN MGos MPkF |
| – 'Golden Globe' | ESwi MPkF NLar |
| – 'Gresham' new | MPkF |
| – 'Horizontalis' | CMen MBlu SBig SLim |
| – 'Jade Butterflies' | CBcs MBlu MBri MPkF NLar SLim |
| – 'Jerry Vercade' new | MPkF |
| – 'King of Dongting' (f) | CAgr CMCN ESwi MBlu SBig |
| – 'Lakeview' (m) | MPkF |
| – 'Mariken' | ELan ESwi GKin MBri MGos MPkF NLar SBig SLim SMad SPoG |
| – 'Mayfield' (m) | SBig |
| – Ohazuki Group (f) | CAgr SBig |
| – Pendula Group | CEnd CMCN ECrN ESwi MBlu MPkF NPal NPri SGol |
| – 'Princeton Sentry' (m) | CDoC SBig SMad |
| – 'Robbie's Twist' | MPkF |
| – 'Saratoga' (m) | CAgr CBcs CDoC CEnd CMCN CPMA ECrN EPfP ESwi MBri MGos MPkF SBig SLim SMad SSpi |
| – 'Sinclair' new | MPkF |
| – 'Tit' | CEnd CMCN CMen EPfP ESwi LRHS MGos NLar SBig |
| – 'Tremonia' | CMCN EPfP MBlu MPkF NLar SBig SLim |
| – 'Troll' | CDoC MBlu NLar SBig SCoo SLim SMad |
| – 'Tubifolia' | CMCN CMen ESwi MBlu MPkF NLar SBig SLim |
| – 'Umbrella' | SBig |
| – Variegata Group (v) | CMCN CMen CPMA ESwi MGos MPkF NLar SBig SLim SPoG |
| – 'W. B.' new | MPkF |

## ginseng see *Panax ginseng*

## *Gladiolus* (*Iridaceae*)

| | |
|---|---|
| sp. | MNrw |
| ***abyssinucus*** | GCal |
| ***acuminatus*** | WCot |
| 'Akuta' (M/E) | CGrW |
| ***alatus*** | ECho |
| – 'Rawsonville' new | ECho |
| 'Alba' (N) | CGrW |
| 'Alexandra' (P) | WCot |
| 'Allosius' (S) | CGrW |
| 'Alpen Glow' (L) | CGrW |
| 'Amanda Mahy' (N) | LAma |
| 'Amsterdam' (G) | CGrW |
| 'Andre Viette' | LLHF WCot |
| ***angustus*** | CDes CGrW WCot |
| ***antakiensis*** | CPou |
| 'Antica' (L) | CGrW |
| 'Antique Lace' (L) | CGrW |
| 'Antique Rose' (M) | WCot |
| 'Anyu S' (L) | CGrW |
| 'Atom' (S/P) | CAvo CBro CFFs CGrW ECho LAma |
| ***aureus*** | WCot |
| Barnard hybrids | CGrW |
| 'Beautiful Angel' | CGrW |
| 'Beauty Bride' (L) | CGrW |
| 'Beauty of Holland' PBR (L) | CGrW |
| 'Big Boss' (G) | CGrW |
| 'Black Jack' | ERCP |
| 'Black Star' new | EPfP SPer |
| 'Blackbird' (S) | CGrW |
| 'Blue Tropic' | CSut |
| 'Bonfire' (G) | CGrW |
| 'Boone' | SMrm WCot |
| × ***brenchleyensis*** | CPen |
| ***brevifolius*** 'Somerset West' | ECho |
| – 'Villiersdorp' new | ECho |
| 'Brittania' (L) | CGrW |
| ***byzantinus*** | see *G. communis* subsp. *byzantinus* |

| |  |  |
|---|---|---|
| | ***caeruleus*** 'Saldanha' | ECho |
| | ***callianthus*** | see *G. murielae* |
| | ***cardinalis*** | CDes CPne CPrp CRDP GBin GCal GGar IBlr LEdu SAga SChr SKHP WCru |
| | ***carinatus*** | CDes CGrW ECho GGar WCot |
| | ***carinatus* × *huttonii*** 'Purple Spray' | WCot |
| | ***carinatus* × *orchidiflorus*** | WCot |
| | 'Carine' (N) | GKev LAma |
| | ***carmineus*** | CGrW ECho LWst WCot |
| | ***carneus*** | CGrW CPen ECho EPot GCal SDeJ |
| | 'Carquirenne' (G) | CGrW |
| | ***caryophyllaceus*** | CGrW ECho |
| | 'Charm' (N/Tub) | CBro CPrp LAma |
| | 'Charming Beauty' (Tub) | ECho LAma |
| | 'Charming Lady' (Tub) | CElw ECho LAma |
| | 'Chartreuse Ruffles' (S) | CGrW |
| | 'Chocolate Smores' (E) | CGrW |
| | 'Cindy' (B) | ECho |
| | ***citrinus*** | see *G. trichonemifolius* |
| | 'Claudia' (N) | CGrW |
| | × ***colvillii*** | CPne IBlr |
| | - 'Albus' | ERCP |
| | - 'The Bride' ♀H3 | CAvo CBro CElw CFFs CMea CPrp EBee EPot GKev LAma LEdu LSRN SDeJ SPhx |
| | 'Comet' (N) | CAvo |
| § | ***communis*** subsp. ***byzantinus*** ♀H4 | Widely available |
| | 'Contessa Queen' | CGrW |
| | 'Coral Dream' (L) | CGrW |
| | 'Costa'[PBR] (L) | CGrW |
| | 'Cotton Queen' (L) | CGrW |
| | ***crassifolius*** | ECho |
| | 'Cream Perfection' (L) | CGrW |
| | 'Creamy Yellow' (S) | CGrW |
| | 'Cristabel' | WCot |
| § | ***dalenii*** | CGrW CPou ECho IBlr WCot |
| | - subsp. ***dalenii*** | CPrp IBlr |
| | - green-flowered | IBlr |
| | - orange-flowered | CDes |
| * | - f. ***rubra*** | IBlr |
| | - yellow-flowered | CDes EBee |
| | 'Daydreamer' (L) | CGrW |
| | ***densifolius*** | ECho |
| | 'Drama' (L) | CGrW |
| | ***ecklonii*** | ECho |
| | - 'Mount Thomas' | ECho |
| | 'Elderberry Wine' (E) | CGrW |
| | 'Elvira' (N) | ECho GKev LAma |
| | 'Emerald Spring' (S) | CGrW WCot |
| | ***equitans*** | CGrW |
| | 'Esta Bonita' (G) | CGrW |
| | 'Evergreen' **new** | ERCP |
| | 'Extasy'[PBR] (L) | CGrW |
| | 'Felicta' (L) | CGrW |
| | 'Finishing Touch'[PBR] (L) | CGrW |
| | ***flanaganii*** | CDes CMea CPBP CPLG CSpe ECho EPot GBin GCal ITim LLHF LWst NSla SChr WAbe WCot WHil |
| | - JCA 261.000 | EBee SKHP |
| | 'Flevo Cosmic' (Min) | CGrW |
| | 'Flevo Dancer' (S) | CGrW |
| | 'Flevo Eclips'[PBR] (G) | CGrW |
| | 'Flevo Eyes'[PBR] (L) | CGrW |
| | 'Flevo Focus' | CGrW |
| | 'Flevo Junior' (S) | CGrW |
| | 'Flevo Libre'[PBR] (L) | CGrW |
| | 'Flevo Primo' (S) | CGrW |
| | 'Flevo Smile' (S) | CGrW WCot |
| | 'Flevo Souvenir'[PBR] (L) | CGrW |
| | 'Flevo Sunset'[PBR] (L) | CGrW |
| | 'Flevo Vito' (Min) | CGrW |
| | ***floribundus*** hort. | ECho |
| | - subsp. ***fasciatus*** **new** | CGrW |
| | ***fourcadei*** | CGrW ECho |
| | 'Frangine' (L) | CGrW |
| | 'French Silk' (L) | CGrW |
| | ***garnieri*** | CDes |
| | ***geardii*** | WCot WHil |
| | 'Gold Struck' (L) | CGrW |
| | 'Good Luck' (N) | CBro |
| | ***gracilis*** | ECho WCot |
| | ***grandis*** | see *G. liliaceus* |
| | 'Green Star' (L) | CGrW |
| | 'Green Woodpecker' (M) | EBee |
| | ***gueinzii*** 'Mossel Bay' | ECho |
| | 'Halley' (N) | CGrW ECho GKev LAma |
| | ***hirsutus*** | CGrW ECho |
| | 'Holland Pearl' (B) | ERCP |
| | 'Huron County' (L) | CGrW |
| | 'Huron Frost' (L) | CGrW |
| | 'Huron Jewel' (M) | CGrW |
| | 'Huron Pleasure' | CGrW |
| | 'Huron Silk' (L) | CGrW |
| | ***huttonii*** | CDes CGrW ECho WCot |
| | ***huttonii* × *tristis*** | CPou |
| | ***huttonii* × *tristis*** var. ***concolor*** | CDes WCot |
| | 'Ibadan'[PBR] (L) | CGrW |
| | 'Ice Cream' | SPer |
| | ***illyricus*** | CGrW CSam ECho GCal WShi |
| | ***imbricatus*** | CGrW ECho |
| | - RS 0572 | LWst |
| | 'Impressive' (N) | CBro LAma |
| | ***inflatus*** | CGrW ECho |
| | - 'Ceres' | ECho |
| | 'Inspector's Choice' (M) | CGrW |
| | ***involutus*** | CGrW |
| | - 'Mossel Bay' | ECho |
| | 'Irish Blessing' (S) | CGrW |
| § | ***italicus*** | CGrW CHid CPen EBee ELan GCal GKev SKHP WHil XLum |
| | 'Jayvee' (S) | CGrW |
| | 'Jester' (L) | CSut |
| | 'Jim S' (G) | CGrW |
| | ***kotschyanus*** | ECho |
| | 'Lady Lucille' (M) | CGrW |
| | 'Lavender Flare' (S) | CGrW |
| | 'Lemon Zest' (M) | CGrW |
| | ***leptosiphon*** | CGrW SGar |
| | - 'Molenaars River' | ECho |
| § | ***liliaceus*** | CGrW ECho WCot |
| | - 'Caledon' | ECho |
| | 'Little Rainbow' (P) | WCot |
| | 'Little Wiggy' (P) | CGrW |
| | ***longicollis*** | ECho |
| | 'Loulou' (G) | CGrW |
| | 'Lowland Queen' (L) | CGrW |
| | 'Lynwood Pinkie' **new** | CMea |
| | 'Mademoiselle de Paris' **new** | ERCP |
| | 'Marj S' (L) | CGrW |
| | ***meliusculus*** | ECho |
| | 'Mexico' | CSut |
| | ***miniatus*** | CDes |
| | 'Mirella' (N) | CAvo CFFs LAma MRav |
| | 'Mon Amour'[PBR] | CGrW |
| | ***montanus*** | CPen |
| | ***mortonius*** | GCal |

| | | |
|---|---|---|
| § | ***murielae*** ♀H3 | CAvo CBro CFFs CGrW CMea EBee ECho EPfP ERCP EWll LAma LEdu LRHS MCot SCoo SPad SPer SPet SPhx SPlb STes WHal WHil WHoo WPtf |
| | 'Murieliae' | see *G. murielae* |
| | 'My Treasure' (L) | CGrW |
| | ***natalensis*** | see *G. dalenii* |
| | 'Nathalie' (N) | CGrW SDeJ |
| | 'Nori' (M) | ERCP |
| | 'Nymph' (N) | CAvo CFFs CMea EPot LAma LEdu SDeJ |
| | 'Oasis'PBR (G) | CGrW |
| | 'Of Singular Beauty' (G) | CGrW |
| § | ***oppositiflorus*** | CPou EBee SChr |
| | – subsp. ***salmoneus*** | see *G. oppositiflorus* |
| | ***orchidiflorus*** | CGrW ECho |
| | 'Oscar' (G) | ERCP |
| | ***palustris*** | CDes CRDP |
| | ***papilio*** | Widely available |
| | – 'David Hills' | GMac NCGa WCot WHal |
| § | – Purpureoauratus Group | CBro CSam EBee IBlr SRms |
| | – 'Ruby' | CAby CDes CMea CPen CPne CPou CPrp CTca EPri GMac IBlr IPot LEdu LSRN NCGa NChi SMad SUsu WCot WHil WHoo |
| | – yellow-flowered | CCse |
| | 'Parade' (G) | CGrW |
| | 'Passos'PBR **new** | ERCP |
| | 'Peach Blossom' (N) **new** | WCot |
| | 'Peach Royale' (L) | CGrW |
| | 'Perseus' (P/Min) | ERCP |
| | 'Perth Pearl' (M) | CGrW |
| | 'Phyllis M' (L) | CGrW |
| | Pilbeam hybrids | CGrW WCot |
| | 'Pink Elegance' (L) | CGrW |
| | 'Pink Lady' (L) | CGrW |
| | 'Plum Tart' (L) | ERCP |
| | 'Powerful Lady' (L) | CGrW |
| | ***primulinus*** | see *G. dalenii* |
| | 'Prins Claus' (N) | CBro CGrW CTca GKev LAma |
| | 'Prinses Margaret Rose' (Min) | CSut |
| | ***priorii*** 'Dasberg' | ECho |
| | 'Priscilla' (L) | MLHP |
| | ***pritzelli*** | CGrW |
| | – 'Quaggasfontein' | ECho |
| | 'Purple Flora' **new** | ERCP SPer |
| | 'Purple Prince' (M) | CGrW WCot |
| | ***purpureoauratus*** | see *G. papilio* Purpureoauratus Group |
| | ***quadrangularis*** | CGrW ECho |
| | ***recurvus*** | CGrW ECho |
| | 'Red Deer' (L) | CGrW |
| | 'Robinetta' (*recurvus* hybrid) ♀H3 | ECho LAma |
| | 'Roma' (L) | CGrW |
| | 'Rose Flame' (L) | CGrW |
| | 'Royal Spire' | CGrW |
| | 'Rusty Red' (P) | CGrW |
| | 'Ruth Ann' | CGrW |
| | 'San Remo'PBR (L) | CGrW |
| | ***saundersii*** | GCal |
| | 'Scarlet Lady' (P) | CGrW |
| | scarlet-flowered **new** | WHil |
| | ***scullyi*** | CGrW |
| | – 'Ceres Karoo' | ECho |
| | ***segetum*** | see *G. italicus* |
| | ***sericeovillosus*** | IBlr |
| | 'Sharkey' (G) | CGrW |
| | 'Show Star' (L) | CGrW |
| | 'Show Stopper' (G) | CGrW |
| | 'Sirael' (L/E) | CGrW WCot |
| | 'Smoke Stack' (L) | CGrW |
| | 'Solveiga' (L/E) | CGrW |
| | 'Sophie'PBR | CGrW |
| | 'Spinners' **new** | IBlr |
| | ***splendens*** | CDes CGrW WCot WPGP |
| | – 'Roggeveld' | ECho |
| | 'Spring Thaw' (L/E) | CGrW |
| | ***stefaniae*** | CGrW |
| | 'Stiena' (L) | CGrW |
| | 'Tan Royale' (P) | CGrW |
| | 'Tante Ann' (M) | CGrW |
| | 'Terry' (G) | CGrW |
| § | ***trichonemifolius*** | CGrW ECho |
| | ***tristis*** | CAby CAvo CBro CDes CElw CGHE CGrW CPen CPne CPou CPrp EBee ECha ECho EDif ELan ELon GBin GCal GKev IPot SAga SDix SUsu WFar WHal WHil WPGP |
| | – var. ***concolor*** | CGrW CPou CPrp EBee WCot |
| | ***undulatus*** | CDes CGrW ECho WCot |
| | ***uysiae*** | CGrW ECho |
| | – 'Gannaga' | ECho |
| | ***vandermerwei*** | CGrW ECho |
| | ***venustus*** | CGrW ECho |
| | 'Video' (L) | CGrW |
| | 'Violetta' (M) | CGrW |
| | ***virescens*** | CGrW |
| | – 'Ceres' | ECho |
| | ***watermeyeri*** | CGrW |
| | ***watsonioides*** | CPou SKHP WCot |
| | 'Wax Ruffles' (L/E) | CGrW |
| | 'White Prosperity' (L) | CSut ERCP |
| | 'Ziporra' (S) | CGrW |

## *Glandularia* see *Verbena*

## *Glaucidium* (*Ranunculaceae*)

| | | |
|---|---|---|
| | ***palmatum*** ♀H4 | CPLG EFEx EPot EWld GEdr GKev GLam LWSt NSla WCru WHal |
| | – 'Album' | see *G. palmatum* var. *leucanthum* |
| § | – var. ***leucanthum*** | EFEx GBin GEdr GKev |

## *Glaucium* (*Papaveraceae*)

| | | |
|---|---|---|
| § | ***corniculatum*** | CAbP CBot CSpe LRHS SPhx |
| | ***flavum*** | CArn CSpe ECha ELan MHer SEND SMrm SPav XSen |
| | – ***aurantiacum*** | see *G. flavum* f. *fulvum* |
| § | – f. ***fulvum*** | ECha LRHS NCGa SDix WCot XSen |
| | – orange-flowered | see *G. flavum* f. *fulvum* |
| | – red-flowered | see *G. corniculatum* |
| | ***grandiflorum*** | SWal |
| | ***phoenicium*** | see *G. corniculatum* |

## *Glaux* (*Primulaceae*)

| | | |
|---|---|---|
| | ***maritima*** | WPer |
| | – dwarf | NWCA |

## *Glebionis* (*Asteraceae*)

| | | |
|---|---|---|
| | ***coronaria*** | MNHC |
| § | ***segetum*** | CHab MNHC |

## *Glechoma* (*Lamiaceae*)

| | | |
|---|---|---|
| | ***hederacea*** | CArn GPoy MHer NMir WHer |
| | – 'Barry Yinger Variegated' (v) | EBee |
| § | – 'Variegata' (v) | SPer SPet XLum |

## *Gleditsia* (*Caesalpiniaceae*)

***caspica*** CArn
***japonica*** EPfP NLar
***triacanthos*** CDul CWib ECrN LEdu SEND SPlb WDin
- 'Calhoun' CAgr
- 'Elegantissima' (v) SPer
- 'Emerald Cascade' CBcs CEnd EBee
- f. ***inermis*** Spectrum = 'Speczam' EBee LRHS MBri
- 'Millwood' CAgr
- 'Rubylace' Widely available
- 'Skyline' LMaj
- 'Sunburst' ♀H4 Widely available

## *Globba* ✿ (*Zingiberaceae*)

***marantina*** LAma
***racemosa*** var. ***hookeri*** HWJCM 471 new WCru
***winitii*** 'Mount Everest' LAma

## *Globularia* (*Plantaginaceae*)

***bellidifolia*** see *G. meridionalis*
***bisnagarica*** GKev
***cordifolia*** ♀H4 ECho EDAr EPot GEdr GKev GLam NBir NMen WFar WPat
- 'Alba' new NHar
× ***indubia*** new IRar
§ ***meridionalis*** CFee EPot EWes GMaP MWat NMen NWCA SAga WPat
- SDR 5444 GKev
- 'Blue Bonnets' GEdr NHar
- 'Hort's Variety' NMen WAbe WPat
***nana*** see *G. repens*
***nudicaulis*** GEdr
***punctata*** CSpe SMrm SRms
***pygmaea*** see *G. meridionalis*
§ ***repens*** EPot GEdr NHar NMen WAbe WPat
***trichosantha*** CFee SRms WFar
***valentina*** GEdr GLam

## *Gloriosa* (*Colchicaceae*)

***lutea*** see *G. superba* 'Lutea'
***rothschildiana*** see *G. superba* 'Rothschildiana'
***superba*** ♀H1 ERCP MBri
- 'Carsonii' ERCP LAma
- 'Greenii' ERCP LAma LWst
§ - 'Lutea' LAma LRHS
§ - 'Rothschildiana' CBcs CRHN EGxp LAma LRHS MOWG SRms
- 'Simplex' CLak
- 'Verschuurii' CLak

## *Gloxinia* (*Gesneriaceae*)

sp. EABi
***nematanthodes*** 'Evita' EShb SUsu
***sylvatica*** EShb WDib

## *Glumicalyx* (*Scrophulariaceae*)

***flanaganii*** GKev
- HWEL 0325 NWCA
***montanus*** CFee

## *Glyceria* (*Poaceae*)

***aquatica variegata*** see *G. maxima* var. *variegata*
***maxima*** CRWN MMuc MSKA NMir NPer SEND SPlb
§ - var. ***variegata*** (v) Widely available
***notata*** SVic
***spectabilis*** 'Variegata' see *G. maxima* var. *variegata*

## *Glycyrrhiza* (*Papilionaceae*)

***echinata*** CArn NLar
§ ***glabra*** CArn CBod CCCN CHby EBtc ELau GPoy MHer MNHC NLar SDix SIde WJek
***glandulifera*** see *G. glabra*
***uralensis*** CArn ELau GPoy MHer SPhx
***yunnanensis*** MHer

## *Glyptostrobus* (*Cupressaceae*)

***pensilis*** CGHE CPLG EGFP WPGP

## *Gmelina* (*Lamiaceae*)

***hystrix*** CCCN

## *Gnaphalium* (*Asteraceae*)

'Fairy Gold' see *Helichrysum thianschanicum* 'Goldkind'
***mackayi*** WAbe
***trinerve*** see *Anaphalis trinervis*

## *Godetia* see *Clarkia*

## *Gomphocarpus* (*Apocynaceae*)

§ ***physocarpus*** CArn CDTJ SBfd

## *Gomphostigma* (*Scrophulariaceae*)

***virgatum*** CPLG EPPr LLWG SAga SMrm SPlb SSvw WCFE WCot WHrl WSHC
- 'White Candy' EBee NLar

## *Gomphrena* (*Amaranthaceae*)

***globosa*** CCCN

## *Goniolimon* (*Plumbaginaceae*)

***collinum*** 'Sea Spray' CMea EDAr MBNS NBre WHil
§ ***incanum*** SMrm
- 'Blue Diamond' EBee
***speciosum*** LLHF
§ ***tataricum*** NBre NLar
§ - var. ***angustifolium*** SRms WPer
- 'Woodcreek' NLar

## *Goniophlebium* (*Polypodiaceae*)

§ ***subauriculatum*** 'Knightiae' WRic

## *Goodia* (*Papilionaceae*)

***lotifolia*** CCCN ESwi

## *Goodyera* (*Orchidaceae*)

***biflora*** EFEx
***pubescens*** EFEx
***schlechtendaliana*** EFEx

## gooseberry see *Ribes uva-crispa*

## *Gordonia* (*Theaceae*)

***axillaris*** see *Polyspora axillaris*

## *Gossypium* (*Malvaceae*)

***herbaceum*** CCCN

## granadilla see *Passiflora quadrangularis*

## granadilla, purple see *Passiflora edulis*

## granadilla, sweet see *Passiflora ligularis*

## grape see *Vitis*

## grapefruit see *Citrus* × *paradisi*

## *Graptopetalum* (*Crassulaceae*)

| | |
|---|---|
| ***bellum*** ♀H1 | CPBP |
| ***filiferum*** | SPlb |
| ***pachyphyllum*** | MSCN |
| § ***paraguayense*** | SEND |

## × *Graptoveria* (*Crassulaceae*)

| | |
|---|---|
| 'Doctor Phillips Pink' | STre |

## *Gratiola* (*Plantaginaceae*)

| | |
|---|---|
| ***officinalis*** | CArn CWan EHon LLWG MHer MSKA |

## *Greenovia* (*Crassulaceae*)

| | |
|---|---|
| § ***aurea*** | ESem NMen SPlb |
| ***diplocycla*** 'Gigantea' | SPlb |

## *Greigia* (*Bromeliaceae*)

| | |
|---|---|
| ***sphacelata*** | IDee |

## *Grevillea* (*Proteaceae*)

| | |
|---|---|
| ***alpina*** 'Olympic Flame' | CBcs CCCN CDoC CPLG CSBt CWib EPfP GBin LRHS MMuc MOWG SBrd SCoo SEND SPoG SRms SVen WBor WFar WGrn |
| ***australis*** new | ECou |
| ***baileyana*** | MOWG |
| ***banksii*** 'Canberra Hybrid' | see *G.* 'Canberra Gem' |
| - var. ***forsteri*** | SPlb |
| ***barklyana*** | MOWG |
| ***baueri*** | MOWG |
| ***beadleana*** | MOWG |
| 'Bonnie Prince Charlie' | MOWG |
| 'Bronze Rambler' | MOWG |
| § 'Canberra Gem' ♀H3-4 | Widely available |
| 'Clearview David' | CCCN CTrC CWGN LRHS LSRN MOWG SCoo SLim SSpi SVen WPat |
| 'Cranbrook Yellow' | CDoC EPfP |
| ***crithmifolia*** | MOWG SPlb |
| 'Elegance' red-flowered | MOWG |
| ***endlicheriana*** | MOWG |
| 'Evelyn's Coronet' | MOWG |
| 'Honey Gem' | MOWG |
| ***iaspicula*** | MOWG |
| ***johnsonii*** | CWSG MOWG |
| ***juniperina*** | CBcs CCCN CPLG CTsd EBee EPfP LRHS MGos SLim SVen |
| - f. ***sulphurea*** | CCCN CDoC CHll CPLG CTrC CTsd ELon EPfP MMuc MOWG SBrd SEND SPlb SPoG WGrn WPat WSHC |
| I ***lanigera*** 'Lutea' | MOWG |
| - 'Mount Tamboritha' | CBcs CCCN CDoC CPLG CTrC EBee EPfP GGar IDee LRHS SPoG SVen WFar |
| - prostrate | MAsh MOWG WCot WGrn WPat |
| § - 'Red Salento'PBR | LRHS |
| ***leucopteris*** | SPlb |
| ***levis*** | MOWG |
| 'Mason's Hybrid' | MOWG |
| 'Moonlight' | MOWG |
| ***olivacea*** | LRHS |
| - 'Apricot Glow' | MOWG |
| 'Orange Marmalade' | MOWG |
| ***paniculata*** | MOWG SPlb |
| 'Pink Lady' | CWGN ECou ELon EPfP LRHS MOWG SCoo |
| 'Poorinda Constance' | MOWG |
| 'Poorinda Peter' | MOWG |
| 'Red Dragon' (v) | LRHS SPtl |
| ***repens*** | MOWG |
| ***rhyolitica*** | MOWG |
| ***robusta*** ♀H1+3 | CTsd EShb MOWG SPlb SSta |
| - 'Red Salento'PBR | see *G. lanigera* 'Red Salento' |
| 'Robyn Gordon' | MOWG |
| 'Rondeau' | CCCN LRHS |
| ***rosmarinifolia*** ♀H3 | CAbb CBcs CDoC CHll CMac CPLG CSBt CTrC CTri CWib EBee EPfP EShb GGar GKin IDee MOWG MWat SArc SBod SCoo SLim SLon SPer SPlb SPoG SSta WCot WFar |
| - 'Desert Flame' | CPLG |
| - 'Jenkinsii' | CDoC CPLG CSBt EBee EPPr EPfP LAst SBfd SLim SSpi |
| 'Sandra Gordon' | MOWG |
| 'Scarlet Sprite' | MOWG |
| § × ***semperflorens*** | CTrC CWib LRHS MMuc MOWG SEND SPlb WGrn |
| 'Spider Man' | LRHS |
| 'Splendour' | MOWG |
| ***thelemanniana*** Spriggs' form | MOWG |
| ***thyrsoides*** | GGal |
| ***tolminsis*** | see *G.* × *semperflorens* |
| ***victoriae*** | CDoC CPne CTsd EBee EPfP GGal GGar MOWG SCoo WCot WPGP |
| - subsp. ***victoriae*** | CPLG |
| - yellow-flowered | LRHS |
| ***williamsonii*** | ECou LRHS MOWG SCoo WGrn WPat |

## *Grewia* (*Malvaceae*)

| | |
|---|---|
| ***occidentalis*** | CDoC MOWG |

## *Greyia* (*Melanthiaceae*)

| | |
|---|---|
| ***sutherlandii*** | CTrC MOWG SGar SPlb |

## *Grindelia* (*Asteraceae*)

| | |
|---|---|
| § ***camporum*** | CWCL SPlb WPer |
| ***chiloensis*** | CAbb ECha SMad WCot XLum |
| ***integrifolia*** | XLum |
| ***robusta*** | see *G. camporum* |
| ***squarrosa*** | WHil |
| ***stricta*** | CArn |

## *Griselinia* ✿ (*Griseliniaceae*)

| | |
|---|---|
| ***littoralis*** ♀H3 | Widely available |
| - 'Bantry Bay' (v) | CAbP CCCN CDoC CTsd CWSG EBee EHoe ELan ESwi LRHS NCGa NWad SEND SLim SPer SPoG SWvt WFar |
| - 'Brodick Gold' | CPLG EQua GGar GKin |
| - 'Crinkles' | CPMA |
| - 'Dixon's Cream' (v) | CBcs CCCN CDul CMac CSBt EBee EPfP GQui IArd IFoB LRHS SGol SLim SLon SPoG SVen |
| - 'Green Jewel' (v) | CBcs CCCN CPMA CTrC CWib ESwi NLar |
| - 'Variegata' (v) ♀H3 | Widely available |
| ***scandens*** | WSHC |

## guava, common see *Psidium guajava*

## guava, purple or strawberry see *Psidium littorale* var. *longipes*

## *Gunnera* ✿ (*Gunneraceae*)

| | |
|---|---|
| ***chilensis*** | see *G. tinctoria* |
| ***cordifolia*** | CPne LLWG |
| ***densiflora*** | GEdr LLWG |
| ***dentata*** | CPne |
| ***flavida*** | LLWG NWCA WGwG |
| ***hamiltonii*** | CAby CSpr ECha EWld GAbr LLWG MAvo NBir NWCA WMoo |
| ***magellanica*** | Widely available |
| - 'Muñoz Gamero' | WShi |
| - 'Osorno' | EBee MMoz |
| ***manicata*** ♀H3-4 | Widely available |
| × ***mixta*** | CPne |
| ***monoica*** | CPne GGar LLWG |
| aff. ***monoica*** | CPne |
| purple-leaved **new** | |
| ***perpensa*** | CBcs CCCN EWTr LLWG WCot |
| ***prorepens*** | CFee CMac CPLG EBee ECha ECou GEdr GGar LLWG NBir SBfd SWat WFar WGwG WMoo WWEG |
| ***scabra*** | see *G. tinctoria* |
| § ***tinctoria*** ♀H4 | CBcs CCCN CHEx CMHG CMac CPLG CWib EBee EBla ECha EHon ELan EPfP GAbr GBin GGar IVic LBMP LRHS NCot NLar SBfd SDix SWat SWvt WFar WPGP |

## *Gymnadenia* (*Orchidaceae*)

| | |
|---|---|
| ***camtschatica*** | NLAp |
| * - f. ***alba*** | LWst |
| ***conopsea*** | ECho EFEx LWst NLAp |
| × ***densiflora*** **new** | NLAp |
| ***odoratissima*** | NLAp |
| - white-flowered | NLAp |

## *Gymnocarpium* (*Woodsiaceae*)

| | |
|---|---|
| ***dryopteris*** ♀H4 | CLAP EFer EFtx GGar GKev GMaP LEdu MMoz MMuc NLar NWCA SRms WAbe WFib WPtf WRic WShi |
| - 'Plumosum' ♀H4 | CBty CKel CLAP EBee EFtx EPfP EPla GBin LRHS NBid NHar NLar WFib WHal WMoo WWEG |
| ***fedtschenkoanum*** | WAbe WRic |
| ***oyamense*** | CLAP EFer EFtx SKHP WRic |
| ***robertianum*** | EFer EWld |

## *Gymnocladus* (*Caesalpiniaceae*)

| | |
|---|---|
| ***dioica*** | CBcs CDul CLnd CMCN EBee EBtc ELan EPfP LRHS MBlu MBri SPer SSpi WDin WPGP |

## *Gymnocoronis* (*Asteraceae*)

| | |
|---|---|
| ***spilanthoides*** **new** | LLWG |
| - 'Variegata' (v) **new** | LLWG |

## *Gymnospermium* (*Berberidaceae*)

| | |
|---|---|
| § ***albertii*** | ECho |

## *Gynandriris* (*Iridaceae*)

| | |
|---|---|
| ***setifolia*** | ECho |
| ***sisyrinchium*** | ECho |
| * - ***purpurea*** | ECho |

## *Gynerium* (*Poaceae*)

| | |
|---|---|
| ***argenteum*** | see *Cortaderia selloana* |

## *Gynostemma* (*Cucurbitaceae*)

| | |
|---|---|
| ***pentaphyllum*** | CAgr |
| - B&SWJ 570 | WCru |

## *Gypsophila* (*Caryophyllaceae*)

| | |
|---|---|
| ***aretioides*** | ECho EPot LRHS NMen |
| § - 'Caucasica' | CPBP ECho EPot GEdr LLHF |
| - 'Compacta' | see *G. aretioides* 'Caucasica' |
| ***briquetiana*** | WPat |
| ***cerastioides*** | CMea CTri ECho ECtt EDAr EPfP EWTr GAbr GGar LBMP LHop LRHS MAsh MRav NGdn NLar NMen NWCA SPlb SRms SWvt WAbe WHoo WNew WPat WPer WPnn |
| ***dubia*** | see *G. repens* 'Dubia' |
| ***fastigiata*** 'Silverstar' | EBee LBuc LRHS LSou SPoG |
| (Festival Series) 'Festival'[PBR] | ECtt |
| - 'Festival Pink' | EBee ECtt GBee GMac LRHS SHar SPoG WFar |
| ***gracilescens*** | see *G. tenuifolia* |
| 'Jolien' (v) | ELan NBPC |
| ***muralis*** 'Garden Bride' | SWvt |
| - 'Gypsy Deep Rose' **new** | LRHS |
| - 'Gypsy Pink' (d) | EPfP SWvt |
| - 'Pink Sugardot' | SBch |
| ***nana*** 'Compacta' | CPBP |
| 'Pacific Rose' | MRav |
| ***pacifica*** | EBee MWea NBre NLar SBfd WPer |
| ***paniculata*** | EBee EPfP NBre NEgg SMrm SRms XLum |
| - 'Bristol Fairy' (d) ♀H4 | CSBt EBee ECha ECtt ELan EPfP GMaP LRHS NLar SPoG SWvt WCAu WWEG XLum |
| - 'Compacta Plena' (d) | EBee ECtt ELan EPfP GMaP LHop LRHS MRav NDov NEgg NGdn SRms WHil |
| - double white-flowered (d) | XLum |
| - 'Fairy Perfect' | EBee IPot |
| - Festival Star = 'Danfestar'[PBR] (Festival Series) | LAst |
| - 'Flamingo' (d) | CBcs EBee ECha IPot LHop MWea NLar SWvt XLum |
| - 'Perfekta' | CBcs EBee SPer |
| - 'Pink Star' (d) | EBee |
| § - 'Schneeflocke' (d) | EBee EPfP GMaP LRHS NBre NLar SPhx SRms WWEG |
| - Snowflake | see *G. paniculata* 'Schneeflocke' |
| - Summer Sparkles = 'Esm Chispa'[PBR] **new** | LBuc |
| ***repens*** ♀H4 | ECtt EPfP GJos MAsh MWat SBch SPlb SWvt WFar WPer XLum |
| - 'Dorothy Teacher' | CMea ECho ECtt LBee LRHS MAsh WGor |
| § - 'Dubia' | ECha ECho ECtt EDAr EPot MAsh MHer MMuc NBlu SEND SPoG SRms WPer WSHC |
| - 'Fratensis' | ECho ECtt LLHF MAsh NMen |
| - Pink Beauty | see *G. repens* 'Rosa Schönheit' |
| § - 'Rosa Schönheit' | EBee ECha EPot LRHS NLar SPer XLum |
| - 'Rosea' | CPBP CTri CWib EBee ECho ECtt EDAr EPfP GJos GMaP LBMP MAsh MMuc MWat NBlu NGdn NWCA SEND SPoG SRms SWvt WFar WHoo XLum |
| - 'Silver Carpet' (v) | WPer |
| - white-flowered | CMea CWib EBee ECho ELan EPfP LRHS NGdn SWvt WPer |
| § 'Rosenschleier' (d) ♀H4 | CMea EBee ECha ECtt ELan EPfP IPot LAst LRHS MCot MRav NCGa NDov NEgg NGdn SBch SPer SRms |

| | |
|---|---|
| | SRot SWvt WHoo WSHC WWEG XLum |
| 'Rosenschleier Variegata' (v) | MAvo WWEG |
| 'Rosy Veil' | see *G.* 'Rosenschleier' |
| § ***tenuifolia*** | EPot GMaP LBee NMen WPat |
| Veil of Roses | see *G.* 'Rosenschleier' |
| 'White Festival'PBR (Festival Series) (d) | EBee GMac LBuc LRHS SPoG WFar |

## *Gyptis* (*Asteraceae*)

| | |
|---|---|
| ***commersonii*** | LHop |

# H

## *Haberlea* (*Gesneriaceae*)

| | |
|---|---|
| ***ferdinandi-coburgii*** | CLAP ECho NMen NWCA |
| - 'Connie Davidson' | GEdr NMen |
| ***rhodopensis*** ♀H4 | CDes CElw CFee ECho GEdr GKev NMen NSla NWCA SRms WAbe WPGP WTin |
| - 'Virginalis' | CElw CLAP NMen NSla WThu |

## *Habranthus* ✿ (*Amaryllidaceae*)

| | |
|---|---|
| ***andersonii*** | see *H. tubispathus* |
| 'Argentine Pink' | EDif |
| ***brachyandrus*** | GCal SRms |
| ***gracilifolius*** | WThu |
| ***howardii*** | ECho |
| ***martinezii*** | CPBP ECho EPot NWCA WCot |
| 'Pinky' | WHil |
| § ***robustus*** ♀H1 | CCCN CPLG CPne EBee ECho EPot EShb LAma LHop NLBP SEND WCot WHil WPGP |
| § ***tubispathus*** ♀H1 | CGHE CYeo EBee ECho EDif EPot GCal NWCA WCot WHil |

## *Hacquetia* (*Apiaceae*)

| | |
|---|---|
| ***epipactis*** ♀H4 | Widely available |
| § - 'Thor' (v) | CDes CLAP EWes GEdr LLHF NMen SUsu WAbe WCot WFar WPGP |
| - 'Variegata' | see *H. epipactis* 'Thor' |

## *Haemanthus* (*Amaryllidaceae*)

| | |
|---|---|
| ***albiflos*** ♀H1 | CHEx CPrp CSpe CTca ECho EOHP EShb LAma LToo SRms STre WCot |
| ***amarylloides*** subsp. ***amarylloides*** | CLak |
| - subsp. ***polyanthes*** | CLak ECho |
| ***barkerae*** | CLak ECho |
| ***carneus*** | ECho |
| ***coccineus*** ♀H1 | CLak ECho |
| ***crispus*** | ECho |
| ***humilis*** | ECho |
| ***kalbreyeri*** | see *Scadoxus multiflorus* subsp. *multiflorus* |
| ***katherinae*** | see *Scadoxus multiflorus* subsp. *katherinae* |
| ***lanceifolius*** | ECho |
| ***montanus*** | CLak ECho |
| ***natalensis*** | see *Scadoxus puniceus* |
| ***pauculifolius*** | ECho |
| ***pubescens*** subsp. ***leipoldtii*** | CLak ECho |
| ***sanguineus*** | ECho |

## *Hakea* (*Proteaceae*)

| | |
|---|---|
| § ***drupacea*** | CBcs CTrC |
| ***epiglottis*** | CTrC ECou |
| ***laurina*** | SPlb |
| ***lissocarpha*** | CTrC |
| § ***lissosperma*** | CDoC ECou EPfP SPlb WPGP |
| ***microcarpa*** | ECou |
| ***nodosa*** | CCCN |
| ***platysperma*** | SPlb |
| § ***salicifolia*** | CCCN SPlb |
| - 'Gold Medal' (v) | CTrC |
| ***saligna*** | see *H. salicifolia* |
| ***sericea*** misapplied | see *H. lissosperma* |
| ***sericea*** Schrad. & J.C.Wendl. | ECou |
| - pink-flowered | SPlb |
| ***suaveolens*** | see *H. drupacea* |
| ***teretifolia*** | CTrC |

## *Hakonechloa* ✿ (*Poaceae*)

| | |
|---|---|
| ***macra*** | CEnt CGHE CKno CSam EBee EHoe EPPr EPla EShb GCal MAvo MLLN MMoz MRav NDov SApp SMad SPhx SPoG WDyG WPGP WSHC |
| § - 'Alboaurea' (v) ♀H4 | CBcs CChe CFee CKno CPLG CWGN EBee ELan EPfP EShb LAst LRHS LSRN MGos MMuc MRav NCGa NPla NWCA SAga SApp SEND STre WFar |
| - 'Albovariegata' (v) | CKno CWan EPPr GCal LEdu MAvo WDyG |
| - 'All Gold' | EBee EPPr EWes GBin LEdu SMad SPoG WCot WWEG |
| - 'Aureola' ♀H4 | Widely available |
| * - 'Mediopicta' (v) | SApp |
| - 'Mediovariegata' (v) | CGHE CWCL EBee EPPr EPla WPGP |
| - 'Naomi' (v) | CWGN EBee EPfP LRHS |
| - 'Nicolas' | CMil CSam CSpe EBee ELon EPfP EWes GBin LLHF LRHS LSRN LSou MCot MLLN NDov NLBP SMad SMrm SPad SPer SPoG WCot WWEG |
| - 'Stripe It Rich' (v) | EWes SBfd SGol |
| - 'Variegata' | see *H. macra* 'Alboaurea' |

## *Halesia* (*Styracaceae*)

| | |
|---|---|
| § ***carolina*** | Widely available |
| - Monticola Group | CBcs CCVT CDul CMCN ELan EPfP GBin IVic MMuc NLar SPer SPur SSpi SWvt |
| - UConn = 'Wedding Bells' | CPMA MBlu |
| - Vestita Group ♀H4 | CDoC CDul CPMA CTho EPfP IDee LRHS MAsh MBlu MBri MGos MRav NLar NVic SPer SPoG SSpi WDin WFar WGob WPat |
| - - 'Rosea' | CBcs CPMA EPfP MBlu |
| ***diptera*** | MBlu NEgg SKHP |
| - Magniflora Group | EPfP MBlu |
| ***tetraptera*** | see *H. carolina* |

## × *Halimiocistus* (*Cistaceae*)

| | |
|---|---|
| ***algarvensis*** | see *Halimium ocymoides* |
| 'Ice Rose' | NBlu |
| § 'Ingwersenii' | CBcs CDoC EBee ELan EWes LRHS MMuc NMun SBfd SPer SPoG SRms |
| ***revolii*** misapplied | see × *H. sahucii* |
| § ***sahucii*** ♀H4 | CBcs CBod CDoC CSBt CTri EBee ECha ELan EPfP LBMP LRHS LTen MAsh MBNS MRav MSwo MWat NPri SBfd SBrd SDys SEND SPer SPoG SPtl SRms STes SWvt WDin WFar |

- Ice Dancer = 'Ebhals'[PBR] (v) — CDoC EBee EPfP LAst MAsh SBfd SPer SWvt
'Susan' — see *Halimium* 'Susan'
§ ***wintonensis*** 🏆H3 — CBcs CDoC EBee ELan EPfP GMaP LRHS MAsh SLon SPer SRms WHar WHHC
§ - 'Merrist Wood Cream' 🏆H3 — CBcs CBod CDoC CMac CSBt EBee ELan EPfP LAst LRHS LSRN MAsh MMuc MRav MSwo NBir SBfd SBrd SEND SLim SPer SPoG SSpi SWvt WDin WFar WPat WSHC

## *Halimium* (*Cistaceae*)

§ ***calycinum*** — CChe CDoC EBee ELan EPfP IVic LRHS MAsh MBri MMuc SAga SBfd SCoo SEND SLim SPer SPoG SWvt WAbe WCFE WDin WGob
***commutatum*** — see *H. calycinum*
N ***halimifolium*** misapplied — see *H.* × *pauanum*, *H.* × *santae*
§ ***lasianthum*** 🏆H3 — CBcs CMac CSBt CWib ELan EPfP LRHS MRav SBfd SLim WKif
- 'Concolor' — CBod CWib LRHS MAsh MSwo SWvt WDin
- subsp. ***formosum*** 'Sandling' — ELan EPfP LRHS MMuc SBrd SLon SRms
***libanotis*** — see *H. calycinum*
§ ***ocymoides*** 🏆H3 — CBcs CDoC CWib ELan EPfP IVic LRHS MMHG MSwo WHar WKif
§ × ***pauanum*** — MMuc
§ 'Susan' 🏆H3 — CBod CDoC ELan EPfP MMHG SCoo SLim SPer SPoG WAbe
§ ***umbellatum*** — CBod EPfP LHop MMuc SEND SPer
***wintonense*** — see × *Halimiocistus wintonensis*

## *Halimodendron* (*Papilionaceae*)

***halodendron*** — CArn CBcs CDul MBlu SBrt SPer WDin

## *Halleria* (*Stilbaceae*)

***lucida*** — CCCN SVen

## *Halocarpus* (*Podocarpaceae*)

§ ***bidwillii*** — CDoC ECou

## *Haloragis* (*Haloragaceae*)

***erecta*** — SVen XLum
- 'Rubra' — WCot WPer
- 'Wellington Bronze' — CEnt CPLG CSpe ECtt EHoe GGar LEdu LRHS MCCP MLHP SDys WBox WHer WMoo XLum

## *Hamamelis* ✿ (*Hamamelidaceae*)

'Amethyst' — CPMA NLar SGol SPtl
'Brevipetala' — CBcs CEnd CPMA NLar
'Danny' — CPMA NLar
'Dishi' **new** — CPMA
'Doerak' — CPMA MBlu
'Fire Blaze' — CPMA
'Girard Orange' — EPfP
× ***intermedia*** 'Advent' — CPMA NLar
- 'Angelly' 🏆H4 — CEnd CPMA IVic MBlu MBri NLar SBir SGol
- 'Aphrodite' 🏆H4 — CPMA EPfP IVic LRHS MBlu MBri MGos MRav NCGa NLar SBir
- 'Arnold Promise' 🏆H4 — Widely available
- 'Aurora' 🏆H4 — CPMA LRHS MBlu MBri NLar
- 'Barmstedt Gold' 🏆H4 — CPMA EPfP IVic LRHS LSRN MAsh MGos MRav NLar SPoG SReu SRms SSpi SSta
- 'Bernstein' — CPMA IVic
- 'Carmine Red' — CMac CPMA NLar
- 'Copper Beauty' — see *H.* × *intermedia* 'Jelena'
- 'Diane' 🏆H4 — Widely available
§ - 'Feuerzauber' — CEnd CMac CSBt CTri LBuc NLar SBir SPer SRms WDin
- Fire Cracker — see *H.* × *intermedia* 'Feuerzauber'
- 'Frederic' — CPMA LRHS MAsh SBir
- 'Gimborn's Perfume' — NLar
- 'Gingerbread' — CPMA LRHS MAsh NLar
- 'Glowing Embers' — CPMA LRHS MAsh
- 'Harlow Carr' — LRHS
- 'Harry' — CPMA IVic LRHS MAsh MBri NLar SBir
- 'Heinrich Bruns' **new** — CPMA
§ - 'Jelena' 🏆H4 — Widely available
- 'John' — MBri
- 'Limelight' — CPMA MBlu NLar
- 'Livia' — CPMA EPfP LRHS MAsh MBri NLar SBir SCoo SPoG SSpi
- Magic Fire — see *H.* × *intermedia* 'Feuerzauber'
- 'Moonlight' — CPMA NLar
- 'Nina' — LRHS MAsh NHol NLar SBir
- 'Ninotchka' **new** — CPMA
- 'Orange Beauty' — CBcs LRHS MBlu SBrd SCoo SGol
- 'Orange Peel' — CPMA EPfP LRHS MAsh MBri NLar SBir SPoG SSta
- 'Ostergold' — CPMA NLar
- 'Pallida' 🏆H4 — Widely available
- 'Primavera' — CPMA CWSG EBee IArd NLar NPCo SBrd SLim
- 'Ripe Corn' — CPMA EPfP LRHS MAsh MBri
- 'Robert' — CPMA EPfP LRHS MAsh MBri SPoG
- 'Rubin' — CPMA EPfP LRHS MAsh MBri NLar SCoo SPoG
- 'Rubinstar' — CPMA
- 'Ruby Glow' — CBcs CMac CWGN CWib EBee ECho EGxp LMaj LSRN MGos NLar NPCo NWea SBfd SCoo SLim SPer WDin
- 'Savill Starlight' — CPMA
- 'Spanish Spider' — MBlu
- 'Strawberries and Cream' — CPMA NLar
- 'Sunburst' — CPMA EPfP LRHS NLar SBrd SGol
- 'Twilight' — CPMA
- 'Vesna' 🏆H4 — CMac CPMA EPfP LRHS MAsh MBlu NLar SBir SCoo SPoG
- 'Westerstede' — CPMA CWSG EBee EPfP IArd LAst LSRN MGos MRav NLar NPla NWea SBfd SBrd SCoo SGol SLim WDin WHar
- 'Wiero' — CPMA NLar
- 'Zitronenjette' — CPMA
***japonica*** — WFar
- 'Pendula' — CPMA MBlu NLar
- 'Rubra' — NPCo
- 'Zuccariniana' — NLar
***mollis*** 🏆H4 — Widely available
- 'Boskoop' — CPMA NLar
- 'Coombe Wood' — CPMA
- 'Goldcrest' — CPMA
- 'Imperialis' **new** — CPMA
- 'Iwado' **new** — CPMA
- 'Jermyns Gold' 🏆H4 — CPMA EPfP LRHS
- 'Kort's Yellow' **new** — CPMA
- 'Wisley Supreme' — CAbP CPMA ELan EPfP LRHS MAsh MBri SGol SPoG SSpi
'Rochester' — CPMA NLar NPCo SBir
***vernalis*** — WDin
- 'Lombarts' Weeping' — NLar
- purple — MBlu NLar

- 'Sandra' ♀H4 CBcs CMCN ELan EPfP LRHS MAsh MBlu MGos MRav NLar SLon SPer SPoG SReu
***virginiana*** CAgr GPoy IDee LLHF MMuc NWea SEND WDin
- 'Mohonk Red' CPMA

## *Hamelia* (*Rubiaceae*)

***patens*** CCCN EShb

## *Hanabusaya* (*Campanulaceae*)

§ ***asiatica*** NCGa NChi SBrt WFar

## *Haplocarpha* (*Asteraceae*)

***rueppellii*** CFee GLam NBro SRms SRot

## *Haplopappus* (*Asteraceae*)

***brandegeei*** see *Erigeron aureus*
***coronopifolius*** see *H. glutinosus*
§ ***glutinosus*** EBee ECha ECho ECtt GEdr NLar NWCA SPlb SRms
***lyallii*** see *Tonestus lyallii*
***prunelloides*** NWCA
- var. ***mustersii*** NGBo WCot
***rehderi*** GJos MWat

## *Hardenbergia* (*Papilionaceae*)

***comptoniana*** ♀H1 CPLG WCot
- shrubby **new** CSpe
***violacea*** ♀H1 CCCN CHII CRHN CSPN CTrC EGxp ELan LRHS MHer SEND SLim SPer WCot
- f. ***alba*** CHII ECou GGar IDee LRHS SEND SLim
- - 'White Crystal' SPer
- - 'White Wanderer' CCCN
- dwarf ECou
- 'Happy Wanderer' CCCN LRHS MOWG SChF
- f. ***rosea*** CCCN EBee LRHS SLim SPer

## *Harpephyllum* (*Anacardiaceae*)

***caffrum*** (F) XBlo

## *Haworthia* ✿ (*Asphodelaceae*)

***attenuata*** EShb
'Black Prince' EPfP EShb SBch
***cooperi*** STre
***cymbiformis*** EPfP STre
***fasciata*** EPfP SEND SWal
***glabrata*** var. ***concolor*** EPfP EShb
***pumila*** ♀H1 SEND
***radula*** EPfP
***tesselata*** see *H. venosa* subsp. *tesselata*
§ ***venosa*** SEND
subsp. ***tesselata*** ♀H1

## hazelnut see *Corylus*

## *Hebe* ✿ (*Plantaginaceae*)

***albicans*** ♀H4 CMac ELan EPfP GGar GKin IFoB LAst LRHS LSRN MBri MGos MRav NBlu NPri SBfd SCoo SLim SPer SPoG STre SWal SWvt WFar XLum
- 'Cobb' ECou
- prostrate see *H. albicans* 'Snow Cover'
* - 'Snow Carpet' CCCN LRHS
§ - 'Snow Cover' EWes LRHS
- 'Snow Drift' see *H. albicans* 'Snow Cover'
§ - 'Sussex Carpet' STre
§ 'Alicia Amherst' CDoy LRHS SPer SRms WCFE
'Amanda Cook' (v) MCCP NPer SGol SPoG
'Amethyst' SBfd
***amplexicaulis*** clone 4 STre
§ 'Amy' ELon GGal LRHS NPer SCoo SPer
× ***andersonii*** CDul EPfP LRHS
§ - 'Andersonii Variegata' (v) LRHS SBfd SRms
- 'Argenteovariegata' see *H.* × *andersonii* 'Andersonii Variegata'
'Andressa Paula' CCCN LRHS
'Anna' **new** EPfP
***anomala*** misapplied see *H.* 'Imposter'
***anomala*** (Armstr.) Cockayne CCCN LRHS
§ ***armstrongii*** ECho GGar SBrd WDin
'Arthur' ECou
'Autumn Glory' CSBt CWSG ELan EPfP LAst LRHS MAsh MGos MLHP MSwo NBir NPri SBfd SBrd SGar SGol SPer SPlb SPoG SWvt WDin XLum
***azurea*** see *H. venustula*
'Azurens' see *H.* 'Maori Gem'
'Baby Blush'PBR LRHS
'Baby Marie' CAbP CAbb CSBt ECho ECou ELan EPfP GKin LRHS LSRN MGos MSwo NBlu NMen NPer SBfd SCoo SPoG SRGP SRms SRot STre SWvt
'Beverley Hills'PBR CSBt LRHS NLar WHar
'Bicolor Wand' CCCN CTsd LRHS
***bishopiana*** ECou EPfP MMuc SCoo
'Black Panther' LAst
'Blue Clouds' ♀H3 LAst LLHF LRHS MSwo SBrd SPer WCFE
§ 'Blue Gem' CTrC SBfd
'Blue Shamrock' SWvt
Blue Star = 'Vergeer 1'PBR EPfP GGar LRHS MAsh NLar SLon SPoG
'Blushing Bride' (v) **new** LRHS
***bollonsii*** GGar
'Boscawenii' ECre
'Bouquet'PBR NEgg
§ 'Bowles's Hybrid' CCCN LRHS MRav MSwo SBod SEND SRms STre
***brachysiphon*** CTrC CTri EPfP MRav SEND SPer WDin
***brevifolia*** LRHS
Bronze Glow = 'Lowglo' **new** LRHS
'Bronzy Baby'PBR (v) SPoG
***buchananii*** ECho EPot GGar MHer NPer STre
§ - 'Fenwickii' ECho NWCA
- 'Minima' ECho EPot
- 'Minor' ambig. GLam
- 'Minor' Hort N.Z. ECho GBin NBir NWCA
***buxifolia*** misapplied see *H. odora*
***buxifolia*** (Benth.) Andersen CMac ELan LHop MMuc NBlu NWea SEND SWal WDin WHar XLum
§ 'Caledonia' ♀H3 CCCN CSBt EPfP LBMP LRHS LSRN MAsh MBri MGos NPer NPri SBfd SCoo SPoG SWvt WFar WHoo XLum
§ ***canterburiensis*** ECou GGar
N 'Carl Teschner' see *H.* 'Youngii'
'Carnea Variegata' (v) EPfP EShb LRHS MSCN SPer SPoG
***carnosula*** GGar NBir SPer WHar
***catarractae*** see *Parahebe catarractae*
'Celine' GGar SBfd SPoG SRGP
'Champagne' CCCN LAst LRHS LSRN NBlu NLar NWad SBfd SCoo SEND XLum

| |  |  |
|---|---|---|
| | Champion = 'Champseiont'[PBR] | EKen LRHS LTen NLar SCoo |
| | 'Charming White' | CChe EQua LRHS LSRN SBfd SWal |
| | ***chathamica*** | ECou GGar LRHS |
| | ***cheesemanii*** | EPot |
| | 'Christabel' | LRHS |
| | 'Claymoddie Blue Seedling' | GGal |
| | 'Clear Skies'[PBR] | ECou LRHS NEgg |
| | 'Colwall' | ECho |
| | 'Conwy Knight' | WAbe |
| | 'County Park' | ECou EWes NMen SWal |
| | 'Cranleighensis' | CTsd SBfd |
| | 'Cupins' | NWCA SWal |
| | ***cupressoides*** | IRar MSCN WDin |
| | - 'Boughton Dome' | CTri ECho EPfP MCot MGos MHer NMen SWal WAbe WCFE WHoo WPer |
| | 'Dazzler' (v) | CAbP |
| | ***decumbens*** | EWes GGar |
| | 'Denise' | LRHS |
| | 'Diamond' | LRHS LSRN SLon |
| | ***dieffenbachii*** | GGar |
| | ***diosmifolia*** | CAbb CBot CDoC ELan LRHS NBlu WAbe WFar |
| | - 'Marie' | SWal |
| | ***divaricata*** | ECou |
| * | - 'Marlborough' | ECou |
| | - 'Nelson' | ECou |
| | 'Donald' **new** | GGar |
| | 'Dorothy Peach' | see *H.* 'Watson's Pink' |
| | 'E.B.Anderson' | see *H.* 'Caledonia' |
| | 'Early Blue' | NBir |
| | 'Edington' | LRHS SPer WCFE |
| | 'Ellie' | LRHS |
| | ***elliptica*** | ECou SBfd |
| | - 'Kapiti' | ECou |
| | - 'Variegata' | see *H.* 'Silver Queen' |
| | 'Emerald Dome' | see *H.* 'Emerald Gem' |
| § | 'Emerald Gem' 🏆H3 | CMac CTri ECho EPfP EShb LRHS LSRN MAsh MBri MGos MHer MMuc MSCN MSwo NLar NMen NWCA SBfd SEND SPer SPlb SPoG STre SWal WPat |
| | 'Emerald Green' | see *H.* 'Emerald Gem' |
| | ***epacridea*** | EWes |
| § | 'Eveline' | CSBt CTri LRHS NBir SPer WKif |
| | ***evenosa*** | GGar |
| | 'Eversley Seedling' | see *H.* 'Bowles's Hybrid' |
| | 'Fairfieldii' | EOHP IRar |
| | 'First Light'[PBR] | CWSG GGar LRHS NPri SGol WHar |
| | 'Fragrant Jewel' | CAbP CWib LRHS SEND SPhx |
| | × ***franciscana*** | ECou |
| | - 'Blue Gem' misapplied | see *H.* × *franciscana* 'Lobelioides', *H.* 'Combe Royal' |
| | - 'Blue Gem' ambig. | ECho ELan EPfP LRHS MRav NBir NPer SBfd SEND SGol SPer SPlb SPoG SRms WHar |
| § | - 'Lobelioides' | GGar |
| | - 'Purple Tips' misapplied | see *H. speciosa* 'Variegata' |
| | - 'Variegata' | see *H.* 'Silver Queen' |
| I | - 'White Gem' | SRms |
| | - yellow-variegated (v) | SPer |
| | 'Franjo' | ECou |
| | 'Frozen Flame' (v) **new** | LBuc SPoG |
| | Garden Beauty Blue = 'Cliv'[PBR] | LBuc LRHS |
| | Garden Beauty Pink = 'Lowink' | LBuc |
| | Garden Beauty Purple = 'Nold'[PBR] | LBuc LRHS |

| |  |  |
|---|---|---|
| | 'Garden Elegance Blue' **new** | LBuc NPri |
| | 'Garden Elegance Blush' **new** | LRHS |
| | 'Garden Elegance Pastel' **new** | LBuc |
| | 'Garden Elegance Pink' **new** | LBuc NPri |
| | 'Garden Elegance Purple' **new** | LBuc |
| | 'Garden Elegance Rose' **new** | LBuc |
| | 'Gauntlettii' | see *H.* 'Eveline' |
| | 'Gibby' | LRHS |
| | ***glaucophylla*** 'Clarence' | ECou GGar |
| I | 'Glaucophylla Variegata' (v) | CTri EPfP LRHS NBir SCoo SPer WKif |
| | 'Godefroyana' | see *H. pinguifolia* 'Godefroyana' |
| | 'Goethe' | SEND |
| | 'Gold Beauty' (v) | LRHS NPri |
| | 'Golden Nugget' | LRHS |
| | 'Goldrush'[PBR] (v) | LBuc SPoG |
| | 'Gran's Favourite' | CCCN LRHS LSRN |
| | 'Great Orme' 🏆H3 | CBot CDul CSBt CWib ECou ELan EPfP GGal GGar LAst LRHS LSRN MAsh MGos MLHP MRav MSwo NPer SBfd SEND SPer SPlb SPoG SWvt WAbe WDin WFar WSFF |
| | 'Green Globe' | see *H.* 'Emerald Gem' |
| | 'Greensleeves' | GGar LRHS |
| | 'Grethe' | SPoG |
| | 'Gruninard's Seedling' | GGar |
| | ***haastii*** | NLar |
| | 'Hadspen Pink' | LRHS |
| | 'Hagley Park' | EPfP LRHS SAga |
| § | 'Hartii' | EPfP LRHS MRav SBfd |
| | 'Heartbreaker'[PBR] (v) | CWSG EGxp ELan GGar LBuc LRHS MAsh MCCP MGos NLar NPri SBfd SCoo SPoG SPtl SWvt |
| | 'Hidcote' | LRHS |
| | 'Hielan Lassie' | LRHS |
| | 'Highdownensis' | LRHS |
| | 'Hinderwell' | NPer |
| | 'Hinerua' | GGar |
| | 'Holywell' | SWal |
| | ***hookeriana*** | see *Parahebe hookeriana* |
| | ***hulkeana*** 🏆H3 | CBot LRHS LSou MHer SAga SWal WKif WPat |
| § | 'Imposter' | SRms |
| | 'Inspiration' | GGar LRHS |
| | ***insularis*** | ECou |
| | 'James Stirling' | see *H. ochracea* 'James Stirling' |
| | 'Jane Holden' | LRHS |
| | 'Janet' | SGar |
| | 'Jean Searle' | LAst |
| | 'Joanna' | ECou |
| § | 'Johny Day' | LRHS |
| | 'Judy' | LRHS |
| | 'Kirkii' | CDul EPfP NLar SBfd SPer SWal XLum |
| | 'Knightshayes' | see *H.* 'Caledonia' |
| | 'La Séduisante' | CTri ECou GGal LRHS MLHP SEND WKif |
| | 'Lady Ann'[PBR] (v) | CSBt CWSG EPfP GGar LRHS NEgg NLar SPoG WHar |
| | 'Lady Ardilaun' | see *H.* 'Amy' |
| | ***laevis*** | see *H. venustula* |
| | ***latifolia*** | see *H.* 'Blue Gem' |
| | 'Lavender Spray' | see *H.* 'Hartii' |
| | 'Lilac Wand' | CTsd |

| |  |  |
|---|---|---|
| | 'Lindsayi' | ECou LRHS |
| | 'Lisa' | EPfP |
| § | 'Loganioides' | GGar |
| | 'Lopen' (v) | ECou |
| | 'Louise' | SGar |
| | ***lyallii*** | see *Parahebe lyallii* |
| | ***lycopodioides*** | EWes WThu |
| | - 'Aurea' | see *H. armstrongii* |
| | 'Lynash' | LRHS |
| | ***mackenii*** | see *H.* 'Emerald Gem' |
| | ***macrantha*** ♀H3 | EPfP LRHS SRms WAbe |
| | ***macrocarpa*** | ECou LRHS |
| | - var. ***latisepala*** | ECou LRHS |
| | 'Magic Summer' **new** | LBuc SPoG |
| § | 'Maori Gem' | GGar NBlu SBfd |
| | 'Margery Fish' | see *H.* 'Primley Gem' |
| | 'Margret' PBR ♀H4 | CSBt CWCL EPfP GGar LAst LBMP LRHS LSRN MAsh MBrN MGos NPri SBfd SCoo SPer SPoG SRGP |
| | 'Marie Antoinette' | GGar LRHS |
| | 'Marjorie' | CDul CMac CTrC ELan EPfP LAst LRHS LSRN MGos MRav MSwo NLar NPer NWea SBfd SBod SPer SPoG SRms WDin |
| | ***matthewsii*** | MAsh WPat |
| | 'Mauve Queen' | LRHS |
| | 'Mauvena' | SPer |
| | 'McKean' | see *H.* 'Emerald Gem' |
| | 'Megan' | ECou |
| | 'Mercury' | ECou |
| | 'Mette' | LLHF |
| | Midnight Sky = 'Lowten' | LBuc LRHS NPri SCoo SPoG SPtl |
| | 'Midsummer Beauty' ♀H3 | CWCL ECou EPfP LAst LRHS LSRN MGos MLHP MRav NBir SBfd SEND SPer SPlb SPoG SWvt WDin WHar WSFF XLum |
| | 'Milmont Emerald' | see *H.* 'Emerald Gem' |
| | 'Misty' | CCCN |
| * | 'Moppets Hardy' | SPer |
| § | 'Mrs Winder' ♀H4 | Widely available |
| | 'Mystery' | ECou SWal |
| | 'Nantyderry' | CCCN LRHS SBrd |
| § | 'Neil's Choice' ♀H4 | CCCN ECou ELon SWal |
| | 'Neopolitan' | LRHS |
| | 'New Zealand' | XLum |
| | 'Nicola's Blush' ♀H4 | Widely available |
| | ***ochracea*** | LRHS SWal |
| § | - 'James Stirling' ♀H4 | CBcs CMac CSBt ECho ELan EPfP EShb GKin LRHS LSRN LTen MAsh MBri MGos MMuc MSwo NBir NLar NPri NWad SBfd SCoo SLim SPer SPlb SPoG SRGP SWvt WDin WFar |
| | 'Oddity' | LRHS |
| § | ***odora*** | CTrC ECou EPfP GGar MMuc SEND STre |
| I | - 'Nana' | EPfP |
| | - 'New Zealand Gold' | LRHS MAsh MMuc SCoo SWal |
| | - 'Summer Frost' | LRHS NWCA |
| | 'Oratia Beauty' ♀H4 | ETod LRHS MRav NLar SEND WHlf |
| | 'Orphan Annie' PBR (v) | CWSG LRHS LSRN SPoG |
| | ***parviflora*** misapplied | see *H.* 'Bowles's Hybrid' |
| § | ***parviflora*** (Vahl) Cockayne & Allan | GGar |
| | - var. ***angustifolia*** | see *H. stenophylla* |
| | - var. ***arborea*** | see *H. parviflora* (Vahl) Cockayne & Allan |
| | - 'Holdsworth' | LRHS SDys |
| | 'Pascal' ♀H4 | CCCN ELan EPfP LRHS LSRN MBri MGos MRav SBfd SCoo SLon SPer SPoG SWvt |
| | 'Pastel Elegance' | LRHS |
| | 'Patti Dossett' | see *H. speciosa* 'Patti Dossett' |
| | ***pauciramosa*** | SRms |
| | 'Pearl of Paradise' PBR | SPoG |
| | ***perfoliata*** | see *Parahebe perfoliata* |
| | 'Perry's Rubyleaf' | NPer |
| | 'Petra's Pink' | CCCN LRHS |
| | 'Pewter Dome' ♀H4 | CMac CSBt ECou EHoe EPfP LHop LRHS MGos MRav SBfd SDix SPer SRms STre SWal SWvt |
| | ***pimeleoides*** | ECou |
| | - 'Glauca' | NPer SGol |
| | - 'Glaucocaerulea' | ECou |
| | - 'Quicksilver' ♀H4 | CAbP CSBt CTri ECou EDAr ELan EPfP GGar LAst LRHS LSRN MGos MMuc MRav MSCN MSwo NBir NPer SBfd SBrd SCoo SPer STre SWal WHar WPat |
| | ***pinguifolia*** | ECou SPlb |
| | - 'Dobson' | LRHS |
| § | - 'Godefroyana' | SWal |
| | - 'Pagei' ♀H4 | Widely available |
| | - 'Sutherlandii' | CBcs CDoC CDul ECho GGar LEdu LRHS LSRN LTen MGos SCoo SWvt WFar |
| | 'Pink Elegance' | LRHS |
| | 'Pink Elephant' (v) ♀H3 | ELan EPfP LBMP LBuc LRHS MAsh NLar NPri SBfd SPoG |
| | 'Pink Fantasy' | CChe LRHS MRav |
| | 'Pink Goddess' | LRHS SRGP |
| | 'Pink Lady' PBR | SGol SPoG |
| | 'Pink Paradise' PBR | CAbP ELan EPfP LRHS SPoG |
| | 'Pink Payne' | see *H.* 'Eveline' |
| | 'Pink Pixie' | LBuc MBri MGos SCoo |
| | 'Pink Princess' | LRHS |
| | 'Pink Wand' | CTsd |
| | ***poppelwellii*** | GLam |
| | 'Porlock Purple' | see *Parahebe catarractae* 'Delight' |
| | 'Pretty in Pink' **new** | LRHS |
| § | 'Primley Gem' | CCCN EQua LRHS |
| | ***propinqua*** | NMen |
| I | 'Prostrata' | CSBt |
| | 'Purple Elegance' **new** | LRHS |
| | 'Purple Emperor' | see *H.* 'Neil's Choice' |
| | 'Purple Paradise' PBR | MBri NEgg SPoG |
| | 'Purple Picture' | ELon |
| | 'Purple Princess' | LRHS SGol |
| | 'Purple Queen' | ELan EPfP EShb LIMB LRHS MCot SEND SPoG |
| | Purple Shamrock = 'Neprock' PBR (v) | EPfP LAst LBuc LRHS LSRN MBri MGos NEgg NLar SBfd SCoo SPer SPoG SWal WHar |
| | 'Purple Tips' misapplied | see *H. speciosa* 'Variegata' |
| | 'Rachel' | LRHS LSRN SLon |
| | ***rakaiensis*** ♀H4 | Widely available |
| | ***ramosissima*** | GGar |
| | ***raoulii*** | NMen WAbe |
| | 'Raven' | LRHS |
| | ***recurva*** | CSam CTri EPfP LRHS MCot MGos MMuc SRms SWal WDin |
| | - 'Boughton Silver' ♀H3 | ELan LRHS SEND |
| | 'Red Edge' ♀H4 | Widely available |
| | 'Red Ruth' | see *H.* 'Eveline' |
| | ***rigidula*** | LRHS MMuc SWal |
| | 'Ronda' | ECou |
| | 'Rose Elegance' | LRHS |
| | 'Rosie' PBR | CSBt LAst LBuc LRHS LSRN NMen SCoo SEND SPer SWvt |
| | 'Royal Blue' | LRHS |
| | 'Royal Purple' | see *H.* 'Alicia Amherst' |

| | | |
|---|---|---|
| | ***salicifolia*** | CCCN CChe CDul CMac CTca ECou ELan EPfP GGar LAst LRHS MDun MGos MRav NWad SBfd SBrd SEND SPlb SRms WFar WGwG XLum |
| | BR 30 | GGar |
| | – 'Snow Wreath' | see *H.* 'Snow Wreath' |
| | 'Sandra Joy' | CCCN LRHS |
| | 'Sapphire' ♀H4 | ECou EPfP LRHS MAsh MGos MWea NBlu NPri SBfd SCoo SWvt WFar |
| | 'Sarana' | CCCN ECou LRHS |
| | ***selaginoides*** hort. | see *H.* 'Loganioides' |
| | 'Shiraz' | LRHS |
| | 'Silver Dollar' (v) | CAbP CCCN CMac CSBt ELan LRHS LTen MGos MMuc NEgg NWad SPer SPoG SWal |
| § | 'Silver Queen' (v) ♀H2 | CMac CSBt ECou ELan EPfP LRHS MAsh MGos NEgg NLar NPer SBfd SEND SPer SPoG |
| | 'Simon Délaux' | ECou LRHS SEND |
| § | 'Snow Wreath' (v) | NWad |
| I | 'Southlandii' | ECho LAst MWhi SGol |
| | ***speciosa*** 'Johny Day' | see *H.* 'Johny Day' |
| § | – 'Patti Dossett' | LRHS |
| | – 'Rangatira' | ECou |
| § | – 'Variegata' (v) | LRHS NPer |
| | 'Spender's Seedling' misapplied | see *H. stenophylla* |
| | 'Spender's Seedling' ambig. | MCot MMuc |
| | 'Spender's Seedling' Hort. | ECou EPfP LRHS MRav SEND SPoG SRms STre |
| | 'Spring Glory' | LRHS |
| § | ***stenophylla*** | EShb GGal MSCN SArc SBfd SDix SEND |
| | – 'White Lady' | GGar |
| | ***stricta*** | ECou LRHS |
| | – var. ***egmontiana*** | LRHS |
| | 'Stuart Fraser' | SWal |
| | ***subalpina*** | CSBt ECho LTen |
| | 'Summer Blue' | LRHS MRav |
| | 'Super Red' | CSBt LRHS SBfd |
| | 'Sussex Carpet' | see *H. albicans* 'Sussex Carpet' |
| | 'Sweet Kim' (v) | CMac LBuc LRHS |
| | 'Tina' | ECou |
| | 'Tom Marshall' | see *H. canterburiensis* |
| | ***topiaria*** ♀H4 | CAbP CChe CSBt CSam ECho ECou EPfP GGar LAst LHop LRHS LTen MBrN MMuc MRav MSwo NBir NBlu SBfd SCoo SEND SPer SPoG STre SWal WFar WGwG |
| | – 'Doctor Favier' | LRHS |
| | ***townsonii*** | ECou LHop LRHS |
| | ***traversii*** | ECou SRms |
| | – 'Mason River' | ECou |
| | – 'Woodside' | ECou |
| | 'Tricolor' | see *H. speciosa* 'Variegata' |
| | 'Trixie' | CCCN ECou LRHS |
| | 'Twisty' | ELan LRHS |
| | 'Valentino'PBR | ELon LRHS NEgg SCoo |
| | 'Veitchii' | see *H.* 'Alicia Amherst' |
| § | ***venustula*** | ECou GGar IArd LRHS MMuc SEND |
| | – 'Patricia Davies' | ECou |
| | ***vernicosa*** ♀H3 | CChe CDul ECho EPfP LRHS MGos MHer NBlu NWad SBfd SCoo SPer SPlb SRot STre SVen SWvt WFar |
| | 'Violet Wand' | LRHS |
| | 'Vogue' | LRHS |
| | 'Waikiki' | see *H.* 'Mrs Winder' |
| § | 'Warley' **new** | LRHS |
| | 'Warley Pink' | LRHS |
| | 'Warleyensis' | see *H.* 'Warley' |
| § | 'Watson's Pink' | LRHS MWea SBrd SPer WKif |
| | 'White Gem' (*brachysiphon* hybrid) ♀H4 | CCCN CWCL ECou LRHS NPer SEND SPer WFar |
| | 'White Heather' | EPfP LRHS NBir SBfd |
| | 'White Paradise'PBR | SPoG |
| | 'Willcoxii' | see *H. buchananii* 'Fenwickii' |
| | 'Wingletye' ♀H3 | CCCN ECho ECou LRHS WGwG XLum |
| | 'Winter Glow' | CCCN LRHS SBfd SCoo |
| | 'Wiri Blush' | LRHS SWvt |
| | 'Wiri Charm' | CAbP CMac CSBt ELon EPfP GGar LAst LRHS MGos MRav MSwo NBlu NEgg SBfd SEND SPoG SWal |
| | 'Wiri Cloud' ♀H3 | CBcs CMac EPfP GGar LRHS MGos MMuc MSwo SBfd SEND SWal |
| | 'Wiri Dawn' ♀H3 | ELan EPfP EWes LRHS MGos MMuc SBfd SEND SWvt |
| | 'Wiri Desire' | CCCN LRHS |
| | 'Wiri Gem' | LRHS MRav |
| | 'Wiri Icing Sugar' | LRHS |
| | 'Wiri Image' | CSBt LRHS NBlu SEND SPoG SWal |
| | 'Wiri Joy' | LRHS SEND SPoG |
| | 'Wiri Mist' | CBcs CDul CTrC GGar LRHS SBfd SCoo SPoG SWal WFar XLum |
| | 'Wiri Prince' | CTrC LRHS |
| | 'Wiri Splash' | CTrC LRHS SGol SPoG |
| | 'Wiri Vision' | CSBt LRHS SEND |
| § | 'Youngii' ♀H3-4 | CMac CSBt CTri ELan EPfP GKin LAst LBMP LRHS MAsh MGos MHer MMuc MRav NBir NMen NPri SBfd SEND SGol SPer SPlb SPoG SRms SWvt WCFE WHoo |

## *Hebenstretia* (*Scrophulariaceae*)

| | | |
|---|---|---|
| | ***dura*** | CPBP |
| | – 'Jeanie' | SDys |
| * | ***quinquinervis*** | LSou |

## *Hedeoma* (*Lamiaceae*)

| | | |
|---|---|---|
| | ***hyssopifolia*** | SPhx |

## *Hedera* ✿ (*Araliaceae*)

| | | |
|---|---|---|
| § | ***algeriensis*** | CDoC SArc WFib |
| | – 'Bellecour' | WFib XLum |
| § | – 'Gloire de Marengo' (v) ♀H3 | Widely available |
| § | – 'Gloire de Marengo' arborescent (v) | SPer |
| | – 'Marginomaculata' (v) ♀H3 | CDoC EPfP EShb LRHS MAsh SBfd SMad WFib |
| | – 'Montgomery' | LRHS LSRN MWht SBfd |
| | – 'Ravensholst' ♀H3 | CMac EShb MRav SGol WFib |
| § | ***azorica*** | EShb WFar WFib |
| | – 'Pico' | EPfP EShb WFib |
| | ***canariensis*** hort. | see *H. algeriensis* |
| | – var. ***azorica*** | see *H. azorica* |
| | – 'Cantabrian' | see *H. maroccana* 'Spanish Canary' |
| | – 'Gloire de Marengo' arborescent | see *H. algeriensis* 'Gloire de Marengo' arborescent |
| | – 'Variegata' | see *H. algeriensis* 'Gloire de Marengo' |
| | ***chinensis*** | see *H. sinensis* var. *sinensis* |
| | – typica | see *H. sinensis* var. *sinensis* |
| § | ***colchica*** ♀H4 | CDul SPer WCFE WDin WFar WFib |
| | – 'Batumi' | MBNS WFib |
| | – 'Dentata' ♀H4 | CHEx MRav MWhi NEgg SGol WFib |
| | – 'Dentata Aurea' | see *H. colchica* 'Dentata Variegata' |
| § | – 'Dentata Variegata' (v) ♀H4 | Widely available |

| | | |
|---|---|---|
| | – 'My Heart' | see *H. colchica* |
| | – 'Paddy's Pride' | see *H. colchica* 'Sulphur Heart' |
| § | – 'Sulphur Heart' (v) ♀H4 | Widely available |
| | – 'Variegata' | see *H. colchica* 'Dentata Variegata' |
| | ***cristata*** | see *H. helix* 'Parsley Crested' |
| § | ***cypria*** | CDoC EWld WFib |
| | ***helix*** | CArn CCVT CMac CRWN CTri MGos NWea WDin WHer WSFF XLum |
| | – 'Adam' (v) | CWib LAst LSRN MAsh MBri STre WFib |
| | – 'Amberwaves' | MBri WFib |
| | – 'Angularis Aurea' ♀H4 | EPfP NBir WFib |
| | – 'Anita' | GBin WFib WGwG |
| § | – 'Anna Marie' (v) | CMac MBri SRms WFib |
| | – 'Anne Borch' | see *H. helix* 'Anna Marie' |
| | – 'Arborescens' | WDin WSFF XLum |
| | – 'Ardingly' (v) | MWhi WFib |
| | – 'Asterisk' | WFib |
| | – 'Atropurpurea' | EPPr GBin WDin WFib |
| | – 'Baby Face' | WFib |
| | – 'Baden-Baden' | EShb |
| | – var. ***baltica*** | WFib |
| | – 'Barabits' Silver' (v) | EPla |
| | – 'Bill Archer' | GBin WFib |
| | – 'Bird's Foot' | see *H. helix* 'Pedata' |
| | – 'Blarney' | WFib |
| | – 'Blue Moon' | WFib |
| | – 'Boskoop' | WFib |
| | – 'Bowles's Ox Heart' | WFib |
| | – 'Bredon' | MRav |
| | – 'Brimstone' (v) | WFib |
| § | – 'Brokamp' | SLPl WFib |
| | – 'Buttercup' | CBcs CDul CMac CTri EBee EHoe ELan EPfP EShb LAst LRHS LSRN MAsh MBri MGos MWhi NBid NHol NWad SAga SBfd SLim SPer SPoG WCFE WDin WFar WFib |
| | – 'Caecilia' (v) ♀H4 | EPfP EQua LRHS MSwo SPer SWvt WCot WFib |
| N | – 'Caenwoodiana' | see *H. helix* 'Pedata' |
| | – 'Caenwoodiana Aurea' | WFib |
| | – 'Calico' (v) | WFib |
| | – 'California Gold' (v) | WFib |
| | – 'Calypso' | WFib |
| | – 'Carolina Crinkle' | GBin MWhi WFib |
| | – 'Cathedral Wall' | WFib |
| § | – 'Cavendishii' (v) | SRms WFib WRHF |
| | – 'Cavendishii Latina' | WCot |
| | – 'Celebrity' (v) | WFib |
| § | – 'Ceridwen' (v) ♀H4 | MBri SDys SPlb WFib |
| | – 'Chalice' | WFib |
| | – 'Cheap Thrills' | WFib |
| | – 'Cheeky' | WFib |
| | – 'Cheltenham Blizzard' (v) | CNat |
| | – 'Chester' (v) | LRHS WFib |
| | – 'Chicago' | CWib WFib |
| | – 'Chicago Variegated' (v) | WFib |
| | – 'Chrysophylla' | MSwo |
| | – 'Clotted Cream' (v) | CMac ECGP ELon LBMP LRHS MAsh MWat WFib |
| | – 'Cockle Shell' | WFib |
| | – 'Colin' | GBin |
| § | – 'Congesta' ♀H4 | CMac GCra NBir SBrd SRms STre WFib |
| | – 'Conglomerata' | CBcs ELan EPla NBir SRms WDin WFib |
| | – 'Conglomerata Erecta' | SRms WCFE WFib |
| | – 'Courage' | WFib WGwG |
| | – 'Crenata' | WFib |
| | – 'Crispa' | MRav |
| | – 'Cristata' | see *H. helix* 'Parsley Crested' |
| | – 'Curleylocks' | see *H. helix* 'Manda's Crested' |
| | – 'Curley-Q' | see *H. helix* 'Dragon Claw' |
| | – 'Curvaceous' (v) | WCot WFib |
| | – 'Cyprus' | see *H. cypria* |
| | – 'Dainty Bess' | CWib |
| | – 'Danish Crown' | WFib |
| | – 'Dead Again' | GBin WCot |
| § | – 'Dealbata' (v) | CMac WFib |
| | – 'Delft' | WFib |
| | – 'Deltoidea' | see *H. hibernica* 'Deltoidea' |
| | – 'Discolor' | see *H. helix* 'Minor Marmorata', *H. helix* 'Dealbata' |
| § | – 'Donerailensis' | MBlu WFib |
| | – 'Don's Papillon' | CNat |
| | – 'Dovers' | WFib |
| § | – 'Dragon Claw' | SDys WFib |
| | – 'Duckfoot' ♀H4 | CDoC EShb GBin MWhi WFib |
| | – 'Egret' | WFib |
| | – 'Eileen' (v) | WFib |
| | – 'Elfenbein' (v) | WFib |
| | – 'Emerald Jewel' | WFib |
| | – 'Erecta' ♀H4 | CDul CTca EPPr EPfP GCal LAst MBlu MGos NHol NWad SBfd SDys SPer SPlb WDin WFar WFib XLum |
| | – 'Erin' | see *H. helix* 'Pin Oak' |
| | – 'Ester' (v) | CBar EQua LAst MAsh SRGP WFib |
| § | – 'Eva' (v) | WDin WFib |
| | – 'Fanfare' | WFib |
| | – 'Fantasia' (v) | EShb MBri WFib |
| | – 'Feenfinger' | SDys WFib WGwG |
| | – 'Ferney' | WFib |
| | – 'Filigran' | NLar WFib WHer |
| | – 'Flashback' (v) | WFib |
| | – 'Flavescens' | WFib |
| | – 'Fluffy Ruffles' | WFib |
| I | – 'Francis Ivy' | WFib |
| | – 'Frizzle' | WFib |
| | – 'Frosty' (v) | WFib |
| | – 'Funny Girl' | WFib |
| | – 'Garland' | WFib |
| | – 'Gavotte' | WFib |
| | – 'Ghost' | WFib |
| | – 'Gilded Hawke' | WFib WGwG |
| | – 'Glache' (v) | WFib |
| | – 'Glacier' (v) ♀H4 | Widely available |
| | – 'Glymii' | GBin WCFE WFar WFib WTin |
| | – 'Gold Harald' | see *H. helix* 'Goldchild' |
| | – 'Gold Ripple' | NLar SEND |
| § | – 'Goldchild' (v) ♀H3-4 | CBar CBcs CDoC CMac EBee EHoe EPfP EShb LAst LRHS LTen MAsh MGos MRav MSwo NBir NBlu NEgg NHol SAga SBfd SLim SPer SPoG SWvt WDin WFib |
| | – 'Goldcraft' (v) | WFib |
| | – 'Golden Ann' | see *H. helix* 'Ceridwen' |
| * | – 'Golden Arrow' | ELan LRHS MAsh |
| | – 'Golden Curl' (v) | CMac EPfP LRHS |
| | – 'Golden Ester' | see *H. helix* 'Ceridwen' |
| | – 'Golden Gate' (v) | LAst WFib |
| | – 'Golden Girl' | SDys WFib |
| | – 'Golden Ingot' (v) ♀H4 | ELan EQua EShb MAsh MWhi SBfd SDys WFib WGwG |
| | – 'Golden Jytte' (v) | WFib |
| | – 'Golden Kolibri' | see *H. helix* 'Midas Touch' |
| | – 'Golden Mathilde' (v) | GBin |
| | – 'Golden Pittsburgh' (v) | WFib |
| | – 'Golden Snow' (v) | WFib |
| | – 'Goldfinch' | MBri WFib |

| |  |  |
|---|---|---|
| | – 'Goldfinger' | EShb MBri WFib |
| | – 'Goldheart' | see *H. helix* 'Oro di Bogliasco' |
| | – 'Goldstern' (v) | MRav MWhi WFib |
| | – 'Gracilis' | see *H. hibernica* 'Gracilis' |
| | – 'Green Finger' | see *H. helix* 'Très Coupé' |
| | – 'Green Ripple' | CBcs CTri EBee EShb LRHS MAsh MGos MRav MSwo MWht NBro NPri SEND SPer SPlb SRms WDin WFar WFib |
| | – 'Greenman' | SDys WFib WGwG |
| | – 'Halebob' | EShb MBri SDys WFib WGwG |
| | – 'Hamilton' | see *H. hibernica* 'Hamilton' |
| | – 'Harald' (v) | CTri CWib MAsh WDin WFib |
| * | – 'Hazel' (v) | WFib |
| | – 'Hedge Hog' | WFib |
| | – 'Heise' (v) | WFib |
| | – 'Heise Denmark' (v) | WFib |
| | – 'Helvig' | see *H. helix* 'White Knight' |
| | – 'Henrietta' | WFib |
| | – 'Hester' | WFib |
| | – 'Hispanica' | see *H. iberica* |
| | – 'Hite's Miniature' | see *H. helix* 'Merion Beauty' |
| | – 'Holly' | see *H. helix* 'Parsley Crested' |
| | – 'Hullavington' | CNat |
| | – 'Humpty Dumpty' | CPLG |
| | – 'Imp' | see *H. helix* 'Brokamp' |
| | – 'Ingelise' (v) | WFib |
| | – 'Ingrid' (v) | WFib |
| | – 'Itsy Bitsy' | see *H. helix* 'Pin Oak' |
| | – 'Ivalace' ♀H4 | CBcs EBee ECha EPfP EShb LTen MAsh MGos MSwo MWhi MWht SDys SRms WDin WFib WTin XLum |
| | – 'Jake' | EShb MBri WFib |
| | – 'Jasper' | WFib |
| | – 'Jersey Doris' (v) | WFib |
| | – 'Jerusalem' | see *H. helix* 'Schäfer Three' |
| | – 'Jester's Gold' | ELan EPfP MAsh MBri SBfd WDin WRHF |
| | – 'Jubilee' (v) | WCFE WFib |
| | – 'Kaleidoscope' | WFib |
| | – 'Kevin' | WFib |
| | – 'Kloster's Joy' | WFib |
| | – 'Knülch' | WFib |
| | – 'Kolibri' (v) | CDoC EBee EPfP EShb LAst MBri MGos NBlu SBfd WFib |
| § | – 'Königer's Auslese' | CDul EShb WFib |
| | – 'Lalla Rookh' | MRav WFib WGwG WHrl |
| | – 'Lemon Swirl' (v) | WFib |
| | – 'Leo Swicegood' | MWhi WFib |
| | – 'Light Fingers' | EPfP LRHS MAsh SDys WFib WGwG WHrl |
| | – 'Limey' | WFib |
| | – 'Little Diamond' (v) | CDoC CMac CTri ELan EPfP LRHS LTen MAsh MBri NHol SLon SWvt WDin WFib WHrl WTin |
| | – 'Little Luzii' | EShb WFib |
| | – 'Liz' | see *H. helix* 'Eva' |
| | – 'Lucille' | WFib |
| | – 'Luzii' (v) | WFib WGwG |
| | – 'Maculata' | see *H. helix* 'Minor Marmorata' |
| § | – 'Manda's Crested' ♀H4 | CDul NLar WFib WGwG |
| | – 'Maple Leaf' ♀H4 | EShb GBin SDys WFib |
| | – 'Maple Queen' | MBri |
| | – 'Marginata' (v) | SRms |
| | – 'Marginata Elegantissima' | see *H. helix* 'Tricolor' |
| | – 'Marginata Minor' | see *H. helix* 'Cavendishii' |
| I | – 'Marmorata' Fibrex | WFib |
| | – 'Masquerade' (v) | WFib WGor |
| | – 'Mathilde' (v) | SBfd WFib |
| | – 'Melanie' ♀H4 | ECha SRGP WFib WGwG |
| | – 'Meon' | WFib |
| § | – 'Merion Beauty' | WFib |
| § | – 'Midas Touch' (v) ♀H3-4 | CWib EPPr EPfP MBri WFib |
| | – 'Mini Ester' (v) | MBri |
| | – 'Mini Heron' | LAst MBri |
| | – 'Minikin' (v) | WCot WFib |
| | – 'Minima' misapplied | see *H. helix* 'Spetchley' |
| | – 'Minima' Hibberd | see *H. helix* 'Donerailensis' |
| | – 'Minima' M.Young | see *H. helix* 'Congesta' |
| § | – 'Minor Marmorata' (v) ♀H4 | CWan WSHC XLum |
| | – 'Mint Kolibri' | EHoe LAst MBri |
| | – 'Minty' (v) | WFib |
| | – 'Misty' (v) | WFib |
| | – 'Mon Premier' | WFib |
| | – 'Needlepoint' | XLum |
| | – 'Niagara Falls' | LRHS |
| | – 'Nigra Aurea' (v) | WFib |
| | – 'Obovata' | WFib |
| N | – 'Oro di Bogliasco' (v) | CDul CMac CTri EBee ECrN EPfP EShb GKin LRHS MBri MRav MSwo NBlu NHol NLar NPri NWad NWea SBfd SEND SPer SPlb SPoG SRms STre SWvt WDin WFar WFib WPat |
| | – 'Ovata' | WFib |
| § | – 'Parsley Crested' ♀H4 | CMac EPfP EQua EShb LRHS MAsh MGos NBid SGol SRms WFib WGwG |
| | – 'Patent Leather' | WFib |
| N | – 'Pedata' | CDul MSwo SDys WFib |
| | – 'Perkeo' | WFib |
| | – 'Persian Carpet' | WFib |
| | – 'Peter' (v) | WFib |
| | – 'Peter Pan' | WFib WGwG |
| | – 'Phantom' | WFib |
| § | – 'Pin Oak' | WDin |
| | – 'Pink 'n' Curly' | WFib |
| | – 'Pink 'n' Very Curly' | WCot |
| § | – 'Pittsburgh' | EShb LTen SBfd WFib |
| | – 'Plume d'Or' | WFib |
| § | – f. ***poetarum*** | EPla MBlu WFib WPat |
| | – – 'Poetica Arborea' | ECha SDix |
| | – 'Poetica' | see *H. helix* f. *poetarum* |
| | – 'Raleigh Delight' (v) | WCot |
| | – 'Ray's Supreme' | see *H. helix* 'Pittsburgh' |
| | – subsp. ***rhizomatifera*** | WFib |
| | – 'Richard John' | WFib |
| | – 'Ritterkreuz' | WFib WGwG |
| | – 'Romanze' (v) | WFib WGwG |
| | – 'Rotunda' | WFib |
| | – 'Russelliana' | WFib |
| | – 'Sagittifolia' misapplied | see *H. helix* 'Königer's Auslese' |
| | – 'Sagittifolia' Hibberd | see *H. hibernica* 'Sagittifolia' |
| | – 'Sagittifolia' ambig. | ECrN LRHS MAsh MMuc |
| | – 'Sagittifolia Variegata' (v) | MBri WFib WRHF |
| | – 'Saint Agnes' | LRHS |
| | – 'Sally' (v) | WFib |
| | – 'Salt and Pepper' | see *H. helix* 'Minor Marmorata' |
| § | – 'Schäfer Three' (v) | CWib WFib |
| | – 'Seabreeze' | WFib |
| | – 'Shadow' | WFib |
| | – 'Shamrock' | EPfP WFib |
| | – 'Shannon' | WFib |
| | – 'Silver Butterflies' (v) | WFib |
| | – 'Silver Ferny' | WFib |
| | – 'Silver King' (v) | MRav MWht WFib WGwG |
| | – 'Silver Queen' | see *H. helix* 'Tricolor' |
| | – 'Spectre' (v) | WHer |
| § | – 'Spetchley' ♀H4 | CMac GCal GGar GKev MAsh MRav MWhi NHol NPer NWad WCot WFib WGwG WHrl WPtf WTin |

- 'Spinosa' SDys WFib
- 'Splashes' WFib
- 'Stuttgart' WFib
- 'Sunrise' WFib
- 'Suzanne' see *H. nepalensis* 'Suzanne'
- 'Tango' ECrN
- 'Tanja' WFib
- 'Teardrop' WFib
- 'Telecurl' WFib
- 'Temptation' (v) WFib
- 'Tenerife' (v) WFib
- 'Tiger Eyes' WFib
- 'Topazolite' (v) WFib
§ - 'Très Coupé' CDoC EShb LRHS MAsh SArc SEND WDin
§ - 'Tricolor' (v) CMac CTri EBee EPfP EShb LRHS MAsh MCot WCFE WFib
- 'Trinity' (v) WFib
- 'Tripod' SDys WFib WGwG
- 'Triton' EPfP WFib
- 'Troll' WFib WPat
- 'Tussie Mussie' (v) WFib
- 'Ursula' (v) EShb WFib
- 'Very Merry' EPPr SDys WFib
* - 'Vitifolium' WFib
§ - 'White Knight' (v) ♀H4 WFib
- 'White Mein Herz' (v) WFib
- 'White Ripple' (v) WFib
- 'White Wonder' WFib
- 'William Kennedy' (v) WFib
- 'Williamsiana' (v) WFib
- 'Woerneri' WFib
- 'Wonder' WFib
- 'Yellow Ripple' EShb LAst MBri SDys WDin WFib
- 'Zebra' (v) WFib
***hibernica*** ♀H4 CCVT CDul CSBt EPfP LBuc MRav MSwo MWhi NBlu NWea SBfd SEWo SGol SPer SRms WDin WFib
- 'Anna Marie' see *H. helix* 'Anna Marie'
- 'Aracena' SLPl
I - 'Arbori Compact' EPfP
- 'Betty Allen' WFib
§ - 'Deltoidea' ♀H4 MWht WCFE WFib
- 'Digitata Crûg Gold' WCru
- 'Ebony' WFib
- 'Glengariff' WFib
§ - 'Gracilis' WFib
§ - 'Hamilton' WFib
- 'Harlequin' (v) WFib
- 'Lobata Major' SRms
- 'Maculata' (v) SLPl WSHC
- 'Palmata' WFib
- 'Rona' WFib WGwG
§ - 'Sagittifolia' CTri EPfP GBin SBfd SRms WDin
- 'Sulphurea' (v) WFib
- 'Variegata' (v) WFib
§ ***iberica*** WFib
***maderensis*** WFib
***maroccana*** 'Morocco' WFib
§ - 'Spanish Canary' WFib
***nepalensis*** WFib
- 'Marble Dragon' see *H. sinensis* var. *sinensis* 'Marble Dragon'
§ - 'Suzanne' WFib
***pastuchovii*** CDoC EShb WFib
- from Troödos, Cyprus see *H. cypria*
- 'Ann Ala' CDoC EPfP GBin WCot WFib WGwG
- 'Lagocetti' WFib
§ ***rhombea*** WCot WFib
- 'Eastern Dawn' WFib
- 'Japonica' see *H. rhombea*
I - f. ***pedunculata*** 'Maculata' CWib
- var. ***rhombea*** 'Variegata' (v) WFib
§ ***sinensis*** var. ***sinensis*** WFib
§ - - 'Marble Dragon' WFib

## *Hedychium* ✿ (*Zingiberaceae*)

CC 6412 EWld
'Anne Bishop' SEND
***aurantiacum*** CBcs CBct CHEx EAmu EBee ETod LAma LEdu NPla SBig XLum
***brevicaule*** B&SWJ 7171 WCru
***chrysoleucum*** CCCN EShb LAma LTen SBst
***coccineum*** ♀H1 CDTJ EAmu EBee ECho EPfP EShb ETod IKil MNrw SBig SPlb XLum
- B&SWJ 5238 WCru
- var. ***angustifolium*** CDes CGHE CRHN EPfP WPGP
- 'Disney' CDTJ EAmu
- 'Tara' ♀H3 CBct CDes CDoC CGHE CHEx CHll CPLG CPne CRHN CSam EAmu EBee EPfP IBlr LEdu LPJP MNrw SArc SBfd SBst SChr WCru WPGP
'Corelli' CHll
***coronarium*** CBct CCCN CDTJ CDes CHll EAmu EBee EPfP EShb GBin IKil LEdu SBig WPGP XBlo XLum
- B&SWJ 3745 WCru
- 'Gold Spot' SKHP
- var. ***maximum*** ETod
- 'Orange Spot' EAmu
- var. ***urophyllum*** IBlr
- - HWJ 604 WCru
***coronarium*** × ***gardnerianum*** SPer
'Daniel Weeks' EBee
***densiflorum*** CBct CCCN CDTJ CDes CHEx CHll CPLG CSpe EAmu EBee ECha EPfP ETod GBin IBlr LEdu MLLN NPla SDix SSpi WCru WPGP XLum
- EN 562 CPLG
- LS&H 17393 CPLG WPGP
- 'Assam Orange' Widely available
- 'Sorung' CPLG LEdu SChr WPGP
- 'Stephen' CAvo CBct CCCN CDTJ CDes CFir CGHE CHEx CPLG CPne CSam EAmu EBee EPfP LEdu MNrw NPal SChr SPlb WPGP
'Devon Cream' CCCN CDTJ CHll CPLG EAmu NPal SChr
'Doctor Moy' (v) CDTJ EAmu EBee SPoG
'Elizabeth' CDes EAmu EBee LEdu
***ellipticum*** CDTJ CHEx EAmu EBee ETod GCal LAma LEdu MNrw SBig SPoG XLum
- B&SWJ 8354 WCru
'Filigree' CPLG EBee LEdu
***flavescens*** CBcs CBct CDTJ EAmu EBee EPfP EShb LAma MNrw SChr WCru
***flavum*** Roxb. EBee XLum
***forrestii*** misapplied CTrC
***forrestii*** Diels CDes CPLG EAmu EBee EShb ETod GCal IBlr LPJP MNrw MREP SArc SPlb WPGP
***gardnerianum*** ♀H1 CBcs CBct CDes CFir CGHE CHEx CHll CPLG CPne CRHN CSam EBee EPfP EShb GBin IDee IKil LAma LEdu MNrw NBir NPla SAdn SArc SBfd SChr SPoG WCru WPGP XLum

| |  |  |
|---|---|---|
| | 'Gold Flame' | CDes EBee LEdu MNrw SChr |
| | ***gracile*** | EAmu LEdu WCru |
| | ***greenii*** | CBct CDoC CFir CHEx CHll CPne CRHN CSam EBee ECho EPfP EShb GBin LEdu MNrw NPla SBfd SBig SChr SDix WBor WCru XLum |
| | ***griffithianum*** | CSpe EAmu EBee EPfP ETod IKil MNrw SBig XLum |
| | – white-flowered | CCCN |
| | 'Hardy Exotics 1' | CHEx |
| | 'Kinkaku' | WDyG |
| | 'Luna Moth' | EAmu WPGP |
| | ***maximum*** | EAmu SChr SKHP WDyG WPGP |
| | – B&SWJ 8261A | WCru |
| | – HWJ 810 | WCru |
| | 'Pink Flame' | EBee LEdu |
| | 'Pink V' | EAmu EBee |
| | pink-flowered | CDes |
| | 'Pradhan' | CFir |
| | × ***raffillii*** | MNrw SBig WCru |
| | 'Samsheri' **new** | CHll |
| | 'Shamshiri' | CCCN |
| | ***spicatum*** | CDTJ CDes CFir CHEx CPLG CRHN GCal GPoy IBlr LEdu MNrw SGar SPoG WCFE |
| | – B&SWJ 7231 | WCru |
| | – BWJ 8116 | WCru |
| | from Sichuan, China | |
| | – CC 1705 | CPLG |
| | – CC 3249 | EBee |
| | – P. Bon. 57188 | CPLG CDes EBee WPGP |
| | – from Salween Valley, China | CPLG |
| | – 'Liberty' | WCru |
| | – 'Singalila' | CDes WCru |
| | 'St Martin's' | CCCN ELon GBin |
| | ***stenopetalum*** B&SWJ 7155 | WCru |
| | ***thyrsiforme*** | EAmu EBee EShb ETod SBig WCru XLum |
| | ***villosum*** | CDTJ EBee ECho |
| | ***wardii*** | CHEx CPLG WPGP |
| | ***yunnanense*** | CDes CFir CHll CRHN EBee LEdu MNrw SBig WPGP |
| | – B&SWJ 9717 | WCru |
| | – BWJ 7900 | WCru |
| | – L 633 | CPLG IBlr |
| | – from Cally Gardens **new** | GCal |

## *Hedysarum* (*Papilionaceae*)

| |  |  |
|---|---|---|
| | ***coronarium*** | CSpe ELan EPfP MCot WCot WKif |
| | ***hedysaroides*** | IKil |
| | ***multijugum*** | CBcs EBee MBlu NPal SPer |
| | ***tauricum*** | SPhx |

## *Heimia* (*Lythraceae*)

| |  |  |
|---|---|---|
| | ***salicifolia*** | CArn ECre EOHP IDee MBlu NMun SEND SGar |

## *Helenium* ✿ (*Asteraceae*)

| |  |  |
|---|---|---|
| | ***autumnale*** | CSBt CTri LSRN MLHP MNHC NChi SMrm SPet SWvt WFar WGwG WMoo |
| | – JLS 8807WI | CSam EPPr |
| | – 'All Gold' | NBPC SWvt |
| I | – 'Cupreum' | SBch |
| § | – Helena Series | SWvt |
| § | – – 'Helena Gold' | EBee EPfP LRHS NBre SBfd WPer |
| | – – 'Helena Rote Töne' | CSpr EBee EPfP LBMP LRHS MWhi SBfd SGar WPer |
| | 'Baronin Linden' | CSam MAvo MSpe |
| | 'Baudirektor Linne' ♀H4 | CSam EBee MSpe SUsu |
| | 'Biedermeier' | CSam CWCL EBee EBla ECtt EShb MRav MSpe NEgg SAga WHlf |
| | ***bigelovii*** | XLum |
| | 'Blütentisch' misapplied | see *H.* 'Riverton Beauty' |
| | 'Blütentisch' Foerster ♀H4 | CHVG CMHG CMea COIW CSam EBee GMaP MSpe MTis NCGa NLar NVic WMnd WWEG |
| | 'Bressingham Gold' | CSam MAvo MNrw MSpe WHrl WWEG |
| | 'Bruno' | CAby CHar CWCL EBee ELan ELon LRHS MArl MSpe MTis NLar |
| | 'Butterpat' ♀H4 | EBee ECtt GBee GCra GMaP GMac LRHS MArl MRav MSpe NCGa NPri NSti SBfd SMrm WWEG |
| | 'Can Can' | CSam MAvo MSpe |
| | 'Chelsey' | CAby CPrp EBee ELan EPfP IBal LHop LRHS LSRN LSou MSpe MTis NBPC NChi NLar NPri NSti WWlt |
| | 'Chesney' | LSou |
| | 'Chipperfield Orange' | CElw CSam ECtt MArl MRav MSpe MTis NBre NGdn NVic WOld WWEG XLum |
| | 'Coppelia' | CSam ECtt LRHS MAsh MRav MSpe NBir NGdn |
| | Copper Spray | see *H.* 'Kupfersprudel' |
| | 'Crimson Beauty' | ECtt ELan MRav |
| | Dark Beauty | see *H.* 'Dunkle Pracht' |
| | 'Dauerbrenner' | CSam MSpe |
| | 'Die Blonde' | EBee MSpe NBre |
| | 'Double Trouble'[PBR] | EBee EPfP IKil LLHF LRHS LSou MBNS MBri MSCN MSpe NBPC NCGa NPri SBfd SPoG STes WCot |
| § | 'Dunkle Pracht' | CElw CMHG CPrp CSam CWGN EBee ECtt LSRN MCot MSpe NBPC NDov NEgg NLar SPoG WCAu WCot WFar WWEG |
| | 'El Dorado' | CSam MSpe MTis |
| | 'Fata Morgana' | EBee ECtt LEdu LLHF MSpe NBre WCAu |
| | 'Feuersiegel' ♀H4 | CAby CSam EBee ECtt MAsh MSpe NBre SUsu WOld WWEG |
| | 'Fiesta' | CAby CSam EBee MSpe NDov WHoo |
| | 'Flammendes Käthchen' | CSam EBee IPot LRHS MAsh MAvo MSpe NBre NDov SAga SHar SMrm SUsu |
| | 'Flammenrad' | CSam EBee MSpe SDys |
| | 'Flammenspiel' | EBee ECtt LRHS MAsh MCot MNrw MSpe MTis NLar |
| | ***flexuosum*** | NBre SPhx |
| | 'Gartensonne' ♀H4 | CSam MSpe NBre SMrm WWEG |
| | 'Gay-go-round' | CSam MSpe |
| | Gold Fox | see *H.* 'Goldfuchs' |
| | 'Gold Intoxication' | see *H.* 'Goldrausch' |
| | Golden Youth | see *H.* 'Goldene Jugend' |
| § | 'Goldene Jugend' | CMea ECtt ELan MRav MSpe WCot WWEG |
| § | 'Goldfuchs' | CSam CWCL LRHS MSpe SDys WCot |
| § | 'Goldlackzwerg' | EBee LRHS MAvo MSpe NBre |
| § | 'Goldrausch' | CHar CSam CWCL EBee EBla ECtt EPfP GBee GCra LRHS LSou MDKP MSpe MTis MWat NBre NGdn NSti SPhx WMoo WOld WWEG |
| | 'Goldreif' | MSpe |
| | 'Hartmut Rieger' | CSam MSpe |
| | 'Helena' misapplied | see *H. autumnale* 'Helena Gold' |
| | 'Helena' Foerster | MSpe NLar WPer |
| | ***hoopesii*** | see *Hymenoxys hoopesii* |

| | | |
|---|---|---|
| | 'Indianersommer' | CCVN CElw CSam CWCL EBee EBla ECtt GMaP LRHS MSpe MTis NBPC NCGa NDov NLar NMRc NOrc SMrm SPer SUsu WCAu WFar WHoo WWEG |
| | 'Jam Tarts' | MSpe WCot |
| | 'July Sun' | NBir |
| | 'Kanaria' | CAby CHVG CPrp EBee EWll GKev GQue LRHS MAsh MLLN MSpe NDov NEgg NLar SAga SMrm SPhx SPoG WMnd WOld |
| | 'Karneol' ♀H4 | CSam MSpe NBre SUsu |
| | 'Kleiner Fuchs' | CSam MSpe NLar WWEG |
| | 'Kokarde' | CSam MAvo MSpe WWEG |
| | 'Königstiger' | CAby CSam EBee ECGP ECtt GQue LRHS LSou MAsh MNrw MSpe MWea NBre NDov SMrm WFar |
| | 'Kugelsonne' | EBee MSpe NBre |
| § | 'Kupfersprudel' | CSam MAvo MSpe MTis |
| | 'Kupferziegel' | CSam MSpe |
| | 'Kupferzwerg' | CSam CWCL EBee ELan IPot MSpe NBre NDov SUsu |
| | 'Lambada' **new** | EBee |
| | 'Lemon Queen' **new** | SAga |
| | 'Loysder Wieck' | EBee ECtt NDov NGdn SPet WHil |
| | 'Luc' | CSam MSpe MTis |
| § | 'Mahagoni' | CSam GBin MSpe |
| | Mahogany | see *H.* 'Mahagoni' |
| | 'Mahogany' | see *H.* 'Goldlackzwerg' |
| | 'Mardi Gras' | ECtt LRHS LSou NCGa NDov SPoG SUsu |
| | 'Margot' | CSam CWCL MSpe MTis NBre SDys SUsu |
| | 'Marion Nickig' | CSam MSpe NDov |
| | 'Meranti' | CMea CSam MAvo MSpe NDov WHlf |
| | 'Mien Ruys' **new** | NDov |
| | 'Moerheim Beauty' ♀H4 | Widely available |
| | 'Moth' | MSpe |
| | 'Orange Beauty' | EBee GQue |
| | 'Patsy' | MSpe |
| | Pipsqueak = 'Blopip' | EBee ECtt LLHF LRHS MSpe NBre NPri SPoG |
| | 'Potter's Wheel' | CAby CSam MSpe NDov WWEG |
| | ***puberulum*** | EBee LRHS MCCP MSpe NBir NLar SPav WHil |
| | 'Puck' **new** | MSpe |
| | 'Pumilum Magnificum' | CHar CSam CWCL EBee EPfP GQue LEdu LHop LRHS MSpe SMad SPer WFar WPGP XLum |
| | 'Ragamuffin' | CSam MSpe SUsu |
| | 'Rauchtopas' | CSam EBee GQue IPot MAvo MSpe NCGa NDov SDys SUsu WPGP |
| | Red and Gold | see *H.* 'Rotgold' Foerster |
| | 'Red Army' | CPrp EKen ELan GMac IBal LRHS LSou MAvo MNrw MSCN MSpe NCGa NGdn SPet |
| | 'Red Glory' | EBee MAsh |
| | 'Red Jewel' | CWGN EBee ECtt ELon IPot LLHF LPla LRHS LSou MSpe MTis NBPC NDov NEgg NGdn NLar NPnk NSti SKHP SMad SMrm SUsu WCAu WCot WCra WMoo WPGP WWEG |
| | 'Ring of Fire' ♀H4 | CSam IPot MSpe |
| § | 'Riverton Beauty' | CSam LLHF MSpe MTis SUsu WCot WHoo |
| | 'Riverton Gem' | CSam ECtt LLHF MNrw MSpe MTis NChi WHoo |
| | 'Rotgold' misapplied | see *H. autumnale* Helena Series |
| § | 'Rotgold' Foerster | CMea ECtt LSRN MSpe NBre NChi SGar SRms WFar WMoo WPer WWEG |
| | 'Rotkäppchen' | CSam |
| | 'Rubinkuppel' | LRHS NCGa |
| | 'Rubinzwerg' ♀H4 | Widely available |
| § | 'Ruby Thuesday' | CAby EBee ECtt EPPr EPfP GQue IKil LLHF LRHS LSRN LSou MBNS MHer MNrw MSpe NBPC NDov NEgg NGdn NLar NOrc NSti SBfd SPoG WCot WWEG |
| | 'Ruby Tuesday' | see *H.* 'Ruby Thuesday' |
| | 'Sahin's Early Flowerer' ♀H4 | Widely available |
| | 'Samtjuwel' | MSpe |
| | 'Septemberfuchs' | LEdu LPla MCot NBre NDov WWEG |
| | 'Septembergold' | MSpe |
| | 'Sonnenkringel' **new** | MSpe |
| | 'Sonnenwunder' | EBee ECha LEdu MLHP MSpe NBre |
| | 'Sophie zur Linden' **new** | CSam |
| | 'Summer Circle' ♀H4 | CSam MSpe |
| | 'Sunshine' | MSpe |
| | 'The Bishop' | CAby COlW CPrp CSam EBee EBla ECtt ELon EPPr EPfP GCra GMac LAst LEdu LRHS MBri MDKP MRav MSCN MSpe NPri SPer SPet SRGP SWvt WFar WHil WMnd WWEG |
| | 'Tip Top' | EBee LBMP SBfd |
| | 'Tresahor Red' | MSpe |
| | 'Vicky' | MSpe |
| | 'Vivace' | CSam MSpe |
| | 'Wagon Wheel' | MSpe WCot |
| | 'Waldhorn' | LRHS MSpe |
| | 'Waltraut' ♀H4 | Widely available |
| | 'Wesergold' ♀H4 | EBee EBla GBBs LLHF LSou MHer MSpe NDov NLar |
| | 'Wonnadonga' | MSpe |
| | 'Wyndley' | Widely available |
| | 'Zimbelstern' | CAby CCse CElw EBee ECha ECtt ELon LHop LRHS MAsh MCot MNFA MRav MSpe MTis NLar SMrm SPhx WAul WFar WPGP WWEG |

## *Heliamphora* ✿ (*Sarraceniaceae*)

| | | |
|---|---|---|
| | ***nutans*** | SHmp |

## *Helianthella* (*Asteraceae*)

| | | |
|---|---|---|
| § | ***quinquenervis*** | CDes GBin GCal LLHF LRHS NLar SPer |

## *Helianthemum* ✿ (*Cistaceae*)

| | | |
|---|---|---|
| | sp. | SVic |
| | 'Albert's Brick' | LIMB |
| | 'Albert's Gold' | LIMB |
| | 'Alice Howarth' | WHoo |
| | ***alpestre serpyllifolium*** | see *H. nummularium* subsp. *glabrum* |
| | 'Amabile Plenum' (d) | GAbr GCal LIMB |
| | 'Amy Baring' ♀H4 | CTri ECho ECtt GAbr LIMB LRHS NWad WPer |
| | 'Annabel' (d) | ECho ECtt GAbr LHop LRHS SSvw WPer |
| | ***apenninum*** | LLHF SRms |
| | 'Apricot' | CTri LIMB |
| | 'Apricot Blush' | LIMB WAbe |
| | 'Baby Buttercup' | CMea GAbr LIMB |
| | 'Banwy Copper' | LIMB |
| | 'Banwy Velvet' | LIMB |
| | 'Beech Park Red' | CTri ECho LIMB MHer SDix WAbe WFar WHoo WKif |

| | | |
|---|---|---|
| | 'Ben Afflick' | ECho ECtt LHop LIMB LRHS SRms WFar |
| | 'Ben Alder' | ECho ECtt GAbr LIMB MHer |
| | 'Ben Attow' | LIMB |
| | 'Ben Dearg' | CMea ECho ECtt LIMB SRms |
| | 'Ben Fhada' | Widely available |
| | 'Ben Heckla' | CSam ECho ECtt EPfP GAbr LHop LIMB LRHS MAsh WPer XLum |
| | 'Ben Hope' | CTri ECho ECtt ELan EPfP LIMB SPer SRGP XLum |
| § | 'Ben Ledi' | CBcs CEnt COlW ECho ECtt ELan EPfP GAbr GEdr GMaP LHop LIMB MAsh MHer MSCN NSla SBfd SEND SPoG SRms SRot WAbe WFar WNew WPer |
| | 'Ben Lomond' | ECho GAbr LIMB |
| | 'Ben Macdhui' | ECtt GAbr LIMB |
| | 'Ben More' | CBcs CEnt CMea COlW ECho ECtt ELan ELon EPfP GAbr GJos GMaP LHop LIMB LRHS MAsh MSCN MSwo NBir SBfd SEND SPoG SRGP SRms SRot WFar WHoo |
| | 'Ben Nevis' | CTri ECho ECtt GAbr GEdr LIMB SRms WFar |
| | 'Ben Vane' | ECho ECtt GAbr LIMB LRHS |
| | 'Big Orange' | LIMB |
| | 'Birch Double' (d) | LIMB |
| | 'Boughton Double Primrose' (d) | CPBP ECho ELan GMaP WHoo WSHC |
| | 'Braungold' | LIMB |
| | 'Bronzeteppich' | LLHF |
| | 'Broughty Beacon' | ECtt GAbr LIMB WGor |
| | 'Broughty Orange' | LIMB |
| | 'Broughty Sunset' | CSam ECtt GAbr LIMB NBir |
| | 'Bunbury' | COlW ECtt ELon GAbr LHop LIMB MBrN NBir SDix SPoG SRms |
| I | 'Butter and Eggs' | LIMB |
| | ***canum* subsp. *balcanicum*** | WAbe |
| | 'Captivation' | GAbr |
| I | 'Carminium Plenum' | LIMB |
| | 'Cerise Queen' (d) | CTri ECha ECho GAbr GKev LAst LHop LIMB MAsh MMHG MSwo SDix SEND SPer SRms WHoo |
| | ***chamaecistus*** | see *H. nummularium* |
| | 'Cheviot' | CMea ECtt GAbr GLam LIMB NBir WHoo WSHC XLum |
| | 'Chichester' | LIMB |
| | 'Chloe's Variegata' (v) | EWes |
| | 'Chocolate Blotch' | ECho GAbr GCra LHop LRHS NWad SAga SBrd SEND SRms WPer |
| | 'Cornish Cream' | ECho ECtt GAbr LBee LIMB |
| | ***croceum*** | LLHF |
| | ***cupreum*** | GAbr |
| | 'David' | LIMB |
| | 'David Ritchie' | LIMB LLHF WHoo |
| | 'Diana' | CMea LIMB SAga |
| | 'Dompfaff' | LIMB |
| | 'Dora' | LIMB |
| | double apricot-flowered (d) | GAbr LIMB |
| | double orange-flowered (d) | LHop |
| | double primrose-flowered (d) | LIMB |
| | double red-flowered (d) | NChi |
| | 'Eisbar' | LIMB |
| | 'Elfenbeinglanz' | LIMB |
| | 'Ellen' (d) | CMea LIMB |
| | 'Etna' | LIMB STre |
| | 'Everton Ruby' | see *H.* 'Ben Ledi' |
| | 'Fairy' | ELan EPfP LLHF |
| | 'Feuerbraund' | LIMB |
| § | 'Fire Dragon' ♀H4 | CMea ECho ECtt ELan EPfP GAbr GMaP GQue LIMB LRHS NBir NWCA SRms WAbe XLum XSen |
| | 'Fireball' | see *H.* 'Mrs C.W. Earle' |
| | 'Firegold' (v) | WAbe WFar |
| | 'Flame' | LIMB |
| | 'Frau Bachtaler' | LIMB |
| | 'Georgeham' | CMea ECho ECtt ELon EPfP LBee LIMB NBir SAga SRms WGor WHoo WPer XLum |
| § | 'Golden Queen' | ECho ECtt EPfP GAbr LAst LIMB MAsh MSwo WFar WPer |
| | 'Hampstead Orange' | CTri |
| | 'Hartswood Ruby' | MBNS |
| | 'Henfield Brilliant' ♀H4 | CHVG CPLG CSam CSpe ECho ECtt ELan EPfP GAbr GEdr LHop LIMB LRHS MRav MSCN NBir SBfd SDix SMad SRms WCot WHoo WPer XLum XSen |
| | 'Highdown' | SRms |
| | 'Highdown Apricot' | ECho ECtt LHop LIMB LLHF LRHS MAsh SPoG WFar |
| | 'Honeymoon' | ECtt EPfP LIMB NWad WPer |
| | 'Ilna's Master' (d) | LIMB |
| | 'Ilona' (d/v) | LIMB |
| | 'Jubilee' (d) ♀H4 | CTri ECho ECtt ELan EPfP GAbr LHop LIMB MAsh MBNS NBir NBlu NChi SPoG SRms WFar WHil |
| | 'Jubilee Variegatum' (v) | ECtt LIMB |
| | 'Karen's Silver' | LIMB WAbe |
| | 'Kathleen Druce' (d) | ECho ECtt EWes GAbr LIMB NWad WHoo |
| | 'Kathleen Mary' | CMea LIMB |
| | 'Lawrenson's Pink' | ECho ECtt GAbr LHop LIMB LRHS MCot SAga SRGP WPer |
| | 'Lemon Queen' | LIMB |
| | 'Lucy Elizabeth' | ECtt LIMB |
| | ***lunulatum*** | CMea ECho LLHF LRHS NMen WAbe WPat |
| | 'Magnificum' | MWat |
| | 'Marianne' | LIMB |
| | 'Mette' | LIMB |
| § | 'Mrs C.W. Earle' (d) ♀H4 | COlW CTri ECho ECtt ELan EPfP GCra LIMB LRHS MAsh MBNS MLLN NEgg SBfd SRms STre WFar WPer |
| | 'Mrs Clay' | see *H.* 'Fire Dragon' |
| | 'Mrs Croft' | LIMB |
| | 'Mrs Hays' | GAbr LIMB |
| | 'Mrs Jenkinson' | LIMB |
| | 'Mrs Lake' | LIMB |
| | 'Mrs Moules' | LIMB SRms |
| | ***mutabile*** | SPlb |
| § | ***nummularium*** | GPoy MHer MNHC NMir WAbe WPat WSFF XSen |
| § | - subsp. ***glabrum*** | WPat |
| | - subsp. ***pyrenaicum*** | NWCA |
| § | - subsp. ***tomentosum*** | GAbr |
| I | 'Oblongatum' | LIMB |
| | ***oelandicum*** | NWCA SRms WAbe |
| | - subsp. ***alpestre*** | NMen |
| | - subsp. ***piloselloides*** | WAbe |
| | 'Old Gold' | ECtt GAbr LIMB SRms WAbe |
| | 'Orange Phoenix' (d) | ECtt EPfP GAbr LIMB MBNS NPri WFar |
| | 'Ovum Supreme' | GAbr LIMB |
| | 'Peach' | LIMB |
| | 'Pershore Orange' | LIMB |
| | 'Pink Angel' (d) | ECtt LIMB MBNS WPer |
| | 'Pink Beauty' | LIMB |

| | | |
|---|---|---|
| | 'Pink Glow' | GAbr LIMB WPer |
| | 'Praecox' | CMea CTri ECho LBee LIMB SRms WHoo |
| | 'Prima Donna' | ELan EPfP NBir |
| | 'Prostrate Orange' | LIMB SRms |
| | 'Raspberry Ripple' | ECho ECtt ELan EPfP EPot LIMB LRHS MAsh SBfd SPoG SRms WFar |
| | 'Razzle Dazzle' (v) | ECtt ELon LLHF SLon SRms WFar |
| | 'Red Dragon' | ECtt EPot GLam LIMB MSCN WAbe |
| | 'Red Orient' | see *H.* 'Supreme' |
| | 'Regenbogen' (d) | CPBP GCal LIMB SEND |
| § | 'Rhodanthe Carneum' ♀H4 | CBar CEnt CMea COIW CSam CTri ECha ECho ECtt ELan EPfP GMaP LBee LHop LIMB LRHS MRav MSwo NBir SAga SBfd SEND SPer SPoG SRot STre WAbe WHil WHoo WNew |
| § | 'Rosakönigin' | ECho ECtt LIMB MHer WAbe |
| | 'Rose of Leeswood' (d) | CMea CTri LBee LIMB NChi NEgg SAga SPoG SRms WFar WHoo WKif WSHC |
| | Rose Queen | see *H.* 'Rosakönigin' |
| | 'Roxburgh Gold' | SRms |
| | 'Rubin' (d) | LIMB |
| | 'Rushfield's White' | LIMB |
| | 'Ruth' | LIMB SEND |
| | 'Saint John's College Yellow' | CSam ECho GAbr LIMB LRHS |
| | 'Salmon Queen' | ECho ECtt GAbr LHop LIMB LRHS SEND SRms WPer |
| * | ***scardicum*** | CMea |
| | 'Schnee' (d) | LIMB |
| | ***serpyllifolium*** | see *H. nummularium* subsp. *glabrum* |
| | 'Shot Silk' | ECtt EWes |
| | 'Snow Queen' | see *H.* 'The Bride' |
| | 'Southmead' | ECho LIMB |
| | 'Sterntaler' | GAbr LIMB LLHF SRms |
| | 'Sudbury Gem' | CTri ECha ECho GAbr LIMB LRHS SEND |
| | 'Sulphur Moon' | ECho LHop LLHF LRHS |
| | 'Sulphureum Plenum' (d) | LIMB |
| | 'Sunbeam' | CSam ECho LIMB SRms |
| | 'Sunburst' | LIMB |
| § | 'Supreme' | ECho ELan EPfP EWes LIMB MAsh SBrd SRms |
| | 'Tangerine' | ECtt GAbr LIMB |
| § | 'The Bride' ♀H4 | Widely available |
| | 'Tigrinum Plenum' (d) | EWes LIMB |
| | 'Tomato Red' | NSla SEND XLum XSen |
| | ***tomentosum*** | see *H. nummularium* subsp. *tomentosum* |
| | ***umbellatum*** | see *Halimium umbellatum* |
| | 'Venustum Plenum' (d) | LIMB |
| | 'Victor' (d) | LIMB |
| | 'Voltaire' | ECho ECtt EPfP LIMB LLHF NWad XLum |
| | 'Watergate Rose' | ECho ECtt MWat NBir |
| | 'Welsh Flame' | LIMB WAbe WFar |
| | 'Windmill Gold' | LIMB |
| | 'Wisley Pink' | see *H.* 'Rhodanthe Carneum' |
| | 'Wisley Primrose' ♀H4 | Widely available |
| | 'Wisley White' | CTri ECha ECho ECtt EPfP LIMB MAsh |
| | 'Wisley Yellow' | ECtt ELan SAga |
| | 'Yellow Queen' | see *H.* 'Golden Queen' |
| I | 'Zonatus' | LIMB |

## *Helianthus* (*Asteraceae*)

| | | |
|---|---|---|
| | sp. | SVic |
| | RCB/Arg CC-3 | WCot |
| | ***angustifolius*** | WFar |
| | ***atrorubens*** | LHop MRav NBPC NBro |
| | - 'Giganteus' | MAvo |
| | 'Bitter Chocolate' | WCot |
| | 'Capenoch Star' ♀H4 | CElw CPrp EBee ECha ECtt GMaP LEdu LRHS MAvo MBri MRav MTis NBPC NBro NLar SDix SLPl SMrm WFar WWEG |
| | 'Capenoch Supreme' | ECtt LRHS |
| | 'Carine' | MAvo MNrw MTis WCot |
| | ***decapetalus*** | CHar MLLN |
| | - Morning Sun | see *H.* 'Morgensonne' |
| | ***divaricatus*** | NBre |
| | 'Dorian Roxburgh' **new** | WCot |
| | × ***doronicoides*** | LRHS |
| | ***giganteus*** **new** | SHar |
| | - 'Sheila's Sunshine' | CAby CBre CElw EBee IPot LHop LRHS NBPC NDov SHar WOld |
| | ***gracilentus*** | NBre |
| | 'Gullick's Variety' ♀H4 | CBre EBee ECtt LLWP NBro NLar STes WOld WWEG XLum |
| | 'Happy Days' | EBee ECtt ELon LSou MAvo MLLN MTis NCGa WCot |
| | 'Hazel's Gold' | ECtt LRHS NBre |
| | ***hirsutus*** | EBee NBre |
| | × ***kellermanii*** | MTis NBre NDov SAga SPhx |
| § | × ***laetiflorus*** | EBee ELan GAbr MWhi NBre NLar NOrc WPer |
| | - 'Grandiflora' **new** | LRHS |
| § | 'Lemon Queen' ♀H4 | Widely available |
| | 'Limelight' | see *H.* 'Lemon Queen' |
| | 'Loddon Gold' ♀H4 | CHar EBee ECtt ELan EPfP EShb LRHS MAvo MRav MSCN MTis NBPC NBir NVic SAga SMrm SRGP WBrk WCot WFar WWEG |
| § | ***maximiliani*** | ELon EWll MDKP SPav SPhx SWal WPer WPtf |
| | ***microcephalus*** | CSam NDov |
| | - 'JS Straffe Prairie Gast' **new** | EBee |
| | 'Miss Mellish' ♀H4 | CAby EBee MSCN WBrk WCot WHoo WWEG |
| | ***mollis*** | CSam EBee LRHS NBre SPav WPer |
| | 'Monarch' ♀H4 | CSam EBee GBee MAvo MDKP MLLN MRav NBre NCGa NLar SMad SMrm WCot WMoo WOld |
| § | 'Morgensonne' | CPrp ECtt MTis MWat WCot WFar |
| | × ***multiflorus*** 'Meteor' | ECtt LRHS NBre WWEG |
| | ***occidentalis*** | WPer |
| | ***orgyalis*** | see *H. salicifolius* |
| | ***quinquenervis*** | see *Helianthella quinquenervis* |
| | ***rigidus*** misapplied | see *H.* × *laetiflorus* |
| § | ***salicifolius*** | Widely available |
| | - 'Low Down'PBR | EBee MCCP |
| | - 'Table Mountain' | EBee WCot |
| | ***scaberrimus*** | see *H.* × *laetiflorus* |
| | 'Soleil d'Or' | EBee ECtt EWll IPot WHal WWEG |
| | ***strumosus*** | WCot |
| | 'Triomphe de Gand' | EBee MRav MTis MWat NDov WFar |
| | ***tuberosus*** | CArn EBee GPoy SVic |
| | - 'Fuseau' | LEdu SVic |
| | - 'Garnet' | LEdu |
| | - 'Sugarball' | LEdu |

## *Helichrysum* (*Asteraceae*)

| | | |
|---|---|---|
| | from Drakensberg Mountains, South Africa | GAbr NWCA |
| | ***adenocarpum*** | SPlb |
| | ***alveolatum*** | see *H. splendidum* |

| |  |  |
|---|---|---|
| | ***ambiguum*** | EPfP |
| | ***amorginum*** | LRHS |
| | 'Pink Sapphire'[PBR] **new** | |
| | - Ruby Cluster = 'Blorub'[PBR] | EBee IRar LRHS NPri SPer SPoG WCot |
| | ***angustifolium*** | see *H. italicum* |
| | - from Crete | see *H. microphyllum* (Willd.) Cambess. |
| § | ***arwae*** | CPBP EPot IRar WAbe |
| | ***basalticum*** | WAbe |
| | ***bellidioides*** | see *Anaphalioides bellidioides* |
| | ***bellum*** | NWCA |
| | 'Coco' | see *Xerochrysum bracteatum* 'Coco' |
| | ***confertum*** | SPlb |
| | ***coralloides*** | see *Ozothamnus coralloides* |
| | 'County Park Silver' | see *Ozothamnus* 'County Park Silver' |
| | 'Dargan Hill Monarch' | see *Xerochrysum bracteatum* 'Dargan Hill Monarch' |
| | ***depressum*** | EPot |
| | 'Elmstead' | see *H. stoechas* 'White Barn' |
| | ***flanaganii*** **new** | GLam |
| | ***fontanesii*** | WHer |
| | ***frigidum*** | CPBP |
| | ***heldreichii*** NS 127 | NWCA |
| | ***hookeri*** | see *Ozothamnus hookeri* |
| § | ***hypoleucum*** | GGar SDix |
| | ***intermedium*** **new** | GLam |
| § | ***italicum*** ♀H3 | CPrp CWan ECha EGHP GPoy MAvo MHer MMuc MNHC NBlu NPri SBfd SEND SPet SPoG SRms WDin WGwG WHfH WJek XLum |
| | - from Crete | NWCA |
| | - 'Dartington' | EGHP EOHP SIde WJek |
| I | - 'Glaucum' | CWib |
| | - 'Korma'[PBR] | CSpe EBee EHoe ELan EPfP EWTr GBin LRHS LSRN LSou MAsh NPri SIde SLon SPoG WJek |
| | - subsp. ***microphyllum*** | see *H. microphyllum* (Willd.) Cambess. |
| | - 'Nanum' | see *H. microphyllum* (Willd.) Cambess. |
| § | - subsp. ***serotinum*** | CBcs EHoe EPfP EPot GGar GPoy MAsh MCot MRav SBfd SLim SMad SPer SRms STre SWal SWvt WDin WPer |
| | ***lanatum*** | see *H. thianschanicum* |
| | ***ledifolium*** | see *Ozothamnus ledifolius* |
| | ***marginatum*** misapplied | see *H. milfordiae* |
| | ***microphyllum*** ambig. | LAst |
| § | ***microphyllum*** (Willd.) Cambess. | EPot MHer MNHC NBlu SIde WJek |
| § | ***milfordiae*** ♀H2-3 | EPot GEdr NSla SRms WPat |
| | ***orientale*** | EPot IRar XSen |
| | ***pagophilum*** | CPBP |
| | ***petiolare*** ♀H2 | EBak ECtt LAst MCot SBfd SGar SPer SPoG |
| | - 'Aureum' | see *H. petiolare* 'Limelight' |
| | - 'Goring Silver' ♀H2-3 | SPet SPoG |
| § | - 'Limelight' ♀H2 | ECtt MCot NBlu NPri SBfd SPer SPet SPoG |
| | - 'Variegatum' (v) ♀H2 | ECtt LAst MCot NPri SBfd SPet SPoG |
| | ***petiolatum*** gold-leaved **new** | LAst |
| | ***plumeum*** | EPot |
| | ***populifolium*** misapplied | see *H. hypoleucum* |
| | ***retortoides*** **new** | GLam |
| | ***rosmarinifolium*** | see *Ozothamnus rosmarinifolius* |
| § | 'Schwefellicht' | EBee ECha EPPr EPfP EShb MLHP SPer WCAu WKif WSHC WWEG |
| | ***selago*** | see *Ozothamnus selago* |
| | ***serotinum*** | see *H. italicum* subsp. *serotinum* |
| | ***sessilioides*** | EPot WAbe |
| § | ***sibthorpii*** | NWCA |
| | 'Skynet' | see *Xerochrysum bracteatum* 'Skynet' |
| § | ***splendidum*** ♀H3 | EPfP LRHS NBro SKHP SLon WDin WPer XSen |
| | - McB 2921 | GLam |
| | aff. ***splendidum*** JJ&JH 401783 | NWCA |
| | ***stoechas*** | CArn |
| § | - 'White Barn' | CSpe NGBo WCot XLum |
| | Sulphur Light | see *H.* 'Schwefellicht' |
| § | ***thianschanicum*** | EDAr SRms XLum XSen |
| | - Golden Baby | see *H. thianschanicum* 'Goldkind' |
| § | - 'Goldkind' | EPfP NBir |
| | ***thyrsoideum*** | see *Ozothamnus thyrsoideus* |
| | ***trilineatum*** | see *H. splendidum* |
| | ***tumidum*** | see *Ozothamnus selago* var. *tumidus* |
| | ***virgineum*** | see *H. sibthorpii* |
| | ***wightii*** B&SWJ 9503 | WCru |
| | ***witbergense*** McB 349 **new** | GLam |
| | ***woodii*** | see *H. arwae* |

## *Helicodiceros* (*Araceae*)

| |  |  |
|---|---|---|
| § | ***muscivorus*** | CHid EBee WCot |

## *Heliconia* ✿ (*Heliconiaceae*)

| |  |  |
|---|---|---|
| | ***caribaea*** 'Burgundy' | see *H. caribaea* 'Purpurea' |
| § | - 'Purpurea' | XBlo |
| | 'Golden Torch' | XBlo |
| | ***indica*** 'Spectabilis' | XBlo |
| | ***latispatha*** 'Orange Gyro' | XBlo |
| * | - 'Red Gyro' | XBlo |
| | ***metallica*** | XBlo |
| | ***psittacorum*** | CCCN |
| | ***rostrata*** | CCCN XBlo |
| | ***schiedeana*** **new** | CHll |
| | - 'Fire and Ice' | EAmu |

## *Helictotrichon* (*Poaceae*)

| |  |  |
|---|---|---|
| | ***pratense*** | CHab EHoe |
| § | ***sempervirens*** ♀H4 | Widely available |
| I | - 'Pendulum' | EBee GBin MAvo |
| | - 'Saphirsprudel' | CCse CSpe EBee LRHS WCot WPGP |

## *Heliophila* (*Brassicaceae*)

| |  |  |
|---|---|---|
| | ***coronopifolia*** | CSpe |

## *Heliopsis* (*Asteraceae*)

| |  |  |
|---|---|---|
| | Golden Plume | see *H. helianthoides* var. *scabra* 'Goldgefieder' |
| | ***helianthoides*** | LRHS MLHP NBre |
| | - 'Limelight' | see *Helianthus* 'Lemon Queen' |
| | - Loraine Sunshine = 'Helhan'[PBR] (v) | EBee LSou NSti WCot |
| | - var. ***scabra*** | CMac MDKP NBPC SRot WMnd XLum |
| | - - 'Asahi' | EBee EBla ECtt ELan EPPr MAvo MCCP MDev NBPC NLar NPri WHoo |
| | - - Ballerina | see *H. helianthoides* var. *scabra* 'Spitzentänzerin' |
| | - - 'Benzinggold' ♀H4 | LSou MRav SMrm |
| | - - 'Bressingham Doubloon' (d) | ECtt |

- - 'Desert King' **new** LRHS
- - Golden Plume see *H. helianthoides* var. *scabra* 'Goldgefieder'
§ - - 'Goldgefieder' ♀H4 EBee EBla EPfP NBPC NBre WFar
- - Goldgreenheart see *H. helianthoides* var. *scabra* 'Goldgrünherz'
§ - - 'Goldgrünherz' EBee NBre
- - 'Hohlspiegel' EBee NBre
- - 'Incomparabilis' MRav
- - 'Patula' EBee
- - 'Prairie Sunset' PBR EBee ECtt NBPC
§ - - 'Sommersonne' CSBt EBee ECtt LRHS MSpe MWhi NGBl NLar NPer NPri SMrm SPer SRms WMnd WWEG XLum
§ - - 'Spitzentänzerin' ♀H4 EBee EBla MAvo NBre
- - 'Summer Nights' CMea CSam EBee EPPr GMac LBMP LRHS LSou MDKP MNFA MSpe NBPC SMrm SPhx
- - Summer Sun see *H. helianthoides* var. *scabra* 'Sommersonne'
- - 'Sunburst' LRHS
- - 'Venus' EBee EBla ECtt LRHS LSou MAvo MBri NBPC NDov NLar NSti WCra WFar
- 'Summer Pink' **new** LSou
- 'Super Dwarf' LSou
- 'Tuscan Sun' **new** ECtt WHil
***orientalis*** LRHS

## *Heliotropium* ✿ (*Boraginaceae*)

§ ***amplexicaule*** SDys
***anchusifolium*** see *H. amplexicaule*
§ ***arborescens*** CArn EPfP EShb MAJR MCot MHom
- 'Chatsworth' ♀H1 CAby CCCN CSev CSpe ECre ECtt ERea EShb MAJR MHom WFar
- 'Chequerboard' ERea MAJR
- 'Dame Alice de Hales' ECtt ERea MAJR MHom
- 'Florence Nightingale' MAJR
- 'Fowa' ERea
- 'Gatton Park' MAJR MHom SMrm
- 'Lord Roberts' ECtt ERea MAJR MHom WWlt
- 'Marine' ECtt SPav WGor
- 'Mary Fox' ERea MAJR MHom
- 'Mrs J.W. Lowther' MAJR MHom
- 'Netherhall White' ERea
- 'President Garfield' ERea MAJR MHom WFar
- 'Princess Marina' ♀H1 EPfP LAst LSou MAJR NLar SPav
- 'Reva' ECtt MAJR MHom
- 'Seifel' ERea
- 'The Queen' ECtt ERea MAJR
- 'The Speaker' ERea MAJR MHom
- 'White Lady' CCCN CSpe ECtt ERea MAJR MHom NLar
- 'White Queen' ECtt MAJR MHom
- 'Woodcote' MAJR MHom
'Baby Blue' NPri
'Butterfly Kisses' **new** EPfP
***peruvianum*** see *H. arborescens*

## *Helipterum* see *Syncarpha*

***anthemoides*** see *Rhodanthe anthemoides*

## *Helleborus* ✿ (*Ranunculaceae*)

***abruzzicus*** WM 0227 MPhe
***abschasicus*** see *H. orientalis* Lam. subsp. *abchasicus*
'Angel Glow' LRHS
§ ***argutifolius*** ♀H4 Widely available
- 'Janet Starnes' (v) MAsh
- 'Little 'Erbert' MAsh
- mottled-leaved see *H. argutifolius* 'Pacific Frost'
§ - 'Pacific Frost' (v) CLAP EBla EWes MAsh WWEG
- 'Red Riding Hood' LRHS
- 'Silver Lace' CBod CFir EBee EBla ELan ELon EPfP EWTr GKev LRHS LSRN MGos MLLN NBir NLar NSti SKHP SPer SPoG
***atrorubens*** misapplied see *H. orientalis* Lam. subsp. *abchasicus* Early Purple Group
***atrorubens*** Waldst. & Kit. CDes MRav
- WM 9028 from Slovenia MPhe
- WM 9805 from Croatia MPhe
- WM 9825 LWst
- spotted form MPhe
× ***ballardiae*** CLAP MAsh WFar
- 'Candy Love' **new** LRHS MBri NLar
- 'HGC Cinnamon Snow' **new** LRHS
- 'HGC Pink Frost' **new** LRHS
***bocconei*** LWst
- subsp. ***bocconei*** see *H. multifidus* subsp. *bocconei*
'Briar Rose' MAsh
***colchicus*** see *H. orientalis* Lam. subsp. *abchasicus*
***corsicus*** see *H. argutifolius*
***croaticus*** LWst WFar
- WM 9313 MPhe
- WM 9810 from Croatia MPhe
***cyclophyllus*** GBin GEdr GMaP MHom MPhe NLar SPer WFar
- HOA 8934 LWst
- HOA 9144 LWst
***dumetorum*** WFar
- WM 0023 LWst
- WM 9209 MPhe
- WM 9832 LWst
- WM 9627 from Croatia MPhe
§ × ***ericsmithii*** Widely available
- 'Bob's Best' CEnd CHid CLAP CYeo ESwi LPla LRHS MAvo MBNS MNrw NPnk SHar SKHP SMrm SPoG WCot
- 'HGC Silvermoon' PBR LRHS MAsh NLar SPoG
- 'Ruby Glow' EPfP LRHS
- 'Snow Love' **new** MBri NLar
- 'Winter Moonbeam' CLAP EPfP LRHS MAsh MCot NCGa SKHP SLon
- 'Winter Sunshine' **new** LRHS SKHP
***foetidus*** ♀H4 Widely available
- 'Chedglow' CNat
- 'Gold Bullion' CLAP MAsh SBfd WFar WWEG
- 'Harvington Pewter' CLAP LRHS MAsh SPoG
- 'Pewter' CLAP
- 'Ruth' MAsh
- 'Sopron' CLAP NLar
- sweet-scented MHom
- Wester Flisk Group CPLG EBee EBla EPPr EPfP GGar IFoB LAst LRHS MAsh MBri MGos MNrw MRav MSwo NPer NPnk NWad SBrd SPoG WCAu WFar WGwG WHoo WPGP
- 'Yorkley' LSRN
Gold Collection see *H.* cultivars with names starting HGC
'HGC Jericho' PBR IVic
'HGC Josef Lemper' PBR IVic LRHS
N × ***hybridus*** Widely available
- 'Albin Otto' LRHS
- 'Amber Queen' (Queen Series) **new** SBfd

| | |
|---|---|
| – anemone-centred | CHid CLAP IFoB LHel LRHS MNrw SPoG WFar |
| – 'Antique Shades' | WFar |
| – 'Apple Blossom' | WFar |
| – apricot-flowered | CLAP WFar WTin |
| – Ashwood Garden hybrids | CPMA EPPr EPfP LRHS MAsh MGos MMuc MRav SCoo SEND SLon SRms WWEG |
| – – anemone-centred | CPMA MAsh |
| – – double-flowered (d) | MAsh |
| – Ballard's Group | CLAP GEdr MWat NCGa SPer WFar WMnd WPnP |
| – 'Black Beauty' | GAbr MWea NEgg NHol NPnk NPri |
| – black-flowered | CLAP GMaP NChi SSth WFar WHoo WTin |
| – 'Blue Lady' (Lady Series) | CBcs COlW EBee EBla EPfP GAbr GBin GEdr IFoB LRHS MBNS MGos MWat MWea NGdn SMad SMrm SPer |
| – 'Blue Metallic Lady' (Lady Series) | COlW CPLG CSpe CWCL EAEE EBee EPfP GAbr GEdr LAst LBMP LHop LRHS MBNS MWat MWhi NEgg NGdn NPri SPer WGwG WWEG |
| – Bradfield hybrids | MCot |
| – – anemone-centred | MCot |
| – – double (d) | MCot |
| – – picotee | MCot |
| – Caborn hybrids | LLWP |
| – 'Cheerful' | NBir |
| – 'Cinderella' (d) **new** | LRHS |
| – 'Clare's Purple' | GBin LSRN SCoo |
| – 'Cosmos' | MBNS |
| – cream-flowered | CLAP CPMA MCCP WFar WTin |
| – dark purple-flowered | LHel SBfd |
| – dark red-flowered | LHel |
| – 'David's Star' (d) | CFir |
| – deep red-flowered | CLAP NChi NHol WFar WTin |
| – double (d) | CLAP CSpe LHop MDun MNrw NPnk WFar WTin |
| – – pink-flowered (d) | LHel |
| – – black-flowered (d) | CPLG IFoB |
| – – green-flowered (d) **new** | LHel |
| – – purple-flowered (d) | LHel |
| – – red-flowered (d) | CPLG MDun |
| – – white-flowered (d) | CPLG IFoB LHel SSth |
| – – yellow-flowered (d) | CPLG IFoB LHel MDun |
| – 'Double Ellen Picotee' (d) **new** | WHlf |
| – 'Double Ellen Red' (d) **new** | WHlf |
| – 'Double Ellen White' (d) **new** | WHlf |
| – Double Ladies, mixed (d) | GAbr MWat |
| – 'Double Vision' (d) | EPPr WWEG |
| – Elizabeth Town red strain **new** | IFro |
| – 'Emerald Queen' (Queen Series) **new** | GQue |
| – 'Farmyard Appleblossom' | WFar |
| – Farmyard anemone-centred | WFar |
| – – apricot | WFar |
| – – black | WFar |
| – – cream | WFar |
| – – cream, dark-eyed | WFar |
| – – cream, spotted | WFar |
| – – dark pink | WFar |
| – – double apricot (d) | WFar |
| – – – black (d) | WFar |
| – – – cream (d) | WFar |
| – – – cream spotted (d) | WFar |
| – – – pink (d) | WFar |
| – – – pink spotted (d) | WFar |
| – – – primrose (d) | WFar |
| – – – primrose spotted (d) | WFar |
| – – – red (d) | WFar |
| – – – slate-grey (d) | WFar |
| – – – white (d) | WFar |
| – – – white spotted (d) | WFar |
| – – green | WFar |
| – – green spotted | WFar |
| – – picotee | WFar |
| – – pink | WFar |
| – – pink spotted | WFar |
| – – plum | WFar |
| – – primrose | WFar |
| – – – dark-eyed | WFar |
| – – – spotted | WFar |
| – – red | WFar |
| – – slate spotted | WFar |
| – – slate-grey | WFar |
| – – veined | WFar |
| – – white | WFar |
| – – – dark-eyed | WFar |
| – – – splash | WFar |
| – – – spotted | WFar |
| – 'Farmyard Woodland' | WFar |
| – 'Gala Queen' (Queen Series) **new** | SBfd |
| – 'Golden Lotus' (d) **new** | WHlf |
| – green-flowered | WFar |
| – 'Green Ripple' | WFar |
| – 'Günther Jürgl' (d) | WFar |
| – 'Harvington Apricots' | EBee LRHS NBir NLar SKHP SLon SPoG |
| – Harvington double dark purple (d) **new** | LRHS |
| – – – pink (d) | CLAP EBee LRHS SKHP SLon SPoG |
| – – – purple (d) | CLAP EBee LRHS NBir NLar SKHP SPoG |
| – – – red (d) | CLAP EBee LRHS NBir NLar SLon SPoG WCra |
| – – – speckled (d) **new** | LRHS |
| – – – white (d) | CLAP EBee LRHS NBir NLar SKHP SLon SPoG WCra |
| – – – yellow (d) | CLAP EBee LRHS NBir NLar SKHP SLon SPoG WCra |
| – – – apricot-flowered (d) **new** | LRHS SPoG |
| – – – lime-green (d) | CLAP |
| – – picotee | CLAP EBee LRHS MGos NBir NLar SKHP SLon SPoG WCra |
| – – pink | EBee LRHS MGos NLar SLon SPoG WCra |
| – – – speckled | EBee MGos NLar SLon SPoG |
| – – red | EBee LRHS MGos MHer NLar SLon SPoG WCra |
| – – speckled | EBee LRHS MHer SLon |
| – – – white | EBee SKHP SLon SPoG |
| – – white | EBee LRHS MGos MHer NLar SKHP SLon SPoG |
| – – yellow | EBee LRHS MGos MHer NLar SKHP SLon SPoG |
| – – – speckled | EBee LRHS MGos MHer NLar SLon SPoG |
| – 'Harvington Shades of the Night' | EBee LRHS MGos MHer NLar SKHP SLon SPoG WCra |
| – 'Harvington Smokey Blues' | LRHS SKHP SLon SPoG |
| – 'Harvington Smokey Double' (d) | EBee |
| – 'Helen Ballard' | GKev NHol |

| | |
|---|---|
| – Hillier hybrids, burgundy | LRHS |
| – – slate | LRHS |
| – – spotted, double-pink (d) | LRHS |
| – – – green | LRHS |
| – – – pink | LRHS |
| – – – white | LRHS |
| – Homelea hybrids, anemone-centred | CRDP |
| – – double (d) | CRDP |
| – 'Ice Queen' (Queen Series) **new** | SBfd |
| – ivory-flowered | WFar |
| – Kaye's garden hybrids | NBPC WMnd |
| – 'Lady Macbeth' | EWes |
| – Lady Series | NSum |
| – large, pink-flowered | WTin |
| – maroon-flowered | WFar |
| – 'Mrs Betty Ranicar' (d) | CBro EPfP EWes GEdr IFoB LBuc LHop LRHS MBNS MGos NCGa NLar NSum WFar WWEG |
| – 'Onyx Odyssey' **new** | WHlf |
| – 'Pamina' | IFoB |
| § – Party Dress Group (d) | CHid EBla ELan ELon IFoB LSRN NLar STes WFar |
| – Picotee Group | NLar SSth WTin |
| – 'Picotee' | CLAP EGxp IFoB LHel WCru WFar WHoo |
| – 'Picotee' double-flowered (d) | LHel |
| – 'Pink Lady' (Lady Series) | EPfP GQue MGos MWat NEgg NGdn NPri SMrm SPer |
| – 'Pink Upstart' | IFoB |
| – pink-flowered | CLAP CPMA GAbr LHel MBNS MCCP MMuc SSth WFar WHoo WTin |
| – pink-red-flowered **new** | LHel |
| – plum-flowered | CLAP MMuc SEND SSth WFar WTin |
| – 'Pluto' | WFar |
| – primrose-flowered | CLAP ECGP ELan MCot MMuc NEgg SBfd SEND WFar WTin |
| – purple-flowered | CLAP CPMA NHol SSth WBor WFar WHoo |
| * – 'Purpurascens' | MCCP |
| – (Queen Series) 'Queen of Hearts' **new** | SBfd |
| – – 'Queen of Spades' **new** | SBfd |
| – – 'Queen of the Night' | CLAP CPLG CWCL EPfP IBal MWhi SPad STes |
| – 'Red Lady' (Lady Series) | CBcs COIW CPLG EAEE EBla EPfP EPot GAbr GBin GQue IBal LAst LHop LRHS LSRN MBNS MGos MWat MWea MWhi NEgg NOrc NPri SMrm SPer GwG WHil |
| – 'Red Spotted' | EPfP GEdr LRHS MWhi WWEG |
| – 'Red Upstart' | IFoB |
| – slaty-blue-flowered | CLAP IFoB LHel SSth WFar |
| – slaty-purple-flowered | WFar |
| – 'Smokey Blue' | EGxp EWTr LRHS SEND |
| – smokey-purple-flowered | ELan LSRN MMuc WFar |
| – 'Speckled Draco' | CPLG |
| § – spotted | CLAP EPfP GMaP MCCP NEgg SBfd SWal WCot WCru WHoo WTin WWEG |
| – – cream | CLAP NBir SSth WTin |
| – – double, pink (d) | LHel |
| – – – white (d) | GBin LHel |
| – – green | CLAP WFar WTin |
| – – ivory | CLAP |
| – – pink | CLAP LHel LRHS MBNS NBir SEND WFar WHoo WTin |
| – – primrose | CLAP ELan WFar WTin |
| – – white | EBla LHel MMuc NBir SSth WFar WTin WWEG |
| – – yellow | LHel |
| – 'Spotted Lady' | GBin |
| – Sunshine selections | GKev IBal |
| – 'Swirling Skirts' | EBla |
| – 'Tricastin' | CHid SPad |
| – 'Tutu' | CWCL EGxp EPfP LBuc LRHS NCGa SPoG |
| – 'Ushba' | CLAP |
| – Washfield double-flowered (d) | CSpe EWTr MGos MLLN SBfd SPer SPoG SRkn SWal WBor WRHF |
| – – white (d) | IFoB |
| – 'White Lady' (Lady Series) | COIW CPLG EBla GEdr GQue IFoB LAst LHop MBNS MGos MWat MWea NEgg NPri SDix SMrm SPer WWEG |
| – 'White Lady Spotted' (Lady Series) | CHVG COIW EPfP GEdr GQue NEgg SDix SPer |
| – white-flowered | LHel SSth WCFE WFar WHoo WTin |
| – white-veined | WFar |
| – Winter Queen strain | WWEG |
| – 'Yellow Lady' (Lady Series) | CBcs EPfP EPot GEdr GQue LHop LRHS MBNS MWat MWea MWhi NEgg NPri SMrm SPer WWEG |
| – yellow-flowered | GMaP IFoB LHel SSth WFar WHoo WTin |
| § 'Ivory Prince'PBR | EPfP LBuc LRHS MAsh SPoG |
| 'Kiwi Black Velvet' | IBal |
| ***liguricus*** | EWTr |
| – WM 0230 | MPhe |
| ***lividus*** ♀H2-3 | CAby CBro CEnt CLAP CSpe EPfP EWes GKev LHop LRHS MPhe NBir SDeJ SKHP SWal SWat WFar |
| – subsp. ***corsicus*** | see *H. argutifolius* |
| – 'Silver Edge' | EPfP |
| – 'White Marble' | GKev SKHP |
| 'Moonshine'PBR | CLAP EKen NLar SLon |
| ***multifidus*** | EBee EPPr NBir WFar |
| § – subsp. ***bocconei*** | LWst MHom NLar WFar |
| – – WM 9719 from Italy | MPhe |
| – – WM 9905 from Sicily | MPhe |
| – subsp. ***hercegovinus*** | CAvo WFar |
| – – WM 0020 | MPhe |
| – – WM 0622 | MPhe |
| – subsp. ***istriacus*** | CBro MAsh WFar |
| – – WM 9322 | MPhe |
| – – WM 9324 | MPhe |
| – subsp. ***multifidus*** | MHom |
| – – WM 9529 | MPhe |
| – – WM 9748 from Croatia | MPhe |
| – – WM 9833 | MPhe |
| ***niger*** ♀H4 | Widely available |
| – Ashwood strain | CLAP MAsh |
| – Blackthorn Group | CLAP NLar |
| – 'David' | IVic |
| – double-flowered (d) | ELan MAsh |
| – 'Eifelturm' | IVic |
| – Harvington hybrids | CLAP LRHS MAsh MBri MHer SPoG |
| – 'HGC Jacob'PBR | IVic LBuc LRHS |
| – 'HGC Joshua'PBR | IVic |
| – 'Ivory Prince'PBR | see *H.* 'Ivory Prince' |
| – Lynda Windsor Group **new** | CRDP |
| – 'Marion' (d) | IFoB |
| – 'Maximus' | CLAP EBee EWes WFar |
| – 'Potter's Wheel' | CDes CLAP CPMA EBee ELan EPfP LRHS MRav NBir NLar |
| – 'Praecox' | EBee EPPr EPfP EWes LRHS |
| – 'Schneeball' | IVic |

| | | |
|---|---|---|
| | - Sunset Group | NLar |
| | - 'White Christmas' | LRHS |
| | - 'White Magic' | CPMA MNrw |
| | × ***nigercors*** ♀H4 | CDes CMac CSpe CYeo ECha ECtt GMaP LHop LPla MAsh MBri MCot SPoG WCot WFar WPGP |
| | - double-flowered (d) | CYeo IBal LSou MAvo MBNS WCot |
| | - 'HGC Green Corsican'PBR | LRHS |
| | - 'Morning's Pride' new | LRHS |
| | - 'Pink Beauty' | LBuc NLar |
| | × ***nigristern*** | see *H.* × *ericsmithii* |
| | ***odorus*** | EWes GMaP IFoB MPhe NLar SPer WFar XLum |
| | - WM 0312 from Bosnia | MPhe |
| | - WM 9415 | MPhe |
| | - WM 9728 from Hungary | MPhe |
| N | ***orientalis*** misapplied | see *H.* × *hybridus* |
| | ***orientalis*** ambig. | CBar CHab ECho LAst LRHS MLLN NPri WPtf |
| | ***orientalis*** Lam. | CBcs CChe EWes LRHS LWst MPhe MSwo SBod STre WCAu XLum |
| § | - subsp. ***abchasicus*** | GEdr NLar SRms WFar |
| | - - WM 9607 | LWst |
| § | - - Early Purple Group | CTri GCal MRav WFar |
| | - subsp. ***guttatus*** misapplied | see *H.* × *hybridus* spotted |
| | - subsp. ***guttatus*** (A. Braun & Sauer) B. Mathew | NChi SRkn |
| | - - IBT 9401-7 | CWCL SEND |
| | - subsp. ***orientalis*** from the Caucasus | LWst |
| | 'Pink Beauty'PBR | EPfP LRHS MBri NLar SLon SPoG |
| | 'Pink Ice' | MAsh |
| | 'Pirouette' | CLAP EPfP LBuc LRHS MAsh |
| | ***purpurascens*** | EBee EPPr EPfP GEdr GMaP IFoB MAsh MMuc MRav NBir SMad SPer WFar WPnP WWEG |
| | - WM 0815 from Romania | MPhe |
| | - WM 9211 from Hungary | MPhe |
| | - WM 9412 | MPhe |
| | - WM 9922 | LWst |
| | 'Silver Dollar' | EWes LSRN MAsh SPoG |
| | 'Snow White' new | MAsh |
| | × ***sternii*** | CBcs CSpe CTri CWCL EBla ELan EPfP EWTr GMaP IFro LRHS MAvo MCot MGos MNrw MWat NEgg NLar NMRc SGar SPer WFar WMnd WMoo WTin |
| | - Aberconwy strain | CLAP |
| | - Ashwood strain | MAsh NLar |
| | - 'Beatrice le Blanc' | MAsh |
| | - Blackthorn Group ♀H3-4 | CPMA ELon EPfP GAbr IFoB LRHS MCot MRav NCGa SBfd SPer SPoG WBrk WFar WPGP |
| | - Blackthorn dwarf strain | CLAP EBee |
| | - 'Boughton Beauty' | CLAP CMea EBee ELan LRHS MAsh NSum |
| | - dwarf | WFar |
| | - pewter-flowered | CAby CSpe |
| | ***thibetanus*** | CFir CLAP CPLG EFEx EWes GEdr LAma MAsh MCot MPhe |
| | ***torquatus*** | CBro EBla LRHS MAsh MPhe SPer WFar WTin |
| | - LD 308 | LWst |
| | - HOA 9115 | LWst |
| | - WM 0609 from Montenegro | MPhe |
| | - WM 0617 from Serbia | MPhe |
| | - WM 9106 from Montenegro | MPhe |
| | - WM 9820 from Bosnia | MPhe |
| | - Caborn hybrids | LLWP |
| | - 'Dido' (d) | CPLG WFar |
| | - double-flowered, from Montenegro (d) | WFar |
| | - - WM 0620 | MPhe |
| | - double-flowered hybrids (d) | WFar |
| | - hybrids | WFar |
| | - Party Dress Group | see *H.* × *hybridus* Party Dress Group |
| | - semi-double-flowered (d) | WFar |
| | - Wolverton hybrids | WFar |
| | 'Verboom Beauty' | LRHS |
| | ***vesicarius*** | EWes MAsh |
| | ***viridis*** | EBee GPoy IFoB MCot NLar SRms WFar WTin |
| | - WM 0444 | MPhe |
| | - subsp. ***occidentalis*** | CBro MHom |
| | - - WM 9401 | MPhe |
| | - - WM 9502 from Germany | MPhe |
| | - subsp. ***viridis*** WM 9723 from Italy | MPhe |
| | Walberton's Rosemary = 'Walhero' | LBuc LRHS MAsh MBri SPoG |
| | 'White Beauty'PBR | CBcs EPPr EPfP EWes LBuc LRHS MBri MGos MRav NLar SPoG |

## *Helonias* (*Melanthiaceae*)

| | | |
|---|---|---|
| | ***bullata*** | EBee GEdr LRHS WCot |

## *Heloniopsis* (*Melanthiaceae*)

| | | |
|---|---|---|
| | ***acutifolia*** B&SWJ 218 | GEdr WCru |
| | - B&SWJ 6817 | WCru |
| | - B&SWJ 6836 | WCru |
| | ***japonica*** | see *H. orientalis* |
| § | ***kawanoi*** | CDes EBee GEdr NMen SKHP WCot WCru |
| | ***koreana*** B&SWJ 4173 new | WCru |
| § | ***orientalis*** | CBro CLAP ECho GCal GEdr GGar NMen WCot WCru |
| | - B&SWJ 6278 | WCru |
| | - B&SWJ 6327 | WCru |
| | - B&SWJ 6380 from Japan | WCru |
| | - from Japan | LWst |
| | - from Korea | EBee EPfP GEdr SChF SKHP SMad |
| | - var. ***breviscapa*** | EBee EPfP LEdu SChF SMad WCru WPGP |
| | - - B&SWJ 5635 | WCru |
| | - - B&SWJ 5873 | WCru |
| | - - B&SWJ 5938 | WCru |
| | - - 'A-so' | WCru |
| | - var. ***flavida*** B&SWJ 11400 new | WCru |
| | - variegated (v) | WCru |
| | - var. ***yakusimensis*** | see *H. kawanoi* |
| | ***tubiflora*** B&SWJ 822 | WCru |
| | - 'Temple Blue' | WCru |
| | ***umbellata*** | CDes CPom EBee EPfP GEdr SKHP SMad WMoo |
| | - B&SWJ 1839 | WCru |
| | - B&SWJ 3732 | CLAP WCru |
| | - B&SWJ 6836 | WCru |
| | - B&SWJ 6846 | WCru |
| | - B&SWJ 7117 | WCru |

## *Helwingia* (*Helwingiaceae*)

| | | |
|---|---|---|
| | ***chinensis*** | NLar SSpi WBor WPGP WPat |
| | ***himalaica*** | CGHE WPGP |
| | ***japonica*** | CBot CHGN EFEx WFar |

## *Helxine* see *Soleirolia*

## *Hemerocallis* ✿ (*Hemerocallidaceae*)

| | |
|---|---|
| 'A Special Lady' **new** | EJBD |
| 'Aabaa' **new** | EWoo |
| 'Aabachee' | EWoo SApp |
| 'Above the Clouds' | EWoo |
| 'Absolute Treasure' | CFwr SBrk |
| 'Absolute Zero' | CFwr EJBD SBrk SPol WAul |
| 'Adah' | SDay |
| 'Added Dimensions' | SApp |
| 'Addie Branch Smith' | EGol SDay |
| 'Adeline Goldner' **new** | CFwr |
| 'Admiral' | CHar |
| 'Admiral's Braid' | EWoo |
| 'Adoration' | SPer |
| 'Africa' | SBrk |
| 'African Chant' | ELan |
| 'Age of Miracles' | SPol |
| 'Ageless Beauty' **new** | EJBD |
| 'Ah Youth' | SApp |
| 'Ahoya' | CBgR |
| 'Alabama Jubilee' | WNHG |
| 'Alakazam' **new** | EWoo |
| 'Alan' | ECtt LRHS MRav |
| 'Alaqua' | CFir LRHS MBNS MNrw SApp SBrk SHar WFar |
| 'Alec Allen' | SBrk |
| 'Alejandro Pavlos' | SApp |
| 'Alien Encounter' | SPol |
| 'Alien's Eye' **new** | CFwr |
| 'All American Baby' | CWat EJBD MBNS MSpe SBrk SPol |
| 'All American Chief' | SBrk |
| 'All American Magic' | SPol |
| 'All American Plum' | CWCL EPfP GBin MBNS MSpe SBrk WAul WHrl |
| 'All American Tiger' | MSpe SBrk SDay |
| 'All American Windmill' | CFwr EWoo |
| 'All Fired Up' | EJBD SBrk SPol |
| 'Allegiance' | WNHG |
| 'Almost Paradise' | SPol |
| 'Alpine Mist' | SDay |
| 'Alpine Rhapsody' | SPol |
| 'Alpine Snow' | EWoo SBrk |
| ***altissima*** | CHEx LPla MNrw SMrm SPhx |
| 'Always Afternoon' | CKel EBee EBla EJBD EWoo MBNS MNrw MSpe NCGa SApp SBrk SPol WAul WCAu WHrl WWEG XSen |
| 'Amadeus' | SApp |
| 'Ambassador' | CBgR |
| 'Amber Classic' | ELon SApp |
| 'American Freedom' **new** | EWoo |
| 'American Revolution' | Widely available |
| 'Amersham' | MNFA SApp |
| 'Amerstone Amethyst Jewel' | SApp |
| 'Amethyst Squid' **new** | EWoo |
| 'Amorous and Glamorous' **new** | EWoo |
| 'Amy' | WWEG |
| 'Anastasia' | SBrk |
| 'Anatomically Correct' **new** | EWoo |
| 'Andrew Christian' | SPol |
| 'Android' | EWoo |
| 'Andy Candy' **new** | CFwr |
| 'Angel Artistry' | SApp SDay |
| 'Angel Curls' | EGol |
| 'Angel Rodgers' | SApp |
| 'Angel Unawares' | SApp WTin |
| 'Aniakchak' **new** | EWoo |
| 'Ann Kelley' | SApp SBrk SDay |
| 'Anna Warner' | ELon MMuc SEND |
| 'Annabelle's Ghost' | CBgR |
| 'Annie Golightly' | SDay |
| 'Annie Welch' | ELon EPfP EPla MBNS MSpe NBre |
| 'Antarctica' | SApp SPol |
| 'Antique Rose' | CKel SBrk SDay |
| 'Anzac' | COlW ECha ECtt EPla GMac LRHS MBNS NBre NGdn NPri SAga SApp SPav SWvt WMoo |
| 'Apache Bandana' | EWoo |
| 'Apache Beacon' | EWoo |
| 'Apache Uprising' | SBrk |
| 'Apache War Feather' **new** | EWoo |
| 'Apollo' **new** | XSen |
| 'Apollodorus' | SBrk |
| 'Apple Court Chablis' | SApp SPol |
| 'Apple Court Champagne' | SApp SPol |
| 'Apple Court Damson' | SApp SPol |
| 'Apple Court Ruby' | SApp SPol |
| 'Apple Crisp' | SApp |
| 'Apple Of My Eye' | EWoo |
| 'Applique' **new** | CFwr |
| 'Après Moi' | EBla EKen MBNS NLar |
| 'Apricot Angel' | SApp |
| 'Apricot Beauty' (d) | CPrp MBNS |
| 'Apricot Butterfly' **new** | EJBD |
| 'Apricotta' | WCot WPnP |
| 'Apron Strings' **new** | CFwr |
| 'Aquamarine Seedling' | SApp |
| 'Arachnephobia' | EWoo |
| 'Arctic Snow' | CBgR CBro CMac EBee EJBD ELon EWoo GMac LRHS MBNS MNrw NBPC NLar SBrk SPol SUsu WAul WPnP |
| 'Arms to Heaven' | EWoo |
| 'Arpeggio' | WHrl |
| 'Arriba' | MNFA NBro |
| 'Artistic Gold' | WTin |
| 'Asian Artistry' | WNHG |
| 'Asiatic Pheasant' | SPol |
| 'Asterisk' | EJBD |
| 'Astral Voyager' **new** | CFwr |
| 'Aten' | CBgR CSpr SBfd WAul |
| 'Athlone' | EWoo |
| 'Atlanta Bouquet' | SBrk |
| 'Atlanta Fringe Benefit' | SApp SDay |
| 'August Frost' | CBgR |
| 'August Orange' | MNFA |
| 'Augusto Bianco' | SApp |
| 'Aunt Wimp' **new** | EWoo |
| 'Authur Vincent' | SPol |
| 'Autumn Jewels' **new** | EWoo |
| 'Autumn Minaret' | EWoo |
| 'Autumn Prince' **new** | EWoo |
| 'Autumn Red' | CBcs EBla GKin LRHS MBNS MMuc MNrw NBir SEND SPol WCot |
| 'Ava Michelle' | SApp |
| 'Avant Garde' | EJBD SApp SPol WCAu |
| 'Avon Crystal Rose' | WNHG |
| 'Awakening Dream' | SBrk |
| 'Awesome Blossom' | GBin LSou MBNS MNrw SMrm WCAu |
| 'Awesome Candy' | EWoo LSRN |
| 'Aztec Firebird' | CFwr EWoo |
| 'Aztec Furnace' | CBro |
| 'Baby Blues' | SDay SPol |
| 'Baby Red Eyes' | CFwr |
| 'Baby Talk' | CFir SMrm |
| 'Badge of Honor' | SApp |
| 'Baja' | MNFA WFar |
| 'Bald Eagle' | WWEG |

| | |
|---|---|
| 'Bali Hai' | COIW GBee GBin LRHS MBNS MSCN SRms WHrl |
| 'Ballerina Girl' | SBrk |
| 'Bam' **new** | EJBD |
| 'Bamboo Blackie' | CBgR EWoo SPol |
| 'Banbury Cinnamon' | MBNS MSpe |
| 'Bandit of Baja' **new** | EJBD |
| 'Bangkok Belle' | CWat SDay |
| 'Banned in Boston' | EWoo MSpe |
| 'Banzai' | CFwr |
| 'Barbara Dittmer' **new** | EJBD |
| 'Barbara Mitchell' | EWoo MBNS MNFA SApp SBrk SDay SHar WAul XSen |
| 'Barbaresco' | SPol |
| 'Barbary Corsair' | MSpe SApp |
| 'Bark At Me' **new** | CFwr |
| 'Barnegat Light' | EWoo |
| 'Barnegat Orange Twister' **new** | CFwr |
| 'Baronet's Badge' | SPol |
| 'Baroni' | ECha |
| 'Bat Signal' **new** | CFwr EWoo |
| 'Bathsheba' | SBrk SPol |
| 'Bea' **new** | EJBD |
| 'Beat the Barons' | SBrk SPol |
| 'Beautiful Edgings' | CFwr EWoo SBrk SDay SPol |
| 'Beauty to Behold' | SApp SBrk SDay |
| 'Becky Lynn' | ECtt MBNS SApp |
| 'Bees Rose' **new** | XSen |
| 'Beijing' | EJBD SBrk |
| 'Bejeweled' | EGol EPla SApp SBrk WTin |
| 'Bela Lugosi' | Widely available |
| 'Believe It' **new** | WNHG |
| 'Bellini' | SBrk |
| 'Ben Lee' | SDay |
| 'Benchmark' | SApp SBrk |
| 'Benedict' | SBrk |
| 'Bengal Bay' | EWoo |
| 'Berlin Lemon' 𝕐$^{H4}$ | MNFA |
| 'Berlin Maize' | SApp |
| 'Berlin Oxblood' | WAul |
| 'Berlin Red' 𝕐$^{H4}$ | CPrp EBee EBla ECha EPla GBee GKin LBMP MNFA MNrw SApp WFar |
| 'Berlin Red Velvet' 𝕐$^{H4}$ | MNFA |
| 'Berlin Tallboy' | SApp SBrk |
| 'Berlin Watermelon' | MBNS |
| 'Bernard Thompson' | SApp |
| 'Bertie Ferris' | MSpe NLar |
| 'Bess Ross' | CMHG MNFA XSen |
| 'Bess Vestal' | MWat |
| 'Best Kept Secret' | EWoo SPol |
| 'Bette Davis Eyes' | CWat EJBD MSpe SApp SBrk SPol |
| 'Betty Benz' | SBrk |
| 'Betty Jenkins' | SBrk SDay |
| 'Betty Lyn' | SApp |
| 'Betty Warren Woods' | SBrk SDay |
| 'Betty Woods' (d) | SBrk SDay |
| 'Betty's Pick' | EWoo |
| 'Beware the Wizard' **new** | CFwr |
| 'Beyond 2000' | CFwr SApp |
| 'Big Apple' | SApp SBrk SDay SPol |
| 'Big Bird' | EWoo GMac LSRN MBNS SApp SBrk WAul |
| 'Big Bird's Friend' **new** | CFwr |
| 'Big Boy' **new** | CBgR |
| 'Big City Eye' | EJBD MBNS SApp SBrk |
| 'Big Golden' | WWEG |
| 'Big Kiss' (d) | SPol |
| 'Big Ross' **new** | EWoo |
| 'Big Smile' | CWCL CWGN EJBD MBNS MNrw MWea NBPC NBro SBrk WFar |
| 'Big Snowbird' | CFwr SBrk |
| 'Big Time Happy' | MBNS SBfd SBrk SPoG |
| 'Bill Norris' | SApp SBrk |
| 'Bird Bath Pink' | SPol |
| 'Birdwing Butterfly' | EWoo SPol |
| 'Bitsy' | EGol ELon LRHS SPet WCot WMnd WWEG |
| 'Black Emanuelle' | CPLG EBee ERCP IKil LAst MBNS MNrw MWhi SBch WPtf |
| 'Black Eye' | SDay WNHG |
| 'Black Eyed Stella' | CKel MBNS WCot |
| 'Black Eyed Susan' | MBNS MSpe SBrk |
| 'Black Friar' **new** | EWoo |
| 'Black Handlebars' **new** | EWoo |
| 'Black Ice' | CFwr EWoo SPol |
| 'Black Knight' | EWoo NLar SRms |
| 'Black Magic' | Widely available |
| 'Black Plush' | EJBD EWoo MSpe SPol |
| 'Black Prince' | CFir EBee EWll EWoo LRHS MBNS NBre NBro WAul |
| 'Black Stockings' **new** | EWes IPot NGBo |
| 'Blackberry Candy' | CSam GKin MBNS MNrw MSpe NWad SBrk WAul WCAu |
| 'Blackthorne' | CFwr |
| 'Blessing' | SBrk SDay SPol |
| 'Blonde is Beautiful' | SBrk SDay |
| 'Blue Moon' | SApp |
| 'Blue Ridge Shepherd Boy' **new** | CFwr |
| 'Blue Sheen' | CBgR CFir CMac CPar EBee ECtt EGol GMaP MBNS MCCP NGdn WFar WMoo |
| 'Blueberry Candy' | ECtt EJBD EWoo MBNS SApp SBrk WAul WHrl |
| 'Blueberry Cream' | CWCL EPfP MBNS MMHG MNrw MSpe SBrk |
| 'Blueberry Sundae' | CWat |
| 'Blue-eyed Butterfly' | EJBD SPol |
| 'Blue-eyed Chris' | WCot |
| 'Blue-eyed Curls' **new** | CFwr |
| 'Blushing Belle' | EBla LRHS MBNS NBro NEgg SApp |
| 'Blutorange' **new** | CFwr |
| 'Bobo Anne' **new** | CWat EJBD |
| 'Bogie and Becall' | SPol |
| 'Bold Encounter' | CFwr |
| 'Bold One' | CMHG SPol |
| 'Bold Ruler' | SPol |
| 'Bold Tiger' | MSpe SDay |
| 'Bonanza' | Widely available |
| 'Boney Maroney' | CBgR CFwr EJBD EWoo SApp SBrk |
| 'Bonheur' **new** | WHrl |
| 'Bonnie Boy' **new** | XLum |
| 'Booger' | SBrk |
| 'Boogie my Woogie Baby' | CFwr EWoo |
| 'Booroobin Magic' | EJBD EWoo |
| 'Border Baby' | ECtt SBrk |
| 'Border Lord' | EWoo |
| 'Born Yesterday' | SApp |
| 'Boulderbrook Serenity' | SDay |
| 'Bourbon Kings' | EBee EGol MBNS MSpe NBre SPav WCAu WHrl |
| 'Bowl of Roses' | SApp |
| 'Bradley Bernard' | SPol |
| 'Braided Edgings' **new** | CFwr |
| 'Brand New Lover' | SApp |
| 'Brass Buckles' | see *H.* 'Puddin' |
| 'Breed Apart' | SPol |
| 'Brenda Newbold' | SPol |

'Brer Rabbit's Baby' EWoo
'Bridget' ELan
'Bright Beacon' SPol
'Bright Spangles' MSpe SApp
'Brilliant Circle' SApp
'Bristol Fashion' SApp
'Broadway Bold Eyes' SPol
'Broadway Image' SBrk
'Broadway Valentine' SApp SBrk XSen
'Brocaded Gown' EJBD ELan SApp SBrk
'Brooklyn Twist' **new** EJBD
'Brookwood Wow' SApp
'Brown Billows' **new** EWoo
'Brown Exotica' EWoo
'Brown Witch' EWoo
'Brunette' SApp
'Bruno Müller' MNFA SApp
'Brushed with Bronze' **new** SPol
'Bubbling Brown Sugar' SDay
'Bubbly' SApp SDay
'Buckyballs' SDay
'Bud Producer' SPol
'Buddha' **new** WCAu
'Buffy's Doll' EBee EJBD MBNS SApp SBrk
'Bug's Hug' **new** EJBD
'Bumble Bee' CWat ECtt MBNS NBre SApp
'Burlesque' SPol WCot
'Burning Daylight' ♀H4 EBee ECtt EPfP EPla LAst LRHS MNFA MNrw MRav MWat NBre NEgg NHol SPer SRms WAul WCFE WCot WFar WWHy
'Burning Embers' SApp
'Bus Stop' SApp SPol
'Butterfly Ballet' SBrk
'Butterfly Charm' CWat
'Butterscotch' WFar
'Butterscotch Ruffles' SDay
'Buzz Bomb' CWat ECtt GBee GKin LRHS LSRN MBNS NEgg NGdn SApp SPer WFar WWEG
'Cabbage Flower' XSen
'Cage' SBrk
'Cajun Christmas' **new** CFwr
'Calico Jack' **new** EJBD
'Calico Spider' EJBD SBrk
'California Sunshine' SApp SPol
'Camden Glory' SApp
'Camden Gold Dollar' EGol SApp SBrk
'Camelot Green' WNHG
'Cameron Quantz' SApp
'Campfire Embers' GBin
'Canadian Border Patrol' CWCL EJBD IBal IPot MBNS MNrw MSCN MWea NLar SApp SBrk SPer SPol WFar WHrl
'Canary Feathers' SApp
'Canary Glow' CTri SMrm WFar
'Canary Wings' CBgR
'Candide' SApp SDay
'Candied Popcorn Perfection' **new** CFwr
'Cantique' SApp SPol
'Capernaum Cocktail' SPol
'Captain Ahab' SApp
'Captive Audience' SBrk
'Capulina' CFwr EWoo
'Cara Mia' CBgR LAst MBNS NBir SPol WFar
'Caramba' EJBD
'Caribbean Jack Dolan' EWoo
'Carolicolossal' ELon SDay SPol
'Carolina Cranberry' ELan
'Carolina Low Country' **new** CFwr
'Caroline Taylor' WHrl
'Carolipiecrust' SApp
'Carrick Wildon' **new** CFwr
'Carrot' CFwr
'Cartwheels' ♀H4 EBee EBla EPfP EPla EShb GKin GMaP LRHS MBNS NBro SBch SPer WFar WMoo WTin
'Casino Gold' SBrk
'Castle Strawberry Delight' SPol
'Catherine Neal' SBrk SPol
'Catherine Woodbery' Widely available
'Cathy's Sunset' CKel CSam EBee EBla ECtt EPla GKin LRHS LSRN MBNS MSpe MWat NBre NBro NEgg NGdn NWad SMrm SRGP
'Cat's Cradle' EJBD
'Cedar Waxwing' EGol MNrw
'Cee Tee' SBrk
'Celebration of Angels' SApp
'Celtic Christmas' CFwr SPol
'Cenla Crepe Myrtle' EWoo
'Cerulean Star' EWoo SApp
'Challenger' EJBD EWoo
'Champagne Memory' SApp
'Chance Encounter' MBNS MSpe
'Charles Johnston' CBgR CKel CMMP EWoo MBNS MNrw SApp SBrk WAul
'Charlie Pierce Memorial' MSpe SBrk SPol
'Charon the Ferryman' **new** CFwr
'Chartreuse Magic' CMHG EGol EPla
'Chartwell' **new** EWoo
'Chasing the Sun' CFwr
'Château Lafite' **new** SPol
'Cheerful Note' WNHG
'Cherokee Patterns' **new** SPol
'Cherry Cheeks' CEnt CFir ECtt EGol ELan ELon EPfP LRHS MBNS MBri MLLN MNrw MRav NBPC NHol SApp SBrk SPol WAul WCAu WCot WFar WMoo WWEG
'Cherry Eyed Pumpkin' EWoo SBrk
'Cherry Kiss' SBrk
'Cherry Ripe' EQua MNFA
'Cherry Smoke' SApp
'Cherry Tiger' MBNS MSpe
'Cherry Valentine' CBcs EBee EJBD MBNS MSpe SApp SBrk
'Chesières Lunar Moth' ELon SApp SPol
'Chesnut Lane' SApp SBrk
'Chester Cyclone' SDay
'Chevron Spider' **new** EJBD
'Chicago Apache' CFir EPfP EWoo MBNS MNFA MWea NBir NHol SApp SBch SBrk SMad SPer SPol SUsu WAul
'Chicago Blackout' CFir CWat ECtt EGol EPfP IPot MSCN NHol SApp WCAu WCot
'Chicago Brave' WAul
'Chicago Cardinal' **new** EJBD
'Chicago Cattleya' CFir EGol SApp WAul
'Chicago Cherry' WNHG
'Chicago Fire' EGol EPfP MBNS NBPC
'Chicago Firecracker' XLum XSen
'Chicago Heirloom' CFir EGol MBNS WAul WCAu
'Chicago Jewel' CFir EGol NSti WAul
'Chicago Knobby' MBNS MNrw SDay
'Chicago Knockout' CFir EGol ELan EPfP EWoo WAul WWEG
'Chicago Mist' WNHG
'Chicago Peach' NBir

'Chicago Petticoats' EGol NHol SApp WAul
'Chicago Picotee Lace' EGol NGdn SApp WWEG
'Chicago Picotee Memories' LRHS MBNS
'Chicago Picotee Promise' WNHG
'Chicago Picotee Queen' SApp SMrs
'Chicago Princess' EGol EWoo
'Chicago Queen' SDay WMnd WNHG
'Chicago Rainbow' CBgR MBNS WAul
'Chicago Rosy' EGol
'Chicago Royal Crown' ECtt LRHS MSpe SBrd
'Chicago Royal Robe' CWCL CWat EGol EJBD ELon EPla EWll MBNS NBid NCGa SPer SWal SWat WCot WTin
'Chicago Ruby' SApp SBrk WWHy
'Chicago Silver' CFir EGol MBNS WAul
'Chicago Star' WNHG
'Chicago Sugarplum' SDay
'Chicago Sunrise' CBgR EBee EBla EGol EPla GMaP MBNS MBri MRav NGdn NHol NOrc SApp SBrk SPet SWvt WCot WPer WWEG
'Chicago Thistle' **new** EJBD
'Chief Four Fingers' **new** EWoo
'Chief Sarcoxie' ♀H4 SApp
'Chief Sequoia' **new** EJBD
'Child of Fortune' SApp SDay
'Children's Festival' EBee ECtt EGol GMaP LPBA LRHS MBNS MRav MSpe NLar SApp SBrk SWvt WFar WMoo
'China Bride' EWoo SApp SBrk SDay SPol
'China Grove Plantation' CFwr
'Chinese Autumn' SApp SBrk
'Chinese Cloisonne' SApp
'Chinese Coral' EWoo
'Chinese Imp' NLar
'Chiricahua Warrior' **new** EWoo
'Chocolate Candy' CWGN EPfP MBNS
'Chocolate Cherry Truffle' SApp
'Choctaw Chick' **new** CFwr
'Chokecherry Mountain' EWoo
'Chorus Line' SApp SBrk SPol WNHG
'Chorus Line Kid' SPol
'Chosen Love' SApp
'Chris Salter' **new** EJBD
'Christine Lynn' WNHG
'Christmas Carol' SApp
'Christmas Is' CBgR CMac COlW CWGN EBee EBla EGol EJBD ELon GBin GKin LRHS LSou MBNS MCot MNrw MSpe NBre SApp SBrk SDay SMrm SPav SPol WAul WCAu WCot WHrl WWEG XSen
'Christmas Ribbon' EWoo
'Christmas Tidings' SApp
'Chute Libre' **new** CFwr
'Ciao' SApp
'Cimarron Knight' EWoo SBrk SPol
'Cindy's Eye' EJBD WCot
'Cinnamon Pleasure' **new** WCAu
'Circle of Beauty' SBrk SPol
'Circles and Stripes' CFwr
***citrina*** CBgR CHid CMac CPLG EBee EJBD EWTr GQue LRHS MAvo MCot NGdn WCot WHrl WTin XLum
***citrina*** × (× ***ochroleuca***) WCot
'Civil Law' SDay
'Civil Rights' SBrk
'Classic Caper' WNHG
'Classic Spider' SApp
'Claudine' SApp
'Cleo' **new** EWoo
'Cleopatra' CPar ELon EWoo SPol WAul
'Clockwork' SBrk
'Clothed in Glory' CWCL EJBD EWoo MBNS MSpe SApp WCot WWEG
'Coburg Fright Wig' EWoo
'Cocktail Party' **new** MBri
'Colonel Joe' **new** EWoo
'Colonial Dame' WTin
'Colour Me Yellow' SApp
'Comanche Eyes' SApp SDay
'Comet Flash' SPol
'Coming Up Roses' CPar ELon SApp SBrk
'Concorde Nelson' **new** CFwr
'Condilla' (d) EJBD SApp SBrk SPol
'Conspicua' SPol
'Contessa' CBro GBin LRHS SPer
'Cool It' CEnt CKel EBee MBNS NBre NCGa NHol SApp WHrl
'Cool Jazz' SApp SBrk SPol
'Copper Dawn' NChi SApp
'Copper Windmill' SPol
'Copperhead' SPol
'Coral Crab' EWoo SApp
'Coral Eye Shadow' EWoo
'Coral Mist' MBNS NBre
'Coral Sparkler' WNHG
'Coral Spider' SPol
'Coral Taco' EWoo
'Corky' ♀H4 Widely available
'Corryton Pink' SPol
'Corsican Bandit' CMMP SDay
'Cosmic Hummingbird' MSpe SApp
'Cosmopolitan' MBNS MCot SBrk
'Côte d'Azur' **new** CFwr
'Country Club' EGol GMaP MBNS NHol SApp SPol WWEG
'Country Melody' SDay
'Court Cavalcade' SBrk
'Court Magician' EWoo MDun MSpe SApp SBrk
'Court Troubadour' SPol
'Courting Trouble' **new** EWoo
'Coyote Moon' SDay
'Cranberry Baby' CWan EJBD SBrk SDay WHoo WNHG WTin
'Cranberry Coulis' CWat MBNS
'Crawleycrow' XSen
'Crazy Larry' **new** EJBD
'Crazy Pierre' EWoo SPol WHrl XSen
'Cream Drop' CPrp EBee EBla ECtt EGol EJBD GMaP GMac LRHS MCot MHer MLLN MRav MSpe NBro NGdn NLar NSti SApp SBrd SBrk SPav WAul WCot WHrl WMoo WTin
'Creation' **new** EWoo
'Creative Edge' WAul
'Creature of the Night' SApp
'Crimson Flood' **new** EWoo
'Crimson Icon' GMac WTin
'Crimson Pirate' CBgR CBre CFwr EBee ELon EWoo LSRN MBNS MSpe NBir NHol NOrc NPro SApp SBfd SBrk SPer SPlb SPol SWat WAul WHrl WMoo WTin
'Crimson Wind' SApp
'Crintonic Shadowlands' **new** SPol
'Cripple Creek' EWoo
'Crispin' **new** EJBD
'Croesus' NHol SRms
'Crystal Pinot' IPot
'Crystalline Pink' SBrk

| | |
|---|---|
| 'Cupid Bow' | EGol |
| 'Cupid's Gold' | SBrk SDay |
| 'Curls' | MBNS SDay |
| 'Curly Cinnamon Windmill' | EJBD SDay SPol |
| 'Curly Pink Ribbons' new | EJBD |
| 'Curly Ripples' | SApp |
| 'Custard Candy' | CWCL CWGN EWoo GKin MBNS MBri MSpe SApp SBfd SBrk SUsu WAul WCAu |
| 'Cute As Can Be' | EJBD |
| 'Cynthia Mary' | ECtt EQua GKin LHop LRHS MBNS MSpe NBro SRGP WFar |
| 'D.R. McKeithan' new | CFwr |
| 'Dad's Best White' | WTin |
| 'Daggy' | SBrk |
| 'Dahlonga Gold' new | EJBD |
| 'Daily Dollar' | EBla LRHS MBNS NGdn SApp |
| 'Dainty Pink' | EGol |
| 'Dallas Spider Time' | MNFA |
| 'Dallas Star' | SApp SPol |
| 'Dan Mahony' | MBNS |
| 'Dan Tau' | CKel EJBD SDay |
| 'Dance Among the Stars' new | CFwr |
| 'Dance Ballerina Dance' | EBee SBrk |
| 'Dancing Crab' new | EWoo |
| 'Dancing Dwarf' | SApp |
| 'Dancing Shiva' | SApp SBrk SDay |
| 'Dancing Summerbird' | SApp SPol |
| 'Daring Deception' | CFir CKel ECtt EJBD ELon IPot LRHS MBNS MNrw MSpe MWea NCGa SApp SMrm SPad WFar WHrl |
| 'Daring Dilemma' | MSpe SPol |
| 'Daring Reflection' | SDay |
| 'Darius' | WNHG |
| 'Dark and Handsome' | MBNS |
| 'Dark Angel' | MSpe |
| 'Dark Avenger' | EBee MBNS SBrk SHar |
| 'Dark Elf' | SApp |
| 'Dark Sprite' new | MSpe |
| 'Dark Star' | SDay |
| 'Darker Shade' | SBrk |
| 'Darkest Night' | SApp SBrk |
| 'Darla Anita' | NGBo SBrk |
| 'David Holman' | WNHG |
| 'David Kirchhoff' | IPot SApp WAul |
| 'Davidson Update' | WNHG |
| 'Dazzle' | SApp |
| 'Dazzling Spider' new | CFwr |
| 'De Colores' | EJBD |
| 'Debary Canary' new | EWoo |
| 'Debussy' | EWoo |
| 'Decatur Ballerina' | WNHG |
| 'Decatur Captivation' | WNHG |
| 'Decatur Cherry Smash' | SDay |
| 'Decatur Dictator' | WNHG |
| 'Decatur Elevator' new | EWoo |
| 'Decatur Imp' | EGol WHrl |
| 'Decatur Jewel' new | WNHG |
| 'Decatur Rhythm' | WNHG |
| 'Decatur Supreme' | WNHG |
| 'Decatur Treasure Chest' | WNHG |
| 'Dee Dee Mac' | SApp |
| 'Delicate Design' | SApp SPol |
| 'Delightsome' | SBrk |
| 'Demetrius' | CWat EJBD MWea SApp |
| 'Dena Marie' new | EJBD |
| 'Dena Marie's Sister' new | CFwr |
| 'Denali' | SBrk |
| 'Derrick Cane' | SPol |
| 'Desdemona' | SPol XLum |

| | |
|---|---|
| 'Desert Bandit' | SApp |
| 'Desert Dreams' | WCot |
| 'Desert Icicle' | CFwr EJBD EWoo |
| 'Designer Gown' | SApp |
| 'Designer Jeans' | SBrk SPol |
| 'Destined to See' | Widely available |
| 'Devil's Footprint' | SDay SPol |
| 'Devon Cream' | SPer |
| 'Devonshire' | SApp SBrk |
| 'Dewberry Candy' | MSpe |
| 'Diabolique' | CFwr EWoo |
| 'Diamond Dust' | CKel EBee ECtt EPla GBee MBNS MSpe NLar SApp SMrm SPer WTin |
| 'Dido' | CTri |
| 'Dipped in Ink' | SPol |
| 'Distant Star' | EWoo |
| 'Diva Assoluta' | SApp |
| 'Divertissment' | CBgR ELon EWoo SApp SDay WHrl |
| 'Do You Know Doris' | EJBD SDay |
| 'Doll House' | SBrk |
| 'Dominic' | CBgR CPar EBee MSpe SApp SBrk SPol WCot WMoo |
| 'Donnie Delight' | SBrk |
| 'Dont Mess with Me' new | CFwr |
| 'Dorethe Louise' | SBrk SPol |
| 'Dorothy McDade' | COlW EWoo MNrw |
| 'Dot Paul' | ELan |
| 'Dottie's Rompers' | EJBD |
| 'Double Action' (d) | SPol |
| 'Double Bold One' (d) new | EJBD |
| 'Double Coffee' (d) | SApp SPav SPol |
| 'Double Corsage' (d) | SApp SPol |
| 'Double Cream' (d) | WCot |
| 'Double Cutie' (d) | NBre NLar SDay WAul |
| 'Double Delicious' (d) | WCot |
| 'Double Doubloon' (d) new | XLum |
| 'Double Dream' (d) | MDev WHrl |
| 'Double Firecracker' (d) | CCVN CWat EGxp IBal MBNS MDun NBro NLar SBrk SMrm XSen |
| 'Double Grapette' (d) | SApp |
| 'Double Layer' (d) | CFwr |
| 'Double Oh Seven' (d) | ELon SApp SPol |
| 'Double Passion' (d) | MBNS |
| 'Double Peach Schnapps' (d) | EJBD SBrk |
| 'Double Red Royal' (d) | XSen |
| 'Double River Wye' (d) | CBgR CFir COlW CWat EBee ECtt EGol EJBD EPfP EShb MBNS MHer MNrw NGdn NMRc NPri SApp SHar SPol SWat WAul WBrk WCot WHoo WHrl WMnd WTin WWEG |
| 'Doublecious' | CWGN |
| § 'Doubloon' (d) | COlW NHol |
| 'Douglas Clark' new | EJBD |
| 'Doug's Red Mercedes' new | EWoo |
| 'Dover Plantation' | CFwr |
| 'Dragon Dreams' | SApp SPol |
| 'Dragon Fire Breath' new | CFwr |
| 'Dragon Heart' | EWoo |
| 'Dragon King' | SPol |
| 'Dragon Lore' | MBNS SBrk |
| 'Dragon's Eye' | CWat EJBD EWoo MSpe SDay SPol |
| 'Dragon's Orb' | CKel |
| 'Dream Baby' | NBre |
| 'Dream Catcher' | EWoo |
| 'Dream Icicle' new | EJBD |
| 'Dream Keeper' | EWoo |
| 'Dreamy Cream' | SBrk |
| 'Dresden Doll' | SPer |
| 'Dripping with Gold' new | EJBD |
| 'Driven Snow' | SApp |

'Drop Cloth' **new** EJBD
'Druid's Chant' EWoo LRHS MSpe
'Duke of Durham' MBNS MNFA MSpe SApp SPhx
***dumortieri*** CAvo CBro ECha EGol ELan GGar LRHS MCoo MCot MRav NBid NBir NGdn SPer WCot WHrl WTin WWhi
– B&SWJ 1283 WCru
'Dune Needlepoint' EJBD SPol
'Dutch Beauty' EPla WFar
'Dutch Gold' MNrw NBro
'Dynasty Pink' SApp
'Earl of Warwick' CBgR
'Earlianna' SPol
'Early to Bed' SBrk
'Earth Angel' SApp SPol
'Easy Ned' EWoo SBrk SPol WTin
'Eat our Wake CFwr
Pintaheads' **new**
'Ebony Prince' **new** EWoo
'Echo Canyon' EWoo
'Ed Murray' EJBD GBin MNFA WAul WCAu
'Edgar Brown' MBNS SBrk
'Edge Ahead' CMac ECtt GKin LRHS MBNS MSpe SBrd SBrk SMrm
'Edge of Darkness' CKel CWGN EPfP IPot MBNS MWea NBro NLar NSti SApp WAul WFar
'Edge of Heaven' **new** CWat
'Edna Spalding' GMac LRHS SApp
'Eenic Allegro' CBro ECtt EGol IBal MBNS SPer WMnd
'Eenie Fanfare' EGol MBNS NBir WAul WWEG
'Eenie Weenie' CBro CFee EBla ECtt EGol EPla GKev IBal MBNS NBro SApp SPer SRms WPer WWEG
'Eenie Weenie Non-stop' ECha EPPr
'Eggplant Ecstasy' **new** CFwr
'Eggplant Electricity' **new** EWoo
'Eggplant Escapade' CBgR SPol
'Egyptian Ibis' EWoo MSpe SPol WMnd WNHG
'Egyptian Queen' CBgR
'El Desperado' CBcs CBgR CMHG COIW CPar CSam EBee ECtt ELon EWoo GBin IPot LRHS LSRN MBNS MNrw MSCN NCGa NEgg SApp SBrk SMad SPav WAul WCAu WCFE WCot WWEG
'El Glorioso' CWat
'El Padre' SApp
'Elaine Farrant' SDay
'Elaine Strutt' MBNS MNFA MNrw SApp SDay SWvt WCot
'Eleanor Frye' **new** EWoo
'Elegant Candy' CBgR CKel CMac EBee EJBD MBNS MSpe NCGa SApp SBrk WCAu
'Eleonor' EPfP MBNS SApp SMrm WFar
'Elfin Daydream' SPol
'Elf's Cap' SDay
'Elijah Sain' **new** SPol
'Elizabeth Anne Hudson' SBrk
'Elizabeth Salter' CWCL EJBD IPot MBNS NLar SApp SBrk SPol SUsu WCAu
'Elizabeth Yancey' EGol
'Eloquent Cay' **new** CFwr
'Elva White Grow' SDay
'Emerald Enchantment' SApp
'Emerald Lady' SPol
'Emily Anne' SApp
'Emily Jaye' SApp
'Emmaus' SApp
'Emperor Butterfly' SApp
'Enchanted April' **new** SPol
'English Cameo' SPol
'English Toffee' SApp
'Enjoy' SBrk
'Entransette' GMac SApp SBrk
'Entrapment' MBNS MSpe SBrk
'Erin Prairie' SApp
***esculenta*** SMad
'Eskimo Kisses' **new** CFwr
'Etched Eyes' EWoo MSpe SPol
'Eternal Blessing' SPol
'Eternity Road' **new** EJBD
'Ethel Smith' SApp
'Etruscan Tomb' SBrk SPol
'Evelyn Claar' CMac
'Evelyn Lela Stout' SApp
'Evening Bell' SApp
'Evening Enchantment' SBrk
'Evening Glow' SApp
'Evening Gown' SPol
'Evening Tulip' **new** CFwr
'Ever So Ruffled' SBrk
'Exotic Dancer' **new** CFwr
'Exotic Love' SDay
'Eye Catching' EWoo
'Eye of Round' CFwr
'Eye on America' **new** EJBD
'Eyes Wide Shut' **new** CFwr
'Eye-yi-yi' SPol
'Ezekiel' EJBD WHrl XSen
'Fabergé' SApp SBrk
'Fabulous Prize' MSpe SApp
'Fairest Love' EBee MBNS MNrw MSpe
'Fairy Charm' SApp SDay
'Fairy Finery' SBrk
'Fairy Summerbird' SApp SBrk
'Fairy Tale Pink' CWat EWoo MNFA SApp SBrk SDay SPol
'Fairy Wings' SPer
'Faith Nabor' SBrk SPol
'Falcon' SPol
'Fall Farewell' WNHG
'Fall Guy' SApp
'Fama' SBrk
'Fan Dancer' EGol
'Fandango' LPla SPer
'Fantasia' **new** EWoo
'Farmer's Daughter' CBgR EJBD EWoo SApp SBrk
'Fashion Model' SApp WPer
'Feather Down' SPol
'Feathered Fascination' SApp
'Feelings' SApp
'Femme Osage' SBrk
'Ferengi Gold' CFwr
'Ferris Wheel' CBgR EWoo SApp
'Festive Art' MSpe SBrk SPol
'Final Touch' CBgR EJBD GMac LTen MBNS MSCN MSpe MWea NBro NGBo SBrk SPol
'Finlandia' MNFA
'Fire and Fog' CFwr EJBD MBNS
'Fire and Wind' **new** CFwr
'Fire from Heaven' SApp
'Fire Tree' SPol
'Fireborn' **new** CFwr
'Fires of Fuji' **new** EJBD
'Firestorm' EWoo SApp SPol
'First Formal' SMrm SPer
'First Picture of You' **new** EJBD
'Flaming Sword' NHol WBrk WRHF

| | | |
|---|---|---|
| | ***flava*** | see *H. lilioasphodelus* |
| | 'Fleeting Fancy' | SBrk |
| | 'Fleishel's Black' **new** | CFwr |
| | 'Flight of the Dragon' | SApp |
| | 'Flower Pavilion' | SPol |
| | 'Floyd Cove' | SBrk SDay |
| | 'Fly Catcher' | CBgR SBrk |
| | 'Flyaway Home' | SPol |
| | 'Flying Saucer' **new** | EWoo |
| | 'Foggy London Town' | CFwr |
| | 'Fol de Rol' | EWoo |
| | 'Fooled Me' | EBee EJBD MBNS MBri MSpe MWea SBrk SPad SPol |
| | 'Foolscap' **new** | EWoo |
| | 'For the Good Times' **new** | EWoo |
| | 'Forbidden Dreams' | EWoo |
| | 'Forgotten Dreams' | EBee MBNS MSpe SBrk |
| | ***forrestii*** | CPLG |
| | 'Forsyth Lemon Drop' | SDay |
| | 'Forsyth White Sentinel' | CFwr SBrk |
| | 'Forty Second Street' | CFir EBee EJBD LRHS MBNS MLLN SApp WFar |
| | 'Fox Ears' **new** | EWoo |
| | 'Fragrant Bouquet' | MSpe SBrk |
| | 'Fragrant Pastel Cheers' | SDay |
| | 'Fragrant Treasure' | ERCP |
| | 'Frances Fay' | SPol WAul |
| | 'Frances Joiner' **new** | EJBD EWoo |
| | 'Francis of Assisi' **new** | CFwr EWoo |
| | 'Francois Verhaert' | EWoo SBrk |
| | 'Frandean' | MNFA |
| | 'Frank Gladney' | MNFA SApp SBrk |
| | 'Frank Smith' **new** | EJBD |
| | 'Frans Hals' | Widely available |
| | 'Fred Ham' | SBrk XSen |
| | 'Free Wheelin'' **new** | EJBD MBri NGBo |
| | 'French Cavalier' **new** | CFwr |
| | 'French Doll' | SApp |
| | 'French Porcelain' | MSpe |
| | 'Fresh Air' **new** | MNrw |
| | 'Fritz Schroer' | CFwr |
| | 'Frosted Encore' | SApp |
| | 'Frosted Pink Ice' **new** | SPol |
| | 'Frosty White' | SDay |
| | 'Frozen Jade' | SBrk |
| | 'Fuchsia Beauty' **new** | SPol |
| | 'Fuchsia Fashion' | SApp |
| | ***fulva*** | CTri ELan NBir NBre SGar SPol SRms WBrk WHrl XSen |
| | - B&SWJ 8647 | WCru |
| N | - 'Flore Pleno' (d) | Widely available |
| N | - 'Green Kwanso' (d) | CBgR CPLG ECGP ECha EPla LBMP LRHS MMHG NVic SMad WAul WFar WPnP WTin |
| | - var. ***kwanso*** | MAvo |
| | - - B&SWJ 6328 | WCru |
| | - 'Kwanso' ambig. (d) | EJBD LRHS NOrc SBrk |
| | - var. ***littorea*** | CMac EPla |
| | - var. ***rosea*** | LRHS SPol WCot |
| § | - 'Variegated Kwanso' (d/v) | CBot CRow CWCL GCal GCra MRav MSCN NBir SMad SUsu WBor WCot WFar WHer WHil WHoo WHrl |
| | 'Fun Fling' | SPol |
| | 'Funky Fuchsia' | EJBD SPol |
| | 'Gadsden Firefly' **new** | CFwr |
| | 'Gadsden Goliath' | CFwr SPol |
| | 'Gadsden Light' | SDay SPol |
| | 'Gala Gown' | SApp |
| | 'Gale Storm' **new** | WNHG |
| | 'Garden Portrait' | EWoo SPol |
| | 'Gaucho' | MNFA |
| | 'Gay Music' | MBNS |
| | 'Gay Octopus' | SPol |
| | 'Gay Rapture' | SPer |
| | 'Gay Troubadour' | EWoo |
| | 'Gemini' | SBrk |
| | 'Geneva Firetruck' | CFwr |
| | 'Gentle Country Breeze' | SApp SBrk SPol |
| | 'Gentle Rose' | SBrk SDay |
| | 'Gentle Shepherd' | Widely available |
| | 'George Cunningham' | ECtt EGol ELan LRHS MRav NBir SMrs SPol WFar |
| | 'George David' | WHrl |
| | 'George Jets On' | SBrk |
| | 'Georgette Belden' | EBla ECGP ECtt GKin LRHS MBNS MBri MMHG MSpe MWea NHol SPol WTin |
| | 'Georgia Cream' (d) | NLar |
| | 'German Ballerina' | SPol |
| | 'Get All Excited' | SPol |
| | 'Ghost Ranch' **new** | EWoo |
| | 'Giant Moon' | CBgR CMHG EBee ECtt ELan EPla LRHS MBNS NCGa NHol SPer SRms WFar WHal |
| | 'Giddy Go Round' | EWoo SPol |
| | 'Gingerbread Man' | SApp SBrk |
| | 'Girl Scout' | SApp |
| | 'Give Me Eight' **new** | EWoo SPol |
| | 'Glacier Bay' | CBgR CWat EJBD MBNS NCGa |
| | 'Glacier Gleam' | MSpe |
| | 'Glazed Heather Plum' | SApp SBrk |
| | 'Gleber's Top Cream' | SApp |
| | 'Glittering Treasure' | LRHS |
| | 'Glomunda' | SApp |
| | 'Glory Bright' **new** | EWoo |
| | 'Glory's Legacy' | SBrk |
| | 'Glowing Heart' | SApp |
| | 'Going Bananas' | WCot |
| | 'Gold Elephant' | CFwr |
| | 'Gold Imperial' | NBre |
| | 'Gold Spider' **new** | EWoo |
| | 'Golden Bell' | NGdn NHol |
| | 'Golden Change' | CFwr |
| | 'Golden Chimes' ♀H4 | Widely available |
| | 'Golden Empress' | SApp |
| | 'Golden Ginkgo' | MBri MSpe SApp |
| | 'Golden Marvel' **new** | EWoo |
| | 'Golden Orchid' | see *H.* 'Doubloon' |
| | 'Golden Peace' | SBrk |
| | 'Golden Prize' | EJBD EPla EWoo GQue NGdn NPri SApp SBrk WCot WFar |
| | 'Golden Scroll' | EJBD MSpe SApp SBrk |
| | Golden Zebra = 'Malja'[PBR] (v) | CWGN ELan EPfP LBuc LRHS MBNS MGos MRav NLar NSti SBrd SPoG WCot |
| | 'Goldeneye' | SApp |
| | 'Golliwog' | CBgR |
| | 'Good Looking' | EGol |
| | 'Gothic Window' | SDay |
| | 'Grace and Favour' | SDay SPol |
| | 'Grace and Grandeur' **new** | EWoo |
| | 'Graceful Eye' | SApp SBrk |
| | 'Grand Masterpiece' | CMMP NGdn SPet WAul |
| | 'Grand Palais' | SApp SBrk |
| | 'Grandiose' | SBrk |
| | 'Grandma Kissed Me' | SPol |
| | 'Granite City Towhead' **new** | CFwr |
| | 'Granny Coot' **new** | EJBD |
| | 'Grape Harvest' **new** | WNHG |

| | |
|---|---|
| 'Grape Magic' | EGol WCot WTin |
| 'Grape Velvet' | CHar CPar CSpe EGol EWoo MCCP MNFA NBre NSti SApp SBch SBrk SRms WAul WCAu WMnd WWEG |
| 'Great Northern' | SApp |
| 'Green Dolphin Street' | SBrk SDay |
| 'Green Dragon' | SPol |
| 'Green Drop' | WFar |
| 'Green Eyed Giant' | MNFA |
| 'Green Eyed Lady' | SDay |
| 'Green Flutter' ♀H4 | CBgR CFwr EBee EJBD EWoo GCal LPla LSRN MBNS MNFA NBir NBre NGdn NSti SApp SPhx SPol WCot WWEG |
| 'Green Goddess' **new** | XLum |
| 'Green Gold' | CMHG |
| 'Green Puff' | NBir SDay |
| 'Green Spider' | CBgR SDay |
| 'Green Spill' **new** | CFwr |
| 'Green Valley' | MNFA |
| 'Green Warrior' | EWoo |
| 'Green Widow' | EWoo SDay |
| 'Greywoods Nautical Nellie' **new** | CFwr |
| 'Greywoods Workhouse Willie' **new** | EWoo |
| 'Grumbly' | ELan WPnP |
| 'Guardian Angel' | WCFE WTin |
| 'Guinea Jubilee' **new** | CFwr |
| 'Gypsy Ballerina' | SApp |
| 'Gypsy Cranberry' | SPol |
| 'Gypsy Prince' | MNFA |
| 'Happy Hopi' | EJBD SApp |
| 'Happy Returns' | CBgR CHid CSBt CTri EBee EBla ECha EGol EJBD ELan EPla EWoo IBal LRHS LSRN MBNS MBri NBPC NEgg NGdn SApp SBrk SRGP SRms WCAu WTin WWEG |
| 'Harbor Blue' | SApp SDay |
| 'Harrods' **new** | EJBD |
| 'Harry Barras' **new** | XLum |
| 'Havana Banana' | SApp |
| 'Hawaiian Nights' | EWoo |
| 'Hawaiian Punch' | EGol |
| 'Hawaiian Purple' | EGol |
| 'Hawk' | ELon SApp SPol |
| 'Hazel Monette' | EGol |
| 'Heady Wine' | MSpe SDay |
| 'Heat Wave' **new** | CFwr |
| 'Heather Green' | SApp |
| 'Heather Hills' **new** | EJBD |
| 'Heavenly Mr Twister' **new** | EWoo |
| 'Heavenly Starfire' **new** | EWoo |
| 'Heavenly Treasure' | SApp SBrk SPol |
| 'Heidi Eidelweiss' | CPLG |
| 'Heirloom Lace' | WFar |
| 'Helaman' **new** | CFwr |
| 'Helena Pulsar' **new** | EJBD |
| 'Helix' | CFwr |
| 'Helle Berlinerin' ♀H4 | MNFA SApp SPol |
| 'Helter Skelter' | SPol |
| 'Hemlock' | GMac |
| 'Her Majesty's Wizard' | CBgR EJBD ELan EWoo MBNS MHer NBro SPol |
| 'Hercules' | NBre |
| 'Heron's Cove' | EWoo |
| 'Hexagon' **new** | EWoo |
| 'Hey There' | SBrk |
| 'High Energy' | SApp |
| 'High Tor' | GBin GQui SHar SPol WHrl WTin |
| 'Highland Belle' | SApp |
| 'Highland Lord' (d) | EPfP MBNS MWea SApp WCAu XSen |
| 'Highland Summerbird' | SApp |
| 'Hightower' **new** | CFwr |
| 'Hillbilly Heart' **new** | CFwr |
| 'His Majesty's Wizard' | SBrk |
| 'Holiday Delight' | MBNS |
| 'Holiday Mood' | ELan SApp |
| 'Holly Dancer' | EWoo SPol |
| 'Honey Jubilee' | SPol |
| 'Honky Tonk Blues' | CFwr |
| 'Hornby Castle' | CBro LRHS NHol |
| 'Hortensia' | EJBD |
| 'Hot Cakes' | SBrk |
| 'Hot Chocolate'PBR | EBee SRGP |
| 'Hot Ticket' | SApp SBrk |
| 'Hot Town' | ELan |
| 'Hot Wheels' | SBrk |
| 'Hot Wire' | MSpe SBrk |
| 'Houdini' | EGol MSpe WMnd |
| 'House of Orange' | SApp SPol |
| 'Howard Goodson' | MNFA |
| 'Howdy' | CFwr |
| I 'How's the Weather up There?' **new** | EWoo |
| 'Hubbles Buddy' **new** | EWoo |
| 'Humdinger' | SBrk WCot |
| 'Hyperion' | CBgR CMac COIW CPrp CSev CTri EBee ECha ECtt EGol EPfP EWoo GKin LAst LEdu MNFA MRav MSpe NBid NGdn NHol SApp SMrs SPer SPoG SUsu WCot WWEG |
| 'Ice Carnival' | CKel ELon EPfP GMac MBNS NBre NGdn NOrc SApp SHar SPet |
| 'Ice Castles' | CTri SApp SBrk WHrl |
| 'Ice Cool' | SApp |
| 'Icecap' | WAul WFar WMoo WPnP |
| 'Icy Lemon' | SBrk |
| 'Ida Duke Miles' | SBrk SDay |
| 'Ida Munson' | EGol |
| 'Ida's Magic' | SApp SBrk WFar |
| 'Iditarod' | EJBD |
| 'If' | EJBD |
| 'Igor' **new** | CFwr EJBD |
| 'Imperator' | CBen LPBA NHol |
| 'Imperial Lemon' | SApp |
| 'Imperial Wizard' **new** | CFwr |
| 'In Depth' (d) | EPfP EWoo MBNS NBro NCGa NLar WCot WHrl |
| 'In Excess' **new** | EJBD |
| 'In Search of Angels' | CFwr |
| 'In Strawberry Time' | WNHG |
| 'Indian Fandango' **new** | EWoo |
| 'Indian Fires' | CFwr |
| 'Indian Giver' | SPol |
| 'Indian Paintbrush' | EWoo MBri NBir SBfd SPol WAul WCAu |
| 'Indigo Moon' | SApp SPol |
| 'Indy Envy' | CFwr |
| 'Inky Fingers' | EJBD SApp |
| 'Inner View' | ECtt MBNS MSpe NLar SApp WMnd |
| 'Inspired Word' | SBrk |
| 'Invitation to Immortality' | EWoo |
| 'Iowa Greenery' **new** | SPol |
| 'Iridescent Jewel' | SDay |
| 'Iris Perry' **new** | EJBD |
| 'Irish Elf' | ELon SApp SHar WTin |
| 'Iron Gate Glacier' | CSpr MBNS XLum |
| 'Isaac' **new** | EJBD |

| |  |  |
|---|---|---|
| | 'Isle of Dreams' | SPol |
| | 'Isleworth' | EWoo |
| | 'Itsy Bitsy Spider' | CBgR CFwr EJBD EWoo |
| | 'Ivelyn Brown' | SPol |
| | 'Jake Russell' | MBNS MNFA |
| | 'Jamaican Jammin" | SPol |
| | 'Jamaican Me Crazy' | EJBD SBrk |
| | 'Jamaican Me Happy' **new** | CFwr EJBD |
| | 'James Clark' | EWoo |
| | 'James Marsh' | CBgR EPfP EWes MBNS MBri MNrw MSpe NSti SApp WAul WCot WMnd |
| | 'Jan Kay' | SDay |
| | 'Janet Gordon' | SBrk SPol |
| | 'Janice Brown' | CKel CWCL CWGN EJBD EWoo LAst LSou MBNS MNFA MSpe MWea NCGa NLar SApp SBrk SDay SPol |
| | 'Jan's Twister' | MNrw SApp SBrk SPol |
| | 'Jason Salter' | EJBD MSpe NCGa SApp SBrk SDay WAul |
| | 'Jay Turman' | SApp SDay |
| | 'Jaybees Lilting Lemon' **new** | EJBD |
| | 'Jazz at the Wool Club' **new** | CFwr |
| | 'Jean' | EJBD SDay |
| | 'Jean Swann' | MBNS SBrk |
| | 'Jedi Dot Pierce' | CFwr MSpe SApp SBrk |
| | 'Jedi Irish Spring' | SApp |
| | 'Jedi Rose Frost' | SApp |
| | 'Jedi Tequila Sunrise' **new** | CFwr |
| | 'Jellyfish Jealousy' | EWoo |
| | 'Jenny Wren' | EBee EBla EJBD EPPr EPla ETod EWoo MBNS MSpe NBre NBro NHol SRGP WAul WWEG |
| | 'Jersey Jim' **new** | EWoo |
| | 'Jersey Spider' | EWoo SDay WCAu |
| | 'Jerusalem' | SBrk SDay |
| | 'Jesse James' | SApp SPol |
| | 'Jessica Lilian' | SBrk |
| | 'Jewel Case' | WNHG |
| | 'Joan Senior' | Widely available |
| | 'Jocelyn's Oddity' | SApp |
| | 'Jockey Club' (d) | ECtt EJBD MBNS |
| | 'Joe Marinello' | SPol |
| | 'John Allen' | CFwr |
| | 'John Bierman' | SBrk |
| | 'John Robert Biggs' | SApp |
| | 'Johnny Come Lately' **new** | EJBD SPol |
| | 'Joie de Vivre' | EWoo |
| | 'Jolly Red Giant' | EWoo |
| | 'Jolly White Giant' **new** | CFwr |
| | 'Jolyene Nichole' | SApp SBrk |
| | 'Jordan' **new** | LSRN |
| | 'Journey to Oz' **new** | EWoo |
| | 'Journey's End' | SDay |
| | 'Jovial' | MSpe SApp SBrk SDay |
| | 'Judah' | SApp |
| | 'Judge Roy Bean' | EJBD EWoo SPol |
| | 'Julie Newmar' | IPot |
| | 'June Melody' **new** | WNHG |
| | 'Jungle Beauty' | CBgR SPol |
| | 'Justin George' | SPol |
| | 'Kachina Firecracker' **new** | CFwr EWoo |
| | 'Kansas Kitten' **new** | EWoo |
| | 'Karateake' **new** | CFwr |
| | 'Karen My Love' **new** | EJBD |
| | 'Karen's Curls' | EWoo SBrk SPol |
| | 'Kasia' | WHrl |
| | 'Katahdin' **new** | EWoo |
| | 'Kate Carpenter' | SBrk SDay SPol |
| | 'Katherine Harris' **new** | CFwr |
| | 'Kathleen Salter' | EWoo |
| | 'Kathryn June Wood' | EWoo |
| | 'Kathy Macartney' | EWoo |
| | 'Katie Elizabeth Miller' | EJBD SBrk SDay |
| | 'Kazuq' | SApp SBrk |
| | 'Kecia' | MNFA |
| | 'Keene' **new** | EWoo |
| | 'Kelly's Girl' | SBrk SPol |
| | 'Kent's Favorite Two' | SBrk |
| | 'Kenyan Sun' **new** | EWoo |
| | 'Kevin Michael Coyne' | EWoo |
| | 'Key to my Heart' **new** | CBgR |
| | 'Key West' **new** | CFwr |
| | 'Kien Mill' **new** | CFwr |
| | 'Kindly Light' | EWoo MNFA SPol |
| | 'King Haiglar' | EGol SApp SBrk |
| | 'King James' **new** | EWoo |
| | 'King's Throne' **new** | WNHG |
| | 'Kiowa Sunset' | MSpe |
| | 'Kisses for Cinderella' **new** | CFwr |
| | 'Kiwi Claret' | MSpe |
| | 'Kolan Dee Jay' **new** | EJBD |
| N | 'Kwanso Flore Pleno' | see *H. fulva* 'Green Kwanso' |
| N | 'Kwanso Flore Pleno Variegata' | see *H. fulva* 'Variegated Kwanso' |
| | 'La Peche' | SDay |
| | 'Lace Cookies' | EWoo |
| | 'Lacy Doily' | EJBD MBri WCAu |
| | 'Lacy Marionette' | EWoo SApp SPol |
| | 'Lady Cynthia' | CKel |
| | 'Lady Fingers' | CBgR EJBD MNFA SDay SPol |
| | 'Lady Hillary' | SApp |
| | 'Lady Inma' | SApp |
| | 'Lady Liz' | MNFA |
| | 'Lady Mischief' | SApp |
| | 'Lady Neva' | CBgR CPar SApp SBrk |
| | 'Ladykin' | SApp SBrk SPol |
| | 'Lake Norman Spider' | EWoo MNFA SApp |
| | 'Lake Norman Sunset' | CFwr |
| | 'Lark Song' | LRHS WFar WHrl |
| | 'Laughing Feather' | EWoo |
| | 'Laughing Giraffe' | EJBD |
| | 'Laura Abdallah' **new** | EJBD |
| | 'Laura Lambert' **new** | SPol |
| | 'Laurena' | EWoo SPol |
| | 'Lavender Arrowhead' | SApp |
| | 'Lavender Deal' | EBee LRHS MNrw WNHG |
| | 'Lavender Flushing' | SApp |
| | 'Lavender Green' **new** | CFwr |
| | 'Lavender Handlebars' | EJBD SBrk |
| | 'Lavender Illusion' | CSev SApp |
| | 'Lavender Light' | EWoo |
| | 'Lavender Memories' | SDay |
| | 'Lavender Plicata' **new** | SPol |
| | 'Lavender Showstopper' **new** | WCAu |
| | 'Lavender Silver Cords' | SPol |
| | 'Lavender Spider' | CBgR SApp |
| | 'Legs Limmer' **new** | EWoo |
| | 'Lemon Bells' ♀H4 | CWat EBee EBla ECGP ECha EPfP EWoo GKin GMaP LRHS MBNS NBro NCGa NGdn SApp SDay |
| | 'Lemon Dessert' | EJBD SBrk |
| | 'Lemon Madeline' **new** | EWoo |
| | 'Lemon Meringue Twist' **new** | EWoo |
| | 'Lemon Mint' | SBrk |
| | 'Lemon Starfish' | SApp |
| | 'Lemonora' | SDay |
| | 'Lenox' | SBrk |
| | 'Leonard Bernstein' | EJBD EWoo SApp SBrk SPol |
| | 'Leslie Renee' **new** | CFwr |

| | |
|---|---|
| 'Let It Rip' | EWoo |
| 'Lexington Avenue' | SPol |
| 'Licorice Candy' | EJBD SBrk |
| 'Light the Way' | ECha GBin |
| 'Light Years Away' | EJBD ELon MBNS MNrw NBro SApp SMrm |
| 'Lil Ledie' | SApp |
| § ***lilioasphodelus*** ♀H4 | Widely available |
| – 'Rowden Golden Jubilee' (v) | CRow |
| 'Lillian Frye' | EGol |
| 'Lilly Dache' | EWoo |
| 'Lilting Belle' | MSpe SBrk SPol |
| 'Lilting Lady' | SApp SDay SPol |
| 'Lilting Lady Red' | SApp |
| 'Lilting Lavender' | WCot |
| 'Lime Frost' | SBrk SPol |
| 'Limited Edition' | EWoo |
| 'Limoncello' | SApp |
| 'Lin Wright' **new** | MSpe |
| 'Linda' | MRav NHol |
| 'Linda Agin' | EWoo |
| 'Lines of Splendor' | EWoo |
| 'Lipstick Print' | SBrk |
| 'Little Angel' | SApp |
| 'Little Audrey' | SApp |
| 'Little Baby Mine' | MSpe |
| 'Little Bee' | NBre |
| 'Little Beige Magic' | EGol |
| 'Little Big Man' | SDay |
| 'Little Bugger' | ELon NLar WWEG |
| 'Little Bumble Bee' | CFir COlW EGol EJBD MBNS SApp WWEG |
| 'Little Business' | MBNS SApp WAul |
| 'Little Cadet' | XLum |
| 'Little Cameo' | EGol |
| 'Little Carpet' | MBNS SPer SPet |
| 'Little Cranberry Cove' | EGol |
| 'Little Dandy' | EGol |
| 'Little Deeke' | COlW SApp SBrk SDay WHrl |
| 'Little Fantastic' | EGol |
| 'Little Fat Cat' | CBgR EJBD SApp |
| 'Little Fat Dazzler' | SApp SBrk SPol |
| 'Little Fellow' | EJBD MBNS |
| 'Little Fruit Cup' | SApp |
| 'Little Grapette' | COlW EGol EPfP ERCP GCra GQue LPla MBNS MSpe NLar NSti SApp SBrk WAul WBrk WCAu WTin WWEG |
| 'Little Greenie' | SDay |
| 'Little Gypsy Vagabond' | CWat SBrk SDay |
| 'Little Heavenly Angel' | COlW SPol |
| 'Little Lavender Princess' | EGol |
| 'Little Maggie' | SApp SDay SPol |
| 'Little Missy' | CBgR COlW CWat EJBD LAst MBNS MSCN NBPC NBre SPet WHoo |
| 'Little Monica' | SApp |
| 'Little Orange Slices' | CFwr |
| 'Little Pink Umbrella' **new** | EJBD |
| 'Little Pumpkin Face' | EGol |
| 'Little Rainbow' | WWEG |
| 'Little Red Hen' | CSam EBla ECGP GKin LRHS MBNS MSpe NBir NBro NEgg NGdn SUsu WFar |
| 'Little Show Stopper' | EWoo MBNS MSpe NBro NLar NMRc |
| 'Little Sweet Sue' | MNFA |
| 'Little Sweet Talk' | SBrk |
| 'Little Toddler' | SApp |
| 'Little Violet Lace' | SDay |
| 'Little Wart' | EGol SDay WHrl |
| 'Little Wine Cup' | Widely available |
| 'Little Wine Spider' | SApp |
| 'Little Witching Hour' | MSpe |
| 'Little Women' | MBNS SDay |
| 'Little Zinger' | GMac SDay |
| 'Littlest Angel' | SDay |
| 'Littlest Clown' | SDay |
| 'Lizard's Purple Fashion' **new** | CFwr |
| 'Lochinvar' | MRav |
| 'Lois Burns' | CFwr EWoo SBrk |
| 'Lollapaloosa' **new** | EJBD |
| 'London Season' **new** | EJBD |
| 'Lonesome Dove' | SBrk SPol |
| 'Long John Silver' | CFwr EJBD |
| 'Long Stocking' | CFwr EJBD EWoo SPol WCot |
| 'Longfields Anwar' **new** | EWoo |
| 'Longfield's Bandit' | EWoo |
| 'Longfield's Beauty' | EWoo MBNS MSpe NCGa SBrk |
| 'Longfield's Glory' | MBNS NBre |
| 'Longfield's Mandy' | MSpe |
| 'Longfield's Maxim' (d) | MBNS |
| 'Longfield's Pearl' | SBrk |
| 'Longfield's Pride' | ECho MBNS SRms WBor |
| 'Longfield's Purple Eye' | NCGa NLar |
| 'Longfield's Tropica' | MBNS |
| 'Longfield's Twins' | EKen MBNS NBPC WCot |
| ***longituba*** B&SWJ 4576 | WCru |
| 'Look at Me' | ELan |
| 'Look Lucky' **new** | CFwr |
| 'Lord Camden' | MNFA |
| 'Lori Goldston' | EWoo MBNS |
| 'Loth Lorien' **new** | CFwr |
| 'Lotsa Dots' **new** | EWoo |
| 'Louise Lemly' **new** | CFwr |
| 'Lourice Abdallah' **new** | EJBD |
| 'Love Glow' | CFir |
| 'Love or Else' **new** | EWoo |
| 'Loving Memories' | SApp |
| 'Lowenstine' | SApp |
| 'Lucille Lennington' | WNHG |
| 'Lucretius' | MNFA |
| 'Luke Senior Junior' | SApp |
| 'Lullaby Baby' | CWat EGol ELan MBNS NLar SApp SDay SPol |
| 'Lurch' **new** | CFwr |
| 'Luscious Honeydew' | WNHG |
| 'Lusty Lealand' | EGol MBNS MNFA SBrk |
| 'Luverne' | SBrk |
| 'Luxury Lace' | CPrp CWat EBla ECtt EGol EJBD ELan EPfP EPla GKin LRHS LSRN MSpe NBir NGdn NPri NWad SPer SPol WAul WCAu WFar WHrl WMoo WPnP WTin XLum XSen |
| 'Lydia Bechtold' | EJBD SBrk |
| 'Lyn Wright' | EWoo |
| 'Lynn Hall' | ECtt EGol EMil MBNS NLar |
| 'Mabel Fuller' | MRav SPer WHrl |
| 'Macbeth' | MBNS SBrk |
| 'Mad Max' | EWoo MSpe SPol |
| 'Madge Cayse' **new** | EJBD |
| 'Mae Graham' | SApp |
| 'Maestro Puccini' | SDay |
| 'Maggie Fynboe' | CBgR SPol |
| 'Magic Amethyst' | CBgR |
| 'Magic Carpet Ride' | SBrk SPol |
| 'Magic Lace' | EWoo SBrk |
| 'Magic of Oz' **new** | CFwr |
| 'Magnificent Eyes' | SPol |

| | |
|---|---|
| 'Magnificent Rainbow' | CBcs SApp |
| 'Mahogany Magic' | EJBD SBrk |
| 'Malachite Prism' | CWGN EJBD NGBo |
| 'Malaysian Masquerade' | SApp |
| 'Malaysian Monarch' | SBrk WMnd WNHG |
| 'Malaysian Spice' | WNHG |
| 'Maleny Blossom' new | EJBD |
| 'Maleny Bright Eyes' | MSpe |
| 'Maleny Chantilly Lace' new | EJBD |
| 'Maleny Debutante' new | EJBD |
| 'Maleny Emperor' new | EJBD |
| 'Maleny Eyecatcher' new | EJBD |
| 'Maleny Flamingo' new | EJBD |
| 'Maleny Mite' | EWoo MSpe |
| 'Maleny Piecrust' | EWoo |
| 'Maleny Sensation' new | EJBD |
| 'Maleny Tapestry' | MSpe |
| 'Maleny Think Big' | EJBD EWoo |
| 'Mallard' | CBgR CWat ECGP ECtt EGol EPla LLWP LRHS MBNS MNFA MRav MSpe NBir SApp SBrk SPer SWat WCot |
| 'Man on Fire' | MBNS |
| 'Manchurian Apricot' | SBrk |
| 'Mandalay Bay Music' | EWoo |
| 'Marble Faun' | SApp SBrk SDay |
| 'Margaret Perry' | CFee CPrp EJBD GBin MNrw WAul |
| 'Maria Callas' new | EJBD |
| 'Marilyn Siwik' new | EJBD |
| 'Marion Caldwell' | SPol |
| 'Marion Vaughn' ♀H4 | CSev EBee ECtt ELan EPfP EWoo GKin GMaP LBMP LHop LRHS MLLN MNFA MSpe NSti SBch SBrk SDix SPer SRGP SSpi WCot WFar WPtf |
| 'Mariska' | SApp SBrk SDay WNHG |
| 'Mark My Word' | SApp |
| 'Marked by Lydia' | CFwr SPol |
| 'Marse Connell' | MSpe |
| 'Martha Adams' | SDay |
| 'Martie Everest' | EWoo |
| 'Martina Verhaert' | CWGN EJBD |
| 'Mary Ethel Anderson' | EJBD EWoo MSpe |
| 'Mary Todd' | EGol MBNS SApp WMnd XSen |
| 'Mary's Gold' | EJBD SBrk SPol |
| 'Mascara Snake' new | EWoo |
| 'Mask Ball' | SBrk |
| 'Mata Hari' | SPol |
| 'Matt' | SBrk |
| 'Mauna Loa' | CSBt CWGN EBee EJBD GQue LRHS MBNS MNFA MNrw MSpe MWea NBre SApp SBrk WAul WCAu WCot |
| 'May May' | SApp SPol |
| 'Meadow Mist' | CBgR EGol |
| 'Meadow Sprite' | SBrk WCot |
| 'Medicine Feather' | CFwr EWoo |
| 'Medieval Guild' | SApp |
| 'Medusa's Glance' new | EWoo |
| 'Mega Stella' | SApp |
| 'Megatrend' new | CFwr |
| 'Melody Lane' | EGol |
| 'Memory Jordan' new | CFwr |
| 'Meno' | EGol |
| 'Mephistopheles' | EWoo |
| 'Merlot Rouge' | WAul |
| 'Merry Maker's Serenade' | MSpe |
| 'Merry Moppet' new | EWoo |
| 'Metaphor' | SApp SBrk XSen |
| 'Michele Coe' | CMMP EBee EBla ECtt EGol EQua GKin LPla LRHS MAvo MBNS MNFA MSpe NBre NBro NCGa NEgg NGdn SApp SRGP WHrl WMoo |
| ***middendorffii*** | CAvo CMac EJBD GMaP LRHS MCoo NSti SMrm WFar WHrl WPnP WThu |
| - 'Major' | CFee |
| 'Midnight Dynamite' | MBNS SBrk |
| 'Midnight Love' | EWoo |
| 'Midnight Magic' | EWoo |
| 'Midnight Mantis' | SPol |
| 'Midnight Raider' | CBgR EWoo |
| 'Mighty Highty Tighty' new | CFwr |
| 'Mighty Mogul' | MNFA SBrd |
| 'Mikado' | CBgR CMac EJBD |
| 'Milady Greensleeves' | EWoo SBrk SPol |
| 'Milanese Mango' | EWoo MSpe |
| 'Mildred Mitchell' | CBgR CFwr CWat EBee EJBD MBNS NLar NMRc SApp SBrk WHlf |
| 'Millie Schlumpf' | SApp SBrk SPol |
| 'Mimosa Umbrella' | SPol |
| 'Ming Lo' | MSpe |
| 'Ming Porcelain' | SApp SBrk SPol WCAu |
| 'Mini Pearl' | CMMP COlW EGol EJBD ELon MBNS MBri MSpe SApp SBrk SPer WPer |
| 'Mini Stella' | CBro ECtt GGar IBal MBNS NBPC NBre NOrc SBrk SPet WAul WFar |
| miniature hybrids | SRms |
| 'Minnie Wildfire' | SPol |
| ***minor*** | CBro EDAr EGol GBin GKev LRHS NGdn SRms |
| - B&SWJ 8841 | WCru |
| 'Miracle Maid' | WNHG |
| 'Miss Jessie' | EWoo MNFA SDay SPol |
| 'Missenden' ♀H4 | CBgR MNFA MNrw SApp |
| 'Mission Moonlight' | EGol |
| 'Missouri Beauty' | MBNS SApp |
| 'Missouri Memories' | SBrk SPol |
| 'Mister Lucky' | MSpe |
| 'Misty Twisty' new | CFwr |
| 'Mitchell Leichhardt' new | EJBD |
| 'Moment of Truth' | NBre |
| 'Monica Marie' | SBrk |
| 'Monica Mead' new | EJBD |
| 'Mont Royal Demitasse' | SPol |
| 'Moon Witch' | SBrk SPol |
| 'Moonbeam' | SApp |
| 'Moonlight Masquerade' | CBgR CWat EBee ECtt EJBD EPfP MMuc NLar SApp SRms |
| 'Moonlight Mist' | SApp SBrk SPol |
| 'Moonlit Caress' | CBgR EBee MBNS NBro SApp SBrk WFar |
| 'Moonlit Crystal' | SApp SPol |
| 'Moonlit Masquerade' | CPar CWGN EWoo GBin GMac MBNS MBri MCCP MLLN MNrw MSCN MSpe NCGa SBch SBrk SEND SPer SPet SPol WAul WCAu WHrl |
| 'Moonlit Pirouette' | SApp |
| 'Moonlit Summerbird' | SPol |
| 'Moonstruck Madness' | CFwr |
| 'Moontraveller' | WCot |
| 'Mormon Spider' | MSpe SApp SPol |
| 'Morning Dawn' | WWEG |
| 'Morning Sun' | MBNS NBre NLar WCot |
| 'Morocco' | CFwr SPol |
| 'Morocco Red' | CBro CCse CTri ELan EPla NBre WWEG |
| 'Morrie Otte' | SPol |

| | |
|---|---|
| 'Moses' Fire' | ECtt EJBD EPfP EWTr MBNS NLar |
| 'Mount Echo Sunrise' | EWoo |
| 'Mount Joy' | SPer |
| 'Mountain Laurel' | EBee ECGP ECtt GKin LRHS LSRN MBNS MCot MRav MSpe NEgg SApp SBrk SPol WTur |
| 'Mountain Top Experience' | EWoo SDay |
| 'Mountain Violet' | SApp |
| 'Move Over Moon' **new** | EJBD |
| 'Mrs David Hall' | CCse |
| 'Mrs Hugh Johnson' | CSev EBee GCra NHol WHrl |
| 'Muffet's Little Friend' | SPol |
| 'Mulberry Frosted Edge' **new** | EWoo |
| ***multiflora*** | LRHS MNFA NHol |
| 'Muscle and Blood' **new** | EWoo |
| 'My Belle' | SBrk |
| 'My Darling Clementine' | SBrk SDay |
| 'My Hope' | SPol |
| 'My Melinda' | MSpe SDay |
| 'My Sweet Rose' | SBrk |
| 'Mynelle's Starfish' | CPar EJBD SBrk SPol |
| 'Mysterious Veil' | EGol |
| 'Nairobi Dawn' | SBrk |
| ***nana*** | CFir EPot GLam |
| 'Nanuq' | SApp SBrk |
| 'Naomi Ruth' | EGol MBNS MSpe SApp WTin |
| 'Nashville' | CBro ELan WHrl |
| 'Nashville Lights' | CBgR SPol |
| 'Nathan Sommers' | EWoo |
| 'Natural Veil' | SPol |
| 'Navajo Princess' | CWat EJBD MBNS MNrw SBrk |
| 'Navajo Rodeo' | EWoo |
| 'Neal Berrey' | SApp SBrk SDay |
| 'Nefertiti' | CBgR ELon MBNS NBir NCGa SAga SPer WAul WTin |
| 'Neon Rose' | EBla GKin MWat SBrk |
| 'Netsuke' | SApp SMrm |
| 'Neusa Gergemann' **new** | EJBD |
| 'Never Get Away' **new** | EJBD |
| 'New Direction' | CFwr EWoo |
| 'New Swirls' | SApp |
| 'New York Follies' | SBrk |
| 'Newberry Borrowed Time' | CFwr |
| 'Neyron Rose' ♀[H4] | CHar EGol EPfP EPla GKin GQue LHop LRHS MBNS MWea NBre NEgg NGdn SBrd WMoo |
| 'Nick's Faith' | WHrl |
| 'Night Beacon' | CBgR ECho ECtt EGol EJBD ELon EWes EWoo GKin GMac IBal MBNS MBri MNrw MSpe NLar SApp SBrk SDay SPol SWal WCAu WHrl |
| 'Night Embers' | EJBD EWoo |
| 'Night Raider' | SApp SBrk |
| 'Night Wings' | EWoo SApp |
| 'Nigrette' | CBen LPBA NHol |
| 'Nile Crane' | CBgR EJBD MBNS MNrw MSpe SApp SBrk SDay SHar SPer WAul |
| 'Nile Plum' | EJBD SApp |
| 'Ninth Millennium' **new** | CFwr |
| 'Nivia Guest' | SApp SDay |
| 'Nob Hill' | CCse EGol EPla GBin LRHS SApp SPol WHrl XLum |
| 'Noble Warrior' | MSpe |
| 'Nona's Garnet Spider' | ELon SApp SPol |
| 'Noonday Dreams' **new** | CFwr |
| 'Nordic Night' | CBgR SPol |
| 'North Star' | SApp |
| 'North Wind Dancer' **new** | EWoo |
| 'Northbrook Star' | MNFA |
| 'Northern Nocturne' **new** | EWoo |
| 'Norton Beauté' | WCot |
| 'Norton Eyed Seedling' | WNHG |
| 'Norton Orange' | MNFA WFar |
| 'Nosferatu' | SPol |
| 'Nova' ♀[H4] | CPrp SApp |
| 'Nuclear Meltdown' **new** | EWoo |
| 'Nuka' | XLum |
| 'Numinous Moments' | SDay |
| 'Nutmeg Elf' | CBgR EWoo SBrk |
| 'Ocean Rain' | SApp SBrk SPol |
| 'Octopus Hugs' | SBrk |
| 'Ode to Oz' **new** | EWoo |
| 'Official Curse' **new** | SPol |
| 'Ojo de Dios' **new** | EWoo |
| 'Old Tangiers' | EJBD EWoo SBrk |
| 'Olive Bailey Langdon' | EGol SApp SBrk SPol WCot |
| 'Oliver Billingslea' | EWoo |
| 'Olympic Showcase' | EJBD SBrk |
| 'Omomuki' | SApp SBrk |
| 'On and On' | GQue LHop MBNS MSpe |
| 'On Pointe' **new** | EWoo |
| 'On Silken Thread' | SPol |
| 'On the Web' | CFwr SApp |
| 'One Last Straw' **new** | EWoo |
| 'Oom Pah Pah' | ECha |
| 'Open Hearth' | CFwr SBrk SDay SPol |
| 'Open my Eyes' **new** | EWoo |
| 'Orange Blossom Special' **new** | EJBD |
| 'Orange Buttons' **new** | WCAu |
| 'Orange Dream' | SDay |
| 'Orange Exotica' | CBgR EJBD |
| 'Orange Grove' **new** | EJBD |
| 'Orange Velvet' | SApp SBrk |
| 'Orangeman' misapplied | EBla EPla MBNS NGdn NHol |
| 'Orchard Sprite' | SApp |
| 'Orchid Beauty' | ECha MLHP WMoo |
| 'Orchid Candy' | EJBD EWoo MBNS NBir SBrk SPol WAul |
| 'Orchid Corsage' | EJBD SApp |
| 'Orchid Lady Slipper' **new** | EJBD EWoo |
| 'Orchid Moonrise' | EWoo |
| 'Oriental Ruby' | EGol |
| 'Orion's Band' **new** | EWoo |
| 'Ostrich Plume' | EJBD |
| 'Ottis Leonard' | CFwr |
| 'Ouachita Beauty' | SPol |
| 'Our Kirsten' | SDay |
| 'Out of Darkness' | EWoo |
| 'Outrageous' | SApp SBrk WNHG |
| 'Over the Top' | MBNS |
| 'Paige Parker' | EGol |
| 'Paige's Pinata' | CFwr MBNS NBPC SApp SBrk |
| 'Paint Your Wagon' | SApp |
| 'Painted Lady' | MNFA SApp |
| 'Painting the Roses Red' **new** | CFwr |
| 'Palace Garden Beauty' | SApp |
| 'Palace Guard' | MNFA |
| 'Palantir' | SApp |
| 'Pale Moon Windmill' **new** | CFwr |
| 'Panama Hattie' | SBrk |
| 'Pandora's Box' | Widely available |
| 'Pantaloons' | SApp |
| 'Pantherette' | SApp SPol |
| 'Paper Butterfly' | MSpe SBrk SPol |
| 'Papoose' **new** | XLum |
| 'Paradise Prince' | EGol |
| 'Pardon Me' | CBro CMHG CMMP EGol EJBD ELan ELon EWoo GGar GKin GMaP |

|  |  |
|---|---|
| | LRHS MBNS MNFA MSpe NBPC NCGa NGdn NHol SApp SBrk SPol SRGP SWal WAul WBor WCAu |
| 'Pardon Me Boy' | SPol |
| 'Parfait' | CBgR EJBD EWoo SPol |
| 'Party Queen' | SDay |
| 'Pas de Deux' | SApp |
| 'Passion's Promise' **new** | CWat |
| 'Pastel Ballerina' | SBrk SDay |
| 'Pastel Classic' | SApp SBrk |
| 'Pastilline' | SPol |
| 'Pat Mercer' | SApp XSen |
| 'Patchwork Puzzle' | EWoo SBrk SPol |
| 'Patricia' | MBNS |
| 'Patricia Fay' | SApp |
| 'Patricia Gentzel Wright' | EWoo |
| 'Patsy Bickers' | EWoo SApp |
| 'Patterns' **new** | SPol |
| 'Paul Weber' | SApp |
| 'Pawn of Prophecy' | SDay |
| 'Peace be Still' **new** | EWoo |
| 'Peach Candy' **new** | EJBD |
| 'Peach Float' | EWoo |
| 'Peach Jubilee' | SPol |
| 'Peach Petticoats' | SBrk |
| 'Peach Yum Yum' **new** | CFwr |
| 'Peacock Curls' | EWoo |
| 'Peacock Maiden' | EWoo SApp SBrk SPol XSen |
| 'Pear Ornament' | EJBD SBrk |
| 'Pearl Lewis' | EJBD SBrk SPol |
| 'Pearl Sherwood' **new** | EWoo |
| 'Peggy Jeffcoat' | CFwr SBrk |
| 'Penelope Vestey' | EBla MBNS MNFA NBir SApp SPol SRGP |
| 'Penny's Worth' | EGol LEdu LRHS MBNS NOrc WAul WCot WFar WHoo XLum |
| 'Perfect Pleasure' | MBNS |
| 'Persian Melon Plus' **new** | WCAu |
| 'Persian Ruby' | SPol |
| 'Persian Shrine' | SPol |
| 'Persnickety' **new** | EJBD |
| 'Petite Ballerina' | SDay |
| 'Phyllis Cantini' **new** | SPol |
| 'Piano Man' | MBNS MSpe MWea NLar SBrk WAul WNHG |
| 'Piccadilly Princess' | EJBD SBrk SDay WAul |
| 'Picket Fences' **new** | CFwr |
| 'Pink Ambrosia' | EWoo |
| 'Pink Attraction' | SApp |
| 'Pink Ballerina' | EGol |
| 'Pink Charm' | CBen CMac COlW EBee ECha ECtt EPPr GKin GMaP LPBA LRHS MBNS NBro NHol SPol |
| 'Pink Circle' | SDay |
| 'Pink Cotton Candy' | EWoo SBrk SDay SPol |
| 'Pink Crinkles' | SBrk |
| 'Pink Damask' ♀H4 | Widely available |
| 'Pink Dream' | EQua MBNS NBir NBre SPol |
| 'Pink Grace' | SPol |
| 'Pink Heaven' | EGol |
| 'Pink Lady' | MNrw MRav SRms |
| 'Pink Lavender Appeal' | EGol WCAu |
| 'Pink Monday' | WNHG |
| 'Pink Pajamas' **new** | CFwr |
| 'Pink Picotee Deluxe' | SBrk |
| 'Pink Picotee Elite' | SBrk |
| 'Pink Piglet' **new** | EJBD |
| 'Pink Prelude' | GBee LRHS MBNS MWat NBro SMrm |
| 'Pink Puff' | MBNS NBir NBre NLar |
| 'Pink Ruffled Love' | CFwr |
| 'Pink Spider' | SDay |
| 'Pink Sundae' | ECha WHrl |
| 'Pink Super Spider' | EWoo MNFA SBrk SPol |
| 'Pink Windmill' | EWoo SDay SPol |
| 'Piping Rock' **new** | CFwr |
| 'Pirate Treasure' | MBNS |
| 'Pirate's Patch' | EWoo SBrk SDay SPol WCot |
| 'Pixie Parasol' | WMnd WNHG |
| 'Pixie Pipestone' | SApp SPol |
| 'Pixie Pleasure' | CFwr |
| 'Pizza' | SDay |
| 'Planet Max' **new** | EWoo |
| 'Platinum and Gold' | CFwr |
| 'Plinko' **new** | CFwr |
| 'Plum Beauty' | NLar |
| 'Plum Candy' | EWoo |
| 'Pocket Change' **new** | EJBD |
| 'Pocket Size' | SApp |
| 'Poetic Dance' | EWoo |
| 'Poinsettia' | EJBD |
| 'Point of Honor' | EWoo |
| 'Pojo' | CFwr SDay |
| 'Pompeian Purple' | EGol |
| 'Pony' | CWat EGol SBrk SPol |
| 'Ponytail Pink' | EGol |
| 'Pookie Bear' | SApp |
| 'Porcelain Pleasure' | SDay |
| 'Prague Spring' | CFwr MNFA MSpe SPol WCAu |
| 'Prairie Belle' | MBNS NBre NLar SApp SPol WFar |
| 'Prairie Blossoms' | CFwr |
| 'Prairie Blue Eyes' | ECtt EGol EJBD GBin MBNS NPri SApp SPlb SPol WAul WCot WHrl WMnd WWEG |
| 'Prairie Charmer' | MMuc SEND WHrl |
| 'Precious d'Oro' **new** | GQue |
| 'Pretty Miss' | ECtt LRHS MBri |
| 'Pretty Peggy' | MNFA |
| 'Preview Party' | WNHG |
| 'Primal Scream' | CFwr SApp SBrk WCot |
| 'Primrose Mascotte' | NBir |
| 'Prince Redbird' | SBrk |
| 'Princess Blue Eyes' | SPol |
| 'Princess Ellen' | SApp |
| 'Princess Lilli' | MBNS |
| 'Princeton Eye Glow' | SDay |
| 'Princeton Point Lace' | SApp |
| 'Prissy Frills' | SPol |
| 'Prize Picotee Deluxe' | SPol |
| 'Prize Picotee Elite' | SPol WTin |
| 'Promising Future' **new** | CFwr |
| 'Prophetess' **new** | CFwr |
| 'Protocol' | MSpe SDay SPol |
| 'Ptarmigan' | SDay |
| § 'Puddin' | CWat SDay WAul |
| 'Pudgie' | SApp |
| 'Pueblo Dreamer' **new** | EWoo |
| 'Pug Yarborough' | SPol |
| 'Pumpkin Kid' | SApp SPol |
| 'Pumpkin Prince' **new** | CFwr |
| 'Puppet Lady' | SApp |
| 'Puppet Show' | SDay |
| 'Pure and Simple' | CFwr SDay SPol |
| 'Pure Country' | CFwr |
| 'Purple Bicolor' | WHrl |
| 'Purple Corsage' | SApp |
| 'Purple Grasshopper' | EWoo |
| 'Purple Oddity' | EWoo SPol |
| 'Purple Pinwheel' | EWoo SPol |

'Purple Rain' CWat LRHS MBNS MWea SApp SPol SWvt
'Purple Rain Dance' SPol
'Purple Waters' MBNS NBre NOrc SPol WPnP
'Pursuit of Excellence' SBrk
'Pyewacket' SApp
'Pygmy Plum' SBrk SDay
'Queen Empress' **new** WNHG
'Queen Lily' WNHG
'Queen of May' MNrw SApp WCot
'Queens Delight' SBrk
'Queens Fancy' SApp
'Queen's Gift' SApp
'Queensland' EJBD SApp
'Quick Results' SApp SBrk
'Quiet Pink' **new** EJBD
'Ra Hansen' EJBD SApp SBrk SDay
'Racing Stripes' **new** CFwr
'Radiant' CBcs
'Radiant Greetings' MNFA XSen
'Radiant Moonbeam' EJBD
'Radiation Biohazard' **new** CFwr
'Rags to Riches' CFwr
'Rainbow Candy' CWGN LLHF MBNS SBrk SPad
'Rainbow Drive' CFwr
'Raindrop' EGol
'Raining Violets' EWoo
'Rajah' CBgR CMac MBNS MSpe NBro SPer WHrl
'Randall Moore' SPol
'Rander's Pride' **new** EWoo
'Rapid Eye Movement' **new** CFwr
'Raspberry Butterflies' **new** EWoo
'Raspberry Candy' CBro EJBD GCra MBNS MNrw MSpe NBro NCGa NHol NOrc SApp SBrk SRms WHrl
'Raspberry Masquerade' **new** CFwr
'Raspberry Pixie' EGol SPol
'Raspberry Star' **new** EWoo
'Raspberry Wine' ECha
'Rave On' SApp SBrk
'Raven Woodsong' EWoo
'Real Wind' CFwr SApp SBrk SPol
'Red Admiral' LRHS
'Red Butterfly' EJBD SPol
'Red Eyed Shocker' **new** CFwr
'Red Flag' CFwr
'Red Hill' **new** EWoo
'Red Joy' SApp
'Red Monarch' **new** EJBD
'Red Pennant' **new** CFwr
'Red Precious' ♀H4 MNFA MNrw SApp WCot
'Red Rain' EWoo
'Red Ribbons' EWoo SDay SPol
'Red Ruby' ERCP
'Red Rum' EJBD EWll MSpe NBro SBfd WMoo WPnP
'Red Skeletons' **new** CFwr
'Red Suspenders' MBNS
'Red Thrill' **new** CFwr
'Red Twister' SBrk SPol
'Red Volunteer' SBrk SPol
'Red Vortex' **new** EJBD
'Reflections in Time' **new** EWoo
'Regal Finale' SDay
'Regal Giant' EWoo
'Regal Vision' SApp
'Regency Dandy' SApp SDay SPol
'Renee' MNrw
'Respighi' SApp SBrk

'Return Trip' SPol
'Revolute' SDay
'Rhode Island Red' CFwr
'Ribbonette' EJBD MBNS MSpe
'Rigamarole' SPol
'Right on Red' [illegible]
'Riptide' SApp
'Rocket City' EJBD ELan SPol
'Rocky Horror' **new** CFwr
'Rococo' SBrk SDay
'Rodeo Sweetheart' CFwr
'Roger Grounds' CBgR SApp SPol
'Roman Toga' **new** CBgR EJBD
'Romanian Rendevous' **new** EWoo
* 'Romantic Rose' EBee MBNS NLar WHrl
'Ron Rousseau' SApp SPol
'Root Beer' WTin
'Rose' EJBD
'Rose Claire' **new** LPla
'Rose Corsage' EWoo
'Rose Emily' EJBD SApp SBrk SDay SPol
'Rose Fever' EWoo
'Rose Roland' NBre
'Roseate Spoonbill' EWoo
'Rosella Sheridan' SBrk
'Roses in Snow' MBNS SBrk SPol
'Roswitha' CWat EJBD SApp SPol
'Rosy Lights' CFwr EWoo SPol
'Rosy Returns' LRHS MBNS NLar SBrk SHar
'Round Midnight' SPol
'Royal Braid' EPfP MBNS MNrw MSpe NCGa NLar SApp SBrk SPer WAul WCot
'Royal Celebration' WCot
'Royal Corduroy' SBrk
'Royal Crown' CSev
'Royal Elk' **new** EWoo
'Royal Hunter' CFwr
'Royal Parade' SDay
'Royal Prestige' SApp XSen
'Royal Robe' CTri
'Royal Saracen' SDay
'Royal Thornbird' CBgR
'Royalty' GCra
'Ruby Moon' **new** CFwr
'Ruby Sentinel' SDay
'Ruby Spider' EJBD ELon EWoo SBrk SDay SPol
'Rue Madelaine' SPol
'Ruffled Apricot' CKel LBMP MBNS MNFA MSpe SBrk SDay WNHG
'Ruffled Carousel' WNHG
'Rumble Seat Romance' WNHG
'Russian Easter' SBrk
'Russian Ragtime' **new** EJBD
'Russian Rhapsody' CKel EJBD SApp SBrk SPol
'Sabie' SApp
'Sabine Baur' CWat EBee EWoo IBal IPot LRHS MBNS MNrw MSpe MWea NLar SApp SBrk WAul WFar
'Sabra Salina' EWoo SBrk
'Sachsen Little Gold' CFwr
'Sachsen Pink Ball' **new** CFwr
'Sachsen Purple Eye' **new** CFwr
'Sachsen Rustic' CFwr
'Sachsen White Giant' CFwr
'Saffron Glow' SDay
* 'Sagamore' SApp
'Saintly' EWoo MSpe
'Salmon Sheen' SDay SPer
'Sammy Russell' Widely available
'Samuel Bell' EWoo

'San Luis Halloween' **new** CFwr
'Sandra Walker' EGol
'Sanford Code Red' **new** CFwr
'Sanford Star Search' **new** CFwr
'Sangre de Cristo' CFwr
'Santa's Little Helper' **new** CFwr
'Santiago' SPol
'Saratoga Pinwheel' **new** SPol
'Satin Clouds' EGol
'Satin Glass' LRHS MNFA
'Satin Glow' ECha MLHP
'Scapes from Hell' **new** EWoo
'Scarlet Flame' ECha WMoo
'Scarlet Oak' MBri SBrk WAul
'Scarlet Orbit' EWoo MSpe SApp SBrk SHar SPol
'Scarlet Prince' WNHG
'Scarlet Ribbons' SPol
'Scatterbrain' CKel SPol
'Schnickel Fritz' NCGa
'School Girl' LRHS
'Scorpio' CBgR SPol
'Scotland' IBal SApp
'Screaming Demon' SPol
'Sea of Love' **new** EJBD
'Sea Siren' **new** CWat
'Sea Swept Dreams' **new** EJBD
'Searcy Marsh' EGol
'Sebastian' MNFA SApp SBrk
'Secret Splendor' SPol
'Secretary's Sand' **new** EWoo
'Segramoor' SApp
'Seminole Blood' SBrk
'Seminole Wind' EWoo SBrk SPol
'Serena Sunburst' CFwr SBrk SPol
'Serenade' **new** EWoo
'Serene Madonna' CFir GBin MWea SBfd SPoG
'Serenity Bay' **new** CFwr
'Serenity Morgan' EPfP MBNS SMrm
'Serge Rigaud' **new** CFwr
'Sergeant Major' **new** EWoo
'Shadowed Pink' WNHG
'Shady Lady' SDay
'Shake the Mountains' **new** CFwr
'Shaman' SApp SBrk SPol
'Shangri La Truffle' **new** CFwr
'She Devil' **new** CFwr
'Shelly Victoria' SDay
'Sherry Lane Carr' EJBD SPol
'Sherwood Gladiator' **new** WNHG
'Shimek September Morning' SPol
'Shimmering Elegance' CFwr
* 'Shocker' EWoo
'Shogun' MBNS
'Shotgun' SPol
'Show Amber' SApp
'Show Girl' EJBD LRHS
'Shuffle the Deck' **new** EWoo
'Significant Other' SApp
'Sigudilla' **new** WNHG
'Silent Sentry' SApp
'Silken Fairy' EGol SDay
'Silken Touch' SApp SBrk SPol
'Siloam Amazing Grace' SApp SBrk SDay
'Siloam Baby Talk' EGol ELon GMac NBir SApp WAul WHoo WMoo WPnP WTin
'Siloam Bertie Ferris' MBNS
'Siloam Bo Peep' EGol SApp WAul
'Siloam Button Box' EGol MBNS WAul WHrl
'Siloam Bye Lo' EGol EWoo MSpe SBrk
'Siloam Cinderella' EGol EJBD SBrk
'Siloam David Kirchhoff' EJBD MBNS MSpe SDay XSen
'Siloam Doodlebug' CBgR CWat EGol MSpe SBrk
'Siloam Double Classic' (d) EGol EJBD SBrk SPol
'Siloam Dream Baby' MBNS MSpe NCGa
'Siloam Edith Sholar' EGol
'Siloam Ethel Smith' EGol SApp SBrk SPol
'Siloam Fairy Tale' CWat EGol
'Siloam French Doll' MBNS NLar SApp
'Siloam French Marble' SBrk SDay
'Siloam Frosted Mint' SApp SBrk
'Siloam Gold Coin' SApp SDay
'Siloam Grace Stamile' CFir MBNS SApp
'Siloam Harold Flickinger' SBrk
'Siloam Helpmate' WNHG
'Siloam Jim Cooper' MSpe SBrk
'Siloam Joan Senior' EGol MBNS
'Siloam John Yonski' SDay
'Siloam June Bug' CBgR EGol ELan SApp WCot
'Siloam Justine Lee' MBNS
'Siloam Kewpie Doll' EGol
'Siloam Little Angel' EGol SApp SPol
'Siloam Little Girl' CWat ECtt EGol SBrk SDay
'Siloam Mama' SApp SBrk
'Siloam Merle Kent' EWoo MSpe SApp SBrk SPol
'Siloam New Toy' EGol EJBD
'Siloam Nugget' SApp
'Siloam Orchid Jewel' EGol
'Siloam Paul Watts' SApp SBrk SPol
'Siloam Peewee' EGol
'Siloam Penny' SApp
'Siloam Pink Glow' EGol SWat WAul
'Siloam Pink Petite' EGol
'Siloam Plum Tree' EGol SApp
'Siloam Pocket Size' EGol SApp
'Siloam Powder Pink' SApp
'Siloam Prissy' EGol SApp
'Siloam Purple Plum' EGol
'Siloam Queen's Toy' SPol
'Siloam Ra Hansen' SApp
'Siloam Red Ruby' EGol
'Siloam Red Toy' EGol
'Siloam Red Velvet' EGol
'Siloam Ribbon Candy' EGol SApp WNHG
'Siloam Rose Dawn' SApp SBrk SPol
'Siloam Royal Prince' EGol EJBD EPfP MSpe SApp
'Siloam Shocker' EGol
'Siloam Show Girl' CWGN EGol EWoo GKin MBNS SApp
'Siloam Spizz' SBrk
'Siloam Sugar Time' EGol
'Siloam Tee Tiny' EGol
'Siloam Tinker Toy' EGol
'Siloam Tiny Mite' EGol SDay WHrl
'Siloam Toddler' EGol
'Siloam Tom Thumb' EGol MBNS MSpe WCAu
'Siloam Ury Winniford' CBro CMac CWan EGol EMil MBNS MCCP MSpe NBre NLar SApp SBrk WAul WHoo WHrl WPnP WTin
'Siloam Virginia Henson' EGol EJBD EWoo NCGa SApp SBrk WWEG
'Silver Ice' EWoo MSpe SApp SBrk SPol
'Silver King' GBin
'Silver Lance' SPol
'Silver Quasar' SBrk SPol
'Silver Trumpet' EGol WWEG
'Silver Veil' WFar
'Simply Divine' **new** CFwr
'Sinbad Sailor' NLar
'Singing in the Sunshine' EWoo

'Sings the Blues' **new** EJBD
'Sir Blackstem' ELon GCal SApp SBrk
'Sir Modred' SPol WNHG
'Sirius' NHol
'Sirocco' WTin
'Sixth Sense' ELon MBNS SBrk SPad WHrl
'Skinwalker' EWoo
'Slapstick' ELon SDay
'Sleepy Hollow' **new** EJBD NGBo
'Slender Lady' CFwr SBrk
'Small World' **new** EWoo
'Small World Tornado' **new** EWoo
'Smith Brothers' SPol
'Smoky Mountain Autumn' EWoo MSpe SApp SBrk SPol
'Smoky Mountain Bell' SApp
'Smuggler's Gold' ECtt SApp
'Snappy Rhythm' MNFA
'Snowed In' EWoo SBrk
'Snowy Apparition' EBla ECtt EWTr GKin LHop LRHS MBNS MBri MNFA MSpe MWhi NWad SApp SPol
'Snowy Eyes' CHid EGol GKin MBNS NCGa NHol SApp SWat WAul WCAu WHrl
'So Excited' SBrk SDay
'So Lovely' EWoo SApp XLum
'So Many Stars' CFwr
'Soft Cashmere' **new** XLum
'Solano Bull's Eye' MLHP
'Someone Special' SBrk SPol
'Someplace Special' SBrk
'Song In My Heart' EWoo
'Song Sparrow' CBro GMac MSCN SApp WPer
'South Seas' LRHS
'Southern Charmer' SBrk
'Southern Prize' SDay
'Sovereign Queen' EGol WNHG
'Spacecoast Dragon Prince' **new** EWoo
'Spacecoast Gator Eye' **new** EJBD IPot
'Spacecoast Peach Fringe' **new** CFwr
'Spacecoast Scrambled' CBcs CWGN EPfP MBNS NLar SBrk
'Spacecoast Starburst' CBcs EJBD IPot MBNS NBro SApp SBrk WCAu WCot WFar
'Spanish Fandango' SPol
'Spanish Glow' SBrk SPol
'Sparkling Dawn' SBrk
'Speak of Angels' SApp SBrk
'Spice Hunter' **new** CFwr
'Spider Breeder' SApp
'Spider Impostor' **new** EJBD
'Spider Man' CFwr MNFA SApp SBrk SDay SPol XSen
'Spider Miracle' EWoo MNFA SBrk SDay SPol
'Spider Red' CWGN EWoo
'Spider Web' EJBD
'Spilled Milk' SPol
'Spindazzle' CBgR CFwr SPol
'Spinne in Lachs' SBrk SPol
'Spiral Charmer' SApp
'Spirit of Sapelo' **new** EWoo
'Spock's Sun' **new** CFwr
'Spode' SApp SDay
'Spooner' CBgR
'Spring Ballerina' SApp
'Spring Willow Song' SDay
'Squash Dolly' EWoo
'Stafford' Widely available
'Staghorn Sumac' EBla GKin LEdu LRHS MBNS MSpe WCAu
'Stanley Baby' **new** EJBD
'Star of Fantasy' CFwr
'Star Twister' CFwr EWoo
'Starling' CFir CPar EGol EWoo MNFA SApp WAul WWEG
'Starman's Quest' SPol
'Stars and Stripes' MNFA
'Starstruck' WNHG
'Startle' CFir CWGN ELon EPfP MBNS MNrw SApp SBrk WCot
'Statuesque' EWoo WFar
'Steely Blue Eyes' **new** EJBD
'Stella de Oro' Widely available
'Stella in Red' **new** EPfP
'Steve Trimmer' **new** CFwr
'Stinnette' WCot
'Stoke Poges' ♀H4 CAvo CBgR CBro EBee EBla EPfP EPla GBin LAst LBMP LHop LRHS LSRN MBNS MNFA MSpe SApp SPer STes SWat
'Stoplight' CBgR EBla ELon LRHS SApp SDay SPol
'Storm of the Century' **new** MNrw
'Storm Over Toledo' **new** CFwr
'Strawberry Candy' CMMP CMac CSBt CWGN ECtt EJBD ELon EWll EWoo LSRN MBNS MBri MSCN MSpe NGdn SApp SBfd SBrk SPer SPet STes WAul WCAu WHoo WHrl WMoo WWEG
'Strawberry Fields Forever' EJBD EWoo MBNS MBri MSpe NLar SBrk SHar SPol
'Strawberry Swirl' MNFA
'Strawberry Velvet' **new** EJBD
I 'Streaker' B. Brown (v) WCot XSen
'Street Urchin' EJBD SPol
'Streets of Heaven' **new** EWoo
'Strider Spider' SApp
'Strutter's Ball' EJBD EWoo IPot MBNS MNFA MSCN MSpe NGdn SApp SBfd SBrk SDay SPer SPol SWat WAul WCAu WMnd
'Sugar Cookie' EWoo SApp SBrk SPol
'Summer Dragon' MBNS SBrk
'Summer Fireworks' **new** EWoo
'Summer Interlude' WMoo
'Summer Jubilee' SApp
'Summer Wine' Widely available
'Sun King' SBrk
'Sunday Gloves' EGol SBrk SPol WNHG
'Sungold Candy' EJBD SApp
'Sunray Brilliance' EWoo
'Super Purple' CKel SApp
'Superlative' EJBD SApp SBrk SPol
'Susan Weber' EJBD EWoo SApp SBrk SPol
'Suzie Wong' MNFA
'Svengali' SPol
'Swan Dance' **new** EJBD
'Sweet Hot Chocolate' LRHS MBNS
'Sweet Pea' EGol EJBD
'Sweet Sugar Candy' EWoo
'Swirling Spider' CBgR EWoo
'Tahitian Waterfall' CFwr
'Tail Feathers' **new** CFwr
'Taj Mahal' ELon EWoo SApp WFar
'Tall Boy' SApp
'Tang' CHid MBNS MMuc NOrc WCAu
'Tangerine Tango' EWoo
'Tango Noturno' SApp SPol
'Tapestry of Dreams' MSpe
'Tarantula' ELon SApp

| | |
|---|---|
| 'Taruga' | EWoo |
| 'Tasmania' | SPer |
| 'Tchao Pantin' | CFwr XSen |
| 'Teahouse Tapestry' **new** | EJBD |
| 'Technical Knockout' **new** | EWoo |
| 'Techny Breeze' | SBrk |
| 'Techny Spider' | SBrk |
| 'Tejas' | CElw ELon NBre SPer |
| 'Ten to Midnight' | SApp |
| 'Tender Shepherd' | EGol |
| 'Tennessee Flycatcher' | EWoo SPol |
| 'Tennessee Williams' **new** | SPol |
| 'Tennyson' **new** | CFwr |
| 'Tet Set' | WNHG |
| 'Tetraploid Stella de Oro' | SDay |
| 'Tetrina's Daughter' ♀H4 | CBgR LRHS NHol SApp SBrk |
| 'Texas Sunlight' | WAul |
| 'Thanks a Bunch' | SBrk SPol |
| 'The Tingler' **new** | EWoo |
| 'Theresa Hall' | WFar |
| 'Thin Man' **new** | CFwr |
| 'Third Witch' **new** | CFwr EWoo |
| 'Three Diamonds' | SPol |
| 'Thumbelina' | ECha WMoo XLum |
| § ***thunbergii*** | CAvo ECha GCal MCoo |
| - 'Ovation' | MBNS |
| 'Thundering Ovation' | CWGN MSpe MWea SBrk |
| 'Thy True Love' | SApp |
| 'Tigereye Spider' | EWoo |
| 'Tigerling' | EWoo MSpe SPol |
| 'Tiger's Eye' | SBrk |
| 'Tigger' | CFwr EJBD |
| 'Time Lord' | SApp XSen |
| 'Time to Believe' | SPol |
| 'Time Together' **new** | EJBD |
| 'Timeless Fire' | SApp SBrk |
| 'Tiny Talisman' | SApp |
| 'Tirade' **new** | CFwr |
| 'Tis Midnight' | WNHG |
| 'Tobacco Road' | EJBD |
| 'Tom Collins' | SBrk |
| 'Tom Wise' | SBrk SPol |
| 'Tomorrow's Song' | SApp SPol |
| 'Tone Poem' | WNHG |
| 'Tonia Gay' | SApp SBrk SPol |
| 'Too Much Fun' | CFwr |
| 'Toodleloo Kangaroo' **new** | EWoo |
| 'Toothpick' | EWoo MSpe SPol |
| 'Tootsie Rose' | SBrk SPol |
| 'Top Honors' | SPol |
| 'Topspin' **new** | EWoo |
| 'Torpoint' | EBla GBee MBNS MRav NEgg SBfd |
| 'Total Eclipse' | SBrk |
| 'Totally Tropical' | SBrk |
| 'Touched by Magic' | CFwr |
| 'Towhead' | MRav WCot |
| 'Toyland' | EGol EPfP MBNS NBir NGdn NLar NPri SPol |
| 'Trahlyta' | CBgR CPar EJBD EWoo MSpe SApp SBrk SDay SPol WHrl WTin |
| 'Treasure of Love' | EWoo |
| 'Tremor' | CFwr |
| 'Trevi Fountain' | EWoo |
| 'Tripoli' **new** | EJBD |
| 'Tropic Sunset' | SBrk |
| 'Tropical Depression' **new** | EWoo |
| 'Tropical Heat Wave' | SApp |
| 'Troubled Sleep' | EWoo |
| 'Truchas Sunrise' **new** | EWoo |
| 'True Glory' | SApp |
| 'True Grit' | SApp SBrk |
| 'True North' **new** | CFwr |
| 'True Pink Beauty' | EWoo |
| 'Truffle Heritage' **new** | CFwr |
| 'Tune the Harp' | SPol |
| 'Tuolumne Fairy Tale' | SPol |
| 'Turkish Turban' | SPol |
| 'Tuscawilla Bill Reed' | EJBD |
| 'Tuscawilla Blackout' | SApp SBrk XSen |
| 'Tuscawilla Dave Talbot' **new** | EJBD |
| 'Tuscawilla Snowdrift' **new** | EJBD |
| 'Tuscawilla Thomas Wilson' **new** | EJBD |
| 'Tuscawilla Tigress' | GKin GMac IKil MBNS MWea NCGa SBrk SMad WAul WHrl |
| 'Tuscawilla Tranquility' **new** | EJBD |
| 'Tutankhamun' | MSpe |
| 'Tutti Frutti Truffle' **new** | CFwr |
| 'Tuxedo' | SApp SPol |
| 'Twenty Third Psalm' | WHal |
| 'Twiggy' | CFwr MSpe |
| 'Twilight Secrets' | LRHS MBNS |
| 'Twirling Pinata' **new** | EWoo |
| 'Twist and Shout' **new** | CFwr |
| 'Twist of Lemon' | CFwr EWoo |
| 'Twister Time' **new** | CFwr |
| 'Two Faces of Love' | SPol |
| 'Two Part Harmony' | CFwr |
| 'Tylwyth Teg' | CFwr SPol |
| 'Ultimate Destiny' **new** | CWat |
| 'Umbrella Parade' | EJBD |
| 'Unchartered Waters' | EJBD MBNS SBrk |
| 'Unforgetable Fire' | EWoo |
| 'Uniquely Different' | SPol |
| 'Upper Class Peach' | SBrk |
| 'Uptown Girl' | SBrk |
| 'Valiant' | EWoo MBNS WHrl |
| 'Vanessa Arden' | SApp |
| 'Vanilla Candy' | MSpe SBrk |
| 'Vanilla Fluff' **new** | EJBD |
| 'Varsity' | CPLG CSpr CWat EGol GMac LRHS NBir SBrk SPer |
| 'Veins of Truth' **new** | CBgR EJBD |
| 'Velvet Shadows' | SDay |
| 'Velvet Widow' **new** | CFwr |
| 'Vendetta' | WNHG |
| 'Vera Biaglow' | EJBD MSpe SApp SBrk SDay SPol |
| 'Very Berry Ice' | SPol |
| 'Vespers' | CAbP EJBD WFar WPnP |
| ***vespertina*** | see *H. thunbergii* |
| 'Veuve Joyeuse' | XSen |
| 'Vi Simmons' | SBrk |
| 'Victoria Aden' | CBro |
| 'Victoria Elizabeth Barnes' | WNHG |
| 'Victorian Collar' | SApp SBrk |
| 'Victorian Lace' | EWoo |
| 'Victorian Ribbons' | CFwr SPol |
| 'Victorian Violet' | SDay |
| 'Video' | SApp SBrk |
| 'Vintage Bordeaux' | ELan SApp WAul |
| 'Vintage Burgundy' | WNHG |
| 'Violet Hour' | EJBD SDay |
| 'Viracocha' | SApp WMnd WNHG |
| 'Virgin's Blush' | SPer |
| 'Vision of Beauty' | SApp |
| 'Vohann' | SApp SBrk |
| 'Waiting in the Wings' | SBrk |
| 'Walking on Sunshine' | SApp SBrk WCot |
| 'Wally Nance' | SApp |

'Walnut Hill' **new** EJBD
'Walt Disney' **new** GKin
'War Paint' SDay
'Warrior Victorious' **new** CFwr
'Watchyl Christmas Widow' **new** CFwr
'Watchyl Cyber Spider' **new** CFwr
'Watchyl Dancing Spider' CFwr
'Watchyl Digital Scream' **new** CFwr
'Watchyl Digital Spider' **new** CFwr
'Watchyl Lavender Blue' **new** CFwr
'Water Witch' CWat EGol SApp STes
'Watermelon Man' EWoo
'Watership Down' EWoo
'Wayside Green Imp' EGol MNrw SApp
'We Love' **new** EWoo
'Weaver's Art' CFwr SPol
'Web Browser' CFwr
'Web Dancer' **new** SPol
'Wedding Band' SBrk
'Wekiwa' **new** EWoo
'Welchkins' WAul
'Welfo White Diamond' SApp SPol
'Wendy Glawson' SApp
'Westward Wind' CFwr EWoo
'What a Day for a Daydream' **new** CFwr
'When Fortune Smiles' SBrk
'When I Dream' SBrk
'Whichford' ♀H4 CBgR CBro CMMP CSam EBee ECha ECtt ELan EPla EWoo GKin LRHS MBNS MNFA MSpe NEgg SMrm SPer SPhx WAul
'Whirling Fury' EWoo SApp
'Whiskey on Ice' SApp
'White Coral' LRHS LSRN MBNS MNFA NBro WFar
'White Edged Madonna' SBch WHrl
'White Lemonade' SApp
'White Pansy' SBrk SDay
'White Perfection' EWoo
'White Temptation' CFir CMMP EGol EJBD EPfP EWoo GBin MNFA MWea NCGa NGdn SApp SBrk WAul WHoo WMnd WNHG XSen
'White Tie Affair' EWoo SApp SBrk SDay
'White Zone' EWoo
'Whooperee' SBrk SDay
'Wideyed' EPla GBin XLum
'Wild about Sherry' CFwr SPol
'Wild and Wonderful' CWGN EJBD WWlt
'Wild Horses' CFwr CWGN EJBD EWes LRHS MNrw SBrk SPad SPol WHrl
'Wild Mustang' MBNS MSpe SBrk
'Wild One' SApp
'Wild Rose Fandango' EWoo
'Wild Winter Wine' **new** CFwr
'Wild Wookie' **new** CFwr
'Wildest Dreams' EWoo
'Wildfire Tango' SApp
'Wilson Spider' SApp SPol
'Wind Beneath My Sails' EWoo
'Wind Frills' SApp SBrk SPol WCAu
'Wind Song' SApp SBrk
'Windmill Yellow' EWoo SBrk
'Window Dressing' EGol EJBD EWoo SBrk
'Winds of Love' EWoo
'Windsor Castle' SApp
'Wine Bubbles' EGol SApp
'Wine Delight' SDay
'Wineberry Candy' EJBD EWoo LHop MBNS MLLN MSpe NLar SApp WAul
'Winged Migration' **new** EWoo
'Wings on High' SApp
'Winnie' EJBD
'Winsome Lady' ECGP ECha ECtt EWTr GKin MBNS MSpe WHrl
'Wisest of Wizards' EJBD MBNS MNrw NCGa SPol WHrl
'Wishing Well' WCot
'Witches Wink' EWoo MSpe
'Without Warning' **new** CBgR
'Women's Work' SApp
'Wood Duck' SApp
'Woodland Spider' SDay
'Woodside Ruby' **new** WNHG
'Xia Xiang' EWoo SBrk
'Xochimilco' WNHG
'Ya Ya Girl' EWoo
'Yabba Dabba Doo' EJBD EWoo SApp SPol
'Yazoo Green Octopus' EWoo
'Yearning Love' SApp
'Yellow Angel' ELon SApp SPol WCot
'Yellow Explosion' SApp
'Yellow Lollipop' EJBD SApp SBrk SDay
'Yellow Mammoth' **new** EJBD
'Yellow Spider' SApp
'Yellow Submarine' EJBD MBNS SBrk
'Yesterday Memories' SBrk
***yezoensis*** **new** EBtc
'You Angel You' EJBD MBNS MSpe SApp SBrk
'Yuma' WNHG
'Zampa' CBgR SDay
'Zara' SPer
'Zenobia' **new** EJBD
'Zimbabwe Sunset' **new** EJBD
'Zuni Thunderbird' EWoo

## *Hemionitis* (*Pteridaceae*)

***arifolia*** WRic

## *Hepatica* (*Ranunculaceae*)

***acutiloba*** CBro CRDP EBee ECho GBBs GEdr LAma MHom MMoz NBir NLar NMen WAbe
- blue-flowered MAsh
- white-flowered MAsh NLar
***americana*** EBee ECho ELan LHop MAsh NBir NPnk
***angulosa*** see *H. transsilvanica*
***henryi*** GEdr LAma MAsh
***insularis*** MAsh
- B&SWJ 859 WCru
***maxima*** GEdr MAsh
- B&SWJ 4344 WCru
× ***media*** 'Ballardii' GEdr IBlr MNFA
- 'Harvington Beauty' CLAP EBee IBlr LRHS MAsh MHom NBir WSHC
§ ***nobilis*** ♀H4 Widely available
- SDR 5301 GKev
- var. ***asiatica*** MAsh NPnk
- blue-flowered ECho GEdr IFoB MAsh NSla WAbe WGwG
- 'Cobalt' CLAP ECho NSla WAbe
- 'Cremar' MAsh
- dark-blue-flowered CLAP
- dwarf white-flowered IFoB
- var. ***japonica*** EPfP EWes GKev LAma LHop MAsh NBir NHol NSla

| | |
|---|---|
| - - 'Akane' | ECho GEdr |
| - - 'Akanezora' (b/d) | GEdr |
| - - 'Akebono' (9/d) | GEdr |
| - - 'Aniju' | GEdr |
| - - 'Asahi' (7/d) | GEdr |
| - - 'Asahizuru' (6/d) | GEdr |
| - - 'Benikanzan' | GEdr |
| - - 'Benioiran' | GEdr |
| - - 'Benisuzume' (1) | GEdr |
| - - 'Bojyou' (5A/d) | GEdr |
| - - 'Dewa' (9/d) | GEdr |
| - - 'Echigobijin' | GEdr |
| - - 'Ensyu' (9/d) | GEdr |
| - - 'Fujimusume' | GEdr |
| - - 'Gosho-zakura' (5A/d) | GEdr |
| - - 'Gyousei' | ECho GEdr |
| - - 'Hakurin' (6/d) | GEdr |
| - - 'Haruka' | GEdr |
| - - 'Harukaze' (5A/d) | GEdr |
| - - 'Haruno-awajuki' (9/d) | GEdr |
| - - 'Hohobeni' (9/d) | GEdr |
| - - 'Houkan' (9/d) | GEdr |
| - - 'Isaribi' (1) | ECho GEdr |
| - - 'Kagura' (5A/d) | GEdr |
| - - 'Kasumino' | ECho GEdr |
| - - 'Kimon' (9/d) | GEdr |
| - - 'Koshino-maboroshi' | GEdr |
| - - 'Kouetsu' | GEdr |
| - - 'Kougyoku' (9/d) | GEdr |
| - - 'Kousei' (9/d) | GEdr |
| - - 'Koushirou' | GEdr |
| - - 'Kuukai' (8/d) | GEdr |
| - - f. ***magna*** | MAsh |
| - - - 'Murasaki-shikibu' (9/d) | GEdr |
| - - - 'Seizan' | GEdr |
| - - - 'Taeka' | GEdr |
| - - 'Mangekyou' | GEdr |
| - - 'Miwaku' (1) | GEdr |
| - - 'Miyuki' (9/d) | GEdr |
| - - 'Murasaki-sakama' (1) | GEdr |
| - - 'Odoriko' (9/d) | GEdr |
| - - 'Okina' (9/d) | GEdr |
| - - 'Ō-murasaki' | ECho GEdr |
| - - 'Orihime' (9/d) | GEdr |
| - - 'Ryokurei' (5A/d) | GEdr |
| - - 'Ryokusetsu' (9/d) | GEdr |
| - - 'Ryokuun' (9/d) | GEdr |
| - - 'Ryougetsu' (1) | GEdr |
| - - 'Sadobeni' (1) | GEdr |
| - - 'Saichou' (7/d) | GEdr |
| - - 'Sakuragari' | GEdr |
| - - Sandan Group (7/d) | GEdr |
| - - 'Sansetsu' (7/d) | GEdr |
| - - 'Sawanemidori' (6/d) | GEdr |
| - - 'Sayaka' (1) | GEdr |
| - - 'Senhime' (9/d) | GEdr |
| - - 'Shikouden' (9/d) | GEdr |
| - - 'Shikouryuu' (9/d) | GEdr |
| - - 'Shirayuki' (9/d) | GEdr |
| - - 'Shirin' (d) | GEdr |
| - - 'Shiun' (9/d) | GEdr |
| - - 'Shoujyouno-homare' (9/d) | GEdr |
| - - 'Sougetsu' (6/d) | ECho GEdr |
| - - 'Subaru' (9/d) | GEdr |
| - - 'Suien' (9/d) | GEdr |
| - - 'Tae' (5A/d) | GEdr |
| - - 'Tamahime' (8/d) | GEdr |
| - - 'Tamakujyaku' | GEdr |
| - - 'Tamamushi' (9/d) | GEdr |
| - - 'Tamao' (1) | GEdr |
| - - 'Tamasaburou' | GEdr |
| - - 'Tenjinbai' (1) | GEdr |
| - - 'Tensei' (9/d) | GEdr |
| - - 'Toki' (9/d) | GEdr |
| - - 'Touryoku' (9/d) | GEdr |
| - - 'Toyama-chiyoiwai' | GEdr |
| - - 'Usugesyou' (9/d) | GEdr |
| - - 'Wakakusa' (9/d) | GEdr |
| - - 'Yahiko' | GEdr |
| - - 'Yahikomuasaki' | GEdr |
| - - 'Yoshinosato' (9/d) | GEdr |
| - - 'Yukishino' | GEdr |
| - - 'Yumegokochi' | GEdr |
| - - 'Yuunami' (1) | GEdr |
| - - 'Yuzuru' (8/d) | GEdr |
| - large, pale blue-flowered | NSla |
| - 'Lilac Picotee' **new** | NSla |
| - mottled leaf | ECho |
| - patterned leaf **new** | NSla |
| - pink-flowered | CLAP ECho MAsh NMen |
| - var. ***pubescens*** | MAsh |
| * - var. ***pyrenaica*** | LEdu MAsh NSla WThu |
| * - - 'Apple Blossom' | CLAP MAsh NBir WAbe |
| - 'Pyrenean Marbles' | CLAP NMen |
| - red-flowered | ECho NMen |
| - Rene's form | WFar |
| - var. ***rubra*** | CLAP ECho NMen NSla |
| - 'Rubra Plena' (d) | GEdr MHom NHar NSla SCnR WPnP |
| - white-flowered | CLAP ECho MAsh NMen |
| 'Sakaya' | ECho |
| 'Shunrin' (d) **new** | CRDP |
| § ***transsilvanica*** ♀H4 | CBro CLAP EBee ECho EPot GAbr GLam LAma MAsh MCot NHol NMen NPnk SMrm WTin |
| - 'Ada Scott' | GEdr |
| - 'Blue Eyes' | EBee ECho GEdr GKev LWst MHom |
| - 'Blue Jewel' | CFir CLAP EBee ECho GBBs GEdr LWst MCot MHom NCGa NLar NMen WCot WPnP |
| - blue-flowered | IBlr MAsh |
| - 'Buis' | CAvo CLAP EBee ECho GEdr GKev LRHS MHom NLar SPhx WPnP |
| - 'Eisvogel' | CLAP ECho GEdr NMen |
| - 'Elison Spence' (d) | GEdr IBlr MCot |
| - 'Lilacina' | ECho GEdr MAsh NSla |
| - 'Loddon Blue' | IBlr |
| - pink-flowered | CLAP ECho MAsh |
| - 'Sieben Bergen' | IBlr |
| - white-flowered | ECho MAsh |
| ***triloba*** | see *H. nobilis* |
| 'Wakana' | GEdr |
| aff. ***yamatutai*** | MAsh |

## *Heptacodium* (*Caprifoliaceae*)

| | |
|---|---|
| ***jasminoides*** | see *H. miconioides* |
| § ***miconioides*** | Widely available |

## *Heptapleurum* see *Schefflera*

## *Heracleum* (*Apiaceae*)

| | |
|---|---|
| ***lehmannianum*** | NBPC WCot |
| ***maximum*** 'Washington Limes' (v) | EWes |
| ***sosnowskyi*** | CSpe |

## *Herbertia* (*Iridaceae*)

| | |
|---|---|
| § ***lahue*** | CDes ECho |

## *Hereroa* (*Aizoaceae*)

***glenensis*** ECho LRHS SPlb

## *Hermannia* (*Malvaceae*)

***flammea*** SPlb
***pinnata*** NMen
***pulchella*** NWCA
***stricta*** CPBP NWCA WAbe WPat

## *Hermodactylus* (*Iridaceae*)

§ ***tuberosus*** CArn CAvo CBro CHid CPrp CTri CWCL ECGP ECha ECho ELan EPfP ERCP GKev LAma MAvo MCot MLLN NMin NWCA SDeJ SMrm WCot WTin
- BS 348 WCot
- MS 76 WCot
- MS 729 WCot
- MS 731 WCot
- MS 821 WCot
- MS 964 WCot
- PB WCot

## *Herniaria* (*Caryophyllaceae*)

***glabra*** CArn EGHP GPoy XLum

## *Hertia* see *Othonna*

## *Hesperaloe* (*Asparagaceae*)

F&M 311.1 WPGP
***parviflora*** CTrC EAmu LEdu SBig SChr SPlb WCot XSen

## *Hesperantha* (*Iridaceae*)

§ ***baurii*** ECho EWld GBin GGar GLam GLin LLHF NMen
***buhrii*** see *H. cucullata* 'Rubra'
***coccinea*** see *Schizostylis coccinea*
***cucullata*** ECho
* - 'Rubra' NWCA
***falcata*** ECho
***grandiflora*** ECho
***huttonii*** ECho EWld GKev GMac LLHF MSCN NBir
***mossii*** see *H. baurii*
***oligantha*** 'Kamiesberg' ECho
***pauciflora*** ECho
§ ***radiata*** GGar
***tysonii*** see *H. radiata*

## *Hesperis* (*Brassicaceae*)

***dinarica*** LRHS
***lutea*** see *Sisymbrium luteum*
***matronalis*** Widely available
- ***alba*** see *H. matronalis* var. *albiflora*
§ - var. ***albiflora*** CPrp CSpe CTri EBee EGHP ELau EPfP MCot MMuc NGdn NPnk SIde SPer STes SWat WBrk WFar WMnd WMoo
- - 'Alba Plena' (d) CAbP EBee ECtt ELan ELon LRHS MCot MNrw NBir NCGa WCot WFar WHer WSHC
- 'Lilacina' SWat
I - 'Variegata' (v) WHil

## *Hessea* (*Amaryllidaceae*)

***breviflora*** ECho
***incana*** 'Pendoornhoek' ECho
***mathewsii*** ECho
***pulcherrima*** ECho
***speciosa*** ECho
***stellaris*** ECho

## *Heteromeles* (*Rosaceae*)

***arbutifolia*** see *H. salicifolia*
§ ***salicifolia*** WWau

## *Heteromorpha* (*Apiaceae*)

***arborescens*** CPLG SPlb SVen

## *Heteropyxis* (*Myrtaceae*)

***natalensis*** EShb

## *Heterotheca* (*Asteraceae*)

***mariana*** see *Chrysopsis mariana*
***pumila*** NWCA
§ ***villosa*** EPPr WCot
- 'Golden Sunshine' CPrp

## *Heuchera* ✿ (*Saxifragaceae*)

'Alan Davidson' MPnt
'Alan Dickenson' new MPnt
'Amber Waves' PBR CPLG EBee ELan EPfP LRHS LSRN MPkF MPnt NBPC NBir NBro NGdn NHol SBfd SGol SPoG SRGP SWvt WFar
§ ***americana*** CEnt ECha MRav NBir SWvt
- var. ***americana*** MPnt
- Dale's strain CBar EHoe IFoB MPnt NLar SPlb SPur SWvt WHrl WMnd WPnP
- 'Eco-magnififolia' CLAP
- 'Harry Hay' CDes CLAP EBee EPPr LPla MPnt NDov SUsu WPGP WSHC
- var. ***hirsuticaulis*** new WPtf
- 'Ring of Fire' EBee ECtt LHop LSRN MPkF NPri SApp SBfd SPav SWvt WFar WWEG
'Amethyst Myst' CLAP CMMP COIW EBee ECtt EPfP GKev LBMP LHop LRHS LSRN MAsh MPkF NPla SBfd SGol SLim SPer SRkn WFar WWEG
'Autumn Haze' PBR MPnt NHol SHeu
'Autumn Leaves' CLAP EBee ECtt GCai LSou MAsh MPkF MPnt NDov NHol NLar NWad SFai SHeu
'Baby's Breath' ECho MPnt
'Bardot' new MPnt
'Beaujolais' PBR CAbP CWGN ECGP ECtt ELon ESwi LSou MBNS MPnt MTis NBir NCGa NLar NSti SEND SHeu WCot
'Beauty Colour' CAbP CLAP CMac CWCL CWGN EBee ECha ECtt ELan EPfP GMaP LHop LRHS LSRN LSqH MAsh MRav NGdn NHol NMyG NWad SBfd SPer SPoG SWvt WFar WMnd
'Berry Smoothie' new CHid CWGN EBee EPPr ESwi LLHF LSRN LSou MBNS MBri MPkF MPnt MTis MWea NLar NPer NPri NWad SBfd SFai SHeu SMrm SPer SPoG SRkn SRot SWvt WGor WHlf
'Binoche' new MPnt
'Birkin' new MPnt
* 'Black Velvet' CLAP EPfP NBre
'Blackberry Jam' CLAP CSpe EBee ECtt GCai MPnt MTis NBir SFai SHeu SWvt WGor
'Blackbird' ♀H4 CLAP CMac EBee MPnt SApp SBrd SFai SHeu SWvt WMnd
'Blackout' CAbP CWGN ECtt MAsh MCot MNrw MPnt MTis SEND SHeu WBrk WCot

| | |
|---|---|
| 'Blood Red' | CLAP EBee LSou MAsh MPkF MPnt NWad SFai SHeu SLim SPoG |
| 'Blood Vein' | NBre NHol SHeu |
| ***bracteata*** | XLum |
| 'Bressingham Glow' | MPnt |
| Bressingham hybrids | CWib GJos IFoB MLHP MMuc NBir NBlu SBfd SEND SPer SRms WFar WPer WWEG |
| 'Bronze Beauty' | MPnt SHeu |
| 'Brownfinch' | SUsu |
| 'Brownies' | CAbP CLAP ECtt ESwi LPla MBNS MPnt SHeu |
| 'Burgundy Frost' ♀H4 | WCot |
| 'Café Olé'PBR | CLAP GCai LSou MPnt SHeu WHer |
| 'Can-can' ♀H4 | CTri CWCL EBee ECtt ELon EPfP GAbr GBin GKev LAst LRHS LSRN LSou MAvo MCot MNrw NBir NEgg NGdn NHol NLar NPri SBfd SHar SPer SWvt WBrk WCFE WCot WWEG |
| 'Canyon Duet' | EAEE EBee LRHS MBNS MPnt NOrc SHeu |
| 'Canyon Pink' | NSti |
| 'Cappuccino' | CLAP EAEE EBee ECtt ELan EPfP LSqH MRav NBro NGdn SBfd SHeu SWvt WFar |
| 'Caramel'PBR | Widely available |
| 'Carmen' **new** | MPnt |
| 'Cascade Dawn' | CLAP CWCL EBee ECtt EPfP LAst LSRN LSou LSqH MRav NBir NHol SBfd SPer SWvt WFar |
| 'Cathedral Windows' | LRHS |
| 'Champagne Bubbles'PBR | SHeu |
| Charles Bloom = 'Chablo' | MPnt |
| 'Chatterbox' | MPnt |
| 'Checkers' | see *H.* 'Quilter's Joy' |
| 'Cherries Jubilee'PBR | CAbP CFir CLAP EBee EBla ELon GMaP LRHS LSRN LSou MAsh NHol NWad SLim WFar |
| 'Cherry Cola' **new** | MPnt |
| * 'Cherry Red' | CLAP |
| 'Chiqui' | MPnt |
| ***chlorantha*** | MPnt NBre |
| 'Chocolate Ruffles'PBR | Widely available |
| 'Chocolate Veil' ♀H4 | EPfP LSRN WWEG |
| 'Christa' | MPnt SHeu |
| 'Cinnabar Silver'PBR | CLAP LSou MAsh MPkF MPnt NBir NCGa NDov SBfd SHeu |
| 'Citronelle' | CLAP CSev CWCL CWGN ECtt ELon LSou MBNS MPnt MTis MWea NDov NPnk SBrd SFai SHeu WCot |
| 'City Lights' | LSou SHeu |
| 'Color Dream'PBR | EBee |
| coral bells | see *H. sanguinea* |
| 'Coral Bouquet' | SHar SHeu WCra |
| 'Coral Cloud' | MPnt MRav |
| Crème Brûlée = 'Tnheu041' (Dolce Series) | Widely available |
| 'Crème Caramel' | CPLG IFoB MPnt SBfd SHar |
| 'Crimson Curls' | CLAP EBee LBuc LRHS LSou MAsh SBfd SHeu SRms SWvt |
| 'Crispy Curly' | NBre SHeu |
| ***cylindrica*** | EPfP LLWP LRHS MPnt MRav NBre WWEG |
| - var. ***alpina*** | GKev NWCA |
| - 'Greenfinch' | CWan EBee ELan EPfP GKev GMaP LSRN MRav MWhi NBir NOrc SHeu SMrm SWat WFar WMnd |
| - 'Hyperion' | MPnt |
| 'Damask' **new** | MPnt |
| 'Dark Beauty'PBR | CCVN CLAP ECtt GKev LBMP LRHS LSRN LSou MAsh MBNS MPkF MTis NHol NLar NPri NWad SBfd SHeu SMrm SPoG SRot |
| 'Dark Secret' | MAsh MPnt SHeu |
| 'David' | MPnt WBrk |
| 'Dennis Davidson' | see *H.* 'Huntsman' |
| 'Dingle Mint Chocolate' | ECtt |
| Ebony and Ivory = 'E and I'PBR | CAbP CBcs CLAP CMMP EBee ECtt EPfP EShb GKev GMaP LBMP LHop LRHS LSRN LSou MCCP MGos NBir NHol NLar NSti SHar SRot SUsu SWvt WFar WWEG |
| 'Eden's Aurora' | WMnd |
| 'Electra' | CLAP CMea EBee ECtt EPPr ESwi LSou MAsh MBNS MBri MPkF MPnt MTis MWea NDov NHol NLar NPnk NPri NWad SBfd SHeu SMrm SPoG SRkn SRot SWvt WHlf |
| 'Electric Lime' **new** | MPnt SHeu |
| ***elegans*** NNS 05-372 | WCot |
| 'Elworthy Rusty' **new** | CElw |
| 'Emperor's Cloak' | ELon LEdu MWhi NLar SHeu SWvt WMoo |
| 'Encore'PBR | EBee MPnt SHeu |
| 'Fantasia'PBR | NHol SHeu |
| 'Fire Chief' **new** | CWGN EBee ECtt ESwi LRHS LSou MAsh MBri MPkF MPnt MTis NLar NPri NWad SFai SHeu SMrm SRot |
| 'Firebird' | MPnt NBir NVic |
| Firefly | see *H.* 'Leuchtkäfer' |
| 'Fireworks'PBR ♀H4 | CAbP EBee ECtt LAst LRHS MBNS MPnt NLar NPri SLim SPer SRot WFar WGor |
| 'Florist's Choice' | MNFA |
| 'French Quarter' **new** | SHeu |
| 'Frosted Violet'PBR | see *H.* 'Frosted Violet Dream' |
| § 'Frosted Violet Dream'PBR | CLAP EBee ECtt EPfP LRHS LSRN LSou MAsh NCGa NDov SBfd SHeu WWEG |
| 'Georgia Peach'PBR | Widely available |
| 'Ginger Ale'PBR | CHar CLAP CWCL CWGN EBee ECha ECtt ESwi EWes GCai LHop LRHS LSou MAsh MBNS MPnt MTis MWea NBir NGdn NHol NPnk NPri NWad SBfd SHeu SPer SWvt WCot WWEG |
| 'Ginger Peach' **new** | MPnt |
| ***glabra*** | MPnt |
| ***glauca*** | see *H. americana* |
| 'Gloire d'Orléans' **new** | XLum |
| 'Green Ivory' | EAEE MPnt MRav SBch WBrk XLum |
| 'Green Spice' | CLAP CWCL EBee ECtt ESwi EWll GBin LBMP LHop LRHS LSou MPkF MPnt NBir NCGa NDov NHol NPla NPnk SBfd SFai SMrm SPer SPoG SRkn SUsu SWvt WGor WHoo |
| 'Green Spire' | CLAP |
| 'Guardian Angel' | CLAP CMac EBee LSou SFai SHeu SPoG SRGP SRkn |
| 'Gypsy Dancer'PBR (Dancer Series) | CLAP ECtt EPfP LSou MAsh MGos MPkF MPnt NGdn NWad SBfd SHeu |
| 'Hailstorm' (v) | MPnt |
| ***hallii*** | MPnt |
| 'Havana' **new** | GCai MPnt SHeu |
| 'Helen Dillon' (v) | EBee GMaP NBir NPnk SRGP SWvt WFar WWEG |
| 'Hercules'PBR | ECtt MPnt SHeu |
| ***hispida*** | MPnt |

| | |
|---|---|
| 'Hollywood'[PBR] | CWCL ECtt EPPr EPfP LBMP LRHS LSRN LSou MAsh MBri MPnt MTis NBir NCGa NWad SBfd SHeu SPoG SRot WFar |
| § 'Huntsman' | MBNS MPnt MRav WFar WMnd |
| 'Jade Gloss'[PBR] | CLAP EPfP LRHS MAsh MPnt SBfd SHeu WWEG |
| 'Kassandra' **new** | EBee LRHS MAsh MPnt SHeu |
| Key Lime Pie = 'Tnheu042'[PBR] (Dolce Series) | Widely available |
| 'Lady in Red' | NBre |
| 'Lady Romney' | XLum |
| § 'Leuchtkäfer' | CWat EBee ECtt EPfP GMaP LAst LHop LRHS MHer MRav MWat MWhi NBir NEgg NMir NOrc SBfd SGol SPer SPlb SRms STes SWal WFar WMnd WMoo WPer WPtf WWEG XLum |
| Licorice = 'Tnheu044'[PBR] (Dolce Series) | CBod CLAP CWCL ECtt LRHS MBNS MBri MGos NBir NLar NPnk NPri SBfd SHeu SLim SRot SWvt WFar WHoo WWEG |
| 'Lime' | CLAP |
| 'Lime Marmalade' | CLAP ECtt GCai LSou MAsh MPkF MPnt NDov NHol NLar NPnk NWad SFai SHeu |
| 'Lime Rickey'[PBR] | Widely available |
| 'Lipstick' **new** | MAsh MPkF MPnt NDov SHeu |
| 'Little Tinker' | NBir |
| 'Magic Color'[PBR] | EBee |
| 'Magic Wand'[PBR] ♀H4 | CAbP ECtt ELon MBNS NEgg SHeu WCot |
| 'Mahogany'[PBR] | CLAP CWCL GCai LRHS LSou MAsh MPkF MPnt MTis NBir NGdn SBfd SFai SHeu SLim STes SWvt |
| 'Malachite' **new** | LRHS |
| 'Marmalade'[PBR] | Widely available |
| 'Mars' | EBee EPfP MPnt SHeu |
| 'Melting Fire' | CBod EDAr ETod GJos LRHS LSou MPkF MPnt MWhi NLar SBfd SHeu |
| 'Metallica' | NGBl SHeu SWal WMoo |
| ***micans*** | see *H. rubescens* |
| ***micrantha*** | GCal MLHP SHeu SRms |
| – var. ***diversifolia*** misapplied | see *H. villosa* |
| – 'Martha's Compact' | WCot |
| § – 'Ruffles' | ECha |
| 'Midas Touch' **new** | GCai LSou MAsh MPkF MPnt SHeu |
| 'Midnight Bayou' **new** | ECtt MBri MPnt MTis NPer SFai SHeu SWvt |
| 'Midnight Rose' | Widely available |
| 'Milan' **new** | MPnt SHeu |
| 'Mini Mouse' | EWes MPnt SHeu |
| 'Mint Frost'[PBR] | CWCL EBee ELan EPfP LSou MPnt MRav NBir NCGa NHol SHeu SMrm SPoG SWvt WFar WWEG |
| 'Mint Julep' **new** | LSou MPnt SHeu |
| 'Miracle' | CLAP ECtt EPfP MAsh MPnt NDov SHeu |
| 'Mocha'[PBR] | CBod CLAP CWGN EBee MBNS MNrw MPnt MWea SBfd SFai SHeu SMrm SPoG STes SWvt |
| 'Molly Bush' ♀H4 | EBee ECtt LRHS NCGa SHeu |
| 'Montrose Ruby' | NBre |
| 'Mother of Pearl' | MPnt |
| 'Mysteria' **new** | LSou MAsh MPkF MPnt SHeu |
| 'Mystic Angel' **new** | MPnt |
| 'Neptune' | EPfP LRHS SHeu |
| 'Oakington Jewel' | EBee ELan |
| 'Obsidian'[PBR] | Widely available |
| 'Orphée' | MPnt |
| 'Paris'[PBR] | CLAP ECtt LRHS LSou MPkF MPnt NDov NWad SBfd SHeu |
| ***parishii*** NNS 93 384 | NWCA |
| ***parvifolia*** var. ***utahensis*** **new** | MPnt |
| 'Peach Flambé'[PBR] | Widely available |
| 'Peachy Keen' | SHeu |
| 'Peppermint Spice'[PBR] (21st Century Collection Series) | EBee LSou MPnt NPnk SGol SHeu |
| 'Persian Carpet' | CHEx CWCL ECtt GMaP MPnt NBir NHol NPri SHeu SWvt WFar WPtf |
| (Petite Series) 'Petite Marbled Burgundy' | EBee ECtt EHoe LAst LLHF LRHS MPnt NDov SHeu SWvt WAul WCot WCra WFar |
| – 'Petite Pearl Fairy' | CAbP EHoe ELan MPnt NGdn SHeu SWvt WFar |
| – 'Petite Pink Bouquet' | EBee ECtt EHoe MPnt SHeu |
| 'Pewter Moon' | CBcs EBee ELan EPfP GMaP LAst LTen MGos MRav MSpe NBir SEND SHeu WFar WTin XLum |
| 'Pewter Veil'[PBR] | EBee EPfP LRHS NPri SHeu WFar WMnd WWEG |
| ***pilosissima*** | NBre XLum |
| 'Pink Lipstick' | NWad |
| 'Pinot Bianco' **new** | MPnt SHeu |
| 'Pinot Gris'[PBR] | CLAP CWGN ECtt LRHS LSou MAsh MNrw MPkF MPnt MTis SHeu WCot |
| 'Pinot Noir' | CLAP MPnt SHeu |
| 'Pistache' | CAbP CWGN ECtt ELon LSou MAvo MBNS MPkF MPnt NCGa NPnk SHeu SPer WCot |
| § 'Pluie de Feu' | CFir ECtt EPPr EPfP LRHS MPnt MRav SMrm WFar XLum |
| 'Plum Pudding'[PBR] | Widely available |
| 'Plum Royale' | CLAP CMac CWGN EBee ECha ECtt ELon EPPr LRHS LSou MAsh MBri MPkF MPnt MSCN NCGa NLar NSti NWad SBfd SFai SHeu SRkn WWEG |
| 'Prince' | CBod ELan EPfP GCai LSRN MAsh MBNS NMRc SApp SFai SHeu SPoG SWvt |
| 'Prince of Silver' | CBod LRHS MBNS SHeu |
| ***pringlei*** | see *H. rubescens* |
| ***pubescens*** | ECho MPnt SHeu XLum |
| ***pulchella*** | EBee LLHF MHer MPnt MWat SHeu SRms |
| – JCA 9508 | NMen |
| 'Purple Mountain Majesty' | CBcs EBee ECtt SHeu WFar |
| 'Purple Petticoats' ♀H4 | CBcs EBee ECtt EPfP LAst LRHS LSou MLHP MNFA MPkF NBre NHol NLar NPnk NPri SHar SLim SMrm WFar |
| 'Quick Silver' | EBla NBir SHeu SWvt WFar |
| § 'Quilter's Joy' **new** | LRHS |
| 'Rachel' | CAbP CWCL EAEE EBee ECtt ELan EPfP GCal GMaP IFoB LRHS LSRN MPnt MRav MWat NBir NGdn NPnk SPer SRGP SWvt WAul WBrk WFar XLum |
| Rain of Fire | see *H.* 'Pluie de Feu' |
| 'Raspberry Regal' ♀H4 | ECtt MRav NBir NSti SHeu SWvt WAul WCot WFar |
| 'Rave On'[PBR] | Widely available |
| 'Red Spangles' | EPfP NBir WWEG |
| 'Regina' ♀H4 | CAbP EBee ECtt EPfP LSRN MPnt NBro SBfd SFai SHeu SWvt WFar |

| | | |
|---|---|---|
| | 'Rhapsody' new | LRHS |
| | ***richardsonii*** | MNrw |
| | 'Rickard' | MPnt |
| | 'Robert' | MPnt |
| | 'Root Beer' new | MPnt |
| § | ***rubescens*** | CAbP ECho NBro NMen WPer WThu |
| | 'Ruby Veil' | EBee LRHS |
| | 'Ruffles' | see *H. micrantha* 'Ruffles' |
| § | ***sanguinea*** | CMac CSBt MRav NBir SBfd WPer |
| | - 'Alba' ♀H4 | EPPr NMRc |
| | - 'Geisha's Fan' | CWCL LSou MPkF MPnt MSpe NEgg NHol NPla SBfd SHeu SPer SWvt |
| | - 'Monet' (v) | EBee MLHP MPnt SHeu |
| | - var. ***pulchra*** | CPBP |
| | - 'Ruby Bells' | CChe EAEE EPPr EPfP LRHS LSRN MCot NLar NPri SHeu |
| | - 'Sioux Falls' | EWes MBNS NBre SHeu |
| | - 'Snow Storm' (v) | ELan EPfP MRav SHeu SPlb WFar WMnd |
| | - 'Splendens' | XLum |
| | - 'Taff's Joy' (v) | EWes |
| | - 'White Cloud' (v) | EPfP NBre SHeu SRms WPer XLum |
| | 'Sashay' ♀H4 | CLAP LSou MAsh MPkF MPnt NLar SGol SHeu |
| | 'Saturn' | LRHS MDev MPnt SHeu SWvt |
| | 'Schneewittchen' | EBee EPfP MPnt MRav |
| | 'Scintillation' ♀H4 | NBre |
| | 'Shamrock' | NBre |
| | 'Shanghai' new | LSou MAsh MPnt SBfd SHeu |
| | 'Shenandoah Mountain' | WWEG |
| | 'Silver Indiana' PBR | EBee LRHS LSRN SHeu |
| | 'Silver Light' PBR | EPfP LRHS SHeu |
| | 'Silver Lode' PBR | SBfd SHeu |
| | 'Silver Scrolls' PBR | Widely available |
| | 'Silver Shadows' | MBrN SHeu |
| | 'Silver Streak' | see × *Heucherella* 'Silver Streak' |
| | 'Smoothie' new | MAsh |
| | 'Snow Angel' | EPfP SHeu WCot |
| | 'Snowfire' (v) | MPnt SHeu |
| | 'Southern Comfort' | CLAP CWCL CWGN EBee ECtt ELon EPPr ESwi LRHS LSou MAsh MBNS MPkF MPnt NCGa NLar NPer NWad SBfd SGol SHeu SLim SMad SPoG SWvt |
| | 'Sparkling Burgundy' | CBod CLAP ECtt EPfP LSou MPkF MPnt SBfd SHeu SWvt |
| | 'Starry Night' PBR | MPnt SBfd SHeu |
| | 'Steel City' | SHeu |
| | 'Stormy Seas' | CMHG EAEE EBee ELan EPfP GCra LRHS MLHP MPkF MRav NBir SBfd SHeu SWvt WFar WPtf WWEG |
| | 'Strawberry Candy' PBR | CBcs CMac CWCL CWGN EAEE EBee ELon GBin GJos LAst LBMP LHop LRHS LSRN LSou MBNS MMHG MPnt MWea NBir NLar NWad SHeu SLim SPer SPoG SRkn |
| | 'Strawberry Swirl' | CElw EBee EBla ECtt EWTr GMaP LRHS MGos MPnt MRav NBir NLar NPri NSti SBfd SHeu SWvt WFar WWEG |
| | Sugar Frosting = 'Pwheu0104' PBR | CBod ECtt EWll GKev LAst LRHS MPnt NCGa SHeu SWvt WFar |
| | 'Sugar Plum' new | LRHS MPnt SHeu |
| | 'Swirling Fantasy' PBR | EBee EPfP EShb GJos LSou MAsh MDev MPnt SHeu SMrm |
| | 'Tara' | MPnt SHeu |
| | 'Tiramisu' PBR | Widely available |
| | 'Van Gogh' | SHeu |
| | 'Vanilla Spice' | MPnt NHol SHeu |
| | 'Veil of Passion' | NBre |
| | 'Velvet Night' | EBee EPfP NBir NBre NHol SHeu SPlb WFar WMnd WPtf WWEG |
| | 'Venus' | CBod CMea CWGN ECtt ELon EPfP EShb GAbr LRHS MBNS MLLN MNrw NCGa NGdn NMRc NSti SEND SHeu SPer SPur WBrk WCot WCra WHoo |
| | 'Vesuvius' PBR | MPnt NCGa SHeu |
| § | ***villosa*** | ECha LRHS MRav SVic XLum |
| | - 'Autumn Bride' | EBee ECtt SHeu |
| | - Bressingham Bronze = 'Absi' PBR | EAEE EBee LRHS SHeu WFar |
| | - 'Chantilly' | EBee |
| | - var. ***macrorhiza*** | EShb LBMP MPnt NBre WMnd WPnP XLum |
| N | - 'Palace Purple' | Widely available |
| | - 'Palace Purple Select' | CBcs CMac CTri CWat CWib LAst MCot NEgg SBfd SEND SLim SWvt WFar |
| | - 'Royal Red' | GMac |
| | 'Whirlwind' | WCAu |
| | 'White Marble' | MPnt |
| | 'White Spires' | LRHS MPnt |
| | 'White Swirls' new | MPnt |
| | 'William How' | MPnt |
| | 'Winter Red' | EAEE EBee LRHS MBNS NEgg SPur |
| | 'Zabeliana' | GBee MPnt |

## × *Heucherella* ✿ (*Saxifragaceae*)

| | | |
|---|---|---|
| | 'Alabama Sunrise' | CLAP CWCL EBee ECtt ELon EPPr ESwi ETod LSou MBri MLLN MPkF MPnt MTis NCGa NHol NPer NPri NWad SBfd SGol SHeu SPoG SRot SUsu SWvt WBor WGor |
| | ***alba*** 'Bridget Bloom' | EBee ECha ELan EPfP EWTr GMaP LRHS MRav NOrc SBfd SRms WCAu WFar |
| § | - 'Rosalie' | EBee ECha GKev LRHS MPnt MRav NBir NBro NPnk NPro SPlb WFar WSHC |
| | 'Birthday Cake' | SHeu |
| | 'Brass Lantern' new | MPnt |
| | 'Burnished Bronze' PBR | EBee ECtt ELon GKev LRHS LSou MPkF NBro NEgg NGdn NHol NLar NPla NWad SBfd SMrm SPoG SRot SWvt WCot WFar |
| | 'Chocolate Lace' PBR | SHeu |
| | 'Cinnamon Bear' | SHeu |
| | 'Dayglow Pink' PBR | CLAP EBla EShb GKev GMaP LSRN MPkF MPnt NBro NHol NLar SHar SHeu SMrm SPoG WFar WGor |
| | 'Fan Dancer' new | SHeu |
| | Gold Strike = 'Hertn041' PBR | CLAP ECtt EWll GJos LRHS MBNS MPnt SHeu SPoG |
| | 'Golden Zebra' | CLAP CWGN ECtt LSou MAsh MAvo MBNS MPkF MPnt MTis NHol NLar NWad SFai SHeu |
| | 'Gunsmoke' new | MPnt |
| | 'Heart of Darkness' PBR | EBee SBfd SHeu WWEG |
| | 'Kimono' PBR ♀H4 | Widely available |
| | 'Ninja' PBR | see *Tiarella* 'Ninja' |
| | 'Party Time' PBR | SHeu |
| | 'Persian Carpet' new | MPnt |
| | Pink Whispers = 'Hertn042' PBR | MPnt SHeu WFar |
| | 'Quicksilver' | CBcs EBee GMaP SHeu SWvt WFar WWEG |
| | 'Ring of Fire' | CMac SWvt WFar |

§ 'Silver Streak' EBee GAbr LRHS MRav NBro SHeu SWvt WFar
'Solar Power' new MPnt
'Stoplight'PBR Widely available
'Sunspot'PBR (v) CLAP ECtt EKen EPfP MGos NBro NSti SGol SHeu WHer
'Sweet Tea' Widely available
'Tapestry' CBar CHid CLAP ECtt GCai LRHS LSou MAsh MBNS MLLN MPkF MPnt MTis NCGa NPla NPnk NSti NWad SBfd SFai SHeu SPoG SRkn SRot SWvt
***tiarelloides*** ♀H4 CMac EPfP WMnd
§ 'Viking Ship'PBR CElw CMHG CMMP EAEE EBee EBla ECha ECtt GKev LBMP LRHS MPnt MRav MTPN NBir NPla SFai SHeu SUsu WFar WPtf WWEG

## *Hexastylis* see *Asarum*

## *Hibanobambusa* (*Poaceae*)

'Kimmei' MMuc SEND
***tranquillans*** CEnt EPla MBrN MMoz MMuc MWht SEND WDyG WJun
- 'Shiroshima' (v) ♀H4 CAbb CDTJ CDoC CEnt EAmu ENBC EPfP EPla LPal MBrN MBri MCCP MMoz MMuc MWhi MWht NPal NVic SApp SBfd SBig SEND WDyG WJun

## *Hibbertia* (*Dilleniaceae*)

***aspera*** CBcs CCCN CRHN CTsd EBee ECre IVic LRHS SBrd WCFE WCot WFar WSHC
§ ***cuneiformis*** CCCN
***obtusifolia*** new EPot
***pedunculata*** WAbe
***procumbens*** WAbe
§ ***scandens*** ♀H1 CCCN CHll CRHN ECou ELan MOWG SEND
***tetrandra*** see *H. cuneiformis*
***volubilis*** see *H. scandens*

## *Hibiscus* ✿ (*Malvaceae*)

***acetosella*** 'Red Shield' CSpe
***coccineus*** EShb MOWG SBrt SMad
- 'Texas Star' new XDel
- 'Texas Star' white-flowered new XDel
***coccineus* × *moscheutos*** new SBrt
***dasycalyx*** new XDel
***fallax*** CHll
'Fantasia'PBR CWGN XDel
'Fireball'PBR new XDel
***grandiflorus*** new XDel
***hamabo*** ELan XDel
***huegelii*** see *Alyogyne huegelii*
'Jazzberry Jam' new XDel
'Kopper King'PBR CWGN MAsh XDel
'Lady Baltimore' new XDel
***lasiocarpus*** XDel
***leopoldii*** SRms
'Lord Baltimore' new XDel
***manihot*** see *Abelmoschus manihot*
***militaris*** SBrt XDel
'Moesiana' MBri
***moscheutos*** CArn CFir EBee SBrt SMad SVic XDel XLum
- 'Blue River II' new XDel
- 'Cranberry Crush' new XDel
- 'Galaxy' NExo WHil XDel XLum
- Luna Series new XDel
- 'Old Yella' new XDel
- Southern Belle Group CHEx XDel
***mutabilis*** MOWG XDel
- double-flowered (d) new XDel
aff. ***mutabilis*** 'Nagoya Pink' XDel
- 'Nagoya White' XDel
Newbiscus Series new XDel
'Old Yella'PBR CWGN
***paramutabilis*** EWes SMad XDel
- red-flowered new XDel
***paramutabilis*** × 'Tosca' new XDel
'Plum Crazy'PBR new XDel
'Pyranees Pink' EMil
***rosa-sinensis*** EBak EShb MBri MOWG SPlb
- 'Big Tango' MOWG
- 'Bimbo' MOWG
- 'Byron Metts' MOWG
- 'Candy' MOWG
- 'Carmen Keene' MOWG
- 'Casablanca' MBri
- 'Cockatoo' MOWG
- 'Cooperi' (v) ♀H1 MOWG
- 'Courier Mail' MOWG
- 'Dorothy Brady' MOWG
- 'Enid Lewis' MOWG
- 'Expo' MOWG
- 'Gina Marie' MOWG
- 'Great White' MOWG
- 'Gwen Mary' MOWG
- 'Helene' LSRN
- 'Holiday' MBri
- 'Holly's Pride' MOWG
- 'June's Joy' MOWG
- 'Kardinal' MBri
- 'Königer' MBri
- 'Lady Flo' MOWG
- 'Lemon Chiffon' (d) MOWG
- 'Linda Pear' MOWG
- 'Love' MOWG
- 'Mrs Andreasen' MOWG
- 'Norman Lee' MOWG
- 'Pink Mist' MOWG
- 'Rhinestone' MOWG
- 'Silver Rose' MOWG
- 'Spanish Lady' MOWG
- 'Sprinkle Rain' MOWG
- 'Tarantella' MOWG
- 'The Path' MOWG
- 'Thelma Bennell' MOWG
- 'Tivoli' MBri
- 'Weekend' MOWG
***schizopetalus*** ♀H1 CCCN MOWG
***sinosyriacus*** 'Lilac Queen' CPLG LRHS SKHP WPGP
- 'Ruby Glow' CPLG LRHS LSRN MGos SKHP WPGP
***striatus*** subsp. ***lambertianus*** new XDel
'Summer Storm' new XDel
'Sweet Caroline' new XDel
***syriacus*** LEdu MNHC WFar
- 'Admiral Dewey' (d) EGxp
- 'Aphrodite' CPMA EPfP
- 'Ardens' (d) CEnd CSBt EBee ELon LAst MGos NLar

| | |
|---|---|
| - Blue Bird | see *H. syriacus* 'Oiseau Bleu' |
| - Blue Chiffon = 'Notwood3'$^{PBR}$ | LBuc MGos SBrd SPoG |
| - 'Boule de Feu' (d) | CWGN ELan |
| - China Chiffon = 'Bricutts' | EBee MAsh |
| - 'Diana' 🏆$^{H4}$ | EPfP EQua LRHS LSRN MAsh MGos MRav SCoo SKHP SLon |
| - 'Dorothy Crane' | EBee LRHS SKHP |
| - 'Duc de Brabant' (d) | CSBt EGxp ELon EPfP MBlu SPer |
| - 'Elegantissimus' | see *H. syriacus* 'Lady Stanley' |
| - 'Hamabo' 🏆$^{H4}$ | CDul CSBt CTri EBee EMil EPfP LAst LRHS LSRN MBri MGos MWat NLar NPri SBfd SBrd SCoo SEND SGol SLim SPer SPoG SWvt WDin WFar |
| - 'Helene' | ELan EQua LSRN MBlu MRav |
| - 'Jeanne d'Arc' (d) | EMil SGol |
| § - 'Lady Stanley' (d) | CMac CSBt SCoo SPer SSta |
| - Lavender Chiffon = 'Notwoodone'$^{PBR}$ 🏆$^{H4}$ | EBee ELan EPfP EWes LRHS LSRN MGos NLar SCoo SEND SPer SPoG |
| - 'Leopoldii' | EQua SBfd SKHP |
| - 'Marina' | EPfP MBlu MRav NLar SBfd SGol |
| - 'Meehanii' misapplied | see *H. syriacus* 'Purpureus Variegatus' |
| - 'Meehanii' (v) 🏆$^{H4}$ | CEnd CSBt EMil EPfP LRHS SCoo SKHP SPer SPoG |
| - 'Monstrosus' | EBee NLar |
| § - 'Oiseau Bleu' 🏆$^{H4}$ | Widely available |
| - Pink Giant = 'Flogi' | CDul EBee ELan EPfP EQua LAst MAsh MBri MGos SPad SPer |
| § - 'Purpureus Variegatus' (v) | CMac CSBt LAst LRHS SPoG |
| - 'Red Heart' 🏆$^{H4}$ | CEnd CMac CPMA CSBt CTri EBee ELan EPfP LAst LRHS MAsh MBri MCCP MMuc MRav NLar SBrd SEND SKHP SLim SPad SPer SPoG SRms SWvt WCFE WDin |
| - Rosalbane = 'Minrosa' | EMil SGol |
| - 'Roseus Plenus' (d) | WDin |
| - Russian Violet = 'Floru' | CBcs CEnd EBee ELan EMil EPfP LAst LRHS MGos SKHP |
| - 'Sanchon Yo' | EPfP LRHS |
| - 'Shintaeyang' | SBrd |
| - 'Speciosus' | SPer |
| - 'Totus Albus' | CMac CSBt SPoG |
| - Ultramarine = 'Minultra' **new** | EMil EPfP |
| - 'Variegatus' | see *H. syriacus* 'Purpureus Variegatus' |
| - 'Violet Clair Double' (d) | CMac |
| - White Chiffon = 'Notwoodtwo'$^{PBR}$ (d) 🏆$^{H4}$ | EBee ELan EMil EPfP EWes LRHS LSRN LTen MAsh MGos MRav NLar SCoo SPer SPoG |
| - 'William R. Smith' 🏆$^{H4}$ | CDul CPMA EBee ELan LAst LRHS MMuc MSwo SBfd SBrd SEND SPer WDin |
| - 'Woodbridge' 🏆$^{H4}$ | Widely available |
| ***tiliaceus*** | XDel |
| ***trionum*** | CSpe SBch WKif WTou |
| - 'Sunny Day' | ELan |

## hickory, shagbark see *Carya ovata*

## *Hieracium* (*Asteraceae*)

| | |
|---|---|
| ***aurantiacum*** | see *Pilosella aurantiaca* |
| ***brunneocroceum*** | see *Pilosella aurantiaca* subsp. *carpathicola* |
| § ***lanatum*** | ECho MDKP NBir |
| ***maculatum*** | see *H. spilophaeum* |
| ***pilosella*** | see *Pilosella officinarum* |
| × ***rubrum*** | LRHS |
| ***scullyi*** | EPPr |
| § ***spilophaeum*** | EHoe GGar MMuc NBid NPer WOut |
| - 'Leopard' | CEnt NBlu SGar |
| ***umbellatum*** | WOut |
| ***villosum*** | CPBP ECho EHoe LRHS NBro WHer |
| ***waldsteinii*** | MDKP |
| ***welwitschii*** | see *H. lanatum* |

## *Hierochloe* (*Poaceae*)

| | |
|---|---|
| ***odorata*** | EPPr GBin GPoy MBNS WHfH XLum |

## hildaberry see *Rubus* 'Hildaberry'

## *Himalayacalamus* (*Poaceae*)

| | |
|---|---|
| ***asper*** | CDTJ WJun |
| ***cupreus*** | WJun |
| * ***equatus*** | EPla |
| § ***falconeri*** | CDTJ CEnt EPla SDix |
| § - 'Damarapa' | CDTJ CEnt EPla MMoz WDyG WJun |
| § ***hookerianus*** | CPLG EAmu EPla SBst WJun |
| - 'Himalaya Blue' | CDTJ CTrC MGos |
| - 'Jim Dawe' | ESwi |
| ***porcatus*** | CDTJ WJun WPGP |

## *Himantoglossum* (*Orchidaceae*)

| | |
|---|---|
| ***hircinum*** | NLAp |

## × *Hippeasprekelia* (*Amaryllidaceae*)

| | |
|---|---|
| 'Red Beauty' | WCot |
| 'Red Star' | CCCN |

## *Hippeastrum* (*Amaryllidaceae*)

| | |
|---|---|
| × ***acramannii*** | GCal WCot |
| ***advenum*** | see *Rhodophiala advena* |
| 'Alasca'$^{PBR}$ **new** | WHlf |
| 'Alfresco'$^{PBR}$ | LAma |
| 'Amputo' | LAma |
| 'Apple Blossom' | LAma MBri SDeJ SGar |
| ***aulicum*** | CPne |
| 'Baby Star' | SDeJ |
| 'Balentino' | WHlf |
| 'Benfica' | LAma |
| ***bifidum*** | see *Rhodophiala bifida* |
| 'Black Beauty' | LAma |
| 'Blossom Peacock' (d) | LAma |
| 'Bogota' | LAma |
| 'Bolero' | LAma |
| 'Bouquet' | LAma |
| 'Britney'$^{PBR}$ | LAma |
| 'Chico' | LAma |
| 'Christmas Gift' | LAma |
| 'Dancing Queen' | LAma |
| 'Emerald' | LAma WCot |
| 'Estella' | LAma |
| 'Fairytale' | MBri SDeJ |
| 'Ferrari' | LAma |
| 'Flaming Peacock' | LAma |
| ***gracile*** 'Pamela' | LAma |
| 'Grandeur' | LAma |
| 'Green Goddess' | LAma |
| 'Helios'$^{PBR}$ | WHlf |
| 'Hercules' | MBri |
| 'Inca' | LAma |
| 'Jewel' (d) | MBri |
| × ***johnsonii*** | CPLG WCot |
| 'La Paz' | LAma |
| 'Lady Jane' | MBri |
| 'Lemon Lime' | LAma |
| 'Liberty' | SDeJ |

| | |
|---|---|
| 'Lima' | LAma |
| 'Lollypop' **new** | WHlf |
| 'Lovely Garden' | LAma |
| 'Loyalty'PBR | LAma |
| 'Merengue' | LAma |
| 'Misty' | LAma |
| 'Mrs Garfield' | LAma |
| 'Naughty Lady' | LAma |
| ***papilio*** ♀H1 | CTca EGxp LAma MMHG |
| 'Picotee' | LAma SDeJ |
| 'Pink Floyd' | LAma |
| ***puniceum*** | LAma |
| 'Quito' | LAma |
| 'Rebecca' | LAma |
| 'Red Lion' | LAma |
| 'Red Peacock' (d) | LAma |
| 'Red Rascal' | WHlf |
| 'Rembrandt van Rijn' | LAma |
| 'Rilona' | LAma SDeJ |
| 'Rosario' | LAma |
| 'Royal Velvet' | LAma |
| 'Ruby Meyer' | LAma |
| 'San Antonio Rose' | EBee WCot WPGP |
| 'Santiago' | LAma |
| ***striatum*** | WCot |
| 'Swan Lake'PBR **new** | WHlf |
| 'Sweet Surrender' | LAma |
| 'Tango' | LAma |
| 'Toughie' | CAby CCse CDes EBee LLHF WCot WPGP |
| ***vittatum*** | LAma |
| 'White Christmas' | LAma |
| 'White Dazzler' | LAma |

## *Hippocrepis* (*Papilionaceae*)

| | |
|---|---|
| § ***comosa*** | CRWN EDAr EWil SSpi |
| § ***emerus*** | CBcs CCCN CMHG CPLG ELan EPfP LAst LHop MGos MMuc NLar SEND STre SVen WSHC |

## *Hippophae* (*Elaeagnaceae*)

| | |
|---|---|
| ***rhamnoides*** ♀H4 | CAlb CArn CBcs CCVT CDul CHab CLnd CMac CRWN CSpe CTri EBee ECrN EHoe ELan EPfP LBuc MBlu MCoo MMuc NWea SBfd SEND SEWo SGol SPlb WDin WFar |
| - 'Frugna' (f) | CAgr |
| - 'Hergo' (f) | CAgr MCoo |
| - 'Juliet' (f) | CAgr |
| - 'Leikora' (f) | CAgr ELan EPfP IVic MBlu MCoo MGos NLar SPer |
| - 'Orange Energy' (f/F) | CAgr MCoo |
| - 'Pollmix' (m) | CAgr ELan EPfP IVic MBlu MCoo MGos NLar SPer |
| - 'Pollmix 3' (m) | MCoo |
| - 'Sirola' | MCoo |
| ***salicifolia*** | CAgr |
| - GWJ 9221 | WCru |
| ***sinensis*** SDR 6006 | GKev |

## *Hippuris* (*Plantaginaceae*)

| | |
|---|---|
| ***vulgaris*** | CBen CWat EHon EWil MSKA NPer WMAq XLum |

## *Histiopteris* (*Dennstaedtiaceae*)

| | |
|---|---|
| ***incisa*** | WRic |

## *Hoheria* ✿ (*Malvaceae*)

| | |
|---|---|
| 'Ace of Spades' **new** | CMHG EBee EPfP SKHP |
| § ***angustifolia*** | ECou EPfP |
| ***angustifolia*** × ***sexstylosa*** **new** | WPGP |
| 'Borde Hill' | CDul CMHG CMac CPMA EBee ECou EPfP IVic LHop LRHS MAsh SKHP SLim SPer SPur SSpi WPat |
| 'County Park' | ECou |
| ***glabrata*** | CBcs CMac ECou EPfP GBin GGal GGar NBir NPal SKHP WPGP |
| 'Glory of Amlwch' ♀H3 | CAbb CBcs CDul CPMA CSam EBee ECou EPfP GQui SChF SKHP SMad SSpi WPGP |
| 'Hill House' | CHll |
| § ***lyallii*** ♀H4 | CCCN CDoC CDul CPLG EBee ECou ELan EPfP GCra IArd IDee LRHS LSRN SPer SSpi SVen WDin |
| - 'Chalk Hills' | ECou |
| - 'Swale Stream' | ECou |
| ***microphylla*** | see *H. angustifolia* |
| ***populnea*** | CBcs CCCN IArd SGar |
| - 'Alba Variegata' (v) | CTrC ECou |
| - 'Holbrook' | CSam |
| - 'Moonlight' | CHGN EMil SPoG |
| - 'Purple Shadow' | ECou |
| - 'Variegata' (v) | ECou |
| 'Purple Delta' | ECou |
| ***sexstylosa*** | CAbb CDoC CDul CHEx CHid CMHG CTho CTri CWSG ECou ELan EPfP EWTr LHop LRHS LSRN MGos NEgg SEND SGar SKHP SPer SPur SSta SWvt |
| - 'Crataegifolia' **new** | CAbb CDul |
| - 'Pendula' | CBcs CMac WDin |
| - 'Stardust' ♀H4 | Widely available |

## *Holarrhena* (*Apocynaceae*)

| | |
|---|---|
| ***pubescens*** | CCCN |

## *Holboellia* (*Lardizabalaceae*)

| | |
|---|---|
| ***angustifolia*** | MBri NLar WCru |
| - subsp. ***linearifolia*** BWJ 8004 | WCru |
| - subsp. ***obtusa*** DJHC 506 | WCru |
| ***brachyandra*** HWJ 1023 | WCru |
| aff. ***chapaensis*** B&SWJ 7250 | WCru |
| ***coriacea*** | CBcs CHll CRHN CSam EBee ELan EPfP IDee LRHS MGos MOWG MRav NLar SKHP SPer WBor WCru |
| - B&SWJ 2818 | WCru |
| ***fargesii*** | EBee LRHS SKHP WCru |
| ***latifolia*** | CAlb CBcs CCCN CHEx CHll CMac CSam CTri EBee ELan GCal LRHS MMuc MOWG NLar SArc SBfd SEND SKHP SLPl SLim SPer SPoG WBor WCFE WCot WCru WFar WPGP |
| - SF 95134 | EPfP |
| - HWJCM 008 | WCru |
| - HWJK 2014 | WCru |
| - HWJK 2213 | WCru |
| - dark-flowered HWJK 2213 | WCru |

## *Holcus* (*Poaceae*)

| | |
|---|---|
| ***lanatus*** | WSFF |
| ***mollis*** 'Albovariegatus' (v) | CWCL EBee ECha EHoe ELan EPPr EPfP GMaP LBMP MWhi NBid NBro NGdn NPer NSti SPlb SRms WFar WMoo WPtf WTin WWEG |
| - 'Jackdaw's Cream' (v) | EPPr |

| | | |
|---|---|---|
| | - 'White Fog' (v) | CChe EBee EHul EPPr MMuc NWad SApp SEND WFar |

## *Holmskioldia* (*Lamiaceae*)

| | | |
|---|---|---|
| * | ***lutea*** | CCCN |
| | ***sanguinea*** | CCCN |

## *Holodiscus* (*Rosaceae*)

| | | |
|---|---|---|
| | ***discolor*** | CBcs CDul EBee ELan EPfP EWTr EWes IDee LRHS MBlu MBri MMuc MRav NLar SCoo SEND SKHP SLon SPer SPlb SPoG SSpi WDin |
| | - var. ***ariifolius*** | EPfP LRHS |
| | ***dumosus*** | EBee NLar |

## *Homalocladium* (*Polygonaceae*)

| | | |
|---|---|---|
| § | ***platycladum*** | EShb |

## *Homeria* (*Iridaceae*)

| | | |
|---|---|---|
| | ***bifida*** 'Roggeveld' | ECho |
| | ***breyniana*** | see *H. collina* |
| | - var. ***aurantiaca*** | see *H. flaccida* |
| | ***britteniae*** | ECho |
| § | ***collina*** | ECho |
| | ***elegans*** | ECho |
| § | ***flaccida*** | ECho |
| | - 'Roggeveld' | ECho |
| | ***hantamensis*** 'Calvinia' | ECho |
| | ***ochroleuca*** | ECho |
| | ***rogersii*** 'Roggeveld' | ECho |
| | ***speciosa*** 'Tanqua' | ECho |

## *Homoglossum* see *Gladiolus*

## *Hordeum* (*Poaceae*)

| | | |
|---|---|---|
| | ***chilense*** | EBee |
| | ***jubatum*** | CKno CSpe CWCL EHoe EWes GKev MSCN MWhi NChi NGdn SApp SEND SPhx SUsu WHil |
| | - from Ussuri | NGBl |
| | - 'Early Pink' | NDov |
| | ***secalinum*** new | CHab |

## *Horkeliella* (*Rosaceae*)

| | | |
|---|---|---|
| | ***purpurascens*** NNS 98-323 | WCot |

## *Horminum* (*Lamiaceae*)

| | | |
|---|---|---|
| | ***pyrenaicum*** | CPom CPrp EBee ECho LBMP MMuc SEND SRms WFar WMoo WOut WPer WPtf WTin |
| I | - f. ***alboviolaceum*** new | EDAr |
| | - dark-flowered | ECho GCal |
| | - pale blue-flowered | MDKP |
| | - 'Rubrum' | EDif |
| | - white-flowered new | GKev |

## horseradish see *Armoracia rusticana*

## *Hosta* ✿ (*Asparagaceae*)

| | | |
|---|---|---|
| | AGSJ 302 | CDes WPGP |
| | 'A Many-Splendored Thing' | EMic IBal |
| | 'Abba Dabba Do' (v) | COIW EBee ECtt EGol EMic LBuc LPla NBPC NEgg NHol SApp |
| | 'Abba Showtime' | IBal |
| | 'Abby' (v) | EGol EMic EPGN IBal NMyG SApp WWEG |
| | 'Abiqua Ariel' | EMic SApp |
| | 'Abiqua Blue Crinkles' | EMic IBal NBir SApp |
| | 'Abiqua Blue Edger' | EMic |
| | 'Abiqua Delight' (v) | IBal |
| | 'Abiqua Drinking Gourd' | EBee EGol EMic EPGN GBin GMaP IBal MHom NMyG SApp WWEG |
| | 'Abiqua Ground Cover' | EGol IBal |
| | 'Abiqua Moonbeam' (v) | CFir EMic EPGN IBal MSwo NGdn NMyG SApp |
| | 'Abiqua Recluse' | EGol EMic SApp |
| | 'Abiqua Trumpet' | EGol EMic IBal NGdn NLar NNor SApp |
| | 'Academy Blushing Recluse' (v) | IBal |
| | 'Ada Reed' | IBal |
| | ***aequinoctiiantha*** | EGol |
| | 'Aksarben' | EMic |
| | 'Alan Titchmarsh' | EPGN |
| | ***albomarginata*** | see *H. sieboldii* 'Paxton's Original' |
| § | 'Albomarginata' (*fortunei*) (v) | CBcs CMac EGol EQua GKev IBal MNrw NBir NGdn SEND SPoG SWvt |
| | 'Alex Summers' | EMic IBal WFar |
| | 'All That Jazz' (v) | EMic IBal |
| | 'Allan P. McConnell' (v) | EGol EMic EPGN GCra IBal MHom NMyG WHal WWEG |
| | 'Allegan Emperor' (v) | IBal |
| | 'Allegan Fog' (v) | EGol EMic EPGN IBal |
| | 'Alligator Shoes' (v) | EGol EMic IBal |
| | 'Alpine Aire' | EMic |
| | 'Alpine Dream' | IBal |
| | 'Alternative' | IBal |
| | 'Alvatine Taylor' (v) | EGol EMic IBal LAst NGdn |
| | 'Amanuma' | EGol EMic IBal MHom |
| | 'Amazing Grace' (v) | EMic IBal |
| | 'Amber Tiara' | EMic IBal |
| | 'American Dream' (v) | EGol EMic EPGN GSec IBal |
| | 'American Halo' | EMic IBal NBPC NLar NMRc |
| | 'American Icon' | EMic IBal |
| | 'American Sweetheart' PBR | EMic IBal SApp |
| | 'Americana' (v) | EMic IBal |
| | 'Amethyst Gem' new | EGol |
| | 'Amy Elizabeth' (v) | EMic IBal |
| | 'Andy Taylor' new | LRHS |
| | 'Anglo Saxon' (v) | IBal |
| | 'Ann Kulpa' (v) | EMic EPGN IBal |
| | 'Anne' (v) | EMic IBal LSRN NMyG |
| | 'Anne Arett' (*sieboldii*) (v) | EPGN |
| | 'Ansly' (v) | IBal |
| | 'Antioch' (*fortunei*) (v) | EGol EMic GQue IBal LPla MRav NBPC NLar WFar |
| | 'Aoba Tsugaru' | IBal |
| | 'Aoki' (*fortunei*) | EMic |
| | 'Aphrodite' (*plantaginea*) (d) | EBee IBal LSou MBNS MCot NGdn NLar SApp SMrm WCot WGwG WWEG |
| | 'Apollo' | NNor |
| | 'Apple Court' | SApp |
| | 'Apple Green' | EMic IBal |
| | 'Apple Pie' | SApp |
| | 'Aqua Velva' | EGol IBal |
| | 'Arc de Triomphe' | EMic IBal SApp |
| | 'Archangel' | EGol |
| | 'Arctic Blast' | EMic IBal |
| | 'Argentea Variegata' (*undulata*) | see *H. undulata* var. *undulata* |
| | 'Aristocrat' (Tardiana Group) (v) | EGol EMic EPGN IBal SApp WFar |
| | 'Asian Beauty' | EGol |
| | 'Aspen Gold' (*tokudama* hybrid) | EMic SApp |
| | 'Athena' (v) | IBal |
| | 'Atlantis' PBR (v) | EMic IBal NGdn |
| | 'August Beauty' | EMic IBal |

|  |  |
|---|---|
| 'August Moon' | Widely available |
| ***aureafolia*** | see *H.* 'Starker Yellow Leaf' |
| 'Aureoalba' (*fortunei*) | see *H.* 'Spinners' |
| 'Aureomaculata' (*fortunei*) | see *H. fortunei* var. *albopicta* |
| 'Aureomarginata' ambig. (v) | SCoo |
| 'Aureomarginata' (*montana*) (v) | CMac EGol EHoe ELan EMic EPGN GCal GMaP IBal MMuc NCGa NEgg NGdn NHol NLar SApp SEND WFar WTin WWEG |
| 'Aureomarginata' (*rohdeifolia*) (v) | EMic |
| § 'Aureomarginata' (*ventricosa*) (v) ♀H4 | ECha EGol EMic EPfP IBal MWat NGdn NMyG SApp WFar WTin |
| 'Aureostriata' (*tardiva*) | see *H.* 'Inaho' |
| 'Aurora Borealis' (*sieboldiana*) (v) | EGol IBal |
| 'Austin Dickinson' (v) | EGol EMic IBal LBuc LRHS NEgg |
| 'Avalanche' | IBal |
| 'Avocado' | IBal |
| 'Azure Mediterranean' | IBal |
| 'Azure Snow' | EGol IBal |
| 'Babbling Brook' | EGol |
| 'Baby Blue' (Tardiana Group) | EMic |
| 'Baby Blue Eyes' | IBal |
| 'Baby Bunting' | EGol EMic EPGN IBal IFoB NBro NLar NNor NPro |
| 'Bali-Hai' **new** | IBal |
| 'Ballerina' | EGol IBal |
| 'Banana Boat' (v) | EGol IBal |
| 'Banana Muffins' | IBal |
| 'Banana Sundae' (v) | IBal |
| 'Band of Gold' | IBal |
| 'Banyai's Dancing Girl' | EGol EMic |
| 'Barbara Ann' (v) | EMic EPGN IBal MBri NGdn NMyG WWEG |
| 'Barbara May' | IBal |
| 'Barbara White' | IBal |
| 'Beauty Little Blue' | EGol IBal |
| 'Beauty Substance' | EGol EMic EPGN IBal NNor |
| 'Beckoning' | EMic IBal |
| 'Bedford Blue' | EMic IBal |
| 'Bedford Rise and Shine' (v) | EGol EMic |
| 'Bedford Wakey-Wakey' | EGol |
| 'Bell Bottom Blues' | IBal |
| ***bella*** | see *H. crassifolia* |
| 'Bennie McRae' | EGol |
| 'Betcher's Blue' | EGol EMic |
| 'Betsy King' | CMac EBee EGol MRav NMyG |
| 'Bette Davis Eyes' | EGol |
| 'Betty' | EGol IBal |
| 'Bianca' | SApp |
| 'Big Boy' (*montana*) | EGol |
| 'Big Chance' | IBal |
| 'Big Daddy' (*sieboldiana* hybrid) (v) | Widely available |
| 'Big John' (*sieboldiana*) **new** | IBal |
| 'Big Mama' | EGol MBNS NLar NPnk SApp |
| 'Big Top' | IBal |
| 'Bigfoot' | EGol |
| 'Biggie' | IBal SApp |
| 'Bill Brinka' (v) | EGol EMic |
| 'Bill Dress's Blue' | IBal |
| 'Birchwood Blue' | EGol |
| 'Birchwood Blue Beauty' | IBal NMyG |
| 'Birchwood Elegance' | NMyG SApp |
| 'Birchwood Gem' | IBal |
| § 'Birchwood Parky's Gold' | CFir CMHG EBee EGol EMic EPfP EWTr GMaP IBal LBMP LRHS MBNS NGdn NHol NNor SApp |

|  |  |
|---|---|
| 'Birchwood Ruffled Queen' | EGol EMic IBal |
| 'Bitsy Gold' | EGol EMic IBal |
| 'Bitsy Green' | EGol |
| 'Bix Blues' | IBal |
| 'Bizarre' | EMic IBal |
| 'Black Beauty' | EGol IBal |
| 'Black Hills' | EGol EMic IBal |
| 'Black Pearl' | IBal |
| 'Blackfoot' | EGol EMic |
| 'Blackjack' (*sieboldiana*) | IBal NMyG SApp |
| 'Blaue Venus' | EGol IBal |
| 'Blaues Boot' | IBal |
| 'Blauspecht' | IBal |
| 'Blaze of Glory' | IBal |
| 'Blazing Saddles' (v) | EMic IBal MBNS |
| 'Blonde Elf' | EGol EMic IBal NEgg NGdn NHol NMyG NNor SApp WWEG |
| 'Blue Angel' misapplied | see *H. sieboldiana* var. *elegans* |
| 'Blue Angel' (*sieboldiana*) ♀H4 | CBar COlW ECtt EGol EHoe ELan EMic EPGN EPfP GBBs GBin GMaP IBal LEdu MHom MSwo NBPC NBid NBir NEgg NGdn NNor NOrc WAul WFar WMnd |
| 'Blue Arrow' | EGol IBal NNor SApp |
| 'Blue Baron' | EMic IBal |
| 'Blue Beard' | IBal |
| 'Blue Belle' (Tardiana Group) | EGol EMic IBal NGdn NPro WTin |
| 'Blue Blush' (Tardiana Group) | EGol EMic GSec IBal NGdn |
| 'Blue Boy' | EGol EMic EWes NMyG NNor |
| 'Blue Cadet' | CBcs CMac EGol EMic EShb GQue IBal IFoB LPBA LRHS MLHP MWhi NBir NGdn NLar NMyG SApp SMrm SPoG WFar WMnd WWEG |
| 'Blue Canoe' | EMic IBal SApp |
| 'Blue Chip' | EMic EPGN IBal SApp |
| 'Blue Clown' | IBal |
| 'Blue Cup' (*sieboldiana*) | MRav |
| 'Blue Danube' (Tardiana Group) | EGol EMic IBal MHom NMyG |
| 'Blue Diamond' (Tardiana Group) | EGol EMic NNor WFar WWEG |
| 'Blue Dimples' (Tardiana Group) | ECtt EGol EMic IBal |
| 'Blue Edger' | EMic IBal NBir |
| 'Blue Eyes' | IBal |
| 'Blue Flame' | EMic IBal |
| 'Blue Frost' | IBal |
| 'Blue Haired Lady' | IBal |
| 'Blue Hawaii' | EMic IBal |
| 'Blue Heart' (*sieboldiana*) | ECha EMic IBal |
| 'Blue Ice' (Tardiana Group) | EGol IBal |
| 'Blue Impression' | EMic |
| 'Blue Ivory' (v) | CBcs IBal NMyG |
| 'Blue Jay' (Tardiana Group) | EGol EMic IBal SApp |
| 'Blue Lady' | EMic IBal |
| 'Blue Mammoth' (*sieboldiana*) | EGol EMic IBal SApp |
| 'Blue Maui' | EMic IBal |
| 'Blue Monday' | EMic |
| 'Blue Moon' (Tardiana Group) | CMea EGol EMic EPfP GKev IBal NGdn NNor WAul |
| 'Blue Mountains' | IBal LBuc |
| 'Blue Mouse Ears' | EGol EMic EPGN EPfP GBin GEdr GQue IBal LLWG MBNS MDev MHom NGdn NHar NMen NMyG NNor NSla SApp SPoG WWEG |
| 'Blue River' (v) | EMic SApp |
| 'Blue Seer' (*sieboldiana*) | EGol EMic |

| | |
|---|---|
| 'Blue Shadows' (*tokudama*) (v) | EMic ESwi NLar SApp WFar |
| 'Blue Skies' (Tardiana Group) | EGol MHom SApp |
| 'Blue Splendor' (Tardiana Group) | IBal |
| 'Blue Umbrellas' (*sieboldiana* hybrid) | EGol ELan EMic EPGN EPfP GMaP IBal LRHS MHom NGdn NLar NMyG NNor SApp SMrm |
| 'Blue Veil' | EGol |
| 'Blue Vision' | EMic EPGN SApp |
| 'Blue Wedgwood' (Tardiana Group) | EBee EGol ELan EMic GQue LPBA LRHS MGos MMuc NGdn NMyG SApp SEND WHil WWEG |
| 'Blue Wonder' | IBal |
| 'Blueberry Tart' | IBal |
| 'Blütenwunder' | SApp |
| 'Bob Deane' (v) | EMic IBal |
| 'Bob Olson' (v) | EGol IBal |
| 'Bobbie Sue' (v) | EGol IBal |
| 'Bold Edger' (v) | EGol EMic |
| 'Bold Intrigue' (v) | IBal |
| 'Bold Ribbons' (v) | EGol EMic GAbr IBal WTin |
| 'Bold Ruffles' (*sieboldiana*) | EGol SApp |
| 'Bolt out of the Blue' | EMic |
| 'Bonanza' | EMic |
| 'Border Bandit' (v) | EGol IBal |
| 'Border Favorite' | EMic IBal |
| 'Border Street' (v) **new** | IBal |
| § 'Borwick Beauty' (*sieboldiana*) (v) | EGol EMic EPGN IBal MSCN NBPC NCGa NGdn NLar NMyG NPnk SApp SPer WAul WWEG |
| 'Bottom Line' (v) | IBal |
| 'Bountiful' | EGol EMic |
| 'Bouquet' | EGol |
| 'Boyz Toy' **new** | EMic |
| 'Brandywine' | IBal |
| 'Brash and Sassy' | IBal |
| 'Brass Ring' (v) | IBal |
| 'Brenda's Beauty' (v) | EGol EMic IBal |
| 'Bressingham Blue' | EBee ECtt EGol EMic GQue IBal LRHS MRav NLar NMyG NNor SApp SWvt WFar WMnd |
| 'Bridal Veil' | IBal |
| 'Bridegroom' | EGol EMic |
| 'Bridgeville' | IBal |
| 'Brigadier' | EGol |
| 'Brigham Blue' | IBal |
| 'Bright Glow' (Tardiana Group) | EGol EMic |
| 'Bright Lights' (*tokudama*) (v) | EGol EMic EPGN GBBs GSec IBal NGdn SApp WFar |
| 'Brim Cup' (v) | EBee EGol ELon EMic EPGN GAbr IBal LAst LSou MBNS NBro NGdn NNor NOrc SApp SBfd SMrm WWEG |
| 'Brooke' | EGol EMic IBal NMyG WWEG |
| 'Brother Ronald' (Tardiana Group) | EGol EMic IBal SApp |
| 'Brother Stefan' | EMic IBal SApp |
| 'Bruce's Blue' | EGol |
| 'Bubba' | IBal |
| 'Buckshaw Blue' | EGol EPGN GSec IBal MDKP NBir NGdn NPro WHrl |
| 'Buckwheat Honey' | IBal |
| 'Bunchoko' | IBal NNor |
| 'Burke's Dwarf' | IBal |
| 'Butter Rim' (*sieboldii*) (v) | EGol |
| 'Cadillac' (v) | EMic |
| 'Caliban' | SApp |
| 'Cally Atom' | GCal IBal |
| 'Calypso' (v) | EGol EMic EPGN IBal LBuc WWEG |
| 'Camelot' (Tardiana Group) | EGol EMic IBal LRHS NGdn |
| 'Cameo' | EMic IBal SApp |
| 'Camouflage' | IBal |
| 'Canadian Blue' | EMic |
| 'Candy Dish' **new** | IBal |
| 'Candy Hearts' | CMHG CSam EGol EMic MHom NNor WTin |
| ***capitata*** | NNor |
| - B&SWJ 588 | WCru |
| 'Captain Kirk' (v) | EMic IBal NGdn NMyG SApp |
| ***caput-avis*** | see *H. kikutii* var. *caput-avis* |
| 'Carder Blue' | EMic |
| 'Carnival' (v) | EGol EMic EPGN IBal NBPC NEgg SApp |
| 'Carol' (*fortunei*) (v) | EGol EMic IBal NEgg NGdn NLar NMyG NNor SApp |
| 'Carolina Blue' | IBal |
| 'Carousel' (v) | EGol IBal |
| 'Carrie' (*sieboldii*) (v) | EGol |
| 'Cascades' (v) | EGol EMic IBal |
| 'Cat and Mouse' | EGol IBal |
| 'Cathedral Windows' (v) | IBal |
| 'Catherine' | IBal LLWG |
| 'Cat's Eyes' (*venusta*) (v) | EGol EMic EPGN IBal NNor SApp |
| 'Celebration' (v) | EGol ELan EMic MDKP WWEG |
| 'Celestial' | IBal |
| 'Celtic Uplands' **new** | EMic |
| 'Center of Attention' | EMic IBal NGdn NMyG SApp |
| 'Cha Cha Cha' | IBal |
| 'Chain Lightning' (v) | IBal |
| 'Challenger' | EMic |
| 'Change of Tradition' (*lancifolia*) (v) | EMic |
| 'Chantilly Lace' (v) | EGol EMic SApp WTin |
| 'Chariots of Fire' (v) | IBal |
| 'Chartreuse Waves' | EGol |
| 'Chartreuse Wiggles' (*sieboldii*) | EGol IBal |
| 'Cheatin' Heart' | EGol EMic IBal WWEG |
| 'Chelsea Babe' (*fortunei*) (v) | EGol |
| 'Cherish' | EGol EMic EPGN IBal NGdn |
| 'Cherry Berry' (v) | CMHG EGol EMic EPGN EPfP GBin IBal LRHS MBNS MLLN MMuc NBro NCGa NEgg NGdn NLar NMyG NPro NWad SApp SBfd SPoG WAul WBor WFar WWEG |
| 'Cherry Tart' | EMic IBal |
| 'Cherub' (v) | EGol IBal |
| 'Chesapeake Bay' | EMic IBal |
| 'Chesterland Gold' | IBal |
| 'Chickadee' (v) | EMic |
| 'Chinese Sunrise' (v) | CWCL EGol EMic EPGN IBal LBuc MHom NMyG NNor SRms |
| 'Chionea' (v) | IBal |
| 'Chiquita' | EGol IBal |
| 'Chodai Ginba' | IBal |
| § 'Chōkō Nishiki' (*montana*) (v) | EGol EMic EPGN EQua IBal LRHS NGdn NMyG NNor SApp SBfd |
| 'Choo Choo Train' | EGol EMic SApp |
| 'Chopsticks' | EMic IBal |
| 'Christmas Candy'[PBR] | EMic EPGN IBal NMyG |
| 'Christmas Cookies' | IBal |
| 'Christmas Lights' (v) | IBal |
| 'Christmas Pageant' (v) | EMic IBal |
| 'Christmas Tree' (v) | CMMP EGol EMic EPGN IBal IFoB LPla LRHS NBPC NEgg NGdn NMyG SApp WMoo WWEG |

| | |
|---|---|
| 'Cinderella' | IBal |
| 'Cinnamon Sticks' | IBal |
| 'Citation' (v) | EGol |
| 'City Lights' | EGol EMic NEgg |
| 'City Slicker' (v) | IBal |
| ***clausa*** | EMic |
| – var. ***normalis*** | GQui NBir NGdn NLar NMyG |
| 'Clear Fork River Valley' | IBal |
| 'Cleopatra' (v) | IBal |
| 'Clifford's Forest Fire' | EMic EPGN IBal NLar WFar |
| 'Clifford's Stingray' (v) | EMic IBal |
| 'Climax' (v) | EMic IBal |
| 'Cloudburst' | IBal |
| 'Clovelly' | IBal |
| 'Clown's Collar' (v) **new** | EMic |
| 'Cody' | EGol IBal |
| 'Collector's Banner' | EGol |
| 'Collector's Choice' | EGol IBal |
| 'Color à la Mode' (v) | IBal |
| 'Color Festival' (v) **new** | EMic IBal |
| 'Color Glory' | see *H.* 'Borwick Beauty' |
| 'Colossal' | EGol EMic |
| 'Columbus Circle' (v) | EGol EMic |
| 'Confused Angel' (v) **new** | IBal |
| 'Cookie Crumbs' (v) | EGol EMic EPGN IBal SApp |
| 'Coquette' (v) | EGol EMic GAbr IBal NMyG |
| 'Corkscrew' | EMic SApp |
| 'Corn Belt' (v) | IBal |
| 'Cotillion' (v) | EGol EMic SApp |
| 'Country Mouse' (v) | EGol EMic IBal |
| 'County Park' | EGol EMic IBal |
| 'Cowrie' (v) | IBal |
| 'Cracker Crumbs' (v) | EGol EMic EPGN GEdr GKev IBal MHom NHar NMyG NNor NSla SApp |
| 'Craig's Temptation' | IBal NMyG |
| § ***crassifolia*** | EMic IBal LRHS XLum |
| 'Crater's Heart' (*venusta*) (v) | IBal |
| 'Cream Cheese' (v) | EGol IBal |
| 'Cream Delight' (*undulata*) | see *H. undulata* var. *undulata* |
| 'Crepe Soul' (v) | EGol IBal |
| 'Crepe Suzette' (v) | EGol EPGN NNor |
| 'Crested Reef' | EGol EMic NMyG |
| 'Crested Surf' (v) | EGol EMic EPGN IBal |
| 'Crinoline Petticoats' | EGol |
| § ***crispula*** (v) $\heartsuit^{H4}$ | CBot EGol EMic EPfP MCot MHom MRav NChi NMyG |
| 'Crown Jewel' (v) | EPGN IBal |
| 'Crown Prince' (v) | EGol IBal |
| § 'Crowned Imperial' (*fortunei*) (v) | CWat EMic NHol |
| 'Crumples' (*sieboldiana*) | EGol |
| 'Crusader' (v) | EGol ELon EMic EPGN IBal LRHS NMyG SApp WFar WWEG |
| 'Crystal Chimes' | IBal |
| 'Crystal Dixie' | EGol IBal SApp |
| 'Cupboard Love' | SApp |
| 'Curlew' (Tardiana Group) | EGol IBal |
| 'Curls' | IBal |
| 'Curtain Call' | IBal |
| 'Cutting Edge' | IBal |
| 'Dab a Green' | IBal |
| 'Daisy Doolittle' (v) | IBal SApp |
| 'Dance with Me' (v) | EMic IBal |
| 'Dancing in the Rain' (v) | CWGN EMic EPGN NBro SApp SMrm WFar |
| 'Dancing Queen' **new** | IBal |
| 'Dark Shadows' | EMic EPGN IBal NGdn |
| 'Dark Star' (v) | EGol EMic EPGN IBal SApp |

| | |
|---|---|
| 'Dark Victory' | IBal |
| 'Dawn' | EGol EMic GSec IBal NMyG |
| 'Dawn's Early Light' | EMic |
| 'Dax' | IBal |
| 'Daybreak' | EGol EMic EPGN IBal MBri NBro SApp |
| 'Day's End' (v) | EGol EMic IBal |
| 'Deane's Dream' | EMic IBal |
| ***decorata*** | EGol EMic |
| 'Deep Blue Sea' | EMic IBal SApp |
| 'Deep Pockets' | IBal |
| 'Déjà Blu' (v) | EMic IBal |
| 'Delia' (v) | EPGN |
| 'Delta Dawn' (v) | EMic IBal NGdn |
| 'Delta Desire' | IBal |
| 'Deluxe Edition' | IBal |
| 'Designer Genes' | EMic IBal SApp |
| 'Devon Blue' (Tardiana Group) | EGol EMic NMyG NNor |
| 'Devon Desire' (*montana*) | NLar |
| 'Devon Discovery' | IBal |
| 'Devon Giant' | EMic IBal NNor SApp |
| 'Devon Gold' | EMic GAbr IBal |
| 'Devon Green' | ELan EMic EPGN GBin IBal LRHS MHom MLLN MMuc NBro NEgg NGdn NLar NMyG NPro SApp SBfd SEND SPoG WAul WFar WHal WHoo WWEG |
| 'Devon Mist' | IBal NNor |
| 'Devon Tor' | IBal |
| 'Dew Drop' (v) | EMic IBal WWEG |
| 'Dewed Steel' **new** | IBal |
| 'Diamond Tiara' (v) | EGol EMic EPGN IBal LRHS NBir NGdn NMyG WWEG |
| 'Diana Remembered' | EGol EMic EPGN IBal WBor |
| 'Dick Ward' | EMic EPGN IBal |
| 'Dillthlum Crystal' | IBal |
| 'Dillie Perkeo' | IBal |
| 'Dilys' | EMic MNrw |
| 'Dimple' | EMic IBal |
| 'Dinky Donna' | IBal |
| 'Dinner Jacket' **new** | SBfd |
| 'Dixie Chick' (v) | EGol EMic IBal NMyG NNor SApp |
| 'Dixie Chickadee' (v) **new** | EGol |
| 'Dixieland Heat' | IBal |
| 'Doctor Fu Manchu' | IBal |
| 'Domaine de Courson' | EMic EPGN SApp WFar |
| 'Don Stevens' (v) | EGol IBal |
| 'Donahue Piecrust' | GSec |
| 'Dorothy' | EMic |
| 'Dorset Blue' (Tardiana Group) | EMic EPGN IBal SApp SBfd |
| 'Dorset Charm' (Tardiana Group) | EGol EMic |
| 'Dorset Flair' (Tardiana Group) | EGol EMic IBal |
| 'Doubloons' | EGol EMic |
| 'Dragon Tails' | EMic IBal LRHS |
| 'Dragon Wings' | IBal |
| 'Dream Queen' (v) | ECtt EMic IBal |
| 'Dream Weaver' (v) | EGol EMic EPGN IBal MHom MNrw NBro NGdn NMyG SApp SPer SPoG WFar WWEG |
| 'Dress Blues' | CMac EMic EPGN IBal |
| 'Drummer Boy' | EGol EMic IBal WWEG |
| 'Duchess' (*nakaiana*) (v) | IBal |
| 'Duke of Cornwall' (v) **new** | IBal |
| 'DuPage Delight' (*sieboldiana*) (v) | EGol EMic IBal NGdn NLar |
| 'Dust Devil' (*fortunei*) (v) | EGol IBal |

| | |
|---|---|
| 'Earth Angel'PBR (v) | EMic EPGN IBal NGdn NMyG SApp |
| 'Edge of Night' | EGol EMic |
| 'Edwin Bibby' | EMic |
| 'El Capitan' (v) | EGol EMic EPGN IBal |
| 'El Niño'PBR (Tardiana Group) (v) | CWGN EGol EMic EPGN IBal LRHS MHom MNrw NBro NGdn NMyG SApp WFar WWEG |
| § 'Elata' | EGol EMic SApp |
| 'Elatior' (*nigrescens*) | EMic IBal LRHS |
| 'Eldorado' | see *H.* 'Frances Williams' |
| 'Eleanor Lachman' (v) | EGol EMic IBal |
| 'Eleanor Roosevelt' | IBal |
| 'Elegans' | see *H. sieboldiana* var. *elegans* |
| 'Elfin Power' (*sieboldii*) (v) | EGol |
| 'Elisabeth' | EMic GBin IBal LSRN |
| 'Elizabeth Campbell' (*fortunei*) (v) | EGol EMic |
| 'Elkheart Lake' | EMic |
| 'Ellen' | EMic |
| 'Ellerbroek' (*fortunei*) (v) | EMic IBal |
| 'Ellie Bee' | IBal |
| 'Elsley Runner' | EGol IBal WWEG |
| 'Elvis Lives' | EGol EMic EPGN GBin IBal LAst NEgg NGdn NLar NMyG NNor NPro |
| 'Embroidery' (v) | EPGN |
| 'Emerald Carpet' | EGol IBal |
| 'Emerald Crown' | IBal |
| 'Emerald Necklace' (v) | EGol |
| 'Emerald Ruff Cut' | EMic IBal SApp |
| 'Emerald Tiara' (v) | EGol EMic EPGN GSec LRHS MLHP NLar NMyG SApp SBfd WTin WWEG |
| 'Emeralds and Rubies' | EGol EMic IBal |
| 'Emily Dickinson' (v) | EBee EGol EMic IBal LRHS MMuc NNor SApp SEND WWEG |
| 'Empress Wu' | IBal |
| 'Encore' | IBal |
| 'English Sunrise' (Tardiana Group) | IBal |
| 'Enterprise' | EMic IBal LLWG NGdn SApp |
| 'Eos' | NLar |
| 'Eric Smith' (Tardiana Group) | EGol EMic IBal MHom NMyG WFar |
| 'Eric's Gold' | EPGN IBal |
| 'Erie Magic' (v) | EGol IBal |
| 'Eskimo Pie' (v) | EBee EMic IBal NGdn SApp SMrm WFar |
| 'Essence of Summer' | EMic EPfP IBal SApp |
| 'Eternal Flame' | EMic IBal |
| 'Eternity' | GSec |
| 'Evelyn McCafferty' (*tokudama* hybrid) | EGol |
| 'Eventide' (v) | EGol |
| 'Everlasting Love' (v) | EGol |
| 'Excitation' | EGol EMic IBal |
| 'Extasy' (v) | EMic IBal NGdn |
| 'Extreme' | IBal |
| 'Eye Candy' (v) | IBal |
| 'Eye Catcher' | EMic |
| 'Eye Declare' (v) | IBal |
| 'Fair Maiden' (v) | IBal NMyG |
| 'Faith' | EMic |
| 'Faithful Heart' (v) | IBal |
| 'Fall Bouquet' (*longipes* var. *hypoglauca*) | EGol |
| 'Fall Emerald' | EMic |
| 'Fallen Angel' | IBal |
| 'Falling Waters' (v) | IBal |
| 'Fan Dance' (v) | EGol EMic IBal |
| 'Fantabulous' (v) | EPGN IBal |
| 'Fantastic' (*sieboldiana* hybrid) | EGol |
| 'Fantasy Island' (v) | EGol EMic IBal |
| 'Fatal Attraction' | IBal |
| 'Feather Boa' | EGol EMic IBal NHar NMyG WWEG |
| 'Fenman's Fascination' | EMic IBal |
| 'Fiesta' (v) | IBal |
| 'Fire and Ice' (v) | Widely available |
| 'Fire Island' | EGol EMic EPGN GBin IBal MHom SApp |
| 'Fireworks' (v) | EBee EGol EMic EPGN EPfP GBin IBal MBNS MDev NBro NGdn NMyG SApp SMrm SPoG |
| 'First Frost' (v) | EMic IBal LRHS MAvo MDev NGdn SApp WWEG |
| 'First Mate' (v) | EMic IBal |
| 'First Moon' **new** | IBal |
| 'Five O'Clock Shadow' (v) | IBal |
| 'Five O'Clock Somewhere' (v) | IBal |
| 'Flame Stitch' (*ventricosa*) (v) | IBal |
| 'Fleet Week' **new** | IBal |
| 'Flemish Gold' **new** | IBal |
| 'Flemish Sky' | EMic IBal NGdn SApp |
| 'Floradora' | EGol EMic NMyG |
| 'Flower Power' | EGol GSec NNor |
| 'Fool's Gold' (*fortunei*) | EMic IBal |
| 'Forest Fireworks' (v) | IBal |
| 'Forest Shadows' | IBal |
| 'Formal Attire' (*sieboldiana* hybrid) (v) | EGol EMic IBal LRHS |
| 'Forncett Frances' (v) | EGol IBal |
| 'Fortis' | see *H. undulata* var. *erromena* |
| ***fortunei*** | EGol EMic NHol NNor WFar |
| § - var. ***albopicta*** (v) ♀H4 | CSam EBee ECha EGol EHoe ELan EMic EPGN EPfP GBin GMaP IBal LBMP LRHS MRav NEgg NGdn NHol NMyG NNor SApp SPer WBrk WFar WHoo WMnd WTin WWEG |
| - - f. ***aurea*** ♀H4 | CMHG CMac ECha EGol EHoe ELan EMic EPla GBin MRav NEgg NLar NMyG SRms WFar WHal |
| - - - dwarf | EMic |
| - - f. ***viridis*** **new** | NNor |
| § - var. ***aureomarginata*** (v) ♀H4 | Widely available |
| - var. ***gigantea*** | see *H. montana* |
| - var. ***hyacinthina*** ♀H4 | EGol EMic EPfP LRHS MRav NGdn NLar SApp WPtf XLum |
| - - variegated (v) | see *H.* 'Crowned Imperial' |
| - var. ***rugosa*** | EMic IBal |
| - 'Shaman' | SApp |
| 'Fountain of Youth' (*kikutii*) | IBal |
| 'Fourth of July' | EGol |
| 'Fragrant Blue' | EBee EGol EMic GBBs IBal NBro NGdn NMyG SApp SPoG XLum |
| 'Fragrant Bouquet' (v) | CMHG EGol ELan EMic EPGN GAbr IBal LAst LRHS LSRN MMuc NCGa NGdn NHol NLar NMyG SEND WPtf WWEG |
| 'Fragrant Dream' | EGol EMic EPfP IBal NLar WWEG |
| 'Fragrant Fire' | EMic IBal SApp |
| 'Fragrant Gold' | EGol EMic |
| 'Fragrant King' | IBal |
| 'Fragrant Star' | EMic IBal SApp |
| 'Fragrant Surprise' (v) | IBal |
| 'Fran Godfrey' | EMic EPGN IBal |
| 'Francee' (*fortunei*) (v) ♀H4 | Widely available |

| | | |
|---|---|---|
| § | 'Frances Williams' (*sieboldiana*) (v) ♀H4 | Widely available |
| | 'Frances Williams Improved' (*sieboldiana*) (v) | EGol EPfP MWat |
| | 'Fresh' (v) | EGol EMic EPGN IBal SApp |
| | 'Fried Bananas' | EGol EMic MBri SApp WWEG |
| | 'Fried Green Tomatoes' | EGol EMic GBin NLar NMyG NNor SApp |
| | 'Fringe Benefit' (v) | EGol EMic GAbr IBal SApp WWEG |
| | 'Frost Giant' (v) **new** | IBal |
| | 'Frosted Dimples' | EMic EPGN IBal |
| | 'Frosted Frolic' (v) **new** | EMic |
| | 'Frosted Jade' (v) | EBee EGol EMic EPGN IBal NLar SApp SBfd SRGP WTin |
| | 'Frosted June' | IBal |
| | 'Frosted Mouse Ears' | EGol EMic IBal |
| | 'Frozen Margarita' | EMic IBal |
| | 'Frühlingsgold' (v) | IBal |
| | 'Fujibotan' (v) | EGol EMic IBal SApp |
| | 'Fulda' | EMic |
| | 'Gaiety' (v) | EGol EMic EPGN |
| | 'Gaijin' (v) | EGol IBal SApp |
| | 'Garden Party' (v) | IBal |
| | 'Garden Treasure' | EGol |
| | 'Garnet Prince' | EGol IBal |
| | 'Gay Blade' (v) | EGol IBal LRHS SApp |
| | 'Gay Feather' (v) | EMic SApp |
| | 'Gay Search' (v) | EPGN IBal |
| | 'Geisha' (v) | EGol EMic IBal LRHS NGdn NMyG NNor NPro SApp WWEG |
| | 'Geisha Satin Ripples' | IBal |
| | 'Gemini Moon' (v) | IBal |
| | 'Gemstone' | IBal |
| | 'Gene's Joy' | EPGN IBal |
| | 'Ghost Spirit' | IBal SApp WFar |
| | 'Gig Harbor' | IBal |
| | 'Gigantea' (*sieboldiana*) | see *H.* 'Elata' |
| | 'Gilt by Association' | IBal |
| | 'Gilt Edge' (*sieboldiana*) (v) | CWat EMic NMyG WWEG |
| | 'Gingee' | IBal |
| | 'Ginko Craig' (v) | CMHG CMac EBee ECha EGol EHoe ELan EMic EPGN EPfP GKev GMaP IBal LPBA MRav NBir NGdn NLar NMyG NNor NSti SApp SBfd SPer SPoG SRGP WFar WMnd WWEG |
| | 'Ginrei' | IBal |
| | 'Ginsu Knife' (v) | EMic IBal |
| | 'Glad Rags' (v) **new** | IBal |
| | 'Glass Hearts' | EMic IBal |
| | ***glauca*** | see *H. sieboldiana* var. *elegans* |
| | 'Glitter' | EMic IBal |
| | 'Glockenspiel' | EGol EMic |
| I | 'Gloriosa' (*fortunei*) (v) | EGol IBal LRHS WFar |
| | 'Glory' | EGol |
| | 'Goddess of Athena' (*decorata*) (v) | EGol |
| | 'Gold Drop' (*venusta* hybrid) | EGol EMic NHol WWEG |
| | 'Gold Edger' | CBcs CMac CPrp EGol EHoe ELan EMic EPfP GMaP IBal MLLN MRav NBir NGdn NLar NMyG NNor NSti SApp WFar WTin WWEG |
| | 'Gold Edger Surprise' (v) | EMic |
| | 'Gold Flush' (*ventricosa*) | EMic |
| § | 'Gold Haze' (*fortunei*) | EGol EMic EPGN IBal MHom NBir NCGa NMyG WWEG |
| | 'Gold Leaf' (*fortunei*) | EGol |
| | 'Gold Regal' | EGol EMic EPGN GBin IBal LRHS MHom NMyG WFar WMnd |
| | 'Gold Rush' | EMic GSec NMyG |

| | |
|---|---|
| 'Gold Standard' (*fortunei*) (v) | Widely available |
| 'Goldbrook' (v) | EGol EMic IBal WTin |
| 'Goldbrook Galleon' | EGol IBal |
| 'Goldbrook Gayle' (v) | EGol |
| 'Goldbrook Gaynor' | EGol IBal |
| 'Goldbrook Genie' | EGol IBal |
| 'Goldbrook Ghost' (v) | EGol |
| 'Goldbrook Girl' | EGol IBal |
| 'Goldbrook Glamour' (v) | EGol IBal |
| 'Goldbrook Gleam' (v) **new** | EGol |
| 'Goldbrook Glimmer' (Tardiana Group) (v) | EGol IBal LRHS |
| 'Goldbrook Glory' | EGol EMic |
| 'Goldbrook Gold' | EGol IBal |
| 'Goldbrook Good Gracious' (v) **new** | EGol |
| 'Goldbrook Grace' | EGol |
| 'Goldbrook Gratis' (v) | EGol IBal |
| 'Goldbrook Grayling' | EGol EMic IBal |
| 'Goldbrook Grebe' | EGol IBal |
| 'Goldbrook Greenheart' | IBal |
| 'Golden Age' | see *H.* 'Gold Haze' |
| 'Golden Anniversary' | EGol IBal |
| 'Golden Ben' | ITim |
| 'Golden Fascination' | EGol |
| 'Golden Fountain' | EMic |
| 'Golden Friendship' | EGol |
| 'Golden Gate' | EGol |
| 'Golden Goal' | IBal |
| 'Golden Guernsey' (v) | EMic |
| 'Golden Isle' | EGol EMic IBal |
| 'Golden Meadows'PBR (*sieboldiana*) | EMic EPGN IBal NGdn SMrm |
| 'Golden Medallion' (*tokudama*) | CMHG EGol ELan EMic IBal NEgg NGdn NMyG WFar |
| 'Golden Nakaiana' | see *H.* 'Birchwood Parky's Gold' |
| 'Golden' (*nakaiana*) | see *H.* 'Birchwood Parky's Gold' |
| 'Golden Oriole' | EGol EMic IBal NMyG NNor WWEG |
| 'Golden Prayers' (*tokudama*) | ECtt EHoe ELan EMic IBal LRHS MRav NBir NBro NEgg NGdn NLar WFar WHal WSHC |
| 'Golden Scepter' | EGol EMic EPGN GSec IBal LRHS NMyG NNor SApp WFar |
| 'Golden Sculpture' (*sieboldiana*) | EGol EMic |
| 'Golden Spider' | EGol EMic WWEG |
| 'Golden Sunburst' (*sieboldiana*) | CPrp EGol ELan IBal NEgg NGdn NLar WFar XLum |
| 'Golden Tiara' (v) ♀H4 | Widely available |
| 'Golden Tusk' | IBal |
| 'Golden Waffles' | CMHG EMic NEgg |
| 'Goldsmith' | EGol SApp |
| 'Gone Fishin'' (v) | IBal |
| 'Goober' | IBal |
| 'Good as Gold' | EMic EPGN IBal NMyG |
| 'Gorgon' | IBal |
| 'Gosan' (*takahashii*) | EGol |
| 'Gosan Hildegarde' | GSec |
| 'Gosan Leather Strap' | IBal |
| ***gracillima*** | EPGN IBal NRya WWEG |
| 'Granary Gold' (*fortunei*) | EGol EPGN GSec |
| 'Grand Canyon' | EMic SApp |
| 'Grand Finale' | IBal |
| 'Grand Forks' | IBal |
| 'Grand Marquee' (v) | EMic GBin IBal NGdn NLar SApp WFar WWEG |
| 'Grand Master' | EGol IBal MDKP SApp |
| 'Grand Prize' (v) | IBal |
| 'Grand Slam' | EGol GSec |

| | |
|---|---|
| 'Grand Tiara' (v) | EGol EMic EPGN GSec IBal SApp |
| 'Grand Total' | IBal |
| 'Grant Park' | IBal |
| 'Gray Cole' (*sieboldiana*) | EGol EMic IBal NMyG |
| 'Great Arrival' | EMic IBal |
| 'Great Escape'PBR (v) | EMic IBal |
| 'Great Expectations' (*sieboldiana*) (v) | CBar CHid CMac COIW EBee EGol EMic EPGN EPfP IBal LRHS LSRN MBNS MHer MNrw NBPC NBro NCGa NGdn NHol NLar NNor NSti SAga SApp SMad SMrm WAul WWEG |
| 'Great Lakes Gold' | IBal |
| 'Green Acres' (*montana*) | EMic IBal LEdu WFar |
| 'Green Angel' (*sieboldiana*) | EGol |
| 'Green Dwarf' | NWCA WFar |
| 'Green Eyes' (*sieboldii*) (v) | EGol EMic IBal |
| 'Green Fountain' (*kikutii*) | EGol EMic NMyG WWEG |
| 'Green Gold' (*fortunei*) (v) | EMic |
| 'Green Lama' | IBal |
| 'Green Mouse Ears' | EGol EMic IBal |
| 'Green Piecrust' | EGol NNor |
| 'Green Sheen' | EGol EMic EPGN NMyG |
| 'Green Summer Fragrance' | IBal |
| 'Green Velveteen' | EGol |
| 'Green Wedge' **new** | GSec |
| 'Green with Envy' (v) | EGol EMic EPGN IBal NNor SApp |
| 'Greensleeves' (v) | IBal |
| 'Grey Ghost' | EMic IBal |
| 'Grey Piecrust' | EGol IBal |
| 'Groo Bloo' **new** | IBal |
| 'Ground Cover Trompenburg' | SApp |
| 'Ground Master' (v) | CMHG CMac EBee ECtt EGol ELan EPfP GCra GMaP IBal IFoB LPBA MRav MSwo NBro NGdn NNor NSti WFar WMoo WPtf WWEG |
| 'Ground Sulphur' | EGol EMic |
| 'Grünherz' | IBal |
| 'Grunspecht' (Tardiana Group) | IBal |
| 'Guacamole' (v) | CBcs ECha ECtt EGol EMic EPGN EPfP GBin IBal IPot LRHS MBri NGdn NLar NMyG NNor NPnk SApp WAul WHoo WTin WWEG |
| 'Guardian Angel' (*sieboldiana*) | EGol EMic EPGN IBal NLar |
| 'Gum Drop' | EMic NNor |
| 'Gun Metal Blue' | EGol IBal |
| 'Gypsy Rose' | EPGN EPfP MBri NGdn NMyG SApp WFar |
| 'Hacksaw' | EMic IBal |
| 'Hadspen Blue' (Tardiana Group) | Widely available |
| 'Hadspen Hawk' (Tardiana Group) | IBal NMyG SApp |
| 'Hadspen Heron' (Tardiana Group) | EGol EMic MHom MWat NMyG WCot XLum |
| 'Hadspen Nymphaea' | EGol IBal |
| 'Hadspen Rainbow' | IBal |
| 'Hadspen Samphire' | EGol EMic EPGN MHom NBir NBro NMyG |
| 'Hadspen White' (*fortunei*) | EMic IBal NLar |
| 'Haku-chu-han' (*sieboldii*) (v) | IBal |
| 'Hakujima' (*sieboldii*) | EGol IBal |
| 'Hakumuo' (v) | IBal |
| § 'Halcyon' (Tardiana Group) ♀H4 | Widely available |
| 'Halo' | EGol |
| 'Hampshire County' (v) | EMic IBal |
| 'Hanky Panky' (v) | EMic IBal NGdn NMyG NSti |
| 'Happily Ever After' (v) | IBal |
| 'Happiness' (Tardiana Group) | EGol EHoe EMic MHom MRav NMyG |
| 'Happy Camper' (v) | IBal |
| 'Happy Hearts' | EGol EMic |
| 'Happy Valley' (v) | IBal |
| 'Harlequin' | SApp |
| 'Harmony' (Tardiana Group) | EGol EMic |
| 'Harpoon' (v) | EMic IBal |
| 'Harriette Ward' | IBal |
| 'Harry van de Laar' | EMic IBal SApp |
| 'Harry van Trier' | EMic GBin |
| 'Hart's Tongue' | IBal |
| 'Harvest Glow' | EGol |
| 'Hawkeye' (v) | IBal |
| 'Hazel' | EMic IBal |
| 'Heart Ache' | EGol |
| 'Heart and Soul' (v) | EGol EMic SApp |
| 'Heart Broken' | IBal |
| 'Heart of Chan' | IBal |
| 'Heart Throb' | EMic |
| 'Heartbeat' (v) | IBal |
| 'Heartleaf' | EMic |
| 'Heart's Content' (v) | EGol IBal |
| 'Heartsong' (v) | EGol EMic NMyG |
| 'Heat Wave'PBR (v) | EMic EPGN GSec IBal SApp |
| 'Heavenly Beginnings' (v) | IBal |
| 'Heavenly Tiara' (v) | IBal |
| 'Heideturm' | EGol |
| 'Helen Doriot' (*sieboldiana*) | EGol EMic |
| 'Helen Field Fischer' (*fortunei*) | CPrp IBal |
| 'Herifu' (v) | EGol EMic |
| 'Herkules' | EMic IBal |
| 'Hertha' (v) | EMic |
| 'Hidden Cove' (v) | EGol IBal |
| 'High Kicker' | EGol IBal |
| 'High Society' (v) | CBcs EBee EMic EPGN EPfP GBin IBal MHom MNrw NGdn NMyG NNor SApp |
| 'High Tide' | IBal |
| 'Hi-ho Silver' (v) | EMic EPGN IBal WWEG |
| 'Hilda Wassman' (v) | EGol |
| 'Hillbilly Blues' (v) | IBal |
| 'Hippodrome' (v) | EMic IBal |
| 'Hirao Elite' | EMic IBal |
| 'Hirao Grande' | GSec |
| 'Hirao Majesty' | EGol |
| 'Hirao Splendor' | EGol NMyG |
| 'Hirao Supreme' | EGol EMic |
| 'His Honor' (v) | IBal |
| 'Holly's Honey' | EGol |
| 'Hollywood Lights' (v) | EMic IBal NGdn |
| 'Holstein' | see *H.* 'Halcyon' |
| 'Holy Molé' (v) | IBal |
| 'Holy Mouse Ears' | EGol EMic IBal |
| 'Honey Moon' | EGol NNor |
| 'Honeybells' ♀H4 | CBcs CMHG CMac CTri EBee ECha EGol ELan EMic EPGN EPfP GBin LHop LPBA MCot MRav NBid NGdn NMyG NNor NSti SApp SPer WFar WPtf WWEG XLum |
| 'Honeysong' (v) | EBee EGol EMic EPGN NNor |
| 'Hoosier Dome' | EMic |
| 'Hoosier Harmony' (v) | EGol EMic |
| 'Hoosier Homecoming' | SApp |
| 'Hope' (v) | EGol IBal SApp |
| 'Hotcakes' | IBal |

| | |
|---|---|
| 'Hotspur' (v) | EMic SApp |
| 'Hush Puppie' | EGol EMic IBal |
| 'Hyacintha Variegata' (*fortunei*) (v) | CMHG CMac NNor |
| 'Hydon Gleam' | EGol EMic IBal |
| 'Hydon Sunset' (*nakaiana*) | CMHG CMMP ECtt EGol EMic EPGN GCra IBal LRHS NBir NHol NMyG NNor NRya NSti NWCA SApp SBch WHal WMnd WPtf WTin WWEG |
| ***hypoleuca*** | EGol EMic |
| 'Hyuga Urajiro' (v) | EMic IBal SApp |
| 'Ice Age Trail' (v) | IBal |
| 'Ice Cream' (*cathayana*) (v) | EGol |
| 'Ice Prancer' **new** | EMic |
| 'Iced Lemon' (v) | EGol EMic IBal NNor |
| 'Illicit Affair' | EGol EMic IBal SApp |
| 'Imp' (v) | EMic IBal |
| § 'Inaho' | EGol LRHS |
| 'Inca Gold' | EGol IBal |
| 'Independence' (v) | EBee EMic EPGN IBal NBro NMyG SApp SPoG WFar |
| 'Indigo' | IBal |
| 'Innisjade' | IBal |
| 'Inniswood' (v) | CWCL ECtt EMic EPGN EPfP IBal IPot MBNS NBro NGdn NLar NSti SApp WFar WMnd WWEG |
| 'Invincible' | EBee EGol EMic GBin IBal LAst NBid NEgg NGdn NLar NMyG NNor SApp SPoG WPtf WTin WWEG |
| 'Iona' (*fortunei*) | EGol EMic EPGN NMyG NNor |
| 'Irische See' (Tardiana Group) | EGol IBal |
| 'Irish Eyes' (v) | IBal |
| 'Iron Gate Delight' (v) | NNor |
| 'Iron Gate Glamour' (v) | EGol IBal |
| 'Iron Gate Special' (v) | EMic |
| 'Iron Gate Supreme' (v) | EMic |
| 'Island Charm' (v) | EGol EMic EPGN IBal LRHS NHar NLar NMyG SApp |
| 'Island Forest Gem' | IBal |
| 'Iszat U Doc' | GSec |
| 'Itsy Bitsy Spider' | EGol |
| 'Ivory Necklace' (v) | IBal |
| 'Iwa Soules' | EGol |
| 'Jack of Diamonds' | IBal |
| 'Jade Cascade' | CFir EGol ELan EMic GBin IBal NBir NEgg NLar SApp SMrm WWEG |
| 'Jade Scepter' (*nakaiana*) | EGol EMic GSec |
| 'Jadette' (v) | EGol GBin |
| 'Janet Day' (v) | EMic IBal SApp |
| 'Janet' (*fortunei*) (v) | EBee EGol EMic GMaP IBal NGdn NMyG NNor |
| 'Janet's Green Sox' | IBal |
| 'Jaws' **new** | IBal |
| 'Jaz' | IBal |
| 'Jerry Landwehr' | EMic IBal |
| 'Jester' | SApp |
| 'Jewel of the Nile' (v) | EMic IBal SApp |
| 'Jim Mathews' | IBal |
| 'Jimmy Crack Corn' | EGol EMic IBal SApp |
| 'Jingle Bells' | IBal |
| 'John Wargo' | EGol |
| 'Johnny Angel' **new** | EMic |
| 'Joker' (*fortunei*) (v) | NNor |
| 'Jolly Green Giant' (*sieboldiana* hybrid) | EMic |
| 'Joseph' | EGol EMic IBal |
| 'Josephine' (v) | NNor |
| 'Journeyman' | EGol EMic IBal |
| 'Journey's End' (v) | EMic IBal SApp |
| 'Joyce Trott' (v) | EMic IBal |
| 'Joyful' (v) | IBal |
| 'Jubilee' (v) | IBal |
| 'Judy Rocco' | IBal |
| 'Juha' (v) | EMic IBal SApp |
| 'Jules' **new** | EPGN |
| 'Julia' (v) | EGol EMic IBal |
| 'Julie Morss' | EGol EMic EPGN GMaP IBal MHom NEgg SApp WWEG |
| 'Jumbo' (*sieboldiana*) | EMic |
| 'June' PBR (Tardiana Group) (v) 🏆H4 | Widely available |
| 'June Fever' PBR (Tardiana Group) | EMic ESwi GBin IBal MDev NBro NGdn NLar SApp SMrm |
| 'Jurassic Park' | EMic IBal MDev |
| 'Just So' (v) | EGol EMic |
| 'Kabitan' | see *H. sieboldii* var. *sieboldii* f. *kabitan* |
| 'Kabuki' | IBal |
| 'Kalamazoo' (v) | EMic |
| 'Karin' | EGol EMic |
| 'Katherine Lewis' (Tardiana Group) (v) | ECtt EMic IBal LRHS LSRN NHol NMyG |
| 'Kath's Gold' | EMic |
| 'Katie Q' (v) | EMic IBal |
| 'Katsuragawa-beni' (v) | EMic IBal |
| 'Kelly' | GSec |
| 'Kelsey' | EGol EMic |
| 'Key Lime Pie' | EMic IBal SApp |
| 'Ki Nakafu Otome' (*venusta*) | IBal |
| 'Kifukurin' (*kikutii*) | see *H.* 'Kifukurin Hyuga' |
| 'Kifukurin' (*pulchella*) (v) | EGol |
| 'Kifukurin' (*venusta*) (v) | EMic |
| § 'Kifukurin Hyuga' (v) | IBal |
| 'Kifukurin Ko Mame' (*gracillima*) (v) | EMic |
| 'Kifukurin Ubatake' (*pulchella*) (v) | EGol EMic EPGN IBal |
| ***kikutii*** | EGol EMic WTin |
| § - var. ***caput-avis*** | EGol EMic |
| - var. ***kikutii*** f. ***leuconota*** | SApp |
| - var. ***polyneuron*** | SApp |
| - var. ***pruinosa*** | SApp |
| § - var. ***yakusimensis*** | CPBP EMic GBin IBal SMad |
| 'Kinbotan' (v) | EGol EMic |
| 'King James' | IBal |
| 'King of Spades' | IBal |
| 'King Tut' | EMic |
| 'Kingfisher' (Tardiana Group) | EGol |
| § 'Kirishima' | EMic NSla |
| 'Kisuji' | see *H.* 'Mediopicta' |
| 'Kitty Cat' | EMic EPGN IBal SApp |
| 'Kiwi Black Magic' | EGol IBal |
| 'Kiwi Blue Baby' | EGol IBal |
| 'Kiwi Blue Ruffles' | IBal |
| 'Kiwi Blue Sky' | IBal |
| 'Kiwi Canoe' | IBal |
| 'Kiwi Cream Edge' (v) | EMic |
| 'Kiwi Fruit' | SApp |
| 'Kiwi Full Monty' (v) | EMic IBal |
| 'Kiwi Gold Rush' | IBal |
| 'Kiwi Hippo' | EGol IBal |
| 'Kiwi Jordan' | IBal |
| 'Kiwi Kaniere Gold' | IBal |
| 'Kiwi Leap Frog' | IBal |
| 'Kiwi Minnie Gold' | IBal |

| | |
|---|---|
| 'Kiwi Parasol' | IBal |
| 'Kiwi Skyscraper' | IBal |
| 'Kiwi Sunlover' | IBal |
| 'Kiwi Sunshine' | IBal |
| 'Klopping Variegated' (v) | EGol EMic |
| 'Knight's Journey' | IBal |
| 'Knockout' (v) | EGol IBal MBNS MNrw MRav NBPC NBro NEgg NGdn NLar NMyG NNor SApp |
| 'Komodo Dragon' | EMic IBal SKHP WTin |
| 'Kong' | IBal |
| 'Konkubine' | EMic |
| 'Korean Snow' | IBal |
| 'Koreana Variegated' (*undulata*) | EMic |
| 'Koriyama' (*sieboldiana*) (v) | EMic |
| 'Krossa Cream Edge' (*sieboldii*) (v) | IBal |
| 'Krossa Regal' ♀H4 | Widely available |
| 'Krugerrand' | IBal |
| 'Lacy Belle' (v) | CSBt EGol EMic EPfP GSec IBal NBro NGdn NPro SBfd |
| 'Lady Godiva' | IBal |
| 'Lady Guineverre' | EMic GSec IBal |
| 'Lady Helen' | EMic |
| 'Lady Isobel Barnett' (v) | EMic IBal NMyG SApp |
| ***laevigata*** | EGol SApp |
| 'Lake Hitchock' | EGol IBal |
| 'Lakeside Accolade' | EGol IBal |
| 'Lakeside April Snow' (v) | EMic |
| 'Lakeside Baby Face' (v) | EMic IBal |
| 'Lakeside Banana Bay' (v) **new** | IBal |
| 'Lakeside Beach Captain' (v) | EMic IBal |
| 'Lakeside Black Satin' | EMic IBal NMyG SApp |
| 'Lakeside Blue Cherub' | EMic GSec IBal |
| 'Lakeside Breaking News' (v) **new** | EMic IBal |
| 'Lakeside Butter Ball' | IBal SApp |
| 'Lakeside Cha Cha' (v) | EGol EMic NMyG |
| 'Lakeside Cindy Cee' (v) | IBal |
| 'Lakeside Coal Miner' | EMic IBal |
| 'Lakeside Contender' | IBal |
| 'Lakeside Cranberry Relish' (v) | IBal |
| 'Lakeside Cricket' (v) | IBal |
| 'Lakeside Cupcake' (v) | EMic IBal |
| 'Lakeside Dimpled Darling' (v) **new** | EGol |
| 'Lakeside Dividing Line' (v) | IBal |
| 'Lakeside Doodad' (v) **new** | IBal |
| 'Lakeside Down Sized' (v) | EGol EMic IBal |
| 'Lakeside Dragonfly' (v) | EMic EPfP IBal |
| 'Lakeside Elfin Fire' | EMic IBal |
| 'Lakeside Feather Light' (v) | IBal |
| 'Lakeside Hoola Hoop' (v) | IBal |
| 'Lakeside Iron Man' | IBal |
| 'Lakeside Kaleidoscope' | EGol EMic IBal |
| 'Lakeside Legal Tender' | IBal |
| 'Lakeside Lime Time' | IBal |
| 'Lakeside Little Gem' | GSec IBal |
| 'Lakeside Little Tuft' (v) | EMic IBal |
| 'Lakeside Lollipop' | EGol EMic EPGN IBal SApp |
| 'Lakeside Looking Glass' | EMic IBal |
| 'Lakeside Love Affaire' | EGol EMic IBal |
| 'Lakeside Maestro' | NLar |
| 'Lakeside Meadow Ice' (v) | IBal |
| 'Lakeside Meter Maid' (v) | IBal |
| 'Lakeside Miss Muffett' (v) | EMic IBal |

| | |
|---|---|
| 'Lakeside Missy Little' (v) | IBal |
| 'Lakeside Neat Petite' | EGol GSec IBal |
| 'Lakeside Ninita' (v) | EGol EMic EPGN GSec IBal NMyG |
| 'Lakeside Old Smokey' | IBal |
| 'Lakeside Party Dress' | IBal |
| 'Lakeside Premier' | EGol EMic IBal |
| 'Lakeside Rhapsody' (v) | EMic IBal |
| 'Lakeside Ring Master' (v) | IBal |
| 'Lakeside Ripples' | IBal |
| 'Lakeside Rocky Top' (v) | IBal |
| 'Lakeside Roy El' (v) | IBal |
| 'Lakeside Scamp' (v) **new** | EMic |
| 'Lakeside Shadows' (v) | IBal |
| 'Lakeside Shockwave' (v) | IBal |
| 'Lakeside Shoremaster' (v) | IBal |
| 'Lakeside Sir Logan' | IBal |
| 'Lakeside Sparkle Plenty' (v) | IBal |
| 'Lakeside Spellbinder' (v) | IBal |
| 'Lakeside Spruce Goose' (v) | IBal |
| 'Lakeside Storm Watch' **new** | IBal |
| 'Lakeside Symphony' (v) | EGol EMic |
| 'Lakeside Tycoon' | IBal |
| 'Lakeside Zinger' (v) | EMic IBal |
| ***lancifolia*** ♀H4 | CMHG CMac EBee ECha EGol ELan EMic GMaP MRav NGdn NMyG NSti SApp SRms WAul WKif WSHC WTin |
| 'Last Dance' (v) | IBal |
| 'Laura Z' | IBal |
| 'Lavender Doll' | IBal |
| 'Lavender Lace' | IBal |
| 'Leading Lady' | IBal |
| 'Leather Sheen' | EGol EMic IBal |
| 'Leatherneck' | IBal |
| 'Lederhosen' | EMic IBal |
| 'Lee Armiger' (*tokudama* hybrid) | EGol |
| 'Lemon Delight' | EGol EMic EPGN GSec IBal NMyG NNor |
| 'Lemon Frost' | IBal |
| 'Lemon Lime' | EGol EMic GBin IBal MHom MNrw NMyG NNor NPro WPat WTin WWEG |
| 'Lemonade' | GBin |
| 'Leola Fraim' (v) | EGol EMic IBal LRHS NMyG |
| 'Let Me Entertain You' | EMic |
| 'Leviathan' | EMic |
| 'Libby' | IBal |
| 'Liberty' PBR (v) | CWGN EMic GBin IBal NBro NGdn NMyG NNor SApp WFar |
| 'Li'l Abner' (v) | IBal |
| * ***lilacina*** | WFar |
| 'Lily Pad' | EPGN IBal |
| 'Lime Fizz' | EGol EMic IBal SApp |
| 'Lime Piecrust' | EGol |
| 'Lime Shag' (*sieboldii* f. *spathulata*) | EGol |
| 'Limey Lisa' | EGol EMic EPGN IBal WWEG |
| 'Linda Sue' (v) | EMic IBal |
| 'Little Aurora' (*tokudama* hybrid) | EGol EMic IBal WWEG |
| 'Little Bit' | IBal |
| 'Little Black Scape' | EGol EMic GBin IBal LSRN MHom NEgg NGdn NHol NLar NMyG NPro |
| 'Little Blue' (*ventricosa*) | EGol EMic |
| 'Little Bo Beep' (v) | EGol |
| 'Little Boy' | IBal |

| | |
|---|---|
| 'Little Caesar' (v) | EGol EMic EPGN IBal |
| 'Little Devil' **new** | IBal |
| 'Little Doll' (v) | EGol |
| 'Little Jay' (v) | EGol EMic IBal SApp |
| 'Little Miss Magic' | IBal |
| 'Little Razor' | EGol |
| 'Little Red Joy' | EGol EMic IBal |
| 'Little Red Rooster' | EMic EPGN IBal NGdn NNor |
| | WWEG |
| 'Little Stiffy' | EGol EMic SApp |
| 'Little Sunspot' (v) | EGol EMic EPGN NHar |
| 'Little Town Flirt' (v) | IBal |
| 'Little White Lines' (v) | EGol EMic EPGN IBal |
| 'Little Willie' (v) **new** | EGol |
| 'Little Wonder' (v) | EGol EMic EPGN IBal WWEG |
| 'Lizard Lick' | IBal |
| 'Lollapalooza' (v) | IBal |
| 'London Fog' (v) | IBal |
| 'Lonesome Dove' (v) | EMic IBal |
| ***longipes*** | EGol GSec SApp |
| – B&SWJ 10806 | WCru |
| ***longissima*** | CMHG WCru |
| 'Lothar the Giant' | IBal |
| 'Louisa' (*sieboldii*) (v) | LRHS |
| 'Love Pat' ♀H4 | CFir EBee EGol EMic EPGN EPfP |
| | GBin GKev IBal LSRN MRav NGdn |
| | NLar NMyG NNor SApp WCAu |
| 'Lovely Loretta' | IBal |
| 'Loyalist' PBR (v) | EMic NLar SApp SPoG WFar WWEG |
| 'Lucy Vitols' (v) | EGol EMic IBal |
| 'Lullabye' | EMic |
| 'Lunar Eclipse' (v) | CHid EMic GSec NEgg SApp |
| | WWEG |
| 'Lyme Regis' (v) **new** | GSec |
| 'Machete' | IBal |
| 'Mack the Knife' | EMic IBal |
| 'Maekawa' | EGol EMic |
| 'Magic Fire' PBR (v) | EMic EPGN EPfP IBal MNrw |
| 'Majesty' | EGol EMic IBal MBri NGdn |
| 'Mama Mia' (v) | CWat EGol EMic EPGN EPfP EQua |
| | IBal MBNS MLLN NBro NGdn NHol |
| | NMyG NWad SBfd SRGP |
| 'Manhattan' | EMic |
| 'Manzo' (v) **new** | EGol |
| 'Maraschino Cherry' | EGol EMic EWTr GBin IBal NEgg |
| | NMyG SApp |
| 'Marble Rim' (v) | EGol |
| 'Mardi Gras' (v) | EMic SApp |
| 'Marge' (*sieboldiana* hybrid) | EMic |
| 'Margin of Error' (v) | EGol EPGN IBal NMyG |
| 'Marginata Alba' misapplied | see *H.* 'Albomarginata' (*fortunei*), |
| | *H. crispula* |
| 'Marginata Alba' ambig. (v) | ECha LPBA NNor |
| 'Marilyn' | EGol EMic GSec IBal |
| 'Marilyn Monroe' | EMic IBal |
| 'Marmalade on Toast' | EMic |
| 'Marquis' (*nakaiana* hybrid) | EGol |
| 'Marrakech' **new** | EMic |
| 'Mary Joe' | EMic IBal |
| 'Mary Marie Ann' | EGol EMic EPGN IBal |
| (*fortunei*) (v) | |
| 'Masquerade' (v) | EGol EMic EPGN IBal NHar NWCA |
| | SApp WFar WHal WThu |
| 'Maui Buttercups' | EMic IBal SApp |
| 'May' | EMic IBal |
| 'Maya' (*fortunei*) (v) | IBal |
| § 'Mediopicta' (*sieboldii*) | EMic |
| 'Mediovariegata' (*undulata*) | see *H. undulata* var. *undulata* |
| 'Medusa' (v) | EGol EMic IBal |
| 'Memories of Dorothy' | EMic IBal |
| 'Mentor Gold' | EGol |
| 'Merlin' (v) | IBal |
| 'Mesa Fringe' (*montana*) | EMic |
| 'Mid Afternoon' | IBal |
| 'Midas Touch' | GBin NEgg NHol NLar NNor |
| 'Middle Ridge' | EMic |
| 'Midnight Ride' | IBal |
| 'Midwest Gold' | MHom SApp |
| 'Midwest Magic' (v) | EGol EMic IBal NLar SApp |
| 'Mieke' (v) | IBal |
| 'Mighty Mouse' (v) **new** | IBal |
| 'Mikawa-no-yuki' | IBal |
| 'Miki' | IBal |
| 'Mildred Seaver' (v) | EGol EMic GAbr IBal LRHS NMyG |
| 'Millennium' | EMic EPGN SApp |
| 'Millie's Memoirs' (v) | IBal |
| 'Ming Jade' | GSec SApp |
| 'Ming Treasure' (v) | IBal |
| 'Minnie Bell' (v) | EGol IBal |
| 'Minnie Klopping' | EMic |
| ***minor*** misapplied f. ***alba*** | see *H. sieboldii* var. *alba* |
| § ***minor*** Maekawa | EBee EGol EPGN GEdr GGar ITim |
| | NMyG WCot WFar XLum |
| – B&SWJ 1209 from Korea | WCru |
| – B&SWJ 8775 from Korea | WCru |
| – B&SWJ 11103 | WCru |
| from Japan **new** | |
| – from Korea | EGol IBal |
| – Goldbrook form | EGol IBal |
| 'Minor' (*ventricosa*) | see *H. minor* Maekawa |
| 'Mint Candy' | IBal |
| 'Mint Julep' (v) | IBal |
| 'Minuet' (v) | IBal |
| 'Minuteman' (*fortunei*) (v) | CFir EBee ECtt EMic EPGN EPfP |
| | IBal IPot LAst MBNS MMuc NBPC |
| | NGdn NLar NNor NOrc NPnk SApp |
| | SBfd SPoG WFar WGor WTin |
| | WWEG |
| 'Miss Ruby' | EMic IBal |
| 'Miss Saigon' (v) | IBal |
| 'Miss Susie' **new** | EMic |
| 'Miss Tokyo' (v) | EMic IBal |
| 'Mississippi Delta' | EMic |
| 'Mister Watson' | EMic IBal SApp |
| 'Misty Waters' (*sieboldiana*) | EMic |
| 'Moerheim' (*fortunei*) (v) | EBee EGol EMic EPGN GBee IBal |
| | WHal WWEG |
| 'Mohegan' | EMic |
| N ***montana*** | EGol EMic GBin |
| – B&SWJ 4796 | WCru |
| – B&SWJ 5585 | WCru |
| – 'Hida no hana' (v) **new** | IBal |
| – f. ***macrophylla*** | EGol IBal |
| 'Moon Glow' (v) | EGol EMic |
| 'Moon River' (v) | EGol EMic EPGN SApp |
| 'Moon Shadow' (v) | EGol |
| 'Moon Waves' | EGol |
| 'Moonbeam' | EShb |
| 'Moonlight' (*fortunei*) (v) | EGol EMic EPGN GMaP GSec IBal |
| | LRHS NMyG NNor SApp |
| 'Moonlight Sonata' | EGol EMic |
| 'Moonstruck' PBR (v) | ECtt EGol EMic EPGN IBal |
| 'Moorheim' | LRHS |
| 'Morning Light' PBR | EBee EGol EMic EPGN EPfP IBal |
| | LBMP MBNS MBri NBro NGdn NLar |
| | NPnk SApp SRkn WBor WCra |
| 'Moscow Blue' | EGol EMic |
| 'Mount Everest' | EMic IBal |
| 'Mount Fuji' (*montana*) | EGol IBal |
| 'Mount Hope' (v) | EGol |

| | |
|---|---|
| 'Mount Kirishima' (*sieboldii*) | see *H.* 'Kirishima' |
| 'Mount Tom' (v) | EGol EMic IBal |
| 'Mountain Fog' (v) | IBal |
| 'Mountain Snow' (*montana*) (v) | CWat EGol SApp |
| 'Mountain Sunrise' (*montana*) | EGol |
| 'Mourning Dove' (v) | EMic IBal |
| 'Mr Big' | IBal NGdn |
| 'Mrs Minky' | EMic EPGN LRHS |
| 'Muffie' (v) | EMic IBal |
| 'Munchkin' (*sieboldii*) | WPat |
| 'My Claire' (v) | IBal |
| 'My Cup of Tea' | IBal |
| 'My Friend Nancy' (v) | EGol |
| 'Mystic Star' | IBal |
| 'Naegato' | SApp |
| ***nakaiana*** | EBee EMic IBal |
| 'Nakaimo' | IBal NHol |
| 'Nameoki' | NHol |
| 'Nana' (*ventricosa*) | see *H. minor* Maekawa |
| 'Nancy' | EMic IBal |
| § 'Nancy Lindsay' (*fortunei*) | CTri EMic IBal NGdn NLar SApp |
| 'Nancy Minks' | EMic IBal |
| 'Neat and Tidy' | IBal |
| 'Neat Splash' (v) | CWCL NBir WWEG |
| 'Neat Splash Rim' (v) | IBal |
| 'Nemesis' (v) | IBal |
| 'Neptune' **new** | EMic |
| 'Niagara Falls' | CFir EGol EMic IBal NGdn |
| 'Nicola' | EGol EMic EPGN IBal MHom |
| 'Night before Christmas' (v) | CFir CHid CMMP CWGN EBee EGol EMic EPGN EWTr IPot LPBA LRHS MNrw NBro NCGa NEgg NGdn NHol NMyG NNor NPnk SApp WHoo WWEG |
| 'Night Life' | EMic IBal |
| ***nigrescens*** | EGol EMic EPGN GGal LRHS NMyG |
| - 'Cally White' | GCal IBal NCGa |
| 'Nokogiryama' | EMic |
| 'None Lovelier' (v) | EMic IBal |
| 'Nor'easter' (v) | IBal |
| 'North Hills' (*fortunei*) (v) | EAEE EBee EGol EMic IBal LRHS NBir NGdn SWvt WWEG |
| 'Northern Exposure' (*sieboldiana*) (v) | CFir EGol EMic EWTr IBal NGdn NMyG SApp |
| 'Northern Halo' (*sieboldiana*) (v) | EMic |
| 'Northern Sunray' (*sieboldiana*) (v) | IBal |
| 'Nougat' (v) | IBal |
| 'Nouzang' | IBal |
| 'Nutty Professor' (v) | IBal |
| 'Oberon' **new** | EGol |
| 'Obscura Marginata' (*fortunei*) | see *H. fortunei* var. *aureomarginata* |
| 'Obsession' | EGol IBal |
| 'Ocean Isle' (v) | IBal |
| 'Oder' | IBal |
| 'Ogon Chirifu Hime' **new** | IBal |
| 'Ogon Koba' **new** | IBal |
| 'O'Harra' | EGol EMic |
| 'Old Faithful' | EGol EMic |
| 'Old Glory'PBR (v) | EGol EMic IBal |
| 'Olga's Shiny Leaf' | EGol EMic |
| 'Olive Bailey Langdon' (*sieboldiana*) (v) | EMic IBal SApp |
| 'Olive Branch' (v) | EGol EMic IBal |
| 'Olympic Edger' | EMic IBal |
| 'Olympic Glacier' (v) | EMic IBal SApp |
| 'Olympic Gold Medal' | IBal |
| 'Olympic Silver Medal' | EMic IBal |
| 'Olympic Sunrise' (v) | EMic IBal |
| 'On Stage' | see *H.* 'Choko Nishiki' |
| 'On the Border' (v) | IBal |
| 'One Man's Treasure' | EMic EPGN GBin IBal MLLN NGdn NMyG SApp |
| 'Ooh La La' (v) | IBal |
| 'Ophir' | EMic IBal |
| 'Ops' (v) | EGol EMic IBal |
| 'Orange Crush' (v) | IBal SApp |
| 'Orange Marmalade' (v) | EMic EPGN IBal NGdn NMyG SApp SBfd |
| 'Orange Slices' | IBal |
| 'Oriana' (*fortunei*) | EGol EMic IBal |
| 'Orion's Belt' (v) | IBal |
| 'Osprey' (Tardiana Group) | EGol |
| 'Oxheart' | EMic |
| 'Oze' (v) **new** | IBal |
| ***pachyscapa*** | EMic |
| 'Pacific Blue Edger' | CFir CMMP EGol EMic MDev MMuc NGdn NNor SApp WAul WWEG |
| 'Pamela Lee' (v) | EMic IBal NGdn NMyG |
| 'Pandora's Box' (v) | EGol EPGN GBin GEdr IBal NHar SApp WCot |
| 'Paradigm' (v) | EBee EGol EMic EPGN IBal NGdn SApp |
| 'Paradise Backstage' (v) | EMic IBal |
| 'Paradise Beach' | EMic IBal |
| 'Paradise Expectations' (*sieboldiana*) (v) | EMic IBal SApp |
| 'Paradise Glory' | EMic IBal |
| 'Paradise Gold Line' (*ventricosa*) (v) | IBal |
| 'Paradise Island' (v) | EMic EPGN IBal MDev NGdn SApp |
| 'Paradise Joyce'PBR | EGol EMic EPGN IBal LRHS NLar NMyG NNor SApp WWEG |
| 'Paradise Ocean' | EMic |
| 'Paradise on Fire' (v) | EMic IBal SApp |
| 'Paradise Parade' (v) | IBal |
| 'Paradise Passion' (v) | IBal |
| 'Paradise Power'PBR | EMic |
| 'Paradise Puppet' (*venusta*) | EMic EPGN IBal NNor SApp WWEG |
| 'Paradise Red Delight' (*pycnophylla*) | EMic IBal |
| 'Paradise Sandstorm' | IBal |
| 'Paradise Standard' (d) | EMic IBal |
| 'Paradise Sunset' | EGol EMic IBal |
| 'Paradise Sunshine' | EMic |
| 'Paradise Surprise' (v) | IBal |
| 'Parhelion' | EMic |
| 'Parky's Prize' (v) | EGol |
| 'Party Favor' | GSec |
| 'Pastures Green' | EGol IBal |
| 'Pastures New' | EGol EMic EQua MHom NMyG SApp WWEG |
| 'Pathfinder' (v) | EGol EMic IBal SApp |
| 'Patricia' | EMic |
| 'Patrician' (v) | EGol EMic EPGN IBal |
| 'Patriot' (v) | Widely available |
| 'Patriot's Fire' (v) | IBal |
| 'Patriot's Green Pride' | IBal |
| 'Paul Revere' (v) | IBal |
| 'Paul's Glory' (v) | EGol EMic EPGN EQua GAbr GBin GMaP IBal LPBA LRHS MBri NBir NGdn NMRc NMyG NNor SApp WFar WWEG |
| 'Peace' (v) | EGol EMic EPGN IBal |
| 'Peacock Strut' | IBal |

|  |  |
|---|---|
| 'Peanut' | EGol EMic IBal |
| 'Pearl Lake' | EBee EGol EMic EPGN GBin IBal MHom NBir NEgg NGdn NHol NLar NMen NMyG NNor SApp SMrm SRGP WTin |
| 'Peedee Absinth' | EMic GSec |
| 'Peedee Elfin Bells' (*ventricosa*) | GSec |
| 'Peedee Laughing River' (v) | IBal |
| 'Pelham Blue Tump' | EGol EMic GSec |
| 'Peppermint Cream' (*cathayana*) | IBal |
| 'Peppermint Ice' (v) | EGol IBal |
| 'Percy' | EMic IBal |
| 'Peridot' (Tardiana Group) | GSec |
| 'Permanent Wave' | EGol GSec |
| 'Perry's True Blue' | EMic |
| 'Peter Pan' | EGol EMic IBal |
| 'Peter the Rock' | IBal |
| 'Pete's Dark Satellite' | EMic IBal |
| 'Pewterware' | EMic IBal |
| 'Phantom' | IBal SApp |
| 'Philadelphia' | IBal |
| 'Phoenix' | EGol EMic NLar SApp |
| 'Photo Finish' (v) | EGol EMic |
| 'Phyllis Campbell' (*fortunei*) | see *H.* 'Sharmon' |
| 'Picta' (*fortunei*) | see *H. fortunei* var. *albopicta* |
| 'Piedmont Gold' | CHid EMic EPGN IBal NBPC SApp WPtf |
| 'Pilgrim' (v) | EBee EGol ELan EMic EPGN IBal NBPC NBro NMyG SApp WFar |
| 'Pineapple Poll' | EGol EMic EPGN NMyG NNor WTin WWEG |
| 'Pineapple Upside Down Cake' (v) | EMic EPGN IBal NBro NLar NMyG WFar |
| 'Pinky' | IBal |
| 'Pinwheel' (v) | IBal |
| 'Pistache' (v) **new** | EMic IBal |
| 'Pizzazz' (v) | EGol EMic IBal LRHS MHom NGdn NHol NLar NMyG SApp WFar WHil WWEG |
| ***plantaginea*** | EMic IBal LEdu LPla LRHS MHom NMyG SSpi WCru WFar WKif |
| – var. ***grandiflora*** | see *H. plantaginea* var. *japonica* |
| § – var. ***japonica*** ♀H4 | CBot CDes ECha EPGN LRHS MRav NLar SApp SMrm WCFE WFar WPGP WWEG |
| 'Platinum Tiara' (v) | EGol EMic GSec IBal NBir NMyG |
| 'Plug Nickel' | EMic IBal |
| 'Polar Moon' (v) | IBal |
| 'Pole Cat' (v) **new** | IBal |
| 'Pooh Bear' (v) | EGol EMic |
| 'Popcorn' | EMic IBal SApp |
| 'Popo' | EGol EMic EPGN IBal SApp |
| 'Potomac Pride' | EGol EMic EPGN NMyG SApp |
| 'Powder Blue' (v) | IBal |
| 'Powderpuff' | IBal |
| 'Prairie Glow' | IBal |
| 'Prairie Sky' | CWGN EMic IBal MDev NGdn |
| 'Praying Hands' (v) | EGol EMic EPGN EPfP GBin IBal IPot LSou MBNS NMyG WWEG |
| 'Prestige and Promise' (v) **new** | IBal |
| 'Pretty Flamingo' | EMic IBal |
| 'Prima Donna' | EMic |
| 'Primavera Primrose' | SApp |
| 'Prince of Wales' | EMic IBal LRHS LSqu NNor SApp SPoG SRkn |
| 'Princess Anastasia' (v) | IBal |
| 'Puck' | EGol |
| 'Punky' (v) | IBal |
| 'Purple Boots' | EMic IBal |
| 'Purple Dwarf' | EGol EMic NLar WCru WHal WWEG |
| 'Purple Glory' | EMic |
| 'Purple Haze' | IBal |
| 'Purple Lady Finger' | GSec WWEG |
| 'Purple Passion' | EGol EMic |
| 'Purple Profusion' | EGol EMic |
| 'Quarter Note' (v) | IBal |
| 'Queen Josephine' (v) | EGol EMic EPGN IBal IPot LRHS MBNS MHom MMuc NCGa NGdn NMyG SApp SBfd SEND SRGP WFar |
| 'Queen of the Seas' | EMic IBal SApp |
| 'Quill' | EMic |
| 'Quilting Bee' | EGol EMic |
| 'Radiant Edger' (v) | EGol EMic EPGN GCra IBal NHol SBfd WWEG |
| 'Radio Waves' | EMic IBal |
| 'Rain Forest' | EMic IBal |
| 'Rainbow's End' (v) | EMic IBal |
| 'Rainforest Sunrise' (v) | EMic IBal LLWG MAvo NGdn SApp |
| 'Rascal' (v) | EGol EMic |
| 'Raspberries and Cream' (v) | IBal |
| 'Raspberry Sorbet' | EGol EMic EPGN IBal |
| ***rectifolia*** | NNor |
| – 'Kinbuchi Tachi' (v) | IBal |
| – 'Ogon Tachi' (v) | EMic IBal |
| 'Red Cadet' | EMic IBal |
| 'Red Dragon' | IBal |
| 'Red Hot Flash' (v) | IBal |
| 'Red Hot Poker' | IBal |
| 'Red Neck Heaven' (*kikutii* var. *caput-avis*) | GSec IBal SApp WTin |
| 'Red October' | ECtt EMic EPGN EPfP GAbr GBin IBal LEdu LSou MBNS MLLN NGdn NLar NMyG NPnk SPoG WCot WFar WWEG |
| 'Red Salamander' | EGol EMic IBal |
| 'Red Stepper' | IBal |
| 'Red Wing' (v) **new** | IBal |
| 'Regal Chameleon' | IBal |
| 'Regal Rhubarb' | EGol IBal |
| 'Regal Splendor' (v) | EGol EMic EPGN GBin LRHS MHom NBro NCGa NGdn NHol NMyG NNor SApp WAul WHoo WMnd |
| 'Reginald Kaye' | EMic |
| 'Remember Me'PBR | CWCL ELan ELon EMic EPGN IBal LSRN MBNS MDev NGdn NHol NLar NMyG NNor NWad SApp SMrm WFar WGor WWEG |
| 'Reptilian' | EGol EMic GSec |
| 'Resonance' (v) | GBee NGdn NLar |
| 'Restless Sea' | EMic IBal |
| 'Reversed' (*sieboldiana*) (v) | EBee EGol ELan EMic EPGN IBal LRHS MDKP NBro NGdn NNor WHal |
| 'Revolution'PBR (v) | EBee EGol EMic EPGN GKev IBal IPot LSRN MMuc NBPC NBro NEgg NGdn NLar NMyG NOrc SApp SPoG WAul WFar WWEG |
| 'Rhapsody' (*fortunei*) (v) | EGol EMic |
| 'Rhapsody in Blue' | EGol IBal |
| 'Rhein' (*tardiana*) | EMic |
| 'Rheingold' (v) | IBal |
| 'Rhinestone Cowboy' (v) **new** | IBal |
| 'Rhythm and Blues' | IBal |
| 'Rich Uncle' | IBal |

| | |
|---|---|
| 'Richland Gold' (*fortunei*) | EGol EMic EPGN GSec NMyG |
| 'Rickrack' | IBal |
| 'Rim Rock' | EMic |
| 'Rippled Honey' | COlW EGol EMic EPGN GSec IBal NMyG NPro SApp |
| 'Rippling Waves' | EGol EMic |
| 'Riptide' | EMic |
| 'Risa' | IBal |
| 'Rising Sun' | EGol |
| 'Risky Business'PBR (v) | IBal |
| 'Robert Frost' (v) | EGol EMic IBal WTin |
| 'Robin Hood' | EMic IBal SApp |
| 'Robusta' (*fortunei*) | see *H. sieboldiana* var. *elegans* |
| 'Robyn's Choice' (v) | EMic |
| 'Rock Island Line' (v) | IBal |
| 'Rock Princess' | IBal |
| ***rohdeifolia*** f. ***albopicta*** | ELan |
| 'Roller Coaster Ride' | IBal |
| 'Ron Damant' | EPGN IBal |
| 'Rootin'-Tootin" (v) | IBal |
| 'Rosedale Golden Goose' | IBal |
| 'Rosedale Knox' | IBal |
| 'Rosedale Lost Dutchman' | IBal SApp |
| 'Rosedale Melody of Summer' (v) | IBal |
| 'Rosedale Misty Magic' (v) | IBal |
| 'Rosedale Richie Valens' | IBal |
| 'Rosedale Spoons' **new** | IBal |
| 'Rosemoor' | EGol IBal |
| 'Rotunda' | EGol |
| 'Rough Waters' | SApp |
| 'Roxsanne' | EMic |
| 'Roy Klehm' (v) | IBal |
| 'Royal Charm' | IBal |
| 'Royal Flush' (v) | IBal |
| 'Royal Golden Jubilee' | EMic EPGN IBal NCGa NMyG |
| § 'Royal Standard' ♀H4 | Widely available |
| 'Royal Super' | EPGN |
| 'Royal Tapestry' (v) | IBal |
| 'Royal Tiara' (*nakaiana*) (v) | EGol IBal |
| 'Royalty' | EGol |
| ***rupifraga*** | EGol |
| 'Rusty Bee' | EMic IBal |
| § 'Sagae' (v) ♀H3-4 | CWat EBee EGol EMic EPGN IBal IPot LRHS MBri MHom MNrw NGdn NNor NPnk SApp SDix SPoG WAul WFar WHoo WWEG |
| 'Saint Elmo's Fire' (v) | EGol EMic EPGN IBal LRHS SApp |
| 'Saint Paul' | EMic IBal |
| 'Saishu Jima' (*sieboldii* f. *spathulata*) | EMic WCru |
| 'Saishu Yahite Site' (v) | EGol |
| 'Salute' (Tardiana Group) | EGol EMic GSec |
| 'Samual Blue' | EGol |
| 'Samurai' (*sieboldiana*) (v) | EGol EMic IBal IPot MRav NBir NBro NGdn NLar NNor SApp |
| 'Sandhill Crane' (v) | IBal |
| 'Sarah Kennedy' (v) | EPGN |
| 'Satisfaction' (v) | EMic |
| 'Savannah' | EGol |
| 'Sazanami' (*crispula*) | see *H. crispula* |
| 'Schwan' | GBin |
| 'Scooter' (v) | EGol EMic |
| 'Sea Beacon' (v) | EGol |
| 'Sea Bunny' | EGol |
| 'Sea Dream' (v) | EGol EMic LRHS NEgg NMyG NNor |
| 'Sea Drift' | EGol |
| 'Sea Fire' | EGol |
| 'Sea Frolic' | EGol |
| 'Sea Gold Star' | EGol NMyG |
| 'Sea Gulf Stream' | EMic |
| 'Sea Hero' | EGol |
| 'Sea Lotus Leaf' | EGol EMic LLWP NLar NNor |
| 'Sea Monster' | EGol IBal |
| 'Sea Nautilus' **new** | GSec |
| 'Sea Octopus' | EGol |
| 'Sea Sapphire' | EGol |
| 'Sea Sunrise' | EPGN |
| 'Sea Thunder' (v) | EGol EMic EPGN |
| 'Sea Yellow Sunrise' | EGol EMic IBal SApp |
| 'Second Wind' (*fortunei*) (v) | EGol EMic EPGN IBal NMyG SApp |
| 'Secret Ambition' (v) **new** | EMic |
| 'Secret Love'PBR | EMic IBal |
| 'Seducer' (v) **new** | IBal |
| 'See Saw' (*undulata*) | EGol EMic SApp |
| 'September Sun' (v) | EGol EMic GSec IBal LRHS NMyG NNor |
| 'Serena' (Tardiana Group) | IBal SApp |
| 'Serendipity' | EGol EMic GAbr MHom |
| 'Shade Beauty' (v) | EGol |
| 'Shade Fanfare' (v) ♀H4 | EGol ELan EMic EPfP IBal LAst LBMP LPla LRHS MBNS MRav MWhi NBir NGdn NLar NSti SApp SPer WFar WMnd WTin WWEG |
| 'Shade Finale' (v) | IBal |
| 'Shade Master' | EGol EMic |
| 'Shade Parade' (v) **new** | IBal |
| 'Shamoa' | SApp |
| § 'Sharmon' (*fortunei*) (v) | EGol ELon EMic EPGN IBal MBNS NEgg NLar NMyG SApp SBfd |
| 'Sharp Dressed Man' | EMic IBal |
| 'Sheila West' | EMic IBal |
| 'Shelleys' (v) | EGol IBal |
| 'Sherborne Profusion' (Tardiana Group) | EMic IBal |
| 'Sherborne Songbird' (Tardiana Group) | EGol IBal |
| 'Sherborne Swan' (Tardiana Group) | EGol IBal |
| 'Sherborne Swift' (Tardiana Group) | EGol EMic GSec LRHS |
| 'Shere Khan' (v) | EGol |
| 'Shining Tot' | EGol LLHF |
| 'Shiny Penny' (v) | EGol EMic IBal WWEG |
| 'Shirley Vaughn' (v) | EGol |
| 'Shogun' (v) | EGol IBal |
| 'Showboat' (v) | EGol EMic IBal LRHS NMyG |
| ***sieboldiana*** | CMac CSBt ECha EGol ELan EMic GCra GLam GMaP LLWP LTen MAvo MRav MSwo NChi NHol SPlb SRms WFar WMoo WWEG XLum |
| § - var. ***elegans*** ♀H4 | Widely available |
| - 'George Smith' | EMic IBal SApp |
| - var. ***mira*** | EMic |
| - var. ***sieboldiana*** | GAuc NGdn |
| ***sieboldiana* × *venusta*** | NGdn |
| ***sieboldii*** | CWat MRav |
| § - var. ***alba*** | EGol IBal |
| § - 'Paxton's Original' (v) ♀H4 | EGol SRms WWEG |
| § - var. ***sieboldii*** f. ***kabitan*** (v) | EGol EMic EPGN NHar SApp WTin WWEG |
| - - f. ***shiro-kabitan*** (v) | EGol EMic EPGN |
| - f. ***spathulata*** | EMic |
| 'Silberpfeil' | EMic IBal |
| 'Silk Kimono' (v) | EGol |
| 'Silver Bay' | EMic |
| 'Silver Bowl' | EGol |
| 'Silver Crown' | see *H.* 'Albomarginata' |
| 'Silver Lance' (v) | EGol EMic |
| 'Silver Lining' | IBal |

|  |  |
|---|---|
| 'Silver Lode' (v) | IBal |
| 'Silver Shadow' (v) | CHid EMic GBin IBal NBir NGdn NHol NNor NWad SApp WPtf |
| 'Silver Spray' (v) | EGol IBal |
| 'Silver Threads and Gold Needles' (v) | IBal |
| 'Silvery Slugproof' (Tardiana Group) | LRHS NMyG SApp |
| 'Singin' the Blues' | IBal |
| 'Singing in the Rain' (v) | IBal |
| 'Sitting Pretty' (v) | EGol EPGN |
| 'Sky Dancer' | EMic IBal |
| 'Sleeping Beauty' | CWGN EMic GQue IBal NGdn NMyG SApp |
| 'Slick Willie' | EGol EMic |
| 'Slim and Trim' **new** | EGol EMic |
| 'Small Parts' | EGol EMic IBal |
| 'Small Sum' | IBal |
| 'Smooth Sailing' (v) | IBal |
| 'Snow Cap' (v) | EBee EGol EMic IBal NGdn NLar NNor NPro SApp WWEG |
| 'Snow Crust' (v) | EGol EMic |
| 'Snow Flakes' (*sieboldii*) | CMac EGol EPGN EPfP EWTr NBro NGdn NLar NPro WFar WWEG |
| 'Snow Mound' | IBal |
| 'Snow Mouse' **new** | EMic |
| 'Snow White' (*undulata*) (v) | EGol IBal |
| 'Snowbound' (v) | IBal |
| 'Snowden' | CPrp ECha EGol EMic EPGN ETod GMaP IBal LRHS MWat NBir NGdn NHol NNor SApp SSpi WAul WCru WWEG |
| 'Snowy Lake' (v) | IBal |
| 'So Sweet' (v) | CAby COIW EBee EGol EHoe ELan EMic EPGN EPfP LBMP LPBA LRHS MHom MSwo NBro NGdn NHol NMyG NNor SApp SBfd SPad SPoG SRGP WWEG |
| 'Solar Flare' | EGol IBal |
| 'Something Blue' | EMic |
| 'Something Different' (*fortunei*) (v) | EGol EPGN |
| 'Sophistication' (v) | EGol |
| 'Southern Gold' | EMic |
| 'Sparkling Burgundy' | EGol EMic |
| 'Sparky' (v) | EGol IBal |
| 'Spartacus' (v) | EMic IBal |
| 'Spartan Glory' (v) | IBal |
| 'Special Gift' | EGol EMic WWEG |
| 'Spellbound' (v) | IBal |
| 'Spilt Milk' (*tokudama*) (v) | EGol EMic EPGN IBal SApp SPoG WHoo |
| § 'Spinners' (*fortunei*) (v) | ECha EGol EMic NNor |
| 'Spinning Wheel' (v) | EGol IBal |
| 'Spring Fling' | EMic IBal |
| 'Spritzer' (v) | EGol EMic GSec IBal MNrw NMyG SApp |
| 'Squash Casserole' | EGol |
| 'Squiggles' (v) | EGol |
| 'Stained Glass' | CBcs EGol ELon EMic EPGN IBal MBri NGdn NMyG NNor SApp WFar |
| 'Star Kissed' | IBal |
| 'Star Light Star Bright' **new** | EMic |
| 'Starburst' stable (v) | IBal |
| 'Stardust' | IBal |
| 'Stargate' | IBal |
| § 'Starker Yellow Leaf' | EMic |
| 'Starship' (v) | IBal |
| 'Stenantha' (*fortunei*) | EMic |
| 'Stenantha Variegated' (*fortunei*) (v) | NHol |
| 'Step Sister' | EMic IBal |
| 'Stepping Out' (v) | EMic IBal |
| 'Stetson' (v) | EMic IBal |
| 'Stiletto' (v) | Widely available |
| 'Stimulation' **new** | IBal |
| 'Stirfry' | EMic GSec |
| 'Stitch in Time' (v) | IBal |
| 'Stolen Kiss' (v) | IBal |
| 'Stonewall' | IBal |
| 'Striker' (v) | EGol IBal |
| 'Striptease' (*fortunei*) (v) | CMac EGol EMic EPGN GBin GQue IBal LRHS MBNS MNrw NGdn NHol NLar NPnk SApp WFar WHoo WWEG |
| 'Sugar and Cream' (v) | CMMP CWat EGol EMic IBal LRHS NGdn NNor |
| 'Sugar and Spice' (v) | EMic IBal |
| 'Sugar Daddy' | EMic IBal |
| 'Sultana' (v) | EMic IBal WWEG |
| 'Sum and Substance' ♀H4 | Widely available |
| 'Sum Cup-o-Joe' (v) | EMic |
| 'Sum it Up' (v) | EMic |
| 'Summer Breeze' (v) | EGol EMic IBal NGdn |
| 'Summer Fragrance' | ECtt EGol EMic GBin IBal LRHS NMyG |
| 'Summer in Georgia' | IBal |
| 'Summer Lovin'' (v) | IBal |
| 'Summer Music' (v) | CWCL EGol EMic EPGN IBal MBri SApp WWEG |
| 'Summer Serenade' (v) | EGol EMic IBal SApp |
| 'Sun Catcher' | EMic |
| 'Sun Glow' | EGol |
| 'Sun Kissed' (v) | IBal |
| 'Sun Power' | EGol EMic EPfP GBin IBal LRHS MBNS NBro NGdn NLar NMyG NSti SApp SBfd SDix SMrm |
| 'Sun Worshipper' | EMic IBal SApp |
| 'Sundance' (*fortunei*) (v) | EGol |
| 'Sunlight Child' | EGol IBal |
| 'Sunnybrook' (v) | IBal |
| 'Sunshine Glory' | EGol EMic |
| 'Super Bowl' | EGol |
| 'Super Nova' (v) | EGol EMic IBal SApp SPoG |
| 'Super Sagae' **new** | EMic |
| 'Surf and Turf' | IBal |
| 'Surprised by Joy' (v) | EGol EMic IBal NNor SApp WWEG |
| 'Susy' | IBal |
| 'Sutter's Mill' | IBal |
| 'Suzuki Thumbnail' | EMic |
| 'Sweet Bo Beep' | EGol GSec LRHS |
| 'Sweet Bouquet' | EMic |
| 'Sweet Home Chicago' (v) | EGol EMic GSec IBal |
| 'Sweet Innocence' (v) | EMic IBal |
| 'Sweet Marjorie' | EGol |
| 'Sweet Standard' | NMyG |
| 'Sweet Sunshine' | EGol |
| 'Sweet Susan' | EGol EMic GBin GSec LPla LSRN LTen MBNS SApp SPer SWvt |
| 'Sweet Tater Pie' | EGol EMic |
| 'Sweetie' (v) | EMic IBal LRHS SApp WWEG |
| 'Sweetness' | IBal |
| 'Swirling Hearts' | EGol GSec |
| 'Swizzle Sticks' | IBal |
| 'T. Rex' | EMic SApp |
| 'Tall Boy' | CSev ECha EGol NBir NNor |
| 'Tamborine' (v) | CWat EGol EPGN IBal LRHS NMyG SApp |
| 'Tango' | EMic IBal |

| |  |  |
|---|---|---|
| | 'Tappen Zee' (v) | IBal |
| | Tardiana Group | EGol ELan MHom NGdn NHol |
| | ***tardiflora*** | EGol EPGN SApp WCot WPGP |
| | 'Tattoo'[PBR] (v) | CWGN EGol EMic EPGN LSRN MBNS MNrw NLar SApp WWEG |
| | 'Tea and Crumpets' (v) | EPGN IBal |
| | 'Tea at Betty's' | EPGN |
| | 'Teaspoon' | EMic IBal NNor SApp |
| | 'Teatime' (v) | EMic IBal |
| | 'Teeny-weeny Bikini' (v) | EMic IBal |
| | 'Templar Gold' | IBal |
| | 'Temple Bells' | EGol |
| | 'Temptation' | EMic IBal SApp |
| | 'Tenryu' | EGol |
| | 'Tequila Sunrise' | IBal |
| | 'Terracotta' | MCri |
| | 'Terry Wogan' | EPGN NNor |
| | 'Tet-a-Poo' | IBal |
| | 'Thai Brass' | SApp |
| | 'The Leading Edge' (v) | IBal |
| | 'The Razor's Edge' | IBal |
| | 'The Shining' | IBal |
| | 'The Twister' | EGol IBal NMyG |
| | 'Theo's Blue' | EMic GSec IBal |
| | 'Thomas Hogg' | see *H. undulata* var. *albomarginata* |
| | 'Thumb Nail' | ECha EGol EMic IBal NNor SApp SCnR |
| | 'Thumbelina' | EGol EMic IBal |
| | 'Thunderbolt'[PBR] (*sieboldiana*) | EGol EMic EPGN IBal MBNS NGdn NLar SApp WFar |
| | 'Tick Tock' (v) | EMic IBal |
| | 'Tickle Me Pink' **new** | EMic |
| | 'Tidewater' | IBal |
| | 'Time Tunnel'[PBR] (*sieboldiana*) (v) | EMic IBal |
| | 'Tiny Tears' | EGol GAbr IBal IFoB |
| | 'Titanic'[PBR] | EMic IBal |
| | 'Toasted Waffles' | WFar |
| | ***tokudama*** | EGol EMic IBal MHom NBir NGdn NHol NNor NSti SApp WFar XLum |
| § | - f. ***aureo-nebulosa*** (v) | EGol EMic EPGN IBal NGdn NSti SRms WMnd |
| | - f. ***flavocircinalis*** (v) | CPrp EGol EMic EPGN GMaP IBal NBPC NBro SApp WFar WHoo WMnd |
| | 'Tom Rex' | IBal |
| | 'Tom Schmid' (v) | EGol EMic IBal NMyG |
| | 'Tom Thumb' | EGol EMic IBal SApp |
| | 'Topaz' | IBal |
| | 'Topscore' | NNor |
| | 'Torchlight' (v) | EGol EMic GSec IBal |
| | ***tortifrons*** | EMic IBal |
| | 'Tortilla Chip' | IBal |
| | 'Tot Tot' | EGol IBal |
| | 'Touch of Class'[PBR] (v) | EMic EPGN IBal NMyG NNor WWEG |
| | 'Touchstone' (v) | GSec IBal LRHS NMyG SApp SWvt WWEG |
| | 'Toy Soldier' | EMic IBal SApp |
| | 'Trail's End' | EMic |
| | 'Tremors' | EMic |
| | 'Trill' | SApp |
| | 'Trixi' (v) | IBal |
| | 'True Blue' | EGol EMic IBal SApp WWEG |
| | 'Tsugaru Komachi' | EMic |
| | 'Tsugaru Komachi Kifukurin' (v) | IBal |
| | 'Turning Point' | EGol |
| | 'Tutu' | EGol |
| | 'Twiggie' | EMic |
| | 'Twilight' (*fortunei*) (v) | EGol EKen EMic EPGN IBal LRHS MBNS MDev NGdn NLar NMyG SApp SWvt WWEG |
| | 'Twilight Time' | IBal |
| | 'Twinkle Toes' | EGol EMic |
| | 'Twist of Lemon' | GBin |
| | 'Twist of Lime' (v) | EGol EMic IBal NNor WWEG |
| | 'Ultramarine' | IBal |
| | 'Ultraviolet Light' | EGol |
| | 'Unchained Melody' | IBal |
| | ***undulata*** | NNor WFar |
| § | - var. ***albomarginata*** | CBcs CMHG CMac COlW CSam EBee EGol ELan EMic EPGN EPfP GMaP LRHS LSRN MAvo MRav MWat NBid NBir NGdn NLar SPer SRms SWvt WFar WMnd WPtf WTin WWEG XLum |
| § | - var. ***erromena*** ♀H4 | EMic GMaP LPBA NNor WHrl |
| § | - var. ***undulata*** (v) ♀H4 | CBot EBee ELan EPGN EPfP GMaP IBal LPBA LRHS MCot MRav MSwo NEgg NGdn NLar NMyG NNor NVic SPer SPoG WFar WWEG |
| | - var. ***univittata*** (v) ♀H4 | ECha EGol EMic GKev LAst MHom MWhi NBir NPro WFar WMoo |
| | 'Unforgettable' | EMic IBal NMyG SApp |
| | 'Upper Crust' (v) | IBal |
| | 'Urajiro Hachijo' (*longipes* var. *latifolia*) | EGol IBal |
| | 'Urajiro' (*hypoleuca*) | EGol |
| | 'Valentine Lace' | EGol EMic IBal |
| | 'Valley's Cathedral' **new** | IBal |
| | 'Valley's Chute the Chute' | EMic IBal |
| | 'Valley's Glacier' (v) **new** | EMic IBal MDev |
| | 'Valley's Vanilla Sticks' | EMic IBal |
| | 'Van Wade' (v) | EGol EMic IBal |
| | 'Vanilla Cream' (*cathayana*) | EGol EMic |
| | 'Variegata' (*gracillima*) | see *H.* 'Vera Verde' |
| | 'Variegata' (*tokudama*) | see *H. tokudama* f. *aureo-nebulosa* |
| | 'Variegata' (*undulata*) | see *H. undulata* var. *undulata* |
| | 'Variegata' (*ventricosa*) | see *H.* 'Aureomarginata' (*ventricosa*) |
| | 'Variegated' (*fluctuans*) | see *H.* 'Sagae' |
| | 'Velvet Moon' (v) | EMic IBal |
| | ***ventricosa*** ♀H4 | CBcs CMac EGol EMic GMaP LPBA MAvo MWhi NGdn SGar WFar |
| | - BWJ 8160 from Sichuan | WCru |
| | - var. ***aureomaculata*** | EGol EMic NBir NNor NSti WFar |
| I | 'Venucosa' | EGol |
| | 'Venus' (d) | CAby IBal LRHS NGdn SApp SMrs SPer WBrk WCot |
| | 'Venus Star' | EGol EMic IBal NMyG |
| | ***venusta*** ♀H4 | CDes CFir EBee ECho EDAr EGol EMic EPGN GCra GEdr IBal MHer MRav NBid NBir NMen NMyG NNor NRya NSti SApp SRot WCot WTin WWEG |
| | - B&SWJ 4389 | WCru |
| | - 'Kin Botan' (v) | GEdr |
| | - 'Porter' | IBal |
| | - 'Red Tubes' | IBal |
| | - ***yakusimensis*** | see *H. kikutii* var. *yakusimensis* |
| § | 'Vera Verde' (v) | GCra GQui IBal NBir NMyG |
| | 'Verdi Valentine' | IBal |
| | 'Verkade's No 1' | IBal |
| | 'Verna Jean' (v) | EGol EMic IBal |
| | 'Veronica Lake' (v) | EGol EMic GSec IBal LRHS NMyG NNor WHal |
| | 'Victory' | EMic IBal |
| | 'Viking Ship' | EMic |
| | 'Vilmoriniana' | EGol EMic IBal |

'Vim and Vigor' IBal
'Vina' IBal
'Viridis Marginata' see *H. sieboldii* var. *sieboldii* f. *kabitan*
'Vulcan' (v) EMic IBal
'Wagtail' (Tardiana Group) EGol EMic IBal
'Wahoo' (*tokudama*) (v) EGol
'War Paint' EMic IBal
'Warwick Ballerina' EGol
'Warwick Comet' (v) EMic IBal SApp
'Warwick Curtsey' (v) EGol EMic GSec IBal
'Warwick Delight' (v) EGol EMic IBal
'Warwick Edge' (v) EGol IBal
'Warwick Essence' EGol EMic
'Warwick Sheen' IBal
'Waukon Thin Ice' **new** EMic
'Waving Winds' (v) EGol IBal LRHS
'Waving Wuffles' EMic IBal NMyG
'Wayside Blue' EMic
'Wayside Perfection' see *H.* 'Royal Standard'
'Website' IBal
'Weihenstephan' (*sieboldii*) EGol EMic
'Weser' EGol
'Wheaton Blue' EMic LRHS
'Whirligig' (v) EMic
'Whirling Dervish' (v) IBal
'Whirlwind' (*fortunei*) (v) EGol EMic EPGN GBin GQue IBal IPot MNrw MRav NBro NEgg NGdn NMyG NNor NOrc SApp SMrm SPad WAul WMnd WWEG
'Whirlwind Tour' (v) EGol IBal SApp
'Whiskey Sour' IBal
'White Bikini' (v) IBal
'White Ceiling' **new** IBal
'White Christmas' (*undulata*) (v) EGol EMic EPGN EQua IBal
'White Dove' (v) EMic IBal
'White Fairy' (*plantaginea*) (d) EMic IBal
'White Feather' (*undulata*) CHid CWGN ELon EPfP MSCN NBir NGdn NMyG NNor SBfd
'White Gold' EGol
'White Knight' IBal
'White On' (*montana*) EMic
'White Ray' **new** IBal
'White Triumphator' (*rectifolia*) EGol EMic GBin IBal
'White Trumpets' EMic
'White Vision' EGol
'Wide Brim' (v) ♀H4 Widely available
'Wiggle Worms' (v) IBal
'William Lachman' (v) NLar
'Wily Willy' IBal
'Wind River Gold' EGol EMic
'Windsor Gold' see *H.* 'Nancy Lindsay'
'Winfield Blue' CMHG EGol EMic IBal
'Winfield Gold' EGol EMic IBal
'Winfield Mist' (v) IBal
'Winsome' (v) EGol IBal
'Winter Lightning' (v) NNor
'Winter Snow' (v) EMic IBal SApp
'Wintergreen' (v) IBal
'Wogon' (*sieboldii*) CMMP EMic GBin GEdr GKev GMaP ITim NMen NSti
'Wogon's Boy' EGol EMic EPGN IBal LRHS WWEG
'Wolverine' (v) EBee ECGP ECtt EGol EHoe EMic EPGN GAbr IBal ITim LPla LRHS LSou MHom NGdn NLBP NMyG SWvt WBrk WCot WWEG
'Woolly Mammoth' (v) IBal
'Wooly Bully' SApp
'Woop Woop' (v) EMic IBal
'World Cup' IBal
'Worldly Treasure' IBal
'Wrinkles and Crinkles' EMic
'Wylde Green Cream' EGol IBal
'Xanadu' (v) IBal
'X-rated' (v) IBal
'Yakushima-mizu' (*gracillima*) EMic IBal NMyG
* ***yakushimana*** NHar NMen
'Yankee Blue' IBal
'Yellow Boa' EGol EMic
'Yellow Edge' (*fortunei*) see *H. fortunei* var. *aureomarginata*
'Yellow Edge' (*sieboldiana*) see *H.* 'Frances Williams'
'Yellow River' (v) EGol EMic EPGN GBin IBal NGdn NMyG NNor SApp
'Yellow Splash' (v) ECha EMic EPGN LRHS MHom NMyG NNor
'Yellow Splash Rim' (v) EGol EMic NCGa
'Yellow Splashed Edged' (v) EMic
'Yellow Submarine' IBal
'Yesterday's Memories' (v) EMic
'Yin' (v) EMic IBal SApp
***yingeri*** EGol SApp WPGP
– B&SWJ 546 WCru
'Zager Blue' EMic
'Zager Green' EMic
'Zager White Edge' (*fortunei*) (v) EGol EMic IBal NMyG SApp WTin
'Zitronenfalter' EGol IBal
'Zodiac' (*fortunei*) (v) IBal
'Zounds' CBot CMHG EBee ECtt EGol EMic EPfP EShb GBin IBal LRHS MRav NGdn NLar NMyG NOrc NSti SApp SBfd SRms WBor WFar WWEG

## *Hottonia* (*Primulaceae*)

***palustris*** CBen EHon ELan EWil LPBA MSKA MWts NPer SWat

## *Houstonia* (*Rubiaceae*)

***caerulea*** L. ECho NPri
– var. ***alba*** SPlb
***longifolia*** EWes
***michauxii*** 'Fred Mullard' EWes

## *Houttuynia* (*Saururaceae*)

***cordata*** GKev GPoy SBfd SDix SWat WFar XLum
§ – 'Boo-Boo' (v) CMac EPfP EPla LBMP NBro SBfd SMrm WFar WWEG
§ – 'Chameleon' (v) Widely available
– 'Fantasy' LLWG
– 'Flame' (v) CMac CWCL LRHS MBri NPri SBfd WWEG
– 'Flore Pleno' (d) CBen CMac CRow CWat ECha EHon ELan EPfP EPla LPBA MCCP MRav MSCN NBir NPer NVic SIde SPer SPlb SRms SWat WFar WHrl WPnP XLum
– 'Joker's Gold' CMac EBee ECtt EPPr EPfP EPla LBMP NVic SMrm SPoG
– 'Pied Piper' CDoC SAga SBfd SPad
– 'Sunshine' EBee
– 'Tequila Sunrise' CHEx
– 'Terry Clarke' see *H. cordata* 'Boo-Boo'
– 'Tricolor' see *H. cordata* 'Chameleon'
– Variegata Group (v) LPBA NBro

## Hovea (Papilionaceae)

| | | |
|---|---|---|
| | ***celsii*** | see *H. elliptica* |
| § | ***elliptica*** | SPlb |
| | ***montana*** | SPlb |

## Hovenia (Rhamnaceae)

| | | |
|---|---|---|
| | ***dulcis*** | CAgr CBcs CMCN EPfP LEdu NLar |
| | - B&SWJ 11024 | WCru |

## Howea (Arecaceae)

| | | |
|---|---|---|
| § | ***belmoreana*** ♀H1 | LPal |
| § | ***forsteriana*** ♀H1 | CCCN LPal NPla XBlo |

## Hoya (Apocynaceae)

| | | |
|---|---|---|
| § | ***australis*** | MOWG |
| | ***bella*** | see *H. lanceolata* subsp. *bella* |
| | ***carnosa*** ♀H1 | CBcs EBak EOHP SEND SRms SWal WWFP |
| | - 'Compacta Regalis' (v) | NPer |
| | - 'Krinkle 8' | NPer |
| | - 'Red Princess' | SAdn |
| | - 'Tricolor' (V) | NPer |
| | ***cinnamomifolia*** | MOWG |
| * | ***compacta*** 'Tricolor' | NPer |
| | ***darwinii*** misapplied | see *H. australis* |
| | ***lacunosa*** | CCCN |
| § | ***lanceolata*** | CBcs EShb SEND SRms |
| | subsp. ***bella*** ♀H1 | |
| | ***linearis*** | MOWG |
| | ***multiflora*** | MOWG |

## huckleberry, garden see *Solanum scabrum*

## Huernia (Apocynaceae)

| | | |
|---|---|---|
| | ***barbata*** | LToo |
| | ***guttata*** new | LToo |
| | ***hislopii*** new | LToo |
| | ***hystrix*** | LToo |
| | ***leachii*** new | LToo |
| | ***levyi*** new | LToo |
| | ***longituba*** | LToo |
| | ***nouhuysii*** new | LToo |
| | ***procumbens*** new | LToo |
| | ***quinta*** | LToo |
| | ***zebrina*** | LToo |

## Humata (Davalliaceae)

| | | |
|---|---|---|
| | ***tyermannii*** | CMen EShb ISha WFib WRic |
| | - 'Selcka' new | CMen |

## Humea see *Calomeria*

| | | |
|---|---|---|
| | ***elegans*** | see *Calomeria amaranthoides* |

## Humulus (Cannabaceae)

| | | |
|---|---|---|
| | ***lupulus*** | CArn CBcs CRWN EGHP EPfP GPoy ILis MNHC NLar NMir SIde WDin WHer |
| | - 'Aureus' ♀H4 | Widely available |
| | - 'Aureus' (f) | CRHN ELon EOHP GCal GKev MCCP SPoG WCot WWFP |
| | - 'Aureus' (m) | MCCP |
| * | - ***compactus*** | GPoy |
| | - 'Fuggle' | CAgr GPoy SDea |
| | - 'Golden Showers' | MCCP |
| | - 'Golden Tassels' (f) | EBee EGHP ELon LBuc LHop LRHS MBri MGos SBfd SEND SPer SPoG |
| | - (Goldings Group) 'Cobbs' | SDea |
| | - - 'Mathons' | CAgr SDea |
| | - 'Hallertauer' | SDea |
| | - 'Prima Donna' | CAgr EBee EGxp GBin LHop MCoo NLar SBfd SCoo SIde SPer SPoG SWvt |
| | - 'Taff's Variegated' (v) | EGHP EWes WSHC |
| | - 'Wye Challenger' | CAgr GPoy MHer |
| | - 'Wye Northdown' | CAgr SDea |

## Hunnemannia (Papaveraceae)

| | | |
|---|---|---|
| | ***fumariifolia*** | CSpe XSen |

## Huodendron (Styracaceae)

| | | |
|---|---|---|
| | ***biaristatum*** | WPGP |
| | ***tibeticum*** | WPGP |

## Hutchinsia see *Pritzelago*

## Hyacinthella (Asparagaceae)

| | | |
|---|---|---|
| | ***acutiloba*** | ECho WCot |
| | ***dalmatica*** 'Grandiflora' | ECho |
| | ***glabrescens*** | WCot |
| | ***heldreichii*** | ECho WCot |
| | ***hispida*** new | WCot |
| | ***lazuliria*** | LWst |
| | ***leucophaea*** | ECho LWst |
| | ***lineata*** | WCot |
| | ***millingenii*** | ECho WCot |
| | ***pallens*** | ECho |
| | ***siirtensis*** new | WCot |

## Hyacinthoides (Asparagaceae)

| | | |
|---|---|---|
| | ***aristidis*** | ECho |
| § | ***hispanica*** | ECho NBir SEND |
| | - 'Alba' | ECho |
| | - subsp. ***algeriensis*** | WCot |
| | - 'Dainty Maid' | ECho WCot |
| | - 'Excelsior' | ECho LRHS |
| | - 'Miss World' | ECho WCot |
| | - 'Mount Everest' | ECho |
| | - 'Queen of the Pinks' | ECho WCot |
| | - 'Rosea' | ECho |
| | - 'White City' | ECho WCot |
| § | ***italica*** ♀H4 | CPom ECho WCot WShi |
| | - BS 380 | WCot |
| § | ***non-scripta*** | CAvo CBct CBro CFFs CHab CTca CTri ECho EPot EWil GKev LAma LRHS MCot MHer MMuc MWat NBir NMen NMir NPri SDeJ SEND SMrm SPad SPer SRms SVic WHer WShi |
| | - 'Alba' | CAvo ECho MMuc NBir SEND |
| | - 'Backkums Blue' new | NMin |
| | - 'Bracteata' | CNat |
| | - 'Rosea' | ECho MMuc SEND |
| | 'Stuart Williams' | CAvo |
| § | ***vicentina*** | WCot |

## Hyacinthus ✿ (Asparagaceae)

| | | |
|---|---|---|
| | ***amethystinus*** | see *Brimeura amethystina* |
| | ***azureus*** | see *Muscari azureum* |
| | ***comosus*** 'Plumosus' | see *Muscari comosum* 'Plumosum' |
| | multi-flowered blue | CAvo SDeJ |
| | multi-flowered pink | SDeJ |
| | multi-flowered white | CAvo SDeJ |
| | ***orientalis*** 'Aiolos' | SPer |
| | - 'Amethyst' | ERCP LAma |
| | - 'Anastasia' | SPhx |
| | - 'Anna Liza' | MBri |
| | - 'Anna Marie' ♀H4 | CBro LAma MBri SDeJ |
| | - 'Apricot Passion' | EPfP |
| | - 'Ben Nevis' (d) | LAma |

| | |
|---|---|
| - 'Blue Giant' | LAma SDeJ |
| - 'Blue Jacket' ♀H4 | CBro LAma MBri SDeJ |
| - 'Blue Magic' | SDeJ |
| - 'Blue Star' | LAma SPhx |
| - 'Carnegie' | CAvo CBro CFFs EPfP ERCP LAma SPhx |
| - 'China Pink' | SDeJ SPer |
| - 'City of Haarlem' ♀H4 | CAvo CBro CFFs EPfP LAma MBri SDeJ SPhx |
| - 'Crystal Palace' (d) | LAma |
| - 'Delft Blue' ♀H4 | CAvo CBro EPfP LAma MBri SDeJ SPer SPhx |
| - 'Fondant' | LAma SDeJ |
| - 'General Köhler' (d) | LAma |
| - 'Gipsy Princess' | LAma |
| - 'Gipsy Queen' ♀H4 | EPfP LAma MBri SDeJ SPer |
| - 'Hollyhock' (d) ♀H4 | LAma SDeJ |
| - 'Jan Bos' ♀H4 | EPfP LAma MBri SDeJ SPer SPhx |
| - 'L'Innocence' ♀H4 | CAvo CBro |
| - 'Miss Saigon' ♀H4 | ERCP |
| - multi-flowered | ERCP |
| - 'Odysseus' | LAma |
| - 'Ostara' ♀H4 | LAma MBri |
| - 'Peter Stuyvesant' | EPfP ERCP LAma |
| - 'Pink Festival' ♀H4 | SPer |
| - 'Pink Pearl' ♀H4 | EPfP LAma MBri SDeJ SPhx |
| - 'Pink Royal' (d) | LAma |
| - 'Purple Sensation'PBR | SPhx |
| - 'Red Magic' | LAma SDeJ |
| - 'Rosette' (d) | LAma |
| - 'Splendid Cornelia' | ERCP SDeJ SPer |
| - 'White Festival' ♀H4 | SPer |
| - 'White Pearl' | LAma MBri SDeJ |
| - 'Woodstock' | CAvo CFFs EPfP ERCP LAma SDeJ SPer SPhx |

## *Hydrangea* ✿ (*Hydrangeaceae*)

| | |
|---|---|
| ***angustipetala*** | see *H. scandens* subsp. *chinensis* f. *angustipetala* |
| ***anomala*** | WCru |
| subsp. ***anomala*** BWJ 8052 from China | |
| - - HWJK 2065 from Nepal **new** | WCru |
| - - 'Winter Glow' | WCru |
| - subsp. ***glabra*** B&SWJ 6804 | WCru |
| - - 'Crûg Coral' | WCru |
| § - subsp. ***petiolaris*** ♀H4 | Widely available |
| - - B&SWJ 5457 | WCru |
| - - B&SWJ 5996 from Yakushima | WCru |
| - - B&SWJ 6081 | WCru |
| § - - var. ***cordifolia*** | NLar WPat |
| - - B&SWJ 11487 | WCru |
| § - - - 'Brookside Littleleaf' | EQua GKin IDee MBri NLar WFar |
| - - dwarf | see *H. anomala* subsp. *petiolaris* var. *cordifolia* |
| * - - var. ***minor*** B&SWJ 5991 | WCru |
| - - 'Mirranda' | CBcs EBee EPfP NBro SGol SMad SPoG SWvt |
| * - - var. ***tiliifolia*** | EBee WFar WSHC |
| - - B&SWJ 4400 | WCru |
| - - B&SWJ 8497 | WCru |
| - - 'Yakushima' | WCru |
| * - subsp. ***quelpartensis*** B&SWJ 8799 | WCru |
| - Semiola = 'Inovalaur' | LLHF LRHS SBfd SKHP SLim WPGP |
| § ***arborescens*** | CArn CPLG MRav WFar WPGP |
| - 'Annabelle' ♀H4 | Widely available |
| - 'Bounty' | MAsh |
| § - subsp. ***discolor*** | WKif WPat |
| - - 'Sterilis' | SHyH WPGP WPat |
| - 'Grandiflora' ♀H4 | CBcs CBot ELan EPfP EQua LSRN MRav MSwo NBro NEgg WDin WPGP |
| - 'Hayes Starburst'PBR | CMil CWGN LLHF LRHS MAsh SCoo SHyH SKHP SPoG SSpi WPGP WPat |
| - 'Hills of Snow' | IVic NLar |
| - 'Picadilly' | NLar |
| - 'Pink Pincushion' | NLar |
| - 'Puffed Green' | NLar |
| - subsp. ***radiata*** | CAbP LRHS MRav SPoG SSpi WCru WFar WPGP |
| - - 'Samantha' | EPfP LRHS |
| - 'Vasterival' | NLar |
| - 'Wesser Falls' | CMil |
| - White Dome = 'Dardom'PBR | NBro |
| ***aspera*** | CMac CTri SHyH SLon SSpi SSta WCru WKif WPGP |
| - HWJCM 452 | WCru |
| - from Gongshan, China | CMil CPLG WPGP |
| - 'Anthony Bullivant' | GKin IArd LRHS NLar SHyH SKHP WPat |
| - Kawakamii Group | CGHE CHEx CMil CPLG CSpe EPla EWTr LRHS NLar SGol SKHP WCru WPGP |
| - - B&SWJ 1420 | WCru |
| - - B&SWJ 3456 | WCru |
| - - B&SWJ 3462 | WCru |
| - - B&SWJ 6702 | WCru |
| - - B&SWJ 6714 | WCru |
| - - B&SWJ 6827 | WCru |
| - - B&SWJ 7025 | WCru |
| - - B&SWJ 7101 | WCru |
| - - 'August Abundance' | WCru |
| - - 'Formosa' **new** | WCru |
| - - 'Maurice Mason' | CPLG |
| - - 'September Splendour' | WCru |
| - Kawakamii Group × ***involucrata*** | WPGP |
| - 'Macrophylla' ♀H3 | CWib EPfP GCal IVic MRav NBlu NPal SHyH SPer WCru WFar WPGP |
| - 'Mauvette' | CMil EPfP LRHS LTen MBlu NBro NLar NPal SGol SPer SSpi WCru |
| - 'Peter Chappell' | CMil CPLG LRHS WPat |
| § - subsp. ***robusta*** | CPLG SLPl WCru WPGP |
| - - GWJ 9430 | WCru |
| - - WWJ 11888 | WCru |
| - 'Rocklon' | NLar WCru |
| - 'Rosthornii' | see *H. aspera* subsp. *robusta* |
| - 'Sam MacDonald' | CPLG LRHS NLar SKHP SSpi WPGP WPat |
| § - subsp. ***sargentiana*** ♀H3 | Widely available |
| - - large-leaved | WCru WPat |
| - subsp. ***strigosa*** | CDul CPLG EPfP SHyH SSpi WCru WPGP WPat |
| - - B&SWJ 8201 | WCru |
| - - HWJ 653 | WCru |
| - - HWJ 737 | WCru |
| - - from Gong Shan, China | CGHE |
| - 'Taiwan' | EQua |
| - 'Taiwan Pink' | EPfP IArd NLar |
| - 'Velvet and Lace' | LBuc NLar |
| § - Villosa Group ♀H3 | Widely available |
| ***cinerea*** | see *H. arborescens* subsp. *discolor*, *H. aspera* subsp. *discolor* |
| 'Cohhii' | ECre |

| | |
|---|---|
| 'Garden House Glory' **new** | CGHE WPGP |
| ***glabrifolia*** | see *H. scandens* subsp. *chinensis* |
| ***glandulosa*** B&SWJ 4031 | WCru |
| aff. ***gracilis*** B&SWJ 3942 | WCru |
| § ***heteromalla*** | CGHE CMHG EWTr GGal SLPl SSpi WPGP |
| - B&SWJ 2142 from India | WCru |
| - B&SWJ 2602 from Sikkim | WCru |
| - BWJ 7657 from China | WCru |
| - GWJ 9337 from Sikkim | WCru |
| - HWJ 938 from Vietnam **new** | WCru |
| - HWJCM 180 | WCru |
| - HWJK 2127 from Nepal | WCru |
| - Bretschneideri Group | EPfP GQui SHyH WCru WFar WPGP |
| - 'Fan Si Pan' | WCru |
| - 'Nepal Beauty' | IVic SGol |
| - 'Snowcap' | EPfP GQui IArd LRHS NLar SHyH SKHP SLPl SSpi WPGP |
| ***hirta*** B&SWJ 5000 | WCru |
| - B&SWJ 11022 | WCru |
| ***indochinensis*** | CPLG |
| - B&SWJ 8307 | WCru |
| - B&SWJ 11717 | WCru |
| ***integerrima*** | see *H. serratifolia* |
| ***integrifolia*** B&SWJ 022 | WCru |
| - B&SWJ 6967 | NLar WCru |
| ***involucrata*** | EPfP GGal LLHF LRHS MMHG SBrt SHyH WDin |
| - dwarf | WCru |
| - 'Hortensis' (d) ♀H3-4 | CMil EPfP MRav NLar SMad SSpi WCru WKif WPGP WSHC |
| - 'Mihara-kokonoe' | CPMA |
| - 'Multiplex' **new** | WCru |
| - 'Plena' (d) | CLAP EBee LRHS MRav NLar SSta WCru WFar WPGP |
| - 'Sterilis' | CMil EPfP WCru |
| - 'Viridescens' | LLHF LRHS WCru WPGP |
| - 'Yokudanka' (d) | GQui MAsh NLar |
| ***kawagoeana*** | WCru |
| var. ***grosseserrata*** B&SWJ 11500 **new** | |
| ***kwangsiensis*** B&SWJ 11717 **new** | WCru |
| - WWJ 11609 | WCru |
| ***lingii*** B&SWJ 11790 **new** | WCru |
| ***lobbii*** | see *H. scandens* subsp. *chinensis* |
| ***longifolia*** B&SWJ 6883 | WCru |
| - CWJ 12413 | WCru |
| ***longipes*** | CMil CPLG GQui WCru WPGP |
| - var. ***fulvescens*** B&SWJ 8188 | WCru |
| ***luteovenosa*** | WCru |
| - B&SWJ 5647 | WCru |
| - B&SWJ 5929 | WCru |
| - B&SWJ 6220 | WCru |
| - B&SWJ 6317 | WCru |
| ***macrophylla*** (H) | GGal |
| - 'AB Green Shadow'PBR | MAsh MMHG SPoG |
| - 'Adria' (H) | NLar SHyH |
| - 'Aduarda' | see *H. macrophylla* 'Mousmée' |
| - 'All Summer Beauty' (H) | CMil MAsh |
| - Alpen Glow | see *H. macrophylla* 'Alpenglühen' |
| § - 'Alpenglühen' (H) | CBcs CPLG CSBt CSpr ELan IVic LRHS SHyH SLim SRms |
| - 'Altona' (H) ♀H3-4 | CBcs EPfP IArd LRHS MAsh MGos MRav NBir NLar SHyH SPer |
| - 'Amethyst' (H/d) | CGHE |
| - 'Ami Pasquier' (H) ♀H3-4 | CDoC CMac COlW CSBt CTri EBee ELan EPfP GGal IVic LRHS LSRN MMuc MRav MSwo NEgg SBrd SCoo SEND SGar SHyH SLim SSpi SWvt |
| * - 'Aureomarginata' (v) | SHyH WCot |
| - 'Ave Maria' (H) | EQua MAsh |
| § - 'Ayesha' (H) | Widely available |
| - 'Bachstelze' (Teller Series) (L) | MAsh SSpi |
| - 'Beauté Vendômoise' (L) | CGHE LRHS NLar SHyH SSpi WPGP |
| - 'Bela'PBR (H) | LRHS |
| - 'Benelux' (H) | CBcs |
| - 'Bicolor' | see *H. macrophylla* 'Harlequin' |
| § - 'Blauer Prinz' (H) | CSam MAsh SHyH |
| § - 'Bläuling' (Teller Series) (L) | CDoC EPfP GKin LSRN SBfd SHyH |
| § - 'Blaumeise' (Teller Series) (L) | CDoC CMHG ELon EPfP EQua LRHS LTen MAsh MBri MDKP MGos MRav NEgg SCoo SHyH SLim SLon SPoG SSpi SWvt WDin WPGP |
| - 'Blue Bonnet' (H) | CChe CDul CSpr EPfP LRHS LSRN MRav SHyH SPer |
| - Blue Butterfly | see *H. macrophylla* 'Bläuling' |
| - Blue Prince | see *H. macrophylla* 'Blauer Prinz' |
| - Blue Sky | see *H. macrophylla* 'Blaumeise' |
| - Blue Tit | see *H. macrophylla* 'Blaumeise' |
| - 'Blue Wave' | see *H. macrophylla* 'Mariesii Perfecta' |
| - Bluebird | see *H. macrophylla* 'Bläuling' |
| - 'Bluebird' misapplied | see *H. serrata* 'Bluebird' |
| - 'Blushing Bride' | GKin LBuc MAsh NPri SBrd SLon SPoG |
| - 'Bodensee' (H) | LTen MBri MMuc SEND SHyH |
| - 'Bouquet Rose' (H) | CWib ECtt LBMP MMuc SEND SHyH |
| - 'Brestenburg' (H) | MAsh |
| - 'Bridal Bouquet' (H) | CDoC |
| - 'Brügg' (H) | LRHS MAsh SHyH SLim SPer WPGP |
| - 'Buchfink' (Teller Series) (L) | SHyH |
| - Cardinal | see *H. macrophylla* 'Kardinal' (Teller Series) |
| § - 'Cardinal Red' (H) | ECre EPfP |
| - 'Chaperon Rouge' (H) | LRHS |
| - 'Colour Fantasy' (H) | MBrN |
| - 'Cordata' | see *H. arborescens* |
| - 'Dandenong' (L) | GQui MAsh |
| - 'Dart's Romance' **new** | SHyH |
| - 'Dart's Song' | NLar |
| - 'Deutschland' (H) | CTri |
| - 'Domotoi' | see *H. macrophylla* 'Setsuka-yae' |
| - Dragonfly | see *H. macrophylla* 'Libelle' |
| * - 'Dwaag Pink' | MRav |
| - 'Eldorado' (H) | SHyH |
| - Endless Summer = 'Bailmer' (H) | EMil EPfP LBuc LRHS MAsh MGos NPri SPoG |
| - Endless Summer Twist-n-Shout = 'Piihm-I' **new** | LBuc SBrd |
| § - 'Enziandom' (H) | CBcs CPLG CSBt GGal MAsh WPGP |
| - 'Etoile Violette' | EQua MAsh |
| - 'Europa' (H) ♀H3-4 | CBcs CPLG LRHS SHyH |
| - 'Fantasia'PBR **new** | NPnk |
| § - 'Fasan' (Teller Series) (L) | EQua MAsh |
| - Firelight | see *H. macrophylla* 'Leuchtfeuer' |
| - Fireworks | see *H. macrophylla* 'Hanabi' |
| - Fireworks Blue | see *H. macrophylla* 'Jōgasaki' |
| - Fireworks Pink | see *H. macrophylla* 'Jōgasaki' |
| - Fireworks White | see *H. macrophylla* 'Hanabi' |
| - Forever and Ever = 'Early Sensation' (Forever and Ever Series) (H) | CMac GKin LBuc |

| Entry | Suppliers |
|---|---|
| – 'Forever Pink' (H) | MAsh NLar |
| § – 'Frau Fujiyo' (Lady Series) (H) | CPLG |
| § – 'Frau Katsuko' (Lady Series) (H) | SPer |
| § 'Frau Mariko' (Lady Series) (H) | MRav |
| § – 'Frau Taiko' (Lady Series) (H) | SPer |
| – 'Frillibet' (H) | CAbP MRav NLar |
| – 'Gartenbaudirektor Kühnert' (H) | SHyH |
| § – 'Générale Vicomtesse de Vibraye' (H) ♀H3-4 | CChe CDoC CDul CEnd CMHG COlW CTri EBee EPfP GGal LRHS MAsh SBrd SDix SHyH SLim SPer SSpi |
| – Gentian Dome | see *H. macrophylla* 'Enziandom' |
| – 'Geoffrey Chadbund' | see *H. macrophylla* 'Möwe' |
| – 'Gertrud Glahn' (H) | SHyH WFar |
| – 'Gimpel' (Teller Series) (L) | MAsh |
| – 'Glowing Embers' (H) | IArd MBNS |
| – Goldrush = 'Nehyosh' (v) | CDul CMil CWGN LRHS NEgg SBfd SLim |
| – 'Goliath' (H) | EPfP GGar |
| § – 'Grant's Choice' (L) | EQua NBro |
| – Great Star = 'Blanc Bleu' | CAlb EPfP LRHS LSRN MAsh SBfd SLim SPur |
| – 'Hamburg' (H) | CTri ECtt EPfP LAst MGos SDix SHyH SLim WFar |
| § – 'Hanabi' (L/d) | CBcs CDoC CEnd CLAP CMil ECre EQua GGal MBlu NLar |
| § – 'Harlequin' (H) | WCot |
| – 'Harry's Red' (H) | MAsh |
| – 'Hatsu-shime' (L) | NLar |
| – 'Heinrich Seidel' (H) | CBcs CTri WMoo |
| – 'Hobergine'PBR (Hovaria Series) (H) | SHyH |
| – 'Holehird Purple' | MAsh |
| – 'Izu-no-hana' (L/d) | CAlb CBcs CLAP CMil ELon LHop MAsh MBlu NLar SHyH SUsu WBor WPGP |
| – 'James Grant' | see *H. macrophylla* 'Grant's Choice' |
| – 'Jofloma' | EQua NLar |
| § – 'Jōgasaki' (L/d) | CBcs CLAP CMil CPLG MAsh MBlu NLar SHyH WPGP |
| – 'Joseph Banks' (H) | CBcs CTri |
| – 'Kardinal' | see *H. macrophylla* 'Cardinal Red' (H) |
| § – 'Kardinal' (Teller Series) (L) | MAsh |
| – 'King George' (H) | CBar CBcs CDoC CDul CSBt EBee EPfP LAst LRHS MGos MMuc NEgg SBfd SBrd SGol SHyH SLim SPer SPoG SWvt WFar WMoo |
| § – 'Klaveren' | CMil MAsh NBro NMun SHyH |
| – 'Kluis Superba' (H) | CBcs CTri GGal SHyH |
| – 'La France' (H) | COlW CTri EBee IVic SBfd SHyH SLim WFar |
| – 'Lady Fujiyo' | see *H. macrophylla* 'Frau Fujiyo' |
| – 'Lady in Red' (L) | CMil |
| – Lady Katsuko | see *H. macrophylla* 'Frau Katsuko' |
| – 'Lady Mariko' | see *H. macrophylla* 'Frau Mariko' |
| – 'Lady Taiko Blue' | see *H. macrophylla* 'Frau Taiko' |
| – 'Lady Taiko Pink' | see *H. macrophylla* 'Frau Taiko' |
| – 'Lanarth White' (L) ♀H3-4 | CBar CBcs CDoC CPLG CSBt CTri ELan EPfP GGal LBMP LRHS MAsh MMuc MSwo NLar SBod SEND SHyH SLPl SLim SPer SRms SSpi SWvt WBor WKif WPGP |
| – 'Lemon Wave' (L/v) | NLar |
| § – 'Leuchtfeuer' (H) | LRHS MGos SHyH WMoo |
| § – 'Libelle' (Teller Series) (L) | CBcs CDoC EPfP LBMP MGos MRav NEgg NLar NMun SBfd SGol SHyH SLim SPer SSpi |
| – 'Lilacina' | see *H. macrophylla* 'Mariesii Lilacina' |
| 'Love You Kiss'PBR (Hovaria Series) (L) | CBcs CMil LBuc LRHS NLar SCoo SHyH SPoG SRGP |
| § – 'Maculata' (L/v) | ELan GQui MSCN WGwG |
| – 'Madame A. Riverain' (H) | NLar SHyH |
| – 'Madame Emile Mouillère' (H) ♀H3-4 | Widely available |
| – 'Maréchal Foch' (H) | CTri GGal NLar |
| – 'Mariesii' (L) | CDoy CMHG CTri CTsd ELan GGal MSwo NLar NMun SDix SHyH SPer |
| § – 'Mariesii Grandiflora' (L) ♀H3-4 | CAlb CSpr CTsd EPfP GGal LRHS NBro SBfd SEND SHyH SPer SRms WDin WFar WMoo |
| § – 'Mariesii Lilacina' (L) ♀H3-4 | CSpr EPfP MMuc SEND SLon SPer SSpi WMoo |
| § – 'Mariesii Perfecta' (L) ♀H3-4 | Widely available |
| – 'Mariesii Variegata' (L/v) | CWib |
| – 'Masja' (H) | CBar ELon GKin IArd IVic LAst MAsh MGos MMuc MRav MSwo NBro NLar SEND SGol SHyH WBor |
| – 'Mathilde Gütges' (H) | CDoC GGal |
| – 'Max Löbner' (H) | LAst SHyH |
| – 'Merveille Sanguine' (H) | CDoC CGHE CMHG CMil CPLG CSpe EMil EPfP EQua GCal GGal IArd IVic LRHS MBri MMuc MRav NCGa NLar SEND SHyH SPoG SWvt WCFE WCot WGrn WKif WPGP WPat WSHC |
| – 'Messalina' (L) | MAsh SHyH |
| – 'Mirai'PBR (H) | CBcs SCoo SHyH WPGP |
| – 'Miss Belgium' (H) | CMac CTri EQua GKin MAsh |
| § – 'Mousmée' (L) | IArd SSpi |
| – 'Mousseline' (H) | MAsh |
| § – 'Möwe' (L) ♀H3-4 | CBcs CDoC CEnd CMil CPLG ECtt ELon EPfP GGal LHop LSRN MAsh MMuc NLar SCoo SDix SEND SGol SHyH SLim SPer SRms SSpi SSta WPat |
| – 'Mrs W.J. Hepburn' | CSBt LAst SHyH SPer |
| § – 'Nachtigall' (Teller Series) (L) | CMil GGal MAsh SHyH |
| – 'Nanping'PBR (Sturdy Series) (L) | EPfP |
| – 'Niedersachsen' (H) | CDoC CTri MRav SHyH |
| – Nightingale | see *H. macrophylla* 'Nachtigall' |
| – 'Nigra' (H) ♀H3-4 | CBcs CMac CPLG CWib ELan ELon EPfP IFoB LRHS MAsh MBri MGos MMuc MRav MSCN NBro NLar SDix SEND SHyH SLim SPer WFar WGrn WGwG WPGP WPat |
| – 'Nikko Blue' (H) | CBcs CTsd EPfP GKin MMuc NBlu SEND SHyH |
| – var. ***normalis*** (L) | CPLG |
| § – 'Nymphe' (H) | SHyH |
| – 'Oregon Pride' (H) | LRHS MAsh WPGP |
| – 'Otaksa' (H) | NLar |
| – 'Papagei' (Teller Series) | SPer |
| – 'Parzifal' (H) ♀H3-4 | CDul |
| – 'Pax' | see *H. macrophylla* 'Nymphe' |
| – 'Pfau' (Teller Series) (L) | ELon MAsh SHyH |
| – Pheasant | see *H. macrophylla* 'Fasan' |
| – 'Pia' (H) | CDoC CMil CPLG ELan LBuc MAsh MGos MMuc MRav NWCA SMad SPer SRms WBor WCru WFar WGrn |
| – Pigeon | see *H. macrophylla* 'Taube' |

| | | |
|---|---|---|
| | - 'Pirate's Gold' | CMil EHoe ELon MAsh WHar WMoo |
| | - 'Prinses Beatrix' (H) | SHyH |
| | - 'Quadricolor' (L/v) | CHll CMac CPLG EHoe GCal GGal MRav SDix SGar SHyH SLim SPer SPlb SRms WCot WSHC |
| | - 'Queen Elizabeth' (H) **new** | GKin |
| | - 'R.F. Felton' (H) | SHyH |
| | - 'Red Baron' | see *H. macrophylla* 'Schöne Bautznerin' |
| | - 'Red Red' (H) | MAsh |
| | - Redbreast | see *H. macrophylla* 'Rotkehlchen' |
| | - 'Regula' (H) | SHyH |
| | - 'Renate Steiniger' (H) | LRHS LTen MGos MMuc MRav SHyH |
| | - 'Romance' | LBuc |
| | - 'Rosea' | MCri |
| | - 'Rosita' (H) | MAsh NBir WFar |
| § | - 'Rotkehlchen' (Teller Series) (L) | CDoC EPfP NEgg SLim SPlb SWvt WDin |
| | - 'Rotschwanz' (Teller Series) (L) | CMil EQua LRHS MAsh WPGP WPat |
| | - 'Sabrina'PBR (H) | CBcs MBri MGos SPoG |
| | - 'Salsa' **new** | MBri |
| | - 'Sandra' (Dutch Ladies Series) (L) | CBcs CMil ELon |
| | - 'Schneeball' (H) | MAsh SHyH |
| § | - 'Schöne Bautznerin' | LRHS MWea NCGa SHyH WMoo |
| | - 'Sea Foam' (L) | NBlu NLar |
| | - 'Selina' | CBcs EPfP LSRN MBri MDKP SBrd SCoo SPoG |
| | - 'Selma'PBR (Dutch Ladies Series) (L) | CBcs MBri |
| § | - 'Setsuka-yae' (L/d) | CMil NLar |
| | - 'Sheila' (Dutch Ladies Series) (L) | CBcs EPfP LSRN MBri SBrd SPoG |
| | - 'Sibilla' (H) | CBcs SPlb |
| | - 'Sindarella' **new** | MBri |
| | - Sister Therese | see *H. macrophylla* 'Soeur Thérèse' |
| § | - 'Soeur Thérèse' (H) | CBar MAsh MMuc NLar SEND SGol SHyH SWvt WGwG |
| | - 'Soraya'PBR (Dutch Ladies Series) (L) | CBcs |
| | - 'Sumida-no-hanabi' (L/d) | WPGP |
| * | - 'Sunset' (L) | CBcs |
| § | - 'Taube' (Teller Series) (L) | CBcs CDoC CMHG CPLG EPfP GGal GQui MAsh NBlu SCoo SHyH SWvt |
| | - 'Teller Pink' | see *H. macrophylla* 'Taube' |
| | - 'Teller Red' | see *H. macrophylla* 'Rotkehlchen' |
| N | - Teller variegated | see *H. macrophylla* 'Tricolor' |
| N | - Teller Weiss | see *H. macrophylla* 'Libelle' |
| | - var. ***thunbergii*** | see *H. serrata* var. *thunbergii* |
| | - 'Tokyo Delight' (L) ♀H3-4 | CGHE CLAP CMil CPLG CTsd LRHS MAsh SHyH WPGP |
| § | - 'Tricolor' (L/v) | CBcs CBot CDoC CDul CTri ELon EQua LAst LRHS MGos MLLN SHyH SLon SPer SPoG WFar WMoo |
| | - 'Variegata' | see *H. macrophylla* 'Maculata' |
| | - 'Veitchii' (L) ♀H3-4 | CBcs CBot CDoy CDul CMHG CPLG CSBt EPfP GGal LRHS MGos MRav MSwo SDix SGar SHyH SPer SSpi WPGP |
| | - 'Vicomte de Vibraye' | see *H. macrophylla* 'Générale Vicomtesse de Vibraye' |
| | - 'Westfalen' (H) ♀H3-4 | CMac IArd SDix |
| I | - 'White Lace' (L) | ELan GKin |
| | - white lacecap (L) | CSpr |
| | - 'White Mop' (H) | CWib |
| | - 'White Wave' | see *H. macrophylla* 'Mariesii Grandiflora' |
| | - 'Zaunkoenig' (L) | MAsh |
| | - 'Zebra'PBR (H) | EPfP MGos SBrd SPoG WCot |
| | - 'Zhuni Hito' | NLar |
| | - 'Zorro'PBR | CBcs CDoC EPfP GKin LRHS MAsh SBfd SCoo SLon SPoG SSpi |
| | - 'Zulu' **new** | MGos |
| | aff. ***mangshanensis*** BWJ 8120 | WCru |
| | ***paniculata*** | CMCN WBor |
| | - B&SWJ 3556 from Taiwan | WCru |
| | - B&SWJ 5413 from Japan | WCru |
| | - B&SWJ 8894 from Japan | WCru |
| | - from Taiwan | SKHP |
| | - 'Ammarin' | GQui LLHF NLar WPat |
| | - Angel's Blush | see *H. paniculata* 'Ruby' |
| | - 'Big Ben' ♀H4 | EPfP GQui MBri NLar SKHP |
| | - 'Brussels Lace' | CAbP EPfP LRHS LSRN MBri MRav NLar SGol SHyH SLon SPoG WGrn WPat |
| | - 'Burgundy Lace' | CBcs EQua MBlu MBri NLar |
| | - 'Chantilly Lace' | CMil LRHS |
| | - Dart's Little Dot = 'Darlido'PBR | IVic LLHF LSRN MAsh NLar WPGP |
| | - 'Dharuma' | GKin LLHF LRHS MAsh SGol WPat |
| | - 'Dolly' | GQui |
| | - Early Sensation = 'Bulk'PBR | GKin LRHS MSwo SKHP WMoo |
| | - 'Everest' | CAbP CMil EPfP LRHS MAsh SHyH WPat |
| | - 'Floribunda' | CGHE ELan EPfP LRHS MAsh SHyH SPoG WPGP |
| | - 'Grandiflora' ♀H4 | Widely available |
| | - 'Great Escape' | NLar |
| | - 'Greenspire' | EPfP LRHS MAsh MBlu MRav SHyH WFar WPat |
| | - 'Harry's Souvenir' | NLar |
| | - 'Kyushu' ♀H4 | Widely available |
| | - 'Last Post' | GQui |
| | - 'Limelight'PBR ♀H4 | Widely available |
| | - 'Mathilde' | NLar |
| | - 'Mega Pearl' | LSRN NLar |
| | - 'Melody' | NLar |
| | - 'Mount Aso' | EWld GQui NBro WPGP |
| | - 'October Bride' | CEnd GQui MBri NLar WPGP |
| | - 'Papillon' | WPGP WPat |
| | - 'Pee Wee' | LLHF NLar |
| | - 'Phantom' ♀H4 | CBcs CMil EMil EPfP GKin LEdu LRHS LSRN LSqu MAsh MBri MDKP MRav NBro NCGa NLar SCoo SHyH SPoG WCot WPGP WPat |
| | - 'Pink Beauty'PBR (H) | CTri LSRN |
| | - Pink Diamond = 'Interhydia' ♀H4 | Widely available |
| | - 'Pink Jewel' | CWib LLHF WPat |
| | - Pinky-Winky = 'Dvppinky'PBR ♀H4 | CWGN EGxp EPPr EPfP GKin GQui IArd IVic LLHF LRHS MBlu NLar SGol SPoG |
| | - 'Praecox' | GQui MRav |
| | - 'Rosy Morn' | LRHS |
| § | - 'Ruby' | CBcs LSRN NPal |
| | - 'Silver Dollar' ♀H4 | EPfP LRHS LSRN MBri |
| | - 'Tardiva' | CBcs CBot CChe CDoC EBee EPfP EWTr GKin GQui LRHS MGos MRav NBro SDix SHyH SPer SRms SWvt WDin WFar WPGP WPat |
| | - 'Tender Rose' | NLar |
| | - 'Unique' ♀H4 | CBcs CDoC CDul CGHE CSpe EBee EPfP EWTr GQui LHop LRHS LSRN MAsh MMuc MRav NBro NCGa |

| |  |  |
|---|---|---|
| | | NLar SCoo SHyH SPer SPoG SSpi |
| | | WBor WDin WFar WGrn WGwG |
| | | WPGP WPat |
| | - Vanille Fraise | CAlb CBcs CDoC CEnd CWGN |
| | = 'Renhy'PBR | EPfP EWTr LDuc LRHS LSRN MAsh |
| | | MBri NCGa SBfd SGol SHyH SPoG |
| | | SWvt WGrn WPGP |
| | - 'Waterfall' | CLAP |
| | - 'White Goliath' | GQui NLar |
| | - 'White Lace' | CBcs NLar |
| | - 'White Lady' | CBcs |
| | - 'White Moth' | CAbP CBcs CWGN EPfP EQua |
| | | LLHF LRHS NBro NLar SHyH WPat |
| | - 'Wim's Red' **new** | EWTr MMHG SGol |
| | - 'Yuan-Yang' | WCru |
| | ***peruviana* × *seemanii*** | CEnd GKin IArd IDee SSta |
| | ***petiolaris*** | see *H. anomala* subsp. *petiolaris* |
| | 'Preziosa' ♀H3-4 | Widely available |
| * | ***quelpartensis*** | CRHN GQui |
| | - B&SWJ 8846 | WCru |
| | ***quercifolia*** ♀H3-4 | Widely available |
| | - 'Alice' | CPMA EPfP EPla ESwi LRHS MAsh |
| | | SGol SSpi WPGP |
| | - 'Alison' | EPfP SGol |
| I | - 'Amethyst' Dirr | SGol |
| | - 'Applause' **new** | IVic LRHS |
| | - 'Back Porch' | SGol |
| | - 'Burgundy' | CBcs CMil CPMA EPfP ESwi IArd |
| | | IVic NLar SGol WPGP |
| | - 'Flore Pleno' | see *H. quercifolia* Snowflake |
| | - 'Harmony' | CMil CPMA EPfP ESwi IArd LRHS |
| | | NLar SKHP SSta WPGP WPat |
| | - 'Ice Crystal' **new** | SGol |
| | - 'Lady Anne' | MRav WPGP |
| | - 'Little Honey' | SGol SSpi |
| | - Little Honey = 'Brihon' | CAbP EPfP LRHS MAsh SPoG |
| * | - 'Pee Wee' | CAbP CBcs CDoC CPMA EPfP LRHS |
| | | MAsh NLar SGol SHyH SKHP SLon |
| | | SPoG SReu SSta WPGP WPat |
| | - 'Sike's Dwarf' | CPMA IVic LTen MPkF MRav SGol |
| | - 'Snow Giant' | CPMA |
| | - Snow Queen | CBcs CDoC CDul CKno CPMA |
| | = 'Flemygea' | EBee ELan EPfP IVic LRHS MAsh |
| | | MBri MGos MPkF MRav NCGa NLar |
| | | SGol SHyH SKHP SLim SPer SPoG |
| | | SWvt WFar WGrn WPGP WPat |
| | - 'Snowdrift' | CMil CPMA |
| § | - Snowflake = 'Brido' (d) | CAbP CBcs CDoC CEnd CMil |
| | | CPMA CSPN CWGN EBee ELan |
| | | EPfP LRHS MAsh MGos MRav NLar |
| | | SHyH SKHP SLon SPer SPoG SSpi |
| | | SSta WPGP WPat |
| | - 'Stardust' | MMHG |
| | - 'Tennessee Clone' | CPMA ESwi NLar |
| | ***sargentiana*** | see *H. aspera* subsp. *sargentiana* |
| | ***scandens*** | NBro |
| | - B&SWJ 5448 | WCru |
| | - B&SWJ 5481 | WCru |
| | - B&SWJ 5496 | WCru |
| | - B&SWJ 5523 | WCru |
| | - B&SWJ 5602 | WCru |
| | - B&SWJ 5893 | WCru |
| | - B&SWJ 5929 | WCru |
| | - B&SWJ 6159 | WCru |
| | - B&SWJ 6317 | WCru |
| § | - subsp. ***chinensis*** | CBcs CPLG WFar |
| | - - B&SWJ 1488 | WCru |
| | - - B&SWJ 3214 | WCru |
| | - - B&SWJ 3410 from Taiwan | WCru |
| | - - B&SWJ 3420 | WCru |
| | - - B&SWJ 3423 | WCru |
| | - - B&SWJ 3487 | WCru |
| | - - B&SWJ 3869 | WCru |
| | - - BWJ 8000 from Sichuan | WCru |
| § | - - f. ***angustipetala*** | WCru |
| | B&SWJ 3454 | |
| | - - - B&SWJ 3553 | WCru |
| | - - - B&SWJ 3667 | WCru |
| | - - - B&SWJ 3733 | WCru |
| | - - - B&SWJ 3814 | WCru |
| | - - - B&SWJ 6038 | WCru |
| | from Yakushima | |
| | - - - B&SWJ 6041 | WCru |
| | - - - B&SWJ 6056 | WCru |
| | - - - B&SWJ 6787 | WCru |
| | - - - B&SWJ 6802 | WCru |
| | - - - B&SWJ 7121 | WCru |
| | - - - B&SWJ 7128 | WCru |
| | - - f. ***formosana*** | WCru |
| | B&SWJ 1488 | |
| | - - - B&SWJ 3271 | WCru |
| | - - - B&SWJ 7058 | EQua NLar WCru |
| | - - - B&SWJ 7097 | NLar WCru |
| | - - f. ***macrosepala*** | WCru |
| | B&SWJ 3423 | |
| | - - - B&SWJ 3476 | WCru |
| | - - - CWJ 12441 | WCru |
| | - - f. ***obovatifolia*** | WCru |
| | B&SWJ 3487b | |
| | - - - B&SWJ 3683 | WCru |
| | - - - B&SWJ 7121 | WCru |
| | - subsp. ***liukiuensis*** | WCru |
| | - - B&SWJ 11471 | WCru |
| | - - B&SWJ 6022 | WCru |
| | - 'Splash' (v) | CMil |
| | ***seemannii*** | Widely available |
| | ***serrata*** | CPLG CTri CWib WDin WKif |
| | - B&SWJ 4817 | WCru |
| | - B&SWJ 6241 | WCru |
| | - B&SWJ 6241A | WCru |
| | - 'Acuminata' | see *H. serrata* 'Bluebird' |
| | - 'Aigaku' (L) | CLAP CPLG |
| | - 'Aka Beni-yama' | GQui |
| | - 'Akabe-yama' | NBro NLar |
| | - Amacha Group | CGHE |
| | - - 'Amagi-amacha' (L) | CMil GQui NBro NLar |
| | - - 'Ō-amacha' | CMil GQui |
| | - 'Amagyana' (L) | CGHE CPLG |
| | - subsp. ***angustata*** **new** | WCru |
| | - Avelroz = 'Dolmyf' | SBfd |
| | - 'Belladonna' | GQui |
| | - 'Belle Deckle' | see *H. serrata* 'Blue Deckle' |
| | - 'Beni-gaku' (L) | CLAP CMil CPLG CTsd EGxp MAsh |
| | | NBro NLar WPGP |
| | - 'Beni-yama' (L) | CGHE CMil GQui WPGP |
| | - 'Blue Billow' (L) | NBro NLar |
| § | - 'Blue Deckle' (L) | CMHG CMac EQua GGal MAsh |
| | | MRav NBro SHyH WPGP |
| § | - 'Bluebird' (L) ♀H3-4 | Widely available |
| | - 'Chiba Cherry-lips' | WCru |
| | - 'Chiri-san Sue' (d) | WCru |
| | - 'Crûg Cobalt' **new** | WCru |
| | - 'Diadem' (L) ♀H3-4 | CMil CPLG EPfP EQua GQui LRHS |
| | | NBro SDix SHyH WPGP |
| | - dwarf white-flowered (L) | WCru |
| | - 'Forget Me Not' | GQui |
| | - 'Fuji Snowstorm' (v) | CMil |
| | - 'Fuji Waterfall' | see *H. serrata* 'Fuji-no-taki' |
| § | - 'Fuji-no-taki' (L/d) | CAbP ELon LLHF NCGa NEgg SMad |
| | | WBor WFar |

| | | |
|---|---|---|
| | – 'Golden Showers' (L) | NBro |
| | – 'Golden Sunlight'PBR (L) | CDoC GQui SLim SWvt |
| | – 'Graciosa' (L) | WPGP WPat |
| | – 'Grayswood' (L) 🏆H3-4 | CBcs CEnd CMac CPLG CSBt EPfP EQua GGal GQui LRHS MAsh MRav NBro SBrd SDix SGar SGol SHyH SLim SPer SSpi WBor WKif WPGP |
| | – 'Hakucho' (L/d) | NBro |
| | – 'Hallasan' misapplied | see *H. serrata* 'Maiko', 'Spreading Beauty' |
| | – 'Hallasan' ambig. | CMil |
| | – 'Hallasan' R. & J. de Belder (L) | CMil |
| | – 'Hime-benigaku' (L) | CLAP CMil MAsh |
| | – 'Impératrice Eugénie' (L) | GQui |
| | – 'Intermedia' (L) | CPLG NBro |
| | – 'Isusai-jaku' (L) | GQui |
| | – 'Kiyosumi' (L) | CDoC CEnd CGHE CLAP CMil CPLG ECre ELon EWTr GGal GQui MAsh NBir SBrt WBor WCot WCru WPGP WPat |
| | – 'Klaveren' | see *H. macrophylla* 'Klaveren' |
| | – 'Koreana' (L) | EQua MAsh |
| | – 'Kurenai' (L) | NBro NLar |
| | – 'Kurohime' (L) | CMil NBro |
| | – 'Macrosepala' (L) | MAsh |
| § | – 'Maiko' (L) | IArd |
| | – 'Midora' | CPLG |
| | – 'Midori' (L) | SHyH |
| | – 'Miranda' (L) 🏆H3-4 | CPLG CSam EPfP LRHS MAsh NBro NLar SHyH SSpi WFar |
| | – 'Miyama-yae-murasaki' (L/d) | CGHE CLAP CMil CPLG CSpe EQua MAsh WPGP |
| | – 'Momo Beni Yama' | CMil |
| | – 'Pretty Maiden' | see *H. serrata* 'Shichidanka' |
| | – 'Professeur Iida' (L) | WPGP |
| § | – 'Prolifera' (L/d) | CGHE CMil WPGP WPat |
| | – 'Pulchella' | see *H. serrata* 'Prolifera' |
| | – 'Ramis Pictis' (L) | EQua GQui NBro NLar WPGP |
| | – 'Rosalba' (L) 🏆H3-4 | CLAP CPLG ECre GGal IVic NBro WFar WSHC |
| | – 'Sapphirine' (L) | GQui |
| § | – 'Shichidanka' (L/d) | NBro WPat |
| | – 'Shichidanka-nishiki' (L/d/v) | CDoC CGHE CPLG ECre GQui SHyH WBor |
| | – 'Shinonome' (L/d) | CLAP CMil CPLG GQui WPGP |
| | – 'Shirofuji' (L/d) | CLAP CMil EWld MAsh WPGP WPat |
| | – 'Shiro-gaku' (L) | MAsh NBro NLar |
| | – 'Shirotae' (L/d) | CMil CPLG WPGP |
| | – 'Shōjō' | MAsh WPat |
| § | – 'Spreading Beauty' (L) | WPGP |
| § | – var. ***thunbergii*** (L) | GQui WFar |
| * | – – 'Plena' (L/d) | GQui WCru |
| | – 'Tiara' (L) 🏆H3-4 | CAbb CDul CMil CPLG GGal IVic LRHS LSRN MAsh NBir NBro NLar NMun SDix SHyH SLim WPGP WPat |
| | – 'Uzu-azisai' | WPGP |
| | – 'Woodlander' (L) | WPat |
| | – 'Yae-no-amacha' (L/d) | CPLG NBro WPGP |
| | – subsp. ***yezoensis*** | CMil GQui NLar |
| | – – 'Hime-Gaku' **new** | CMil |
| § | ***serratifolia*** | CHEx CPLG EPfP EPla IArd SSpi SSta WCru WFar WPGP |
| | – HCM 98056 | WCru |
| | ***sikokiana*** | CLAP |
| | – B&SWJ 5035 | WCru |
| | – B&SWJ 5855 | WCru |
| | – B&SWJ 11174 | WCru |
| | – B&SWJ 11381 | WCru |
| | 'Silver Slipper' | see *H. macrophylla* 'Ayesha' |
| | ***tiliifolia*** | see *H. anomala* subsp. *petiolaris* |
| | ***villosa*** | see *H. aspera* Villosa Group |
| | ***xanthoneura*** | see *H. heteromalla* |
| | 'You and Me' | MGos SCoo |
| | 'Zambia' | EPfP MGos SBrd SPoG WCot |

## *Hydrastis* (*Ranunculaceae*)

| | | |
|---|---|---|
| | ***canadensis*** | CArn GPoy LEdu |

## *Hydrocharis* (*Hydrocharitaceae*)

| | | |
|---|---|---|
| | ***morsus-ranae*** | CBen CHab CRow CWat EHon EWil LPBA MSKA MWts NPer SWat WPnP |

## *Hydrocleys* (*Alismataceae*)

| | | |
|---|---|---|
| | ***nymphoides*** | LLWG XBlo |

## *Hydrocotyle* (*Araliaceae*)

| | | |
|---|---|---|
| | ***asiatica*** | see *Centella asiatica* |
| | ***sibthorpioides*** 'Crystal Confetti' (v) | EPPr LLWG |
| | ***vulgaris*** | CWat EWil |

## *Hydrophyllum* (*Boraginaceae*)

| | | |
|---|---|---|
| | 'Spring Silver' | SKHP |

## *Hylomecon* (*Papaveraceae*)

| | | |
|---|---|---|
| * | ***hylomecoides*** | WCru |
| § | ***japonica*** | CLAP ECho ELan EWld GBBs GCra GEdr LEdu LRHS NBir NLBP NMen NRya WCru WFar |

## *Hylotelephium* see *Sedum*

## *Hymenanthera* see *Melicytus*

## *Hymenocallis* (*Amaryllidaceae*)

| | | |
|---|---|---|
| | 'Advance' | ECho LAma |
| § | ***caroliniana*** | ECho |
| | × ***festalis*** 🏆H1 | CCCN ECho EPfP LAma SPav WFar |
| | – 'Zwanenburg' | CGrW ECho |
| | ***harrisiana*** | CCCN CTca ECho EPfP WCot |
| | ***littoralis*** 'Variegata' | SPoG |
| § | ***longipetala*** | ECho |
| | ***occidentalis*** | see *H. caroliniana* |
| | 'Sulphur Queen' 🏆H1 | CGrW ECho SPav |

## *Hymenolepis* (*Asteraceae*)

| | | |
|---|---|---|
| | ***parviflora*** | see *Athanasia parviflora* |

## *Hymenosporum* (*Pittosporaceae*)

| | | |
|---|---|---|
| | ***flavum*** | EShb MOWG |

## *Hymenoxys* (*Asteraceae*)

| | | |
|---|---|---|
| | ***grandiflora*** | see *Tetraneuris grandiflora* |
| § | ***hoopesii*** | CMHG EBee EBla EGxp ELan EPfP GMaP LHop LRHS NBPC NBir NChi NEgg NPri SPer SPoG SRms WCot WFar WMnd WPer WWEG |

## *Hyophorbe* (*Arecaceae*)

| | | |
|---|---|---|
| | ***lagenicaulis*** | LPal |
| | ***verschaffeltii*** | LPal |

## *Hyoscyamus* (*Solanaceae*)

| | | |
|---|---|---|
| | ***niger*** | CArn GPoy MNHC |
| | ***reticulatus*** **new** | WCot |

## *Hypericum* ✿ (*Hypericaceae*)

| | | |
|---|---|---|
| | CC 4131 | CPLG |

| |  |  |
|---|---|---|
| | CC 4544 | CPLG |
| | ***acmosepalum*** | WPat |
| | ***aegypticum*** | ECho ECtt MAsh MHer NMen SBrt WAbe WFar WPer WThu |
| | ***amblycalyx*** | WAbe |
| | ***androsaemum*** | CArn CRWN ECha ELan MHer MRav MSwo NPer WDin WHfH WMoo WOut |
| § | – 'Albury Purple' | ELan EShb MRav NLar WMoo XLum |
| | – 'Autumn Blaze' | CBcs |
| § | – 'Dart's Golden Penny' | SPer |
| | – 'Excellent Flair' | NLar |
| § | – f. ***variegatum*** 'Mrs Gladis Brabazon' (v) | NBir NLar NPla WCot WHrl |
| | ***athoum*** | NBir WAbe WThu |
| | ***balearicum*** | WAbe XSen |
| | ***barbatum*** | WFar |
| § | ***beanii*** | GAuc |
| | ***bellum*** | EBee GCal SLon |
| | ***buckleyi*** | WAbe |
| | ***calycinum*** | CBcs CDul CMac CTri ECrN ELan ELon EPfP LBuc MGos MMuc MRav MWat NBlu NWea SBfd SEND SGol SPer SWvt WDin WGwG WMoo XLum |
| | – 'Brigadoon' | LRHS MAsh SGol |
| | – 'Senior' | LAst |
| | ***cerastioides*** | CMea CTri CWib EDif NGdn SRms WAbe WFar WPat WPer XSen |
| | ***coris*** | EWes MWat NMen SRms |
| | ***cuneatum*** | see *H. pallens* |
| | × ***cyathiflorum*** 'Gold Cup' | CMac LRHS MAsh |
| | × ***dummeri*** 'Peter Dummer' | NLar |
| | 'Eastleigh Gold' | CMac |
| | 'Elite Baby Green' | EPfP |
| | 'Elite Mayor' | EPfP |
| | 'Elite Sweet Lion' | EPfP |
| | ***elodes*** | CWat EWil LLWG MSKA |
| | ***empetrifolium*** 'Prostratum' | see *H. empetrifolium* subsp. *tortuosum* |
| § | – subsp. ***tortuosum*** | EWes |
| | ***foliosum*** NJM 08.031 **new** | WPGP |
| | ***forrestii*** ♀$^{H4}$ | EBee MMuc SEND WFar |
| N | ***fragile*** misapplied | see *H. olympicum* f. *minus* |
| | ***frondosum*** 'Buttercup' | NLar |
| | – 'Sunburst' | EBee EPfP |
| N | 'Gemo' | ECrN |
| | 'Gold Penny' | see *H. androsaemum* 'Dart's Golden Penny' |
| | 'Golden Beacon' | CBre CEnd CSpe LAst LRHS LSou NEgg NLar SBfd SPad SPoG WCot |
| | ***grandiflorum*** | see *H. kouytchense* |
| | ***henryi*** | MSnd SLPl |
| | – L 753 | SRms |
| | 'Hidcote' ♀$^{H4}$ | Widely available |
| | 'Hidcote Variegated' (v) | LRHS MAsh MCCP SLim SRms WFar |
| | ***hirsutum*** | CHab NMir |
| | × ***inodorum*** 'Albury Purple' | see *H. androsaemum* 'Albury Purple' |
| | – 'Autumn Surprise'$^{PBR}$ | NEgg NHol WHar |
| | – 'Dream' | NLar |
| | – 'Elstead' | ECtt ELan EPfP MGos MMHG MRav MWat NHol NLar NWea WDin |
| | – 'Hysan' | GGar |
| | – Magical Cherry = 'Kolmcherrip' **new** | EPfP |
| | – 'Rheingold' | MAsh |
| | – 'Ysella' | MRav |
| | ***japonicum*** | ECho EWes |
| | ***kalmianum*** | EWes WCot |
| | ***kamtschaticum*** | XLum |
| | ***kelleri*** | ITim |
| § | ***kouytchense*** ♀$^{H4}$ | CDul CMCN EBee ELon EPfP EQua EWes GQui LHop LRHS MAsh MMuc MRav SEND SPoG WCFE WCot WHrl WKif WPat |
| | ***lancasteri*** | EPfP LRHS MAsh SPoG WPat |
| | ***leschenaultii*** misapplied | see *H. addingtonii*, *H.* 'Rowallane' |
| | ***maclarenii*** | EWes |
| | Magical Beauty = 'Kolmbeau'$^{PBR}$ | ELon NHol NLar NPnk |
| | Magical Red = 'Kolmred'$^{PBR}$ | NLar SPoG |
| | Miracle Fantasy = 'Hymirfan' **new** | NLar |
| | Miracle Summer = 'Hymirsum' | EPfP NLar |
| | Miracle Wonder = 'Hymirwon' **new** | NLar |
| | × ***moserianum*** ♀$^{H4}$ | CBar CDul CMac EBee EPfP LRHS MRav NPer SLon SPer SRms WDin |
| | – 'Daybreak' | LRHS MAsh SPoG |
| § | – 'Tricolor' (v) | Widely available |
| | – 'Variegatum' | see *H.* × *moserianum* 'Tricolor' |
| | 'Mrs Brabazon' | see *H. androsaemum* f. *variegatum* 'Mrs Gladis Brabazon' |
| | ***nummularium*** | NBir NMen WAbe |
| | ***oblongifolium*** | CPLG |
| | – CC 4546 | WCot |
| | ***olympicum*** ♀$^{H4}$ | CEnt CTri ECha ECho ELan EPfP GJos LRHS MAsh MBrN MMuc MWat SEND SPer SRms SWvt WAbe WDin WFar WNew XLum XSen |
| | – 'Grandiflorum' | see *H. olympicum* f. *uniflorum* |
| § | – f. ***minus*** | CTri ECho ECtt NBlu NGdn SPlb SRms WHrl WPer XLum |
| § | – – 'Sulphureum' | CBot CChe CPrp ECho ELon EWes GMaP LRHS MLHP NBir SPer SRms SWvt WCFE |
| | – – 'Variegatum' (v) | CWan EWes LBee NBir SPoG SWvt WPat |
| § | – f. ***uniflorum*** | ECho NBro NVic |
| | – – 'Citrinum' ♀$^{H4}$ | CMea ECha ECtt EPfP LBee LRHS MRav MWat NBro SRot WAbe WCot WHoo WKif WPat |
| | ***orientale*** | EWes |
| § | ***pallens*** | ECho NMen WAbe |
| | ***patulum*** var. ***henryi*** Veitch ex Bean | see *H. beanii* |
| | ***perforatum*** | CArn CBod CHab CHby CWan EPfP EWil GPoy MHer MNHC NMir NMun SEND SIde WHer WHfH WJek WMoo WSFF |
| | ***polyphyllum*** | see *H. olympicum* f. *minus* |
| | – 'Citrinum' | see *H. olympicum* f. *minus* 'Sulphureum' |
| | – 'Grandiflorum' | see *H. olympicum* f. *uniflorum* |
| | ***prolificum*** | ECtt MMHG WCFE |
| | ***quadrangulum*** L. | see *H. tetrapterum*, *H. maculatum*, *H.* × *desetangsii* |
| | ***reptans*** misapplied | see *H. olympicum* f. *minus* |
| | ***reptans*** Dyer | CMea ECho EWes |
| § | 'Rowallane' ♀$^{H3}$ | CEnd CTri GCal SDix SMrm SSpi |
| | 'Sonnenbrut' **new** | SLPl |
| | ***stellatum*** | WFar |
| | ***subsessile*** | CPLG |
| | 'Sungold' | see *H. kouytchense* |
| § | ***tetrapterum*** | CArn LLWG |
| | ***tomentosum*** | XSen |
| | ***trichocaulon*** | EWes |

| | |
|---|---|
| ***uralum*** HWJ 520 | WCru |
| ***xylosteifolium*** | SLon |

## *Hypocalymma* (*Myrtaceae*)

| | |
|---|---|
| ***angustifolium*** | MOWG |

## *Hypocalyptus* (*Papilionaceae*)

| | |
|---|---|
| ***sophoroides*** | SPlb |

## *Hypochaeris* (*Asteraceae*)

| | |
|---|---|
| ***maculata*** | WHer |
| ***radicata*** | CHab EWil NMir |

## *Hypocyrta* see *Nematanthus*

## *Hypoestes* (*Acanthaceae*)

| | |
|---|---|
| ***aristata*** | CPLG EShb |
| - white-flowered | WHil |
| § ***phyllostachya*** (v) ♀H1 | EShb |
| ***sanguinolenta*** misapplied | see *H. phyllostachya* |

## *Hypolepis* (*Dennstaedtiaceae*)

| | |
|---|---|
| ***ambigua*** | WRic |
| ***millefolium*** | GGar LRHS WCot |
| ***punctata*** | EFer |
| ***rufobarbata*** | WRic |

## *Hypoxis* (*Hypoxidaceae*)

| | |
|---|---|
| ***hemerocallidea*** 'Bloemfontein' | ECho |
| ***hirsuta*** | CCCN ECho WCot |
| ***hygrometrica*** | ECho ECou IBal NMen WThu |
| ***iridiflora*** | see *H. obtusa* |
| ***krebsii*** | ECho LLHF |
| § ***obtusa*** | LLHF |
| - 'Harrismith' | ECho |
| ***parvula*** | CFee CTca NMen |
| - var. ***albiflora*** | ITim |
| § - - 'Hebron Farm Biscuit' | CBro CCCN ECho EWes GEdr WAbe WFar |
| ***rigidula*** 'Harrismith' | ECho |
| ***villosa*** | ECho |

## *Hypoxis* × *Rhodohypoxis* see × *Rhodoxis*

| | |
|---|---|
| ***H. parvula* × *R. baurii*** | see × *Rhodoxis hybrida* |

## *Hypsela* (*Campanulaceae*)

| | |
|---|---|
| sp. | CFee |
| ***longiflora*** | see *H. reniformis* |
| § ***reniformis*** | ECho EDAr GAbr GGar LBee LLWG LRHS MAsh MRav NWCA WFar |

## *Hyssopus* ✿ (*Lamiaceae*)

| | |
|---|---|
| ***officinalis*** | CArn CHby CSev ECha EGHP ELan ELau EPfP GPoy LBuc LHop MBri MCot MHer MLHP MNHC MRav NBir SBfd SEND SIde SPlb SPoG SVic SWal WHfH WJek WPer XLum XSen |
| - f. ***albus*** | CWan ECha EGHP ELau EPfP EWhm GPoy MHer MNHC SIde SPlb WHfH WJek WPer XLum XSen |
| - subsp. ***aristatus*** | CArn EBee ELau ELon EPfP EWhm GPoy LLWP LRHS MHer MNHC SBrt SIde SPoG WJek XLum XSen |
| - 'Blaue Wolke' | GBin |
| - 'Roseus' | CEnt ECha EGHP ELau EPfP EWhm GPoy LLWP MHer MNHC SEND SIde SPoG WJek WPer WSHC XLum XSen |

## *Hysterionica* (*Asteraceae*)

| | |
|---|---|
| ***pulchella*** new | CPBP |

## *Hystrix* (*Poaceae*)

| | |
|---|---|
| ***patula*** | CKno CSam EHoe EPPr EShb LLWP MLLN MMoz MNrw MWhi SPlb SSvw WPer WTin XLum |

# I

## *Iberis* (*Brassicaceae*)

| | |
|---|---|
| ***aurosica*** subsp. ***cantabrica*** new | GKev |
| - 'Sweetheart' | EDAr GEdr WFar |
| ***candolleana*** | see *I. pruitii* Candolleana Group |
| ***commutata*** | see *I. sempervirens* |
| 'Correvoniana' | MAsh |
| ***gibraltarica*** | ECho SRms WGor |
| - 'Betty Swainson' | EWld SBch SMrm SPhx SUsu |
| § ***pruitii*** Candolleana Group | ECho GEdr NMen WAbe WFar |
| ***saxatilis*** | ECho LRHS WThu |
| ***semperflorens*** | WCFE WWEG |
| § ***sempervirens*** ♀H4 | CMea CTri CWib ECho ELan EPfP IFoB LAst MAsh MMuc MWat NBro NOrc NVic SEND SRms SWal WCFE WFar WHoo WPer XLum |
| - 'Compacta' | ECho |
| - 'Elfenreigen' | GCal |
| - 'Fischbeck' | SRot |
| - 'Golden Candy' | CTri EHoe MAvo SPoG WFar |
| - 'Little Gem' | see *I. sempervirens* 'Weisser Zwerg' |
| - 'Pygmaea' | ECho NMen |
| - Schneeflocke | see *I. sempervirens* 'Snowflake' |
| - 'Snow Cushion' | EDAr GEdr WWEG |
| § - 'Snowflake' ♀H4 | CBar ECho ELon EPfP GEdr IFoB MAsh MWat NBlu NBre NPri SBch SPer SPoG SWvt WFar WRHF XLum |
| - 'Tahoe' new | EDAr |
| § - 'Weisser Zwerg' | CMea ECha ECho ECtt ELan GEdr LBee MHer MRav MWat NMen NRya SBch SPoG SRms WHoo |

## *Ichthyoselmis* (*Papaveraceae*)

| | |
|---|---|
| § ***macrantha*** | CDes CEnt CLAP ECha EPfP EWld GCra LAma LHop MNrw WCru WPGP WSHC |

## *Idesia* (*Salicaceae*)

| | |
|---|---|
| ***polycarpa*** | CAbP CDul CMCN EPfP LHop MMuc NLar SSpi WDin WFar WPat |

## *Ilex* ✿ (*Aquifoliaceae*)

| | |
|---|---|
| N × ***altaclerensis*** | WFar |
| - 'Atkinsonii' (m) | WWHy |
| - 'Balearica' (f) | SBrd |
| - 'Barterberry' (f) | WWHy |
| § - 'Belgica Aurea' (f/v) ♀H4 | CAlb CBcs CDoC CPMA CTho EBee EPfP EQua MBri MSwo NHol NWea WFar WWHy |
| - 'Camelliifolia' (f) ♀H4 | CAlb CDul CTho EBee ELan EPfP LMaj MBlu MBri MWat NEgg NLar NPCo NWea SBrd SGol WFar WWHy |
| - 'Camelliifolia Variegata' (f/v) new | CMac |
| - 'Golden King' (f/v) ♀H4 | Widely available |

| |  |  |
|---|---|---|
| | - 'Hendersonii' (f) | NPCo SBrd WWHy |
| | - 'Hodginsii' (m) ♀$^{H4}$ | CTri MRav WFar WWHy |
| | - 'Lady Valerie' (f/v) | IArd WWHy |
| | - 'Lawsoniana' (f/v) ♀$^{H4}$ | Widely available |
| | - 'Marnockii' (f) | WWHy |
| | - 'Purple Shaft' (f) | CMCN EQua MBlu |
| | - 'Ripley Gold' (f/v) | LRHS MBri WWHy |
| | - 'Silver Sentinel' | see *I.* × *altaclerensis* 'Belgica Aurea' |
| | - 'W.J. Bean' (f) | WWHy |
| | - 'Wilsonii' (f) | EPfP NLar NPCo NWea WWHy |
| | ***aquifolium*** ♀$^{H4}$ | CBar CBcs CCVT CDul CHab CPMA CRWN CSBt CTho CTri CWib EBee ECrN EPfP MBri MGos MMuc MRav MSwo NLar NPri NWea SBfd SEND SEWo SGol SPer WDin WMoo WMou |
| | - 'Alaska' (f) | CAlb CCVT CDoC CDul CMCN CPMA LAst LBuc MAsh NLar NSti SBfd SGol SWvt WFar WGob WWHy |
| | - 'Amber' (f) ♀$^{H4}$ | CTri EQua NPCo WWHy |
| | - 'Angustifolia' (f) | LRHS WCFE WFar WWHy |
| | - 'Angustifolia' (m or f) | EPfP MWat SPoG WFar |
| | - 'Angustimarginata Aurea' (m/v) | NPCo |
| | - 'Argentea Longifolia' (m/v) | WWHy |
| § | - 'Argentea Marginata' (f/v) ♀$^{H4}$ | Widely available |
| § | - 'Argentea Marginata Pendula' (f/v) | CDoC CMac CTri ELan EPfP LRHS MAsh MRav NLar NWea SPer SRms WFar WPat WWHy |
| | - 'Argentea Pendula' | see *I. aquifolium* 'Argentea Marginata Pendula' |
| | - 'Argentea Variegata' | see *I. aquifolium* 'Argentea Marginata' |
| | - 'Atlas' (m) | CBcs CDoC LBuc WWHy |
| | - 'Aurea Marginata' (f/v) | CAlb CMac EPfP LBuc MGos NPCo SEWo WCFE WDin WFar WPat |
| | - 'Aurea Marginata Pendula' (f/v) | CDoC WPat |
| | - 'Aurea Marginata Stricta' (f/v) | WWHy |
| | - 'Aurea Regina' | see *I. aquifolium* 'Golden Queen' |
| | - 'Aureovariegata Pendula' | see *I. aquifolium* 'Weeping Golden Milkmaid' |
| | - 'Aurifodina' (f) | NPCo WWHy |
| | - 'Bacciflava' (f) | CAlb CBcs CDoC CDul CMac CTho CTri ELan ELon EPfP IArd LMaj LTen MBlu MBri MGos MRav NEgg NLar NPCo NWea SLim SPer SPoG SRms SWvt WCFE WDin WFar WWHy |
| | - 'Bokrijk' (f/v) | WWHy |
| | - 'Bowland' (f/v) | NHol |
| | - 'Chris Whittle' | NHol |
| | - 'Cookii' (f) | WWHy |
| | - 'Crassifolia' (f) | CWib IArd SMad WWHy |
| | - 'Crispa' (m) | WWHy |
| § | - 'Crispa Aurea Picta' (m/v) | WWHy |
| | - 'Crispa Aureomaculata' | see *I. aquifolium* 'Crispa Aurea Picta' |
| | - 'Elegantissima' (m/v) | CPMA SCoo WWHy |
| | - 'Fastigiata Sartori' | NLar |
| | - 'Ferox' (m) | ELan EPfP LRHS SPer SPoG WDin WWHy |
| | - 'Ferox Argentea' (m/v) ♀$^{H4}$ | Widely available |
| * | - 'Ferox Argentea Picta' (m/v) | WFar WWHy |
| | - 'Ferox Aurea' (m/v) | CDoC CPMA CWib EBee ELan ELon EPfP EPla MAsh NEgg NPCo SBrd SPer WWHy |
| § | - 'Flavescens' (f) | CBot EPfP EQua MBlu NPCo SBrd |
| | - 'Frogmore Silver' (m/v) | EQua |
| | - 'Gold Flash' (f/v) | LRHS MGos NEgg NLar WDin WWHy |
| I | - 'Golden Hedgehog' | LRHS SPer SPoG WWHy |
| | - 'Golden Milkboy' (m/v) | CAlb CMac ELan EPfP MAsh MGos SGol WDin WPat WWHy |
| § | - 'Golden Queen' (m/v) ♀$^{H4}$ | CDoC CMac CWib IArd MGos NBir NPCo SRms WPat WWHy |
| | - 'Golden Tears' (f/v) | WWHy |
| | - 'Golden van Tol' (f/v) | CAlb CBcs CDoC CSBt CTri CWSG ECrN ELan ELon EPfP LAst LRHS LTen MAsh MBlu MGos MSwo NEgg NLar NPCo SCoo SGol SRms WDin WGob WMoo WWHy |
| | - 'Green Minaret' | IVic |
| § | - 'Green Pillar' (f) | EPfP WWHy |
| | - 'Green Spire' | see *I. aquifolium* 'Green Pillar' |
| | - 'Handsworth New Silver' (f/v) ♀$^{H4}$ | Widely available |
| | - 'Harpune' (f) | IArd WWHy |
| § | - 'Hascombensis' | CDoC LHop NMen NWea WWHy |
| | - 'Hastata' (m) | CWib IArd IDee MRav WWHy |
| | - 'Ingramii' (m/v) | WWHy |
| | - 'Integrifolia' (f) | WWHy |
| | - 'J.C. van Tol' (f) ♀$^{H4}$ | Widely available |
| | - 'Latispina' (f) | WWHy |
| | - 'Laurifolia' (m) | IArd |
| | - 'Lichtenthalii' (f) | IArd IVic NPCo |
| | - 'Madame Briot' (f/v) ♀$^{H4}$ | Widely available |
| | - moonlight holly | see *I. aquifolium* 'Flavescens' |
| | - 'Myrtifolia' (f) | NEgg NPCo |
| | - 'Myrtifolia' (m) | ELan EPfP GCal MGos NEgg NLar NPCo SCoo SMad WFar WMoo WWHy |
| | - 'Myrtifolia Aurea' (m/v) | NEgg SWvt WFar WGob |
| | - 'Myrtifolia Aurea Maculata' (m/v) ♀$^{H4}$ | CDoC CPMA CSam CTri EBee ELan EPfP LRHS MAsh NEgg NPCo NWea SMad SPoG SWvt WFar WPat WWHy |
| | - 'Ovata' (m) | WWHy |
| | - 'Ovata Aurea' (m/v) | WWHy |
| | - 'Pendula' (f) | MRav |
| | - 'Pendula Mediopicta' | see *I. aquifolium* 'Weeping Golden Milkmaid' |
| | - 'Pyramidalis' (f) ♀$^{H4}$ | CDoC CDul CMac CTri EBee ELan EWTr LRHS MAsh MBri MGos NLar NPCo NWea SBrd SGol SRms WDin WFar WMoo WWHy |
| | - 'Pyramidalis Aureomarginata' (f/v) | CDoC MBri NLar |
| | - 'Pyramidalis Fructu Luteo' (f) ♀$^{H4}$ | MAsh SBrd |
| | - 'Recurva' (m) | CMac WWHy |
| | - 'Rederly' (f) | WWHy |
| | - 'Rubricaulis Aurea' (f/v) | NLar NPCo WGob WWHy |
| | - 'Scotica' (f) | NWea WWHy |
| | - Siberia = 'Limsi'[PBR] (f) | IVic WWHy |
| | - 'Silver King' | see *I. aquifolium* 'Silver Queen' |
| | - 'Silver Milkboy' (f/v) | ELan EPfP MBlu WFar WWHy |
| | - 'Silver Milkmaid' (f/v) | CDoC EBee EPfP LAst LRHS NEgg NHol SBrd SLim SPer SWvt WGob WMoo WMou WWHy |
| § | - 'Silver Queen' (m/v) ♀$^{H4}$ | Widely available |
| | - 'Silver Sentinel' | see *I.* × *altaclerensis* 'Belgica Aurea' |
| | - 'Silver van Tol' (f/v) | CDoC CPMA ELan LAst MAsh NEgg NLar NPCo NPer NWea WFar WWHy |
| | - 'Somerset Cream' (f/v) | CPMA CTri CWib WWHy |

| | | |
|---|---|---|
| | - 'Sterntaler' | IVic |
| § | - 'Weeping Golden Milkmaid' (f/v) | MRav WPat |
| | - 'White Cream' (m/v) | IVic MBri |
| | - 'Wichtel' | IVic |
| | - 'Yellow Star' (f/v) | IVic |
| | × ***aquipernyi*** Dragon Lady = 'Meschick' (f) | CAlb CDoC NLar NPCo WWHy |
| | × ***attenuata*** | WFar |
| | - 'Sunny Foster' (f/v) | CDoC CMCN EPfP EPla WFar |
| § | ***bioritsensis*** | CMCN CTri |
| | 'Brilliant' (f) | NPCo |
| | China Boy = 'Mesdob' (m) | LMaj |
| | 'Clusterberry' (f) | NPCo |
| | ***colchica*** | CMCN |
| | ***cornuta*** | EPfP ERom WFar |
| | - B&SWJ 8756 | WCru |
| | - 'Burfordii' (f) | IArd |
| | - 'Ira S. Nelson' (f/v) | IArd IDee |
| | ***crenata*** | CMCN CTri ERom GCra MGos NHol NWea STrG WDin WFar |
| * | - 'Akagi' | WFar |
| | - 'Aureovariegata' | see *I. crenata* 'Variegata' |
| | - 'Convexa' (f) ♀H4 | CAlb EPfP MAsh MRav NEgg NPCo NWea WFar WGwG WPat |
| | - 'Convexed Gold' (f/v) | LRHS MBri SPoG |
| | - 'Dwarf Pagoda' (f) | IVic |
| | - 'Fastigiata' (f) | CDoC EPfP LRHS MAsh MBri MGos NHol NLar SCoo SLim SPer SPoG WFar |
| * | - 'Glory Gem' (f) | CBcs |
| | - 'Golden Gem' (f/v) ♀H4 | CAlb CDoC CDul CSBt CTri EBee ELan ELon EPfP IVic LAst LRHS LTen MAsh MGos NWea SCoo SGol SLim SPer SPoG SWvt WDin WFar WGwG WPat WWHy |
| * | - 'Green Hedge' | CAlb LBuc |
| | - 'Helleri' (f) | EPfP WPat |
| | - 'Hetzii' (f) | NLar |
| | - 'Ivory Tower' (f) | NEgg NPCo |
| | - 'Luteovariegata' | see *I. crenata* 'Variegata' |
| | - 'Mariesii' (f) | CMac EBee MBlu |
| I | - 'Pyramidalis' (f) | MRav NWea |
| | - 'Rotundifolia' (m) | CAlb |
| § | - 'Shiro-fukurin' (f/v) | CMCN CMHG ELan EPfP GQue LRHS |
| | - 'Snowflake' | see *I. crenata* 'Shiro-fukurin' |
| | - 'Stokes' (m) | NLar |
| § | - 'Variegata' (v) | CMac EPfP EPla LRHS |
| | ***dimorphophylla*** | CBcs CDoC CMac SMad |
| | ***dipyrena*** | CBcs IArd |
| | 'Doctor Kassab' (f) | CMCN |
| | 'Elegance' (f) | MBlu WFar |
| | 'Good Taste' (f) | CDoC WFar WWHy |
| | ***hascombensis*** | see *I. aquifolium* 'Hascombensis' |
| | ***hookeri*** | CDoC |
| | 'Indian Chief' (f) | NLar NPCo WFar |
| | ***insignis*** | see *I. kingiana* |
| § | ***kingiana*** | WFar |
| | × ***koehneana*** | CBot CDul ELan |
| | - 'Chestnut Leaf' (f) ♀H4 | CCVT CDoC CFee CLnd CMCN EBtc EPfP EQua MRav NPCo SSta WFar WGrn WMou WWHy |
| | - 'Wirt L. Winn' (f) | WWHy |
| | ***latifolia*** | CBcs CHEx CMCN NLar SMad WPGP |
| * | 'Little Diamond' | LSRN |
| | 'Lydia Morris' (f) | CSam WFar |
| | ***maximowicziana*** var. ***kanehirae*** | CBcs WWHy |
| | × ***meserveae*** Blue Angel = 'Conang' (f) | CBcs CDoC CDul CMac CWSG EBee ELan EPfP IFoB MBri MRav MWat NEgg NHol NLar NPCo NWea SPoG SRms WDin WFar WMoo WWHy |
| | - Blue Bunny = 'Meseal' (f) | IVic |
| | - 'Blue Girl' (f) | CTri |
| | - Blue Maid = 'Mesid' (f) | EWTr NLar NPCo WWHy |
| | - Blue Prince = 'Conablu' (m) | CBcs CDoC CDul CMac EBee ELan LBuc LRHS MBlu NEgg NHol NLar NWea SLim SPer SPoG WDin WFar WWHy |
| | - Blue Princess = 'Conapri' (f) | CBcs CMac ELan EPfP LBuc LRHS MBlu MRav NHol NLar NPCo NPri NSti NWea SCoo SLim SPer SPoG WDin WMoo WWHy |
| | - Blue Stallion = 'Mesan' (m) | CAlb CDoC |
| | - Castle Spire = 'Hachfee'PBR | IVic NLar |
| | - Castle Wall = 'Hecken Star'PBR | IVic |
| | - Golden Girl = 'Mesgolg' (f) | WWHy |
| | - 'Golden Prince' (m) **new** | IArd |
| | - 'Goliath' (f) | WWHy |
| | - 'Heckenpracht'PBR | IVic |
| | ***myrtifolia*** | CMac MAsh MRav NPri |
| | 'Nellie R. Stevens' (f) | CAlb CDoC ECrN LMaj LTen NLar NWea SCoo WWHy |
| | ***opaca*** | CMCN |
| | ***perado*** subsp. ***perado*** | CBcs NPCo |
| | - subsp. ***platyphylla*** | CBcs CMCN MBlu SArc WWHy |
| | ***pernyi*** | CDoC CMCN CMac CTri EPfP LRHS MAsh SBrd SLon SPoG WFar WWHy |
| | - var. ***veitchii*** | see *I. bioritsensis* |
| | ***rugosa*** | WWHy |
| | 'September Gem' (f) | CMCN NPCo |
| | ***serrata*** | CMac CMen |
| | - 'Koshobai' | CMen |
| | - 'Leucocarpa' | CMen |
| | ***spinigera*** | CBcs |
| | ***suaveolens*** | CMCN |
| | ***verticillata*** | CMCN LRHS NEgg WDin WFar |
| | - (f) | CBcs EPfP MMHG NLar NWea WFar |
| | - (m) | EPfP MMHG NLar NWea |
| | - 'Christmas Cheer' (f) | WFar |
| | - 'Maryland Beauty' (f) | CPMA |
| | - 'Southern Gentleman' (m) | CPMA MBlu |
| | - 'Winter Gold' (f) | CPMA |
| | - 'Winter Red' (f) | CMCN CPMA EBee LTen MBlu |
| | ***vomitoria*** | CMCN EBtc EShb |
| | × ***wandoensis*** | CMCN WWHy |
| | 'Washington' (f) | NWad WWHy |
| | ***yunnanensis*** | GQui IArd |

## *Iliamna* see *Sphaeralcea*

## *Illicium* (*Schisandraceae*)

| | |
|---|---|
| ***anisatum*** | CBcs CDoC CMac CPLG EPfP IGor NLar WFar WPGP WSHC |
| ***floridanum*** | CBcs CPne EPfP GKin MBri NLar SBrt SSpi WPat |
| - f. ***album*** | EPfP |
| - 'Halley's Comet' | NLar |
| ***henryi*** | CDoC CGHE CMHG CPLG CWib EPfP NLar SSpi WPGP WSHC |
| aff. ***henryi*** | CBcs |
| ***majus*** WWJ 11919 **new** | WCru |
| ***simonsii*** | CPLG MBlu |

- BWJ 8024 WCru
'Woodland Ruby' NLar

## *Ilysanthes* see *Lindernia*

## *Impatiens* ✿ (*Balsaminaceae*)

CC 4980 CPLG
DJHC 98115 CDes WCru WPGP
***apiculata*** GCal
***arguta*** CDes CFir CLAP CPLG CPom CSpe EBee EPPr EShb GCal MDKP SBrt WPGP
***auricoma*** WCot
- 'Jungle Gold' EShb
***auricoma* × *bicaudata*** EShb WDib
***bicaudata*** new CSpe
***congolensis*** CCCN
'Fiesta Salmon'PBR see *I.* 'Sparkler Salmon'
***flanaganae*** CFir WPGP
***forrestii*** CLAP
***gomphophylla*** CFir
(Harmony Series) Harmony Dark Red = 'Danhardkrd' WGor
- Harmony Orange Star WGor
- Harmony Pink Smile = 'Danhar267' WGor
- Harmony Raspberry Cream = 'Danharras' WGor
- Harmony Violet = 'Danharvio' WGor
***keilii*** WDib
***kerriae*** B&SWJ 7219 WCru
***kilimanjari*** subsp. ***kilimanjari*** CDoC CSpe GCal
- 'Pink Candy' CSpe
***kilimanjari* × *pseudoviola*** CDoC CFee CSpe
***langbianensis*** HWJ 1054 WCru
'Linda's White' GCal
***macrophylla*** B&SWJ 10157 WCru
***namchabarwensis*** CDes CPom CSpe MCot SBch WCot WPGP
***niamniamensis*** CHll EBak EShb WCot WDib
- 'Congo Cockatoo' CDTJ CDoC CHEx CTsd EOHP GCal NPer SRms
- 'Golden Cockatoo' (v) CDTJ CDoC CHll EBak EShb
***noli-tangere*** WSFF
***omeiana*** CCCN CDes CFir CHEx CLAP CPom EBee EPPr ESwi EWld GCal GEdr IGor LEdu LRHS MNrw MSCN NLar NMyG SBch SBig SUsu WBor WCot WCru WHil WPGP WPtf
- DJH C98492 WCru
- 'Ice Storm' GCal
- silver-leaved CDes CHEx CLAP CSpe MDKP WCru WPGP
***parasitica*** WDib
***platypetala*** B&SWJ 9722 WCru
***pseudoviola*** SDix
***puberula*** CFir
- HWJK 2063 CDes EBee WCru WPGP
***repens*** ♀H1 WDib
***rothii*** CFir CPom EShb GCal
'Salmon'PBR (Fiesta Series) see *I.* 'Sparkler Salmon'
***scabrida*** CSpe
***sodenii*** CDTJ CFir CSpe EShb GCal SBHP WDib
§ 'Sparkler Salmon'PBR (Fiesta Series) (d) LAst
***stenantha*** CFir
***tinctoria*** CFir CGHE CHEx CHll CPLG CPom CSpe EBee EShb GCal GCra MNrw WCot WPGP WWlt
- subsp. ***elegantissima*** CFee
- subsp. ***tinctoria*** IFro
***tuberosa*** EShb WDib
***ugandensis*** CFir GCal
***uniflora*** CDes CFir EBee GCal WPGP
Velvetea = 'Secret Love' CCCN
***walleriana*** Fiesta Orange Spice = 'Balfieorce' (Fiesta Series) (d) LAst

## *Imperata* (*Poaceae*)

***cylindrica*** CMen XLum
- 'Red Baron' see *I. cylindrica* 'Rubra'
§ - 'Rubra' Widely available

## *Incarvillea* (*Bignoniaceae*)

***arguta*** CBot LLHF
***brevipes*** see *I. mairei*
***compacta*** BWJ 7620 WCru
***delavayi*** CBcs CBot CSBt CWib EBee ECha ECho ELan ELon EPfP EPot GAuc GMaP MGos MRav MSCN MWhi NBPC NBir NLar NVic SPad SPer SPoG SRms SWvt WFar XLum
- 'Alba' see *I. delavayi* 'Snowtop'
- 'Bees' Pink' EBee EDAr EPot GGar GKev LRHS NLar
- 'Rose' LRHS
§ - 'Snowtop' CBot EBee ELan EPfP EPot GCal GKev GMaP LRHS LTen NBPC NBir NLar SPer SWvt WCot WFar WWEG XLum
***forrestii*** GKev
***grandiflora*** EBee ELan GKev
***lutea*** BWJ 7784 WCru
§ ***mairei*** CTsd ECho EDAr EPfP GEdr GLam LRHS NLar WHil WPer XLum
- SDR 3028 GKev
- var. ***mairei*** f. ***multifoliata*** see *I. zhongdianensis*
- pink-flowered GCal
***olgae*** EPfP NLar
***sinensis*** 'Cheron' CSpe
***younghusbandii*** GEdr
- CC 5973 GKev
§ ***zhongdianensis*** CPBP EBee GEdr GKev LRHS MDKP NWCA
- ACE 1600 GLam
- BWJ 7692 WCru
- BWJ 7978 EDAr WCru

## *Indigofera* (*Papilionaceae*)

***amblyantha*** ♀H4 CBcs CPLG EBee ELon EPfP LRHS MBlu MBri MMHG NLar SEND SKHP SPlb SSpi WDin WSHC
***australis*** MOWG
***balfouriana*** WSHC
- BWJ 7851 WCru
***cassioides*** WCru
***decora*** f. ***alba*** EPfP
***dielsiana*** EPfP MWea WKif WPGP
'Dosua' SEND SLPl
***gerardiana*** see *I. heterantha*
***hebepetala*** EPfP SKHP WPGP WSHC
§ ***heterantha*** ♀H4 Widely available

| | |
|---|---|
| - from China | MBri |
| ***himalayensis*** | CMHG CPLG |
| - Yu 10941 | WPGP WSHC |
| - 'Silk Road' | EPfP LBuc LRHS MBri MGos |
| ***kirilowii*** | EPfP MBri MOWG NLar WPGP WSHC |
| ***pendula*** | CMHG CPLG CWGN EPfP LRHS MOWG SEND SSpi WKif WPGP WSHC |
| - B&SWJ 7741 | WCru |
| ***potaninii*** | CMac CPLG EPfP LRHS MOWG SBrt WHer |
| ***pseudotinctoria*** | CCCN EPfP MHer SEND SRms |
| ***subverticillata*** | EBee WPGP WSHC |
| ***tinctoria*** | CArn |

## *Indocalamus* (*Poaceae*)

| | |
|---|---|
| ***latifolius*** | EPPr EPla MMoz MMuc MWht NLar WJun |
| - 'Hopei' | EPla |
| ***longiauritus*** | EPla |
| ***solidus*** | see *Bonia solida* |
| § ***tessellatus*** ♀H4 | CAbb CDoC CEnt CHEx EAmu ELon ENBC EPfP EPla MBri MCCP MMoz MWht NGdn NLar SEND SMad WDyG WFar WJun WMoo WPGP WPnP |
| - f. ***hamadae*** | EPla MMoz MWht WDyG WJun |

## *Inula* (*Asteraceae*)

| | |
|---|---|
| ***acaulis*** | WCot |
| ***barbata*** | LRHS |
| ***cordata*** new | LRHS |
| ***crithmoides*** | WHer |
| ***dysenterica*** | see *Pulicaria dysenterica* |
| ***ensifolia*** | CBcs ELan GJos MDKP MNFA NBro NWCA SLPl WWEG XLum |
| - 'Compacta' | ECho GCal LRHS |
| - 'Gold Star' | CMac EBee ECho MBNS MRav MWat NBPC NBid NBir NEgg SPet SPoG WFar WMnd WPer WWEG |
| ***glandulosa*** | see *I. orientalis* |
| ***helenium*** | CArn CHab CHby CPrp CSev EBee ELau GAbr GPoy ILis LEdu LPBA MHer MNHC NBPC NBid NBir NLar NMir SPoG SRms WGwG WHer WHfH WJek WMoo WPer |
| - 'Goliath' | SMrm |
| ***hirta*** | NBre WPer |
| ***hookeri*** | CBre CChe CMea CSam CSev EBee ECha ELan GCal GJos GMaP GMac IFro LEdu MLHP MLLN MMuc MNFA NBid NChi NDov NHol NPer NSti SAga SDix SEND WAbb WBrk WFar |
| - GWJ 9033 | WCru |
| ***macrocephala*** misapplied | see *I. royleana* |
| ***magnifica*** | Widely available |
| - 'Sonnenstrahl' ♀H4 | SEND SPhx |
| ***oculus-christi*** | CDes EBee EWes NBre WCot |
| - MESE 437 | EPPr |
| § ***orientalis*** | CMea EBee EPfP GJos MBri MNFA NBre NGBl NLar SPad WFar WJek WMnd WPer WWEG |
| ***racemosa*** | CTca EPPr EPla EWes GBin GCal IBlr MNrw NBid SMrm SPlb WBor WFar |
| - 'Sonnenspeer' | EBee GMac NBid NBre NLar SLPl SMad WPer WPtf |
| ***rhizocephala*** | MDKP WPer |
| § ***royleana*** | CEnt GCal GMac MDKP MNrw MRav NBre |
| ***salicina*** | EBee |

## *Iochroma* (*Solanaceae*)

| | |
|---|---|
| § ***australe*** | CHll CSpe EWld IRar LRHS MOWG SGar SVen |
| § - 'Andean Snow' | CHll CPLG EShb |
| § - 'Bill Evans' | CPLG EShb |
| ***cyaneum*** | CCCN CDoC CHll EWld MOWG SBrd WHil |
| - purple-flowered | CHll |
| ***gesnerioides*** | WCot |
| - 'Coccineum' | CCCN CDoC CHll |
| - - B&SWJ 10255 | WCru |
| § ***grandiflorum*** | CCCN CDoC CHll CSev MOWG SEND SGar |
| ***warscewiczii*** | see *I. grandiflorum* |

## *Ipheion* ✿ (*Alliaceae*)

| | |
|---|---|
| 'Alberto Castillo' | Widely available |
| ***dialystemon*** | ECho EPot LLHF WAbe |
| ***hirtellum*** | WCot |
| 'Jessie' | CBro CDes CMea CPom CPrp EBee ECho EPot ERCP LAma LHop LLHF LRHS MNrw NMen NMin WCot WHil |
| 'Rolf Fiedler' ♀H2-3 | Widely available |
| ***sellowianum*** | CDes SCnR WCot |
| ***sessile*** | CDes ECho |
| § ***uniflorum*** | CBro CTri EBee ECha ECho LAma LEdu MNrw MRav NMen NWCA SBch SEND SMrm SPer SRms WAbb WAul WBrk WCot WFar WPer WTin |
| - 'Album' | CBro CPom CPrp EBee ECha ECho EPPr EPot ERCP EWes GKev LEdu LRHS MNrw MRav WCot WHal WHil |
| - 'Charlotte Bishop' | Widely available |
| - 'Froyle Mill' ♀H4 | CAvo CBro CMea CPom CPrp EBee ECho ELon EPPr EPot ERCP EWes GKev LEdu LHop LLWP LRHS MNrw MRav NMen SAga SPhx SUsu WCot WFar WHil WHoo WTin |
| - subsp. ***tandiliense*** | CDes |
| - 'Wisley Blue' ♀H4 | Widely available |
| yellow-flowered | CDes |

## *Ipomoea* (*Convolvulaceae*)

| | |
|---|---|
| ***acuminata*** | see *I. indica* |
| ***alba*** | CCCN EShb |
| ***batatas*** 'Black Tone' new | EShb |
| - 'Blackie' | EShb ESwi WFar |
| - 'Margarita' | EShb ESwi |
| - 'Pink Frost' (v) | EShb |
| - (Sweet Caroline Series) 'Sweet Caroline Bronze'PBR new | ESwi |
| - - 'Sweet Caroline Sweetheart Light Green'PBR new | ESwi |
| - - 'Sweet Caroline Sweetheart Purple'PBR new | ESwi |
| ***bolusiana*** | LToo |
| ***carnea*** | CCCN MOWG |
| ***coccinea*** var. ***hederifolia*** | see *I. hederifolia* |
| § ***hederifolia*** | CCCN |
| × ***imperialis*** 'Sunrise Serenade' | CCCN |

| | |
|---|---|
| § ***indica*** ♀H1 | CCCN CHEx CHll CRHN EShb MOWG MREP SPer |
| ***learii*** | see *I. indica* |
| § ***lobata*** | CSpe LSou SBch |
| 'Milky Way' | CCCN |
| ***muellerii*** | CCCN |
| × ***multifida*** | CSpe |
| ***purpurea*** | CSpe SBch |
| 'Kniola's Black Night' | |
| ***quamoclit*** | CSpe |
| ***tricolor*** | MNHC |
| ***tuberosa*** | see *Merremia tuberosa* |
| ***versicolor*** | see *I. lobata* |

## *Ipomopsis* (*Polemoniaceae*)

| | |
|---|---|
| § ***aggregata*** | GKev |
| – subsp. ***aggregata*** | GKev |
| NNS 07-277 | |

## *Iresine* (*Amaranthaceae*)

| | |
|---|---|
| ***herbstii*** | EShb |
| – 'Aureoreticulata' | EShb |
| 'Shiny Rose Purple' | LBuc |

## *Iris* ✿ (*Iridaceae*)

| | |
|---|---|
| AC 4413 from Tibet | GAuc |
| AC 4450 from Tibet | GAuc |
| AC 4471 from Tibet | GAuc |
| AC 4490 from Tibet | GAuc |
| AC 4623 from Tibet | GAuc |
| AC 4674 from Tibet | GAuc |
| 'Abbey Chant' (IB) | CIri XSen |
| 'Abbey Road' (TB) | WViv |
| 'Ablaze' (MDB) | WViv |
| 'About Town' (TB) | WCAu |
| 'Above the Clouds' (TB) | WViv |
| 'Absolute Treasure' (TB) **new** | EWoo |
| 'Ace' (MTB) | ESgI |
| 'Acoma' (TB) | EWoo WViv |
| 'Action Front' (TB) | EAEE EBee EBla EIri ESgI ETod EWoo LHop LRHS MAvo SBfd WWEG |
| 'Actress' (TB) | CAby CWGN EAEE EBla ETod LBuc LRHS LSRN |
| ***acutiloba*** **new** | LWst |
| – subsp. ***lineolata*** | LWst |
| 'Adobe Rose' (TB) | ESgI WViv XSen |
| 'Adventuress' (TB) | EWoo WViv XSen |
| 'African Wine' | WAul |
| 'After Dark' (TB) | CKel |
| 'Afternoon Delight' (TB) | CWCL ESgI EWoo WCAu WViv |
| 'Again and Again' (TB) **new** | EWoo |
| 'Agatha Christie' (IB) | WCAu |
| 'Agnes James' (CH) ♀H3 | CBro |
| 'Ahwahnee Princess' (SDB) | EWoo |
| 'Aichi-no-kagayaki' (SpH) | WCot |
| 'Air Up There' (TB) | CIri |
| 'Alabaster Unicorn' (TB) | ESgI |
| 'Albatross' (TB) | SMrm |
| ***albicans*** ♀H4 | CMea ECho LEdu SEND |
| ***albomarginata*** | ECho LWst |
| 'Alcazar' (TB) | ESgI EWoo LSRN SWat WMnd WWEG |
| 'Aldo Ratti' (TB) | ESgI |
| 'Alene's New Love' (IB) **new** | EWoo |
| 'Alene's Other Love' (SDB) | WCAu |
| 'Alenette' (TB) | WCAu |
| 'Alerte Rose' (TB) | WViv |
| 'Alexia' (TB) ♀H4 | CKel |
| 'Alice Harding' (TB) | ESgI |
| 'Alida' (Reticulata) | CBro ECho EPot ERCP GKev LAma LLHF |
| 'Alizes' (TB) ♀H4 | CIri ESgI EWoo WCAu WViv XSen |
| 'All Night Long' (TB) | CIri EWoo |
| 'All That Magic' (SDB) **new** | EWoo |
| 'Allison Elizabeth' (BB) ♀H4 | WAul |
| 'Alsterquelle' (SDB) | WTin |
| 'Amadora' (TB) | CKel EIri |
| 'Amas' (TB) | EWoo |
| 'Amazing Grace' (TB) **new** | EWoo |
| 'Ambassadeur' (TB) | EBee EWoo |
| 'Amber Queen' (DB) | EBee EBla ECtt ELan EPfP NBir NGdn SPer |
| 'Ambersand' (IB) | SIri |
| 'Ambroisie' (TB) ♀H4 | ESgI ETod EWoo WViv |
| 'Amelia Bedeila' (IB) | SIri |
| 'American Patriot' (IB) | CKel WCAu |
| 'Amethyst Dancer' (TB) | WCAu |
| 'Amethyst Flame' (TB) | ECho ESgI NBre SRms |
| 'Amherst Blue' (IB) | SIri |
| 'Amherst Bluebeard' (SDB) | SIri |
| 'Amherst Glacier' (IB) | WCAu |
| 'Amherst Jester' (BB) | SIri WAul |
| 'Amherst Moon' (SDB) | SIri |
| 'Amherst Mustard' (SDB) | SIri |
| 'Amherst Purple Ribbon' (SDB) | SIri WCAu |
| 'Amherst Sweetheart' (SDB) | SIri |
| 'Amigo' (TB) | ESgI EWoo |
| 'Amphora' (SDB) | CBro |
| 'Ancient Echoes' (TB) | ESgI |
| 'Andalou' (TB) ♀H4 | CWCL ESgI EWoo WViv XSen |
| 'Angel Heart' (IB) **new** | EWoo |
| 'Angel Unawares' (TB) | WCAu |
| 'Angel's Tears' | see *I. histrioides* 'Angel's Tears' |
| 'Angel's Touch' (TB) | ESgI |
| ***anglica*** | see *I. latifolia* |
| 'Anna Belle Babson' (TB) | ESgI |
| 'Annabel Jane' (TB) | CKel COIW CWan WCAu |
| 'Anne Elizabeth' (SDB) | CBro |
| 'Annikins' (IB) ♀H4 | CKel |
| 'Anniversary Celebration' (TB) | CKel |
| 'Announcement' (TB) | CIri |
| 'Antarctique' (IB) | ESgI WViv |
| 'Antiope' (RC) **new** | GKev |
| 'Antler Road' (TB) **new** | CIri |
| 'Anvil of Darkness' (TB) | CIri EWoo |
| 'Aphrodisiac' (TB) | WViv XSen |
| ***aphylla*** | GBin WThu |
| 'Apollo' (Dut) | CAvo CFFs GKev |
| 'Appledore' (SDB) | CBro |
| 'Appointer' (SpH) | GBin NChi |
| 'Apricorange' (TB) ♀H4 | CKel |
| 'Apricot Drops' (MTB) ♀H4 | ESgI WAul WCAu |
| 'Apricot Frosty' (BB) | ESgI XSen |
| 'Apricot Silk' (IB) | CCCN SBfd SEND WWEG |
| 'Apricot Topping' (BB) | WAul WCAu |
| 'Aqua Taj' (IB) | WAul |
| 'Arab Chief' (TB) | CKel |
| 'Arabi Pasha' (TB) | ESgI |
| 'Arc de Triomphe' (TB) | ESgI |
| 'Arctic Age' (TB) | WViv |
| 'Arctic Express' (TB) | ESgI |
| 'Arctic Fancy' (IB) ♀H4 | CKel |
| 'Arctic Night' **new** | WCAu |
| 'Arctic Sunrise' (TB) | ESgI |
| ***arenaria*** | see *I. humilis* |
| 'Armageddon' (TB) | ESgI |
| 'Arnold Sunrise' (CH) ♀H3 | GAbr |

| | | | | |
|---|---|---|---|---|
| | 'Around Midnight' (TB) | LRHS WCAu | | 'Batik' (BB) | WCot WViv XSen |
| | 'Arpège' (TB) | XSen | | 'Batman' (TB) | CIri |
| | 'Art Deco' (TB) | SIri WViv XSen | | 'Baubles and Beads' (MTB) | ESgI |
| | 'Art School Angel' (TB) | CIri | | 'Bayberry Candle' (TB) | CIri ESgI |
| | 'As de Coeur' (TB) | ESgI XSen | | 'Be Happy' (SDB) | WViv |
| | 'Ascension Crown' (TB) | ESgI | | 'Be Mine' (TB) | CIri |
| | 'Ask Alma' (IB) | ESgI WViv XSen | | 'Beach Girl' (TB) new | EWoo |
| | 'Astrid Cayeux' (TB) | ESgI WViv | | 'Beatrice Cherbuy' (TB) | WViv |
| * | 'Atlantique' (TB) | CKel | | 'Bedtime Story' (IB) | SSvw SWat WCot WViv WWEG XSen |
| | 'Attention Please' (TB) | CKel ELan WWEG | | 'Bee Wings' (MDB) | WViv |
| | ***attica*** | CBro CPBP ECho LLHF NRya WThu | | 'Beechfield' new | LRHS |
| | - J&JA 583.900 | NWCA | | 'Bee's Knees' (SDB) ♀H4 | SIri |
| | - lemon-flowered | CPBP WThu | | 'Before the Storm' (TB) | CIri CKel ELon ESgI GBin WCAu XSen |
| § | ***aucheri*** ♀H2 | ECho EPot ERCP GKev LLHF LWst NMin | | 'Beguine' (TB) | ESgI |
| | - 'Blue Jay' new | LWst | | 'Being Busy' (SDB) | ESgI |
| | - 'Blue Tit' new | LWst | | 'Bel Avenir' (TB) | WViv |
| | - indigo-flowered | GKev LWst | | 'Bel Azur' (IB) | ESgI EWoo WViv |
| | - 'Leylek Ice' | GAuc | | 'Bel Esprit' (TB) | ESgI |
| | - 'Leylek Lilac' | LWst | | 'Belise' (Spuria) ♀H4 | WAul WCot |
| | - 'Olof' new | LWst | | 'Belle de Nuit' (TB) | EWoo WViv |
| | - 'Snow Princess' | ECho LWst | | 'Belvi Queen' (TB) | MNrw |
| | - 'Snow White' | ECho GAuc GKev LWst | | 'Ben a Factor' (MTB) | ESgI |
| | - 'Turkish Ice' | LWst | | 'Benton Caramel' | EMal EWoo |
| | - white-flowered new | LWst | | 'Benton Cordelia' (TB) | EMal |
| | 'Aunt Corley' (TB) | CIri | | 'Benton Daphne' (TB) | EMal EWoo |
| | 'Aunt Josephine' (TB) | ESgI | | 'Benton Dierdre' (TB) | ELon SRms |
| | 'Aurean' (IB) | CKel | | 'Benton Evora' (TB) | EMal EWoo |
| | 'Aurelie' (TB) | SIri WViv | | 'Benton Nigel' (TB) | EMal EWoo WCAu |
| | 'Austrian Sky' (SDB) | CAby CMac EBee EBla ECtt LHop LRHS SMrm SPhx STes WAul WCot | | 'Benton Olive' (TB) new | EWoo |
| | 'Autumn Apricot' (TB) | EWoo | | 'Benton Primrose' (TB) new | EWoo |
| | 'Autumn Circus' (TB) | EWoo WAul WCAu WViv | | 'Benton Sheila' (TB) | ECha |
| | 'Autumn Echo' (TB) | ESgI XSen | | 'Benton Susan' (TB) new | EWoo |
| | 'Autumn Encore' (TB) | EWoo MHer SBfd | | 'Beotie' (TB) new | EWoo |
| | 'Autumn Leaves' (TB) | ESgI | | 'Berkeley Gold' (TB) | CSBt EBee EBla ECtt ELan EShb EWes LRHS MAsh NOrc SBfd SPer SWat WWEG |
| | 'Autumn Maple' (SDB) | ESgI | | | |
| | 'Autumn Tryst' (TB) | ESgI EWoo | | | |
| | 'Autumn Wine' (BB) new | CIri | | 'Berlin Tiger' (SpH) ♀H4 | CRow EPPr EPfP GBin LLWG MWts NLar SApp WHil |
| | 'Avalon Sunset' (TB) | EIri ESgI WViv | | | |
| | 'Avanelle' (IB) | GBin NBre WHil | | 'Bermuda Triangle' (BB) | CIri SDys WAul |
| | 'Awesome Blossom' (TB) | ESgI | | 'Best Bet' (TB) | ESgI EWoo WCAu |
| | 'Az Ap' (IB) | ELon WCAu WHil | | 'Bethany Claire' (TB) | ESgI WCAu |
| | 'Aztec Sun' (TB) | WViv | | 'Betty Cooper' (Spuria) | WAul |
| | 'Babbling Brook' (TB) | ESgI XSen | | 'Betty Simon' (TB) | CKel CWCL ESgI ETod EWoo WViv XSen |
| | 'Baboon Bottom' (BB) | CIri | | | |
| | 'Baby Bengal' (BB) | EWoo XSen | | 'Beverly Sills' (TB) | EAEE EPfP ESgI EWoo GBin LSou MRav SRGP WAul WGwG WHil WViv XSen |
| | 'Baby Blessed' (SDB) | CBro WCAu | | | |
| | 'Baby Prince' (SDB) | ESgI | | | |
| | 'Baccarat' (TB) | WCAu | | 'Bewilderbeast' (TB) | XSen |
| | 'Bach Toccata' (MTB) new | SDys | | 'Bianco' (TB) | WCAu WWEG |
| | 'Back in Black' (TB) | CKel | | 'Bibury' (SDB) ♀H4 | WCAu |
| | 'Badlands' (TB) | WCAu | | 'Big Dipper' (TB) | ECtt ESgI WViv |
| | 'Bal Masqué' (TB) | WViv XSen | | 'Big Melt' (TB) | CKel |
| | ***baldschuanica*** | LWst | | 'Big Squeeze' (TB) | WViv |
| | 'Ballerina' (TB) | NBir | | ***biglumis*** | see *I. lactea* |
| | 'Ballistic' (SDB) | WCAu | | ***biliottii*** | CBro |
| | 'Ballyhoo' (TB) | WCAu XSen | | 'Billie the Brownie' (MTB) | ESgI |
| | 'Baltic Star' (TB) new | EWoo | | 'Bishop's Robe' (TB) | SSvw |
| | 'Banbury Beauty' (CH) ♀H3 | MAvo | | 'Black as Night' (TB) | XSen |
| | 'Banbury Melody' (CH) | MAvo | N | 'Black Beauty' (Dut) | EPfP |
| | 'Banbury Ruffles' (SDB) | ESgI WAul WViv | | 'Black Beauty' (TB) | MWat SPer |
| | 'Bang' (TB) | CKel | | 'Black Dragon' (TB) | CCCN CHid NLar XSen |
| | 'Bangles' (MTB) ♀H4 | ESgI SDys WCAu | | 'Black Flag' (TB) | XSen |
| | 'Banshee' (IB) new | WAul | | 'Black Gamecock' (La) | CAby CFir CWCL ELan IPot LPBA MBNS MNrw MSCN MWts NBro NLar NOrc SKHP SMrm SSvw WMAq |
| | 'Bar de Nuit' (TB) | ESgI EWoo | | | |
| | 'Barbara's Kiss' (Spuria) | CIri | | | |
| | ***barbatula*** BWJ 7663 | WCru | | | |
| | ***barnumae*** | LWst | | 'Black Hills' (TB) | EBee |
| | 'Baroque Prelude' (TB) | CKel | | 'Black Hope' (TB) new | CIri |

| |  |  |
|---|---|---|
| | 'Black Ink' (TB) | COIW |
| | 'Black Knight' (TB) | MRav NLar WKif |
| | 'Black Magic' (IB) **new** | EWoo |
| | 'Black Night' (IB) | MWea SRGP WWEG |
| | 'Black Sergeant' (TB) ♀H4 | CKel |
| | 'Black Stallion' (MDB) | ESgI |
| | 'Black Suited' (TB) | CIri |
| | 'Black Swan' (TB) | CMac EBla ECha ECtt ELan EPfP ESgI EShb EWoo GCal LAst LRHS LSRN MCot NBre NGdn SBfd SPer SPoG STes WCot WHil XSen |
| | 'Black Taffeta' (TB) | CKel |
| | 'Black Tie Affair' (TB) | ESgI EWoo WViv XSen |
| | 'Blackbeard' (BB) ♀H4 | CKel |
| | 'Blackcurrant' (IB) | WAul |
| | 'Blackout' (TB) | ESgI EWoo SIri |
| | 'Blast' (IB) | CKel WViv |
| | 'Blatant' (TB) | ESgI EWoo WCAu XSen |
| | 'Blazing Light' (TB) | ESgI XSen |
| | 'Blazing Sunrise' (TB) | ESgI |
| | 'Blenheim Royal' (TB) | ESgI EWoo WCAu WViv XSen |
| | 'Blowing Bubbles' (TB) | CIri |
| | 'Blue Beret' (MDB) | WViv |
| | 'Blue Bossa' (CH) ♀H4 | WAul |
| | 'Blue Boy' (IB) **new** | EWoo |
| | 'Blue Crusader' (TB) | WViv |
| | 'Blue Denim' (SDB) | ECho ECtt EPfP GCal MRav NBir NPnk WBor WHil WTin WWEG |
| | 'Blue Eyed Brunette' (TB) | ESgI WCAu |
| | 'Blue Gown' (TB) | EWoo |
| | 'Blue Hendred' (SDB) | NBir WCAu |
| | 'Blue Lamp' (TB) | CKel |
| | 'Blue Line' (SDB) ♀H4 | NBre |
| | 'Blue Luster' (TB) ♀H4 | ESgI |
| | 'Blue Note Blues' (TB) | WCAu |
| | 'Blue Pigmy' (SDB) | CPBP CWat EBla ECtt LRHS NGdn NLar SBfd SPer |
| | 'Blue Pools' (SDB) | NBir WTin |
| | 'Blue Reflection' (TB) | ESgI |
| | 'Blue Rhythm' (TB) | CKel EBla ELan ELon EPfP EWoo GMaP LRHS MRav NBre SBfd SBrd SCoo SPer SPhx SSvw WCAu WMnd WWEG |
| | 'Blue Sapphire' (TB) | ESgI EWoo WCAu |
| | 'Blue Shimmer' (TB) | CSBt EBee EBla ECha ELan EPfP ESgI EShb ETod EWoo LRHS LSRN MCot NCGa NGdn SBch SBfd SPer SWat WCAu WGwG |
| | 'Blue Staccato' (TB) | CKel ESgI WCAu XSen |
| | 'Blue Suede Shoes' (TB) | ESgI EWoo LSRN WViv XSen |
| | 'Bluebird Wine' (TB) | WCAu |
| | 'Blushing Moon' (TB) | WAul |
| | 'Bob Nichol' (TB) ♀H4 | CKel |
| | 'Bockingford' (MTB) | SIri |
| | 'Bohemia Sekt' (TB) | CKel |
| | 'Bohemian' (TB) | CWCL WViv |
| | 'Bold Fashion' (TB) | WViv |
| | 'Bold Gold' (TB) | WViv |
| | 'Bold Look' (TB) | ESgI |
| | 'Bold Pretender' (La) | ELan EPfP MBNS NLar SKHP WHil |
| | 'Bold Print' (IB) | CAby CWan EAEE EBee EBla ELon LAst LRHS LSRN NCGa SBfd SPoG WAul WCAu WWEG |
| | 'Bollinger' | see *I.* 'Hornpipe' |
| | 'Bonbon Acidulé' (TB) | WViv |
| | 'Bonnie Davenport' (TB) | CIri |
| I | 'Bonny' (MDB) | CBro |
| | 'Bonus Bucks' (TB) | CKel |
| | 'Boo' (SDB) | CKel CPBP WCAu XSen |
| | 'Bouzy Bouzy' (TB) | ESgI XSen |
| | ***bracteata*** | CPBP IGor |
| | – NNS 04-223 | WCot |
| | – NNS 07-282 | GKev |
| | ***bracteata* × *thompsonii*** **new** | IGor |
| | 'Braggadocio' (TB) | WViv |
| | 'Braggin' Rights' (TB) **new** | CIri |
| | 'Braithwaite' (TB) | CAby CKel CWGN EBee EBla ELan ESgI EShb EWoo LRHS NBre SBfd SBrd SPer SPur SRms SWat WAul WCAu WKif |
| | 'Brannigan' (SDB) | CBro NBir SMrm |
| | 'Brasero' (TB) | CWCL ECtt EWoo WViv |
| | 'Brash' (SDB) | WViv |
| | 'Brasilia' (TB) | NBir NBre |
| | 'Brassie' (SDB) | CBro MBNS NPnk WHil WWEG XSen |
| | 'Brave New World' (TB) ♀H4 | CIri |
| | 'Breakers' (TB) ♀H4 | CKel ESgI EWoo |
| | 'Breaking Point' (TB) **new** | CIri |
| § | 'Bride' (DB) | WMnd |
| | 'Bride's Blush' (TB) | CIri |
| | 'Bride's Halo' (TB) | EWoo LSRN WViv XSen |
| * | 'Brigantino' (BB) | ESgI |
| | 'Bright Button' (SDB) | CKel ESgI EWoo |
| | 'Bright Chic' (SDB) | ESgI |
| | 'Bright Fire' (TB) | EIri WViv |
| | 'Bright Spring' (DB) | WViv |
| | 'Bright Vision' (SDB) | ESgI |
| | 'Bright White' (MDB) | CBro CKel ECho |
| N | 'Bright Yellow' (DB) | MRav |
| | 'Brighteyes' (IB) | LRHS SRms |
| | 'Brindisi' (TB) | ESgI XSen |
| | 'Brise de Mer' (TB) | ESgI XSen |
| | 'Bristo Magic' (TB) | XSen |
| | 'Bristol Gem' (TB) | XSen |
| | 'Broad Shoulders' (TB) | WCAu |
| | 'Broadband' (TB) **new** | WCAu |
| | 'Broadleigh Angela' (CH) | CBro |
| | 'Broadleigh Ann' (CH) | CBro |
| | 'Broadleigh Carolyn' (CH) ♀H3 | CBro CElw |
| N | 'Broadleigh Clare' (CH) | CBro |
| | 'Broadleigh Dorothy' (CH) | CBro MAvo |
| | 'Broadleigh Eleanor' (CH) **new** | CBro |
| | 'Broadleigh Elizabeth' (CH) | CBro |
| N | 'Broadleigh Emily' (CH) | CBro |
| | 'Broadleigh Fenella' (CH) **new** | CBro |
| N | 'Broadleigh Jean' (CH) | CBro |
| | 'Broadleigh Joan' (CH) | CBro |
| | 'Broadleigh Lavinia' (CH) | CBro MAvo MRav |
| | 'Broadleigh Mitre' (CH) | CBro CElw GMac |
| | 'Broadleigh Nancy' (CH) | CBro |
| | 'Broadleigh Peacock' (CH) | CBro EShb WSHC |
| | 'Broadleigh Penny' (CH) | CBro |
| N | 'Broadleigh Rose' (CH) | CBro CElw EPyc LRHS MBrN MRav SApp SMrm WSHC |
| | 'Broadway Baby' (IB) | ESgI WAul WViv |
| | 'Bronzaire' (IB) ♀H4 | CKel EIri ESgI WCAu WGwG |
| | 'Bronze Beauty' (Dut) | ERCP LAma SBch |
| | 'Bronze Beauty' van Tubergen (*boogiana* hybrid) | EPfP MWat NBir SDeJ |
| | 'Bronzed Aussie' (TB) | CIri |
| | 'Bronzed Violet' (TB) | CKel |
| | 'Brother Carl' (TB) | XSen |
| | 'Bruce' (TB) **new** | WCAu |

| | Name | Suppliers |
|---|---|---|
| N | 'Brummit's Mauve' (TB) | WCAu |
| | 'Bruno' (TB) | LSRN NLar |
| | 'Brussels' (TB) | ESgI |
| | 'Bubbly Mood' (TB) | EWoo |
| | ***bucharica*** misapplied | see *I. orchioides* Carrière |
| | ***bucharica*** ambig. | CAvo EBla ECho ELon IFro MNrw NCGa SDeJ SMrm WBor |
| § | ***bucharica*** Foster $\Upsilon^{H3-4}$ | CBro CSam ECho EPfP EPot GKev LAma |
| * | - 'Baldschuan Yellow' (J) | LWst |
| | - 'Princess' | ECho |
| * | - 'Top Gold' | ECho |
| | ***bucharica* × *orchioides*** | ECho LWst |
| | ***bucharica* × *warleyensis*** | LWst |
| | 'Buckwheat' (TB) | EWoo SIri WViv |
| | 'Bugleboy Blues' (TB) **new** | CIri |
| | 'Buisson de Roses' (TB) | ESgI WViv XSen |
| | ***bulleyana*** | ECho GAuc GEdr GKev NWCA SRms |
| | - BWJ 7912 | WCru |
| | - SSSE 8 | GLam |
| | - SSSE 82 | GLam |
| | - black-flowered | CPLG GKev |
| | - - SDR 1792 | EBee |
| | - - SDR 4775 | GKev |
| | 'Bumblebee Deelite' (MTB) $\Upsilon^{H4}$ | CKel CPMA WCAu |
| | ***bungei*** | GAuc |
| | 'Burgermeister' (TB) | WViv XSen |
| | 'Burgundy Party' (TB) | ESgI XSen |
| | 'Burka' (TB) | ESgI |
| | 'Burning Bright' (TB) | WViv |
| | 'Burnt Toffee' (TB) | ESgI WAul WViv XSen |
| | 'Burst' (TB) | CKel |
| | 'Buto' (TB) | EWoo |
| | 'Butter Pecan' (IB) | WCAu |
| | 'Buttermere' (TB) | SRms |
| | 'Butterpat' (IB) | ESgI |
| | 'Butterscotch Carpet' (SDB) | WCAu |
| | 'Butterscotch Kiss' (TB) | CMac EBee EBla ECGP ELan LHop LRHS MBNS MRav MWea NBir NLar SBfd SPer |
| | 'Bye Bye Blues' (TB) | ESgI XSen |
| | 'Cabaret Royale' (TB) | ESgI EWoo XSen |
| | 'Cable Car' (TB) | CKel CWCL ECtt ESgI EWoo WCAu WViv |
| | 'Cache of Gold' (SDB) | EWoo |
| | 'Cajun Rhythm' (TB) | WViv XSen |
| | 'Caliente' (TB) | CWGN EKen EPfP ESgI MCot MRav MWhi WCAu XSen |
| | 'California Dreamin'' (TB) | CIri |
| | 'California Gold' (TB) | WWEG |
| | 'California Style' (IB) | ESgI WViv XSen |
| § | Californian hybrids | CElw CPBP EPot GCra LRHS MCot NBir WCFE WCot |
| | 'Caliph' (TB) | WViv |
| | 'Calm Stream' (TB) $\Upsilon^{H4}$ | CKel WCAu |
| | 'Calypso Beat' (TB) | WViv |
| | 'Calypso Mood' (TB) | XSen |
| | 'Cambridge Blue' | see *I.* 'Monspur Cambridge Blue' |
| | 'Cameliard' (TB) **new** | EWoo |
| | 'Camelot Rose' (TB) | XSen |
| | 'Cameo Blush' (BB) | EWoo XSen |
| | 'Cameo Queen' (SDB) $\Upsilon^{H4}$ | CIri |
| | 'Cameo Wine' (TB) | CPMA ECtt ESgI WViv XSen |
| | 'Cameroun' (TB) | ESgI EWoo |
| | 'Campbellii' | see *I. lutescens* 'Campbellii' |
| | ***canadensis*** | see *I. hookeri* |
| | 'Canadian Streaker' (TB/v) | WCot |
| | 'Candy Rock' (IB) | CIri EWoo WCAu |

| | Name | Suppliers |
|---|---|---|
| | 'Candylane' (MTB) | CKel |
| | 'Cannington Apricot' (IB) | CKel |
| | 'Cannington Ochre' (SDB) | CBro |
| | 'Cannington Skies' (IB) | CKel |
| | 'Cannonball' (TB) | EWoo |
| | 'Can't Touch This' (TB) **new** | WCAu |
| | 'Cantab' (Reticulata) | CAby CAvo CBro ECho EPot ERCP GBin GKev LAma SDeJ SMrm SPhx |
| | 'Caprice' (TB) | EWoo |
| | 'Capricious' (TB) | ESgI |
| | 'Capricious Candles' (TB) **new** | CIri |
| | 'Captain Indigo' (IB) | CKel ESgI WCAu |
| | 'Caption' (TB) | ESgI |
| | 'Captive Sun' (SDB) **new** | CWGN EAEE EPfP LRHS SIri |
| | 'Caramel' (TB) | XSen |
| | 'Carenza' (BB) | CKel |
| | 'Caribbean Dream' (TB) | EWoo WViv XSen |
| | 'Carnaby' (TB) | EBla ESgI LAst LRHS MBri MRav MWea NCGa SBfd STes WCAu WViv WWEG XSen |
| | 'Carnival Time' (TB) | CMac CWGN EBee EBla ECtt EShb LBuc LRHS MCot MWea NCGa SBfd SMrm SPer STes WAul XSen |
| | 'Carolina Gold' (TB) | XSen |
| | 'Carolyn Rose' (MTB) $\Upsilon^{H4}$ | NBre SMrm |
| * | 'Caronte' (IB) | ESgI |
| | 'Carriwitched' (IB) | CKel |
| | 'Casbah' (TB) | XSen |
| | 'Cascade Springs' (TB) | WViv XSen |
| | 'Cascade Sprite' (SDB) | SRms |
| | 'Casual Joy' (TB) **new** | CIri |
| | 'Catalyst' (TB) | XSen |
| | 'Cat's Eye' (SDB) | WViv |
| | ***caucasica*** | CMac |
| | 'Cayenne Capers' (TB) | ESgI |
| N | 'Cedric Morris' | EWes |
| | 'Cee Jay' (IB) $\Upsilon^{H4}$ | EWoo WViv |
| | 'Cee Tee' | EWoo XSen |
| | 'Celebration Song' (TB) | CWCL ESgI SIri WAul WCAu WViv XSen |
| | 'Celestial Glory' (TB) | XSen |
| | 'Cercle Bleu' (TB) | WViv |
| | 'Cerdagne' (TB) | ESgI XSen |
| | 'Cerf-Volant' (TB) | SIri WViv |
| | ***chamaeiris*** | see *I. lutescens* subsp. *lutescens* |
| | 'Champagne Elegance' (TB) | ECtt EIri EPri ESgI EWoo NBir WViv XSen |
| | 'Champagne Encore' (IB) | ESgI EWoo |
| | 'Champagne Frost' (TB) | XSen |
| | 'Champagne Waltz' (TB) | CWCL WViv XSen |
| | 'Chance Beauty' (SpH) $\Upsilon^{H4}$ | WViv |
| | 'Change of Pace' (TB) | ESgI WViv XSen |
| | 'Changing Winds' (TB) | WViv |
| | 'Chanted' (SDB) | ESgI EWoo WCAu WViv XSen |
| | 'Chantilly' (TB) | EBee EBla ELan EPfP EWoo LRHS MCot MRav NBir NGdn NLar SPer SWat WFoF |
| | 'Chapeau' (TB) | ESgI WCAu |
| | 'Chapel Bells' (TB) | CKel |
| | 'Charlotte Maria' (TB) | CKel |
| | 'Charmaine' (TB) | XSen |
| | 'Chartreuse Ruffles' (TB) | ECtt EWoo SIri |
| | 'Chasing Rainbows' (TB) | SDys WCAu |
| | 'Chaste White' (TB) | ESgI |
| | 'Château d'Auvers-sur-Oise' (TB) | SIri WViv |
| | 'Chelsea Bleu' (TB) | WViv |
| | 'Cher' (TB) | LSRN WViv |
| N | 'Cherished' (TB) | GBin WWEG |

| | Name | Suppliers |
|---|---|---|
| | 'Cherokee Lace' (Spuria) | WTin |
| | 'Cherry Garden' (SDB) | CAby CBro CKel CPBP EAEE EBee |
| | | EBla ECho ECtt ELan EPfP EShb |
| | | EWes GMaP LEdu LRHS MAsh |
| | | MBNS MRav NBir NGdn NPnk |
| | | NWCA SDGI SDeJ WAul WBor WHil |
| | | WWEG WWFP |
| | 'Cherrywood' (SDB) | CBro |
| | 'Cherub's Smile' (TB) | ESgI XSen |
| | 'Cheryl Ann O'Leary' (TB) | CIri |
| | 'Chevalier de Malte' (TB) | ESgI WViv |
| | 'Chickee' (MTB) ♀H4 | CKel |
| | 'Chicken Little' (MDB) | CBro |
| I | 'Chieftain' (SDB) | MRav |
| | 'China Dragon' (TB) | SWat XSen |
| | 'China Nights' (TB) | ESgI |
| | 'China Seas' (TB) | NBre |
| | 'Chinese Coral' (TB) **new** | XSen |
| | 'Chinese Treasure' (TB) | XSen |
| | 'Chinook Winds' (TB) | ESgI WCAu |
| | 'Chivalry' (TB) | ESgI WTin |
| | 'Chocolate Marmalade' (TB) | ECtt WViv |
| | 'Chocolate Moose' (TB) | CIri |
| | 'Chocolate Vanilla' (TB) | ESgI |
| | 'Chorus Girl' (TB) | CKel |
| | 'Chou Bleu' (TB) | WViv |
| | 'Christmas Angel' (TB) | WCAu |
| | Chrysofor Group | CAby |
| | ***chrysographes*** ♀H4 | CBro CHid CMac CWCL EBla EPfP |
| | | EPri EWll GMac IKil LAst LRHS |
| | | MCCP MHer MLHP MLLN MMuc |
| | | MRav MSCN NBPC NPnk NPri NSti |
| | | SPoG SRot SWal WFar |
| I | - 'Black Beauty' | CFir ECho EPfP GAbr |
| | - 'Black Gold' | EPri |
| I | - 'Black Knight' | CBot CCse CPLG EDAr ELon EPfP |
| | | GCal GCra GGar ITim LHop MDun |
| | | NChi NLar SMad SWat WBor |
| | | WGwG WMnd |
| | - black-flowered | Widely available |
| * | - 'Ellenbank Nightshade' | GMac |
| N | - 'Inshriach' | LEdu |
| N | - 'Kew Black' | CPLG ECho EShb LEdu NBir WHer |
| | | WWEG |
| | - 'Mandarin Purple' | GCal GMac MBri MSpe SPer SWat |
| | | WMoo |
| | - 'Rob' | ECho |
| § | - 'Rubella' | CRow ECho GCra GMac WFar |
| * | - 'Rubens' | GCal |
| | - 'Rubra' | see *I. chrysographes* 'Rubella' |
| N | - 'Tsiri' | NWCA |
| | - yellow-flowered | WFar |
| | ***chrysographes* × *forrestii*** | GBin NBir |
| | ***chrysophylla*** | IGor |
| | - NNS 04.225 | CPBP |
| | - NNS 05-387 | WCot |
| | 'Chubby Cheeks' (SDB) | CKel WCAu |
| | 'Chuckwagon' (TB) | ESgI |
| | 'Church Stoke' (SDB) | WCAu |
| N | 'Cider Haze' (TB) | CKel |
| | 'Ciel et Mer' (TB) | EWoo WViv |
| | 'Cimarron Rose' (SDB) | ESgI WAul WViv |
| | 'Cimarron Strip' (TB) | EPfP WWEG XSen |
| | 'Cinnabar Red' (Spuria) | WAul |
| | 'Cinnamon Apples' (MDB) | ESgI |
| | 'Circus Stripes' (TB) | XSen |
| | 'Cirrus Veil' (SDB) | WCAu |
| | 'Citoyen' (TB) | XSen |
| | 'Citronnade' (TB) | WViv |

| | Name | Suppliers |
|---|---|---|
| | 'City Lights' Harrell (TB) | WCAu |
| | 'Claire Doodle' (MTB) | ESgI |
| | 'Clairette' (Reticulata) | ECho EPot LAma NMin SDeJ |
| | 'Clara Garland' (IB) ♀H4 | CKel WCAu |
| | 'Clarence' (TB) | CKel ESgI EWoo XSen |
| | ***clarkei*** | CPrp WFar |
| | - B&SWJ 2122 | WCru |
| | - CC 2751 | CPLG NWCA WCot |
| | 'Classic Edition' (TB) | WViv |
| | 'Classic Hues' (TB) | ESgI |
| | 'Classic Look' (TB) | ESgI WViv |
| | 'Clay's Caper' (SDB) | NBre |
| N | 'Cleo' (TB) | CKel NBir |
| | 'Cleo Murrell' (TB) | ESgI EWoo |
| | 'Cliffs of Dover' (TB) | CKel EIri EKen ESgI EWoo GCal |
| | | MCot SGar SRms |
| | 'Close Shave' (TB) | CIri |
| | 'Cloud Ballet' (TB) **new** | EWoo |
| | 'Cloud Mistress' (IB) | ESgI WViv |
| | 'Cloud Pinnacle' (IB) | CKel |
| | 'Cloudcap' (TB) | SRms |
| | 'Clown Around' (TB) | CIri |
| | 'Clownerie' (TB) | EWoo WViv |
| | 'Clyde Redmond' (La) ♀H4 | WAul WMAq |
| | 'Coalignition' (TB) | CIri ETod EWoo WCAu |
| | 'Cocktail' (TB) | WViv |
| | 'Codicil' (TB) | EIri ESgI EWoo WViv XSen |
| | 'Coeur d'Or' (TB) | WViv |
| | 'Colery' **new** | LRHS |
| | 'Colette Thurillet' (TB) | ESgI WViv XSen |
| | ***collettii*** | ECho GKev LWSt |
| | 'Color Glory' (TB) | WViv |
| | 'Color Me Blue' (TB) | WCAu |
| | 'Color Splash' (TB) | XSen |
| | 'Colorific' (La) | EPfP NBro NLar WHil |
| | 'Colortart' (TB) | XSen |
| | 'Combo' (SDB) | CKel |
| | 'Coming Up Roses' (TB) | XSen |
| | 'Con Fuoco' (TB) | ESgI XSen |
| | 'Concertina' (IB) | CIri EWoo WCAu |
| | 'Condottiere' (TB) | WViv |
| | 'Confetti' (TB) | MBri |
| | ***confusa*** ♀H3 | CHEx CSev EWld GGal IFro LEdu |
| | | SArc SBig SGar SMad WFar XSen |
| N | - 'Martyn Rix' | CBct CDes CGHE CHEx CHid CPou |
| | | EBee ELon EPfP GCal IGor MLHP |
| | | WCot WFar WGwG WHer WMnd |
| | | WPGP WPer |
| | 'Congo Bongo' (BB) | WAul |
| | 'Conjuration' (TB) | ESgI EWoo WViv |
| | 'Constant Wattez' (IB) | CKel EBee ESgI NLar |
| | 'Consummation' (MTB) | WHil |
| | 'Copatonic' (TB) | ESgI |
| | 'Copper Classic' (TB) | ESgI WViv |
| | 'Cops' (SDB) | ESgI |
| | 'Coquetterie' (TB) | ESgI WViv |
| | 'Coral Point' (TB) | EWoo WCAu |
| | 'Coral Sunset' (TB) | WViv XSen |
| | 'Cordoba' (TB) | WCAu XSen |
| | 'Corps de Ballet' (TB) | CIri |
| | 'Côte d'Or' (TB) | WViv XSen |
| | 'Count Dracula' (TB) | CIri |
| | 'Country Charm' (TB) | WViv |
| | 'County Town Red' (TB) | SIri |
| | 'Coup de Soleil' (TB) | EWoo WViv |
| | 'Court Magician' (SDB) | SIri |
| | 'Cozy Calico' (TB) | ESgI |
| | 'Crackles' (TB) | CKel |
| | 'Cracklin Burgundy' (TB) | XSen |
| | 'Crackling Caldera' (TB) | WAul |

| | Name | Suppliers |
|---|---|---|
| | 'Cranapple' (BB) ♕$^{H4}$ | WAul |
| | 'Cranberry Ice' (TB) | ELon EWoo XSen |
| | 'Cranbrook' (IB) ♕$^{H4}$ | SIri |
| | 'Cream and Peaches' (SDB) | SIri WViv |
| | 'Cream Beauty' (Dut) | GKev LAma SPhx |
| | 'Cream Soda' (TB) ♕$^{H4}$ | CKel |
| | 'Crème d'Or' (TB) | ESgI |
| | 'Crème Glacée' (TB) | ESgI WViv |
| | ***cretensis*** | see *I. unguicularis* subsp. *cretensis* |
| | 'Crimson King' (IB) **new** | EWoo |
| | 'Crinoline' (TB) | CKel XSen |
| | 'Crisis' (TB) | CIri |
| | 'Crispette' (TB) | WCAu |
| | ***cristata*** ♕$^{H4}$ | CPBP EPot GEdr LLHF NHar NLar |
| | | SRms |
| | - 'Alba' | GCal LLHF WAbe WThu |
| | ***cristata* × *lacustris*** | NMen |
| | ***crocea*** ♕$^{H4}$ | GBin GKev |
| | 'Croftway Lemon' (TB) | COIW ELon |
| | 'Cross Current' (TB) | WCAu |
| | 'Crowned Heads' (TB) | CKel ESgI WCAu WViv XSen |
| | 'Crownette' (SDB) | CKel |
| | 'Crushed Velvet' (TB) | WCAu |
| | 'Crystal Glitters' (TB) | ESgI WViv |
| | 'Crystal Phoenix' **new** | CRow |
| | 'Cumulus' (TB) | EWoo WViv |
| | ***cuniculiformis*** | ECho GAuc |
| | 'Cup Race' (TB) | WCAu XSen |
| | 'Cupid's Cup' (SDB) | ESgI |
| | 'Curio' (MDB) | WViv |
| | 'Curlew' (IB) | WCAu |
| | 'Cutie' (IB) | ESgI EWoo WViv |
| | 'Cyanea' (DB) | ECho GEdr |
| | ***cycloglossa*** | ECho EPot GKev LLHF LWst WCot |
| | 'Dakota Smoke' (TB) **new** | EWoo |
| | 'Dale Dennis' (DB) | XSen |
| | 'Dance Away' (TB) | ESgI WViv |
| | 'Dance for Joy' (TB) | XSen |
| | 'Dancer's Veil' (TB) | CHar CKel CMac ECtt ELon ESgI |
| | | LRHS MRav NBre SBrd SPer |
| | 'Dancing Lilacs' (MTB) | ESgI |
| | 'Dandy' (TB) | ESgI |
| | ***danfordiae*** | CAvo CBro CFFs ECho EPfP EPot |
| | | ERCP GKev LAma LRHS NWad |
| | | SDeJ SGar SMrm WFar WGwG |
| | 'Danger' (TB) | ESgI |
| | 'Dangerous Mood' (TB) **new** | EWoo |
| | 'Dante's Inferno' (TB) | EWoo |
| | 'Dardanus' (RC) | ECho EPot ERCP LLHF SDeJ WCot |
| | 'Dark Chocolate' (TB) | EWoo |
| | 'Dark Crystal' (SDB) | ESgI EWoo |
| | 'Dark Rosaleen' (TB) ♕$^{H4}$ | NBre |
| | 'Dark Spark' (SDB) | WCAu |
| | 'Dark Vader' (SDB) | ESgI WAul WCAu WViv |
| | 'Darkness' (IB) | SIri |
| | 'Darkside' (TB) | XSen |
| | ***darwasica*** | LWst |
| | 'Dash Away' (SDB) | ESgI SIri WViv |
| | 'Dashing' (TB) | EWoo |
| | 'Dauber's Delight' | CIri |
| | 'Daughter of Stars' (TB) | ESgI EWoo |
| | 'Dauntless' (TB) | ESgI EWoo |
| | 'David Guest' (IB) | CKel |
| | 'Dawn of Fall' (TB) | ESgI |
| | 'Dawning' (TB) ♕$^{H4}$ | ESgI EWoo WViv |
| | 'Dazzling Gold' (TB) | ESgI WViv XSen |
| | 'Death by Chocolate' (SDB) | ESgI WAul |
| § | ***decora*** | NWCA |
| | 'Deep Black' (TB) | CAby CKel CPar CWGN EBla ELan |
| | | EPfP GBin IPot LAst LRHS LSRN |
| | | MBNS MCot MRav MWat NCGa |
| | | NLar NOrc SBfd SPer SPoG SWat |
| | | WAul WCAu WCot |
| | 'Deep Caress' (TB) | ESgI |
| | 'Deep Pacific' (TB) | MBri WCAu |
| | 'Deep Space' (TB) | WCAu |
| | 'Deft Touch' (TB) | CKel WCAu WViv XSen |
| | ***delavayi*** ♕$^{H4}$ | ECho EWes GAuc GLam GMaP IBlr |
| | | MLLN WRHF |
| | - SDR 50 | CPLG GKev |
| N | - 'Didcot' | LRHS |
| | 'Delicate Lady' (IB) ♕$^{H4}$ | CKel |
| | 'Delirium' (IB) | WAul WViv |
| | 'Delta Blues' (TB) | EWoo WViv |
| | 'Delta Butterfly' (La) | WMAq |
| | 'Demelza' (TB) | CKel |
| | 'Demi-Deuil' (TB) **new** | EWoo |
| | 'Demon' (SDB) | CKel CPMA XSen |
| | 'Denys Humphry' (TB) | CKel WCAu |
| | 'Deputé Nomblot' (TB) | ESgI EWoo |
| | 'Derwentwater' (TB) | SRms |
| | 'Desert Dream' (AB) | GGar |
| I | 'Desert Dream' (Sino-Sib) | GAbr |
| | 'Desert Echo' (TB) | MHer XSen |
| | 'Desert Orange' (SDB) | WViv |
| | 'Desert Song' (TB) | CKel WCAu |
| | 'Destination' (Spuria) ♕$^{H4}$ | CIri |
| | 'Devil David' (TB) | CIri |
| | 'Devil May Care' (IB) | CIri EWoo WAul |
| | 'Devil's Lake' (TB) | WViv |
| | 'Devil's Spoon' (TB) | CIri |
| | 'Devonshire Cream' (TB) | CIri |
| | 'Diabolique' (TB) ♕$^{H4}$ | EWoo WViv XSen |
| | 'Diamond Ring' (TB) **new** | SDys |
| | 'Diligence' (SDB) ♕$^{H4}$ | CKel |
| | 'Disco Jewel' (MTB) | ESgI |
| | 'Ditto' (MDB) | WViv |
| | 'Diversion' (TB) | ESgI |
| | 'Divine' (TB) | CKel |
| | 'Dixie Darling' (TB) | ESgI XSen |
| | 'Dixie Pixie' (SDB) | WCAu WTin |
| | 'Dogrose' (TB) | EWoo |
| | ***dolichosiphon*** | GAuc |
| | aff. ***dolichosiphon*** | GAuc |
| | 'Doll' (IB) | EWoo |
| | 'Dolly Madison' (TB) | ESgI |
| | 'Don Juan' (TB) | ESgI |
| | 'Donegal' (IB) | WViv |
| | 'Don't Touch' (TB) | CIri |
| | 'Doodads' (TB) | ESgI |
| | 'Dorcas Lives Again' (TB) | WHil |
| | 'Dorothy' (TB) | SBch |
| | 'Dotted Swiss' (TB) **new** | XSen |
| | 'Double Bubble' (TB) | EWoo |
| | 'Double Byte' (SDB) | XSen |
| | 'Double Click' (TB) **new** | EWoo |
| | 'Double Espoir' (TB) | ESgI WViv XSen |
| | 'Double Lament' (SDB) | CBro |
| | 'Double Mini' | EWoo |
| | 'Double Shot' (TB) | EWoo |
| | 'Double Vision' (TB) | EWoo XSen |
| | 'Double Your Fun' (IB) | WAul |
| | 'Douce Reverie' (TB) | WViv |
| | ***douglasiana*** ♕$^{H4}$ | ECho GCal MHer NWCA WFar |
| | | WOut WWEG |
| | - 'Cape Ferrelo' | SKHP |
| | 'Dover Beach' (TB) | SGar SIri |
| | 'Draco' (TB) | ESgI XSen |
| | 'Drake Carne' (TB) | CKel |
| | 'Dream Express' (TB) | WViv |

| | | |
|---|---|---|
| | 'Dream Indigo' (IB) | CKel EWoo WCAu XSen |
| | 'Dream Lover' (TB) | ESgI |
| | 'Dreamsicle' (TB) | EWoo SIri WViv |
| | 'Dreamy' (TB) **new** | EWoo |
| | 'Dresden Candleglow' (IB) | WCAu |
| | 'Dualtone' (TB) | CKel SAga |
| | 'Dunlin' (MDB) | CBro ECho NBir |
| | 'Dural White Butterfly' (La) | CHid LPBA MSCN |
| | 'Durham Dream' (TB) | CIri |
| | 'Dusky Challenger' (TB) | CKel CPMA ESgI EWoo WCAu WViv XSen |
| | 'Dusky Evening' (TB) | ESgI XSen |
| | 'Dutch Chocolate' (TB) | ESgI ETod EWes EWoo WViv XSen |
| | 'Dwight Enys' (TB) ♀H4 | CKel |
| | 'Dynamite' (TB) | EWoo XSen |
| | 'Dyonisos' (TB) | WViv |
| | 'Eagle's Flight' (TB) | CKel XSen |
| | 'Earl of Essex' (TB) | WCAu XSen |
| | 'Early Frost' (IB) | CKel WViv |
| | 'Early Light' (TB) ♀H4 | ESgI WCAu |
| | 'Easter' (SDB) | SIri |
| | 'Eastertime' (TB) | ESgI WViv |
| | 'Easy' (MTB) **new** | SIri |
| | 'Easy Grace' (TB) | EWoo |
| | 'Eau Vive' (TB) | WViv |
| | 'Ebony Echo' (TB) | EWoo |
| | 'Echo de France' (TB) | ESgI EWoo XSen |
| | 'Ecstatic Echo' (TB) | ESgI WViv |
| | 'Edge of Winter' (TB) | CKel SIri XSen |
| | 'Edith Wolford' (TB) | CCCN CWCL ECtt ESgI EWoo GBin MWea SRGP WViv WWEG XSen |
| N | 'Ed's Blue' (DB) | ELan |
| | 'Edward' (Reticulata) | CBro ECho EPfP EPot GKev LAma LRHS MWat NMin SDeJ SMrm |
| | 'Edward of Windsor' (TB) | ELan GMaP NLar SRGP WMnd |
| | 'Effervescence' (TB) | WViv |
| | 'Eggnog' (TB) | EWoo |
| | 'El Tovar' (TB) **new** | EWoo |
| | 'Eldorado' (TB) **new** | EWoo |
| | 'Eleanor Clare' (IB) ♀H4 | CKel |
| | 'Eleanor Hill' (Spuria) | WAul |
| | 'Eleanor Roosevelt' (IB) | EWoo |
| | 'Eleanor's Pride' (TB) | CKel ESgI WCAu |
| | 'Electrique' (TB) | WCAu |
| | 'Elegans' (TB) | MCot |
| | ***elegantissima*** | see *I. iberica* subsp. *elegantissima* |
| | 'Elizabeth Arden' (TB) | CKel |
| | 'Elizabeth of England' (TB) | COIW CSpr GKev SRGP WWEG |
| | 'Elizabeth Poldark' (TB) | ESgI XSen |
| | 'Ella' (IB) | CSpr |
| * | 'Ellenbank Damselfly' | GMac |
| | 'Elsa Sass' (TB) | ESgI |
| | 'Elsie Petty' (IB) | SIri |
| N | 'Elvinhall' | CBro |
| | 'Empress of India' (TB) | EBee |
| | 'Encre Bleue' (IB) | ESgI WViv |
| | 'Endless Love' (TB) | EIri WViv |
| | 'English Charm' (TB) | ESgI EWoo WAul WViv XSen |
| | 'English Cottage' (TB) | COIW ELon GBin GCal LSRN LTen MWat NLar SMrm WCAu WSHC WWEG XSen |
| | 'Ennerdale' (TB) | SRms |
| | 'Ennoble' (TB) | ESgI |
| | 'Enriched' (MTB) ♀H4 | SIri |
| § | ***ensata*** ♀H4 | CBcs CBro CHEx COIW CWat ELan EPfP EWTr LPBA LRHS MHer MMuc MNrw NBro NLar SPlb SRms SWat WCFE WFar |
| N | – 'Activity' | CRow GBin NBro SHar WFar WWEG |
| | – 'Agrippine' | SKHP |
| | – 'Alba' | ECha |
| | – 'Aldridge Prelude' | WAul |
| | – 'Aldridge Snow Maiden' ♀H4 | WAul |
| | – 'Aldridge Visitor' ♀H4 | WAul |
| | – 'Alpine Majesty' ♀H4 | CIri |
| | – 'Apollo' | CBen CRow |
| | – 'Artist' | NBro |
| | – 'Asian Warrior' | LRHS NLar |
| | – 'August Emperor' | EKen LAst SMrm WCAu |
| | – 'Azuma-kagami' | CFir EBee EKen ELan EPfP MNrw |
| | – 'Azure' | CSpr |
| N | – 'Barnhawk Sybil' | SKHP |
| | – 'Barr Purple East' ♀H4 | CHid CPrp CRow |
| | – 'Blue Beauty' **new** | CSpr |
| I | – 'Blue King' | NBro SPet |
| I | – 'Blue Peter' | CBen CRow |
| | – 'Blue Pompon' | WViv |
| | – 'Blue Prince' | CBen |
| N | – 'Blush' | NBro |
| | – 'Butterflies in Flight' | CRow |
| | – 'Caprician Butterfly' ♀H4 | CMHG CSpr EPfP GBin LRHS MBri WCAu |
| N | – 'Carnival Prince' | CFir NBro WFar WMoo WPnP |
| | – 'Cascade Crest' | SWat WAul |
| | – 'Cascade Spice' | WAul |
| | – 'Center of Interest' | MSCN NBir NCGa |
| * | – 'Chico Geisho' | WAul |
| | – 'Chitose-no-tomo' | CRow |
| | – 'Chiyodajō' | CKel |
| | – 'Continuing Pleasure' ♀H4 | WAul |
| | – 'Crepe Paper' | WFar |
| N | – 'Cry of Rejoice' | EBee ECho ECtt NBre NBro SWat WFar |
| | – 'Crystal Halo' | CIri LRHS WCAu |
| | – 'Dace' | GAbr GBin |
| | – 'Dancing Waves' | CRow |
| I | – 'Darling' | CRow EBee ECho EPfP MBri MMuc NBro NLar SEND SRGP SWat WFar WMoo WWEG |
| | – 'Diamant' | GBin |
| | – 'Dramatic Moment' | WFar WWEG |
| I | – 'Dresden China' | CRow |
| N | – 'Eden's Blue Pearl' | CHid |
| N | – 'Eden's Blush' | MLHP |
| N | – 'Eden's Charm' | ELan EPfP GBin LPBA |
| N | – 'Eden's Paintbrush' | ELan EPfP SPer WHil |
| N | – 'Eden's Picasso' | CFir ELan IPot |
| N | – 'Eden's Purple Glory' | CHid GBin WCot WTin |
| N | – 'Eden's Starship' | CFir |
| | – 'Electric Rays' | WAul |
| I | – 'Emotion' | CMac EBee NBro WAul WFar WPnP |
| | – 'Epimetheus' | WViv |
| | – 'Evening Episode' | WViv |
| | – 'Exstase' | WViv |
| I | – 'Fortune' | MBri WAul |
| | – 'Fractal Blue' | CIri |
| | – 'Freckled Geisha' | CIri EBee ELon IPot LRHS NBir |
| | – 'Frilled Enchantment' ♀H4 | IPot WCAu |
| * | – 'Galathea' | CPrp |
| | – 'Geisha Gown' | WViv |
| N | – 'Gipsy' | EBee |
| | – 'Gold Bound' | SKHP |
| N | – 'Gracieuse' | EBee ELan EPfP GBin LRHS MSCN NBro NLar SUsu SWat WFar WPnP WWEG |
| | – 'Gusto' | CMHG EBee ELon EPfP IPot MBri MNrw MWts NBro SPoG SWat WBor |

| | | |
|---|---|---|
| | - 'Haru-no-umi' | CKel |
| | - 'Hercule' | CHid CPLG CRow GAbr NBir |
| | - Higo hybrids | LRHS |
| | - Higo white | SPer |
| * | - 'Himatsuri' | CMHG |
| N | - 'Hokkaido' | CBen CRow |
| | - 'Hoshi-akari' **new** | WBor |
| | - hybrids | EHon ESgI |
| * | - 'Innocence' | CKel CMac NBre NLar SWat WAul WFar WMoo |
| | - 'Iso-no-nami' | CDes EBee NBro WAul |
| * | - 'Jitsugetsu' | CFir CMHG NLar |
| | - 'Jocasta' **new** | MBri |
| N | - 'Jodlesong' | WFar |
| | - 'Kalamazoo' | WFar |
| | - 'Katy Mendez' ♀H4 | CSpr WAul |
| * | - 'Kiyo-tsura' | CKel |
| * | - 'Kiyo-zuru' | EPfP MWts |
| N | - 'Kogesho' | EBee EPfP LRHS MNrw NBro NLar |
| N | - 'Koh Dom' | SPer |
| | - 'Kongo San' | WFar |
| | - 'Kuma-funjin' | CPLG CRow |
| | - 'Kumo-no-obi' | CMHG CSpr EBee EBla GGar NBro NPnk SPoG SWat |
| * | - 'Kunshikoku' | NLar |
| | - 'Lace Ruff' | EBee MBri |
| | - 'Lady in Waiting' | EPfP GBin MBri NLar SMrm SWal WHil |
| | - 'Landscape at Dawn' | CRow |
| N | - 'Laughing Lion' | EBee EBla ECtt MBri NBro WAul WFar WMoo WWEG |
| | - 'Light at Dawn' | CEnt CMHG EPfP MLLN NBPC NBro WAul WBor WFar WMoo |
| N | - 'Lilac Blotch' | SPer |
| I | - 'Loyalty' | EBla ECho SRGP WFar |
| | - 'Mancunian' ♀H4 | CKel |
| I | - 'Mandarin' | CBen CRow |
| | - 'Midsummer Reverie' | CRow WViv |
| N | - 'Momozomo' | LLHF NBro NLar |
| § | - 'Moonlight Waves' | CHid CMHG CPLG CPrp CRow EAEE EBee EBla ELan EPPr EPfP EShb GAbr GCra GGar GKin GMaP GMac LRHS MCot MWts NBro NGdn NHol SMrm SPoG SWat WAul WFar |
| | - 'Murasame' ♀H4 | CMHG WAul |
| | - 'Ocean Mist' | CHid ECtt NBro WViv |
| | - 'Oku-banri' | CHEx CPLG CPrp EShb |
| | - 'Ol' Man River' ♀H4 | WAul |
| | - 'Oriental Eyes' | GBin NGdn NLar WAul |
| | - pale mauve-flowered | NBir SPer |
| | - 'Pastel Princess' | WAul |
| | - 'Pin Stripe' | MBri MWts NLar SUsu SWat WAul WBor WMoo |
| | - 'Pink Frost' | CRow EBee ELan EPPr EPfP EWll GCal LBMP LHop LRHS MWts NBro WFar WTin |
| | - 'Pinkerton' | CIri |
| | - 'Pleasant Earlybird' | WAul |
| | - 'Pleasant Journey' | ECtt |
| | - 'Prairie Frost' | NLar SMrm |
| | - 'Prairie Noble' | EBee NBro NLar |
| N | - 'Purple Glory' | ELan |
| | - purple-flowered | SPer |
| | - 'Queen's Tiara' | ELon |
| | - 'Rakka-no-Utage' | NLar |
| | - 'Ranpo' | CRow |
| I | - 'Red Dawn' | CBen |
| I | - 'Reveille' | EBee NBro SWat WAul |
| | - 'Rivulets of Wine' | CIri |
| § | - 'Rose Queen' ♀H4 | Widely available |
| | - 'Rowden Amir' | CRow |
| | - 'Rowden Autocrat' | CRow |
| | - 'Rowden Begum' | CRow |
| | - 'Rowden Caliph' | CRow |
| | - 'Rowden Consul' | CRow |
| | - 'Rowden Dauphin' | CRow |
| | - 'Rowden Dictator' | CRow |
| | - 'Rowden Emperor' | CRow |
| | - 'Rowden King' | CRow |
| | - 'Rowden Knave' | CRow |
| | - 'Rowden Knight' | CRow |
| | - 'Rowden Mikado' | CRow |
| | - 'Rowden Naib' | CRow |
| | - 'Rowden Nuncio' | CRow |
| | - 'Rowden Pasha' | CRow |
| | - 'Rowden Prince' | CRow |
| | - 'Rowden Queen' | CRow |
| | - 'Rowden Shah' | CRow |
| | - 'Rowden Sultana' | CRow |
| I | - 'Royal Banner' | EBee MBri NBro WAul WFar |
| | - 'Royal Crown' | ECho XLum |
| | - 'Royal Pageant' | CMHG EBee NBPC NBro |
| I | - 'Ruby King' | LEdu WAul |
| | - 'Ruffled Dimity' | CBcs EBee IPot LRHS MLLN NBPC WHil |
| | - 'Sandsation' | CIri |
| | - 'Sapphire Star' | CKel |
| | - 'Sea of Amethyst' | MWts |
| | - 'Sennyo-no-hora' | CPrp |
| I | - 'Sensation' | CMHG CWCL ECho ECtt EWTr GBin MBri SMrm SWat WAul WWEG |
| | - 'Snowy Hills' | WAul XLum |
| | - 'Sorcerer's Triumph' | GBin GGar LRHS WFar WViv |
| | - var. ***spontanea*** | SWat |
| | - - B&SWJ 1103 | WCru |
| | - - B&SWJ 8699 | WCru |
| | - 'Springtime Melody' | WAul |
| I | - 'Star' | CBen |
| | - 'Stippled Ripples' | IPot MWts SPoG |
| | - 'Summer Snowflake' | WViv |
| | - 'Summer Storm' ♀H4 | CKel SPer |
| | - 'Taga-sode' | WViv |
| | - 'Taketori-hime' (v) **new** | XLum |
| | - 'The Great Mogul' ♀H4 | CKel CRow |
| | - 'Tropic Showers' | WViv |
| | - 'Umi-kaze' | NLar |
| | - 'Variegata' (v) ♀H4 | Widely available |
| N | - 'Velvety Queen' | CPrp WAul |
| | - 'Waka-murasaki' | NBro |
| I | - 'White Ladies' | CSBt EWll SWat WWEG |
| I | - 'White Pearl' | CRow |
| | - white-flowered | WFar |
| | - 'Wine Ruffles' | CMHG EBee LSRN SIri SMrm |
| | - 'Worley Pink' | WViv |
| | - 'Yako-no-tama' | CRow WMoo |
| | - 'Yamato Hime' | CMHG EPfP NLar |
| N | - 'Yedo-yeman' | WFar |
| | - 'Yezo-nishiki' | GBin NBro |
| N | - 'Yu Nagi' | SPer |
| | 'Entertainer' (TB) | EWoo |
| | 'Epicenter' (TB) | XSen |
| | 'Eramosa Skies' (SDB) | WCAu |
| | 'Erect' (IB) | CKel |
| | 'Esoteric' (SDB) | ESgI |
| | 'Etched Apricot' (TB) | WCAu |
| | 'Eternal Bliss' (TB) | EWoo WViv |
| | 'Evening Drama' (TB) **new** | WCAu |
| | 'Evening Gown' (TB) | XSen |

| | Name | Suppliers |
|---|---|---|
| | 'Evening Pond' (MTB) | CKel |
| | 'Ever After' (TB) | ECtt ESgI EWoo WViv XSen |
| | 'Evergreen Hideaway' (TB) | CIri |
| | 'Everything Plus' (TB) | ESgI XSen |
| | 'Exclusivity' (TB) | ESgI |
| | 'Exotic Isle' (TB) | ECtt ESgI WViv XSen |
| | 'Extra' (BB) | CPBP LLHF WViv |
| | 'Extra Innings' (TB) **new** | EWoo |
| | 'Eye Magic' (IB) ♀H4 | CKel XSen |
| | 'Eye of Tiger' (Dut) | see *I.* 'Tigereye' |
| | 'Eyebright' (SDB) ♀H4 | CBro WCAu |
| | 'Fabuleux' (TB) | SIri WViv |
| | 'Faenelia Hicks' (La) | WMAq |
| | 'Falconeer' (TB) **new** | CIri |
| | 'Fall Empire' (TB) | EWoo |
| | 'Fall Enterprise' (TB) | CIri |
| | 'Fall Fiesta' (TB) | ESgI WViv XSen |
| | 'Fancy Brass' (TB) | SIri |
| | 'Fancy Dress' (TB) | SIri WViv |
| | 'Fanfaron' (TB) | ESgI XSen |
| | 'Fanfreluche' (TB) | WViv |
| | 'Farleigh Damson' (SDB) **new** | SIri |
| | 'Fashion Holiday' (IB) | SIri |
| | 'Fashion Lady' (MDB) | CBro ECho |
| | 'Fashion Statement' (TB) | WViv |
| | 'Fashionably Late' (TB) | WViv |
| | 'Fathom' (IB) | WCAu |
| | 'Favori' **new** | EWoo |
| | 'Feature Attraction' (TB) | WViv |
| | 'Feminine Charm' (TB) | MRav WCAu |
| | ***fernaldii*** | GAuc |
| | 'Festive Skirt' (TB) | CKel |
| | 'Feu du Ciel' (TB) ♀H4 | ESgI EWoo WViv XSen |
| | 'Fierce Fire' (IB) ♀H4 | CKel |
| | 'Fiesta Time' (TB) | CWCL ECtt EWoo WViv XSen |
| | 'Filibuster' (TB) | WCAu |
| | ***filifolia*** var. ***latifolia*** | NMin |
| | 'Film Festival' (TB) | ESgI |
| | 'Finalist' (TB) | WCAu WViv XSen |
| | 'Firebeard' (TB) | CIri |
| | 'Firebug' (IB) | ESgI WViv XSen |
| | 'Firecracker' (TB) | MRav |
| | 'First Interstate' (TB) | CWCL ESgI WViv XSen |
| | 'First Movement' (TB) | ESgI |
| | 'First Romance' (SDB) | LSRN SIri WViv |
| | 'Fit the Bill' (TB) | EWoo WViv |
| | 'Five Star Admiral' (TB) | XSen |
| | 'Flaming Dragon' (TB) | XSen |
| | 'Flaming Victory' (TB) | ESgI XSen |
| | ***flavescens*** | ESgI EWoo SBch WCAu XSen |
| | 'Fleur Collette Louise' (La) | CIri |
| | 'Flight of Fantasy' (La) | CKel |
| | 'Flight to Mars' (TB) | CIri |
| | 'Flirting' (SDB) | WViv |
| | 'Flirting Again' (SDB) ♀H4 | SIri WViv |
| | 'Floorshow' (TB) | XSen |
| § | 'Florentina' (IB/TB) ♀H4 | CArn CBro CHby COIW ECGP EOHP ESgI EWoo GCal GPoy ILis MNHC MRav NBid NBir SEND SIde WCAu WHer XSen |
| | 'Florentine Silk' (TB) **new** | WCAu |
| | 'Floridor' (TB) **new** | EWoo |
| | 'Flumadiddle' (IB) | CBro CKel |
| | 'Flushed Delight' (TB) | CIri |
| | 'Flute Enchantée' (TB) | CIri XSen |
| | 'Flutter-By' (TB) **new** | EWoo |
| | 'Focus' (TB) | XSen |
| | ***foetidissima*** ♀H4 | Widely available |
| | - 'Aurea' | GQue WCot |
| | - ***chinensis*** | see *I. foetidissima* var. *citrina* |
| § | - var. ***citrina*** | CBre CFir ECGP EPfP EPla EWld GAbr GCal GCra IBlr NLar SChr SUsu SWal WCot WGwG |
| | - 'Citrina' | EPri SLPl |
| | - 'Fructu Albo' | GBin NSti |
| | - var. ***lutescens*** | CHid EPPr |
| | - 'Variegata' (v) ♀H4 | CElw CHar ECtt EPfP MAvo MCCP MSCN NBir NPer WBor WCot WWFP |
| | - yellow-seeded | GCal WTin |
| | 'Foghound' (TB) | WCAu |
| | 'Foggy Dew' (TB) | EAEE EShb LRHS MWea NCGa NPnk |
| | 'Folie Douce' (TB) | WViv |
| | 'Fondation Van Gogh' (TB) | ESgI XSen |
| | 'Foolish Fancy' (TB) | EWoo SIri |
| | 'Footloose' (TB) | SIri WViv XSen |
| | 'Forest Hills' (TB) | LRHS |
| | 'Forest Light' (SDB) | CBro ESgI |
| | 'Forever Blue' (SDB) | WCAu WViv |
| | 'Forever Gold' (TB) | EWoo XSen |
| * | 'Forever Trevor' (CH) | SPhx |
| | 'Forever Yours' (TB) | WAul |
| | 'Forge Fire' (TB) | ESgI |
| | ***formosana*** | ECho |
| | - B&SWJ 3076 | WCru |
| | ***forrestii*** ♀H4 | CHid CPLG ECho GAbr GAuc GBin GCal GCra ITim LEdu LPBA MBri MHer MMuc NBPC NBir NBro NGdn SRot WAbe |
| | 'Fort Apache' (TB) | ESgI EWes EWoo |
| | 'Fortunata' (TB) | XSen |
| | 'Fortunate Son' **new** | EWoo WCAu |
| | 'Fortune Teller' (TB) | CKel |
| | 'Fourfold Blue' (SpH) | GBin |
| | 'Foxy Lady' (TB) | ESgI EWoo |
| | 'Framboise' (TB) | WViv XSen |
| | 'Frances Iva' (TB) | EWoo |
| | 'Francheville' (TB) **new** | EWoo |
| | 'Frank Elder' (Reticulata) | ECho EPot GKev LAma LLHF MRav SDeJ |
| | 'Frans Hals' (Dut) | GKev MMHG MNrw |
| | 'Freedom Flight' (TB) | CIri |
| | 'French Can Can' (TB) | EWoo SIri WViv |
| | 'French Horn' (TB) | CIri |
| | 'French Rose' (TB) | CKel |
| | 'Fresno Calypso' (TB) | ESgI WCAu XSen |
| | 'Friday Blues' (BB) **new** | WAul |
| | 'Frigiya' (Spuria) | WAul |
| | 'Frimousee' (TB) | ESgI WViv |
| | 'Fringe Benefits' (TB) | ESgI |
| | 'Frison-roche' (TB) | CWCL ESgI WViv |
| | 'Frisounette' (TB) | ESgI |
| | 'Fritillary Flight' (IB) ♀H4 | CKel SAga |
| | 'Frontier Lady' (TB) | CIri |
| | 'Frontier Marshall' (TB) | XSen |
| | 'Frost and Flame' (TB) | EBla ECtt ELan LBMP LBuc LRHS MAsh MCot MRav NBir NLar SBfd SPer SPoG SWat WAul WWEG |
| | 'Frost Echo' (TB) | EWoo |
| | 'Frosted Angel' (SDB) | CBro |
| | 'Frosted Biscuit' (TB) ♀H4 | CKel |
| | 'Frosted Fantasy' (TB) | CIri |
| | 'Frosted Velvet' (MTB) | WCAu |
| | 'Frosty Jewels' (TB) | ESgI XSen |
| | 'Fruit Cocktail' (IB) | CKel CRDP WViv XSen |
| | ***fulva*** ♀H3 | CDes CPrp CRow EBee GCal MMHG MWts NBir NBro NSti WBor WCot WHil WTin |
| | - 'Marvell Gold' (La) | CRow |

| | Name | Suppliers |
|---|---|---|
| | × ***fulvala*** ♀H4 | CDes CFir EWes GBin NBir NSti WTin |
| | – 'Violacea' | LRHS |
| | 'Fumo negli Occhi' (TB) | ESgI |
| | 'Funambule' (TB) | EWoo WViv |
| | 'Furnaceman' (SDB) | CBro MBri |
| | 'Futuriste' (TB) | SIri WViv |
| | 'Gai Luron' (TB) | WWEG |
| | 'Gallant Moment' (TB) | ECtt EWoo SIri WViv XSen |
| | 'Galleon Gold' (SDB) | CKel |
| | 'Galway' (IB) | SIri WViv XSen |
| | 'Garnement' (TB) | WViv |
| | 'Gay Head' (TB) **new** | EWoo |
| | 'Gay Parasol' (TB) | WViv |
| N | 'Gelbe Mantel' (Sino-Sib) | CBot CHid EBee NBir NBro NSti WFar |
| | 'Gemstar' (SDB) | WViv |
| | 'Gemstone Walls' (TB) | ESgI |
| | 'Gentius' (TB) | WMnd |
| | 'Gentle Grace' (SDB) | ESgI |
| | 'George' (Reticulata) ♀H4 | CAby CAvo CBro CFFs ECho EPfP EPot ERCP GKev LAma NMin NWad SPhx WBrk WHoo |
| | 'George Smith' (TB) | ESgI |
| | 'Gerald Darby' | see *I.* × *robusta* 'Gerald Darby' |
| | 'Gérard Brière' (TB) | WViv |
| | 'Germaine Perthuis' (TB) **new** | EWoo |
| | ***germanica*** ♀H4 | MMuc SEND WCAu |
| | – var. ***florentina*** | see *I.* 'Florentina' |
| N | – 'Mel Jope' | NBir |
| § | – 'Nepalensis' | WCAu |
| | – 'The King' | see *I. germanica* 'Nepalensis' |
| | 'Gertrude' (TB) | EWoo |
| | 'Ghost Train' (TB) | EWoo WViv |
| | 'Gingerbread Man' (SDB) | CBro CMea CPBP ESgI EWoo MBrN SWal WCAu |
| | 'Gingersnap' (TB) **new** | EWoo |
| | 'Glacier' (TB) | ECho |
| | 'Glacier Gold' (TB) | XSen |
| | 'Glad Rags' (TB) | ESgI XSen |
| | 'Gladbeck Yellow' (TB) **new** | EWoo |
| | 'Gladys Austin' (TB) | XSen |
| | 'Glory Bound' (TB) | WViv |
| | 'Gnu' (TB) | XSen |
| | 'Gnus Flash' (TB) | CIri |
| | 'Goddess of Green' (IB) **new** | EWoo |
| | 'Godfrey Owen' (TB) | CKel WCAu |
| | 'Godsend' (TB) | CIri CKel |
| | 'Going Home' (TB) ♀H4 | SIri |
| | 'Going My Way' (TB) | ESgI EWoo LSou SIri WCAu WViv WWEG XSen |
| | 'Gold Burst' (TB) | XSen |
| | 'Gold Country' (TB) | ESgI XSen |
| | 'Gold Galore' (TB) | WViv |
| | 'Gold of Autumn' (TB) | CKel SMrm |
| | 'Goldberry' (IB) | WCAu |
| | 'Golden Alien' (TB) | CIri |
| | 'Golden Alps' (TB) | SRms WCAu |
| | 'Golden Beauty' **new** | GKev |
| | 'Golden Child' (SDB) | ESgI XSen |
| | 'Golden Encore' (TB) | CKel WCAu |
| | 'Golden Fair' (SDB) | NBir |
| | 'Golden Forest' (TB) | GBin MWea |
| | 'Golden Immortal' (TB) | EWoo WViv |
| | 'Golden Panther' (TB) | WCAu |
| | 'Golden Planet' (TB) | CKel |
| | 'Golden Violet' (SDB) | ESgI |
| | ***goniocarpa*** | WAbe |
| | – KR 3739 | GEdr |
| | 'Good Looking' (TB) | ESgI WCAu |
| | 'Good Show' (TB) | EWoo WViv XSen |
| | 'Good Vibrations' (TB) | SIri WViv XSen |
| | 'Goodbye Heart' (TB) | ESgI EWoo LSRN WViv |
| | 'Gordon' (Reticulata) | CAvo CFFs ECho EPfP EPot ERCP GKev LAma MWat SMrm |
| | ***gormanii*** | see *I. tenax* |
| | 'Gosh' (SDB) | CKel |
| | 'Gossip' (SDB) | CBro |
| | 'Got Milk' (TB) | WViv |
| | 'Gracchus' (TB) | EWoo LRHS WCAu |
| | ***gracilipes*** | LWst |
| | ***gracilipes*** × ***lacustris*** | GAuc GEdr WAbe |
| | ***graeberiana*** | ECho EPot GKev LWst SDeJ |
| | – white fall | LWst |
| | – yellow fall | ECho LWst |
| | ***graminea*** ♀H4 | CAvo CBro CHid CMac CPne CRow EBee ECha ECho ELan EPPr EPfP EPri GKev IFro LLWP LRHS NBir NMen NSti NWCA SBch SEND WAul WCot |
| | – var. ***pseudocyperus*** | GCal NMRc SDys |
| | ***graminifolia*** | see *I. kerneriana* |
| | 'Granada Gold' (TB) | SRms XSen |
| | 'Grand Amiral' (TB) | EWoo WViv |
| | 'Grand Circle' (TB) | CIri EWoo |
| | 'Grand Waltz' (TB) | XSen |
| | 'Grape Accent' (TB) **new** | EWoo |
| | 'Grape Cordial' (SDB) **new** | WAul |
| | 'Grape Jelly' (TB) | WViv |
| | 'Grapelet' (MDB) | CPBP WCAu WViv |
| | 'Grapeshot' (TB) | CIri |
| | 'Great Gatsby' (TB) | CKel |
| | 'Great Lakes' (TB) | ESgI EWoo |
| | 'Grecian Skies' (TB) | ESgI |
| | 'Green Ice' (TB) | CKel MRav |
| | 'Green Prophecy' (TB) | CKel |
| | 'Green Spot' (SDB) ♀H4 | CBro CKel EBee EBla ECho ECtt ELan LHop LRHS MRav NBir NLar NWCA SBrd SDeJ SPer SPhx WAul |
| | 'Green Streak' (TB) | CIri |
| | 'Grenade' (TB) | WViv |
| | 'Gringo' (TB) | WCAu |
| | 'Gwyneth Evans' (BB) ♀H4 | CKel |
| | 'Gypsy Beauty' (Dut) | CAvo CFFs EPfP GKev LAma MWat SBch |
| | 'Gypsy Jewels' (TB) | CKel ESgI LTen XSen |
| | 'Gypsy Romance' (TB) ♀H4 | EIri ESgI EWoo SIri WCAu WViv |
| | 'Habit' (TB) | EWoo WAul WCAu |
| | 'Hafnium' (SDB) | CKel |
| | 'Hakuna Matata' (AB) **new** | SDys |
| | ***halophila*** | see *I. spuria* subsp. *halophila* |
| | 'Handshake' (TB) ♀H4 | WViv |
| | 'Happenstance' (TB) | ESgI EWoo WViv |
| | 'Happy Again' (TB) | WViv |
| | 'Happy Birthday' (TB) | ESgI |
| | 'Happy Mood' (IB) ♀H4 | NBre WCAu |
| | 'Harbor Blue' (TB) | CKel MWat SWat WCAu WWEG |
| * | 'Hareknoll' | NWCA |
| | 'Harlow Gold' (IB) | ESgI |
| | 'Harmony' (Reticulata) | CAby CAvo CBro CFFs ECho EPfP EPot GKev LAma MBri NWad SMrm SPhx |
| | 'Harriette Halloway' (TB) | EBla EPfP EShb ETod LRHS LSRN MAvo NLar SMrm SRGP WCot |
| | ***hartwegii*** | ECho |
| | – NNS 05-394 | WCot |
| | – subsp. ***hartwegii*** | GAuc IGor |
| | – subsp. ***pinetorum*** | GAuc IGor |
| | 'Harvest King' (TB) | ECtt ESgI WViv XSen |

| | | |
|---|---|---|
| | 'Harvest of Memories' (TB) | ESgI EWoo WWEG |
| | 'Haut les Voiles' (TB) | CWCL WViv |
| | 'Haute Couture' (TB) | WViv XSen |
| | 'Haviland' (TB) | WViv XSen |
| | 'Headcorn' (MTB) ♀H4 | SIri WAul |
| | 'Headline Banner' (IB) | EWoo WCAu |
| | 'Heartbeat Away' (TB) | CIri |
| | 'Heartbreak Point' (TB) | EWoo |
| | 'Heart's Radiance' (MTB) **new** | SDys |
| | 'Heather Sky' (TB) | CIri |
| | 'Heaven's Edge' (TB) | WCAu |
| | 'Helen Boehm' (TB) | ESgI WViv |
| | 'Helen Collingwood' (TB) | ESgI EWoo |
| | 'Helen Dawn' (TB) ♀H4 | SIri |
| | 'Helen McGregor' (TB) | CKel ESgI EWoo |
| | 'Helen Proctor' (IB) | ESgI EWoo WCot XSen |
| | 'Helene C.' (TB) | EWoo WViv XSen |
| | 'Helge' (IB) | COIW ECho NBre SWat |
| | 'Hellcat' (IB) | EWoo WAul WCAu WViv |
| | 'Hello Darkness' (TB) ♀H4 | ESgI EWoo WCAu WCot WViv XSen |
| | 'Hell's Fire' (TB) | EWoo GBin WCAu |
| | 'Hemstitched' (TB) | EWoo |
| | 'Her Majesty' (TB) **new** | EWoo |
| | 'Hercules' (Reticulata) | ECho LAma NMin |
| | 'Heure Bleue' (TB) | EWoo WViv |
| | ***hexagona*** | GAuc |
| | 'Hey There' (MDB) | WViv |
| | 'Hi' (IB) | CIri |
| | 'High Barbaree' (TB) | EWoo |
| | 'High Blue Sky' (TB) | WCAu |
| | 'High Command' (TB) | CKel SMrm |
| | 'High Ho Silver' | ESgI |
| | 'High Impact' (TB) | EWoo |
| | 'High Roller' (TB) ♀H4 | CIri |
| | 'High Stakes' (TB) | WViv |
| | 'Highline Amethyst' (Spuria) | EPri WAul |
| | 'Hildegarde' (Dut) | SDeJ |
| | 'His Royal Highness' | WCAu |
| | 'Hissy-Fit' (IB) | CKel |
| | ***histrio*** | ECho EPot GAuc |
| | - subsp. ***aintabensis*** | ECho GKev LAma |
| | ***histrioides*** | ECho GAuc |
| § | - 'Angel's Tears' (Reticulata) | CAvo ECho GKev NMin |
| | - 'Halkis' (Reticulata) | EPot ERCP GKev LAma NMin |
| | - 'Lady Beatrix Stanley' | CBro ECho EPot ERCP GBin LAma NMen NMin |
| N | - 'Major' | CDes ECho GKev LAma NMin |
| N | - 'Michael Tears' | ECho |
| | - var. ***sophenensis*** | ECho |
| | 'Hocus Pocus' (SDB) | CWGN EAEE ECho EWoo LRHS WAul WViv |
| | 'Hold That Tiger' (TB) **new** | EWoo |
| | 'Holden Clough' (SpH) ♀H4 | CBot CPLG CPrp CRow ELan EPfP EPla GBin GCra GMaP LEdu MLLN MRav NBir NEgg NGdn NSti WAul WBrk WCAu WFar WHer WPtf WSHC WWEG |
| | 'Holden's Child' | MWts WHil |
| | × ***hollandica*** hort. | NBir |
| | 'Hollywood Nights' (TB) **new** | EWoo |
| | 'Holy Night' (TB) | CKel |
| | 'Honey Behold' (SDB) | CKel |
| | 'Honey Glazed' (IB) | ESgI WAul WViv |
| | 'Honeylove' (SDB) **new** | SDys |
| | 'Honeymoon Suite' (TB) | EWoo WViv |
| | 'Honeyplic' (IB) ♀H4 | SIri |
| | 'Honington' (SDB) | WCAu |
| | 'Honky Tonk Blues' (TB) | CKel ESgI LSRN WViv |
| | 'Honky Tonk Hussy' (BB) | CKel |
| | 'Honorabile' (MTB) | EWoo SMrm WCAu |
| | ***hoogiana*** ♀H3 | ECho EPot GKev LRHS |
| | - 'Purpurea' | ECho |
| § | ***hookeri*** | CPBP EBee ELan GAuc GBin GBuc GGar GKev GMac IGor LEdu MGos NBPC SMrm |
| | ***hookeriana*** | LRHS MMuc |
| | 'Horizon Bleu' (TB) | EWoo |
| § | 'Hornpipe' (TB) | WCAu |
| | 'Hortensia Rose' (TB) | SIri |
| | 'Hot Spiced Wine' (TB) **new** | EWoo |
| | 'Hot to Trot' (TB) | ESgI |
| | 'Howard Weed' (TB) | MNrw |
| | 'Huckleberry Fudge' (TB) | WAul XSen |
| | 'Hula Hands' (IB) **new** | CIri |
| | 'Hula Moon' (TB) | ESgI |
| § | ***humilis*** | GKev |
| | ***hyrcana*** | ECho |
| | 'I Repeat' (TB) | ESgI XSen |
| | 'I Seek You' (TB) | ESgI |
| | ***iberica*** | ECho GAuc |
| § | - subsp. ***elegantissima*** | ECho LWst |
| | - subsp. ***iberica*** | LWst |
| § | - subsp. ***lycotis*** | LWst |
| | 'Ice Dancer' (TB) ♀H4 | CKel |
| | 'Iced Tea' (TB) ♀H4 | CIri |
| | 'Ida' (Reticulata) | ECho LAma |
| | 'Idol' (TB) | EWoo |
| | 'Ila Crawford' (Spuria) ♀H4 | XSen |
| | 'I'll Be Back' (IB) **new** | WAul |
| | ***illyrica*** | see *I. pallida* |
| | ***imbricata*** | GKev |
| | 'Imbue' (SDB) | ESgI WViv |
| | 'Immortality' (TB) | CKel CWGN EKen ESgI WCAu WCot WWEG XSen |
| | 'Imperative' (IB) **new** | EWoo SIri |
| | 'Imperator' (Dut) | ECho |
| | 'Imperial Bronze' (Spuria) | WAul WCAu |
| | 'Impetuous' (BB) ♀H4 | CKel |
| | 'Imprimis' (TB) | ESgI EWoo XSen |
| | 'In Concert' (TB) **new** | SMrm |
| | 'In Limbo' (IB) | CKel |
| | 'In Love' (TB) | XSen |
| | 'In Reverse' (TB) | WViv |
| | 'In Town' (TB) | ESgI EWoo XSen |
| | 'Incentive' (TB) | ECtt EWoo |
| * | 'Incoscente' (TB) | ESgI |
| | 'Indian Chief' (TB) | CCCN CWCL EPfP ESgI EWoo GBin LTen MRav SPur WCAu WWEG |
| | 'Indian Hills' (TB) **new** | EWoo |
| | 'Indian Idyll' (IB) | CKel EWoo |
| | 'Indian Jewel' (SDB) | ECho |
| | 'Indian Pow Wow' (SDB) | CRDP CSev |
| N | 'Indiana Sunset' (TB) | CKel |
| | 'Indigo Flight' (IB) | CKel |
| | 'Indigo Princess' (TB) | CKel EWoo WViv XSen |
| | 'Indigo Seas' (TB) **new** | EWoo |
| | 'Indiscreet' (TB) | WViv |
| | 'Infernal Fire' (TB) | CIri |
| | 'Inferno' (TB) | EWoo WViv |
| | 'Infinite Grace' (TB) | ESgI |
| | 'Inner Vision' (TB) | WViv |
| | 'Innocent Devil' (TB) | CIri |
| | 'Innocent Pink' (TB) | ESgI |
| | ***innominata*** | CAvo ECha ECho EPot GAbr GAuc GKev IBlr LHop LRHS NBir NBro NMen SRms WCot WWEG |
| | - JCA 1:460:800 | GEdr |
| | - NNS 01-407 | WCot |

| | | |
|---|---|---|
| | - apricot-flowered | IBlr |
| | - Ballyrogan hybrids | IBlr |
| | - bronze-flowered | MMuc SEND |
| | - dwarf **new** | NMen |
| | - 'Peacock' | GEdr |
| | - yellow-flowered | NMen NRya |
| | 'Inscription' (SDB) | CPBP ECho |
| | 'Interpol' (TB) | ESgI EWoo XSen |
| | 'Intrepid' (TB) | CWCL WViv |
| | 'Invicta Daybreak' (IB) | SIri |
| | 'Invicta Garnet' (SDB) **new** | SIri |
| | 'Invicta Gold' (SDB) | SIri |
| | 'Invitation' (TB) | ESgI |
| | 'Irisades' (TB) | WViv |
| | 'Irish Chant' (SDB) | WCAu |
| | 'Irish Moss' (SDB) | WViv |
| | 'Irish Tune' (TB) | ESgI |
| | 'Iron Eagle' (TB) **new** | CIri |
| | 'Isabelle' **new** | LSRN XSen |
| | 'Island Dancer' (TB) | WViv |
| | 'Island Sunset' (TB) | ESgI EWoo SIri WViv |
| | 'Isoline' (TB) | ESgI |
| | 'J.S. Dijt' (Reticulata) | CAvo CBro CFFs ECho EPfP EPot ERCP GKev LAma MBri MGos SPhx |
| | 'Jabal' (SDB) | SIri WViv |
| | 'Jack Attack' (La) **new** | MSCN |
| | 'Jacquessiana' | EWoo |
| | 'Jade Mist' (SDB) | ECho |
| | 'Jaguar Blue' (TB) | EWoo WCAu |
| | 'Jane Phillips' (TB) ♀H4 | Widely available |
| | 'Jane Taylor' (SDB) | CBro |
| | 'Janet Lane' (BB) | CKel SAga |
| | 'Janine Louise' (TB) ♀H4 | CKel |
| | ***japonica*** ♀H3 | CHEx CPLG ECho EPfP NLar NPer WAul WOut XLum XSen |
| | - B&SWJ 8921 | WCru |
| | - 'Bourne Graceful' | CAby CPLG |
| | - 'Ledger' | CAby CDes CHll CMac CPLG CPrp ECha ELan EPfP IGor MRav SEND SHom SMad WWFP |
| N | - 'Rudolph Spring' | GCal WWFP |
| § | - 'Variegata' (v) ♀H3 | CAby CBot CBro CChe CDes CHEx CKel CPrp ECha ELan ELon ESwi GGar MHer NBro NPer SAga SArc SBfd SEND SMad WHil WWFP XSen |
| | 'Jasper Gem' (MDB) | ECho NBir |
| | 'Java Bleue' (TB) | WViv |
| | 'Jayceetee' (TB) | CIri |
| | 'Jazz Festival' (TB) | EWoo SIri WViv XSen |
| | 'Jazzamatazz' (SDB) | ESgI WViv |
| | 'Jazzed Up' (TB) | WViv XSen |
| | 'Je l'Adore' (TB) | EWoo WViv |
| | 'Jean Cayeux' (TB) | ESgI EWoo |
| | 'Jean Guymer' (TB) | ESgI EWoo NBir |
| | 'Jeanne Price' (TB) | EWoo LSRN WCAu WViv |
| | 'Jelly Belly' (SDB) | EWoo |
| | 'Jennie Grace' (SDB) | SIri |
| | 'Jeremy Brian' (SDB) ♀H4 | WCAu |
| | 'Jesse Lee' (SDB) | CKel |
| | 'Jesse's Song' (TB) | ESgI XSen |
| | 'Jet Black' (TB) **new** | EWoo |
| | 'Jet-Setter' (TB) | CIri |
| | 'Jeunesse' (TB) | ESgI |
| | 'Jewel Baby' (SDB) | CBro CKel |
| | 'Jeweler's Art' (SDB) | EWoo WViv |
| | 'Jiansada' (SDB) | CBro |
| | 'Jigsaw' (TB) | ESgI XSen |
| | 'Joanna' (TB) | GKev LSRN NLar WWEG |
| | 'John' (IB) | CKel LSRN |
| | 'Joli Coeur' (TB) | ESgI EWoo WViv |
| | 'Joy Boy' (SDB) | ESgI |
| | 'Joyce' (Reticulata) | CBro ECho EPfP EPot GKev LAma MBri NLar SDeJ SMrm SPhx |
| | 'Joyce Terry' (TB) | CWan ESgI |
| | 'Joyful' (SDB) | ESgI WViv |
| | 'Jubilant Spirit' (Spuria) | EWes |
| | 'Jubilation' (TB) | EWoo |
| | 'Jubilé Rainier III' (TB) | WViv |
| | 'Jubilee Gem' (TB) | CKel SAga |
| | 'Jud Paynter' (TB) | CKel |
| | 'Julia Vennor' (TB) | CKel |
| | 'Juliet' (TB) | ESgI |
| | 'Jump Start' (IB) | EWoo WCAu |
| | 'Junaluska' (TB) **new** | EWoo |
| | 'June Prom' (IB) | EAEE LRHS SRGP |
| | 'Jungle Fires' (TB) | WCAu |
| | 'Jungle Shadows' (BB) | EWoo MRav NBir WCAu |
| | 'Jungle Warrior' (SDB) | CKel |
| | 'Jurassic Park' (TB) | ESgI EWoo WCAu XSen |
| | 'Juris Prudence' (TB) | ESgI |
| | 'Jus d'Orange' (TB) | WViv |
| | 'Just Before Dawn' (TB) | WViv |
| | 'Just Dance' (IB) | ESgI |
| | 'Just Jennifer' (BB) | WAul WCAu |
| | ***kaempferi*** | see *I. ensata* |
| | 'Kangchenjunga' (TB) | ESgI |
| | 'Karen' (TB) | LSRN WViv |
| | 'Kashmir White' (TB) | EWoo |
| | ***kashmiriana*** | CBcs ECre |
| | 'Katharine Hodgkin' (Reticulata) ♀H4 | Widely available |
| | - dark-flowered **new** | NMin |
| | 'Katie-Koo' (IB) ♀H4 | CKel |
| | 'Katy Petts' (SDB) | ESgI WCAu |
| | 'Kayleigh-Jayne Louise' (TB) | CKel |
| | 'Kelway Renaissance' (TB) | CKel |
| | ***kemaonensis*** | GAuc |
| | 'Ken's Choice' (TB) ♀H4 | CKel |
| | 'Kent Blackguard' (IB) | SIri |
| | 'Kent Compote' (IB) | SIri |
| | 'Kent Pride' (TB) | CSBt CWGN EAEE EBee EBla ECha ECtt EPfP ESgI EShb ETod EWoo GBin IPot LRHS MCot MRav MWat SBfd SBrd SGar SPer SPoG SWat WAul WTin |
| | 'Kentish Icon' (SDB) **new** | SIri |
| | 'Kentucky Derby' (TB) | WViv XSen |
| § | ***kerneriana*** ♀H4 | LRHS MLLN NBir |
| | 'Kharput' (IB) | EWoo |
| | 'Kildonan' (TB) | WCAu |
| | 'Kind Word' (TB) | WViv |
| | 'King's Jester' (TB) | EWoo |
| | ***kirkwoodii*** | ECho LWst |
| | 'Kiss of Summer' (TB) ♀H4 | ESgI SDys WAul |
| | 'Kissing Circle' (TB) | ESgI EWoo SBfd |
| | 'Kiwi Slices' (SDB) | CPBP ESgI |
| | 'Knick Knack' (MDB) | CBro CMea CPBP EBla ECho ELan EPfP GAbr GKev LBee MRav NWCA SMrs SPhx SPoG |
| | 'Kona Nights' (BB) | ESgI |
| | ***koreana*** | GAuc |
| | ***korolkowii*** | ECho |
| | - from Kazakhstan **new** | GAuc |
| | 'Kuh-e-Abr' **new** | GKev |
| | 'La Belle Aube' (TB) | ESgI |
| | 'La Meije' (TB) | SIri WViv |
| | 'La Senda' (Spuria) | WCot |
| | 'La Vie en Rose' (TB) | ESgI WViv |
| | 'Lace Legacy' (TB) | ECtt EWoo LSRN WViv |
| | 'Laced Cotton' (TB) | ESgI XSen |

| | | |
|---|---|---|
| | 'Laced Lemonade' (SDB) | MBri |
| § | ***lactea*** ♀H4 | GAuc NWCA XSen |
| | – var. ***lactea*** | GAuc |
| | ***lacustris*** ♀H4 | CBro NMen WAbe XSen |
| | 'Lacy Snowflake' (TB) | LHop |
| | 'Lady Essex' (TB) | EWoo |
| | 'Lady Friend' (TB) | ESgI WViv XSen |
| | 'Lady Gale' (IB) | CKel |
| | 'Lady in Red' (SDB) | ESgI WCAu |
| | 'Lady Mohr' (AB) | CKel |
| | 'Lady of Fatima' (TB) | ESgI |
| | 'Lady R' (SDB) | ECho |
| | ***laevigata*** ♀H4 | CRow ECha ECho EHon ELan EPfP GAuc ITim LPBA MMuc MRav NBro NPer SEND SGar SPer SWat WFar WMAq WMoo WPnP WShi WWEG |
| | – var. ***alba*** | CRow ECha ECho EHon ELan EPfP EWTr GAuc LPBA MMuc MRav SWat WFar WMoo |
| | – 'Atropurpurea' | CRow |
| | – 'Colchesterensis' | CRow EPri NGdn NPer SWat WMAq |
| I | – 'Dorothy' | LPBA NGdn |
| N | – 'Dorothy Robinson' | LRHS SWat |
| | – 'Elegant' | see *I. laevigata* 'Weymouth Elegant' |
| * | – 'Elgar' | WMAq |
| | – 'Liam Johns' | CRow |
| | – 'Midnight' | see *I. laevigata* 'Weymouth Midnight' |
| | – 'Mottled Beauty' | CRow |
| | – 'Rashomon' | CRow |
| | – 'Regal' | CWat |
| | – 'Richard Greaney' | CRow |
| | – 'Rose Queen' | see *I. ensata* 'Rose Queen' |
| | – 'Rowden Seaspray' | CRow |
| | – 'Rowden Starlight' | CRow |
| I | – 'Snowdrift' | CRow CWat LPBA LRHS NBir NGdn NLar NPer SPer SWat WFar WMAq WPnP |
| | – 'Variegata' (v) ♀H4 | CBen CRow CWat EAEE ECha ECho EHoe EPfP EPla LLWG LPBA MWts NBro NGdn NPer SPer SWat WMAq WMoo WTin |
| | – 'Violet Garth' | CRow |
| | – 'Weymouth' | see *I. laevigata* 'Weymouth Blue' |
| § | – 'Weymouth Blue' | CRow |
| § | – 'Weymouth Elegant' | CRow |
| § | – 'Weymouth Midnight' | CMil CRow LPBA SWat |
| N | 'Langport Chapter' (IB) | CKel ESgI |
| N | 'Langport Chief' (IB) | CKel |
| N | 'Langport Claret' (IB) | CKel ESgI |
| N | 'Langport Curlew' (IB) | CKel ESgI |
| N | 'Langport Duchess' (IB) | ESgI WTin |
| N | 'Langport Fairy' (IB) | CKel ESgI |
| N | 'Langport Finch' (IB) | NBir |
| N | 'Langport Flame' (IB) | CKel ESgI EWoo SAga WTin |
| N | 'Langport Haze' (IB) | ESgI |
| N | 'Langport Hope' (IB) | CKel ESgI |
| N | 'Langport Jane' (IB) | CKel |
| N | 'Langport Lady' (IB) | CKel |
| N | 'Langport Lord' (IB) | ESgI |
| | 'Langport Minstrel' (IB) | CKel ESgI |
| N | 'Langport Pearl' (IB) | CKel |
| | 'Langport Phoenix' (IB) | CKel |
| N | 'Langport Pinnacle' (IB) | CKel |
| N | 'Langport Robe' (IB) | ESgI |
| N | 'Langport Smoke' (IB) | CKel |
| | 'Langport Snow' (IB) | CKel |
| N | 'Langport Song' (IB) | CKel ESgI |
| N | 'Langport Star' (IB) | CKel ESgI |

| | | |
|---|---|---|
| | 'Langport Storm' (IB) | CKel EAEE EBla ESgI LRHS MRav WAul WTin |
| N | 'Langport Sun' (IB) | CKel ESgI |
| N | 'Langport Swift' (IB) | CKel |
| | 'Langport Sylvia' (IB) | CKel |
| N | 'Langport Tartan' (IB) | CKel |
| N | 'Langport Violet' (IB) | CKel ESgI |
| | 'Langport Vista' (IB) | CKel SAga |
| | 'Langport Warrior' (IB) | CKel |
| | 'Langport Wren' (IB) ♀H4 | CAby CBro CKel EAEE EPfP EPri ESgI GCal GQue LAst LRHS MBri MCot NBir SBch SBfd WAul WTin WWEG |
| | 'Lark Ascending' (TB) | WViv |
| | 'Lark Rise' (TB) ♀H4 | CKel |
| | 'Last Hurrah' **new** | EWoo |
| | 'Late Liftoff' (TB) **new** | CIri |
| § | ***latifolia*** ♀H4 | ECho MMuc NMin SEND WShi |
| | – 'Duchess of York' | ECho GKev |
| | – 'Isabella' | ECho GKev |
| | – 'King of the Blues' | ECho GKev |
| | – 'Mansfield' | ECho |
| | – 'Montblanc' | ECho GKev |
| | – 'Queen of the Blues' (Eng) | ECho |
| | – wild-collected | GCal |
| | 'Latin Lady' (TB) | ESgI |
| | 'Latin Lark' (TB) | ESgI |
| | 'Laura Jean' (TB) | EWoo |
| | 'Laura Louise' (La) | SKHP |
| | 'Lava Moonscape' (TB) | CIri |
| | 'Lavandulacea' (TB) **new** | EWoo |
| | 'Lavender Park' (TB) | ESgI |
| | ***lazica*** ♀H4 | CAbP CBct CBro CHll CMac CPrp CRow CSpe EAEE EBee EPPr EPfP EPot ESgI GKev IBlr LEdu LRHS MRav NBir NCGa NSti NWCA SEND WCot WGwG WSHC |
| | – 'Joy Bishop' | CPMA WCot |
| * | – 'Richard Nutt' | CPMA ELon WCot |
| N | – 'Turkish Blue' | CPrp GBin IBlr |
| | 'Lazuline' **new** | LWst |
| | 'Leda's Lover' (TB) | ESgI |
| | 'Legato' (TB) | ESgI |
| * | 'Lemon Beauty' (TB) | LHop |
| | 'Lemon Brocade' (TB) | ESgI EWoo MBri WViv |
| | 'Lemon Fever' (TB) | ESgI |
| | 'Lemon Flare' (SDB) | EIri MRav SRms |
| | 'Lemon Flurry' (IB) | SBch |
| | 'Lemon Ice' (TB) | CAby EBla ECha EPfP LBuc LRHS MWea SBfd SPer |
| | 'Lemon Lyric' (TB) | ESgI |
| | 'Lemon Mist' (TB) | ESgI |
| * | 'Lemon Peel' (IB) | CKel |
| | 'Lemon Pop' (IB) | WCAu |
| | 'Lemon Puff' (MDB) | CBro WCAu |
| | 'Lemon Tree' (TB) | WCAu |
| | 'Lemon Whip' (IB) | EWoo |
| N | 'Lena' (SDB) | CBro |
| | 'Lenkoran' (Spuria) **new** | WAul |
| | 'Lenna M' (SDB) | CKel CPBP ECho |
| | 'Lenora Pearl' (BB) | ESgI EWoo XSen |
| | 'Lent A. Williamson' (TB) | GMaP WWEG |
| | 'Lenten Prayer' (TB) | WViv |
| | 'Leprechaun's Delight' (SDB) | CKel |
| | 'Leprechaun's Purse' (SDB) | WCAu WViv |
| | 'Let's Elope' (IB) | ESgI |
| | 'Licorice Fantasy' (TB) | ESgI |
| | 'Licorice Stick' (TB) | XSen |

'Light Beam' (TB) XSen
'Light Cavalry' (IB) ESgI EWoo
'Light Laughter' (IB) WCAu
'Light Rebuff' (TB) EWoo
'Lightning Streak' (TB) WViv
'Lightshine' (TB) WViv
'Lilac Times' EWoo
'Lilli-white' (SDB) CAby CKel CWat EBee EBla ELan LRHS MBNS MRav SBfd SPhx SPoG WWEG
'Lilting' (TB) XSen
'Lima Colada' (SDB) NBre
'Limbo' (SpH) CRow
'Lime Fizz' (TB) ESgI XSen
'Limelight' (TB) SRms
'Little Black Belt' (SDB) EWoo SIri
'Little Blackfoot' (SDB) ESgI WCAu WCot
'Little Blue-eyes' (SDB) ESgI WCAu
'Little Bluets' (SDB) ESgI
'Little Dandy' (SDB) ECho
'Little Dogie' (SDB) ECho
'Little Dream' (SDB) WCAu
'Little Episode' (SDB) ESgI
'Little Firecracker' (SDB) WCAu
'Little Paul' (MTB) ESgI
'Little Rosy Wings' (SDB) CBro CPBP
'Little Shadow' (IB) MRav SRms WWEG
'Little Showoff' (SDB) ESgI
'Little Snowman' **new** LRHS
'Little Tilgates' (CH) ♀H3 WCot
'Local Color' (TB) ESgI EWoo SIri WViv XSen
'Lodore' (TB) SRms
'Logo' (IB) WCAu
'Lohengrin' (TB) EWoo
'Lollipop' (SDB) ESgI SIri WViv
'London Pride' (TB) EWoo
***longipetala*** EWes NBir
'Loop the Loop' (TB) CMac EBee EWoo LAst MNrw MWea NBre SCoo SPoG SWat WViv
'Loose Valley' (MTB) ♀H4 SIri
'Lord Warden' (TB) EBla ECGP ECtt LRHS MCot MWea SAga SPur
'Loreley' (TB) ESgI
'Lorenzaccio de Médicis' (TB) ESgI EWoo
'Lorilee' (TB) ESgI
'Lothario' (TB) WFoF
'Lotus Land' (TB) WCAu
'Louis d'Or' (TB) ♀H4 WViv
'Louvois' (TB) ESgI EWoo NLar
'Love Power' (BB) **new** WAul
'Love the Sun' (TB) ESgI XSen
'Lovely Again' (TB) MRav WCAu
'Lovely Leilani' (TB) ESgI
'Lovely Light' (TB) MBri
'Lovely Señorita' (TB) WViv
'Love's Tune' (IB) EBla LBuc LRHS MAsh SRGP SWat
'Loyalist' (TB) EWoo SIri WViv
'Lucky Charm' (MTB) CMea
'Lucky Devil' (Spuria) ♀H4 CIri
'Lucy's Gift' (MTB) ♀H4 SRGP WAul
'Lugano' (TB) ESgI EWoo
'Lula Marguerite' (TB) **new** EWoo
'Luli-Ann' (SDB) ♀H4 CKel
'Lullaby of Spring' (TB) CKel
'Lumarco' (TB) EWoo WViv
'Lumière d'Automne' (TB) ESgI XSen
'Luminosity' (TB) ESgI
'Luna di Miele' (BB) ESgI
'Lunar Frost' (IB) SIri WViv
***lutescens*** ♀H4 ECho EPot GAuc GCra
§ – 'Campbellii' ECho
§ – subsp. ***lutescens*** XSen
'Luxor Gold' (TB) **new** EWoo
***lycotis*** see *I. iberica* subsp. *lycotis*
'Lyrique' (BB) CKel WAul
'Ma Mie' (IB) ESgI EWoo WViv
***maackii*** GEdr
– from Ussuri River GAuc
***macrosiphon*** IGor
'Madame Louis Aureau' (TB) **new** EWoo
'Madeira Belle' (TB) ESgI EWoo WViv
'Madeleine Frances' (SDB) SIri
'Mady Carriere' (TB) **new** EWoo
'Magharee' (TB) ESgI
'Magic Kingdom' (TB) CIri
'Magic Man' (TB) XSen
'Magical Encounter' (TB) EWoo WViv
***magnifica*** ♀H3-4 ECho ELon GKev
N – 'Agalik' ECho
– 'Alba' ECho
* 'Mahogany Mix' (Dut) LAma
'Maisie Lowe' (TB) ESgI EWoo
'Making Eyes' (SDB) ESgI WCAu
'Mallow Dramatic' (TB) WViv
'Man About Town' (TB) WCAu
I 'Mandarin' (TB) ESgI WViv
'Mandarin Purple' (Sino-Sib) CAby EBee GGar NGdn
***mandshurica*** CPBP
'Mango Entree' (TB) WCAu
'Many Mahalos' WAul
'Maple Treat' (TB) WViv
'Mara' (IB) CKel
'Marbre Bleu' (TB) WViv
'Marcel Turbat' (TB) ESgI WViv
'Marche Turque' (TB) ESgI EWoo
'Margrave' (TB) EWoo WViv XSen
'Marguérite' (Reticulata/v) ECho ERCP
***mariae*** **new** LWst
'Marie José Nat' (TB) WViv
'Mariposa Autumn' (TB) EWoo SIri WViv
'Mariposa Skies' (TB) ESgI
'Mariposa Wizard' (IB) WAul
'Marmalade Skies' (BB) WCAu
'Maroon Caper' (IB) SBch
'Martyn Rix' see *I. confusa* 'Martyn Rix'
'Mary Constance' (IB) ♀H4 CKel
'Mary Frances' (TB) ESgI LSRN WViv XSen
'Mary Geddes' (TB) **new** EWoo
'Mary McIlroy' (SDB) ♀H4 CBro CKel WTin
'Maslon' (MTB) ESgI
'Master Plan' (TB) WViv
'Master Touch' (TB) ELon XSen
'Masterwork' (TB) **new** CIri
'Matinata' (TB) CKel XSen
'Matt McNames' (TB) **new** EWoo
'Maui Moonlight' (IB) ♀H4 CKel ESgI EWoo NLar SAga WAul WCAu
'Mauna Loa Fire' (TB) EWoo
'May Melody' (TB) WCAu
'Maya Mint' (MDB) LLHF
'Meadow Court' (SDB) CBro CKel WCAu WWEG
'Media Luz' (Spuria) WCAu
'Medici Prince' (TB) EWoo
'Medway Valley' (MTB) ♀H4 SIri WCAu
'Megabucks' (TB) WViv
'Meg's Mantle' (TB) ♀H4 CKel
***mellita*** see *I. suaveolens*
'Melon Honey' (SDB) CKel ELon MAvo SAga WCAu

| | Name | Suppliers |
|---|---|---|
| | 'Menton' (SDB) | CKel |
| | 'Mer du Sud' (TB) ♀H4 | EIri ESgI EWoo LRHS WCot WViv XSen |
| * | 'Merebrook Blue Lagoon' (La) | WMAq |
| | 'Merebrook Jemma J' (La) | WMAq |
| * | 'Merebrook Lemon Maid' (La) | WMAq |
| | 'Merebrook Malvern Shadow' (La) | WMAq |
| | 'Merebrook Purpla' (La) | WMAq |
| * | 'Merebrook Rusty Red' (La) | WMAq |
| * | 'Merebrook Snowflake' (La) | WMAq |
| | 'Merebrook Sunnyside Up' (La) | WMAq |
| | 'Merry Dance' (SDB) | CKel |
| | 'Mesmerizer' (TB) | ESgI WViv |
| | 'Metaphor' (TB) | WCAu |
| | 'Mezza Cartuccia' (IB) | ESgI |
| | 'Michael Paul' (SDB) ♀H4 | ESgI |
| I | 'Midnight Blue' (MDB) | CBro |
| | 'Midnight Caller' (TB) | ESgI EWoo XSen |
| | 'Midnight Majesty' (TB) **new** | EWoo |
| | 'Midnight Mango' | see *I.* 'Midnight Web' |
| | 'Midnight Oil' (TB) | CIri EWoo WViv |
| § | 'Midnight Web' (IB) ♀H4 | CKel |
| | 'Midsummer Night's Dream' (IB) | EWoo WAul WViv |
| | 'Mighty Mouse' | EWoo |
| | ***milesii*** ♀H4 | CPLG GLam IGor NBir WSHC |
| | – CC 4590 | CHid |
| | 'Millennium Falcon' (TB) | WAul |
| | 'Mini Big Horn' (IB) | CIri |
| | 'Mini-Agnes' (SDB) | CBro |
| | 'Minnis Bay' (SDB) **new** | SIri |
| | 'Miss Carla' (IB) | NBre |
| | 'Miss Nellie' (BB) | CKel |
| | ***missouriensis*** ♀H4 | CAvo CMac EBee IGor NBid |
| | 'Mister Matthew' (TB) ♀H4 | CKel |
| | 'Mister Roberts' (SDB) | ESgI |
| | 'Mistigri' (IB) | WViv |
| | 'Mme Chéreau' (TB) | ESgI EWoo WCAu |
| | 'Mme Louis Aureau' (TB) | ESgI |
| | 'Moby Grape' (TB) **new** | GKev |
| | 'Monet's Blue' (TB) | EWoo WViv |
| | 'Monsieur-Monsieur' (TB) | ESgI |
| | Monspur Group | WCot |
| § | 'Monspur Cambridge Blue' (Spuria) ♀H4 | MWat |
| | 'Moon Journey' (TB) | SIri WAul WViv |
| | 'Moon Sparkle' (IB) | CKel |
| | 'Moonbeam' (TB) | CKel |
| | 'Moonlight Waves' | see *I. ensata* 'Moonlight Waves' |
| | 'Moonlit Waves' (TB) | CKel |
| | 'Moonstruck' (TB) | EWoo |
| | 'Morning's Blush' (SDB) ♀H4 | CIri |
| | 'Morwenna' (TB) ♀H4 | CKel |
| | 'Mote Park' (MTB) | WAul |
| | 'Mother Earth' (TB) | ESgI EWoo WAul |
| | 'Mountain Majesty' (TB) | ESgI |
| | 'Mountain Music' | EWoo |
| | 'Mousquetaire' (IB) | WViv |
| | 'Mrs Horace Darwin' (TB) | CFir SWat WMnd |
| | 'Mrs Tait' (Spuria) | NChi |
| | 'Mukaddam' (TB) | CIri |
| | 'Mulberry Rose' (TB) | CFee NChi |
| | 'Mulled Wine' (TB) | ESgI |
| | 'Must Unite' (TB) | WCAu |
| | 'My Honeycomb' (TB) | WCAu |
| | 'My Kayla' (SDB) | ESgI |
| N | 'My Seedling' (MDB) | CBro |
| | 'Myra' (SDB) | ESgI XSen |
| | 'Mysterieux' (TB) | SIri WViv |
| | 'Mystic Beauty' (Dut) | LAma |
| | 'Mystic Dragon' (TB) **new** | SDys |
| | 'Naivasha' (TB) | CKel |
| | 'Nancy' (TB) | SApp |
| | 'Nancy Hardy' (MDB) | CBro |
| | 'Naples' (TB) | ESgI WViv |
| | ***narcissiflora*** | WCot |
| | 'Nassak' (TB) **new** | EWoo |
| | 'Natascha' (Reticulata) | ECho EPot LAma NMin NWad SDeJ SPhx |
| | 'Natchez Trace' (TB) | EPri XSen |
| | 'Navajo Code' (TB) | CIri |
| | 'Navajo Jewel' (TB) | ESgI EWoo XSen |
| | 'Nectar' (IB) | ESgI |
| | 'Needlecraft' (TB) | NBre XSen |
| | 'Needlepoint' (TB) | ESgI |
| | 'Negro Modelo' (SDB) | WCAu |
| | 'Neige de Mai' (TB) | ESgI WViv |
| * | 'Nel Jupe' (TB) | LRHS NLar |
| | ***nepalensis*** | see *I. decora* |
| | ***nertschinskia*** | see *I. sanguinea* |
| | 'Neutron Dance' (TB) | WViv |
| | 'New Centurion' (TB) | EWoo WViv XSen |
| | 'New Day Dawning' (TB) | CIri |
| | 'New Idea' (MTB) | ESgI WCAu |
| | 'New Leaf' (TB) | WCAu |
| | 'New Snow' (TB) | WCAu |
| | 'Next in Line' **new** | EWoo |
| | 'Next Millenium' (TB) **new** | EWoo |
| | 'Nibelungen' (TB) | CPMA ELon MNrw MWea NBre WFar WGwG XSen |
| | 'Nice 'n' Nifty' (IB) | WTin |
| | 'Nicola Jane' (TB) ♀H4 | CKel |
| | ***nicolai*** | GKev |
| | – RM 8276 | LWst |
| | 'Night Edition' (TB) | CPMA ESgI EWoo XSen |
| | 'Night Game' (TB) | EWoo WViv XSen |
| | 'Night Owl' (TB) | CKel ELan ELon ESgI LAst LHop MCot MHer SPoG |
| | 'Night Ruler' (TB) | ESgI EWoo WViv |
| | 'Night Shift' (IB) | NBre WViv |
| | 'Nightfall' (TB) | EBee |
| | 'Nightmare' (TB) | CIri |
| | 'Nights of Gladness' (TB) | ESgI |
| | ***nigricans*** | LWst |
| | 'Noble Lady' (TB) | CIri |
| * | 'Noces Blanches' (IB) | ESgI |
| | 'Noctambule' (TB) | EWoo WViv |
| | 'Noon Siesta' (TB) | ESgI |
| | 'Nora Eileen' (TB) ♀H4 | CKel |
| | 'Nordica' (TB) | ESgI WViv |
| | 'Norfolk Belle' (TB) ♀H4 | WAul |
| | 'North Downs' (BB) | SIri |
| | 'Northern Jewel' (IB) | SIri WViv |
| | 'Northwest Pride' (TB) | EWoo WViv |
| | 'Nuee d'Orage' (TB) **new** | EWoo |
| | 'Nuit de Noces' (TB) | WViv |
| | 'Oasis Angel' (TB) | CIri |
| | 'Oasis Dragon' (TB) | CIri |
| | 'Oblivion' (IB) **new** | WAul |
| | 'Obsidian' (TB) | CIri WAul |
| | 'Ocean Depths' (TB) | ESgI |
| | 'Ocelot' (TB) | ESgI |
| | 'Ochraurea' (Spuria) | SMrm |
| | 'Ochre Doll' (SDB) | CBro CKel |
| | ***ochroleuca*** | see *I. orientalis* Mill. |

| | | |
|---|---|---|
| | 'O'Cool' (IB) | CKel |
| | 'October Storm' (IB) | EWoo |
| | 'Oh Jamaica' (TB) | XSen |
| | 'Oh So Cool' (MTB) | ESgI |
| | 'Oiseau Lyre' (TB) | ESgI |
| | 'Oklahoma' (TB) | EWoo |
| | 'Oktoberfest' (TB) | ESgI XSen |
| | 'Ola Kalá' (TB) | EAEE EBla ESgI EWll GMaP LRHS MCot NBre NLar SPer WCAu WWEG XSen |
| | 'Old Black Magic' (TB) | ESgI XSen |
| | 'Old Flame' (TB) | XSen |
| | 'Olympiad' (TB) | ESgI XSen |
| | 'Olympic Challenge' (TB) | ESgI MRav |
| | 'Olympic Torch' (TB) | ESgI |
| | 'Ominous Stranger' (TB) | ESgI WCAu |
| | 'Once Again' (TB) | EWoo XSen |
| | 'One Desire' (TB) | XSen |
| | 'Open Sky' (SDB) | EWoo SIri WViv XSen |
| | 'Orageux' (IB) | CWCL ESgI SIri WViv |
| | 'Orange Caper' (SDB) | EBla ECtt EPfP ESgI MRav NGdn NLar SBfd |
| | 'Orange Embers' (TB) | WViv |
| | 'Orange Encore' (SDB) | WAul |
| | 'Orange Harvest' (TB) | EWoo XSen |
| | 'Orange King' (TB) **new** | EWoo |
| N | 'Orange Plaza' | WHil |
| | 'Orange Pop' (BB) | WAul |
| | 'Orange Tiger' (SDB) | WViv |
| | 'Orchardist' (TB) | CKel |
| | 'Orchidarium' (TB) | CKel |
| | 'Orchidea Selvaggia' (TB) | ESgI |
| | ***orchioides*** misapplied | see *I. bucharica* Foster |
| § | ***orchioides*** Carrière | GKev |
| | - 'Aktash' | LWst |
| | - 'Baschkhizilsai' **new** | LWst |
| | - deep yellow-flowered | LWst |
| | - dwarf | LWst |
| N | - 'Urungachsai' | EPot LWst |
| | ***orchioides*** × ***warleyensis*** | LWst |
| | 'Oregon Skies' (TB) | ESgI ETod EWoo WViv |
| | 'Oreo' (TB) | CIri WCAu |
| | 'Oriental Baby' (IB) | CKel |
| | 'Oriental Beauty' (Dut) | CAvo GKev LAma SBch SPhx WCot WFar |
| | 'Oriental Touch' (SpH) | CRow |
| | ***orientalis*** Thunb. | see *I. sanguinea* |
| | ***orientalis*** ambig. | CAvo EPyc EWes SLPl |
| § | ***orientalis*** Mill. ϒ$^{H4}$ | CBot EWTr GAuc GCal LRHS NLar SGar WCru WDyG XSen |
| | - 'Alba' | see *I. sanguinea* 'Alba' |
| | 'Orinoco Flow' (BB) ϒ$^{H4}$ | CHar CKel ESgI |
| | 'Orloff' (TB) | ESgI |
| | 'Oro Antico' (TB) | CIri |
| | 'Osage Buff' (TB) | CKel |
| | 'Osay Canuc' (TB) | CIri |
| | 'Ostrogoth' (TB) | CIri |
| | 'Othello' (TB) **new** | EWoo |
| | 'Oulo' (TB) | ESgI XSen |
| | 'Our House' (TB) | ESgI |
| | 'Ouragan' (TB) | WViv |
| | 'Out Yonder' (TB) | WCAu |
| | 'Ovation' (TB) | ESgI |
| | 'Over Easy' (SDB) | CKel |
| | 'Overjoyed' (TB) | XSen |
| | 'Overnight Sensation' (TB) | EWoo WViv |
| | 'O'What' (SDB) | ESgI |
| | 'Oxford Tweeds' (SDB) | ESgI |
| | 'Ozark Maid' (MTB) **new** | SDys |
| | 'Ozone Alert' (TB) | CIri |
| | Pacific Coast hybrids | see *I.* Californian hybrids |
| | 'Pacific Mist' (TB) | WCAu WViv |
| | 'Pacific Panorama' (TB) | ESgI XSen |
| | 'Pagan Dance' (TB) | EWoo |
| | 'Pagan Goddess' (TB) | EWoo |
| | 'Pagan Pink' (TB) | CIri XSen |
| | 'Paint It Black' (TB) | ETod EWoo WViv XSen |
| | 'Pale Shades' (IB) ϒ$^{H4}$ | CBro CKel CPBP |
| | 'Palissandro' (TB) | ESgI |
| § | ***pallida*** | EBee ESgI EWoo GMaP MCCP MRav MWat SEND SRms WCAu WMnd XSen |
| § | - 'Argentea Variegata' (TB/v) | CSBt CWCL EBee ECha EHoe EPfP EShb EWoo GKev GMaP LAst LRHS MAsh MBrN MBri MCot MNFA MRav NBir NBro SBfd SBrd SPer SPoG WAul WHoo WWEG XSen |
| | - 'Aurea' | see *I. pallida* 'Variegata' Hort. |
| | - 'Aurea Variegata' | see *I. pallida* 'Variegata' Hort. |
| | - subsp. ***cengialtii*** | NWCA XSen |
| | - var. ***dalmatica*** | see *I. pallida* subsp. *pallida* |
| § | - subsp. ***pallida*** ϒ$^{H4}$ | CBot CKel CPLG CWan EAEE ECGP ECha ELan GCal LRHS MBri SDix SPer |
| | - 'Variegata' misapplied | see *I. pallida* 'Argentea Variegata' |
| § | - 'Variegata' Hort. (v) ϒ$^{H4}$ | CAby CBcs CBot CBro CHar CMac CWat EBee ECha ELan EPfP ESgI LRHS MBri MCot MRav NBPC NSti SDix SPer SPet SPlb SRot SWvt WCFE WCot WFar WWEG XSen |
| | 'Palm Springs' (IB) | NMin |
| | 'Paltec' (IB) | CPou |
| | 'Pane e Vino' (TB) | ESgI |
| | 'Pansy Top' (SDB) | SIri |
| | 'Paradise' (TB) | CKel |
| | ***paradoxa*** | ECho LWst |
| | 'Paricutin' (SDB) | CBro |
| | 'Paris Lights' (TB) | XSen |
| | 'Parisien' (TB) | CWCL EIri WViv |
| | 'Parts Plus' (IB) | CIri |
| | 'Party Dress' (TB) | CAby CMac CSam EBee EBla ELan EPfP LRHS MRav MWhi NBir NGdn NLar SBfd SPer SPoG SRms STes SWat WCot |
| | 'Pastel Charm' (SDB) | NPnk WMnd |
| | 'Patches' (TB) | ESgI |
| | 'Patina' (TB) | ECtt EIri ESgI ETod EWoo WAul WCAu WViv |
| | 'Patterdale' (TB) | NBir NBre |
| | 'Paul Black' (TB) ϒ$^{H4}$ | CIri |
| | 'Pauline' (Reticulata) | CAvo CBro ECho EPfP ERCP GKev LAma LRHS MWat SMrm SPhx |
| | 'Peaceful Waters' (TB) | ECtt EWoo WViv XSen |
| | 'Peach Eyes' (SDB) | CBro CKel |
| | 'Peach Jam' (TB) **new** | WHlf |
| | 'Peach Picotee' (TB) | ESgI WViv XSen |
| | 'Peach Spot' (TB) | CPMA |
| | 'Peachy Face' (IB) | XSen |
| | 'Pearls of Autumn' (TB) | WCAu |
| | 'Pearly Dawn' (TB) | EBla ECtt LRHS SPer SRGP SWat WWEG |
| | 'Peau de Pêche' (TB) | WViv |
| * | 'Pêche Melba' (TB) | ESgI XSen |
| | 'Pegaletta' (La) | NBro |
| | 'Peggy Chambers' (IB) ϒ$^{H4}$ | CSpr |
| | 'Pele' (SDB) | ESgI |
| | 'Penny a Pinch' (TB) | WWEG |
| | 'Pepita' (SDB) | EWoo SIri WViv |
| | 'Perfect Interlude' (TB) | ECtt EIri WViv XSen |
| | 'Performer' (MTB) **new** | SIri |

| | | |
|---|---|---|
| | 'Perfume Shop' (IB) | CKel |
| | 'Persan' (TB) **new** | EWoo |
| | 'Persian Berry' (TB) | WCAu XSen |
| | 'Persian Gown' (TB) | EWoo |
| | 'Petal Pushers' (TB) **new** | CIri |
| | 'Pétillant' (TB) | EWoo WViv |
| | 'Petit Caprice' (TB) | WViv |
| | 'Petit Tigre' (IB) | WViv |
| | 'Petite Monet' (MTB) | ESgI |
| | 'Pharaoh's Daughter' (IB) | EWoo SIri |
| | 'Phil Keen' (TB) ♀H4 | CKel |
| | 'Philippa Baughen' (Spuria) ♀H4 **new** | CIri |
| N | 'Picadee' | EBla EPfP MWea |
| | 'Piero Bargellini' (TB) | ESgI |
| | 'Pigeon' (SDB) | XSen |
| | 'Pinewood Charmer' (CH) | CElw |
| | 'Pinewood Sunshine' (CH) | MAvo |
| | 'Pink Attraction' (TB) | ESgI XSen |
| | 'Pink Bubbles' (BB) | XSen |
| | 'Pink Charm' (TB) | EAEE EBla EPfP LBuc LRHS NCGa SBfd SMrm SPlb SPoG WAul |
| | 'Pink Confetti' (TB) | ESgI EWoo WViv XSen |
| | 'Pink Fawn' (SDB) | ESgI |
| | 'Pink Formal' (TB) | ESgI |
| | 'Pink Horizon' (TB) | EPfP XSen |
| | 'Pink Kitten' (IB) | WCAu WGwG XSen |
| N | 'Pink Lavender' (TB) | ELon |
| | 'Pink Parchment' (BB) ♀H4 | CKel |
| | 'Pink Pele' (IB) | ESgI WAul |
| | 'Pink Pinafore' (TB) **new** | EWoo |
| | 'Pink Pussycat' (TB) | MBri |
| | 'Pink Reprise' (BB) | EWoo |
| | 'Pink Rose' (TB) | WViv |
| | 'Pink Swan' (TB) | ESgI WViv XSen |
| | 'Pink Taffeta' (TB) | ESgI XSen |
| | 'Pinnacle' (TB) | CKel ESgI GCal SWat |
| | 'Pipes of Pan' (TB) | ESgI WCAu |
| | 'Pirate's Patch' (SDB) | ESgI |
| | 'Pirate's Quest' (TB) | ESgI EWoo WViv XSen |
| | 'Piroska' (TB) ♀H4 | ESgI SGar WViv XSen |
| * | 'Piu Blue' (TB) | ESgI |
| | 'Pixie' (DB) | GKev |
| | 'Pixie' (Reticulata) ♀H4 | ECho ELan EPot LAma NLar SDeJ SMrm |
| | ***planifolia*** | CMea LWSt |
| | 'Platinum' (TB) | WCAu |
| | 'Pledge Allegiance' (TB) | ECtt ESgI EWoo WViv |
| | 'Plickadee' (SDB) | CBro |
| | 'Pluie d'Or' (TB) | ESgI |
| | 'Plum Fun' (TB) | WViv |
| | 'Plum Lucky' (SDB) | SIri WViv |
| | 'Plum Wine' (SDB) | CKel CPMA |
| | 'Plumeri' (TB) **new** | EWoo |
| | 'Poesie' (TB) | WViv |
| | 'Pogo' (SDB) | CAby EBla ECho ECtt ELan EPfP EPot ETod GMaP LRHS MMHG MRav NBir NWCA SBfd SBrd SDeJ SMrm SRms |
| | 'Polished Manners' (TB) | WViv |
| | 'Pond Lily' (TB) | ESgI |
| | 'Pookanilly' (IB) | CPMA WViv |
| | 'Poppa John' (TB) | CIri |
| | 'Portfolio' (TB) | ESgI |
| | ***potaninii*** | GAuc |
| | 'Powder Blue Cadillac' (TB) | CKel |
| | 'Power Point' (TB) | CIri |
| | 'Power Surge' (TB) | EWoo |
| | 'Prairie Sunset' (TB) | EWoo |
| | 'Precious Heather' (TB) ♀H4 | CKel |
| | 'Presence' (TB) | SIri WViv |
| | 'Pretender' (TB) | WCAu |
| | 'Pretty Please' (TB) | ESgI |
| | 'Prime Power' (TB) **new** | EWoo |
| | 'Prince Indigo' (TB) | MRav |
| | 'Prince of Burgundy' (IB) ♀H4 | CIri |
| | 'Princess Beatrice' (TB) | EWoo WCAu |
| | 'Princess Sabra' (TB) ♀H4 | CKel |
| | 'Princesse Caroline de Monaco' (TB) | CWCL ESgI EWoo WViv |
| | ***prismatica*** | GKev |
| | - ***alba*** | IGor |
| | 'Private Treasure' (TB) | WViv |
| | 'Prodigy' (MDB) | WViv |
| | 'Professor Blaauw' (Dut) ♀H4 | CAvo CFFs EPfP GKev SPhx |
| | 'Progressive Attitude' (TB) | EPri |
| | 'Protocol' (IB) | CKel WViv |
| | 'Prototype' (TB) | CIri |
| | 'Proud Tradition' (TB) | SIri WCAu WViv XSen |
| | 'Provençal' (TB) | CKel CPMA CWCL ECtt ESgI ETod EWoo WAul WCAu WViv XSen |
| | 'Prudy' (BB) ♀H4 | CKel |
| | 'Prunelle' (IB) | WViv |
| | ***pseudacorus*** ♀H4 | Widely available |
| | - B&SWJ 5018 from Japan | WCru |
| | - from Korea | CRow |
| | - 'Alba' | CPrp EBee GBin GCal MRav MWts NGdn SWat |
| | - var. ***bastardii*** | CRow CWat EBee ECha ELon EPfP ESgI LPBA MSKA NPer SLon SPer SWat WBrk WFar WMoo WPnP WTin WViv XLum |
| | - 'Beuron' | CRow |
| | - cream-flowered | NBir SWat WAul |
| N | - 'Crème de la Crème' | ELon GBin GQue NLar NSti WHil |
| | - 'Donau' **new** | CSpr |
| | - 'Esk' | GBin GCal |
| N | - 'Flore Pleno' (d) | CBot CPrp CRow EBee ECho ESgI GCra LPBA MSKA NLar NPer WBrk WCot WFar WPnP WWEG |
| N | - 'Golden Daggers' | CRow |
| I | - 'Golden Fleece' | SPer |
| | - 'Golden Queen' | CRow |
| | - 'Ilgengold' | CRow |
| N | - 'Ivory' | CRow CSpr |
| | - 'Krill' | WHil |
| | - 'Mandchurica' | XBlo |
| * | - ***nana*** | CRow |
| | - 'Roccapina' | GBin |
| | - 'Roy Davidson' ♀H4 | CBro CPrp CRow GBin GCal IBlr LPBA NLar WCot WFar WHil WTin WViv |
| N | - 'Sulphur Queen' | WCot |
| | - 'Sun Cascade' | CRow |
| N | - 'Tiger Brother' | CBro WBrk |
| | - 'Tiggah' | CRow |
| N | - 'Turnipseed' | WCot WTin |
| | - 'Variegata' (v) ♀H4 | Widely available |
| | - white-flowered, from Lake Michigan | WTin |
| * | ***pseudocapnoides*** (J) | LWSt |
| | 'Pulse Rate' (SDB) | CBro |
| | ***pumila*** | CPBP LRHS MCot MWat NWCA |
| | - 'Alba' (DB) | CPBP |
| | - f. ***atroviolacea*** | CKel ESgI SMrm WMnd |
| * | - 'Caerulea' | GAuc |
| N | - 'Gelber Mantel' | NBir |
| N | - 'Lavendel Plicata' | NBro |

| | Name | Suppliers |
|---|---|---|
| | – 'Nicola' | NWCA |
| | – 'Violacea' (DB) | SRms |
| | – yellow-flowered | SWal |
| | 'Pumpin' Iron' (SDB) ♀H4 | CKel CPMA ESgI |
| | 'Punch' (BB) | WAul |
| | 'Punchline' (TB) | CWCL ECtt WViv |
| | 'Punk' (MDB) | CIri |
| | 'Puppet Baby' (MDB) | WViv |
| | ***purdyi*** | IGor |
| | 'Pure As Gold' (TB) | CWCL ESgI EWoo WViv XSen |
| | 'Purple Gem' (Reticulata) | ECho EPfP EPot GKev LAma SPhx |
| | 'Purple People Eater' (TB) | CIri |
| | 'Purple Sensation' (Dut) | ECho SDeJ |
| | 'Purr for Mints' (TB) new | CIri |
| | 'Quaker Lady' (TB) | ESgI EWoo SIri |
| | 'Quantum Leap' (TB) | CIri |
| | 'Quark' (SDB) | CBro CKel CPBP |
| | 'Quechee' (TB) | CWCL EAEE EBee EBla EPfP ESgI ETod EWoo GMaP IPot LBuc LRHS LSRN MAvo MCot MRav NCGa NLar SBrd SMrm SPer STes SWat WAul WGwG |
| | 'Queen in Calico' (TB) | ESgI WViv |
| | 'Queen of Angels' (TB) new | WCAu |
| | 'Queen of Hearts' (TB) | XSen |
| | 'Queen of May' (TB) | ESgI EWoo |
| | 'Queen's Circle' (TB) ♀H4 | CIri |
| | 'Queen's Ivory' (SDB) | SMrs |
| | 'Queen's Prize' (SDB) | SIri WViv |
| | 'Rabbit's Foot' (SDB) | LSRN WViv |
| | 'Radiant Apogee' (TB) | ECtt EIri ESgI WViv |
| | 'Radiant Burst' (IB) | SIri |
| | 'Rain Dance' (SDB) ♀H4 | ESgI |
| | Rainbow Grand Mixture | SDeJ |
| | 'Rainbow Rim' (SDB) | ESgI |
| | 'Rajah' (TB) | CAby EBee EBla ELan EPfP ESgI EShb EWoo GMaP LRHS LSRN MCot MLHP MMHG MRav NCGa NOrc SBfd SBrd SPer SPoG SPur WMnd |
| | 'Ramblin' Rose' | WViv |
| | 'Rameses' (TB) | ESgI EWoo |
| | 'Rancho Rose' (TB) | CKel XSen |
| | 'Rapture in Blue' (TB) | EWoo WViv |
| | 'Rare Edition' (IB) | CKel ESgI EWoo NBir NBre WAul WViv XSen |
| | 'Rare Quality' (TB) | WAul WViv XSen |
| | 'Rare Treat' (TB) | XSen |
| | 'Raspberry Acres' (IB) | MRav WCAu |
| | 'Raspberry Blush' (IB) ♀H4 | CAby CKel CPar EAEE EBla EIri EPfP GBin IPot LBMP LRHS LSou MAsh MRav NBre NCGa NGdn SAga SPur STes SWat WAul WWFP XSen |
| | 'Raspberry Frost' (TB) new | EWoo |
| | 'Ravenous' (TB) | WViv |
| | 'Ravissant' (TB) | WViv |
| | 'Razoo' (SDB) | CKel |
| | 'Re La Blanche' (TB) | WViv |
| | 'Real Coquette' (SDB) | SIri WViv |
| | 'Realm' (TB) | ESgI |
| | 'Rebecca Perret' (TB) | WViv |
| | 'Rebus' (SDB) | SIri |
| | 'Red at Night' (TB) | WAul |
| | 'Red Atlast' (MDB) | ESgI |
| | 'Red Canyon Glow' (TB) | CIri |
| | 'Red Flash' (TB) | ESgI |
| | 'Red Hawk' (TB) | WViv |
| | 'Red Heart' (SDB) | ESgI MRav WHil WTin WWEG XSen |

| | Name | Suppliers |
|---|---|---|
| | 'Red Orchid' (IB) | ELan NBre SRms WCAu WWEG |
| | 'Red Revival' (TB) | MRav WCAu |
| N | 'Red Rum' (TB) | CKel EWes |
| | 'Red Tornado' (TB) | ESgI |
| | 'Red Zinger' (IB) | CPMA ESgI EWoo WAul WViv |
| | 'Redelta' (TB) | XSen |
| | 'Redondo' (IB) new | EWoo |
| | 'Reflets Safran' (TB) | SIri WViv XSen |
| | 'Reg Wall' (TB) ♀H4 | CIri |
| | 'Regal Surprise' (SpH) ♀H4 | CRow WAul |
| | 'Regards' (SDB) | CBro GEdr XSen |
| § | ***reichenbachii*** | CPBP EPot LLHF NWCA WThu |
| | 'Reincarnation' (TB) | EWoo |
| | 'Reminiscence' (MTB) | ESgI |
| | 'Renewal' (TB) | EWoo |
| | 'Renown' (TB) | ESgI EWoo |
| | 'Repartee' (TB) | ESgI EWoo XSen |
| | 'Replicator' (SDB) new | EWoo |
| | ***reticulata*** ♀H4 | ECho ELan EPfP LRHS SDeJ SEND SMrm SPer WGwG |
| | – var. ***bakeriana*** | ECho NMin |
| | – 'Spring Time' | ECho GKev LAma NMin SDeJ |
| N | – 'Violet Queen' | ECho |
| | 'Return to Bayberry' (TB) | CIri |
| | 'Return to Sender' (TB) | EWoo |
| | 'Réussite' (TB) new | EWoo |
| | 'Rhages' (TB) new | EWoo |
| | 'Rheinfels' (TB) new | EWoo |
| | 'Rheingauperle' (TB) new | EWoo |
| | 'Rime Frost' (TB) | WCAu |
| | 'Ringer' (SDB) | ESgI WViv |
| | 'Ringo' (TB) | CKel ESgI EWoo LSRN MRav |
| | 'Rio de Oro' (TB) | WViv |
| | 'Rip City' (TB) | ESgI EWoo WViv |
| | 'Ripple Chip' (SDB) | WTin |
| | 'Rippling River' (TB) | WViv |
| | 'Rippling Waters' (TB) | ESgI |
| | 'Rising Moon' (TB) | EWoo SIri WViv |
| | 'Ritz' (SDB) | WWEG |
| | 'Rive Gauche' (TB) | ESgI |
| | 'Riverbuds' | SIri WCAu |
| | 'Robe d'Été' (TB) | CWCL WViv |
| § | × ***robusta*** 'Dark Aura' ♀H4 | MAvo MWts WCot WTin WViv |
| § | – 'Gerald Darby' ♀H4 | Widely available |
| | – 'Mountain Brook' | CRow LLWG |
| | – 'Nutfield Blue' | WTin |
| * | – 'Purple Fan' | LLWG |
| | 'Rock Star' (TB) | CIri |
| § | 'Rocket' (TB) | CAby EBla EPfP GMaP LBuc LRHS MRav MWea NBir NBre SMrm SPer WAul |
| | 'Rocket Master' (TB) | ESgI |
| | 'Roman Carnival' (TB) | EWoo |
| | 'Roman Rhythm' (TB) | EWoo |
| | 'Romance' (TB) | EWoo WViv |
| | 'Romano' (Dut) | LRHS |
| | 'Romantic Evening' (TB) | EIri ESgI EWoo WViv XSen |
| | 'Romantic Mood' (TB) | CKel WViv |
| | 'Romney Marsh' (IB) | SIri |
| | 'Ron' (TB) | EWoo |
| | 'Rondo' (TB) | ECtt |
| | 'Rosalie Figge' (TB) | ESgI EWoo WCot WViv |
| | 'Rosé' (TB) | LSRN WViv |
| | 'Rose Queen' | see *I. ensata* 'Rose Queen' |
| | 'Rose Unique' (IB) new | EWoo |
| | 'Rose-Marie' (TB) new | EWoo |
| | 'Rosemary's Dream' (MTB) | ESgI NBre |
| | 'Rosemohr' (TB) new | EWoo |
| | ***rosenbachiana*** | ECho LWst |
| | – 'Darwas' new | LWst |

| | | |
|---|---|---|
| | – deep purple-flowered | LWst |
| N | – 'Harangon' | ECho LWst |
| | – 'Tovil-Dara' **new** | LWst |
| | 'Roseplic' (TB) | ESgI LRHS WViv |
| | 'Rosette Wine' (TB) | ESgI |
| | 'Rosy Veil' (TB) | EWoo |
| | 'Rosy Wings' (TB) | ECho ESgI EWoo |
| | 'Roucoulade' (TB) | SIri WViv |
| | 'Rouge Gorge' (TB) | WViv |
| | 'Rougissant' | WViv |
| | 'Roulette' (TB) | MBri |
| N | 'Roy Elliott' | NMen |
| | 'Royal Courtship' (TB) | ESgI |
| | 'Royal Crusader' (TB) | CCse CPMA EWoo XSen |
| | 'Royal Elegance' (TB) | SIri WViv |
| | 'Royal Intrigue' (TB) | SIri WViv |
| | 'Royal Magician' (SDB) | WTin |
| | 'Royal Satin' (TB) | CHid MNrw WGwG |
| | 'Royal Tapestry' (TB) | NBre |
| | 'Royalist' (TB) | CKel |
| | 'Rubacuori' (TB) | ESgI EWoo |
| | 'Ruban Bleu' (TB) | ESgI WViv |
| | 'Rubistar' (TB) | ESgI EWoo |
| | 'Ruby Chimes' (IB) | ESgI WCAu |
| | 'Ruby Contrast' (TB) | WCAu |
| | 'Ruby Eruption' | WViv |
| | ***rudskyi*** | see *I. variegata* |
| | 'Ruée vers l'Or' (TB) | ESgI |
| | 'Ruffled Goddess' (TB) | WViv |
| | 'Russet Crown' (TB) | CKel |
| | 'Rustic Cedar' (TB) | ESgI WViv |
| | 'Rustic Royalty' (TB) | WViv |
| | 'Rustler' (TB) | ESgI |
| | 'Rusty Beauty' (Dut) | LAma |
| | 'Rusty Magnificence' (TB) | EWoo WViv |
| | 'Ruth Rowlands' (TB) | EWoo |
| | ***ruthenica*** | ECho GBin GLam WCot |
| | – var. ***nana*** | CPLG GKev |
| | 'Ryan James' (TB) | CKel |
| | 'Sable' (TB) | EBee EBla ELan EPfP ESgI ETod EWoo GMaP LBuc LRHS LSRN MAsh MCot MRav MWat NLar NOrc SEND SMrm SPer WAul WCAu WWEG |
| | 'Sable Night' (TB) | CHar CKel ESgI |
| | 'Sager Cedric' (TB) | WCAu |
| | 'Saint Crispin' (TB) | EPfP GCra GMaP LRHS MRav SBfd SPer SPoG WGwG |
| | 'Sally Jane' (TB) | WCAu |
| | 'Salonique' (TB) | NBre NLar |
| | 'Saltwood' (SDB) | CBro NBre SIri |
| | 'Sam Carne' (TB) | WCAu |
| | × ***sambucina*** **new** | XSen |
| | 'San Gabriel' (TB) **new** | EWoo |
| | 'San Leandro' (TB) | MBri |
| | 'San Leon' (DB) | GBin |
| | 'Sandro' (TB) | WViv |
| | 'Sandstone Sentinel' (BB) | CIri |
| | 'Sandy Caper' (IB) | WCAu WTin |
| | 'Sangone' (IB) | ESgI |
| § | ***sanguinea*** 🏆$^{H4}$ | CMCN LEdu |
| § | – 'Alba' | IBlr |
| | – 'Nana Alba' | CSpr GBin IBlr |
| § | – 'Snow Queen' | CAvo CBcs EBee ELan EPfP EPla EPri EShb EWTr GBin GGar GKev GMaP LPBA LRHS MBri MGos MSCN NCGa NPri NSti SPer SWat WCot WMnd WMoo WWEG |
| | 'Santana' (TB) | ECtt |
| | 'Sapphire Beauty' (Dut) | SDeJ |

| | | |
|---|---|---|
| | 'Sapphire Gem' (SDB) | CKel ESgI EWoo LSRN WAul WCAu WViv |
| | 'Sapphire Hills' (TB) | WCAu WViv XSen |
| | 'Sarah Taylor' (SDB) 🏆$^{H4}$ | CBro ECho EWoo |
| * | 'Sarajaavo' (AB) | CKel |
| | ***sari*** | ECho LWst |
| | 'Sass with Class' (SDB) | CKel WTin |
| | 'Saturday Night Live' (TB) | ESgI |
| | 'Scene Stealer' (TB) | WViv |
| | ***schachtii*** | CPBP |
| | 'Scottish Warrior' (TB) | CIri |
| | 'Scribe' (MDB) | CBro NBir WCAu |
| | 'Sea Double' (TB) | WWEG |
| | 'Sea Fret' (SDB) | CBro |
| | 'Sea Monster' (SDB) | CPMA SIri |
| | 'Sea of Joy' (TB) | XSen |
| | 'Sea Wisp' (La) | NBro SKHP |
| | 'Seakist' (TB) | WViv |
| | 'Season Ticket' (IB) | ESgI WViv XSen |
| | 'Seastone' (SDB) | WCAu |
| | 'Second Look' (TB) | XSen |
| | 'Second Wind' (TB) | ECtt EWoo |
| | 'Secret Melody' (TB) | WViv XSen |
| | 'Secret Rites' (TB) | CIri |
| | 'Self Evident' (MDB) | LLHF |
| | 'Seminole' (TB) **new** | EWoo |
| | 'Semola' (SDB) | ESgI |
| | 'Senlac' (TB) | EPfP NLar WMnd |
| | 'September Replay' (TB) | EWoo |
| | ***serbica*** | see *I. reichenbachii* |
| | 'Serene Moment' (TB) | SIri WViv |
| | 'Serenity Prayer' (SDB) | EWoo WCAu WViv |
| | ***setosa*** 🏆$^{H4}$ | CBro CMac CTri CWCL EBee ECho EKen GAuc GCra GKev GMaP IGor LEdu LPBA LRHS MNrw SBfd |
| | – ***alba*** | NLar NWCA |
| | – var. ***arctica*** | LEdu NWCA WPer |
| I | – 'Baby Blue' | LRHS |
| | – subsp. ***canadensis*** | see *I. hookeri* |
| | – dark violet-flowered **new** | EPri |
| | – 'Kosho-en' | MBri |
| | – var. ***nana*** | see *I. hookeri* |
| | 'Severn Side' (TB) 🏆$^{H4}$ | CKel |
| | 'Shadows of Night' (TB) **new** | EWoo |
| | 'Shahryar' **new** | LWst |
| | 'Shakespeare's Sonnet' (SDB) | ESgI |
| | 'Shameless' (IB) | NBre |
| | 'Shampoo' (IB) | CKel SIri WCAu |
| | 'Shaun Emmerson' (TB) | CIri |
| | 'Shawano' (TB) **new** | EWoo |
| | 'Sheer Class' (SDB) | WViv |
| | 'Sheila Ann Germaney' (Reticulata) | ECho EPot GKev LAma LLHF LWst NHol NMen NMin NWad WCot |
| | 'Shelford Giant' (Spuria) 🏆$^{H4}$ | NEgg |
| | 'Sherbet Lemon' (IB) 🏆$^{H4}$ | CKel WCAu |
| | 'Shirley Chandler' (IB) 🏆$^{H4}$ | SIri |
| | 'Short Distance' (IB) | EWoo SIri WViv |
| | ***shrevei*** | see *I. virginica* var. *shrevei* |
| | 'Shurton Brook' (TB) | CKel |
| | 'Shurton Inn' (TB) | CKel WCAu |
| | ***sibirica*** 🏆$^{H4}$ | CAvo CMHG COIW CWat EDAr EHon ESgI GAbr GBBs GKev LAma LAst LLWP MLHP MMuc NChi NVic SEND SPlb WBrk WCot WFar WHer WMoo WShi |
| | – 'Ahrtalwein' | GBin |
| | – 'Ann Dasch' | WAul |
| | – 'Annemarie Troeger' 🏆$^{H4}$ | GMac NBre SMrm |
| | – 'Atlantic Crossing' | SIri WAul |

| | Name | Suppliers |
|---|---|---|
| | - 'Atoll' | WViv |
| | - 'Baby Sister' | CMHG EBla GAbr GBin GGar GMac LSRN NBre NBro SRGP SWat WAul WViv |
| | - 'Banish Misfortune' | CIri WAul |
| | - 'Beaumaris' | GMac |
| | - 'Berlin Bluebird' | CGHE |
| | - 'Berlin Purple Wine' | EPri WViv |
| | - 'Berlin Ruffles' ♀H4 | CIri EWes GBin WViv |
| | - 'Berlin Sky' | ESgI EWes |
| | - 'Berliner Overture' | GBin |
| | - 'Bickley Cape' | WWEG |
| | - 'Blaue Milchstrasse' ♀H4 | GBin |
| | - 'Blaumacher' | WViv |
| | - 'Blue Burgee' | ECha |
| I | - 'Blue Butterfly' | CPrp ELan EPfP LLWG MDev MNrw MSCN NGdn |
| | - 'Blue King' | CHid CKel EBee EBla ELan EPfP GBin GMaP MRav NBro NGdn SBrd SMrm SPer WMnd WMoo WWEG |
| | - 'Blue Mere' | MCot WAul |
| | - 'Blue Moon' | CPrp EBee EWll GBin MSCN WFar |
| | - 'Blue Pennant' | GBin |
| | - 'Blue Reverie' | EPPr ESgI WViv |
| N | - 'Blue Sceptre' | IBlr |
| | - 'Blue Seraph' | GBin |
| | - 'Blueberry Fair' | CIri |
| | - 'Bournemouth Ball Gown' | SIri |
| | - 'Bracknell' | WBor |
| | - 'Bridal Jig' | EBee |
| | - 'Butter and Sugar' ♀H4 | Widely available |
| | - 'Caesar' | CRow SDys SRms |
| | - 'Caesar's Brother' | CFir CHid CPrp ECGP ELan EPfP GBin IBlr LRHS MNFA NBro SBfd SBrd SMrm SPer SPet SWal SWat WCAu WHoo WNew WWEG WWlt |
| | - 'Cambridge' ♀H4 | CAby EBee EBla ECGP EIri GBin LRHS MNFA NBre SWat WAul WCAu WFar WHoo WPtf |
| | - 'Chandler's Choice' | EWes |
| | - 'Chartreuse Bounty' | EBee EPri EWes GAbr GBin GQue ITim MLLN NBPC NLar NSti WPtf WViv |
| | - 'Circle Round' | CSpe |
| | - 'Cleedownton' ♀H4 | WAul |
| | - 'Cleve Dodge' | CPMA ESgI SIri WViv XLum |
| | - 'Contrast in Styles' | EPri LLWG LSou MAvo MSCN WBor |
| | - 'Coquet Waters' | NBid |
| | - 'Coronation Anthem' | WAul WViv |
| | - 'Dance Ballerina Dance' | CFir CHid CRow CWCL EBee EPfP EPri EWTr GGar GQue LLWG LRHS NBPC NMRc SMrm WFar |
| | - 'Dancing Nanou' | NBre SBfd SWat |
| | - 'Dark Desire' | MRav WAul |
| | - 'Dear Delight' | EPPr LLHF LRHS WBor WFar |
| | - 'Dear Dianne' | CHid CKel ECha NBre |
| | - 'Dirigo Black Velvet' | CIri |
| | - 'Double Standards' | CIri EPri |
| | - 'Dragonfly' | GMac |
| | - 'Dreaming Orange' | ECtt EWTr EWll WViv |
| | - 'Dreaming Spires' ♀H4 | CPMA ESgI SIri WCot WViv |
| | - 'Dreaming Yellow' ♀H4 | Widely available |
| | - 'Dunkler Wein' | EWes |
| | - 'Ego' | CAvo CHid CYeo EBee ECha ELon EWTr GAbr GBin MGos NBro SWat WMoo WViv |
| | - 'Ellenbank Sapphire' | GBin |
| | - 'Ellesmere' | NGdn |
| | - 'Emma Ripeka' | WAul |
| | - 'Emperor' | CRow CWat NBre NSti SWat |
| | - 'Eric the Red' | IBlr |
| | - 'Erste Sahne' | GBin |
| | - 'Ewen' | CHid CPou CRow GBin GKin GMaP IBlr LEdu MNrw NGdn SMrm SWat WCot WFar WWEG WWlt |
| | - 'Flight of Butterflies' | Widely available |
| | - 'Fourfold Lavender' | EWes NLar WAul |
| | - 'Fourfold White' | ESgI |
| N | - 'Gerbel Mantel' | GBin GKin GMac MSpe SPet WFar |
| | - 'Golden Edge' | GQue MAvo MLLN WViv WWlt |
| * | - 'Goldkind' | WAul |
| | - grey-flowered | SApp |
| | - 'Gull's Wing' | LHop MLLN |
| | - 'Harpswell Hallelujah' | SBch |
| | - 'Harpswell Happiness' ♀H4 | CPrp EBee EPfP GCra SBch SWat WAul WMoo WViv |
| | - 'Harpswell Haze' | ECha WMoo WViv |
| | - 'Helen Astor' | CRow CTri EShb MRav SApp SWal SWat |
| N | - 'Himmel von Komi' | GBin |
| | - 'Hohe Warte' ♀H4 | GBin |
| | - 'Höhenflug' | GBin |
| | - 'Hubbard' | CEnt CPMA EBee EPri EShb GBin LLWG MLLN MNrw NBro SBch |
| | - 'Illini Charm' | CHid EWll NBro SSvw WFar WMoo |
| | - 'Isabelle' | LSRN |
| | - 'Jac-y-do' | EWes |
| | - 'Jewelled Crown' | EWTr WFar |
| | - 'Kabluey' | CIri |
| | - 'Kathleen Mary' ♀H4 | WAul |
| | - 'Kent Arrival' | SIri |
| | - 'Lady Vanessa' | CPou GAbr GBin MLLN MRav NBro NSti SMrm WAul |
| § | - 'Lake Niklas' | EBee ELon GBin NCGa |
| | - 'Langthorns Pink' | CCse ELan MRav |
| | - 'Laurenbuhl' | CPLG |
| | - 'Lavendelwein' ♀H4 | GBin |
| | - 'Lavender Bounty' | CHid EBla NBre NBro SPet WViv |
| | - 'Lavender Fair' | CIri |
| | - 'Limeheart' | CPou CSev ELan LLHF |
| | - 'Little Blue' | WAul |
| N | - 'Little Twinkle Star' | EWTr GBin NPro WFar |
| | - 'Marilyn Holmes' | GQue WCot |
| | - 'Marshmallow Frosting' | WFar |
| § | - 'Melton Red Flare' | CMHG EBee EBla EHon ELan EPPr EShb GBin LRHS LSou MBNS MSpe SDys SMrm SPoG WFar |
| | - 'Memphis Memory' | EBee ELan GBin GCra MNrw MSCN NGdn NLar SBch SPer |
| | - 'Mesa Pearl' | CIri |
| I | - 'Mint Fresh' | WViv |
| | - 'Moon Silk' | EBee ECtt EPri GBin LLHF LLWG LRHS WCot WFar |
| | - 'Mountain Lake' | CAby EPPr EShb GBin LRHS MSpe SWat WCot WFar |
| | - 'Mrs Rowe' | CFee CPou CRow EBla EIri LLWP MRav MWat SWat WAul WFar |
| | - 'Mrs Saunders' | WAul |
| | - 'Navy Brass' | EPri NBre WViv |
| | - new hybrids **new** | WOut |
| | - 'Night Breeze' | EPri SIri WViv |
| | - 'Niklas Sea' | see *I. sibirica* 'Lake Niklas' |
| | - 'Nottingham Lace' | LLHF SWat |
| | - 'Oban' ♀H4 | ESgI |
| | - 'Orville Fay' | GMac WBor WCot WFar |
| | - 'Other Worlds' | WAul |
| | - 'Ottawa' | CPou CRow CWat EBee ECGP ELan LRHS MBNS SWat WFar |
| | - 'Outset' | ELon SSvw WWEG |

I - 'Pageant' WCot
- 'Papillon' CSev CTri EBee EBla ECtt ELan ELon GAbr GGar LHop LRHS MLLN MWat NBir NBro NGdn NSti SApp SMrm SPer SWat WBor WFar WPnP
N - 'Pearl Queen' WCot WFar
- 'Percheron' CPMA CSpr ESgI SIri WViv
- 'Perfect Vision' ♀H4 CIri
- 'Perry's Blue' CBcs CMac CSBt EBee EHon EPfP EPri EWTr GGar GKin GMaP LRHS LTen MGos MRav NBir NBro NGdn NPer SBfd SPer SPoG SRms SSvw SWat WAul WFar WMnd WPtf
I - 'Perry's Favourite' CFee CRow
- 'Persimmon' misapplied see *I. sibirica* 'Tycoon'
- 'Persimmon' ambig. CAby CFir CHid CYeo EBla ECtt GCra GKin LRHS MWat SWat WFar WMoo
- 'Peter Hewitt' ♀H4 CIri WAul
- 'Pink Haze' CRow EPfP ESgI GBin MBri MLLN MMuc NBro SEND WViv WWEG
- 'Pirate Prince' NPer
- 'Pleasures of May' **new** WBor
- 'Plissée' ♀H4 GBin
- 'Pounsley Purple' CPou EPri
- 'Primrose Cream' WCot
- 'Prussian Blue' ♀H4 CIri GBin
- 'Purple Mere' CSpr WAul WFar
- 'Redflare' see *I. sibirica* 'Melton Red Flare'
N - 'Regality' CWCL GBin MHer MMuc NBro SEND
- 'Regency Belle' ♀H4 SIri
- 'Regency Buck' MSCN SBch WCot
- 'Rikugi-sakura' EBee EBla EPri GBin LLHF NBPC NBro WCot
- 'Roanoke's Choice' CElw EWes GAbr GBin NCGa WBor WFar
- 'Roaring Jelly' EBee EPri EWes LRHS NLar WCot WViv
- 'Roger Perry' CFee
- 'Rosselline' ♀H4 GBin
I - 'Royal Blue' ECha SWat
- 'Ruby Wine' CFir EPri LEdu NLar
- 'Ruffled Velvet' ♀H4 Widely available
- 'Ruffles Plus' EPri MLLN
- 'Salamander Crossing' CIri
- 'Savoir Faire' ECha
- 'Sea Horse' WAul
- 'Sea Shadows' ESgI NBir
- 'Shaker's Prayer' ♀H4 CIri CPrp EWes GAbr MBrN WAul
- 'Shall We Dance' ♀H4 CIri EWes WAul
- 'Shirley Pope' ♀H4 EBee EWes GAbr GBin LRHS MBri MNFA NCGa NSti WAul WCot WFar WMoo WNew WWEG
- 'Shirley's Choice' CSpr EPri SIri WViv
- 'Showdown' ECtt GMaP SAga SWat WFar
- 'Silver Edge' ♀H4 Widely available
- 'Simple Gifts' ♀H4 CIri
- 'Sky Wings' CRow ECha GQue MArl WMoo
- 'Snow Prince' CSpr EPri WAul
- 'Snow Queen' see *I. sanguinea* 'Snow Queen'
- 'Snowcrest' CBre SBfd
- 'Soft Blue' ♀H4 NBre WAul
N - 'Southcombe White' CRow GBin NGdn WWEG
- 'Sparkle' WAul
- 'Sparkling Rosé' Widely available
- 'Star Cluster' WFar
- 'Stephen Wilcox' WAul
- 'Steve' CPar EWes GMac NBro SWat
- 'Steve Varner' EWTr WFar WViv
- 'Strawberry Fair' ♀H4 CIri
- 'Summer Revels' EPri LLWG
- 'Summer Sky' CBre CIri LEdu MSCN NCGa SWat WAul WCot WTin WWEG
- 'Super Ego' WCot WViv
- 'Sutton Valence' SIri WAul
- 'Swank' CSpr WAul
- 'Taldra' WAul
- 'Tal-y-Bont' WAul WFar
- 'Tanz Nochmal' GBin
- 'Teal Velvet' ECha EPri WFar WViv
- 'Temper Tantrum' CEnt CKel CPrp EBee MBNS MBri
- 'Tropic Night' Widely available
§ - 'Tycoon' EShb GBin IBlr LRHS SMrm SPer
- 'Velvet Night' ECtt
- 'Vi Luihn' CBcs ECha WAul WMoo
- 'Victorian Secret' **new** LRHS MBri
- 'Viel Creme' ♀H4 GBin
- 'Viel Schnee' GBin
N - 'Violet Skies' GBin
- 'Visual Treat' SIri
- 'Wall Street Blues' WAul
- 'Waterloo' WAul
- 'Wealden Butterfly' ♀H4 SIri WAul
- 'Wealden Carousel' SIri
- 'Wealden Mystery' SIri WAul
- 'Wealden Skies' SIri WAul
- 'Welcome Return' CElw GAbr GBin GQue MBNS MMuc NBro NLar SEND SUsu SWat WFar WMoo
N - 'Welfenfürstin' GBin
- 'Welfenprinz' ♀H4 WAul
I - 'White Queen' EBla ESgI SWat
I - 'White Swan' EPri
- 'White Swirl' ♀H4 Widely available
- 'Wisley White' NBre
- 'Yankee Consul' WAul
- 'Zakopane' ♀H4 EWes
- 'Zweites Hundert' GMac NBre WFar
'Sibirica Alba' ECha EPfP EPri EShb GBBs LLWP SWat WBrk WCFE WFar
'Sibirica Baxteri' CFee WAul
'Sibtosa Princess' (SpH) WViv
***sichuanensis*** CPLG
***sieboldii*** see *I. sanguinea*
'Sierra Blue' (TB) ESgI
'Sierra Grande' (TB) WViv XSen
'Sierra Nevada' (Spuria) SMrm XSen
'Sign of Leo' (TB) XSen
***sikkimensis*** NWCA
'Silent Strings' (IB) MBri
'Silicon Prairie' (TB) ESgI
'Silkirim' (TB) CKel
'Silver Shower' (TB) EWoo WViv
'Silverado' (TB) CKel ECtt ESgI EWoo WCAu WViv
'Silvery Beauty' (Dut) GKev LAma MBri NBir SDeJ SPhx
***sindjarensis*** see *I. aucheri*
'Sindpers' (Juno) ♀H3 LWst
'Sinister Desire' (IB) EWoo WViv
***sintenisii*** ♀H4 CBro CPBP CYeo ECho LWst NWCA WTin XSen
'Sir Michael' (TB) ESgI EWoo
'Siva Siva' (TB) MRav
'Six Pack' (TB) CIri
'Sixteen Candles' (IB) EWoo
'Sixtine C' (TB) SIri WViv
'Skating Party' (TB) CKel ESgI EWoo WViv XSen
'Skiers' Delight' (TB) NBre
'Sky Hooks' (TB) XSen

'Sky Tracery' (MTB) **new** SDys
'Skyfire' (TB) CWCL ESgI EWoo MWea WViv WWEG
'Skylark's Song' (TB) EIri EWoo WViv
'Slap Bang' (SDB) ESgI
'Sleepy Time' (MDB) WViv
'Slovak Prince' (TB) CIri
'Small Sky' (SDB) CBro
'Smart Aleck' (TB) ECtt EWoo WViv
N 'Smart Girl' (TB) CKel EIri
'Smart Move' (TB) CWCL WViv
'Smiling Angel' (TB) WViv
'Smiling Faces' (TB) WCAu WViv
'Smitten Kitten' (IB) **new** LSRN
'Smokey Dream' (TB) CKel
'Smokey Salmon' (TB) CKel
'Snow and Wind' (TB) WAul
'Snow Cloud' (TB) EWoo
'Snow Fiddler' (MTB) EWoo
'Snow Plum' (IB) SIri WViv
'Snow Season' (SDB) WViv
'Snow Tracery' (TB) MAsh MBri NCGa NPnk
'Snow Troll' (SDB) WCAu
'Snowcone' (IB) ESgI EWoo
'Snowdrift' (*laevigata*) see *I. laevigata* 'Snowdrift'
'Snowmound' (TB) CCCN CKel ESgI EWoo
'Snowy Owl' (TB) 🏆H4 CKel SAga WCAu
'Snugglebug' (SDB) CPBP EWoo
'Social Event' (TB) ESgI XSen
'Soft Return' EWoo
'Solar Fire' (TB) CIri
'Solent Breeze' SBch
'Solid Mahogany' (TB) MRav
'Somerset Blue' (TB) 🏆H4 CKel
N 'Somerset Vale' (TB) SMrm
'Somerton Brocade' (SDB) CKel
'Somerton Dance' (SDB) CKel
'Son of Sun' (Spuria) CIri
'Song of Norway' (TB) ECtt EIri ESgI EWoo WViv XSen
'Sopra il Vulcano' (BB) ESgI EWoo
'Sortilege' (TB) WViv
'Sostenique' (TB) ESgI
'Southern Clipper' (SDB) MBri
'Southland' (IB) **new** EWoo
'Souvenir de Madame Gaudichau' (TB) EWoo
'Sparkplug' (SDB) ESgI
'Spartan' (TB) CKel
'Special Feature' (TB) CIri WViv
'Speck So' (MTB) ESgI
'Spellbreaker' (TB) ESgI EWoo WViv
'Spiced Cider' (TB) WViv
'Spiced Custard' (TB) CKel EIri ESgI EWoo
'Spicy Cajun' (La) WHil
'Spinning Wheel' (TB) SIri
'Spirit of Memphis' (TB) XSen
'Spirit World' (TB) WViv
'Splashacata' (TB) WViv XSen
'Splashdown' (Sino-Sib) SWat
'Splat' (IB) **new** CIri
'Spreckles' (TB) ESgI
'Spring Blush' (MTB) **new** SIri
'Spring Festival' (TB) WCAu
'Spring Kiss' (TB) SIri WViv
'Spun Gold' (TB) ESgI EWoo
***spuria*** CMac CPou WCot
§ - subsp. ***halophila*** GAuc
- subsp. ***ochroleuca*** see *I. orientalis* Mill.
- subsp. ***sogdiana*** GAuc
- subsp. ***spuria*** GAuc

'St Louis Blues' (TB) ESgI XSen
'St Petersburg' (TB) EWoo WViv
'Stairway to Heaven' (TB) ESgI WCAu
'Stapleford' (SDB) CBro
'Staplehurst' (MTB) 🏆H4 SIri WAul
'Star Prince' (SDB) ESgI
'Star Shine' (TB) CKel ESgI WCAu
'Starcrest' (TB) ESgI EWoo WViv
'Stardate' (SDB) CKel
'Stardock' (TB) EWoo
'Starlette Rose' (TB) EWoo WViv
'Starlight Express' (TB) **new** EWoo
'Starring' (TB) CIri EWoo WAul
'Starship' (TB) ESgI XSen
'Starship Enterprise' (TB) CIri
'Starwoman' (IB) WAul WCAu
'Staten Island' (TB) ESgI SEND SRms WCAu WTin
'Stella Polaris' (TB) CWan ELon
'Stellar Lights' (TB) EIri EWoo WCAu
'Stepping Out' (TB) 🏆H4 CAby CPar CWGN EAEE EBee EBla EPfP ESgI GBin LBMP LRHS MCot MWea NBre NCGa WAul WBor
'Stinger' (SDB) 🏆H4 CIri
'Stingray' (TB) CIri ESgI
'Stitch in Time' (TB) EIri EWoo WViv
'Stockholm' (SDB) CKel
***stolonifera*** ECho
- 'Zwanenburg Beauty' ECho
'Stop the Music' (TB) XSen
'Storm Center' (TB) EWoo
'Stormy Circle' (SDB) WCAu
'Strawberry Love' (IB) 🏆H4 CKel
'Striking' (TB) EWoo WViv
'Study In Black' (TB) XSen
***stylosa*** see *I. unguicularis*
§ ***suaveolens*** CPou ECho NMen
* - var. ***flavescens*** LWst
* - var. ***violacea*** ECho EPot GCal LWst
'Succès Fou' (TB) EWoo SIri WViv
'Sudden Impact' (TB) WViv
'Sugar' (IB) WCAu
'Sugar Magnolia' (TB) EWoo WViv
'Sultan's Palace' (TB) CWCL ECho ESgI EWoo LRHS LTen NBPC WViv WWEG XSen
'Sumatra' (TB) ESgI
'Summer Holidays' (TB) XSen
'Summer's Smile' (TB) ESgI EWoo
'Summertime Blues' (TB) EWoo
'Sun Ada Beach' (TB) CIri
'Sun Doll' (SDB) 🏆H4 CKel
'Sunblaze' (TB) **new** WCAu
'Sundown Red' (IB) NBir
'Sunny and Warm' (TB) CKel
'Sunny Dawn' (IB) 🏆H4 CKel WViv
'Sunny Disposition' (TB) XSen
'Sunny Side Up' LWst
'Sunnyside Delight' (TB) WCAu
'Sunol' (TB) **new** EWoo
'Sunshine Boy' (IB) CKel
'Superstition' (TB) 🏆H4 EIri ELan ESgI EWes EWoo GBin LRHS MRav SMrm WCAu WCot WViv WWEG XSen
'Supreme Sultan' (TB) ESgI ETod EWoo WCAu WViv XSen
'Susan Bliss' (TB) CKel EBee ELan EPfP ESgI EWoo NBre WCAu
'Susan Gillespie' (IB) 🏆H4 CKel
'Suspicion' (TB) CIri WViv
'Swain' (TB) ESgI

| | Name | Suppliers |
|---|---|---|
| | 'Swazi Princess' (TB) | CKel ESgI |
| | 'Sweertii' | EWoo |
| | 'Sweet Kate' (SDB) ℽ[H4] | WCAu |
| | 'Sweet Lena' (TB) | ESgI |
| | 'Sweet Musette' (TB) | WCAu WViv |
| | 'Sweeter than Wine' (TB) | ESgI EWoo MRav WViv |
| | 'Swingtown' (TB) | EWoo WCAu |
| | 'Swizzle' (IB) | XSen |
| | 'Sybil' (TB) | GBin GCra GLam NHar |
| | 'Sylvan' (TB) | XSen |
| | 'Sylvia Murray' (TB) | WCAu |
| | 'Symphony' (Dut) | ECho NBir SDeJ |
| | 'Syncopation' (TB) | CKel ESgI WViv XSen |
| | 'Tabac Blond' (TB) | EWoo WViv |
| | 'Taco Supreme' (TB) | EWoo |
| | 'Tact' (IB) **new** | SIri |
| | 'Tahitian Pearl' (TB) | CIri |
| | 'Take Me Away' (TB) **new** | SDys |
| | 'Tall Chief' (TB) | WCAu |
| | 'Tamerlan' (TB) **new** | EWoo |
| | 'Tan Tingo' (IB) | XSen |
| N | 'Tanex' | ECho |
| | 'Tangerine Sky' (TB) | EWoo WViv |
| | 'Tangfu' (IB) | ESgI |
| | 'Tango Music' (SpH) ℽ[H4] | GBin |
| | 'Tantara' (SDB) | XSen |
| | 'Tantrum' (IB) | WAul WCAu XSen |
| | 'Tanya' (TB) **new** | EWoo |
| | 'Tanzanian Tangerine' (TB) | WCAu |
| | 'Tarheel Elf' (SDB) | ESgI |
| | 'Tarn Hows' (TB) | ESgI SRms WCAu |
| | 'Tchin Tchin' (IB) | WViv |
| | 'Teasaucer Hill' (MTB) ℽ[H4] **new** | SIri |
| | ***tectorum*** | CCse CHEx GAuc GBin GKev LRHS NWCA SDix WAul WCot XSen |
| | - BWJ 8191 | WCru |
| | - 'Alba' | WThu XSen |
| | - 'Variegata' misapplied | see *I. japonica* 'Variegata' |
| | - 'Variegata' (v) | NSti |
| | 'Tell Fibs' (SDB) | CBro CKel |
| | 'Temple Gold' (TB) | CKel NPer |
| | 'Temple Meads' (IB) | ESgI |
| | 'Templecloud' (IB) ℽ[H4] | CHar CKel |
| | 'Tempting Fate' (TB) | EWoo WViv |
| § | ***tenax*** | CPBP ECho GAuc GEdr NWCA |
| | - subsp. ***tenax*** **new** | IGor |
| | 'Tennessee Woman' (TB) | CIri |
| | 'Tennison Ridge' (TB) | WCAu |
| | ***tenuissima*** subsp. ***tenuissima*** | GAuc IGor NMen |
| | 'Terre de Couleur' (TB) | WViv |
| | 'Terre de Feu' (TB) | ESgI WViv |
| | 'Thaïs' (TB) | ESgI |
| | 'The Black Douglas' (TB) | EWoo |
| | 'The Bride' | see *I.* 'Bride' |
| | 'The Citadel' (TB) | ELon |
| | 'The Red Douglas' (TB) | ESgI EWoo |
| | 'The Rocket' | see *I.* 'Rocket' |
| | 'Theatre' (TB) | ESgI |
| | 'Theodolinda' (TB) **new** | EWoo |
| | 'Third Charm' (SDB) | CBro |
| | 'Third World' (SDB) | CBro |
| | 'This and That' (IB) | WCAu |
| | ***thompsonii*** | IGor |
| | - J&JA 1.461.800 | NWCA |
| | - NNS 05-416 | WCot |
| | 'Thornbird' (TB) ℽ[H4] | ECtt EIri ESgI EWoo WCAu WViv |
| | 'Three Cherries' (MDB) | CBro CPBP ECho WViv |
| | 'Thriller' (TB) | ESgI EWoo XSen |
| | 'Throb' (TB) | WViv |
| | ***thunbergii*** | see *I. sanguinea* |
| | 'Thunder Echo' (TB) | ESgI WViv |
| | 'Thundering Hills' (TB) | CKel |
| | 'Tide's In' (TB) | ECtt ESgI EWoo WViv |
| | 'Tiffany' (TB) | EWoo WTin |
| | 'Tiger Butter' (TB) | ESgI |
| | 'Tiger Honey' (TB) | CIri WViv |
| | 'Tiger Shark' (TB) | CIri |
| § | 'Tigereye' (Dut) | ERCP GKev LAma |
| | ***tigridia*** | CPLG |
| | 'Time Piece' (TB) | CKel |
| | 'Tinkerbell' (SDB) | CPBP GMaP LRHS NBir NGdn SDeJ |
| | 'Tintinara' (TB) ℽ[H4] | CKel |
| | 'Tishomingo' **new** | EWoo |
| | 'Titan's Glory' (TB) ℽ[H4] | ESgI EWoo LEdu MRav WCot WViv |
| | 'To the Point' (TB) | CIri |
| | 'Toile de Jouy' (TB) | WViv |
| | 'Tollong' ℽ[H4] | IKil |
| | 'Tom Johnson' (TB) ℽ[H4] | EWoo |
| | 'Tom Tit' (TB) | WCAu |
| | 'Tomorrow's Child' (TB) | ESgI EWoo WViv |
| | 'Toni Lynn' (MDB) | ECho |
| | 'Toots' (SDB) | ECho WTin |
| | 'Top Flight' (TB) | ELan LRHS SPer SRms |
| | 'Top Gun' (TB) | CPMA WViv |
| N | 'Topolino' (TB) | CKel GBin SAga |
| | 'Topsy Turvy' (MTB) | NBre |
| | 'Torchlight' (TB) | SEND |
| | 'Torero' (TB) | EWoo SIri WViv |
| | 'Total Eclipse' (TB) | SRms |
| | 'Totally Cool' (SDB) | LSRN SIri WViv |
| | 'Touch of Mahogany' (TB) | WCAu |
| | 'Tourbillon' (TB) | WViv |
| | 'Toy Clown' (SDB) **new** | EWoo |
| | 'Tracy Tyrene' (TB) | ESgI WViv |
| | 'Trade Secret' (TB) | CIri |
| | 'Trails West' (TB) | ESgI EWoo WViv |
| | 'Trapel' (TB) | ESgI |
| | 'Treccia d'Oro' (TB) | ESgI |
| | 'Trencavel' (TB) | ESgI |
| | 'Trenwith' (TB) | CKel |
| | 'Trillion' (TB) | CIri |
| | 'Triple Whammy' (TB) | ESgI XSen |
| | 'Triplicate' (SDB) | SMrm |
| | 'Tropical Butterfly' (TB) **new** | EWoo |
| | 'Tropical Magic' (TB) | WViv |
| | 'True Charm' (TB) **new** | EWoo |
| | 'True Navy' (SDB) | WViv |
| | ***tuberosa*** | see *Hermodactylus tuberosus* |
| | 'Tumultueux' (TB) | ESgI EWoo WViv |
| | 'Tut's Gold' (TB) | ECtt ESgI WCAu WViv |
| | 'Tuxedo' (TB) | XSen |
| | ***typhifolia*** | GAuc |
| | 'Tyrian Dream' (IB) | WCAu |
| | 'UFO' (TB) **new** | CIri |
| | 'Ultimate' (SDB) | CIri |
| | 'Uncle Charlie' (TB) **new** | WCAu |
| § | ***unguicularis*** ℽ[H4] | Widely available |
| | - 'Abington Purple' | CAvo CBro CPMA EIrl |
| | - 'Alba' | CAvo CBct CPLG ECha ESgI XSen |
| N | - 'Bob Thompson' | CAvo CBro SAga |
| § | - subsp. ***cretensis*** | ECho GKev NMen SKHP WAbe WHil XSen |
| N | - 'Diana Clare' | CPMA WCot |
| | - from Lady Gibson | GEdr |
| N | - 'Marondera' | CAvo CPMA |
| | - 'Mary Barnard' ℽ[H4] | CAvo CBro CFee CHar CPMA CPou CTca ECGP ECha ECho GEdr IBlr NBir NMen SBrd SSvw WMnd |

| | | |
|---|---|---|
| N | – 'Oxford Dwarf' | CBro ECho LLHF |
| N | – 'Palette' | ELan |
| § | – 'Walter Butt' | CAvo CBro CPMA ECGP NBir WCot WFar |
| | ***uromovii*** | MArl |
| | 'Ursula Warleggan' (TB) | CKel |
| | 'Vague à l'Ame' (TB) | ESgI EWoo WViv |
| | 'Val de Loire' | EWoo |
| | 'Vamp' (IB) | CKel EWoo SIri WViv XSen |
| | 'Vandal Spirit' (TB) | ESgI EWoo |
| | 'Vanilla Skies' (TB) | WCAu |
| | 'Vanity' (TB) ♀H4 | ESgI WViv XSen |
| | 'Vanity's Child' (TB) | WCAu XSen |
| § | ***variegata*** ♀H4 | GLam IGor XSen |
| | 'Vegas Heat' (BB) | CIri |
| | 'Velvet Dusk' (TB) **new** | EWoo |
| | 'Velvet Purple' | XBlo |
| | 'Verdissant' (IB) | WViv |
| | 'Verity Blamey' (TB) | CKel |
| | ***verna*** | EPot |
| | ***versicolor*** ♀H4 | CArn CBen CRow CWat EHon GBin GKev GMaP IBlr LPBA MGos MMuc MNHC MNrw MWts NWCA SEND SPlb SRms SWat WBrk WFar WMAq WMoo WPnP WShi WTin WViv |
| | – 'Between the Lines' | CRow WViv |
| | – 'Candystriper' | WViv |
| | – 'China West Lake' | CRow |
| | – 'Claret Cup' | CPou WWEG |
| | – 'Dottie's Double' | CRow |
| * | – 'Georgia Bay' | CRow |
| | – 'Kermesina' | CRow CWat EBee ECha EHon ELan ESgI GBin GGar IBlr LLWG LPBA MBri MGos MWts NPer NSti SRms SWat WBrk WFar WMAq WMoo WPnP |
| | – 'Mysterious Monique' | CCse CDes CWat LLWG |
| | – 'Party Line' | SIri |
| | – 'Rosea' | CRow |
| | – 'Rowden Allegro' | CRow |
| | – 'Rowden Aria' | CRow |
| | – 'Rowden Cadenza' | CRow |
| | – 'Rowden Calypso' | CRow |
| | – 'Rowden Cantata' | CRow |
| | – 'Rowden Concerto' | CRow |
| | – 'Rowden Harmony' | CRow |
| | – 'Rowden Lullaby' | CRow |
| | – 'Rowden Lyric' | CRow |
| | – 'Rowden Mazurka' | CRow |
| | – 'Rowden Melody' | CRow |
| | – 'Rowden Nocturne' | CRow |
| | – 'Rowden Pastorale' | CRow |
| | – 'Rowden Prelude' | CRow |
| | – 'Rowden Refrain' | CRow |
| | – 'Rowden Rondo' | CRow |
| | – 'Rowden Sonata' | CRow |
| | – 'Rowden Symphony' | CRow |
| | – 'Rowden Waltz' | CRow |
| | – 'Silvington' | CRow |
| | – 'Whodunit' | CRow |
| | 'Vert Galant' (TB) | ESgI |
| | 'Via Domitia' (TB) | ESgI |
| | 'Vibrant' (TB) | ESgI WCAu |
| | 'Vibrations' (TB) | ESgI |
| | ***vicaria*** | ECho GKev LWst |
| | – RM 8269 | LWst |
| * | – 'Hodji-obi-garm' | LWst |
| | – 'Morgiana' **new** | LWst |
| * | – 'Prominence' | LWst |
| I | – 'Sina' | LWst |
| | 'Victoria Falls' (TB) | ESgI EWoo WCAu |
| | 'Vigilante' (TB) | EWoo |
| | 'Vin Nouveau' (TB) | WViv XSen |
| | 'Vinho Verde' (IB) ♀H4 | CKel |
| | 'Vino Rosso' (SDB) | ESgI |
| | 'Violet Beauty' (Reticulata) | ECho ERCP GKev LAma NWad |
| | 'Violet Classic' (TB) | WCAu |
| | 'Violet Harmony' (TB) | ESgI |
| | 'Violet Icing' (TB) ♀H4 | CKel |
| | 'Violet Rings' (TB) | WCAu WViv |
| * | 'Violet Tiara' | LHop |
| | 'Viper' (IB) | CIri EWoo |
| | 'Virginia Bauer' (TB) | EWoo |
| | ***virginica*** 'De Luxe' | see *I.* × *robusta* 'Dark Aura' |
| I | – 'Pink Butterfly' | MDev |
| | – 'Pond Crown Point' | CRow |
| | – 'Pond Lilac Dream' | CRow |
| N | – 'Purple Fan' | CRow |
| § | – var. ***shrevei*** | CRow WViv |
| | 'Vision in Pink' (TB) **new** | WCAu |
| | 'Visual Arts' (TB) | WViv |
| | 'Visual Intrigue' (TB) **new** | EWoo |
| | 'Vitafire' (TB) | ECtt EWoo WViv |
| | 'Vitality' (IB) | ELon ESgI |
| | 'Vitrail' (IB) | WViv |
| | 'Viva Mexico' (TB) **new** | EWoo |
| | 'Vive la France' (TB) | ESgI WViv |
| | 'Voilà' (IB) | ESgI |
| | 'Volts' (SDB) | CKel XSen |
| | 'Voluminous' (TB) | CIri |
| | 'Volute' (TB) | ESgI WViv |
| I | 'Vonnies Wedding Iris' | ELon |
| | 'Voyage' (SDB) | EWoo XSen |
| | 'Wabash' (TB) | ELan ESgI LRHS WCAu WTin XSen |
| | 'Walter Butt' | see *I. unguicularis* 'Walter Butt' |
| | 'War Chief' (TB) | ESgI MRav |
| | 'War Sails' (TB) | EWoo SIri WCAu WViv |
| | 'Warbler' (IB) **new** | EWoo |
| | ***warleyensis*** | ECho LWst |
| | 'Warrior King' (TB) | EWoo |
| | 'Waters Of Miraba' (BB) **new** | EWoo |
| | ***wattii*** | CPLG GCal WCot |
| | 'Waxen Image' (IB) | WAul |
| | 'Way to Go' (TB) | CIri |
| | 'Wealden Canary' (Spuria) | WAul |
| | 'Wealden Elegance' (Spuria) | WAul |
| | 'Wealden Sunshine' (Spuria) | WAul |
| | 'Webmaster' (SDB) **new** | SIri |
| | 'Wedding Vow' (TB) | CKel EIri |
| | 'Wedgwood' (Dut) | NBre |
| | 'Welch's Reward' (MTB) ♀H4 | CKel ESgI |
| | 'Well Suited' (SDB) | EWoo WViv |
| | 'Wench' (TB) | EWoo |
| | 'Westar' (SDB) ♀H4 | CKel EIri |
| | 'Westpointer' (TB) | CIri |
| | 'Westwell' (SDB) | WCAu |
| | 'What Again' (SDB) | XSen |
| | 'Wheels' (SDB) | WTin |
| | 'White City' (TB) | EAEE EBla ECGP EPfP ESgI EWoo GMaP LRHS MCot MRav MWat MWhi NPer SBfd SMrm SPer SRms SWat WCAu WMnd |
| | 'White Excelsior' (Dut) | ECho |
| | 'White Gem' (SDB) | EWoo |
| | 'White Knight' (TB) | EBee ELan EPfP NBre WMnd WWEG |
| | 'White Reprise' (TB) | ESgI XSen |
| | 'White van Vliet' (Dut) | SDeJ |

| | | |
|---|---|---|
| | 'White Wine' (MTB) | WCAu |
| | 'White-Wave' | XBlo |
| | 'Whole Cloth' (TB) | ESgI |
| N | 'Wild Echo' (TB) | CKel |
| | 'Wild Jasmine' (TB) | ECtt WViv |
| | 'Wild Ruby' (SDB) | CKel |
| | 'Wild West' (TB) | CKel |
| | 'Wild Wings' (TB) | EWoo MCot NCGa STes WViv WWEG |
| | ***willmottiana*** | ECho LWst |
| | - 'Alba' | ECho |
| | ***wilsonii*** ♀H4 | CPLG GAuc |
| | 'Windjammer Seas' (TB) | SDys WAul |
| | 'Winds Of Change' (TB) new | EWoo |
| | 'Winemaster' (TB) | ECtt EWoo SIri |
| | 'Winesap' (TB) new | EWoo |
| | 'Wings of Peace' (TB) | CIri |
| | 'Winner's Circle' (TB) | SMrm |
| | ***winogradowii*** ♀H4 | CBro ECho GKev LAma LLHF NMin WAbe |
| | 'Winter Crystal' (TB) ♀H4 | CKel |
| | 'Winter Olympics' (TB) | CAby EAEE EBee ESgI EShb LBuc LRHS MRav STes |
| | 'Winter Pearl' (IB) new | EWoo |
| | 'Wintry Sky' (TB) | WCAu |
| | 'Wishful Thinking' (TB) | SIri WViv |
| | 'Wisteria Sachet' (IB) | WCAu |
| | 'Witch's Wand' (TB) | EWoo |
| | 'Wondrous' (TB) | ESgI |
| | 'World Class' (TB) new | EWoo |
| | 'World Premier' (TB) | WViv |
| | 'Wrangler' (IB) | EWoo SIri |
| | 'Wyomissing' (TB) new | EWoo |
| | 'Xillia' (IB) | CKel |
| | ***xiphioides*** | see *I. latifolia* |
| | ***xiphium*** | ECho |
| | 'Yaquina Blue' (TB) | ESgI WCAu WViv |
| | 'Yellow and White' | GAbr |
| | 'Yellow Flirt' (MTB) | WCAu |
| | 'Yellow Moon' (J) | LWst |
| | 'Yes' (TB) | CPMA ESgI WViv |
| | 'Yosemite Nights' (TB) new | EWoo |
| | 'Yosemite Star' (TB) new | EWoo |
| | 'Youth Dew' (TB) | EWoo |
| | 'Yo-yo' (SDB) | STes |
| | 'Zantha' (TB) | ESgI XSen |
| | 'Zen' | LRHS |
| | ***zenaidae*** | GKev |
| | - ARJA 9715 | LWst |
| | - 'Dessert' new | LWst |
| | - 'Flagship' | LWst |
| | 'Zero' (SDB) ♀H4 | CKel WViv |
| | 'Zing Me' (IB) | WViv |

## *Isatis* (*Brassicaceae*)

| | | |
|---|---|---|
| | ***tinctoria*** | CArn CBod CHab CHby CRWN CSev EOHP GJos GPoy ILis MHer MNHC NPnk SIde SPav SSvw WHfH WJek XLum |
| | - var. ***indigotica*** | CArn |

## *Ischyrolepis* (*Restionaceae*)

| | | |
|---|---|---|
| § | ***subverticillata*** | CAbb CCtw CHEx CTrC |

## *Ismene* see *Hymenocallis*

## *Isodon* (*Lamiaceae*)

| | | |
|---|---|---|
| | ***calycinus*** | SPlb |
| | ***longitubus*** | WCot |
| | - B&SWJ 11027 | WCru |

## *Isolepis* (*Cyperaceae*)

| | | |
|---|---|---|
| § | ***cernua*** | CBen CMil CWat EHoe MBri MSKA MWts NOak SBfd SCoo SHDw WFar WMAq WTch |

## *Isoloma* see *Kohleria*

## *Isomeris* see *Cleome*

## *Isoplexis* (*Plantaginaceae*)

| | | |
|---|---|---|
| | ***canariensis*** | CAbb CBcs CBot CCCN CDTJ CHEx CHll CRHN CSpe EBee ESwi EWll SAga SEND SGar SPlb SPoG SVen WBox WCFE WWlt |
| | ***isabelliana*** | CCCN CDTJ EShb |
| | ***sceptrum*** | CAbb CBot CCCN CDTJ CHEx CHll CPLG SPlb SVen WPGP |

## *Isopogon* (*Proteaceae*)

| | | |
|---|---|---|
| | ***anemonifolius*** | SPlb |
| | ***anethifolius*** | SPlb |

## *Isopyrum* (*Ranunculaceae*)

| | | |
|---|---|---|
| | ***biternatum*** | NLar |
| | ***dicarpon*** | see *Dichocarpum dicarpon* |
| | ***nipponicum*** | CLAP CPom GEdr WCru WPGP |
| | ***stoloniferum*** | WCru |
| | ***thalictroides*** | EPot LLHF |

## *Isotoma* (*Campanulaceae*)

| | | |
|---|---|---|
| | sp. | SWvt |
| § | ***axillaris*** | CSpe LAst NPer SCoo SPer SPet SPoG |
| | - 'Fairy Carpet' | GAbr SRms |
| | ***fluviatilis*** | NLar |

## *Itea* (*Iteaceae*)

| | | |
|---|---|---|
| | ***chinensis*** | CPLG |
| | ***ilicifolia*** ♀H3 | Widely available |
| * | - 'Rubrifolia' | LRHS SLon SPoG |
| | ***japonica*** 'Beppu' | SLPl SSpi |
| | ***virginica*** | CAbP CBcs CMCN EBee ELan MRav NPal SLim SLon WFar |
| § | - 'Henry's Garnet' | CAbP CDoC CEnd CMCN CMac CPMA CSBt EBee ECrN EPfP GBin LAst LEdu LRHS MBri MGos NCGa NLar NPri SBfd SLim SPoG SRGP SSpi SWvt WDin WGwG |
| | - Little Henry = 'Sprich'PBR | CHGN CMac CSBt ELan ELon IVic LRHS LSRN NLar SPtl |
| | - 'Long Spire' | CPMA IArd NLar WDin |
| | - 'Merlot' | CPMA NLar |
| | - 'Sarah Eve' | CMCN CPMA NLar SRGP |
| | - 'Saturnalia' | NLar WDin |
| | - Swarthmore form | see *I. virginica* 'Henry's Garnet' |
| | ***yunnanensis*** | CPLG MBlu NLar SSpi |

## *Ixeris* (*Asteraceae*)

| | | |
|---|---|---|
| | ***stolonifera*** new | XLum |

## *Ixia* (*Iridaceae*)

| | | |
|---|---|---|
| | ***aurea*** 'Saldanha' | ECho |
| | 'Blue Bird' | CFir ECho LAma SMrm WHil |
| | ***capillaris*** 'Citrusdal' | ECho |
| | 'Castor' | CAvo CPrp ECho WHil |
| | ***curta*** | ECho |
| | ***dubia*** | ECho |
| | ***flexuosa*** | ECho |
| | 'Gemini' | ECho |

| | |
|---|---|
| 'Giant' | CAvo CTca ECho WHil |
| 'Hogarth' | CPrp ECho LAma WHil |
| 'Holland Glory' | ECho |
| ***latifolia*** var. ***latifolia*** | ECho |
| ***longituba*** 'Citrusdal' | ECho |
| ***lutea*** | ECho |
| 'Mabel' | CAvo ECho WCot |
| ***maculata*** | ECho |
| ***marginifolia*** | ECho |
| from Komsberg **new** | |
| 'Marquette' | ECho |
| ***metelerkampiae*** | ECho |
| - 'Goudini' **new** | ECho |
| ***monadelpha*** | ECho |
| ***orientalis*** | ECho |
| ***paniculata*** | ECho |
| 'Panorama' | ECho WHil |
| ***polystachya*** | ECho |
| - var. ***longistylis*** | ECho |
| - var. ***lutea*** | ECho |
| ***pumilio*** | WCot |
| ***purpureorosea*** 'Saldanha' | ECho |
| ***rapunculoides*** | ECho |
| - var. ***rigida*** | ECho |
| - var. ***subpendula*** | ECho |
| 'Rose Emperor' | ECho LAma SDeJ SMrm WHil |
| ***scillaris*** var. ***subundulata*** | ECho |
| 'Spotlight' | ECho WHil |
| ***thomasiae*** | WCot |
| ***trifolia*** | ECho |
| 'Venus' | CFir CTca ECho LAma WHil |
| ***versicolor*** | ECho |
| ***viridiflora*** | CDes ECho WCot |
| - var. ***minor*** | ECho |
| 'Vulcan' | CPrp ECho |
| 'Yellow Emperor' | CAvo CTca ECho WHil |

## *Ixiolirion* (*Ixioliriaceae*)

| | |
|---|---|
| ***montanum*** | CHid ECho |
| ***pallasii*** | see *I. tataricum* |
| § ***tataricum*** | ECho LAma MCot |
| - Ledebourii Group | CAvo CFFs |

## *Ixora* (*Rubiaceae*)

| | |
|---|---|
| ***chinensis*** 'Apricot Queen' | MOWG |
| 'Golden Ball' | MOWG |
| 'Pink Malay' | MOWG |

# J

## *Jaborosa* (*Solanaceae*)

| | |
|---|---|
| ***integrifolia*** | CDes CFir CPLG EBee ELan LEdu LRHS MAvo SUsu WCot WPGP XLum |

## *Jacaranda* (*Bignoniaceae*)

| | |
|---|---|
| ***acutifolia*** misapplied | see *J. mimosifolia* |
| § ***mimosifolia*** | CBcs CCCN CHII ELan EShb GQui MOWG MREP SPlb |

## *Jacobinia* see *Justicia*

## *Jamesbrittenia* (*Scrophulariaceae*)

| | |
|---|---|
| Sumatra Indigo = 'Yagemon' | MNrw |

## *Jamesia* (*Hydrangeaceae*)

| | |
|---|---|
| ***americana*** | NLar |

## *Jasione* (*Campanulaceae*)

| | |
|---|---|
| § ***heldreichii*** | LRHS NBir SRms |
| ***jankae*** | see *J. heldreichii* |
| § ***laevis*** | ECho GAbr GKev SRms WWFP |
| § - 'Blaulicht' | CMHG EBee ECha EPfP GGar LRHS MBNS MMuc NBPC NBlu NEgg NLar SBfd SMrm SPlb WMoo |
| - Blue Light | see *J. laevis* 'Blaulicht' |
| ***montana*** | ECho MNHC WFar WPnn WSFF |
| ***perennis*** | see *J. laevis* |

## *Jasminum* ✿ (*Oleaceae*)

| | |
|---|---|
| CC 4728 | CPLG |
| ***adenophyllum*** | CTyn MOWG |
| ***affine*** | see *J. officinale* f. *affine* |
| ***angulare*** ♀H1 | CPLG CRHN CTyn ERea EShb MOWG SEND |
| ***azoricum*** ♀H1 | CCCN CDoC CRHN CTrC CTyn ELan EPfP ERea EShb NPal |
| ***beesianum*** | Widely available |
| ***bignoniaceum*** | CTyn |
| ***blinii*** | see *J. polyanthum* |
| ***dispermum*** | CRHN |
| ***diversifolium*** | see *J. subhumile* |
| ***farreri*** | see *J. humile* f. *farreri* |
| ***floridum*** | EWes |
| ***fruticans*** | CMac EBee ELon EPfP LRHS SEND WCru XLum |
| ***giraldii*** hort. | see *J. humile* f. *farreri* |
| ***grandiflorum*** misapplied | see *J. officinale* f. *affine* |
| ***grandiflorum*** L. | IDee |
| - 'De Grasse' ♀H1 | CRHN CTyn ERea EShb MOWG |
| ***heterophyllum*** | see *J. subhumile* |
| ***humile*** | CEnt CPLG EQua GAuc SEND WFar WKif |
| § - f. ***farreri*** | CTyn MBri |
| - var. ***glabrum*** | see *J. humile* f. *wallichianum* |
| § - 'Revolutum' ♀H4 | Widely available |
| § - f. ***wallichianum*** | CTyn |
| - - B&SWJ 2559 | WCru |
| § ***laurifolium*** f. ***nitidum*** | CTyn ERea MOWG |
| § ***mesnyi*** ♀H2-3 | CCCN CDoy CEnt CMac CPLG CRHN CTri CTyn CWib EBak EBee ELan EPfP ERea IGor IVic MOWG MRav SAga SBfd SEND SPer STre SVen WSHC |
| ***multiflorum*** | CCCN MOWG |
| ***multipartitum*** | CTyn EShb |
| - bushy | CSpe CTyn |
| ***nitidum*** | see *J. laurifolium* f. *nitidum* |
| § ***nudiflorum*** ♀H4 | Widely available |
| - 'Argenteum' | see *J. nudiflorum* 'Mystique' |
| - 'Aureum' | CTyn EBee ELan EPla LRHS MAsh MBNS MRav NSti SLim SPer SPoG SRms WCot |
| * - 'Compactum' | MAsh |
| § - 'Mystique' (v) | ELan LRHS MAsh NLar SLon SPer SPoG WCot |
| ***odoratissimum*** | ERea EShb MOWG |
| ***officinale*** ♀H4 | Widely available |
| - CC 1709 | WMoo |
| § - f. ***affine*** | CBcs CCCN CRHN CSPN CSam CTri CTyn CWSG CWib EBee ELan ELon EPfP LAst LRHS MRav SCoo SDix SLim SRms WCru WFar |
| § - 'Argenteovariegatum' (v) ♀H4 | Widely available |
| - 'Aureovariegatum' | see *J. officinale* 'Aureum' |

| | |
|---|---|
| § – 'Aureum' (v) | CBcs CBot CChe CDoC CHby CMac CTyn CWSG CWib EBee ECtt ELan EPfP LBMP LRHS MAsh MBri MHer MREP MSCN NBir NHol SBfd SCoo SLim SLon SMad SPer SRms WPat |
| – 'Clotted Cream' PBR | see *J. officinale* 'Devon Cream' |
| – 'Crûg's Collection' | CTyn WCru |
| § – 'Devon Cream' PBR | CBcs CCCN CSBt CTyn CWGN EPfP EShb LAst LBuc LRHS LSRN MAsh MBri MGos MREP MWea NHol NLar NPri SBfd SCoo SLim SPer SPoG WCot WPat |
| – Fiona Sunrise = 'Frojas' PBR | Widely available |
| – 'Grandiflorum' | see *J. officinale* f. *affine* |
| – 'Inverleith' ♀H4 | CCCN CDoC CMac CTrC CTyn CWSG EBee ELan EPfP EShb IArd LAst LBMP LHop LRHS MAsh MBNS MBri MGos MRav SBfd SCoo SLim SMad SPad SPer SPoG WFar WGrn WSHC |
| – 'Variegatum' | see *J. officinale* 'Argenteovariegatum' |
| ***parkeri*** | CBcs CCCN CMac CMea CTri CTyn EBee ECho ELon EPfP EPot GEdr GMaP LRHS MBNS NLar NMen WFar WPat WRHF |
| § ***polyanthum*** ♀H1-2 | CArn CBcs CPLG CRHN CSBt CTrC CTri CTyn EBak EBee ELan EPfP ERea ERom EShb LRHS MBri MOWG NEgg NPal SBfd SEND SLim SPer SRms |
| – dark red-leaved | CPLG IVic WPGP |
| – 'Greenholm' (v) **new** | CTyn |
| ***primulinum*** | see *J. mesnyi* |
| ***reevesii*** hort. | see *J. humile* 'Revolutum' |
| ***sambac*** ♀H1 | CCCN CDoC CHII CRHN CTyn EAmu ELan EPfP EShb MOWG |
| – 'Bangkok Peony' (d) | ERea |
| – 'Grand Duke of Tuscany' (d) | ERea MOWG |
| – 'Maid of Orleans' (d) ♀H1 | ERea MOWG |
| ***sieboldianum*** | see *J. nudiflorum* |
| ***stenalobium*** | CTyn MOWG |
| × ***stephanense*** | Widely available |
| § ***subhumile*** | IRar |

## *Jatropha* (*Euphorbiaceae*)

| | |
|---|---|
| ***integerrima*** | CCCN |
| ***multifida*** | SPlb |

## *Jeffersonia* (*Berberidaceae*)

| | |
|---|---|
| ***diphylla*** | CArn CBro CDes CLAP EBee ECho EPPr EPri GAbr GGar LAma LEdu LRHS MMoz MNFA MNrw NBir NLar NMyG NWCA WAbe WCru WFar |
| ***dubia*** | CBro CFir CLAP ECho EWes GEdr LEdu LRHS MNrw NBir NHar NMen NWCA WAbe WCru |

## jostaberry see *Ribes* × *culverwellii*

## *Jovellana* (*Calceolariaceae*)

| | |
|---|---|
| ***punctata*** | CCCN CDoC CMac CPLG EBee SPlb |
| ***repens*** | CFir |
| ***sinclairii*** | CHII CPLG ECou LLHF SBrd SMrm SUsu |
| ***violacea*** ♀H3 | CAbP CAbb CBcs CCCN CDoC CEnt CMac CPLG CTrC CTsd CWib EBee EPfP GCal GGal GGar ITim LRHS SArc SMad SUsu SVen WAle WCru WPGP WPat WSHC WWlt |

## *Jovibarba* ✿ (*Crassulaceae*)

| | |
|---|---|
| § ***allionii*** | CMea CTri CWil EDAr EPot LAst LBMP LRHS MAsh MHer MSCN NHol NPri WAbe WFar WHal WHoo WIvy WPer WTin |
| – 'Oki' | ECho LRHS |
| ***allionii*** × ***hirta*** | CWil MSCN NMen SDys SFgr |
| § ***arenaria*** | CWil GAbr NMen XLum |
| – from Passo di Monte Croce Carnico | CWil |
| 'Autumn Fires' | MSCN |
| * ***echiniformis*** **new** | XLum |
| 'Emerald Spring' | NMen SFgr |
| § ***heuffelii*** | ECho LRHS MDun NHol NMen WIvy WPer |
| – 'Aga' | NHol WIvy |
| – 'Aiolos' | NHol |
| – 'Alemene' | NHol |
| – 'Almkroon' | NHol |
| – 'Angel Wings' | CWil LRHS NHol NMen WHoo |
| § – 'Apache' | CWil |
| – 'Aquarius' | CWil WIvy |
| – 'Artemis' | NHol |
| – 'Aurora' | NHol |
| – 'Be Mine' | CWil WGor |
| – 'Beacon Hill' | CWil WIvy |
| – 'Belcore' | CWil WIvy |
| – 'Benjamin' | CWil NHol |
| – 'Bermuda' | WIvy |
| – 'Bermuda Sunset' | NHol |
| – 'Big Red' | NHol |
| – 'Blaze' | CWil |
| – 'Brandaris' | NHol SDys |
| – 'Brocade' | MSCN NHol WIvy |
| – 'Bronze Ingot' | CWil WCot |
| – 'Bulgarien' | CWil |
| – 'Cakor' | NHol |
| § – 'Cherry Glow' | CWil NHol |
| – 'Chocoleto' | WTin |
| – 'Cleopatra' | NHol |
| – 'Copper King' | CWil WIvy |
| – 'Dunbar Red' | NHol |
| – 'Fandango' | CWil MHom WIvy |
| – 'Gento' | NHol |
| – 'Geronimo' | NHol |
| – 'Giuseppi Spiny' | MHom NHol WTin |
| – var. ***glabra*** | LRHS WHoo |
| – – from Anabakanak | CWil MHom NHol WTin |
| – – from Anthoborio | CWil NMen WTin |
| – – from Backovo | NHol |
| – – from Galicica | NHol |
| – – from Haila, Montenegro/Kosovo | CWil NHol NMen SFgr WIvy |
| – – from Jakupica, Macedonia | CWil WIvy |
| – – from Ljuboten | CWil NHol NMen WTin |
| – – from Osljak | CWil |
| – – from Pasina Glava | CWil |
| – – from Rhodope | CWil MHom NHol |
| – – from Treska Gorge, Macedonia | CWil NMen WTin |
| – – from Vitse, Greece | WIvy |
| § – – 'Cameo' | NHol WIvy |
| – 'Gold Rand' | NHol |

| | | |
|---|---|---|
| | - 'Grand Slam' | CWil |
| | - 'Green Land' | CWil |
| | - 'Greenstone' | CWil MHom NHol NMen WAbe WIvy WTin |
| | - 'Harmony' | CWil NHol |
| | - 'Henry Correvon' | CWil |
| | - 'Hot Lips' | CWil |
| | - 'Hot Stuff' | ESem |
| | - 'Hystyle' | WIvy |
| | - 'Ikaros' | NHol |
| | - 'Inferno' | MHom NHol |
| § | - 'Inge' | ESem NMen |
| | - 'Iole' | WIvy |
| | - 'Ithaca' | NHol |
| | - 'Iuno' | CWil NHol |
| | - 'Jade' | CWil NMen WIvy |
| | - 'Kapo' | WIvy |
| | - var. ***kopaonikensis*** | CWil LRHS MHom NMen |
| | - 'Mary Ann' | MHom WIvy |
| | - 'Miller's Violet' | CWil WIvy WTin |
| | - 'Mink' | CWil |
| | - 'Minuta' | CWil NHol NMen WIvy WTin |
| | - 'Mystique' | CMea CWil LRHS NMen WIvy |
| | - 'Nannette' | CWil |
| | - 'Nobel' | NHol |
| | - 'Opele' | NHol |
| | - 'Orion' | CMea CWil NHol NMen |
| | - 'Pink Skies' | CWil WIvy |
| | - 'Pink Star' **new** | CWil |
| | - 'Prisma' | CWil WIvy WTin |
| | - 'Purple Haze' | WIvy |
| | - 'Red Rose' | CWil |
| | - 'Serenade' | CWil WGor |
| | - 'Springael's Choice' | CWil |
| | - 'Sungold' | NHol |
| | - 'Suntan' | CWil NHol WIvy |
| | - 'Sylvan Memory' | CWil WGor |
| | - 'Tan' | CWil NHol WTin |
| | - 'Torrid Zone' | WIvy WTin |
| | - 'Tuxedo' | CWil |
| | - 'Vesta' | CWil |
| | - 'Violet' | SDys WIvy |
| § | ***hirta*** | CWil EDAr GAbr NHol NMen SFgr STre WPer XLum |
| | - from Wintergraben | SPlb |
| § | - subsp. ***borealis*** | CWil NHol |
| | - subsp. ***glabrescens*** | EPot |
| | - - from Belianske Tatry | CWil |
| | - - from High Tatra | XLum |
| | - - from Smeryouka | CWil |
| I | - 'Glauca' | SFgr |
| | - 'Hedgehog' | SFgr |
| | - var. ***neilreichii*** | ECho LRHS MHom |
| | - 'Preissiana' | LBee NHol NMen SFgr WIvy WTin |
| | - 'Purpurea' | ESem XLum |
| | - 'Rax' | SFgr |
| § | ***sobolifera*** | CHEx CWil EDAr EPot NHol NMen SFgr SPlb WAbe WHal WIvy WPer XLum |
| | - 'August Cream' | LBee LRHS |
| | - 'Bronze Globe' | SFgr |
| | - 'Green Globe' | ECho LRHS SDys WTin |
| | - 'Miss Lorraine' | SFgr |

## *Juania* (*Arecaceae*)

| | | |
|---|---|---|
| | ***australis*** | EAmu |

## *Juanulloa* (*Solanaceae*)

| | | |
|---|---|---|
| | ***aurantiaca*** | see *J. mexicana* |
| § | ***mexicana*** | MOWG |

## *Jubaea* (*Arecaceae*)

| | | |
|---|---|---|
| § | ***chilensis*** | CBcs CBrP CPHo EAmu IDee LPJP LPal SBig SChr SPlb |
| | ***spectabilis*** | see *J. chilensis* |

## *Juglans* ✿ (*Juglandaceae*)

| | | |
|---|---|---|
| § | ***ailanthifolia*** | CMCN EGFP |
| | - var. ***cordiformis*** 'Brock' (F) | CAgr |
| | - - 'Campbell Cw3' (F) | CAgr |
| | - - 'Fodermaier' seedling | CAgr |
| | - - 'Rhodes' (F) | CAgr |
| | ***ailanthifolia*** × ***cinerea*** | see *J.* × *bixbyi* |
| § | × ***bixbyi*** | CAgr |
| | ***cinerea*** (F) | CMCN LMaj |
| | - 'Beckwith' (F) | CAgr |
| | - 'Booth' seedlings (F) | CAgr |
| | - 'Craxezy' (F) | CAgr |
| | - 'Kenworthy' seedling | CAgr |
| | - 'Myjoy' (F) | CAgr |
| | ***hindsii*** | EBtc |
| | ***mandshurica*** BWJ 8097 from China | WCru |
| | - RWJ 9905 from Taiwan | WCru |
| * | - subsp. ***sieboldiana*** B&SWJ 11026 | WCru |
| | ***microcarpa*** | CMCN |
| | ***nigra*** (F) ♀H4 | CBcs CCVT CDul CLnd CMCN CMac CSBt CTho CWib EBee ECrN ELan EPfP GTwe LAst LRHS MAsh MBri MGos NWea SDea SEND SGol SPer WCFE WDin WFar WMou |
| | - 'Bicentennial' (F) | CAgr |
| | - 'Emma Kay' (F) | CAgr |
| | - 'Laciniata' | EPfP ERea MBlu MBri WPat |
| | - 'Purpurea' | WPat |
| | - 'Thomas' (F) | CAgr |
| | - 'Weschke' (F) | CAgr |
| | ***regia*** (F) ♀H4 | Widely available |
| | - 'Axel' (F) | CAgr |
| | - 'Broadview' (F) | CAgr CEnd CSBt CTho ELan EPom ERea GTwe LAst LBuc LRHS MBlu MBri MCoo MGos NEgg NWea SCoo SDea SEWo SKee SPer SVic WHar |
| | - 'Buccaneer' (F) | CAgr CTho ECrN EPom GTwe SDea SKee WHar |
| | - 'Chandler' (F) | CAgr |
| | - 'Corne du Périgord' (F) | CAgr |
| | - 'Ferjean' (F) | CAgr |
| | - 'Fernette'PBR (F) | CAgr WHar |
| | - 'Fernor' (F) | CAgr WHar |
| | - 'Franquette' (F) | CAgr ECrN GTwe MCoo WDin WHar |
| | - 'Hansen' (F) | CAgr |
| | - 'Hartley' (F) | CAgr |
| | - 'Jupiter' (F) | CAgr |
| | - 'Laciniata' | CDul WPat |
| | - 'Lara' (F) | CAgr GTwe |
| | - 'Mayette' (F) | CAgr ECrN WDin |
| | - 'Meylannaise' (F) | CAgr |
| | - number 16 (F) | CAgr WHar |
| | - 'Parisienne' (F) | CAgr SGol |
| | - 'Plovdivski' (F) | CAgr MBri WHar |
| | - 'Proslavski' (F) | CAgr CDul MBri WHar |
| | - 'Purpurea' | CMCN MBlu MBri |
| | - 'Rita' (F) | CAgr LBuc MBri |
| | - 'Ronde de Montignac' (F) | CAgr |
| | - 'Saturn' (F) | CAgr |

| | | |
|---|---|---|
| | - 'Soleze' (F) | CAgr |
| | - 'Sorrento' (F) | CCCN |
| | ***sieboldiana*** | see *J. ailanthifolia* |

## jujube see *Ziziphus jujuba*

## *Juncus* (*Juncaceae*)

| | | |
|---|---|---|
| | ***articulatus*** | XLum |
| | ***bulbosus*** | CNat CRWN |
| | 'Curly Gold Strike' (v) | LRHS MSKA SBfd |
| § | ***decipiens*** 'Curly-wurly' | CFee CSpe EBee EHoe EPfP EPla EWes LPBA LRHS NOak SWal SWat |
| | - 'Spiralis' | see *J. decipiens* 'Curly-wurly' |
| I | - 'Spiralis Nana' | NWCA |
| | ***effusus*** | CHEx CRWN CWat EHon EWil LPBA MSKA NPer SBfd SWat WMAq XLum |
| | - 'Carman's Japanese' | CKno |
| | - 'Gold Strike' (v) | CWat EPPr LLWG |
| § | - f. ***spiralis*** | CBen CFee CRow CSpe CWat EHoe EHon ELan EPfP GKev LPBA LRHS LTen NBir NLar NOak NWsh SBfd SLim SPer SPlb SPoG SVic WFar WHal WMAq WPGP WPnP XLum |
| § | - - 'Unicorn'$^{PBR}$ | EBee EPPr LRHS SApp SBfd SPoG WWEG |
| | ***ensifolius*** | CKno CRow CWat EHoe EWes LPBA MMHG MSKA MWts NPer |
| | ***filiformis*** 'Spiralis' | EBee SApp WWEG |
| | ***inflexus*** | CBen CRWN CWat EHon EWil MSKA SEND SWat |
| | - 'Afro' | EBee ELan EPfP MCCP NBro NOak SPlb SWal WHal WWEG |
| | ***pallidus*** | EPPr GCal |
| | ***patens*** 'Carman's Gray' | CKno CWCL EPPr EPla GCal GQue LRHS MAvo MMoz NGdn NHol NNor NOak NWad NWsh SApp WMoo WPtf WWEG |
| | - 'Elk Blue' | CKno WWEG |
| | 'Unicorn'$^{PBR}$ | see *J. effusus* f. *spiralis* 'Unicorn' |
| | ***xiphioides*** | EHoe EPla |

## *Junellia* (*Verbenaceae*)

| | | |
|---|---|---|
| | ***azorelloides*** F&W 9344 | WAbe |
| § | ***micrantha*** | GEdr |
| | ***odonnellii*** | WAbe |
| | ***wilczekii*** | WFar |

## *Juniperus* ✿ (*Cupressaceae*)

| | | |
|---|---|---|
| | ***chinensis*** | CMen |
| | - 'Aurea' 🏆$^{H4}$ | CBcs CMac EHul LRHS MGos |
| § | - 'Blaauw' 🏆$^{H4}$ | CDoC CMac CMen EHul MGos SGol STre WEve WFar |
| | - 'Blue Alps' | CPMA ECho EHul LRHS MGos MMuc NEgg NHol NLar SCoo SEND SGol SLim WDin WEve WFar |
| | - 'Densa Spartan' | see *J. chinensis* 'Spartan' |
| | - 'Echiniformis' | CKen |
| | - 'Expansa Aureospicata' (v) | CDoC CKen ECho EHul EPfP MGos SEND SLim SPoG SRms |
| § | - 'Expansa Variegata' (v) | CDoC CWib ECho EHul EPfP MGos SRms WDin WFar |
| | - 'Ferngold' | CDoC MGos |
| | - 'Itoigawa' | CMen |
| | - 'Japonica Variegata' (v) | EPla |
| § | - 'Kaizuka' 🏆$^{H4}$ | EHul LBee NLar SCoo SGol SLim SMad STre |
| | - 'Kaizuka Variegata' | see *J. chinensis* 'Variegated Kaizuka' |
| | - 'Kuriwao Gold' | see *J.* × *pfitzeriana* 'Kuriwao Gold' |
| | - 'Obelisk' 🏆$^{H4}$ | EHul MGos |
| | - 'Oblonga' | CDoC EHul |
| § | - 'Parsonsii' | STre |
| | - 'Plumosa Aurea' 🏆$^{H4}$ | EHul WDin WFar |
| | - 'Plumosa Aureovariegata' (v) | CKen |
| | - 'Pyramidalis' 🏆$^{H4}$ | CDoC ECho EHul EPfP MAsh NPri SCoo SRms WDin WFar |
| | - 'Robust Green' | ECho NLar SEND |
| | - 'San José' | CMen EHul LRHS MAsh SCoo WDin |
| § | - var. ***sargentii*** | CMen STre |
| | - 'Shimpaku' | CKen CMen NLar |
| § | - 'Spartan' | EHul |
| | - 'Stricta' | CSBt EHul LBee LRHS MGos SGol SLim WDin |
| | - 'Sulphur Spray' | see *J.* × *pfitzeriana* 'Sulphur Spray' |
| | - 'Torulosa' | see *J. chinensis* 'Kaizuka' |
| § | - 'Variegated Kaizuka' (v) | ECho EHul WFar |
| | ***communis*** | CArn CDul CHab CRWN EHul GPoy MNHC NWea SIde WAbe |
| | - (f) | SIde |
| | - 'Arnold' | CDul MGos |
| | - 'Arnold Sentinel' | CKen |
| | - 'Atholl' | CKen |
| | - 'Barton' | MGos NLar |
| | - 'Barton Gem' **new** | NWad |
| | - 'Berkshire' | CKen WThu |
| | - 'Brien' | CDoC CKen |
| | - 'Brynhyfryd Gold' | CKen |
| | - 'Compressa' 🏆$^{H4}$ | Widely available |
| § | - 'Constance Franklin' (v) | EHul STre |
| | - 'Corielagan' | CKen MBri NLar |
| | - 'Cracovia' | CKen |
| | - var. ***depressa*** | GPoy SGol |
| | - 'Depressa Aurea' | CKen CSBt ECho EHul EPla LBee MGos WFar |
| | - 'Depressed Star' | ECho EHul SPoG WGor |
| | - 'Derrynane' | EHul |
| | - 'Effusa' | CKen |
| | - 'Gelb' | see *J. communis* 'Schneverdingen Goldmachangel' |
| | - 'Gold Cone' | CKen ECho EHul EPfP EPla LBee LRHS MAsh MGos SLim SPoG STre WDin WFar |
| | - 'Golden Showers' | see *J. communis* 'Schneverdingen Goldmachangel' |
| | - 'Goldschatz' **new** | LAst SPoG |
| | - 'Green Carpet' 🏆$^{H4}$ | CDoC CKen CMen ECho EHul EPfP EPla GKin LBuc LRHS MAsh NEgg NHol SCoo SLim SPoG WCFE WDin |
| | - 'Haverbeck' | CKen |
| | - 'Hibernica' 🏆$^{H4}$ | CDul CSBt CTri ECho EHul EPfP LAst LRHS MGos NWea SBfd SLPl SLim SPer SPoG WDin WEve |
| | - 'Hibernica Aurea' | CMac |
| | - 'Hibernica Variegata' | see *J. communis* 'Constance Franklin' |
| | - 'Hornibrookii' 🏆$^{H4}$ | EHul MGos NWea SRms STre WDin |
| | - 'Horstmann' | GKin NLar |
| I | - 'Horstmann's Pendula' | CDoC |
| | - 'Kenwith Castle' | CKen |
| | - 'Meyer' | GKin |
| | - 'Prostrata' | WFar |
| | - 'Pyramidalis' | SPlb |
| | - 'Rakete' **new** | IVic |
| | - 'Repanda' 🏆$^{H4}$ | CBcs CDoC CMac CSBt CWib ECho EHul EPfP GGar LAst LRHS MAsh MGos SCoo SGol SLim SPer SPoG SRms WDin WEve WFar |
| § | - var. ***saxatilis*** | LAst |

| |  |  |
|---|---|---|
| § | – 'Schneverdingen Goldmachangel' | EPla LRHS MAsh MGos NLar SLim SPoG |
| | – 'Sentinel' | CDoC EHul EPfP LRHS SLim WCFE WDin WEve WMou |
| | – 'Sieben Steinhauser' | CKen |
| | – 'Silver Mist' | CKen |
| | – 'Spotty Spreader' (v) | LRHS SLim SPoG |
| | – Suecica Group | EHul NLar NWea |
| | – – 'Suecica Aurea' | EHul |
| | – 'Zeal' | CKen |
| | ***conferta*** | see *J. rigida* subsp. *conferta* |
| | – var. ***maritima*** | see *J. taxifolia* |
| | ***davurica*** | EHul |
| | – 'Expansa' | see *J. chinensis* 'Parsonsii' |
| | – 'Expansa Albopicta' | see *J. chinensis* 'Expansa Variegata' |
| | – 'Expansa Variegata' | see *J. chinensis* 'Expansa Variegata' |
| | ***excelsa*** subsp. ***polycarpos*** | CMen |
| | 'Fitz Kukuri Gold' | MMuc |
| | ***foetidissima*** | CMen |
| | × ***gracilis*** 'Blaauw' | see *J. chinensis* 'Blaauw' |
| | 'Grey Owl' $\mathbb{Y}^{H4}$ | ECho EHul ELan EPfP LRHS NWea SCoo SEND SGol SLim SRms STre WDin WFar |
| | ***horizontalis*** | NWea |
| § | – 'Andorra Compact' | ECho NLar SCoo |
| | – 'Andorra Variegata' (v) **new** | ECho |
| | – 'Bar Harbor' | CKen CMac EHul MGos NWea |
| § | – 'Blue Chip' | ECho EHul ELan EPfP EPla LBee LRHS MGos NBir SCoo SLim SPer SPoG WDin |
| | – 'Blue Horizon' **new** | LRHS |
| | – 'Blue Moon' | see *J. horizontalis* 'Blue Chip' |
| | – 'Blue Pygmy' | CKen |
| | – 'Blue Rug' | see *J. horizontalis* 'Wiltonii' |
| | – 'Douglasii' | CKen EHul |
| | – 'Emerald Spreader' | CKen ECho EHul ELan |
| | – 'Glacier' | CKen |
| | – Glauca Group | EHul MGos NWea SPoG WDin |
| | – 'Glomerata' | CKen |
| | – 'Golden Carpet' | ECho ELan EPfP LBuc MGos NLar SPoG |
| | – 'Golden Spreader' | CDoC |
| | – 'Grey Pearl' | CKen EHul |
| | – 'Hughes' | EHul LBee NWea |
| | – Icee Blue = 'Monber' | CKen ECho GKin MAsh NLar SLim SPoG |
| | – 'Jade River' | EHul |
| | – 'Limeglow' | CDoC CKen ECho EPfP LRHS MGos NEgg NLar SCoo SLim SPer SPoG WGor |
| | – 'Mother Lode' | CKen |
| | – 'Neumann' | CKen |
| | – 'Plumosa Compacta' | see *J. horizontalis* 'Andorra Compact' |
| | – 'Prince of Wales' | EHul MAsh MGos NLar WEve |
| | – var. ***saxatilis*** misapplied | see *J. communis* var. *saxatilis* |
| | – 'Turquoise Spreader' | CSBt EHul NWea SGol |
| | – 'Venusta' | see *J. virginiana* 'Venusta' |
| | – 'Villa Marie' | CKen |
| § | – 'Wiltonii' $\mathbb{Y}^{H4}$ | EHul |
| | – 'Winter Blue' | LBee LRHS SLim SPer |
| | – 'Youngstown' | ECho WFar |
| | – 'Yukon Belle' | CKen |
| N | × ***media*** | see *J.* × *pfitzeriana* |
| § | × ***pfitzeriana*** | CDul SGol WEve |
| | – 'Armstrongii' | EHul |
| | – 'Blaauw' | see *J. chinensis* 'Blaauw' |
| | – 'Blue and Gold' (v) | CKen ECho EHul |
| | – 'Blue Cloud' | see *J. virginiana* 'Blue Cloud' |
| § | – 'Carbery Gold' | CBcs CDoC CDul CMac CSBt ECho EHul EPla GKin LBee LRHS MAsh MGos SCoo SLim SPoG WEve WFar |
| | – 'Daub's Frosted' | SLim |
| | – 'Gold Coast' | CDoC CKen CSBt ECho EHul EPfP LBee MBri MGos NLar SGol SLim SPer WDin WEve |
| | – Gold Sovereign = 'Blound'$^{PBR}$ | LBee MAsh MGos |
| * | – 'Golden Joy' | LRHS SLim SPoG |
| | – 'Golden Saucer' | SCoo |
| | – 'Goldkissen' | NLar |
| | – 'King of Spring' | SLim |
| § | – 'Kuriwao Gold' | CMac EHul GKin LRHS MAsh MGos NLar NPri SCoo SEND SGol SPoG WFar |
| | – 'Mint Julep' | CSBt ECho EHul LTen MGos SCoo SGol SLim WDin WEve WFar |
| | – 'Mordigan Gold' | WEve |
| | – 'Old Gold' $\mathbb{Y}^{H4}$ | CKen ECho EHul EPfP GKin LBee MGos NEgg NPri NWea SCoo SEND SGol SLim SPlb SPoG SRms WDin WEve WFar |
| | – 'Old Gold Carbery' | see *J.* × *pfitzeriana* 'Carbery Gold' |
| | – 'Pfitzeriana' | see *J.* × *pfitzeriana* 'Wilhelm Pfitzer' |
| | – 'Pfitzeriana Aurea' | ECho EHul EPfP MGos NWea SGol WDin WEve WFar |
| | – 'Pfitzeriana Compacta' $\mathbb{Y}^{H4}$ | EHul SCoo |
| | – 'Pfitzeriana Glauca' | EHul SCoo |
| § | – 'Sulphur Spray' $\mathbb{Y}^{H4}$ | CDul CWib ECho EHul EPla LAst MAsh MGos MMuc SEND SGol SLim SRms WCFE WDin WEve WFar |
| § | – 'Wilhelm Pfitzer' | EHul EPfP NWea |
| § | ***pingii*** 'Glassell' | CDoC MAsh NLar |
| | – 'Hulsdonk Yellow' | SLim |
| § | – var. ***wilsonii*** | CDoC CKen NLar |
| | ***procera*** | WPGP |
| | ***procumbens*** 'Bonin Isles' | LRHS SPoG |
| | – 'Nana' $\mathbb{Y}^{H4}$ | CDoC CKen CMac CSBt ECho EHul EPfP EPla LAst LBee LRHS MAsh MGos NEgg NHol SCoo SLim SPoG WCFE WDin WEve WFar |
| | ***recurva*** | CDoC |
| | – 'Castlewellan' | CDoC NLar |
| | – var. ***coxii*** | CDoC CMac EHul MGos NHol SMad SRms WCFE |
| § | – 'Densa' | CDoC CKen EHul |
| | – 'Nana' | see *J. recurva* 'Densa' |
| | ***rigida*** | CMen NLar |
| § | – subsp. ***conferta*** | CMac ECho LBee SEND SGol WEve |
| | – – 'All Gold' | SLim |
| * | – – 'Blue Ice' | CKen GKev WFar |
| | – – 'Blue Pacific' | ECho EHul MBri NLar SGol WCFE WFar |
| | – – 'Blue Tosho' | CDul NLar SPoG |
| | – – 'Emerald Sea' | EHul |
| | – – 'Schlager' | LRHS SLim |
| | – – 'Silver Mist' | CKen |
| | ***sabina*** | NWea |
| § | – 'Blaue Donau' | EHul |
| | – Blue Danube | see *J. sabina* 'Blaue Donau' |
| | – 'Broadmoor' | EHul |
| | – 'Buffalo' | EHul |
| | – 'Knap Hill' | see *J.* × *pfitzeriana* 'Wilhelm Pfitzer' |
| | – 'Mountaineer' | see *J. scopulorum* 'Mountaineer' |
| | – 'Rockery Gem' | EHul LRHS SLim SPoG WGor |
| | – 'Skandia' | CKen |
| | – 'Tamariscifolia' | CBcs CWib ECho EHul GGar GKin LBee LRHS LTen MAsh MGos NWea |

| | |
|---|---|
| | SEND SGol SLim SPer SPoG WCFE WDin WEve WFar |
| - 'Variegata' (v) | EHul |
| ***sargentii*** | see *J. chinensis* var. *sargentii* |
| ***scopulorum*** | CKen |
| - 'Blue Arrow' | CDoC CDul CKen CSBt CWib ECho ECrN ELan EPfP EPla GKin LAst LBee LRHS MAsh MBri MGos NEgg NHol NLar NPCo NWea SCoo SGol SLim SPer WBor WDin WEve WFar |
| - 'Blue Banff' | CKen |
| - 'Blue Heaven' | EHul SRms |
| - 'Blue Pyramid' | EHul |
| - 'Boothman' | EHul |
| - 'Moonglow' | EHul |
| § - 'Mountaineer' | EHul |
| - 'Mrs Marriage' | CKen |
| - 'Silver Star' (v) | EHul |
| - 'Skyrocket' | CBcs CCVT CDul CMac CSBt CTri CWib ECho ECrN EHul EPfP GGal LAst LBee MGos NPCo NWea SEND SPlb WBor WCFE WDin WEve WFar |
| - 'Snow Flurries' | SLim |
| - 'Springbank' | EHul WCFE |
| - 'Wichita Blue' | EHul EPfP IVic WEve |
| ***squamata*** | Widely available |
| 'Blue Carpet' ♀H4 | |
| - 'Blue Spider' | CKen LRHS SCoo SLim |
| - 'Blue Star' ♀H4 | Widely available |
| - 'Blue Star Variegated' | see *J. squamata* 'Golden Flame' |
| - 'Blue Swede' | see *J. squamata* 'Hunnetorp' |
| - 'Chinese Silver' | EHul SLim |
| - 'Dream Joy' | CKen LRHS NLar NWad SCoo SLim SPoG |
| - 'Filborna' | CKen LBee LRHS SLim |
| - 'Glassell' | see *J. pingii* 'Glassell' |
| § - 'Golden Flame' (v) | CKen |
| - 'Holger' ♀H4 | CDoC CDul CMac CSBt ECho EHul EPfP EPla GEdr LAst LBee LRHS MAsh MBri MGos SCoo SGol SLim SPoG WEve |
| § - 'Hunnetorp' | NHol |
| - 'Loderi' | see *J. pingii* var. *wilsonii* |
| - 'Meyeri' | CBcs EHul GKev NWea SCoo SGol STre WDin WFar |
| - 'Wilsonii' | see *J. pingii* var. *wilsonii* |
| § ***taxifolia*** | CSBt GGar |
| § ***virginiana*** 'Blue Cloud' | EHul LRHS LTen SLim WGor |
| - 'Burkii' | EHul WEve |
| - 'Frosty Morn' | CKen EHul WFar |
| - 'Glauca' | EHul NWea |
| - 'Golden Spring' | CKen |
| - 'Helle' | see *J. chinensis* 'Spartan' |
| - 'Hetzii' | EHul NLar NWea WDin WFar |
| - 'Hillspire' | EHul |
| - Silver Spreader = 'Mona' | CKen EHul |
| - 'Sulphur Spray' | see *J.* × *pfitzeriana* 'Sulphur Spray' |
| § - 'Venusta' | CKen |

## *Jurinea* (*Asteraceae*)

| | |
|---|---|
| ***glycacantha*** | LRHS |
| ***ledebourii*** | LRHS |

## *Jurinella* see *Jurinea*

## *Jussiaea* see *Ludwigia*

## *Justicia* (*Acanthaceae*)

| | |
|---|---|
| ***aconitiflora*** | WHil |
| ***adhatodoides*** | WHil |
| ***americana*** | LLWG |
| ***aurea*** | EShb SMad WHil |
| § ***brandegeeana*** ♀H1 | CCCN EShb MOWG |
| - 'Lutea' | see *J. brandegeeana* 'Yellow Queen' |
| - variegated (v) | EShb |
| - yellow-flowered **new** | EShb |
| § - 'Yellow Queen' | EShb |
| § ***carnea*** | CHll EBak EShb MOWG SAga SMad WCot WHil |
| - 'Alba' | CCCN EShb WHil |
| - dark-leaved **new** | CHll |
| ***guttata*** | see *J. brandegeeana* |
| 'Penrhosiensis' | EShb WHil |
| ***petioloris*** subsp. ***bowiei*** | WHil |
| ***pohliana*** | see *J. carnea* |
| ***rizzinii*** ♀H1 | CCCN CHll MOWG SMad WHil |
| ***scheidweileri*** | EShb |
| ***spicigera*** | EShb WHil |
| ***suberecta*** | see *Dicliptera sericea* |

## *Kadsura* (*Schisandraceae*)

| | |
|---|---|
| ***coccinea*** B&SWJ 11793 | WCru |
| ***japonica*** | CBcs EShb |
| - B&SWJ 1027 | WCru WPGP |
| - B&SWJ 4463 from Korea | WCru |
| - B&SWJ 11109 from Japan | WCru |
| - 'Fukurin' (v) | NLar |
| - 'Variegata' (v) | CCCN EPfP LRHS SEND WSHC |
| - white fruit | CBcs |

## *Kaempferia* ✿ (*Zingiberaceae*)

| | |
|---|---|
| ***rotunda*** | CCCN LAma LEdu |

## *Kageneckia* (*Rosaceae*)

| | |
|---|---|
| ***oblonga*** | SPlb |

## *Kalanchoe* (*Crassulaceae*)

| | |
|---|---|
| ***beharensis*** ♀H1 | CAbb CCCN CDTJ EShb LToo STre |
| - 'Fang' | CDTJ |
| - 'Rusty' | CDTJ CSpe |
| ***daigremontiana*** | SRms STre |
| § ***delagoensis*** | CCCN EShb STre |
| ***fedtschenkoi*** | EShb STre |
| ***humilis*** | EShb |
| ***laciniata*** | EShb |
| ***marmorata*** ♀H1 | EShb |
| ***orgyalis*** | EShb |
| ***porphyrocalyx*** | EOHP |
| ***prolifera*** **new** | EShb |
| ***pubescens*** | EShb |
| ***pumila*** ♀H1 | EShb EWoo SBch SPet STre |
| ***rhombopilosa*** | EShb |
| ***scandens*** | EShb |
| 'Kalahari Survivor' **new** | |
| ***sexangularis*** | EShb |
| 'Tessa' ♀H1 | SRms STre WCot |
| ***thyrsiflora*** | EShb STre |
| - 'Bronze Sculpture' | CAbb |
| ***tomentosa*** ♀H1 | EShb WCot |
| ***tubiflora*** | see *K. delagoensis* |

## *Kalimeris* (*Asteraceae*)

| | |
|---|---|
| § ***incisa*** | EBee MMuc MRav WBor |
| - 'Alba' | EBee ECha LHop NLar SSvw WFar XLum |

| | | |
|---|---|---|
| | - 'Blue Star' | EBee ECha EWll LHop LRHS NLar WCAu WFar WPtf WSHC |
| | - 'Charlotte' | EBee EWes NBre NDov |
| | - 'Madiva' | CSam EBee ECha LHop LPla NDov |
| | - 'Nana Blue' | NDov |
| | ***intricifolia*** | NBre |
| § | ***mongolica*** | CDes CMac EBee ECha MMuc NBre SEND WFar WSHC |
| | - 'Antonia' | NDov |
| § | ***pinnatifida*** | EBee EPPr LRHS |
| | - 'Hortensis' | ECtt NBPC |
| § | ***yomena*** 'Shogun' (v) | CPrp EBee ECha EHoe ELan EPfP EShb LRHS NBir NBre NLar SAga SMrm WFar WPer WSHC WWEG XLum |
| | - 'Variegata' | see *K. yomena* 'Shogun' |

## *Kalmia* ✿ (*Ericaceae*)

| | | |
|---|---|---|
| | ***angustifolia*** ♀$^{H4}$ | SRms WDin WFar |
| | - f. ***rubra*** ♀$^{H4}$ | CBcs CDoC CDul EBee ELan EPfP LRHS MAsh MGos NLar NPri SBfd SPer SReu WFar |
| I | - 'Rubra Nana' | CMac |
| | ***latifolia*** ♀$^{H4}$ | CBcs CEnd ELan EPfP LRHS LSou MGos MMuc NPri NWea SEND SPer SWvt WDin WFar |
| | - 'Bullseye' | NLar |
| | - 'Carousel' | CBcs CCCN GEdr NLar WFar |
| | - 'Clementine Churchill' | CMac |
| | - 'Freckles' ♀$^{H4}$ | ELan EPfP NPCo SPoG WFar |
| | - 'Fresca' | NPCo |
| | - 'Galaxy' | IVic |
| | - 'Ginkona' **new** | IVic |
| | - 'Kaleidoscope' | IVic |
| | - 'Minuet' | CCCN CDoC CEnd EPfP GEdr LRHS MGos MLea MMuc MPkF NLar NPCo SLim SPoG SSpi SWvt WFar |
| | - 'Mitternacht' | IVic |
| | - f. ***myrtifolia*** | LRHS WFar |
| | - - 'Elf' | CEnd EPfP GEdr IVic MAsh MGos MPkF NLar SLim WFar |
| | - 'Nancy' | NLar WFar |
| | - 'Nipmuck' | CMac |
| | - 'Olympic Fire' ♀$^{H4}$ | CEnd IVic MGos MPkF MRav NLar SLim |
| | - 'Olympic Wedding' **new** | NLar |
| | - 'Ostbo Red' | CDoC CDul CEnd CMac EPfP GEdr IVic LRHS MGos MLea MPkF NCGa NPCo SPoG SReu SSpi SWvt WFar |
| | - 'Peppermint' | IVic MPkF SLim |
| | - 'Pink Charm' ♀$^{H4}$ | IVic |
| | - 'Pink Frost' | NLar NPCo WFar |
| | - 'Pinwheel' | CEnd MPkF NLar SLim |
| | - 'Quinnipiac' | MPkF |
| | - 'Richard Jaynes' | WFar |
| | - 'Sarah' | MLea NPCo |
| | - 'Snowdrift' | NLar WFar |
| | ***polifolia*** | CBcs EPfP NHar NMen SPer WThu |
| | - var. ***compacta*** | WSHC |
| | - f. ***leucantha*** | NHar NMen WThu |

## × *Kalmiothamnus* (*Ericaceae*)

| | | |
|---|---|---|
| | ***ornithomma*** 'Cosdon' | WThu |

## *Kalopanax* (*Araliaceae*)

| | | |
|---|---|---|
| | ***pictus*** | see *K. septemlobus* |
| § | ***septemlobus*** | CBcs CDul ELan EPfP GBin NLar |
| | - var. ***magnificus*** B&SWJ 10900 **new** | WCru |
| | - f. ***maximowiczii*** | CDoC EBee EPfP IVic MBlu |

## *Kelseya* (*Rosaceae*)

| | | |
|---|---|---|
| | ***uniflora*** | WAbe |

## *Kennedia* (*Papilionaceae*)

| | | |
|---|---|---|
| | ***beckxiana*** | MOWG |
| | ***coccinea*** | CCCN SVen |
| | ***macrophylla*** | CBcs |
| | ***nigricans*** | CCCN MOWG |
| | ***prostrata*** | SPlb |
| | ***rubicunda*** | CCCN CRHN |

## *Kentia* (*Arecaceae*)

| | | |
|---|---|---|
| | ***belmoreana*** | see *Howea belmoreana* |
| | ***forsteriana*** | see *Howea forsteriana* |

## *Kentranthus* see *Centranthus*

## *Kerria* (*Rosaceae*)

| | | |
|---|---|---|
| | ***japonica*** (d) | see *K. japonica* 'Pleniflora' |
| | ***japonica*** misapplied single | see *K. japonica* 'Simplex' |
| | - 'Albescens' | CBot WFar |
| | - 'Golden Guinea' ♀$^{H4}$ | CMac CPLG ECtt ELan EPfP EWTr GGal IFro LRHS MAsh MGos MNrw MRav MSwo SBfd SCoo SPer SRms SWvt WDin WFar |
| § | - 'Picta' (v) | CDul CWib EBee ECrN ELan EPfP LRHS MGos MRav MSwo SBfd SGol SLim SLon SPer SPoG SRms WDin WFar WSHC |
| § | - 'Pleniflora' (d) ♀$^{H4}$ | Widely available |
| § | - 'Simplex' | CMac CPLG GGal NWea WDin WFar |
| | - 'Variegata' | see *K. japonica* 'Picta' |

## *Khadia* (*Aizoaceae*)

| | | |
|---|---|---|
| | ***acutipetala*** | CCCN |

## *Kirengeshoma* (*Hydrangeaceae*)

| | | |
|---|---|---|
| | ***palmata*** ♀$^{H4}$ | Widely available |
| | - Koreana Group | Widely available |

## *Kitaibela* (*Malvaceae*)

| | | |
|---|---|---|
| | ***vitifolia*** | CPLG CSpe EBee ELan GCal MLLN NBid SBrt SEND SGar SPav SPlb WPer WPtf WTcb |

## *Kitchingia* see *Kalanchoe*

## kiwi fruit see *Actinidia deliciosa*

## *Kleinia* (*Asteraceae*)

| | | |
|---|---|---|
| | ***articulata*** | see *Senecio articulatus* |
| | ***repens*** | see *Senecio serpens* |

## *Knautia* (*Caprifoliaceae*)

| | | |
|---|---|---|
| § | ***arvensis*** | CArn CHab CHll CRWN EPfP EWil MHer MMuc MNHC NLan NLar NMir NPnk SEND WFar WHer WMoo WSFF |
| | - 'Rachael' | CElw |
| | ***dipsacifolia*** | SHar |
| | 'Jardin d'en Face' | EPfP LRHS WCot |
| § | ***macedonica*** | Widely available |
| | - 'Crimson Cushion' | CSpe ECtt LSou WCot WFar |
| | - 'Mars Midget' | CHll CPLG CSam CSpe EBee ELan ELon EPfP EShb ETod GQue LAst LBMP LRHS LSRN LSou MGos MLHP MWat NBPC NLar SAga |

| | |
|---|---|
| | SPoG SUsu SWvt WFar WHoo WPtf WSHC WWEG |
| – Melton pastels | COIW CPLG EBee EPfP EShb GJos LBMP LRHS LSRN LSou MGos NBPC NBlu NLar NPer SPet SPoG [illegible] SWat SWvt WFar WWEG |
| – pink-flowered | CSam |
| – 'Red Knight' | EPfP MBNS MSCN |
| – red-flowered | CWib |
| – short | CAbP ECtt SPad |
| – tall, pale-flowered | SPhx |
| – 'Thunder and Lightning' new | EBee |
| ***sarajevensis*** | EBee SUsu |
| § ***tatarica*** | NBre |

# *Knightia* (*Proteaceae*)

| | |
|---|---|
| ***excelsa*** | IDee |

# *Kniphofia* ✿ (*Asphodelaceae*)

| | |
|---|---|
| sp. | SBod SVic |
| 'Ada' | EBla EWTr EWes |
| ***albescens*** | SGar SPlb |
| 'Alcazar' | CBcs CDes CElw CPrp EBee EBla ECtt EPfP LSRN MAvo MBri MHer MSCN SBfd SPer SRkn SWvt WCAu WCot WFar WMnd WWEG |
| * ***alpina*** new | LRHS |
| 'Amber' | NBre |
| 'Ample Dwarf' | ECtt WCot |
| 'Amsterdam' | MWat SHar |
| ***angustifolia*** | SPlb |
| 'Apricot' | EPla |
| 'Apricot Souffle' | EPri WCot |
| 'Apricots and Cream' | WCot |
| 'Atlanta' | LRHS SBfd |
| 'Barton Fever' | WCot |
| ***baurii*** | CPLG IGor SPlb |
| 'Bees' Jubilee' | MNrw WHoo |
| 'Bees' Lemon' | Widely available |
| 'Bees' Sunset' ♀H4 | CAvo CDes GCra GQue LPla MNFA MNrw SUsu WCot WWEG |
| 'Bengal Fire' | LRHS |
| 'Bicolor' | ECtt NSti |
| 'Bitter Chocolate' | WCot |
| 'Bob's Choice' | WCot |
| 'Border Ballet' | LBMP LHop LRHS NBir NBre NGdn NLar SWat WFar |
| ***brachystachya*** | ELon GAbr GBin GCal SPlb WCot |
| 'Bressingham Comet' | EBee EBla ECtt LRHS MBri MRav NBir NCGa SRms |
| 'Bressingham Gleam' | WCot |
| Bressingham hybrids | IFoB |
| Bressingham Sunbeam = 'Bresun' | EBla ECtt NBir WCot WWEG |
| 'Bressingham Yellow' | EPPr |
| Bridgemere hybrids | WFar |
| 'Brimstone' Bloom ♀H4 | Widely available |
| ***bruceae*** | EPri |
| ***buchananii*** | CDes |
| 'Buttercup' ♀H4 | CAvo LSRN WSHC WTin |
| 'Candlelight' | CCse CDes COIW ECtt EPri LRHS NBre SBfd SDys SUsu |
| 'Candlemass' | CTca SBfd |
| 'Carole's Crush' | WCot |
| ***caulescens*** ♀H3-4 | Widely available |
| – 'Cally Compact' | GCal |
| – 'Coral Breakers' | CPLG CTca EBee ECtt GBin LRHS NEgg SBfd SDix SKHP SMad SPer SPoG WCot |
| – 'John May' | EBee ECtt LRHS WCot |
| – short | ECha |
| 'Chichi' | MAvo WCot |
| ***citrina*** | CFir CTrC EPfP GCra LAst LRHS MAvo MBrN NBre NLar NBir WCot WHil XLum |
| 'C.M. Prichard' misapplied | see *K. rooperi* |
| 'C.M. Prichard' Prichard | WCot |
| 'Cobra' | EBla GBin MRav SBfd SUsu WCAu WCot WHil |
| 'Comet' | ECtt |
| 'Coral Sceptre' | LPla WCot |
| 'Corallina' | WFar |
| 'Dingaan' | CSam EBee ECtt GBin GQue MNrw NBir NEgg SAga WCot WFar |
| 'Dorset Sentry' | CAbP CAbb CChe COIW EBee EBla ECtt ELon EPfP GAbr GCal LRHS MCot MGos MNrw NBir NEgg NLar NOrc NSti SAga SBfd SKHP WCAu WCot WFar WWEG |
| 'Dropmore Apricot' | LSRN |
| 'Drummore Apricot' | CMHG EAEE EBee ECha ECtt ELan GCal LRHS LSRN LSou MLLN MRav NBir NCGa NEgg NSti SEND SPoG WCot WFar WPtf |
| I 'Earliest of All' | EBee |
| 'Early Buttercup' | CTca MRav SBfd WCot WFar |
| ***ensifolia*** | CTca ECtt GKev NGdn SRms WMnd XLum |
| 'Ernest Mitchell' | MRav WCot |
| Express hybrids | NBre NLar XLum |
| 'Fairyland' | NGBl SGar WBrk WFar WTin |
| 'Fiery Fred' | EBla ELan LRHS MRav NBre SBfd SMrm WCot |
| 'Firefly' new | LRHS |
| 'First Sunrise'PBR | EBee ECtt EWll NCGa |
| 'Flamenco' | CChe COIW EBee EDAr EWll LRHS NBre NGdn SBfd SPet WRHF WWEG |
| 'Frances Victoria' | WCot |
| ***galpinii*** misapplied | see *K. triangularis* subsp. *triangularis* |
| ***galpinii*** ambig. | SPer WWEG |
| ***galpinii*** Baker ♀H4 | CBot MRav NBre SEND SRms |
| 'Gilt Bronze' | WCot |
| 'Gladness' | ECtt MAvo MRav NBir NBre NCGa NSti WCot WWEG |
| 'Goldelse' | NBir WCot |
| 'Goldfinch' | CCse CSam MRav |
| ***gracilis*** | LEdu |
| 'Green and Cream' | MNrw |
| 'Green Jade' | Widely available |
| 'Green Lemon' | NBre |
| 'H.E. Beale' | ECtt GCal WCot |
| 'Hen and Chickens' | EBee ECtt MAvo MNrw WCot |
| ***hirsuta*** | CFir EShb GBin SPad WCot WSHC |
| – JCA 3.461.900 | SKHP |
| – 'Fire Dance' new | LRHS |
| – 'Traffic Lights' | GBin |
| 'Hollard's Gold' | WCot |
| 'Ice Queen' | CAvo CFir CPar EBee ECha ECtt ELon EPPr LAst LRHS MAvo MHer MMuc MRav NChi NGdn NLar SBfd SEND SMad SRms SSvw SWvt WCAu WCot WTin WWEG |
| ***ichopensis*** | CDes MAvo WPGP |
| 'Incandesce' | WCot |
| 'Ingénue' | WCot |
| 'Innocence' | EBla NBre |

| |  |  |
|---|---|---|
| | 'Jenny Bloom' | CAby CMHG CMac COIW CTca EBla ECtt ELan ELon EPfP EShb EWTr GAbr GCal GMaP ITim LAst LRHS MRav NBPC NEgg NLar SPer SRGP SWat WCot WFar WMnd WWEG |
| | 'Jess's Delight' | WCot |
| | 'John Benary' | CHar CTca EAEE EBee EBla ECtt GBBs GMaP IKil LRHS LSou MCot MLLN NBir NEgg NGdn NLar SBfd SBrd SEND SMrm SPer SPoG WCot WFar WKif WTin WWEG |
| | 'Jonathan' | WCot |
| | ***laxiflora*** | EPri WPGP |
| | 'Lemon Ice' | WCot |
| | 'Light of the World' | see *K. triangularis* subsp. *triangularis* 'Light of the World' |
| | ***linearifolia*** | CPLG CTrC GCra MLLN MNrw SGar SPlb WCot |
| | 'Little Elf' | SDys |
| | 'Little Maid' | Widely available |
| | 'Lord Roberts' | CDes EBee GCal MRav SBfd SDix SMad WCot WPGP |
| I | 'Luna' Brown | WCot |
| | ***macowanii*** | see *K. triangularis* subsp. *triangularis* |
| | 'Maid of Orleans' | CRow WCot |
| | 'Mermaiden' | CFir CMHG CRow CSam EBee ECtt LAst LSou MNrw WCAu WCot WFar |
| | 'Minister Verschuur' | EBee EBla ECtt GQue MBri NBre WFar WMnd |
| | 'Modesta' | WSHC |
| | 'Moonstone' | ECtt WCot |
| | 'Mount Etna' | WCot |
| | ***multiflora*** | CTca ECtt |
| | 'Nancy's Red' | Widely available |
| | ***nelsonii*** Mast. | see *K. triangularis* subsp. *triangularis* |
| | 'Nobilis' | see *K. uvaria* 'Nobilis' |
| | ***northiae*** ♀$^{H4}$ | Widely available |
| | - JCA 3.462.600 | WCot |
| | 'November Glory' | CTca WCot |
| | 'Old Court Seedling' | GGal WCot |
| | 'Olympic Torch' | WCot |
| | 'Painted Lady' | CAvo COIW CSam CTca CTri CYeo EBee ECGP ECtt EPfP GAbr GMaP MNrw MRav MTis NCGa NLar WCot |
| | ***pauciflora*** | SDys WCot |
| | 'Percy's Pride' | Widely available |
| | 'Pfitzeri' | SRms |
| | × ***praecox*** | LRHS MAvo SGar WCFE WCot |
| | 'Prince Igor' misapplied | see *K. uvaria* 'Nobilis' |
| | 'Prince Igor' Prichard | EBee GAbr MLHP MRav MWea NBir SMad WCot |
| | ***pumila*** | LLHF |
| | 'Raging Inferno' | WCot |
| | 'Red Rocket' **new** | EBee |
| | 'Rich Echoes' | WCot |
| | ***ritualis*** | LSou SKHP |
| § | ***rooperi*** ♀$^{H4}$ | Widely available |
| | - 'Cally Giant' | GCal |
| | - 'Cally Torch' | GCal |
| I | - 'Torchlight' | CPne |
| | 'Royal Castle' | GMaP LRHS MRav NBir NGdn NOrc SEND WFar WWEG XLum |
| | 'Royal Standard' ♀$^{H4}$ | CBcs CMac CPrp EBee EBla ELan EPfP EShb LRHS LSRN MCot MRav NCGa NLar SBfd SPer SWvt WCot WFar WMnd WWEG |
| | ***rufa*** Baker | SUsu |
| | - - CD&R 1032 | SGar |
| | 'Safranvogel' | ECtt MAvo SMad WCot |
| | 'Samuel's Sensation' Samuel ♀$^{H4}$ | CFir EBee EBla ELan MRav NLar NSti SEND SRGP WCot WWEG |
| | ***sarmentosa*** | CTrC SGar SPlb WCot |
| | 'September Sunshine' | MRav |
| | 'Sherbet Lemon' | CTca CYeo ECtt GQue MLLN MNrw WCot |
| | 'Shining Sceptre' | CSam CTca EBee ECha ECtt MRav MSCN NLar SBfd SGar SMad SWvt WAul WWEG |
| | 'Springtime' | WCot |
| | 'Star of Baden Baden' | CDes NBir SEND SMad WCot WWEG |
| | 'Strawberries and Cream' | CAvo CBcs CFir COIW CTca CWCL CYeo EBee ECha ECtt EPfP GBin GQue LAst MAvo SAga SBfd SPer WCot |
| | ***stricta*** | WCot |
| | 'Sunningdale Yellow' ♀$^{H4}$ | CCse CDes COIW CYeo EBee EBla ECha EPfP GMaP MAvo MLHP SRms WCot WHoo WWEG |
| | 'Tawny King' | Widely available |
| | 'Tetbury Torch' PBR | CWGN EAEE EBee EBla ECGP ECtt GBin LHop LRHS LSou MAvo MLLN NCGa NLar WAul WPtf WWEG |
| | ***thomsonii*** | GCal NGdn |
| | - var. ***snowdenii*** misapplied | see *K. thomsonii* var. *thomsonii* |
| | - var. ***snowdenii*** ambig. | CPLG WPGP |
| § | - var. ***thomsonii*** | CBot CEnt ECGP SAga SUsu WCot WHal |
| | 'Timothy' | Widely available |
| | 'Toffee Nosed' ♀$^{H4}$ | Widely available |
| | 'Torchbearer' | NBre WCot WFar |
| | ***triangularis*** | EPfP EShb MBlu NCGa WFar XLum |
| § | - subsp. ***triangularis*** | CBro COIW EPfP GCal LAst LRHS LSRN MRav SMrm SRms SWat WCot |
| § | - - 'Light of the World' | CHar CSpe CTca EAEE EBee ECtt GAbr LEdu LSou MAvo MBlu NBPC NBir NCGa NLar SMad SRms SUsu SWvt WCot WFar WGrn WPtf WWEG |
| | 'Tubergeniana' | WCot |
| | 'Tuckii' | SRms |
| | ***typhoides*** | CDes NBir SPlb WCot |
| | ***tysonii*** | SPlb |
| | ***uvaria*** | CTrC LRHS NBir NVic SEND SRms WCot WMnd XSen |
| | - 'Grandiflora' | MWhi NPri SBfd WFar |
| § | - 'Nobilis' ♀$^{H4}$ | Widely available |
| | 'Vanilla' | CFir EBee GBin LAst LRHS LSRN MAvo MMuc MRav NGdn NLar SBfd SEND WAul WWEG |
| | 'Vincent Lepage' | EBee NLar |
| | 'White Trust' | WCot |
| | 'Wol's Red Seedling' | CAby CAvo CBct CEnt COIW CSam CYeo EBee EBla ECtt ELon EWTr GAbr LSou MAvo MCot MNrw NBPC NCGa NEgg NGdn NLar SBfd SMrm WCot WGrn WGwG WHoo |
| | 'Wrexham Buttercup' | CAby COIW CSam EBee EBla ECtt ELan EPfP GAbr GBin GMaP GMac GQue LRHS LSRN MCot MNrw MRav NLar SBfd SMrm SUsu WCot WHal WWEG WWlt |
| | 'Yellow Hammer' Slieve Donard | CSam EBee MMuc NBre SBfd SEND WFar |
| | 'Zululandii' | WCot |

## *Knowltonia* (*Ranunculaceae*)

| | | |
|---|---|---|
| | ***filia*** | CPLG |

## *Koeleria* (*Poaceae*)

| | | |
|---|---|---|
| | ***cristata*** misapplied | see *K. macrantha* |
| | ***glauca*** | CPrp CWib EBee ECha EHoe EHul EPPr EPfP EPla GMaP LEdu LRHS LTen MBNS MWhi NBro NGdn NWsh SBfd SLim SMrm SPlb SWvt WFar WMnd WWEG XLum |
| § | ***macrantha*** | NBre NLar SPhx XLum |
| | ***pyramidata*** | SMea XLum |
| | ***vallesiana*** | EHoe LRHS SMea |
| | - 'Mountain Breeze' **new** | EPPr |

## *Koelreuteria* (*Sapindaceae*)

| | | |
|---|---|---|
| | ***bipinnata*** | CMCN LEdu |
| | ***paniculata*** ♀H4 | Widely available |
| | - 'Coral Sun'PBR | CGHE CMHG CPLG LRHS MBlu MBri MGos NLar SMad WPGP WPat |
| | - 'Fastigiata' | CMCN EBee EPfP MBlu MBri SCoo SSpi WHar |
| | - 'Rosseels' | NLar |
| | - 'September' | EPfP |

## *Kohleria* (*Gesneriaceae*)

| | | |
|---|---|---|
| | 'Cybele' | EABi WDib |
| | 'Dark Velvet' | WDib |
| | ***eriantha*** ♀H1 | CDoC EShb WDib |
| | ***hirsuta*** | WDib |
| | 'Jester' ♀H1 | EABi WDib |
| | 'Marquis de Sade' | EABi |
| | 'Red Ryder' | EABi |
| | 'Ruby Red' | WDib |
| § | 'Sunrise'PBR | WDib |
| | 'Sunshine'PBR | see *K.* 'Sunrise' |
| | ***warscewiczii*** ♀H1 | EABi WDib |

## *Kolkwitzia* (*Caprifoliaceae*)

| | | |
|---|---|---|
| | ***amabilis*** | CDoy CPLG CSBt CTri ECGP ELan EPfP GQue MGos NWea SGol SPlb SRms WCFE WDin WHar WMoo |
| | - 'Maradco' | CMac CPMA CWSG EPfP MAsh MRav NLar NPro WPat |
| | - 'Pink Cloud' ♀H4 | Widely available |

## **kumquat** see *Fortunella*

## *Kunzea* (*Myrtaceae*)

| | | |
|---|---|---|
| | ***ambigua*** | ECou ESwi IDee MOWG SPlb |
| | - pink-flowered | ECou |
| | - prostrate | ECou |
| | ***baxteri*** | ECou ESwi MOWG |
| | ***ericifolia*** | SPlb |
| § | ***ericoides*** | CTsd ECou GGar MOWG |
| | - 'Auckland' | ECou |
| | - 'Bemm' | ECou |
| | ***parvifolia*** | ECou MOWG |
| | ***pomifera*** | ECou |
| | ***recurva*** | CTsd |

# L

## *Lablab* (*Papilionaceae*)

| | | |
|---|---|---|
| § | ***purpureus*** | LSou SHDw |
| | - 'Ruby Moon' | CSpe |

## + *Laburnocytisus* (*Papilionaceae*)

| | | |
|---|---|---|
| | 'Adamii' | CDul CLnd CMac CPMA EBee ECrN ELan EPfP LAst LSRN MGos MPkF MRav NLar SMad SPer |

## *Laburnum* ✿ (*Papilionaceae*)

| | | |
|---|---|---|
| | ***alpinum*** | EPfP NWea SPlb |
| | - 'Pendulum' | CDoC CDul CLnd ELan LSRN MAsh MBri MGos MRav NEgg NPri SCrf SGol SLim SPer SPoG |
| § | ***anagyroides*** | CDul CWib LMaj MMuc NMun NWea SEND SRms WDin |
| | ***vulgare*** | see *L. anagyroides* |
| | × ***watereri*** 'Vossii' ♀H4 | Widely available |

## *Lachenalia* (*Asparagaceae*)

| | | |
|---|---|---|
| | ***alba*** 'Nieuwoudtville' | ECho |
| | ***algoensis*** | ECho |
| § | ***aloides*** | CDoC CGrW CTca ECho EPot GKev NMen |
| | - var. ***aurea*** ♀H1 | CTca ECho EPot SBch WCot |
| I | - var. ***luteola*** | ECho |
| | - 'Nelsonii' | ECho WCot |
| | - 'Pearsonii' | ECho GKev |
| | - var. ***quadricolor*** ♀H1 | CDes CGrW CPrp CTca ECho WCot |
| | - var. ***vanzyliae*** ♀H1 | WCot |
| | ***angelica*** 'Agterkop' | ECho |
| | ***anguinea*** | ECho |
| | ***arbuthnotiae*** 'Somerset West' | ECho |
| | ***attenuata*** | ECho |
| | ***barkeriana*** | ECho |
| | ***bolusii*** | ECho |
| § | ***bulbifera*** ♀H1 | CTca ECho WCot |
| | - 'George' ♀H1 | ECho |
| | ***capensis*** | ECho |
| | ***carnosa*** | ECho |
| | ***cernua*** 'Goudini' | ECho |
| | ***comptonii*** | ECho |
| | ***congesta*** 'Roggeveld' | ECho |
| | ***contaminata*** ♀H1 | CGrW CPrp ECho EPfP WCot |
| | ***doleritica*** | ECho |
| | ***elegans*** | ECho GKev |
| | - var. ***membranacea*** | ECho |
| | - var. ***suaveolens*** | ECho |
| | ***fistulosa*** | ECho |
| | - 'Klein Drakenstein' | ECho |
| | ***framesii*** | ECho |
| | 'Fransie'PBR | ECho |
| | ***gillettii*** | ECho |
| | ***glaucophylla*** | ECho |
| | ***hirta*** | ECho |
| | ***juncifolia*** | ECho |
| | - var. ***juncifolia*** | ECho |
| | ***kliprandensis*** 'Kliprand' | ECho |
| | ***lactosa*** | ECho |
| | ***latimerae*** | ECho |
| | ***leipoldtii*** | ECho |
| | 'Lemon Ripple' (v) | WCot |
| | ***liliiflora*** | CGrW ECho |
| | ***longibracteata*** | ECho |
| | ***longituba*** | WCot |
| | ***marginata*** | ECho |
| | ***mathewsii*** | ECho |
| | ***maximilianii*** | GKev |
| | - 'Cederberg' | ECho |
| | ***mediana*** | ECho |
| | ***montana*** | ECho |

| | |
|---|---|
| ***muirii*** 'Bredasdorp' | EСho |
| ***multifolia*** | ECho |
| ***mutabilis*** | CTca ECho WCot |
| 'Namakwa' (African Beauty Series) | CTca ECho |
| ***namaquensis*** | ECho |
| ***namibiensis*** | ECho |
| ***nardoubergensis*** | ECho |
| ***neilii*** | ECho |
| ***nervosa*** | ECho |
| ***obscura*** | ECho WCot |
| ***orchioides*** var. ***glaucina*** | ECho WCot |
| ***orthopetala*** | CDes ECho GKev WCot |
| ***pallida*** | ECho |
| ***peersii*** 'Betty's Bay' | ECho |
| ***pendula*** | see *L. bulbifera* |
| ***polyphylla*** | ECho |
| ***polypodantha*** 'Varsputs' | ECho |
| ***purpureocoerulea*** 'Darling' | ECho |
| ***pusilla*** | ECho WCot |
| ***pustulata*** ♀H1 | CTca ECho EPot WCot |
| - blue-flowered | CGrW ECho GKev |
| - 'Meerlust' | ECho |
| - yellow-flowered | CTca ECho |
| ***reflexa*** | ECho EPot |
| 'Robijn' | CPrp ECho WCot |
| 'Rolina' | ECho |
| 'Romaud' | ECho WCot |
| 'Romelia'PBR | ECho WCot |
| 'Ronina' (African Beauty Series) | CPrp ECho GKev WCot |
| 'Rosabeth' | ECho WCot |
| ***rosea*** | ECho EPot GKev |
| ***rubida*** | CDes CGrW ECho WCot |
| 'Rupert' (African Beauty Series) | CPrp ECho GKev WCot |
| ***salteri*** 'Elim' | ECho |
| ***splendida*** | ECho |
| ***stayneri*** | CLak |
| ***thomasiae*** | ECho |
| ***trichophylla*** | ECho |
| ***tricolor*** | see *L. aloides* |
| ***unicolor*** | ECho WCot |
| ***unifolia*** | ECho |
| ***variegata*** 'Mamre' | ECho |
| ***violacea*** | ECho |
| - var. ***glauca*** | ECho |
| ***viridiflora*** ♀H1 | CTca ECho EPot GKev SBch WCot |
| ***xerophila*** | ECho |
| ***youngii*** 'Humansdorp' | ECho |
| ***zebrina*** | ECho |
| - f. ***densiflora*** 'Tanqua' | ECho |
| ***zeyheri*** | ECho |

## *Lactuca* (*Asteraceae*)

| | |
|---|---|
| ***alpina*** | see *Cicerbita alpina* |
| ***perennis*** | CPom EPPr LRHS NLar WCot WHer |
| ***virosa*** | CArn |

## *Lagarostrobos* (*Podocarpaceae*)

| | |
|---|---|
| § ***franklinii*** | CBcs CDoC IArd IDee STre |
| - 'Fota' (f) | WThu |
| - 'Picton Castle' (m) | WThu |

## *Lagerstroemia* (*Lythraceae*)

| | |
|---|---|
| ***indica*** ♀H1 | CCCN CDul EGxp EPfP ERom EShb SEND SPlb SSpi SVen WSHC |
| - 'Berlingot Menthe' | SEND |
| - Dynamite = 'Whit II' | LRHS SSpi |
| - Little Chief hybrids | EShb |
| - 'Nana Lavendula' | LRHS |
| - 'Red Imperator' | SEND |
| - 'Rosea' | CBcs SEND |
| - 'World's Fair' | LRHS |
| ***subcostata*** CWJ 12352 | WCru |

## *Lagunaria* (*Malvaceae*)

| | |
|---|---|
| ***patersonii*** | CHll WPGP |

## *Lagurus* (*Poaceae*)

| | |
|---|---|
| ***ovatus*** ♀H3 | CKno EHoe GJos NGBl SAdn SBch |

## *Lallemantia* (*Lamiaceae*)

| | |
|---|---|
| ***canescens*** | CPBP |

## *Lamiastrum* see *Lamium*

## *Lamium* ✿ (*Lamiaceae*)

| | |
|---|---|
| ***album*** | CArn CHab MWat NMir |
| - 'Friday' (v) | NBir WHer WWEG |
| ***flexuosum*** | EBee EPPr |
| § ***galeobdolon*** | CArn CTri CWib EShb LRHS MHer SRms WHer |
| § - 'Florentinum' (v) | CMac CWan EBee ECha EPfP MMuc MRav SEND WFar WPer WWEG |
| - 'Hermann's Pride' | EBee EHoe ELon EPfP GMaP LBMP LRHS MAvo MMuc MNFA NBir NBlu NDov NMir SAga SMrm SPer SPoG SRms SWvt WAul WFar WHoo WMoo WWEG XLum |
| - 'Kirkcudbright Dwarf' | EBee EWes GBin NBre XLum |
| § - 'Silberteppich' | ECha ELan MRav XLum |
| - 'Silver Angel' | XLum |
| - Silver Carpet | see *L. galeobdolon* 'Silberteppich' |
| - 'Variegatum' | see *L. galeobdolon* 'Florentinum' |
| ***garganicum*** subsp. ***garganicum*** | CPom EWes LPla |
| ***luteum*** | see *L. galeobdolon* |
| ***maculatum*** | MMuc NChi SEND SRms WFar |
| - 'Album' | EBee ELan EPfP LBMP LRHS SHar SPer SRms |
| - 'Anne Greenaway' (v) | EBee EWes SPet WWEG |
| § - 'Aureum' | EHoe ELan SMrm SPet SWvt WFar XLum |
| - 'Beacon Silver' | CMac CWib EBee ECha ELan EPfP LRHS LTen MGos MHer MLHP MSCN MWhi NBir SPer SPet SPlb SPoG SRGP SRms SWvt WFar XLum |
| - 'Beedham's White' | NBir |
| - 'Brightstone Pearl' | EWes MAvo |
| - 'Cannon's Gold' | ECtt ELan EWes LRHS SWvt WWEG |
| - 'Chequers' ambig. | LBMP LRHS NBPC NBre SPer |
| - 'Elaine Franks' | CSam |
| - 'Elisabeth de Haas' (v) | EBee EWes NBre |
| - 'Forncett Lustre' | EWes |
| - 'Forncett White Lustre' | NBre |
| - 'Gold Leaf' | see *L. maculatum* 'Aureum' |
| - Golden Anniversary = 'Dellam'PBR (v) | ELan ELon LAst LSRN NBro SWvt WFar |
| - 'Golden Nuggets' | see *L. maculatum* 'Aureum' |
| - 'Ickwell Beauty' (v) | WWEG |
| - 'James Boyd Parselle' | CMea CSam NBre WHal |
| - 'Margery Fish' | SRms |
| - 'Orchid Frost' | CHid ECGP EWll LRHS MAvo |
| - Pink Chablis = 'Checkin'PBR | LRHS |
| - 'Pink Nancy' | CBot MLLN SWvt |
| - 'Pink Pearls' | CSBt LRHS NBre SHar SMrm SPet WFar WMoo WWEG |

| | | |
|---|---|---|
| | – 'Pink Pewter' | EBee ECha ECtt EHoe ELan ELon EPfP EShb GMaP LBMP LRHS MMuc SPer SPlb SPoG SUsu WWEG XLum |
| | – 'Purple Winter' | EPPr |
| | – 'Red Nancy' | [illegible] XLum |
| § | – 'Roseum' | CWib EBee ELan EPfP LBMP LRHS LTen MCot MRav MWat NChi SGar SPer WMoo XLum |
| | – 'Shell Pink' | see *L. maculatum* 'Roseum' |
| | – 'Silver Shield' | EWes |
| | – 'Sterling Silver' | CSam EBee GQue NBre |
| | – 'White Nancy' ♀H4 | Widely available |
| | – 'Wootton Pink' | MHer NBir NLar SSvw SWvt |
| | ***orvala*** | Widely available |
| | – 'Album' | CBod CBot CDes CLAP CPrp EBee ELan EPPr LEdu LRHS NBir NLar SHar SMrm WHer WPGP WPtf WTin |
| | – pink-flowered | CLAP CSpe |
| | – 'Silva' | CCVN CDes CLAP CSam EBee EPPr EPfP GBin LEdu LRHS NBre NCGa WCot WSHC |
| | ***sandrasicum*** | CPBP |

## *Lampranthus* (*Aizoaceae*)

| | | |
|---|---|---|
| | sp. | EDAr NWCA SBod |
| | ***aberdeenensis*** | see *Delosperma aberdeenense* |
| | ***aurantiacus*** | CBcs CHEx SPet |
| | 'Bagdad' | CHEx |
| | ***blandus*** | CBcs CCCN |
| | 'Blousey Pink' | CHEx SVen |
| § | ***brownii*** | CBcs CCCN ECho ELan ELon LRHS SEND SPet SPlb WPnn |
| | ***coccineus*** | SPet |
| | ***deltoides*** | see *Oscularia deltoides* |
| | ***edulis*** | see *Carpobrotus edulis* |
| | ***glaucus*** | SEND |
| | ***multiradiatus*** | SEND |
| | ***oscularis*** | see *Oscularia deltoides* |
| | 'Pink' **new** | WPnn |
| | purple-flowered | EShb |
| | ***roseus*** | CCCN CHEx ECho IRar LRHS SPet WNew |
| | 'Salmon Pink' **new** | WPnn |
| | 'Shanklin' **new** | SVen |
| | ***spectabilis*** | CBcs CCCN CTri ELon SArc SBfd SPet WNew WPnn |
| | – orange-flowered | WNew |
| | – purple-flowered **new** | WNew |
| | – 'Tresco Apricot' | CCCN ECho |
| | – 'Tresco Brilliant' | CCCN CHEx SEND SPet SWvt WPnn |
| | – 'Tresco Fire' | CCCN CDoC ELon SVen |
| | – 'Tresco Orange' | CCCN WPnn |
| | – 'Tresco Peach' | CCCN |
| | – 'Tresco Red' | CCCN ELon SEND SWvt WNew WPnn |
| | – white-flowered | SVen WPnn |
| | – yellow-flowered | WNew WPnn |
| | ***spiniformis*** **new** | SGar |
| | 'Sugar Pink' | CHEx SEND |

## *Lamprocapnos* (*Papaveraceae*)

| | | |
|---|---|---|
| § | ***spectabilis*** ♀H4 | Widely available |
| | – 'Alba' ♀H4 | Widely available |
| | – 'Gold Heart'PBR | CBcs EBee ECha EPfP LRHS MAsh MGos MRav NLar NSti SBfd SGol SPoG WCot |
| | – 'Valentine' **new** | EBee |

## *Lamprothyrsus* (*Poaceae*)

| | | |
|---|---|---|
| | ***hieronymi*** CDPR 3096 | EPPr |
| | – RCB RA K2-2 | WCot |

## *Lancea* (*Phrymaceae*)

| | | |
|---|---|---|
| | ***tibetica*** | NWCA |

## *Lantana* (*Verbenaceae*)

| | | |
|---|---|---|
| | 'Calippo Tutti Frutti' **new** | LSou |
| | ***camara*** | CArn ELan EPfP EShb SRms WFar |
| | – 'Kolibri' | LAst |
| | – orange-flowered | CCCN |
| | – pink-flowered | CCCN EShb |
| | – red-flowered | CCCN |
| | – 'Sonja' | LAst |
| | – variegated (v) | EShb |
| | – white-flowered | CCCN EShb |
| | – yellow-flowered | EShb |
| | 'Goldsome' | SEND |
| § | ***montevidensis*** | EShb |
| * | – ***alba*** | EShb |
| | 'Red and Gold' | SEND |
| | ***sellowiana*** | see *L. montevidensis* |
| | 'Spreading Sunset' | MOWG |

## *Lapageria* ✿ (*Philesiaceae*)

| | | |
|---|---|---|
| | ***rosea*** ♀H3 | CBcs CCCN CDoy CPLG CPne CRHN CTsd EPfP MDun NLar SAdn WFar WPGP |
| | – var. ***albiflora*** | CRHN SAdn |
| | – 'Avalanche' | CBcs |
| | – 'Flesh Pink' | CPLG CRHN |
| | – 'Tierra del Fuego' | CBcs |
| | – 'Torres del Paine' | CBcs |

## *Lapeirousia* (*Iridaceae*)

| | | |
|---|---|---|
| | ***anceps*** | CPBP ECho |
| | ***corymbosa*** | ECho |
| | ***cruenta*** | see *Anomatheca laxa* |
| | ***divaricata*** | ECho |
| | ***fabricii*** 'Grey's Pass' | ECho |
| | ***fastigiata*** | ECho |
| | ***jacquinii*** 'Gilberg' | ECho |
| | ***laxa*** | see *Anomatheca laxa* |
| | ***montana*** 'Danielskuil' | ECho |
| | ***plicata*** 'Nieuwoudtville' | ECho |
| | ***pyramidalis*** 'Worcester' | ECho |

## *Lapiedra* (*Amaryllidaceae*)

| | | |
|---|---|---|
| | ***martinezii*** | ECho WCot |

## *Lapsana* (*Asteraceae*)

| | | |
|---|---|---|
| | ***communis*** 'Inky' | CNat |

## *Larix* ✿ (*Pinaceae*)

| | | |
|---|---|---|
| | ***decidua*** ♀H4 | CBcs CCVT CDoC CDul CMen CRWN ECrN ELan EPfP MGos MMuc NEgg NWea SEND SPer SPlb WDin WEve WFar WMou |
| | – 'Corley' | CKen MBlu NLar SLim |
| | – 'Croxby Broom' | CKen |
| § | – var. ***decidua*** | WFar |
| | – 'Globus' | LRHS NLar SLim |
| | – 'Grott' | NLar |
| | – 'Horstmann Recurved' | LRHS NLar SCoo SLim |
| | – 'Kornik' | NLar |
| | – 'Krejci' | NLar SLim |
| | – 'Little Bogle' | CKen MAsh NHol NLar |
| | – 'Oberförster Karsten' | CKen NLar |

| | | |
|---|---|---|
| | - 'Pendula' | CBcs WFar |
| | - 'Puli' | CEnd EBee LRHS MAsh MBlu MGos NHol NLar NPri SCoo SLim SPer SPoG WFar |
| | - 'Schwarzenburg' | NLar |
| | × ***eurolepis*** | see *L.* × *marschlinsii* |
| | ***europaea*** DC. | see *L. decidua* var. *decidua* |
| | ***gmelinii*** var. ***olgensis*** | NLar |
| | - 'Tharandt' | CKen LRHS SLim |
| § | ***kaempferi*** ♀H4 | CCVT CDoC CDoy CDul CLnd CMen CTri ELan EPfP LBuc LMaj LRHS MAsh MMuc NWea SCoo SEWo SLim SPer STre WDin WEve WFar WMou |
| | - 'Bambino' | CKen |
| | - 'Bingman' | CKen |
| | - 'Blue Ball' | CKen NLar SLim WEve |
| | - 'Blue Dwarf' | CDoC CKen LRHS MAsh MBri MGos SCoo SLim SPoG WEve WFar |
| | - 'Blue Haze' | CKen |
| | - 'Blue Rabbit' | CKen LRHS |
| | - 'Blue Rabbit Weeping' | LRHS MGos SCoo SLim SPoG WDin |
| | - 'Cruwys Morchard' | CKen |
| | - 'Cupido' | LRHS SLim |
| | - 'Diane' | CEnd CKen LRHS MAsh MBlu MGos NHol NLar SLim SPoG WFar |
| | - 'Elizabeth Rehder' | CKen |
| | - 'Grant Haddow' | CKen |
| | - 'Grey Pearl' | CKen MAsh NLar WFar |
| | - 'Hanna's Broom' | LRHS SLim |
| | - 'Hobbit' | CKen |
| * | - 'Jakobsen's Pyramid' | CDoC CMen LRHS MAsh SCoo SLim SPoG WEve WFar |
| | - 'Lobby Dosser' | LRHS |
| | - 'Nana' | CKen LRHS NLar SLim WFar |
| I | - 'Nana Prostrata' | CKen |
| | - 'Pendula' | CDul CEnd EPfP MBlu MGos NHol NLar SPer SPoG |
| | - 'Peve Tunnis' | NLar |
| | - 'Stiff Weeping' | CTri LRHS MBlu MPkF NLar NPCo SCoo SLim |
| | - 'Swallow Falls' | CKen |
| | - 'Varley' | CKen |
| | - 'Wehlen' | CKen |
| | - 'Wolterdingen' | CKen LRHS MBlu NLar SLim |
| | - 'Yanus Olieslagers' | CKen |
| | ***laricina*** 'Arethusa Bog' | CKen NLar SLim |
| | - 'Bear Swamp' | CKen SLim WFar |
| | - 'Bingman' | CKen |
| | - 'Hartwig Pine' | CKen |
| | - 'Newport Beauty' | CKen |
| | ***leptolepis*** | see *L. kaempferi* |
| § | × ***marschlinsii*** | CCVT GBin MMuc NWea |
| | - 'Domino' | CKen SLim |
| | - 'Gail' | CKen |
| | - 'Julie' | CKen |
| | 'Varied Directions' | SCoo SLim |

## *Laserpitium* (*Apiaceae*)

| | | |
|---|---|---|
| | ***latifolium*** | EPPr |
| § | ***siler*** | CArn EBee MAvo SPhx SPlb WSHC |

## *Lasiagrostis* see *Stipa*

## *Lasiospermum* (*Asteraceae*)

| | |
|---|---|
| ***bipinnatum*** | SPlb |

## *Lastreopsis* (*Dryopteridaceae*)

| | |
|---|---|
| ***glabella*** | WRic |
| ***hispida*** | ESwi WRic |
| ***microsora*** | WRic |

## *Latania* (*Arecaceae*)

| | |
|---|---|
| ***loddigesii*** | LPal |
| ***verschaffeltii*** | LPal |

## *Lathyrus* ✿ (*Papilionaceae*)

| | | |
|---|---|---|
| § | ***articulatus*** | SBch |
| § | ***aureus*** | CDes CLAP CMac CPom CSpe EBee GCal IFro LRHS MCot MHer NBid NBir NChi NSti SKHP SMrm SSvw SUsu WAul WCAu WFar WHal WHoo WKif WPGP WViv WWEG |
| | - 'Cally Variegated' (v) | GCal |
| | ***chilensis*** | CFir LLHF |
| | ***chloranthus*** | SPav |
| | ***cirrhosus*** | CDes WPGP |
| | ***clymenum articulatus*** | see *L. articulatus* |
| | ***cyaneus*** misapplied | see *L. vernus* |
| | ***davidii*** | CDes CPom EBee EWes EWld GCal LLHF WSHC |
| | ***fremontii*** hort. | see *L. laxiflorus* |
| | ***gmelinii*** | NLar |
| | ***grandiflorus*** | CSev CTri ECGP NLar SDix SSvw SWat WCot |
| | ***heterophyllus*** | EBee |
| | ***incurvus*** | MPet |
| | ***inermis*** | see *L. laxiflorus* |
| | ***japonicus*** | EBee |
| | 'Lamorna's Love' | WViv |
| | ***latifolius*** ♀H4 | CArn CRHN CRWN EBee EPfP LAst MWat MWhi NPer NWad SPoG SRms SVic SWal WBrk WFar WHer WPer XLum |
| § | - 'Albus' ♀H4 | CBot CTri ELan SPav SRms XLum |
| | - deep pink-flowered | MHer NLar NSti |
| | - pale pink-flowered | NSti |
| | - Pink Pearl | see *L. latifolius* 'Rosa Perle' |
| | - 'Red Pearl' | CBcs ECtt ELan EPfP GAbr LBuc LRHS LSRN MBri MCot NPri SEND SPav SPer SPlb SPoG SSvw WPer |
| § | - 'Rosa Perle' ♀H4 | CBcs CTri EBee ECha ECtt LBMP LHop LRHS LSRN MBri MCot MLHP MNHC MRav NBir NLar NPer NPri SMrm SPer SSvw WCAu WHil WMoo WWEG XLum |
| | - Weisse Perle | see *L. latifolius* 'White Pearl' |
| | - 'White Pearl' misapplied | see *L. latifolius* 'Albus' |
| § | - 'White Pearl' ♀H4 | CBcs ECha EPfP GAbr GCal LBMP LRHS LSRN MBri MCot MHer MNHC MRav NBir NLar NPer NPri NSti SMrm SPer SPoG SSvw WCAu WFar WPer |
| § | ***laxiflorus*** | CDes CPom EBee MCCP SSvw WPGP WSHC |
| | ***linifolius*** | EBee NLar WHfH WPGP |
| | ***maritimus*** | NLar |
| | ***montanus*** | GPoy |
| | ***nervosus*** | CSpe EBee EWes SBch SBrt SEND SRms |
| | ***neurolobus*** | CPom EBee WHil |
| | ***niger*** | CSpe EBee GMac LHop LSou MCot MHer MMHG NLar SSvw WFar WKif WWEG |
| | ***odoratus*** | NBlu SVic |
| | - 'Dancing Queen' | MPet |
| | - 'Lucinda Jane' **new** | MPet |
| | - 'Mammoth Mixed' | MPet |
| | - 'Matucana' | CSpe MWat SBch WBrk |
| | - Winter Elegance Series | MPet |

***odoratus* × *belinensis* 'Erewhon'** new — MPet
- × – 'Navy' new — MPet
***palustris*** — EBee NLar
***polyphyllus*** — EBee MPet NSti
***pratensis*** — CHab EBee NMir WSFF
***pubescens*** — EBee MPet
***roseus*** — GCal WSHC WViv
***rotundifolius*** ♀H4 — EBee GLog MNrw WFar WHoo
– 'Tillyperone' — SSvw
***sativus*** — CHid CSpe ELan
– f. ***albus*** — CSpe
***sylvestris*** — EBee NLar SBch SEND WBrk
***tingitanus*** — CSpe
– 'Roseus' — CSpe SBch
***transsylvanicus*** — CPom EBee SPhx
***tuberosus*** — CAby CArn EBee WCot WSHC
'Tubro' — EBee
***venetus*** — CPom EBee GCal MNrw MWea WSHC
§ ***vernus*** ♀H4 — Widely available
– 'Alboroseus' ♀H4 — CLAP EBee ELan ELon EPfP GCal GCra GGar GMaP IFro LHop MAvo MBri MCCP MHer MNrw NBir NChi NPnk SAga SMrm SPhx SPoG SWat SWvt WCot WFar WHoo WViv
– var. ***albus*** — CLAP WCot WPGP
– ***aurantiacus*** — see *L. aureus*
– 'Caeruleus' — CLAP ECGP MNFA WHoo WPGP
* – 'Cyaneus' — SAga SWat WCot
I – 'Filifolius' — CSpe
– 'Flaccidus' — CAby SBrt WCot WKif WTin
* – 'Gracilis' — WViv
– 'Madelaine' — WCot
– purple-flowered — LRHS MMuc SEND
– 'Rainbow' — CLAP EPfP GAbr LRHS NWCA SMrm WFar WHil WWEG
– 'Rosenelfe' — CBot CMea EBee MCot MDKP NPri SMrm SPhx WCot WHal WPGP WSHC XLum
– f. ***roseus*** — EBee ECha GAbr LRHS MMuc MRav NBir NCGa SEND SRms WBrk WCot
– 'Spring Beauty' — CLAP
– 'Spring Melody' — MRav WCot WPat
– 'White Wisps' — WCot

## *Latua* (Solanaceae)

***pubiflora*** new — WAle

## *Laurelia* (Atherospermataceae)

§ ***sempervirens*** — CBcs CTrC IArd NMun WPGP
***serrata*** — see *L. sempervirens*

## *Laureliopsis* (Atherospermataceae)

***philippiana*** — IArd

## *Laurentia* see *Isotoma*

## *Laurus* (Lauraceae)

§ ***azorica*** — CBcs
***canariensis*** — see *L. azorica*
***nobilis*** ♀H4 — Widely available
– f. ***angustifolia*** — CMac CTsd EOHP GGal IDee LRHS MBlu MHer MRav NLar SArc SEND SPoG
– 'Aurea' ♀H4 — CBcs CDul CMac EBee ELan ELon EPfP LHop LRHS MBlu MGos MHer MMuc NEgg NLar SEND SLim SLon SPer SPoG SWvt WDin WFar WMoo
– clipped pyramid — LSRN
– 'Crispa' — MRav
– 'Sunspot' (v) — WCot
– variegated (v) — CMac

## *Lavandula* ✿ (Lamiaceae)

'After Midnight' — see *L.* 'Avonview'
'Alba' — see *L. angustifolia* 'Alba', *L.* × *intermedia* 'Alba'
'Alba' ambig. — CWib SAdn SIde SPer SWat WPer
'Alexandra'PBR — SBfd
× ***allardii*** (Gaston Allard Group) 'African Pride' — SVen
§ ***angustifolia*** — CArn CBar CCVT CWCL CWib EBee ELau EPfP EWTr GPoy LBuc LRHS LSRN MBri MGos MHer MWat NGdn NPer NPri SBfd SDow SLim SPlb SVic WFar XLum XSen
– 'Alba' misapplied — see *L. angustifolia* 'Blue Mountain White'
§ – 'Alba' — CChe EPfP GPoy LBuc LSRN LTen MHer MRav MSwo NMen SBch SLon SPlb WDin WFar WJek
– 'Alba Nana' — see *L. angustifolia* 'Nana Alba'
– 'Arctic Snow' — CBcs CEnt CHab EGHP LRHS LSRN MHer MSwo MWat NBPC NDov NGdn NLLv NPri SDow SFai SPoG WLav
– 'Ashdown Forest' — CWan EGHP EWhm LRHS MHer MLHP MNHC SAdn SAga SBch SDow SIde SPer WHoo WJek WLav
– 'Backhouse Purple' — SDow
– 'Beechwood Blue' ♀H4 — SDow WLav
– 'Betty's Blue' — SDow
– Blue Cushion = 'Lavandula Schola'PBR — EPfP LRHS LSRN MAsh SDow SFai WFar WLav
– Blue Ice = 'Dow3'PBR — CSev EGHP LRHS LSou MNHC MTis NBPC NGdn SDow SFai SLim WLav
§ – 'Blue Mountain White' — NLLv SDow WLav
– 'Blue Rider' — EWTr LRHS MTis NGdn SWal WLav
– 'Blue River'PBR — WFar
– Blue Scent = 'Syngablusc' — LRHS
§ – 'Bowles's Early' — EGHP SAga WFar
– 'Bowles's Grey' — see *L. angustifolia* 'Bowles's Early'
– 'Bowles's Variety' — see *L. angustifolia* 'Bowles's Early'
– 'Cedar Blue' — CSev CWan EGHP ELau EPfP EWhm MHer SBfd SDow SHDw SIde WFar WJek WLav
– 'Coconut Ice'PBR — CWCL CWSG NLLv WLav
– 'Compacta' — SDow WLav
– 'Dwarf Blue' — EPfP LSRN WFar
– 'Elizabeth' — LRHS LSRN SDow SFai SPoG SRGP WLav
– 'Ellagance Ice' — LRHS
– 'Ellagance Purple' new — LRHS
– 'Ellagance Sky' — LRHS
– 'Folgate' — CArn ECtt EGHP ELau EPfP LSou MHer MNHC NGdn SDow SGol SIde WFar WHoo WJek WLav WMnd
– 'Fring A' — SDow
– Garden Beauty = 'Lowmar'PBR (v) — LBuc LRHS NPri SPoG
– 'Granny's Bouquet' — LSRN SBfd
§ – 'Hidcote' ♀H4 — Widely available
– 'Hidcote Pink' — CEnt CWCL CWib EGHP EPfP LSRN LSou MHer MNHC MRav NGdn SDow SPer SWat WFar WMnd WPer
– 'Hidcote Superior' — LBMP LSRN NGdn
– 'Imperial Gem' ♀H4 — Widely available

| | | |
|---|---|---|
| | - 'Jean Davis' | see *L. angustifolia* 'Rosea' |
| | - 'Lady' | NPer SBfd SWal WPer |
| | - 'Lady Ann' | CWCL NLLv SDow WLav |
| I | - 'Lavender Haze' **new** | SFai |
| | - 'Lavenite Petite' PBR | EGHP EPfP LLHF LRHS LSRN NBPC NLLv NLar SDow SFai SPoG WLav |
| | - Little Lady = 'Batlad' | CMea CSev EBee ECtt EGHP ELon EPfP LAst LBMP LRHS LSRN MAsh MSwo NBPC NLLv NLar SAll SFai SGol SLim WLav |
| | - Little Lottie = 'Clarmo' 🏆H4 | CWCL ELon LSRN MHer SDow SIde SWvt WLav |
| | - 'Loddon Blue' 🏆H4 | CEnt CWCL EGHP EPfP EWhm LBMP LRHS SAdn SDow SFai SIde WLav |
| § | - 'Loddon Pink' 🏆H4 | CWCL CWan EGHP ELan EPfP GMaP LRHS MAsh MLHP MMuc MNHC MRav NGdn SAdn SEND SFai WFar WLav |
| | - 'Luberon' **new** | XSen |
| | - 'Lullaby Blue' **new** | SDow |
| | - 'Maillette' | EGHP NGdn SDow SIde SPet WLav |
| | - 'Mellisa Lilac' PBR | CBcs CSBt CSev LBMP LRHS LSRN LSou MGos MHer MNHC SDow SFai SPoG SRkn WLav |
| | - 'Miss Donnington' | see *L. angustifolia* 'Bowles's Early' |
| | - 'Miss Katherine' PBR 🏆H4 | CWCL EBee ECtt EGHP ELan EPfP LHop LRHS LSRN MAsh NBPC NLar SDow SPer SPoG WLav |
| | - Miss Muffet = 'Scholmis' 🏆H4 | CWCL EBee LLHF SDow WLav |
| | - 'Mont Ventoux' **new** | XSen |
| | - 'Munstead' | Widely available |
| § | - 'Nana Alba' 🏆H4 | CArn CMea CWan ECha EGHP ELan ELon EPfP GMaP GPoy LRHS MAsh MHer MNHC MWat SBch SDow SPer SWvt WHoo WJek XSen |
| | - 'Nana Atropurpurea' | SDow |
| | - 'No 9' | SDow |
| | - 'Oxford Gem' **new** | SFai |
| | - 'Pacific Blue' | LRHS |
| | - 'Peter Pan' | CWCL ECtt EGHP ELau LSRN MHer NDov NGdn SBch SDow WLav |
| | - 'Princess Blue' | CWCL EBee ELan EWhm LRHS MAsh SAga SDow SFai SIde WFar WLav WPer |
| § | - 'Rosea' | Widely available |
| | - 'Royal Purple' | CBcs CHab CWCL EBee EGHP EWes LSou NGdn SDow SFai SIde SWvt WLav |
| | - 'Royal Velvet' | SDow |
| | - 'Saint Jean' | SDow |
| | - 'Silver Mist' | CMea EPfP GGar WHer |
| | - 'Thumbelina Leigh' PBR | LBMP SDow SFai |
| | - 'Twickel Purple' | CBcs CWCL EBee EGHP EPfP LHop LRHS LSRN MNHC MRav NGdn SBfd SDow SFai SIde SPer SVen SWat SWvt WFar WLav XSen |
| | - 'Walberton's Silver Edge' | see *L.* × *intermedia* Walberton's Silver Edge |
| | - 'Wendy Carlile' 🏆H4 | CSev EPfP |
| | - 'White Horse' | EGHP |
| | ***aristibracteata*** | MHer WLav |
| § | 'Avonview' | EGHP EWhm MHer SDow WHoo WLav |
| | 'Ballerina' | SDow |
| § | 'Bee Brilliant' PBR | EWhm WLav |
| § | 'Bee Cool' PBR | EWhm MHer WLav |
| § | 'Bee Happy' | CWCL EWhm NBir WJek WLav |
| § | 'Bee Pretty' | EWhm |
| | 'Blue Star' | EGHP EPfP EWhm LRHS NGdn SAll WFar WGwG |
| | 'Bowers Beauty' | LRHS |
| | ***buchii*** var. ***buchii*** | SDow WLav |
| | - var. ***gracilis*** | CSpe |
| | 'Bulls Cross' **new** | WLav |
| | Butterfly Garden = 'Avenue' PBR | CWSG |
| | ***canariensis*** | MHer SDow SVen WLav |
| | × ***chaytoriae*** 'Gorgeous' | SDow |
| | - 'Richard Gray' 🏆H3-4 | CArn CBar EBee EGHP LSRN MHer MNHC NCGa SBfd SDow SLim SSvw WAbe WLav WMnd XSen |
| § | - 'Sawyers' 🏆H4 | Widely available |
| | - 'Silver Sands' | LBMP LSRN LSou SBfd SFai SPoG |
| | × ***christiana*** | CArn EGHP EShb LRHS SBfd SDow SFai SHDw WJek WKif WLav |
| | 'Cornard Blue' | see *L.* × *chaytoriae* 'Sawyers' |
| | ***dentata*** | CEnt CSev EShb GCal MNHC MRav SAdn SEND SGar WJek |
| § | - var. ***candicans*** | CSev EShb MHer MNHC NLLv SAga SBch SBfd SDow WJek WLav |
| | - var. ***dentata*** 'Dusky Maiden' | SDow WLav |
| | - - 'Ploughman's Blue' | CWCL SVen WGwG WLav |
| | - - f. ***rosea*** | SDow |
| | - - 'Royal Crown' 🏆H2-3 | MHer WFar WLav |
| | - - 'Silver Queen' | WLav |
| | - silver-leaved | see *L. dentata* var. *candicans* |
| | 'Devonshire Compact' | CSBt EWhm LRHS NGdn SBch WJek |
| | 'Devonshire Compact White' | EWhm |
| | 'Fathead' | CBcs CChe CWCL EBee ECtt EGHP ELan EPfP LRHS LSRN LSou MGos MHer MNHC MTis NBir NEgg NGdn NPri SAdn SCoo SDow SFai SGol SLim SPoG WJek WLav |
| | × ***ginginsii*** 'Goodwin Creek Grey' | MHer NLLv SDow WGwG WLav |
| | 'Hazel' | CEnd EPfP LRHS |
| | 'Helmsdale' PBR | Widely available |
| | ***heterophylla*** misapplied | see *L.* × *heterophylla* Viv. Gaston Allard Group |
| § | ***heterophylla*** Viv. Gaston Allard Group | EGHP EShb NLLv WLav |
| | 'Hidcote Blue' | see *L. angustifolia* 'Hidcote' |
| § | × ***intermedia*** | WFar |
| | - 'Abrialii' | NLLv SDow |
| § | - 'Alba' 🏆H4 | CBot CMea EPfP MHer MMuc MNHC SAga SDow SEND XSen |
| | - 'Arabian Night' | see *L.* × *intermedia* 'Impress Purple', 'Sussex' |
| § | - Dutch Group | CSBt CWCL CWan CWib EPfP MAsh MRav MSwo SBfd SCoo SDow SFai SLim SPer SPoG SWat WFar WPer |
| | - 'Edelweiss' | CBar CWan EGHP EPfP LRHS LSou MRav MTis NEgg NGdn NLLv SAll SDow SGol SWal WLav XSen |
| | - 'Fragrant Memories' | EBee EGHP EPfP SDow SIde WLav |
| | - Goldburg = 'Burgoldeen' (v) | EPfP EWhm MRav MWat |
| | - 'Grappenhall' misapplied | see *L.* × *intermedia* 'Pale Pretender' |
| | - 'Grey Hedge' | CWan EGHP EWhm SAga WLav |
| | - 'Gros Bleu' | SDow WLav XSen |
| | - 'Grosso' | Widely available |
| | - 'Hidcote Giant' 🏆H4 | CArn EPfP NPer SAdn SDow WKif WLav |
| § | - 'Impress Purple' | LBuc MNHC NLLv SDow WLav |

| | | |
|---|---|---|
| | - 'Lullingstone Castle' | CBod EGHP EWhm SDow WGwG WJek WLav |
| | - 'Old English' misapplied | see *L. × intermedia* 'Seal' |
| | - 'Old English' | SDow |
| | - Old English Group | CArn CBod ELau MMuc MNHC SEND WHoo WJek WLav |
| § | - 'Pale Pretender' | CArn CSBt CSam CTri EGHP MHer MSwo SDow SPer SWal WFar WJek WMnd WPnn XSen |
| § | - 'Seal' | CArn EGHP ELau EWhm GMaP MNHC SDow SPer WFar WJek WMnd XSen |
| § | - 'Sussex' ♀H4 | SDow WLav XSen |
| | - 'Twickel Purple' | CWib ECtt EGHP EWes LSRN SBrd SGol SWat WJek WMnd |
| § | - Walberton's Silver Edge = 'Walvera' (v) | CSBt EPfP LBuc LRHS MGos MWat NEgg SBfd SCoo SDow SFai SIde SLim SPoG |
| | 'Jamboree' | WLav |
| | 'Jean Davis' | see *L. angustifolia* 'Rosea' |
| | ***lanata*** ♀H3 | CBot ECha GPoy MHer WJek WLav |
| § | ***latifolia*** | CArn XSen |
| I | 'Lavender Lace' | CWSG EGHP LSRN SCoo |
| | 'Loddon Pink' | see *L. angustifolia* 'Loddon Pink' |
| | 'Madrid' | NBlu |
| | 'Madrid Blue' | see *L.* 'Bee Happy' |
| | 'Madrid Pink' | see *L.* 'Bee Pretty' |
| | 'Madrid Purple'PBR | see *L.* 'Bee Brilliant' |
| | 'Madrid White'PBR | see *L.* 'Bee Cool' |
| | 'Marshwood'PBR | CTri EBee EPfP SCoo SDow SIde SLim |
| | ***minutolii*** | SDow |
| | ***multifida*** | CSev MHer WLav |
| | - 'Blue Wonder' | IFro |
| | ***officinalis*** | see *L. angustifolia* |
| | 'Passionné' | CWSG LRHS WLav |
| § | ***pedunculata*** subsp. ***pedunculata*** ♀H3-4 | Widely available |
| | - - 'James Compton' | CWib ECha LRHS MAsh NBir NGdn |
| | - - 'Wine' | CBcs |
| | - subsp. ***sampaiana*** 'Purple Emperor' | LRHS WLav |
| | - - 'Roman Candles' | WLav |
| | ***pinnata*** | CSev CSpr EPfP LRHS MHer MNHC SDow |
| | 'Pippa White' | NLLv |
| | 'Pretty Polly' | CBcs EGHP EPfP LBMP LRHS LSou NBPC NLLv SDow SFai SRkn WLav |
| | 'Pukehou' | EPfP LRHS NLLv SCoo SDow WLav |
| | 'Regal Splendour'PBR | CSBt CWCL ECtt EGHP ELan EPfP LRHS LSRN LSou MAsh MGos MHer MNHC NLLv NPri SCoo SDow SFai SLim SPoG WLav |
| | Rocky Road = 'Fair09'PBR | EGHP LBMP LRHS LSRN MGos NBPC NGdn NLLv SDow SFai SRkn WLav |
| | 'Rosea' | see *L. angustifolia* 'Rosea' |
| | ***rotundifolia*** | SDow |
| | 'Roxlea Park' | CWCL |
| | 'Russian Anna' | LSRN |
| | 'Saint Brelade' | CWCL EPfP LRHS NLLv SDow WLav |
| | 'Silver Edge' | see *L. × intermedia* Walberton's Silver Edge |
| | 'Somerset Mist' | EWhm WLav |
| N | ***spica*** nom. rejic. | see *L. angustifolia*, *L. latifolia*, *L. × intermedia* |
| | - 'Hidcote Purple' | see *L. angustifolia* 'Hidcote' |
| | ***stoechas*** ♀H3-4 | Widely available |
| | - from Corsica **new** | LRHS |
| | - var. ***albiflora*** | see *L. stoechas* subsp. *stoechas* f. *leucantha* |
| | - 'Anouk'PBR | LRHS NGdn SPoG |
| | - 'Blueberries and Cream' | CSev EGHP LRHS LSou SFai |
| | - 'Boysenberry Ruffles'PBR (Ruffles Series) | LRHS LSRN |
| | - 'Lace' | LSRN WLav |
| | - Lilac Wings = 'Prolil'PBR | EGHP EPfP LLHF LRHS LSRN SCoo SFai WLav |
| | - (Little Bee Series) Little Bee Blue and White = 'Florvendula Blue White' | CAby LBuc MTis |
| | - - Little Bee Deep Purple **new** | LRHS |
| | - - Little Bee Deep Rose **new** | LRHS |
| | - - Little Bee Lilac = 'Florvendula Lilac' | CWSG LRHS MTis |
| | - - Little Bee Rose = 'Florvendula Rose' | CWSG LBuc LRHS MHer MTis |
| | - subsp. ***luisieri*** 'Tickled Pink'PBR | CWCL ECtt EGHP |
| | - 'Night of Passion' | LRHS SDow |
| | - 'Papillon' | see *L. pedunculata* subsp. *pedunculata* |
| | - subsp. ***pedunculata*** | see *L. pedunculata* subsp. *pedunculata* |
| | - 'Purley' | CWan |
| | - 'Rocky Red' | CSev LSRN |
| | - 'Silver Anouk' | LRHS |
| § | - subsp. ***stoechas*** f. ***leucantha*** | CBot CSev CWCL CWan CWib ECha EPfP LRHS MNHC MSwo MWat SBfd SDow SPer WFar |
| | - - - 'Snowman' | CBcs CChe CHab CSBt EGHP EGxp EPfP LRHS MHer MWat NBPC SAdn SBfd SCoo SFai SLim SPoG SWvt WDin WFar |
| | - - 'Liberty' | NLLv |
| | - - 'Provençal' | LRHS SCoo |
| | - - 'Purple Wings' | EPfP LRHS LSou MAsh MGos SFai SLim SRkn |
| | - - f. ***rosea*** 'Kew Red' | CBcs CTri CWan EBee EGHP GGar LBMP LSRN MGos MHer MNHC NBPC SAdn SDow SFai SLim SWvt WGwG WJek WLav |
| | - 'Victory' | LRHS SPoG |
| | - 'With Love' | LRHS SDow |
| | 'Sugar Plum' | WLav |
| | Tiara = 'Fair 10'PBR | CSBt EGHP EPfP LRHS LSRN MGos NBPC NLLv NPri SCoo SDow SFai SGar SLim SPoG WLav |
| | 'Van Gogh' | SDow |
| | ***vera*** misapplied | see *L. × intermedia* Dutch Group |
| | ***vera*** DC. | see *L. angustifolia* |
| | ***viridis*** | CArn CChe ELan ELau ELon EPfP LRHS MHer NLLv NPer SDow WAbe WJek WLav |
| | 'Whero Iti' | SDow |
| | 'Willow Vale' ♀H3-4 | CMea CTri CWCL EPfP EWhm LBMP LRHS LSRN MAsh MHer MLHP NLLv SAga SDow SFai SWvt WJek |
| | 'Willowbridge Calico'PBR | NGdn WLav |

## *Lavatera* (*Malvaceae*)

| | |
|---|---|
| ***arborea*** | CArn SChr SEND WHer |
| - 'Rosea' | see *L. × clementii* 'Rosea' |
| - 'Variegata' (v) | ELan NPer NSti SDix SEND SGar WCot |

| | | |
|---|---|---|
| | ***bicolor*** | see *L. maritima* |
| | ***cachemiriana*** | CBod EQua LRHS NBir NPer WPer |
| | Chamallow = 'Inovera'PBR | EPfP LBuc LRHS LSRN LSou MGos SBrd SPoG |
| | × ***clementii*** 'Barnsley' | Widely available |
| | - 'Barnsley Baby' | ELon LBuc LRHS NGdn NLar NPer NPri SPer SWvt WHil WRHF |
| | - 'Blushing Bride' | CDoC EBee ELon EPfP LBMP LRHS LSRN MBri MGos NLar SBfd SEND SPer SPoG |
| | - 'Bredon Springs' ♀H3-4 | CBar CDoC CDul CSBt CWSG EBee ECha ECtt EPfP LHop LRHS LSRN MAsh MMuc MSwo NGdn NHol NLar SBrd SEND SGol SLim SPer SWvt WFar WHar |
| | - 'Burgundy Wine' ♀H3-4 | CBar CBcs CMac EBee ELan EPfP LRHS MAsh MBri MGos MSwo NBir NEgg NGdn NHol NLar NPer NPri SAga SBfd SBrd SLim SLon SPer SPoG SWvt WDin WFar WKif |
| | - 'Candy Floss' ♀H3-4 | EBee EPfP LRHS MAsh MGos NBir NLar NPer SGol WDin |
| | - 'Kew Rose' | CDoC EBee LRHS MMuc MSwo NPer SEND SLim SRms |
| | - 'Lavender Lady' | ECtt LHop NPer SEND |
| | - 'Lisanne' | LRHS MSwo NHol SGol SMrm |
| | - 'Mary Hope' | EPfP LRHS MAsh |
| | - Memories = 'Stelav' | GBin LRHS LSRN NLar SLim |
| | - 'Pavlova' | CPLG |
| § | - 'Rosea' ♀H3-4 | CBcs CDul CMac CWSG EBee ECtt EPfP GGar LAst LRHS LSRN MAsh MGos NBir NEgg NHol NPri SBfd SBod SGol SLon SPer SPoG SWvt WDin WFar |
| | - 'Shorty' | WFar |
| § | - 'Wembdon Variegated' (v) | NPer |
| | 'Grey Beauty' | LHop MAsh |
| § | ***maritima*** ♀H2-3 | CBot CDoC CMHG CMac CPLG CRHN ECtt ELan EPfP LHop LRHS MCot SBfd SEND SPer SPoG SWvt WCFE WFar WKif WSHC |
| | ***oblongifolia*** | CBot |
| N | ***olbia*** | CTri SPlb SRms |
| | - 'Eye Catcher' | EBee IVic LRHS MSwo NLar SPer SPoG SWal |
| | - 'Lilac Lady' | EBee ECha ELan EPfP LRHS MGos SLim SPer WFar WKif WSHC |
| § | - 'Pink Frills' | CBot EBee MGos SWvt WCot WSHC WWlt |
| | 'Peppermint Ice' | see *L. thuringiaca* 'Ice Cool' |
| | 'Pink Frills' | see *L. olbia* 'Pink Frills' |
| | 'Rosea' | see *L.* × *clementii* 'Rosea' |
| | 'Sweet Dreams'PBR | NLar |
| N | ***thuringiaca*** | GCal NNor WFar |
| | - 'First Light' **new** | EDAr |
| § | - 'Ice Cool' | CBot ECha ECtt GCal MGos NDov SWvt WFar WKif |
| | - Red Rum = 'Rigrum'PBR | CChe CMac EPfP GBin LAst LBuc LLHF LRHS LSRN MAsh MGos NEgg NHol NLar NPri SBrd SEND SHar SLim SPoG SWvt WFar WHar |
| | 'Variegata' | see *L.* × *clementii* 'Wembdon Variegated' |
| | 'White Angel'PBR | NDov NLar |
| | 'White Satin'PBR | NLar |

## *Lecanthus* (*Urticaceae*)

| | | |
|---|---|---|
| | ***peduncularis*** | CHEx |

## *Ledebouria* (*Asparagaceae*)

| | | |
|---|---|---|
| | ***adlamii*** | see *L. cooperi* |
| | ***concolor*** misapplied | see *L. socialis* |
| § | ***cooperi*** | CDes CYeo ECho ELan EPri ITim LEdu LHop LRHS SUsu WPGP WTcb |
| | ***ovalifolia*** | ECho |
| § | ***socialis*** | ECho LToo MCot SBHP SBch SPet STre |
| | ***violacea*** | see *L. socialis* |

## × *Ledodendron* (*Ericaceae*)

| | | |
|---|---|---|
| § | 'Arctic Tern' ♀H4 | CDoC CSBt CTri ECho GGar GLam GQui LMil MGos MLea NMun SPer |

## *Ledum* (*Ericaceae*)

| | | |
|---|---|---|
| | ***glandulosum*** SIN 1828 | GLin |
| § | ***groenlandicum*** | GGar GKin MLea NLar SPer WDin WFar WSHC |
| | - 'Compactum' | IVic NLar WFar |
| | - 'Helma' | IVic NLar |
| | - 'Lenie' | NLar |
| | ***palustre*** | GPoy NLar WThu |

## *Legousia* (*Campanulaceae*)

| | | |
|---|---|---|
| | ***pentagonica*** 'Midnight Stars' | CSpe |

## *Leiophyllum* (*Ericaceae*)

| | | |
|---|---|---|
| | ***buxifolium*** ♀H4 | EPfP NLar SSpi WThu |
| | - var. ***hugeri*** | GBin |
| | - 'Maryfield' | WAbe |

## *Lembotropis* see *Cytisus*

## *Lemna* (*Araceae*)

| | | |
|---|---|---|
| | ***gibba*** | NPer |
| | ***minor*** | CWat LPBA MSKA NPer SWat |
| | ***trisulca*** | CWat EHon LPBA MSKA NPer SWat |

## lemon see *Citrus limon*

## lemon balm see *Melissa officinalis*

## lemon grass see *Cymbopogon citratus*

## lemon verbena see *Aloysia citrodora*

## *Leonotis* (*Lamiaceae*)

| | | |
|---|---|---|
| | ***leonitis*** | see *L. ocymifolia* |
| | ***leonurus*** | CBcs CBod CCCN CDTJ CHEx CHGN CHll ECre EPfP EShb EWes LRHS MNrw SBrd SMad SMrm SPoG WHil XLum |
| | - var. ***albiflora*** | CCCN WHil |
| | ***nepetifolia*** | CHll |
| | - var. ***nepetifolia*** 'Staircase' | CCCN SPav |
| § | ***ocymifolia*** | CCCN CPLG LSou WPGP |
| | - var. ***raineriana*** | CHll |

## *Leontice* (*Berberidaceae*)

| | | |
|---|---|---|
| | ***albertii*** | see *Gymnospermium albertii* |

## *Leontochir* (*Alstroemeriaceae*)

| | | |
|---|---|---|
| | ***ovallei*** | CCCN |

## *Leontodon* (*Asteraceae*)

| | | |
|---|---|---|
| | ***autumnalis*** | CHab EWil NMir |

***hispidus*** CHab NMir
§ ***rigens*** EBee LRHS MLHP MMuc MNrw NBid NBir SDix SMrm WFar WMoo
- 'Girandole' see *L. rigens*

## *Leontopodium* (*Asteraceae*)

***alpinum*** CTri CWib ECho EPfP GAbr GEdr GKev LRHS MAsh NBlu NWCA SPlb SPoG SRms WPer XLum
- 'Mignon' ECho EWes GEdr GLam GMaP WAbe WFar WHoo
***coreanum*** GKev
§ ***ochroleucum*** var. ***campestre*** MDKP NLar XLum
***palibinianum*** see *L. ochroleucum* var. *campestre*
***souliei*** XLum

## *Leonurus* (*Lamiaceae*)

***artemisia*** see *L. japonicus*
***cardiaca*** CArn CWan GPoy MHer MNHC SIde WHfH
§ ***japonicus*** CArn MMuc
***macranthus*** EFEx
- var. ***alba*** EFEx
***sibiricus*** misapplied see *L. japonicus*
***sibiricus*** L. CArn GCal SSvw

## *Leopoldia* (*Hyacinthaceae*)

***comosa*** see *Muscari comosum*
***tenuiflora*** see *Muscari tenuiflorum*

## *Lepechinia* (*Lamiaceae*)

***bella*** SDys
***chamaedryoides*** CHll CPLG CSpe
***floribunda*** CSev WHil
***hastata*** CCse CDoC CPom CSpe MSpe MWea SBHP WJek WTcb WWlt
***salviae*** EPPr EPri SEND SUsu

## *Lepidium* (*Brassicaceae*)

***campestre*** CArn CHab
***latifolium*** CArn LEdu

## *Lepidothamnus* (*Podocarpaceae*)

§ ***laxifolius*** WThu

## *Lepidozamia* (*Zamiaceae*)

***peroffskyana*** CBrP LPal

## *Leptecophylla* (*Ericaceae*)

§ ***juniperina*** ECou
- 'Nana' WThu
§ - subsp. ***parvifolia*** ECou

## *Leptinella* (*Asteraceae*)

***atrata*** subsp. ***luteola*** EBee EPfP GEdr NWCA
'County Park' ECho ECou EDAr MMuc
***dendyi*** ECho ECou EWes GEdr MHer NMen NSla
***dioica*** CTrC GBin
***filicula*** ECou
***hispida*** see *Cotula hispida* (DC.) Harv.
§ ***minor*** ECou EDAr WMoo
***pectinata*** subsp. ***villosa*** CC 475 NWCA
§ ***potentillina*** CTri EBee ECha ECho EHoe GBin GEdr MBNS NLar NRya SRms WMoo WPer WPtf XLum
§ ***pyrethrifolia*** ECho EDAr GEdr GGar NMen
- 'Macabe' ECou
§ ***rotundata*** ECou
§ ***serrulata*** ECho
§ ***squalida*** ECha ECho EDAr EPPr GBin MWat NLar NRya NSti STre WMoo
§ - 'Platt's Black' Widely available
***traillii*** GAbr GGar MMuc

## *Leptocarpus* (*Restionaceae*)

***similis*** ECou
- BR 70 GGar

## *Leptocodon* (*Campanulaceae*)

***gracilis*** EWld
- HWJK 2155 WCru

## *Leptodactylon* (*Polemoniaceae*)

§ ***californicum*** CPBP

## *Leptopteris* (*Osmundaceae*)

***hymenophylloides*** WRic
***superba*** WRic

## *Leptospermum* ✿ (*Myrtaceae*)

***argenteum*** CBcs
'Centaurus' WFar
***citratum*** see *L. petersonii*
'Confetti' ECou
'Copper Sheen' CBcs CTrC
'County Park Blush' ECou ELon
***cunninghamii*** see *L. myrtifolium*
'Electric Red' (Galaxy Series) CEnd LRHS SLim
***ericoides*** see *Kunzea ericoides*
***flavescens*** misapplied see *L. glaucescens*
***flavescens*** Sm. see *L. polygalifolium*
§ ***glaucescens*** ECou SPlb
§ ***grandiflorum*** CTrC ELan EPfP GGar MOWG SSpi SVen WSHC
***grandifolium*** ECou LRHS
'Havering Hardy' ECou
***humifusum*** see *L. rupestre*
***juniperinum*** CBcs CTrC SPlb
'Karo Pearl Star' CBcs CTrC
'Karo Spectrobay'PBR CBcs
***laevigatum*** 'Yarrum' ECou
§ ***lanigerum*** CBcs CMHG CPLG CTrC CTri CTsd ECou EPfP GAbr GGar MOWG SPlb SPoG SVen
- 'Cunninghamii' see *L. myrtifolium*
- 'Wellington' ECou
***liversidgei*** CChe ECou IVic
***macrocarpum*** MOWG
***minutifolium*** ECou
***morrisonii*** ECou
§ ***myrtifolium*** CTrC CTri ECou EPla EWes GGar MOWG SPer
- 'Newnes Forest' ECou
***myrtifolium*** × ***scoparium*** ECou
***nitidum*** CBcs CTrC ECou MOWG SPlb
- 'Cradle' ECou
§ ***petersonii*** CArn ECou EOHP EShb MHer MOWG
- 'Chlorinda' ECou
***phylicoides*** see *Kunzea ericoides*
'Pink Surprise' ECou MOWG
§ ***polygalifolium*** CBcs CTrC ECou SPlb SRms
***prostratum*** see *L. rupestre*
***pubescens*** see *L. lanigerum*
'Red Cascade' SWvt
***rodwayanum*** see *L. grandiflorum*

| | |
|---|---|
| ***rotundifolium*** | CTrC ECou |
| § ***rupestre*** ♀H4 | CDoC CTrC CTri ECou EPot NHar SPlb SRms WFar WSHC |
| ***rupestre* × *scoparium*** | ECou |
| ***scoparium*** | CArn CBcs CTsd ECou ELau ERom MNHC SPlb SVen WDin WJek |
| - 'Adrianne' | ELan EPfP LRHS MRav |
| - 'Album' | CTrC |
| - 'Appleblossom' | CEnd SGol SLim |
| - 'Autumn Glory' | EBee SLim |
| - 'Avocet' | ECou |
| - 'Blossom' (d) | CBcs CMac ECou LRHS MOWG |
| - 'Burgundy Queen' (d) | CBcs CMac CSBt ECou |
| - 'Chapmanii' | CMHG |
| - 'Coral Candy' | CBcs LRHS MMuc MOWG SEND |
| - 'County Park Pink' | ECou |
| - 'County Park Red' | ECou |
| - 'Crimson Glory' (d) | CSBt |
| - 'Elizabeth Jane' | GGar |
| - 'Essex' | ECou |
| - 'Fantasia' | ECou |
| - 'Fred's Red' | WPat |
| - 'Gaiety Girl' (d) | CSBt |
| - var. ***incanum*** | CTrC ECou MOWG |
| 'Keatleyi' ♀H3 | |
| - - 'Wairere' | ECou |
| - 'Jubilee' (d) | CBcs CMac SLim |
| - 'Kerry' | CAbP |
| - 'Leonard Wilson' (d) | CTri ECou |
| - 'Lyndon' | ECou |
| - 'Martini' | CAbb CBcs CDoC CMac CSBt CTrC EPfP GKev LRHS MOWG |
| - 'McLean' | ECou |
| - 'Moko' | ECou |
| - (Nanum Group) 'Kea' | CBcs ECou MHer MMuc MRav SEND |
| - - 'Kiwi' ♀H3 | CAbP CAbb CBcs CCCN CDoC CDul CSBt CTrC CWSG ECou ELan ELon EPfP EWes GQui LRHS MAsh SLim WFar |
| - - 'Nanum' | ECou NMen |
| - - 'Pipit' | EWes ITim WAbe |
| - - 'Tui' | CSBt CTrC ECou |
| - 'Nichollsii' ♀H3 | GQui SVen WSHC |
| - 'Nichollsii Nanum' ♀H2-3 | ITim SRms WAbe WPat WThu |
| - 'Pink Cascade' | CAbb CBcs CMac CTrC CTri CWib GAbr LRHS SEND SLim |
| - 'Pink Damask' | IVic SLim SWvt |
| - 'Pink Falls' | ECou |
| - 'Pink Frills' | ECou |
| - 'Pink Queen' | LRHS |
| - 'Pink Splash' | ECou |
| - 'Pom Pom' | LRHS |
| - var. ***prostratum*** hort. | see *L. rupestre* |
| - 'Red Damask' (d) ♀H3 | Widely available |
| - 'Red Falls' | CBcs CPLG CTrC ECou |
| - 'Redpoll' | ECou |
| - 'Roseum' | MRav |
| * - 'Ruby Wedding' | ELan EPfP LRHS LSRN MAsh SPoG |
| - var. ***scoparium*** | GGar |
| - 'Silver Spire' | MOWG |
| - 'Snow Flurry' | CTrC EPfP LRHS MMuc SEND SGol SLim SPoG SVen |
| - 'Snow White' | LRHS |
| - 'Spectro Silver Ice' **new** | CBcs |
| - 'Wingletye' | ECou |
| - 'Winter Cheer' (d) | LRHS SGol |
| - 'Wiri Joan' (d) | CAbb CBcs |
| - 'Wiri Linda' | CMac |
| - 'Zeehan' | ECou |
| ***sericeum*** | ECou MOWG |
| 'Silver Sheen' ♀H3 | CEnd ECou ELan EPfP LRHS MAsh NLar SBrd SPoG WPGP |
| 'Snow Column' | ECou |
| ***sphaerocarpum*** | ECou |
| ***squarrosum*** | CTrC |
| 'Sugar Candy' **new** | CEnd |
| ***turbinatum*** | ECou |
| - 'Thunder Cloud' | ECou |
| 'Wellington Dwarf' | ECou |

## *Leschenaultia* (*Goodeniaceae*)

| | |
|---|---|
| ***biloba*** | ECou |
| - 'Sky Blue' | ECou |

## *Lespedeza* (*Papilionaceae*)

| | |
|---|---|
| ***bicolor*** | CCCN CSpe EBee ELon LRHS MMuc NPal SEND SKHP WCFE WDin WFar WSHC |
| ***buergeri*** | EPfP LRHS MMHG NLar WSHC |
| ***japonica*** | SPlb |
| ***thunbergii*** ♀H4 | Widely available |
| - 'Albiflora' | CAbP EBee LRHS WPGP WSHC |
| - 'Avalanche' | NLar |
| - 'Edo-shibori' | NLar |
| - 'Summer Beauty' | CBcs EPPr EPfP LRHS MGos |
| - 'White Fountain' | LRHS SBrd SKHP SPoG |
| ***tiliifolia*** | see *Desmodium elegans* |

## *Leucadendron* (*Proteaceae*)

| | |
|---|---|
| ***argenteum*** | CBcs CCCN CHEx CTrC SPlb |
| ***daphnoides*** | SPlb |
| ***discolor*** | SPlb |
| ***eucalyptifolium*** | CTrC SPlb |
| ***galpinii*** | CTrC |
| 'Inca Gold' | CTrC MOWG |
| ***laureolum*** | CCCN |
| 'Maui Sunset' | CTrC |
| 'Mrs Stanley' | CTrC MOWG |
| 'Safari Sunset' | CBcs CCCN CDoC CTrC EAmu SBig |
| 'Safari Sunshine' | CTrC |
| ***salicifolium*** | SPlb |
| ***salignum*** | CCCN |
| - 'Early Yellow' | CTrC |
| - 'Fireglow' | CDoC CTrC MOWG |
| ***strobilinum*** | CDoC |

## *Leucaena* (*Mimosaceae*)

| | |
|---|---|
| ***leucocephala*** **new** | SPlb |

## *Leucanthemella* (*Asteraceae*)

| | |
|---|---|
| § ***serotina*** ♀H4 | Widely available |
| - 'Herbststern' | NLar |

## *Leucanthemopsis* (*Asteraceae*)

| | |
|---|---|
| § ***alpina*** | ECho |
| ***hosmariensis*** | see *Rhodanthemum hosmariense* |

## *Leucanthemum* ✿ (*Asteraceae*)

| | |
|---|---|
| 'Angel' | CMea NPri WGrn |
| ***atlanticum*** | see *Rhodanthemum atlanticum* |
| ***catananche*** | see *Rhodanthemum catananche* |
| ***graminifolium*** | EPfP LRHS WPer |
| ***hosmariense*** | see *Rhodanthemum hosmariense* |
| ***mawii*** | see *Rhodanthemum gayanum* |
| ***maximum*** misapplied | see *L.* × *superbum* |
| § ***maximum*** (Ramond) DC. | MMuc NBro NPer |
| - ***uliginosum*** | see *Leucanthemella serotina* |
| ***nipponicum*** | see *Nipponanthemum nipponicum* |

| | | |
|---|---|---|
| | 'Osiris Neige' **new** | NLar |
| | 'Sante' **new** | CCVN LBuc |
| | 'Sunshine Peach' | LBuc SPad SRot |
| § | × ***superbum*** | CMac MHer MLHP MMuc NBlu NVic SEND WFar |
| | - 'Aglaia' (d) ♀H4 | Widely available |
| | - 'Alaska' | CAni CPLG EBee EBla EPfP LAst LHop LRHS MCot NGdn SBfd SPer SPur SWvt WFar WPer WWEG |
| | - 'Amelia' | NBre NLar SRGP |
| | - 'Andernach' | CAni |
| | - 'Anita Allen' (d) | CAni CElw CFee CPrp EBee EBla MAvo NBre WCot WFar WPer WWEG |
| | - 'Anna Camilla' | CAni |
| | - 'Antwerp Star' | NBre NLar |
| | - 'Banwell' | CAni |
| | - 'Barbara Bush' (v/d) | ECtt NBir SRGP SWvt |
| § | - 'Beauté Nivelloise' | CAni CCVN CPrp CWCL EBee EBla ECtt EPfP GBin GMac IPot MAvo MDKP MMuc MSpe NBPC NBre NCGa NLar NPri SMad SWat WFar WPer WPtf WWEG |
| | - 'Becky' | CCse CMac CWan EBee ECha ELon EWes LLHF LRHS LSRN LSou MAvo NBre NLar NPro SPoG SRGP SSvw WWEG |
| | - 'Bishopstone' | CAni CSam EBee ECtt ELan LBMP LEdu MSpe NBre NCGa SMrm WPer WWEG |
| | - 'Brightside' | GQue LRHS |
| | - Broadway Lights = 'Leumayel' PBR | ECtt EGxp IPot LRHS MBri MSCN NBir SPoG SUsu WGrn WHil WWEG |
| | - 'Christine Hagemann' | CAni CPrp EBee ECtt EWes GBin MAvo MDKP MRav NCGa NLar SHar WWEG |
| | - 'Cobham Gold' (d) | CAni CWCL NBre NOrc SUsu |
| | - 'Coconut Ice' | WPer WWEG |
| | - 'Colwall' | CAni WWEG |
| | - 'Crazy Daisy' | CAni CMMP CTri CWib EBee LRHS NBre NLar NPri SRot SWal SWvt WHrl WWEG |
| | - 'Crazy Daisy Butterfly' | LAst |
| | - 'Devon Mist' | CAni |
| | - 'Dipsy Daisy' | WPer |
| | - 'Droitwich Beauty' | CAni CPrp ECtt LLHF MAvo WCFE WHoo WWEG |
| | - 'Duchess of Abercorn' | CAni CSam |
| | - 'Dwarf Snow Lady' | NBre NLar |
| | - 'Easton Lady' | CAni |
| | - 'Eclipse' | CAni MAvo WWEG |
| | - 'Edgebrook Giant' | CAni MAvo WWEG |
| | - 'Edward VII' | CAni |
| | - 'Eisstern' | CDes EBee LEdu MAvo WWEG |
| | - 'Elworthy Sparkler' | CElw MAvo WWEG |
| | - 'Esther Read' (d) | CMMP EBee EBla ECtt ELan EPfP GBin GMaP LBMP LRHS LSRN MAvo MCCP MLLN MMuc NBro NCGa NEgg SPoG SRGP SRms STes SWat SWvt WCot WFar WMnd WWEG |
| | - 'Etoile d'Anvers' | EBee |
| § | - 'Everest' | CAni CSam NBre SRms WWEG |
| | - 'Exhibition' | NBre WWEG |
| | - 'Fiona Coghill' (d) | CAni CElw CPrp CWGN EAEE EBee EBla ECtt EPfP GBin LBMP LRHS LSou MAvo MDKP MHer MNrw MSpe NBir NCGa NEgg NGdn NLar NVic WCot WHlf WHoo WWEG |
| | - 'Firnglanz' | CAni GBin MAvo WWEG |
| | - 'Flore Pleno' (d) | SPlb |
| | - 'Goldrausch' PBR | Widely available |
| | - 'Gruppenstolz' | CAni EBee GBin |
| | - 'H. Seibert' | CAni CPrp EBla MAvl MAvo WWEG |
| | - 'Harry' | CAni |
| | - 'Highland White Dream' PBR | LRHS WFar |
| | - 'Horace Read' (d) | CAni CElw CPrp ECtt ELan NBir SAga SBch SWvt WPer WWEG |
| | - 'Jennifer Read' | CAni CPrp MAvo MSpe WCot WWEG |
| § | - 'John Murray' (d) | CAni EWes MAvo MDKP MTis NBir SMrm WAbb WCot WWEG |
| | - 'Little Miss Muffet' | CSBt CWGN EAEE EBee EBla ECtt GGar LAst LLHF LRHS LSou MBNS NCGa NPro NWad WWEG |
| | - 'Little Princess' | see *L.* × *superbum* 'Silberprinzesschen' |
| | - 'Majestic' | CAni |
| | - 'Manhattan' | CAni CCse EBee EBla EWes GBin NBre |
| | - 'Margaretchen' | CAni EBee MAvo WWEG |
| | - 'Marion Bilsland' | CAni MDKP MSpe MTis NCGa NChi WBrk |
| | - 'Marion Collyer' | CAni |
| | - 'Mayfield Giant' | CAni CTri WPer |
| | - 'Mount Everest' | see *L.* × *superbum* 'Everest' |
| | - 'Octopus' | CAni MAvo WBrk WWEG |
| | - 'Old Court' | see *L.* × *superbum* 'Beauté Nivelloise' |
| | - 'Phyllis Smith' | CAni COIW EBee EBla ECtt GMac LSRN MAvo MBri MHer MLLN MRav MSCN MSpe NCGa NGdn SAga SMad SMrm SPer SPoG STes SUsu WAbb WBrk WCAu WCot WFar WMoo WWEG |
| | - 'Polaris' | EBee LRHS MBNS NBre WMoo XLum |
| | - 'Rags and Tatters' | CAni ECtt EWes MAvo WWEG |
| | - 'Rijnsburg Glory' | WPer |
| | - 'Schwabengruss' | CAni |
| | - 'Shaggy' | see *L.* × *superbum* 'Beauté Nivelloise' |
| § | - 'Silberprinzesschen' | CAni COIW CSBt EBee EBla ELon EPfP GJos LRHS NEgg NPri SBfd SPlb SRms WFar WMoo WPer WWEG XLum |
| | - 'Silver Spoon' | EPfP WPer |
| | - 'Snehurka' | CAni EBee EBla LLHF LRHS LSou MAvo MTis SPoG SUsu WCot WWEG |
| | - 'Snow Lady' | EBee NEgg NPer NPri SBfd SRms WFar |
| | - 'Snowcap' | CHid EBla ECha EPfP LRHS MRav NEgg SWvt WCAu WTin |
| | - 'Snowdrift' | CAni CMMP MAvo NBre NLar SBfd WCot WPer WWEG |
| | - 'Snowstorm' **new** | MAvo |
| § | - 'Sonnenschein' | Widely available |
| | - 'Starburst' (d) | SRms |
| | - 'Stina' | EBee GBin MAvo WWEG |
| | - 'Summer Snowball' | see *L.* × *superbum* 'John Murray' |
| | - 'Sunny Killin' | CAni WTin |
| | - 'Sunny Side Up' PBR | EBee ECtt MBri NBPC NCGa NLar WWEG |
| | - Sunshine | see *L.* × *superbum* 'Sonnenschein' |
| | - 'T.E. Killin' (d) ♀H4 | CKno CPrp CSam EBee EBla ECha ECtt EPfP GGar LBMP LRHS MBri |

| | |
|---|---|
| | MRav SPoG WCot WFar WWEG WWlt |
| - 'White Iceberg' (d) | CAni WPer |
| - 'Wirral Pride' | CAni CCVN CHar ELon EPfP MAvo WBrk WMnd WWEG |
| - 'Wirral Supreme' (d) ♀H4 | Widely available |
| 'Tizi-n-Test' | see *Rhodanthemum catananche* 'Tizi-n-Test' |
| § ***vulgare*** | CArn CHab CMac CRWN EPfP EShb EWil LEdu MHer MNHC NLan NMir SBch SIde WHer WJek WMoo WSFF WShi XLum |
| - 'Filigran' | EShb LRHS SIde |
| § - 'Maikönigin' | WHrl XLum |
| - May Queen | see *L. vulgare* 'Maikönigin' |
| - 'Sunny' | CBre EBla EWes |
| 'White Knight' | LRHS NBre NLar NPri |

## *Leucochrysum* (*Asteraceae*)

| | |
|---|---|
| ***albicans*** subsp. ***alpinum*** | GKev |

## *Leucocoryne* (*Alliaceae*)

| | |
|---|---|
| ***alliacea*** | ECho |
| 'Andes' | CCCN ECho |
| 'Caravelle' | ECho |
| hybrids | CGrW ECho |
| ***ixioides*** | ECho |
| * - ***alba*** | ECho |
| - 'Blue Ocean' **new** | GKev |
| ***purpurea*** ♀H1 | CGrW ECho |

## *Leucogenes* (*Asteraceae*)

| | |
|---|---|
| ***grandiceps*** | NSla WAbe |
| ***leontopodium*** | GGar NSla WAbe |
| ***tarahaoa*** | WAbe |

## *Leucogenes* × *Raoulia* see × *Leucoraoulia*

## *Leucojum* ✿ (*Amaryllidaceae*)

| | |
|---|---|
| ***aestivum*** | CBcs CFee CTri EBee ECGP ECho EPfP EWil GCal ITim LAma LHop MAvo MCot MMuc NEgg NHol SEND SMrm SRms WBor WCot WFar WShi |
| - 'Gravetye Giant' ♀H4 | Widely available |
| ***autumnale*** | see *Acis autumnalis* |
| ***longifolium*** | see *Acis longifolia* |
| ***roseum*** | see *Acis rosea* |
| ***tingitanum*** | see *Acis tingitana* |
| ***trichophyllum*** | see *Acis trichophylla* |
| ***valentinum*** | see *Acis valentina* |
| ***vernum*** ♀H4 | Widely available |
| - var. ***carpathicum*** | CLAP ECha ECho GEdr MRav NMen |
| - var. ***vagneri*** | CLAP EBee ECha GEdr IGor SDys WSHC WTin |

## *Leucophyllum* (*Scrophulariaceae*)

| | |
|---|---|
| ***frutescens*** | MOWG |

## *Leucophysalis* (*Solanaceae*)

| | |
|---|---|
| ***sinense*** BWJ 8093 | WCru |

## *Leucophyta* (*Asteraceae*)

| | |
|---|---|
| § ***brownii*** | WCot |

## *Leucopogon* (*Ericaceae*)

| | |
|---|---|
| § ***colensoi*** | WPat WThu |
| § ***fraseri*** | ECou GEdr NHar WPat WThu |
| - bronze-leaved | NHar |
| § ***parviflorus*** | ECou |

## × *Leucoraoulia* (*Asteraceae*)

| | |
|---|---|
| § ***loganii*** | NWCA WAbe |

## *Leucosceptrum* (*Lamiaceae*)

| | |
|---|---|
| ***canum*** | CPLG |
| - GWJ 9424 | WCru |
| ***japonicum*** B&SWJ 10804 | WCru |
| - B&SWJ 10981 | WCru |
| - 'Golden Angel' | WCot |
| ***stellipilum*** | WCru |
| var. ***formosanum*** B&SWJ 1926 | |
| - - RWJ 9907 | WCru |
| - var. ***tosaense*** B&SWJ 8892 | WCru |

## *Leucospermum* (*Proteaceae*)

| | |
|---|---|
| ***cordifolium*** | MOWG |
| 'Scarlet Ribbon' | CCCN |

## *Leucothoe* (*Ericaceae*)

| | |
|---|---|
| ***axillaris*** 'Curly Red'PBR | CBcs CWSG EBee ELan EPfP IVic LBuc LRHS MAsh MCCP MGos MMHG NCGa NLar SBfd SLim SLon SPoG SWvt |
| - 'Scarletta' | see *L.* Scarletta |
| Carinella = 'Zebekot' | EPfP LRHS NLar SBfd SPoG |
| ***davisiae*** | NLar |
| § ***fontanesiana*** ♀H4 | CMCN CMac EPfP GGal |
| - 'Rainbow' (v) | Widely available |
| - 'Rollissonii' ♀H4 | MRav SRms |
| ***keiskei*** | EPfP |
| - 'Royal Ruby' | EPfP LSou MGos NEgg NLar SGol SLim SPoG WDin WFar WMoo |
| Lovita = 'Zebonard' | EBee EPfP IVic LRHS MBri MGos MRav NHol NLar SBfd SCoo |
| ***populifolia*** | see *Agarista populifolia* |
| Red Lips = 'Lipsbolwi'PBR | CDoC ELan EPfP IVic MGos NPla |
| § Scarletta = 'Zeblid' | Widely available |
| ***walteri*** | see *L. fontanesiana* |

## *Leuzea* (*Asteraceae*)

| | |
|---|---|
| ***centaureoides*** | see *Stemmacantha centaureoides* |

## *Levisticum* (*Apiaceae*)

| | |
|---|---|
| ***officinale*** | CArn CBod CHby CPrp CSev EGHP ELau EPfP GAbr GGar GPoy LEdu MHer MMuc MNHC NPri SBfd SDix SEND SIde SPlb SVic SWat WHer WHfH WJek WPer |

## *Lewisia* ✿ (*Portulacaceae*)

| | |
|---|---|
| 'Archangel' | NRya |
| Ashwood Carousel hybrids | CTri ECho MAsh NHar |
| 'Ashwood Pearl' | MAsh |
| 'Ben Chace' | MAsh |
| Birch strain | CBcs ECho ELan |
| ***brachycalyx*** ♀H2 | CPBP ECho EWes LLHF MAsh NWCA WPer |
| - pink | MAsh |
| ***cantelovii*** | MAsh |
| ***columbiana*** | MAsh WPer |
| - 'Alba' | MAsh |
| - subsp. ***columbiana*** NNS 07-430 | NWCA |
| - 'Rosea' | GKev NSla |
| - subsp. ***rupicola*** | LLHF MAsh |
| - subsp. ***wallowensis*** | MAsh NMen NWCA |

| | | |
|---|---|---|
| | ***congdonii*** | MAsh |
| | 'Constant Comment' | SEND |
| | ***cotyledon*** 🏆H4 | CWCL ECho EDAr GAbr GKev LLHF LRHS NBlu NSla WFar |
| | - f. ***alba*** | MAsh NWCA |
| | - - 'Snowstorm' | LLHF |
| | - 'Ashwood Ruby' | MAsh |
| | - Ashwood strain | ECho EPfP EWes LBee LRHS MAsh SRms WGor |
| | - 'Brannan Bar' | MAsh |
| | - 'Bright Eyes' | GKev |
| | - var. ***cotyledon*** NNS 05-430 | NWCA |
| | - Crags hybrids | SRms |
| | - double-flowered (d) | GKev |
| | - 'Fransi' | GEdr NLar |
| | - var. ***howellii*** | LLHF SRms WGor |
| | - hybrid | ECho EPot GGar LHop SPoG WGor |
| | - 'John's Special' | MAsh |
| | - magenta-flowered | ECho MAsh NWCA |
| § | - 'Regenbogen' | NWCA WGor WPer |
| | - Sunset Group 🏆H4 | ECho EPfP GLam LAst MHer NLar NWCA SRms WNew WPer WRHF |
| | - violet-flowered | GKev |
| | 'George Henley' | ECho EPfP EWes LLHF MAsh NMen NRya NWCA WAbe WGor |
| | ***leeana*** | MAsh |
| | 'Little Peach' | CPBP GGar GKev WGor WPer |
| | 'Little Plum' | CMea CPBP ECho EDAr EPfP EPot GGar GKev ITim MDKP NLar NRya NWCA WGor WHoo WPer |
| § | ***longipetala*** | ECho |
| § | ***nevadensis*** | ECho EDAr EPot GEdr GGar GLam ITim LRHS MAsh NMen NRya NWCA SRms WHoo WPer |
| I | - 'Alba' | GKev |
| | - ***bernardina*** | see *L. nevadensis* |
| | - 'Rosea' | MAsh NWCA |
| | ***oppositifolia*** 'Richeyi' | GKev |
| | 'Pinkie' | CPBP LLHF MAsh NMen |
| | ***pygmaea*** | CWCL ECho EWes GEdr GLam ITim LAst LRHS MAsh MHer MWat NBir NMen NRya NSla |
| | - subsp. ***longipetala*** | see *L. longipetala* |
| | Rainbow mixture | see *L. cotyledon* 'Regenbogen' |
| | 'Rawreth' | LLHF |
| | ***rediviva*** | CPBP EWes GEdr LLHF MAsh WAbe |
| | - subsp. ***minor*** | EPot |
| | ***serrata*** | LLHF MAsh |
| | ***sierrae*** | GLam |
| | 'Trevosia' | MAsh |
| | ***tweedyi*** 🏆H2 | CPBP ECho EPfP LHop LRHS MAsh NWCA |
| | - 'Alba' | MAsh WAbe |
| | - 'Elliott's Variety' | MAsh NWCA |
| | - lemon-flowered | NWCA |
| | - 'Rosea' | ECho LHop LRHS NWCA |

## *Leycesteria* (*Caprifoliaceae*)

| | | |
|---|---|---|
| | ***crocothyrsos*** | CAbP CBcs CHid CWib ELan EPfP GAbr LAst MDKP NLar |
| | ***formosa*** 🏆H4 | Widely available |
| | - brown-stemmed | IFoB |
| | - Golden Lanterns ='Notbruce'[PBR] | CDoC CMac CSBt EBee ELan EPfP EQua LBuc LRHS LSRN LTen MAsh MBri MDun MGos MMHG MMuc NEgg NLar SBfd SCoo SLim SPoG SPtl SWvt WBor WFar WMoo |
| | - 'Golden Pheasant' (v) | EHoe NExo |
| | - 'Purple Rain' | EBee EQua EWes LBuc LRHS LTen NLar SBfd SLim |
| | 'Gold Leaf' | MDKP |

## *Leymus* (*Poaceae*)

| | | |
|---|---|---|
| | from Falkland Islands | EPPr |
| § | ***arenarius*** | Widely available |
| | ***hispidus*** | see *Elymus hispidus* |
| | 'Niveus' | EHul |

## *Lhotzkya* see *Calytrix*

## *Liatris* (*Asteraceae*)

| | | |
|---|---|---|
| | ***aspera*** | EBee NBre NLar |
| | ***elegans*** | EBee EPfP NBre NLar SPlb |
| | ***ligulistylis*** | EBee LRHS MSCN NBPC NBre NLar SPhx |
| | ***mucronata*** | NLar |
| | ***punctata*** | EBee LRHS NBre |
| | ***pycnostachya*** | CRWN EBee NLar SRms |
| | ***scariosa*** 'Alba' | CMea SMrm |
| § | ***spicata*** | Widely available |
| | - 'Alba' | CMac CPrp CSBt CSpe EBee ECha ECtt ELan EPfP GKev LAma LAst LEdu LSRN MAvo MNFA MNrw MSCN NBPC NBre NGdn NLar NPri SBfd SPer SPet SPlb STes WPer XLum |
| | - ***callilepis*** | see *L. spicata* |
| | - 'Floristan Violett' | CTri EBee EPfP GMaP LBMP LRHS MAvo MHer MLLN MWat NEgg NLBP NLar SCoo SPlb SPoG SWal SWvt WFar WGwG WMnd WMoo WPer WWEG XLum |
| | - 'Floristan Weiss' | CTri EBee EPPr EPfP ERCP GMaP LBMP LRHS MAvo MHer MLLN MRav MWat MWhi NBPC NCGa NLar SPoG SWal SWvt WFar WGwG WMnd WMoo WPer WWEG |
| | - Goblin | see *L. spicata* 'Kobold' |
| § | - 'Kobold' | Widely available |
| | ***squarrosa*** | LRHS |

## *Libanotis* (*Umbelliferae*)

| | | |
|---|---|---|
| | ***montana*** | see *Seseli libanotis* |

## *Libertia* ✿ (*Iridaceae*)

| | | |
|---|---|---|
| | HCM 98.089 | WPGP |
| | 'Amazing Grace' | CDes EBee GCal GMac SBch |
| | 'Ballyrogan Blue' | CDes |
| * | ***breunioides*** | CDes CPLG WPGP |
| | ***caerulescens*** | CCCN CMac COIW CPLG EBee ECho EPfP EPla EShb GGar IFoB LRHS NBid NBir NCGa SGar SMrm WAle WFar WHer WMoo |
| | ***chilensis*** | see *L. formosa* |
| | ***elegans*** | CPLG |
| § | ***formosa*** | Widely available |
| | - brown-stemmed | IFoB |
| | ***grandiflora*** 🏆H4 | Widely available |
| | - stoloniferous | GGar |
| | 'Highlander' **new** | LBuc LRHS NWad |
| | ***ixioides*** | CBcs EBee ECha ECho ECou EShb LEdu MAvo MCot NSti SBfd SLPl WPGP WRHF |
| | - 'Goldfinger' (v) | Widely available |
| | - hybrid | SDix |
| | - 'Tricolor' | GAbr GGar GKev LRHS MMuc WMoo WPat |
| | 'Nelson Dwarf' | EBee EPPr GCal |

| | |
|---|---|
| ***paniculata*** | CPLG WSHC |
| ***peregrinans*** | Widely available |
| - 'Gold Leaf' | CBcs CBod CCCN CChe CElw CPMA CPrp CSpe CTri CTsd CWGN EBee LAst LHop LRHS MRav NOak SMad SWvt WFar WHoo WMoo |
| - 'Gold Stripe' | CHar EPPr LRHS |
| * ***procera*** | CDes CSpe EBee LEdu LRHS SKHP WPGP WSHC |
| ***pulchella*** | EBee |
| ***sessiliflora*** | CFee CPLG EBee NBir WFar |
| - RB 94073 | SMad |
| Shackleton hybrid | WFar |
| 'Taupo Blaze' | CBcs CKno CMac CPrp CSpe CWGN EBee EWll LRHS LSRN LSou NHol NSti SBfd SGol SHar SKHP SLon |
| 'Taupo Sunset' PBR | CCCN CPLG EBee ELon ETod EWes GBin LAst LRHS LSou MBNS MLLN MPkF NBir NOak NPnk SBfd SGol SKHP SWvt |
| ***tricococca*** HCM 98.089 | CDes EBee |

## *Libocedrus* (*Cupressaceae*)

| | |
|---|---|
| ***chilensis*** | see *Austrocedrus chilensis* |
| ***decurrens*** | see *Calocedrus decurrens* |

## *Libonia* see *Justicia*

## *Licuala* (*Arecaceae*)

| | |
|---|---|
| ***spinosa*** | LPal |

## *Ligularia* ✿ (*Asteraceae*)

| | |
|---|---|
| ***amplexicaulis*** GWJ 9404 | WCru |
| 'Britt Marie Crawford' PBR | Widely available |
| 'Cheju Charmer' | ELon LEdu WCru WWEG |
| ***clivorum*** | see *L. dentata* |
| § ***dentata*** | CRow EBee ECtt GAuc GGal MMuc NBro NLar SBfd SRms SWat WFar |
| - 'Dark Beauty' | EWll MMuc MWhi NBre WMnd |
| - dark-leaved | WWEG |
| - 'Desdemona' ♀H4 | Widely available |
| - 'Enkelrig' | EBee |
| - 'Midnight Lady' | NBre |
| - 'Orange Princess' | NPer WPer |
| - 'Orange Queen' | NBre WFar |
| - 'Osiris Fantaisie' (v) | CAbP CAbb COIW CPLG EBee ECtt EWes GAbr GBin IPot ITim LLHF MAsh MNrw NMyG NSti SPoG SUsu WBor WCot WCra WPnP WWEG |
| - 'Othello' | CBct CFir CRow EBee EBla ECtt EHon EPfP EShb LAst LRHS MSCN NBPC NBid NCGa NEgg NGdn NLar NPri SBfd SPav SPet SPoG SWat SWvt WBor WCAu WFar WWEG WWlt |
| - 'Sommergold' | ECha |
| - 'Twilight' | ECtt MBNS |
| § ***fischeri*** | CBct ECha LEdu NBre WPer |
| - B&SWJ 1158 | WFar |
| - B&SWJ 2570 | WCru |
| - B&SWJ 4381 | WCru |
| - B&SWJ 4478 | WCru |
| - B&SWJ 5653 | WCru |
| - B&SWJ 8802 | WCru |
| 'Gold Torch' | ECtt |
| 'Granito' new | MAsh |
| § 'Gregynog Gold' ♀H4 | EBee ECha ECtt EPfP GAbr GMaP LRHS LTen MRav MWhi MWts NBro NCGa NLar NOrc SPav SPer WFar WWEG WWlt |
| × ***hessei*** | GMaP MMuc NLar SWat WFar |
| ***hodgsonii*** | CKno EBla EPPr LEdu LRHS WPer |
| - B&SWJ 10855 | WCru |
| - SSSE 106 | GLam |
| - SSSE 307 | GLam |
| ***intermedia*** | WFar |
| - B&SWJ 606a | WCru |
| ***japonica*** | CHar CLAP CRow ECha GCra LEdu LMaj LRHS MWhi NLar WFar |
| - B&SWJ 2883 | WCru |
| - 'Rising Sun' | CLAP CPLG GEdr WCru |
| 'Laternchen' PBR | EBee GGar IBal MBri NBPC |
| 'Little Rocket' PBR | CPLG EBee ECtt EKen GBin MBNS MBri NBro NGdn NLar |
| ***macrophylla*** | LRHS WFar |
| 'Osiris Café Noir' | EBee ECtt IPot MAsh |
| 'Osiris Pistache' (v) new | ECtt |
| × ***palmatiloba*** | see *L.* × *yoshizoeana* 'Palmatiloba' |
| § ***przewalskii*** ♀H4 | Widely available |
| - 'Light Fingered' | NBre |
| ***sibirica*** | CSam EShb GAbr LRHS NLar WFar WMoo WPer WWEG |
| - B&SWJ 4383 | WCru |
| - B&SWJ 5806 | WCru |
| - B&SWJ 5841 | WCru |
| - var. ***speciosa*** | see *L. fischeri* |
| ***smithii*** | see *Senecio smithii* |
| ***speciosa*** | see *L. fischeri* |
| ***stenocephala*** | EBee LRHS MCot NBro NGdn NLar SHar SWat WFar WTcb XLum |
| - B&SWJ 283 | WCru |
| 'Sungold' | CMac CSam EBee EBla ECtt GBin LRHS NCGa NGdn |
| ***tangutica*** | see *Sinacalia tangutica* |
| 'The Rocket' ♀H4 | Widely available |
| ***tussilaginea*** | see *Farfugium japonicum* |
| - 'Aureo-maculata' | see *Farfugium japonicum* 'Aureomaculatum' |
| ***veitchiana*** | CDoy CFir CRow EBla EPfP GAbr GCal GGar LAst LEdu NCGa SPav SWat WFar |
| ***vorobievii*** | CSpr GAbr GAuc GCal NLar |
| 'Weihenstephan' | GCal |
| ***wilsoniana*** | CBct CFir CHEx CRow ECtt LLWG MMuc MRav NBre NMun SEND SPav SWat WCAu WFar |
| § × ***yoshizoeana*** 'Palmatiloba' | CHEx EBee EBla ELan ELon EPla GBee GCal LEdu MRav SPhx SWat WFar WWEG |
| 'Zepter' | CMHG EBee EBla ECtt GCal GQue LLWG MBNS MWhi MWts NEgg NLar NWad SMrm WCot WFar WWEG |

## *Ligusticum* (*Apiaceae*)

| | |
|---|---|
| ***lucidum*** | CMCN EBee EPfP IVic SPhx WPGP |
| ***porteri*** | CArn |
| § ***scoticum*** | CArn CElw EBee EOHP EShb EWTr EWes GPoy ILis MCot MDKP MHer NBPC NPnk SUsu WFar WHrl WJek WPtf |
| ***striatum*** B&SWJ 7259 | WCru |

## *Ligustrum* ✿ (*Oleaceae*)

| | |
|---|---|
| ***chenaultii*** | see *L. compactum* |
| § ***compactum*** | NLar |

| | | |
|---|---|---|
| § | ***delavayanum*** | EBtc EPfP ERom MGos NLar SArc STrG WFar |
| | – B&L 12083 | CPLG EQua |
| | ***ibota*** | EBtc NLar |
| | ***ionandrum*** | see *L. delavayanum* |
| | ***japonicum*** | ECHN LRHS LTen MMuc SEND SGol SPer WDin WFar |
| I | – 'Aureum' | MGos |
| | – 'Coriaceum' | see *L. japonicum* 'Rotundifolium' |
| * | – 'Coriaceum Aureum' | LRHS |
| | – 'Macrophyllum' | EPfP |
| § | – 'Rotundifolium' | CAbP CBcs CDoC CDul CFee CHEx CMac CPLG CSam EBee ELan EMil EPfP IVic LRHS MAsh MGos MRav NLar SBfd SCoo SMad SPer SPoG WCFE WFar |
| | – 'Silver Star' (v) | EBee MGos NLar SEND SLon |
| § | – 'Texanum' | CAlb EWes MMuc NLar SEWo WCFE |
| * | – 'Texanum Argenteum' | SGol |
| | – 'Variegatum' (v) | LMaj SGol |
| | ***lucidum*** ♀H4 | CCVT CDoC CDul CSBt CTri EBee ELan EWTr IDee LAst MGos MMuc MRav NLar NWea SArc SBfd SBrd SEND SGol SPer SWvt WDin WFar |
| | – Guiz 296 | CPLG |
| | – 'Excelsum Superbum' (v) ♀H4 | CMac CPMA ECrN ELan EPfP LAst LHop MGos SGol SSpi |
| | – 'Golden Wax' | CPMA MRav SSpi |
| | – 'Tricolor' (v) | CPMA ELan EPfP LRHS MAsh NLar SBfd SPer SPoG SSpi SWvt WDin WFar |
| | ***obtusifolium*** 'Dart's Perfecta' | SLPl |
| | ***ovalifolium*** | Widely available |
| § | – 'Argenteum' (v) | CBcs CCVT CDoC CDul CMac CTri CWib EBee ECrN EHoe LBuc LRHS MMuc MWat NEgg NLar SBfd SEND SGol SLim SPer SPoG SWvt WDin WFar |
| | – 'Aureomarginatum' | see *L. ovalifolium* 'Aureum' |
| § | – 'Aureum' (v) ♀H4 | Widely available |
| | – 'Lemon and Lime' (v) | CDoC EHoe EPfP LRHS SCoo SWvt WPat WRHF |
| | – 'Variegatum' | see *L. ovalifolium* 'Argenteum' |
| | ***quihoui*** ♀H4 | CHGN EBee ECre ELan EPfP IDee LHop LRHS NLar SDix SEND SKHP SLon SMad SPer SSpi WFar WPat |
| | ***sempervirens*** | EPfP |
| | ***sinense*** | CMCN EPfP GLin MRav SBfd WFar |
| | – 'Multiflorum' | CWib WFar |
| | – var. ***stauntonii*** | NLar |
| | – 'Variegatum' (v) | CPMA EBee EPla EWes LHop MMuc MRav SPer |
| | – 'Wimbei' | WFar |
| | ***strongylophyllum*** | CDoC CPLG WFar |
| | ***texanum*** | see *L. japonicum* 'Texanum' |
| | ***tschonoskii*** | NLar |
| | ***undulatum*** 'Lemon Lime and Clippers' | LRHS MAsh MWea NLar NPri SDix SLim |
| | 'Vicaryi' | CPMA ELan EPfP EPla EQua EWTr MGos NHol NPro SEND SGol WFar |
| | ***vulgare*** | CBcs CCVT CDul CHab CMac CRWN CTri CWan ECrN EPfP LAst LBuc LRHS MMuc MSwo NWea SEND SEWo SWvt WDin WMou WSFF |
| | – 'Aureovariegatum' (v) | CNat |
| | – 'Lodense' | EBtc |
| | ***walkeri*** | GAuc |

# *Lilium* ✿ (*Liliaceae*)

| | | |
|---|---|---|
| | 'Acapulco' (VII-/d) | LAma MCri NGdn SDeJ |
| | African Queen Group (VI/a) ♀H4 | ERCP LAma LRHS NLar SCoo SPer SRms |
| | – 'African Queen' (VIb-c/a) | CBro MCri |
| | 'Algarve' (VIIIa-b/c) | MBri |
| | 'Altari' (VIIIa-b/b) | MCri |
| | ***amabile*** (IXc/d) | GAuc |
| | – var. ***luteum*** (IXc/d) | GAuc MCri |
| | ***amoenum*** (IXc/b) | GAuc |
| | 'Anastasia' (VIIIb-c/b-d) | LAma |
| | 'Apeldoorn' (Ia/b) | MCri NNor |
| | 'Apollo' (Ia-b) ♀H4 | CBro LAma NNor SDeJ |
| | 'Arena' (VIIa/b) | EPfP LRHS MCri SCoo WFar |
| | 'Ariadne' (Ic-d) | CDes |
| | Asiatic hybrids (I) | LAma NGdn SGar |
| | ***aurantiacum*** new | GAuc |
| | ***auratum*** (IXb/c) | CDoy ECho EFEx EPfP GAuc GKev WGwG |
| | – 'Gold Band' | see *L. auratum* var. *platyphyllum* |
| | – 'Perfection' (IX b/c) new | LRHS |
| § | – var. ***platyphyllum*** (IXb/c) | GAuc MCri NNor |
| | – – B&SWJ 4824 | WCru |
| | – – B&SWJ 5041 | WCru |
| | – var. ***virginale*** (IXb/c) | GAuc MCri |
| | 'Avignon' (Ia/b) | MCri |
| | 'Bach' (VIIIa-b/b) | MBri |
| | Backhouse hybrids | see *L.* × *dalhansonii* Backhouse Group |
| | ***bakerianum*** (IXc/b) | LAma |
| | – var. ***aureum*** (IXc/b) | GAuc |
| | – var. ***delavayi*** (IXc/b) | GAuc |
| | 'Barbaresco' (VIIa-b/b) | SCoo |
| | 'Barcelona' (Ia/b-c) | NNor |
| | Bellingham Group (IVc/d) | GEdr |
| | 'Bergamo' (VIIb/b) | EPfP SCoo WFar |
| | 'Black Beauty' (VIIIb-c/d) | CAvo CFFs EPfP GGar GKev LAma LRHS MCri NNor SDeJ |
| | 'Black Dragon' | see *L. leucanthum* var. *centifolium* 'Black Dragon' |
| | 'Black Pearl' new | EPfP SPer |
| | 'Black Tie' (VIIa-b/b) | MCri |
| | ***bolanderi*** (IXb-c/a) | GAuc |
| | ***bosniacum*** | GAuc |
| | 'Bright Star' (VIb-c/c) | LAma MCri |
| | ***brownii*** (IXb-c/a) | ECho LAma LWSt MCri |
| | – var. ***viridulum*** new | GAuc |
| | ***bulbiferum*** (IXa/b) | ECho GAuc |
| | 'Burgundy Splash' (I) | LAma |
| | 'Butter Pixie'[PBR] (Ia/b) | NNor WGor |
| | ***callosum*** (IXc/d) | GAuc |
| § | ***canadense*** (IXc/a) | CBro CDes CRDP GAuc LAma WCru |
| | – var. ***coccineum*** (IXc/a) | CRDP |
| | – var. ***flavum*** | see *L. canadense* |
| | ***candidum*** (IXb/a) ♀H4 | CAvo CBcs CBro CTca CTri CWCL EBee ECha ECho EGHP ELan EPfP EPot ERCP GAuc GKev LAma LAst MCri MHer NLar SDeJ SEND SRms XLum |
| | 'Capuchino' (Ia-b/c) | LAma MCri |
| | ***carniolicum*** | see *L. pyrenaicum* subsp. *carniolicum* |
| | 'Casa Blanca' (VIIb/b-c) ♀H4 | CAvo CBro CFFs EPfP GKev LAma MCri NBir NLar NNor SCoo SDeJ WFar |
| | 'Casa Rosa' | see *L.* × *parkmanii* 'Rote Horn' |
| | 'Centerfold' (Ia-b/b) | LAma NNor |

| | |
|---|---|
| ***cernuum*** (IXc/d) | CAvo ECho GAuc GKev LAma MCri SPer |
| * - 'Album' | ECho GAuc |
| ***chalcedonicum*** (IXb-c/d) | GAuc |
| ***ciliatum*** **new** | GAuc LWst |
| Citronella Group (Ic/d) | CAvo ECGP ECho LAma MCri SDeJ WFar |
| ***columbianum*** (IXc/d) | ECho GAuc NMen WHal |
| - B&SWJ 9564 | WCru |
| - dwarf (IXc/d) | GAuc NMen |
| 'Con Amore' (VIIb/b) | SCoo WFar |
| 'Conca d'Or'$^{PBR}$ (VIIIb/b) | LAma |
| ***concolor*** (IXa/c) | GAuc LRHS |
| - var. ***pulchellum*** (IXa/c) | GAuc |
| - var. ***stictum*** (IXa/c) | GAuc |
| 'Connecticut King' (Ia/b) | LAma MCri |
| 'Corina' (Ia/b) | NNor |
| 'Côte d'Azur' (Ia/b-c) | LAma NBlu NNor |
| 'Coulance' (VII-/d) | LRHS |
| 'Crimson Pixie' (Ia/b) | CBro NGdn SPet |
| × ***dalhansonii*** (IIc/d) | SPhx WCot |
| § - Backhouse Group (IIc/d) | CAvo |
| § - 'Marhan' (IIc/d) | ECho |
| - 'Mrs R.O. Backhouse' (IIc/d) | ECho GEdr |
| § ***dauricum*** (IXa/b) | GAuc |
| - from Amur Region, Russia **new** | GAuc |
| - var. ***alpinum*** **new** | GAuc MCri |
| ***davidii*** (IXc/d) | CPLG EBee ECho GAuc GEdr GKev LAma MCri WCru |
| - var. ***macranthum*** (IXa/b) **new** | GAuc |
| - var. ***unicolor*** | GAuc |
| § - var. ***willmottiae*** (IXc/d) | GAuc MCri WCot WCru |
| 'Dimention' (I) | LAma |
| ***distichum*** (IXb-c/d) | GAuc |
| - B&SWJ 794 | WCru |
| - B&SWJ 4465 | WCru |
| 'Dizzy' (VIIa-b/b-c) | MCri NNor |
| ***duchartrei*** (IXc/d) | CDes CDoy CPLG ECho GAuc GEdr LAma NSla WCru |
| - from Gansu, China | GAuc |
| 'Ebony' (Ic/d) | LAma |
| 'Electric' (Ia/b-c) | MCri NNor |
| 'Elodie'$^{PBR}$ (1a/b) | CAvo CFFs LAma |
| ***euxanthum*** (IX) | GAuc |
| 'Eyeliner'$^{PBR}$ | LAma |
| 'Fancy Joy' (Ia/b-c) | MBri |
| 'Fangio' (VIIIa/b) | NNor |
| ***fargesii*** (IXc/d) | GAuc |
| 'Fata Morgana' (Ia/b) 🏆$^{H4}$ | LAma NNor SCoo |
| 'Fire King' (Ib/d) | EPfP LAma MCri SCoo SDeJ SRms WFar |
| ***formosanum*** (IXb/a) | GAuc LRHS MCri WCot |
| - RWJ 10005 | WCru |
| * - var. ***album*** **new** | GAuc |
| - var. ***pricei*** (IXb/a) | CAby ECho ELan EPot GAuc GEdr GGar LRHS MHer NMen NSla NWCA SPoG |
| * - - f. ***album*** **new** | GAuc |
| - - 'Snow Queen' (Vb/a) | SDeJ |
| 'Garden Party' (VIIb/b) 🏆$^{H4}$ | LSou NLar SDeJ WFar |
| 'Glossy Wings' (VIIIa-b/b) | NNor |
| 'Golden Joy' (Ia/-) | MBri |
| Golden Splendor Group (VIb-c/a) 🏆$^{H4}$ | LAma MCri SCoo SDeJ |
| 'Graffity' (I) | LAma |
| 'Gran Paradiso' (Ia/b) | MCri SRms |
| 'Grand Cru' (Ia/b) 🏆$^{H4}$ | LRHS MCri NNor SDeJ |
| Green Magic Group (VI-/a) | NNor |
| ***hansonii*** (IX/b-c/d) | ECha ECho GAuc GEdr LAma MCri |
| - B&SWJ 4756 from Aomori, Japan | WCru |
| - B&SWJ 8506 | WCru |
| - B&SWJ 8528 | WCru |
| * - f. ***rubrum*** **new** | GAuc |
| ***henryi*** (IXc/d) 🏆$^{H4}$ | CAvo EBee ECho EPfP GAuc GKev LAma MCri NLar NNor SDeJ WCot WCru |
| - var. ***citrinum*** (IXc/d) | GAuc |
| 'Hit Parade' (VII) | SDeJ |
| × ***hollandicum*** (Ia/b) | MCri |
| 'Hot Lips' (VIIb/b-d) | EPfP |
| ***humboldtii*** (IXc/d) | GAuc |
| - subsp. ***ocellatum*** (IXc/d) | GAuc |
| 'Ibarra' (Ia/b) | MCri |
| 'Italia' (Ia) | LRHS |
| 'Ivory Pixie' (Ia/b) | GKev SPet |
| 'Jacqueline' | LRHS |
| ***japonicum*** (IXb/a) | EFEx GAuc |
| - 'Albomarginatum' (IXb/a/v) | GEdr |
| 'Journey's End' (VIIb/c) | LAma |
| § 'Joy' (VIIa-b/b) 🏆$^{H4}$ | LAma MCri NNor |
| § ***kelleyanum*** (IXc/d) | GAuc |
| ***kelloggii*** (IXc/d) | GAuc |
| ***kesselringianum*** (IXc/d) | GAuc |
| - from W. Caucasus, Russia **new** | GAuc |
| 'King Pete' (Ib/b-c) 🏆$^{H4}$ | SDeJ |
| 'Lady Alice' (VI-/d) | WGwG |
| § ***lancifolium*** (IXc/d) | CArn CHid GBin WBrk WFar |
| - B&SWJ 4352 | WCru |
| - var. ***flaviflorum*** (IXc/d) | GAuc MCri |
| - 'Flore Pleno' (IXc/d) | EPPr GAuc GCal GGar LHop LRHS MHer MMHG NBir NNor SMrm WCot WCru WFar WHil WTin |
| * - var. ***forrestii*** (IX) | GAuc MCri |
| - Forrest's form (IX) | LRHS |
| - var. ***fortunei*** (IXc/d) | GAuc GCal SDix |
| - - B&SWJ 539 | WCru |
| - pink-flowered | SDeJ |
| - 'Splendens' (IXc/d) 🏆$^{H4}$ | CBro EBee ECGP ECho EPfP GAuc GKev LAma MCri NBid NNor SDeJ SPhx |
| * - ***viridulum*** | GAuc |
| ***lankongense*** (IXc/d) | CWCL EPot GAuc GEdr LAma MCri WCru |
| - BWJ 7691 | WCru |
| 'Latvia' (Ia/b) | MCri |
| 'Le Rêve' | see *L.* 'Joy' |
| ***ledebourii*** (IXc/d) | GAuc |
| ***leichtlinii*** (IXc/d) | CBro ECho EPot GAuc GKev LRHS MCri |
| - B&SWJ 4519 | WCru |
| - 'Iwashimiza' (IXc/d) | MCri |
| - var. ***maximowiczii*** (IXc/d) | GAuc |
| 'Lemon Pixie'$^{PBR}$ (Ia/b) | LAma SPet |
| ***leucanthum*** (IXb-c/a) | GAuc LAma LWst |
| - var. ***centifolium*** (IXb-c/a) | GAuc MCri WCru |
| - - BWJ 8130 | WCru |
| § - - 'Black Dragon' (IXb-c/a) | MCri |
| ***lijiangense*** (IXc/d) | GAuc GEdr MCri |
| 'Little John' (VIIa-b/b) | MBri SPer |
| Lollypop = 'Holebibi' (Ia/b) | EPfP MBri NNor SCoo SPet |
| ***longiflorum*** (IXb/a) 🏆$^{H2-3}$ | EBee ECho GAuc LAma MCri SCoo |
| - B&SWJ 11376 | WCru |
| - 'Memories' | MBri |

|  |  |
|---|---|
| § – 'White American' (Vb/a) | CBro ECho LRHS SPer |
| – 'White Heaven'$^{PBR}$ (Vb/a) | EPfP |
| ***lophophorum*** (IXc/b) | EPot GAuc LAma |
| – var. ***linearifolium*** (IXc/b) | GAuc |
| 'Lovely Girl' (VII /b) | CSut SDeJ |
| 'Luxor' (Ib) | MCri NBir |
| ***mackliniae*** (IXc/a) | CWCL EBee ECho EPot GAuc GCal GCra GEdr GMaP GMac ITim NBir NMen WAbe WHal |
| – from Nagaland, India **new** | GAuc |
| – robust habit | GGar |
| × ***maculatum*** (Ia/b) **new** | GAuc |
| 'Mambo'$^{PBR}$ (VII) | LAma |
| 'Marco Polo' (Ia/-) | SCoo SDeJ WFar |
| 'Marhan' | see *L.* × *dalhansonii* 'Marhan' |
| ***martagon*** (IXc/d) $\Upsilon^{H4}$ | CBro CFir CTca CWCL EBee ECha ECho ELan EPot ERCP EWil GAuc GEdr GKev GPoy LAma LRHS MCot NBir NLar NPnk SDeJ SGar SRms WAul WCot WFar WPnP WShi WTin |
| – var. ***albiflorum*** (IXc/d) | GAuc |
| – var. ***album*** (IXc/d) $\Upsilon^{H4}$ | CAvo CBro CWCL EBee ECho ELan EPfP EPot GAuc GEdr GKev GMaP LAma LRHS NBir NChi SDeJ WPtf WShi |
| – var. ***cattaniae*** (IXc/d) | EPot GAuc MCri WCot |
| – var. ***daugavense*** (IXc/d) | LWst |
| – var. ***pilosiusculum*** (IXc/d) | GAuc |
| – 'Plenum' (IXc/d) | WCot WKif |
| – var. ***sanguineo-purpureum*** (IXc/d) | GAuc |
| ***medeoloides*** (IXc/d) | ECho EFEx GAuc NMen |
| 'Mediterrannee' (VIIb/d) | NNor |
| ***michiganense*** (IXc/d) | GAuc |
| 'Miss Feya' (VIII) | LAma |
| 'Miss France' (VIIb/b-c) | EPfP |
| 'Miss Lucy'$^{PBR}$ (VIIa-b/b c) | CHid LAma |
| 'Miss Rio' (VII) | SCoo |
| 'Mona Lisa' (VIIb/b-c) | EPfP GKev LAma LRHS LSou MBri MCri NGdn NNor SDeJ WFar |
| ***monadelphum*** (IXc/d) | ECho GAuc LAma NLar SDeJ |
| 'Monte Negro' (Ia/b) | CBro LRHS MCri NGdn |
| * ***montegena*** (IX) **new** | GAuc |
| 'Montreux' (Ia/b-c) | LAma |
| 'Mount Duckling' **new** | GKev |
| 'Muscadet'$^{PBR}$ (VIIa-b/b) | CSut EPfP LAma NGdn SDeJ |
| § ***nanum*** (IXc/b) | ECho GAuc GEdr LAma LWst NMen WAbe WCru WHal |
| – AGS/ES | NMen LWst |
| – EMAK 670 | LWst |
| – from Bhutan (IX) | GAuc NMen WCru |
| – var. ***flavidum*** (IXc/b) | GEdr LWst NMen |
| – – hybrids | LWst |
| ***neilgherrense*** (IX) | GAuc |
| ***nepalense*** (IXc/a) | CAby CBcs CBro CFir CHid CPLG CTca EBee EBla ECho EPot ERCP GAuc GEdr GGar GMac LAma MCri MDun WCot WCru WFar XLum |
| – B&SWJ 2985 | WCru |
| – CC 3663 | WCot |
| 'Nerone' (Ia/b) | CHid NNor |
| 'Netty's Pride' (Ia/b-c) | CAvo CFFs CHid EPfP ERCP MCri SPer |
| 'New Wave' (Ia/b) | NBlu |
| ***nobilissimum*** (IXa-b/a) | EFEx |
| 'Nove Cento' (Ia/b) $\Upsilon^{H4}$ | MCri SDeJ |
| 'Odeon' (VI-/a) | MCri |
| 'Olivia' (Ia) | LAma MCri |
| Olympic Group (VI-/a) | MCri |
| 'Orange Electric' (Ia/b) | SDeJ |
| 'Orange Pixie' (Ia/b) | MCri NBlu NNor SCoo SPet WGor |
| 'Orange Twinkle' (Ib-c/b) | SDeJ |
| * Oriental Superb Group | NGdn |
| § ***oxypetalum*** (IXb-c/b) | ECho GAuc LWst |
| – var. ***insigne*** (IXb-c/b) | ECho GAuc GBin GEdr GGar LWst NMen WAbe WCru WHal |
| ***papilliferum*** (IXc/d) | LAma |
| ***pardalinum*** (IXc/d) $\Upsilon^{H4}$ | CBro CWCL ECho ELan ERCP GAuc LWst MCot WCru WHal |
| – var. ***giganteum*** (IXc/d) | EPfP MCri MNrw WTin |
| – subsp. ***shastense*** (IXc/d) | NMen |
| § – subsp. ***vollmeri*** (IXc/d) | GAuc NMen WCru |
| § – subsp. ***wigginsii*** (IXc/d) | GAuc MCri |
| × ***parkmanii*** Imperial Silver Group (VIIb/c) | LAma |
| § – 'Rote Horn' (VIIIb/a) | MCri |
| – 'Sam' (VIIb/c) $\Upsilon^{H4}$ | EPfP |
| ***parryi*** (IXb-c/a) | GAuc WHal |
| ***parvum*** (IXa-b/a) | ECho GAuc |
| – var. ***hallidayi*** | GAuc |
| 'Patricia's Pride' | MCri |
| 'Peach Pixie' (Ia/b) | NBir SCoo |
| ***pensylvanicum*** | see *L. dauricum* |
| ***philadelphicum*** (IXa/b) | GAuc |
| – var. ***andinum*** (IXa/b) | GAuc |
| ***philippinense*** (IXa-b/a) | CDes LAma MCri WPGP |
| Pink Perfection Group (VIb/a) $\Upsilon^{H4}$ | CAvo CBro EPfP ERCP LAma LRHS MCri NNor SCoo SPer WFar |
| 'Pink Pixie'$^{PBR}$ (Ia/b) | NNor SPet |
| 'Pink Tiger' (VIIIb/c) | CAvo MCri NNor WGor |
| 'Pink Twinkle' | CBro |
| ***poilanei*** HWJ 681 | WCru |
| – WWJ 11679 | WCru |
| ***polyphyllum*** | GLin |
| ***pomponium*** (IXc/d) | GAuc |
| ***primulinum*** var. ***burmanicum*** (IXc/a) | GAuc |
| – var. ***ochraceum*** (IXc/a) | GAuc LAma MCri WCru |
| § ***pumilum*** (IXc/d) $\Upsilon^{H4}$ | EBee ECho EPot ERCP GAuc GKev LAma MCri |
| ***pyrenaicum*** (IXc/d) | CAby ECho GAuc IBlr LWst MCri WPGP WShi |
| § – subsp. ***carniolicum*** (IXc/d) | GAuc MCri |
| – – var. ***jankae*** (IX) | GAuc |
| – subsp. ***pyrenaicum*** f. ***rubrum*** (IXc/d) | GAuc |
| Red Band Group (VII-/b) | WFar |
| 'Red Carpet' (Ia/b) | MCri NBir NNor SDeJ |
| Red Rum = 'Zanlorum' | MBri |
| 'Red Star' | LRHS |
| ***regale*** (IXb/a) $\Upsilon^{H4}$ | CArn CAvo CBro CDoy CFFs CFir CMea CTca EBee ECha ELan EPfP ERCP GAuc GGar GKev LAma LRHS MCot MCri NLar NNor SDeJ SPer WCot WFar |
| – 'Album' (IXb/a) | CAvo EBee ERCP GAuc GKev LAma LRHS MCri NLar NNor SCoo SDeJ WCot WFar WGwG XLum |
| § – 'Royal Gold' (IXb/a) | GAuc MCri |
| 'Reinesse' (Ia/b) | MBri |
| 'Rina's Twinkle' | LRHS |
| 'Robert Swanson' | LAma |
| 'Robina' (VIIIa-b/b-c) | LAma WCot |
| 'Rodolfa'$^{PBR}$ (VIIIa-b/-) | LSou |
| 'Roma' (Ia/b) | NBir |
| 'Rosefire' (Ia/b) | NNor |
| 'Rosemary North' (Ic/d) | CDes |
| 'Rosita' (Ia/b-c) | WFar |

| | |
|---|---|
| ***rosthornii*** (IXc/d) | CPLG GAuc GEdr LAma LWst WCot WCru |
| 'Royal Fantasy' (VIII) | NNor |
| 'Royal Gold' | see *L. regale* 'Royal Gold' |
| ***rubellum*** (IXb/a) | EFEx GAuc |
| ***rubescens*** (IXa/a) | GAuc |
| * 'Rubina' | MCri |
| 'Ruud' (VIIb/b-c) | LAma |
| ***sachalinense*** (IXa/b) | GAuc |
| - RBS 0235 | EPPr |
| 'Salmon Twinkle' (Ib-c/c) | LRHS SDeJ WFar |
| 'San Vincenzo' new | EPfP |
| ***sargentiae*** (IXb-c/a) | GAuc MCri NMen WCot WCru |
| 'Scheherazade' (VIIIc/d) | LAma MCri |
| 'Set Point' (VIIb/b) | SDeJ |
| ***shastense*** | see *L. kelleyanum* |
| 'Silly Girl' (Ia/-) | NNor |
| § 'Snow Crystal' (Ia/b) | EPfP |
| ***souliei*** (IXc/a-b) | GAuc |
| 'Souvenir'PBR (VIIa-b/b) | NGdn |
| 'Spark' | NNor |
| ***speciosum*** (IXb-c/d) | GAuc |
| - B&SWJ 4847 | WCru |
| - B&SWJ 4924 | WCru |
| - var. ***album*** (IXb-c/d) | EBee ECho EPfP GAuc GKev LEdu MCri NBir SDeJ |
| - var. ***gloriosoides*** (IXb-c/d) | GAuc LAma |
| - var. ***rubrum*** (IXb-c/d) | EBee ECha ECho EPfP GAuc GKev LAma MCri NBir SPer SRms |
| § - 'Uchida' (IXb-c/d) | CPLG EPfP GAuc MCri |
| 'Sphinx' (Ia/d) | CAbP NNor WCot |
| 'Spring Pink' (Ia) | ERCP |
| 'Staccato' (Ia/c) | MCri |
| 'Star Gazer' (VIIa/c) | CBro CSut ELan LAma LRHS MCri NBlu NNor SCoo SDeJ WFar |
| 'Starfighter' (VIIa-b/c) | EPfP GKev MCri SDeJ SPet |
| 'Sterling Star' (Ia/b) | MCri NNor |
| Stones = 'Holebobo' (Ia/b) | NNor |
| 'Sulphur King' | WCot |
| ***sulphureum*** (IXb-c/a) | GAuc LAma MCri |
| 'Sumatra' (VIIb/b) | LAma |
| 'Sun Ray' (Ia/b) | MCri NBlu |
| ***superbum*** (IXc/d) | CBro EBee GAuc LAma WCot WCru WPGP |
| 'Sweet Surrender' (Ib-c/c-d) | EPfP MCri NNor SDeJ |
| 'Sweet-kiss' (Ia-b/b) | MBri |
| ***szovitsianum*** (IXc/d) new | GAuc |
| - subsp. ***ponticum*** (IXc/d) new | GAuc |
| ***taliense*** (IXc/d) | ECho GAuc GEdr LAma MCri WCru |
| ***tenuifolium*** | see *L. pumilum* |
| 'Tiger Woods' (VII) | LAma |
| ***tigrinum*** | see *L. lancifolium* |
| 'Time Out'PBR (VIIa-b/b-c) | EPfP |
| 'Tom Pouce' (VIIa/b) | EPfP MCri |
| 'Touch' (VIIb/-) | MCri |
| Triumphator ) = 'Zanlophator'PBR (VIIIb/a-b | EPfP MCri NNor |
| ***tsingtauense*** (IXa/c) | GAuc MCri |
| - B&SWJ 519 | WCru |
| - B&SWJ 4263 | WCru |
| - B&SWJ 4698 | WCru |
| 'Uchida Kanoka' | see *L. speciosum* 'Uchida' |
| 'Venture' (1a) new | NNor |
| 'Vermeer' (Ia-b/b-c) | LRHS WFar |
| 'Victory Joy' | MBri |
| 'Vivaldi' (Ia/b) | SDeJ |
| ***vollmeri*** | see *L. pardalinum* subsp. *vollmeri* |
| ***wallichianum*** (IXb/a) | EBee ECho EPot GAuc LAma XLum |
| ***wardii*** (IXc/d) | CPLG |
| ***washingtonianum*** (IXb/a) | GAuc |
| - var. ***purpurascens*** (IXb/a-b) | GAuc |
| 'White American' | see *L. longiflorum* 'White American' |
| 'White Paradise' (V) | SCoo |
| White Pixie | see *L.* 'Snow Crystal' |
| 'White Twinkle' (Ia-b/b) | CAvo SDeJ |
| ***wigginsii*** | see *L. pardalinum* subsp. *wigginsii* |
| ***willmottiae*** | see *L. davidii* var. *willmottiae* |
| ***wilsonii*** var. ***luteum*** new | MCri |
| ***xanthellum*** var. ***luteum*** (IXb-c/d) | CDes WCru |
| 'Yellow Electric' new | MCri |

## lime see *Citrus aurantiifolia*

## lime, djeruk see *Citrus amblycarpa*

## lime, Philippine see × *Citrofortunella microcarpa*

## *Limnanthes* (*Limnanthaceae*)

| | |
|---|---|
| ***douglasii*** ♀H4 | CArn EPfP SIde |
| - subsp. ***rosea*** | CSpe |

## *Limnobium* (*Hydrocharitaceae*)

| | |
|---|---|
| sp. | LLWG |

## *Limonium* (*Plumbaginaceae*)

| | |
|---|---|
| ***bellidifolium*** | CMea ECha EDAr MWat WPer WTin |
| 'Blauer Diamant' | NBre |
| ***chilwellii*** | ECGP LRHS SEND |
| ***cosyrense*** | CMea GEdr MHer NMen WPer |
| ***dregeanum*** | WThu |
| ***dumosum*** | see *Goniolimon tataricum* var. *angustifolium* |
| ***gmelinii*** | SPlb WPer |
| * - subsp. ***hungaricum*** | NLar XLum |
| ***gougetianum*** | LLHF WPer |
| ***latifolium*** | see *L. platyphyllum* |
| ***minutum*** | NWCA |
| ***perezii*** | CFir WPer |
| § ***platyphyllum*** | CArn CHar CKno CMea EBee EPPr EPfP GMaP LHop LRHS MHer MWat NBPC NChi NMir NPri SAga SBfd SEND SGar SPer SPoG SRms STes WAul WCAu WHoo WPer WTin WWEG |
| - 'Robert Butler' | CPrp GCal |
| - 'Violetta' | EBee ECGP ECha ELan EPfP GCal LAst LRHS MBri MRav NOrc SPer SPoG WHoo |
| ***speciosum*** | see *Goniolimon incanum* |
| ***tataricum*** | see *Goniolimon tataricum* |
| ***vulgare*** | WHer |

## *Linaria* (*Plantaginaceae*)

| | |
|---|---|
| ***aeruginea*** | CSpe |
| - 'Neon Lights' | CSpe EDAr EDif LRHS NGdn SBfd |
| - subsp. ***nevadensis*** 'Gemstones' | SBch |
| ***alpina*** | CSpe ECtt NRya NSla SRms |
| ***anticaria*** 'Antique Silver' | LSou MRav WPtf WWEG |
| Blue Lace = 'Yalin' | LSou |
| ***cymbalaria*** | see *Cymbalaria muralis* |

| | |
|---|---|
| § ***dalmatica*** | EBee ECha ELan EPPr GGar IFro MWea NBid NBre SBch WCot WMoo WPer WWEG |
| ***dalmatica* × *purpurea*** | WCot |
| × ***dominii*** 'Carnforth' | SBch SHar WCot WWEG |
| – 'Yuppie Surprise' | CHid NBir SWvt |
| ***genistifolia*** | MDKP |
| – subsp. ***dalmatica*** | see *L. dalmatica* |
| ***hepaticifolia*** | see *Cymbalaria hepaticifolia* |
| * ***lobata alba*** | ECho SPlb |
| ***nevadensis*** 'Grenada Sol' | MWea |
| ***origanifolia*** | see *Chaenorhinum origanifolium* |
| ***pallida*** | see *Cymbalaria pallida* |
| 'Peachy' **new** | CSpe |
| ***pilosa*** | see *Cymbalaria pilosa* |
| ***purpurea*** | COIW CTri EBee EHoe ELan EPfP IFoB LRHS MHer MMuc MNHC NBPC NBro NPer NPri NVic SEND SPhx SRms WCot WMoo WPer WSFF |
| – 'Alba' | see *L. purpurea* 'Springside White' |
| – 'Brown's White Strain' **new** | MLLN SPad |
| – 'Canon Came' **new** | CNat |
| – 'Canon Went' | Widely available |
| – pink-flowered | CSpe |
| – 'Radcliffe Innocence' | see *L. purpurea* 'Springside White' |
| § – 'Springside White' | EBee ECha ECtt EWTr LBMP LRHS MBri NBir NGdn NPri SBch SPhx SSvw WAul WCAu WCot WPer WWEG XLum |
| – 'Thurgarton Beauty' | MDKP |
| ***repens*** | CPom MNrw WCot WHer |
| × ***sepium*** | WCot |
| ***triornithophora*** | CFir CSpr ECha LBMP LRHS MHer MWea SBfd SPlb WKif WMoo |
| – 'Pink Budgies' | LSou |
| – purple-flowered | WMoo |
| – 'Rosea' | CSpe |
| ***vulgaris*** | CArn CHab EWil MDKP MHer MNHC NMir WHer WHfH WJek |
| – 'Peloria' | MDKP |
| 'Winifrid's Delight' | NBre |

## *Lindelofia* (*Boraginaceae*)

| | |
|---|---|
| ***anchusoides*** misapplied | see *L. longiflora* |
| ***anchusoides*** (Lindl.) Lehm. | EPPr NBid |
| § ***longiflora*** | EBee GCal GCra GMaP |

## *Lindera* (*Lauraceae*)

| | |
|---|---|
| ***benzoin*** | CBcs CMac EPfP LRHS MBlu WDin |
| ***erythrocarpa*** | EPfP |
| – B&SWJ 6271 | WCru |
| – B&SWJ 8730 | WCru |
| ***megaphylla*** | CBcs CHEx |
| ***obtusiloba*** ♀H4 | CAbP EPfP SSpi |
| – B&SWJ 8723 | WCru |
| – B&SWJ 11054 | WCru |
| ***praecox*** | EPfP |
| – B&SWJ 10802 | WCru |
| – B&SWJ 10953 from north Japan | WCru |
| – B&SWJ 11125 from south Japan **new** | WCru |
| ***reflexa*** | CGHE EPfP NLar |
| ***sericea*** B&SWJ 11123 | WCru |
| – B&SWJ 11141 | WCru |
| – var. ***lancea*** B&SWJ 11071 | WCru |
| – – B&SWJ 11118 | WCru |
| ***strychnifolia*** | EPfP |
| ***triloba*** | SSpi |
| – B&SWJ 5570 | WCru |
| – B&SWJ 11121 | WCru |
| – B&SWJ 11466 | WCru |
| ***umbellata*** B&SWJ 10881 | WCru |
| – var. ***membranacea*** B&SWJ 6227 | WCru |
| – – B&SWJ 10837 | WCru |

## *Lindernia* (*Linderniaceae*)

| | |
|---|---|
| ***grandiflora*** | LLWG |

## *Linnaea* (*Caprifoliaceae*)

| | |
|---|---|
| ***borealis*** | ILis WAbe |
| – subsp. ***americana*** | NHar NWCA WAbe |

## *Linum* (*Linaceae*)

| | |
|---|---|
| ***arboreum*** ♀H4 | GKev LLHF WAbe WPat |
| – NS 529 | NWCA |
| ***campanulatum*** | WThu |
| ***capitatum*** | WPat |
| ***dolomiticum*** | WPat |
| ***flavum*** | EPfP GKev XSen |
| – 'Compactum' | CMea EBee ECho GGar GKev LLHF SRms WCot |
| 'Gemmell's Hybrid' ♀H4 | ECho EWes MDKP NBir NMen WAbe WPat WThu |
| ***leonii*** | LRHS |
| ***monogynum*** | ECou |
| § – var. ***diffusum*** | ECou |
| – 'Nelson' | see *L. monogynum* var. *diffusum* |
| ***narbonense*** | CCse CSam EDif LBMP LRHS SBch SPhx |
| – 'Heavenly Blue' | NCGa WKif |
| § ***perenne*** | CArn CRWN EBee ECha ELan EPfP GMaP MAsh MHer MNHC NLar SIde SPer SPoG WJek WPer WWEG |
| – 'Album' | EBee ECha ELan EPfP NLar SPer WJek WPer |
| § – 'Blau Saphir' | EBee GQue MWat NLar |
| – Blue Sapphire | see *L. perenne* 'Blau Saphir' |
| – 'Himmelszelt' | LBMP NLar |
| – subsp. ***lewisii*** | NBir |
| – 'Nanum Diamond' | NLar |
| – 'Nanum Sapphire' | see *L. perenne* 'Blau Saphir' |
| – 'White Diamond' | SPoG |
| ***sibiricum*** | see *L. perenne* |
| ***suffruticosum*** subsp. ***salsoloides*** 'Nanum' | WPat WThu |
| ***uninerve*** | WAbe |

## *Lippia* (*Verbenaceae*)

| | |
|---|---|
| sp. | SWvt |
| ***canescens*** | see *Phyla nodiflora* var. *canescens* |
| ***chamaedrifolia*** | see *Verbena peruviana* |
| ***citriodora*** | see *Aloysia citrodora* |
| ***dulcis*** | CArn EOHP |
| ***nodiflora*** | see *Phyla nodiflora* |
| ***repens*** | see *Phyla nodiflora* |

## *Liquidambar* ✿ (*Altingiaceae*)

| | |
|---|---|
| ***acalycina*** | CDul CLnd CPMA EBee ELan EMil EPfP LRHS MGos MRav NLar SBir SCoo SGol SLim SPoG SSpi SSta WPGP WPat |
| – 'Burgundy Flush' | CPMA NLar SSta |
| – 'Spinners' | LRHS SSpi |
| ***formosana*** | CDul CEnd CMCN CMac EBee EPfP IArd LAst MGos MSnd NPCo SBir SGol SSta WPGP |

- 'Afterglow' CPMA SSta
- 'Ellen' CPMA SSta
- 'Gail' **new** SSta
- Monticola Group CPMA EPfP SBir SSta
- 'Woodleigh' SSta

***orientalis*** CDul CMCN CPMA EPfP EWTr LLHF NPCo SBir SSta

***styraciflua*** Widely available
- 'Andrew Hewson' CAbP CLnd CPMA EBee EPfP LRHS MAsh MBlu NLar SBir SReu SSta
- 'Anja' CPMA MBlu SBir SSta WPat
- 'Anneke' CPMA SBir SSta
- 'Aurea' see *L. styraciflua* 'Variegata' Overeynder
- 'Aurea Variegata' see *L. styraciflua* 'Variegata' Overeynder
- 'Aurora' CPMA SBir SLim
- 'Brodsman' NLar
- 'Burgundy' CLnd CPMA LLHF MBlu SBir SSta WPat
- 'Elstead Mill' CAbP
- 'Festeri' CEnd SBir SSta WPat
- 'Festival' CLnd CPMA MBlu SSta
- 'Frosty' (v) CPMA
- 'Globe' see *L. styraciflua* 'Gum Ball'
- 'Gold Beacon' **new** MPkF
- 'Golden Treasure' (v) CBcs CDul CMCN CPMA LRHS MAsh MBri MGos NLar SPer SPoG SReu SSta WPat
- 'Goldmember' CPMA SSta
- 'Granary Sunset' SBir SSta
- § - 'Gum Ball' CEnd CLnd CMCN CPMA ELon EPfP ERom EWes LLHF MGos NLar NPCo SBir SLim SSta WPat
- Happidaze = 'Hapdell' CEnd CPMA NLar SBir SSta WPat
- 'Jennifer Carol' CPMA NLar SBir SSta
- 'Kia' CAbP CEnd CPMA LLHF NLar SBir WPat
- 'Kirsten' CPMA
- 'Lane Roberts' ♀H4 Widely available
- 'Manon' (v) CDoC CEnd CPMA SBir SLim
- 'Midwest Sunset' CPMA MBlu WPat
- 'Moonbeam' (v) CEnd CPMA EBee NLar SBir SLim SSta WPat
- 'Moraine' CPMA SBir
- 'Naree' CPMA NLar SBir SSta
- 'Oconee' CEnd EPfP MAsh SSta WPat
- 'Paarl' (v) CPMA
- 'Palo Alto' CEnd CPMA LLHF LRHS MAsh MBlu SBir SCoo SLim SSta WPGP WPat
- 'Parasol' CAbP CEnd CLnd CPMA NLar NPCo SBir SSta
- 'Pendula' CLnd CPMA MBlu SBir SSta
- 'Penwood' CPMA NLar SSta
- 'Professor Louwjan' **new** NLar
- 'Red Sunset' **new** SSta
- 'Rotundiloba' CLnd CMCN CPMA EPfP LEdu LLHF MAsh SBir SSta WPat
- 'Schock's Gold' CPMA MAsh SSta WPat
- 'Silver King' (v) CMCN CMac CPMA EBee ECrN LRHS MBri MGos MMHG NLar NPCo SCoo SLim SPer SReu SSta WFoF WPat
- 'Slender Silhouette' CAbP CPMA EBee EPfP GKin LLHF LRHS MAsh MBlu NLar SBir SCoo SGol SLim SPoG SReu SSpi SSta WMou WPat
- 'Stared' CDul CEnd CLnd CPMA EBee LTen MBlu MBri NLar SBir SCoo SPoG SSta WPGP WPat
- 'Thea' CAbP CLnd CPMA EMil EPfP LRHS MAsh MBlu SBir SSta
- § - 'Variegata' Overeynder (v) CBcs CBot CDul CLnd CMac CPMA EBee ELan EPfP LRHS MAsh MGos SLim SSta WDin WPat
- 'White Star' (v) CPMA SSta
- 'Woorby Rose' SBir SSta
- 'Worplesdon' ♀H4 Widely available

## *Liriodendron* ✿ (*Magnoliaceae*)

'Chapel Hill' MBlu NLar

***chinense*** CBcs CDul CGHE CMCN EPfP MBlu SGol WFar WPGP

***chinense × tulipifera*** WPGP

'Doc Deforce's Delight' MBlu

***tulipifera*** ♀H4 Widely available
- 'Ardis' CMCN
- 'Arnold' SGol
- 'Aureomarginatum' (v) ♀H4 Widely available
- 'Fastigiatum' CDoC CDul CEnd CLnd CMCN CMac CTho EBee ECrN ELan EPfP GKin LRHS MAsh MBlu MBri MGos NLar SSta WPat
- 'Glen Gold' CEnd GKin MBlu
- 'Purgatory' MBlu

## *Liriope* ✿ (*Asparagaceae*)

'Big Blue' see *L. muscari* 'Big Blue'

§ ***exiliflora*** CEnd CLAP NLar WCot WWEG
- 'Ariaka-janshige' (v) LRHS WWEG
- Silvery Sunproof misapplied see *L. spicata* 'Gin-ryu', *L. muscari* 'Variegata'

§ ***gigantea*** CLAP EPPr SWat

***graminifolia*** misapplied see *L. muscari*

***hyacinthifolia*** see *Reineckea carnea*

***koreana*** EBee EPPr GCal
- B&SWJ 8821 WCru

'Majestic' CBct CHar CLAP WFar WHoo

'Minnow' WCot

***minor*** CMac

§ ***muscari*** ♀H4 Widely available
- B&SWJ 561 WCru
- 'Alba' see *L. muscari* 'Monroe White'
- Amethyst = 'Liptp' NPri
- § - 'Big Blue' CBar CBct CLAP CMac CPLG EBee ECtt ELon EPPr EPfP EPri EShb LEdu LHop LRHS LSRN MRav MSwo NLar SBfd SEND SUsu SWvt WCFE WMoo WWEG
- 'Christmas Tree' CLAP EPPr WHoo WMoo WWEG
- 'Evergreen Giant' see *L. gigantea*
- 'Gold-banded' (v) CBct CLAP EBee EPfP LHop LRHS NSti WCot WFar WWFP
- 'Goldfinger' CPLG EBee EPla WPGP
- 'Ingwersen' CPLG EBee ECho ELon EPPr EPfP LRHS NMRc XLum
- 'John Burch' (v) CBct CLAP CPLG EBee ELon EShb MCCP NLar NOak SMad WGrn WWEG
- 'Majestic' misapplied see *L. exiliflora*
- 'Moneymaker' EBee ECtt EPPr LRHS
- § - 'Monroe White' CBct CLAP CMac CPLG EBee EBla ECha ELon EPPr EPfP EShb EWTr LAst LEdu LRHS MRav NBid NLar NOak SPet WAul WFar WWEG
- 'Okina' (v) EBee ECtt ELon EWes MAvo MCot SMad SPer SPlb WCot
- 'Paul Aden' EPfP WPGP
- 'Pee Dee Ingot' CWGN EBee ECtt EShb LRHS LSou NGdn NLar

- 'Royal Purple' CBct CHar CLAP EBee ELon EPPr EPfP NBPC NGdn NLar SBfd WCot WGrn
- 'Silver Ribbon' CBro CLAP CWGN EBee EBla EPfP EWhm GQue LAst LBMP LRHS LSRN MGos NGdn NOak NSti SBch WWEG
- 'Super Blue' new EPPr
- 'Superba' WCot
§ - 'Variegata' (v) Widely available
- variegated, white-flowered (v) CDes CFir ECho
- 'Webster Wideleaf' EBee
'New Wonder' LEdu
***platyphylla*** see *L. muscari*
'Samantha' ECha NOak SBch
***spicata*** EBee ECho SWat WWEG XLum
- 'Alba' ECho MRav WTin
§ - 'Gin-ryu' (v) CBct CLAP CMac CPLG CPrp EBee ECtt ELon EPPr EShb EWes LEdu LSRN MCCP MRav NLar SLPl SMad WCot XLum
- 'Silver Dragon' see *L. spicata* 'Gin-ryu'
- 'Small Green' WWEG

## *Listera* (*Orchidaceae*)

***ovata*** WHer

## *Litchi* (*Sapindaceae*)

***chinensis*** CCCN

## *Lithocarpus* ✿ (*Fagaceae*)

***cleistocarpa*** new CHEx
***edulis*** CGHE CHEx CPLG SArc SKHP WPGP

## *Lithodora* (*Boraginaceae*)

§ ***diffusa*** ECho MWat SGol SRot
- 'Alba' CTri ECho GEdr MGos NBlu SPer SPoG WFar
- 'Cambridge Blue' NWad
- 'Compacta' EWes WAbe WPat
§ - 'Grace Ward' ♀H4 EPfP MMuc WAbe WFar WPat
§ - 'Heavenly Blue' ♀H4 Widely available
- 'Inverleith' ECho EWes LLHF
- 'Pete's Favourite' ECtt WAbe WPat
- 'Picos' CMea CPBP ECho GGar NLar NMen NSla WAbe WFar WPat WThu
- 'Star' PBR CMHG CMea ECtt EPfP GGar LRHS MAvo NLar SCoo SPer SPoG SRot SWvt
***fruticosa*** CArn
× ***intermedia*** see *Moltkia* × *intermedia*
§ ***oleifolia*** ♀H4 ECho EPot LLHF LRHS MWat NBir NMen SBch
***rosmarinifolia*** CSpe WCFE
***zahnii*** ECho EPot LLHF LRHS WFar WPat
- 'Azureness' CPBP CSpe WAbe

## *Lithophragma* (*Saxifragaceae*)

***parviflorum*** EWes NLar NWCA WAbe

## *Lithospermum* (*Boraginaceae*)

***diffusum*** see *Lithodora diffusa*
***doerfleri*** see *Moltkia doerfleri*
'Grace Ward' see *Lithodora diffusa* 'Grace Ward'
'Heavenly Blue' see *Lithodora diffusa* 'Heavenly Blue'
***officinale*** CArn GPoy NMir
***oleifolium*** see *Lithodora oleifolia*
***purpureocaeruleum*** see *Buglossoides purpurocaerulea*

## *Litsea* (*Lauraceae*)

***glauca*** see *Neolitsea sericea*
***japonica*** SVen

## *Littonia* (*Colchicaceae*)

***modesta*** CRHN ECho

## *Livistona* (*Arecaceae*)

***australis*** EAmu LPal
***chinensis*** ♀H1 CPHo EAmu LPal SBig SChr
***decora*** EAmu LPal
***mariae*** EAmu LPal
***nitida*** EAmu SChr
***saribus*** EAmu

## *Lloydia* (*Liliaceae*)

***serotina*** GAuc

## *Loasa* (*Loasaceae*)

***triphylla*** var. ***volcanica*** EWes WSHC

## *Lobelia* (*Campanulaceae*)

B&SWJ 8220 from Vietnam WCru
***aberdarica*** CHEx
***angulata*** see *Pratia angulata*
***angustifolia*** CHll
***bequeartii*** GCal
***bridgesii*** CDTJ CPLG EWes EWld EWll GCal GGal GGar LLHF NGBl WAle WHer WHil WKif WMoo WPGP
§ ***cardinalis*** ♀H3 CArn CBen CHEx CMac CRWN EBla EHon ELon EPfP GAbr GMaP LPBA LRHS MMuc NBlu NLar NPer SMrm SPer SPet SPlb SRms SWat SWvt WFar WMAq
- 'Bee's Flame' CFir CPrp CWGN EPla GGar LBMP LRHS MCot MRav MSpe NBre NEgg NGdn SAga SPad SUsu SWat
§ - 'Elmfeuer' CMHG EBee EHoe EPfP EShb LAst LSou MWat NLar NPri SBfd SMrm SPlb SWvt WFar XLum
- 'Eulalia Berridge' CAby EBee ECtt NPnk SMrm WFar WSHC
- subsp. ***graminea*** var. ***multiflora*** CFir
§ - 'Queen Victoria' ♀H3 Widely available
N - 'Russian Princess' misapplied CAby EGxp LRHS LSou MAsh NGdn NPnk SWvt WCAu WWEG WWlt
***chinensis*** LLWG
'Cinnabar Deep Red' see *L.* × *speciosa* 'Fan Tiefrot'
'Cinnabar Rose' see *L.* × *speciosa* 'Fan Zinnoberrosa'
Compliment Blue see *L.* × *speciosa* 'Kompliment Blau'
Compliment Deep Red see *L.* × *speciosa* 'Kompliment Tiefrot'
Compliment Purple see *L.* × *speciosa* 'Kompliment Purpur'
Compliment Scarlet see *L.* × *speciosa* 'Kompliment Scharlach'
***dortmanna*** GAuc
Elizabeth Strangman selection NDov
***erinus*** Big Blue = 'Weslobigblue' PBR LAst
- 'Kathleen Mallard' (d) CCCN ECtt SWvt
- 'Purple Star' LBMP LSou
- 'Richardii' see *L. richardsonii*
- 'Sailor Star' LAst
***excelsa*** CSpr EShb GGar MTPN SGar SPav WAle WFar

- B&SWJ 9513 WCru
Fan Deep Red see *L.* × *speciosa* 'Fan Tiefrot'
Fan Deep Rose see *L.* × *speciosa* 'Fan Orchidrosa'
Fan Salmon see *L.* × *speciosa* 'Fan Lachs'
'Flamingo' see *L.* × *speciosa* 'Pink Flamingo'
***fulgens*** see *L. cardinalis*
- Saint Elmo's Fire see *L. cardinalis* 'Elmfeuer'
× ***gerardii*** see *L.* × *speciosa*
***gibberoa*** CDTJ CHEx
'Gladys Lindley' NLar
***grandidentata*** F&M 133 WPGP
'Hadspen Purple'PBR see *L.* × *speciosa* 'Hadspen Purple'
'Hot Tiger' LAst LBMP
***inflata*** CArn EOHP GPoy
***kalmii*** WPer
***laxiflora*** CHid CHll SAga SHom
- B&SWJ 9064 WCru
- F&M 71 GCal
- var. ***angustifolia*** CDTJ CHEx CPrp CSam EBee ECtt EPfP EWld GCal LRHS MSpe SMrm SPav SPoG SRms WAle WWlt
***linnaeoides*** SPlb
'Lipstick' WWEG
***montana*** EWld
- B&SWJ 8220 WCru
***pedunculata*** see *Pratia pedunculata*
'Periwinkle Blue' **new** LAst
'Pink Passion' LRHS
***polyphylla*** ECtt MSCN WAle
'Queen Victoria' see *L. cardinalis* 'Queen Victoria'
§ ***richardsonii*** ♀H1+3 ECtt LAst NBlu SWvt
'Royal Velvet' IPot
***seguinii*** B&SWJ 7065 WCru
***sessilifolia*** CPLG EBee GMac LLWG LPBA WCot WPer
- B&SWJ 8875 WCru
***siphilitica*** Widely available
- 'Alba' CEnt CSam EBee EBla EPfP GCal LPBA LRHS SBch SBfd SPav SRms SWat SWvt WBor WFar WHrl WMnd WMoo WPer WShi XLum
- blue-flowered CSpe MMuc NCGa NLar SWat SWvt
- 'Rosea' MNrw
'Sonia' SWat
§ × ***speciosa*** CEnt IKil MHer NBre SMrm SVic SWat WBor WFar WMoo WSHC XLum
- 'Butterfly Blue' EBee LBMP SPad
- 'Butterfly Rose' SRot
- 'Cherry Ripe' CPrp GCra LLHF NHol
- 'Dark Crusader' CPrp EBee ECGP ECtt ELan EPfP LAst LBMP LRHS MCot MSCN MWhi NHol SAga SWat WMnd
- (Fan Series) 'Fan Blau' EPfP LRHS NBir NBlu WWEG
- - 'Fan Burgundy' CEnt CPrp EPfP LRHS NGdn NLar SPet WHil
§ - - 'Fan Lachs' EPfP NBPC SAga SPet
§ - - 'Fan Orchidrosa' ♀H3-4 CHEx EPfP EWTr LRHS NBir NGdn NLar SPet SRot
- - 'Fan Scharlach' ♀H3-4 EBee EPfP LRHS MAvo MGos NBir NLar SGar SPoG SRot SWvt WCFE WDyG WHil WShi
§ - - 'Fan Tiefrot' ♀H3-4 EPfP MWea NBlu SPet SRms SWat SWvt WCot WPer
§ - - 'Fan Zinnoberrosa' ♀H3-4 CEnt CFir CMMP EBee SRms SRot SWvt WMoo WPer
- 'Grape Knee-high' EBee EPfP GCra LLHF LSRN SWat
§ - 'Hadspen Purple'PBR CAby CMHG CSpe CWGN EBee ELan EPfP IPot LRHS LSRN MAsh MBri MCCP MCot MWea NCGa NDov NHol NSti SHar SWat SWvt WWlt
- 'Kimbridge Beet' CMac
- Kompliment Series WWEG
§ - - 'Kompliment Blau' CFir CWat SPet SWvt WPer
§ - - 'Kompliment Purpur' MNrw SPet SWvt
§ - - 'Kompliment Scharlach' ♀H3-4 CAby EBee EPfP LHop MNrw NHol NPer SPer SPet SWvt WFar WMnd WPer WWEG
§ - - 'Kompliment Tiefrot' CWat MNrw NLar SPet SWvt WPer
- 'Monet Moment' EBee EBla EWes GCal SPoG SWvt
- 'Pauline' ECtt
- 'Pink Elephant' ♀H4 GCra MDKP NBre SHar WFar WWEG
§ - 'Pink Flamingo' CMMP EBla NLar SPer SWat WFar WMoo WShi
- 'Purple Towers' NBre
- 'Rosenkavalier' EBee ECtt LRHS MCot NDov WFar
- 'Rosy Pink' SMrm
- 'Ruby Slippers' EBee ECtt ELan EPfP LAst LSRN NCGa SWat WFar WWEG
N - 'Russian Princess' purple-flowered CFir CPrp CTri EBee ECtt EHoe ELan LAst LBMP LHop LPBA LSou MBri MCCP MCot MHer MSCN MSpe NCGa NHol SAga SBfd SMrm SPer WFar WMnd WMoo
- 'Sparkle deVine' WFar
- 'Sparkling Burgundy' **new** LRHS
- 'Sparkling Ruby' LBuc MCot
- 'Tania' Widely available
§ - 'Vedrariensis' Widely available
- 'Wildwood Splendor' WFar
- 'Will Scarlet' LRHS SAga
'Star Sky' LSou
'Tania's Sister' **new** WGrn
***treadwellii*** see *Pratia angulata* 'Treadwellii'
***tupa*** Widely available
- JCA 12527 IBlr MTPN
- Archibald's form CPLG GCra WCot
***urens*** CRDP WPGP
***valida*** EWld SGar SWvt WFar
- 'True Blue' CWGN SBrd SWvt
***vedrariensis*** see *L.* × *speciosa* 'Vedrariensis'
***wollastonii*** SPlb

## *Lobularia* (*Brassicaceae*)

***maritima*** ECtt

## *Loeselia* (*Polemoniaceae*)

***mexicana*** CHll

## loganberry see *Rubus* × *loganobaccus*

## *Lomandra* (*Asparagaceae*)

***confertifolia*** ECou
- 'Wingarra' EHoe NOak
***filiformis*** Savanna Blue = 'Lfm500' ESwi LSou NOak
***hystrix*** SPlb
***longifolia*** ECou GCal LEdu SPlb
- 'Kulnura' ECou
- Nyalla = 'Lm400'PBR **new** LHop
- 'Orford' ECou
- Tanika = 'Lm300'PBR EBee ESwi GBin LTen MWea NOak

## *Lomaria* see *Blechnum*

## *Lomatia* (*Proteaceae*)

***dentata*** LRHS

| |  |  |
|---|---|---|
| | ***ferruginea*** | CBcs CDoC CPLG CTsd EPfP GBin GGal IDee SArc SKHP WCru WPGP |
| | ***fraseri*** | EPfP LRHS SBrd SSpi |
| | ***hirsuta*** | SKHP |
| | ***longifolia*** | see *L. myricoides* |
| § | ***myricoides*** | CBcs CCCN CDoC CPLG CTsd ELan EPfP LRHS MBri NLar SKHP SLon SPer SSpi |
| | ***tinctoria*** | CBcs CDoC CPLG EPfP IDee SArc SSpi |

## *Lomatium* (*Apiaceae*)

| |  |  |
|---|---|---|
| | ***foeniculaceum*** subsp. ***fimbriatum*** NNS 06-349 | WCot |
| | ***grayi*** | SPhx |

## *Lonicera* ✿ (*Caprifoliaceae*)

| |  |  |
|---|---|---|
| | sp. | CMen |
| | B&SWJ 2654 from Sikkim | WCru |
| | KR 291 | ELon |
| | SDR 6044 | GKev |
| § | ***acuminata*** | CFir EBee LRHS |
| | - B&SWJ 3480 | WCru |
| | - B&SWJ 6743 | WCru |
| | - B&SWJ 6815 | WCru |
| | ***alberti*** | CDul MBNS MMuc NLar |
| | ***alseuosmoides*** | EBee EBla IArd LRHS NLar SAga SKHP SLon SPoG WCru WPGP WSHC |
| | × ***americana*** misapplied | see *L.* × *italica* Tausch |
| § | × ***americana*** (Miller) K. Koch | CBcs CRHN EPfP MAsh MGos MMuc MRav MSwo MWhi NLar NWea SEND SGar SKHP SLim SRms WBor |
| § | × ***brownii*** 'Dropmore Scarlet' | Widely available |
| | - 'Fuchsioides' misapplied | see *L.* × *brownii* 'Dropmore Scarlet' |
| | - 'Fuchsioides' K. Koch | WSHC |
| | ***caerulea*** | MRav STre |
| | - var. ***altaica*** | LEdu |
| | - var. ***edulis*** | CAgr LEdu MCoo |
| | - var. ***kamtschatica*** | CAgr NLar |
| § | ***caprifolium*** ♀H4 | CDoC CRHN EBla ELan EPfP LRHS MAsh NLar SBrd SPer |
| | - 'Anna Fletcher' | CRHN CSPN LSRN NHaw WCFE |
| | - 'Cornish Cream' | SGol |
| | - f. ***pauciflora*** | see *L.* × *italica* Tausch |
| | ***chaetocarpa*** | CEnd MRav WSHC |
| | ***chamissoi*** | NLar |
| | 'Clavey's Dwarf' | see *L.* × *xylosteoides* 'Clavey's Dwarf' |
| | 'Copper Beauty'PBR | CAlb EPPr LBuc LSRN LSou SLim |
| | ***crassifolia*** | SBrt WCot |
| | - 'Little Honey' | CWCL EPPr MMHG MRav WCot |
| | ***deflexicalyx*** | EPfP NLar |
| | 'Early Cream' | see *L. caprifolium* |
| | ***elisae*** | CAbP CMac CPMA EPfP IDee NLar WPat WSHC |
| | ***etrusca*** | CFir MRav |
| | - 'Donald Waterer' ♀H4 | CRHN EPfP LRHS LSRN NLar WFar WGor |
| | - 'Michael Rosse' | ELan IArd LRHS MBNS SKHP SRms |
| | - 'Superba' ♀H4 | CRHN EBee ECtt ELan EPfP LRHS MAsh NLar SEND SLim SPer SPoG WFar WSHC |
| | 'Fire Cracker' | SLon |
| | ***flexuosa*** | see *L. japonica* var. *repens* |
| | ***fragrantissima*** | Widely available |
| | ***giraldii*** misapplied | see *L. acuminata* |
| | ***giraldii*** Rehder | CBot EBee EPfP MAsh MRav SBrd SLim |
| | ***glabrata*** | SCoo SLim |
| | - B&SWJ 2150 | WCru |
| | ***glehnii*** | GAuc |
| | 'Golden Trumpet' | CWGN LRHS LSRN |
| | ***grata*** | see *L.* × *americana* (Miller) K. Koch |
| | × ***heckrottii*** | CDoC CRHN CSBt ECtt MGos NLar WDin |
| § | - 'American Beauty' | EBee NBlu |
| | - 'Gold Flame' misapplied | see *L.* × *heckrottii* 'American Beauty' |
| | - 'Gold Flame' ambig. | CChe GKin LSRN LTen NLar |
| | - 'Gold Flame' hort. | CDul CMac COIW EBee ELan EPfP LBuc LRHS MAsh MBri MGos MRav NBlu NHol SBfd SLim SPer SRms WDin WFar WMoo WSHC |
| § | ***henryi*** | Widely available |
| | - B&SWJ 8109 | WCru |
| | - Sich 1489 | WPGP |
| | - 'Copper Beauty' | CAlb CEnd CFir EQua GKin LHop LRHS LSRN MAsh MGos MRav NLar SGol SLon SPoG WDin WPGP |
| | - var. ***subcoriacea*** | see *L. henryi* |
| | ***hildebrandiana*** | CCCN CHII CPLG CRHN EShb LRHS MOWG SKHP WPGP |
| | 'Honey Baby'PBR | ELon EPfP LLHF LRHS MAsh MBlu NHol NWad |
| | ***insularis*** | see *L. morrowii* |
| | ***involucrata*** | CFee CHII CMCN CMHG CPLG CWib EPPr GQui LHop MBNS MBlu MMuc NChi SEND SPer WCFE WDin WFar |
| | - var. ***ledebourii*** | CEnt ELan EPfP LAst LLHF LRHS MRav SDys SKHP WGob |
| | - 'Orange Dwarf' | SKHP |
| | × ***italica*** ambig. | NPer SPer |
| § | × ***italica*** Tausch ♀H4 | CRHN CSam CTri ECtt LRHS MBNS MSwo NEgg NPer SCoo SKHP WDin WFar WPnn |
| § | - Harlequin = 'Sherlite'PBR (v) | CBot CMac CSPN EGxp EHoe EPfP GKin LRHS LSRN MAsh MGos SLim SPlb SRms SWvt WCot |
| | ***japonica*** | CCVT CMen |
| § | - 'Aureoreticulata' (v) | CDul CMac CWib ECrN EHoe ELan ELon EPfP EShb LRHS LSRN MGos MRav MWhi NPer SGar SGol SPer SPet SRms STre WDin WFar |
| | - 'Cream Cascade' | COIW EBee LRHS MSwo NLar SCoo SGol |
| | - 'Dart's Acumen' | CRHN |
| | - 'Dart's World' | CAlb LRHS MBri WFar |
| | - 'Halliana' ♀H4 | Widely available |
| | - 'Hall's Prolific' | CDoC CDul CSBt CWSG EBee ECrN ELan EPfP LBuc LRHS LSRN MAsh MBlu MBri MGos MHer MRav MSwo MWat NBlu NEgg SBfd SGol SLim SPad SPoG SWvt WDin WFar |
| § | - 'Horwood Gem' (v) | EBee ECtt LSRN NLar SCoo SLim WFar |
| | - 'Maskerade' (v) | LLHF NBro NLar |
| | - 'Mint Crisp'PBR (v) | CMac CSBt CWGN CWSG ECrN ECtt ELan EPfP LAst LRHS LSRN LSou MAsh MBri MGos NLar SBfd SGol SLim SLon SPad SPer SPoG SWvt WDin WFar |
| | - 'Peter Adams' | see *L. japonica* 'Horwood Gem' |
| § | - var. ***repens*** ♀H4 | Widely available |
| | - 'Variegata' | see *L. japonica* 'Aureoreticulata' |
| | ***korolkowii*** | CBot CPMA EBee EPPr EPfP MBNS NBir NLar SPoG WCFE WSHC |

|  |  |
|---|---|
| - 'Blue Velvet' | MCoo NLar |
| - var. ***zabelii*** misapplied | see *L. tatarica* 'Zabelii' |
| - var. ***zabelii*** (Rehder) Rehder | ELan |
| ***lanceolata*** BWJ 7935 | WCru |
| ***maackii*** | CHll CMCN CPMA EBee EPPr EPfP IGor MRav NLar WCFE |
| - f. ***podocarpa*** | SPoG |
| * ***macgregorii*** | CMCN |
| ***macrantha*** B&SWJ 11687 | WCru |
| - WWJ 11606 | WCru |
| 'Mandarin' | CDoC ELan LRHS MAsh MBlu MGos MRav NLar SCoo SGol SLim SWvt WPat WSHC |
| ***maximowiczii*** var. ***sachalinensis*** | NLar |
| § ***morrowii*** | CMCN GAuc |
| ***myrtillus*** | GAuc NLar |
| ***nitida*** | CAlb CBar CBcs CCVT CDul CMac CMen CSBt CTri ECrN EPfP NWea SBfd SEWo SGol SPer STre SWal WDin WFar WHar |
| - 'Baggesen's Gold' ♀H4 | Widely available |
| - 'Eden Spring' | NPro |
| - Edmée Gold = 'Briloni' | MAsh |
| - 'Elegant' | WDin |
| - 'Fertilis' | SPer |
| - 'Lemon Beauty' (v) | Widely available |
| - 'Lemon Queen' | CWib ELan MMuc MSwo SEND |
| - 'Lemon Spreader' | CBcs |
| § - 'Maigrün' | CAlb CBar CBcs CCVT CDul EPfP MSwo NPro SBfd SPer STre SWvt WDin WFar |
| - Maygreen | see *L. nitida* 'Maigrün' |
| - 'Red Tips' | EHoe EPPr EPfP EPla GKin MGos SBfd SCoo WDin WFar WMoo |
| - 'Silver Beauty' (v) | CDul CMac CWib EBee EHoe EPfP LAst LHop MGos MRav MSwo NBlu NEgg NHol SAga SBfd SGar SPer SPlb SRms STre SWvt WDin WFar WMoo |
| - 'Twiggy' (v) | CAlb CDoC CSBt EDAr EHoe ELon LBuc LRHS MAsh NEgg NHol NLar SBfd WGrn |
| ***periclymenum*** | CArn CCVT CDul CRWN CTri GPoy MHer MLHP MRav NLar NMir NWea SPlb WDin WPnn WSFF |
| - 'Belgica' misapplied | see *L.* × *italica* Tausch |
| - 'Belgica' | Widely available |
| - Caprilia Imperial = 'Inov86' | SBfd |
| - 'Florida' | see *L. periclymenum* 'Serotina' |
| - 'Graham Thomas' ♀H4 | Widely available |
| - 'Harlequin' PBR | see *L.* × *italica* Harlequin |
| - 'Heaven Scent' | LBuc LSRN MNHC NLar WFar WGwG WPnn |
| - 'Honeybush' | CDoC CPMA CSPN CWGN LBMP LRHS MAsh MBri MGos NHol SLim WMoo |
| - 'La Gasnérie' | SLim WPnn |
| - 'Munster' | WPnn WSHC |
| - 'Purple Queen' | CChe |
| - 'Red Gables' | CWan ELon LSRN MBNS MGos NLar SCoo SEND SLim WCot WGor WKif WPnn |
| - 'Scentsation' PBR | CMac CSBt CWGN EPfP LAst LBuc LRHS MAsh MBri NLar SCoo SLon SPoG |
| N - 'Serotina' ♀H4 | Widely available |
| * - ***sulphurea*** | WFar |

|  |  |
|---|---|
| - 'Sweet Sue' | COlW CRHN CSPN CSpe EBee ECtt ELan ELon EPfP LBuc LRHS LSRN MAsh MBNS MBri MGos MLHP MSwo NEgg NHol SCoo SPoG SWvt WFar WMoo |
| - yellow | NEgg |
| ***pileata*** | CBcs CCVT CDoy CDul CMac CSBt CTri EBee ECrN EHoe ELan EPfP EShb LBuc LRHS MGos MSwo MWhi NPer NWea SBfd SGol SPer SPoG SRms STre WCFE WDin WFar WHar |
| - 'Moss Green' | CBod CDoC |
| - 'Pilot' | SLPl |
| - 'Silver Lining' (v) | EPla |
| - 'Stockholm' | SLPl |
| ***pilosa*** Willd. F&M 207 | WPGP |
| × ***purpusii*** | CDoC CHll CMac COlW CRHN CTri CWSG CWib EBee ECrN EPfP EWTr LSRN MBNS MGos MLHP MWat SBfd SPer SPoG SRms WCFE WFar WSHC |
| - 'Spring Romance' | CMac |
| - 'Winter Beauty' ♀H4 | Widely available |
| ***ramosissima*** | NLar |
| ***saccata*** | CPMA EPfP |
| ***sempervirens*** ♀H4 | CBot CMac CRHN CSBt MBNS MRav WFar WSHC |
| - 'Cedar Lane' | CRHN LRHS |
| - 'Dropmore Scarlet' | see *L.* × *brownii* 'Dropmore Scarlet' |
| - 'Leo' | CSPN CWGN |
| N - f. ***sulphurea*** | EPfP WSHC |
| - - 'John Clayton' | LRHS SKHP |
| ***setifera*** | CBot |
| - 'Daphnis' | CPMA EPfP |
| ***similis*** var. ***delavayi*** ♀H4 | CBot CChe CRHN CSPN CWGN EBee ELan EPfP LRHS MAsh MBri MNHC MRav NEgg SBfd SBrd SDix SEND SLPl SPoG SRms WCot WCru WFar WPGP WSHC |
| ***splendida*** | CBot WSHC |
| 'Spring Bouquet' | LRHS |
| ***standishii*** | CTri EBee WDin WFar |
| - 'Budapest' | LEdu LLHF LRHS MAsh MBlu MBri NLar SPoG WPat |
| ***stenantha*** | IGor |
| ***subaequalis*** | CGHE |
| - Og 93.329 | SKHP WPGP WSHC |
| Sweet Isabel = 'Genbel' PBR | EPfP LBuc LRHS NCGa SKHP |
| ***syringantha*** | CArn CRHN EBee ECrN ELan EPfP LAst LEdu MBri MGos MMuc MNrw MRav MWhi NEgg NLar NPro SEND SLPl SPer WBor WCFE WDin WFar WSHC |
| - 'Grandiflora' | GQui |
| ***tatarica*** | CHll CMCN CWib EBee MRav WFar |
| - 'Alba' | CPMA EPPr |
| - 'Arnold Red' | CBcs EBee ELan EPPr EPfP MBlu MHer NLar SEND WBor WDin |
| - 'Hack's Red' | CWib EBee EPPr EPfP LHop LRHS LSou MRav SAga SCoo SKHP SPer SPoG SVen SWvt WCot WDin WFar |
| - 'Rosea' | EPPr WCot |
| § - 'Zabelii' | EPfP |
| × ***tellmanniana*** | Widely available |
| - 'Joan Sayers' | LSRN SCoo SLim WCFE |
| ***thibetica*** | MBlu SPer WFar |
| ***tianschanica*** | GAuc |
| ***tragophylla*** ♀H4 | CDoC CDoy CSBt ELan EPfP GGal LRHS LSRN MAsh MBNS MBri |

| | |
|---|---|
| | MRav SBrd SCoo SEND SLim SPer SPoG SSpi SWvt WDin WSHC |
| - 'Maurice Foster' | ELan EPfP MBNS WSHC |
| - 'Pharaoh's Trumpet' | EPfP LRHS MAsh SLon |
| ***webbiana*** | ELan |
| × ***xylosteoides*** | WFar |
| § - 'Clavey's Dwarf' | EBee EPPr GKin LLHF NHol |
| ***xylosteum*** | CArn EBee NLar WFar |

## *Lophomyrtus* (*Myrtaceae*)

| | |
|---|---|
| § ***bullata*** | CAbP CDTJ CTrC CTsd GQui SPer WFar |
| - 'Matai Bay' | CBcs CTrC |
| § × ***ralphii*** | MHer |
| - 'Black Pearl' | EShb LBuc LRHS SBfd SLim SPtl |
| - 'Gloriosa' (v) | CDoC CTrC EPfP |
| - 'Kathryn' | CBcs CDoC EBee ELan EMil EPfP LRHS NLar SPoG SRGP SSpi |
| - 'Krinkly' | SVen |
| - 'Little Star' (v) | CDoC CTrC LRHS SPoG WPat |
| - Logan's form (v) | CBcs LRHS |
| - 'Multicolor' (v) | CBcs CTrC EBee EPfP LRHS NPri SLim |
| - 'Pixie' | CBcs CDoC CFee CTrC EPfP LRHS MAsh SPoG SVen WPat |
| - 'Red Dragon' | CBcs CTrC CTsd CWSG IDee LEdu LRHS LSou MAsh WFar WPat |
| - 'Red Pixie' | CDoC |
| - 'Red Wing' | LRHS |
| § - 'Traversii' (v) | SPoG |
| - 'Tricolor' (v) | WFar |
| - 'Variegata' (v) | MHer |
| - 'Wild Cherry' | CTrC GGar LRHS |

## *Lophosoria* (*Dicksoniaceae*)

| | |
|---|---|
| ***quadripinnata*** | CBty CDTJ CFir CKel EAmu SBig WPGP WRic |

## *Lophospermum* (*Plantaginaceae*)

| | |
|---|---|
| 'Cream Delight' | CCCN |
| § ***erubescens*** ♀H2-3 | CBot CRHN GMac SBch SGar |
| § 'Magic Dragon' | LSou SVic |
| § 'Red Dragon' | CCCN EShb SBch SGar |
| § ***scandens*** | CCCN CRHN ELan |
| 'Summer Cream' **new** | LAst |
| 'Wine Red' | LAst |

## loquat see *Eriobotrya japonica*

## *Loropetalum* (*Hamamelidaceae*)

| | |
|---|---|
| ***chinense*** | CWib |
| - Black Pearl | see *L. chinense* 'Pearl' |
| - 'China Pink' | CBcs |
| - 'Ming Dynasty' | CAbP CTrC MAsh SSta |
| - 'Pearl' | CWSG |
| - 'Rose Blush' | ECho SHeu |
| - f. ***rubrum*** | CBcs CPLG CWib |
| - - 'Blush' | CPMA SBfd SBrd SSpi |
| - - 'Burgundy' | CTrC MPkF |
| - - 'Daybreak's Flame' | CPMA CTrC EGxp LRHS MPkF SSta WGob |
| - - 'Fire Dance' | CAbP CBcs CCCN CDoC CHll CPMA CTrC EGxp ELon EPfP IDee LRHS MAsh MGos SBfd SHeu SPoG SPtl SSpi SWvt WCot WFar WGrn WHlf WPat |
| - - 'Fire Glow' | IDee LRHS |
| - - 'Pipa's Red' | MGos MPkF |
| - 'Snowdance' | CAbP |
| - 'Tang Dynasty' | CTrC ESwi LRHS MMuc SSta |

## *Lotus* (*Papilionaceae*)

| | |
|---|---|
| ***berthelotii*** | CCCN CDTJ CHEx ECtt ELan EOHP MCot SBfd SPet |
| - deep red-flowered ♀H1+3 | SBfd SWvt |
| ***berthelotii*** × ***maculatus*** ♀H1+3 | CCCN EShb MSCN |
| ***corniculatus*** | CArn CHab EWil MCoo MHer MMuc MNHC NLan NMir SEND SIde WSFF XLum |
| - 'Plenus' (d) | NLar WPer |
| 'Gold Flash' | SBfd |
| ***hirsutus*** ♀H3-4 | Widely available |
| - 'Brimstone' (v) | CWSG CWib ECtt LHop LRHS SBfd SPer SPoG SWvt XSen |
| - Little Boy Blue = 'Lisbob'PBR | CSBt EBee EPfP LRHS LSou LSqu MAsh SBfd SSpi |
| - 'Lois' | EBee EPfP LHop LRHS MDKP SPoG WPGP |
| ***jacobaeus*** | EShb MCot |
| ***maculatus*** | EOHP MOWG SMrm SPet |
| ***maritimus*** | CPom SRot |
| ***pedunculatus*** | see *L. uliginosus* |
| ***pentaphyllus*** | NLar XSen |
| ***tetragonolobus*** | CPom SPhx SVic |
| § ***uliginosus*** | CHab EWil MCoo NMir WSFF |

## lovage see *Levisticum officinale*

## *Loxostigma* (*Gesneriaceae*)

| | |
|---|---|
| ***kurzii*** GWJ 9342 | WCru |

## *Ludwigia* (*Onagraceae*)

| | |
|---|---|
| ***uruguayensis*** | LPBA |

## *Luetkea* (*Rosaceae*)

| | |
|---|---|
| ***pectinata*** | GEdr NRya |

## *Luma* (*Myrtaceae*)

| | |
|---|---|
| § ***apiculata*** ♀H3 | Widely available |
| § - 'Glanleam Gold' (v) ♀H3 | Widely available |
| - 'Nana' **new** | LEdu WJek |
| - 'Penlee' | WJek |
| - 'Saint Hilary' (v) | GGar LRHS SBfd WJek |
| - 'Variegata' (v) | CMHG CTri SAga SLim |
| § ***chequen*** | CBcs CFee EBee GGar IDee LEdu LRHS MHer NLar WFar WJek WMoo |

## *Lunaria* (*Brassicaceae*)

| | |
|---|---|
| § ***annua*** | MNHC NPri SIde SWat WHer WJek WSFF |
| - var. ***albiflora*** ♀H4 | MMuc NBir SEND SWat WCot |
| I - - 'Alba Variegata' (v) | CSpe WBrk WTin |
| - 'Chedglow' | CNat |
| - 'Corfu Blue' | CSpe EDif |
| - 'Munstead Purple' | CSpe |
| - 'Nettleton' **new** | CNat |
| - 'Variegata' (v) | NBir SWat WCot WHer |
| - violet-flowered | NBir |
| ***biennis*** | see *L. annua* |
| ***rediviva*** | CSpe EBee ECGP ECha EPPr EPla GAbr GBin GCal GCra GGar IBlr IFro LEdu LRHS MMuc NBid NPer NSti WCot WFar WHer WPGP |
| - 'Partway White' | WCot |

## *Lunathyrium* (*Woodsiaceae*)

| | |
|---|---|
| ***pycnosorum*** | ISha WRic |

## *Lupinus* ✿ (*Papilionaceae*)

| | |
|---|---|
| B&SWJ 10309 from Guatemala | WCru |
| 'African Sunset' | CWCL |
| ***albus*** | CArn |
| 'Animal' | CWCL |
| 'Approaching Storm' | SMrm |
| ***arboreus*** ♀H4 | Widely available |
| - blue and white-flowered | NChi |
| - 'Blue Boy' | ELan LSRN |
| - blue-flowered | CHar CTrC CWCL GGar MCot MWat NBPC SBfd SPer SPlb SPoG SWvt WFar |
| - 'Chelsea Blue' | EPfP LRHS |
| - mixed | CArn |
| - prostrate | MDKP MMHG |
| - 'Rhubarb and Custard' | CWCL |
| - 'Snow Queen' | CWCL LRHS NChi SPer SPoG |
| - 'Sulphur Yellow' | SWvt |
| - white-flowered | CSpe GCal GGar SPlb |
| - yellow and blue-flowered | NBir SRkn |
| - yellow-flowered | CTrC ELan GGar MCot MLHP WWEG |
| ***arboreus* × *variicolor*** | CHid |
| ***arcticus*** | CSpe |
| Band of Nobles Series ♀H4 | ECtt WFar |
| 'Beefeater' | CWCL EBee |
| 'Bishop's Tipple' | CWCL EWes |
| 'Blossom'PBR | CWCL IPot LRHS LSRN MBri |
| 'Blue Streak' | CWCL |
| ***bogotensis*** B&SWJ 10761 | WCru |
| 'Brimstone' | CWCL |
| 'Bruiser' | CWCL |
| 'Bubblegum' | CWCL |
| 'Camelot Blue' | EPfP |
| 'Carmen' | CWCL |
| 'Chameleon' | CWCL |
| ***chamissonis*** | CHll CSpe CWCL ELan EWes LHop LRHS MCot SMrm SPer SPhx WFar |
| 'Chandelier' (Band of Nobles Series) | CBcs CSBt CTri EBee ECtt ELan EPfP LRHS MBri MCot MLLN MNHC MWat NBir NBlu NGBl NPri SBfd SBrd SMrm SPer SPoG SWal SWvt WCAu WFar WMnd XLum |
| ***costaricensis*** B&SWJ 10487 | WCru |
| 'Desert Sun' | CWCL EBee |
| Dwarf Gallery hybrids | WMoo |
| 'Dwarf Lulu' | see *L.* 'Lulu' |
| Gallery Series | CSBt SCoo SPlb WFar |
| - 'Gallery Blue' | ECtt ELan EPfP LRHS LSRN NBlu NLar NPri NVic SBrd SCoo SMrm SPer SPoG WFar |
| - 'Gallery Pink' | ELan EPfP LRHS NLar NPri SCoo SMrm SPer SPoG WFar |
| - 'Gallery Red' | ECtt ELan EPfP GAbr LRHS NBlu NLar NPri NVic SCoo SMrm SPer SPoG WFar |
| - 'Gallery Rose' | ELan LSRN SPoG |
| - 'Gallery White' | ELan EPfP GAbr LRHS NBlu NLar NPri NVic SCoo SPer SPoG WFar |
| - 'Gallery Yellow' | ECtt ELan EPfP GAbr LRHS NLar NPri NVic SMrm SPer SPoG |
| 'Gladiator' | CWCL EWes |
| 'Imperial Robe' | CWCL |
| 'Inspiration' | CWCL |
| 'Ivory Chiffon' | GBin |
| 'Le Gentilhomme' (Band of Nobles Series) | MCot XLum |
| 'Lindy Lou' | CWCL |
| § 'Lulu' | ECtt EPfP LRHS MWat SBfd SBrd SPer SPoG SWvt WFar WMoo |
| 'Manhattan Lights'PBR | CWCL EWes IPot LRHS MBri |
| 'Masterpiece' | CWCL GBin LRHS MBri MWea |
| Minarette Group | CTri ECtt SPet SRms WFar |
| 'Morello Cherry' | CWCL |
| 'Mrs Perkins' | SMrm |
| 'My Castle' (Band of Nobles Series) | CBcs CSBt CTri EBee ECtt ELan EPfP LRHS LSRN MBri MGos MNHC MWat NGBl NPri SBfd SBrd SPer SPoG SWal SWvt WCAu WFar WMnd WMoo XLum |
| 'Neptune' | CWCL |
| 'Noble Maiden' (Band of Nobles Series) | CBcs CPrp CSBt CTri EBee ECtt ELan EPfP LRHS LSRN MBri MCot MLLN MNHC MWat NGBl NPri SBfd SMrm SPer SPoG SWal SWvt WCAu WFar WMnd WMoo XLum |
| ***nootkatensis*** | GLog GMac LRHS |
| 'Pauly' | CWCL |
| 'Pen and Ink' | CWCL |
| ***perennis*** | LRHS |
| 'Persian Slipper'PBR | CWCL EWes GBin IPot LRHS MBri |
| 'Pluto' | CWCL |
| 'Polar Princess' | EWes GBin LRHS SWat |
| ***propinquus*** | CEnt SPhx |
| 'Red Arrow' | CWCL |
| 'Red Rum'PBR | CWCL GBin LRHS MBri |
| 'Redhead' | CWCL |
| 'Rote Flamme' | CPrp EWes GBin SMrm XLum |
| Russell hybrids | CSBt EPfP LAst MHer MLHP MMuc SBfd SEND SGar SPet SPlb SRms SVic SWvt WFar |
| 'Saffron'PBR | CWCL GBin LRHS LSRN |
| 'Salmon Star'PBR | CWCL GBin LRHS |
| 'Sand Pink' | EWes |
| 'Silver Fleece' **new** | WHer |
| 'Snowgoose' | CWCL |
| 'Tequila Flame' | CWCL EBee GBin LRHS |
| 'Terracotta' | CWCL |
| ***texensis*** | CSpe |
| 'The Chatelaine' (Band of Nobles Series) | CBcs CSBt EBee ECtt ELan EPfP GBin LAst LRHS LSRN MBri MCot MNHC MWat NBir NBlu NGBl NPri SBfd SBrd SMrm SPer SPoG SWal SWvt WCAu WFar WMnd WMoo XLum |
| 'The Governor') (Band of Nobles Series | CBcs CSBt CTri EBee ECtt ELan EPfP GAbr GBin LRHS LSRN MBri MNHC MWat NGBl NPri SBfd SBrd SMrm SPer SPoG SWal SWvt WCAu WFar WMnd WMoo XLum |
| 'The Page' (Band of Nobles Series) | CBcs EBee ELan EPfP LRHS LSRN MBri MCot MLLN MNHC MWat NPri SBfd SMrm SPer SPoG SWal SWvt WCFE WFar WMnd WMoo XLum |
| 'Thundercloud' | CDes SMrm |
| 'Towering Inferno' | CWCL EWes |
| ***variicolor*** | CHid SMad |
| ***varius*** | CSpe |
| subsp. ***orientalis*** **new** | |

## *Luzula* (*Juncaceae*)

| | |
|---|---|
| ***alpinopilosa*** | EPPr MMHG |
| × ***borreri*** | EPPr |
| - 'Botany Bay' (v) | ECtt EPPr EPla GBin NHol WWEG |
| 'Engel' **new** | EPPr |
| ***lactea*** | LRHS |
| ***luzuloides*** | GQui WPtf |

| | | |
|---|---|---|
| | - 'Schneehäschen' | GBin GCal NWsh |
| | ***maxima*** | see *L. sylvatica* |
| | ***nivalis*** | GAbr |
| | ***nivea*** | Widely available |
| | - 'Lucius' | LTcn |
| | - 'Schattenkind' | EBee |
| | ***pedemontana*** **new** | EPPr SMea |
| | ***pilosa*** | EPla GCal |
| | - 'Igel' | EBee GBin LEdu NBid SLPl SMad WWEG |
| | ***purpureosplendens*** | LEdu |
| | ***rufa*** | ECou |
| § | ***sylvatica*** | CHEx CRWN CRow ELan EPPr EPfP EPla LEdu LRHS MLLN MMoz MMuc MRav NBro NMir NOrc SBfd SEND WDin WFar WHer WShi WWEG XLum |
| | - 'A. Rutherford' | see *L. sylvatica* 'Taggart's Cream' |
| | - 'Aurea' | CHEx CKno ECha EPPr EPfP EPla LAst LBMP LRHS MMoz MRav NBid NOak NSti SApp STre WCot WFar WGrn WMoo WPtf |
| | - 'Aureomarginata' | see *L. sylvatica* 'Marginata' |
| I | - 'Auslese' | EPPr EPfP WMoo |
| | - 'Barcode' (v) | CNat |
| | - 'Hohe Tatra' | Widely available |
| § | - 'Marginata' (v) | Widely available |
| * | - f. ***nova*** | ELon EPPr LRHS |
| | - 'Schattenlicht' | EBee |
| | - 'Solar Flair' **new** | MWhi |
| § | - 'Taggart's Cream' (v) | EHoe EPla GGar MBNS NBid NHol SApp WGrn WMoo WWEG |
| | - 'Tauernpass' | EBee EHoe EPPr EPla GCal SLPl |
| | - 'Wäldler' | EPPr MBNS NHol |
| | ***ulophylla*** | ECou EDAr GBin NWCA |

# *Luzuriaga* (*Luzuriagaceae*)

| | | |
|---|---|---|
| | ***polyphylla*** HCM 98202 | WCru |
| | ***radicans*** | CCCN CFee IBlr WCru WSHC |
| | - RH 0602 | WCru |

# *Lychnis* (*Caryophyllaceae*)

| | | |
|---|---|---|
| | ***alpina*** | CMac EBee ECho EDAr EPfP GLam GMaP MAsh MSCN NBlu NGdn NVic SGar WFar XLum |
| | - 'Alba' | NBir |
| | - 'Rosea' | NBir |
| | - 'Snow Flurry' | EDAr NLar |
| § | × ***arkwrightii*** | ECha ELan LRHS WFar |
| | - 'Orange Zwerg' | CWCL MBNS SMrm WHal |
| | - 'Vesuvius' | CBcs CMac CWGN EAEE EBee LRHS MWat NBPC NBir NPnk SGar SMrm SPad SPer SRms STes WMnd WPer WWEG XLum |
| | ***chalcedonica*** $\Psi^{H4}$ | Widely available |
| | - var. ***albiflora*** | EBee NBro NMRc SMrm WBrk WCAu WFar WMoo WPer |
| | - 'Carnea' | LRHS MBNS NBre NGdn SMrm SPhx WBrk WCAu WPer WWEG |
| | - 'Dusky Salmon' | MDKP NBPC WOut |
| | - 'Flore Pleno' (d) | EBee ELan EShb GCal NLar WFar |
| | - 'Morgenrot' | LRHS MCCP MLLN NBPC |
| | - 'Pinkie' | ELan NLar |
| | - 'Rauhreif' | MWat NBre SPhx XLum |
| | - 'Rosea' | EBee EPfP LRHS NBir WFar WHrl WMoo WPer |
| * | - 'Salmonea' | NBir SRms |
| | - 'Summer Sparkle Pink' | SWal |
| | ***cognata*** | GMac MDKP |
| | - B&SWJ 4234 | WCru |
| § | ***coronaria*** $\Psi^{H4}$ | Widely available |
| | - MESE 356 | SPhx |
| | - 'Abbotswood Rose' | see *L.* × ***walkeri*** 'Abbotswood Rose' |
| | - 'Alba' $\Psi^{H4}$ | Widely available |
| | - 'Angel's Blush' | CSpr MDKP NBir SPav SPer SRkn WRHF |
| | - Atrosanguinea Group | CBre EBee EWTr GMaP IBlr LRHS MLLN MRav MSCN MSpe NEgg NGdn NPri NSti NWad SPer |
| | - 'Blood Red' | CSpe |
| | - 'Cerise' | MArl MDKP NBir |
| | - 'Dancing Ladies' | WMnd |
| | - Gardeners' World = 'Blych' (d) | CBcs CDes CSpe EBee ECtt ELon EWes LRHS LSou MBNS MLLN MTis NBPC NGdn NSti SMrm SPer SSvw SUsu WBrk WCot WFar |
| | - 'Hutchinson's Cream' (v) | NBir NPro |
| | - Oculata Group | CSpe EBee ECtt EPfP LEdu SBfd SMrm SPav SPet SPlb WFar WKif WMoo WWEG |
| § | ***coronata*** var. ***sieboldii*** | MWea SBrt |
| | ***dioica*** | see *Silene dioica* |
| | ***flos-cuculi*** | CArn CBen CEnt CHab CPom CRWN CWat EBee ECho EHon EPfP EWil LEdu LPBA MHer MMuc MNHC NLan NMir NPri SEND WHer WMAq WMoo WPnP WSFF XLum |
| | - var. ***albiflora*** | CBre LPBA MSKA NBro NLar WHer WMnd WMoo |
| | - Jenny = 'Lychjen'$^{PBR}$ (d) | CAby CChe CWCL EBee ELan GQue LAst LBMP LLWG LRHS MBNS MNrw MTis NBPC NPnk NSti SBfd SHar SPoG SRkn STes SUsu WCot WGrn |
| | - 'Little Robin' | EDAr LLWG |
| | - 'Nana' | ECho EDAr GAbr IFro MMuc MSKA NGdn NLar NWCA SBch |
| | - 'White Robin' | CBod CBre CEnt GMac GQue IFro IKil LBMP LEdu LRHS MBNS NCGa NGdn NPri SPoG WAul WBor WFar WPtf |
| | ***flos-jovis*** $\Psi^{H4}$ | ECha EPfP GJos LRHS NBir NLar SRms WMoo XLum |
| | - 'Alba' | WPtf |
| | - 'Hort's Variety' | LRHS MRav NBir |
| | - 'Minor' | see *L. flos-jovis* 'Nana' |
| § | - 'Nana' | LRHS MSCN SBch |
| | - 'Peggy' | EShb LRHS NBre NGdn NLar |
| | ***fulgens*** | NBre |
| | × ***haageana*** | EBee NLar SRms |
| | - 'Lumina Bronze Leaf Red' **new** | LRHS |
| | 'Hill Grounds' | CDes WCot |
| | ***lagascae*** | see *Petrocoptis pyrenaica* subsp. *glaucifolia* |
| | ***miqueliana*** | SPhx WMoo |
| | 'Molten Lava' | EBee MRav NBlu NLar WPer |
| | 'Red Star' **new** | LRHS |
| | 'Rollie's Favorite' | EBee ECtt NDov SPoG WBor WHil |
| * | ***sikkimensis*** | EBee NBre |
| | 'Terry's Pink' | NCGa WFar |
| § | ***viscaria*** | CArn ECha GCra GJos SBch SGar WFar WMoo WTin |
| | - 'Alba' | EBee ECha NBre NBro SBch XLum |
| | - ***alpina*** | see *L. viscaria* |
| § | - subsp. ***atropurpurea*** | CAby ECtt EWes LSou NBre SBHP SRms WHrl WPtf |
| | - MESE 66 | ECtt |
| | - 'Feuer' | CSpr EBee EWes GJos LRHS NLar NVic WMoo |

- 'Firebird' EWes NBre
- 'Plena' (d) NBir SRkn
- 'Schnee' CSpr LRHS NEgg
- 'Splendens' EPfP NBPC SPet XLum
- 'Splendens Plena' (d) ♀H4 EBee NBre NBro SUsu WFar

§ × *walkeri* 'Abbotswood Rose' ♀H4 IBlr

§ ***yunnanensis*** EBee GKev NBid SBHP SPhx WPtf XLum
- ***alba*** see *L. yunnanensis*

## *Lycianthes* (*Solanaceae*)

***quichensis*** B&SWJ 10395 WCru

§ ***rantonnetii*** CAlb CBcs CCCN CHll ELan EPfP EShb IDee LRHS MOWG SBrd SEND SPer SPoG WWlt
- 'Royal Robe' CRHN
- 'Variegatum' (v) CHll EShb MSCN WCot

## *Lycium* (*Solanaceae*)

***barbarum*** CAgr CCCN CSpe EPfP EWes LBuc LEdu LRHS MCoo SBfd SEND SMad SPlb SPoG SVic WHar

***chinense*** CArn CMen NLar

## *Lycopodium* (*Lycopodiaceae*)

***clavatum*** GPoy

## *Lycopsis* see *Anchusa*

## *Lycopus* (*Lamiaceae*)

***americanus*** CArn

***europaeus*** CArn CHab ELau EWil GPoy LLWG WGwG WHer

## *Lycoris* (*Amaryllidaceae*)

***albiflora*** ECho

***aurea*** EBee ECho GKev

***incarnata*** ECho

***radiata*** CCCN EBee ECho GBin

***sanguinea*** ECho

***sprengeri*** ECho

***squamigera*** ECho

## *Lygodium* (*Lygodiaceae*)

***japonicum*** ISha NBid WFib WRic

## *Lyonia* (*Ericaceae*)

***ligustrina*** NLar

***mariana*** NLar

## *Lyonothamnus* (*Rosaceae*)

***floribundus*** CCCN CDoC CGHE CPLG NLar

subsp. ***aspleniifolius*** SArc SGar SSpi WFar WPGP

## *Lysichiton* (*Araceae*)

sp. GGal

***americanus*** ♀H4 Widely available

***americanus* × *camtschatcensis*** ECha

***camtschatcensis*** ♀H4 Widely available

## *Lysimachia* ✿ (*Primulaceae*)

***albescens*** CPLG GKev SGar WHer

§ ***atropurpurea*** CHar CSpe EBee ELan EPfP GJos LRHS SBfd SPer SPlb WCot WMnd WWEG
- 'Beaujolais' EShb GJos GQue LRHS LSRN NBPC NPri SPav WHil
- 'Geronimo' CSpe

***barystachys*** CPrp GMac LPla LRHS MRav NPnk SHar WCot WFar WOut WWEG

Candela = 'Innlyscand' LSou MBri SMrm SPoG WHil

***candida*** WCot

***ciliata*** CMHG CMac EBee ECha EHoe ELan GMaP MNrw NBir NGdn SWat WCot WFar WMnd

§ - 'Firecracker' ♀H4 Widely available
- 'Purpurea' see *L. ciliata* 'Firecracker'

***clethroides*** ♀H4 Widely available
- 'Geisha' (v) EBee ECtt EWes LLHF WCot
- 'Lady Jane' CFir CSpr SRms

§ ***congestiflora*** LAst NPer SPet
- HWJ 846 WCru
- 'Golden Falls' LAst LSou
- 'Outback Sunset'PBR (v) LAst

***ephemerum*** Widely available

***fortunei*** EBee EWld LRHS MWat SBch

***hybrida*** WCot

***japonica*** CFee

var. ***minutissima***

***lichiangensis*** CPLG EDAr GKev LRHS NBir SGar WMoo

***lyssii*** see *L. congestiflora*

***mauritiana*** LRHS

'Midnight Sun' LSou

***minoricensis*** CEls CFir ELan SWat

***nemorum*** EWil
- subsp. ***azorica*** WCot
- 'Pale Star' CBre CDes EBee

***nummularia*** COlW CSBt CTri CWat ECtt EHon EPfP EWil GPoy LPBA MMuc NBir SGol SWat WBrk WHfH
- 'Aurea' ♀H4 Widely available

***paridiformis*** WCot
- var. ***stenophylla*** CPLG
- - DJHC 704 CDes EBee WCot

***punctata*** misapplied see *L. verticillaris*

***punctata*** L. CRow CSBt EBee ECha EHon EPfP GMaP MHer MMuc MRav MWat NBPC NBro NHol NMir NPer SBfd SEND SGar SPer SPlb SRms SWat WBrk WCAu WFar WMAq WMoo WPer WPnP

§ - 'Alexander' (v) Widely available
- 'Gaulthier Brousse' MTis WCot WWEG
- Golden Alexander = 'Walgoldalex'PBR (v) LRHS MBNS MBri MLLN MMuc MTis NHol NLar SBfd SPoG WFar WWEG
- 'Golden Glory' (v) MAvo WCot
- 'Hometown Hero' EBee
- 'Ivy Maclean' (v) EBee SWvt WCot WWEG
- 'Variegata' see *L. punctata* 'Alexander'
- ***verticillata*** see *L. verticillaris*

'Purpurea' see *L. atropurpurea*

***pyramidalis*** WHrl WPtf WWEG

***quadrifolia*** EBee

Snow Candles = 'L9902' CCVN COlW EBee LHop

***thyrsiflora*** CWat EBee EHon GAuc NPer SWat WCot WMAq

§ ***verticillaris*** CTri WCot

***vulgaris*** CArn CHab CRWN EWil LPBA MSKA SIde WFar WJek WMoo
- subsp. ***davurica*** WCot
- - B&SWJ 8632 WCru

## *Lysionotus* (*Gesneriaceae*)

***gamosepalus*** B&SWJ 7241 WCru

aff. ***kwangsiensis*** HWJ 643 WCru

'Lavender Lady' CSpe WHil

| | |
|---|---|
| ***pauciflorus*** | CDes WAbe WSHC |
| - B&SWJ 189 | WCru |
| - B&SWJ 303 | WCru |
| - B&SWJ 335 | WCru |
| ***serratus*** | MWea |
| - HWJK 2426 | WCru |

## *Lythrum* (*Lythraceae*)

| | |
|---|---|
| ***alatum*** | NDov |
| ***anceps*** | NBre NLar |
| ***salicaria*** | Widely available |
| - 'Augenweide' **new** | XLum |
| - 'Blush' ♀H4 | Widely available |
| § - 'Feuerkerze' ♀H4 | CAby CKno CMea CPrp EAEE EBee ECtt ELan ELon EPfP IPot LAst LBMP LHop LRHS LSou MBri MCot MLLN MRav MSpe MWts NBir NEgg NSti NVic SAga SPer WFar WWEG |
| - Firecandle | see *L. salicaria* 'Feuerkerze' |
| - 'Happy' | ELon LRHS |
| - 'Lady Sackville' | EBee ECtt ELon EPPr GBin GMaP IPot LRHS MCot NLar SMrm WSHC |
| - 'Morden Pink' | CChe EBee MBri MDKP MMuc NLar SEND SPhx SSvw WFar WPtf |
| - 'Prichard's Variety' | CAby CKno WPGP |
| - 'Robert' | Widely available |
| - 'Robin' | EBee LLHF LRHS MAsh MCot NPri SRot SWvt |
| - 'Rose' | ELan NBir SWvt |
| - 'Stichflamme' | SMrm |
| - 'Swirl' | EBee ECtt LLWG MDKP NBre NDov NLar SHar SMrm WFar |
| - 'The Beacon' | CMHG EBee MDKP NLar SRms |
| - 'Zigeunerblut' | CElw CKno CMHG EBee ELon EPPr MDKP MRav NLar SMrm SPhx SSvw SWat |
| ***virgatum*** | CMHG NDov SPhx SSvw SUsu WCFE WMoo WOut WSHC |
| - 'Dropmore Purple' | CHar CSam EBee ECtt ELon EPPr EPfP LAst LBMP LHop LLWG LRHS LSRN MAsh MBri MCot MDKP MRav MSpe NDov NEgg NPri SAga SPhx WCAu WCot WFar WPnP WSHC XLum |
| - 'Rose Queen' | ECha ECtt MDKP MRav NDov WFar WPer |
| - 'Rosy Gem' | CMMP EBee ECtt EPfP GMaP LAst LRHS MWat MWhi NBPC NBro SRms SWvt WCFE WFar WPer WWEG |
| - 'The Rocket' | CAby CMMP CSam CTri EBee EPPr EPfP GBee LAst LRHS MRav MSpe NBro NDov SPer SWvt |

## *Lytocaryum* (*Arecaceae*)

| | |
|---|---|
| § ***weddellianum*** ♀H1 | LPal |

# M

## *Maackia* (*Papilionaceae*)

| | |
|---|---|
| ***amurensis*** | CBcs CHGN ELan EPfP IArd IDee IVic LRHS MBri WSHC |
| - var. ***buergeri*** | CDul |
| ***chinensis*** | MBlu MBri NLar |

## *Macbridea* (*Lamiaceae*)

| | |
|---|---|
| ***caroliniana*** | WPGP |

## mace, English see *Achillea ageratum*

## *Macfadyena* (*Bignoniaceae*)

| | |
|---|---|
| ***uncata*** | MOWG |
| § ***unguis-cati*** | CCCN CRHN EShb SGar |

## *Machaerina* (*Cyperaceae*)

| | |
|---|---|
| ***rubiginosa*** 'Variegata' (v) | CKno LLWG |
| ***sinclairii*** | ECou |

## *Machilus* see *Persea*

## *Mackaya* (*Acanthaceae*)

| | |
|---|---|
| § ***bella*** ♀H1 | CHll EShb WHil |

## *Macleaya* (*Papaveraceae*)

| | |
|---|---|
| ***cordata*** misapplied | see *M.* × *kewensis* |
| § ***cordata*** (Willd.) R. Br. ♀H4 | COlW EBee ELan EPfP LHop LRHS MBri MSCN MWhi NBPC NBir NOrc NPri SBfd SPer SPlb SPoG SRms WCAu WCot WFar WMnd WMoo XLum |
| - 'Celadon Ruffles' | GBin |
| § × ***kewensis*** | CWan MLLN SMrm |
| - 'Flamingo' ♀H4 | CPrp EBee ECha ECtt GQue LAst LRHS MBNS MLLN MNFA NGdn SMrm SWvt WHoo WWEG |
| § ***microcarpa*** | EHoe SGar SWat WWEG |
| - 'Kelway's Coral Plume' ♀H4 | Widely available |
| - 'Spetchley Ruby' | GBin MRav SPhx SUsu WCot WPGP WWEG |
| 'Plum Tassel' | WCot |

## *Maclura* (*Moraceae*)

| | |
|---|---|
| ***pomifera*** | CArn CBcs EBee IVic NLar SPlb WDin WFar |
| - 'Pretty Woman' | NLar |
| ***tricuspidata*** | EGFP |

## *Macrodiervilla* see *Weigela*

## *Macropidia* (*Haemodoraceae*)

| | |
|---|---|
| ***fuliginosa*** 'Bush Eclipse' (Bush Gems Series) | MOWG |

## *Macropiper* (*Piperaceae*)

| | |
|---|---|
| § ***excelsum*** | CHEx ECou |

## *Macrozamia* (*Zamiaceae*)

| | |
|---|---|
| ***communis*** | CBrP EAmu LPal |
| ***diplomera*** | CBrP |
| ***dyeri*** | see *M. riedlei* |
| ***glaucophylla*** | CBrP |
| ***johnsonii*** | CBrP |
| ***lucida*** | CBrP |
| ***miquelii*** | CBrP |
| ***moorei*** | CBrP LPal |
| ***mountperiensis*** | CBrP |
| § ***riedlei*** | CBrP LPal |

## *Maddenia* (*Rosaceae*)

| | |
|---|---|
| ***hypoleuca*** | NLar |

## *Madia* (*Asteraceae*)

| | |
|---|---|
| ***elegans*** | WHer |

## *Maesa* (*Primulaceae*)

| | |
|---|---|
| ***japonica*** | CPLG |

| | |
|---|---|
| - CWJ 12371 | WCru |
| ***montana*** | CPLG |

## *Magnolia* ✿ (*Magnoliaceae*)

| | |
|---|---|
| ***acuminata*** | CBcs CDul CMCN EPfP LMaj NLar WDin |
| - 'Blue Opal' | CBcs CPMA |
| * - 'Kinju' | CEnd CPMA NLar |
| - 'Koban Dori' | CBcs CPMA |
| - large yellow-flowered | NLar |
| - 'Moegi Dori' | NLar |
| - 'Patriot' | SKHP |
| - 'Patriot' × (× ***brooklynensis*** 'Yellow Bird') | CPMA |
| - 'Seiju' | CPMA |
| § - var. ***subcordata*** | CBcs NLar |
| - - 'Miss Honeybee' | CBcs CPMA |
| - - 'Mister Yellowjacket' | CPMA |
| 'Advance' | CBcs CPMA |
| 'Albatross' | CDoC CEnd WPGP |
| 'Alex' | CPMA SSta |
| 'Alixeed' | CPMA |
| ***alternifolia*** **new** | NHim |
| 'Amber' | CPMA |
| 'Ambrosia' | CBcs CPMA |
| ***amoena*** | CTho |
| - 'Multiogeca' | CBcs CWib EGxp |
| 'Anilou' | CPMA |
| 'Ann' 🏆H4 | CPLG MGos NLar |
| 'Anna' | CPMA |
| 'Anne Rosse' | WPGP |
| 'Anticipation' | CEnd CPMA |
| 'Apollo' | CBcs CDoC CPMA LSRN SKHP WPGP |
| 'Archangel' | CPMA |
| ***ashei*** | see *M. macrophylla* subsp. *ashei* |
| 'Asian Artistry' | CPMA |
| 'Athene' | CBcs CDoC CEnd CPMA WPGP |
| 'Atlas' | CBcs CDoC CEnd CPMA CTho ERea NHim WPGP |
| 'Aurora' | CBcs CDoC CPMA |
| 'Banana Split' | CPMA NHim |
| 'Betty' 🏆H4 | CBcs CDoC CDul CMac EPfP GEdr LRHS LSRN MGos NLar NMun NPla SKHP SLim SSta WDin WFar |
| 'Big Dude' | CEnd CPMA IArd LSRN |
| ***biondii*** | CBcs LSRN NLar |
| 'Black Beauty' | CBcs CPMA |
| Black Tulip = 'Jurmag1'PBR | CBcs EBee ELan EPfP ERea LBuc LRHS MGos SBrd SCoo WPGP |
| 'Blushing Belle' | CPMA |
| 'Brenda' | CPMA |
| × ***brooklynensis*** | NPal |
| - 'Evamaria' | CBcs CTho |
| - 'Golden Joy' | CDoC CPMA |
| - 'Hattie Carthan' | CBcs CPMA NLar |
| - 'Woodsman' | CBcs NLar |
| - 'Yellow Bird' | CBcs CDoC CEnd CPMA CTho EBee EPfP GKin IArd LSRN MBlu MBri MGos NCGa NEgg NHol NLar NPal SKHP WDin |
| 'Butterbowl' | CBcs CPMA |
| 'Butterflies' | CBcs CDoC CDul CEnd CPMA CTho EBee ELan ELon EPfP LRHS LSRN MBlu MDun MGos NLar SGol SKHP SLim SSta WFar WGob |
| 'Caerhays Belle' | CBcs CPMA NHim NLar SKHP SSpi SSta |
| 'Caerhays New Purple' | CLnd |
| 'Caerhays Surprise' | CBcs CEnd CPMA SKHP SSpi SSta |
| ***campbellii*** | CBcs CMCN ELan EPfP SKHP SSpi WFar |
| - Alba Group | CEnd IDee WFar WPGP |
| - - 'Sir Harold Hillier' | CPMA |
| - 'Ambrose Congreve' **new** | WPGP |
| - 'Betty Jessel' | CPMA WPGP |
| - 'Darjeeling' | CBcs CDoC CPMA LRHS SKHP |
| - 'John Gallagher' **new** | SKHP |
| - 'Lamellan Pink' | CTho |
| - 'Lamellan White' | CTho |
| - subsp. ***mollicomata*** | CEnd CHEx EPfP IArd WFar |
| - - 'Lanarth' | CBcs CEnd CPMA LRHS |
| - 'Queen Caroline' **new** | WPGP |
| - (Raffillii Group) 'Charles Raffill' | CBcs CDoC CDul CLnd ELan EPfP LRHS MGos SLim WDin WPGP |
| - - 'Kew's Surprise' | CBcs CDoC CPMA WPGP |
| ***campbellii*** × ***sprengeri*** **new** | WPGP |
| 'Candy Cane' | CPMA |
| 'Carlos' | CPMA |
| ***cathcartii*** HWJ 874 | WCru |
| ***cavaleriei*** var. ***platypetala*** **new** | CPLG |
| 'Cecil Nice' | CCVT CDoC |
| Chameleon | see *M.* 'Chang Hua' |
| ***champaca*** | CCCN |
| § 'Chang Hua' | CPMA NLar |
| ***chapensis*** | CBcs IArd SKHP |
| 'Charles Coates' | CPMA EPfP NLar WPGP |
| ***chevalieri*** B&SWJ 11802 | WCru |
| - DJHV 06037 | WCru |
| - HWJ 533 | WCru |
| - HWJ 621 | WCru |
| 'China Dream' | EGxp |
| China Town = 'Jing Ning' | CPMA NLar |
| 'Chinese Magic' | EGxp |
| 'Columbus' | CPMA SKHP WPGP |
| 'Columnar Pink' | NLar |
| ***compressa*** | CCCN EPfP |
| 'Coral Lake' | CPMA SKHP |
| ***cordata*** | see *M. acuminata* var. *subcordata* |
| 'Cotton Rose' | EGxp |
| 'Crystal Chalice' | CPMA SSta |
| 'Cup Cake' | CPMA |
| 'Curly Locks' | CPMA |
| ***cylindrica*** misapplied | see *M.* 'Pegasus' |
| ***cylindrica*** ambig. | CBcs IArd |
| ***cylindrica*** E.H.Wilson | EPfP IArd |
| - 'Bjuv' | CPMA |
| 'Daphne' | CBcs CPMA LRHS MAsh NLar SBrd SKHP SPoG SSta |
| 'Darrell Dean' | CPMA |
| 'David Clulow' | CBcs CPMA ERea LRHS SKHP SSta WPGP |
| ***dawsoniana*** | EPfP NLar |
| - 'Barbara Cook' | CPMA |
| - 'Valley Splendour' **new** | SSta |
| 'Daybreak' | CBcs CPMA IArd MBlu NPal SGol SSpi SSta WPGP |
| 'Deborah' **new** | CPMA |
| ***decidua*** **new** | SKHP |
| ***delavayi*** | CBcs CBrP CDoy CDul CHEx CMCN EGFP EPfP IArd SArc SSpi WPGP |
| § ***denudata*** 🏆H3-4 | CBcs CDoy CDul CMCN CTho CWib EGxp EPfP IArd LMaj LRHS MBlu MGos NLar SSpi SSta WDin WFar |
| - 'Double Diamond' | CPMA |

| | |
|---|---|
| - 'Dubbel' | CBcs NHim |
| - 'Forrest's Pink' | CBcs LRHS |
| - Fragrant Cloud = 'Dan Xin' | CBcs CPMA CWib EGxp MBri NHim NLar |
| - 'Gere' | CBcs CPMA |
| - 'Ghost Ship' | CPMA |
| - late-flowered **new** | SKHP |
| - 'Rubiflora' | SSta |
| - Yellow River = 'Fei Huang' | CBcs CEnd CPMA CWib EGxp LSou MBri NLar NPal |
| ***doltsopa*** | CBcs CCCN CGHE CHEx CPLG EPfP SKHP SSta WPGP |
| - 'Silver Cloud' | CBcs CDoC CPLG |
| 'Doctor M. Oesthook' **new** | SSta |
| 'Early Rose' | CPMA |
| 'Eleanor May' | CPMA |
| 'Elegance' | CPMA |
| 'Elisa Odenwald' | CPMA NHim |
| 'Elizabeth' 🏆$^{H4}$ | CBcs CDoC CMCN CPMA CTho ELan EPfP ERea IArd LAst LMil LRHS LSRN MAsh MBlu MDun MGos NLar NPal SKHP SPer SSpi SSta SWvt |
| § ***ernestii*** | CPLG CWib |
| 'Eskimo' | CPMA SKHP SSpi |
| 'Felicity' | CPMA |
| Felix Jury = 'Jurmag2'$^{PBR}$ | ELan EPfP ERea LRHS SSpi WPGP |
| ***figo*** | CBcs CCCN CDoC CPLG EBee EPfP LRHS SKHP SSta WPGP |
| - var. ***crassipes*** | CBcs |
| ***figo* × *laevifolia*** | SKHP |
| 'Fireglow' | CPMA CTho |
| 'Flamingo' | CPMA |
| aff. ***floribunda*** var. ***tonkinensis*** DJHV06 105 | WCru |
| - - WWJ 12003 | WCru |
| ***fordiana*** | CBcs CPLG |
| § ***foveolata*** | CBcs CWib SSpi |
| - WWJ 11929 | WCru |
| 'Frank Gladney' | CPMA |
| 'Frank's Masterpiece' | CPMA SKHP |
| ***fraseri*** | SKHP |
| - var. ***pyramidata*** | SKHP |
| 'Galaxy' 🏆$^{H4}$ | CBcs CDoC CDul CEnd CMac CPMA ELon EPfP ERea IArd LMil LRHS MAsh MGos NLar SBrd SEWo SLim SSpi SSta WDin WGob |
| 'Genie' | CBcs CDoC |
| 'George Henry Kern' | CBcs CDoC CDul GEdr IArd IDee LRHS MBri MGos NEgg NLar NMun NPCo SLdr SSpi WCFE WDin WFar WGob |
| 'Gladys Carlson' | CPMA |
| ***globosa*** | CBcs CPLG WFar WGob |
| 'Gold Crown' | CBcs CPMA |
| 'Gold Star' | CBcs CDoC CEnd CPMA CTho EMil EPfP LRHS MGos NCGa NLar SKHP SSpi SSta |
| 'Golden Endeavour' | CPMA |
| 'Golden Gala' | CPMA |
| 'Golden Gift' | CPMA LRHS MAsh SBrd SSpi |
| 'Golden Pond' | CPMA |
| 'Golden Rain' | CPMA |
| 'Golden Sun' | CBcs CPMA NLar |
| 'Goldenship' | EGxp |
| 'Goldfinch' | CPMA |
| I × ***gotoburgensis*** Chollipo clone **new** | WPGP |
| - clone 2 | CPMA |
| ***grandiflora*** | CMCN CWib EGxp EPfP ESwi LEdu LRHS LSRN MGos MRav NEgg NLar SBfd SEWo WDin WFar |
| - 'Blanchard' | CBcs CPMA |
| - 'Bracken's Brown Beauty' | SGol |
| - 'Charles Dickens' | CPMA |
| - 'Edith Bogue' | CBcs CDul CPMA EQua GKin LMil MGos NEgg NPCo SGol WGob |
| - 'Exmouth' 🏆$^{H3-4}$ | Widely available |
| - 'Ferruginea' | CBcs CPMA CTho LRHS |
| - 'François Treyve' | EPfP EQua LRHS LTen SBfd |
| - 'Galissonière' | CBcs CCVT CWib ECrN EPfP ERom LMaj LRHS LTen MGos MREP SBfd SGol SKHP SLim SSpi SWvt WDin WFar WPGP |
| - 'Galissonière Nana' | LMaj |
| - 'Goliath' | CBcs CDul CEnd CHEx ELan EPfP LRHS SBfd SEWo SKHP SLdr SLim SPer SSpi WPGP |
| - 'Harold Poole' | CBcs CPMA |
| - 'Kay Paris' | CPMA EPfP LRHS SKHP SSpi |
| - 'Little Gem' | CBcs CDoC CPMA ELan EPfP LRHS MGos SSpi |
| - 'Mainstreet' | CPMA |
| - 'Monlia' | CPMA |
| - 'Nannetensis' | CPMA EQua LRHS |
| - 'Overton' | CPMA |
| - 'Russet' | CPMA |
| - 'Saint Mary' | CBcs CPMA |
| - 'Samuel Sommer' | CBcs CPMA SSpi |
| - 'Symmes Select' | CPMA |
| - 'Treyvei' | CPMA |
| - 'Victoria' 🏆$^{H3-4}$ | CBcs CDoC CDul CPMA CTho ELan ELon EPfP LMil LRHS LSRN MAsh MBlu MGos MWat NHim NLar SGol SLim SPer SPoG SReu SSpi SSta WFar WGob WPGP |
| 'Green Bee' | CPMA |
| 'Green Mist' | CPMA LRHS SSpi |
| 'Hawk' | WPGP |
| 'Heaven Scent' 🏆$^{H4}$ | Widely available |
| 'Helen Fogg' | CPMA |
| ***heptapeta*** | see *M. denudata* |
| 'Honey Flower' | CPMA NLar |
| § 'Hong Yur' | CEnd CPMA NPal |
| 'Hot Flash' | CBcs CPMA |
| 'Hot Lips' | CPMA |
| ***hypoleuca*** | see *M. obovata* Thunb. |
| 'Ian's Red' | CBcs CDoC CPMA |
| § ***insignis*** | CBcs CHEx CPLG SKHP SSpi WPGP |
| - B&SWJ 11800 | WCru |
| 'Iolanthe' | CBcs CDoC CEnd CGHE CMCN CPMA CTho ELan ERea MAsh MBri MGos NLar SSpi SSta WFar WPGP |
| 'Iufer' | CPMA SSta |
| 'J.C. Williams' | CBcs CDoC CPMA CTho WPGP |
| 'Jack Fogg' | MPkF SKHP |
| 'Jane' 🏆$^{H4}$ | CDoC CMac CPMA ELan EPfP LMil LRHS MAsh MGos MRav SPer |
| 'Jersey Belle' | CPMA |
| 'Joe McDaniel' | CBcs CPMA ERea NHim NLar SKHP |
| 'John Bond' **new** | SSta |
| 'John Congreve' **new** | WPGP |
| 'Joli Pompom' | CPMA |
| 'Judith Zuk' **new** | SSta |
| 'Judy' | NLar |
| 'Kate Brook' | NLar |
| × ***kewensis*** 'Wada's Memory' | see *M. salicifolia* 'Wada's Memory' |

| | |
|---|---|
| ***kobus*** | CBcs CDoy CDul CLnd CMCN CTho CTsd EPfP GKin LMaj MBlu MMuc NLar NWea SEWo SLdr WDin WFar WGob |
| - var. ***borealis*** | CPMA |
| - 'Esveld Select' | CPMA SSpi |
| - 'Janaki Ammal' | CPMA |
| § - 'Norman Gould' | CDoC CPMA EPfP MBri NLar NPla SSta WDin |
| - 'Octopus' **new** | CPMA |
| - pink-flowered **new** | CPMA |
| - 'White Elegance' | CPMA |
| - 'Wisley Star' **new** | SSta |
| ***laevifolia*** | CBcs SKHP WPGP WSHC |
| - arborescent | SKHP |
| - 'Dali Velvet' | CPLG |
| - 'Gail's Favourite' | LRHS SSpi |
| - 'Kneehigh' | SSpi |
| - 'Velvet and Cream' **new** | WPGP |
| - 'Willow Leaf' | SKHP |
| 'Laura Saylor' | CPMA |
| 'Leda' | CPMA SSta |
| 'Legacy' | CPMA NLar SKHP WPGP |
| 'Legend' | CPMA EPfP |
| 'Lennarth Jonsson' | CPMA |
| § ***liliiflora*** | CBcs GKin NHim |
| - 'Darkest Purple' | CPMA |
| § - 'Nigra' ♀H4 | Widely available |
| - 'Raven' **new** | SKHP |
| * 'Limelight' | CPMA SSpi WPGP |
| × ***loebneri*** | CBcs NEgg |
| - 'Ballerina' | CDoC NLar |
| - 'Donna' | CPMA EPfP LRHS MAsh NLar SKHP SSpi SSta |
| - 'Encore' | CPMA |
| - 'Leonard Messel' ♀H4 | Widely available |
| - 'Lesley Jane' | CPMA |
| - 'Merrill' ♀H4 | Widely available |
| - 'Neil McEacharn' | CPMA |
| - 'Pink Cloud' | CPMA |
| - 'Powder Puff' | CPMA |
| - 'Raspberry Fun' | CPMA |
| - 'Snowdrift' | CPMA NLar SSta |
| - 'Star Bright' | CPMA |
| - 'White Stardust' | CPMA |
| - 'Wildcat' | CPMA NLar |
| - 'Willow Wood' | CPMA |
| 'Lois' | CBcs CPMA EPfP ERea LRHS LSRN MAsh NLar SKHP SPoG SSpi SSta WPGP |
| 'Lombardy Rose' | NLar |
| ***lotungensis*** | NLar |
| 'Lotus' | CPMA |
| 'Lucy Carlson' | CPMA |
| ***macclurei*** | CBcs |
| ***macrophylla*** | CBcs CBrP CMCN CMac EPfP IDee LRHS MBlu MPkF NLar SArc SKHP WPGP |
| § - subsp. ***ashei*** | CBcs SKHP WPGP |
| - subsp. ***ashei*** × ***virginiana*** | CPMA |
| ***macrophylla*** × ***macrophylla*** subsp. ***ashei*** | SKHP |
| ***macrophylla*** × ***sieboldii*** | CPMA |
| 'Mag's Pirouette' | SKHP |
| 'Malin' | CPMA |
| 'Manchu Fan' | CBcs CPMA EMil EPfP ERea IArd LRHS LSRN LTen NLar SKHP SLim SSpi |
| § 'March Til Frost' | CPMA WPGP |
| 'Margaret Helen' | CBcs CDoC CPMA |
| 'Marj Gossler' | CPMA |
| 'Marjorie Congreve' **new** | WPGP |
| 'Mark Jury' | SKHP WPGP |
| 'Mary Bee' **new** | SKHP |
| 'Mary Nell' | CPMA |
| 'Maryland' | CPMA CWib EQua SKHP SSpi |
| ***maudiae*** | CBcs CDoC CGHE CPLG EPfP IArd NLar SKHP SSpi WPGP |
| 'Maxine Merrill' | CPMA IDee SSta |
| 'May to Frost' | see *M.* 'March Til Frost' |
| 'Milky Way' ♀H4 | CBcs CDoC CGHE CMHG CPMA CTho MGos SKHP SSpi SSta WPGP |
| 'Moondance' | CPMA |
| 'Morning Calm' **new** | SKHP |
| 'Nimbus' | CPMA SKHP SSpi |
| ***nitida*** | CBcs |
| ***obovata*** Diels | see *M. officinalis* |
| § ***obovata*** Thunb. ♀H4 | CAlb CBcs CDul CMCN CPMA CTho EPfP IDee MGos NLar NWea SSpi SSta WDin WMou WPGP |
| ***odora*** | CWib |
| § ***officinalis*** | CBcs EPfP NLar WFar |
| - var. ***biloba*** | CGHE EPfP NLar WPGP |
| 'Old Port' | CBcs |
| 'Olivia' | CPMA |
| 'Peachy' | CBcs CPMA NLar |
| § 'Pegasus' | CBcs CEnd CPMA LRHS SKHP SSpi SSta WDin |
| 'Peppermint Stick' | CBcs SSta |
| 'Peter Smithers' | CPMA WFar |
| 'Phelan Bright' | CPMA |
| 'Phillip Tregunna' | CBcs CTho SKHP |
| 'Phil's Masterpiece' | CPMA |
| 'Pickard's Stardust' | EPfP |
| 'Pickard's Sundew' | see *M.* 'Sundew' |
| 'Piet van Veen' | CPMA |
| 'Pink Delight' | CPMA |
| 'Pink Goblet' | LRHS NHim |
| 'Pink Surprise' | CPMA |
| 'Pinkie' ♀H4 | CBcs CPMA EMil LSRN MGos NEgg NLar SSpi SSta WGob |
| 'Pirouette' | CPMA EPfP LLHF LRHS NHim SSpi SSta |
| 'Porcelain Dove' | CPMA NHim SSpi |
| 'Pretty Lee' | EGxp |
| 'Princess Margaret' | CBcs CDoC CPMA |
| × ***proctoriana*** | CAbP CDoC CGHE LMil LRHS NLar SChF SKHP WPGP |
| - Gloster form | NLar |
| - 'Robert's Dream' | CPMA LRHS MAsh SSpi SSta |
| - 'Slavin's No 44' | CPMA |
| 'Purple Globe' | CPMA SKHP |
| 'Purple Sensation' | CBcs CPMA |
| ***quinquepeta*** | see *M. liliiflora* |
| 'Raspberry Ice' | CBcs CDoC CMHG CMac CSam CTho EPfP LMil LRHS MAsh NLar SLim WFar WGob |
| 'Raspberry Swirl' | SSta |
| 'Red As' | CBcs |
| 'Red as Red' | CDoC |
| 'Red Baron' **new** | CPMA |
| 'Red Lion' | CPMA |
| 'Ricki' | CBcs CPMA EMil EPfP LSRN MBlu MGos NLar NMun WFar |
| 'Roseanne' | CPMA |
| ***rostrata*** | CBcs CGHE ELan SKHP WPGP |
| 'Rouged Alabaster' | CDoC NLar |

| |  |  |
|---|---|---|
| | 'Royal Crown' | CBcs CDoC EPfP EQua IDee LRHS MRav NEgg NLar NPCo SLim |
| | 'Ruby' | CBcs CPMA |
| | ***salicifolia*** ♀$^{H3-4}$ | CBcs CMCN EPfP SSpi SSta |
| | - var. ***concolor*** | CPMA |
| | - 'Jermyns' | CPMA |
| | - 'Louisa Fete' | CPMA |
| * | - 'Rosea' | CPMA |
| | - upright | WPGP |
| | - 'Van Veen' | CPMA |
| § | - 'Wada's Memory' ♀$^{H4}$ | CAlb CDoC CDul CMCN CPLG CPMA CTho ELan EMil EPfP ERea EWTr LMil LRHS MAsh MBri MMuc NLar SEND SKHP SLdr SSpi SSta WDin WFar WGob |
| | - 'Windsor Beauty' | CPMA ERea NHim |
| | ***sargentiana*** | CBcs |
| | - 'Broadleas' | CPMA |
| | - var. ***robusta*** | CBcs CEnd CMCN ELan EPfP MGos NLar SSpi WDin WFar |
| | - - 'Blood Moon' | CPMA |
| | - - 'Multipetal' | WPGP |
| | - - 'Trengwainton Glory' | ERea NHim |
| | 'Satisfaction' | CDul CPMA NLar NPal |
| | 'Sayonara' ♀$^{H4}$ | CBcs CPMA EPfP ERea SSpi WDin |
| | 'Schmetterling' | see *M.* × *soulangeana* 'Pickard's Schmetterling' |
| | 'Serene' | CBcs CEnd CPMA EPfP MGos SSpi SSta WPGP |
| | 'Shirazz' | CBcs CDoC CPMA SKHP WPGP |
| | ***sieboldii*** | CBcs CDul CGHE CLnd CMCN CMac CPMA CTho ELan EPfP GKin IDee LRHS LSRN MBlu MBri MDun MGos NLar SKHP SLim SPad SSpi SSta WDin WFar WPGP |
| | - B&SWJ 4127 | WCru |
| | - 'Colossus' | CPMA MBlu SKHP SSta |
| | - 'Genesis' | CPMA |
| | - 'Genesis' × ***tripetala*** | CPMA |
| | - 'Genesis' × ***virginiana*** new | CPMA |
| | - 'Michiko Renge' | CPMA NLar |
| | - 'Min Pyong-gal' | CPMA |
| | - 'Pride of Norway' | CPMA |
| | - subsp. ***sinensis*** | CBcs CDoC CPMA CTho ELan EPfP MBlu NLar WDin WPGP |
| I | - - 'Grandiflora' new | CPMA |
| | 'Sir Harold Hillier' | CBcs WPGP |
| | 'Snow Goose' | CPMA |
| | 'Solar Flair' | CBcs CPMA IArd SKHP |
| | × ***soulangeana*** | Widely available |
| | - 'Alba Superba' | CBcs CDoC CTri EPfP MBlu MGos MRav SLim SPer WFar |
| | - 'Alexandrina' | EPfP NLar |
| | - 'Amabilis' | SBfd |
| | - 'Brozzonii' ♀$^{H3-4}$ | CBcs CDoC CMac EPfP GCra IArd IVic LMil LRHS MGos NEgg NLar NPCo |
| | - 'Burgundy' | CBcs CBot CDoC NPCo WFar |
| | - 'Fukuju' | CPMA |
| | - 'Lennei' ♀$^{H3-4}$ | CBcs CDoC CMCN CMac CSBt EBee EPfP GEdr LAst LRHS MBri MGos MSwo NLar SLim SPer SRms WFar |
| | - 'Lennei Alba' ♀$^{H3-4}$ | CBcs CDoC CMCN CMac WFar WGob |
| | - 'Nigra' | see *M. liliiflora* 'Nigra' |
| § | - 'Pickard's Schmetterling' | CDoC LMil LRHS MAsh NHim |
| | - 'Pickard's Snow Queen' | CPMA |
| | - 'Pickard's Sundew' | see *M.* 'Sundew' |
| | - 'Picture' | CBcs CDoC CMac CTri NLar WDin WGob |
| | - Red Lucky | see *M.* 'Hong Yur' |
| | - 'Rosea' | LMaj |
| | - 'Rubra' misapplied | see *M.* × *soulangeana* 'Rustica Rubra' |
| § | - 'Rustica Rubra' ♀$^{H3-4}$ | CBcs CDoC CDul CMCN CMac CTri EBee ELan EPfP LAst LMil LRHS LSRN MAsh MBri MGos NLar NVic SGol SPer SPoG SReu SSpi WCFE WDin WFar WGob |
| | - 'San José' | LMil LRHS MAsh NHim NLar WFar |
| | - 'Speciosa' | NMun SSta |
| | - 'Superba' | CMac SBfd |
| | - 'Verbanica' | CAlb CCVT LMil LRHS MAsh |
| | 'Spectrum' | CBcs CDoC CEnd CPMA EMil ERea LRHS MBri MGos NLar SKHP SLdr SSpi SSta |
| | ***sprengeri*** | CWib |
| | - 'Copeland Court' | CPMA NHim SSta |
| | - var. ***diva*** | CBcs CEnd CPLG EPfP NLar SKHP WPGP |
| | - - 'Burncoose' | CBcs CDoC |
| | - - 'Dark Diva' | CPMA |
| | - - 'Diva' | GGal NHim WPGP |
| | - - 'Eric Savill' | CPMA SKHP SSpi SSta WPGP |
| | - - 'Lanhydrock' | CPMA SSta WPGP |
| | - - 'Westonbirt' | WPGP |
| | - var. ***elongata*** | CPMA SKHP |
| | - 'Marwood Spring' | CMHG SKHP SSta WPGP |
| | 'Spring Rite' | CPMA |
| | 'Star Wars' ♀$^{H4}$ | CBcs CDoC CEnd CPLG CPMA CTho ELan EPfP ERea LMil LRHS LTen MAsh MBri MGos NLar SBrd SKHP SPoG SSpi SSta WPGP |
| | 'Stellar Acclaim' | CBcs CPMA |
| | ***stellata*** ♀$^{H4}$ | Widely available |
| | - 'Centennial' | CDoC CPMA CTho MBri NLar SSta WFar |
| | - 'Chrysanthemumiflora' | CPMA EGxp EPfP SKHP |
| | - 'Dawn' | CPMA |
| | - 'Jane Platt' | CPMA ELan EPfP EWes LMil LRHS MBri MGos SKHP SPoG SSpi SSta |
| | - f. ***keiskei*** | CBcs CEnd CPMA EPfP MGos NHol NLar SKHP |
| | - 'Kikuzaki' | CPMA |
| | - 'King Rose' | CBcs CDoC CPMA CTsd EPfP LAst MAsh NHim SPoG |
| | - 'Massey' | CPMA |
| | - 'Norman Gould' | see *M. kobus* 'Norman Gould' |
| | - 'Rosea' | CBar CMCN CPMA CTho ELan ELon GEdr GKev IVic LMil MDun MGos MRav MSwo NEgg NLar SKHP WDin |
| | - 'Rosea Massey' | CPMA WFar |
| | - 'Royal Star' | Widely available |
| | - 'Scented Silver' | CPMA LRHS MAsh SPoG |
| | - 'Shi-banchi Rosea' | CPMA |
| | - 'Waterlily' ♀$^{H4}$ | CBcs CMCN CMac CPMA CTho ELan ELon EPfP GKev LAst LMil LRHS LSRN LTen MAsh MBlu NHim NLar NPCo SKHP SLim SPer SPoG SSpi SSta WDin WFar WGob WPGP |
| | 'Summer Solstice' | CBcs CPMA NHim |
| | 'Sun Ray' | CBcs CPMA |
| | 'Sunburst' | CBcs CPMA |
| | 'Sundance' | CBcs CPMA NLar |
| § | 'Sundew' | CDoC CTsd EPfP EQua IArd MGos NHim NLar NPCo |
| | 'Sunrise' | CBcs |
| | 'Sunsation' | CBcs CDoC CPMA SSta |

| | |
|---|---|
| 'Sunspire' | CBcs CPMA NLar |
| 'Suntown' | CPMA |
| 'Susan' ΨH4 | Widely available |
| 'Susanna van Veen' | CBcs CDoC CEnd CPMA WPGP |
| 'Swedish Star' | CPMA |
| 'Sweet Merlot' | CBcs CDoC CPMA |
| 'Sweet Valentine' | CBcs CPMA |
| 'Sweetheart' | CPMA SSpi |
| 'Theodora' | NLar |
| × ***thompsoniana*** | CBcs CMCN EPfP NLar SSpi |
| - 'Olmenhof' | IArd |
| 'Thousand Butterflies' | CBcs CPMA |
| 'Tina Durio' | SKHP |
| 'Todd Gresham' | CPMA |
| 'Todd's Forty Niner' | CPMA |
| 'Touch of Pink' | CBcs NLar |
| 'Tranquility' | CBcs CPMA SKHP |
| 'Trewidden Belle' | CEnd |
| ***tripetala*** | CBcs CMCN CPLG ELan EPfP MDun NLar SKHP SSpi SSta WDin WPGP |
| - 'Bloomfield' | CPMA |
| 'Ultimate Yellow' | CPMA NLar |
| 'Valley Scorcher' **new** | SSta |
| × ***veitchii*** | CBcs CDul EPfP |
| - 'Peter Veitch' | CTho |
| ***virginiana*** | CBcs CMCN CPMA EPfP IArd IDee NLar SBig SKHP SSpi WDin WPGP |
| - 'Aiken County' **new** | SKHP |
| - 'Green Shadow' **new** | SGol |
| - 'Havener' | SKHP |
| - 'Henry Hicks' | CPMA |
| - 'Moonglow' | CPMA |
| - 'Pink Halo' | CPMA |
| - 'Satellite' | CPMA |
| 'Vulcan' | CBcs CDoC CEnd CPMA ELan EPfP MBri NHol SCoo |
| × ***watsonii*** | see *M.* × *wieseneri* |
| 'White Mystery' **new** | CPMA |
| § × ***wieseneri*** | CBcs CGHE CPMA EBee ELan EPfP ERea IArd LRHS MBlu NLar SKHP SPer SSpi WFar WPGP |
| - 'Aashild Kalleberg' | CPMA SKHP SSpi |
| - 'Lupo Osti' **new** | SKHP |
| - 'William Watson' **new** | SSta |
| ***wilsonii*** ΨH4 | Widely available |
| - 'Gwen Baker' | CEnd |
| 'Yaeko' | CPMA |
| 'Yellow Fever' | CBcs CPMA CTho |
| 'Yellow Garland' | CPMA |
| 'Yellow Lantern' | CAbP CBcs CDoC CEnd CPMA EPfP LMil LRHS LSRN MAsh MBlu NLar SPoG SSpi SSta |
| 'Yellow Sea' | CPMA |
| ***yunnanensis*** ambig. | CCCN MBri MPkF SSpi |
| ***zenii*** 'Pink Parchment' | CPMA |

## × *Mahoberberis* (*Berberidaceae*)

| | |
|---|---|
| ***aquisargentii*** | CMac EBee ECrN EPfP GCal LRHS MMuc MRav SEND SKHP WFar |
| 'Dart's Desire' | NLar |
| 'Dart's Treasure' | EPla |
| 'Magic' | NLar |
| ***miethkeana*** | LRHS SRms WDin |
| ***neubertii*** | NLar |

## *Mahonia* ✿ (*Berberidaceae*)

| | |
|---|---|
| § ***aquifolium*** | CBcs CDul CMac EBee ECrN MGos MMuc MRav NWea SGol SPer SPlb SReu WDin |
| - 'Apollo' ΨH4 | CMac CSBt CWib ELan EPfP LAst LHop LRHS LSRN MAsh MGos MRav MWat NEgg NLar SCoo SEND SPer SPoG WDin |
| - 'Atropurpurea' | CMac CSBt ELan EPfP EPla NLar SPer WDin |
| - 'Cosmo Crawl' | LRHS |
| - 'Euro' | NLar |
| - 'Fascicularis' | see *M.* × *wagneri* 'Pinnacle' |
| - 'Green Ripple' | CPMA EPfP NLar |
| - 'Orange Flame' | CPMA EPfP NLar |
| - 'Smaragd' | CDoC CMac ELan EPfP LRHS LSRN MBlu MGos MRav SLPl |
| - 'Versicolor' | EPla MBlu |
| ***bealei*** | see *M. japonica* Bealei Group |
| 'Bokrafoot'PBR | EPfP LRHS MAsh MBlu SLon SSta |
| ***confusa*** | CDoC CGHE CHEx EPla LLHF LRHS NLar SKHP SMad WFar WPGP |
| ***eutriphylla*** | see *M. trifolia* |
| ***fortunei*** | CBcs IDee MBlu NLar WSHC |
| - 'Winter Prince' | NLar |
| ***gracilipes*** | CGHE CHEx EPfP EPla GCal MBlu MDun NLar SKHP SLon SPoG SSpi WPGP |
| ***japonica*** ΨH4 | Widely available |
| § - Bealei Group | CAlb CBcs CDul CSBt EBee ELan ELon EPfP EPla LAst LRHS MAsh MGos MRav MSwo NHol NPer NPla NWea SBfd SCoo SGol SKHP SLim SWvt WDin WFar |
| - 'Gold Dust' | CMac NLar NWea |
| - 'Hiemalis' | see *M. japonica* 'Hivernant' |
| § - 'Hivernant' | EPfP LTen MGos NEgg NWea |
| ***lanceolata*** | WPGP |
| ***leschenaultii*** B&SWJ 9535 | WCru |
| × ***lindsayae*** 'Cantab' **new** | WPGP |
| ***lomariifolia*** ΨH3 | CBcs CBot CHEx EPfP EWes GCal LRHS MAsh MBlu SArc SBfd SBrd SKHP SPoG SSpi |
| ***longibracteata*** **new** | WPGP |
| × ***media*** 'Buckland' ΨH4 | CAlb CBcs CDul CHab CMac CSam CTrC EBee EPfP MRav NCGa NEgg NLar SBfd SDix SPer SRms WPat |
| - 'Charity' | Widely available |
| - 'Hope' | NLar |
| - 'Lionel Fortescue' ΨH4 | CAlb CBcs CEnd CMac CSBt CSam CTrC EBee ELan EPfP GKin LHop LRHS MAsh MCoo MRav NCGa NEgg SBfd SDix SKHP SPer SPoG SSpi WCFE |
| - 'Winter Sun' ΨH4 | Widely available |
| ***nervosa*** | CMac EPfP MBlu NEgg NLar WCru WDin |
| - B&SWJ 9562 | WCru |
| ***nitens*** | CBcs |
| - 'Cabaret'PBR **new** | EPfP EWTr LRHS MMHG |
| * ***nitida*** | WPGP |
| ***oiwakensis*** B&SWJ 371 | WCru |
| - B&SWJ 3660 | WCru |
| ***pallida*** | SKHP SSpi WPGP |
| ***pinnata*** misapplied | see *M.* × *wagneri* 'Pinnacle' |
| ***pinnata*** ambig. | EPfP |
| ***pinnata*** (Lag.) Fedde 'Ken S. Howard' **new** | NLar |
| - 'Maurice Foster' **new** | NLar |
| ***repens*** | GCal NLar NMun |
| × ***savilliana*** | EPla WPGP |
| - 'Commissioner' | CWib |
| Sioux = 'Bokrasio'PBR | LRHS MAsh SPoG |

§ ***trifolia*** GCal
***trifoliolata*** var. ***glauca*** CEnd CPMA NLar
× ***wagneri*** 'Fireflame' GCal
- 'Hastings Elegant' CPMA IDee NLar
- 'Moseri' NLar SSpi WPat
§ - 'Pinnacle' ♀H4 ELan EPfP EPla LRHS MAsh NLar SPer SPoG WDin
- 'Sunset' CPMA GKin MBlu NLar
- 'Undulata' EPfP LRHS MBlu NLar SPer SRms

## *Maianthemum* (*Asparagaceae*)

***amoenum*** LEdu
- B&SWJ 10390 WCru
***atropurpureum*** WCru
***bicolor*** CDes LEdu SWat
***bifolium*** CAvo CBct CDes CHid CMac EBee ECho GCra LEdu MAvo MMoz MNrw NBro NMen SBch SRms WCru WPtf WTin WWEG XLum
§ - subsp. ***kamtschaticum*** CLAP EBee ECha EPPr EPot LEdu LRHS LWst MAvo NLar NRya WCot WTin
- - B&SWJ 4360 WCru
- - CD&R 2300 WCru
* - - var. ***minimum*** GCal
***canadense*** EBee ECho EPot GCal GGar MNrw NBid NMen WCru WHil WPnP
***chasmanthum*** see *M. bifolium* subsp. *kamtschaticum*
***comaltepecense*** B&SWJ 10215 WCru
***dilatatum*** see *M. bifolium* subsp. *kamtschaticum*
***flexuosum*** LEdu
- B&SWJ 9069 WCru
- B&SWJ 9079 WCru
- B&SWJ 9150 WCru
aff. ***flexuosum*** B&SWJ 9026 WCru
- B&SWJ 9055 WCru
***formosanum*** B&SWJ 349 EPPr WCru
***forrestii*** WCru
***fuscum*** GBin WCru
- var. ***cordatum*** WCru
***gigas*** B&SWJ 10470 WCru
***henryi*** ECho GEdr LEdu WCru
***japonicum*** LEdu
- B&SWJ 1179 WCru
- B&SWJ 4714 WCru
***oleraceum*** CBct CPLG GBin GEdr LEdu MMoz WCot WFar
- B&SWJ 2148 WCru
- purple-flowered **new** GEdr
***paniculatum*** B&SWJ 9137 WCru
- B&SWJ 9140 WCru
- purple-flowered B&SWJ 9139 **new** WCru
pendent, B&SWJ 10305 from Guatemala WCru
***purpureum*** G-W&P 150 EPPr
***racemosum*** ♀H4 Widely available
- subsp. ***amplexicaule*** GBin GCal
- - 'Emily Moody' CBct CDes CPLG CPou EBee EPPr EPfP EPla SKHP WPGP
- dwarf ECho
- 'Wisley Spangles' LRHS
aff. ***salvinii*** B&SWJ 9000 WCru
- B&SWJ 9088 WCru
- B&SWJ 10402 WCru
***scilloideum*** B&SWJ 10407 WCru
* - var. ***roseum*** B&SWJ 10335 **new** WCru
***stellatum*** CAvo CBct EBee ECha ECho EPPr EPfP EPla EPot GAuc GBBs GBin GCal LEdu LHop LRHS MAvo NChi NLar SMad SMrm WCru WFar WGwG WHil WPnP WTin XLum
***szechuanicum*** WCru
***tatsienense*** CBct CPLG WCru WFar

## *Maihuenia* (*Cactaceae*)

***poeppigii*** SPlb WCot

## *Maireana* (*Amaranthaceae*)

***georgei*** SPlb

## *Malacothamnus* (*Malvaceae*)

***fremontii*** MDKP

## *Malus* ✿ (*Rosaceae*)

§ 'Adirondack' CLnd EPfP LRHS MAsh MBlu MBri MMuc MWat NLar SCoo SEND SLim SPoG WJas
'Admiration' see *M.* 'Adirondack'
× ***adstringens*** 'Almey' ECrN
- 'Hopa' CDul
- 'Simcoe' EBee LLHF
'Aldenhamensis' see *M.* × *purpurea* 'Aldenhamensis'
'Amberina' CLnd
× ***arnoldiana*** LMaj
× ***atrosanguinea*** 'Gorgeous' CDul CLnd CTho EBee ECrN GTwe LRHS LSRN MAsh MGos MSwo NLar NWea SCoo SEWo SKee SLim SPer SPoG WDin WJas WMou
***baccata*** CDul CMCN CTho GTwe MMuc NWea SCoo SEND SPlb
- 'Dolgo' EPom SKee WHar
- 'Lady Northcliffe' CLnd SFam
- var. ***mandshurica*** CTho
- 'Street Parade' LMaj
aff. ***baccata*** MAsh NWea
§ ***bhutanica*** CDul CLnd MAsh SCrf
- 'Mandarin' MBri NLar SCoo
***brevipes*** CLnd CTho LRHS SCoo
- 'Wedding Bouquet' CWSG ERea MAsh MWat NLar SEWo
'Butterball' CDul CLnd CTho EBee ECrN EPfP ERea LAst LMaj LTen NWea SCoo SLim SPer WDin WHar WJas WMou
'Candymint Sargent' CLnd
'Cave Hill' CLnd
* 'Cheal's Weeping' CMac LAst MMuc NEgg
Coccinella = 'Courtarou' MMuc SGol WDin
'Comtessa de Paris' EPfP LRHS LTen MAsh
'Coralburst' MAsh MBri
***coronaria*** var. ***dasycalyx*** 'Charlottae' (d) CDul CLnd EBee EPfP SPer SPur
- 'Elk River' MAsh SCoo
'Crimson Brilliant' CLnd
'Crittenden' EBee ECrN MAsh MRav SLim
* 'Directeur Moerlands' CCVT CDoC EBee ECrN EPfP IArd SBfd SPur WDin
***domestica*** 'Acklam Russet' (D) SKee
- 'Acme' (D) ECrN MCoo SDea
- 'Adams's Pearmain' (D) CCAT CTho CTri ECrN ERea GTwe LRHS MAsh MCoo SDea SFam SKee WHar WWct
- 'Admiral' (D) ECrN ERea

| |  |  |
|---|---|---|
| | – 'Akane' (D) | SDea |
| § | – 'Alexander' (C) | SKee |
| | – 'Alfriston' (C) | CAgr SKee |
| § | – 'Alkmene' (D) ♀H4 | CAgr ECrN SDea SKee |
| | – 'All Doer' (D/C/Cider) | CCAT CTho |
| | – 'Allen's Everlasting' (D) | GTwe SDea SKee |
| | – 'Allington Pippin' (D) | CSBt CTho CTri ECrN LRHS SDea SFam SKee WHar |
| | – 'American Mother' | see *M. domestica* 'Mother' |
| | – 'Ananas Reinette' (D) | ECrN SKee |
| | – 'Anna Boelens' (D) | SDea |
| | – 'Annie Elizabeth' (C) | CAgr CCAT CTho CWib ECrN GTwe LAst LRHS MCoo SDea SFam SKee SVic WHar WJas WWct |
| | – 'Anniversary' (D) | SDea |
| | – 'Ard Cairn Russet' (D) | ECrN SDea SKee |
| | – 'Arthur Turner' (C) ♀H4 | CCVT CTri ECrN EPom GTwe LAst LBuc MWat SCrf SDea SFam SKee WHar WJas |
| | – 'Ashmead's Kernel' (D) ♀H4 | CAgr CBod CCAT CDul CSBt CTho CTri CWSG CWib ECrN EPfP EPom ERea GTwe LBuc LRHS MAsh MCoo MRav MWat NWea SCrf SDea SFam SKee SLim SVic WHar WJas WWct |
| | – 'Ashton Bitter' (Cider) | CCAT CTho CTri GTwe |
| | – 'Ashton Brown Jersey' (Cider) | CCAT |
| | – 'Autumn Pearmain' (D) | SDea WHar |
| | – 'Aynho Scarlet' (F) **new** | LBuc |
| | – 'Baker's Delicious' (D) | ECrN SDea SKee WHar |
| | – 'Ballerina Flamenco' (F) **new** | MAsh |
| | – 'Ball's Bittersweet' (Cider) | CCAT CTho ERea |
| | – 'Balsam' | see *M. domestica* 'Green Balsam' |
| | – 'Banana Pippin' | CEnd |
| | – 'Banns' (D) | ECrN ERea |
| | – 'Bardsey' (D) | CAgr EPom ERea LBuc WGwG WHar |
| | – 'Barnack Beauty' (D) | CTho CTri SKee |
| | – 'Barnack Orange' (D) | SKee |
| | – 'Baumann's Reinette' (D) | SKee |
| | – 'Baxter's Pearmain' (D) | ECrN ERea SDea SKee |
| | – 'Beauty of Bath' (D) | CAgr CCAT CCVT CDoC CDul CTho CTri CWib ECrN ELan GTwe LAst LBuc SDea SFam SKee SPer WHar WJas |
| | – 'Beauty of Hants' (D) | ECrN |
| | – 'Beauty of Kent' (C) | SDea SKee |
| | – 'Beauty of Moray' (C) | GQui SKee |
| | – 'Bedwyn Beauty' (C) | CTho |
| | – 'Beeley Pippin' (D) | GTwe SDea SKee |
| | – 'Bell Apple' (Cider/C) | CCAT CTho |
| | – 'Belle de Boskoop' (C/D) ♀H4 | CAgr CCAT ECrN GTwe MCoo SDea SKee |
| | – 'Belvoir Seedling' (D/C) | SKee |
| | – 'Bembridge Beauty' (F) | SDea |
| | – 'Ben's Red' (D) | CAgr CBod CCAT CEnd CTho |
| | – 'Bess Pool' (D) | MCoo SDea SFam |
| | – 'Bewley Down Pippin' | see *M. domestica* 'Crimson King' (Cider/C) |
| | – 'Bickington Grey' (Cider) | CTho |
| | – 'Billy Down Pippin' (F) | CTho |
| | – 'Bismarck' (C) | CCAT ECrN SKee |
| | – 'Black Dabinett' (Cider) | CCAT CEnd CTho |
| | – 'Black Tom Putt' (C/D) | CTho |
| | – 'Blenheim Orange' (C/D) ♀H4 | Widely available |
| | – 'Bloody Ploughman' (D) | ECrN GTwe LRHS SKee SLon WHar |
| | – 'Blue Pearmain' (D) | SDea |
| | – 'Blue Sweet' (Cider) | CTho |
| | – Bolero = 'Tuscan'PBR (D/Ball) | MCoo SDea SKee |
| | – 'Boston Russet' | see *M. domestica* 'Roxbury Russet' |
| | – 'Bountiful' (C) | CAgr CCAT CDoC CDul CSBt CTri CWSG CWib ECrN EPom GTwe LRHS LSRN MBri NLar SDea SKee SLim WHar WWct |
| | – 'Braddick Nonpareil' (D) | SKee |
| | – 'Braeburn' (D) | CAgr CCAT CSut CTri ECrN EPom ERea LAst LBuc LRHS MAsh SBfd SCrf SDea SEWo SFam SKee SPer WHar WJas |
| | – 'Braintree Seedling' (D) | ECrN |
| | – 'Bramley's Seedling' (C) ♀H4 | Widely available |
| | – 'Bramley's Seedling' clone 20 | CDoC CMac ERea MBri NLar SCoo SDea SLim SPoG WHar WWct |
| | – 'Bramshott Rectory' (D/C) | SKee |
| | – 'Bread Fruit' (C/D) | CEnd CTho |
| | – 'Breakwell's Seedling' (Cider) | CCAT CTho |
| | – 'Bridgwater Pippin' (C) | CCAT CTho |
| | – 'Bright Future' (D) **new** | LBuc MCoo WWct |
| | – 'Broad-eyed Pippin' (C) | SKee |
| | – 'Broadholm Beauty' | EPom MAsh WHar |
| | – 'Brookes's' (D) | WHar |
| | – 'Brown Snout' (Cider) | CCAT CTho |
| | – 'Brownlees Russet' (D) | CAgr CCAT CTho CTri GTwe LRHS MCoo NEgg NWea SDea SFam SKee WHar |
| | – 'Brown's Apple' (Cider) | CAgr CCAT GTwe |
| | – 'Brown's Seedling' (D) **new** | SKee |
| | – 'Broxwood Foxwhelp' (Cider) | CCAT |
| | – 'Burn's Seedling' (D) | CTho |
| | – 'Burrowhill Early' (Cider) | CTho |
| | – 'Bushey Grove' (C) | SDea |
| | – 'Buttery Do' | CCAT CTho |
| | – 'Byfleet Seedling' (C) | SKee |
| | – 'Cadbury' | CCAT |
| | – 'Calville Blanc d'Hiver' (D) | SKee |
| | – 'Cambusnethan Pippin' (D) | GQui SKee |
| | – 'Camelot' (Cider/C) | CCAT |
| | – 'Cap of Liberty' (Cider) | CCAT |
| | – 'Captain Broad' (D/Cider) | CCAT CEnd CTho |
| | – 'Captain Kidd' (D) | EPom SKee WHar |
| | – 'Captain Smith' (F) | CEnd |
| | – 'Carlisle Codlin' (C) | GTwe NLar NWea SDea SKee |
| | – 'Caroline' (D) | ECrN |
| | – 'Carswell's Orange' (D) | SKee |
| | – 'Catherine' (C) | ECrN |
| | – 'Catshead' (C) | CAgr CCAT CTri ECrN GQui MAsh SDea SKee WHar WWct |
| | – 'Caudal Market' (F) **new** | LBuc |
| | – 'Cellini' (C/D) | SDea |
| | – 'Cevaal' (D) **new** | WWct |
| | – 'Charles Ross' (C/D) ♀H4 | Widely available |
| | – 'Charlotte'PBR (C/Ball) | SDea |
| | – 'Chaxhill Red' (Cider/D) | CCAT CTho |
| | – 'Cheddar Cross' (D) | CAgr CCVT CTri ECrN |
| | – 'Chelmsford Wonder' (C) | SKee |
| | – 'Chisel Jersey' (Cider) | CAgr CCAT CTri SKee |
| | – 'Chivers Delight' (D) | CAgr CCAT CSBt ECrN ERea GTwe LRHS MCoo SDea SKee WHar WJas |
| | – 'Chorister Boy' (D) | CTho |

| |  |  |
|---|---|---|
| | – 'Christmas Pearmain' (D) | CAgr CTho ECrN GTwe SDea SFam SKee |
| | – 'Cider Lady's Finger' (Cider) | CCAT SKee |
| | – 'Cissy' (D) | WGwG |
| | – 'Claygate Pearmain' (D) ♀H4 | CAgr CCAT CTho CTri ECrN GTwe LRHS MCoo SDea SFam SKee SVic WHar |
| | – 'Clopton Red' (D) | ECrN |
| | – 'Clydeside' | GQui |
| | – 'Coat Jersey' (Cider) | CCAT |
| | – 'Cobra' | LBuc LRHS MAsh MBri MCoo WHar |
| | – 'Cockle Pippin' (D) | CAgr CTho SDea SKee |
| | – 'Coeur de Boeuf' (C/D) | SKee |
| | – 'Coleman's Seedling' (Cider) | CTho |
| | – 'Collogett Pippin' (C/Cider) | CCAT CEnd CTho |
| | – 'Colonel Vaughan' (C/D) | SKee |
| | – 'Cornish Aromatic' (D) | CAgr CBod CCAT CTho CTri GTwe SCrf SDea SFam SKee WHar |
| | – 'Cornish Gilliflower' (D) | CAgr CBod CCAT CDul CTho ECrN LRHS MCoo SDea SFam SKee WHar |
| | – 'Cornish Honeypin' (D) | CEnd CTho SKee |
| | – 'Cornish Longstem' (D) | CAgr CEnd CTho |
| | – 'Cornish Mother' (D) | CEnd CTho |
| | – 'Cornish Pine' (D) | CEnd CTho SDea |
| | – 'Coronation' (D) | SDea SKee |
| | – 'Corse Hill' (D) | CCAT CTho |
| | – 'Costard' (C) | GTwe SKee |
| | – 'Cottenham Seedling' (C) | SKee |
| | – 'Coul Blush' (D) | SKee |
| | – 'Court of Wick' (D) | CAgr CCAT CTho ECrN SKee SVic WHar |
| | – 'Court Pendu Plat' (D) | CAgr CCAT CTho LBuc MAsh MWat NWea SDea SFam SKee WHar WJas WWct |
| | – 'Court Royal' (Cider) | CCAT |
| | – 'Cox Cymraeg' (D) | WGwG |
| | – 'Cox's Orange Pippin' (D) | Widely available |
| | – 'Cox's Pomona' (C/D) | SDea SKee WHar |
| | – 'Cox's Rouge de Flandres' (D) | SKee |
| | – 'Cox's Selfing' (D) | CDoC CTri CWSG CWib EPfP EPom GTwe LBuc LRHS MAsh MBri MGos MNHC SCrf SDea SKee SPer SPoG WHar WJas |
| | – 'Crawley Beauty' (C) | CAgr CCAT GTwe SDea SFam SKee WHar |
| | – 'Crimson Beauty of Bath' (D) | CAgr |
| | – 'Crimson Bramley' (C) | CCAT LAst |
| | – 'Crimson Cox' (D) | SDea |
| § | – 'Crimson King' (Cider/C) | CAgr CCAT |
| | – 'Crimson King' (D) | CAgr |
| | – 'Crimson Peasgood' (C) | SKee |
| | – 'Crimson Queening' (D) | WHar |
| | – 'Crimson Victoria' (Cider) | CTho |
| | – Crispin | see *M. domestica* 'Mutsu' |
| | – 'Croen Mochyn' (D) **new** | WGwG |
| § | – 'Crowngold' (D) | EPom GTwe |
| | – 'Cutler Grieve' (D) | SDea |
| | – Cybèle = 'Delrouval' | LRHS |
| | – 'Dabinett' (Cider) | CAgr CCAT CTho CTri ERea GTwe LBuc SCrf SDea SKee WHar WWct |
| | – 'D'Arcy Spice' (D) | CAgr CCAT ECrN EPfP ERea MCoo MWat SDea SFam SKee WHar WWct |
| | – 'Deacon's Blushing Beauty' (C/D) | SDea |
| | – 'Deacon's Millennium' | SDea |
| | – 'Decio' (D) | SKee |
| | – Delbarestivale = 'Delcorf' (red) (D) ♀H4 | LRHS |
| | – 'Devon Crimson Queen' (D) | CTho |
| | – 'Devonshire Buckland' (C) | CEnd CTho |
| | – 'Devonshire Crimson Queen' (D) | SDea |
| | – 'Devonshire Quarrenden' (D) | CAgr CCAT CDul CEnd CTho LRHS SDea SFam SKee SVic WHar WJas |
| | – 'Diamond' (D) | WGwG |
| | – 'Discovery' (D) ♀H4 | Widely available |
| | – 'Doctor Harvey' (C) | ECrN ERea SFam SKee |
| | – 'Doctor Kidd's Orange Red' | see *M. domestica* 'Kidd's Orange Red' |
| | – 'Don's Delight' (C) | CTho |
| | – 'Dove' (Cider) | CCAT |
| | – 'Downton Pippin' (D) | WHar |
| | – 'Dredge's Fame' (D) | CTho |
| | – 'Duchess of Oldenburg' (C/D) | SKee |
| | – 'Duchess's Favourite' (D) | SKee |
| | – 'Dufflin' (Cider) | CCAT CTho |
| | – 'Duke of Cornwall' (C) | CTho |
| | – 'Duke of Devonshire' (D) | CTho CTri SDea SFam SKee |
| N | – 'Dumeller's Seedling' | see *M. domestica* 'Dummellor's Seedling' |
| § | – 'Dummellor's Seedling' (C) ♀H4 | CCAT CTri SDea SKee WHar |
| | – 'Dunkerton Late Sweet' (Cider) | CCAT CCVT CTho LBuc |
| | – 'Dunn's Seedling' (D) | SDea |
| § | – 'Dutch Mignonne' (D) | ECrN SKee |
| | – 'Dymock Red' (Cider) | CCAT LBuc |
| | – 'Early Blenheim' (D/C) | CCAT CEnd CTho |
| | – 'Early Bower' (D) | CEnd |
| | – 'Early Julyan' (C) | GQui SKee |
| | – 'Early Victoria' | see *M. domestica* 'Emneth Early' |
| | – Early Windsor | see *M. domestica* 'Alkmene' |
| | – 'Early Worcester' | see *M. domestica* 'Tydeman's Early Worcester' |
| | – 'East Lothian Pippin' (C) | GQui |
| | – 'Easter Orange' (D) | GTwe |
| | – 'Ecklinville' (C) | SDea |
| | – 'Eden' | LBuc |
| | – 'Edith Hopwood' (D) | ECrN |
| | – 'Edward VII' (C) ♀H4 | CCAT GTwe MAsh SCrf SDea SFam SKee WHar WWct |
| | – 'Egremont Russet' (D) ♀H4 | Widely available |
| | – 'Ellis' Bitter' (Cider) | CCAT CTho GTwe SKee SVic |
| | – 'Ellison's Orange' (D) ♀H4 | CAgr CCAT CDul CMac CSBt CTri CWib ECrN EPfP ERea GTwe LAst LBuc LRHS MMuc MWat NWea SDea SFam SKee SPer SVic WHar WJas WWct |
| | – 'Elstar' (D) ♀H4 | CCVT CWib ECrN EPom GTwe LAst LRHS SDea SKee WHar |
| | – 'Elton Beauty' (D) | SDea SKee |
| § | – 'Emneth Early' (C) ♀H4 | CAgr ECrN ERea GTwe SDea SFam SKee WJas WWct |
| | – 'Emperor Alexander' | see *M. domestica* 'Alexander' |
| | – 'Empire' (D) | LAst SKee |
| | – 'Encore' (C) | SDea |
| | – 'Endsleigh Beauty' (D) | CEnd |
| | – 'English Codlin' (C) | CCAT CTho CTri ERea |
| | – 'Epicure' | see *M. domestica* 'Laxton's Epicure' |
| | – 'Ernie's Russet' (D) | SDea |
| | – 'Eros' (D) | ECrN |
| | – 'Essex Pippin' (D) | ECrN |

- 'Evening Gold' (C) SDea
- 'Eve's Delight' (D) SDea
- 'Excelsior' (C) ECrN
- 'Exeter Cross' (D) CCAT ECrN SDea SFam
- 'Eynsham Challenger' (F) **new** LBuc
- 'Fair Maid of Devon' (Cider) CAgr CCAT CEnd CTho
- 'Fairfield' (D) CTho
- 'Falstaff'PBR (D) ♀H4 CAgr CCAT CDul ECrN EPfP EPom GTwe LSRN MGos NPri SCoo SDea SKee WHar WJas
- 'Farmer's Glory' (D) CAgr CTho
- 'Feltham Beauty' (D) LBuc
- 'Fiesta'PBR (D) ♀H4 Widely available
- 'Fillbarrel' (Cider) CCAT
- 'Firmgold' (D) SDea
- 'Flame' (D) ECrN SKee
- 'Flamenco'PBR see *M. domestica* 'Obelisk'

§ - 'Flower of Kent' (C) SCrf SDea SKee
- 'Forfar' see *M. domestica* 'Dutch Mignonne'
- 'Forge' (D) CAgr SDea SKee
- 'Fortune' see *M. domestica* 'Laxton's Fortune'
- 'Foxwhelp' (Cider) LBuc SKee
- 'Francis' (D) ECrN
- 'Frederick' (Cider) CCAT CTho
- 'French Crab' (C) SDea
- 'Freyberg' (D) SKee
- 'Fuji' (D) SDea SKee
- 'Gala' (D) CMac CSBt EPom GTwe LAst SCoo SCrf SDea SFam SKee SLim WHar
- 'Galloway Pippin' (C) GQui GTwe SKee
- 'Garnet' (D) ECrN
- 'Gascoyne's Scarlet' (D) CCAT SDea SFam SKee WHar WJas
- 'Gavin' (D) CAgr SDea SKee
- 'Genesis II' (D/C) SDea
- 'Genet Moyle' (C/Cider) CTri WHar
- 'George Carpenter' (D) SDea
- 'George Cave' (D) CTho ECrN GTwe MCoo SDea SFam SKee WHar WJas
- 'George Neal' (C) ♀H4 CAgr SDea SFam
- 'Gilliflower of Gloucester' (D) CTho
- 'Gin' (Cider) CCAT
- 'Gladstone' (D) CAgr CTho SKee WHar WWct

§ - 'Glass Apple' (C/D) CCAT CEnd CTho
- 'Gloria Mundi' (C) SDea SKee
- 'Gloster '69' (D) SDea SKee
- 'Gloucester Royal' (D) CTho
- 'Gloucester Underleaf' CTho
- 'Golden Ball' CTho
- 'Golden Bittersweet' (D) CAgr CTho
- 'Golden Bromham' (F) **new** LBuc
- 'Golden Delicious' (D) ♀H4 CCVT CDul CSBt CWib ECrN ELan EPfP LAst MMuc SBfd SCrf SDea SEWo SKee SVic WHar
- 'Golden Glow' (C) SDea
- 'Golden Harvey' (D) CAgr CCAT SKee
- 'Golden Jubilee' CEnd
- 'Golden Knob' (D) CCAT CTho SKee
- 'Golden Noble' (C) ♀H4 CAgr CCAT CTho CTri ECrN ERea GTwe MCoo SDea SFam SKee
- 'Golden Nugget' (D) CAgr SKee
- 'Golden Pippin' (C) CAgr CCAT SKee WHar
- 'Golden Reinette' (D) GTwe SFam SKee
- 'Golden Russet' (D) CAgr ECrN GTwe SDea SKee WHar
- 'Golden Spire' (C) MCoo SDea SKee WHar
- 'Gooseberry' (C) LSRN
- 'Gooseberry Apple' (Ronald's) (F) **new** LBuc
- 'Goring' (Cider) CTho
- 'Granny Smith' (D) CBcs CDul CLnd CWib ECrN GTwe LAst LRHS LSRN SCrf SDea SKee SPer SVic WHar
- 'Gravenstein' (D) CCAT GQui SDea SFam SKee

§ - 'Green Balsam' (D) CTri
- 'Green Kilpandy Pippin' (C) GQui
- 'Green Roland' ECrN ERea
- 'Greensleeves'PBR (D) ♀H4 CAgr CCAT CDoC CDul CMac CSBt CTri CWib ECrN EPfP EPom GTwe LAst LRHS MGos MMuc NLar SDea SKee SLim WHar WJas WWct
- 'Grenadier' (C) ♀H4 CAgr CCAT CDoC CSBt CTri ECrN GTwe LRHS MGos MMuc SDea SFam SKee SLon SVic WHar WJas
- 'Gwell Na Mil' (D) **new** WGwG
- 'Hagloe Crab' LBuc
- 'Halstow Natural' (Cider) CAgr CTho
- 'Hambledon Deux Ans' (C) SDea SFam SKee
- 'Hangy Down' (Cider) CCAT CTho
- Harmonie = 'Delorina' LRHS

§ - 'Harry Master's Jersey' (Cider) CAgr CCAT CTho CTri ERea SDea SKee WHar
- 'Harvester' (D) CTho
- 'Harvey' (C) SDea
- 'Hawthornden' (C) GQui GTwe SKee
- 'Herefordshire Redstreak' ERea WHar
- 'Herefordshire Russet'PBR CDul CWSG EPom LBuc LRHS MAsh MBri MCoo SKee SLim WHar WJas WWct
- 'Herring's Pippin' (D) CTri GTwe LBuc SDea
- 'High View Pippin' (D) SKee
- 'Hoary Morning' (C) CCAT CTho ECrN SDea SKee
- 'Hocking's Green' (C/D) CAgr CCAT CEnd CTho
- 'Holland Pippin' (C) WHar
- 'Hollow Core' (C) CAgr CTho
- 'Holstein' (D) CTho SDea SKee
- 'Honey Pippin' (D) ECrN
- 'Honey String' (F) CCAT
- 'Horneburger Pfannkuchen' (C) SKee
- 'Horsford Prolific' (D) ECrN ERea SKee
- 'Horsham Russet' (D) ERea
- 'Howgate Wonder' (C) CAgr CCAT CCVT CDul CSBt CWib ECrN ERea GTwe LAst LBuc LRHS MAsh MMuc SCrf SDea SFam SKee SPer SVic WHar WJas WWct
- 'Hubbard's Pearmain' (D) ECrN SKee
- 'Hunter's Majestic' (D/C) ECrN
- 'Hunt's Duke of Gloucester' (D) CTho LBuc
- 'Idared' (D) ♀H4 CCAT CWib ECrN SDea SKee SVic WHar
- 'Improved Dove' (Cider) CCAT
- 'Improved Keswick' (C/D) CEnd CTho
- 'Improved Lambrook Pippin' (Cider) CCAT CTho CTri
- 'Improved Redstreak' (Cider) CTho
- 'Ingall's Red' (D) **new** SKee
- 'Ingrid Marie' (D) SDea SKee
- 'Irish Peach' (D) CAgr CCAT CTri ECrN ERea GTwe LRHS MCoo SDea SFam SKee WHar
- 'Isaac Newton's Tree' see *M. domestica* 'Flower of Kent'
- 'Isle of Wight Pippin' (D) LBuc SDea
- 'Isle of Wight Russet' (D) SDea

| | | |
|---|---|---|
| | – 'Jackson's' | see *M. domestica* 'Crimson King' (Cider/C) |
| | – 'James Grieve' (D) ♀H4 | Widely available |
| | – 'Jerseymac' (D) | SDea |
| | – 'Jester' (D) | ECrN GTwe SDea SKee |
| | – 'Joaneting' (D) | CAgr |
| | – 'John Standish' (D) | CAgr CCAT CTri ERea GTwe SDea |
| | – 'John Toucher's' | see *M. domestica* 'Crimson King' (Cider/C) |
| | – 'Johnny Andrews' (Cider) | CAgr CTho |
| | – 'Johnny Voun' (D) | CEnd CTho |
| | – 'Jonagold' (D) ♀H4 | CTri CWib ECrN ELan EPom GTwe NLar SBfd SCrf SDea SFam SKee SPer SVic WWct |
| | – 'Jonagold Crowngold' | see *M. domestica* 'Crowngold' |
| § | – 'Jonagored'PBR (D) | MAsh SDea SKee WHar |
| | – 'Jonared' (D) | GTwe |
| | – 'Jonathan' (D) | CMac SDea SKee |
| | – 'Jordan's Weeping' (C) | ERea SDea |
| | – 'Josephine' (D) | SDea |
| | – 'Jubilee' | see *M. domestica* 'Royal Jubilee' |
| | – 'Julie's Late Golden' (F) | CTri |
| | – 'Jumbo' | LRHS MAsh MBri MCoo SKee WHar WJas |
| | – 'Jupiter'PBR (D) ♀H4 | CAgr CSBt CTri CWib ECrN GTwe LAst LSRN MAsh SBfd SDea SKee SLon WHar WJas |
| | – 'Kapai Red Jonathan' (D) | SDea |
| | – 'Karmijn de Sonnaville' (D) | SDea SKee |
| § | – 'Katja' (D) | CAgr CCAT CCVT CDoC CDul CMac CTri CWib ECrN ERea GKin GTwe LBuc MAsh MMuc NEgg NLar SBfd SCoo SDea SEWo SKee SPer WHar WJas WWct |
| | – Katy | see *M. domestica* 'Katja' |
| | – 'Kent' (D) | ECrN ERea GTwe MCoo NLar SCrf SDea |
| | – 'Kentish Fillbasket' (C) | SKee |
| | – 'Kerry Pippin' (D) | SKee |
| | – 'Keswick Codlin' (C) | CTho ECrN GTwe MBri MCoo NEgg NLar NWea SDea SKee WHar WJas |
| § | – 'Kidd's Orange Red' (D) ♀H4 | CAgr CCAT CMac CTri ECrN EPfP EPom GQui GTwe LBuc LRHS MWat SBfd SCrf SDea SFam SKee SLon WHar WWct |
| | – 'Kill Boy' | CTho |
| | – 'Killerton Sharp' (Cider) | CTho |
| | – 'Killerton Sweet' (Cider) | CTho |
| | – 'King Byerd' (C/D) | CCAT CEnd CTho |
| | – 'King Luscious' (D) | SDea |
| § | – 'King of the Pippins' (D) ♀H4 | CCAT CTho CTri ECrN GTwe MCoo SCrf SDea SFam SKee SVic WHar |
| | – 'King of Tompkins County' (D) | SFam |
| | – 'King Russet' (D) ♀H4 | SDea |
| | – 'King's Acre Pippin' (D) | CCAT SDea SFam WHar |
| | – 'Kingston Bitter' (Cider) | CTho |
| | – 'Kingston Black' (Cider/C) | CCAT CEnd CTho CTri ECrN GTwe LBuc SDea SKee |
| | – 'Kirton Fair' (D) | CTho |
| | – 'Knobby Russet' (D) | SKee |
| | – 'Lady Henniker' (D) | CCAT CTho ECrN GTwe SDea SKee WHar |
| | – 'Lady of the Wemyss' (C) | GQui SKee |
| | – 'Lady Sudeley' (D) | CTho SDea SKee |
| | – 'Lady's Finger' (C/D) | CEnd |
| | – 'Lady's Finger of Lancaster' (C/D) | SKee |
| | – 'Lady's Finger of Offaly' (D) | SDea |
| | – 'Lake's Kernel' (D) | CTho |
| | – 'Lane's Prince Albert' (C) ♀H4 | CAgr CCAT CSBt ECrN GTwe MGos MBri MWat NWea SCoo SCrf SDea SFam SKee SVic WHar WJas |
| | – 'Langley Pippin' (D) | SDea |
| § | – 'Langworthy' (Cider) | CCAT CTho |
| | – 'Lass o' Gowrie' (C) | GQui SKee |
| § | – 'Laxton's Epicure' (D) ♀H4 | CAgr CDul ECrN GTwe LAst SDea SFam SKee WHar |
| § | – 'Laxton's Fortune' (D) ♀H4 | CCAT CMac CSBt CTri CWib ECrN GTwe LAst SCrf SDea SFam SKee WHar WJas WWct |
| | – 'Laxton's Pearmain' (D) | MCoo SFam |
| | – 'Laxton's Royalty' (D) | SDea |
| § | – 'Laxton's Superb' (D) | CBcs CCAT CCVT CDul CMac CSBt CTri CWib ECrN ERea GKin GTwe LAst LBuc LHop LRHS MCoo NPri NWea SBfd SCrf SDea SEWo SKee SLim SPer SVic WHar WJas WWct |
| | – 'Leathercoat Russet' (D) | CAgr CCAT CTri SKee |
| | – 'Lemon Pippin' (C) | CCAT ECrN SDea WHar |
| | – 'Lemon Pippin of Gloucestershire' (D) | CTho |
| | – 'Liberty' (D) | SDea |
| | – 'Limberland' (C) | CTho |
| | – 'Limelight' (D) | ERea LBuc LRHS MAsh MBri MCoo NLar SBfd SCoo SKee SLim WHar |
| | – 'Link Wonder' | CEnd |
| | – 'Lodgemore Nonpareil' (D) | LBuc |
| | – 'Lodi' (C) | SDea |
| | – 'London Pearmain' (D) | ECrN |
| | – 'London Pippin' (C) | CAgr CTho |
| | – 'Longkeeper' (D) | CAgr CEnd CTho |
| | – 'Longney Russet' | LBuc |
| | – 'Longstem' (Cider) | CTho |
| | – 'Lord Burghley' (D) | SDea SKee |
| | – 'Lord Derby' (C) | CAgr CCAT CDul CMac CTho CWib ECrN EPom GTwe LRHS SCrf SDea SFam SKee SVic WHar WWct |
| | – 'Lord Grosvenor' (C) | SKee WHar |
| | – 'Lord Hindlip' (D) | LRHS SDea SFam WWct |
| | – 'Lord Lambourne' (D) ♀H4 | CAgr CCAT CDoC CDul CMac CSBt CSut CTri CWib ECrN EPfP GTwe LAst LRHS LSRN MAsh MCoo MGos MWat SBfd SCrf SDea SFam SKee SPer WHar WJas WWct |
| | – 'Lord of the Isles' (F) | CAgr CCAT |
| | – 'Lord Stradbroke' (C) | ECrN SKee |
| | – 'Lord Suffield' (C) | CTri ECrN SKee |
| | – 'Lucombe's Pine' (D) | CAgr CCAT CEnd CTho ECrN SVic |
| | – 'Lucombe's Seedling' (D) | CTho |
| | – 'Lynn's Pippin' (D) | ECrN |
| | – 'Mabbott's Pearmain' (D) | SDea |
| | – 'Maclean's Favourite' (D) | ECrN |
| | – 'Madresfield Court' (D) | SDea WWct |
| | – 'Maggie Sinclair' (D) | GQui |
| | – 'Maid of Kent' | CCAT |
| | – 'Major' (Cider) | CCAT |
| | – 'Maldon Wonder' (D) | ECrN |
| | – 'Malling Kent' (D) | ERea SDea SFam |
| | – 'Manaccan Primrose' (C/D) | CEnd |
| | – 'Mannington's Pearmain' (D) | SKee |
| | – 'Margil' (D) | CCAT SDea SFam SKee WHar |
| | – 'Marriage-maker' (D) | SKee |
| | – 'Maxton' (D) | ECrN |

| | |
|---|---|
| – 'May Queen' (D) | SDea SFam |
| – 'Maypole'PBR (D/Ball) | LAst MGos SDea WJas |
| – 'McIntosh' (D) | SKee |
| – 'Médaille d'Or' (Cider) | SKee |
| – 'Melon' (D) | SDea |
| – 'Melrose' (D) | ECrN SVic |
| – 'Merchant Apple' (D) | CCAT CTho CTri |
| – 'Mère de Ménage' (C) | SFam WHar |
| – 'Meridian'PBR (D) | CAgr CDoC ECrN LRHS SDea |
| – 'Merton Knave' (D) | SDea SFam |
| – 'Merton Russet' (D) | SDea |
| – 'Merton Worcester' (D) | ECrN SDea SKee |
| – 'Michaelmas Red' (D) | GTwe NEgg SKee |
| – 'Michelin' (Cider) | CAgr CCAT CTri ERea GTwe SDea SKee WHar WWct |
| – 'Miller's Seedling' (D) | SKee |
| – 'Millicent Barnes' (D) | SDea |
| – 'Mollie's Delicious' (D) | SKee |
| – 'Monarch' (C) | CAgr CCAT CTri ECrN GTwe SDea SFam SKee |
| – 'Montfort' (D) | ECrN |
| – 'Morgan's Sweet' (C/Cider) | CCAT CEnd CTho CTri SDea SKee |
| – 'Moss's Seedling' (D) | SDea |
| § – 'Mother' (D) ♀H4 | CAgr CCAT CTri ECrN GTwe SCrf SDea SKee |
| § – 'Mutsu' (D) | CCAT CTri ECrN LBuc SCrf SDea SKee SPer |
| – 'Nancy Jackson' (C) | SKee |
| – 'Nant Gwrtheyrn' (D) | WGwG |
| – 'Nettlestone Pippin' (D) | SDea |
| – 'Newton Wonder' (D/C) ♀H4 | CAgr CCAT CDoC CDul CSBt CTho CTri CWib ECrN GTwe LAst LRHS MCoo MGos SCrf SDea SFam SKee WHar WJas |
| – 'Newtown Pippin' (D) | SDea |
| – 'Nine Square' (D) | CCAT CTho |
| – 'Nittany Red' (D) | SDea |
| – 'No Pip' (C) | CTho |
| – 'Nolan Pippin' (D) | ECrN |
| – 'Nonpareil' (D) | SKee WHar |
| – 'Norfolk Beauty' (C) | ECrN ERea SKee |
| – 'Norfolk Beefing' (C) | ECrN ERea SDea SFam SKee |
| – 'Norfolk Royal' (D) | CDoC ECrN ERea GTwe SDea SKee |
| – 'Norfolk Royal Russet' (D) | ECrN ERea LRHS |
| – 'Norfolk Winter Coleman' (C) | ERea SKee |
| – 'North Aston Nonpareil' (F) **new** | LBuc |
| – 'Northcott Superb' (D) | CTho |
| – 'Northern Greening' (C) | SKee WHar |
| § – 'Northwood' (Cider) | CCAT CTho SKee |
| – 'Nutmeg Pippin' (D) | CCAT ECrN SDea SFam |
| – Nuvar Freckles (D) | SKee |
| – Nuvar Golden Elf | SKee |
| – Nuvar Golden Hills (D) | SKee |
| – Nuvar Home Farm (D) | SKee |
| – Nuvar Melody (D) | SKee |
| – 'Oaken Pin' (D) | CCAT CTho |
| § – 'Obelisk'PBR (D) | LRHS NPri SDea SKee |
| – 'Old Pearmain' (D) | SDea WHar |
| – 'Old Somerset Russet' (D) | CCAT CTho |
| – 'Opalescent' (D) | SKee |
| – 'Orin' (D) | SKee |
| – 'Orkney Apple' (F) | SKee |
| – 'Orleans Reinette' (D) | CAgr CCAT CDul CTho CTri CWib ECrN GTwe LBuc LRHS MAsh MWat NEgg SCrf SDea SFam SKee WHar WJas |
| – 'Oslin' (D) | SKee |
| – 'Otava'PBR | SKee |
| – 'Owen Thomas' (D) | CTri |
| – 'Paignton Marigold' (Cider) | CTho |
| – 'Pascoe's Pippin' (D/C) | CTho |
| – 'Payhembury' (C/Cider) | CAgr CTho CTri |
| – 'Pear Apple' (D) | CAgr CEnd CTho |
| – 'Pearl' (D) | SDea |
| – 'Peasgood's Nonsuch' (C) ♀H4 | CAgr CCAT CDoC ECrN ERea GTwe MAsh NEgg SCrf SDea SFam SKee SLon |
| – 'Pendragon' (D) | CTho |
| – 'Penhallow Pippin' (D) | CTho |
| – 'Peter Lock' (C/D) | CAgr CCAT CEnd CTho SKee |
| – 'Peter's Pippin' (D) | SDea |
| – 'Peter's Seedling' (D) | SDea |
| – 'Pethyre' (Cider) | CCVT |
| – 'Phelp's Favourite' (D) **new** | LBuc |
| – 'Pig Aderyn' (C) | WGwG |
| – 'Pig's Nose Pippin' (D) | CEnd |
| – 'Pig's Nose Pippin' Type III (D) | CAgr CCAT CTho |
| – 'Pig's Snout' (Cider/C/D) | CCAT CEnd CTho |
| – 'Pine Apple Russet' | CAgr ERea |
| – 'Pinova'PBR (D) | CAgr SKee WHar |
| – 'Pitmaston Pine Apple' (D) | CCAT CTho CTri ECrN ERea LAst LRHS MAsh MCoo MWat SCrf SDea SFam SKee SLon WHar WWct |
| – 'Pixie' (D) ♀H4 | CCAT CWib EPom GTwe LRHS MWat SBfd SDea SFam SKee SLon WHar WJas WWct |
| – 'Plum Vite' (D) | CAgr CTho CTri |
| – 'Plymouth Cross' (D) **new** | SKee |
| – 'Plympton Pippin' (C) | CEnd CTho CTri |
| – Polka = 'Trajan'PBR (D/Ball) | SDea SKee |
| – 'Polly' (C/D) | CEnd |
| – 'Polly Prosser' (D) | SKee |
| – 'Polly Whitehair' (C/D) | CCAT CTho SDea |
| – 'Poltimore Seedling' | CTho |
| – 'Pomeroy of Somerset' (D) | CCAT CTho CTri |
| – 'Ponsford' (C) | CAgr CCAT CTho |
| – 'Port Allen Russet' (C/D) | GQui |
| – 'Port Wine' | see *M. domestica* 'Harry Master's Jersey' |
| – 'Porter's Perfection' (Cider) | CCAT ERea |
| – 'Prince Charles' (D) | SKee |
| – 'Princesse' | ECrN SDea SKee |
| – 'Profit' | CTho |
| – 'Quarry Apple' (C) | CTho |
| – 'Queen' (C) | CAgr CTho ECrN SKee |
| – 'Queen Caroline' (C) | SKee |
| – 'Queen Cox' (D) | CTri ECrN EPom LSRN SDea SKee SLon |
| – 'Queen Cox' self-fertile | CSut CWib EPom ERea LSRN SDea SWvt WHar |
| – 'Queens' (D) | CTho |
| – 'Quench' (D/Cider) | CTho |
| – 'Rajka' (D) | SKee WWct |
| – 'Red Alkmene' (D) | MBri |
| – 'Red Belle de Boskoop' (D) | CAgr |
| – 'Red Bramley' (C) | CWib |
| – 'Red Charles Ross' (C/D) | SDea |
| – 'Red Delicious' (D) | SCrf SKee |
| – 'Red Devil' (D) | CAgr CMac CTri CWSG ECrN EPom GTwe LAst MAsh MBri SBfd SCoo SDea SKee SLim SLon WHar WJas WWct |
| – 'Red Ellison' (D) | CTho CTri ECrN ERea GTwe SDea |

|  |  |
|---|---|
| – 'Red Falstaff'PBR (D) | CAgr CCAT CCVT CDoC CDul CMac ECrN EPfP ERea GKin LBuc LRHS LSRN MAsh MBri MCoo NLar SBfd SKee SLim SLon SPer SPoG WHar WWct |
| – 'Red Fuji' (D) | SDea |
| – 'Red James Grieve' | LSRN |
| – 'Red Jersey' (Cider) | CCAT |
| – 'Red Joaneting' (D) | SKee WHar |
| – 'Red Jonagold'PBR | see *M. domestica* 'Jonagored' |
| – 'Red Jonathan' (D) | SDea |
| – 'Red Miller's Seedling' (D) | ECrN SCrf SDea |
| – 'Red Rattler' (D) | CTho |
| – 'Red Roller' (D) | CTho |
| – 'Red Ruby' (F) | CTho |
| – 'Red Victoria' (C) | GTwe |
| – 'Red Windsor' (F) | CMac EPom ERea LBuc LRHS MAsh NLar SCoo SKee SLim SPoG WHar WJas |
| – 'Redcoat Grieve' (D) | SDea |
| – 'Redsleeves' (D) | CAgr ECrN GTwe SDea SKee |
| – 'Redstrake' (Cider) | CCAT |
| – Regali = 'Delkistar'PBR | LRHS |
| – 'Reine des Reinettes' | see *M. domestica* 'King of the Pippins' |
| – 'Reinette Descardre' (D) | SVic |
| – 'Reinette d'Obry' (Cider) | CCAT |
| – 'Reinette du Canada' (D) | SKee |
| – 'Reinette Rouge Etoilée' (D) | SDea |
| – 'Reverend Greeves' (C) | SDea |
| – 'Reverend McCormick' (F) | CTho |
| – 'Reverend W. Wilks' (C) | CAgr CDoC CDoy CSBt CTri ECrN ERea LAst LRHS MAsh MBri SCrf SDea SFam SKee WHar WJas WWct |
| – 'Ribston Pippin' (D) ♀H4 | CCAT CTho CTri CWib ECrN ERea GTwe LBuc LRHS MCoo MWat SCrf SDea SFam SKee SLon WHar WJas WWct |
| – 'Rival' (D) | CAgr SDea |
| – 'Robert Blatchford' (C) | ECrN |
| – 'Rome Beauty' (D) | SDea |
| – 'Rosemary Russet' (D) ♀H4 | CAgr CCAT CTho ERea GTwe MCoo SCrf SDea SFam SKee WHar WWct |
| – 'Ross Nonpareil' (D) | CAgr GTwe SDea SKee WHar |
| – 'Rosy Blenheim' (D) | ECrN |
| – 'Rough Pippin' (D) | CCAT CEnd |
| – 'Roundway Magnum Bonum' (D) | CAgr CTho SDea |
| § – 'Roxbury Russet' (D) | SKee |
| – 'Royal Gala' (D) ♀H4 | ECrN EPom LAst LBuc SDea SLon |
| § – 'Royal Jubilee' (C) | CCAT |
| – 'Royal Russet' (C) | CEnd ECrN SDea |
| – 'Royal Somerset' (C/Cider) | CCAT CTho CTri |
| – 'Rubinette' (D) | ECrN SDea |
| – Rubinette Rosso (F) = 'Rafzubex'PBR | LRHS |
| – 'Rubinola'PBR | SKee WWct |
| – 'Saint Ailred' | SKee |
| – 'Saint Cecilia' (D) | SDea WGwG |
| § – 'Saint Edmund's Pippin' (D) ♀H4 | CDul CTho ECrN ERea GTwe LRHS MCoo SCrf SDea SFam SKee |
| – 'Saint Edmund's Russet' | see *M. domestica* 'Saint Edmund's Pippin' |
| – 'Saint Magdalen' (D) | SKee |
| – 'Saltcote Pippin' (D) | SKee |
| – 'Sam Young' (D) | CAgr SKee |
| – 'Sandlands' (D) | SDea |
| – 'Sandringham' (C) | ECrN ERea |
| – 'Sanspareil' (D) | CAgr LBuc SKee |
| – 'Santana' (D) | SKee |
| – 'Saturn' (D) | CAgr CCVT CTri ERea GTwe SDea SKee WHar WWct |
| – 'Saw Pits' (F) | CAgr CEnd |
| – 'Scarlet Nonpareil' (D) | SDea |
| – 'Scotch Bridget' (C) | NBid SCoo SKee WHar |
| – 'Scotch Dumpling' (C) | GKin GTwe MCoo WHar |
| – 'Scrumptious'PBR (D) ♀H4 | CAgr CCVT CDoC CDul CMac EPfP EPom ERea GKin LBuc LRHS LSRN MAsh MBri NLar NWea SBfd SCoo SEWo SKee SLim SLon SPer SPoG WHar WJas |
| – 'Sercombe's Natural' (Cider) | CTho |
| – 'Severn Bank' (C) | CCAT CTho |
| – 'Sheep's Nose' (C) | CCAT CTho SDea |
| – 'Shenandoah' (C) | SKee |
| – 'Shilling' (F) **new** | LBuc |
| – 'Sidney Strake' (C) | CAgr CEnd |
| – 'Sir Isaac Newton's' | see *M. domestica* 'Flower of Kent' |
| – 'Sir John Thornycroft' (D) | SDea |
| – 'Slack Ma Girdle' (Cider) | CCAT CTho |
| – 'Smart's Prince Arthur' (C) | SDea |
| – 'Snell's Glass Apple' | see *M. domestica* 'Glass Apple' |
| – 'Somerset Lasting' (C) | CCAT CTri |
| – 'Somerset Redstreak' (Cider) | CCAT CTho CTri GTwe WHar |
| – 'Sops in Wine' (C/Cider) | CCAT CTho SVic |
| – 'Sour Bay' (Cider) | CAgr CTho |
| – 'Sour Natural' | see *M. domestica* 'Langworthy' |
| – 'Spartan' (D) | CCAT CCVT CDoC CMac CSBt CTri CWib ECrN ELan GKin GTwe LAst LRHS MAsh MCoo MGos NPri SBfd SCrf SDea SFam SKee SPer SVic WHar WJas WWct |
| – 'Spencer' (D) | CTri ECrN |
| – 'Spotted Dick' (Cider) | CTho |
| – 'Spout Apple' | LBuc |
| – 'Stable Jersey' (Cider) | CCAT |
| – 'Stamford Pippin' (D) | SDea |
| – 'Stanway Seedling' (C) | ECrN |
| – 'Star of Devon' (D) | CCAT CEnd SDea |
| – 'Stark' (D) | SDea |
| – 'Starking' (D) | ECrN |
| – 'Stark's Earliest' (D) | SVic |
| – 'Stembridge Cluster' (Cider) | CCAT |
| – 'Stembridge Jersey' (Cider) | CCAT |
| – 'Steyne Seedling' (D) | SDea |
| – 'Stirling Castle' (C) | CAgr GQui SKee |
| – 'Stobo Castle' (C) | GQui SKee |
| – 'Stockbearer' (C) | CTho |
| – 'Stoke Edith Pippin' (D) | WHar |
| – 'Stoke Red' (Cider) | CCAT CTho SKee |
| – 'Strawberry Pippin' (D) | CTho |
| – 'Striped Beefing' (C) | ECrN ERea SKee |
| – 'Sturmer Pippin' (D) | CCAT CSBt CTri ECrN GTwe MWat SCrf SDea SFam SKee WHar |
| * – 'Sugar Apple' | CTho |
| – 'Sugar Bush' (C/D) | CTho |
| – 'Sugar Loaf' | see *M. domestica* 'Sugar Apple' |
| – 'Summer Golden Pippin' (D) | SKee |
| – 'Summer Stubbard' (D) | CCAT |
| – 'Summerred' (D) | ECrN EMil |
| – 'Sunburn' (D) | ECrN |
| – 'Sunnydale' (D/C) | SDea |
| – 'Sunrise'PBR (D) | SKee WHar |

- 'Sunset' (D) ♀H4 — Widely available
- 'Suntan' (D) ♀H4 — CCAT CMac CWib ECrN LAst SDea SKee
- 'Superb' — see *M. domestica* 'Laxton's Superb'
- 'Surprise' (D) — GTwe
- 'Sweet Alford' (Cider) — CCAT CTho ECrN
- 'Sweet Bay' (Cider) — CAgr CTho
- 'Sweet Cleave' (Cider) — CTho
- 'Sweet Coppin' (Cider) — CCAT CTho CTri
- 'Sweet Society' (D) — LBuc LRHS MAsh MCoo WHar WJas
- 'Tale Sweet' (Cider) — CCAT CTho
- 'Tamar Beauty' (F) — CEnd
- 'Tan Harvey' (Cider) — CCAT CEnd CTho
- 'Taunton Cross' (D) — CAgr
- 'Taunton Fair Maid' (Cider) — CCAT CTho
- 'Taylor's' (Cider) — CCAT SDea
- 'Ten Commandments' (D/Cider) — CCAT SDea WWct
- 'Tewkesbury Baron' (D) — CTho
- 'The Rattler' (F) — CEnd
- 'Thomas Rivers' (C) — SDea
- 'Thorle Pippin' (D) — SKee
- 'Tidicombe Seedling' (D) — CTho
- 'Tom Putt' (C) — CAgr CCAT CCVT CTho CTri CWib ECrN GTwe LBuc SDea SKee WHar WJas WWct
- 'Tommy Knight' (D) — CAgr CCAT CEnd CTho
- 'Topaz'PBR (D) — SKee
- 'Totnes Apple' (D) — CTho
- 'Tower of Glamis' (C) — GQui GTwe SKee
- Town Farm Number 59 (Cider) — CTho
- 'Transparent Codlin' — LBuc
- 'Tregonna King' (C/D) — CCAT CEnd CTho
- 'Tremlett's Bitter' (Cider) — CAgr CCAT CTho SDea SKee SVic
- 'Trwyn Mochyn' (C) — WGwG
- § 'Tydeman's Early Worcester' (D) — CAgr CLnd CWib ECrN GTwe SDea SVic WWct
- 'Tydeman's Late Orange' (D) — CMac ECrN EMil ERea GTwe LAst LRHS MCoo SDea SFam SKee WHar
- 'Upton Pyne' (C/D) — CCAT CTho SDea
- 'Vallis Apple' (Cider) — CCAT CTho
- 'Veitch's Perfection' (C/D) — CTho
- 'Venus Pippin' (C/D) — CEnd
- 'Vicar of Beighton' (D) — ECrN ERea
- 'Vicary's Late Keeper' — CTho
- 'Vickey's Delight' (D) — SDea
- 'Vileberie' (Cider) — CCAT
- 'Vista-bella' (D) — ECrN SDea SKee
- 'Wadey's Seedling' (D) **new** — SKee
- 'Wagener' (D) — ECrN SDea SKee
- 'Waltham Abbey Seedling' (C) — ECrN
- Waltz = 'Telamon'PBR (D/Ball) — SDea SKee
- 'Warner's King' (C) ♀H4 — CCAT CTho CTri SCrf SDea SKee WHar
- 'Warrior' (F) — CCAT CTho
- 'Wealthy' (D) — SDea
- 'Wellington' (C) — see *M. domestica* 'Dummellor's Seedling'
- 'Wellington' (Cider) — CAgr CTho
- 'Welsh Russet' (D) — SDea
- 'West View Seedling' (D) — ECrN
- 'Wheeler's Russet' (D) — LBuc
- 'White Alphington' (Cider) — CTho
- 'White Close Pippin' (Cider) — CTho
- 'White Jersey' (Cider) — CCAT
- 'White Joaneting' (D) — CCAT
- 'White Melrose' (C) — GTwe LRHS SDea SKee
- 'White Transparent' (C/D) — SDea
- 'Whitpot Sweet' (F) — CEnd
- 'Wick White Styre' (Cider) — CTho
- 'William Crump' (D) — CCAT CTho ECrN SDea SFam SKee WHar WWct
- 'Winston' (D) ♀H4 — CAgr CCAT CCVT CMac CSBt CTri ECrN GTwe MCoo NWea SDea SFam SKee SVic WHar WWct
- 'Winter Banana' (D) — ECrN LRHS MCoo SDea SKee SVic WHar
- 'Winter Gem' (D) — CAgr CCVT CDul ECrN EMil EPom ERea LAst LBuc SDea SKee WHar WJas
- 'Winter Lawrence' (F) — CTho
- 'Winter Lemon' (C/D) — GQui
- 'Winter Majetin' (C) — ECrN ERea SKee
- 'Winter Peach' (D/C) — CAgr CEnd CTho ECrN
- 'Winter Pearmain' (D) — SKee WHar
- 'Winter Quarrenden' (D) — SDea
- 'Winter Queening' (D/C) — SDea
- 'Winter Stubbard' (C) — CTho
- 'Woodbine' — see *M. domestica* 'Northwood'
- 'Woodford' (C) — ECrN
- 'Woolbrook Pippin' (D) — CAgr CEnd CTho
- 'Woolbrook Russet' (C) — CEnd CTho ECrN
- 'Worcester Pearmain' (D) ♀H4 — Widely available
- 'Wormsley Pippin' (D) — ECrN
- 'Wyatt's Seedling' — see *M. domestica* 'Langworthy'
- 'Wyken Pippin' (D) — CCAT ECrN GTwe SDea SFam SKee
- 'Yarlington Mill' (Cider) — CAgr CCAT CTho CTri SDea SKee SVic WWct
- 'Yellow Ingestrie' (D) — ERea LRHS MAsh MCoo SFam SKee WHar WJas WWct
- 'Yellow Styre' (Cider) — CTho
- 'Yorkshire Greening' (C) — WHar
- 'Zabergäu Renette' (D) — SKee

'Donald Wyman' — CLnd EPfP SCoo
'Echtermeyer' — see *M.* × *gloriosa* 'Oekonomierat Echtermeyer'
§ 'Evereste' ♀H4 — Widely available
***florentina*** — CLnd CTho EBee EPfP LLHF SSpi
- 'Rosemoor' — EBee
- 'Skopje' — EPfP WMou
***floribunda*** ♀H4 — Widely available
'Gardener's Gold' — CEnd CTho
§ × ***gloriosa*** 'Oekonomierat Echtermeyer' — SDea SGol WDin
'Golden Gem' — EMil EPfP GTwe MAsh SEWo SLim SPer
'Golden Hornet' — see *M.* × *zumi* 'Golden Hornet'
'Harry Baker' — CCVT CEnd EBee EMil EPfP EPom ERea LRHS MAsh MBlu MBri NLar SCoo SLim SPoG WJas WWct
× ***hartwigii*** **new** — CLnd
'Hillieri' — see *M.* × *scheideckeri* 'Hillieri'
***hupehensis*** ♀H4 — CDoy CDul CEnd CLnd CMCN CSBt CTho EBee ECrN EPfP LHop MBlu MGos MRav NWea SCrf SFam SPer WPat
'Hyde Hall Spire' — MAsh SCoo
'Indian Magic' — CLnd MAsh MBri
Jelly King = 'Mattfru' **new** — LRHS MBri NLar
'John Downie' (C) ♀H4 — Widely available
'Kaido' — see *M.* × *micromalus*
***kansuensis*** — CLnd EPfP
'Kemp' **new** — SDea

| |  |  |
|---|---|---|
| | 'Laura' | CDul EPfP EPom LRHS LSRN MAsh MBri NLar SCoo SKee SLim SLon SPoG WJas |
| | 'Liset' **new** | WMou |
| | 'Louisa' | CWSG MAsh NWea SCoo SGol |
| | × ***magdeburgensis*** | CCVT CDul CLnd CSBt |
| | 'Marshal Ōyama' | CTho |
| | 'Mary Potter' | CLnd |
| § | × ***micromalus*** | NLar |
| | × ***moerlandsii*** | CLnd |
| | - 'Liset' | CDul CEnd CSBt CWib EBee ECrN MRav NEgg SCoo SEWo SFam SPer SPoG WFar |
| § | - 'Profusion' | CBcs CDul CMac CTri EBee ECrN ELan EWTr MGos MMuc MRav MSwo NPri NWea SBfd SCrf SEND SGol SPer SWvt WDin WFar WJas |
| | - 'Profusion Improved' | CEnd CSBt CWSG LRHS MAsh MWat SCoo SWvt WHar |
| | 'Mokum' | CCVT LMaj LTen |
| | 'Molten Lava' | CLnd MAsh |
| | ***niedzwetzkyana*** | CLnd CTho GAuc |
| | Nuvar Carnival | SKee |
| | Nuvar Dusty Red | SKee |
| | Nuvar Marble | SKee |
| | Nuvar Red Lantern | SKee |
| | ***orthocarpa*** | CLnd |
| | Perpetu | see *M.* 'Evereste' |
| | 'Pink Glow' | CEnd CLnd CSBt EPom ERea MAsh MBlu NLar SBfd SCoo SEWo SLim SPer SPoG WHar |
| | 'Pink Mushroom' | NLar |
| | 'Pink Perfection' | CDoC CEnd EBee ECrN NWea |
| | Pom'Zaï = 'Courtabri' | CDoC |
| | 'Pond Red' | CLnd |
| | 'Prairie Fire' | CDul CLnd LRHS MAsh MBri SCoo SLim SPoG |
| | ***prattii*** | CLnd CTho EPfP |
| | 'Princeton Cardinal' | CLnd EPfP SCoo SLim |
| | 'Professor Sprenger' | see *M.* × *zumi* 'Professor Sprenger' |
| | 'Profusion' | see *M.* × *moerlandsii* 'Profusion' |
| | ***prunifolia*** | MBlu |
| | - var. ***rinkii*** | CLnd |
| | ***pumila*** 'Cowichan' | ECrN |
| | - 'Dartmouth' | CDul CLnd CSBt CSam CTri ECrN NEgg NPCo SFam |
| | - 'Montreal Beauty' | CLnd WJas |
| | 'Purple Prince' **new** | CLnd |
| § | × ***purpurea*** 'Aldenhamensis' | SDea WDin WHar |
| | - 'Eleyi' | CDul LAst NWea WDin |
| | - 'Lemoinei' | CLnd ECrN |
| | - 'Neville Copeman' | CCVT CDoC CDul CLnd EBee ECrN EPom EWTr SBfd SPur WJas WMou |
| | - 'Pendula' | see *M.* × *gloriosa* 'Oekonomierat Echtermeyer' |
| | 'R.J. Fulcher' | CTho |
| | 'Ralph Shay' | CLnd |
| | 'Red Ace' | CDul |
| | 'Red Barron' | CLnd |
| | 'Red Glow' | CLnd EBee ECrN MAsh MMuc SEND WJas |
| | 'Red Jade' | see *M.* × *scheideckeri* 'Red Jade' |
| | 'Red Obelisk' | CWSG MAsh MBri SCoo SPoG |
| | 'Red Peacock' | CLnd |
| | 'Resi'PBR **new** | WWct |
| | 'Robinson' | CLnd |
| § | × ***robusta*** | CLnd GTwe LSRN NWea SBfd SCrf SLon |
| | - 'Red Sentinel' ♀H4 | Widely available |
| | - 'Red Siberian' | SDea SPer |
| | - 'Yellow Siberian' | CLnd |
| | ***rockii*** | GAuc |
| | 'Royal Beauty' ♀H4 | CDoC CDul CLnd CWib EBee EPfP GTwe LAst LRHS MAsh MBri MGos MSwo SBfd SCoo SCrf SLon SPer WDin WHar WMou |
| | 'Royalty' | CBcs CDul CLnd CMac CSBt EBee ECrN ELan GTwe LAst LBuc LRHS MGos MRav MSwo MWat NEgg NPla SBfd SCrf SEND SEWo SGol SPer SPoG WDin WHar WJas |
| | 'Rudolph' | CCVT CDul CLnd EBee ECrN EWTr GKin LBuc LMaj LRHS MAsh MGos SCoo SEWo SLim SPer SPoG WJas |
| | 'Ruth Ann' | CLnd |
| | ***sargentii*** | CDul CTho ECrN NWea SFam |
| | - 'Tina' | CLnd CWSG MAsh |
| | 'Satin Cloud' | CLnd |
| § | × ***scheideckeri*** 'Hillieri' | CDul CLnd ECrN SFam |
| § | - 'Red Jade' | CDul CMCN CTri CWib EBee ECrN ELan GTwe MGos MMuc MRav MSwo MWat NEgg NPri NWea SBfd SEND SPer WDin WFar WJas |
| | Siberian crab | see *M.* × *robusta* |
| | ***sieboldii*** | see *M. toringo* |
| | ***sieversii*** **new** | CDul |
| | 'Silver Drift' | CLnd |
| | 'Snowcloud' | CDul CLnd EBee ECrN MAsh SLim SPer |
| | 'Street Parade' | CLnd |
| | × ***sublobata*** | CLnd |
| | 'Sun Rival' | CCVT CDoC CDul CEnd CLnd CSBt EPfP GTwe MAsh MBlu MBri NLar SBfd SCoo SLim SPoG WHar WJas |
| | ***sylvestris*** | CCVT CDul CHab CLnd CRWN ECrN EPfP LBuc MMuc MRav NLar NWea SEND SEWo SPer WDin WMou |
| § | ***toringo*** | CLnd CTho ECrN EPfP LMaj MBlu MBri WSHC |
| I | - var. ***arborescens*** | CLnd CTho |
| | - 'Browers' | LMaj |
| | - 'Scarlett' | IArd LRHS MBri NLar NWea SCoo SLim SPoG WJas |
| | - 'Wintergold' | MMuc |
| | ***toringoides*** | see *M. bhutanica* |
| | ***transitoria*** ♀H4 | CDoC CDul CEnd CLnd CTho EBee ECrN ELan EMil EPfP LRHS MAsh MBlu MBri NWea SCoo SFam SSpi WMou WPGP |
| | - 'Thornhayes Tansy' | CTho LRHS SLim SPoG |
| | ***trilobata*** | CLnd CTho EBee ELan EMil EPfP LMaj MBlu MGos MMuc SCoo SEND |
| | - 'Guardsman' | LRHS MBri NLar SSpi |
| | ***tschonoskii*** ♀H4 | CDoC CDul CMCN CMac CSBt CTho CTri CWib EBee ECrN ELan EPfP GTwe LAst LMaj LRHS MBlu MBri MGos MMuc NPri NWea SBfd SEND SPer SWvt WDin WJas WMou |
| | 'Van Eseltine' | CDul CSBt CWib EBee ECrN EPfP MAsh MMuc MWat SFam WHar WJas WPat |
| | 'Veitch's Scarlet' | CDoy CDul CLnd CSBt GTwe NEgg NPCo SFam |
| | Weeping Candied Apple = 'Weepcanzam' | CLnd |
| | 'White Star' | CCVT CDoC CDul CLnd CSBt EBee ECrN SBfd SLim SLon |

'Winter Gold' CDul EBee LMaj MMuc SCrf
'Wisley Crab' CLnd LRHS SDea SFam SLon
***yunnanensis*** EPfP GAuc
- var. ***veitchii*** CTho
× ***zumi*** var. ***calocarpa*** CLnd CTho
§ - 'Golden Hornet' ♀H4 Widely available
§ - 'Professor Sprenger' CLnd CSam EPfP LMaj MBri SCoo

## *Malva* (*Malvaceae*)

***alcea*** var. ***fastigiata*** CMac EBee ECGP NBro SRms WFar WPer XLum
***bicolor*** see *Lavatera maritima*
'Gibbortello' LRHS
***moschata*** CArn CBcs CPrp CRWN EBee ECtt ELan EPfP EWil GJos GPoy MHer MMuc MNHC NBPC NLar NMir SIde SPer SPlb SWat WHer WJek WMoo XLum
- f. ***alba*** ♀H4 Widely available
- 'Appleblossom' CBod CSpr EBee
- 'Romney Marsh' see *Althaea officinalis* 'Romney Marsh'
- ***rosea*** EPfP GMaP NBPC NBlu NEgg NPer SBfd SPoG SWvt
- 'White Perfection' ELon
***pusilla*** CCCN
'Sweet Sixteen' EBee ECtt NBPC WHil
***sylvestris*** CArn EWil NBro SWat WFar WHfH WJek WMoo
- 'Blue Fountain'PBR LSou NBPC WHil WKif
- 'Brave Heart' SPav SWvt
- Marina = 'Dema'PBR ELan NLar WFar
- subsp. ***mauritiana*** NPer WMoo
- - 'Bibor Fehlo' CSpe CSpr
- 'Mystic Merlin' SPav
- 'Perry's Blue' NPer
- 'Primley Blue' CBot EBee ECtt ELan EPfP GMaP MRav NBPC NPer WFar WNew
- 'Windsor Castle' NBPC
- 'Zebrina' CSpr EBee EPfP NPer SWvt WFar WMoo

## *Malvastrum* (*Malvaceae*)

× ***hypomadarum*** see *Anisodontea* × *hypomadara* (Sprague) D.M. Bates
***lateritium*** CMea CRHN CSpe CTri EBee ELan EPfP EPri GBin LAst LHop LRHS MAvo NBir NSti SMad SMrm SPet SPhx SRms SUsu WHal WHil WHoo WPGP WPer WPtf WSHC XLum

## *Malvaviscus* (*Malvaceae*)

***arboreus*** CHll

## mandarin see *Citrus reticulata* Mandarin Group

## *Mandevilla* (*Apocynaceae*)

§ × ***amabilis*** CCCN
- 'Alice du Pont' ♀H1 CCCN CSpe ELan EShb LRHS MOWG
- 'Passion Pink' (Parfait Series) (d) **new** LRHS
× ***amoena*** see *M.* × *amabilis*
***boliviensis*** ♀H1 CCCN CRHN CSpe ELan LRHS MOWG
§ ***laxa*** ♀H2 CBot CCCN CHEx CHGN CHll CRHN CSpe ECre ELan ERea EShb IDee IRar LRHS MOWG SAga SGar SVen WHrl WPGP WSHC
- 'Snowbird' ERea
***sanderi*** CCCN EShb
- 'Rosea' CSpe
***splendens*** ♀H1 CCCN CHll MOWG
***suaveolens*** see *M. laxa*
Sundaville Pink = 'Sunmandecripi'PBR LSou
Sundaville Red = 'Sunmandecrim'PBR LAst LSou
Sweet Passion (Perlavilla Series) **new** LRHS

## *Mandragora* (*Solanaceae*)

***autumnalis*** SMad WCot
§ ***officinarum*** CArn CEls CRDP GCal GPoy SMad WCot

## *Manettia* (*Rubiaceae*)

***inflata*** see *M. luteorubra*
§ ***luteorubra*** CCCN CHll ELan

## *Manfreda* see *Agave*

## × *Mangave* see *Agave*

'Macha Mocha' see *Agave* 'Macha Mocha'

## *Mangifera* (*Anacardiaceae*)

***indica*** (F) CCCN EAmu

## *Manglietia* see *Magnolia*

***yunnanensis*** see *Magnolia insignis*

## mango see *Mangifera indica*

## *Manihot* (*Euphorbiaceae*)

***carthaginensis*** SPlb
***esculenta*** 'Variegata' EAmu

## *Maranta* (*Marantaceae*)

***leuconeura*** var. ***erythroneura*** ♀H1 XBlo
- var. ***kerchoveana*** ♀H1 XBlo

## *Marattia* (*Marattiaceae*)

***salicina*** WRic

## *Marchantia* (*Marchantiaceae*)

***polymorpha*** CArn

## *Margyricarpus* (*Rosaceae*)

§ ***pinnatus*** CFee GEdr NWCA WPer
***setosus*** see *M. pinnatus*

## *Mariscus* see *Cyperus*

## marjoram, pot see *Origanum onites*

## marjoram, sweet see *Origanum majorana*

## marjoram, wild, or oregano see *Origanum vulgare*

## *Marrubium* (*Lamiaceae*)

§ ***bourgaei*** var. ***bourgaei*** 'All Hallow's Green' EBee ECha ECtt LHop LRHS MRav NEgg XSen
***candidissimum*** see *M. incanum*
***cylleneum*** EWll
* - 'Velvetissimum' XSen
§ ***incanum*** XSen
***libanoticum*** WPer
***supinum*** CArn

| | |
|---|---|
| ***vulgare*** | CArn GPoy MHer MNHC SIde WJek XLum |

## *Marsdenia* (*Apocynaceae*)

| | |
|---|---|
| ***formosana*** CWJ 12354 new | WCru |

## *Marshallia* (*Asteraceae*)

| | |
|---|---|
| ***grandiflora*** | CDes EBee SUsu |
| ***mohrii*** | EBee |
| ***trinerva*** | ELon WHil |

## *Marsilea* (*Marsileaceae*)

| | |
|---|---|
| ***angustifolia*** new | LLWG |
| ***quadrifolia*** variegated (v) | LLWG |

## *Mascarena* see *Hyophorbe*

## *Massonia* (*Asparagaceae*)

| | |
|---|---|
| ***depressa*** | ECho |
| - 'Branvlei Dam' | ECho |
| - 'Reitfontein Gamoep' | ECho |
| ***echinata*** | ECho WCot |
| aff. ***echinata*** | ECho WCot |
| ***jasminiflora*** | ECho |
| ***pustulata*** | ECho WCot |
| ***pygmaea*** subsp. ***kamiesbergensis*** | ECho |
| - subsp. ***pygmaea*** | ECho |

## *Mathiasella* (*Apiaceae*)

| | |
|---|---|
| ***bupleuroides*** | CHid LSou |
| - 'Green Dream' | CAbP CAby CAvo CBcs CBod CBre CMea CSpe EBee ECtt EWll GBin LRHS MLLN MPnt NCGa NPnk SDix SLon SPoG SUsu WCot |

## *Matricaria* (*Asteraceae*)

| | |
|---|---|
| ***chamomilla*** | see *M. recutita* |
| ***parthenium*** | see *Tanacetum parthenium* |
| § ***recutita*** | CArn GPoy MNHC |
| ***tchihatchewii*** | XSen |
| 'White Star' new | EPfP |

## *Matteuccia* (*Onocleaceae*)

| | |
|---|---|
| ***orientalis*** | CBty CDTJ CDes CKel CLAP EFer EPfP GCal GEdr GGar GMaP LRHS LWst NBid NLar NMyG NOrc SPad WFar WMoo WPnP WRic WWEG XLum |
| ***pensylvanica*** | CLAP EBee MMoz WRic |
| ***struthiopteris*** ♀H4 | Widely available |
| * - 'Depauperata' | CLAP |
| - 'Jumbo' | CBty CCCN CLAP EBee ISha LRHS |
| - 'The King' | WCot |

## *Matthiola* (*Brassicaceae*)

| | |
|---|---|
| ***fruticulosa*** 'Alba' | CDes LEdu WPGP |
| - subsp. ***perennis*** | NSti WHal |
| ***incana*** | LRHS MArl SPad WCFE WFar WKif WRHF |
| - ***alba*** | CHid ECha ELan LSou MMuc NCGa SEND SMad SPav WCot |
| - purple-flowered | SEND |
| ***montana*** | LLHF |
| white-flowered perennial | CArn CSev CSpe MAvo MLHP MSCN NPer |

## *Maurandella* (*Plantaginaceae*)

| | |
|---|---|
| § ***antirrhiniflora*** | EWld |

## *Maurandya* (*Plantaginaceae*)

| | |
|---|---|
| § ***barclayana*** | CBot CDTJ CHll MBri SGar |
| - ***alba*** | CBot |
| 'Bridal Bouquet' | CCCN GMac LSou |
| ***erubescens*** | see *Lophospermum erubescens* |
| ***lophantha*** | see *Lophospermum scandens* |
| ***lophospermum*** | see *Lophospermum scandens* |
| 'Magic Dragon' | see *Lophospermum* 'Magic Dragon' |
| 'Red Dragon' | see *Lophospermum* 'Red Dragon' |

## *Maytenus* (*Celastraceae*)

| | |
|---|---|
| ***boaria*** | CBcs CMCN EPfP GBin GGal IArd IDee LEdu MBri MGos NLar SArc SEND WSHC |
| ***disticha*** | LEdu |
| ***magellanica*** | WFar |

## *Mazus* (*Phrymaceae*)

| | |
|---|---|
| ***novae-zeelandiae*** | CTrC |
| ***reptans*** | EBee ECho EDAr EPfP MSKA NLBP NLar NPer NWCA XLum |
| - B&SWJ | GEdr |
| - 'Albus' | EBee ECho EPfP GGar LLWG MSKA NLar SPlb XLum |
| - 'Blue' | LLWG |

## *Mecardonia* (*Plantaginaceae*)

| | |
|---|---|
| 'Goldflake' | CCCN |
| 'Sundona Early Yellow' | LAst |

## *Meconopsis* ✿ (*Papaveraceae*)

| | |
|---|---|
| ***baileyi*** | see *M. betonicifolia* |
| Ballyrogan form | GEdr |
| § ***betonicifolia*** ♀H4 | CBcs CGHE CSBt CTri CWCL EBee ELan EPau EPfP GAbr GCra GKev GKin ITim LRHS MBri MCot MDun NBPC NBir NEgg NLar NPal NSla NSum SPoG WCAu WFar WMoo |
| - var. ***alba*** | CSpr EBee ELan GCra GKev LRHS NGdn NLar NSum |
| - 'Glacier Blue' | GCra |
| - 'Hensol Violet' | CSpr GCra GKev GMac NLar NSum |
| - violet-flowered | ITim |
| ***cambrica*** | CCCN CMac CPLG CTri ELan EPfP EWil GGar GJos MMuc NPri SGar WBrk WFar WHer WPtf |
| - 'Anne Greenaway' (d) | WCot |
| - var. ***aurantiaca*** | SBch WFar |
| - ***flore-pleno*** (d) | WCot WFar |
| - - orange-flowered (d) | NBir WCot |
| § - 'Frances Perry' | EWld GCal WCot WFar |
| - 'Muriel Brown' (d) | GCal |
| - 'Rubra' | see *M. cambrica* 'Frances Perry' |
| ***chelidoniifolia*** | EWld GBee GCra IGor NBid WCru WFar |
| × ***cookei*** | GEdr GMac |
| N Fertile Blue Group | ITim |
| N - 'Blue Ice' | see *M.* (Fertile Blue Group) 'Lingholm' |
| N - 'Lingholm' | Widely available |
| - 'Mop-head' | GEdr |
| § George Sherriff Group | GCal GCra GEdr NBir |
| - 'Ascreavie' | GEdr GKev GMaP |
| - 'Barney's Blue' | GMaP |
| - 'Branklyn' ambig. | CGHE GEdr LRHS WFar WPGP |
| - 'Dalemain' | GMaP |
| - 'Huntfield' | GBin GEdr GMaP |
| - 'Jimmy Bayne' | GBin GEdr GMaP |

| | | |
|---|---|---|
| | ***grandis*** misapplied | see *M.* George Sherriff Group |
| | - GS 600 | see *M.* George Sherriff Group |
| | ***grandis*** ambig. | CHar GEdr GLin WFar |
| | - 'Tromso' | GEdr |
| | (Infertile Blue Group) 'Bobby Masterton' | GCra GEdr GKev |
| | - 'Crewdson Hybrid' | GEdr GMaP |
| | - 'Dawyck' | see *M.* (Infertile Blue Group) 'Slieve Donard' |
| | - 'Maggie Sharp' | GEdr |
| | - 'Mrs Jebb' | GCra GEdr GMaP |
| § | - 'Slieve Donard' ♀H4 | GCal GCra GEdr GKev GKin GMaP LRHS |
| | ***integrifolia*** | CCCN GEdr WAbe WFar |
| N | ***napaulensis*** misapplied | GCra GEdr ITim LHop NLar WMoo |
| | - from Solu Khumbu **new** | GCra |
| | - pink-flowered | GBin NGdn WFar |
| | - red-flowered | CBcs ITim |
| | ***nudicaulis*** | see *Papaver nudicaule* |
| | ***paniculata*** | ITim LRHS |
| | - from Bhutan | GCra |
| | - from Ghunsa, Nepal | CLAP |
| | - ginger foliage | CHid CSpr |
| | ***quintuplinervia*** ♀H4 | CLAP GCra NBir NHar NSla |
| | - Farrer's form **new** | GKev |
| | ***racemosa*** | GAbr |
| | ***regia*** misapplied | WMoo |
| | × ***sheldonii*** misapplied (fertile) | see *M.* Fertile Blue Group |
| | × ***sheldonii*** misapplied (sterile) | see *M.* Infertile Blue Group |
| | × ***sheldonii*** ambig. | CBcs CHar EBee GAbr ITim MCot MDun NBPC NBir NLar NPer WFar |
| | 'Stewart Annand' | GEdr |
| | ***superba*** | WAbe |
| | ***villosa*** | CSpr GCra GLin WFar |
| | ***wallichii*** ambig. **new** | GLin |
| | 'Willie Duncan' | GMaP |
| | ***wilsonii*** | GLin |
| | subsp. ***australis*** **new** | |

## *Medicago* (*Papilionaceae*)

| | |
|---|---|
| ***arborea*** | CArn SEND SPlb |
| ***lupulina*** | CHab |
| ***sativa*** | NLar WHer WSFF |

## *Medinilla* (*Melastomataceae*)

| | |
|---|---|
| ***magnifica*** ♀H1 | CCCN MBri |

## medlar see *Mespilus germanica*

## *Meehania* (*Lamiaceae*)

| | |
|---|---|
| ***cordata*** | CDes EBee |
| ***fargesii*** | CLAP |
| ***urticifolia*** | EPPr GCal GEdr WSHC |
| - B&SWJ 1210 | WCru |
| - 'Wandering Minstrel' (v) | WCot |

## *Megaskepasma* (*Acanthaceae*)

| | |
|---|---|
| ***erythrochlamys*** | SVen |

## *Melaleuca* (*Myrtaceae*)

| | | |
|---|---|---|
| | ***acerosa*** | MOWG |
| | ***acuminata*** | SPlb |
| | ***alternifolia*** | CArn CBcs CCCN CTsd ECou EOHP GPoy IDee MHer MOWG SEND SPlb SVen WHer WHfH |
| | ***armillaris*** | CBcs CCCN CDoC IDee MOWG SEND SGar SPlb |
| | - pink-flowered | MOWG |
| | ***blaeriifolia*** | ECou |
| | ***bracteata*** | ECou |
| | ***citrina*** | MOWG |
| | ***coccinea*** | MOWG |
| | ***cuticularis*** | SPlb |
| | ***decora*** | MOWG |
| | ***decussata*** | CBcs ECou MOWG SPlb |
| § | ***diosmatifolia*** | CBcs CPLG |
| | ***elliptica*** | MOWG |
| | ***ericifolia*** | CTri CTsd GLin MOWG SEND SPlb |
| | ***erubescens*** | see *M. diosmatifolia* |
| | ***filifolia*** | MOWG |
| | ***fulgens*** | MOWG SPlb |
| | - apricot-flowered | MOWG |
| * | - 'Hot Pink' | MOWG |
| | - purple-flowered | MOWG |
| | ***gibbosa*** | CPLG CTrC ECou ELan IDee LRHS LSou MOWG SEND WSHC |
| | ***huegelii*** | MOWG |
| | ***hypericifolia*** | CDoC CPLG ECou MOWG SPlb |
| | ***incana*** | MOWG |
| | ***lateritia*** | ECou MOWG |
| | ***linariifolia*** | CCCN ECou SPlb |
| | ***nesophila*** | ECou EShb IDee MOWG SPlb |
| | ***pentagona*** var. ***subulifolia*** | ECou |
| | ***platycalyx*** | MOWG |
| | ***pulchella*** | ECou MOWG |
| | ***pungens*** | SPlb |
| | ***pustulata*** | ECou MOWG |
| | ***radula*** | MOWG |
| | ***spathulata*** | MOWG |
| | ***squamea*** | CTsd GGar IDee SEND SPlb |
| * | ***squarmania*** | MOWG |
| | ***squarrosa*** | CPLG CTrC ECou IDee LRHS MOWG SPlb SVen |
| | ***thymifolia*** | ECou LRHS MOWG SPlb WAbe |
| | ***viridiflora*** | GQui |
| | ***wilsonii*** | ECou IDee |

## *Melandrium* see *Vaccaria*

| | |
|---|---|
| ***rubrum*** | see *Silene dioica* |

## *Melanoselinum* (*Apiaceae*)

| | | |
|---|---|---|
| § | ***decipiens*** | CAbb CArn CHEx CSpe EWes GGar LEdu WCot WPGP |

## *Melasphaerula* (*Iridaceae*)

| | | |
|---|---|---|
| | ***graminea*** | see *M. ramosa* |
| § | ***ramosa*** | CBre ECho |

## *Melastoma* (*Melastomataceae*)

| | |
|---|---|
| sp. | CCCN |
| ***malabathricum*** | MOWG |

## *Melia* (*Meliaceae*)

| | | |
|---|---|---|
| § | ***azedarach*** | CArn CBcs CCCN EBee EPfP EShb GPoy SEND SPlb |
| | - B&SWJ 7039 | WCru |
| | - var. ***japonica*** | see *M. azedarach* |

## *Melianthus* (*Melianthaceae*)

| | |
|---|---|
| ***comosus*** | CDTJ CHid CTsd EAmu EBee ELan EPri EShb ESwi EWes NLar SCoo SPlb WCot |
| ***major*** ♀H3 | Widely available |
| ***minor*** | CFir CHid |
| ***villosus*** | CFir CHGN EWes MCCP SGar SPlb WHil WPGP |

## *Melica* (*Poaceae*)

| | |
|---|---|
| ***altissima*** 'Alba' | EHoe MLHP |
| - 'Atropurpurea' | CWCL EBee ECha EHoe EPPr LEdu LHop LLWP LRHS MCot MMoz MNrw MWat MWhi NBid NLar SEND SGar SPlb WBox WFar WFoF WMnd WMoo WPtf WWEG |
| ***ciliata*** | EHoe EPPr MMoz MWhi WMnd WPtf WWEG XLum |
| ***macra*** | EHoe EPPr SApp |
| ***nutans*** | CWCL EBee EHoe EPPr EPla EShb GQue NMRc NWCA NWsh SBch SMrm |
| ***penicillaris*** | EPPr |
| ***transsilvanica*** 'Atropurpurea' | EBee MMuc |
| - 'Red Spire' | CWib EShb MBNS MWhi SBfd SGol SHDw SMea SMrm WMoo XLum |
| ***uniflora*** | NOak |
| - f. ***albida*** | ECha EHoe EPPr GCal MAvo NDov SLPl SUsu WCot WSHC |
| - 'Variegata' (v) | CBre ECGP ECha EHoe ELon EPPr EPla GCal MMoz SUsu WCot WMoo WTin WWEG |

## *Melicope* (*Rutaceae*)

| | |
|---|---|
| ***ternata*** | ECou |

## *Melicytus* (*Violaceae*)

| | |
|---|---|
| ***alpinus*** | ECou |
| ***angustifolius*** | ECou |
| ***crassifolius*** | ECou WFar |
| ***obovatus*** | ECou NLar |
| ***ramiflorus*** | CHEx ECou |

## *Melilotus* (*Papilionaceae*)

| | |
|---|---|
| ***officinalis*** | CArn CHab GPoy SIde WHer |
| - subsp. ***albus*** | CArn |

## *Melinis* (*Poaceae*)

| | |
|---|---|
| ***nerviglumis*** | CKno LEdu MAvo |
| - 'Savannah' | CWib |

## *Meliosma* (*Sabiaceae*)

| | |
|---|---|
| ***cuneifolia*** | CBcs NLar |
| ***dilleniifolia*** subsp. ***tenuis*** | CPLG |
| ***myriantha*** | SSpi |

## *Melissa* ✿ (*Lamiaceae*)

| | |
|---|---|
| ***officinalis*** | CArn CHab CPbn CTri CWan ELau GJos GMaP GPoy MBri MHer MNHC NBir NBlu SBfd SEND SIde SPlb SVic WHfH WJek |
| - 'All Gold' | CBre CPbn CSev ECha EHoe ELan ELau EOHP MNHC NBid NBlu NVic SPer SPoG |
| - subsp. ***altissima*** new | WBox |
| § - 'Aurea' (v) | CArn CFee CPLG CPrp CSev CWan ELan ELau GCra GMaP GPoy MBri MHer MMuc MNHC MRav NBid NBir NBro SBfd SEND SIde SPer SPoG SRms WFar WJek WMnd WMoo XLum |
| * - 'Compacta' | CPbn GPoy |
| - 'Lime Balm' | CPbn EOHP |
| - 'Quedlinburger Niederliegende' | CArn CPbn |
| N - 'Variegata' misapplied | see *M. officinalis* 'Aurea' |

## *Melittis* (*Lamiaceae*)

| | |
|---|---|
| ***melissophyllum*** | CAby CArn CLAP CMea CPom CRDP CSpe EBee ELon LEdu LRHS LFou MNrw MHav MWea NMen SRms SSvw SUsu WCot WOut |
| - subsp. ***albida*** | EBee WCot |
| - 'Apple Blossom' new | CDes |
| - pink-flowered | CLAP SUsu WCot WPtf |
| - 'Royal Velvet Distinction'[PBR] | CSpe EBee MRav WCot WHil |

## *Melliodendron* (*Styracaceae*)

| | |
|---|---|
| ***xylocarpum*** | CPLG |

## *Menispermum* (*Menispermaceae*)

| | |
|---|---|
| ***canadense*** | CTri GPoy |
| ***davuricum*** | GKin NLar |

## *Menstruocalamus* (*Poaceae*)

| | |
|---|---|
| ***sichuanensis*** | WPGP |

## *Mentha* ✿ (*Lamiaceae*)

| | |
|---|---|
| sp. | CHab |
| SJ 2075 | WCot |
| from Jamaica | CArn |
| ***angustifolia*** Corb. | see *M.* × *villosa* |
| ***angustifolia*** Host | see *M. arvensis* |
| ***angustifolia*** ambig. | CPbn SIde |
| ***aquatica*** | CArn CBen CHab CPbn CRow CWat EHon EPfP EWil GPoy LEdu LPBA MHer MNHC MWts NMir NPer SIde SPlb SVic SWat WHer WMAq WMoo WPnP WSFF XLum |
| § - var. ***crispa*** | CPbn SIde |
| - krause minze | see *M. aquatica* var. *crispa* |
| - 'Mandeliensis' | CPbn |
| § ***arvensis*** | CArn CPbn ELau MHer SIde |
| - 'Banana' | CPbn EGHP LEdu MHer MNHC SIde WJek |
| - var. ***piperascens*** | LEdu MHer SIde WJek |
| § - - 'Sayakaze' | CArn ELau |
| - var. ***villosa*** | CPbn |
| ***asiatica*** | CPbn ELau MHer SIde |
| 'Berries and Cream' | LEdu WJek |
| 'Betty's Slovakian' | CPbn |
| Bowles's mint | see *M.* × *villosa* var. *alopecuroides* Bowles's mint |
| * ***brevifolia*** | CPbn SIde WHer |
| ***cervina*** | CArn CBen CPbn CWat EHon LEdu LPBA MHer MSKA NLar SIde SWat WJek XLum |
| * - ***alba*** | CPbn LLWG LPBA MHer MSKA NLar WMAq |
| I 'Chocolate Peppermint' | EWhm LLWG NBir WHer |
| ***citrata*** | see *M.* × *piperita* f. *citrata* |
| 'Clarissa's Millennium' | CPbn SIde |
| ***cordifolia*** | see *M.* × *villosa* |
| ***corsica*** | see *M. requienii* |
| ***crispa*** L. (1753) | see *M. spicata* var. *crispa* |
| ***crispa*** L. (1763) | see *M. aquatica* var. *crispa* |
| ***crispa*** ambig. × (× ***piperita***) | CArn CPbn |
| 'Dionysus' | CPbn SIde |
| × ***dumetorum*** | CPbn |
| 'Eau de Cologne' | see *M.* × *piperita* f. *citrata* |
| eucalyptus mint | CPbn EGHP ELau MHer WGwG |
| ***gattefossei*** | CArn |
| × ***gentilis*** | see *M.* × *gracilis* |

| | | |
|---|---|---|
| § | × ***gracilis*** | CArn CHby CPbn EGHP ELau NPri SIde |
| | – 'Aurea' | see *M.* × *gracilis* 'Variegata' |
| § | – 'Variegata' (v) | CPbn CSev CWan ECha ELau GGar GPoy ILis LEdu MCot MHer MNHC NPri NVic SPlb SWal WFar WHer WPer XLum |
| | ***haplocalyx*** | CArn ELau SIde |
| * | 'Hillary's Sweet Lemon' | CPbn ELau MHer SIde |
| | 'Julia's Sweet Citrus' | CPbn MHer SIde |
| * | ***lacerata*** | SIde |
| | lavender mint | EGHP ELau GPoy LEdu MHer MNHC WJek |
| § | ***longifolia*** | CPbn CWan ELau LEdu MMuc SEND SIde SPlb WHer |
| | – Buddleia Mint Group | CArn CPbn EBee EGHP ELau GGar LEdu MHer MRav SIde WJek XLum |
| | – – variegated (v) | LEdu WJek |
| | – subsp. ***capensis*** | WBox |
| | – dwarf | CPbn |
| | – subsp. ***schimperi*** | LEdu SIde WJek |
| | – silver-leaved | CArn CPbn ELau LEdu MHer MMuc MNHC NBlu NLar SEND WJek |
| * | – 'Variegata' (v) | CPbn ELau |
| | aff. ***longifolia*** new | WBox |
| | Nile Valley mint | CArn ELau EWhm LEdu SHDw SIde |
| | × ***piperita*** | CArn CHab CHby CPbn CSev CWan ECha EGHP EHoe ELau GGar GJos GPoy ILis LHop MBri MCot MHer MNHC NPri NVic SPlb WPer |
| | – 'Black Mitcham' | CArn CPbn XLum |
| | – black peppermint | CHby CPbn EGHP EPfP EWhm LEdu LLWG MMuc MNHC NBir NBlu NLar SEND SWal WGwG WJek |
| § | – f. ***citrata*** | Widely available |
| | – – from Portugal | CPbn |
| * | – – 'Basil' | CPbn CWan EGHP ELau LEdu MHer MNHC MRav NBlu SBfd SHDw SIde WGwG WJek XLum |
| | – – 'Bergamot' | CPbn |
| | – – 'Chocolate' | CArn CPbn CWan EGHP ELau EOHP EPfP GGar GJos ILis LEdu MHer MNHC SBfd SHDw SIde SPlb WGwG WJek |
| | – – 'Grapefruit' | CPbn CWan EGHP EWhm LSou MNHC SWal WGwG WJek |
| | – – 'Lemon' | CPbn CWan EGHP ELau EWhm GGar GPoy LEdu MBri MHer MNHC SBfd SHDw SIde WGwG WJek WPer |
| | – – 'Lime' | CPbn CWan EGHP EWhm ILis LBuc LEdu LSou MHer SBfd SHDw SIde SPlb WGwG WJek |
| | – – 'Orange' | CPbn EGHP LEdu MHer MMuc MNHC SEND WHil WJek |
| | – – 'Reverchonii' | CPbn SIde |
| | – – 'Swiss Ricola' | MHer SIde |
| | – 'Logee's' (v) | CPbn SIde WHer |
| | – f. ***officinalis*** | CPbn ELau SIde |
| | – var. ***ouweneellii*** Belgian mint | CPbn SIde |
| | – 'Reine Rouge' | CPbn SIde |
| | – 'Swiss' | EGHP EWhm LEdu NLar WJek |
| I | – Swiss mint | CArn CPbn |
| * | – white-flowered | CArn CPbn |
| | 'Polynesian Mint' | CPbn |
| | ***pulegium*** | CArn CHby CPbn CRWN CSev CTri CWan ELau EWil GPoy LLWG MHer MNHC MSKA NPri SIde SPlb SRms SVic WBox WHer WHfH WJek WPer |
| | – 'Upright' | CArn CPbn GPoy MHer SBfd SHDw SIde WJek WPer |
| § | ***requienii*** | Widely available |
| | ***rotundifolia*** misapplied | see *M. suaveolens* |
| | ***rotundifolia*** (L.) Hudson | see *M.* × *villosa* |
| | ***rubra*** var. ***raripila*** | see *M.* × *smithiana* |
| | 'Russian' curled leaf | CPbn |
| | 'Russian' plain leaf | CPbn |
| | 'Sayakaze' | see *M. arvensis* var. *piperascens* 'Sayakaze' |
| § | × ***smithiana*** | CArn CPbn CWan EGHP ELau GPoy MHer MNHC MRav NBir WHer WJek WPer |
| | – 'Capel Ulo' (v) | ELau |
| | 'South of France' | CPbn |
| § | ***spicata*** | CArn CHby COlW CPbn CPrp CSev CTri CWan EGHP ELau GJos GPoy ILis MBri MCot MHer MMuc MNHC NBlu NPri SEND SPlb SRms SWal WHer WJek WPer XLum |
| | – Algerian fruity | CPbn SIde |
| | – 'Austrian' | CPbn |
| * | – 'Brundall' | CPbn ELau ILis SIde |
| | – 'Canaries' | CPbn |
| * | – var. ***crispa*** | CArn CPbn CWan ECha EGHP ELau GGar LEdu LHop MHer MMuc MNHC NHol NRya SBfd SIde SPlb WJek WPer |
| | – – 'Moroccan' | CArn CPbn CPrp CSev EGHP ELau EOHP GAbr GGar GJos GPoy LEdu MHer MMuc MNHC NPri NVic SBfd SEND SHDw SIde STre WJek |
| | – – 'Persian' | CPbn |
| | – 'Guernsey' | CPbn SBfd SHDw SIde |
| | – 'Irish' | CPbn |
| | – 'Kentucky Colonel' | CPbn LEdu |
| | – 'Mexican' | CArn CPbn |
| | – 'Newbourne' | CPbn ELau SIde |
| | – 'Pharaoh' | CArn CPbn |
| | – 'Rhodos' | CPbn |
| | – 'Russian' | EGHP NHol SIde |
| | – 'Small Dole' (v) | SBfd SHDw |
| | – 'Spanish' | LEdu |
| | – 'Spanish Furry' | CPbn MHer SIde |
| | – 'Spanish Pointed' | CPbn ELau SIde WJek |
| | – 'Tashkent' | CArn CHby CPbn EGHP ELau EOHP EWhm LEdu MHer MNHC SBfd SHDw SIde WGwG WJek |
| | – subsp. ***tomentosa*** | CPbn |
| * | – 'Variegata' (v) | CPbn SBfd SHDw WGwG |
| | – 'Verte Blanche' | CPbn |
| § | ***suaveolens*** | CArn CHby CPbn CWan EGHP ELau GJos GMaP GPoy ILis MBri MHer MLHP MMuc MNHC NBlu SBfd SIde SPlb SVic SWal WJek WPer WSFF |
| * | – 'Grapefruit' | EGHP |
| | – 'Jokka' | CPbn EBee |
| * | – 'Mobillei' | CPbn SIde |
| * | – 'Pineapple' | LBuc WGwG WJek |
| | – subsp. ***timija*** | CPbn ELau LEdu SIde WJek |
| | – 'Variegata' (v) | CArn COlW CPbn CPrp CTri CWan ECha EHoe ELau GMaP GPoy LEdu MBri MCot MHer MNHC MRav NBlu NHol NPri NVic SBfd SIde SPlb SRms SWal WHer WPer XLum |
| | 'Sweet Pear' | MHer |
| | ***sylvestris*** L. | see *M. longifolia* |
| * | ***verona*** | CPbn |
| | × ***verticillata*** | WJek |

| | |
|---|---|
| § × ***villosa*** | CArn CPbn MMuc SEND SIde |
| § – var. ***alopecuroides*** Bowles's mint | CBre CPbn CPrp EGHP ELau GGar GPoy ILis LEdu MHer MNHC NBir SBfd SIde STre SWat WGwG WHer WJek |
| ***viridis*** | see *M. spicata* |

## *Mentzelia* (*Loasaceae*)

| | |
|---|---|
| ***decapetala*** | CSpe |

## *Menyanthes* (*Menyanthaceae*)

| | |
|---|---|
| ***trifoliata*** | CBen CRow CWat EHon EWil GPoy LLWG LPBA MCCP MMuc MSKA MWts NLar NPer WFar WHal WMAq WSFF XLum |

## *Menziesia* (*Ericaceae*)

| | |
|---|---|
| ***alba*** | see *Daboecia cantabrica* f. *alba* |
| ***ciliicalyx*** var. ***multiflora*** | EPfP |
| – 'Slieve Donard' | CMac |
| ***ferruginea*** | IVic |
| ***polifolia*** | see *Daboecia cantabrica* |
| 'Spring Morning' | WAbe |

## *Mercurialis* (*Euphorbiaceae*)

| | |
|---|---|
| ***perennis*** | GPoy WHer WHfH WSFF WShi |

## *Merendera* (*Colchicaceae*)

| | |
|---|---|
| ***attica*** | ECho |
| ***eichleri*** | see *M. trigyna* |
| ***filifolia*** | ECho |
| § ***montana*** | CPBP ECho EPot LWSt WIvy |
| ***pyrenaica*** | see *M. montana* |
| ***raddeana*** | see *M. trigyna* |
| ***robusta*** | LWSt |
| ***sobolifera*** | NWCA WCot |
| § ***trigyna*** | ECho |
| – bright pink-flowered | LWSt |
| – white-flowered clone | LWSt |

## *Merremia* (*Convolvulaceae*)

| | |
|---|---|
| § ***tuberosa*** | MOWG |

## *Mertensia* (*Boraginaceae*)

| | |
|---|---|
| ***ciliata*** | CCse SWat |
| § ***maritima*** | CBot CSpe CWCL ECho GBee GEdr GPoy LEdu NBir NWCA SPlb WFar WHoo WWEG |
| – subsp. ***asiatica*** | see *M. maritima* |
| ***primuloides*** | GAuc LLHF |
| ***pterocarpa*** | see *M. sibirica* |
| ***pulmonarioides*** | see *M. virginica* |
| § ***sibirica*** | CLAP CSpe NLar SPlb |
| § ***virginica*** ♀H4 | CBot CBro CLAP CSpe CWCL EBee ECho ECtt ELan EPfP EWTr LAma LEdu MMoz NBir NLar NPnk NPri NWCA SRms WFar |

## *Merwilla* (*Asparagaceae*)

| | |
|---|---|
| § ***plumbea*** | WCot |

## *Merxmuellera* see *Rytidosperma*

## *Mesembryanthemum* (*Aizoaceae*)

| | |
|---|---|
| 'Basutoland' | see *Delosperma nubigenum* |
| ***brownii*** | see *Lampranthus brownii* |

## *Mespilus* ✿ (*Rosaceae*)

| | |
|---|---|
| ***germanica*** (F) | CBcs CDul CLnd CMCN CTri EBee ECrN ELan EWTr IDee LMaj LTen MWat NEgg NPla SLon WDin WFar WMou WPat |
| – 'Bredase Reus' (F) | SKee |
| – 'Dutch' (F) | ERea SDea SFam SKee |
| – 'Iranian' (F) | SKee |
| – 'Large Russian' (F) | CAgr ERea |
| – 'Macrocarpa' (F) | SKee |
| – 'Monstrous' (F) | SDea |
| – 'Nottingham' (F) | Widely available |
| – 'Royal' (F) | CAgr ERea LRHS MBri MCoo SCoo SKee WHar |
| – 'Westerveld' (F) | CLnd NLar SKee |

## *Metanarthecium* (*Nartheciaceae*)

| | |
|---|---|
| ***luteo-viride*** new | LWSt |

## *Metapanax* (*Araliaceae*)

| | |
|---|---|
| ***davidii*** | IRar SLon |
| ***delavayi*** | SBig |

## *Metaplexis* (*Apocynaceae*)

| | |
|---|---|
| ***japonica*** B&SWJ 8459 | WCru |

## *Metarungia* (*Acanthaceae*)

| | |
|---|---|
| ***longistrobus*** | GFai |

## *Metasequoia* ✿ (*Cupressaceae*)

| | |
|---|---|
| ***glyptostroboides*** ♀H4 | Widely available |
| – 'All Bronze' | NLar |
| – 'Emerald Feathers' | SLim |
| – 'Fastigiata' | see *M. glyptostroboides* 'National' |
| – 'Gold Rush' | Widely available |
| – 'Golden Dawn' | NLar SLim |
| – 'Green Mantle' | EHul |
| – 'Little Creamy' | NLar |
| – 'Little Giant' | MBlu |
| – 'Matthaei Broom' | LRHS NLar SLim SPoG |
| – 'McCracken's White' (v) | NLar SLim |
| – 'Miss Grace' | MAsh NLar SLim |
| § – 'National' | MBlu |
| – 'Ōgon' new | SGol |
| – 'Schirrmann's Nordlicht' new | SLim |
| – 'Sheridan Spire' | CEnd MBlu |
| – 'Spring Cream' | NLar |
| – 'Waasland' | MBlu |
| – 'White Spot' (v) | MBlu NPCo SLim WEve |

## *Metrosideros* (*Myrtaceae*)

| | |
|---|---|
| ***carminea*** | CCCN CTsd |
| § ***excelsa*** | CHII CTsd EBak ECou ESwi |
| – 'Aurea' | ECou |
| – 'Parnell' | CBcs CCCN |
| – 'Scarlet Pimpernel' | MOWG |
| – 'Vibrance' | CCCN |
| ***kermadecensis*** | ECou |
| – 'Red and Gold' | CBcs CDoC |
| – 'Twisty' (v) | CBcs |
| – 'Variegata' (v) | CBcs CDoC ECou EPfP SMrm |
| ***lucida*** | see *M. umbellata* |
| 'Moon Maiden' | MOWG |
| Moonlight = 'Lowmoo' new | LRHS SLim |
| 'Pink Lady' | CTrC |
| ***robusta*** | CCCN CHEx MREP |
| – ***aureovariegata*** | CCCN EShb |
| § 'Springfire' | CCCN LRHS MOWG |
| × ***subtomentosa*** 'Mistral' | ECou |
| 'Thomasii' | see *M.* 'Springfire' |
| ***tomentosa*** | see *M. excelsa* |

| | |
|---|---|
| § ***umbellata*** | CBcs CCCN CDoC CDul CHEx CTrC CTsd EBee ECou GGar |
| - Gold Nugget = 'Lownug' **new** | LRHS MSCN SLim SPtl |
| ***villosa*** | MOWG |

## *Meum* (*Apiaceae*)

| | |
|---|---|
| ***athamanticum*** | CArn CSpe EBee EDAr GCal GPoy ILis LPla MAvo MCot MRav SPhx WFar WPer WTin |

## *Michauxia* (*Campanulaceae*)

| | |
|---|---|
| ***campanuloides*** | CSpe |
| ***tchihatchewii*** | CCCN CDTJ CSpe MWea NGBl |

## *Michelia* see *Magnolia*

| | |
|---|---|
| ***fulgens*** | see *Magnolia foveolata* |
| ***wilsonii*** | see *Magnolia ernestii* |
| ***yunnanensis*** | see *Magnolia laevifolia* |

## *Microbiota* (*Cupressaceae*)

| | |
|---|---|
| ***decussata*** ♀H4 | CBcs CDoC CKen CMac CSBt ECho EHul EPla LAst LBee LRHS MGos MMuc MWat NHol NWea SEND SLim SPoG WEve WFar |
| - 'Gold Spot' | CDoC SLim SPoG |
| - 'Jakobsen' | CDoC CKen |
| - 'Trompenburg' | CKen |

## *Microcachrys* (*Podocarpaceae*)

| | |
|---|---|
| ***tetragona*** | CDoC ECho ECou EHul EPla LRHS SCoo WThu |

## *Microcoelum* see *Lytocaryum*

| | |
|---|---|
| ***weddellianum*** | see *Lytocaryum weddellianum* |

## *Microglossa* (*Asteraceae*)

| | |
|---|---|
| ***albescens*** | see *Aster albescens* |

## *Microlaena* see *Ehrharta*

## *Microlepia* (*Dennstaedtiaceae*)

| | |
|---|---|
| ***speluncae*** | EShb |
| ***strigosa*** | CBty CCCN CLAP LLHF LRHS WRic |

## *Micromeria* (*Lamiaceae*)

| | |
|---|---|
| ***corsica*** | see *Acinos corsicus* |
| ***croatica*** | NMen |
| ***dalmatica*** | XLum |
| ***fruticosa*** | CArn WJek |
| ***graeca*** | CArn |
| ***rupestris*** | see *M. thymifolia* |
| § ***thymifolia*** | NMen SPlb |
| ***viminea*** | see *Satureja viminea* |

## *Microseris* (*Asteraceae*)

| | |
|---|---|
| ***ringens*** hort. | see *Leontodon rigens* |

## *Microsorum* (*Polypodiaceae*)

| | |
|---|---|
| ***diversifolium*** | see *Phymatosorus diversifolius* |
| ***scolopendria*** **new** | CBty |

## *Microtropis* (*Celastraceae*)

| | |
|---|---|
| ***petelotii*** HWJ 719 | WCru |

## *Mikania* (*Asteraceae*)

| | |
|---|---|
| ***araucana*** | LSou |

## *Milium* (*Poaceae*)

| | |
|---|---|
| ***effusum*** 'Aureum' ♀H4 | Widely available |
| - var. ***esthonicum*** | EPPr |
| - 'Yaffle' (v) | CBod CBre CKno EBee ECha EPPr EPla EShb LEdu MWat SGar SSvw SUsu WCot WPnP |

## *Millettia* (*Papilionaceae*)

| | |
|---|---|
| ***japonica*** 'Hime Fuji' | NLar |
| murasaki-natsu-fuji | see *M. reticulata* |
| § ***reticulata*** | CPLG |

## *Mimosa* (*Mimosaceae*)

| | |
|---|---|
| ***pudica*** | CCCN CDTJ WTou |

## *Mimulus* (*Phrymaceae*)

| | |
|---|---|
| sp. | SVic |
| 'Andean Nymph' | see *M. naiandinus* |
| § ***aurantiacus*** ♀H2-3 | CBot CElw CMac CSpe CTri EBak ECtt LHop LRHS MAsh NBir NPer SAga SBch SBfd SGar SPlb SUsu |
| × ***bartonianus*** | see *M.* × *harrisonii* |
| ***bifidus*** 'Trish' | CSpe SAga SUsu |
| - 'Verity Buff' | MAsh |
| § - 'Verity Purple' | EDif |
| - 'Wine' | see *M. bifidus* 'Verity Purple' |
| × ***burnetii*** | ECho LPBA SRms |
| ***cardinalis*** ♀H3 | CEnt EBee ELan EPfP LPBA MNrw MSKA NBir NMRc WFar WMoo WWEG |
| - 'Dark Throat' | SGar |
| - gold-flowered | WHil |
| - 'Red Dragon' | SBHP WHrl |
| ***cupreus*** 'Minor' | ECho |
| - 'Whitecroft Scarlet' ♀H4 | ECho ELan EPfP SRms |
| ***eastwoodiae*** | GKev |
| 'Eleanor' | ECtt LSou SAga SGar SHom SUsu |
| 'Frost' | EDif |
| ***glutinosus*** | see *M. aurantiacus* |
| - ***atrosanguineus*** | see *M. puniceus* |
| - ***luteus*** | see *M. aurantiacus* |
| § ***guttatus*** | NMir NPer SRms WMoo WPnP |
| § × ***harrisonii*** | EPfP EWes LSou SAga |
| 'Highland Orange' | ECho EPfP NBlu SPlb SPoG WGor |
| 'Highland Pink' | ECho EPfP SPlb SPoG WGor |
| 'Highland Pink Rose' | WFar |
| 'Highland Red' ♀H4 | ECho ECtt EPfP GGar GKev LPBA NBlu SPlb SPoG SRms WFar WNew |
| 'Highland Yellow' | ECho ECtt GKev LPBA NBlu SPlb SPoG WFar |
| hose-in-hose (d) | NPer |
| 'Inca Sunset' | EWes |
| ***langsdorffii*** | see *M. guttatus* |
| ***lewisii*** ♀H3 | CHll SRms |
| ***longiflorus*** | CBot MAsh |
| 'Lothian Fire' | CWat |
| ***luteus*** | CWat EHon LPBA NHol NPer SPlb WBrk WFar WMAq XLum |
| § - 'Gaby' (v) | LPBA |
| - 'Variegatus' | see *M. luteus* 'Gaby' |
| - 'Variegatus' ambig. (v) | NPer |
| 'Malibu Orange' | EPfP |
| ***minimus*** | ECho |
| ***moschatus*** | EBee LLWG |
| § ***naiandinus*** ♀H3 | CEnt GKev SPlb SRms |
| 'Orange Glow' | LLWG WHal |
| orange hose-in-hose (d) | NBir |
| § 'Orkney Gold' (d) | ECtt |
| 'Popacatapetl' | CSpe EDif LHop MAsh SBHP SHom SUsu |

| | | |
|---|---|---|
| | 'Prairie Buff' **new** | EDif |
| | 'Prairie Caramel' | EDif |
| | 'Prairie Cerise' | EDif |
| | 'Prairie Citron' | EDif |
| | 'Prairie Coral' | EDif |
| | 'Prairie Dawn' **new** | EDif |
| | 'Prairie Frost' **new** | EDif |
| | 'Prairie Lilac Frost' | EDif |
| | 'Prairie Pink' **new** | EDif |
| | 'Prairie Scarlet' **new** | EDif |
| | 'Prairie Sunrise' **new** | EDif |
| | 'Prairie Sunshine' | EDif |
| | 'Prairie Violet' | EDif |
| | ***primuloides*** | ECho EWes LLWG SPlb |
| | - var. ***linearifolius*** NNS 07-355 | NWCA |
| | 'Puck' | ECho SPoG |
| § | ***puniceus*** | CBot CTri EDif IRar LHop SBHP SHom SMrm SRkn |
| | 'Quetzalcoatl' | LHop |
| | ***ringens*** | CBen CWat EDif EHon LPBA MSKA NBir NPer SPlb SRms WFar WHil WMAq WMoo WWEG |
| | 'Threave Variegated' (v) | MRav NBir WFar |
| | ***tilingii*** | CPBP |
| | 'Vortex' | LSou |
| | 'Wine Red' | see *M. bifidus* 'Verity Purple' |
| | 'Wisley Red' | ECho SRms |
| | yellow hose-in-hose | see *M.* 'Orkney Gold' |

## *Mina* see *Ipomoea*

## mint, apple see *Mentha suaveolens*

## mint, Bowles's see *M.* × *villosa* var. *alopecuroides*

## mint, curly see *M. spicata* var. *crispa*

## mint, eau-de-Cologne see *M.* × *piperita* f. *citrata*

## mint, ginger see *M.* × *gracilis*

## mint, horse or long-leaved see *M. longifolia*

## mint, pennyroyal see *M. pulegium*

## mint (peppermint) see *M.* × *piperita*

## mint, round-leaved see *M. suaveolens*

## mint (spearmint) see *M. spicata*

## *Minuartia* (*Caryophyllaceae*)

| | | |
|---|---|---|
| | ***capillacea*** | ECho |
| | ***caucasica*** | see *M. circassica* |
| § | ***circassica*** | NWCA |
| | ***laricifolia*** | NMen XSen |
| | ***parnassica*** | see *M. stellata* |
| § | ***stellata*** | EPot NMen WPat |
| § | ***verna*** | ECho NMen |
| | - subsp. ***caespitosa*** | CTri ECho |
| | - - 'Aurea' | see *Sagina subulata* var. *glabrata* 'Aurea' |

## *Mirabilis* (*Nyctaginaceae*)

| | | |
|---|---|---|
| | ***dichotoma*** **new** | EShb |
| | ***jalapa*** | CArn CPLG CWCL EPfP LAma LEdu SEND SRms WHil WTou |
| | - 'Buttermilk' | CCCN |
| | - red-flowered | SEND WTou |
| | - white-flowered | CSpe WTou |
| | - yellow-flowered | WTou |
| | ***longiflora*** | WHil |

## *Miscanthus* ✿ (*Poaceae*)

| | | |
|---|---|---|
| | sp. | MBNS |
| | ***capensis*** | SPlb |
| | ***chejuensis*** B&SWJ 8803 | WCru |
| | 'Dronning Ingrid' | CKno EBee EPPr XLum |
| | 'Elfin' | CKno |
| | ***flavidus*** B&SWJ 6749 | WCru |
| | ***floridulus*** misapplied | see *M.* × *giganteus* |
| | ***floridulus*** ambig. | CFir EBee MMuc MNrw SEND SPlb WFar XLum |
| | ***floridulus*** (Labill.) Warb. ex K. Schum. & Lauterb. HWJ 522 | WCru |
| § | × ***giganteus*** | CHar CKno CSpe EHoe ELon EPPr GCal GKev GQue MCCP MMoz MMuc MNrw MWat NDov NVic NWsh SApp SDix SEND SMad SVic WCot WFar WPGP WWEG |
| | - 'Gilt Edge' (v) | CKno EPPr MAvo NWsh SApp |
| | - 'Gotemba' (v) | EBee ELon EPPr EWes NWsh SApp |
| | 'Golden Bar' | EPla NGdn SBrd WCra |
| | 'Gotemba Gold' | SApp |
| | 'Mount Washington' | SApp |
| | ***nepalensis*** | CDes CElw CEnt CHVG CKno CPLG ECha ECre EHoe EPGN EWes GCal LEdu MAvo MLLN MNrw NOak SDix SUsu |
| | - 'Shikola' | WCru |
| § | ***oligostachyus*** 'Afrika' | CHar CKno EPPr LHop MAvo WPGP XLum |
| I | - 'Nanus Variegatus' (v) | CKno EHoe EWes LEdu MMoz WCot WPGP WWEG |
| | 'Pos' | SApp |
| § | 'Purpurascens' | CKno COIW CWCL ECha EHoe EShb LBMP LPla LRHS LSRN MAvo MWhi NOak SApp SGol SPer WCot WMoo WTin |
| | ***sacchariflorus*** misapplied | see *M.* × *giganteus* |
| | ***sacchariflorus*** ambig. | CBcs CDul CHEx CKno EBee ECha ELan EPfP EPla EShb LPBA LRHS MBrN MSCN NGdn SBfd SPer WFar WMoo XLum |
| | ***sacchariflorus*** (Maxim.) Hack. | MMuc MWhi WWEG |
| | ***sinensis*** | CEnt CHEx CTri EBla LEdu MMoz NGBl NOak WDin WMoo WWEG |
| | - 'Abundance' | CKno |
| | - 'Adagio' | CHar CKno EAEE EBee EHoe EPPr GBin GQue LBMP LEdu LRHS LTen MWhi NDov SHDw SLPl SMea WCot XLum |
| | - 'Afrika' | see *M. oligostachyus* 'Afrika' |
| | - 'Andante' | CKno |
| | - 'Arabesque' | EPPr MMoz NLar SApp WWEG XLum |
| | - 'Augustfeder' | CHar EBee EPPr LEdu SMea WWEG XLum |
| | - 'Autumn Light' | CKno EPPr SMea XLum |
| | - 'Ballerina' | CHar |
| | - 'Blütenwunder' | CHar CKno EBee EPfP |
| | - 'China' | Widely available |
| | - var. ***condensatus*** | LRHS LSou |
| | - - 'Cabaret' (v) | Widely available |
| | - - 'Central Park' | see *M. sinensis* var. *condensatus* 'Cosmo Revert' |
| § | - - 'Cosmo Revert' | LEdu MMoz NWsh WDyG |

| | | |
|---|---|---|
| | - - 'Cosmopolitan' (v) ♀H4 | Widely available |
| | - - 'Emerald Giant' | see *M. sinensis* var. *condensatus* 'Cosmo Revert' |
| | - 'David' | EBee ELon EPPr LEdu MAvo MBNS |
| | - 'Dixieland' (v) | CHar CKno EHoe ELan EPPr IFoB LEdu LRHS MBri MMoz NWsh SApp WWEG XLum |
| | - 'Emmanuel Lepage' | CHar CKno EBee EPPr LRHS XLum |
| | - 'Etincelle' | CKno EWes XLum |
| | - 'Federriese' | XLum |
| | - 'Ferner Osten' | Widely available |
| | - 'Flamingo' ♀H4 | Widely available |
| | - 'Flammenmeer' | CHar XLum |
| | - 'Gaa' | SApp |
| | - 'Gearmella' | EPPr LEdu LRHS MAsh NWsh XLum |
| | - 'Gewitterwolke' ♀H4 | CHar EPPr EWes LRHS XLum |
| | - 'Ghana' ♀H4 | CHar CKno EBee ELon EPPr LHop LRHS MAvo NLar SUsu XLum |
| | - 'Giraffe' | CDTJ CDes CHar CKno EBee EWes LEdu WPGP WWEG XLum |
| | - 'Gnome' | CKno EAEE EBee EHoe EPPr LRHS MMHG MWhi NDov NLar WWEG |
| | - 'Gold Bar'PBR (v) | CChe CElw CKno CMea CWGN EBee ECha ECtt EHoe ELon EPPr EPfP LEdu LRHS LSRN LSou MAsh MBNS NCGa NGdn NWad NWsh SBfd SPer SPoG SUsu WCot WMoo WWEG |
| | - 'Goldfeder' (v) | EHoe XLum |
| | - 'Goliath' | CHar CKno EHoe ELan ELon EPPr GQue IPot LBMP LEdu LRHS MBNS NWsh WFar WWEG XLum |
| | - 'Gracillimus' | Widely available |
| | - 'Gracillimus Nanus' | CKno |
| | - 'Graziella' | CEnd CFir CHar CKno CSam CWCL CWib EBee EBla EHoe EPPr EPfP EPla LEdu LRHS LTen MBri MMoz MWhi NGdn NOak NOrc SLPl SPer SRms WBor WPGP XLum |
| | - 'Grosse Fontäne' ♀H4 | CFir CWCL EBee EBla EHoe ELan EPPr LEdu LRHS LSRN NWsh WAul WCot WMoo WWEG XLum |
| | - 'Gutenberg Gold' | XLum |
| | - 'Haiku' | CHar CKno EPPr LEdu LRHS NDov XLum |
| | - 'Helga Reich' | EWes LRHS SApp |
| | - 'Hercules' | LRHS MAvo MMoz SApp XLum |
| | - 'Hermann Müssel' | CHar CKno EBee EPPr EWes GBin LEdu LPla LRHS NDov SMea XLum |
| | - 'Hinjo' (v) | CElw CHGN CHar EBee ECGP ECha ECtt EHoe ELon EPPr GBin GQue LBMP LEdu LRHS LSou NGdn NLar NWsh SApp WCot WCra WFar WPGP WWEG |
| I | - 'Jubilaris' (v) | EPPr EWes |
| | - 'Juli' | XLum |
| | - 'Kaskade' ♀H4 | CHar CKno CWCL EBee EHoe EPPr IPot LEdu MAsh MMoz MMuc MWhi NDov SApp SEND SUsu WFar WMoo WWEG XLum |
| | - 'Kirk Alexander' (v) | SApp |
| | - 'Kleine Fontäne' ♀H4 | Widely available |
| | - 'Kleine Silberspinne' ♀H4 | Widely available |
| | - 'Krater' | CHar CKno EHoe EPPr LEdu LPla MAsh MBrN SDys SGar SMea SWat XLum |
| | - 'Kupferberg' | CHar XLum |
| § | - 'Little Kitten' | CHar CKno EBee LEdu NWsh SMad SMea WMoo WPGP WWEG XLum |
| | - 'Little Zebra'PBR (v) | CKno EBee EPPr EPfP LHop LSRN MAsh NOak NWsh SRms |
| | - 'Malepartus' | Widely available |
| | - 'Morning Light' (v) ♀H4 | Widely available |
| | - hybrids | SGol |
| | - 'Nippon' | CDes CElw CFir CKno CPrp CWCL EAEE EBee EBla EHoe EPPr LEdu LPla LRHS MMoz MWhi NBro NDov NGdn NOrc NWsh SDys SMrm SPer WPGP WWEG XLum |
| | - 'Nishidake' | CHar XLum |
| | - 'November Sunset' | EPPr EWes MMoz XLum |
| | - 'Overdam' | NGdn XLum |
| | - 'Pagel's Pride' **new** | LRHS |
| | - 'Poseidon' | EPPr LRHS MAvo NChi SDys SMad XLum |
| | - 'Positano' | CKno MMoz WPGP XLum |
| | - 'Professor Richard Hansen' | CHar CKno GBin LRHS NDov XLum |
| | - 'Pünktchen' (v) | CHar CKno CWCL EAEE EAmu EBee ECha EHoe EPPr GBin LBMP LEdu LRHS MAvo NCGa NOak SApp SBfd SHDw SMad SRms WFar WMoo WPnP WTin WWEG XLum |
| | - 'Purple Fall' **new** | LRHS |
| | - var. ***purpurascens*** misapplied | see *M.* 'Purpurascens' |
| | - 'Red Chief' | EPPr EWes |
| | - 'Rigoletto' (v) | EPPr LRHS SApp |
| | - 'Roland' | CHar CKno EBee EPPr GBin LRHS NWsh SPhx XLum |
| | - 'Roterpfeil' | CHar EBee EPPr |
| | - 'Rotfeder' | EPPr SBfd XLum |
| | - 'Rotfuchs' | CHar EBee LPla LRHS SAga WFar XLum |
| | - 'Rotsilber' | CHar CKno CPrp CSpe CWib EBee ECha EHoe EPPr EPla GMaP IArd LEdu LRHS MAsh MAvo MMuc MRav MWhi NDov NOak NWsh WFar WHoo WMoo WPnP WPtf WWEG XLum |
| I | - 'Russianus' | NWsh |
| | - 'Samurai' | CEnt CHar EPPr GMaP GQue MAvo |
| | - 'Sarabande' | CHar CKno EBee EHoe EHul ELan EPPr IPot NDov NWsh SApp WFar WMoo XLum |
| | - 'Septemberrot' ♀H4 | CHVG CHar CPrp CWCL EBee LEdu MMuc SEND |
| § | - 'Silberfeder' ♀H4 | Widely available |
| | - 'Silberpfeil' (v) | EHoe NWsh |
| | - 'Silberspinne' | CCse EBla EPla LEdu MWat NDov NGdn SApp SBfd SMea SPlb WAul WDin XLum |
| | - 'Silberturm' | CHar EBee EPPr LPla |
| | - Silver Feather | see *M. sinensis* 'Silberfeder' |
| | - 'Silver Stripe' | EPPr |
| | - 'Sioux' | CEnt CHar EBee EHoe EPPr EPfP EShb GBin LBMP LEdu LRHS MBNS MMoz NCGa NWsh SPer SUsu WTin WWEG |
| | - 'Sirene' | CFir CHar EAEE EBee EHoe EPPr GQue LRHS MBNS MBlu MBri MSpe NWsh SMrm WFar XLum |
| | - 'Spätgrün' | CHar |
| | - 'Strictus' (v) ♀H4 | Widely available |
| | - 'Tiger Cub' (v) | CWCL EWes LRHS MAvo SApp |

| | |
|---|---|
| - 'Undine' ♀H4 | CFir CHar CKno CMea EBee EBla ECha EHoe ELan EPPr LEdu LRHS MLLN MMoz MSnd NWsh SLPl WMoo XLum |
| - 'Variegatus' (v) | Widely available |
| - 'Vorläufer' | CHar EBee EHoe EPPr NWsh XLum |
| [illegible] | [illegible] |
| - 'Wetterfahne' | CHar LEdu XLum |
| § - 'Yaku-jima' | CHar CSam EBee ECha EPPr LHop MWhi SMea |
| - 'Yakushima Dwarf' | Widely available |
| - 'Zebrinus' (v) ♀H4 | Widely available |
| - 'Zwergelefant' | CHar MMoz XLum |
| I 'Spartina' | SApp |
| ***tinctorius*** 'Nanus Variegatus' misapplied | see *M. oligostachyus* 'Nanus Variegatus' |
| ***transmorrisonensis*** | CHar CKno EBee EHoe ELan EPPr MAvo MLLN MMoz NWsh SApp SWal WBox WCot WTin WWEG XLum |
| - B&SWJ 3697 | WCru |
| ***yakushimensis*** | see *M. sinensis* 'Yaku-jima', *M. sinensis* 'Little Kitten' |

## *Mitchella* (*Rubiaceae*)

| | |
|---|---|
| ***repens*** | CBcs EBee GBin IVic WCru |
| ***undulata*** B&SWJ 10928 | WCru |
| * - f. ***quelpartensis*** B&SWJ 4402 | WCru |

## *Mitella* (*Saxifragaceae*)

| | |
|---|---|
| ***breweri*** | CFir CHid CMac ECha GCal GGar MRav SBch SRms WFar WMoo WOut WPnP WTin |
| ***caulescens*** | ECha NBro WMoo |
| ***diphylla*** | EPPr |
| ***formosana*** B&SWJ 125 | EPPr WCru |
| × ***inami*** B&SWJ 11122 | WCru |
| ***japonica*** B&SWJ 4971 | WCru |
| ***kiusiana*** | CLAP |
| - B&SWJ 5888 | WCru |
| ***makinoi*** | CLAP EBee EWld |
| - B&SWJ 4992 | WCru |
| ***ovalis*** | EBee EPPr |
| ***pauciflora*** B&SWJ 6361 | WCru |
| ***stylosa*** B&SWJ 5669 | WCru |
| ***yoshinagae*** B&SWJ 4893 | CHid GEdr WCru WMoo WPtf |

## *Mitraria* (*Gesneriaceae*)

| | |
|---|---|
| ***coccinea*** | CBcs CCCN CDoy CEnt CHll CMac CPLG CTsd CWib ECho ELan GAbr GKev LSou MBlu MDun NMun SArc SLon SPer SPlb SSpi WAle |
| - Clark's form | CTrC LAst NLar |
| - 'Lake Caburgua' | CCCN CSpe ELon EWld GCal GGal GGar IArd IDee NLar NSti WAle |
| - 'Lake Puyehue' | CAbb CBcs CCCN CDoC CFee CPLG EBee EPfP GQui LHop LRHS MAsh MGos SPoG SWvt WAle WCru WFar WGwG WSHC |

## *Moehringia* (*Caryophyllaceae*)

| | |
|---|---|
| ***muscosa*** | WCot |

## *Molinia* (*Poaceae*)

| | |
|---|---|
| ***altissima*** | see *M. caerulea* subsp. *arundinacea* |
| 'Autumn Charm' **new** | CKno |
| ***caerulea*** | CRWN CWib EPPr MBlu NChi NGBl |
| § - subsp. ***arundinacea*** | CKno CWCL ECha EPPr MMuc NLar SApp SLPl WPtf WWEG XLum |
| - - 'Bergfreund' | CKno CSam EBee EHoe EPPr MAvo NWsh SApp SUsu WDyG WMoo |
| - - 'Black Arrow' **new** | NDov |
| - - 'Cordoba' | CKno EPPr GQue NDov SPhx XLum |
| - - 'Fontäne' | CSam EBee EHoe EPPr GCal GQue LEdu LPla NDov NWsh SApp SPhx |
| - - 'Karl Foerster' | Widely available |
| - - 'Skyracer' | CCVN CChe CKno COIW CPrp CSam EBee EBla EHoe EPPr EPfP GCal GQue MAvo MMoz MWhi NVic NWsh SMad SPhx WCot WFar WGrn WMoo WWEG |
| - - 'Staefa' | EHoe |
| - - 'Transparent' | Widely available |
| - - 'Windsaule' | CKno EBee EPPr SPhx |
| - - 'Windspiel' | CKno CSam CSpe CWCL EAEE EBee ECha EHoe EPPr IKil LEdu LRHS MAvo MBri MNrw MWat NDov NWsh SApp SMrm SPhx SWal WCot WMoo WPGP WPtf XLum |
| - - 'Zuneigung' | CKno CSam EPPr LPla MAvo SApp SPhx |
| - subsp. ***caerulea*** 'Carmarthen' (v) | EHoe EPPr SApp SUsu WHal WPnP WWEG |
| - - 'Claerwen' (v) | ECha EPPr GCal SPhx WMoo |
| - - 'Coneyhill Gold' (v) | EPPr |
| - - 'Dauerstrahl' | CKno EBee EPPr GBin GCal GQue LPla MAvo MNrw NDov |
| - - 'Edith Dudszus' | CKno COIW CWCL EAEE EBee ECha EHoe ELon EPPr GQue IPot LPla LRHS MAvo MBrN MBri MNFA NDov NGdn NHol NOrc NWsh SApp SPer WCot WGrn WMoo WWEG |
| - - 'Heidebraut' | CBod EAEE EBee EBla EHoe EPPr GBin GQue MBri MRav NBro NDov NOrc SApp SBfd SPhx WFar WMoo WWEG |
| - - 'Moorflamme' | CKno CSam EBee EHoe EPPr MAvo NDov SPhx |
| - - 'Moorhexe' | Widely available |
| - - 'Overdam' | MMuc MNrw NDov SEND |
| - - 'Poul Petersen' | CHar CKno EPPr NDov SPhx |
| - - 'Strahlenquelle' | CSam EBee ELan EPPr GCal GQue LPla MAvo MNFA MWat NBro NDov SPhx WWEG |
| - - 'Variegata' (v) ♀H4 | Widely available |
| - 'Dark Defender' **new** | SPhx |
| - 'Showers of Gold' **new** | SPhx |
| - 'Winterfreude' | NDov |
| ***litoralis*** | see *M. caerulea* subsp. *arundinacea* |
| 'Nearly-see-Through' **new** | SSvw |

## *Molopospermum* (*Apiaceae*)

| | |
|---|---|
| ***peloponnesiacum*** | CAby CSpe GCal LEdu NLar SPhx WCru WPnP WPtf WSHC |

## *Moltkia* (*Boraginaceae*)

| | |
|---|---|
| § ***doerfleri*** | GCal NBir NChi |
| § × ***intermedia*** ♀H4 | CMea IRar SAga SBch WFar WPat |
| ***petraea*** | LLHF LRHS MWat WFar |

## *Moluccella* (*Lamiaceae*)

| | |
|---|---|
| ***laevis*** 'Pixie Bells' | CSpe |

## *Monachosorum* (*Dennstaedtiaceae*)

| | |
|---|---|
| ***henryi*** | WRic |

## *Monarda* (*Lamiaceae*)

| | |
|---|---|
| 'Adam' | EBee GCal LRHS LSRN MPkF NBre NGdn NLar WSHC |
| 'Amethyst' | ECtt EWes SIde |
| 'Aquarius' | CAby EBee EGHP EPPr IKil LRHS MMuc MSpe NDov SEND SHar SPet WCAu XLum |
| ***austromontana*** | see *M. citriodora* subsp. *austromontana* |
| 'Baby Spice' | EBee |
| § 'Balance' | EBee ECtt EGHP EPfP GCal LAst LRHS MCot MRav MSpe NBro NDov NGdn NHol NSti SMrm WFar WSHC WWEG XLum |
| 'Beauty of Cobham' ♀H4 | CAby CHar CPrp CWCL EAEE EBee ECha ELan EPfP GMaP LEdu MBri MCot MHer MSpe NDov NHol NLar SBch SMad SPer SPhx WBor WHlf WWEG WWlt XLum |
| 'Blaukranz' | NBre |
| § 'Blaustrumpf' | CElw EBee ECtt ELon EPfP EWes GBBs GQue LRHS NLar SPer WSHC |
| Blue Stocking | see *M.* 'Blaustrumpf' |
| Bowman | see *M.* 'Sagittarius' |
| ***bradburyana*** | NBre NLar |
| 'Cambridge Scarlet' ♀H4 | Widely available |
| 'Capricorn' | NBre WWEG XLum |
| 'Cherokee' | WFar |
| 'Chippawa' | LRHS |
| ***citriodora*** | ECtt GPoy LRHS NSti SGar SIde SRms SWat WBox XLum |
| § - subsp. ***austromontana*** | CSpe NBir SBch SIde SVic WFar |
| - - 'Bee's Favourite' | SPad |
| 'Comanche' | EBee EWes NDov WFar |
| 'Croftway Pink' ♀H4 | Widely available |
| ***didyma*** | CArn CHar CWan EGHP EPfP NBlu NBro SBfd SWat WJek |
| - 'Coral Reef' | EWes WWEG |
| - 'Duddiscombe' | CAby CSam CWCL MSpe |
| - 'Goldmelise' | WMoo |
| - 'Pink Lace'PBR | GKev LSou MAsh MBri MNrw NCGa NLar STes WHlf |
| 'Earl Grey' | GAbr MSpe NDov |
| 'Elsie's Lavender' | CAby EBee LPla LRHS NDov NLar WWEG |
| 'Elworthy' | CElw |
| 'Fireball'PBR | CCVN CPrp CWCL EBee ECtt ELon GAbr LEdu LLHF LRHS LSou MNrw MTis NBPC NCGa NHol NLar NPri SBfd WBor WHil |
| § 'Fishes' | CMac EAEE EBee ECtt EGHP ELan EPPr EWes IKil LRHS MCot MRav MSpe NDov NGdn NHol NLar SMrm SPet STes WFar WSHC WWEG |
| ***fistulosa*** | CArn CMac GPoy MHer MNHC WJek WMoo XLum |
| 'Gardenview Scarlet' ♀H4 | Widely available |
| Gemini | see *M.* 'Twins' |
| 'Gewitterwolke' | CAby CSam EBee MSpe SDys |
| 'Hartswood Wine' | EWes SMad SMrm WPer WWEG |
| 'Heidelerche' | EPPr |
| 'Jacob Cline' | EPPr GBin IPot MAsh MSpe NBre NCGa NDov SPhx STes WPtf WWEG |
| 'Kardinal' | EBee GBin LRHS NDov NLar |
| Libra | see *M.* 'Balance' |
| 'Loddon Crown' | CHar COIW CPrp ECtt GQue LRHS MBri MDKP NHol NLar SBfd SHar SIde WCAu WSHC WWEG |
| 'Mahogany' | CPrp EBee ELan GMaP IKil LRHS MNrw MRav SPer WSHC WWEG |
| 'Marshall's Delight' ♀H4 | CPrp CSam EBee ECtt EWTr EWes EWhm LRHS LSou MRav MTis NLar SGar SMrm WCAu WFar |
| 'Melissa' | LSRN NBre NLar |
| ***menthifolia*** | CArn EBee GCal MCot SMrm |
| 'Mohawk' | CAby CPrp EAEE EBee ECtt EPPr EWhm LRHS MSpe MWat NDov NGdn NHol NOrc SDix WWEG |
| 'Mrs Perry' | EWes |
| 'Neon' | MTis NDov SPhx |
| 'Night Rider' | EWes |
| 'On Parade' | CSam EAEE EBee ECtt LRHS MMHG MSpe MTis NDov NGdn NHol |
| 'Othello' | CSam LRHS NDov |
| 'Ou Charm' | EBee EWes MMHG NDov NLar SMrm WFar |
| 'Panorama' | ECtt NLar SPet SPlb WMoo |
| 'Panorama Red Shades' (Panorama Series) | CWib MNHC MSCN SPet WCFE |
| 'Pawnee' | LRHS NDov |
| Petite Delight = 'Acpetdel' | CBcs EBee ECtt EGHP EHoe ELan LHop LSou MAsh MPkF NHol NLar SMad WFar WWEG |
| 'Petite Pink Supreme' | EBee |
| 'Pink Supreme'PBR | EGHP EPfP GAbr GQue LSou MTis NCGa NLar NPri SBfd WHil |
| 'Pink Tourmaline' | EWhm MTis NDov NHol SMrm WWEG |
| Pisces | see *M.* 'Fishes' |
| 'Poyntzfield Pink' | GPoy |
| Prairie Night | see *M.* 'Prärienacht' |
| § 'Prärienacht' | CAby CHar CPrp CSBt CSam EBee ECha ELan EPfP LRHS MCot MHer MSpe NBPC NBro NGdn NHol NPri SBch SPer SPlb SRms STes SWvt WCAu WFar WPer WSHC WWEG |
| ***punctata*** | CArn ELan LBMP MCot NGdn SWat WFar |
| 'Raspberry Wine' | ECtt EPPr MSpe |
| 'Ruby Glow' | CAby CSam CWCL EBee LRHS LSRN MArl MBri MMHG NDov NGdn NHol SAga SMrm SPhx |
| § 'Sagittarius' | EAEE EBee MMHG MSpe NGdn NHol NSti SPur |
| 'Saxon Purple' | CSam MTis NDov NLar |
| § 'Schneewittchen' | CAby CWCL EBee ECha ECtt EGHP ELan EPfP LRHS MGos MHer MRav NHol NLar NPri NSti SIde SPer SWvt WFar WWEG |
| 'Scorpion' | CWCL EBee ECtt ELan EPPr LEdu LRHS MCot MMuc MRav MSpe NBPC NBir NEgg NGdn NLar NOrc SEND SMrm SPet SPhx SWvt WCAu WGwG WSHC WWlt XLum |
| 'Shelley' | ECha |
| 'Sioux' | EBee EWes WFar |
| 'Snow Maiden' | see *M.* 'Schneewittchen' |
| 'Snow Queen' | EBee ECtt EPPr LRHS MLLN MSpe MWat NGdn NHol NPro SMrm SPur STes |
| Snow White | see *M.* 'Schneewittchen' |
| 'Squaw' ♀H4 | Widely available |
| 'Talud' ♀H4 | EBee MSpe NDov |
| § 'Twins' | CWCL EBee EGHP EPPr LSRN NLar SWvt WSHC WWEG |

| | | |
|---|---|---|
| | 'Velvet Queen' | LSou |
| | 'Vintage Wine' | CAby CWCL ECtt NDov WFar |
| | 'Violacea' | NHol |
| | 'Violet Queen' ♀H4 | CWCL EAEE EBee ECtt ELan EWes GQue LRHS MCot MLLN NBre NPro SCoo SMrm WFar WWlt |
| | 'Violette' new | CSam |
| | 'W[illegible] Purple' new | [illegible] EWes |

## *Monardella* (*Lamiaceae*)

| | | |
|---|---|---|
| | ***macrantha*** | CPBP |
| | ***nana*** subsp. ***tenuiflora*** | CPBP |
| | ***odoratissima*** | CArn |
| | ***viridis*** subsp. ***saxicola*** | CPBP |

## *Monochoria* (*Pontederiaceae*)

| | | |
|---|---|---|
| § | ***hastata*** | LLWG MSKA |

## *Monopsis* (*Campanulaceae*)

| | | |
|---|---|---|
| | ***unidentata*** | CSpe |

## *Monstera* (*Araceae*)

| | | |
|---|---|---|
| | ***deliciosa*** (F) ♀H1 | MBri XBlo |
| | - 'Variegata' (v) ♀H1 | MBri |

## *Montbretia* see *Crocosmia*

## *Montia* (*Portulacaceae*)

| | | |
|---|---|---|
| | ***perfoliata*** | see *Claytonia perfoliata* |
| | ***sibirica*** | see *Claytonia sibirica* |

## *Moraea* (*Iridaceae*)

| | | |
|---|---|---|
| | ***algoensis*** new | WCot |
| | ***alticola*** | CPne ECho GCal GGar WHer |
| § | ***aristata*** | CDes ECho WCot |
| § | ***bellendenii*** | ECho WCot |
| | ***bifida*** from Roggeveld new | ECho |
| | ***bipartita*** | WCot |
| | ***calcicola*** | ECho |
| | ***ciliata*** | ECho WCot |
| | ***citrina*** | ECho |
| | ***comptonii*** | WCot |
| | ***crispa*** from Roggeveld new | ECho |
| | ***fergusoniae*** 'Swellendam' | ECho |
| | ***flaccida*** from Roggeveld new | ECho |
| | ***fugacissima*** | ECho |
| | ***gigandra*** | ECho WCot |
| | ***glaucopsis*** | see *M. aristata* |
| | ***huttonii*** | CCCN CFir CPBP CSpe CTca EDif EPPr EPri GAbr MHer SMad WCot WHil WKif WSHC |
| | - from Eastern Cape new | ECho |
| | ***inclinata*** 'Howick' | ECho |
| | ***incurva*** | ECho |
| | ***iridioides*** | see *Dietes iridioides* |
| | ***longiaristata*** 'Caledon' | ECho |
| | ***loubseri*** | WCot |
| | ***lurida*** | WCot |
| | - 'Bredasdorp' | ECho |
| | ***macronyx*** 'Komsberg' | ECho |
| | ***marlothii*** | ECho |
| | ***mediterranea*** | ECho |
| | ***neglecta*** | ECho |
| | ***papilionacea*** 'Gordon's Bay' | ECho |
| | ***pavonia*** var. ***lutea*** | see *M. bellendenii* |
| | ***polystachya*** | CGrW ECho |
| | ***robusta*** | GCal |
| | ***serpentina*** | ECho |
| | ***setifolia*** | ECho |
| | ***spathacea*** | see *M. spathulata* |
| § | ***spathulata*** | CPLG CTca ECho GCal LEdu WCot WKif |
| | ***speciosa*** from Tanqua new | ECho |
| | ***tortilis*** 'Nababeep' | ECho |
| | ***tricolor*** | ECho WCot |
| | ***trifida*** 'Sentinel Peak' | ECho |
| | ***tripetala*** 'Riverlands' | ECho |
| | ***tulbaghensis*** | EBee WCot |
| | ***unibracteata*** 'Sentinel Peak' | ECho |
| | ***vegeta*** | CPBP ECho WCot |
| | ***versicolor*** 'Paarl' | ECho |
| | ***villosa*** | ECho WCot |

## *Moricandia* (*Brassicaceae*)

| | | |
|---|---|---|
| | ***arvensis*** | WCot |

## *Morina* (*Caprifoliaceae*)

| | | |
|---|---|---|
| * | ***afghanica*** | GAbr |
| | ***alba*** | GCra GLam |
| | ***longifolia*** | Widely available |
| | ***persica*** | EWes EWld SPhx |
| | ***polyphylla*** | GPoy |

## *Morinda* (*Rubiaceae*)

| | | |
|---|---|---|
| | ***umbellata*** WWJ 11688 | WCru |

## *Morisia* (*Brassicaceae*)

| | | |
|---|---|---|
| | ***hypogaea*** | see *M. monanthos* |
| § | ***monanthos*** | EPot MAsh NBlu NWCA SRot WFar |
| | - 'Fred Hemingway' | ECho ECtt ITim LRHS NMen NSla WAbe WThu |

## *Morus* ✿ (*Moraceae*)

| | | |
|---|---|---|
| | ***alba*** | CAgr CArn CBcs CCVT CDul CLnd CMCN CTho CWib EBee ECrN ELan EPfP ERea GTwe LBuc LHop LMaj MGos SDea SMrm WDin WFar |
| | - 'Issai' | LRHS |
| | - 'Laciniata' | EBee |
| | - 'Macrophylla' | CMCN NLar |
| | - 'Nana' | NLar |
| | - 'Pendula' | CDoC CDul CEnd CLnd CMac CTho CTri EBee ECrN ELan ERea GTwe LAst LRHS MAsh MBlu MBri NLar SBfd SCoo SLim WDin |
| | - 'Platanifolia' | LMaj MBlu |
| | - var. ***tatarica*** | CAgr LEdu NLar |
| § | ***bombycis*** | MAsh SEND |
| | 'Capsrum' (F) | CAgr |
| | 'Carmen' (F) | CAgr |
| | 'Illinois Everbearing' (F) | CAgr ECrN ERea |
| | 'Italian' (F) | CAgr |
| | 'Ivory' (F) | CAgr |
| | ***kagayamae*** | see *M. bombycis* |
| | ***latifolia*** 'Spirata' | NLar SEND |
| | ***nigra*** (F) ♀H4 | Widely available |
| § | - 'Chelsea' (F) | CDul CEnd CTho CTri EBee ECrN EPfP EPom ERea GTwe LRHS MBri MGos NWea SCoo SEWo SKee SPer SPoG WHar |
| | - 'Jerusalem' (F) | LRHS MCoo WHar |
| | - 'King James' | see *M. nigra* 'Chelsea' |
| | - 'Large Black' (F) | EPom |
| | ***rubra*** | CAgr NLar |
| | - 'Nana' | NLar |
| | 'Wellington' (F) | CAgr CEnd ECrN NPri |

## *Mosla* (*Lamiaceae*)

| | | |
|---|---|---|
| | ***dianthera*** | EBee EWld GCal MAvo MNrw WSHC |

## *Muehlenbeckia* (*Polygonaceae*)

| | | |
|---|---|---|
| | ***astonii*** | CDoC ECou LRHS |
| | ***australis*** | ECou |
| | ***axillaris*** misapplied | see *M. complexa* |
| § | ***axillaris*** Walp. | CBcs CTri ECou GGar SBig |
| | - 'Mount Cook' (f) | ECou |
| | - 'Ohau' (m) | ECou |
| § | ***complexa*** | CBcs CDoC CHEx CHll CMac CTrC CTri CWib EBee ECou EPfP EShb ETod LRHS LTen NLBP NSti SArc SEND SLim SLon SPer SPoG SWvt WCFE WPGP WSHC XLum |
| | - (f) | ECou |
| | - 'Nana' | see *M. axillaris* Walp. |
| | - small-leaved | ETod |
| | - 'Spotlight' PBR (v) | EShb |
| | - var. ***trilobata*** | CBcs CHEx CTrC EPla EShb ESwi GCal SSta WDyG XLum |
| | - 'Ward' (m) | ECou |
| | ***ephedroides*** | ECou |
| | - 'Clarence Pass' | ECou |
| * | - var. ***muricatula*** | ECou |
| | ***gunnii*** | ECou |
| | ***platyclados*** | see *Homalocladium platycladum* |

## *Muhlenbergia* (*Poaceae*)

| | | |
|---|---|---|
| | ***capillaris*** | EPPr GCal SBfd SHDw SMrm WBox |
| | ***dubia*** | WPGP |
| | ***dumosa*** | CKno |
| | ***glomerata*** | WBox |
| | ***japonica*** 'Cream Delight' (v) | EHoe EPPr LEdu SBfd SHDw |
| | ***lindheimeri*** | CKno EPPr GCal SMea WCot |
| | ***mexicana*** | LEdu SRms |
| | ***rigens*** | CKno GCal SApp WPGP |

## *Mukdenia* (*Saxifragaceae*)

| | | |
|---|---|---|
| | ***acanthifolia*** | CDes CLAP WCru |
| | ***rossii*** | CAby CLAP EBee ELon EPla GCal IFro LEdu MNrw NBid NLar NMyG NPnk SMad WCru WPGP WSHC WThu WTin XLum |
| | - 'Crimson Fans' | see *M. rossii* 'Karasuba' |
| | - dwarf | CDes CLAP GCal MNrw |
| § | - 'Karasuba' | CLAP CWGN EBee GEdr LSou MAvo NLar NMyG NPnk SPoG WHil |
| | - 'Ōgon' | CLAP |
| | - 'Shishiba' | GEdr |
| | - variegated (v) | WWEG |

## mulberry see *Morus*

## *Murraya* (*Rutaceae*)

| | | |
|---|---|---|
| * | ***elliptica*** | MOWG |
| | ***exotica*** | see *M. paniculata* |
| | ***koenigii*** | EOHP GPoy |
| § | ***paniculata*** | CArn GPoy MHer |

## *Musa* ✿ (*Musaceae*)

| | | |
|---|---|---|
| | from Yangtze Valley, China | LPJP |
| | from Yunnan, China | see *M. itinerans* 'Yunnan' |
| § | ***acuminata*** | LRHS MBri |
| | - 'Siam Ruby' (AA Group) (F) | EAmu |
| § | - 'Dwarf Cavendish' (AAA Group) (F) ♀H1 | CDoC EAmu ELan LRHS LTen NPla SBst SPer SPlb XBlo |
| | - 'Grand Nain' | EAmu |
| | × ***acuminata*** 'Zebrina' | |
| | - 'Williams' (AAA Group) (F) | EAmu XBlo |
| | - 'Zebrina' ♀H1+3 | CDTJ EAmu LRHS SBst XBlo |
| | ***balbisiana*** | EAmu SBst |
| | ***basjoo*** ♀H3-4 | Widely available |
| | - 'Little Prince' | LRHS |
| I | - 'Rubra' | CCCN EAmu ESwi |
| | - 'Sakhalin' | SAdn |
| | 'Blue Java' | see *M.* 'Ice Cream' |
| | ***cavendishii*** | see *M. acuminata* 'Dwarf Cavendish' |
| § | ***coccinea*** ♀H1 | XBlo |
| | ***ensete*** | see *Ensete ventricosum* |
| | 'Helen' | EAmu LPJP |
| | ***hookeri*** | see *M. sikkimensis* |
| § | 'Ice Cream' (ABB Group) **new** | EAmu |
| * | ***iterans glaucum*** | CDTJ |
| | ***itinerans*** | WCot |
| § | - 'Yunnan' | EAmu |
| | ***lasiocarpa*** | CDTJ CDoC CHEx CHll EAmu EShb ESwi ETod LRHS MBri NPal NPla SBfd SBig SBst SPlb WGwG |
| | ***nana*** misapplied | see *M. acuminata* 'Dwarf Cavendish' |
| | ***nana*** Lour. | see *M. acuminata* |
| | ***ornata*** ♀H1 | CCCN XBlo |
| | × ***paradisiaca*** 'Ney Poovan' (AB Group) (F) | CCCN EAmu |
| | - 'Orinoco' (ABB Group) (F) | EAmu |
| | - 'Rajapuri' (AAB Group) (F) | EAmu |
| § | ***sikkimensis*** | CDTJ EAmu ELan ESwi ETod EWes LPJP SBig SBst SChr SPlb WFar XBlo |
| | - 'Red Tiger' | CCCN CDTJ EAmu |
| | 'Tropicana' | XBlo |
| | ***uranoscopus*** misapplied | see *M. coccinea* |
| | ***velutina*** ♀H1+3 | CCCN CDoC EAmu SBig SBst |

## *Muscari* ✿ (*Asparagaceae*)

| | | |
|---|---|---|
| | PF | NWCA |
| | 'Aleyna' | ECho NMin |
| | ***ambrosiacum*** | see *M. muscarimi* |
| | ***anatolicum*** | ECho |
| | ***armeniacum*** ♀H4 | CBro CTri ECho EPfP LRHS MBri MMuc SEND SPer SRms WCot WFar WShi |
| | - 'Argaei Album' | ECho EPot LAma |
| | - 'Atlantic' | ECho EPfP LRHS |
| | - 'Blue Pearl' | ECho GKev |
| | - 'Blue Spike' (d) | CBro CTca EBla ECho EPfP GKev LAma MBri NBir NEgg SDeJ SPer WCot WFar WGwG |
| | - 'Bright Eyes' | GKev |
| | - 'Cantab' | ECho GKev SDeJ |
| | - 'Christmas Pearl' ♀H4 | ECho GKev SPhx WCot |
| | - 'Côte d'Azur' | GKev |
| | - 'Dark Eyes' | ECho EPfP SMrm SPer WFar |
| | - 'Early Giant' | ECho SDeJ |
| | - 'Fantasy Creation' | EBla ECho EPot SDeJ |
| | - 'Gul' | WCot |
| | - 'Heavenly Blue' | ECho |
| | - 'New Creation' | ECho |
| | - 'Peppermint' | CTca ECho EPfP EPot ERCP LAma NMin SPhx WCot |
| | - 'Saffier' ♀H4 | ECho LAma SPhx WCot |
| | - 'Valerie Finnis' | CAby CAvo CBre CBro CFFs CMea CTca EBla ECho EPPr EPfP EPot ERCP GEdr GMaP LAma |

| | | |
|---|---|---|
| | | MLLN MNrw NLar SAga SDeJ SMrm SPer SPhx WAul WBrk WCot WHil |
| | ***aucheri*** ♀[H4] | ECho LAma NRya |
| * | – var. ***bicolor*** | WCot |
| | – 'Blue Magic' | ECho EPot ERCP LAma |
| | – 'Ocean Magic' | CBro ECho GKev LAma NLar |
| § | – 'Tubergenianum' | ECho LRHS |
| | – 'White Magic' | CAvo ECho ERCP LAma WCot |
| § | ***azureum*** ♀[H4] | CAvo CBro CTca ECho ELan EPfP ERCP GMaP LAma LEdu NLar NMen NWCA SPhx WCot |
| | – 'Album' | EBla ECho LAma LRHS SPhx WBrk WCot |
| | 'Baby's Breath' | see *M.* 'Jenny Robinson' |
| | 'Big Smile' | GKev WCot |
| | 'Blue Dream' | ECho |
| | 'Blue Eyes' | ECho WCot |
| | 'Blue Star' | ECho GKev |
| | ***botryoides*** | CAvo ECho LAma LEdu |
| | – 'Album' | CAvo CBro CFFs CTca CTri EBla ECho EPfP LAma MBri SDeJ SMrm SPer SRms WBor WCot WShi |
| | ***caucasicum*** | ECho WCot |
| | ***chalusicum*** | see *M. pseudomuscari* |
| | ***coeleste*** KPPZ 90-318 **new** | LWst |
| | ***commutatum*** | ECho |
| § | ***comosum*** | CArn CBro ECho EPfP ERCP LEdu MCot NEgg NWCA WCot |
| | – 'Monstrosum' | see *M. comosum* 'Plumosum' |
| § | – 'Plumosum' | CAvo EBla ECho ELan EPfP GKev LAma LEdu MBri MLLN SDeJ WCot WHil |
| | 'Cupido' | GKev |
| | ***dionysicum*** | ECho |
| | – HOA 8965 | ECho LWst WCot |
| | ***grandifolium*** | NWCA |
| | – JCA 689.450 | WCot |
| | ***inconstrictum*** | ECho |
| | 'Ivor's Pink' | WCot |
| § | 'Jenny Robinson' ♀[H4] | CMil EBla IFoB SCnR SMad WCot |
| | ***latifolium*** ♀[H4] | CAby CBro CTca EBla ECho EPfP EPot ERCP GAuc GGar LAma LRHS MWat NEgg NLar SBch SDeJ SMrm SPhx WBor WCot WTin |
| * | – 'Blue Angels' | NBir |
| § | ***macrocarpum*** | CAvo CBro CTca EBcc ECha ECho EPot GAuc LAma LRHS WAbe WCot |
| | – 'Golden Fragrance'[PBR] | CHid ECho ERCP GKev IFoB LAma MCot MNrw MWea NMin SDeJ WCot WHil |
| | ***mirum*** | ECho |
| | ***moschatum*** | see *M. muscarimi* |
| | 'Mount Hood' | CTca EBla ECho ERCP IPot LRHS MWea SDeJ WBor |
| § | ***muscarimi*** | CAvo CBro CFFs CTca ECho IFoB LAma LEdu MCot NLar NWCA SDeJ WCot |
| | – var. ***flavum*** | see *M. macrocarpum* |
| § | ***neglectum*** | ECho ITim LAma NLar SEND WCot WShi |
| | ***pallens*** | ECho NMin NWCA WCot |
| | ***paradoxum*** | see *Bellevalia paradoxa* |
| | ***parviflorum*** | ECho |
| § | ***pseudomuscari*** ♀[H4] | WCot |
| | ***racemosum*** | see *M. neglectum* |
| | 'Rosy Sunrise' **new** | WCot |
| | 'Sky Blue' | ECho WCot |
| | 'Superstar' | ECho LEdu WCot |
| § | ***tenuiflorum*** | ECho WCot |
| | aff. ***tenuiflorum*** JCA 0.691.251 | WCot |
| | ***tubergenianum*** | see *M. aucheri* 'Tubergenianum' |
| | 'White Beauty' | ECho SPhx |
| | 'Winter Amethyst' **new** | WCot |

## *Muscarimia* (*Asparagaceae*)

| | | |
|---|---|---|
| | ***ambrosiacum*** | see *Muscari muscarimi* |
| | ***macrocarpum*** | see *Muscari macrocarpum* |

## *Musella* see *Musa*

## *Mussaenda* (*Rubiaceae*)

| | | |
|---|---|---|
| | 'Tropic Snow' | CCCN |

## *Musschia* (*Campanulaceae*)

| | | |
|---|---|---|
| | ***wollastonii*** | WHer |

## *Mutisia* (*Asteraceae*)

| | | |
|---|---|---|
| | ***ilicifolia*** | WHil |
| | ***retusa*** | see *M. spinosa* var. *pulchella* |
| § | ***spinosa*** var. ***pulchella*** | GGal |

## *Myoporum* (*Scrophulariaceae*)

| | | |
|---|---|---|
| | ***acuminatum*** | see *M. tenuifolium* |
| | ***debile*** | see *Eremophila debilis* |
| | ***laetum*** | CAbb CBcs CPLG CTrC SVen |
| | ***sandwicense*** **new** | SVen |
| § | ***tenuifolium*** | SVen |

## *Myosotidium* (*Boraginaceae*)

| | | |
|---|---|---|
| § | ***hortensia*** | CBcs CBct CGHE CSpe CYeo EBee ECre ELan EPfP EWes GBin GCal GGar GKev IKil ITim LRHS MCot WCot WGwG WPGP WWlt |
| | – 'True Blue' | CHid |
| | ***nobile*** | see *M. hortensia* |

## *Myosotis* (*Boraginaceae*)

| | | |
|---|---|---|
| | from Eyre Mountains, New Zealand | GEdr NWCA |
| | ***alpestris*** 'Ruth Fischer' | NBir |
| | ***colensoi*** | ECou NMen NWCA |
| | ***explanata*** | NMen |
| | ***macrantha*** | GBin |
| | My Oh My = 'Myomark'[PBR] | ECtt LSou NPri |
| | ***palustris*** | see *M. scorpioides* |
| | ***pulvinaris*** | ECou WAbe |
| | ***rakiura*** | SBch |
| § | ***scorpioides*** | CBen CHab CWat EHon EWil LPBA MMuc MNrw MSKA MWts NMir SCoo SPer SPlb SRms SWat WBrk WMAq WMoo WPnP XLum |
| | – 'Alba' | LPBA MSKA |
| | – 'Ice Pearl' | ECha |
| | – Maytime = 'Blaqua' (v) | LLWG NBir |
| | – 'Mermaid' | CBen CRow CWat ECha LLWG LPBA SBch SDix SWat WPer |
| | – 'Pinkie' | CWat LLWG LPBA MSKA SWat |
| | – 'Snowflakes' | CWat SWat |
| | – variegated (v) | MSKA |
| | ***sylvatica*** | CRWN EWil MMuc NMir |
| | – 'Pompadour' | NBlu |
| | – 'Victoria Blue' (Victoria Series) | NBlu |
| | 'Unforgettable' (v) | NBro |

## *Myosurus* (*Ranunculaceae*)

| | | |
|---|---|---|
| | ***minimus*** | CRDP |

## *Myrica* (*Myricaceae*)

| | | |
|---|---|---|
| | ***californica*** | NLar |
| | ***cerifera*** | CArn NLar |
| | ***gale*** | CAgr CRWN GPoy GQue IVic MCoo MGos NLar SBfd SPoG SWat WDin WFar WGwG WHfH |
| | ***pensylvanica*** | GAuc IVic NLar |
| | ***rubra*** | CAgr |

## *Myricaria* (*Tamaricaceae*)

| | | |
|---|---|---|
| | ***germanica*** | NLar |

## *Myriophyllum* (*Haloragaceae*)

| | | |
|---|---|---|
| | ***propinquum*** | LLWG |
| * | 'Red Stem' | LPBA |
| | ***spicatum*** | EHon EWil MSKA WMAq |
| | ***verticillatum*** | CWat SCoo |

## *Myrrhidendron* (*Apiaceae*)

| | | |
|---|---|---|
| | ***glaucescens*** B&SWJ 10699 | WCru |

## *Myrrhis* (*Apiaceae*)

| | | |
|---|---|---|
| | ***odorata*** | CArn CBod CBre CHby COlW CSev CSpe CWan EBee ECha ELau GPoy IFro ILis MHer MMuc MNHC NBPC NPri SBfd SEND SIde SPad WAul WHer WJek WPer WPtf WWFP |
| | - 'Forncett Chevron' | GCal LEdu |

## *Myrsine* (*Primulaceae*)

| | | |
|---|---|---|
| | ***africana*** | CBcs CWib EShb |
| | ***aquilonia*** | ECou |
| | ***australis*** | SVen |
| | ***divaricata*** | CTrC ECou SVen |
| | ***nummularia*** | WThu |

## *Myrteola* (*Myrtaceae*)

| | | |
|---|---|---|
| § | ***nummularia*** | GAbr NHar NMen WAbe WThu |

## *Myrtus* (*Myrtaceae*)

| | | |
|---|---|---|
| | ***apiculata*** | see *Luma apiculata* |
| | ***bullata*** | see *Lophomyrtus bullata* |
| | ***chequen*** | see *Luma chequen* |
| | ***communis*** ♀H3 | Widely available |
| | - 'Flore Pleno' (d) | ELau EOHP MHer |
| | - 'Jenny Reitenbach' | see *M. communis* subsp. *tarentina* |
| | - 'Merion' | WJek |
| | - 'Microphylla' | see *M. communis* subsp. *tarentina* |
| | - 'Nana' | see *M. communis* subsp. *tarentina* |
| | - 'Pyewood Park' | WJek |
| § | - subsp. ***tarentina*** ♀H3 | Widely available |
| | - - 'Compacta' | LRHS |
| | - - 'Microphylla Variegata' (v) | CBcs EGHP EShb GQui LRHS MHer MNHC SBfd SPer WJek |
| I | - - 'Variegata' (v) | EOHP EPfP EWhm SEND SPoG |
| | - 'Tricolor' | see *M. communis* 'Variegata' |
| § | - 'Variegata' (v) | Widely available |
| | ***dulcis*** | see *Austromyrtus dulcis* |
| | 'Glanleam Gold' | see *Luma apiculata* 'Glanleam Gold' |
| | ***lechleriana*** | see *Amomyrtus luma* |
| | ***luma*** | see *Luma apiculata* |
| | ***nummularia*** | see *Myrteola nummularia* |
| * | ***paraguayensis*** | CTrC |
| | × ***ralphii*** | see *Lophomyrtus* × *ralphii* |
| | 'Traversii' | see *Lophomyrtus* × *ralphii* 'Traversii' |
| | ***ugni*** | see *Ugni molinae* |

# N

## *Nananthus* (*Aizoaceae*)

| | | |
|---|---|---|
| | ***aloides*** new | MSCN |
| | ***vittatus*** | WAbe |

## *Nandina* (*Berberidaceae*)

| | | |
|---|---|---|
| | ***domestica*** ♀H3 | Widely available |
| | - B&SWJ 4923 | WCru |
| | - B&SWJ 11113 | WCru |
| | - 'Fire Power' ♀H3 | Widely available |
| | - 'Gulf Stream' | CBcs GBin |
| | - 'Harbor Dwarf' | CDoC CEnd EBee LRHS MAsh SBfd SLim SPoG WFar |
| | - var. ***leucocarpa*** | CMCN NLar |
| | - 'Nana' | see *N. domestica* 'Pygmaea' |
| | - 'Nana Purpurea' | EPla GCal |
| | - Plum Passion = 'Monum' | LBuc LRHS MAsh SPoG |
| § | - 'Pygmaea' | CMen SGol WDin |
| | - 'Richmond' | CDul CEnd EBee ELan EPfP LAst LRHS MAsh MGos NLar SBfd SLim SPer SPoG SRkn SWvt WFar WPat |
| | - 'Wood's Dwarf' | CBcs |

## *Nannorrhops* (*Arecaceae*)

| | | |
|---|---|---|
| | ***ritchiana*** | LPal |

## *Napaea* (*Malvaceae*)

| | | |
|---|---|---|
| | ***dioica*** | WCot |

## *Narcissus* ✿ (*Amaryllidaceae*)

| | | |
|---|---|---|
| | 'Abba' (4) ♀H4 | CQua |
| | 'Aberfoyle' (2) ♀H4 | CQua |
| | 'Abstract' (11a) | CQua |
| | 'Accent' (2) ♀H4 | CQua |
| | 'Accomplice' (3) | IRhd |
| | 'Achduart' (3) | CQua |
| | 'Achentoul' (4) | CQua |
| | 'Achnasheen' (3) | CQua |
| | 'Acropolis' (4) | CQua EPfP SDeJ |
| | 'Actaea' (9) ♀H4 | CBro CQua CTca EPfP MBri SDeJ SEND |
| | 'Acumen' (2) | CQua |
| | 'Admiration' (8) | CQua |
| | 'Advocat' (3) | CQua |
| | 'African Sunset' (3) | IRhd |
| | 'Agnes Mace' (2) | IRhd |
| | 'Ahwahnee' (2) | CQua IRhd |
| | 'Ainley' (2) | CQua |
| | 'Aintree' (3) | CQua |
| | 'Aircastle' (3) | CQua |
| | 'Airtime' (2) new | IRhd |
| | 'Akepa' (5) | CQua |
| | 'Albatross' (3) | CQua GCro |
| | 'Albus Plenus Odoratus' | see *N. poeticus* 'Plenus' ambig. |
| | 'All Rounder' (3) | IRhd |
| | 'Alpine Glow' (1) | CQua |
| | 'Alpine Winter' (1) | IRhd |
| | 'Alston' (2) | IRhd |
| | 'Alto' (2) | IRhd |
| | 'Altruist' (3) | CQua ERCP |
| | 'Altun Ha' (2) | CQua IRhd |
| | 'Altun Ha Gold' (2) new | CQua |
| | 'Amabilis' (3) new | GCro |
| | 'Amazing Grace' (2) | IRhd |
| | 'Amber Castle' (2) | CQua |
| | 'Ambergate' (2) | CQua LAma |

| | |
|---|---|
| 'Ambergris Caye' (1) | CQua |
| 'American Goldfinch' (7) | CQua |
| 'American Heritage' (1) | CQua IRhd |
| 'American Robin' (6) | CQua |
| 'American Shores' (1) | CQua IRhd |
| 'Amstel' (4) | CQua |
| 'Andalusia' (6) | CQua |
| 'Andrew's Choice' (7) ♀$^{H4}$ | CQua |
| 'Angel' (3) | CQua |
| 'Angel Face' (3) | CQua IRhd |
| 'Angelito' (3) ♀$^{H4}$ | IRhd |
| Angel's tears | see *N. triandrus* subsp. *triandrus* var. *triandrus* |
| 'Angel's Wings' (2) | CQua |
| 'Angkor' (4) | CQua |
| 'An-gof' (7) | CQua |
| 'Ann Sonia' (4) | IRhd |
| 'Anna Panna' (3) | IRhd |
| 'Annequin' (3) | CQua |
| 'Apollo Gold' (10) **new** | GKev |
| 'Apotheose' (4) | CQua SDeJ |
| 'Applins' (2) | IRhd |
| 'Apricot' (1) | CBro |
| 'Apricot Blush' (2) | CQua |
| 'Apricot Whirl' (11a) | CQua |
| 'April Love' (1) | CQua |
| 'April Snow' (2) | CBro CQua |
| 'April Tears' (5) ♀$^{H4}$ | NMin |
| 'Ara' (6) **new** | CQua |
| 'Aranjuez' (2) | CQua |
| 'Arctic Gem' (3) | CQua |
| 'Arctic Gold' (1) ♀$^{H4}$ | CQua LAma |
| 'Ardress' (2) | CQua |
| 'Areley Kings' (2) | CQua |
| 'Argosy' (1) | CQua |
| 'Arid Plains' (3) | IRhd |
| 'Ariel'$^{PBR}$ (8) **new** | GKev |
| 'Arish Mell' (5) | CQua |
| 'Arkle' (1) ♀$^{H4}$ | CQua SDeJ |
| 'Arleston' (2) | IRhd |
| 'Armada' (2) ♀$^{H4}$ | CQua |
| 'Armidale' (3) | IRhd |
| 'Armoury' (4) | CQua |
| 'Arndilly' (2) | CQua |
| 'Arpege' (2) | CQua |
| 'Arran Isle' (2) | IRhd |
| 'Arrowhead' (6) | NMin |
| 'Arthurian' (1) | CQua IRhd |
| 'Articol' (11a) | CQua |
| 'Arwenack' (11a) | CQua |
| 'Ashmore' (2) | CQua IRhd |
| 'Ashton Wold' (2) | CQua |
| 'Asila' (2) | IRhd |
| 'Assertion' (2) | IRhd |
| § ***assoanus*** (13) | CBro ECho EPot GKev LAma MNrw MSSP NMen NMin SPhx |
| 'Astropink' (11a) | CQua |
| § ***asturiensis*** (13) ♀$^{H3-4}$ | CSam ECho NMin |
| – giant form | see *N. asturiensis* 'Wavertree' |
| § – 'Navarre' Gathorne-Hardy (1) | WCot |
| § – 'Wavertree' (1) | CQua NMin |
| ***asturiensis* × *cyclamineus*** | NMen |
| 'Atlas Gold' | see *N. romieuxii* 'Atlas Gold' |
| 'Atricilla' (11a) | IRhd |
| 'Auchrannie' (2) | IRhd |
| 'Audubon' (2) | CQua SDeJ |
| 'Aunt Betty' (1) | CQua |
| 'Auntie Eileen' (2) | CQua |
| 'Auspicious' (2) | IRhd |

| | |
|---|---|
| 'Avalanche' (8) ♀$^{H3}$ | CQua GCro NMin SDeJ |
| 'Avalanche of Gold' (8) | CQua |
| 'Avalon' (2) | CQua |
| 'Azocor' (1) | IRhd |
| 'Baby Boomer' (7) | LAma NMin |
| 'Baby Moon' (7) | CQua CTca EPfP EPot ERCP GEdr GKev LAma MBri NMin SDeJ SPhx |
| 'Back Flash' (2) | CQua |
| 'Badanloch' (3) | CQua |
| 'Badbury Rings' (3) ♀$^{H4}$ | CQua |
| 'Bala' (4) | CQua |
| 'Balalaika' (2) | CQua |
| 'Baldock' (4) | CQua |
| 'Ballydorn' (9) | IRhd |
| 'Ballygarvey' (1) | CQua |
| 'Ballygowan' (3) | IRhd |
| 'Ballynichol' (3) | CQua |
| 'Ballyrobert' (1) | CQua |
| 'Baltic Shore' (3) | IRhd |
| 'Balvenie' (2) | CQua |
| 'Bandesara' (3) | CQua IRhd |
| 'Bandit' (2) | CQua |
| 'Banker' (2) | CQua |
| 'Banstead Village' (2) | CQua |
| 'Bantam' (2) ♀$^{H4}$ | CBro CQua NMin |
| 'Barbary Gold' (2) | CQua |
| 'Barlow' (6) | CQua |
| 'Barnesgold' (1) | IRhd |
| 'Barnham' (1) | CQua |
| 'Barnsdale Wood' (2) | CQua |
| 'Barnum' (1) ♀$^{H4}$ | IRhd |
| 'Barrett Browning' (3) | EBla SDeJ |
| 'Barrii' (3) | CQua |
| 'Bartley' (6) | CQua |
| 'Bath's Flame' (3) | CAvo CQua GCro WShi |
| 'Bear Springs' (4) | IRhd |
| 'Bear's Gold' (4) **new** | CQua |
| 'Beaulieu' (1) **new** | CQua |
| 'Beautiful Dream' (3) | CQua |
| 'Bebop' (7) | CBro |
| 'Bedruthan' (2) | CQua |
| 'Beersheba' (1) | CQua |
| 'Belbroughton' (2) | CQua |
| 'Belcanto' (11a) | CQua SDeJ |
| 'Belfast Lough' (1) | IRhd |
| 'Belisana' (2) | SDeJ |
| 'Bell Rock' (1) | CQua |
| 'Bell Song' (7) | CAvo CBro CFFs CQua EPfP ERCP GKev LSou SDeJ WShi |
| 'Bella Estrella' (11a) **new** | ERCP |
| 'Belzone' (2) | CQua |
| 'Ben Aligin' (1) | CQua |
| 'Ben Hee' (2) ♀$^{H4}$ | CQua |
| 'Berceuse' (2) | CQua IRhd |
| 'Bere Ferrers' (4) | CQua |
| 'Bergerac' (11a) | CQua |
| 'Bernardino' (2) | CQua GCro |
| 'Beryl' (6) | CBro CQua EPot NMin |
| 'Best Friend' (3) **new** | CQua |
| 'Best Seller' (1) | SPer |
| 'Bethal' (3) | CQua |
| 'Betsy MacDonald' (6) | CQua |
| 'Biffo' (4) | CQua |
| * 'Big Cycla' (6) | ECho |
| 'Bikini Beach' (2) | IRhd |
| 'Bilbo' (6) | CBro CQua |
| 'Billy Graham' (2) | CQua |
| 'Binkie' (2) | CBro CQua SPer |
| 'Birchwood' (3) | CQua |
| 'Birdsong' (3) | CQua |

| | |
|---|---|
| 'Birma' (3) | LAma SDeJ |
| 'Bishops Light' (2) | CQua |
| 'Bittern' (12) | CQua SDeJ |
| 'Blair Athol' (2) | CQua |
| 'Blarney' (3) | CQua |
| 'Blisland' (9) | CQua |
| 'Blossom' (4) | CQua |
| 'Blue Danube' (1) | CQua |
| 'Blushing Maiden' (4) | CQua |
| 'Bob Spotts' (2) | CQua |
| 'Bobbysoxer' (7) | CBro CQua NMin |
| 'Bobolink' (2) | CQua |
| 'Boconnoc' (2) **new** | CQua |
| 'Bodelva' (2) | CQua |
| 'Bodwannick' (2) | CQua |
| 'Bold Prospect' (1) | CQua |
| 'Bolton' (7) | CBro |
| 'Bon Viveur' (11a) | IRhd |
| 'Bonython' (1) **new** | GCro |
| 'Bosbigal' (11a) | CQua |
| 'Boscastle' (7) | CQua |
| 'Boscoppa' (11a) | CQua |
| 'Boslowick' (11a) 🏆$^{H4}$ | CQua |
| 'Bosmeor' (2) | CQua |
| 'Bossa Nova' (3) | CQua |
| 'Bossiney' (11a) | CQua |
| 'Bosvale' (11a) | CQua |
| 'Bosvigo' (11a) | CQua |
| 'Boulder Bay' (2) 🏆$^{H4}$ | CQua |
| 'Bouzouki' (2) | IRhd |
| 'Bowles's Early Sulphur' (1) | CRow |
| 'Boyne Bridge' (1) | IRhd |
| 'Brandaris' (11a) | CQua |
| 'Bravoure' (1) 🏆$^{H4}$ | CQua SDeJ |
| 'Brentswood' (8) | CQua |
| 'Bridal Crown' (4) 🏆$^{H4}$ | EPfP LAma SPer |
| 'Bright Flame' (2) | CQua |
| 'Bright Spot' (8) | CQua |
| 'Brilliancy' (3) | CQua |
| 'Brindaleena' (2) | IRhd |
| 'Brindle Pink' (2) | IRhd |
| 'Broadland' (2) | CQua |
| 'Broadway Star' (11b) | LAma SDeJ |
| 'Brodick' (3) | CQua IRhd |
| 'Bronzewing' (1) | IRhd |
| 'Brookdale' (1) | CQua |
| 'Brooke Ager' (2) 🏆$^{H4}$ | IRhd |
| 'Broomhill' (2) 🏆$^{H4}$ | CQua |
| 'Broughshane' (1) **new** | CQua |
| 'Brunswick' (2) | CQua |
| 'Bryanston' (2) 🏆$^{H4}$ | CQua |
| 'Bryher' (3) | CQua |
| 'Buckshead' (4) **new** | CQua |
| 'Budock Bells' (5) | CQua |
| 'Budock Water' (2) | CQua |
| 'Bugle Major' (2) | CQua |
| ***bulbocodium*** (13) 🏆$^{H3-4}$ | CBro GKev ITim LBee LEdu LRHS NWCA SMrm SRms |
| - from Atlas Mountains, Morocco | MSSP |
| § - subsp. ***bulbocodium*** (13) | CBro |
| § - - var. ***citrinus*** (13) | LRHS SSpi |
| - - - MS 577 | MSSP |
| - - var. ***conspicuus*** (13) | CBro CHar CPMA CQua CTca ECho EPfP EPot ERCP GEdr GKev LAma MSSP NMen NMin NRya SDeJ SGar WCot XLum |
| * - - var. ***filifolius*** (13) | CBro |
| - - var. ***nivalis*** (13) | ECho EPot GKev ITim |
| - - var. ***pallidus*** (13) | GEdr |
| § - - var. ***tenuifolius*** (13) | EPot NMen |
| - var. ***filifolius*** | MSSP |
| § - Golden Bells Group (10) | CAvo CBro CHid CQua CTri CWCL ECho EPot GKev MBri NHol NMin SDeJ |
| - 'Ice Warrior' | SKHP |
| - var. ***mesatlanticus*** | see *N. romieuxii* subsp. *romieuxii* var. *mesatlanticus* |
| - subsp. ***obesus*** (13) | ECho GKev MSSP WCot |
| § - - 'Diamond Ring' | CQua EPot ITim LAma MSSP NMin |
| - subsp. ***praecox*** (13) | CBro ECho LRHS WCot |
| - - var. ***paucinervis*** (13) | ECho |
| - subsp. ***tananicus*** | see *N. cantabricus* subsp. *tananicus* |
| - subsp. ***vulgaris*** | see *N. bulbocodium* subsp. *bulbocodium* |
| ***bulbocodium* × *romieuxii*** | WCot |
| 'Bunchie' (5) | CQua |
| 'Bunclody' (2) | CQua |
| 'Bunting' (7) 🏆$^{H4}$ | CQua |
| 'Burning Bush' (3) | IRhd |
| 'Burning Ring' (3) **new** | IRhd |
| 'Burntollet' (1) | CQua |
| 'Burravoe' (1) | CQua |
| 'Burt House' (2) **new** | IRhd |
| 'Busselton' (3) | IRhd |
| 'Bute Park' (4) **new** | CQua |
| 'Butter and Eggs' (4) **new** | CAvo |
| 'Butterscotch' (2) | CQua |
| 'C.J. Backhouse' (2) | CQua GCro |
| 'Cabernet' (2) | IRhd |
| 'Cacatua' (11a) | IRhd |
| 'Cadgwith' (2) | CQua |
| 'Cairntoul' (3) | CQua |
| 'Calamansack' (2) | CQua |
| I ***calcicola*** 'Idol' (7) | CQua EPot NMin |
| 'California Rose' (4) | CQua IRhd |
| 'Camaraderie' (2) | IRhd |
| 'Camden' (1) **new** | CQua |
| 'Camelot' (2) 🏆$^{H4}$ | CQua EPfP SDeJ SPer |
| 'Cameo Angel' (2) | CQua |
| 'Cameo King' (2) | CQua |
| 'Cameo Marie' (3) | CQua |
| 'Camilla Duchess of Cornwall' (2) **new** | CQua |
| 'Camoro' (10) | MSSP NMen |
| 'Campernelli' (7) **new** | CQua |
| 'Campernelli Plenus' | see *N.* × *odorus* 'Double Campernelle' |
| 'Campion' (9) | CQua IRhd |
| ***canaliculatus*** Gussone | see *N. tazetta* subsp. *lacticolor* |
| 'Canaliculatus' (8) | CBro CQua CTri ECho EPfP ERCP GKev LAma MBri SDeJ SEND SMrm SPer |
| 'Canary' (7) | CQua |
| 'Canarybird' (8) | CQua WShi |
| 'Canasta' (11a) | CQua |
| 'Candida' (4) | CQua |
| 'Canisp' (2) | CQua |
| 'Cantabile' (9) 🏆$^{H4}$ | CQua |
| ***cantabricus*** (13) | ECho |
| - subsp. ***cantabricus*** (13) | NMin NRya |
| - - var. ***foliosus*** (13) 🏆$^{H2}$ | ECho EPot GKev NMen SCnR WAbe WCot |
| § - subsp. ***tananicus*** (13) | ECho EPot |
| 'Cantatrice' (1) | CQua |
| 'Canterbury' (5) **new** | CQua |
| 'Canticle' (9) | IRhd |
| 'Capax Plenus' | see *N.* 'Eystettensis' |

| | |
|---|---|
| 'Cape Cornwall' (2) | CQua |
| 'Cape Helles' (3) | IRhd |
| 'Cape Point' (2) | IRhd |
| 'Capisco' (3) | CQua |
| 'Caramba' (2) | CQua |
| 'Carbineer' (2) | CQua GCro SDeJ |
| 'Carclew' (6) | CQua |
| 'Cardiff' (2) | CQua |
| 'Cardinham' (3) | CQua |
| 'Cargreen' (9) | CQua |
| 'Carib Gipsy' (2) ♀H4 | CQua IRhd |
| 'Caribbean Snow' (2) | CQua |
| 'Carlton' (2) ♀H4 | CQua EPfP GKev LAma SDeJ |
| 'Carnearny' (3) | CQua |
| 'Carnkeeran' (2) | CQua |
| 'Carnkief' (2) | CQua |
| 'Carnyorth' (11a) | CQua |
| 'Carole Lombard' (3) | CQua |
| 'Carolina Dale' (2) **new** | IRhd |
| 'Carwinion' (2) | CQua |
| 'Casiah' (2) **new** | CQua |
| 'Cassata' (11a) | EPfP LAma NBir SDeJ |
| 'Castanets' (8) | IRhd |
| 'Casterbridge' (2) | CQua IRhd |
| 'Catalyst' (2) | IRhd |
| 'Catistock' (2) | CQua |
| 'Causeway Sunset' (2) | IRhd |
| 'Causeway Sunshine' (1) | IRhd |
| 'Cavalli King' (4) **new** | CQua |
| 'Cavalryman' (3) | IRhd |
| 'Cawdron' (2) | CQua |
| 'Caye Chapel' (3) | CQua |
| 'Cazique' (6) | CQua |
| × ***cazorlanus*** (13) | MSSP NSla |
| 'Ceasefire' (2) | IRhd |
| 'Cedar Hills' (3) | CQua |
| 'Cedric Morris' (1) | CDes CLAP ECha NDov |
| 'Celestial Fire' (2) | CQua |
| 'Celtic Gold' (2) | CQua |
| 'Centrefold' (3) | CQua |
| 'Cernuus Plenus' (4) | CQua |
| 'Cha-cha' (6) | CBro CQua |
| 'Changing Colors' (11a) | CQua |
| 'Chanson' (1) ♀H4 | CQua IRhd |
| 'Chanterelle' (11a) | EBla LAma |
| 'Chantilly' (2) | CQua |
| 'Chapman's Peak' (2) | IRhd |
| 'Charity May' (6) ♀H4 | CQua |
| 'Charleston' (2) | CQua |
| 'Charlie Connor' (1) | CQua |
| 'Chasseur' (2) | IRhd |
| 'Chaste' (1) | CQua IRhd |
| 'Chat' (7) | CQua |
| 'Cheer Leader' (3) | CQua |
| 'Cheerfulness' (4) ♀H4 | CAvo CFFs CQua LAma MBri SDeJ |
| 'Cheesewring' (3) | CQua |
| 'Cheetah' (1) | CQua IRhd |
| 'Chelsea Girl' (2) | CQua |
| 'Cheltenham' (2) | CQua |
| 'Chenoweth' (2) | CQua |
| 'Chérie' (7) | CQua |
| 'Cherish' (2) | CQua |
| 'Cherry Glow' (3) | IRhd |
| 'Cherrygardens' (2) | CQua IRhd |
| 'Chesapeake Bay' (1) | CQua |
| 'Chesterton' (9) ♀H4 | CQua |
| 'Chickadee' (6) | CBro CQua |
| 'Chicken Hill' (1) | CQua |
| 'Chickerell' (3) | CQua |
| 'Chief Inspector' (1) | IRhd |
| 'Chiloquin' (1) | CQua |
| 'China Doll' (2) | CQua |
| 'Chinchilla' (2) | CQua IRhd |
| 'Chingah' (1) | IRhd |
| 'Chinita' (8) | CBro CQua EPfP GCro |
| 'Chipper' (5) | CBro CQua NMin |
| 'Chit Chat' (7) ♀H4 | CQua EPot NMin |
| 'Chiva' | CBro CHid GKev LLHF NMin |
| 'Chobe River' (1) | CQua IRhd |
| 'Chorus Line' (8) | IRhd |
| 'Churchfield Bells' (5) | CQua |
| 'Churston Ferrers' (4) | CQua |
| 'Chy Noweth' (2) | CQua |
| 'Chysauster' (2) | CQua |
| 'Cinco de Mayo' (2) | CQua |
| 'Cisticola' (3) | IRhd |
| ***citrinus*** | see *N. bulbocodium* subsp. *bulbocodium* var. *citrinus* |
| 'Citron' (3) | CQua |
| 'Citronita' (3) | CQua |
| 'Clare' (7) | CBro CQua IRhd NMin |
| 'Claverley' (2) | CQua |
| 'Clearbrook' (2) | CQua |
| 'Cloud Nine' (2) | CBro |
| 'Clouded Yellow' (2) | CQua IRhd |
| 'Clouds Hill' | CQua |
| 'Clouds Rest' (2) | IRhd |
| 'Clovelly Ayr' (9) **new** | CQua |
| 'Codlins and Cream' | see *N.* 'Sulphur Phoenix' |
| 'Coker's Frome' (9) **new** | CQua |
| 'Coldbrook' (2) | CQua |
| 'Colin's Joy' (2) | CQua |
| 'Coliseum' (2) | IRhd |
| 'Colleen Bawn' (1) | CQua NMin |
| 'Colley Gate' (3) | CQua |
| 'Colliford' (2) | CQua |
| 'Colorama' (11a) | CQua |
| 'Colourful' (2) | IRhd |
| 'Columbus' (2) | CQua |
| 'Colville' (9) | CQua |
| 'Comal' (1) | CQua |
| 'Compressus' | see *N.* × *intermedius* 'Compressus' |
| 'Compton Court' (3) | IRhd |
| 'Conestoga' (2) | CQua IRhd |
| 'Congress' (11a) | CQua |
| 'Conly' (3) | CQua |
| 'Conowingo' (11a) | CQua |
| 'Conspicuus' (3) | CAvo CQua GCro |
| 'Conspicuus' ambig. | CQua LAma |
| 'Content' (1) | CQua |
| 'Cool Autumn' (2) | CQua |
| 'Cool Crystal' (3) | CQua |
| 'Cool Evening' (11a) | CQua IRhd |
| 'Cool Pink' (2) | CQua |
| 'Cool Shades' (2) | CQua |
| 'Coolmaghery' (2) | IRhd |
| 'Coombe Creek' (6) | CQua |
| 'Copper Nob' (2) | IRhd |
| 'Copper Rings' (3) | CQua |
| 'Copperfield' (2) | CQua |
| 'Cora Ann' (7) | CBro |
| 'Coral Fair' (2) | CQua |
| 'Corbiere' (1) | CQua IRhd |
| 'Corbridge' (2) | CQua |
| 'Corky's Song' (2) | CQua |
| 'Cornet' (6) | CQua |
| 'Cornish Chuckles' (12) ♀H4 | CBro CQua |
| 'Cornish Sun' (2) | CQua |
| 'Cornish Vanguard' (2) ♀H4 | CQua |
| 'Coroboree' | IRhd |

| | |
|---|---|
| 'Corofin' (3) | CQua |
| 'Coromandel' (2) | IRhd |
| 'Corozal' (3) | CQua |
| 'Cosmic Dance' (3) | IRhd |
| 'Cotinga' (6) | CQua NMin |
| 'Countdown' (2) | CQua |
| 'Coverack Glory' (2) | CQua |
| 'Crackington' (4) 🏆H4 | CQua IRhd |
| 'Cragford' (8) | SDeJ |
| 'Craig Stiel' (2) | CQua |
| 'Creag Dubh' (2) | CQua |
| 'Creed' (6) | CQua |
| 'Crenver' (3) | CQua GCro |
| 'Crevenagh' (2) | IRhd |
| 'Crewenna' (1) | CAvo CQua |
| 'Crill' (7) | CQua |
| 'Crimson Chalice' (3) | CQua IRhd |
| 'Cristobal' (1) | CQua |
| 'Crock of Gold' (1) | CQua |
| 'Croesus' (2) | CQua GCro |
| 'Crofty' (6) | CQua |
| 'Croila' (2) | CQua |
| 'Crowndale' (4) | CQua IRhd |
| 'Crugmeer' (11a) | CQua |
| 'Cryptic' (1) | CQua IRhd |
| 'Crystal Arrow' (6) **new** | CQua |
| 'Crystal Star' (2) | CQua |
| 'Cudden Point' (2) | CQua |
| 'Cul Beag' (3) | CQua |
| 'Culmination' (2) | CQua |
| 'Cultured Pearl' (2) | CQua |
| 'Cum Laude' (11a) | ERCP |
| 'Curlew' (7) 🏆H4 | CQua GKev SDeJ |
| 'Curly' (2) | SDeJ |
| 'Curlylocks' (7) **new** | NMin |
| ***cyclamineus*** (13) 🏆H4 | CBro CDes CRDP CWCL LRHS MSSP NMen SCnR SKHP SRms |
| 'Cyclope' (1) | CQua |
| ***cypri*** (8) | CQua |
| 'Cyros' (1) | CQua |
| 'Dailmanach' (2) | CQua IRhd |
| 'Dailmystic' (2) | IRhd |
| 'Dallas' (3) | CQua |
| 'Dalmeny' (2) **new** | CQua |
| 'Dambuster' (4) | IRhd |
| 'Damson' (2) | CQua GCro |
| 'Dan du Plessis' (8) | CQua |
| 'Dancing Queen' (2) | IRhd |
| 'Dardanelles' (2) | IRhd |
| 'Dateline' (3) | CQua |
| 'David Alexander' (1) | CQua |
| 'David Mills' (2) | CQua |
| 'Dawn Brooker' (2) **new** | CQua |
| 'Dawn Call' (2) | IRhd |
| 'Dawn Run' (2) | IRhd |
| 'Dawn Sky' (2) | CQua |
| 'Daydream' (2) 🏆H3 | CQua |
| 'Daymark' (8) | CQua |
| 'Dayton Lake' (2) | CQua |
| 'Debutante' (2) | CQua |
| 'December Bride' (11a) | CQua |
| 'Decision' (2) | IRhd |
| 'Defence Corps' (1) | IRhd |
| 'Delia' (6) | IRhd |
| 'Dell Chapel' (3) | CQua |
| 'Delnashaugh' (4) | CQua ERCP LAma SPer |
| 'Delos' (3) | CQua |
| 'Delphin Hill' (4) | IRhd |
| 'Delta Flight' (6) | IRhd |
| 'Demand' (2) | CQua |
| 'Demeanour' | IRhd |
| 'Demmo' (2) | CQua |
| 'Dena' (3) | IRhd |
| 'Denali' (1) | IRhd |
| 'Descant' (1) | IRhd |
| 'Desdemona' (2) 🏆H4 | CQua SDeJ |
| 'Desert Bells' (7) | CQua NMin |
| 'Desert Orchid' (2) | CQua |
| 'Dewy Dell' (3) | IRhd |
| 'Diamond Ring' | see *N. bulbocodium* subsp. *obesus* 'Diamond Ring' |
| 'Dick Wilden' (4) | CQua EBla GKev |
| 'Dickcissel' (7) 🏆H4 | CQua ERCP SPhx |
| 'Dignitary' (2) | IRhd |
| 'Dimity' (3) | CQua |
| 'Dimple' (9) | CQua |
| 'Dinkie' (3) | CBro |
| 'Disquiet' (1) | CQua |
| 'Diversity' (11a) | IRhd |
| 'Doctor Hugh' (3) 🏆H4 | CQua IRhd |
| 'Doctor Jazz' (2) | CQua |
| 'Doll Baby' (7) | NMin |
| 'Doombar' (1) | CQua |
| 'Dora Allum' (2) | CQua |
| 'Dorchester' (4) | CQua IRhd |
| 'Dorneywood' (1) | IRhd |
| 'Double Campernelle' | see *N.* × *odorus* 'Double Campernelle' |
| 'Double Itzim' (4) **new** | NMin |
| double pheasant eye | see *N. poeticus* 'Plenus' ambig. |
| double Roman | see *N.* 'Romanus' |
| 'Double White' (4) | CQua |
| 'Doubleday' (4) | CQua IRhd |
| 'Doublet' (4) | CQua |
| 'Doubtful' (3) | CQua |
| 'Dove Wings' (6) 🏆H4 | CQua |
| 'Dover Cliffs' (2) | CQua |
| 'Downlands' (3) | CQua |
| 'Downpatrick' (1) | CQua |
| 'Dragon Run' (2) | CQua |
| 'Drama Queen' (11a) | IRhd |
| 'Dream Catcher' (2) | IRhd |
| 'Dreamlight' (3) | CQua |
| 'Drumlin' (1) 🏆H4 | IRhd |
| ***dubius*** (13) | CBro ECho EPot |
| 'Duchess of Westminster' (2) **new** | GCro |
| 'Duiker' (6) | IRhd |
| 'Dulcimer' (9) | CQua |
| 'Dunadry Inn' (4) | IRhd |
| 'Dunkeld' (2) | CQua |
| 'Dunkery' (4) | CQua IRhd |
| 'Dunley Hall' (3) | CQua IRhd |
| 'Dunmurry' (1) | CQua |
| 'Dunskey' (3) | CQua |
| 'Dupli Kate' (4) | IRhd |
| 'Dusky Lad' (2) | IRhd |
| 'Dusky Maiden' (2) | IRhd |
| 'Dutch Delight' (2) | IRhd |
| 'Dutch Lemon Drops' (5) 🏆H4 | CQua |
| 'Dutch Master' (1) 🏆H4 | CQua LAma SDeJ SPer |
| 'Early Bride' (2) | CQua |
| 'Early Splendour' (8) | CQua |
| 'Earthlight' (3) | CQua |
| 'Easter Moon' (2) | CQua |
| 'Eastern Dawn' (2) | CQua SDeJ |
| 'Eastern Promise' (2) | CQua |
| 'Eaton Song' (12) 🏆H4 | CBro CQua |
| 'Ebony' (1) | CQua |

| |  |  |
|---|---|---|
| | 'Eddy Canzony' (2) | CQua |
| | 'Edenderry' (1) | IRhd |
| | 'Edgbaston' (2) | CQua |
| | 'Edge Grove' (2) | CQua |
| | 'Editor' (2) | IRhd |
| | 'Edward Buxton' (3) | CQua |
| | 'Egard' (11a) | CQua |
| | 'Egmont King' (2) | CQua |
| | 'Eland' (7) | CQua |
| | 'Elburton' (2) | CQua |
| | 'Electrus' (11a) | IRhd |
| | 'Elegans' (3) **new** | GCro |
| | ***elegans*** (13) | ECho EPot |
| | 'Elf' (2) | CBro CQua |
| | 'Elfin Gold' (6) | CQua |
| | 'Elizabeth Ann' (6) | CQua |
| | 'Elka' (1) | CAvo CBro CQua MSSP NMin |
| | 'Ella D' (2) | CQua |
| | 'Elphin' (4) | CQua |
| | 'Elrond' (2) | CQua |
| | 'Elven Lady' (2) | CQua |
| | 'Elvira' (8) | CQua WShi |
| | 'Emcys' (6) | EPot NMin |
| | 'Emerald Pink' (3) | CQua |
| | 'Emily' (2) | NMin |
| | 'Eminent' (3) | CQua |
| | 'Emperor' (1) | CQua GCro |
| | 'Emperor's Waltz' (6) | IRhd |
| | 'Empire' (2) **new** | GCro |
| | 'Empress of Ireland' (1) ♀H4 | CQua IRhd |
| | 'English Caye' (1) | CQua |
| | 'Ensemble' (4) | CQua |
| | 'Enterprise' (4) | CQua |
| | 'Epona' (3) | CQua |
| | 'Erin' (3) **new** | CQua |
| | 'Erlicheer' (4) | CQua SDeJ |
| | 'Escapee' (2) | IRhd |
| | 'Estrella' (3) | CQua |
| | 'Ethereal Beauty' (2) | IRhd |
| | 'Ethos' (1) | IRhd |
| § | ***eugeniae*** (13) | WCot |
| | 'Euryalus' (1) | CQua |
| | 'Evangeline' (3) **new** | GCro |
| | 'Eve Robertson' (2) | CQua |
| | 'Evelyn Roberts' (11a) **new** | CQua |
| | 'Evening' (2) | CQua |
| | 'Evesham' (3) | CQua IRhd |
| | 'Eyeglass' (3) | CQua IRhd |
| | 'Eyelet' (3) | CQua IRhd |
| | 'Eype' (4) | IRhd |
| | 'Eyrie' (3) | CQua IRhd |
| § | 'Eystettensis' (4) | CBro CRDP IBlr |
| | 'Fair Head' (9) | CQua |
| | 'Fair Prospect' (2) | CQua |
| | 'Fair William' (2) | CQua |
| | 'Fairgreen' (3) | CQua |
| | 'Fairlawns' (3) | CQua |
| | 'Fairmile' (3) | CQua |
| | 'Fairy Chimes' (5) | CBro CQua |
| | 'Fairy Footsteps' (3) | CQua IRhd |
| | 'Fairy Island' (3) | CQua |
| | 'Fairy Spell' (3) | IRhd |
| | 'Fairy Tale' (3) | CQua |
| | 'Falconet' (8) ♀H4 | CBro CQua EPfP SPer |
| | 'Falmouth Bay' (3) | CQua |
| | 'Falstaff' (2) | CQua |
| | 'Fanline' (11a) | CQua |
| | 'Far Country' (2) | CQua |
| I | 'Fashion' (11b) | CQua |
| | 'Fashion Model' (2) | IRhd |

| |  |  |
|---|---|---|
| | 'Fastidious' (2) | CQua |
| | 'February Gold' (6) ♀H4 | CAvo CBro CFFs CQua CTri EPfP EPot ERCP GKev LAma MBri NBir SDeJ SEND SPer SPhx SRms WShi |
| | 'February Silver' (1) | CBro EPot ERCP LAma SDeJ |
| | 'Felindre' (9) | CQua EPot |
| | 'Feline Queen' (1) | IRhd |
| | 'Feock' (3) | CQua |
| | ***fernandesii*** (13) | ECho GEdr ITim NMin SCnR WCot WThu |
| | - var. ***cordubensis*** (13) | CBro ECho EPot GEdr |
| | - var. ***cordubensis*** × ***jonquilla*** | NMin |
| | 'Ferndown' (3) | CQua IRhd |
| | 'Ferral' (4) | IRhd |
| | 'Fertile Crescent' (7) | CQua |
| | 'Feu de Joie' (4) **new** | GCro |
| | 'Ffitch's Ffolly' (2) | CQua |
| | 'Filoli' (1) | CQua IRhd |
| | 'Finchcocks' (2) | CQua |
| | 'Fine Gold' (1) | CQua |
| | 'Fine Romance' (2) | CQua |
| | 'Finland' (2) | CQua |
| | 'Fiona Linford' (3) | IRhd |
| | 'Fiona MacKillop' (2) | IRhd |
| | 'Fire Tail' (3) | CQua WShi |
| | 'First Born' (6) | CQua NMin |
| | 'First Formal' (3) | CQua |
| | 'First Hope' (6) | CQua |
| | 'Flambards Village' (4) | CQua |
| | 'Flirt' (6) | CQua |
| | 'Flomay' (7) | NMin |
| | 'Florida Manor' (3) | IRhd |
| | 'Flower Record' (2) | LAma |
| | 'Flusher' (2) | CQua |
| | 'Flycatcher' (7) | CQua |
| | 'Flying Colours' (4) | IRhd |
| | 'Flying High' (3) | CQua |
| | 'Foff's Way' (1) | CQua |
| | 'Foresight' (1) | CQua |
| | 'Forge Mill' (2) | CQua |
| | 'Fortescue' (4) | IRhd |
| | 'Fortissimo' (2) | SPer |
| | 'Fortune' (2) | CQua LAma MBri SDeJ |
| | 'Fossie' (4) | CQua |
| | 'Foundling' (6) ♀H4 | CBro CQua |
| | 'Foxfire' (2) | CQua |
| | 'Foxhunter' (2) | CQua |
| | 'Fragrant Breeze' (2) | SDeJ |
| | 'Fragrant Rose' (2) | CQua ERCP IRhd |
| | 'Frances Delight' (11a) **new** | CQua |
| | 'Francolin' (1) | IRhd |
| | 'Frank' (9) | IRhd |
| | 'Freedom Rings' (2) | CQua |
| | 'Freedom Stars' (11a) ♀H4 | IRhd |
| | 'Fresco' (11a) | IRhd |
| | 'Fresh Field' (2) | CQua |
| | 'Fresh Lime' (1) | CQua |
| | 'Fresno' (3) | IRhd |
| | 'Frigid' (3) | CQua |
| | 'Frogmore' (6) | CQua |
| | 'Front Royal' (2) | CQua |
| | 'Frosted Pink' (2) | IRhd |
| | 'Frostkist' (6) | CBro CQua |
| | 'Frosty Morn' (5) | NMin |
| | 'Frou-frou' (4) | CQua |
| | 'Frozen Jade' (1) | CQua |
| | 'Fruit Cup' (7) | CQua EPfP SDeJ |
| | 'Fuco' (1) | CQua NMin |
| | 'Full House' | SDeJ |

| | |
|---|---|
| 'Fulwell' (4) | CQua |
| 'Furbelow' (4) | CQua |
| 'Furnace Creek' (2) | IRhd |
| 'Fynbos' (3) | IRhd |
| ***gaditanus*** (13) | CBro |
| 'Gamebird' (1) | IRhd |
| 'Garden News' (3) | IRhd |
| 'Garden Opera' (7) ♀H4 | CQua |
| 'Garden Princess' (2) | CBro |
| 'Garden Treasure' (2) | IRhd |
| 'Gatecrasher' (1) | IRhd |
| 'Gay Cavalier' (4) | CQua |
| 'Gay Kybo' (4) ♀H4 | CQua |
| 'Gay Song' (4) | CQua |
| ***gayi*** (13) | CQua WShi |
| 'Geevor' (4) | CQua |
| 'Gellymill' (2) | CQua |
| 'Gemini Girl' (2) | CQua |
| 'George Leak' (2) | CQua |
| 'Georgie Girl' (6) | CQua |
| 'Geranium' (8) ♀H4 | CBro CQua EPfP ERCP GCro LAma SDeJ SPer WShi |
| 'Gettysburg' (2) | CQua |
| 'Gillan' (11a) | CQua |
| 'Gin and Lime' (1) ♀H4 | CQua |
| 'Gipsy Moon' (2) | CQua |
| 'Gipsy Queen' (1) | CBro CQua ECha EPot NMin |
| 'Gironde' (11) | CQua |
| 'Glacier' (1) | CQua |
| 'Glasnevin' (2) | CQua |
| 'Glen Cassley' (3) | CQua |
| 'Glen Clova' (2) | CQua |
| 'Glendermott' (2) | CQua |
| 'Glenside' (2) | CQua |
| 'Glissando' (2) | CQua |
| 'Gloria Mundi' (2) **new** | GCro |
| 'Gloriosus' (8) | CQua |
| 'Glover's Reef' (1) | CQua |
| 'Glowing Pheonix' (4) | CQua |
| 'Glowing Red' (4) | CQua |
| 'Goff's Caye' (2) | CQua IRhd |
| 'Golant' (2) | CQua |
| 'Gold Bond' (2) | CQua IRhd |
| 'Gold Cache' (11a) | CQua |
| 'Gold Charm' (2) | CQua |
| 'Gold Convention' (2) ♀H4 | CQua IRhd |
| 'Gold Ingot' (2) ♀H4 | IRhd |
| 'Gold Medallion' (1) | CQua |
| 'Gold Top' (2) | CQua |
| 'Golden Amber' (2) | CQua |
| 'Golden Aura' (2) ♀H4 | CQua |
| 'Golden Bear' (4) | CQua |
| 'Golden Bells' | see *N. bulbocodium* Golden Bells Group |
| 'Golden Cheer' (2) | CQua |
| 'Golden Dawn' (8) ♀H3 | CQua EPfP |
| 'Golden Ducat' (4) | CQua LAma MBri NBir |
| 'Golden Flute' (2) | IRhd |
| 'Golden Gamble' (11a) | IRhd |
| 'Golden Goal' (2) | IRhd |
| 'Golden Halo' (2) | CQua |
| 'Golden Harvest' (1) | CQua LAma |
| 'Golden Incense' (7) | CQua |
| 'Golden Jewel' (2) ♀H4 | CQua |
| 'Golden Joy' (2) | CQua |
| 'Golden Lion' (1) | CQua EPfP |
| 'Golden Marvel' (1) | CQua |
| 'Golden Orbit' (4) | CQua |
| 'Golden Phoenix' (4) | CQua |
| 'Golden Rain' (4) | CQua |
| 'Golden Rapture' (1) ♀H4 | CQua |
| 'Golden Sceptre' (7) | CBro |
| 'Golden Sheen' (2) | CQua |
| 'Golden Splash' (11a) | IRhd |
| 'Golden Spur' (1) | CQua LAma |
| 'Golden Torch' (2) | CQua |
| 'Golden Twins' (7) **new** | CQua |
| 'Golden Vale' (1) ♀H4 | CQua |
| 'Goldfinger' (1) ♀H4 | CQua IRhd |
| 'Goldhanger' (2) | CQua |
| 'Goldsithney' (2) | CBro |
| 'Golitha Falls' (2) | CQua |
| 'Good Fella' (2) | CQua |
| 'Good Measure' (2) | CQua |
| 'Goonbell' (2) | CQua |
| 'Goose Green' (3) | GKev |
| 'Gorran' (3) | CQua |
| 'Gossmoor' (4) | CQua |
| 'Grace Note' (3) | CQua |
| 'Grand Monarque' | see *N. tazetta* subsp. *lacticolor* 'Grand Monarque' |
| 'Grand Opening' (4) | IRhd |
| 'Grand Primo Citronière' (8) | CQua |
| 'Grand Prospect' (2) | CQua |
| 'Grand Soleil d'Or' (8) | CQua ERCP LAma SDeJ |
| 'Great Expectations' (2) | CQua |
| 'Greatwood' (1) | CQua |
| 'Greek Surprise' (4) | IRhd |
| 'Green Chartreuse' (2) | CQua |
| 'Green Island' (2) | SDeJ |
| 'Green Lawns' (9) **new** | CQua |
| 'Green Lodge' (9) | IRhd |
| 'Green Pearl' (3) **new** | NMin |
| 'Greenodd' (3) | CQua |
| 'Greenpark' (9) | IRhd |
| 'Grenoble' (2) | CQua |
| 'Gresham' (4) | CQua IRhd |
| 'Gribben Head' (4) | CQua |
| 'Groundkeeper' (3) | IRhd |
| 'Guiding Spirit' (4) **new** | CQua |
| 'Gulliver' (3) | CQua GCro |
| 'Gunwalloe' (11a) | CQua |
| 'Guy Wilson' (2) | CQua |
| 'Gwennap' (1) | CQua |
| 'Gwinear' (2) | CQua |
| 'Habari' (4) **new** | IRhd |
| 'Hacienda' (1) | CQua |
| 'Half Moon Caye' (2) | CQua |
| 'Halley's Comet' (3) | CQua IRhd |
| 'Halloon' (3) | CQua |
| 'Halvose' (8) | CBro |
| 'Halzephron' (2) | CQua |
| 'Hambledon' (2) ♀H4 | CQua |
| 'Hampton Court' (2) | CQua |
| 'Happy Dreams' (2) | IRhd |
| 'Happy Fellow' (2) | CQua |
| 'Happy Valley' (2) | IRhd |
| 'Harbour View' (2) | IRhd |
| 'Harmony Bells' (5) | CBro CQua |
| 'Harp Music' (2) | IRhd |
| 'Harpers Ferry' (1) | CQua |
| 'Hartlebury' (3) | CQua |
| 'Havelock' (2) **new** | GCro |
| 'Hawangi' (3) | IRhd |
| 'Hawera' (5) ♀H4 | CAvo CBro CFFs CHid CMea CQua CTca CTri EPfP EPot ERCP GAbr GKev LAma LSou MBri SDeJ SPer SPhx WShi |
| 'Heamoor' (4) ♀H4 | CQua |

| | |
|---|---|
| ***hedraeanthus*** (13) | ECho EPot |
| - SG 15 | WCot |
| 'Helford Dawn' (2) | CQua |
| 'Helford Sunset' (2) | CQua |
| 'Helios' (2) | CQua GCro |
| ***hellenicus*** | see *N. poeticus* var. *hellenicus* |
| ***henriquesii*** | see *N. jonquilla* var. *henriquesii* |
| 'Henry Irving' (1) | CQua GCro |
| 'Hero' (1) | CQua |
| 'Heslington' (3) | CQua |
| 'Hexameter' (9) | CQua |
| 'Hexworthy' (3) | CQua |
| 'Hibernian' (4) | IRhd |
| 'Hicks Mill' (1) | CQua |
| 'High Society' (2) 🏆H4 | CQua |
| 'Highfield Beauty' (8) 🏆H4 | CQua |
| 'Highgrove' (1) | CQua |
| 'Highlite' (2) | CQua |
| 'Hihitahi' (2) | CQua |
| 'Hilda's Pink' (2) | CQua |
| 'Hill Head' (9) | IRhd |
| 'Hillstar' (7) 🏆H4 | CQua NMin SDeJ |
| ***hispanicus*** (13) | ECho |
| 'Hocus Pocus' (3) | IRhd |
| 'Holland's Glory' (4) **new** | GCro |
| 'Hollypark' (3) | IRhd |
| 'Holme Fen' (2) | CQua |
| 'Home Fires' (2) | CQua |
| 'Homestead' (2) 🏆H4 | IRhd |
| 'Honey Pink' (2) | CQua |
| 'Honeybird' (1) | CQua |
| 'Honeyorange' (2) | IRhd |
| 'Hoopoe' (8) 🏆H4 | CQua GKev |
| 'Horace' (9) | CQua |
| 'Horn of Plenty' (5) | CBro CQua |
| 'Hornpipe' (1) | IRhd |
| 'Hors d'Oeuvre' (8) | CBro |
| 'Horsfieldii' (1) **new** | GCro |
| 'Hospodar' (2) | CQua GCro |
| 'Hot Affair' (2) | IRhd |
| 'Hot Gossip' (2) | CQua |
| 'Hotspur' (2) | CQua |
| 'Hugh Town' (8) | CAvo CQua SEND |
| 'Hugus' (7) | CQua |
| 'Hullabaloo' (2) | IRhd |
| 'Hummingbird' (6) **new** | EPot |
| 'Hunting Caye' (2) | CQua |
| 'Huntley Down' (1) | CQua |
| 'Ice Chimes' (5) | CQua |
| 'Ice Dancer' (2) | CQua |
| 'Ice Diamond' (4) | CQua |
| 'Ice Follies' (2) 🏆H4 | CQua EPfP GKev LAma MBri NBir SDeJ SPer |
| 'Ice King' (4) | EBla NBir SDeJ |
| 'Ice Wings' (5) 🏆H4 | CAvo CBro CFFs CQua EPot NMin WShi |
| 'Idless' (1) | CQua |
| 'Immaculate' (2) | CQua |
| 'Inara' (4) | CQua |
| 'Inca' (6) | CQua |
| 'Inchbonnie' (2) | CQua |
| × ***incomparabilis*** | SEND |
| 'Independence Day' (4) | CQua |
| 'Indian Maid' (7) 🏆H4 | CQua IRhd |
| 'Indora' (4) | CQua |
| 'Inner Glow' (2) | IRhd |
| 'Innisidgen' (8) | CQua |
| 'Innovator' (4) | CQua |
| 'Innuendo' (2) | IRhd |
| 'Inny River' (1) | IRhd |
| 'Interim' (2) | CQua |
| × ***intermedius*** (13) | CBro CQua NMin WAbe WCot |
| § - 'Compressus' (8) | CBro CQua |
| 'Intrigue' (7) 🏆H4 | CQua |
| 'Invercassley' (3) | CQua |
| 'Ireland's Eye' (9) | CQua |
| 'Irene Copeland' (4) | CQua |
| 'Irish Fire' (2) | CQua |
| 'Irish Light' (2) | CQua |
| 'Irish Luck' (1) | CQua |
| 'Irish Minstrel' (2) 🏆H4 | CQua |
| 'Irish Mist' (2) | CQua |
| 'Irish Rum' (2) | CQua |
| 'Irish Wedding' (2) | CQua |
| 'Isambard' (4) | CQua |
| 'Island Pride' (8) | CQua |
| 'Islander' (4) | CQua |
| 'Ita' (2) | IRhd |
| 'Itzim' (6) 🏆H4 | CBro CQua SDeJ |
| ***jacetanus*** (13) | MSSP NMin |
| 'Jack Snipe' (6) 🏆H4 | CAvo CBro CFFs CHid CQua ECho EPfP EPot GKev LAma MBri SDeJ SEND WShi |
| 'Jack Wood' (11a) | CQua |
| 'Jackadee' (2) | CQua IRhd |
| 'Jacob Maurer' (6) **new** | CQua |
| 'Jake' (3) | IRhd |
| 'Jamage' (8) | CQua |
| 'Jamaica Inn' (4) | CQua |
| 'Jamboree' (2) | CQua |
| 'Jammin' (3) | IRhd |
| 'Janelle' (2) | CQua |
| 'Janet's Gold' (2) **new** | IRhd |
| 'Jantje' (11a) | CQua |
| 'Jauno' (1) | IRhd |
| 'Javelin' (2) | CQua |
| 'Jeanine' (2) | CQua |
| 'Jeanne Bicknell' (4) | CQua |
| 'Jedna' (2) | CQua |
| 'Jenny' (6) 🏆H4 | CAvo CBro CMea CQua EBla ERCP GKev LAma MCot NBir SDeJ SPhx WShi |
| 'Jersey Carlton' (2) | CQua |
| 'Jersey Lace' (2) | CQua |
| 'Jersey Roundabout' (4) | CQua |
| 'Jersey Star' (4) **new** | CQua |
| 'Jersey Torch' (4) | CQua |
| 'Jetfire' (6) 🏆H4 | CMea CQua ECho EPfP EPot ERCP GKev LAma LRHS LSou SDeJ SPer WShi |
| 'Jezebel' (3) | CBro |
| 'Jimmy Noone' (1) | CQua |
| 'Jim's Gold' (2) | CQua |
| 'Jingle Bells' (4) | CQua |
| 'Jodi' (11b) | IRhd |
| 'Jodi's Sister' (11a) | IRhd |
| 'Johanna' (5) | CBro |
| 'John Daniel' (4) | CQua |
| 'John Evelyn' (2) **new** | GCro |
| 'John Lanyon' (3) | CQua |
| 'John Philip Sousa' (2) | CQua |
| 'Johnny Dodds' (1) **new** | CQua |
| 'John's Delight' (3) | CQua |
| ***jonquilla*** (13) 🏆H4 | CBro CQua EPot GKev LAma LEdu NMin WShi |
| § - var. ***henriquesii*** (13) | CQua ECho GKev NMin SCnR SPhx |
| 'Joppa' (7) | CQua |
| 'Joy Bishop' | see *N. romieuxii* 'Joy Bishop' |
| 'Joybell' (6) | CQua |
| 'Juanita' (2) | SDeJ |

| | |
|---|---|
| 'Jules Verne' (2) | CQua |
| 'Julia Jane' | see *N. romieuxii* 'Julia Jane' |
| 'Juliet Firstbrook' (2) **new** | CQua |
| 'Jumblie' (12) ♀H4 | CBro CQua EPfP EPot GKev LAma LRHS MBri SDeJ |
| 'Jumbo Gold' (1) | CTri |
| ***juncifolius*** Req. ex Lag. | see *N. assoanus* |
| 'June Lake' (2) | CQua IRhd |
| 'Junior Miss' (12) | NMin |
| 'Kabani' (9) | CQua |
| 'Kaka Point' (2) | IRhd |
| 'Kalimna' (1) | CQua |
| 'Kamau' (9) | IRhd |
| 'Kamms' (1) | CQua |
| 'Kamura' (2) | CQua |
| 'Kanchenjunga' (1) | CQua |
| 'Kate Davies' (2) **new** | CQua |
| 'Katherine Jenkins' (7) | CQua |
| 'Kathleen Smith' (7) **new** | CQua |
| 'Kathy A' | IRhd |
| 'Kathy's Clown' (6) | CQua |
| 'Katie Heath' (5) | EPfP ERCP SDeJ SPer |
| 'Katrina Rea' (6) | CQua |
| 'Kaydee' (6) ♀H4 | CQua IRhd SPhx |
| 'Kea' (6) | CQua |
| 'Keats' (4) | CBro CQua NMin |
| 'Kebaya' (2) | CQua |
| 'Kedron' (7) | ERCP |
| 'Kelly Bray' (1) | CQua |
| 'Kenellis' (10) | CBro CQua EPot GEdr |
| 'Kernow' (2) | CQua |
| 'Kidling' (7) | CQua EPot NMin |
| 'Killara' (8) | CQua |
| 'Killigrew' (2) | CQua GCro |
| 'Killivose' (3) | CQua |
| 'Kilmood' (2) | CQua |
| 'Kiltonga' (2) | IRhd |
| 'Kilworth' (2) | CQua |
| 'Kimmeridge' (3) | CQua |
| 'King Alfred' (1) | CQua EPfP SDeJ SEND SPer |
| 'King Size' (11a) | CQua |
| 'Kinglet' (7) | CQua |
| 'King's Grove' (1) ♀H4 | CQua |
| 'Kings Pipe' (2) | CQua |
| 'Kingscourt' (1) ♀H4 | CQua |
| 'Kingsleigh' (1) | IRhd |
| 'Kingsmill Lake' (2) | CQua |
| 'Kirklington' (2) | CQua |
| 'Kit Hill' (7) | CQua |
| 'Kitten' (6) | CQua |
| 'Kiwi Magic' (4) | CQua IRhd |
| 'Kiwi Solstice' (4) | CQua |
| 'Kiwi Sunset' (4) | CQua |
| 'Knightsbridge' (1) | CQua |
| 'Knocklayde' (3) | CQua |
| 'Knowehead' (2) | CQua |
| 'Knowing Look' (3) | IRhd |
| 'Kokopelli' (7) ♀H4 | CBro CQua NMin |
| 'Koomooloo' (2) | CQua |
| 'Korora Bay' (1) | IRhd |
| 'La Riante' (3) | CQua |
| 'La Vella' (2) | CQua |
| 'Ladies' Choice' (7) | IRhd |
| 'Ladies' Favorite' (7) | IRhd |
| 'Lady Alice' (7) | CQua |
| 'Lady Ann' (2) | IRhd |
| 'Lady Be Good' (2) | CQua |
| 'Lady Diana' (2) | CQua |
| 'Lady Emily' (2) | CQua |
| 'Lady Eve' (11a) | IRhd |
| 'Lady Godiva' (3) **new** | GCro |
| 'Lady Hilaria' (2) | CQua |
| 'Lady Margaret Boscawen' (2) | CQua GCro |
| 'Lady Serena' (9) | CQua |
| 'Lake District' | IRhd |
| 'Lake Tahoe' (2) | IRhd |
| 'Lalique' (3) | CQua |
| 'Lamanva' (2) | CQua |
| 'Lamlash' (2) | IRhd |
| 'Lanarth' (7) | CBro GCro |
| 'Lancaster' (3) | CQua |
| 'Landewednack Lady' (4) | CQua |
| 'Langarth' (11a) | CQua |
| 'Lapwing' (5) | IRhd |
| 'Larkelly' (6) | CBro CQua |
| 'Larkhill' (2) | CQua |
| 'Larkwhistle' (6) ♀H4 | LAma SDeJ |
| 'Latchley' (2) | CQua |
| 'Latchley Meadows' (2) **new** | CQua |
| 'Laurelbank' (2) **new** | IRhd |
| 'Lauren' (3) | IRhd |
| 'Laurens Koster' (8) | CQua |
| 'Lava Flow' (3) | IRhd |
| 'Lavender Lass' (6) | CQua |
| 'Lavender Mist' (2) | CQua |
| 'Lazy River' (1) | CQua |
| 'Leading Light' (2) | CQua |
| 'Lee Moor' (1) | CQua |
| 'Lemon Beauty' (11b) | CQua EBla SDeJ |
| 'Lemon Drizzle' (2) | CQua |
| 'Lemon Drops' (5) | CMea ECho EPot ERCP NMin SDeJ SPhx |
| 'Lemon Grey' (3) | IRhd |
| 'Lemon Haze' (2) | CQua |
| 'Lemon Silk' (6) | CBro CQua ECho NMin |
| 'Lemon Snow' (2) | IRhd |
| 'Lemonade' (3) | CQua |
| 'Lennymore' (2) | CQua IRhd |
| 'Lewis George' (1) | CQua |
| 'Libby' (2) | IRhd |
| 'Liberty Bells' (5) | CBro CQua ECho LAma MBri |
| 'Liebeslied' (3) | CQua |
| 'Life' (7) | CQua |
| 'Lifeline' (1) | IRhd |
| 'Lighthouse' (3) | CQua |
| 'Lighthouse Reef' (1) | CQua IRhd |
| 'Lilac Charm' (6) | CQua IRhd |
| 'Lilac Hue' (6) | CBro |
| 'Lilac Mist' (2) | CQua |
| 'Lilliput' ambig. | CQua |
| 'Lily-May Bostock' (6) **new** | CQua |
| 'Limbo' (2) | CQua IRhd |
| 'Limehurst' (2) | CQua |
| 'Limequilla' (7) | CQua |
| 'Limpopo' (3) | IRhd |
| 'Lindsay Joy' (2) | CQua |
| 'Lintie' (7) | CQua |
| 'Lisbarnett' (3) | IRhd |
| 'Lisnamulligan' (3) | IRhd |
| 'Lisnaruddy' (3) | IRhd |
| 'Little Alice' (4) **new** | IRhd |
| 'Little Beauty' (1) ♀H4 | CBro CQua LAma NMin |
| 'Little Dancer' (1) | CBro CQua |
| 'Little Dorr' (4) | IRhd |
| 'Little Flik' (12) **new** | NMin |
| 'Little Jewel' (3) | CQua |
| 'Little Karoo' (3) | IRhd |
| 'Little Meg' (7) **new** | CQua |
| 'Little Rosie' (2) | IRhd |

| | |
|---|---|
| 'Little Rusky' (7) | CBro CQua NMin |
| 'Little Sentry' (7) | CBro CQua NMin |
| 'Little Soldier' (10) | CQua NMin |
| 'Little Spell' (1) | CQua |
| 'Little Tyke' (2) | CQua |
| 'Little Witch' (6) | CBro CQua EPfP GKev LAma SDeJ SPhx WShi |
| 'Littlefield' (7) | CQua |
| 'Livelands' (1) | CQua |
| 'Liverpool Festival' (2) | CQua |
| 'Lobularis' | see *N. lobularis* (Haw.) Schult. & Schult. f. |
| ***lobularis*** misapplied | see *N. nanus* |
| § ***lobularis*** (Haw.) Schult. & Schult. f. | CAvo CBro CFFs CQua CTca CTri ECho EPot GKev LRHS MBri SDeJ SEND SPer SPhx |
| 'Loch Alsh' (3) | CQua IRhd |
| 'Loch Assynt' (3) | CQua |
| 'Loch Brora' (2) | CQua |
| 'Loch Coire' (3) | CQua |
| 'Loch Fada' (2) | CQua |
| 'Loch Hope' (2) | CQua |
| 'Loch Leven' (2) | CQua |
| 'Loch Loyal' (2) | CQua |
| 'Loch Lundie' (2) | CQua |
| 'Loch Maberry' (2) | CQua |
| 'Loch Naver' (2) | CQua |
| 'Loch Owskeich' (2) ♀H4 | CQua |
| 'Loch Stac' (2) | CQua |
| 'Logan Rock' (7) | CQua |
| 'Longitude' (1) | IRhd |
| 'Lordship' (1) | CQua |
| 'Lorikeet' (1) | CQua |
| 'Lothario' (2) | LAma MBri |
| 'Lough Gowna' (1) | IRhd |
| 'Louise de Coligny' (2) **new** | ERCP |
| 'Love Call' (11a) | CQua |
| 'Loveny' (2) | CQua |
| 'Lubaantun' (1) | CQua |
| 'Lucifer' (2) | CQua GCro WShi |
| 'Lucky Chance' (11a) | IRhd |
| 'Lulworth' (2) **new** | GCro |
| 'Lundy Light' (2) | CQua |
| 'Lynher' (2) | CQua |
| 'Lyrebird' (3) | CQua |
| 'Lyric' (9) | CQua |
| 'Lysander' (2) | CQua |
| 'Madam Speaker' (4) | CQua |
| 'Madame Plemp' (1) **new** | GCro |
| 'Madison' (4) | CQua |
| 'Maelor' **new** | SEND |
| 'Magic Moment' (3) | CQua |
| 'Magician' (2) | CQua IRhd |
| 'Magna Carta' (2) | CQua |
| 'Magnet' (1) | LAma |
| 'Magnificence' (1) | CQua |
| 'Mai's Family' (6) | CQua |
| 'Majestic Star' (1) | CQua |
| 'Major' (2) **new** | GCro |
| 'Mallee' (11a) ♀H4 | IRhd |
| 'Malpas' (3) | CQua |
| 'Malvern City' (1) | CQua |
| 'Mamma Mia' (4) | IRhd |
| 'Manaccan' (1) | CQua |
| 'Mangaweka' (6) | CQua |
| 'Manly' (4) ♀H4 | CQua ERCP |
| 'Mantle' (2) | CQua |
| 'Marabou' (4) | CQua |
| 'Margaret Herbert' (7) **new** | CQua |
| 'Maria Pia' (11a) | IRhd |
| 'Marie Curie Diamond' (7) ♀H4 | CQua |
| 'Marieke' (1) | LAma |
| 'Marilyn Anne' (2) | CQua |
| 'Marjorie Hine' (2) | CQua |
| 'Marjorie Treveal' (4) | CQua |
| 'Marlborough' (2) | CQua |
| 'Marlborough Freya' (2) | CQua |
| 'Marshfire' (2) | CQua |
| 'Martha Washington' (8) | CBro CQua |
| 'Martinette' (8) | CQua CTca MBri SDeJ |
| 'Martinsville' (8) | CQua |
| 'Mary Copeland' (4) | CQua |
| 'Mary Kate' (2) | CQua IRhd |
| 'Mary Lou' (6) | IRhd |
| 'Mary Plumstead' (5) **new** | NMin |
| 'Mary Rosina' | CQua |
| 'Mary Veronica' (3) | CQua |
| 'Marzo' (7) | CQua IRhd NMin |
| 'Matador' (8) | CQua IRhd |
| 'Mawla' (1) | CQua |
| 'Max' (11a) | CQua |
| 'Maximus Superbus' (1) | CQua |
| 'Maya Dynasty' (2) | CQua |
| 'Mayor's Choice' (11a) **new** | CQua |
| 'Maywood' (11a) **new** | CQua |
| 'Mazzard' (4) | CQua |
| 'Media Girl' (2) | IRhd |
| × ***medioluteus*** (13) | CBro CQua NMin |
| 'Medusa' (8) | CBro GCro |
| 'Melancholy' (1) | CQua |
| 'Melbury' (2) | CQua |
| 'Meldrum' (1) | CQua |
| 'Memento' (1) | CQua |
| 'Menabilly' (4) | CQua |
| 'Mên-an-Tol' (2) | CQua |
| 'Menehay' (11a) ♀H4 | CQua |
| 'Mereworth' (2) | CQua |
| 'Merlin' (3) ♀H4 | CQua LAma SDeJ |
| 'Merry Bells' (5) | CQua |
| 'Merrymeet' (4) | CQua |
| 'Mersing' (3) | CQua |
| 'Merthan' (9) | CQua |
| 'Michaels Gold' (2) | CQua |
| 'Midas Touch' (1) | CQua |
| 'Midget' | see *N. nanus* 'Midget' |
| 'Mike Pollock' (8) | CQua |
| 'Milan' (9) | CQua |
| 'Millennium Sunrise' (2) | CQua |
| 'Millennium Sunset' (2) | CQua |
| 'Milly's Magic' (2) | CQua |
| Minicycla Group (6) | ECho MSSP WAbe |
| ***minimus*** misapplied | see *N. asturiensis* |
| 'Minnow' (8) ♀H3 | CAvo CBro CFFs CMea CQua ECho EPfP EPot ERCP GKev LAma MBri NBir SDeJ SPer SPhx |
| ***minor*** (13) ♀H4 | CBro CQua ECha ECho EPot GKev LAma NMin WCot WShi |
| - 'Douglasbank' (1) | ITim |
| - 'Little Gem' (1) ♀H4 | CBro CQua CTri EPfP LAma SPhx |
| - var. ***pumilus*** 'Plenus' | see *N.* 'Rip van Winkle' |
| - Ulster form | IBlr MSSP |
| 'Mint Julep' (3) ♀H4 | SPhx |
| 'Minute Waltz' (6) | CQua |
| 'Mirar' (2) | CQua |
| 'Misquote' (1) | CQua |
| 'Miss Klein' | CQua NMin |
| 'Miss Muffit' (1) | CAvo CQua |
| 'Mission Bells' (5) ♀H4 | CQua IRhd SPhx |
| 'Mission Impossible' (11a) | CQua |

| |  |  |
|---|---|---|
| | 'Mist of Avalon' (4) **new** | CQua |
| | 'Misty Glen' (2) ♀H4 | CQua |
| | 'Misty Moon' (3) | CQua |
| | 'Mite' (6) ♀H4 | CBro CQua EPot LAma LLHF NMin |
| | 'Mithrel' (11a) | CQua |
| | 'Mitylene' (2) | CQua GCro |
| | 'Mitzy' | LLHF NMin |
| | 'Modern Art' (2) | CQua |
| | 'Molly Mop' (12) **new** | CQua |
| | 'Mondragon' (11a) | CQua |
| | 'Mongleath' (2) | CQua |
| | 'Monks Wood' (1) | CQua |
| | 'Monksilver' (3) | CQua |
| | 'Montclair' (2) | CQua |
| | 'Montego' (3) | CQua |
| | 'Montroig' (2) | IRhd |
| | 'Moon Dream' (1) | CQua |
| | 'Moon Ranger' (3) | CQua |
| | 'Moon Shadow' (3) | CQua |
| | 'Moon Valley' (2) | IRhd |
| | 'Moonstruck' (1) | CQua |
| | 'Morab' (1) | CQua |
| | 'Moralee' (4) | IRhd |
| | 'Morvah Lady' (5) | CQua |
| | 'Morval' (2) | CQua |
| | ***moschatus*** (13) ♀H4 | CBro CQua ECho EPot LAma NMin SPhx WCot WShi |
| | 'Motmot' | CQua |
| | 'Mount Fuji' (2) | CQua |
| | 'Mount Hood' (1) ♀H4 | EPfP GKev LAma NBir SDeJ SEND SPer |
| | 'Mount Rainier' (1) | CQua |
| | 'Movie Star' (2) | IRhd |
| | 'Mowser' (7) | CQua |
| | 'Mr Julian' (6) | CQua |
| | 'Mrs Langtry' (2) | GCro WShi |
| | 'Mrs R.O. Backhouse' (2) | CQua EBla WShi |
| | 'Mulatto' (1) | GCro |
| | 'Mullion' (3) | CQua |
| | 'Mulroy Bay' (1) | CQua IRhd |
| | 'Murlough' (9) | CQua |
| | 'Muscadet' (2) | CQua |
| | 'My Sunshine' (2) | CQua |
| | 'My Sweetheart' (3) | CQua |
| | 'Mystic' (3) | CQua |
| | 'Naivasha' (2) | IRhd |
| | 'Namraj' (2) | CQua |
| | 'Nancegollan' (7) | CBro CQua |
| | 'Nangiles' (4) | CQua |
| | 'Nanpee' (7) | CQua |
| | 'Nansidwell' (2) | CQua |
| | 'Nanstallon' (1) | CQua |
| § | ***nanus*** | CWCL |
| § | - 'Midget' (1) | CBro CQua ECho ERCP GKev LAma SKHP |
| | 'Narrative' (2) | IRhd |
| | 'Navarre' Gathorne-Hardy | see *N. asturiensis* 'Navarre' Gathorne-Hardy |
| | 'Nederburg' (1) | IRhd |
| | 'Neon Light' (2) | CQua |
| | 'Nessa' (7) **new** | CQua |
| | 'Nether Barr' (2) | CQua |
| | ***nevadensis*** (13) | SKHP |
| | 'New Hope' (3) | CQua |
| | 'New Life' (3) | CQua |
| | 'New Paris' (2) | CQua |
| | 'New Penny' (3) | CQua IRhd |
| | 'New World' (2) | CQua |
| | 'New-Baby' (7) | CQua CTca EPfP EPot NMin |
| | 'Newcastle' (1) | CQua |
| | 'Newcomer' (3) | CQua |
| | 'Night Music' (4) | CQua IRhd |
| | 'Nightcap' (1) | CQua |
| | 'Nirvana' (7) | CBro |
| | 'Niveth' (5) | CQua |
| § | ***nobilis*** (13) | CQua EPot |
| | - var. ***nobilis*** (13) | NMin |
| | 'Nonchalant' (3) | CQua IRhd |
| | 'Norma Jean' (2) | CQua |
| | 'Nor-nor' (2) | CBro |
| | 'North Liberty' (2) | CQua |
| | 'North Rim' (2) | CQua |
| | 'Noss Mayo' (6) | CBro CQua |
| | 'Notre Dame' (2) ♀H4 | CQua IRhd |
| | 'Numen Rose' (2) | IRhd |
| | Nylon Group (10) | CBro ECho EPot GEdr MSSP WCot |
| | - yellow-flowered (10) | ECho |
| | 'Oadby' (1) | CQua |
| | 'Oak Wood Sprite' (1) **new** | NMin |
| | 'Obdam' (4) | EBla SDeJ |
| | 'Obelisk' (11a) | CQua |
| | 'Obsession' (2) | CQua |
| | ***obvallaris*** (13) ♀H4 | CAvo CBro CFFs CQua CTca ECho EPfP EPot ERCP EWil GKev NMin SDeJ SPer SPhx WHer WShi |
| | 'Ocarino' (4) | CQua |
| | 'Ocean Blue' (2) | IRhd |
| | 'Odd Job' | CQua |
| | × ***odorus*** (13) | WShi |
| § | - 'Double Campernelle' (4) | CQua ECho SDeJ WShi |
| | - 'Plenus' (d) | ERCP |
| | 'Oecumene' (11a) | CQua |
| | 'Ohau Lights' (1) | CQua |
| | old pheasant's eye | see *N. poeticus* var. *recurvus* |
| | 'Ombersley' (1) | CQua |
| | 'Orange Tint' (2) | CQua |
| | 'Orange Walk' (3) | CQua IRhd |
| | 'Orangery' (11a) | EBla LAma |
| | 'Orbital Pink' (3) | IRhd |
| | 'Orchard Place' (3) | CQua |
| | 'Oregon Bells' (7) | CQua |
| | 'Oregon Pioneer' (2) | IRhd |
| | 'Orkney' (2) | CQua |
| | 'Ormeau' (2) ♀H4 | CQua |
| | 'Ornatus Maximus' (9) **new** | NMin |
| | 'Oryx' (7) ♀H4 | CQua |
| | 'Osceola' (2) | CQua |
| | 'Osmington' (2) | CQua |
| | 'Ouma' (1) | CQua |
| | 'Outline' (2) | IRhd |
| | 'Ouzel' (6) | CQua |
| | 'Owyhee' (2) | CQua |
| | 'Oykel' (3) | CQua |
| | 'Oz' (12) | CQua LLHF |
| | ***pachybolbus*** | NMin |
| | 'Pacific Coast' (8) ♀H4 | CQua EPfP LAma NMin |
| | 'Pacific Mist' (11a) | CQua |
| | 'Pacific Rim' (2) | CQua IRhd |
| | 'Painted Desert' (3) | CQua |
| | 'Palace Pink' (2) | IRhd |
| | 'Pale Sunlight' (2) | CQua |
| | ***pallidiflorus*** (13) | ECha |
| | 'Palmares' (11a) | CQua SDeJ |
| | 'Pamela Hubble' (2) | CQua |
| | 'Pamela Joan' (2) | CQua |
| | 'Pampaluna' (11a) | CQua |
| | 'Panache' (1) | CQua |
| | 'Pandemonium' (3) | IRhd |
| | ***panizzianus*** (13) | CQua |

| |  |  |
|---|---|---|
| | 'Panorama Pink' (3) | IRhd |
| | 'Paper White' | see *N. papyraceus* |
| | 'Paper White Grandiflorus' (8) | CQua EPfP MBri SPer |
| | 'Papillon Blanc' (11b) | ERCP |
| | 'Papua' (4) $\Upsilon^{H4}$ | CQua |
| § | ***papyraceus*** (13) | CAvo CQua CTca GKev LAma NMin |
| | 'Paradigm' (4) | IRhd |
| | 'Paramour' (4) | IRhd |
| | 'Parcpat' (7) | CBro |
| | 'Parisienne' (11a) | EBla |
| | 'Park Springs' (3) | CQua |
| | 'Parkdene' (2) | CQua |
| | 'Party Time' (2) | IRhd |
| | 'Passionale' (2) $\Upsilon^{H4}$ | CQua EPfP LAma NBir |
| | 'Pastiche' (2) | CQua |
| | 'Pat Brown' (2) **new** | CQua |
| | 'Patabundy' (2) | CQua |
| | 'Pathos' (3) | IRhd |
| | 'Patois' (9) | CQua IRhd |
| | 'Patrick Hacket' (1) $\Upsilon^{H4}$ | CQua |
| | 'Paula Cottell' (3) | NMin |
| | 'Pay Day' (1) | CQua |
| | 'Peach Prince' (4) | CQua |
| | 'Pearl Wedding' (3) | CQua |
| | 'Pearlshell' (11a) | CQua |
| | 'Peeping Tom' (6) $\Upsilon^{H4}$ | CBro ECho ERCP LAma SDeJ SRms |
| | 'Peggy's Gift' (3) | IRhd |
| | 'Pelynt' (3) | CQua |
| | 'Pemboa' (1) | CQua |
| | 'Pencrebar' (4) | CAvo CBro CHid CQua EPot LAma NMin SDeJ WShi |
| | 'Pend Oreille' (3) | CQua |
| | 'Pengarth' (2) | CQua |
| | 'Penjerrick' (9) | CQua |
| | 'Penkivel' (2) $\Upsilon^{H4}$ | CQua |
| | 'Pennance Mill' (2) | CQua |
| | 'Pennine Way' (1) | CQua |
| | 'Penny Perowne' (7) | CQua |
| | 'Pennyfield' (2) | CQua |
| | 'Penpol' (7) | CBro CQua |
| | 'Penril' (6) | CQua |
| | 'Penstraze' (7) | CQua |
| | 'Pentewan' (2) | CQua GCro |
| | 'Pentille' (1) | CQua |
| | 'Pentire' (11a) | CQua |
| | 'Penvale' | CQua |
| | 'Peppercorn' (6) | CQua |
| | 'Percuil' (6) | CQua |
| | 'Perdredda' (3) | CQua |
| | ***perez-chiscanoi*** (13) | SKHP |
| | 'Perimeter' (3) | CQua |
| | 'Peripheral Pink' (2) | CQua |
| | 'Perky' 1970 (6) | NMin |
| | 'Perlax' (11a) | CQua |
| | 'Perpetuation' (7) | CQua |
| | 'Personable' (2) | CQua |
| | 'Petanca' (5) | IRhd |
| | 'Peter Chown' (11a) **new** | CQua |
| | 'Petit Four' (4) | EBla LAma SDeJ |
| | 'Petrel' (5) | CBro CQua EPot ERCP GKev NMin SDeJ SPhx |
| | 'Phalarope' (6) | CQua |
| | 'Phantom' (11a) | CQua |
| | 'Phil's Gift' (1) | CQua |
| | 'Phinda' (2) | IRhd |
| | 'Phoenician' (2) | CQua |
| | 'Picatou' (3) | IRhd |
| | 'Picoblanco' (2) | CBro CQua NMin |
| | 'Pigeon' (2) | CQua |
| | 'Pineapple Prince' (2) $\Upsilon^{H4}$ | CQua |
| | 'Pink Angel' (7) | CQua |
| | 'Pink Champagne' (4) | CQua |
| | 'Pink Charm' (2) | CQua |
| | 'Pink China' (2) | CQua |
| | 'Pink Clover' (2) | CQua |
| | 'Pink Evening' (2) | CQua |
| | 'Pink Formal' (11a) | CQua |
| | 'Pink Gilt' (2) | IRhd |
| | 'Pink Glacier' (11a) | CQua |
| | 'Pink Holly' (11a) | CQua |
| | 'Pink Ice' (2) | CQua |
| | 'Pink Pageant' (4) | CQua IRhd |
| | 'Pink Paradise' (4) | CQua IRhd |
| | 'Pink Parasol' (1) | SDeJ |
| | 'Pink Perry' (2) | IRhd |
| | 'Pink Sapphire' (2) | CQua |
| | 'Pink Silk' (1) | CQua |
| | 'Pink Surprise' (2) | CQua |
| | 'Pink Tango' (11a) | CQua |
| | 'Pinza' (2) $\Upsilon^{H4}$ | CQua |
| | 'Pipe Major' (2) | CQua EPfP |
| | 'Pipers Barn' (7) | CQua |
| | 'Piper's End' (3) | CQua |
| | 'Piper's Gold' (1) | CQua |
| | 'Pipestone' (2) | CQua |
| | 'Pipit' (7) $\Upsilon^{H4}$ | CAvo CBro CFFs CMea CQua ECho EPfP EPot ERCP GAbr GKev LAma MBri MNrw NBir NMin SDeJ WShi |
| | 'Piraeus' (4) | IRhd |
| | 'Pismo Beach' (2) | CQua |
| | 'Pitchroy' (2) | CQua |
| | 'Pitt's Diamond' (3) | CQua |
| | 'Pixie's Sister' (7) $\Upsilon^{H4}$ | CQua NMin |
| | 'Pledge' (1) | NMin |
| | ***poeticus*** (13) | WHer |
| § | – var. ***hellenicus*** (13) | CBro CQua |
| | – old pheasant's eye | see *N. poeticus* var. *recurvus* |
| | – var. ***physaloides*** (13) | CQua |
| | – 'Plenus' misapplied | see *N.* 'Tamar Double White' |
| § | – 'Plenus' ambig. (4) | CBro CQua EPot ERCP GQui SDeJ WShi |
| § | – var. ***recurvus*** (13) $\Upsilon^{H4}$ | CArn CAvo CBro CFFs CQua CTca ECho EPfP ERCP GKev LAma NBir SDeJ SEND SPhx WShi |
| | 'Poet's Way' (9) | CQua |
| | 'Pol Crocan' (2) | CQua IRhd |
| | 'Pol Dornie' (2) | CQua |
| | 'Pol Voulin' (2) | CQua IRhd |
| | 'Polar Ice' (3) | CMea CQua LAma SDeJ SPhx |
| | 'Polar Morn' (3) | CQua |
| | 'Polglase' (8) | CBro |
| | 'Polgooth' (2) | CQua |
| | 'Polly's Pearl' (8) | CQua |
| | 'Polnesk' (7) | CBro |
| | 'Polonaise' (2) | CQua |
| | 'Polwheveral' (2) | CQua |
| | ***polyanthus*** from Morocco | WCot |
| | 'Pomona' (3) | GCro |
| | 'Pooka' (3) | IRhd |
| | 'Poppy's Choice' (4) | CQua |
| | 'Pops Legacy' (1) | CQua IRhd |
| | 'Port Noo' (3) **new** | CQua |
| | 'Porthchapel' (7) | CQua |
| | 'Portloe Bay' (3) | CQua |
| | 'Portrush' (3) | CQua |
| | 'Potential' (1) | CQua |
| | 'Powerstock' (2) | IRhd |
| | 'Praecox' (9) | CBro CQua |

| |  |  |
|---|---|---|
| | 'Prairie Fire' (3) | CQua IRhd |
| | 'Pratincole' (3) | IRhd |
| | 'Preamble' (1) | CQua |
| I | 'Precocious' (2) ♀H4 | CQua |
| | 'Premiere' (2) | CQua |
| | 'Presidential Pink' (2) | CQua |
| | 'Pretty Baby' (3) | CQua |
| | 'Pride of Cornwall' (8) | CBro CQua |
| | 'Primrose Beauty' (4) | CQua |
| | 'Princeps' (1) | CQua GCro |
| | 'Princess Zaide' (3) | CQua |
| | 'Princeton' (3) | CQua |
| | 'Printal' (11a) | SDeJ |
| | 'Prism' (2) | CQua |
| | 'Problem Child' (2) | IRhd |
| | 'Probus' (1) | CQua |
| | 'Professor Einstein' (2) | EPfP SDeJ |
| | 'Prologue' (1) | CQua |
| | 'Prototype' (6) | IRhd |
| | 'Proud Fellow' (1) | IRhd |
| | 'Proverbial Pink' (2) | IRhd |
| | 'Prussia Cove' (2) | CQua |
| | ***pseudonarcissus*** (13) ♀H4 | CHab CQua CRow EWil GKev LAma MMuc SEND SPhx WHer WShi |
| | - subsp. ***eugeniae*** | see *N. eugeniae* |
| | - subsp. ***nobilis*** | see *N. nobilis* |
| | - 'O'Mahoney' | see *N. pseudonarcissus* 'The O'Mahoney' |
| | - subsp. ***pseudonarcissus*** (4) | CQua |
| § | - 'The O'Mahoney' | WCot |
| | 'Ptolemy' (1) | GCro |
| | 'Pueblo' (7) | CQua SDeJ |
| | 'Pukenui' (4) **new** | CQua |
| | 'Pulsar' (2) | IRhd |
| | ***pumilus*** ambig. | CQua ECho NMin SDeJ WShi |
| | 'Punchline' (7) ♀H4 | CQua |
| | 'Puppet' (5) | CQua |
| | 'Purbeck' (3) ♀H4 | CQua IRhd |
| | 'Quail' (7) ♀H4 | CQua CTca EPfP GKev LAma LSou MBri |
| | 'Quasar' (2) ♀H4 | CQua |
| | Queen Anne's double daffodil | see *N.* 'Eystettensis' |
| | 'Queen Juliana' (1) | CQua |
| | 'Queen Mum' (1) | CQua |
| | 'Queen of Spain' (10) | CQua NMin |
| | 'Queen of the North' (3) **new** | GCro |
| | 'Queen's Guard' (1) | IRhd |
| | 'Quick Step' (7) | CQua |
| | 'Quiet Day' (2) | CQua |
| | 'Quiet Hero' (3) | IRhd |
| | 'Quiet Man' (1) | IRhd |
| | 'Radiant Gem' (8) | CQua |
| | ***radiiflorus*** (13) | EPot |
| | - var. ***poetarum*** (13) | CBro CQua GCro |
| | 'Radjel' (4) | CQua |
| | 'Rainbow' (2) ♀H4 | CQua SPer |
| | 'Rame Head' (1) | CQua |
| | 'Rameses' (2) | CQua |
| | 'Ransom' (4) | IRhd |
| | 'Raoul Wallenberg' (2) | EPfP |
| | 'Rapid Stride' (6) | IRhd |
| | 'Rapture' (6) ♀H4 | CBro CQua IRhd NMin |
| | 'Rashee' (1) | CQua |
| | 'Raspberry Ring' (2) | CQua |
| | 'Rathowen Gold' (1) | CQua |
| | 'Ravenhill' (3) | CQua |
| | 'Rebekah' (4) | CQua |

| |  |  |
|---|---|---|
| | 'Recital' (2) | CQua |
| | 'Red Coat' (2) | CQua |
| | 'Red Devon' (2) ♀H4 | CQua SDeJ SPer |
| | 'Red Era' (3) | CQua |
| | 'Red Legend' (2) | CQua |
| | 'Red Lips' (2) | CQua |
| | 'Red Reed' (1) | IRhd |
| | 'Red Socks' (6) | CQua |
| | 'Red Spartan' (2) | CQua |
| | 'Refrain' (2) | CQua |
| | 'Regal Bliss' (2) | CQua |
| | 'Reggae' (6) ♀H4 | CBro CQua WShi |
| | 'Rembrandt' (1) | CQua |
| | 'Rendezvous Caye' (2) | CQua |
| | 'Repertoire' (3) **new** | IRhd |
| | 'Replete' (4) | CQua EBla |
| | 'Reprieve' (3) | CQua |
| | ***requienii*** | see *N. assoanus* |
| | 'Resistasol' (1) | IRhd |
| | 'Resolute' (2) **new** | GCro |
| | 'Reverse Image' (11a) | CQua |
| | 'Ribald' (2) | IRhd |
| | 'Ridgecrest' (3) | IRhd |
| | ***rifanus*** | see *N. romieuxii* subsp. *romieuxii* var. *rifanus* |
| | 'Rijnveld's Early Sensation' (1) ♀H4 | CAvo CBro CFFs CMea CQua ECha ERCP SEND WCot |
| | 'Rikki' (7) | CBro CQua NMin |
| | 'Rima' (1) | CQua |
| | 'Rimmon' (3) | CQua |
| | 'Ring Fence' (3) | IRhd |
| | 'Ringhaddy' (3) | IRhd |
| | 'Ringing Bells' (5) | CQua |
| | 'Ringleader' (2) | CQua |
| | 'Ringmaster' (2) | CQua |
| | 'Ringmer' (3) | CQua |
| | 'Rio Bravo' (2) | IRhd |
| | 'Rio Gusto' (2) | IRhd |
| | 'Rio Lobo' (2) | IRhd |
| | 'Rio Rondo' (2) | IRhd |
| | 'Rio Rouge' (2) | IRhd |
| § | 'Rip van Winkle' (4) | CAvo CBro CQua CTca EBla EPfP EPot ERCP GCro IFro LAma MBri SDeJ SGar WShi |
| | 'Rippling Waters' (5) ♀H4 | CBro CQua LAma |
| | 'Ristin' (1) | CQua |
| | 'Rival' (6) | CQua |
| | 'River Dance' (2) | IRhd |
| | 'River Queen' (2) | CQua IRhd |
| | 'Rockall' (3) | CQua |
| | 'Rockery White' (1) | NMin |
| | 'Rocoza' (2) | IRhd |
| | 'Roger' (6) | CBro CQua |
| | 'Rogue' (2) | CBro |
| | 'Romance' (2) ♀H4 | LAma |
| § | 'Romanus' (4) | CQua |
| | ***romieuxii*** (13) ♀H2-3 | CBro CDes CPBP ITim LRHS MSSP SCnR WCot |
| | - JCA 805 | EPot LWst |
| | - SB&L 237 | WCot |
| | - SF 370 | WCot |
| | - subsp. ***albidus*** (13) | ECho EPot WCot |
| | - - SF 110 | WCot |
| § | - - var. ***zaianicus*** (13) | ECho |
| | - - - SB&L 82 | MSSP WCot |
| I | - - - f. ***lutescens*** (13) | GEdr |
| § | - 'Atlas Gold' (10) | EPot GEdr SCnR |
| § | - 'Joy Bishop' (10) | GEdr NMen SCnR |
| § | - 'Julia Jane' (10) | ECho EPot GKev ITim NMin SCnR WCot |

|  |  |
|---|---|
| - subsp. ***romieuxii*** (13) | GKev |
| § - - var. ***mesatlanticus*** (13) | WCot |
| § - - var. ***rifanus*** (13) | ECho GKev |
| - - B 8929 | WCot |
| § - 'Treble Chance' (10) | EPot |
| 'Rory's Glen' (2) | CQua |
| 'Rosannor Gold' (11a) | CQua |
| 'Roscarrick' (6) | CQua |
| 'Rose of May' (4) | CQua WShi |
| 'Rose of Tralee' (2) | CQua |
| 'Rose Royale' (2) | CQua |
| 'Rose Sheen' (2) | CQua |
| 'Rose Villa' (2) | CQua |
| 'Rosedown' (5) | CBro |
| 'Rosemerryn' (2) | CQua |
| 'Rosemoor Gold' $\mathbb{Y}^{H4}$ | CBro CQua |
| 'Rosemullion' (4) | CQua |
| 'Rosevine' (3) | CQua |
| 'Roseworthy' (2) | EBla |
| 'Rosy Trumpet' (1) | CBro |
| 'Rosy Wonder' (2) | CQua |
| 'Round Oak' (1) new | CQua |
| 'Roxton' (4) | IRhd |
| 'Royal Ballet' (2) | CQua |
| 'Royal Connection' (8) | CQua |
| 'Royal Marine' (2) | CQua |
| 'Royal Princess' (3) | CQua |
| 'Royal Regiment' (2) | CQua |
| 'Rubh Mor' (2) | CQua |
| 'Ruby Red' (2) | CQua |
| 'Ruby Rose' (4) | IRhd |
| 'Ruby Wedding' (2) | IRhd |
| 'Rubythroat' (2) | CQua |
| 'Ruddy Duck' | IRhd |
| 'Ruddy Rascal' (2) | IRhd |
| 'Rugulosus' (7) $\mathbb{Y}^{H4}$ | CBro CQua ECho |
| * 'Rugulosus Flore Pleno' (d) | ECho |
| 'Rumpus' (3) | IRhd |
| 'Runkerry' (4) | IRhd |
| ***rupicola*** (13) | CBro CQua CWCL ECho EPot GKev MSSP NMen NMin NWCA SCnR SPhx |
| § - subsp. ***watieri*** (13) | CBro CQua ECho EPot GKev ITim MSSP NMin SPhx WCot |
| 'Rustom Pasha' (2) | CQua GCro |
| 'Rytha' (2) | CQua |
| 'Saberwing' (5) | CQua |
| 'Sabine Hay' (3) | CQua ERCP |
| 'Sabrosa' (7) $\mathbb{Y}^{H4}$ | CBro CQua NMin |
| 'Sacré Coeur' (2) | IRhd |
| 'Sagana' (9) | CQua |
| 'Sagitta' (1) $\mathbb{Y}^{H4}$ | CQua |
| 'Sailboat' (7) $\mathbb{Y}^{H4}$ | CQua SPer |
| 'Saint Agnes' (8) | CQua |
| 'Saint Budock' (1) | CQua |
| 'Saint Day' (5) | CQua |
| 'Saint Dilpe' (2) | CQua |
| 'Saint Keverne' (2) $\mathbb{Y}^{H4}$ | CQua EPfP SDeJ SEND SPer |
| 'Saint Keyne' (8) | CQua |
| 'Saint Olaf' (3) new | GCro |
| 'Saint Patrick's Day' (2) | CQua EBla LAma SDeJ |
| 'Saint Peter' (4) | CQua |
| 'Saint Petroc' (9) | CQua |
| 'Saint Piran' (7) | CQua |
| 'Salakee' (2) | CQua |
| 'Salcey Forest' (1) | CQua |
| 'Salmon Trout' (2) | CQua |
| 'Salome' (2) $\mathbb{Y}^{H4}$ | CQua EBla LAma NBir SDeJ SEND |
| 'Salute' (2) | CQua |

|  |  |
|---|---|
| 'Samantha' (4) | CQua |
| 'Samaria' (3) | CBro |
| 'Sancerre' (11a) | CQua |
| 'Sandycove' (2) | CQua |
| 'Santa Claus' (4) | CQua |
| 'Sarah Dear' (2) | CQua |
| 'Sarah Markillie' (11a) new | CQua |
| 'Sargeant's Caye' (1) | CQua |
| 'Satchmo' (1) | CQua |
| 'Satsuma' (1) | CQua |
| 'Saturn' (3) | CQua |
| 'Savoir Faire' (2) | IRhd |
| ***scaberulus*** (13) | EPot |
| 'Scarlet Chord' (2) | CQua |
| 'Scarlet Elegance' (2) | CQua |
| 'Scarlet Gem' (8) | SDeJ |
| 'Scarlett O'Hara' (2) | CQua |
| 'Scented Breeze' (2) | IRhd |
| 'Scilly Spring' (8) | CAvo |
| 'Scilly White' (8) | CQua |
| 'Scorrier' (2) | CQua |
| 'Scrumpy' (2) | CQua |
| 'Sea Dream' (3) | CQua |
| 'Sea Gift' (7) | CBro |
| 'Sea Green' (9) | CQua |
| 'Sea Legend' (2) | CQua |
| 'Sea Princess' (3) | CQua |
| 'Sea Shanty' (2) | IRhd |
| 'Seagull' (3) | CAvo CQua GCro LAma WShi |
| 'Sealing Wax' (2) | CQua |
| 'Segovia' (3) $\mathbb{Y}^{H4}$ | CBro CQua EBla EPot LAma NMin SCnR SGar SPer SPhx |
| 'Sempre Avanti' (2) | LAma MBri SDeJ |
| 'Seraglio' (3) | CQua |
| 'Serena Beach' (4) | IRhd |
| 'Serena Lodge' (4) $\mathbb{Y}^{H4}$ | CQua IRhd |
| ***serotinus*** (13) | ECho EPot GKev |
| 'Sextant' (6) | CQua |
| 'Shangani' (2) | IRhd |
| 'Sheelagh Rowan' (2) | CQua IRhd |
| 'Sheer Joy' (6) | CQua IRhd |
| 'Shepherd's Hey' (7) | CQua EPfP |
| 'Sherborne' (4) $\mathbb{Y}^{H4}$ | CQua |
| 'Sherpa' (1) | IRhd |
| 'Sheviock' (2) | CQua |
| 'Shindig' (2) | IRhd |
| 'Shining Light' (2) | CQua |
| 'Shockwave' (2) | CQua |
| 'Shortcake' (2) | CQua |
| 'Shrimp Boat' (11a) | IRhd |
| 'Sidhe' (5) | CQua |
| 'Sidley' (3) | CQua IRhd |
| 'Signet Ring' (3) new | IRhd |
| 'Signorina' (2) | IRhd |
| 'Silent Valley' (1) $\mathbb{Y}^{H4}$ | CQua |
| 'Silk Cut' (2) | CQua |
| 'Silkwood' (3) | CQua |
| 'Silver Bells' (5) | CQua |
| 'Silver Chimes' (8) | CAvo CBro CQua CTca ECho EPfP LAma NBir SDeJ SPhx |
| 'Silver Convention' (1) | CQua |
| 'Silver Crystal' (3) | IRhd |
| 'Silver Kiwi' (2) | CQua |
| 'Silver Minx' (1) | CQua |
| 'Silver Plate' (11a) | CQua |
| 'Silver Shell' (11a) | CQua |
| 'Silver Smiles' (7) | SPhx |
| 'Silver Standard' (2) | CQua |
| 'Silver Surf' (2) | CQua IRhd |
| 'Silversmith' (2) | CQua |

| | |
|---|---|
| 'Silverthorne' (3) | CQua |
| 'Silverwood' (3) | CQua IRhd |
| 'Singing Pub' (3) | IRhd |
| 'Sinopel' (3) | LAma SDeJ |
| 'Sir Samuel' (2) | CQua |
| 'Sir Watkin' (2) | CQua GCro |
| 'Sir Winston Churchill' (4) 🏆H4 | CQua EPfP LAma SDeJ SPer |
| 'Sissy' (6) | CQua |
| 'Skerry' (2) | CQua |
| 'Skilliwidden' (2) 🏆H4 | CQua |
| 'Skookum' (3) | CQua |
| 'Skywalker' (2) | IRhd |
| 'Slieveboy' (1) | CQua |
| 'Slipstream' (6) | IRhd |
| 'Small Fry' (1) | CQua |
| 'Small Talk' (1) 🏆H4 | CQua NMin |
| 'Smiling Maestro' (2) | CQua |
| 'Smokey Bear' (4) | CQua |
| 'Smooth Sails' (3) | CQua |
| 'Snipe' (6) | CQua NMin WShi |
| 'Snoopie' (6) | CQua |
| 'Snow Bunting' (7) | CBro |
| 'Snowcrest' (3) | CQua |
| 'Snowshill' (2) | CQua |
| 'Soft Focus' (2) | IRhd |
| 'Solar System' (3) | IRhd |
| 'Solar Tan' (3) | CQua |
| 'Soleil d'Or' (8) | CQua |
| 'Solera' (2) | IRhd |
| 'Solferique' (2) | CQua |
| 'Soloist' (2) | IRhd |
| 'Solveig's Song' (12) | WAbe |
| 'Sonata' (9) | CQua |
| 'Songket' (2) | CQua |
| 'Sophie Girl' (2) | CQua |
| 'Soprano' (2) | CQua IRhd |
| 'Sorcerer' (3) | CQua |
| 'South Street' (2) | CQua |
| 'Southease' (2) | CQua |
| 'Southern Gem' (2) **new** | GCro |
| 'Spaniards Inn' (4) | CQua |
| 'Sparkling Tarts' (8) | CQua |
| 'Sparnon' (11a) | CQua |
| 'Sparrow' (6) | CQua |
| 'Special Envoy' (2) 🏆H4 | CQua |
| 'Speenogue' (1) | IRhd |
| 'Spellbinder' (1) 🏆H4 | CQua MBri |
| 'Spencer Tracy' | CQua |
| 'Spin Doctor' (3) | IRhd |
| 'Spindletop' (3) 🏆H4 | IRhd |
| 'Spirit of Rame' (3) | CQua |
| 'Split Image' (2) | IRhd |
| 'Split Vote' (11a) | IRhd |
| 'Sportsman' (2) | CQua |
| 'Spring Dawn' (2) | EPfP LSou SPer |
| 'Spring Glory' (1) **new** | GCro |
| 'Spring Morn' (2) | IRhd |
| 'Spring Sunset' (2) | IRhd |
| 'Spun Honey' (4) | CQua |
| 'Stadium' (2) | LAma |
| 'Stainless' (2) | SPhx |
| 'Stann Creek' (1) | CQua |
| 'Stanway' (3) | CQua |
| 'Star Glow' (2) | CQua |
| 'Star Quality' (3) | IRhd |
| 'Starfire' (7) | CQua |
| 'State Express' (2) | CQua |
| 'Steenbok' (3) | IRhd |
| 'Stella' (2) | GCro GKev WShi |

| | | |
|---|---|---|
| | 'Stella Glow' (3) | IRhd |
| | 'Stenalees' (6) | CQua |
| | 'Step Child' (6) | CQua |
| | 'Step Forward' (7) | CQua |
| | 'Stilton' (9) | CQua GCro |
| | 'Stinger' (2) | CQua |
| | 'Stint' (5) 🏆H4 | CBro CQua SPhx |
| | 'Stocken' (7) | CBro CQua MSSP NMin |
| | 'Stoke Charity' (2) | CQua |
| | 'Stoke Doyle' (2) | CQua |
| | 'Stormy Weather' (1) | CQua |
| | 'Stratosphere' (7) 🏆H4 | CQua NMin |
| | 'Strines' (2) | CQua |
| | 'Suave' (3) | CQua |
| | 'Subtle Shades' (2) | IRhd |
| | 'Sugar and Spice' (3) | CQua |
| | 'Sugar Bird' (2) | IRhd |
| | 'Sugar Cups' (8) | CQua |
| | 'Sugar Loaf' (4) | CQua |
| | 'Sugarbush' (7) | CBro WShi |
| | 'Suisgill' (4) | CQua |
| | 'Sukey' (6) **new** | CQua |
| § | 'Sulphur Phoenix' (4) | CQua GCro WShi |
| | 'Summer Solstice' (3) | IRhd |
| | 'Sumo Jewel' (6) | CQua |
| | 'Sun Disc' (7) 🏆H4 | CBro CMea CQua CSam CTri ECho GKev LAma LSou MBri NMin SDeJ WShi |
| | 'Sunday Chimes' (5) | CQua |
| | 'Sundial' (7) | CBro CQua GKev LAma NMin |
| | 'Sunrise' (3) | CQua GCro |
| | 'Sunstroke' (2) | CQua |
| | 'Suntory' (3) | CQua |
| | 'Suntrap' (2) | IRhd |
| | 'Surfside' (6) 🏆H4 | CQua |
| | 'Surprise Packet' (2) | IRhd |
| | 'Surrey' (2) | CQua |
| | 'Suzie Dee' (6) | IRhd |
| | 'Suzie's Sister' (6) | IRhd |
| | 'Suzy' (7) 🏆H4 | CBro SDeJ |
| | 'Swaledale' (2) | CQua |
| | 'Swallow' (6) | CQua LAma SDeJ |
| | 'Swallow Wing' (6) | IRhd |
| | 'Swanpool' (3) | CQua |
| | 'Swanvale' (1) | CQua |
| | 'Swedish Fjord' (2) | CQua |
| | 'Sweet Blanche' (7) | CQua |
| | 'Sweet Lorraine' (2) | CQua |
| | 'Sweet Memory' (2) | CQua |
| | 'Sweet Pepper' (7) | CBro |
| | 'Sweet Sue' (3) | CQua |
| | 'Sweetness' (7) 🏆H4 | CAvo CBro CFFs CQua LAma WPtf WShi |
| | 'Swift Arrow' (6) 🏆H4 | CQua |
| | 'Swing Wing' (6) | CQua |
| | 'Sydling' (5) | CQua |
| I | 'Sylph' G.E. Mitsch (1) | CQua |
| | 'Taffeta' (10) | CBro WCot |
| | 'Tahiti' (4) 🏆H4 | CQua EPfP LAma SDeJ |
| | × ***taitii*** | CAvo CQua NMin |
| | 'Talgarth' (2) | CQua |
| § | 'Tamar Double White' | CBro |
| | 'Tamar Fire' (4) 🏆H4 | CQua |
| | 'Tamar Lad' (2) | CQua |
| | 'Tamar Lass' (3) | CQua |
| | 'Tamar Snow' (2) | CQua |
| | 'Tamara' (2) | CQua |
| | 'Tangent' (2) | CQua |
| | 'Tarlatan' (10) | CBro |
| | 'Tarnished Gold' (2) | CQua |

| |  |  |
|---|---|---|
| | 'Tasgem' (4) | CQua |
| | 'Taslass' (4) | CQua |
| | 'Tater-du' (5) | CQua |
| | ***tazetta*** (13) | ECho |
| | - subsp. ***italicus*** from France | SEND |
| § | - subsp. ***lacticolor*** (13) | CQua ERCP LAma SDeJ |
| § | - - 'Grand Monarque' (8) | CBro CQua |
| | - subsp. ***ochroleucus*** (13) | CQua |
| * | - var. ***odoratus*** | CQua NMin WPtf |
| | 'Teal' (1) | CQua |
| | 'Tehidy' (3) | CQua |
| § | 'Telamonius Plenus' (4) | CAvo CBro CQua IGor SEND WCot WShi |
| | 'Temba' (1) | IRhd |
| | 'Temple Cloud' (4) | IRhd |
| | ***tenuifolius*** | see *N. bulbocodium* subsp. *bulbocodium* var. *tenuifolius* |
| | × ***tenuior*** (13) | NMin |
| | 'Terracotta' (2) | CQua IRhd |
| | 'Terrapin' (3) | IRhd |
| | 'Tête-à-tête' (12) ♀H4 | CAvo CBro CFFs CHar CQua CTca CWCL EPfP EPot ERCP GAbr GKev LAma LRHS LSou MBri MNHC SDeJ SEND SPer |
| | 'Texas' (4) | CQua GCro |
| | 'Thalia' (5) | CAvo CBro CFFs CQua CTca EPfP ERCP GKev LAma MBri MCot NBir NHol SDeJ SEND SPer SPhx WShi |
| | 'The Alliance' (6) ♀H4 | CBro CQua |
| | 'The Caley' (2) **new** | CQua |
| | 'The Grange' (1) | CQua |
| | 'The Knave' (6) | CQua |
| | 'The Little Gentleman' (6) | NMin |
| | 'The O'Mahoney' | see *N. pseudonarcissus* 'The O'Mahoney' |
| | 'Thistin' (1) | IRhd |
| | 'Thoresby' (3) | CQua |
| | 'Thoughtful' (5) | CBro CQua |
| | 'Tibet' (2) | CQua |
| | 'Tickled Pink' (11a) **new** | IRhd |
| | 'Tideford' (2) | CQua |
| | 'Tidy Tippet' (2) | IRhd |
| | 'Tiercel' (1) | CQua |
| | 'Tiffany Jade' (3) | CQua |
| | 'Tiger Moth' (6) | CQua |
| | 'Timolin' (3) | CQua |
| | 'Tinderbox' (2) | IRhd |
| | 'Tinhay' (7) | CQua |
| | 'Tiny Bubbles' (12) **new** | NMin |
| | 'Tiritomba' (11a) | CQua |
| | 'Titania' (6) | CQua |
| | 'Tittle-tattle' (7) | CQua |
| | 'Toby' (2) | SDeJ |
| | 'Toby the First' (6) | CAvo CQua |
| | 'Tommora Gold' (2) | CQua |
| | 'Tommy White' (2) | CQua |
| | 'Top Hit' (11a) | CQua |
| | 'Topolino' (1) ♀H4 | CAvo CBro CFFs CQua EPot LAma |
| | 'Toretta' (3) | IRhd |
| | 'Torianne' (2) ♀H4 | CQua |
| | 'Torridon' (2) | CQua |
| | 'Toto' (12) ♀H4 | CBro CQua ERCP MBri SPhx |
| | 'Tracey' (6) ♀H4 | CQua LAma |
| | 'Treasure Hunt' (2) | IRhd |
| | 'Trebah' (2) ♀H4 | CQua |
| | 'Treble Chance' | see *N. romieuxii* 'Treble Chance' |
| | 'Treble Two' (7) | CQua |
| | 'Trecara' (3) | CQua |
| | 'Trefusis' (1) | CQua |
| | 'Trehane' (6) | CQua |
| | 'Trelawney Gold' (2) | CQua |
| | 'Trelissick' | CQua |
| | 'Tremough Dale' (11a) | CQua |
| | 'Trena' (6) ♀H4 | CQua ERCP NMin |
| | 'Trendy Trail' (3) | IRhd |
| | 'Trentagh' (3) **new** | IRhd |
| | 'Trenwith' (1) **new** | CQua |
| | 'Tresamble' (5) | CBro CQua LAma SDeJ |
| | 'Trevaunance' (6) | CQua |
| | 'Treverva' (6) | CQua |
| | 'Treviddo' (2) | CQua |
| | 'Trevithian' (7) ♀H4 | CAby CBro CQua EBla LAma SDeJ WShi |
| | 'Trewarvas' (2) | CQua |
| | 'Trewirgie' (6) | CQua |
| | 'Trewoon' (4) | CQua |
| | ***triandrus*** var. ***albus*** | see *N. triandrus* subsp. *triandrus* var. *triandrus* |
| | - subsp. ***triandrus*** (13) | MSSP |
| § | - - var. ***triandrus*** (13) | CQua CWCL |
| | 'Tricollet' (11a) | SDeJ |
| | 'Trident' (3) | CQua |
| | 'Trielfin' (5) | IRhd |
| | 'Trigonometry' (11a) ♀H4 | CQua |
| | 'Tripartite' (11a) ♀H4 | CQua GKev NMin SDeJ |
| | 'Triple Crown' (3) ♀H4 | CQua IRhd |
| | 'Tristram' (2) | CQua |
| | 'Tropic Isle' (4) | CQua |
| | 'Tropical Heat' (2) | IRhd |
| | 'Trousseau' (1) | CQua |
| | 'Troutbeck' (3) | CQua |
| | 'Tru' (3) | CQua |
| | 'Truculent' (3) | CQua |
| | 'Trueblood' (3) | IRhd |
| | 'Trumpet Warrior' (1) ♀H4 | CQua IRhd |
| | 'Tryst' (2) | CQua |
| | 'Tudor Minstrel' (2) | CQua |
| | 'Tuesday's Child' (5) ♀H4 | CQua |
| | 'Tullynagee' (3) | IRhd |
| | 'Tunis' (2) **new** | GCro |
| | 'Turncoat' (6) | CQua |
| | 'Tutankhamun' (2) | CQua |
| | 'Tweeny' (2) | CQua |
| | 'Twink' (4) | CQua |
| | 'Tyee' (2) | CQua |
| | 'Tyrian Rose' (2) | CQua IRhd |
| | 'Tyrone Gold' (1) ♀H4 | CQua IRhd |
| | 'Tyrree' (1) | IRhd |
| | 'Tywara' (1) | CQua |
| | 'Ulster Bank' (3) | CQua |
| | 'Ulster Bride' (4) | CQua |
| | 'Ultimus' (2) | CQua |
| | 'Uncle Bill' (1) | CQua |
| | 'Uncle Duncan' (1) | CQua IRhd |
| | 'Unique' (4) ♀H4 | CQua EBla LAma SDeJ |
| | 'Unsurpassable' (1) | CQua GCro LAma |
| | 'Upalong' (12) | CQua |
| | 'Upshot' (3) | CQua |
| | 'Urchin' (2) | IRhd |
| | 'Utiku' (6) | CQua |
| | 'Vahu' (2) | CQua |
| | 'Val d'Incles' (3) | CQua IRhd |
| | 'Valdrome' (11a) | CQua EBla |
| | 'Valinor' (2) | CQua |
| | 'Valley Dew' (2) | CQua |
| | 'Valley Glow' (2) | CQua |
| | 'Van Sion' | see *N.* 'Telamonius Plenus' |

| | |
|---|---|
| 'Vanellus' (11a) $\Upsilon^{H4}$ | IRhd |
| 'Vantage' (2) **new** | CQua |
| 'Vaticaan' (1) | SDeJ |
| 'Velvet Spring' (2) | CQua |
| 'Vendell' (3) **new** | IRhd |
| 'Veneration' (1) | CQua |
| 'Verdin' (7) | CQua |
| 'Verger' (3) | LAma MBri SDeJ |
| 'Vernal Prince' (3) $\Upsilon^{H4}$ | CQua |
| 'Verona' (3) $\Upsilon^{H4}$ | CQua |
| 'Verran Rose' (2) | IRhd |
| 'Vers Libre' (9) | CQua |
| 'Version' (1) | IRhd |
| 'Vice-President' (2) $\Upsilon^{H4}$ | CQua |
| 'Victoria' (1) | CQua |
| 'Victorious' (2) | CQua |
| 'Vienna Woods' (9) **new** | CQua |
| 'Vigil' (1) $\Upsilon^{H4}$ | CQua |
| 'Viking' (1) $\Upsilon^{H4}$ | CQua |
| 'Village Green' (3) **new** | IRhd |
| 'Violetta' (2) | CQua |
| 'Virginia Waters' (3) | CQua |
| 'Vivash' (4) **new** | IRhd |
| 'Volare' (2) | CQua |
| 'Volcanic Rim' (3) | IRhd |
| 'Vulcan' (2) $\Upsilon^{H4}$ | CQua |
| 'W.P. Milner' (1) | CAvo CBro CQua EBla EPfP EPot ERCP LAma NMin SDeJ SEND SMrm SPhx WShi |
| 'Wadavers' (2) | CQua |
| 'Waif' (6) | CQua |
| 'Waldon Pond' (3) | CQua |
| 'Waldorf Astoria' (4) | CQua IRhd |
| 'Walton' (7) | CQua |
| 'War Dance' (3) | IRhd |
| 'Warbler' (6) $\Upsilon^{H4}$ | CQua LAma NMin |
| 'Warm Day' (2) | IRhd |
| 'Warm Welcome' (2) | IRhd |
| 'Warmington' (3) | CQua |
| 'Watamu' (3) | IRhd |
| 'Waterperry' (7) | CBro LAma SEND |
| 'Watership Down' (2) | CQua |
| 'Watersmeet' (4) | CQua |
| ***watieri*** | see *N. rupicola* subsp. *watieri* |
| 'Wave' (4) | CQua |
| 'Wavelength' (3) | IRhd |
| 'Wavertree' | see *N. asturiensis* 'Wavertree' |
| 'Waxwing' (5) | CQua |
| 'Wayward Lad' (3) | IRhd |
| 'Wee Bee' (1) | CQua |
| 'Weena' (2) | CQua |
| 'Welcome' (2) | CQua |
| 'Welsh Rugby Union' (1) **new** | CQua |
| 'West Post' (3) | IRhd |
| 'Westward' (4) | CQua |
| 'Whang-hi' (6) | CQua |
| 'Wheal Bush' (4) | CQua |
| 'Wheal Coates' (7) $\Upsilon^{H4}$ | CQua |
| 'Wheal Honey' (1) | CQua |
| 'Wheal Jane' (2) | CQua |
| 'Wheal Kitty' (7) | CQua |
| 'Wheal Rose' (4) | CQua |
| 'Wheatear' (6) | CQua IRhd NMin |
| 'Whetstone' (1) | CQua |
| 'Whisky Galore' (2) | CQua |
| 'Whisky Mac' (2) | CQua |
| 'White Emperor' (1) | CQua GCro |
| 'White Empress' (1) | CQua |
| 'White Giant' **new** | GKev |
| 'White Ideal' (1) | CQua |
| 'White Lady' (3) | CAvo CFFs CQua GCro LAma WShi |
| 'White Lion' (4) $\Upsilon^{H4}$ | CQua LAma |
| 'White Majesty' (1) | CQua |
| 'White Marvel' (4) | CQua |
| 'White Nile' (2) | CQua |
| 'White Prince' (1) | CQua |
| 'White Star' (1) | CQua |
| 'White Tea' (2) | CQua |
| 'White Tie' (3) | CQua |
| 'Wicklow Hills' (3) | CQua |
| 'Widgeon' (2) | CQua |
| 'Wild Honey' (2) | CQua |
| 'Will Scarlett' (2) | CQua |
| ***willkommii*** (13) | CBro CQua MSSP NMin |
| 'Wimbledon County Girl' (2) $\Upsilon^{H4}$ | CQua |
| 'Wind Song' (2) | CQua |
| 'Winged Victory' (6) | CQua |
| 'Winholm Jenni' (3) | CQua |
| 'Winifred van Graven' (3) | CQua |
| 'Winter Waltz' (6) | CQua |
| 'Wisley' (6) $\Upsilon^{H4}$ **new** | CQua ERCP |
| 'Witch Doctor' (3) | IRhd |
| 'Witch Hunt' (4) | IRhd |
| 'Woodcock' (6) | CQua |
| 'Woodland Prince' (3) | CQua |
| 'Woodland Star' (3) | CQua |
| 'Woodley Vale' (2) | CQua |
| 'Woolsthorpe' (2) | CQua |
| 'World Class' (5) | CQua |
| 'Xit' (3) | CAvo CBro CQua GKev NMin SPhx |
| 'Xunantunich' (2) | CQua IRhd |
| 'Yellow Belles' (5) | IRhd |
| 'Yellow Cheerfulness' (4) $\Upsilon^{H4}$ | CQua EPfP LAma MBri SDeJ |
| 'Yellow Minnow' (8) | CQua |
| 'Yellow River' (1) | LAma |
| 'Yellow Xit' (3) | CQua NMin |
| 'Yoley's Pond' (2) | CQua |
| 'York Minster' (1) | CQua IRhd |
| 'Young American' (1) | CQua |
| 'Young Blood' (2) | CQua IRhd |
| 'Your Grace' (2) | CQua |
| 'Yum-Yum' (3) | IRhd |
| ***zaianicus*** | see *N. romieuxii* subsp. *albidus* var. *zaianicus* |
| 'Zekiah' (1) | CQua |
| 'Zion Canyon' (2) | CQua |
| 'Ziva' (8) | CAvo CFFs ERCP SDeJ |
| 'Zwynner' (2) | IRhd |

## *Nardostachys* (*Caprifoliaceae*)

| | |
|---|---|
| ***grandiflora*** | GPoy |

## *Nardus* (*Poaceae*)

| | |
|---|---|
| ***stricta*** | CRWN |

## *Nassauvia* (*Asteraceae*)

| | |
|---|---|
| ***gaudichaudii*** | WAbe |

## *Nassella* (*Poaceae*)

| | |
|---|---|
| ***cernua*** | WPGP |
| ***poeppigiana*** | see *Stipa poeppigiana* |
| ***pulchra*** | WPGP |
| ***tenuissima*** | see *Stipa tenuissima* |
| ***trichotoma*** | CKno CMea EHoe EPPr SLim SPoG WHal WPGP |

## *Nasturtium* (*Brassicaceae*)

| | |
|---|---|
| 'Banana Split' | CCCN |
| ***officinale*** | EWil MSKA SVic SWat |

## Natal plum see *Carissa macrocarpa*

## *Nauplius* (*Asteraceae*)

| | |
|---|---|
| ***sericeus*** | CSpe |

## nectarine see *Prunus persica* var. *nectarina*

## *Nectaroscordum* (*Alliaceae*)

| | |
|---|---|
| sp. | WFoF |
| § ***siculum*** | CAvo CBre CBro CFFs CMea CTri CWCL ECho ELan ERCP GCra GKev LLWP LRHS MCot MLLN MWat NBPC NBir NChi NDov NLar SDeJ SGar SMrm SPer SPhx WBor WFar WHoo |
| § - subsp. ***bulgaricum*** | CAby CTca ECha EPfP EPot IBlr ITim LRHS MMoz MNrw NLar SPhx WAbb WCot WTin XLum |
| ***tripedale*** | CAvo CMea ECho |

## *Neillia* (*Rosaceae*)

| | |
|---|---|
| ***affinis*** | CDul CPLG EBee EPfP EWTr IDee LLHF LRHS NBid NLar SCoo SWvt WCot WDin |
| ***longiracemosa*** | see *N. thibetica* |
| ***sinensis*** | NLar |
| § ***thibetica*** | Widely available |
| ***thyrsiflora*** HWJ 505 | WCru |
| var. ***tunkinensis*** | |

## *Nelumbo* (*Nelumbonaceae*)

| | |
|---|---|
| ***nucifera*** | XBlo |

## *Nematanthus* (*Gesneriaceae*)

| | |
|---|---|
| 'Apres' | WDib |
| 'Black Magic' | WDib |
| 'Christmas Holly' | WDib |
| 'Freckles' | WDib |
| § ***gregarius*** ♀H1 | EBak SEND WDib |
| § - 'Golden West' (v) | WDib |
| - 'Variegatus' | see *N. gregarius* 'Golden West' |
| 'Lemon and Lime' | WDib |
| ***radicans*** | see *N. gregarius* |
| 'Tropicana' ♀H1 | WDib |

## *Nemesia* (*Scrophulariaceae*)

| | |
|---|---|
| Amelie = 'Fleurame'[PBR] | EPfP SPoG |
| (Aromatica Series) Aromatica Royal = 'Balaroyal'[PBR] | LAst |
| - Aromatica Deep Blue = 'Balardeblu' | NPri |
| - Aromatica Rose Pink = 'Balarropi'[PBR] | LAst NPri |
| Berries and Cream = 'Fleurbac'[PBR] | EPfP LBuc LSou MSCN MWea NPri SBrd SPoG |
| 'Blue Button' | LAst |
| § Bluebird = 'Hubbird'[PBR] | CHll |
| § ***caerulea*** | WPer |
| § ***denticulata*** ♀H3-4 | CPrp EPfP GBee LHop LRHS NEgg SAga SCoo SPoG WFar WFoF WHlf XLum |
| - 'Confetti' | see *N. denticulata* |
| - 'Maggie' | LBuc LRHS |
| 'Fleurie Blue' | EPfP SPoG |
| ***foetens*** | see *N. caerulea* |
| 'Fragrant Cloud' | ELan LSou MNrw |
| 'Fragrant Gem' | LSRN |
| ***fruticans*** misapplied | see *N. caerulea* |
| Golden Eye = 'Yateye'[PBR] | EPfP LSRN LSou MPnt SLon |
| Ice Pink = 'Fleuripi' | SPoG |
| 'Innocence' ♀H3 | CPrp MAsh SCoo SPoG |
| (Karoo Series) Karoo Blue = 'Innkablue'[PBR] | LSou SCoo |
| - Karoo Dark Blue = 'Innemkadab' **new** | LSou |
| - Karoo Pink = 'Innkapink'[PBR] | SBfd |
| - Karoo Violet Ice = 'Innemkavic' **new** | LSou |
| - Karoo White = 'Innkarwhi'[PBR] | LSou SMrm |
| (Maritana Series) Blue Lagoon = 'Pengoon'[PBR] | LSRN SBfd SCoo |
| - Candy Girl = 'Pencand'[PBR] | SCoo |
| -Honey Girl = 'Penhon'[PBR] | LSRN SCoo |
| - Maritana Sky Lagoon = 'Pensky' | SCoo |
| - Sugar Girl = 'Pensug'[PBR] | EPfP LSRN |
| Melanie = 'Fleuron' ♀H3 | EPfP |
| Nemesis Orange = 'Wesneo' | LAst |
| (Nuvo Series) 'Nuvo Blue Bicolour' | LSou |
| - 'Nuvo Blue' | LSou WGor |
| - 'Nuvo Carmine' | LSou WGor |
| - 'Nuvo Rose' | LSou WGor |
| 'Orchard Blue' | EPfP |
| 'Provencal Dusky Blue' | EPfP SPoG |
| 'Provencal Dusky Pink' | EPfP SPoG |
| Pure Lagoon = 'Penpur'[PBR] | LHop SBfd |
| Raspberries and Cream = 'Fleurrac' **new** | LBuc SBrd SPoG |
| 'Rose Wings' | EPfP |
| 'Sugar Almond' **new** | WHlf |
| 'Sugar Plum'[PBR] | EPfP LRHS SLon |
| (Sunsatia Series) Sunsatia Blackberry = 'Inuppink'[PBR] | SBfd SCoo |
| - Sunsatia Cranberry = 'Intraired'[PBR] | SCoo |
| - Sunsatia Lemon = 'Intraigold'[PBR] | SCoo |
| - Sunsatia Peach = 'Inupcream' | SCoo |
| ***sylvatica*** | CSpe |
| 'Vanilla Cream' **new** | LBuc |
| 'Vanilla Lady' **new** | LAst |
| Vanilla Mist = 'Grega'[PBR] | CChe EPfP LRHS LSou SLon SPoG |
| 'White Wings' | EPfP |
| 'Wisley Vanilla' | EPfP SPoG |

## *Nemophila* (*Boraginaceae*)

| | |
|---|---|
| ***menziesii*** 'Penny Black' | CSpe |

## *Neodypsis* (*Arecaceae*)

| | |
|---|---|
| ***decaryi*** | see *Dypsis decaryi* |

## *Neolepisorus* (*Polypodiaceae*)

| | |
|---|---|
| ***lancifolius*** | CPLG |

## *Neolitsea* (*Lauraceae*)

***glauca*** see *N. sericea*
***polycarpa*** WCru
KWJ 12309 new
§ ***sericea*** CBcs SSpi WSHC

## *Neomarica* ✿ (*Iridaceae*)

***caerulea*** CDes EBee WCot
***gracilis*** CLak

## *Neopanax* (*Araliaceae*)

§ ***arboreus*** CDoC CHEx CTrC CTsd ECou LEdu SBig
***colensoi*** CTrC
§ ***laetus*** CDoC CHEx CTrC ECou LEdu SArc SBig

## *Neoregelia* (*Bromeliaceae*)

***carolinae*** (Meyendorffii Group) 'Meyendorffii' XBlo
'Hojo Rojo' XBlo
'Marconfos' XBlo

## *Neoshirakia* (*Euphorbiaceae*)

***japonica*** EPfP MBlu WPGP WPat
- B&SWJ 8744 WCru

## *Neottia* (*Orchidaceae*)

***ovata*** NLAp

## *Neottianthe* (*Orchidaceae*)

***cucullata*** EFEx

## *Nepenthes* ✿ (*Nepenthaceae*)

***alata*** CSWC NChu
***alata* × *ventricosa*** SHmp
***aristolochioides*** SHmp
***bongso*** SHmp
***copleandii*** CSWC
***densiflora*** SHmp
***diatas*** SHmp
***ephippiata*** SHmp
***fusca*** SHmp
***fusca* × *maxima*** SHmp
× ***hookeriana*** SHmp
***izumiae*** SHmp
***lowii*** SHmp
***macfarlanei*** SHmp
***maxima mixta*** SHmp
***maxima* × *talangensis*** SHmp
***mikei*** SHmp
***ovata*** SHmp
***rajah*** SHmp
***ramispina*** SHmp
'Rebecca Soper' SHmp
***sanguinea*** SHmp
***sibuyanensis*** SHmp
***singalana*** SHmp
***spectabilis*** SHmp
***talangensis*** new SHmp
***talangensis* × *veitchii*** new SHmp
***tobaica*** SHmp
***truncata*** highland form SHmp
- 'King of Spades' × ***truncata*** 'Queen of Hearts' new SHmp
***ventricosa*** SHmp

## *Nepeta* ✿ (*Lamiaceae*)

sp. LAst
from China EWes
from Ethiopia GCal
***amethystina*** new XSen
'Blue Beauty' see *N. sibirica* 'Souvenir d'André Chaudron'
* ***buddlejifolium*** MSCN NLar
***camphorata*** SIde SMrm
***cataria*** CArn CPrp CTri CWan EGHP ELau GJos GPoy MHer MNHC NBro NPri SBfd SIde SVic WHfH WJek WMoo
§ - 'Citriodora' CArn CBot CHar EGHP ELan GPoy MHer SIde SPhx WJek XLum
***citriodora*** Dum. see *N. cataria* 'Citriodora'
***clarkei*** EBee EPPr GMaP IFro MDKP MMuc MTis NDov SBfd SEND SIde SWat WFar WHil WHrl WMoo
'Dropmore' LRHS
§ × ***faassenii*** ♀H4 Widely available
- 'Alba' COIW CSpr EBee ECtt EGHP EPfP EWhm LAst MMuc NBPC NBre NLar SBfd SEND WFar WHil WJek WWEG XSen
- 'Blauknirps' NBre
- 'Kit Cat' CSpe ECGP GCal LHop LRHS LSRN MNrw MTis NDov WCAu WFar
- 'Select' WPtf
***glechoma*** 'Variegata' see *Glechoma hederacea* 'Variegata'
***govaniana*** Widely available
***granatensis*** new XSen
***grandiflora*** MMuc MSpe NBre SIde WFar WHrl WPtf
- 'Blue Danube' EBee NDov SIde
- 'Bramdean' CElw CMea EBee ECtt EPfP EWes LRHS MCot MTis SAga SBch SPhx WWEG XLum
- 'Dawn to Dusk' Widely available
- 'Pool Bank' EBee ECtt EWes GCal LPla MAvo MTis NBre SGar SIde SMrm WHil XLum
- 'Wild Cat' EBee EPfP MAvo MBri MTis SPur WCAu WFar
***hederacea*** 'Variegata' see *Glechoma hederacea* 'Variegata'
***italica*** SIde
***kubanica*** LPla
'Lamendi' new NDov
***lanceolata*** see *N. nepetella*
***latifolia*** SIde
- 'Super Cat' EBee
'Lilac Cloud' NBir
* ***longipes*** hort. CPrp EBee EPfP LAst LEdu LHop LRHS MCot MRav NCGa NGdn NSti SMrm SPer SWat WAul WCAu WFar WHal WMnd WPer WWEG
***macrantha*** see *N. sibirica*
'Maurice' new NDov
***melissifolia*** SBch WPer
***mussinii*** misapplied see *N.* × *faassenii*
***mussinii*** Spreng. see *N. racemosa*
§ ***nepetella*** NBir WFar
***nervosa*** CSpe EBee ECha ELan EPfP LAst MCot MNHC NBPC NBro NLar NPri NSti SBfd SPer WFar WJek WMnd WSHC WWEG
- 'Blue Carpet' CSpe NEgg
- 'Blue Moon' EBee EPfP EWes LRHS LSou NBid SPoG WFar
- 'Forncett Select' CSam MRav NBre SMrm

| | | |
|---|---|---|
| | - 'Pink Cat' | EPfP LRHS LSou MDKP MNHC NLar SRkn WWEG |
| § | ***nuda*** | CSam EBee ECha ECtt MDKP SHar SIde WFar WHil WHrl |
| | - 'Accent' | GBin |
| | - subsp. ***albiflora*** | ECha |
| * | - 'Anne's Choice' | EBee GBin SIde |
| * | - 'Grandiflora' | NBre NLar WMoo |
| | - 'Purple Cat' | EBee EPfP GBin LLHF LSou SIde WFar |
| | - 'Snow Cat' | EBee GBin SIde SPhx |
| | ***pannonica*** | see *N. nuda* |
| | ***parnassica*** | ECtt MLLN MMuc MSpe MTis NBPC NLar SEND SIde SMrm SPav WBox WFar WHil WHrl WMnd WMoo WPer WPtf |
| | ***phyllochlamys*** | CBot CPBP WAbe XSen |
| | Pink Candy | EWll WHil |
| | 'Porzellan' | EBee LPla SMrm |
| § | ***prattii*** | CSpe MWat NLar NPro SIde WWEG |
| § | ***racemosa*** ♀H4 | CArn CBot CHby CMac CPbn CSev CWan ELau EPfP GBBs GJos LRHS MCot MLHP MNHC MRav MSCN NBlu SGar SIde WMoo XLum |
| | - RCB AM 3 | WCot |
| | - ***alba*** | SBfd WFar XLum |
| | - 'Amelia' | MSpe WHil |
| | - 'Blue Ice' | SIde |
| | - 'Grog' | SIde |
| | - 'Little Titch' | CBod EBee ECtt EPfP GCra LRHS LSRN MCot NLar SIde SMrm SPoG SWat WFar WWEG |
| | - 'Senior' **new** | MAsh |
| | - 'Snowflake' | CBcs CMea CPrp EBee ELan ELon EPfP EShb GMaP LRHS MAsh MCot MHer MTis NBir NCGa SAga SIde SMrm SPer SPoG SWvt WCAu WFar |
| | - 'Superba' | NBre WCot WFar |
| | - 'Toria' **new** | NDov |
| | - 'Walker's Low' | Widely available |
| * | 'Rae Crug' | ECtt EWes |
| | ***reichenbachiana*** | see *N. racemosa* |
| § | ***sibirica*** | COlW EBee ECha ELan EPfP GMac LEdu MHer MMuc MRav MSCN NBid NBro NLar NPri SBch SBfd SRkn WCAu WCot WFar WHal WJek WPer WPtf XLum |
| § | - 'Souvenir d'André Chaudron' | CSam CWCL EBee ECtt ELan EPfP GMaP LAst LHop LRHS MBri MCot MRav MTis NVic SBch SMrm SPer SPoG WCAu WCot WFar WHil WWEG |
| | 'Six Hills Giant' | Widely available |
| | ***stewartiana*** | EPPr LLHF MRav WCAu WMoo |
| | - BWJ 7999 | WCru |
| | ***subsessilis*** | Widely available |
| | - 'Blue Dreams' | ELon LBMP NLar SHar SPhx WHil XLum |
| | - 'Candy Cat' | EBee EPfP MDKP NBPC NBre SBHP SPoG |
| | - 'Cool Cat' | EBee EPfP LSRN MDKP NBre NLar NPro SIde SPoG WFar |
| | - Nimbus = 'Yanim'PBR | EBee MPnt |
| | - 'Pink Dreams' | ELon EPfP GBee GJos LBMP LRHS MHer MSpe WHil XLum |
| | - pink-flowered | ECha SMrm WWEG |
| | - 'Sweet Dreams' | CHar CKno EAEE EBee ECtt EPfP EWTr LBMP LEdu LHop LRHS MCot MDKP MRav MTis NCGa NLar NPro NSti WFar WMnd |
| | - 'Washfield' | IPot LHop SAga |
| | ***transcaucasica*** | MSCN NBre NLar WMnd WMoo |
| | 'Blue Infinity' | WWEG |
| | ***troodii*** | MDKP SIde |
| | ***tuberosa*** | CArn CBod CSpe ECha EKen LRHS MHer MRav SBch SIde SMad SPav WBox WCot WMnd WMoo WTcb XSen |
| | 'Veluws Blauwtje' | EBee |
| | ***yunnanensis*** | EBee EPPr LEdu LPla SMrm WHil WOut WPGP WPer |

# *Nephrolepis* (*Lomariopsidaceae*)

| | |
|---|---|
| ***auriculata*** | WRic |
| ***cordifolia*** | WRic |
| ***duffii*** | EShb WRic |
| ***falcata*** | WRic |
| ***pendula*** | WRic |

# *Nephrophyllidium* (*Menyanthaceae*)

| | |
|---|---|
| ***crista-galli*** | IBlr |

# *Nerine* ✿ (*Amaryllidaceae*)

| | | |
|---|---|---|
| | 'Afterglow' | EBee ECho LAma LRHS SGar WCot |
| | 'Alexandra' | WCot |
| | ***alta*** | see *N. undulata* Alta Group |
| | ***angustifolia*** | CPen |
| | 'Aries' | WCot |
| | 'Aurora' | ECho WCot |
| | 'Baghdad' | ECho WCot |
| | 'Belladonna' | WCot |
| | 'Bennett-Poë' | WCot |
| | 'Berlioz' | WCot |
| | 'Blanchefleur' | WCot |
| | ***bowdenii*** ♀H3-4 | Widely available |
| | - 'Alba' | CBro LRHS |
| | - 'Alba' ambig. | CBgR CBro CFir CPrp CTca EBee ECho ELan EPot ERCP SCoo WCot |
| | - 'Albivetta' | CAby CBgR EBee ECho WCot |
| | - 'Blanca Perla' **new** | WCot |
| I | - 'Chris Sanders' | WCot |
| | - 'Codora' | see *N.* 'Codora' |
| | - 'E.B. Anderson' | EBee WCot WHil |
| | - 'Ella K' **new** | EPot SPer |
| | - 'Isabel' | CBro CPrP EPot EPri LRHS |
| | - 'Linda Vista' | WCot |
| | - 'Manina' | CCse WCot |
| | - 'Marjorie' | EMal |
| | - 'Mark Fenwick' | CBcs CBro CDes ECha WCot WOld |
| | - 'Marnie Rogerson' | CBro CPne WCot |
| § | - 'Mollie Cowie' (v) | CCse CPrp GCal IBlr NCGa WCot WCru WHil WSHC |
| | - 'Nikita' | CBgR CPen ECho EPot EPri ERCP LRHS |
| | - 'Ostara' | CBgR CPrp EBee EPot ERCP LRHS WCot |
| | - 'Patricia' **new** | EPot LRHS |
| | - 'Pink Frostwork' | WCot |
| | - 'Pink Surprise' | CDes WCot |
| | - 'Porlock' | EBee |
| § | - 'Quinton Wells' | CPrp CTca SCnR SPhx WCot WHil |
| | - 'Rowie' | CBgR CPrp EPot EPri LRHS |
| | - 'Ted Allen's Early' | EBla |
| | - 'Variegata' | see *N. bowdenii* 'Mollie Cowie' |
| | - 'Wellsii' | see *N. bowdenii* 'Quinton Wells' |
| | 'Canasta' | WCot |
| | 'Cardinal' | WCot |
| | 'Carnival' | WCot |
| | 'Carolside' | WCot |
| | 'Caryatid' | WCot |
| | 'Catherine' | WCot |

| | | |
|---|---|---|
| | 'Catkin' | WCot |
| | 'Christmas' | WCot |
| | 'Clarabel' | WCot |
| | 'Clent Charm' | WCot |
| § | 'Codora' | CCCN CPen EBee ECho LHop LSou SPer WCot |
| | 'Corlette' | WCot |
| | ***corusca*** 'Major' | see *N. sarniensis* var. *corusca* |
| | 'Cranfield' | WCot |
| | 'Cynthia Chance' | WCot |
| | 'Dame Alice Godman' | WCot |
| | 'Diana Oliver' | WCot |
| | 'Doris Vos' | WCot |
| | 'Druid' | WCot |
| | 'Elspeth' | WCot |
| | 'Enchantress' | WCot |
| | 'Eve' | WCot |
| | 'Evelyn Emmett' | WCot |
| | 'Exbury Red' | WCot |
| | ***filamentosa*** misapplied | see *N. filifolia* |
| | ***filamentosa*** ambig. | CBro CLak ECho |
| § | ***filifolia*** | CPBP CPen ECho EPot ITim NWCA WAbe |
| | ***flexuosa*** | see *N. undulata* Flexuosa Group |
| | 'Fucine' | CDes EBee WCot |
| | 'Gaiety' | WCot |
| | ***gracilis*** | ECho WCot |
| | 'Grilse' | WCot |
| | 'Hamlet' | WCot |
| | 'Harlequin' | WCot |
| | 'Hera' | CBro SPhx WCot |
| | 'Hertha Berg' | WCot |
| * | ***hirsuta*** | ECho WAbe |
| | ***humilis*** | ECho WCot |
| | - Breachiae Group | SBch |
| | ***huttoniae*** | CLak ECho |
| | 'Iman' | WCot |
| | 'Innominata' | WCot |
| | 'Isobel' | CPrp EPot LRHS |
| | 'Janet' | WCot |
| | 'Jenny Wren' | WCot WHil |
| | 'Joan' | WCot |
| I | 'Judith' Norris | WCot |
| | 'Kashmir' | CDes WCot |
| | 'Killarney' | WCot |
| | 'King Leopold' | WCot |
| | 'King of the Belgians' | ECho LAma WCot |
| | 'Kinn McIntosh' | CDes WCot |
| | ***krigei*** | CPen ECho |
| | 'Kyoto' | WCot |
| | 'Lady Cynthia Colville' | WCot |
| | 'Lady Eleanor Keane' | WCot |
| | 'Lady Havelock-Allen' | WCot |
| | 'Lady Llewellyn' | WCot |
| | 'Lady St Aldwyn' | WCot |
| | ***laticoma*** | ECho WCot |
| | 'Lawlord' | CDes WCot |
| | 'Leila Hughes' | WCot |
| | 'Lucinda' | WCot |
| | 'Lyndhurst Salmon' | WCot |
| | 'Mansellii' | CBro GKev SKHP WCot |
| | 'Maria' | CBgR WCot |
| | 'Mars' | WCot |
| | ***masoniorum*** | CBro CPen ECho NMen SBch WCot |
| | 'Miss E. Cator' | WCot |
| | 'Miss Florence Brown' **new** | WCot |
| | 'Miss Frances Clarke' | WCot |
| | 'Mrs Cooper' | WCot |
| | 'Mrs Dent Brocklehurst' | WCot |
| | 'Nena' | WCot |
| | 'November Cheer' | ECho |
| | ***peersii*** | WCot |
| | 'Pink Triùmph' | CAbP CBcs CBgR EBee EBla ECho ERCP EShb GQui IBlr LAma LHop LRHS WCot WHoo |
| | 'Plymouth' | SChr WCot |
| | ***pudica*** | CLak SBch |
| | - pink-flowered | WCot |
| | ***pusilla*** | CLak |
| | 'Quivotina' **new** | WCot |
| | 'Red Pimpernel' | ECho LAma |
| | 'Regina' | WCot |
| | 'Rushmere Star' | CBgR EBee SChr WCot |
| | 'Ruth' | WCot |
| | ***sarniensis*** ♀H2-3 | CBro CPne ECha ECho EPot EPri GKev LRHS SKHP WCot WHil |
| * | - 'Alba' | WCot |
| * | - 'Borde Hill White' | WCot |
| § | - var. ***corusca*** | LAma |
| | - - 'Major' | ECho SChr WCot |
| | - var. ***curvifolia*** f. ***fothergillii*** | CAvo ECho WCot |
| | - late, dull red-flowered | CDes |
| | 'Shardlow Beauty' **new** | WCot |
| | 'Smokey Special' | WCot |
| | 'Snowflake' | WCot |
| | 'Stephanie' | CBgR CBro CCCN CTca EBee ECho ERCP EShb LAma LHop LRHS LSou SWal WCot WFar WHoo |
| | 'Timoshenko' | WCot |
| | ***undulata*** | CAby CBgR CBro CCCN CPen CPne CTca ECha ECho EPri GCal LAma LSou SPer WCot WHil |
| * | - 'Alba' | ECho |
| § | - Alta Group | WCot |
| § | - Flexuosa Group | CPne ECho MRav |
| | - - 'Alba' | CBgR CBro CDes CPen EBee ECha ECho EPri EWTr EWll MRav WAbe WCot |
| | 'Vicky' | WCot |
| | 'Virgo' | ECho LAma |
| | 'White Swan' | ECho |
| | 'Wolsey' | ECho WCot |
| | 'Zeal Giant' ♀H3-4 | CAvo CBro CFFs CPne ECho GCal WCot |
| | 'Zeal Grilse' | CDes CPne |

## *Nerium* ✿ (*Apocynaceae*)

| | | |
|---|---|---|
| | ***oleander*** misapplied | see *N. oleander* 'Soeur Agnès' |
| | ***oleander*** L. | CAbb CArn CBcs CEls CHll CTri EBak ELan EShb LRHS MMuc NLar SChr SEND SPer SPlb SPoG SRms |
| | - 'Album' | CEls CTri |
| | - 'Album Plenum' (d) | CEls |
| | - 'Alsace' | CEls |
| | - 'Altini' | CEls |
| | - 'Angiolo Pucci' | CEls |
| * | - 'Atlas' | XSen |
| | - 'Bousquet d'Orb' | CEls |
| § | - 'Carneum Plenum' (d) | CEls |
| | - 'Cavalaire' (d) | CEls XSen |
| * | - 'Clare' | MOWG |
| * | - 'Claudia' | SEND |
| | - 'Cornouailles' | CEls |
| | - 'Docteur Golfin' | CEls |
| | - 'Emile Sahut' | CEls |
| | - 'Emilie' | CEls |
| | - 'Flavescens Plenum' (d) | CEls EShb XSen |
| | - 'Géant des Batailles' (d) | CEls MOWG |
| | - 'Hardy Red' | CEls |

- 'Hawaii' CEls
- 'Isle of Capri' MOWG
- 'J.R.' CEls
- 'Jannoch' CEls
- 'Louis Pouget' (d) CEls
- 'Madame Allen' (d) CEls EShb
- 'Magaly' SEND
- 'Maresciallo Graziani' CEls
- 'Margaritha' CEls
- 'Marie Gambetta' CEls
- 'Mont Blanc' (d) CEls XSen
- 'Mrs Roeding' see *N. oleander* 'Carneum Plenum'
- 'Nana Rosso' CEls
- 'Oasis' (d) CEls
- subsp. ***oleander*** CEls
- 'Papa Gambetta' CEls
- 'Petite Pink' CEls
- 'Petite Red' CEls
- 'Petite Salmon' CEls
- 'Pink Beauty' SEND
- 'Professeur Granel' (d) CEls EShb
- 'Provence' (d) CEls MOWG
- 'Red Beauty' **new** XSen
- 'Rosario' (d) EShb
- 'Rose des Borrels' (d) CEls
- 'Rosée du Ventoux' (d) CEls MOWG
- 'Roseum' CEls
- 'Roseum Plenum' (d) CEls CRHN SEND
- 'Rosita' CEls
- salmon-flowered SEND
- 'Sealy Pink' CEls

* - 'Snowflake' MOWG

§ - 'Soeur Agnès' CEls

- 'Soleil Levant' CEls
- 'Souvenir d'Emma Schneider' CEls
- 'Souvenir des Iles Canaries' CEls
- 'Splendens' (d) MOWG
- 'Splendens Giganteum' (d) CEls EShb
- 'Splendens Giganteum Variegatum' (d/v) CEls
- 'Tito Poggi' CEls
- 'Variegatum' (v) ♀H1+3 CBot CHll EShb LRHS
- 'Variegatum Plenum' (d/v) WCot
- 'Villa Romaine' CEls XSen
- 'Ville de Carpentras' (d) CEls
- white-flowered SEND

## *Nertera* (*Rubiaceae*)

***balfouriana*** ECou

## *Neviusia* (*Rosaceae*)

***alabamensis*** NLar

## *Nicandra* (*Solanaceae*)

***physalodes*** CArn CHby GBee ILis NBir NVic SMrm WSFF
- 'Splash of Cream' (v) CCCN
- 'Violacea' CSpe SRms SWvt

## *Nicotiana* (*Solanaceae*)

***alata*** CSpe EPfP WSFF
***glauca*** CCCN CDTJ CHGN CHll CSpe EShb EWTr NGBo SPav SPlb
***knightiana*** CDTJ CSpe
***langsdorffii*** ♀H3 CSpe SPav
- 'Hot Chocolate' CSpe

'Lime Green' ♀H3 CSpe
***mutabilis*** CHll CSpe MWea SBch SPhx
***suaveolens*** CBre SPhx
***sylvestris*** ♀H3 CDTJ CSpe CWSG ELan EPfP NPri SBfd SEND SPav SPoG SWvt WTou
***tabacum*** CArn SPav
- var. ***macrophylla*** CDTJ

'Tinkerbell' CSpe

## *Nidularium* (*Bromeliaceae*)

***innocentii*** XBlo

## *Nierembergia* (*Solanaceae*)

***frutescens*** see *N. scoparia*
§ ***repens*** CDoy ECho EDAr NLar
***rivularis*** see *N. repens*
§ ***scoparia*** CSpr

## *Nigella* (*Ranunculaceae*)

***papillosa*** 'African Bride' CSpe
- 'Midnight' CSpe

## *Nigritella* see *Gymnadenia*

## *Nipponanthemum* (*Asteraceae*)

§ ***nipponicum*** CSam CWan EBee ECho GBin GCal IVic LAst NSti SRms WHil XLum

## *Noccaea* see *Thlaspi*

## *Nolina* (*Asparagaceae*)

***bigelovii*** WPGP
***durangensis*** F&M 333 WPGP
***longifolia*** EAmu
***microcarpa*** WCot
***nelsonii*** SPlb WPGP
- F&M 307 WPGP

***parryi*** subsp. ***wolfii*** WPGP
***parviflora*** NJM 05.010 WPGP
***texana*** CTrC NWCA

## *Nomocharis* (*Liliaceae*)

***aperta*** CPLG GCra GEdr GGar GLin LAma WCru
- ACE 2271 LWst
- CLD 229 LWst
- CLD 524 LWst

× ***finlayorum*** LWst
***mairei*** see *N. pardanthina*
***meleagrina*** GAuc LAma LWst WAbe
***nana*** see *Lilium nanum*
***oxypetala*** see *Lilium oxypetalum*
§ ***pardanthina*** GAuc GGar GMac WAbe
- CLD 1490 LWst
- f. ***punctulata*** LWst WCru

***saluenensis*** LWst WAbe

## *Nonea* (*Boraginaceae*)

***lutea*** LSou NOrc NSti WHal

## *Nothochelone* see *Penstemon*

## *Nothofagus* ✿ (*Nothofagaceae*)

§ × ***alpina*** CBcs CMCN GBin WDin
***antarctica*** CBcs CCVT CDul CLnd CMCN CTho ECrN ELan EPfP EWTr GKin LTen MBlu MBri MGos NPal NWea WDin
- 'Benmore' **new** NLar

***betuloides*** CBcs CMCN GBin IArd IDee SPlb
***cunninghamii*** CTrC IArd SPlb

| | |
|---|---|
| ***dombeyi*** | CBcs CDoC CDul CLnd CMCN EPfP GBin IArd MBlu NWea SArc WPGP |
| ***fusca*** | CDoC IArd |
| ***glauca*** | CBcs CDul IArd |
| × ***leonii*** new | IArd |
| ***menziesii*** | CTrC |
| ***nitida*** | CBcs GBin IArd IDee |
| ***obliqua*** | CBcs CDul CMCN GAbr GBin SPlb WAle WDin |
| ***procera*** misapplied | see *N.* × *alpina* |
| ***pumilio*** | CBcs GBin |
| ***solandri*** | GGar |
| - var. ***cliffortioides*** | NMun |

## *Notholaena* see *Cheilanthes*

## *Notholirion* (*Liliaceae*)

| | |
|---|---|
| ***bulbuliferum*** | EBee ECho GAuc GCra |
| - Cox 5074 | LWSt |
| - SDR 2865 | GKev |
| ***campanulatum*** | EBee ECho GAuc LWSt |
| ***macrophyllum*** | EBee ECho GAuc LWSt |
| ***thomsonianum*** | ECho LWSt |

## *Nothoperanema* (*Dryopteridaceae*)

| | |
|---|---|
| ***squamisetum*** | WRic |

## *Nothoscordum* (*Alliaceae*)

| | |
|---|---|
| sp. | GCal |
| ***gracile*** | CFir |
| ***montevidense*** | LWSt |
| ***neriniflorum*** | see *Caloscordum neriniflorum* |
| ***ostenii*** | SCnR |
| ***strictum*** | EBee ECho |

## *Nuphar* (*Nymphaeaceae*)

| | |
|---|---|
| ***advenum*** | LPBA |
| ***japonica*** | CRow NLar |
| var. ***variegata*** (v) | |
| ***lutea*** | CBen CHab CRow EHon EWil LPBA SCoo SWat |

## *Nuxia* (*Stilbaceae*)

| | |
|---|---|
| ***congesta*** | EShb |
| ***floribunda*** | EShb |

## *Nylandtia* (*Polygalaceae*)

| | |
|---|---|
| ***spinosa*** | SPlb |

## *Nymphaea* ✿ (*Nymphaeaceae*)

| | |
|---|---|
| ***alba*** (H) | CBen CHab CRWN CRow CWat EHon EWil GQue LPBA MSKA NBir SCoo SVic SWat WMAq WPnP |
| 'Albatros' misapplied | see *N.* 'Hermine' |
| § 'Albatros' Latour-Marliac (H) | CWat LPBA MSKA NPer SWat WPnP |
| 'Albatross' | see *N.* 'Albatros' Latour-Marliac, *N.* 'Hermine' |
| * 'Albida' | WMAq XBlo |
| 'Almost Black' (H) | CBen MSKA |
| 'Amabilis' (H) | CBen CRow LPBA MSKA SWat WMAq |
| 'American Star' (H) | CBen SWat WMAq |
| 'Andreana' (H) | CWat LLWG LPBA MSKA SWat |
| 'Arc-en-ciel' (H) | CBen LPBA SCoo SWat WMAq |
| 'Arethusa' (H) | LPBA |
| 'Atropurpurea' (H) | CBen LLWG LPBA MSKA NPer SWat WMAq |
| 'Attraction' (H) | CBen CRow EHon LPBA MSKA NPer SCoo SVic SWat WMAq XBlo |
| 'Aurora' (H) | CBen GQue LPBA SVic SWat WMAq WPnP |
| 'Barbara Davies' (H) | LLWG |
| 'Barbara Dobbins' (H) | CBen LLWG LPBA MSKA |
| 'Bateau' (H) | CBen LLWG |
| 'Bernice Ikins' (H) | MSKA |
| 'Brakeleyi Rosea' (H) | LPBA MSKA WMAq |
| 'Burgundy Princess' (H) | CWat LLWG MSKA NPer |
| ***candida*** (H) | CBen EHon MSKA MWts NPer WMAq |
| 'Candidissima' (H) | SWat |
| § ***capensis*** (T/D) | XBlo |
| 'Carolina Sunset' (H) | LLWG |
| 'Caroliniana Nivea' (H) | CBen EHon |
| 'Caroliniana Perfecta' (H) | CBen LPBA MSKA SWat |
| 'Celebration' (H) | LLWG MSKA |
| 'Charlene Strawn' (H) | CWat LLWG LPBA WMAq |
| 'Charles de Meurville' (H) | CBen CRow LPBA MSKA NPer SVic WMAq WPnP |
| 'Château le Rouge' (H) | LLWG |
| 'Clyde Ikins' (H) | MSKA |
| 'Colonel A.J. Welch' (H) | CBen EHon LPBA MSKA NPer SCoo SWat WMAq |
| 'Colorado' (H) | CBen LLWG MSKA NPer |
| ***colorata*** | see *N. capensis* |
| 'Colossea' (H) | CBen CWat LPBA MSKA NPer WPnP |
| 'Comanche' (H) | CBen MSKA NPer WMAq |
| 'Conqueror' (H) | CBen IArd LPBA MSKA NPer SCoo SVic SWat |
| § 'Darwin' (H) | CBen CWat LPBA MSKA NPer SLon SWat WMAq WPnP |
| × ***daubenyana*** (T/D) | ECho |
| 'David' (H) | CBen LLWG |
| 'Denver' (H) | LLWG MSKA |
| 'Deva' (H) | CBen |
| 'Ellisiana' (H) | CBen LLWG LPBA MSKA NPer SWat |
| 'Escarboucle' (H) ♀H4 | CBen CRow CWat EHon LPBA MSKA NLar NPer SCoo SVic SWat WMAq WPnP XBlo |
| 'Esmeralda' (H) | SWat |
| § 'Fabiola' (H) | CBen CRow EHon LPBA MSKA NPer SCoo WMAq |
| 'Fiesta' | CBen MSKA |
| 'Fire Crest' (H) | CBen GQue LPBA MSKA NPer SCoo SVic SWat WMAq |
| 'Fireball' (H) | MSKA |
| 'Fritz Junge' (H) | CBen |
| 'Froebelii' (H) | CBen CRow CWat EHon LPBA MSKA NPer SWat WMAq |
| 'Fulva' (H) | LLWG |
| 'Galatée' (H) | CBen MSKA |
| 'Geisha Girl' | MSKA |
| 'Georgia Peach' (H) | LLWG MSKA |
| 'Gladstoniana' (H) ♀H4 | CBen CRow EHon LPBA MSKA NPer SCoo SWat WMAq |
| 'Gloire du Temple-sur-Lot' (H) | CBen EHon NPer SWat WMAq |
| 'Gloriosa' (H) | CBen LPBA NPer SCoo SWat WPnP |
| 'Gold Medal' (H) | CBen LLWG MSKA |
| 'Gonnère' (H) ♀H4 | CBen CRow CWat EHon LPBA MSKA MWts NPer SLon SWat WMAq WPnP |
| 'Graziella' (H) | CBen LPBA MSKA WMAq |
| 'Gypsy' (H) | LLWG |
| 'Hal Miller' (H) | LLWG |
| 'Hassell' (H) | LLWG |
| 'Helen Fowler' (H) | SWat WMAq |
| × ***helvola*** | see *N.* 'Pygmaea Helvola' |
| § 'Hermine' (H) | CBen MSKA NPer SWat WMAq |
| 'Highlight' | LLWG |

| |  |  |
|---|---|---|
| | 'Hollandia' misapplied | see *N.* 'Darwin' |
| | 'Hollandia' Koster (H) | CBen SWat |
| | 'Indiana' (H) | CBen LPBA MSKA NPer WMAq |
| | 'Inner Light' | LLWG MSKA |
| | 'J.C.N. Forestier' (H) | CBen |
| | 'James Brydon' (H) ♀H4 | CBen CHid CRow CWat EHon LPBA MSKA NLar NPer SCoo SLon SVic SWat WMAq WPnP |
| | 'Jean de Lamarsalle' (H) | LLWG |
| | 'Jerusalem Dawn' | MSKA |
| § | 'Joanne Pring' (H) | SWat |
| | 'Joey Tomocik' (H) | CBen CWat LLWG LPBA MSKA SCoo WMAq WPnP |
| | 'King of the Blues' (T/D) | MSKA |
| | 'Lactea' (H) | CBen LLWG |
| | 'Laydekeri Fulgens' (H) | CBen LPBA MSKA SWat WMAq |
| | 'Laydekeri Lilacea' (H) | CBen CRow LPBA SWat WMAq |
| | 'Laydekeri Purpurata' (H) | LPBA SWat |
| | 'Laydekeri Rosea' misapplied | see *N.* 'Laydekeri Rosea Prolifera' |
| § | 'Laydekeri Rosea Prolifera' (H) | CBen LPBA |
| | 'Lemon Chiffon' (H) | CBen MSKA |
| | 'Lemon Mist' | LLWG MSKA |
| | 'Lily Pons' (H) | CBen MSKA |
| | 'Limelight' | SWat |
| | 'Liou' (H) | CBen LLWG MSKA |
| | 'Little Sue' (H) | LLWG MSKA |
| | 'Livingstone' (H) | LLWG |
| | 'Lucida' (H) | CBen LPBA MSKA SWat WMAq |
| | 'Madame Wilfon Gonnère' (H) | CBen CWat EHon LPBA MSKA MWts NPer SVic SWat WMAq |
| | 'Marliacea Albida' (H) | CBen CWat EHon LPBA MSKA NPer SWat WMAq WPnP XBlo |
| | 'Marliacea Carnea' (H) | CBen CRow EHon LPBA MSKA NPer SCoo SWat WMAq |
| § | 'Marliacea Chromatella' (H) ♀H4 | CBen CHid CRow CWat EHon GQue LPBA MSKA MWts NLar SCoo SVic SWat WMAq WPnP XBlo |
| | 'Marliacea Flammea' (H) | CBen |
| | 'Marliacea Rosea' (H) | CBen MSKA SWat WMAq XBlo |
| | 'Marliacea Rubra Punctata' (H) | LPBA |
| | 'Mary' (H) | LLWG |
| | 'Masaniello' (H) | CBen CRow EHon LPBA MSKA SWat WMAq |
| | 'Maurice Laydeker' (H) | CBen LLWG |
| | 'Maxima' | see *N.* 'Odorata Maxima' |
| | 'Mayla' | CBen LLWG LPBA MSKA NPer |
| § | 'Météor' (H) | CBen MSKA WMAq |
| | ***mexicana*** | MSKA |
| | 'Millennium Pink' | MSKA |
| | 'Moorei' (H) | CBen LPBA MSKA SWat WMAq |
| | 'Mrs Richmond' misapplied | see *N.* 'Fabiola' |
| | 'Mrs Richmond' Latour-Marliac (H) | CBen SWat XBlo |
| | 'Neptune' (H) | LLWG |
| | 'Newchapel Beauty' | WMAq |
| | 'Newton' (H) | CBen LLWG MSKA SWat WMAq |
| | 'Nigel' (H) | LLWG MSKA SWat |
| | 'Norma Gedye' (H) | CBen CWat LPBA MSKA SWat WMAq |
| | 'Odalisque' (H) | CBen |
| § | ***odorata*** (H) | CBen CRow EHon LPBA MSKA SCoo WMAq |
| § | - var. ***minor*** (H) | CBen CRow LPBA MSKA SWat WMAq |
| | - 'Pumila' | see *N. odorata* var. *minor* |
| | - subsp. ***tuberosa*** (H) | CBen LPBA |
| | 'Odorata Alba' | see *N. odorata* |
| § | 'Odorata Maxima' (H) | WMAq |
| | 'Odorata Sulphurea' (H) | SWat WPnP |
| § | 'Odorata Sulphurea Grandiflora' (H) | CBen CRow LPBA MSKA SCoo SWat XBlo |
| § | 'Odorata Turicensis' (H) | LPBA MSKA |
| | 'Odorata William B. Shaw' | see *N.* 'W.B. Shaw' |
| | 'Pam Bennett' (H) | CBen LLWG |
| | 'Panama Pacific' (T/D) | XBlo |
| | 'Patio Joe' | LLWG MSKA |
| | 'Paul Hariot' (H) | CWat LPBA MSKA NPer SWat WMAq WPnP |
| | 'Peace Lily' | LLWG MSKA |
| | 'Peach Glow' | LLWG MSKA |
| | 'Peaches and Cream' (H) | MSKA |
| | Pearl of the Pool (H) | SWat |
| | 'Perry's Baby Red' (H) | CBen CWat LLWG MSKA MWts NPer SCoo WMAq |
| | 'Perry's Crinkled Pink' (H) | CBen |
| | 'Perry's Double White' (H) | MSKA NPer WPnP |
| | 'Perry's Double Yellow' | MSKA |
| | 'Perry's Dwarf Red' (H) | CBen MSKA |
| | 'Perry's Fire Opal' (H) | MSKA NPer |
| | 'Perry's Orange Sunset' | MSKA |
| | 'Perry's Pink' (H) | SWat WMAq |
| | 'Perry's Red Beauty' (H) | CBen |
| | 'Perry's Red Bicolor' (H) | LLWG |
| | 'Perry's Red Glow' (H) | MSKA |
| | 'Perry's Red Wonder' (H) | CBen |
| | 'Perry's Viviparous Pink' (H) | CBen |
| | 'Perry's White Star' (H) | LLWG |
| | 'Perry's Yellow Sensation' | see *N.* 'Yellow Sensation' |
| | 'Peter Slocum' (H) | CBen SWat |
| | 'Phoebus' (H) | CBen SWat |
| | 'Picciola' (H) | LLWG |
| | 'Pink Domino' | MSKA |
| | 'Pink Grapefruit' (H) | XBlo |
| | 'Pink Opal' (H) | CBen CWat LPBA |
| | 'Pink Peony' (H) | MSKA |
| | 'Pink Pumpkin' (H) | LLWG |
| | 'Pink Sensation' (H) | CBen LLWG MSKA NPer SLon SWat WMAq |
| | 'Pink Sparkle' (H) | LLWG |
| | 'Pink Sunrise' (H) | MSKA |
| | 'Pöstlingberg' (H) | LLWG LPBA |
| | 'Princess Elizabeth' (H) | CBen EHon LLWG LPBA |
| | 'Pygmaea Alba' | see *N. tetragona* |
| § | 'Pygmaea Helvola' (H) ♀H4 | CBen CHid CRow CWat GQue LPBA MSKA MWts NLar NPer SCoo SLon SVic SWat WMAq WPnP |
| | 'Pygmaea Rubis' (H) | CRow LPBA SWat WMAq |
| | 'Pygmaea Rubra' (H) | CBen CWat MSKA MWts NLar NPer SCoo SVic WMAq WPnP |
| | 'Ray Davies' (H) | CBen LLWG |
| | 'Red Paradise' (H) | MSKA |
| | 'Red Spider' (H) | LPBA MSKA NPer SVic |
| | 'Rembrandt' misapplied | see *N.* 'Météor' |
| | 'Rembrandt' Koster (H) | CBen LPBA |
| | 'René Gérard' (H) | CBen CWat EHon GQue LPBA MSKA NPer SWat WMAq WPnP |
| | 'Rosanna Supreme' (H) | LLWG SWat |
| | 'Rose Arey' (H) | CBen LPBA MSKA NPer SCoo SVic SWat WMAq |
| | 'Rose Magnolia' (H) | CWat SWat |
| | 'Rosea' (H) | LPBA |
| | 'Rosennymphe' (H) | CBen LPBA MSKA NPer SWat WMAq WPnP |
| | 'Rosy Morn' (H) | CBen LLWG MSKA |
| | 'Shady Lady' | MSKA |
| | 'Sioux' (H) | CBen EHon LPBA MSKA NPer SVic WMAq XBlo |

'Sirius' (H) CBen LLWG LPBA MSKA SWat
'Snow Princess' LPBA WPnP
'Solfatare' (H) LLWG
'Splendida' (H) WMAq
'Starbright' LLWG
'Starburst' (H) MSKA
'Steven Strawn' (H) LLWG
'Sultan' (H) MSKA
'Sunny Pink' LLWG MSKA
'Sunrise' see *N.* 'Odorata Sulphurea Grandiflora'
§ ***tetragona*** (H) CRow CWat LPBA MWts NPer WMAq
- 'Alba' see *N. tetragona*
- 'Johann Pring' see *N.* 'Joanne Pring'
'Texas Dawn' (H) CBen CWat LLWG MSKA SLon WMAq
'Thomas O'Brian' LLWG
'Tuberosa Flavescens' see *N.* 'Marliacea Chromatella'
'Tuberosa Richardsonii' (H) CBen EHon MSKA NPer WPnP
'Turicensis' see *N.* 'Odorata Turicensis'
'Vésuve' (H) LLWG MSKA SWat
'Virginalis' (H) CBen LLWG LPBA MSKA NPer SWat WMAq
'Virginia' (H) LLWG
§ 'W.B. Shaw' (H) CBen EHon LPBA MSKA NPer SWat WMAq
'Walter Pagels' (H) LLWG MWts WMAq
'Weymouth Red' (H) CBen
'White Sultan' (H) CWat LLWG MSKA
'William Doogue' (H) MSKA
'William Falconer' (H) CBen CWat LPBA MSKA NPer SWat
'Wow' (H) MSKA
'Yellow Queen' (H) MSKA
§ 'Yellow Sensation' (H) CBen
'Yul Ling' (H) LLWG MSKA SWat
'Zeus' MSKA

## *Nymphoides* (*Menyanthaceae*)

***indica*** XBlo
***peltata*** CBen CHab CWat EHon EWil MSKA NLar NPer SCoo SVic WMAq WPnP
§ - 'Bennettii' LPBA

## *Nyssa* ✿ (*Nyssaceae*)

***aquatica*** CBcs SSta
***leptophylla*** SBir SSta
***sinensis*** ♀H4 CAbP CBcs CDoC CDoy CDul CMCN CMac CTho ELan EPfP LRHS MAsh MBlu SBir SPer SSpi SSta
- 'Jim Russell' SBir SSta
- Nymans form SBir
***sylvatica*** ♀H4 Widely available
- 'Autumn Cascades' EPfP LRHS MBlu NLar SBir SSpi SSta WPGP
- var. ***biflora*** SSta
- 'Dirr' SSpi
- 'Haymen's Red' see *N. sylvatica* Red Rage
- 'Isabel Grace' LRHS MAsh MBri SBir SSpi
- 'Jermyns Flame' CAbP EPfP LRHS MAsh SBir SSpi SSta
- Jolly = 'Yiping' (v) **new** MPkF
- 'Miss Scarlet' (f) NLar SBir SSta
- 'Pendula' SSta
§ - Red Rage = 'Haymanred' MPkF
- 'Red Red Wine' CGHE EPfP NLar SBir SSta WPGP
- 'Sheffield Park' CAbP LRHS MAsh SBir SLim
- 'Wildfire' LRHS MPkF SBir SGol SSpi
- 'Windsor' EPfP LRHS MAsh SBir
- 'Wisley Bonfire' (m) CAbP CGHE EBee ECrN EPfP LRHS MAsh NLar SBir SPoG SSpi SSta WPGP
***ursina*** CBcs

# O

## *Oakesiella* see *Uvularia*

## *Ochagavia* (*Bromeliaceae*)

sp. NPal
***carnea*** RCB RA S-2 EBee LSou
§ ***litoralis*** CMac SMad
* ***rosea*** CHEx SPlb

## *Ochna* (*Ochnaceae*)

***serrulata*** CCCN

## *Ocimum* (*Lamiaceae*)

'African Blue' CArn CBod CSpe EGHP ELau EOHP GPoy LSou MHer NBlu NPri SPoG
§ ***americanum*** EGHP WJek
- 'Meng Luk' see *O. americanum*
***basilicum*** CArn CSev ELau GPoy NBlu NPri SBfd SIde SWat WJek
- 'Anise' see *O. basilicum* 'Horapha'
- 'Ararat' EGHP ELau
- ***camphorata*** see *O. kilimandscharicum*
- 'Cinnamon' EGHP ELau MNHC SBfd SHDw WJek
- 'Gecofure' ELau
- 'Genovese' EGHP ELau MHer MNHC NVic
- 'Genovese Special Select' ELau
- 'Glycyrrhiza' see *O. basilicum* 'Horapha'
- 'Green Globe' EGHP MNHC
- 'Green Ruffles' ELau EPfP MNHC WJek
- 'Holy' see *O. tenuiflorum*
§ - 'Horapha' CArn EGHP ELau MHer MNHC SIde WJek
* - 'Horapha Nanum' EGHP WJek
- 'Magic Michael' ELau
- 'Magic Mountain' SPoG
- 'Magic White' EGHP SPoG
- 'Mexican' ELau
- 'Mrs Burns' EGHP WJek
- 'Napolitano' CBod EGHP ELau SIde SWat WJek
- 'New Guinea' ELau
- 'Osmin' PBR ELau
- 'Pistou' ELau
- 'Purple Delight' ELau
- var. ***purpurascens*** CSev NBlu SIde
- - 'Dark Opal' CBod EGHP MNHC SBfd SHDw
- - 'Purple Ruffles' EPfP MNHC SIde SWat WJek
- - 'Red Rubin' MHer MNHC WJek
- var. ***purpurascens*** × ***kilimandscharicum*** CSpe GPoy
- 'Queenette' ELau
- 'Sweet Genovase' SVic
- 'Thai' see *O. basilicum* 'Horapha'
***canum*** see *O. americanum*
× ***citriodorum*** EGHP MNHC SBfd SHDw SIde WJek
- 'Lime' EGHP MNHC
- 'Pesto Perpetuo' EGHP
- 'Siam Queen' EGHP ELau MHer WJek

| | | |
|---|---|---|
| | ***gratissimum*** | ELau |
| § | ***kilimandscharicum*** | ELau GPoy |
| | ***minimum*** | CBod EGHP ELau MHer MNHC SBfd SIde WJek |
| | ***sanctum*** | see *O. tenuiflorum* |
| | 'Spice' | EGHP ELau |
| | 'Spicy Globe' | ELau |
| § | ***tenuiflorum*** | CArn EGHP ELau GPoy MNHC SBfd SHDw SIde WJek |

## *Odontonema* (*Acanthaceae*)

| | | |
|---|---|---|
| | ***schomburgkianum*** | CCCN WHil |
| | ***tubaeforme*** | CCCN |

## *Oemleria* (*Rosaceae*)

| | | |
|---|---|---|
| | ***cerasiformis*** | CBcs CHGN CPMA CTri EBee EBtc EPfP EPla LRHS NLar SSpi WCot WSHC |

## *Oenanthe* (*Apiaceae*)

| | | |
|---|---|---|
| | ***fistulosa*** | EWil LLWG MSKA |
| | ***javanica*** 'Flamingo' (v) | CWat ELan EPfP GCal GGar LEdu LPBA MSKA MWts NBro WFar WMAq WSHC XLum |
| | ***lachenalii*** | LLWG SDix |
| | ***pimpinelloides*** | CHab LLWG |

## *Oenothera* ✿ (*Onagraceae*)

| | | |
|---|---|---|
| § | ***acaulis*** | CBot CMea CPBP CSpe CSpr MDKP MNrw SBch WCFE WCot WPGP |
| § | - 'Aurea' | XLum |
| | - 'Lutea' | see *O. acaulis* 'Aurea' |
| | 'Apricot Delight' | EHoe GJos LRHS MLLN STes WMnd WMoo |
| § | ***biennis*** | CArn CSev CWan EGHP ELan EWil GAbr GPoy MHer NBro SBfd SGar SIde SPhx WBrk WFar WHer WJek WSFF |
| | - SDR 6501 | GKev |
| | ***bistorta*** | see *Camissonia bistorta* |
| | 'Blood Orange' | MDKP SMrm |
| | ***caespitosa*** | GKev |
| | ***childsii*** | see *O. speciosa* |
| | ***cinaeus*** | see *O. fruticosa* subsp. *glauca* |
| | 'Cold Crick' | EBee |
| | 'Colin Porter' | MDKP WHrl WMoo |
| | ***coryi*** | LRHS |
| | 'Crown Imperial' | CMac EBee LEdu LRHS LSou MArl NHol SHar SLon SPer SPoG |
| | Crown of Gold = 'Lishal' | ELan LLHF |
| § | ***elata*** subsp. ***hookeri*** | EWes NBre |
| | ***erythrosepala*** | see *O. glazioviana* |
| | 'Finlay's Fancy' | WCru |
| § | ***fruticosa*** | NLar SEND SPlb XSen |
| | - 'African Sun' PBR | EBee EWes SRot |
| | - 'Camel' (v) | MDKP NPro SMrm WHrl WWEG XLum |
| | - Fireworks | see *O. fruticosa* 'Fyrverkeri' |
| § | - 'Fyrverkeri' ♀H4 | CBcs CMea CPrp EBee ECtt ELan GMaP LEdu LHop LRHS MRav NGdn NHol NVic SPer SWvt WAul WCAu WMnd WWEG XLum |
| § | - subsp. ***glauca*** ♀H4 | CElw CEnt EPfP MDKP MNrw NBPC SBfd SMrm SRms WJek WPer |
| | - - 'Erica Robin' (v) | CChe CMea CPrp ECtt EHoe LRHS LSou MNrw MRav NEgg NGdn SAga SMad SMrm SRot SWvt WCot WHil WHoo WWEG |
| | - - 'Frühlingsgold' (v) | ECtt |
| | - - 'Longest Day' | MBrN |
| | - - Solstice | see *O. fruticosa* subsp. *glauca* 'Sonnenwende' |
| § | - - 'Sonnenwende' | CBre CElw CEnt EBee LRHS NLar NPro WMoo WWEG XLum |
| | - 'Lady Brookeborough' | MRav |
| | - 'Michelle Ploeger' | NBre SUsu |
| | - 'Yellow River' | CElw EBee |
| | - 'Youngii' | CWan EPfP LEdu MCCP WJek WTel WWEG |
| | ***glabra*** Miller | see *O. biennis* |
| | ***glabra*** misapplied | ECha NSti |
| § | ***glazioviana*** | MNHC NBir |
| | ***hookeri*** | see *O. elata* subsp. *hookeri* |
| | ***kunthiana*** | CEnt ECha ECho MDKP MHer NWCA WMnd WMoo |
| | - 'Glowing Magenta' | SPoG WHil |
| | ***lamarckiana*** | see *O. glazioviana* |
| | 'Lemon Sunset' | CCVN LSou SWal WHil WHlf WMoo |
| | ***linearis*** | see *O. fruticosa* |
| § | ***macrocarpa*** ♀H4 | Widely available |
| | - subsp. ***fremontii*** | XSen |
| | - - 'Silver Wings' | EBee SMrm SPhx |
| | - subsp. ***incana*** | CMea CSpe NBre SPhx WHoo |
| | - 'Yellow Queen' | GJos |
| * | ***minima*** | MDKP |
| | ***missouriensis*** | see *O. macrocarpa* |
| | ***muricata*** | NBre |
| | ***oakesiana*** | SPhx |
| | ***odorata*** misapplied | see *O. stricta* |
| | ***odorata*** Hook. & Arn. | see *O. biennis* |
| | - cream-flowered | CSpe |
| | ***organensis*** | CDes EBee WPGP |
| | ***pallida*** 'Innocence' | CBot NBre |
| § | ***perennis*** | CEnt NBre NPro SRms WPer XLum |
| | ***pumila*** | see *O. perennis* |
| | ***rosea*** | CMea |
| | 'Silky Orchid' | ELon |
| § | ***speciosa*** | CMHG EBee NBre SEND SPhx WFar WJek XLum |
| * | - 'Alba' | EBee EWes |
| | - var. ***childsii*** | see *O. speciosa* |
| | - 'Pink Petticoats' | ECha NPer SWat |
| | - 'Rosea' | CBot ECho LAst LEdu SPlb SWat |
| | - 'Siskiyou' | CSpe EAEE EBee ECtt EPfP EShb EWld IPot LEdu LRHS LSou NBro NPri SCoo SGar SMrm SPer SRot SUsu XLum |
| | - Twilight = 'Turner01' PBR (v) | EBee |
| | - 'Woodside White' | ELon SMrm |
| § | ***stricta*** | CHar CMea GCal WBrk |
| * | - 'Moonlight' | SGar |
| | - 'Sulphurea' | CHar CMHG CMea ECGP ELan EWld GCal GMaP IFro MNFA NPer SBch SGar SMrm SPhx WAbb WCot |
| | 'Summer Sun' | EAEE EBee LRHS NBre SPoG WCAu |
| | ***taraxacifolia*** | see *O. acaulis* |
| | ***tetragona*** | see *O. fruticosa* subsp. *glauca* |
| | - var. ***fraseri*** | see *O. fruticosa* subsp. *glauca* |
| | ***versicolor*** | CSev WCFE |
| | - 'Sunset Boulevard' | CPom CSpe GCal LRHS MBNS MMuc SBfd SGar SPad SPer WBor WFar WMoo XLum |

## *Olea* (*Oleaceae*)

| | | |
|---|---|---|
| | ***europaea*** (F) | Widely available |
| | - subsp. ***africana*** | CTrC WPGP |
| | - 'Aglandau' (F) | CAgr |
| | - 'Arbequina' (F) | CDoy ETod SBig |
| | - 'Bouteillan' (F) | CAgr |
| | - 'Cailletier' (F) | CAgr |

| | | |
|---|---|---|
| | – 'Chelsea Physic Garden' (F) | CDoC CDoy |
| § | – 'Cipressino' (F) | ESwi MGos SBfd SBig |
| | – 'Cornicabra' (F) | ETod |
| | – 'El Greco' (F) | CBcs |
| | – subsp. ***europaea*** var. ***sylvestris*** | SEND |
| | – 'Fastigiata' | SBfd |
| | – 'Frantoio' (F) | CAgr CDoy SBfd SBig |
| | – 'Hojiblanca' (F) | CDoy SBig |
| | – 'Leccino' (F) | CDoy SBig |
| | – 'Manzanillo' (F) | ETod |
| | – subsp. ***maroccana*** NJM 06.008 **new** | WPGP |
| | – 'Maurino' (F) | SBig |
| | – 'Peace' | CDoy |
| | – 'Pendolino' (F) | SBig |
| | – 'Picual' (F) | CDoy ETod SBig |
| | – 'Pyramidalis' | see *O. europaea* 'Cipressino' |
| | – 'Serrana' | ETod |
| | – 'Villalonga' | ETod |

## *Olearia* ✿ (*Asteraceae*)

| | | |
|---|---|---|
| | ***albida*** misapplied | see *O.* 'Talbot de Malahide' |
| | ***albida*** Hook.f. | GGar |
| | – var. ***angulata*** | CTrC |
| | ***algida*** | ECou GGar |
| | ***angustifolia*** | GGar |
| | ***arborescens*** | GGar |
| | ***argophylla*** | CPLG ECou GGar |
| | ***avicenniifolia*** | CBcs CMac CTrC ECou GGar SEND |
| | ***bullata*** | ECou |
| | ***canescens*** | CPne |
| | × ***capillaris*** | CDoC ECou GGar |
| | ***chathamica*** | GGar |
| § | ***cheesemanii*** | CBcs CDoC CMHG CPLG CTrC GGal GGar LRHS NLar SVen |
| | ***coriacea*** | ECou GGar |
| | 'County Park' | ECou |
| | ***erubescens*** | CDoC |
| | ***erubescens*** × ***ilicifolia*** | SVen |
| | 'Fish Supper' **new** | GGar |
| | ***floribunda*** | CTrC GGar |
| | ***frostii*** | GGar |
| | ***furfuracea*** | ECou GLin SEND |
| | ***glandulosa*** | ECou GGar |
| | ***gunniana*** | see *O. phlogopappa* |
| | × ***haastii*** | Widely available |
| | – 'McKenzie' | ECou ELon |
| | 'Havering Blush' | ECou |
| | ***hectorii*** | ECou |
| § | 'Henry Travers' | CBcs CCCN CPLG EPfP GGar GQui NMun |
| | ***ilicifolia*** | CDoC EPfP GGar IDee LRHS NLar |
| | ***insignis*** | see *Pachystegia insignis* |
| | ***ledifolia*** | GGar |
| | ***lepidophylla*** | ECou |
| | – 'Silver Knight' | NLar |
| | – silver-leaved | ECou |
| | ***lirata*** | ECou GGar |
| | ***macrodonta*** ♀H3 | Widely available |
| | – 'Intermedia' | GGar |
| | – 'Major' | CCCN GGal GGar LTen NLar |
| | – 'Minor' | CBcs CCCN CDoC CMac CTrC ELan EPfP GBin GGar GQui SPlb |
| § | × ***matthewsii*** | GGar |
| | × ***mollis*** misapplied | see *O.* × *matthewsii* |
| | × ***mollis*** (Kirk) Cockayne | CMac GQui LRHS SPer |
| | – 'Zennorensis' ♀H3 | CBcs CCCN CDoC EPfP GGar IArd IDee MOWG NLar WDin |
| | ***moschata*** | GGar |
| | ***moschata*** × ***nummularifolia*** var. ***cymbifolia*** | GGar |
| | ***nummularifolia*** | CBcs CCCN CDoC CHll CTrC CTri ECou ELan EPfP EPla GGar GKin IVic LRHS NLar SEND SPer SPoG STre SVen SWvt WDin WFar |
| | – var. ***cymbifolia*** | ECou |
| | – hybrids | ECou |
| | – 'Little Lou' | ECou |
| | ***odorata*** | ECou NLar WFar |
| | ***oleifolia*** | see *O.* 'Waikariensis' |
| | ***paniculata*** | CDoC CMHG CTrC CTri CTsd EPfP GGar IVic LRHS MBlu SEND |
| § | ***phlogopappa*** | CTri ECou EWld GGar GLin SVen WKif |
| | – 'Comber's Blue' | CBcs CCCN ELan EPfP GGal GGar GKin IVic LRHS LSRN MAsh SCoo SLim SPer |
| § | – 'Comber's Pink' | CBcs CBod CCCN CDoC CPLG ELan ELon EPfP GGar GKin LRHS LSRN NPer NSti SAga SCoo SLim SPer SPoG WGrn WSHC |
| | – 'Rosea' | see *O. phlogopappa* 'Comber's Pink' |
| | – 'Sawtooth' | GGar |
| | – Splendens Group | WFar |
| I | – var. ***subrepanda*** (DC.) J.H.Willis | CTrC GGal GGar |
| | – 'Tournaig Titch' | GGar |
| | ***ramulosa*** | CCCN CDoC CPLG |
| | – 'Blue Stars' | CMac ECou SLon WGrn |
| | – var. ***ramulosa*** | ECou |
| | ***rani*** misapplied | see *O. cheesemanii* |
| | ***rani*** Druce | CTrC |
| * | ***rossii*** | CTrC GGar |
| | × ***scilloniensis*** misapplied | see *O. stellulata* DC. |
| | × ***scilloniensis*** ambig. | CBcs EHoe SAga SGar SPoG WFar |
| | × ***scilloniensis*** Dorrien-Smith ♀H3 | CCCN CTsd GGar MRav |
| | – 'Compacta' | CBcs |
| | – 'Master Michael' | CBot CCCN CDoC CTri ELon EPfP IVic LRHS MAsh MOWG SBfd SPer SPoG WCFE WGrn WPGP WSHC |
| | ***semidentata*** misapplied | see *O.* 'Henry Travers' |
| | ***solandri*** | CCCN CDoC CMac CTrC CTsd ECou EHoe GGar LRHS SBrd SDix SEND SPer STre |
| | – 'Aurea' | CBcs GQui |
| | 'Stardust' | CTrC LRHS |
| | ***stellulata*** misapplied | see *O. phlogopappa* |
| § | ***stellulata*** DC. | CBot CMac CPLG CSBt CWSG CWib ECou EPfP GGal LRHS MAsh MOWG SCoo SDix SLim SPer WDin WFar WSHC |
| | – 'Michael's Pride' | CPLG |
| | – var. ***rugosa*** | ECou |
| § | 'Talbot de Malahide' | GGar |
| | ***traversii*** | CBcs CBod CCCN CDoC CMHG CSBt CTrC CTsd EBee EPfP GGal GGar LRHS SBfd SEND WHer |
| | – 'Tweedledee' (v) | CChe |
| | – 'Tweedledum' (v) | CBod CCCN CDoC CWib ECou EHoe GGar SBfd |
| | – 'Variegata' (v) | CBcs CTrC CTsd GGar SEND |
| | ***virgata*** | CCCN CHEx ECou GBin GGar GQui IDee LEdu MCot WCot |
| | – var. ***laxiflora*** | CTrC WHer |
| | – var. ***lineata*** | CDoC ECou GGar NLar SEND WDin WHer WSHC |

- - 'Dartonii' CBcs CBod CDoC ECou EPfP GGar LRHS SLPl SPlb SPoG SVen
§ 'Waikariensis' CBot CMHG CMac CPLG CTrC ECou GGar GKin IDee IVic LRHS MSCN SEND SLon SPoG WCFE WDin

## *Oligoneuron* see *Solidago*

## *Oligostachyum* (*Poaceae*)

***lubricum*** see *Semiarundinaria lubrica*
***oedogonatum*** WPGP

## olive see *Olea europaea*

## *Olsynium* (*Iridaceae*)

§ ***douglasii*** ♀H4 CBro CMea LLHF NMen NRya NSla WCot
- 'Album' CWCL ELon EPot GAbr GBin GEdr LLHF NHar NMen NRya NSla WHal
- dwarf GEdr
- var. ***inflatum*** EWes
§ ***filifolium*** GAbr NWCA
§ ***junceum*** CSpe MDKP WPGP
- F&W 8666 CPBP
***scirpoideum*** LLHF
***trinerve*** B&SWJ 10459 WCru

## *Omphalodes* ✿ (*Boraginaceae*)

***cappadocica*** ♀H4 CElw CEnt EBee EPot EShb IFoB LBMP LEdu LRHS MMuc NBro NPer NSla NSum NWCA SRms SWat WBrk WFar WKif WPat
- 'Alba' CMac
- 'Anthea Bloom' NEgg
- 'Blue Rug' NBPC
- 'Cherry Ingram' ♀H4 Widely available
- 'Lilac Mist' CLAP EBee EWTr LLWP MRav SRms SSvw SWat SWvt WTin WWEG
- 'Parisian Skies' CDes CLAP
- 'Starry Eyes' Widely available
§ ***linifolia*** ♀H4 CSpe MCot NMen SBch
- ***alba*** see *O. linifolia*
***luciliae*** CLAP
- var. ***cilicica*** WFar
***nitida*** CSpe GGar LRHS MMuc MNrw NLBP NRya WWEG
***verna*** Widely available
- 'Alba' Widely available
- 'Elfenauge' EBee NBir NLar NRya SMrm SSvw WCot WWEG
- ***grandiflora*** WCot

## *Oncostema* see *Scilla*

## onion see *Allium cepa*

## *Onixotis* (*Colchicaceae*)

***stricta*** CLak WCot

## *Onobrychis* (*Papilionaceae*)

***viciifolia*** WTcb

## *Onoclea* (*Onocleaceae*)

***sensibilis*** ♀H4 Widely available
- copper-leaved CHEx CPMA CRow WPGP

## *Ononis* (*Papilionaceae*)

***repens*** CArn NMir
***rotundifolia*** CPom
***spinosa*** MHer SMrm SPhx WFar WPer XLum

## *Onopordum* (*Asteraceae*)

***acanthium*** CArn EBee ECha ELan EPfP GAbr GMaP LRHS MHer MWat NBid NEgg NVic SDfd SIde SPhx WCAu WCot WFar WHer WMnd
***arabicum*** see *O. nervosum*
§ ***nervosum*** ♀H4 CSpe NBPC SEND

## *Onosma* (*Boraginaceae*)

***alborosea*** CCse ECha GCal GCra SAga SEND WKif WPat WSHC
***helvetica*** GEdr
***nana*** WAbe

## *Onychium* (*Pteridaceae*)

***japonicum*** CBty CPLG EFer EFtx GQui SRms WAbe WRic
***lucidum*** WCot

## *Ophiopogon* ✿ (*Asparagaceae*)

ACE 2362 NMen
BWJ 8244 from Vietnam WCru
from India GCal
'Black Dragon' see *O. planiscapus* 'Nigrescens'
***bodinieri*** CBct ECho EShb EWes LEdu
- B&L 12505 CLAP EBee EPPr EPla
***caulescens*** B&SWJ 8230 WCru
- B&SWJ 11813 WCru
aff. ***caulescens*** HWJ 590 WCru WPGP
***chingii*** EBee EPPr GCal LEdu SCnR
***clarkei*** MMoz
***formosanus*** CPrp GBin
- B&SWJ 3659 WCru
'Gin-ryu' see *Liriope spicata* 'Gin-ryu'
***graminifolius*** see *Liriope muscari*
***intermedius*** CBct CSpe EPPr EShb GGar NLar WAbe WCot
- GWJ 9387 WCru
§ - 'Argenteomarginatus' ECho EWes
- 'Variegatus' see *O. intermedius* 'Argenteomarginatus'
§ ***jaburan*** CMac ECho EWTr LBMP LEdu WMoo
- 'Variegatus' see *O. jaburan* 'Vittatus'
§ - 'Vittatus' (v) ECho EHoe ELan EPfP EWes LEdu MCCP MGos MTis WCot WFar
***japonicus*** CMac ECho EPPr EPfP EPla EShb GPoy LEdu STre XLum
- B&SWJ 1871 WCru
- 'Albus' CLAP ECho EPri MWat
- 'Compactus' CDoC EBee WPGP
- 'Gyoku-Ryu' GCal
- 'Kigimafukiduma' CMac CPLG EBee LRHS MRav WCot
- 'Kyoto' EBee EPPr ESwi
- 'Minor' CBct CChe CEnd CKno ELon EPPr EPfP EPla NLar WPGP WWEG XLum
- 'Nanus Variegatus' (v) CDes EBee NChi
- 'Nippon' CPrp EBee ECho EHoe EPPr GGar LRHS NGdn
- 'Tama-ryu' WAbe WPat
* - 'Tama-ryu Number Two' ECho EPPr
* - 'Variegatus' (v) CDTJ CKno CMac CPrp ECho LEdu SLPl
***longifolius*** 'Takashi-shimomura' (v) WCot
***parviflorus*** GWJ 9387 WCru

| | |
|---|---|
| - HWJK 2093 | WCru |
| ***planiscapus*** | CEnd CFee CKno CMHG CPLG CSam CSev EBee ECho EPPr EPla NBro SBfd SPad STre WMoo |
| * - 'Albovariegatus' | WCot WFar |
| - 'Black Beard' | WCot |
| - 'Green Dragon' | ELan |
| - 'Kansu' | WCot |
| - ***leucanthus*** | EPPr SLPl WCot |
| - 'Little Tabby' (v) | CDes CLAP EBee ECho EPla MDKP MMoz MWhi NPro WAbe WCot WDyG WGrn WHal WTin WWEG |
| * - ***minimus*** | ECho |
| § - 'Nigrescens' ♀H4 | Widely available |
| - 'Silver Ribbon' | ECho MDKP SGar |
| ***scaber*** B&SWJ 1842 | WCru |
| - B&SWJ 3655 | WCru |
| 'Spring Gold' | EShb |

## *Ophrys* (*Orchidaceae*)

| | |
|---|---|
| ***apifera*** | CFir NLAp WHer |
| ***apifera × holoserica*** | NLAp |
| ***apifera × scolopax*** | NLAp |
| ***fuciflora*** | NLAp |
| ***heldreichii*** | NLAp |
| ***insectifera*** | NLAp |
| ***reinholdii*** | NLAp |
| ***speculum*** | NLAp |
| ***sphegodes*** | NLAp |
| ***strausii*** | NLAp |

## *Oplopanax* (*Araliaceae*)

| | |
|---|---|
| ***horridus*** | CArn |
| - B&SWJ 9551 | WCru |

## *Opopanax* (*Apiaceae*)

| | |
|---|---|
| ***chironium*** | CArn LEdu |

## *Opuntia* (*Cactaceae*)

| | |
|---|---|
| sp. | SArc |
| ***compressa*** | see *O. humifusa* |
| ***erinacea*** var. ***utahensis*** × ***polycantha*** NNS 99-263 | WCot |
| ***fragilis*** new | SKHP XSen |
| § ***humifusa*** | CDTJ EAmu EGxp ETod SChr SMad WCot XLum XSen |
| § ***polyacantha*** | SChr SPlb XSen |
| ***rhodantha*** | see *O. polyacantha* |

## orange, sour or Seville see *Citrus aurantium*

## orange, sweet see *Citrus sinensis*

## *Orbea* (*Apocynaceae*)

| | |
|---|---|
| ***cooperi*** | LToo |
| ***gerstneri*** new | LToo |
| ***halipedicola*** | LToo |
| ***knobelii*** | LToo |
| ***lugardii*** | LToo |
| ***paradoxa*** new | LToo |
| ***pulchella*** | LToo |
| ***semota*** new | LToo |
| ***speciosa*** | LToo |
| ***tapscottii*** new | LToo |
| ***ubomboensis*** new | LToo |
| § ***variegata*** ♀H1 | EShb LToo STre |

## *Orchis* (*Orchidaceae*)

| | |
|---|---|
| ***anthropophora*** | EFEx NLAp |
| ***elata*** | see *Dactylorhiza elata* |
| ***foliosa*** | see *Dactylorhiza foliosa* |
| ***fuchsii*** | see *Dactylorhiza fuchsii* |
| ***italica*** | NLAp |
| ***laxiflora*** | see *Anacamptis laxiflora* |
| ***maculata*** | see *Dactylorhiza maculata* |
| ***maderensis*** | see *Dactylorhiza foliosa* |
| ***majalis*** | see *Dactylorhiza majalis* |
| § ***mascula*** | ECho NLAp WHer |
| ***militaris*** | NLAp |
| ***morio*** | see *Anacamptis morio* |
| ***purpurea*** | NLAp |
| ***simia*** | NLAp |

## oregano see *Origanum vulgare*

## *Oreomyrrhis* (*Apiaceae*)

| | |
|---|---|
| ***argentea*** | GKev NMen SPhx |

## *Oreopteris* (*Thelypteridaceae*)

| | |
|---|---|
| § ***limbosperma*** | SRms WRic |

## *Oreorchis* (*Orchidaceae*)

| | |
|---|---|
| ***patens*** | LWst |

## *Origanum* ✿ (*Lamiaceae*)

| | |
|---|---|
| from Kalamata | SEND |
| ***acutidens*** | XSen |
| ***amanum*** ♀H2-3 | CPBP ECho EPot EWes MDKP NBir NMen NSla SBch WAbe WPat |
| - var. ***album*** | ECho LLHF NSla SBch WAbe |
| × ***applii*** | ELau |
| 'Barbara Tingey' | CPBP CRDP ECho ELan EWes ITim LBee MNrw NWCA SPhx WCFE |
| 'Bristol Cross' | MHer XSen |
| 'Buckland' | CPrp CRDP ECho ECtt EPot MHer NMen NWCA SPhx WAbe WSHC |
| ***caespitosum*** | see *O. vulgare* 'Nanum' |
| § ***calcaratum*** | ECho LLHF SUsu WPat |
| 'Carol's Delight' | MHer |
| ***creticum*** | see *O. vulgare* subsp. *hirtum* |
| ***dictamnus*** | CMea ECho GPoy LLHF MHer SBfd SHDw WJek XSen |
| 'Dingle Fairy' | CMMP CWCL EBee ECho EDAr ELon EPot EWes MHer MNrw NBir SBch SIde SRot WGwG WMoo XSen |
| ***ehrenbergii*** new | XSen |
| 'Emma Stanley' | WAbe |
| 'Frank Tingey' | ECho LLHF |
| 'Gold Splash' | CPbn EPfP SIde WMoo |
| ***heracleoticum*** L. | see *O. vulgare* subsp. *hirtum* |
| 'Hot and Spicy' | CPbn LBuc MHer WJek WWEG XSen |
| 'Ingolstadt' | SPhx |
| 'Kent Beauty' | CKno CMea CSpe CWCL EBee ECho ECtt ELan EPfP EShb GCal LAst LRHS LSou MHer MLLN MSCN NBir NMen NWCA SBfd SPhx SUsu SWvt WAbe WJek WKif WPat WSHC XSen |
| 'Kent Beauty Variegated' (v) | ECho |
| ***kopetdaghense*** | WBox |
| ***laevigatum*** ♀H3 | CMHG ECho ELan EPfP EPot GBee MHer NBro NMir NPer NWCA SIde SUsu WKif WMoo WPer WSHC XSen |
| - 'Herrenhausen' ♀H4 | Widely available |
| - 'Hopleys' | CMea CPbn CPrp CSev CTri EBee ECha ELan EPfP GCal LAst LHop LRHS MHer MMuc MRav MWat |

NBir NCGa NDov NWCA SBfd SEND SPer WGwG WHoo WPer WSHC XSen
- 'Joanne' **new** NWCA
- 'Purple Charm' EDAr MNHC NBre SIde
'Lynda Windsor' CRDP
***majorana*** CArn CHab CPbn CSev ELan ELau MHer MNHC SIde SWat WJek WPer
I - 'Aureum' GKev
- Pagoda Bells = 'Lizbell'PBR SIde SMrm SRot WHoo
'Marchants Seedling' SPhx
***microphyllum*** CFee CPbn EDAr NMen XSen
***minutiflorum*** ECho LLHF
'Norton Gold' CBre EBee ECha ECtt LRHS MHer NBre NPer SIde WWEG
'Nymphenburg' CFee LSou SIde WHer
***onites*** CHby CPbn CWan ELau ILis MHer MNHC NBlu SBfd SIde SPlb WBrk WGwG WJek WPer
Overseas Farm hybrid MHer
'Rosenkuppel' CMea CPbn EBee ECha ECtt EGHP ELan EPot GCal LHop LRHS MHer MLHP MRav SBch SPer SPhx SPlb WJek WMoo WPer WPnn WTin WWEG
'Rotkugel' CMHG CPrp ELon WCFE WCru WWEG
***rotundifolium*** ♀H4 CMea EBee ECho ELan LLHF MDKP MHer NBir SBch XSen
- hybrid MDKP
***scabrum*** subsp. ***pulchrum*** 'Newleaze' SBch
***syriacum*** CArn XSen
'Tinpenny Pink' WTin
***tournefortii*** see *O. calcaratum*
***virens*** CArn ILis
***vulgare*** CArn CHab COlW CPbn CRWN CSev CWan EWil GJos GMaP GPoy MHer MMuc MNHC NBro NLan NMir NPri SBfd SEND SGar SIde SPlb SVic SWal WHer WJek WPer WSFF
- from Israel ELau
- 'Acorn Bank' CArn CBod CPbn CPrp EBee ELau EWes GGar LRHS MNHC NHol NLar SIde SPoG WGwG WHer WJek
- var. ***album*** ELau
- 'Aureum' ♀H4 Widely available
- 'Aureum Crispum' CPbn CPrp CWan ECha ELau GPoy ILis NBid NBlu SBch SBfd SIde SWat WJek
- 'Compactum' CArn CMea CPbn CPrp CSev EBee ECha EGHP ELau EPot GCal GGar GPoy ILis LEdu MHer MNHC NBir NSla NWCA SIde SPlb SWat WGwG WJek WMoo WPer WTin XLum XSen
- 'Corinne Tremaine' (v) NBir
- 'Country Cream' (v) Widely available
- ***formosanum*** B&SWJ 3180 WCru
§ - 'Gold Tip' (v) CEnt CMea CPbn CSev EBee ELau MCot MHer MNHC NWad SBfd SIde SPlb SWat WFar WHer WJek WWEG
- 'Golden Shine' CMMP EHoe EWes SIde
§ - subsp. ***hirtum*** CArn CHby CPbn GPoy SPlb WJek WPer
- - 'Greek' CBod CEnt CPrp CWan EGHP ELau MHer MNHC SBfd SEND WGwG
§ - 'Nanum' LRHS WJek
- 'Nyamba' GPoy
- 'Polyphant' (v) CPbn CSev LSou NBir WJek XLum XSen
- 'Thumble's Variety' CElw CMea CPrp EAEE EBee ECha EHoe EPfP GCal GGar LHop LRHS MAsh MBri MHer MRav NHol NWad SAga SIde SPoG SSvw SWat WCFE WMnd WMoo WWEG XLum XSen
- 'Tomintoul' GPoy
- 'Variegatum' see *O. vulgare* 'Gold Tip'
- 'White Charm' CPbn NHol NWad SIde
'Z'Attar' MHer SIde WJek

## *Orixa* (*Rutaceae*)

***japonica*** CBot CPLG GAuc MBri NLar WFar WPGP
- 'Variegata' (v) LLHF LRHS NLar

## *Orlaya* (*Apiaceae*)

***grandiflora*** CBre CFir CSpe LBMP MWea SBch SUsu WCot WFar WHal WHil WWFP

## *Ornithogalum* (*Asparagaceae*)

***arabicum*** CBro CCCN CFir CHid ECho GKev LAma MBri
***arcuatum*** WCot
***balansae*** see *O. oligophyllum*
***caudatum*** see *O. longibracteatum*
***chionophilum*** EBee ECho
***dubium*** ♀H1 CBro ECho LRHS
***fimbriatum*** ECho
***lanceolatum*** ECho WCot
§ ***longibracteatum*** CHEx EBee ECho GAuc SChr WGwG
***maculatum*** ECho
***magnum*** CAvo CBro CFFs CMea EBee ECho EPot ERCP GAuc GKev MCot MNrw SPad SPhx WCot
***multifolium*** 'Loeriesfontein' ECho
***nanum*** see *O. sigmoideum*
***narbonense*** EBee ECho GAuc GKev MMHG SPhx WCot
***nutans*** ♀H4 CAvo CBro CFFs CHid CPrp CTca EBee ECho EPfP EPot GCal GKev LAma LRHS MAvo MCot MNrw NBir NMRc NMen NWCA SDeJ SEND SPhx WCot WFar
§ ***oligophyllum*** EBee ECho EPfP EPot MMHG MNrw NMen NWCA
§ ***orthophyllum*** ECho
***ponticum*** ECho
***pyramidale*** CPom EBee ECho EPot GAuc GMac MNrw SPhx
***pyrenaicum*** CAvo ECha WCot WShi
***reverchonii*** EBee ECho EPot SPhx
***saundersiae*** EBee ECho
***sibthorpii*** see *O. sigmoideum*
§ ***sigmoideum*** EBee
***sintenisii*** EBee ECho
***suaveolens*** 'Saldanha' ECho
***tenuifolium*** see *O. orthophyllum*
- subsp. ***aridum*** ECho LWst

| | |
|---|---|
| ***thyrsoides*** ♀H1 | CCCN ECho EPfP LAma LRHS |
| ***ulophyllum*** | ECho |
| ***umbellatum*** | CAvo CBro CFFs CTca CTri ECho EPfP GKev GPoy LAma LHop MBri MCot MNrw NMen SDeJ SEND SMrm SPer SRms WFar WHil WPer WShi |

## *Ornithoglossum* (*Colchicaceae*)

| | |
|---|---|
| ***viride*** | CLak |

## *Orontium* (*Araceae*)

| | |
|---|---|
| ***aquaticum*** | CWat EHon LLWG LPBA MSKA MWts NLar NPer SWat WMAq WPnP |

## *Orostachys* (*Crassulaceae*)

| | |
|---|---|
| ***furusei*** | WFar |
| § ***spinosa*** | EWes GKev NMen NWCA SPlb WCot WFar |

## *Orthrosanthus* (*Iridaceae*)

| | |
|---|---|
| ***chimboracensis*** | CFir EWld MDKP MWea NLar WFar WPer |
| - JCA 13743 | CPou |
| ***laxus*** | CFir ECou LLHF MAvo MCot NBir SEND SHom SMad WMoo WNew WWEG |
| ***multiflorus*** | CBro CDes CSpe EPri |
| ***polystachyus*** | CAby CCVN CSpe CTsd CWCL CYeo EWld MWea SMrm WSHC |

## *Orychophragmus* (*Brassicaceae*)

| | |
|---|---|
| ***violaceus*** | CCCN |

## *Oryzopsis* (*Poaceae*)

| | |
|---|---|
| ***hymenoides*** 'Rimrock' new | SPhx |
| ***lessoniana*** | see *Anemanthele lessoniana* |
| ***miliacea*** | CKno CSpe EBee ECha EHoe EPPr MMoz NDov NWsh SEND SUsu WCot WPGP WWEG |
| ***paradoxa*** | EPPr |

## *Oscularia* (*Aizoaceae*)

| | |
|---|---|
| § ***deltoides*** ♀H1-2 | CCCN CHEx NWCA SVen |

## *Osmanthus* (*Oleaceae*)

| | |
|---|---|
| ***armatus*** | CAbP CBcs CMac EPfP NLar SGol SPur WFar |
| § × ***burkwoodii*** ♀H4 | Widely available |
| § ***decorus*** | CBcs CMac CTri EBee ELan EPfP EWTr MGos MRav MWea NLar NWea SBrt SGol SPer WDin WFar |
| ***delavayi*** ♀H4 | Widely available |
| - 'George Gardner' | CMac |
| - 'Latifolius' | CPMA LRHS MAsh SLon SPer SPoG WFar |
| ***forrestii*** | see *O. yunnanensis* |
| × ***fortunei*** | CPLG EBee EPfP LAst LLHF LRHS MMuc SEND WFar |
| ***fragrans*** | CBcs CDoC CMCN GBin MBri SLon |
| - f. ***aurantiacus*** | GBin |
| - 'Fudingzhu' | GBin |
| - 'Latifolius' | CBcs |
| - f. ***thunbergii*** | GBin |
| § ***heterophyllus*** | CBcs CDul CMac EBee ECrN EPfP EWTr MGos MRav NLar SGol SPer SRms SSta WDin WFar |
| § - all gold | CAbP CDoC IVic |
| - 'Argenteomarginatus' | see *O. heterophyllus* 'Variegatus' |
| § - 'Aureomarginatus' (v) | CBcs CDoC CMHG CTsd EBee EHoe ELon GKin NWea SLon SPer WCFE |
| - 'Aureus' misapplied | see *O. heterophyllus* all gold |
| - 'Aureus' Rehder | see *O. heterophyllus* 'Aureomarginatus' |
| § - 'Goshiki' (v) | Widely available |
| N - 'Gulftide' ♀H4 | CDul EBee EPfP LRHS MAsh MGos NLar SCoo WFar |
| - 'Kembu' (v) | NLar |
| - 'Myrtifolius' | CMac NLar |
| - 'Ōgon' | EPfP |
| - 'Purple Shaft' | CAbP ELan EPfP LRHS MAsh |
| - 'Purpureus' | CBcs CBot CDoC CDul CMHG CMac CWib EBee EHoe ELon MBri MGos MSwo NLar SCoo SEND SGol SLim SLon SPer SPoG SSpi WCFE WDin |
| - 'Rotundifolius' | CBcs CMac NLar |
| - Tricolor | see *O. heterophyllus* 'Goshiki' |
| § - 'Variegatus' (v) ♀H4 | Widely available |
| ***ilicifolius*** | see *O. heterophyllus* |
| ***rigidus*** | NLar |
| ***serrulatus*** | CBot NLar |
| ***suavis*** | NLar |
| § ***yunnanensis*** | CMHG EPfP MBlu MBri NLar SArc WFar WPGP WPat |

## × *Osmarea* see *Osmanthus*

| | |
|---|---|
| ***burkwoodii*** | see *Osmanthus* × *burkwoodii* |

## *Osmaronia* see *Oemleria*

## *Osmitopsis* (*Asteraceae*)

| | |
|---|---|
| ***asteriscoides*** | GFai |

## *Osmorhiza* (*Apiaceae*)

| | |
|---|---|
| ***aristata*** B&SWJ 1607 | WCru |

## *Osmunda* ✿ (*Osmundaceae*)

| | |
|---|---|
| sp. | CCCN |
| ***cinnamomea*** ♀H4 | CBty CCCN CKel CLAP CWCL EBee EWes GBin GCal ISha LRHS LTen NLar NMyG WRic |
| ***claytoniana*** ♀H4 | CLAP EFer GBin GLin ISha LRHS NLar NMyG WCru WPnP WRic XLum |
| ***japonica*** | CHid CLAP GBin ISha LWSt NMyG |
| ***regalis*** ♀H4 | Widely available |
| - from southern USA | CLAP |
| - 'Cristata' ♀H4 | CBty CFwr CLAP EBee ELan EPfP GBin LRHS MBri MMoz MRav NBid NLar NMyG SWvt WFib WRic |
| - 'Purpurascens' | CLAP CPrp CWCL EBee ELan ELon EPfP GQui LBMP LRHS MAvo MGos MRav NBid NBir NHol NLar SBfd SGol SWat WFar WFib WMoo WPGP WPnP WRic WWEG XLum |
| - var. ***spectabilis*** | CCCN CLAP ISha LRHS WRic |
| - 'Undulata' | WFib |

## *Osteomeles* (*Rosaceae*)

| | |
|---|---|
| ***subrotunda*** | MBri WKif |

## *Osteospermum* (*Asteraceae*)

| | |
|---|---|
| 'African Queen' | see *O.* 'Nairobi Purple' |
| 'Almach' (Springstar Series) | LSou SMrm |

| | | |
|---|---|---|
| | 'Arusha'$^{PBR}$ (Cape Daisy Series) | LSou |
| | (Astra Series) | WGor |
| | 'Astra Pink' **new** | |
| | - 'Astra Pink Silver' | SVen |
| | - 'Astra Purple Spoon' | WGor |
| | 'Astra Violet' | WGor |
| | - 'Astra Yellow' **new** | LAst |
| | Banana Symphony = 'Sekiin47' (Symphony Series) | CCCN LAst SMrm |
| | ***barberae*** misapplied | see *O. jucundum* (Phillips) Norlindh |
| | 'Blue Streak' | CCCN |
| | 'Brickell's Hybrid' | see *O.* 'Chris Brickell' |
| | 'Buttermilk' ♀$^{H1+3}$ | CCCN CSpr ELan SVen WWlt |
| | 'Cannington John' | CCCN LSRN |
| | 'Cannington Roy' | CBar CBcs CCCN COlW CSam EBee ECtt ELan EPfP GAbr LSRN SBrd SPoG WAbe WNew |
| | ***caulescens*** misapplied | see *O.* 'White Pim' |
| § | 'Chris Brickell' | GCal |
| | compact white-flowered | CHEx |
| | ***ecklonis*** | CBcs CCCN CDTJ CHll CMac CTri EBee EPfP GGar GMaP NBro NGdn SPoG WPer |
| | - var. ***prostratum*** | see *O.* 'White Pim' |
| | 'Giles Gilbey' (v) | CCCN MBNS |
| | 'Gold Sparkler' (v) | SEND |
| | 'Gweek Variegated' (v) | CCCN |
| | 'Helen Dimond' | LBuc LRHS |
| | 'Hopleys' ♀$^{H3-4}$ | MHer SEND |
| | 'Iced Gem' | LBuc LRHS |
| | 'Irish' | EPot IGor LSou SMrm |
| § | ***jucundum*** (Phillips) Norlindh ♀$^{H3-4}$ | CChe CEnt CMea CTri CWCL ECha EPfP LRHS LSRN MAvo MLHP MRav NBir NPer SEND SMrm SPlb SRms WBrk |
| | - 'Blackthorn Seedling' ♀$^{H3-4}$ | CCCN CMea CWGN EBee GGar IVic NGdn SAga |
| | - var. ***compactum*** | CHEx CMac EBee ELan ELon EPfP GCal LAst LRHS LSRN MBri NPer NPri SBrd SMrm SPer SPoG SPur SWvt WAbe WHil WHoo WNew WPat |
| | - 'Killerton Pink' | WPer |
| | - 'Langtrees' ♀$^{H3-4}$ | SMrm |
| | - 'White Moon' | GGar |
| | 'Keia' (Springstar Series) | CCCN |
| | 'La Mortola' | GCal |
| § | 'Lady Leitrim' ♀$^{H3-4}$ | CBar CCCN CWGN EBee ECha ELan ELon EPfP GCra GGar LHop LSRN MGos MSpe NPer SAga SPer SPoG SWvt WAbe WFar WHlf WNew WPtf |
| | 'Lemon Symphony'$^{PBR}$ (Symphony Series) | CBcs |
| | 'Mango Symphony' (Symphony Series) **new** | MBNS |
| | Milk Symphony = 'Seiremi' (Symphony Series) | CCCN CWCL |
| § | 'Nairobi Purple' | CBcs CCCN CFee CHEx CMea COlW CWCL EBee ELan EPfP ESwi MBNS MBri NPri SEND SMrm SWvt WBor WHil WNew |
| | Nasinga Cream = 'Aknam'$^{PBR}$ (Cape Daisy Series) | CCCN |
| | Nasinga Purple = 'Aksullo' (Cape Daisy Series) | CSpr EPfP |
| | ***oppositifolium*** | CCCN |
| | Orange Symphony = 'Seimora'$^{PBR}$ (Symphony Series) | CBcs CCCN LAst MBNS SMrm |
| | 'Pale Face' | see *O.* 'Lady Leitrim' |
| | 'Peggyi' | see *O.* 'Nairobi Purple' |
| | 'Pink Whirls' ♀$^{H1+3}$ | CCCN |
| | 'Port Wine' | see *O.* 'Nairobi Purple' |
| | 'Seaside' (Side Series) | EPfP |
| | 'Silver Sparkler' (v) ♀$^{H1+3}$ | CCCN CDTJ ELan MHer SVen |
| | 'Snow Pixie' | CMea CSpe CWGN LHop NPri SWvt WHil |
| | Sonja = 'Sunny Sonja'$^{PBR}$ | EPfP |
| | 'Sparkler' | CCCN CHEx |
| | Springstar Series | CBcs |
| | 'Stardust'$^{PBR}$ | EPfP LBuc LRHS NPer SCoo SPoG |
| | (Sunbrella Series) | LSou |
| | 'Sunbrella Orange' **new** | |
| | - 'Sunbrella Pink' **new** | LSou |
| | - 'Sunbrella Purple' **new** | LSou |
| | - 'Sunbrella Salmon' **new** | LSou |
| | 'Sunny Amanda'$^{PBR}$ | LSou |
| | 'Sunny Dark Florence' | LSou SVen WRHF |
| | 'Sunny Dark Martha' | EPfP |
| | 'Sunny Davina' | LSou SVen |
| | 'Sunny Serena'$^{PBR}$ | LSou |
| | 'Sunny Sheila' | LSou WGor |
| * | 'Superbum' | CHEx |
| I | 'Superbum' × 'Lady Leitrim' | CHEx |
| | 'Tauranga' | see *O.* 'Whirlygig' |
| | 'Tresco Peggy' | see *O.* 'Nairobi Purple' |
| | 'Tresco Pink' | CCCN |
| | 'Tresco Purple' | see *O.* 'Nairobi Purple' |
| | 'Weetwood' ♀$^{H3-4}$ | CCCN CWGN EBee ECtt ELan GCal GGar LHop LRHS MHer MLHP SAga SBrd SPer SPoG SWvt WAbe WFar |
| § | 'Whirlygig' ♀$^{H1+3}$ | CCCN CSpr |
| § | 'White Pim' ♀$^{H3-4}$ | CDTJ CHll ELan ELon MAvo NPer SDix SEND SMrm SPer SUsu |
| | 'Wine Purple' | see *O.* 'Nairobi Purple' |
| | 'Wisley Pink' | NEgg |
| | 'Zaurak' (Springstar Series) | CCCN CWCL |
| | 'Zulu' (Cape Daisy Series) | CCCN |

## *Ostrowskia* (*Campanulaceae*)

| | |
|---|---|
| ***magnifica*** | LWst |

## *Ostrya* (*Betulaceae*)

| | |
|---|---|
| ***carpinifolia*** | CBcs CDul CLnd CMCN CTho CWib ECrN EMil EPfP EWTr LRHS MBlu MMuc NLar NWea SGol SWvt |
| ***japonica*** | CDul CMCN NLar |
| ***virginiana*** | EPfP |

## *Othonna* (*Asteraceae*)

| | |
|---|---|
| sp. | XLum |
| ***cheirifolia*** | CBot CCCN CSpe EHoe ELan EWes NBir SAga SEND WBrk WPer WSHC WWEG XLum XSen |

## *Othonnopsis* see *Othonna*

## *Ourisia* (*Plantaginaceae*)

| | |
|---|---|
| × ***bitternensis*** 'Cliftonville Canary' | WAbe |
| - 'Cliftonville Crimson' **new** | WAbe |
| - 'Cliftonville Damask' **new** | WAbe |
| - 'Cliftonville Lemon' | WAbe |
| - 'Cliftonville Ling' | WAbe |

- 'Cliftonville Old Rose' **new** WAbe
- 'Cliftonville Pink' WAbe
- 'Cliftonville Roset' WAbe
***caespitosa*** var. ***gracilis*** GGar
***coccinea*** EBee GAbr GCra GEdr GGar GKev GMac NBir NMen NWCA WAbe
***crosbyi*** GEdr
'Loch Ewe' CPLG GAbr GBin GGar
***macrophylla*** GGar LLHF
***microphylla*** WAbe
- f. ***alba*** WAbe
- 'Hollowcliffe' **new** WAbe
***modesta*** GBin
***polyantha*** WAbe WFar
'Cliftonville Scarlet'
'Snowflake' ♀H4 GAbr GBin GEdr GGar NBir NLBP NMen WAbe

## *Oxalis* (*Oxalidaceae*)

sp. NMen
from Mount Stewart WMoo
***acetosella*** CRWN EWil MHer NMir WHer WShi
- var. ***subpurpurascens*** IFro MMHG WCot
***adenophylla*** ♀H4 CElw CMea CPLG CTri ECho EPfP EPot GAbr GKev GMaP ITim LAma LHop LRHS MAsh MAvo NBlu NEgg NHol NLar NMen NWCA SDeJ SPoG WFar WHoo WPer
***adenophylla*** × ***enneaphylla*** see *O.* 'Matthew Forrest'
'Anne Christie' **new** CPBP
***anomala*** ECho WCot
***arenaria*** F&W 10584 WCot
§ ***articulata*** LRHS NPer SEND WCot XLum
- 'Alba' SEND WCot XLum
I - f. ***crassipes*** 'Alba' WCot
- 'Festival' WCot
'Black Velvet' (Xalis Series) ECtt
***bowiei*** CPBP ECho EPot
- 'Amarantha' ECho
***brasiliensis*** CPBP ECho EPot
***deppei*** see *O. tetraphylla*
§ ***depressa*** CTri ECho EPot EWes GEdr LLHF MSCN NBir NMen NRya NSla SRms WFar
***eckloniana*** ECho
- var. ***sonderi*** EBee ECho WCot
***enneaphylla*** ♀H4 CElw ECho ELon EPot GAbr GGar LRHS NMen NRya SBch WFar
- 'Alba' CMea CPBP ECho GEdr GGar NMen NSla NWCA
- subsp. ***ibari*** ECho EPot GEdr ITim NMen NSla
- 'Minutifolia' LLHF NMen NRya NSla
- 'Rosea' ECho EPot GKev ITim NLar NRya NSla SBch
- 'Sheffield Swan' ECho GEdr LLHF NMen NSla
- 'Ute' EPot
***falcatula*** WCot
'Fanny' EBee ECho
***flava*** CGrW ECho WCot
***floribunda*** misapplied see *O. articulata*
***fourcadei*** ECho WCot
***glabra*** CPBP
***griffithii*** LWst
- double-flowered (d) GEdr LWst
'Gwen McBride' CPBP NMen
***hedysaroides*** CCCN GCal
'Hemswell Knight' CPBP NMen SBch
***hirta*** CPBP EPot
- 'Gothenburg' CPBP EBee ECho GKev NMen SBch
***imbricata*** CPBP ECho LLHF
***inops*** see *O. depressa*
'Ione Hecker' ♀H4 CMea CPBP ECho ELon EPot GEdr GGar GKev ITim NHar NLar NMen NRya NWCA
'Irish Mist' (v) CHid EBee ECho WCot WHil
'Jess's Pink Treasure' (v) WCot
* ***karroica*** ECho NMen WCot
§ ***laciniata*** ECho GKev NHar NMen
- hybrids NHar
***lactea*** double-flowered see *O. magellanica* 'Nelson'
***lasiandra*** CCCN ECho
§ ***latifolia*** CPBP
***loricata*** ECho NMen
***magellanica*** CRow CSpe CTri ECho EDAr GGar LBee LRHS NChi SPlb WFar WMoo WPer
- 'Flore Pleno' see *O. magellanica* 'Nelson'
§ - 'Nelson' (d) CSpe EBee ECho EWes GAbr GCal GGar GMac LBee MMuc NBir NPer WMoo WPer WPtf
***mallobolba*** 'Citrino' CPBP WAbe
***massoniana*** CPBP ECho EPot NMen WAbe WCot WHil
§ 'Matthew Forrest' EPot NMen WCot
§ ***megalorrhiza*** CHEx SChr
§ ***melanosticta*** CBro CPBP ECho EPot LLHF SDeJ WCot
***monophylla*** ECho
***namaquana*** ECho
***obtriangulata*** ECho
***obtusa*** ECho NMen SCnR
- apricot-flowered WCot
***oregana*** CDes CHid CMac CRow EBee ECho ELon GGar GMac SPhx WCot WCru WPGP WSHC
- 'Klamath Ruby' WSHC
- f. ***smalliana*** EWes WCru
***palmifrons*** CPBP ECho EPot LLHF
***perdicaria*** CBro CPBP ECho EPot EWes LRHS WAbe WFar
***pes-caprae*** CGrW
***polyphylla*** EBee ECho
- var. ***pentaphylla*** CPBP EPot
§ ***purpurea*** ECho MWea WAbe
- 'Ken Aslet' see *O. melanosticta*
***regnellii*** see *O. triangularis* subsp. *papilionacea*
***semiloba*** ECho GCal NCGa
Slack Top hybrids **new** NSla
***speciosa*** see *O. purpurea*
***spiralis*** subsp. ***vulcanicola*** CCCN LSou SDix WDyG
- - 'Burgundy' NPri
***squamata*** CPBP LLHF WPat
***squamoso-radicosa*** see *O. laciniata*
***stipularis*** ECho LLHF
***succulenta*** Barnéoud see *O. megalorrhiza*
***succulenta*** ambig. CHll
'Sunny' ECho
'Sunset Velvet' WCot
§ ***tetraphylla*** CBro CPLG EBee ECho LAma NPer
* - ***alba*** ECho
- 'Iron Cross' CCVN CHEx CHid EBee ECho EPot GAbr LAma NBir NPnk SDeJ SWal WPer
'Tina' CPBP
***triangularis*** CCCN CHEx CPLG ECho EOHP EPot LAma MAvo NBir NPer WFar

- 'Birgit' EBee ECho
- Burgundy Wine = 'JR Oxburwi' (Xalis Series) CWGN ECtt NPer
- 'Cupido' EBee ECho GGar WPer
- 'Mijke' EBee ECho NMRc

§ subsp. ***papilionacea*** ♀H1 EBee ECho LAma NMRc
- - 'Atropurpurea' CSpe EBee LHop SDeJ

* - - ***rosea*** WCot
- subsp. ***triangularis*** CHid EBee ECho NCGa

***tuberosa*** GPoy ILis LEdu
'Ute' CPBP GEdr NMen NSla
***valdiviensis*** MDKP
***versicolor*** ♀H1 CPBP ECho EPot NBir NMen SCnR WAbe WCot
***vespertilionis*** Zucc. see *O. latifolia*
I 'Waverley Hybrid' NMen
***zeekoevleyensis*** WCot

## *Oxycoccus* see *Vaccinium*

## *Oxydendrum* ✿ (*Ericaceae*)

***arboreum*** CAbP CBcs CDoC CEnd CMCN EBee EPfP IDee IVic LRHS MAsh MBri MMuc NLar SCoo SPer SSpi SSta WDin WFar WPGP
- 'Chameleon' SSta

## *Oxylobium* (*Papilionaceae*)

***ellipticum*** GAbr GGar

## *Oxypetalum* (*Apocynaceae*)

***caeruleum*** see *Tweedia caerulea*
***solanoides*** EBee

## *Oxyria* (*Polygonaceae*)

***digyna*** GGar

## *Oxytropis* (*Papilionaceae*)

***purpurea*** LLHF
***shokanbetsuensis*** LLHF

## *Ozothamnus* (*Asteraceae*)

***antennaria*** WSHC
§ ***coralloides*** ♀H2-3 ECou EPot WAbe
§ 'County Park Silver' EWes GEdr GLam ITim MDKP NWCA WPat
§ ***hookeri*** CBcs CDoC EBee ECou GGar LRHS MBrN MRav SPer WJek WPat
§ ***ledifolius*** ♀H4 CBcs CDoC EBee ELan EPfP GGar MBri NBir SLon SPer WAbe WDin WPat
§ ***rosmarinifolius*** CBcs CDoC CTsd EBee ELan EPfP GGar LRHS MAsh MSwo NChi SBfd SPer WDin WFar
- 'Kiandra' ECou
- 'Silver Jubilee' ♀H3 CBcs CDoC CEnd CEnt CSBt EBee ECrN ELan EPfP GBin GCal LRHS MAsh MBri MGos MRav MSwo NSti SAga SLim SLon SPer SPlb SRkn WDin

***scutellifolius*** ECou
***secundiflorus*** GGar
§ ***selago*** ECou WCot WPat WThu
§ - var. ***tumidus*** ITim WPat WThu
'Sussex Silver' CDoC GGar
'Threave Seedling' CDoC EBee ELan GBin IVic MAsh MMuc SPer
§ ***thyrsoideus*** WFar

# P

## *Pachyphragma* (*Brassicaceae*)

§ ***macrophyllum*** CBcs CSev EBee ECGP ECha ELan ELon GCal IBlr NCGa NLar NMRc NSti WCot WCru WPGP WSHC

## *Pachyphytum* (*Crassulaceae*)

***bracteosum*** new MSCN
***oviferum*** SChr

## *Pachypodium* (*Apocynaceae*)

***bispinosum*** LToo
× ***succulentum*** new
***geayi*** ♀H1 EAmu
***lamerei*** ♀H1 EAmu
***succulentum*** LToo

## *Pachysandra* (*Buxaceae*)

***axillaris*** CLAP GCal SKHP WCot
- BWJ 8032 WCru
- 'Crûg's Cover' EWld WCru

***procumbens*** CLAP EBee EPla LHop NLar SKHP WCot WCru
- 'Angola' (v) WCot

***stylosa*** CHEx MRav NLar SMad
***terminalis*** Widely available
- 'Green Carpet' ♀H4 Widely available
- 'Green Sheen' ECha EPPr EPfP ESwi EWTr LRHS MBri WFar
- 'Variegata' (v) ♀H4 Widely available

## *Pachystachys* (*Acanthaceae*)

***lutea*** ♀H1 CCCN

## *Pachystegia* (*Asteraceae*)

§ ***insignis*** CBrP LRHS
- Daizea = 'Hardec' LBuc

## *Pachystima* see *Paxistima*

## *Paederota* (*Plantaginaceae*)

***lutea*** NWCA WAbe

## *Paeonia* ✿ (*Paeoniaceae*)

'Age of Gold' (S) GBin WCAu
'Age of Victoria' GBin
***albiflora*** see *P. lactiflora*
'America' GBin
'Anna Marie' (S) GBin
***anomala*** CFir GEdr LWst MHom MPhe NLar WCot
§ - var. ***anomala*** GBin
- var. ***intermedia*** GCal

***arietina*** see *P. mascula* subsp. *arietina*
'Athena' GBin
***aurelia*** GKev MNrw
***banatica*** see *P. officinalis* subsp. *banatica*
'Banquet' (S) GBin WCAu
§ 'Bartzella' (d) CKel ELan GBin WCAu WHlf
***beresowskii*** EBee LWst
'Black Panther' (S) GBin WCAu
'Black Pirate' (S) CKel
'Blaze' GMaP LRHS MBri MSCN NCGa NSti
Blue and Purple Giant see *P. suffruticosa* 'Zi Lan Kui'
'Border Charm' GBin WHlf
'Boreas' (s) GBin

| | | |
|---|---|---|
| | 'Bravura' | GBin |
| | 'Bride's Dream' | GBin |
| | 'Brocaded Gown' (S) | GBin |
| | ***broteroi*** | SKHP WCot |
| | ***brownii*** | EPot |
| | 'Buckeye Belle' (d) | CKel EBee ELan EPfP EWTr GBin LRHS LSRN MHom MNrw MRav MWea NCGa SHar SPer SWat WCAu WCot WWEG |
| | 'Burma Midnight' | GBin |
| | 'Burma Ruby' | GBin WCAu |
| | ***californica*** | CFir |
| | 'Callie's Memory' | CKel GBin WCAu WHlf |
| | ***cambessedesii*** ♀H2-3 | CBro CSpe EBee EPot GEdr GKev LRHS NBir NMen NWCA SSpi SUsu WAbe WCot WKif |
| | - dwarf | EPot |
| | 'Canary Brilliant'PBR | GBin WCAu |
| | 'Cardinal's Robe' | GBin |
| | 'Carina' | GBin |
| | ***caucasica*** | see *P. mascula* subsp. *mascula* |
| | 'Chalice' | GBin |
| | × ***chamaeleon*** | GKev SKHP |
| | 'Cheddar Royal' | GBin |
| | 'Cherry Ruffles' | GBin |
| | 'Chinese Dragon' (S) | CKel WCAu |
| | 'Chocolate Soldier' | GBin |
| | 'Claire de Lune' | CKel GBin MBri SHar WCAu |
| | 'Claudia' | WCAu |
| | 'Command Performance' | GBin |
| | 'Copper Kettle' | CKel |
| | 'Cora Louise' | CKel GBin WCAu WHlf |
| | 'Coral Charm' | CKel GBin SKHP WCAu WCot |
| | 'Coral Fay' | GBin WCAu |
| | 'Coral Sunset' | CKel GBin NLar SMrm |
| | 'Coral Supreme' | GBin |
| | ***corallina*** | see *P. mascula* subsp. *mascula* |
| | ***coriacea*** | EBee LWst |
| | - var. ***atlantica*** | CBro |
| | 'Court Jester' | GBin |
| | Crimson Red | see *P. suffruticosa* 'Hu Hong' |
| | 'Cytherea' | MHom |
| | 'Dancing Butterflies' | see *P. lactiflora* 'Zi Yu Nu' |
| | 'Daredevil' (S) | GBin |
| | ***daurica*** | see *P. mascula* subsp. *triternata* |
| | ***decomposita*** | MPhe |
| | ***decora*** | see *P. peregrina* |
| | ***delavayi*** (S) ♀H4 | Widely available |
| | - BWJ 7775 | WCru |
| | - SDR 4259 | GKev |
| | - SDR 4327 | GKev |
| | - from China (S) | MPhe |
| | - var. ***angustiloba*** f. ***alba*** (S) | CPLG |
| § | - - f. ***angustiloba*** (S) | EPot GKev SSpi WCot |
| | - - - 'Coffee Cream' (S) | CKel |
| § | - - f. ***trollioides*** (S) | CPLG |
| § | - var. ***delavayi*** f. ***lutea*** (S) | CCVT CDul CSpe EBee EPfP GAbr GAuc IFro LEdu LRHS MAsh MGos NBir NEgg SBrd SGar SLon SPhx SPoG SRms STre SUsu WAul WFar WHar WHoo WTin |
| | - var. ***lutea*** | see *P. delavayi* var. *delavayi* f. *lutea* |
| | - 'Mrs Colville' (S) | GBin GCal |
| | - 'Mrs Sarson' (S) | CHid CSpe ELan EWes EWll GBin NCGa NHol NLar SWat |
| | - Potaninii Group | see *P. delavayi* var. *angustiloba* f. *angustiloba* |
| | - 'Tapestry' | CSpe |
| | - Trollioides Group | see *P. delavayi* var. *angustiloba* f. *trollioides* |
| | ***delavayi* × *suffruticosa*** | LSRN |
| | 'Diana Parks' | CKel GBin |
| | Drizzling Rain Cloud | see *P. suffruticosa* 'Shiguregumo' |
| | 'Early Bird' | GBin NLar |
| | 'Early Glow' | GBin |
| | 'Early Scout' | GBin MHom WCAu WCot |
| | 'Echt Klasse' | GBin |
| | 'Eden's Perfume' | GBin LRHS MBri |
| | 'Elizabeth Foster' | GBin |
| | 'Ellen Cowley' | GBin WCAu |
| | ***emodi*** | CAvo CKel GKev SHar |
| | 'Etched Salmon' | GBin |
| | 'Ezra Pound' (S) | GBin |
| | 'F. Koppius' | CKel |
| | 'Fairy Princess' | GBin WAul WCAu |
| | 'Firelight' | GBin |
| | 'First Arrival' | CKel GBin WCAu WHlf |
| | 'First Dutch Yellow' | see *P.* 'Garden Treasure' |
| | 'Flame' | CKel EBee EPfP EWTr GBin MHom MNrw MWea NLar SPoG WAul |
| | 'Fuchsia Cuddles' | GBin |
| § | Gansu Group (S) | CKel ELan MPhe |
| | - 'Bai Bi Fen Xia' (S) | MPhe |
| | - 'Bai Bi Lan Xia' (S) | MPhe |
| | - 'Bing Shan Xue Lian' (S) | MPhe |
| | - 'Cheng Xin' (S) | MPhe |
| | - 'Fen He' (S) | MPhe |
| | - 'Fen Jin Yu Zhu' (S) | MPhe |
| | - 'Feng Xian' (S) | MPhe |
| | - 'He Hua Deng' (S) | MPhe |
| | - 'He Ping Lian' (S) | MPhe |
| | - 'Hei Feng Die' (S) | MPhe |
| | - 'Hei Tian E' (S) | MPhe |
| | - 'Hei Xuan Feng' (S) | MPhe |
| | - 'Hong Lian' (S) | MPhe |
| | - 'Hong Xia Ying Xue' (S) | MPhe |
| | - 'Huang He' (S) | MPhe |
| | - 'Hui He' (S) | MPhe |
| | - 'Jiao Rong' (S) | MPhe |
| | - 'Jin Cheng Ming Yue' (S) | MPhe |
| | - 'Ju Hua Fen' (S) | MPhe |
| | - 'Lan Hai Yiu Bo' (S) | MPhe |
| | - 'Lan He' (S) | MPhe |
| | - 'Lan Tian Meng' (S) | MPhe |
| | - 'Li Xiang' (S) | MPhe |
| | - 'Lian Chun' (S) | MPhe |
| | - 'Long Yuan Hong' (S) | MPhe |
| | - 'Mo Hai Yin Bo' (S) | MPhe |
| | - 'Mo Hai Yin Zhou' (S) | MPhe |
| | - 'Shu Sheng Peng Mo' (S) | MPhe |
| | - 'Tao Hua Nu' (S) | MPhe |
| | - 'Tie Mian Wu Si' (S) | MPhe |
| | - 'Xiang Lu Zi Yan' (S) | MPhe |
| | - 'Xiong Mao' (S) | MPhe |
| | - 'Xue Hai Bing Xin' (S) | MPhe |
| | - 'Xue Lian' (S) | MPhe |
| | - 'Ye Guang Bei' (S) | MPhe |
| | - 'Yu Ban Xiu Qiu' (S) | MPhe |
| | - 'Yu Guan Lan Dai' (S) | MPhe |
| | - 'Yu Lu Lian Dan' (S) | MPhe |
| | - 'Yu Rong Dan Xin' (S) | MPhe |
| | - 'Zi Die Ying Feng' (S) | MPhe |
| | - 'Zi Hai Yin Bo' (S) | MPhe |
| | - 'Zong Ban Bai' (S) | MPhe |
| | Gansu Mudan Group | see *P.* Gansu Group |
| § | 'Garden Treasure' | GBin WCAu WHlf |
| | 'Gold Standard' | GBin WAul |
| | 'Golden Bowl' | CKel GBin |

| | |
|---|---|
| 'Golden Dream' | see *P.* 'Bartzella' |
| 'Golden Isles' | CKel |
| 'Golden Thunder' | CKel |
| 'Golden Wings' | GBin |
| 'Grace Root' | GBin |
| Green Dragon Lying on a Chinese Inkstone | see *P. suffruticosa* 'Qing Long Wo Mo Chi' |
| 'Hephestos' (S) | GBin |
| 'Heritage' | GBin |
| 'Hillary' | CKel GBin WCAu |
| 'Ho-gioku' | GBin |
| 'Horizon' | GBin |
| ***humilis*** | see *P. officinalis* subsp. *microcarpa* |
| 'Illini Belle' | GBin |
| 'Illini Warrior' | WAul |
| 'In the Mood' | GBin |
| ***intermedia*** | WCot |
| 'Isani Gidui' | see *P. lactiflora* 'Isami-jishi' |
| ***japonica*** misapplied | see *P. lactiflora* |
| ***japonica*** ambig. | GEdr |
| ***japonica*** (Makino) Miyabe & Takeda B&SWJ 10985 | WCru |
| 'Jay Cee' | GBin |
| ***jishanensis*** | MPhe |
| 'Joseph Rock' | see *P. rockii* |
| 'Joyce Ellen' | GBin |
| 'Jubilation' | GBin |
| 'Julia Rose' | CKel GBin WCAu WHlf |
| 'Kamikaze' | CKel |
| 'Kathryn Ann' | GBin |
| ***kavachensis*** | EBee GCal LWst |
| 'Kinkaku' | see *P.* × *lemoinei* 'Souvenir de Maxime Cornu' |
| 'Kinko' | see *P.* × *lemoinei* 'Alice Harding' |
| 'Kinshi' | see *P.* × *lemoinei* 'Chromatella' |
| 'Kintei' | see *P.* × *lemoinei* 'L'Espérance' |
| 'Koikagura' | CKel |
| 'Kokamon' | CKel |
| § ***lactiflora*** | CArn GCal GKev LWst MLLN MPhe MRav WCot |
| - 'Abalone Pearl' | GBin |
| - 'Adolphe Rousseau' | CBcs CKel EBee NLar WCAu |
| * - 'Afterglow' | CKel |
| - 'Agida' | GBin LRHS MRav |
| - 'Agnes Mary Kelway' | CKel |
| - ***alba*** | MLLN WBor |
| - 'Albert Crousse' | CBcs CKel GBin MRav NBir SWat WCAu |
| - 'Alexander Fleming' | EBee MBNS MWea NBir SMrm SWat WCAu |
| - 'Algae Adamson' | CKel |
| - 'Alice Harding' | GBin WCAu |
| - 'Amibilis' | WCAu |
| - 'Angel Cheeks' | CKel GBin MBri WCAu |
| - 'Anna Pavlova' | CKel MRav |
| - 'Antwerpen' | LRHS |
| - 'Arabian Prince' | CKel |
| - 'Argentine' | EBee |
| - 'Asa Gray' | CKel |
| - 'Auguste Dessert' | CKel GBin WCFE WCot |
| § - 'Augustin d'Hour' | CKel |
| - 'Aureole' | CKel MRav |
| - 'Avalanche' | CKel EPfP GBin NBPC NLar SHar SMrm |
| - 'Ballerina' | CKel MRav |
| - 'Barbara' | CKel NCGa WCAu |
| - 'Baroness Schröder' | EBee ELan GBin |
| - 'Barrington Belle' | EPfP GBin WCAu |
| - 'Barrymore' | CKel |
| - 'Beacon' | CKel |
| - 'Beatrice Kelway' | CKel |
| - 'Belle Center' | GBin WCAu |
| - 'Bernice Carr' | GBin |
| - 'Best Man' | MBri NGdn WCAu |
| - 'Bethcar' | CKel |
| - 'Bev' | GBin |
| - 'Big Ben' | GBin SHar |
| - 'Blaze of Beauty' | CKel |
| - 'Bluebird' | CKel |
| - 'Blush Queen' | ELan WCAu |
| - 'Border Gem' | LRHS MRav |
| - 'Bouchela' | EBee |
| - 'Boule de Neige' | EWll NLar |
| - 'Bower of Roses' | CKel |
| - 'Bowl of Beauty' ♀H4 | Widely available |
| - 'Bowl of Cream' | CKel EBee GBin SMrm SWat SWvt WCAu |
| - 'Bracken' | CKel |
| - 'Bridal Gown' | GBin |
| - 'Bridal Veil' | CKel |
| - 'Bridesmaid' | CKel MRav |
| - 'British Beauty' | CKel |
| - 'Bunker Hill' | CKel GBin LRHS SBfd SWvt WHil |
| - 'Bu-te' | GBin |
| - 'Butter Bowl' | GBin |
| - 'Candeur' | CKel |
| - 'Cang Long' | CKel |
| - 'Captivation' | CKel |
| - 'Carnival' | CKel |
| - 'Caroline Allain' | CKel |
| - 'Carrara' | GBin |
| - 'Cascade' | CKel |
| - 'Catherine Fontijn' | CKel GBin |
| - 'Charles Burgess' **new** | WCAu |
| - 'Charles' White' | CKel GBin NBPC |
| - 'Charm' | GBin WCAu |
| - 'Cheddar Charm' | GBin WAul |
| - 'Cheddar Cheese' | WCot |
| - 'Cheddar Supreme' | GBin |
| - 'Chestine Gowdy' | CKel |
| - 'Chief Wapello' | GBin |
| - 'Chippewa' | GBin |
| - 'Chun Xiao' | CKel |
| - 'Circus Circus' | GBin |
| - 'Claire Dubois' | CKel GBin |
| - 'Cora Stubbs' | MBri |
| - 'Couronne d'Or' | GBin |
| - 'Crimson Glory' | CKel |
| - 'Crinkles Linens' | GBin |
| - 'Dawn Crest' | CKel |
| - 'Dayspring' | CKel |
| - 'Daystar' | MRav |
| - 'Decorative' | CKel |
| - 'Delachei' | CKel |
| - 'Denise' | MRav |
| - 'Dinner Plate' | GBin MBri SPer WCAu |
| - 'Do Tell' | GBin MBri NCGa NGdn NLar SPer WCAu |
| - 'Docteur H. Barnsby' | CKel |
| - 'Doctor Alexander Fleming' | CKel LRHS MDev SHar SRot STes SWat SWvt WHoo |
| - 'Dominion' | CKel |
| - 'Don Juan' | CKel |
| - 'Doreen' | CKel GBin MMHG NCGa SHar WCAu |
| - 'Dorothy Welsh' | CKel |
| - 'Dragon' | CKel |
| - 'Duchesse de Nemours' ♀H4 | Widely available |

| | |
|---|---|
| - 'Edulis Superba' | CKel EBee ELan EWTr GBin LRHS LSRN MBNS MRav NPer SPer |
| - 'Elizabeth Stone' | CKel |
| - 'Ella Christine Kelway' | CKel |
| - 'Elsa Sass' | GBin NCGa SHar WCAu |
| - 'Emma Klehm' | GBin WCAu |
| - 'Emperor of India' | CKel |
| - 'Enchantment' | CKel |
| - 'English Princess' | CKel |
| - 'Ethereal' | CKel |
| - 'Evelyn Tibbets' | GBin |
| - 'Evening Glow' | CKel |
| - 'Evening World' | CKel |
| - 'Fairy's Petticoat' | WCAu |
| - 'Fashion Show' | CKel |
| - 'Félix Crousse' ♀$^{H4}$ | CBcs CKel CMac CTri ELan GBin GMaP LRHS LSRN MBNS MDev MRav MSCN NBir SPer SWat WCAu |
| - 'Felix Supreme' | GBin |
| - 'Fen Chi Jin Yu' | CKel |
| - 'Festiva Maxima' ♀$^{H4}$ | CKel CSBt CTri EBee ELan EPfP GBin LRHS MBri NBir NEgg NLar SBfd SMrm SPer SRkn SRot SWat SWvt WCAu WHil WHoo WWEG |
| - 'Festiva Supreme' | GBin |
| - 'Florence Nicholls' | GBin |
| - 'France' | CKel |
| - 'Fuji-no-mine' | GBin |
| - 'Garden Lace' | GBin |
| - 'Gardenia' | CKel EBee EPfP GBin NLar |
| - 'Gay Paree' | CKel EWTr GBin NCGa NLar SHar SPer WCAu |
| - 'Gayborder June' | CKel |
| - 'Gene Wild' | GBin |
| - 'Général Joffre' | MRav |
| - 'Général MacMahon' | see *P. lactiflora* 'Augustin d'Hour' |
| - 'General Wolfe' | CKel |
| - 'Germaine Bigot' | CKel GBin MRav WCAu |
| - 'Gertrude' | GBin |
| - 'Gladys McArthur' | GBin |
| - 'Gleam of Light' | CKel |
| - 'Globe of Light' | GBin |
| - 'Go-Daigo' | GBin |
| - 'Goldmine' | GBin |
| - 'Great Sport' | MRav |
| - 'Green Lotus' | WAul |
| - 'Gypsy Girl' | CKel |
| - 'Hakodate' | CKel |
| - 'Heartbeat' | CKel |
| - 'Helen Hayes' | GBin |
| - 'Henri Potin' | GBin |
| - 'Henry Bockstoce' | CKel GBin |
| - 'Her Grace' | CKel |
| - 'Herbert Oliver' | CKel |
| - 'Hermione' | CKel GBin WCAu |
| - 'Honey Gold' | CKel ELan GBin WAul WCAu |
| - 'Hot Chocolate' **new** | WCAu |
| - 'Huang Jin Lun' | CKel |
| - 'Hyperion' | CKel |
| - 'Immaculée' | CKel EBee EPfP GBin LRHS LSRN MBri NCGa SPoG |
| - 'Inspecteur Lavergne' | CKel EBee LRHS MSCN MWea NGdn SPer STes WAul WCAu WCot WWEG |
| - 'Instituteur Doriat' | CKel GBin |
| § - 'Isami-jishi' | GBin |
| - 'Jacorma' | CFir GBin |
| - 'Jacques Doriat' | CKel |
| - 'James Kelway' | CKel GBin |
| - 'Jan van Leeuwen' | CKel EBee EPfP GBin GMaP MBri SPer WCAu WCot |
| - 'Jappensha-ikhu' | GBin |
| - 'Jeanne d'Arc' | CKel |
| - 'Jin Chi Yu' | CKel |
| - 'Joy of Life' | CKel |
| - 'Judith Eileen' | GBin |
| - 'June Morning' | CKel |
| - 'June Rose' | WCAu |
| - 'Kakoden' | GBin |
| - 'Kansas' | CKel EBee ELan EPfP GBin LRHS MBri NBir NGdn NLar SMrm SPoG WCAu WCot WFar |
| - 'Karen Gray' | GBin |
| - 'Karl Rosenfield' | CKel CSBt EBee EPfP GBBs LAst LRHS LSRN MNrw MRav MSCN NEgg NLar SBfd SBrd SHar SPer SPoG SRms SRot STes SWvt WBor WFar WHil WHoo WWEG XSen |
| - 'Kathleen Mavoureen' | CKel |
| - 'Kelway's Betty' | CKel |
| - 'Kelway's Brilliant' | CKel |
| - 'Kelway's Circe' | CKel |
| - 'Kelway's Daystar' | CKel |
| - 'Kelway's Exquisite' | CKel |
| - 'Kelway's Glorious' | CKel EBee EPfP GBin MBNS MRav NLar WCAu WGwG |
| - 'Kelway's Lovely' | CKel GBin |
| - 'Kelway's Lovely Lady' | CKel |
| - 'Kelway's Majestic' | CKel MRav |
| - 'Kelway's Scented Rose' | CKel |
| - 'Kelway's Supreme' | CKel SWat |
| - 'King of England' | GBin |
| - 'Knighthood' | CKel |
| - 'Kocho-jishi' | CKel |
| - 'Königswinter' | GBin |
| § - 'Koningin Wilhelmina' | EBee GBin MNrw |
| - 'Krinkled White' | CKel EBee EWTr GBBs GBin LRHS MHom MMHG MRav NLar NSti SBfd SHar SKHP SUsu WAul WCAu WCot WWEG |
| - 'La Belle Hélène' | CKel |
| - 'La France' | GBin |
| - 'La Lorraine' | CKel |
| - 'Lady Alexandra Duff' ♀$^{H4}$ | CKel EPfP GBin LRHS MRav MWea NBir NCGa NGdn SMrm SWvt WCAu WWEG |
| - 'Lady Ley' | CKel |
| - 'Lady Mayoress' | CKel |
| - 'Lady Orchid' | EPfP MSCN NGdn WCAu |
| - 'Lady Romilly' | MRav |
| - 'Lancaster Imp' | GBin WAul |
| - 'Langport Triumph' | CKel |
| - 'Largo' | WCAu |
| - 'Laura Dessert' ♀$^{H4}$ | CKel EBee GBin MWea NCGa WCAu |
| - 'Le Cygne' | GBin |
| - 'L'Éclatante' | CKel GBin LRHS WGwG |
| - 'Legion of Honor' | CKel |
| - 'Lemon Ice' | CKel |
| - 'Lemon Queen' | GBin |
| - 'L'Étincelante' | GBin |
| - 'Lights Out' | GBin |
| - 'Lillian Wild' | GBin |
| - 'Little Medicineman' | EBee GBin WBor |
| - 'Lois Kelsey' | GBin WCAu |
| - 'Longfellow' | CKel GBin |
| - 'Lord Kitchener' | CKel GBin LRHS |
| - 'Lorna Doone' | CKel |

- 'Lotus Queen' GBin WCAu
- 'Louis van Houtte' CKel NEgg SBfd
- 'Lyric' CKel
- 'Madame Ducel' CKel
- 'Madame Emile Debatène' CKel MBNS NOrc WBor
- 'Madame Gaudichau' MAvo
- 'Madame Jules Dessert' EBee
- 'Madelon' CKel
- 'Maestro' GBin
- 'Magenta Moon' **new** WCAu
- 'Magic Orb' CKel
- 'Mandarin's Coat' GBin
- 'Margaret Truman' CKel WCAu
- 'Marie Lemoine' CKel GBin LRHS WCAu WCot
- 'Mary Elizabeth' GBin
- 'Masterpiece' CKel MRav
- 'May Treat' GBin WCAu
- 'Merry Mayshine' GBin
- 'Midnight Sun' GBin WCAu
- 'Mischief' MRav WCAu
- 'Miss America' EPfP GBin WCAu WCot
- 'Miss Eckhart' CKel EBee GBin WCAu
- 'Miss Mary' EPfP EWTr
- 'Missie's Blush' GBin
- 'Mister Ed' GBin WCAu
- 'Mistral' CKel
- 'Monsieur Jules Elie' ♀H4 CKel EBee EPfP GBin LRHS MBri MHom MSCN NBPC NGdn SBfd SPer WAul WCAu WHoo WWEG
- 'Monsieur Martin Cahuzac' CKel GBin LRHS
- 'Moon River' EPfP GBin MSCN WCAu WHoo
- 'Mother's Choice' CKel GBin LSRN NGdn NLar WCAu WHil
- 'Mr G.F. Hemerik' CKel GBin WCot
- 'Mrs Franklin D. Roosevelt' GBin WCAu
- 'Mrs J.V. Edlund' GBin
- 'My Pal Rudy' GBin
- 'Myrtle Gentry' GBin
- 'Nancy Nicholls' WCAu
- 'Nancy Nora' MBri NGdn SPer
- 'Neomy Demay' CKel GBin
- 'Neon' NCGa
- 'Nice Gal' WCAu
- 'Nick Shaylor' CKel GBin WCAu
- 'Nippon Beauty' EBee GBin MMHG NCGa SBfd SHar SKHP WCot
- 'Noemie Demay' LRHS
- 'Norma Volz' GBin
- 'Nymphe' CKel MRav NLar WAul WCAu
- 'Orlando Roberts' GBin
- 'Ornament' CKel
- 'Orpen' CKel
- 'Paola' CKel
- 'Paul Bunyan' GBin
- 'Paul M. Wild' CKel WCAu

* - 'Pecher' CKel NLar NPer
- 'Peter Brand' CKel GBin NBPC NLar
- 'Philippe Rivoire' CKel
- 'Pillow Talk' CKel GBin MBri NCGa SPer WCAu
- 'Pink Cameo' NLar WCot
- 'Pink Dawn' EPfP MBri WCAu
- 'Pink Delight' WCAu
- 'Pink Parfait' GBin LRHS SPer WCAu
- 'Pink Princess' GBin WCAu
- 'Plainsman' GBin
- 'Port Royale' CKel
- 'President Franklin D. Roosevelt' LRHS SWat
- 'Président Poincaré' CKel MRav SWat
- 'President Taft' see *P. lactiflora* 'Reine Hortense'
- 'Primevère' CKel EBee EPfP EWll GBin MWea NBir NCGa NLar SHar SPer WWEG
- 'Qi Hua Lu Shuang' CKel
- 'Qing Wen' CKel
- 'Queen Victoria' GBin
- 'Queen Wilhelmina' see *P. lactiflora* 'Koningin Wilhelmina'
- 'Raoul Dessert' WCAu
- 'Raspberry Sundae' CKel ELan GBin MRav NLar SPer STes WCAu
- 'Ray Payton' GBin
- 'Red Dwarf' CKel
- 'Red Rover' CKel
- 'Red Sarah Bernhardt' ELan SMrm WWEG

§ - 'Reine Hortense' CKel GBin LRHS MRav SHar WWEG
- 'Renato' GBin STes
- 'Sante Fe' CKel EPfP NCGa WCAu
- 'Sarah Bernhardt' ♀H4 Widely available
- 'Scarlet O'Hara' CMac GBin NGdn SPer WCAu
- 'Schaffe' GBin
- 'Sea Shell' EPfP GBin GMaP WCAu
- 'Shawnee Chief' GBin
- 'Shen Tao Hua' CKel
- 'Shimmering Velvet' CKel
- 'Shirley Temple' (d) CKel EBee ELan GBin LRHS LTen MBNS MBri MRav NBir NGdn SBfd SBrd SPoG WCAu WWEG
- 'Silver Flare' CKel
- 'Soft Salmon Joy' GBin
- 'Solange' CKel GBin LRHS NLar SMrm WCAu
- 'Sorbet' CKel EBee EPfP NBPC NBir NCGa NLar NPer SBfd STes WBor WWEG
- 'Spellbinder' GBin
- 'Starlight' CKel EWTr GBin LRHS SHar STes WCAu WCot
- 'Strephon' CKel
- 'Sweet Melody' GBin
- 'Sword Dance' CKel EWll GBBs GBin
- 'The Mighty Mo' GBin
- 'The Nymph' LRHS NBir WWEG
- 'Tom Eckhardt' CKel EKen GBin SPer
- 'Top Brass' CBot CKel GBin MBri MRav NLar WCAu WWEG
- 'Topeka Garnet' GBin
- 'Translucient' CKel
- 'Victoire de la Marne' CKel
- 'Violet Dawson' GBin
- 'Vivid Rose' GBin
- 'Vogue' CKel GBin MRav NCGa SWvt WCAu
- 'W.F. Turner' **new** CKel
- 'Walter Faxon' GBin
- 'West Elkton' GBin
- 'Westerner' GBin
- 'White Grace' **new** WCAu
- 'White Rose of Sharon' CKel
- 'White Sands' GBin
- 'White Wings' CBcs CKel CMac CTri EBee ELan EPfP GBin LRHS MAvo MWea NBPC NLar SPoG STes SWat SWvt WAul WCAu WCot
- 'Whitleyi Major' ♀H4 MPhe WCot
- 'Wilbur Wright' GBin
- 'Wine Red' GBin
- 'Wladyslawa' GBin LRHS NLar SHar
- 'Xue Feng' CKel
- 'Yan Fei Chu Yu' CKel
- 'Yan Zi Dian Yu' CKel
- 'Zhong Sheng Feng' GBin
- 'Zhu Sha Dian Yu' CKel

§ - 'Zi Yu Nu' LSRN

| | |
|---|---|
| - 'Zuzu' | GBin WAul WCAu |
| 'Lafayette Escadrille' (S) | WCAu |
| 'Late Windflower' | CKel GCra MHom |
| 'Leda' (S) | GBin |
| 'Legion of Honour' | GBin |
| × ***lemoinei*** (S) | GBin WHal |
| § - 'Alice Harding' (S) | CKel WCAu |
| § - 'Chromatella' (S) | CKel LAma |
| - 'High Noon' (S) | CKel MPhe NBPC SKHP SWat WCAu |
| § - 'L'Espérance' (S) | LAma WCAu |
| - 'Marchioness' (S) | CKel WCAu |
| § - 'Souvenir de Maxime Cornu' (S) | CKel EPfP LAma SKHP SPer WCAu |
| 'Lemon Dream' PBR | CKel |
| 'Lilith' (S) | GBin |
| ***lithophila*** | see *P. tenuifolia* subsp. *lithophila* |
| 'Little Red Gem' | GBin |
| ***lobata*** 'Fire King' | see *P. peregrina* |
| 'Lois Arleen' | WCAu |
| 'Lovebirds' | GBin |
| ***ludlowii*** (S) ♀H4 | Widely available |
| ***lutea*** | see *P. delavayi* var. *delavayi* f. *lutea* |
| ***macrophylla*** | MPhe |
| 'Magenta Gem' | WAul |
| 'Mai Fleuri' | WCAu |
| ***mairei*** | CFir CPLG MPhe |
| 'Many Happy Returns' | GBin |
| ***mascula*** | CBro EPfP GKev GLam LLHF LWst NBir SHar WCot WWEG |
| - from Sicily | MPhe |
| § - subsp. ***arietina*** | GKev MWat WCot |
| - subsp. ***bodurii*** | LWst |
| - subsp. ***hellenica*** from Sicily | MPhe |
| § - subsp. ***mascula*** | GBin GKev LWst WCot |
| - - from Georgia | MPhe |
| § - subsp. ***russoi*** | EPot GEdr LWst WCot WThu |
| - - from Sardinia | MPhe |
| - - 'Picotee' | GBin |
| § - subsp. ***triternata*** | GBin GKev LRHS MPhe WCot |
| - - RS 125/80 | LWst |
| 'Mikuhino-akebono' | CKel |
| ***mlokosewitschii*** ♀H4 | Widely available |
| - 'Pearl Rose' | GBin |
| ***mollis*** | see *P. officinalis* subsp. *villosa* |
| 'Morning Lilac' | WCAu |
| 'Murad of Hershey Bar' (S) | GBin |
| 'My Love' | GBin |
| 'Nova' | GBin |
| ***obovata*** ♀H4 | CFir GAuc LRHS MPhe WCot |
| - var. ***alba*** ♀H4 | CPLG GBin GEdr GKev LLHF WAbe WCot WThu |
| - 'Grandiflora' | LRHS |
| - var. ***willmottiae*** | CPLG MPhe |
| ***officinalis*** | CArn GAuc GCra GKev |
| - WM 9821 from Slovenia | MPhe |
| - from NW Croatia | LWst |
| - 'Alba Plena' | CPou LRHS MRav NEgg SWvt WCAu WWEG |
| - 'Anemoniflora Rosea' ♀H4 | GBin LRHS MBri MHom SWvt WCAu |
| § - subsp. ***banatica*** | LWst MHom MPhe WCot |
| - 'China Rose' | GBin |
| - subsp. ***humilis*** | see *P. officinalis* subsp. *microcarpa* |
| - 'Lize van Veen' | GBin |
| § - subsp. ***microcarpa*** | WCot |
| - 'Mutabilis Plena' | IBlr |
| - 'Rosea Plena' ♀H4 | CKel CMac EBee ECtt EPfP GBin GMaP LAst LRHS MRav NEgg SPer SWat SWvt WCAu WCot WFar WWEG |
| - 'Rubra Plena' ♀H4 | CKel CPou CTri EBee ECtt EPfP GAbr GBin GCra GMaP LAst LHop LRHS MBri MHom MRav NEgg NGdn SEND SPer SRms STes SWat SWvt WCAu WCot WFar WHil |
| § - subsp. ***villosa*** | CKel ELan GBin GKev WCAu WFar |
| 'Old Faithful' | GBin |
| 'Old Rose Dandy' | GBin |
| 'Oriental Gold' | CKel |
| ***ostii*** (S) | CKel CPLG EPfP MPhe SKHP |
| § - 'Feng Dan Bai' (S) | CKel GBin MPhe |
| 'Pageant' | GBin |
| 'Paladin' | GBin |
| ***papaveracea*** | see *P. suffruticosa* |
| ***paradoxa*** | see *P. officinalis* subsp. *microcarpa* |
| 'Pastel Splendor' | CKel GBin WCAu |
| 'Paula Fay' | CKel EPfP GBin MRav STes WCAu WCot |
| 'Peachy Rose' | GBin |
| § ***peregrina*** | CAby CBro CKel ECho EWll GBin GEdr MPhe NLar SKHP SSpi WAbe WCAu WCot |
| - 'Fire King' | CKel |
| § - 'Otto Froebel' ♀H4 | GBin GCra NLar |
| - 'Sunshine' | see *P. peregrina* 'Otto Froebel' |
| 'Pink Hawaiian Coral' | CKel GBin NLar WCot |
| 'Pink Vanguard' | GBin |
| 'Postilion' | GBin |
| ***potaninii*** | see *P. delavayi* var. *angustiloba* f. *angustiloba* |
| 'Prairie Charm' | GBin |
| 'Prairie Moon' | GBin WCot |
| ***qiui*** | MPhe |
| 'Red Charm' | CKel GBin MBri NCGa WCAu |
| 'Red Glory' | GBin |
| 'Red Magic' | NBPC NLar SMrm SPoG WFar |
| 'Renown' (S) | CKel |
| 'Requiem' | GBin |
| § ***rockii*** (S) | CBcs CKel CSpe EPfP GAuc GBin MPhe |
| - from Tianshui, Gansu | MPhe |
| - from Wenshian, Gansu | MPhe |
| - hybrid | see *P.* Gansu Group |
| - subsp. ***linyanshanii*** (S) | MPhe |
| aff. ***rockii*** (S) | ELan GAuc |
| 'Roman Gold' | CKel |
| ***romanica*** | see *P. peregrina* |
| 'Rose Garland' | GBin |
| 'Roselette' | GBin |
| 'Roselette's Child' | GBin |
| Rouge Red | see *P. suffruticosa* 'Zhi Hong' |
| 'Roy Pehrson's Best Yellow' | GBin |
| ***ruprechtiana*** | GKev LWst WCot |
| ***russoi*** | see *P. mascula* subsp. *russoi* |
| 'Scarlet Heaven' | CKel GBin WCAu WHlf |
| 'Shimano-fuji' | CKel |
| 'Shining Light' | GBin |
| 'Show Girl' | GBin |
| 'Showanohokori' | CKel |
| 'Silver Dawn' | GBin |
| ***sinensis*** | see *P. lactiflora* |
| ***sinjianensis*** | see *P. anomala* var. *anomala* |
| 'Soshi' | GBin |
| 'Spring Carnival' (S) | GBin |
| 'Squirt' | GBin |
| 'Stardust' | WCAu |

***steveniana*** EBee LWst MHom MPhe WCot
§ ***suffruticosa*** (S) CWib ELan GKev MGos SSpi
- 'Akashigata' (S) CKel
- 'Alice Palmer' (S) CKel
I - 'Better than Snow Tower' (S) **new** LRHS
- Bird of Rimpo see *P. suffruticosa* 'Rimpo'
- Black Dragon Brocade see *P. suffruticosa* 'Kokuryū-nishiki'
- Brocade of the Naniwa see *P. suffruticosa* 'Naniwa-nishiki'
- 'Burgundy Wine' (S) GBin
- 'Cardinal Vaughan' (S) CKel
- 'Dou Lu' (S) CKel
- Double Cherry see *P. suffruticosa* 'Yae-zakura'
- 'Duchess of Kent' (S) CKel
- 'Duchess of Marlborough' (S) CKel
- 'Er Qiao' (S) CKel
- Eternal Camellias see *P. suffruticosa* 'Yachiyo-tsubaki'
- Flight of Cranes see *P. suffruticosa* 'Renkaku'
- Floral Rivalry see *P. suffruticosa* 'Hana-kisoi'
- 'Frost on Peach Blossom' (S) LRHS
- 'Fuji Zome Goromo' (S) CKel
* - 'Glory of Huish' (S) CKel
- 'Godaishu' (S) CKel GBin LAma SKHP SPer
- 'Guardian of the Monastry' (S) GBin
- 'Hai Huang' (S) **new** WKif
§ - 'Hakuo-jisi' (S/d) CKel EPfP WCAu
§ - 'Hana-daijin' (S) LAma
§ - 'Hana-kisoi' (S) CKel GBin LAma WCAu
- 'Haru-no-akebono' (S) CKel
§ - 'Higurashi' (S) EPfP
§ - 'Hu Hong' (S) LTen
§ - 'Huang Hua Kui' (S) CKel
- 'Hu's Family Red' (S) LRHS
- Jewel in the Lotus see *P. suffruticosa* 'Tama-fuyo'
- Jewelled Screen see *P. suffruticosa* 'Tama-sudare'
- 'Jia Ge Jin Zi' (S) CKel
- 'Jing Ge' (S) **new** WKif
- 'Jitsugetsu-nishiki' (S) CKel
- 'Joseph Rock' see *P. rockii*
- Kamada Brocade see *P. suffruticosa* 'Kamada-nishiki'
§ - 'Kamada-fuji' (S) CKel
§ - 'Kamada-nishiki' (S) CKel
§ - 'Kaow' (S) CKel
- King of Flowers see *P. suffruticosa* 'Kaow'
- King of White Lions see *P. suffruticosa* 'Hakuo-jisi'
- 'Kinkaku' see *P.* × *lemoinei* 'Souvenir de Maxime Cornu'
- 'Kinshi' see *P.* × *lemoinei* 'Alice Harding'
- 'Kokucho' (S) CKel
§ - 'Kokuryū-nishiki' (S) CKel GBin LAma LRHS SKHP SPer
- 'Koshi-no-yuki' (S) CKel
- 'Lan Bao Shi' (S) WKif
- Magnificent Flower see *P. suffruticosa* 'Hana-daijin'
- 'Montrose' (S) CKel
* - 'Mrs Shirley Fry' (S) CKel
- 'Mrs William Kelway' (S) CKel
§ - 'Naniwa-nishiki' (S) CKel
- 'Nigata Akashigata' (S) CKel
- Pride of Taisho see *P. suffruticosa* 'Taisho-no-hokori'
- 'Princess Chiffon' (S) GBin
§ - 'Qing Long Wo Mo Chi' (S) CKel
- 'Reine Elisabeth' (S) CKel
§ - 'Renkaku' (S) CKel SKHP SPer
§ - 'Rimpo' (S) CKel EPfP GBin LAma SKHP SPer
- subsp. ***rockii*** see *P. rockii*
- 'Rou Fu Rong' (S) LTen
§ - 'Shiguregumo' (S) CKel
- 'Shimadaigin' (S) CKel
- 'Shimane-chōjuraku' (S) CKel GBin
- 'Shimane-hakugan' (S) CKel
- 'Shimane-seidai' (S) CKel
- 'Shimanishiki' (S) CKel SKHP SPer
- 'Shin Shima Kagayaki' (S) CKel
- 'Shintoyen' (S) CKel
- 'Sumi-no-ichi' (S) CKel
- 'Superb' (S) CKel
§ - 'Taisho-no-hokori' (S) CKel
§ - 'Taiyo' (S) CKel EPfP LAma SKHP SPer
§ - 'Tama-fuyo' (S) CKel
§ - 'Tama-sudare' (S) CKel
- The Sun see *P. suffruticosa* 'Taiyo'
- Twilight see *P. suffruticosa* 'Higurashi'
- Wisteria at Kamada see *P. suffruticosa* 'Kamada-fuji'
- 'Wu Long Peng Sheng' (S) CKel GBin
- 'Xue Ta' (S) CKel LRHS
§ - 'Yachiyo-tsubaki' (S) CKel LAma SKHP
§ - 'Yae-zakura' (S) LAma WCAu
- 'Yan Long Zi Zhu Pan' (S) CKel
- 'Yin Hong Qiao Dui' (S) CKel
- 'Ying Ri Hong' (S) **new** WKif
- 'Yoshinogawa' (S) CKel EPfP
- 'Yu Ban Bai' (S) WKif
- 'Zha Sha Lei' (S) GBin
- 'Zhao Fen' (S) LRHS NBPC NPer
§ - 'Zhi Hong' (S) CKel
- 'Zhu Sha Lei' (S) CKel
- 'Zi Er Qiao' (S) CKel
§ - 'Zi Lan Kui' (S) CKel
'Sunshine' see *P. peregrina* 'Otto Froebel'
* ***szowitsianum*** **new** EPot
'Taiheko' CKel
'Ten' i' CKel
***tenuifolia*** CAby CBot CPMA EWll GAuc GBin GCal GKev LRHS MHom NMen NSla SKHP SMad WCot
- subsp. ***carthalinica*** MPhe
§ - subsp. ***lithophila*** LWst MHom MPhe
- 'Plena' EPot GEdr MHom
- 'Rosea' GBin
'Thunderbolt' (S) WCAu
***tomentosa*** MHom MPhe
'Tria' (S) GBin
***turcica*** GBin
'Vanilla Twist' WAul
***veitchii*** CAby EPfP GAuc GCal GEdr GKev GLam GMaP MHom NBid NMen SSpi
- from China MPhe
- pale-flowered GCal
- var. ***woodwardii*** CAvo CFir ECho EPot GBin GCra GKev NWCA SSpi WCAu
'Vesuvian' CKel WCAu
'Viking Full Moon' GBin WCAu
'White Emperor' WCAu
White Phoenix see *P. ostii* 'Feng Dan Bai'
'Wine Angel' GBin
***wittmanniana*** CBot GBin GCal WCAu WCot
'Xiang Yu' LRHS
'Yellow Crown' CKel GBin SHar WCAu
'Yellow Dream' GBin
'Yellow Emperor' GBin
Yellow Flower of Summer see *P. suffruticosa* 'Huang Hua Kui'
'Yellow Gem' GBin

## *Paesia* (*Dennstaedtiaceae*)

***scaberula*** CDes CLAP GGar NBir SSpi WFib

## *Paliurus* (*Rhamnaceae*)

| | |
|---|---|
| ***spina-christi*** | CArn CBcs IDee NLar SLon |

## *Pallenis* (*Asteraceae*)

| | |
|---|---|
| § ***maritima*** | CCCN |

## *Pamianthe* (*Amaryllidaceae*)

| | |
|---|---|
| ***peruviana*** | ERea |

## *Panax* (*Araliaceae*)

| | |
|---|---|
| ***ginseng*** | GPoy |
| ***japonicus*** | GPoy WCru |
| - BWJ 7932 | WCru |

## *Pancratium* (*Amaryllidaceae*)

| | |
|---|---|
| ***maritimum*** | CArn ECho GKev SDeJ |

## *Pandanus* (*Pandanaceae*)

| | |
|---|---|
| ***utilis*** | EAmu LPal |

## *Pandorea* (*Bignoniaceae*)

| | |
|---|---|
| ***jasminoides*** | CCCN CDoC CHll CRHN CTri CTsd EBak EBee EShb EWld MOWG |
| § - 'Charisma' (v) | CBcs CCCN CHll EPfP EShb LSou MOWG SEND SLim SPer SPoG |
| - 'Lady Di' | CCCN MOWG |
| - 'Rosea' | CCCN |
| - 'Rosea Superba' Y$^{H1}$ | CBcs CHEx CRHN SEND SLim |
| - 'Variegata' | see *P. jasminoides* 'Charisma' |
| ***lindleyana*** | see *Clytostoma calystegioides* |
| ***pandorana*** | CHll CRHN SLim SMrm |
| - 'Golden Showers' | CBcs CCCN CDoC CRHN MOWG MRav SEND SLim |

## *Panicum* (*Poaceae*)

| | |
|---|---|
| ***amarum*** 'Dewey Blue' | CKno EPPr |
| ***bulbosum*** | CKno EHoe EPPr EPla |
| ***clandestinum*** | EBee EHoe EPPr EWes MWhi SMea WWEG XLum |
| ***miliaceum*** 'Purple Majesty' | CWib |
| - 'Violaceum' | CKno CSpe |
| ***virgatum*** | CRWN CTri SMrm WMnd WPer WWEG XLum |
| - 'Blue Tower' | CKno ELon EPPr MAvo SApp SMea |
| - 'Cloud Nine' | CKno EBee EPPr MAvo MSnd NOak SApp SUsu WHal |
| - 'Dallas Blues' | CDes CKno CPrp EBee EBla ECha EHoe EPPr EWes LEdu LHop LRHS MAvo MCot MRav NOak NWsh SApp SHDw SMrm SPer WFar WMoo WPGP XLum |
| - 'Farbende Auslese' | MAvo |
| - 'Hänse Herms' | CKno EBee EHoe EPPr MAvo MWhi SApp SMea WFar WTin WWEG |
| - 'Heavy Metal' | Widely available |
| - 'Heiliger Hain' | CHar CSpe EBee EPPr LHop MAvo WCot |
| I - 'Kupferhirse' | CKno EBee EPPr |
| - 'Northwind' | CKno EBee EPPr LRHS MAvo SApp SHDw SPhx WFar |
| - 'Pathfinder' | SApp |
| - 'Prairie Sky' | CKno CPrp CWCL EAEE EBee EHoe ELon EPPr LEdu LRHS MAvo MBri NBro NLar SDix SMea SUsu WAul WFar WMoo WPGP WTin |
| - 'Red Cloud' | CKno |
| - 'Red Metal' | IPot |
| - 'Rehbraun' | EBee EHoe EPPr EPfP LEdu LHop LRHS LTen NMRc NOak NWsh SAga SApp SGol WCAu WFar WTin WWEG |
| - 'Rotstrahlbusch' | CKno CPrp CWib EBee EBla EHoe EPPr GMaP MAvo MWhi NOak NOrc NWsh SPer SWal WCot WMnd WMoo WPGP WWEG |
| - 'Rubrum' | CKno ECha EHoe ELan EPPr EPfP MAvo MRav MWat SApp SDix WMoo |
| - 'Shenandoah' | Widely available |
| - 'Squaw' | CHar CKno CPrp CWCL CWib EAEE EBee EBla EHoe EPPr EPfP IPot LRHS MAsh MMuc MSpe NOak NOrc NWsh SApp SEND SMad SWal WCot WDyG WFar WMoo WTin WWEG XLum |
| - 'Strictum' | EBee EHoe EHul EPPr EWes GQue LEdu LPla LRHS NLar SApp SPhx SUsu WMoo |
| - 'Warrior' | Widely available |
| - 'Wood's Variegated' (v) | WCot |

## *Papaver* ✿ (*Papaveraceae*)

| | |
|---|---|
| ***aculeatum*** | CTca |
| ***alboroseum*** | LRHS |
| 'Alpha Centauri' (SPS) | LLHF SWat WHoo |
| ***alpinum*** | CSpe GJos LRHS MAsh NBlu NGdn NSla SPet SWal SWat WFar |
| - 'Flore Pleno' (d) | NBir |
| ***amurense*** | SWat |
| ***anomalum album*** | CSpe |
| ***atlanticum*** | NBro NGdn SPlb |
| - 'Flore Pleno' (d) | CSpe IFro NBro NGdn WCot WFar |
| 'Aurora' (SPS) | SWat |
| 'Beyond Red' (SPS) | SWat |
| ***bracteatum*** | see *P. orientale* var. *bracteatum* |
| 'Bright Star' (SPS) | SWat |
| ***burseri*** | SRot |
| 'Cathay' (SPS) | SWat |
| ***commutatum*** Y$^{H4}$ | CSpe ELan GAbr SPhx SWat |
| ***corona-sancti-stephani*** | SWat |
| 'Danish Flag' | NNor |
| 'Eccentric Silk' (SPS) | SWat |
| ***fauriei*** | GKev |
| § 'Fire Ball' (d) | ECha GCal LHop NBid NBro SWat WMnd WWEG |
| 'Heartbeat'[PBR] (SPS) | IPot MAsh SWat |
| ***heldreichii*** | see *P. pilosum* subsp. *spicatum* |
| ***hybridum*** 'Flore Pleno' (d) | LRHS NSti SWat |
| 'Jacinth' (SPS) | CDes LLHF MAvo SWat WCot |
| ***lateritium*** | CHid CPou SRms |
| - 'Nanum Flore Pleno' | see *P.* 'Fire Ball' |
| 'Lauffeuer' | ELon SWat |
| 'Matador'[PBR] Y$^{H4}$ | NNor WBor WCot |
| 'Medallion' (SPS) | CDes EPri LLHF SWat WCot WHoo |
| § ***miyabeanum*** | CSpe ECho ELan GKev LRHS MAsh MMuc SRot WFar WPer |
| - ***tatewakii*** | see *P. miyabeanum* |
| ***nanum*** 'Flore Pleno' | see *P.* 'Fire Ball' |
| § ***nudicaule*** | ELan |
| - 'Aurora Borealis' | CSpe |
| - Champagne Bubbles Group | NNor SPet SWat WFar |
| - - 'Champagne Bubbles Orange' | NPri |
| - - 'Champagne Bubbles Pink' | NPri |

| | | |
|---|---|---|
| | - - 'Champagne Bubbles White' | NPri |
| | - - 'Champagne Bubbles Yellow' | NPri |
| | - var. ***croceum*** 'Flamenco' | NNor |
| | Garden Gnome Group | see *P. nudicaule* Gartenzwerg Group |
| § | - Gartenzwerg Group ΨH4 | COlW CSpe EPfP LRHS MBri NBlu NGdn SBfd SBrd SPet SPlb SPoG SRot WFar WGor WWEG |
| | - 'Matador' | GAbr GGar NLar |
| | - 'Pacino' | CMea EWll NLar SPet WFar |
| | - 'Summer Breeze' | SPet |
| | - 'Summer Breeze Orange' ΨH4 | NPri |
| | - 'Summer Breeze Yellow' | NPri |
| | - Wonderland Series | NNor SPet |
| | - - 'Wonderland Orange' | NPri |
| | - - 'Wonderland Pink Shades' | NPri |
| | - - 'Wonderland White' | LRHS NPri |
| | ***orientale*** | CBcs EPfP NBlu SRms SWat WFar WPer |
| | - 'Abu Hassan' | SWat |
| | - 'Aglaja' ΨH4 | CAby CElw CKno EBee ECtt ELon GBin LRHS NEgg NGdn NSti SAga SMad SMrm SUsu SWat WCot WHoo |
| | - 'Aladin' | SWat |
| | - 'Ali Baba' | GCra SWat |
| | - 'Alison' | SWat |
| | - 'Allegro' | CMea CSBt EBee ECtt EPfP GAbr GMaP LAst LRHS MBNS MBri NGdn NVic SBfd SPer SPlb SVic SWat SWvt WWEG XLum |
| | - 'Arwide' | SWat |
| | - 'Aslahan' | ECha ELon MRav SWat |
| | - 'Atrosanguineum' | SWat |
| | - 'Avebury Crimson' | MWat SWat |
| | - 'Baby Kiss'[PBR] | ECtt NLar SWat |
| | - 'Ballkleid' | ECha ELon SWat |
| | - 'Beauty Queen' | EBee ECha LRHS MRav NGdn SDix SWat |
| | - 'Bergermeister Rot' | SWat |
| | - 'Big Jim' | SWat |
| | - 'Black and White' ΨH4 | ECha ELan EPfP GMaP LRHS MNrw MRav NBPC NEgg SApp SPer SWat |
| | - 'Blackberry Queen' | ECtt SWat |
| | - 'Blickfang' | SWat |
| | - 'Bolero' | ECtt NGdn NLar |
| | - 'Bonfire' | LSou |
| | - 'Bonfire Red' | EBee SWat WCAu |
| § | - var. ***bracteatum*** ΨH4 | NBir SWat WMoo |
| | - 'Brilliant' | EBee GJos LRHS LTen MWat NBre NGdn SWat WFar WMoo XLum |
| | - 'Brooklyn' (New York Series) | ECtt IPot LRHS LSRN MAvo SWat |
| | - 'Burning Heart' | ECtt LRHS MAsh MSCN NLar SBfd SPer SPoG |
| | - 'Carmen'[PBR] | ELon GAbr MAsh MNrw MSCN NBPC WCot |
| * | - 'Carneum' | LRHS NBre NLar WWEG |
| | - 'Carnival' | EBee NBre SWat |
| | - 'Casino' | NGdn |
| | - 'Catherina' | NBre SWat |
| | - 'Cedar Hill' | EBee ECtt EWes GCal GMac MRav MWat NBre NGdn SMrm SWat |
| | - 'Cedric Morris' ΨH4 | ECha ELan EPPr GMaP MArl MRav SWat WCot WHoo WMnd |
| | - 'Central Park' (New York Series) | WFar |
| I | - 'Charming' pink-flowered | CAby EBee ECtt NCGa NGdn SMrm SPhx SWat |
| | - 'Charming' red-flowered | LRHS |
| | - 'China Boy' | SWat WHrl |
| | - 'Clochard' | CElw SWat WCot |
| | - 'Coral Reef' | MHer MLHP SAga SWat WMoo WRHF |
| | - 'Corrina' | SWat |
| | - 'Curlilocks' | CPar EBee ECtt ELan ELon EPfP LRHS MRav MWat NGdn SBfd SPer SRms SWat SWvt WHoo WWEG |
| | - 'Derwisch' | ELon SWat |
| * | - 'Diana' | SWat |
| | - 'Double Pleasure' | EBee ECtt MSCN NBre SWat WHrl |
| | - double red shades (d) | NGdn |
| | - 'Doubloon' (d) | EBee NBre NGdn SWat |
| | - 'Dwarf Allegro' | WMnd |
| | - 'Dwarf Allegro Vivace' | LRHS |
| | - 'Earl Grey' | SWat |
| | - 'Effendi' ΨH4 | MAvo SUsu SWat WCot |
| | - 'Elam Pink' | SWat WCot |
| | - 'Erste Zuneigung' | ECha ELon SWat |
| | - 'Eskimo Pie' | SWat |
| | - 'Fancy Feathers'[PBR] | ECtt NBPC NGdn NLar SWat |
| | - 'Fatima' | CDes SWat |
| | - 'Feuerriese' | SWat |
| | - 'Feuerzwerg' | SWat |
| | - 'Fiesta' | ELon NBre SWat |
| | - 'Flamenco' | CBcs ECtt ELon NGdn SWat |
| | - 'Flamingo' | ELon MSCN SWat |
| | - 'Flore Pleno' (d) | NGdn |
| | - 'Forncett Summer' | CPar ECtt ELon GMac MRav NBre NGdn NLar SMrs SPer SWat WCAu WHoo WHrl WTin WWEG |
| | - 'Frosty' (v) | SHar |
| | - 'Fruit Punch' | GJos SWal |
| | - 'Garden Glory' | EBee ECtt ELon GCra GMac LRHS LSRN MArl NBre NGdn SMrs SWat WCAu |
| | - 'Glowing Embers' | ECtt SWat |
| | - 'Glowing Rose' | ELon MDKP NBre SWat |
| | - Goliath Group | ECha ELan ELon LRHS MRav NBro NVic SDix SRms SWat WFar WMnd WWEG |
| | - - 'Beauty of Livermere' | Widely available |
| § | - - 'Beauty of Livermere' clonal | ELon WCot |
| | - 'Graue Witwe' | ELon SApp SWat WHrl WTin |
| | - 'Guardsman' | see *P. orientale* (Goliath Group) 'Beauty of Livermere' clonal |
| | - 'Halima' | NBre SWat |
| | - 'Harlem' (New York Series) | CElw CSpe CWCL EBee IPot NGdn NPnk SWat WHil |
| | - 'Harvest Moon' (d) | CMac EBee ECtt LRHS NPer SWat WHal WWEG |
| | - 'Heidi' | SWat |
| | - 'Hewitt's Old Rose' | NBre |
| | - 'Hula Hula' | ECha ELon SWat |
| | - 'Indian Chief' | EBee GMac IPot MDev MLLN NBPC NLar NPer NPri SMrm SRot WFar WWEG |
| | - 'Inferno'[PBR] | NLar |
| | - 'John III' ΨH4 | SPhx SWat |
| | - 'John Metcalf' | EBee ECtt EPPr LRHS NBre NSti SMrs SWat WCot |
| | - 'Juliane' | CAby ECha ECtt ELon NSti SWat WCot WTin |
| | - 'Karine' ΨH4 | CDes CElw CSam CWCL EBee ECha ELan EPPr EPfP GMaP GMac LRHS MNrw NGdn NLar SPoG SWat WCAu WHoo WTin |

- 'Khedive' (d) ♀H4 CWCL EBee SWat
- 'King George' SWat
- 'King Kong' MAvo NBPC NLar
- 'Kleine Tänzerin' CSam ECtt GMac LRHS LSou MHer MLLN MMuc MRav MSCN NBre NPri NSti SAga SWat WCAu WCot
- 'Kollebloem' SWat
- 'Lady Frederick Moore' LRHS NBre NLar SWat WWEG
- 'Lady Roscoe' NBre SWat
- 'Ladybird' EPfP LRHS NBre
- 'Laffeuer' SUsu
- 'Lambada' SWat
- 'Lauren's Lilac' EAEE EBee ECtt ELon LBMP LRHS LSRN MSpe NBre NCGa SMrs SWat
- 'Leuchtfeuer' ♀H4 CDes ECha LRHS NBre SWat
- 'Lighthouse' ♀H4 CWCL SWat
- 'Lilac Girl' CMac EBee ECha ECtt ELon GMaP MLLN NLar SApp SWat WHrl
- 'Little Candyfloss'PBR NLar SWat
- 'Louvre' COlW EBee ECtt ELon GAbr MAvo NLar SPoG SWat WCot WFar
- 'Maiden's Blush' ECtt NBre NSti SWat
- 'Mandarin'PBR WCot
- 'Manhattan' (New York Series) CElw CSam EBee ECtt ELon EPfP EWes GMac MNrw NEgg NGdn NPnk NSti SPer SPoG STes SWat WCot WHrl
- 'Marcus Perry' EBee ECtt EWes GMaP LRHS NEgg NGdn SBfd SPoG SWat WCAu WFar
- 'Marlene' **new** IPot MSCN
- 'Mary Finnan' CTca EAEE NBre SWat
- 'Master Richard' SWat
- 'May Queen' (d) EWes IBlr MRav NBre NBro NLar NSti SWat WCot WHrl WPnn
- 'May Sadler' NBre NLar SWat
- 'Midnight' ELon NBre SWat
- 'Miss Piggy'PBR ECtt IKil LLHF NGdn WCot WHil
- 'Mrs H.G. Stobart' SWat
- 'Mrs Marrow's Plum' see *P. orientale* 'Patty's Plum'
- 'Mrs Perry' CMac CMea CSBt CSam EBee ECtt ELan GMaP IFro LRHS MLLN MWat NGdn NPer NPri SPer SRms SWat WBrk WCAu WFar WHil WMnd WTin
- 'Nanum Flore Pleno' see *P.* 'Fire Ball'
- 'Noema' SWat
- 'Olympic Flame' (d) SWat
- 'Orange Glow' EBee MLLN SWat WMoo
- 'Orangeade Maison' NBre SWat
- 'Oriana' NBre SWat
- 'Oriental' SWat
- 'Pagode' **new** NCGa
- 'Pale Face' SWat
- 'Papillon'PBR CBcs EBee WFar
- 'Paradiso' **new** MSCN NCGa
- § 'Patty's Plum' Widely available
- 'Perry's White' Widely available
- 'Peter Pan' ELon NBPC NBre SWat
- 'Petticoat' ECtt ELan NBre SWat
- 'Picotée' EBee ECtt ELan EShb LRHS LSou MRav NBPC NEgg NLar NPri SPer SPoG SRot SWat SWvt WCAu WFar WHil WMoo WWEG
- 'Pink Lassie' NBre SWat
- 'Pink Panda' SWat
- 'Pink Pearl'PBR NBPC NCGa SWat WCot
- 'Pink Ruffles'PBR CBcs EBee SWat WCot
- 'Pinnacle' CDes EBee ELon NBPC SMrm SWat WFar
- 'Pizzicato' CEnt CWib LBMP LRHS MBri NNor NPer SBfd SGar SPet SWal SWat WFar WMoo WRHF WWEG
- 'Place Pigalle' (Parisienne Series) CDes EBee ELon EPfP LHop LSou MAvo MLLN NBPC NEgg NGdn NPri SMad SPer SPoG SWat WCot WHil
- 'Polka' SWat
- 'Prince of Orange' SWat WWEG
- Princess Victoria Louise see *P. orientale* 'Prinzessin Victoria Louise'
- 'Prinz Eugen' ELon GMaP NBre SWat
- § 'Prinzessin Victoria Louise' EBee EPfP GMaP LAst LRHS NGdn NLar NNor SGar SPoG SWat WBrk WFar WPer WWEG XLum
- 'Prospero' NBre
- 'Queen Alexandra' CSpr LBMP NGdn NLar WWEG XLum
- 'Raspberry Queen' CAby CDes CFir CMea EBee ECtt ELan ELon EWTr GMaP GMac MArl MLLN MRav MWat NBPC NLar NSti SApp SBfd SMrm SWat WCot WFar WHal WHoo WMnd WTin WWEG
- 'Raspberry Ruffles' NBre SWat
- 'Rembrandt' CAby MDKP NBre SMrm SWat WPer
- 'Rose Queen' NBre WCot
- 'Rosenpokal' NGdn SWat
- 'Roter Zwerg' ECha ELon SWat
- 'Royal Chocolate Distinction' CElw CSpe CWCL EBee ECtt ELon EPPr EPfP LSRN MAvo MLLN MWea NBPC NLar SBfd SPoG SWat
- 'Royal Wedding' Widely available
- 'Ruffled Patty'PBR EBee ECtt MAsh NCGa SMrm
- * 'Saffron' CAby SWat
- 'Salmon Glow' (d) SWat WFar WPer WWEG
- 'Salome' SWat
- 'Scarlet King' CMac LRHS NOrc SWat
- 'Scarlett O'Hara'PBR (d) EBee ECtt EPfP LLHF NPri SWat WBor WFar
- 'Showgirl' ELon MLLN NBre SWat
- * 'Silberosa' SWat
- 'Sindbad' ECtt ELon GMac MRav NEgg SWat
- 'Snow Goose' EBee ELon MCot MLLN SWat WCot WHoo
- 'Spätzünder' NBre SWat
- 'Springtime' ELon EWes GMac LAst MRav NGdn SWat WTin
- 'Staten Island' (New York Series) ECtt MAvo MNrw
- Stormtorch see *P. orientale* 'Sturmfackel'
- § 'Sturmfackel' NBre SWat
- 'Suleika' SWat
- 'Sultana' ECha ELon GMac MArl MWat SWat
- 'Sunset'PBR SWat
- 'The Promise' NBre SWat
- 'Tiffany' ECtt ELon GAbr GMac LSRN MAvo MCot MTis NEgg NGdn SMrm SPer STes SWat WCot WWEG
- 'Trinity' SWat
- 'Türkenlouis' EBee ECGP ECtt ELon EPfP GAbr GCra GMaP GMac LAst LRHS LSRN MRav MSCN MWat NBPC NGdn NLar SMrm SPad SWat WCAu WCot WFar WHil WHoo WTin WWEG
- 'Turkish Delight' EBee ECtt ELon GCra GMaP LRHS LSRN MAvo MLLN MMuc MRav

| | |
|---|---|
| | NBir NLar NPri SBfd SWat SWvt WCAu WFar WMnd WWEG |
| – 'Tutu' | SWat |
| – 'Victoria Dreyfuss' | SWat |
| – 'Viola' | SWat |
| – 'Violetta' | SWat |
| – 'Walking Fire' | MNrw |
| – 'Water Babies' | SWat |
| – 'Watermelon' | ECtt IPot LRHS NBPC NLar SMrm SPad SPer SWat WFar WHoo |
| – 'White Karine' | GMac |
| – 'White Ruffles' | EBee ECtt EWTr GMac IKil NCGa SWat |
| – 'Wild Salmon' | NBre |
| – 'Wisley Beacon' | ELon SWat |
| – 'Wunderkind' | EBee ECtt LRHS SWat |
| 'Party Fun' | CSpe SWal |
| ***paucifoliatum*** | WHrl |
| ***pilosum*** | SWat WTin |
| § – subsp. ***spicatum*** | CFir CMea CSev CSpe ECha ELon LHop LPla NBir WCot WFar WMoo |
| ***rhaeticum*** | GKev |
| 'Rhapsody in Red' (SPS) | SWat |
| ***rhoeas*** | CArn CHab GJos GPoy MNHC NNor WJek |
| – Angels' Choir Group (d) | NNor SWat |
| – Mother of Pearl Group | CSpe MCot SWat |
| – Shirley Group | NNor |
| ***rupifragum*** | CEnt ECha LEdu MSCN SGar SVic WFar WPer WPnn |
| – 'Double Tangerine Gem' | see *P. rupifragum* 'Flore Pleno' |
| § – 'Flore Pleno' (d) | CSpe LRHS MHer NCGa WBrk WFar WMoo |
| – 'Tangerine Dream' | SPet |
| 'Serena' (SPS) | SWat |
| 'Shasta' (SPS) | LLHF SWat WCot |
| 'Snow White' (SPS) | SWat |
| ***somniferum*** | CArn ELau GPoy SVic SWat |
| – (Laciniatum Group) 'Crimson Feathers' | NNor |
| – – 'Swansdown' (d) | CSpe |
| – 'Lauren's Grape' **new** | CSpe |
| – Paeoniiflorum Group (d) | SWat |
| – – 'Black Beauty' (d) | CSpe SVic SWat |
| – 'Pink Chiffon' | SWat |
| – subsp. ***setigerum*** | NNor |
| – single white-flowered | CSpe |
| – 'White Cloud' (d) | SWat |
| 'Tequila Sunrise' (SPS) | CDes SWat |
| 'The Cardinal' | NBre |
| 'The Falklands' (SPS) | SWat |
| ***triniifolium*** | CSpe EDif LRHS SPhx |
| – RCBAM -10 | WCot |
| 'Vesuvius' (SPS) | SWat |
| 'Viva' (SPS) | SWat |
| 'Waltzing Elizabeth' **new** | WHlf |

## papaya (paw paw) see *Carica papaya*

## *Parabenzoin* see *Lindera*

## *Parachampionella* see *Strobilanthes*

## *Paradisea* (*Asparagaceae*)

| | |
|---|---|
| ***liliastrum*** ♀H4 | CBro CHid CPrp EBee ECho EPPr EPri GCal IGor NBid NChi |
| – 'Major' | ECho SPhx |
| ***lusitanica*** | CAvo CBro CDes CHid CMHG CPom CSam CSpe CTca EBee ECho EPri GCal IBlr LEdu MCot SPhx WHoo WPGP WTin |

## *Parahebe* (*Plantaginaceae*)

| | |
|---|---|
| 'Angela' | MSCN |
| 'Betty' | GGar |
| × ***bidwillii*** | GJos MHer NWCA SRms SRot |
| – 'Kea' | CFee ECou ECtt MDKP SRot WPer |
| ***canescens*** | ECou |
| § ***catarractae*** | CHar CMHG CPLG CTri CWib ECho ECou EPfP GAbr GCra MLHP MRav MSCN MWat NBir NBro WAle WFar WKif WMnd WPer |
| – from Chatham Island | EWes |
| – 'Baby Blue' | CAbP |
| – blue-flowered | CDoC CHar SPer |
| – 'County Park' | ECou |
| – 'Cuckoo' | ECou |
| § – 'Delight' ♀H3 | CPLG ECou EWes GCal GGar GMaP GQue LHop LRHS MHer NPer SDix SRot WFar |
| – subsp. ***diffusa*** | ECou NPer NWCA |
| – – 'Annie' | ECou |
| – 'Miss Willmott' | SPer SPlb WPer |
| – 'Porlock' | CBar CMea GKev |
| – 'Porlock Purple' | see *P. catarractae* 'Delight' |
| – 'Rosea' | ECho MAsh WFar |
| – white-flowered | CBot CSpe IRar MLHP WPer |
| § ***formosa*** | SVen |
| – erect | GGar |
| 'Gillian' | WPer |
| 'Greencourt' | see *P. catarractae* 'Delight' |
| § ***hookeriana*** | GGar |
| § – var. ***olsenii*** | GGar |
| 'Jean' | GGar |
| 'Joy' | EWes |
| 'Julia' | GGar |
| ***linifolia*** | CTri |
| – 'Blue Skies' | EPot |
| § ***lyallii*** | CBot ECho EPfP GGal GJos GMaP LAst MCot MHer MMuc MRav MSwo MWat NBlu NLBP NWCA SEND SPlb SRms WKif |
| – 'Glacier' | ECou |
| – 'Julie-Anne' ♀H3 | GCal LRHS |
| – 'Rosea' | CTri WPer |
| – 'Summer Snow' | ECou |
| 'Mervyn' | CTri MDKP WPer |
| ***olsenii*** | see *P. hookeriana* var. *olsenii* |
| § ***perfoliata*** ♀H3-4 | Widely available |
| – dark blue-flowered | XLum |
| 'Snow Clouds' | CBar CMea GKev LHop LRHS SBch SDix SRot SUsu WAle WFar |
| 'Snowcap' | CDoC LAst LRHS MRav SPlb |

## *Parajubaea* (*Arecaceae*)

| | |
|---|---|
| ***cocoides*** | LPal |
| ***torallyi*** var. ***torallyi*** | EAmu |

## *Parakmeria* see *Magnolia*

## *Paranomus* (*Proteaceae*)

| | |
|---|---|
| ***reflexus*** | SPlb |

## *Paraquilegia* (*Ranunculaceae*)

| | |
|---|---|
| ***adoxoides*** | see *Semiaquilegia adoxoides* |
| § ***anemonoides*** | CPLG WAbe |
| ***grandiflora*** | see *P. anemonoides* |

## Parasenecio (Asteraceae)

| | |
|---|---|
| **delphiniifolius** | GEdr |
| - B&SWJ 5789 | WCru |
| - B&SWJ 10885 | WCru |
| - B&SWJ 11189 | WCru |
| - B&SWJ 11415 | WCru |
| **farfarifolius** var. **acerinus** B&SWJ 11549 new | WCru |
| - - B&SWJ 11554 | WCru |
| - var. **bulbifer** | WCru |
| **hastatus** var. **farfarifolius** | see *P. maximowiczianus* |
| **kiusianus** B&SWJ 11460 | WCru |
| § **maximowiczianus** B&SWJ 11468 new | WCru |
| **mortonii** GWJ 9419 | WCru |
| - HWJK 2214 | WCru |
| **tebakoensis** B&SWJ 11167 | WCru |
| - B&SWJ 11536 | WCru |
| aff. **yatabei** B&SWJ 11117 | WCru |

## Paraserianthes (Mimosaceae)

| | |
|---|---|
| **distachya** | see *P. lophantha* |
| § **lophantha** ♀H1 | CHEx CPLG CSpr EBak ELan EShb MOWG SEND |

## Parasyringa see *Ligustrum*

## Parathelypteris (Thelypteridaceae)

| | |
|---|---|
| **beddomei** | WRic |

## × Pardancanda (Iridaceae)

| | |
|---|---|
| **norrisii** | EBee EWes LRHS SBfd |
| - 'Dazzler' | CSpe MLLN NLBP SPad |

## Pardanthopsis (Iridaceae)

| | |
|---|---|
| **dichotoma** | EWes |

## Parietaria (Urticaceae)

| | |
|---|---|
| **judaica** | CArn GPoy WHer WSFF |

## Paris ✿ (Melanthiaceae)

| | |
|---|---|
| **chinensis** | WCru |
| - B&SWJ 265 from Taiwan | WCru |
| **cronquistii** | CLAP |
| **delavayi** | WCru |
| **fargesii** | GAuc LAma WCru |
| - var. **brevipetalata** | WCru |
| - var. **petiolata** | WCru |
| **forrestii** | WCru |
| **incompleta** | CLAP GCal WCru |
| - VVTR.1755 | LWst |
| **japonica** | LAma LWst WCru |
| **lancifolia** B&SWJ 3044 from Taiwan | WCru |
| **mairei** | WCru |
| **polyphylla** ♀H4 | CArn CBct CBro CFir CLAP EBee ECho GAuc GBin GEdr LAma LRHS LWst MNrw SPhx WAbe WCru WFar WPnP WSHC WShi |
| - B&SWJ 2125 | WCru |
| - Forrest 5945 | GCal |
| - HWJCM 475 | WCru |
| - var. **alba** | CFir |
| - var. **stenophylla** | CFir EBee LAma WCru |
| * - var. **yunnanensis alba** | GCal |
| **quadrifolia** | CLAP CSpe ECho EPfP EWil GCal GPoy MAvo NHar NLar NMen NMyG SPhx SSpi WBor WCru WHer WPGP WPnP WShi WTin |
| **tetraphylla** | GEdr LWst WCru |
| **thibetica** | CFir LWst WCru |
| - var. **apetala** | WCru |
| **verticillata** | CLAP GAuc GEdr LAma LWst WCru |
| - 'Ryokutei' (d) | WCru |

## Parnassia (Celastraceae)

| | |
|---|---|
| **nubicola** | GKev |

## Parochetus (Papilionaceae)

| | |
|---|---|
| § **africanus** ♀H2 | CHid ELon |
| **communis** misapplied | see *P. africanus* |
| **communis** ambig. | CFee CFir CPLG MSCN NPer XLum |
| - B&SWJ 7215 from the Golden Triangle | WCru |
| - from Himalaya | GCra |
| * - 'Blue Gem' | CCCN CSpe |
| - dark-flowered | GGar |

## Paronychia (Caryophyllaceae)

| | |
|---|---|
| **argentea** | WPat |
| § **capitata** | CTri SRms |
| **kapela** | SPlb XSen |
| - 'Binsted Gold' (v) | WPer XLum XSen |
| § - subsp. **serpyllifolia** | GBin NRya XLum |
| **nivea** | see *P. capitata* |
| **serpyllifolia** | see *P. kapela* subsp. *serpyllifolia* |

## Parrotia (Hamamelidaceae)

| | |
|---|---|
| **persica** ♀H4 | Widely available |
| - 'Biltmore' | CPMA |
| - 'Burgundy' | CPMA NLar |
| - 'Felicie' | CPMA EPfP NLar |
| - 'Globosa' | NLar |
| - 'Jodrell Bank' | CPMA MBlu NLar |
| § - 'Lamplighter' (v) | CPMA |
| - 'Pendula' | CMCN CPMA EPfP SSta |
| - 'Summer Bronze' | LRHS MAsh SSpi |
| - 'Vanessa' | CBcs CDoC CMCN CPMA EPfP EWes GBin GKin IArd LRHS LTen MAsh MBlu MGos NLar NPal SGol SLPl SPoG SPur SSta WDin WFar WMou |
| - 'Variegata' | see *P. persica* 'Lamplighter' |

## Parrotiopsis (Hamamelidaceae)

| | |
|---|---|
| **jacquemontiana** | CBcs CPMA IVic MBlu NLar SSpi |

## Parrya (Brassicaceae)

| | |
|---|---|
| **menziesii** | see *Phoenicaulis cheiranthoides* |

## parsley see *Petroselinum crispum*

## Parsonsia (Apocynaceae)

| | |
|---|---|
| **capsularis** | ECou |
| **heterophylla** | ECou |

## Parthenium (Asteraceae)

| | |
|---|---|
| **integrifolium** | CArn EBee GPoy LRHS SPhx |

## Parthenocissus (Vitaceae)

| | |
|---|---|
| § **henryana** ♀H4 | Widely available |
| **himalayana** | CBcs |
| - 'Purpurea' | see *P. himalayana* var. *rubrifolia* |
| § - var. **rubrifolia** | CWCL EBee ELan LRHS LTen MRav NLar SBfd SLim SLon SPoG WCru WFar WGrn |
| **inserta** misapplied | see *P. quinquefolia* |

| | | |
|---|---|---|
| | ***inserta*** ambig. | CMac CTsd NLar |
| | ***laetevirens*** | NLar |
| § | ***quinquefolia*** ♀H4 | Widely available |
| | - var. ***engelmannii*** | CBcs EBee LAst LBuc SBfd SPer WCFE |
| | - 'Guy's Garnet' | WCru |
| | Star Showers = 'Monham' (v) | EBee LRHS NLar |
| | ***semicordata*** B&SWJ 6551 | WCru |
| | ***striata*** | see *Cissus striata* |
| | ***thomsonii*** | see *Cayratia thomsonii* |
| § | ***tricuspidata*** ♀H4 | CCVT EBee ECtt EHoe EPfP MGos MMuc SGol SPer WDin WFar |
| | - 'Beverley Brook' | LBuc LRHS LSRN MBri NLar SPer SRms WFar |
| | - 'Crûg Compact' | WCru |
| | - 'Fenway Park' | MGos MRav NLar |
| | - 'Green Spring' | CBcs IArd MGos NLar SPer |
| | - 'Lowii' | CMac EPfP LBuc LRHS MBlu MGos MRav NLar SLon SPer |
| | - 'Minutifolia' | SPer |
| | - 'Robusta' | CHEx SBfd |
| § | - 'Veitchii' | Widely available |

## *Pasithea* (*Hemerocallidaceae*)

| | |
|---|---|
| ***caerulea*** | CAvo WCot |

## *Paspalum* (*Poaceae*)

| | |
|---|---|
| ***glaucifolium*** | LEdu |
| ***quadrifarium*** | CKno CMHG EPPr |

## *Passerina* (*Thymelaeaceae*)

| | |
|---|---|
| ***montana*** | NWCA |

## *Passiflora* ✿ (*Passifloraceae*)

| | | |
|---|---|---|
| | RCB/Arg R-7 | WCot |
| | 'Aafue' **new** | CTyn |
| | 'Abigail' **new** | CTyn |
| | ***actinia*** | CRHN CTyn |
| | 'Adularia' | CCCN CTyn |
| | ***alata*** (F) ♀H1 | CCCN CTyn EGxp |
| | - 'Shannon' (F) | CTyn |
| | × ***alatocaerulea*** | see *P.* × *belotii* |
| | 'Allardii' | CCCN CTyn ERea |
| | ***amalocarpa*** | CTyn |
| § | 'Amethyst' ♀H1 | CCCN CRHN CSBt CSPN CTyn EAmu EShb LHop LRHS LSRN MREP MRav SPad SPoG WFar WPGP |
| | ***amethystina*** misapplied | see *P.* 'Amethyst' |
| § | ***amethystina*** Mikan | CBcs ECre ERea |
| | ***ampullacea*** (F) | CTyn |
| | 'Anastasia' | CCCN CTyn |
| | 'Andy' | CCCN CTyn |
| | 'Anemona' | CTyn |
| | ***anfracta*** | CTyn |
| | 'Angelo Blu' | CCCN CTyn |
| | 'Annette' **new** | CTyn |
| | ***antioquiensis*** misapplied | see *P.* × *exoniensis* |
| | ***antioquiensis*** ambig. | CBcs CDoC MOWG SEND |
| | ***antioquiensis*** ambig. × (× ***exoniensis*** 'Hill House') | CHll |
| | ***antioquiensis*** ambig. × ***mixta*** | CTrC |
| | ***antioquiensis*** Karst ♀H2 | CHll CRHN GGal IDee |
| | ***apetala*** | CTyn |
| | 'Ariane' **new** | CCCN |
| | × ***atropurpurea*** | CCCN CTyn |
| § | ***aurantia*** | CTyn LRHS |
| | 'Aurora' | CTyn |
| | ***banksii*** | see *P. aurantia* |
| | 'Barborea' | CTyn |
| | 'Beaky' **new** | CTyn |
| § | × ***belotii*** | CCCN CRHN CTyn EQua EShb LRHS SLim |
| | - 'Impératrice Eugénie' | see *P.* × *belotii* |
| | 'Betty Myles Young' | CRHN CTyn |
| | ***biflora*** ambig. | CTyn |
| | 'Blaumilch' | CTyn |
| | 'Blue Bird' | CCCN CTyn |
| | 'Blue Moon' | CCCN CTyn |
| | 'Byron Beauty' | CCCN CTyn |
| | 'Cacita' | CTyn |
| § | ***caerulea*** ♀H3 | Widely available |
| | - 'Clear Sky' PBR | CCCN CTyn LRHS |
| | - 'Constance Elliott' | Widely available |
| | - ***rubra*** | CSBt WFar |
| | × ***caeruleoracemosa*** | see *P.* × *violacea* |
| | × ***caponii*** | CCCN |
| | ***capsularis*** | CTyn |
| | 'Celine' **new** | CTyn |
| | ***chinensis*** | see *P. caerulea* |
| | ***citrifolia*** | CCCN EGxp |
| | ***citrina*** | CTyn EShb LRHS MOWG SLim |
| | ***colinvauxii*** | CTyn |
| | × ***colvillii*** | CHll CTyn |
| | ***conzattiana*** | CTyn |
| | 'Coordination' | CCCN |
| § | ***coriacea*** | CTyn |
| | 'Corry Rooymans' **new** | CTyn |
| | 'Crimson Tears' | CTyn |
| | 'Crimson Trees' | CCCN |
| I | 'Curiosa' | CTyn |
| | 'Debby' | CCCN CTyn |
| | × ***decaisneana*** (F) | CCCN CTyn |
| | 'Eclipse' | CTyn |
| | Eden = 'Hil Pas Eden' PBR | CCCN CSBt CTyn EAmu EBee LRHS MBri SCoo SLim SRkn |
| | ***edulis*** (F) | CAgr CBcs CCCN CTyn ELau SVic |
| | - f. ***flavicarpa*** (F) | CTyn |
| | - 'Golden Star' **new** | CTyn |
| | - 'Norfolk' (F) | CTyn |
| | ***eichleriana*** | CTyn |
| | ***elegans*** | CTyn |
| | 'Empress Eugenie' | see *P.* × *belotii* |
| | 'Erik' | CTyn |
| | 'Everywhere' **new** | CTyn |
| | 'Excel' | CTyn |
| § | × ***exoniensis*** ♀H1 | CBot CCCN CHll CRHN CSBt CTyn ECre |
| | 'Fairylights' | CCCN |
| | 'Fledermouse' | CTyn |
| | 'Flirtation' **new** | CTyn |
| | 'Flying V' | CCCN CTyn |
| | ***foetida*** | CTyn |
| | ***gracilis*** | CTyn |
| | 'Grand Duchess' **new** | CCCN |
| | ***hahnii*** | CTyn EAmu |
| | ***helleri*** | CTyn |
| | ***herbertiana*** (F) | CTyn |
| | ***holosericea*** | CTyn |
| | ***incarnata*** (F) | CAgr CArn CTyn SPlb |
| | 'Incense' (F) ♀H1 | CCCN CTyn SPlb WFar |
| | 'Inspiration' | CTyn |
| | 'Inverleith' | CTyn |
| | 'Jeanette' | CTyn |
| | 'Jelly Joker' | CCCN CTyn |
| | ***jorullensis*** | CTyn |
| | 'Justine Lyons' | CRHN CTyn |
| | ***kalbreyeri*** | CTyn |

| | | |
|---|---|---|
| | ***karwinskii*** | CCCN |
| | 'Kate Adie' | CTyn |
| | × ***kewensis*** | CCCN CTyn |
| | - 'Déjà Vu' | CTyn |
| | 'Lady Margaret' | CTyn EGxp LRHS |
| | 'Lambiekins' | CRHN CTyn |
| § | ***ligularis*** (F) | CTyn |
| | 'Lilac Lady' | see *P.* × *violacea* 'Tresederi' |
| | 'Little Dot Beardshaw' **new** | CTyn |
| | 'Lolly' **new** | CTyn |
| | ***lowei*** | see *P. ligularis* |
| | ***maliformis*** (F) | CHll |
| | ***manicata*** (F) | CTyn |
| | 'Maria' | CCCN |
| | 'Mary Jane' | CCCN |
| I | ***matthewsii*** 'Alba' | CRHN |
| | 'Mavis Mastics' | see *P.* × *violacea* 'Tresederi' |
| | ***mayana*** | see *P. caerulea* |
| | 'Mini Lamb' | CRHN CTyn |
| | ***mixta*** (F) | CCCN CTyn SEND |
| | ***mollissima*** misapplied | see *P. tarminiana* |
| | ***mollissima*** ambig. (F) | CCCN CHll CTyn MOWG SPlb |
| | ***mollissima*** (Kunth) L.H. Bailey (F) ♀H1 | CRHN |
| | ***morifolia*** | CTyn |
| | ***mucronata*** | CTyn |
| | ***murucuja*** | CCCN CTyn |
| | ***naviculata*** | CTyn |
| | 'New Incense' | CTyn |
| | ***obtusifolia*** | see *P. coriacea* |
| | 'Olga' **new** | CTyn |
| | ***onychina*** | see *P. amethystina* Mikan |
| | ***organensis*** | CTyn |
| | 'Oriental Sunset' | CTyn |
| I | ***pardifolia*** | CTyn |
| | 'Peter Lawerence' | CCCN |
| | 'Pink Nightmare' | CTyn |
| | × ***piresiae*** | CCCN CTyn |
| | 'Precioso' **new** | CTyn |
| | ***punctata*** | CTyn |
| | 'Pura Vida 1' | CTyn |
| | 'Pura Vida 2' | CTyn |
| | 'Purple Haze' | CCCN CTyn CWib EBee NBlu NEgg NLar |
| | 'Purple Pendulum' **new** | CTyn |
| | 'Purple Rain' | CCCN CTyn |
| | ***quadrangularis*** (F) ♀H1 | CCCN CHll CWSG ERea |
| | ***quinquangularis*** | CBcs CTyn |
| | ***racemosa*** ♀H2 | CCCN CTyn LAst MNHC |
| | - 'Buzios' **new** | CCCN |
| | ***reflexiflora*** | CTyn |
| | ***rubra*** | CCCN CTyn SLim |
| | 'Saint Rule' | CTyn |
| | 'Sammie B' **new** | CTyn |
| | 'Sancap' | CTyn |
| | ***sanguinolenta*** | CTyn |
| | - 'Maria Rosa' **new** | CTyn |
| | 'Sapphire' | CTyn |
| | ***serratifolia*** | CTyn |
| | ***sexocellata*** | see *P. coriacea* |
| | 'Simply Red' | CCCN CTyn |
| | 'Smythiana' | CTyn |
| | 'Star of Bristol' ♀H2 | CTyn SLim |
| | 'Star of Clevedon' | CTyn |
| | 'Star of Kingston' | CCCN CTyn |
| | 'Star of Surbiton' | CRHN CTyn |
| | ***suberosa*** | CTyn |
| | ***subpeltata*** | CTyn |
| | 'Sunburst' | CCCN CHEx CTyn |
| | 'Surprise' | CTyn |
| § | ***tarminiana*** (F) | CSBt |
| | 'Temptation' | CTyn |
| | ***tetrandra*** | CPLG ECou |
| | 'Tinalandia' | CTyn |
| | × ***tresederi*** | see *P.* × *violacea* 'Tresederi' |
| | ***tricuspis*** | CTyn |
| | ***trifasciata*** | CCCN |
| | - 'El Indio' **new** | CTyn |
| | ***trisecta*** | CTyn |
| | ***tulae*** | CTyn LRHS |
| | ***umbilicata*** | CTyn |
| | 'Venus' **new** | CTyn |
| § | × ***violacea*** ♀H1 | CBcs CRHN SGar WFar |
| | - 'Eynsford Gem' | CCCN CTyn EAmu |
| | - 'Lilac Lady' | see *P.* × *violacea* 'Tresederi' |
| | - 'Sabin' **new** | CCCN CTyn |
| § | - 'Tresederi' | CCCN SEND WFar |
| | - 'Victoria' | CCCN CSBt CTyn EBee NLar SLim |
| | ***vitifolia*** 'Scarlet Flame' (F) | CTyn |
| | 'White Lightning' | LBuc LRHS LSqu SBfd SLim SPoG SWvt |
| | 'White Star' | CTyn |
| | 'White Wedding' **new** | CCCN CTyn |
| | 'Wilgen K Verhoeff' **new** | CTyn |

## passion fruit see *Passiflora*

## passion fruit, banana see *Passiflora mollissima* (Kunth) L.H. Bailey

## *Pastinaca* (*Apiaceae*)

| | |
|---|---|
| ***sativa*** | CHab SVic |

## *Patersonia* (*Iridaceae*)

| | |
|---|---|
| ***occidentalis*** | LRHS SPlb |

## *Patrinia* ✿ (*Caprifoliaceae*)

| | | |
|---|---|---|
| | ***gibbosa*** | CSam CSpe GEdr GKev LRHS MLHP MMHG NLar WFar WMoo WPat WPnP |
| | - B&SWJ 874 | WCru |
| | ***scabiosifolia*** | CDes CHll CKno CSpe EBee ECha ECtt GAbr GCal LRHS MNFA NBir NLar NPri SPhx SUsu WAul WFar WHoo WMoo WPGP WTcb |
| | - B&SWJ 8740 | WCru |
| | - 'Nagoya' | MNrw |
| | ***triloba*** | CRDP CSpe ECho GCal GEdr LRHS LSou MMHG SUsu WFar WMoo WPnP WWFP |
| * | - 'Minor' | ECho |
| | - var. ***palmata*** | GKev WDyG WFar WMoo WPnP |
| | ***villosa*** | CPLG EBee GCal LRHS MMHG NGdn NLar SSvw |

## *Paulownia* (*Paulowniaceae*)

| | |
|---|---|
| ***catalpifolia*** | LLHF MBri NLar |
| ***elongata*** | CBcs LLHF NLar |
| ***fortunei*** | CDul IVic MBlu NLar SEND SPlb |
| - Fast Blue = 'Minfast' | CHGN CPLG EPfP ESwi LLHF LSRN SBfd SGol SLim WHar WMou |
| ***kawakamii*** RWJ 9909 | WCru |
| ***taiwaniana*** B&SWJ 7134 | WCru |
| ***tomentosa*** ♀H3 | Widely available |
| - 'Coreana' | CHll |
| - - B&SWJ 8503 | WCru |

## *Pavonia* (*Malvaceae*)

| | |
|---|---|
| ***missionum*** | CSpe |

| | |
|---|---|
| ***multiflora*** ambig. | CCCN |
| ***praemorsa*** | CBot CSpe |
| ***strictiflora*** | CCCN |
| * ***volubilis*** | CCCN |

## paw paw (false banana) see *Asimina triloba*

## paw paw (papaya) see *Carica papaya*

## *Paxistima* (*Celastraceae*)

| | |
|---|---|
| ***canbyi*** | WPat WThu |

## peach see *Prunus persica*

## pear see *Pyrus communis*

## pear, Asian see *Pyrus pyrifolia*

## pecan see *Carya illinoinensis*

## *Pedicularis* (*Orobanchaceae*)

| | |
|---|---|
| SDR 2931 | GKev |
| ***superba*** SDR 1960 | GKev |

## *Peganum* (*Nitrariaceae*)

| | |
|---|---|
| ***harmala*** | CArn |

## *Pelargonium* (*Geraniaceae*)

| | |
|---|---|
| 'A.M. Mayne' (Z/d) | WFib |
| 'Abb and Mab' (Sc) | MBPg |
| 'Abba' (Z/d) | WFib |
| 'Abbie Hillier' (R) | LDea |
| 'Abel Carrière' (I/d) | SKen |
| ***abrotanifolium*** (Sc) | EWoo MBPg MHer SSea WFib WGwG |
| 'Abundance' (Sc) | CSev LDea |
| ***acetosum*** | CSev EWoo GCal MHer SMrm |
| 'Acushla by Brian' (Sc) | MBPg |
| 'Ada Green' (R) | LDea WFib |
| 'Ada Sutterby' (Dw/d) | SKen |
| 'Adam's Quilt' (Z/C) | SKen |
| 'Adele' (Min/d) | ESul |
| 'Ade's Elf' (Z/St) | NFir SSea |
| 'Aerosol' (Min) | ESul |
| 'Ailsa' (Min/d) | ESul SKen |
| 'Ainsdale Beauty' (Z) | SSea WFib |
| 'Ainsdale Duke' (Z) | NFir |
| 'Ainsdale Eyeful' (Z) | WFib |
| 'Ainsdale Happiness' (Z/d) | SSea |
| 'Akela' (Min) | ESul |
| 'Alan Shellard' (Z/d/v) | ESul |
| 'Alan West' (Z/St) | SSea |
| Alba = 'Fisalb' (Z/d) | SKen |
| 'Alberta' (Z) | SKen |
| ***alchemilloides*** | CRHN |
| 'Alcyone' (Dw/d) | ESul SKen WFib |
| 'Alde' (Min) | NFir SKen SSea WFib |
| 'Aldenham' (Z) | WFib |
| 'Aldham' (Min) | ESul WFib |
| 'Aldwyck' (R) | ESul LDea WFib |
| 'Alex' (Z) | SKen |
| 'Alex Kitson' (Z) | WFib |
| 'Alex Mary' (R) | ESul |
| 'Algenon' (Min/d) | ESul WFib |
| I 'Alice' (Min) | WFib |
| 'Alice Greenfield' (Z) | NFir |
| 'Alison' (Dw) | ESul |
| 'Alison Field' (R) | LDea |
| 'Alma' (Dw/C) | ESul |
| ***alpinum*** | MHer |
| 'Altair' (Min/d) | ESul |
| 'Amari' (R) | WFib |
| 'Amazon' (R) | ESul |
| 'Ambrose' (Min/d) | ESul WFib |
| Amelit = 'Pacameli'PBR (I/d) | LAst NPri SSea WGor |
| 'American Prince of Orange' (Sc) | MBPg |
| 'Amethyst' (R) | ESul LDea SCoo SPet WFib |
| § Amethyst = 'Fisdel'PBR (I/d) ♀H1+3 | SKen |
| 'Amour' (R) | ESul |
| I 'Amy' (Dw) | WFib |
| 'Andrew Salvidge' (R) | LDea |
| 'Androcles' (A) | LDea |
| 'Angela' (R) | ESul |
| 'Angela Read' (Dw) | ESul |
| 'Angela Thorogood' (R) | ESul |
| 'Angela Woodberry' (Z) | WFib |
| (Angeleyes Series) | LAst NPri |
| Angeleyes Bicolor = 'Pacbicolor'PBR (A) | |
| - Angeleyes Burgundy = 'Pacburg'PBR (A) | LAst SSea |
| - Angeleyes Josie (A) | SKen |
| - Angeleyes Orange = 'Paccrio'PBR (A) | EWoo LSou MWea SUsu |
| - Angeleyes Randy (A) | SSea |
| - Angeleyes Velvet Duet (A) | LAst |
| 'Angelique' (Dw/d) | ESul WFib |
| 'Anglia' (Dw) | ESul |
| 'Ann Field' (Dw/d) | ESul |
| 'Ann Hoystead' (R) ♀H1+3 | ESul NFir WFib |
| 'Ann Redington' (R) | ESul |
| 'Anna' (Dw) | ESul |
| 'Anna Lisa Pope' (R) **new** | MGbk |
| 'Anna Scheen' (Min) | ESul |
| 'Anne' (I/d) | WFib |
| 'Annsbrook Aquarius' (St) | ESul NFir |
| 'Annsbrook Beauty' (A/C) | ESul NFir WFib |
| 'Annsbrook Capricorn' (St/d) | ESul |
| 'Annsbrook Fruit Sundae' (A) | LDea |
| 'Annsbrook Jupitor' (Z/St) | ESul NFir |
| 'Annsbrook Mars' (St/C) | ESul |
| 'Annsbrook Mulberry Blotch' (Z/v) **new** | MGbk |
| 'Annsbrook Peaches' (Min) | ESul |
| 'Annsbrook Pluto' (Z/St) | ESul |
| 'Annsbrook Venus' (Z/St) | ESul |
| 'Anthony Ayton' (R) | ESul |
| Anthony = 'Pacan'PBR (Z/d) | LAst |
| (Antik Series) Antik Pink = 'Tikpink'PBR (Z) | MWea |
| - Antik Violet = 'Tikvio'PBR (Z) | MWea |
| 'Antoine Crozy' (Z × I/d) | WFib |
| 'Antoinette' (Min) | ESul |
| 'Antonnia Scammell' (St/d) | ESul |
| 'Apache' (Z/d) ♀H1+3 | WFib |
| 'Apollo' (R) | ESul |
| ***appendiculatum*** | MHer |
| 'Apple Betty' (Sc) | EWoo MBPg WFib |
| 'Apple Blossom Rosebud' (Z/d) ♀H1+3 | EShb ESul MBri MCot MHer NEgg SKen SMrm SSea WBrk WFib |
| 'Appleblossom' (Angeleyes Series) | LAst WGor |
| 'Appledram' (R) | LDea |
| 'Apri Parmer' (Min) | ESul |
| 'Apricot' (Z/St) | ESul LAst |
| 'April Hamilton' (I) | WFib |

| |  |  |
|---|---|---|
| | 'April Showers' (A) | LDea WFib |
| | 'Aquarell' (R) | ESul |
| | 'Archie Pope' (R) **new** | MGbk |
| | 'Arctic Frost' | WFib |
| | 'Arctic Glitter' (Z/St) **new** | ESul |
| § | 'Arctic Star' (Z/St) | CSpe ESul MCot NFir SKen SSea WBrk WFib |
| | 'Ardens' | CHll CSev CSpe EBee ESul EWoo LSou MCot MHer NFir SMrm SSea SUsu SWvt WCot WFib WWFP |
| | 'Ardwick Cinnamon' (Sc) | ESul EWoo MBPg MHer NFir WFib |
| | ***aridum*** | WCot |
| | (Aristo Series) Aristo Apricot = 'Regapri' (R) | LAst |
| | - Aristo Beauty = 'Regbeauty'$^{PBR}$ (R) | LAst LSou |
| | - Aristo Clara Schumann (R) | LAst |
| | - Aristo Clarina = 'Regli'$^{PBR}$ (R) | LAst |
| | - Aristo Red Velvet = 'Regvel'$^{PBR}$ (R) | LAst |
| | - Aristo Schoko = 'Regschoko' (R) | LAst |
| | - Aristo Velvet (R) | LSou |
| | 'Arizona' (Min/d) | SKen |
| | 'Arnside Fringed Aztec' (R) | LDea MHer WFib |
| | 'Aroma' (Sc) | EWoo MBPg |
| | 'Ashby' (U/Sc) | CWCL EWoo MBPg MHer NFir SBch SSea |
| | 'Ashfield Jubilee' (Z/C) | NFir SKen |
| | 'Ashfield Monarch' (Z/d) ♀H1+3 | NFir |
| | 'Ashfield Serenade' (Z) ♀H1+3 | SKen SSea WFib |
| | 'Ashley Stephenson' (R) | WFib |
| | 'Askham Fringed Aztec' (R) ♀H1+3 | ESul LDea WFib |
| | ***asperum*** Ehr. ex Willd. | see *P.* 'Graveolens' |
| | 'Astrakan' (Z/d) | SSea |
| | 'Athabasca' (Min) | ESul |
| | 'Atlantic Burgundy' | CWCL MCot |
| § | 'Atomic Snowflake' (Sc/v) | CFee ESul LDea MBPg MCot MNHC SIde SKen SPet WFib |
| | 'Atrium' (U) | MHer WFib |
| | 'Attar of Roses' (Sc) ♀H1+3 | CArn CHby CRHN ESul LDea MBPg MCot MHer NFir NPri SBch SGar SIde SKen SSea WBrk WFib WGwG |
| | 'Aubusson' (R) | ESul |
| | 'Audrey Clifton' (I/d) | SKen |
| | 'Auntie Billie' (A) | LDea |
| | 'Aurelia' (A) | LDea |
| | 'Aurora' (Z/d) | LAst LSou SKen SSea WGor |
| | ***australe*** | CRHN CSpe EWoo MCot SBch SChr SVen WFib |
| | 'Australian Bute' (R) | ESul |
| | 'Australian Mystery' (R/Dec) | CSpe ESul NFir WFib |
| | 'Autumn Colours' (Min) | ESul |
| | 'Autumn Haze' (R) | ESul |
| | 'Aztec' (R) ♀H1+3 | ESul LDea NFir WFib |
| | 'Baby Bird's Egg' (Min) | CSpe ESul WFib |
| | 'Baby Brocade' (Min/d) | ESul WFib |
| | 'Baby Harry' (Dw/v) | WFib |
| | 'Baby Helen' (Min) | ESul |
| | 'Baby James' (Min) | ESul |
| | 'Baby Snooks' (A) | LDea |
| | 'Babylon' (R) | ESul |
| | 'Badley' (Dw) | ESul |
| | Balcon Imperial | see *P.* 'Roi des Balcons Impérial' |
| | 'Balcon Lilas' | see *P.* 'Roi des Balcons Lilas' |

| |  |  |
|---|---|---|
| | 'Balcon Rose' | see *P.* 'Hederinum' |
| | 'Balcon Rouge' | see *P.* 'Roi des Balcons Impérial' |
| | 'Balcon Royale' | see *P.* 'Roi des Balcons Impérial' |
| | 'Ballerina' (R) | see *P.* 'Carisbrooke' |
| I | 'Ballerina' (Min) | WFib |
| | 'Bandit' (Min) | ESul |
| | 'Bantam' (Min/d) | ESul WFib |
| | 'Barbara Houghton' (Dw/d) | WFib |
| | 'Barbara Lambert' (Z/St) **new** | MGbk |
| § | 'Barbe Bleu' (I/d) | NFir SKen SSea WFib |
| | 'Barcelona' (R) | ESul |
| | 'Barham' (Min/d) | ESul |
| | 'Barking' (Min/z) | ESul NFir |
| | 'Barnston Dale' (Dw/d) | ESul NFir |
| | 'Bath Beauty' (Dw) | CSpe SKen |
| | 'Baylham' (Min) | ESul |
| | 'Beacon Hill' (Min) | ESul |
| | 'Beatrice Cottington' (I/d) | SKen WFib |
| | 'Beau Geste' (R) | ESul |
| | 'Beauty of Eastbourne' misapplied | see *P.* 'Lachskönigin', *P.* 'Eastbourne Beauty' |
| | 'Beauty of El Segundo' (Z/d) | SKen |
| | 'Beidermeier' (R) | ESul |
| | 'Belinda Adams' (Min/d) ♀H1+3 | NFir SSea |
| | Belladonna = 'Fisopa' (I/d) | SCoo |
| | 'Belle Ville Red Star' | MCot |
| | 'Belvedere' (R) | ESul |
| | 'Bembridge' (Z/St/d) | NFir SSea WFib |
| | 'Ben Franklin' (Z/d/v) ♀H1+3 | ESul NFir SSea |
| | 'Ben Matt' (R) | ESul WFib |
| | 'Ben Nevis' (Dw/d) | ESul |
| | 'Ben Picton' (Z/d) | WFib |
| | 'Bentley' (Dw) | ESul |
| | 'Berkswell Beacon' (A) | LDea |
| | 'Berkswell Blush' (A) | LDea |
| | 'Berkswell Bonanza' (A) | LDea |
| | 'Berkswell Calypso' (A) | LDea |
| | 'Berkswell Carnival' (A) | LDea |
| | 'Berkswell Champagne' (A) | LDea |
| | 'Berkswell Charm' (A) | LDea |
| | 'Berkswell Dainty' (A) | LDea |
| | 'Berkswell Debonair' (A) | LDea |
| | 'Berkswell Fondant' (A) | LDea |
| | 'Berkswell Gaiety' (A) | LDea |
| | 'Berkswell Gipsy' (A) | LDea |
| | 'Berkswell Jester' (A) | LDea |
| | 'Berkswell Lace' (A) | LDea MHer |
| | 'Berkswell Nocturne' (A) | LDea |
| | 'Berkswell Petticote' (A) | LDea |
| | 'Berkswell Pixie' (A) | LDea |
| | 'Berkswell Rosette' (A) | LDea |
| | 'Berkswell Sparkler' (A) | LDea |
| | 'Berkswell Trinket' (A) | LDea |
| | 'Berkswell Windmill' (A) | LDea |
| | 'Berliner Balkon' (I) | SKen |
| | Bernardo = 'Guiber'$^{PBR}$ (I/d) | LAst |
| | 'Bernice Ladroot' | ESul LDea |
| | 'Beromünster' (Dec) | ESul EWoo MHer NFir WFib |
| | 'Bert Pearce' (R) | ESul LDea WFib |
| | 'Beryl Read' (Dw) | ESul |
| | 'Beryl Reid' (R) | ESul LDea WFib |
| | 'Berylette' (Min/d) | ESul SKen |
| | 'Bess' (Z/d) | ESul |
| | 'Bett Rickaby' (R) | LDea |
| | 'Bette Shellard' (Z/d/v) | NFir |
| | 'Betty Catchpole' (Z) **new** | EWoo |
| | 'Betty Merry' (R) | LDea |

|  |  |
|---|---|
| 'Betty Read' (Dw) | ESul |
| 'Betty West' (Min/d) | ESul |
| ***betulinum*** | EWoo WFib |
| 'Betwixt' (Z/v) | SKen SSea |
| 'Bianca' (Min/d) | ESul |
| 'Big Apple' (Sc) | MBPg |
| 'Bildeston' (Dw/C) | ESul WFib |
| 'Bill West' (I) | SSea WFib |
| 'Billie Read' (Dw/d) | ESul |
| 'Bingo' (Min) | ESul |
| 'Bird Dancer' (Dw/St) ♀H1+3 | CSpe ESul MHer MNHC NFir SBch SSea SWal WBrk |
| (Birdbush Series) 'Birdbush Andy Pandy' (Sc) | MBPg |
| - 'Birdbush Beautiful' (Sc) | MBPg |
| - 'Birdbush Belinda' (Sc) | MBPg |
| - 'Birdbush Bella' (Sc) | MBPg |
| - 'Birdbush Betty' (Sc) | MBPg |
| - 'Birdbush Billy' (Sc) | MBPg |
| - 'Birdbush Blanco' (Sc) | MBPg |
| - 'Birdbush Blush' (Sc) | MBPg |
| - 'Birdbush Bobby' (Sc) | MBPg |
| - 'Birdbush Bold and Beautiful' (Sc) | MBPg |
| - 'Birdbush Bolero' (Sc) | MBPg |
| - 'Birdbush Bonny' (Sc) | MBPg |
| - 'Birdbush Bountiful' (Sc) | MBPg |
| - 'Birdbush Bramley' (Sc) | MBPg |
| - 'Birdbush Brandy' (Sc) | MBPg |
| - 'Birdbush Brilliant' (Sc) | MBPg |
| - 'Birdbush Champion' (Sc) **new** | MBPg |
| - 'Birdbush Chloe' (St) | MBPg |
| - 'Birdbush Claire Louise' (Sc) | MBPg |
| - 'Birdbush Dawndew' (Sc) | MBPg |
| - 'Birdbush Eleanor' (Z) | MBPg WFib |
| - 'Birdbush Julie Anne' (Sc) | MBPg |
| - 'Birdbush Kay Lye' (Sc) | MBPg |
| - 'Birdbush Lemonside' (Sc) | MBPg |
| - 'Birdbush Limey' (Sc) | MBPg |
| - 'Birdbush Linda Creasey' (Sc) | MBPg |
| - 'Birdbush Marion Louise' (Sc) | MBPg |
| - 'Birdbush Matty' | MBPg |
| - 'Birdbush Miriam' (Sc) | MBPg |
| - 'Birdbush Nutty' (Sc) | MBPg |
| - 'Birdbush Pink and Perky' (U) | MBPg |
| - 'Birdbush Pinky' (Sc) | MBPg |
| - 'Birdbush Suzy' (Sc) **new** | MBPg |
| - 'Birdbush Sweetness' (Sc) | MBPg |
| - 'Birdbush Tiny Tot' (Sc) | MBPg |
| - 'Birdbush Too Too O' (Sc) | MBPg |
| - 'Birdbush Velvet' (Sc) | MBPg |
| - 'Birdbush Victoria' (Sc) | MBPg |
| 'Birthday Girl' (R) | WFib |
| 'Bitter Lemon' (Sc) | ESul EWoo MBPg |
| 'Black Butterfly' | see *P.* 'Brown's Butterfly' |
| 'Black Knight' (A) **new** | NFir |
| 'Black Knight' (R) | CSpe EWoo MHer |
| 'Black Knight' Lea (Dw/d/C) | ESul NFir |
| 'Black Moth' | EWoo |
| 'Black Prince' (R/Dec) | CSpe EWoo NFir WFib |
| 'Black Top' (R) | ESul |
| 'Black Velvet' (R) | ESul EWoo LDea MCot |
| 'Black Vesuvius' | see *P.* 'Red Black Vesuvius' |
| 'Blackberry Yhu' (Dec/R) | ESul |
| 'Blackcurrant Yhu' (Dec) | NFir |
| 'Blackdown Delight' (Z) | NFir |
| 'Blackdown Sensation' (Dw/Z) | NFir |
| 'Blakesdorf' (Dw) | ESul |
| Blanca = 'Penwei'PBR (Dark Line Series) (Z/d) | LAst LBMP |
| Blanche Roche = 'Guitoblanc' (I/d) | LAst LBMP LSou NPri SCoo |
| § 'Blandfordianum' (Sc) | EWoo LDea MHer |
| 'Blandfordianum Roseum' (Sc) | EWoo LDea |
| 'Blaze Away' | SSea |
| 'Blazonry' (Z/v) | SKen SSea WFib |
| 'Blendworth' (R) | LDea |
| 'Blue Beard' | see *P.* 'Barbe Bleu' |
| 'Blue Orchid' (R) | ESul |
| 'Blue Peter' (I/d) | SKen |
| Blue Sybil = 'Pacblusy'PBR (I/d) | LAst LSou NPri |
| Blue Wonder = 'Pacbla'PBR (Z/d) | LAst WGor |
| Blue-Blizzard = 'Fisrain'PBR (I) | SCoo |
| 'Blushing Bride' (I/d) | SKen |
| 'Blushing Emma' (Dw/d) | ESul |
| 'Bob Hall' (St) | ESul |
| 'Bob Newing' (Min/St) | ESul WFib |
| 'Bobberstone' (Z/St) | WFib |
| 'Bold Appleblossom' (Z) | WFib |
| 'Bold Carmine' (Z/d) | NFir |
| 'Bold Carousel' (Z/d) | WFib |
| 'Bold Cherub' (Z/d) **new** | MGbk |
| 'Bold Flame' (Z/d) | WFib |
| 'Bold Gem' (Z/d) **new** | MGbk |
| 'Bold Limelight' (Z/d) | WFib |
| 'Bold Melody' (Z) | SSea |
| 'Bold Pixie' (Dw/d) | WFib |
| 'Bold Princess' (Z/d) **new** | MGbk |
| 'Bold Sunrise' (Z/d) | NFir |
| 'Bold Sunset' (Z/d) | NFir WFib |
| 'Bold White' (Z) | NFir |
| 'Bolero' (U) ♀H1+3 | NFir WFib |
| 'Bon Bon' (Min/St) | WFib |
| 'Bonito' (I/d) | SSea |
| 'Bonnie Austin' (St) | ESul |
| 'Bonny' (Min/St) | ESul |
| 'Bosham' (R) | ESul LDea WFib |
| 'Both's Snowflake' (Sc/v) | MBPg |
| ***bowkeri*** | WFib |
| 'Brackenwood' (Dw/d) ♀H1+3 | ESul NFir |
| 'Bramford' (Dw) | ESul |
| Bravo = 'Fisbravo'PBR (Z/d) | WFib |
| 'Bredon' (R) ♀H1+3 | ESul |
| 'Brenda' (Min/d) | ESul WFib |
| 'Brenda Hyatt' (Dw/d) | ESul WFib |
| 'Brettenham' (Min) | ESul |
| 'Brian West' (Min/St/C) | ESul WFib |
| 'Brian West Butterfly' (Z/St) | MGbk WFib |
| 'Briarlyn Beauty' (A) | LDea MBPg |
| 'Briarlyn Moonglow' (A) | ESul LDea |
| 'Bridesmaid' (Dw/d) | ESul NFir SKen |
| 'Bright Eyes' ambig. (Dw) | WFib |
| 'Brightstone' (Z/d) | WFib |
| 'Brightwell' (Min/d) | ESul |
| 'Brilliant' (Dec) | WFib |
| 'Brilliantine' (Sc) | CSev ESul EWoo MBPg MHer WFib WGwG |
| 'Bristol' (Z/v) | SSea |
| 'Britannia' (R) | LDea |

|  |  |
|---|---|
| 'Brixworth Pearl' (Z) | WFib |
| 'Brockbury Scarlet' (Ca) | WFib |
| 'Bronze Corinne' (Z/C/d) | SKen SPet |
| 'Brook's Purple' | see *P.* 'Royal Purple' |
| 'Brookside Astra' (Z/Dw) **new** | ESul |
| 'Brookside Betty' (Dw/C/d) | ESul |
| 'Brookside Bolero' (Z) | ESul |
| 'Brookside Candy' (Dw/d) | ESul |
| 'Brookside Champagne' (Min/d) | ESul |
| 'Brookside Fiesta' (Min/d) | ESul |
| 'Brookside Flamenco' (Dw/d) | ESul WFib |
| 'Brookside Free Spirit' (Min/D) | ESul |
| 'Brookside Melody' (Min/D) | ESul |
| 'Brookside Polka' (Dw/D) | ESul |
| 'Brookside Primrose' (Min/C/d) | ESul NFir SKen WFib |
| 'Brookside Romeo' (Z/Dw) **new** | ESul |
| 'Brookside Rosita' (Min) | ESul |
| 'Brookside Serenade' (Dw) | ESul WFib |
| 'Brookside Spitfire' (Dw/d) | ESul |
| 'Brookside Tango' (Min/D) | ESul |
| § 'Brown's Butterfly' (R) | ECtt ESul NFir WFib |
| 'Brunswick' (Sc) | ESul EWoo LDea MHer SMrm WFib |
| 'Bucklesham' (Dw) | ESul |
| 'Bullfinch' (R) | ESul |
| 'Bumblebee' (Dw) | ESul |
| 'Burgenlandmädel' (Z/d) | SKen |
| 'Burgundy' (R) | LBMP |
| 'Burns Country' (Dw) | NFir |
| 'Burstall' (Min/d) | ESul |
| 'Bushfire' (R) 🏆H1+3 | ESul EWoo WFib |
| 'Butley' (Min) | ESul |
| Butterfly = 'Fisam'[PBR] (I) | NFir SCoo |
| 'Button 'n' Bows' (I/d) | WFib |
| 'Cal' | see *P.* 'Salmon Irene' |
| Calais = 'Paclai'[PBR] | LAst |
| 'California Brilliant' (U) | MHer |
| 'Calignon' (Z/St) | WFib |
| 'Camphor Rose' (Sc) | ESul MBPg NFir SSea |
| 'Can-can' (I/d) | WFib |
| 'Candy' (Min/d) | ESul |
| 'Candy Kisses' (D) | ESul |
| Candy Rose = 'Pacdy'[PBR] | LAst |
| ***canescens*** | see *P.* 'Blandfordianum' |
| 'Cape Beauty' | EWoo |
| 'Capel' (Dw/d) | ESul |
| ***capitatum*** | CArn MBPg MHer MNHC WFib |
| 'Capri' (Sc) | MBPg WFib |
| 'Capricorn' (Min/d) | ESul |
| 'Captain Starlight' (A) | CRHN ESul EWoo LDea MBPg MHer NFir SKen SSea WFib |
| 'Caravan' (A) | LDea |
| 'Cardinal' | see *P.* 'Kardinal' |
| 'Cardington' (St/Dw) | ESul |
| 'Carefree' (U) | NFir WFib |
| § 'Carisbrooke' (R) 🏆H1+3 | ESul LDea WFib |
| 'Carl Gaffney' | LDea |
| 'Carmel' (Z) | WFib |
| 'Carnival' (R) | see *P.* 'Marie Vogel' |
| ***carnosum*** | MHer |
| 'Carol' (R) | ESul |
| 'Carol Gibbons' (Z/d) | NFir WFib |
| 'Carol Helyar' (Z/d) | WFib |
| 'Caroline' (Dec) | ESul |
| 'Caroline Plumridge' (Dw) | ESul |
| 'Caroline Schmidt' (Z/d/v) | LAst MCot NFir SKen SSea WBrk WFib |
| 'Carolyn' (Dw) | ESul |
| 'Carolyn Dean' (St) | NFir |
| 'Carolyn Hardy' (Z/d) | WFib |
| Cascade Lilac | see *P.* 'Roi des Balcons Lilas' |
| Cascade Pink | see *P.* 'Hederinum' |
| 'Catford Belle' (A) 🏆H1+3 | ESul LDea |
| 'Cathay' (Z/St) | ESul NFir |
| 'Cathy' (R) | NFir |
| ***caucalifolium*** subsp. ***caucalifolium*** | MHer |
| - subsp. ***convolvulifolium*** | WFib |
| 'Cayucas' (I/d) | SKen |
| 'Celebration' (Z/d) | ESul |
| 'Cézanne' (R) | ESul MCot WFib |
| 'Chantilly Claret' (R) | LDea |
| 'Chantilly Lace' (R) | ESul |
| 'Charity' (Sc) 🏆H1+3 | ESul LDea MBPg MCot MHer NFir SKen WFib |
| 'Charlie Boy' (R) | LDea |
| 'Charlotte Amy' (R) | LDea |
| 'Charlotte Bidwell' (Min) | ESul |
| 'Charlotte Bronte' (Dw/v) | WFib |
| 'Charm' (Min) | ESul |
| 'Charmay Alf' (A) | LDea |
| 'Charmay Aria' (A) | LDea |
| 'Charmay Bagatelle' (A) | LDea |
| 'Charmay Electra' (A) | LDea |
| 'Charmay Marjorie' (A) | LDea |
| 'Charmay Snowflake' (Sc/v) | ESul MBPg |
| 'Chattisham' (Dw/C) | ESul NFir |
| 'Chelmondiston' (Min/d) | ESul |
| 'Chelsea Gem' (Z/d/v) 🏆H1+3 | SKen SSea WFib |
| 'Chelsea Morning' (Z/d) | WFib |
| 'Chelsea Star' (Z/d/v) | MGbk |
| 'Chelsworth' (Min/d) | ESul |
| 'Cherie' (R) | ESul |
| 'Cherie Bidwell' (Dw/d/v) | ESul |
| 'Cherie Maid' (Z/v) | SSea |
| 'Cherry' (Min) | WFib |
| 'Cherry Baby' (Dec) | NFir |
| 'Cherry Cocktail' (Z/d/v) | NFir |
| 'Cherry Hazel Ruffled' (R) | ESul |
| 'Cherry Orchard' (R) | ESul LDea WFib |
| 'Cherry Sundae' (Z/d/v) | ESul |
| 'Chew Magna' (R) | WFib |
| 'Chi-Chi' (Min) | ESul |
| 'Chieko' (Min/d) | WFib |
| 'Chime' (Min/d) | ESul |
| 'China Doll' (Dw/d) | WFib |
| 'Chinz' (R) | NFir |
| § 'Chocolate Peppermint' (Sc) | CRHN CSev ESul EWoo LDea MBPg MHer MNHC NFir SIde SSea SWal WBrk WFib |
| 'Chocolate Tomentosum' | see *P.* 'Chocolate Peppermint' |
| 'Chocolate Twist' (St/C) **new** | LAst |
| 'Chris' **new** | LAst |
| 'Chrissie' (R) | ESul WFib |
| 'Christina Beere' (R) | LDea |
| 'Cindy' (Dw/d) | ESul WFib |
| 'Citriodorum' (Sc) 🏆H1+3 | LDea MBPg MCot MHer WFib |
| 'Citronella' (Sc) | CRHN LDea MBPg WFib WGwG |
| ***citronellum*** (Sc) | MBPg |
| 'City of Bath' | CWCL |
| 'Clara Read' (Dw) | ESul |
| 'Claret Rock Unique' (U) | EWoo MBPg SKen SSea WFib |

|  |  |
|---|---|
| 'Clarissa' (Min) | ESul |
| 'Clatterbridge' (Dw/d) | ESul NFir |
| 'Claude Read' (Dw) | ESul |
| 'Claudette' (Min) | ESul |
| 'Claudius' (Min) | ESul |
| 'Claydon' (Dw/d) | ESul NFir |
| 'Claydon Firebird' (R) | ESul |
| 'Clorinda' (U/Sc) | CRHN EShb ESul EWoo MBPg MCot MHer MNHC SBch SIde SKen SSea SWal WFib WGwG |
| 'Clovelly Rose' | CWCL |
| 'Clown' (R) | ESul |
| 'Coconut Ice' (Dw) | ESul |
| Coco-Rico (I) | SKen |
| 'Coddenham' (Dw/d) | ESul WFib |
| 'Cola Bottles' **new** | NPer |
| § 'Colonel Baden-Powell' (I/d) | WFib |
| 'Colwell' (Min/d) | WFib |
| 'Concolor Lace' | see *P.* 'Shottesham Pet' |
| 'Confetti' (R) | ESul |
| 'Conner' (Min) | NFir |
| 'Contrast' (Z/C/v) | CWCL MBri NEgg SCoo SKen SPoG SSea WFib |
| 'Cook's Peachblossom' | WFib |
| 'Copdock' (Min/d) | ESul |
| 'Copthorne' (U/Sc) ♀H1+3 | CRHN CSpe ESul EWoo LDea MBPg MCot MHer NFir SSea WFib |
| 'Coral Frills' (Min/d) | ESul |
| ***cordifolium*** | CRHN EWoo WFib |
| - var. ***rubrocinctum*** | ESul NFir |
| ***coriandrifolium*** | see *P. myrrhifolium* var. *coriandrifolium* |
| 'Cornell' (I/d) | WFib |
| ***cortusifolium*** | MHer |
| 'Corvina' (R) | WFib |
| 'Cottenham Beauty' (A) | ESul LDea NFir |
| 'Cottenham Belle' (A) | ESul |
| 'Cottenham Bliss' (A) | ESul SUsu |
| 'Cottenham Charm' (A) | ESul LDea |
| 'Cottenham Cheer' (A) | ESul |
| 'Cottenham Cynthia Haird' (A) | ESul |
| 'Cottenham Delight' (A) | ESul LDea NFir |
| 'Cottenham Gem' (A) | ESul |
| 'Cottenham Glamour' (A) | ESul MHer NFir |
| 'Cottenham Harmony' (A) | ESul LDea |
| 'Cottenham Jubilee' (A) | ESul LDea MHer |
| 'Cottenham Magic' (A) | ESul |
| 'Cottenham Mervyn Haird' (A) | ESul |
| 'Cottenham Special' (A) **new** | ESul |
| 'Cottenham Star' (A) | ESul |
| 'Cottenham Surprise' (A) | ESul LDea NFir |
| 'Cottenham Treasure' (A) | ESul LDea |
| 'Cottenham Triumph' (A) | ESul |
| 'Cottenham Wonder' (A) | ESul NFir |
| 'Cotton Candy' (Min/d) | ESul |
| 'Cottontail' (Min) | ESul WFib |
| ***cotyledonis*** | WFib |
| 'Countess Mariza' | see *P.* 'Gräfin Mariza' |
| 'Countess of Scarborough' | see *P.* 'Lady Scarborough' |
| 'Country Girl' (R) | SPet |
| 'Cover Girl' (Z/d) | WFib |
| 'Cowes' (St/Min/d) | ESul |
| 'Cramdon Red' (Dw) | SKen WFib |
| 'Cransley Blends' (R) | ESul |
| 'Cransley Star' (A) | LDea WFib |
| 'Cream 'n' Green' (R/v) | NFir |
| 'Creamery' (d) | WFib |
| 'Creamy Nutmeg' (Sc/v) | EShb ESul EWoo LDea MHer NFir SSea WBrk |
| 'Creeting St Mary' (Min) | ESul |
| 'Creeting St Peter' (Min) | ESul |
| 'Crimson Fire' (Z/d) | MBri |
| 'Crimson Unique' (U) ♀H1+3 | CSpe EWoo MCot MHer SKen SSea WFib |
| § ***crispum*** (Sc) | GPoy MBPg NEgg |
| § - 'Golden Well Sweep' (Sc/v) | MBPg WFib |
| - 'Major' (Sc) | ESul MCot SKen WFib |
| - 'Peach Cream' (Sc/v) | ESul MBPg WFib |
| - 'Prince Rupert' (Sc) | MBPg |
| - 'Variegatum' (Sc/v) ♀H1+3 | CRHN GPoy LDea MBPg MCot MHer NFir SBch SIde SPet SSea WFib |
| ***crithmifolium*** | MHer |
| 'Crocketta' (I/d/v) | NFir SKen |
| 'Crocodile' (I/C/d) | ECtt EShb MHer NFir SKen SSea WBrk WFib |
| 'Crowfield' (Min/d) | ESul WFib |
| 'Crown Jewels' (R) | LDea |
| 'Crystal Palace Gem' (Z/v) | SKen SSea WFib |
| 'Crystal West' (Min/St) | ESul |
| ***cucullatum*** | ESul SSea WFib |
| - 'Flore Pleno' | MHer WFib |
| - subsp. ***strigifolium*** | EWoo |
| 'Culpho' (Min/C/d) | ESul |
| 'Cupid' (Min/Dw/d) | WFib |
| 'Cyril Read' (Dw) | ESul |
| § 'Czar' (Z/C) | SCoo |
| 'Dainty Lassie' (Dw/v) | ESul |
| 'Dainty Maid' (Sc) | CSpe ESul MBPg NFir |
| 'Dale Queen' (Z) | WFib |
| 'Dallimore' (Dw) | ESul |
| 'Danielle Marie' (A) | LDea |
| 'Danton' (Z/d) | WFib |
| 'Dark Ascot' (Dec) | ESul |
| 'Dark Red Irene' (Z/d) | SKen WFib |
| 'Dark Secret' (R) | CSpe ESul LDea SMrm WFib |
| 'Dark Venus' (R) | ESul EWoo LDea WFib |
| Dark-Red-Blizzard = 'Fisblizdark' (I) | CWCL EWoo |
| 'Darmsden' (A) ♀H1+3 | ESul LDea NFir SSea |
| 'David John' (Dw/d) | ESul |
| 'David Mitchell' (Min/Ca/d) | ESul |
| 'Davina' (Min/d) | ESul WFib |
| 'Dawn Star' (Z/St) | ESul NFir |
| 'Deacon Arlon' (Dw/d) | ESul SKen |
| 'Deacon Avalon' (Dw/d) | WFib |
| 'Deacon Barbecue' (Z/d) | ESul SKen WFib |
| 'Deacon Birthday' (Z/d) | ESul WFib |
| 'Deacon Bonanza' (Z/d) | ESul SKen SSea WFib |
| 'Deacon Clarion' (Z/d) | ESul SKen WFib |
| 'Deacon Constancy' (Z/d) | ESul |
| 'Deacon Coral Reef' (Z/d) | ESul WFib |
| 'Deacon Finale' (Z/d) | ESul |
| 'Deacon Fireball' (Z/d) | ESul WFib |
| 'Deacon Flamingo' (Z/d) | ESul |
| 'Deacon Gala' (Z/d) | ESul WFib |
| 'Deacon Golden Bonanza' (Z/C/d) | ESul WFib |
| 'Deacon Golden Gala' (Z/C/d) | ESul SKen |
| 'Deacon Golden Lilac Mist' (Z/C/d) | ESul WFib |
| 'Deacon Jubilant' (Z/d) | ESul SKen |
| 'Deacon Lilac Mist' (Z/d) | ESul SSea WFib |
| 'Deacon Mandarin' (Z/d) | ESul SKen WFib |
| 'Deacon Minuet' (Z/d) | ESul NFir WFib |

| | |
|---|---|
| 'Deacon Moonlight' (Z/d) | ESul |
| 'Deacon Peacock' (Z/C/d) | ESul WFib |
| 'Deacon Picotee' (Z/d) | ESul SKen WFib |
| 'Deacon Regalia' (Z/d) | ESul WFib |
| 'Deacon Romance' (Z/d) | ESul |
| § 'Deacon Summertime' (Z/d) | ESul WFib |
| 'Deacon Sunburst' (Z/d) | ESul |
| 'Deacon Suntan' (Z/d) | ESul |
| 'Deacon Trousseau' (Z/d) | ESul WFib |
| 'Dean's Delight' (Sc) | LDea MBPg |
| 'Debbie' (A) | LDea |
| 'Debbie Parmer' (Dw/d) | ESul |
| 'Debbie Thrower' (Dw) | ESul |
| 'Deborah Miliken' (Z/d) | ESul NFir WFib |
| 'Decora Lavender' | see *P.* 'Decora Lilas' |
| § 'Decora Lilas' (I) | ECtt LAst NPri SKen SPet |
| 'Decora Mauve' | see *P.* 'Decora Lilas' |
| 'Decora Pink' | see *P.* 'Decora Rouge' |
| 'Decora Red' | see *P.* 'Decora Rouge' |
| § 'Decora Rose' (I) | ECtt LAst NPri SPet |
| § 'Decora Rouge' (I) | ECtt SPet |
| 'Decora Scarlet' (I) | SKen |
| 'Decora Stellena' (I/v) | LAst |
| 'Deerwood Darling' (Min/v/d) | WFib |
| 'Deerwood Lavender Lad' (Sc) | CSev ESul EWoo LDea MBPg MHer SSea WFib |
| 'Deerwood Lavender Lass' | ESul LDea MBPg MHer |
| 'Deerwood Pink Puff' (St/d) | WFib |
| 'Delightful' (R) | WFib |
| 'Delli' (R) | MHer NFir NPer SMrm WFib |
| 'Delta' (Min/d) | ESul |
| 'Denebola' (Min/d) | ESul |
| 'Dennis Hunt' (Z/C) | NFir |
| ***denticulatum*** | MHer SKen SSea |
| § - 'Filicifolium' (Sc) | CRHN EShb ESul LDea MBPg MHer SSea WFib |
| 'Diana Hull' | MBPg |
| 'Diana Palmer' (Z/d) | SKen |
| 'Diane' (Min/d) | ESul |
| 'Diane Louise' (d) | SSea |
| 'Dibbinsdale' (Z) | ESul NFir |
| ***dichondrifolium*** (Sc) | CSev CSpe MBPg MHer NFir SSea WFib |
| ***dichondrifolium* × *reniforme*** (Sc) | ESul NFir |
| 'Didi' (Min) | SKen |
| 'Dinky' (Min/d) | ESul |
| 'Display' ambig. (Dw/v) | WFib |
| 'Distinction' (Z) | MHer NFir SKen SPoG SSea WFib |
| 'Dollar Bute' (R) | ESul |
| 'Dollar Princess' (Z/C) | SKen |
| 'Dolly Read' (Dw) | ESul |
| 'Dolly Varden' (Z/v) Υ[H1+3] | ESul NFir SKen SSea WFib |
| 'Don's Helen Bainbridge' (Z/C) | NFir |
| 'Don's Mona Noble' (Z/C) | NFir |
| 'Don's Richard A. Costain' (Z/C) | NFir |
| 'Don's Seagold' (Z/C) | NFir |
| 'Don's Silva Perle' (Dw/v) | SKen |
| 'Don's Southport' (Z/v) | NFir |
| 'Don's Swanland Girl' (Min) | ESul |
| 'Don's Wensleydale' (Dw/C) | ESul |
| 'Dorcus Bingham' (Sc) | MBPg |
| 'Doreen' (Z/d) | MGbk |
| 'Doris Hancock' (R) | WFib |
| 'Doris Shaw' (R) | ESul |
| 'Dorothy May' (A) | LDea SKen |

| | |
|---|---|
| 'Dot Fowler' (R) | LDea |
| 'Double Bird's Egg' (Z/d) | SKen |
| 'Double Grace Wells' (Min/d) | ESul |
| 'Double Lilac White' (I/d) | SKen |
| 'Double Orange' (Z/d) | SKen |
| 'Double Pink' (R/d) | WFib |
| 'Dovedale' (Dw/C) | ESul WFib |
| 'Dovepoint' (Dw/2) | NFir |
| 'Downlands' (Z/d) | WFib |
| 'Dresden China' (R) | ESul LDea |
| 'Dresden Pippa Rosa' (Z) | SKen |
| 'Dresden White' (Dw) | WFib |
| Dresdner Apricot = 'Pacbriap'[PBR] (I/d) | NPri |
| 'Dubai Star' (Z) **new** | MGbk |
| 'Duchess of Devonshire' (U) | WFib |
| 'Duke of Edinburgh' | see *P.* 'Hederinum Variegatum' |
| 'Dulcie' (Min) | ESul |
| 'Dunkery Beacon' (R) | ESul WFib |
| 'Dusty Rose' (Min) | ESul |
| 'E. Dabner' (Z/d) | SKen WFib |
| 'Earl of Chester' (Min/d) Υ[H1+3] | WFib |
| 'Earliana' (Dec) | LDea SUsu |
| 'Earlsfour' (R) | LDea |
| 'East Sussex' (Dw/C) | ESul |
| § 'Eastbourne Beauty' (I/d) | SKen |
| 'Easter Promise' (R) | ESul |
| ***echinatum*** | EWoo MHer |
| - 'Album' | SSea WFib |
| 'Eclipse' (Dw/d) | SKen |
| 'Eclipse' (I/d) | SKen |
| 'Eden Gem' (Min/d) | WFib |
| 'Edith Stern' (Dw/d) | ESul |
| 'Edmond Lachenal' (Z/d) | WFib |
| 'Edward Humphris' (Z) | SKen |
| 'Edwards Michael' (A) | LDea |
| 'Eileen' (Min/d) | ESul |
| 'Eileen Nancy' (Z) | NFir |
| 'Eileen Postle' (R) Υ[H1+3] | WFib |
| 'Eileen Stanley' (R) | LDea |
| 'Elaine' (R) | LDea |
| 'Elaine Thompson' (R) | LDea |
| Elbe Silver = 'Pensil' (I) | LAst NFir SCoo |
| 'Electra' (Z/d) | SKen |
| 'Elizabeth Angus' (Z) | SKen WFib |
| 'Elizabeth Read' (Dw) | ESul |
| 'Ella Martin' (St) | ESul |
| 'Elmfield' (St/Min/d) | ESul |
| 'Elmsett' (Dw/C/d) | ESul NFir SSea WFib |
| 'Elna' (Min) | ESul |
| 'Els' (Dw/St) | ESul SKen WBrk |
| 'Elsi' (I × Z/d/v) | WFib |
| 'Elsie Gillam' (St) | ESul WFib |
| 'Elsie Hickman' (R) | ESul LDea |
| 'Elsie Portas' (Z/C/d) | ESul SKen |
| 'Embassy' (Min) | ESul WFib |
| 'Emerald' (I) | SKen |
| Emilia = 'Pactina'[PBR] | LAst |
| 'Emma Game' (Z/St) | WFib |
| 'Emma Hössle' | see *P.* 'Frau Emma Hössle' |
| 'Emma Jane Read' (Dw/d) | ESul WFib |
| 'Emma Louise' (Z) | SKen |
| 'Emmy Sensation' (R) | LDea |
| 'Emperor Nicholas' (Z/d) | SSea |
| 'Empress' (Z) | SKen |
| 'Ena' (Min) | ESul |
| 'Enchantress' (I) | SKen |
| 'Encore' (Z/d/v) | SSea |

***endlicherianum*** WCot WWFP
'Endsleigh' (Sc) MBPg SBch
'Enid Brackley' (R) ESul
'Erwarton' (Min/d) ESul NFir
'Escapade' (Min/d) ESul
'Eskay Gold' (A) WFib
'Eskay Jewel' (A) WFib
'Eskay Ruby' (A) MHer
'Eskay Sugar Candy' (A) WFib
'Eskay Verglo' (A) WFib
'Espresso Coffee' (R) **new** ESul
Evening Glow = 'Bergpalais'PBR LAst
'Evka'PBR (I/v) CWCL LAst SCoo SSea
***exstipulatum*** EShb EWoo SSea
'Fabiola' LAst
'Fair Dinkum' (Z/v) ESul
'Fair Ellen' (Sc) ESul LDea MBPg MHer WFib
'Fairlee' (DwI) WFib
'Fairy Lights' (Dw/St) ESul NFir
'Fairy Orchid' (A) ESul LDea WFib
'Fairy Queen' LDea MHer
'Falkenham' (Min) ESul
'Falkland Brother' (Z/C/v) WFib
'Falkland Hero' (Z/v) NFir
'Fallen Angel' (Z/St) WFar
'Fandango' (Z/St) ESul NFir SMrm WFib
'Fanny Eden' (R) CWCL EWoo WFib
'Fantasia' white-flowered (Dw/d) 🏆H1+3 ESul WFib
'Fareham' (R) 🏆H1+3 LDea WFib
'Feneela' (Dw/d) ESul
'Fenland' (R) ESul
'Fenland Queen' (A) ESul
'Fenton Farm' (Dw/C) ESul NFir
'Festal' (Min/d) ESul
'Feuerriese' (Z) SKen
'Fiat' (Z/d) SKen
'Fiat Queen' (Z/d) SKen WFib
'Fiat Supreme' (Z/d) SKen
'Fiery Sunrise' (R) ESul LDea
'Fifth Avenue' (R) ESul WFib
'Filicifolium' see *P. denticulatum* 'Filicifolium'
'Fir Trees Audrey B' (St) NFir
'Fir Trees Betty' (U) **new** NFir
'Fir Trees Echoes of Pink' (A) EWoo
'Fir Trees Eileen' (St) NFir SMrm
'Fir Trees Ele' (A/v) NFir
'Fir Trees Fantail' (Min) NFir
'Fir Trees Flamingo' (Dw) NFir
'Fir Trees Jack' (Z/Dw) NFir
'Fir Trees Janet' (Dw) NFir
'Fir Trees Jennifer' (R/Dec) NFir
'Fir Trees John Grainger' (Z/v) NFir
'Fir Trees Mark' (R/Dec/v) NFir
'Fir Trees Nan' (R/Dec) NFir
'Fir Trees Pink Pom-Pom' (Dw/St/C/d) NFir
'Fir Trees Ruby Wedding' (C) NFir
'Fir Trees Silver Wedding' (Z/C/d) NFir
'Fir Trees Sparkler' (Min/C) NFir
'Fir Trees Val' (Z) NFir
'Fire Dancer' (R) ESul
'Fire Dragon' (Z/St/d) SKen SSea
'Firefly' (Min/d) ESul
'Firestone' (Dw) ESul
(Fireworks Series) LAst SBfd
Fireworks Cherry = 'Fiwocherry'PBR (Z)
- Fireworks Cherry-white = 'Fiwocher'PBR (Z) LAst SSea
- Fireworks Light Pink = 'Fiwopink'PBR (Z/St) SBfd SWal
- Fireworks Red-white = 'Fiworewhi'PBR (Z) SBfd
- Fireworks White = 'Fiwowit'PBR (Z) SBfd
'First Blush' (R) WFib
'First Love' (Z) NFir
First Yellow = 'Pacyell' **new** WGor
'Flakey' (I/d/v) 🏆H1+3 ESul
'Flaming Katy' (Min) ESul NFir
'Flarepath' (Z/C/v) NFir
'Flash' (Min) ESul
'Flecks' (Min/St) ESul
'Fleur-de-lys' (A) LDea
'Fleurette' (Min/d) ESul SKen
'Fleurisse' (Z) WFib
'Flirt' (Min) WFib
'Floral Cascade' (Fr/d) SSea
'Florence Hunt' (R) NFir
'Floria Moore' (Dec) ESul EWoo NFir SSea
'Flower Basket' (R/d) ESul EWoo LDea
(Flower Fairy Series) LAst
Flower Fairy Berry = 'Sweberry'PBR
- Flower Fairy Rose = 'Swero'PBR (Z) LAst LSou
- Flower Fairy Violet = 'Swevio'PBR **new** LAst
- Flower Fairy White Splash = 'Swewhi' (Z) LAst LSou
'Flower of Spring' (Z/v) 🏆H1+3 SKen SSea
'Flowton' (Dw/d) ESul
'Foxhall' (Dw) ESul
Foxy = 'Pacfox'PBR (Z) LSou
***fragrans*** SWal
Fragrans Group (Sc) CRHN CSev ESul EWoo GPoy MBPg MCot MHer SKen SPet SSea WFib WGwG
§ - 'Fragrans Variegatum' (Sc/v) CSev ESul MBPg NFir SKen SWal WBrk WFib
- 'Snowy Nutmeg' see *P.* (Fragrans Group) 'Fragrans Variegatum'
'Fraiche Beauté' (Z/d) WFib
'Francis Gibbon' (Z/d) WFib
'Francis James' (Z) WFib
'Francis Kelly' (R) ESul
'Francis Parmenter' (MinI/v) LAst
'Francis Parrett' (Min/d) 🏆H1+3 ESul SKen WFib
'Francis Read' (Dw/d) ESul
'Frank Hazel' **new** NFir
'Frank Headley' (Z/v) 🏆H1+3 ESul LAst MCot MWea NPer NVic SCoo SIde SKen SMrm SSea SWal WFib
§ 'Frau Emma Hössle' (Dw/d) ESul WFib
'Freak of Nature' (Z/v) ESul MHer NFir SKen SSea WFib
'Frensham' (Sc) ESul LDea MBPg MHer WFib
'Freshfields Suki' (Dw) NFir
'Freshwater' (St/C) ESul SSea WFib
'Freston' (Dw) ESul
'Friary Wood' (Z/C/d) ESul NFir WFib

| | | |
|---|---|---|
| | 'Friesdorf' (Dw/Fr) | ESul MCot MHer NFir SKen WBrk WFib |
| | 'Frills' (Min/d) | ESul |
| | 'Fringed Angel' (A) | CFee |
| | 'Fringed Apple' (Sc) | LDea MBPg |
| | 'Fringed Aztec' (R) ♀H1+3 | CWCL ESul LDea NFir SPet WFib |
| | 'Fringed Jer'Ray' (A) | LDea SSea |
| | 'Frosty' misapplied | see *P.* 'Variegated Kleine Liebling' |
| | 'Frosty Petit Pierre' | see *P.* 'Variegated Kleine Liebling' |
| | 'Frühlingszauber Lila' (R) | ESul |
| | 'Fruity' (Sc) | MBPg |
| | ***fruticosum*** | EWoo WFib |
| | 'Fuji' (R) | NFir |
| | ***fulgidum*** | ESul EWoo MCot WFib |
| | 'Funny Girl' (R) | ESul |
| | 'Fynn' (Dw) | ESul |
| | 'Gabriel' (A) | ESul EWoo LDea |
| | 'Gaiety Girl' (A) | ESul |
| | 'Galilee' (I/d) ♀H1+3 | SKen |
| | Galleria Sunrise = 'Sunrise' (R) | ESul LDea |
| | 'Galway Star' (Sc/v) ♀H1+3 | MBPg MHer WFib |
| | 'Garland' (Dw/d) | ESul |
| | 'Garnet' (Z/d) | ESul |
| | 'Garnet Rosebud' (Min/d) | ESul NFir WFib |
| | 'Gartendirektor Herman' (Dec) | ESul EWoo NFir WFib |
| | 'Gatwig' | LAst |
| | 'Gaudy' (Z) | WFib |
| | 'Gay Baby' (DwI) | ESul |
| | 'Gay Baby Supreme' (DwI) | ESul |
| | 'Gemini' (Z/St/d) | CWCL NFir WFib |
| | 'Gemma' (R) | ESul NFir |
| | 'Gemma Jewel' (R) ♀H1+3 | ESul |
| I | 'Gemstone' (Min) | ESul |
| | 'Gemstone' (Sc) ♀H1+3 | CSev LDea MBPg MHer |
| | 'Genie' (Z/d) | SKen WFib |
| | 'Gentle Georgia' (R) | WFib |
| | 'Geofbar' (R) | ESul |
| | 'Geoff May' (Min) | ESul |
| | 'Georgia' (R) | WFib |
| | 'Georgia Mai Read' | ERea |
| | 'Georgia Peach' (R) | WFib |
| | 'Georgie' (R) | LDea |
| | 'Georgina Blythe' (R) ♀H1+3 | WFib |
| | (Gerainbow Series) 'Gerainbow Neon' (I) **new** | LAst |
| | - 'Gerainbown Orange' (I) **new** | LAst |
| | - 'Gerainbow Red' (I) **new** | LAst |
| | - 'Gerainbow White' (I) **new** | LAst |
| | 'Gerald Portas' (Dw/C) | ESul |
| | 'Gerald Wells' (Min) | ESul |
| | 'Geraldine' (Min) | ESul |
| | 'Gesa' | LAst |
| | 'Gess Portas' (Z/v) | ESul |
| | 'Giant Butterfly' (R) | ESul |
| | 'Giant Oak' (Sc) | ESul MBPg |
| | ***gibbosum*** | EWoo MHer SSea WFib WGwG |
| | 'Gilbert West' (Z) | SKen |
| | 'Gilda' (R/v) | LDea |
| | 'Gill' (Min/Ca) | ESul |
| | 'Ginger Frost' (Sc/v) | WFib WGwG |
| | 'Ginger Rogers' (Z) | NFir |
| | 'Glacier Claret' (Z) | WFib |
| | 'Glacier Crimson' (Z) | SKen |
| | 'Glacis'[PBR] (Quality Series) (Z/d) | LAst LSou SSea |
| | 'Gladys Evelyn' (Z/d) | WFib |
| | 'Gladys Stevens' (Min/d) | ESul |
| | 'Gladys Weller' (Z/d) | WFib |
| | ***glaucum*** | see *P. lanceolatum* |
| | 'Glen Sheree' (R) | ESul |
| | 'Gloria Pearce' (R) | ESul LDea |
| | 'Glowing Embers' (R) | ESul LDea |
| § | ***glutinosum*** | WFib |
| | 'Goblin' (Min/d) | ESul SKen WFib |
| | 'Godshill' (R) | LDea |
| | Golden Angel[PBR] | see *P.* 'Sarah Don' |
| | 'Golden Baby' (Dw/I/C) | ESul WFib |
| | 'Golden Brilliantissimum' (Z/v) | ESul SSea WFib |
| | 'Golden Butterfly' (Z/C) | ESul |
| | 'Golden Chalice' (Min/v) | ESul NFir WFib |
| | 'Golden Clorinda' (U/Sc/C) | CRHN LDea MBPg NFir SSea |
| | 'Golden Ears' (Dw/St/C) | NFir NPer WFib |
| | 'Golden Edinburgh' (I/v) | WFib |
| | 'Golden Everaarts' (Dw/C) | ESul |
| | 'Golden Fleece' (Dw/C/d) | ESul |
| | 'Golden Gates' (Z/C) | ESul SKen |
| | 'Golden Harry Hieover'[3] (Z/C) ♀H1+ | ESul MBri SSea |
| | 'Golden Lilac Gem' (I/d) | WFib |
| | 'Golden Lilac Mist' | SKen |
| | 'Golden Oldie' (Sc) | MHer |
| | 'Golden Petit Pierre' (Min/C) | ESul SSea |
| | 'Golden Princess' (Min/C) | WFib |
| | 'Golden Roc' (Min/C) | ESul |
| | 'Golden Square' (Dw/St) | WFib |
| | 'Golden Staphs' (Z/St/C) | ESul MHer NFir SSea WFib |
| | 'Golden Stardust' (Z/St) | ESul |
| | 'Golden Wedding' (Z/d/v) | NFir |
| | 'Golden Well Sweep' | see *P. crispum* 'Golden Well Sweep' |
| | 'Goldilocks' (A) | ESul |
| | 'Goldstone Copper' (Min/d) **new** | MGbk |
| | 'Gooseberry Leaf' | see *P. grossularioides* |
| | 'Gordano Midnight' (R) | EWoo |
| | 'Gordon Quale' (Z/d) | WFib |
| | 'Gosbeck' (A) | SSea WFib |
| | 'Gosbrook Clifford Taylor' (Min/d) **new** | MGbk |
| | 'Gosbrook Gillian Martin' (Min/d) **new** | MGbk |
| | 'Gosbrook Robyn Louise' (Z/St/d) **new** | MGbk |
| | 'Gosbrook Snowcap' (Z/St/d) **new** | MGbk |
| | 'Gothenburg' (R) | ESul |
| | 'Gottweig' (Z) | ESul |
| | 'Grace' (A) | LDea |
| | 'Grace Thomas' (Sc) ♀H1+3 | CSev LDea MBPg MHer WFib |
| | 'Grace Wells' (Min) | ESul WFib |
| § | 'Gräfin Mariza' (Z/d) | SKen |
| | 'Grand Slam' (R) | CWCL ESul LDea NFir WFib |
| | 'Grandad Mac' (Dw/St) | ESul NFir SSea |
| | ***grandiflorum*** | CSpe EWoo MCot MHer WFib |
| | 'Grandma Ross' (R) | ESul |
| | 'Grandma Thompson' (R) | ESul |
| | 'Granny Hewitt' (Min/d) | ESul |
| | ***graveolens*** *sensu* J.J.A. van der Walt | LDea SBch WFib |
| § | 'Graveolens' (Sc) | ESul GPoy MBPg MHer SSea SWal WBrk WFib |
| | 'Graveolens Minor' (Sc) **new** | EWoo |

| | |
|---|---|
| 'Great Bricett' (Dw/d) | ESul |
| 'Great Glemham Lemon' (Sc) **new** | EWoo |
| 'Green Ears' (Z/St) | ESul |
| 'Green Eyes' (I/d) | MHer SKen |
| 'Green Goddess' (I/d) | SKen |
| 'Green Gold Petit Pierre' (Min) | ESul |
| 'Green Silver Galaxy' (St) | ESul |
| § 'Greengold Kleine Liebling' (Min/C/v) | ESul SKen |
| 'Greengold Petit Pierre' | see *P.* 'Greengold Kleine Liebling' |
| 'Greetings' (Min/v) | ESul MBri SSea WFib |
| 'Grey Lady Plymouth' (Sc/v) | ESul EWoo LDea MBPg MCot MHer WFib |
| 'Grey Sprite' (Min/v) | ESul WFib |
| § ***grossularioides*** | EOHP MBPg MHer |
| - 'Coconut' | MBPg |
| 'Grozser Garten' (Dw) | ESul |
| 'Grozser Garten Weiss' (Dw) | ESul |
| 'Guardsman' (Dw) | ESul |
| 'Guernsey Flair' (Z) | CSpe LAst LSou MCot |
| 'Gustav Emich' (Z/d) | SKen |
| 'Gwen' (Min/v) | NFir |
| 'H. Rigler' (Z) | SKen |
| 'Hadleigh' (Min) | ESul |
| 'Halo' (R) | ESul |
| § 'Hannaford Star' (Z/St) | WFib |
| 'Hannah West' (Z/C) | SSea |
| 'Hansen's Pinkie' (R) | EWoo |
| 'Hansen's Wild Spice' (Sc) | MBPg |
| 'Happy Anniversary' (Dw/C) **new** | NFir |
| 'Happy Appleblossom' (Z/v/d) | NFir SKen |
| (Happy Face Series) | NPri |
| Happy Face Amethyst = 'Penrad'[PBR] (I) | |
| - Happy Face Mex = 'Pacvet'[PBR] (I) | LAst NPri |
| - Happy Face Scarlet = 'Penhap'[PBR] (I) | LAst |
| - Happy Face Velvet Red = 'Pachafvel'[PBR] (I) | LAst NPri |
| - Happy Face White = 'Pacfali' (I) | LAst NPri |
| 'Happy Thought' (Z/v) 𝕐H1+3 | ESul MBri MCot NFir NVic SCoo SKen SSea WFib |
| 'Harbour Lights' (R) | ESul LDea WFib |
| 'Harewood Slam' (R) | ESul WFib |
| 'Harkstead' (Dw) | ESul |
| 'Harlequin' (Dw) | ESul |
| 'Harlequin Mahogany' (I/d) | SKen |
| § 'Harlequin Miss Liver Bird' (I) | SKen |
| 'Harlequin Picotee' (I/d) | SKen |
| 'Harlequin Pretty Girl' (I × Z/d) | WFib |
| 'Harlequin Rosie O'Day' (I) | SKen WFib |
| 'Harriet Le Hair' (Z) | SKen |
| 'Harvard' (I/d) | WFib |
| 'Havenstreet' (Dw/St) | ESul |
| ***havlasae*** | ECou |
| 'Hazel' (R) | MSCN WFib |
| 'Hazel Burtoff' (R) | ESul LDea |
| 'Hazel Candy' (R) | ESul |
| 'Hazel Cherry' (R) | ESul LDea WFib |
| 'Hazel Chick' (R) | ESul |
| 'Hazel Choice' (R) | ESul LDea NFir |
| 'Hazel Gypsy' (R) | ESul LDea |
| 'Hazel Harmony' (R) | ESul LDea |
| 'Hazel Henderson' (R) | LDea |
| 'Hazel Herald' (R) | ESul |
| 'Hazel Orchid' (R) | ESul |
| 'Hazel Perfection' (R) | NFir |
| 'Hazel Ripple' (R) | ESul |
| 'Hazel Rose' (R) | LDea |
| 'Hazel Satin' (R) | LDea |
| 'Hazel Star' (R) | ESul WFib |
| 'Hazel Stardust' (R) | ESul NFir |
| § 'Hederinum' (I) | LSou |
| § 'Hederinum Variegatum' (I/v) | MCot NFir SPet WFib |
| 'Heidi' (Min/d) | ESul |
| 'Helen Christine' (Z/St) | ESul NFir WFib |
| 'Hemingstone' (A) | LDea |
| 'Hemley' (Sc) | LDea |
| 'Henhurst Gleam' (Dw/d) | ESul |
| 'Henley' (Min/d) | ESul |
| 'Henry Weller' (A) | ESul MBPg NFir WFib |
| 'Hermione' (Z/d) | WFib |
| Hidemi = 'Pachide' (Z) **new** | WGor |
| 'High Fidelity' (R) | ESul |
| 'Highfields Appleblossom' (Z) | SKen |
| 'Highfields Attracta' (Z/d) | SKen WFib |
| 'Highfields Candy Floss' (Z/d) | NFir |
| 'Highfields Choice' (Z) | SKen |
| 'Highfields Comet' (Z) | SKen |
| 'Highfields Contessa' (Z/d) | SKen WFib |
| 'Highfields Delight' (Z) | WFib |
| 'Highfields Fancy' (Z/d) | NFir SKen |
| 'Highfields Festival' (Z/d) | NFir SKen WFib |
| 'Highfields Joy' (Z/d) | SKen |
| 'Highfields Melody' (Z/d) | WFib |
| 'Highfields Pride' (Z) | SKen WFib |
| 'Highfields Prima Donna' (Z/d) | SKen |
| 'Highfields Snowdrift' (Z) | SKen |
| 'Highfields Sugar Candy' (Z/d) | SKen WFib |
| 'Highfields Symphony' (Z) | WFib |
| 'Hilbre Island' (Z/C/d) | NFir |
| 'Hildegard' (Z/d) | SKen |
| 'Hills of Snow' (Z/v) | MBri MHer SKen SSea WFib |
| 'Hillscheider Amethyst'[PBR] | see *P.* Amethyst = 'Fisdel' |
| 'Hindoo' (R × U) | CSpe EWoo NFir SSea WFib |
| 'Hindoo Rose' (U) | NFir |
| 'Hintlesham' (Min) | ESul |
| ***hispidum*** | MHer |
| 'Hitcham' (Min/d) | ESul WFib |
| 'Holbrook' (Dw/C/d) | ESul NFir WFib |
| 'Holt Beauty' | EWoo |
| 'Honeywood Lindy' (R) | ESul |
| 'Honeywood Lindy Variegated' (R/v) | ESul |
| 'Honeywood Margaret' (R) | ESul |
| 'Honeywood Suzanne' (Min/Fr) | ESul NFir SKen |
| 'Honne Frühling' (Z) | SKen |
| 'Honneas' (Dw) | ESul |
| 'Honnestolz' (Dw) | ESul SKen |
| 'Hope Valley' (Dw/C/d) 𝕐H1+3 | ESul NFir SKen |
| 'Horace Parsons' (R) | WFib |
| 'Horace Read' (Dw) | ESul |
| 'Horning Ferry' (Dw) | ESul |
| 'House and Garden' (R) | NFir |
| 'Hula' (R × U) | EWoo |
| 'Hulda Conn' (Z/Ca/d) | WFib |
| 'Hulverstone' (Dw/St) | ESul |

| |  |  |
|---|---|---|
| | 'Hunter's Moon' (Z/C) | NFir |
| | 'Hurdy-gurdy' (Z/d/v) | ESul |
| | 'Ian Read' (Min/d) | ESul |
| | 'Ibiza' (Dw/C) | ESul |
| | 'Icing Sugar' (I/d) | ESul WFib |
| | 'Immaculatum' (Z) | WFib |
| | 'Imperial'$^{PBR}$ (R) | LAst |
| | 'Imperial Butterfly' (A/Sc) | CRHN ESul EWoo LDea NFir SSea WFib |
| | 'Inca' (R) | ESul |
| | 'Inspiration' (R) | ESul |
| | ***ionidiflorum*** | CSpe EShb MBPg MCot MHer MNHC SAga SPhx |
| | 'Ipswich Town' (Dw/d) | ESul |
| | 'Irene' (Z/d) 🏆$^{H1+3}$ | SKen WFib |
| | 'Irene Collet' (R) | LDea |
| | 'Irene Picardy' (Z/d) | SKen |
| | 'Irene Toyon' (Z) 🏆$^{H1+3}$ | SKen WFib |
| | 'Isidel' (I/d) 🏆$^{H1+3}$ | SKen WFib |
| | 'Islington Peppermint' (Sc) | MBPg NFir SBch WFib |
| | 'Isobel Eden' (Sc) | LDea MBPg |
| | 'Italian Gem' (I) | SKen |
| | 'Ivalo' (Z/d) | SKen WFib |
| | 'Ivory Snow' (Z/d/v) | ESul NFir WFib |
| | 'Jacey' (Z/d) | SKen |
| | 'Jack of Hearts' (I × Z/d) | WFib |
| | 'Jack Simmons' (Z/d/Dw) | ESul |
| | 'Jack Wood' (Z/d) | NFir WFib |
| § | 'Jackie' (I/d) | EShb MBri WFib |
| | 'Jackie Davies' (R) | EWoo |
| | 'Jackie Gall' | see *P.* 'Jackie' |
| | 'Jackie Totlis' (Z/St) | WFib |
| | 'Jackpot Wild Rose' (Z/d) | WFib |
| | 'Jacqueline' (Z/d) | SKen |
| | 'Jacqui Caws' (Dw) | ESul |
| | 'Jake Brougham' (St) | ESul |
| | 'Jane Biggin' (Dw/C/d) | ESul SKen |
| | 'Janet Dean' (R) | LDea |
| | 'Janet Hofman' (Z/d) | WFib |
| | 'Janet Kerrigan' (Min/d) | ESul WFib |
| | 'Jasmin' (R) | ESul |
| | 'Jaunty' (Min/d) | ESul |
| | 'Jayne' (Min/d) | ESul |
| | 'Jayne Eyre' (Min/d) | ESul SKen WFib |
| | 'Jazzy' (Min/St) | ESul |
| | 'Jean Bart' (I) | SSea |
| | 'Jean Caws' (Z/St) | WFib |
| | 'Jean Marion' (R) | LDea |
| | 'Jean Oberle' (Z/d) | SKen |
| | 'Jeanie Hunt' (Z/C/d) | NFir |
| | 'Jeanne' (Z) | WFib |
| § | 'Jeanne d'Arc' (I/d) | SKen WFib |
| | 'Jenifer Read' (Dw) | ESul |
| | 'Jennifer' (Min) | ESul |
| | 'Jennifer Strange' (R) | ESul |
| | 'Jericho' (Z/St/v) | ESul |
| | 'Jer'Ray' (A) | ESul EWoo LDea NFir SSea WFib |
| | 'Jessel's Unique' (U) | MHer SPet |
| | 'Jewel'$^{PBR}$ (R) | ESul |
| | 'Jimbar' (R) | ESul |
| | 'Jinny Reeves' (R) | LDea |
| | 'Jip's Freda Burgess' (Z/C/d) | NFir |
| | 'Jip's Nippy' (Dw) | NFir |
| | 'Jip's Pip' (Z/C/d) | NFir |
| | 'Jip's Rosy Glow' (Min/d) | ESul NFir |
| | 'Jip's Twink' (Iv/v) | NFir |
| | 'Joan Cashmere' (Z/d) | ESul |
| | 'Joan Fontaine' (Z) | WFib |
| | 'Joan Hayward' (Min) | ESul |
| | 'Joan Morf' (R) | ESul EWoo NFir WFib |
| | 'Joan of Arc' | see *P.* 'Jeanne d'Arc' |
| | 'Joan Sharman' (Min) | ESul |
| | 'John's Pride' (Dw) | MBri NFir |
| | 'Joseph Haydn' (R) | ESul |
| | 'Joseph Wheeler' (A) | ESul LDea |
| | 'Joy' (I) | SPet |
| | 'Joy' (R) 🏆$^{H1+3}$ | CSpe ESul LDea NFir WFib |
| I | 'Joy' (Z/d) | LAst SKen |
| | 'Joy Lucille' (Sc) | ESul LDea MBPg |
| | 'Joyful' (Min) | ESul |
| | 'Jubilant' (R) | ESul |
| | 'Judy Read' (Dw) | ESul |
| | 'Juliana' (R) | LAst LDea |
| | 'Julie Bannister' (R) | ESul |
| | 'Julie Smith' (R) | ESul WFib |
| | 'Julie's Delight' (Sc) | MHer |
| | 'June Filbey' (R) | LDea |
| | 'Jungle Night' (R) | ESul |
| | 'Juniper' (Sc) | MBPg |
| | 'Jupiter' (Min/d) | SKen |
| | 'Jupiter' (R) | ESul |
| | 'Just Bella' (d) | NFir |
| | 'Just Beth' (Z/C/d) | NFir |
| | 'Just Joss' (Dw/d) | NFir |
| | 'Just Rita' (A) | SSea |
| | 'Just William' (Min/C/d) | ESul WFib |
| | 'Kamahl' (R) | ESul WFib |
| § | 'Kardinal' (Z/d) | SPet |
| | 'Karen' (Dw/C) | LAst LSou |
| | 'Karl Hagele' (Z/d) | SKen WFib |
| | 'Karl Offenstein' (R) | ESul |
| | 'Karmin Ball' | WFib |
| | 'Karrooense' | see *P. quercifolium* |
| | 'Kathleen' (Min) | ESul |
| | 'Kathleen Gamble' (Z) | SKen WFib |
| | 'Kathryn' (Min) | ESul |
| | 'Kathryn Portas' (Z/v) | ESul |
| | 'Kathy Kirby' (R) | ESul |
| | 'Katie' (R) | EWoo |
| | 'Katie Hillier' (R) | LDea |
| | 'Katrine' | CWCL LAst NPri |
| | 'Kayleigh Aitken' (R) | CWCL |
| | 'Kayleigh West' (Min) | ESul SSea |
| | 'Keepsake' (Min/d) | ESul WFib |
| | 'Keith Vernon' (Z) | NFir |
| | 'Kelly Brougham' (St/Dw) | ESul |
| | 'Ken Lea' (Z/v) | ESul |
| | 'Ken Lea Butterfly' (Z/d) **new** | MGbk |
| | 'Ken Salmon' (Dw/d) | ESul |
| | 'Kenny's Double' (Z/d) | WFib |
| | 'Kensington' (A) | LDea |
| | 'Kerensa' (Min/d) | ESul SKen WFib |
| | 'Kershy' (Min) | ESul |
| | 'Kesgrave' (Min/d) | ESul WFib |
| | 'Kettlebaston' (A) 🏆$^{H1+3}$ | LDea WFib |
| | 'Kewense' (Z) | EShb |
| | 'Kimono' (R) | ESul NFir |
| | 'Kinder Gaisha' (R) | NFir |
| | 'King Edmund' (R) | ESul LDea NFir |
| | 'King of Balcon' | see *P.* 'Hederinum' |
| | 'King of Denmark' (Z/d) | WFib |
| | 'King Solomon' (R) | LDea WFib |
| | 'Kirton' (Min/d) | ESul |
| § | 'Kleine Liebling' (Min) | ESul WFib |
| | 'Knaves Bonfire' (R) | ESul |
| | 'Krista' (Min/d) | ESul WFib |
| | 'Kyoto' (R) | NFir |
| | 'Kyra' (Min/d) | ESul WFib |
| | 'L.E.Wharton' (Z) | SKen |

| | | |
|---|---|---|
| | 'La France' (I/d) $\Upsilon^{H1+3}$ | MCot SKen WFib |
| | 'La Paloma' (R) | ESul WFib |
| | Laced Red Mini Cascade = 'Achspen' (I) | NFir |
| § | 'Lachskönigin' (I/d) | SKen SPet WFib |
| | 'Lady Ilchester' (Z/d) | SKen WFib |
| | 'Lady Love Song' (R) | ESul NFir WFib |
| | 'Lady Mary' (Sc) | ESul EWoo MBPg MCot MHer |
| | 'Lady Mavis Pilkington' (Z/d) | WFib |
| | 'Lady Plymouth' (Sc/v) $\Upsilon^{H1+3}$ | CRHN CSpe EPfP EShb ESul EWoo LDea MBPg MCot MHer MNHC MSCN NEgg NFir SBfd SKen SPet SSea SWal WFib WGwG |
| § | 'Lady Scarborough' (Sc) | ESul EWoo MBPg MHer WFib |
| | 'Lady Woods' (Z) | SSea |
| | ***laevigatum*** | MHer |
| | 'Lakeland' (I) | ESul SKen SSea |
| | 'Lakis' (R) | LDea |
| | 'Lamorna' (R) | ESul LDea |
| | 'Lancastrian' (Z/d) | WFib |
| § | ***lanceolatum*** | MHer |
| | 'Langley' (R) | ESul |
| | 'Lanham Royal' (Dw/d) | ESul |
| | 'Lara Aladin' (A) | LDea |
| | 'Lara Ballerina' | NFir SBch |
| | 'Lara Candy Dancer' (Sc) $\Upsilon^{H1+3}$ | CRHN ESul LDea MBPg SBch WFib |
| | 'Lara Jester' (Sc) | EWoo WFib |
| | 'Lara Maid' (A) $\Upsilon^{H1+3}$ | WFib |
| | 'Lara Nomad' (Sc) | LDea MBPg |
| | 'Lara Rajah' (R) **new** | EWoo |
| | 'Lara Starshine' (Sc) $\Upsilon^{H1+3}$ | ESul EWoo MHer NFir WFib |
| | 'Lara Waltz' (R/d) | WFib |
| | 'Lark' (Min/d) | ESul |
| | 'Larkfield' (Z/v) | SSea |
| N | 'Lass o' Gowrie' (Z/v) | ESul NFir SKen |
| | 'Lateripes' (I) | SKen |
| | 'Latte Coffee' (R) | ESul |
| | 'Laura Parmer' (Dw/St) | ESul |
| | 'Laura Wheeler' (A) | LDea |
| | 'Laurel Hayward' (R) | WFib |
| | 'Lauren Alexandra' (Z/d) | WFib |
| | Lauretta = 'Pacamla'$^{PBR}$ (Quality Series) (Z/d) | LAst |
| | Lavenda = 'Penlava'$^{PBR}$ (Dark Line Series) (Z/d) | LAst |
| | 'Lavender Grand Slam' (R) $\Upsilon^{H1+3}$ | ESul LDea NFir |
| | 'Lavender Harewood Slam' (R) | ESul LDea |
| | 'Lavender Mini Cascade'$^{PBR}$ | see *P.* Lilac Mini Cascade |
| | 'Lavender Sensation' (R) | WFib |
| | 'Lawrenceanum' | ESul EWoo WFib |
| | 'Layham' (Dw/d) | ESul |
| | 'L'Élégante' (I/v) $\Upsilon^{H1+3}$ | EWoo MCot MHer SKen SSea SWal WFib |
| | 'Lemon Air' (Sc) | ESul MBPg |
| | 'Lemon Crisp' | see *P. crispum* |
| | 'Lemon Fancy' (Sc) | LDea MBPg MCot MHer NFir WFib |
| | 'Lemon Kiss' (Sc) | CSpe EWoo MBPg |
| | 'Lemon Meringue' (Sc) | MBPg |
| | 'Lemon Toby' (Sc) | MBPg |
| | 'Len Chandler' (Min) | ESul |
| | 'Lenore' (Min/d) | ESul |
| | 'Leo' (Min) | ESul |
| | 'Leonie Holbrow' (Min) | ESul |
| | 'Lesley Judd' (R) | ESul |
| | 'Leslie William Burrows' | EWoo |
| | Lila Compakt-Cascade | see *P.* 'Decora Lilas' |
| | Lilac Cascade | see *P.* 'Roi des Balcons Lilas' |
| | 'Lilac Domino' | see *P.* 'Telston's Prima' |
| | 'Lilac Elaine' (R) | LDea |
| | 'Lilac Gem' (Min/I/d) | MCot SKen |
| | 'Lilac Gemma' (R) | ESul |
| | 'Lilac Jewel' (R) | ESul |
| | 'Lilac Joy' (R) | ESul |
| § | Lilac Mini Cascade = 'Lilamica'$^{PBR}$ (I) | ESul LAst NFir |
| | 'Lili Marlene' (I) | SKen SPet |
| | 'Lilian' (Min) | ESul SKen |
| | 'Lilian Pottinger' (Sc) | CRHN CSev ESul EWoo LDea MBPg MHer NFir SKen SSea |
| | 'Lilian Woodberry' (Z) | WFib |
| | Lilly = 'Paclill'$^{PBR}$ | LAst NPri |
| | 'Limoneum' (Sc) | CSev MBPg MHer |
| | 'Linda' (R) | ESul |
| | 'Lindsey' (Min) | ESul |
| | 'Lindy Portas' (I/d) | SKen |
| | 'Lipstick' (St) | WFib |
| | 'Lisa' (Min/C) | ESul WFib |
| | 'Lisa Jo' (St/v/Dw/d) | WFib |
| | 'Little Alice' (Dw/d) $\Upsilon^{H1+3}$ | ESul NFir WFib |
| | 'Little Blakenham' (A) | ESul LDea SSea |
| | 'Little Fi-fine' (Dw/C) | ESul |
| | 'Little Gem' (Sc) | MBPg MHer SSea WFib |
| | 'Little Jim' (Min/d) | NFir |
| | 'Little Jip' (Z/d/v) | ESul NFir WFib |
| | 'Little Lisa' (Dw) | ESul |
| | 'Little Margaret' (Min/v) | ESul |
| | 'Little Primular' (Min) | ESul |
| | 'Little Spikey' (St/Min/d) | ESul WFib |
| | 'Lively Lady' (Dw/C) | ESul |
| | 'Liverbird' | see *P.* 'Harlequin Miss Liver Bird' |
| | 'Lizzie Hillier' (R) | LDea |
| | ***longicaule*** | MBPg |
| | 'Lord Baden-Powell' | see *P.* 'Colonel Baden-Powell' |
| | 'Lord Bute' (R) $\Upsilon^{H1+3}$ | CSpe ECtt ESul EWoo LAst LDea MCot MHer MSCN NFir NPer SBch SBrd SGar SIde SKen SMrm SPet SSea SUsu SVen WFib WGwG |
| | 'Lord Constantine' (R) | LDea |
| | 'Lord de Ramsey' | see *P.* 'Tip Top Duet' |
| | 'Lord Roberts' (Z) | WFib |
| | 'Loretta' (Dw) | ESul |
| | 'Lorna' (Dw/d) | ESul LAst |
| | 'Lorraine' (Dw) | ESul |
| | 'Lotta Lundberg' (Dw/Z/St/d) | ESul |
| | Lotus = 'Floscala' (Z/d) | LAst |
| | 'Lotusland' (Dw/St/C) | NFir WFib |
| | 'Louise' (Min) | ESul |
| I | 'Louise' (R) | ESul NFir |
| | 'Louise Waddington' (Min/St) | ESul |
| | 'Love Song' (R/v) | ESul LDea NFir WFib |
| | 'Love Story' (Z/v) | ESul |
| | 'Loveliness' (Z) | WFib |
| * | 'Loverly' (Min/d) | ESul |
| | 'Lovesdown' (Dw/St) | ESul |
| | 'Lowood' (R) | ESul |
| | 'Lucie Caws' (St/d) | ESul |
| | 'Lucilla' (Min) | ESul |
| | 'Lucinda' (Min) | ESul |
| | 'Lucy' (Min) | ESul |
| | 'Lucy Gunnett' (Z/d/v) | ESul NFir |
| | 'Lucy Jane' (R) | ESul |
| | ***luridum*** | WCot |
| | 'Lustre' (R) | ESul |
| | 'Lyewood Bonanza' (R) | CWCL ESul WFib |

| | | |
|---|---|---|
| | 'Lyric' (Min/d) | ESul SKen WFib |
| | 'Mabel Grey' (Sc) ♀H1+3 | CRHN CSev CSpe EShb ESul EWoo MBPg MCot MHer MNHC NFir NPer SBch SIde SKen SSea WFib |
| § | 'Madame Auguste Nonin' (U/Sc) | ESul MHer NFir SKen WFib |
| | 'Madame Butterfly' (Z/d/v) | ESul NFir SKen |
| | 'Madame Crousse' (I/d) ♀H1+3 | EWoo WFib |
| | 'Madame Fournier' (Dw/C) | ESul |
| | 'Madame Hibbault' (Z) | SKen |
| | 'Madame Layal' (A) | EWoo MHer NFir SBch WFib |
| | 'Madame Margot' | see *P.* 'Hederinum Variegatum' |
| | 'Madame Salleron' (Min/v) ♀H1+3 | LDea LSou WBrk |
| | 'Madame Thibaut' (R) | LDea |
| | 'Madge Taylor' (R) | NFir |
| | 'Magaluf' (I/C/d) | SSea |
| | 'Magda' (Z/d) | ESul |
| | ***magenteum*** | ESul |
| | 'Magic Lantern' (Z/C) | NFir |
| | 'Magic Moments' (R) | ESul |
| | 'Magnum' (R) | WFib |
| | 'Maid of Honour' (Min) | ESul |
| | 'Mairi' (A) | LDea WFib |
| | 'Majesta' (Z/d) | SKen |
| | 'Majorca' (Dw/C) | ESul |
| | 'Maloya' (Z) | SKen |
| | 'Mamie' (Z/d) | SKen |
| | 'Mandarin' (R) | ESul |
| | 'Mangles' Variegated' (Z/v) | WFib |
| | 'Mantilla' (Min) | ESul SKen |
| | 'Manx Maid' (A) | ESul LDea NFir |
| | 'Maple Leaf' (Sc) | EWoo MBPg |
| | 'Marble Sunset' | see *P.* 'Wood's Surprise' |
| | 'Marchioness of Bute' (R/Dec) | LDea MHer NFir WFib |
| | 'Maréchal MacMahon' (Z/C) | SKen SSea |
| | 'Margaret Harris' (A) | ESul |
| | 'Margaret Parmenter' (I/C) | ESul |
| | 'Margaret Pearce' (R) | LDea |
| | 'Margaret Soley' (R) ♀H1+3 | LDea WFib |
| | 'Margaret Waite' (R) | ESul WFib |
| | 'Margery Stimpson' (Min/d) | ESul WFib |
| | 'Maria Wilkes' (Z/d) | WFib |
| | 'Marie Rober' (R) | ESul |
| | 'Marie Thomas' (Sc) | LDea MBPg SBch SSea |
| § | 'Marie Vogel' (R) | ESul |
| | Marimba = 'Fisrimba'PBR | SCoo |
| | 'Marion' (Min) | ESul |
| | 'Mariquita' (R) | ESul WFib |
| | 'Marja' (R) | LDea |
| | 'Mark' (Dw/d) | WFib |
| | 'Marmalade' (Min/d) | ESul WFib |
| | 'Marquis of Bute' (R/v) | ESul NFir |
| | 'Martha Parmer' (Min) | ESul |
| | 'Martin Parrett' (Min/d) | WFib |
| | 'Martin's Splendour' (Min) | ESul |
| | 'Martlesham' (Dw) | ESul |
| | 'Mary' (R) | ESul |
| | 'Mary Caws' (Dw/Z/d) | ESul |
| | 'Mary Ellen Tanner' (Min/d) | ESul |
| | 'Mary Harrison' (Z/d) | WFib |
| | 'Mary Read' (Min) | ESul |
| | 'Mary Webster' (Min) | ESul |
| | 'Masquerade' (Min) | ESul |
| | 'Masquerade' (R) | ESul SPet |
| | 'Master Paul' (Z/v) | ESul |
| | 'Masterpiece' (Z/C/d) | SKen |

| | | |
|---|---|---|
| | 'Maureen' (Min) | ESul |
| | 'Mauve Beauty' (I/d) | SKen WFib |
| | (Maverick Series) 'Maverick Red' (Z) | LAst |
| | - 'Maverick Violet' (Z) | LAst |
| | - 'Maverick White' (Z) | LAst |
| | 'Maxime Kovalevski' (Z) | WFib |
| | 'Maxine' (Z/C) | NFir |
| | 'May Day' (R) | LDea WFib |
| | 'May Magic' (R) | ESul NFir WFib |
| | 'Mayfield County Girl' (R) | ESul |
| | 'Meadowside Dark and Dainty' (St) | NFir SKen WFib |
| | 'Meadowside Harvest' (Z/St/C) | NFir WFib |
| | 'Meadowside Julie Colley' (Dw) | NFir |
| | 'Meadowside Midnight' (St/C) | WFib |
| | 'Medallion' (Z/C) | SSea |
| | 'Meditation' (Min) | ESul |
| | 'Medley' (Min/d) | WFib |
| | 'Megan Hannah' (Dw/c/d) | NFir |
| | 'Meike' (R) | ESul |
| | 'Melanie' (Min) | ESul |
| | 'Melanie' (R) | ESul LDea |
| | 'Melanie Day' (St) | NFir |
| * | 'Melissa' (Min) | ESul |
| | 'Melissa' (R) | ESul |
| | 'Melody'PBR (Tempo Series) (Z/d) | LAst |
| | 'Memento' (Min/d) | ESul WFib |
| | 'Mendip' (R) | WFib |
| | 'Mendip Anne' (R) | NFir |
| | 'Mendip Barbie' (R) | NFir |
| | 'Mendip Blanche' (R) | NFir |
| | 'Mendip Candy Floss' (R) | ESul |
| | 'Mendip Lorraine' (R) | ESul NFir |
| | 'Mendip Louise' (R) | NFir |
| | 'Mendip Sarah' (R) | NFir |
| | 'Menorca' (Dw/C/d) | ESul WFib |
| | 'Meon Maid' (R) | ESul LDea WFib |
| | 'Mere Casino' (Z) | WFib |
| | 'Mere Greeting' (Z/d) | WFib |
| | 'Mere Seville' (Z) | WFib |
| | 'Merle Seville' (Z/d) | SKen |
| | 'Mexica Tomcat' (I/d) | LAst |
| | 'Mexically Rose' (R) | ESul |
| | 'Mexican Beauty' (I) | SKen WFib |
| | 'Mexicana' | see *P.* 'Rouletta' |
| | 'Mexicanerin' | see *P.* 'Rouletta' |
| | 'Michael' (A) | ESul LDea MHer NFir SUsu |
| | 'Michelle' (Min/C) | LDea |
| | 'Michelle West' (Min) | ESul WFib |
| | 'Midas Touch' (Dw/C/d) | ESul |
| | 'Mikado' (R) | ESul |
| | 'Milden' (Dw/Z/C) | ESul NFir |
| | 'Millbern Clover' (Min/d) | ESul |
| | 'Millbern Sharna' (Min/d) | ESul |
| | 'Millfield Gem' (I/d) | WFib |
| | 'Millfield Rose' (I/d) | EWoo |
| | 'Mimi' (Dw/C/d) | ESul |
| | 'Mina Lorenzen' (R) | ESul |
| | 'Mini-Czech' (Min/St) | ESul WBrk |
| | 'Minnie' (Z/d/St) | WBrk |
| | 'Minstrel Boy' (R) | ESul EWoo LDea SSea WFib |
| | 'Minx' (Min/d) | WFib |
| | 'Miranda' (Dw) | ESul |
| | 'Miriam' (A) | ESul |
| | 'Miss Australia' (R/v) | LDea MBPg |

| | |
|---|---|
| 'Miss Burdett Coutts' (Z/v) | ESul MHer SKen SSea WFib |
| 'Miss McKinsey' (Z/St/d) | NFir |
| 'Miss Muffett' (Min/d) | WFib |
| § 'Miss Stapleton' | EWoo MHer WFib |
| 'Miss Wackles' (Min/d) | ESul |
| 'Misterioso' (R) | EWoo WFib |
| 'Misty Morning' (R) | EWoo WFib |
| 'Modesty' (Z/d) | SKen WFib |
| 'Mohawk' (R) | ESul NFir WFib |
| 'Mole' | see *P.* 'The Mole' |
| ***mollicomum*** | WCot |
| 'Mona Lisa'PBR | ESul |
| 'Monarch' (Dw/v) | ESul |
| 'Monica Bennett' (Dw) | ESul SKen |
| 'Monkwood Charm' (R) | ESul |
| 'Monkwood Rhapsody' (R) | ESul |
| 'Monkwood Rose' (A) | LDea NFir |
| 'Monkwood Sprite' (R) | ESul |
| 'Monsal Dale' (Dw/C/d) | ESul SKen |
| 'Monsieur Ninon' misapplied | see *P.* 'Madame Auguste Nonin' |
| § 'Monsieur Ninon' (U) | CRHN WFib |
| 'Mont Blanc' (Z/v) | ESul WFib |
| 'Montague Garabaldi Smith' (R) | WFib |
| 'Moon Maiden' (A) | ESul EWoo LDea WFib |
| 'Moor' (Min/d) | ESul |
| 'Moppet' (Min/d) | ESul |
| 'Morello'PBR (R) | ESul |
| 'More's Victory' (U/Sc) | SSea |
| 'Morning Cloud' (Min/d) | ESul |
| 'Morse' (Z) | SKen |
| 'Morval' (Dw/C/d) ♀H1+3 | ESul WFib |
| 'Morwenna' (R) | ESul LDea MHer NFir SMrm WFib |
| 'Mosaic Gay Baby' (I/v/d) | WFib |
| 'Mountie' (Dw) | ESul |
| 'Mozart' (R) | ESul |
| 'Mr Everaarts' (Dw/d) | ESul |
| 'Mr Henry Cox' (Z/v) ♀H1+3 | ESul MHer NFir SKen WFib |
| 'Mr Wren' (Z) | SKen SSea WFib |
| 'Mrs Cannell' (Z) | WFib |
| 'Mrs Dumbrill' (A) | ESul LDea |
| 'Mrs Eve Scott' (Z/d) **new** | MGbk |
| 'Mrs Farren' (Z/v) | MCot SKen |
| 'Mrs G.H. Smith' (A) | ESul LDea MBPg NFir SSea WFib |
| 'Mrs Innes Rogers' (R) | ESul |
| 'Mrs J.C. Mappin' (Z/v) ♀H1+3 | SKen |
| 'Mrs Kingsbury' (U) | SKen WFib |
| 'Mrs Langtry' (R) | LDea |
| 'Mrs Lawrence' (Z/d) | SKen |
| 'Mrs Martin' (I/d) | WFib |
| 'Mrs May Last' (Z/St/v) **new** | MGbk |
| 'Mrs McKenzie' (Z/St) | WFib |
| 'Mrs Parker' (Z/d/v) | ESul NFir SKen WFib |
| 'Mrs Pat' (Dw/St/C) | NFir |
| 'Mrs Pollock' (Z/v) | LAst MCot MWea NEgg NVic SCoo SSea WBrk WFib |
| 'Mrs Quilter' (Z/C) ♀H1+3 | MBri NVic SKen SMrm SSea WBrk WFib |
| 'Mrs Salter Bevis' (Z/Ca/d) | ESul WFib |
| 'Mrs Strang' (Z/d/v) | SKen SSea |
| 'Mrs Taylor' (Sc) | MBPg |
| 'Mrs W.A.R. Clifton' (I/d) | LDea SKen WFib |
| ***mutans*** | WFib |
| § 'Mutzel' (I/v) | NFir |
| 'My Chance' (Dec) | NFir WFib |
| § ***myrrhifolium*** var. ***coriandrifolium*** | MHer NFir WCot WFib |
| 'Mystery' (U) ♀H1+3 | CWCL NFir SSea WFib |
| 'Nacton' (Min) | ESul |
| 'Nancy Grey' (Min) | ESul NFir |
| 'Nancy Mac' (St) | ESul |
| 'Narina' (I) | SCoo |
| 'Natalie' (Dw) | ESul |
| 'Naughton' (Min) | ESul |
| 'Noalt L' = 'Tenca'PBR (I/d) | MPri |
| 'Needham Market' (A) | ESul LDea WFib |
| 'Neene' (Dw) | ESul |
| 'Neil Clemenson' (Sc) | WFib |
| 'Neil Jameson' (Z/v) | SKen |
| 'Nell Smith' (Z/d) | WFib |
| 'Nellie' (R) | ESul LDea |
| 'Nellie Green' (R) | LDea |
| 'Nellie Nuttall' (Z) | WFib |
| 'Nervosum' (Sc) | ESul MBPg |
| 'Nervous Mabel' (Sc) ♀H1+3 | ESul LDea MHer WBrk WFib |
| 'Nettlecombe' (Min/St) | ESul |
| 'Nettlestead' (Dw/d) | ESul |
| 'Nettlestone' (Dw/d) | ESul |
| 'Nettlestone Star' (Min/St) | ESul |
| 'Neville West' (Z) | SSea |
| 'New Day' (A) | LDea |
| 'New Life' (Z) | ESul NFir |
| 'Newbridge' (St/Min/d) | ESul |
| 'Newtown' (Min/St) | ESul |
| 'Nicola Buck' (R) | LDea NFir |
| 'Nicor Star' (Min) | ESul WFib |
| 'Nikki' (A) | LDea |
| 'Nimrod' (R) | LDea |
| 'Noche' (R) | ESul SMrm |
| 'Noel' (Z/Ca/d) | WFib |
| 'Noele Gordon' (Z/d) | WFib |
| 'Nono' (I) | WFib |
| 'Notting Hill Beauty' (Z) | SKen |
| ***oblongatum*** | NFir |
| 'Occold Embers' (Dw/C) | ESul NFir |
| 'Occold Lagoon' (Dw/d) | ESul |
| 'Occold Orange Tip' (Min/d) | ESul |
| 'Occold Profusion' (Dw/d) | ESul NFir |
| 'Occold Shield' (Dw/C/d) | ESul LAst NEgg NFir SSea WBrk WFib |
| 'Occold Tangerine' (Z) | WFib |
| 'Occold Volcano' (Dw/C/d) | WFib |
| ***odoratissimum*** (Sc) | ESul EWoo GPoy LDea MBPg MHer NFir SKen SSea WFib WGwG |
| 'Odyssey' (Min) | WFib |
| 'Offton' (Dw) | ESul |
| 'Old Orchard' (A) | LDea |
| 'Old Rose' (Z/d) | WFib |
| 'Old Spice' (Sc/v) | ESul EWoo LDea MBPg MCot NFir SWal WFib WGwG |
| 'Oldbury Duet' (A/v) | ESul LAst LDea MBPg MHer NFir SSea |
| 'Olga Shipstone' (Sc) | MBPg |
| 'Oliver Welfare' (Dw/C) | ESul |
| 'Olivia' (R) | WFib |
| 'Onalee' (Dw) | ESul WFib |
| 'Opera House' (R) | WFib |
| 'Orange Fizz' (Sc) | ESul EWoo MHer NFir |
| 'Orange Fizz' (Z/d) | LDea |
| 'Orange Imp' (Dw/d) | ESul |
| 'Orange Parfait' (R) | WFib |
| 'Orange Princeanum' (Sc) | MBPg |
| 'Orange Ruffy' (Min) | ESul |
| 'Orange Splash' (Z) | SKen |
| 'Orangeade' (Dw/d) | SKen WFib |
| 'Orchid Clorinda' (Sc) | MBPg WFib |

| | |
|---|---|
| 'Orchid Paloma' (Dw/d) | ESul SKen |
| 'Oregon Hostess' (Dw) | ESul |
| 'Oriental Delight' (R) | ESul |
| 'Orion' (Min/d) | ESul SKen SSea WFib |
| 'Orsett' (Sc) ♀$^{H1+3}$ | LDea |
| 'Osna' (Z) | SKen |
| 'Otto's Red' (R) | NFir |
| 'Our Amy' (Z/d) | SSea |
| 'Our Gynette' (Dec) | EWoo SSea |
| 'Overchurch' (Dw) | NFir |
| 'Oyster' (Dw) | ESul |
| PAC cultivars | see under selling name |
| 'Paddie' (Min) | ESul |
| 'Page Boy' (Dw/Z/d/v) | ESul |
| 'Pagoda' (Z/St/d) | ESul MHer SKen WFib |
| 'Paisley Red' (Z/d) | NFir WFib |
| 'Pam Craigie' (R) | LDea |
| 'Pamela' (R) | ESul |
| 'Pamela Vaughan' (Z/St) | WFib |
| 'Pampered Lady' (A) | LDea NFir |
| ***panduriforme*** | WFib |
| ***papilionaceum*** | CHEx CRHN EWoo MCot MHer SSea WFib |
| 'Parisienne' (R) | ESul EWoo LDea WFib |
| 'Parmenter Pink' (Min) | ESul |
| 'Party Dress' (Z/d) | SKen WFib |
| 'Pascal' (Z) | SKen |
| 'Pat Hannam' (St) | WFib |
| 'Paton's Unique' (U/Sc) ♀$^{H1+3}$ | CRHN EWoo MBPg MCot MHer NFir SPet SSea WCot WFib |
| 'Patricia Andrea' (T) | ESul NFir NPer WFib |
| 'Patricia O'Reilly' (R) | LDea |
| 'Patricia Read' (Min) | ESul |
| 'Patsy 'Q'' (Z/C) | SKen |
| 'Paul Crampel' (Z) | MCot MHer SSea WFib |
| 'Paul Gotz' (Z) | SKen |
| 'Paul West' (Min/d) | CFee ESul SBch |
| 'Pauline' (Min/d) | ESul SSea |
| 'Pauline Harris' (R) | LDea |
| 'Pax' (R) | LDea |
| 'Peace' (Min/C) | ESul WFib |
| 'Peace Palace' (Dw) | ESul |
| 'Peach Princess' (R) | ESul NFir |
| 'Peaches and Cream' (R) | MBPg |
| 'Peacock' | LDea |
| 'Pearl Eclipse' (I) | SKen |
| Pearl Necklace | see *P.* 'Perlenkette' |
| 'Peggy Clare' (Dw/St) | ESul |
| 'Peggy Sue' (R) | ESul LDea |
| PELFI cultivars | see under selling name |
| ***peltatum*** | WFib |
| 'Penny' (Z/d) | SKen WFib |
| 'Penny Dixon' (R) | NFir |
| 'Penny Lane' (Z) | WFib |
| 'Penny Serenade' (Dw/C) | ESul SKen |
| 'Pensby' (Dw) | ESul NFir |
| 'Peppermint Lace' (Sc) | CSev EWoo MBPg |
| 'Peppermint Scented Rose' (Sc) | MBPg MSCN |
| 'Peppermint Star' (Z/St) | ESul SSea |
| 'Percy Hunt' (R) | NFir |
| 'Perfect' (Z) | WFib |
| § 'Perlenkette' (Z/d) | MHer |
| Perlenkette Orange = 'Orangepen'$^{PBR}$ (Quality Series) (Z/d) | LAst |
| Perlenkette Sabine (Quality Series) (Z/d) | LAst |
| 'Pershore Princess' | WBrk |
| 'Persian King' (R) | LDea |
| 'Persian Ruler' (Min) | ESul |
| 'Persimmon' (Z/St) | WFib |
| 'Petals' (Z/v) | SKen |
| 'Peter Beard' (Dw/d) | ESul |
| 'Peter Godwin' (R) | ESul WFib |
| 'Peter Read' (Dw/d) | ESul |
| 'Peter's Choice' (R) | ESul LDea WFib |
| 'Peter's Luck' (Sc) ♀$^{H1+3}$ | ESul MBPg |
| 'Petit Pierre' | see *P.* 'Kleine Liebling' |
| 'Petite Blanche' (Dw/d) | SSea WFib |
| 'Philomel' (I/d) | SPet |
| 'Phlox New Life' (Z) | ESul |
| 'Phyllis' (U/v) | ESul EWoo MBPg MHer NFir SSea |
| 'Phyllis' (Z) | MCot |
| 'Phyllis Brooks' (R) | ESul |
| 'Phyllis Read' (Min) | ESul |
| 'Phyllis Richardson' (R/d) | ESul |
| 'Phyllis Variegated' (v) | MSCN WCot |
| 'Picotee' | MHer |
| 'Pin Mill' (Min/d) | ESul |
| 'Pink Aura' (Min/St) | ESul SSea |
| 'Pink Aurore' (U) | WFib |
| 'Pink Blush' (Min/St) | ESul |
| 'Pink Bonanza' (R) | ESul NFir WFib |
| 'Pink Bouquet' (R) | ESul |
| 'Pink Capitatum' | see *P.* 'Pink Capricorn' |
| § 'Pink Capricorn' (Sc) | CRHN ESul EWoo MBPg WFib |
| 'Pink Cascade' | see *P.* 'Hederinum' |
| 'Pink Champagne' (Sc) | CRHN ESul MCot MHer |
| 'Pink Countess Mariza' (Z) | SKen |
| 'Pink Dolly Varden' (Z/v) | WFib |
| 'Pink Fondant' (Min/d) | ESul WFib |
| 'Pink Gay Baby' | see *P.* 'Sugar Baby' |
| 'Pink Golden Ears' (Dw/St/C) | ESul |
| 'Pink Golden Harry Hieover' (Z/C) | ESul |
| 'Pink Happy Thought' (Z/v) | MSCN SSea SWal WFib |
| 'Pink Hindoo' (Dec) | EWoo |
| 'Pink Ice' (Min/d) | ESul NFir |
| 'Pink Margaret Pearce' (R) | ESul |
| 'Pink Mini Cascade' | see *P.* 'Rosa Mini-cascade' |
| 'Pink Needles' (Min/St) | ESul WFib |
| 'Pink Rambler' (Z/d) | SKen WFib |
| 'Pink Raspail' (Z/d) | SSea |
| 'Pink Rosebud' (I/d) | SKen |
| 'Pink Rosebud' (Z/d) | SSea WFib |
| 'Pink Snow' (Min/d) | ESul |
| 'Pink Sparkler' (Dw/St/C) | ESul |
| 'Pink Splash' (Min/d) | ESul |
| 'Pink Tiny Tim' (Min) | ESul |
| 'Pippa' (Min/Dw) | ESul NFir |
| 'Pixie' (Min) | ESul |
| 'Playmate' (Min/St) | ESul WFib |
| 'Plum Rambler' (Z/d) | EShb SKen SSea WBrk WFib |
| 'Poetesse' (A) | LDea |
| 'Polestar' (Min/St) | ESul |
| 'Polka' (U) | ESul EWoo MBPg NFir WFib |
| 'Pompeii' (R) | NFir WFib |
| 'Poquita' (Sc) | MBPg MSCN |
| 'Porchfield' (Min/St) | ESul WBrk |
| 'Portsmouth' (R) | ESul |
| 'Potpourri' (Min) | SKen |
| 'Potter Heigham' (Dw) | ESul |
| 'Powder Puff' (Dw/d) | WFib |
| 'Presto' (Dw/St) | ESul |
| 'Preston Park' (Z/C) | SKen WFib |
| 'Pretty Girl' (I) | MCot |
| 'Pretty Petticoat' (Z/d) | WFib |
| 'Pretty Polly' (Sc) | LDea WFib |

| | |
|---|---|
| 'Prim' (Dw/St/d) | ESul WFib |
| 'Prince of Orange' (Sc) | CArn CSev ESul EWoo GPoy LDea MBPg MCot MHer MWea NFir SBch SIde SPet SSea SWal WFib WGwG |
| 'Princeanum' (Sc) ♀H1+3 | MBPg WFib |
| 'Princess Abigail' (Dw/d) | NFir |
| 'Princess Alexandra' (Z/d/v) | ESul NFir |
| 'Princess Anne' (Z) | CSpe |
| 'Princess Josephine' (R) | LDea WFib |
| 'Princess of Balcon' | see *P.* 'Roi des Balcons Lilas' |
| 'Princess of Wales' (R) | ESul LDea WFib |
| 'Princess Virginia' (R/v) | ESul LDea WFib |
| 'Priory Coral' (Z/St/v) **new** | MGbk |
| 'Priory Salmon' (St/d) | EShb ESul |
| 'Priory Star' (St/Min/d) | ESul WFib |
| 'Prosperity' (Sc) | LDea MBPg |
| ***pseudoglutinosum*** | WFib |
| 'Purple Ball' | see *P.* Purpurball |
| 'Purple Emperor' (R) | ESul LDea WFib |
| 'Purple Flare' (St) | ESul |
| 'Purple Heart' (Dw/St/C) | ESul NFir |
| 'Purple Rambler' (Z/d) | ESul |
| 'Purple Rogue' (R) | WFib |
| Purple Sybil = 'Pacpursyb' **new** | LAst |
| 'Purple Unique' (U/Sc) | EShb ESul EWoo MCot MHer NFir SKen SSea WFib |
| § Purpurball (Z/d) | SKen |
| Purpurball 2 = 'Penbalu'PBR (Quality Series) (Z/d) | LAst |
| 'Pygmalion' (Z/d/v) | SSea WFib |
| 'Quakeress' (R) | ESul |
| 'Quakermaid' (Min) | ESul |
| 'Quantock' (R) | ESul WFib |
| 'Quantock Angelique' (A) | NFir |
| 'Quantock Beauty' (A) | ESul LDea |
| 'Quantock Blonde' (A) | LDea |
| 'Quantock Candy' (A) | EWoo NFir |
| 'Quantock Clare' (A) | NFir |
| 'Quantock Classic' (A) | EWoo NFir |
| 'Quantock Darren' (A) | NFir |
| 'Quantock Double Dymond' (A) **new** | NFir |
| 'Quantock Jayne' (A) | ESul |
| 'Quantock Kendy' (A) | CWCL ESul LDea NFir |
| 'Quantock Kirsty' (A) | EWoo LDea NFir |
| 'Quantock Louise' (A) | NFir |
| 'Quantock Marjorie' (A) | CWCL ESul LDea MBPg NFir SSea |
| 'Quantock Matty' (A) | ESul LDea NFir |
| 'Quantock May' (A) | LDea NFir |
| 'Quantock Medoc' (A) | ESul LDea |
| 'Quantock Millennium' (A) | CWCL ESul LDea |
| 'Quantock Mr Nunn' (A) | NFir |
| 'Quantock Perfection' (A) | NFir |
| 'Quantock Philip' (A) | ESul |
| 'Quantock Rory' (A) | LDea |
| 'Quantock Rory Paul' (A) | NFir |
| 'Quantock Rose' (A) | ESul LDea |
| 'Quantock Sally' (A) (d) **new** | NFir |
| 'Quantock Sapphire' (A) | LDea |
| 'Quantock Sarah' (A) | ESul |
| 'Quantock Shirley' (A) | ESul LDea |
| 'Quantock Star' (A) | CWCL LDea NFir |
| 'Quantock Ultimate' (A) | ESul NFir |
| 'Queen of Denmark' (Z/d) | SKen WFib |
| 'Queen of Hearts' (I × Z/d) | WFib |
| 'Queen of Sheba' (R) | LDea |
| 'Queen of the Lemons' | EWoo |
| N ***quercifolium*** (Sc) | CRHN CSev GPoy MBPg MNHC NFir SKen WFib |
| - variegated (v) | MBPg SKen |
| ***quinquelobatum*** | CSpe |
| 'R.A.Turner' (Z/d) | WFib |
| 'Rachel' (Min) | ESul |
| ***radens*** (Sc) | WFib |
| 'Rads Star' (Z/St) | ESul NFir WFib |
| 'Radula' (Sc) ♀H1+3 | CSev ESul LDea MBPg MHer MNHC SBch SSea SWal WFib |
| 'Radula Roseum' (Sc) | EWoo MBPg SSea WFib |
| 'Ragamuffin' (Dw/d) | ESul |
| 'Rager's Pink' (Dw/d) | ESul |
| 'Rager's Star' (Dw) | ESul |
| 'Rager's Veri-Star' (Min/C) | ESul |
| 'Raphael' (A) | LDea |
| 'Raspberry Ripple' (A) | ESul LDea NFir WFib |
| 'Raspberry Surprise' (R) | ESul SSea |
| 'Raspberry Yhu' (R) | ESul |
| 'Ray Bidwell' (Min) | ESul NFir WFib |
| 'Raydon' (Min) | ESul |
| 'Reba' | ESul |
| 'Rebecca' (Min/d) | ESul WFib |
| 'Red Admiral' (Min/d/v) | ESul SKen |
| § 'Red Black Vesuvius' (Min/C) | ESul SKen SSea WFib |
| 'Red Cactus' (St) | NFir |
| 'Red Capri' (Sc) | MBPg |
| 'Red Cascade' (I) ♀H1+3 | WFib |
| 'Red Glitter' (Dw/St) | ESul |
| 'Red Ice' (Min/d) | ESul NFir |
| 'Red Magic Lantern' (Z/C) | SKen |
| 'Red Pandora' (z) | NFir WFib |
| 'Red Rambler' (Z/d) | ESul SKen WBrk WFib |
| 'Red Robin' (R) | WCot |
| 'Red Silver Cascade' | see *P.* 'Mutzel' |
| 'Red Spider' (Dw/Ca) | ESul WFib |
| 'Red Starstorm' (Dw/St) | ESul |
| 'Red Startel' (Z/St/d) | SKen WFib |
| 'Red Susan Pearce' (R) | ESul WFib |
| Red Sybil = 'Pensyb'PBR (I/d) | LAst NPri |
| 'Red Velvet' (R) | LBMP |
| 'Red Witch' (Dw/St/d) | ESul MHer SSea WBrk WFib |
| Red-Blizzard = 'Fizzard' (I) | MCot SCoo |
| § Red-Mini-Cascade = 'Rotemica' (I) | ESul LAst SKen WFib |
| 'Redondo' (Dw/d) | ESul WFib |
| 'Reflections' (Z/d) | WFib |
| 'Reg 'Q'' (Z/C) | NFir |
| 'Regina' (Z/d) | SKen WFib |
| 'Rembrandt' (R) | WFib |
| 'Renate Parsley' | CDes ESul MBPg MCot MHer NFir SSea WFib |
| 'Rene Roué' (Dw/d/v) | ESul NFir |
| ***reniforme*** | GPoy MBPg MHer SSea SUsu SWal WFib |
| - 'Sue S' **new** | CSpe |
| 'Retah's Crystal' (Z/v) | ESul |
| 'Reverend David Harley' (Z) **new** | NFir |
| 'Rhian Harris' (A) | LDea |
| 'Rhineland' (I) | SKen |
| Rhodonit = 'Paccherry'PBR (I/d) | LAst |
| 'Richard Gibbs' (Sc) | LDea MBPg MHer |
| 'Richard Key' (Z/d/C) | WFib |
| 'Richard Upward' (Z/d) **new** | MGbk |
| 'Ricky Black Velvet' (A) | LDea |
| 'Ricky Cheerful' (A) | LDea |
| Ricky = 'Pacric' | LAst |
| 'Ricky Promise' (A) | LDea |

| | |
|---|---|
| 'Ricky Ruby' (A) | LDea |
| 'Ricky Susan' (R) | LDea |
| 'Ridsdale' (Z/Dw) **new** | ESul |
| 'Rietje van der Lee' (A) | ESul WFib |
| 'Rigel' (Min/d) | ESul NFir SKen |
| 'Rigi' (I/d) | MBri SKen |
| 'Rimey' (St) | NFir |
| 'Rimfire' (R) | CWCL ESul EWoo LDea MHer NFir WFib |
| 'Rimfire Dark' (R) | ESul |
| 'Rio Grande' (I/d) | MHer NFir SKen SPet WFib |
| 'Rising Sun' | NFir |
| 'Rita Scheen' (A/v) | ESul SSea |
| 'Ritchie' (R) | ESul |
| 'Robbie Hare' (R) | ESul |
| 'Robe'[PBR] (Quality Series) (Z/d) | LAst |
| 'Rober's Lemon Rose' (Sc) | CRHN ESul MBPg MCot MHer SIde SSea WBrk |
| 'Rober's Salmon Coral' (Dw/d) | ESul |
| 'Robert Fish' (Z/C) | ESul SCoo |
| 'Robert McElwain' (Z/d) | WFib |
| 'Robin' (R) | LDea SSea |
| 'Robin' (Sc) | MBPg |
| 'Robin's Unique' (U) | EWoo MHer WFib |
| 'Robyn Hannah' (St/d) | NFir |
| 'Rockwell Sophie' (A) **new** | ESul |
| ***rodneyanum*** | CDes |
| 'Rogue' (R) | WFib |
| 'Roi des Balcons' | see *P.* 'Hederinum' |
| 'Roi des Balcons Des Rameaux' (I) | SKen |
| § 'Roi des Balcons Impérial' (I) ♀H1+3 | SKen |
| § 'Roi des Balcons Lilas' (I) ♀H1+3 | WFib |
| 'Roi des Balcons Mauve' (I) | SKen |
| 'Roi des Balcons Rose' | see *P.* 'Hederinum' |
| 'Roller's Echo' (A) | ESul LDea WFib |
| 'Roller's Pioneer' (I/v) | EWoo SAga SKen |
| 'Roller's Satinique' (U) ♀H1+3 | MHer |
| 'Roller's Shadow' (A) | ESul LDea |
| 'Rollisson's Unique' (U) | MHer SSea WFib |
| 'Romeo' (R) | CSpe EWoo |
| 'Rookley' (St/d) | ESul NFir |
| § 'Rosa Mini-cascade' (I) | ESul LAst NFir |
| 'Rosaleen' (Min) | ESul |
| 'Rosalie' (R) | ESul |
| 'Rose Bengal' (A) | ESul LDea WFib |
| 'Rose Jewel' (R) | ESul |
| 'Rose of Amsterdam' (Min/d) | ESul WFib |
| 'Rose Paton's Unique' (U/Sc) | SMrm |
| 'Rose Pope' (R) **new** | MGbk |
| 'Rose Silver Cascade' (I) | MCot MHer |
| 'Rose Startel' (Z/St) | SKen |
| 'Rosebud Supreme' (Z/d) | ESul WFib |
| 'Rosette' (Dw/d) | SKen |
| 'Rosina Read' (Dw/d) | ESul |
| 'Rosmaroy' (R) | ESul LDea WFib |
| 'Rospen' (Z/d) | SKen |
| 'Rosy Dawn' (Min/d) | WFib |
| 'Rosy Morn' (R) | NFir |
| 'Rote Mini-cascade' | see *P.* Red-Mini-Cascade |
| § 'Rouletta' (I/d) | LAst SKen SWal WFib |
| 'Royal Ascot' (R) | ESul LDea NFir SMrm SPet SSea |
| 'Royal Black Rose' | MCot MWea |
| 'Royal Carpet' (Min/d) | ESul |
| 'Royal Celebration' (R) | ESul |
| 'Royal Court' (R) | LDea |
| 'Royal Hussar' (R) | ESul |
| 'Royal Knight' (R) | ESul |
| 'Royal Magic' (R) | ESul LDea |
| 'Royal Majesty' (R) | ESul |
| 'Royal Norfolk' (Min/d) | ESul NFir SKen |
| 'Royal Oak' (Sc) ♀H1+3 | CRHN CSev ESul LDea MBPg MCot MHer MNHC MWea SBch SPet SSea SVen SWal WFib |
| 'Royal Prince' (R) | ESul |
| § 'Royal Purple' (Z/d) | WFib |
| 'Royal Sovereign' (Z/C/d) | LDea |
| 'Royal Surprise' (R) | ESul EWoo NFir |
| 'Royal Wedding' (R) | ESul |
| 'Royal Winner' (R) | LDea |
| 'Ruben' (d) | LAst LSou |
| 'Ruby' (Min/d) | ESul WFib |
| 'Ruby Orchid' (A) | LDea |
| 'Ruby Wedding' (Z) | ESul |
| 'Ruffled Velvet' (R) | EWoo |
| 'Rushmere' (Dw/d) | ESul WFib |
| 'Rushmoor Golden Rosebud' (Z) **new** | MGbk |
| 'Rushmoor Jazz' (Z/St/v) **new** | MGbk |
| 'Rushmoor Rhapsody' (St) **new** | MGbk |
| 'Rushmoor Wind Chimes' (Z/St) **new** | MGbk |
| 'Rusty' (Dw/C/d) | ESul |
| 'Saint Elmo's Fire' (St/Min/d) | MHer SSea WFib |
| 'Saint Helen's Favourite' (Min) | ESul |
| Saint Malo = 'Guisaint' (I) | NFir |
| 'Sally Read' (Dw/d) | ESul |
| 'Salmon Beauty' (Dw/d) | WFib |
| 'Salmon Black Vesuvius' (Min/C) | ESul |
| § 'Salmon Irene' (Z/d) | WFib |
| Salmon Princess = 'Pacsalpri'[PBR] | LAst LSou |
| 'Salmon Queen' | see *P.* 'Lachskönigin' |
| 'Saltford' (R) | ESul |
| 'Samantha' (R) | ESul WFib |
| 'Samantha Stamp' (Dw/d/C) | WFib |
| Samelia = 'Pensam'[PBR] (Dark Line Series) (Z/d) | LAst LBMP SWal WGor |
| 'Sammi Caws' (St) | ESul |
| 'Sancho Panza' (Dec) ♀H1+3 | CSpe ESul LDea SKen SSea WFib |
| 'Sandford' (Dw/St) | ESul |
| 'Sandown' (Dw/d) | ESul |
| 'Sandra Lorraine' (I/d) | WFib |
| 'Sanguineum' | CSev CSpe |
| 'Sanibel' (Min/d) **new** | MGbk |
| 'Santa Maria' (Z/d) | SKen |
| 'Santa Paula' (I/d) | SKen |
| § 'Sarah Don'[PBR] (A/v) | SKen WFib |
| 'Sarah Hunt' (Min/d) | NFir |
| 'Sarah Jane' (Sc) | MBPg |
| 'Sassa'[PBR] (Quality Series) (Z/d) | LAst |
| 'Satsuki' (R) | ESul NFir |
| 'Scarborough Fair' (A) | NFir |
| 'Scarlet Gem' (Z/St) | WBrk WFib |
| 'Scarlet Pet' (U) | CFee CRHN ESul MBPg NFir SMrm |

'Scarlet Pimpernel' (Z/C/d) ESul
'Scarlet Rambler' (Z/d) EShb SMrm SSea WFib
'Scarlet Unique' (U) CRHN EWoo MCot SKen SSea SUsu WFib
***schizopetalum*** WFib
§ 'Schneekönigin' (I/d) SKen
'[illegible]' MHer NFir WFib
'Scottow Star' (Z/C) WFib
'Seale Star' (Dw/St/C) SSea
'Seaview Silver' (Min/St) WFib
'Seaview Sparkler' (Z/St) WFib
'Secret Love' (Sc) LDea MBPg
'Seeley's Pansy' (A) EWoo LDea MHer WFib
'Sefton' (R) 𝕐H1+3 ESul LDea WFib
'Selena' (Min) LDea
'Semer' (Min) ESul SKen
'Shalfleet' (Min/St) ESul
'Shan Hoy' (Dw) **new** NFir
'Shanks' (Z) NFir
'Shannon' EWoo SBch WFib
'Sharon' (Min/d) ESul
'Sheila' (Dw) ESul
'Shelley' (Dw) ESul SKen
'Shirley Ash' (A) LDea WFib
'Shirley Gillam' (Z/St/v) ESul
Shocking Orange = 'Pacshorg' **new** LAst
Shocking Pink = 'Pensho'PBR (Quality Series) (Z/d) LAst
Shocking Violet = 'Pacshovi'PBR (Quality Series) (Z/d) LAst
'Shogan' (R) NFir
'Shorwell' (Dw/C/d) ESul
§ 'Shottesham Pet' (Sc) ESul EWoo MBPg MHer MNHC
'Shrubland Pet' (U/Sc) SKen SSea
'Shrubland Rose' (Sc) SSea
***sidoides*** CEnt CSpe ESul EWoo GPoy MBPg MCot MHer MWea NFir SBch SMrm SPhx SSea SVen WCot WFib WGwG
- black-flowered CTca SBrt
- 'Sloe Gin Fizz' CSpe
Sidonia = 'Pensid'PBR (Dark Line Series) (Z/d) LAst WGor
'Sienna' (R) ESul NFir
'Sil Claudio'PBR (Z) LAst
'Sil Falko'PBR (I) LSou WGor
'Sil Frauke'PBR (Z) LAst
'Sil Friesia'PBR (Z) LAst
'Sil Hero'PBR (Z) LAst WGor
'Sil Lenja' (Z) **new** LAst
'Sil Linus'PBR (Z) LSou
'Sil Liske'PBR (Z) LAst
'Sil Magnus' (Z) **new** LAst
'Sil Malaika'PBR (I) LSou
'Sil Okka' LAst
'Sil Pia'PBR (I) LAst LSou
'Sil Quirin'PBR (I) **new** LAst
'Sil Raiko'PBR LAst
'Sil Renko'PBR (Z) LAst
'Sil Rumika'PBR LAst
'Sil Sören' LAst
'Sil Tedo'PBR (Z) LAst
'Sil Teske'PBR (I) LAst
'Sil Tomke'PBR (I) LAst LSou
'Sil Wittje'PBR (I) LAst
'Silver Anne' (R/v) ESul NFir
'Silver Dawn' (Min/St) ESul
'Silver Delight' (v/d) WFib
'Silver Dusk' (Min/St) ESul
'Silver Glitter' (Dw/St) ESul
'Silver Kewense' (Dw/v) NFir WFib
'Silver Lady' (Z/d/v) **new** MGbk
'Silver Leaf Rose' (Sc) MBPg
'Silver Rimfire' (R) ESul
'Silver Snow' (Min/St/d) ESul WFib
'Silver Splash' (Z/v) **new** MGbk
'Silver Wings' (Z/v) ESul NFir
'Simon Portas' (I/d) SKen
'Simon Read' (Dw) ESul
'Sir Colin' (Z) SSea
'Skelly's Pride' (Z) SKen WFib
'Skies of Italy' (Z/C/d) MBri SKen SSea WFib
'Small Fortune' (Min/d) ESul SKen
'Snape' (Min) ESul
'Sneezy' (Min) ESul NFir
'Snow Cap' (MinI) NFir
'Snow Flurry' (Sc) WBrk
Snow Queen see *P.* 'Schneekönigin'
'Snow White' (Min) ESul
'Snowbaby' (Min/d) ESul WFib
'Snowberry' (R) ESul
'Snowbright' (St/d) ESul
'Snowdrift' (I/d) WFib
'Snowflake' (Min) see *P.* 'Atomic Snowflake'
'Snowstorm' (Z) SKen WFib
'Sofie' see *P.* 'Decora Rose'
'Solent Waves' (R) ESul
'Solferino' (A) ESul LDea
Solidor (I/d) 𝕐H1+3 NFir
'Somersham' (Min) ESul WFib
'Something Special' (Z/d) NFir WFib
'Sonata' (Dw/d) ESul
'Sophia' (Z) LAst
'Sophie' (R) ESul
Sophie Casade see *P.* 'Decora Rose'
'Sophie Caws' (St) ESul
'Sophie Dumaresque' (Z/v) MBri NFir SKen SSea WFib
'Sophie Emma' (Z) **new** NFir
'Sophie Marion' (Dw/Z) **new** MGbk
'Sorcery' (Dw/C) ESul SKen
'Sound Appeal' (A) ESul LDea
'South African Sun' (Z/d) MGbk
'South American Bronze' (R) 𝕐H1+3 SMrm WFib
'Southern Belle' (A) LDea SSea
'Southern Belle' (Z/d) WFib
'Southern Charm' (Z/v) NFir
'Southern Cherub' (A) LDea
'Southern Damsel' (R) ESul
'Southern Fairy' (A) ESul
'Southern Festival' (Dw) ESul
'Southern Flamenco' (R) ESul
'Southern Frills' (A) ESul
'Southern Galaxy' (Min/St) ESul
'Southern Gem' (Min/d) ESul
'Southern Michaela' (A) ESul
'Southern Peach' (Min/d) ESul
'Southern Posy' (Dw) ESul
'Southern Purity' (Min) ESul
'Southern Rosina' (Dw) ESul
'Southern Scheen' (A) ESul
'Southern Siewigy' (Dec) ESul
'Southern Starlight' (A) ESul
'Souvenir' (R) ESul LDea
'Souvenir de Prue' EWoo
'Spanish Angel' (A) 𝕐H1+3 CWCL ESul LDea MHer NFir SSea WFib

| | | |
|---|---|---|
| | 'Spanish Banks' (Z/St/v) | ESul |
| | 'Spellbound' (R) | WFib |
| | 'Spital Dam' (Dw/d) | ESul NFir |
| | 'Spitfire' (Z/Ca/d/v) | ESul WFib |
| | 'Spithead Cherry' (R) | LDea |
| § | 'Splendide' | CRHN CSpe EPfP EShb ESul MBPg MHer MSCN NFir SPoG SSea SWvt WFib |
| | 'Splendide' white-flowered | MBPg |
| | 'Spot-on-bonanza' (R) | ESul NFir WFib |
| | 'Spring Park' (A) | ESul MHer SSea WFib |
| | 'Springfield Alba' (R) | ESul |
| | 'Springfield Black' (R) | ESul LDea MCot |
| | 'Springfield Glory' (Z) **new** | MGbk |
| | 'Springfield Joy' (R) | ESul |
| | 'Springfield Pearl' (R) | ESul |
| | 'Springfield Purple' (R) | ESul |
| | 'Springfield Unique' (R) | ESul |
| I | 'Springtime' (R) | ESul |
| | 'Springtime' (Z/d) | SKen WFib |
| | 'Sproughton' (Dw) | ESul |
| | 'Stacey' (R) | ESul |
| | 'Stadt Bern' (Z/C) | LAst MBri NFir SKen |
| | 'Stan Shaw' (R) | LDea |
| | × ***stapletoniae*** | see *P.* 'Miss Stapleton' |
| | 'Star Flair' (St/Min/d) | ESul |
| | 'Star Flecks' (St) | NFir |
| | 'Star of Persia' (Z/Ca/d) | WFib |
| | 'Star Storm' (St/d) | ESul |
| | 'Starlet' (Ca) | WFib |
| | 'Starlight' (R) | WFib |
| | 'Starlight Magic' (A) ♀H1+3 | ESul LDea |
| | 'Starry Eyes' (Dw) | ESul |
| | 'Startel Salmon' (Z/St) | MHer |
| | 'Stella Ballerina' | SMrm |
| | 'Stella Read' (Dw/d) | ESul |
| | 'Stellar Arctic Star' | see *P.* 'Arctic Star' |
| | 'Stellar Cathay' (Z/St/d) | SSea |
| | 'Stellar Hannaford Star' | see *P.* 'Hannaford Star' |
| | 'Stephen Read' (Min) | ESul |
| | 'Stewart Meehan' (R) | LDea |
| | 'Stolen Kisses' (Min/D) | ESul |
| | 'Strawberries and Cream' (Z/St) | NFir |
| | 'Strawberry Fayre' (Dw/St) | WFib |
| | 'Strawberry Sundae' (R) | ESul LDea WFib |
| | 'Stringer's Delight' (Dw/v) | ESul |
| | 'Stringer's Souvenir' (Dw/d/v) | SSea |
| | 'Stuart Mark' (R) | LDea |
| | 'Stutton' (Min) | ESul |
| | 'Suffolk Agate' (R) | ESul |
| | 'Suffolk Amethyst' (A) | ESul |
| | 'Suffolk Coral' (R) | ESul |
| | 'Suffolk Emerald' (A) | ESul |
| | 'Suffolk Garnet' (Dec) | ESul |
| | 'Suffolk Jade' (Min) | ESul |
| | 'Suffolk Jet' (Min) | ESul |
| | 'Suffolk Salmon' (R) | ESul |
| § | 'Sugar Baby' (DwI) | ECtt ESul LAst MBri MHer SKen WFib |
| | 'Summer Cloud' (Z/d) | WFib |
| | 'Summertime' (Z/d) | see *P.* 'Deacon Summertime' |
| | 'Sun Rocket' (Dw/d) | WFib |
| | 'Sundridge Moonlight' (Z/C) | WFib |
| | 'Sundridge Surprise' (Z) | WFib |
| | 'Sunny Jim' (Z) | SSea |
| | 'Sunraysia' (Z/St) | WFib |
| | 'Sunridge Moonlight' (Dw) | NFir |
| | 'Sunset Snow' (R) | ESul WFib |
| | 'Sunspot' (Min/C) | NFir |
| | 'Sunspot Kleine Liebling' (Min) | SSea WFib |
| | 'Sunspot Petit Pierre' (Min/v) | WFib |
| | 'Sunstar' (Min/d) | ESul WFib |
| | 'Super Rose' (I) | SKen SPet |
| | 'Supernova' (Z/St/d) | ESul SKen WFib |
| | 'Surcouf' (I) | WFib |
| | 'Surfing Purple' | LSou |
| | 'Surfing Red' | LSou |
| | 'Susan Hillier' (R) | LDea |
| | 'Susan Payne' (Dw/d) | ESul MHer |
| | 'Susan Pearce' (R) | ESul LDea |
| | 'Susan Read' (Dw) | ESul |
| | 'Susie 'Q'' (Z/C) | SKen SSea |
| | 'Sussex Delight' (Min) | SPet |
| | 'Sussex Gem' (Min/d) | ESul SKen WFib |
| | 'Sussex Lace' | see *P.* 'White Mesh' |
| | 'Swanland Lace' (I/d/v) | WFib |
| | 'Swedish Angel' (A) | LDea NFir WFib |
| | 'Sweet Lady Mary' (Sc) | MBPg |
| | 'Sweet Mimosa' (Sc) ♀H1+3 | CHVG CRHN ESul EWoo MCot MHer NEgg NFir SBch SSea SWal WBrk WFib WGwG |
| | 'Sweet Miriam' (Sc) | LDea MBPg |
| | 'Sweet Sixteen' | WFib |
| | 'Sweet Sue' (Min) | ESul |
| | 'Swilland' (A) | LDea WFib |
| | 'Sybil Bradshaw' (R) | LDea |
| | 'Sybil Holmes' (I/d) | LAst MBri SKen SPet WFib |
| | 'Sylbar' (R) | ESul |
| | 'Sylvia' (R) | ESul |
| | 'Sylvia Marie' (d) | SKen |
| | 'Taffety' (Min) | ESul WFib |
| | 'Tamie' (Dw/d) | ESul NFir |
| | 'Tammy' (Dw/d) | ESul |
| | 'Tangerine' (Min/Ca/d) | ESul WFib |
| | 'Tangerine Elf' (St) | WFib |
| | 'Tanzy' (Min) | ESul |
| | 'Tapriz' (R) | ESul |
| | 'Tara Caws' (Z) | ESul |
| | 'Taspo' (R) | ESul |
| | 'Tattingstone' (Min) | ESul |
| | 'Tattoo' (Min) | ESul |
| | 'Tazi' (Dw) | ESul |
| | 'Ted Dutton' (R) | ESul |
| | 'Telstar' (Min/d) | ESul SKen |
| § | 'Telston's Prima' (R) | ESul |
| | 'Tenderly' (Dw/d) | ESul |
| | 'Tenerife Magic' (MinI/d) | ESul |
| | ***tetragonum*** | CRHN EWoo MBPg MHer SSea WFib |
| | 'The Alde' | EWoo |
| | 'The Axe' (A) | LDea |
| | 'The Barle' (A) ♀H1+3 | LDea WFib |
| | 'The Boar' (Fr) ♀H1+3 | EShb EWoo MCot WFib |
| | 'The Bray' (A) | LDea |
| | 'The Creedy' (A) | LDea |
| | 'The Culm' (A) | ESul EWoo LDea SSea WFib |
| | 'The Czar' | see *P.* 'Czar' |
| | 'The Dart' (A) | LDea |
| | 'The Heddon' (A) | LDea |
| | 'The Joker' (I/d) | WFib |
| | 'The Kenn-Lad' (A) | EWoo LDea |
| | 'The Lowman' (A) | LDea |
| | 'The Lyn' (A) | ESul LDea |
| § | 'The Mole' (A) | ESul LDea MHer WFib |
| | 'The Okement' (A) | LDea |

| |  |  |
|---|---|---|
| | 'The Otter' (A) | ESul LDea |
| | 'The Speaker' (Z/d) | SKen |
| | 'The Tamar' (A) | CFee EWoo LDea MHer |
| | 'The Tone' (A) ♀H1+3 | LDea |
| | 'The Yar' (Z/St) | WFib |
| | 'Thomas' (Sc) | MBPg |
| | 'Thomas Earle' (Z) | WFib |
| | 'Thomas Gerald' (Dw/C) | ESul SKen |
| | 'Tilly' (Min) | NFir |
| | 'Tim' (Min) | ESul |
| | 'Timothy Clifford' (Min/d) | ESul |
| | 'Tinkerbell' (A) | LDea |
| § | 'Tip Top Duet' (A) ♀H1+3 | ESul EWoo LDea MHer NFir SKen SMrm SSea WFib |
| | 'Tirley Garth' (A) | WFib |
| | 'Tomcat'[PBR] (I/d) | LAst NPri SKen SSea |
| | ***tomentosum*** (Sc) ♀H1+3 | CHEx CSev CSpe EShb ESul EWoo GPoy LDea MBPg MCot MHer MNHC NFir SBch SKen SSea WFib WGwG |
| | - 'Chocolate' | see *P.* 'Chocolate Peppermint' |
| | 'Tomgirl' (A) | NPri |
| | Tomgirl = 'Pactomgi'[PBR] (I × Z/d) | LAst SSea |
| | 'Tommay's Delight' (R) | LDea |
| | 'Tony' (Min) | ESul |
| | 'Topan' (R) | ESul |
| | 'Topcliffe' (Dw/St) | ESul |
| | 'Topscore' (Z/d) | SKen WFib |
| | 'Tornado' (R) | ESul NFir WFib |
| | 'Torrento' (Sc) | ESul LDea MBPg MHer WFib |
| | 'Tortoiseshell' (R) | WFib |
| | 'Toscana Okka' (Toscana Series) (I) | LAst LSou SPet |
| | 'Tracy' (Min/d) | ESul NFir |
| | ***transvaalense*** | EWoo NFir |
| | 'Treasure Chest' (Z) | SKen |
| | 'Treasure Trove' (Z/v) | NFir |
| | ***tricolor*** misapplied | see *P.* 'Splendide' |
| | ***tricolor*** Curt. | NFir |
| | ***tricuspidatum*** | CSpe EWoo WCot |
| | ***trifidum*** | EWoo MBPg SSea WFib |
| | 'Trimley' (Dw/d) | ESul |
| | 'Trinket' (Min/d) | WFib |
| | 'Triomphe de Nancy' (Z/d) | WFib |
| | ***triste*** | EWoo MHer SSea SUsu WCot WFib |
| | 'Trudie' (Dw/Fr) | ESul MHer SKen WBrk WFib |
| | 'Trulls Hatch' (Z/d) | SKen |
| | 'Tu Tone' (Dw/d) | ESul |
| | 'Tuddenham' (Min/d) | ESul |
| | 'Tuesday's Child' (Dw/C) | ESul SKen |
| | 'Tunias Perfecta' (R) | ESul |
| | 'Turkish Coffee' (R) | ESul NFir WFib |
| | 'Turkish Delight' (Dw/C) | ESul NFir WFib |
| | 'Turtle's Surprise' (Z/d/v) | SKen WBrk |
| | 'Tuyo' (R) | WFib |
| | 'Tweedle-Dum' (Dw) | ESul |
| | 'Tweenaway' (Dw) | ESul MGbk |
| | 'Twinkle' (Min/d) | ESul WFib |
| | 'Tyabb Princess' (R) | EWoo |
| | 'Ullswater' (Dw/C) | ESul |
| | 'Unique Aurore' (U) | MHer SKen |
| | 'Unique Mons Ninon' | see *P.* 'Monsieur Ninon' |
| | 'Urban White' (Dec) | WFib |
| | 'Urchin' (Min/St) | ESul NFir WFib |
| | 'Ursula Key' (Z/c) | SKen WFib |
| | 'Ursula's Choice' (A) | WFib |
| | 'Val Merrick' (Dw/St) | WFib |
| | 'Valencia' (R) | ESul |
| | 'Valentina' (Min/d) | ESul |
| | 'Valentine' (Z/C) | ESul WFib |
| | 'Valerie Susan' (R) | LDea |
| | 'Vancouver Centennial' (Dw/St/C) ♀H1+3 | ESul MBri MCot MHer NEgg NFir SCoo SKen SSea WBrk WFib |
| | 'Vandersea' | EWoo |
| | 'Variegated Attar of Roses' (Sc/v) | MBPg |
| | 'Variegated Clorinda' (Sc/v) | WFib |
| | 'Variegated Fragrans' | see *P.* (Fragrans Group) 'Fragrans Variegatum' |
| | 'Variegated Joy Lucille' (Sc/v) | MBPg |
| § | 'Variegated Kleine Liebling' (Min/v) | ESul SSea WFib |
| | 'Variegated Madame Layal' (A/v) ♀H1+3 | WFib |
| | 'Variegated Petit Pierre' (Min/v) | MHer WFib |
| | 'Variegated Wootton's Unique' (v) | EWoo |
| | 'Vasco da Gama' (Dw/d) | ESul |
| | 'Vectis Blaze' (I) | EWoo |
| | 'Vectis Cascade' | EWoo |
| | 'Vectis Dazzler' (Z/St/d) **new** | MGbk |
| | 'Vectis Dream' (St) | ESul |
| | 'Vectis Embers' (Z/d/v) **new** | MGbk |
| | 'Vectis Fanfare' (St/d) | ESul |
| | 'Vectis Finery' (St/d) | ESul NFir |
| | 'Vectis Glitter' (Z/St) | ESul NFir SSea WBrk WFib |
| | 'Vectis Pink' (Dw/St) | WFib |
| | 'Vectis Purple' (Z/d) | WFib |
| | 'Vectis Sparkler' (Dw/St) | ESul NFir |
| | 'Vectis Spider' (Dw/St) | ESul |
| | 'Vectis Starbright' (Dw/St) | WFib |
| | 'Vectis Volcano' (Z/St) | WFib |
| | 'Velvet Duet' (A) ♀H1+3 | LAst LDea NFir |
| | 'Venus' (Min/d) | ESul |
| | 'Vera Dillon' (Z) | SKen |
| | 'Verdale' (A) | LDea WFib |
| | 'Verity Palace' (R) | ESul WFib |
| | 'Verona' (Z/C) | MBri SKen SSea |
| | 'Verona Contreras' (A) | CWCL ESul LDea NFir WFib |
| | 'Veronica' (Z/d) | SKen |
| | 'Vic Claws' (Dw/St) | NFir |
| | 'Vicki' (R) **new** | EWoo |
| | 'Vicki Town' (R) | WFib |
| | 'Vicky Claire' (R) | ESul EWoo LDea NFir SMrm WFib |
| | Vicky = 'Pacvicky'[PBR] (I) | LAst NPri |
| | 'Vickybar' (R) | ESul |
| | Victor = 'Pacvi'[PBR] (Quality Series) (Z/d) | LAst LBMP LSou |
| | 'Victoria' (Z/d) | LAst SKen |
| | 'Victoria Regina' (R) | ESul LDea |
| | 'Viking' (Min/d) | SKen |
| | 'Village Hill Oak' (Sc) | ESul LDea MBPg |
| | Ville de Dresden = 'Pendresd'[PBR] (I) | EWoo |
| | 'Ville de Paris' | see *P.* 'Hederinum' |
| | 'Vina' (Dw/C/d) | SKen WFib |
| | 'Vincent Gerris' (A) | ESul LDea |
| | Vinco = 'Guivin'[PBR] (I/d) | LAst WGor |
| | ***violareum*** misapplied | see *P.* 'Splendide' |
| | 'Violet Lambton' (Z/v) | WFib |
| I | 'Violetta' (R) | WFib |
| | 'Virginia' (R) | LDea SPet |
| | 'Viscossisimum' (Sc) | MHer |
| | ***viscosum*** | see *P. glutinosum* |
| | 'Vivat Regina' (Z/d) | WFib |

| | |
|---|---|
| 'Voodoo' (U) 🏆H1+3 | CSpe EWoo ESul LAst MBPg MCot MHer NFir SMrm SPet SSea SUsu WCot WFib |
| 'Wallis Friesdorf' (Dw/C/d) | ESul |
| 'Wantirna' (Z/v) | ECtt MHer NFir SSea |
| 'Warrenorth Coral' (Z/C/d) | ESul WFib |
| 'Warrenorth Pearl' (Z/d) **new** | MGbk |
| 'Warrenorth Platinum' (Z/v/d) **new** | ESul MGbk |
| 'Warrenorth Red Beryl' (Dw/Z/d/v) | ESul |
| 'Warrenorth Rubellite' (Z/v) | ESul MGbk |
| 'Warrenorth Spinel' (Min/Z/d/v) | ESul |
| 'Washbrook' (Min/d) | ESul NFir |
| 'Watersmeet' (R) | LDea |
| 'Waveney' (Min) | ESul |
| 'Wayward Angel' (A) 🏆H1+3 | ESul LDea WFib |
| 'Wedding Royale' (Dw/d) | WFib |
| 'Welcome' (Z/d) | WFib |
| 'Welling' (Sc) | ESul LDea MBPg MHer NFir |
| 'Wendy Anne' | SKen |
| 'Wendy Jane' (Dw/d) | WFib |
| 'Wendy Read' (Dw/d) | ESul WFib |
| 'Wendy-O' (R) | LDea |
| 'Wensum' (Min/d) | ESul |
| 'Westdale Appleblossom' (Z/d/C) | ESul SSea WBrk WFib |
| 'Westerfield' (Min) | ESul |
| 'Westside' (Z/d) | WFib |
| 'Westwood' (Z/St) | WFib |
| 'Wherstead' (Min) | ESul |
| 'Whisper' (R) | EWoo WFib |
| 'White Bird's Egg' (Z) | WFib |
| 'White Boar' (Fr) | CSpe EShb EWoo WFib |
| 'White Bonanza' (R) | ESul WFib |
| 'White Cascade' (I) **new** | SKen |
| 'White Charm' (R) | ESul LDea |
| 'White Chiffon' (R) | ESul |
| 'White Christmas' (Min/St) | ESul |
| 'White Duet' (A) | LDea |
| 'White Eggshell' (Min) | ESul WFib |
| 'White Feather' (Z/St) | MHer |
| 'White Glory' (R) 🏆H1+3 | ESul NFir |
| 'White Lively Lady' (Dw/C) | ESul |
| § 'White Mesh' (I/v) | ECtt MBri NFir SKen |
| 'White Prince of Orange' (Sc) | MBPg |
| 'White Roc' (Min/d) | ESul |
| 'White Unique' (U) | SBch SKen SPet SSea WFib |
| 'White Velvet Duet' (A) | ESul |
| White-Blizzard = 'Fisbliz'PBR | SCoo |
| 'Wickham Lad' (R) | LDea |
| Wico = 'Guimongol'PBR (I/d) | CWCL LAst WGor |
| 'Wild Spice' (Sc) | LDea |
| 'Wilf Vernon' (Min/d) | ESul |
| 'Wilhelm Kolle' (Z) | WFib |
| 'Wilhelm Langath' | SCoo WBrk |
| 'Willa' (Dec) | WFib |
| 'Winner' **new** | LAst |
| 'Winnie Read' (Dw/d) | ESul |
| 'Wirral Target' (Z/d/v) | ESul |
| 'Wispy' (Dw/St/C) | ESul |
| 'Witnesham' (Min/d) | ESul |
| 'Wolverton' (Z) | WFib |
| § 'Wood's Surprise' (Min/I/d/v) | ESul SKen SPet SWal |
| 'Wootton's Unique' | CSev CSpe EWoo |
| 'Wychwood' (A/Sc) | EWoo LDea |
| 'Wyck Beacon' (I/d) | SKen |
| 'Yale' (I/d) 🏆H1+3 | MBri SKen WFib |
| 'Yhu' (R) | ESul NFir SMrm WFib |
| 'Yolanda' (Dw/C) | ESul |
| 'York Minster' (Dw/v) | SKen |
| 'Yvonne' (Z) | WFib |
| 'Zama' (R) | NFir |
| 'Zena' (Dw) | ESul |
| 'Zinc' (Z/d) | WFib |
| 'Zoe' (A) | LDea |
| 'Zofia Pope' (R) **new** | MGbk |
| ***zonale*** | WFib |
| 'Zulu King' (R) | WFib |
| 'Zulu Warrior' (R) | WFib |

## *Peliosanthes* (*Asparagaceae*)

| | |
|---|---|
| ***arisanensis*** B&SWJ 3639 | WCru |
| ***caesia*** B&SWJ 5183 | WCru |

## *Pellaea* (*Pteridaceae*)

| | |
|---|---|
| ***andromedifolia*** | WRic |
| ***atropurpurea*** | CLAP WFib |
| § ***calomelanos*** | WRic |
| ***falcata*** | CLAP EShb WRic |
| ***hastata*** | see *P. calomelanos* |
| ***rotundifolia*** 🏆H2 | CBty CLAP EShb LRHS STre WRic |
| ***viridis*** | WPGP WRic |
| - var. ***macrophylla*** | WRic |

## *Pellionia* see *Elatostema*

## *Peltandra* (*Araceae*)

| | |
|---|---|
| ***alba*** | see *P. sagittifolia* |
| § ***sagittifolia*** | CRow |
| ***undulata*** | see *P. virginica* (L.) Schott |
| § ***virginica*** (L.) Schott | CRow LPBA NLar NPer SWat |
| - 'Snow Splash' (v) | CRow |

## *Peltaria* (*Brassicaceae*)

| | |
|---|---|
| ***alliacea*** | CSpe LEdu |

## *Peltiphyllum* see *Darmera*

## *Peltoboykinia* (*Saxifragaceae*)

| | |
|---|---|
| § ***tellimoides*** | CLAP GCal GEdr GKev NBir WFar WMoo WPnP |
| ***watanabei*** | CAby CDes CLAP CSpe EBee GEdr LEdu LRHS NLar WCot WCru WMoo WPGP |

## *Pennantia* (*Pennantiaceae*)

| | |
|---|---|
| ***baylisiana*** | ECou |
| ***corymbosa*** | ECou |
| - 'Akoroa' | ECou |
| - 'Woodside' | ECou |

## *Pennellianthus* see *Penstemon*

## *Pennisetum* ✿ (*Poaceae*)

| | |
|---|---|
| × ***advena*** 'Eaton Canyon' | see *P. setaceum* 'Eaton Canyon' |
| § ***alopecuroides*** | CEnd CHar CWCL EBee EHoe EPfP LRHS MBrN MLLN MSCN MWat NGdn SApp SLim SPer SPlb SWat SWvt WDin WFar WWEG XLum |
| - B&SWJ 11434 | WCru |
| - Autumn Wizard | see *P. alopecuroides* 'Herbstzauber' |
| - 'Black Beauty' | CSpe |
| - 'Cassian's Choice' | CKno CSam EBee EHoe ELon EWes SMrm |
| - 'Caudatum' | CKno EBee SApp |

| | | |
|---|---|---|
| | - f. ***erythrochaetum*** | EBee |
| | - - 'Ferris' | WCru |
| | - 'Foxtrot' | IPot MAvo |
| | - 'Gelbstiel' | EPPr |
| | - 'Hameln' | Widely available |
| § | - 'Herbstzauber' | CFir CKno CSam EBee EHoe EPfP |
| | | LHop LRHS MAvo WCot [illegible] |
| | - 'Little Bunny' | CKno CWCL CWib EBee EHoe |
| | | ELan EPPr EPfP EQua GCal IVic |
| | | LRHS LSRN LTen NGdn NLar SApp |
| | | SMea SWvt WDin WFar WWEG |
| | - 'Little Honey' (v) | CKno EBee MBNS MBri NLar XLum |
| | - 'Magic' | ELon EPPr MAvo MDKP WWEG |
| | - 'Moudry' | CKno CPLG CSam EBee EHoe ELon |
| | | EPPr EPfP LRHS MAvo MBri NSti |
| | | SBfd SHDw XLum |
| | - 'National Arboretum' | CKno EHoe EPPr LEdu SApp WCot |
| | - var. ***purpurascens*** | CWCL |
| | - 'Reborn' **new** | MAvo |
| | - 'Red Head' | CKno CMea CSam CSpe ELon EWes |
| | | IPot LRHS LSou MAvo MBNS NBPC |
| | | WCot |
| | - f. ***viridescens*** | CKno COIW ECha EHoe ELan |
| | | EPPr EPfP EShb LEdu LRHS |
| | | MRav MWhi NWsh SApp SDix |
| | | SMad SMrm SPhx WPer WPnP |
| | | WPtf WWEG XLum |
| | - 'Weserbergland' | CKno CSam EBee EHoe EPPr LRHS |
| | | SApp WWEG |
| | - 'Woodside' | CKno CWCL EBee EHoe EPPr EQua |
| | | LEdu MBNS SApp SMad |
| | ***compressum*** | see *P. alopecuroides* |
| | 'Fairy Tails' | CKno |
| | ***flaccidum*** | CSam EBee EHul EPPr |
| | ***glaucum*** 'Purple Baron' | SBfd |
| | - 'Purple Majesty' | MNrw NBlu NGBl SBfd SMrm |
| | ***incomptum*** | EHoe NWsh XLum |
| | - purple-flowered | CFir MMoz |
| | ***longistylum*** misapplied | see *P. villosum* |
| | ***macrourum*** | Widely available |
| | - 'Short Stuff' **new** | CKno |
| | - 'Tail Feathers' | CPrp |
| | ***massaicum*** 'Red Bunny Tails' | ELon LRHS |
| | - 'Red Buttons' | see *P. thunbergii* 'Red Buttons' |
| | ***orientale*** 🏆H3 | CKno COIW CPrp CSpe CWCL |
| | | EBee ECha EHoe EPfP LHop LRHS |
| | | MNrw MRav NBir NWsh SApp |
| | | SEND SGar SMad SMrm SPer SPhx |
| | | SUsu WCot WDin WHoo WKif |
| | | WWEG XLum |
| | - 'Karley Rose' PBR | CKno EBee EHoe EWes IPot LHop |
| | | LRHS MAvo MWhi NDov NPnk |
| | | NWsh SBfd SPhx SSvw SUsu WGrn |
| | | WWEG |
| I | - 'Robustum' | CDes EPPr MAvo SApp WPGP |
| | - 'Shenandoah' | SApp |
| | - 'Shogun' | CKno CSam EBee EPPr MAvo WCot |
| | - 'Tall Tails' | CHar CKno EBee ECGP EHoe EPPr |
| | | EWes LEdu LRHS MAvo MWhi |
| | | NBPC NPnk NSti SMea WWEG |
| | | XLum |
| | 'Paul's Giant' | CKno SApp |
| | ***rueppellii*** | see *P. setaceum* |
| § | ***setaceum*** 🏆H3 | CKno CWib NWsh SBfd SHDw SIde |
| § | - 'Eaton Canyon' | LRHS |
| | - 'Emelia Mae' | SBfd SHDw |
| | - 'Fireworks' (v) **new** | SBfd SPad |
| | - 'Rubrum' 🏆H4 | CAbb CBcs CKno CPLG CWCL |
| | | EShb LAst LSRN MGos NWsh SAga |
| | | SBfd SCoo SHDw SMad SMrm SPoG |
| | | SRkn SRot SWvt WCot |
| | - 'Titch' **new** | SHDw |
| | ***thunbergii*** **new** | LRHS |
| § | - 'Red Buttons' | CKno ECha EHoe ELon EPPr LEdu |
| | | MAvo MDKP MSCN SBfd SHDw |
| | | SMea SPhx SSvw SUsu WGrn WHoo |
| § | ***villosum*** 🏆H3 | Widely available |
| | - 'Cream Falls' | LRHS |

## pennyroyal see *Mentha pulegium*

## *Penstemon* ✿ (*Plantaginaceae*)

| | | |
|---|---|---|
| | sp. | SVic |
| | NJM 09.028 | WPGP |
| | P&C 150 | CFee |
| | 'Abberley' | MBNS WPer |
| | 'Abbey Dore' | SLon |
| | 'Abbotsmerry' | ECtt EPfP MBNS MCot SAga SGar |
| | | SLon |
| | 'Agnes Laing' | LPen MBNS SPlb |
| § | 'Alice Hindley' 🏆H3 | Widely available |
| | ***alpinus*** | LRHS MAsh |
| § | 'Andenken an Friedrich Hahn' 🏆H4 | Widely available |
| § | ***angustifolius*** | MNrw SRms |
| | 'Apple Blossom' misapplied | see *P.* 'Thorn' |
| | 'Apple Blossom' 🏆H3-4 | Widely available |
| | ***arizonicus*** | see *P. whippleanus* |
| | 'Ashton' | LPen MBNS SAga |
| | 'Audrey Cooper' | CChe MBNS |
| | 'Axe Valley Pixie' | MLLN SAga |
| | ***azureus*** | CFir |
| | - NNS 02-065 | NWCA |
| | - subsp. ***azureus*** | CFir |
| | - - NNS 05-527 | GKev |
| | 'Baby Lips' | LLHF |
| | 'Barbara Barker' | see *P.* 'Beech Park' |
| § | ***barbatus*** | CBot CFee ELan SRms WFar |
| | - 'Cambridge Mixed' | LAst |
| | - subsp. ***coccineus*** | CFir LPen MBNS NChi NLar SPhx |
| | - 'Iron Maiden' | LRHS NBPC |
| | - 'Jingle Bells' | EAEE EPfP LPen MDKP NBPC |
| | | SMrm SPav |
| | - orange-flowered | SPlb |
| | - 'Peter Catt' | MDKP SMrm |
| | - Pinacolada Series | LRHS |
| | - var. ***praecox*** | CBot EPfP MBNS SRot WPer |
| | - - f. ***nanus*** | SRms |
| | - - - 'Rondo' | LRHS NBlu NLar |
| | ***barrettiae*** | LLHF |
| | 'Beckford' | EPfP EShb LLHF MBNS |
| § | 'Beech Park' 🏆H3 | EPfP EWes LPen MBNS NBir |
| | 'Bisham Seedling' | see *P.* 'White Bedder' |
| | 'Blackbird' | Widely available |
| | 'Blue Spring' misapplied | see *P. heterophyllus* 'Blue Spring' |
| | 'Blueberry Fudge' (Ice Cream Series) | CWGN MBri MTis WHlf |
| | 'Bodnant' | LAst LLHF LSou MBNS SAga WHoo |
| | | WPer WWEG |
| | ***bradburii*** | see *P. grandiflorus* |
| | 'Bredon' | MBNS SAga WBrk |
| | ***bridgesii*** | see *P. rostriflorus* |
| | 'Bubblegum' (Ice Cream Series) | WHlf |
| | 'Burford Purple' | see *P.* 'Burgundy' |
| | 'Burford Seedling' | see *P.* 'Burgundy' |
| | 'Burford White' | see *P.* 'White Bedder' |
| § | 'Burgundy' | CFir CMac CPrp CSam CWCL EBee |
| | | ECtt ELon GBBs GMaP LLWP LPen |

| | | |
|---|---|---|
| | | LRHS MCot NBir NPer NPri SAga SBch SGar SMrm SPer SPoG SRms WFar WPer XLum |
| | ***caeruleus*** | see *P. angustifolius* |
| | ***californicus*** | WAbe WFar XSen |
| § | ***campanulatus*** | EPfP EPot EWes GEdr MHer NMen SAga SRms WFar WPer |
| | - PC&H 147 | CFee |
| | - PC&H 148 | SGar |
| | - ***pulchellus*** | see *P. campanulatus* |
| | - ***roseus*** misapplied | see *P. kunthii* |
| | 'Candy Pink' | see *P.* 'Old Candy Pink' |
| | ***cardwellii*** NNS 07-385 | EPPr GKev |
| | ***cardwellii*** × ***davidsonii*** | WAbe |
| | 'Castle Forbes' | EPyc GMac LPen MBNS SAga SRms WPer |
| | 'Cathedral Rose' | EPfP LRHS |
| | 'Catherine de la Mare' | see *P. heterophyllus* 'Catherine de la Mare' |
| | 'Centra' | LPen MBNS XLum |
| | 'Charles Rudd' | CAby CWCL EBee ECtt ELon EPfP LPen LRHS LSRN MBNS SAga SRGP SRms SWal SWvt WCot |
| § | 'Cherry' ♀H3 | GBee GMac LPen MBNS SGar SHar SMrm SPlb WPer WWEG |
| | 'Cherry Ripe' misapplied | see *P.* 'Cherry' |
| § | 'Chester Scarlet' ♀H3 | CWCL ECtt GMac LPen MBNS MRav SDix SGar SLon WCFE WPer XLum |
| | 'Choirboy' | EWes |
| | ***cinicola*** | LLHF |
| | 'Claret' | SAga |
| | ***cobaea*** | GKev SPhx WPer |
| | 'Comberton' | ECtt MBNS SAga |
| | ***confertus*** | CTri ECho EPot LPen MBNS NChi NMen SRms WPer |
| | - NNS 94-95 | NWCA |
| | - RCB/MO A-7 | WCot |
| | 'Connie's Pink' ♀H3 | ECtt LPen MBNS SGar SLon SRms WWEG |
| | 'Cottage Garden Red' | see *P.* 'Windsor Red' |
| § | 'Countess of Dalkeith' | CBcs CHVG COIW ECtt ELan EWes LLWP LPen MCot MLLN MRav SAga SGar SPer SPlb SRms SUsu SWvt WCot WFar |
| | ***crandallii*** | CPBP |
| § | - subsp. ***taosensis*** | MRav SMrm |
| | ***cristatus*** | see *P. eriantherus* |
| * | ***cyananthus*** var. ***utahensis*** | WCot |
| | ***cyaneus*** | GKev |
| | ***davidsonii*** | ECho EWes NMen WAbe WFar WPat WThu |
| | - var. ***davidsonii*** | WAbe |
| | - var. ***menziesii*** ♀H4 | GEdr LRHS |
| | - - 'Microphyllus' | GEdr LLHF NHar WAbe |
| | - var. ***praeteritus*** | GEdr MDKP |
| | 'Dazzler' | CMMP CWCL LPen MBNS SAga SWal SWvt WPer |
| | 'Devonshire Cream' | CWCL ECtt LPen MBNS SAga |
| | ***diffusus*** | see *P. serrulatus* |
| | ***digitalis*** | CRWN GCal LPen LRHS MBNS NWCA WFar WPer |
| § | - 'Husker Red' | Widely available |
| | - 'Joke' | IPot |
| | - 'Mystica' | EDif EWll LBuc |
| | - 'Purpureus' | see *P. digitalis* 'Husker Red' |
| | - 'Ruby Tuesday' | EWes SUsu WPGP |
| | - white-flowered | SRms |
| | ***discolor*** pale lavender-flowered | NBir WFar |
| § | 'Drinkstone Red' | ECtt EPfP LPen MBNS NChi SDix WPer |
| | 'Drinkwater Red' | see *P.* 'Drinkstone Red' |
| | ***eatonii*** | NBPC |
| | (Elgar Series) 'Elgar Crown of India' **new** | EBee |
| | - 'Elgar Firefly' **new** | EBee |
| | - 'Elgar Nimrod' **new** | EBee |
| | 'Ellenbank Amethyst' | GMac |
| | 'Ellenbank Cardinal' | GMac |
| | 'Ellwood Red Phoenix' | MBNS |
| | 'Elmley' | EPfP MBNS WCot |
| § | ***eriantherus*** | LLHF |
| | Etna = 'Yatna' | ECtt EPfP GKev LHop LPen LRHS MBNS NEgg SAll SBfd SMrm SRms WHlf |
| | ***euglaucus*** | EBee GKev LLHF |
| | - NNS 07-397 | GKev |
| § | 'Evelyn' ♀H4 | Widely available |
| | 'Evelyn' × 'Papal Purple' | LPen SBch |
| | 'Fanny's Blush' | SAga |
| | 'Firebird' | see *P.* 'Schoenholzeri' |
| | 'Flame' | LPen MBNS SAga SLon WPer WWEG |
| | 'Flamingo' | CWCL EBee ECtt EPfP EWes GBBs LAst LPen LRHS LSRN MBNS NBir NLar NPri SAga SBfd SGar SMrm SPet SPoG SRms SWvt WFar WHoo WWEG |
| | ***fruticosus*** | WAbe WFar |
| | - var. ***scouleri*** | CSpe WAbe WThu |
| | f. ***albus*** ♀H4 | |
| | - - 'Amethyst' | GEdr WAbe |
| | - var. ***serratus*** 'Holly' | NMen |
| | Fujiyama = 'Yayama'PBR | CWGN ECtt EPfP LBMP LHop LPen LRHS SAll SBfd SRms STes SWvt WFar WHlf |
| | 'Garden Red' | see *P.* 'Windsor Red' |
| | 'Garnet' | see *P.* 'Andenken an Friedrich Hahn' |
| | ***gentianoides*** B&SWJ 10271 | WCru |
| | 'Geoff Hamilton' | CElw CWGN EBee ECtt EPfP LPen LSRN MBNS SAga SPoG |
| | 'George Elrick' | LPen WHoo |
| § | 'George Home' ♀H3 | CWCL ECtt ELon EWes LPen MBNS SMrm SRms |
| | 'George Moon' | EPfP LRHS MWea SPad |
| | 'Ghent Purple' | CFee |
| | 'Gilchrist' | ECtt SLon |
| | ***glaber*** | CMHG CMea GBee GMac LHop LLWP LPen LSRN SPlb WKif WPer |
| | - 'Roundway Snowflake' | CWGN SHar SPhx |
| | - white-flowered | SGar |
| | 'Gloire des Quatre Rues' | MBNS XLum |
| | ***gormanii*** | SGar |
| | ***gracilis*** | WPer |
| § | ***grandiflorus*** | CFir EBee SBfd SPhx |
| | 'Great Witley' | WPer |
| | ***grinnellii*** | WFar |
| | ***hallii*** | EPot EWes WPat |
| | ***hartwegii*** ♀H3-4 | LPen WPer |
| | - 'Albus' | LPen SBch SGar SHar |
| | - 'Picotee Red' | CWCL LPen LRHS |
| | - 'Tubular Bells Rose' | NGBl SPet |
| | 'Helenetti' | SDys |
| | ***heterodoxus*** NNS 93-564 | NWCA |
| § | ***heterophyllus*** | CMea LPen MNrw MSCN NBir NGBl SBrt SPet SRkn SRms WCot WPer |

| |  |  |
|---|---|---|
| | – 'Blue Eye' | MBrN |
| | – 'Blue Gem' | CTri NMen WHil |
| § | – 'Blue Spring' | CBot CSpe EBee ECtt EPfP LPen LRHS MRav NLar SPhx WAbe WWEG |
| § | 'Catherine de la Mare' 🏆$^{H4}$ | ELan LHop LPen LRHS LSRN MHer MMuc MWat NBir SAga SBch SPer SRGP SWvt WFar WHrl WKif WWEG |
| | – 'Electric Blue' | CWCL LRHS NBlu SGar SWal |
| | – 'Heavenly Blue' | Widely available |
| | – 'Jeanette' | CMea |
| | – 'Les Holmes' | LPen |
| | – 'Misty Blue Shades' | LRHS |
| | – subsp. ***purdyi*** | EPyc |
| | – 'Roundway White' | WCot |
| | – 'True Blue' | see *P. heterophyllus* |
| | – 'Züriblau' | CFir EPfP GAbr SPhx SPlb |
| | aff. ***heterophyllus*** **new** | SBrt |
| § | 'Hewell Pink Bedder' 🏆$^{H3}$ | CHar COlW EBee ECtt EPfP LPen LRHS MBNS NLar NPri SGar SMrm SRms SWvt WFar WMnd WPer |
| | 'Hewitt's Pink' | CBcs ECtt SLon |
| | ***hidalgensis*** **new** | CDes |
| | 'Hidcote Pink' 🏆$^{H3-4}$ | Widely available |
| | 'Hidcote Purple' | CElw NGdn SHar WHoo XLum |
| * | 'Hidcote White' | LIMB MHer SAga SWvt WWEG |
| | 'Hillview Pink' | SLon |
| | 'Hillview Red' | MBNS |
| § | ***hirsutus*** | SGar WFar WPer |
| | – f. ***albiflorus*** | WAbe |
| | – var. ***pygmaeus*** | CMea EBee ECho EShb MHer NBlu NMen NWCA SAll SGar SPhx SPlb WAbe WHoo |
| * | – – f. ***albus*** | NWCA SPhx WHoo |
| | 'Hopleys Variegated' (v) | CWGN LRHS MBNS SWvt |
| | ***idahoensis*** | EDAr |
| | ***isophyllus*** 🏆$^{H3-4}$ | LPen SAga SEND WFar WPer |
| | 'James Bowden' | MBNS |
| | Jean Grace = 'Penbow' | CSpe NDov WHlf |
| | 'Jessica' | CWGN SAga |
| | 'Jingle Bells' | NLar |
| | 'John Booth' | MBNS |
| | 'John Nash' misapplied | see *P.* 'Alice Hindley' |
| | 'John Nash' | ECtt MHer SAga SRms |
| | 'John Spedan Lewis' | SLon |
| | 'Joy' | ECtt EPyc LPen MBNS SAga WPer |
| | 'Juicy Grape' (Ice Cream Series) | MBri MTis WHlf |
| | 'June' | see *P.* 'Pennington Gem' |
| | 'Kate Gilchrist' | SLon |
| | Kilimanjaro = 'Yajaro' | EPfP LRHS SRms |
| | 'King George V' | Widely available |
| | 'Knight's Purple' | ECtt MBNS |
| | 'Knightwick' | LPen MBNS WPer |
| § | ***kunthii*** | EBee GEdr LLWP LPen MDKP WPer |
| | – upright | SGar |
| § | ***laetus*** subsp. ***roezlii*** | ECho EPot GGar GLam LRHS MAsh |
| § | 'Le Phare' | LPen MBNS WPer XLum |
| | 'Lilac and Burgundy' | LPen MBNS MLLN SRms SWal SWvt WFar WWEG |
| | 'Lilac Frost' | ECtt LLHF MWhi WPer |
| | 'Lilliput' | CMea GKev LHop LIMB NPri SBfd SPet WHil WHoo |
| | ***linarioides*** | WPat |
| | – 'Marilyn Ross' | ECtt MBNS |
| | 'Little Witley' | WPer |
| | 'Lord Home' | see *P.* 'George Home' |
| | 'Louise Wilson' **new** | WHlf |

| |  |  |
|---|---|---|
| | 'Lucinda Gilchrist' | SLon |
| | ***lyallii*** | ELan GKev LPen WHil WPer |
| | 'Lynette' | LPen MBNS SBch SPlb WPer |
| | 'Macpenny's Pink' | ECtt EPyc LPen MBNS SAga |
| | 'Madame Golding' | GMac LPen MBNS SGar SPlb WPer |
| | 'Malvern Springs' | MBNS |
| | 'Margery Fish' 🏆$^{H3}$ | CElw ECtt EPyc EWes LPen WPer WWEG |
| | 'Martley' | WPer |
| | 'Marylin' **new** | WHlf |
| | 'Maurice Gibbs' 🏆$^{H3}$ | CBcs CMMP CWCL ECtt EPfP EPyc EWes LHop LPen LSRN MBNS MLLN NBPC SAga SGar SRGP SRms WMnd WWEG |
| | 'Melting Candy' (Ice Cream Series) | WHlf |
| | ***mensarum*** | WCot |
| | Mexicali hybrids | LPen MLLN WFoF |
| | × ***mexicanus*** 'Sunburst Amethyst' | LRHS SBfd SPad WPer |
| | – 'Sunburst Ruby' | LRHS SBfd |
| | 'Midnight' | CSam ECtt ELan EPfP GBBs LPen MBNS MRav SAga SEND SGar STes SWvt WCFE WCot WMnd WPer WWEG |
| | (Minibird Series) 'Minibird Lavender' **new** | LRHS |
| | – 'Minibird Lilac' **new** | LRHS |
| | – 'Minibird Pink' **new** | LRHS |
| | – 'Minibird Purple' **new** | LPen |
| | 'Mint Pink' | SAga |
| | 'Modesty' | EPfP LPen MBNS SAga SRms WPer |
| | 'Mother of Pearl' | CBcs CFir CWCL EPfP EShb GMaP GMac LHop LPen LRHS LSRN MBNS MCot MLLN MSwo MWat NBPC SPer SPlb SRkn SRms SWvt WFar WMoo WPer WWEG WWlt |
| | 'Mrs Miller' | LPen MBNS |
| | 'Mrs Morse' | see *P.* 'Chester Scarlet' |
| | 'Mrs Oliver' | EWes |
| | ***multiflorus*** | LPen |
| § | 'Myddelton Gem' | LPen MWat SRms WCot WFoF |
| | 'Myddelton Red' | see *P.* 'Myddelton Gem' |
| | ***newberryi*** 🏆$^{H4}$ | SAga |
| | – f. ***humilior*** | EPot |
| § | – subsp. ***sonomensis*** | GEdr WAbe WFar |
| * | 'Newbury Gem' | LPen LSRN MBNS SRGP SWvt WFar |
| | 'Oaklea Red' | EPyc SEND |
| § | 'Old Candy Pink' | LPen MBNS SWvt WPer |
| | 'Osprey' 🏆$^{H3}$ | CMac CWCL EBee ECtt ELan EPfP EShb EWes LAst LPen LRHS MBNS NBPC NBir NGdn SBfd SMrm SRms STes SWvt WHoo WMnd WPer WWEG |
| | ***ovatus*** | CFir CMac CSpe EBee ELan EWTr GBBs LPen NBre NLar SGar SPhx SRms |
| | 'Overbury' | ECtt LPen MBNS SAga SRms |
| | ***palmeri*** | SBrt |
| | 'Papal Purple' | LLWP LPen MBNS MHer NBir SAga SLon SPhx SRms WFar XLum |
| | 'Patio Bells Pink' | LPen MLHP SBfd |
| | Patio Bells Red = 'Yapbred' | LPen SBfd |
| | 'Patio Bells Shell' | CSpe LHop SLon SMrm WHlf |
| | ***payettensis*** NNS 07-414 | GKev |
| | 'Peace' | LPen MBNS MRav SLon WHoo |
| § | 'Pennington Gem' 🏆$^{H3}$ | CPrp ELan GMac GQue LLWP LPen MHer MSCN NBir SPer SRms SWvt WPer WWlt |
| | 'Pensax' | WPer |

| | |
|---|---|
| 'Pensham Amelia Jane' | CCVN CWGN EBee ECtt ELon EPfP LHop LPen LRHS LSRN LSou MAsh MBNS MBri MSCN MTis MWea NCGa SAga SAll SPer SRGP SRkn SWal SWvt WHil WHlf |
| 'Pensham Arctic Fox' | ECtt LHop LRHS SAga SLon |
| 'Pensham Arctic Sunset' | ECtt SAga SLon WHrl |
| 'Pensham Avonbelle' | MBNS SRms |
| 'Pensham Bilberry Ice' | ECtt EPyc MBNS SWvt WMnd |
| 'Pensham Blackberry Ice' | ECtt EPfP EPyc LPen LSou MBNS SAll SRms WMnd |
| 'Pensham Blueberry Ice' | ECtt EPyc LPen LSou MBNS SWvt WFar WMnd |
| 'Pensham Bow Bells' | SAga |
| 'Pensham Capricorn Moon' | ECtt NLar SLon SRGP |
| 'Pensham Charlotte Louise' | ECtt ELon LRHS MAsh MTis NLar SAll SWal |
| 'Pensham Claret' | WFar |
| 'Pensham Czar' | CCVN EBee ECtt EPfP LHop LRHS LSou LSqH MAsh MBNS MBri MCot MTis MWea NCGa SAga SAll SLon SPer SRkn SRms SWvt WHil WHlf WHrl |
| 'Pensham Dorothy Wilson' | EPyc SMrm SRGP |
| 'Pensham Edith Biggs' | CHVG CWCL ECtt EPfP WFar WMoo |
| 'Pensham Eleanor Young' | EBee ECtt LSou MBNS MTis MWea SAll SGar SRGP SWal SWvt WHlf |
| 'Pensham Freshwater Pearl' | CElw SAga SRms WHlf WHoo |
| 'Pensham Great Expectations' | EBee |
| 'Pensham Jessica Mai' | ECtt ELon LRHS LSou MAsh MTis NCGa SPer SRkn SWvt WHil |
| 'Pensham Just Jayne' | CWGN EBee ECtt ELon EPfP EPyc LRHS LSRN MBNS MLLN SAll SLon SRGP SRkn SRms SWvt WHil WHoo WMnd |
| 'Pensham Kay Burton' | EPfP EPyc SRGP WMnd |
| 'Pensham Laura' | CCVN CWGN EAEE EBee ECtt EPfP LHop LPen LRHS LSRN LSqH MAsh MBNS MBri MLLN MTis MWea SAga SAll SPer SRGP SRkn SWvt WHil WHlf |
| 'Pensham Loganberry Ice' | LSou MBNS MBri SAga SLon |
| 'Pensham Marjorie Lewis' | WMnd |
| 'Pensham Miss Wilson' | SAga SRms |
| 'Pensham Petticoat' | EBee SUsu |
| 'Pensham Plum Jerkum' | CWGN EBee ECtt ELon EPfP EPyc LHop LRHS LSou MBNS MBri MCot MWea NLar SAga SAll SPer SRkn SWal SWvt WHil WMnd WMoo |
| 'Pensham Raspberry Ice' | MBNS MBri WMnd |
| 'Pensham Saint James's' | WHlf |
| 'Pensham Son of Raven' | SAga |
| 'Pensham Tayberry Ice' | CSpr ECtt EPyc MBNS WMnd |
| 'Pensham Tiger Belle Coral' | NChi SAga |
| 'Pensham Victoria Plum' | CElw EShb MHer SHar WHoo |
| 'Pensham Wedding Bells' | SRms WFar |
| 'Pensham Wedding Day' | CWCL EBee EPfP LHop LPen LSRN LSou MBNS MBri NLar SAga SAll SPer SPoG SRGP WHlf |
| 'Persham Skies' **new** | WHlf |
| 'Pershore Carnival' | SRms WHrl |
| 'Pershore Fanfare' | LPen SAga WHrl |
| 'Pershore Pink Necklace' | CWCL ECtt LPen LRHS SAga SRms SWvt WCot WHlf WWEG |
| 'Phare' | see *P.* 'Le Phare' |
| 'Phoenix Red' (Phoenix Series) **new** | WCFE |
| 'Phyllis' | see *P.* 'Evelyn' |
| ***pinifolius*** ♀H4 | CFir CMea CTri ECho EDAr EPot GKev LHop LRHS MAsh MLLN NHar SGar SPhx SPoG WFar WHoo WPat XLum XSen |
| - 'Compactum' **new** | GKev |
| - dwarf | XSen |
| - 'Mersea Yellow' | CFir CMea ECho ECtt EDAr EPfP EPot GEdr GKev LHop LRHS MAsh NHar NWCA SAga SPhx SPlb SPoG WFar WPat WPer XLum XSen |
| - 'Wisley Flame' ♀H4 | ECho EPfP EPot EWes GEdr GLam MBNS MHer MSCN MWat NRya NWCA XSen |
| 'Pink Bedder' | see *P.* 'Hewell Pink Bedder', 'Sutton's Pink Bedder' |
| 'Pink Endurance' | LPen MBNS SRkn WHal WPer |
| 'Pink Ice' | LPen |
| 'Port Wine' ♀H3 | CElw CMea CSam CTri CWCL ELon EPfP GMaP LPen LRHS LSRN MCot MWat NBPC NBir SPer SPoG SRms SWal SWvt WKif WMnd WPer WWEG |
| 'Powis Castle' | ECtt EWes WPer |
| 'Pretty Petticoat' | IPot |
| 'Primrose Thomas' | SAga |
| 'Priory Purple' | MBNS WPer |
| ***procerus*** | SBrt WPer |
| - var. ***brachyanthus*** | GKev |
| § - var. ***formosus*** | GEdr GKev NMen WAbe WFar |
| - - NNS 01-345 | NWCA |
| § - 'Roy Davidson' ♀H4 | CMea CYeo EPot LBee LRHS NHar NMen SAga WAbe WFar WPat |
| - var. ***tolmiei*** | EPot GCal GEdr NMen |
| ***pubescens*** | see *P. hirsutus* |
| ***pulchellus*** Greene | see *P. procerus* var. *formosus* |
| ***pulchellus*** Lindl. | see *P. campanulatus* |
| 'Purple and White' | see *P.* 'Countess of Dalkeith' |
| 'Purple Bedder' | CHar COIW EBee EPfP LPen LRHS LSRN MLHP MWat NBir SBfd SMrm SPoG SRkn SRms SWvt WCFE WFar WGor |
| 'Purple Passion' | CElw EBee EPfP EWes LRHS WCAu WWEG |
| 'Purple Pixie' | LPen WCot |
| 'Purple Sea' | SGar |
| 'Purpureus Albus' | see *P.* 'Countess of Dalkeith' |
| ***purpusii*** | LLHF |
| 'Raspberry Ripple' | MBri MTis |
| 'Raven' ♀H3 | CBar CMac CSam CWCL EBee ECtt EPfP EShb GCra LAst LBMP LHop LLWP LPen LRHS MCot MHer NBPC NChi SAll SEND SPer SRms SWvt WCAu WFar WHal WPer WWEG WWlt |
| 'Razzle Dazzle' | LPen MBNS SPlb SRms WCot WPer |
| 'Red Emperor' | ECtt LPen SPlb WPer WWEG |
| 'Red Knight' | CWCL GCra LPen MBNS |
| 'Red Riding Hood' PBR | EPfP |
| 'Red Sea' | SGar |
| 'Rich Purple' | EPyc MBNS SPlb |
| 'Rich Ruby' | CAby CWCL CWGN EBee ECtt ELan EPfP EWes LLWP LPen LRHS MCot NBir SAga SPlb SRGP SWvt WCot WPer WWEG |
| ***richardsonii*** | WPer |
| - NNS 00-623 | NWCA |
| 'Ridgeway Red' | MBNS |
| ***roezlii*** Regel | see *P. laetus* subsp. *roezlii* |
| 'Ron Sidwell' | SGar SLon WCFE |
| § ***rostriflorus*** | LLHF |

| | | |
|---|---|---|
| | 'Rosy Blush' | LPen MBNS SAga SPlb |
| | 'Roundhay' | CFee |
| | 'Roy Davidson' | see *P. procerus* 'Roy Davidson' |
| | 'Royal White' | see *P.* 'White Bedder' |
| | 'Rubicundus' ♀H3 | CWCL CWGN EBee ELan EPfP LPen LRHS LSRN MBNS SAga SBfd SWvt WCot WFar WMnd WWlt |
| | 'Ruby' misapplied | see *P.* 'Schoenholzeri' |
| | 'Ruby Field' | EPyc GBee MSCN WCFE |
| | 'Ruby Gem' | LPen |
| | ***rupicola*** ♀H4 | EPot GEdr LHop LRHS |
| | - 'Albus' | NSla |
| | - 'Conwy Lilac' | WAbe |
| | - 'Conwy Rose' | WAbe |
| | 'Russian River' | CPrp EAEE EBee ECtt EPPr EPfP EPyc EWes LHop LPen LRHS LSRN MBNS SGar SPlb SWvt WPer |
| | 'Samsong' **new** | WCFE |
| * | Saskatoon hybrids | LHop |
| | - rose-flowered | SLon |
| | Scarlet Queen | see *P.* 'Scharlachkönigin' |
| § | 'Scharlachkönigin' | ECtt |
| § | 'Schoenholzeri' ♀H4 | Widely available |
| § | ***serrulatus*** | EWes |
| | - 'Albus' | SPhx |
| | 'Shell Pink' | LPen WPer |
| * | 'Sherbourne Blue' | LPen SAga WCot WPer |
| * | 'Shrawley' | WPer |
| | 'Sissinghurst Pink' | see *P.* 'Evelyn' |
| | 'Six Hills' | WAbe WPat |
| | 'Skyline' | EPfP |
| | ***smallii*** | CDes CEnt EBee EPPr EShb EWes LPen LRHS LSRN NBPC SAll SPhx SRkn WPGP WPer |
| | 'Snow Storm' | see *P.* 'White Bedder' |
| | 'Snowflake' | see *P.* 'White Bedder' |
| | ***sonomensis*** | see *P. newberryi* subsp. *sonomensis* |
| | 'Sour Grapes' misapplied | see *P.* 'Stapleford Gem' |
| | 'Sour Grapes' ambig. | CAby CChe CMea MCot MGos MLLN NGdn SAll SMrm STes WWEG |
| § | 'Sour Grapes' M. Fish ♀H3-4 | Widely available |
| | 'Southcombe Pink' | LPen |
| | 'Southgate Gem' | CWCL GBee LPen MBNS MWat SRms SWvt |
| | 'Souvenir d'Adrian Regnier' | LPen MBNS SGar |
| | 'Souvenir d'André Torres' misapplied | see *P.* 'Chester Scarlet' |
| | ***speciosus*** subsp. ***kennedyi*** | CPBP |
| | ***spectabilis*** **new** | SBrt |
| § | 'Stapleford Gem' ♀H3 | CBot CWCL ECtt ELan LPen LRHS MCot MLHP MLLN MRav MWhi NCGa NChi NPri SAga SMrm SPer SPet SPlb SRms SWvt WCot WFar WHlf WHoo WMnd WMoo WWEG |
| | 'Strawberries and Cream' (Ice Cream Series) | MBri MTis NLar WHlf |
| | ***strictus*** | CFir EBee EPPr EShb LPen MBNS SGar SRms WPer |
| | - 'Bandera' | WFar |
| | Stromboli = 'Yaboli' | LRHS |
| § | 'Sutton's Pink Bedder' | MBNS SPlb |
| | 'Sweet Cherry' (Ice Cream Series) | MBri MTis |
| | tall pink-flowered | see *P.* 'Welsh Dawn' |
| N | 'Taoensis' | EWes MBNS SGar |
| | ***taosensis*** | see *P. crandallii* subsp. *taosensis* |
| | 'Ted's Purple' **new** | WHlf |
| | ***teucrioides*** | EPot |
| | - JCA 1717050 | CPBP |
| | 'The Juggler' | CChe ECtt EPfP LPen MBNS MLLN SWvt WFar WMnd |
| § | 'Thorn' | CWGN ECtt ELan EShb LPen LRHS MWat NBir SAga SEND SPer SPhx SRms SWal SWvt WWEG |
| | 'Threave Pink' | CWCL EBee ECtt LLWP LRHS MBNS MRav SEND SHar SMrm SPer SWvt WWEG |
| | 'Thundercloud' | ECtt LPen |
| | 'Torquay Gem' | LLHF LPen MBNS WCot WPer |
| | 'True Sour Grapes' | see *P.* 'Sour Grapes' M. Fish |
| | ***tubaeflorus*** | SPhx |
| | 'Tubular Bells Red' | NGBl |
| | ***utahensis*** | CBot GBee SAga |
| | 'Vanilla Plum' (Ice Cream Series) | MBri MTis WHil |
| | ***venustus*** | GKev SRms |
| | Vesuvius = 'Yasius' | EAEE ECtt EPfP EPyc LPen LRHS NEgg SBfd SGar SMrm SRms SWal WFar WHlf |
| | ***virens*** | CPBP WPer |
| | ***virgatus*** 'Blue Buckle' | EBee IPot NBir SPlb WFar |
| | 'Wallington Pink' **new** | LRHS |
| § | 'Welsh Dawn' | CEnt LPen MBNS |
| § | ***whippleanus*** | GEdr LRHS WAbb |
| § | 'White Bedder' ♀H3 | Widely available |
| | 'Whitethroat' Sidwell | LPen MBNS SAga |
| I | 'Whitethroat' purple-flowered | SMrm WPer |
| | 'Willy's Purple' | ECtt MBNS |
| § | 'Windsor Red' | CTri EBee ECtt EPfP LPen LRHS MBNS NBPC SBfd SRms SWal SWvt |
| | 'Woodpecker' | CAby ECtt LPen MAvo MBNS SAga SGar SRms SUsu SWal |

## *Pentachondra* (*Ericaceae*)

| | | |
|---|---|---|
| | ***pumila*** | IBlr |

## *Pentaglottis* (*Boraginaceae*)

| | | |
|---|---|---|
| § | ***sempervirens*** | CArn EPfP MHer WSFF |

## *Pentagramma* (*Pteridaceae*)

| | | |
|---|---|---|
| | ***triangularis*** | WRic |

## *Pentapanax* see *Aralia*

## *Pentapterygium* see *Agapetes*

## *Pentas* (*Rubiaceae*)

| | | |
|---|---|---|
| | ***lanceolata*** | CCCN ELan EShb |
| | - white-flowered **new** | EShb |

## *Penthorum* (*Saxifragaceae*)

| | | |
|---|---|---|
| | ***sedoides*** | LLWG |

## pepino see *Solanum muricatum*

## peppermint see *Mentha* × *piperita*

## *Peranema* (*Dryopteridaceae*)

| | | |
|---|---|---|
| | ***cyatheaodes*** **new** | WRic |

## *Perezia* (*Asteraceae*)

| | | |
|---|---|---|
| | ***recurvata*** | NWCA |

## *Pericallis* (*Asteraceae*)

| | | |
|---|---|---|
| | ***aurita*** | CRHN |
| | × ***hybrida*** Senetti Series | MGos NPer NPri SPoG |

| | | |
|---|---|---|
| | - - Senetti Blue Bicolor = 'Sunseneribuba'PBR | MGos SPoG |
| | - - Senetti Magenta Bicolor = 'Sunsenereba'PBR | MGos SPoG |
| | ***lanata*** ambig. | CRHN IRar |
| § | ***lanata*** (L'Hér.) B. Nord. | CHll EShb |
| | - Kew form | CSpe SMrm |

## *Perilla* (*Lamiaceae*)

| | | |
|---|---|---|
| § | ***frutescens*** var. ***crispa*** ♀H2 | CArn CSpe |
| | - green-leaved | ELau |
| | - var. ***japonica*** | GPoy |
| | - var. ***nankinensis*** | see *P. frutescens* var. *crispa* |
| | - var. ***purpurascens*** | CArn ELau WJek |
| | - 'Shizo Green' | CSpe |

## *Periploca* (*Apocynaceae*)

| | |
|---|---|
| ***graeca*** | CBcs CMac CRHN SLon |
| ***purpurea*** B&SWJ 7235 | WCru |
| ***sepium*** | CPLG |

## *Peristrophe* (*Acanthaceae*)

| | |
|---|---|
| ***speciosa*** | ECre |

## *Pernettya* see *Gaultheria*

| | |
|---|---|
| ***mucronata*** | see *Gaultheria mucronata* |

## *Perovskia* (*Lamiaceae*)

| | |
|---|---|
| ***abrotanoides*** | LRHS XLum |
| ***atriplicifolia*** | CArn CBcs CBot CMea ELan EWTr MHer MNHC NSti WKif WMnd WPer XSen |
| - 'Blue Shadow' | LRHS |
| - Lacey Blue = 'Lisslitt' **new** | LRHS |
| - 'Little Spire'PBR | CAbP CBar CHar CMac CSBt CSpe EBee EHoe EPfP EWes GBin GMaP GQue LRHS LSRN MAsh NBPC NBid NLar SBfd SGol SPer SPoG SRkn WKif WSHC |
| 'Blue Haze' | GCal LRHS |
| 'Blue Spire' ♀H4 | Widely available |
| 'Filigran' | EBee LBMP LRHS LSou MWhi NDov SBfd SPoG WFar WPat XSen |
| 'Hybrida' | CAlb LRHS SBfd |
| 'Longin' | NDov SPoG |

## *Persea* (*Lauraceae*)

| | |
|---|---|
| ***americana*** | CCCN |
| ***indica*** | CCCN |
| ***japonica*** B&SWJ 8410 | WCru |
| ***lingue*** | CBcs IDee |
| ***thunbergii*** | CBcs CHEx |

## *Persicaria* (*Polygonaceae*)

| | | |
|---|---|---|
| | B&SWJ 11268 from Sumatra | WCru |
| § | ***affinis*** | CBcs CBen CSBt EBee GAbr MWhi NBro NSti NVic SWat WBrk WFar WMoo |
| | - 'Darjeeling Red' ♀H4 | Widely available |
| | - 'Dimity' | see *P. affinis* 'Superba' |
| | - 'Donald Lowndes' ♀H4 | CChe CEnt CHVG CMac COIW CTri CYeo EBee ELan EPfP GMaP IVic LAst LPBA LRHS LSRN MHer MNrw MRav SPer SPoG SRGP SRms SWat SWvt WFar WMoo WPer WWEG |
| | - 'Kabouter' | EBee GBin IPot NLar |
| | - 'Ron McBeath' | LRHS |
| § | - 'Superba' ♀H4 | Widely available |
| | ***alata*** | see *P. nepalensis* |
| | ***alpina*** | CDes CSpe ECha ELan EPPr EWTr GBin GMaP IPot LEdu LRHS MAvo MCot MRav NCGa NDov SBch SDix SPhx WCot WFar WMoo WWEG |
| | ***amphibia*** | CRow EWil LLWG MSKA SWat XLum |
| § | ***amplexicaulis*** | CBre CHVG CKno CPrp CRow CSpe ELan EWes GMaP MCot MHer MLLN MMuc NOrc WBor WFar WGwG WMoo WTin XLum |
| | - 'Alba' | CElw CHar CKno CPrp CRow CSam EBee ECha ELon EPPr GCal GGar LRHS MCot MLLN MRav MSpe NDov SMrm SPhx SWat WBor WCAu WCot WFar WMnd WMoo WPnP WTin WWEG |
| | - 'Arun Gem' | see *P. amplexicaulis* var. *pendula* |
| | - 'Atrosanguinea' | CKno CMac CRow CTri EBee ECha ELan EPla GGar LRHS MMuc MNFA MRav MSpe NBir NLar NVic SEND SPer SRms SWat SWvt WCAu WFar WOld WWEG |
| | - 'Baron' | CRow |
| | - 'Blackfield'PBR | CBct EBee ECtt ELon EPPr GQue LRHS LSou MBNS MLLN NDov NLar WCot |
| | - 'Blush Clent' | WHoo WTin |
| | - 'Clent Charm' | NChi WWEG |
| | - 'Cottesbrooke Gold' | CRow ECtt |
| | - 'Dikke Floskes' | CRow |
| | - 'Eastfield' (v) | WCot |
| | - 'Fascination' **new** | WCot |
| | - 'Fat Domino'PBR | GBin IPot NDov NLar |
| | - 'Firedance' | CKno EBee EHoe ELon EPPr GBin GQue IPot NDov SMrm SPhx SWat WCot |
| | - 'Firetail' ♀H4 | Widely available |
| | - 'High Society' | EBee |
| | - 'Inverleith' | CBct CBre CDes CHar CKno CRow EBee ECGP ECha ECtt EPPr EPla GBin GGar GMaP GQue LBMP LRHS MAvo MLLN MMuc MSpe SPhx WCot WMoo WOut WPGP WPnP |
| I | - 'Jo and Guido's Form' | EBee ELon NDov NLar SUsu WCAu WFar |
| | - 'JS Caliente' **new** | EBee ECtt GQue NCGa WCot |
| | - 'Orange Field' | EBee EPPr GQue LRHS |
| * | - var. ***pendula*** | CRow EBee EPPr GQue NBir WFar WMoo |
| | - - HWJK 2255 | EBla WCru |
| | - 'Pink Elephant' | CSam EBee EPPr GBee GBin GQue NDov NLar WWEG |
| | - 'Pink Lady' | CRow NLar |
| | - 'Rosea' | Widely available |
| | - 'Rowden Gem' | CRow WMoo |
| | - 'Rowden Jewel' | CRow |
| | - 'Rowden Rose Quartz' | CRow |
| | - 'September Spires' | NDov |
| | - 'Summer Dance' | EBee ECtt EPPr GQue LPla NBre NDov NLar |
| | - Taurus = 'Blotau' | CDes CElw CKno CSam EBee ECha EPPr GBin LRHS MBri NLar NSti WCAu WFar WPGP WPnP WTin WWEG |
| § | ***bistorta*** | CArn CRow ELau GPoy MHer MMuc MNHC MWhi NBir NLar SEND SRms SWat WOut |

| | |
|---|---|
| - subsp. ***carnea*** | CRow EBee EBla ECha EHoe ELon GGar LPla LRHS MBNS MDKP MMuc MSpe NBir NBro NDov WFar WMoo |
| - 'Hohe Tatra' | CDes CRow LRHS NDov WFar WMoo |
| - 'Superba' ♀H4 | Widely available |
| ***campanulata*** | CElw CRow EBee ECha ECtt EHoe GAbr GGar GMaP IFro MMuc MRav MSpe MWhi NBro NEgg SEND SPer WFar WMoo WOld WOut WRHF |
| - Alba Group | CElw EBee GBin GGar NBro WMoo |
| - var. ***lichiangense*** | GBin |
| - 'Madame Jigard' | CRow GBin |
| - 'Rosenrot' | CBre CRow LRHS NBir NHol SWat WFar WOld WWEG |
| - 'Southcombe White' | CRow EPla LRHS WPer WWEG |
| § ***capitata*** | CRow LLWG SRms WMoo XLum |
| - 'Pink Bubbles' | ECtt EHoe SPet SWvt |
| ***chinensis*** B&SWJ 11268 | WCru |
| ***conspicua*** | EBee NBre |
| ***dshawachischwilii*** | SUsu |
| * ***elata*** | CSpr LRHS |
| ***emodi*** | CRow |
| ***hydropiper*** 'Fastigiata' | CArn |
| * ***kahil*** | WCot |
| * ***macrophylla*** | WFar |
| - CC 5790 | GKev |
| I - 'Cally Strain' | GCal |
| ***microcephala*** | CRow EWes |
| - 'Red Dragon'PBR | Widely available |
| - var. ***wallichii*** | CRow |
| ***milletii*** | NLar WCru WFar WWEG |
| § ***mollis*** | CRow LRHS WDyG WPGP |
| ***nakaii*** | EBee |
| ***neofiliformis*** | EShb MWhi |
| § ***nepalensis*** | CPLG CRow EBee EPPr EShb MAvo MSpe |
| 'October Pink' **new** | CSam |
| § ***odorata*** | CArn EGHP ELau EOHP GPoy ILis MHer MNHC SBfd SHDw SIde WJek |
| ***orientalis*** | CSpe SMrm SUsu |
| ***polystachya*** | see *P. wallichii* |
| 'Red Baron' | EPPr |
| § ***runcinata*** | CRow EBee GGar MMuc NBir NLar WFar WMoo |
| - Needham's form | CRow |
| ***scoparia*** | see *Polygonum scoparium* |
| ***sphaerostachya*** Meisn. | see *P. macrophylla* |
| ***tenuicaulis*** | CBre CEnt CRow EPla GBin GEdr GGar NLar SBch WCru WFar WMoo |
| § ***tinctoria*** | EOHP WSFF |
| § ***vacciniifolia*** ♀H4 | CBcs COIW CPrp CRow CSBt CTri EBee ECha ECho ECtt EHoe GAbr GGar LAst LHop MHer MLHP MMuc NBir SDix SPer SPlb SRms SWat SWvt WAbe WFar WMoo WWEG |
| - 'Ron McBeath' | CRow |
| § ***virginiana*** | CRow ECtt GCal LRHS WMoo |
| - var. ***filiformis*** | CHEx CSpe EBee ECtt GBin GQue LBMP LPla MMoz NBPC SBfd SBrt SWvt WCot WDyG WHil WPtf WTcb WWEG |
| - - 'Ballet' | WCot |
| - - 'Batwings' | ESwi LRHS |
| - - Compton's form | CBct CHEx CRow ECha EPPr EPfP EShb GCal LHop LPla LRHS MMoz SBrt WAul WCot WHil |
| - - 'Lance Corporal' | CMac CRow EHoe EPPr EShb GBin GQue MAvo NLar SMrm WMnd WMoo |
| - - 'Moorland Moss' | WMoo |
| - Variegated Group (v) | CBot CRow ECha EPla EShb MBNS WMoo WOld |
| - - 'Painter's Palette' (v) | Widely available |
| - white-flowered | CKno EPPr |
| ***vivipara*** | NLar |
| § ***wallichii*** | CRow EBee MMuc NLar SDix SEND SWat WCot WMoo WPtf WWEG XLum |
| § ***weyrichii*** | GCal NBir NBro NLar WFar WMoo XLum |

## **persimmon** see *Diospyros virginiana*

## **persimmon, Japanese** see *Diospyros kaki*

## *Petalostemon* see *Dalea*

## *Petamenes* see *Gladiolus*

## *Petasites* (*Asteraceae*)

| | |
|---|---|
| ***albus*** | GPoy MHer NLar |
| ***formosanus*** B&SWJ 3025 | LEdu |
| ***fragrans*** | EBee ELan MHer SWat WFar XLum |
| § ***frigidus*** var. ***palmatus*** | EBee LEdu NLar |
| - - JLS 86317CLOR | SMad |
| ***hybridus*** | EBee LEdu MSKA SWat WMAq WSFF |
| * - 'Variegatus' (v) | XLum |
| ***japonicus*** | CBcs GPoy |
| - var. ***giganteus*** | CArn CHEx CMac CRow ECha ELan EPfP LEdu NVic SWat WCru |
| § - - 'Nishiki-buki' (v) | CHEx CMac CRow EBee EPPr EPla EWld GQue MHer MLLN MSKA NBir NEgg NSti SMad WBor WFar WWEG |
| - - 'Variegatus' | see *P. japonicus* var. *giganteus* 'Nishiki-buki' |
| - f. ***purpureus*** | EPPr EWes |
| ***palmatus*** | see *P. frigidus* var. *palmatus* |
| ***paradoxus*** | CDes CLAP EPPr EWes EWld LEdu MLLN WCot |

## × *Petchoa* (*Solanaceae*)

| | |
|---|---|
| (Supercal Series) | LAst |
| Supercal Cherry **new** | |
| - SuperCal Neon Rose = 'Kakegawa S89'PBR **new** | LSou |
| - SuperCal Terracotta = 'Kakegawa S91'PBR | LSou |
| - SuperCal Vanilla Blush = 'Sakpxc005' **new** | LAst |

## *Petrea* (*Verbenaceae*)

| | |
|---|---|
| ***volubilis*** | CCCN CHII |

## *Petrocallis* (*Brassicaceae*)

| | |
|---|---|
| ***lagascae*** | see *P. pyrenaica* |
| § ***pyrenaica*** | NWCA WAbe |
| - ***alba*** | WAbe |

## *Petrocoptis* (*Caryophyllaceae*)

| | |
|---|---|
| ***pseudoviscosa*** | GKev WPat |
| ***pyrenaica*** | SRms |
| § - subsp. ***glaucifolia*** | GKev NBir |

## *Petrocosmea* (*Gesneriaceae*)

| | |
|---|---|
| ***begoniifolia*** | WAbe |
| ***formosa*** 'Crûg's Capricious' | WCru |
| ***forrestii*** | WAbe |

***grandiflora*** WAbe
- 'Crème de Crûg' WCru
***iodioides*** WAbe
***kerrii*** WCot
- B&SWJ 6634 WAbe
aff. ***martini*** WAbe
***minor*** CPBP WAbe
***rosettifolia*** WAbe
***sericea*** WAbe

## *Petrophytum* (*Rosaceae*)

***caespitosum*** EPot WAbe
***cinerascens*** NWCA WAbe
§ ***hendersonii*** WAbe

## *Petrorhagia* (*Caryophyllaceae*)

'Pink Starlets' EPfP LHop
***saxifraga*** ♀H4 CSpe ECho EDAr EHoe LBMP SRms SWal WMoo WPnn
- 'Alba Plena' (d) **new** CSpe

## *Petroselinum* (*Apiaceae*)

§ ***crispum*** CArn EGHP GPoy ILis MNHC NBlu SBfd SIde SPoG SWal WJek WPer
- 'Bravour' ♀H4 ELau MHer
- 'Champion Moss Curled' SVic
- 'Darki' EGHP ELau NPri
- French CArn ELau MHer MNHC NPri NVic SPoG WJek
- 'Hank' (v) CNat
- 'Italian' see *P. crispum* var. *neapolitanum* plain-leaved
§ - var. ***neapolitanum*** plain-leaved ELau SBfd SIde SPoG SVic
- 'Super Moss Curled' NVic SWal
§ - var. ***tuberosum*** MHer MNHC SIde SVic
***hortense*** see *P. crispum*
***tuberosum*** see *P. crispum* var. *tuberosum*

## *Petteria* (*Papilionaceae*)

***ramentacea*** EBtc NLar

## *Petunia* (*Solanaceae*)

Candyfloss = 'Kercan'PBR (Tumbelina Series) (d) LSou NPri
(Cascadias Series) Cascadias Bicolor Pastel = 'Dancasbipas'PBR **new** NPri
- Cascadias Rim Violet **new** NPri
Cherry Ripple = 'Kerripcherry' (Tumbelina Series) (d) LSou NPri
Clara = 'Kerclara' (Tumbelina Series) (d) **new** LSou
'Corona Amethyst' (Corona Series) **new** NPri
'Empaurea' LAst NPri
Joanna (Tumbelina Series) LAst LSou
Julia = 'Kerjul'PBR (Tumbelina Series) (d) LAst
Katrina = 'Kerkat'PBR (Tumbelina Series) (d) LAst
(Littletunia Series) Littletunia Bicolour Illusion **new** LSou
- Littletunia Breezy Pink = 'Dantun2' **new** LSou
- Littletunia Sweet Pink = 'Dantun3' **new** LSou
- Littletunia Ultra Purple **new** LSou
Melissa = 'Kermelis'PBR (Tumbelina Series) (d) LAst LSou
(Mini Me Series) 'Mini Me Lilac Vein' **new** LAst
- 'Mini Me Pink Star' LAst
***patagonica*** WAbe
Priscilla = 'Kerpril'PBR (Tumbelina Series) (d) LAst LSou NPri
Rosy Ripple = 'Kerriprosy' (Tumbelina Series) (d) LAst
(Surfinia Series) Surfinia Baby Pinkmorn = 'Sunbapimo'PBR LSou
- Surfinia Blue Picotee **new** LSou
- Surfinia Blue = 'Sunblu' LAst LSou NPri WGor
- Surfinia Blue Vein = 'Sunsolos'PBR LAst LSou WGor
- Surfinia Burgundy = 'Keiburtel'PBR LAst NPri WGor
- Surfinia Crazy Pink = 'Sunrovein'PBR LAst NPri
- Surfinia Double Blue Star = 'Sunsurfelevi' (d) **new** NPri
- Surfinia Hot Pink = 'Marrose'PBR LSou WGor
- Surfinia Hot Red = 'Sunhore'PBR NPri
- Surfinia Lime = 'Keiyeul'PBR LAst LSou NPri WGor
- Surfinia Pastel 2000 = 'Sunpapi'PBR WGor
- Surfinia Pink Ice = 'Hakice'PBR (v) LAst NPri WGor
- Surfinia Purple = 'Shihi Brilliant' ♀H3 LAst LSou NPri WGor
- Surfinia Red = 'Keirekul'PBR LAst NPri WGor
- Surfinia Rose Vein = 'Sunrove'PBR LAst WGor
- Surfinia Sky Blue = 'Keilavbu'PBR ♀H3 LAst NPri WGor
- Surfinia Sweet Pink = 'Sunsurfmomo' LSou
- Surfinia Vanilla = 'Sunvanilla'PBR LSou
- Surfinia Victorian Yellow = 'Sunpatiki'PBR LAst NPri
- Surfinia White = 'Kesupite' LAst
Susanna (Tumbelina Series) **new** LAst
Victoria = 'Kervic'PBR (Tumbelina Series) LAst LSou
(Viva Series) 'Viva Amethyst' LSou
- 'Viva Burgundy' LSou
- 'Viva Dark Purple Vein' LSou
- 'Viva Hot Pink' LSou
- 'Viva Red' LSou
- 'Viva Violet' (d) LSou

## *Peucedanum* (*Apiaceae*)

***japonicum*** B&SWJ 8816B WCru
***officinale*** NLar SPlb
***ostruthium*** GPoy LEdu NCGa WCFE WPtf

\- 'Daphnis' (v) CElw CSpe EBee EPPr LEdu LPla MAvo MMoz NChi NLar NMRc NPro WCot WHrl WWFP XLum
***praeruptorum*** CArn
***siamicum*** B&SWJ 6487 WCru
***verticillare*** CArn EBee GQue ITim LRHS MAvo MCot MLLN NChi SDix SKHP SPhx WSHC WWEG

## *Peumus* (*Monimiaceae*)
***boldus*** CBcs IArd IDee

## *Phacelia* (*Boraginaceae*)
***tanacetifolia*** SPhx

## *Phaedranassa* (*Amaryllidaceae*)
BKBlount 2623 WCot
***carmiolii*** WCot
***cinerea*** ECho WCot
***dubia*** ECho WCot
* ***montana*** ECho
***tunguraguae*** ECho
***viridiflora*** ECho WCot

## *Phaedranthus* see *Distictis*

## *Phaenocoma* (*Asteraceae*)
***prolifera*** SPlb

## *Phaenosperma* (*Poaceae*)
***globosa*** CSam CSpe EHoe EPPr EWes LEdu MAvo NWsh SPhx WBox WCot WPGP XLum

## *Phagnalon* (*Asteraceae*)
***saxatile*** RCB RL -21 WCot

## *Phaiophleps* see *Olsynium*
***nigricans*** see *Sisyrinchium striatum*

## *Phalaris* (*Poaceae*)
***arundinacea*** MBNS MSKA SPlb SVic SWat WTin
\- cream-flowered WWEG
\- 'Elegantissima' see *P. arundinacea* var. *picta* 'Picta'
\- var. ***picta*** CDul CHEx CTri CWCL CWib MSKA NBid NBir NPer SApp SPoG WDin WFar XLum
\- - 'Arctic Sun' (v) CKno ELon EPPr LLWG SBfd SDix SPoG
\- - 'Aureovariegata' (v) CBcs MRav NGdn NPer SWat WMoo XLum
\- - 'Feesey' (v) Widely available
\- - 'Luteopicta' (v) EBee EHoe EPPr EPfP MMuc SEND WTin XLum
\- - 'Luteovariegata' (v) NGdn
§ - - 'Picta' (v) ♀H4 COlW EBee ELan EPfP EPla LPBA LRHS MMuc SBfd SEND SPer SWal SWat WMoo
\- - 'Streamlined' (v) EPPr EPla LLWG NWsh SLPl WFar
\- - 'Tricolor' (v) EHoe EPla LLWG

## *Phalocallis* (*Iridaceae*)
§ ***coelestis*** WPGP

## *Phanerophlebia* (*Dryopteridaceae*)
***caryotidea*** see *Cyrtomium caryotideum*
***falcata*** see *Cyrtomium falcatum*
***fortunei*** see *Cyrtomium fortunei*

## *Pharbitis* see *Ipomoea*

## *Phaseolus* (*Papilionaceae*)
***caracalla*** see *Vigna caracalla*
***vulgaris*** 'Yin Yang' LSou

## *Phedimus* see *Sedum*

## *Phegopteris* (*Thelypteridaceae*)
§ ***connectilis*** EFer EFtx SRms WAbe WRic
***decursive-pinnata*** CDes CLAP EFtx LRHS NLar NMyG WFib WPnP WRic

## *Phellodendron* ✿ (*Rutaceae*)
***amurense*** CBcs CCCN CDul CMCN EBee ELan EPfP GAuc GBin IArd IVic LEdu NLar NMun SEND WBor WDin WPGP
\- B&SWJ 11000 WCru
\- var. ***sachalinense*** CBcs
***japonicum*** B&SWJ 11175 WCru

## *Phenakospermum* (*Strelitziaceae*)
***guianense*** XBlo

## *Pherosphaera* (*Podocarpaceae*)
***fitzgeraldii*** CKen WThu

## *Philadelphus* ✿ (*Hydrangeaceae*)
SDR 2823 CPLG
SDR 4862 GKev
SDR 4946 CPLG GKev
***argyrocalyx*** SBrd
'Avalanche' CMHG CPLG EBee NLar NPro SEND SPer SRms WDin WFar
'Beauclerk' ♀H4 CDoC CDul CTri EBee EPfP GGal GQui IVic LRHS MAsh MBri MGos MRav NBro NEgg NHol NWea SBrd SKHP SLim SPer SRms SWvt WDin WPat
'Belle Etoile' ♀H4 Widely available
'Bicolore' NLar
'Bouquet Blanc' MRav NLar SRms WPat
***brachybotrys*** EPfP MRav
'Buckley's Quill' (d) ECrN EPfP EQua EWes LRHS MRav SGol SWvt WGrn
'Burfordensis' CWSG EPfP LAst MRav SEND
aff. ***calvescens*** MRav
\- BWJ 8005 WCru
***coronarius*** CBcs CDul EPfP LBuc MLHP MMuc MWhi NWea SEND SPer WDin
\- 'Aureus' ♀H4 Widely available
\- 'Bowles's Variety' see *P. coronarius* 'Variegatus'
§ - 'Variegatus' (v) ♀H4 CDul CMHG CPMA CWib ELan EPfP EPla LAst LHop LRHS MAsh MGos MMuc MRav MSwo NBir SLim SPoG WCFE WCot WDin WFar WKif WMoo WPat WSHC
***coulteri*** WPGP
'Coupe d'Argent' MRav
'Dainty Lady' LRHS
'Dame Blanche' (d) EPfP MRav
***delavayi*** CGHE EPfP GGal SKHP WPGP
\- var. ***melanocalyx*** GCra MRav WPGP
\- - B&L 12168 WPGP
\- 'Nymans' CPLG EPfP SKHP WKif
'Enchantement' (d) MRav SDix
'Erectus' CSBt CWib EBee ELon EPfP LEdu LRHS MGos MRav SKHP SLim SPer SPoG WDin WPat
'Etoile Rose' WMoo

| | | |
|---|---|---|
| | 'Frosty Morn' (d) | CBcs EPfP LRHS MMuc MRav NBro SEND SPer |
| | ***incanus*** B&SWJ 8616 | WCru |
| § | 'Innocence' (v) | CBot CMac CPLG EBee ECrN EHoe ELan EPfP EWTr LAst LBMP LRHS MAsh MBri MGos MMuc MRav MSwo NLar NPro SAga SBfd SBrd SEND SKHP SLim SPad SPer SPoG WFar |
| | 'Innocence Variegatus' | see *P.* 'Innocence' |
| § | ***insignis*** | MRav |
| | 'Kelmarsh' | SLPl |
| | × ***lemoinei*** | CBcs CDul CTri EWTr LBMP MGos MWat NLar WDin WFar |
| I | - 'Lemoinei' | NWea |
| | ***lewisii*** | CPLG |
| | - L1896 | CPLG |
| | 'Limestone' | MRav |
| | ***maculatus*** | CGHE CPLG SKHP WPGP WPat |
| | 'Mexican Jewel' | |
| | - 'Scented Storm' new | CMHG CSam |
| | ***madrensis*** | CGHE LHop MRav |
| | - F&M 326 | WPGP |
| | 'Manteau d'Hermine' (d) ♀H4 | Widely available |
| | 'Marjorie' | NLar |
| | ***mexicanus*** | CBcs GCal WSHC |
| | - B&SWJ 10253 | WCru |
| | - 'Rose Syringa' | CGHE CPLG SKHP SSta WPGP |
| | ***microphyllus*** | CBot CDul CMCN CTri EBee ELan EPfP LAst MAsh MGos MRav MWhi SKHP SLon SPer SPhx SSpi WKif WPGP WPat WSHC |
| | 'Miniature Snowflake' (d) | CSpe MAsh SEND WPat |
| | 'Minnesota Snowflake' (d) | CBcs ECtt EQua EWes LBuc LRHS LSRN MMuc MRav NEgg NHol NLar NPro SBfd SGol SPur WDin WFar |
| | 'Mont Blanc' | CBcs GKin MRav WFar |
| | 'Mrs E.L. Robinson' (d) | CMac EBee ECtt ELon LAst LLHF LRHS MAsh MGos NEgg NLar WBor WPat |
| | ***myrtoides*** | WCru |
| | B&SWJ 10436 new | |
| | 'Natchez' (d) | CMac ECtt ELon MAsh NLar WDin WPat |
| | 'Oeil de Pourpre' | MRav |
| | ***palmeri*** | CGHE WPGP WPat |
| | ***pekinensis*** | CPLG |
| | 'Perryhill' | MRav |
| | 'Polar Star' | ELon GBin IArd WKif |
| | ***purpurascens*** | CPLG EPfP EWes GQui LLHF MRav SChF SKHP WPGP WPat |
| | - BWJ 7540 | WCru |
| | × ***purpureomaculatus*** | LLHF MAsh MRav WPat |
| | ***satsumi*** | SLPl |
| | - B&SWJ 10811 | WCru |
| | - B&SWJ 11004 | WCru |
| | ***schrenkii*** | NLar |
| | - B&SWJ 8465 | WCru |
| § | 'Silberregen' | CDul CMac CSam ELon EPfP LRHS MAsh MGos MMuc MRav NLar NPro SLim SRms SWvt WFar WPat |
| | Silver Showers | see *P.* 'Silberregen' |
| | 'Snow Velvet' | EPfP LLHF LRHS |
| | 'Snowbelle' (d) | EBee LBMP LRHS MAsh MBri NBro NHol NLar SKHP SWvt |
| | 'Snowflake' | WMoo |
| | 'Souvenir de Billiard' | see *P. insignis* |
| | ***subcanus*** | CPLG |
| | - L 524 | CPLG WPGP |
| | 'Sybille' ♀H4 | CDul CMHG EPfP EWTr LHop LRHS MAsh MRav MSwo SDix SKHP SPer SRms SSpi WPat WSHC |
| | ***tenuifolius*** | NLar SLPl |
| | ***tomentosus*** | CPLG |
| | - B&SWJ 2707 | WCru |
| | - GWJ 9215 | WCru |
| | 'Virginal' (d) | Widely available |
| | 'Voie Lactée' | MRav |
| | White Icicle = 'Bialy Sopel' | CCCN |
| | White Rock = 'Pekphil' | CDoC CMac EPfP LLHF LRHS LSRN MRav SKHP SLim SPer WPat |
| | 'Yellow Cab' | CWSG NEgg NLar SLim |
| | 'Yellow Hill' | CMac EPfP LRHS NEgg NLar SBfd SKHP SLim |
| | ***zeyheri*** | SLPl |

## *Philesia* (*Philesiaceae*)

| | | |
|---|---|---|
| | ***buxifolia*** | see *P. magellanica* |
| § | ***magellanica*** | CPLG IBlr SSpi WAbe WCru WSHC |
| | - 'Rosea' | CWib EPfP IBlr SSpi |

## *Phillyrea* (*Oleaceae*)

| | | |
|---|---|---|
| | ***angustifolia*** | CDul CGHE CMCN EBee ELan EPfP ERom LRHS MBri MGos MRav NLar SBfd SBig SEND SPer SSpi WDin WFar WPGP WSHC XSen |
| | - f. ***rosmarinifolia*** | CCCN CPLG ELan EPfP EPla LAst NLar SLPl WFar |
| | - - 'French Fries' | WPGP |
| | ***decora*** | see *Osmanthus decorus* |
| § | ***latifolia*** | CDul EGFP ELan EPfP GGal LRHS MWea NLar SArc SBfd SBrd SEND SSpi WDin WFar WPGP |
| I | - 'Rodrigueziensis' | WCFE |
| | ***media*** | see *P. latifolia* |

## *Philodendron* (*Araceae*)

| | | |
|---|---|---|
| | ***bipinnatifidum*** ♀H1 | EAmu SEND XBlo |
| * | ***rubrum*** | XBlo |
| | ***scandens*** 'Mica' | XBlo |
| | ***xanadu*** | XBlo |

## *Philotheca* (*Rutaceae*)

| | | |
|---|---|---|
| | ***buxifolia*** | ECou |
| | - 'Cascade of Stars' | MOWG |

## *Phlebodium* (*Polypodiaceae*)

| | | |
|---|---|---|
| § | ***aureum*** ♀H1 | CSpe WRic |
| | - 'Mandaianum' | WRic |
| | ***pseudoaureum*** | WCot |

## *Phleum* (*Poaceae*)

| | | |
|---|---|---|
| | ***bertolonii*** | CRWN |
| | ***phleoides*** new | LRHS |
| | ***pratense*** | EHoe NMir WSFF |

## *Phlomis* ✿ (*Lamiaceae*)

| | | |
|---|---|---|
| * | ***anatolica*** | LRHS NLar |
| * | - 'Lloyd's Variety' | CAbP CSam ELan LRHS MAsh SEND SPer |
| | ***angustifolia*** | LRHS |
| | ***anisodonta*** white-flowered | XSen |
| | ***armeniaca*** | XSen |
| | ***atropurpurea*** BWJ 7922 | WCru |
| | ***bourgaei*** | XSen |
| | ***bovei*** subsp. ***maroccana*** | CBot IFro SEND WHal XLum XSen |
| | ***capitata*** | XSen |

**cashmeriana** CBcs CBot CFir CSam ECha EHoe EPfP LBMP LSou MMuc NLar SBfd SKHP SMad SPhx WCFE WWEG
**chrysophylla** ♀H3 CAbP CBot ECha ELan EPfP LRHS MAsh MRav NLar SBrd SDix SEND SPer WCFE XSen
**cretica** XSen
**crinita** EBee XSen
**cypria** XSen
'Edward Bowles' CDul ECha LRHS LSRN MRav NBid SKHP SLPl SWvt XSen
* 'Elliot's Variety' CPLG
**fruticosa** ♀H4 Widely available
– white-flowered ECrN
**grandiflora** CBot SEND XSen
**herba-venti** XSen
**italica** Widely available
– 'Pink Glory' CMac
**lanata** ♀H3-4 CAbP EBee ELan EPfP LRHS NLar SBrt SPer WCFE WKif XSen
– 'Pygmy' CHVG NPro XSen
'Le Sud' XSen
**leucophracta** SVen XSen
**longifolia** CBot EBee EPfP LHop LRHS LSou MNrw NLar SEND SKHP SPer SSvw WGrn XSen
– var. **bailanica** CSam EPfP LRHS SMrm
**lunariifolia** XSen
**lychnitis** XSen
**lycia** XSen
**macrophylla** SPhx
**monocephala** XSen
**nissolei** XSen
**platystegia** XSen
**purpurea** CAbP CArn CBot CPLG CSam EBee ELan EPfP LRHS MAsh MNrw NBir SBfd SEND WCot WGrn XSen
– **alba** CBot EPfP XSen
– subsp. **almeriensis** CCse CPom XSen
– subsp. **caballeroi** XSen
§ **russeliana** ♀H4 Widely available
– 'Mosaic' (v) MAvo WCAu WCot XSen
**samia** Boiss. see *P. russeliana*
**samia** L. CKno CSpe EBee LBMP LHop LRHS NBPC NBir NChi NGdn NLar SKHP WOut WPtf XSen
– 'Green Glory' WTin
**taurica** EPfP LRHS NBPC
**tuberosa** CArn CBcs CBot CFir CKno CPou EBee EPPr EPfP LEdu LRHS LSRN MMuc NGdn NLar SBfd SPet WFar WGwG WHoo WMnd WPtf XSen
– 'Amazone' EBee ECha EPfP LHop MLLN MRav NBid NCGa NDov NOrc NPnk NSti SMad SWal WCot WFar WMnd XSen
– 'Bronze Flamingo' CKno EBee ECGP EPfP ETod LAst LRHS LSou MAvo MNrw MRav NBPC NBid NOrc SKHP SMrm SPoG SPur WMnd WPer WWEG
**viscosa** misapplied see *P. russeliana*

## *Phlox* ✿ (*Polemoniaceae*)

**adsurgens** ♀H4 MAsh
– 'Mary Ellen' ITim
– 'Wagon Wheel' CMea CWCL ECho ECtt EPot EWes GGar ITim LRHS NHar NWCA SMrm SPlb SRms SRot WCFE WFar
**amplifolia** EBee NBre WFar
× **arendsii** 'Andrew' WCot
– 'Anja' WCot
– 'Babyface' LSou MSCN NGdn
– 'Dougal' WCot
– 'Dylan' WCot
– 'Early Star' EBee LSou
– 'Eyecatcher' NBro NGdn
– 'Gary' WCot
– 'Lilac Girl' NBre
– 'Lisbeth' WCot
– 'Luc's Lilac' CAby CPrp ECtt GBin LLHF LRHS MSpe NBro NEgg NGdn NSti SMrm SPhx SPoG STes WAul WWlt
§ – 'Miss Jill' (Spring Pearl Series) EPfP LRHS MSCN NBPC NHol SPet WCot WTin
§ – 'Miss Karen' (Spring Pearl Series) LRHS NBro
§ – 'Miss Margie' (Spring Pearl Series) LEdu NBir
§ – 'Miss Mary' (Spring Pearl Series) ECtt EPfP GMaP MDKP MSpe
§ – 'Miss Wilma' (Spring Pearl Series) EPfP GMaP LRHS
– 'Paul' WCot
– 'Ping Pong' NBPC NBre STes
– 'Pink Attraction' MNrw NBro NCGa
– 'Purple Star' EBee
– 'Roger' **new** WCot
– 'Rosa Star' NBre
**austromontana** EPot GKev ITim NWCA NWad
**bifida** CPBP ECho
– 'Alba' ECho LLHF WFar
– blue-flowered ECho SUsu
– 'Colvin's White' ECho XLum
– 'Frohnleiten' NHar WPer
– 'Minima Colvin' ECho ECtt EPot GKev
– 'Ralph Haywood' CMea CWCL ECtt EPot ITim
– 'Starbrite' WFar
– 'Starcleft' WHoo
– 'Thefi' EWes MNrw
'Black Buttes' GEdr
**borealis** see *P. sibirica* subsp. *borealis*
* – **arctica** EPot GLam
**caespitosa** CMea EWes
– subsp. **pulvinata** see *P. pulvinata*
– 'Zigeunerblut' CPBP EPot NHar
**canadensis** see *P. divaricata*
**carolina** subsp. **angusta** SUsu
– 'Bill Baker' ♀H4 Widely available
– 'Magnificence' EBee EWes GMac MDKP NLar SMad SPhx WCot WSHC
– 'Miss Lingard' ♀H4 CSam CWCL EBee ECtt LBMP LRHS LSou MCot MSpe NBid NBir NGdn NLar NSti SMrm WAul WCot WFar WRHF WWEG
'Casablanca' MAvo NDov
'Charles Ricardo' EWes GMac LRHS WHoo
'Chattahoochee' see *P. divaricata* subsp. *laphamii* 'Chattahoochee'
§ **condensata** WPat
Coral Flame (Flame Series) **new** LRHS LSou SRkn
**covillei** see *P. condensata*
'Daniel's Cushion' see *P. subulata* 'McDaniel's Cushion'
**diffusa** EPot WAbe
§ **divaricata** ♀H4 SPlb XLum
– 'Blue Dreams' CFir ECtt LRHS MNrw SUsu WFar WHal WWlt
– 'Blue Perfume' CPrp EBee ECtt LSou NBro NGdn NLar SMrm WFar

|  |  |
|---|---|
| - 'Clouds of Perfume' | CMMP CWCL EAEE ECtt GMaP LRHS LSRN LSou MSCN MSpe NDov NEgg NLar NPnk SMrm SPoG STes SWvt WFar WGwG WWEG |
| - 'Dirigo Ice' | ECho LHop LRHS NLar WFar WSHC |
| - 'Eco Texas Purple' | CPrp ECtt MSCN NCGa WFar WSHC WWlt |
| - 'Fuller's White' | CWCL ECtt LRHS |
| - subsp. ***laphamii*** | CBot EWes NWCA WFar |
| § - - 'Chattahoochee' ♀H4 | CBcs CBot CPrp CSpe CWCL ECho ECtt ELan EPfP EPot EWes GMac LHop LRHS MAsh MCot MWat NBPC NLar SMrm SPoG SRot SWvt WCFE WFar WHoo |
| § - 'Louisiana Purple' | WSHC |
| - 'May Breeze' | ECho GCra GMaP LHop LRHS MNrw MSCN NPnk SUsu WFar WSHC WWEG WWlt |
| - 'Plum Perfect' | ECtt LLHF WFar |
| * - 'White Perfume' | CMMP CPrp CWCL EBee EWes LRHS LSou MDKP NBro NCGa NLar SMrm SPet STes WFar WWEG |
| ***douglasii*** | NWCA SRms |
| - 'Alba' | GJos |
| - 'Apollo' | CTri ECho ECtt LLHF NHar NMen |
| - 'Boothman's Variety' ♀H4 | CPBP ECha ECho ECtt EDAr ELan EPfP EPot ITim MLHP MWat NMen SRms |
| - 'Crackerjack' ♀H4 | CMea CTri ECho ECtt EDAr ELan ELon EPfP EPot GAbr GJos GMaP ITim LRHS MAsh MHer MLHP NBir NEgg NMen NSla NWCA SPoG SRGP WAbe WFar |
| - 'Eva' | CMMP CPBP ECho ECtt EDAr EPot GMaP ITim LRHS LSRN MAsh MSCN NBir NLar NMen NPri NSla NWCA NWad SRGP WFar WNew |
| - 'Georg Arends' | ECtt GJos |
| - 'Ice Mountain' | CMea CYeo ECho ECtt ELan EPot GMaP NEgg NWCA NWad SPoG SRot WFar WNew |
| - 'Iceberg' ♀H4 | GJos NMen |
| - 'J.A. Hibberson' | EPot |
| - 'Lilac Cloud' | CYeo ECho ECtt EDAr GJos NPro |
| - Lilac Queen | see *P. douglasii* 'Lilakönigin' |
| - 'Lilac Wonder' | CPBP |
| § - 'Lilakönigin' | CTri |
| - 'Napoleon' | CPBP ECho ECtt EPot ITim LLHF NMen NWad |
| - 'Ochsenblut' | ECho EPot GLam LLHF LRHS MHer MLHP MSCN NHar NLar WAbe |
| - 'Red Admiral' ♀H4 | CYeo ECho ECtt EPfP EWes GKev GMaP MAsh MWat NLar WCFE WFar WRHF |
| - 'Rose Cushion' | ECho EDAr EWes MHer |
| - 'Rose Queen' | ECho |
| - 'Rosea' | CMea ECho EDAr ELan LRHS MAsh NMen WFar WNew |
| - 'Silver Rose' | ECho MWat NWCA |
| - 'Sprite' | SRms |
| - 'Tycoon' | see *P. subulata* 'Tamaongalei' |
| - 'Violet Queen' | ECho EWes WFar WPat |
| - 'Waterloo' | CMea ECho ECtt EPot ITim LRHS MAsh NMen |
| I - 'White Admiral' | CTri CYeo ECho ECtt EPot LSRN |
| - 'Zeigeurnerblut' | CMea WAbe |
| ***drummondii*** 'Classic Cassis' | LSou SPoG WHlf |
| 'Fancy Feelings' (Feelings Series) | NBro |
| ***glaberrima*** 'Morris Berd' | CDes EBee |
| ***idahoensis*** | SPhx |
| 'Kelly's Eye' ♀H4 | CMMP ECho ECtt EPot GEdr LRHS NBir NHar SPoG WFar |
| ***kelseyi*** | GLam NWCA WAbe WPat |
| - 'Lemhi Purple' | CPBP |
| - 'Rosette' | ECho MDKP WFar WPer |
| Light Pink Flame = 'Bareleven'PBR | ECtt EPfP LRHS SPoG WHil |
| Lilac Flame = 'Barten'PBR | EPfP SPoG WHil |
| ***longifolia*** subsp. ***brevifolia*** | CPBP |
| 'Louisiana' | see *P. divaricata* 'Louisiana Purple' |
| ***maculata*** | NOrc WPer |
| - 'Alpha' ♀H4 | CPrp CSam CWCL EBee ECha ECtt EPfP GCal GCra GGar GMaP LRHS MSpe NCGa NHol NLar NOrc SKHP SPer SWvt WAul WFar WSHC WWlt |
| - Avalanche | see *P. maculata* 'Schneelawine' |
| - 'Delta' | EBee EPPr EPfP LRHS NBPC NCGa NHol NLar SBfd SPer SRkn SWvt WFar |
| - 'Natascha' | Widely available |
| - 'Omega' ♀H4 | CAby CMac CPLG CPrp EAEE EBee ECtt GAbr GGar LHop LRHS MCot MNrw MSpe NBPC NGdn NHol NLar NPnk SBfd SKHP SMad SPer SPoG SWvt WAul WCAu WFar WSHC WWEG |
| - 'Princess Sturdza' ♀H4 | SDix WCot |
| - 'Reine du Jour' | CSam ELon GMac IVic LPla MDKP NDov SAga SMrm SPhx WSHC |
| - 'Rosalinde' | CPrp EBee ECtt ELon LRHS NHol NLar SBfd SRGP STes SWvt WCAu WFar WSHC WWEG |
| § - 'Schneelawine' | SPlb |
| 'Matineus' | SPhx |
| 'Millstream' | see *P.* × *procumbens* 'Millstream' |
| 'Millstream Blue' | EPfP |
| 'Millstream Jupiter' | ECho |
| 'Minnie Pearl' | EWes SKHP |
| ***nana*** 'Mary Maslin' | WAbe |
| ***nivalis*** 'Nivea' | EPot GJos |
| ***paniculata*** | ECha GCra NBid NDov SDix WCot WTin |
| - var. ***alba*** | SDix WCot WTin |
| - 'Alba Grandiflora' ♀H4 | GMaP MAvo MNrw WCot WHoo |
| - 'Alexandra' **new** | MSCN |
| - 'All in One' | ECtt LSou |
| - 'Amethyst' misapplied | see *P. paniculata* 'Lilac Time' |
| - 'Amethyst' Foerster | CFir CSam GQue LAst LRHS MWhi NBir NLar NOrc SPet SWat WCAu WFar |
| I - 'Aureovariegata Undulata' (v) | WCot |
| - 'Balmoral' | EBee ECtt EPfP GCra LRHS MLHP MRav MSpe MWat NEgg NSti SBfd SMrs SWat SWvt WWEG |
| - 'Barnwell' | SWat |
| - 'Becky Towe'PBR (v) | CWGN EBee ECtt ELon LHop LLHF LRHS LSou MNrw NEgg NLar WCot |
| - 'Betty Margarite' **new** | NDov |
| - 'Blauer Morgen' | IPot |
| - 'Blue Boy' | COlW EBee ECtt EPfP GKev GMaP LAst LRHS MDKP NBir NBro NEgg NLar SKHP SMrm SWvt WCot WFar WMnd |
| - 'Blue Evening' | CAby |
| - 'Blue Ice' ♀H4 | EBee ELan NBro |

| |  |  |
|---|---|---|
| | – 'Blue Paradise' | Widely available |
| | – 'Blushing Bride' | SRms |
| | – 'Border Gem' | CAby CBcs CMac EBee ECtt LRHS |
| | | MCot MRav MSpe MWat NChi |
| | | NDov NHol NLar NVic SDix SPur |
| | | SWat SWvt WBrk WHrl WSHC |
| | | WWEG |
| | – 'Branklyn' | GCra LRHS |
| | – 'Brigadier' ♈H4 | CPrp CTri EBee ECtt ELan GMaP |
| | | LRHS MCot MDKP MSpe MWat |
| | | NEgg NGdn NVic SBfd SMrm SPer |
| | | SRms WFar |
| | – 'Bright Eyes' ♈H4 | Widely available |
| | – 'Burgi' | SDix |
| | – 'Candy Floss' | ELon LLHF |
| | – 'Cardinal' | NDov |
| | – 'Caroline van den Berg' | SRms |
| | – 'Cecil Hanbury' | NLar SRms |
| | – 'Chintz' | SRms |
| | – 'Cinderella' | ECtt |
| | – 'Cool Best' | NDov |
| § | – 'Cool of the Evening' | WKif |
| | – 'Coral Queen' **new** | MSpe |
| | – 'Cosmopolitan' | LSou MAsh MNrw |
| | – Count Zeppelin | see *P. paniculata* 'Graf Zeppelin' |
| | – 'Crème de Menthe' (v) | CWGN |
| | – 'Danielle' | CSBt LSou WHil WHlf |
| | – 'Darwin's Choice' | see *P. paniculata* 'Norah Leigh' |
| | – 'David' | Widely available |
| | – 'Delilah'PBR | MAsh NPri |
| | – 'Discovery' | EBee EWes LRHS MCot MRav MSpe |
| | | NEgg SBfd SPur STes SWat |
| | – 'Doghouse Pink' | SDix |
| | – 'Dresden China' | MAvo SWat |
| § | – 'Düsterlohe' | CElw CSBt CSam ECtt GQue NBir |
| | | NDov NLar NSti SMrm SPer STes |
| | | SWat WCAu WCot WHil WHoo |
| | | XLum |
| | – 'Düsterlohe Zwerg' **new** | NDov |
| | – 'Eclaireur' misapplied | see *P. paniculata* 'Düsterlohe' |
| | – 'Eclaireur' Lemoine | SWat |
| | – 'Eden's Crush' | NBre NVic |
| | – 'Eden's Flash' | CElw ECtt LRHS MSpe NBre |
| | – 'Elisabeth' (v) | ECtt EPfP LSRN SRGP WHil |
| | – 'Elizabeth Arden' | ECtt MSpe NLar SWat |
| | – 'Elizabeth Campbell' | GCal |
| | – 'Empty Feelings' (Feelings Series) | NBro |
| | – 'Etoile de Paris' | see *P. paniculata* 'Toits de Paris' Symons-Jeune |
| | – 'Europa' | EBee ECtt ELan MCot NBir NGdn |
| | | NLar SPer WCAu WFar |
| | – 'Eva Cullum' | EBee ECtt EPfP GCra GMaP LHop |
| | | LRHS MArl MAvo MCot MSpe |
| | | NBPC NHol NLar SBfd SPer SPet |
| | | SWat WCot WWEG WWlt |
| | – 'Eventide' ♈H4 | CAby CMac CSam CWCL EBee |
| | | ECGP ECtt EPfP EWTr LRHS MArl |
| | | MCot MLLN MNrw MRav MSpe |
| | | MWat SBfd SPer SPet SWat WPtf |
| | – 'Excelsior' | MRav |
| | – 'Ferris Wheel' | LSou |
| | – 'Flamingo' | EBee ECtt EWTr LRHS NLar SWvt |
| | – 'Fondant Fancy'PBR | LSou NLar SPoG |
| | – 'Franz Schubert' | CAby CSam EBee ECtt EPfP |
| | | GCra LRHS MCot MLHP MRav |
| | | MSpe MWat NBir NGdn NLar |
| | | NSti SBfd SGar SPer SPhx STes |
| | | SWat SWvt WCot WFar WKif |
| | | WWEG WWlt |
| § | – 'Frau Alfred von Mauthner' | ECtt SMrm |
| | – 'Frosted Elegance' (v) | WWEG |
| | – 'Fujiyama' | see *P. paniculata* 'Mount Fuji' |
| | – 'Glamis' | MWat |
| | – 'Goldmine'PBR (v) | ELan LSou MCCP MNrw |
| § | – 'Graf Zeppelin' | ECtt ELan LRHS SRms SRot XLum |
| | – 'Grenadine Dream'PBR | LLHF LSou MBri NVic SPoG |
| | – 'Harlequin' (v) | CBcs CWGN EBee ECha ECtt ELon |
| | | GMaP LRHS NBPC NBid NBro NEgg |
| | | NLar NSti SPer SPoG WCot WFar |
| | | WWEG WWlt |
| | – 'Hesperis' | CCse EBee ECha ELon GBin GQue |
| | | NDov NLar SMrm SPhx WFar |
| | – 'Iris' | SMrm SRms WCot |
| | – 'Jade' **new** | CWGN ECGP ECtt ELon NDov NSti |
| | | WCot |
| | – 'Judy' | LSRN NBro |
| | – 'Jules Sandeau' | LRHS |
| § | – 'Juliglut' | CSpr SWat WCot |
| | – July Glow | see *P. paniculata* 'Juliglut' |
| | – 'Junior Bouquet' | ECtt NLar |
| | – 'Junior Dance' | ECtt NLar SRot |
| | – 'Junior Dream' | ECtt NLar SRot |
| | – 'Junior Fountain' | ECtt NLar |
| | – 'Katarina' | CElw ECtt NLar |
| | – 'Katherine' | CHar NLar |
| | – 'Kirchenfürst' | CElw IPot LRHS MSpe NBir SBfd |
| | | SMrm |
| | – 'Kirmesländler' | ECtt GBin NLar SWat |
| | – 'Lads Pink' | SDix |
| | – 'Lady Clare' | SRms |
| | – 'Landhochzeit' | GBin WFar |
| * | – 'Laura' | CMMP EBee ECtt EPfP IPot LRHS |
| | | NBPC NBro NCGa NPri NVic SMrm |
| | | SPet SRGP SRkn STes SWvt WBor |
| | | WFar WHoo WMnd WTin |
| § | – 'Lavendelwolke' | CSam GCal NBir NLar SWat |
| | – Lavender Cloud | see *P. paniculata* 'Lavendelwolke' |
| | – 'Le Mahdi' ♈H4 | ELan MRav SRms SWat |
| | – 'Lichtspel' | LPla NDov SAga SPhx |
| | – 'Lila Miniatur' **new** | NDov |
| § | – 'Lilac Time' | EBee ECtt EWTr LSRN MDKP |
| | | MMuc NLar SEND SWat SWvt |
| | | WWEG |
| | – 'Little Boy' | CElw ECtt MDKP MNrw NLar WFar |
| | – 'Little Laura' | CElw CWGN EBee ECtt LRHS LSRN |
| | | MCCP MSpe MWea NLar NOrc |
| | | NPri SPoG WCot |
| | – 'Little Princess' | ELon LLHF LRHS NLar SMrm SRGP |
| | | WMnd |
| | – 'Little Sara' | NDov |
| | – 'Lizzy'PBR | NLar |
| | – 'Logan Black' **new** | GCal |
| | – 'Magic Blue' **new** | LSou |
| | – 'Magical Dream' **new** | CWGN |
| | – 'Magical Favourite' **new** | CWGN |
| | – 'Manoir d'Hézèques' | WCot |
| | – 'Mary Christine' (v) | CDes NBid |
| | – 'Mary Fox' | CSam |
| | – 'Maud Stella Dagley' **new** | MSpe |
| | – 'Mia Ruys' | MArl MLHP |
| | – 'Midnight Feelings' (Feelings Series) | NBro NLar |
| | – 'Mies Copijn' | GMaP WFar |
| | – 'Milly van Hoboken' | WKif |
| | – 'Miss Elie' | LAst NBre NGdn WFar |
| | – 'Miss Holland' | LAst MWea NBPC NGdn SPet STes |
| | | WWEG |
| | – 'Miss Jessica' | LAst STes |

| |  |  |
|---|---|---|
| | - 'Miss Jill' | see *P.* × *arendsii* 'Miss Jill' |
| | - 'Miss Karen' | see *P.* × *arendsii* 'Miss Karen' |
| | - 'Miss Kelly' | CMMP LRHS LSou MSpe MWat MWea SRGP WHoo |
| | - 'Miss Margie' | see *P.* × *arendsii* 'Miss Margie' |
| | - 'Miss Mary' | see *P.* × *arendsii* 'Miss Mary' |
| | - 'Miss Pepper' | CWCL ECtt ELon LSou MMuc MSpe NGdn NLar SEND SMrm SRkn WBor WFar WHil |
| | - 'Miss Universe' | NBre WHil WWEG |
| | - 'Miss Wilma' | see *P.* × *arendsii* 'Miss Wilma' |
| | - 'Monica Lynden-Bell' | Widely available |
| | - 'Mother of Pearl' 🏆H4 | CAby EBee ECtt ELan GQue IPot LRHS MSpe MWat NEgg NVic SPer SUsu WFar WWEG |
| § | - 'Mount Fuji' 🏆H4 | Widely available |
| | - 'Mount Fujiyama' | see *P. paniculata* 'Mount Fuji' |
| | - 'Mrs A.E. Jeans' | SRms |
| | - 'Natural Feelings'[PBR] (Feelings Series) | ELan NBro NLar |
| | - 'Newbird' | ECtt MSpe SRms WWEG |
| | - 'Nicky' | see *P. paniculata* 'Düsterlohe' |
| § | - 'Norah Leigh' (v) | Widely available |
| | - 'Orange Perfection' | see *P. paniculata* 'Prince of Orange' |
| | - 'Othello' | CAby CSam EBee ECGP ECtt LRHS MSpe NSti SBfd SMrs SUsu WFar WMnd WWlt |
| | - 'Otley Choice' | EBee ECtt LRHS MRav MWat NLar NVic SWat |
| | - 'Otley Purple' | MHer |
| | - 'P.D. Williams' | WCot |
| | - 'Pastorale' | WCot |
| | - 'Peppermint Twist' | CWCL CWGN EBee ELon GKev LRHS LSou MAsh MBri MMuc MNrw MTis MWea NEgg NLar NPri SMad SPoG SPur SWvt WCot WHil |
| | - 'Picasso' | ECtt LSou |
| | - 'Pina Colada' | LSou MAsh MBri SPoG WHil |
| | - Pink Eye Flame = 'Barthirtyfive'[PBR] | EPfP LSou MTis SHar SKHP SPoG WHil |
| | - 'Pink Posie' (v) | WCot |
| | - Pink Red Eye Flame | EPfP LRHS LSou SPoG |
| | - 'Pinky Hill' | CElw CSBt LSou NPri |
| | - 'Pleasant Feelings'[PBR] (Feelings Series) | NBro |
| | - 'Popeye' | ECtt LPla NLar |
| | - 'Prime Minister' | ELon |
| § | - 'Prince of Orange' 🏆H4 | Widely available |
| | - 'Prospero' Foerster 🏆H4 | CHar CSam EBee LRHS MCot MSpe NBid SRkn SWat |
| | - Purple Eye Flame = 'Barthirtythree'[PBR] | LLHF LRHS LSou MTis SBfd SHar SKHP WHil |
| | - 'Purple Kiss' | LSou MBri WHil |
| | - 'Rainbow' | ELon |
| | - 'Rectory Pink' **new** | MSpe |
| | - 'Red Caribbean' **new** | LSou MAsh MBri |
| | - 'Red Feelings' (Feelings Series) | NBro |
| | - 'Red Flame' | CWGN ECtt EPfP LRHS LSou MTis SBfd SKHP SPoG WCot WHil |
| | - 'Red Riding Hood' | ECtt LAst LSou MSCN NBPC SPet SRkn |
| | - 'Reddish Hesperis' | NDov |
| | - 'Rembrandt' | CPLG LRHS LTen |
| | - 'Rijnstroom' | CBcs EBee ECha ECtt ELon LRHS MArl NLar SMrm SRot WBrk WFar |
| | - 'Robert Poore' | ELon GBin |
| | - 'Rosa Pastell' | CAby CEnd ELon IPot LPla LSou MTis SAga SMrm SPer SPoG SUsu WCot WWlt |
| | - 'Rowie' | NBid |
| | - 'Rubymine' (v) | LLHF |
| | - 'Sandringham' | EBee EPfP LRHS MArl MLHP MRav MSpe NBir NHol SBfd SPer SPoG SWvt |
| § | - 'Schneerausch' | LPla SPhx WCot |
| | - 'Septemberglut' | NLar |
| | - 'Sir Malcolm Campbell' | MAvo |
| | - 'Skylight' | EBee LRHS LSRN NBre NBro NVic SBfd SDix |
| | - 'Snow White' | NBre NVic |
| | - Snowdrift | see *P. paniculata* 'Schneerausch' |
| | - 'Speed Limit 45' | WCot |
| | - 'Spitfire' | see *P. paniculata* 'Frau Alfred von Mauthner' |
| | - 'Starburst' | EBee NBro |
| | - 'Starfire' 🏆H4 | Widely available |
| | - 'Starfire Purple' **new** | LRHS |
| | - 'Starlight' | NHar |
| | - 'Steeple Bumpstead' | LSou WCot |
| | - 'Sternhimmel' | LPla |
| | - 'Strawberry Daiquiri' | LSou MAsh SPoG |
| | - 'Sweet Melody' **new** | MAsh |
| | - 'Swizzle' | LSou MAsh MBri MLLN SPoG WBor WHil |
| | - 'Tenor' | CDes CFir CHar CMac CTri EBee ECtt ELon EPfP LAst LRHS MCot MDKP NHol NLar NPri SBfd SPet SPoG SWvt WFar WGwG WWEG |
| | - 'Tequila Sunrise' **new** | MAsh MBri |
| | - 'The King' | EBee ECtt LRHS MDKP NBro NLar SWat WHlf WSHC |
| | - 'Tiara' (d) | CWGN ECtt LSou MAsh MTis SPer SWvt WCot |
| | - 'Toits de Paris' misapplied | see *P. paniculata* 'Cool of the Evening' |
| | - 'Toits de Paris' ambig. | MAvo |
| § | - 'Toits de Paris' Symons-Jeune | WSHC |
| | - 'Uspekh' | CAby COlW CSam EBee ECtt EPPr EWes LRHS MCot MDKP MRav MSpe NBro NOrc SAga SBfd SMrs SPer SUsu WFar WGwG WWEG |
| | - 'Utopia' | CDes CSam ELon LPla NLar SMrm SPhx SUsu WCot |
| | - 'Van Gogh' | CCse |
| | - 'Velvet Flame' | LSou MWea SHar SKHP WHil |
| | - 'Violetta Gloriosa' | CAby ELon LPla SMrm |
| | - 'Watermelon Punch' | LSou MAsh MBri |
| | - 'Wendy House' | LEdu LLHF MNrw |
| | - 'Wenn Schon Denn Schon' | GBin |
| | - 'White Admiral' 🏆H4 | CAby CBcs CWCL EBee ECtt ELan ELon EPfP GAbr GCra GKev GMaP LHop LRHS LSqH MCot MHer MSpe MWat NEgg SBfd SPer SPhx SPoG SRms SWat SWvt WMnd WSHC WWEG |
| | - White Flame = 'Bartwentynine'[PBR] | ECtt EPPr EPfP LRHS LSou MTis SBfd SBrd SKHP WHil |
| | - 'Wilhelm Kesselring' | EBee ECtt ELon NBre WBor |
| | - 'Windsor' 🏆H4 | CBar EBee ECtt ELon EPfP GCal LRHS MSpe NDov NEgg NLar SBfd SCoo SPoG SRms SWvt WCAu WFar WWEG |
| | 'Petticoat' | CMea ECtt EPot MDKP NHar SBch WFar |
| | ***pilosa*** | EDAr NPro |
| | Pink Flame = 'Bartwelve'[PBR] | EPfP LLHF LRHS LSou SBfd SPoG |

| | | |
|---|---|---|
| | 'Pride of Rochester' | ECtt GJos LHop LRHS |
| § | × ***procumbens*** | ECtt |
| | 'Millstream' ♀$^{H4}$ | |
| | - 'Variegata' (v) | ECha ECho ECtt MDKP NBlu NWCA SPlb SRot SUsu |
| § | ***pulvinata*** | WAbe |
| | Purple Flame = 'Barfourteen'$^{PBR}$ | EPfP LRHS LSou SBla SHar SPoG |
| | × ***rugelii*** | EPot |
| | 'Sherbet Cocktail'$^{PBR}$ | CSpr CWGN EKen MWea NLar NMRc WCot WHil WPtf |
| § | ***sibirica*** subsp. ***borealis*** | EDAr WAbe |
| | 'Sileniflora' | EPot |
| | ***stolonifera*** | IFro MNrw |
| I | - 'Alba' | EBee EPfP |
| | - 'Ariane' | CWCL ECha EWld LSou MCot SBch WCFE |
| | - 'Blue Ridge' ♀$^{H4}$ | CPLG ECha ECtt EPPr EPfP LRHS LSRN MRav SRms |
| | - 'Bob's Motley' (v) | ECtt |
| | - 'Fran's Purple' | EWld MNrw NBro SBch WCFE |
| | - 'Home Fires' | EBee ECho ECtt EPfP LEdu LRHS NBro SMrm SPlb WFar XLum |
| | - 'Mary Belle Frey' | CEnt |
| | - 'Montrose Tricolor' (v) | NBre NBro |
| | - 'Pink Ridge' | NBir |
| | - 'Purpurea' | CWCL EBee EPfP LEdu LSou |
| | - 'Violet Vere' | LRHS |
| | ***subulata*** | ECho ECtt EDAr EPfP EPot GLam |
| | 'Alexander's Surprise' | LBee LRHS MAsh NBir NLar SPlb SRGP |
| | - 'Amazing Grace' | CTri CWCL CYeo ECho EDAr EPfP EPot EWes LAst LHop LRHS MAsh SPoG WAbe |
| | - 'Apple Blossom' | EDAr EPot SPet SPoG SRms WFar |
| | - 'Atropurpurea' | EDAr EPfP LIMB LRHS MAsh SPoG XLum |
| | - 'Bavaria' | LLHF |
| | - Beauty of Ronsdorf | see *P. subulata* 'Ronsdorfer Schöne' |
| | - 'Betty' | ECtt MAsh |
| | - 'Blue Eyes' | see *P. subulata* 'Oakington Blue Eyes' |
| | - 'Bonita' | CPBP ECho ECtt EPot GJos LRHS MAsh MMuc NLar SEND XLum |
| | - 'Bressingham Blue Eyes' | see *P. subulata* 'Oakington Blue Eyes' |
| | - 'Candy Stripe' | see *P. subulata* 'Tamaongalei' |
| | - 'Cavaldes White' | SPoG |
| | - 'Drumm' | see *P. subulata* 'Tamaongalei' |
| | - 'Emerald Cushion' | CTri CWCL ECho ECtt EDAr ELon GKev LRHS MDKP MWat NLar WCFE WHoo WNew |
| | - 'Emerald Cushion Blue' | CPLG CTri CYeo ECho EPfP GJos LAst LIMB LRHS MAsh NBir NMen NPnk NPri NPro SBch SPlb SPoG WAbe WFar WPer |
| | - 'Fairy' | WPer |
| | - 'Fort Hill' | NHar |
| | - 'G.F. Wilson' | see *P. subulata* 'Lilacina' |
| * | - 'Holly' | ECtt EPot ITim LLHF NHol NWad |
| | - 'Jupiter' | ECho |
| | - 'Kimono' | see *P. subulata* 'Tamaongalei' |
| § | - 'Lilacina' | CMea ECho ECtt MAsh MWat |
| § | - 'Maischnee' | CTri ECho ECtt MAsh MWat SPlb WFar |
| | - 'Marjorie' | CYeo ECho ECtt GJos LBee MAsh MHer NBir NWCA SPoG SRGP WFar WNew |
| | - May Snow | see *P. subulata* 'Maischnee' |
| § | - 'McDaniel's Cushion' ♀$^{H4}$ | Widely available |
| | - 'Mikado' | see *P. subulata* 'Tamaongalei' |
| | - 'Millstream Daphne' **new** | LRHS |
| | - 'Moonlight' | ECtt EDAr GJos |
| | - 'Nettleton Variation' (v) | CYeo ECho EDAr EPfP EPot EWes GKev LHop LRHS MAsh MDKP NBlu NLar SPlb SPoG |
| § | - 'Oakington Blue Eyes' | CTri LRHS MAsh SRms |
| | - 'Pink Pearl' | EWes |
| | - 'Purple Beauty' | CMea CWCL ECho EPot GGar GJos LIMB LLHF LRHS MSCN NHar NWad SPoG STes WCFE WFar WPer WSHC |
| | - 'Red Wings' ♀$^{H4}$ | ECho ECtt EPfP MAsh SRms |
| § | - 'Ronsdorfer Schöne' | EPot LBee LLHF MSCN NBir |
| | - 'Samson' | EDAr LSRN MAsh MMuc SEND |
| | - 'Sarah' | LLHF |
| | - 'Scarlet Flame' | CBar CMea ECho ECtt EDAr EPfP EPot MAsh NHol NPri SRGP WFar |
| | - 'Snow Queen' | see *P. subulata* 'Maischnee' |
| | - 'Snowflake' | MSCN |
| | - 'Starglow' | MAsh |
| § | - 'Tamaongalei' | CMea CTri CWCL CYeo EDAr ELon EPfP EPot EWes GEdr GGar GJos GMaP LAst LRHS MMuc MSCN NHol SEND SPet STes WCFE WHil WNew WPer XLum |
| | - 'Temiskaming' | CTri ECho ECtt EDAr EWes LBee LHop LRHS MLHP NMen SRms WAbe WSHC |
| | - 'Tschernobyl' | EPot |
| | - 'White Delight' | CBar CMea ECho ECtt EDAr EPfP GJos LAst LBee LRHS MAsh NBlu NMen SPet SPoG STes WFar WPer |
| | - 'Winifred' | NEgg |
| | 'Sweet William' | MSpe NEgg SRGP |
| | 'Swirly Burly' | GQue |
| | 'Tiny Bugles' | WPat |
| | Violet Flame = 'Barsixtyone' **new** | LRHS |
| | White Eye Flame = 'Barsixty' **new** | LRHS |
| | 'White Kimono' | LHop LRHS |
| | 'Zwergenteppich' | LLHF WPer |

## *Phoenicaulis* (*Brassicaceae*)

| | | |
|---|---|---|
| § | ***cheiranthoides*** | LLHF |

## *Phoenix* (*Arecaceae*)

| | | |
|---|---|---|
| | ***canariensis*** ♀$^{H1+3}$ | CBcs CPLG CTrC CWSG CWib EAmu EPfP IVic LPJP LPal LRHS MBri MCCP MMuc MREP SArc SBfd SBst SEND SLim SPlb SPoG STrG WFar |
| | ***dactylifera*** (F) | EAmu LPal SBig |
| | ***reclinata*** | EAmu NPal XBlo |
| | ***roebelenii*** ♀$^{H1+3}$ | CBrP CDTJ CDoC EGxp LPal LRHS MBri SBig |
| | - 'Multistem' | XBlo |
| | ***rupicola*** | EAmu LPal |
| | ***sylvestris*** | EAmu LPal |
| | ***theophrasti*** | CPHo EAmu LPJP LPal |

## *Phormium* ✿ (*Hemerocallidaceae*)

| | | |
|---|---|---|
| § | 'Alison Blackman'$^{PBR}$ | CAlb CBcs CChe CDoC CKno COIW CTrC EBee ESwi IVic LHop LRHS LSRN MBri MCCP MGos MREP MRav NPla SBfd SBrd SCoo SEND SPoG SRkn SWvt WCot |
| | 'Amazing Red' | CTrC ESwi SBfd |
| | 'Apricot Queen' (v) | CAbb CAlb CBcs CCCN CDoC CSBt CTrC CWib EBee EPfP ESwi GQui |

LRHS LSRN LTen MAsh MBri MGos MWat NEgg NLar SBfd SEND SLim SPer SPoG SRkn WFar WPat

'Back in Black' ELon MPnt SBfd SRkn WCot

'Black Edge' MRav

'Black Rage' **new** CBcs

Black Velvet = 'Seivel' NPla SBfd

'Bronze Baby' Widely available

'Buckland Ruby' CDoC

'Carousel' CTrC ESwi

'Chocolate Fingers' CBcs WCot

'Chocomint' **new** CTrC

***colensoi*** see *P. cookianum*

§ ***cookianum*** CHEx CTrC EPfP GGar GKev SArc WFar

- 'Black Adder'[PBR] CBcs ESwi LBuc LRHS LSRN MDev SBfd SPoG

- dwarf SLPl

- 'Flamingo' (v) CAlb CBcs CCCN CDTJ CSBt CTrC EBee ELan ELon EPfP ESwi LRHS LSou MBri MGos NLar SBfd SEND SLim SPer SPoG SRkn WCFE WPat

- subsp. ***hookeri*** 'Cream Delight' (v) ♀H3-4 Widely available

- - 'Tricolor' (v) ♀H3-4 Widely available

'Copper Beauty' WDyG

'Crimson Devil' CTrC MREP NPri SBfd

Dark Avocado = 'Westado'[PBR] **new** IBal

'Dark Delight' CBcs CDoC

'Dazzler' (v) CBcs CDoC LAst LSRN

'Duet' (v) ♀H3 CCCN CDoC CTrC CWib EBee EHoe ELon EPfP ESwi LHop LRHS NLar SEND SWvt

'Dusky Chief' CSBt CTrC EPfP ESwi LRHS

'Dusky Princess' ESwi LRHS

'Emerald Isle' CDoC

'Evening Glow' (v) CBcs CCCN CSBt CTrC EBee ELan EPfP ESwi ETod LRHS LSRN MAsh MBri MGos MREP SBfd SEND SPoG SRkn SWvt WCot WGrn WPat

'Firebird' ESwi LSRN SAga SWvt

'Glowing Embers' CBcs COlW CTrC EAmu ELon ESwi IVic

'Gold Ray' CBcs CTrC EBee ELon ESwi LRHS MBri MREP NLar NPri SBfd SCoo SWvt WCot WGrn

'Gold Sword' (v) CCCN CDoC CMHG CSBt CTrC EBee EPfP ESwi LRHS MAsh MDev NEgg SBfd

'Golden Alison'[PBR] see *P.* 'Alison Blackman'

'Green Sword' CCCN

'Jack Spratt' (v) CBcs ECou EHoe ELan MNHC SWvt

'Jester' (v) Widely available

'Limelight' SBfd SWvt

§ 'Maori Chief' CSBt ELan EPfP ESwi LRHS SWvt WFar WGrn WPat

§ 'Maori Maiden' (v) CAlb CBcs CCCN CChe CDoC CDul CTrC CTri EBee EHoe EPfP ESwi LAst MGos MREP MRav SRkn SWvt WFar

§ 'Maori Queen' (v) CBcs CCCN CChe CDTJ CDoC COlW CSBt CTrC EBee ELan EPfP ESwi LRHS MBri MGos MSwo NBid NPri SBfd SBrd SCoo SEND SLPl SPer SPoG SRkn SWvt WFar

§ 'Maori Sunrise' (v) CBcs CCCN CDoC CTrC EBee ELon EPfP ESwi IArd LAst LRHS LSRN MBrN MGos MRav NPla SBfd SCoo SLim SPer SWvt WFar

'Margaret Jones'[PBR] CCCN CKno CTrC EBee LSRN SLim

'Merlot'[PBR] EGxp NPri

'Moonraker' **new** CTrC

'Pink Panther' (v) Widely available

'Pink Stripe' (v) CBcs CDoC CMHG CSBt EAmu EBee EQua ESwi GGar LRHS MGos MLLN NPri SBfd SPoG SWvt WCot

'Platt's Black' Widely available

'Rainbow Chief' see *P.* 'Maori Chief'

'Rainbow Maiden' see *P.* 'Maori Maiden'

'Rainbow Queen' see *P.* 'Maori Queen'

'Rainbow Sunrise' see *P.* 'Maori Sunrise'

'Red Fingers' **new** CBcs

'Red Sensation' ELon EPfP LRHS

I 'Rubrum' CTrC ESwi LRHS

'Stormy Dawn' WCot

'Sundowner' (v) ♀H3 Widely available

'Sunset' (v) CBcs CCCN CSBt IFoB LAst SWvt WCot

'Surfer' (v) CBcs EHoe LHop MBri MCCP MLLN WGrn

'Surfer Boy' LAst LTen

'Surfer Bronze' CBcs CCCN CSBt EBee ETod LSou SBfd

'Surfer Green' CCCN ESwi SBfd

'Sussex Velvet' SCoo SLim

***tenax*** ♀H4 Widely available

- 'All Black'[PBR] LBuc LRHS MGos SCoo

- 'Atropurpureum' CEnt CHEx LAst SGol

- 'Bronze' SWvt

- 'Chocolate Dream' EPfP

- 'Co-ordination' CBcs CCCN EBee EPfP GGar SBfd

- 'Darkside' WCot

- 'Deep Purple' CHEx

- dwarf SLPl

I - 'Giganteum' CHEx

- 'Joker' **new** CTrC

* - ***lineatum*** MMuc SEND

- Purpureum Group ♀H3-4 Widely available

- Sweet Mist = 'Phos2' LBMP NOak

- 'Variegatum' (v) ♀H3-4 CDTJ CDoy CTrC EBee ELon EPfP ETod LPal LRHS MGos MMuc SArc SBfd SEND SEWo SPer SRms WFar

- 'Veitchianum' (v) CDoy SPer

'Thumbelina' CBcs CCCN ESwi IFoB MAsh WPat

'Tom Thumb' CBcs WDin

'Wings of Gold' ESwi ETod IBal

'Yellow Wave' (v) ♀H3 Widely available

## *Photinia* ✿ (*Rosaceae*)

***arbutifolia*** see *Heteromeles salicifolia*

***beauverdiana*** IRar WWau

- var. ***notabilis*** EPfP NLar

***davidiana*** CMac CTri ELan EPfP MRav NLar SPer SRms WDin WFar WWau

- 'Palette' (v) CBcs CDul CEnd CMac CWib EBee EHoe ELan EPfP LAst LHop LRHS MAsh MGos MMuc MSwo NEgg NPri SBfd SBrd SLim SMad SPer SPoG SRms SWvt WFar WHar WMoo

- var. ***undulata*** 'Fructu Luteo' CAbP CDul EPla GGal MMuc MRav NLar SEND WFar WWau

- - 'Prostrata' CMac CTri ELan EQua MRav NLar WFar WWau

× ***fraseri*** CMCN WWau

- 'Allyn Sprite'[PBR] NEgg SBfd

I - 'Atropurpurea Nana' MGos

- 'Birmingham' CMac EWes WDin

| | | |
|---|---|---|
| | - 'Canivily' | CEnd CTrC EMil EWes IVic LRHS NLar SBfd SGol SLim |
| * | - 'Ilexifolium' | ESwi |
| | - 'Little Red Robin' | CAlb CChe CSBt EGxp EHoe EShb IVic LBuc LRHS LSRN MAsh MCCP MWea NHol NLar NPal SAdn SBfd SGol SLim SLon SPad SPoG SWvt |
| | - Pink Marble = 'Cassini' (v) | CEnd LBuc SBfd SLon |
| | - 'Purple Peter' | CEnd |
| | - 'Red Robin' 🏆$^{H4}$ | Widely available |
| | - 'Red Select' | CAlb EQua LBuc NPri WPat |
| | - 'Robusta' | CMac CTrC EPfP LRHS SWvt |
| I | - 'Robusta Compacta' | CAlb MWea WFar |
| | ***glabra*** | SArc WWau |
| § | - 'Parfait' (v) | CAbP ELan LRHS MAsh SLon WFar WWau |
| | - 'Pink Lady' | see *P. glabra* 'Parfait' |
| | - 'Rubens' | ELan EPfP LRHS MAsh MRav SPer WWau |
| | - 'Variegata' | see *P. glabra* 'Parfait' |
| | ***integrifolia*** HWJ 946 **new** | WCru |
| | ***lasiogyna*** | CMCN |
| | ***lucida*** | WCru |
| | ***microphylla*** B&SWJ 11837 | WCru |
| | - HWJ 564 | WCru |
| | ***niitakayamensis*** | IGor |
| | ***parvifolia*** | EPfP |
| | 'Redstart' | CAbP CMac EBee EPfP LSou MGos NEgg NLar NPro SEND SLim SLon SPer SWvt WMoo |
| § | ***serratifolia*** | CAbP CBcs CBot CDul CHEx EPfP NLar SArc SBfd SEND SPer WFar WWau |
| I | - 'Compacta' | WFar |
| | - 'Jenny' | CDul CTrC IVic LRHS LSou NEgg NLar |
| | ***serrulata*** | see *P. serratifolia* |
| | - Curly Fantasy = 'Kolcurl'$^{PBR}$ | EMil IVic LBuc LRHS MGos MRav NLar SPoG WWau |
| | Super Hedge = 'Branpara'$^{PBR}$ | CTrC LRHS LSou WHar WWau |
| | 'Super Red' | CAlb CSBt MNHC NLar SLim |
| | ***villosa*** 🏆$^{H4}$ | CAbP CDul CGHE CTho GAuc WWau |
| | - B&SWJ 8665 | WCru |
| | - var. ***coreana*** B&SWJ 8789 **new** | WCru |
| | - var. ***laevis*** | CPLG EPfP WWau |
| | - - B&SWJ 8877 | WCru |
| | - f. ***maximowicziana*** | EPfP GAuc |
| * | - var. ***zollingeri*** B&SWJ 8903 | WCru |

## *Phragmites* (*Poaceae*)

| | | |
|---|---|---|
| | from Sichuan, China | EPPr |
| § | ***australis*** | CBen CRWN CWat LPBA MSKA NLar NMir SVic SWat WMAq WPnP XLum |
| | - subsp. ***australis*** var. ***striatopictus*** | EPPr |
| | - - 'Variegatus' (v) | CBen CKno CWCL CWat EBee EHoe EPPr EPla EShb LLWG LPBA LRHS MMuc MWhi NBir NLar NWsh SEND SMad WFar WWEG XLum |
| | - subsp. ***pseudodonax*** | EPPr MMoz |
| | ***communis*** | see *P. australis* |
| | ***karka*** | EPPr |
| | - 'Candy Stripe' (v) | CBen EPPr MSKA |

## *Phuopsis* (*Rubiaceae*)

| | | |
|---|---|---|
| § | ***stylosa*** | CHVG CSev CTri EBee ECha ELan ELon EPfP GAbr GMaP IFoB LRHS LSou MHer MLHP MMuc MSCN NBid NBir NBro NChi SPoG SRms WCAu WFar WMoo WPer XLum |
| | - 'Purpurea' | CElw MNrw MRav NChi NDov |

## *Phygelius* ✿ (*Scrophulariaceae*)

| | | |
|---|---|---|
| | ***aequalis*** | CFee CTca MRav WMoo |
| | - ***albus*** | see *P. aequalis* 'Yellow Trumpet' |
| | - 'Aureus' | see *P. aequalis* 'Yellow Trumpet' |
| | - Cedric Morris form | SHom |
| | - 'Cream Trumpet' | see *P. aequalis* 'Yellow Trumpet' |
| | - 'Indian Chief' | see *P.* × *rectus* 'African Queen' |
| | - 'Pink Trumpet' | SCoo SMrm SPet |
| | - 'Sani Pass' | CPrp ECtt ELon EPfP GMaP LSRN MHer MRav SCoo SEND SHom SPet SPlb SRms SWvt WCot |
| | - 'Trewidden Pink' 🏆$^{H4}$ | CWib EBee ELan ELon EPfP LAst LHop MHer MSCN NGdn SBfd SHom SLim SWvt WHoo WMnd WMoo WWEG XLum |
| § | - 'Yellow Trumpet' 🏆$^{H3-4}$ | CFee CSBt CTca CWib EBee ELan ELon EPfP EPla GMaP LSRN MAsh MCCP MLHP SBfd SEND SGar SHom SLim SPad SPer SPet SWal SWvt WFar WHoo WMnd WMoo WWEG XLum |
| | ***aequalis*** × ***capensis*** | see *P.* × *rectus* |
| | (Candy Drops Series) Candy Drops Cream = 'Kerphycrem'$^{PBR}$ **new** | LRHS |
| | - Candy Drops Purple = 'Kerphypur'$^{PBR}$ | MCCP SGar SVic |
| | - Candy Drops Salmon Orange = 'Kerphysalm'$^{PBR}$ | LRHS MCCP |
| | - Candy Drops Tangerine = 'Kerphytan' **new** | LRHS |
| | - Candy Drops Yellow | MCCP |
| § | ***capensis*** 🏆$^{H3-4}$ | CDoy CDul CHll CWib ELan EPfP GCra GGal MHer NLar SBch SGar SHom SPet SRms WFar WMnd |
| | - McB 2925 | GLam |
| | - ***coccineus*** | see *P. capensis* |
| | - orange-flowered | LHop SHom |
| | Cherry Ripe = 'Blacher'$^{PBR}$ | LSou |
| | 'Golden Gate' | see *P. aequalis* 'Yellow Trumpet' |
| | 'Midas Touch' | ELon MAsh NLar NPri |
| | New Sensation = 'Blaphy'$^{PBR}$ | ECtt EPfP LRHS MNrw SPoG SWvt |
| | 'Passionate'$^{PBR}$ **new** | MCCP NLar |
| § | × ***rectus*** | EPla |
| § | - 'African Queen' 🏆$^{H3-4}$ | CFee EBee ECtt ELan EPfP MLHP MRav MSwo NBir NGdn SEND SHom SMad SPlb SWvt WFar WKif WMnd WMoo WWEG |
| | - 'Aylesham's Pride' | SHom |
| | - 'Devil's Tears' 🏆$^{H4}$ | CBcs EBee ELan EPfP LAst LRHS NEgg NLar SBfd SEND SHom SLim SPad SWvt WMnd WMoo |
| | - 'Fantasia' **new** | SHom |
| | - 'Ivory Twist' | ELon LHop LRHS SHom |
| | - 'Jodie Southon' | LSou SHom SUsu WCot |
| * | - 'Logan's Pink' | LSRN |
| | - 'Moonraker' | CHll CTri EBee ECtt ELan EPfP LAst LHop LRHS MBri MHer MRav NEgg NGdn NLar SBfd SEND SHom SMrm SPlb SRms WFar WKif WMoo XLum |

- 'Pink Elf' ELan
- 'Raspberry Swirl' LRHS SHom
- 'Salmon Leap' ♀H4 CBcs CTri EBee ELan EPfP LAst LRHS LSRN MBNS MGos MRav NEgg NLar SBfd SEND SHom SLim SMrm SPlb SWal SWvt WFar WMnd WMoo WWEG
- Somerford Funfair Apricot = 'Yapapr' SWvt
- Somerford Funfair Coral = 'Yapcor'PBR CDoC EAEE EBee EPfP MBri NEgg NLar SLim SRkn SWvt WFar
- Somerford Funfair Cream = 'Yapcre'PBR CDoC EBee EPfP LBMP LRHS MNHC NEgg NLar NPri SGar SLim SMrm SRkn SWvt WFar
- Somerford Funfair Orange = 'Yapor'PBR EBee LBMP LRHS MBri NLar NPri SLim SPoG SWvt WFar
- Somerford Funfair Wine = 'Yapwin' EBee ELan EPfP EShb LRHS LSou MAsh MBNS MBri NEgg NLar NPri SBfd SLim SMrm SPoG SWvt WFar
- Somerford Funfair Yellow = 'Yapyel'PBR EBee LRHS SLim SPoG SWvt
- 'Sunshine' EBee ELan MDKP SHom SMrm WCot
- 'Sweet Dreams' LRHS SHom
§ - 'Winchester Fanfare' CSBt ECtt ELan EPfP GMaP LRHS MGos MRav NGdn NVic SEND SLim SMrm SPer SWvt WFar WKif WMoo WWEG
- 'Winton Fanfare' see *P.* × *rectus* 'Winchester Fanfare'

## *Phyla* (*Verbenaceae*)

***lanceolata*** LLWG
§ ***nodiflora*** CEls ECha NWCA WJek WPer
- 'Alba' MMuc SEND
§ - var. ***canescens*** WHal XLum

## × *Phylliopsis* (*Ericaceae*)

'Coppelia' ♀H4 GEdr NHar WAbe WPat
***hillieri*** 'Askival' WThu
- 'Pinocchio' NHar WPat WThu
'Hobgoblin' WAbe WThu
'Mermaid' ITim NHar WThu
'Sprite' WPat
'Sugar Plum' CCCN CWSG LRHS NHar NLar SWvt WThu
'Swanhilde' WAbe

## *Phyllitis* see *Asplenium*

## *Phyllocladus* (*Podocarpaceae*)

***alpinus*** CDoC ECou NHol NLar NWad

## *Phyllodoce* (*Ericaceae*)

***aleutica*** ECho NHar SRms WThu
***caerulea*** ♀H4 ECho
- ***japonica*** see *P. nipponica*
- 'Murray Lyon' NHar WThu
- 'W.M. Buchanan's Peach Seedling' NHar
***empetriformis*** ECho SRms WThu
§ ***nipponica*** ♀H4 GKev NHar NMen WThu

## *Phyllostachys* ✿ (*Poaceae*)

***angusta*** EPla MWht SBig WJun
***arcana*** EPla WJun
- 'Luteosulcata' CEnt EPla GBin MMoz MMuc MWht NLar NPal SEND WJun
§ ***atrovaginata*** EPla SGol WJun
***aurea*** ♀H4 Widely available
- 'Albovariegata' (v) CDTJ ENBC EPla LRHS WJun
- 'Flavescens Inversa' EPla MWht SEND WJun
- 'Holochrysa' CDTJ EPla MMuc MWht WJun WPGP
- 'Koi' CDTJ CEnt EPla LPal MMoz MWht NPal SBig SGol WJun WPGP
***aureocaulis*** see *P. aureosulcata* f. *aureocaulis*, *P. vivax* f. *aureocaulis*
***aureosulcata*** CWib ENBC EPfP EPla LEdu MMoz MWht WJun WMoo
- f. ***alata*** see *P. aureosulcata* f. *pekinensis*
- 'Argus' EPla
§ - f. ***aureocaulis*** ♀H4 Widely available
- 'Harbin' EPla
- 'Harbin Inversa' CDTJ EPla
- 'Lama Tempel' CDTJ EPla WPGP
§ - f. ***pekinensis*** EPla MMoz NLar SBig
- f. ***spectabilis*** ♀H4 Widely available
***bambusoides*** CDTJ EPla SBig SDix WJun
- 'Albovariegata' (v) EPla ETod
- 'Allgold' see *P. bambusoides* 'Holochrysa'
- 'Castilloni Inversa' EAmu EPla ETod EWes LEdu LPal MMoz MWht WJun
- 'Castillonii' CBcs CEnt EAmu ENBC EPla EWes LEdu LPal MMoz MMuc MWht NLar NPal SBig SDix SEND WJun WPGP
- 'Castillonis Inversa Variegata' (v) WJun
§ - 'Holochrysa' CDTJ CDoC CEnt EPla MMoz MMuc MWht NPal SEND WJun WPGP
- 'Katashibo' EPla
- 'Kawadana' (v) EPla WJun
- f. ***lacrima-deae*** CAgr CDTJ CTrC EPfP EPla GBin
- 'Marliacea' EPla SBig WJun
- 'Subvariegata' EPla
- 'Sulphurea' see *P. bambusoides* 'Holochrysa'
- 'Tanakae' CDTJ ENBC MMoz NLar SBig
- 'Violascens' EPla SBig
***bissetii*** Widely available
***circumpilis*** EPla
***congesta*** misapplied see *P. atrovaginata*
***decora*** EPla MMoz MMuc MWht NLar NPal SEND WDyG WJun
***dulcis*** CEnt EPfP EPla LPJP MWht SBig WDyG WJun
§ ***edulis*** CAgr CDTJ CTrC ELon EPla MMoz MWht SArc SBig WJun
- 'Bicolor' WJun
§ - 'Heterocycla' XBlo
- f. ***pubescens*** see *P. edulis*
***fimbriligula*** EPla WJun
***flexuosa*** CEnt EPla LRHS MWht SGol WJun
***glauca*** CDTJ EPla ETod MMoz MWht NLar NPal SBig WDyG
- f. ***yunzhu*** EPla MWht WJun
'Green Groove' **new** NHim
***heteroclada*** CAgr CDTJ CEnt WJun
- 'Solid Stem' misapplied see *P. purpurata* 'Straight Stem'
***heterocycla*** see *P. edulis* 'Heterocycla'
- f. ***pubescens*** see *P. edulis*
***humilis*** CDul CEnt ENBC EPla MCCP MGos MMoz MMuc MWhi MWht NLar NPal SBig SEND WJun
***incarnata*** WJun
***iridescens*** EPla ETod NLar SBig WJun
***kwangsiensis*** EPla
***lithophila*** EPla
***lofushanensis*** EPla
***mannii*** EPla MWht
***meyeri*** EPla

***nidularia*** EPla MMoz SBig WDyG WJun
- f. ***farcta*** EPla
***nigella*** EPla
***nigra*** ♀H4 Widely available
- 'Boryana' CDoC CEnt EAmu EPfP EPla MGos MMoz MMuc MWht SBig SEND SWvt WFar WJun WMoo WPGP
- 'Fulva' EPla
'Hale' EPla MWht
- f. ***henonis*** ♀H4 EAmu ENBC EPla LPal MMoz MMuc MREP MWht NLar SBig SEND SGol WDyG WJun WPGP
- 'Megurochiku' ENBC EPla MWht WJun
- f. ***nigra*** EPla
- f. ***punctata*** CDoC ENBC EPla MAvo MMuc MWht NGdn SEND WDyG WJun WMoo
- 'Tosaensis' EPla
- 'Wisley' EPla
***nuda*** EAmu EPla MMoz MMuc MWht NLar NPal SEND WJun
- f. ***localis*** EPla MWht
***parvifolia*** CEnt EPla MWht WJun
***platyglossa*** EPla
***praecox*** EPla ETod WJun
- f. ***notata*** EPla
- f. ***viridisulcata*** EAmu EPla WJun
***prominens*** EPla
***propinqua*** CDoC CDul EPla GBin MMoz MMuc MWht WJun
- 'Li Yu Gan' EPla
* ***pubescens*** 'Mazel' SPlb
§ ***purpurata*** 'Straight Stem' EPla MWht
***rubicunda*** EPla WJun
***rubromarginata*** CDTJ CEnt EPla MMuc MWht NLar WJun
'Shanghai 3' EAmu ETod
***stimulosa*** EPla MWht WJun
***sulphurea*** CDTJ
- 'Houzeau' EPla MMuc SEND
- 'Mitis' LMaj
- 'Robert Young' EPla
§ - f. ***sulphurea*** WJun
- 'Sulphurea' see *P. sulphurea* f. *sulphurea*
§ - f. ***viridis*** EPla SBig
***violascens*** CBcs CEnt EPla MMoz MWht SBig WJun
***virella*** EPla
***viridiglaucescens*** CDTJ EBee EPfP EPla ETod MBrN MMoz MMuc MWht NLar SBig SEND WJun
***viridis*** see *P. sulphurea* f. *viridis*
***vivax*** EPfP EPla GQui LEdu MMoz MWht NLar SBig SEND WJun
§ - f. ***aureocaulis*** ♀H4 Widely available
- - 'Huanwenzii' CDTJ CTrC EAmu ENBC EPla ETod MGos MMoz MWht NPla WJun
- 'Katrin' LEdu
* - 'Sulphurea' EPla XBlo

## × *Phyllothamnus* (*Ericaceae*)

***erectus*** WAbe WPat

## *Phymatosorus* (*Polypodiaceae*)

§ ***diversifolius*** CGHE WCot WPGP

## *Phymosia* (*Malvaceae*)

§ ***umbellata*** CBot MOWG

## *Phyodina* see *Callisia*

## *Physalis* (*Solanaceae*)

***alkekengi*** ♀H4 CTri NBir NLar SWvt WFar XLum
- var. ***franchetii*** CArn CDoy CMac CSBt EBee ECha ELan EPfP LAst LRHS MAvo MHer MWat NBPC NBir NBro NEgg NGdn NPri NVic SBfd SMad SPer SPoG SRms WFar WMnd WOld WPer
- - dwarf LRHS NLar
- - 'Gigantea' ECGP MNHC NGBl NLar SPlb
- - 'Gnome' see *P. alkekengi* var. *franchetii* 'Zwerg'
- - 'Variegata' (v) ECtt EPla EWes LEdu MMuc NPro SEND WOld
§ - - 'Zwerg' EWll LRHS
***angulata*** B&SWJ 7016 LLHF WCru
***campanula*** B&SWJ 10409 WCru
***edulis*** see *P. peruviana*
§ ***peruviana*** (F) CCCN SBfd SHDw SVic

## *Physocarpus* (*Rosaceae*)

'Burning Embers' **new** LBuc
***malvaceus*** EWes
***monogynus*** NLar
***opulifolius*** CDul MAsh
- 'Angel Gold' EPfP SBfd
- 'Center Glow' MGos
- Coppertina PBR see *P. opulifolius* Diable D'Or
- 'Dart's Gold' ♀H4 Widely available
§ - Diable D'Or = 'Mindia' PBR CAlb CDoC EMil EPfP LBuc LRHS MBlu MBri NEgg NPla SBfd SGol WMoo
- 'Diabolo' PBR ♀H4 Widely available
- Lady in Red = 'Tuilad' PBR CMac CSBt EBee EShb EWes LAst LHop LRHS LSqu MAsh MGos MPkF MWea NHol NLBP NLar SHar SKHP SLim SLon SPoG SPtl SRkn WMoo WPat
§ - 'Luteus' CBot CDoC CWib MRav SRms WDin WFar WMoo
- Summer Wine = 'Seward' PBR EPfP EWes
- 'Tilden Park' EBee SGol
***ribesifolius*** 'Aureus' see *P. opulifolius* 'Luteus'

## *Physochlaina* (*Solanaceae*)

***orientalis*** NLar SPhx

## *Physoplexis* (*Campanulaceae*)

§ ***comosa*** ♀H2-3 EPot NMen NSla WAbe

## *Physostegia* (*Lamiaceae*)

***angustifolia*** GQui NBre
I 'Aquatica' LLWG
§ ***virginiana*** CSBt CTri GMaP LHop LRHS MLLN SBfd SGar SPoG SRms SWat WBrk WCFE WFar WRHF XLum
- 'Alba' CBot COlW CSBt CTri EBee ELon GAbr GJos GMaP LEdu LRHS MLLN NBPC NChi NLar SMrm SPet SPlb WHrl XLum
§ - 'Crown of Snow' CFir CMMP EBee ECtt EPfP MHer MRav MSCN MWat NPri SBfd SHar SPoG SWal SWvt WFar WHil WPer
- 'Galadriel' EBee
- 'Grandiflora' CFir
- 'Miss Manners' CMac EAEE EBee ECGP ECtt LRHS MBri MCot NBre NCGa NGdn NLar SRGP SUsu

- 'Olympic Gold' (v) MDKP MRav
- 'Red Beauty' EBee MDKP NBPC
- 'Rose Crown' SPer
- 'Rose Queen' COlW CTri MWat NBre NChi NPri SBfd
- 'Rosea' CBot EBee EPfP GJos IFoB MDKP MMuc NBPC NBre NGdn SHar SPoG SWal SWvt WFar WHrl WPer WWEG
- Schneekrone see *P. virginiana* 'Crown of Snow'
- 'Snow Queen' see *P. virginiana* 'Summer Snow'
- var. ***speciosa*** WFar
§ - - 'Bouquet Rose' CPrp EBee ECGP ECha EPfP LEdu LRHS MCot MNFA MRav NBir NLar SPer SWvt WCAu WFar WGwG WMoo WWEG XLum
- - Rose Bouquet see *P. virginiana* var. *speciosa* 'Bouquet Rose'
- - 'Variegata' (v) CHar CMac COlW CSBt EBee ECha ECtt EHoe ELan ELon EPfP LHop MRav NBPC NBir NGdn NPnk SPer SRms SWat WBrk WCot WFar WHoo WMnd WSHC WWEG XLum
§ - 'Summer Snow' ♀H4 CBcs CPrp EBee ECha ELan EPfP LHop LRHS NHol NLar SPer SRms SWat WBrk WCot WFar WMnd
- 'Summer Spire' ELan LRHS NHol WFar
- 'Vivid' ♀H4 Widely available
- 'Wassenhove' SMrm

## *Phyteuma* (*Campanulaceae*)

***balbisii*** see *P. cordatum*
***comosum*** see *Physoplexis comosa*
§ ***cordatum*** EDif GJos
***hemisphaericum*** ECho
***humile*** EDAr LRHS WThu
***nigrum*** ECho LLHF NBid WBor WPGP
***orbiculare*** GEdr
***scheuchzeri*** CSpe EBee ECho EPfP EWld GEdr LRHS NSla NWCA SGar SMad SRms SRot WHoo WPGP XLum
***sieberi*** CPBP
***spicatum*** NBro

## *Phytolacca* (*Phytolaccaceae*)

***acinosa*** GKev GPoy NLar SWat WBox
- HWJ 647 WCru
§ ***americana*** CArn CSev ELan EPfP ESwi GKev GPoy MBNS MHer MNHC NLar SIde SRms SWat WAbb WBox WFar WJek WMnd WMoo WSFF XLum
- B&SWJ 1000 WCru
- B&SWJ 8817A WCru
- 'Silberstein' (v) CBct EBee ECtt ESwi MBNS NLar WCot WHer WHil WWlt
- 'Variegata' (v) MMHG NBir
***bogotensis*** WBox
***chilensis*** WBox
***clavigera*** see *P. polyandra*
***decandra*** see *P. americana*
***dioica*** CHEx CPLG LEdu
***esculenta*** LEdu LHop SEND
***icosandra*** B&SWJ 8988 WCru
- B&SWJ 9033 WCru
- Purpurascens Group B&SWJ 11251 WCru
***insularis*** WBox
***japonica*** B&SWJ 3005 NBid WCru
- B&SWJ 3522 WCru
'Laka Boom' LHop WHil
***octandra*** B&SWJ 9514 WCru
- B&SWJ 10151 WCru
§ ***polyandra*** NBid NBro SRms
***rivinoides*** B&SWJ 10264 WCru
***rugosa*** B&SWJ 10263 WCru

## *Picea* (*Pinaceae*)

§ ***abies*** CCVT CDul CLnd CMac CSBt CTri CWib EHul EPfP LAst LBuc MBri MGos MMuc NEgg NWea SCoo SEND SLim SPer SPoG WDin WEve WMou
- 'Acrocona' ECho EHul MBlu MBri MGos NLar WEve
- 'Archer' CKen
- 'Argenteospica' (v) NHol NPCo
- 'Aurea' MGos NPCo WEve
- 'Capitata' CKen NLar
- 'Clanbrassiliana' CKen ECho MGos NLar NWad SCoo WEve WFar
- Compacta Group LBee NPCo
I - 'Congesta' CKen
- 'Crippsii' CKen
I - 'Cruenta' CKen SLim
- 'Cupressina' CKen
- 'Diffusa' CKen NLar SCoo
- 'Dumpy' CKen MGos NLar NWad
- 'Ellwangeriana' NLar WEve
- 'Excelsa' see *P. abies*
- 'Fahndrich' CKen CMen
- 'Finedonensis' MGos NLar WEve
- 'Formanek' CDoC CKen CMen NLar
- 'Four Winds' CKen NLar
- 'Frohburg' CKen MGos NLar NPri
- 'Globosa Nana' LAst MGos
- 'Gold Drift' **new** NLar
- 'Gregoryana' CKen CMac
- 'Heartland Gem' CKen
- 'Himfa' NLar
- 'Horace Wilson' CKen CMen
- 'Humilis' CKen
- 'Hystrix' CMen NHol NLar NWad
- 'Inversa' CDul CKen IVic MBlu MGos NLar SLim WEve
- 'J.W. Daisy's White' see *P. glauca* 'J.W. Daisy's White'
- 'Jana' CKen
- 'Kral' CKen
- 'Little Gem' ♀H4 CDoC CKen CMen ECho EHul EPla GEdr LBee LRHS MAsh NHol NLar NWad NWea SCoo SLim SPer SPoG WEve WFar
- 'Marcel' CKen
- 'Maxwellii' EHul
- 'Mikulasovice' NLar
- 'Nana Compacta' CKen CMen ECho EHul LAst MAsh WFar
- 'Nidiformis' ♀H4 CDoC CKen CMac CMen CSBt CTri EHul LAst LRHS NHol NPCo NWea SCoo SGol SLim SPer SPoG SRms WDin WEve WFar
- 'Norrkoping' CKen
- 'Ohlendorffii' CKen ECho EHul MGos NLar SCoo
- 'Pachyphylla' CKen
- 'Pseudomaxwellii' NLar
- 'Pumila Nigra' ECho EHul LRHS MGos SLim
- 'Pusch' CKen CMen NLar SLim
- 'Pygmaea' CKen MGos NLar
- 'Reflexa' MAsh NPCo WEve
- 'Remontii' NWea
- 'Repens' MBlu

|  |  |
|---|---|
| - 'Rydal' | CBcs CDoC CDul CKen MAsh MBri MGos NHol NLar NWea SLim WEve |
| - 'Saint James' | CKen |
| - 'Saint Mary's Broom' | CMen |
| - 'Silberkugel' | NLar |
| - 'Sonnenberg' | NLar |
| - 'Starý Smolivec' | NLar |
| - 'Tompa' | LRHS MBri NLar SLim |
| - 'Vermont Gold' | CKen NLar |
| - Will's Dwarf | see *P. abies* 'Wills Zwerg' |
| § - 'Wills Zwerg' | SGol |
| ***ajanensis*** | GAuc |
| § ***alcoquiana*** var. ***alcoquiana*** | NWea SLim |
| - var. ***reflexa*** | MPkF |
| ***asperata*** | NWea |
| ***bicolor*** | see *P. alcoquiana* var. *alcoquiana* |
| ***breweriana*** ♀H4 | CCVT CDoC CDul CMac EHul EPfP GKin IDee LEdu MBlu MGos MMuc MRav NEgg NPCo NPri NWea SEND SLim SPoG SSta WCFE WDin WEve WFar WMou |
| - 'Emerald Midget' | NLar |
| - 'Kohout's Dwarf' | CKen |
| ***chihuahuana*** | SLim |
| ***engelmannii*** | CDul NWea |
| - 'Compact' | ECho |
| - subsp. ***engelmannii*** | CKen NPCo |
| - 'Jasper' | NLar |
| - 'Lace' | NLar |
| ***glauca*** | CDul NWea WEve |
| - Alberta Blue = 'Haal'PBR | CKen LRHS MAsh WEve WFar |
| - var. ***albertiana*** 'Alberta Globe' | CDoC CSBt ECho EHul EPla EPot GKin LBee LRHS MAsh MBri MGos NBlu NEgg NHol NWad SCoo SLim SPoG WEve WFar |
| - - 'Conica' | Widely available |
| - - 'Gnome' | CKen WEve |
| - - 'Laurin' | CKen EPla MGos NPCo NWad WEve |
| - - 'Tiny' | CKen NWad WEve WGor |
| - 'Arneson's Blue Variegated' (v) | CDoC CKen LRHS MAsh MBri SLim WFar WGor |
| - 'Biesenthaler Frühling' | NLar SLim |
| - 'Blue Planet' | CKen IVic NLar |
| - 'Coerulea' | NPCo |
| I - 'Coerulea Nana' | NLar |
| - 'Cy's Wonder' | CKen |
| - 'Echiniformis' ♀H4 | CKen GKin LBee MBri |
| - var. ***glauca*** | WEve |
| - 'Goldilocks' | CKen MBri |
| § - 'J.W. Daisy's White' | CBcs CDoC CKen ECho EHul EPfP EPla GKin LRHS MAsh MGos NEgg NHol NLar NWad SCoo SLim SPer SPoG WEve WFar WGor |
| - 'Jean Dilly' **new** | NLar |
| - 'Julian Potts Monstrosa' | NLar |
| - 'Lilliput' | CKen EHul MBri MGos NLar NWad WGor |
| § - 'Nana' | CKen |
| - 'Piccolo' | CBcs CKen LRHS MGos NHol NLar SLim WEve |
| - 'Pixie' | CKen WEve |
| - 'Rainbow's End' (v) | CKen ECho LRHS MGos NLar SLim WFar |
| - 'Sander's Blue' | CKen ECho EHul EPfP EPla GKin LBee LRHS MBri MGos SLim WEve WFar |
| - 'Zuckerhut' | GKin LRHS MBri |
| ***glehnii*** 'Sasanosei' | CKen |
| - 'Shimezusei' | CKen |
| ***jezoensis*** | CKen CMen MGos NWea |
| - 'Aurea' | SLim |
| - subsp. ***hondoensis*** | CMen |
| - 'Marianbad' | CKen |
| - 'Yatsabusa' | CKen CMen |
| ***koraiensis*** | CDul GAuc NWea |
| ***kosteri*** 'Glauca' | see *P. pungens* 'Koster' |
| ***koyamae*** 'Bedgebury Cascade' | SLim |
| ***likiangensis*** | CDul CMCN EPfP NWea |
| - var. ***balfouriana*** | see *P. likiangensis* var. *rubescens* |
| § - var. ***rubescens*** | LRHS MGos SLim |
| ***mariana*** | GGar NWea |
| - 'Aureovariegata' (v) | WFar |
| - 'Austria Broom' | CKen |
| - 'Bill Archer' **new** | NWad |
| - 'Fastigiata' | CKen |
| - 'Nana' ♀H4 | CDoC CKen CMac CMen ECho EHul EPfP EPot GEdr LRHS MAsh MMuc NHol NWad NWea SBrd SCoo SEND SLim SPoG WDin WEve WFar |
| I - 'Pygmaea' | CKen NWad |
| × ***mariorika*** 'Machala' | MBri MGos |
| ***morrisonicola*** | CKen |
| ***obovata*** | GAuc |
| - var. ***coerulea*** | GAuc NLar |
| ***omorika*** ♀H4 | CBcs CCVT CDul CMCN CTho MGos MMuc NWea SEND WCFE WDin WEve WFar |
| - 'de Ruytee' **new** | IVic |
| - 'Frohnleiten' | CKen |
| - 'Frondenberg' | CKen |
| - 'Karel' | CKen MBri NLar |
| - 'Minimax' | CKen |
| - 'Nana' ♀H4 | EHul LRHS MGos NPCo SCoo SLim SPoG WCFE WEve WFar |
| - 'Pendula' ♀H4 | CDoC LRHS MBlu NLar NPal SLim SSta WEve |
| - 'Pendula Bruns' | LRHS NLar SLim SPoG |
| - 'Peve Tijn' | LRHS NLar SPoG |
| - 'Pimoko' | CKen LRHS MBri MGos NLar NPCo SCoo SLim |
| - 'Pimpf' | IVic |
| - 'Pygmy' | CKen |
| - 'Schneverdingen' | CKen |
| - 'Tijn' | CKen SLim |
| - 'Treblitsch' | CKen NLar |
| ***orientalis*** ♀H4 | CDul NWea WThu |
| - 'Aurea' (v) ♀H4 | CMac EHul ELan EPla MBri MGos NHol NLar NPri SCoo SLim WDin |
| - 'Aureospicata' | CDoC CTho MAsh MBlu NLar NPCo NPal SCoo WEve |
| - 'Bergman's Gem' | CKen |
| - 'Early Gold' (v) | MBri WFar |
| - 'Golden Start' | LRHS MBri NLar SLim |
| - 'Jewel' | CKen |
| - 'Kenwith' | CKen |
| - 'Kosteri' **new** | MAsh |
| - 'Mount Vernon' | CKen |
| - Nana Group | GKin |
| - 'Professor Langner' | CKen MAsh SLim |
| - 'Skylands' | CKen ELan LRHS MAsh MBri MGos NHol NLar SLim SPoG WEve |
| - 'Tom Thumb' | CKen NLar SLim |
| - 'Wittboldt' | ECho MBri |
| ***pungens*** | WDin WEve |
| - 'Baby Blueeyes' | WFar |
| - 'Blaukissen' | CKen |

| | | |
|---|---|---|
| | – 'Blue Pearl' | NLar |
| | – 'Blue Trinket' | ECho |
| | – 'Edith' | CKen ECho LRHS NLar NPCo SLim SPer WFar |
| | – 'Egyptian Pyramid' **new** | ECho |
| | – 'Endtz' | ECho |
| | – 'Erich Frahm' | ECho LTen MAsh MBri MGos WFar |
| | – 'Fat Albert' | ECho LRHS MGos NEgg NLar NPCo NWea SLim WFar |
| | – 'Frieda' | LRHS SLim |
| | – Glauca Group | CDul CLnd CMac MMuc NWea SCoo SEND SPoG WDin WEve WFar WMou |
| | – – 'Glauca Procumbens' | CMen NLar NWea |
| § | – – 'Glauca Prostrata' | EHul SLim WEve |
| | – 'Glauca Globosa' | see *P. pungens* 'Globosa' |
| | – 'Globe' | CKen CMen |
| I | – 'Globosa' ♀H4 | CBcs CKen CSBt ECho EHul EPla LAst LRHS MAsh MBri MGos NPCo NPri NWea SCoo SLim SPer SPoG SRms WEve WFar |
| | – 'Gloria' | CKen SLim |
| | – 'Hoopsii' ♀H4 | CDoC CDul CSBt ECho EHul EPfP EPla GKin IVic LMaj LRHS MAsh MBri MGos NEgg NLar NPCo NPri NWea SLim SPoG SWvt WDin WEve WFar |
| | – 'Hoto' | EHul MGos |
| | – 'Hunnewelliana' | EPfP |
| | – 'Iseli Fastigiate' | ECho GKin LRHS MAsh MBri MGos NPCo SCoo SLim SPer SPoG WEve |
| | – 'Iseli Foxtail' | LAst NLar |
| § | – 'Koster' ♀H4 | CSBt ECho EHul EPfP LAst MGos NEgg NPri NWea SLim SPoG SRms WDin WEve WFar WMou |
| | – 'Koster Fastigiata' | NEgg |
| | – 'Lucky Strike' | CKen MBri MGos NLar |
| | – 'Maigold' (v) | CKen IVic NLar SLim |
| | – 'Moerheimii' | ECho EHul NLar WEve |
| | – 'Montgomery' | CKen ECho NLar WEve |
| | – 'Mrs Cesarini' | CKen NLar |
| | – 'Nimety' | CKen |
| | – 'Oldenburg' | NEgg NLar NPCo NWea SLim |
| | – 'Procumbens' | CKen |
| | – 'Prostrata' | see *P. pungens* 'Glauca Prostrata' |
| | – 'Prostrate Blue Mist' | WEve |
| | – 'Rovelli's Monument' | ECho NLar |
| | – 'Saint Mary's Broom' | CKen NLar NPCo |
| | – 'Schovenhorst' | ECho EHul WFar |
| | – 'Snowkiss' | NPCo WFar |
| | – 'Spek' | MGos |
| | – 'Thomsen' | ECho EHul |
| | – 'Thuem' | ECho EHul EPfP MGos NLar NPCo SPoG WFar |
| | – 'Waldbrunn' | CKen ECho WEve |
| | – 'Wendy' | CKen |
| | ***purpurea*** | WEve |
| | ***retroflexa*** | GAuc NWea |
| | ***rubens*** | NLar NWea WEve |
| | ***schrenkiana*** | CMCN |
| | ***sitchensis*** | CDul NWea |
| | – 'Papoose' | see *P. sitchensis* 'Tenas' |
| | – 'Pévé Wiesje' | NLar |
| | – 'Silberzwerg' | CKen LRHS NLar SLim SPoG |
| | – 'Strypemonde' | CKen |
| § | – 'Tenas' | CKen LRHS NLar SLim SPoG |
| | ***smithiana*** | CDul NLar NWea WEve |
| | – 'Sunray' | LRHS SLim |
| | ***wilsonii*** | CKen NLar |

## *Picrasma* (*Simaroubaceae*)

| | | |
|---|---|---|
| | ***ailanthoides*** | see *P. quassioides* |
| § | ***quassioides*** | EPfP MBri WPGP |

## *Picris* (*Asteraceae*)

| | | |
|---|---|---|
| | ***echioides*** | CArn WHer |

## *Picrorhiza* (*Plantaginaceae*)

| | | |
|---|---|---|
| | ***kurrooa*** | GPoy |

## *Pieris* (*Ericaceae*)

| | | |
|---|---|---|
| | 'Balls of Fire' | CMac |
| | 'Bert Chandler' | CMac GKin |
| | 'Firecrest' ♀H4 | CMHG MMuc NLar SEND SSpi |
| | 'Flaming Silver' (v) ♀H4 | Widely available |
| | 'Forest Flame' ♀H4 | Widely available |
| | ***formosa*** B&SWJ 2257 | WCru |
| | – var. ***forrestii*** | CDoC CWib GLin |
| | – – 'Charles Michael' | CPLG |
| | – – 'Jermyns' | CMac MRav |
| | – – 'Wakehurst' ♀H3 | CAbP CDul CMac CPLG CTri ELon EPfP GKin LRHS MAsh MGos MRav MSnd SPer SPoG SSpi WFar |
| | Havila = 'Mouwsvila' (v) | CMac MAsh MGos NHol NWad WFar |
| | ***japonica*** | CMac GGal MGos SArc SReu WDin |
| | – 'Astrid' | IVic |
| | – 'Bisbee Dwarf' | NHol |
| | – 'Blush' ♀H4 | MAsh MBri NHol |
| | – 'Bonfire' | CCCN CEnd ELan EQua GAbr IVic LRHS MBri MGos MMuc NEgg NLar SBfd SEND SLim SPoG |
| | – 'Brookside Miniature' | NHol |
| | – 'Carnaval' (v) | CCCN CDoC CEnd CMac CSBt CWib ELan ELon GAbr IVic LBuc LRHS LSRN MAsh MGos MMuc NLar NPCo SBfd SCoo SLim SPer SPoG SWvt WFar |
| | – 'Cavatine' ♀H4 | CMHG IVic |
| § | – 'Christmas Cheer' | CMac EQua LSRN LSou MAsh NLar WFar WMoo |
| | – 'Cupido' | CDoC IVic MAsh MGos NHol NLar SBfd SLim SPoG WFar |
| | – 'Debutante' ♀H4 | CBcs CWib ELan GKin IVic LRHS MAsh MBri MGos NHol NLar NPCo NPri SBfd SCoo SSpi SWvt WFar |
| | – 'Don' | see *P. japonica* 'Pygmaea' |
| | – 'Dorothy Wyckoff' | MAsh NHol |
| | – 'Flaming Star' | SWvt |
| | – 'Flamingo' | CMac GEdr MAsh NHol |
| | – 'Grayswood' ♀H4 | NHol WFar |
| I | – 'Katsura' | CBcs CDoC CMac CSBt CWSG ELan EPfP GKin IVic LAst LBuc LMil LRHS LSRN LSou LSqu MAsh MBlu MBri MGos NEgg NHol NLar SBfd SCoo SLim SPer SPoG SSpi SWvt |
| | – 'Little Heath' (v) ♀H4 | Widely available |
| | – 'Little Heath Green' ♀H4 | CChe CDoC CMac ELon GKin MAsh MGos MMuc NEgg NPCo SBfd SPer SPoG SWvt WFar WMoo |
| | – 'Minor' | NWad WThu |
| | – 'Mountain Fire' ♀H4 | Widely available |
| | – 'Passion' PBR | CEnd IVic MGos SBfd |
| | – 'Pink Delight' ♀H4 | CAbP CDoC LMil LRHS LSRN LSou MRav NEgg NMun SBfd SRms |
| | – 'Prelude' ♀H4 | CSBt CWSG GKev LRHS MAsh MSnd NLar NMen WAbe WFar |

| | |
|---|---|
| – 'Purity' 🏆H4 | CBcs CDoC CMHG CMac LRHS MGos NEgg SBfd SLim SReu SSta SWvt WDin WFar WGwG WHar |
| § – 'Pygmaea' | CMac GKev NWad SSta WThu |
| – 'Red Mill' | CEnd IVic MAsh SLim SPer SSpi WFar |
| – 'Rondo' | IVic |
| – 'Rosalinda' | LTen MAsh MGos NLar WFar |
| – 'Sarabande' 🏆H4 | GKin IVic MAsh MGos MMuc NLar |
| – 'Scarlett O'Hara' | CSBt |
| – Taiwanensis Group | GGar GKin LRHS MAsh MMuc NLar SBfd SRms WFar |
| – 'Temple Bells' | CSBt LTen MGos SBfd |
| – 'Valley Rose' | CGHE CSBt ELan ELon GKin IVic LLHF MAsh MGos NLar NMun SPoG SSpi WFar |
| – 'Valley Valentine' 🏆H4 | CBcs CDoC CDul CEnd CMac CSBt CWib EPfP GEdr IVic LRHS LSRN MAsh MBri MGos MMuc NBlu NPCo SBfd SCoo SEND SLim SPer SPoG SReu SSta SWvt WFar |
| – 'Variegata' misapplied | see *P. japonica* 'White Rim' |
| – 'Variegata' ambig. | NLar |
| – 'Variegata' (Carrière) Bean (v) | CMHG EPfP LRHS MGos MRav NBlu NHol SBfd SPoG WDin WFar WHar |
| – 'Wada's Pink' | see *P. japonica* 'Christmas Cheer' |
| – 'White Pearl' | CAbP CMac EPfP IVic MAsh MGos |
| § – 'White Rim' (v) 🏆H4 | CDul CMac MAsh NHol SPlb WFar |
| – 'William Buchanan' | NHol WThu |
| – var. ***yakushimensis*** | NLar |
| ***nana*** | WThu |
| 'Tilford' | CMac |

## *Pilea* (*Urticaceae*)

| | |
|---|---|
| § ***microphylla*** | EBak EShb |
| ***muscosa*** | see *P. microphylla* |
| ***peperomioides*** 🏆H1 | CSev |

## *Pileostegia* (*Hydrangeaceae*)

| | |
|---|---|
| ***viburnoides*** 🏆H4 | Widely available |
| – B&SWJ 3565 | WCru |
| – B&SWJ 3570 from Taiwan | WCru |
| – B&SWJ 7132 | WCru |

## *Pilosella* (*Asteraceae*)

| | |
|---|---|
| § ***aurantiaca*** | CArn CRWN ELan EWil LEdu MHer MNHC NBid NOrc NPri SGar SIde WCot WFar WHer WMoo WOut WSFF |
| § – subsp. ***carpathicola*** | GGar MMuc |
| § ***officinarum*** | NRya |

## *Pilularia* (*Marsileaceae*)

| | |
|---|---|
| ***globulifera*** | MSKA |

## *Pimelea* (*Thymelaeaceae*)

| | |
|---|---|
| ***coarctata*** | see *P. prostrata* |
| ***drupacea*** | IArd IDee |
| ***ferruginea*** | ECou WAbe |
| – 'Magenta Mist' | MOWG |
| ***filiformis*** | ECou |
| ***ligustrina*** | GGar |
| ***oreophila*** | WThu |
| § ***prostrata*** | CTrC CTri ECou EPot WPer WThu |
| – 'Misty Blue' | CTrC |
| – f. ***parvifolia*** | ECou |
| ***sericeovillosa*** | WThu |
| ***tomentosa*** | ECou LRHS |

## *Pimpinella* (*Apiaceae*)

| | |
|---|---|
| ***anisum*** | CArn SIde SVic |
| ***bicknellii*** | WPGP |
| ***major*** 'Rosea' | CDes CPLG CPom CSpe EBee EPPr GAbr GCal GMac LHop LRHS LSou MAvo MLLN NBPC NCGa NChi NDov NGdn NOrc SMrm SPer SUsu WCot WFar WHal WPGP |
| ***minima rosea*** | NDov |
| ***saxifraga*** | CHab NBre |

## pineapple see *Ananas comosus*

## pineapple guava see *Acca sellowiana*

## *Pinellia* (*Araceae*)

| | |
|---|---|
| ***cordata*** | CPom EBee LEdu MDKP NMen SChF WCot WCru |
| ***pedatisecta*** | CDes EBee GEdr MDKP MMoz SChF WCot WFar |
| ***pinnatisecta*** | see *P. tripartita* |
| ***ternata*** | EBee GEdr LEdu NLar NMen WFar WPnP |
| – B&SWJ 3532 | WCru |
| § ***tripartita*** | CFee CPLG EBee ECho EPPr MDKP WCot |
| – B&SWJ 1102 | WCru |
| – 'Dragon Tails' (v) | SKHP |
| – 'Purple Face' | WCru |

## *Pinguicula* (*Lentibulariaceae*)

| | |
|---|---|
| ***crassifolia*** | CHew |
| ***cyclosecta*** | CHew CSWC |
| ***debbertiana*** | SHmp |
| ***ehlersiae*** | EFEx |
| ***esseriana*** | EFEx |
| ***grandiflora*** | CSWC EECP EFEx NMen NRya |
| ***hemiepiphytica*** | CHew |
| ***heterophylla*** | CHew |
| ***jaumavensis*** | CHew |
| ***lauana*** | CHew SHmp |
| ***longifolia*** subsp. ***longifolia*** | EFEx |
| ***macrophylla*** | CHew |
| ***macrophylla*** × ***zecheri*** | SHmp |
| ***moranensis*** var. ***caudata*** | EFEx |
| – ***moreana*** | EFEx |
| – ***superba*** | EFEx |
| ***rotundiflora*** | CHew SHmp |
| ***vulgaris*** | EFEx WHer |
| 'Weser' | CSWC NChu |

## pinkcurrant see *Ribes rubrum* (P)

## *Pinus* ✿ (*Pinaceae*)

| | |
|---|---|
| ***albicaulis*** 'Flinck' | CKen |
| – 'Nana' | see *P. albicaulis* 'Noble's Dwarf' |
| – 'No. 3' | CKen |
| § – 'Noble's Dwarf' | CKen |
| ***aristata*** | CDul CLnd CMen EHul MAsh MGos NMun STre WDin WEve |
| – 'Cecilia' | CKen |
| – 'Kohout's Mini' | CKen |
| – 'Sherwood Compact' | CKen MAsh MBri NLar SLim |
| – 'So Tight' | CKen |
| ***armandii*** | CAgr CDoC CDul CMCN CTrC STre WPGP |
| – 'Gold Tip' | CKen |
| ***austriaca*** | see *P. nigra* subsp. *nigra* |

| | | |
|---|---|---|
| N | ***ayacahuite*** | CKen |
| | – var. ***veitchii*** **new** | WPGP |
| | ***balfouriana*** dwarf | CKen |
| | ***banksiana*** | CDul |
| | – 'Arctis' | NLar |
| | – 'Chippewa' | CKen |
| I | – 'Compacta' | CKen |
| | – 'H.J.Welch' | CKen |
| | – 'Manomet' | CKen |
| | – 'Neponset' | CKen |
| | – 'Schneverdingen' | CKen |
| | – 'Schoodic' | LRHS NLar SLim SPoG |
| | – 'Uncle Fogy' | MGos |
| | – 'Wisconsin' | CKen |
| | ***bhutanica*** **new** | WPGP |
| | ***brutia*** | IGor |
| | – var. ***eldarica*** | GAuc |
| | ***bungeana*** | CDoC CDul CLnd EPfP MBlu SLPl WEve |
| | – 'Diamant' | CKen |
| | – 'June's Broom' | CKen |
| | ***cembra*** | CAgr CDul CLnd NLar NWea STre WEve |
| | – 'Aurea' | see *P. cembra* 'Aureovariegata' |
| § | – 'Aureovariegata' (v) | ECho LRHS NPCo WEve |
| | – 'Barnhourie' | CKen |
| | – 'Blue Mound' | CKen |
| | – 'Chalet' | CKen |
| | – 'Compacta Glauca' | MBri |
| | – Glauca Group | WEve |
| * | – 'Griffithii' | WDin |
| | – 'Inverleith' | CKen |
| | – 'Jermyns' | CKen |
| | – 'King's Dwarf' | CKen |
| | – 'Ortler' | CKen NLar |
| | – 'Roughills' | CKen |
| | – 'Stricta' | CDoC CKen |
| | – witches' broom | CKen |
| | ***cembroides*** NJM 09.022A | WPGP |
| | ***contorta*** | CBcs CDoC CDul MGos NWea SPlb WDin WWau |
| | – 'Asher' | CKen |
| | – 'Chief Joseph' | CKen MAsh NLar |
| | – 'Frisian Gold' | CKen SLim |
| | – var. ***latifolia*** | CDul CLnd WDin |
| | – 'Spaan's Dwarf' | CKen LRHS MAsh MGos NLar SCoo SLim SPoG WEve |
| | – 'Taylor's Sunburst' | CKen MAsh |
| | ***coulteri*** ♀H4 | CDul CMCN SBig SBrd SKHP WWau |
| | ***densiflora*** | CDul CMCN CMac GAuc IGor STre |
| | – 'Alice Verkade' | CDoC CMen EHul LRHS MAsh MBri NLar SCoo SLim WEve WFar |
| | – 'Aurea' | LRHS MGos NLar SLim |
| | – 'Golden Ghost' | MAsh NLar SLim |
| | – 'Haybud' **new** | ECho |
| | – 'Jane Kluis' | CKen CMen ECho EHul EPla LRHS LTen NLar SCoo SLim WEve WFar |
| | – 'Jim Cross' | CKen |
| | – 'Low Glow' | CKen ECho LRHS NLar NPCo SLim |
| | – 'Oculus-draconis' (v) | LRHS MGos NEgg NLar SLim WEve WFar |
| | – 'Pendula' | CKen LRHS NEgg NLar SCoo SLim WEve WFar |
| | – 'Umbraculifera' | CMen GKin MAsh MGos NLar NPCo SSta WEve WFar |
| § | ***devoniana*** | LRHS SLim |
| | 'Edsal Wood' **new** | NLar |
| | ***edulis*** | CAgr GAuc |
| | – 'Juno' | CKen |
| | ***elliottii*** | SBig |

| | | |
|---|---|---|
| | – var. ***densa*** | CKen |
| | ***engelmanii*** 'Glauca' | WFar |
| | ***fenzeliana*** | CKen |
| | ***flexilis*** | CDul IGor NWea |
| | – 'Blackfoot' | NLar |
| | – 'Cesarini Blue' **new** | NLar |
| | – 'Firmament' | LRHS NLar SLim |
| | – 'Glenmore Dwarf' | CKen |
| | – 'Nana' | CKen |
| | – 'Piute' **new** | NLar |
| | – 'Tara Mae' | NLar |
| | – 'Tarryall' | CKen |
| | – 'Tinby Temple' | NLar |
| | – 'Vanderwolf's Pyramid' | CDoC MAsh MBri NLar |
| | – WB No 1 | CKen |
| | – WB No 2 | CKen |
| | ***funebris*** **new** | IGor |
| | ***gerardiana*** | CDul GAuc |
| | ***greggii*** | CDul |
| | – NJM 09.014 | WPGP |
| | ***griffithii*** | see *P. wallichiana* |
| | ***halepensis*** | CDul GAuc |
| § | ***hartwegii*** NJM 09.029 | WPGP |
| § | ***heldreichii*** ♀H4 | CDoC CDul GKin MGos NWea WFar |
| | – 'Aureospicata' | NLar WEve |
| | – 'Compact Gem' | CDoC CKen MBri MGos NLar SCoo SLim WEve |
| | – 'Dolce Dorme' | CKen NLar |
| | – 'Groen' | CKen |
| | – 'Kalous' | NLar |
| | – var. ***leucodermis*** | see *P. heldreichii* |
| | – – 'Irish Bell' | NLar |
| | – – 'Pirin 7' | NLar |
| | – 'Malink' | CKen IVic LRHS SLim |
| | – 'Ottocek' | CKen |
| | – 'Pygmy' | CKen WGor |
| | – 'Pyramid' | NLar |
| | – 'Satellit' | CKen EHul LRHS MAsh MGos NLar NPCo SCoo SLim WEve |
| | – 'Schmidtii' | see *P. heldreichii* 'Smidtii' |
| § | – 'Smidtii' ♀H4 | CDoC CKen CMen ECho LRHS MAsh MBri MGos NLar SLim WEve |
| | – 'Zwerg Schneverdingen' | CKen NLar NPCo |
| | × ***holfordiana*** | CDoC WPGP |
| | ***jeffreyi*** ♀H4 | CDul CMCN CTho GAuc NWea |
| | – 'Joppi' | CKen NLar SLim |
| | ***koraiensis*** | GAuc GKin LRHS MBlu |
| | – 'Bergman' | CKen |
| | – 'Dragon Eye' | CKen SLim |
| | – 'Jack Corbit' | CKen |
| | – 'Shibamichi' (v) | CKen |
| | – 'Silver Lining' | NPCo |
| | – 'Silveray' | NLar |
| | – 'Silvergrey' | CKen |
| | – 'Spring Grove' **new** | NLar |
| | – 'Winton' | CKen NLar |
| | ***leucodermis*** | see *P. heldreichii* |
| | ***magnifica*** | see *P. devoniana* |
| * | ***meyerei*** | GAuc |
| | ***monophylla*** 'Tioga Pass' | NLar |
| | ***montezumae*** misapplied | see *P. hartwegii* |
| | ***montezumae*** Lamb. | SArc |
| | – NJM 09.016 | WPGP |
| | – 'Sheffield Park' **new** | SLim |
| | ***monticola*** 'Pendula' | CKen |
| | – 'Pygmy' | see *P. monticola* 'Raraflora' |
| § | – 'Raraflora' | CKen |
| | – 'Skyline' | NLar WEve |
| | – 'Windsor Dwarf' | CKen |

| | | |
|---|---|---|
| | ***mugo*** | CArn CBcs CDul CMac CTri EHul MGos NWea SEND WBor WDin WEve WFar |
| | - 'Allgau' | CKen NLar |
| | - 'Amber Glow' | NLar |
| | - 'Benjamin' | CKen EPla MGos NLar |
| | - 'Bisley Green' | ECho NLar |
| | - 'Brownie' | CKen |
| | - 'Carsten' | CKen ECho MGos SCoo SLim WEve |
| | - 'Carsten's Wintergold' | CDoC EMil LRHS MAsh MBri NLar SPoG WEve |
| | - 'Chameleon' | NLar |
| | - 'Columbo' | NLar |
| | - 'Corley's Mat' | CKen LAst NHol NLar SLim WEve |
| | - 'Devon Gem' | NPCo |
| | - 'Dezember Gold' | LRHS NLar SLim |
| | - 'Flanders Belle' | LRHS SLim |
| | - 'Gnom' | CDul EHul GKin MAsh MBri MGos NEgg NLar NPCo SCoo WDin WEve WFar |
| | - 'Gold Star' | CMen EPla SLim |
| | - 'Golden Glow' | CKen ECho LRHS MBri NLar SCoo SLim |
| | - 'Heinis Triumph' | MBri |
| | - 'Hesse' | ECho SCoo |
| | - 'Hoersholm' | CKen |
| | - 'Hulk' | CKen |
| | - 'Humpy' | CKen CMen ECho LRHS MAsh MBri MGos NPCo SCoo SLim WCFE WEve WFar |
| | - 'Ironsides' | CKen |
| | - 'Jacobsen' | CKen NLar |
| | - 'Janovsky' | CKen |
| | - 'Kamila' | NLar |
| | - 'Kissen' | CKen MBri MGos NLar SLim WEve |
| | - 'Klosterkotter' | MGos NLar WFar |
| | - 'Kobold' | NEgg WFar |
| | - 'Krauskopf' | CKen |
| | - 'Laarheide' | ECho WEve |
| | - 'Laurin' | CKen |
| | - 'Little Lady' | NLar |
| | - 'Marand' | NLar |
| | - 'March' | CKen |
| | - 'Mini Mops' | CKen NLar WEve |
| | - 'Minikin' | CKen MBri |
| | - 'Mops' ♀H4 | CDul CMac CMen ECho EHul EPfP LRHS LTen MAsh MBlu MBri MGos NHol NPCo NWea SBfd SCoo SLim SPer SPoG SSta WDin WEve WFar |
| | - 'Mops Midget' | CMen MAsh MBri NPCo WEve |
| | - 'Mops Snezna' | NLar |
| | - var. ***mughus*** | see *P. mugo* subsp. *mugo* |
| § | - subsp. ***mugo*** | GAuc NWea SGol WCFE WFar |
| | - 'Mumpitz' | CKen |
| | - 'Northern Lights' | CKen |
| | - 'Ophir' | CBcs CDul CKen CMen EHul EPfP EPla LAst LRHS MAsh MBri MGos NLar SCoo SLim SPer SSta WDin WEve WFar |
| | - 'Pal Maleter' (v) | ECho LRHS NLar NPCo SCoo SLim SPoG |
| | - 'Paradekissen' | NPCo |
| | - 'Paul's Dwarf' | CKen |
| | - 'Picobello' | LRHS MAsh NLar SLim |
| | - 'Piggelmee' | CKen IVic NLar |
| | - Pumilio Group ♀H4 | CDoC CDul CLnd EHul MGos MMuc NWea SBfd STre WCFE WDin WFar WMoo |
| | - var. ***rostrata*** | see *P. mugo* subsp. *uncinata* |
| | - 'Rushmore' | CKen |
| | - 'Schweiser Tourist' **new** | ECho |
| | - 'Spaan' | CKen |
| | - 'Sunshine' (v) | CKen NLar |
| | - 'Suzi' | CKen |
| | - 'Trompenburg' | NPCo |
| | - 'Tuffet' | MGos NLar |
| | - 'Uelzen' | CKen NLar |
| § | - subsp. ***uncinata*** | GAuc LMaj NWea SLim WFar |
| | - - 'Grüne Welle' | CKen NLar SLim |
| | - - 'Paradekissen' | CKen NLar |
| | - 'Varella' | CKen IVic LRHS NLar SCoo SLim |
| | - 'White Tip' | CKen ECho |
| | - 'Winter Gold' | CKen ECho EHul EPfP EPla LAst MGos NLar NPCo NWea SSta WEve WFar |
| | - 'Winter Sun' | MAsh NLar |
| | - 'Winzig' | CKen |
| | - 'Zundert' | CKen ECho MGos NLar SPoG WEve |
| | - 'Zwergkugel' | CKen |
| | ***muricata*** ♀H4 | CDoC CDul CLnd MGos NWea |
| | ***nigra*** ♀H4 | CBcs CDul CLnd CMac CTri LMaj LRHS MGos SBfd SGol WDin WEve WMou |
| | - var. ***austriaca*** | see *P. nigra* subsp. *nigra* |
| | - 'Bambino' | CKen |
| | - 'Black Prince' | CKen LRHS MGos NLar NPCo SCoo SLim SPoG WEve WFar WGor |
| | - var. ***calabrica*** | see *P. nigra* subsp. *laricio* |
| | - var. ***caramanica*** | see *P. nigra* subsp. *pallasiana* |
| N | - 'Cebennensis Nana' | CKen |
| | - var. ***corsicana*** | see *P. nigra* subsp. *laricio* |
| * | - 'Fastigiata' | NPCo |
| | - 'Frank' | CKen LRHS NLar SLim |
| | - 'Green Tower' | NLar |
| | - 'Hornibrookiana' | CKen NLar |
| | - 'Komet' | IVic NLar SCoo SLim |
| § | - subsp. ***laricio*** ♀H4 | CCVT CDoC CDul CKen CMac LRHS MGos MMuc NWea SEND WWau |
| | - - 'Aurea' | MBlu |
| | - - 'Bobby McGregor' | CKen |
| | - - 'Globosa Viridis' | NEgg NPCo |
| | - - 'Goldfingers' | CKen NLar |
| | - - 'Moseri' | CKen |
| | - - 'Pygmaea' | CKen WFar |
| | - - 'Spingarn' | CKen |
| | - - 'Talland Bay' | CKen |
| | - - 'Wurstle' | CKen |
| | - subsp. ***maritima*** | see *P. nigra* subsp. *laricio* |
| | - 'Nana' | MBri NLar |
| § | - subsp. ***nigra*** | CCVT CDoC CLnd CTho LBuc MGos MMuc NLar NWea SBfd SEND SEWo SGol WFar WWau |
| | - - 'Birte' | CKen |
| | - - 'Bright Eyes' | NLar SCoo SLim SPoG WEve |
| | - - 'Helga' | CKen NLar |
| | - - 'Schovenhorst' | CKen |
| | - - 'Skyborn' | CKen |
| | - - 'Strypemonde' | CKen NPCo |
| | - - 'Yaffle Hill' | CKen NLar |
| | - 'Obelisk' | CKen NLar |
| § | - subsp. ***pallasiana*** | CDul |
| | - - 'Pyramidalis' | CDoC NLar |
| | - 'Pierrick Bregeon' PBR | LRHS |
| | - 'Richard' | CKen LRHS NLar |
| | - 'Rondello' | NLar |
| | - 'Spielberg' | NLar |
| | ***palustris*** | CDoC CDul CLnd SBig SKHP |
| | ***parviflora*** | CDul GGar SPlb WDin WThu |
| | - 'Aaba-jo' | CKen |

- 'Adcock's Dwarf' ♀H4 CDoC CKen LRHS MBri MGos NLar NPCo SCoo SLim SPoG WEve
- 'Al Fordham' CKen
- 'Aoi' CKen CMen
- 'Ara-kawa' CKen CMen
- 'Atco-goyo' CKen
- Azuma-goyo Group CKen CMen
I - 'Baasch's Form' CKen MGos NLar
- 'Bergman' CDoC MAsh NLar
- 'Blauer Engel' CDoC MBlu MGos NLar
- 'Blue Giant' EPla IArd LTen MBri NLar
- 'Blue Lou' NLar
- 'Bonnie Bergman' CDoC CKen NLar WEve
- 'Brevifolia' NLar
- 'Chikusa Goten' NLar
- 'Dai-ho' CKen
- 'Daisetsusan' CKen
- 'Doctor Landis Gold' CKen
- 'Dougal' CKen
- 'Fukai' (v) CKen MGos NLar
- 'Fukiju' CKen
- Fukushima-goyo Group CKen CMen
- 'Fuku-zu-mi' CKen IVic NLar WEve
- 'Fu-shiro' CKen
- 'Gimborn's Ideal' IVic NLar
- 'Gin-sho-chuba' CKen
- Glauca Group EHul MAsh MBlu MBri MGos NPCo SGol SKHP WEve WFar
I - 'Glauca Nana' CKen
- 'Goldilocks' CKen MAsh NLar
- 'Green Wave' CKen
- 'Gyok-ke-sen' CKen
- 'Gyo-ko-haku' CKen
- 'Gyokuei' CKen
- 'Gyokusen Sämling' CKen NLar
- 'Gyo-ku-sui' CKen CMen
- 'H2' CKen
- 'Hagaromo Seedling' CKen CMen NLar
- 'Hakko' CKen
- 'Hatchichi' CKen
- 'Hatsumari' NLar
- 'Ibo-can' CKen CMen
- 'Ichi-no-se' CKen
- 'Iri-fune' CKen
- Ishizuchi-goyo Group CKen
- 'Ka-ho' CKen
- 'Kanrico' CKen
- 'Kanzan' CKen
- 'Kin-po' NLar
- 'Kiyomatsu' CKen NLar
- 'Kobe' CKen NLar WEve
- 'Kokonoe' CKen CMen
- 'Kokuho' CKen NLar
- 'Koraku' CKen
- 'Kusu-dama' CKen
- 'Meiko' CKen CMen
- 'Michinoku' CKen
- 'Momo-yama' CKen
- 'Myo-jo' CKen
- Nasu-goyo Group CKen
- 'Negishi' CDoC CKen CMen LRHS MAsh MBri NLar SCoo SLim WEve
- 'Nellie D.' NLar
- 'Ogon-janome' CKen MAsh SLim
- 'Ossorio Dwarf' CKen
- var. ***pentaphylla*** IVic
- 'Regenhold' CKen
- 'Richard Lee' CKen
- 'Ryo-ku-ho' CKen
- 'Ryu-ju' CKen NLar
- 'Sa-dai-jin' CKen
- 'San-bo' CKen MGos
§ - 'Saphir' CKen
- 'Schoon's Bonsai' CDoC NLar
- 'Setsugekka' CKen NLar
- 'Shika-shima' CKen
- 'Shimada' CKen
- Shiobara-goyo Group CKen
- 'Shirobana' NLar
- 'Shizukagoten' CKen MBri
- 'Shu-re' CKen
- 'Sieryoden' CKen
- 'Smout' CKen
- 'Tani-mano-uki' CKen
- 'Tempelhof' LMaj NHol NLar NPCo
- 'Tenysu-kazu' CKen
- 'Tokyo Dwarf' CKen
- 'Tribune' NLar
- 'Walker's Dwarf' CKen
- 'Watnong' CKen
- 'Zelkova' CMen
- 'Zui-sho' CKen

***patula*** ♀H2-3 CBcs CCCN CDoC CDul CHll CLnd CMCN EPfP IDee LAst LRHS SArc SBfd SBig SBrd SCoo SLim SPlb STre WEve WPGP

***peuce*** GAuc GLin IGor NLar NWea STre
- 'Arnold Dwarf' CKen
- 'Cesarini' CKen
- 'Thessaloniki Broom' CKen

***pinaster*** ♀H4 CBcs CDoC CDul CLnd MMuc SEND
- subsp. ***escarena*** new WWau

***pinea*** ♀H4 CAgr CArn CCVT CDoC CDul CKen CLnd CTho ELau EPfP IVic LHop LMaj LRHS MGos MMuc NPri SArc SBfd SCoo SEND SEWo SGol SLim SPlb WEve WPGP
- 'Queensway' CKen

***ponderosa*** ♀H4 CDul CLnd GAuc NWea WEve
- var. ***scopulorum*** NWea

***pseudostrobus*** WPGP
- NJM 09.009A WPGP

***pumila*** 'Buchanan' CKen
- 'Draijer's Dwarf' LRHS SCoo SLim WEve
- 'Dwarf Blue' NLar
- 'Glauca' ♀H4 CDoC CKen MAsh NLar
- 'Globe' MAsh MBri NLar SLim
- 'Jeddeloh' CKen
- 'Knightshayes' CKen
- 'Pinocchio' CKen
- 'Säntis' CKen
- 'Saphir' see *P. parviflora* 'Saphir'

***radiata*** ♀H3-4 CBcs CCVT CDoC CDul CLnd CMac CTrC CTri ECrN ELan LRHS MMuc NWea SArc SBfd SBrd SCoo SEND STre WDin WEve WFar WWau
- Aurea Group CDoC CDul CKen ECho LRHS MAsh MGos NEgg NPCo SCoo SLim SPoG WEve WFar
- 'Bodnant' CKen
- 'Isca' CKen
- 'Marshwood' (v) CKen SLim

***resinosa*** 'Don Smith' CKen
- 'Joel's Broom' CKen
- 'Nana' NLar
- 'Quinobequin' CKen

***rigida*** CMac

***roxburghii*** WPGP

***sabineana*** GAuc

| |  |  |
|---|---|---|
| | × ***schwerinii*** | CDoC CKen MBri |
| | - 'Wiethorst' | CKen IArd IDee LRHS MBri NLar SLim SPoG |
| | ***sibirica*** 'Blue Smoke' | CKen |
| | - 'Mariko' | CKen |
| | ***strobiformis*** 'Coronado' | CKen |
| | - 'Loma Linda' | CKen |
| | ***strobus*** | CAlb CBcs CCVT CDul CLnd CMen MGos MMuc NWea SEND SLim WDin WEve WFar |
| § | - 'Alba' | SLim |
| | - 'Amelia's Dwarf' | CKen |
| | - 'Anna Fiele' | CKen MBri |
| | - 'Bergman's Mini' | CKen NLar |
| | - 'Bergman's Pendula Broom' | CKen |
| I | - 'Bergman's Sport of Prostrata' | CKen |
| | - 'Beth' | CKen |
| | - 'Bloomer's Dark Globe' | CKen |
| | - 'Blue Shag' | LRHS MGos NLar SCoo SLim SPer SPoG |
| | - 'Brevifolia' | CKen |
| | - 'Cesarini' | CKen |
| | - 'Compacta' | NPCo |
| | - 'Contorta' | CDoC |
| | - 'Densa' | CKen |
| | - 'Dove's Dwarf' | CKen |
| | - 'Ed's Broom' | CKen |
| | - 'Elkins Dwarf' | CKen NHol NLar |
| | - 'Fastigiata' | CKen MBri |
| | - 'Golden Showers' | NLar |
| | - 'Green Curls' | CKen |
| | - 'Green Twist' | MAsh NLar |
| | - 'Greg' | CKen |
| | - 'Hershey' | CKen |
| | - 'Hillside Gem' | CKen |
| | - 'Himmelblau' | IDee MBlu MBri NLar SLim |
| | - 'Horsford' | CDoC CKen LRHS NLar SLim |
| | - 'Jericho' | CKen NLar |
| | - 'Julian Pott' | CKen |
| | - 'Julian's Dwarf' | CKen |
| | - 'Krügers Lilliput' | LRHS NLar SLim |
| | - 'Louie' | CKen LRHS NLar SLim |
| | - 'Macopin' | NLar |
| | - 'Mary Butler' | CKen NLar |
| | - 'Merrimack' | CKen NLar |
| | - 'Minima' | CDoC CDul CKen LRHS MBlu MBri MGos NLar NPCo SCoo SLim SPoG WGor |
| | - 'Minuta' | CKen |
| | - 'Nana' | see *P. strobus* Nana Group |
| § | - Nana Group | MGos NPri WEve |
| | - 'Nana Compacta' | LRHS |
| | - 'Nivea' | see *P. strobus* 'Alba' |
| | - 'Northway Broom' | CKen LRHS SLim |
| | - 'Pendula' | CKen SMad |
| | - 'Pendula Broom' | CKen |
| | - 'Radiata' | CTri EHul LRHS NLar |
| I | - 'Radiata Aurea' | LRHS |
| | - 'Reinshaus' | CKen |
| | - 'Sayville' | CKen |
| | - 'Sea Urchin' | CKen LRHS SLim SPoG |
| | - 'Secrest' | NLar |
| | - 'Stowe Pillar' | NLar SLim |
| | - 'Tiny Kurls' | MAsh NLar SLim |
| I | - 'Tortuosa' | NLar |
| | - 'Torulosa' | MBlu SMad |
| | - 'Uncatena' | CKen |
| | - 'Verkade's Broom' | CKen |
| | - 'Wendy' | NLar |
| | ***sylvestris*** ♀H4 | Widely available |
| | - 'Abergeldie' | CKen |
| | - 'Alderly Edge' | CMen WEve WFar |
| | - 'Andorra' | CKen |
| § | - 'Argentea' | CMen SLim |
| | - 'Aurea' | see *P. sylvestris* Aurea Group |
| § | - Aurea Group ♀H4 | CDul CKen CMac CMen ECho EHul EMil LRHS MAsh MBlu MBri NEgg NHol NLar NPCo NPri NWea SCoo SLim SPer SPoG SSta WEve WFar |
| | - 'Avondene' | CKen |
| | - 'Bergfield' | CMen NLar |
| | - 'Beuvronensis' ♀H4 | CMen ECho MGos NEgg NLar NPCo SCoo SLim WEve |
| | - 'Blue Sky' | NLar SLim |
| | - 'Bonna' | LRHS SCoo SLim |
| | - 'Brevifolia' | MGos |
| | - 'Buchanan's Gold' | CKen |
| | - 'Burghfield' | CKen CMen WFar |
| | - 'Chantry Blue' | CMen ECho EHul LRHS MAsh MBri MGos NEgg NLar NPCo SCoo SLim WEve WFar |
| | - 'Clumber Blue' | CKen |
| | - 'Compressa' | SLim |
| | - 'Dereham' | CKen |
| | - 'Doone Valley' | CKen MGos NEgg NPCo WEve WFar |
| | - 'Edwin Hillier' | see *P. sylvestris* 'Argentea' |
| | - Fastigiata Group | CDoC CDul CEnd CKen CMac CMen IDee LRHS MGos NPCo SCoo SLim SPoG WCFE WEve WFar |
| | - 'Frensham' | CKen EPla MAsh MBri MGos NLar NPCo WEve WFar |
| | - 'Globosa' | NPCo |
| | - 'Gold Coin' | CDoC CDul CKen CMen EPfP LRHS MAsh MGos NEgg NHol NLar NPCo SCoo SLim SPoG WEve WFar |
| | - 'Gold Medal' | CKen SLim WEve WFar |
| | - 'Grand Rapids' | CKen |
| | - 'Gwydyr Castle' | CKen |
| | - 'Helsey Dwarf' | NLar |
| | - 'Hillside Creeper' | CKen LRHS NLar SCoo SLim SPoG WEve |
| | - 'Humble Pie' | CKen |
| | - 'Inverleith' (v) | EHul MGos SCoo SLim SPoG WEve WFar |
| | - 'Jeremy' | CKen ECho NEgg NHol NPCo SCoo SLim SPoG WEve |
| | - 'John Boy' | CMen NLar |
| | - 'Kelpie' | LRHS SCoo |
| | - 'Kenwith' | CKen |
| | - 'Kosice' | NLar |
| | - 'Lakeside Dwarf' | CMen |
| | - 'Lodge Hill' | CMen ECho LRHS MAsh NPCo SCoo SLim WEve |
| | - 'Longmoor' | CKen MGos NLar |
| | - 'Martham' | CKen CMen WEve |
| | - 'Mitsch Weeping' | CKen |
| * | - 'Moseri' | MAsh NPCo |
| | - 'Mount Vernon Blue' | NLar |
| | - 'Munches Blue' | CKen |
| | - 'Nana' misapplied | see *P. sylvestris* 'Watereri' |
| | - 'Nana Compacta' | CMen |
| § | - 'Nisbet's Gem' | CKen CMen |
| | - 'Padworth' | CMen MGos NLar |
| | - 'Peve Heiheks' | NLar |
| | - 'Peve Miba' | NLar |
| I | - 'Pine Glen' | CKen |
| | - 'Piskowitz' | CKen |

| | | |
|---|---|---|
| | – 'Pixie' | CKen MGos NLar |
| I | – 'Prostrata' | NPCo SCoo |
| | – 'Pygmaea' | SLim |
| | – 'Pyramidalis Compacta' | ECho |
| | – 'Repens' | CKen |
| | – 'Saint George' | CKen |
| | – 'Saxatilis' | CKen CMen WEve |
| | – subsp. ***scotica*** | GQue NWea |
| | – 'Scott's Dwarf' | see *P. sylvestris* 'Nisbet's Gem' |
| | – 'Scrubby' | NLar |
| | – 'Sentinel' | CKen SLim |
| | – 'Skjak I' | CKen NLar |
| | – 'Skjak II' | CKen LRHS SCoo |
| | – 'Skogbygdi' | NLar |
| | – 'Slimkin' | CKen |
| | – 'Spaan's Slow Column' | CKen LRHS SCoo SLim |
| | – 'Tage' | CKen |
| | – 'Tanya' | CKen |
| | – 'Tilhead' | CKen |
| | – 'Treasure' | CKen MBri |
| | – 'Trefrew Quarry' | CKen |
| | – 'Troll Guld' | NLar SLim |
| § | – 'Watereri' | EHul LAst LRHS LTen MBri MGos NHol NLar NPri SCoo SLim WDin WFar |
| | – 'Westonbirt' | CKen CMen EHul MAsh NLar WEve |
| | – 'Wolf Gold' | CKen |
| | – 'Xawrey 1' | NLar |
| | ***tabuliformis*** | CDul CMCN NMun STre |
| | ***taeda*** | CDul EPfP WPGP |
| | ***taiwanensis*** | CDoC CDul |
| | ***thunbergii*** | CDul CLnd CMCN CMen ELan GAuc MGos MMuc NWea SEND STre |
| | – 'Akame' | CKen CMen |
| | – 'Akame Yatsabusa' | CMen |
| | – 'Aocha-matsu' (v) | CKen CMen NLar |
| | – 'Arakawa-sho' | CKen CMen |
| | – 'Banshosho' | CKen CMen LRHS MGos NLar SLim WEve |
| | – 'Beni-kujaku' | CKen CMen |
| | – 'Compacta' | CKen CMen |
| | – var. ***corticosa*** 'Fuji' | CMen |
| | – – 'Iihara' | CMen |
| | – 'Dainagon' | CKen CMen |
| | – 'Eechee-nee' | CKen |
| | – 'Hayabusa' | CMen |
| | – 'Iwai' | CMen |
| | – 'Janome' | CMen |
| | – 'Katsuga' | CMen |
| | – 'Kotobuki' | CKen CMen NLar NPCo WEve WFar |
| | – 'Koyosho' | CMen |
| | – 'Kujaku' | CKen CMen |
| | – 'Kyokko' | CKen CMen |
| | – 'Kyushu' | CKen CMen |
| | – 'Maijima' | NLar |
| | – 'Mikawa' | CMen MBlu |
| | – 'Miyajuna' | CKen CMen |
| | – 'Nishiki-ne' | CKen CMen |
| | – 'Nishiki-tsusaka' | CMen |
| | – 'Oculus-draconis' (v) | CMen NPCo |
| | – 'Ōgon' | CKen CMen LRHS NLar SLim |
| | – 'Porky' | CKen CMen |
| § | – 'Sayonara' | CMen LRHS MAsh MBri NLar SCoo SLim SPoG |
| | – 'Senryu' | CKen CMen |
| | – 'Shinsho' | CKen CMen |
| | – 'Shio-guro' | CKen CMen |
| | – 'Suchiro' | NEgg NPCo |
| | – 'Suchiro Yatabusa' | CKen CMen |
| | – 'Sunsho' | CKen CMen |
| | – 'Taihei' | CKen CMen |
| I | – 'Thunderhead' | CDoC CKen CMen LRHS NLar SLim |
| | – 'W.B.' | CKen |
| | – 'Yatsubusa' | see *P. thunbergii* 'Sayonara' |
| | – 'Ye-i-kan' | CKen |
| | – 'Yoshimura' | CMen |
| | – 'Yumaki' | CKen CMen MGos |
| | ***torreyana*** | GAuc |
| | ***uncinata*** | see *P. mugo* subsp. *uncinata* |
| | – 'Etschtal' | CKen |
| | – 'Hexe' | NHol |
| | – 'Jezek' | CKen NLar SLim |
| | – 'Leuco-like' | CKen |
| | – 'Litomysl' | NLar |
| | – 'Offenpass' | CKen |
| | – 'Susse Perle' | CKen |
| | ***virginiana*** | GAuc |
| | – 'Wate's Golden' | CKen NLar |
| § | ***wallichiana*** ♀H4 | Widely available |
| | – 'Densa' | NLar SLim |
| | – 'Densa Hill' | LRHS |
| | – 'Frosty' | CKen |
| | – 'Nana' | CKen LRHS NLar SCoo SLim SPoG WEve |
| | – 'Umbraculifera' | MBri |
| | – 'Winter Light' new | NLar |
| | – 'Zebrina' (v) | MBlu MGos NLar |
| | ***yunnanensis*** | CDoC WBor |

## *Piper* (*Piperaceae*)

| | |
|---|---|
| ***auritum*** | GPoy |
| ***excelsum*** | see *Macropiper excelsum* |

## *Piptanthus* (*Papilionaceae*)

| | | |
|---|---|---|
| | ***forrestii*** | see *P. nepalensis* |
| | ***laburnifolius*** | see *P. nepalensis* |
| § | ***nepalensis*** | CBcs CBot CDul CSpe EBee ELan EMil EPau EPfP GGar LHop LRHS MGos MOWG MSCN NBid NLar SGar SMad SPer SPoG SRms |
| | ***tomentosus*** | MMHG WPGP |

## *Pistacia* (*Anacardiaceae*)

| | |
|---|---|
| ***chinensis*** | EBtc EPfP WPGP |
| ***lentiscus*** | CArn CBcs ERom SEND XSen |
| ***terebinthus*** | XSen |

## *Pistia* (*Araceae*)

| | |
|---|---|
| ***stratiotes*** | CBen LPBA MSKA NPer SCoo |

## *Pitavia* (*Rutaceae*)

| | |
|---|---|
| ***punctata*** new | IArd |

## *Pitcairnia* (*Bromeliaceae*)

| | |
|---|---|
| ***bergii*** | CHll |
| ***heterophylla*** | WCot |

## *Pittosporum* ✿ (*Pittosporaceae*)

| | | |
|---|---|---|
| | ***anomalum*** | CTrC ECou MOWG |
| | – (f) | ECou |
| | – (m) | ECou |
| | – 'Falcon' | ECou |
| | – 'Raven' (f) | ECou |
| | – 'Starling' (m) | ECou |
| * | ***argyrophyllum*** | LTen |
| | 'Arundel Green' | CDoC EJRN EPfP LRHS LSRN MAsh SBfd SLim SRms SWvt |
| | ***bicolor*** | CTsd GGal GQui WPGP |
| | ***buchananii*** | SGar SVen |

| | |
|---|---|
| ***colensoi*** | ECou |
| - 'Cobb' (f) | ECou |
| - 'Wanaka' (m) | ECou |
| 'Collaig Silver' | LRHS MAsh SBfd SPoG |
| ***crassifolium*** | CBcs CCCN CHEx CHGN CTrC CTsd ECou EWld LRHS |
| - 'Havering Dwarf' (f) | ECou |
| - 'Napier' (f) | ECou |
| - 'Variegatum' (v) | CCCN WPat |
| ***crassifolium* × *tenuifolium*** | see *P.* × *intermedium* |
| 'Crinkles' (f) | ECou |
| ***daphniphylloides*** | CHEx ELan |
| - B&SWJ 6789 | WCru |
| - RWJ 9913 | WCru |
| 'Dark Delight' (m) | ECou |
| 'Essex' (f/v) | ECou EJRN |
| ***eugenioides*** | CHEx CSam GGar |
| - 'Mini Green' | CAlb SBfd |
| - 'Platinum' (v) | CBcs CCCN LRHS |
| - 'Variegatum' (v) ♀H3 | CAlb CBty CCCN CChe CDoC CDul CHEx CMac CTrC EBee EHoe EJRN EPfP EWTr GGar GQui IArd LRHS MBri MGos NLar SBfd SEND SKHP SLim SPer SPoG SVen WGob WSHC |
| 'Garnettii' (v) ♀H3 | Widely available |
| ***heterophyllum*** | ECou ECrN ELan EWes SEND |
| - variegated (v) | EBtc ECou LRHS MAsh SEND SPoG |
| 'Holbrook' (v) | CSam |
| 'Humpty Dumpty' | ECou EJRN |
| ***illicioides* var. *angustifolium* B&SWJ 6771** | WCru |
| - - RWJ 9846 | WCru |
| - var. ***illicioides*** B&SWJ 6712 | WCru |
| × ***intermedium*** | CWib ECou SWvt |
| - 'Craxten' (f) | CCCN ECou EJRN LRHS |
| ***michiei*** | ECou |
| - (f) | ECou |
| - (m) | ECou |
| - 'Jack' (m) | ECou |
| - 'Jill' (f) | ECou |
| 'Nanum Variegatum' | see *P. tobira* 'Variegatum' |
| ***obcordatum*** | ECou |
| - var. ***kaitaiaense*** | ECou |
| ***oblongilimbum*** DJHV 06137 **new** | WCru |
| 'Oliver Twist' | LRHS LSRN SBfd SCoo SMad SPtl |
| ***omeiense*** | ECou EWes SKHP |
| 'Peter Pan' | EJRN |
| ***pimeleoides*** var. ***reflexum*** (m) | ECou |
| 'Purple Princess' | EJRN |
| ***ralphii*** | CCCN CTsd ECou |
| - 'Green Globe' | SKHP |
| - 'Variegatum' (v) | CCCN CGHE EPla LRHS SKHP SSpi WPGP |
| ***ralphii* × *tenuifolium*** | ECou |
| 'Saundersii' (v) | EQua SCoo |
| 'Tadina Gold' | SEND |
| ***tenuifolium*** ♀H3 | Widely available |
| - 'Abbotsbury Gold' (f/v) | CAbb CAlb CBty CCCN CDoC CDul CMac CTri EBee ECou EHoe ELan EPfP EWTr EWes LRHS MGos MREP MSwo SBfd SBrd SEND SGol SLim SPer SWvt WGob WSHC |
| - 'Atropurpureum' | ELan |
| - 'Brockhill Compact' **new** | LRHS |
| - 'County Park' | CCCN LRHS WFar |
| - 'County Park Dwarf' | CBty ECou EJRN EQua MAsh |
| - 'County Park Green' | ELon |
| - 'Deborah' (v) | ECou EJRN |
| - 'Dixie' | ECou |
| § - 'Eila Keightley' (v) | CMHG EJRN |
| - 'Elizabeth' (m/v) | CAbP CBcs CDoC CMac CTrC EBee ECou EHoe EJRN EPfP IArd LAst LRHS LSRN MAsh MBri MGos MREP NLar NMun SBfd SEND SLim SPoG WGob |
| - 'Emerald Star' **new** | STes |
| - 'French Lace' | CAlb CBcs CCCN EBee ECou EJRN ELan GBin LRHS NLar SBfd SEND WFar |
| - 'Gold Star' | CAlb CChe CDoC CWSG ECou EGxp EHoe ELan ELon EPfP LBMP LRHS MAsh MGos SBfd SCoo SLim SPer SPoG SWvt WFar WGob WMoo |
| - 'Golden Cut' | NLar |
| - 'Golden King' | CAlb CCCN CDoC CMHG CMac CSBt EJRN EPfP LRHS MAsh NEgg NPla SBfd SLim SRms |
| - 'Golden Princess' (f) | ECou EJRN |
| - 'Golf Ball' PBR | CBcs CDoC CTrC GBin LRHS |
| - 'Green Elf' | ECou EJRN |
| - 'Green Thumb' | CMac EBee ELan |
| - 'Irene Paterson' (m/v) ♀H3 | Widely available |
| - 'James Stirling' | CCCN ECou EPfP |
| - 'John Flanagan' | see *P. tenuifolium* 'Margaret Turnbull' |
| - 'Limelight' (v) | CBcs CSBt CSPN EBtc LHop LRHS LSRN MGos MREP NHol SLim SPoG |
| - 'Loxhill Gold' | CAbP CCCN CWSG IArd LRHS MGos NPla SEND SGol |
| § - 'Margaret Turnbull' (v) | CBcs CTrC ECou EJRN ELan EWes GKin LRHS LSRN MBri MGos SGol |
| - 'Marjory Channon' (v) | EBee ELan EPfP LRHS LSRN SPtl |
| - 'Mellow Yellow' | CAbP |
| - 'Moonlight' (v) | CAlb CBcs CTrC EBee EHoe LRHS WDin |
| - 'Mountain Green' | CMac SBfd |
| - 'Nutty's Leprechaun' | CCCN ELan |
| - 'Pompom' | CCCN IVic LRHS SRms |
| - 'Purpureum' (m) | CBty CCCN CDul CMac CSBt CSam CTri EBee EHoe EPfP GBin LAst LRHS LSRN MBri MREP NEgg NLar SBfd SBrd SCoo SEND SLim SPer SPoG SRms |
| - 'Silver Magic' (v) | CAlb CBcs CChe EBee EJRN EPfP LRHS MGos NLar SBfd WGob |
| - 'Silver Princess' (f) | ECou EJRN |
| - 'Silver Queen' (f/v) ♀H3 | Widely available |
| - 'Silver Sheen' (m) | CBcs EBee ECou LRHS SBfd |
| - 'Stevens Island' | CBcs CPMA CTrC LRHS MGos |
| - 'Stirling Gold' (f/v) | ECou EPfP EWes |
| - 'Sunburst' | see *P. tenuifolium* 'Eila Keightley' |
| - 'Tandara Gold' (v) | CAlb CBcs CBty CCCN CDoC CDul CSBt CTrC EBee ECou EHoe EJRN ELan ELon EPfP LBMP LRHS LSRN MAsh MGos SBfd SCoo SLim SPoG WCot WFar WGob |
| - 'Tiki' (m) | CBcs CCCN CTrC ECou LRHS |
| - 'Tom Thumb' ♀H3 | Widely available |
| - 'Tresederi' (f/m) | CCCN CTrC CTsd EBee ECou WFar |
| - 'Variegatum' (m/v) | CAlb CBar CBcs CDoC CSBt EBee ECou EQua LRHS LSRN MGos MSwo SLim SPer SPoG SWvt WGob |
| - 'Victoria' (v) | CBcs CCCN CDoC CTrC EBee LRHS LSRN MGos SLim SPoG WFar |

| | | |
|---|---|---|
| | - 'Warnham Gold' (m) ♀H3 | CBty CDoC CMac CWib EBee ECou EJRN ELan EPfP GKin IVic LRHS MAsh MGos SBfd SLim SPer SPoG SSpi WFar |
| | - 'Wendle Channon' (m/v) | CAlb CBty CCCN CMHG CMac CSBt EBee ECou EHoe EPfP EQua LRHS SGol SLim SPer WGob WSHC |
| | - 'Wrinkled Blue' | CBcs CTrC LRHS MAsh MRav SBfd SPoG |
| | ***tobira*** ♀H3 | Widely available |
| | - B&SWJ 4362 | LAst |
| * | - 'Cuneatum' | CCCN CDoC CPLG CWGN ELan EPfP LHop LRHS LSRN SKHP |
| * | - 'Nanum' | CAlb CBcs CCCN CDoC CMac EBee ELan EPfP ERom ETod LRHS LTen MGos MOWG SArc SBfd SLim SPer SPoG WDin WFar |
| § | - 'Variegatum' (v) ♀H2-3 | CAlb CBcs CBot CCCN CHll CMac CSam CWGN EBee ELan EPfP IVic LHop LRHS LSRN MGos NLar SAga SBfd SEND SKHP SLim SLon SPer SPoG SSta WSHC |
| | 'Trim's Hedger' **new** | CTho |
| | ***truncatum*** | EWes |
| | ***undulatum*** | CHEx |
| | ***viridiflorum*** | EShb |

## *Plagianthus* (*Malvaceae*)

| | | |
|---|---|---|
| | ***betulinus*** | see *P. regius* |
| | ***divaricatus*** | CBcs CTrC |
| | ***lyallii*** | see *Hoberia lyallii* |
| § | ***regius*** | CBcs SBig |

## *Plagiorhegma* see *Jeffersonia*

## *Planera* (*Ulmaceae*)

| | | |
|---|---|---|
| | ***aquatica*** | EGFP |

## *Plantago* (*Plantaginaceae*)

| | | |
|---|---|---|
| | ***asiatica*** 'Variegata' (v) | NBro |
| | ***coronopus*** | ELau |
| | ***lanceolata*** | CHab NMir WHfH WSFF |
| | - 'Golden Spears' | CBre EBee |
| | - 'Keer's Pride' (v) | WCot |
| | - 'Streaker' (v) | WCot |
| | ***major*** 'Atropurpurea' | see *P. major* 'Rubrifolia' |
| | - 'Bowles's Variety' | see *P. major* 'Rosularis' |
| | - 'Frills' | WBox |
| § | - 'Rosularis' | CArn CRow CSpe EBee ILis LEdu MHer NBro NChi NPri SPav WBox WHer |
| § | - 'Rubrifolia' | CArn CHid CRow CSpe EShb MBNS MHer NBid NBro NChi NDov NLBP WBox WHer WMoo |
| | ***maritima*** | WHer |
| | ***media*** | CHab MHer |
| | ***psyllium*** L. | CArn |
| | ***rosea*** | see *P. major* 'Rosularis' |
| | ***uniflora*** Hook. f. | WCot |

## *Platanthera* (*Orchidaceae*)

| | | |
|---|---|---|
| | ***chlorantha*** | NLAp |
| | ***hologlottis*** | EFEx |
| | ***metabifolia*** | EFEx LWst NLAp |

## *Platanus* ✿ (*Platanaceae*)

| | | |
|---|---|---|
| | × ***acerifolia*** | see *P.* × *hispanica* |
| § | × ***hispanica*** ♀H4 | CBcs CCVT CDul CLnd CMCN EBee ECrN EPfP EWTr LAst LBuc LMaj MGos MMuc NWea SEND SEWo SGol SPer WDin WFar WMou |
| | - 'Pyramidalis' | ECrN |
| | - 'Suttneri' (v) | WMou |
| | ***orientalis*** ♀H4 | CCVT CDul CLnd CMCN CTho EBee EPfP LEdu NLar SLPl WDin |
| | - 'Cuneata' | ECrN |
| § | - f. ***digitata*** ♀H4 | CDoC CDul CLnd CMCN CTho EBee EPfP MBlu WFar |
| | - var. ***insularis*** | WPGP |
| | - 'Laciniata' | see *P. orientalis* f. *digitata* |
| | - 'Minaret' | CDul |
| | - 'Mirkovec' | CDoC IArd MBri SMad SPer |
| | ***racemosa*** | EGFP |

## *Platycarya* (*Juglandaceae*)

| | | |
|---|---|---|
| | ***strobilacea*** | CBcs CMCN NLar |

## *Platycerium* (*Polypodiaceae*)

| | | |
|---|---|---|
| | ***alcicorne*** misapplied | see *P. bifurcatum* |
| § | ***bifurcatum*** ♀H1 | CCCN MBri WRic XBlo |
| | 'Lemoinei' | WRic |

## *Platycladus* (*Cupressaceae*)

| | | |
|---|---|---|
| § | ***orientalis*** 'Aurea Nana' ♀H4 | CDoC CKen CMac CSBt CWib ECho EHul EPfP LBee LRHS MAsh MGos NBlu NWea SGol SLim SPoG WDin WEve WFar |
| | - 'Autumn Glow' | CKen SCoo WGor |
| | - 'Beverleyensis' | NLar WEve |
| | - 'Caribbean Holiday' | MAsh |
| | - 'Collen's Gold' | EHul |
| | - 'Conspicua' | CKen CSBt CWib ECho EHul SPoG |
| | - 'Elegantissima' ♀H4 | EHul LRHS |
| | - 'Franky Boy' | CDoC ECho LAst LRHS MGos NHol NLar SLim SPoG |
| | - 'Golden Pygmy' | CKen MAsh |
| | - 'Juniperoides' | EHul |
| | - 'Kenwith' | CKen |
| | - 'Lemon 'n' Lime' | WEve |
| | - 'Magnifica' | EHul |
| | - 'Meldensis' | CDoC CTri EHul |
| | - 'Minima' | EHul WGor |
| | - 'Minima Glauca' | CKen |
| | - 'Morgan' | NLar WEve |
| | - 'Purple King' | SCoo |
| I | - 'Pyramidalis Aurea' | LBee SCoo WEve |
| | - 'Raffles' | WBor |
| | - 'Rosedalis' | CKen CSBt ECho EHul EPfP LBee LRHS MAsh SCoo |
| | - 'Sanderi' | WCFE |
| | - 'Shirley Chilcott' | MAsh |
| | - 'Sieboldii' | EHul |
| | - 'Southport' | LBee |
| | - 'Summer Cream' | CKen EHul |
| | - 'Westmont' (v) | CKen NLar |

## *Platycodon* ✿ (*Campanulaceae*)

| | | |
|---|---|---|
| | ***grandiflorus*** ♀H4 | CArn CTri EBee ECha ELau EPfP GKev LHop LRHS MHer NBlu SRms WHoo |
| | - 'Albus' | CBro CMac EBee EPfP LRHS SPer SWvt WHoo WPer |
| | - Apoyama Group ♀H4 | GKev NMen WHoo WPer |
| | - - 'Fairy Snow' | EBee ELan EShb LBMP NBre NPnk SMrm WHoo WSHC |
| | - (Astra Series) 'Astra Blue' | ELon EPfP SPoG SRot WHoo |
| | - - 'Astra Pink' | SPoG |
| | - - 'Astra White' | SPoG |
| | - 'Blaue Glocke' | NBre |
| | - 'Blue Pearl' | WHoo |

| | | |
|---|---|---|
| | - 'Blue Star'[PBR] | LRHS |
| | - 'Fuji Blue' | EBee ELon MAvo NLar SPad WHoo WWEG XLum |
| | - 'Fuji Pink' | CPrp EAEE ELan ELon EPfP LAst LHop LRHS MAvo MRav NLar SMrm SPad SWvt WHoo WWEG XLum |
| | - 'Fuji White' | ELan ELon NLar WWEG XLum |
| | - 'Hakone' | LAst MRav WHoo |
| | - 'Hakone Blue' | NBre NLar SMrm |
| * | - 'Hakone Double Blue' (d) | EAEE ELan MBNS SRms WCAu |
| | - 'Hakone White' | CPrp EBee EPfP LAst LRHS MRav NLar NMen WHoo |
| | - 'Mariesii' ♀H4 | CBro CDoy CMea CSBt EAEE EBee EPfP LRHS MNHC NBir NEgg NMen SEND SPer SPlb SRms SWvt WHoo WPer WSHC WWEG WWlt |
| | - Mother of Pearl | see *P. grandiflorus* 'Perlmutterschale' |
| | - 'Park's Double Blue' (d) | SAga |
| § | - 'Perlmutterschale' | CPrp EAEE EBee EPfP LBMP MRav WAul WHoo |
| | - 'Pink Star' | LRHS |
| | - ***pumilus*** | GKev NChi NWCA WHoo |
| | - ***roseus*** | GKev |
| | - 'Sentimental Blue' | CMac CWib NLar SPet XLum |
| | - 'Shell Pink' | see *P. grandiflorus* 'Perlmutterschale' |
| | - 'Willy' **new** | XLum |
| | - 'Zwerg' | EShb LBMP NBre |

## *Platycrater* (*Hydrangeaceae*)

| | | |
|---|---|---|
| | ***arguta*** | WCru |
| | - B&SWJ 6266 | WCru |

## *Plectocephalus* (*Asteraceae*)

| | | |
|---|---|---|
| | ***varians*** | GCal |

## *Plectranthus* (*Lamiaceae*)

| | | |
|---|---|---|
| | sp. | LAst |
| | from Puerto Rico | CArn |
| | ***ambiguus*** | EOHP |
| | - 'Manguzuku' | EOHP |
| | - 'Nico' | EOHP |
| | - 'Umigoye' | EOHP |
| | ***amboinicus*** | CArn EOHP WHil WJek |
| * | - 'Variegatus' (v) | EOHP |
| | - 'Well Sweep Wedgewood' (v) | EOHP |
| | ***argentatus*** ♀H2 | CDoC CPom CSev CSpe EOHP EShb IDee MCot SDix SEND SGar SRkn WKif WWlt |
| | - 'Hill House' (v) | CHll CPne EOHP |
| | ***australis*** misapplied | see *P. verticillatus* |
| | ***barbatus*** 'Vicki' | CPne |
| | ***behrii*** | see *P. fruticosus* |
| | Blue Angel = 'Edelblau' (Cape Angels Series) | EOHP |
| | ***caninus*** | SPoG |
| | ***ciliatus*** | CPne EOHP EShb SGar SRkn WWlt |
| | - 'All Gold' | CPne |
| | - 'Easy Gold' | CPne EOHP |
| | - 'Sasha' (v) | CCCN CDoC CHll ECtt EShb SPet |
| | 'Cloud Nine' | EOHP |
| | ***coleoides*** 'Marginatus' | see *P. forsteri* 'Marginatus' |
| | - 'Variegatus' | see *P. madagascariensis* 'Variegated Mintleaf' |
| | Cuban oregano | EOHP |
| | ***ecklonii*** | EOHP WDyG |
| | - 'Medley Wood' | EOHP |
| | ***ernstii*** | EOHP |
| | ***excisus*** | CDes WPGP |
| § | ***forsteri*** 'Marginatus' | EOHP |
| | 'Frills' | CPne EOHP |
| § | ***fruticosus*** | CPne EOHP |
| | - 'Behr's Pride' | EOHP |
| | - 'James' | EOHP |
| | ***hadiensis*** var. ***tomentosus*** 'Carnegie' | EOHP |
| | - - green-leaved | EOHP |
| | - - 'Penge' (v) | EOHP |
| I | - 'Variegata' (v) | CPne |
| | - var. ***woodii*** | EOHP |
| | ***madagascariensis*** | CPne EOHP |
| | - gold-leaved | EOHP |
| | - 'Lothlorien' (v) | EOHP |
| § | - 'Variegated Mintleaf' (v) ♀H1 | EOHP MNHC SPet SRms WJek |
| | 'Marble Ruffles' | EOHP EShb |
| | menthol-scented, large-leaved | EOHP |
| | - small-leaved | EOHP |
| | Mona Lavender = 'Plepalila'[PBR] | GFai |
| | ***mutabilis*** | EOHP |
| | ***neochilus*** | CSpe |
| § | ***oertendahlii*** ♀H1 | EBak EOHP |
| | - silver-leaved | EOHP |
| | ***ornatus*** | EOHP NPla SWal |
| | - 'Pee Off' | EOHP |
| | - variegated (v) | EOHP NPla |
| | ***prostratus*** | EOHP |
| | ***purpuratus*** large-leaved | EOHP |
| | - small-leaved | EOHP |
| | ***rehmannii*** | EOHP |
| | ***saccatus*** | EOHP WCot |
| | subsp. ***longitubus*** | |
| | - subsp. ***pondoensis*** | EOHP |
| | 'Silver Shield' | SBrd WHrl |
| | ***sinensis*** | LRHS |
| | ***spicatus*** | EOHP |
| | - 'Nelspruit' | EOHP |
| | ***strigosus*** | EOHP |
| | Swedish ivy | see *P. verticillatus*, *P. oertendahlii* |
| § | ***thyrsoideus*** | ECre EOHP |
| § | ***verticillatus*** | EOHP |
| | - 'Barberton' | EOHP |
| | - 'Pink Surprise' | EOHP |
| | Vick's plant | EOHP |
| | ***zatarhendii*** | EOHP |
| | ***zuluensis*** | CArn CCse CDoC CPne EOHP EShb SBch SBrd SRkn WBor |
| | - dark-leaved | EOHP |
| | - 'Sky' | EOHP |
| | - 'Symphony' | CFee |

## *Pleioblastus* (*Poaceae*)

| | | |
|---|---|---|
| § | ***argenteostriatus*** 'Okinadake' (v) | EPla |
| § | - f. ***pumilus*** | CDoC EHoe EPfP EPla MBlu MMuc MWht SPlb WFar WJun |
| | ***auricomus*** | see *P. viridistriatus* |
| | - 'Vagans' | see *Sasaella ramosa* |
| § | ***chino*** | EPla |
| | - f. ***angustifolius*** | see *P. chino* 'Murakamianus' |
| | - var. ***argenteostriatus*** | see *P. argenteostriatus* 'Okinadake' |
| | - f. ***aureostriatus*** (v) | EPla MMoz |
| | - f. ***elegantissimus*** | CDoC CEnt CFir EPfP EPla MGos MMoz MMuc NLar SBig SEND WJun WMoo WPnP |
| | - var. ***hisauchii*** | EPla MWht WJun |

| | | |
|---|---|---|
| | – 'Kimmei' | EPla MMuc |
| § | – 'Murakamianus' | GBin |
| | ***fortunei*** | see *P. variegatus* 'Fortunei' |
| | 'Gauntlettii' | see *P. argenteostriatus* f. *pumilus* |
| | ***glaber*** 'Albostriatus' | see *Sasaella masamuneana* 'Albostriata' |
| | ***gramineus*** | EPla IArd |
| § | ***hindsii*** | EPla GBin MMoz MMuc SEND |
| § | ***humilis*** | ENBC MWhi SEND |
| | – var. ***pumilus*** | see *P. argenteostriatus* f. *pumilus* |
| | ***kongosanensis*** 'Aureostriatus' (v) | EPla |
| | ***linearis*** | CAbb EAmu EPla LPal LRHS MMoz MWht NLar SBig WJun WMoo |
| | ***longifimbriatus*** | see *Sinobambusa intermedia* |
| | ***oleosus*** | EPla |
| § | ***pygmaeus*** | CBcs CDoC CDul CTri EHoe EHul ELan ENBC EPla GAbr LEdu MBrN MGos MMoz MMuc MWhi NBro NGdn NLar NWCA SGol SRms WFar WMoo |
| § | – 'Distichus' | CEnt EHul ENBC EPPr EPla MGos MMuc MWht NGdn NLar SEND WJun WMoo |
| § | – 'Mirrezuzume' | CPLG WFar |
| * | – var. ***pygmaeus*** 'Mini' | SEND |
| § | ***simonii*** | GBin LRHS MMuc MWht NLar SEND |
| | – 'Variegatus' (v) | EPla LRHS NGdn SPer WJun |
| § | ***variegatus*** (v) ♀H4 | CBcs CDoC CEnt EHoe EHul ELan ELon ENBC EPfP EPla LEdu LRHS MBrN MGos MWht NGdn SArc SBfd SDix SLim SPlb SWal SWvt WDin WFar WJun WMoo XBlo |
| § | – 'Fortunei' (v) | EPla MMuc SEND SGol |
| | – 'Tsuboii' (v) | CAbb CDTJ CDoC EPPr EPla GQui LPal MAvo MBrN MBri MMoz MWhi MWht NLar SGol WFar WJun WMoo WPnP |
| § | ***viridistriatus*** ♀H4 | Widely available |
| | – 'Chrysophyllus' | EPla |
| | – f. ***variegatus*** (v) | SAga SWvt WMoo |
| | ***yixingensis*** | EPla |

# *Pleione* ✿ (*Orchidaceae*)

| | | |
|---|---|---|
| | sp. | NDav |
| | **Adams gx** | LYaf |
| | ***albiflora*** | CFwr |
| | **Alishan gx** 'Merlin' | LYaf |
| | – 'Mother's Day' | LYaf |
| | – 'Mount Fuji' | LYaf |
| | **Asama gx** 'Red Grouse' | GEdr LYaf |
| | **Askia gx** | GEdr LYaf |
| | ***aurita*** | CFwr EPot GEdr LYaf |
| | **Bandai-san gx** | LYaf |
| | – 'Sand Grouse' | LYaf |
| | × ***barbarae*** | EPot LYaf |
| | **Barcena gx** | EPot LYaf |
| | **Berapi gx** 'Purple Sandpiper' | EPot LYaf |
| | **Betty Arnold gx** | LYaf |
| | **Brigadoon gx** | EPot LYaf |
| | – 'Stonechat' | EPot LYaf |
| | **Britannia gx** 'Doreen' | EPot LYaf |
| § | ***bulbocodioides*** | EPot GEdr LYaf |
| | – 'New Forest' | GEdr |
| § | – 'Yunnan' | EPot GEdr |
| | **Burnsall gx** | GEdr |
| | **Captain Hook gx** | LYaf |
| | ***chunii*** | EFEx GEdr LAma LYaf |
| | **Danan gx** | LYaf |
| | **Deriba gx** | EPot LYaf |
| | **Eastfield gx** 'Purple Emperor' | LYaf |
| | **Eiger gx** | LYaf |
| | – cream-flowered | LYaf |
| | **El Pico gx** 'Goldcrest' | EPot |
| | – 'Kestrel' | EPot |
| | – 'Pheasant' | EPot LYaf |
| | **Erebus gx** 'Brambling' **new** | EPot |
| | – 'Redpoll' | GEdr LYaf |
| | **Etna gx** 'Bullfinch' | EPot |
| | ***formosana*** ♀H2 | CFir CPne ECho EFEx EPot GEdr GGar LAma LEdu WFar WPGP |
| | – Alba Group | CFwr ECho WFar |
| | – – 'Claire' | GEdr LEdu LYaf |
| | – – 'Snow Bunting' | LEdu LYaf |
| | – 'Blush of Dawn' | GLin LYaf |
| | – 'Greenhill' | LYaf |
| | – 'Pitlochry' | LYaf |
| | – (Pricei Group) 'Oriental Grace' | LYaf |
| | – – 'Oriental Splendour' | GEdr LYaf |
| | – 'Snow White' | LEdu LYaf WPGP |
| | ***forrestii*** | CFwr ECho EFEx EPot LAma |
| | **Fuego gx** | EPot |
| | **Ganymede gx** | LYaf |
| | **Gerry Mundey gx** | GEdr |
| | – 'Tinney's Firs' | LYaf |
| § | ***grandiflora*** | CFwr GEdr LYaf |
| | **Harlequin gx** 'Norman' | LYaf |
| | **Hekla gx** 'Locking Stumps' | GEdr |
| | – 'Partridge' | LYaf |
| | – 'Partridge' × **Zeus Weinstein gx** **new** | GEdr |
| | ***hookeriana*** | LWst |
| | ***humilis*** | LWst LYaf |
| | **Irazu gx** 'Cheryl' | EPot |
| | **Jorullo gx** 'Long-tailed Tit' | GEdr LYaf |
| | **Keith Rattray gx** 'Kelty' | LYaf |
| | **Kenya gx** | LYaf |
| | – 'Bald Eagle' | LYaf |
| | **Krakatoa gx** 'Wheatear' | LYaf |
| | **Lascar gx** 'Dipper' **new** | LYaf |
| | **Leda gx** | LYaf |
| | **Lhasa gx** 'Blushes' **new** | LYaf |
| | ***limprichtii*** ♀H2 | CFwr ECho EFEx EPot LWst LYaf |
| | **Lyn Butterfield gx** **new** | LYaf |
| | ***maculata*** | EFEx LWst |
| | **Marion Johnson gx** | LYaf |
| | **Mauna Loa gx** | LYaf |
| | – 'Glossy Starling' | LYaf |
| | **Mawenzi gx** | LYaf |
| | **Novarupta gx** 'Goshawk' **new** | LYaf |
| | – 'Raven' | LYaf |
| | **Orinoco gx** 'Gemini' | GEdr |
| | **Orizaba gx** | LYaf |
| | – 'Fish Eagle' | LYaf |
| | **Paricutin gx** | LYaf |
| | ***pinkepankii*** | see *P. grandiflora* |
| | **Piton gx** | EPot LYaf |
| § | ***pleionoides*** | EPot LYaf |
| | ***pogonioides*** misapplied | see *P. pleionoides* |
| | ***pogonioides*** (Rolfe) Rolfe | see *P. bulbocodioides* |
| | ***praecox*** | LWst |
| | **Quizapu gx** 'Peregrine' | LYaf |
| | **Rakata gx** | EPot GEdr |
| | – 'Locking Stumps' **new** | EPot GEdr |
| | – 'Redwing' | LYaf |

| | |
|---|---|
| - 'Rock Dove' | LYaf |
| - 'Shot Silk' | LYaf |
| - 'Skylark' | GEdr LYaf |
| **San Salvador gx** | LYaf |
| **Sangay gx** | LYaf |
| **Santorini gx** | LYaf |
| - 'Yellow Wagtail' | LYaf |
| ***saxicola*** | CFwr LYaf |
| ***scopulorum*** | EFEx |
| **Shantung gx** | CFir EPot LAma |
| - 'Ducat' | EPot LYaf |
| - 'Gerry Mundey' | LYaf |
| - 'Ridgeway' | EPot LYaf |
| - 'Silver Anniversary' | LYaf |
| **Sharon Ann Winter gx** | LYaf |
| **Sorea gx** | GEdr |
| **Soufrière gx** | LYaf |
| ***speciosa*** Ames & Schltr. | see *P. pleionoides* |
| **St Helens gx** new | LYaf |
| **Stromboli gx** 'Fireball' | EPot |
| **Surtsey gx** | EPot |
| - 'Stephanie Rose' | EPot |
| **Taal gx** 'Red-tailed Hawk' | LYaf |
| × ***taliensis*** | LYaf |
| **Tarawera gx** | LYaf |
| **Toff gx** | LYaf |
| **Tolima gx** 'Moorhen' | LEdu LYaf |
| **Tongariro gx** | CPBP EPot |
| **Ueli Wackernagel gx** | GEdr |
| **Versailles gx** | EPot |
| - 'Bucklebury' ♀H2 | EPot LYaf |
| **Vesuvius gx** | EPot |
| - 'Grey Wagtail' | LYaf |
| - 'Leopard' | LYaf |
| - 'Phoenix' | EPot LYaf |
| - 'Tawny Owl' | GEdr LYaf |
| **Volcanello gx** 'Honey Buzzard' | GEdr LYaf |
| - 'Song Thrush' | EPot LYaf |
| **Whakari gx** | LYaf |
| 'Wharfedale Pine Warbler' | LYaf |
| ***yunnanensis*** misapplied | see *P. bulbocodioides* 'Yunnan' |
| ***yunnanensis*** ambig. | LAma |
| ***yunnanensis*** (Rolfe) Rolfe | LYaf |
| **Zeus Weinstein gx** | GEdr LYaf |
| - 'Desert Sands' | GEdr |

## *Pleiospilos* (*Aizoaceae*)

| | |
|---|---|
| ***compactus*** ♀H1 | WCot |

## *Pleomele* see *Dracaena*

## *Pleurospermum* (*Apiaceae*)

| | |
|---|---|
| from Nepal | WCot |
| aff. ***album*** KWJ 12281 | WCru |
| aff. ***amabile*** BWJ 7886 | WCru |
| ***benthamii*** B&SWJ 2988 | WCru |
| - SSSE 50 | GLam |
| ***brunonis*** | GKev |
| ***calcareum*** B&SWJ 8008 | WCru |
| ***yunnanense*** BWJ 7952A | WCru |

## plum see *Prunus domestica*

## *Plumbago* (*Plumbaginaceae*)

| | |
|---|---|
| § ***auriculata*** ♀H1-2 | CBcs CCCN CHEx CRHN CSBt CTri CWCL CWSG EBak ELan EPfP EPri EShb LRHS MOWG NPal SEND SMrm SPer SPoG SRms SVic WCFE |
| - f. ***alba*** ♀H1-2 | CBot CHEx CRHN CSev EPfP EShb MOWG SEND |
| * - ***aurea*** | MRav |
| - 'Crystal Waters' | CCCN ERea EShb |
| - dark blue-flowered | CSpe |
| 'Escapade Blue' (Turquoise Series) | NPri |
| ***capensis*** | see *P. auriculata* |
| § ***indica*** ♀H1 | CCCN MOWG |
| - ***rosea*** | see *P. indica* |
| ***larpentiae*** | see *Ceratostigma plumbaginoides* |

## *Plumeria* (*Apocynaceae*)

| | |
|---|---|
| sp. | WSFF |
| ***rubra*** ♀H1 | CCCN LRHS MOWG XBlo |
| - f. ***acutifolia*** | MOWG |
| - 'Golden Glow' new | XBlo |
| - 'Velvet Red' new | XBlo |

## *Pneumatopteris* (*Thelypteridaceae*)

| | |
|---|---|
| ***pennigera*** | WRic |

## *Poa* (*Poaceae*)

| | |
|---|---|
| ***alpina*** | NLar SMea XLum |
| - var. ***nodosa*** | SWal |
| ***chaixii*** | EHoe EPPr EPla NLar XLum |
| ***cita*** | GMaP |
| ***colensoi*** | CKno EBee EHoe EPPr GAbr MAvo |
| × ***jemtlandica*** | EHoe EPPr |
| ***labillardierei*** | CKno CWCL EBee ECha EHoe EPPr GGar MAvo MMuc NWsh SEND SPer SUsu WDyG WMoo XLum |
| ***pratensis*** | CHab |
| ***trivialis*** | CRWN |
| I 'Variegata' (v) | SApp |

## *Podalyria* (*Papilionaceae*)

| | |
|---|---|
| ***calyptrata*** | GFai SPlb |
| ***sericea*** | SPlb |

## *Podocarpus* ✿ (*Podocarpaceae*)

| | |
|---|---|
| ***acutifolius*** | CBcs CDoC ECou GGar IGor STre |
| - (f) | ECou |
| - (m) | ECou |
| ***andinus*** | see *Prumnopitys andina* |
| 'Autumn Shades' (m) | ECou |
| 'Blaze' (f) | CBcs CDoC ECou LEdu LRHS MBrN NHol NLar SCoo SLim SPoG WFar |
| ***chilinus*** | see *P. salignus* |
| 'Chocolate Box' (f) | ECou MAsh NWad SLim |
| 'County Park Fire'[PBR] (f) | CBcs CDoC CWSG ECho ECou EHul EPfP ESwi LAst LRHS MGos NEgg NHol NLar NWad SCoo SLim SPoG SWvt WEve WFar WGor |
| 'County Park Treasure' | ECou |
| ***cunninghamii*** | ECou |
| - 'Kiwi' (f) | ECou MGos |
| - 'Roro' (m) | CBcs CDoC ECou |
| ***cunninghamii*** × ***nivalis*** (f) | ECou |
| ***dacrydioides*** | see *Dacrycarpus dacrydioides* |
| ***elongatus*** | CTrC |
| - 'Blue Chip' | CBcs |
| ***ferrugineus*** | see *Prumnopitys ferruginea* |
| 'Flame' | CDoC ECho ECou EHul MAsh NLar NPCo |
| 'Havering' (f) | CDoC ECou MGos |
| ***henkelii*** | CTrC EShb GGar |
| 'Jill' (f) | ECou |

| | |
|---|---|
| ***latifolius*** | ECou EShb GCal |
| ***lawrencei*** | EHul GGar WThu |
| - (f) | ECou |
| - 'Alpine Lass' (f) | ECou |
| - 'Blue Gem' (f) | CDoC ECou EPla LRHS MAsh MGos MMuc SCoo SEND SLim WFar |
| - 'Kiandra' | ECou |
| - 'Kosciuszko' | ECou |
| - 'Pine Lake' | ECou |
| - 'Red Tip' | CDoC LRHS SCoo SLim STre WGor |
| 'Lucky Lad' | ECou |
| 'Macho' (m) | ECou |
| ***macrophyllus*** | CDoC CHEx ERom EShb SArc SMad STre WFar |
| - (m) | ECou WFar |
| - 'Aureus' | CBcs |
| 'Maori Prince' (m) | CDoC ECou MGos |
| ***nivalis*** | CBcs CDul CMac CTrC ECou EPla GCal GGar SRms STre WThu |
| - 'Arthur' (m) | ECou |
| - 'Bronze' | CDoC ECou EPla GCal MGos |
| - 'Christmas Lights' (f) | CKen ECou |
| - 'Clarence' (m) | ECou |
| - 'Cover Girl' | LRHS SPoG |
| - 'Green Queen' (f) | ECou |
| - 'Hikurangi' | CDoC |
| - 'Jack's Pass' (m) | ECho ECou WFar |
| - 'Kaweka' (m) | ECou |
| - 'Kilworth Cream' (v) | CBcs CDoC CMen ECho ECou ESwi LRHS MGos NHol NLar SLim SPoG SWvt WGor |
| - 'Little Lady' (f) | ECou |
| - 'Livingstone' (f) | ECou |
| - 'Lodestone' (m) | ECou |
| - 'Moffat' (f) | CBcs CDoC ECou |
| - 'Otari' (m) | CDoC ECou MAsh NLar |
| - 'Park Cover' | ECou |
| - 'Princess' (f) | ECou MBrN |
| - 'Ruapehu' (m) | CDoC ECou EPla |
| - 'Trompenburg' | NLar |
| ***nubigenus*** | CBcs |
| 'Orangeade' (f) | CBcs CDoC MGos NHol NLar |
| 'Red Embers' | CDoC ECho ECou ESwi NEgg SCoo WFar WGor |
| * 'Redtip' | CMen |
| § ***salignus*** ♀H3 | CBcs CDoC CHEx CPLG EPla GGal IDee LRHS NMun SArc SLim WAle WFar WSHC |
| - (f) | ECou WFar |
| - (m) | ECou |
| 'Soldier Boy' | ECou |
| ***spicatus*** | see *Prumnopitys taxifolia* |
| 'Spring Sunshine' (f) | CBcs CDoC ECou EPla MGos NLar |
| ***totara*** | CBcs CBrP CTrC ECou GGar LEdu WFar |
| - 'Albany Gold' | CTrC |
| - 'Aureus' | CBcs CDoC ECou EPla WFar |
| - 'Pendulus' | CDoC ECou |
| 'Young Rusty' (f) | CBcs CDoC ECou EPla MAsh MGos NHol WEve |

## *Podophyllum* (*Berberidaceae*)

| | |
|---|---|
| sp. | LWst WBor |
| ***aurantiocaule*** | CPLG |
| § ***delavayi*** | CBct CFir CLAP CPLG EBla ECho GEdr MDun NLar SKHP WAbe WCot WCru |
| ***difforme*** | CBct CLAP GEdr SKHP WCru |
| ***emodi*** var. ***chinense*** | see *Sinopodophyllum hexandrum* var. *chinense* |
| ***hexandrum*** | see *Sinopodophyllum hexandrum* |
| - var. ***chinense*** | see *Sinopodophyllum hexandrum* var. *chinense* |
| 'Kaleidoscope' (v) | CBct CLAP CMil EBee ESwi GEdr NCGa NGBo NLar NPnk WCot |
| ***peltatum*** | CAby CArn CBct CBro CDes CHid CLAP CWCL EBee EBla ECho EWTr EWld GAbr GBBs GEdr GPoy LAma LEdu NLar NMyG NSti SPhx WBor WCru WFar WPGP WPnP |
| - var. ***peltatum*** f. ***deamii*** | EBee |
| ***pleianthum*** | CAby CBct CDes CLAP CSpr GEdr LRHS NLar WCru |
| - B&SWJ 282 from Taiwan | WCru |
| - short | WCru WFar |
| ***veitchii*** | see *P. delavayi* |
| ***versipelle*** | CLAP LEdu LWst SKHP WCru |
| - 'Spotty Dotty'PBR | CBct CLAP CPLG EBee ESwi GQue LRHS MMHG MMoz NGBo NLar NPnk NSti SHeu SMad WCot |

## *Podranea* (*Bignoniaceae*)

| | |
|---|---|
| § ***ricasoliana*** | CRHN LRHS MOWG SPoG WBor |

## *Pogonatherum* (*Poaceae*)

| | |
|---|---|
| * ***distichum*** | XBlo |

## *Pogonia* (*Orchidaceae*)

| | |
|---|---|
| sp. | NDav |

## *Pogostemon* (*Lamiaceae*)

| | |
|---|---|
| from An Veleniki Herb Farm, Pennsylvania | CArn |
| § ***cablin*** | EOHP GPoy |
| ***patchouly*** | see *P. cablin* |

## *Polemonium* ✿ (*Polemoniaceae*)

| | |
|---|---|
| ***ambervicsii*** | see *P. pauciflorum* subsp. *hinckleyi* |
| 'Apricot Beauty' | see *P. carneum* 'Apricot Delight' |
| N ***archibaldiae*** ♀H4 | NBir SRms |
| 'Blue Pearl' | CMea ELan EPfP GJos LRHS MBri MNrw NBro NGdn NLar SBfd SGar SMrm WCra WFar |
| § ***boreale*** | EBee LRHS SWvt WMoo |
| - 'Heavenly Habit' | EBee GJos LRHS MBNS NGdn WJek WWEG XLum |
| ***brandegeei*** misapplied | see *P. pauciflorum* |
| § ***brandegeei*** Greene | CCVN |
| - subsp. ***mellitum*** | see *P. brandegeei* Greene |
| § ***caeruleum*** | Widely available |
| - 'Bambino Blue' | EBee LRHS NBlu NBre SWvt |
| - 'Blue Bell' | LRHS |
| - Brise d'Anjou = 'Blanjou'PBR (v) | CMMP CMac CMea EBee ECtt ELan EPfP EShb EWes GAbr LRHS MAsh MBri NBir NGdn SBfd SMad SPer SWvt WFar WWEG |
| - subsp. ***caeruleum*** f. ***album*** | CBre CSBt CWCL ECha ELan EPfP GAbr GKev MBNS MHer MRav NBro SBfd SPer SPoG SRms STes WMoo XLum |
| - 'Filigree Clouds' | LRHS MAvo NGdn NLar SMrm |
| - 'Filigree Skies' | GCal LRHS NGdn NLar |
| - var. ***grandiflorum*** | see *P. caeruleum* subsp. *himalayanum* |
| § - subsp. ***himalayanum*** | CSpe GAbr WJek WMoo |
| - 'Humile' | see *P.* 'Northern Lights' |
| - 'Idylle' | GMac |
| - 'Pam' (v) | CDes |

| | |
|---|---|
| – 'Snow and Sapphires' (v) | MBri NPer SWvt |
| – white-flowered | GJos MMuc |
| ***carneum*** | CTri CWan ECha GCal GMaP LRHS MNrw NLar SPer WFar WMoo |
| § – 'Apricot Delight' | EBee GJos MNrw NBir NGdn SBfd GGar GIde GPer GPoG [illegible] WFar WHer WJek WPer WPnP WPtf WWEG |
| ***cashmerianum*** | see *P. caeruleum* subsp. *himalayanum* |
| ***chartaceum*** | LLHF |
| 'Churchills' | CBre EBee WPGP WSHC |
| 'Dawn Flight' | WFar |
| 'Eastbury Purple' | CElw CWCL |
| 'Elworthy Amethyst' | CElw WPGP |
| ***eximium*** | LLHF |
| ***foliosissimum*** misapplied | see *P. archibaldiae* |
| ***foliosissimum*** A. Gray var. ***albiflorum*** | see *P. foliosissimum* var. *alpinum* |
| § – var. ***alpinum*** | NBir |
| – 'Cottage Cream' | CDes WCot WPGP |
| – var. ***foliosissimum*** | EWes |
| 'Glebe Cottage Lilac' | CHar GCra NBir SBch WPGP |
| 'Hannah Billcliffe' | CDes CElw EBee ECtt EWes MBrN MTis NCot WPGP |
| 'Heaven Scent' **new** | EBee |
| 'Heavenly Blue' | ECtt |
| § 'Hopleys' | GCal LHop WFar |
| × ***jacobaea*** | EBee WCot WPGP |
| 'Katie Daley' | see *P.* 'Hopleys' |
| 'Lambrook Mauve' ♀H4 | Widely available |
| ***mellitum*** | see *P. brandegeei* Greene |
| 'North Tyne' | NChi |
| § 'Northern Lights' | CDes CMea CSev CWCL EBee ECGP ECtt ELon EWes GAbr MCot MLLN MNrw MTis NDov SBch STes SUsu WCot WFar WMoo WPGP WWFP |
| 'Norwell Mauve' | MNrw |
| § ***pauciflorum*** | CEnt EBee ECtt EPfP GGar IFro LRHS NBir SPer WFar WJek WKif WMoo |
| § – subsp. ***hinckleyi*** | LRHS NLBP |
| § – subsp. ***pauciflorum*** | SGar SPav |
| – silver-leaved | see *P. pauciflorum* subsp. *pauciflorum* |
| – 'Sulphur Trumpets' | SWvt |
| – subsp. ***typicum*** | see *P. pauciflorum* subsp. *pauciflorum* |
| 'Pink Beauty' | CMac EBee ELan EPfP LBMP NBre NGdn STes WWEG |
| ***pulchellum*** Salisb. | see *P. reptans* |
| ***pulchellum*** Turcz. | see *P. caeruleum* |
| ***pulchellum*** Willd. | EDAr |
| ***pulcherrimum*** misapplied | see *P. boreale*, *P. boreale* 'Tricolor' |
| ***pulcherrimum*** Hook. | GCal NBro WPer |
| – subsp. ***pulcherrimum*** | LLHF |
| § ***reptans*** | CArn GPoy LRHS MHer NBro WAul WFar WMoo WPtf XLum |
| – 'Album' | see *P. reptans* 'Virginia White' |
| – 'Firmament' | EBee MAvo WPGP |
| * – 'Sky Blue' | NBro |
| – 'Stairway to Heaven' PBR (v) | Widely available |
| – 'Touch of Class' (v) | EBee LSou NLar |
| § – 'Virginia White' | CBre CDes CElw CMea CSev EBee EWes MAvo MTis NChi SUsu WFar WPGP |
| – 'White Pearl' | NPri |
| × ***richardsonii*** misapplied | see *P.* 'Northern Lights' |
| × ***richardsonii*** Graham | see *P. boreale* |
| 'Sapphire' | CBre ELan LRHS |
| 'Sonia's Bluebell' | CDes CElw CWCL EBee ECGP ECtt EPPr EWes GBin MDKP MNrw MTis NDov NLar NSti SBch STes WPGP |
| 'Thuddingworth' | WFar |
| ***viscosum*** | GKev |
| ***yezoense*** | CBre NBre WFar |
| – var. ***hidakanum*** Bressingham Purple = 'Polbress' | CSev EBee ECtt ELan EWes GBin LHop LRHS MAsh MBNS MBri NCGa NDov NLar NOrc NPri NWad SBfd SMrm SPer WFar |
| – – 'Purple Rain' | Widely available |

## *Polianthes* (*Asparagaceae*)

| | |
|---|---|
| ***elongata*** | WCot |
| § ***geminiflora*** | WCot |
| ***tuberosa*** ♀H1-2 | CBcs CCCN EPfP WCot XLum |
| – 'The Pearl' (d) | LAma WCot WHil WPGP XLum |

## *Poliomintha* (*Lamiaceae*)

| | |
|---|---|
| ***bustamanta*** | NBir SPhx WCot WSHC |

## *Poliothyrsis* (*Salicaceae*)

| | |
|---|---|
| ***sinensis*** ♀H4 | EPfP IArd IDee MBri NLar SSpi WPGP |

## *Pollia* (*Commelinaceae*)

| | |
|---|---|
| ***japonica*** | EShb ESwi EWes EWld |

## *Polygala* (*Polygalaceae*)

| | |
|---|---|
| ***calcarea*** | LLHF WPat |
| – 'Lillet' ♀H4 | ECho EWes GEdr LHop LLHF LRHS NLar NMen WAbe WFar WPat WThu |
| ***chamaebuxus*** ♀H4 | CBcs MAsh MDKP MGos NLar NSla SPoG SRms WGwG |
| I – ***alba*** | LBee LRHS NLar SChF WAbe |
| § – var. ***grandiflora*** ♀H4 | CBcs CFir ECho EPfP EPot GAbr GEdr GGar GKev IVic LBee LRHS MAsh MGos MWat NMen NSla SChF SPoG WAbe WFar WGwG WPat WSHC |
| – 'Kamniski' | NLar |
| – 'Loibl' | EPot |
| – 'Purpurea' | see *P. chamaebuxus* var. *grandiflora* |
| – 'Rhodoptera' | see *P. chamaebuxus* var. *grandiflora* |
| § × ***dalmaisiana*** ♀H1 | CAbb CCCN CHEx CHll CRHN CSpe CWGN EPfP EPri SEND SGar SPad SPlb WAbe WCFE |
| ***myrtifolia*** | CCCN CTrC GFai MGos NWCA SMrm SPlb |
| – Bibi Pink = 'Polylap' | LRHS |
| – 'Grandiflora' | see *P.* × *dalmaisiana* |
| ***virgata*** | CCCN |

## *Polygonatum* ✿ (*Asparagaceae*)

| | |
|---|---|
| ACE 1753 | EPot |
| CC-5729 | EWld |
| ***acuminatifolium*** | EBla |
| ***altelobatum*** B&SWJ 286 | EBla WCru |
| – B&SWJ 1886 | WCru |
| ***arisanense*** B&SWJ 3839 | WCru |
| § ***biflorum*** | Widely available |
| – dwarf | EBla EPla |
| ***canaliculatum*** | see *P. biflorum* |
| ***cathcartii*** B&SWJ 2429 | WCru |

| |  |  |
|---|---|---|
| | ***cirrhifolium*** | CCse CDes CFir CLAP CPom EBee EBla ELan EPot GBin GEdr GGar MMoz MNrw SKHP WCru WPGP |
| | - red-flowered | NLar WCot WFar |
| | ***commutatum*** | see *P. biflorum* |
| | 'Corsley' | CPou |
| | ***cryptanthum*** | EBla WCru |
| | ***curvistylum*** | CAby CAvo CBct CFir CLAP CPom EBla ECha EPPr GEdr IFoB IGor MNFA NCGa NLar NRya SPhx WCru WFar WHil WSHC |
| | - CLD 761 | GEdr |
| | ***cyrtonema*** misapplied | see *Disporopsis pernyi* |
| | ***cyrtonema*** Hua B&SWJ 271 | WCru |
| * | ***desoulavyi*** var. ***yezoense*** B&SWJ 764 | EBla WCru |
| | ***falcatum*** misapplied | see *P. humile* |
| | ***falcatum*** A. Gray | EBee NRya WHer |
| | - B&SWJ 1077 | EBla WCru |
| | - silver-striped | CLAP GEdr |
| | - - B&SWJ 5101 | WCru |
| | - 'Variegatum' | see *P. odoratum* var. *pluriflorum* 'Variegatum' |
| | 'Falcon' | see *P. humile* |
| | ***filipes*** | WCru |
| | ***fuscum*** | WCru |
| | ***geminiflorum*** | CBct CLAP CPom EBla IGor LRHS WCru WFar |
| | - McB 2448 | CLAP GEdr |
| | ***giganteum*** | see *P. biflorum* |
| | ***glaberrimum*** | CBct EBla IPot WCot WFar |
| § | ***graminifolium*** | CAby CBct CLAP CPBP CPom EBla ECho GEdr LRHS SCnR WCot WCru WThu |
| | - G-W&P 803 | ECho EPot IPot NMen |
| § | ***hirtum*** | CAby CBct CLAP CPom CPrp EBla ECho EPPr EPla IFoB LEdu MAvo MMoz WCru WFar WTin |
| | - BM 7012 | EBla ECho EBee |
| | ***hookeri*** | CAby CBct CBro CMac CPLG EBee EBla ECho EDAr EPPr EPot GEdr GGar ITim NBid NCGa NHol NLar NMen NMyG NRya NSla NWCA SPhx SRot WCru WFar WHil WWEG |
| | - McB 1413 | GEdr |
| § | ***humile*** | CBct CLAP EBee EBla ECho EPPr EPfP GCal GGar IBal LHop LWst MAvo NGdn NLar NMen NMyG NPnk WAul WCru WFar WHil XLum |
| I | - 'Variegatum' (v) | CMac |
| § | × ***hybridum*** ♀$^{H4}$ | Widely available |
| | - 'Betberg' | CAvo CBct CFir CLAP CRow EBla ECha EPPr MAvo NBir WCot |
| | - 'Flore Pleno' (d) | CBct EBla ELon WHer |
| | - 'Nanum' | CAby CBct CHid EBla WCot |
| | - 'Purple Katie' | MAvo |
| § | - 'Striatum' (v) | Widely available |
| | - 'Variegatum' | see *P.* × *hybridum* 'Striatum' |
| | - 'Wakehurst' | EBla |
| | - 'Weihenstephan' | EBee EBla GCal |
| | - 'Welsh Gold' (v) | CAvo |
| | ***inflatum*** | EBee ECho WCru |
| | - B&SWJ 922 | EBla WCru |
| | ***involucratum*** | ECho WCru |
| | - B&SWJ 4285 | WCru |
| | ***japonicum*** | see *P. odoratum* |
| | ***kingianum*** | WHil |
| | - yellow-flowered B&SWJ 6545 | WCru |
| | - - B&SWJ 6562 | WCru |
| | 'Langthorn's Variegated' (v) | ELan |
| | ***lasianthum*** | LWst WCru |
| | - B&SWJ 671 | WCru |
| | ***latifolium*** | see *P. hirtum* |
| | ***leptophyllum*** KEKE 844 | GEdr |
| | ***maximowiczii*** | CPom EBee EPPr GCal WCru |
| | 'Multifide' | EBee |
| | ***multiflorum*** misapplied | see *P.* × *hybridum* |
| | ***multiflorum*** L. | Widely available |
| | - CC 4572 | WCot |
| | - ***giganteum*** hort. | see *P. biflorum* |
| * | - 'Ramosissima' | EBla |
| * | ***nanum*** 'Variegatum' (v) | CBcs ECho |
| | ***nodosum*** | EBla WCru |
| | ***obtusifolium*** | EBla |
| § | ***odoratum*** ♀$^{H4}$ | CAvo CBct CBro CPom CRow EBee EBla ECho EPla GMaP NBid NLar NPnk NRya SWal WCru WFar WHil WPnP WWEG |
| | - 'Angel's Wings' | MAvo |
| § | - dwarf | ECho LEdu |
| | - 'Flore Pleno' (d) ♀$^{H4}$ | CAvo CDes CLAP CPom CRDP EBla ECha ECho EPla LEdu MAvo MMoz SCnR WCot WFar WHoo WTin |
| | - 'Grace Barker' | see *P.* × *hybridum* 'Striatum' |
| | - Kew form | EPot |
| | - var. ***pluriflorum*** | EBee |
| § | - - 'Variegatum' (v) ♀$^{H4}$ | Widely available |
| | - 'Red Stem' | ECho WCru |
| | - 'Silver Wings' (v) | CBct CLAP EBla ECha NBir NLar |
| | - var. ***thunbergii*** new | WCru |
| | - 'Ussuriland' | EPPr GCal |
| | - 'Ussuriland Roundleaf' new | GCal |
| | ***officinale*** | see *P. odoratum* |
| | ***oppositifolium*** | WFar |
| | - B&SWJ 2537 | EBla WCru |
| § | ***orientale*** | CAvo CBct CLAP EBla ECho ELau WFar |
| | ***pluriflorum*** | see *P. graminifolium* |
| | ***polyanthemum*** | see *P. orientale* |
| | ***prattii*** | EBla ECho WCru |
| | - CLD 325 | GEdr |
| | ***pubescens*** | CBct EBee ECho LEdu WCru WThu |
| | ***pumilum*** | see *P. odoratum* dwarf |
| | ***punctatum*** | CRDP LEdu WFar |
| | - B&SWJ 2395 | CBct EBla WCru |
| | ***roseum*** | CDes CLAP CPom EPPr GEdr MAvo MMoz WCru WHer WPGP |
| | ***sewerzowii*** | EBla EPPr EPla |
| | ***sibiricum*** | CAvo CBct CPom CRDP EBla GEdr IGor WCru WFar |
| | - DJHC 600 | CDes EBee WCot WPGP |
| | ***stenanthum*** | LWst |
| | - B&SWJ 5727 | EBla WCru |
| | ***stenophyllum*** | CAvo EBla WCru |
| | ***stewartianum*** | CLAP EPPr NRya |
| | aff. ***tessellatum*** B&SWJ 9752 | WCru |
| | ***tonkinense*** | LEdu |
| | - B&SWJ 8246 | EBla WCru |
| | - HWJ 551 | EBla WCru WFar |
| | - HWJ 567 | WCru |
| | - white-flowered HWJ 861 new | WCru |
| | ***verticillatum*** | CBct CBro CGHE CHid CRow EBla ECha EPfP EPla EPot IFoB LBMP LEdu MNFA MNrw MRav SKHP SMad WCru WFar WPGP |
| | - CLD 1308 | EPPr |
| | - 'Giant One' | IPot |

| | |
|---|---|
| – 'Himalayan Giant' | CHid EBla ECho LWst WFar WPnP |
| * – 'Roseum' | CAvo |
| – 'Rubrum' | CAby CArn CBct CLAP CRow EBee EBla EPPr EPla GEdr IGor LEdu LRHS MAvo NBid NChi NLar SPhx WCot WCru WHil |
| – 'Serbian Dwarf' | CBct CHid EBee EBla ECho LEdu |
| aff. ***verticillatum*** | CSpe |
| ***wardii*** | WCot |
| aff. ***wardii*** | WCot |
| – B&SWJ 6599 | WCru |
| ***zanlanscianense*** | CBct EBla IGor WCru WFar |

## *Polygonum* (*Polygonaceae*)

| | |
|---|---|
| ***affine*** | see *Persicaria affinis* |
| ***amplexicaule*** | see *Persicaria amplexicaulis* |
| ***aubertii*** | see *Fallopia baldschuanica* |
| ***aviculare*** | CArn |
| ***baldschuanicum*** | see *Fallopia baldschuanica* |
| ***bistorta*** | see *Persicaria bistorta* |
| ***capitatum*** | see *Persicaria capitata* |
| ***compactum*** | see *Fallopia japonica* var. *compacta* |
| ***equisetiforme*** misapplied | see *P. scoparium* |
| ***filiforme*** | see *Persicaria virginiana* |
| ***molle*** | see *Persicaria mollis* |
| ***multiflorum*** | see *Fallopia multiflora* |
| ***odoratum*** | see *Persicaria odorata* |
| ***polystachyum*** | see *Persicaria wallichii* |
| ***runciforme*** | see *Persicaria runcinata* |
| § ***scoparium*** | CRow EHoe EPPr EPla ESwi SDys WFar WOld XLum |
| ***tinctorium*** | see *Persicaria tinctoria* |
| ***vacciniifolium*** | see *Persicaria vacciniifolia* |
| ***weyrichii*** | see *Persicaria weyrichii* |

## *Polylepis* (*Rosaceae*)

| | |
|---|---|
| ***australis*** | CSpe EPla ESwi LEdu MBri SEND SMad WCot WCru |
| – tall | WPGP |

## *Polymnia* (*Asteraceae*)

| | |
|---|---|
| ***sonchifolia*** | LEdu |

## *Polypodium* ✿ (*Polypodiaceae*)

| | |
|---|---|
| ***aureum*** | see *Phlebodium aureum* |
| – 'Glaucum' | CSpe WCot |
| ***australe*** | see *P. cambricum* |
| § ***cambricum*** | EBee EFer WCot WFib WRic WTin |
| – 'Barrowii' | CLAP WAbe WFib |
| I – 'Cambricum' ♀H4 | CLAP GCal WAbe WRic |
| – 'Conwy' **new** | WFib |
| – 'Cristatum' | CLAP WFib |
| – (Cristatum Group) 'Grandiceps Forster' | CLAP |
| – – 'Grandiceps Fox' ♀H4 | WFib |
| – 'Hornet' | GBin WFib |
| – 'Macrostachyon' | CLAP GBin NBid NMyG WFib |
| – 'Oakleyae' | EFtx WCot |
| – 'Omnilacerum Oxford' | CLAP |
| – 'Prestonii' | CDes WAbe WCot WFib |
| – Pulcherrimum Group | CLAP WAbe WRic |
| – – 'Pulcherrimum Addison' | CDes GBin WAbe WCot WFib WPGP |
| – – 'Pulchritudine' | CLAP WAbe WCot |
| – 'Richard Kayse' | CDes CLAP EBee WAbe WCot WFib WPGP |
| – Semilacerum Group | WRic |
| – – 'Carew Lane' | WFib |
| – – 'Falcatum O'Kelly' | CDes |
| – – 'Robustum' | WFib |
| – 'Whilharris' ♀H4 | CLAP CRDP WAbe |
| I × ***coughlinii*** bifid | WFib |
| ***formosanum*** | WRic |
| ***glycyrrhiza*** | CLAP GPoy WFib WRic |
| – bifid | see *P.* × *coughlinii* bifid |
| – 'Longicaudatum' ♀H4 | CLAP GBin MWhi NMyG WAbe WCot WFib WRic |
| – 'Malahatense' | CLAP |
| – 'Malahatense' (sterile) | CDes WAbe WPGP |
| ***interjectum*** | CLAP EFer LRHS MMoz NVic WPnP WRic |
| – 'Cornubiense' ♀H4 | CHVG CLAP GEdr MMoz NBid NBir NVic WAbe WTin |
| – 'Glomeratum Mullins' | WFib |
| × ***mantoniae*** | WFib WIvy |
| – 'Bifidograndiceps' | NBid WFib WRic |
| ***scouleri*** | CBty CLAP EFer NBro WPGP |
| ***subauriculatum*** 'Knightii' | see *Goniophlebium subauriculatum* 'Knightiae' |
| ***vulgare*** | Widely available |
| – 'Bifidocristatum' | see *P. vulgare* 'Bifidomultifidum' |
| – 'Bifidomulticeps' | WCot |
| § – 'Bifidomultifidum' | CBty CLAP CWCL EWTr GBin GCal GEdr LLWP LRHS MCCP MGos MRav NLar WCot WWEG |
| * – 'Congestum Cristatum' | SRms |
| – 'Cornubiense Grandiceps' | GCal SRms WIvy WRic |
| * – 'Cornubiense Multifidum' | EBee WCot |
| – 'Elegantissimum' | NBid WFib |
| – 'Parsley' | WCot |
| – 'Trichomanoides Backhouse' | CLAP GCal WAbe WFib |
| 'Whitley Giant' | WCot |

## *Polypompholyx* see *Utricularia*

## *Polyspora* (*Theaceae*)

| | |
|---|---|
| § ***axillaris*** | CCCN |
| ***longicarpa*** WWJ 11604 **new** | WCru |
| ***speciosa*** B&SWJ 11750 | WCru |
| – WWJ 11934 | WCru |

## *Polystichum* ✿ (*Dryopteridaceae*)

| | |
|---|---|
| ***acrostichoides*** | CBty CDTJ CDes CKel CLAP CMHG EBee GEdr LRHS MBri NLar NMyG SBfd WPGP WRic XLum |
| ***aculeatum*** ♀H4 | CLAP CRWN EBee ECha EFer ELan EPfP EShb GMaP LAst LRHS LTen MBri MCot MGos MMuc NBid NEgg NLar NOrc SEND SRms SWvt WFib WMoo WRic WWEG XLum |
| I – Densum Group | EFer |
| – Grandiceps Group | EFer |
| – 'Portia' | WFib |
| ***andersonii*** | CLAP EFtx WRic |
| ***bissectum*** | CPLG |
| ***braunii*** | CBcs CMHG CWCL EBee EFtx EGol EQua GBin GMaP IKil LRHS MMoz MMuc NBid NLar SBfd SEND WFib WPnP WRic WWEG XLum |
| ***caryotideum*** | see *Cyrtomium caryotideum* |
| ***chilense*** | WRic |
| ***deltodon*** | WRic |
| ***dracomontanum*** | WRic |
| × ***dycei*** | CBty ISha LRHS WRic |
| ***falcatum*** | see *Cyrtomium falcatum* |
| ***falcinellum*** | GLin |
| ***fortunei*** | see *Cyrtomium fortunei* |
| ***imbricans*** | CLAP |

| | | |
|---|---|---|
| | ***interjectum*** | MRav |
| | ***lentum*** | NBir |
| | ***lepidocaulon*** | WRic |
| | ***makinoi*** | CBty CCCN CLAP EBee ETod LRHS NBid WFib WRic |
| | ***munitum*** ♀H4 | Widely available |
| | ***neolobatum*** | EFtx WFib |
| | - BWJ 8182 | WCru |
| | ***parvipinnulum*** | WRic |
| | ***piceopalaceum*** | WRic |
| | ***polyblepharum*** ♀H4 | Widely available |
| | - 'Jade' | LRHS LTen |
| | ***proliferum*** misapplied | see *P. setiferum* Acutilobum Group |
| | ***proliferum*** ambig. | CBty EAmu WPtf |
| | ***proliferum*** (R. Br.) C. Presl | CLAP EFtx GCal SBig WFib WPGP WRic |
| * | ***- plumosum*** | LAst SPad SWvt |
| | ***retrorsopaleaceum*** | WRic |
| | ***richardii*** | GBin SBig WRic |
| | ***rigens*** | CBty CLAP CPrp EBee EFer LAst LRHS LSou NLar NMyG SBfd SRms SRot WCru WFib WRic WWEG |
| | ***setiferum*** ♀H4 | Widely available |
| § | - Acutilobum Group | CLAP CMHG CPrp EBee ECha GMaP LRHS NHol SDix SGol SMad SPer SRms WBor WMoo WPGP WPnP WRic |
| | - Congestum Group | GBin MMoz NCGa NEgg NHol NLar SBfd SPer SRms WFib WPat WRic |
| | - - 'Congestum' | CBty CLAP CWCL EBee EFtx ELan EPPr EPfP IKil LRHS LTen MRav MWhi NBir NGdn NHol NMyG SPoG WGor WMoo XLum |
| | - - 'Congestum Cristatum' | LAst |
| | - 'Cristatopinnulum' | CGHE CLAP NHar WPGP |
| | - Cristatum Group | CLAP SRms |
| | - Cruciatum Group | CLAP |
| | - Divisilobum Group | CBcs CFee CLAP CMHG EFer ELan LPBA MCot MGos MLHP MMoz MWhi SRms STre WAul WFar WFib WHoo WIvy WKif WPGP WRic WTin |
| | - - 'Caernarvon' | CLAP EFtx |
| | - - 'Dahlem' | CBty CDoC CEnt CLAP EBee ECha EFer ELan ELon EPfP GMaP LRHS LSRN MCot MMoz MWhi SPer SPoG SUsu WFib WKif WMoo WPnP WPtf WRic WWEG |
| | - - 'Divisilobum Densum' ♀H4 | CLAP EPfP MMuc NBir NOrc |
| | - - 'Divisilobum Iveryanum' ♀H4 | CLAP EFer SRms WFib |
| | - - 'Divisilobum Laxum' | CLAP |
| | - - 'Divisilobum Wollaston' | CDTJ CKel CLAP CWCL ETod GBin LRHS MRav NBid NLar |
| | - - 'Herrenhausen' | Widely available |
| | - - 'Madame Patti' | MMoz |
| | - - 'Mrs Goffey' | CGHE WFib WPGP |
| | - Foliosum Group | CLAP EFer |
| | - 'Gracile' | LTen MRav NBir |
| | - 'Grandiceps' | CGHE CLAP EFer ELan WPGP |
| | - 'Hamlet' | WFib |
| | - 'Helena' | WFib |
| | - 'Hirondelle' | SRms |
| | - Lineare Group | WFib |
| | - Multilobum Group | CLAP SRms WFib |
| | - 'Othello' | WFib |
| | - Perserratum Group | GBin NBid WFib |
| | - 'Plumo-Densum' | see *P. setiferum* 'Plumosomultilobum' |
| | - 'Plumosodensum' | see *P. setiferum* 'Plumosomultilobum' |
| | - Plumosodivisilobum Group | CLAP ECha EGol GBin LSou NBid WFib |
| | - - 'Baldwinii' | CLAP WFib |
| | - - 'Bland' | WFib |
| I | - 'Plumosomultilobum' | CBty CGHE CLAP CWCL EBee EFtx EPfP GBin LAst LBMP MCot MGos MMoz NBir NLar SBfd SMad WCot WFib WGwG WHoo WMoo WPat WPnP WRic |
| I | - (Plumosomultilobum Group) 'Plumosomultilobum Densum' | LRHS SEND WCot WWEG |
| | - Plumosum Group | CGHE CLAP CMHG CSpe EFer EFtx LTen NOrc SArc SRot |
| | - - dwarf | CSBt MMuc |
| * | - ***plumosum grande*** 'Moly' | SRms |
| | - 'Portmeirion' | CLAP |
| | - Proliferum Group | see *P. setiferum* Acutilobum Group |
| * | - 'Proliferum Wollaston' | CBcs CBty CPrp EBee ETod MMoz MMuc WWEG |
| | - 'Pulcherrimum Bevis' ♀H4 | CAby CBty CDes CHid CLAP CMea EBee ECGP ELon ESwi GBin MAvo MRav NGdn NMyG SDix SMad SUsu SWvt WCot WFib WKif WPGP WPat WPnP WRic |
| | - Rotundatum Group | CBty CLAP |
| | - - 'Cristatum' | CLAP |
| | - - 'Rotundatum Ramosum' | CLAP |
| | - 'Smith's Cruciate' | CLAP GBin LLHF WFib |
| | - 'Wakeleyanum' | EFer SRms |
| | ***tsussimense*** ♀H4 | Widely available |
| | ***vestitum*** | CLAP CTrC EFtx GBin MMoz SBig WRic |
| | ***yunnanense*** | WRic |

## *Polyxena* (*Asparagaceae*)

| | | |
|---|---|---|
| * | ***brevifolia*** | ECho |
| | ***corymbosa*** | ECho NMen |
| § | ***ensifolia*** | ECho LLHF WCot |
| | ***longituba*** | CPBP ECho WCot |
| | ***odorata*** | ECho NRya |
| | ***paucifolia*** | ECho |
| | ***pygmaea*** | see *P. ensifolia* |

## *Pomaderris* (*Rhamnaceae*)

| | | |
|---|---|---|
| | ***apetala*** | CPLG |
| | ***elliptica*** | CPLG ECou |
| | ***kumeraho*** | CCCN |

## pomegranate see *Punica granatum*

## *Poncirus* (*Rutaceae*)

| | | |
|---|---|---|
| § | ***trifoliata*** | CAgr CArn CBcs CCCN CDoC CDul EBee ELan EPfP GBin IDee IVic LEdu LRHS MBlu MRav NEgg NWea SArc SMad SPer SPlb SPoG SVic WDin WFar WPGP WSHC |
| | - 'Flying Dragon' | SMad |

## *Ponerorchis* (*Orchidaceae*)

| | | |
|---|---|---|
| | ***graminifolia*** | LAma LWst |

## *Pontederia* (*Pontederiaceae*)

| | | |
|---|---|---|
| | ***cordata*** ♀H4 | CBen CHEx CRow CWat EHon ELan EPfP LPBA MSKA MWts NPer SCoo SPlb SWat WFar WMAq WPnP XLum |

| | |
|---|---|
| – f. ***albiflora*** | CRow CWat EPfP LPBA MWts NLar WMAq XLum |
| – 'Blue Spires' | MSKA |
| § – var. ***lancifolia*** | CBen CRow LPBA MNrw MSKA MWts NPer SWat WTin |
| – 'Pink Pons' | CRow LPBA MSKA NLar |
| ***hastata*** | see *Monochoria hastata* |
| ***lanceolata*** | see *P. cordata* var. *lancifolia* |

## *Populus* ✿ (*Salicaceae*)

| | |
|---|---|
| × ***acuminata*** | WMou |
| ***alba*** | CAlb CBcs CCVT CDoC CDul CLnd CMac CSBt CTho CTri CWib ECrN LBuc NWea SBfd SEWo SGol SPer WDin WMou |
| – 'Bolleana' | see *P. alba* f. *pyramidalis* |
| – 'Nivea' | MMuc SEND |
| § – f. ***pyramidalis*** | SRms WMou |
| § – 'Raket' | CCVT CLnd CTho ECrN ELan SPer |
| – 'Richardii' | EBtc MAsh WCot WFar WMou |
| – Rocket | see *P. alba* 'Raket' |
| § 'Balsam Spire' (f) ♀H4 | CAlb CDoC CDul CLnd CTho WDin WMou |
| § ***balsamifera*** | CCVT CDoC CSBt CTri MGos SBfd SPer SRms WCot WDin WFar |
| – 'Vita Sackville West' | MBlu |
| × ***berolinensis*** | CDoC |
| × ***canadensis*** | ECrN |
| § – 'Aurea' ♀H4 | CDul CLnd CTho CWib ECrN MGos MRav NEgg SPer WDin WFar WMou |
| – 'Aurea' × (× ***jackii*** 'Aurora') | WDin |
| – 'Columbia' | WMou |
| – 'Eugenei' (m) | WMou |
| – 'Robusta' (m) | CCVT CDoC CDul CLnd CTri LBuc NWea WDin WMou |
| – 'Serotina' (m) | CDoC CDul WDin WMou |
| × ***candicans*** misapplied | see *P.* × *jackii* |
| × ***canescens*** | CDoC CLnd NWea WDin |
| ***deltoides*** 'Fuego' **new** | SGol |
| × ***generosa*** 'Beaupré' | WMou |
| § × ***jackii*** (f) | WDin |
| – 'Aurora' (f/v) | CBcs CCVT CDul CLnd CMac CSBt ELan LBuc MGos MMuc NPri NWea SBfd SGol SPer SRms WDin WFar WHar WMou |
| ***lasiocarpa*** ♀H4 | CGHE CMCN CPLG CTho ELan EPfP IArd MBlu MRav SLPl WMou WPGP |
| ***nigra*** | CDul CHab CLnd CMac CTho EPfP NWea WDin WSFF |
| – (f) | ECrN SLPl |
| – (m) | SLPl |
| – subsp. ***betulifolia*** | CCVT CDul CHab CLnd CWan NWea WDin WMou |
| – – (f) | EBtc WMou |
| – – (m) | EBtc WMou |
| § – 'Italica' (m) ♀H4 | CAlb CCVT CDoC CDul CLnd CMac CSBt CTho CTri CWib EBee ECrN ELan LBuc MGos NWea SBfd SEWo SPer SRms WDin WMou |
| – 'Italica Aurea' | see *P. nigra* 'Lombardy Gold' |
| § – 'Lombardy Gold' (m) | CEnd |
| – 'Pyramidalis' | see *P. nigra* 'Italica' |
| 'Serotina Aurea' | see *P.* × *canadensis* 'Aurea' |
| ***simonii*** 'Fastigiata' | WMou |
| ***szechuanica*** | WMou |
| § – var. ***tibetica*** | WMou |
| ***tacamahaca*** | see *P. balsamifera* |
| 'Tacatricho 32' | see *P.* 'Balsam Spire' |
| ***tremula*** ♀H4 | CCVT CDoC CDul CHab CLnd CMac CRWN CSBt CTho CTri CWib ECrN ELan GAbr LBuc NWea SBfd SEND SEWo SPer WDin WHar WMou WSFF |
| § – 'Erecta' | CDul CEnd CLnd CTho LMaj MBlu MBri SMad WFar WMou |
| – 'Fastigiata' | see *P. tremula* 'Erecta' |
| – 'Pendula' (m) | CEnd CTho ECrN IDee WDin WMou |
| ***trichocarpa*** | CDul LMaj SPer |
| – 'Fritzi Pauley' (f) | CDul CTho WMou |
| ***violascens*** | see *P. szechuanica* var. *tibetica* |
| ***yunnanensis*** | WMou |

## *Porophyllum* (*Asteraceae*)

| | |
|---|---|
| ***ruderale*** | CArn ELau |

## *Portulaca* (*Portulacaceae*)

| | |
|---|---|
| ***oleracea*** | CArn MHer MNHC SIde SVic WJek |
| – var. ***aurea*** | MNHC WJek |

## *Portulacaria* (*Didiereaceae*)

| | |
|---|---|
| ***afra*** | EShb |
| – 'Variegata' (v) | EShb |

## *Potamogeton* (*Potamogetonaceae*)

| | |
|---|---|
| ***crispus*** | CBen CWat EHon MSKA WMAq WSFF |
| ***natans*** | MSKA SEND |
| ***pectinatus*** | CWat |

## *Potentilla* ✿ (*Rosaceae*)

| | |
|---|---|
| CC 5780 | GKev |
| ***alba*** | CTri EBee ECha ECho ELan GCal GMac MLHP MRav MWat NChi WAul |
| ***alchemilloides*** | CMac LRHS WPer |
| ***alpicola*** | WPer |
| ***ambigua*** | see *P. cuneata* |
| ***anglica*** | CArn |
| ***anserina*** | CArn MHer NMir WHer XLum |
| – 'Golden Treasure' (v) | EBee WHer |
| ***anserinoides*** | WMoo WPer |
| ***arbuscula*** misapplied | see *P. fruticosa* 'Elizabeth' |
| – 'Beesii' | see *P. fruticosa* 'Beesii' |
| 'Arc-en-ciel' | Widely available |
| ***argentea*** | CRWN GAuc LRHS MBNS SPlb WFar XLum |
| ***arguta*** | EBee NBre |
| ***argyrophylla*** | see *P. atrosanguinea* var. *argyrophylla* |
| – 'Alfred Salter' | LRHS |
| ***atrosanguinea*** | Widely available |
| § – var. ***argyrophylla*** | CFir COIW CSam CWCL EBee ECha ELan EPfP GCal LRHS MMuc NBPC NBir NBro NChi SEND SRms STes WAul WFar WMoo XLum |
| – – 'Golden Starlit' **new** | LRHS |
| – – 'Scarlet Starlit' **new** | LRHS NCGa |
| – 'Fireball' (d) | EPfP GJos LRHS WPer |
| – var. ***leucochroa*** | see *P. atrosanguinea* var. *argyrophylla* |
| * – 'Sundermannii' | CSpr LLHF |
| ***aurea*** | ECho ECtt EPfP NWCA WBrk WNew WPat |
| – 'Aurantiaca' | EWes NBlu NLar NPro |
| § – subsp. ***chrysocraspeda*** | NMen |
| § – 'Goldklumpen' | ECtt MRav NPro |

| |  |  |
|---|---|---|
| | 'Blazeaway' | EBee ECtt LRHS LSou MArl MBNS NGdn NPro SPoG WFar |
| | ***brevifolia*** | NWCA |
| | ***calabra*** | CSpr EBee ECha EWes WHer |
| § | ***cinerea*** | CTri ECho LBee LLHF LRHS |
| | ***collina*** | LLHF |
| § | ***crantzii*** | CMea SRms |
| | - 'Nana' | see *P. crantzii* 'Pygmaea' |
| § | - 'Pygmaea' | ECho ECtt EPfP NBir NMen |
| § | ***cuneata*** ♀H4 | ECho GAbr GKev MMuc NWCA SEND WPer |
| | ***davurica*** 'Abbotswood' | see *P. fruticosa* 'Abbotswood' |
| | ***delavayi*** | LRHS MNrw |
| | ***detommasii*** | LLHF |
| | - MESE 400 | EBee |
| | ***dickinsii*** | NMen |
| | 'Emilie' (d) | CSpe EBee ECtt GAbr GCal GMac LRHS MAvo MBNS MLLN MNrw NBPC NLar NMRc NPro SWvt WBor WCot WFar WHil WWlt |
| § | ***erecta*** | CRWN CWan GPoy MNHC WHfH WNew |
| | ***eriocarpa*** | EBee ECho EPau GEdr NMen NSla WAbe WPat |
| | - CC 6352 | GKev |
| | - var. ***tsarongensis*** | WAbe |
| | 'Esta Ann' | CMac EBee ECtt EPPr LHop MArl MAvo MBNS MCot NCGa NDov NPro SRGP |
| | 'Etna' | CAby CEnt CHar CKno EBee ECtt ELan LRHS MLHP MNFA MNrw NBir NLar NPnk SPad WHrl WMoo WPer WPtf |
| | 'Everest' | see *P. fruticosa* 'Mount Everest' |
| | 'Fireflame' | ECha MRav NBre NCGa NLar WMoo |
| | ***fissa*** | MNrw NBir NBre SPhx |
| | 'Flambeau' (d) | CWCL EBee ECtt EShb GGar GKin IPot LHop LPla LRHS MArl MNFA MRav NBre NGdn NLar NPro WMoo |
| | 'Flamenco' | CSam CTri CWCL ECtt GMac MArl MBNS MBri MLHP MNrw MRav NBir NCGa SUsu WAbb WFar WMoo |
| | ***fragariiformis*** | see *P. megalantha* |
| | ***fruticosa*** | LBuc NWea |
| § | - 'Abbotswood' ♀H4 | Widely available |
| | - 'Abbotswood Silver' (v) | MSwo WMoo |
| | - 'Annette' | CMac MBrN NPro |
| | - 'Apple Blossom' | CWib |
| | - var. ***arbuscula*** hort. | see *P. fruticosa* 'Elizabeth' |
| | - 'Argentea Nana' | see *P. fruticosa* 'Beesii' |
| | - 'Baby Bethan'PBR (d) | LLHF NHol WFar |
| § | - 'Beesii' | ELan EPfP GGar |
| | - 'Bewerley Surprise' | NBir |
| | - 'Chelsea Star' ♀H4 | CMac LRHS LSRN MAsh MGos SBfd |
| | - 'Chilo' (v) | NEgg WMoo |
| | - var. ***dahurica*** 'Hersii' | see *P. fruticosa* 'Snowflake' |
| | - - 'Rhodocalyx' | WFar |
| | - 'Dart's Golddigger' | CTri NWad |
| | - 'Daydawn' | CBcs CDoC CDul CMac CTri CWSG EBee ECtt ELan EPfP LHop LRHS MAsh MLHP MRav MSwo NBir NEgg NHol NLar NWad SGol SLim SPer SRms SWvt WDin WFar WMoo |
| § | - 'Elizabeth' | CBar CBcs CDoC CDul CWib EBee ELan EPfP LAst LRHS LSRN MGos MMuc MNHC MSwo NHol NWea SBfd SGol SPer SPoG SRms SWvt WCFE WDin WFar WMoo |
| | - 'Farreri' | see *P. fruticosa* 'Gold Drop' |
| | - 'Floppy Disc' | ELan EPfP |
| | - 'Glenroy Pinkie' | EPfP MRav NLar |
| § | - 'Gold Drop' | CMac NHol |
| | - 'Golden Spreader' | LRHS |
| | - 'Goldfinger' | CChe CDoC CMac CSBt CWSG EBee ELan EPfP LHop LRHS MAsh MGos MMuc MRav MSwo MWat NEgg NHol SBrd SCoo SEND SLim SPer SPlb SPoG WDin WFar |
| | - Goldkugel | see *P. fruticosa* 'Gold Drop' |
| | - 'Goldstar' | CBar CDul CWSG EQua IArd LRHS MGos NHol NPri SBfd SCoo SEND SLon WFar |
| | - 'Goldteppich' | LBuc |
| | - 'Goscote' | MGos |
| | - 'Grace Darling' | CAbP ELan EPfP EWes GGar NBir NEgg NHol NLar SRGP SWvt WMoo |
| | - 'Groneland' ♀H4 | EPfP LRHS MAsh SBrd SCoo SPoG |
| | - 'Haytor's Orange' | CWib |
| | - 'Hopleys Little Joker' | WFar |
| | - 'Hopleys Orange' ♀H4 | CDoC CWSG EBee ELon EPfP EWes LHop LRHS MMuc MWat NHol NPri SCoo SEND SGol WFar WGor WMoo |
| | - 'Hurstbourne' | NPro |
| | - 'Jackman's Variety' ♀H4 | CWib EPfP LRHS MAsh SRms |
| | - 'Katherine Dykes' | CDoC CDul CTri CWib EBee EPfP GKin LAst LBMP LRHS LSRN MAsh MGos MNHC NEgg NWea SCoo SLim SPer SPoG SRms WDin WFar WHar WMoo |
| * | - 'King Cup' ♀H4 | LRHS MAsh SBrd |
| § | - 'Klondike' | CBcs CSBt EBee MMuc NEgg NWea EBee |
| | - 'Kobold' | EBee |
| * | - 'Lemon and Lime' | LRHS NBir NPro |
| | - 'Limelight' ♀H4 | CSBt EBee ELan EPfP GKin LRHS MAsh MBri MRav MSwo NHol WFar |
| | - 'Longacre Variety' | CMac CTri EQua IArd MSwo NWea |
| | - 'Lovely Pink'PBR | see *P. fruticosa* 'Pink Beauty' |
| § | - 'Maanelys' | CSBt ELan EQua NHol NWea SPer SRms WDin WMoo |
| | - 'Macpenny's Cream' | CMac |
| § | - 'Manchu' | CDoC CMac MRav MWat SPer SRms |
| | - Mango Tango = 'Uman'PBR | CDoC CSBt EBee LRHS LSRN MNHC |
| § | - Marian Red Robin = 'Marrob'PBR ♀H4 | CDoC CSBt CWib EBee ELan EPfP GKin LAst LRHS MAsh MBri MRav MSwo MWat NEgg NHol NPri NWea SBrd SCoo SLim SLon SPer SPoG SWvt WDin |
| | - 'McKay's White' | NLar |
| | - 'Medicine Wheel Mountain' ♀H4 | ELan EWes IArd LRHS MAsh MGos MRav NHol NLar NPro NWad SCoo SLim SPer SPoG |
| | - Moonlight | see *P. fruticosa* 'Maanelys' |
| § | - 'Mount Everest' | CTri EQua MMuc NWea SEND SLon SRms |
| | - 'Nana Argentea' | see *P. fruticosa* 'Beesii' |
| | - 'New Dawn' | CDoC EWTr GKin WFar |
| | - 'Orangeade' | EPfP LRHS MAsh NLar SBrd SCoo SPoG |
| * | - 'Peachy Proud' | NPro |
| § | - 'Pink Beauty'PBR ♀H4 | CDoC CSBt CWSG EBee EGxp ELan EPfP GKin LRHS LSRN MAsh MBrN MBri MMuc MNHC MRav NCGa NEgg NHol NPri SBfd SCoo SEND SPer SPoG SWvt WHar WMoo |
| | - 'Pink Pearl' | WMoo |

| |  |  |
|---|---|---|
| | – 'Pink Queen' | NLar |
| | – 'Pink Whisper' | NPro NWad |
| | – 'Pretty Polly' | ELan LAst LRHS MGos MSwo NHol NLar WDin WFar WMoo |
| | – 'Primrose Beauty' ♀H4 | CDoC CDul CMac EBee ECrN ELan EPfP LAst LBMP LRHS LSRN MAsh MMuc MRav MSwo NEgg NHol SCoo SEND SLPl SLim SPer SPlb WDin WFar WMoo |
| § | – Princess = 'Blink' | CBcs CDul CWSG ELan EPfP LBMP LRHS MAsh MRav NEgg NHol SCoo SGol SLim SRms WDin WFar WMoo |
| | – 'Red Ace' | Widely available |
| | – Red Robin PBR | see *P. fruticosa* Marian Red Robin |
| | – 'Royal Flush' | NHol |
| | – 'Setting Sun' new | LBuc |
| | – 'Snowbird' | EPfP MGos NPro SLim WFar |
| § | – 'Snowflake' | CBcs WMoo |
| | – 'Sommerflor' ♀H4 | EPfP EQua LRHS MAsh NCGa SBrd |
| | – 'Sophie's Blush' | CChe MRav NHol NWea WDin WSHC |
| | – 'Summer Dawn' new | LBuc |
| | – 'Summer Sorbet' | LRHS |
| | – 'Sunset' | CBcs CMac CWib EBee ECrN ELan EPfP GKin LSRN MGos NBir NEgg NHol NWea SAga SCoo SLim SPer SRms WFar WMoo |
| | – 'Tangerine' | Widely available |
| | – 'Tilford Cream' | CDoC CSBt CTri EBee ELan EPfP GKin LAst LBMP LRHS LSRN MSwo NBir NEgg NHol SGol SPer SPoG SRms WDin WFar WMoo |
| | – 'Tom Conway' | CMac NLar |
| | – var. ***veitchii*** | CDoy CSBt |
| | – 'Vilmoriniana' | CBot CTri ELan EPfP GCal LRHS MAsh MLHP MRav NWea SPer SPoG SSpi SWvt WSHC |
| | – 'Whirligig' | CMac |
| | – 'Wickwar Beauty' | CWib |
| | – 'Yellow Bird' ♀H4 | LRHS MAsh MGos |
| | 'Gibson's Scarlet' ♀H4 | Widely available |
| | ***glandulosa*** | NBre SMad WBrk |
| | 'Gloire de Nancy' (d) | CWCL EBee LBMP MRav NBir NChi NLar WCot |
| | 'Gold Clogs' | see *P. aurea* 'Goldklumpen' |
| | ***gracilis*** | EBee GMac |
| | 'Helen Jane' | GBee GJos LRHS MBNS MHer MSpe NBir NLar SAga STes WFar WMnd WPtf |
| | ***heptaphylla*** | NBre |
| | 'Herzblut' | NLar |
| | × ***hopwoodiana*** | Widely available |
| | × ***hybrida*** 'Jean Jabber' | EBee GMac MRav NLar NPro SRGP |
| | ***hyparctica*** | MDKP |
| | 'Jack Elliot' | NPro |
| | ***kurdica*** new | XLum |
| | ***leuconota*** new | LRHS |
| | 'Light My Fire' | EBee ECtt EKen LLHF MAvo MBNS MBri |
| § | 'Majland' | NDov |
| | 'Mandshurica' | see *P. fruticosa* 'Manchu' |
| | 'Maynard's' | see *P.* 'Majland' |
| § | ***megalantha*** ♀H4 | Widely available |
| | – 'Gold Sovereign' | EAEE EPfP LRHS LSou NPro SPoG |
| | 'Melton' | EBee MNrw NBir |
| * | 'Melton Fire' | CEnt CWan ECtt EPfP EShb GBee GJos GKin GQue LAst LRHS MNHC NBir SGar WFar WMnd WMoo |
| | 'Monarch's Velvet' | see *P. thurberi* 'Monarch's Velvet' |

| |  |  |
|---|---|---|
| | 'Monsieur Rouillard' (d) | CSam CWCL EBee ECtt GCra IPot LRHS MArl MCot MNrw MRav MWat NGdn WHoo WMnd |
| | 'Mont d'Or' | MRav |
| | ***montana*** | WPer |
| | ***morefieldii*** | CPBP |
| | ***nepalensis*** | CEnt EHor LAst MLHP NBPC NDov NChi NPro XLum |
| | – 'Flammenspiel' | WFar |
| | – 'Master Floris' | WFar WHal |
| § | – 'Miss Willmott' ♀H4 | Widely available |
| | – 'Ron McBeath' | Widely available |
| | – 'Roxana' | CFir EBee ELan LRHS MRav NBro NLar SRGP WAbb WFar WMoo WPer |
| | – 'Shogran' | COlW EBee GAbr GJos GLam GQue LAst LBMP MBNS NBPC NHol NLar NVic WHrl WPtf |
| § | ***neumanniana*** | CPBP CSpr NBir NPri |
| | – 'Goldrausch' | LEdu MRav |
| § | – 'Nana' | ECho ECtt EPot GGar LBee MHer MWat NMen NRya SPlb SRms WFar WMoo WPat XLum |
| | – white-flowered | LAst |
| | ***nevadensis*** | CTri ECho GEdr MAsh SRms |
| | ***nitida*** | EPot GEdr MAsh NMen SRms WAbe |
| | – 'Alba' | ECho EPot NMen |
| | – 'Lissadell' | EPot |
| | – 'Rubra' | CFir CMea ECho EDAr MWat NBir NWCA SRms WAbe WPat |
| | ***nivalis*** | ECho |
| | ***norvegica*** | GAuc |
| | ***ovina*** var. ***ovina*** NNS 06-491 new | GKev |
| | ***palustris*** | CWat EBee LLWG NLar NMir WMoo XLum |
| | ***parvifolia*** 'Klondike' | see *P. fruticosa* 'Klondike' |
| | ***pedata*** | LLWP NChi XLum |
| | ***pensylvanica*** | LLHF |
| | 'Pink Panther' | see *P. fruticosa* Princess |
| | aff. ***polyphylla*** CHP&W 314 | GKev |
| | ***recta*** | COlW CSpr MArl NPri WTou XLum |
| | – 'Alba' | CEnt GMaP LAst NBre NEgg WPtf |
| | – 'Citrina' | see *P. recta* var. *sulphurea* |
| | – 'Macrantha' | see *P. recta* 'Warrenii' |
| § | – var. ***sulphurea*** | CAby CEnt EWTr GMac LAst MCot MHer MLHP MMuc MNFA MNrw NBir NBre NLar SAga SBch SEND SPhx WBrk WFar WHal WHoo WHrl WMnd WMoo WPer WPtf WTin XLum |
| § | – 'Warrenii' | CSBt EBee EPla GMaP LAst LRHS MRav NBPC NBir NEgg SPer SPoG SRms WFar WHal WHrl WMoo WPer XLum |
| | ***reptans*** | CArn CRWN |
| | 'Roxanne' (d) | LRHS MHer |
| | ***rupestris*** | CMea ECha MHer NBPC NLar NSti SGar WCAu WFar WHal WMoo WPer WPtf |
| | ***simplex*** | EBee |
| | ***speciosa*** | EWes WMoo |
| | ***sterilis*** | CHid WHer WSFF |
| * | ***sundermanii*** | WHrl |
| | ***tabernaemontani*** | see *P. neumanniana* |
| | ***ternata*** | see *P. aurea* subsp. *chrysocraspeda* |
| | ***thurberi*** | LRHS MCot MMHG MNFA MNrw NLar SPhx WMoo XLum |
| § | – 'Monarch's Velvet' | Widely available |
| | ***tommasiniana*** | see *P. cinerea* |

× ***tonguei*** ♀H4 — Widely available
***tormentilla*** — see *P. erecta*
'Twinkling Star' — EBee WPtf
***uniflora*** — LLHF
***verna*** — see *P. neumanniana*
– 'Pygmaea' — see *P. neumanniana* 'Nana'
'Versicolor Plena' (d) — NLar
***villosa*** — see *P. crantzii*
'Volcan' — CWCL EBee ECtt ETod EWes GQue MBri NPro SUsu WAbb WCAu WFar WHal
'White Queen' — GMac MNrw MRav NBre SHar SPur
'William Rollisson' ♀H4 — Widely available
***willmottiae*** — see *P. nepalensis* 'Miss Willmott'
'Yellow Queen' — CBcs CMac CTri GKin GMaP LHop MNrw MRav NHol NLar SPer WCAu WFar

## *Poterium* see *Sanguisorba*

***sanguisorba*** — see *Sanguisorba minor*

## *Pratia* (*Campanulaceae*)

§ ***angulata*** — CDoy
– 'Jack's Pass' — NEgg
§ – 'Treadwellii' — ECha ECho EPfP GEdr GGar LRHS SPlb WHal
§ ***pedunculata*** — CBar CPLG CTri ECha ECho ECou ECtt EDAr ELan EPfP GGar LBee LLWG LRHS MAsh NChi NRya SPet SPlb SRms SRot WFar WMoo WPer WPtf
I – 'Alba' **new** — WBrk
– 'County Park' — CBar CEnt CMea CSpe CTri CYeo ECha ECho ECou ECtt EDAr ELan EPfP GAbr GGar LBMP LLWG LRHS MAsh MMuc SPlb SPoG SRms SRot WHoo WMoo WPer XLum
– 'Tom Stone' — ECtt
– 'White Stars' — ECho EDAr LLWG

## *Premna* (*Verbenaceae*)

* ***vanrensburgii*** — CCCN

## *Preslia* see *Mentha*

## *Primula* ✿ (*Primulaceae*)

sp. — SVic
SDR 4735 (Cy) — GKev
***acaulis*** — see *P. vulgaris*
'Adrian Jones' (Au) — IPen NHol WAbe
***advena*** var. ***euprepes*** — see *P. euprepes*
'Alan Robb' (Pr/Prim/d) — ECtt EPfP NGdn SPer SRGP WFar
'Alexina' (*allionii* hybrid) (Au) — MFie NHar
***algida*** (Al) — ECho
§ ***allionii*** (Au) ♀H2 — IPen NSum WAbe
– HNG 12 (Au) — ITim
– 'Agnes' (Au) — NMen
– 'Aire Waves' — see *P.* × *loiseleurii* 'Aire Waves'
– var. ***alba*** (Au) — IPen
– 'Allen Moonbeam' (Au) — ITim
– 'Allen Queen' (Au) — IPen
– 'Anna Griffith' (Au) — CPBP IPen MFie WAbe
– 'Anne' (Au) — IPen
– 'Aphrodite' (Au) — NHar
– 'Apple Blossom' (Au) — GAbr GKev
– 'Archer' (Au) — IPen ITim NWad
– 'Ares' (Au) — NHar
– 'Aries Violet' (Au) — NHar
– 'Austen' (Au) — GLam
– 'Avalanche' (Au) — IPen WAbe
– 'Beryl' (Au) — IPen
– 'Biddy' (Au) — IPen
– 'Bill Martin' (Au) — EPot IPen ITim NWad
– 'Blood Flake' (Au) — IPen
– Burnley form (Au) — NWad
– 'Circe's Flute' (Au) — NHar
– 'Cissie' (Au) — IPen ITim
– 'Crowsley Variety' (Au) — NMen NWCA
– 'Crusader' (Au) — WThu
– 'Crystal' (Au) — WAbe
– 'DA No2' (Au) **new** — EPot
– 'Duncan' (Au) — ITim
§ – 'Edinburgh' (Au) — IPen ITim NWad
– 'Edrom' (Au) — IPen ITim
– 'Elizabeth Baker' (Au) — IPen ITim MFie
– 'Elizabeth Burrow' (Au) — WAbe
– 'Elizabeth Earle' (Au) — EPot ITim WAbe
– 'Elliott's Large' — see *P. allionii* 'Edinburgh'
– 'Elliott's Variety' — see *P. allionii* 'Edinburgh'
– 'Emily Jane' (Au) — IPen
– 'Eureka' (Au) — CPBP
– 'Eveline Burrow' (Au) — WAbe
– 'Fanfare' (Au) — GKev IPen NHar
– 'Frank Barker' (Au) — IPen
– 'Gavin Brown' (Au) — IPen ITim
– 'Gilderdale Glow' (Au) — CPBP
– 'Giuseppi's Form' — see *P. allionii* 'Mrs Dyas'
– 'Grandiflora' (Au) — ITim
– 'Hannah' (Au) **new** — EPot
– 'Hartside' (Au) — NWad
– 'Hartside 6' (Au) — IPen ITim NHar
– 'Hartside 12' (Au) — IPen
– 'Hazey' (Au) — ITim
– 'Hocker Edge' (Au) — GLam ITim NWad
– 'Io 2' (Au) — NHar
– 'Ion's Amethyst' (Au) — NHar
– 'Isobel' (Au) — IPen
– 'James' (Au) — IPen
– 'Jan' (Au) — IPen
– 'Joe Elliott' (Au) — IPen
– K R W — see *P. allionii* 'Ken's Seedling'
§ – 'Kath Dryden' (Au) — GKev IPen ITim LLHF
§ – 'Ken's Seedling' (Au) — IPen
– 'Little O' (Au) — WAbe
– 'Louise' (Au) — IPen
– 'Lucy' (Au) — IPen NHar
– 'Malcolm' (Au) — IPen
– 'Margaret Earle' (Au) — IPen WAbe
– 'Marjorie Wooster' (Au) — IPen ITim MFie NWCA
– 'Martin' (Au) — IPen ITim
– 'Mary Anne' (Au) — WAbe
– 'Mary Berry' (Au) — CPBP IPen MFie NWad
– 'Maurice Dryden' (Au) — IPen WAbe
– 'Molly' (Au) — IPen
§ – 'Mrs Dyas' (Au) — IPen NWad WAbe
– 'Neon' (Au) — IPen
– 'Neptunes Wave' (Au) — NHar
– 'Nettleton 855' (Au) **new** — EPot
– 'New Dawn' (Au) — NHar
– 'Pale Venus' (Au) — IPen NHar
– 'Peggy Wilson' (Au) — EWld NLar NWad WThu
– 'Pennine Pink' (Au) — IPen
– 'Perkie' (Au) — IPen
– 'Phoebe's Moon' (Au) — IPen NHar
– 'Pink Ice' (Au) — ITim MFie
– 'Pinkie' (Au) — IPen WAbe
– 'Praecox' (Au) — IPen
– 'Raymond Wooster' (Au) — IPen NWad
– 'Scimitar' (Au) — IPen MFie
– 'Serendipity' (Au) — IPen

- 'Snowflake' (Au) CPBP IPen NWCA WAbe
- (thrum, white) (Au) IPen
- 'Tranquillity' (Au) ITim NHar
- 'Travellers' (Au) IPen
- 'William Earle' (Au) CPBP IPen ITim
***allionii* × *auricula*** misapplied 'Blairside Yellow' (Au) ECho IPen NSum WFar
***allionii* × *auricula*** misapplied 'Old Red Dusty Miller' (Au) ECho NWad
***allionii* × *clusiana*** (Au) ECho
***allionii* × *hirsuta*** (Au) NWad
***allionii* × *pedemontana*** see *P.* × *sendtneri*
***allionii* × *pubescens*** (Au) ECho
***allionii* × *pubescens*** 'Harlow Car' (Au) GAgs
***allionii*** × 'Lismore Jewel' (Au) NWCA
***allionii*** × 'Lismore Treasure' (Au) CPBP MFie NWCA
***allionii*** × 'Snow Ruffles' (Au) IPen ITim MFie
***allionii*** × 'White Linda Pope' (Au) IPen MFie NHar
***alpicola*** (Si) ♀H4 CAby CFee CLAP CWCL GAbr GAuc GEdr GGar GKev IPen LPBA LRHS NBid NBro NCGa NGdn NSum NWCA SBfd
- var. ***alba*** (Si) GAuc GEdr GGar GKev IPen LRHS MNrw NBid SEND
§ - var. ***alpicola*** (Si) CLAP GCra GEdr GKev IPen MMuc MNrw SEND
- hybrids (Si) STes WMoo
- 'La Luna' (Si) MMuc SEND
- var. ***luna*** see *P. alpicola* var. *alpicola*
- var. ***violacea*** (Si) CAby CFir CLAP GAbr GCra GGar GKev IPen LRHS MMuc MNrw NBid SEND WFar WHil WPer
'Altaica' see *P. elatior* subsp. *meyeri*
***altaica grandiflora*** see *P. elatior* subsp. *meyeri*
***amethystina*** (Am) WAbe
***amoena*** see *P. elatior* subsp. *meyeri*
'Amy Smith' **new** WThu
***angustifolia*** (Pa) NWCA
***anisodora*** see *P. wilsonii* var. *anisodora*
'Annemijne' GEdr WCot
I 'Appleblossom' (Pr/Prim/d) **new** CSpr
'April Rose' (Pr/Prim/d) NBid
× ***arctotis*** see *P.* × *pubescens*
'Arduaine' (Pe) **new** CDes
***aurantiaca*** (Pf) CFir GEdr GKev IPen
***aureata*** (Pe) WAbe
***auricula*** ambig. (Au) CTsd NBlu
***auricula*** L. (Au) ♀H4 EDAr IPen LRHS MFie NBro SPer SPet SPlb SPoG WAbe
- SDR 2705 GKev
- SDR 5507 GKev
- subsp. ***balbisii*** see *P. auricula* L. subsp. *ciliata*
- subsp. ***bauhinii*** (Au) GAuc
§ - subsp. ***ciliata*** (Au) GKev GLam
- subsp. ***olgae*** (Or) GKev
***auricula*** misapplied (Au) GAgs
- '2nd Vic' (Au/S) SPop WFar
- A74 (Au) SEND STre SWal
- K85 (Au/S) ITim SPop
- 'Abdor' (Au/St) SPop
- 'Abundance' (Au/A) SPop
- 'Achates' (Au/A) IPen
- 'Admiral' (Au/A) EWoo WCre
- 'Adrian' (Au/A) GAgs IPen MFie NBro NDro SPop WCre
- 'Aga Khan' (Au/A) SPop
- 'Agamemnon' (Au/A) EWoo MFie WCre
- 'Alamo' (Au/A) MFie NDro WCre
- 'Alan Ball' (Au) WCre
- 'Alan Ravenscroft' (Au/A) MFie SPop WFar
- 'Albert Bailey' (Au/d) EWoo GAbr GAgs GCai IPen ITim MFie NDro NEgg SPop WCre WHil
- 'Albury' (Au/d) IPen
- 'Alchemist' (Au/S) **new** IPen WCre
- 'Alexandra Georgina' (Au/A) MFie
- 'Alf' (Au/A) IPen MFie NDro SPop
- 'Alfred Niblett' (Au/S) IPen
- 'Alice' (Au/d) **new** IPen
- 'Alice Haysom' (Au/S) CWCL ELan EWoo GAbr GAgs GCai IPen MAsh NDro SPop WCre WFar
- 'Alicia' (Au/A) EWoo GAbr GAgs MFie NDro SPop WCre
- 'Alison Jane' (Au/A) CPBP IPen MFie NDro WCre WHil
- 'Alison Telford' (Au/A) WHil
- 'Allensford' (Au/A) WCre
- alpine mixed (Au/A) EPfP SRms
- 'Amber Light' (Au/S) SPop
- 'Amber Waves' (Au) GAbr
- 'Amicable' (Au/A) EWoo GAgs MFie NDro SPop WCre WHil
- 'Ancient Society' (Au/A) EWoo GAbr GAgs IPen MFie NDro SPop WFar
- 'Andrea Julie' (Au/A) GAgs IPen MFie NDro SPop WCre WHil
- 'Andrew Hunter' (Au/A) MFie NDro SPop
- 'Andy Cole' (Au/A) EWoo NDro SPop
- 'Angel Eyes' (Au/St) SPop
- 'Angel Islington' (Au/S) NDro
- 'Angela Gould' (Au) GAbr MFie
- 'Angela Short' (Au/St) NDro SPop
- 'Angostura' (Au/d) SPop
- 'Ann Taylor' (Au/A) IPen
- 'Anne Hyatt' (Au/d) GAbr NDro
- 'Annie Tustin' (Au/S) SPop
- 'Antoc' (Au/S) EWoo SPop
- 'Anwar Sadat' (Au/A) EWoo GAbr MFie NDro WCre WFar WHil
- 'Apple Blossom' (Au/B) NDro
- 'Applecross' (Au/A) IPen ITim NDro SPop WCre WFar WHil
- 'April Moon' (Au/S) MAsh MFie NDro SPop
- 'April Tiger' (Au/St) EWoo
- 'Aquarium' (Au/d) **new** SPop
- 'Arctic Fox' (Au) MFie
- 'Argus' (Au/A) EWoo GAbr GAgs IPen MAsh MFie NDro SPop WCre WHil
- 'Arthur Delbridge' (Au/A) MFie NDro WFar WHil
- 'Arundel Cross' (Au) IPen NEgg
- 'Arundell' (Au/S/St) CPBP CWCL GAbr GAgs GCai IPen MAsh MFie SPop WCre WFar WHil
- 'Arwen' (Au/A) SPop
- 'Ashcliffe Gem' (Au/A) NDro
- 'Astolat' (Au/S) EBee GAbr GAgs GKev IPen ITim NDro SPop WCre WHil
- 'Athene' (Au/S) IPen NDro SPop
- 'Atlantic' (Au/S) NDro NEgg
- 'Aubergine' (Au/B) NDro
- 'Aurora' (Au/A) EDAr MFie NDro WCre
- 'Austin' (Au/A) IPen SPop
- 'Autumn Fire' (Au/A) EWoo SPop
- 'Aviemore' (Au/A) WCre

- 'Avon Carrier' (Au/d) SPop
- 'Avon Citronella' (Au) SPop
- 'Avon Twist' (Au/d) SPop
- 'Avril' (Au/A) IPen NDro SPop WCre
- 'Avril Hunter' (Au/A) GAgs IPen MFie NDro SPop WCre
- 'Awesome' (Au/St) **new** SPop
- 'Bacchante' (Au/d) SPop
- 'Bacchus' (Au/A) MFie NDro SPop
- 'Baggage' (Au) GAbr SPop
- 'Balbithan' (Au/B) GAbr
- 'Baltic Amber' (Au) MFie SPop
- 'Bank Error' (Au/S) **new** IPen NDro
- 'Barbarella' (Au/S) IPen MFie NDro SPop WCre
- 'Barbarian' (Au) WFar
- Barnhaven doubles (Au/d) CWCL GAbr NSum
- 'Barnhaven Gold' (Au) IPen
- 'Barr Beacon' (Au/A) NDro
- 'Basilio' (Au/S) NDro
- 'Basuto' (Au/A) IPen ITim MFie NDro SPop WCre
- 'Beatrice' (Au/A) CTri EWoo GAbr GCai IPen MFie NDro SPop WCre WFar WHil
- 'Bedford Lad' (Au/A) WCre
- 'Beechen Green' (Au/S) EWoo GAbr GAgs GCai IPen ITim MAsh NDro SPop WCre
- 'Behold' (Au) WCre
- 'Belgravia Gold' (Au/B) NDro
- 'Bellamy Pride' (Au/B) GAbr IPen NDro SPop WCre
- 'Belle Zana' (Au/S) EWoo GAgs IPen MFie NDro SPop
- 'Ben Lawers' (Au/S) SPop
- 'Ben Wyves' (Au/S) SPop WCre
- 'Bendigo' (Au/S) EWoo MFie SPop
- 'Bengal Rose' (Au/S) SPop
- 'Benno' (Au/St) **new** NDro
- 'Benny Green' (Au/S) IPen SPop WCre
- 'Beppi' (Au) WHil
- 'Bethan McSparron' (Au/B) NDro
- 'Bewitched' (Au/A) MFie NDro
- 'Bilbo Baggins' (Au/A) NDro SPop
- 'Bill Bailey' (Au/d) GAbr NDro SPop WCre
- 'Bilton' (Au/S) SPop WCre
- 'Bingley Folk' (Au/B) SPop
- 'Bizarre' (Au) GAgs WCre
- 'Black Ice' (Au/S) NDro
- 'Black Jack'PBR (Au/d) GKin LRHS
- 'Blackfield' (Au/S) SPop
- 'Blackhill' (Au/S) MFie SPop
- 'Blackpool Rock' (Au/St) CWCL
- 'Blairside Yellow' (Au/B) ECho EWes LLHF NDro WAbe
- 'Blakeney' (Au/d) GCai MFie NDro
- 'Blossom' (Au/A) GAbr MFie WFar
- 'Blue Bonnet' (Au/A/d) EWoo GAbr GAgs NDro SPop WCre
- 'Blue Boy' (Au/S) NDro
- 'Blue Chips' (Au/S) GAgs NDro SPop WCre
- 'Blue Cliffs' (Au/S) IPen SPop
- 'Blue Fire' (Au/S) SPop
- 'Blue Heaven' (Au/A) IPen NDro SPop WCre
- 'Blue Jean' (Au/S) GAbr IPen MFie NDro SPop
- 'Blue Nile' (Au/S) NDro SPop WCre
- 'Blue Skies' (Au/St) SPop
- 'Blue Velvet' (Au/B) GAbr GAgs IPen LLHF NBro NDro WCre WPat
- 'Blue Wave' (Au/d) MSCN SPop
- 'Blue Yodeler' (Au/A) GAgs MFie NDro SPop WCre WHil
- 'Blush Baby' (Au/St) EWoo GAbr GAgs NDro SPop
- 'Bob Dingley' (Au/A) WCre
- 'Bob Lancashire' (Au/S) CWCL GAbr GAgs IPen ITim MFie NDro SPop WCre
- 'Bold Tartan' (Au/St) IPen
- 'Bonanza' (Au/S) SPop
- 'Bookham Firefly' (Au/A) GAbr GAgs IPen MFie NDro SPop WCre WFar WHil
- 'Bookham Star' (Au/S) NDro SPop
- 'Border Bandit' (Au/B) SPop
- 'Border Beauty' (Au/St) **new** NDro
- 'Border Tawny' (Au/B) NDro
- 'Boromir' (Au/A) EWoo NDro
- 'Bradford City' (Au/A) CWCL LRHS NDro SPop
- 'Bradmore Bluebell' (Au) NDro
- 'Bramley Rose' (Au/B) SPop
- 'Bran' (Au/B) NDro
- 'Brasso' (Au) MFie NDro SPop
- 'Brazil' (Au/S) EBee IPen ITim MFie NDro SPop WCre WHil
- 'Brazos River' (Au/A) EWoo MFie
- 'Breckland Joy' (Au/A) NDro
- 'Brenda's Choice' (Au/A) IPen MFie NDro SPop WCre WFar
- 'Bright Eyes' (Au/A) IPen MFie NDro WCre
- 'Bright Ginger' (Au/S) **new** EWoo
- 'Brimstone and Treacle' (Au/d) **new** SPop
- 'Broad Gold' (Au/A) MFie SPop WCre
- 'Broadwell Gold' (Au/B) GAbr NDro NLar SPop WCre
- 'Brookfield' (Au/S) GAgs IPen ITim MAsh MFie NDro SPop WCre
- 'Broughton' (Au/S) MFie SPop
- 'Brown Ben' (Au) GAgs MFie WFar
- 'Brown Bess' (Au/A) GAbr GAgs GCai IPen ITim MAsh MFie NDro WCot WCre WFar
- 'Brownie' (Au/B) CWCL GAbr GAgs NBir NDro SPop WHil
- 'Bucks Green' (Au/S) GAbr NDro SPop
- 'Bunty' (Au/A) MFie
- 'Bush Baby' (Au/B) NDro
- 'Butterwick' (Au/A) EWoo GAbr GAgs GMaP IPen MFie NDro NEgg SPop WCre
- 'C.G. Haysom' (Au/S) GAbr MFie NDro SPop WCre
- 'C.W. Needham' (Au/A) IPen MFie NDro SPop WCre
- 'Calypso' (Au/d) SPop
- 'Cambodunum' (Au/A) IPen MFie NDro SPop WCre WFar WHil
- 'Camelot' (Au/d) EBee ELan EWoo GAgs GCai MFie NBro NDro SPop WCre WFar WHil
- 'Cameo' (Au/A) WCre
- 'Cameo Beauty' (Au/d) NDro SPop
- 'Candida' (Au/d) IPen MFie NDro SPop WCre
- 'Candy Stripe' (Au/St) SPop
- 'Caramel' (Au/A) IPen
- 'Cardinal Red' (Au/d) NDro SPop
- 'Carmel' (Au/D) SPop
- 'Carole' (Au/A) MFie NDro SPop WCre WFar
- 'Carreras' (Au) MFie
- 'Carzon' (Au/A) NDro
- 'Ceri Nicolle' (Au/B) NDro
- 'Chaffinch' (Au/S) EWoo GAbr IPen NDro SPop
- 'Chamois' (Au/B) GAbr IPen MFie NDro
- 'Chanel' (Au/S) SPop
- 'Channel' (Au/S) WCre
- 'Charles Bronson' (Au/d) GAbr MFie NDro
- 'Charles Rennie' (Au/B) MFie NDro SPop
- 'Checkmate' (Au) MFie SPop
- 'Chelsea Bridge' (Au/A) EWoo IPen MFie NDro SPop WCre WHil
- 'Cheops' (Au/A) IPen MFie NDro NEgg
- 'Cherry' (Au/S) GAgs IPen NDro WCre
- 'Cherry Picker' (Au/A) MFie NDro SPop WCre WFar
- 'Cheyenne' (Au/S) EWoo GAbr GAgs MFie NDro WCre WFar
- 'Chiffon' (Au/S) CPBP EWoo IPen MAsh NDro SPop
- 'Chiquita' (Au/d) SPop

- 'Chloë' (Au/S) IPen NDro
- 'Chorister' (Au/S) CPBP EBee GAbr GAgs GCai IPen ITim MFie NDro WCre WHil
- 'Chyne' (Au) EWoo
- 'Cicero' (Au/A) MFie SPop
- 'Cindy' (Au/A) NDro
- 'Cinnamon' (Au/d) EWoo GAgs ITim MAsh MFie NDro SPop WCre
- 'Cinnamon' (Au/S) GAbr WHil
- 'Citron-Ella' (Au/d) **new** SPop
- 'Clare' (Au/S) IPen MFie NDro SPop WCre
- 'Clatter-Ha' (Au/d) MAsh WHil
- 'Claudia Taylor' (Au) SPop
- 'Cloud Nine' (Au/S) **new** WCre
- 'Clouded Yellow' (Au/S) SPop WHil
- 'Cloudy Bay' (Au) LRHS NDro WFar
- 'Clunie' (Au/S) IPen NDro WCre
- 'Clunie II' (Au/S) GAgs IPen WFar
- 'Cobden Meadows' (Au/A) WCre
- 'Coffee' (Au/S) GAgs IPen MFie NDro SPop WCre WFar
- 'Colbury' (Au/S) NDro SPop
- 'Colonel Champney' (Au/S) EWoo NDro SPop WCre
- 'Comet' (Au/S) IPen NDro
- 'Connaught Court' (Au/A) EWoo IPen NDro WCre
- 'Conquistador' (Au/A) **new** NDro
- 'Conservative' (Au/S) GAbr IPen NDro WFar
- 'Consett' (Au/S) EWoo IPen MFie SPop WHil
- 'Cooper's Gold' (Au/B) NDro
- 'Coppi' (Au/A) EWoo IPen NDro SPop
- 'Coral' (Au/S) EWoo NDro
- 'Cornish Cream' (Au/B) IPen NDro
- 'Cornmeal' (Au/S) EWoo GAgs ITim MFie NDro WCre
- 'Corntime' (Au/S) SPop WCre
- 'Corporal Jones' (Au/S) SPop WCre
- 'Corporal Kate' (Au/St) WCre
- 'Corrie Files' (Au/d) MFie
- 'Cortina' (Au/S) CPBP CWCL ECho EWoo GAbr GAgs GCai IPen MFie NDro SPop WCre WFar WHil
- 'County Park Red' (Au/B) NDro
- 'Coventry Street' (Au/S) MAsh MFie NDro SPop
- 'Crackley Tagetes' (Au/d) ECho
- 'Craig Dhu' (Au/B) SPop
- 'Craig Vaughan' (Au/A) MFie NDro SPop
- 'Cranborne' (Au/A) SPop
- 'Crecy' (Au/A) MFie SPop
- 'Crimple' (Au/S) NDro SPop
- 'Crimson Glow' (Au/d) EWoo GAbr GAgs MFie NDro SPop
- 'Crinoline' (Au/S) NDro SPop
- 'Cuckoo Fair' (Au/S) GAbr GAgs IPen SPop WCre
- 'Cuddles' (Au/A) MFie NDro
- 'Curry Blend' (Au/B) NDro
- 'Cutie Pie' (Au/St) IPen WCre
- 'Cuttlefish' (Au/St) SPop
- 'Daftie Green' (Au/S) EWoo GAbr GAgs IPen NDro WCre
- 'Dakota' (Au/S) EWoo MFie
- 'Dales Red' (Au/B) EWoo GAbr GAgs IGor IPen MFie NDro NLar SPop WCre WHil
- 'Dan Tiger' (Au/St) EWoo MFie NDro SPop
- 'Daniel' (Au/A) NDro
- 'Dark Eyes' (Au/d) EWoo GAbr GAgs MFie NDro SPop
- 'Dark Red' (Au/S) IPen
- 'David Beckham' (Au/d) SPop
- 'Deckchair' (Au/St) NDro SPop
- 'Delilah' (Au/d) GAbr GAgs ITim MFie NDro SPop WHil
- 'Denna Snuffer' (Au/d) GAbr NDro
- 'Derrill' (Au/B) **new** SPop
- 'Devon Cream' (Au/d) ECho MFie NDro SPop WFar
- 'Diane' (Au/A) MFie NDro
- 'Dick Rogers' (Au/B) NDro
- 'Digby' (Au/d) EWoo NDro
- 'Digit' (Au/d) NDro
- 'Dilemma' (Au/A) SPop
- * - 'Dill' (Au/A) IPen NDro SPop WHil
- 'Dilly Dilly' (Au/A) NDro SPop
- 'Divint Dunch' (Au/A) GAgs IPen MFie NDro SPop WCre WFar WHil
- 'Doctor Duthie' (Au/S) SPop
- 'Doctor Lennon's White' (Au/B) GAgs IPen MFie NDro SPop WCre WHil
- 'Dolly Viney' (Au/d) GAbr
- 'Donhead' (Au/A) MFie NDro SPop WCre WFar WHil
- 'Donna Clancy' (Au/S) EWoo SPop
- 'Doreen Stephens' (Au/A) MFie NDro WFar
- 'Doris Jean' (Au/A) MFie WFar
- 'Doublet' (Au/d) ECho GAbr GAgs GCai IPen MFie NDro SPop WCre WFar WHil
- 'Doubloon' (Au/d) ECho
- 'Doublure' (Au/d) EWoo GAbr NDro SPop WCre WHil
- 'Douglas Bader' (Au/A) EWoo GAbr MFie NDro SPop WCre WHil
- 'Douglas Black' (Au/S) EWoo GAbr GAgs MFie NDro SPop WCre WHil
- 'Douglas Green' (Au/S) EWoo IPen NDro
- 'Douglas White' (Au/S) MFie SPop
- 'Dovedale' (Au/S) NDro
- 'Dowager' (Au/A) MFie
- Downtown Doubles (Au/d) SPop
- 'Doyen' (Au/d) EWoo IPen MAsh MFie WFar
- 'Dream' (Au/St) **new** SPop
- 'Dubarii' (Au/A) MFie
- 'Duchess of Malfi' (Au/S) SPop
- 'Duke of Edinburgh' (Au/B) NDro
- * - 'Dusky' (Au) WFar
- 'Dusky Girl' (Au/A) NDro
- 'Dusky Maiden' (Au/A) EWoo GAgs GCai MFie NDro SPop WCre WHil
- 'Dusky Yellow' (Au/B) ECho NDro
- 'Dusty Miller' (Au/B) ECho LRHS MRav NBir
- 'Eastern Promise' (Au/A) GAgs GCai MFie NDro SPop WFar WHil
- 'Ed Spivey' (Au/A) NDro WCre
- 'Eden Alexander' (Au/B) MFie NDro
- 'Eden Blue Star' (Au/B) EWoo SPop
- 'Eden Carmine' (Au/B) MFie
- 'Eden David' (Au/B) MFie SPop WHil
- 'Eden Goldfinch' (Au/B) **new** SPop
- 'Eden Greenfinch' (Au/B) **new** SPop
- 'Eden Lilactime' (Au/B) **new** SPop
- 'Eden Moonlight' (Au/B) WHil
- 'Edith Major' (Au/d) CPBP MFie SPop
- 'Eglinton' (Au) WCre
- 'Eileen K' (Au/S) NDro
- 'Elf Star' (Au/A) SPop
- 'Elizabeth Ann' (Au/A) GAbr NDro SPop
- 'Ellen Thompson' (Au/A) EWoo GAbr GAgs MFie NDro SPop WCre WFar
- 'Elsie' (Au/A) WCre
- 'Elsie May' (Au/A) MAsh MFie NDro SPop WCre
- 'Elsinore' (Au/S) IPen WCre
- 'Embley' (Au/S) NDro SPop WCre
- 'Emery Down' (Au/S) NDro SPop
- 'Emily' (Au/d) IPen
- 'Emma Louise' (Au) IPen
- 'Emmett Smith' (Au/A) NBro NDro

– 'Emorydown' (Au/S) **new** WCre
– 'Enigma' (Au/S) SPop
– 'Enlightened' (Au/A) MFie
– 'Envy' (Au/S) MFie
– 'Erica' (Au/A) IPen MFie NDro SPop WCre WHil
– 'Erjon' (Au/S) MFie NDro SPop
– 'Error' (Au/S) MFie
– 'Esso' (Au/S) NDro
– 'Ethel' (Au) NDro WCre
– 'Ethel Wild' (Au/d) **new** SPop
– 'Eve Guest' (Au/A) NDro
– 'Eventide' (Au/S) SPop
– 'Everest Blue' (Au/S) GAbr GAgs SPop WCre
– 'Excalibur' (Au/d) EWoo GAgs NDro SPop WFar
– (Exhibition Series) 'Exhibition Blau' (Au/B) LRHS
– – 'Exhibition Gelb' (Au/B) LRHS
– – 'Exhibition Rot' (Au/B) LRHS
– 'Eyeopener' (Au/A) IPen MFie NDro SPop WCre WHil
– 'Fabuloso' (Au/St) SPop
– 'Fairy' (Au/A) NDro
– 'Fairy Moon' (Au/S) IPen
– 'Falcon' (Au/S) SPop
– 'Fanciful' (Au/S) EWoo MFie NDro WHil
– 'Fancy Free' (Au) SPop
– 'Fanfare' (Au/S) EWoo MAsh MFie NDro SPop
– 'Fanny Meerbeck' (Au/S) GAbr GCai IPen MFie NDro SPop WFar
– 'Faro' (Au/S) MAsh NDro SPop WCre
– 'Favourite' (Au/S) EWoo GAbr GAgs IPen ITim MAsh MFie NDro SPop WCre WFar WHil
– 'Fen Tiger' (Au/St) SPop
– 'Fennay' (Au/S) EWoo
– 'Ferrybridge' (Au/A) IPen
– 'Fiddler's Green' (Au/d) CPBP EWoo GAbr GAgs NDro SPop
– 'Figaro' (Au/S) GAbr GAgs MFie NDro SPop WCre
– 'Finchfield' (Au/A) GAbr IPen MFie NDro
– 'Firecracker' (Au) IPen
– 'Firenze' (Au/A) MFie SPop
– 'Firsby' (Au/d) NDro SPop WCre
– 'First Lady' (Au/A) NDro SPop
– 'First Light' (Au/B) **new** NDro
– 'Fishtoft' (Au/d) MFie
– 'Fitzroy' (Au/d) SPop
– 'Fleet Street' (Au/S) NDro
– 'Fleminghouse' (Au/S) GAbr MFie NDro SPop WCre
– 'Florence Brown' (Au/S) IPen
– 'Forest Burgundy' (Au/d) SPop
– 'Forest Cappuccino' (Au/d) SPop
– 'Forest Duet' (Au/d) SPop
– 'Forest Fire' (Au/d) SPop
– 'Forest Lemon' (Au/d) SPop
– 'Forest Sunlight' (Au/d) **new** SPop
– 'Fradley' (Au/A) IPen MFie NDro
– 'Frank Bailey' (Au/d) MAsh SPop
– 'Frank Crosland' (Au/A) MFie NDro WCre WFar
– 'Frank Jenning' (Au/A) NDro
– 'Frank Taylor' (Au/S) EWoo
– 'Fred Booley' (Au/d) EWoo GAbr GAgs IPen MAsh MFie NDro SPop WCre WFar WHil
– 'Fred Livesley' (Au/A) NDro
– 'Fresco' (Au/A) SPop
– 'Frittenden Yellow' (Au/B) NDro SPop WFar
– 'Frosty' (Au/S) NDro WCre
– 'Fuller's Red' (Au/S) ITim NDro SPop WCre WFar WHil
– 'Funny Valentine' (Au/d) IPen MFie SPop
– 'G.L. Taylor' (Au/A) IPen NDro
– 'Gaia' (Au/d) SPop
– 'Gail Atkinson' (Au/A) SPop
– 'Galen' (Au/A) WCre WFar
– 'Ganymede' (Au/d) SPop
– 'Gay Crusader' (Au/A) GAbr GAgs IPen MFie NDro SPop WCre WFar
– 'Gee Cross' (Au/A) GAbr IPen NDro
– 'Geldersome Green' (Au/S) GCai NDro SPop WCre WFar
– 'Gemini' (Au/S) GLin NDro
– 'General Champney' (Au) WCre
– 'Generosity' (Au/A) MFie NDro WCre
– 'George Edge' (Au/B) NDro
– 'George Harrison' (Au/B) GAbr GAgs NDro SPop
– 'George Jennings' (Au/A) MFie NDro
– 'George Swinford's Leathercoat' (Au/B) GAbr NDro
– 'Geronimo' (Au/S) GAbr IPen MAsh MFie NDro SPop WCre
– 'Ghost Grey' (Au) WCre
– 'Gizabroon' (Au/S) CPBP CWCL EWoo GAbr GAgs LRHS MFie NDro NEgg SPop WCre WFar
– 'Gleam' (Au/S) CWCL EBee ECho EDAr LLHF MFie NDro SPop WCre WFar WHil
– 'Glencoe' (Au/S) EWoo
– 'Gleneagles' (Au/S) EWoo IPen NDro SPop WCre
– 'Glenelg' (Au/S) EWoo GAbr GAgs ITim MFie NDro SPop WCre WHil
– 'Glenluce' (Au/S) EWoo SPop
– 'Gnome' (Au/B) GAbr IPen NDro
– 'Gold Blaze' (Au/S) NDro
– 'Gold Seal' (Au/d) SPop
– 'Gold Seam' (Au/A) EWoo MFie
– 'Golden Boy' (Au/A) MFie
– 'Golden Chartreuse' (Au/d) EWoo GAbr
– 'Golden Fleece' (Au/S) EWoo GAbr MFie NDro SPop
– 'Golden Harvest' (Au/A) SPop
– 'Golden Hill' (Au/S) MAsh SPop
– 'Golden Hind' (Au/d) EWoo GAgs MFie NBro NDro SPop WCre
– 'Golden Splendour' (Au/d) EWoo GAgs IPen ITim MAsh MFie NDro SPop WCre WFar WHil
– 'Golden Wedding' (Au/A) IPen MFie SPop
– 'Goldie' (Au/S) NDro
– 'Goldthorn' (Au/A) WCre
– 'Gollum' (Au/A) MFie NDro SPop
– 'Good Report' (Au/A) EWoo GAgs MAsh MFie NDro SPop WFar WHil
– 'Goody Goody' (Au/St) SPop
– 'Gorey' (Au/A) MFie NDro WCre WHil
– 'Gorgeous George' (Au/St) SPop
– 'Grabley' (Au/S) SPop
– 'Grandad's Favourite' (Au/B) NDro SPop
– 'Green Abundance' (Au/B) **new** EWoo
– 'Green Finger' (Au/S) MFie SPop
– 'Green Frill' (Au) GAgs NDro
– 'Green Heart' (Au/S) **new** SPop
– 'Green Isle' (Au/S) GAbr IPen MFie NDro SPop WCre WFar
– 'Green Jacket' (Au/S) IPen SPop WCre
– 'Green Meadows' (Au/S) GAgs SPop
– 'Green Parrot' (Au/S) GAbr NDro SPop WCre WHil
– 'Green Shank' (Au/S) EWoo GAgs IPen NDro SPop WFar WHil
– 'Greenfield's Fancy' (Au) EBee
– 'Greenfinch' (Au/S) **new** EWoo
– 'Greenheart' (Au/S) SPop
– 'Greenpeace' (Au/S) GAbr GAgs NDro SPop
– 'Greswolde' (Au/d) SPop
– 'Greta' (Au/S) CWCL ECho EWoo GAbr GAgs IPen ITim NDro SPop WFar WHil
– 'Gretna Green' (Au/S) SPop
– 'Grey Bonnet' (Au/S) SPop

- 'Grey Edge' (Au) ECho
- 'Grey Friar' (Au/S) SPop
- 'Grey Hawk' (Au/S) IPen MFie SPop
- 'Grey Lag' (Au/S) SPop WHil
- 'Grey Monarch' (Au/S) GAbr MAsh MFie NDro SPop WCre
- 'Grizedale' (Au/S) SPop
- 'Grüner Veltliner' (Au/S) NDro SPop WCre
- 'Guinea' (Au/S) EWoo GAbr IPen ITim NDro SPop
- 'Gwen' (Au/A) NDro SPop WCre
- 'Gwen Baker' (Au/d) MFie NDro SPop WCre
- 'Gwenda' (Au/A) SPop WHil
- 'Gypsy Rose Lee' (Au/A) MFie
- 'Habanera' (Au/A) NDro SPop WCre WFar
- 'Haffner' (Au/S) NDro SPop
- 'Hallmark' (Au/A) MFie
- 'Handsome Lass' (Au/St) SPop
- 'Harlequin' (Au/B) NDro
- 'Harmony' (Au/B) MFie NBro
- 'Harry Hotspur' (Au/A) EWoo GAgs IPen MFie NDro SPop WFar WHil
- 'Harry 'O'' (Au/S) MFie NDro SPop WCre
- 'Harthorpeburn' (Au/B) **new** NDro
- 'Harvest Glow' (Au/S) IPen NDro SPop WHil
- 'Hawkwood' (Au/S) CPBP CWCL GAbr GAgs IPen MAsh MFie NDro NEgg SPop WFar
- * 'Hazel' (Au/A) IPen MFie NDro SPop WCre WHil
- 'Headdress' (Au/S) GAbr MFie SPop WCre
- 'Heady' (Au/A) EWoo MFie NDro
- 'Heart of Gold' (Au/A) MAsh MFie SPop
- 'Hebers' (Au) NDro SPop
- 'Helen' (Au/S) GAbr IPen MFie NDro SPop WCre WHil
- 'Helen Barter' (Au/S) MFie NDro SPop
- 'Helen Ruane' (Au/d) EBee EWoo GAgs GKev SPop WCre WFar
- 'Helena' (Au/S) IPen MAsh MFie NDro SPop WFar WHil
- 'Helena Dean' (Au/d) SPop
- 'Her Nibs' (Au/St) MAsh
- 'Hermia' (Au/A) MFie SPop
- 'Hetty Woolf' (Au/S) NDro SPop WCre
- 'Hew Dalrymple' (Au/S) EWoo NDro SPop
- 'High Hopes' (Au) NDro
- 'Highland Park' (Au/A) NDro SPop
- Hillview selection (Au) **new** WHil
- 'Hinton Admiral' (Au/S) CWCL EWoo IPen NDro SPop
- 'Hinton Fields' (Au/S) CPBP CSev CWCL EBee EShb GAbr GAgs IPen LRHS MAsh MFie NDro NEgg NWCA SPop WCre WFar WHil
- 'Hobby Horse' (Au) EWoo ITim NDro
- 'Holyrood' (Au/S) GAbr IPen NDro SPop
- 'Honey' (Au/d) GAbr NBro NDro NEgg SPop
- 'Hopleys Coffee' (Au/d) GAbr NDro SPop WCre
- 'Howard Telford' (Au/A) MFie NDro SPop
- 'Hurstwood Midnight' (Au) MFie
- 'Iago' (Au/S) NDro SPop
- 'Ian Greville' (Au/A) IPen MFie NDro SPop WCre
- 'Ibis' (Au/S) WCre
- 'Ice Maiden' (Au/A) EWoo GAbr MFie NDro SPop
- 'Idmiston' (Au/S) CWCL EWoo GAbr MAsh MFie NDro SPop WCre WFar WHil
- 'Ilona' (Au/d) SPop
- 'Imari Stripe' (Au/St) MAsh
- 'Immaculate' (Au/A) MFie SPop WCre WHil
- 'Impassioned' (Au/A) MFie SPop WCre WFar
- 'Impeccable' (Au/A) MFie
- 'Imperturbable' (Au/A) MFie NDro SPop
- 'Indian Love Call' (Au/A) GAbr GAgs IPen ITim MFie NDro SPop WCre WFar WHil
- 'Iris Scott' (Au/A) NDro
- 'Isabella' (Au/A) NDro
- 'Jack Dean' (Au/A) MFie SPop WCre WFar WHil
- 'Jack Redfern' (Au/A) NDro
- 'Jack Wood' (Au/S) NDro
- 'James Arnot' (Au/S) IPen MFie NDro SPop WFar
- 'Janet' (Au) ECho GEdr
- 'Janet Watts' (Au) GAgs
- 'Janie Hill' (Au/A) GAbr MFie SPop WCre
- 'Jean Fielder' (Au/A) SPop
- 'Jean Walker' (Au/B) SPop
- 'Jeanne' (Au/A) MFie
- 'Jeannie Telford' (Au/A) MFie SPop WCre WHil
- 'Jenny' (Au/A) GEdr IPen MFie NDro SPop WCre WFar
- 'Jersey Bounce' (Au/A) NDro
- 'Jilting Jessie' (Au/St) NDro SPop
- 'Joan Curtis' (Au/d) SPop
- 'Joan Elliott' (Au/A) GAbr
- 'Joanne' (Au/A) GAbr MFie NDro SPop WCre
- 'Joe Perks' (Au/A) EWoo IPen MFie NBro NDro SPop WFar WHil
- 'Joel' (Au/S) EWoo GAgs IPen MFie NDro SPop WCre
- 'Johann Bach' (Au/B) SPop
- 'John Stewart' (Au/A) MFie SPop
- 'John Wayne' (Au/A) GAbr MAsh MFie NDro WCre WFar
- 'John Woolf' (Au/S) NDro
- 'Jonathon' (Au/A) EWoo NDro
- 'Jorvic' (Au/S) NDro
- 'Joy' (Au/A) CWCL IPen LLHF MAsh NDro SPop WCre WFar
- 'Joyce' (Au/A) GAbr GAgs IPen MFie NDro SPop WCre WFar
- 'Judith' (Au/B) NDro
- 'Judy Borman' (Au/d) **new** GAgs NDro
- 'Julia' (Au/S) NDro
- 'Julie Nuttall' (Au/B) NDro
- 'June' (Au/A) NDro SPop
- 'Jungfrau' (Au/d) NDro
- 'Jupiter' (Au/S) NDro SPop
- 'K S' (Au/S) NDro
- 'Karen Cordrey' (Au/S) EBee ECho EWoo GAbr GAgs GKev IPen ITim MFie NDro SPop WCre WFar WHil
- 'Karen McDonald' (Au/A) MFie NDro SPop
- 'Kate Haywood' (Au/B) NDro
- 'Kath Dryden' see *P. allionii* 'Kath Dryden'
- 'Kelso' (Au/A) MFie
- 'Ken Chilton' (Au/A) MFie NDro SPop WFar WHil
- 'Kentucky Blues' (Au/d) SPop
- 'Kercup' (Au/A) MFie NDro SPop WCre
- 'Kevin Keegan' (Au/A) MFie SPop WHil
- 'Key West' (Au/A) SPop
- 'Khachaturian' (Au/A) NDro
- 'Kilby' (Au/A) SPop
- 'Kim' (Au/A) IPen MFie NDro WCre
- 'Kingcup' (Au/A) MFie NDro SPop WCre
- 'Kingfisher' (Au/A) EWoo GAbr GAgs ITim MFie NDro SPop WHil
- 'Kingpin' (Au/St) NDro
- 'Kintail' (Au/A) MFie
- 'Kiowa' (Au/S) SPop
- 'Kirklands' (Au/d) EWoo ITim MFie NDro SPop
- 'Kohinoor' (Au) MFie
- 'Königin der Nacht' (Au/St) MFie NDro SPop WCre
- 'Lady Daresbury' (Au/A) MFie NDro SPop WFar
- 'Lady Day' (Au/d) SPop
- 'Lady Diana' (Au/S) NDro
- 'Lady Emma Monson' (Au/S) NDro SPop

- 'Lady Joyful' (Au/S) WCre
- 'Lady of the Vale' (Au/A) NDro
- 'Lady Zoë' (Au/S) GAgs MAsh MFie NDro SPop WCre
- 'Lambert's Gold' (Au) SPop
- 'Lamplugh' (Au/d) IPen
- 'Lancelot' (Au/d) EWoo SPop
- 'Landy' (Au/A) MFie NDro SPop WCre
- 'Langley Park' (Au/A) GAgs IPen MAsh MFie NDro SPop WCre WHil
- 'Laptop' (Au/St) **new** SPop
- 'Lara' (Au/A) MFie
- 'Laredo' (Au/A) EWoo
- 'Larry' (Au/A) EWoo GAgs MFie NDro SPop WCre WFar
- 'Last Chance' (Au/St) SPop
- 'Lavender Lady' (Au/B) IPen NDro NEgg
- 'Laverock' (Au/S) MFie NBir NBro NEgg WCre WHil
- 'Laverock Fancy' (Au/S) IPen ITim NDro
- 'Lazy River' (Au/A) EWoo NDro WCre
- 'Leather Jacket' (Au) GAbr WHil
- 'Leathercoat' (Au) **new** EWoo
- 'Lechistan' (Au/S) GAbr IPen ITim MAsh MFie NDro SPop WCre WHil
- 'Lee' (Au/A) IPen NDro WCre
- 'Lee Clark' (Au/A) MFie
- 'Lee Paul' (Au/A) EWoo GAbr IPen MAsh MFie NDro SPop WCre WHil
- 'Lee Sharpe' (Au/A) EWoo IPen MFie NDro SPop
- 'Lemmy Getatem' (Au/d) NDro SPop
- 'Lemon Drop' (Au/S) EWoo MAsh NBro NDro SPop
- 'Lemon Sherbet' (Au/B) GAgs NDro SPop WHil
- 'Lemonade' (Au) GAgs
- 'Lepton Jubilee' (Au/S) GAbr NDro
- 'Lester' (Au/d) SPop
- 'Leverton' (Au/d) EWoo SPop
- 'Lewis Telford' (Au/A) SPop
- 'Lich' (Au/S) NDro
- 'Lichfield' (Au/A/d) IPen SPop WCre
- 'Light Hearted' (Au/A) CWCL MFie NDro WFar
- 'Likely Lad' (Au/St) SPop
- 'Lila' (Au/S) EWoo NDro
- 'Lilac Domino' (Au/S) EWoo GAbr GAgs IPen ITim MFie NDro NEgg SPop WFar
- 'Lilac Ladywood' (Au/D) **new** SPop
- 'Lillian Hill' (Au/A) EWoo MFie
- 'Lima' (Au/d) MFie
- 'Limelight' (Au/A) NDro SPop
- 'Limelight' (Au/S) IPen
- 'Lincoln Bullion' (Au/d) SPop
- 'Lincoln Charm' (Au/D) GAbr SPop
- 'Lincoln Chestnut' (Au/d) SPop
- 'Lincoln Glow' (Au/D) **new** SPop
- 'Lincoln Imp' (Au/d) SPop
- 'Lincoln Imperial' (Au/d) SPop
- 'Lincoln Major' (Au/d) SPop
- 'Lindley' (Au/S) GAgs ITim MAsh NDro SPop
- 'Ling' (Au/A) MFie NDro SPop WCre
- 'Linnet' (Au/B) NDro
- 'Lintz' (Au/B) MAsh MFie NDro SPop
- 'Linze 2' (Au/S) MFie NDro
- 'Lisa' (Au/A) EWoo IPen MFie NDro SPop WCre WFar WHil
- 'Lisa Clara' (Au/S) EWoo GAbr IPen ITim MAsh MFie NDro SPop WCre WFar
- 'Lisa's Smile' (Au/S) EWoo MFie NDro SPop
- 'Little Rosetta' (Au/d) GAbr NDro
- 'Lockyer's Gem' (Au/B/St) NDro NEgg
- 'Lockyer's Green' (Au) **new** EWoo
- 'Lolita' (Au/St) SPop
- 'Lord Saye and Sele' (Au/St) CWCL EWoo GAbr IPen ITim MAsh MFie NCGa NDro NEgg SPop WCre WHil
- 'Louisa Woolhead' (Au/d) SPop
- 'Lovebird' (Au/S) CPBP CWCL GAbr MAsh MFie NDro SPop
- 'Lucy Locket' (Au/B) CWCL EWoo IPen LRHS NDro NEgg NLar WCre WHil
- 'Ludlow' (Au/S) GAbr
- 'Lupy Minstrel' (Au/S) NDro SPop
- 'Lusty Lad' (Au/St) **new** SPop
- 'Lynn Cooper' (Au) SPop WFar
- 'MacWatt's Blue' (Au/B) GAbr GAgs IGor IPen MFie NDro SPop WCre
- 'Madelaine Palmer' (Au/d) SPop
- 'Maggie' (Au/S) GAbr NDro SPop WCre
- 'Magnolia' (Au/B) WCre
- 'Mandarin' (Au/A) CWCL GAbr GAgs MFie NDro SPop WCre WFar WHil
- 'Margaret' (Au/S) GAbr
- 'Margaret Faulkner' (Au/A) GAbr MFie NDro WCre
- 'Margaret Irene' (Au/A) IPen SPop WCre
- 'Margaret Martin' (Au/S) IPen MFie NDro SPop WCre
- 'Margery Thompson' (Au/d) SPop
- 'Margot Fonteyn' (Au/A) GAbr MFie SPop
- 'Marie Crousse' (Au/d) CMea CPBP EWoo GMaP MFie NDro SPop WCre WFar
- 'Marigold' (Au/d) WFar
- 'Marion Howard Spring' (Au/A) MFie WCre
- 'Marion Tiger' (Au/St) NDro
- 'Mark' (Au/A) IPen MAsh MFie NBro NDro SPop WCre WFar
- 'Marmion' (Au/S) EWoo GAbr IPen ITim MFie NDro SPop WCre WFar WHil
- 'Martin Fish' (Au) WCre
- 'Martin Luther King' (Au/S) NDro
- 'Mary' (Au/d) GAbr NDro SPop
- 'Mary Zach' (Au/S) EWoo MFie NDro SPop WHil
- 'Matthew Yates' (Au/d) CMea EBee GAbr IPen ITim MAsh MFie NDro SPop WCot WCre WHil
- 'Maureen Millward' (Au/A) IPen MFie NDro SPop WCre
- 'May' (Au/A) WCre
- 'Mazetta Stripe' (Au/S/St) GAbr ITim MFie NBro NDro NLar SPop
- 'Meadowlark' (Au/A) EWoo MFie NDro SPop WCre WFar
- 'Mease Tiger' (Au/St) GAbr
- 'Mellifluous' (Au) MFie WCre WFar WHil
- 'Melody' (Au/S) IPen SPop
- 'Mere Peppermint' (Au) **new** EWoo
- 'Merlin' (Au/A) EBee IPen
- 'Merlin' (Au/S) MFie
- 'Merlin Stripe' (Au/St) CWCL IPen NDro SPop WCre WHil
- 'Mermaid' (Au/d) NDro
- 'Merridale' (Au/A) MFie WCre
- 'Mersey Tiger' (Au/S) EWoo ITim MAsh MFie NDro SPop WCre WHil
- 'Metha' (Au/A) NDro
- 'Metis' (Au/d) SPop
- 'Michael' (Au/S) MFie SPop
- 'Michael Wattam' (Au/S) MFie SPop
- 'Mick' (Au/A) MFie WCre
- 'Midland Marvel' (Au/St) SPop
- 'Mikado' (Au/S) IPen MAsh MFie WCre
- 'Milkmaid' (Au/A) MFie WMAq
- 'Millicent' (Au/A) MFie WFar WHil
- 'Mink' (Au/A) MFie NDro WFar

| | | |
|---|---|---|
| | – 'Minley' (Au/S) | CPBP GAbr ITim MFie NBir NBro NDro NEgg SPop WCre |
| | – 'Minstead' (Au/S) | SPop |
| | – 'Minstrel' (Au/S) | MFie NDro WCre |
| | – 'Mipsie Miranda' (Au/d) | SPop |
| | – 'Mirandinha' (Au/A) | MFie |
| | – 'Miriam' (Au/A) | SPop |
| | – 'Mish Mish' (Au/d) | GAbr NDro WHil |
| | – 'Miss Bluey' (Au/d) | EWoo NDro SPop |
| | – 'Miss Newman' (Au/A) | SPop |
| | – 'Miss Pinky' (Au) | NDro SPop |
| | – 'Mojave' (Au/S) | EWoo GAbr GAgs IPen ITim MFie NDro NEgg SPop WCre WHil |
| | – 'Mollie Langford' (Au/A) | MFie NDro SPop WHil |
| I | – 'Molly' (Au) **new** | NWCA |
| | – 'Moneymoon' (Au/S) | EWoo GAgs IPen NDro WCre |
| | – 'Monica' (Au/A) | MFie |
| | – 'Monk' (Au/S) | MFie NDro WHil |
| | – 'Monmouth Star' (Au/St) | NDro |
| | – 'Moody Cow' (Au/St) | MAsh |
| | – 'Moon Fairy' (Au/S) | NDro SPop |
| | – 'Moonglow' (Au/S) | EWoo NDro |
| | – 'Moonrise' (Au/S) | EWoo NDro |
| | – 'Moonriver' (Au/A) | EWoo SPop WCre WFar WHil |
| | – 'Moscow' (Au/S) | SPop |
| | – 'Moselle' (Au/S) | MAsh NDro |
| | – 'Mr A' (Au/S) | EWoo NDro SPop WHil |
| | – 'Mr Bojangles' (Au/d) | SPop |
| | – 'Mr Greenfingers' (Au) | WCre |
| | – 'Mrs Dargan' (Au/d) | NDro |
| | – 'Mrs J.H. Watson' (Au) | WCre |
| | – 'Mrs L. Hearn' (Au/A) | EWoo GAbr IPen ITim NDro SPop WHil |
| | – 'Mrs Lowry' (Au/B) | NDro |
| | – 'Mrs R. Bolton' (Au/A) | WCre WFar |
| | – 'Mrs Robinson' (Au/St) **new** | NDro |
| | – 'Mrs Wilson' (Au) **new** | GAbr |
| | – 'Murray Lakes' (Au/A) | NDro |
| | – 'Murray Lanes' (Au/A) | EWoo |
| | – 'Mustard Sauce' (Au/B) | NDro |
| | – 'My Buddy' (Au/St) | SPop |
| | – 'My Fair Lady' (Au/A) | MFie NDro |
| | – 'My Friend' (Au/B) | NDro |
| | – 'Mystery' (Au) **new** | GAbr |
| | – 'Nancy Dalgetty' (Au/B) | NDro |
| | – 'Naniconan' (Au/A) | NDro |
| | – 'Nankenan' (Au/S) | ITim MFie NDro |
| | – 'Neat and Tidy' (Au/S) | EWoo GAbr GAgs MFie NDro SPop WCre WFar |
| | – 'Nefertiti' (Au/A) | EWoo IPen MFie NDro SPop WCre WHil |
| | – 'Nessun Dorma' (Au/A) | EWoo NDro SPop |
| | – 'Neville Telford' (Au/S) | GAbr IPen MAsh MFie NDro SPop WFar |
| | – 'Nick Drake' (Au/d) | SPop |
| | – 'Nickity' (Au/A) | GAbr GAgs IPen ITim MAsh MFie NDro SPop WCre WFar WHil |
| | – 'Nicola Jane' (Au/A) | EWoo SPop |
| | – 'Nigel' (Au/d) | EWoo GAbr ITim MFie NDro |
| | – 'Night and Day' (Au/S) | NDro SPop |
| | – 'Nightwink' (Au/S) | MFie |
| | – 'Nil Amber' (Au) | SPop |
| | – 'Nina' (Au/A) | NDro |
| | – 'No 21' (Au/S) | NDro SPop |
| | – 'Nocturne' (Au/S) | IPen NBro NDro SPop WCre |
| | – 'Noelle' (Au/S) | EWoo IPen |
| | – 'Nona' (Au/d) | EWoo NDro SPop |
| | – 'Nonchalance' (Au/A) | MFie NDro SPop WHil |
| | – 'Norma' (Au/A) | MFie NDro |
| | – 'Nymph' (Au/d) | EWoo GAbr GAgs MFie NDro SPop WHil |
| | – 'Oake's Blue' (Au/S) | NDro |
| | – 'Oban' (Au/S) | NDro SPop |
| | – 'Oikos' (Au/B) | SPop |
| | – 'Ol' Blue Eyes' (Au/St) | SPop |
| | 'Old Black Isle Dusty Miller' (Au/B) | NDro |
| | – 'Old Clove Red' (Au/B) | EWoo GAbr GAgs MFie NDro WCre WHil |
| | – 'Old Cottage Blue' (Au/B) | GAbr NDro WFar |
| | – 'Old Dublin Blue' (Au/B) | NDro |
| | – 'Old England' (Au/S) | EWoo MFie NDro SPop |
| | – 'Old Gold' (Au/S) | GAbr IPen NDro WFar |
| | – 'Old Gold Dusty Miller' (Au/B) | NDro |
| | – 'Old Irish Blue' (Au/B) | NDro NEgg WCre |
| | – 'Old Irish Green' (Au/B) | GAbr NDro |
| | – 'Old Irish Scented' (Au/B) | GAbr IPen NBro NDro WHil |
| | – 'Old Irish Yellow' (Au/B) | NDro NEgg |
| | – 'Old Mustard' (Au/B) | NDov NDro |
| | – 'Old Pink Dusty Miller' (Au/B) | GAbr IPen NDro |
| § | – 'Old Purple Dusty Miller' (Au/B) | GAbr |
| | – 'Old Red' (Au) | GAgs |
| | – 'Old Red Dusty Miller' (Au/B) | GAbr LLHF NDro SPop WHil |
| | – 'Old Red Elvet' (Au/S) | GAbr NDro SPop |
| | – 'Old Smokey' (Au/A) | EWoo NDro SPop WHil |
| | – 'Old Suffolk Bronze' (Au/B) | GAgs NDro |
| | – 'Old Timer' (Au/S) **new** | SPop |
| | – 'Old Yellow Dusty Miller' (Au/B) | EWes EWoo GAbr IGor IPen NBro NDro NLar NRya WCre WHil WThu |
| | – 'Olivia' (Au/d) | SPop |
| | – 'Olton' (Au/A) | IPen MFie |
| | – 'Optimist' (Au/St) | EWoo SPop WCre |
| | – 'Opus One' (Au/A) | EWoo |
| | – 'Orb' (Au/S) | IPen MAsh MFie NDro SPop WCre WHil |
| | – 'Orlando' (Au/S) | MFie NDro SPop |
| | – 'Orwell Tiger' (Au/St) | EWoo GAgs IPen SPop WCre |
| | – 'Osbaston Bullseye' (Au/St) **new** | SPop |
| | – 'Osbourne Green' (Au/B) | EWoo GAbr GAgs IGor MFie NDov NDro SPop WCre WHil |
| | – 'Ossett Saphire' (Au/A) | NDro SPop |
| | – 'Overdale' (Au/A) | NDro |
| | – 'Paddlin Madeleine' (Au/A) | EWoo NDro |
| | – 'Paleface' (Au/A) | GAgs IPen MFie NDro WCre |
| | – 'Pam Tiger' (Au/St) | WCre |
| | – 'Paphos' (Au/d) | SPop |
| | – 'Paradise Yellow' (Au/B) | EWoo GAbr GEdr MFie NDro NEgg SPop |
| | – 'Paragon' (Au/A) | ITim MFie WHil |
| | – 'Party Time' (Au/S) | IPen |
| | – 'Pastiche' (Au/A) | MFie NDro WCre |
| | – 'Pat' (Au/S) | SPop |
| | – 'Pat Barnard' (Au) | IPen |
| | – 'Pat Mooney' (Au/d) | NDro |
| | – 'Patience' (Au/S) | GAgs ITim NDro SPop WHil |
| | – 'Patricia Barras' (Au/S) | EWoo |
| | – 'Pauline' (Au/A) | EWoo MFie |
| | – 'Pavarotti' (Au/A) | NDro SPop |
| | – 'Pegasus' (Au/d) | EWoo NDro SPop |
| | – 'Peggy' (Au/A) | GAbr WHil |
| | – 'Pequod' (Au/A) | NDro SPop |
| | – 'Petite Hybrid' (Au) | EPot |

|  |  |
|---|---|
| – 'Phantom' (Au/D) | SPop |
| – 'Pharaoh' (Au/A) | CWCL EWoo GAbr GAgs MFie NDro SPop WFar |
| – 'Phyllis Douglas' (Au/A) | IPen MFie NDro NEgg SPop WCre WHil |
| – 'Piccadilly' (Au/S) | MFie |
| – 'Pierot' (Au/A) | IPen MFie NDro SPop WCre WHil |
| – 'Piers Telford' (Au/A) | CPBP CWCL EWoo GAbr GAgs IPen ITim LRHS MFie NDro NEgg NLar SBch SPop WCre WHil |
| – 'Piglet' (Au/D) | GAbr GAgs NDro SPop |
| – 'Pimroagh' (Au/A) **new** | EWoo |
| – 'Pink Fondant' (Au/d) | GAbr NDro |
| – 'Pink Hint' (Au/B) | NDro |
| – 'Pink Lady' (Au/A) | GAbr MFie NBro NDro SPop WHil |
| – 'Pink Lilac' (Au/A/S) | NDro |
| – 'Pinkerton' (Au/d) **new** | SPop |
| – 'Pinkie' (Au/A) | WHil |
| – 'Pinkie Dawn' (Au/B) | NDro WCre |
| – 'Pinstripe' (Au) | EWoo GAbr GAgs IPen NDro SPop WCre WHil |
| – 'Pioneer Stripe' (Au/S) | GAbr GAgs IPen SPop WCre |
| – 'Pippin' (Au/A) | CPBP CWCL GAbr GAgs IPen MFie NBro NDro SPop WCre WFar WHil |
| – 'Pixie' (Au/A) | EWoo IPen MFie |
| – 'Plain Jane' (Au) | MAsh |
| – 'Playboy' (Au/A) | NDro SPop |
| – 'Polestar' (Au/A) | MFie NDro SPop WCre WFar WHil |
| – 'Polly' (Au/B) **new** | GAgs NDro |
| – 'Pop's Blue' (Au/S/d) | NEgg SPop |
| – 'Portree' (Au/S) | GAbr SPop |
| – 'Pot o' Gold' (Au/S) | CPBP EBee ECho EWoo GAgs IPen ITim MAsh MFie NDro NEgg SPop WCre WFar WHil |
| – 'Prague' (Au/S) | IPen MAsh MFie NBir NDro SPop WCre |
| – 'Pretender' (Au/A) | MFie SPop |
| – 'Pride of Poland' (Au/S) | SPop |
| – 'Prince Bishop' (Au/S) | NDro SPop |
| – 'Prince Charming' (Au/S) | GAgs IPen ITim MFie NDro SPop |
| – 'Prince John' (Au/A) | MFie NBro NDro SPop WCre WFar WHil |
| – 'Proctor's Yellow' (Au/B) | NDro |
| – 'Prometheus' (Au/d) | EWoo MAsh MFie NDro NRya SPop WCre WHil |
| – 'Prosperine' (Au/S) | SPop WCre |
| – 'Purple Dusty Miller' | see *P. auricula* 'Old Purple Dusty Miller' |
| – 'Purple Emperor' (Au/A) | MFie |
| – 'Purple Frills' (Au) | MFie |
| – 'Purple Haze' (Au) | SPop |
| – 'Purple Lovely' (Au) | MFie SPop |
| – 'Purple Promise' (Au) | GAbr ITim |
| – 'Purple Prose' (Au/St) | MFie SPop |
| – 'Purple Royale' (Au/B) | NDro |
| – 'Purple Sage' (Au/S) | EWoo MFie NDro |
| – 'Purple Velvet' (Au/S) | CWCL IPen NDro SPop |
| – 'Quality Chase' (Au/A) | NDro |
| – 'Quatro' (Au/d) | EWoo SPop |
| – 'Queen Alexandra' (Au/B) | GAbr NDro WHil |
| – 'Queen Bee' (Au/S) | GAbr MFie NDro SPop WCre WFar |
| – 'Queen's Bower' (Au/S) | SPop WCre |
| – 'Queenswood' (Au/S) **new** | WCre |
| – 'Quintessence' (Au/A) | MFie WCre |
| – 'R.L. Bowes' (Au/A) | NDro |
| – 'Rabley Heath' (Au/A) | GAgs MFie NDro SPop WCre |
| – 'Rachel' (Au/A) | EWoo WCre |
| – 'Radiant' (Au/A) | IPen |
| – 'Rag Doll' (Au/S) | NDro |
| – 'Rajah' (Au/S) | EBee ECho EWoo GAbr GAgs IPen ITim LRHS MFie NDro NEgg NLar SPop WCre WFar WHil |
| – 'Raleigh Stripe' (Au/St) | EWoo GAbr GAgs IPen ITim WCre |
| – 'Ralph's Tan' (Au/B) | NDro |
| – 'Rameses' (Au/A) | IPen MFie NDro WCre |
| – 'Rebecca Baker' (Au/d) | SPop |
| – 'Red Admiral' (Au) | NDro SPop |
| – 'Red and White Stripe' (Au/S/St) | WFar |
| – 'Red Arrows' (Au) | SPop |
| – 'Red Beret' (Au/S) | SPop |
| – 'Red Bordeaux' (Au/S) | NDro |
| – 'Red Carpet' (Au/S) **new** | SPop |
| – 'Red Embers' (Au/S) | SPop |
| – 'Red Ensign' (Au/B) | NDro |
| – 'Red Gauntlet' (Au/S) | EWoo GAbr GAgs IPen MFie MRav NDro SPop WCre WFar |
| – 'Red Mark' (Au/A) | MFie SPop WHil |
| – 'Red Sonata' (Au/S) | SPop |
| – 'Red Vulcan' (Au) | WCre |
| – 'Red Wire' (Au/St) | MAsh NDro SPop |
| – 'Redcar' (Au/A) | MFie NDro WCre |
| – 'Reddown Bat' (Au/d) **new** | SPop |
| – 'Redstart' (Au/B) | ITim |
| – 'Redstart' (Au/S) | GAgs IPen ITim WHil |
| – 'Regency' (Au/A) | NDro |
| – 'Regency Dandy' (Au/St) | SPop |
| – 'Regency Emperor' (Au/St) | SPop |
| – 'Regency Saint Clements' (Au/St) | SPop |
| – 'Reknown' (Au/A) **new** | WCre |
| – 'Remus' (Au/S) | CPBP ECho ELan EWoo GAbr GAgs IPen ITim LLHF MAsh MFie NDro NEgg SPop WCre WFar WHil |
| – 'Renata' (Au/S) | NDro |
| – 'Rene' (Au/A) | EWoo GAbr IPen MFie NDro WCre |
| – 'Renown' (Au/A) | IPen NDro |
| – 'Reynardyne' (Au/d) | SPop |
| – 'Riatty' (Au/d) | GAbr NDro SPop |
| – 'Richard Shaw' (Au/A) | IPen SPop |
| – 'Ring of Bells' (Au/S) | SPop |
| – 'Risdene' (Au) | IPen WCre |
| – 'Robbo' (Au/B) | NDro |
| – 'Robert Green' (Au/S) **new** | EWoo SPop |
| – 'Roberto' (Au/S) | MAsh |
| – 'Robin Hood Stripe' (Au/St) | NDro SPop |
| – 'Robinette' (Au/d) | GAbr SPop |
| – 'Rock Sand' (Au/S) | EWoo GAbr MFie NDro WFar WHil |
| – 'Rodeo' (Au/A) | EWoo GAbr IPen SPop WPat |
| – 'Rolts' (Au/S) | ECho EWoo GAbr GAgs GKev IPen MAsh MFie NBro NDro SPop WCre WFar WHil |
| – 'Rondy' (Au/S) | MFie SPop WHil |
| – 'Ronny Simpson' (Au) | WCre |
| – 'Rosalie' (Au) | SPop |
| – 'Rosalie Edwards' (Au/S) | MFie SPop WCre |
| – 'Rose Conjou' (Au/d) | EWoo GAbr GAgs IPen MFie NDro SPop WFar |
| – 'Rose Kaye' (Au/A) | GAbr IPen NDro SPop WCre |
| – 'Rosebud' (Au/S) | EWoo GAbr NDro SPop |
| – 'Rosemarket Rackler' (Au/B) | NDro SPop |
| – 'Rosemary' (Au/S) | EWoo ITim MAsh MFie NDro SPop WCre WHil |
| – 'Rosewood' (Au) | SPop WCre |
| – 'Rosie' (Au/S) | NDro |
| – 'Rowena' (Au/A) | IPen MFie NBro NDro SPop WCre |
| – 'Roxborough' (Au/A) | GAgs IPen |

- 'Roxburgh' (Au/A) MFie NDro SPop WCre
- 'Roy Keane' (Au/A) IPen MFie SPop
- 'Royal Mail' (Au/S) MFie NDro SPop WCre
- 'Royal Marine' (Au/S) MFie SPop
- 'Royal Scot' (Au/S) **new** WCre
- 'Royal Velvet' (Au/S) GAbr GAgs IPen NDro WHil
- 'Ruby Hyde' (Au/B) EWoo GAbr NDro
- 'Ruby Sutton' (Au/d) **new** EWoo
- 'Ruddy Duck' (Au/S) **new** WCre
- 'Rumbled' (Au/St) MAsh
- 'Rusty Dusty' (Au) GAbr
- 'Rusty Red' (Au/B) NDro
- 'Saginaw' (Au/A) EWoo
- 'Sailor Boy' (Au/S) MFie NDro SPop
- 'Saint Boswells' (Au/S) GAbr NDro SPop
- 'Saint Elmo' (Au/A) MFie SPop
- 'Salad' (Au/S) GAbr
- 'Sale Green' (Au/S) MFie SPop
- 'Sally' (Au/A) MFie
- 'Sam Brown' (Au/S) **new** NDro
- 'Sam Gamgee' (Au/A) NDro
- 'Sam Hunter' (Au/A) NDro SPop
- 'Samantha' (Au/A) EWoo WCre
- 'Samantha' (Au/d) **new** SPop
- 'Sandhills' (Au/A) MAsh MFie WCre WHil
- 'Sandmartin' (Au/S) MFie
- 'Sandra' (Au/A) ELan GAbr GAgs IPen MAsh MFie NDro SPop WCre WHil
- 'Sandra's Lass' (Au/A) EWoo SPop
- 'Sandwood Bay' (Au/A) EWoo GAbr GAgs MFie NBro NDro NEgg SPop WCre WHil
- 'Sarah Gisby' (Au/d) MFie NDro SPop
- 'Sarah Lodge' (Au/d) EWoo GAbr IPen MAsh NDro SPop WCre
- 'Satchmo' (Au/S) NDro
- 'Satin Doll' (Au/d) MFie NDro SPop
- 'Scipio' (Au/S) NDro SPop
- 'Scorcher' (Au/S) IPen MFie NDro SPop
- 'Searchlight' (Au) WCre
- 'Second Victory' (Au) CPBP NDro WCre WHil
- 'Serenity' (Au/S) MFie NDro SPop WCre
- 'Sergeant Wilson' (Au) SPop
- 'Shalford' (Au/d) EWoo GAbr MFie NDro SPop WCre WFar WHil
- 'Sharman's Cross' (Au/S) MFie
- 'Sharon Louise' (Au/S) IPen NDro SPop WCre
- 'Sheila' (Au/S) GAbr MAsh NDro SPop WCre WFar WHil
- 'Shere' (Au/S) EWoo MFie NDro SPop WCre
- 'Shergold' (Au/A) MFie WCre
- 'Sherwood' (Au/S) CWCL IPen MAsh MFie NDro SPop
- 'Shirley' (Au/S) SPop
- 'Shotley' (Au/A) MFie SPop
- 'Show Bandit' (Au/St) SPop
- 'Showtime' (Au/S) NDro
- 'Sibsey' (Au/d) CWCL MAsh NDro SPop
- 'Silmaril' (Au) SPop
- 'Silver Rose' (Au) WCre
- 'Silverway' (Au/S) EWoo MAsh NDro SPop WCre WHil
- 'Simply Red' (Au) IPen MAsh MFie NDro SPop
- 'Sir John' (Au/A) MAsh MFie WFar WHil
- 'Sir John Hall' (Au) MFie
- 'Sirbol' (Au/A) EWoo IPen MFie NDro SPop WCre WFar WHil
- 'Sirius' (Au/A) CWCL EWoo GAbr IPen MFie NDro SPop WCre WFar
- 'Skylark' (Au/A) GAbr GAgs IPen NDro SPop WCre WHil
- 'Skyliner' (Au/A) NDro
- 'Slack Top Red' (Au) **new** NSla
- 'Slim Whitman' (Au/A) NDro SPop
- 'Slioch' (Au/S) EWoo GAbr IPen MAsh MFie NDro SPop WCre
- 'Smart Tar' (Au/S) WCre
- 'Smoothy' (Au/St) **new** SPop
- 'Snooty Fox' (Au/A) GAbr IPen MFie SPop WCre
- 'Snooty Fox II' (Au/A) MFie NDro
- 'Snowy Owl' (Au/S) GAbr MFie NDro SPop WCre
- 'Soliloquy' (Au) MAsh
- 'Soncy Face' (Au/A) MFie SPop WCre
- 'Sonia Nicolle' (Au/B) NDro
- 'Sonny Boy' (Au/A) NDro SPop
- 'Sophie' (Au/d) SPop
- 'South Barrow' (Au/d) GAbr SPop WCre WHil
- 'Southport' (Au) **new** GAbr
- 'Sparky' (Au/A) MFie NDro
- 'Spitfire' (Au/S) MFie
- 'Spokey' (Au) IPen
- 'Spring Meadows' (Au/S) EWoo GAbr MAsh MFie NDro NEgg SPop
- 'Springtime' (Au/A) SPop
- 'Standish' (Au/d) GAbr
- 'Stant's Blue' (Au/S) IPen MFie NBro NDro WCre WFar
- 'Star Spangle' (Au/St) **new** NDro
- 'Star Wars' (Au/S) GAbr MAsh MFie NDro SPop WCre
- 'Star Wars II' (Au) GAgs
- 'Stardust' (Au/S) **new** WCre
- 'Starling' (Au/B) EWoo IPen NDro SPop
- 'Starry' (Au/S) NDro
- 'Starsand' (Au/S) **new** WCre
- 'Stella' (Au/S) NDro
- 'Stella Coop' (Au/d) NDro
- 'Stoney Cross' (Au/S) SPop
- 'Stonnal' (Au/A) MFie NDro SPop WHil
- 'Stormin Norman' (Au/A) EWoo MFie NDro SPop WHil
- 'Stormy Weather' (Au/St) SPop
- 'Striped Ace' (Au/St) NDro SPop WCre WHil
- 'Stripey' (Au/d) IPen WCre
- 'Stromboli' (Au/d) NDro SPop
- 'Stuart West' (Au/A) WCre
- 'Sue' (Au/A) MFie SPop WCre WFar
- 'Sue Ritchie' (Au/D) **new** SPop
- 'Suede Shoes' (Au/S) SPop
- 'Sugar Plum Fairy' (Au/S) EWoo GAbr NDro SPop WHil
- 'Summer Sky' (Au/A) SPop WCre
- 'Summer Wine' (Au/A) EWoo MFie SPop
- 'Sumo' (Au/A) EWoo GAbr GAgs MFie NDro SPop WCre WFar WHil
- 'Sunflower' (Au/A/S) EWoo GAbr ITim MAsh MFie NDro SPop WCre
- 'Sunlit Tiger' (Au/S) **new** EWoo
- 'Sunsplash' (Au) WCre
- 'Sunstar' (Au/S) NDro
- 'Super Para' (Au/S) EWoo GAbr IPen MFie NDro SPop WHil
- 'Superb' (Au/S) MFie NDro
- 'Susan' (Au/A) MFie NDro SPop WCre
- 'Susannah' (Au/d) CWCL EWoo GAbr GAgs GMaP IPen MFie NDro SPop WCre WFar WHil
- 'Sweet Georgia Brown' (Au/A) MFie SPop
- 'Sweet Pastures' (Au/S) CPBP GAbr IPen MFie NDro SPop WCre
- 'Swiss Royal Velvet' (Au/B) NDro
- 'Sword' (Au/d) CPBP CWCL EWoo GAbr GAgs IPen ITim MAsh MFie NDro SPop WCre WFar WHil
- 'Symphony' (Au/A) EWoo MFie NDro SPop WCre WFar WHil

- 'T.A. Hadfield' (Au/A) EWoo GAgs MFie NDro SPop WFar WHil
- 'Taffeta' (Au/S) CWCL LRHS NDro SPop WCre WHil
- 'Tall Purple Dusty Miller' (Au/B) SPop
- 'Tally-ho' (Au/A) NDro
- 'Tamino' (Au/S) IPen MFie NDro SPop
- 'Tarantella' (Au/A) GAbr MFie NDro SPop
- 'Tawny Owl' (Au/B) NBro
- 'Tay Tiger' (Au/St) GAbr MAsh MFie SPop WHil
- 'Teawell Pride' (Au/d) EWoo SPop
- 'Ted Gibbs' (Au/A) MFie NDro SPop WCre
- 'Ted Roberts' (Au/A) ITim MFie NDro SPop WCre WFar
- 'Teem' (Au/S) GAbr IPen MAsh NDro SPop WCre
- 'Temeraire' (Au/A) MFie
- 'Tenby Grey' (Au/S) SPop WCre
- 'Terpo' (Au/A) MFie NDro
- 'The Argylls' (Au/St) SPop
- 'The Baron' (Au/S) GAgs IPen ITim MFie NDro SPop WCre WFar WHil
- 'The Bishop' (Au/S) IPen SPop WHil
- 'The Bride' (Au/S) ITim MFie NDro SPop WCre
- 'The Cardinal' (Au/d) EWoo
- 'The Czar' (Au/A) MFie NDro SPop
- 'The Egyptian' (Au/A) IPen NDro SPop WHil
- 'The Lady Galadriel' (Au/A) NDro
- 'The Maverick' (Au/S) MFie SPop
- 'The Raven' (Au/S) EWoo GAbr GAgs ITim MAsh MFie SPop WCre
- 'The Sneep' (Au/A) EWoo GAgs IPen MFie NDro SPop WCre WFar
- 'The Snods' (Au/S) EWoo IPen MFie NDro SPop
- 'The Wrekin' (Au/S) SPop
- 'Thetis' (Au/A) EWoo MFie SPop WCre WFar
- 'Thisbe' (Au/A) NDro
- 'Three Way Stripe' (St) EWoo GAbr GAgs WCre WHil
- 'Thunderstorm' (Au) MAsh
- 'Thutmoses' (Au/A) NDro
- 'Tiger Tim' (Au/St) EWoo
- 'Tim' (Au) GAbr IPen SPop
- 'Tim's Fancy' (Au/S) NDro
- 'Tinkerbell' (Au/S) IPen MFie SPop WCre WFar
- 'Titania' (Au) SPop
- 'Toffee Crisp' (Au/A) EWoo IPen NDro SPop
- 'Tom Farmer' (Au) WCre
- 'Tomboy' (Au/S) IPen MAsh NDro SPop
- 'Toolyn' (Au/S) EWoo NDro
- 'Tosca' (Au/S) CWCL GAbr GAgs IPen MAsh NDro SPop WCre WFar WHil
- 'Trafalgar Square' (Au/S) **new** GAbr GAgs NDro
- 'Trish' (Au) GAbr
- 'Trojan' (Au/S) WCre
- 'Trouble' (Au/d) EWoo GAbr GMaP IPen MAsh MFie NDro SPop WCre WHil
- 'Troy Aykman' (Au/A) MFie NDro SPop
- 'Trudy' (Au/S) EWoo GAbr IPen ITim MAsh MFie NDro SPop WCre WHil
- 'True Briton' (Au/S) IPen MFie NDro SPop WCre
- 'Trumpet Blue' (Au/S) MFie SPop WFar WHil
- 'Tudor Rose' (Au/S) NDov NDro
- 'Tumbledown' (Au/A) EWoo MFie SPop
- 'Tummel' (Au/A) EWoo MFie NDro SPop WHil
- 'Turnberry' (Au/S) SPop
- 'Twiggy' (Au/S) NDro SPop
- 'Typhoon' (Au/A) EWoo IPen MFie SPop WCre
- 'Uncle Arthur' (Au/A) MFie
- 'Unforgettable' (Au/A) MFie
- 'Upper Crust' (Au/St) SPop
- 'Upton Belle' (Au/S) IPen MAsh MFie NDro SPop WCre WFar
- 'Ushba' (Au/d) SPop
- 'V2 Green' (Au/S) **new** WCre
- 'Valerie' (Au/A) IPen MFie SPop WCre
- 'Valerie Clare' (Au) MFie
- 'Vee Too' (Au/A) GAbr MFie NDro SPop WCre WFar WHil
- 'Vega' (Au/A) SPop
- 'Velvet Moon' (Au/A) MFie WFar
- 'Venetian' (Au/A) GAgs MFie NDro SPop WFar WHil
- 'Vera' (Au/A) NDro SPop
- 'Verdi' (Au/A) SPop
- 'Vesuvius' (Au/d) IPen NDro SPop
- 'Victoria' (Au/S) SPop
- 'Victoria de Wemyss' (Au/A) IPen MFie WCre WHil
- 'Violet Surprise' (Au/St) **new** NDro
- 'Vulcan' (Au/A) MAsh MFie NBro
- 'W. Muller' (Au) **new** NBro
- 'Walhampton' (Au/S) SPop
- 'Walton' (Au/A) CPBP GAbr MAsh MFie NDro SPop WCre WFar
- 'Walton Heath' (Au/d) GAgs IPen MAsh MFie NDro SPop WCre WFar
- 'Waltz Time' (Au/A) MFie
- 'Warpaint' (Au/St) NDro
- 'Warwick' (Au/S) MFie NDro SPop
- 'Wayward' (Au/S) WCre
- 'Wedding Day' (Au/S) EWoo ITim MFie NDro
- 'Wentworth' (Au/A) IPen
- 'Whistle Jacket' (Au/S) MFie NDro SPop
- 'White Ensign' (Au/S) EWoo GAbr IPen NDro SPop WCre WFar WHil
- 'White Satin' (Au/S) **new** SPop WCre
- 'White Water' (Au/A) MFie NDro SPop WCre WHil
- 'White Wings' (Au/S) EWoo IPen ITim MFie NDro SPop WCre
- 'Whitecap' (Au/S) NDro SPop
- 'Wichita Falls' (Au/A) NDro
- 'Wide Awake' (Au/A) NDro SPop
- 'Wild and Grey' (Au/S) NDro
- 'Wilf Booth' (Au/A) MFie SPop WFar
- 'William Gunn' (Au/d) MFie SPop
- 'Wincha' (Au/S) EWoo MFie NDro NEgg SPop WCre WFar
- 'Windways Mystery' (Au/B) NDro
- 'Winifrid' (Au/A) GAbr NDro SPop WCre WFar
- 'Witchcraft' (Au) SPop WCre
- 'Woodlands Lilac' (Au/B) NDro
- 'Woodmill' (Au/A) EWoo IPen MFie NDro SPop WHil
- 'Wookey Hole' (Au/A) MFie SPop
- 'Wor Jackie' (Au/S) SPop
- 'Wycliffe Harmony' (Au/B) NDro
- 'Wycliffe Midnight' (Au/B) GAbr NDro
- 'Wye Hen' (Au/St) SPop
- 'Wye Lemon' (Au/S) SPop
- 'X2' (Au) WHil
- 'Yitzhak Rabin' (Au/A) WHil
- 'Yorkshire Grey' (Au/S) IPen MFie NBro SPop
- 'Zambia' (Au/d) GAbr MFie NDro WCre
- 'Zimmer' (Au/St) SPop
- 'Zircon' (Au/S) SPop

'Barbara Barker' (Au) GEdr NMen
'Barbara Midwinter' (Pr) CDes EBee GAbr GEdr GLam NHar SHar WAbe WCot

| |  |  |
|---|---|---|
| | Barnhaven Blues Group (Pr/Prim) ♀H4 | EBla GAbr NCGa NSum |
| | Barnhaven doubles (Pr/Prim/d) | CWCL |
| | Barnhaven Gold-laced Group | see *P.* Gold-laced Group Barnhaven |
| | Barnhaven hybrids | NSum |
| | 'Beatrice Wooster' (Au) | EPot GAbr GAgs IPen MFie NWCA WFar |
| | 'Beeches' Pink' | GAbr NHar NSum |
| | ***beesiana*** (Pf) | Widely available |
| | - CLD 1018 | GLam |
| | (Belarina Series) 'Belarina Butter Yellow' (Pr/Prim/d) | CAby CPLG CWCL EPfP EWll GAbr MBNS NLar NPnk SRot |
| | - 'Belarina Cobalt Blue' (Pr/Prim/d) | CAby CPLG CWCL CWGN EPot EWll MBNS MFie NGdn NPnk SMrm SRot |
| | - 'Belarina Cream' (Pr/Prim/d) | CAby CPLG CWCL ELon EWll LLHF MFie NGdn NPnk SMrm SRot WBor WCot |
| | - 'Belarina Pink Ice' (Pr/Prim/d) | CAby CWCL EWll LHop MBNS NLar NPnk |
| | - 'Belarina Rosette Nectarine' (Pr/Prim/d) | CAby CPLG CWCL ECtt ELon EPot EWll GAbr MBNS MFie NLar NPnk SMrm WPtf |
| | 'Belinda' | ITim |
| | ***bellidifolia*** (Mu) | GEdr IPen NGdn |
| | ***beluensis*** | see *P.* × *pubescens* 'Freedom' |
| | × ***berninae*** (Au) | GAgs |
| § | - 'Windrush' (Au) | WAbe |
| | 'Bewerley White' | see *P.* × *pubescens* 'Bewerley White' |
| | ***bhutanica*** | see *P. whitei* 'Sherriff's Variety' |
| | 'Big Red Giant' (Pr/Prim/d) | ECtt |
| | ***bileckii*** | see *P.* × *forsteri* 'Bileckii' |
| | 'Blue Julianas' (Pr) | NCGa NSum |
| | 'Blue Riband' (Pr/Prim) | CDes EBee LLHF WFar |
| | 'Blue Ribbon' **new** | IGor |
| | 'Blue Sapphire' (Pr/Prim/d) | CSpe GAbr MFie NDov |
| | 'Blutenkissen' (Pr/Prim) | GAbr GEdr |
| | 'Bon Accord Cerise' (Pr/Poly/d) | GAbr |
| | 'Bon Accord Purple' (Pr/Poly/d) | WFar |
| | ***boothii*** (Pe) | NSum |
| | - ***alba*** (Pe) | LLHF NHar |
| | - subsp. ***repens*** (Pe) | CEnt MNrw |
| | 'Boothman's Ruby' | see *P.* × *pubescens* 'Boothman's Variety' |
| | ***bracteata*** (Bu) | WAbe |
| § | ***bracteosa*** (Pe) | GKev ITim |
| | Bressingham (Pf) | WFar |
| | ***brevicula*** (Cy) SDR 4452 | GKev |
| | - SDR 4770 | GKev |
| | 'Broadwell Milkmaid' | IPen WAbe |
| | 'Broadwell Oliver' (Au) | IPen ITim |
| | 'Broadwell Pink' (Au) | IPen |
| | 'Broadwell Ruby' (Au) | WAbe |
| | 'Broadwell Violet' | EPot IPen |
| | 'Broxbourne' | EPot MFie |
| | 'Buckland Wine' (Pr/Prim) | CElw |
| | × ***bulleesiana*** (Pf) | Widely available |
| | - Moerheim hybrids (Pf) | WFar |
| | ***bulleyana*** (Pf) ♀H4 | Widely available |
| | - ACE 2484 | SWat |
| | - SDR 4261 | GKev |
| | ***burmanica*** (Pf) | EBee GEdr GGar GKev GLam IPen MMuc NWCA SWat WFar WMoo |
| | - SDR 5801 | GKev |
| | 'Butter's Bronze' (Pr/Prim) | GAbr |
| | 'Butterscotch' (Pr/Prim) | NCGa NSum WHil |
| | 'Caerulea Plena' (Pr/Prim) | GCal NBid |
| | ***calderiana*** | GKev |
| | subsp. ***calderiana*** (Pe) **new** | |
| | - subsp. ***strumosa*** (Pe) | GKev |
| | Candelabra hybrids (Pf) | CBre CBro CAbe [illegible] ITim [illegible] NBir NGdn SMrm SPet SWal SWat WFar WHil WOut WPtf |
| | Candelabra hybrids orange-flowered (Pf) | SMrm |
| | Candy Pinks Group (Pr/Prim) | NCGa NSum WHil |
| | ***capitata*** (Ca) | CMMP CMac EBee ECho EPfP GCal GKev IPen MSCN NWCA SPer WFar WWFP |
| | - CC 3843 | GKev |
| | - CC 4847 | GKev |
| | - dark-flowered (Ca) | WCot |
| | - subsp. ***mooreana*** (Ca) | CFir CHid CLAP CPLG CPrp CTsd IPen LRHS NGdn NSum SMrm SPet SPlb SRot XLum |
| | - 'Norverna Blue' (Ca) | CSpr |
| | 'Captain Blood' (Pr/Prim/d) | CDes EKen EPfP GAbr IPot WFar |
| | Carnation Victorians Group (Pr/Poly) | NCGa |
| | ***carniolica*** (Au) | GKev WCot |
| | ***cernua*** (Mu) | GKev IPen |
| § | ***chionantha*** (Cy) ♀H4 | CLAP CWCL EPfP GAuc GCra GGar GKev MMuc NBPC NBir NCGa NGdn NSum SBfd WAbe WFar WPtf |
| | - SDR 4426 | GKev |
| | - SDR 4610 | SEND |
| | - SDR 4847 | GKev |
| | - subsp. ***chionantha*** (Cy) | GKev IPen |
| | - cream-flowered | MMuc |
| § | - subsp. ***melanops*** (Cy) | GAuc |
| § | - subsp. ***sinoplantaginea*** (Cy) SDR 5904 | GKev |
| § | - subsp. ***sinopurpurea*** (Cy) | CLAP CWCL EBee GGar GKev IPen MDKP MMuc NBir NCGa NLar NSum SPer WAbe |
| | - - SDR 4418 | GKev |
| | ***chungensis*** (Pf) | CLAP CWCL EBee EPfP GCra GEdr GGar GKev IPen MMuc NBPC NGdn NHol NSum SBfd SWvt WAbe WMoo |
| § | ***chungensis*** × ***pulverulenta*** (Pf) | CHid CLAP GEdr GKev NBPC NHol NLar WMnd WWEG |
| | × ***chunglenta*** | see *P. chungensis* × *P. pulverulenta* |
| | 'Cisca' | WCot |
| | 'Clarence Elliott' (Au) | CDes CPBP GLam IPen ITim MFie NHar NMen NWCA NWad WAbe WFar WThu |
| | ***clarkei*** (Or) | GEdr WAbe |
| | ***clusiana*** 'Murray-Lyon' (Au) | NMen |
| | ***cockburniana*** (Pf) ♀H4 | EBla GAuc GEdr GGar GKev GQui IPen LRHS NCGa NGdn SWat WAbe WFar |
| | - SDR 1967 | EBee |
| | - 'Edrom Primrose' (Pf) **new** | GEdr |
| | - hybrids (Pf) | SWat |
| | - 'Kevock Sunshine' (Pf) | GKev IPen |
| | ***concholoba*** (Mu) | GKev |
| | 'Corporal Baxter' (Pr/Prim/d) | EPfP GGar GMac LLHF |
| | ***cortusoides*** (Co) | CLAP EBee EPfP GAbr GCra GKev GLam IPen LRHS |

|  |  |
|---|---|
| Cowichan (Pr/Poly) | CElw |
| Cowichan Amethyst Group (Pr/Poly) | CDes CWCL EBee NCGa |
| Cowichan Blue Group (Pr/Poly) | NCGa NSum |
| Cowichan Garnet Group (Pr/Poly) | CDes CWCL EWoo NCGa NSum |
| Cowichan Red Group (Pr/Poly) | WFar |
| Cowichan Venetian Group (Pr/Poly) | CDes CWCL NCGa NSum WFar |
| Cowichan Yellow Group (Pr/Poly) | CDes NCGa NSum |
| 'Coy' (Au) | ITim WAbe |
| Crescendo Series (Pr/Poly) | GAbr WHil |
| 'Crimson Velvet' (Au) | GAbr IPen ITim WThu |
| ***crispa*** | see *P. glomerata* |
| ***cuneifolia*** subsp. ***heterodonta*** (Cu) | GEdr |
| ***daonensis*** (Au) | GAgs |
| ***darialica*** (Al) | GKev LLHF |
| 'Dark Rosaleen' (Pr/Poly) | CPLG CWGN EBee ECtt GAbr GEdr IGor ITim LLHF MBNS MFie MNrw NBPC NCGa NDov SSvw SUsu WCot |
| 'David Valentine' (Pr) | EBla GAbr WAbe WCot |
| 'Dawn Ansell' (Pr/Prim/d) | CDes CRow CSpe CWCL EBla ECtt EPfP GAbr IGor MFie MRav NBir NCGa NDov NLar SBch SRGP WFar WHer |
| Daybreak Group (Pr/Poly) | CWCL NCGa |
| ***deflexa*** (Mu) | EPot IPen |
| ***denticulata*** (De) ♀H4 | Widely available |
| - CC 4629 | GKev |
| - var. ***alba*** (De) | CBcs CBen CTri CWat EBee ECha ECho EPfP GAbr GCra GGar GKev GMaP MFie MLLN NBid NGdn NHol NLar NPri SMrm SPer SPoG WMoo WPer WWEG |
| - blue-flowered (De) | CWCL ECho GAbr NLar NPri SMrm WFar |
| - 'Bressingham Beauty' (De) | LRHS |
| - 'Glenroy Crimson' (De) | CLAP EBee LLHF |
| - 'Karryann' (De/v) | WCot WHil |
| - lilac-flowered (De) | ECho EHon NPri SMrm WWEG |
| - purple-flowered (De) | ECho WMoo |
| - red-flowered (De) | ECho GGar MFie NBir WMoo |
| - 'Ronsdorf' (De) | ELon LBMP NBPC NLar |
| - 'Rubin' (De) | CWCL CWat ECho EHon GAbr GMaP MBrN MLHP NChi NLar SMrm SPer SPoG SRms WPer WWEG XLum |
| - 'Rubinball' (De) | NHol |
| ***deorum*** (Au) | GKev |
| × ***deschmannii*** | see *P.* × *vochinensis* |
| 'Desert Sunset' (Pr/Poly) | CWCL NCGa WHil |
| 'Devon Cream' (Pr/Prim) | WFar |
| ***diantha*** SDR 4841 | GKev |
| 'Don Keefe'PBR | CBod EBee ECtt GAbr GBin GEdr GMac LLHF LSou MBNS NBPC NGdn NLar NPnk WCot WWlt |
| 'Dorothy' (Pr/Poly) | MRav |
| 'Double Lilac' | see *P. vulgaris* 'Lilacina Plena' |
| 'Duchess of York' (Pr/Poly) | GAbr LLWP WCot |
| 'Duckyls Red' (Pr/Prim) | WHal |
| 'Dusky Lady' | CLAP MBri WFar |
| 'Early Bird' (*allionii* hybrid) (Au) | IPen ITim MFie |
| 'Easter Bonnet' (Pr/Prim) | NBid WCot |
| ***edgeworthii*** | see *P. nana* |
| § ***elatior*** (Pr) ♀H4 | CMac CRWN CRow CSev EBee ECho GKev MHer MNHC MNrw NChi NEgg NLar NMen NPnk NPri SBch SBfd SPer SPoG SWvt WBrk WCot WFar WHil WPtf |
| - SDR 5439 | GKev |
| - SDR 6327 | GKev |
| - hose-in-hose (Pr/d) | NBid |
| - hybrids (Pr) | EPfP MWat SPlb |
| I - 'Jessica' (Pr) | WCot |
| § - subsp. ***meyeri*** (Pr) | GKev LLHF NSla |
| - subsp. ***pallasii*** (Pr) | GAuc |
| 'Elizabeth Browning' | GAbr WCot |
| 'Elizabeth Killelay'PBR (Pr/Poly/d) | CBct CElw CMea CPLG CWCL CWGN EBee EBla ECtt ELan GEdr GMaP LSou MFie MLLN NBPC NBir NChi NDov NEgg NGdn NLar NPnk NSti SPer SSvw SUsu WCot WFar WKif |
| 'Ellen Page' (Au) | MFie |
| 'Ethel Barker' (Au) | IPen ITim MFie NWad |
| 'Eugénie' (Pr/Prim/d) | ECtt LLHF NCGa SRGP |
| § ***euprepes*** | GKev |
| 'Fairy Rose' (Au) | IPen NWad WAbe |
| ***farinosa*** (Al) | IPen NGdn NSum WAbe WFar |
| ***fasciculata*** (Ar) | NWCA |
| - CLD 345 | WAbe |
| 'Fire Opal' | LRHS |
| Firefly Group (Pr/Poly) | NCGa WCot |
| § ***firmipes*** (Si) | EWes IPen |
| § ***flaccida*** (Mu) | GAuc GEdr GGar GKev IPen NCGa SBfd WAbe |
| Flamingo Group (Pr/Poly) | NCGa WHil |
| ***florida*** (Y) | GKev |
| - SDR 5954 | GKev |
| ***florindae*** (Si) ♀H4 | Widely available |
| - SDR 4626 | GKev |
| - bronze-flowered (Si) | GQui NBir SWat |
| - buff-flowered (Si) | GAuc |
| - hybrids (Si) | CMac GAbr GEdr GMaP ITim NCGa NHol NSti SMrm |
| - Keillour hybrids (Si) | CLAP NGdn NLar |
| - magenta-flowered (Si) | MDKP |
| - 'Muadh' (Si) | MMuc SEND |
| - orange-flowered (Si) | CSam GCal GMac IPen LLWG MDKP MNrw WFar WMoo |
| - peach-flowered (Si) | CSpe MDKP |
| - 'Ray's Ruby' (Si) | CHar CLAP GEdr MDKP MNrw NBir NGdn SWat |
| - red-flowered (Si) | CAby GBin GGar GKev IPen LLWG MMuc NBid NLar NSum WFar |
| - terracotta-flowered (Si) | CSpr NGdn |
| Footlight Parade Group (Pr/Prim) | NCGa |
| ***forbesii*** (Mo) CC 4084 | CPLG |
| ***forrestii*** (Bu) | GAuc IPen WAbe |
| - SDR 4304 | CPLG |
| § × ***forsteri*** 'Bileckii' (Au) | NBir NWCA |
| - 'Dianne' (Au) | EDAr GAbr GKev NBro NRya NWCA WAbe |
| 'Francisca' (Pr/Poly) | Widely available |
| 'Freckles' (Pr/Prim/d) | SWat |
| ***frondosa*** (Al) ♀H4 | ECho GCra GKev IPen MLHP NMen NWCA SBch WAbe |
| Fuchsia Victorians Group (Pr/Poly) | CWCL |
| 'Garnet' (*allionii* hybrid) (Au) | MFie |
| 'Garryarde Crimson' | GEdr LLHF |
| 'Garryarde Guinevere' | see *P.* 'Guinevere' |
| ***gaubana*** (Sp) | GKev |

| | | |
|---|---|---|
| | ***gemmifera*** (Ar) | GKev GLam |
| | – SSSE 242 | GKev |
| | – var. ***monantha*** (Ar) | GKev |
| | ***geraniifolia*** (Co) | CLAP GCra GEdr GKev |
| § | 'Gigha' (Pr/Prim) | CDes CLAP CWCL EBee GCal |
| | 'Gilded Ginger' | CWCL NCGa |
| | 'Ginger Spice' (Au) new | NDro |
| | ***glaucescens*** (Au) | NSum |
| § | ***glomerata*** (Ca) | GKev IPen |
| | – SDR 3924 | GKev |
| | 'Glowing Embers' (Pf) | GKev LLHF NBir |
| | ***glutinosa*** All. | see *P. allionii* |
| | Gold-laced Group (Pr/Poly) | Widely available |
| § | – Barnhaven (Pr/Poly) | EBla GAbr NBPC NBir |
| | – Beeches strain (Pr/Poly) ♀H4 | CWCL |
| | ***gracilipes*** (Pe) | CLAP GLam MDKP WAbe |
| | – GOS 146 | GEdr |
| | – L&S 1166 | CLAP |
| | – early-flowering (Pe) | GCra WAbe |
| | – late-flowering (Pe) | CLAP GCra |
| | – 'Major' | see *P. bracteosa* |
| | – 'Minor' | see *P. petiolaris* Wall. |
| | ***graminifolia*** | see *P. chionantha* |
| | Grand Canyon Group (Pr/Poly) | CWCL NCGa |
| | ***grandis*** (Sr) | GLam IPen |
| | 'Groenekan's Glorie' (Pr/Prim) | GAbr GEdr NBir NSum WFar |
| § | 'Guinevere' (Pr/Poly) ♀H4 | CPLG CSam CSpe EBee EBla EHoe GAbr GEdr GMaP IGor LSou MBri NBPC NBid NBir NBro NDov NSla NSum SPlb SPoG WCot WFar WHil WPat |
| | 'Hall Barn Blue' (Pr/Prim) | EPot GAbr GEdr GMaP MFie NBPC NHar NMyG WCot WHil |
| § | ***halleri*** (Al) | IPen MDKP NSum WAbe |
| | – 'Longiflora' | see *P. halleri* |
| | aff. ***handeliana*** | GKev |
| | Harbinger Group (Pr/Prim) | CWCL |
| | Harbour Lights mixture (Pr/Poly) | CWCL NCGa |
| | Harlow Carr hybrids (Pf) | EPfP GQui NCGa NSla WHil WMoo |
| | Harvest Yellows Group (Pr/Poly) | CWCL NCGa WCot |
| | 'Hazel's White' | GKev ITim |
| | 'Helmswell Abbey' (Au) | GAgs |
| | ***helodoxa*** | see *P. prolifera* |
| | 'Hemswell Blush' (Au) | CSpe GKev GLam ITim NLar WCre |
| | 'Hemswell Ember' (Au) | CPBP GAgs NRya NWad |
| | ***heucherifolia*** (Co) | GAuc IPen |
| | – SDR 3224 | GKev |
| | ***hidakana*** (R) | GEdr |
| | 'High Point' (Au) | NMen WAbe |
| | ***hirsuta*** (Au) | GAgs GKev IPen SEND WAbe |
| | – 'Lismore Snow' (Au) | NHar NWad |
| | – red-flowered (Au) | EBee GAgs GKev MMuc |
| | hose-in-hose (Pr/Poly/d) | MNrw |
| | 'Hyacinthia' (Au) | GAgs IPen MFie NLar NWCA WThu |
| | ***ianthina*** | see *P. prolifera* |
| | ***incana*** (Al) | GKev |
| | Indian Reds Group (Pr/Poly) | CWCL |
| | 'Ingram's Blue' (Pr/Poly) | CDes GAbr WCot |
| | Inshriach hybrids (Pf) | CMHG LRHS WFar |
| | ***integrifolia*** (Au) | GEdr |
| § | 'Inverewe' (Pf) ♀H4 | CRow GBin GCra GKev GQui NBir NBre NMun SUsu |
| | ***involucrata*** | see *P. munroi* |
| | ***ioessa*** (Si) | EWes GCra GKev GQui NGdn |
| | – var. ***hopeana*** (Si) | GKev |
| | 'Iris Mainwaring' (Pr/Prim) | ECtt GAbr GCra GEdr GKev LLHF MCot |
| | ***irregularis*** (Pe) | WAbe |
| | Jack in the Green Group (Pr/Poly) | CLAP CWCL MNrw WBor WFar WMoo |
| | – red-flowered (Pr/Poly) new | WHil |
| | – white-flowered (Pr/Poly) | IFro |
| | 'Jackie Richards' (Au) | GLam MFie NWad |
| | ***jaffreyana*** (Pu) | EPot |
| | aff. ***jaffreyana*** new | EPot |
| | ***japonica*** (Pf) | CMHG CSam ECha GAuc GGar GQui IPen LPBA LRHS MSCN NBro NGdn NHol SPer SWat WAbe WFar WMoo |
| | – 'Alba' (Pf) | CPrp CTri EBee EPfP GAuc GCal GEdr GGar IPen MFie NGdn NPri NWad SPer WAbe WFar WHil WWEG |
| | – 'Apple Blossom' (Pf) | Widely available |
| * | – 'Carminea' (Pf) | CHid COlW EBee GEdr GGar GKev IPen MFie MSCN NBro NGdn NLar NWad WFar WHil WPnP |
| | – 'Fuji' (Pf) | NBro |
| | – 'Fuji' hybrids (Pf) | NLar |
| | – hybrids (Pf) | CMac GCra MRav |
| | – 'Jim Saunders' (Pf) | SLon |
| | – 'Merve's Red' (Pf) | EBee SUsu |
| | – 'Miller's Crimson' (Pf) ♀H4 | Widely available |
| | – 'Oriental Sunrise' (Pf) | CCVN CMil GKev LLHF NSum |
| | – pale pink-flowered (Pf) | ITim NSum |
| | – 'Peninsula Pink' (Pf) | IPen |
| | – 'Pink Pagoda' (Pf) | ITim |
| | – 'Pinkie' (Pf) | IPen |
| | – 'Postford White' (Pf) ♀H4 | Widely available |
| | – Redfield strain (Pf) | IPen |
| | – red-flowered (Pf) | IPen WAbe |
| | – 'Splendens' (Pf) | IPen |
| | – 'Valley Red' (Pf) | GKev IPen ITim LRHS WHil |
| | ***jesoana*** (Co) | LLHF |
| | – B&SWJ 618 | WCru |
| | – var. ***pubescens*** (Co) | EBee |
| | 'Joan Hughes' (*allionii* hybrid) (Au) | WAbe |
| | 'Joanna' | ECou |
| | 'Johanna' (Pu) | GAbr GEdr GGar GKev LLHF NGdn NHar NPnk NSum NWCA WAbe |
| | 'John Fielding' (Sr × Pr) | CBro CElw EBee GAbr GEdr MCot WCot |
| | 'Jo-Jo' (Au) | GLam MFie WAbe |
| | ***juliae*** (Pr) | ECho EDAr GEdr GLam LRHS NBid NHar NPnk NSum NWCA SPlb WAbe |
| I | – 'Millicent' (Pr) | WCot |
| | – white-flowered (Pr) | NSum |
| | 'Juliana's Fireflies' (Pr/Poly) new | CWCL |
| | 'Ken Dearman' (Pr/Prim/d) | ECtt EPfP NBir SRGP |
| | ***kialensis*** SDR 6004 (Y) new | GKev |
| | 'Kinlough Beauty' (Pr/Poly) | CAby GAbr GEdr GMaP LLHF LRHS NPnk |
| § | ***kisoana*** (Co) | CLAP CPLG EBla IPen LLHF LRHS WCru |
| | – var. ***alba*** (Co) | CLAP |
| | – var. ***shikokiana*** | see *P. kisoana* |
| | – 'Velvet' (Co) | CLAP GEdr |
| | 'Kusum Krishna' | GEdr NHar NMen |
| | 'Lady Greer' (Pr/Poly) ♀H4 | CMac CSam EBee EDAr EPfP GAbr GEdr GKev GMaP IGor LLWP MCot |

| |  |  |
|---|---|---|
| | | MHer NChi NGdn NHar NLar NRya NSum SAga SUsu WFar WHer |
| | 'Lambrook Mauve' (Pr/Poly) **new** | GAbr |
| | ***latisecta*** (Co) | GEdr IPen WCot |
| § | ***laurentiana*** (Al) | CTsd GAuc GKev GLam NMen |
| | 'Lea Gardens' (*allionii* hybrid) (Au) | IPen MFie NWad |
| | 'Lee Myers' (*allionii* hybrid) (Au) | EPot IPen MFie |
| | ***leucophylla*** | see *P. elatior* |
| | 'Lilac Domino' (Au) | IPen WCre |
| | 'Lilian Harvey' (Pr/Prim/d) | CSpr SPer |
| | 'Lindum Malcolm's Mate' **new** | CPBP |
| | 'Lindum Moonlight' | MFie |
| | 'Lindum Wedgwood' (Au) | IPen |
| | 'Lingwood Beauty' (Pr/Prim) | CSam GAbr WAbe |
| I | 'Linnet' (Pe) | GKev |
| | 'Lismore' (Au) | GAgs |
| | 'Lismore 79/7' **new** | NWad |
| | 'Lismore Bay' (Au) | GKev |
| | 'Lismore Jewel' (Au) | NMen |
| | 'Lismore Sunshine' | NHar WThu |
| | 'Lismore Treasure' (Au) | NMen |
| | 'Lismore Yellow' (Au) | CPBP EPot NHar NWCA WAbe |
| | Lissadel hybrids (Pf) | NCGa |
| | 'Little Egypt' (Pr/Poly) | CWCL NCGa NSum |
| | ***littoniana*** | see *P. vialii* |
| | × ***loiseleurii*** 'Aire Mist' (Au) | GKev IPen NHar NMen NRya NSum NWCA NWad WAbe WHil WThu |
| § | - 'Aire Waves' (Au) | CWCL ITim NHar NMen NWad |
| | - 'Pink Aire Mist' (Au) | WHil |
| | - 'White Waves' (Au) | IPen |
| | ***longiflora*** | see *P. halleri* |
| | ***luteola*** (Or) | ECho GKev LLHF NGdn NSum WFar WPer |
| | ***macrocalyx*** | see *P. veris* |
| | ***macrophylla*** (Cy) | GLam |
| | 'MacWatt's Claret' (Pr/Poly) | GAbr LLWP |
| | 'MacWatt's Cream' (Pr/Poly) | EBee EBla GAbr GCra GEdr LRHS SSvw WCot WHil |
| | ***magellanica*** (Al) | NGdn WAbe |
| | 'Maisie Michael' | LLHF WAbe WHil |
| | ***malacoides*** (Mo) | GKev |
| | ***marginata*** (Au) ♀$^{H4}$ | CPne ECho GAbr GEdr IPen LHop LRHS MFie MMuc NSla NSum SBch SEND WAbe WFar |
| | - from the Dolomites (Au) | NWad |
| | - 'Adrian Evans' (Au) | GLam ITim |
| | - 'Adrian Jones' (Au) | ITim |
| | - 'Alba' (Au) | MFie NBro NRya NWad WFar WThu |
| | - 'Ardfearn' (Au) | GAgs |
| | - 'Baldock's Purple' (Au) | IPen |
| | - 'Barbara Clough' (Au) | GEdr IPen ITim MFie NWad WFar |
| | - 'Beamish' (Au) ♀$^{H4}$ | NBro NRya NSla NWad |
| | - 'Beatrice Lascaris' (Au) | MFie NRya WThu |
| | - 'Caerulea' (Au) | MFie NWad |
| | - 'Clear's Variety' (Au) | IPen ITim |
| | - 'Doctor Jenkins' (Au) | IPen ITim NLar NRya NWad |
| | - 'Drake's Form' (Au) | IPen NLar NRya |
| | - dwarf (Au) | ECho GEdr LRHS MFie |
| | - 'Earl L. Bolton' | see *P. marginata* 'El Bolton' |
| § | - 'El Bolton' (Au) | IPen NWad WAbe |
| | - 'Elizabeth Fry' (Au) | IPen MFie |
| | - 'F.W. Millard' (Au) | CWCL |
| | - 'Grandiflora' (Au) | IPen NWad |
| | - 'Highland Twilight' (Au) | IPen NSla WAbe |
| | - 'Holden Variety' (Au) | IPen ITim MFie NHol NRya NWad WAbe |
| | - 'Ivy Agee' (Au) | IPen NRya |
| | - 'Janet' (Au) | GEdr WCre |
| | - 'Jenkins Variety' (Au) | ECho |
| | - 'Kesselring's Variety' (Au) | CMMP ECho GEdr GLam IPen MFie NWad WAbe WFar WTin |
| | - 'Laciniata' (Au) | ECho IPen LRHS |
| | - lilac-flowered (Au) | IPen |
| | - 'Linda Pope' (Au) ♀$^{H4}$ | GAgs GKev IPen NBir NHar NSla NSum WAbe |
| | - maritime form (Au) | IPen |
| | - 'Millard's Variety' (Au) | IPen ITim NWad |
| | - 'Miss Fell' (Au) | GAgs IPen |
| | - 'Mrs Carter Walmsley' (Au) | NRya |
| | - 'Mrs Gatenby' (Au) | NWCA |
| | - 'Nancy Lucy' (Au) | WAbe |
| | - 'Napoleon' (Au) | GEdr IPen MFie MSCN |
| | - 'Prichard's Variety' (Au) ♀$^{H4}$ | ECho GEdr IPen ITim MFie MSCN NRya NWCA WAbe WFar |
| | - 'Rosea' (Au) | IPen |
| | - 'Sheila Denby' (Au) | IPen ITim |
| | - 'The President' (Au) | GAgs |
| | - violet-flowered (Au) | ECho |
| | - 'Waithman's Variety' (Au) | IPen NRya |
| | - wild-collected (Au) | MFie NWad |
| | 'Maria Talbot' (*allionii* hybrid) (Au) | IPen NWCA |
| | 'Marianne Davey' (Pr/Prim/d) | MRav WKif |
| | 'Marie Crousse' (Pr/Prim/d) | CWCL EPfP NWCA SRGP WFar WHal |
| | Marine Blues Group (Pr/Poly) | CWCL NCGa NSum |
| | 'Maris Tabbard' (Au) | IPen NLar |
| | 'Mars' (*allionii* hybrid) (Au) | IPen MFie NRya NWad |
| | 'Marven' (Au) | GEdr IPen |
| | 'Mary Anne' | GAbr |
| | ***maximowiczii*** (Cy) | GLam IPen MMHG NGdn SPad WHil |
| | ***melanops*** | see *P. chionantha* subsp. *melanops* |
| | × ***meridiana*** (Au) | NWad |
| § | - 'Miniera' (Au) | IPen MFie |
| | 'Mexico' | LLHF |
| | Midnight Group | CWCL NCGa |
| | 'Miniera' | see *P.* × *meridiana* 'Miniera' |
| | ***minima*** (Au) | NBro NLar WAbe |
| | - SDR 5517 | GKev |
| | - var. ***alba*** (Au) | NLar NRya |
| | ***minima*** × ***wulfeniana*** | see *P.* × *vochinensis* |
| | 'Miss Indigo' (Pr/Prim/d) | ECtt EPfP GAbr GMaP MFie MRav NDov NLar NWCA SBch SGar SPer WFar |
| | ***mistassinica*** (Al) | GKev |
| | - var. ***macropoda*** | see *P. laurentiana* |
| | ***miyabeana*** (Pf) | GKev IPen |
| | ***modesta*** var. ***faurieae*** (Al) | EPot GAuc GKev IPen NWCA |
| | 'Moorland Apricot' | WMoo |
| | ***moupinensis*** | CLAP CPLG GAbr GEdr WAbe |
| * | 'Mrs Eagland' | GAbr |
| | 'Mrs Frank Neave' (Pr/Prim) | GEdr IPen |
| | 'Mrs McGillivray' (Pr/Prim) | GAbr |
| § | ***munroi*** (Ar) | CDes GEdr GKev IPen NHar WAbe |
| | - CC 5311 | EWld |
| | - SDR 6121 | GKev |
| § | - subsp. ***yargongensis*** (Al) | GAuc GKev GLam IPen |
| | - - SDR 1932 | GKev |
| | - - SDR 3096 | GKev |
| | - - SDR 6158 | GKev |
| | ***muscarioides*** (Mu) | GKev IPen WAbe |

|  |  |
|---|---|
| Muted Victorians Group (Pr/Poly) | NCGa NSum WHil |
| § ***nana*** (Pe) | IPen WAbe |
| – 'Alba' (Pe) | WAbe |
| ***nepalensis*** | see *P. tanneri* subsp. *nepalensis* |
| 'Netta Dennis' (Pr) | NHar WAbe |
| New Pinks Group (Pr/Poly) | CWCL NCGa NSum |
| ***nipponica*** (Su) | GEdr |
| ***nivalis*** Pallas | see *P. chionantha* |
| ***nivalis*** ambig. | NSum |
| 'No Eye Cow' | WPGP |
| ***nutans*** Delavay ex Franch. | see *P. flaccida* |
| 'Old Port' (Pr/Poly) | CElw CSam GKev LLWP NMen NSum SBch |
| Old Rose Victorians Group (Pr/Poly) | NSum |
| 'Oriental Sunset' | MDKP |
| Osiered Amber Group (Pr/Prim) | NSum |
| ***palinuri*** (Au) | IPen |
| ***palmata*** (Co) | GEdr GKev |
| 'Paris '90' (Pr/Poly) | CWCL NCGa NSum |
| ***parryi*** (Pa) | GKev SBfd |
| – NNS 04-422 | WCot |
| – NNS 04-423 | WCot |
| – NNS 06-494 | NWCA |
| ***pedemontana*** (Au) | NWCA |
| – 'Alba' (Au) | MFie WPat WThu |
| 'Perle von Bottrop' (Pr/Prim) | GAbr GEdr WCot |
| 'Peter Klein' (Or) | LLHF WAbe WTin |
| ***petiolaris*** misapplied | see *P.* 'Redpoll' |
| § ***petiolaris*** Wall. (Pe) | GCra GEdr ITim NHar NSum WAbe |
| – Sherriff's form | see *P.* 'Redpoll' |
| 'Petticoat' | GMac NCGa |
| 'Pink Aire' (Au) | MFie NMen NRya |
| 'Pink Fairy' (Au) | IPen |
| 'Pink Ice' (*allionii* hybrid) (Au) | CPBP GKev MFie NRya NWad |
| ***poissonii*** (Pf) | CBen CTri ELan EPfP GAuc GCra GEdr GGar GKev GQui IBal IPen LPBA LRHS NGdn SBfd WAbe WShi WTcb |
| – ACE 2030 | EPot |
| – SDR 3201 | GKev |
| – SDR 5126 | GKev |
| – SDR 5959 | GKev |
| polyanthus (Pr/Poly) | WFar |
| ***polyneura*** (Co) | GEdr GGar GLam IPen MSnd NGdn WHil |
| – SDR 4728 | GKev |
| 'Port Wine' (Pr) | EBla GAbr GCra |
| 'Powdery Pink' | LRHS |
| ***prenantha*** (Pf) | GKev WAbe |
| § ***prolifera*** (Pf) 𝕐H4 | CMHG CWCL EBee ECha EPfP GCra GEdr GGar GKev GQui IPen LPBA LRHS MMuc NCGa NGdn NVic SPer SWat WAbe WMoo |
| § × ***pubescens*** (Au) 𝕐H4 | IPen MHer NDro NGdn WPer |
| – 'Apple Blossom' (Au) | GAgs IPen MFie |
| § – 'Bewerley White' (Au) | EBee ECho EPfP GAgs IPen NDro WCre WFar |
| – 'Blue Wave' (Au) | IPen MFie |
| § – 'Boothman's Variety' (Au) | CTri ECho EPfP GKev ITim MFie NSla WFar WHoo WTin |
| – 'Carmen' | see *P.* × *pubescens* 'Boothman's Variety' |
| – 'Chamois' (Au) | MFie |
| – 'Christine' (Au) | CDes CMea GAgs IPen ITim MFie NBir NSum WCot |
| – 'Deep Mrs Wilson' (Au) | CPBP MFie |
| – 'Faldonside' (Au) | IPen MFie NPnk NSum WCre WHil WThu |
| § – 'Freedom' (Au) | CTri ECho GAgs GKev IPen MFie NBir NLar NSla |
| – 'George Harrison' (Au) | MFie |
| – 'Harlow Car' (Au) | CMea CPBP GQui IPen MFie NSum NWCA WFar WTin |
| – 'Hazel's White' (Au) | GAgs |
| – 'Henry Hall' (Au) | NWCA |
| – 'Joan Danger' (Au) | IPen ITim |
| – 'Joan Gibbs' (Au) | GLam IPen ITim MFie WCre |
| – 'Kath Dryden' (Au) | ITim |
| – 'Lilac Fairy' (Au) | IPen ITim NPnk NWad WThu |
| – 'Mrs J.H. Wilson' (Au) | GEdr MFie NRya |
| – 'Pat Barwick' (Au) | IPen MFie NDro NRya WTin |
| – 'Peggy Fell' (Au) | WHil |
| – 'Rufus' (Au) | EWes GAbr GAgs NDro WThu |
| – 'S.E. Matthews' (Au) | GAgs |
| – 'Sid Skelton' (Au) | IPen |
| – 'Snowcap' (Au) | IPen ITim |
| – 'Sonya' (Au) | IPen |
| – 'The General' (Au) | CTri IPen ITim MFie SPop |
| § – 'Wedgwood' (Au) | GAbr IPen ITim MFie WHil |
| – 'Winifred' (Au) | EWoo GAgs NDro SPop |
| – yellow-flowered (Au) | IPen |
| ***pulverulenta*** (Pf) 𝕐H4 | Widely available |
| – Bartley hybrids (Pf) 𝕐H4 | CBot GMac ITim LRHS LSou NSum |
| ***purdomii*** **new** | GKev |
| 'Quaker's Bonnet' | see *P. vulgaris* 'Lilacina Plena' |
| 'Rachel Kinnen' (Au) | GAbr IPen MFie WFar |
| 'Ramona' (Pr/Poly) | CWCL NCGa |
| 'Ravenglass Vermilion' | see *P.* 'Inverewe' |
| 'Red Ruffles' (Pr/Poly/d) **new** | GAbr |
| § 'Redpoll' (Pe) | CLAP LLHF NHar WAbe |
| ***reidii*** (So) | GEdr NSla |
| – var. ***williamsii*** (So) | IPen |
| 'Reverie' (Pr/Poly) | CWCL NCGa NSum |
| 'Rheniana' (Au) | IPen MFie NLar NRya |
| 'Romeo' (Pr/Prim) | CLAP WCot |
| ***rosea*** (Or) 𝕐H4 | CAby CBot CElw EBee ECho EPfP GAuc GEdr IPen MAsh MFie MMuc NBid NBir NVic |
| – CC 5260 | GKev |
| – 'Delight' | see *P. rosea* 'Micia Visser-de Geer' |
| – 'Gigas' (Or) | LRHS WFar |
| – 'Grandiflora' (Or) | CMac CPrp ECho EHon EPfP GGar GKev LPBA LRHS NCGa NWCA SBfd SPoG SRms SWal SWat WFar WHil WPer XLum |
| § – 'Micia Visser-de Geer' (Or) | WTin |
| I 'Rowena' | GAbr GCra LLHF WCot |
| 'Roy Cope' (Pr/Prim/d) | EPfP GAbr NBir SRGP WFar |
| ***rubra*** | see *P. firmipes* |
| ***rusbyi*** (Pa) | GKev NWCA |
| – subsp. ***ellisiae*** (Pa) | IPen |
| 'Saracen' **new** | MFie |
| ***scandinavica*** (Al) | GAuc |
| § 'Schneekissen' (Pr/Prim) | CFee CWCL EBee EGHP GAbr GCra GEdr LRHS MHer NBro NChi NMyG NPro WHil |
| ***scotica*** (Al) | GAuc GLin GPoy NSla NWCA WAbe |
| ***secundiflora*** (Pf) | CAby CLAP CWCL EBee ELan GCra GGar GKev GLam LLWG LPBA MCot MMuc NBir NGdn SBfd SPer SPlb SWat WAbe WFar WHoo WMoo |
| – SDR 4435 | GKev |
| § × ***sendtneri*** (Au) | MFie |
| × ***serrata*** | see *P.* × *vochinensis* |

***serratifolia*** SDR 5165(Pf) GKev
***sibthorpii*** see *P. vulgaris* subsp. *sibthorpii*
***sieboldii*** (Co) ♀H4 CEnt CSpr GKev MCot MLHP MNrw NMen NSla NWCA SBch SRms SUsu WAbe WFar
– 'Aimayama' (Co) **new** NHar
– 'Akinoysool' (Co) MAsh WFar
– 'Ankoan' (Co) WFar
– 'Asahi' (Co) WFar
– 'Asahigata' (Co) **new** NHar
– 'Ayanami' (Co) WFar
– 'Bide-a-Wee Blue' (Co) NBid
– 'Bijyonomai' (Co) WFar
I – 'Blue Lagoon' (Co) EBee LLHF MMHG NLar
– 'Blue Shades' (Co) IPen NMen
– blue-flowered (Co) CLAP CWCL NMen WHil
– 'Blush' (Co) CLAP WWEG
– 'Boykavitch' (Co) **new** NHar
– 'Bureikou' (Co) NHar WFar
– 'Carefree' (Co) CLAP IPen LLHF NBro NLar NMen
– 'Cherubim' (Co) CLAP EBee GCra LLHF MMHG WHil
– 'Daiminnisiki' (Co) **new** NHar
– 'Dancing Ladies' (Co) CLAP CMil EBla IPen NBro NHar WFar
– 'Dart Rapids' (Co) CDes
– 'Duane's Choice' (Co) CDes CLAP EBee NHar SBch WHil
– 'Edasango' (Co) WFar
– 'Edomurasaki' (Co) WFar
– 'Galaxy' (Co) NBro
– 'Geisha Girl' (Co) CFir CLAP CSpe EBla MRav NLar WAbe WFar WHil WWEG
– 'Ginhukurin' (Co) NHar WFar
– 'Godaisyo' (Co) WFar
– 'Hantack Botanic Garden' (Co) **new** NHar
– 'Hatagarasi' (Co) WFar
– 'Hatusugato' (Co) **new** NHar
– 'Higurasi' (Co) **new** NHar
– 'Higurias' (Co) WFar
– 'Hinokoromo' (Co) WFar
– 'Hujikosi' (Co) WFar
– 'Hukiageakura' (Co) **new** NHar
– 'Hutaezuru' (Co) WFar
– 'Inikina White' (Co) WFar
– 'Inokima Minoura' WFar
– 'Izuto' (Co) WFar
– 'Jyuuyuunoutage' (Co) NHar WFar
– 'Kaedegari' (Co) WFar
– 'Kansenden' (Co) WFar
– 'Karagoromo' (Co) WFar
– 'Koba-no-fue' (Co) **new** NHar
– 'Kokoroiki' (Co) WFar
– 'Kosijimoyuki' (Co) WFar
– 'Kotonosirabe' (Co) WFar
– 'Kourohou' (Co) WFar
– 'Kurama' (Co) WFar
– 'Lacewing' WHil
– f. ***lactiflora*** (Co) CLAP IPen NBro NMen SRot WFar WPGP WTin
– 'Lilac Sunbonnet' (Co) CLAP EPfP LLHF NHar NWCA WFar
– 'Lisujyanome' (Co) WFar
– 'Maiougi' (Co) WFar
– 'Makazebeni' (Co) WFar
– 'Managuruma' (Co) WFar
– 'Manakoora' (Co) CLAP EBee IPen NBro NSum WFar WHil
– 'Mangetu' (Co) WFar
– 'Masasino' (Co) WFar
– 'Matso-no-yuki' (Co) **new** NHar
– 'Matunoyuki' (Co) WFar
– 'Mihonokoji' (Co) WFar
– 'Mikado' (Co) CLAP EBee GCra IPen WFar WHil WWEG
– 'Mikininonomare' (Co) WFar
– 'Mitanohikari' (Co) WFar
– 'Miyakowakare' (Co) WFar
– 'Miyuki' (Co) WFar
– 'Momotidori' (Co) **new** NHar
– 'Musasi' (Co) WFar
– 'Myoutiriki' (Co) WFar
– 'Nankinkozakura' (Co) **new** NHar
– 'Noboruko' (Co) **new** NHar
– 'Nuretubame' (Co) **new** NHar
– 'Okinanotomo' (Co) **new** NHar
– 'Okinatomo' (Co) WFar
– 'Oshibori' (Co) **new** NHar
– 'Pago-Pago' (Co) CDes CLAP EBee IPen NBro NWCA WFar WHil
– 'Pink Laced' (Co) WFar
– pink-flowered (Co) CWCL NBir
– 'Rasyoumon' (Co) WFar
– 'Rock Candy' (Co) NHar WFar
– 'Saiun' (Co) **new** NHar
– 'Sakuragana' (Co) WFar
– 'Sasanari' (Co) WFar
– 'Sekidaiko' (Co) **new** NHar
– 'Senyuu' (Co) WFar WHil
– 'Seraphim' (Co) CLAP EBee MMHG NLar SBch WWEG
– 'Seto-no-ume' (Co) **new** NHar
– 'Shiokemuri' (Co) **new** NHar
– 'Shirousagi' (Co) NHar WFar
– 'Sikoubai' (Co) WFar
– 'Sinipukurn' (Co) WFar
– 'Sinnkirou' (Co) WFar
– 'Sinseiu' (Co) WFar
– 'Siritonbo' (Co) WFar
– 'Sitikenjin' (Co) WFar
– 'Snowdrop' (Co) LSou NCGa WCot
– 'Snowflake' (Co) CDes CLAP EBee MMHG NLar NMen NSla SBch WAbe WFar
– 'Sotodorihime' (Co) WFar
– 'Sousiarai' (Co) NHar WFar
– 'Spring Blush' (Co) GEdr
– 'Spring Rose' (Co) GEdr
– 'Spring Song' (Co) GEdr
– 'Sumida No Hatu' (Co) WFar
– 'Sumisonegawa' (Co) WFar
– 'Sumizomegenji' (Co) **new** NHar
– 'Sweetie' (Co) WFar
– 'Syunkou' (Co) WFar
– 'Syutyuka' (Co) WFar
– 'Tagonoura' (Co) NHar WFar
– 'Tah-ni' (Co) CMil NBro NSum
– 'Taoyami' (Co) **new** NHar
– 'Tatutanoy' (Co) WFar
– 'Tidoriasobi' (Co) WFar
– 'Tokinohina' (Co) WFar
– 'Toyonoharu' (Co) NHar WFar
– 'Tukinomiyaka' (Co) WFar
– 'Turunokegoromo' (Co) **new** NHar
– 'Winter Dreams' (Co) CLAP CWCL NBid NBro NHar NSum WFar WHil
– 'Yukiguruma' (Co) WFar
– 'Yuuhibeni' (Co) **new** NHar
***sikkimensis*** (Si) ♀H4 CEnt EBee ECho EPot GAuc GEdr GGar GKev IPen LRHS MSnd NGdn NSum SBfd SBrt SPer SPoG WFar WPnP

| |  |  |
|---|---|---|
| | – CC&McK 1022 | GQui |
| | – from Bhutan | GCra LEdu |
| | – 'Claret' (Si) **new** | GEdr |
| | – var. ***pseudosikkimensis*** (Si) | IPen |
| | – – SDR 4528 | GKev |
| | – var. ***pudibunda*** (Si) | GEdr |
| | – 'Ruby Shades' (Si) **new** | GEdr |
| | aff. ***sikkimensis*** (Si) | CBot NCGa NGdn |
| | Silver-laced Group (Pr/Poly) | ECGP LBMP NLar SPoG SWvt WFar |
| | 'Silverwells' (Pf) | GEdr |
| | ***simensis*** (Sp) | GKev |
| | ***sinoplantaginea*** | see *P. chionantha* subsp. *sinoplantaginea* |
| | ***sinopurpurea*** | see *P. chionantha* subsp. *sinopurpurea* |
| | 'Siobhan' | WCot |
| | 'Sir Bedivere' (Pr/Prim) | CDes GAbr GKev NHar WCot |
| | ***smithiana*** | see *P. prolifera* |
| | 'Snow Carpet' | see *P.* 'Schneekissen' |
| | 'Snow White' (Pr/Poly) | GEdr MRav |
| | Snowcushion | see *P.* 'Schneekissen' |
| | 'Snowruffles' | ITim |
| | ***sonchifolia*** (Pe) | CFir CLAP |
| | ***sorachiana*** | see *P. yuparensis* |
| | 'Sorbet' | CWCL NCGa |
| | 'Sparkling Eyes' | WCot |
| | ***spectabilis*** (Au) | GEdr GKev |
| | Spice Shades Group (Pr/Poly) | NCGa |
| | 'Stonewash' | LRHS |
| | 'Stradbrook Charm' (Au) | CPBP CWCL EPot MFie WFar WThu |
| | 'Stradbrook Dainty' (Au) | MFie NWad WFar |
| | 'Stradbrook Dream' (Au) | EPot ITim MFie WFar |
| | 'Stradbrook Lilac Lustre' (Au) | MFie |
| | 'Stradbrook Lucy' (Au) | EPot IPen ITim NWad WFar |
| | 'Stradbrook Mauve Magic' (Au) | MFie |
| | ***stricta*** (Al) | GKev |
| | Striped Victorians Group (Pr/Poly) | NCGa NSum WHil |
| | 'Sue Jervis' (Pr/Prim/d) | CSpe CWCL MRav NBir NLar NSum SPer WHal |
| | ***suffrutescens*** (Su) | WAbe |
| | 'Sunshine Susie' (Pr/Prim/d) | CSpr EPfP MRav SPer SRGP WHil |
| | ***takedana*** (Bu) | LLHF |
| | 'Tango' (Pr/Prim) | NCGa NSum |
| | ***tangutica*** (Cy) | IPen |
| § | ***tanneri*** subsp. ***nepalensis*** (Pe) | GKev |
| | 'Tantallon' (Pe) | CLAP LLHF NHar |
| | Tartan Reds Group (Pr/Prim) | CWCL |
| | 'Tawny Port' (Pr/Poly) | CLAP GAbr NBro |
| | 'Tie Dye' (Pr/Prim) | CDes EBla GBin MNrw NBPC NGBo NLar SPoG WCot WFar WKif |
| | 'Tinney's Moonlight' (Pe) | NHar |
| | 'Tipperary Purple' (Pr/Prim) | GAbr GEdr GLam |
| | 'Tomato Red' (Pr/Prim) | CDes EBee GAbr WCot |
| | 'Tony' (Au) | CPBP IPen MFie WAbe |
| | 'Top Affair' (Au/d) | IPen |
| | 'Torchlight' (Pr/Prim/d) | IGor |
| | 'Tournaig Pink' (Pf) | GGar |
| | 'Val Horncastle' (Pr/Prim/d) | CSpr ECtt EPfP GMaP GMac MFie NDov NLar SPer WCot |
| | Valentine Victorians Group (Pr/Poly) | NCGa |
| | × ***venusta*** | GKev |
| | 'Vera Maud' (Pr) | NCGa NSum |
| § | ***veris*** (Pr) ♀H4 | Widely available |
| | – subsp. ***columnae*** (Pr) | EBee |
| | – feather-petalled (Pr) | WCot |
| | – hybrids (Pr) | LBMP MLLN SGar |
| | – 'Katy McSparron' (Pr/d) | CMca CPLG GAbr GCra LSou NDov SPer WBor WCot |
| | – subsp. ***macrocalyx*** (Pr) | NWCA WCot |
| | – orange-flowered (Pr) | MHer WMoo |
| | – red-flowered (Pr) | CAby CSpr NBid NGdn SPer SWal WMoo |
| | – 'Sunset Shades' (Pr) | ECGP EGHP NGdn NLar SBch WFar |
| | ***vernalis*** | see *P. vulgaris* |
| | ***verticillata*** (Sp) | IPen |
| § | ***vialii*** (So) ♀H4 | Widely available |
| | – JJH 061072 | GKev |
| | ***violacea*** SDR 6150 (Mu) | GKev |
| | Violet Victorians Group (Pr/Poly) | NCGa |
| § | × ***vochinensis*** (Au) | CFee NWCA |
| § | ***vulgaris*** (Pr/Prim) ♀H4 | Widely available |
| | – var. ***alba*** (Pr/Prim) | CRow NSla WBrk |
| | – 'Alba Plena' (Pr/Prim) | CRow GAbr GCal GGar MBri NSum WPtf |
| | – green-flowered | see *P. vulgaris* 'Viridis' |
| § | – 'Lilacina Plena' (Pr/Prim/d) | CBot CDes CWCL EBee EPfP GCal IFro IGor LLHF MRav NCGa NDov NSum SPer WFar |
| § | – subsp. ***sibthorpii*** (Pr/Prim) ♀H4 | CAby CMHG CSam EBee EBla ECho EGHP GAbr GEdr IPen ITim LLWP LRHS MCot MFie MHer MLHP MNrw MRav NBro NChi NDov NMyG SKHP SRms WCot WHil |
| | – 'Slack's Crimson Beauty' (Pr/Prim) **new** | NSla |
| | – 'Taigetos' (Pr/Prim) | CBro CPLG |
| § | – 'Viridis' (Pr/Prim/d) | CFir EBla EOHP MNrw |
| | ***walshii*** (Mi) | WAbe |
| | ***waltonii*** (Si) | CCVN CLAP CWCL EBee EDAr GKev IPen MDKP MMuc MNrw NBPC NCGa SBfd SPoG |
| | – hybrids (Si) | MCot NWCA |
| | 'Wanda' (Pr/Prim) ♀H4 | CBcs CTri EBla ECho GAbr GCra LBMP LLWP MCot MFie MHer MMuc NBid NDov NPnk NVic SEND SRGP SRms WBrk WCFE WCot WFar WHil WTin |
| | Wanda Group (Pr/Prim) | ECho SPoG SVic |
| | 'Wanda Grace' | NPnk |
| | 'Wanda Hose-in-hose' (Pr/Prim/d) | EBla GAbr GCra GLam LLWP MMHG NBir NChi SSvw WHer WHil |
| | 'Wanda Jack-in-the-Green' (Pr/Prim) | CLAP WCot WFar |
| | ***wardii*** | see *P. munroi* |
| | ***warshenewskiana*** (Or) | CLAP ECtt GEdr GGar GKev NHar NMen NRya NWCA WAbe |
| | ***watsonii*** (Mu) | EWes GKev NHar SWat |
| | – ACE 1402 | IPen |
| | – SDR 1626 | GKev |
| | – SDR 1673 | GKev |
| | 'Wedgwood' | see *P.* × *pubescens* 'Wedgwood' |
| | 'Welsh Blue' | CSpe |
| | 'Wharfedale Bluebell' (Au) | IPen NBir NWCA WAbe WThu |
| | 'Wharfedale Buttercup' (Au) | IPen NHar NWad |
| | 'Wharfedale Butterfly' (Au) | ITim NWad |
| | 'Wharfedale Crusader' (Au) | IPen |

| | | |
|---|---|---|
| | 'Wharfedale Gem' (*allionii* hybrid) (Au) | ITim MFie NWad |
| | 'Wharfedale Ling' (*allionii* hybrid) (Au) | CPBP GLam ITim MFie NLar NWad |
| | 'Wharfedale Sunshine' (Au) | CPBP GKev IPen ITim NWad |
| | 'Wharfedale Superb' (*allionii* hybrid) (Au) | ITim NWCA |
| | 'Wharfedale Village' (Au) | IPen WAbe WThu |
| | 'White Linda Pope' (Au) | GAgs NMen NWad |
| | 'White Wanda' (Pr/Prim) | GAbr NDov |
| | 'White Waves' (*allionii* hybrid) (Au) | ITim |
| | ***whitei*** (Pe) | LRHS |
| § | - 'Sherriff's Variety' (Pe) | CLAP |
| | 'William Genders' (Pr/Poly) | GAbr GEdr |
| | ***wilsonii*** (Pf) | CSam CTri CTsd LLWG MCot MDKP NBPC NGdn SWat |
| § | - var. ***anisodora*** (Pf) | CLAP GKev GQui IPen NGdn WHrl WPtf |
| | 'Windrush' | see *P.* × *berninae* 'Windrush' |
| | 'Winter White' | see *P.* 'Gigha' |
| | 'Wisley Crimson' | see *P.* 'Wisley Red' |
| § | 'Wisley Red' (Pr/Prim) | CElw LRHS |
| | ***wulfeniana*** (Au) | GEdr GKev |
| | ***yargongensis*** | see *P. munroi* subsp. *yargongensis* |
| | ***yunnanensis*** (Y) | NLar |
| § | ***yuparensis*** (Al) | IPen NWCA WHil |
| | - white-flowered (Al) | GKev |
| | ***zambalensis*** (Ar) | GKev IPen |
| | - SDR 1611 | GKev |
| | - SDR 1716 | GKev |
| | 'Zenobia' | WCre |

## *Prinsepia* (*Rosaceae*)

| | | |
|---|---|---|
| | ***sinensis*** | CArn CBcs CFee MBlu NLar SLon WSHC |
| | ***utilis*** | CTrC |

## *Prionosciadium* (*Apiaceae*)

| | | |
|---|---|---|
| | ***thapsoides*** B&SWJ 10345 | WCru |

## *Pritchardia* (*Arecaceae*)

| | | |
|---|---|---|
| | ***affinis*** | XBlo |
| | ***pacifica*** | XBlo |

## *Pritzelago* (*Brassicaceae*)

| | | |
|---|---|---|
| | ***alpina*** | GEdr NBlu NSla NWCA |

## *Prostanthera* (*Lamiaceae*)

| | | |
|---|---|---|
| | ***aspalathoides*** | CCCN CTsd EWes MOWG |
| | 'Badja Peak' | CTrC CTsd LRHS MAsh MOWG |
| | ***baxteri*** | ECou MOWG |
| | ***chlorantha*** | MOWG |
| | ***cuneata*** ♀H4 | Widely available |
| | - 'Alpine Gold' | CMHG CWSG GKev LRHS WFar |
| | - Kew form | WPGP |
| * | ***digitiformis*** | CTsd ECou MOWG |
| | ***incisa*** | CTsd SGar SHDw |
| | - 'Rosea' | EOHP WKif |
| | 'La Provence' PBR | LRHS |
| | ***lasianthos*** | CCCN CDoC CEnt CHVG CHll CTsd EWes LRHS MOWG SAga SHDw SPlb SVen WCFE WJek |
| | - 'Kallista Pink' | CTsd MOWG |
| | - var. ***subcoriacea*** | CPLG |
| | ***latifolia*** | CTsd |
| | ***magnifica*** | MOWG |
| | 'Mauve Mantle' | MOWG |
| | ***melissifolia*** | CArn CTsd |
| § | - var. ***parvifolia*** | CBcs CCCN |
| | 'Mint Royale' | LRHS |
| | ***nivea*** | ECou |
| | ***ovalifolia*** ♀H2 | CCCN ECou GGar IRar MOWG WJek |
| I | - 'Variegata' (v) | CBcs CCCN CHGN CMac CPLG CTrC CTsd ECou GGar LRHS MOWG SPoG WCFE WGrn |
| | ***phylicifolia*** | CAbb |
| | 'Poorinda Ballerina' | CAlb CDoC CTsd EBee ECou EOHP GGar LRHS MGos MOWG SLim SPoG SRkn WFar |
| | 'Poorinda Petite' | CCCN CDoC CTsd LRHS |
| | ***rotundifolia*** ♀H2 | CAbb CCCN CHEx CSev CTri CTsd CWSG EBee ECho EGHP EOHP ESwi MNHC MOWG MSCN SBrd SPer SVen WCFE WGrn |
| | - 'Chelsea Girl' | see *P. rotundifolia* 'Rosea' |
| § | - 'Rosea' ♀H2 | CCCN CDoC CTrC CTsd ECou GGar LRHS MOWG SEND SPoG |
| | ***scutellarioides*** 'Lavender Lady' | ECou |
| | ***sericea*** | LRHS |
| | ***sieberi*** misapplied | see *P. melissifolia* var. *parvifolia* |
| | ***sieberi*** Benth. | CTrC CTsd MOWG |
| | ***walteri*** | CCCN LRHS MOWG |

## *Protea* (*Proteaceae*)

| | | |
|---|---|---|
| | ***aurea*** | SPlb |
| | ***burchellii*** | SPlb |
| | ***coronata*** | SPlb |
| | ***cynaroides*** | CBcs CCCN CCtw CHEx CTrC EAmu LTen MOWG SBig SPlb |
| | ***effusa*** | SPlb |
| | ***eximia*** | CBcs CCCN EAmu SPlb |
| | ***grandiceps*** | CCCN SPlb |
| | ***lacticolor*** | SPlb |
| | ***laurifolia*** | SPlb |
| | ***nana*** | SPlb |
| | ***neriifolia*** | CCCN SPlb |
| | ***obtusifolia*** | SPlb |
| | 'Pink Ice' | CTrC |
| | ***repens*** | SPlb |
| | ***scolymocephala*** new | SPlb |
| | ***subvestita*** | CTrC SPlb |
| | ***susannae*** | SPlb |
| | ***venusta*** | CTrC |

## *Prumnopitys* (*Podocarpaceae*)

| | | |
|---|---|---|
| § | ***andina*** | CDoC IArd IDee LRHS NMun SLim WThu |
| | ***elegans*** | see *P. andina* |
| § | ***ferruginea*** | IGor |
| § | ***taxifolia*** | CDoC CTrC ECou |

## *Prunella* (*Lamiaceae*)

| | | |
|---|---|---|
| § | ***grandiflora*** | CHby CPrp ECha SBfd SPer SWat WFar WWEG |
| | - 'Alba' | CSpr EBee ECha EGHP EPfP GMaP LRHS MNFA NLar SPer WFar |
| | - 'Bella Deep Rose' | WFar |
| | - 'Blue Loveliness' | GBee SWvt |
| | - 'Carminea' | EBee ECtt SPer |
| | - light blue-flowered | NLar WFar WOut |
| | - 'Loveliness' ♀H4 | CDoC CMac EBee ECha ECtt GMaP MLLN MNFA MRav NBro NGdn NSti NVic SPer SPlb SRGP WCAu WFar |
| | - 'Pagoda' | CEnt CSpe NBre NLar |

| | |
|---|---|
| – 'Pink Loveliness' | CPrp SRms WWEG |
| – 'Rosea' | EBee EPfP |
| – 'Rubra' | EGHP GAbr NLar WPer |
| – violet-flowered | EPfP LRHS |
| – 'White Loveliness' | CMac CPrp WWEG |
| ***hyssopifolia*** | XSen |
| ***incisa*** | see *P. vulgaris* |
| * 'Inshriach Ruby' | GBin |
| Summer Daze = 'Binsumdaz' **new** | LSou NSti SPoG |
| § ***vulgaris*** | CArn CHab CRWN GPoy MHer MNHC NLan NMir WHer WHfH WJek WMoo |
| – f. ***leucantha*** | WHer |
| – 'Marbled White' (v) | NWad |
| – 'Rose Pearl' **new** | LRHS |
| × ***webbiana*** | see *P. grandiflora* |
| – 'Gruss aus Isernhagen' | EBee |

## *Prunus* ✿ (*Rosaceae*)

| | |
|---|---|
| 'Accolade' ♀H4 | Widely available |
| § 'Amanogawa' ♀H4 | Widely available |
| ***amygdalus*** | see *P. dulcis* |
| ***armeniaca*** 'Alfred' (F) | ERea GTwe MGos SDea SFam SKee SPer WHar |
| – var. ***ansu*** 'Flore Pleno' (d) | LAst |
| – 'Blenheim' (F) | ERea |
| – 'Bredase' (F) | CWib ERea SDea |
| – 'De Nancy' | see *P. armeniaca* 'Gros Pêche' |
| – 'Early Moorpark' (F) | CAgr CWib EPfP ERea GTwe LAst LRHS MAsh MBri SDea SEND SLon WHar |
| – 'Farmingdale' (F) | ERea SDea |
| – Flavorcot = 'Bayoto'PBR (F) | CAgr CSut EPfP EPom MCoo SKee SPer |
| – 'Garden Aprigold' (F) | MGos SPoG |
| – 'Goldcot' (F) | CAgr CTho ERea LRHS MAsh MBri MCoo SDea SKee WHar |
| – 'Golden Glow' (F) | CAgr CTho EPom ERea GTwe LRHS MBri MCoo MWat SKee WHar |
| – 'Goldrich' (F) | CAgr |
| § – 'Gros Pêche' (F) | SVic |
| – 'Hargrand' (F) | CAgr SVic |
| – 'Harogem' (F) | CAgr |
| – 'Hemskirke' (F) | SKee |
| – 'Hongaarse' (F) | SDea |
| – 'Isabella' (F) | CAgr ERea |
| – 'Moniqui' (F) | ERea |
| – 'Moorpark' (F) ♀H3 | CEnd CSBt CTri CWib ERea GTwe LBuc MGos MMuc MRav SBfd SDea SKee SPer |
| – 'New Large Early' (F) | ERea SDea SEND SKee |
| – 'Petit Muscat' (F) | ERea |
| – 'Tomcot' (F) | CAgr CTho CTri EPom LBuc LSRN MAsh MBri MCoo SFam SKee SLim WHar |
| – 'Tross Orange' (F) | CWib SDea |
| ***avium*** ♀H4 | Widely available |
| – 'Amber Heart' (F) | SKee |
| – 'Bigarreau Gaucher' (F) | SKee WHar |
| § – 'Bigarreau Napoléon' (F) | GTwe LSRN SCrf SKee SVic |
| – 'Birchenhayes' | see *P. avium* 'Early Birchenhayes' |
| – 'Black Eagle' (F) | SKee |
| – 'Black Elton' (F) | SKee |
| – 'Black Heart' (F) | CWib MMuc SEND |
| – 'Black Tartarian' (F) | SKee |
| – 'Bottlers' | see *P. avium* 'Preserving' |
| – 'Bradbourne Black' (F) | SCrf SKee WHar |
| – 'Bullion' (F) | CEnd CTho |
| – 'Burcombe' (F) | CEnd CTho |
| – Celeste = 'Sumpaca'PBR (D) | CAgr CTri EMil GTwe LRHS MBri MCoo NLar SDea SFam SKee SLim SPoG WHar |
| – 'Cherokee' | see *P. avium* 'Lapins' |
| – 'Colney' (F) ♀H4 | ERea GTwe NLar SFam SKee WJas |
| – 'Dun' (F) | CTho |
| § – 'Early Birchenhayes' (F) | CEnd CTho |
| – 'Early Rivers' (F) | CSBt CWib ECrN GTwe LAst LSRN NLar SDea SKee SVic WHar WWct |
| – 'Elton Heart' (F) | SKee |
| – 'Emperor Francis' (F) | SKee |
| – 'Fastigiata' | WHar |
| – 'Fice' (F) | CBod CEnd CTho |
| – 'Florence' (F) | SKee |
| – 'Governor Wood' (F) | GTwe SKee |
| – 'Grandiflora' | see *P. avium* 'Plena' |
| – 'Greenstem Black' (F) | CTho |
| – 'Hannaford' (D/C) | CTho |
| – 'Hertford' (F) ♀H4 | SFam SKee WHar |
| – 'Inga' (F) | SFam SKee |
| – 'Ironsides' (F) | SKee |
| – 'Kentish Red' (F) | SKee |
| – 'Kordia' (D) | EPom GTwe SFam SKee WHar |
| § – 'Lapins' (F) | CAgr CDul CTho CTri ECrN EPfP EPom GTwe LAst MAsh MBri NLar SDea SFam SKee SPoG WHar WJas WWct |
| – 'May Duke' | see *P.* × *gondouinii* 'May Duke' |
| – 'Merchant' (F) ♀H4 | ECrN SKee |
| – 'Merton Bigarreau' (F) | WHar |
| – 'Merton Favourite' (F) | SKee |
| – 'Merton Glory' (F) | CAgr CDul CSBt ECrN ERea GTwe MAsh MGos SCrf SEND SFam SKee SLim WHar WWct |
| – 'Merton Late' (F) | SKee |
| – 'Merton Marvel' (F) | SKee |
| – 'Merton Premier' (F) | SKee SVic |
| – 'Merton Reward' | see *P.* × *gondouinii* 'Merton Reward' |
| – 'Nabella' (F) | MAsh WJas |
| – 'Napoléon' | see *P. avium* 'Bigarreau Napoléon' |
| – 'Noble' (F) | SKee |
| – 'Noir de Guben' (F) | ECrN SKee WHar |
| – 'Noir de Meched' (D) | SKee |
| – 'Old Black Heart' (F) | SKee |
| – 'Penny'PBR (F) | CAgr CDul EPom SKee WHar |
| § – 'Plena' (d) ♀H4 | Widely available |
| § – 'Preserving' (F) | CTho |
| – 'Regina' (F) | CSut SFam |
| – 'Ronald's Heart' (F) | SKee |
| – 'Roundel Heart' (F) | SKee WHar |
| – 'Small Black' (F) | CBod CTho |
| – 'Stella' (F) ♀H4 | Widely available |
| – 'Stella Compact' (F) | CWib LAst LSRN SDea WHar |
| – 'Summer Sun' (D) ♀H4 | CAgr CDul CSut CTho CTri EPfP EPom ERea GTwe LBuc LRHS MAsh MBri MCoo NLar SBfd SCoo SDea SFam SKee SLim SPoG WHar WWct |
| – 'Summit' (F) | SKee |
| – 'Sunburst' (D) | CAgr CCVT CDul CEnd CMac CTho CTri CWib ECrN GTwe LBuc LRHS LSRN MAsh MBri SBfd SCoo SDea SEWo SFam SKee SLim SPer SPoG SVic SWvt WHar WJas WWct |
| – 'Sweetheart' (F) | CAgr CDul GTwe LRHS LSRN MAsh MBri SKee SLim SPoG WHar |
| – 'Sylvia' (F) | CAgr SFam |
| – 'Turkish Black' (F) | SKee |
| – 'Van' (F) | CSBt ECrN GTwe SFam SKee WHar |

| |  |  |
|---|---|---|
| | – 'Vega' (F) | CAgr ERea GTwe LBuc SKee WHar WJas |
| | – 'Waterloo' (F) | SKee |
| | – 'White Heart' (F) | CWib ECrN SKee |
| | 'Beni-yutaka' | CCVT LAst LRHS MAsh MBri SCoo SLim SPoG |
| | ***besseyi*** | CAgr |
| | 'Blaze' | see *P. cerasifera* 'Nigra' |
| | × ***blireana*** (d) ♀$^{H4}$ | CDul CEnd CTri ECrN EPfP LAst MAsh MBri MGos MMuc MRav MSwo MWat NLar NWea SBfd SCoo SPer SPoG WFar WHar |
| | – 'Saling Hall' (d) | ERea |
| | 'Blushing Bride' | see *P.* 'Shogetsu' |
| | ***campanulata*** 'Felix Jury' | EBee SSpi |
| | 'Candy Floss' | see *P.* 'Matsumae-beni-murasaki' |
| | ***cerasifera*** | CDul CHab CRWN CTri ECrN EPfP GAbr LBuc NWea SPer SVic WDin |
| | – 'Cherry Plum' (F) | CTri ECrN MMuc SDea SKee |
| | – 'Crimson Dwarf' | MBri SCoo SWvt |
| | – 'First' (F) | CAgr |
| | – 'Golden Sphere' (F) | CAgr CTho CTri LRHS SLim WHar |
| | – 'Gypsy' (F) | CAgr CTho LRHS SLim SPoG WHar |
| | – 'Hessei' (v) | MAsh MBri MRav SBfd |
| | – 'Kentish Red' (F) | SEND |
| § | – Myrobalan Group (F) | ECrN MRav SDea SVic |
| | – – 'Magda Jensen' (C) | CAgr |
| § | – 'Nigra' ♀$^{H4}$ | Widely available |
| | – 'Pendula' | ECrN SWvt WFar |
| § | – 'Pissardii' | CDul CWib ECrN EPfP LAst LMaj LSRN MMuc NWea SCoo SFam SLim SLon SWvt WFar WJas WMou |
| | – 'Ruby' **new** | CAgr MBri |
| | – 'Spring Glow' | CCVT CDul CEnd EBee EPfP LRHS MAsh MSwo SBfd SCoo SLim SLon |
| | ***cerasus*** 'Maynard' | LSRN |
| | – 'Montmorency' (F) | SKee |
| | – 'Morello' (C) ♀$^{H4}$ | Widely available |
| | – 'Nabella' (F) | SKee |
| | – 'Rhexii' (d) | CDul ECrN MAsh MBri NEgg NPCo |
| | 'Cheal's Weeping' | see *P.* 'Kiku-shidare-zakura' |
| | Chocolate Ice | see *P.* 'Matsumae-fuki' |
| § | 'Chōshū-hizakura' | LAst |
| § | × ***cistena*** ♀$^{H4}$ | CDul CSBt EBee ELan EPfP LAst LRHS MBri MGos MSwo NPri SBfd SBrd SCoo SGol SPlb SPoG SWvt WDin |
| | – 'Crimson Dwarf' | see *P.* × *cistena* |
| | 'Collingwood Ingram' | EBee LRHS MBri MGos SLim SPoG |
| | ***conradinae*** | see *P. hirtipes* |
| | 'Daikoku' | EBee |
| | ***davidiana*** | SPlb |
| | ***domestica*** 'Allgroves Superb' (D) | ERea |
| | – 'Angelina Burdett' (D) | ERea GTwe SDea SKee |
| | – 'Anna Späth' (C/D) | SKee |
| | – 'Ariel' (C/D) | SDea SKee |
| | – 'Autumn Compote' (C) | SKee |
| | – 'Avalon' (D) | CAgr CCAT CCVT GTwe LBuc SDea SFam SKee WHar |
| | – 'Beauty' (D) | CSut |
| | – 'Belgian Purple' (C) | SKee |
| | – 'Belle de Louvain' (C) | CTho CTri GTwe SDea SKee WHar WWct |
| | – 'Birchenhayes' (F) | CEnd |
| | – 'Black Diamond' | see *P. salicina* 'Black Diamond' |
| | – 'Blaisdon Red' (C) | CTho GTwe WHar |
| | – 'Blue Rock' (C/D) ♀$^{H4}$ | SKee |
| | – 'Blue Tit' (C/D) ♀$^{H4}$ | CAgr CTho EPom ERea GTwe SDea SEND SKee WHar WWct |
| | – 'Bonne de Bry' (D) | SKee |
| | – 'Brandy Gage' (C/D) | SKee |
| | – 'Bryanston Gage' (D) | CTho SKee |
| | – 'Burbank's Giant' | see *P. domestica* 'Giant Prune' |
| | – 'Burcombe' (F) | CEnd |
| | – 'Cambridge Gage' (D) ♀$^{H4}$ | CAgr CCVT CDoC CDul CTri CWib ECrN EPfP EPom ERea GTwe LAst LRHS MAsh MBri MMuc MWat SBfd SCoo SDea SEND SEWo SFam SKee SLim SPer SPoG WHar WJas WWct |
| | – 'Chrislin' (F) | CAgr CTho |
| | – 'Coe's Golden Drop' (D) | CCAT ERea GTwe LAst MBri MGos MRav SDea SFam SKee SPer WHar WWct |
| | – 'Count Althann's Gage' (D) | ERea GTwe NEgg SDea SFam SKee WWct |
| | – 'Cox's Emperor' (C) | SKee |
| | – 'Crimson Drop' (D) | ERea SKee |
| | – 'Cropper' | see *P. domestica* 'Laxton's Cropper' |
| | – 'Curlew' (C) | SDea SKee |
| | – 'Czar' (C) ♀$^{H4}$ | Widely available |
| | – 'Delikya' (D) | ERea |
| | – 'Denbigh Plum' (D) | WGwG |
| | – 'Denniston's Superb' | see *P. domestica* 'Imperial Gage' |
| | – 'Diamond' (C) | SKee |
| | – 'Dittisham Black' (C) | CAgr CTho |
| | – 'Dittisham Ploughman' (C) | CTho SKee |
| | – 'Dunster Plum' (F) | CAgr CBod CTho CTri CWib |
| | – 'Early Favourite' (D/C) | ERea |
| | – 'Early Green Gage' (D) | NEgg |
| | – 'Early Laxton' (C/D) ♀$^{H4}$ | ERea GTwe LAst SDea SEND SFam SKee |
| | – 'Early Prolific' | see *P. domestica* 'Rivers's Early Prolific' |
| | – 'Early Rivers' | see *P. domestica* 'Rivers's Early Prolific' |
| | – 'Early Transparent Gage' (C/D) | CCAT CMac CSBt CTho CTri ERea GTwe LBuc LRHS MBri MCoo SCoo SDea SFam SKee WHar |
| | – 'Early Victoria' (C/D) | SDea |
| | – 'Edda' (D) | WHar |
| | – 'Edwards' (C/D) ♀$^{H4}$ | CTri CWib GTwe NEgg SDea SKee |
| | – 'Excalibur' (D) | CAgr GTwe LBuc SDea SFam SKee WHar |
| § | – German Prune Group (C) | MCoo SKee |
| § | – 'Giant Prune' (C) | GTwe MMuc SDea SEND SFam SKee |
| I | – 'Godshill Big Sloe' (F) | SDea |
| | – 'Godshill Blue' (C) | SDea |
| | – 'Godshill Minigage' (F) | SDea |
| | – 'Golden Transparent' (D) | GTwe LAst MCoo SFam SKee |
| | – 'Goldfinch' (D) | GTwe MCoo SKee |
| | – 'Gordon Castle' | WHar |
| | – Green Gage Group | see *P. domestica* Reine-Claude Group |
| | – 'Grey Plum' (F) | CAgr CBod CTho |
| | – 'Guinevere' (F) | CAgr LRHS MBri WHar |
| | – 'Guthrie's Late Green' (D) | SKee |
| | – 'Haganta'$^{PBR}$ (F) **new** | CAgr |
| | – 'Hays' (C/D) | ERea |
| | – 'Herman' (C/D) | CAgr EMil ERea GTwe LAst LRHS MBri MCoo SDea SFam SKee WHar |
| | – 'Heron' (F) | GTwe SKee WHar |
| | – 'Impérial Epineuse' (D) | SKee |
| § | – 'Imperial Gage' (C/D) ♀$^{H4}$ | CAgr CCAT CSBt CTho CTri EPom ERea GTwe MAsh MGos NLar SDea SEND SFam SKee WHar |
| | – 'Italian Prune' (F) | MCoo |
| | – 'Jan James' (F) | CEnd |

| |  |  |
|---|---|---|
| | - 'Jefferson' (D) ♀H4 | CAgr GTwe NLar SDea SFam SKee SVic WHar |
| * | - 'Jubilaeum' (D) | CAgr CSut EPom GTwe LRHS SCoo SEWo SFam SKee |
| | - 'Kea' (C) | CAgr CBod CTho SKee |
| | - 'Kirke's' (D) | CCAT CTho GTwe SDea SFam SKee WHar |
| | - 'Landkey Yellow' (F) | CAgr CTho |
| | - 'Langley Gage' (F) | CAgr SDea |
| | - 'Late Muscatelle' (D) | ERea SKee |
| | - 'Late Transparent Gage' (D) | SKee |
| § | - 'Laxton's Cropper' (C) | CTri GTwe SKee WHar |
| | - 'Laxton's Delight' (D) ♀H4 | GTwe |
| | - 'Laxton's Gage' (D) | SDea SKee |
| I | - 'Liegel's Apricot' | SKee |
| | - 'Mallard' (D) ♀H4 | SKee WHar |
| | - 'Manaccan' (C) | CAgr CBod CTho |
| | - 'Marjorie's Seedling' (C) ♀H4 | Widely available |
| | - 'McLaughlin' (D) | SKee |
| | - 'Merton Gage' (D) | SKee |
| | - 'Merton Gem' (C/D) | SKee |
| | - 'Monarch' (C) | SKee |
| | - Old English gage | EPom LAst MAsh SBfd |
| | - 'Olympia' (C/D) | SKee |
| | - 'Ontario' (C/D) | SKee |
| | - 'Opal' (D) ♀H4 | CAgr CCAT CCVT CDoC CDul CMac CWSG CWib EPom ERea GTwe LBuc LRHS MBri MGos MMuc MWat NLar NWea SCoo SCrf SDea SEND SFam SKee SLim SPoG WHar WWct |
| | - 'Orleans' (C) | SKee |
| | - 'Oullins Gage' (C/D) ♀H4 | Widely available |
| | - 'Pershore' (C) ♀H4 | CAgr CWib GTwe LAst MBri NEgg SDea SFam SKee WHar WWct |
| | - 'Pond's Seedling' (C) | CSBt SDea SKee |
| | - 'President' (C/D) | SDea SEND SKee |
| | - 'Priory Plum' (D) | SDea |
| | - 'Purple Pershore' (C) | CAgr CTri CWib GTwe NEgg SDea SFam SKee WHar WWct |
| | - 'Quetsche d'Alsace' | see *P. domestica* German Prune Group |
| | - 'Reeves' (C) ♀H4 | GTwe SFam SKee WHar |
| | - 'Reine-Claude Dorée' | see *P. domestica* Reine-Claude Group |
| § | - Reine-Claude Group (C/D) | CSBt GTwe MGos SDea SFam SKee SLim SPer |
| | - - 'Old Green Gage' | see *P. domestica* (Reine-Claude Group) 'Reine-Claude Vraie' |
| | - - 'Reine-Claude de Bavais' (D) | CCAT CTho CTri ERea GTwe SDea SFam SKee WHar |
| | - - 'Reine-Claude de Vars' (D) | SVic |
| | - - 'Reine-Claude Violette' (D) | ERea SKee |
| § | - - 'Reine-Claude Vraie' (C/D) | CAgr CCVT CMac CSBt CWib EPfP ERea LBuc LRHS LSRN NPri WJas |
| § | - - 'Willingham Gage' (C/D) | CMac ERea GTwe LRHS WHar |
| § | - 'Rivers's Early Prolific' (C) | CAgr CCAT CSBt CTho CTri ERea GTwe LRHS LSRN MAsh NWea SCoo SDea SFam SKee WHar WWct |
| | - 'Royale de Vilvoorde' (D) | SKee |
| | - 'Sanctus Hubertus' (D) ♀H4 | CTri ERea GTwe SDea SKee WHar WWct |
| | - 'Seneca' (D) | WHar |
| | - 'Severn Cross' (D) | GTwe SKee |
| | - 'Stanley' (C/D) | SVic |
| | - 'Stella' | CCVT CDul LAst LSRN NEgg NPri SLim WHar |
| | - 'Stella's Star' | LBuc LRHS MCoo |
| | - 'Swan' (C) | GTwe SKee WHar WWct |
| | - 'Syston White' | MGos |
| | - 'Thames Cross' (D) | CSut SKee |
| | - 'Transparent Gage' (D) | SKee |
| | - 'Upright' (F) | CEnd |
| | - 'Utility' (D) | SKee |
| | - 'Valor' (C/D) ♀H4 | WHar |
| | - 'Verity' (D/C) | SKee |
| | - 'Victoria' (C/D) ♀H4 | Widely available |
| | - 'Violetta'PBR (C/D) | CAgr GTwe SFam WHar |
| | - 'Warwickshire Drooper' (C) | CAgr CTho CWib ERea GTwe NEgg NLar SBfd SDea SFam SKee SLon WHar WWct |
| | - 'Washington' (D) | SDea SKee |
| | - 'White Magnum Bonum' (C) | SDea |
| | - 'Willingham' | see *P. domestica* (Reine-Claude Group) 'Willingham Gage' |
| § | ***dulcis*** | CDul CLnd CTri CWib EPfP EPom EWTr LAst LRHS MGos MREP MWat NWea SBfd SCoo SCrf SDea SEND SFam SWvt WDin |
| | - 'Ai' (F) | CAgr |
| | - 'Ardechoise' (F) | CAgr |
| | - 'Ferraduel' (F) | CAgr |
| | - 'Ferragnes' (F) | CAgr |
| | - 'Lauranne' (F) | CAgr |
| | - 'Mandaline' (F) | CAgr |
| * | - 'Phoebe' (F) | CAgr |
| | - 'Supernova' (F) | CCCN |
| | - 'Tuono' (F) | CCCN |
| | Easter Bonnet = 'Comet'PBR | CTri EPfP LRHS |
| | Fragrant Cloud | see *P.* 'Shizuka' |
| | 'Fugenzō' | CDoy CSBt |
| | ***glandulosa*** 'Alba Plena' (d) | CEnd CMac CSBt LBMP SGol SPlb SPoG SRms SWvt WCFE WDin |
| | - 'Rosea Plena' | see *P. glandulosa* 'Sinensis' |
| § | - 'Sinensis' (d) | CEnd CPLG CSBt SPoG SRms WDin |
| § | × ***gondouinii*** 'May Duke' (F) | SKee SVic WHar |
| § | - 'Merton Reward' (F) | ERea |
| | 'Gyoikō' | CEnd |
| | 'Hally Jolivette' | CEnd ELan GKin MAsh SPoG WDin |
| | 'Hillieri Spire' | see *P.* 'Spire' |
| | 'Hilling's Weeping' | EBee SLon |
| § | ***hirtipes*** | CEnd CLnd |
| | 'Hisakura' | see *P.* 'Choshu-hizakura' |
| | 'Hokusai' | CDul EPfP LRHS SGol |
| | Hollywood | see *P.* 'Trailblazer' |
| | 'Horinji' | EBee MBri SCoo |
| | 'Ichiyo' (d) ♀H4 | CDul EBee ECrN EPfP LAst MBri SCoo SCrf SPoG |
| | ***incisa*** | CTri NEgg NWea |
| | - 'Ariane' | LMaj |
| | - 'Beniomi' | MRav |
| | - 'February Pink' | CPMA MRav SGol WDin |
| | - 'Fujima' | CSBt EBee LAst SBfd |
| | - 'Kojo-no-mai' | Widely available |
| | - 'Mikinori' | CEnd CMac CSBt EPfP MAsh MBlu NLar SCoo WFar |
| | - 'Oshidori' (d) | CMac CSBt EPfP LRHS MBri MGos MRav NEgg NLar SLim SRms |
| | - 'Pendula' | SCoo |
| | - 'Praecox' ♀H4 | CHGN CSBt CTho EPfP LRHS MWat SCoo |
| | - 'The Bride' | CDul CEnd LRHS MAsh MBri SCoo |
| § | - f. ***yamadae*** | CPMA LBMP NLar |
| | ***insititia*** (F) | CRWN |

| |  |  |
|---|---|---|
| | - 'Blue Violet Damson' (F) | CAgr MCoo SKee WHar |
| § | - 'Bradley's King Damson' (C) | MAsh MCoo SKee WHar |
| | - bullace (C) | NWea SDea |
| | - 'Countess' (C) | CTri |
| | - 'Dittisham Damson' (C) | CTho |
| | - 'Farleigh Damson' (C) ♀$^{H4}$ | CAgr CWib ERea GTwe LAst LBuc LRHS MMuc NWea SBfd SDea SFam SKee SPer SVic WHar WJas WWct |
| | - 'Godshill Damson' (C) | SDea |
| | - 'Golden Bullace' | see *P. insititia* 'White Bullace' |
| | - 'King of Damsons' | see *P. insititia* 'Bradley's King Damson' |
| | - 'Langley Bullace' (C) | CAgr CDul ERea GTwe NLar SKee WHar |
| | - 'Lisna' (C) | CTri |
| | - 'Merryweather Damson' (C) | Widely available |
| | - 'Mirabelle de Nancy' (C) | CAgr CTho CTri ERea GTwe LAst LMaj SDea SFam SKee SLim WHar |
| | - 'Mirabelle de Nancy' red (C) | SDea |
| | - 'Mirabelle Ruby' (F) **new** | LRHS |
| § | - 'Prune Damson' (C) ♀$^{H4}$ | CAgr CDoC CTho CTri EPom GTwe LBuc LRHS MAsh MBri MMuc MWat NLar SBfd SDea SEND SFam SKee SPer WHar WJas WWct |
| | - 'Shepherd's Bullace' (C) | CAgr CTho ERea SKee |
| | - 'Shropshire Damson' | see *P. insititia* 'Prune Damson' |
| | - 'Small Bullace' (C) | CAgr SKee |
| § | - 'White Bullace' (C) | CAgr ERea |
| | - 'Yellow Apricot' (C) | ERea SKee |
| § | ***jamasakura*** | CDul |
| | 'Jō-nioi' | CDul CEnd CTho MBri |
| § | 'Kanzan' ♀$^{H4}$ | Widely available |
| § | 'Kiku-shidare-zakura' ♀$^{H4}$ | Widely available |
| | Korean hill cherry | see *P. verecunda* |
| | 'Kulilensis Ruby' | LSRN SLPl |
| | 'Kursar' ♀$^{H4}$ | CDul CLnd CSBt CTho CTri EBee EPfP GKin LRHS LSRN MAsh MBri NLar NWea SBfd SCoo SCrf SLim SLon SPer SPoG SWvt WMou |
| | ***laurocerasus*** ♀$^{H4}$ | CBcs CCVT CChe CDul CMac CPMA CWSG EBee ECrN ELan EPfP EShb GKin LAst MGos MMuc MRav NWea SBrd SEND SGol SPer SPoG SReu WFar WMoo WMou WWau |
| | - 'Angustifolia' | WDin |
| | - 'Aureovariegata' | see *P. laurocerasus* 'Taff's Golden Gleam' |
| | - 'Camelliifolia' | CMac CTri EPla EQua MBlu WCFE WWau |
| N | - 'Castlewellan' (v) | CAlb CBot CDoC CDul CTri EPfP EPla LAst LHop LRHS MGos MRav MSwo NLar NPro SBfd SDix SLim SPer SPoG SSta WDin WFar WGrn WHar WMoo WWau |
| | - 'Caucasica' | CEnd LTen NLar SBfd SGol WWau |
| | - 'Cherry Brandy' | MRav SGol SLPl WDin WWau |
| | - Dart's Lowgreen | see *P. laurocerasus* Low 'n' Green |
| | - Etna = 'Anbri'$^{PBR}$ | CMac EBee EPfP LBuc LRHS LSou MAsh MBri MWat SWvt WMou WWau |
| | - 'Gajo'$^{PBR}$ | NLar NPro SPer WWau |
| | - Genolia = 'Mariblon'$^{PBR}$ | SGol |
| | - 'Green Marble' (v) | CPMA CTri EBee EHoe WWau |
| | - 'Herbergii' | MAsh NLar |
| § | - 'Latifolia' | CHEx EQua SLPl WWau |
| § | - Low 'n' Green = 'Interlo' | MRav |
| | - 'Magnoliifolia' | see *P. laurocerasus* 'Latifolia' |
| | - 'Mano' | NLar |
| | - 'Marbled White' | see *P. laurocerasus* 'Castlewellan' |
| | - 'Miky' | CPMA |
| | - 'Mischeana' | SLPl |
| | - 'Mount Vernon' | CTri LBuc MBlu WDin WWau |
| | - 'Novita' | CWSG EPfP |
| | - 'Otto Luyken' ♀$^{H4}$ | Widely available |
| | - 'Prostrata' | NWad |
| | - 'Reynvaanii' | CPMA MBri SLPl |
| | - 'Rotundifolia' | CAlb CBar CDoC CMac CSBt CTri CWib EBee ELan EPfP LBuc LRHS LSRN MBri MGos MSwo NEgg NLar NWea SBfd SEWo SGol SLim SPoG SRms SWvt WDin WHar WMoo |
| | - 'Schipkaensis' | SLPl |
| § | - 'Taff's Golden Gleam' (v) | CPMA WWau |
| | - 'Van Nes' | CPMA EBee MAsh NLar WDin WWau |
| | - 'Variegata' misapplied | see *P. laurocerasus* 'Castlewellan' |
| | - 'Variegata' ambig. (v) | CWib SRms |
| | - 'Whitespot' | MMuc |
| | - 'Zabeliana' | CAlb CDul CMac CTri EBee EPfP MSwo NEgg NHol NWad NWea SPer SRms WDin WFar WWau |
| | ***litigiosa*** | CEnd EBee SCoo |
| | 'Little Pink Perfection' | CDul MBri SCoo |
| | ***lusitanica*** ♀$^{H4}$ | Widely available |
| | - subsp. ***azorica*** | CDoC CPLG EQua LRHS MRav WFar WPGP |
| | - 'Myrtifolia' | CAlb CBar CDul CTri EBee EPfP EQua LRHS MBri MRav SBfd SGol SLon SWvt WCFE WDin WMoo |
| | - 'Variegata' (v) | CBar CBot CDul CMac CTri CWib EBee ELan ELon LAst LHop MGos MLHP MMuc MRav MSwo SBfd SDix SEND SGol SLim SPer SPoG SSta SWvt WDin WFar WMoo |
| | ***maackii*** | MMuc SEND SSpi WDin |
| | - 'Amber Beauty' | CBcs CDoC CDul EBee ECrN EPfP GBin GKin LMaj LSRN MRav SBfd SGol SLon WDin WFar |
| | 'Mahogany Lustre' | see *P. serrula* 'Mahogany Lustre' |
| | ***mandshurica*** | ERea |
| | ***maritima*** | GAuc |
| § | 'Matsumae-beni-murasaki' | EBee ERea NLar SCoo |
| | 'Matsumae-beni-tamanishiki' | LRHS |
| § | 'Matsumae-fuki' | CWSG ERea LRHS LSRN MBri NWea SBfd SLim |
| § | 'Matsumae-hanagasa' | CEnd LRHS MBri NLar WMou |
| | ***maximowiczii*** B&SWJ 10967 | WCru |
| | ***mexicana*** **new** | EGFP |
| | 'Mount Fuji' | see *P.* 'Shirotae' |
| | ***mume*** | CMCN CMen WDin |
| | - 'Beni-chidori' | CEnd CMac CWib EBee EPfP IVic LRHS MAsh MBlu MBri MGos NLar SCoo SLim SPoG WCot WJas |
| § | - 'Omoi-no-mama' (d) | CEnd CMen |
| | - 'Omoi-no-wac' | see *P. mume* 'Omoi-no-mama' |
| | ***myrobalana*** | see *P. cerasifera* Myrobalan Group |
| | ***nipponica*** var. ***kurilensis*** 'Brilliant' | CBcs CSBt LRHS MAsh MBri MGos NLar SBfd SPoG |
| | - - 'Ruby' | CBcs LSRN MBri MGos NEgg WFar |
| | 'Okamé' ♀$^{H4}$ | Widely available |
| | 'Okame Harlequin' (v) | SLim |
| | 'Okumiyako' misapplied | see *P.* 'Shogetsu' |
| | ***padus*** | CCVT CDul CHab CLnd CMac CRWN CSBt CTri ECrN LBuc MGos |

| | |
|---|---|
| | MMuc MSwo NWea SEND SEWo WDin WMou |
| - 'Albertii' | CCVT MBri SCoo |
| - 'Colorata' ♀H4 | CBcs CDoC CDul CEnd CMac CTho EBee ECrN ELan EWTr LHop LMaj MAsh MGos NLar SCoo SGol SPer SWvt WCot WDin WFar WPat |
| - 'Grandiflora' | see *P. padus* 'Watereri' |
| - 'Purple Queen' | CEnd ECrN EQua SGol |
| § - 'Watereri' ♀H4 | CCVT CDoC CDul CEnd CMCN CMac CTho CWib EBee ECrN ELan EPfP EWTr LAst LHop LMaj NWea SCoo SEWo SGol SLim SPer SPoG WDin WMou |
| 'Pandora' ♀H4 | CCVT CDul CLnd EBee ECrN EPfP LAst LRHS MAsh MBri MGos MMuc MRav MSwo NPCo NWea SBfd SCoo SEND SEWo SPer WFar |
| ***pendula*** | SCrf |
| - var. ***ascendens*** 'Rosea' | EBee |
| § - 'Pendula Rosea' ♀H4 | CDoC CDul CEnd CTri CWib EPfP SCrf WFar WJas |
| § - 'Pendula Rubra' ♀H4 | CCVT CDoC CDul CLnd CMac CSBt CWib EBee EPfP LAst LHop LRHS MBri MGos MSwo SBfd SCoo SLim SPer SPoG WFar WMou WPat |
| § - 'Stellata' | LRHS MBri |
| ***pensylvanica*** | LMaj |
| ***persica*** 'Amsden June' (F) | CWib EBtc ERea GTwe MCoo NLar SDea SFam SKee WHar |
| - 'Avalon Pride' (F) | CAgr CSut EPfP ERea LBuc MCoo |
| - 'Barrington' (F) | ERea |
| - 'Bellegarde' (F) | ERea GTwe SDea SFam |
| - 'Bonanza' (F) | ERea LSRN |
| - 'Cardinal' (F/d) | ERea |
| - 'Darling' (F) | SVic |
| - 'Dixi Red' (F) | CAgr ERea |
| - 'Doctor Hogg' (F) | ERea SDea |
| - 'Duke of York' (F) ♀H3 | CTri ERea GTwe SDea SFam |
| - 'Dymond' (F) | ERea |
| - 'Early Alexander' (F) | ERea |
| - 'Flat China' (F) | ERea |
| - 'Foliis Rubris' (F) | CDul LRHS |
| - 'Francis' (F) | SKee |
| - 'Garden Lady' (F) | ERea GTwe SLim SPoG WHar |
| - 'Hale's Early' (F) | ERea GTwe MRav MWat SFam SKee SLim SPer WHar |
| - 'Hylands' (F) | ERea SDea |
| - 'Johnny Brack' (F) | ERea |
| - 'Kestrel' (F) | ERea |
| - 'Madison' (F) | ERea |
| - 'Melred' (F) | MGos |
| - 'Natalia' (F) | SDea |
| - var. ***nectarina*** Crimson Gold (F) | SDea |
| - - 'Early Blaze' (F) | ERea |
| - - 'Early Gem' (F) | ERea SDea |
| - - 'Early Rivers' (F) ♀H3 | ERea GTwe LSRN SDea |
| - - 'Elruge' (F) | ERea GTwe SDea |
| - - 'Fantasia' (F) | EPfP ERea SDea |
| - - 'Fire Gold' (F) | ERea SDea |
| - - 'Flavortop' (F) | EPfP ERea SPer |
| - - 'Garden Beauty' (F/d) | MGos SPoG |
| - - 'Humboldt' (F) | CAgr ERea GTwe SDea SFam SKee WHar |
| - - 'John Rivers' (F) | GTwe SDea SPer |
| - - 'Lord Napier' (F) ♀H3 | CAgr CDoC CSBt CTri CWSG CWib EPfP EPom ERea LAst LBuc LRHS MAsh MGos MMuc MWat SDea SEND SFam SKee SLim SPer SVic WHar |
| - - 'Nectared' (F) | CWib ERea |
| - - 'Nectarella' (F) | ERea LSRN SLim WHar |
| - - 'Pineapple' (F) | CAgr CTri ERea GTwe SDea SFam SKee SPoG WHar |
| - - 'Red Gold' (F) | ERea |
| - - 'Ruby Gold' (F) | ERea SDea |
| 'Terrace Ruby' (F) | MGos SPoG |
| - - 'Violette Hâtive' (F) | ERea |
| - 'Peregrine' (F) ♀H3 | CAgr CSBt CTri CWSG CWib EPfP EPom ERea GTwe LAst LBuc LRHS LSRN MAsh MBri MGos MMuc MWat SDea SEND SFam SKee SLim SPer SPoG WHar WJas |
| - 'Pink Peachy' (F) | NLar |
| - 'Purpurea' | GKin |
| - 'Red Haven' (F) | CAgr CWib ERea GTwe SDea SKee SVic WHar |
| - 'Red Top' (F) <u>**new**</u> | EPfP |
| - 'Redwing' (F) | CAgr ERea |
| - 'Reliance' (F) | SDea |
| - 'Robin Redbreast' (F) | CAgr SDea |
| - 'Rochester' (F) ♀H3 | CAgr CSBt CTri CWSG CWib EPom ERea GTwe LAst LRHS LSRN MBri MMuc SDea SEND SFam SKee SLim SPer SPoG WHar |
| - 'Royal George' (F) | GTwe SFam SPer |
| - 'Saturne' (F) | ERea SKee WHar |
| - 'Springtime' (F) | ERea SDea |
| - 'Terrace Amber' (F) | MGos SPoG |
| - 'Terrace Diamond' (F) | MGos SPoG |
| - 'Terrace Garnet' (F) | MGos |
| - 'White Peachy' (F) | NLar |
| × ***persicoides*** 'Ingrid' (F) | CAgr EBtc LBuc LRHS MBri MCoo SCoo WHar |
| - 'Pollardii' (F) | MMuc NWea WJas |
| - 'Robijn' (F) | CAgr EPom LBuc MCoo SVic |
| - 'Spring Glow' (F) | CDoC ERea LAst MBri MMuc MWea NWea SEND WJas |
| 'Petite Noir' | LRHS |
| 'Pink Parasol' | see *P.* 'Matsumae-hanagasa' |
| 'Pink Perfection' ♀H4 | CBcs CDul CLnd CSBt CWib EBee ECrN EPfP LAst LRHS MBri MGos MWat NLar SBfd SPer WDin WFar WHar WJas |
| 'Pink Shell' ♀H4 | CAbP EBee EPfP MAsh MBri SPur |
| ***pissardii*** | see *P. cerasifera* 'Pissardii' |
| 'Pissardii Nigra' | see *P. cerasifera* 'Nigra' |
| ***prostrata*** | GAuc |
| * - var. ***discolor*** | NLar |
| ***pumila*** var. ***depressa*** | MRav NLar NPro |
| 'Rebecca' | SPoG |
| 'Royal Burgundy' (d) | CCVT CDul CEnd CLnd CMac CWGN EBee EMil EPfP ERea LAst LRHS LSRN MAsh MBri MDun MGos MWat SBfd SCoo SEWo SLim SPer SPoG WFar WHar |
| ***rufa*** | CDul CLnd CPMA CTho EBee EBtc GKin SKHP SSpi |
| ***salicina*** | ERea |
| - 'Beauty' | ERea |
| § - 'Black Diamond' (F) | SDea |
| - 'Methley' (D) | ERea SPoG WHar |
| - 'Satsuma' (F) | ERea |
| - 'Shiro' (D) | ERea |
| ***sargentii*** ♀H4 | Widely available |
| - 'Charles Sargent' | LRHS |
| - 'Columnaris' | MAsh MBri |
| - 'Rancho' | CLnd SCoo SLim SPer SPoG WFar |

| | | |
|---|---|---|
| | × ***schmittii*** | CCVT ECrN MMuc SCoo SEND SPer WJas |
| | 'Sekiyama' | see *P.* 'Kanzan' |
| | ***serotina*** | CDul NLar |
| § | ***serrula*** ♀H4 | Widely available |
| | - Branklyn form | MGos |
| | - Dorothy Clive form | EBee LSRN |
| § | - 'Mahogany Lustre' | WFar WPat |
| | - var. ***tibetica*** | see *P. serrula* |
| | ***serrula*** × ***serrulata*** | CBcs CTho |
| | ***serrulata*** 'Erecta' | see *P.* 'Amanogawa' |
| | - 'Grandiflora' | see *P.* 'Ukon' |
| | - 'Longipes' | see *P.* 'Shogetsu' |
| | - 'Miyako' misapplied | see *P.* 'Shogetsu' |
| N | - var. ***pubescens*** | see *P. verecunda* |
| | - 'Rosea' | see *P.* 'Kiku-shidare-zakura' |
| | - var. ***spontanea*** | see *P. jamasakura* |
| | 'Shidare-zakura' | see *P.* 'Kiku-shidare-zakura' |
| | 'Shimizu-zakura' | see *P.* 'Shogetsu' |
| | 'Shirofugen' ♀H4 | CBcs CDoC CDul CLnd CMCN CMac CSBt CTho CWSG CWib EBee ECrN EPfP GKin LBuc LRHS LSRN MAsh MBri MMuc MRav MWat SBfd SEND SGol SPer WDin WFar WHar WJas |
| § | 'Shirotae' ♀H4 | Widely available |
| § | 'Shizuka' | CWSG CWib LAst LRHS MBri NLar SBfd SCoo SLim SPer |
| § | 'Shōgetsu' ♀H4 | CBcs CDul CEnd CLnd CSBt CTho EBee ELan EPfP LAst LMaj LRHS MAsh MBri MMuc MRav NEgg NLar SBfd SEWo SFam SLim SPer SPoG WDin |
| | 'Shosar' | CEnd CWib ECrN LAst NLar SCoo SPer |
| | × ***sieboldii*** 'Caespitosa' | SCoo |
| | 'Snow Goose' | CDoC EBee LAst LMaj LRHS NEgg SCoo SEND SGol WFar |
| | 'Snow Showers' | CCVT CEnd CMac EBee LRHS LSRN MAsh MBri MGos MMuc MWat NWea SBfd SEND SPer SPoG |
| | ***spinosa*** | CCVT CDoC CDul CHab CMac CRWN CTri ECrN EPfP EShb GAbr LAst LBuc LSRN MAsh MBlu NLar NWea SBfd SEWo SPer SPoG SVic WDin WFar WMou WSFF |
| | - 'Plena' (d) | CEnd CTho MBlu |
| | - 'Purpurea' | CDul CTho MAsh MBlu MBri NLar WDin WFar WMou |
| § | 'Spire' ♀H4 | Widely available |
| | × ***subhirtella*** | LAst |
| | - var. ***ascendens*** | see *P. pendula* var. *ascendens* |
| | - 'Autumnalis' ♀H4 | Widely available |
| | - 'Autumnalis Rosea' ♀H4 | Widely available |
| | - 'Falling Stars' | SLon |
| | - 'Fukubana' | CLnd CMac EBee ECrN EPfP MAsh NLar |
| | - 'Pendula' misapplied | see *P. pendula* 'Pendula Rosea' |
| | - 'Pendula Plena Rosea' (d) | LAst |
| | - 'Pendula Rosea' | see *P. pendula* 'Pendula Rosea' |
| | - 'Pendula Rubra' | see *P. pendula* 'Pendula Rubra' |
| N | - 'Rosea' | CLnd MRav |
| | - 'Stellata' | see *P. pendula* 'Stellata' |
| | 'Taihaku' ♀H4 | Widely available |
| | 'Taki-nioi' | ECrN |
| | ***tenella*** | CAgr ECha ELan SEND WCot |
| | - 'Fire Hill' | CPMA CWib ECho ELan EPfP LRHS LSRN MGos MRav SPer WCFE WCot WDin WJas |
| | ***tibetica*** | see *P. serrula* |
| | 'Tiltstone Hellfire' **new** | MBri |
| | ***tomentosa*** | CAgr LLHF MAsh SEND |
| § | 'Trailblazer' (C/D) | CEnd CLnd CSBt ECrN IVic LAst MSwo SLon SPer WMou |
| | ***triloba*** | CBcs CWib ECha ECrN EGxp LAst MBlu NWea WDin |
| | - 'Multiplex' (d) | MGos SPoG SRms WJas |
| § | 'Ukon' ♀H4 | CBcs CDoC CDul CLnd CMCN CMac CTho CTri EBee ECrN EPfP LRHS MAsh MBri MGos MMuc MRav MWat NEgg NLar NWea SBfd SCrf SEND SGol SPer WDin WFar WHar |
| | 'Umineko' | CCVT CDoC CLnd CWib ECrN GQue MGos MMuc SEND SLPl SPer WDin WHar |
| § | ***verecunda*** | CLnd NWea WJas |
| | ***virginiana*** 'Schubert' | CDul CLnd EBee ECrN SCoo WFar WJas WMou WPat |
| | 'White Cloud' | CDul |
| | 'Woodfield Cluster' **new** | IArd |
| | ***yamadae*** | see *P. incisa* f. *yamadae* |
| | × ***yedoensis*** | CCVT CDul EBee LMaj MAsh MBri MRav SBfd SLon SPer |
| | - 'Ivensii' | CBcs CDul CSBt CWib EBee LMaj MMuc NEgg NWea SCoo SEND SPer WDin |
| | - 'Pendula' | see *P.* × *yedoensis* 'Shidare-yoshino' |
| | - 'Perpendens' | see *P.* × *yedoensis* 'Shidare-yoshino' |
| § | - 'Shidare-yoshino' | CCVT CDul CLnd CSBt EBee ECrN LAst LRHS MAsh MBri MGos MRav MSwo MWat NWea SBfd SLim SLon |
| § | - 'Somei-Yoshino' ♀H4 | CCVT CLnd CTho CTri ECrN EPfP LAst MBri NWea SLim SPer WDin WHar WJas |
| | 'Yoshino' | see *P.* × *yedoensis* 'Somei-Yoshino' |
| | 'Yoshino Pendula' | see *P.* × *yedoensis* 'Shidare-yoshino' |

## *Psacalium* (*Asteraceae*)

| | | |
|---|---|---|
| | ***pinetorum*** B&SWJ 10269 | WCru |

## *Pseuderanthemum* (*Acanthaceae*)

| | | |
|---|---|---|
| | ***carruthersii*** var. ***atropurpureum*** 'Rubrum' | LSou |
| | ***laxiflorum*** | CCCN |
| | ***reticulatum*** orange-flowered | CCCN |

## *Pseudocydonia* (*Rosaceae*)

| | | |
|---|---|---|
| § | ***sinensis*** | CAgr CMen NLar |

## *Pseudofumaria* see *Corydalis*

| | | |
|---|---|---|
| | ***alba*** | see *Corydalis ochroleuca* |
| | ***lutea*** | see *Corydalis lutea* |

## *Pseudogynoxys* (*Asteraceae*)

| | | |
|---|---|---|
| § | ***chenopodioides*** | CCCN CSpe ELan |

## *Pseudolarix* (*Pinaceae*)

| | | |
|---|---|---|
| § | ***amabilis*** ♀H4 | CBcs CDoC CMCN CTho ECrN EHul EPfP GBin GQue LRHS MBlu MBri MMuc MPkF NHol NPCo NWea SBfd SCoo SKHP SLim SMad SPoG SSpi STre WFar |
| | ***kaempferi*** | see *P. amabilis* |

## *Pseudomuscari* see *Muscari*

## Pseudopanax (Araliaceae)

| | |
|---|---|
| (Adiantifolius Group) | CBcs CDoC CHEx CTrC ESwi GQui |
| 'Adiantifolius' | SEND SVen |
| - 'Cyril Watson' ♀H1 | CBcs CDoC CHEx ELan LRHS LTen SBig SVen |
| ***arboreus*** | see *Neopanax arboreus* |
| ***chathamicus*** | CDoC CHEx SArc |
| ***crassifolius*** | CAbb CBcs CBot CBrP CCCN CDTJ CHEx CTrC EAmu ESwi GBin IDee LRHS SArc SBig |
| - var. ***trifoliolatus*** | CHEx |
| ***discolor*** | ECou IDee LEdu |
| ***ferox*** | CAbb CBcs CBrP CDTJ CTsd EAmu ESwi GBin SArc SBig SMad SVen |
| 'Forest Gem' | CDoC |
| ***laetus*** | see *Neopanax laetus* |
| ***lessonii*** | CBcs CBrP CHEx ECou ELan |
| - 'Gold Splash' (v) ♀H1 | CBcs CDoC CHEx CTrC ELan IVic LRHS SBig SEND SVen |
| - 'Goldfinger' | CBcs |
| - 'Nigra' | CTrC |
| - 'Rangitira' | CBcs CDoC CTrC GBin LRHS SBig |
| 'Linearifolius' | CHEx CTrC IDee LEdu |
| 'Purpureus' ♀H1 | CDoC CTrC ESwi SEND SVen |
| 'Sabre' | CBcs CDoC CHEx CTrC LRHS |
| 'Trident' | CDoC CHEx CMHG CTrC ECou LEdu SBig SVen |

## Pseudophoenix (Arecaceae)

| | |
|---|---|
| * ***nativo*** | MBri |
| ***sargentii*** | EAmu |

## Pseudosasa (Poaceae)

| | |
|---|---|
| ***amabilis*** misapplied | see *Arundinaria gigantea* |
| § ***amabilis*** (McClure) Keng f. | CEnt EPla WFar |
| § ***japonica*** ♀H4 | Widely available |
| § - 'Akebonosuji' (v) | CEnt EPla MWht WJun WPGP |
| I - var. ***pleioblastoides*** | EPla MWht |
| - 'Tsutsumiana' | CHEx ELon EPla MMoz MWht NLar SBig WJun |
| - 'Variegata' | see *P. japonica* 'Akebonosuji' |
| ***orthotropa*** | see *Sinobambusa orthotropa* |
| ***usawai*** | EPla WJun |
| ***viridula*** | MWht |

## Pseudotsuga (Pinaceae)

| | |
|---|---|
| § ***menziesii*** ♀H4 | CBcs CDul CLnd ECrN EPfP MBlu MMuc NWea SEND WDin WFar |
| - 'Bhiela Lhota' | CKen NLar |
| - 'Blue Wonder' | CKen |
| - 'Densa' | CKen |
| - 'Fastigiata' | CKen |
| - 'Fletcheri' | CKen SLim |
| - 'Geijsteren' | NLar |
| - var. ***glauca*** | CDul |
| - 'Glauca Pendula' | CKen |
| I - 'Gotelli's Pendula' | CKen |
| - 'Graceful Grace' | CKen |
| - 'Idaho Gem' | CKen |
| - 'Julie' | CKen |
| - 'Knaphill' | NLar |
| - 'Little Jamie' | CKen |
| - 'Lohbrunner' | CKen |
| - 'McKenzie' | CKen |
| - 'Nana' | CKen |
| - 'Oudemansii' | NLar |
| - Pendula Group | NPCo |
| - 'Stairii' | CKen |
| - 'Uwes Golden' | NLar |
| ***taxifolia*** | see *P. menziesii* |

## Pseudowintera (Winteraceae)

| | |
|---|---|
| § ***colorata*** | CBcs CDoC CMac CPLG CTrC CWib GAbr GCal GGar GKin LRHS MPkF MRav NLar NPnk NWad WFar |
| - 'Marjorie Congreve' | IDee LRHS |
| - 'Moulin Rouge' | CBcs |
| - 'Mount Congreve' | CBcs GKin IArd MBri NLar |
| - 'Red Leopard' | LBuc LRHS NLar |

## Psidium (Myrtaceae)

| | |
|---|---|
| ***cattleyanum*** | see *P. littorale* var. *longipes* |
| ***guajava*** (F) | CCCN ERea SPlb XBlo |
| ***littorale*** (F) | ERea |
| § - var. ***longipes*** (F) | CCCN ERea XBlo |

## Psilotum (Psilotaceae)

| | |
|---|---|
| ***nudum*** | ECou |

## Psoralea (Papilionaceae)

| | |
|---|---|
| * ***fleta*** new | SPlb |
| ***glabra*** | SPlb |
| ***glandulosa*** | CArn SPlb WSHC |
| ***oligophylla*** | SPlb |
| ***pinnata*** | CPLG CTrC IRar |

## Psychotria (Rubiaceae)

| | |
|---|---|
| ***capensis*** | CPLG |

## Ptelea (Rutaceae)

| | |
|---|---|
| ***trifoliata*** | CArn CBcs CDul CLnd CMac CWib EMil EPfP MBlu MBri SPer SRms SSpi WDin WPGP |
| - 'Aurea' ♀H4 | CAbP CBcs CBot CEnd CLnd CMac CPLG CPMA EBee ELan EPfP EWTr GBin LHop LRHS MAsh MBlu MBri NLar SPer SPoG SSpi WDin WPGP |
| - 'Fastigiata' | EPfP |

## Pteracanthus see *Strobilanthes*

## Pteridophyllum (Papaveraceae)

| | |
|---|---|
| ***racemosum*** | EFEx GEdr LWst WCru |

## Pteris (Pteridaceae)

| | |
|---|---|
| from Yunnan | CLAP |
| § ***actiniopteroides*** | WCot |
| ***angustipinna*** B&SWJ 6738 | WCru |
| ***cretica*** ♀H1+3 | CHEx SArc |
| - var. ***albolineata*** ♀H1 | CBty GQui LRHS SRms XBlo |
| - 'Mayi' (v) new | CBty |
| - var. ***nervosa*** new | WRic |
| - 'Ouvradii' | ISha |
| - 'Rowei' | CBty LRHS XBlo |
| - 'Wimsettii' | CBty LRHS |
| ***dentata*** | WRic |
| ***ensiformis*** 'Evergemiensis' (v) new | CBty |
| ***gallinopes*** | CLAP |
| * ***hendersonii*** | GLin |
| ***henryi*** | see *P. actiniopteroides* |
| ***multifida*** | WRic |
| ***nipponica*** | WRic |
| ***quadriaurita*** | WRic |
| * ***staminea*** | XBlo |
| ***tremula*** | EFtx GQui SRms WRic |
| ***tricolor*** | CBty WRic |
| ***umbrosa*** | WRic |
| ***wallichiana*** | CGHE CHEx CLAP WPGP |

## *Pterocarya* ✿ (*Juglandaceae*)

| | |
|---|---|
| ***fraxinifolia*** ♀H4 | CBcs CCVT CDul CLnd CMCN CTho EBee ECrN EGFP EPfP GQui IArd IDee LMaj MBlu MMuc SEND WDin |
| - IDS 02 | WHCr |
| ***macroptera*** var. ***insignis*** | WPGP |
| × ***rehderiana*** | CTho MBlu WMou |
| ***stenoptera*** | CBcs CDTJ CMCN CTho EGFP NLar |
| - 'Fern Leaf' | EPfP MBlu WMou WPGP |

## *Pterocephalus* (*Caprifoliaceae*)

| | |
|---|---|
| ***depressus*** | CPBP WPat |
| ***parnassi*** | see *P. perennis* |
| § ***perennis*** | CMea ECho MHer NBir NMen NRya SRms WAbe WHoo |
| - subsp. ***perennis*** | WHrl |
| ***pinardii*** | WAbe |

## *Pterodiscus* (*Pedaliaceae*)

| | |
|---|---|
| sp. **new** | LToo |
| ***aurantiacus*** | LToo |
| ***luridus*** **new** | LToo |
| ***ngamicus*** | LToo |

## *Pterostylis* (*Orchidaceae*)

| | |
|---|---|
| ***coccina*** | ECho |
| ***curta*** | ECho LLHF |

## *Pterostyrax* (*Styracaceae*)

| | |
|---|---|
| ***corymbosa*** | CBcs CPMA IArd IDee MBlu NLar SSpi WFar |
| ***hispida*** ♀H4 | CAbP CBcs CDoC CDul CHGN CMCN CMac CPMA CWib EPfP EPla GBin IArd IDee LRHS MBlu MGos MRav NLar SChF SPoG SSpi WDin WFar WPGP |

## *Ptilostemon* (*Asteraceae*)

| | |
|---|---|
| ***afer*** | CCse |
| § ***diacantha*** | ELan IFoB LRHS MSCN |
| ***echinocephalus*** | EWll MDKP |

## *Ptilotrichum* see *Alyssum*

## *Ptilotus* (*Amaranthaceae*)

| | |
|---|---|
| ***exaltatus*** | SPlb |

## *Pueraria* (*Papilionaceae*)

| | |
|---|---|
| ***montana*** var. ***lobata*** | CArn |

## *Pulicaria* (*Asteraceae*)

| | |
|---|---|
| § ***dysenterica*** | CArn CHab EWil NMir SIde WSFF |

## *Pulmonaria* (*Boraginaceae*)

| | |
|---|---|
| ***angustifolia*** ♀H4 | CMac EBee EPfP GMaP MNrw NOrc SRms WTin |
| * - ***alba*** | IFoB |
| - 'Azurea' | CBro CElw CTca EBee ELan EPPr EPfP GAbr GMaP IGor LRHS MCot MMuc MRav NBro NLar SBfd SMrm SPer SRms WFar WMnd |
| - 'Blaues Meer' | CSam ECtt EPfP GAbr WCru |
| - 'Munstead Blue' | CElw CLAP CMac MCot MRav NRya SRms |
| 'Apple Frost' | EBee LRHS NLar SGol WWEG |
| 'Baby Blue' | SHeu |
| 'Barfield Regalia' | CMHG IGor LLHF NSti SDys WCru |
| 'Benediction' | CDes LLHF MNrw NSti |
| 'Beth's Pink' | ECha WFar |
| 'Blauer Hügel' | CElw LLHF NSti |
| 'Blauhimmel' | CElw GCra |
| 'Blue Buttons' | CFir ECtt EPla WWEG |
| 'Blue Crown' | CElw CLAP CSev EBee EWes |
| 'Blue Ensign' | Widely available |
| 'Blue Moon' | see *P. officinalis* 'Blue Mist' |
| 'Bonnie' | CMea |
| 'Botanic Hybrid' | WCru |
| 'Bubble Gum'PBR **new** | SHeu |
| Cally hybrid | CElw CLAP GCal NBre WCru |
| 'Cedric Morris' | CElw |
| 'Chintz' | CLAP CSam MAvo SMrm |
| 'Cleeton Red' | NSti |
| 'Coral Springs' | EBee LLHF NLar |
| 'Corsage' | ECtt |
| 'Cotton Cool' | CGHE CLAP CMac CPrp CTca EAEE EBee ECha ECtt EShb GGar IPot LBMP LRHS MBNS MCot MSpe MWhi NEgg NOrc NSti NWad SBfd SPer SUsu WCAu WFar WMoo |
| 'Crawshay Chance' | CElw |
| 'De Vroomen's Pride' (v) | WMnd |
| 'Diana Clare' | Widely available |
| 'Elworthy Rubies' | CElw EPPr |
| 'Emerald Isles' | SWvt |
| 'Excalibur' | ECtt NLar |
| 'Fiona' | WWEG |
| 'Glacier' | CBro CTca EBee EPfP LRHS MNrw NSti SAga WWEG |
| 'Hazel Kaye's Red' | LLWP |
| 'Highdown' | see *P.* 'Lewis Palmer' |
| 'Ice Ballet' (Classic Series) | EBee SHeu |
| 'Joan's Red' | CElw WTin |
| § 'Lewis Palmer' ♀H4 | CBro CElw CMHG CMea CSam CTca EBee ELan GCal GMaP LRHS MAvo MNrw NBir NHol NLar SBrd SPoG SRGP SRms WBrk WCFE WCot WCru WHoo WTin WWEG |
| 'Little Star' | ECtt LRHS NSti SRGP SUsu WCru WFar |
| ***longifolia*** | CArn CBot CFee CHar CPrp EAEE EBee ECha EHoe ELan EPfP GAbr GKev LRHS NBir NLar NOrc NSti WBrk WFar |
| § - 'Ankum' | CElw CLAP CSam EPfP MRav NBir NSti WWEG |
| - 'Ballyrogan Blue' | IBlr |
| - 'Bertram Anderson' | CPrp CTca EBee ECtt ELon GMaP LRHS NBir NLar NVic SBfd SPer SRGP SRms SWvt WBrk WCAu WCru WFar WMnd WWEG |
| - subsp. ***cevennensis*** | CLAP EBee LRHS MBri MLLN NCGa NLar NSti WPtf WWEG |
| - 'Coen Jansen' | see *P. longifolia* 'Ankum' |
| - 'Dordogne' | CLAP MAsh NBir NLar |
| - 'Howard Eggins' | EBee |
| 'Majesté' | CLAP CWib EBee ECha EHoe ELan EPfP EWes GMaP IFro LAst LHop LRHS MRav NBPC NBir NCGa NEgg NOrc NSti SApp SBfd SPer SPoG WBrk WCAu WCot WFar WMnd WWEG |
| 'Margery Fish' ♀H4 | CBro CHar CLAP CSam EBee EPfP LRHS SPer WMnd |
| 'Mary Mottram' | CElw ECtt ELan NBir NSti WCot WMnd |
| 'Matese Blue' | CLAP |

| | |
|---|---|
| 'Mawson's Blue' | CElw CLAP EWes GMac MRav MSpe MWea NBir NChi SWvt WBrk WMoo WRHF WSHC |
| 'May Bouquet'[PBR] | LLHF |
| 'Melancholia' | IBlr |
| 'Merlin' | CLAP SKHP |
| § 'Milchstrasse' | CLAP |
| Milky Way | see *P.* 'Milchstrasse' |
| ***mollis*** | CBot CLAP EBee ECGP GCal MNrw NSti WCru |
| - 'Royal Blue' | MRav |
| - 'Samobor' | CLAP |
| 'Moonstone' | CElw CLAP |
| 'Mountain Magic'[PBR] | ECtt LRHS SIde |
| 'Mournful Purple' | ELon |
| 'Mrs Kittle' | CFir CMMP EBee IFoB LRHS MRav NBir NSti WBrk WCAu WFar WMnd WWEG |
| 'Netta Statham' | LLHF NSti |
| 'Nürnberg' | WWEG |
| ***officinalis*** | CArn CBro CHby IFoB MLHP MNHC NChi NVic SIde WBrk WFar |
| - 'Alba' | WBrk |
| § - 'Blue Mist' | CBro CLAP EBee ELan GMaP MLLN NBir WBrk WCot WHoo WMnd WMoo WTin |
| - 'Bowles's Blue' | see *P. officinalis* 'Blue Mist' |
| - Cambridge Blue Group | EBee GMaP LRHS MRav MWat NBir WCot WPtf |
| - 'Marjorie Lawley' | LRHS |
| - 'Stillingfleet Gran' | LLHF |
| - 'White Wings' | CElw CLAP EBee MRav NLar SIde WFar |
| - 'Wuppertal' | EBee |
| 'Oliver Wyatt's White' | CLAP EBee SRGP |
| Opal = 'Ocupol' | Widely available |
| 'Pink Haze'[PBR] | CAbP CYeo ECtt LPla MLLN NSti SBfd SHeu SPoG SWvt WBrk WCot |
| 'Polar Splash' | EBee GBin LRHS SIde WFar |
| 'Raspberry Splash'[PBR] | CLAP ECtt EGxp LRHS MTis NLar SGol SHeu SIde SMrm SPoG |
| * 'Rowlatt Choules' | MAvo |
| 'Roy Davidson' | CLAP CSam CTca EBee ECGP ECtt EPfP GMac IGor LHop LRHS MLLN NBir NCGa NDov NSti SRGP SRms SWvt WFar WPtf WWEG |
| ***rubra*** ♀H4 | CBcs CElw CHab CPom ECha ELan EShb GAbr LBMP LLWP MLHP MMuc MNrw NBid NOrc NSti SEND SRms WCAu WFar WTin |
| - var. ***alba*** | see *P. rubra* var. *albocorollata* |
| § - var. ***albocorollata*** | CBre EBtc GAbr MLLN NBid SHar WBrk WFar WWEG |
| - 'Ann' | CLAP WFar |
| - 'Barfield Pink' | CBro ELan GCal IFro MLLN NBir NLar WCru |
| - 'Bowles's Red' | CBot CMac EBee ECtt EPfP IFoB LAst LRHS MNrw MRav NBir NCGa NGdn NPnk SHeu SIde SPer STes WFar WGwG WMnd |
| - 'David Ward' (v) | Widely available |
| - 'Rachel Vernie' (v) | CLAP CPou MAvo WBrk |
| - 'Redstart' | CBro CMac CSBt CSam CTca EBee ECtt EPfP GKev IGor LEdu LHop LRHS MLLN MNrw MRav NBPC NBir NEgg NGdn NLar NVic SRms SWat SWvt WBrk WFar WMnd WMoo WWEG |
| § ***saccharata*** | ECha ELan GMaP IFro MMuc NEgg NPnk SEND SIde SRms WFar |
| - 'Alba' | CBro CElw ECha MMuc SRms |
| - Argentea Group ♀H4 | CBro CSev CTri EBee ELan EPfP GMaP LRHS MLLN MRav NGdn WBrk WCot WWEG |
| - 'Dora Bielefeld' | CElw CLAP EBee ECha ECtt EPPr EPfP EWTr GMaP LLWP LRHS MCot MNrw MRav NBPC NBir NCGa NGdn NHol NSti SBfd SMrm SPer SRGP SWvt WFar WHil WHoo WMnd |
| - 'Frühlingshimmel' | CBro CElw EBee ECtt ELon EPfP LRHS MAsh MNrw MRav NDov NSti SBrd WFar |
| - 'Glebe Cottage Blue' | CElw ECGP |
| - 'Leopard' | CEnt CLAP CMac CSam CTca CWCL EBee ECha ECtt GMaP LRHS MLLN MNrw NBir NLar SApp SRGP WBrk WCot WFar WHoo WWEG WWlt |
| - 'Mrs Moon' | CTri CWib EBee ECtt ELon EPfP GMaP LAst LRHS LTen MWat NBPC NLar NOrc NPri SBfd SPer SRGP SWvt WCAu WHil WMnd WWEG |
| - 'Old Rectory Silver' | CLAP NBir |
| - 'Picta' | see *P. saccharata* |
| - 'Pink Dawn' | CMHG WMnd |
| - pink-flowered | WCru |
| - 'Reginald Kaye' | EBee ECha EWes MNrw |
| - 'Silverado'[PBR] | EBee ECtt GEdr LRHS MAsh MLLN NLar NOrc |
| - 'Stanhoe' | EWes |
| 'Saint Ann's' | CElw LLHF NSti WCru |
| 'Samurai' | GBin GEdr NSti WPtf |
| 'Silver Sabre' | IBlr |
| 'Silver Surprise' | WCot |
| 'Sissinghurst White' ♀H4 | Widely available |
| 'Smoky Blue' | CLAP EBee ECtt EPfP EWTr MRav NBPC SMrm SWat WFar WMnd WWEG |
| 'Spilled Milk' | NLar |
| 'Stillingfleet Meg' | CLAP EAEE EBee ECtt LAst LHop LRHS MLLN MNrw NHol NSti NWad SRGP WFar WPtf |
| 'Tim's Silver' | ECtt |
| 'Trevi Fountain' | CLAP EBee ECtt EShb GJos GKev LRHS MTis SHeu SIde SPoG WCot WPtf |
| 'Vera May' ♀H4 | EBee MAvo |
| 'Victorian Brooch'[PBR] | CLAP EBee ECtt GAbr GKev GQue LSou MNrw MTis NEgg NLar NPri SHeu SIde WFar WPtf WWEG |
| 'Weetwood Blue' | CBre CLAP CTca EBee EPfP MNrw |
| 'Wisley White' | CElw |

## *Pulsatilla* (*Ranunculaceae*)

| | |
|---|---|
| ***alba*** | CBro GKev NWCA |
| ***albana*** | CBro ECho LHop LLHF LRHS |
| - 'Lutea' | GKev LLHF |
| ***alpina*** | CBot ECho NGdn SRms WPat |
| § - subsp. ***apiifolia*** ♀H4 | GKev GMac IFro |
| - subsp. ***sulphurea*** misapplied | see *P. alpina* subsp. *apiifolia* |
| ***ambigua*** | GKev GLam LLHF |
| ***bungeana*** | GKev |
| subsp. ***bungeana*** new | |
| ***caucasica*** | CBro ECho LRHS |
| ***cernua*** | CBro LHop |
| × ***gayeri*** | NBir |
| ***georgica*** | EDAr GEdr |
| ***halleri*** ♀H4 | EBee |

| | | |
|---|---|---|
| | - subsp. ***slavica*** ♀H4 | GEdr LLHF |
| | - subsp. ***taurica*** | LRHS |
| | ***lutea*** | see *P. alpina* subsp. *apiifolia* |
| | ***montana*** | LLHF NMen SPlb |
| § | ***patens*** | EDAr LLHF NGdn |
| | - subsp. ***flavescens*** | EDAr |
| | ***pratensis*** | GPoy SRms |
| | - subsp. ***nigricans*** | LHop LRHS WFar |
| I | - 'Semiplena' | MMoz |
| | ***rubra*** | EGHP GKev NGdn SPad SRot WGwG |
| | ***turczaninovii*** | GKev GMac LLHF LRHS |
| § | ***vernalis*** ♀H2 | EPot NLar NSla |
| | ***violacea*** | CBcs |
| § | ***vulgaris*** ♀H4 | Widely available |
| | - 'Alba' ♀H4 | Widely available |
| | - 'Barton's Pink' | CBro ECho EWes LHop LLHF LRHS SRot |
| | - 'Blaue Glocke' | GEdr LRHS MCot MWat NPri SHar SMrm SWvt WFar WHil WRHF XSen |
| | - 'Eva Constance' | CBro ECho LHop LLHF LRHS WAbe |
| | - 'Gotlandica' | LLHF |
| | - subsp. ***grandis*** | CBot LRHS NMen |
| | - - 'Budapest' | CRDP |
| | - - 'Papageno' | CBot CSpe EAEE EBee ECho ELon GAbr GEdr GMaP LBMP LRHS MAvo NCGa NDov NLar NSla SRot WFar WHil |
| | - Heiler hybrids | CPrp EAEE LRHS MRav NCGa NDov NEgg NGdn NSla |
| | - 'Perlen Glocke' **new** | EDAr |
| | - pink-flowered **new** | NSla |
| | - Red Clock | see *P. vulgaris* 'Röde Klokke' |
| § | - 'Röde Klokke' | EBee ECtt EPot GEdr GKev LRHS MCot MWat MWhi NBPC NPri NWCA SHar SMrm SWvt WHil XLum XSen |
| | - ***rosea*** | GAbr |
| | - Rote Glocke | see *P. vulgaris* 'Röde Klokke' |
| | - var. ***rubra*** | CMea EBee ECho ELan EPPr EPfP GMaP LRHS MBri MHer MNHC MRav NBPC NBir NBlu NLar NSla SBfd SGar SPer SPet SPoG SRms SRot STes WBor WFar WHoo WWlt |
| § | - 'Weisse Schwan' | GMaP NMen SRot |
| | - 'White Bells' | GEdr |
| | - White Swan | see *P. vulgaris* 'Weisse Schwan' |
| | ***zimmermannii*** | NWCA |

## *Pultenaea* (*Papilionaceae*)

| | |
|---|---|
| ***juniperina*** | SPlb |

## pummelo see *Citrus maxima*

## *Punica* (*Lythraceae*)

| | |
|---|---|
| ***granatum*** | CBcs CHEx CMen EAmu EPfP ERom IDee LRHS MGos MOWG MREP SBrd SLim STre SVic WSHC |
| - 'André le Roi' (F) | SLPl |
| - 'Chico' | SEND |
| - 'Fina Tendral' | CCCN ERea |
| - 'Flore Pleno' | see *P. granatum* f. *plena* 'Rubrum Flore Pleno' |
| - 'Legrelleae' (F/d) | SEND SLPl |
| - 'Maxima Rubra' | EShb XSen |
| - var. ***nana*** ♀H3 | CAgr CArn CCCN CMen EBtc ELau EOHP EPfP EShb LEdu LRHS MREP SMrm SRms WPat |
| - f. ***plena*** (d) | CBcs LRHS MRav WCFE WPat |
| - - 'Flore Pleno Luteo' (d) | LRHS |
| - - 'Rubrum Flore Pleno' (d) ♀H3 | SEND |
| - 'Provence' | XSen |
| * - 'Striata' | MOWG |

## *Puschkinia* (*Asparagaceae*)

| | | |
|---|---|---|
| | ***scilloides*** | ECho NBir |
| | - 'Aragat's Gem' | ECho LWst |
| | - large-flowered clone **new** | LWst |
| § | - var. ***libanotica*** | ECho EPfP EPot GKev LAma LEdu MAvo SDeJ SMrm SPer WRHF WShi |
| | - - 'Alba' | ECho EPot GKev LAma SPer WCot |
| | - 'Snowdrift' **new** | LWst |

## *Puya* (*Bromeliaceae*)

| | |
|---|---|
| ***alpestris*** | CBrP CCCN CTrC EAmu EShb ETod SArc SBig WCot WPGP |
| ***berteroana*** | CBcs CCCN CDTJ CDoC CHEx EShb ETod SPlb |
| ***chilensis*** | CAbb CBcs CCCN CDTJ CDoC CHEx EAmu LRHS SPlb |
| ***coerulea*** | CCCN CDTJ CFir EAmu ELon EWld SPlb |
| ***laxa*** | SChr |
| ***mirabilis*** | CDTJ ESwi |
| - RCB/Arg L-3 | WCot |
| ***spathacea*** RCB/Arg S-2 | WCot |
| ***venusta*** | CCCN CDTJ ETod SPlb |

## *Pycnanthemum* (*Lamiaceae*)

| | |
|---|---|
| ***muticum*** | CArn MSCN |
| ***pilosum*** | CArn EBee ELau MHer NBre NLar SIde SWal XLum |
| ***tenuifolium*** | NBre NLar |
| ***virginianum*** | GCal SPhx |

## *Pycnostachys* (*Lamiaceae*)

| | |
|---|---|
| ***reticulata*** | EOHP |
| ***urticifolia*** | ECre EOHP EWes |

## *Pygmea* see *Chionohebe*

## *Pyracantha* (*Rosaceae*)

| | | |
|---|---|---|
| | Alexander Pendula = 'Renolex' | LHop MRav MSwo SRms WFar |
| | ***angustifolia*** | NMun WCFE |
| § | ***atalantioides*** | SPlb WCFE |
| | 'Brilliant' | EPfP SCoo WRHF |
| | 'Buttercup' | EPla |
| § | ***coccinea*** 'Lalandei' | CMac |
| | - 'Red Column' | Widely available |
| | - 'Red Cushion' | MRav SRms |
| | Dart's Red = 'Interrada' | CSBt SBfd SLim SPoG WHar |
| | 'Fiery Cascade' | LRHS SPoG SRms |
| | ***gibbsii*** | see *P. atalantioides* |
| | 'Golden Charmer' ♀H4 | CDul CMac EBee ECtt EPfP LRHS MAsh MGos MSwo NEgg NLar NPri NWea SBfd SCoo SGol SLPl SPer SPoG SRms SWvt WDin WFar WGwG WRHF |
| | 'Golden Glow' | SLim |
| | 'Golden Sun' | see *P.* 'Soleil d'Or' |
| | 'Harlequin' (v) | MAsh SGol WFar |
| | 'Knap Hill Lemon' | MBlu |
| | 'Mohave' | CChe CMac CTri EBee ECrN ELan ELon LRHS MAsh MWat NPri SCoo SGol SLim SRms SWvt WDin |
| | 'Mohave Silver' (v) | CMac CWSG ELan LAst LBMP LRHS MAsh SBfd |
| | 'Molten Lava' | MBri |

| | |
|---|---|
| 'Monrovia' | see *P. coccinea* 'Lalandei' |
| 'Navaho' | EPfP |
| 'Orange Charmer' | CBar CMac CTri EBee ELan LHop LRHS MAsh MGos MWat NLar SPer SPlb STre WFar |
| 'Orange Glow' ♀H4 | Widely available |
| 'Renault d'Or' | SLPl |
| ***rogersiana*** ♀H4 | CDul ECrN EPfP MRav WFar |
| - 'Flava' ♀H4 | CDul CSBt EBee EPfP LRHS MAsh NEgg SBfd SPoG SWvt |
| 'Rosedale' | LRHS WHar |
| Saphyr Jaune = 'Cadaune'PBR | CAlb CBar CBcs CCVT CDoC CEnd CSBt CWSG EBee ECrN EMil EPfP LRHS LTen MAsh MGos MRav NCGa NLar NPri SCoo SGol SPer |
| Saphyr Orange = 'Cadange'PBR ♀H4 | CAlb CBar CBcs CCVT CDoC CEnd CMac CSBt CWSG EBee EMil EPfP LRHS LTen MAsh MBri MGos MRav NEgg NLar SCoo SGol SPer |
| Saphyr Rouge = 'Cadrou'PBR ♀H4 | CAlb CBar CBcs CCVT CDoC CEnd CMac CSBt CWSG EBee ECrN ELan EMil EPfP LTen MBri MGos MMuc MRav NLar NPri SCoo SEND SGol SPer SWvt WFar |
| 'Shawnee' | CMac CWib MAsh MSwo MWat |
| § 'Soleil d'Or' | CBar CTri CWib EBee ECrN ECtt ELan EPfP LAst LBuc LRHS MAsh MMuc MRav NBlu NLar SBrd SEND SEWo SGol SLPl SLim SLon SPer SPlb SWvt WDin WFar WHar |
| 'Sparkler' (v) | CMac EGxp EHoe SLim WFar |
| 'Teton' ♀H4 | CMac CWSG EBee ELan EPfP EPla LAst LRHS MAsh MSwo MWat NEgg NWea SGol SPoG SRms WDin WFar |
| 'Ventoux Red' | SCoo |
| 'Watereri' | NWea SLPl WFar |
| 'Yellow Sun' | see *P.* 'Soleil d'Or' |

## *Pyrenaria* (*Theaceae*)

| | |
|---|---|
| ***spectabilis*** | see *Tutcheria spectabilis* |

## *Pyrethropsis* see *Rhodanthemum*

## *Pyrethrum* see *Tanacetum*

## *Pyrola* (*Ericaceae*)

| | |
|---|---|
| ***minor*** | NMen |
| ***rotundifolia*** | LEdu WHer |

## *Pyrostegia* (*Bignoniaceae*)

| | |
|---|---|
| ***venusta*** | CCCN MOWG |

## *Pyrrosia* (*Polypodiaceae*)

| | |
|---|---|
| ***hastata*** new | CMen |
| ***lingua*** | CMen WPGP WRic |
| ***polydactyla*** | CMen WRic |

## *Pyrus* ✿ (*Rosaceae*)

| | |
|---|---|
| ***amygdaliformis*** var. ***cuneifolia*** | CLnd SCoo |
| ***betulifolia*** | CMCN |
| ***calleryana*** 'Bradford' | CLnd |
| - 'Capital' | LMaj |
| - 'Chanticleer' ♀H4 | Widely available |
| - 'Chanticleer' variegated (v) | CDul CLnd MAsh |
| ***communis*** (F) | CCVT CDul CTri LBuc NWea SPer SPlb WMou |
| - 'Abbé Fétel' (D) | SKee |
| - 'Baronne de Mello' (D) | CTho SFam |
| - 'Beech Hill' (F) | CDul CLnd EBee ECrN SGol SPer |
| - 'Belle Guérandaise' (D) | SKee |
| - 'Belle Julie' (D) | SKee |
| - 'Bergamotte Esperen' (D) | SKee |
| - 'Beth' (D) ♀H4 | CAgr CDoC CMac CSBt CTri CWib ECrN EPfP ERea GTwe LAst LBuc LRHS MAsh MBri MGos NLar NPri SDea SFam SKee SLim SPer WHar WWct |
| - 'Beurré Alexandre Lucas' (D) | SKee |
| - 'Beurré Bedford' (D) | SKee |
| - 'Beurré Clairgeau' (C/D) | SKee |
| - 'Beurré d'Amanlis' (D) | SKee |
| - 'Beurré d'Avalon' (D) | SKee |
| - 'Beurré de Beugny' (D) | SKee |
| - 'Beurré Diel' (D) | SKee |
| - 'Beurré Dumont' (D) | CAgr SFam |
| - 'Beurré Giffard' (D) | CAgr |
| - 'Beurré Hardy' (D) ♀H4 | CAgr CCVT CDoC CDul CMac CSBt CTho CTri CWib ECrN ERea GTwe LAst LRHS MAsh MBri MCoo MMuc MWat NEgg NLar SBfd SDea SEND SFam SKee WHar WWct |
| - 'Beurré Mortillet' (D) | SKee |
| § - 'Beurré Precoce Morettini' (D) | SDea |
| - 'Beurré Six' (D) | SKee |
| - 'Beurré Superfin' (D) ♀H4 | ECrN GTwe MCoo SFam SKee WHar |
| - 'Bianchettone' (D) | SKee |
| - 'Bishop's Thumb' (D) | SDea SKee |
| - 'Black Worcester' (C) | GTwe MAsh SDea SFam SKee WHar WJas WWct |
| - 'Blakeney Red' (Perry) | SDea SKee WHar |
| - 'Blickling' (D) | SKee |
| - 'Brandy' (Perry) | CAgr SDea SKee WHar |
| - 'Bristol Cross' (D) | CAgr GTwe SKee |
| - 'Calebasse Bosc' (D) | SKee |
| - 'Catillac' (C) ♀H4 | CAgr GTwe SFam SKee WHar |
| - 'Charneaux' (F) | SVic |
| - 'Chaumontel' (D) | SKee |
| - 'Clapp's Favourite' (D) | CTho ECrN SKee SVic |
| - 'Concorde'PBR (D) ♀H4 | Widely available |
| - 'Conference' (D) ♀H4 | Widely available |
| - 'Deacon's Pear' (D) | SDea |
| - Delbardélice = 'Deleté' | LRHS |
| - 'Devoe' (D) | SDea |
| - 'Docteur Jules Guyot' (D) | CAgr ECrN SDea SKee |
| - 'Doyenné d'Été' (D) | ERea MCoo SFam SKee |
| - 'Doyenné du Comice' (D) ♀H4 | Widely available |
| - 'Doyenné Georges Boucher' (D) | SKee |
| - 'Duchesse d'Angoulême' (D) | SKee |
| - 'Durondeau' (D) | ERea GTwe SDea SFam SKee |
| - 'Emile d'Heyst' (D) | GTwe MCoo WHar |
| - 'Fertility' (D) | CLnd ERea |
| - 'Fertility Improved' | see *P. communis* 'Improved Fertility' |
| - 'Fondante d'Automne' (D) | CAgr CTho LRHS WHar |
| - 'Forelle' (D) | ERea SKee |
| - 'Glou Morceau' (D) | CAgr ECrN ERea GTwe MCoo MWat SDea SFam SKee WHar |
| - 'Glow Red Williams' (D) | SFam |
| - 'Gorham' (D) ♀H4 | CAgr CTho ECrN GTwe MCoo SFam SKee WHar |
| - 'Green Horse' (Perry) | CCAT |
| - 'Green Pear of Yair' (D) | SKee |

| | |
|---|---|
| - 'Hacon's Imcomparable' (D) | SKee |
| - 'Harley Gum' (F) **new** | WHar |
| - 'Harrow Delight' (D) | SDea |
| - 'Harvest Queen' (D/C) | CAgr SDea |
| - 'Hellen's Early' (Perry) | CCAT SKee WHar |
| - 'Hendre Huffcap' (Perry) | CCAT WHar |
| - 'Hessle' (D) | CAgr GTwe MCoo NWea SDea SFam SKee |
| § - 'Improved Fertility' (D) | CAgr CDoC GTwe SDea |
| - Invincible = 'Delwinor' (D/C) | CAgr CDul CSut CTho EPom LBuc LRHS MAsh MBri MCoo SLim WHar |
| - 'Jargonelle' (D) | CAgr CTho ECrN GTwe SDea SFam SKee WHar |
| - 'Jeanne d'Arc' (D) | SVic |
| - 'Joséphine de Malines' (D) 🏆$^{H4}$ | CAgr GTwe SDea SFam SKee WHar |
| - 'Judge Amphlett' (Perry) | WHar |
| - 'Kieffer' (C) | CAgr |
| - 'Laxton's Foremost' (D) | CAgr SKee |
| - 'Laxton's Satisfaction' (D) | SFam |
| - 'Légipont' (F) | CAgr |
| - 'Louise Bonne of Jersey' (D) 🏆$^{H4}$ | CAgr CDoC CMac CTri ECrN GTwe LAst MGos SDea SFam SKee WHar WWct |
| - 'Marguérite Marillat' (D) | SDea SKee |
| - 'Marie-Louise' (D) | SKee WHar |
| - 'Merton Pride' (D) | CAgr CTho GTwe MCoo MWat SDea SFam SKee WHar |
| - 'Moonglow' | CAgr ERea SDea |
| - 'Moorcroft' (Perry) | SKee |
| - 'Morettini' | see *P. communis* 'Beurré Precoce Morettini' |
| - 'Nouveau Poiteau' (C/D) | CAgr ECrN GTwe SKee |
| - 'Nuvar Celebration' (F) **new** | SKee |
| - 'Nye Russet Bartlett' (F) | CAgr |
| - 'Olivier de Serres' (D) | SKee |
| - 'Onward' (D) 🏆$^{H4}$ | CAgr CDul CLnd CTho CTri CWib ECrN EPom GTwe MAsh MBri NEgg NLar NWea SDea SFam SKee WHar WWct |
| - 'Ovid' (D) | CAgr |
| § - 'Packham's Triumph' (D) | CAgr CDoC CTri CWib ECrN GTwe LAst SDea SKee SVic WHar |
| - 'Passe Crassane' (D) | SKee |
| - 'Pear Apple' (D) | SDea |
| - 'Pero Nobile' | SKee |
| - 'Pitmaston Duchess' (C/D) 🏆$^{H4}$ | ECrN GTwe MCoo SDea SFam SKee WHar |
| - 'Précoce de Trévoux' (D) | WHar |
| - 'Red Comice' (D/C) | GTwe SKee |
| - 'Red Sensation Bartlett' (D/C) | GTwe LBuc LRHS SKee |
| - 'Robin' (C/D) | ERea SDea SKee |
| - 'Santa Claus' (D) | SDea SFam SKee |
| - 'Seckel' (D) | SFam SKee |
| - 'Shipova' (F) **new** | LRHS |
| - 'Sierra' (D) | CAgr |
| - 'Snowdon Queen' (D) | WGwG |
| - 'Souvenir du Congrès' (D) | CAgr |
| - 'Swan's Egg' (D) | SKee |
| - 'Terrace Pearl' | MGos SPoG |
| - 'Tettenhall Dick' (C/D) **new** | LRHS |
| - 'Thompson's' (D) | SFam SKee |
| - 'Thorn' (Perry) | CAgr SKee WHar |
| - 'Triomphe de Vienne' (D) | SFam |
| - 'Triumph' | see *P. communis* 'Packham's Triumph' |
| - 'Uvedale's St Germain' (C) | SFam SKee |
| - 'Verbelu' | SKee |
| - 'Vicar of Winkfield' (C/D) | ECrN GTwe SDea SKee |
| - 'Williams' Bon Chrétien' (D/C) 🏆$^{H4}$ | Widely available |
| - 'Williams Red' (D/C) | GTwe |
| - 'Winnal's Longdon' (Perry) | WHar |
| - 'Winter Nelis' (D) | CAgr CTri CWib ECrN GTwe LRHS SDea SFam SKee WHar |
| - 'Zéphirin Grégoire' (D) | SKee |
| ***cordata*** | CDul CTho |
| ***elaeagnifolia*** | CDul CEnd SLim |
| var. ***kotschyana*** | |
| - 'Silver Sails' | CLnd EBee EMil LAst LRHS MBlu MBri MGos NLar SCoo SPur SSpi |
| ***nivalis*** | CDul CLnd CTho EBee ECrN EPfP LMaj LRHS MRav SCoo SPer SPur |
| - 'Catalia' | CEnd EBee MAsh MBri NPal SCoo |
| ***pashia*** | EBee LRHS NLar |
| ***pyraster*** | CDul CHab |
| ***pyrifolia*** | GAuc |
| - '20th Century' | see *P. pyrifolia* 'Nijisseiki' |
| - 'Chojuro' (F) | ERea |
| - 'Hosui' (F) | CAgr SVic |
| - 'Kosui' (F) | ERea SVic |
| - 'Kumoi' (F) | LRHS MAsh SDea SKee WHar |
| § - 'Nijisseiki' (F) | SVic |
| - 'Shinko' (F) | CAgr ERea |
| - 'Shinseiki' (F) | CAgr CLnd ERea MAsh SDea SKee WHar |
| - 'Shinsui' (F) | SDea SKee |
| * ***salicifolia*** var. ***orientalis*** | CTho |
| - 'Pendula' 🏆$^{H4}$ | Widely available |
| ***ussuriensis*** | GAuc |

# Q

## *Qiongzhuea* see *Chimonobambusa*

## *Quercus* ✿ (*Fagaceae*)

| | |
|---|---|
| ***acerifolia*** | EPfP |
| ***acherdophylla*** | SBir |
| § ***acuta*** | CBcs |
| ***acutifolia*** | SBir |
| ***acutifolia*** × ***mexicana*** | SBir |
| ***acutissima*** | CBcs CDul CMCN EGFP EPfP SBir |
| ***aegilops*** | see *Q. ithaburensis* subsp. *macrolepis* |
| ***affinis*** | EPfP SBir |
| ***agrifolia*** | CBcs CDul CMCN EBtc EGFP |
| ***ajudaghiensis*** | see *Q. hartwissiana* |
| ***alba*** | CMCN WDin |
| ***aliena*** | CDul CMCN SBir |
| ***alnifolia*** | CDul |
| ***arkansana*** | CMCN SBir |
| × ***atlantica*** | SBir |
| ***austrina*** | CMCN SBir |
| × ***beadlei*** | see *Q.* × *saulii* |
| ***berberidifolia*** | CMCN SBir |
| ***bicolor*** | CDul CLnd CMCN EPfP SBir WDin |
| × ***bimundorum*** | SBir |
| § - 'Crimschmidt' | EPfP MBlu MBri |
| ***borealis*** | see *Q. rubra* |
| ***breweri*** | see *Q. garryana* var. *breweri* |
| ***buckleyi*** | CDul CMCN MBri SBir |

| | | |
|---|---|---|
| | × ***bushii*** | CMCN EPfP MBlu MBri SBir |
| | – 'Seattle Trident' **new** | MBlu |
| | ***canariensis*** 🏆H4 | CBcs CDul CLnd CMCN CTho EPfP WMou WPGP |
| | ***castaneifolia*** | CDul CMCN WDin |
| | – 'Green Spire' 🏆H4 | CMCN EPfP IArd MBlu SBir SEND SMad |
| | ***cerris*** | CBcs CCVT CDoC CDul CLnd CMCN EBee ECrN ELan EPfP EWTr LAst LMaj MGos MMuc NWea SEND SPer WDin WFar |
| | – 'Afyon Lace' | MBlu MBri |
| § | – 'Argenteovariegata' (v) | CBcs CDul CEnd CMCN CPMA EBee ELan EPfP IArd MAsh MBlu MBri MPkF SBir SMad WCot WPat |
| | – 'Marmor Star' | SEND |
| | – 'Variegata' | see *Q. cerris* 'Argenteovariegata' |
| | – 'Wodan' | EPfP MBlu |
| | ***chenii*** | CDul CMCN EGFP SBir |
| | ***chrysolepis*** | CMCN EPfP |
| | ***coccifera*** | CGHE CMCN EPla SSpi WDin WPGP |
| | ***coccinea*** | CBcs CDul CMCN CTho CTri EBee ECrN EPfP MBlu MMuc MWht NEgg NWea SBir SEWo SLim SPer SPoG WDin WPat |
| | – 'Splendens' 🏆H4 | CDoC CDul CEnd CHII CMCN CPMA CTri EBee ELan EPfP LRHS MAsh MBlu MBri SMad SPer WDin WPat |
| | ***conspersa*** | SBir |
| | ***crassifolia*** **new** | CMCN |
| | Crimson Spire | see *Q. × bimundorum* 'Crimschmidt' |
| | ***crispipilis*** | SBir |
| | ***dalechampii*** | CMCN SBir |
| | ***dentata*** | CDul CMCN |
| | – 'Carl Ferris Miller' | CBcs CMCN EPfP LLHF MBlu MBri SBir WMou WPGP WPat |
| | – 'Pinnatifida' | CMCN EPfP IDee MBlu MPkF SMad WPat |
| | – 'Sir Harold Hillier' | MBlu MBri |
| | – subsp. ***yunnanensis*** | SBir |
| | ***dilatata*** ambig. **new** | SBir |
| | ***dolicholepis*** | SBir |
| | 'Doring's Zweizack' | SBir |
| | ***douglasii*** | CMCN SSpi |
| | – G 261 | WPGP |
| | ***dumosa*** | CMCN |
| | – G 315 | WPGP |
| | – G 316 | WPGP |
| | ***elliottii*** | SBir |
| | ***ellipsoidalis*** | CDul CMCN SBir |
| | – 'Hemelrijk' | EPfP IArd MBlu MBri SBir |
| | × ***exacta*** **new** | SBir |
| | ***fabrei*** | CMCN SBir |
| | ***faginea*** | CDul EGFP |
| | ***falcata*** | CDul CMCN EBtc SBir |
| | – var. ***pagodifolia*** | see *Q. pagoda* |
| | × ***fernaldii*** | CMCN EPfP MBlu |
| | ***frainetto*** | CDoC CDul CLnd CMCN CTho EBee ECrN ELan EPfP LMaj NWea SEND SPer WDin WMou |
| | – 'Hungarian Crown' 🏆H4 | CMCN EPfP MBlu MMuc SBir |
| | – 'Tortworth' | SMad WMou |
| | – 'Trump' | CLnd CMCN |
| | ***franchetii*** **new** | SBir |
| | ***gambelii*** | CMCN EGFP |
| | ***garryana*** | CMCN |
| § | – var. ***breweri*** | EGFP |
| | – var. ***fruticosa*** | see *Q. garryana* var. *breweri* |
| | ***georgiana*** | CDul CMCN EPfP SBir |
| | ***gilva*** | SBir |
| | ***glandulifera*** | see *Q. serrata* Thunb. |
| § | ***glauca*** | CBcs CDul CMCN EPfP NLar SArc SBir WPGP |
| | ***graciliformis*** | SBir |
| | ***gravesii*** | CMCN EPfP SBir |
| | ***greggii*** **new** | SBir |
| | ***grisea*** | CMCN |
| § | ***hartwissiana*** | SBir |
| | × ***hastingsii*** | CMCN SBir |
| | ***havardii*** **new** | CMCN |
| | × ***hawkinsiae*** | SBir |
| | × ***haynaldiana*** | SBir |
| | ***hemisphaerica*** | CDul EPfP SBir |
| | × ***heterophylla*** | CMCN EPfP SBir |
| | × ***hickelii*** | CMCN EPfP SBir |
| | ***hinckleyi*** | WDin |
| § | × ***hispanica*** | CLnd |
| | – 'Ambrozyana' | CMCN WDin |
| | – 'Bloemendaal' | MBlu MBri |
| | – 'Diversifolia' | CMCN EPfP IArd MBlu |
| | – 'Fulhamensis' | CMCN MBlu MBri SBir WMou |
| § | – 'Lucombeana' 🏆H4 | CBcs CDul CHGN CMCN CSBt CTho EBee EPfP IArd IDee MBlu SBir SPer |
| § | – 'Pseudoturneri' | CBcs CDul EBee EWTr IArd MBlu |
| | – 'Suberosa' | CTho |
| | – 'Waasland Select' | MBri SBir |
| | – 'Wageningen' | CMCN MBri SBir |
| | ***hypoleucoides*** | EPfP |
| | ***ilex*** 🏆H4 | Widely available |
| | – 'Fordii' | SBir |
| | ***ilicifolia*** | CMCN EPfP SBir |
| | ***imbricaria*** | CDul CMCN EPfP SBir |
| | ***incana*** Roxb. | see *Q. leucotrichophora* |
| § | ***ithaburensis*** subsp. ***macrolepis*** | CMCN LEdu SBir |
| | – – 'Hemelrijk Silver' | MBlu SBir |
| | × ***jackiana*** | EPfP |
| | ***john-tuckeri*** G 271 | WPGP |
| | ***kelloggii*** | CBcs CMCN SBir WPGP |
| | × ***kewensis*** | CMCN LMaj SBir |
| | ***laceyi*** | CMCN |
| | ***laevigata*** | see *Q. acuta* |
| | ***laevis*** | CDul CMCN EPfP SBir |
| | 'Langtry' | SBir |
| § | ***laurifolia*** | CDul CMCN EGFP EPfP SBir |
| | ***laurina*** | SBir |
| § | ***leucotrichophora*** | CDul CMCN SBir WCFE |
| | ***liaotungensis*** | see *Q. wutaishanica* |
| | × ***libanerris*** | SBir |
| | – 'Rotterdam' | CMCN SBir |
| | ***libani*** | CDul CMCN EPfP WDin |
| | ***lobata*** | CMCN EGFP LEdu |
| | × ***lucombeana*** | see *Q. × hispanica* |
| | – 'William Lucombe' | see *Q. × hispanica* 'Lucombeana' |
| | × ***ludoviciana*** | CMCN EPfP SBir |
| | ***lyrata*** | CDul CMCN SGol |
| | ***macranthera*** | CMCN EPfP MBri SBir |
| | ***macrocarpa*** | CDul CMCN EPfP |
| | ***macrolepis*** | see *Q. ithaburensis* subsp. *macrolepis* |
| | ***marilandica*** | CDul CEnd CMCN EPfP IArd MBlu SBir |
| | 'Mauri' | MBri |
| | ***mexicana*** | CDul SBir |
| § | ***michauxii*** | CDul CMCN EPfP MBlu |
| | ***mongolica*** | CDul MBlu SBir |

| |  |  |
|---|---|---|
| | - subsp. ***crispula*** var. ***grosseserrata*** | CMCN |
| | ***muhlenbergii*** | CDul CMCN MBlu MPkF SBir |
| | × ***mutabilis*** | SBir |
| | ***myrsinifolia*** | see *Q. glauca* |
| | ***myrtifolia*** | EPfP SBir |
| | ***nigra*** | CDul CMCN MBri NLar SBir |
| | - 'Beethoven' | MBlu MBri SBir |
| I | - 'Nyewoodii' | SBir |
| | ***nuttallii*** | see *Q. texana* |
| | ***obtusa*** | see *Q. laurifolia* |
| | ***oglethorpensis*** | SBir |
| | ***pacifica*** G 301 | WPGP |
| | - G 305 | WPGP |
| | - G 313 | WPGP |
| § | ***pagoda*** | CMCN IGor SBir |
| | ***palustris*** ♀H4 | CCVT CDoC CDul CLnd CMCN CTho EBee ECrN ELan EPfP EWTr IArd LMaj MAsh MBlu MMuc NEgg NLar NWea SBir SEWo SGol SPer WDin |
| | - 'Green Dwarf' | CMCN MBlu |
| | - 'Pendula' | CEnd CMCN |
| | - 'Silhouette' | CPMA SBir |
| | - 'Swamp Pygmy' | CMCN EPfP MBlu |
| | - 'Windischleuba' | MBlu |
| | ***pannosa*** new | SBir |
| | ***parvula*** var. ***parvula*** | SBir |
| | - var. ***shrevei*** | SBir |
| § | × ***pauciloba*** | CMCN |
| | ***pedunculata*** | see *Q. robur* |
| | ***pedunculiflora*** | see *Q. robur* subsp. *pedunculiflora* |
| § | ***petraea*** ♀H4 | CAlb CDoC CDul CHab CLnd ECrN EPfP GAbr MBlu NLar NWea SGol SPer WDin WFar WMou |
| | - 'Acutiloba' | SBir |
| § | - 'Insecata' | CDul CEnd CMCN EPfP MBlu |
| | - 'Laciniata' | see *Q. petraea* 'Insecata' |
| § | - 'Purpurea' | CMCN MBlu |
| | - 'Rubicunda' | see *Q. petraea* 'Purpurea' |
| § | ***phellos*** | CDul CLnd CMCN EBee EBtc ECrN EPfP EWTr MBlu MBri SBir SLPl WDin |
| | ***phillyreoides*** | CBcs CDul CMCN EPfP SBir SLPl |
| | ***polymorpha*** | CDul CMCN MBri |
| | Pondaim Group | CMCN WMou |
| | ***pontica*** | CBcs CMCN EPfP LLHF MBlu MPkF WPat |
| | ***prinoides*** | CMCN |
| | ***prinus*** misapplied | see *Q. michauxii* |
| § | ***prinus*** L. | CMCN EPfP |
| | ***pubescens*** | CMCN |
| | ***pumila*** Michx. | see *Q. prinus* L. |
| | ***pumila*** Walt. | see *Q. phellos* |
| | ***pungens*** new | CMCN |
| | ***pyrenaica*** | CDul CLnd CMCN CTho EBtc MBri |
| | - 'Pendula' | CMCN EPfP WDin |
| | Regal Prince | see *Q.* × *warei* 'Long' |
| | ***rhysophylla*** | CBcs CDul CMCN EPfP MBlu SBir WPGP |
| | - 'Maya' | ELan IArd MBri MPkF SBir |
| | × ***riparia*** | SBir |
| § | ***robur*** ♀H4 | Widely available |
| | - 'Argenteomarginata' (v) | CDul CMCN MBlu WPat |
| | - 'Atropurpurea' | IArd MGos MPkF NWea WDin |
| | - 'Compacta' | MBlu |
| | - 'Concordia' | CBcs CDul CEnd CLnd CMCN EBee EBtc ELan EPfP MAsh MBlu MPkF NLar SKHP WDin |
| | - 'Dissecta' | CMCN |
| | - 'Facrist' | SBir |
| | - f. ***fastigiata*** | CDoC CDul CLnd CTho EBee ECrN EPfP IVic MGos NWea SBir SGol SLPl SLim SPer WDin WFar |
| | - - 'Koster' ♀H4 | CDul CMCN CMac CTri EPfP LMaj MBlu |
| | - 'Fennessyi' | IArd |
| | - 'Filicifolia' misapplied | see *Q. robur* 'Pectinata' |
| | - 'Filicifolia' | CEnd WPat |
| | - var. ***haas*** | CDul |
| | - - 'Cankiri' | SBir |
| | - 'Irtha' | EPfP |
| | - 'Menhir' | LLHF MBlu WPat |
| § | - 'Pectinata' | EPfP MBlu WDin |
| § | - subsp. ***pedunculiflora*** | CMCN SBir |
| | - 'Pendula' | CEnd CMCN MBlu |
| | - 'Purpurascens' | CEnd CMCN |
| | - 'Purpurea' | MBlu |
| | - 'Raba' | CMCN |
| | - 'Rita's Gold' | MBri |
| § | - 'Salfast' | MBlu |
| | - 'Salicifolia Fastigiata' | see *Q. robur* 'Salfast' |
| | - Sherwood oak clone | SMad |
| | - 'Strypemonde' | CMCN |
| | - 'Timuki' | MBlu |
| | - f. ***variegata*** (v) | CPMA |
| | - - 'Fürst Schwarzenburg' (v) | MBlu |
| | - 'Zeeland' | SBir |
| | ***robur*** × ***macrocarpa*** × ***virginiana*** | SBir |
| | ***rotundifolia*** | CAgr CMCN EPfP WPGP |
| § | ***rubra*** ♀H4 | Widely available |
| | - 'Aurea' | CDul CEnd CMCN CPMA EBee EPfP MBlu |
| | - 'Boltes Gold' | CPMA MBlu MBri |
| | - 'Cyrille' | SBir |
| | - 'Magic Fire' | EPfP MBlu NLar SBir |
| | - 'Red Queen' | MBlu |
| * | - 'Sunshine' | CMCN MBlu WPat |
| | ***rugosa*** | CMCN SBir |
| | × ***runcinata*** | SBir |
| | ***salicina*** | WPGP |
| | ***sartorii*** | SBir |
| § | × ***saulii*** | CMCN SBir |
| | × ***schochiana*** | EPfP MBlu MBri |
| | × ***schuettei*** | SBir |
| | ***semecarpifolia*** | MBlu |
| § | ***serrata*** Thunb. | CMCN EGFP EPfP MBri SBir |
| | ***sessiliflora*** | see *Q. petraea* |
| | ***shumardii*** | CDul CMCN EPfP MBlu MBri NLar SBir SGol |
| | ***sinuata*** subsp. ***breviloba*** | SBir |
| | ***stellata*** | CBcs CMCN EPfP SBir |
| | ***suber*** | CAgr CBcs CCVT CDoC CDul CLnd CMCN CTho EBee ELan EPfP EPla IArd LEdu LMaj MGos MMuc MREP SArc SEND WDin WPGP |
| | - 'Sopron' | EPfP MBlu |
| § | ***texana*** | CMCN EPfP SBir |
| | - New Madrid Group | EPfP MBlu MBri SBir |
| | ***tomentella*** new | SBir |
| | ***trojana*** | CDul CMCN SBir |
| | ***turbinella*** | CMCN |
| | × ***turneri*** | CDoC CLnd CMCN CTho EPfP MBri WDin WMou |
| | - 'Pseudoturneri' | see *Q.* × *hispanica* 'Pseudoturneri' |
| | ***undulata*** Torr. | see *Q.* × *pauciloba* |
| | ***variabilis*** | CDul CMCN EPfP SGol |
| | ***velutina*** | CBcs CDul CLnd CMCN CPMA CTho EPfP NLar SBir |

| | |
|---|---|
| - 'Albertsii' | CPMA MBlu |
| - 'Oakridge Walker' | MBlu |
| - 'Rubrifolia' | CMCN CPMA EPfP |
| ***virginiana*** | CBcs CDul CMCN SBir |
| × ***warburgii*** | EPfP |
| × ***warei*** | SBir |
| § - 'Long' | EPfP MBlu MPkF |
| - 'Windcandle' | MBlu SBir |
| ***wislizeni*** | CDul CMCN SBir |
| - G 265 | CBcs WPGP |
| § ***wutaishanica*** | CBcs CMCN |

## *Quillaja* (*Quillajaceae*)

| | |
|---|---|
| ***saponaria*** | CArn CBcs CCCN IDee WAle |

## quince see *Cydonia oblonga*

## *Quisqualis* (*Combretaceae*)

| | |
|---|---|
| ***indica*** | CCCN MOWG |

# R

## *Racosperma* see *Acacia*

## *Ramonda* (*Gesneriaceae*)

| | |
|---|---|
| § ***myconi*** ♀H4 | CLAP CPBP ECho EPot EWes GEdr LLHF NLar NMen NSla NWCA SChF SRms WAbe |
| - var. ***alba*** | CLAP ECho GEdr WThu |
| - 'Jim's Shadow' | WAbe |
| - 'Rosea' | CLAP |
| ***nathaliae*** ♀H4 | CLAP ECho WAbe WThu |
| - 'Alba' | CLAP NSla WAbe |
| ***pyrenaica*** | see *R. myconi* |
| ***serbica*** | NSla WThu |

## *Randia* (*Rubiaceae*)

| | |
|---|---|
| ***formosa*** | CCCN |

## *Ranunculus* (*Ranunculaceae*)

| | |
|---|---|
| ***abnormis*** | WAbe WCot |
| ***aconitifolius*** | EBee ECha ECho GCra GMaP NLar SHar SWat WHal WMnd WMoo WSHC |
| - 'Flore Pleno' (d) ♀H4 | CFir CSpe EBee ECha ECho EPfP GAbr GBBs GBin GCal GMaP GMac IGor IPot LRHS MLHP MRav NBir NPnk SRms WBor WCot WFar WHer WMoo WPnP WSHC |
| ***acris*** | CHab EWil NBir NLan NMir NPer |
| - subsp. ***acris*** 'Stevenii' | CFee EPPr IGor LPla SDix WHal WSHC |
| - 'Citrinus' | CElw GBin LRHS MMHG NCGa NRya WHal WMoo |
| - 'Flore Pleno' (d) ♀H4 | CDes CElw CFee CWCL EBee ECha ECho ELan EPfP GBin GQue LLWG LRHS MCot MRav NBid NBro NGdn NRya NWad SRms WFar WHil WMoo XLum |
| - 'Hedgehog' | ECho EPPr LSou MMHG NDov |
| - 'Sulphureus' | CBre ECha WFar WHal |
| ***alpestris*** | ECho GEdr NMen NRya |
| ***amplexicaulis*** | CMea EBee ELon EPot GLam GMaP NHar NMen |
| ***aquatilis*** | CWat EHon MSKA MWts SWat WMAq WPnP WSFF |
| × ***arendsii*** 'Moonlight' | CElw CRDP LRHS SUsu |
| ***asiaticus*** | ERCP |
| ***baurii*** | ECho |
| ***bilobus*** | NMen |
| § ***bulbosus*** 'F.M. Burton' | NRya WCot |
| - ***farreri*** | see *R. bulbosus* 'F.M. Burton' |
| - 'Speciosus Plenus' | see *R. constantinopolitanus* 'Plenus' |
| ***calandrinioides*** ♀H2-3 | EBee ECho EWes NBir WAbe WCot |
| - SF 137 | WCot |
| § ***constantinopolitanus*** 'Plenus' (d) | CElw EWld GCal MRav NBid NBro NRya WCot WFar WMoo |
| ***cortusifolius*** | SWat WSHC |
| ***crenatus*** | ECho GAuc GEdr NMen NRya |
| ***creticus*** | ECho |
| ***extorris*** 'Flore Pleno' | EBee WCot |
| ***ficaria*** | CArn CTri ESwi EWil MHer WHer WShi |
| - 'Aglow in the Dark' | CHid |
| - var. ***albus*** | CHid CSam ELon LEdu NRya |
| - anemone-centred | see *R. ficaria* 'Collarette' |
| - 'Art Nouveau' | CDes |
| - 'Ashen Primrose' | EBee |
| § - var. ***aurantiacus*** | ECha ECho MRav NLar NRya SPhx SRms WFar |
| - 'Bowles's Double' | see *R. ficaria* 'Double Bronze', 'Picton's Double' |
| - 'Brambling' | CBre CHid CLAP ECho LEdu MRav NLar SBch SSvw |
| - 'Brazen Child' | MDKP SHar |
| - 'Brazen Daughter' | ECho |
| - 'Brazen Hussy' | Widely available |
| - 'Broadleas Black' | ECho |
| - subsp. ***bulbilifer*** 'Chedglow' | MDKP WCot |
| - 'Choc Ice' new | SSvw |
| - 'Chocolate Cream' | ECho |
| § - subsp. ***chrysocephalus*** | ECha ELon IFro NRya SBch WCot WFar |
| - 'Coffee Cream' | EBee |
| § - 'Collarette' (d) | CHid EBee ECho ELon EPot IGor LEdu MHer NBir NLar NMen NRya WFar |
| - 'Coppernob' | CHid ECho ELon MDKP SBch WCot WFar |
| - 'Corinne Tremaine' | WHer |
| - 'Cupreus' | see *R. ficaria* var. *aurantiacus* |
| - 'Damerham' (d) | CHid |
| - 'Deborah Jope' | SUsu |
| § - 'Double Bronze' (d) | CHid EBee ECho LEdu MDKP MHer NBir NLar NRya SHar |
| - double cream-flowered | see *R. ficaria* 'Double Mud' |
| § - 'Double Mud' (d) | CHid CLAP ECho IFro LEdu NLar NRya SHar WFar WHal WSHC |
| - double yellow-flowered | see *R. ficaria* Flore Pleno Group |
| - double, green-eyed (d) | CHid LEdu |
| - 'Dusky Maiden' | ECho NLar SBch WFar |
| - 'E.A. Bowles' | see *R. ficaria* 'Collarette' |
| - 'Elan' (d) | CDes EBee |
| § - Flore Pleno Group (d) | CFee CHid CTri ECha ECho ELan ELon EPPr NRya NSti SBch SRms WCot WFar |
| - 'Fried Egg' | ECho |
| - 'Granby Cream' | ECho |
| - 'Green Mantle' | ECho |
| - 'Green Petal' | CHid EBee ECho EPPr LEdu MCot MDKP MHer NBir NLar NRya SSvw WHal WHer WHil |
| - 'Holly' | see *R. ficaria* 'Holly Green' |
| § - 'Holly Green' | ECho |
| - 'Hyde Hall' | ECho SBch WFar |
| - 'Jake Perry' | CDes MNrw |

| | | |
|---|---|---|
| | - 'Jane's Dress' | CHid |
| | - 'Ken Aslet Double' (d) | CDes EBee LEdu MHer NLar WHal |
| | - 'Lambrook Black' | WHer |
| | - 'Lambrook Variegated' (v) | EPPr |
| | - 'Lemon Queen' | CHid |
| | - 'Leo' | MDKP |
| | - subsp. ***major*** | see *R. ficaria* subsp. *chrysocephalus* |
| | - 'Melanie Jope' | EBee |
| | - 'Mobled Jade' | CHid |
| | - 'Monksilver' | IFro |
| | - 'Mud' | MDKP |
| | - 'Newton Abbot' | CBre |
| I | - 'Nigrifolia' | MDKP |
| | - 'Old Master' | NCGa WCot |
| | - 'Orange Sorbet' | LEdu MNrw NLar |
| § | - 'Picton's Double' (d) | NRya |
| | - 'Primrose' | CHid NLar NRya |
| | - 'Primrose Elf' | EBee ECha |
| | - 'Ragamuffin' (d) | CDes EBee LEdu |
| | - 'Randall's White' | EBee EPfP MCot MRav NCGa SHar WFar WPtf |
| | - 'Richard and Val' | WCot |
| | - 'Salad Bowl' (d) | ECho |
| | - 'Salmon's White' | CBre EBee ECho ELan ELon EPPr MRav NBir NLar NRya SHar WFar WHal WHer WPtf |
| | - 'Sheldon Silver' | CHid |
| | - 'Silver Collar' | LEdu |
| | - 'Torquay Elf' | EBee |
| | - 'Tortoiseshell' | CHid EBee MDKP WFar WPtf |
| | - 'Wisley Double' | see *R. ficaria* 'Double Bronze', *R. ficaria* 'Wisley Double White' |
| | - 'Wisley White' | NSti |
| | - 'Witchampton' | CDes EBee |
| | - 'Yaffle' | CHid EBee ECho MDKP |
| | ***flammula*** | CBen CHab CRow CWat EHon LPBA MSKA SWat WPnP |
| | - subsp. ***minimus*** | CRow |
| | ***gouanii*** | NRya |
| | ***gramineus*** ♀H4 | CFir CSpe CWCL EBee ECho EDAr GBin GEdr GMaP LBee LRHS MNrw MWat NMen NRya SMrm SPhx SRms SUsu WCAu WFar WHil WPer |
| | - 'Pardal' | SCnR WCot WFar |
| * | ***guttatus*** | NMen |
| | ***hederaceus*** | EWil LLWG |
| | ***illyricus*** | EBee ECha EDAr EPPr LRHS NRya WAbe WHal |
| | ***kochii*** | EBee ECho EPot |
| | ***lanuginosus*** | EPPr |
| | ***lingua*** | MCCP SPlb WSFF |
| | - 'Grandiflorus' | CBen CRow EHon GQue LPBA MSKA NPer SWat WHal WMAq WPnP |
| | ***lyallii*** | GGar GKev |
| | ***macauleyi*** | GEdr |
| | ***millefoliatus*** | CPBP ECho NMen WAbe |
| | ***montanus*** double-flowered (d) | CPBP SHar WCot |
| | - 'Molten Gold' ♀H4 | ECho ECtt GMaP MMHG MRav NRya |
| | ***nivicola*** | LRHS WCot |
| | ***parnassiifolius*** | GEdr NMen WAbe |
| | ***platanifolius*** | LPla |
| | ***psilostachys*** new | LRHS |
| | ***pyrenaeus*** | NMen |
| | ***repens*** 'Buttered Popcorn' (v) | CRow LLWG LRHS NLar WMoo |
| | - 'Cat's Eyes' (v) | EBee |
| | - 'Gloria Spale' | CBre CRow |
| | - var. ***pleniflorus*** (d) | CBre CRow LLWG LRHS SPhx SRot WFar |
| | - 'Snowdrift' (v) | CDes EBee LEdu |
| | - 'Timothy Clark' (d) | CBre |
| | ***rhomboideus*** | LRHS |
| | ***seguieri*** | ECho LRHS WAbe |
| | ***serbicus*** | EBee |
| | ***speciosus*** 'Flore Pleno' | see *R. constantinopolitanus* 'Plenus' |

## *Ranzania* (*Berberidaceae*)

| | |
|---|---|
| ***japonica*** | WCru |

## *Raoulia* (*Asteraceae*)

| | | |
|---|---|---|
| | ***australis*** misapplied | see *R. hookeri* |
| | ***australis*** Hook.f. ex Raoul | CEnt CYeo EDAr EPot GEdr GGar GKev ITim MAsh MWat NWCA |
| § | - Lutescens Group | ECha ECho GLam SMad |
| | ***glabra*** | EPot |
| | ***haastii*** | ECou |
| § | ***hookeri*** | CMea ECha ECho EPot GAbr ITim MAsh NWCA SMad SPlb SRms WPat WThu |
| | - var. ***laxa*** | EWes |
| | × ***loganii*** | see × *Leucoraoulia loganii* |
| | ***lutescens*** | see *R. australis* Lutescens Group |
| | ***petriensis*** | WAbe |
| | × ***petrimia*** 'Margaret Pringle' | WAbe |
| | ***subsericea*** | EWes NMen |
| | ***tenuicaulis*** | ECha EPot SPlb |

## raspberry see *Rubus idaeus*

## *Ratibida* (*Asteraceae*)

| | |
|---|---|
| ***columnifera*** | CRWN EBee EPfP SPet SPhx |
| - f. ***pulcherrima*** | CSpe EPfP LRHS SMad SPet SPhx XLum |
| - - 'Red Midnight' new | EBee |
| - - 'Red Midget' | CSpe EDif LRHS MSpe SBfd SPet SPhx SUsu |
| ***pinnata*** | CEnt CRWN CSam CSpe EBee EPfP LSRN NBir SPet SPhx SPlb WCot WMnd XLum |

## *Ravenala* (*Strelitziaceae*)

| | |
|---|---|
| ***madagascariensis*** | EAmu LPal SPlb XBlo |

## *Ravenea* (*Arecaceae*)

| | |
|---|---|
| ***rivularis*** | CCCN EAmu LPal XBlo |

## *Rechsteineria* see *Sinningia*

## redcurrant see *Ribes rubrum* (R)

## *Rehderodendron* (*Styracaceae*)

| | |
|---|---|
| ***macrocarpum*** | WPGP |

## *Rehmannia* (*Plantaginaceae*)

| | | |
|---|---|---|
| | ***angulata*** misapplied | see *R. elata* |
| § | ***elata*** ♀H2 | CBot CFir CSam CSpe ELan EPfP IDee LAst LBMP LHop LLWP LRHS MHer MNHC NOrc SGar WFar WHil WTcb WWEG WWlt XLum |
| | ***glutinosa*** ♀H3 | CSpe EWTr WCot |
| | ***piasezkii*** | WPGP |

## *Reineckea* (*Asparagaceae*)

| | | |
|---|---|---|
| § | ***carnea*** | CAby CFee CFir CHid CHll CPLG EBee ECha ELan EPPr EPla GEdr GGar GKev LEdu LRHS MMuc NLar |

| | | |
|---|---|---|
| | | NSti SDys SEND SPlb SUsu WCot WCru WPGP WPtf WTin XLum |
| | - B&SWJ 4808 | ELon WCru |
| | - SDR 330 | EBee EPPr GKev |
| | - 'Baoxing Booty' | EBla WCru |
| | 'Crûg's Broadleaf' | EBla WCru |
| | - RBGE form **new** | GEdr |
| | - 'Variegata' (v) | EShb WCot |
| | aff. ***carnea*** from Sichuan | WCot |

## *Reinwardtia* (*Linaceae*)

| | | |
|---|---|---|
| § | ***indica*** | CCCN CHII CPLG EShb SAdn SMrm |
| | ***trigyna*** | see *R. indica* |

## *Remusatia* (*Araceae*)

| | | |
|---|---|---|
| | ***hookeriana*** B&SWJ 2529 | WCru |

## *Reseda* (*Resedaceae*)

| | | |
|---|---|---|
| | ***alba*** | MHer |
| | ***lutea*** | SIde |
| | ***luteola*** | CHab CHby EWil GPoy MHer WHer WHfH WSFF |

## *Restio* (*Restionaceae*)

| | | |
|---|---|---|
| | ***festuciformis*** | CPrp EHoe GCal |
| | ***quadratus*** | CCtw |
| | ***subverticillatus*** | see *Ischyrolepis subverticillata* |
| | ***tetraphyllus*** | CAbb CCtw CFir CHid CTrC CTsd EHoe GBin GCal GGar IDee SPlb SPoG WDyG |

## *Reynoutria* see *Fallopia*

## *Rhamnus* (*Rhamnaceae*)

| | | |
|---|---|---|
| | ***alaternus*** var. ***angustifolia*** | WFar |
| § | - 'Argenteovariegata' (v) ♀H4 | Widely available |
| | - 'Variegata' | see *R. alaternus* 'Argenteovariegata' |
| | ***cathartica*** | CCVT CDul CHab CLnd CTri ECrN EPfP EShb LBuc NLar NWea SEWo WDin WMou WSFF |
| | ***frangula*** | see *Frangula alnus* |
| | ***imeretina*** | WPGP WPat |
| | ***pallasii*** | NLar |
| | ***pumila*** | NLar |
| | ***taquetii*** | NLar |

## × *Rhaphiobotrya* (*Rosaceae*)

| | | |
|---|---|---|
| § | 'Coppertone' | EPfP SArc SCoo SEND |

## *Rhaphiolepis* (*Rosaceae*)

| | | |
|---|---|---|
| | × ***delacourii*** | CMHG CWib EBee ECrN ELan EPfP LAst SEND SRms |
| | - 'Coates' Crimson' | CDoC CTsd EBee ELan EPfP IVic LAst LHop LRHS SEND WPat WSHC |
| | - Enchantress = 'Moness' | CSam CTsd ELan EPfP LRHS MAsh MRav SLon |
| | - 'Pink Cloud' | CBcs EPfP LRHS |
| | - 'Spring Song' | SLon |
| | ***indica*** | ERom SEND |
| | - B&SWJ 8405 | WCru |
| | - 'Coppertone' | see × *Rhaphiobotrya* 'Coppertone' |
| | - Springtime = 'Monme' | CBcs IVic LRHS SPur WDin |
| | ***umbellata*** ♀H2-3 | CBcs CBot CFee CHEx CSam CTri CWib EBee ELan EPfP LAst LHop LRHS SBrt SEND SLon SVen WFar WPGP WPat WSHC |
| | - f. ***ovata*** B&SWJ 4706 | WCru |

## *Rhaphithamnus* (*Verbenaceae*)

| | | |
|---|---|---|
| | ***cyanocarpus*** | see *R. spinosus* |
| § | ***spinosus*** | CBcs EPfP GBin LRHS |

## *Rhapidophyllum* (*Arecaceae*)

| | | |
|---|---|---|
| | ***hystrix*** | CBrP LPal NPal |

## *Rhapis* ✿ (*Arecaceae*)

| | | |
|---|---|---|
| § | ***excelsa*** ♀H1 | CCCN EAmu LPal WCot XBlo |
| | ***multifida*** | LPal |

## *Rhazya* (*Apocynaceae*)

| | | |
|---|---|---|
| | ***orientalis*** | see *Amsonia orientalis* |

## *Rheum* ✿ (*Polygonaceae*)

| | | |
|---|---|---|
| | CC 5243 | EWld |
| | GWJ 9329 from Sikkim | WCru |
| | SDR 1863 | GKev |
| | SDR 5004 | GKev |
| | SDR 5919 | GKev |
| | from India | GCal |
| § | 'Ace of Hearts' | Widely available |
| | 'Ace of Spades' | see *R.* 'Ace of Hearts' |
| | ***acuminatum*** | EBee |
| | - HWJCM 252 | WCru |
| | - HWJK 2354 | WCru |
| | ***alexandrae*** | EWes GCal MMHG NChi |
| | - SDR 2924 | EBee |
| | - SDR 4602 | GKev |
| | - SDR 4757 | GKev |
| | - SDR 6031 | GKev |
| | ***altaicum*** | LEdu |
| | 'Andrew's Red' | GTwe |
| § | ***australe*** | CAgr CArn CFir CSpe EBee GCal LEdu LPBA NBro NLar WCot WFar WHoo WMnd XLum |
| | 'Cally Dwarf' **new** | GCal |
| | 'Cally Giant' **new** | GCal |
| N | × ***cultorum*** | see *R.* × *hybridum* |
| | ***delavayi*** | GCal |
| | ***emodi*** | see *R. australe* |
| | ***forrestii*** | GAuc |
| § | × ***hybridum*** | SEND |
| | - from Burston Hall | LRHS |
| | - from Gledhill **new** | LRHS |
| | - from Hartley **new** | LRHS |
| | - from Holt **new** | LRHS |
| | - from Isle of Ely Horticultural Institute | LRHS |
| | - from Maldon, Essex **new** | LRHS |
| | - from Ramsden **new** | LRHS |
| | - from Sherburn Park | LRHS |
| | - 'Amerikanske Kaempe' | LRHS |
| | - 'Amstel Seedling' | LRHS |
| | - 'Appleton's Forcing' | LRHS |
| | - 'Baker's All Season' | GTwe LRHS |
| | - 'Bedford Scarlet' | LRHS |
| | - 'Brandy Carr Scarlet' | ECrN EGHP MRav |
| | - 'Brown's Crimson' | LRHS |
| | - 'Brown's Red' | LRHS |
| | - 'Canada Red' | GTwe LRHS |
| | - 'Carter's Forcing' | LRHS |
| | - 'Cawood Advance' | LRHS |
| | - 'Cawood Castle' | LRHS |
| | - 'Cawood Delight' | GTwe LRHS |
| | - 'Cawood Ensign' | LRHS |
| | - 'Cawood Oak' | LRHS |
| | - 'Champagne' | CAgr ECrN EGHP EPfP EPom GTwe LBuc LRHS SPer SWal |
| * | - 'Champagne Rood' | LRHS |
| | - 'Collis's Ruby' | LRHS |
| | - 'Goutt's Red Stick' | LRHS |

- 'Crimson Queen' LRHS
- 'Crimson Wine' LRHS
- 'Cutbush's Seedling' LRHS
- 'Dawe's Challenge' LRHS
- 'Daw's Champion' GTwe LRHS
- 'Donkere Bloedrede Zoet' LRHS
- 'Drust's Red' **new** LRHS
- 'Early Champagne' LRHS
- 'Early Cherry' GTwe LRHS
- 'Early Devon' LRHS
- 'Early Mitchell' LRHS
- 'Early Superb' LRHS
- 'Early Victoria' LRHS
- 'Exhibition Red' LRHS
- 'Fenton's Special' CTri EGHP GTwe LRHS MCoo MRav
- * – 'Frambozenrood Limburg' LRHS
- 'Fulton's Strawberry Surprise' 🏆H4 GTwe LRHS
- 'German Wine' LRHS
- 'Giant Grooveless Crimson' LRHS
- 'Glaskin's Perpetual' CAgr CWib LBuc LRHS MAsh SWal
- 'Goliath' LRHS MCoo
- 'Grandad's Favorite' 🏆H4 LRHS
- 'Green Jam' LRHS
- 'Greengage' GTwe LRHS
- 'Guardsman' LRHS
- 'Hadspen Crimson' CBct WCot
- 'Hammond's Early' GTwe LRHS
- 'Harbinger' GTwe LRHS
- 'Hawke's Champagne' 🏆H4 GTwe LRHS
- 'Holsteiner Blut' EPfP LRHS
- 'Irish Apple' **new** LRHS
- 'Kentville' LRHS
- 'Larne' LRHS
- 'Laxton's No 1' LRHS
- 'Linnaeus' LRHS
- 'Livingstone'PBR LRHS
- 'Mac Red' 🏆H4 GTwe
- 'Marshall's Early' LRHS
- 'McDonald' LRHS
- 'Merton's Banner' LRHS
- 'Merton's Broadleaf' LRHS
- 'Merton's Foremost' LRHS
- 'Merton's Yardstick' LRHS
- 'Mikoot' **new** LRHS
- 'Mira' **new** LRHS
- 'Mitchell's Early Albert' LRHS
- 'Mitchell's Royal Albert' LRHS
- 'Mrs McKenzie' LRHS
- 'Perpetual' LRHS
- 'Pink Champagne' **new** EPfP
- 'Prince Albert' EGHP GTwe LRHS NEgg
- * – 'Ras Versteeg' LRHS
- 'Raspberry Red' EPom LRHS NBlu
- 'Red Champagne' EGHP EPfP LBuc LRHS
- 'Red Prolific' GTwe
- 'Red Victoria' **new** LRHS
- 'Reed's Champagne' LRHS
- 'Reed's Early Superb' 🏆H4 GTwe LRHS
- 'Reed's Red' **new** LRHS
- 'Riverside Giant' LRHS
- 'Rosenhagen' LRHS
- 'Ruby' LRHS
- 'Saint Kevin' LRHS
- 'Seedling Le Grice' **new** LRHS
- 'Seedling Piggot' LRHS
- 'Stein's Champagne' 🏆H4 GTwe LRHS
- 'Stockbridge' LRHS
- 'Stockbridge Arrow' CSut CTri EGHP GTwe LRHS NEgg
- 'Stockbridge Bingo' GTwe LRHS
- 'Stockbridge Cropper' LRHS
- 'Stockbridge Emerald' GTwe LRHS
- 'Stockbridge Guardsman' GTwe
- 'Stockbridge Harbinger' LRHS
- 'Stockbridge Smith' LRHS
- 'Stott's Monarch' LRHS
- 'Strawberry' GTwe LRHS NBir
- 'Strawberry Red' LRHS
- 'Strawberry Taylor' **new** LRHS
- 'Sutton's Cherry Red' GTwe LRHS
- 'The Appleton' LRHS
- 'The Sutton' CWib GTwe LRHS
- 'Timperley Early' 🏆H4 CDoC CMac CSBt CTri CWib EGHP EMil EPfP EPom GTwe LRHS LSRN MAsh MGos MMuc MRav NEgg NPri SBfd SCoo SDea SEND SKee SLim SPer SPoG WGwG WHar
- 'Tingley Cherry' GTwe
- 'Valentine' LRHS
- 'Victoria' CAgr CDoC CSBt CTri CWib EGHP ELau EMil EPfP EPom GTwe LBuc LRHS LSRN MAsh MCoo MGos MHer MNHC SDea SLim SPoG SVic SWal WHar
- 'Vinrabarber Svenborg' LRHS
- 'Vroege Engelse' LRHS
- 'Zwolle Seedling' GTwe

***kialense*** CBct CDes LEdu NBid NSti WPGP WWEG
***officinale*** CArn CBct CHEx EBee GCal LRHS MBri SIde SWat
***palmatum*** CArn CBcs EBee ECha ELan EPfP GCra LPBA LRHS MGos MNHC MRav NGdn SWat WFar
- 'Atropurpureum' see *R. palmatum* 'Atrosanguineum'
- § – 'Atrosanguineum' 🏆H4 CBct CBot CFir CMac EBee ECha ELan EPfP EPla EShb GCal IFro LBMP LPBA LRHS MBri MGos MMuc MRav NBid NBro NEgg NWad SEND SPlb SPoG SWat WCru WMnd
- 'Bowles's Crimson' CBct LRHS MBri MGos MRav NBid WCot
- 'Red Herald' CBct LBuc LRHS WCot WWEG
- 'Rubrum' CBct EBee LRHS MCCP NBir NHol WFar
- 'Savill' LRHS MBri MRav WWEG
- var. ***tanguticum*** Widely available
- – 'Rosa Auslese' WHil

***rhaponticum*** NLar
***ribes*** WCot WCru
***tataricum*** LEdu

## *Rhinanthus* (*Orobanchaceae*)

***minor*** CHab GJos

## *Rhodanthe* (*Asteraceae*)

§ ***anthemoides*** CPBP ECou IRar SEND

## *Rhodanthemum* (*Asteraceae*)

'African Eyes' ECho EPfP LRHS MBrN MBri MGos NPri SBrd SPoG SRot SUsu SVen WNew
§ ***atlanticum*** ECho EWes
§ ***catananche*** CCCN ECho EPot EWes MBNS SRot

| | | |
|---|---|---|
| § | – 'Tizi-n-Test' | ECho |
| | – 'Tizi-n-Tichka' | CPBP ECho EWes LRHS |
| § | ***gayanum*** | CCCN ECho EWes IRar |
| | – 'Flamingo' | see *R. gayanum* |
| § | ***hosmariense*** 🏆$^{H4}$ | CCCN CMea ECha ECho EDAr ELan EPfP EPot GGar GMaP LHop LRHS MCot MWat NBlu NPri NSla SCoo SEND SPer SPoG SRms SRot WAbe WHoo WPat |

## *Rhodiola* (*Crassulaceae*)

| | | |
|---|---|---|
| | CC 5344 | GKev |
| | CC 6359 | EWld |
| | ***amabilis*** | GAuc |
| | ***bupleuroides*** HWJK 2258 | WCru |
| | ***crassipes*** | see *R. wallichiana* |
| | ***cretinii*** HWJK 2283 | WCru |
| § | ***fastigiata*** | EBee GCal GKev NMen NWCA |
| | – BWJ 7544 | WCru |
| § | ***heterodonta*** | ECha ELan LRHS MRav WCot |
| | ***himalensis*** misapplied | see *R.* 'Keston' |
| | ***himalensis*** (D. Don) Fu | CTri |
| | – HWJK 2258 | WCru |
| § | ***integrifolia*** NNS 95-458 | NWCA |
| | – subsp. ***integrifolia*** | EDAr |
| § | ***ishidae*** | CTri |
| § | 'Keston' | CTri XLum |
| § | ***pachyclados*** | ECho ECtt EDAr GGar GJos GLam GMaP LBee LRHS MHer MMuc NBir NRya NWad SEND SGar SPlb SRot SWal SWvt WAbe WFar WOut WPer XLum |
| | aff. ***purpureoviridis*** | WFar |
| | – BWJ 7544 | WCru |
| | ***rhodantha*** | NSla |
| § | ***rosea*** | Widely available |
| | ***semenovii*** | NLar |
| | ***sinuata*** HWJK 2318 | WCru |
| | – HWJK 2326 | WCru |
| § | ***trollii*** | ECho EPot LRHS SPlb WAbe |
| § | ***wallichiana*** | MLHP NBid |
| | – GWJ 9263 | WCru |
| | – HWJK 2352 | WCru |

## *Rhodochiton* (*Plantaginaceae*)

| | | |
|---|---|---|
| § | ***atrosanguineus*** 🏆$^{H1-2}$ | CCCN CEnd CHll CSpe ELan EPfP GBee GGar GMac IDee LRHS MAsh MOWG MSCN NPri SGar SLon SPer SPoG |
| | ***volubilis*** | see *R. atrosanguineus* |

## *Rhodocoma* (*Restionaceae*)

| | | |
|---|---|---|
| | ***arida*** | CCCN CCtw |
| | ***capensis*** | CAbb CCCN CCtw CFir CPen CPrp CTrC CTsd GBin GCal LRHS |
| | ***foliosa*** | IDee |
| | ***gigantea*** | CCCN CCtw CFir CPen CTrC EAmu ETod GBin IDee SPlb |

## *Rhododendron* ✿ (*Ericaceae*)

| | | |
|---|---|---|
| | sp. | GKin SEWo |
| | 'A.J. Ivens' | see *R.* 'Arthur J. Ivens' |
| | 'Abegail' | SLdr |
| | ***aberconwayi*** | LMil SReu |
| | – 'His Lordship' | LMil MSnd |
| | 'Addy Wery' (EA) 🏆$^{H3-4}$ | CDoC ECho GKin MGos SLdr SPer |
| | ***adenogynum*** | LMil MSnd |
| § | – Adenophorum Group F 20444 | SLdr |
| | ***adenophorum*** | see *R. adenogynum* Adenophorum Group |
| | ***adenopodum*** | MSnd |
| | 'Admiral Piet Hein' | SReu |
| | 'Adonis' (EA/d) | CBcs CMac LMil NLar SBrd SLdr |
| | 'Adriaan Koster' (hybrid) | SHea |
| | 'Advance' (EA) | MSnd SLdr |
| | ***aeruginosum*** | see *R. campanulatum* subsp. *aeruginosum* |
| | ***aganniphum*** | MSnd |
| | – var. ***flavorufum*** | MSnd |
| | – 'Rusty' | MSnd |
| | 'Aida' (R/d) | CSBt SReu |
| | 'Aksel Olsen' | CTri GEdr LRHS MAsh |
| | 'Aladdin' (EA) | CMac ECho NEgg WFar |
| | Aladdin Group | SReu |
| | Albatross Group | LMil SReu |
| | 'Albatross Townhill Pink' | LMil |
| | 'Albert Schweitzer' 🏆$^{H4}$ | CDoC CWri LMil NLar SLdr SLim WFar |
| | ***albertsenianum*** | MSnd |
| | ***albrechtii*** (A) | IVic LMil SLdr |
| | – Whitney form (A) | LMil |
| | 'Album Elegans' | MSnd |
| | 'Alexander' (EA) 🏆$^{H4}$ | IVic LMil LSRN MAsh MGos SLdr |
| | 'Alexis' | IVic |
| | 'Alfred' | NMun |
| | 'Alice' (EA) | SLdr |
| | 'Alice' (hybrid) 🏆$^{H4}$ | CMac CSBt LMil SHea SLdr |
| | 'Alison Johnstone' | GGal SHea WThu |
| | Alison Johnstone Group | CBcs LMil MSnd SLdr SReu |
| | Alpine Gem Group | GQui |
| | 'Altair' (K) **new** | SHea |
| § | ***alutaceum*** var. ***iodes*** | MSnd |
| § | – var. ***russotinctum*** | MDun MSnd NHim |
| | – – R 158 | SLdr |
| | ***amagianum*** (A) | LMil NHim |
| | Amalfi Group | LMil |
| | 'Amber Rain' (A) | SHea |
| | ***ambiguum*** | LMil MSnd |
| I | – 'Crosswater' | LMil |
| | – 'Jane Banks' | LMil |
| | 'Ambrosia' (EA) | CSBt |
| | 'Ambush' **new** | SHea |
| | 'America' | SHea WFar |
| | 'Amity' | CSBt CWri ECho LMil MAsh MMuc MSnd NPCo WFar WGwG |
| | 'Amoenum Coccineum' (EA/d) | IVic MAsh MSnd SLdr SReu |
| | Amor Group | SHea |
| | 'Amoretto' | IVic |
| | 'Anah Kruschke' | MAsh SPoG |
| | 'Analin' | see *R.* 'Anuschka' |
| | 'Anchorite' (EA) | SLdr |
| | 'Androcles' | LMil |
| | 'Angelo' | IVic LMil |
| | Angelo Group | CWri LMil SReu |
| | Anita Group | SHea |
| | 'Anna Baldsiefen' | ELon GKin MGos NHim NMun NPCo SLim SPoG SReu |
| | 'Anna Kauser' | MSnd |
| | 'Anna Rose Whitney' | CBcs CTri CWri LRHS LTen MAsh MGos MSnd NEgg SLim |
| | 'Annabella' (K) 🏆$^{H4}$ | MDun NLar |
| | ***annae*** | LMil NHim NMun |
| | 'Anne Frank' (EA) | MGos WFar |
| | 'Anne Teese' | LMil |
| | 'Anneke' (A) | EPfP LMil NLar SPoG SReu SSta WFar |
| | 'Anouk' (EA) | NMun |

| |  |  |
|---|---|---|
| | ***anthopogon*** | LMil |
| | - subsp. ***hypenanthum*** | MDun |
| | - - 'Annapurna' | ITim WAbe |
| | 'Antilope' (Vs) | CBcs CWri ECho LMil MAsh MDun MGos MLea MMuc NEgg NLar SHea SLdr SPer SReu SSta |
| | 'Antonio' | LMil |
| § | 'Anuschka' | MAsh MMuc |
| | ***anwheiense*** | SHea |
| | ***apodectum*** | see *R. dichroanthum* subsp. *apodectum* |
| | 'Apotrophia' | SLdr |
| | 'Apple Blossom' ambig. | CMac GKin MSnd |
| | 'Apple Blossom' Wezelenburg (M) | NBlu SLdr |
| N | 'Appleblossom' (EA) | see *R.* 'Ho-o' |
| | 'Apricot Blaze' (A) | MDun SReu SSta |
| | 'Apricot Fantasy' | LMil MDun |
| | 'Apricot Nectar' (V) | MDun |
| | 'Apricot Surprise' | CTri LRHS MAsh |
| | 'April Chimes' | WThu |
| | 'April Gem' | IVic |
| | 'April Rose' | IVic |
| | 'April Showers' (A) | LMil LRHS |
| | 'Aquamarin' | IVic |
| | 'Arabesk' (EA) | GKin LMil MAsh MBri MGos SLdr WFar |
| | ***araiophyllum*** KR 4029 | LMil |
| | - KR 7483 | LMil |
| | ***arborescens*** (A) | LMil |
| | - pink-flowered (A) | LMil |
| | ***arboreum*** | CDoC CHEx IDee LMil MDun MSnd NHim SReu |
| | - subsp. ***arboreum*** | MSnd |
| | - 'Blood Red' | MSnd |
| | - subsp. ***cinnamomeum*** | CDoC GGar LMil MSnd SLdr SReu |
| | - - var. ***album*** | MSnd NMun SReu |
| | - - var. ***roseum*** 'Tony Schilling' | GKin LMil NLar SReu |
| | - subsp. ***delavayi*** | LMil MSnd |
| | - - KR 3909 | LMil |
| | - - var. ***delavayi*** | GLin |
| | - - var. ***peramoenum*** AC 5577 | GLin |
| | - 'Heligan' | CWri SReu |
| § | - subsp. ***nilagiricum*** | GLin |
| | - var. ***roseum*** | NHim SHea |
| | 'Arctic Regent' (K) | GQui |
| | 'Arctic Tern' | see × *Ledodendron* 'Arctic Tern' |
| § | ***argipeplum*** | MSnd |
| | 'Argosy' $\Upsilon^{H4}$ | LMil SReu |
| | ***argyrophyllum*** | MSnd SLdr |
| | - subsp. ***argyrophyllum*** | SLdr |
| | - subsp. ***nankingense*** | CDoC IDee LMil MDun MSnd SLdr |
| | 'Chinese Silver' $\Upsilon^{H4}$ | SReu |
| | ***arizelum*** | IDee LMil LRHS MAsh MDun MSnd |
| | - subsp. ***arizelum*** Rubicosum Group | LMil |
| | 'Arkona' | IVic |
| | 'Arneson Gem' (M) | CBcs CDoC LMil MAsh MMuc SEND SLdr |
| | 'Arpege' (Vs) | LMil SReu |
| | 'Arthur Bedford' | CBcs SLdr SReu |
| § | 'Arthur J. Ivens' | SLdr |
| | 'Arthur Osborn' | SLdr SSpi |
| | 'Arthur Stevens' | MSnd SLdr |
| | 'Asa-gasumi' (Kurume) (EA) | NHim SLdr |
| | ***asterochnoum*** | MSnd |
| | 'Astrid' | IVic LMil LSRN |
| | 'Astronaut' (K) **new** | SHea |

| |  |  |
|---|---|---|
| | ***atlanticum*** (A) | GKev LMil SReu SSta |
| | - 'Seaboard' (A) | LMil |
| | ***augustinii*** | CWri GGal IDee LMil MLea MSnd SLdr SSpi SSta |
| | - compact EGM 293 | LMil |
| § | - 'Electra' $\Upsilon^{H3-4}$ **new** | LRHS NLar |
| § | - Electra Group | CDoC GGar LMil MLea SLdr |
| | - Exbury best form | LMil SReu |
| | - pale lilac-flowered | SLdr |
| * | - 'Trewithen' | LMil |
| I | - 'Werrington' | CPLG SLdr SReu |
| § | ***aureum*** | WThu |
| | ***auriculatum*** | LMil MDun MSnd NHim SLdr SReu SSta |
| | - Reuthe's form | SReu |
| | ***auritum*** | MSnd SLdr |
| | 'Aurora' (K) | SLdr |
| | ***austrinum*** (A) | LMil LRHS NLar |
| | - yellow-flowered (A) | LMil |
| | 'Avalanche' $\Upsilon^{H4}$ | LMil SReu |
| | Avocet Group | LMil |
| | 'Award' | LMil |
| | 'Ayah' | LMil |
| | Azor Group | SHea |
| | Azrie Group | SLdr |
| § | 'Azuma-kagami' (Kurume) (EA) | LMil LSRN WFar |
| | 'Azurika' | IVic |
| | 'Azurro' | LMil NLar |
| | B.B.C. Group | LMil |
| | 'B. de Bruin' | SHea |
| | 'Babette' | see *R.* (Volker Group) 'Babette' |
| | 'Babuschka' | LMil |
| | 'Baden-Baden' | CMac CTri ECho GEdr GKin GLam MAsh MDun MGos MSnd NEgg NLar NMun SLdr SPoG WFar |
| | 'Bagshot Ruby' | SHea |
| | ***baileyi*** | MSnd NHim |
| * | 'Baker's Lavender' (EA) | CTrh |
| | 'Bakkarat' (K) **new** | SHea |
| | 'Balalaika' | MDun |
| | 'Bali' | MDun |
| | 'Ballerina' (K) | SHea |
| | 'Balzac' (K) | CDoC ECho GKin MAsh MBri MGos NEgg SHea SPer SPur SReu |
| | 'Banana Boat' | IVic |
| | 'Banana Ripe' | MDun |
| | 'Bandoola' | SReu |
| | 'Barbara Coats' (EA) | SLdr |
| | ***barbatum*** | CDoC CHEx GGar LMil MDun MSnd |
| | - B&SWJ 2160 | WCru |
| | - B&SWJ 2237 | WCru |
| | - B&SWJ 2624 | WCru |
| | 'Barbecue' (K) | LMil |
| | 'Barmstedt' | CWri MAsh |
| | 'Barnaby Sunset' | LMil LRHS |
| | 'Bartholo Lazzari' (G) **new** | SReu SSta |
| | 'Bashful' $\Upsilon^{H4}$ | CBcs CSBt ECho EPfP MGos SLdr |
| § | ***basilicum*** | CDoC IDee LMil NHim NLar SLdr |
| | - AC 616 | MSnd |
| | - KR 7532 | LMil |
| | - KR 7540 | LMil |
| | ***bauhiniiflorum*** | see *R. triflorum* var. *bauhiniiflorum* |
| | ***beanianum*** | MSnd NHim |
| | - compact | see *R. piercei* |
| | 'Beatrice Keir' | LMil MSnd SReu |
| | 'Beattie' (EA) | SLdr |
| | 'Beau Brummell' | LRHS |

| | |
|---|---|
| Beau Brummell Group | LMil |
| 'Beaulieu' (K) | SHea |
| 'Beaulieu Manor' | GQui |
| 'Beautiful Day' | MDun |
| 'Beautiful Dreamer' | MDun |
| 'Beauty of Littleworth' | SHea SReu |
| 'Beaver' (EA) | MMuc |
| 'Beefeater' × ***yakushimanum*** | SLdr |
| ***beesianum*** | MSnd |
| 'Beethoven' (EA) ♀H3-4 | MSnd SLdr |
| 'Belami' **new** | IVic |
| 'Belkanto' | CDoC GKin |
| 'Belle Heller' | SLdr |
| 'Bengal' | ECho GEdr GLam LRHS LSRN SLdr SLim |
| 'Bengal Beauty' (EA) | SLdr |
| 'Bengal Fire' (EA) | CMac |
| 'Beni-giri' (EA) | CMac |
| 'Bergensiana' | SReu |
| 'Bergie Larson' | CBcs ECho IVic LMil MAsh MDun MLea MMuc NPCo SLdr |
| 'Berg's 10' | MLea |
| 'Berg's Yellow' | CWri ECho LMil MGos MLea MMuc MSnd WFar |
| 'Bernstein' | LMil LRHS MAsh NLar WFar |
| 'Berryrose' (K) ♀H4 | CBcs CMac CSBt CTri CWri ECho EPfP GKin LMil MAsh MGos MMuc MSnd NLar SLdr SPer SReu WFar |
| 'Betty Anne Voss' (EA) | ECho LSRN MAsh MGos SCoo SLdr |
| 'Betty Wormald' | CMac CSBt CWri ECho LMil MBri MGos MLea MMuc NMun SHea SLdr SPer |
| ***bhutanense*** KR 8233 | LMil |
| Bibiani Group | SHea |
| 'Bijou de Ledeberg' (EA) | CMac |
| 'Billy Budd' | SLdr |
| 'Birthday Girl' | ECho ELon LMil LSRN MAsh MDun MLea NHim SBod SLdr |
| Biskra Group | LMil |
| 'Blaauw's Pink' (EA) ♀H3-4 | CDoC CMac CSBt ECho ELon EPfP GKin GQui LMil MBri MGos MMuc MSnd NPCo SEND SLdr SPer SPlb SPoG SReu SRms WFar |
| 'Black Knight' (EA) | SLdr |
| 'Black Magic' | CDoC CWri GKin LMil |
| 'Black Sport' | MLea |
| Blaue Donau | see *R.* 'Blue Danube' |
| 'Blazecheck' | SCoo |
| 'Blewbury' ♀H4 | IVic LMil SLdr SReu SSta |
| 'Blue Bell' | SHea |
| 'Blue Boy' | CDoC LMil |
| 'Blue Chip' | SLdr |
| § 'Blue Danube' (EA) ♀H3-4 | CDoC CMac CSBt CTri ECho ELon EPfP GKin IVic LMil LRHS MAsh MBri MGos MMuc MSnd NBlu NPCo NPri SLdr SLim SPer SPoG SReu SSta WFar |
| 'Blue Diamond' | CMac CSBt ECho ELon LSRN MGos NPCo SLdr SPer SPoG WGwG |
| Blue Diamond Group | CBcs ECho EPfP MDun MGos MSnd SReu SRms |
| 'Blue Monday' (EA) | SLdr |
| 'Blue Moon' (EA) | ELon LMil LRHS SBrd SLdr |
| 'Blue Peter' ♀H4 | CSBt CWri ECho ELon EPfP LMil LRHS MAsh MDun MGos MLea NLar SLdr SReu SSta |
| 'Blue Pool' | LMil |
| 'Blue Star' | GGar MDun NMen |
| 'Blue Steel' | see *R. fastigiatum* 'Blue Steel' |

| | |
|---|---|
| Blue Tit Group | CBcs CDoC CSBt EPfP LRHS MDun MSnd SLim SReu SSta STre |
| Bluebird Group | CMac CSBt MGos SRms |
| 'Bluerettia' | CDoC CWri MMuc |
| 'Blutopia' | LMil |
| 'Bob Bovee' | NLar |
| 'Bob's Blue' | MDun |
| 'Boddaertianum' | SHea SLdr SReu |
| 'Bodnant Yellow' | LMil |
| Bohlken's Lupinberg | IVic |
| 'Bonfire' | SHea SLdr SReu |
| 'Bo-peep' | GQui LMil SLdr |
| Bo-peep Group | CBcs |
| 'Boskoop Ostara' | CBcs LMil MGos |
| 'Bouquet de Flore' (G) ♀H4 | CDoC EPfP LMil MLea SReu |
| 'Bow Bells' ♀H4 | ECho EPfP GEdr LMil LRHS MAsh MBri MSnd NBlu NHim NLar NPri SHea SLdr WFar |
| Bow Bells Group | MDun MGos MLea |
| 'Bow Street' | SHea |
| ***brachycarpum*** | GKev GLin |
| 'Brazier' (EA) | SLdr |
| 'Brazil' (K) | CSBt SHea |
| 'Bremen' | LMil |
| ***brevinerve*** **new** | MSnd |
| 'Bric-à-brac' | SLdr WThu |
| Bric-à-brac Group | CBcs |
| 'Bridesmaid' (O) | EPfP |
| 'Bright Forecast' (K) | CWri IVic MLea SHea SLdr |
| 'Brigitte' | CWri IVic LMil LRHS LSRN MAsh MDun SLdr |
| 'Brilliant' (hybrid) | MGos WFar |
| 'Brilliant Blue' (EA) | MAsh |
| 'Brilliant Crimson' (EA) | SLdr |
| 'Britannia' | CSBt CWri EPfP LMil SReu WFar |
| 'Brocade' | MSnd SHea SLdr |
| 'Bronze Fire' (A) | SLdr SReu SSta |
| 'Brown Eyes' | ECho GKin MMuc SLdr WFar |
| 'Bruce Brechtbill' ♀H4 | CDoC CWri ECho GKin LMil MAsh MBri MGos MMuc NPCo SEND SLdr SReu SSta |
| 'Bruce Hancock' (Ad) | ECho ELon MMuc SLdr |
| 'Bruns Diamant' | IVic |
| § 'Bruns Gloria' | LMil |
| 'Bruns Schneewitchen' | SPoG SReu |
| 'Buccaneer' (EA) | SLdr |
| ***bullatum*** | see *R. edgeworthii* |
| 'Bullfinch' (K) **new** | SHea |
| 'Bungo-nishiki' (EA/d) | CMac WThu |
| ***bureavii*** ♀H4 | CBcs GLin IDee LMil MDun MGos MSnd NHim SReu SSta |
| ***bureavii*** × ***yakushimanum*** | SReu |
| ***bureavioides*** | LMil MSnd SReu |
| 'Burletta' | IVic LMil |
| ***burmanicum*** | MDun SLdr |
| 'Busuki' | LMil |
| 'Butter Brickle' | LMil MLea SLdr WFar |
| 'Butter Yellow' | ECho |
| 'Buttered Popcorn' | MDun |
| 'Butterfly' | LMil SHea |
| 'Buttermint' | ECho GQui MGos MLea WFar |
| 'Buzzard' (K) | LMil |
| ***calendulaceum*** (A) | LMil |
| - red-flowered (A) | LMil |
| - yellow-flowered (A) | LMil |
| Calfort Group | SLdr |
| ***callimorphum*** | LMil |
| - var. ***myiagrum*** | MSnd |
| ***calophytum*** ♀H4 | LMil MSnd NHim SLdr |

| | | |
|---|---|---|
| | - EGM 343 | LMil |
| | ***calostrotum*** | CWri NMun WAbe |
| | - 'Gigha' ♀H4 | LMil MAsh MGos SLdr |
| § | - subsp. ***keleticum*** ♀H4 | CDoC GEdr GKev GLam MDun MGos NMun WFar |
| | - - R 58 | LMil |
| § | - - Radicans Group | GEdr GLam MDun MLea WAbe WThu |
| | - - - USDAPI 59182/R11188 | MLea |
| | - subsp. ***riparium*** | GLin |
| | - - Calciphilum Group | WThu |
| § | - - Nitens Group | CDoC GBin GLam MAsh NMen WAbe |
| | ***caloxanthum*** | see *R. campylocarpum* subsp. *caloxanthum* |
| | Calstocker Group | LMil |
| | ***campanulatum*** | LMil LRHS MDun MSnd SReu WAbe |
| | - CC 5124 | GKev |
| | - HWJCM 195 | WCru |
| § | - subsp. ***aeruginosum*** | LMil MDun MSnd SLdr SReu |
| | - 'Knaphill' | MSnd |
| | ***campylocarpum*** | IDee LMil MDun MSnd SReu |
| | - from East Nepal | MDun |
| § | - subsp. ***caloxanthum*** | LMil MDun |
| | - - KR 6152 | LMil |
| § | - - Telopeum Group | MSnd |
| | ***campylogynum*** ♀H4 | CBcs LMil MLea NMen NMun NPCo SSpi WAbe |
| | - 'Album' | see *R.* 'Leucanthum' |
| | - black-flowered | IVic |
| | - 'Bramble' | MDun |
| | - Charopoeum Group | MDun WThu |
| | - - 'Patricia' | ECho EPot LLHF LMil MDun NLar NWCA SLdr |
| | - (Cremastum Group) 'Bodnant Red' | WThu |
| | - Myrtilloides Group | CDoC ECho GKev GQui LMil MAsh MDun MGos MSnd NMen NMun SReu WAbe WThu |
| | - salmon pink-flowered | ECho GEdr |
| | ***camtschaticum*** | GAuc LMil WThu |
| | - var. ***albiflorum*** | NMen |
| | ***canadense*** f. ***albiflorum*** (A) | LMil |
| | - dark-flowered (A) | LMil |
| | ***canescens*** (A) | LMil |
| | 'Cannon's Double' (K/d) ♀H4 | CBcs CWri GKin LMil MAsh MBri MGos MLea NLar SLdr SPer |
| | 'Canzonetta' (EA) ♀H4 | ECho ELon IVic LMil LRHS MAsh MGos MMuc NMun SLdr |
| | 'Caractacus' | WFar |
| | 'Carat' (A) | NLar SReu |
| | ***cardiobasis*** | see *R. orbiculare* subsp. *cardiobasis* |
| | Carita Group | SHea |
| | 'Carita Golden Dream' | LMil |
| | 'Carita Inchmery' | SHea |
| | 'Carmen' | CWri ECho EPot GEdr GKev GKin GLam LMil MAsh MDun MGos MLea MSnd NMun NPCo SBrd SLdr SReu SRms |
| | 'Carmine' | MSnd |
| | 'Caroline Allbrook' ♀H4 | CWri ECho IDee MAsh MDun MGos MLea NEgg NLar SLdr |
| | 'Caroline de Zoete' | SHea |
| | 'Caruso' | IVic |
| | 'Cary Ann' | CBcs CTri CWri LMil MAsh SLdr SReu WFar |
| | 'Casablanca' (EA) | SLdr |
| | 'Cassata' | LMil |
| | 'Cassley' (Vs) | LMil |
| | ***catawbiense*** | GKev GLin SLdr |
| | 'Catawbiense Album' | CTri MAsh WFar |
| | 'Catawbiense Boursault' | SLdr WFar |
| | 'Catawbiense Grandiflorum' | CWri MAsh NMun WFar |
| | 'Catharine van Tol' | LMil SBrd |
| | 'Caucasicum Pictum' | LMil MSnd SLdr |
| | 'Cayenne' (EA) | SLdr |
| | 'Cecile' (K) ♀H4 | CBcs CDoC CMac CWri ECho GKin LMil LSRN MAsh MBri MDun MGos MMuc NBlu SEND SLdr SPer SReu |
| | 'Celestial' (EA) | CMac |
| | ***cephalanthum*** | LMil |
| | - subsp. ***cephalanthum*** SBEC 0751 | WThu |
| | - - Crebreflorum Group | LMil WAbe WThu |
| | - - - Week's form | ITim |
| | ***cerasinum*** | LMil MSnd |
| | - 'Cherry Brandy' | MSnd |
| | - 'Coals of Fire' | MSnd |
| | 'Cetewayo' ♀H4 | CWri LMil SReu |
| | ***chaetomallum*** | see *R. haematodes* subsp. *chaetomallum* |
| | ***chamaethomsonii*** var. ***chamaethomsonii*** | MSnd |
| | ***chameunum*** | see *R. saluenense* subsp. *chameunum* |
| § | 'Champagne' ♀H3-4 | CSBt EPfP LMil LRHS MAsh MDun NMun SHea SReu |
| | 'Chanel' (Vs) | MDun SReu SSta |
| | 'Chanticleer' (EA) | SLdr SReu |
| | ***chapaense*** | see *R. maddenii* subsp. *crassum* |
| | 'Chariots of Fire' (EA) | LMil |
| | ***charitopes*** | LMil |
| | - F 25570 | LMil |
| § | - subsp. ***tsangpoense*** | GQui NMun |
| * | 'Charlotte de Rothschild' (A) | SLdr |
| | 'Cheer' | CWri MAsh MMuc NEgg SEND SLdr SLim WFar |
| | 'Chelsea Reach' (K/d) | SHea SLdr |
| | 'Chelsea Seventy' | MAsh MSnd SLdr |
| | 'Chenille' (K/d) | SHea SLdr |
| | 'Cherie' (EA) | MAsh |
| | 'Cherokee' (EA) | MSnd NHim SLdr |
| | 'Cherries and Cream' | LMil |
| | 'Cherry Drops' (EA) | MAsh |
| | 'Cherry Float' | MDun |
| | 'Chetco' (K) | LMil |
| | 'Chevalier Félix de Sauvage' ♀H4 | LMil SHea SReu |
| | 'Chikor' | CBcs ECho GKin MAsh MBri MGos MSnd WFar WThu |
| | 'Chinchilla' (EA) | GQui |
| | 'Chink' | CBcs MSnd SLdr |
| | 'Chionoides' | CMac LMil SLdr |
| | 'Chipmunk' (EA/d) | LRHS MAsh |
| | 'Chippewa' (EA) | CTri IVic LMil |
| | 'Chocolate Ice' (K/d) | SHea |
| | 'Choremia' ♀H3 | LMil MLea SHea SReu |
| | 'Chorus Line' | MDun |
| | 'Christina' (EA/d) | LMil MMuc SReu |
| | 'Christmas Cheer' (EA/d) | see *R.* 'Ima-shojo' |
| | 'Christmas Cheer' (hybrid) | CBcs CDoC CMac CSBt CWri GGal GKin LMil MAsh MGos MLea MSnd NLar SLdr SReu |
| | ***chrysanthum*** | see *R. aureum* |
| | ***chrysodoron*** | LMil |
| | ***ciliatum*** | CBcs LMil SLdr |
| | 'Cilpinense' ♀H3-4 | CMac CSBt CWri ECho EPfP GKev LMil LRHS MMuc NBlu NLar NPri SEND SHea SLdr SPoG SReu WGwG |

| |  |  |
|---|---|---|
| | Cilpinense Group | CBcs MDun MSnd SPer WFar |
| | ***cinnabarinum*** | LMil MDun MSnd SLdr |
| | - subsp. ***cinnabarinum*** BL&M 234 | LMil MDun |
| | - - Blandfordiiflorum Group | LMil MSnd |
| § | - - 'Conroy' | CBcs CTsd LMil MDun |
| | - - 'Nepal' | LMil |
| | - - Roylei Group | LMil MDun NHim NMun |
| | - - - 'Magnificum' | MDun |
| | - - - 'Vin Rosé' | LMil MDun |
| § | - subsp. ***tamaense*** | NHim |
| | - 'Wasgau' | IVic |
| § | - subsp. ***xanthocodon*** | CBcs LMil MDun MSnd NHim |
| § | - - Concatenans Group | LMil MDun MSnd NHim NMun SLdr |
| | - - - KW 5874 | LMil |
| | - - - 'Amber' | MDun |
| | - - Purpurellum Group | MDun MSnd |
| | Cinnkeys Group | MDun |
| | Cinzan Group | LMil |
| | 'Circus' | MDun |
| | ***citriniflorum*** | LMil |
| | - R 108 | LMil |
| | - Brodick form | LMil |
| | - var. ***citriniflorum*** | LMil MSnd |
| | - var. ***horaeum*** **new** | MSnd |
| | 'Clarice' (K) **new** | SHea |
| | 'Claudine' | IVic |
| | ***clementinae*** | MSnd |
| | - F 25705 | LMil |
| | - SDR 3230 | GKev |
| | 'Cliff Garland' | GQui LMil |
| | 'Coccineum Speciosum' (G) ♀H4 | CDoC CMac CSBt GKin LMil SLdr SReu SSta |
| | ***coeloneuron*** | LMil |
| | - EGM 334 | LMil |
| | 'Colin Kenrick' (K/d) | SHea |
| | 'Colonel Coen' | CWri ELon GKin LMil LRHS MBri MGos MLea MMuc NLar SBrd SLdr |
| | Colonel Rogers Group | SReu |
| | 'Colyer' (EA) | SLdr |
| | ***concatenans*** | see *R. cinnabarinum* subsp. *xanthocodon* Concatenans Group |
| | ***concinnum*** | NMun SLdr |
| | - Pseudoyanthinum Group | GQui MDun SLdr |
| | 'Conroy' | see *R. cinnabarinum* subsp. *cinnabarinum* 'Conroy' |
| | 'Conversation Piece' (EA) | SLdr |
| | 'Conyan Apricot' **new** | SLdr |
| | ***cookeanum*** | see *R. sikangense* var. *sikangense* Cookeanum Group |
| | 'Cool Haven' **new** | LMil |
| | 'Coral Reef' | SLdr |
| | 'Coral Sea' (EA) | MDun SReu |
| | ***coriaceum*** | LMil MSnd SLdr |
| | - R 120 | MSnd |
| | 'Corinna' | IVic |
| | 'Corneille' (G/d) ♀H4 | CSBt LMil SPer SReu SSta |
| | Cornish Early Red Group | see *R.* Smithii Group |
| | 'Cornish Red' | see *R.* Smithii Group |
| | 'Corona' | SHea |
| | 'Coronation Day' | LMil SReu |
| | 'Coronation Lady' (K) | SHea |
| | ***coryanum*** 'Chelsea Chimes' | MSnd |
| | 'Cosmopolitan' | CWri LMil MGos MMuc SEND SPoG WMoo |
| | 'Costa del Sol' | MSnd |
| | Cote Group (A) | SLdr |
| | 'Cougar' | MDun |
| | 'Countess of Derby' | SHea SLdr SReu |
| | 'Countess of Haddington' ♀H2 | CBcs LMil SLdr |
| | 'Countess of Stair' | WFar |
| | 'Cowslip' | LRHS |
| | Cowslip Group | CTri CWri LMil MAsh MDun MGos MLea MSnd |
| | 'Cranbourne' | SReu |
| | 'Crane' ♀H4 | EPfP GQui IVic LLHF LMil LRHS MAsh NPri SLdr |
| | ***crassum*** | see *R. maddenii* subsp. *crassum* |
| | 'Cream Crest' | GKin GQui LMil SLdr SLim WFar |
| | 'Cream Glory' | MDun |
| | 'Creamy Chiffon' | CWri ECho MGos MLea NHim NLar WGwG |
| § | 'Creeping Jenny' | ECho GGal GGar MSnd SLdr |
| | 'Crest' ♀H3-4 | CWri LMil MGos |
| | 'Crete' ♀H4 | LMil |
| | 'Crimson Pippin' | LMil |
| | ***crinigerum*** | IDee LMil MDun |
| | - var. ***crinigerum*** | MSnd |
| | - var. ***euadenium*** | MSnd |
| | 'Crinoline' (EA) | SLdr |
| | 'Crinoline' (K) | SReu |
| | Crossbill Group | CBcs SLdr |
| | 'Crossroads' | MSnd |
| | 'Crosswater Belle' | IDee LMil |
| | 'Crosswater Red' (K) | LMil |
| | 'Csárdás' | IVic |
| | ***cumberlandense*** (A) | IDee LMil |
| | - 'Sunlight' (A) | LMil |
| | 'Cunningham's Snow White' | IVic |
| | 'Cunningham's White' | CBcs CSBt CTri CWri ELan EPfP LMil LTen MAsh MDun MGos MMuc MSnd NPri SEND SLdr SLim SPoG SReu WFar |
| | 'Curlew' ♀H4 | CBcs CMac CSBt GEdr GKev GKin GLam LMil MAsh MBri MGos MSnd NLar SLdr SReu SSpi WFar |
| | ***cyanocarpum*** | MSnd |
| | 'Cynthia' ♀H4 | CBcs CMac CSBt CWri ECho EPfP LMil LSRN MDun MGos MSnd NEgg SLdr SPer SReu SSta |
| | 'Dagmar' | IVic |
| | Damaris Group | SLdr |
| | 'Damaris Logan' | see *R.* 'Logan Damaris' |
| | 'Damozel' | SHea SLdr |
| | 'Danger' (K) | SHea SLdr |
| | 'Danuta' | IVic |
| | 'Daphne Daffarn' | SHea |
| | 'Daphne Millais' | SHea |
| | 'Dartmoor Pixie' | WThu |
| | ***dasycladum*** | see *R. selense* subsp. *dasycladum* |
| | ***dasypetalum*** | MDun |
| | 'David' ♀H4 | SHea |
| | ***davidii*** | LMil |
| | ***davidsonianum*** ♀H3-4 | LMil MSnd NHim SLdr SSpi |
| | - Bodnant form | LMil MDun |
| | - 'Caerhays Blotched' | SLdr |
| | - 'Caerhays Pink' | SLdr |
| | - 'Ruth Lyons' | LMil |
| | 'Daviesii' (G) ♀H4 | CBcs CDoC CSBt CTri CWri ECho ELan EPfP GKin GQui LMil MAsh MBri MLea MMuc MSnd NPCo SLdr SPer SReu SSpi WFar |
| | 'Day Dream' | SHea SLdr |
| N | 'Daybreak' | see *R.* 'Kirin' |
| | 'Daybreak' (K) | GQui SHea |
| | 'Dear Barbara' **new** | LMil |

| |  |  |
|---|---|---|
| | 'Dear Grandad' (EA) | CTri LMil LSRN SCoo |
| | 'Dear Grandma' | LMil LSRN |
| | 'Dearest' (EA) | LRHS MAsh NPri |
| | 'Debutante' | NHol SHea |
| | ***decorum*** 🏆[H4] | CDoC LLHF LMil LRHS MDun MSnd SLdr SReu SSpi |
| | – SDR 5026 | GKev |
| | – 'Cox's Uranium Green' | SReu |
| § | – subsp. ***diaprepes*** | MSnd SLdr |
| | – – 'Gargantua' | SReu |
| | – late-flowering | LMil |
| | ***decorum* × *yakushimanum*** | SLdr SReu |
| | ***degronianum*** | NHim |
| § | – subsp. ***degronianum*** | LMil MSnd |
| § | – subsp. ***heptamerum*** | MDun |
| | – – var. ***heptamerum*** **new** | MSnd |
| | – – 'Ho Emma' | IDee LMil MDun |
| | – – 'Oki Island' | LMil |
| | – 'Rae's Delight' | IDee LMil |
| | ***deleiense*** | see *R. tephropeplum* |
| | 'Delicatissimum' (O) | CBcs CDoC CWri ECho GKin GQui MGos MLea MMuc MSnd NEgg NLar NPCo SEND SHea SLdr SPer WGwG |
| | 'Delta' | NLar SLdr SLim |
| | ***dendrocharis*** | NHim |
| | – Cox 5016 | WAbe |
| | 'Denise' **new** | IVic |
| * | 'Denny's Rose' (A) | LMil MDun SReu |
| | 'Denny's Scarlet' | MDun SReu SSta |
| | 'Denny's White' (A) | LMil NHol SReu SSta |
| | ***denudatum*** | GLin LMil MSnd |
| | – EGM 294 | LMil |
| | ***desquamatum*** | see *R. rubiginosum* Desquamatum Group |
| | × ***detonsum*** | MSnd |
| | 'Dexter's Champagne' | MDun |
| | 'Dexter's Spice' | MDun |
| | 'Dexter's Springtime' | MDun |
| | 'Dexter's Vanilla' | MDun |
| | 'Diabolo' (K) | SHea |
| | Diamant Group lilac-flowered (EA) | ECho LMil MLea |
| | – pink-flowered (EA) | ECho MGos MLea NBlu |
| § | – purple-flowered (EA) | ECho MGos MLea |
| § | – red-flowered (EA) | ECho MLea SLdr |
| | – rosy red-flowered (EA) | ECho |
| | – white-flowered (EA) | ECho MLea |
| | 'Diamant Purpur' | see *R.* Diamant Group purple-flowered |
| | 'Diamant Rot' | see *R.* Diamant Group red-flowered |
| | 'Diane' | CMac |
| | ***diaprepes*** | see *R. decorum* subsp. *diaprepes* |
| | ***dichroanthum*** | LMil MDun SReu |
| § | – subsp. ***apodectum*** | LMil MSnd |
| | – subsp. ***dichroanthum*** | MSnd |
| § | – subsp. ***scyphocalyx*** | LMil LTen MSnd NLar |
| | ***dictyotum*** | see *R. traillianum* var. *dictyotum* |
| | ***didymum*** | see *R. sanguineum* subsp. *didymum* |
| | 'Dietrich' | WFar |
| | ***dignabile*** | MSnd |
| | ***dimitrum*** | MDun |
| | 'Diorama' (Vs) | GKin LMil SReu SSta |
| | ***discolor*** | see *R. fortunei* subsp. *discolor* |
| | 'Django' | IVic |
| | 'Doc' | CBcs CMac EPfP MAsh MDun MGos SLdr SReu WFar |
| | 'Doctor A. Blok' | SLdr |
| | 'Doctor M. Oosthoek' (M) 🏆[H4] | CSBt GKin SReu |
| | 'Doctor Stocker' | MSnd |
| | 'Doctor V.H. Rutgers' | MDun WFar |
| | 'Doncaster' | WFar |
| | 'Donna Hardgrove' | MDun |
| | 'Dopey' 🏆[H4] | CBcs CSBt CWri ECho ELon EPfP LMil LRHS MAsh MBri MDun MGos MLea MSnd NEgg NHol SLdr SLim SPoG SReu |
| | 'Dora Amateis' 🏆[H4] | CBcs CDoC ECho IVic LMil LRHS MAsh MBri MGos MMuc NPri SBrd SLdr SLim SReu |
| | Dormouse Group | CBcs ECho GGar LMil MAsh MMuc NLar SReu WFar |
| | 'Dorothy Corston' (K) | SHea |
| | 'Double Beauty' (EA/d) | SReu SSta |
| | 'Double Damask' (K/d) 🏆[H4] | SHea SLdr |
| | 'Double Date' (d) | SLdr |
| | double yellow-flowered (A/d) | SLdr |
| | 'Douggie Betteridge' | MSnd |
| | 'Douglas McEwan' | SLdr |
| | Dragonfly Group | SReu |
| | 'Dreamland' 🏆[H4] | CBcs CDoC CSBt CWri ECho LMil LRHS MAsh MDun MGos MLea MSnd NLar SLim SPoG SReu WFar |
| | 'Drury Lane' (K) | GQui LMil LRHS |
| | ***dryophyllum*** misapplied | see *R. phaeochrysum* var. *levistratum* |
| | 'Dufthecke'[PBR] | see *R.* White Dufthecke |
| | 'Dusky Dawn' | SLdr |
| | 'Dusky Orange' | MDun SReu |
| | 'Düsselfeuer' | IVic |
| | 'Dusty Miller' | LRHS MAsh MBri MDun MGos MSnd NLar SLdr |
| | 'Earl of Athlone' | SHea SReu |
| | 'Earl of Donoughmore' | SReu |
| | 'Ebony Pearl' | CBcs ECho ELon GBin IVic MGos MMuc SLdr WGwG |
| | ***eclecteum*** | LMil MSnd |
| | 'Edeltraud' **new** | IVic |
| § | ***edgeworthii*** 🏆[H2-3] | CBcs SLdr WAbe |
| | 'Edith Bosley' | NLar |
| | 'Edmund de Rothschild' | NMun |
| | 'Edna Bee' (EA) | LMil |
| | 'Egret' 🏆[H4] | ECho EPot GEdr GKev GLam LMil MDun MGos MLea MSnd NLar SLdr WThu |
| | 'Eider' | MAsh SLdr |
| | 'Eileen' | LMil |
| N | 'Eisenhower' (K) **new** | SHea |
| | 'El Camino' | ECho MMuc MSnd NPCo SEND SLdr |
| | 'El Greco' | SLdr |
| | Eldorado Group | GQui |
| | 'Eleanore' **new** | SLdr |
| | 'Electra' | see *R. augustinii* 'Electra' |
| | ***elegantulum*** | LMil MDun MSnd |
| | 'Elisabeth Hobbie' 🏆[H4] | ECho LMil |
| | 'Eliska' | IVic |
| | 'Elizabeth' | CTri CTsd CWri ECho IVic LRHS LSRN MGos MSCN MSnd NPri SBod SHea |
| | Elizabeth Group | CBcs LMil MAsh SLdr SPer SReu WFar |
| N | 'Elizabeth' (EA) | CMac CSBt EPfP MGos SLdr |
| | 'Elizabeth Jenny' | see *R.* 'Creeping Jenny' |
| | 'Elizabeth Lockhart' | ECho GQui MDun MGos NMun |

|  |  |
|---|---|
| 'Elizabeth Red Foliage' | CTri LMil LRHS MAsh MBri SPer SReu |
| Elsae Group | NMun |
| 'Elsie Lee' (EA/d) 🏆$^{H3-4}$ | CSBt CTrh ECho LMil MAsh MGos MMuc NPCo SLdr |
| 'Elsie Pratt' (A) | NHol SHea |
| 'Emasculum' | LMil SLdr |
| 'Ember Glow' | NMun |
| 'Emma Williams' | CBcs |
| 'Endsleigh Pink' | CBcs LMil MMuc |
| ***eriogynum*** | see *R. facetum* |
| 'Ernest Inman' | LMil SLdr |
| ***erosum*** | MSnd |
| 'Eruption' | IVic |
| 'Esmeralda' | CMac |
| 'Etna' (EA) | MSnd SLdr |
| 'Etta Burrows' | CWri MDun |
| ***euchroum*** | MSnd |
| ***eudoxum*** | MSnd NHim |
| 'Europa' | SReu |
| ***eurysiphon*** | MSnd |
| 'Eva Goude' (K) | SHea |
| 'Evelyn Hyde' (EA) | SLdr |
| 'Evening Fragrance' (A) | LMil |
| 'Everbloom' (EA) | SLdr |
| 'Everest' (EA) | SPoG |
| 'Everestianum' | SHea |
| Exburiense Group | MMuc |
| 'Exbury Calstocker' | LMil |
| 'Exbury Lady Chamberlain' | MSnd |
| 'Exbury Naomi' | LMil |
| 'Exbury White' (K) | GQui |
| ***excellens*** | IDee LMil |
| ***eximium*** | see *R. falconeri* subsp. *eximium* |
| 'Exotic' | MDun |
| 'Exquisitum' (O) 🏆$^{H4}$ | CBcs CDoC CWri ECho EPfP GKin LMil MBri NLar SLdr SPer |
| ***exquisitum*** | see *R. oreotrephes* Exquisitum Group |
| 'Extraordinaire' **new** | SReu |
| ***faberi*** | LMil |
| 'Fabia' 🏆$^{H3}$ | CMac GKin LMil LRHS MDun MSnd NMun SHea SLdr |
| Fabia Group | CWri |
| § 'Fabia Tangerine' | MLea |
| 'Fabia Waterer' | LMil |
| § ***facetum*** | IDee LMil MSnd |
| - KR 7593 | LMil |
| 'Faggetter's Favourite' 🏆$^{H4}$ | LMil MDun SHea SReu SSta |
| Fairy Light Group | LMil |
| ***falconeri*** 🏆$^{H3-4}$ | CBcs CDoC CHEx CHll CWri LMil MDun MGos MLea MSnd NHim NPCo SLdr SPer |
| - from East Nepal | MDun |
| § - subsp. ***eximium*** | CDoC IDee LMil MDun MSnd NLar |
| 'Fanal' (K) | MBri |
| 'Fanny' | see *R.* 'Pucella' |
| 'Fantastica' 🏆$^{H4}$ | CDoC CWri ELan ELon EPfP IDee IVic LMil LRHS MAsh MBri MDun MGos MLea NLar NPCo NPri SLdr SLim SPoG |
| ***fargesii*** | see *R. oreodoxa* var. *fargesii* |
| ***farinosum*** **new** | NHim |
| ***farrerae*** **new** | NHim |
| 'Fashion' (EA) | SLdr |
| ***fastigiatum*** | GEdr LMil MSnd NMun SLdr |
| - SBEC 804/4869 | WThu |
| § - 'Blue Steel' 🏆$^{H4}$ | CBcs CTri ECho ELon GAbr GKin IVic LMil LRHS MAsh MDun MGos NPCo SLdr SPlb WPat |
| 'Fastuosum Flore Pleno' (d) 🏆$^{H4}$ | CBcs CMac CSBt CWri EPfP LMil MDun MGos MLea MSnd NLar SHea SLdr SPer SReu SSta WFar |
| 'Fatima' | LMil |
| 'Favor Major' (K) **new** | SHea |
| 'Favorite' ambig. (EA) | NMun SLdr |
| 'Fawley' (K) | SHea SLdr |
| 'Fénelon' (G) | SReu SSta |
| ***ferrugineum*** | LMil MGos |
| - 'Plenum' (d) | MDun |
| 'Festivo' | MDun |
| 'Feuerwerk' (K) | IVic SHea |
| ***fictolacteum*** | see *R. rex* subsp. *fictolacteum* |
| Fire Bird Group | SHea SLdr |
| 'Fireball' (K) 🏆$^{H4}$ | CBcs CDoC CTri CWri EPfP GKev GKin LMil MAsh MBri MGos MLea MMuc NLar NMun SEND SLdr SPer SPoG |
| 'Fireglow' (EA) | CSBt GKin LMil WFar |
| 'Firelight' (hybrid) | GKin LMil |
| 'Firetail' | SHea |
| 'Flaming Bronze' | SReu |
| 'Flaming Gold' | EPfP LRHS MAsh |
| § ***flammeum*** (A) | LMil |
| 'Flanagan's Daughter' | LMil MAsh |
| 'Flautando' | IVic LMil |
| Flava Group | see *R.* Volker Group |
| ***flavidum*** 'Album' | WThu |
| aff. ***flinckii*** AC 5441 | GLin |
| ***floccigerum*** | LMil MSnd |
| 'Floradora' (M) | SReu |
| 'Floriade' × ***yakushimanum*** | SLdr |
| ***floribundum*** | LMil MSnd SLdr |
| 'Florida' (EA/d) 🏆$^{H3-4}$ | CMac LMil SLdr SReu WFar |
| 'Flower Arranger' (EA) | LMil MAsh SCoo |
| ***formosum*** | CBcs GQui SLdr |
| ***forrestii*** KR 6113 | LMil |
| - subsp. ***forrestii*** | LMil |
| - - Repens Group | LMil |
| - - - 'Seinghku' | WThu |
| - Tumescens Group | WThu |
| Fortune Group | SLdr |
| ***fortunei*** | IVic LMil MDun SLdr |
| § - subsp. ***discolor*** 🏆$^{H4}$ | LMil MSnd SLdr |
| - - (Houlstonii Group) 'John R. Elcock' | LMil |
| - - var. ***kwangfuense*** AC 5208 | LMil |
| - - 'Nymphenrose' | IVic |
| - 'Lu-Shan' | MDun |
| - 'Mrs Butler' | see *R. fortunei* 'Sir Charles Butler' |
| § - 'Sir Charles Butler' | LMil |
| 'Fox Hunter' | SLdr |
| 'Fragrantissimum' 🏆$^{H2-3}$ | CAby CBcs CEnd CMac CSBt CTsd CWri GGal IDee LMil MRav NLar NMun SKHP SLdr |
| Francis Hanger Group | SReu |
| 'Frank Galsworthy' 🏆$^{H4}$ | LMil SReu |
| 'Fred Peste' | CDoC ECho GKin LMil MAsh MDun MGos MLea MMuc MSnd NLar NPCo SEND SLim |
| 'Fred Wynniatt' | MSnd SLdr |
| 'Freda' (EA) **new** | SLdr |
| 'Freya' (R/d) | LMil LSRN |
| 'Fridtjof Nansen' (A) | SLdr |
| 'Frigate' (EA) | SLdr |
| 'Frills' (K/d) | SHea |
| 'Frome' (K) | SHea |
| 'Frosted Orange' (EA) | LMil MAsh |

| |  |  |
|---|---|---|
| | 'Frühlingsbeginn' | IVic |
| | 'Fulbrook' | LMil |
| | ***fulgens*** | GLin LMil MDun MSnd |
| | ***fulvum*** ♀H4 | CDoC GKin LMil MDun MSnd NLar SReu SSta |
| | - KR 7614 | LMil |
| | - subsp. ***fulvoides*** | LMil MSnd |
| § | 'Fumiko' (EA) | CBcs CSBt ELon LMil LRHS MAsh MGos MLea MMuc NLar NMun NPCo WFar |
| | 'Furnivall's Daughter' ♀H4 | CMac CSBt CWri ECho EPfP LMil MDun MGos MMuc MSnd NLar SEND SHea SLdr SPer SReu SSta WFar |
| | 'Fusilier' | SHea SReu |
| | 'Gabrielle Hill' (EA) | MAsh SLdr |
| | 'Gaiety' (EA) | LMil SLdr SReu |
| | ***galactinum*** | IDee LMil MDun NHim |
| | 'Galathea' (EA) | MMuc |
| | 'Gallipoli' (K) | SHea |
| | 'Gandy Dancer' | CWri MLea |
| | 'Garden State Glow' (EA/d) | SLdr |
| | 'Garibaldi' | SHea |
| | 'Garnet' | SHea |
| | 'Gartendirektor Glocker' | CWri ECho IVic MAsh MDun MSnd SLim |
| | 'Gartendirektor Rieger' ♀H4 | CWri IVic LMil MDun SHea SReu |
| | 'Gauche' (A) | GQui SLdr |
| | 'Gaugin' | GQui |
| | 'Geisha Lilac' | see *R.* 'Hanako' |
| | 'Geisha Orange' | see *R.* 'Satschiko' |
| | 'Geisha Pink' | see *R.* 'Momoko' |
| | 'Geisha Purple' | see *R.* 'Fumiko' |
| | 'Geisha Red' | see *R.* 'Kazuko' |
| | 'Geisha White' | see *R.* 'Hisako' |
| | 'Gena Mae' (A/d) | SLdr |
| | 'General Eisenhower' | SHea SReu |
| | 'General Eric Harrison' | SLdr |
| | 'General Practitioner' | MSnd NMun SLdr |
| | 'General Wavell' (EA) | CMac MSnd SLdr |
| | 'Gene's Favourite' | SReu |
| | 'Genoveva' | LMil |
| | 'Geoffrey Millais' | LMil |
| | 'Georg Arends' (Ad) | EPfP LRHS MAsh SLdr |
| | 'George Hyde' (EA) | LRHS LSRN MAsh SCoo |
| | 'George Johnstone' | SLdr |
| | 'George's Delight' | MSnd |
| § | × ***geraldii*** | SLdr |
| | 'Germania' | LMil LRHS MAsh NHim NPri SPoG SReu |
| | Gertrud Schäle Group | CDoC CTri GEdr NBlu SHea |
| | 'Gibraltar' (K) ♀H4 | CBcs CDoC CMac CSBt CTri CWri EPfP GKin LMil LRHS MAsh MBri MDun MGos NBlu NLar SLdr SLim SPer SReu SSta WFar |
| | Gibraltar Group | CTri |
| | ***giganteum*** | see *R. protistum* var. *giganteum* |
| | 'Gilbert Mullie' (EA) | LMil NBlu SLim |
| | 'Gill's Crimson' | SHea SReu |
| | 'Ginger' (K) | CSBt CWri GKin LMil SBrd |
| | 'Ginny Gee' ♀H4 | CBcs CDoC CSBt CWri ECho EPfP GEdr GGar GKev GKin GLam IVic LMil LRHS MAsh MBri MDun MGos MLea MMuc MSnd NEgg NLar SLdr SPoG SReu SSta WFar WPat |
| § | 'Girard's Hot Shot' (EA) | ECho GQui MAsh MGos SReu WFar |
| | 'Girard's Hot Shot' variegated (EA/v) | ECho LMil MAsh MMuc NMun |

| |  |  |
|---|---|---|
| | ***glanduliferum*** EGM 347 | LMil |
| | ***glaucophyllum*** | LMil MDun MSnd NHim NMun WThu |
| | - B&SWJ 2638 | WCru |
| | - Borde Hill form | LMil |
| | - var. ***glaucophyllum*** | MSnd |
| § | - subsp. ***tubiforme*** | NMun |
| | 'Gletschernacht' | IVic |
| | ***glischrum*** | MSnd NHim |
| | - subsp. ***glischroides*** | LMil |
| | 'Glockenspiel' (K/d) | SHea SLdr |
| | 'Gloria' | see *R.* 'Bruns Gloria' |
| | 'Gloria Mundi' (G) | SHea |
| | 'Glory of Littleworth' (Ad) | LMil |
| | 'Glowing Embers' (K) | CBcs CDoC CMac CTri CWri ECho GKin MAsh MBri MDun MLea NHol SHea SLdr SLim SPer SPur SReu SSta |
| | 'Goblin' | MSnd SLdr |
| | 'Gog' (K) | CSBt SHea |
| | 'Goldcrest' (A) **new** | SHea |
| | 'Golden Belle' | MAsh |
| | 'Golden Coach' | CWri ECho MGos MLea MSnd SBod SLdr SPer |
| | 'Golden Eagle' (K) | CBcs CDoC ECho GGar GKin LMil MAsh MDun MGos MSnd NLar SHea SReu SSta WMoo |
| | 'Golden Flare' (A) | CBcs CDoC CSBt CWri ECho GKin LRHS MAsh MBri MGos MLea MMuc NBlu NEgg NMun NPCo SLdr SPoG |
| | 'Golden Gate' | CDoC CSBt ECho MLea MMuc NLar NMun WFar |
| | 'Golden Hind' (A) **new** | SHea |
| | 'Golden Horn' **new** | SLdr |
| | 'Golden Horn' (K) | GQui SHea |
| | 'Golden Lights' (A) | CWri ECho GKin LMil MBri MGos MLea NEgg NPCo WGwG |
| § | (Golden Oriole Group) 'Talavera' | LMil SSpi |
| | 'Golden Princess' | LMil |
| | 'Golden Ruby' | CBcs ECho MLea NHim NMun SPer |
| | 'Golden Splendour' | LMil SLdr |
| | 'Golden Sunset' (K) | CMac ECho LMil MAsh MBri MGos MLea NHol NLar SHea SLdr |
| | 'Golden Torch' ♀H4 | CBcs CDoC CSBt CWri ECho EPfP GGar LMil LRHS MAsh MBri MDun MGos MLea MSnd NLar SLdr SLim SPer SPoG SReu SSta WFar |
| | 'Golden Wedding' | CBcs CSBt CWri ECho ELon LMil LSRN MAsh MDun MGos MMuc MSnd NPCo SBod SLdr SPer |
| | 'Golden Wit' | MAsh MMHG MMuc NEgg |
| | 'Goldfinch' (K) | SHea |
| | 'Goldflimmer' (v) | CDoC EPfP GKin LMil LRHS MAsh MGos MMuc NLar NPri SLim SPoG WFar |
| | 'Goldfort' | SReu |
| | 'Goldika' | LMil |
| | 'Goldkollier' | IVic |
| | 'Goldkrone' ♀H4 | CWri ELon EPfP LMil MAsh MGos MLea SPer SPoG SReu |
| | 'Goldpracht' (K) | IVic |
| | Goldschatz = 'Goldprinz' | IVic LMil |
| | 'Goldsworth Orange' | CSBt CWri ECho MGos MSnd SBod SLdr |
| | 'Goldsworth Orange' × ***insigne*** **new** | MAsh |
| | 'Goldsworth Yellow' | CSBt |
| | 'Goldtopas' (K) | GKin LMil LRHS SBrd |

| | | |
|---|---|---|
| | 'Golfer' | CWri LMil |
| | 'Gomer Waterer' ♀H4 | CDoC CMac CSBt CWri ECho EPfP LMil LRHS LTen MAsh MBri MDun MGos MMuc MSnd NLar SLdr SPer SPoG SReu SSta WFar |
| | ***gongushunense*** **new** | NHim |
| | 'Gordian' | MDun |
| | Gowenianum Group (Ad) | LMil |
| | 'Grace Seabrook' | CSBt CTri CWri ECho MDun MGos MMuc MSnd NPCo SBod SLdr SPer SReu |
| | 'Graciosum' (O) | SReu |
| | 'Graffito' | IVic LMil |
| | 'Graham Thomas' | LMil SReu |
| | 'Grand Slam' | ECho GAbr MLea MSnd |
| | ***grande*** | MSnd SLdr |
| | - pink-flowered | MSnd |
| | ***gratum*** | see *R. basilicum* |
| | 'Graziella' | LMil MDun |
| | 'Greensleeves' | LMil LRHS |
| | 'Greenway' (EA) | CBcs SLdr |
| | 'Grenadier' | LMil SHea |
| | ***griersonianum*** | CBcs LMil MDun MSnd NMun |
| | ***griersonianum* × *yakushimanum*** | SLdr |
| | ***griffithianum*** | MSnd NHim SLdr |
| | 'Gristede' ♀H4 | ECho LMil MGos NHim SBrd SReu |
| | ***groenlandicum*** | see *Ledum groenlandicum* |
| | 'Grosclaude' | CMac SHea |
| | 'Grouse' × ***keiskei*** var. ***ozawae*** 'Yaku Fairy' | ECho |
| | 'Grumpy' | CBcs CSBt CWri ECho LMil LRHS MAsh MBri MGos NHim SLdr SReu |
| | 'Gumpo' (EA) | CMac SLdr |
| | 'Gumpo Pink' (EA) | SLdr |
| | 'Gumpo White' (EA) | LRHS MAsh MGos NLar NMun |
| | 'Gunter Dinger' **new** | IVic |
| | 'Gwenda' (EA) | CTri SLdr |
| | 'Gwendoline' **new** | SReu SSta |
| | 'Gwillt-king' | CBcs |
| | ***habrotrichum*** | LMil |
| | 'Hachmann's Anastasia' | LMil |
| | 'Hachmann's Brasilia' | MDun |
| | 'Hachmann's Charmant' | LMil SPoG |
| | 'Hachmann's Constanze' | LMil |
| | 'Hachmann's Diadem' | LMil |
| | 'Hachmann's Eskimo' | LMil |
| | 'Hachmann's Feuerschein' | LMil |
| | 'Hachmann's Junifeuer' | IVic LMil SReu |
| | 'Hachmann's Kabarett' | LMil LRHS NLar |
| | 'Hachmann's Marianne' | LMil |
| | 'Hachmann's Marlis' ♀H4 | LMil SReu |
| § | 'Hachmann's Polaris' ♀H4 | CDoC LMil MBri NLar SLdr |
| | 'Hachmann's Porzellan' ♀H4 | LMil |
| § | 'Hachmann's Rokoko' (EA) | LMil NMun |
| | 'Hachmann's Topsi' | IVic |
| | ***haematodes*** | IDee LMil LRHS MDun MSnd SLdr SRms |
| § | - subsp. ***chaetomallum*** | LMil MSnd |
| | - subsp. ***haematodes*** | LMil |
| | 'Halfdan Lem' | CBcs CDoC ECho GKin LMil LTen MAsh MBri MGos MLea MMuc MSnd SEND SLdr SLim SPer SReu SSta |
| | 'Hallelujah' | IVic MAsh |
| | 'Halopeanum' | SHea SLdr |
| | 'Hamlet' (M) | LMil |
| | 'Hampshire Belle' | LMil |
| | 'Hana-asobi' (EA) | MSnd |
| § | 'Hanako' (EA) | MGos MLea NBlu |
| | ***hanceanum*** Nanum Group | CBcs |
| | 'Hanger's Flame' (A) | LMil |
| | 'Hansel' | CDoC CWri ECho GQui LMil MAsh MDun MMuc SLdr WFar |
| | Happy Group | CMac ECho |
| | 'Hardijzer Beauty' (Ad) | MSnd SLdr |
| | 'Harkwood Moonlight' | LMil |
| | 'Harkwood Red' (EA) | SLdr |
| | Harry White's hybrid (A) **new** | SReu SSta |
| | 'Harvest Moon' (K) | SCoo SHea SLdr SSta |
| | 'Harvest Moon' (hybrid) | CSBt MMuc |
| | 'Hatsu-giri' (EA) | CMac LMil MSnd SLdr SPoG SReu |
| | Hawk Group | SLdr |
| | 'Heather Macleod' (EA) | SLdr |
| | ***heatheriae*** | LMil NHim |
| | - KR 6176 | IDee LMil |
| | Hebe Group | NMun |
| | 'Heidi'PBR (EA) | SLdr |
| | 'Helen Close' (EA) | SLdr |
| | 'Helen Curtis' (EA) | SLdr |
| | 'Helene Schiffner' ♀H4 | LMil SReu |
| | ***heliolepis*** | LMil |
| | ***hemidartum*** | see *R. pocophorum* var. *hemidartum* |
| | × ***hemigynum*** | MSnd |
| | ***hemsleyanum*** | IDee LMil MDun MSnd NHim SLdr |
| | ***heptamerum*** | see *R. degronianum* subsp. *heptamerum* |
| | 'Herbert' (EA) | CMac SLim |
| | 'Herbstzauber' **new** | LMil |
| | 'Heureuse Surprise' (G) | SLdr |
| | 'High Summer' | LMil |
| | 'Hilda Margaret' | SReu |
| | 'Hille' | LMil |
| | 'Hinamayo' | see *R.* (Obtusum Group) 'Hinomayo' |
| | 'Hino-crimson' (EA) ♀H3-4 | CBcs CDoC CMac CSBt CTri ELon GKin LMil LRHS MAsh MBri MGos MMuc NHim NHol SEND SLdr SPer SPoG SReu SSta WFar |
| | 'Hinodegiri' (EA) | CMac CSBt SLdr SReu WFar |
| | 'Hino-scarlet' (EA) | CBcs |
| | ***hippophaeoides*** | GKev LMil MDun MSnd SLdr WAbe WFar |
| | - Yu 13845 | LMil MDun |
| | - 'Bei-ma-shan' | see *R. hippophaeoides* 'Haba Shan' |
| | - 'Blue Silver' | EGxp IVic LMil MAsh NLar NMun |
| § | - 'Haba Shan' ♀H4 | LMil MDun WThu |
| | - var. ***hippophaeoides*** Fimbriatum Group | NMun |
| | ***hirsutum*** | LMil |
| | - f. ***albiflorum*** | SReu |
| | - 'Flore Pleno' (d) | ECho GEdr MDun |
| | ***hirtipes*** | MSnd NHim |
| § | 'Hisako' (EA) | GEdr |
| | ***hodgsonii*** | LMil MDun MSnd SLdr |
| | - 'Poet's Lawn' | MSnd |
| | 'Holden' | WFar |
| | 'Homebush' (K/d) ♀H4 | CBcs CDoC CMac CTri CWri EPfP GKev LMil MAsh MBri MDun MGos NPCo SLdr SPer SReu SSta |
| | 'Honey Butter' | LMil SLim |
| | 'Honeysuckle' (K) | SHea SReu SSta |
| § | 'Ho-o' (EA) | NLar SLdr |
| | 'Hoppy' | CBcs CSBt CWri LMil MAsh MDun MGos MLea MMuc MSnd NLar NMun SEND SLdr SLim SPoG |

| | Name | Suppliers |
|---|---|---|
| | 'Horizon Monarch' 🏆H3-4 | CDoC CWri GKin IVic LMil LRHS MBri MDun MLea NLar SLdr SLim SReu |
| | 'Hortulanus H. Witte' (M) | CSBt SReu WFar |
| | 'Hot Shot' | see *R.* 'Girard's Hot Shot' |
| | 'Hot Shot Variegated' (EA/v) | CDoC NEgg SLdr |
| | 'Hotei' 🏆H4 | CDoC CSBt CWri ECho EPfP GKin LMil MAsh MDun MGos NEgg NPCo SLdr SPer SReu WFar |
| | 'Hotspur' (K) | CSBt CWri ECho GBin MGos NLar SLdr |
| | 'Hotspur Red' (K) 🏆H4 | CDoC GKev GKin LMil MAsh NEgg NPCo SHea SReu WMoo |
| | 'Hotspur Yellow' (K) | SReu |
| | ***huanum*** | LMil |
| | - EGM 316 | LMil |
| | 'Hugh Koster' | CSBt SLdr |
| | aff. ***huidongense*** KR 7315 | LMil |
| | 'Hullaballoo' | LMil |
| | 'Humboldt' | WFar |
| | Humming Bird Group | CBcs CMHG GEdr LMil MDun SRms |
| | ***hunnewellianum*** | MSnd |
| | 'Hussar' | CWri |
| | 'Huzza' | LMil |
| | 'Hyde and Seek' | GQui |
| | 'Hydie' (EA/d) | SPoG |
| | 'Hydon Dawn' 🏆H4 | CBcs CDoC CWri LMil MAsh MGos MLea MSnd SHea SLdr SPer SReu SSta |
| | 'Hydon Hunter' 🏆H4 | MSnd SHea SLdr SReu SSta |
| | 'Hydon Pink' | SHea |
| | 'Hydon Velvet' | LMil SReu |
| | ***hylaeum*** | MSnd |
| | Hyperion Group | SReu SSta WFar |
| | ***hyperythrum*** | MSnd NMun |
| | 'Ice Cube' | ECho MLea MMuc NHim NLar NMun SEND SLdr WFar |
| | 'Iceberg' | see *R.* 'Lodauric Iceberg' |
| | 'Idealist' | CWri SReu |
| | 'Ightham Gold' | SReu |
| | 'Ightham Peach' | SReu |
| | 'Ightham Purple' | SReu |
| | 'Ightham Yellow' | CWri SHea SLdr SReu |
| | 'Igneum Novum' (G) | SReu |
| | 'Ilam Carmen' (K) **new** | SHea |
| § | 'Ilam Melford Lemon' (A) | LMil |
| § | 'Ilam Ming' (A) | LMil |
| | 'Ilam Violet' | LMil |
| | 'Imago' (K/d) | LMil SLdr |
| § | 'Ima-shojo' (EA/d) | CMac LSRN MGos |
| | ***imberbe*** **new** | MSnd |
| | ***impeditum*** | CBcs CSBt CWib ECho EPot GEdr GKev GQui MAsh MGos MLea MMuc MSnd NWCA SLdr SPer SReu SSta WFar |
| | - 'Blue Steel' | see *R. fastigiatum* 'Blue Steel' |
| | - 'Indigo' | GGar GKin LLHF MAsh MGos NPCo SLdr WAbe |
| | - 'Pygmaeum' | GEdr NHar WAbe WThu |
| | - Reuthe's form | SReu |
| | - 'Williams' | NMun |
| | 'Impi' | NMun SReu |
| | Impi Group | MDun |
| § | ***indicum*** 'Macranthum' (EA) | SLdr |
| | Inkarho Lilac Dufthecke = 'Rhodunter 149'PBR **new** | LMil |
| | ***insigne*** 🏆H4 | GLin LMil MSnd NLar |
| | - Reuthe's form | SReu |
| | ***insigne*** × ***yakushimanum*** | SReu |

| | Name | Suppliers |
|---|---|---|
| | Intrepid Group | SReu |
| | ***iodes*** | see *R. alutaceum* var. *iodes* |
| | 'Irene Koster' (O) 🏆H4 | CDoC CSBt CWri EPfP GKin LMil MAsh MBri MLea NEgg NLar SLdr SLim SSpi |
| | 'Irohayama' (EA) 🏆H3-4 | CMac ELon EPfP GQui LMil LRHS MAsh MMuc NPri SLdr SPer |
| | ***irroratum*** | LMil |
| | - subsp. ***irroratum*** | MSnd |
| * | - subsp. ***kontumense*** var. ***ningyuenense*** | GLin |
| | - 'Polka Dot' | LMil |
| | - subsp. ***yiliangense*** EGM 339 | LMil |
| | 'Isabel' | NPri |
| | 'Isabel' (EA) | LRHS MAsh |
| | 'Isabel Pierce' | CWri |
| | Isabella Group | WFar |
| | 'Ivette' (EA) | CMac |
| | 'Izabelle' (EA) | MBri |
| | 'J.C. Williams' | CBcs |
| | 'J.G. Millais' | SLdr |
| | 'J.J. de Vink' | SHea |
| | 'J.M. de Montague' | see *R.* 'The Hon. Jean Marie de Montague' |
| | 'Jacksonii' | SHea |
| | 'Jalisco Eclipse' | LMil MSnd |
| | 'Jalisco Elect' | CWri |
| | 'Jalisco Emblem' | SLdr |
| | 'Jalisco Janet' | LMil SHea SLdr |
| | 'James Burchett' 🏆H4 | LMil SLdr SReu |
| | 'James Gable' (EA) | MAsh SLdr |
| | 'Jan Dekens' | SReu |
| | 'Janet Blair' | CWri MDun |
| | 'Janet Rhea' (EA) | SLdr |
| | 'Janet Ward' | SReu |
| | ***japonicum*** (A. Gray) Valcken | see *R. molle* subsp. *japonicum* |
| | ***japonicum*** Schneider var. ***japonicum*** | see *R. degronianum* subsp. *heptamerum* |
| | - var. ***pentamerum*** | see *R. degronianum* subsp. *degronianum* |
| | 'Jean Marie Montague' | see *R.* 'The Hon. Jean Marie de Montague' |
| | 'Jeff Hill' (EA) | ECho MMuc SEND SLdr SReu |
| | 'Jenny' | see *R.* 'Creeping Jenny' |
| | 'Jeremy Davies' | SReu |
| | 'Joan Paton' (A) | SLdr |
| | 'Joanna' | MMuc |
| | 'Jocelyne' | LMil |
| | 'Jock' | SLdr |
| | Jock Group | CBcs CMHG |
| | 'Jock Brydon' (O) | LMil SHea |
| | 'Johann Sebastian Bach' (EA) | SLdr |
| | 'Johanna' (EA) 🏆H4 | CDoC CTri EPfP IVic LMil LRHS MAsh MMHG NHol NLar NPri SLdr SPer SReu |
| | 'John Cairns' (EA) | CMac MSnd SLdr |
| | 'John Walter' | SHea |
| | 'John Waterer' | SHea WFar |
| | 'Johnny Bender' | SLdr |
| | ***johnstoneanum*** | CBcs LMil NHim NMun SLdr |
| | - KW 7732 | SLdr |
| | - 'Double Diamond' (d) | LMil |
| | 'Jolie Madame' (Vs) | CWri ECho GKin LMil LRHS MAsh MBri MLea MMuc NLar NPri SLdr SPur SReu SSta |
| | 'Joseph Baumann' (G) | SLdr |
| | 'Joseph Hill' (EA) | ECho ELon MGos MMuc SReu |
| | 'Josephine Klinger' (G) | SReu |

| | | |
|---|---|---|
| | 'Jubilant' | LMil SHea |
| | 'Jubilee' | SLdr |
| | 'June Fire' (A) | MDun SReu |
| | ***kaempferi*** (EA) | LMil SLdr |
| | – 'Damio' | see *R. kaempferi* 'Mikado' |
| § | – 'Mikado' (EA) | LMil SLdr SReu |
| | – orange-flowered (EA) | CMac |
| | 'Kalinka' | LMil MAsh NLar SLdr SPoG |
| | 'Karen Triplett' | LMil |
| | 'Karin' | MDun SLdr |
| | 'Kasane-kagaribi' (EA) | SLdr |
| | 'Kate Waterer' ♀H4 | MDun MGos SReu WFar |
| N | 'Kathleen' de Rothschild (K) | SHea |
| | 'Kathleen' van Nes (EA) | SLdr |
| | 'Katisha' (EA) | SLdr |
| | 'Katy Watson' | SReu SSta |
| § | 'Kazuko' (EA) | MGos NBlu WFar |
| | 'Keija' (EA) | SLdr |
| | ***keiskei*** | LLHF NMun |
| | – var. ***ozawae*** 'Yaku Fairy' ♀H4 | ITim LMil WAbe WThu |
| | ***keleticum*** | see *R. calostrotum* subsp. *keleticum* |
| | 'Kelsay's Double' **new** | MLea |
| | 'Kentucky Colonel' | SLdr |
| | 'Kermesinum' (EA) | CTri MAsh MGos NMun NWad SLdr SLim SPlb SReu |
| I | 'Kermesinum Album' (EA) | SReu |
| I | 'Kermesinum Rosé' (EA) | CSBt ECho ELon LMil MGos MLea SLdr SLim SReu |
| | ***kesangiae*** | LMil MDun |
| | – AC 5343 | LMil |
| | Kewense Group | CSBt |
| | ***keysii*** | MDun |
| | – EGM 064 | LMil |
| | 'Kilian' (A) | MAsh |
| | 'Kilimanjaro' | LMil SReu |
| | 'King Fisher' | NMun |
| | 'King George' Loder | see *R.* 'Loderi King George' |
| § | 'Kirin' (Kurume) (EA/d) | CBcs CMac LMil SLdr |
| | 'Kirishima' (EA) | SRms |
| | 'Kirsten Begeer' | IVic |
| | ***kiusianum*** (EA) ♀H4 | LMil MSnd SReu SRms |
| I | – 'Album' (EA) | LMil SReu |
| | – 'Hillier's Pink' (EA) | LMil |
| | 'Kiwi Majic' | LMil MDun |
| | 'Klondyke' (K) ♀H4 | CBcs CSBt CTri EPfP GKin LMil LRHS MAsh MGos NLar NPri SHea SLdr SReu |
| | 'Kluis Sensation' ♀H4 | CMac CSBt MDun MSnd SLdr SReu |
| | 'Kluis Triumph' | SReu |
| | 'Knap Hill Apricot' (K) | LMil SHea |
| | 'Knap Hill Red' (K) | CDoC LMil SHea |
| | 'Knap Hill Yellow' (K) **new** | SHea |
| | 'Kobold' (EA) | SLdr |
| | 'Koichiro Wada' | see *R. yakushimanum* 'Koichiro Wada' |
| | 'Kokardia' | LMil NHim NLar |
| | 'Kokette' | IVic |
| | ***kongboense*** | WAbe |
| | 'Königstein' (EA) | LMil |
| § | 'Koningin Emma' (M) | GKin LMil NLar |
| | 'Konsonanz' **new** | IVic |
| | 'Koster's Brilliant Red' (M) | CSBt EPfP MGos SReu SSta |
| § | 'Kure-no-yuki' (EA/d) | LMil MAsh MMuc |
| | 'Lackblatt' | see *R.* (Volker Group) 'Lackblatt' |
| | ***lacteum*** | LMil MDun |
| | 'Lady Alice Fitzwilliam' ♀H2-3 | CBcs CMHG CMac CTsd GKin IDee LMil |
| | 'Lady Chamberlain Salmon Trout' | see *R.* 'Salmon Trout' |
| | 'Lady Clare' (K) **new** | SHea |
| | 'Lady Clementine Mitford' ♀H4 | CSBt CWri ECho EPfP GQui LMil MAsh MBri MDun MGos MLea MMuc SEND SHea SLdr SPer SReu |
| | 'Lady Eleanor Cathcart' | SHea SLdr |
| | 'Lady Linda' | MSnd |
| | 'Lady Louise' (EA) | SLdr |
| | 'Lady Robin' (EA) | SLdr |
| | 'Lady Romsey' ♀H4 | LMil MSnd SLdr |
| | 'Lamplighter' | SHea SReu |
| | ***lanatoides*** | LMil |
| § | ***lanatum*** | ECho LMil MDun |
| | – Flinckii Group | see *R. lanatum* |
| | 'Langworth' | CWri ECho GQui LMil MGos MLea MMuc MSnd SLdr SReu |
| | ***lanigerum*** | LMil MDun MSnd SReu |
| | 'Lanzette' | IVic |
| | 'Lapwing' (K) | SHea SLdr |
| | 'Late Love' (EA) | CDoC |
| | Laura Aberconway Group | SHea SLdr |
| | 'Lavender Brilliant' (EA) | SLdr |
| | 'Lavender Girl' ♀H4 | CMac LMil MSnd NMun SLdr SReu SSta |
| | 'Lavender Queen' | SPoG |
| | 'Lavendula' | IVic |
| | 'Lea Rainbow' | MLea |
| | 'Ledifolium' | see *R.* × *mucronatum* |
| | 'Ledifolium Album' | see *R.* × *mucronatum* |
| | 'Lee's Dark Purple' | CSBt CWri LMil WFar |
| | 'Lee's Scarlet' | LMil |
| | 'Lemon Dream' | LMil MAsh MDun NLar NPri SLdr SLim |
| | 'Lemon Lights' (A) | LMil |
| | 'Lemon Marmalade' | MDun |
| | 'Lemon Meringue' | LMil |
| | 'Lemonora' (M) | CBcs GKin |
| | 'Lem's 45' | CBcs CWri ECho SLdr |
| | 'Lem's Cameo' ♀H3 | LMil SReu SSta |
| | 'Lem's Monarch' ♀H4 | CBcs CDoC CWri ELon LMil MBri MGos MLea MMuc NHim SLdr SReu SSta |
| | 'Lem's Tangerine' | CDoC LMil |
| | 'Lemur' (EA) | ECho GEdr GLam MLea NBlu WThu |
| | 'Leni' | LRHS MAsh |
| | 'Leo' (EA) | GQui MSnd SLdr |
| | 'Leonardslee Giles' | SLdr |
| | 'Leonardslee Primrose' | SLdr |
| | Leonore Group | LMil |
| | ***lepidostylum*** | CBcs CMac LMil LRHS MDun SReu WFar |
| | ***lepidotum*** | MDun |
| | – yellow-flowered McB 110 | WThu |
| | ***leptopeplum*** **new** | NHim |
| | Letty Edwards Group | CSBt |
| § | 'Leucanthum' | WThu |
| | ***leucaspis*** | GGal MDun NMun SLdr WAbe |
| | 'Leuchtpolster' | IVic |
| | 'Lewis Monarch' | GQui |
| | 'Lila Pedigo' | CWri ECho MAsh MGos NHim SPer WFar |
| | 'Lilac Time' (EA) | SLdr |
| | 'Lilactina' **new** | SLdr |
| | 'Lilliput' (EA) | MAsh |
| | 'Lily Marleen' (EA) | CTri SCoo |
| | 'Linda' ♀H4 | CBcs CTri ECho EPfP LMil LRHS LSRN MAsh MBri MGos MMuc SLdr |
| I | 'Linda Lee' (EA) | SLdr |
| | 'Linda R' (EA) | NPri |
| | ***lindleyi*** | CBcs GQui NHim |

| | | |
|---|---|---|
| | – 'Dame Edith Sitwell' | LMil |
| | 'Linearifolium' | see *R. stenopetalum* 'Linearifolium' |
| | 'Linnet' (K/d) | SHea SLdr |
| | 'Lionel's First' | LMil |
| | Lionel's Triumph Group | LMil |
| | 'Lissabon' | IVic |
| | 'Little Beauty' (EA) | SLdr |
| | 'Little Ben' | ECho GEdr MDun |
| | 'Loch o' the Lowes' | MGos WFar |
| | 'Loch Rannoch' | WFar |
| | 'Lochinch Spinbur' | GQui |
| | Lodauric Group | SReu |
| § | 'Lodauric Iceberg' ♀H3-4 | LMil MSnd SReu |
| | 'Lodbrit' | SReu |
| | Loderi Group | SLdr |
| | 'Loderi Fairy Queen' | SLdr |
| | 'Loderi Game Chick' ♀H3-4 | SLdr SReu |
| | 'Loderi Georgette' | SLdr |
| | 'Loderi Helen' | SLdr |
| § | 'Loderi King George' ♀H3-4 | CBcs CDoC CHll CMac CSBt CWri ECho GKin IVic LMil MDun MGos MLea MSnd NLar SLdr SPer SReu SSta WGwG |
| | 'Loderi Patience' | SLdr |
| | 'Loderi Pink Coral' | LMil SLdr |
| | 'Loderi Pink Diamond' ♀H3-4 | CDoC CWri LMil SLdr |
| | 'Loderi Pink Topaz' ♀H3-4 | SLdr |
| | 'Loderi Pretty Polly' | CWri SLdr |
| | 'Loderi Princess Marina' | SLdr |
| | 'Loderi Sir Edmund' | MSnd SLdr |
| | 'Loderi Sir Joseph Hooker' | MSnd SLdr |
| | 'Loderi Titan' | SLdr SReu |
| | 'Loderi Venus' ♀H3-4 | MSnd SLdr SReu SSta |
| | 'Loderi White Diamond' | SLdr |
| | 'Loder's White' ♀H3-4 | CWri LMil MLea SHea SLdr SReu SSta |
| § | 'Logan Damaris' | SReu |
| | ***longesquamatum*** | MSnd |
| | ***longipes*** | LMil MSnd SLdr |
| | – EGM 336 | LMil |
| | – var. ***chienianum*** | MSnd |
| | ***lopsangianum*** | NHim |
| | 'Lord Roberts' ♀H4 | CBcs CDoC CMac CSBt CTri CWri ECho EPfP GAbr IVic LMil MAsh MGos MLea MMuc MSnd NEgg NLar SEND SHea SLdr SLim SPer SReu WFar WMoo |
| | 'Loreley' | IVic NLar |
| | 'Lori Eichelser' | GEdr |
| | 'Louis Pasteur' | SReu |
| | 'Louisa' (EA) | MAsh |
| | 'Louise Dowdle' (EA) | SLdr |
| | 'Lovely William' | CMac LMil MSnd SLdr |
| | 'Luisella' | IVic |
| | 'Lullaby' (EA) | SLdr |
| | 'Lunar Queen' | SLdr |
| | ***luteiflorum*** | MSnd |
| | ***lutescens*** | CBcs LMil MDun MSnd SLdr SReu SSta WAbe WThu |
| | – 'Bagshot Sands' ♀H3-4 | LMil SLdr |
| | – 'Exbury' | CPLG |
| | ***luteum*** (A) ♀H4 | Widely available |
| | × ***lysolepis*** | NMun |
| * | 'Mac Ovata' | CMac |
| | 'Macarena' | IVic |
| | ***maccabeanum*** ♀H3-4 | CBcs CDoC CWri GGar GKev GKin IDee LMil LRHS MDun MLea MMuc MSnd NLar NPCo SLdr SPer SReu SSpi SSta WFar |

| | | |
|---|---|---|
| | – Reuthe's form | SReu |
| | ***macranthum*** | see *R. indicum* 'Macranthum' |
| | 'Macranthum Roseum' (EA) | MMHG |
| | ***macrosmithii*** | see *R. argipeplum* |
| | ***maculiferum*** | NHim |
| | 'Madame Ad. van Hecke' (EA) | CTri GKin IVic LMil MAsh MBri MMuc SLdr SLim WFar |
| | 'Madame Galle' | NBlu |
| | 'Madame Masson' | CDoC CTri CWri ECho LMil LRHS MAsh MBri MDun MGos MLea MMuc MSnd NLar NPCo NPri SPer SReu SSta WFar |
| | ***maddenii*** | CDoC LMil |
| § | – subsp. ***crassum*** | CBcs CPLG GLin IVic MSnd SKHP SLdr |
| § | – subsp. ***maddenii*** Polyandrum Group | CBcs GGal GQui NMun |
| | 'Madeleine' (K) **new** | SHea |
| | 'Mademoiselle Masson' | WFar |
| | 'Maggie' | IVic |
| | 'Magic Flute' (EA) | LRHS MAsh MGos |
| I | 'Magic Flute' (V) | LMil SCoo |
| | 'Magnificum' (O) | SHea SLdr |
| | ***magnificum*** | SReu |
| | 'Mai-ogi' (EA) | IVic |
| | 'Maischnee' (EA) | IVic |
| | 'Maja' (G) | SReu SSta |
| § | ***makinoi*** ♀H4 | IDee LLHF LMil LRHS MDun NHim SReu SSpi SSta WAbe |
| | – 'Fuju-kaku-no-matsu' | MGos |
| | 'Makiyak' | LMil |
| | 'Malahat' | MSnd |
| | ***mallotum*** | IDee LMil LRHS MDun MSnd NHim NMun SReu |
| | 'Manda Sue' | MMuc |
| | Mandalay Group | SHea |
| | 'Mandarin Lights' (A) | LMil MBri |
| | 'Maraschino' (EA) | IVic |
| | 'Marathon Gold' **new** | IVic |
| | 'Marcel Ménard' | CDoC LMil LRHS MAsh NLar NPri SLdr SReu WFar |
| | 'Marchioness of Lansdowne' | SHea |
| | 'Mardi Gras' | CDoC NEgg NLar NPCo SLdr |
| | Margaret Dunn Group | CWri |
| | 'Margaret Falmouth' | SReu |
| | Margaret Findlay Group **new** | NMun |
| | 'Maricee' | WAbe |
| | 'Marie Curie' | LMil SReu |
| | 'Marie Hoffman' | LMil |
| | 'Marilee' (EA) | CDoC ECho ELon IVic LRHS MAsh MGos SLdr |
| | Mariloo Group | LMil MSnd |
| | 'Marina' (K) **new** | SHea |
| | 'Marion Merriman' (K) | SHea |
| | 'Marion Street' ♀H4 | LMil SReu |
| | 'Markeeta's Prize' ♀H4 | CDoC CWri ECho EPfP GAbr LMil LRHS MAsh MBri MDun MGos MLea MMuc NPri SHea SLdr SLim SReu |
| | 'Marley Hedges' | LMil |
| | 'Marlies' (A) | MBri SLdr |
| | 'Marmot' (EA) | ECho GLam MLea |
| | 'Mars' | SLdr |
| | 'Marsalla' | LMil |
| | 'Martha Hitchcock' (EA) | SRms |
| | 'Martha Isaacson' (Ad) ♀H4 | CWri LMil MGos SLdr SReu |
| | ***martinianum*** | SLdr |
| | 'Maruschka' (EA) | IVic LMil LRHS MAsh |
| | 'Mary Claire' (K) **new** | SHea |

| | Name | Suppliers |
|---|---|---|
| | 'Mary Helen' (EA) | LRHS MAsh SCoo SLim |
| | 'Mary Poppins' (K) | GKin LMil LSRN MAsh SCoo SLdr SLim WMoo |
| | 'Master of Elphinstone' (EA) | SLdr |
| | 'Matador' | IVic LMil MSnd SHea SLdr |
| | Matador Group | SReu |
| | 'Maxi' (EA) | IVic |
| § | 'Maxwellii' (EA) | CMac SLdr |
| | 'May Day' ♀H3-4 | CMac MAsh NEgg NLar SHea SLdr |
| | May Day Group | CBcs CWri MDun MGos MSnd |
| | 'Mayor Johnstone' | CTri MAsh NPri |
| | 'Mazurka' (K) | IVic SHea SLdr |
| | Medea Group | SLdr |
| | Medusa Group | SHea |
| | 'Megan' (EA) | ECho ELon LSRN MAsh MGos MMuc NLar SLdr WGwG |
| | ***megaphyllum*** | see *R. basilicum* |
| | ***megeratum*** | NHim SLdr |
| | - 'Bodnant' | ITim WAbe WThu |
| | ***mekongense*** | see *R. viridescens* Rubroluteum Group |
| | var. ***mekongense*** Rubroluteum Group | |
| | - - Viridescens Group | see *R. viridescens* |
| | 'Melford Lemon' | see *R.* 'Ilam Melford Lemon' |
| | 'Melidioso' | LMil |
| | 'Melina' (EA/d) | LMil |
| | 'Mendosina' | IVic |
| | ***mengtszense*** | MSnd |
| | 'Mephistopheles' (K) new | SHea |
| | 'Merganser' ♀H4 | GEdr LMil MLea SReu WThu |
| | 'Merlin' (EA) | SLdr |
| | ***metternichii*** | see *R. degronianum* subsp. *heptamerum* |
| | - var. ***pentamerum*** | see *R. degronianum* subsp. *degronianum* |
| | 'Mi Amor' | LMil |
| | 'Miami' (A) | SLdr |
| | 'Michael Hill' (EA) | MAsh |
| | 'Michael Waterer' | MSnd SLdr |
| | 'Michael's Pride' | CBcs GQui LMil |
| | ***micranthum*** | MDun |
| | ***microgynum*** | MSnd |
| | - Gymnocarpum Group | MSnd |
| | ***microleucum*** | see *R. orthocladum* var. *microleucum* |
| | 'Midnight Mystique' | MDun SReu |
| | 'Midsummer' | IVic SHea |
| | 'Midsummer Mermaid' (A) | LMil |
| | 'Mikado' (EA) | see *R. kaempferi* 'Mikado' |
| | 'Milton' (R) | LMil |
| | 'Mimi' (EA) | CMac |
| | 'Mindy's Love' | LMil MDun NHim |
| | 'Ming' | see *R.* 'Ilam Ming' |
| | 'Minikin' (K) new | SHea |
| | 'Minterne Cinnkeys' | MDun |
| | ***minus*** | GQui |
| | - var. ***minus*** (Carolinianum Group) 'Epoch' | LMil |
| | 'Miss Muffet' (EA) | SLdr |
| | 'Moerheim' ♀H4 | CBcs CWri ECho LRHS MGos MMuc NPCo NPri SLdr SLim SReu |
| § | 'Moerheim's Pink' | LMil MSnd SLdr |
| | 'Moidart' (Vs) | LMil |
| § | ***molle*** subsp. ***japonicum*** (A) | LMil |
| | - subsp. ***molle*** (A) | LMil |
| | ***mollicomum*** | NHim |
| | Mollis orange-flowered (M) | GKin SRms |
| | Mollis pink-flowered (M) | GKin NBlu SRms |
| | Mollis red-flowered (M) | GKin NBlu SRms |
| | Mollis salmon-flowered (M) | GQui |
| | Mollis yellow-flowered (M) | GKin GQui NBlu SRms |
| | 'Molly Ann' | ECho LSRN MGos MSnd NLar |
| | 'Molten Gold' (v) | LMil MAsh |
| § | 'Momoko' (EA) | MAsh |
| | ***monosematum*** | see *R. pachytrichum* var. *monosematum* |
| | ***montroseanum*** | CDoC LMil MDun MSnd NHim SLdr |
| | 'Moon Maiden' (EA) | ECho ELon GQui MMuc NLar SLdr |
| | 'Moonshine Bright' | MDun |
| | Moonstone Group | MLea |
| | 'Moonstone Pink' | MSnd SLdr |
| | 'Moonstone Yellow' | MSnd |
| | 'Moonwax' | SLdr |
| § | 'Morgenrot' | IVic MGos NLar SReu WFar |
| | ***morii*** | MDun |
| | 'Morning Cloud' ♀H4 | ECho EPfP LMil LRHS MAsh NHol SLdr SLim SReu |
| | 'Morning Magic' | MDun |
| | Morning Red | see *R.* 'Morgenrot' |
| | 'Moser's Maroon' | CWri ECho MGos MLea SLdr SPoG |
| | 'Motet' (K/d) | SHea |
| | 'Mother's Day' (EA) ♀H4 | CDoC CMac CSBt CTri ECho EPfP GKin GQui LMil LRHS LSRN MAsh MBri MGos MMuc NBlu NEgg NHol NPCo NPri SEND SLdr SLim SPer SPoG SReu SSta WFar |
| | 'Mount Everest' | LMil SReu SSta |
| | 'Mount Rainier' (K) | SLdr |
| | 'Mount Saint Helens' (A) | LMil NLar SLdr SLim |
| | 'Mount Seven Star' | see *R. nakaharae* 'Mount Seven Star' |
| | ***moupinense*** | GLin MSnd SLdr SReu |
| | 'Mrs A.C. Kenrick' | SHea SLdr |
| | 'Mrs A.T. de la Mare' ♀H4 | CWri LMil MDun SHea SReu SSta |
| | 'Mrs Betty Robertson' | CMac ECho MGos MMuc SLdr |
| | 'Mrs Charles E. Pearson' ♀H4 | CSBt LMil MSnd NLar SHea SLdr |
| | 'Mrs Davies Evans' ♀H4 | CWri SReu SSta |
| | 'Mrs Donald Graham' | SReu |
| | 'Mrs E.C. Stirling' | SRms |
| | 'Mrs Emil Hager' (EA) | SLdr |
| | 'Mrs Furnivall' ♀H4 | CBcs CDoC CWri ECho LMil MGos MLea MMuc NLar SLdr SReu |
| | 'Mrs G.W. Leak' | CSBt LMil MDun MLea SHea SReu |
| | 'Mrs J.C. Williams' ♀H4 | LMil |
| | 'Mrs J.G. Millais' | LMil SHea |
| | 'Mrs James Horlick' | CWri |
| | 'Mrs Kingsmill' | SLdr |
| | 'Mrs Lionel de Rothschild' ♀H4 | CWri SReu |
| | 'Mrs P.D. Williams' | SReu |
| | 'Mrs Peter Koster' (M) | SLdr WFar |
| | 'Mrs R.S. Holford' ♀H4 | MSnd SHea SLdr |
| | 'Mrs T.H. Lowinsky' ♀H4 | CDoC CMac CSBt ECho GKin LMil MAsh MDun MGos MLea MMuc MSnd NHim NLar SEND SHea SLdr SLim SPer SReu SSta |
| § | × ***mucronatum*** (EA) | CBcs MSnd SLdr SRms |
| | 'Mucronatum' | see *R.* × *mucronatum* |
| | ***mucronulatum*** | CBcs MSnd |
| | - B&SWJ 786 | WCru |
| | - 'Cornell Pink' ♀H4 | WFar |
| | 'Muncaster Hybrid' | NMun |
| | 'Muncaster Mist' | MSnd |
| | 'Nabucco' (A) | EPfP MMuc SEND |
| | ***nakaharae*** (EA) | MSnd NHim SLdr SReu WAbe |
| | - 'Mariko' (EA) | WAbe WThu |
| § | - 'Mount Seven Star' (EA) ♀H4 | ECho LMil MGos NWad SLdr WAbe |
| § | - orange-flowered (EA) | ECho LMil LRHS MAsh MGos MMuc SLdr SReu |

| | Name | Suppliers |
|---|---|---|
| | - pink-flowered (EA) | ECho MGos MMuc NLar SLdr SPer SReu SSta |
| | - red-flowered (EA) | ECho MGos |
| | 'Nakahari Orange' | see *R. nakaharae* orange-flowered |
| | ***nakotiltum*** | MSnd |
| | 'Nancor' | CBcs |
| | 'Nancy' (EA) | MAsh |
| | 'Nancy Buchanan' (K) | SLdr |
| | 'Nancy Evans' ♀H3-4 | CDoC CSBt ECho EPfP GKin LMil LSRN MAsh MDun MLea NLar NPCo NPri SBrd SLdr SLim SReu SSpi WFar |
| | 'Nancy of Robinhill' (EA) | SReu |
| | 'Nancy Waterer' (G) ♀H4 | EPfP LMil NLar SPoG SReu |
| | 'Nanki Poo' (EA) | SLdr |
| | 'Naomi' (EA) | GQui MSnd SLdr |
| | Naomi Group | CWri MSnd |
| | 'Naomi Hope' | LMil |
| | 'Naomi Nautilus' | LMil |
| | 'Naomi Pink Beauty' | LMil |
| | 'Narcissiflorum' (G/d) ♀H4 | CSBt EPfP GKin LMil NLar SReu SSta |
| | 'Naselle' | SReu |
| | 'Nassau' (EA/d) | LMil |
| | ***neriiflorum*** | MDun MSnd |
| § | - subsp. ***phaedropum*** | MDun |
| | 'Nestor' | SReu |
| | 'Netty Koster' | SLdr |
| | 'Newcomb's Sweetheart' | LMil |
| | 'Niagara' (EA) ♀H3-4 | CMac LMil MGos SLdr SPoG |
| | 'Nichola' (EA) | LSRN |
| | 'Nico' (EA) | CMac LRHS MAsh |
| | 'Nicoletta' | IVic LMil LRHS |
| | 'Night Sky' | CDoC ECho LMil LRHS MAsh MDun MGos MMuc MSnd NLar NPCo SLdr |
| | 'Nightingale' | SReu |
| | ***nilagiricum*** | see *R. arboreum* subsp. *nilagiricum* |
| | 'Nishiki' (EA) | CMac |
| | ***nitens*** | see *R. calostrotum* subsp. *riparium* Nitens Group |
| | ***nitidulum*** var. ***omeiense*** | MSnd |
| § | ***nivale*** subsp. ***nivale*** | ITim |
| | ***niveum*** ♀H4 | LMil MSnd NHim SReu |
| | - B&SWJ 2611 | WCru |
| | - B&SWJ 2659 | WCru |
| | - B&SWJ 2675 | WCru |
| | ***nobleanum*** | see *R.* Nobleanum Group |
| § | Nobleanum Group | LMil MLea MSnd SLdr SSta |
| | 'Nobleanum Album' | LMil SReu SSta |
| | 'Nobleanum Coccineum' | SReu |
| | 'Nobleanum Venustum' | CSBt LMil SReu SSta |
| | 'Nordlicht' (EA) | SLdr |
| | 'Norfolk Candy' | LMil LRHS MDun NLar |
| | 'Noriko' (EA) | SLdr |
| N | 'Norma' (R/d) ♀H4 | SReu |
| | 'Northern Hi-Lights' (A) | GKin LMil MBri NLar SLdr SLim |
| | 'Nova Zembla' | CBcs CDoC CTri ECho EPfP LMil LRHS MAsh MGos MMuc NEgg SEND SLim SPer SPoG SReu SSta |
| | ***nudiflorum*** | see *R. periclymenoides* |
| | ***nudipes*** | LMil |
| | ***nuttallii*** | GLin LMil |
| | 'Oban' | GEdr GLam WAbe WThu |
| | Obtusum Group (EA) | MSnd SLdr |
| | - 'Amoenum' (EA/d) | CBcs CDoC CMac CSBt ECho LMil MGos MSnd NMun SBfd SLdr SPer WFar |
| N | - 'Hinomayo' (EA) ♀H3-4 | CMac CTri EPfP GKin GQui LMil MSnd NHim NMun SLdr SReu |
| | ***occidentale*** (A) ♀H4 | GGal GKin LMil MDun SHea |
| | - SIN 1830 | GLin |
| | ***ochraceum*** | LMil |
| | 'Odee Wright' | CTri CWri LRHS MAsh SLdr |
| | 'Odoratum' (Ad) | MLea |
| | 'Oh! Kitty' | CWri ECho MLea NPCo SLdr |
| | 'Old Copper' | CWri |
| | 'Old Gold' (K) | ECho SHea SLdr SReu |
| | 'Old Port' ♀H4 | CWri LMil |
| | 'Olga' ♀H4 | CBcs LMil SHea SReu SSta |
| | 'Olga Niblett' (EA) | SReu |
| | 'Olin O. Dobbs' | IVic |
| | 'Olive' | SLdr |
| | 'Olympic Flame' (EA) | LMil |
| | 'Olympic Sunrise' | LMil |
| § | 'One Thousand Butterflies' | MSnd SLdr |
| | 'Ophelia' (EA) | SLdr |
| | 'Orange Beauty' (EA) ♀H3-4 | CBcs CDoC CMac CSBt ECho MAsh MGos MSnd SLdr SReu WFar |
| | 'Orange Flirt' | MDun |
| | 'Orange King' (EA) | LMil MGos SPoG |
| | 'Orange Sunset' | MDun |
| | 'Orangeade' (K) | SHea |
| | ***orbiculare*** ♀H3-4 | LMil MSnd NMun |
| § | - subsp. ***cardiobasis*** | NHim |
| | - Sandling Park form | SReu |
| | 'Orchid Lights' | LRHS MAsh |
| | 'Oregon' (EA) | SLdr |
| | Oregonia Group | LMil |
| | ***oreodoxa*** | LMil |
| § | - var. ***fargesii*** ♀H4 | LMil MSnd |
| | - var. ***oreodoxa*** | LMil |
| | ***oreotrephes*** | CBcs IVic LMil MSnd SHea SLdr SReu |
| § | - Exquisitum Group | SLdr |
| | - 'Pentland' | LMil |
| | 'Orient' (K) | SHea |
| § | ***orthocladum*** var. ***microleucum*** | GKev WThu |
| | 'Oryx' (O) | SHea SLdr |
| | 'Osaraku Seedling' (EA) | EPfP LRHS |
| | 'Osmar' ♀H4 | MGos MSnd SReu |
| | 'Ostara' | MDun MGos |
| | 'Osterschnee' | IVic |
| | 'Oudijk's Favorite' | SLdr |
| | 'Oudijk's Sensation' | CBcs CWri ECho GQui MAsh MGos MMuc NHim NPCo SEND SHea SLdr |
| | ***ovatum*** | MSnd |
| | 'Oxydol' (K) | IVic MMuc SHea SLdr |
| | ***pachysanthum*** ♀H4 | CDoC CWri GKin IDee LMil MDun MSnd NMun SLdr SReu SSpi |
| | - 'Crosswater' | LMil LRHS MDun NLar |
| | ***pachysanthum*** × ***yakushimanum*** | SReu |
| | ***pachytrichum*** | NHim SLdr |
| § | - var. ***monosematum*** | MSnd |
| | 'Pacific Gold' | MDun |
| | 'Palestrina' (EA) ♀H3-4 | CBcs CMac CSBt ECho EPfP GKin MAsh MGos MMuc NLar NPCo SEND SLdr SPer SReu SSta WFar |
| | 'Pallas' (G) | GKin SReu |
| | ***paludosum*** | see *R. nivale* subsp. *nivale* |
| | 'Pancake' | CMac |
| | 'Panda' (EA) ♀H4 | CSBt CTri ECho EPfP GLam LMil LRHS MAsh MLea NPri SReu |
| | 'Papaya Punch' | LMil |

'Paprika Spiced' CWri ECho LMil MAsh MDun MGos MLea NHim NLar NPCo SLdr WFar
'Parkfeuer' (A) IVic LMil
***parmulatum*** LMil
- KW 5876 LMil
'Patty Bee' ♀H4 CBcs CSBt CTri CWri ECho EPfP EPot GEdr GGar GKev GLam IDee ITim LMil LRHS MAsh MBri MDun MGos MLea NLar NPri SLdr SLim SPoG SReu SSpi SSta WFar
***patulum*** see *R. pemakoense* Patulum Group
'Pavane' (K) SHea
'Peep-bo' (EA) SLdr
'Peeping Tom' MDun SReu
***pemakoense*** CSBt MSnd SLdr SReu WThu
§ - Patulum Group SLdr
'Pemakofairy' WAbe WThu
Penelope Group SReu
'Penheale Blue' ♀H4 CWri GKin LMil MDun
'Penny Tomlin' SReu SSta
***pentaphyllum*** (A) LMil NMun
'Percy Wiseman' ♀H4 CBcs CDoC CSBt CWri ECho EPfP GGar GKin LMil LRHS MAsh MBri MGos MLea MMuc MSnd NEgg SLdr SLim SPer SPoG SReu SSta WFar
'Perfect Lady' LMil
§ ***periclymenoides*** (A) GKev LMil
'Persil' (K) ♀H4 CBcs CMac CSBt CTri CWri ECho EPfP GKev GKin LMil LRHS MAsh MBri MDun MGos MLea MMuc NBlu NLar SCoo SEND SLdr SReu SSta
'Peter Gable' (EA) SLdr
'Peter John Mezitt' see *R.* (PJM Group) 'Peter John Mezitt'
'Peter Koster' (hybrid) GKin SLdr WFar
'Peter Koster' (M) SHea WFar
'Petrouchka' (K) SHea
***phaedropum*** see *R. neriiflorum* subsp. *phaedropum*
***phaeochrysum*** MSnd SLdr
- var. ***agglutianum*** **new** NHim
§ - var. ***levistratum*** MSnd SLdr
'Phalarope' GEdr GLam SLdr SReu
'Phyllis Korn' CWri LMil LTen SLdr
'Picotee' (K) **new** LMil
§ ***piercei*** LMil MSnd
Pilgrim Group LMil
'Pineapple Delight' MDun
***pingianum*** SLdr
'Pink Bride' SLdr
'Pink Cameo' CWri
'Pink Cherub' ♀H4 ECho ELon LMil MAsh SLdr SReu
'Pink Delight' GQui MAsh
I 'Pink Delight' (K) GKin MBri MGos NLar SHea SLdr
'Pink Delight' (V) MMuc
'Pink Drift' CSBt ECho LMil MDun MGos MMuc NPCo SLdr SPer
'Pink Gin' LMil LRHS NHim
'Pink Mimosa' (Vs) SLdr
'Pink Pancake' (EA) ♀H4 ECho ELon EPfP GKin LMil LRHS MAsh MGos MMuc NPri SBrd SLdr
'Pink Pearl' (EA) see *R.* 'Azuma-kagami'
'Pink Pearl' (hybrid) CBcs CMac CSBt CTri CWri ECho EPfP LMil MAsh MBri MGos MMuc MSnd NLar NPri SHea SLdr SPer SPoG SReu SSta WFar
'Pink Pebble' ♀H3-4 CBcs CPLG ELon MLea SLdr
'Pink Perfection' CMac MGos MSnd SHea SLdr WFar
'Pink Polar Bear' GKin LMil LRHS
'Pink Rosette' LMil
'Pink Ruffles' (K) SHea SLdr
'Pinkerton' LMil
'Pintail' LMil LRHS MAsh
'Pippa' (EA) CMac
'PJM Elite' NLar
§ (PJM Group) 'Peter John Mezitt' ♀H4 SLdr
'PJM Regal' IVic
'Pleasant White' (EA) NMun
***pocophorum*** MSnd NHim
§ - var. ***hemidartum*** MSnd
'Point Defiance' CWri ECho LMil MDun MSnd
'Polar Bear' ♀H3-4 CBcs CHll CSBt GKin IVic LMil LRHS MGos NHim SLdr SReu
'Polar Bear' (EA) MDun SLdr
Polar Bear Group CWri ECho LMil MLea MSnd
'Polaris' see *R.* 'Hachmann's Polaris'
'Polaris' (EA) LRHS SReu
'Polarnacht' CDoC GKin LMil LRHS MAsh
***poluninii*** KR 8231 LMil
***polyandrum*** see *R. maddenii* subsp. *maddenii* Polyandrum Group
§ ***polycladum*** Scintillans Group SLdr
***polylepis*** MSnd
'Polynesian Sunset' MDun
***ponticum*** CBcs CDul CMac CTri CWri MGos SBfd WFar
- 'Foliis Purpureis' SReu
§ - 'Variegatum' (v) CBcs CMac CSBt CTri EPfP LMil LRHS MAsh MDun MGos MLea MSnd NPri SBfd SBrd SLdr SPoG SRms SSta WFar
'Popocatapetl' SReu
'Praecox' ♀H4 CBcs CSBt ECho ELon EPfP GKev GKin LMil LRHS MAsh MDun MGos MMuc NBlu NLar NPri SLdr SLim SPer SPoG SReu SSta WFar
***praestans*** GKin IDee LMil MDun MSnd SLdr
***prattii*** NHim
- 'Perry Wood' LMil
***preptum*** SLdr
'President Roosevelt' (v) CSBt EPfP GKin LRHS MAsh MDun MGos MLea NMun NPri SPer SPoG SReu WFar
'Pridenjoy' LMil
***primuliflorum*** MSnd WAbe
- 'Doker-La' LMil
'Prince Camille de Rohan' LMil SHea
'Princess Alice' CBcs SLdr WAbe
'Princess Anne' ♀H4 CBcs CMHG ECho GEdr LMil MAsh MDun MGos MLea NMun SLdr SLim SPer SPoG SReu SSta
'Princess Galadriel' SLdr
'Princess Juliana' ECho MGos MMuc
'Princess Margaret of Windsor' (K) GQui LMil
***principis*** LMil SLdr
- 'Lost Horizon' CDoC LMil MSnd SLdr
§ - Vellereum Group SLdr
§ ***prinophyllum*** (A) GKin LMil LRHS
'Prins Bernhard' (EA) SLdr
'Prinses Juliana' (EA) MMuc SLdr SReu WFar
'Professor Hugo de Vries' ♀H4 SHea SLdr
***prostratum*** see *R. saluenense* subsp. *chameunum* Prostratum Group
§ ***protistum*** var. ***giganteum*** SReu

| Name | Suppliers |
|---|---|
| ***prunifolium*** (A) | LMil |
| ***przewalskii*** | MSnd |
| ***pseudochrysanthum*** ♀H4 | IDee LMil MSnd SReu |
| 'Psyche' (EA) | MDun |
| 'Ptarmigan' ♀H3-4 | ECho GEdr GLam LMil MAsh MGos MMuc MSnd NPri SLdr SReu WFar WPat |
| ***pubicostatum*** | GLin MSnd |
| § 'Pucella' (G) ♀H4 | CWri |
| 'Pulchrum Maxwellii' | see *R.* 'Maxwellii' |
| ***pumilum*** | GKev WAbe WThu |
| 'Puncta' | SLdr |
| 'Purple Cushion' (EA) | LRHS MAsh NPri |
| 'Purple Diamond' | see *R.* Diamant Group purple-flowered |
| 'Purple Gem' | SPoG |
| purple Glenn Dale (EA) | SLdr |
| 'Purple Heart' | LMil |
| 'Purple Passion' PBR **new** | SLdr |
| 'Purple Queen' (EA/d) | MAsh |
| 'Purple Splendor' (EA) | CMac MMuc SLdr |
| 'Purple Splendour' ♀H4 | CBcs CSBt CWri ECho ELon EPfP GAbr LMil MDun MGos MLea MMuc NEgg NPCo SLdr SPer SReu SSta WFar |
| 'Purple Triumph' (EA) ♀H3 | LMil SLdr SSta |
| 'Purpurtraum' (EA) ♀H4 | IVic LMil |
| 'Quail' | LMil SLdr |
| Quaver Group | SRms |
| 'Queen Alice' | LMil MDun NLar |
| Queen Emma | see *R.* 'Koningin Emma' |
| 'Queen Louise' (K) **new** | SHea |
| 'Queen of Hearts' | LMil SHea SLdr SReu |
| 'Queen Souriya' | SReu |
| 'Quentin Metsys' (R) | SLdr SReu SSta |
| ***quinquefolium*** (A) | LMil MSnd |
| 'Rabatz' **new** | LMil |
| 'Raby' (A) | LMil |
| ***racemosum*** ♀H4 | CBcs LMil MDun MSnd SLdr |
| - 'Rock Rose' ♀H3-4 | LMil |
| 'Racine' (G) | SLdr SReu SSta |
| ***radicans*** | see *R. calostrotum* subsp. *keleticum* Radicans Group |
| 'Radistrotum' | IVic |
| 'Raimunde' (K) | IVic |
| 'Ramapo' ♀H4 | CDoC ECho EPfP GKev LMil LRHS MAsh MBri MDun MGos MSnd SLdr SLim SPer SReu |
| 'Raoul Millais' | LMil |
| 'Raphael de Smet' (G/d) | SReu |
| 'Razorbill' ♀H4 | CDoC ECho GKin LMil MGos SLdr SLim |
| ***recurvoides*** | IDee LMil MDun MSnd SLdr SReu |
| ***recurvum*** | see *R. roxieanum* var. *roxieanum* |
| 'Red Dawn' | LRHS |
| 'Red Delicious' | CWri LMil SLdr |
| 'Red Diamond' | see *R.* Diamant Group red-flowered |
| 'Red Fountain' (EA) | ECho MMuc |
| 'Red Jack' | CWri LMil |
| 'Red Pimpernel' (EA) | ELan SLdr |
| 'Red Sunset' (A) | SLdr |
| 'Red Velour' | MSnd SLdr |
| 'Redwing' (EA) | CDoC MAsh SLdr |
| 'Rennie' (A) | ECho GKin MGos MLea MMuc SHea |
| 'Renoir' ♀H4 | CSBt LMil SLdr SReu |
| ***reticulatum*** (A) | LMil MSnd SReu |
| 'Reuthe's Purple' | SReu WAbe WThu |
| 'Rêve d'Amour' (Vs) | MDun SReu SSta |
| ***rex*** | CDoC GKin LMil MDun SLdr |

| Name | Suppliers |
|---|---|
| - EGM 295 | LMil |
| § - subsp. ***fictolacteum*** ♀H3-4 | CDoC GKin IDee LMil LRHS MDun MSnd NHim NLar NMun SLdr SReu |
| - - Miniforme Group | MDun |
| - subsp. ***gratum*** | LMil |
| - subsp. ***rex*** ♀H3-4 **new** | MSnd |
| ***rex × yakushimanum*** | SReu |
| 'Rex' (EA) | MAsh SLdr SPoG WFar |
| 'Ria Hardijzer' | LMil |
| 'Ribera' (R) | SLdr |
| ***rigidum*** | GLin |
| * - ***album*** | LMil |
| 'Ring of Fire' | CWri ECho IVic LMil MDun MGos MLea MSnd NHim SLdr |
| 'Ripe Corn' | MSnd |
| 'Ripples' (EA) | CTrh |
| ***ririei*** | LMil SLdr SReu |
| - AC 2036 | LMil |
| 'Robert Croux' | MSnd SLdr |
| 'Robert Seleger' | GKin LMil LRHS MAsh MMuc SReu |
| 'Robert Whelan' (A) | SReu |
| 'Robin Hill Frosty' (EA) | SLdr |
| 'Robin Hill Gillie' (EA) | SLdr |
| 'Robinette' | CBcs CWri ECho MAsh |
| 'Rocket' | CDoC CTri ECho MAsh MGos MLea MMuc SHea SLdr SLim SPoG |
| 'Roehr's Peggy Ann' (EA) | IVic LMil |
| 'Rokoko' | see *R.* 'Hachmann's Rokoko' |
| (Romany Chai Group) 'Romany Chai' | SHea |
| 'Romany Chal' | SHea |
| 'Rosa' (EA) | LMil LRHS |
| 'Rosa Mundi' | CSBt |
| Rosalind Group | CMac |
| 'Rosalinda' (EA) | SLdr |
| 'Rosata' (Vs) ♀H4 | GKin SLdr SReu SSta |
| 'Rose Bud' | CSBt CTri |
| 'Rose Elf' | WThu |
| 'Rose Glow' (A) | SReu |
| 'Rose Gown' | SReu |
| 'Rose Greeley' (EA) | CDoC ECho GQui SLdr SLim SPer SReu WFar WGwG |
| 'Rose Haze' (Vs) | SLdr SReu |
| 'Rose Torch' (A) | SReu |
| 'Rosebud' (EA/d) ♀H3-4 | CBcs CMac MGos NHol SLdr SReu |
| ***roseum*** | see *R. prinophyllum* |
| 'Roseum Elegans' | CDoC MAsh SLdr SLim WFar |
| 'Rosy Dream' | CWri ECho MAsh MMuc MSnd |
| 'Rosy Fire' (A) | LMil SReu |
| 'Rosy Lea' | MLea |
| 'Rosy Lights' (A) | CTri LMil NLar SLdr |
| 'Rotglocke' | IVic |
| 'Rothenburg' | SLdr |
| ***rothschildii*** | CDoC IDee LMil MSnd NHim SLdr |
| 'Rotkäppchen' | IVic |
| 'Rouge' | SHea |
| ***roxieanum*** | LMil MSnd SLdr |
| - var. ***oreonastes*** ♀H4 | LMil MSnd SSta |
| - - Nymans form | SReu |
| § - var. ***roxieanum*** | NHim |
| 'Royal Command' (K) | CTri CWri GKin LMil SHea |
| 'Royal Lodge' (K) | SHea |
| 'Royal Mail' | SHea |
| 'Royal Ruby' (K) | CWri ECho MAsh MGos MMuc SHea SLdr |
| 'Roza Stevenson' | LMil |
| 'Rubicon' | CWri ECho GQui MAsh MMuc MSnd SLdr |
| ***rubiginosum*** | CBcs LMil MSnd NHim |
| - SDR 5142 | GKev |

| Name | Suppliers |
|---|---|
| § – Desquamatum Group | CBcs SLdr |
| – pink-flowered | LMil |
| – white-flowered | LMil |
| 'Rubinetta' (EA) | LMil WFar |
| ***rubroluteum*** | see *R. viridescens* Rubroluteum Group |
| 'Ruby F. Bowman' | SReu |
| 'Ruby Hart' | CBcs LSRN MMuc MSnd SReu |
| 'Ruddy Duck' (K) new | SHea |
| 'Rumba' (K) | SHea |
| ***russatum*** ♀H4 | EPfP LMil MDun MSnd NMun SLdr SSpi WFar |
| – blue-black-flowered | GKin LMil |
| – 'Purple Pillow' | CSBt |
| Russautinii Group | MSnd SLdr |
| Russellianum Group | GGal |
| ***russotinctum*** | see *R. alutaceum* var. *russotinctum* |
| 'Ryde Heron' (EA) | SLdr |
| 'Sabina' (EA) | SLdr |
| 'Sacko' | CWri LLHF LMil MAsh MDun SLim |
| 'Saffron Queen' | CBcs CTsd MMuc SLdr |
| 'Sahara' (K) | LMil SHea |
| 'Saint Breward' | GQui MDun MSnd NMun SLdr |
| 'Saint Merryn' ♀H4 | CBcs CWri ECho MDun MMuc SLdr |
| 'Saint Minver' | SLdr |
| 'Saint Tudy' | MDun SLdr |
| 'Salmon Queen' (M) | WFar |
| 'Salmon Sander' (EA) | SLdr |
| § 'Salmon Trout' | LMil |
| 'Salmon's Leap' (EA/v) | CMac CSBt LMil LRHS MAsh MBri SLdr SReu WFar |
| ***saluenense*** | LMil MSnd SLdr WThu |
| § – subsp. ***chameunum*** | GKev |
| § – – Prostratum Group | WAbe |
| 'Sammetglut' | CWri |
| 'Samuel Taylor Coleridge' (M) | GKin NLar |
| 'Sang de Gentbrugge' (G) | SReu |
| ***sanguineum*** | LMil MDun MSnd SLdr |
| § – subsp. ***didymum*** | MDun MSnd |
| – subsp. ***sanguineum*** var. ***haemaleum*** | LMil MSnd |
| – – – F 21732 | CWri |
| – – var. ***himertum*** R 1006 | MSnd |
| – – var. ***sanguineum*** F 25521 | LMil |
| 'Santa Maria' (EA) | ECho ELon LMil LSRN MBri MGos SLdr SReu SSta |
| 'Sapphire' | MAsh MDun SRms WThu |
| 'Sappho' | CBcs CMac CSBt CWri ECho EPfP GBin GKin LMil MDun MGos MLea MSnd NEgg NPCo SLdr SPer SReu SSta WFar WGwG |
| 'Sapporo' | LMil |
| 'Sarah Boscawen' | SReu |
| ***sargentianum*** | NHar WAbe WThu |
| 'Sarled' ♀H4 | GLam ITim LMil NHar SHea WPat WThu |
| Sarled Group | SRms WAbe |
| 'Saroi' (EA) | SLdr |
| 'Satan' (K) ♀H4 | CSBt MDun SHea SReu |
| § 'Satschiko' (EA) ♀H4 | CSBt LRHS MAsh MGos NBlu NHim NMun SLdr |
| 'Satsop Surprise' | SLdr |
| Satsuki type (EA) | ECho SLdr |
| 'Saturnus' (M) | GKin |
| § ***scabrifolium*** var. ***spiciferum*** | NMun SLdr WAbe |
| 'Scandinavia' | SHea |
| 'Scarlet Pimpernel' (K) | SHea |
| 'Scarlet Wonder' ♀H4 | CBcs CDoC CMHG CSBt CWri ECho EPfP GAbr GKev GKin LMil LRHS MAsh MBri MDun MGos NBlu NPri SHea SLdr SPoG SReu WFar |
| 'Sceptre' (K) new | SHea |
| ***schistocalyx*** F 17637 | MSnd |
| ***schlippenbachii*** (A) | LMil MSnd SLdr |
| – 'Sid's Royal Pink' (A) | LMil |
| 'Schneeperle' (EA) | LMil LRHS SBrd |
| ***scintillans*** | see *R. polycladum* Scintillans Group |
| 'Scintillation' | CWri LMil LTen MAsh MBri MGos MLea MMuc MSnd NLar SLdr |
| ***scopulorum*** | MMuc SLdr |
| 'Scout' (EA) | MAsh NMun SLdr |
| ***scyphocalyx*** | see *R. dichroanthum* subsp. *scyphocalyx* |
| 'Seb' | SLdr |
| 'Second Honeymoon' | CBcs CWri ECho MLea MSnd NHim SLdr WFar |
| 'Seikai' (EA) | SLdr |
| ***seinghkuense*** CCH&H 8106 | LMil |
| § ***selense*** subsp. ***dasycladum*** | MSnd |
| ***semibarbatum*** | GLin |
| ***semnoides*** | LMil SLdr |
| 'Sennocke' | LMil |
| 'September Song' | CBcs CMac CSBt CWri ECho GAbr LMil LRHS MAsh MDun MGos MLea MMuc NHol NLar NPCo SEND SLdr WFar |
| ***serotinum*** | GLin LMil |
| ***serpyllifolium*** (A) | CBcs NMun SLdr |
| 'Sesterianum' | CMHG SLdr |
| 'Seta' | CAbP CBcs SHea SLdr WThu |
| Seta Group | SReu |
| 'Seven Stars' | CSBt |
| 'Seville' | SHea |
| 'Shamrock' | CDoC EPfP GEdr GLam LRHS MAsh MBri MGos MLea NBlu NEgg NMun SLdr SLim SPoG WFar |
| 'Shanty' (K/d) | SHea |
| 'Sheila' (EA) | CSBt MAsh NPri |
| 'Shelley' (EA) new | LSRN |
| ***sherriffii*** | MSnd |
| 'Shiko' (EA) | MAsh |
| 'Shiko Lavender' (A) | SPoG |
| Shilsonii Group | LMil SReu |
| 'Shi-no-noe' (EA) | SLdr |
| 'Shrimp Girl' | GKin MAsh MDun MSnd SLdr |
| ***sichotense*** | GAuc |
| ***siderophyllum*** | GLin MSnd NMun |
| ***sikangense*** | MSnd SLdr |
| – var. ***exquisitum*** | GLin |
| § – var. ***sikangense*** Cookeanum Group | SLdr |
| 'Silbervelours' | IVic |
| § 'Silberwolke' ♀H4 | IVic LMil MAsh SReu |
| Silver Cloud | see *R.* 'Silberwolke' |
| 'Silver Edge' | see *R. ponticum* 'Variegatum' |
| 'Silver Glow' (EA) | CMac |
| 'Silver Jubilee' ♀H4 | CBcs LMil |
| 'Silver Moon' (EA) | SLdr SPer |
| 'Silver Queen' (EA) | ECho ELon LMil MGos NEgg SLdr SPer |
| 'Silver Sixpence' | CBcs CSBt ECho EPfP LRHS LSRN MAsh MBri MGos MMuc MSnd NPCo SEND SLdr |

| | |
|---|---|
| 'Silver Skies' | LMil |
| 'Silver Slipper' (K) ♀H4 | CBcs GKin LMil MAsh MLea NHol NLar SHea SLdr SPoG SReu SSta WFar |
| 'Silverwood' (K) | LMil |
| 'Silvester' (EA) | CTri LMil LRHS MAsh MBri MGos NMun SLdr SReu |
| 'Simona' | LMil SReu |
| ***simsii*** (EA) | CMac LMil SLdr |
| ***sinofalconeri*** | GGar LMil |
| - KR 7342 | LMil |
| - SEH 229 | LMil |
| ***sinogrande*** ♀H3 | CAbb CBcs CDoC CHEx CHll CWri ELon GGar GKin IDee LMil LRHS MDun MLea MMuc NLar NMun NPCo SLdr SPer WFar |
| - KR 4027 | GAbr LMil |
| 'Sir Charles Lemon' ♀H3-4 | CDoC CWri ECho GAbr LMil MAsh MGos MLea MSnd NMun NPCo SHea SLdr SPer SReu |
| 'Sir Robert' (EA) | MAsh SLdr |
| 'Sleepy' | CBcs CSBt ECho MAsh MGos MSnd |
| ***smirnowii*** | IDee LMil MSnd SReu |
| ***smithii*** | see *R. argipeplum* |
| § Smithii Group | CWri |
| 'Sneezy' | CBcs CSBt CWri ECho EPfP LMil LRHS MAsh MGos MSnd SLdr SLim WFar |
| 'Snipe' | CBcs CTri ECho GEdr LMil LRHS MAsh MBri MGos SLdr SLim SReu |
| 'Snow' (EA) | SLdr |
| 'Snow Crown' (*lindleyi* hybrid) | MAsh MLea |
| 'Snow Hill' (EA) | GQui LMil MGos SLdr |
| 'Snow Lady' | CBcs ECho EPfP EPot GEdr GGar GKin GLam GQui MAsh MDun MGos MMuc SLdr SPoG SReu |
| 'Snow Pearl' | MAsh |
| 'Snow Queen' | ELan LMil |
| Snow Queen Group | SReu |
| 'Snowbird' (A) | GGal LMil SLdr |
| 'Snowflake' (EA/d) | see *R.* 'Kure-no-yuki' |
| 'Snowstorm' | MMuc NPCo |
| 'Snowwhite' (EA) | LMil LRHS |
| 'Soft Lips' (K) **new** | SHea |
| 'Soho' (EA) | GQui |
| 'Soir de Paris' (Vs) | CSBt GKin IVic LMil MBri MDun MLea MMuc NLar SEND SLdr SReu SSta WFar WGwG |
| 'Soldier Sam' | SReu |
| 'Solidarity' | ECho MAsh MBri MGos SLdr WBor |
| 'Solway' (Vs) | LMil |
| 'Sommerduft' (A) | IVic |
| 'Son de Paris' (A) | GQui |
| 'Sonata' | CWri GGal MDun SReu |
| 'Songbird' | LMil MAsh MSnd SLdr |
| 'Sophie Hedges' (K/d) | SLdr |
| ***sororium*** (V) | LMil |
| - KR 3085 | LMil |
| ***souliei*** | IDee LMil SSpi |
| 'Southern Cross' | SLdr |
| 'Souvenir de D.A. Koster' | SLdr |
| 'Souvenir de Doctor S. Endtz' ♀H4 | SHea SLdr |
| 'Souvenir of Anthony Waterer' ♀H4 | SHea SReu |
| 'Souvenir of W.C. Slocock' | SReu |
| 'Spätlese' | IVic |
| ***speciosum*** | see *R. flammeum* |
| 'Spek's Orange' (M) ♀H4 | GKin |
| ***sperabile*** | NHim |
| - var. ***weihsiense*** | MSnd SLdr |
| ***sphaeranthum*** | see *R. trichostomum* |
| ***sphaeroblastum*** | MSnd |
| - var. ***wumengense*** | GLin |
| - - KR 1481 | MSnd |
| ***spiciferum*** | see *R. scabrifolium* var. *spiciferum* |
| 'Spicy Lights' (A) | LMil |
| ***spilotum*** | NHim |
| 'Spinner's Glory' | MAsh |
| 'Spitfire' | MDun NHol |
| 'Spring Beauty' (EA) | CMac MSnd SLdr SReu |
| 'Spring Magic' | MSnd SLdr |
| 'Spring Pearl' | see *R.* 'Moerheim's Pink' |
| 'Spring Rose' | SLdr |
| 'Spring Sunshine' | LMil |
| 'Springday' | CMac |
| 'Squirrel' (EA) ♀H4 | CDoC ECho GEdr GKin GLam LMil MAsh MGos MLea SLdr SLim SReu |
| Stadt Essen Group | LMil SLdr |
| 'Stadt Westerstede' | LMil |
| ***stamineum*** | MSnd NHim |
| 'Starbright Champagne' | LMil |
| 'Statuette' | IVic MDun |
| § ***stenopetalum*** 'Linearifolium' (EA) | CMac ITim LMil NMun SLdr WAbe |
| ***stenophyllum*** | see *R. makinoi* |
| ***stewartianum*** | LMil SLdr |
| 'Stewartstonian' (EA) | CMac ELon SReu WFar |
| 'Stoat' (EA) | GQui |
| 'Stopham Girl' (A) | LMil |
| 'Stopham Lad' (A) | LMil |
| 'Stour' (K) **new** | SHea |
| 'Strategist' | SHea SLdr |
| 'Strawberry Cream' | LRHS MAsh |
| 'Strawberry Ice' (K) ♀H4 | CBcs CDoC CSBt CWri ECho EPfP GKin LMil LRHS MAsh MBri MGos MMHG MMuc NEgg SLdr SPer SReu WMoo |
| 'Strawberry Sundae' | MLea MMuc NEgg SLdr |
| ***strigillosum*** | GLin MSnd |
| - Reuthe's form | SReu |
| ***suberosum*** | see *R. yunnanense* Suberosum Group |
| ***succothii*** | SLdr |
| 'Suede' | MDun |
| 'Suga-no-ito' (EA) | SLdr |
| 'Summer Blaze' (A) | SLdr SReu |
| 'Summer Dawn' | LMil |
| 'Summer Flame' | SReu |
| 'Summer Fragrance' (O) ♀H4 | LMil MDun SReu SSta |
| 'Summer Snow' | IVic MDun |
| 'Sun Chariot' (K) | CBcs LMil MAsh MMHG |
| 'Sun of Austerlitz' | SHea SLdr |
| Sunkist Group **new** | SLdr |
| (Sunrise Group) 'Sunrise' | MSnd SLdr |
| 'Sunset Pink' (K) | SLdr |
| 'Sunte Nectarine' (K) ♀H4 | ECho GKin GQui IDee LMil MBri MLea MMuc NLar SHea SLdr |
| 'Surprise' ambig. (EA) | CDoC CTri SLdr |
| 'Surrey Heath' | CBcs CDoC CSBt CWri ECho EPfP LMil MAsh MDun MGos MMuc MSnd NLar NMun SLdr SLim |
| 'Susan' (EA) | MSnd |
| 'Susan' J.C. Williams ♀H4 | CSBt CWri LMil MDun SPer SReu |
| 'Susannah Hill' (EA) | CDoC MGos SLdr |
| ***sutchuenense*** | IDee LMil MSnd NHim |
| - var. ***geraldii*** | see *R.* × *geraldii* |

'Swamp Beauty' CWri ECho MAsh MDun MGos MLea MMuc MSnd SLdr WGwG
'Swansong' (EA) CMac SLdr
'Sweet Simplicity' CWri SHea SLdr
'Sweet Sue' MSnd SLdr
'Swift' ECho GLam GQui LLHF LMil LRHS MAsh MBri MMuc NPCo SLdr
'Sword of State' (K) CWri
'Sylphides' (K) CMac
'T.S. Black' (EA) SLdr
'Taka-no-tsukasa' (EA) SLdr
***taliense*** LMil MDun
- SDR 1804 NHim
Tally Ho Group SHea
***tamaense*** see *R. cinnabarinum* subsp. *tamaense*
'Tama-no-utena' (EA) SLdr
'Tanager' (EA/k) SLdr
'Tangerine' see *R.* 'Fabia Tangerine'
'Tangiers' (K) SHea SLdr
'Tarantella' NEgg
'Taurus' ♀H4 CDoC CWri ECho ELon GKin IVic LMil LRHS MAsh MDun MGos MMuc MSnd NPCo SLdr
'Tay' (K) SLdr
'Teal' ECho GEdr GLam MGos MLea
'Ted Millais' **new** LMil
'Teddy Bear' CWri LMil MDun MLea
***telopeum*** see *R. campylocarpum* subsp. *caloxanthum* Telopeum Group
'Temple Belle' CBcs ECho MDun NBlu SLdr
'Tender Heart' (K) SLdr
'Teniers' (R) **new** SReu SSta
§ ***tephropeplum*** MSnd NHim
- Deleiense Group see *R. tephropeplum*
'Tequila Sunrise' LMil
'Terra-cotta' LMil
'Terra-cotta Beauty' (EA) WPat WThu
'Tessa' CBcs ECho ELon MMuc SLdr
Tessa Group LMil
'Tessa Roza' (EA) ♀H4 GKev GQui
***thayerianum*** MSnd
§ 'The Hon. Jean Marie de Montague' ♀H4 CWri ELon EPfP GKin LMil MAsh MBri MDun MGos MLea MMuc MSnd NLar SLdr SPer SReu
***thomsonii*** CDoC GKin IDee LMil MDun MSnd SLdr SReu
- B&SWJ 2465 WCru
- B&SWJ 2638 WCru
'Thor' SReu
'Thousand Butterflies' see *R.* 'One Thousand Butterflies'
'Thunderstorm' SReu
***thymifolium*** NHim
'Tibet' ♀H3-4 GQui LMil MDun
'Tidbit' ♀H4 CMac LMil MGos MLea MSnd SLdr
'Tinsmith' (K) SLdr
'Titian Beauty' CBcs CDoC CSBt CWri ECho EPfP LMil LRHS MAsh MGos MMuc MNHC MSnd NEgg NPCo NPri SLdr SLim SPer WBor WFar WMoo
'Titness Delight' SLdr
'Tit-Willow' (EA) LRHS MAsh SCoo
'Tolkien' SReu
'Tom Hyde' (EA) LSRN
'Top Banana' SLdr
'Torchlight' (EA) LMil LRHS
'Toreador' (EA) MSnd SLdr
'Tornado' MAsh WFar
'Torridon' (Vs) LMil
Tortoiseshell Group **new** NMun
'Tortoiseshell Champagne' see *R.* 'Champagne'
'Tortoiseshell Orange' ♀H3-4 CSBt CWri LMil MDun NLar SHea SLim SPoG SReu SSta
'Tortoiseshell Salome' SHea
'Tortoiseshell Wonder' ♀H3-4 CSBt EPfP LMil LRHS MAsh NPri SHea
'Toucan' (K) CSBt SHea SLdr
'Tower Beauty' (A) SHea SLdr
'Tower Dainty' (A) SHea
'Tower Daring' (A) SHea
'Tower Dragon' (A) LMil SHea SLdr
***traillianum*** LMil MSnd
§ - var. ***dictyotum*** NHim
'Treecreeper' GKin LMil SLdr
'Tregedna Red' SReu
'Trewithen Orange' SLdr
***trichanthum*** 'Honey Wood' LMil SLdr
***trichocladum*** NMun
§ ***trichostomum*** SSpi WAbe
- Ledoides Group LMil
***triflorum*** LMil NHim
§ - var. ***bauhiniiflorum*** CBcs SLdr
- var. ***triflorum*** Mahogani Group MSnd
'Trill' (EA) SLdr
'Trinidad' MDun
'Tromba' LMil
'Troupial' (K) SHea
***tsangpoense*** see *R. charitopes* subsp. *tsangpoense*
***tsariense*** IDee LMil MSnd
- var. ***trimoense*** LMil MSnd
- - KW 8288 LMil
***tubiforme*** see *R. glaucophyllum* subsp. *tubiforme*
'Tuffet' (EA) SLdr SReu
'Tunis' (K) LRHS MAsh NPri
'Turaço' LMil MGos SLdr
'Twilight Pink' SLdr
'Ulrike Jost' IVic
'Umpqua Queen' (K) SLdr
***ungernii*** MSnd SLdr
'Unique' (G) ECho EPfP MGos MMuc SPer
'Unique' (*campylocarpum* hybrid) ♀H4 CBcs MAsh MBri MSnd SHea SLdr SReu
'Unique Marmalade' ECho LMil MAsh MMuc NLar SLdr
***uvariifolium*** LMil MSnd NHim
var. ***griseum***
- 'Reginald Childs' LMil
***valentinianum*** CBcs MSnd NMun SLdr
- F 24347 MSnd
'Van' LMil NLar SLim
'Van Houttei Flore Pleno' (G) SLdr SReu SSta
'Van Nes Sensation' LMil
Vanessa Group GGal LMil
'Vanessa Pastel' ♀H3-4 CMac LMil MDun SReu
***vaseyi*** (A) ♀H3-4 GLin LMil
- SDR 2209 GKev
- white-flowered (A) LMil
'Vayo' (A) SLdr
***veitchianum*** NHim
***vellereum*** see *R. principis* Vellereum Group
***venator*** MSnd
'Venetian Chimes' CSBt ECho MGos MSnd NMun SLdr SPoG
***vernicosum*** CWri MSnd NHim
'Veryan Bay' CBcs
'Vespers' (EA) CTrh
'Victoria Hallett' SLdr SReu

| Name | Suppliers |
|---|---|
| 'Vida Brown' (EA/d) | CMac SLdr SReu WThu |
| 'Vinecourt Dream' (M) | GKin MBri MLea MMuc NLar SEND |
| 'Vinecourt Duke' (R/d) | CWri ECho GKin MAsh MMuc NEgg NLar NPCo |
| 'Vinecourt Troubador' (K/d) | LMil MAsh NPCo |
| 'Vineland Dream' (K/d) | CWri ECho GKin |
| 'Vineland Fragrance' | SLdr |
| 'Vintage Rosé' 🏆$^{H4}$ | LMil MLea SLdr |
| 'Violetta' (EA) | SLdr |
| 'Violette Funken' | LMil |
| 'Virginia Richards' | SLdr |
| Virginia Richards Group | CWri MAsh MBri MGos |
| § ***viridescens*** | MSnd NHim NMun WThu |
| - 'Doshong La' | LMil |
| § - Rubroluteum Group | SLdr |
| 'Viscosepalum' (G) | SHea SLdr |
| ***viscosum*** (A) 🏆$^{H4}$ | GQui IVic LMil MDun MLea MMHG SHea SPer SReu WGwG |
| - 'Grey Leaf' (Vs) | LMil |
| - var. ***montanum*** (A) | IBlr |
| - f. ***rhodanthum*** (A) | LMil |
| - 'Roseum' (Vs) | LMil SHea |
| 'Viscount Powerscourt' | SLdr |
| 'Viscy' 🏆$^{H4}$ | CSBt CWri ECho EPfP GKin GQui IVic LMil LRHS MAsh MDun MGos MMuc MSnd NLar SLdr |
| § Volker Group | CWri LMil LRHS MAsh MBri SReu SSta WFar |
| § - 'Babette' | LMil |
| § - 'Lackblatt' | LMil MBri MGos MSnd |
| 'Vulcan' 🏆$^{H4}$ | LMil MLea |
| 'Vuyk's Rosyred' (EA) 🏆$^{H4}$ | CBcs CDoC CMac CTri GKin GQui LMil MAsh MGos NHol NWad SLdr SPer SPoG SReu WFar |
| 'Vuyk's Scarlet' (EA) 🏆$^{H4}$ | CBcs CDoC CMac CSBt CTri EPfP GKin GQui LRHS MAsh MGos MMuc MSnd NHol NPri NWad SEND SLdr SPer SPlb SPoG SReu SSta WFar |
| 'W.E. Gumbleton' (M) | SReu |
| 'W.F.H.' 🏆$^{H4}$ | CWri IDee LMil MSnd SLdr SSpi |
| 'Walküre' | LMil SBrd |
| ***wallichii*** | LMil MSnd SLdr |
| - Heftii Group | GLin |
| Walloper Group | NMun |
| 'Wallowa Red' (K) | ECho GBin LMil MBri MLea MMuc SEND SLdr |
| 'Wally Miller' | ECho MAsh SReu WFar |
| ***wardii*** | LMil LRHS MDun MSnd SHea SLdr |
| - KR 5268 | LMil |
| - L&S 5679 | MSnd |
| - var. ***wardii*** Litiense Group | NHim |
| 'Ward's Ruby' (EA) | CTrh SLdr |
| ***wasonii*** | LMil MSnd |
| - SIN 1852 | GLin |
| - f. ***rhododactylum*** | MSnd |
| 'Water Baby' (A) | LMil |
| 'Water Girl' (A) | LMil |
| 'Waterfall' | SLdr |
| ***watsonii*** | MSnd |
| 'Waxwing' | SHea |
| 'Wee Bee' 🏆$^{H4}$ | CDoC CSBt ECho EPfP EPot GEdr GGar GKin GLam LLHF LMil MAsh MLea NMun NPCo SLdr SLim SReu |
| 'Wendy' | MAsh |
| 'Westminster' (O) | LMil LRHS |
| 'Weston's Pink Diamond' (d) | LMil |
| 'Whidbey Island' | LMil |
| 'Whisperingrose' | GEdr GLam LMil NBlu |
| 'White Brocade' | SSta |
| § White Dufthecke = 'Rhodunter 48'$^{PBR}$ | LMil |
| 'White Frills' (EA) | ECho NLar SLdr |
| 'White Glory' **new** | SLdr |
| 'White Grandeur' (EA) | CTrh |
| 'White Jade' (EA) | SLdr |
| 'White Lady' (EA) | SLdr |
| 'White Lights' (A) 🏆$^{H4}$ | EPfP LMil LRHS NLar NPri |
| 'White Perfume' (A) | MDun SReu SSta |
| 'White Rosebud' (EA) | SReu WFar |
| 'White Swan' (hybrid) | CBcs SReu |
| 'White Swan' (K) | GKin MGos MMuc SHea SLdr |
| 'White Wings' | GQui |
| 'Whitethroat' (K/d) 🏆$^{H4}$ | CWri ECho EPfP GQui LMil MAsh MMHG MMuc NEgg SBrd SEND SLdr SPer SReu SSta |
| 'Whitney's Dwarf Red' | SLdr |
| 'Wigeon' | LMil |
| ***wightii*** | GLin MSnd |
| 'Wild Affair' | MDun |
| 'Wilgen's Ruby' | CDoC CSBt LMil MGos MSnd SLdr SLim WFar |
| 'Willbrit' | CBcs CWri ECho MAsh MGos SLdr |
| 'William III' (G) | SLdr |
| ***williamsianum*** 🏆$^{H4}$ | CBcs CMac ECho GBin GLam LMil MAsh MDun MLea MSnd SLdr SReu SRms SSpi WFar |
| - 'Andrea' | IVic |
| - Caerhays form | CPLG LMil |
| 'Willy' (EA) | LMil SLdr |
| ***wiltonii*** 🏆$^{H4}$ | IDee LMil MDun NLar SLdr |
| 'Windlesham Scarlet' | SLdr |
| 'Windsor Hawk' | CWri |
| 'Windsor Lad' | SReu |
| 'Windsor Sunbeam' (K) | CWri |
| 'Winsome' (hybrid) 🏆$^{H3}$ | CBcs CTsd GGal GKin SHea SLdr |
| Winsome Group | CMac CWri MAsh MDun MSnd |
| 'Winston Churchill' (M) | SReu SSta |
| I 'Winter Green' (EA) | MMuc |
| 'Wintergreen' (EA) | MMuc SEND |
| 'Winterpurpur' | IVic |
| 'Wishmoor' | SReu |
| 'Wisley Blush' | LMil |
| 'Wombat' (EA) 🏆$^{H4}$ | CTri EPfP LMil LRHS MAsh MGos NHim NLar NPri SLdr SReu |
| ***wongii*** | GQui MSnd SLdr |
| 'Woodcock' | SHea SLdr |
| 'Wren' | ECho EPot GEdr GKev GLam IVic LMil LRHS MAsh MGos MLea MMuc NMun SBrd SLdr SReu WThu |
| 'Wryneck' (K) | SHea SLdr SReu |
| 'Wye' (K) | SLdr |
| ***xanthocodon*** | see *R. cinnabarinum* subsp. *xanthocodon* |
| 'Yaku Angel' | IVic MDun |
| 'Yaku Incense' | ECho LMil MAsh MLea MMuc MSnd NLar SLdr |
| 'Yaku Prince' | ECho MAsh MGos MMuc NHim SLdr WFar |
| ***yakushimanum*** | CBcs CMHG CSBt CWri ECho GGar GKin LMil MBri MDun MGos MLea MMuc MSnd NHol NLar SLdr SPer SReu SSta WFar |
| - 'Edelweiss' 🏆$^{H4}$ | LMil LRHS |
| - Exbury form | CMac SReu |
| - FCC form | see *R. yakushimanum* 'Koichiro Wada' |

| | |
|---|---|
| § – 'Koichiro Wada' ♀H4 | CMac CPLG EPfP IDee IVic LMil LRHS MDun MGos NLar SLdr SPoG SReu |
| – 'Snow Mountain' | SReu |
| 'Yaye' (EA) | SLdr |
| 'Yellow Cloud' (A) | ECho LMil MLea NPCo |
| 'Yellow Cloud' (K) | MMuc |
| 'Yellow Hammer' ♀H4 | CBcs CMac ECho GKin LMil MBri MDun NLar NMun SLdr WFar |
| Yellow Hammer Group | CWri GGar MGos MSnd SPer SReu SSta |
| 'Yoga' (K) | SHea |
| 'Yol' | SLdr |
| ***yungningense*** F 16282 | GLam |
| ***yunnanense*** | CBcs CWri GGal GGar GKev LMil MSnd NMun SLdr SSpi |
| – SDR 4217 | GKev |
| – SDR 4957 | GKev |
| – 'Openwood' ♀H3-4 | IDee LMil NLar |
| – 'Red Throat' | SLdr |
| – red-blotched | LMil |
| § – Suberosum Group | SLdr |
| – white-flowered | LMil |
| aff. ***yunnanense*** | IDee |
| ***zaleucum*** | LMil NMun |
| – AC 685 | MDun |
| – var. ***zaleucum*** **new** | MSnd |

# *Rhodohypoxis* ✿ (*Hypoxidaceae*)

| | |
|---|---|
| 'Andromeda' | EWes |
| ***baurii*** ♀H4 | CAvo CCCN CMea CPBP ECho GEdr GLam IBal ITim LRHS MAsh MLLN NBir NMen NSla NWCA SPoG SRms WAbe WFar WNew XLum |
| – 'Abigail' | EWes |
| – 'Alba' | CMea CRDP ECho IBal NMen |
| – 'Albrighton' | CRDP CTri ECho EWes GEdr GLam IBal ITim LAma LRHS NHol NMen WAbe WPat |
| – 'Apple Blossom' | CPen CTca CYeo ECho ELon EPot EWes IBal ITim LBee LRHS NHol NMen SCnR SMrm WAbe WFar |
| – 'Badger' | NWad WAbe |
| – var. ***baurii*** | EWes LBee |
| – 'Bridal Bouquet' (d) | EWes NHol WAbe WFar |
| – 'Coconut Ice' | EPot EWes |
| – var. ***confecta*** | CPen ECho EWes NHol |
| – 'Daphne Mary' | EWes |
| – 'David Scott' | EWes |
| – 'Dawn' | CPen CYeo ECho EPot EWes GEdr IBal LAma LRHS NMen WAbe WFar |
| – 'Douglas' | CPen CYeo ECho EPfP EPot EWes GEdr IBal ITim LAma NHol NMen WAbe WFar |
| – 'Dulcie' | CPen ECho EWes GEdr SCnR SUsu WAbe WFar |
| – 'Emily Peel' | ECho EPot EWes ITim LLHF NHol WAbe |
| – 'Eva-Kate' | ECho EWes ITim LAma WAbe WFar WPat |
| – 'Fred Broome' | CPBP CTca ECho EWes GEdr LAma NHol NMen WAbe WFar WPat |
| – 'Goliath' | EWes |
| – 'Harlequin' | ECho EWes GEdr IBal LAma NHol NMen NWad WAbe WFar |
| § – 'Helen' | ECho EWes GEdr IBal NHol WAbe WFar |
| – 'Jacqueline Potterton' | EPot |
| – 'Kitty' **new** | EWes |
| – 'Lily Jean' (d) | CEnt CRDP CTri CYeo ECho ELon EPfP EWes GEdr IBal LRHS NWCA WCot WFar |
| – 'Luna' | EWes |
| – 'Margaret Rose' | CTca ECho EWes IBal ITim LLHF NHol NMen WAbe WFar |
| – 'Mars' | EWes NHol |
| – 'Monique' **new** | EWes |
| – 'Pearl' | ECho LRHS |
| – 'Perle' | CYeo ECho EWes GEdr NHol NSla NWad SCnR WAbe |
| – 'Pictus' (v) | CRDP ECho EWes GEdr IBal LAma LBee LRHS NHol WAbe WFar WPat |
| – 'Pink Pearl' | EWes IBal NHol WAbe |
| – pink-flowered | MMuc SEND |
| – var. ***platypetala*** | CRDP CYeo ECho EPfP EPot EWes GEdr GLam IBal NHol NMen NWad WAbe WFar XLum |
| – var. ***platypetala*** × ***milloides*** | IBal LLHF NHol WAbe |
| – – – Burtt 6981 | EWes |
| – 'Rebecca' | ECho EWes |
| – 'Red King' | EWes IBal |
| – red-flowered | ECho LRHS MMuc SPlb |
| – 'Ruth' | CEnt ECho EPfP EWes IBal LAma NHol WAbe WFar |
| – 'Susan Garnett-Botfield' | ECho EWes GEdr IBal NMen WAbe WFar |
| – 'Tetra Red' | CEnt ECho EPot EWes LRHS NHol NMen WAbe WFar |
| – 'The Bride' | EWes |
| – white-flowered | CTca ECho EPot NMen |
| 'Betsy Carmine' | CCCN CPen ELon GEdr IBal NWad WAbe WFar |
| 'Blush' | CYeo |
| 'Bright Eyes' (d) | CRDP EWes |
| 'Burgundy' | ITim LRHS |
| 'Candy Stripe' | ECho EWes GEdr LRHS |
| 'Carina' | ECho EWes |
| 'Cayasan' | WAbe |
| 'Confusion' | EWes NHol WAbe WFar |
| 'Dainty Dee' (d) | EWes |
| ***deflexa*** | CPBP CPen CRDP CYeo ECho EWes GEdr GKev GLam IBal ITim LRHS NHol NSla NWCA NWad SCnR SMrm WAbe WFar |
| 'Donald Mann' | ECho EWes LLHF NHol NMen WAbe |
| 'Dusky' | ECho EWes GEdr |
| 'E.A. Bowles' | CPen ECho EWes IBal ITim NMen NSla NWCA WAbe WFar |
| 'Ellicks' | IBal |
| 'Garnett' | ECho EWes IBal NMen WAbe |
| 'Goya' (d) | ECho NWCA WPat |
| 'Great Scot' | CYeo EWes GEdr GGar ITim LRHS NMen WAbe WFar |
| 'Hebron Farm Biscuit' | see *Hypoxis parvula* var. *albiflora* 'Hebron Farm Biscuit' |
| 'Hebron Farm Cerise' | see × *Rhodoxis* 'Hebron Farm Cerise' |
| 'Hebron Farm Pink' | see × *Rhodoxis hybrida* 'Hebron Farm Pink' |
| 'Hinky Pinky' | GEdr |
| 'Holden Rose' (d) | ECho NHol NWad |
| hybrids | CWCL ELan MWat |
| 'Jupiter' | GEdr |
| 'Kiwi Joy' (d) | CRDP CWCL CYeo EPot EWes GEdr GGar IBal LLHF NHol NMen NWad WAbe WFar |

| | |
|---|---|
| 'Knockdolian Red' | NHol |
| 'Lily Fan' | WFar |
| 'Midori' | EWes GEdr SUsu |
| ***milloides*** | CEnt CRDP CTca ECho EPfP EPot EWes GEdr IBal ITim LBee LRHS NHol NMen NWCA NWad WAbe WFar |
| - 'Claret' | CEnt CRDP CSam CYeo ECho EWes ITim LLHF LRHS NHol SUsu WAbe WFar WPat |
| - 'Damask' | CRDP EWes |
| - 'Drakensberg Snow' | EWes |
| - giant | ECho WFar |
| - 'Super Milloides' **new** | LRHS |
| 'Monty' | ECho EWes GEdr ITim WAbe |
| 'Mystery' | EWes NHol WAbe |
| 'Naomi' | ECho EWes |
| 'New Look' | ECho EWes GEdr IBal LLHF LRHS NMen NWad SMrm WAbe WFar WGor |
| 'Ori Zuru' | GEdr |
| 'Pearl White' | ECho |
| 'Pink Ice' | GEdr IBal |
| 'Pink Star' | WFar |
| 'Pinkeen' | ECho EPot EWes GEdr IBal LLHF WAbe WFar |
| 'Pinkie' | EPot IBal |
| 'Pintado' | EWes GEdr NWad WAbe |
| 'Raspberry Ice' | ECho NHol |
| 'Rosie Lee' | EWes WAbe |
| 'Shell Pink' | EWes IBal ITim NHol NWad WAbe |
| 'Snow' | EWes |
| 'Snow White' | EWes NHol |
| 'Starlett' | CYeo EWes LRHS NHol |
| 'Starry Eyes' (d) | CRDP ECho EWes |
| 'Stella' | CCCN ECho EPot EWes GEdr IBal NHol NMen NWad WAbe |
| 'Tetra Pink' | ECho EWes IBal NHol NWad SMrm WAbe |
| 'Tetra Rose' | GEdr WFar |
| 'Tetra White' | see *R. baurii* 'Helen' |
| ***thodiana*** | CRDP ECho EPot EWes GEdr GLam IBal NHol NMen SCnR WAbe WFar |
| 'Twinkle Star Mixed' | ECho LRHS |
| 'Two Tone' | EWes |
| 'Venetia' | CMea ECho IBal NHol NWad SBch WAbe |
| 'Westacre Picotee' | EWes |
| 'Wild Cherry Blossom' | ECho EWes |

## *Rhodohypoxis* × *Hypoxis* see × *Rhodoxis*

| | |
|---|---|
| ***R. baurii*** × ***H. parvula*** | see × *Rhodoxis hybrida* |

## *Rhodophiala* (*Amaryllidaceae*)

| | | |
|---|---|---|
| § | ***advena*** | EPot |
| | ***bagnoldii*** | WCot |
| § | ***bifida*** | SCnR WCot |
| | ***chilensis*** F&W 9700 | WCot |
| | ***elwesii*** F&W 10734 | WCot |
| | ***fulgens*** F&W 10299 | WCot |
| | 'Harry Hay' | WCot |
| | ***montana*** | CFee |
| | ***rosea*** | LAma |
| * | ***serotina*** F&W 9586 | WCot |
| | ***splendens*** | WCot |

## *Rhodora* see *Rhododendron*

## *Rhodothamnus* (*Ericaceae*)

| | |
|---|---|
| ***sessilifolius*** | WThu |

## *Rhodotypos* (*Rosaceae*)

| | | |
|---|---|---|
| | ***kerrioides*** | see *R. scandens* |
| § | ***scandens*** | CBot CDul CPLG CTri CWib EBee ELan EPfP EPla EShb EWTr GKin IGor LRHS MBri MMHG MMuc NHol NLar SEND SLon SPoG SSpi WCru WSHC |

## × *Rhodoxis* ✿ (*Hypoxidaceae*)

| | | |
|---|---|---|
| | 'Anne Crock' | CYeo LRHS |
| | 'Aurora' | EWes |
| | 'Bloodstone' | EWes NHol |
| | 'Hebron Farm Biscuit' | see *Hypoxis parvula* var. *albiflora* 'Hebron Farm Biscuit' |
| § | 'Hebron Farm Cerise' | CCCN CYeo ELon EWes GEdr NMen NWCA WFar WNew |
| | 'Hebron Farm Rose' | LLHF |
| § | ***hybrida*** | CPen ECho EWes IBal NMen NWCA SMrm WAbe XLum |
| | - 'Aya San' | CYeo EWes |
| § | - 'Hebron Farm Pink' | CBro CYeo ECho EWes GEdr IBal NHol NMen SCnR WAbe WFar |
| | - 'Hebron Farm Red Eye' | CCCN CYeo ELon EWes GEdr NWCA SCnR WAbe WFar |
| | - 'Pink Stars' | CYeo |
| | 'Little Pink Pet' | EWes |

## *Rhoeo* see *Tradescantia*

## *Rhopalostylis* (*Arecaceae*)

| | |
|---|---|
| ***baueri*** | CBrP LPal |
| ***sapida*** | CBrP CTrC LPal |
| - 'East Cape' | SBig |

## rhubarb see *Rheum* × *hybridum*

## *Rhus* (*Anacardiaceae*)

| | | |
|---|---|---|
| | ***ambigua*** B&SWJ 3656 | WCru |
| | - large-leaved B&SWJ 10884 | WCru |
| § | ***aromatica*** | CArn EBtc ELan LRHS NLar |
| | ***chinensis*** | CMCN EPfP NLar |
| | - var. ***roxburghii*** | SSpi |
| | ***copallina*** | EBtc ELan EPfP |
| | ***coriaria*** | CArn EPfP NLar |
| | ***cotinus*** | see *Cotinus coggygria* |
| | ***glabra*** | CArn CBcs CDoC EBtc EPfP MGos SPer WDin |
| | - 'Laciniata' misapplied | see *R.* × *pulvinata* Autumn Lace Group |
| | - 'Laciniata' ambig. | MMuc |
| | - 'Laciniata' Carrière | NLar |
| | ***glauca*** | EShb |
| N | ***hirta*** | see *R. typhina* |
| | ***incisa*** | SPlb |
| | ***integrifolia*** | CArn |
| | ***krebsiana*** | WHil |
| | ***magalismontana*** | EShb |
| | ***potaninii*** | CBod EPfP LRHS MAsh SBfd |
| § | × ***pulvinata*** Autumn Lace Group | EPfP MGos WFar WPat |
| | - - 'Red Autumn Lace' ♀H4 | LBuc LRHS MBlu MBri MRav SBfd SPer SPoG |
| § | ***radicans*** | CArn GPoy WHer |
| | ***succedanea*** | CDTJ SSpi |
| | ***toxicodendron*** | see *R. radicans* |
| | ***trilobata*** | see *R. aromatica* |
| N | ***typhina*** ♀H4 | CBcs CDoC CDul CHEx CLnd CMac CTri EBee ECrN ELan EPfP GKin LRHS MAsh MGos MMuc |

MRav NEgg NLar NWea SArc SBfd SEND SGol SPer SPoG SSta WDin WFar
§ - 'Dissecta' 🏆H4 — CBcs CDoC CDul CLnd CMac EBee ECrN ELan EPfP LAst LRHS MBri MGos MRav MWat NEgg NLar NPri SBfd SEND SGol SPer WDin WFar
- 'Laciniata' hort. — see *R. typhina* 'Dissecta'
- Radiance = 'Sinrus'[PBR] — EBee LRHS MAsh MBlu SPoG
- Tiger Eyes = 'Bailtiger'[PBR] — EBee ELan EMil EPfP GKin LBuc LRHS MAsh MBlu MBri MGos NLar NPri SCoo SMad SPtl SWvt
§ ***verniciflua*** — EGFP NLar SSpi

## *Rhynchelytrum* see *Melinis*

## *Rhynchospora* (*Cyperaceae*)

***alba*** — GAuc
***colorata*** — CRow LLWG NPer SHom WHal
***latifolia*** — CKno SHDw

## *Ribes* ✿ (*Grossulariaceae*)

***alpinum*** — CPLG MRav MWht NWea SPer SRms WDin WOut
- 'Aureum' — CAbP EHoe NEgg WCot WDin
***americanum*** — SBfd
- 'Variegatum' (v) — EHoe ELan WPat
***aureum*** hort. — see *R. odoratum*
'Ben Hope'[PBR] (B) — CAgr EPom MAsh MCoo SCoo SWvt WHar WWFS
'Black Velvet' (D) — CAgr MCoo
§ × ***culverwellii*** (F) — CAgr CBod CCCN CWib EMil GTwe LBuc LEdu LSRN MAsh NLar SDea SPoG SVic WHar WWFS
***divaricatum*** — CAgr GPri LEdu
***gayanum*** — CPMA NLar
***glaciale*** — NLar
× ***gordonianum*** — Widely available
***griffithii*** **new** — LEdu
- GWJ 9331 — WCru
jostaberry — see *R.* × *culverwellii*
***laurifolium*** — CBcs CBot CDoC CDul CEnd CHGN CMHG CPLG CTri ELan EQua MRav NLar SBrt WDin WFar WSHC
- (f) — CMac EPfP
- (m) — EPfP WPat
- 'Mrs Amy Doncaster' — CMac WCot WPat
- Rosemoor form — CDoC CSam SPoG WPGP
***menziesii*** — CHll EWes NLBP WCot
***nigrum*** — LTen
- 'Baldwin' (B) — CDoC CTri ECrN EPfP LRHS MAsh NLar SDea SKee SLim SPer SPoG WHar
- 'Barchatnaja' (B) — CAgr
- 'Ben Alder'[PBR] (B) — CAgr CWib LRHS MAsh SCoo SDea WWFS
- 'Ben Connan'[PBR] (B) 🏆H4 — CAgr CMac CSBt CWib EPfP EPom ERea GPri GTwe LBuc LRHS LSRN MAsh MBri MGos MMuc NLar SCoo SDea SKee SLim SPoG SWvt WHar WWFS
- 'Ben Gairn'[PBR] (B) — CAgr CSBt MCoo WHar WWFS
- 'Ben Lomond'[PBR] (B) 🏆H4 — CAgr CMac CSBt CTri CWib ECrN EPfP GPri GTwe LBuc LRHS LSRN MAsh MGos MRav NEgg NPri SDea SEND SKee SPer SVic WHar
- 'Ben More' (B) — CAgr CWib MBri
- 'Ben Nevis' (B) — CAgr CTri CWib SDea SKee
- 'Ben Sarek' (B) 🏆H4 — CAgr CDoC CMac CSBt CSut CTri CWib ECrN EMil EPfP ERea GTwe LBuc LRHS LSRN MAsh MGos MRav NLar SBfd SDea SKee SLim SPer SPoG SWvt WHar WWFS
- 'Ben Tirran'[PBR] (B) — CAgr CDoC CSBt CWib ERea LBuc LRHS LSRN MAsh MBri MGos NLar SBfd SCoo SPoG SWvt WHar WWFS
- 'Big Ben' (B) **new** — CSut EPom
- 'Black Reward' (B) — CAgr MCoo
- 'Boskoop Giant' (B) — CAgr GTwe NEgg SLim SPer WHar
* - 'Byelorussian Sweet' (B) — CAgr
- 'Consort' (B) — CAgr
- 'Ebony' — EMil ERea SLon
* - 'Hystawneznaya' (B) — CAgr
- 'Jet' (B) — CAgr GTwe NEgg
* - 'Kosmicheskaya' (B) — CAgr
- 'Loch Ness' (B) **new** — WHar
- 'Pilot Alexander Mamkin' (B) — CAgr
- 'Seabrook's' (B) — CAgr
- 'Titania' (B) — LRHS SPoG
- 'Tsema' (B) — MCoo
- 'Wellington XXX' (B) — CAgr GTwe LBuc SPer
§ ***odoratum*** — CBcs CDoC CDul CSBt CWib EBee ECrN ELan ELon EPfP LRHS MGos MMuc MRav NCGa NLar NWea SBfd SEND SGar SKHP SPer SPoG SRms SSpi WDin WFar WHar WSHC
- 'Crandall' — CAgr LEdu
'Pink Perfection' — CMCN
***praecox*** — CBcs MMuc SEND
***rubrum*** 'Blanka' (W) — CAgr CSut GPri LRHS SBfd
- 'Cascade' (R) — CAgr
- 'Cherry' (R) — CAgr MCoo
- 'Hollande Rose' (P) — GTwe
- 'Jonkheer van Tets' (R) 🏆H4 — CAgr CMac CSBt CWib EPfP EPom GPri GTwe IArd LRHS LSRN MAsh MCoo MMuc NLar SDea SEND SKee SLim SPer WHar WWFS
- 'Junifer' (R) — CAgr GTwe SKee
- 'Laxton's Number One' (R) — CAgr CTri GPri GTwe LRHS LSRN MAsh MNHC NLar SDea SLim SPer SPoG WGwG WHar
- 'Laxton's Perfection' (R) — MCoo
- 'Red Lake' (R) 🏆H4 — CAgr CTri CWib EPfP ERea GPri GTwe LBuc LRHS MGos NEgg NLar NPri SDea SKee SPer SPoG
- 'Redstart' (R) — CAgr CSBt CTri CWib GTwe LBuc LRHS MAsh NLar SKee SPoG WHar WWFS
- 'Rondom' (R) — CAgr SDea SVic
- 'Rosetta' (R) — MCoo
- 'Rovada' (R) — CAgr CSBt CSut CWib EPom ERea GPri GTwe LSRN MAsh SBfd SKee WHar WWFS
- 'Roxby Red' (R) — MCoo
- 'Stanza' (R) 🏆H4 — CAgr GTwe MCoo MMuc SDea SEND
- 'Transparent' (W) — GTwe
§ - 'Versailles Blanche' (W/C) — CAgr CMac CSBt CTri CWib EPfP EPom GPri GTwe LBuc LRHS LSRN MAsh MBri MGos MMuc NPri SDea SEND SKee SLim SPer SPoG WHar
- 'White Dutch' (W) — ERea MCoo
- 'White Grape' (W) 🏆H4 — ERea GTwe
- 'White Pearl' (W) — MCoo SDea SVic
- White Versailles — see *R. rubrum* 'Versailles Blanche'
- 'Wilson's Long Bunch' (R) — GTwe

| | |
|---|---|
| ***sanguineum*** | CDul CWCL NEgg WFar WMoo |
| - 'Brocklebankii' | CMac CPLG ELan LEdu MGos MRav NLar SAga SBrd SLim SPer WBor WCFE WPat WSHC |
| - double-flowered | see *R. sanguineum* 'Plenum' |
| - 'Elkington's White' | LBuc LRHS |
| - 'Flore Pleno' | see *R. sanguineum* 'Plenum' |
| - 'King Edward VII' | Widely available |
| - 'Koja' | EBee GBin LBuc LRHS LSRN MGos SPoG WPat |
| - 'Lombartsii' | MRav |
| § - 'Plenum' (d) | CBot |
| - 'Poky's Pink' | CMac LLHF MRav |
| - 'Pulborough Scarlet' ♀$^{H4}$ | Widely available |
| - 'Red Bross' | SWvt |
| - 'Red Pimpernel' | EPfP LBMP LRHS LSRN MAsh MBNS SBrd SCoo SPoG SWvt |
| - 'Tydeman's White' | CPLG CSBt ELan EPfP MGos NPri WSHC |
| - var. ***variegata*** | CMac |
| - White Icicle = 'Ubric' ♀$^{H4}$ | CBcs CBot CDoC CEnd CTri CWib EBee EPfP EWTr LAst LBMP LRHS MAsh MBlu MHer MRav MWat NBir NLar NPri SBrd SLim SPer SPoG SSpi SWvt WFar WPat |
| ***speciosum*** ♀$^{H3}$ | Widely available |
| ***uva-crispa*** 'Achilles' (D) | GTwe |
| - 'Admiral Beattie' (F) | GTwe NEgg |
| - 'Annelii' (F) | CAgr |
| - 'Bedford Red' (C/D) | GTwe |
| - 'Bedford Yellow' (C/D) | GTwe |
| - 'Beech Tree Nestling' (D) | GTwe |
| - 'Blucher' (D) | GTwe |
| - 'Bright Venus' (D) | GTwe |
| - 'Broom Girl' (D) | GTwe |
| - 'Captivator' (C) | CSBt GTwe LBuc MAsh NEgg SDea |
| - 'Careless' (C/D) ♀$^{H4}$ | CSBt EMil GTwe LRHS LSRN MGos MNHC NLar SDea SKee SPer SPoG WHar |
| - 'Cook's Eagle' (C) | GTwe |
| - 'Cousen's Seedling' (D) | GTwe |
| - 'Criterion' (D) | GTwe |
| - 'Crown Bob' (C/D) | GTwe |
| - 'Dan's Mistake' (D) | GTwe |
| - 'Drill' (D) | GTwe |
| - 'Early Sulphur' (D) | GTwe SDea |
| - 'Firbob' (D) | GTwe NEgg |
| - 'Forester' (D) | GTwe |
| - 'Freedom' (C) | GTwe |
| - 'Gipsy Queen' (D) | GTwe |
| - 'Glenton Green' (D) | GTwe |
| - 'Golden Drop' (D) | GTwe |
| - 'Green Gem' (C/D) | GTwe |
| - 'Green Ocean' (D) | GTwe |
| - 'Greenfinch' (C) ♀$^{H4}$ | CAgr GTwe WWFS |
| - 'Guido' (F) | GTwe |
| - 'Gunner' (C/D) | GTwe NEgg |
| - 'Heart of Oak' (F) | GTwe |
| - 'Hedgehog' (D) | GTwe |
| - 'Hero of the Nile' (D) | GTwe |
| - 'High Sheriff' (D) | GTwe |
| - 'Hinnonmäki' (F) | CAgr LBuc MAsh SPer |
| - 'Hinnonmäki Grön' (F) | CMac CSBt EPfP LRHS LSRN WHar |
| - 'Hinnonmäki Gul' (D) | CAgr CMac CSBt CSut CTri EMil EPfP EPom ERea GTwe LBuc LRHS MAsh MGos NLar SBfd SDea SKee SPer SPoG SVic WHar |
| - 'Hinnonmäki Röd' (C/D) | CAgr CMac CTri EMil EPfP EPom ERea GTwe LBuc LRHS LSRN MAsh MBri MCoo NLar SBfd SDea SPer SPoG SVic WHar |
| - 'Howard's Lancer' (C/D) | GTwe SDea |
| - 'Invicta' (C/D) ♀$^{H4}$ | Widely available |
| - 'Ironmonger' (D) | GTwe |
| - 'Jubilee' (C/D) | LBuc |
| - 'Keen's Seedling' (D) | GTwe |
| - 'Keepsake' (C/D) | GTwe SDea |
| - 'King of Trumps' (F) | GTwe |
| - 'Lancashire Lad' (C/D) | GTwe |
| - 'Langley Gage' (D) | GTwe MCoo NEgg |
| - 'Laxton's Amber' (D) | GTwe |
| - 'Leveller' (D) ♀$^{H4}$ | CTri GTwe LAst LBuc LRHS MAsh MCoo MGos SDea SPer WHar |
| - 'London' (C/D) | GTwe |
| - 'Lord Derby' (C/D) | GTwe |
| - 'Martlet' (F) | CAgr GTwe LRHS MCoo SLim WWFS |
| - 'May Duke' (C/D) | SDea |
| - 'Mitre' (D) | GTwe |
| - 'Pax'$^{PBR}$ (D) | CAgr CDoC CSut EPfP GTwe LBuc LRHS NLar SDea SKee SLim SPoG WWFS |
| - 'Peru' (D) | GTwe |
| - 'Pitmaston Green Gage' (D) | GTwe |
| - 'Plunder' | GTwe |
| - 'Queen of Trumps' (D) | GTwe |
| - var. ***reclinatum*** 'Aston Red' | see *R. uva-crispa* 'Warrington' |
| - 'Red Champagne' (D) | GTwe |
| - 'Rifleman' (D) | GTwe |
| - 'Rokula'$^{PBR}$ (C/D) | CDoC GTwe LRHS MBri SLim |
| - 'Rosebery' (D) | GTwe |
| - 'Scotch Red Rough' (D) | GTwe |
| - 'Scottish Chieftan' (D) | GTwe |
| - 'Snow' (F) | EPfP SCoo |
| - 'Snowdrop' (D) | GTwe |
| - 'Spinefree' (C) | GTwe |
| - 'Surprise' (D) | GTwe |
| - 'Telegraph' (F) | GTwe |
| - 'Tom Joiner' (F) | GTwe |
| - 'Victoria' (C/D) | GTwe |
| § - 'Warrington' (F) | GTwe |
| - 'Whinham's Industry' (C/D) ♀$^{H4}$ | CMac CSBt CTri GPri GTwe LAst LBuc LRHS LSRN MAsh MGos MMuc MRav NEgg NPri SDea SEND SPer WGwG WHar |
| - 'White Lion' (C/D) | GTwe |
| - 'White Transparent' (C) | GTwe |
| - 'Whitesmith' (C/D) | CTri GTwe MCoo SDea |
| - 'Woodpecker' (D) | GTwe NEgg |
| - 'Xenia' **new** | EPom |
| - 'Yellow Champagne' (D) | GTwe |
| ***valdivianum*** | WCot |
| ***viburnifolium*** | NLar SBrt |
| 'Worcesterberry' (C) | MGos SDea SPer |

## *Richea* (*Ericaceae*)

| | |
|---|---|
| ***dracophylla*** | GLin |

## *Ricinocarpos* (*Euphorbiaceae*)

| | |
|---|---|
| ***pinifolius*** | ECou |

## *Ricinus* (*Euphorbiaceae*)

| | |
|---|---|
| ***communis*** | CDTJ MLLN SBfd SPlb |
| - 'Carmencita' ♀$^{H3}$ | MNHC SGar |
| - 'Carmencita Pink' | CDTJ |
| - 'Carmencita Red' | CDTJ EShb NPri SBfd |
| - 'Dominican Republic' | CDTJ |

- 'Gibsonii' CDTJ SBst SMrm
- 'Impala' CDTJ SBst SMrm
- 'New Zealand Black' CDTJ CSpe
- 'Zanzibariensis' CDTJ CSpe EShb

## *Rigidella* see *Tigridia*

## *Riocreuxia* (*Apocynaceae*)

***torulosa*** CCCN SPlb

## *Robinia* (*Papilionaceae*)

× ***ambigua*** SKHP SSpi
§ ***boyntonii*** LSRN
§ ***hispida*** CDul CEnd CLnd CWib ECrN ELan EPfP EWTr MBlu NLar SPer WDin WJas
- 'Macrophylla' CEnd
- 'Rosea' misapplied see *R. boyntonii*, *R. elliottii*, *R. hispida*
- 'Rosea' ambig. CBcs CBot EBee
***kelseyi*** CDul EBee EWes SPer
× ***margaretta*** Casque Rouge see *R.* × *margaretta* 'Pink Cascade'
§ - 'Pink Cascade' CCVT CDoC CDul CEnd CLnd CMac CTri EPfP LAst LMaj MAsh MBlu MGos MREP SBfd SCoo SCrf SEND SGol SLim SPer WDin WFoF
***pseudoacacia*** CCVT CDul CLnd ELan LBuc MCoo NEgg SEND SGol SPlb WDin WFar
- 'Bessoniana' CDul EBee LAst LMaj
- 'Frisia' ♀$^{H4}$ Widely available
- 'Inermis' hort. see *R. pseudoacacia* 'Umbraculifera'
§ - 'Lace Lady'$^{PBR}$ CSBt CWSG ELan EPfP LRHS MAsh MBri MGos NLar SBrd SCoo SLim SPoG
- 'Rozynskiana' CDul
- 'Tortuosa' CEnd EBee EBtc ELan LAst MBlu MGos SBfd SPer
- 'Twisty Baby'$^{PBR}$ see *R. pseudoacacia* 'Lace Lady'
§ - 'Umbraculifera' CDul CLnd LMaj LTen MBri MGos SCoo
- 'Unifoliola' LMaj
× ***slavinii*** 'Hillieri' ♀$^{H4}$ CDoC CDul CEnd EBee ELan EPfP EWTr LRHS LSRN MAsh MBlu MBri MGos NLar SBfd SCrf SEND SLon SPer SPoG

## *Rochea* see *Crassula*

## *Rodgersia* ✿ (*Saxifragaceae*)

ACE 2303 SDix
CLD 1432 CPLG
***aesculifolia*** ♀$^{H4}$ Widely available
- green bud IBlr
- var. ***henrici*** CLAP CRow MRav NBro NMyG SWat WHoo WMoo
- - hybrid CHid EBee EWTr NHol NLar SBrd WAul WWEG XLum
- pink-flowered SSpi
- 'Red Dawn' IBlr
- 'Red Leaf' GCal IFoB
'Badenweiter' ECha
'Blickfang' IBlr
'Bloody Mary' CBcs CElw EBee EPPr SKHP
'Borodin' EBee
Cally strain GCal
'Dark Pokers' **new** EPPr NLar
'Die Anmutige' CLAP CRow
'Die Schöne' CLAP EBee GBin NLar
'Die Stolze' EBee GBin LEdu LLWG MBrN
'Elfenbeinturm' IBlr
'Fascination' IBlr
'Herkules' CSam EBee ECha ECtt EHoe ELon GBin GCal GMaP IFoB LHop LSou MBNS MMuc NEgg NLBP NLar SKHP SSpi WCot WCra WPnP WWEG WWFP
'Irish Bronze' ♀$^{H4}$ CLAP CPrp EAEE EBee ELan GBin GQue LBMP LRHS LSRN MAvo NPnk WAul WCAu WFar WMoo WPnP WWEG
'Koriata' IBlr
'Kupfermond' CRow IBlr NBir
'La Blanche' CAby CMil EBee ECtt ELon LEdu LRHS NCGa NEgg NGdn SPer WCot WCra WPnP WWEG
'Maigrün' IBlr
***nepalensis*** CLAP LRHS MDun
- EMAK 713 CLAP IBlr WPGP
- HWJK 2140 WCru
'Panache' IBlr
'Parasol' CBro CLAP CMac GBin IBlr NBir NHol SKHP SSpi WPGP
***pinnata*** Widely available
- B&SWJ 7741A CBcs WCru WFar
- L 1670 CDes CLAP CPLG ELan IBlr SSpi WPGP
- SDR 3301 GKev
- 'Alba' GCal IBlr NHol
- 'Buckland Beauty' CDes IBlr SSpi WMoo WPGP
- 'Cally Coffee' GCal
- 'Cally Salmon' EWes GCal IBlr
- 'Chocolate Wing' Widely available
- 'Crûg Cardinal' GCal WCru
- 'Elegans' CFir EBee EHoe ELan EPfP EPla GKev GMaP IBlr LBMP LEdu LRHS MRav NEgg NHol NOrc SPer SWvt WGwG WPnP
- 'Fireworks'$^{PBR}$ CFir CHid CLAP EBee ECtt ELan GBin IPot LEdu MBri MSCN SPer WFar WHil
- 'Jade Dragon Mountain' IBlr SKHP
- 'Maurice Mason' CLAP CPLG ECtt GKev IBlr LTen NLar WWEG
- 'Mont Blanc' IBlr
- Mount Stewart form IBlr
- 'Perthshire Bronze' IBlr
- pink-flowered WCru
- 'Rosea' IBlr
- 'Superba' ♀$^{H4}$ Widely available
- white-flowered GAbr SWat WCru
***pinnata*** × ***sambucifolia*** IBlr
***podophylla*** ♀$^{H4}$ Widely available
- B&SWJ 10818 WCru
- B&SWJ 10823 WCru
- 'Braunlaub' CLAP EBee GQue LLWG NBro SMad WFar WMoo WPnP WWEG
- 'Bronceblad' IBlr
- Donard selection GBin IBlr MBri
- 'Rotlaub' CAby CDes CLAP CRow EBee GBin IBlr IPot WBor WMoo
- 'Smaragd' CDes CLAP CRow EBee GBin GCal IBlr MRav NBir NLar
***purdomii*** hort. CLAP GCal WCot WPGP
'Reinecke Fuchs' IBlr
'Rosenlicht' CRow
'Rosenzipfel' IBlr
***sambucifolia*** CBcs CLAP CMac CRow EBee EWTr GBBs GBee GCal LEdu LLWG LRHS MLHP MMuc NBir NEgg NLar

| | |
|---|---|
| | NSti SEND SWat WCAu WFar WMoo WPnP WWEG XLum |
| - B&SWJ 7899 | WCru |
| - dwarf pink-flowered | IBlr |
| - dwarf white-flowered | IBlr |
| - large red-stemmed | NBir |
| - 'Mountain Select' | EBee GCal WFar |
| ***tabularis*** | see *Astilboides tabularis* |

## *Roemeria* (*Papaveraceae*)

| | |
|---|---|
| ***hybrida*** **new** | CSpe |

## *Rohdea* (*Asparagaceae*)

| | |
|---|---|
| ***japonica*** | CHEx LRHS WCot WPGP |
| - B&SWJ 4853 | WCru |
| - B&SWJ 5091 | WCru |
| - 'Godaishu' (v) | WCot |
| - 'Gunjaku' (v) | WCot |
| - 'Lance Leaf' | LEdu |
| - long-leaved | WCot WFar |
| - 'Miyakonojo' (v) | WCot |
| - 'Talbot Manor' (v) | EBla WCot |
| - 'Tama-jishi' (v) | WCot |
| - 'Tuneshige Rokujo' (v) | WCot |
| ***tonkinensis*** HWJ 562 | WCru |
| ***watanabei*** B&SWJ 1911 | WCru |

## *Romanzoffia* (*Boraginaceae*)

| | |
|---|---|
| § ***sitchensis*** | CTri |
| ***suksdorfii*** Greene | see *R. sitchensis* |
| ***tracyi*** | CDes CLAP GEdr GGar GKev NRya |
| ***unalaschcensis*** | CLAP NWCA SRms |

## *Romneya* (*Papaveraceae*)

| | |
|---|---|
| ***coulteri*** ♀H4 | Widely available |
| § - var. ***trichocalyx*** | CFir CGHE |
| § - 'White Cloud' ♀H4 | EBee ELan SChF SMad WPGP |
| × ***hybrida*** | see *R. coulteri* 'White Cloud' |
| ***trichocalyx*** | see *R. coulteri* var. *trichocalyx* |

## *Romulea* (*Iridaceae*)

| | |
|---|---|
| ***amoena*** 'Nieuwoudtville' | ECho |
| ***austinii*** 'Komsberg' | ECho |
| § ***autumnalis*** | ECho |
| ***barkerae*** 'Paternoster' | ECho |
| ***biflora*** 'Vanrhynsdorp' | ECho |
| ***bulbocodium*** | CBro ECho WAbe |
| - var. ***clusiana*** | ECho |
| - var. ***crocea*** | ECho |
| * - 'Knightshayes' | NWCA SCnR |
| ***citrina*** from Tweerivier | ECho |
| - 'Kamiesberg' | ECho |
| ***columnae*** | ECho |
| - subsp. ***columnae*** | ECho |
| ***congoensis*** | GCal |
| ***cruciata*** var. ***cruciata*** 'Riverlands' | ECho |
| - var. ***intermedia*** 'Somerset West' | ECho |
| ***dichotoma*** | ECho |
| ***discifera*** 'Grasberg' | ECho |
| ***diversiformis*** 'Komsberg' | ECho |
| ***eximia*** | ECho |
| ***flava*** var. ***minor*** 'Dassenberg' | ECho |
| - 'Rawsonville' | ECho |
| ***hirsuta*** var. ***cuprea*** 'Rawsonville' | ECho |
| - var. ***hirsuta*** 'Klipheuwel' | ECho |
| - var. ***zeyheri*** 'Malmesbury' | ECho |
| ***hirta*** | ECho |
| ***kamisensis*** | ECho |
| ***leipoldtii*** | ECho |
| ***linaresii*** | ECho |
| ***longipes*** 'Coega' | ECho |
| ***longituba*** | see *R. macowanii* |
| * ***luteoflora*** var. ***sanguinea*** | ECho NMen |
| § ***macowanii*** | ECho |
| ***montana*** | ECho |
| ***namaquensis*** | ECho |
| ***nivalis*** | ECho |
| ***obscura*** var. ***blanda*** | ECho |
| - var. ***obscura*** | ECho |
| - var. ***subtestacea*** | ECho |
| ***pratensis*** | ECho |
| ***ramiflora*** | CPBP CPLG ECho |
| ***rosea*** | ECho |
| - var. ***rosea*** 'Caledon' | ECho |
| - var. ***speciosa*** | see *R. autumnalis* |
| ***sanguinalis*** from Tweerivier | ECho |
| ***setifolia*** var. ***aggregata*** 'Rawsonville' | ECho |
| ***sladenii*** 'Gifberg' | ECho |
| ***stellata*** 'Nardouwsberg' | ECho |
| ***subfistulosa*** from Roggeveld | ECho |
| ***tabularis*** | ECho NWCA |
| ***tempskyana*** | CPBP ECho |
| ***tetragona*** var. ***flavandra*** 'Matjiesfontein' | ECho |
| ***tortuosa*** subsp. ***aurea*** 'Komsberg' | ECho |
| - var. ***tortuosa*** 'Botuin' | ECho |
| ***toximontana*** 'Gifberg' | ECho |
| ***triflora*** 'Riverlands' | ECho |
| ***unifolia*** from Roggeveld | ECho |

## *Rondeletia* (*Rubiaceae*)

| | |
|---|---|
| ***amoena*** | MOWG |

## *Rorippa* (*Brassicaceae*)

| | |
|---|---|
| ***amphibia*** | LLWG MSKA |
| ***nasturtium-aquaticum*** | WMAq |

## *Rosa* ✿ (*Rosaceae*)

| | |
|---|---|
| A Shropshire Lad = 'Ausled'PBR (S) | LRHS LStr MAus MBri NEgg SMrm SSea SWCr |
| A Whiter Shade of Pale = 'Peafanfare'PBR (HT) | ESty MAus SWCr |
| Abbeyfield Gold = 'Korquelda'PBR (F) | SWCr |
| Abbeyfield Rose = 'Cocbrose'PBR (HT) ♀H4 | GCoc MRav SMrm SPer |
| Abbie's Rose (F) **new** | SWCr |
| Abigaile = 'Tanelaigib' (F) | LSRN |
| Abraham Darby = 'Auscot'PBR (S) | CTri EBee EPfP GCoc LRHS LSRN LStr MAsh MAus MBri MRav MWat NEgg NLar SEND SMrm SPer SPoG SWCr |
| Absent Friends = 'Dicemblem'PBR (F) | ESty IDic |
| Absolutely Fabulous = 'Wekvossutono'PBR (F) | CGro CSBt EBee ECnt ESty GCoc LBuc LRHS LSRN LShp LStr MAsh MBri MWat NPri SCoo SMrm SPer SPoG SWCr |
| Accademia = 'Baracc'PBR (S) | EBee ECnt |
| ***acicularis*** | GAuc |

'Adam' (ClT) — LSRN
'Adam Messerich' (Bb) — SLon
Adam's Rose = 'Wekromico' (F) — LSRN
'Adélaïde d'Orléans' (Ra) 𝕐H4 — CRHN LRHS MAus MBri MRav SEND SFam SPer SWCr
'Aglaia' (Ra) — CPou MAus
'Agnes' (Ru) 𝕐H4 — CGro ELon EPfP EWTr GCoc IArd MAus MRav MWat NLar SPer SRGP
'Agnès Schilliger' — MRav SMrm
'Aimée Vibert' (N) — CSam EWTr MAus MCot MRav NLar SEND SPer
'Alain Blanchard' (G) — CPou EBee GCoc MAus
Alan Titchmarsh = 'Ausjive'[PBR] (S) — CSBt ESty LRHS LSRN MAsh MAus MBri SCoo SPer SWCr
× ***alba*** (A) — ECrN
§ – 'Alba Maxima' (A) — EWTr GCoc LRHS MAus MRav NLar SEND SPer SWCr
§ – 'Alba Semiplena' (A) 𝕐H4 — GCoc LRHS MAus SPer SWCr
– Celestial — see *R.* 'Céleste'
– 'Maxima' — see *R.* × *alba* 'Alba Maxima'
'Albéric Barbier' (Ra) 𝕐H4 — CRHN CSBt CSam CTri EBee ECnt ELan EPfP EWTr GCoc LRHS LStr MAsh MAus MBri MRav MWat NBir NPri NWea SEND SMad SMrm SPer SPoG SSea SWCr
'Albertine' (Ra) 𝕐H4 — Widely available
'Alchymist' (S/Cl) — CPou EPfP LRHS LTen MAus MBri MRav NLar SEND SPer WBor
Alec's Red = 'Cored' (HT) — CBcs CSBt CTri CWSG GCoc LAst LRHS LSRN LStr MAsh MAus MRav MWat SMrm SPer SPoG SRGP SWCr
Alexander = 'Harlex' (HT) 𝕐H4 — CGro GCoc LSRN LStr MAus MRav SEND SPer SSea SWCr
'Alexander von Humboldt' (Cl) — NLar
Alexander's Issie = 'DIcland' (F) — IDic
'Alexandre Girault' (Ra) — CRHN LRHS MAus MBri NLar SEND SPer SWCr
'Alfred de Dalmas' misapplied — see *R.* 'Mousseline'
'Alfresco'[PBR] (ClHT) — CSBt SSea
Alibaba = 'Chewalibaba' (Cl) — EBee ECnt ESty MAsh
'Alida Lovett' (Ra) — MAus
Alison = 'Coclibee'[PBR] (F) — GCoc LSRN SWCr
§ 'Alister Stella Gray' (N) — EPfP EWTr MAus MBri MCot MMuc NEgg NLar SEND SLon SMad SPer SSea SWCr
'Allen Chandler' (ClHT) — MAus
§ Alnwick Castle = 'Ausgrab'[PBR] (S) — EPfP LRHS LStr MAus MBri SCoo SMrm SPer SSea SWCr
'Aloha' (ClHT) 𝕐H4 — CBcs CGro CTri EBee ELon EPfP ESty EWTr GCoc LAst LRHS LStr MAsh MAus MBri MCot MRav NLar SEND SMrm SPer SPoG SSea SWCr
***alpina*** — see *R. pendulina*
'Alpine Sunset' (HT) — CTri ELon ESty MAsh MRav SPer SPoG SWCr
***altaica*** Willd. — see *R. spinosissima*
Altissimo = 'Delmur' (Cl) — CGro EBee LRHS MAus SEND SPer SSea SWCr
'Amadis' (Bs) — MAus
Amanda = 'Beesian' (F) — ESty LSRN
'Amazing Grace' (HT) — SWCr
'Ambassador Nogami' (S) — EBls
Amber Abundance = 'Harfizz'[PBR] (Abundance Series) (S) — ESty MRav
Amber Cover = 'Poulbambe'[PBR] (Towne & Country Series) (GC) — SWCr
Amber Nectar = 'Mehamber'[PBR] (F) — MAsh
Amber Queen = 'Harroony' (F) 𝕐H4 — CGro CSBt CTri EBee EPfP GCoc IArd LStr MAsh MAus MBri MRav SMrm SPer SWCr
***amblyotis*** RBS 0262 — NLar
Ambridge Rose = 'Auswonder' (S) — MAus
'Amélia' — see *R.* 'Celsiana'
Amelia = 'Poulen011'[PBR] (Renaissance Series) (S) — ECnt SWCr
'American Pillar' (Ra) — CGro CSBt CTri CWSG ECnt ELan EPfP EWTr LRHS LStr MAsh MAus MMuc MRav NLar SEND SPer SPoG SSea SWCr WBor WKif
'Amy Robsart' (RH) — MAus
'Anaïs Ségalas' (G) — MAus
'Andersonii' (*canina* hybrid) — MAus
***anemoniflora*** — see *R.* × *beanii*
Angela = 'Grifgela' — LSRN
Angela Rippon = 'Ocaru' (Min) — CSBt SPer
'Angela's Choice' (F) — LSRN
Anisley Dickson = 'Dickimono' (F) 𝕐H4 — SPer
Ann = 'Ausfete'[PBR] (S) — LSRN MAus
Ann Henderson = 'Fryhoncho' (F) — LSRN
Anna Ford = 'Harpiccolo' (Min/Patio) 𝕐H4 — LStr SPer
Anna Livia = 'Kormetter'[PBR] (F) 𝕐H4 — EBls ECnt
Anne Boleyn = 'Ausecret'[PBR] (S) — LRHS MAsh MAus MBri NEgg SCoo
'Anne Dakin' (ClHT) — MAus
Anne Harkness = 'Harkaramel' (F) — MAus SPer
Antique '89 = 'Kordalen'[PBR] (ClF) — MAsh
Antique = 'Antike' (F) **new** — CPou
Aperitif = 'Macwaira'[PBR] (HT) — ESty
Aphrodite = 'Tanetidor' — ESty
apothecary's rose — see *R. gallica* var. *officinalis*
'Apricot Nectar' (F) — GCoc MAus SPer
'Apricot Silk' (HT) — CTri SPer
Apricot Sunblaze = 'Savamark' (Min) — CSBt
Archbishop Desmond Tutu = 'Beafatty' **new** — EBls
'Archiduc Joseph' misapplied — see *R.* 'Général Schablikine'
'Arethusa' (Ch) — EBee SLon
§ ***arkansana*** var. ***suffulta*** — GAuc
Art Nouveau = 'Pejamark' (F) **new** — ESty
'Arthur Bell' (F) 𝕐H4 — CGro CSBt CTri ELon EPfP ESty GCoc IArd LAst LRHS LStr MAsh MAus MRav MWat NEgg NPri SMrm SPer SPoG SRGP SSea SWCr WBor
'Arthur de Sansal' (DPo) — EWTr MAus WBor
Artistic Licence = 'Guesmarble' **new** — SWCr
***arvensis*** — CCVT CHab CRWN LBuc MAus NWea
'Assemblage des Beautés' (G) — MAus

| | | |
|---|---|---|
| | 'Astra Desmond' (Ra) | WTin |
| | Attleborough = 'Beaat' (ClHT) **new** | EBls |
| | Audrey Wilcox = 'Frywilrey' (HT) | CSBt |
| | 'Auguste Gervais' (Ra) | MAus |
| | Austrian copper rose | see *R. foetida* 'Bicolor' |
| | Austrian yellow | see *R. foetida* |
| | 'Autumn' (HT) | LSRN |
| | 'Autumn Delight' (HM) | EBee EWTr |
| | Autumn Fire | see *R.* 'Herbstfeuer' |
| | 'Autumnalis' | see *R.* 'Princesse de Nassau' |
| | 'Avignon' (F) | EBee |
| | Avon = 'Poulmulti'PBR (GC) ♀H4 | ELan EPfP GCoc MRav SPer SWCr |
| | Awakening = 'Probuzení' (ClHT) | EBee ECGP EWTr NLar SWCr |
| | 'Ayrshire Splendens' | see *R.* 'Splendens' |
| | 'Baby Bio' (F/Patio) | ESty SWCr |
| | 'Baby Faurax' (Poly) | MAus |
| | Baby Gold Star (Min) | see *R.* 'Estrellita de Oro' |
| | Baby Love = 'Scrivluv'PBR (yellow) (Min/Patio) ♀H4 | CTri MAus |
| | Baby Masquerade = 'Tanba' (Min) | GCoc MRav MWat SPer SWCr |
| | Babyface = 'Rawril'PBR (Min) | ESty |
| | 'Ballerina' (HM/Poly) ♀H4 | CGro CSBt CTri EBee ECnt ELan EPfP ESty GCoc LRHS LSRN LStr MAsh MAus MBri MRav MWat NEgg NLar NPri SMad SMrm SPer SSea SWCr WBor WKif |
| | Ballindalloch Castle = 'Cocneel'PBR (F) | GCoc |
| | 'Baltimore Belle' (Ra) | CRHN MAus |
| | ***banksiae*** (Ra) | CFee CPou SRms |
| | - ***alba*** | see *R. banksiae* var. *banksiae* |
| § | - var. ***banksiae*** (Ra/d) | CBot CDul CHll CPou CSBt CTri EBee ELan EPfP ERea GQui LStr MAus SLon SPer WCot XSen |
| | - 'Lutea' (Ra/d) ♀H3 | Widely available |
| | - 'Lutescens' (Ra) | CHll ERea |
| | - var. ***normalis*** (Ra) | CBot CSBt MAus SKHP SLon WCot WHer |
| I | - 'Rosea' | NLar |
| | 'Bantry Bay' (ClHT) | CSBt EBee ELan LSRN LStr SEND SLon SPer SSea SWCr |
| | Barbara Austin = 'Austop'PBR (S) | MAus |
| | Barbara Windsor = 'Ganleon'PBR (F) | EBee GCoc SWCr |
| | Barkarole = 'Tanelorak'PBR (HT) | CSBt ESty LStr SWCr |
| | 'Baron Girod de l'Ain' (HP) | ELon ESty LAst LRHS MAus MMuc MRav NEgg NLar SEND SMrm SPer SWCr WBor |
| | 'Baroness Rothschild' ambig. | see *R.* Baronne Edmond de Rothschild, Baronne Edmond de Rothschild, Climbing |
| | 'Baroness Rothschild' (HP) | see *R.* 'Baronne Adolph de Rothschild' |
| | 'Baroness Rothschild' (HT) | see *R.* Baronne Edmond de Rothschild |
| § | 'Baronne Adolph de Rothschild' (HP) | MAus MRav |
| § | Baronne Edmond de Rothschild = 'Meigriso' (HT) | EWTr |
| § | Baronne Edmond de Rothschild, Climbing = 'Meigrisosar' (Cl/HT) | CSBt |
| | 'Baronne Prévost' (HP) | MAus SFam |
| | Baroque Floorshow = 'Harbaroque'PBR (S) | MRav |
| | Barry Stephens = 'Horcabellero' (HT) | LSRN |
| | 'Bashful' (Poly) | CGro |
| § | × ***beanii*** (Ra) | IFro |
| | Beatrix Potter **new** | EBls |
| | 'Beau Narcisse' (G) | MAus |
| | Beautiful Britain = 'Dicfire' (F) | LStr MRav SWCr |
| | Beautiful Sunrise = 'Bostimebide'PBR (ClPatio) | SWCr |
| § | Bella = 'Pouljill'PBR (Renaissance Series) (S) | CPou |
| | 'Belle Amour' (A × D) | MAus |
| | Belle Blonde = 'Menap' (HT) | SPer |
| | 'Belle de Crécy' (G) ♀H4 | CPou CSam CTri LRHS LStr MAsh MAus MMuc NPri SEND SFam SKHP SMrm SPer SWCr |
| | 'Belle des Jardins' misapplied | see *R.* × *centifolia* 'Unique Panachée' |
| | Belle Epoque = 'Fryyaboo'PBR (HT) | CGro GCoc LStr SMrm SWCr |
| | 'Belle Isis' (G) | MAus MRav SPer |
| | 'Belle Poitevine' (Ru) | MCot |
| | 'Belle Portugaise' (ClT) | MAus |
| | Belmonte = 'Harpearl'PBR (F) **new** | LRHS |
| § | 'Belvedere' (Ra) | CPou MAus SPer WBor |
| | Benita = 'Dicquarrel' (HT) | IDic |
| | Benjamin Britten = 'Ausencart'PBR (S) | CSBt EPfP LRHS MAus MBri NEgg |
| | Benson and Hedges Gold = 'Macgem' (HT) | CWSG |
| | Benson and Hedges Special = 'Macshana' (Min) | ECGP |
| | Berkshire = 'Korpinka'PBR (GC) ♀H4 | GCoc LStr NLar SWCr |
| | Beryl Joyce = 'Tan96145'PBR (HT) | ESty SWCr |
| | Best of Friends = 'Pouldunk'PBR (HT) | LSRN SWCr |
| | Best Wishes = 'Chessnut'PBR (ClHT/v) | CSBt EBls GCoc LBuc LSRN |
| | Betty Boop = 'Wekplapic'PBR (F) | SRGP |
| | 'Betty Prior' (F) | GCoc |
| § | Bewitched = 'Poulbella'PBR (Castle Series) (F) | ECnt EPfP MAsh SWCr |
| | Bianco = 'Cocblanco' (Patio/Min) | GCoc MAus MRav MWat |
| | Big Purple = 'Stebigpu'PBR (HT) | ECnt ESty |
| | Birthday Boy = 'Tan97607'PBR (HT) | CGro ESty LSRN LStr MRav SWCr |
| | Birthday Girl = 'Meilasso'PBR (F) | CSBt ESty LBuc LSRN LStr MAsh MRav MWat NPri SCoo SMrm SRGP SSea SVic SWCr |
| | Birthday Wishes = 'Guesdelay' (HT) | CTri LRHS LSRN MAsh MBri SWCr |
| | Bishop Elphinstone = 'Cocjolly' (F) | GCoc |
| | Black Baccara = 'Meidebenne'PBR (HT) | CPou EGxp ESty SMrm SWCr |
| | Black Beauty = 'Korfleur' (HT) | MAus |
| | 'Black Ice' (F) | GCoc SPer SWCr |

'Black Jack' (Ce) — see *R.* 'Tour de Malakoff'
'Blairii Number Two' (ClBb) $\Upsilon^{H4}$ — CSam EPfP MAus MRav NEgg NLar SEND SPer
'Blanche Double de Coubert' (Ru) $\Upsilon^{H4}$ — CDul CSBt CSam CTri EBee ECnt ELan EPfP GCoc LBuc LSRN LStr MAus NEgg NLar SEND SMrm SPer SSea SWCr
'Blanche Moreau' (CeMo) — MAus NLar SKHP SLon SPer
'Blanchefleur' (Ce × G) — MAus MRav
'Blesma Soul' (HT) — CSBt
'Blessings' (HT) $\Upsilon^{H4}$ — CBcs CGro CSBt CTri GCoc LBuc LSRN LStr MAsh MAus MGos MRav SMrm SPer SRGP SWCr
'Bleu Magenta' (Ra) $\Upsilon^{H4}$ — EBee IArd MAus MRav NLar SEND SMrm SWCr WKif
'Bloomfield Abundance' (Poly) — CPou ECGP EPfP MAus MRav SPer SWCr WHer
'Blossomtime' (Cl) — SMad SPer
Blue for You = 'Pejamblu'$^{PBR}$ (F) — CGro EBee ECnt ESty GCoc LRHS LStr MAsh MAus MBri SCoo SMrm SPoG SWCr
Blue Moon = 'Tannacht' (HT) — CTri ELan GCoc MGos MRav SPer SPoG
Blue Peter = 'Ruiblun'$^{PBR}$ (Min) — ESty
'Blush Hip' (A) — MAus
'Blush Noisette' — see *R.* 'Noisette Carnée'
'Blush Rambler' (Ra) — CSBt EPfP EWTr MAus MMuc SEND SPer
'Blushing Lucy' (Ra) — MTPN SMrm
Blythe Spirit = 'Auschool'$^{PBR}$ (S) — MAus MBri NEgg
'Bobbie James' (Ra) $\Upsilon^{H4}$ — CTri EBee EPfP GCoc LRHS LStr MAus MBri MRav NEgg NLar SPer SPoG SRGP SSea SWCr
Bonica = 'Meidomonac' (GC) $\Upsilon^{H4}$ — CSam CTri ECnt ELan EPfP ESty EWTr GCoc LRHS LShp LStr MAsh MAus MBri MCot MRav MWat NEgg NLar NPri SEND SMrm SPer SPoG SSea SWCr WKif
§ Bonita = 'Poulen009'$^{PBR}$ (Renaissance Series) (S) — ECnt
Boogie-Woogie = 'Poulyc006'$^{PBR}$ (Courtyard Series) (ClHT) — ECnt MAsh MBri SWCr
'Born Again' — MRav
'Botzaris' (D) — SFam
'Boule de Neige' (Bb) — CBcs CGro CTri EBee ECnt ELan ELon EPfP GCoc LRHS LSRN LStr MAus MBri MRav MWat NLar SFam SMrm SPer SWCr
'Bouquet d'Or' (N) — MAus NLar
'Bouquet Tout Fait' misapplied — see *R.* 'Nastarana'
'Bouquet Tout Fait' (N) — EBee
Bow Bells = 'Ausbells' (S) — MAus
Bowled Over = 'Tandolgnil'$^{PBR}$ (F) — ESty GCoc SWCr
§ ***bracteata*** — CHII CRHN ECre EWes GQui MAus
Brass Ring — see *R.* Peek-a-boo
Brave Heart = 'Horbondsmile' (F) — MAus MRav SPoG
Breath of Life = 'Harquanne'$^{PBR}$ (ClHT) — CGro CSBt ELan LStr MAus MRav SPer SWCr
Breathtaking = 'Hargalore'$^{PBR}$ (HT) — ESty SWCr
Bredon = 'Ausbred' (S) — MAus
§ 'Brenda Colvin' (Ra) — MAus
'Brian's Star' (F) — GCoc LSRN
Bride and Groom = 'Smi 10-98' (HT) **new** — ESty
Bride = 'Fryyearn'$^{PBR}$ (HT) — ESty GCoc LSRN LStr MRav SWCr
Bridge of Sighs = 'Harglowing'$^{PBR}$ (Cl) — ECnt ESty LShp LStr MAsh MBri SPoG SSea SWCr
Bright Fire = 'Peaxi'$^{PBR}$ (ClHT) — SPer SSea SWCr
Bright Future = 'Kirora'$^{PBR}$ (Cl) — ECnt ESty
Bright Smile = 'Dicdance' (F/Patio) — MAus MRav SPer
Brilliant Pink Iceberg = 'Probril' (F) — LStr SWCr
Britannia = 'Frycalm'$^{PBR}$ (HT) — ECnt MAsh
Broadlands = 'Tanmirsch'$^{PBR}$ (GC) — GCoc NLar SLon SWCr
Brother Cadfael = 'Ausglobe'$^{PBR}$ (S) — EBls LRHS LStr MAus MBri NEgg NLar SCoo SPer SSea SWCr
Brown Velvet = 'Maccultra'$^{PBR}$ (F) — ESty SPer SWCr
§ ***brunonii*** (Ra) — CPLG EWes MAus
- CC 4515 — WCot
- CC 5147 — GKev
- 'Betty Sherriff' (Ra) — GGar
§ - 'La Mortola' (Ra) — MAus MRav NLar SPer
Brush-strokes = 'Guescolour' (F) — ESty SWCr
'Buff Beauty' (HM) $\Upsilon^{H4}$ — CSBt CSam CTri CWSG EBee ECnt ELan EPfP EWTr GCoc LAst LRHS LSRN LStr MAsh MAus MRav MWat NEgg NLar NPri SFam SMad SPer SSea SWCr WCFE
'Bullata' — see *R.* × *centifolia* 'Bullata'
§ 'Burgundiaca' (G) — MAus
Burgundian rose — see *R.* 'Burgundiaca'
Burgundy Ice = 'Prose'$^{PBR}$ (F) — CGro CSBt EBee EBls ECnt ESty GCoc LBuc LShp LStr MRav SCoo SMad SMrm SPoG SWCr
'Burgundy Rose' — see *R.* 'Burgundiaca'
'Burma Star' (F) — GCoc SWCr
burnet, double pink — see *R. spinosissima* double pink-flowered
burnet, double white — see *R. spinosissima* double white-flowered
Bush Baby = 'Peanob'$^{PBR}$ (Min) — SWCr
Buttercup = 'Ausband'$^{PBR}$ (S) — LRHS MAus
Buxom Beauty = 'Korbilant'$^{PBR}$ (HT) — ECnt ESty GCoc LRHS MAsh MBri MGos MWat SCoo SPoG SWCr
'C.F. Meyer' — see *R.* 'Conrad Ferdinand Meyer'
***californica*** (S) — GAuc MAus
- 'Plena' — see *R. nutkana* 'Plena'
'Callisto' (HM) — CSam MAus SWCr
§ Calypso = 'Poulclimb'$^{PBR}$ (ClHT) — ECnt SWCr
'Camayeux' (G) — CPou ECnt MAus NLar SMrm SPer
Cambridgeshire = 'Korhaugen'$^{PBR}$ (GC) — LStr MAus SPer SSea SWCr
Camille Pisarro = 'Destricol' (F) — MRav
'Canary Bird' — see *R. xanthina* 'Canary Bird'
***canina*** (S) — CArn CCVT CDul CHab CLnd CRWN CTri ECrN EPfP LBuc MAus MRav NWea SEWo SPer SPoG WMou
'Cantabrigiensis' (S) $\Upsilon^{H4}$ — CSam EPfP MAus NLar SLon SPer SSea
Canterbury = 'Ausbury' (S) — MAus
'Capitaine Basroger' (CeMo) — MAus

|  |  |
|---|---|
| 'Capitaine John Ingram' (CeMo) 🏆H4 | MAus SEND SLon |
| 'Captain Christy' | see *R.* 'Climbing Captain Christy' |
| 'Captain Scarlet' (ClMin) | ESty |
| 'Cardinal de Richelieu' (G) 🏆H4 | CBcs CPou CSam CTri EBee ELon EPfP EWTr GCoc GCra LAst LRHS LSRN LShp LStr MAsh MAus MBri MCot MRav MWat NEgg NLar SEND SFam SMrm SPer SPoG SWCr |
| Cardinal Hume = 'Harregale' (S) | EBee ESty |
| Carefree Days = 'Meirivouri' (Patio) | EPfP LRHS MAsh MBri NPri SMrm SPoG |
| Caribbean Dawn = 'Korfeining'PBR (Patio) | MAsh |
| Caring for You ambig. | LSRN |
| Caring for You = 'Coclust'PBR (HT) | GCoc |
| 'Carmenetta' (S) | NHaw |
| 'Carol' (Gn) | see *R.* 'Carol Amling' |
| § 'Carol Amling' (F) | LSRN |
| ***carolina*** | SLPl |
| 'Caroline Testout' | see *R.* 'Madame Caroline Testout' |
| Caroline Victoria = 'Harprior'PBR (HT) **new** | LRHS LSRN SWCr |
| Carris = 'Harmanna'PBR (HT) **new** | ESty |
| Cascade = 'Poulskab'PBR (ClMin) | ECnt |
| § Casino = 'Macca' (ClHT) | CTri EBee ELon GCoc LAst LBuc MAsh MRav SPer |
| 'Castle Apricot'PBR | see *R.* Lazy Days |
| 'Castle Cream' | see *R.* Perfect Day |
| 'Castle Fuchsia Pink'PBR | see *R.* Bewitched = 'Poulbella' |
| Castle of Mey = 'Coclucid' (F) | GCoc |
| 'Castle Peach'PBR | see *R.* Imagination = 'Pouldron' |
| 'Castle Shrimp Pink'PBR | see *R.* Fascination = 'Poulmax' |
| 'Castle Yellow'PBR | see *R.* Summer Gold |
| 'Catherine Mermet' (T) | MAus |
| § 'Cécile Brünner' (Poly) 🏆H4 | CTri ELan GCoc LRHS LSRN LStr MAus MCot NLar SMad SMrm SPer SSea SWCr |
| Celebration 2000 = 'Horcoffitup'PBR (S) | MAus |
| § 'Céleste' (A) 🏆H4 | EPfP EWTr GCoc LStr MAus MRav NLar SEND SFam SPer |
| 'Célina' (CeMo) | LSRN |
| 'Céline Forestier' (N) 🏆H3 | CPou EBee EWTr MAus MRav NLar SEND SPer SPoG |
| § 'Celsiana' (D) | CPou CSam EWTr LSRN MAus SFam SPer |
| Centenaire de Lourdes = 'Delge' (F) | EBee |
| Centenary = 'Koreledas'PBR (F) 🏆H4 | SPer |
| § × ***centifolia*** (Ce) | CArn LRHS MAus MRav SMad SPer |
| § - 'Bullata' (Ce) | MAus |
| § - 'Cristata' (Ce) 🏆H4 | ECnt ELon LRHS LStr MAus MRav NLar SEND SFam SPer SWCr WBor |
| § - 'De Meaux' (Ce) | MAus MRav NLar SPer |
| § - 'Muscosa' (CeMo) | GCoc LStr MRav MWat SEND SFam |
| - 'Parvifolia' | see *R.* 'Burgundiaca' |
| § - 'Shailer's White Moss' (CeMo) | MAus SFam |
| - 'Spong' (Ce) | MAus |
| § - 'Unique' (Ce) | MAus NLar |
| § - 'Unique Panachée' (Ce) | CPou MAus |
| 'Centifolia Variegata' | see *R.* × *centifolia* 'Unique Panachée' |
| Centre Stage = 'Chewcreepy'PBR (S/GC) | MAsh MAus |
| 'Cerise Bouquet' (S) 🏆H4 | MAus MRav SPer |
| 'Champagne Dream' (Patio) | SWCr |
| § Champagne Moments = 'Korvanaber'PBR (F) | CBcs CSBt EBee EBls ECnt ELan EPfP ESty GCoc LRHS LSRN LStr MAsh MAus MGos MRav MWat NPri SPer SPoG SSea SWCr |
| 'Champneys Pink Cluster' (China hybrid) | LRHS MAus |
| Chandos Beauty = 'Harmisty'PBR (HT) | EBee ECnt ESty GCoc LRHS LStr MAsh SWCr |
| 'Chanelle' (F) | SDix SPer |
| Chantal Merieux = 'Masmaric' (Generosa Series) (S) | MRav |
| Chapeau de Napoléon | see *R.* × *centifolia* 'Cristata' |
| Charles Austin = 'Ausles' (S) | MAus MRav SMrm |
| Charles Darwin = 'Auspeet'PBR (S) | EPfP MAsh MAus MBri NEgg SCoo SPer SWCr |
| Charles de Gaulle | see *R.* Katherine Mansfield |
| 'Charles de Mills' (G) 🏆H4 | CSam CTri EBee ECnt ELan EPfP EWTr GCoc GCra LRHS LShp LStr MAus MBri MRav MWat NLar SFam SKHP SPer SRGP SWCr |
| Charles Rennie Mackintosh = 'Ausren'PBR (S) | CSBt LRHS MAus MBri NEgg SWCr |
| Charlie's Rose = 'Tanellepa' (HT) | ESty LSRN SWCr |
| Charlotte = 'Auspoly'PBR (S) 🏆H4 | EPfP ESty LRHS LSRN MAus MBri NEgg SCoo SEND SMrm SPer SSea SWCr |
| Charmant = 'Korpeligo'PBR (Min) | LRHS |
| Charmian = 'Ausmian' (S) | MAus |
| Charming Cover = 'Poulharmu'PBR (Towne & Country Series) (GC/S) | MAsh |
| Chartreuse de Parme = 'Delviola' (S) | ESty MRav |
| 'Château de Clos-Vougeot' (HT) | IArd |
| Chatsworth = 'Tanotax'PBR (Patio/F) | MRav SMrm SPer SSea SWCr |
| Chaucer = 'Auscer' (S) | MAus |
| § Cheek to Cheek = 'Poulslas'PBR (Courtyard Series) (ClMin) | MAsh SWCr |
| Cheerful Charlie = 'Cocquimmer'PBR (F) | LSRN MRav |
| CheriePBR | see *R.* Songs of Praise |
| Cherry Brandy '85 = 'Tanryrandy'PBR (HT) | CSBt |
| Cheshire = 'Fryelise'PBR (HT) | GCoc |
| Cheshire = 'Korkonopi'PBR (County Rose Series) (S) | MAus SWCr |
| 'Cheshire Life' (HT) | MAus |
| Chianti = 'Auswine' (S) | EBee MAus NLar |
| Chicago Peace = 'Johnago' (HT) | GCoc SWCr |
| Child of AchievementPBR | see *R.* Bella |
| Child of My Heart = 'Beapeace' (HT) | EBls |

Childhood Memories = 'Ferho' (ClHM) — SWCr
Chilterns = 'Kortemma'[PBR] (GC) — SWCr
'Chinatown' (F/S) ♀H4 — CGro CSBt CTri LStr MAsh MAus MRav SMrm SPer SWCr
***chinensis*** misapplied — see *R.* × *odorata*
- 'Minima' *sensu stricto* hort. — see *R.* 'Pompon de Paris'
- 'Mutabilis' — see *R.* × *odorata* 'Mutabilis'
- 'Old Blush' — see *R.* × *odorata* 'Pallida'
Chloe = 'Poulen003'[PBR] (Renaissance Series) (S) — CPou EBee ECnt LSRN SLon SWCr
'Chloris' (A) — MMuc
'Chorus Girl' (F) — MBri
Chris Beardshaw = 'Wekmeredoc'[PBR] (HT) — SWCr
Chris = 'Kirsan'[PBR] (ClHT) — EBee ECnt ESty GCoc LSRN MAus SWCr WGor
Christopher = 'Cocopher' (HT) — GCoc SWCr
Christopher Columbus = 'Meinronsse' (HT) — IArd MMuc
Christopher Marlowe = 'Ausjump'[PBR] (S) — LRHS MAsh MAus MBri SCoo
Cider Cup = 'Dicladida'[PBR] (Min/Patio) ♀H4 — ESty IDic LStr MAus SWCr
'Cinderella' (Min) — CSBt
Cinderella = 'Korfobalt' (ClS) — CPou SWCr
City Lights = 'Poulgan'[PBR] (Patio) — CSBt
City of Carlsbad[PBR] — see *R.* Hanky Panky
'City of Leeds' (F) — MAsh SPer
City of London = 'Harukfore'[PBR] (F) — CSBt SPer SWCr
City of York = 'Direktör Benschop' (ClHT) — MCot
Clair Matin = 'Meimont' (ClS) — CPou MAus
Claire Austin = 'Ausprior'[PBR] (S) — EPfP ESty LRHS MAus MBNS MBri SSea SWCr
'Claire Jacquier' (N) — MAus MMuc SPer SWCr
Claire Rose = 'Auslight'[PBR] (S) — LSRN MAus MRav SMrm SPer
'Clarence House' (Cl) — EBls
Claret = 'Frykristal'[PBR] (HT) — CGro ECnt ESty GCoc LStr SWCr
Clarinda = 'Cocsummery'[PBR] (F) — GCoc
Claude Monet = 'Jacdesa' (HT) — MRav SPoG
'Clementina Carbonieri' (T) — NLar
Cleo = 'Beebop' (HT) — LSRN
'Cliff Richard' (F) — ESty LBuc LSRN SWCr
'Climbing Alec's Red' (ClHT) — ELon
'Climbing Allgold' (ClF) — SLon
'Climbing Arthur Bell' (ClF) ♀H4 — CSBt CTri ESty GCoc LAst LBuc MAsh SPer SPoG SSea SWCr
'Climbing Ballerina' (Ra) — CSBt GCoc SWCr
'Climbing Blue Moon' (ClHT) — GCoc LBuc SWCr
§ 'Climbing Captain Christy' (ClHT) — MAus
'Climbing Cécile Brünner' (ClPoly) ♀H4 — CSBt CTri EBee ECnt EPfP LSRN LStr MAus MBri MCot MRav NLar SEND SPer SPoG SSea SWCr
'Climbing Château de Clos-Vougeot' (ClHT) — MAus
'Climbing Christine' (ClHT) — MAus
§ 'Climbing Columbia' (ClHT) — ERea EShb SPer
'Climbing Crimson Glory' (ClHT) — CPou GCoc MAus MBri
§ 'Climbing Devoniensis' (ClT) — CPou
'Climbing Ena Harkness' (ClHT) — CTri ELon GCoc MAus MBri MRav SEND SPer SPoG SSea SWCr
'Climbing Etoile de Hollande' (ClHT) ♀H4 — CSBt CSam CTri CWSG EPfP GCoc LStr MAsh MAus MBri MRav SEND SFam SMad SPer SPoG SSea SWCr
Climbing Fragrant Cloud = 'Colfragrasar' (ClHT) — CBcs ELan
'Climbing Home Sweet Home' (ClHT) — LSRN
'Climbing Iceberg' (ClF) ♀H4 — CGro CSBt CTri EBee ELan EPfP ESty GCoc IArd LSRN LStr MAsh MAus MMuc MRav MWat NEgg NLar SMrm SPer SPoG SSea SWCr
'Climbing Jazz'[PBR] — see *R.* That's Jazz
'Climbing la France' (ClHT) — MRav
§ 'Climbing Lady Hillingdon' (ClT) ♀H3 — ECGP EPfP LRHS MAus MBri MRav NEgg NLar SEND SPer SWCr WBor
'Climbing Lady Sylvia' (ClHT) — CSBt EBee LRHS MAus MBri SPer
'Climbing Little White Pet' — see *R.* 'Félicité Perpétue'
'Climbing Madame Abel Chatenay' (ClHT) — MAus
'Climbing Madame Butterfly' (ClHT) — MAus NLar SPer
'Climbing Madame Caroline Testout' (ClHT) — CPou CTri MAus MRav SEND SPer
§ 'Climbing Madame Edouard Herriot' (ClHT) — MAus
'Climbing Masquerade' (ClF) — CTri GCoc LBuc MAus MRav NEgg SEND SPer SSea SWCr
'Climbing Mrs Herbert Stevens' (ClHT) — LRHS MAsh MAus MRav SEND SMrm SPer SWCr
'Climbing Mrs Sam McGredy' (ClHT) ♀H4 — CSBt MAus
'Climbing Niphetos' (ClT) — MAus
'Climbing Ophelia' (ClHT) — MAus SEND SPer
Climbing Orange Sunblaze = 'Meiji Katarsar'[PBR] (ClMin) — SPer
§ 'Climbing Paul Lédé' (ClT) — MAus SEND SWCr
'Climbing Peace' (ClHT) — SPer
§ 'Climbing Pompon de Paris' (ClMinCh) — CBot CTri MAus MRav SEND SLPl SMrm SPer
'Climbing Ruby Wedding' — LSRN
'Climbing Shot Silk' (ClHT) ♀H4 — SPer SWCr
§ 'Climbing Souvenir de la Malmaison' (ClBb) — CPou MAus SPer
'Climbing White Cloud'[PBR] — see *R.* White Cloud = 'Korstacha'
Cloud Nine = 'Fryextra'[PBR] (HT) — ECnt GCoc
'Colby School' (F) — EBls
Colchester Beauty = 'Cansend' (F) — ECnt
Colchester Castle = 'Poulcs008'[PBR] (Patio) — ECnt
colonial white — see *R.* 'Sombreuil'
'Columbia' — CPou
'Columbian' — see *R.* 'Climbing Columbia'
'Commandant Beaurepaire' (Bb) — MAus
common moss — see *R.* × *centifolia* 'Muscosa'
Commonwealth Glory = 'Harclue'[PBR] (HT) — SWCr
'Compassion' (ClHT) ♀H4 — CSBt CTri CWSG EBee ECnt ELan EPfP ESty GCoc GKin IArd LAst

| | | |
|---|---|---|
| | | LRHS LSRN LStr MAsh MAus MBri MRav MWat NEgg NLar NPri SMrm SPer SPoG SRGP SSea SWCr WBor |
| * | 'Compassionate' (F) | MRav |
| | 'Complicata' (G) ♀H4 | CTri EPfP EWTr LRHS LStr MAus MBri MCot MRav NLar SEND SKHP SPer SSea SWCr |
| | 'Comte de Chambord' misapplied | see *R.* 'Madame Knorr' |
| | Comtes de Champagne = 'Ausufo'[PBR] (S) | LRHS MAus MBri SCoo |
| | 'Comtesse Cécile de Chabrillant' (HP) | CPou EBee MAus |
| | 'Comtesse de Lacépède' misapplied | see *R.* 'Du Maître d'Ecole' |
| § | 'Comtesse de Murinais' (DMo) | MAus SFam |
| | Comtesse de Ségur = 'Deltendre' (S) | MRav |
| § | 'Comtesse du Caÿla' (Ch) | MAus |
| | Concert[PBR] | see *R.* Calypso |
| | 'Conditorum' (G) | SFam |
| | Congratulations = 'Korlift' (HT) | CSBt ECnt GCoc IArd LBuc LSRN LStr MAus MGos MRav NPri SMrm SPer SRGP SSea SVic SWCr |
| | Connie = 'Boselftay'[PBR] (F) | EGxp GCoc LSRN |
| § | 'Conrad Ferdinand Meyer' (Ru) | CSBt EBee SMrm SPer |
| | Conservation = 'Cocdimple'[PBR] (Min/Patio) | GCoc SMrm SWCr |
| | Constance Finn = 'Hareden'[PBR] (F) | MRav SWCr |
| | 'Constance Spry' (ClS) ♀H4 | CTri EBee ELan EPfP LRHS LStr MAus MBri MMuc MRav MWat NEgg NLar NPri SEND SMrm SPer SWCr |
| § | 'Cooperi' (Ra) | CAbP CWib EWTr MAus MCot SPer SSea SWCr WPGP |
| | Cooper's Burmese | see *R.* 'Cooperi' |
| | 'Coral Cluster' (Poly) | MAus |
| | Coral Palace[PBR] | see *R.* Imagination = 'Pouldron' |
| | Cordelia = 'Ausbottle'[PBR] (S) | MAus MBri |
| | 'Cornelia' (HM) ♀H4 | CBcs CSBt CSam CTri EBee EPfP EWTr GCoc IArd LAst LSRN LStr MAsh MAus MCot MRav MWat NLar SFam SMad SPer SRGP SSea SWCr |
| | Coronation Street = 'Wekswetrup' (F) | LSRN |
| | Corvedale = 'Ausnetting'[PBR] (S) | LRHS MAus |
| | cottage maid | see *R.* × *centifolia* 'Unique Panachée' |
| | Cottage Rose = 'Ausglisten'[PBR] (S) | CGro LRHS LSRN MAus MBri MRav SMrm SWCr |
| | Countess Celeste[PBR] | see *R.* Imagination = 'Pouldron' |
| | 'Coupe d'Hébé' (Bb) | MAus |
| | Courage = 'Poulduf'[PBR] (HT) | ECnt |
| | Courvoisier = 'Macsee' (F) | CSBt |
| | 'Cramoisi Picotée' (G) | MAus |
| | 'Cramoisi Supérieur' (Ch) | MAus |
| | Crathes Castle = 'Cocathes' (F) | GCoc |
| | Crazy for You = 'Wekroalt'[PBR] (F) | ESty LSRN MAsh SRGP SSea SWCr |
| | Cream Abundance = 'Harflax'[PBR] (Abundance Series) (F) | EBee ESty LStr SWCr |
| | Crème Anglaise = 'Ganang'[PBR] (ClHT) | GCoc |

| | | |
|---|---|---|
| | Crème Brûlée = 'Ganbru'[PBR] (Cl) | GCoc |
| | Crème de la Crème = 'Gancre'[PBR] (ClHT) | CSBt EBee EBls ECnt ELon ESty GCoc MAus MRav SPer SPoG SSea SWCr |
| | 'Crépuscule' (N) | MAus NLar SWCr |
| | Cressida = 'Auscress' (S) | MAus |
| | crested moss | see *R.* × *centifolia* 'Cristata' |
| | Cricri = 'Meicri' (Min) | MAus |
| | Crimson Cascade = 'Fryclimbdown'[PBR] (ClHT) | ESty GCoc LRHS MAsh MBri MRav SPer SPoG SSea SWCr |
| | crimson damask | see *R. gallica* var. *officinalis* |
| | 'Crimson Descant' (ClHT) | ECnt SWCr |
| | 'Crimson Glory' (HT) | GCoc MAsh SMrm |
| | 'Crimson Shower' (Ra) ♀H4 | CSam CTri EBee LRHS MAus MBNS MBri MMuc MRav NEgg SEND SMrm SPer SWCr WHer |
| | 'Cristata' | see *R.* × *centifolia* 'Cristata' |
| | Crocus Rose = 'Ausquest'[PBR] (S) | EBee EPfP LRHS LStr MAus MBri MRav MWat NEgg SMrm SPer SWCr |
| | Crown Princess Margareta = 'Auswinter'[PBR] (S) | ECnt EPfP ESty LRHS MAus MBri NEgg SCoo SMad SPer SSea SWCr |
| | cuisse de nymphe | see *R.* 'Great Maiden's Blush' |
| | 'Cupid' (ClHT) | MAus SPer |
| I | 'Cutie' (Patio) | ESty SWCr |
| | Cymbeline = 'Auslean' (S) | SPer |
| | Dacapo = 'Poulcy012'[PBR] (Courtyard Series) (ClPatio) | ECnt |
| | 'D'Aguesseau' (G) | MAus |
| | 'Daily Mail' | see *R.* 'Climbing Madame Edouard Herriot' |
| | 'Dainty Bess' (HT) | EBee MAus SSea SWCr |
| | 'Dale Farm' (F/Patio) **new** | ESty |
| | × ***damascena*** var. ***bifera*** | see *R.* × *damascena* var. *semperflorens* |
| § | – var. ***semperflorens*** (D) | MRav NLar SSea SWCr |
| | – 'Trigintipetala' misapplied | see *R.* 'Professeur Emile Perrot' |
| § | – 'Versicolor' (D) | SPer SSea SWCr |
| | Dame Wendy = 'Canson' (F) | MAus |
| | Dames de Chenonceau = 'Delpabra' (S) | MRav |
| | 'Danaë' (HM) | CSam MAus |
| | Dancing Queen = 'Fryfeston' (ClHT) | ECnt ESty GCoc LRHS MAsh MBri SWCr |
| | Danny Boy = 'Dicxcon'[PBR] (Patio) | IDic LSRN WGor |
| | 'Danse du Feu' (ClF) | CBcs CSBt CTri CWSG ELan EPfP LAst LRHS LStr MAsh MAus MRav NPri SPer SPoG SWCr |
| | Dapple Dawn = 'Ausapple' (S) | MAus |
| | Darcey Bussell = 'Ausdecorum'[PBR] (S) | CSBt EPfP ESty LRHS MAsh MAus MBri SSea SWCr |
| | 'Dart's Defender' (Ru) | SLPl |
| | David Whitfield = 'Gana'[PBR] (F) | GCoc LSRN |
| | ***davidii*** | MAus |
| | Dawn Chorus = 'Dicquasar'[PBR] (HT) ♀H4 | CGro CSBt CWSG EPfP ESty GCoc IDic LRHS LStr MAsh MBri MRav MWat SPer SPoG SWCr |
| | 'Daybreak' (HM) | CTri MAus |
| | 'De Meaux' | see *R.* × *centifolia* 'De Meaux' |
| | 'De Meaux, White' | see *R.* 'White de Meaux' |
| § | 'De Resht' (DPo) ♀H4 | CPou CTri EBee ECnt EPfP GCoc LRHS MAsh MAus MCot MRav MWat NLar SMrm SPer SWCr |
| | 'Dear Daughter' (F) **new** | ESty |

| |  |  |
|---|---|---|
| | 'Dearest' (F) | CBcs CSBt GCoc MRav SPer SWCr |
| | Deb's Delight = 'Legsweet'[PBR] (F) | LSRN |
| | 'Debutante' (Ra) | CSam EBee EWTr LRHS MAus |
| | 'Deep Secret' (HT) 🏆[H4] | CBcs CSBt CTri CWSG ECnt ELon EPfP ESty GCoc LRHS LStr MAsh MRav NPri SPer SPoG SRGP SSea SWCr |
| | 'Delambre' (DPo) | MAus |
| | Della Balfour = 'Harblend'[PBR] (ClHT) | SWCr |
| | Dentelle de Malines = 'Lenfro' (S) | MAus |
| | Desert Island = 'Dicfizz'[PBR] (F) | GCoc IDic |
| | 'Designer Sunset' (Patio) | MAsh SWCr |
| § | 'Desprez à Fleur Jaune' (N) | EBee IArd LRHS MAsh MAus MGos MRav NEgg NLar SEND SFam SPer SWCr |
| | 'Devon Maid' (ClHT) | SWCr |
| | 'Devoniensis' (ClT) | see *R.* 'Climbing Devoniensis' |
| | Diamond Anniversary = 'Morsixty' (Min) | LSRN |
| | 'Diamond Celebration' | LSRN SWCr |
| | Diamond Days Forever = 'Fryjess'[PBR] (F) | ESty LSRN SWCr |
| | 'Diamond Jubilee' (HT) | CSBt GCoc SWCr |
| | Diamond = 'Korgazell'[PBR] (Patio) | ESty GCoc LSRN LStr MAsh |
| | 'Diamond Wishes'[PBR] | see *R.* Misty Hit |
| | Dick's Delight = 'Dicwhistle' (GC) | ESty LSRN SWCr |
| | Dizzy Heights = 'Fryblissful'[PBR] (ClHT) | GCoc MAsh MAus MRav SPer SWCr |
| | Doc = 'Degenhard' (Poly) | CGro |
| | 'Docteur Grill' (T) | MAus |
| | Doctor Goldberg = 'Gandol' (HT) | GCoc |
| | Doctor Jackson = 'Ausdoctor' (S) | MAus |
| | Doctor Jo = 'Fryatlanta'[PBR] (F) | SWCr |
| | 'Doctor W. Van Fleet' (Ra/Cl) | MAus |
| | 'Don Charlton' (HT) | NEgg |
| | 'Don Juan' (ClHT) | SWCr |
| | 'Dopey' (Poly) | CGro |
| | 'Doreen' (HT) | LSRN |
| | 'Doris Tysterman' (HT) | CGro CTri GCoc LBuc LStr MAus SPer SRGP |
| | Dorothy = 'Cocrocket'[PBR] (F) | GCoc LSRN MRav |
| | 'Dorothy Perkins' (Ra) | CGro CTri LRHS MAus MRav MWat NLar NPer SPer |
| | 'Dortmund' (S) 🏆[H4] | EPfP EWTr GCoc MAus NLar SPer SWCr |
| | Double Delight = 'Andeli' (HT) | ESty GCoc LSRN SPer SWCr |
| | Douglas = 'Cocfresco' (F) **new** | GCoc |
| | Dream Lover = 'Peayetti'[PBR] (Patio) | ESty SWCr |
| | 'Dreaming Spires' (Cl) | SPer SWCr |
| | Drummer Boy = 'Harvacity'[PBR] (F/Patio) | GCoc SPer |
| § | 'Du Maître d'Ecole' (G) | ELon LRHS MAus MRav WHer |
| | Dublin Bay = 'Macdub' (ClF) 🏆[H4] | CSBt CTri ECnt ELan EPfP GCoc IArd LAst LRHS LStr MAsh MBri MCot MRav MWat NLar SEND SMrm SPer SSea SWCr WBor |
| | 'Duc de Guiche' (G) 🏆[H4] | CSam MAsh MAus MMuc SEND SFam SLon SPer WHer |
| | Duchess of Cornwall = 'Tan97157' (HT) | CSBt SWCr |
| | 'Duchess of Portland' | see *R.* 'Portlandica' |
| | Duchess of York[PBR] | see *R.* Sunseeker |
| | 'Duchesse d'Angoulême' (Ce × G) | MAus SFam |
| | 'Duchesse de Buccleugh' (G) | MAus MRav |
| § | 'Duchesse de Montebello' (G) 🏆[H4] | CSam EWTr MAus NLar SFam SLon SMrm SPer |
| | 'Duchesse de Verneuil' (CeMo) | MAus SFam |
| | 'Duke of Edinburgh' (HP) | MAus |
| | 'Duke of Windsor' (HT) | SPer |
| | 'Dundee Rambler' (Ra) | MAus |
| | 'Dupontii' (S) | GCoc MAus MMuc SFam SKHP SPer |
| | Durrell = 'Tan02876' **new** | SWCr |
| | 'Dusky Maiden' (F) | EBee MAus MCot SWCr |
| | Dusty Springfield = 'Horluvdust' (F) | LBuc |
| | 'Dutch Gold' (HT) | GCoc MAus SPer |
| | Dynamite | see *R.* High Flyer |
| | 'E.H. Morse' | see *R.* 'Ernest H. Morse' |
| | 'Easlea's Golden Rambler' (Ra) 🏆[H4] | EBee ECGP EPfP LRHS MAus MRav NEgg NLar SLon |
| | Easy Going = 'Harflow'[PBR] (F) | IArd MAsh MRav SWCr |
| | ***ecae*** | MAus |
| | 'Eddie's Jewel' (*moyesii* hybrid) | LSRN MAus |
| | 'Eden Rose' (HT) | GCoc |
| | Eden Rose '88 = 'Meiviolin'[PBR] (ClHT) | CPou EBee MCot SPer SWCr |
| | Edith Holden = 'Chewlegacy'[PBR] (F) | SPer |
| | 'Edward Hyams' (*persica* hybrid) | MAus |
| | Edward's Rose = 'Smi73/7/97' (F) | ESty |
| | ***eglanteria*** | see *R. rubiginosa* |
| | Eglantyne = 'Ausmak'[PBR] (S) 🏆[H4] | CSBt EBls EPfP ESty GCoc LRHS MAsh MAus MBri MRav SMrm SPer SPoG SSea SWCr |
| | 'Eleanor' (Patio) | LSRN |
| | Eleanor Masson = 'Cocdesire' **new** | GCoc |
| | Eleanor = 'Poulberin'[PBR] (S) | ECnt SLon SWCr |
| § | ***elegantula*** 'Persetosa' (S) | MAus NLar SKHP |
| | Elfe = 'Tanelfe' (HT) | NHaw |
| § | Elina = 'Dicjana' (HT) 🏆[H4] | EBee ECnt ELon GCoc LStr MAus MRav SPer SWCr |
| | Elizabeth = 'Coctail'[PBR] (F) | GCoc |
| | 'Elizabeth Harkness' (HT) | MAus SPer |
| | Elizabeth of Glamis = 'Macel' (F) | CTri GCoc SPer SWCr |
| | Elizabeth Stuart = 'Maselstu' (Generosa Series) (S) | LSRN MRav |
| | Elle = 'Meibderos'[PBR] (HT) | ESty LSRN SWCr |
| | Ellen = 'Auscup' (S) | LSRN MAus |
| | 'Ellen Willmott' (HT) | EBee EWTr MAus MCot SPer |
| | 'Elmshorn' (S) | CBcs |
| | Eloise = 'Kirsandra'[PBR] (HT) | ESty |
| | Elspeth Marshall = 'Coczefma' (HT) | GCoc |
| | Emilien Guillot = 'Masemgui' (Generosa Series) (S) | MRav SMrm |

| |  |  |
|---|---|---|
| | Emily = 'Ausburton' (S) | LSRN |
| | 'Emily Gray' (Ra) | CGro ECnt EPfP EWTr LSRN LStr MAsh MAus MRav SPer SWCr |
| | Emily Victoria = 'Boshipeacon' (F) | GCoc LSRN |
| | 'Emma Wright' (HT) | MAus |
| | 'Emmerdale' (F) | LBuc |
| | 'Empereur du Maroc' (HP) | EWTr MAus MRav |
| | Empress Michiko = 'Dicnifty'[PBR] (HT) | ESty IDic |
| | 'Ena Harkness' (HT) | CTri ELan GCoc LRHS SRGP SWCr |
| | English Elegance = 'Ausleaf' (S) | MAus |
| | English Garden = 'Ausbuff'[PBR] (S) | CGro CTri EPfP LSRN MAus MRav SLon SMrm SPer |
| | 'English Miss' (F) ♀H4 | CSBt ECnt EPfP ESty LRHS LStr MAsh MAus MRav SMrm SPer SPoG SWCr |
| | English Sonnet[PBR] | see *R.* Samaritan |
| | 'Eos' (*moyesii* hybrid) | MAus |
| | 'Erfurt' (HM) | EBee EWTr MAus SWCr |
| § | 'Ernest H. Morse' (HT) | CSBt CTri GCoc MRav SPer SPoG SSea SWCr |
| | 'Ernest May' (HT) | SSea |
| | Escapade = 'Harpade' (F) ♀H4 | MAus |
| | Especially for You = 'Fryworthy'[PBR] (HT) | CSBt ELon ESty GCoc LSRN LStr MBri MWat NPri SCoo SRGP SSea SWCr |
| | Essex = 'Poulnoz'[PBR] (GC) | MRav SPer SPoG SWCr |
| § | 'Estrellita de Oro' (Min) | SPer |
| | 'Etain' (Ra) | EBee ECnt |
| § | 'Étendard' (ClHT) | GCoc MRav SPer SPoG SWCr |
| | Eternal Flame = 'Korassenet'[PBR] (F) | MAsh MBri |
| | Eternally Yours = 'Macspeego'[PBR] (HT) | EBee ECnt ESty |
| | 'Ethel' (Ra) | CPou LSRN |
| | 'Étoile de Hollande' (HT) | ELan LRHS MBNS NEgg NLar SLon |
| | 'Eugénie Guinoisseau' (Mo) | CPou |
| | Euphoria = 'Intereup'[PBR] (GC/S) | IDic SWCr |
| | 'Europeana' (F) | GCoc |
| | 'Evangeline' (Ra) | MAus |
| | Evelyn = 'Aussaucer'[PBR] (S) ♀H4 | CSBt EPfP ESty GCoc LRHS LSRN MAsh MAus MBri MRav MWat NEgg NLar SMad SMrm SPer SWCr |
| § | Evelyn Fison = 'Macev' (F) | CSBt CTri ELan GCoc LSRN MAus MRav SPer SWCr |
| | 'Evelyn May' (HT) **new** | EBls |
| | Evening Light = 'Tarde Gris' (ClMin) | MBri |
| | 'Excelsa' (Ra) | CSBt CTri EPfP IArd MAsh MRav NWea SPoG |
| | Exception (Ru) | see *R.* 'Rotes Meer' |
| | Eye Paint = 'Maceye' (F) | MAus |
| | 'Eyecatcher' (F) | ECnt |
| | Eyes for You = 'Pejbigeye' **new** | ESty |
| | 'F.E. Lester' | see *R.* 'Francis E. Lester' |
| § | 'F.J. Grootendorst' (Ru) | NEgg SPer |
| | Fair Bianca = 'Ausca' (S) | MAus |
| | Fairy Prince = 'Harnougette' (GC) | ESty |
| | Fairy Queen = 'Sperien' (Poly/GC) | IDic LBuc MAsh |
| | 'Fairy Rose' | see *R.* 'The Fairy' |
| | Fairy Snow = 'Holfairy' (S) | SWCr |
| | Faithful Friend = 'Beachallenge' (S) | EBls |
| | Falstaff = 'Ausverse'[PBR] (S) | CSBt EBee ELon EPfP LRHS LSRN LStr MAus MBNS MBri MGos MRav NEgg SMrm SPer SPoG SSea SWCr |
| | 'Fantin-Latour' (*centifolia* hybrid) ♀H4 | CTri EBee ECnt ELan EPfP GCoc GCra LAst LRHS LStr MAus MBri MCot MRav MWat NEgg NLar SEND SFam SMad SPer SSea SWCr WKif |
| | ***farreri*** var. ***persetosa*** | see *R. elegantula* 'Persetosa' |
| | Fascination = 'Jacoyel' (Castle Series) (HT) | LStr MBri SCoo |
| § | Fascination = 'Poulmax'[PBR] (F) ♀H4 | CSBt ECnt EPfP LRHS MAsh MRav SPer SRGP SWCr |
| | Father's Favourite = 'Gandoug'[PBR] (F) | GCoc LSRN SWCr |
| § | Favourite Hit = 'Poululv'[PBR] (Patio) | MAsh |
| | ***fedtschenkoana*** misapplied | MAus SPer |
| | ***fedtschenkoana*** Regel | SLPl |
| | Fée des Neiges | see *R.* Iceberg |
| | 'Felicia' (HM) ♀H4 | CSBt CSam CTri EBee ECnt ELan EPfP EWTr GCoc LRHS LStr MAsh MAus MCot MRav MWat NLar SEND SFam SKHP SMad SMrm SPer SWCr WKif |
| | 'Félicité Parmentier' (A × D) ♀H4 | LRHS MAus MBri MRav MWat NLar SFam SPer SWCr |
| § | 'Félicité Perpétue' (Ra) ♀H4 | CBcs CSBt ELan EPfP GCoc LRHS LShp LStr MAsh MAus MBri MRav NEgg NLar SEND SFam SPer SPoG SSea SWCr |
| | 'Fellemberg' (ClCh) | MAus |
| | Fellowship = 'Harwelcome'[PBR] (F) ♀H4 | ESty GCoc LStr MAus MRav SCoo SSea SWCr |
| | 'Ferdinand Pichard' (Bb) ♀H4 | CPou CSBt CTri ECnt ELon EPfP ESty EWTr GCoc LAst LRHS MAus MBri MCot MRav NEgg NLar SEND SKHP SPer SPoG SSea SWCr WFoF WKif |
| | Ferdy = 'Keitoli'[PBR] (GC) | EWTr MRav SPer |
| | Fergie = 'Ganfer'[PBR] (F/Patio) | SWCr |
| | ***ferruginea*** | see *R. glauca* Pourr. |
| | Festival = 'Kordialo'[PBR] (Patio) | ESty LStr MRav SPer SPoG SWCr |
| | Fetzer Syrah Rosé = 'Harextra'[PBR] (S) | ESty |
| | Fiery Hit = 'Poulfiry'[PBR] (PatioHit Series) (Min/Patio) | LRHS |
| | Fiery Sunblaze = 'Meineyta'[PBR] (Min) | SWCr |
| | ***filipes*** | GAuc |
| | - 'Brenda Colvin' | see *R.* 'Brenda Colvin' |
| § | - 'Kiftsgate' (Ra) ♀H4 | Widely available |
| § | 'Fimbriata' (Ru) | CPou ECGP ELon EWTr MAus NLar SPer WBor |
| | Financial Times Centenary = 'Ausfin' (S) | MAus |
| | Fiona = 'Meibeluxen' (S/GC) | LSRN |
| | First Great Western = 'Oracharpam'[PBR] (HT) | ESty LStr SMrm SWCr |
| | 'Fisher and Holmes' (HP) | EBee MAus |
| | Fisherman's Friend = 'Auschild'[PBR] (S) | MAus |
| | Flashdance = 'Poulyc004'[PBR] (ClMin) | ECnt SWCr |

Flirt = 'Korkopapp'PBR MAsh
'Flora' (HT) MAus
'Flora McIvor' (RH) NHaw
'Flore' (Ra) CRHN
'Florence Mary Morse' (S) SDix
Florence Nightingale = 'Ganflor'PBR (F) GCoc SPer
'Flower Carpet Amber' IBal LRHS MAsh SCoo SPoG SWCr
'Flower Carpet Coral'PBR (GC) CGro GCoc IBal LRHS MAsh MBri SCoo SWCr
Flower Carpet Gold = 'Noalesa'PBR (GC) ECnt GCoc LRHS MAsh MBri SPoG SWCr
Flower Carpet PinkPBR see *R.* Pink Flower Carpet
Flower Carpet Red Velvet = 'Noare'PBR (GC/S) CGro ECnt ELan EPfP GCoc IBal LStr MAsh MBri NPri SCoo SPer SPoG SWCr
Flower Carpet Ruby (GC) LRHS MAsh SCoo SPoG
Flower Carpet Scarlet = 'Noa83100b'PBR (GC) **new** MAsh
§ Flower Carpet Sunshine = 'Noason'PBR (GC) CGro ELan LRHS LStr MAsh SCoo SPer
Flower Carpet White = 'Noaschnee'PBR (GC) ♀H4 CGro CTri ECnt ELan EPfP GCoc LRHS LStr MAsh MAus MBri NPri SCoo SPer SPoG SWCr
Flower Power = 'Frycassia'PBR (Patio) CSBt ECnt ELon ESty GCoc LRHS LStr MAsh MAus MRav MWat SPoG SWCr
Flower Power Gold = 'Fryneon' (Patio) **new** ESty
§ ***foetida*** (S) EBee MAus
§ - 'Bicolor' (S) MAus
§ - 'Persiana' (S) MAus SPer
***foliolosa*** SLPl
Fond Memories = 'Kirfelix'PBR (Patio) ESty LSRN LStr SWCr
For You With Love = 'Fryjangle' (Patio) GCoc LBuc LSRN
Forever Royal = 'Franmite' (F) ESty
Forget Me Not = 'Coccharm'PBR (HT) GCoc
***forrestiana*** MAus
'Fountain' (HT) MAus SPer SWCr
Fragrant Cloud = 'Tanellis' (HT) CTri CWSG ELon EPfP ESty GCoc LRHS LStr MAsh MAus MBri MCot MGos MRav NPri SMrm SPer SPoG SWCr
'Fragrant Delight' (F) ♀H4 CSBt ELan GCoc LStr MAus MRav SPer SPoG
Fragrant Dream = 'Dicodour'PBR (HT) CGro ESty IDic LStr MRav SMrm SWCr
Fragrant Gold = 'Tandugoft' (HT) SSea
Fragrant Memories = 'Korpastato'PBR (HT) CSBt MGos SCoo SKHP SWCr
Fragrant Vision = 'Beadick' (S) **new** EBls
'Francesca' (HM) EWTr GCoc LSRN MAus SFam SPer
Francine Austin = 'Ausram'PBR (S/GC) LRHS MAus MBri NEgg SPer
'Francis Dubreuil' (T) MCot
§ 'Francis E. Lester' (HM/Ra) ♀H4 CRHN CSam ELan EPfP EWTr LRHS MAus MBri MCot MMuc NLar SEND SMrm SPer SRGP SSea SWCr
× ***francofurtana*** misapplied see *R.* 'Impératrice Joséphine'
- 'Empress Josephine' see *R.* 'Impératrice Joséphine'
'François Juranville' (Ra) ♀H4 CPou CRHN EPfP GGal LAst LRHS LShp LStr LTen MAus MBri MMuc MRav NLar SEND SLon SPer SWCr
§ 'Frau Karl Druschki' (HP) EBee MAus
'Fred Loads' (F) ♀H4 MAus MCot MRav
Freddie Mercury = 'Batmercury' (HT) LSRN NEgg
Free Spirit = 'Fryjeru'PBR (F) ECnt GCoc
Freedom = 'Dicjem' (HT) ♀H4 CTri EBee EBls ECnt GCoc LStr MAus MRav SPer SRGP SVic
'Frensham' (F) GCoc SSea SWCr
Friend for Life = 'Cocnanne'PBR (F) ♀H4 GCoc LSRN MRav
Friends Forever = 'Korapriber' (F) EPfP GCoc
'Fritz Nobis' (S) ♀H4 EBee GCoc LStr MAus MRav NLar SPer WKif
Frothy = 'Macfrothy'PBR (Patio) ECnt ESty
'Fru Dagmar Hastrup' (Ru) ♀H4 CDul CSBt CTri EBee ECnt ELan EMil EPfP GCoc LBuc LRHS LStr MAus NEgg NLar SEND SMad SPer SWCr
'Frühlingsduft' (SpH) EWTr
'Frühlingsgold' (SpH) ♀H4 CBcs ELan EWTr GCoc LRHS LStr MAus MRav NLar NWea SPer
'Frühlingsmorgen' (SpH) EWTr GCoc LStr MAus SLon SMad SPer
Fulton Mackay = 'Cocdana'PBR (HT) GCoc
Fyvie Castle = 'Cocbamber' (HT) GCoc
§ ***gallica*** var. ***officinalis*** (G) ♀H4 CArn CPrp CSam CTri EBee EPfP GCoc GPoy LRHS MAsh MAus MBri MRav MWat NLar SFam SKHP SPer SSea SWCr
§ - 'Versicolor' (G) ♀H4 Widely available
Galway Bay = 'Macba' (ClHT) GCoc LRHS MAsh MRav SPer SWCr
§ Garden News = 'Poulrim'PBR (HT) ECnt
'Gardeners Glory'PBR (ClHT) ECnt ESty LRHS SMad
Gardeners' Joy = 'Beadrum' (S) **new** EBls
'Gardenia' (Ra) EBee LRHS MAus MMuc NLar SEND SPer
'Gardiner's Pink' (Ra) MCot
'Garnette Carol' see *R.* 'Carol Amling'
'Garnette Pink' see *R.* 'Carol Amling'
'Gaujard' see *R.* Rose Gaujard
'Gelbe Dagmar Hastrup'PBR see *R.* Yellow Dagmar Hastrup
'Général Jacqueminot' (HP) MAus
'Général Kléber' (CeMo) MAus SFam
§ 'Général Schablikine' (T) MAus NLar
Genesis = 'Fryjuicy'PBR (Patio) ECnt ESty MAsh MBri SWCr
N ***gentiliana*** misapplied see *R.* 'Polyantha Grandiflora'
N ***gentiliana*** H. Lév. & Variot see *R. multiflora* var. *cathayensis*
Gentle Hermione = 'Ausrumba'PBR (S) LRHS MAus MBri SWCr
Gentle Touch = 'Diclulu'PBR (Min/Patio) CSBt IDic LBuc MRav SMad SPer SPoG
Geoff Hamilton = 'Ausham'PBR (S) EPfP ESty LRHS LSRN LStr MAus MBNS MBri NEgg SCoo SMrm SPer SSea SWCr
'Georg Arends' (HP) MAus
George Best = 'Dichimanher'PBR (Patio) ESty IDic LBuc LSRN SWCr
'George Dickson' (HT) MAus
'Georges Vibert' (G) MAus
'Geranium' (*moyesii* hybrid) ♀H4 CBcs CDul CSam CTri EBee ELan EPfP EWTr GCoc IArd LRHS LStr

|  |  |
|---|---|
| | MAsh MAus MBri MRav NLar SEND SPer SSea SWCr WBor |
| Gerbe d'Or | see *R.* Casino |
| 'Gerbe Rose' (Ra) | MAus |
| Gertrude Jekyll = 'Ausbord'[PBR] (S) 🏆[H4] | Widely available |
| 'Ghislaine de Féligonde' (Ra/S) | CPou CSam EPfP EWTr GCoc LStr MAus MCot NLar SEND SPer SWCr |
| Ghita[PBR] | see *R.* Millie |
| Ginger Syllabub = 'Harjolina'[PBR] (ClHT) | EBee ECnt ELon ESty GCoc SPoG SWCr |
| Gingernut = 'Coccrazy'[PBR] (Patio) | SWCr |
| Gipsy Boy | see *R.* 'Zigeunerknabe' |
| ***giraldii*** | GAuc |
| Glad Tidings = 'Tantide'[PBR] (F) | CSBt CWSG MRav SPer SWCr |
| Glamis Castle = 'Auslevel'[PBR] (S) | CBcs CTri EPfP LRHS LStr MAsh MAus MBri NEgg SCoo SMrm SPer SWCr |
| ***glauca*** ambig. | GCra MHer MLLN NLar |
| § ***glauca*** Pourr. (S) 🏆[H4] | Widely available |
| 'Glenfiddich' (F) | CSBt CTri CWSG GCoc LStr MAus MBri MRav SPer SWCr |
| Glenshane = 'Dicvood' (GC/S) | MRav |
| Global Beauty = 'Tan 94448' (HT) | MRav SWCr |
| 'Gloire de Dijon' (ClT) | CGro CSBt CTri CWSG EBee ECnt ELan EPfP EWTr GCoc LAst LRHS LSRN LStr MAus MBri MCot MRav NEgg NLar NPri SPer SPoG SSea SWCr |
| 'Gloire de Ducher' (HP) | MAus |
| 'Gloire de France' (G) | EWTr MAus MRav WHer |
| 'Gloire de Guilan' (D) | MAus |
| 'Gloire des Mousseuses' (CeMo) | LRHS MAus SFam |
| 'Gloire du Midi' (Poly) | MAus |
| 'Gloire Lyonnaise' (HP) | MMuc SLon |
| 'Gloria Mundi' (Poly) | NEgg |
| Gloriana = 'Chewpope'[PBR] (ClMin) | CGro ECnt ESty LRHS MAsh MAus MBri MRav MWat SCoo SKHP SMrm SPer SPoG SSea SWCr |
| Glorious = 'Interictira'[PBR] (HT) | ESty IDic SWCr |
| 'Glory of Seale' (S) | SSea |
| Glowing Amber = 'Manglow' (Min) | ESty |
| ***glutinosa*** | see *R. pulverulenta* |
| Gold Rush = 'Jacrebin'[PBR] (F) **new** | ESty GCoc |
| Gold Symphonie = 'Macfraba' (Min) | MAsh |
| 'Golden Anniversary' (Patio) | LRHS LStr MAsh SPer SPoG SWCr |
| 'Golden Autumn' (HT) **new** | LSRN |
| Golden Beauty = 'Korberbeni'[PBR] (F) | ESty GCoc MAsh MBri |
| Golden Celebration = 'Ausgold'[PBR] (S) 🏆[H4] | CGro CSBt CTri CWSG ECnt EPfP ESty GCoc LRHS LSRN LStr MAsh MAus MBri MRav NLar SMrm SPer SPoG SRGP SSea SWCr |
| 'Golden Chersonese' (S) | MAus |
| Golden Future = 'Horanymoll'[PBR] (ClHT) | MAus SWCr |
| Golden Gate = 'Korgolgat'[PBR] (ClHT) | ECnt ESty LStr MAus SWCr |

|  |  |
|---|---|
| Golden Jewel = 'Tanledolg'[PBR] (F/Patio) | ESty MAsh MBri SPoG |
| Golden Jubilee = 'Cocagold' (HT) | GCoc MRav SWCr |
| Golden Kiss = 'Dicalways'[PBR] (HT) | IDic |
| Golden Memories = 'Korholesea'[PBR] (F) | CBcs CGro CSBt EBls ESty GCoc LRHS LStr MAsh MGos MRav SCoo SPer SWCr |
| 'Golden Rambler' | see *R.* 'Alister Stella Gray' |
| 'Golden Showers' (Cl) 🏆[H4] | CGro CSBt CTri CWSG EBee ELan EPfP GCoc LRHS LSRN LStr LTen MAsh MAus MBri MRav MWat NEgg NLar NPri SMad SMrm SPer SPoG SSea SWCr |
| Golden Smiles = 'Frykeyno'[PBR] (F) | ECnt ESty GCoc MAsh |
| Golden Trust = 'Hardish'[PBR] (Patio) | LStr MWat |
| Golden Wedding Anniversary (F) **new** | LSRN |
| Golden Wedding = 'Arokris'[PBR] (F) | CGro CSBt CTri CWSG EBee ECnt ELan EPfP ESty GCoc IArd LRHS LSRN LStr MAsh MAus MGos MRav MWat NEgg NPri SMrm SPer SPoG SRGP SSea SVic SWCr |
| 'Golden Wedding Celebration' (F) | ESty LSRN SWCr |
| 'Golden Wings' (S) 🏆[H4] | CTri ELan EPfP GCoc LStr MAus MRav NLar SKHP SPer SSea SWCr |
| Golden Years = 'Harween'[PBR] (F) | ESty |
| 'Goldfinch' (Ra) | EBee ELan EPfP LRHS LStr MAus MBri MRav NEgg NLar SEND SPer SPoG SWCr |
| Goldstar = 'Candide' (HT) | ECnt |
| Good as Gold = 'Chewsunbeam'[PBR] (ClMin) | CSBt ECnt ESty LStr MBri SPer SRGP SSea SWCr |
| Good Life = 'Cococircus'[PBR] (HT) | GCoc SCoo SPer |
| Good Luck = 'Burspec' (F/Patio) | SPer |
| Good Wishes[PBR] | see *R.* Favourite Hit |
| Gordon Snell = 'Dicwriter' (F) | IDic |
| Gordon's College = 'Cocjabby'[PBR] (F) 🏆[H4] | ESty GCoc |
| 'Grace Abounding' (F) | LSRN |
| Grace = 'Auskeppy'[PBR] (S) | CSBt EBee EPfP ESty LRHS LSRN LStr MAus MBri NEgg SMrm SPer SRGP SSea SWCr |
| Gracious Queen = 'Bedqueen' (HT) | GCoc SWCr |
| 'Graciously Pink' (Min) | MAsh |
| Graham Thomas = 'Ausmas' (S) 🏆[H4] | CGro CSBt CTri EBee ECnt EPfP ESty GCoc LAst LRHS LSRN LStr MAus MBri MCot MRav MWat NEgg NLar NPri SEND SMad SMrm SPer SPoG SSea SWCr WKif |
| Grande Amore = 'Korcoluma'[PBR] (HT) | CSBt LRHS LSRN MBri |
| 'Grandma' (F) | LSRN |
| 'Grandpa Dickson' (HT) | CBcs GCoc MAsh MAus MRav SPer SRGP |
| Granny's Favourite (Patio/F) | LSRN |
| Great Expectations = 'Jacdal' (F) | SPoG |

| | | |
|---|---|---|
| | Great Expectations = 'Lanican' (HT) | CBcs |
| | Great Expectations = 'Mackalves'PBR (F) | EPfP ESty GCoc IArd LBuc LStr MAsh MRav SCoo SPer SWCr |
| § | 'Great Maiden's Blush' (A) | GCoc MRav NLar SFam |
| | 'Great News' (F) | MAus |
| | Greenall's Glory = 'Kirmac'PBR (F/Patio) | MAus MRav |
| | Greetings = 'Jacdreco'PBR (F) | IDic LBuc MAsh MRav SMrm SRGP |
| | Grenadine = 'Poulgrena'PBR (HT) | ECnt |
| | 'Grootendorst' | see *R.* 'F.J. Grootendorst' |
| | 'Grootendorst Supreme' (Ru) | SPer |
| | Grosvenor House (HT) **new** | EBls |
| | Grouse = 'Korimro'PBR (S/GC) ♀H4 | EPfP MAus NLar SEND SLon SMrm SPer |
| | Grumpy = 'Burkhardt' (Poly) | CGro |
| | 'Gruss an Aachen' (Poly) | EPfP LStr MAus MCot NLar SPer SWCr |
| | 'Gruss an Teplitz' (China hybrid) | MAus SPer |
| | 'Guinée' (ClHT) | CSBt EBee ELan ELon EPfP EWTr LAst LRHS LStr MAsh MAus MCot MRav NPri SMrm SPer SPoG SSea |
| | 'Gustav Grünerwald' (HT) | MAus |
| | Guy Savoy = 'Delstrimen'PBR (F) | ESty MRav |
| | Guy's Gold = 'Harmatch'PBR (HT) **new** | ESty LRHS |
| | Gwen Mayor = 'Cocover'PBR (HT) | GCoc |
| | Gwent = 'Poulurt'PBR (GC) | CSBt ELan LSRN LStr SEND SPer |
| § | ***gymnocarpa*** var. ***willmottiae*** | MAus SPer SSea |
| | Gypsy Boy | see *R.* 'Zigeunerknabe' |
| | 'Hakuun' (F/Patio) ♀H4 | MAus |
| | 'Hamburger Phönix' (Ra) | CGro SPer |
| | Hampshire = 'Korhamp'PBR (GC) | MAus |
| | Hand in Hand = 'Haraztec'PBR (Patio/Min) | MAsh MWat SPoG |
| | Händel = 'Macha' (ClHT) ♀H4 | CGro CSBt CTri CWSG ELan EPfP GCoc LAst LRHS LStr MAsh MRav MWat NEgg NLar SPer SPlb SPoG SSea SWCr |
| § | Hanky Panky = 'Wektorcent'PBR (F) | CGro EBls ESty GCoc LRHS MAsh MBri MRav SCoo SWCr |
| | Hannah Gordon = 'Korweiso' (F) | EBls ECnt SPer SWCr |
| | 'Hansa' (Ru) | EBee ECGP EMil GCoc LBuc MAus SPer SWCr |
| | 'Happy' (Poly) | CGro |
| | Happy Anniversary = 'Bedfranc'PBR | LSRN SWCr |
| | Happy Anniversary = 'Delpre' (F) | CGro CTri LRHS LStr MAsh MBri MRav SPoG |
| | 'Happy Birthday' (Min/Patio) | CGro CWSG ESty LBuc LSRN LStr SPoG SWCr |
| | Happy Child = 'Auscomp'PBR (S) | MAus |
| | Happy Days = 'Harquad'PBR **new** | MAsh |
| | Happy Retirement = 'Tantoras'PBR (F) | CGro ESty GCoc LSRN LStr MAsh MRav SCoo SPoG SSea SWCr |
| § | × ***harisonii*** 'Harison's Yellow' (SpH) | MAus SPer |
| § | – 'Lutea Maxima' (SpH) | MAus |
| § | – 'Williams Double Yellow' (SpH) | GCoc MAus |
| | Harlow Carr ambig. | LRHS |
| | Harlow Carr = 'Aushouse'PBR | EPfP LRHS MAus MWat SCoo SMrm SPer |
| | Harlow Carr = 'Kirlyl' (F) | MBri |
| | 'Harry Edland' (F) | SSea SWCr |
| | 'Harry Wheatcroft' (HT) | CGro GCoc MAus SPer |
| | Harvest Fayre = 'Dicnorth'PBR (F) | IDic SPer |
| | Havana Hit = 'Poulpah032'PBR | LRHS SWCr |
| | 'Headleyensis' (S) | EWTr MAus SLon |
| | Heart of Gold = 'Coctarlotte'PBR (HT) | ECnt ESty GCoc MRav |
| | Heather Austin = 'Auscook'PBR (S) | MAus |
| | Heavenly Rosalind = 'Ausmash'PBR (S) | MAus |
| § | 'Hebe's Lip' (D×RH) | MAus |
| | 'Helen Knight' (*ecae* hybrid) (S) | MAsh MAus SSea |
| | ***helenae*** | CTri MAus NLar SPer |
| | ***hemisphaerica*** (S) | MAus |
| § | 'Henri Martin' (CeMo) | GCoc MAsh MAus NEgg NLar SKHP SLon SMrm SPer |
| | Henri Matisse = 'Delstrobla' (HT) | ESty MRav SPoG |
| | Henrietta Barnett = 'Harmaxim'PBR (F) **new** | LRHS |
| | 'Henry Nevard' (HP) | MAus |
| | Her Majesty = 'Dicxotic'PBR (F) | IDic |
| § | 'Herbstfeuer' (RH) | CPou SPer |
| | Heritage = 'Ausblush' (S) | CGro CTri EBee ELan ELon EPfP LStr MAus MBri MRav MWat NEgg NLar NPri SEND SLon SMrm SPer SPoG SSea |
| | 'Hermosa' (Ch) | MAus MRav |
| | Hero = 'Aushero' (S) | MAus |
| | Hertfordshire = 'Kortenay'PBR (GC) ♀H4 | ELan MAus MRav SEND SPer SWCr |
| | × ***hibernica*** | MAus |
| | 'Hidcote Gold' (S) | MAus |
| § | 'Hidcote Yellow' (Cl) | EBee LRHS SPer |
| | Hide and Seek = 'Diczodiac'PBR (F) | IDic |
| | High Flier = 'Fryfandango'PBR (ClHT) | SWCr |
| § | High Flyer = 'Jacsat' (ClHT) | SRGP |
| | High Hopes = 'Haryup'PBR (ClHT) ♀H4 | EPfP GCoc LStr MAsh MAus SPer SPoG SSea SWCr |
| | 'Highdownensis' (*moyesii* hybrid) (S) | ELan MAus SPer |
| | Highfield = 'Harcomp' (ClHT) | MAus SPer |
| | Highgrove = 'Hornightshade' (Cl) **new** | EBls |
| | Hilda Murrell = 'Ausmurr' (S) | MAus |
| | 'Hillieri' (*moyesii* hybrid) | MAus |
| | 'Hippolyte' (G) | MAus |

| |  |  |
|---|---|---|
| | Hole-in-one = 'Horeagle' (F) | LSRN |
| | holy rose | see *R.* × *richardii* |
| | 'Homère' (T) | MAus |
| | Honey Bunch = 'Cocglen'PBR (F) | MRav SPer SRGP |
| | Honey Dijon = 'Weksproulses'PBR (F) | CSBt EBee ECnt ESty GCoc SWCr |
| | Honeybun = 'Tan98264'PBR (Patio) | ESty SWCr |
| | 'Honorine de Brabant' (Bb) | CPou MAus NLar SPer SWCr |
| | Horatio Nelson = 'Beahor' (S) **new** | EBls |
| | Hospitality = 'Horcoff'PBR (F) | ESty |
| | Hot Chocolate = 'Wekpaltez' (F) | CGro CSBt EBee EBls ECnt EGxp ELan ELon EPfP ESty GCoc LBuc LRHS LStr MAsh MBri MRav NPri SCoo SMad SMrm SPer SPoG SRGP SSea SWCr WBor |
| | Hot Stuff = 'Maclarayspo' (Min) | SWCr |
| | 'Hugh Dickson' (HP) | CPou LSRN MAus NLar |
| | ***hugonis*** | see *R. xanthina* f. *hugonis* |
| | - 'Plenissima' | see *R. xanthina* f. *hugonis* |
| | Humanity = 'Harcross'PBR (F) | MRav SMrm |
| | Hyde Hall = 'Ausbosky'PBR (S) | LRHS MAsh MAus SCoo |
| | I Love You = 'Geelove' (HT) | LBuc |
| | Ice Cream = 'Korzuri'PBR (HT) ♀H4 | CSBt CWSG EBee ECnt ESty GCoc LStr MAus MRav SPoG SWCr |
| § | Iceberg = 'Korbin' (F) ♀H4 | CBcs CGro CSBt CTri CWSG EBee ECnt EPfP ESty GCoc LAst LRHS LStr MAsh MAus MGos MRav MWat NPri NWea SMrm SPer SPoG SSea SWCr |
| | 'Illusion' (ClF) | SWCr |
| § | Imagination = 'Pouldron'PBR (F) | MAsh |
| § | 'Impératrice Joséphine' ♀H4 | CSam LRHS MRav NLar SFam |
| | In Memory Of | LSRN |
| | Indian Summer = 'Peaperfume'PBR (HT) ♀H4 | CSBt CWSG ELon GCoc LRHS MAsh MRav MWat SMrm SPoG SWCr |
| | Indianna Mae = 'Beacrunch' (S) | EBls |
| | 'Indigo' (DPo) | CPou ELon MAus |
| | Ingrid Bergman = 'Poulman'PBR (HT) ♀H4 | CTri ECnt EPfP GCoc LRHS LSRN LStr MAsh MBri MGos MRav SMrm SPer SPoG SRGP SWCr |
| | Innocence = 'Cocoray'PBR (Patio) | GCoc |
| | Intrigue = 'Korlech' (F) | LStr |
| | Invincible = 'Runatru' (F) | GCoc LBuc |
| | 'Ipsilanté' (G) | MAus |
| | 'Irène Watts' (Ch) | CPou ECre EPfP LSRN NLar SKHP SWCr |
| | 'Irene's Delight' (HT) | LSRN |
| | Iris = 'Coczero' (HT) | GCoc LSRN |
| | Iris = 'Ferecha' (HT) | LSRN SWCr |
| | Irish Eyes = 'Dicwitness'PBR (F) | CBcs CWSG EBee EPfP ESty GCoc IArd IDic LRHS LStr MAsh MBri MRav MWat SCoo SPer SSea SWCr |
| | Irish Hope = 'Harexclaim'PBR (F) | SWCr |
| | Irish Wonder | see *R.* Evelyn Fison |
| | Isabella = 'Poulisab'PBR (Renaissance Series) (S) | CPou CTri ECnt SLon SWCr |
| | IsisPBR (HT) | see *R.* Silver Anniversary = 'Poulari' |
| | Isn't She Lovely = 'Diciluvit'PBR (HT) | EBee ECnt ESty GCoc IDic LSRN MAsh MBri SWCr |
| | 'Ispahan' (D) ♀H4 | CFee EPfP LRHS MAus MBri NEgg NLar SFam SLPl SLon SPer |
| | Ivor's Rose = 'Beadonald' (S) **new** | EBls |
| | Ivory Castle = 'Guesoverlay' (HT) **new** | SWCr |
| | Jack's Wish = 'Kirsil' (HT) | LSRN |
| § | × ***jacksonii*** 'Max Graf' (GC/Ru) | LRHS MAus NLar |
| | - Red Max GrafPBR | see *R.* Rote Max Graf |
| | Jacobite rose | see *R.* × *alba* 'Alba Maxima' |
| | Jacqueline du Pré = 'Harwanna'PBR (S) ♀H4 | EBee ECnt EPfP ESty GCoc LSRN MAus MCot MRav MWat NLar SLon SPer SSea SWCr |
| | Jacquenetta = 'Ausjac' (S) | MAus |
| N | 'Jacques Cartier' misapplied | see *R.* 'Marchesa Boccella' |
| | James Galway = 'Auscrystal'PBR (S) | CSBt CWSG LRHS LStr MAus MBri NEgg SCoo SSea |
| | 'James Mason' (G) | MAus |
| | 'James Mitchell' (CeMo) | MAus |
| | 'James Veitch' (DPoMo) | MAus |
| | Janet = 'Auspishus'PBR (S) | LRHS LSRN MAus MBri SSea SWCr |
| | 'Janet's Pride' (RH) | MAus |
| § | 'Japonica' (CeMo) | MAus |
| § | Jardins de Bagatelle = 'Meimafris' (HT) | LSRN MRav |
| | Jasmina = 'Korcentex'PBR (ClHT) | CPou EBee EPfP ESty MGos SWCr |
| | 'Jaune Desprez' | see *R.* 'Desprez à Fleur Jaune' |
| | Jayne Austin = 'Ausbreak'PBR (S) | CSBt CWSG LRHS MAus SPer |
| | JazzPBR (Cl) | see *R.* That's Jazz |
| | 'Jazz' (F) | LSRN |
| | Jean = 'Cocupland'PBR (Patio) | GCoc LSRN |
| | 'Jean Mermoz' (Poly) | MAus |
| | 'Jeanne de Montfort' (CeMo) | MAus |
| | 'Jenny Duval' misapplied | see *R.* 'Président de Sèze' |
| | Jenny's Rose = 'Cansit' (F) | EBee ECnt GCoc LSRN SWCr |
| | Jill's Rose = 'Ganjil'PBR (F) | GCoc LSRN SWCr |
| | Joan Beales = 'Beaagile' (S) **new** | EBls |
| | Joëlle Marouani = 'Masjoma' (Generosa Series) (S) | MRav SMrm |
| | John Clare = 'Auscent'PBR (S) | MAus |
| | John Gibb = 'Coczorose' (F) | GCoc |
| | 'John Gwilliam' | MAvo |
| | 'John Hopper' (HP) | MAus SWCr |
| | 'John Innes' **new** | EBls |
| | Joie de Vivre = 'Korfloci 01'PBR **new** | CSBt ECnt ESty LStr |
| | 'Josephine Bruce' (HT) | CBcs CSBt LSRN |
| | 'Joseph's Coat' (ClS) | GCoc IArd LBuc LStr SRGP SWCr |
| | 'Jubilee Celebration' (F) | EPfP |
| | Jubilee Celebration = 'Aushunter'PBR (S) | CSBt EPfP ESty LRHS MAsh MAus MBri SSea |
| | Jude the Obscure = 'Ausjo'PBR (S) | CSBt ESty LRHS MAus MBri NEgg SWCr |
| | 'Julia's Rose' (HT) | LSRN LStr MAus SPer SWCr |
| | Julio Iglesias = 'Meistemon'PBR | LSRN |
| | 'Juno' (Ch) | CPou MAus |
| | 'Just for You' (F) | SWCr |
| | Just for You = 'Moryou' (Min) | LSRN |
| | 'Just Jenny' (Min) | LSRN |

| |  |  |
|---|---|---|
| | 'Just Joey' (HT) ♀H4 | CBcs CGro CSBt CWSG EBee ECnt ELan EPfP GCoc IArd LRHS LStr MAsh MAus MBri MRav MWat NEgg NPri SMrm SPer SPoG SRGP SSea SWCr |
| | 'Katharina Zeimet' (Poly) | CTri EBee GCoc MAus NLar |
| § | Katherine Mansfield = 'Meilanein' (HT) | CSBt |
| | 'Kathleen' (HM) | LSRN |
| | 'Kathleen Harrop' (Bb) | ELon EWTr LRHS LStr MAus MMuc NLar SEND SFam SMrm SPer SRGP SSea SWCr |
| | Kathleen Jane = 'Horcoed' (S/F) | LSRN |
| | Kathleen's Rose = 'Kirkitt' (F) | LSRN |
| | Kathryn McGredy = 'Macauclad' (HT) | ESty |
| | Kathryn Morley = 'Ausclub'PBR (F) | MAus |
| | 'Katie' (ClF) | GCoc LSRN SWCr |
| N | 'Kazanlik' misapplied | see *R.* 'Professeur Emile Perrot' |
| | Keep Smiling = 'Fryflorida' (HT) | GCoc LBuc LStr MAsh SRGP SWCr |
| | 'Keith Maughan' (Cl) | EBls |
| § | Kent = 'Poulcov'PBR (Towne & Country Series) (S/GC) ♀H4 | CSBt ECnt ELan EPfP ESty GCoc LSRN LStr MRav MWat NLar SEND SMrm SPer SSea SWCr |
| | Kew Gardens = 'Ausfence' (S) | LRHS MAus |
| | 'Kew Rambler' (Ra) | CRHN CSam EBee MAus MMuc MRav NLar SFam SLon SPer |
| | 'Kiftsgate' | see *R. filipes* 'Kiftsgate' |
| | 'Kim' (Patio) | LSRN |
| | Kind Regards = 'Peatiger' (F) | LSRN |
| | King's Macc = 'Frydisco'PBR (HT) | CGro GCoc LRHS MAsh MAus MWat |
| | 'King's Ransom' (HT) | CSBt GCoc MRav SPer SPoG SWCr |
| | Knirps = 'Korverlandus'PBR (GC) | SWCr |
| | Knock Out = 'Dadler' (F) | MAsh |
| § | 'Königin von Dänemark' (A) ♀H4 | EBee ECnt ELon EPfP EWTr GCoc LRHS MBri MRav MWat NEgg NLar SKHP SMrm SPer SSea SWCr |
| | Korona = 'Kornita' (F) | SPer |
| | 'Korresia' (F) | CSBt CTri ECnt EPfP ESty GCoc LStr MAsh MAus MBri MRav MWat SPer SPoG SWCr |
| | 'Kronprinzessin Viktoria von Preussen' (Bb) | MAus |
| | L.D. Braithwaite = 'Auscrim'PBR (S) ♀H4 | CBcs ELan EPfP GCoc LRHS LStr MAus MBNS MBri MRav NLar NPri SMad SPer SWCr |
| | 'La Belle Sultane' | see *R.* 'Violacea' |
| | 'La France' (HT) | MAus |
| | 'La Mortola' | see *R. brunonii* 'La Mortola' |
| | 'La Perle' (Ra) | CRHN |
| | 'La Reine Victoria' | see *R.* 'Reine Victoria' |
| | 'La Rubanée' | see *R.* × *centifolia* 'Unique Panachée' |
| | La Sévillana = 'Meigekanu' (F/GC) | SPer WCot |
| | 'La Ville de Bruxelles' (D) ♀H4 | CSam EWTr MAus SLon SPer |
| | Lady Emma Hamilton = 'Ausbrother'PBR (S) | EPfP ESty LRHS MAus MBri SCoo SPer SWCr |
| | 'Lady Gay' (Ra) | WBor |
| | 'Lady Godiva' (Ra) | MAus |
| | 'Lady Hillingdon' (ClT) | see *R.* 'Climbing Lady Hillingdon' |

| |  |  |
|---|---|---|
| | 'Lady Hillingdon' (T) | MAus |
| | 'Lady Iliffe' (HT) | GCoc SWCr |
| | Lady MacRobert = 'Coclent' (F) | GCoc |
| § | Lady Meillandina = 'Meilarco' (Min) | CSBt |
| | Lady of Megginch = 'Ausvolume'PBR (S) | ESty LRHS MAus MBri SSea |
| | Lady of Shalott = 'Ausnyson' (S) | LRHS MAus |
| | Lady Penelope = 'Chewdor'PBR (ClHT) | CSBt |
| § | 'Lady Penzance' (RH) ♀H4 | CBcs CHab MAus SPer |
| | Lady Rachel = 'Candoodle' (F) | EBee ECnt |
| | Lady Rose = 'Korlady' (HT) | MAsh |
| | Lady Sunblaze | see *R.* Lady Meillandina |
| | 'Lady Sylvia' (HT) | CTri MAsh MAus NEgg SPer |
| | Lady Taylor = 'Smitling' (F/Patio) | ESty |
| | 'Lady Waterlow' (ClHT) | MAus NLar |
| | ***laevigata*** (Ra) | MAus MMuc NLar |
| | L'Aimant = 'Harzola'PBR (F) ♀H4 | CSBt ESty GCoc LStr MAus MRav SWCr |
| | 'Lamarque' (N) | CPou EWTr MAus |
| | Lancashire = 'Korstesgli'PBR (GC) ♀H4 | ECnt ESty GCoc LSRN LStr MAus MRav SMrm SWCr |
| | Laura Ford = 'Chewarvel'PBR (ClMin) ♀H4 | CGro CTri LRHS LStr MAsh MAus MGos MRav MWat SPer SPoG SRGP SSea |
| | 'Laura Louisa' (Cl) | EBee EWTr |
| | 'Laure Davoust' (Ra) | CPou MMuc |
| | Lavender Ice = 'Tan04249' (F) | EBee ECnt SWCr |
| | 'Lavender Jewel' (Min) | MAus |
| | 'Lavender Lassie' (HM) ♀H4 | CPou CSam EBee MAus NLar SPer SSea SWCr |
| | Lavender Parfum de Provence = 'Meibriacus'PBR (HT) | ESty |
| | Lavender Symphonie = 'Meiptima' (Patio) | ESty |
| | Lavender Symphonies | SMrm |
| | LaviniaPBR | see *R.* Lawinia |
| § | Lawinia = 'Tanklewi' (ClHT) ♀H4 | CSBt EPfP LStr MAsh MRav SPer SWCr |
| | 'Lawrence Johnston' | see *R.* 'Hidcote Yellow' |
| § | Lazy Days = 'Poulkalm'PBR (F) | ECnt MAsh |
| | 'Le Rêve' (Cl) | EWTr |
| | 'Le Vésuve' (Ch) | CPou EWTr MAus |
| | Lea = 'Poulren019' | ECnt |
| | Leah Tutu = 'Hornavel' **new** | EBls |
| | Leander = 'Auslea' (S) | MAus |
| | Leaping Salmon = 'Peamight'PBR (ClHT) | CGro CSBt ELan ELon ESty GCoc LAst LSRN LStr MAus MRav SPer SWCr |
| | 'Leda' (D) | ELon MAus NLar SFam SPer |
| | 'Lemon Pillar' | see *R.* 'Paul's Lemon Pillar' |
| | Léonardo de Vinci = 'Meideauri'PBR (F) | CSBt |
| | 'Léontine Gervais' (Ra) | CRHN LRHS MAus MBri NLar |
| | 'Leo's Eye' | CPou EPfP |
| | Leslie's Dream = 'Dicjoon' (HT) | IDic |
| | 'Leverkusen' (ClF) ♀H4 | EWTr LRHS MAus MRav NLar SEND SMrm SPer SWCr |
| | Lichfield Angel = 'Ausrelate'PBR (S) | LRHS MAsh MAus MBri SCoo |

| |  |  |
|---|---|---|
| | Lichtkönigin Lucia = 'Korlillub' (S) | EBee SSea |
| | Life Begins at 40! = 'Horhohoho' (F) | LSRN SWCr |
| | Light Fantastic = 'Dicgottago' (F) | ESty GCoc IDic MAsh |
| | 'Lilac Dream' (F) | SWCr |
| | Lilac Rose = 'Auslilac' (S) | MAus |
| | Lilian Austin = 'Ausli' (S) | MAus |
| | Liliana = 'Poulsyng'[PBR] (S) | EBee ECnt SLon SWCr |
| | Lilli Marlene = 'Korlima' (F) | CSBt ECGP GCoc SPer |
| | Lincoln Cathedral = 'Glanlin'[PBR] (HT) | SPer |
| | Lincolnshire Poacher = 'Glareabit' (HT) | NEgg |
| | Lincolnshire Yellow Belly | ESty |
| | Lion's Fairy Tale[PBR] | see *R.* Champagne Moments |
| | Lisa = 'Kirdisco' (F) | LSRN |
| | Little Amy = 'Battamy' (Min) | LSRN |
| | 'Little Buckaroo' (Min) | SPer |
| | Little Cherub = 'Tan00814'[PBR] (Patio) | SWCr |
| | 'Little Flirt' (Min) | MAus |
| | 'Little Gem' (DPMo) | MAus |
| | Little Jackie = 'Savor' (Min) | LSRN |
| | Little Rambler = 'Chewramb'[PBR] (MinRa) ♀H4 | CSBt ECnt ESty GCoc LStr MAus MBri MGos MMuc MRav MWat SCoo SMrm SPer SSea SWCr |
| | 'Little White Pet' | see *R.* 'White Pet' |
| | Little Woman = 'Diclittle'[PBR] (Patio) | IDic LStr |
| | 'Lolabelle' | CPou |
| | 'Long John Silver' (Cl) | MAus SSea |
| | ***longicuspis*** misapplied | see *R. mulliganii* |
| | ***longicuspis*** Bertol. (Ra) AC 2097 | GGar |
| § | - var. ***sinowilsonii*** (Ra) | GCal GGar MAus |
| | aff. ***longicuspis*** | SWCr |
| | Lord Byron = 'Meitosier' (ClHT) | LStr SSea SWCr |
| | 'Lord Penzance' (RH) | SPer |
| | Lorna = 'Cocringer' (F) | GCoc LSRN |
| | 'L'Ouche' misapplied | see *R.* 'Louise Odier' |
| | 'Louis Gimard' (CeMo) | MAus SFam |
| | 'Louis XIV' (Ch) | EBee MCot |
| § | 'Louise Odier' (Bb) | CTri EBee ECnt ELon EPfP GCoc IArd LRHS LStr MAus MBri MCot MRav MWat NLar SFam SPer SSea SWCr |
| | Love & Peace = 'Baipeace'[PBR] (HT) | ELan ESty MAsh SPoG SWCr |
| | Love Knot = 'Chewglorious'[PBR] (ClMin) | CSBt ECnt ELon ESty LRHS MAsh MRav MWat SCoo SRGP SSea SWCr WGor |
| § | Lovely Bride = 'Meiratcan'[PBR] (Patio) | LRHS MAsh MBri SPoG SWCr |
| | Lovely Fairy = 'Spevu'[PBR] (Poly/GC) | IDic |
| | Lovely Lady = 'Dicjubell'[PBR] (HT) ♀H4 | CSBt EBls ECnt ESty GCoc IDic LBuc LSRN LStr MAus MRav MWat SRGP SSea SWCr |
| | Lovely Meidiland[PBR] | see *R.* Lovely Bride |
| | 'Lovers' Meeting' (HT) | GCoc MRav SPer SRGP SSea SWCr |
| | Loving Memory = 'Korgund' (HT) | CGro CSBt CWSG ECnt ESty GCoc IArd LSRN LStr MGos MRav NPri SPer SPoG SRGP SVic SWCr |
| | Lucetta = 'Ausemi' (S) | MAus |
| | ***luciae*** var. ***onoei*** | EPot |
| | 'Lucky' (F) | CGro CWSG EBee EPfP ESty LRHS LShp LStr NPri SMrm SPer |
| | Lucky! = 'Frylucy' (F) | CSBt ECnt GCoc LBuc LSRN MAsh MBri SCoo SMad SPoG SSea SWCr |
| | Lucy = 'Kirlis' (F) | LSRN |
| | 'Lutea Maxima' | see *R.* × *harisonii* 'Lutea Maxima' |
| | Lyda Rose = 'Letlyda' (S) **new** | EBls |
| | 'Lykkefund' (Ra) | MAus |
| | 'Mabel Morrison' (HP) | MAus |
| | Macartney rose | see *R. bracteata*, *R.* The McCartney Rose |
| | Macmillan Nurse = 'Beamac' (S) | EBls ESty |
| | 'Macrantha' (Gallica hybrid) | MAus |
| | ***macrophylla*** | MAus |
| | - B&SWJ 2603 | WCru |
| § | - 'Master Hugh' ♀H4 | MAus |
| | 'Madame Abel Chatenay' (HT) | MAus |
| | 'Madame Alfred Carrière' (N) ♀H4 | Widely available |
| | 'Madame Alice Garnier' (Ra) | CPou MMuc SPer |
| | 'Madame Bravy' (T) | MAus |
| | 'Madame Butterfly' (HT) | MAus SPer |
| § | 'Madame Caroline Testout' (HT) | CTri LRHS SEND SMad SPoG |
| | 'Madame de la Roche-Lambert' (DPMo) | CPou MAus |
| | 'Madame de Sancy de Parabère' (Bs) | EWTr IArd MAus SWCr |
| | 'Madame Driout' (ClT) | CPou EBee |
| | 'Madame Ernest Calvat' (Bb) | CPou |
| | 'Madame Eugène Résal' misapplied | see *R.* 'Comtesse du Cayla' |
| | Madame Figaro = 'Delrona' (S) | MRav |
| § | 'Madame Grégoire Staechelin' (ClHT) ♀H4 | CTri ECnt ELan EPfP LAst LRHS LSRN LStr MAus MBri MRav NEgg SMrm SPer SPlb SWCr |
| | 'Madame Hardy' (ClD) ♀H4 | CPou CSBt ECnt EPfP GCoc LRHS LStr MAus MBri MRav MWat NChi NEgg NLar SFam SMrm SPer SSea SWCr |
| | 'Madame Isaac Pereire' (ClBb) ♀H4 | CSBt CTri EBee ECnt EPfP GCoc LRHS LStr MAus MBri MCot MRav MWat NLar NPri SFam SMad SMrm SPer SPoG SSea SWCr |
| | 'Madame Jules Gravereaux' (ClT) | MAus |
| § | 'Madame Knorr' (DPo) ♀H4 | CPou ECnt ELon EPfP LRHS MCot MRav MWat NLar SMrm SPer SSea SWCr |
| | 'Madame Laurette Messimy' (Ch) | MAus |
| | 'Madame Lauriol de Barny' (Bb) | GCoc MAus MRav NLar SFam SLon |
| | 'Madame Legras de Saint Germain' (A × N) | CPou EBee EWTr LRHS MAus NLar SFam SPer |
| | 'Madame Louis Lévêque' (DPMo) | CPou NLar |
| | 'Madame Pierre Oger' (Bb) | CTri EBee ECnt LRHS LStr MAus MRav SKHP SPer SWCr |
| | 'Madame Plantier' (A × N) | CPou EWTr MAus MRav NLar SEND SPer |
| | 'Madame Zöetmans' (D) | MAus |
| | 'Madeleine Seltzer' (Ra) | ECGP |
| | 'Madge' (HM) | SDix |
| | Magic Carpet = 'Jaclover'[PBR] (S/GC) ♀H4 | CWSG ELan GCoc IDic MAus MGos MRav MWat SMrm SPer SSea SWCr |

| |  |  |
|---|---|---|
| | Magic Hit = 'Poulhi004' (Min) | SWCr |
| | 'Magnifica' (RH) | LRHS MAus |
| | 'Maid of Kent'PBR (Cl) | CSBt MAus SCoo SPer SWCr |
| | 'Maiden's Blush' (A) ♀H4 | CArn CTri ELan LRHS MAsh MAus SFam SPer SSea SWCr |
| | 'Maiden's Blush, Great' | see *R.* 'Great Maiden's Blush' |
| | 'Maigold' (ClPiH) ♀H4 | CBcs CGro CTri ECnt ELan EPfP GCoc LRHS LStr MAsh MAus MCot MRav NLar SEND SMad SPer SWCr |
| | Make a Wish = 'Mehpat'PBR (Min/Patio) | ESty LStr |
| | Maltese rose | see *R.* 'Cécile Brünner' |
| | Malvern Hills = 'Auscanary'PBR (Ra) | CSBt EPfP GCoc LRHS MAsh MAus MBri SPer SSea SWCr |
| | Mamma Mia! = 'Fryjolly'PBR (HT) | ECnt ESty GCoc LBuc MAsh MBri NPri SPoG SWCr |
| | Mandarin = 'Korcelin'PBR (Min) | ESty LStr MRav |
| | 'Manning's Blush' (RH) | MAus |
| | Many Happy Returns = 'Harwanted'PBR (F) ♀H4 | CBcs CGro CSBt CWSG ECnt ELan EPfP GCoc LRHS LSRN LStr MAsh MGos MRav MWat NPri SPer SPoG SRGP SSea SVic SWCr |
| | 'Marbrée' (DPo) | MAus |
| | 'Märchenland' (F) | MAus |
| § | 'Marchesa Boccella' (DPo) ♀H4 | CPou CSam CTri EPfP EWTr GCoc LRHS MBri MCot NLar NPri SEND SPer SPoG SSea SWCr WBor |
| | 'Maréchal Davoust' (CeMo) | MAus SFam |
| | 'Maréchal Niel' (N) | ERea EShb MAus SPer |
| | 'Margaret' (HT) | GCoc |
| | Margaret Merril = 'Harkuly' (F) ♀H4 | CBcs CGro CSBt CTri CWSG EBee ECnt ELan ELon EPfP ESty GCoc IArd LRHS LSRN LStr MAsh MAus MBri MRav NPri SPer SPoG SRGP SSea SWCr |
| | 'Marguerite Hilling' (S) ♀H4 | CTri EPfP MAus MRav NLar SMad SPer |
| | 'Mariae-Graebnerae' | SLPl |
| | 'Marie Louise' (D) | EBee MAus SFam |
| | 'Marie Pavič' (Poly) | CPou MAus |
| | 'Marie van Houtte' (T) | MAus |
| | 'Marie-Jeanne' (Poly) | MAus |
| | Marinette = 'Auscam'PBR (S) | MAus |
| | Marjorie Fair = 'Harhero' (Poly/S) ♀H4 | EPfP ESty GCoc MAsh MAus MRav SWCr |
| | Marjorie Marshall = 'Hardenier'PBR | MRav |
| | 'Marlena' (F/Patio) | GCoc MAus |
| | Marry Me = 'Dicwonder'PBR (Patio) ♀H4 | ESty IDic |
| | 'Martian Glow' (F) | NLar |
| | 'Martin Frobisher' (Ru) | MAus |
| I | 'Mary' (Poly) | LStr |
| | Mary Magdalene = 'Ausjolly'PBR (S) | MAus |
| | 'Mary Manners' (Ru) | NLar |
| | Mary Rose = 'Ausmary' (S) ♀H4 | CGro CSBt CTri CWSG EBee ELan EPfP GCoc LRHS LSRN LStr MAus MBri MRav MWat NLar NPri SMrm SPer SPoG SSea SWCr WKif |
| | 'Mary Wallace' (Cl) | MAus |
| | Mary Webb = 'Auswebb' (S) | MAus |
| | 'Masquerade' (F) | CTri ELan GCoc SMrm SPer SSea SWCr |
| | 'Master Hugh' | see *R. macrophylla* 'Master Hugh' |
| | Matawhero MagicPBR | see *R.* Simply the Best |
| | 'Max Graf' | see *R.* × *jacksonii* 'Max Graf' |
| | 'Maxima' | see *R.* × *alba* 'Alba Maxima' |
| | 'May Queen' (Ra) | CPou LRHS MAus MBri MRav NLar SEND SFam SPer SWCr |
| | Mayor of Casterbridge = 'Ausbrid'PBR (S) | LRHS MAus |
| | 'McCartney Rose'PBR | see *R.* The McCartney Rose |
| | 'Meg' (ClHT) | EWTr LRHS LSRN MAus MCot MMuc SRGP |
| | 'Meg Merrilies' (RH) | MAus NLar |
| | 'Meicobius'PBR | see *R.* Terracotta = 'Meicobuis' |
| | Melody Maker = 'Dicqueen'PBR (F) | IDic |
| | 'Memories Are Made of This' (F) | GCoc |
| | Memory Lane = 'Peavoodoo'PBR (F) | LSRN SWCr |
| | 'Mermaid' (Cl) ♀H3-4 | CBcs CDul CGro CSBt EBee ECnt ELon EPfP LHop LStr MAus MBri MCot NLar SEND SMrm SPer SPoG SSea SWCr |
| § | 'Mevrouw Nathalie Nypels' (Poly) ♀H4 | CTri LRHS LStr MAus MMuc MRav NLar SPer SWCr WKif |
| | 'Michèle Meilland' (HT) | MAus |
| | × ***micrugosa*** | MAus |
| | - 'Alba' | MAus |
| | Middlesborough Football Club = 'Horflame' (HT) | LSRN |
| § | Millie = 'Poulren013'PBR (Renaissance Series) (S) | ECnt LRHS LSRN MAsh MBri NPri SPoG SWCr |
| | Millionaire = 'Peazara' (F) | LSRN |
| | 'Minnehaha' (Ra) | MAus |
| | ***mirifica stellata*** | see *R. stellata* var. *mirifica* |
| | Mischief = 'Macmi' (HT) | LSRN SPer |
| | Miss Alice = 'Ausjake'PBR (S) | MAus MBri SWCr |
| | Miss Dior = 'Harencens'PBR (S) | MRav |
| | 'Miss Edith Cavell' (Poly) | MAus |
| | Missing You = 'Horcakebread' (F) | SWCr |
| § | 'Mister Lincoln' (HT) | SPer SWCr |
| | Mistress Quickly = 'Ausky'PBR (S) | MAus |
| § | Misty Hit = 'Poulhi011'PBR (PatioHit Series) (Patio) | ECnt LRHS LSRN MAsh SWCr |
| | Molineux = 'Ausmol'PBR (S) ♀H4 | CSBt EBee EPfP LRHS MAsh MAus MBri SWCr |
| | Monsieur Pélisson = 'Pélisson' | SFam |
| | Moody Blue = 'Fryniche' (HT) <u>**new**</u> | ECnt ESty GCoc |
| | Moonbeam = 'Ausbeam' (S) | MAus |
| | 'Moonlight' (HM) | CSam CTri EBee ELan EWTr GCoc MAus MRav SMrm SPer SWCr |
| | Moonshine = 'Tan97123'PBR (HT) | ESty |
| | 'Morgengruss' (Cl) | GCoc SPer SWCr |
| | 'Morletii' (Bs) | EWTr MMuc MRav |
| | 'Morning Jewel' (ClF) ♀H4 | GCoc SPer SWCr |
| | Morning Mist = 'Ausfire' (S) | MAus SSea |
| § | 'Morsdag' (Poly/F) | LSRN LStr SVic |
| | Mortimer Sackler = 'Ausorts'PBR (S) | LRHS MAus MBri SCoo |
| | ***moschata*** (Ra) | MAus MRav NLar |
| | - 'Autumnalis' | see *R.* 'Princesse de Nassau' |
| | - var. ***nepalensis*** | see *R. brunonii* |
| | Mother's Day | see *R.* 'Morsdag' |
| I | 'Mother's Day' | SRGP |
| | Mother's Joy = 'Horsiltrop' (F) | LSRN |

| |  |  |
|---|---|---|
| | Mountain Snow = 'Aussnow' (Ra) | LRHS MAus MBri |
| | Mountbatten = 'Harmantelle' (F) 🏆H4 | ELan EPfP LStr MAsh MAus MRav NPri SPer SPoG SSea SWCr |
| § | 'Mousseline' (DPoMo) | CPou MAus MCot MRav NLar SFam SPer |
| | 'Mousseuse du Japon' | see *R.* 'Japonica' |
| | ***moyesii*** (S) | CDoy CTri ELan EWTr GCra MAus NEgg NWea SKHP SPer |
| | 'Mr Bluebird' (MinCh) | MAus |
| | 'Mr Lincoln' | see *R.* 'Mister Lincoln' |
| | 'Mrs Anthony Waterer' (Ru) | EBee MAus SPer |
| | 'Mrs Arthur Curtiss James' (ClHT) | EBee MMuc |
| | Mrs Doreen Pike = 'Ausdor'PBR (Ru) | MAus |
| | 'Mrs Honey Dyson' (Ra) | CPou |
| | 'Mrs John Laing' (HP) | EPfP LRHS MAus NLar SFam SLon SPer SWCr |
| | 'Mrs Oakley Fisher' (HT) | EWTr MAus MCot SDix SMrm SPer SWCr |
| | 'Mrs Paul' (Bb) | MAus |
| | 'Mrs Sam McGredy' (HT) | LRHS NEgg SSea |
| | 'Mrs Yamada' (Bb) **new** | EBls |
| | 'Mullard Jubilee' (HT) | SWCr |
| § | ***mulliganii*** (Ra) 🏆H4 | EBee EPfP GKin SPer SWCr |
| | ***multibracteata*** (S) | MAus |
| | ***multiflora*** (Ra) | LBuc MAus |
| § | - var. ***cathayensis*** (Ra) | WBor |
| § | - 'Grevillei' (Ra) | EBee MMuc SPer |
| | - 'Platyphylla' | see *R. multiflora* 'Grevillei' |
| | - wild-collected **new** | GCal |
| | Mum in a MillionPBR | see *R.* Millie |
| | MummyPBR | see *R.* Newly Wed |
| | Mum's Blessing = 'Guesimage' (F) **new** | SWCr |
| | ***mundi*** | see *R. gallica* 'Versicolor' |
| | Munstead Wood = 'Ausbernard'PBR (S) | LRHS MAus SSea |
| | 'Murjami' | EBls |
| | 'Muscosa Alba' | see *R.* × *centifolia* 'Shailer's White Moss' |
| | 'Mutabilis' | see *R.* × *odorata* 'Mutabilis' |
| | My Everything = 'Coccastle'PBR (F) | ESty GCoc |
| | My Mum = 'Webmorrow'PBR (F) | EGxp ESty GCoc LBuc LSRN SWCr |
| | My Valentine = 'Mormyval' (Min) | LSRN LStr MAsh SPoG SWCr |
| | Myriam = 'Cocgrand' (HT) | GCoc LSRN |
| | Mystery Girl = 'Dicdothis'PBR (HT) | EBee ECnt ESty GCoc IDic LBuc |
| | Mystique = 'Kirmyst' (F) | EBls |
| | Nahéma = 'Deléri' (ClHT) | MRav SMrm SWCr |
| | Nancy = 'Poulninga'PBR (Renaissance Series) | LSRN |
| | 'Narrow Water' (Ra) | CPou NLar SWCr |
| § | 'Nastarana' (N) | NLar |
| | 'Nathalie Nypels' | see *R.* 'Mevrouw Nathalie Nypels' |
| | 'National Trust' (HT) | CBcs CTri GCoc IArd MAsh SPer |
| | 'Nelson's Pride' (F) | EBls |
| | 'Nestor' (G) | EWTr MAus |
| | 'Nevada' (S) 🏆H4 | CSBt CTri ECnt ELan EPfP EWTr GCoc IArd LRHS LStr MAus MRav NLar SPer SSea SWCr WKif |
| | Never Forgotten = 'Gregart' (HT) | LSRN |
| | New Age = 'Wekbipuhit'PBR (F) | CSBt |
| | New Arrival | see *R.* 'Red Patio' |

| |  |  |
|---|---|---|
| | New Beginnings = 'Korprofko' (F) | GCoc SSea |
| § | 'New Dawn' (Cl) 🏆H4 | Widely available |
| | 'New Home' | LSRN |
| | New Life = 'Cocwarble'PBR (F) | GCoc |
| | New Zealand = 'Macgenev'PBR (HT) | SWCr |
| § | Newly Wed = 'Dicwhynot'PBR (Patio) | IDic LBuc LStr MAsh SPoG |
| | News = 'Legnews' (F) | MAus SWCr |
| | Nice Day = 'Chewsea'PBR (ClMin) 🏆H4 | CGro CWSG ELon EPfP ESty LRHS LStr MAsh MRav MWat SPer SPoG SRGP SSea SWCr |
| | 'Nicola' (F) | GCoc LSRN |
| | Night Light = 'Poullight'PBR (Courtyard Series) (Cl) | ECnt MRav |
| | Night Sky = 'Dicetch'PBR (F) | IDic SSea |
| | Nina = 'Mehnina'PBR (S) | LSRN SWCr |
| | Nina = 'Poulren018' (Renaissance Series) (S) | ECnt |
| | ***nitida*** | MAus NWea SEND SLPl SPer WHer |
| | Noble Antony = 'Ausway'PBR (S) | LRHS LStr MAus MBri SMrm |
| § | 'Noisette Carnée' (N) | CSam EBee EPfP GCra LRHS LStr MBNS MCot MRav NLar SLPl SPer SSea SWCr |
| | Norfolk = 'Poulfolk'PBR (GC) | ESty NLar SMrm SPer |
| | 'Northern Lights' (HT) | GCoc |
| | 'Norwich Pink' (S) | MAus |
| | Norwich Theatre Royal = 'Beacalm' (S) | EBls |
| | Nostalgia = 'Savarita' (Min) | MAsh MAus |
| | Nostalgie = 'Taneiglat'PBR (HT) | CSBt EBls ECnt EGxp ELon ESty GCoc LStr MBri MRav SPoG SSea SWCr |
| | 'Nozomi' (ClMin/GC) 🏆H4 | CGro CTri ELan EPfP ESty GCoc MAus MRav NLar NWCA SMrm SPer |
| | 'Nuits de Young' (CeMo) 🏆H4 | GCoc LRHS MAus SEND SFam SKHP |
| | 'Nur Mahal' (HM) | MAus |
| | Nurse Tracey Davies = 'Frykookie'PBR (F) **new** | ESty |
| | ***nutkana*** (S) | MAus |
| § | - 'Plena' (S/D) 🏆H4 | EPfP EWTr GCoc NLar SKHP |
| | 'Nymphenburg' (HM) | EBee SPer |
| | 'Nyveldt's White' (Ru) | MAus |
| | Octavia Hill = 'Harzeal'PBR (F) | EBee MRav NLar SPer SWCr |
| § | × ***odorata*** | SVic |
| § | - 'Mutabilis' (Ch) 🏆H3-4 | CRHN CTri EBee ECre EPfP EWTr GCoc GGal LRHS MAus MCot MRav SEND SKHP SMad SMrm SPer SSea SWCr WCFE WCot WKif XSen |
| § | - 'Pallida' (Ch) | EPfP LRHS MAsh MCot MRav SPer SSea SWCr WBor |
| § | - Sanguinea Group (Ch) | XSen |
| | - - 'Bengal Crimson' (Ch) | ECGP EWTr LRHS LSRN SKHP SLon WCot WKif |
| | - - 'Bob's Beauty' (Ch) | WCot |
| § | - 'Viridiflora' (Ch) | EBee MAus SLon SPer SSea WCot WHer |
| | Odyssey = 'Franski'PBR (F) | ESty SWCr |
| | 'Oeillet Flamand' | see *R.* 'Oeillet Parfait' |
| § | 'Oeillet Parfait' (G) | MAus |
| | ***officinalis*** | see *R. gallica* var. *officinalis* |
| | old blush China | see *R.* × *odorata* 'Pallida' |
| | old cabbage | see *R.* × *centifolia* |
| | Old John = 'Dicwillynilly' (F) | IDic |

old pink moss rose — see *R.* × *centifolia* 'Muscosa'
Old Port = 'Mackati'[PBR] (F) — IArd
old red moss — see *R.* 'Henri Martin'
old velvet moss — see *R.* 'William Lobb'
'Old Velvet Rose' — see *R.* 'Tuscany'
old yellow Scotch (SpH) — see *R.* × *harisonii* 'Williams Double Yellow'
Olivia = 'Wekquahofa' (HT) **new** — LSRN
'Olympic Flame' **new** — MAsh
Olympic Spirit = 'Peaprince' (F) **new** — LRHS MAsh MBri
'Omar Khayyám' (D) — MAus MRav
***omeiensis*** — see *R. sericea* subsp. *omeiensis*
One Promise = 'Frannite'[PBR] — MBri
Open Arms = 'Chewpixcel'[PBR] (ClMin) ♀H4 — ESty MAus MBri SMad SMrm SPer SSea SWCr
'Ophelia' (HT) — EBee LRHS MAus
'Orange Sensation' (F) — CTri MAus
§ Orange Sunblaze = 'Meijikatar'[PBR] (Min) — CSBt SPer
Oranges and Lemons = 'Macoranlem'[PBR] (S/F) — CGro CSBt EBls ECnt ELan ESty GCoc LStr MAsh MAus SPoG SSea SWCr
Othello = 'Auslo'[PBR] (S) — MAus SLon SMrm
'Our Beth' (S) — EBls
'Our Dream' (Patio) — MAsh
Our George = 'Kirrush' (Patio) — LSRN
Our Jubilee = 'Coccages' (HT) — ESty LBuc SVic
Our Molly = 'Dicreason' (GC/S) — IDic LSRN SWCr
Oxfordshire = 'Korfullwind'[PBR] (GC) ♀H4 — LStr MRav MWat
Paddy Stephens = 'Macclack'[PBR] (HT) — SWCr
Painted Moon = 'Dicpaint' (HT) — ESty
Panache = 'Poultop'[PBR] (Patio/Min) — ECnt LStr SWCr
'Papa Gontier' (T) — MAus
Papa Meilland = 'Meisar' (HT) — CGro CSBt GCoc MAus SPer
Paper Anniversary (Patio) — LSRN
Papi Delbard = 'Delaby' (ClHT) — MRav
§ 'Para Ti' (Min) — SPer
I 'Parade' (Cl) ♀H4 — MAus MRav SMad SWCr
'Parkdirektor Riggers' (F) — CSam EBee LStr MAus MBri NLar SMrm SPer SWCr
Parky = 'Harpresto'[PBR] (S) **new** — LRHS
Parson's pink China — see *R.* × *odorata* 'Pallida'
Partridge = 'Korweirim'[PBR] (GC) — MAus SPer
***parvifolia*** — see *R.* 'Burgundiaca'
Pas de Deux = 'Poulhult'[PBR] (Courtyard Series) (ClF) — MAsh
Pascali = 'Lenip' (HT) — CTri GCoc MAus MRav MWat SMrm SPer SSea
Pat Austin = 'Ausmum'[PBR] (S) ♀H4 — CSBt CTri ECnt ELon EPfP GCoc LRHS LSRN LStr LTen MAsh MAus MBNS MBri MRav MWat NEgg NLar SEND SMrm SPer SPoG SRGP SWCr
Patricia = 'Korpatri' (F) — SWCr
'Paul Lédé' (ClT) — see *R.* 'Climbing Paul Lédé'
Paul McCartney[PBR] (HT) — see *R.* The McCartney Rose
'Paul Neyron' (HP) — EWTr MAus SPer
'Paul Noël' (Ra) **new** — MAus
'Paul Ricault' (Ce × HP) — MAus
Paul Shirville = 'Harqueterwife'[PBR] (HT) ♀H4 — ELan ELon MAus SPer SRGP SWCr
'Paul Transon' (Ra) ♀H4 — CPou CRHN EBee EPfP LRHS MBri MMuc NEgg NLar SEND SPer SWCr WHer
'Paulii Rosea' (Ru/GC) — MAus
'Paul's Himalayan Musk' (Ra) ♀H3-4 — CPLG CRHN CSBt CSam CTri EBee ECnt EPfP GKin IArd LRHS LStr MAus MBri MRav NEgg NLar SEND SFam SMad SMrm SPer SPoG SSea SWCr WBor WKif
§ 'Paul's Lemon Pillar' (ClHT) — LAst LRHS MAus NLar SMrm SPer SSea
'Paul's Scarlet Climber' (Cl/Ra) — CGro CSBt ELan LAst LStr MAsh MAus MRav NPri SEND SPer SRGP
'Paul's Single White Perpetual' (Ra) — MMuc
'Pax' (HM) — CPou MAus WKif
Peace = 'Madame A. Meilland' (HT) ♀H4 — CGro CSBt CTri ECnt ELan EPfP ESty GCoc LRHS LSRN LStr MAsh MAus MBri MRav MWat NEgg NPri SMrm SPer SPoG SRGP SSea SWCr WBor
Peace Sunblaze (Min) — see *R.* Lady Meillandina
Peacekeeper = 'Harbella'[PBR] (F) — CSBt MRav
Peach Blossom = 'Ausblossom' (S) — MAus
'Peach Grootendorst' (Ru) — CPou
Peachy = 'Macrelea' (HT) — LRHS MAsh
§ Pearl Abundance = 'Harfrisky'[PBR] (F) — ESty SWCr
Pearl Anniversary = 'Whitston'[PBR] (Min/Patio) — CSBt ESty LSRN LStr MRav SWCr
Pearl Drift = 'Leggab' (S) — MAus SMrm SPer SWCr
Pearl = 'Korterschi'[PBR] (F) — GCoc LRHS SWCr
Peaudouce — see *R.* Elina
§ Peek-a-boo = 'Dicgrow' (Min/Patio) — SPer
Peer Gynt = 'Korol' (HT) — SWCr
Pegasus = 'Ausmoon'[PBR] (S) — LRHS MAus SSea
§ ***pendulina*** — LBuc MAus
'Penelope' (HM) ♀H4 — CSBt CSam CTri EBee ECnt ELan EPfP EWTr GCoc LRHS LSRN LStr MAsh MAus MBri MCot MRav MWat NLar NPri SEND SFam SMad SPer SRGP SSea SWCr WKif
Penny Lane = 'Hardwell'[PBR] (ClHT) ♀H4 — CSBt ECnt ELon EPfP ESty GCoc LAst LRHS LStr MAsh MAus MBri MRav MWat NLar SCoo SPer SPoG SSea SWCr
× ***penzanceana*** — see *R.* 'Lady Penzance'
Peppermint Splash — see *R.* Rachel Louise Moran
Perception = 'Harzippee'[PBR] (HT) — SWCr
Perdita = 'Ausperd' (S) — ESty MAus MRav
Perennial Blue = 'Mehr9601' (Ra) — ESty GCoc SSea SWCr
Perennial Blush = 'Mehbarbie'[PBR] (Ra) — ESty GCoc SWCr
§ Perfect Day = 'Poulrem' (F) — ECnt
'Perle des Jardins' (T) — MAus

§ 'Perle d'Or' (Poly) ♀H4 — ECGP MAus MMuc NLar SDix SLon SMad SPer
Perpetually Yours = 'Harfable'PBR (Cl) — CGro LStr MRav MWat SCoo
Persian yellow — see *R. foetida* 'Persiana'
Peter Pan = 'Chewpan'PBR (Min) — MAsh MAus MWat SWCr
Peter Pan = 'Sunpete' (Patio) — EPfP LRHS NPri SPoG
'Petite de Hollande' (Ce) — MAus NLar SPer
'Petite Lisette' (Ce × D) — MAus NLar
'Petito' (F) — SMrm
Phab Gold = 'Frybountiful'PBR (F) — ESty GCoc MAsh
Pheasant = 'Kordapt'PBR (GC) — GCoc MAus SPer SWCr
Phillipa = 'Poulheart'PBR (S) — LSRN
Phoebe (Ru) — see *R.* 'Fimbriata'
'Phyllis Bide' (Ra) ♀H4 — EBee ECGP EPfP GCoc IArd LRHS LStr MAus MBri MCot NLar SEND SPer SSea SWCr
Piccadilly = 'Macar' (HT) — CGro CSBt CTri GCoc MRav SPer SWCr
Piccolo = 'Tanolokip' (F/Patio) — CGro ESty LStr MBri MRav SWCr
'Picture' (HT) — MAus SPer
Pigalle '84 = 'Meicloux' (F) — SWCr
'Pilgrim'PBR — see *R.* The Pilgrim
***pimpinellifolia*** — see *R. spinosissima*
- double yellow-flowered — see *R.* × *harisonii* 'Williams Double Yellow'
- 'Harisonii' — see *R.* × *harisonii* 'Harison's Yellow'
- 'Lutea' — see *R.* × *harisonii* 'Lutea Maxima'
Pink Abundance = 'Harfrothy'PBR (Abundance Series) (F) — ESty LStr MAus
Pink Bells = 'Poulbells' (GC) — SPer
'Pink Bouquet' (Ra) — CRHN
'Pink Favorite' (HT) — CSBt SPer
Pink Fizz = 'Poulycool' (ClPatio) — ECnt
§ Pink Flower Carpet = 'Noatraum'PBR (GC) ♀H4 — CGro CSBt CTri ECnt ELan GCoc IBal LRHS LStr MAsh MAus MBri NPri SCoo SEND SPer SPoG SWCr
'Pink Garnette' — see *R.* 'Carol Amling'
'Pink Grootendorst' (Ru) ♀H4 — EPfP GCoc LRHS MAus NEgg NLar SPer SWCr
§ Pink Hit = 'Poultipe'PBR (Min/Patio) — ECnt LRHS LSRN MAsh MBri SWCr
Pink Knock Out = 'Radcon' (S) **new** — MAsh
'Pink Leda' (D) **new** — EBee
'Pink Medley' (F) — MAsh MBri
pink moss — see *R.* × *centifolia* 'Muscosa'
'Pink Parfait' (F) — GCoc SPer
Pink Peace = 'Meibil' (HT) — SWCr
Pink Perfection = 'Korpauvio'PBR (HT) **new** — ESty
'Pink Perpétué' (Cl) — CBcs CGro CSBt CTri ECnt ELan EPfP GCoc LRHS LStr MAsh MAus MRav SMrm SPer SPoG SSea SWCr
'Pink Pins' — LRHS
'Pink Prosperity' (HM) — MAus
Pink Skyliner = 'Franwekpink'PBR (ClS) — EBls
Pirouette = 'Poulyc003'PBR (Cl) — ECnt MAsh SWCr
'Plaisanterie' (HM) — MAus
'Playboy' (F) — GCoc
Playtime = 'Morplati' (F) — MAus
Pleine de Grâce = 'Lengra' (S) — MAus
Poetry in Motion = 'Harelan'PBR (HT) — EBls
Polar Star = 'Tanlarpost' (HT) — CSBt ECnt GCoc LBuc LStr MRav MWat SPer SWCr
× ***polliniana*** — SLPl
'Polly' (HT) — GCoc LSRN
§ 'Polyantha Grandiflora' (Ra) — MAus
***pomifera*** — see *R. villosa* L.
'Pompon Blanc Parfait' (A) — MAus
'Pompon de Bourgogne' — see *R.* 'Burgundiaca'
'Pompon de Paris' (ClMinCh) — see *R.* 'Climbing Pompon de Paris'
§ 'Pompon de Paris' (MinCh) — WAbe
'Pompon Panaché' (G) — MAus
Port Sunlight = 'Auslofty'PBR (HM) — LRHS MAus
Portland rose — see *R.* 'Portlandica'
§ 'Portlandica' (Po) — CTri LRHS SPer
Portmeirion = 'Ausguard'PBR (S) — MAus SCoo
Pot o' Gold = 'Dicdivine' (HT) — SPer SWCr
Pour Toi — see *R.* 'Para Ti'
prairie rose — see *R. setigera*
'Precious Memories' (Min) — LSRN
Precious Memories = 'Dichello'PBR (F) — ESty GCoc IDic
'Precious Platinum' (HT) — SPer
§ 'Président de Sèze' (G) ♀H4 — CPou CSam MAus NLar SFam SPer
Pretty in Pink = 'Dicumpteen'PBR (GC) — ECnt IDic SWCr
Pretty Jessica = 'Ausjess' (S) — CGro LSRN MAus MRav SMrm SPer
Pretty Lady = 'Scrivo'PBR (F) ♀H4 — MAus
Pretty Polly = 'Meitonje'PBR (Min) ♀H4 — CGro EPfP ESty GCoc LRHS LStr MAsh MBri MRav MWat SMrm SPer SPoG SRGP SWCr
Pretty Sunrise = 'Meipelmel'PBR (S) **new** — MAsh
Pride of England = 'Harencore'PBR (HT) — EBls GCoc
Pride of Scotland = 'Macwhitba' (HT) — GCoc
'Prima Ballerina' (HT) — CGro CSBt CTri CWSG GCoc LStr MAsh SPer SSea
***primula*** (S) ♀H3-4 — EShb GCoc MAus NLar SPer
'Prince Camille de Rohan' (HP) — EBee MAus
'Prince Charles' (Bb) — MAus NLar WKif
Prince Regent = 'Genpen' (S) — SSea
Princess Alexandra of Kent = 'Ausmerchant'PBR — EPfP ESty MAus MBri SSea
Princess Alexandra = 'Pouldra'PBR (Renaissance Series) (S) — CTri ECnt EPfP SWCr
Princess = 'Canfound'PBR (HT) — ECnt
Princess Nobuko = 'Coclistine'PBR (HT) — GCoc
'Princess of Wales' (HP) — EPfP
Princess of Wales = 'Hardinkum'PBR (F) ♀H4 — EPfP GCoc LRHS LStr MAsh MBri MRav SCoo SPer SWCr
Princess Royal = 'Dicroyal'PBR (HT) — IDic

§ 'Princesse de Nassau' (Ra) MAus SEND SKHP
'Princesse Louise' (Ra) CRHN MAus SFam
'Princesse Marie' misapplied see *R.* 'Belvedere'
'Pristine' (HT) MAus
§ 'Professeur Emile Perrot' (D) CArn SMad
'Prolifera de Redouté' misapplied see *R.* 'Duchesse de Montebello'
Proper Job = 'Tan02733' (HT) **new** SWCr
'Prosperity' (HM) ♀$^{H4}$ CSam CTri EBee EPfP EWTr GCoc LRHS MAus MCot MRav NLar SLon SPer SPoG SWCr
Prospero = 'Auspero' (S) MAus NLar SEND
§ ***pulverulenta*** GAuc
Pure Bliss = 'Dictator'$^{PBR}$ (HT) IDic SWCr
Pure Gold = 'Harhappen'$^{PBR}$ (F) CSBt
'Purezza' (Ra) LRHS NLar
Purple Skyliner = 'Franwekpurp'$^{PBR}$ (ClS) EBls ESty SMrm
Purple Tiger = 'Jacpurr'$^{PBR}$ (F) ESty IDic LStr SMrm SWCr
Quaker Star = 'Dicperhaps' (F) IDic
quatre saisons see *R.* × *damascena* var. *semperflorens*
Queen Elizabeth see *R.* 'The Queen Elizabeth'
Queen Mother = 'Korquemu'$^{PBR}$ (Patio) ♀$^{H4}$ CSBt ELan GCoc LStr MAus MRav SPer SPoG SWCr
'Queen of Bourbons' (Bb) MAus NLar
Queen of Denmark see *R.* 'Königin von Dänemark'
Queen of Sweden = 'Austiger'$^{PBR}$ (S) EBee ECnt LRHS MAsh MAus MBri SPer SWCr
'Rachel' (HT) EBls LSRN
§ Rachel Louise Moran = 'Jacdrama'$^{PBR}$ (HT) **new** ESty
Rachel = 'Tangust'$^{PBR}$ (HT) CSBt ESty LStr MRav SPoG SWCr
Rachel's Delight = 'Beadimple' (S) EBls
Racy Lady = 'Dicwaffle'$^{PBR}$ (HT) IDic
Radio Times = 'Aussal'$^{PBR}$ (S) MAus
'Radway Sunrise' (S) EBls
'Ragamuffin' (Patio) LShp
Rainbow Magic = 'Dicxplosion'$^{PBR}$ (Patio) IDic
Rainbow Sunblaze = 'Meigenpi'$^{PBR}$ (Min) **new** ESty MAsh
'Rambling Rector' (Ra) ♀$^{H4}$ Widely available
Rambling Rosie = 'Horjasper'$^{PBR}$ (Ra) CGro EBls ECnt EPfP ESty GCoc LSRN MAus SWCr
'Ramona' (Ra) MAus SWCr
'Raspberry Royale' (F/Patio) LRHS MAsh
'Raubritter' ('Macrantha' hybrid) ECGP EPfP LRHS MAus MMuc SWCr
Ray of Hope = 'Cocnilly'$^{PBR}$ (F) GCoc
Ray of Sunshine = 'Cocclare'$^{PBR}$ (Patio) GCoc
'Raymond Carver' (S) EBls
'Raymond Chenault' (S) CGro GCoc SWCr
Rebecca (Patio) ESty LSRN
'Rebecca Claire' (HT) LSRN SWCr
Rebecca Mary = 'Dicjury' (F) IDic
Reconciliation = 'Hartillery'$^{PBR}$ (HT) SRGP SWCr
Red Abundance$^{PBR}$ see *R.* Songs of Praise
Red Blanket = 'Intercell' (S/GC) MAus SPer
Red Coat = 'Auscoat' (F) MAus
Red Devil = 'Dicam' (HT) ESty GCoc MAsh SCoo SPoG
Red Drift = 'Meigalpio' (GC) **new** MAsh
Red Eden Rose = 'Meidrason'$^{PBR}$ (Cl) ESty SSea SWCr
Red Finesse = 'Korvillade'$^{PBR}$ (F) MAsh
'Red Grootendorst' see *R.* 'F.J. Grootendorst'
Red Hat Lady = 'Harpeep'$^{PBR}$ (F) **new** LRHS
'Red Max Graf'$^{PBR}$ see *R.* Rote Max Graf
Red Medley = 'Noapu'$^{PBR}$ (Min) MAsh MBri
red moss see *R.* 'Henri Martin'
Red New Dawn see *R.* 'Étendard'
§ 'Red Patio' (F/Patio) LSRN
Red Rascal = 'Jacbed'$^{PBR}$ (S/Patio) CSBt ELon IDic
red rose of Lancaster see *R. gallica* var. *officinalis*
'Red Wing' (S) MAus
Redouté = 'Auspale'$^{PBR}$ (S) LRHS MAus
Reflections = 'Simref' (F) SWCr
Regensberg = 'Macyoumis'$^{PBR}$ (F/Patio) MAus MBri SPer SWCr
'Reine des Centfeuilles' (Ce) SFam
'Reine des Violettes' (HP) CGro CPou ELon EPfP GCoc IArd LRHS LStr MAsh MAus MBri MCot MRav MWat NLar SPer SWCr
§ 'Reine Victoria' (Bb) EPfP GCoc LRHS LStr MAus MBri SPer SWCr
Remember Me = 'Cocdestin' (HT) ♀$^{H4}$ CGro CSBt CWSG ECnt ESty GCoc IArd LSRN LStr MAus MBri MGos MRav NEgg NPri SPer SPoG SRGP SWCr
§ Remember = 'Poulht001'$^{PBR}$ (HT) ECnt EPfP LRHS MAsh SWCr
Remembrance = 'Harxampton'$^{PBR}$ (F) ♀$^{H4}$ CTri CWSG EBls ESty GCoc LRHS LSRN LStr MAsh MRav NPri SPer SPoG SRGP SWCr
Renaissance = 'Harzart'$^{PBR}$ (HT) CSBt GCoc LStr SWCr
'René André' (Ra) CPou CRHN EBee MAus NLar
'René d'Anjou' (CeMo) LRHS MAus
'Rescht' see *R.* 'De Resht'
'Rêve d'Or' (N) MAus MCot SLon SPer
'Réveil Dijonnais' (ClHT) MAus
Rhapsody in Blue = 'Frantasia'$^{PBR}$ (S) CGro CSBt CWSG EBee ECnt ELan ELon EPfP ESty GCoc LAst LRHS LStr MAsh MAus MBri MGos MRav MWat NPri SCoo SMad SMrm SPer SPoG SSea SWCr WHlf
§ × ***richardii*** GCoc MAus MRav NLar
Rick Stein = 'Tan96205'$^{PBR}$ (HT) LSRN LStr SWCr
'Rival de Paestum' (T) MAus
'River Gardens' NPer
Rob Roy = 'Cocrob' (F) GCoc SPer
Robbie Burns = 'Ausburn' (SpH) MAus

| |  |  |
|---|---|---|
| | 'Robert le Diable' (Ce × G) | MAus NLar |
| | Rockabye Baby = 'Dicdwarf' (Patio) | ESty IDic SWCr |
| | 'Roger Lambelin' (HP) | MAus |
| | Romance = 'Tanezamor'PBR (S) | LSRN MRav |
| | 'Rosa Mundi' | see *R. gallica* 'Versicolor' |
| | Rosabell = 'Cocceleste'PBR (F/Patio) | ESty GCoc |
| | 'Rose à Parfum de l'Haÿ' (Ru) | CTri |
| | 'Rose Ball' (S) | EBls |
| § | 'Rose d'Amour' (S) ♀H4 | CFee |
| | 'Rose de Meaux' | see *R.* × *centifolia* 'De Meaux' |
| | 'Rose de Meaux White' | see *R.* 'White de Meaux' |
| | 'Rose de Rescht' | see *R.* 'De Resht' |
| | Rose des Cisterciens = 'Delarle' (HT) **new** | ESty |
| | 'Rose des Maures' misapplied | see *R.* 'Sissinghurst Castle' |
| | 'Rose du Maître d'Ecole' | see *R.* 'Du Maître d'Ecole' |
| | 'Rose du Roi' (HP/DPo) | ELon LRHS MAus |
| | 'Rose du Roi à Fleurs Pourpres' (HP) | MAus |
| § | Rose Gaujard = 'Gaumo' (HT) | GCoc MAsh |
| | Rose of Picardy = 'Ausfudge' (S) | LRHS MAus MBri SSea |
| | 'Rose-Marie Viaud' (Ra) | CFee CPou CSam MAus MMuc |
| | Rosemary Harkness = 'Harrowbond'PBR (HT) | ESty LStr MRav SMrm SPer |
| | 'Rosemary Rose' (F) | SPer |
| | Rosemoor = 'Austough'PBR (S) | CSBt LRHS MAus MBri SSea |
| | 'Roseraie de l'Haÿ' (Ru) ♀H4 | Widely available |
| | Roses des Cistercians = 'Deltisse' | MRav |
| | Rosie = 'Benros' (Min) **new** | LSRN |
| | Rosy Cushion = 'Interall' (S/GC) ♀H4 | GCoc MAsh MAus MCot SLon SPer |
| | Rosy Future = 'Harwaderox' (F/Patio) | CSBt SWCr |
| | 'Rosy Mantle' (ClHT) | CSBt SPer SWCr |
| § | Rotary Sunrise = 'Fryglitzy' (HT) | CSBt MBri |
| § | Rote Max Graf = 'Kormax'PBR (GC/Ru) | CDul EPfP NLar |
| § | 'Rotes Meer' (Ru) | EBls |
| | Rouge Royale = 'Meikarouz' (HT) **new** | ESty |
| | ***roxburghii*** (S) | EPfP LEdu MAus |
| | - f. ***normalis*** (S) | CFee |
| | - 'Plena' | see *R. roxburghii* f. *roxburghii* |
| § | - f. ***roxburghii*** (d/S) | MAus |
| | 'Royal Albert Hall' (HT) | GCoc |
| | Royal CopenhagenPBR | see *R.* Remember = 'Poulht001' |
| | 'Royal Occasion' (F) | SPer |
| | Royal William = 'Korzaun'PBR (HT) ♀H4 | CGro CSBt CWSG ELan ESty GCoc LSRN LStr MAsh MAus MBri MGos MRav SPer SWCr |
| § | ***rubiginosa*** | CArn CCVT CDul CRWN EPfP GPoy IFro ILis LBuc MAus MRav NWea SFam SPer WMou |
| | ***rubrifolia*** | see *R. glauca* Pourr. |
| | 'Rubrotincta' | see *R.* 'Hebe's Lip' |
| | ***rubus*** (Ra) | MAus |
| | Ruby Anniversary = 'Harbonny'PBR (Patio) | CSBt CWSG EBls ESty LBuc LRHS LSRN LStr MAsh MRav SCoo SPoG SRGP SVic SWCr |
| | Ruby Celebration = 'Peawinner'PBR (F) | EBls ESty MRav SWCr |
| | Ruby Ruby | see *R.* Ruby Slippers |
| § | Ruby Slippers = 'Weksactrumi' (Min) | LRHS MAsh MBri SPoG |
| | 'Ruby Wedding' (HT) | CBcs CGro CSBt CTri CWSG ECnt ELan EPfP GCoc IArd LRHS LSRN LStr MAsh MAus MBri MGos MRav MWat NPri SMrm SPer SPoG SSea SVic SWCr |
| | 'Ruby Wedding Anniversary' (F) | LSRN |
| | ***rugosa*** (Ru) | CBar CDul CLnd CTri ECrN EPfP GGar LBuc LRHS MAus MBri MHer MRav MSnd NWea SBfd SGol SPlb SVic SWCr WMou |
| | - 'Alba' (Ru) ♀H4 | CBcs CCVT CDul CHab CTri EBee ECnt ELan EPfP GBin GCoc LAst LBuc LRHS LStr MAus MCot MRav NWea SBfd SBrd SGol SMrm SPer SPoG SSea SVic SWCr WBor |
| | - 'Rubra' (Ru) ♀H4 | CBcs CCVT CHab CTri CWib EPfP GCoc LAst LBuc LStr SBfd SEWo SMrm SPer SPoG SSea SVic |
| | - Sakhalin form | MCCP |
| | 'Rugosa Atropurpurea' (Ru) | SBfd |
| | 'Rural England' (Ra) | EBls |
| | Rushing Stream = 'Austream' (GC) | MAus |
| | 'Russelliana' (Ra) | EBee MAus MMuc SFam WKif |
| | Safe Haven = 'Jacreraz'PBR (F) | IDic LBuc |
| | Saint Alban = 'Auschesnut'PBR (S) | MAus |
| | Saint Boniface = 'Kormatt' (F/Patio) | CSBt |
| | 'Saint Catherine' (Ra) | CFee |
| | Saint Cecilia = 'Ausmit'PBR (S) | LStr MAus |
| | Saint Edmunds RosePBR | see *R.* Bonita |
| | Saint Ethelburga = 'Beabimbo' (S) | EBls MCot |
| | Saint John = 'Harbilbo' (F) | CSBt MRav |
| | Saint John's rose | see *R.* × *richardii* |
| | Saint Mark's rose | see *R.* 'Rose d'Amour' |
| | 'Saint Nicholas' (D) | MAus |
| | Saint Richard of Chichester = 'Harklement'PBR (S) **new** | LRHS |
| | Saint Swithun = 'Auswith'PBR (S) | EPfP LRHS MAus MBri SSea |
| | 'Salet' (DPMo) | MAus |
| | 'Sally Holmes' (S) ♀H4 | ECnt EPfP EWTr GCoc LRHS MAus MRav MWat SEND SLon SMad SPer SWCr |
| | Sally Kane = 'Frygroovy'PBR (HT) | CGro ECnt |
| | Sally's Rose = 'Canrem' (HT) | EBee ECnt GCoc LSRN |
| | SalsaPBR | see *R.* Cheek to Cheek |
| | Salvation = 'Harlark'PBR (F) | EBee ESty SWCr |
| § | Samaritan = 'Harverag'PBR (HT) | CSBt ESty MRav SPoG SWCr |
| | ***sancta*** | see *R.* × *richardii* |
| | 'Sander's White Rambler' (Ra) ♀H4 | CRHN CSam CTri ECGP EPfP LRHS MAus MBri MRav NLar SPer SWCr |
| | Sandra = 'Carsandra' | EPfP SLon |
| | Sandra = 'Poulen055'PBR (Renaissance Series) (S) | LSRN |
| | 'Sanguinea' | see *R.* × *odorata* Sanguinea Group |
| | Sarah (HT) | see *R.* Jardins de Bagatelle |
| | 'Sarah van Fleet' (Ru) | CTri EBee EPfP GCoc IArd LStr MAus MMuc MRav MWat NEgg NLar SMad SMrm SPer SPoG |
| | Sarah, Duchess of YorkPBR | see *R.* Sunseeker |

| |  |  |
|---|---|---|
| | Savoy Hotel = 'Harvintage'PBR (HT) ♀H4 | ECnt GCoc LStr MAus MRav SMrm SPer SPoG SWCr |
| | 'Scabrosa' (Ru) ♀H4 | EBee ECnt EPfP GCoc LRHS MAsh MAus NLar SLon SPer SPoG |
| | Scarborough Fair = 'Ausoran' (S) | MAus MBri |
| | Scarlet Fire | see *R.* 'Scharlachglut' |
| | Scarlet Glow | see *R.* 'Scharlachglut' |
| | Scarlet Hit = 'Poulmo'PBR (PatioHit Series) (Min/Patio) | ECnt LRHS LSRN SWCr |
| | Scarlet Patio = 'Kortingle'PBR (Patio) | ESty MAsh MWat |
| | Scarlet Queen Elizabeth = 'Dicel' (F) | CBcs LBuc MRav |
| | 'Scented Air' (F) | SPer |
| | Scented Carpet = 'Chewground'PBR (GC) | ECnt MAus SWCr |
| | Scented Memory = 'Poulht002'PBR (HT) | ECnt MBri |
| | Scentimental = 'Wekplapep'PBR (F) | ESty LRHS LStr MAsh MBri MRav SCoo SSea SWCr |
| | Scent-sation = 'Fryromeo'PBR (HT) | CWSG GCoc LRHS LStr MAsh MBri MRav SCoo SPoG SWCr |
| | Scepter'd Isle = 'Ausland'PBR (S) ♀H4 | CSBt EBee LRHS MAsh MAus MBri SCoo SPer SSea SWCr |
| § | 'Scharlachglut' (ClS) ♀H4 | CPou MRav SPer |
| * | ***schmidtiana*** | CFee |
| | Schneewittchen | see *R.* Iceberg |
| § | 'Schneezwerg' (Ru) ♀H4 | EBee GCoc MAus MRav NLar SPer SSea SWCr |
| | 'Schoolgirl' (ClHT) | CBcs CSBt CTri CWSG ELan EPfP GCoc LAst LRHS LStr MAsh MRav NEgg SPer SPoG SSea SWCr |
| | 'Schratel' | LRHS |
| | 'Scintillation' (S/GC) | MAus |
| | Scotch rose | see *R. spinosissima* |
| | Scotch yellow (SpH) | see *R.* × *harisonii* 'Williams Double Yellow' |
| | 'Seagull' (Ra) ♀H4 | CGro CTri CWSG ECnt EPfP ESty LAst LRHS LSRN LStr MAsh MAus MRav MWat NLar NWea SLon SMad SMrm SPer SPoG SWCr WHer |
| | 'Seale Pink Diamond' (S) | SSea |
| | 'Sealing Wax' (*moyesii* hybrid) | EBee NLar |
| | 'Semiplena' | see *R.* × *alba* 'Alba Semiplena' |
| | ***sericea*** (S) | CFee MAus |
| | - var. ***morrisonensis*** B&SWJ 7139 | WCru |
| § | - subsp. ***omeiensis*** BWJ 7550 | WCru |
| | - - f. ***pteracantha*** (S) | CDul CSBt ELan EPfP GCoc LTen MAus MRav NLar NSti NWea SPer SSea |
| | - - - 'Atrosanguinea' (S) | CArn |
| | ***sertata*** | GAuc |
| § | ***setigera*** | MAus |
| | ***setipoda*** (S) | MAus |
| | seven sisters rose | see *R. multiflora* 'Grevillei' |
| | Seventh Heaven = 'Fryfantasy'PBR (HT) | GCoc SWCr |
| | Sexy Rexy = 'Macrexy'PBR (F) ♀H4 | CGro CSBt EPfP ESty GCoc LSRN LStr MAsh MAus MBri MRav SMrm SPer SPoG SWCr |
| | 'Shailer's White Moss' | see *R.* × *centifolia* 'Shailer's White Moss' |
| | Sharifa Asma = 'Ausreef'PBR (S) | CSBt EBee ELan ELon LRHS LStr MAus MBri MRav NEgg NLar SLon SPer SWCr |
| | Sheila's Perfume = 'Harsherry' (F) | CGro ECnt ESty GCoc LRHS LSRN LStr MAsh MRav SPer SPoG SRGP SWCr |
| | Shine On = 'Dictalent'PBR (Patio) ♀H4 | CSBt ECnt ESty IDic LBuc LStr MAsh MWat SPoG SWCr |
| | Shining Light = 'Cocshimmer'PBR (Patio) | [illegible] |
| | Shocking Blue = 'Korblue' (F) | CSBt SPer |
| | Shona = 'Dicdrum' (F) | IDic |
| | Showtime = 'Baitime' (ClS) | MAsh |
| | Shrimp Hit = 'Poulshrimp'PBR (Patio) | ECnt |
| | 'Shropshire Lass' (S) | MAus |
| | Silver Anniversary ambig. | LSRN |
| § | Silver Anniversary = 'Poulari'PBR (HT) ♀H4 | CGro CSBt CTri CWSG EBee EBls ECnt ELan GCoc LRHS LSRN LStr MAsh MAus MGos MRav MWat NPri SCoo SMrm SPer SPoG SSea SVic SWCr |
| | 'Silver Jubilee' (HT) ♀H4 | CGro CSBt EPfP GCoc IArd LRHS LStr MAsh MAus MRav SPer SPoG SVic SWCr |
| | 'Silver Lining' (HT) | ELon SRGP |
| | 'Silver Moon' (Cl) | CRHN |
| | 'Silver Wedding' (HT) | ELan GCoc IArd MAus MRav NBir NEgg SMrm SPer SRGP SVic SWCr WBor |
| | 'Silver Wedding Celebration' (F) | CTri ESty |
| | Silver WishesPBR | see *R.* Pink Hit |
| | Simba = 'Korbelma' (HT) | LSRN |
| | 'Simplex Multiflora' | CWib |
| | Simply Heaven = 'Diczombie'PBR (HT) | ESty GCoc IDic |
| § | Simply the Best = 'Macamster'PBR (HT) | CGro CSBt CWSG EBls ECnt ELan ELon ESty GCoc LSRN LStr MAsh MAus MGos MRav MWat NPri SCoo SMrm SPer SPoG SRGP SWCr |
| | ***sinowilsonii*** | see *R. longicuspis* var. *sinowilsonii* |
| | 'Sir Cedric Morris' (Ra) | NLar SSea |
| | Sir Clough = 'Ausclough' (S) | MAus |
| | Sir Edward Elgar = 'Ausprima'PBR (S) | MAus |
| I | 'Sir Galahad' white-flowered (F) | MRav |
| | Sir John Betjeman = 'Ausvivid' (S) | EPfP LRHS MAus |
| | Sir John Mills = 'Beadaffy' (Cl) **new** | EBls |
| | 'Sir Joseph Paxton' (Bb) | MAus |
| | Sir Paul Smith = 'Beapaul' (ClHT) | EBls |
| | Sir Walter Raleigh = 'Ausspry' (S) | MAus MRav MWat SMrm |
| § | 'Sissinghurst Castle' (G) | MAus |
| | Sister Elizabeth = 'Auspalette'PBR (S) | MAus MBri SCoo |
| | Skylark = 'Ausimple'PBR (S) | LRHS MAus MBri |
| | 'Skyrocket' | see *R.* 'Wilhelm' |
| | 'Sleepy' (Poly) | CGro |
| | Smarty = 'Intersmart' (S/GC) | MAus SPer |
| | 'Sneezy' (Poly) | CGro |
| | Snow Carpet = 'Maccarpe' (Min/GC) | MAus |
| | 'Snow Dwarf' | see *R.* 'Schneezwerg' |

Snow Goose = 'Auspom'PBR (ClS) — CSBt EPfP MAus MBri SSea
Snow Hit = 'Poulsnows'PBR (Min/Patio) — ECnt SWCr
'Snow Queen' — see *R.* 'Frau Karl Druschki'
Snow Sunblaze = 'Meigovin' (Min) — CSBt
Snowball = 'Macangeli' (Min/GC) — LSRN
Snowcap = 'Harfleet'PBR (Patio) — ESty SMrm
'Snowdon' (Ru) — LRHS MAsh MAus
Soft Cover = 'Poultco10' — MAsh
'Soldier Boy' (Cl) — CPou SWCr
§ Solo Mio = 'Poulen002'PBR (Renaissance Series) (S) — EBee ECnt
§ 'Sombreuil' (ClT) — EPfP IArd LRHS MAus MBri MRav NEgg NLar SPer SSea SWCr
Something Special = 'Macwyo'PBR (HT) — ESty SWCr
Song and Dance = 'Frydishy'PBR (HT) — ESty GCoc SWCr
§ Songs of Praise = 'Harkimono'PBR (Abundance Series) (F) — ESty MAsh SWCr
Sonia — see *R.* Sweet Promise
'Sophia'PBR — see *R.* Solo Mio = 'Poulen002'
'Sophie's Perpetual' (ClCh) — CPou GCoc MAus SLon SPer SWCr
Sophy's Rose = 'Auslot'PBR (S) — LRHS LSRN MAus MBNS MBri NEgg SPer SSea SWCr
***soulieana*** (Ra/S) ♀H3-4 — EWTr MAus
'Soupert et Notting' (DPoMo) — LRHS MAus MRav SPer
'Southampton' (F) ♀H4 — LSRN LStr MAsh MAus SPer SSea SWCr
'Souvenir de Claudius Denoyel' (ClHT) — SPer
'Souvenir de Jeanne Balandreau' (HP) — CPou
'Souvenir de la Malmaison' (ClBb) — see *R.* 'Climbing Souvenir de la Malmaison'
'Souvenir de la Malmaison' (Bb) — EPfP GCoc MAus MCot MRav MWat NLar SEND SPer
Souvenir de Louis Amade = 'Delilac' (S) — MRav SMrm
'Souvenir de Madame Léonie Viennot' (ClT) — MAus MRav
'Souvenir de Saint Anne's' (Bb) — EWTr MAus
'Souvenir di Castagneto' (HP) — MRav
'Souvenir du Docteur Jamain' (ClHP) — CPou CSBt EBee ECGP ELan ELon EPfP ESty EWTr GCoc LRHS LStr MAus MCot MRav NLar SFam SMrm SPer SPoG SSea SWCr WKif
Spangles = 'Ganspa'PBR (F) — GCoc
'Spanish Beauty' — see *R.* 'Madame Grégoire Staechelin'
SparklerPBR — see *R.* Kent
Sparkling Scarlet = 'Meihati' (ClF) — ELan MAsh
Special Anniversary = 'Whastiluc'PBR (HT) — CGro CSBt EPfP ESty GCoc LRHS LSRN MAsh MBri MRav NPri SCoo SMrm SPoG SRGP SWCr
Special Child = 'Taniripsa'PBR (F/Patio) — ECnt GCoc LStr SWCr
Special Event = 'Meibrelon' (HT) — ESty
Special Friend = 'Kirspec'PBR (Patio) — CWSG ESty GCoc LSRN LStr SWCr
Special Occasion = 'Fryyoung'PBR (HT) — ESty GCoc MBri MRav SMrm SWCr
Special Son (F) **new** — ESty
'Spectabilis' (Ra) — CPou SKHP
SpellboundPBR — see *R.* Garden News
Spice of Life = 'Diccheeky'PBR (F/Patio) — IDic
§ ***spinosissima*** — CDul LBuc MAus NWea SGol SPer SSea WCot
- 'Andrewsii' ♀H4 — MAus MRav
§ - double pink-flowered — SKHP WBor
§ - double white-flowered — ECha GCoc IGor MAus SSea
- 'Dunwich Rose' — EPfP GCoc MAus NLar SKHP SPer
- 'Falkland' — ECha GCra MAus
- 'Glory of Edzell' — MAus
- 'Marbled Pink' — MAus
- 'Mary, Queen of Scots' — MAus SRms
- 'Mrs Colville' — MAus
- 'Ormiston Roy' — MAus
- 'Single Cherry' — MAus SSea
- 'William III' — EWes GCra MAus SLPl
Spirit of Freedom = 'Ausbite'PBR (S) — ESty LRHS MAsh MAus MBri NEgg SSea
§ 'Splendens' (Ra) — MMuc SEND SLPl
St Helena = 'Canlish' (F) — ECnt
'Stanwell Perpetual' (SpH) — CSam EPfP EWTr GCoc LStr MAsh MAus MRav MWat NLar SEND SFam SPer SSea SWCr
'Star Performer'PBR (ClPatio) — CSBt ECnt EPfP ESty MAsh SPoG SRGP SSea SWCr
Stardust = 'Peavandyke'PBR (Patio/F) — ESty
Starlight Express = 'Trobstar'PBR (Cl) — LRHS MAsh MBri MRav SCoo SMrm SPer SPoG
Starry Eyed = 'Horcoexist' (Patio) — SWCr
'Stars 'n' Stripes' (Min) — MAus
Stella (HT) — GCoc LSRN
***stellata*** — MAus
§ - var. ***mirifica*** — MAus
Strawberries and Cream = 'Geestraw' (Min/Patio) — ELan ESty
Strawberry Fayre = 'Arowillip'PBR (Min/Patio) — ESty MRav SPoG
Strawberry Hill = 'Ausrimini'PBR (S) — CSBt EBee ECnt ESty LRHS MAus MBri SCoo SSea
Stunning = 'Poulpm004'PBR (HT) — SWCr
§ Sue Hipkin = 'Harzazz'PBR (HT) — ESty SWCr
Suffolk = 'Kormixal'PBR (S/GC) — CGro CSBt ELan GCoc LStr MAus MRav SEND SPer SSea
***suffulta*** — see *R. arkansana* var. *suffulta*
Sugar and Spice = 'Peaallure'PBR (Patio) — MAus
Sugar Baby = 'Tanabagus'PBR (Patio) — ESty SWCr
Sugar 'n' Spice = 'Tinspice' (Min) — MRav
Suma = 'Harsuma' (GC) — ESty SMrm
Summer Beauty = 'Kororbe'PBR (F) — ECnt
Summer Fever = 'Tan99106' (Patio) — SWCr
Summer Fragrance = 'Tanfudermos'PBR (Castle Series) (HT) — ELon
§ Summer Gold = 'Poulreb'PBR (F) — ECnt ESty MAsh SWCr

Summer Love = 'Franluv' (F) CBcs
Summer Song = 'Austango'PBR (S) EPfP ESty LRHS MAus MBri SWCr
Summer Wine = 'Korizont'PBR (Cl) ♀H4 CSBt EBee ECnt EPfP GCoc LRHS MAsh MGos SCoo SPer SPoG SWCr
Summertime = 'Chewlarmoll'PBR (Patio/Cl) CGro CSBt EBee EBls ECnt ELan GCoc LRHS LStr MAsh MAus MRav MWat NPri SCoo SMrm SPer SPoG SSea
Sun Hit = 'Poulsun'PBR (PatioHit Series) (Min/Patio) CSBt ECnt LRHS MRav SWCr
'Sunblaze'PBR see *R.* Orange Sunblaze
Sunblest = 'Landora' (HT) LRHS MAsh MRav
Sunfire = 'Jacko' (F) **new** ECnt
Sunrise = 'Kormarter'PBR (Cl) CGro EPfP ESty MBri MWat SWCr
§ Sunseeker = 'Dicracer'PBR (F/Patio) EPfP IDic LRHS MAsh MRav SPoG SWCr
Sunset Boulevard = 'Harbabble'PBR (F) ♀H4 ECnt GCoc LStr MAsh MAus MBri MRav SCoo SPer SWCr
Sunset CelebrationPBR see *R.* Warm Wishes
Sunshine Abundance **new** SWCr
Sunsplash = 'Cocweaver'PBR (F) MRav
Super Dorothy = 'Heldoro' (Ra) LSRN MAus SSea SWCr
Super Elfin = 'Helkleger'PBR (Ra) ♀H4 EBee GCoc LBuc LStr MAus MRav SMrm SPer SSea SWCr
Super Excelsa = 'Helexa' (Ra) EBee ESty LRHS LStr MAus SSea SWCr
Super Fairy = 'Helsufair'PBR (Ra) ECnt GCoc LStr MAus MRav SMad SPer SSea SWCr
Super Sparkle = 'Helfels'PBR (Ra) EBee LStr SSea
§ Super Star = 'Tanorstar' (HT) GCoc LStr MAus MRav SRGP SWCr
Super Trouper = 'Fryleyeca' (F) CSBt EBee ECnt ESty GCoc LStr SCoo SWCr
'Surpasse Tout' (G) MAus
Surprise = 'Presur'PBR (HT) SWCr
Surrey = 'Korlanum'PBR (GC) ♀H4 CSBt ELan EPfP ESty GCoc LSRN LStr MAus MRav MWat NLar SPer SSea SWCr
Susan = 'Poulsue' (S) EBee ECnt LSRN SLon SWCr
Sussex = 'Poulave'PBR (GC) CSBt GCoc LStr MRav SMrm SPer SWCr
Swan = 'Auswhite' (S) MAus
Swan Lake = 'Macmed' (Cl) EBee ECnt ELan EPfP GCoc LBuc LStr MRav NLar NPri SMrm SPer SWCr
Swany = 'Meiburenac' (Min/GC) ♀H4 ESty LSRN MAus SPer SWCr
Sweet Caroline = 'Micaroline' (Min) LSRN
Sweet Cover = 'Poulweeto'PBR (Towne & Country Series) MAsh
Sweet Dream = 'Fryminicot'PBR (Patio) ♀H4 CGro CSBt CTri ECnt ELan EPfP ESty GCoc LAst LSRN LStr MAsh MAus MBri MRav MWat NPri SMad SMrm SPer SPoG SRGP SSea SWCr
'Sweet Fairy' (Min) CSBt
Sweet Haze = 'Tan97274'PBR (F) CSBt EPfP ESty GCoc LRHS LStr MAsh MRav SCoo SWCr
Sweet Juliet = 'Ausleap'PBR (S) CSBt ELon ESty LRHS MAus SPer SWCr
* 'Sweet Lemon Dream' (Patio) CTri
Sweet Magic = 'Dicmagic'PBR (Min/Patio) ♀H4 CGro CSBt CTri EPfP GCoc IDic LStr MAsh MBri MRav NPri SPoG
Sweet Memories = 'Whamemo' (Patio) CTri ECnt ELon EPfP ESty LRHS LStr MAsh MBri SCoo SMrm SPer SPoG SRGP SWCr
Sweet Parfum de Provence = 'Meiclusif'PBR (HT) ESty
Sweet Pretty see *R.* The Charlatan
§ Sweet Promise = 'Meihelvet' (GC) SPer
Sweet Remembrance = 'Kirr' (HT) LStr SCoo
'Sweet Revelation'PBR see *R.* Sue Hipkin
'Sweet Wonder' (Patio) EPfP MAsh MBri SPoG
N Sweetheart = 'Cocapeer' (HT) GCoc
'Sweetie' (Patio) ESty SWCr
***sweginzowii*** GAuc MAus
'Sydonie' (HP) EBee
'Sylvia Dot' (F) LSRN
'Sympathie' (ClHT) GCoc MGos SPer SSea SWCr
Tall Story = 'Dickooky' (F) ♀H4 EBee SWCr
Tam O'Shanter = 'Auscerise' (S) **new** LRHS MAus
Tamora = 'Austamora' (S) MAus
Tango Showground = 'Chewpattens'PBR (GC) SSea
Tatoo = 'Poulyc002'PBR (ClPatio) EBee
Tatton = 'Fryentice'PBR (F) EBls ESty MAus MRav SMrm SWCr
Tawny Tiger = 'Frygolly'PBR (F) CGro GCoc SWCr
Tea Clipper = 'Ausrover'PBR (S) CSBt ESty LRHS MAus MBri SCoo SSea
Tear Drop = 'Dicomo'PBR (Min/Patio) IDic LBuc LStr SMrm SPer SWCr
Teasing Georgia = 'Ausbaker'PBR (S) EBee ECnt EPfP ESty LRHS LSRN MAus MBri SCoo SRGP SSea SWCr
Temptress = 'Korramal' (ClS) EPfP MAsh
Tenacious = 'Macblackpo'PBR (F) ESty LStr SWCr
Tequila Sunrise = 'Dicobey'PBR (HT) ♀H4 CGro CTri EBls ELan EPfP ESty GCoc IDic LRHS LStr MAsh MAus MRav SMrm SPer SWCr
§ Terracotta = 'Meicobuis'PBR (HT) ESty SWCr
Tess of the d'Urbervilles = 'Ausmove'PBR (S) ESty LRHS LStr MAus MBri NEgg SCoo SMrm SPer SWCr
'Tessa' (F) GCoc LSRN
Thank You = 'Chesdeep'PBR (Patio) ESty LBuc LStr SMrm SRGP SWCr
§ That's Jazz = 'Poulnorm'PBR (Courtyard Series) (ClF) ECnt MAsh MBri MWat SWCr
The Alexandra Rose = 'Ausday'PBR (S) MAus SEND SSea
The Alnwick RosePBR see *R.* Alnwick Castle
The Attenborough Rose = 'Dicelope'PBR (F) IDic
'The Bishop' (Ce × G) MAus
'The Bishop of Bradford' (ClPiH) EBee ECnt
§ The Charlatan = 'Meiguimov' (S) MAsh
The Compass Rose = 'Korwisco'PBR (S) EPfP

| |  |  |
|---|---|---|
| | The Countryman = 'Ausman'PBR (S) | LRHS LStr MAus SSea |
| | The Dark Lady = 'Ausbloom'PBR (S) | MAsh MAus MBri NEgg SPer |
| § | 'The Fairy' (Poly) 🏆H4 | CSBt CTri EBee ECnt ELan EPfP GCoc LAst LRHS LStr MAsh MAus MRav MWat NLar SBfd SEND SMad SMrm SPer SSea SWCr WCFE |
| | 'The Garland' (Ra) 🏆H4 | CRHN EPfP LRHS MAus MBri MMuc NLar SFam SPer SWCr |
| | The Generous Gardener = 'Ausdrawn'PBR (S) | EPfP LRHS MAsh MAus MBri SCoo SPer SWCr |
| | The Gold Award Rose = 'Poulac008' (Palace Series) (Patio) | ECnt |
| | The Herbalist = 'Aussemi' (S) | LRHS MAus SSea |
| | The Ingenious Mr Fairchild = 'Austijus'PBR (S) | LRHS MAus MBri SCoo |
| | The Jubilee Rose = 'Poulbrido'PBR (F) | EBee ECnt SCoo |
| | The Maidstone Rose = 'Kordauerpa' (S) | SCoo |
| | 'The Margaret Coppola Rose'PBR | see *R.* White Gold |
| | The Mayflower = 'Austilly'PBR (S) | CSBt LRHS LStr MAsh MAus MBri SMrm |
| § | The McCartney Rose = 'Meizeli'PBR (HT) | SWCr |
| | 'The New Dawn' | see *R.* 'New Dawn' |
| | The Nun = 'Ausnun' (S) | MAus |
| | The Painter = 'Mactemaik'PBR (F) | LSRN LStr |
| § | The Pilgrim = 'Auswalker'PBR (S) | CSBt EPfP ESty LRHS LStr MAus MBri SEND SMrm SPer SSea SWCr |
| | The Prince = 'Ausvelvet'PBR (S) | MAus NLar SLon SMrm SPer |
| | The Prince's Trust = 'Harholding'PBR (Cl) | LStr MAsh MAus SPoG |
| | 'The Prioress' (S) | MAus |
| § | 'The Queen Elizabeth' (F) | CBcs CGro CSBt CTri CWSG GCoc LSRN LStr MAsh MAus MBri MRav MWat NPri SPer SWCr WBor |
| | The Reeve = 'Ausreeve' (S) | MAus |
| | The Rotarian | see *R.* Rotary Sunrise |
| I | 'The Rugby Rose' (HT) | GCoc LSRN |
| | The Shepherdess = 'Austwist'PBR (S) | LRHS MAus MBri SSea |
| | The Soham RosePBR | see *R.* Pearl Abundance |
| | The Squire = 'Ausquire' (S) | MAus |
| | The Times Rose = 'Korpeahn'PBR (F) 🏆H4 | ECnt GCoc LStr MAus MRav SPer SWCr |
| | The Wedgwood Rose = 'Ausjosiah' (ClS) | LRHS MAus |
| | The Wren = 'Kormamtiza'PBR (F/Patio) | EPfP |
| | 'Thelma' (Ra) | MAus |
| | 'Thérèse Bugnet' (Ru) | MAus |
| | Thinking of You = 'Frydandy'PBR (HT) | EBls ESty GCoc LRHS LStr MAsh MAus NPri SRGP SVic SWCr |
| | 'Thisbe' (HM) | CPou EBee MAus SPer |
| | Thomas Barton = 'Meihirvin' (HT) | LStr |
| | 'Threave' (Bb) | CPou |
| | Three Cheers = 'Dicdomino'PBR (F) | IDic |
| | Three Wishes = 'Poulpak038' (Patio) | MAsh MBri |
| | threepenny bit rose | see *R. elegantula* 'Persetosa' |
| | Thumbs Up = 'Hornothing' (S) | EBls |
| | ***tibetica*** | GAuc |
| | Tickled Pink = 'Fryhunky'PBR (F) | CSBt EBls EPfP ESty GCoc LRHS LSRN LShp MAsh MBri MRav MWat SCoo SMrm SPer SPoG SRGP SWCr |
| | Times Past = 'Harhilt'PBR (ClHT) | ELon ESty GCoc LStr MRav SPoG SWCr |
| | 'Tina Turner' (HT) | LSRN |
| | Tintinara = 'Dicuptight'PBR (HT) | ECnt IDic |
| | Tip Top = 'Tanope' (F/Patio) | SPer |
| | 'Tipo Ideale' | see *R.* × *odorata* 'Mutabilis' |
| | 'Tipsy Imperial Concubine' (T) | EBls |
| | 'Toby Tristam' (Ra) | CRHN |
| | Together Forever = 'Dicecho'PBR (F) | GCoc IDic MAsh |
| | 'Tom Marshall' | EBee LSRN |
| | Top Marks = 'Fryministar'PBR (Min/Patio) | CGro CSBt GCoc LStr MRav MWat SCoo SPer SWCr |
| | Topaz JewelPBR | see *R.* Yellow Dagmar Hastrup |
| | Toprose = 'Cocgold'PBR (F) | GCoc MAsh |
| | 'Topsi' (F/Patio) | SPer |
| § | 'Tour de Malakoff' (Ce) | CPou LRHS MAus MRav NLar SFam SMrm SPer |
| | Tradescant = 'Ausdir'PBR (S) | MAus |
| | 'Treasure Trove' (Ra) | CRHN LRHS MAus NLar SMrm SWCr |
| | Trevor Griffiths = 'Ausold'PBR (S) | MAus |
| | 'Tricolore de Flandre' (G) | MAus |
| | 'Trier' (Ra) | CPou EBee MAus |
| | 'Trigintipetala' misapplied | see *R.* 'Professeur Emile Perrot' |
| | 'Triomphe de l'Exposition' (HP) | MAus |
| | 'Triomphe du Luxembourg' (T) | MAus |
| | ***triphylla*** | see *R.* × ***beanii*** |
| | Troika = 'Poumidor' (HT) 🏆H4 | CSBt ELan EPfP GCoc LRHS LStr MAsh MAus MBri MRav SMrm SPer SPoG SWCr |
| | Troilus = 'Ausoil' (S) | MAus |
| | 'Tropicana' | see *R.* Super Star |
| | Trumpeter = 'Mactru' (F) 🏆H4 | CSBt CTri EBee ECnt GCoc IArd LRHS LStr MAsh MAus MBri MRav MWat SPer SPoG SSea SWCr |
| § | 'Tuscany' (G) | GCoc MAus SPer |
| | 'Tuscany Superb' (G) 🏆H4 | CPou CSBt CSam CTri EBee EPfP GCra LAst LRHS MAus MBri MRav NChi NLar SEND SFam SKHP SMrm SPer SSea SWCr WKif |
| | Twenty-one Again! = 'Meinimo'PBR (HT) | LSRN SWCr |
| | Twice in a Blue Moon = 'Tan96138'PBR (HT) | CGro CSBt EBee EBls ECnt ESty GCoc LBuc LRHS MBri MRav MWat SCoo SMrm SPoG SSea SWCr |
| | Twist = 'Poulstri'PBR (Courtyard Series) (ClPatio) | CGro EBee ECnt ESty MWat |
| | Tynwald = 'Mattwyt' (HT) | LStr SPer |
| | 'Ulrich Brünner' | see *R.* 'Ulrich Brünner Fils' |
| § | 'Ulrich Brünner Fils' (HP) | MAus |
| | 'Unique Blanche' | see *R.* × *centifolia* 'Unique' |
| | Valencia = 'Koreklia'PBR (HT) 🏆H4 | MAus |

| |  |  |
|---|---|---|
| | Valentine Heart = 'Dicogle'[PBR] (F) ♀H4 | CSBt ESty IArd IDic LSRN MAsh MAus MBri MRav SPoG SRGP SWCr |
| | Vanilla Twist = 'Dicghost' (F) | IDic |
| | Varenna Allen = 'Harmode'[PBR] (F) | ECnt |
| | 'Variegata di Bologna' (Bb) | EBee EPfP LRHS MAus MMuc MRav SLon SMrm SSea SWCr |
| | 'Vatertag' (Min) | LSRN |
| | 'Veilchenblau' (Ra) ♀H4 | CRHN CSBt CSam ECnt ELan EPfP GCoc LRHS LStr MAus MCot MRav NEgg NLar NPri SEND SMrm SPer SPoG SSea SWCr WBor WKif |
| | Velvet Fragrance = 'Fryperdee'[PBR] (HT) | CGro CSBt CWSG ECnt ESty GCoc LStr MAus MRav SMrm SPoG SWCr |
| | 'Venusta Pendula' (Ra) | MAus |
| | ***versicolor*** | see *R. gallica* 'Versicolor' |
| | Versigny = 'Masversi' (Generosa Series) (S) | MRav |
| | 'Vick's Caprice' (HP) | MAus NLar |
| | 'Vicomtesse Pierre du Fou' (ClHT) | MAus |
| | Victoria Joy = 'Diciwill' (F) | IDic |
| | Viking Princess[PBR] | see *R.* Imagination = 'Pouldron' |
| | 'Village Maid' | see *R.* × *centifolia* 'Unique Panachée' |
| § | ***villosa*** L. | CArn |
| § | 'Violacea' (G) | EBee MAus |
| | 'Violette' (Ra) | CPou CRHN EWTr LRHS LTen MAus SPer SWCr |
| | ***virginiana*** ♀H4 | CFee GAuc GCal MAus NWea SPer |
| | - 'Plena' | see *R.* 'Rose d'Amour' |
| | 'Viridiflora' | see *R.* × *odorata* 'Viridiflora' |
| | Waltz = 'Poulkrid'[PBR] (Courtyard Series) (ClPatio) | ECnt |
| | ***wardii*** var. ***culta*** | MAus |
| | Warm Welcome = 'Chewizz'[PBR] (ClMin) ♀H4 | CGro CWSG ECnt EPfP ESty GCoc LRHS LSRN LStr MAsh MAus MBri MGos MRav SMad SMrm SPer SPoG SRGP SSea SWCr |
| § | Warm Wishes = 'Fryxotic'[PBR] (HT) ♀H4 | CSBt ECnt ESty GCoc LRHS LSRN LStr MAsh MAus MBri MGos MRav MWat SPoG SRGP SSea SWCr |
| | 'Warrior' (F) | GCoc SPer |
| | Warwick Castle = 'Auslian'[PBR] (S) | MAus |
| | 'Weavers Way' (HT) **new** | EBls |
| | ***webbiana*** | MAus SKHP |
| | Wedding Celebration = 'Poulht006' (HT) | ECnt SWCr |
| | 'Wedding Day' (Ra) | CRHN CSBt CSam CTri CWSG EBee ECnt ELan EPfP ESty EWTr GCoc LEdu LRHS LSRN LStr MAsh MAus MBri MGos MRav MWat NEgg NLar NPri SEND SMrm SPer SSea SWCr |
| | Wee Cracker = 'Cocmarris'[PBR] (Patio) | ESty GCoc SWCr |
| | Wee Jock = 'Cocabest' (F/Patio) | GCoc SMrm |
| | 'Weetwood' (Ra) | CRHN |
| | Weisse Wolcke[PBR] | see *R.* White Cloud = 'Korstacha' |
| | Well-Being = 'Harjangle'[PBR] (S) | CSBt ELon ESty SWCr |
| | 'Wendy Cussons' (HT) | CGro CTri GCoc MRav SPer SWCr |
| | Wenlock = 'Auswen' (S) | MAus SPer |
| | 'West Country Millennium' (F) | GCoc |
| | Westerland = 'Korwest' (S) ♀H4 | ECGP GCoc MRav SMad SWCr WCot |
| | Where the Heart Is = 'Cocoplan'[PBR] (HT) | ESty |
| | Whisky Mac = 'Tanky' (HT) | CBcs CSBt CTri ELan GCoc MRav NPri SMrm SPer SPoG |
| | 'White Bath' | see *R.* × *centifolia* 'Shailer's White Moss' |
| | 'White Christmas' (HT) | GCoc |
| § | White Cloud = 'Korstacha'[PBR] (S/ClHT) ♀H4 | CSBt EPfP ESty LRHS MAsh MWat SKHP SPoG SWCr |
| | White Cloud = 'Savacloud' (Min) | MBri |
| | 'White Cockade' (Cl) | CPou ESwi GCoc SMrm SPer SWCr |
| | White Cover[PBR] | see *R.* Kent |
| § | 'White de Meaux' (Ce) | MAus |
| | White Diamond = 'Interamon'[PBR] (S) | ECnt GCoc IDic LBuc |
| § | White Gold = 'Cocquiriam'[PBR] (F) | CSBt GCoc MRav |
| | White Meidiland = 'Meicoublan'[PBR] (S/GC) | LRHS MAsh |
| | white moss | see *R.* 'Comtesse de Murinais', *R.* × *centifolia* 'Shailer's White Moss' |
| | White Parfum de Provence = 'Meidiaphaz' (HT) | CSBt ESty |
| | 'White Patio' (Min/Patio) **new** | MAsh |
| § | 'White Pet' (Poly) ♀H4 | CSBt CTri EBee ECnt EPfP GCoc LRHS LStr MBri MCot MRav SEND SMrm SPer SWCr |
| | white Provence | see *R.* × *centifolia* 'Unique' |
| | white rose of York | see *R.* × *alba* 'Alba Semiplena' |
| | White Skyliner = 'Franwekwhit'[PBR] (ClS) | EBls |
| | White Star = 'Harquill' (Cl) **new** | ECnt ESty |
| | 'White Wings' (HT) | EBee EWTr SPer WKif |
| N | ***wichurana*** (Ra) | GCal GLin MAus SKHP |
| | - 'Cally Anemone' (Ra) | GCal |
| | - 'Variegata' (Ra/v) | EPot |
| * | - 'Variegata Nana' (Ra/v) | MRav |
| | 'Wickwar' (Ra) | EWTr GCal GGal |
| | Wife of Bath = 'Ausbath' (S) | MAus |
| | Wild Edric = 'Aushedge'[PBR] (Ru) | LRHS MAus MBri SCoo |
| | Wild Rover = 'Dichirap'[PBR] (F) | ESty IDic LRHS LStr MAsh MBri SSea |
| | Wild Thing = 'Jactoose'[PBR] (S) | IDic MAsh |
| | Wildeve = 'Ausbonny'[PBR] (S) | LRHS MAsh MAus MBri |
| | Wildfire = 'Fryessex' (Patio) | ECnt ELon ESty LRHS MAsh MAus MBri MWat SMrm SPoG SWCr |
| § | 'Wilhelm' (HM) | MAus MRav SPer |
| | 'Will Scarlet' (HM) | MAus |
| | 'William Allen Richardson' (N) | MAus |
| | 'William Cobbett' (F) | SSea |
| § | 'William Lobb' (CeMo) ♀H4 | CGro CPou CRHN EPfP LRHS LStr MAsh MAus MBri MCot MRav NChi NEgg NLar SPer SWCr WKif |
| | William Morris = 'Auswill'[PBR] (S) | CSBt LRHS MAsh MAus MBri NEgg SSea SWCr |
| | William Shakespeare 2000 = 'Ausromeo'[PBR] (S) | CSBt EBee ECnt EPfP ESty LStr MAsh MAus MBNS MBri NEgg SCoo SSea SWCr |
| | William Shakespeare = 'Ausroyal'[PBR] (S) | LRHS SMrm SPer |
| | 'William Tyndale' (Ra) | CSam EBee |
| | 'Williams' Double Yellow' | see *R.* × *harisonii* 'Williams Double Yellow' |

| | |
|---|---|
| ***willmottiae*** | see *R. gymnocarpa* var. *willmottiae* |
| Wilton = 'Eurosa' | SWCr |
| Wiltshire = 'Kormuse'[PBR] (S/GC) ♀[H4] | CSBt ECnt ESty LSRN LStr MRav SEND SLon SSea SWCr |
| Winchester Cathedral = 'Auscat'[PBR] (S) | CGro CSBt CTri EBee ECnt ELon EPfP ESty EWTr GCoc LRHS LSRN LStr MAsh MAus MBri MRav MWat NEgg NLar SMad SMrm SPer SSea SWCr |
| Windflower = 'Auscross' (S) | MAus |
| Windrush = 'Ausrush' (S) | MAus SPer |
| Wine and Dine = 'Dicuncle' (GC) | EBls |
| Wise Portia = 'Ausport' (S) | MAus |
| Wisley 2008 = 'Ausbreeze' (S) | CSBt ECnt EPfP LRHS MAsh MAus SSea |
| Wisley = 'Ausintense'[PBR] (S) | SCoo |
| With All My Love = 'Coczodiac'[PBR] (HT) | CSBt ESty GCoc LStr |
| With Love = 'Andwit' (HT) | SWCr |
| With Thanks = 'Fransmoov'[PBR] (HT) | ESty SRGP SWCr |
| Wonderful News = 'Jonone'[PBR] (Patio) | CGro ESty MWat |
| Wonderful = 'Poulpmt005'[PBR] (HT) | ECnt SWCr |
| § ***woodsii*** | MAus |
| - var. ***fendleri*** | see *R. woodsii* |
| Worcestershire = 'Korlalon'[PBR] (GC) | GCoc MAus MRav SPer SSea SWCr |
| Wordly Wishes = 'Poulpah023' (Patio) | MAsh |
| Wymondham Abbey = 'Beadevil' (ClHT) | EBls |
| § ***xanthina*** 'Canary Bird' (S) ♀[H4] | Widely available |
| § - f. ***hugonis*** ♀[H4] | CTri MAus SKHP SPer |
| 'Yellow Cécile Brünner' | see *R.* 'Perle d'Or' |
| Yellow Charles Austin = 'Ausyel' (S) | MAus |
| § Yellow Dagmar Hastrup = 'Moryelrug'[PBR] (Ru) | EWTr SPer |
| Yellow Floorshow = 'Harfully'[PBR] (GC) | MRav |
| Yellow Flower Carpet[PBR] | see *R.* Flower Carpet Sunshine |
| 'Yellow Mutabilis' | EBls |
| 'Yellow Patio' (Min/Patio) | LStr MAsh NPri SSea SWCr |
| yellow Scotch | see *R.* × *harisonii* 'Williams Double Yellow' |
| Yellow Sunblaze = 'Meitrisical' (Min) | CSBt |
| 'Yesterday' (Poly/F/S) ♀[H4] | EWTr MAsh MAus NLar SLon |
| Yokohama = 'Keihayokoki' (HT) **new** | EBls |
| York and Lancaster | see *R.* × *damascena* 'Versicolor' |
| Yorkshire = 'Korbarkeit'[PBR] (GC) | GCoc LStr MRav |
| 'Yorkshire Lady' (HT) | NEgg |
| You are my Sunshine = 'Frykwango' (HT) | ECnt ESty GCoc LBuc MAsh MBri |
| Young Lycidas = 'Ausvibrant' (S) | CSBt MAus SSea |
| Young Princess = 'Tan02670' **new** | SWCr |
| 'Yvonne Rabier' (Poly) ♀[H4] | MAus MRav NLar SLon SPer |
| 'Zéphirine Drouhin' (Bb) | Widely available |
| § 'Zigeunerknabe' (S) | EBee ECnt GCoc MAus MRav NLar SKHP SPer |

## *Roscoea* ✿ (*Zingiberaceae*)

| | |
|---|---|
| ACE 2539 | GEdr |
| CC 6142 | EWld |
| ***alpina*** | CAby CBro CLAP CPLG CPrp EBee ECho EPot GEdr GGar GKev LWst NGdn NMen NWCA WCru |
| - CC 1820 | IBlr |
| - CC 3667 | EPPr GEdr |
| - 'Leaping Salmon' | CFir |
| - pink-flowered | IBlr |
| - purple-flowered | IBlr |
| - short | WCru |
| § ***auriculata*** | CAvo CBct CBro CFir CFwr CLAP EBee ECho EPfP EPot EShb GCal GEdr GGar IBlr IFoB LWst MCot MLHP NHar NMyG NPnk NWCA SChF SKHP WCot WCru WFar WHar WSHC |
| - B&SWJ 2594 | WCru |
| - brown-stemmed × ***purpurea*** | IBlr |
| - early-flowering | IBlr NCot WCru |
| - 'Floriade' | CDes CLAP EBee GMac IBlr LRHS LWst SPoG |
| - green-stemmed × ***purpurea*** | IBlr |
| - late-flowering | WCru |
| - 'Special' | CLAP |
| - 'White Cap' | EBee LWst |
| ***auriculata*** × ***australis*** | IBlr |
| ***auriculata*** × ***capitata*** | IBlr |
| ***australis*** | CFir CSam ELon GEdr MNrw NMyG WCru WHil |
| - pink-flowered KW 22124 | IBlr |
| - purple-flowered KW 22124 | IBlr |
| ***australis*** × ***humeana*** | IBlr |
| 'Ballyrogan Lavender' | IBlr |
| 'Ballyrogan Purple' | IBlr |
| 'Beesiana' | see *R.* × *beesiana* Gestreept Group |
| × ***beesiana*** Cream Group | CBct CDes CFwr CLAP EBee ELon EPfP EWld GEdr IBlr LEdu MMHG NBir NGdn NPnk SKHP WCru WPGP |
| - Dark Group | ELon IBlr |
| § - Gestreept Group | CAby CAvo CBct CBro CFir CFwr CHEx CLAP CMea EBee ECtt EPot GEdr GGar IBlr LAma LWst MCot MRav NHar NHol NWCA SBrd SKHP WCru WFar WHar WWEG |
| § - 'Monique' | CDes CLAP EBee IBlr LEdu LWst NHar NMyG WPGP |
| Blackthorn strain | IBlr |
| ***brandisii*** misapplied | see *R. tumjensis* |
| ***capitata*** | CLAP IBlr |
| ***cautleyoides*** ♀[H4] | Widely available |
| - CLD 772 | IBlr |
| I - 'Alba' | NGdn |
| - var. ***cautleyoides*** f. ***atropurpurea*** | IBlr |
| - - - 'Giraffe' | IBlr |
| - - white-flowered | CRDP |
| - 'Crûg's Late Lemon' **new** | WCru |
| - 'Doge Purple' | IBlr |
| - dwarf, from Kew **new** | LRHS |
| - 'Early Purple' | CDes CLAP ECho WPGP |
| - 'Early Yellow' | EBee LWst |
| - 'Himalaya' | CLAP EBee LWst |

| | |
|---|---|
| – 'Jeffrey Thomas' | CBct CFwr CLAP CSam EBee ECha ECho ELon EPPr EPot GCal GEdr IBlr LWst MLHP NMyG SRGP WCot |
| – 'Kew Beauty' ♀H4 | CDes CFir CLAP CMea CPLG CRDP CYeo EBee EPfP GCal GEdr LRHS LSou MMoz NCGa NGdn NMyG SKHP WCot WPGP |
| – late, lavender-flowered | IBlr |
| – late, yellow-flowered | IBlr NCot |
| – 'Lemon Giraffe' | IBlr |
| – 'Pennine Purple' | IBlr NHar |
| – plum-flowered | IBlr |
| – var. ***pubescens*** | IBlr |
| – 'Purple Giant' | CLAP LWst NMyG SKHP WCot |
| – purple-flowered | CAby IBlr NHar |
| – 'Reinier' | CAby CLAP EBee GCal IBlr LWst SKHP WCot |
| – f. ***sinopurpurea*** | IBlr |
| – 'Vanilla' | EBee LEdu LWst NMyG SKHP |
| – 'Washfield Purple' | IBlr |
| – 'Yeti' | CLAP EBee LWst NMyG SKHP |
| ***cautleyoides* × *humeana*** | CLAP IBlr LWst NCot WHar |
| ***cautleyoides* × *scillifolia*** f. ***atropurpurea*** | IBlr |
| ***debilis*** var. ***debilis*** | IBlr |
| ***forrestii*** f. ***forrestii*** | IBlr |
| – f. ***purpurea*** | IBlr |
| – f. ***purpurea* × *humeana*** | IBlr |
| 'Gestreept' | see *R.* × *beesiana* Gestreept Group |
| ***humeana*** ♀H4 | CAby CBct CBro CLAP ECho GAuc GEdr LAma LRHS LWst MBri NMyG WCFE WCot WThu |
| – ACE 2539 | IBlr |
| – f. ***alba*** | IBlr |
| – cream-flowered | LWst |
| – Forrest's form | IBlr |
| – lavender-flowered | IBlr |
| – 'Long Acre Sunrise' | CLAP WPGP |
| – f. ***lutea*** | CLAP GEdr IBlr |
| – pink-flowered | IBlr |
| – 'Purple Streaker' | CAby CDes CLAP EBee WPGP |
| – 'Rosemoor Plum' | CDes CLAP GEdr WPGP |
| – 'Snowy Owl' | CLAP |
| – f. ***tyria*** | EBee IBlr |
| – – 'Inkling' | LWst |
| 'Ice Maiden' | IBlr |
| 'Monique' | see *R.* × *beesiana* 'Monique' |
| 'Petite Purple' | IBlr |
| ***praecox*** | IBlr |
| – BWJ 7848 | WCru |
| ***procera*** misapplied | see *R. auriculata* |
| ***procera*** Wall. | see *R. purpurea* |
| 'Purple King' | EBee LWst |
| § ***purpurea*** | Widely available |
| – CC 1757 | IBlr |
| – CC 3628 | CPLG IBlr |
| – CC 3667 | WCot |
| – HWJK 2020 | WCru |
| – HWJK 2169 | WCru |
| – HWJK 2175 | WCru |
| – HWJK 2400 | WCru |
| – HWJK 2407 | WCru |
| – KW 13755 | IBlr |
| – MECC 2 | IBlr |
| – MECC 10 | IBlr |
| – f. ***alba*** | GEdr |
| – bronze-leaved | CAby |
| – 'Brown Peach' **new** | LRHS |
| – 'Brown Peacock' | CDes CLAP IBlr LWst SKHP WPGP |
| – 'Cinnamon Stick' | WCru |
| – 'Dalai Lama' | LWst |
| – var. ***gigantea*** | CLAP |
| – – CC 1757 | IBlr MNrw |
| – green-stemmed | LWst |
| – 'Himalayan Delight' | IBlr |
| – 'Nico' | CLAP EBee ELan IBlr LRHS LWst SKHP |
| – 'Niedrig' | EBee IBlr SKHP |
| – 'Peacock' | CLAP EBee IBlr LWst NMyG SKHP WFar |
| – 'Peacock Eye' | CLAP IBlr LRHS LWst SKHP |
| – var. ***procera*** | see *R. purpurea* |
| – 'Red Foot' | LWst |
| – red-stemmed | LWst |
| – Rosemoor form | CLAP LWst |
| – f. ***rubra*** 'Red Gurkha' | CDes CLAP IBlr |
| – short | CLAP IBlr |
| – tall | CLAP WCru WPGP |
| – 'Typico' | IBlr |
| – 'Vannin' | WCru |
| – 'Vincent' | EBee LWst WCot |
| – 'Wisley Amethyst' | CLAP CYeo GEdr IBlr LRHS LWst MBri NCot SKHP SPtl WCra |
| ***schneideriana*** | IBlr MMoz WThu |
| – robust form | IBlr |
| ***scillifolia*** | CBro CFir CPBP ECho GKev LAma LHop LRHS NBir NGdn NMen WHar |
| – f. ***atropurpurea*** | CAby CDes CPom GEdr IBlr NMyG WAul WCru WPGP WThu WWEG |
| – f. ***scillifolia*** | CDes CYeo EBee GEdr IBlr IFoB NMen NMyG WCot WCru WHar WThu |
| aff. ***scillifolia*** purple-flowered | IBlr |
| ***tibetica*** | CFir CLAP EBee GEdr GKev IBlr WCru WThu |
| – ACE 2538 | IBlr WCru |
| – BWJ 7878 | WCru |
| – f. ***atropurpurea*** BWJ 7640 **new** | WCru |
| aff. ***tibetica*** | IBlr |
| – f. ***albo-purpurea*** | IBlr |
| § ***tumjensis*** | CLAP EBee EWes IBlr LWst WPGP |
| 'Two Tone' **new** | IBlr |
| ***wardii*** | CPLG IBlr |

## **rosemary** see *Rosmarinus officinalis*

## *Rosenia* (*Asteraceae*)

| | |
|---|---|
| ***humilis*** | CPBP |

## *Rosmarinus* ✿ (*Lamiaceae*)

| | |
|---|---|
| sp. | CHab |
| ***corsicus*** 'Prostratus' | see *R. officinalis* Prostratus Group |
| ***lavandulaceus*** misapplied | see *R. officinalis* Prostratus Group |
| × ***noeanus*** **new** | XSen |
| ***officinalis*** | Widely available |
| – SDR 5234 | GKev |
| – var. ***albiflorus*** | CArn CSev ELau EOHP EPfP EWhm GPoy LRHS MHer MNHC SBfd SDow SHDw SLim SPlb STre WGwG WJek XSen |
| – – 'Lady in White' | CSBt EBee ELan EPfP LRHS MHer SBrd SDow SEND SPer WGwG WJek |
| – 'Alderney' | MHer SDow |
| § – var. ***angustissimus*** 'Benenden Blue' ♀H4 | CSBt CWan CWib EBee EPfP GPoy SBfd SDix SPer SPlb SPoG WGwG WJek WPnn WRHF |

| | |
|---|---|
| - - 'Corsican Blue' | CArn EBee ELan EPfP GPoy MHer MNHC MRav SBfd SGol SHDw SIde SPad SPer WPer |
| - 'Aureovariegatus' | see *R. officinalis* 'Aureus' |
| § - 'Aureus' (v) | EOHP WJek |
| - 'Baby P.J.' | EOHP |
| - 'Baie d'Audierne' | XSen |
| - 'Barbecue' PBR | EGHP ELau SIde |
| - 'Blue Lagoon' | EGHP ELau EOHP EWhm LRHS MHer MNHC MSCN SIde WGwG WHer WJek WPnn |
| - 'Blue Rain' | CBar CBod EGHP MHer SIde WHfH WPnn |
| - 'Boule' | CArn ELau MHer SDow WGwG WJek XSen |
| - 'Capercaillie' | SDow |
| - 'Collingwood Ingram' | see *R. officinalis* var. *angustissimus* 'Benenden Blue' |
| - 'Cottage White' | WGwG WHer |
| - dwarf, blue-flowered | ELau |
| - 'Farinole' | CArn ELau MNHC |
| - 'Fastigiatus' | see *R. officinalis* 'Miss Jessopp's Upright' |
| - 'Fota Blue' | CArn CBod CTsd CWib EGHP ELau IArd IGor LRHS MHer MNHC SAga SBfd SDow SGol SHDw SIde SPoG SWvt WFar WGwG WJek WPnn |
| - 'Foxtail' | LRHS WJek |
| - 'Frimley Blue' | see *R. officinalis* 'Primley Blue' |
| - 'Genges Gold' (v) | MHer SBfd |
| - 'Golden Rain' | see *R. officinalis* 'Joyce DeBaggio' |
| - 'Gorizia' | CBcs EHoe SDow WGwG WPnn |
| - 'Green Ginger' | CBod CPrp EGHP ELan ELau EOHP EPfP GBin LHop LRHS MAsh MHer MNHC MRav MSCN NPer SBrd SDow SPer SPoG SVen WGwG WJek WMnd WPnn |
| - 'Guilded' | see *R. officinalis* 'Aureus' |
| - 'Haifa' | CBod EBtc ECtt EGHP ELau EWhm GGar LRHS NLBP SIde WJek WPnn |
| - 'Henfield Blue' | SBfd SHDw |
| - 'Iden Blue' | SIde |
| - 'Iden Blue Boy' | CSpe SIde |
| - 'Iden Pillar' | SIde |
| § - 'Joyce DeBaggio' (v) | MHer SDow WGwG WHer |
| - 'Knightshayes Blue' **new** | LRHS |
| - 'Lady in Blue' | WGwG |
| - ***lavandulaceus*** | see *R. officinalis* Prostratus Group |
| - 'Lilies Blue' | GPoy |
| - 'Lockwood Variety' | see *R. officinalis* (Prostratus Group) 'Lockwood de Forest' |
| - 'Majorca Pink' | CBcs CHab CSBt CSam CSpe CWan ELau GGar LRHS MHer MNHC NPri SDow SIde SPer WGwG WJek XLum |
| - 'Marenca' | ELau MNHC |
| - 'McConnell's Blue' ♀H4 | CAlb CArn CDoC CPrp EBee ELan ELau IGor LHop LRHS MAsh MGos MNHC SBfd SDow SHDw WFar WGwG WHer WHoo WJek WPGP |
| § - 'Miss Jessopp's Upright' ♀H4 | Widely available |
| - 'Pat Vlasto' | SUsu |
| - 'Pointe du Raz' | CAbP EBee ELan EPfP LRHS MAsh SChF |
| § - 'Primley Blue' | CBcs CMea CSam CSev CTsd ECtt ELau MNHC MRav SBrd SGol SIde WFar WJek WPer |
| § - Prostratus Group | Widely available |
| - - 'Capri' | CAbP CDul CSBt ECtt EGHP ELau EPfP LRHS MBrN MHer SPoG WJek |
| - - 'Gethsemane' | SIde WGwG |
| - - 'Jackman's Prostrate' | CBcs CHab ECtt |
| § - - 'Lockwood de Forest' | WGwG WHer |
| - - 'Sheila Dore' | SPlb SVen |
| - f. ***pyramidalis*** | see *R. officinalis* 'Miss Jessopp's Upright' |
| - ***repens*** | see *R. officinalis* Prostratus Group |
| - 'Rex' | ELau |
| - 'Roman Beauty' PBR | CBcs LAst LRHS LSRN SLim SPoG SWvt |
| - 'Roseus' | CArn CEnt CPrp CWib EBee ELan ELau EPfP GPoy LHop LRHS MAsh MHer MNHC NEgg SBfd SDow SEND SLim SPoG WGwG WHer WJek WMnd WPer WPnn |
| - 'Russell's Blue' | WFar |
| - 'Salem' | CBod MHer |
| - 'Sea Level' | CBod ELau MHer WGwG |
| - 'Severn Sea' ♀H4 | Widely available |
| - 'Shimmering Stars' | SDow |
| - 'Silver Sparkler' | WPat |
| - Silver Spires = 'Wolros' | MNHC WFar |
| - 'Sissinghurst Blue' ♀H4 | CArn CDul CWan EBee ECha ECrN ELan ELau EPfP LRHS MAsh MHer MLHP MNHC MRav SBfd SBrd SDow SGol SIde SLim SPer SPlb SRms SWvt WGwG WJek |
| - 'Sissinghurst White' | MMuc WGwG |
| - 'Sorcerer's Apprentice' | WGwG |
| - 'South Downs Blue' | SBfd SHDw |
| - 'Spanish Snow' | WGwG |
| - 'Sudbury Blue' | ELau EPfP MNHC SBfd SDow SHDw WFar WJek WPnn XSen |
| - 'Trusty' | CWan |
| - 'Tuscan Blue' | CDoC CPLG ECha ECtt ELan ELau EPfP GGar LRHS MHer MNHC MSwo NEgg NPri SBfd SDow SGol SIde SPad SPer SRms WAle WFar WGwG WHfH WJek WPGP WPnn XSen |
| - 'Variegatus' | see *R. officinalis* 'Aureus' |
| - 'Vicomte de Noailles' | XSen |
| - 'Wilma's Gold' **new** | EBee |
| ***repens*** | see *R. officinalis* Prostratus Group |
| Salcombe form **new** | CHll |
| 'Sappho' | CHll |

## *Rostrinucula* (*Lamiaceae*)

| | |
|---|---|
| B&SWJ 11739 from northern Vietnam | WCru |
| ***dependens*** | ECre EPfP EWes NLar |
| ***sinensis*** | CPLG |

## *Rosularia* ✿ (*Crassulaceae*)

| | |
|---|---|
| sp. | MWat |
| from Sandras Dag | CWil LBee LRHS |
| § ***aizoon*** | ECho LRHS |
| ***alba*** | see *R. sedoides* var. *alba* |
| ***alpestris*** from Rhotang Pass | WThu |
| § ***chrysantha*** | ECho EDAr LRHS NMen SPlb |
| - number 1 | CWil |
| ***crassipes*** | see *Rhodiola wallichiana* |
| ***hirsuta*** **new** | EPot |

| | |
|---|---|
| ***libanotica*** RCB RL 20 | WCot |
| ***lineata*** RCB RL C-5 | WCot |
| ***pallida*** A. Berger | see *R. chrysantha* |
| ***pallida*** Stapf | see *R. aizoon* |
| ***pallida*** ambig. | SFgr |
| ***sedoides*** | CWil MMuc |
| § – var. ***alba*** | ECho EDAr EPot GGar WNew |
| ***sempervivum*** | CWil ECho EWes NMen |
| § – subsp. ***glaucophylla*** | CWil WAbe WThu |
| ***spathulata*** hort. | see *R. sempervivum* subsp. *glaucophylla* |

# *Rotala* (*Lythraceae*)

| | |
|---|---|
| ***indica*** **new** | LLWG |

# *Rubia* (*Rubiaceae*)

| | |
|---|---|
| ***peregrina*** | CArn GPoy |
| ***tinctorum*** | CArn CHab CHby EOHP GPoy MHer SWat WHfH WSFF |

# *Rubus* ✿ (*Rosaceae*)

| | |
|---|---|
| RCB/Eq C-1 | WCot |
| SDR 4635 | GKev |
| ***alceifolius*** Poir. | CFee SDys |
| ***arcticus*** | EBee ECtt EPPr GAuc GEdr GGar NHar NLar SRms SRot SSvw WCru WPat WThu XLum |
| – subsp. ***stellatus*** | GAuc |
| × ***barkeri*** | ECou |
| 'Benenden' ♀H4 | Widely available |
| 'Betty Ashburner' | CAgr CBcs CDoC CDul EPPr GQui LAst MGos MRav MWhi SLPl SPer WDin WMoo XLum |
| ***biflorus*** ♀H4 | EPfP EWes LEdu MBlu MMuc SEND WPGP |
| 'Black Butte' | CSut EPom GPri LRHS SDea SLon SVic |
| 'Boatsberry' | SDea |
| 'Boysenberry' (F) **new** | LRHS |
| boysenberry, thornless (F) | CMac EMil ERea GPri GTwe LBuc LSRN NPri SDea SPer |
| ***buergeri*** B&SWJ 5555 | WCru |
| ***calophyllus*** | CDul WPGP |
| ***calycinoides*** Hayata | see *R. rolfei* |
| ***calycinoides*** Kuntze | EBtc SGol |
| ***chamaemorus*** | GAuc GPoy |
| ***cockburnianus*** (F) | CArn CBcs CTri CWib EBee ECrN ELan EPfP GCra GKin IFoB LBuc MRav MSwo NLar NSti NWea SPer SPlb SRms WDin WFar |
| – 'Goldenvale' ♀H4 | CDoC CDul EBee EHoe EPfP EPla GQui IFro LHop LRHS MBlu MGos MMuc MRav MSwo MWhi NBir NEgg NLar NSti SEND SLon SMrm SPer SPoG WDin WFar WTin |
| ***crataegifolius*** | LEdu MRav WPat |
| ***deliciosus*** | WFar |
| 'Emerald Spreader' | WMoo |
| ***fockeanus*** misapplied | see *R. rolfei* |
| ***formosensis*** B&SWJ 1798 | WCru |
| N ***fruticosus*** agg. | NWea WSFF |
| – 'Adrienne' (F) | CAgr CSBt LRHS MAsh MBri WHar |
| – 'Ashton Cross' (F) | CDoC GTwe LBuc |
| – 'Bedford Giant' (F) | CSBt GTwe LRHS LSRN MAsh MGos MMuc SEND SKee SLim SPoG WHar |
| – 'Black Satin' (F) | CAgr LRHS MCoo NLar NPri SDea SVic |
| – 'Chester' (F) | LRHS SBfd SKee |
| – 'Godshill Goliath' (F) | SDea |
| – 'Helen' (F) | CAgr CSut GPri MCoo SDea |
| – 'Himalayan Giant' (F) | GTwe MRav NEgg NLar SDea |
| – 'John Innes' (F) | GPri MCoo |
| – 'Kotata' (F) | ERea MRav |
| – 'Loch Maree' (F/d) **new** | LRHS SLon |
| – 'Loch Ness'PBR (F) ♀H4 | CAgr CMac CWib EPom GPri GTwe IArd LBuc LRHS LSRN MCoo SCoo SDea SKee WHar |
| – 'Loch Tay'PBR (F) | EPom GPri SBfd SPer |
| – 'Merton Thornless' (F) | CSBt CWib ERea GTwe LSRN MAsh MGos WHar |
| – 'No Thorn' (F) | SDea |
| – 'Oregon Thornless' (F) | CAgr CCVT CDoC CSBt CWib ECrN EPfP GTwe LRHS LSRN MAsh MBri MRav NEgg NLar SCoo SDea SKee SLim SPoG SRms WHar |
| – 'Parsley Leaved' (F) | SDea |
| * – 'Sylvan' (F) | MCoo MMuc |
| – 'Thornfree' (F) | CAgr CDoC CTri LRHS MMuc NLar SDea SKee SLim |
| – 'Variegatus' (v) | CBot CMac CRDP MBlu WCot |
| – 'Waldo' (F) | CAgr CSBt CWib ECrN LBuc LSRN MAsh MBri MGos NPri SDea WHar |
| aff. ***gachetensis*** B&SWJ 10603 | WCru |
| 'Glencoe' (F) | GPri |
| 'Golden Showers' | CWib |
| ***henryi*** | CBot EBla ESwi IGor LRHS MRav NSti WCot |
| – var. ***bambusarum*** | EPla ESwi MRav WCru |
| 'Hildaberry' (F) | GPri |
| ***hupehensis*** | SLPl |
| ***ichangensis*** | CBcs CBot EPla ESwi LEdu |
| ***idaeus*** | GPoy |
| – 'All Gold' (F) ♀H4 | CAgr CSut EMil ERea GPri LRHS MAsh MCoo MNHC SBfd SCoo SPer SVic WHar |
| – 'Aureus' (F) | ECha ELan EPla EWes MRav NBid WCot WFar |
| – 'Autumn Bliss' (F) ♀H4 | Widely available |
| – 'Autumn Treasure' (F) **new** | CSut LRHS NPri SLon |
| – 'Black Jewel' (F) | LRHS |
| – 'Cascade Delight' (F) **new** | CSut EPom |
| – 'Fallgold' (F) | CWib EPfP MMuc SEND SKee SPoG |
| – 'Glen Ample'PBR (F) ♀H4 | Widely available |
| – 'Glen Clova' (F) | CAgr CSBt CTri CWib ECrN GTwe LSRN MAsh MGos MNHC MRav NLar SBfd SKee SLim SPer SPoG SVic WHar |
| – 'Glen Doll'PBR (F) **new** | CAgr LBuc LRHS MCoo SCoo |
| – 'Glen Lyon'PBR (F) | CWib GKin LBuc MAsh MBri SCoo WHar |
| – 'Glen Magna'PBR (F) ♀H4 | CAgr CSBt CWSG CWib ERea GKin LRHS MAsh MBri NLar SCoo SDea SKee SLim SPoG |
| – 'Glen Moy'PBR (F) ♀H4 | CAgr CSBt CTri CWib ECrN EPfP ERea GPri GTwe LRHS LSRN MAsh MGos NEgg SCoo SDea SKee SLim WHar WWFS |
| – 'Glen Prosen'PBR (F) ♀H4 | CAgr CSBt CWib ECrN EPfP GKin GTwe LRHS LSRN MAsh MBri MGos MNHC MRav NEgg NPri SCoo SDea SKee SLim SPer SPlb WHar |

| | |
|---|---|
| - 'Glen Rosa' (F) | ERea |
| - 'Heritage' (F) | CWib MAsh SCoo |
| - Himbo Top = 'Rafzaqu'PBR (F) | GPri |
| - 'Joan J'PBR (F) ♀H4 | CMac CSut EMil ERea GPri |
| - 'Julia' (F) | GTwe MCoo |
| - 'Leo'PBR (F) ♀H4 | CSBt CTri CWib GTwe MAsh SCoo SKee SPer WHar |
| - 'Mac Black' (F) | LRHS |
| - 'Malling Admiral' (F) ♀H4 | CSBt CTri CWib EPom GTwe LSRN MAsh SCoo SKee SPer |
| - 'Malling Delight' (F) | CSBt CWib MAsh SCoo SPlb |
| - 'Malling Jewel' (F) ♀H4 | CSBt CWib EPom GTwe LBuc LSRN MAsh SDea SKee SPer WHar WWFS |
| - 'Malling Promise' (F) | CWib |
| - 'Octavia'PBR (F) | CAgr CSBt EMil EPom LBuc LRHS MAsh MCoo NLar SLim SPoG WHar WWFS |
| - 'Polka'PBR (F) ♀H4 | EPom GPri LBuc LRHS LSRN MAsh MCoo SCoo SKee SLim SVic WHar |
| - 'Summer Gold' (F) | GTwe |
| - 'Tulameen' (F) ♀H4 | CAgr CSBt CWib EMil EPom GPri LRHS LSRN MAsh MBri MNHC NLar SBfd SCoo SKee SLim SPer SPoG SVic WWFS |
| - 'Valentina' (F) | GPri SVic |
| - 'Zeva Herbsternte' (F) | CWib MAsh |
| ***illecebrosus*** (F) | XLum |
| ***irenaeus*** | EBla LEdu LRHS SEND SSpi |
| Japanese wineberry | see *R. phoenicolasius* |
| 'Jermyn's Jubilee' | SLPl |
| 'Karaka Black'PBR | GPri LBuc SVic |
| 'Kenneth Ashburner' | CDoC NLar WTin |
| ***laciniatus*** | EPla |
| - 'Thornless Evergreen' **new** | NBlu |
| ***lineatus*** | CBot CDTJ CDoC CSpe CWib EBee EPfP EWes LRHS MCot MMuc NSti SBrd SKHP WCru WDin WPGP |
| - B&SWJ 11261 from Sumatra | WCru |
| - HWJ 892 from Vietnam | ESwi WCru |
| - HWJK 2045 from Nepal | GQui WCru |
| - from Nepal | GCra |
| × ***loganobaccus*** 'Brandywine' | GPri SDea |
| - 'Ly 59' (F) ♀H4 | ECrN EPfP GTwe MMuc MRav SDea SKee SPer SRms |
| - 'Ly 654' (F) ♀H4 | CSBt EPom GTwe LBuc MBri NEgg NPri SDea SPer WHar |
| - thornless (F) | CAgr CTri CWSG CWib EPom GPri GTwe LRHS MAsh SBfd SDea SPoG SVic |
| ***ludwigii*** | WBox |
| 'Malling Minerva' (F) | CMac CSut EPom ERea WWFS |
| 'Margaret Gordon' | MRav |
| ***microphyllus*** 'Variegatus' (v) | MRav |
| § ***nepalensis*** | CAgr CDoC GKev LEdu |
| - from Nepal | GCra |
| ***nutans*** | see *R. nepalensis* |
| ***occidentalis*** 'Ebony' **new** | LRHS |
| - 'Haut' | GPri |
| - 'Jewel' | GPri |
| ***odoratus*** | CPLG EBee ELan EPPr EPfP EWTr LEdu MBlu MRav NBid NPal SPer WFar WTin |
| 'Ouachita' (F) | SPer |
| ***palmatus*** var. ***coptophyllus*** | MMuc |
| ***parviflorus*** | CArn |
| - double-flowered (d) | EPPr WCru |
| - 'Sunshine Spreader' | EHoe LEdu WPat |
| ***parvus*** | GGar LEdu |
| ***pectinellus*** var. ***trilobus*** | CFee EWld WCot |
| - - B&SWJ 1669B | NLar WCru |
| ***peltatus*** | CGHE NLar WPGP |
| ***pentalobus*** | see *R. rolfei* |
| § ***phoenicolasius*** | CAgr CBod CCCN CDul CHGN CMac EPfP EPla EWTr GTwe LEdu LHop LRHS MBlu MCoo MRav NLar SDea SGol SPer SPoG SVic WAbb WPGP |
| § ***rolfei*** | CTri GEdr |
| - B&SWJ 3546 from Taiwan | WCru |
| - B&SWJ 3878 from the Philippines | WCru |
| - 'Emerald Carpet' | CAgr NLar |
| ***rosifolius*** | CSpe |
| - 'Coronarius' (d) | CFee CSpe ECrN ELan LSou MRav NLar NPro WCot WFar |
| ***sachalinensis*** | GAuc |
| ***sanctus*** | CNat |
| ***setchuenensis*** | CFee CMCN EBla EWes NLar |
| 'Silvan' (F) ♀H4 | GPri GTwe SEND |
| ***spectabilis*** | CBcs CWib ELan EPPr EPla LEdu MMuc MRav WFar WSHC |
| - 'Flore Pleno' | see *R. spectabilis* 'Olympic Double' |
| § - 'Olympic Double' (d) | Widely available |
| ***splendidissimus*** B&SWJ 2361 | ESwi WCru |
| ***squarrosus*** | ECou |
| * ***stelleri*** | GAuc |
| 'Sunberry' (F) | CCCN GTwe SDea |
| ***swinhoei*** B&SWJ 1735 | WCru |
| ***taiwanicola*** | LEdu LLHF |
| - B&SWJ 317 | EDAr ESwi GBin GEdr WCru |
| - CWJ 12400 | WCru |
| Tayberry Group (F) ♀H4 | CSBt CTri ECrN GTwe LSRN MGos NLar NPri SPer SRms SVic WHar |
| - 'Buckingham' (F) | CSut EMil EPom GPri GTwe LBuc LRHS SBfd SVic |
| - 'Medana Tayberry' (F) | CAgr EPfP ERea GPri LRHS MAsh MBri SDea SKee SPoG |
| § ***thibetanus*** ♀H4 | Widely available |
| - 'Silver Fern' | see *R. thibetanus* |
| ***treutleri*** B&SWJ 2139 | WCru |
| ***tricolor*** | CAgr CBcs CDul CSBt CTri CWib EBee ECrN EPfP EShb GKin MBlu MCoo MMuc MRav MSwo NEgg NHol NLar SBfd SDix SGol SPer WDin WMoo |
| ***trilobus*** B&SWJ 9096 | WCru |
| 'Tummelberry' (F) | EMil GPri GTwe LRHS MCoo SBfd SVic |
| ***ulmifolius*** 'Bellidiflorus' (d) | GCal MBlu MRav MSwo WAbb WHrl |
| ***ursinus*** | SBfd |
| 'Veitchberry' (F) | CDoy GPri |
| ***xanthocarpus*** | NLar XLum |
| 'Youngberry' (F) | SDea |
| 'Youngberry' thornless (F) | GPri |

## *Rudbeckia* ✿ (*Asteraceae*)

| | |
|---|---|
| Autumn Sun | see *R. laciniata* 'Herbstsonne' |
| 'Berlin' **new** | EBee WCot |

| | | |
|---|---|---|
| | ***deamii*** | see *R. fulgida* var. *deamii* |
| | 'Dublin' **new** | EBee |
| | ***fulgida*** 'City Garden' | NDov NLar |
| § | - var. ***deamii*** ♀H4 | Widely available |
| | - 'Early Bird Gold' **new** | NDov NLar SBfd |
| | - var. ***fulgida*** | CAby CMea EBee EPfP MAvo SBfd SMad SPoG |
| § | - var. ***speciosa*** ♀H4 | CKno CMMP CPrp EBee ECha ECtt ELan EPfP GAbr MMuc MSpe NBPC SBch SEND SPhx SPlb SRms SWal WFar WMoo WOut WPer WPtf WTin WWEG XLum |
| | - var. ***sullivantii*** 'Goldsturm' ♀H4 | Widely available |
| | - - 'Pot of Gold' | LSou |
| | - Viette's Little Suzy = 'Blovi' | EBee |
| | ***gloriosa*** | see *R. hirta* |
| | 'Golden Jubilee' | LRHS |
| | ***grandiflora*** 'Sundance' | CSam EBee GMac LRHS SBfd SPhx WPtf |
| | - 'Sunshine' | NDov |
| § | ***hirta*** | CHar LRHS MNHC NBir SVic |
| | - 'Autumn Colours' (mixed) | CMea |
| | - 'Cappuccino' **new** | MSCN |
| | - 'Cherokee Sunset' (d) | CSpe |
| | - 'Cherry Brandy' | LRHS NPri SPhx |
| | - 'Chim Chiminee' | NGBl |
| | - 'Goldilocks' | CBar |
| | - 'Indian Summer' ♀H3 | SPav SPhx |
| | - 'Irish Eyes' | SPav |
| | - 'Marmalade' | EPfP LRHS NGBl |
| | - 'Prairie Sun' | ELon EPfP LRHS NGBl |
| | - 'Sonora' | NGBl |
| | - 'Tiger Eye' **new** | LRHS |
| | - 'Toto' ♀H3 | SPav SWvt |
| | July Gold | see *R. laciniata* 'Juligold' |
| | ***laciniata*** | CElw CHVG CKno CMac EBee ELan GCal GQue LEdu MDKP MLLN MMuc NCGa NDov NGBl NLar NOrc SBfd SPhx WCot WMoo WOld WWEG XLum |
| | - 'Golden Glow' | see *R. laciniata* 'Hortensia' |
| | - 'Goldkugel' (d) ♀H4 **new** | MSpe |
| | - 'Goldquelle' (d) ♀H4 | CWCL EBee ECha ECtt ELan EPfP EShb GMaP LHop LRHS MSpe NBPC NGdn NOrc NPri NWad SBrd SMrm SPer SPoG SRms SRot STes SWvt WBor WCot WFar WMnd WWEG XLum |
| § | - 'Herbstsonne' ♀H4 | Widely available |
| § | - 'Hortensia' (d) | EBee GQue MAvo MLLN MRav MSpe WBrk WHoo WOld WWEG |
| § | - 'Juligold' | CPrp EBee LBMP LRHS MBNS NBre NDov NEgg NGdn SMrm SPoG WFar WWEG WWFP |
| | - 'Starcadia Razzle Dazzle' | WCot WWEG |
| | ***maxima*** | CKno CSpe EBee ECha GMac IFoB LEdu LHop LRHS MAvo MBri MSpe NCGa NLar NSti SBfd SKHP SMad SMrm SPhx SPlb SUsu WBor WCAu WCot WFar WWEG XLum |
| | ***missouriensis*** | EBee LRHS SBfd SUsu |
| | ***mollis*** | EBee NBre |
| | ***newmannii*** | see *R. fulgida* var. *speciosa* |
| | ***nitida*** | EBee EShb |
| | ***occidentalis*** | GKev LRHS NBre NLar |
| | - 'Black Beauty' PBR | EBee EPfP WMnd |
| | - 'Green Wizard' | CMac CWib EBee ECtt ELan EPfP LRHS MCot MLHP NDov NLar NPri NSti SBfd SGar SPav SPer SPoG SRms WFoF WPGP WTin WWEG |
| * | ***paniculata*** | EBee LLHF NBre WCot |
| | 'Peking' **new** | [illegible] |
| | ***purpurea*** | see *Echinacea purpurea* |
| | ***speciosa*** | see *R. fulgida* var. *speciosa* |
| | ***subtomentosa*** | CDes CSam EBee EWes GCal LPla MDKP MNFA NBre NDov NPnk NSti WOld XLum |
| | - 'Henry Eilers' | ECtt ELan EPfP GQue IKil LRHS LSou MBri MMHG NPnk SBfd SKHP SPoG SUsu WCAu WHil |
| | 'Takao' | EBee LSou MDKP |
| | ***triloba*** ♀H4 | CDes CMea CSam EBee ECha EPPr EPfP EShb LEdu LRHS MNrw MSpe NDov NGdn NPnk SMad SMrm SMrs SPhx SUsu WCAu WFar WMoo WPGP WTcb WTin |
| | - 'Prairie Glow' **new** | EDAr |
| | 'Vitamin C' **new** | EBee |

## rue see *Ruta graveolens*

## *Ruellia* (*Acanthaceae*)

| | | |
|---|---|---|
| | ***amoena*** | see *R. brevifolia* |
| § | ***brevifolia*** | ECre EShb |
| | ***humilis*** | EBee EPPr EShb GMac NDov NLar WHil |
| | ***macrantha*** | CCCN EShb WHil |
| | ***makoyana*** ♀H1 | CSev EShb MBri WHil |
| | - pink-flowered **new** | WHil |
| | - white-flowered **new** | WHil |
| | ***tweediana*** | EShb WHil |

## *Rulingia* (*Malvaceae*)

| | |
|---|---|
| ***hermanniifolia*** **new** | ECou MOWG |

## *Rumex* (*Polygonaceae*)

| | |
|---|---|
| ***acetosa*** | CArn CHab CHby CSev CWan EGHP ELau GPoy MCoo MHer MMuc MNHC NBir SBfd SEND SIde WHer WJek WSFF |
| - 'Abundance' | ELau |
| - subsp. ***acetosa*** 'Saucy' (v) | LEdu WCot |
| - 'De Belleville' | CPrp |
| - 'Profusion' | GPoy MHer |
| - subsp. ***vinealis*** | EBee |
| ***acetosella*** | CArn CHab EWil NMir WSFF |
| ***alpinus*** | EBee LEdu SPhx WCot |
| ***crispus*** | ELau |
| ***flexuosus*** | CSpe CSpr EBee EPPr GCal MDKP NLar WJek |
| ***hydrolapathum*** | CArn CHab LPBA MMuc MSKA SEND SPlb WSFF |
| ***patientia*** | CArn CHab ELau |
| ***sanguineus*** | CTri EShb LPBA MSKA NBlu NLar SBfd WFar WMAq WTcb |
| - var. ***sanguineus*** | CArn CElw CRow CSev EBee ELan IFoB MHer MNHC MNrw NBro NPri WHer |
| 'Schavel' | LEdu |
| ***scutatus*** | CArn CHby CSev ELau GPoy MNHC SBfd SIde SPlb WHer WHfH WJek |
| - 'Silver Shield' | CBod CRow ELau LEdu MHer SIde WJek |

## *Rumohra* (*Dryopteridaceae*)

| | |
|---|---|
| ***adiantiformis*** ♀H1 | CCCN EFtx ISha LRHS SEND WFib WPGP WRic |
| – RCB/Arg D-2 | WCot |

## *Ruscus* ✿ (*Asparagaceae*)

| | |
|---|---|
| ***aculeatus*** | CArn CBcs CDul CMac CRWN ELan EPfP ERom GPoy IDee LEdu LTen MGos MRav NLar NWad NWea SArc SBfd SLim SPlb SRms WBor WDin WPGP WRHF |
| – (f) | WFar |
| – (m) | WCFE |
| – hermaphrodite | EPfP EPla EWes GCal MBri SEND SMad WPGP WPat WThu |
| – var. ***aculeatus*** 'Lanceolatus' (f) | GCal |
| – var. ***angustifolius*** | EPla LEdu |
| – – (f) | EPla |
| – 'Christmas Berry' | ELan EPfP NLar |
| – 'John Redmond'PBR | CHid CSBt EGxp ELan ELon EPfP EWes LAst LHop LLHF LRHS LSqu MAsh MMuc NHol NLar NMun NWad SBfd SCoo SEND SKHP SLon SPer SPoG SSpi WBor WCot WFar WPGP |
| * – 'Wheeler's Variety' (f/m) | CPMA MRav WPGP |
| ***hypoglossum*** | EPla MMuc SEND WCot WPGP |
| ***racemosus*** | see *Danae racemosa* |

## *Ruspolia* (*Acanthaceae*)

| | |
|---|---|
| ***hypocrateriformis*** | CCCN |
| ***seticalyx*** | EShb |

## *Russelia* (*Plantaginaceae*)

| | |
|---|---|
| § ***equisetiformis*** ♀H1 | EShb MOWG |
| – 'Lemon Falls' | EShb MOWG |
| ***juncea*** | see *R. equisetiformis* |

## *Ruta* (*Rutaceae*)

| | |
|---|---|
| ***chalepensis*** | CArn XLum XSen |
| ***corsica*** | CArn XLum |
| ***graveolens*** | CArn CHab CWan EPfP GPoy NBlu SBfd SIde SWal WJek XLum |
| – 'Jackman's Blue' | CBcs CPrp CSev CTri EHoe ELan EOHP EPfP GMaP GPoy LAst MGos MHer MNHC MRav MSwo NLar SBfd SLim SRms WMnd XLum |
| – 'Variegata' (v) | CBot CWan ELan EOHP MNHC NPer |

## *Ruttya* (*Acanthaceae*)

| | |
|---|---|
| ***fruticosa*** | CCCN |
| – 'Scholesii' | EShb |

## × *Ruttyruspolia* (*Acanthaceae*)

| | |
|---|---|
| ***lutea*** | CCCN |
| 'Phyllis van Heerden' | MOWG |

## *Rytidosperma* (*Poaceae*)

| | |
|---|---|
| * ***arundinaceum*** | EShb |

# S

## *Sabal* (*Arecaceae*)

| | |
|---|---|
| § ***bermudana*** | EAmu |
| ***causiarum*** | EAmu |
| ***etonia*** | LPal |
| § ***mexicana*** | EAmu |
| ***minor*** | CBrP CHEx CPHo EAmu LPal MREP NPal SBig SPlb |
| ***palmetto*** | CDoC EAmu LPal |
| ***princeps*** | see *S. bermudana* |
| ***rosei*** | LPal |
| ***texana*** | see *S. mexicana* |
| ***uresana*** | LPal |

## *Sabatia* (*Gentianaceae*)

| | |
|---|---|
| ***kennedyana*** | LRHS |

## *Saccharum* (*Poaceae*)

| | |
|---|---|
| ***arundinaceum*** | CKno |
| § ***baldwinii*** | EPPr GCal |
| ***brevibarbe*** var. ***contortum*** | EPPr GCal |
| ***ravennae*** | EPPr SApp SEND SMad SMrm SPlb WCot |
| ***strictum*** (Baldwin) Nutt. | see *S. baldwinii* |

## *Sadleria* (*Blechnaceae*)

| | |
|---|---|
| ***cyatheoides*** | WRic |

## sage see *Salvia officinalis*

## sage, annual clary see *Salvia viridis*

## sage, biennial clary see *Salvia sclarea*

## sage, pineapple see *Salvia elegans*

## *Sageretia* (*Rhamnaceae*)

| | |
|---|---|
| § ***thea*** | CMen STre |
| ***theezans*** | see *S. thea* |

## *Sagina* (*Caryophyllaceae*)

| | |
|---|---|
| ***subulata*** | ECho EHoe LRHS SVic |
| § – var. ***glabrata*** 'Aurea' | CMea CTri ECha ECho ECtt EDAr GMaP SPoG SRms WFar WPer |

## *Sagittaria* (*Alismataceae*)

| | |
|---|---|
| 'Bloomin Babe' | CRow |
| ***graminea*** | LLWG |
| – 'Crushed Ice' (v) | CRow MWts |
| ***japonica*** | see *S. sagittifolia* |
| ***latifolia*** | LLWG LPBA MWts NPer |
| * ***leucopetala*** 'Flore Pleno' (d) | NLar NPer |
| § ***sagittifolia*** | CBen CRow CWat EHon EWil LLWG LPBA MSKA WMAq WPnP |
| – 'Flore Pleno' (d) | CWat LPBA WMAq |
| – var. ***leucopetala*** | WMAq |
| ***subulata*** | XLum |

## *Saintpaulia* (*Gesneriaceae*)

| | |
|---|---|
| 'Aca's Pink Delight' | WDib |
| 'Aca's Red Ember' (v) | WDib |
| 'Allegro Appalachian Trail' | WDib |
| 'Alliance' (v) | WDib |
| 'Always Pink' new | WDib |
| 'Aly's Rosy Baby' new | WDib |
| 'Arctic Frost' (d) | WDib |
| 'Baby's Breath' | WDib |
| 'Bahamian Sunset' (d) | WDib |
| 'Baker Pink Star' new | WDib |
| 'Beacon Trail' | WDib |

'Beate' WDib
'Beatrice Trail' WDib
'Betty Stoehr' WDib
'Blackie Bryant' WDib
'Blue Dragon' (d) WDib
'Blue Tail Fly' **new** WDib
'Blushing Trail' **new** WDib
'Bob Serbin' (d) WDib
'Buffalo Hunt' (d) WDib
'Candy Swirls' WDib
'Cathedral' WDib
'Chantaspring' **new** WDib
'Cherries 'n' Cream' WDib
'Chiffon Fiesta' WDib
'Chiffon Moonmoth' WDib
'Chiffon Vesper' WDib
'Coral Sparkle Trail' WDib
'Crimson Ice' WDib
'Deer Trail' WDib
'Delft' (d) WDib
'Desir' **new** WDib
'Dubois Othello' (v) WDib
'Electric Dreams' WDib
'Emerald Love' WDib
'Falling Raindrops' WDib
'Fantinci' WDib
'Favorite Child' WDib
'Flashy Angel' (v) WDib
'Fun Trail' WDib
'Genetic Blush' WDib
'Gillian' (d) WDib
'Golden Eye' WDib
'Golden Glow' (d) WDib
'Grandmother's Halo' WDib
'Green Ice' WDib
'Green Lace' (d) **new** WDib
'Halo's Aglitter' WDib
'Happy Cricket' WDib
'Indigo Ruffles' **new** WDib
'Irish Flirt' (d) WDib
'King's Trail' (d) WDib
'Kostina Fantaziya' **new** WDib
'Lemon Drop' (d) WDib
'Lemon Whip' (d) WDib
'Lis' WDib
'Little Axel' WDib
'Lollipop' WDib
'Looking Glass' WDib
'Louisiana Lagniappe' WDib
'Louisiana Lullaby' (d) **new** WDib
'Love Spots' WDib
'Lucky Lee Ann' (d) WDib
'Luminescence' WDib
'Lyon's Paprika' **new** WDib
'Lyon's Plum Pudding' WDib
'Mac's Black Jack' **new** WDib
'Mac's Carnival Clown' WDib
'Mac's Circus Clown' WDib
'Mac's Coral Cutie' WDib
'Mac's Exquisite Extravaganza' WDib
'Mac's Just Jeff' (d/v) WDib
'Mac's Nocturne' (d) WDib
'Mair' WDib
'Ma's Corsage' WDib
'Ma's Lily Pad' WDib
'Ma's Winter Moon' WDib
'Midget Lilian' (v) WDib
'Midnight Flame' (d) WDib
'Midnight Magic' WDib
'Midnight Rascal' (d) WDib
'Midnight Waltz' (d) WDib
'Milky Way Trail' WDib
'Minnie Mine' **new** WDib
'Minstrel's Mary Ruth' WDib
'Mosaique' WDib
'Motley Crew' WDib
'Ness' Antique Red' WDib
'Ness' Bangle Blue' **new** WDib
'Ness' Cherry Smoke' **new** WDib
'Ness' Crinkle Blue' (d) WDib
'Ness' Dynomite' **new** WDib
'Ness' Midnight Fantasy' WDib
'Ness' Satin Rose' **new** WDib
'Ness' Sno Fun' WDib
'Ness' Viking Maiden' WDib
'Newtown Ohio' WDib
'Ode to Beauty' WDib
'Okie Easter Bunny' WDib
'Oksana' **new** WDib
'Optimara Little Inca' **new** WDib
'Optimara Little Seneca' **new** WDib
'Otoe' (d) WDib
'Persian Swirl' WDib
'Pink Duchess' (d) WDib
'Pink Wink' **new** WDib
'Pixie Blue' WDib
'Pixie Pink' WDib
'Pixie Show-off' WDib
'Powder Keg' (d) WDib
'Powwow' (d/v) WDib
'Rain Man' WDib
'Rainbow's Limelight' (d) WDib
'Rainbow's Quiet Riot' WDib
'Ramblin' Amethyst' WDib
'Ramblin' Angel' (d) WDib
'Ramblin' Dots' WDib
'Ramblin' Lassie' WDib
'Ramblin' Magic' (d) WDib
'Ramblin' Sunshine' WDib
'Rapid Transit' (d) WDib
'Rare Tapestry' WDib
'Raspberry Crisp' WDib
'Red Lantern' (d) WDib
'Red Summit' WDib
'Rhapsodie Clementine' WDib
'Rhapsodie Mars' **new** WDib
'Rhapsodie Rosalie' **new** WDib
'Robert Mayer' WDib
'Rob's Bamboozle' (d) WDib
'Rob's Blue Cat' **new** WDib
'Rob's Blue Socks' WDib
'Rob's Boo Hoo' **new** WDib
'Rob's Calypso Beat' (d) WDib
'Rob's Chilly Willy' (d/v) **new** WDib
'Rob's Cloudy Skies' (d) WDib
'Rob's Dandy Lion' (d/v) WDib
'Rob's Denim Demon' (d/v) WDib
'Rob's Dust Storm' (d) WDib
'Rob's Gundaroo' (d) WDib
'Rob's Hallucination' WDib
'Rob's Heebie Jeebie' **new** WDib

| | |
|---|---|
| 'Rob's Hopscotch' (d) | WDib |
| 'Rob's Hot Tamale' **new** | WDib |
| 'Rob's Ice Ripples' (d) | WDib |
| 'Rob's Jitterbug' | WDib |
| 'Rob's June Bug' (d/v) | WDib |
| 'Rob's Loose Goose' (d) | WDib |
| 'Rob's Love Bite' (d) | WDib |
| 'Rob's Mad Cat' (d) | WDib |
| 'Rob's Peedletuck' | WDib |
| 'Rob's Pink Buttercups' (v) **new** | WDib |
| 'Rob's Rinky Dink' (d) | WDib |
| 'Rob's Ruff Stuff' | WDib |
| 'Rob's Sarsparilla' (d) | WDib |
| 'Rob's Scarecrow' **new** | WDib |
| 'Rob's Scrumptious' | WDib |
| 'Rob's Seduction' (d/v) | WDib |
| 'Rob's Shadow Magic' (d/v) | WDib |
| 'Rob's Smarty Pants' (d) | WDib |
| 'Rob's Sticky Wicket' (d) | WDib |
| 'Rob's Toorooka' (d) | WDib |
| 'Rob's Twinkle Blue' (d) | WDib |
| 'Rob's Vanilla Trail' (d) | WDib |
| 'Rob's Wooloomooloo' (d) | WDib |
| 'Roll Along Blue' (d) | WDib |
| 'Ruffled Red' | WDib |
| 'Santa Anita' | WDib |
| ***shumensis*** | WDib |
| 'Sky Bells' (v) | WDib |
| 'Sweet Amy Sue' (d) | WDib |
| 'Taffeta Blue' (d) | WDib |
| 'Taffeta Petticoats' | WDib |
| 'Teen Thunder' | WDib |
| 'The Madam' | WDib |
| 'Twist 'n' Shout' | WDib |
| 'Warm Sunshine' | WDib |
| 'Whirligig Star' | WDib |
| 'Wisteria' (d) | WDib |
| 'Witch Doctor' (d) **new** | WDib |
| 'Yesterday's Child' | WDib |

## *Salicornia* (*Amaranthaceae*)

| | |
|---|---|
| ***europaea*** | SVic |

## *Salix* ✿ (*Salicaceae*)

| | | |
|---|---|---|
| | ***acutifolia*** | ELan WDin |
| | - 'Blue Streak' (m) ♀H4 | CEnd CWiW CWon EPfP EPla EWes MBlu NBir NLar SBrd SWat WFar WMou |
| | - 'Pendulifolia' (m) | SGol |
| | 'Aegma Brno' (f) | CWon WMou |
| | ***aegyptiaca*** | CDoC CWon EBtc MBlu NWea WMou |
| | ***alba*** | CCVT CDul CHab CLnd CWiW ECrN GGal LBuc LMaj NWea SEWo SGol WDin WJPR WMou |
| | - f. ***argentea*** | see *S. alba* var. *sericea* |
| | - 'Aurea' | CTho CWon WIvy WMou |
| | - 'Belders' (m) | CWon |
| | - var. ***caerulea*** | CDul CLnd CWon NWea WMou |
| | - - 'Wantage Hall' (f) | CWiW CWon |
| | - 'Cardinalis' (f) | CWiW CWon SWat |
| | - 'Chermesina' hort. | see *S. alba* var. *vitellina* 'Britzensis' |
| | - 'Dart's Snake' | CWon ELan EPfP EPla MAsh MBrN MRav NLar WCot |
| | - 'Drakonburg' **new** | CWon |
| | - 'Flame' **new** | CWon |
| | - 'Golden Ness' | LRHS MAsh MBlu |
| | - 'Hutchinson's Yellow' | CDoC CTho CWon MGos NLar SBrd SCoo SLim WDin |
| | - 'Liempde' (m) | NWea |
| | - 'Raesfeld' (m) | CWiW CWon |
| § | - var. ***sericea*** ♀H4 | CBcs CDul CLnd CTho CWon EPfP MBlu MRav NLar NWea SPer WDin WIvy WMou |
| | - 'Splendens' | see *S. alba* var. *sericea* |
| | - 'Tristis' misapplied | see *S.* × *sepulcralis* var. *chrysocoma* |
| § | - 'Tristis' ambig. | CCVT CLnd CTri CWon ELan MAsh MBri MGos MRav MSwo NLar NWea SEND SEWo SLim SRms SWat WDin WFar WHar |
| | - 'Tristis' Gaudin | MMuc |
| | - var. ***vitellina*** ♀H4 | CDul CTri CWon EPfP GQue LBuc MBNS MBrN NLar NWea SGol SLon SWat WDin WIvy |
| § | - - 'Britzensis' (m) ♀H4 | Widely available |
| | - - 'Nova' | SWat |
| | - 'Vitellina Pendula' | see *S. alba* 'Tristis' ambig. |
| | - 'Vitellina Tristis' | see *S. alba* 'Tristis' ambig. |
| § | - var. ***vitellina*** 'Yelverton' | CWon LRHS MAsh SBrd SPoG SWat |
| | ***alba*** × ***amygdaloides*** × ***nigra*** | CWon |
| § | ***alpina*** | ECho NBir NHar |
| | 'Americana' | CWiW CWon |
| | ***amplexicaulis*** | CWon |
| | - 'Pescara' (m) | CWiW |
| | ***amygdaloides*** | CWiW CWon |
| | 'Aokautere' | see *S.* × *sepulcralis* 'Aokautere' |
| | ***apennina*** 'Cisa Pass' | CWon |
| | ***apoda*** | CWon |
| | - (m) | WPer |
| | ***appendiculata*** **new** | CWon |
| § | ***arbuscula*** | CWon ECho GAuc NLar NWCA WDin |
| | ***arenaria*** | see *S. repens* var. *argentea* |
| | ***aurita*** | CWon GAuc NLar NWea |
| | ***babylonica*** | CDul CEnd CWon WMou |
| | - 'Annularis' | see *S. babylonica* 'Crispa' |
| | - 'Bijdorp' | MBri NLar |
| § | - 'Crispa' | CWon ELan LHop LRHS MBri MTPN MWts SMad SPoG WFar |
| | - 'Pan Chih-kang' | CWiW NLar |
| | - var. ***pekinensis*** | CWon |
| | - - 'Pendula' | NLar |
| | - - 'Snake' | CWon |
| § | - - 'Tortuosa' ♀H4 | Widely available |
| * | - 'Tortuosa Aurea' | MCCP SGol SWvt |
| | × ***balfourii*** | CWon |
| | ***bebbiana*** | CWon |
| | ***bicolor*** | CWon NWea |
| | 'Blackskin' (f) | CWiW |
| | ***bockii*** | EBtc ELan LLHF LRHS MMuc SKHP WFar |
| § | 'Bowles's Hybrid' | WMou |
| | 'Boydii' (f) ♀H4 | CWon ECho EPfP EPot GEdr ITim LEdu MGos NBir NMen NRya NSla SRms WAbe WFar WPat |
| § | 'Boyd's Pendulous' (m) | CWib |
| | ***burjatica*** | CWon |
| | - 'Germany' | CWon |
| | - 'Korso' | CWon |
| | ***caesia*** | NWCA WIvy |
| | × ***calodendron*** (f) | CWon |
| | ***candida*** | CWon GAuc |
| | ***cantabrica*** | CWon |
| | ***caprea*** | CBcs CCVT CDul CHab CLnd CTri CWon ECrN EPfP LBuc LMaj NWea SEWo SPer STre WDin WMou WSFF |

| | | |
|---|---|---|
| | - 'Black Stem' | CDul |
| § | - 'Kilmarnock' (m) | Widely available |
| | - var. ***pendula*** (m) | see *S. caprea* 'Kilmarnock' (m) |
| | - 'Silberglanz' | CWon |
| | ***caprea* × *lanata*** | CWon |
| | × ***capreola*** | CWon |
| | ***cashmiriana*** | CWon GAuc GEdr WPat |
| | ***caspica*** | CWon |
| | - ***rubra nana*** | SWat |
| | × ***cernua*** | NWCA |
| | ***chaenomeloides*** | CWon |
| | 'Chrysocoma' | see *S.* × *sepulcralis* var. *chrysocoma* |
| | ***cinerea*** | CBcs CDoC CTri CWon LBuc NWea SEWo STre WDin WJPR WMou |
| | - 'Bude' | CWon |
| | - subsp. ***oleifolia*** × ***phylicifolia*** | CWon |
| | - 'Tricolor' (v) | CWon NPro |
| | ***cordata*** | CWon SLPl WDin |
| | - 'Purpurescens' | CWon |
| | × ***cottetii*** | GAuc WDin |
| | ***daphnoides*** | CCVT CDoC CDul CLnd CMac CWon EPPr EPfP LRHS MGos MMuc MSwo NWea SEND SGol SPer SRms SWat WDin WFar WJas WMou WSFF |
| | - 'Aglaia' (m) | CBcs CWon GQue WIvy |
| | - 'Continental Purple' | CWon |
| | - 'Henry' **new** | CWon |
| | - 'Lady Aldenham' | CWon |
| | - 'Meikle' (f) | CWiW SWat |
| | - 'Netta Statham' (m) | CWiW CWon |
| | - 'Ovaro Udine' (m) | CWiW |
| | - 'Oxford Violet' (m) | CWon NWea WIvy |
| | - 'Pendulifolia' | CWon |
| | - 'Purple Heart' | CWon |
| | - 'Sinker' | WIvy |
| | - 'Stewartstown' | CWiW |
| | - 'Wynter Bloom' | CWon |
| | × ***dasyclados*** | CWon |
| | - 'Grandis' | NWea |
| | ***discolor*** | CWon |
| | ***discolor*** × ***elaeagnos*** **new** | CWon |
| § | × ***doniana*** 'Kumeti' | CWiW CWon |
| | 'E.A. Bowles' | see *S.* 'Bowles's Hybrid' |
| | × ***ehrhartiana*** | CNat CWon |
| § | ***elaeagnos*** | CCVT CDoC CLnd CTho CTri ECrN EPfP MBrN MMuc SEND SLon SPer SWat WDin WFar WMou |
| § | - subsp. ***angustifolia*** ♀H4 | CBcs CDul CWon ELan EPfP MMuc MRav MSwo NLar NPCo NWea SEND SRms WIvy |
| | - 'Angustifolia' | see *S. elaeagnos* subsp. *angustifolia* |
| | 'Elegantissima' | see *S.* × *pendulina* var. *elegantissima* |
| | × ***erdingeri*** | CWon EPla |
| | ***eriocephala*** 'American Mackay' (m) | CWiW |
| | - 'Green USA' | CWon |
| | - 'Kerksii' (m) | CWiW CWon |
| | - 'Mawdesley' (m) | CWiW CWon |
| | - 'Russelliana' (f) | CWiW CWon |
| § | 'Erythroflexuosa' | CBcs CDoC CDul CEnd CWon EBee ELan EPPr EPfP LAst LBMP LHop MAsh MGos MMuc MRav NWea SBfd SGol SLim SMad SPer SPoG SWat WDin WFar WHer WPat |

| | | |
|---|---|---|
| | ***exigua*** | Widely available |
| | ***fargesii*** | CAbP CBot CDoC CDul CEnd CFee CMac CWon ELan EPfP IDee LEdu LHop LRHS MAsh MBlu MGos MRav NBid NEgg NPCo SBrd SDix SEND SKHP SSpi WCru WFar WPGP WPat |
| | ***fargesii* × *magnifica*** | WPGP |
| § | × ***finnmarchica*** | GAuc GEdr NWCA WAbe |
| | × ***forbyana*** | CWon |
| | ***formosa*** | see *S. arbuscula* |
| | ***fragilis*** | CCVT CDul CHab CLnd LMaj MRav NWea WDin WJPR WMou |
| | - var. ***decipiens*** **new** | CWon |
| § | - var. ***furcata*** | CTri CWon GBin GKev NWCA WPat |
| | - 'Legomey' | WIvy |
| | × ***fruticosa*** 'McElroy' (f) | CWiW CWon |
| | ***fruticulosa*** | see *S. fragilis* var. *furcata* |
| | 'Fuiri-koriyanagi' | see *S. integra* 'Hakuro-nishiki' |
| | ***furcata*** | see *S. fragilis* var. *furcata* |
| | ***gilgiana*** **new** | CWon |
| | ***glabra*** | CWon |
| | ***glauca*** | CNat |
| | ***glaucophylloides*** | CWon |
| | ***glaucosericea*** | EPla |
| | 'Golden Curls' | see *S.* 'Erythroflexuosa' |
| | ***gracilistyla*** | CTho CWon ECrN NWea SCoo SLPl WMou |
| § | - 'Melanostachys' (m) | Widely available |
| | × ***grahamii*** 'Moorei' (f) | NWCA |
| | × ***greyi*** | NPro NWCA |
| | ***hastata*** (f) | SWat |
| | - 'Wehrhahnii' (m) ♀H4 | CBcs CWon ECho ELan EPfP GCra GKev IVic LEdu MBlu MMuc MRav MSwo NBir NPCo NWea SPer SWat WCFE WDin WFar |
| | ***helvetica*** ♀H4 | CBcs CMac CWon ECho EGxp ELan EPfP GAbr IVic MBlu MMuc MRav NBir NEgg NLar NWea SBrd SEND SPer WDin WFar WPat |
| | ***herbacea*** | ECho GAuc GEdr NMen WAbe |
| | ***hibernica*** | see *S. phylicifolia* |
| I | ***himalayas*** | CWon |
| | × ***hirtei*** 'Delamere' | CWon |
| | - 'Rosewarne' | CWon |
| | ***hookeriana*** | CDul CLnd CTho CWon EBee ELan MBlu MBrN MBri NLar SLPl SSpi WCFE WIvy WMou WPGP WTin |
| | ***humilis*** var. ***microphylla*** | CWon |
| | ***incana*** | see *S. elaeagnos* |
| | ***integra*** | CWon |
| | - 'Albomaculata' | see *S. integra* 'Hakuro-nishiki' |
| | - 'Flamingo'[PBR] | SPoG |
| § | - 'Hakuro-nishiki' (v) | Widely available |
| | - 'Pendula' (f) | CEnd MAsh MBri |
| | ***irrorata*** | CDul CLnd CWon EPfP LRHS MBlu MRav MSwo SWat |
| | 'Jacquinii' | see *S. alpina* |
| | ***kinuyanagi*** (m) | CWon ELan WIvy |
| § | ***koriyanagi*** | CWiW CWon |
| | 'Kumeti' | see *S.* × *doniana* 'Kumeti' |
| | 'Kuro-me' | see *S. gracilistyla* 'Melanostachys' |
| | × ***laestadiana*** | GAuc |
| | ***laggeri*** | CWon |
| | ***lanata*** ♀H4 | CBcs CBot CMac CMea CWon ECho ELan ELon EPfP EWTr GAuc GKev MAsh MGos MRav NBir NEgg |

| |  |  |
|---|---|---|
| | | NHol NLar NMen NWCA NWea SPer SWat WCFE WDin WFar |
| | - 'Drake's Hybrid' | NMen |
| | - 'Mrs Mac' (m) | CWon |
| | ***lapponum*** | CWon GAuc GEdr GGar NLar NWCA NWea SRms WAbe |
| | - (m) | EBee |
| | ***lasiandra*** | CWon |
| | × ***laurina*** (f) | CWon |
| § | ***lindleyana*** | CWon |
| | ***lucida*** | CWon |
| | ***mackenzieana*** | CWon |
| | ***magnifica*** ♀H4 | CDul CEnd CGHE CLnd CTho CWon EBee ELan EPfP EPla EWTr LEdu LRHS MSnd NWea SKHP SMad SSpi SWat WDin WFar WMou WPGP |
| | 'Mark Postill' (f) | CDoC CWon EBee EMil GBin LRHS MBNS MMuc |
| | ***matsudana*** 'Tortuosa' | see *S. babylonica* var. *pekinensis* 'Tortuosa' |
| | - 'Tortuosa Aureopendula' | see *S.* 'Erythroflexuosa' |
| | 'Melanostachys' | see *S. gracilistyla* 'Melanostachys' |
| | × ***meyeriana*** | CWon WIvy |
| | - 'Daza' | CWon |
| | - 'Lumley' (f) | CWiW |
| | ***mielichhoferi*** | CWon |
| | ***miyabeana*** | CWon |
| I | - 'Purpurascens' **new** | CWon |
| | ***miyabeana*** × ***schwerinii*** **new** | CWon |
| | × ***mollissima*** | CWiW |
| | var. ***hippophaifolia*** 'Jefferies' (m) | |
| | - - 'Notts Spaniard' (m) | CWiW |
| | - - 'Stinchcombe' | WIvy |
| | - - 'Trustworthy' (m) | CWiW CWon |
| | - 'Pheasant Brown' | CWon |
| | - 'Q83' **new** | CWon |
| | - var. ***undulata*** 'Kottenheider Weide' (f) | CWiW CWon |
| | ***moupinensis*** | CWon EPfP MBri WAbe |
| | - EDHCH 97.319 | WPGP |
| | aff. ***moupinensis*** from Vietnam | WPGP |
| § | ***myrsinifolia*** | MBlu MMuc WGrn |
| | - subsp. ***alpicola*** | CWon |
| | - 'Cotinifolia' | CWon |
| | - 'Faucille' | CWon |
| | ***myrsinites*** var. ***jacquiniana*** | see *S. alpina* |
| | ***myrtilloides*** 'Pink Tassels' (m) | ECho GEdr NHar NWCA |
| | ***myrtilloides*** × ***repens*** | see *S.* × *finnmarchica* |
| | ***nakamurana*** var. ***yezoalpina*** | CFee CWon EBee ELan EWes GEdr GQui IVic LRHS MBlu MMuc MRav NHar NHol NLar NWCA WAbe WFar WPat |
| | ***nepalensis*** | see *S. lindleyana* |
| | ***nigra*** | CWon |
| | ***nigricans*** | see *S. myrsinifolia* |
| | ***nivalis*** | see *S. reticulata* subsp. *nivalis* |
| | × ***ovata*** | NMen NWCA |
| | × ***pendulina*** **new** | CWon |
| § | - var. ***elegantissima*** | CTho CWon SWat |
| | ***pentandra*** | CBot CDul ECrN NWea WDin WFar WJPR WMou |

| |  |  |
|---|---|---|
| | - 'Dark French' | CWon |
| | - 'Patent Lumley' | CWiW CWon |
| | ***petiolaris*** | CWon |
| | 'Phillip's Fancy' | NWCA |
| § | ***phylicifolia*** | NWea WJPR WMou |
| | - 'Malham' (m) | CWiW CWon |
| § | ***purpurea*** | CCVT CDul NWea SRms WDin WGwG WJPR WMou |
| | - 'Brittany Green' (f) | CWiW CWon |
| | - 'Continental Reeks' | CWiW CWon WIvy |
| | - 'Dark Dicks' (f) | CWiW CWon NLar WIvy WSFF |
| | - 'Dicky Meadows' (m) | CWiW CWon WIvy |
| * | - 'Elegantissima' | CWon |
| | - 'Goldstones' | CWiW NLar WIvy |
| | - f. ***gracilis*** | see *S. purpurea* 'Nana' |
| | - 'Green Dicks' | CWiW CWon WIvy |
| | - 'Helix' | see *S. purpurea* |
| | - 'Howki' (m) | CWon WMou |
| | - 'Irette' (m) | CWiW CWon |
| | - 'Jagiellonka' (f) | CWiW CWon WIvy |
| | - var. ***japonica*** | see *S. koriyanagi* |
| | - subsp. ***lambertiana*** | CWiW CWon WIvy |
| | - 'Lancashire Dicks' (m) | CWiW |
| | - 'Leicestershire Dicks' (m) | CWiW |
| | - 'Light Dicks' | CWiW CWon |
| | - 'Lincolnshire Dutch' (f) | CWiW |
| § | - 'Nana' | EPfP MMuc NLar NWea SEND SLPl SLon SPur STre WFar WMoo |
| | - 'Nancy Saunders' (f) | CTho CWiW CWon EHoe EPla GCal MBNS MBlu MBrN MRav NBir NLar NPro NSti SCoo WCot WIvy |
| I | - 'Nicholsonii Purpurascens' | CWon |
| | - 'Pendula' ♀H4 | CCVT CDul CEnd CWon EBee ECrN LRHS MAsh MBri MGos MSwo NPri NWea SBfd SPer SPoG WDin |
| | - 'Procumbens' | CWon |
| | - 'Read' (f) | CWiW |
| | - 'Reeks' (f) | CWiW CWon |
| | - 'Richartii' (f) | CWiW CWon |
| | - 'Uralensis' (f) | CWiW CWon |
| | ***pyrenaica*** | EWes WAbe |
| | ***pyrenaica*** × ***retusa*** | ECho |
| | ***pyrifolia*** | CWon NWea |
| | ***rehderiana*** | CWon |
| | ***reinii*** | CWon |
| | ***repens*** | EWTr GAuc NLar NWea SRms STre SWat WDin WGwG WKif |
| | - from Saint Kilda | GLam |
| § | - var. ***argentea*** | CWon ELan EPfP EWes GAuc LRHS MMuc MRav NWea SPer STre WDin WFar |
| | - 'Armando' PBR | NLar |
| | - 'Iona' (m) | NLar |
| | - ***pendula*** | see *S.* 'Boyd's Pendulous' (m) |
| | - 'Voorthuizen' (f) | ECho WDin |
| | ***reticulata*** ♀H4 | ECho EPot NBir NMen NSla WAbe |
| § | - subsp. ***nivalis*** | EPot NWCA |
| | ***retusa*** | CTri GAuc NBir |
| | ***retusa*** × ***serpyllifolia*** | NWCA |
| | 'Robin Redbreast' | CWon |
| | ***rosmarinifolia*** misapplied | see *S. elaeagnos* subsp. *angustifolia* |
| | × ***rubens*** 'Basfordiana' (m) | CDoC CDul CLnd CTho CWiW CWon EWes MBNS SWat WMou |
| | - 'Bouton Aigu' | CWiW CWon |
| | - 'Farndon' | CWiW |

- 'Farndon Red' CWon
- 'Flanders Red' (f) CWiW CWon
- 'Fransgeel Rood' (m) CWiW CWon
- 'Glaucescens' (m) CWiW CWon
- 'Golden Willow' CWiW CWon
- 'Hutchinson's Brown' CWon
- 'Jaune de Falaise' CWiW CWon
- 'Jaune Hâtive' CWiW
- 'Laurina' CWiW
- 'Natural Red' (f) CWiW CWon
- 'Parsons' CWiW CWon
- 'Rouge Ardennais' CWiW CWon
- 'Rouge Folle' CWiW
- 'Russet' (f) CWiW

**× *rubra*** CWiW
- 'Abbey's Harrison' (f) CWiW
- 'Continental Osier' (f) CWiW CWon
- 'Eugenei' (m) CDul CWon ECrN GQui MBlu SWat WIvy
- 'Fidkin' (f) CWiW CWon
- 'Harrison's' (f) CWiW CWon
- 'Harrison's Seedling A' (f) CWiW
- 'Mawdesley' CWiW CWon
- 'Mawdesley Seedling A' (f) CWiW
- 'Pyramidalis' CWiW CWon

***sachalinensis*** 'Kioryo' CWon
***salviifolia*** CWon
**× *savensis*** CWon
Scarlet Curls = 'Scarcuzam' CWon WPat
***schwerinii*** CWon
- 'Carin Ehrenberg' CWon
- 'Hilliers' CWon

***scouleriana*** CWon
**× *sepulcralis*** NWea
§ - 'Aokautere' CWiW CWon
- 'Caradoc' CWiW CWon

§ - var. ***chrysocoma*** Widely available
**× *sericans*** CWon
**× *seringeana*** CWon
***serissaefolia*** CWon
***serpyllifolia*** CTri NHar NMen WPat WThu
- 'Chamonix' **new** NSla

***serpyllum*** see *S. fragilis* var. *furcata*
'Setsuka' see *S. udensis* 'Sekka'
***silesiaca*** CWon
**× *simulatrix*** GAuc NWCA
***sitchensis*** NWea
**× *smithiana*** CLnd CWon NWea
**× *stipularis*** (f) NWea
'Stuartii' NMen SRms
***subfragilis*** GEdr
***subopposita*** CWon EBee EBtc ELan EWes MMuc WAbe WGwG
***thomasii*** GAuc
***triandra*** CWon WJPR WMou
- 'Black German' (m) CWiW
- 'Black Hollander' (m) CWiW CWon NLar WIvy
- 'Black Maul' CWiW
- 'Brilliant' CWon
- 'Champion B' CWon
- 'Grisette de Falaise' CWiW CWon
- 'Grisette Droda' (f) CWiW CWon
- var. ***hoffmanniana*** CWon
- 'Houghton's Black' CWon
- 'Light French' CWon
- 'Long Bud' CWiW
- 'Noir de Challans' CWiW CWon
- 'Noir de Touraine' CWiW CWon
- 'Noir de Villaines' (m) CWiW CWon WIvy
- 'Oliveacea' CWon
- 'Rouge d'Orléans' CWon EBtc
- 'Sarda d'Anjou' CWiW
- 'Semperflorens' (m) CWon NLar
- 'Whissander' CWiW CWon WIvy
- 'Zwarte Driebast' CWon

**× *tsugaluensis*** 'Ginme' (f) CWon ELPl
***udensis*** NWea
§ - 'Sekka' (m) CWon ELan EPPr EPfP LTen MBlu MMuc NBir NWea STre SWat WFar WIvy WMou
***uva-ursi*** WAbe
***viminalis*** CCVT CLnd CMac CWon ECrN EPfP LBuc NWea SEWo SVic WDin WJPR WMou WSFF
- 'Black Satin' CWon
- 'Brown Merrin' WIvy
- 'Gigantea' (m) CWon
- 'Green Gotz' CWiW WIvy
- 'Reader's Red' (m) WIvy
- 'Regalis' CWon
- 'Riefenweide' WIvy
- 'Romanin' CWon
- 'Suffolk Osier' **new** CWon
- 'Yellow Osier' WIvy

***vitellina*** 'Pendula' see *S. alba* 'Tristis' ambig.
***waldsteiniana*** CWon GAuc NWCA
**× *wimmeriana*** SRms
'Yelverton' see *S. alba var. vitellina* 'Yelverton'

## *Salsola* (*Amaranthaceae*)

***soda*** CArn ELau

## *Salvia* ✿ (*Lamiaceae*)

sp. CHab
ACE 2172 SPin
CC 6306 GKev
CD&R 1141 SPin
CD&R 1162 CAby EPyc SPhx
CD&R 1458 SPin
CD&R 1495 SPin
CD&R 3071 SPin
PC&H 226 SPin
***acetabulosa*** see *S. multicaulis*
***adenophora*** SPin XSen
***aerea*** CPom
***aethiopis*** EWes SDix SPav SPin XSen
§ ***africana*** EPyc SPin WDyG WHil XSen
***africana-caerulea*** see *S. africana*
***africana-lutea*** see *S. aurea*
***agnes*** EPyc SPin
***algeriensis*** CSpe SBch
'Allen Chickering' XSen
***amarissima*** SPin XSen
'Amber' LHop SBrt SPin SUsu XSen
***ambigens*** see *S. guaranitica* 'Blue Enigma'
***ampelophylla*** B&SWJ 10751 SPin WCru
§ ***amplexicaulis*** EPyc MWea NLar SMrm SPin WPer XSen
***amplifrons*** SPin
***angustifolia*** Cav. see *S. reptans*
***angustifolia*** Mich. see *S. azurea*
'Anthony Parker' MAJR SAga SDys WOut XSen
***apiana*** CArn EOHP EPyc MHer SAga SGar SPin WHfH XSen
***arenaria*** SPin
***argentea*** ♀H3 CArn CBcs CSpe EBee EBla ECha ECtt ELan EPfP GMaP

| | |
|---|---|
| | LRHS MSpe SBfd SBrd SGar SMad SPav SPer SPin SWat WCAu WFar WJek WKif WMnd WWEG XLum XSen |
| ***arizonica*** | CFir EPyc GCal LHop MAsh SDys SPin XSen |
| ***aspera*** | SPin XSen |
| ***atrocyanea*** | CAby CSpe EPyc EWes EWld MAJR MAsh SDys SGar SPin WCot WHal WKif WWlt XSen |
| § ***aurea*** | CHll CSev CSpe EShb SAga SBch SGar SPin SPlb SVen XLum XSen |
| - 'Kirstenbosch' | CAby CDes CSev EBee ECtt EPyc EWld GBin SDys SGar SPin WGwG WKif WPGP WPer XSen |
| ***aurita*** | SPin |
| - var. ***galpinii*** | SPin XSen |
| ***austriaca*** | SPin XSen |
| § ***azurea*** | CRWN EPyc LRHS SMrm SPin WWlt XSen |
| - var. ***grandiflora*** | SPin |
| ***bacheriana*** | see *S. buchananii* |
| § ***barrelieri*** | SPin SUsu XSen |
| 'Bee's Bliss' | XSen |
| 'Belhaven' | EWld GCal SPin |
| ***bertolonii*** | see *S. pratensis* Bertolonii Group |
| ***bicolor*** | see *S. barrelieri* |
| 'Black Knight' | CDes CWGN EPyc SDys SPin WPGP |
| ***blancoana*** | CBot CMea ECha ELau EPyc MCot MHer SDys SPin |
| ***blepharophylla*** | ECtt EGHP EPyc EShb LHop MCot MHer MSCN NDov SPav SPin SPoG SRkn WAle XSen |
| - 'Diablo' | ECtt SAga SDys SPin |
| - 'Painted Lady' | CWGN MAsh SDys SPin WWlt |
| 'Blue Chiquita' | CWGN SDys SPin |
| 'Blue Sky' | EWld |
| ***bracteata*** | SPin XSen |
| ***brandegeei*** | SPin |
| ***broussonetii*** | SPin XSen |
| § ***buchananii*** ♀H1+3 | CHll CSam EBee ECtt EGHP EPyc EShb LHop MAsh MHer MLLN MRav NDov SAga SPav SPin SPoG SRkn SWal WFar XSen |
| ***bulleyana*** misapplied | see *S. flava* var. *megalantha* |
| ***bulleyana*** Diels | CPLG CSev EWes EWld GKev LEdu MDKP MMHG MNrw WCru WFar XSen |
| ***cacaliifolia*** ♀H1+3 | CPLG CRHN ECtt EGHP EPyc EWld GCal MAsh MHer MSCN SBch SGar SPer SPin SRkn WSHC WWlt XSen |
| ***cadmica*** | SPin WHil |
| ***caerulea*** misapplied | see *S. guaranitica* 'Black and Blue' |
| ***caerulea*** L. | see *S. africana* |
| ***caespitosa*** | NMen SPin XSen |
| ***campanulata*** | CPom CPou EWld SPin |
| - B&SWJ 9232 | WCru |
| - DJHC C394 | SPin |
| - GWJ 9294 | SPin WCru |
| - aff. var. ***hirtella*** GWJ 9397 **new** | WCru |
| ***canariensis*** | CSpe EShb IDee SPin WOut XSen |
| - f. ***albiflora*** | XSen |
| - f. ***candidissima*** | SPin XSen |
| ***candelabrum*** ♀H3-4 | CAbP CArn CSev CSpe EWes MHer SAga SBch SPav SPin WKif WWlt XSen |
| ***candidissima*** | XSen |
| ***canescens*** | XSen |
| ***cardinalis*** | see *S. fulgens* |
| ***carduacea*** | SPin |
| ***carnea*** | EWld MHom SPin |
| - from Valle de Bravo, Mexico | EPyc SDys |
| ***castanea*** | LRHS SPin |
| ***caudata*** | SPin XSen |
| ***cedrosensis*** | SDys |
| § ***chamaedryoides*** | CPBP CSev CWGN EGHP EPyc MHom NDov SDys SGar SPet SPhx SPin WPGP XLum XSen |
| - var. ***isochroma*** | EPyc IRar MAsh SDys SGar SPin XSen |
| - 'Marine Blue' | MAsh MCot SDys SPin |
| - silver-leaved | CSpe NDov SPin WHil XLum |
| aff. ***chamaedryoides*** B&SWJ 9032 from Guatemala | SPin WCru |
| ***chamelaeagnea*** | EPyc GFai SDys SPin XSen |
| ***chapalensis*** | MAJR SPin WWlt |
| ***chiapensis*** | MAJR MAsh SDys SPin WWlt XSen |
| ***chinensis*** | see *S. japonica* |
| ***chionophylla*** | SPin |
| 'Christine Yeo' | CAby EBee ECtt EGHP ELon EPfP EPri EPyc EWld GGar MAsh MDKP MSpe SAga SBch SDys SEND SGar SPin SUsu SWal WHil WHoo WMnd WPGP XSen |
| ***cinnabarina*** | SPin |
| ***cleistogama*** misapplied | see *S. glutinosa* |
| ***clevelandii*** | EWes MHer SPav SPin WJek XSen |
| - 'Winnifred Gilman' | CWGN SDys |
| ***clinopodioides*** | SPin |
| ***coahuilensis*** misapplied | see *S. greggii* × *serpyllifolia* |
| ***coahuilensis*** ambig. | CAby EPyc EShb LSou MAsh MAvo SGar SKHP SMrm SPin SRkn WSHC XLum |
| ***coahuilensis*** Fernald | LHop LRHS |
| ***coccinea*** | CBot SPin |
| - 'Brenthurst' | SDys SPin |
| - 'Coral Nymph' (Nymph Series) | ECtt EPyc SDys SPav SPin |
| - 'Forest Fire' | EPyc SDys |
| - 'Lactea' | CBot |
| - 'Lady in Red' (Nymph Series) ♀H3 | ECtt SDys SPav |
| * - 'Snow Nymph' (Nymph Series) | ECtt EPyc |
| ***columbariae*** | SPin |
| ***concolor*** misapplied | see *S. guaranitica* |
| ***concolor*** Lamb. ex Benth. | CDes EPyc EWld GCal GGar MHom SPin WPGP WSHC XSen |
| ***confertiflora*** | Widely available |
| ***corrugata*** | CBcs CDes CFir CPne CRHN CSpe EBee ECtt EPyc EShb EWld GCal LRHS MAsh MHer SAga SDys SPin SRkn SWal WAle WPGP WWlt XSen |
| 'Crème Caramel' | CWGN ECtt EPyc MAsh MHom SDys |
| ***cruickshanksii*** | SPin |
| aff. ***curtiflora*** B&SWJ 10356 | WCru |
| ***curviflora*** | EPyc SDys SPin XSen |

| | | |
|---|---|---|
| | ***cyanescens*** | CMea CPBP EPot EPyc SBch SPin XSen |
| | ***cyanicalyx*** | EPyc SDys SPin XSen |
| | ***cyclostegia*** | CPLG |
| | ***daghestanica*** | SDys SPin XSen |
| | 'Dale Blue' | EWld |
| I | ***[illegible]*** SDR 4332 | CPLG EBee |
| | ***darcyi*** misapplied | see *S. roemeriana* |
| | ***darcyi*** J. Compton | CAby CHll CPLG CSpe EPyc EWes EWld MCot SDys SPin WHil WSHC WWlt XSen |
| | ***davidsonii*** | SPin |
| | 'Dear Anja' | see *S.* × *sylvestris* 'Dear Anja' |
| | ***decumbens*** | SPin |
| | ***dentata*** | SDys SPin XSen |
| | ***desoleana*** | SPin WHil XSen |
| | 'Didi' | NDov |
| | ***digitaloides*** | XSen |
| | - BWJ 7777 | SPin WCru |
| | 'Dinah' **new** | SUsu |
| | ***discolor*** ♀H1 | CBot CFir CPne CSev CSpe ECtt ELan EPyc ERea EWld GCal MAsh MCot MHer MLLN SAga SDys SEND SPet SPin SUsu SWal WWlt XSen |
| * | - ***nigra*** | CArn CCse |
| | ***disermas*** | SDys SPin SPlb XSen |
| | - pink-flowered | SPin |
| | ***disjuncta*** | SPin XSen |
| | - 'Chimbango' | SDys |
| | ***divinorum*** | EOHP GPoy LEdu WHfH XSen |
| | ***dolichantha*** | CCVN CFir EBee EPyc LRHS MCot MDKP MMuc NBir NLar SEND SPin WHer WMoo WPtf |
| | - pale blue/white-flowered | SEND |
| | ***dolomitica*** | SPav SPin |
| | ***dombeyi*** | CAby CHll CPne EPyc EWld SDys SPin |
| | ***dominica*** | CArn SPin XSen |
| | ***dorisiana*** | EOHP MAsh SDys SPin SVen XSen |
| | ***dorrii*** | XSen |
| | 'Dorset Wonder' **new** | NDov |
| | 'Dyson's Crimson' **new** | SDys |
| | ***eigii*** | SPin XSen |
| | ***eizi-matudae*** | EPyc SPin |
| | ***elegans*** | ELau EWes GCra MAJR MHom SAga XSen |
| | - 'Golden Delicious' | CWGN ECtt EWes LSou MHer MNHC SBfd SPin WHer WWlt |
| | - 'Honey Melon' | CAby CHVG EGHP EPyc MAsh SDys SUsu |
| § | - 'Scarlet Pineapple' | Widely available |
| | - 'Sonoran Red' | CAby SDys |
| | - 'Tangerine' | CArn CPrp CWan EGHP ELau EOHP EPyc LSou MHer MNHC MSpe NLBP SBfd SPin SWal WGwG WJek |
| | ***evansiana*** | XSen |
| | - BWJ 8013 | SPin |
| | 'Eveline' | CSev CWGN ECtt LRHS NCGa NLar |
| | ***excelsa*** | SPin XSen |
| | 'Fairy Tale' | CWGN |
| | ***fallax*** | SPin XSen |
| | ***farinacea*** | EPfP SPin WHil |
| | - 'Azul' **new** | WHil |
| | - 'Strata' | SDys |
| | - 'Victoria' ♀H3 | LRHS SDys SGar WHrl |

| | | |
|---|---|---|
| § | ***flava*** var. ***megalantha*** | ELan LEdu LSRN SPin XSen |
| | - - BWJ 7974 | WCru |
| | ***florida*** | SPin XSen |
| | ***forreri*** | EBee EPyc MAsh NDov SBHP SDys SEND SPin WPGP XSen |
| | - 'Karen Dyson' | SDys |
| § | ***forsskaolii*** | Widely available |
| | - white-flowered | SPin |
| § | ***fruticosa*** | CArn ELau EPyc LRHS SIde SLon SPin XSen |
| § | ***fulgens*** ♀H3 | EGHP EPyc EWld ILis MAsh SAga SBHP SGar SPin SRkn WFar WWlt XSen |
| | ***gesneriiflora*** | ECtt EPyc EWld SDys SGar SPin XSen |
| | - 'Tequila' | MAJR SPin WWlt |
| | ***gilliesii*** | SPin |
| | ***glabrescens*** | SPin |
| | - B&SWJ 11152 | WCru |
| * | - var. ***robusta*** B&SWJ 11147 | WCru |
| | ***glechomifolia*** | SPin XSen |
| § | ***glutinosa*** | CArn CMac CSpe EBee EPyc EWld GCal GMac LRHS MCot MNrw NBro SAga SPav SPin SWal WCAu WCot WPer WTcb XSen |
| | ***graciliramulosa*** | SPin XSen |
| | ***gracilis*** | SPin |
| | ***grahamii*** | see *S. microphylla* var. *microphylla* |
| | ***gravida*** | SPin |
| | 'Great Comp' **new** | SDys |
| | ***greggii*** | ECtt EGHP EPyc EWes LRHS MHer WPer WTcb XLum XSen |
| | - CD&R 1148 | MCot SDys |
| | - 'Alba' | EGHP EPyc MHer SAga SDys SPin WHil XLum XSen |
| | - 'Blush Pink' | see *S. microphylla* 'Pink Blush' |
| | - 'Caramba' (v) | EBee EGHP EPyc LHop LRHS SAga SPet WHil |
| | - 'Devon Cream' | see *S. greggii* 'Sungold' |
| | - 'Icing Sugar' | CCVN ECtt EPPr EPyc LRHS MAsh MCot MTis NCGa NDov NPri SPet SPoG SRkn SUsu WBor WHil WPer |
| | - 'Lipstick' | CPLG ECtt MAsh |
| | - 'Magenta' | WHil |
| | - 'Magnet' | SPin |
| | - (Navajo Series) 'Navajo Bright Red' | EPyc |
| * | - - 'Navajo Cream' | EPyc |
| * | - - 'Navajo Dark Purple' | EPyc SAga |
| | - - Navajo Pink = 'Rfds019' | SVen |
| * | - - 'Navajo Purple' | EPyc MCot |
| | - - Navajo Salmon Red = 'Rfds016' | EPyc |
| * | - - 'Navajo White' | EPyc |
| | - 'Peach' misapplied | see *S.* × *jamensis* 'Pat Vlasto' |
| | - 'Peach' | CWGN EGHP ELau EPfP EPyc MAsh MHer SAga SEND SGar SPet SPoG WMnd WPGP WWlt XLum XSen |
| | - 'Pink Preference' | MAsh |
| | - 'Raspberry Red' | MCot XLum |
| | - 'Sierra San Antonio' | see *S.* × *jamensis* 'Sierra San Antonio' |
| | - 'Sparkler' (v) | EPfP LRHS MAsh SLon SPoG |
| | - 'Stormy Pink' | CDes CHll CSam CSpe CWGN EPyc LRHS MAsh MCot MSpe |

| | | |
|---|---|---|
| | | NDov SAga SUsu WIvy WPGP WSHC WWlt XSen |
| § | – 'Sungold' | CWGN ECtt EGHP EPfP EPyc EShb LRHS MAsh NDov SDys SHom SPin SSvw SUsu WHil WMnd WWlt XSen |
| | – variegated (v) | EHoe XSen |
| | – yellow-flowered | XLum |
| | ***greggii* × *lycioides*** | see *S. greggii* × *serpyllifolia* |
| § | ***greggii* × *serpyllifolia*** | CAbP CSpe EPyc MAsh MCot NDov NPri SDys SGar SPin WPGP |
| | ***grewiifolia*** | SPin |
| § | ***guaranitica*** | CBcs CBot CEnt CHEx ECtt EShb EWld GQui LRHS MHer SAga SDys SPav SPer SPin SWal WKif WPGP WWlt XLum XSen |
| | – 'Argentina Skies' | CHGN CSpe EPPr EPyc MSpe SAga SDys SMrm SPin WWlt XSen |
| § | – 'Black and Blue' | Widely available |
| § | – 'Blue Enigma' 𝕐H3-4 | Widely available |
| | – 'Brazil' **new** | LRHS |
| | – 'Indigo Blue' | ECtt EPfP MAsh SPin WWlt |
| | – 'Purple Splendor' | EShb EWld MHer |
| | – purple-flowered | CSam |
| | ***haematodes*** | see *S. pratensis* Haematodes Group |
| | ***haenkei*** | SPin XSen |
| | – 'Prawn Chorus' | CSpe CWGN LRHS MAJR MAsh SPin WWlt |
| | ***heerii*** | SPin |
| | ***heldreichiana*** | SPin XSen |
| | ***henryi*** | SPin |
| | ***hians*** | CPLG CPom EBee GCra MDKP NLar SBfd SGar SPav SPin SRms WPer XLum |
| | – CC 1787 | CPLG |
| | ***hierosolymitana*** | CHid LRHS XSen |
| | ***hirtella*** | SPin |
| | ***hispanica*** misapplied | see *S. lavandulifolia* |
| | ***hispanica*** L. | CSam SPin |
| | ***holwayi*** | SPin XSen |
| | – B&SWJ 8995 | WCru |
| | ***horminum*** | see *S. viridis* var. *comata* |
| | ***huberi*** | XSen |
| | 'Huntsman's Red' | IRar |
| | ***inconspicua*** | SPin |
| | ***indica*** | SPin XSen |
| | 'Indigo Spires' | CHll CMHG CPLG CSpe CWGN ECre ECtt EPyc EShb EWld MAsh MCot MHom NDov SAga SDys SMrm SPhx SPin SUsu WSHC WWlt XLum XSen |
| | ***interrupta*** | MCot MHer SAga SPin XSen |
| | ***involucrata*** 𝕐H3 | CFir CPom CSev CSpe EPyc GCra MCot MHom NBro SDys SPin SVen WHrl WSHC XSen |
| | – 'Bethellii' 𝕐H3-4 | CArn CBot CMHG CPne CSev EBee ECtt ELan EPfP EPyc EShb LRHS MAsh MHer SAga SDix SGar SKHP SMrm SPav SPin SRkn WKif WWlt XLum XSen |
| | – 'Boutin' 𝕐H3 | EPyc MAJR MAsh MHom SAga SDys WWlt |
| § | – 'Hadspen' | CBot CDes CFir CHll CRHN CSam CSpe EWes GCal MAJR SPin XLum XSen |
| | – 'Joan' | CWGN EPyc MAsh SDys SPin SUsu WWlt |
| | – 'Mrs Pope' | see *S. involucrata* 'Hadspen' |
| * | – var. ***puberula*** | MAJR MHom SPin XSen |
| | ***iodantha*** | SDys SPin |
| | – 'Louis Saso' | SPin |
| | ***iodochroa*** | EBee |
| | – B&SWJ 10252 | CDes SPin WCru WPGP |
| | × ***jamensis*** | CWGN EBee ELau EWes MWea NPri SDys SPin |
| | – 'California Sunset' | EWld MAsh SUsu |
| | – 'Cherry Queen' | CSpe CWGN EBee EPyc MAsh SAga SDys SPin WWlt XSen |
| | – 'Dark Dancer' | CAby CSpe CWGN MAsh SDys SPhx WWlt XSen |
| | – 'Desert Blaze' (v) | CAbP CDes CWGN ECtt EGHP EPyc LBuc LRHS MCot MHer NCGa SDys SMrm SPin WCot WGrn WPGP WTcb WWlt XLum |
| | – 'Devantville' | NDov XLum |
| | – 'Dysons' Orangy Pink' | CSpe NDov SAga |
| | – 'El Durazno' | WTcb |
| § | – 'Hot Lips' | Widely available |
| | – 'James Compton' | EPyc SDys SMrm |
| | – 'Kentish Pink' **new** | SDys |
| | – 'La Luna' | CDes CEnt CPom CSam ECtt EPfP EPyc LHop MAsh MCot MHer MHom MSCN NDov SDys SGar SPin SUsu WIvy WMnd WPGP WPer WSHC WTcb XLum XSen |
| | – 'La Siesta' | EBee EGHP EPyc SAga SDys WTcb XSen |
| | – 'La Tarde' | CEnt CTri EGHP EPyc MAsh MHom SBch WTcb WWlt XSen |
| | – 'Los Lirios' 𝕐H3-4 | CPom CSpe CTri EPyc SAga SMrm SPin WIvy WWlt |
| | – 'Maraschino' | CAby EBee EPfP EPyc LRHS MAsh SDys SPin WHil WMnd WWlt XLum XSen |
| * | – 'Mauve' | EPyc NDov |
| | – 'Moonlight Over Ashwood' (v) | EPyc MAsh SBHP SPin WSHC WWlt |
| | – 'Moonlight Serenade' | CAby EPyc MAsh MWea SAga SBch SDys |
| § | – 'Pat Vlasto' | EPyc MWea SDys SPin |
| | – 'Peter Vidgeon' | CWGN EPyc SDys SPin SUsu WWlt |
| | – 'Pleasant Pink' | CSev EPyc MAsh SPin XSen |
| | – 'Plum Wine' | WWlt |
| | – 'Raspberry Royale' 𝕐H3-4 | CAby CDes CPom CSev CWGN EBee ECtt EGHP EPfP EPyc LHop LRHS MAsh MCot MHer MLLN SEND SGar SMrm SPav SPin WIvy WMnd WSHC WTcb XSen |
| | – 'Red Velvet' | CAby CSpe ECtt EGHP ELon EPyc EWld MAsh MHom SUsu WHrl WSHC WWlt XSen |
| | – 'Señorita Leah' | CWGN EPyc MAsh SDys SUsu |
| § | – 'Sierra San Antonio' | CDes CWGN EPfP EPyc LRHS MAsh MHom MWea NDov SAga SBHP SDys SMrm SUsu WPGP WTcb XLum XSen |
| | – 'Stormy Sunrise' **new** | SDys |
| § | – 'Trebah' | CPom CSpe ECre EPyc EShb MAsh MCot MHom MWea SDys SGar SMrm SPin SPoG SRot WHil WIvy WPGP WSHC WWlt XSen |
| | – 'Trenance' | CSpe ECre EPyc LHop MAvo MHom SAga SBch SDys SGar SPin SRot WHil WIvy WWlt XSen |
| | – white-flowered | SPin |
| § | ***japonica*** | SPin XSen |

| | | |
|---|---|---|
| | - 'Alba' | SPin |
| | 'Jean's Purple Passion' | EPyc SDys SPin |
| | ***judaica*** | CMac SPin WGrn |
| | ***jurisicii*** | CWib EBee EPyc LRHS MAsh SBrt SEND SGar SPav SPin WJek WSHC XLum XSen |
| | 'Alba' | XSen |
| | - pink-flowered | CSpe SPin XSen |
| | ***karwinskyi*** | SPin XSen |
| | - B&SWJ 9081 | WCru |
| | ***keerlii*** | SPin XSen |
| | ***koyamae*** | LRHS SPin |
| | - B&SWJ 10919 | WCru |
| | 'Lady Strybing' | SPin |
| | ***lanceolata*** | CSpe SPin WWlt XSen |
| | ***lanigera*** | SPin |
| | 'Lararsha' new | SDys |
| | ***lasiantha*** | SPin XSen |
| § | ***lavandulifolia*** | CArn EBee ECha ECho EGHP ELan ELau EPfP EWes GGar GPoy LRHS MAsh MHer MLHP MNHC MRav SBrd SIde SMrm SPer SPin WGwG WHoo WJek WKif WPer WWlt XLum XSen |
| | ***lavanduloides*** | SPin |
| | - B&SWJ 9053 | WCru |
| | ***lemmonii*** | see *S. microphylla* var. *wislizeni* |
| | ***leptophylla*** | see *S. reptans* |
| | ***leucantha*** ♀H1 | CArn CPne CSev CSpe ELan EPyc EShb MAsh MCot MHer MRav MSCN SAga SBrd SDys SEND SPav SPin SPlb SRkn SVen SWal WCot WTcb XSen |
| | - 'Eder' (v) | MAJR MAsh SDys SPin |
| | - 'Midnight' | CSam EShb IFoB SDys |
| | - 'Purple Velvet' | ECtt EGHP EPyc GGar MAJR MAsh MHer MHom SDix SDys SPin SUsu WWlt XSen |
| | - 'San Marcos Lavender' | CSev SPin |
| | - 'Santa Barbara' | CHll CWGN LRHS MAsh SDys XSen |
| | ***leucocephala*** | CSev SGar SPin XSen |
| | ***leucophylla*** | XSen |
| | - NNS 01-375 | SPin WCot |
| | ***littae*** | SPin XSen |
| | ***longispicata*** | SPin |
| | ***longistyla*** | SPin WPGP XSen |
| * | ***luzentzii*** F&W 11499 | IFoB |
| | ***lycioides*** misapplied | see *S. greggii* × *serpyllifolia* |
| | ***lycioides*** A. Gray | CAbP CHll LRHS SEND SPhx SPin |
| | ***lyrata*** | EOHP SGar SPin XSen |
| | - 'Burgundy Bliss' | see *S. lyrata* 'Purple Knockout' |
| § | - 'Purple Knockout' | EBee EGHP EPfP EPyc LAst NLBP SBfd SGar SMrm SPhx SPin WHer WPtf XSen |
| | - 'Purple Vulcano' | see *S. lyrata* 'Purple Knockout' |
| | ***macellaria*** misapplied | see *S. microphylla* |
| | ***macellaria*** Epling | CSam |
| | ***macrophylla*** | GCal MLLN SPin WPGP XSen |
| | - Cally selection new | SPin |
| | - 'Wendy's Surprise' new | WWlt |
| | ***macrosiphon*** | SPin |
| | 'Madeline' new | LSou |
| | ***madrensis*** | EPyc SPin XSen |
| | - 'Dunham' | GCal SDys WWlt |
| | 'Magic Potion' | CWGN |
| | ***melissodora*** | SPin |
| | ***mellifera*** | CArn SPin XSen |
| | ***merjamie*** 'Mint-sauce' | LRHS WFar |
| | ***mexicana*** | SPin |
| | - B&SWJ 10288 | WCru |
| | - T&K 550 | CBot |
| | - 'Lollie Jackson' | MAJR WWlt |
| | - var. ***mexicana*** | XSen |
| | - var. ***minor*** | EPyc EWld MAJR SDys SPin |
| | - 'Snowflake' | MAJR XSen |
| | - 'Tula' | SDys |
| | ***meyeri*** | CPom EPyc EWld MAJR MHom SPin WWlt |
| § | ***microphylla*** | CArn CChe CMHG CMac CPom CPrp CTri CWan ELau EOHP EWes LAst LHop MAvo MHer MSCN NSti SPet SVen WPer XLum |
| | - CD&R 1141 | SPin |
| | - F&M 157 | WPGP |
| | - 'Belize' | EGHP MAsh MSpe NDov SUsu WHil WWlt |
| | - 'Cerro Potosi' | CCse CPom CSev CSpe EGHP ELon EPyc LRHS MAsh SAga SDys SGar SMrm SPin SUsu WCFE WIvy WWlt XLum |
| | - 'Hot Lips' | see *S.* × *jamensis* 'Hot Lips' |
| | - 'Huntington' | EOHP EPyc SPin XSen |
| | - hybrid, purple-flowered | CPom |
| | - 'Kew Red' ♀H3-4 | CFir CHVG EGHP EWld MNrw MWea SBch SPin WHil WHoo WPGP |
| | - 'La Trinidad' | XSen |
| I | - 'Lutea' | MAsh SUsu |
| | - 'Maroon' | CSpe CWGN EPyc SDys SUsu |
| § | - var. ***microphylla*** | Widely available |
| | - - 'La Foux' | EPyc MCot MWea SBch SDys SMrm SPhx SPoG XLum XSen |
| | - - 'Newby Hall' ♀H3-4 | CAby CDes CPom ECtt EGHP EPyc EShb EWes MWea SDys SPhx WPGP XSen |
| N | - var. ***neurepia*** | see *S. microphylla* var. *microphylla* |
| | - 'Orange Door' | EPyc SDys XSen |
| | - 'Oregon Peach' | EPfP LRHS |
| | - 'Oxford' | EGHP SPin |
| § | - 'Pink Blush' ♀H3-4 | CAby CBot EBee ECtt EGHP ELan EPfP EPyc LRHS MAsh MCot MHer MHom SEND SMrm SPin SRkn WHil WIvy WKif WPGP WPer WSHC WTcb WWlt XSen |
| | - 'Pleasant View' ♀H3-4 | EPyc WWlt XSen |
| | - 'Robin's Pride' | EPyc SDys SUsu |
| | - 'Rodbaston Current Purple' | MSpe |
| | - 'Rodbaston Red' new | WWlt |
| § | - 'Ruth Stungo' (v) | ECre IRar |
| | - 'San Carlos Festival' | CDes CPom EGHP EPyc MAsh NCGa SBch SDys SPhx SPin SUsu WPGP WWlt XSen |
| | - 'Trelawny Rose Pink' | see *S.* 'Trelawney' |
| | - 'Trelissick Creamy Yellow' | see *S.* 'Trelissick' |
| | - 'Trewithen Cerise' | see *S.* 'Trewithen' |
| | - 'Variegata' splashed | see *S. microphylla* 'Ruth Stungo' |
| | - 'Violette' | EPfP EPyc |
| | - 'Wild Watermelon' | CAby CWGN EPfP EPyc MAsh SAga SDys WWlt XSen |
| § | - var. ***wislizeni*** | CPom EPyc SPin |
| | - 'Zaragoza' | SPin |
| | ***microstegia*** | XSen |
| | ***miltiorhiza*** | CArn CSpe SPin XSen |
| | ***miniata*** | CSev CSpe EPyc MAJR SBHP SDys SPin XSen |

| | | |
|---|---|---|
| | ***misella*** | CSpe SPin |
| | ***mohavensis*** | SPin |
| | ***moorcroftiana*** | EPyc |
| | ***moschata*** | SPin |
| | 'Mrs Beard' | XSen |
| | ***muelleri*** misapplied | see *S. greggii* × *serpyllifolia* |
| | ***muelleri*** Epling | EBee EPyc |
| | ***muirii*** | SPin |
| | 'Mulberry Jam' | Widely available |
| § | ***multicaulis*** ♀H4 | EPyc MAsh SPin XSen |
| | ***munzii*** | CFir SPin XSen |
| * | ***murrayi*** | CAbP SPin |
| | Mystic Spires Blue = 'Balsalmisp'PBR | CSpe CWGN EPyc |
| | ***namaensis*** | CSev SGar SPin WHil XSen |
| | ***nana*** B&SWJ 10272 | SPin WCru WHil |
| | ***napifolia*** | EBee LRHS NLar SAga SPav SPhx SPin XSen |
| | - 'Baby Blue' **new** | LRHS |
| | 'Nazareth' | MAsh SPin XSen |
| | 'Nel' | LHop MAvo |
| | ***nemorosa*** | EPyc LRHS SPin SRms XLum XSen |
| | - 'Amethyst' ♀H4 | CHar EBee ELon EPfP GBBs IKil LAst LRHS MLLN MRav NDov SDys SMrm SPhx WCAu WCot WKif WWEG WWlt |
| | - 'Blaureiter' **new** | LRHS |
| | - Blue Mound | see *S.* × *sylvestris* 'Blauhügel' |
| | - 'Caradonna' | Widely available |
| | - East Friesland | see *S. nemorosa* 'Ostfriesland' |
| | - 'Indigo Friesland' **new** | LRHS |
| | - 'Kleine Amethyst' | NDov |
| | - 'Lubecca' ♀H4 | EBee ECtt ETod GQue LHop LRHS MCot MSpe NDov NEgg NGdn NLar SPer WFar WMnd WWEG XSen |
| | - Marcus = 'Haeumanarc'PBR | EBee ECtt ELan EPfP EPyc LAst LBMP LRHS LSRN LSou MBNS MBri NBPC NDov NLar SBfd SDys WFar WSHC |
| | - 'Midsummer' | EWld |
| § | - 'Ostfriesland' ♀H4 | Widely available |
| | - 'Phoenix Pink' | SPhx |
| | - 'Pink Beauty' | MWat |
| | - 'Pink Friesland'PBR | EBee ECtt EPPr GQue LRHS LSou MGos NDov NPri |
| | - 'Plumosa' | see *S. nemorosa* 'Pusztaflamme' |
| | - 'Porzellan' ♀H4 | ECtt |
| § | - 'Pusztaflamme' ♀H4 | EBee ECha ECtt EPPr EPfP GQue LRHS LSou MSpe NOrc SPoG SUsu WCAu WWEG |
| | - 'Rose Queen' | ECtt LAst MWat NBir SDys SPer SWat WCot WFar XLum XSen |
| | - 'Rosenwein' | CAby EBee LRHS MDKP MNrw NBPC NGdn SMrm SPhx XSen |
| | - 'Royal Distinction' | EBee ECtt |
| | - 'Schneekönig' | LSou |
| | - 'Schwellenburg' | EBee ECtt LHop LRHS LSou NBPC NLar SPad SUsu WCot |
| I | -(Sensation Series) 'Sensation Blue Improved' **new** | LRHS |
| | - - 'Sensation Blue' **new** | IPot |
| I | - - 'Sensation Deep Rose Improved' **new** | LRHS |
| | - - 'Sensation Rose' | CCVN CWGN EBee GBin LLHF LRHS LSou MAsh NDov WCot |
| | - - 'Sensation Sky Blue' **new** | LRHS |
| | - - 'Sensation White' **new** | CSev CWGN |
| § | - subsp. ***tesquicola*** | ECha EPyc LSRN MNFA MWhi NBPC NGdn NLar SMrm SPhx WFar |
| | - 'Wesuwe' | EBee ELon EPPr ETod NDov |
| | ***neurepia*** | see *S. microphylla* var. *microphylla* |
| * | ***nevadensis*** **new** | SPin |
| | 'Newe Ya'ar' | EPfP LRHS |
| | ***nilotica*** | LRHS SPin XSen |
| | ***nipponica*** B&SWJ 5829 | SPin WCru |
| | - 'Fuji Snow' (v) | EPyc |
| | - var. ***trisecta*** | SPin |
| | ***nubicola*** | CPLG GPoy SPin WHil XSen |
| | - BWJ 7639 | WCru |
| | - CC 4607 | EBee |
| | - CC 4762 | NLar |
| | ***nutans*** | SPin XSen |
| | ***oblongifolia*** B&SWJ 10315 | WCru |
| | ***officinalis*** | Widely available |
| | - 'Albiflora' | CArn CBod CBot ECtt EOHP SPin WJek XSen |
| N | - 'Aurea' ambig. | CWib GPoy |
| | - 'Berggarten' | CArn CPrp EBee ECha ELau EPfP GCal LEdu LHop MCot MHer MRav SDix SPhx SPin WHer WJek WMnd XLum XSen |
| § | - broad-leaved | CBot ELau EWhm MHer SWat WJek |
| | - 'Crispa' | EOHP SPin XSen |
| | - 'Extrakta' | EWhm SPhx |
| | - 'Grete Stolze' | SEND |
| | - 'Growers Friend' | LBMP |
| § | - 'Icterina' (v) ♀H4 | Widely available |
| | - 'Kew Gold' | MRav |
| | - ***latifolia*** | see *S. officinalis* broad-leaved |
| | - narrow-leaved | see *S. lavandulifolia* |
| | - 'Nazareth'PBR | ELau WJek XSen |
| | - ***prostrata*** | see *S. lavandulifolia* |
| | - 'Purpurascens' ♀H4 | Widely available |
| | - 'Robin Hill' | ECtt EWhm GQue LSou NBre NDov |
| | - 'Rosea' | CArn EOHP WJek XSen |
| | - 'Tricolor' (v) | Widely available |
| | - 'Variegata' | see *S. officinalis* 'Icterina' |
| | - variegated (v) | ECho MHer |
| | ***ombrophila*** | SPin |
| | ***omeiana*** BWJ 8062 | SPin WCru WFar |
| | - 'Crûg Thundercloud' | WCru |
| | ***oppositiflora*** misapplied | see *S. tubiflora* |
| | ***oppositiflora*** ambig. | EPyc MAJR SAga SDys SPin XSen |
| | ***orbignaei*** | SPin XSen |
| | ***oxyphora*** | EPyc SDys SPin XSen |
| | ***pachyphylla*** | SPin XSen |
| | ***palaestina*** | XSen |
| § | ***patens*** ♀H3 | Widely available |
| | - 'Alba' misapplied | see *S. patens* 'White Trophy' |
| | - 'Blue Angel' | EWes IFoB MSwo SPad SPet WIvy WWEG |
| | - 'Cambridge Blue' ♀H3 | Widely available |
| | - 'Chilcombe' | CSam ECtt EPyc MCot MHer MSpe SDys SPin WIvy WOut WWlt XSen |
| | - 'Dot's Delight' | CPLG CSpe CWGN ECtt EGHP EPyc EWes LHop LRHS MAsh NCGa NPri SAga SBch SHar SMrm SPin SRkn SUsu WHoo |
| | - 'Guanajuato' | CBcs CPLG CSam CSpe EBee ECtt EGHP EPyc EWes IFoB MAsh MHer MLLN NLar NPri SBfd SDys SMad SMrm SPin SRkn |

| | |
|---|---|
| | SRot WCot WHil WHoo WSHC WWlt |
| - large | CSpe SUsu |
| - lavender-flowered | MLLN SBch |
| - light blue-flowered **new** | EPfP |
| - 'Oxford Blue' | see *S. patens* |
| - 'Pink Ice' | CPom CSpe EPyc WHil |
| - pink-flowered | MSpe SPin |
| - 'Royal Blue' | see *S. patens* |
| § - 'White Trophy' | CBcs CPLG CPrp ECtt EGHP ELan EPyc EWld LRHS SDys SMrm SPer SPin WFar WHil WIvy WOut |
| ***pauciserrata*** | SPin |
| 'Penny's Smile' | EPyc SPin SUsu WWlt |
| ***penstemonoides*** | SDys |
| 'Peru Blue' | CSpe EPyc EWld SDys |
| 'Phyllis' Fancy' | CSam CSpe CWGN EPyc MAsh SDys SPlb SUsu WSHC XSen |
| ***pinguifolia*** | SPin |
| ***pisidica*** | SPin XSen |
| ***plectranthoides*** | SPin XSen |
| ***pogonochila*** | SPin XSen |
| ***polystachya*** | SPin XSen |
| - B&SWJ 8985 | WCru |
| ***pomifera*** | SPin XSen |
| * 'Powis Castle' | MHom |
| ***praeclara*** | SPin WHil |
| ***pratensis*** | CArn CWib EBee EGHP ELan EPyc GJos MHer MNHC NChi SGar SPin XSen |
| - 'Albiflora' | CDes |
| § - Bertolonii Group | EPyc SPin XSen |
| § - Haematodes Group ♀H4 | ELan EPyc MNrw NLar SPav SPin SRms |
| - 'Indigo' ♀H4 | CDes CPrp EBee ECtt EPfP GMaP LRHS LSou MCot MRav NDov NEgg NLar SPhx SPin SPoG SUsu WCot WMnd WPGP |
| - 'Lapis Lazuli' | CDes EPyc EWes NBre SPhx SUsu WFar |
| - 'Pink Delight'PBR | EBee ECtt EPfP LRHS NCGa NDov NLar SPoG |
| - 'Rose Rhapsody' (Ballet Series) | CAby EBee EPPr EPyc LBMP LRHS MHer NCGa SPhx WCAu WFar WHil XSen |
| - 'Rosea' | ECha SPhx SPin |
| - 'Swan Lake' (Ballet Series) | CAby EPPr EPyc LRHS NCGa NChi NLar SAga SPhx SPin SPlb SSvw WCAu WHil XSen |
| - 'Sweet Esmeralda' (Ballet Series) | EBee EPyc LRHS NCGa NGdn NLar SPhx |
| - 'Tenorei' | LRHS |
| - 'Twilight Serenade' (Ballet Series) | CAby EBee ECtt EPyc EWTr LRHS MAvo NCGa SBfd WHil |
| ***pratensis* × *transylvanica*** | GJos |
| ***procurrens*** | SPin XSen |
| ***prostrata*** | EOHP |
| ***prunelloides*** | SPin XSen |
| ***przewalskii*** | CPLG CPom EPyc EWld LRHS NMRc SAga SPhx SPin WPer WTcb |
| - ACE 1157 | WCru |
| - BWJ 7920 | SPin WCru |
| - var. ***mandarinorum*** **new** | LRHS |
| ***pubescens*** | SPin |
| ***pulchella*** | MAJR SPin |
| 'Purple Majesty' | CHll CSam CSev CWGN EPyc EShb LHop MAvo SAga SDys SMrm SPhx SPin SRkn WKif WWlt |
| 'Purple Queen' | CAby EPyc LRHS LSou SBrd SDys WWlt |
| ***purpurea*** | LBMP LSRN SPin |
| ***radula*** | SPin XSen |
| ***ranzaniana*** | SPin XSen |
| ***raymondii*** | SPin XSen |
| subsp. ***mairanae*** | |
| ***recognita*** | CBot SPin WSHC XSen |
| ***recurva*** | SPin |
| red-flowered B&SWJ 10375 from Guatemala | WCru |
| ***reflexa*** | SPin |
| ***regeliana*** misapplied | see *S. virgata* Jacq. |
| ***regeliana*** Trautv. | LRHS NBir SPin XSen |
| ***regla*** | CAby EGHP LRHS SDys SPin WHil WPGP XSen |
| - 'Jame' | SPin |
| - 'Mount Emory' | SPin |
| - 'Royal' | SPin |
| ***repens*** | EBee EPyc SDys SPhx SPin XSen |
| - var. ***repens*** | SGar XSen |
| § ***reptans*** | SPin XSen |
| - from Western Texas | CWGN SDys SUsu |
| ***retinervia*** | SPin |
| ***ringens*** | SDys SPin XSen |
| ***riparia*** misapplied | see *S. rypara* |
| ***roborowskii*** | SPin |
| § ***roemeriana*** ♀H3 | CSpe EBee EPyc IFoB SBch SBrt SDys SPin WPGP |
| - 'Bordeaux Steel Blue' **new** | LRHS |
| - 'Hot Trumpets' | WHil |
| - 'Red Dwarf' **new** | LRHS |
| ***roscida*** | SPin |
| 'Rose Queen' ambig. | MRav |
| 'Royal Bumble' | EPyc LHop MAvo NDov WPGP XLum XSen |
| 'Royal Crimson Distinction'PBR | EPPr IPot |
| ***rubescens*** | SDys SPin XSen |
| ***rubiginosa*** | SPin XSen |
| ***runcinata*** | EPyc SPin |
| ***rutilans*** | see *S. elegans* 'Scarlet Pineapple' |
| § ***rypara*** | CPom SDys SPin XSen |
| ***sagittata*** | EPyc GCal SDys SPin WHil WWlt XSen |
| 'Sally Fun Blue' **new** | LSou |
| 'Sally Light Blue' **new** | LSou |
| * ***sauntia*** | SPin |
| (Savannah Series) 'Savannah Purple' | LRHS SRot |
| - 'Savannah Red' **new** | LRHS |
| - 'Savannah Salmon Rose' | IFoB LRHS SRot |
| ***scabra*** | CSpe EPyc SDys SPin XSen |
| ***schlechteri*** | SPin |
| ***sclarea*** | CArn CHab CHby ECtt EGHP GPoy LRHS MHer MNHC NGdn SIde SPin WHfH WJek XLum XSen |
| - var. ***sclarea*** | EBla ECtt |
| - var. ***turkestanica*** hort. | CPom CSev CSpe EBee ECtt ELan EPfP LRHS LSRN MCot MRav NEgg NGdn SBfd SEND SGar SMad SMrm SPav SPer SWat WCAu WKif WMnd XLum XSen |
| - var. ***turkestaniana*** Mottet | EWTr MSpe NBPC WWEG |
| § - 'Vatican White' | CSpe EBee EPfP LRHS MSpe SBch SMrm WJek WMnd XLum XSen |

| |  |  |
|---|---|---|
| | - white-bracted | CWib NLar SPin SWvt |
| * | ***scordifolia*** | SPin |
| | ***scutellarioides*** | SPin XSen |
| | ***semiatrata*** misapplied | see *S. chamaedryoides* |
| | ***semiatrata*** ambig. | EPyc IFoB |
| | ***semiatrata*** Zucc. | CDes CSpe EWld SAga SDys SPin XSen |
| | 'Serenade' | LRHS NDov SPhx |
| | ***serpyllifolia*** | SDys SPin WHil WOut XSen |
| | ***sessei*** | SPin XSen |
| | ***setulosa*** | SPin XSen |
| | 'Shame' | NDov |
| | 'Silas Dyson' | CAby CDes CSpe CWGN ECtt EPyc EWld LRHS MAvo MHom MWea NDov SAga SBch SDys SPhx SPin SSvw SUsu WOut WPGP WWlt |
| | 'Silke's Dream' | CAby CDes CPom CWGN EBee ECtt EPyc EWld MAsh MWea NDov SBHP SBch SDys SPin SUsu WPGP WWlt XSen |
| | ***sinaloensis*** | EPyc MAsh SPin WFar XSen |
| | ***smithii*** new | SPin |
| | ***somalensis*** | SDys SPin WHil XSen |
| | ***sonomensis*** | XSen |
| | ***spathacea*** ♀H3-4 | SDys SPhx SPin |
| | - 'Avis Keedy' new | SPin |
| | ***spinosa*** | XSen |
| | ***splendens*** | SPin |
| | - 'Dancing Flame' (v) | EPyc |
| | - 'Helen Dillon' | EPyc SPin |
| | - 'Jimi's Good Red' | CSpe |
| | - 'Peach' | SPin |
| | - 'Salsa Burgundy' (Salsa Series) | WWlt |
| | - 'Vanguard' ♀H3 | LAst |
| § | - 'Van-Houttei' ♀H3 | CSam ECre EPyc EShb EWld GCal SDys SPin SVen WWlt |
| | ***sprucei*** | SPin XSen |
| | ***squalens*** | SPin |
| | ***stachydifolia*** | SPin XSen |
| § | ***staminea*** | LRHS SDys SPin |
| | ***stenophylla*** | SPin WHil XSen |
| | 'Stephanie' | EPyc SDys |
| | ***steppos*a** | SPin |
| | ***stolonifera*** new | CSpe SDys |
| | ***stoteonifera*** | SPin |
| | ***striata*** | SPin |
| | - red-flowered new | SPin |
| | ***styphelus*** | SDys SPin |
| | ***subpalmatinervis*** | SPin |
| | ***subrotunda*** | EPyc EWld SDys SPin |
| | ***summa*** | CPBP |
| | × ***superba*** ♀H4 | CBot CPrp CSBt EBee ECtt ELan EPfP EPyc LRHS LSRN MBri MWat SBfd SDix SPer SRms WCAu WGwG WHoo |
| | - 'Adora Blue' new | LRHS |
| | - 'Adrian' | CMHG EBee ECtt EPfP LRHS LSRN LSou MSpe MWea SPoG WGwG |
| | - 'Merleau' | LRHS |
| | - 'Merleau Rose' | EBee LRHS WGor |
| * | - 'Rosea' | EBee |
| | - 'Rubin' ♀H4 | ECtt MBNS NBre SMrm SPhx |
| I | - 'Superba' | CSev ECha ECtt MRav SMrm SPhx SRkn |
| | × ***sylvestris*** | LSRN SGar SPin |
| § | - 'Blauhügel' ♀H4 | CHar EBee ECha ECtt ELan EPfP EShb EWTr LSou MArl MCot MSpe NDov NPri SMrm SPhx WCAu WHoo WPer WWEG |
| § | - 'Blaukönigin' | EBee ELon EPfP GMaP LAst LBMP LRHS MWat NGBl NLar NVic SBfd SPer SPet SPlb SPoG SWvt WPer WWEG XSen |
| | - Blue Queen | see *S.* × *sylvestris* 'Blaukönigin' |
| § | - 'Dear Anja' | EBee IPot LHop NCGa NDov SPhx WHlf |
| | - 'Lye End' | ECtt MWat WCot |
| § | - 'Mainacht' ♀H4 | Widely available |
| | - May Night | see *S.* × *sylvestris* 'Mainacht' |
| | - 'Negrito' | EBee EWll NGdn NLar SMrm |
| | - 'Rhapsody in Blue'PBR | CAbP EBee LRHS MBNS NDov NLar WCot WFar |
| | - 'Rose Queen' | EBee ECha ECtt ELan ELon EPfP EWTr LHop LRHS NGBl NOrc SBfd SCoo SPet SPhx SPoG SWvt WPer WWEG |
| | - 'Rügen' | EBee ELon EPyc |
| | - 'Schneehügel' | CMac CSBt EBee ECha EHoe ELan ELon EPPr EPfP GMaP LAst LRHS MBNS MRav MSpe NBre NEgg NPri NPro SMrm SPer WCAu WHil WMnd WWEG XSen |
| | - 'Tänzerin' ♀H4 | EBee ELon EPPr EPyc LRHS NDov SDys SUsu WHlf |
| | - 'Viola Klose' | CHar CPrp CWGN EAEE EBee ECha ECtt LRHS LSRN MBri MCot MSpe NGdn NLar |
| | ***tachiei*** hort. | see *S. forsskaolii* |
| | 'Tammy' | SPin |
| | ***taraxacifolia*** | SDys SPin WHil XSen |
| | ***tarayensis*** | SPin |
| | ***tesquicola*** | see *S. nemorosa* subsp. *tesquicola* |
| | ***tianschanica*** | SPin |
| | ***tiliifolia*** | SPav SPin SRms |
| | ***tingitana*** | SPin XSen |
| | ***tomentosa*** | SPin XSen |
| | ***transcaucasica*** | see *S. staminea* |
| | ***transsylvanica*** | MSpe SGar SMrm SPav SPhx SPin STes WPer WPtf WTcb XSen |
| | - 'Baumgartenii' new | LRHS |
| | - 'Blue Spire' | CMea EBee ECtt GQue MCot MWhi SPav SPur |
| | 'Trebah Lilac White' | see *S.* × *jamensis* 'Trebah' |
| § | 'Trelawney' | EPPr EPyc MHom SDys SPin SRkn SRot WBor WWlt XSen |
| § | 'Trelissick' | ECre ECtt EPPr EPyc LHop MAsh MHom MTis MWea SEND SPet SPin SRkn SRot WBor WHil WWlt |
| § | 'Trewithen' | CPLG CPom ECre ECtt EPyc MHom SPin SPoG SRkn SRot WHil XSen |
| | ***trijuga*** | SPin |
| | ***triloba*** | see *S. fruticosa* |
| | ***tubifera*** | SPin |
| § | ***tubiflora*** ♀H1+3 | CSpe EPyc EWld MAJR MAsh SPin XSen |
| | ***uliginosa*** ♀H3-4 | Widely available |
| | - 'African Skies' | CChe EBee IPot MNrw SPin |
| | - 'Ballon Azur' | CSpe NDov SDys WSHC |
| | ***urica*** | MAJR SDys SPin XSen |
| | - short | CSpe SDys |
| | ***uruapana*** new | SPin |
| | 'Valerie' | CAby EPyc SDys SPin |
| | 'Van-Houttei' | see *S. splendens* 'Van-Houttei' |
| | ***variana*** new | SPin |
| | 'Vatican City' | see *S. sclarea* 'Vatican White' |

| |  |  |
|---|---|---|
| | ***verbenaca*** | CArn EPyc ITim LRHS MHer SPin WCAu |
| | - pink-flowered | SPhx |
| | ***verticillata*** | EBee EPyc LEdu NLar SDys SPin XSen |
| § | - 'Alba' | CAbP EBee ECtt EPfP GJos GQue LRHS MCot MRav NGdn NLar SPer SPin WCAu XSen |
| | - subsp. ***amasiaca*** | SGar |
| | - 'Endless Love' | LSou NDov |
| | - 'Hannay's Blue' | EPPr MAvo NDov SMrm SUsu |
| | - 'Hannay's Purple' | EPPr |
| | - 'Purple Rain' | Widely available |
| | - 'Smouldering Torches' | LHop LPla NDov SPhx |
| | - 'White Rain' | see *S. verticillata* 'Alba' |
| | ***villicaulis*** | see *S. amplexicaulis* |
| § | ***virgata*** Jacq. | EBee SGar SPin XSen |
| | ***viridis*** | CHby MNHC SPin |
| § | - var. ***comata*** | EGHP MCot SIde WJek |
| | - var. ***viridis*** | WHrl |
| | ***viscosa*** ambig. | EPyc SGar WBox |
| | ***viscosa*** Jacq. | SPin WHil XSen |
| | ***vitifolia*** | CSpe EPyc |
| | - B&SWJ 10236 | SPin WCru |
| | ***wagneriana*** | SPin |
| | 'Waverly' | CDes CHll CRHN CSam EBee EPyc EWld MAJR MAsh MAvo MCot MHer SAga SBch SDys SUsu WWlt XSen |
| | × ***westerae*** | SPin |
| | ***xalapensis*** | SPin |
| | ***yunnanensis*** | SPin |
| | - BWJ 7874 | WCru |
| | aff. ***yunnanensis*** | SPin |

## *Salvinia* (*Salviniaceae*)

| |  |  |
|---|---|---|
| | sp. | LPBA |
| | ***natans*** | LLWG MSKA |

## *Sambucus* (*Adoxaceae*)

| |  |  |
|---|---|---|
| | ***adnata*** | SDix WFar |
| | ***caerulea*** | see *S. nigra* subsp. *caerulea* |
| | ***callicarpa*** | NLar WCot |
| | ***chinensis*** | WCot |
| | ***coraensis*** | see *S. williamsii* subsp. *coreana* |
| | ***ebulus*** | LEdu NLar SMad WCot WSFF |
| | ***formosana*** | WCot |
| * | ***himalayensis*** | WCot |
| | ***mexicana*** B&SWJ 10349 | WCot WCru |
| | ***miquelii*** | WCot |
| | ***nigra*** | CArn CBcs CCVT CDul CHab ECrN GPoy LBuc NWea SBfd SEWo SIde WDin WFar WMou WSFF |
| | - 'Albomarginata' | see *S. nigra* 'Marginata' |
| | - 'Albovariegata' (v) | CMac SEND WCot WMoo |
| * | - 'Ardwall' | CAgr GCal WCot |
| N | - 'Aurea' ♀H4 | CBcs CDul CMac CSBt CWan ELan EPfP MRav NWea SPer WCot WDin WFar WMoo |
| | - 'Aureomarginata' (v) | ECrN ELan EPPr EPfP MRav NLar NSti SBfd WCFE WCot WFar |
| | - 'Bradet' | CAgr NLar WCot |
| | - 'Cae Rhos Lligwy' | CAgr WCot |
| § | - subsp. ***caerulea*** | EPfP WCot |
| | - subsp. ***canadensis*** 'Adams' (F) | WCot |
| | - - 'Aurea' | CWib WCot WHar |
| | - - 'John's' | CAgr WCot |
| | - - 'Maxima' | EWes SMad SMrm WCot |
| | - - 'Rubra' **new** | WCot |
| | - - 'York' (F) | CAgr WCot |
| | - 'Castledean' | WCot |
| | - 'Dolomite' (v) **new** | WCot |
| | - 'Donau' | CAgr WCot |
| | - 'Frances' (v) | EPPr WCot |
| | - 'Franzi' | CAgr WCot |
| | - 'Fructu Luteo' | NLar WCot |
| | - 'Godshill' (F) | CAgr SDea WCot |
| | - 'Haschberg' | CAgr WCot |
| | - 'Heterophylla' | see *S. nigra* 'Linearis' |
| | - 'Hillier's Dwarf' **new** | WCot |
| | - 'Ina' | CAgr WCot |
| | - 'Körsör' (F) | NLar WCot |
| | - f. ***laciniata*** ♀H4 | CDul ELan EPPr EPfP EPla GCal LRHS MBlu MMuc MRav NLar NSti NWea SDix SLon SPer WCFE WCot WDin WFar WPGP |
| § | - 'Linearis' | CPMA ELan EPla MRav NLar WCot WPGP |
| | - 'Long Tooth' | CDul WCot |
| | - 'Lutea Punctata' **new** | WCot |
| | - 'Madonna' (v) | CMac EBee LTen MBlu MGos MRav NLBP NLar SBfd SMad SPer WCot |
| § | - 'Marginata' (v) | CDul CWan CWib EHoe MHer MRav SDix SPer WCot WDin WFar |
| | - 'Marion Bull' (v) | CDul WCot |
| I | - 'Marmorata' | NLar WCot |
| | - 'Mint Julep' **new** | WCot |
| I | - 'Monstrosa' | NLar WCot |
| | - 'Nana' | WCot |
| | - 'Naomi' **new** | WCot |
| | - 'Norfolk Speckled' (v) **new** | WCot |
| | - 'Plena' (d) | WCot |
| | - f. ***porphyrophylla*** 'Black Beauty'PBR | see *S. nigra* f. *porphyrophylla* 'Gerda' |
| | - - 'Black Lace'PBR | see *S. nigra* f. *porphyrophylla* 'Eva' |
| | - - 'Dart's Greenlace' **new** | WCot |
| § | - - 'Eva'PBR | Widely available |
| § | - - 'Gerda'PBR ♀H4 | Widely available |
| § | - - 'Guincho Purple' | CBcs CDul CMac CTri EBee ELan EPPr EPfP MHer MRav NLar NWea SGol SPlb WCot WDin WFar WMoo |
| | - - 'Purple Pete' | CDul WCot |
| | - - 'Thundercloud' | CBcs CDul CMHG EWes LBMP LRHS MAsh MBri MNrw NChi NLar NPro WCot WFar WMoo |
| | - 'Pulverulenta' (v) | CWib EPPr EPla GCal LHop MRav NLBP NLar SPer WCot WFar |
| | - 'Purpurea' | see *S. nigra* f. *porphyrophylla* 'Guincho Purple' |
| | - 'Pyramidalis' | CPMA EPla NLar WCot |
| | - 'Riese aus Vossloch' **new** | WCot |
| | - 'Robert Piggin' (v) | WCot |
| | - var. ***rotundifolia*** **new** | WCot |
| | - 'Sambu' (F) | CAgr WCot |
| | - 'Samdal' (F) | CAgr WCot |
| | - 'Samidan' (F) | CAgr WCot |
| | - 'Samnor' (F) | CAgr WCot |
| | - 'Sampo' (F) | CAgr WCot |
| | - 'Samyl' (F) | CAgr WCot |
| | - 'Stormy Dawn' **new** | WCot |
| * | - 'Tenuifolia' | MRav |
| | - 'Urban Lace' | CAgr WCot |
| | - 'Variegata' | see *S. nigra* 'Marginata' |
| | - f. ***viridis*** | CAgr WCot |

| | |
|---|---|
| ***palmensis*** new | WCot |
| ***racemosa*** | EPfP NWea WCot |
| - 'Aurea' | EHoe |
| - 'Crûg Lace' | WCru |
| - 'Goldenlocks' | EWes MSwo NLar WCot |
| - subsp. ***kamtschatica*** | WCot |
| - 'Plumosa Aurea' | CBcs CSBt CWib EBee ELan EPfP GCra LRHS MBri MRav MSwo NLar NWea SLim WCot WDin WFar |
| - var. ***pubens*** new | WCot |
| § - var. ***sieboldiana*** | WCot |
| - 'Sutherland Gold' 🏆H4 | Widely available |
| - 'Tenuifolia' | CPMA ELan EPfP NLar WCot |
| ***sieboldiana*** | see *S. racemosa* var. *sieboldiana* |
| ***tigranii*** | NLar WCot |
| § ***williamsii*** subsp. ***coreana*** | CDul WCot |

## *Samolus* (*Primulaceae*)

| | |
|---|---|
| ***repens*** | ECou LLHF |
| ***valerandi*** | LLWG |

## *Sandersonia* (*Colchicaceae*)

| | |
|---|---|
| ***aurantiaca*** | CAvo CFFs CPne ECho EPot ERCP LAma SMad SUsu |

## *Sanguinaria* (*Papaveraceae*)

| | |
|---|---|
| ***canadensis*** | Widely available |
| - f. ***multiplex*** (d) | CLAP ECho GEdr IFro NBir WSHC |
| - - 'Plena' (d) 🏆H4 | Widely available |

## *Sanguisorba* ✿ (*Rosaceae*)

| | |
|---|---|
| DJHC 535 | NLar SUsu |
| § ***albiflora*** | CCVN CDes CHar CKno EBee EBla ELan EShb LBMP LPla MAvo MRav NGdn NLar NPro SEND SMrm SPhx SWat WCAu WFar WHil WMoo WOut WPGP |
| 'All Time High' | NDov |
| ***applanata*** | WCot |
| ***armena*** | CElw EBee EBla EWes MAvo MLLN MNrw SSvw WTin |
| ***benthamiana*** | CHEx |
| 'Blackthorn' | NDov |
| 'Burr Blanc' | MAvo SPhx |
| ***canadensis*** | CDes CKno CMac CRow EBee EBla ECha ECtt EPPr EPfP GCal GMaP GPoy LPla MAvo NBir NDov NLar NSti NVic SPer SPhx SWat WAul WFar WMoo WOld WOut WTin WWEG |
| 'Cangshan Cranberry' | MAvo |
| * ***caucasica*** | EBee EPPr EWes LEdu LPla NBre SPhx |
| 'Chocolate Tip' | EBee EBla ECtt IPot NBro |
| ***hakusanensis*** | CDes CHar CKno EBee EBla GBBs GCal GKev IFro IPot LEdu MAvo MNFA MNrw NBir NBre NBro NChi NPro SUsu WCot WFar WPGP WSHC WTin |
| - B&SWJ 8709 | EBla WCru |
| 'John Coke' | NLar |
| ***magnifica*** | CDes EWes GCal LEdu SUsu WCot WPGP |
| - ***alba*** | see *S. albiflora* |
| ***menziesii*** | Widely available |
| - 'Dali Marble' (v) | CCVN EBee EBla ECtt EPPr NBPC NLar SPoG |
| - 'Wake Up' | NDov |
| § ***minor*** | CArn CHby CPrp EBee EBla EGHP ELau EWil GPoy MAvo MHer MNHC NBro NMir SIde SPhx SPlb WGwG WHer WJek WMoo |
| - subsp. ***minor*** | CHab |
| ***obtusa*** | Widely available |
| - 'Chatto' | EBee ECha |
| - silver-leaved | MAvo |
| - white-flowered | CDes MAvo MMuc WPGP |
| ***officinalis*** | CArn CHab CKno COlW CWan EBee EBla EHoe EWil GQue MHer MNFA NMir NPro SPer SPhx SWat WCAu WFar WMoo WWEG |
| - CDC 262 | EPPr SSvw |
| - CDC 282 | CSpe SPhx |
| - CDC 292 | GQue WCot |
| - from Mongolia | LEdu |
| - 'Arnhem' | CCse CKno EBla EPPr LEdu LPla LRHS NDov SMrm SPhx SUsu WCot WPGP WTin |
| - 'False Tanna' | CWib WFar |
| - 'Lemon Splash' (v) | EBee EBla LEdu MAvo WCot |
| - 'Martin's Mulberry' | CDes EWes MAvo NDov |
| - 'Pink Tanna' | CDes CElw CKno CPrp EBee EBla EPPr GBBs LEdu MAvo MCot MDKP MGos MMuc MNFA NBid NBre NBro NSti SEND SMrm SPhx SUsu WCAu WCot WMoo WTin WWEG |
| - 'Red Thunder' | CKno CSpe EBee ECtt EPPr IPot LRHS MAvo NCGa NDov NLar WCAu WWEG |
| - 'Shiro-fukurin' (v) | EBee EWes MAvo NLar WCot WHer WSHC |
| ***parviflora*** | see *S. tenuifolia* var. *parviflora* |
| ***pimpinella*** | see *S. minor* |
| 'Pink Brushes' | EBla LPla MAvo NDov NLar |
| 'Rock and Roll' | ECtt EPPr GQue IPot MAvo NLar |
| ***sitchensis*** | see *S. stipulata* |
| § ***stipulata*** | EBee GCal LPla MAvo MNrw WCAu |
| - var. ***riishirensis*** | EBee MAvo |
| 'Tanna' | Widely available |
| 'Tanna' seedling | EPPr EShb |
| ***tenuifolia*** | CEnt EBla GBBs GCal IFro MCot MHer NChi NLar SBHP SMrm SPhx |
| - var. ***alba*** | CKno CPrp EBee EBla EPPr EWes EWll GCal GQue MAvo MCot MRav NDov NGdn NPro SMad SPhx WCot WFar WMoo WOld WWEG |
| - - 'Korean Snow' | MAvo MNFA NDov SPhx SUsu |
| - 'Big Pink' | GCal MAvo MNrw |
| § - var. ***parviflora*** | CDes EBee LEdu MAvo MNrw NLar WPGP WTin |
| - - white-flowered | EBla |
| - 'Pink Elephant' | CHar CKno EBee EBla ECtt EPPr EWTr GBin GMac GQue LEdu MAvo NDov NLar SHar SMad WCAu WMoo WPGP WTin WWFP |
| - 'Pink Tickler' | NDov |
| - var. ***purpurea*** | CDes WCAu |
| - 'Purpurea' | CKno EBee EBla EPPr LEdu MAvo MDun NLar SPhx WCot WFar WPGP |
| - 'Stand Up Comedian' | EBee LEdu MAvo NLar WWEG |
| - 'Sturdy Guard' | EBee IPot |

| | |
|---|---|
| - 'White Elephant' | EBla |
| - 'White Tanna' **new** | EPPr |

## *Sanicula* (*Apiaceae*)

| | |
|---|---|
| ***europaea*** | GPoy WHer WTin |

## *Sansevieria* (*Asparagaceae*)

| | |
|---|---|
| ***trifasciata*** | EShb |
| 'Moonshine' 🏆[H1] | |

## *Santolina* (*Asteraceae*)

| | |
|---|---|
| ***benthamiana*** | XSen |
| § ***chamaecyparissus*** 🏆[H4] | Widely available |
| - var. ***corsica*** | see *S. chamaecyparissus* 'Nana' |
| - 'Double Lemon' (d) | EPfP |
| - subsp. ***insularis*** **new** | XSen |
| - 'Lambrook Silver' | CDoC EBee ECtt EOHP EPfP LBMP LRHS MAsh NLar SBfd SCoo SLim SPoG WJek |
| - 'Lemon Queen' | CArn CDoC EBee EPfP LRHS MAsh MGos MNHC MSwo NBir NLar SBfd SIde SWat WFar WGwG WJek |
| - subsp. ***magonica*** | WAbe |
| § - 'Nana' 🏆[H4] | CBar CMHG CPrp EPfP LRHS MAsh MHer MRav MSwo SPoG SRms SWat WGrn WPer |
| - 'Pretty Carroll' | CAbP EBee ECtt ELan EPfP GGar LRHS LSRN LTen MAsh MBri NLar SBrd SIde WFar WJek |
| - 'Small-Ness' | CMea EBee ECho ELan EPfP EWes GEdr LRHS MAsh MHer NSla SPer STre SWvt WJek WPer WSHC |
| - 'Weston' | ECho |
| ***incana*** | see *S. chamaecyparissus* |
| * ***lindavica*** | XSen |
| ***pectinata*** | see *S. rosmarinifolia* subsp. *canescens* |
| ***pinnata*** | CArn MHer MLHP WPer |
| § - subsp. ***neapolitana*** 🏆[H4] | CArn CSBt CSev CWib EBee ECha ELan EPfP MBri MMuc MNHC SDix SEND SIde WMnd WWEG |
| - - cream-flowered | see *S. pinnata* subsp. *neapolitana* 'Edward Bowles' |
| § - - 'Edward Bowles' | Widely available |
| - - 'Sulphurea' | CArn CMea EBee EPfP LRHS MAsh SBfd SPer SPhx WKif WPer |
| ***rosmarinifolia*** | CArn CChe CDoC CDul CWan GPoy LRHS MMuc MRav MSCN SEND SLon SPlb SPoG SRms STre |
| § - subsp. ***canescens*** | EPfP WPer XSen |
| - 'Lemon Fizz' | EBee EHoe ELan EMil EPPr LBMP LRHS LSou NCGa NPri SBfd SBrd SCoo SPer SPoG SPtl SWvt |
| § - subsp. ***rosmarinifolia*** | CPrp CSev ECha ECrN ELan EPfP MHer MRav SBfd SDix SIde SPer SWvt WDin WFar WGwG WHoo WJek XSen |
| - - 'Primrose Gem' 🏆[H4] | CBcs CDoC CMHG CPrp CSBt CSam CTri EBee ECha ECrN EPfP LHop LRHS MAsh MMuc MRav MSwo MWat NLar NPri SBfd SEND SPer SPoG SWvt WHoo WJek |
| - - white-flowered | SSvw XSen |
| Shades of Jade = 'Sant101' **new** | WRHF |
| ***tomentosa*** | see *S. pinnata* subsp. *neapolitana* |
| ***virens*** | see *S. rosmarinifolia* subsp. *rosmarinifolia* |
| ***viridis*** | see *S. rosmarinifolia* subsp. *rosmarinifolia* |

## *Sanvitalia* (*Asteraceae*)

| | |
|---|---|
| Aztekengold = 'Starbini'[PBR] | LAst WGor |
| 'Little Sun' | SPet |
| ***procumbens*** 'Irish Eyes' | CSpe |
| 'Sunbini'[PBR] | CCCN CSpe LSou NPri |

## *Saponaria* (*Caryophyllaceae*)

| | |
|---|---|
| × ***boissieri*** | EPot |
| 'Bressingham' 🏆[H4] | CPBP ECho ECtt EDAr EPfP EPot LBee NMen WAbe WPat |
| Bressingham hybrid | LRHS MAsh |
| ***caespitosa*** | EDAr EWes |
| × ***lempergii*** 'Max Frei' | CAbP CSam EBee ELon EPPr LSou MCot MRav SAga SPhx WCot WSHC |
| ***ocymoides*** 🏆[H4] | Widely available |
| - 'Alba' | ECha WFar XLum |
| - 'Snow Tip' | ECho EDAr EPfP NGdn NLar SBch XLum |
| ***officinalis*** | CArn CBre CPbn CWan GPoy MHer MLHP MNHC SIde SPlb SWal WFar WHer WJek WMoo WPer WPtf |
| - 'Alba Plena' (d) | CBre EBee EWTr GGar LRHS MMuc NLar SEND SHar WFar WHer WPer WPtf WTin XLum |
| - 'Betty Arnold' (d) | ECtt EWes GMac MHer WCot WFar WTin |
| § - 'Dazzler' (v) | WWEG |
| - 'Rosea Plena' (d) | Widely available |
| - 'Rubra Plena' (d) | CAby CPrp ELan EWes MMuc MSCN MWhi NBre SHar WHer WTin |
| - 'Variegata' | see *S. officinalis* 'Dazzler' |
| × ***olivana*** 🏆[H4] | CPBP ECho ECtt MAsh NLar NMen XLum |
| 'Rosenteppich' | CPBP ECtt WPat |
| ***zawadskii*** | see *Silene zawadskii* |

## *Saposhnikovia* (*Apiaceae*)

| | |
|---|---|
| ***divaricata*** | CArn |

## *Sarcocapnos* (*Papaveraceae*)

| | |
|---|---|
| ***enneaphylla*** | LSRN |

## *Sarcococca* ✿ (*Buxaceae*)

| | |
|---|---|
| ***confusa*** 🏆[H4] | Widely available |
| ***hookeriana*** 🏆[H4] | EPfP GKin IFoB LSRN LTen MBlu MDun MSwo NLar NPri SBfd WFar WPGP |
| - B&SWJ 2585 | WCru |
| - HWJK 2393 | WCru |
| - Sch 1160 | CPLG |
| - Sch 2396 | CPLG EPla |
| - var. ***digyna*** 🏆[H4] | Widely available |
| - - 'Purple Stem' | CPLG CPMA CTri EPfP EPla GKin LRHS MGos MRav NLar NPnk SBfd SCoo SPoG WCru WDin |
| * - - 'Schillingii' | CPMA WCru |
| - var. ***hookeriana*** | CPMA LSRN |
| - - GWJ 9369 | WCru |
| - - HWJK 2102 | WCru |
| - var. ***humilis*** | Widely available |
| ***orientalis*** | CAbP CMCN CPLG CPMA EBee ELan ELon EPfP EPla LRHS MAsh MGos NLar SPoG SSpi WFar WPGP WPat |

| | |
|---|---|
| 'Roy Lancaster' | see *S. ruscifolia* var. *chinensis* 'Dragon Gate' |
| ***ruscifolia*** | CBcs CDoy CDul CHab CMCN CMHG CMac CPLG CPMA CSBt EBee ECrN ELan EPfP EPla GKin LAst LRHS MAsh MGos MRav NEgg SEND SLim SLon SPer SRms SSpi WCru WFar |
| - var. ***chinensis*** ♀H4 | CPMA CSam EPfP EPla SLon WCru WFar WPGP |
| - - L 713 | EPla |
| § - - 'Dragon Gate' | CDoC CGHE CPLG CPMA CSam EBee ELan EPfP EPla LLHF LRHS LSRN MAsh NLar SChF SLim SLon SPoG SReu WCru WPGP WPat |
| ***saligna*** | CBcs CPMA EBee EBtc EPfP LRHS NLar SLon WCru |
| - MF P2056 | WCru |
| ***trinervia*** B&SWJ 9500 **new** | WCru |
| ***vagans*** B&SWJ 7285 | WCru |
| ***wallichii*** | CGHE CPLG MBlu SEND SPoG WPGP WPat |
| - B&SWJ 2291 | CPMA WCru |
| - GWJ 9427 | WCru |
| ***zeylanica*** var. ***brevifolia*** GWJ 9480 | WCru |

## *Sarmienta* (*Gesneriaceae*)

| | |
|---|---|
| ***repens*** ♀H2 | CGHE CPLG WAbe WPGP |

## *Sarothamnus* see *Cytisus*

## *Sarracenia* ✿ (*Sarraceniaceae*)

| | |
|---|---|
| × ***ahlesii*** | CHew |
| ***alata*** | CHew CSWC EECP MCCP NChu SHmp WSSs |
| - all green | SHmp |
| - 'Black Tube' | WSSs |
| - heavily veined | SHmp WSSs |
| - pubescent | EECP NChu WSSs |
| - 'Red Lid' | EECP NChu WSSs |
| - 'Red Lid' × ***flava*** red pitcher | EECP |
| - wavy lid | SHmp WSSs |
| - white-flowered | WSSs |
| ***alata*** × ***flava*** var. ***maxima*** | CSWC NChu |
| × ***areolata*** | CHew CSWC NChu WSSs |
| × ***catesbyi*** ♀H1 | CHew CSWC NChu SHmp WSSs |
| × ***courtii*** | CSWC NChu |
| 'Dixie Lace' | CSWC |
| × ***excellens*** ♀H1 | CSWC NChu WSSs |
| × ***exornata*** | CSWC NChu SPlb |
| × ***farnhamii*** | CSWC EECP NChu |
| ***flava*** ♀H1 | CSWC MCCP MREP NChu WSSs |
| - all green giant | see *S. flava* var. *maxima* |
| - var. ***atropurpurea*** | EECP WSSs |
| - 'Burgundy' | WSSs |
| - var. ***cuprea*** | CSWC NChu SHmp WSSs |
| - var. ***flava*** | CHew EECP WSSs |
| § - var. ***maxima*** | CHew CSWC EECP NChu WSSs |
| - var. ***ornata*** | CHew CSWC EECP NChu SHmp WSSs |
| - var. ***rubricorpora*** | CHew EECP NChu SHmp WSSs |
| - var. ***rugelii*** | CHew EECP SHmp WSSs |
| - veinless | CSWC |
| × ***harperi*** | CSWC NChu |
| 'Juthatip Soper' | SHmp WSSs |
| 'Ladies in Waiting' | CSWC |
| ***leucophylla*** ♀H1 | CHew CSWC NChu SHmp SPlb WSSs |
| - from Okaloosa Co., Florida | SHmp |
| - 'Deer Park Alabama' | SHmp |
| - green | WSSs |
| - green and white | WSSs |
| - pubescent | WSSs |
| - 'Schnell's Ghost' | WSSs |
| - 'Tarnok' | WSSs |
| ***leucophylla*** × ***oreophila*** | CSWC EECP NChu |
| ***leucophylla*** × (× ***popei***) | EECP |
| 'Lynda Butt' | CSWC SHmp WSSs |
| 'Mardi Gras' **new** | CSWC |
| × ***miniata*** | EECP SHmp |
| ***minor*** | CSWC EECP NChu SHmp WSSs |
| - var. ***minor*** | CHew |
| § - 'Okee Giant' | CSWC NChu WSSs |
| - var. ***okefenokeensis*** | CHew |
| - 'Okefenokee Giant' | see *S. minor* 'Okee Giant' |
| ***minor*** × ***oreophila*** | CSWC |
| × ***mitchelliana*** ♀H1 | SHmp WSSs |
| × ***moorei*** | CHew WSSs |
| - 'Brook's Hybrid' | CHew CSWC EECP NChu WSSs |
| ***oreophila*** | CHew CSWC NChu SHmp WSSs |
| ***oreophila*** × ***purpurea*** subsp. ***venosa*** | CSWC NChu |
| × ***popei*** | CSWC NChu |
| ***psittacina*** | CHew CSWC EECP NChu SHmp WSSs |
| * - f. ***heterophylla*** | CSWC |
| ***purpurea*** | MREP SPlb |
| - subsp. ***purpurea*** | CHew CSWC MCCP NChu SHmp WSSs |
| - - f. ***heterophylla*** | CSWC WSSs |
| - subsp. ***venosa*** | CHew CSWC SHmp WSSs |
| - - var. ***burkii*** | CSWC NChu WSSs |
| × ***readii*** | SHmp WSSs |
| × ***rehderi*** | SHmp |
| ***rubra*** | CSWC EECP NChu WSSs |
| - subsp. ***alabamensis*** | CHew CSWC NChu SHmp WSSs |
| - subsp. ***gulfensis*** | CHew CSWC NChu SHmp WSSs |
| * - - f. ***heterophylla*** | CSWC WSSs |
| - subsp. ***jonesii*** | CSWC EECP NChu WSSs |
| * - - f. ***heterophylla*** | CSWC WSSs |
| - subsp. ***rubra*** | CHew CSWC WSSs |
| - subsp. ***wherryi*** | CHew CSWC EECP NChu WSSs |
| - - giant | WSSs |
| - - yellow-flowered | CSWC WSSs |
| × ***swaniana*** | SHmp |
| 'Umlanftiana' | CSWC |
| × ***wrigleyana*** ♀H1 | MREP |

## *Saruma* (*Aristolochiaceae*)

| | |
|---|---|
| ***henryi*** | CAby CLAP CPom LEdu MAvo SBrt SUsu WCot WCru WPGP WSHC |

## *Sasa* (*Poaceae*)

| | |
|---|---|
| ***chrysantha*** misapplied | see *Pleioblastus chino* |
| ***disticha*** 'Mirrezuzume' | see *Pleioblastus pygmaeus* 'Mirrezuzume' |
| ***glabra*** f. ***albostriata*** | see *Sasaella masamuneana* 'Albostriata' |
| ***kagamiana*** | NLar |
| ***kurilensis*** | EPla LPal MWhi MWht WFar WJun |
| § - 'Shima-shimofuri' (v) | EPPr EPfP EPla MMoz MWht WJun |

| | |
|---|---|
| - 'Shimofuri' | see *S. kurilensis* 'Shima-shimofuri' |
| - short | EPla |
| ***nana*** | see *S. veitchii* f. *minor* |
| ***nipponica*** | WJun |
| ***oshidensis*** | EPla |
| § ***palmata*** | CDul CWib EHoe MCCP MMuc MWhi SBfd SEND SLim WDin WFar WHer |
| - f. ***nebulosa*** | CBcs CBct CDoC CFir CHEx ENBC EPfP EPla EWes MBrN MMoz MWht NLar SArc WDyG WFar WJun WMoo |
| ***quelpaertensis*** | EPla MWht |
| ***tessellata*** | see *Indocalamus tessellatus* |
| ***tsuboiana*** | CBcs CDoC ENBC EPla GQui LPal LRHS MMoz MWht NGdn NLar SBig SGol WDyG WFar WMoo WPnP |
| § ***veitchii*** | CBcs CDoy CKno CTrC ECha EHoe ENBC EPfP EPla MMoz MMuc MRav MWht NLar SEND SGol SPer WDin WFar WJun WMoo |
| § - f. ***minor*** | MCCP WMoo |

## *Sasaella* (*Poaceae*)

| | |
|---|---|
| ***glabra*** | see *S. masamuneana* |
| § ***masamuneana*** | ENBC EPla WDyG |
| § - 'Albostriata' (v) | CDoC CEnt CWib ENBC EPPr EPla LEdu LPal LRHS MCCP MMoz MMuc MWht NGdn SBig SEND WDyG WFar WJun WMoo WPGP |
| - f. ***aureostriata*** (v) | EPla MMoz NPal |
| § ***ramosa*** | CHEx EPla MCCP MWht WDin |

## *Sassafras* (*Lauraceae*)

| | |
|---|---|
| ***albidum*** | CArn CBcs CCCN CMCN EBee EPfP LRHS MAsh MBri SBfd SKHP SLon SSpi WPGP |
| ***tzumu*** | WPGP |

## satsuma see *Citrus unshiu*

## *Satureja* ✿ (*Lamiaceae*)

| | |
|---|---|
| ***coerulea*** ♀H4 | CWan EWes NBir XSen |
| ***douglasii*** | EOHP SBfd SHDw WJek |
| - 'Indian Mint'PBR | CArn EGHP MHer |
| ***hortensis*** | CBod ELau GPoy ILis MHer MNHC SBfd SIde WJek |
| - 'Selektion' | LLWP |
| ***intricata*** new | XSen |
| ***macedonica*** | LLWP |
| ***montana*** | CArn CHby CWan EGHP ELau GKev GPoy ILis ITim LLWP MBri MHer MNHC NMen SBfd SDix SEND SIde SRms SVic WHfH WJek WPer XSen |
| * - ***citriodora*** | GPoy LLWP MHer XSen |
| § - subsp. ***illyrica*** | WJek WPer XLum XSen |
| - 'Purple Mountain' | GPoy LLWP MHer |
| - ***subspicata*** | see *S. montana* subsp. *illyrica* |
| ***obovata*** new | XSen |
| ***parnassica*** | LLWP WPer |
| ***repanda*** | see *S. spicigera* |
| ***seleriana*** | SDys |
| § ***spicigera*** | CArn CBod CPBP CPrp ELau EPot LEdu LLWP MHer NBir NMen SIde WJek WPer XLum |
| ***spinosa*** new | XSen |
| ***thymbra*** | CArn SBfd SHDw XSen |
| § ***viminea*** | EOHP |

## *Saurauia* (*Actinidiaceae*)

| | |
|---|---|
| ***subspinosa*** | CHEx |

## *Sauromatum* (*Araceae*)

| | |
|---|---|
| ***guttatum*** | see *S. venosum* |
| § ***venosum*** | CArn CDes CPLG EAmu EBee ECho EShb GCal LAma LEdu LRHS NLar SBig SBrd WCot WCru WPGP |
| - CC 3810 | WCot |

## *Saururus* (*Saururaceae*)

| | |
|---|---|
| ***cernuus*** | CBen CHEx CRow CWat EHon ELan LLWG LPBA MSKA MWts SRms SWat WMAq |
| ***chinensis*** | CRow LLWG |

## *Saussurea* (*Asteraceae*)

| | |
|---|---|
| ***costus*** | CArn GPoy |
| aff. ***superba*** | GKev |

## savory, summer see *Satureja hortensis*

## savory, winter see *Satureja montana*

## *Saxegothaea* (*Podocarpaceae*)

| | |
|---|---|
| ***conspicua*** | CBcs CDoC CDul GBin NLar |

## *Saxifraga* ✿ (*Saxifragaceae*)

| | |
|---|---|
| McB 1377 (7) | NMen WAbe |
| McB 1377/1 (7) new | NWad |
| McB 1377/2 (7) | NWad |
| SEP 45 | NMen |
| 'Ada' (× *petraschii*) (7) | NMen |
| 'Aemula' (× *borisii*) (7) | NMen |
| 'Affinis' (× *petraschii* ) (7) | CPBP NMen |
| ***aizoides*** (9) | ECho |
| - SDR 5497 | GKev |
| - var. ***atrorubens*** (9) | ECho GKev |
| ***aizoon*** | see *S. paniculata* |
| 'Aladdin' (× *borisii*) (7) | NMen |
| 'Alan Hayhurst' (8) | CPBP GEdr WAbe WFar |
| 'Alan Martin' (× *boydilacina*) (7) | ECho NLar NMen |
| 'Alba' ambig. | LRHS |
| 'Alba' (× *apiculata*) (7) | ECho EDAr MAsh MHer NMen NRya SPlb WFar WPat |
| 'Alba' (× *arco-valleyi*) | see *S.* 'Ophelia' |
| 'Alba' (*oppositifolia*) (7) | ECho ELan EWes ITim NWCA NWad WAbe |
| 'Alba' (*sempervivum*) | see *S.* 'Zita' |
| 'Albert Einstein' (× *apiculata*) (7) | NMen |
| 'Albertii' (*callosa*) | see *S.* 'Albida' |
| § 'Albida' (*callosa*) (8) | ECho WAbe |
| 'Albrecht Dürer' (Lasciva Group) (7) | WAbe |
| 'Aldebaran' (× *borisii*) (7) | NMen |
| 'Aldo Bacci' (Milford Group) (7) | NMen |
| 'Alfons Mucha' (7) | NMen WPat |
| 'Allendale Acclaim' (× *lismorensis*) (7) | NMen |
| 'Allendale Accord' (*diapensioides* × *lilacina*) (7) | NMen |
| 'Allendale Allure' (*aretiodes* × *stolitzkae*) (7) | NMen |

| | |
|---|---|
| 'Allendale Amber' (7) | NMen |
| 'Allendale Andante' (× *arco-valleyi*) (7) | NMen |
| 'Allendale Angel' (× *kepleri*) (7) | NMen WAbe |
| 'Allendale Argonaut' (7) | NMen |
| 'Allendale Ballad' (7) | NMen WAbe |
| 'Allendale Ballet' (7) | NMen |
| 'Allendale Bamby' (× *lismorensis*) (7) | EPot NMen |
| 'Allendale Banshee' (7) | NMen |
| 'Allendale Beau' (× *lismorensis*) (7) | CPBP NMen |
| 'Allendale Beauty' (*aretiodes* × *cinerea*) (7) | CPBP NMen |
| 'Allendale Betty' (× *lismorensis*) (7) | EPot NMen |
| 'Allendale Billows' (7) | NMen |
| 'Allendale Blossom' (× *limorensis*) (7) | NMen |
| 'Allendale Bonny' (7) | NMen WAbe |
| 'Allendale Boon' (× *izari*) (7) | NMen |
| 'Allendale Bounty' (7) | NMen |
| 'Allendale Bravo' (× *lismorensis*) (7) | NMen WAbe |
| 'Allendale Cabal' (7) | NMen |
| 'Allendale Carol' (7) | NMen |
| 'Allendale Celt' (× *novacastelensis*) (7) | NMen |
| 'Allendale Charm' (Swing Group) (7) | CPBP NMen WAbe |
| 'Allendale Chick' (7) | NHar NMen |
| 'Allendale Comet' (7) | NMen |
| 'Allendale Dance' (7) | NMen |
| 'Allendale Desire' (7) | NMen WAbe |
| 'Allendale Divine' (7) | NMen WAbe |
| 'Allendale Dream' (7) | EPot NMen |
| 'Allendale Duo' (*aretiodes* × *georgei*) (7) | NMen WAbe |
| 'Allendale Elegance' (7) | NMen |
| 'Allendale Elf' (7) | ITim NMen |
| 'Allendale Elite' (7) | NMen |
| 'Allendale Enchantment' (7) | NMen |
| 'Allendale Envoy' (7) | NMen WAbe |
| 'Allendale Epic' (*ferdinandi-cobirgi* × *wendelboi*) (7) | NHar NMen WAbe |
| 'Allendale Fairy' (7) | NHar NMen |
| 'Allendale Fame' (7) | NMen |
| 'Allendale Fancy' (7) | WAbe |
| 'Allendale Frost' (7) | NMen |
| 'Allendale Garnet' (7) | NMen |
| 'Allendale Ghost' (7) | NMen |
| 'Allendale Goblin' (7) | NMen NWCA WAbe |
| 'Allendale Grace' (7) | NMen WAbe |
| 'Allendale Gremlin' (7) | NMen |
| 'Allendale Harvest' (7) | NMen |
| 'Allendale Hobbit' (*matta-florida* × *polueminiana*) (7) | NHar NMen WAbe |
| 'Allendale Host' (*andersonii* × *poluminiana*) (7) | WAbe |
| 'Allendale Icon' (× *polulacina*) (7) | WAbe |
| 'Allendale Imp' (7) | WAbe |
| 'Allendale Ina' (7) | NHar NMen WAbe |
| 'Allendale Joy' (× *wendelacina*) (7) | NMen |
| 'Allendale King' **new** | NMen |
| 'Allendale Magic' **new** | NMen |
| 'Allendale Pearl' (× *novacastelensis*) (7) | NMen |
| 'Allendale Ruby' (7) | NMen |
| 'Allendale Snow' (× *rayei*) (7) | NMen |
| 'Alpenglow' (7) | NMen |
| ***alpigena*** (7) | WAbe |
| 'Amitie' (× *gloriana*) (7) | CFee NMen |
| ***andersonii*** (7) | NMen NRya |
| 'Andrea Cesalpino' (Renaissance Group) (7) | NMen |
| ***angustifolia*** Haw. | see *S. hypnoides* |
| 'Anna' (× *fontanae*) (7) | WAbe |
| 'Anne Beddall' (× *goringiana*) (7) | NMen WAbe |
| 'Antonio Vivaldi' (7) | NMen WAbe |
| × ***apiculata*** *sensu stricto* hort. | see *S.* 'Gregor Mendel' |
| 'Apple Blossom' (15) | ECtt GKev NPro NRya WGor |
| 'Arabella' (× *edithae*) (7) | ECho |
| § 'Arco' (× *arco-valleyi*) (7) | NMen |
| × ***arco-valleyi*** *sensu stricto* hort. | see *S.* 'Arco' |
| × ***arendsii*** purple-flowered (15) | SGar SPlb |
| § 'Aretiastrum' (× *boydii*) (7) | NMen |
| ***aretioides*** (7) | NMen |
| 'Argia Romani' (7) | NMen |
| 'Ariel' (× *hornibrookii*) (7) | NMen |
| 'Arthur' (× *anglica*) (7) | NMen |
| 'Asahi' (*fortunei*) (5) | IVic |
| 'Assimilis' (× *petraschii*) (7) | EPot NMen |
| 'Aufheiter von Eri' (*fortunei*) (5) | IVic |
| 'August Hayek' (× *leyboldii*) (7) | NMen |
| 'Aurea' (*umbrosa*) | see *S.* 'Aureopunctata' |
| 'Aurea Maculata' (*cuneifolia*) | see *S.* 'Aureopunctata' |
| § 'Aureopunctata' (× *urbium*) (11/v) | CMac CTri ECha ECho ELan GKev GMaP LBMP LRHS MHer MLHP MRav NDov SBfd SPer SPlb SPoG SRms STre WMoo XLum |
| 'Autumn Tribute' (*fortunei*) (5) | CLAP WAbe WFar |
| 'Ayako' (*fortunei*) (5) **new** | NHar |
| 'Ayer's Rock' (7) | WAbe |
| 'Balcana' (*paniculata*) (8) | WAbe |
| 'Baldensis' | see *S. paniculata* var. *minutifolia* |
| 'Beatles' (7) **new** | EPot |
| § 'Beatrix Stanley' (7) | ECho LRHS MAsh MHer NMen NRya NWad WGor |
| 'Becky Foster' (× *borisii*) (7) | NMen |
| 'Bellisant' (× *hornibrookii*) (7) | NMen |
| 'Beni-komachi' (*fortunei*) **new** | NHar |
| 'Berenika' (× *bertolonii*) (7) | EPot NMen |
| 'Beryl' (× *anglica*) (7) | NMen |
| 'Bettina' (× *paulinae*) (7) | NMen |
| × ***biasolettoi*** *sensu stricto* hort. | see *S.* 'Phoenix' |
| × ***bilekii*** (7) | ECho NMen |
| 'Birch Yellow' | see *S.* 'Pseudoborisii' |
| 'Black Beauty' (15) | MHer |

| |  |  |
|---|---|---|
| | 'Black Ruby' (*fortunei*) (5) | Widely available |
| | 'Blackberry and Apple Pie' (*fortunei*) (5) | CBct CBod CElw CLAP CPLG EBee ECtt EPfP GAbr GEdr IBal ITim IVic LRHS MBrN MLHP MNrw NHar NMen NMyG SBch SBfd SPet SWvt WAul WCot WFar WMoo WWEG |
| | 'Blaník' (× *borisii*) (7) | NMen |
| | 'Blanka' (× *borisii*) (7) | NMen |
| | 'Bob Hawkins' (15/v) | EDAr LRHS NWad |
| § | 'Bodensee' (× *hofmannii*) (7) | WPat |
| | 'Bohdalec' (× *megaseiflora*) (7) | NMen |
| | 'Bohemia' (7) | ECho NLar NMen |
| | × ***borisii*** *sensu stricto* hort. | see *S.* 'Sofia' |
| | 'Bornmuelleri' (7) | NMen |
| | 'Boston Spa' (× *elisabethae*) (7) | ECho ECtt LRHS MAsh MHer NLar NMen SPlb WPat |
| | 'Brailes' (× *poluanglica*) (7) | NMen |
| | 'Brendan' | NMen |
| | 'Brian Arundel' (Magnus Group) (7) | NMen |
| | 'Bridget' (× *edithae*) (7) | ECho LRHS NMen |
| | 'Brimstone' (7) | NMen WAbe |
| | 'Brno' (× *elisabethae*) (7) | NMen |
| | 'Brookside' (*burseriana*) (7) | NMen |
| | ***brunoniana*** | see *S. brunonis* |
| § | ***brunonis*** (1) CC 5315 | GKev |
| | - CC&McK 108 | NWCA |
| | 'Bryn Llwyd' | WAbe |
| | ***bryoides*** (10) | ECho |
| | 'Buchholzii' (× *fleischeri*) (7) **new** | NMen |
| | × ***burnatii*** (8) | LRHS NMen NPro NSla WAbe WGor |
| | ***burseriana*** (7) | ECho WAbe WGor |
| | 'Buster' (× *hardingii*) (7) | NMen |
| | 'Buttercup' (× *kayei*) (7) | EPot ITim NWCA WHoo |
| | × ***byam-groundsii*** (7) | WFar |
| | × ***caesia*** misapplied (× *fritschiana*) | see *S.* 'Krain' |
| | ***caesia*** L. (8) | SRms WAbe |
| § | ***callosa*** (8) 🏆H4 | ECho EDAr GEdr MDKP MHer MLHP NMen WAbe WFar WPat WTin |
| | - subsp. ***callosa*** (8) | ECho |
| § | - - var. ***australis*** (8) | GJos GKev NBro NMen |
| | - var. ***lantoscana*** | see *S. callosa* subsp. *callosa* var. *australis* |
| | - ***lingulata*** | see *S. callosa* |
| | 'Cambridge Seedling' (7) | NMen |
| | 'Camyra' (7) | WAbe |
| | × ***canis-dalmatica*** | see *S.* 'Canis-dalmatica' |
| § | 'Canis-dalmatica' (× *gaudinii*) (8) 🏆H4 | ECho ECtt EPot GEdr GGar GJos LRHS NHar NMen NWCA NWad WGor WPer |
| § | 'Carmen' (× *elisabethae*) (7) | NMen WAbe |
| § | 'Carniolica' (*paniculata*) (8) | NBro NHol NMen NWCA |
| | ***carolinica*** | see *S.* 'Carniolica' (*paniculata*) |
| | ***cartilaginea*** | see *S. paniculata* subsp. *cartilaginea* |
| | 'Castor' (× *bilekii*) (7) | NMen |
| | 'Caterhamensis' (*cotyledon*) (8) | NHar |
| | 'Cathy Reed' (× *polulacina*) (7) | NMen |
| | ***caucasica*** (7) | ECho WAbe |
| | ***cebennensis*** (15) 🏆H2 | EPot NMen NRya |
| | ***cespitosa*** (15) | NMen WAbe |
| | 'Chambers' Pink Pride' | see *S.* 'Miss Chambers' |
| | 'Charles Chaplin' (7) | ECho NHar NMen WAbe |
| | 'Charles Darwin' (7) **new** | EPot |
| | 'Cheap Confections' (*fortunei*) (4) | CBct CLAP EBee ECtt GBee LLHF NMen SBch SBfd WBor WCot WFar WMoo WOld WPGP WWEG |
| § | ***cherlerioides*** (10) | NRya WFar |
| | 'Cherry Pie' (*fortunei*) (5) | CBct CLAP EBee GEdr LLHF LRHS NBir NHar NMyG WCot |
| | 'Cherrytrees' (× *boydii*) (7) | NMen WAbe |
| * | 'Chetwynd' (*marginata*) (7) | NMen |
| | 'Chez Nous' (× *gloriana*) (7/v) | NMen |
| | 'Chodov' (7) | EPot NMen |
| | 'Christine' (× *anglica*) (7) | ECho NMen |
| | ***cinerea*** (7) | NMen WAbe |
| | - McB 1376 | NWad |
| | 'Cio-Cio-San' (Vanessa Group) (7) | NMen |
| | 'Citronella' (7) | ECho WAbe |
| | 'Claire Felstead' (*cinerea* × *poluniniana*) (7) | NMen |
| | 'Clare' (× *anglica*) (7) | NMen |
| § | 'Clarence Elliott' (*umbrosa*) (11) 🏆H4 | CMea CTri ECho EWes GAbr GCal GKev GMaP MDKP MHer NDov NHol NMen NRya NVic NWCA STre WFar WPat WWEG |
| | 'Claude Monet' (Impressio Group) (7) | WAbe |
| | 'Claudia' (× *borisii*) (7) | NMen |
| | 'Cleo' (× *boydii*) (7) | NMen |
| | 'Cloth of Gold' (*exarata* subsp. *moschata*) (15) | ECha ECho EDAr ELan GKev GMaP LRHS MAsh MHer NHol NMen NRya NSla NWad SPlb SPoG SRms WAbe WFar |
| | ***cochlearis*** (8) | CTri GEdr LRHS MAsh NBro NMen NSla SBch STre WAbe WPer |
| | 'Cockscomb' (*paniculata*) (8) | ECho GEdr GLam NHar NMen NRya NWad WAbe |
| | ***columnaris*** (7) | NMen WAbe |
| | 'Combrook' (× *poluanglica*) (7) | NMen |
| | 'Coningsby Queen' (× *hornibrookii*) (7) | NMen |
| | ***continentalis*** (15) | NWCA |
| | 'Conwy Snow' (*fortunei*) (5) | CLAP NHar WAbe WFar |
| | 'Conwy Star' (*fortunei*) (5) | CLAP NHar WAbe WFar |
| | 'Coolock Gem' (7) | NMen WAbe |
| | 'Coolock Jean' (7) | NMen WAbe |
| | 'Coolock Kate' (7) | NMen WAbe |
| | 'Cordata' (*burseriana*) (7) | NMen |
| | 'Corona' (× *boydii*) (7) | NMen |
| | 'Correnie Claret' (15) | EWes GLam |
| | 'Correvoniana' misapplied | see *S.* 'Lagraveana' |
| | 'Correvoniana' Farrer (*paniculata*) (8) | EDAr EPot MHer MSCN SEND WFar |
| | ***cortusifolia*** (5) | CLAP CSpr ECho |
| | - B&SWJ 5879 | WCru |
| | - var. ***stolonifera*** (5) | ECho GCal |
| | - - B&SWJ 6205 | WCru |
| | 'Cotton Crochet' (*fortunei*) (5/d) | CAbP CBct EBee ECtt GEdr LRHS NHar NMyG SBfd SHeu WBor WCot WFar WMoo WOld |
| | ***cotyledon*** (8) | ECho WAbe WCFE WPer |
| § | 'Cranbourne' (× *anglica*) (7) 🏆H4 | CMea ECho LRHS MAsh NMen NWCA WPat |

| | | |
|---|---|---|
| | 'Cream' (*paniculata*) (8) | ECho |
| | 'Cream Seedling' (× *elisabethae*) (7) | ECho MAsh NMen |
| | 'Crenata' (*burseriana*) (7) | EPot NMen |
| | 'Crimscote-love' (*poluanglica*) (7) | NMen |
| | 'Crimson Diall' (× *irvingii*) (7) | NMen |
| | 'Crimson Rose' (*paniculata*) | see *S.* 'Rosea' (*paniculata*) |
| § | ***crustata*** (8) | ECho GLam MDKP NHar NMen WAbe WThu |
| | - var. ***vochinensis*** | see *S. crustata* |
| | 'Crystal Pink' (*fortunei*) (5/v) | CBct CPLG ECtt GAbr GBBs GEdr IFoB LRHS MNrw NHar NMen NMyG NPnk NSla WCot WFar WGrn WOld |
| | 'Crystalie' (× *biasolettoi*) (7) | LRHS NMen NRya WPat |
| | 'Cultrata' (*paniculata*) (8) | NBro |
| | 'Cumulus' (*iranica* hybrid) (7) ♀H4 | EDAr NMen WAbe |
| | ***cuneata*** (15) | NHol |
| § | ***cuneifolia*** (11) | ECho GGar LBee MHer MLHP MWat NWCA NWad WFar WPer |
| | - var. ***capillipes*** | see *S. cuneifolia* subsp. *cuneifolia* |
| § | - subsp. ***cuneifolia*** (11) | ECtt GJos |
| * | - var. ***subintegra*** (11) | ECho |
| | 'Cuscutiformis' (*stolonifera*) (5) | CAby CElw CHid CPLG EBla EWld GEdr LRHS MLLN MSCN SBch SMrm SRms WBor WBox WCru WPGP XLum |
| | ***dahurica*** | see *S. cuneifolia* |
| | 'Dainty Dame' (× *arco-valleyi*) (7) | NMen NWCA |
| | 'Dana' (× *megaseiflora*) (7) | NMen |
| | 'Dartington Double' (15/d) | EWes WFar |
| | 'David' (7) | NMen |
| | 'Dawn Frost' (7) | EPot NMen |
| | 'Delia' (× *hornibrookii*) (7) | ITim NMen |
| § | 'Denisa' (× *pseudokotschyi*) (7) | NMen |
| | ***densa*** | see *S. cherlerioides* |
| | 'Dentata' (× *geum*) | see *S.* 'Dentata' (× *polita*) |
| § | 'Dentata' (× *polita*) (11) | CSpe ECha ECho GCal GGar WMoo WWEG |
| | 'Dentata' (× *urbium*) | see *S.* 'Dentata' (× *polita*) |
| | ***desoulavyi*** (7) | NMen |
| | 'Diana' ambig. | NLar |
| | ***diapensioides*** (7) | NMen WAbe |
| | ***dinnikii*** (7) | EPot NMen WAbe |
| | × ***dinninaris*** (7) | NMen |
| | 'Dobruška' (× *irvingii*) (7) | NMen |
| | 'Doctor Clay' (*paniculata*) (8) | EPot GEdr GKev LRHS NHar NMen NRya SPlb WAbe |
| | 'Doctor Ramsey' (8) | ECho ECtt EWes GEdr LRHS NBro NHol NMen NWad WAbe WGor WPnn |
| | 'Don Giovanni' (7) | NMen |
| | 'Donald Mann' (15) | EWes |
| | 'Donnington Chalice' | NMen |
| | 'Donnington Gold' | NMen |
| | 'Donnington Veil' | NMen |
| | 'Dorothy Milne' (7) | NMen |
| | 'Drakula' (*ferdinandi-coburgi*) (7) | ECho LRHS NMen |
| | 'Dubarry' (15) | EWes NRya |
| | 'Dulcimer' (× *petraschii*) (7) | NMen |
| | 'Edgar Irmscher' (7) | NMen |
| | 'Edith' (× *edithae*) (7) | ECho LRHS |
| | 'Edward Elgar' (× *megaseiflora*) (7) | NMen |
| | 'Egmont' (7) | NMen |
| | 'Elf' (7) | see *S.* 'Beatrix Stanley' |
| | 'Eliot Hodgkin' (× *millstreamiana*) (7) | NMen |
| | × ***elisabethae*** *sensu stricto* hort. | see *S.* 'Carmen' |
| | × ***elisabethae*** Sünd. (7) | EDAr NWCA |
| | 'Elizabeth Sinclair' (× *elisabethae*) (7) | EPot GKev NMen |
| | 'Ellie Brinckerhoff' (× *hornibrookii*) (7) | NMen |
| | 'Elliott's Variety' | see *S.* 'Clarence Elliott' (*umbrosa*) |
| | ***epiphylla*** BWJ 8177 (5) **new** | WCru |
| § | 'Ernst Heinrich' (× *heinrichii*) (7) | NMen |
| | 'Esther' (× *burnatii*) (8) | CMea ECho GEdr GKev LRHS MAsh NMen NWCA SRGP WAbe WPnn |
| § | 'Eulenspiegel' (× *geuderi*) (7) | NMen NWad |
| | 'Eva Hanzliková' (× *izari*) (7) | NMen WAbe |
| | ***exarata*** (15) | NMen WAbe |
| § | - subsp. ***moschata*** (15) | NBir |
| | - - 'Elf' (15) | ECtt EPfP NMen SRms WGor |
| | fair maids of France | see *S.* 'Flore Pleno' |
| | 'Fairy' (*exarata* subsp. *moschata*) (15) | CMea ECtt GLam NBir |
| | 'Faldonside' (× *boydii*) (7) ♀H4 | MAsh NMen NRya WPat |
| | 'Falstaff' (*burseriana*) (7) | NRya |
| | × ***farreri*** hort. | see *S.* 'Reginald Farrer' |
| § | 'Faust' (× *borisii*) (7) | NMen |
| | 'Favorit' (× *bilekii*) (7) | NMen |
| § | ***federici-augusti*** subsp. ***grisebachii*** (7) ♀H2-3 | ECho GKev LRHS NSla WAbe WFar |
| | 'Ferdinand' (× *hofmannii*) (7) | NMen |
| | ***ferdinandi-coburgi*** (7) ♀H4 | ECtt NMen NRya SBch WAbe |
| § | - subsp. ***chrysosplenifolia*** var. ***rhodopea*** (7) | ECho EPot LRHS NMen |
| | - var. ***pravislavii*** | see *S. ferdinandi-coburgi* subsp. *chrysosplenifolia* var. *rhodopea* |
| | - var. ***radoslavoffii*** | see *S. ferdinandi-coburgi* subsp. *chrysosplenifolia* var. *rhodopea* |
| | 'Findling' (15) | EPfP LRHS MAsh NMen NWad SPoG WAbe |
| | 'Firebrand' (× *kochii*) (7) | NMen WAbe |
| | 'Five Color' (*fortunei*) | see *S.* 'Go-nishiki' |
| § | ***flagellaris*** (1) | NMen WAbe |
| | 'Flavescens' misapplied | see *S.* 'Lutea' (*paniculata*) |
| | × ***fleischeri*** (7) | NMen |
| § | 'Flore Pleno' (*granulata*) (15/d) | CFir CRDP EWes NBir SUsu WAbe WFar |
| | 'Flowers of Sulphur' | see *S.* 'Schwefelblüte' |
| | 'Flush' (× *petraschii*) (7) | NMen WAbe |
| | ***fortunei*** (5) ♀H4 | CHEx CLAP CMac ECho GAbr GMaP NBir NPnk SRms WAbe |
| | - B&SWJ 6346 | WCru |
| | - f. ***alpina*** (5) | CLAP |
| | - - from Hokkaido (5) | CLAP WCru |
| | - var. ***koraiensis*** (5) B&SWJ 8688 | WCru |
| | - 'Musgrove Pink' | CLAP |
| | - var. ***obtusocuneata*** (5) | CLAP ECho LLHF NMen WAbe |

|  |  |
|---|---|
| – f. ***partita*** (5) | CLAP GEdr WCru |
| – var. ***pilosissima*** (5) B&SWJ 8557 | WCru |
| – pink-flowered (5) | CLAP WAbe WFar |
| – var. ***suwoensis*** (5) | CLAP |
| 'Foster's Gold' (× *elisabethae*) (7) | NMen WAbe |
| 'Four Winds' (15) | EWes MAsh SPoG |
| 'Francesco Redi' (Renaissance Group) | NMen WAbe |
| 'Francis Cade' (8) | EPot GAbr WAbe |
| 'Frank Sinatra' (× *poluanglica*) (7) | NMen |
| 'Franz Liszt' (7) | WAbe |
| 'Franzii' (× *paulinae*) (7) | NMen |
| 'Freckles' | CYeo GKev |
| 'Frederik Chopin' (7) | NMen WAbe |
| 'Friar Tuck' (× *boydii*) (7) | NMen NWad |
| 'Friesei' (× *salmonica*) (7) | EPot NMen |
| × ***fritschiana*** (8) | NMen |
| 'Fumiko' (*fortunei*) (5) | CLAP WAbe WCru |
| 'Funkii' (× *petraschii*) (7) | NMen |
| 'Gaertneri' (× *mariae-theresiae*) (7) | NMen |
| 'Gaiety' (15) | ECho LRHS SPoG WFar |
| 'Galahad' (× *elizabethae*) (7) | NMen |
| 'Galaxie' (× *megaseiflora*) (7) | NMen |
| 'Ganymede' (*burseriana*) (7) | NMen |
| 'Gelber Findling' (7) | EPot WAbe |
| 'Gelbes Monster' (*fortunei*) (5) | IVic |
| 'Gem' (× *irvingii*) (7) | NMen |
| 'General Joffre' (15) | see *S.* 'Maréchal Joffre' |
| 'Geoff Wilson' (× *biasolettoi*) | NMen |
| 'George Gershwin' (Blues Group) (7) | NMen |
| ***georgei*** (7) | EPot NMen WAbe |
| 'Gertie Pritchard' (× *megaseiflora*) | see *S.* 'Mrs Gertie Prichard' |
| × ***geuderi*** *sensu stricto* hort. | see *S.* 'Eulenspiegel' |
| § × ***geum*** (11) | CHid MRav WFar WMoo |
| – Dixter form (11) | ECha WFar WWEG |
| 'Gleborg' (15) | EWes GAbr SPoG |
| 'Gloria' (*burseriana*) (7) ♀H4 | ECho LRHS MAsh NMen WPat |
| 'Gloriana' | see *S.* 'Godiva' |
| × ***gloriana*** *sensu stricto* hort. (7) | see *S.* 'Godiva' |
| 'Gloriosa' (× *gloriana*) (7) | see *S.* 'Godiva' |
| 'Glückliches Mädchen' (*fortunei*) (5) | IVic |
| § 'Godiva' (× *gloriana*) (7) | NMen WAbe |
| 'Gold Dust' (× *eudoxiana*) (7) | ECho MAsh NMen NRya |
| 'Gold Mound' | WNew |
| 'Golden Falls' (15/v) | EWes LRHS SPlb SPoG |
| Golden Prague (× *pragensis*) | see *S.* 'Zlatá Praha' |
| § 'Go-nishiki' (*fortunei*) (5) | GEdr LLHF NHar NMyG |
| 'Gorges du Verdon' (8) | GKev |
| 'Goring White' (7) | NMen |
| 'Gothenburg' (7) | NMen WAbe WPat |
| 'Grace' (× *arendsii*) (15/v) | see *S.* 'Seaspray' |
| 'Grace Farwell' (× *anglica*) (7) | ECho NLar NMen NRya NWCA WHoo |
| 'Grandiflora' (*burseriana*) (7) | NMen |
| ***granulata*** (15) | CRWN ECho EDAr GJos NMir NSla WAbe WFar |
| 'Gratoides' (× *grata*) (7) | NMen |
| § 'Gregor Mendel' (× *apiculata*) (7) ♀H4 | CMea CSam CYeo ECho ECtt EPot LRHS NLar NMen SRms WAbe WFar WHoo |
| ***grisebachii*** | see *S. federici-augusti* subsp. *grisebachii* |
| 'Haagii' (× *eudoxiana*) (7) | CTri ECho MAsh NLar NMen |
| 'Hare Knoll Beauty' (8) | ECho GKev LRHS NHar NMen NRya NSla WAbe |
| 'Harley' (7) | NMen |
| 'Harlow Car' (7) | NMen NSla |
| 'Harold Bevington' (*paniculata*) (8) | GEdr |
| 'Harold Lloyd' (7) | NMen |
| 'Harry Marshall' (× *irvingii*) (7) | NMen NWad |
| 'Hartswood White' (15) | MWat |
| 'Harvest Moon' (*stolonifera*) (5) | CHEx WBor WHer |
| 'Hedwig' (× *malbyana*) (7) | NMen |
| × ***heinreichii*** *sensu stricto* hort. | see *S.* 'Ernst Heinrich' |
| 'Heisel Kurenai' (*fortunei*) (5) | IVic |
| 'Hi-Ace' (15/v) | ECtt EDAr MHer SPlb |
| 'Hime' (*stolonifera*) (5) | WCru |
| 'Hindhead Seedling' (× *boydii*) (7) | LRHS NMen |
| ***hirsuta*** (11) | EBla EWTr EWld GGar LRHS MMuc WCru |
| 'Hirsuta' (× *geum*) | see *S.* × *geum* |
| 'Hirtella' Ingwersen (*paniculata*) (8) | EPot |
| 'Hirtifolia' (*paniculata*) (8) | GJos |
| 'His Majesty' (× *irvingii*) (7) | EPot NMen WFar |
| 'Hiten' (*fortunei*) | GKev |
| 'Hitomebore' (*fortunei*) (5) **new** | NHar |
| 'Hocker Edge' (× *arco-valleyi*) (7) | ITim NMen |
| 'Holden Seedling' (15) | ECtt EWes |
| 'Honington' (× *poluanglica*) (7) | NMen |
| × ***hornibrookii*** (7) | WPat |
| ***hostii*** (8) | ECho EDAr GKev NWad WTin |
| – subsp. ***hostii*** (8) | GAuc GEdr GLam XLum |
| – – var. ***altissima*** (8) | STre |
| – subsp. ***rhaetica*** (8) | GBin NBro NMen WAbe |
| 'Hradčany' (× *megaseiflora*) (7) | NMen |
| 'Hsitou Silver' (*stolonifera*) (5) | CFee EPPr MDKP SPhx |
| 'Hunscote' (× *poluanglica*) (7) | NMen |
| hybrid JB 11 | NMen |
| § ***hypnoides*** (15) | NMir SPoG WAbe |
| ***hypostoma*** (7) | WAbe |
| 'Iceland' (*oppositifolia*) (7) | EWes WAbe |
| 'Icicle' (× *elisabethae*) (7) | NMen |
| 'Idlecote' | NMen |
| 'Ignaz Dörfler' (× *doerfleri*) (7) | NMen WAbe |
| ***imparilis*** (5) | CLAP GEdr WCru |
| 'Ingeborg' (15) | CElw ECha |
| ***iranica*** (7) | NMen |
| 'Irene Bacci' (× *baccii*) (7) | NMen |
| × ***irvingii*** *sensu stricto* hort. | see *S.* 'Walter Irving' |
| × ***irvingii*** Hort. ex A.S. Thomps. (7) | ECho EPot |

'Ivana' (× *caroliquarti*) (7) NMen WAbe
'Jan Neruda' (× *megaseiflora*) (7) CPBP NMen
'Jan Palach' (× *krausii*) (7) CMea EPot NMen
'Jason' (× *elisabethae*) (7) EPot NMen
'Jenkinsiae' (× *irvingii*) (7) ♀H4 CFee CYeo ECho EDAr LRHS MAsh NMen NRya NWad SEND WAbe WPat
'Joachim Barrande' (× *siluris*) (7) EPot
§ 'Johann Kellerer' (× *kellereri*) (7) CFee EPot WAbe
'John Byam-Grounds' (Honor Group) (7) WAbe
'John Tomlinson' (*burseriana*) (7) NMen
'Jorg' (× *biasolettoi*) (7) EPot
'Josef Čapek' (× *megaseiflora*) (7) NMen
'Josef Mánes' (× *borisii*) (7) NMen
'Joy' see *S.* 'Kaspar Maria Sternberg'
'Judith Shackleton' (× *abingdonensis*) (7) NMen WAbe
'Juliet' see *S.* 'Riverslea'
§ ***juniperifolia*** (7) CMea CYeo ECho EDAr GAbr MAsh NWCA SRms
'Jupiter' (× *megaseiflora*) (7) NMen
'Kampa' (7) NMen
'Kanna' (*fortunei*) (5) IVic
***karadzicensis*** (7) NMen
'Karasin' (7) NMen
'Karel Čapek' (× *megaseiflora*) (7) ECho EPot LRHS NMen NRya NWad WAbe
'Karel Stivín' (× *edithae*) (7) NMen
'Karlštejn' (× *borisii*) (7) EPot
§ 'Kaspar Maria Sternberg' (× *petraschii*) (7) LRHS NMen WPat
'Kath Dryden' (7) ECho ECtt GEdr GKev ITim NWad
'Kathleen' (× *polulacina*) (7) EPot WAbe WFar
'Kathleen Pinsent' (8) ♀H4 ECho NWCA
× ***kellereri*** *sensu stricto* hort. see *S.* 'Johann Kellerer'
'Ken McGregor' (7) NMen WAbe
'Kestoniensis' (× *salmonica*) (7) NMen
'Kew Gem' (× *petraschii*) (7) ECho NMen
'Kewensis' (× *kellereri*) (7) NMen WAbe
'Kineton' (× *poluanglica*) (7) ITim NMen
'King Lear' (× *bursiculata*) (7) ECho LRHS NMen
'Kinki Purple' (*stolonifera*) (5) ELon EShb EWld GGar WCru WPGP
'Knapton Pink' (15) ECtt EDAr EPfP MAsh NPro NRya SPoG WAbe WFar
'Knebworth' (8) ECho
* 'Koigokora' (*fortunei*) (5) NHar
'Kokaku' (*fortunei*) LLHF
'Kon Tiki' (7) WAbe
* 'Kosumosu' (*fortunei*) (5) NHar WOld
'Koukan' (*fortunei*) (5) IVic
§ 'Krain' (× *fritschiana*) (8) ECho GEdr
'Krákatit' (× *megaseiflora*) (7) NMen
'Krasava' (× *megaseiflora*) (7) ITim NMen
'Kyrilli' (× *borisii*) (7) NMen
'Labe' (× *arco-valleyi*) (7) CPBP NMen WAbe
'Ladislav Čelakovský' (7) NMen
'Lady Beatrix Stanley' see *S.* 'Beatrix Stanley'
'Lagraveana' (*paniculata*) (8) ♀H4 ECho EDAr LRHS NRya WGor
'Laka' (7) **new** EPot
× ***landaueri*** *sensu stricto* hort. see *S.* 'Leonore'
'Lemon Hybrid' (× *boydii*) (7) NMen
'Lemon Spires' (7) NMen WAbe
'Lenka' (× *byam-groundsii*) (7) NMen
'Leo Gordon Godseff' (× *elisabethae*) (7) ECho LRHS NMen
§ 'Leonore' (× *landaueri*) (7) ECho LRHS WFar
'Letchworth Gem' (× *urbium*) (11) ECho GCal NWCA
'Licht des Cerise' (*fortunei*) (5) IVic
'Lidice' (7) NMen WAbe WHoo
'Lilac Time' (× *youngiana*) (7) NMen WAbe
***lilacina*** (7) NMen WPat WThu
'Limelight' (*callosa* subsp. *callosa* var. *australis*) (8) WAbe
'Lindau' (7) NMen
***lingulata*** see *S. callosa*
'Lismore Carmine' (× *lismorensis*) (7) EPot NMen
'Lismore Gem' (× *lismorensis*) (7) ECho NMen
'Lismore Mist' (× *lismorensis*) (7) NMen
'Lismore Pink' (× *lismorensis*) (7) NMen
'Lissadell' (*callosa*) (8) GKev IFoB ITim
* 'Little Piggy' (*epiphylla*) (5) CDes GEdr WCru
'Lizzy' (7) **new** EPot
'Lohengrin' (× *hoerhammeri*) (7) NMen
'Long Acre Pink' (*fortunei*) (5) CLAP
***longifolia*** (8) ECho EPot GKev NSla
– hybrids GKev
'Louis Armstrong' (Blues Group) (7) NMen WAbe
Love Me see *S.* 'Miluj Mne'
***lowndesii*** (7) WAbe
'Loxley' (*poluanglica*) (7) GEdr NMen
'Ludmila Šubrová' (× *bertolonii*) (7) NMen
'Luschtinetz' (15) GLam
'Lutea' (*aizoon*) see *S.* 'Lutea' (*paniculata*)
'Lutea' (*diapensioides*) see *S.* 'Wilhelm Tell', 'Primulina'
'Lutea' (*marginata*) see *S.* 'Faust'
'Lutea' ambig. GJos
§ 'Lutea' (*paniculata*) (8) ♀H4 ECho EDAr EHoe GEdr GGar GMaP NBro NHol NWad WFar
§ 'Luteola' (× *boydii*) (7) ♀H4 WAbe
'Lužnice' (× *poluluteopurpurea*) (7) NMen
***macedonica*** see *S. juniperifolia*
'Magdalena' (× *thomasiana*) (7) NMen
'Magna' (*burseriana*) (7) NMen
'Maigrün' (*fortunei*) (5) **new** NHar

| |  |  |
|---|---|---|
| | 'Maiko' (*fortunei*) (5) **new** | NHar |
| | 'Major' (*cochlearis*) (8) ♀H4 | WGor |
| | 'Major Lutea' | see *S.* 'Luteola' |
| | 'Maly Trpaslík' (*vandellii* × *sempervivum*) (7) | WAbe |
| | 'Mangekyo' (*fortunei*) (5) | IVic |
| | 'Marc Chagall' (Decora Group) (7) | NMen WAbe |
| § | 'Maréchal Joffre' (15) | GAbr NEgg |
| | 'Margarete' (× *borisii*) (7) | NMen |
| | ***marginata*** (7) | WAbe |
| | - var. ***balcanica*** | see *S. marginata* subsp. *marginata* var. *rocheliana* |
| | - subsp. ***marginata*** var. ***boryi*** (7) | NMen WAbe |
| | - - var. ***coriophylla*** (7) | EPot NMen NWCA WAbe |
| § | - - var. ***rocheliana*** (7) | ITim NMen |
| | 'Maria Callas' (× *poluanglica*) (7) | WAbe WGor |
| | 'Maria Luisa' (× *salmonica*) (7) | CFee CPBP NMen WPat |
| | 'Marianna' (× *borisii*) (7) | CMea EPot NMen |
| | 'Marie Stivínová' (× *borisii*) (7) | EPot |
| | 'Maroon Beauty' (*stolonifera*) (5) | EBee ECtt EPPr MDKP NBre NGBo SPhx WCot |
| | 'Mars' (× *elisabethae*) (7) | NMen |
| | 'Marshal Joffre' (15) | see *S.* 'Maréchal Joffre' (15) |
| | 'Marsilio Ficino' (Milford Group) (7) | NMen |
| § | 'Martha' (× *semmleri*) (7) | NMen |
| | 'Mary Golds' (Swing Group) (7) | EDAr GKev ITim NLar WGor |
| | ***matta-florida*** (7) | NMen |
| | 'May Queen' (7) | NMen |
| | × ***megaseiflora*** *sensu stricto* hort. | see *S.* 'Robin Hood' |
| | 'Melrose' (× *salmonica*) (7) | NMen |
| | ***mertensiana*** (6) | GEdr NBir WCru |
| | 'Meteor' (7) | NRya NSla |
| | ***micranthidifolia*** (4) | CLAP WPGP |
| | 'Mikuláš Koperník' (× *zenittensis*) (7) | WAbe |
| | 'Millstream' (8) | NWCA |
| | 'Millstream Cream' (× *elisabethae*) (7) | ECho NMen |
| § | 'Miluj Mne' (× *poluanglica*) (7) | ECho NMen WHoo |
| | 'Minor' (*cochlearis*) (8) ♀H4 | ECho GKev LRHS NHar NMen NWCA WGor WPat |
| | 'Mirko Webr' (Harmonia Group) (*aretioides* × *cinerea*) (7 | NMen WAbe |
| § | 'Miss Chambers' (× *urbium*) (11) | WCot WMoo WSHC |
| | 'Momo Sekisui' (*fortunei*) (5) | IVic |
| | 'Momo Tarou' (*fortunei*) (5) **new** | NHar |
| | 'Mona Lisa' (× *borisii*) (7) | NMen WAbe |
| | 'Monarch' (8) ♀H4 | GAbr WAbe |
| | 'Moonlight' (× *boydii*) | see *S.* 'Sulphurea' |
| | 'Morava' (7) | NMen |
| | ***moschata*** | see *S. exarata* subsp. *moschata* |
| | Mossy Group (15) | LRHS |
| * | 'Mossy Pink' | NBlu SPoG |
| | 'Mossy Red' | SPoG WNew |
| | 'Mossy Triumph' | see *S.* 'Triumph' |
| | 'Mossy White' | GAbr WNew |
| | 'Mother of Pearl' (× *irvingii*) (7) | ECho NMen |
| | 'Mother Queen' (× *irvingii*) (7) | NMen WPat |
| | 'Mount Nachi' (*fortunei*) (5) | CBct CDes CElw CWCL EBee EPfP EWes GAbr GEdr GMaP IBal IVic LRHS MLHP NBro NMen NMyG SPlb SUsu WAbe WCot WFar WMoo WPGP WPer WWEG |
| § | 'Mrs Gertie Prichard' (× *megaseiflora*) (7) | NMen |
| | 'Mrs Helen Terry' (× *salmonica*) (7) | NMen |
| | 'Mrs Leng' (× *elisabethae*) (7) | MDKP NMen |
| | 'Myra' (× *anglica*) (7) | ECho NMen NWCA WHoo WPat |
| | 'Myra Cambria' (× *anglica*) (7) | NMen NWad |
| | 'Myriad' (7) | NMen |
| | 'Nancye' (× *goringiana*) (7) | EPot ITim NMen WAbe |
| | 'Nimbus' (*iranica*) (7) | NMen |
| | 'Niobe' (× *pulvilacina*) (7) | NMen |
| | 'Nisi' (*fortunei*) (5) | IVic |
| | 'Norvegica' (*cotyledon*) (8) | WAbe |
| | 'Nottingham Gold' (× *boydii*) (7) | EPot NMen NWad |
| | 'Obristii' (× *salmonica*) (7) | NMen NRya |
| § | ***obtusa*** (7) | EPot MHer NMen WAbe |
| | 'Ochroleuca' (× *elisabethae*) (7) | NMen |
| | 'Odysseus' (*sancta*) (7) | NMen |
| | 'Olymp' (*scardica*) (7) | NMen |
| | 'Omar Khayyám' **new** | NMen |
| | 'Opalescent' (7) | NMen |
| § | 'Ophelia' (× *arco-valleyi*) (7) | NMen |
| | ***oppositifolia*** (7) | MWat NSla SPlb SRms WAbe WFar |
| I | - 'Holden Variety' (7) | NRya NWad |
| | - 'Le Bourg d'Oisans' (7) | WAbe |
| | - subsp. ***oppositifolia*** var. ***latina*** (7) | ECho |
| | 'Oriole' (× *boydii*) (7) | NMen |
| | 'Orjen' (*paniculata* var. *orientalis*) (8) | GEdr |
| | 'Ottone Rosai' (Toscana Group) (7) | NMen |
| | 'Oxhill' (7) | NMen |
| § | ***paniculata*** (8) | ECho EDAr EHoe GGar GKev GMaP MAsh MDKP MHer MWat NSla SPlb SRms WAbe WFar WHoo WNew |
| § | - subsp. ***cartilaginea*** (8) | GKev WAbe |
| | - - 'Atropurpurea' (8) **new** | NHar |
| | - subsp. ***kolenatiana*** | see *S. paniculata* subsp. *cartilaginea* |
| § | - var. ***minutifolia*** (8) | CPBP CTri CYeo ECho LRHS MAsh MSCN MWat NBro NHar NMen NRya NSla NWCA SPlb WAbe |
| | ***paradoxa*** (15) | ECho GEdr LRHS NWad WGor |
| | 'Parcevalis' (× *finnisiae*) (7 × 9) | WAbe |
| | 'Parsee' (× *margoxiana*) (7) | NMen |
| | 'Paula' (× *paulinae*) (7) | NMen |
| | 'Peach Blossom' (7) | NMen |
| | 'Peach Melba' (7) | CPBP EPot ITim NLar NMen WAbe WFar |
| * | 'Peachy Head' | NMen WAbe |

| |  |  |
|---|---|---|
| | 'Pearly Gates' (× *irvingii*) (7) | NMen |
| | 'Pearly Gold' (15) | NRya WFar |
| | 'Pearly King' (15) | GMaP MAsh WAbe WFar |
| | × ***pectinata*** Schott, Nyman & Kotschy | see *S.* 'Krain' |
| | ***pedemontana*** (15) | GKev |
| | 'Penelope' (× *boydilacina*) (7) | ECho LRHS NLar NMen WHoo WPat |
| | ***pensylvanica*** (4) | GCal GCra |
| | 'Perikles' (7) | NMen |
| | 'Peter Burrow' (× *poluanglica*) (7) ♀H4 | CPBP ECho ITim NMen |
| | 'Peter Pan' (15) | EDAr EPfP GJos GMaP LRHS MAsh MHer NBlu NMen NRya NWad SPoG WFar WNew WPat |
| | 'Petra' (7) | EPot ITim NMen WFar |
| § | 'Phoenix' (× *biasolettoi*) (7) | ECho LRHS WThu |
| | 'Pilatus' (× *boydii*) (7) | NMen |
| | 'Pink Cloud' (*fortunei*) (5) | CLAP NHar WAbe WFar |
| | 'Pink Haze' (*fortunei*) (5) | CLAP NHar WAbe |
| | 'Pink Mist' (*fortunei*) (5) | CLAP NHar WAbe WFar |
| | 'Pink Pagoda' (*nipponica*) (5) | CDes CLAP EBee GEdr WCot WCru WPGP |
| | 'Pink Pearl' (7) | NMen SBch |
| | 'Pink Star' (× *boydilacina*) (7) **new** | GKev |
| | 'Pixie' (15) | CTri ECtt LRHS MAsh NMen NRya NWad SPoG SRms |
| | 'Pixie Alba' | see *S.* 'White Pixie' |
| | 'Plena' (*granulata*) | see *S.* 'Flore Pleno' |
| | 'Polar Drift' | NHar WAbe |
| | 'Pollux' (× *boydii*) (7) | NMen |
| | ***poluniniana*** (7) | WAbe |
| | ***poluniniana*** × 'Winifred' (× *poluanglica*) (7) | ECho EPot |
| | 'Pompadour' (15) | NPro |
| | 'Popelka' (subsp. *marginata* var. *rocheliana*) (7) | LRHS NMen |
| | ***porophylla*** (7) | NMen |
| | - var. ***thessalica*** | see *S. sempervivum* f. *stenophylla* |
| | aff. ***porophylla*** (7) | NWCA |
| | 'Precious Piggy' (*epiphylla*) (5) | WCru |
| | 'Primrose Bee' (× *apiculata*) (7) | ITim |
| | 'Primrose Dame' (× *elisabethae*) (7) | ECho MDKP NMen WAbe |
| | 'Primulaize' (9 × 11) | MWat NMen |
| | 'Primulaize Salmon' (9 × 11) | NHar WHoo WPer |
| § | 'Primulina' (× *malbyana*) (7) | NMen |
| § | 'Primuloides' (*umbrosa*) (11) ♀H4 | ECho EDAr MMuc NMen SEND SRms SWvt WFar |
| | 'Prince Hal' (*burseriana*) (7) | ECho EDAr EPot LRHS NMen |
| | 'Princess' (*burseriana*) (7) | ECho EDAr LRHS NMen |
| | 'Probynii' (*cochlearis*) (8) | EPot MWat NMen NWad WAbe |
| | 'Prospero' (× *petraschii*) (7) | NMen |
| | × ***prossenii*** *sensu stricto* hort. | see *S.* 'Regina' |
| | × ***proximae*** 'Květy Coventry' (7) | EPot |
| § | 'Pseudoborisii' (× *borisii*) (7) | NMen |
| | × ***pseudokotschyi*** *sensu stricto* hort. | see *S.* 'Denisa' |
| | 'Pseudoscardica' (× *wehrhahnii*) (7) | NMen |
| | 'Pseudo-valdensis' (*cochlearis*) (8) | WAbe |
| | ***pubescens*** (15) | WAbe |
| | - subsp. ***iratiana*** (15) | CPBP |
| | 'Punctatissima' (*paniculata*) (8) **new** | NHar |
| * | ***punctissima*** | NWad |
| | 'Pungens' (× *apiculata*) (7) | EPot NMen |
| | 'Purple Piggy' (*epiphylla*) (5) | CLAP WCru |
| | 'Purpurea' (*fortunei*) | see *S.* 'Rubrifolia' |
| § | 'Pygmalion' (× *webrii*) (7) | WGor |
| | 'Pyramidalis' (*cotyledon*) (8) | EPfP EWTr SRms |
| | 'Pyrenaica' (*oppositifolia*) (7) | ECho NMen |
| | ***quadrifaria*** (7) | WAbe |
| | 'Quarry Wood' (× *anglica*) (7) | NMen |
| | 'Radvan Horný' (× *cullinanii*) (7) | WAbe |
| | 'Rainsley Seedling' (8) | EPot GKev ITim NBro NMen |
| | ***ramulosa*** (7) | NMen WAbe |
| | 'Red Poll' (× *poluanglica*) (7) | NMen NRya |
| * | 'Regent' | WAbe |
| § | 'Regina' (× *prossenii*) (7) | EPot MHer NMen |
| § | 'Reginald Farrer' (Silver Farreri Group) (8) ♀H4 | GEdr |
| | ***retusa*** (7) | NMen WAbe |
| | 'Rex' (*paniculata*) (8) | CYeo EPot NWad |
| | ***rhodopetala*** (7) | ECho |
| § | 'Riverslea' (× *hornibrookii*) (7) | CPBP NMen WAbe |
| § | 'Robin Hood' (× *megaseiflora*) (7) | CFee CPBP EPot NMen WHoo WPat |
| | 'Rokujō' (*fortunei*) (5) | CLAP EBee IVic NLar NPnk NPro SHeu WFar |
| | 'Romeo' (× *hornibrookii*) (7) | NMen |
| | ***rosacea*** (15) | EDAr |
| | 'Rosea' (*cortusifolia*) (5) | CLAP NHar |
| § | 'Rosea' (*paniculata*) (8) ♀H4 | GMaP LBMP NBro NMen NSla SEND SRms WFar |
| | 'Rosea' (× *stuartii*) (7) | NMen |
| | 'Rosemarie' (7) | ECho NMen |
| | 'Rosenzwerg' (15) | WFar |
| | 'Rosina Sündermann' (× *rosinae*) (7) | ECho EPot NMen |
| | 'Rote Stadt' (*fortunei*) (5) | IVic |
| | ***rotundifolia*** (12) | EBee ECha GMaP MDKP SBfd |
| | 'Roy Clutterbuck' (7) | NMen |
| | 'Rubra' (*aizoon*) | see *S.* 'Rosea' (*paniculata*) |
| § | 'Rubrifolia' (*fortunei*) (5) | CLAP CSpe EBee ECha ECtt EHoe GAbr GEdr IBal LAst LRHS MBri MCot NMen NMyG NPnk SAga SMad SPet SWvt WAbe WBor WCot WCru WFar WMoo WWEG |
| * | 'Ruby Red' | NPro |
| * | 'Ruby Wedding' (*cortusifolia*) (5) | CLAP WCru WFar |
| | ***rufescens*** (5) | GEdr |
| | - BWJ 7510 | WCru |
| | - BWJ 7684 | GEdr WCru |
| | 'Rusalka' (× *borisii*) (7) | NMen |
| | 'Russell V. Prichard' (× *irvingii*) (7) | NMen NWad |
| | 'Ruth Draper' (*oppositifolia*) (7) | WAbe WFar |

| |  |  |
|---|---|---|
| | 'Ruth McConnell' (15) | CMea SBch |
| | 'Sabrina' (× *fallsvillagensis*) (7) | NMen |
| | 'Saint John's' (8) | ECho GEdr WAbe |
| | 'Saint Kilda' (*oppositifolia*) (7) | ITim |
| | × ***salmonica*** *sensu stricto* hort. | see *S.* 'Salomonii' |
| § | 'Salomonii' (× *salmonica*) (7) | GKev NMen SRms |
| | 'Samo' (× *bertolonii*) (7) | NMen |
| | ***sancta*** (7) | ECho EPot GLam LRHS NMen SRms WAbe |
| | - subsp. ***pseudosancta*** | see *S. juniperifolia* |
| | - - var. ***macedonica*** | see *S. juniperifolia* |
| | 'Sandpiper' (7) | NMen |
| | 'Sara Sinclair' (× *arco-valleyi*) (7) | CMea |
| | 'Šárka' (7) | NMen |
| | ***sarmentosa*** | see *S. stolonifera* |
| | 'Sartorii' | see *S.* 'Pygmalion' |
| | 'Saturn' (× *megaseiflora*) (7) | NMen WFar |
| | 'Sázava' (× *poluluteopurpurea*) (7) | NMen |
| | ***scardica*** (7) | EPot NBro NMen WAbe |
| | - var. ***dalmatica*** | see *S. obtusa* |
| § | 'Schelleri' (× *petraschii*) (7) | NMen |
| | 'Schöne Mädchen' (*fortunei*) (5) | IVic |
| § | 'Schwefelblüte' (15) | ECho GMaP LRHS NWCA WPat |
| | ***scleropoda*** (7) | NMen |
| § | 'Seaspray' (× *arendsii*) (15/v) | EWes |
| | 'Seissera' (*burseriana*) (7) | NMen |
| | 'Semafor' (Holenka's Miracle Group) (× *megaseiflora*) (7) | NMen |
| | × ***semmleri*** *sensu stricto* hort. | see *S.* 'Martha' |
| | ***sempervivum*** (7) | NGdn NMen WAbe WTin |
| § | - f. ***stenophylla*** (7) | ECho MHer |
| | ***sendaica*** (5) | WCru |
| | - B&SWJ 7448 | CLAP GEdr |
| | 'Sergio Bacci' (7) | NMen |
| | 'Sherlock Holmes' (7) | WAbe |
| | 'Shinkunomai' (*fortunei*) (5) | IVic |
| | 'Shiragiku' (*fortunei*) (5) **new** | NHar |
| | 'Silver Beads' (*paniculata*) (8) **new** | NHar |
| § | 'Silver Cushion' (15/v) | CMea CTri ECho EDAr ELan LRHS MAsh MBrN NBlu NEgg SBch SPlb SPoG WAbe WFar WNew |
| | 'Silver Edge' (× *arco-valleyi*) (7) | NMen |
| | 'Silver Maid' (× *engleri*) (8) | GEdr NMen NSla WAbe |
| | 'Silver Mound' | see *S.* 'Silver Cushion' |
| | 'Silver Velvet' (*fortunei*) (5) | CLAP CMil ECtt GEdr IFoB LRHS NMyG SHeu WBor WCot |
| | 'Sir Douglas Haig' (15) | NWad |
| | 'Sissi' (7) | CPBP NMen |
| | 'Slack's Ruby Southside' (Southside Seedling Group) ♀H4 | MDKP NMen NSla WAbe WFar |
| | 'Slack's Sensation' **new** | NSla |
| | 'Slack's Supreme' **new** | NHar NSla |
| | 'Slzy Coventry' (× *proximae*) (7) | EPot WAbe |
| | 'Snowcap' (*pubescens*) (15) | EPot NMen WAbe |
| | 'Snowdon' (*burseriana*) (7) | NMen |
| | 'Snowflake' (8) (Silver Farreri Group) ♀H4 | WAbe |
| § | 'Sofia' (× *borisii*) (7) | EPot NMen WFar |
| | 'Sorrento' (*marginata*) (7) | NMen |
| | Southside Seedling Group (v) ♀H4 | Widely available |
| | - 'Southside Red' **new** | GLam |
| | - 'Southside Star' ♀H4 | WAbe WFar |
| | 'Soyokaze' (*fortunei*) (5) **new** | NHar |
| | ***spathularis*** (11) | CEnt |
| | 'Splendens' (*oppositifolia*) (7) ♀H4 | CYeo ECho EPfP NHar NWCA SRms WAbe WPat |
| | 'Spotted Dog' | see *S.* 'Canis-dalmatica' |
| | 'Sprite' (15) | SPoG |
| | ***spruneri*** (7) | ECho LRHS NMen WAbe |
| | - var. ***deorum*** (7) | NMen |
| | 'Stansfieldii' (*rosacea*) (15) | MAsh NMen SPlb SPoG WFar |
| | ***stenophylla*** subsp. ***stenophylla*** | see *S. flagellaris* |
| | ***stolitzkae*** (7) | NMen WAbe |
| § | ***stolonifera*** (5) ♀H2 | CArn CCVN CEnt CHEx CSpe ECho EShb EWTr GBin NBro NPnk SDix SWvt WCot WFar WMoo WPnn |
| | - large-flowered (5) | WCot WGrn |
| | ***stribrnyi*** (7) | NMen WAbe |
| | - JCA 861-400 | NWCA |
| | 'Sturmiana' (*paniculata*) (8) | NMen SRms |
| | 'Sue Drew' (*fortunei*) (5) | LLHF |
| | 'Sue Tubbs' | GKev |
| | 'Suendermannii' (× *kellereri*) (7) | ECho LRHS |
| | 'Suendermannii Major' (× *kellereri*) (7) | ECho LRHS NRya |
| | 'Sugar Plum Fairy' (*fortunei*) (5) | EShb IVic LRHS SPer WCot |
| § | 'Sulphurea' (× *boydii*) (7) | ECho LRHS MAsh NMen NWad WPat |
| | 'Sunset' (*anglica*) (7) | WAbe |
| | 'Swan' (× *fallsvillagensis*) (7) | NMen |
| | 'Sylva' (× *elisabethae*) (7) | NMen |
| | 'Symons-Jeunei' (8) | GEdr WAbe |
| | 'Tábor' (× *schottii*) (7) | NMen |
| | 'Tamatsuzuri' (*fortunei*) (5) | IVic |
| | 'Tamayura' (*fortunei*) (5) | CLAP |
| | 'Teide' (Swirly Group) (7) | NMen |
| | 'Tenerife' (Swirly Group) (7) | CPBP NMen |
| | 'Theoden' (*oppositifolia*) (7) ♀H4 | CMea ECho EWes NHar NWCA WAbe |
| | 'Theresa Cooper' (7) **new** | EPot |
| | 'Theresia' (× *mariae-theresiae*) (7) | NMen |
| | 'Theseus' (7) | CPBP |
| | 'Thorpei' (× *gusmusii*) (7) | NMen |
| | 'Timmy Foster' (× *irvingii*) (7) | NMen |
| | ***tolmiei*** (3) | WAbe |
| | ***tombeanensis*** (7) | NMen |
| | 'Tricolor' (*stolonifera*) (5) ♀H2 | CHEx EBak |
| § | 'Triumph' (× *arendsii*) (15) | ECtt EPfP GMaP MAsh NEgg SPoG |
| | 'Tully' (× *elisabethae*) (7) | WGor WPat |
| | 'Tumbling Waters' (8) ♀H4 | CPBP ECho EPot GAbr LRHS NHol NMen WAbe WFar WGor WPat WThu |
| § | 'Tvoje Píseň' (× *poluanglica*) (7) | GKev NMen WHoo |

| | | |
|---|---|---|
| § | 'Tvůj Den' (× *polulacina*) (7) | NMen WAbe |
| § | 'Tvůj Polibek' (× *poluanglica*) (7) | MDKP NMen |
| § | 'Tvůj Přítel' (× *poluanglica*) (7) | NMen |
| § | 'Tvůj Úsměv' (× *poluanglica*) (7) | NLar NMen |
| § | 'Tvůj Úspech' (× *poluanglica*) (7) | EPot NMen WAbe |
| | 'Tycho Brahe' (× *doerfleri*) (7) | NMen WAbe |
| | 'Tysoe' (7) | ITim NMen |
| | ***umbrosa*** (11) | CMac CTri EBee ECho ECrN EDAr LAst LEdu LRHS MMuc MRav NDov SBfd SEND SPlb SPoG SRms STes SWvt WFar WMoo XLum |
| * | - ***subinteger*** | SEND |
| | 'Unique' | see *S.* 'Bodensee' |
| | × ***urbium*** (11) ♀H4 | CHEx CTri EBee ECho ELan EPfP EWTr GMaP LEdu SBfd SPer SRms STre WBrk WCAu WFar WPer WWEG |
| | 'Vaccariana' (*oppositifolia*) (7) | ECho EPot |
| | 'Václav Hollar' (× *gusmusii*) (7) | NMen |
| | 'Vahlii' (× *smithii*) (7) | NMen |
| | 'Valborg' | see *S.* 'Cranbourne' |
| | 'Valentine' | see *S.* 'Cranbourne' |
| | 'Valerie Finnis' | see *S.* 'Aretiastrum' |
| | 'Valerie Keevil' (× *anglica*) (7) | NMen |
| | 'Variegata' (*umbrosa*) | see *S.* 'Aureopunctata' |
| I | 'Variegata' (*cuneifolia*) (11/v) | ECho ECtt EPfP GGar LRHS NBlu NHol NVic NWad SPet SPlb SPoG WFar WMoo WPer |
| I | 'Variegata' (× *urbium*) (11/v) | EBee ECho EPfP GGar LAst LRHS MSpe NLar SRms WFar WNew WWEG |
| | 'Večerní Hvězda' | WAbe |
| | ***veitchiana*** (5) | GEdr NBro |
| | 'Verona' (× *caroli-langii*) (7) | WAbe |
| | 'Vesna' (× *borisii*) (7) | NMen |
| | 'Vincent van Gogh' (× *borisii*) (7) | EPot NMen |
| | 'Vladana' (× *megaseiflora*) (7) | CPBP ECho LRHS NMen |
| | 'Vlasta' (7) | NMen |
| | 'Vlasta Burian' (7) | WAbe |
| | 'Vltava' (7) | NMen |
| | 'Volgeri' (× *hofmannii*) (7) | NMen |
| | 'Vreny' (8) | GKev |
| | 'Vysoké Mýto' (7) | EPot WAbe |
| | 'Wada' (*fortunei*) (5) | CAbP CDes CLAP EAEE EBee ECtt ELon GEdr LAst LRHS MCot MNrw MSpe NBir NMyG SPer WBor WCot WFar WOld WPGP WSHC WWEG |
| | 'Waithman's Variety' (8) | GEdr |
| | 'Wallacei' (15) | NMen |
| | 'Walpole's Variety' (8) | WAbe WPer |
| | 'Walter Ingwersen' (*umbrosa*) (11) | SRms |
| § | 'Walter Irving' (× *irvingii*) (7) | NMen WAbe |
| | 'Warmes Herz' (*fortunei*) (5) | IVic |
| | 'Wartosque' (*callosa*) (8) | EPot |
| | 'Weisser Zwerg' (15) | NMen |
| | 'Wellesbourne' (× *abingdonensis*) (7) | ITim |
| | 'Welsh Dragon' (15) | WAbe |
| | 'Welsh Red' (15) | WAbe WFar |
| | 'Welsh Rose' (15) | WAbe |
| | ***wendelboi*** (7) | NMen |
| | 'Wendrush' (× *wendelacina*) (7) | NMen |
| | 'Wendy' (× *wendelacina*) (7) | NMen |
| | 'Wheatley Gem' (7) | NMen |
| | 'Wheatley Lion' (× *borisii*) (7) | NMen |
| | 'Wheatley Rose' (7) | ECho LRHS |
| | 'White Alice' | NBlu |
| | 'White Cap' (× *boydii*) (7) | NMen |
| | 'White Imp' (7) | NMen |
| § | 'White Pixie' (15) | ECtt EDAr EPfP GMaP MAsh MHer NPro NRya NWad SPlb SPoG SRms WFar WNew |
| | 'White Star' (× *petraschii*) | see *S.* 'Schelleri' |
| | 'Whitehill' (8) ♀H4 | CMea CPBP ECho ECtt ELan GEdr GJos GMaP LRHS MAsh MDKP NBro NHol NMen NRya NSla NWCA NWad SBch SPet WFar WHoo WNew WPat WTin |
| § | 'Wilhelm Tell' (× *malbyana*) (7) | NMen |
| | 'William Shakespeare' (Blues Group) (7) | WAbe |
| | 'Winifred' (× *anglica*) (7) | ECho NMen |
| | 'Winifred Bevington' (8 × 11) ♀H4 | ECho EDAr EPot GEdr LHop LRHS MMuc NBro NMen NRya NWad WAbe WFar WHoo WPer WPnn |
| | 'Winston Churchill' (15) | CElw CTri ECho LRHS MAsh NHol NWad |
| | 'Winston Churchill Variegata' (15/v) | NWad |
| | 'Winton' (× *paulinae*) (7) | NMen |
| | 'Wisley' (*federici-augusti* subsp. *grisebachii*) (7) ♀H2-3 | EPot GKev NMen WPat |
| | 'Woodside Ross' (15) | ECtt |
| | 'Yellow Rock' (7) | NMen NRya |
| | 'Youkuy' (*fortunei*) (5) | IVic |
| | Your Day | see *S.* 'Tvůj Den' |
| | Your Friend | see *S.* 'Tvůj Přítel' |
| | Your Good Fortune | see *S.* 'Tvůj Úspech' |
| | Your Kiss | see *S.* 'Tvůj Polibek' |
| | Your Smile | see *S.* 'Tvůj Úsměv' |
| | Your Song | see *S.* 'Tvoje Píseň' |
| | Your Success | see *S.* 'Tvůj Úspech' |
| | 'Yunagi' (*fortunei*) (5) | IVic NHar WOld |
| | × ***zimmeteri*** (8 × 11) | ECho NMen |
| § | 'Zita' (*sempervivum*) (7) **new** | NMen |
| § | 'Zlatá Praha' (× *pragensis*) (7) | NMen NRya WAbe |
| | 'Zlin' (× *leyboldii*) (7) | NMen |

## *Scabiosa* (*Caprifoliaceae*)

| | | |
|---|---|---|
| | ***africana*** | CElw EBee EWes SHar WCot |
| | - 'Jocelyn' **new** | SHar |
| | ***alpina*** L. | see *Cephalaria alpina* |
| | ***argentea*** | EBee EWes LEdu WPGP |
| | ***atropurpurea*** | SPav |
| | - 'Ace of Spades' | CWCL EDif MCot SMad SPav WPGP |
| | - 'Beaujolais Bonnets' | LRHS NPri SPer WHrl |
| § | - 'Chile Black' | Widely available |

| | | |
|---|---|---|
| § | - 'Chilli Pepper' | CWCL EPfP LHop LRHS MBri NLar |
| § | - 'Chilli Sauce' | CWCL EPfP LHop LRHS NLar SPoG |
| | - 'Derry's Black' | CSpe |
| | - 'Fire King' | MWea |
| | - 'Nona' | LLHF |
| | - 'Peter Ray' | CElw WWlt |
| | - 'Salmon Queen' | NLar |
| | ***banatica*** | see *S. columbaria* |
| | 'Barocca' **new** | LRHS |
| | 'Blue Diamonds' | LRHS MHer |
| | 'Blue Mound' **new** | WHer |
| | Burgundy Bonnets = 'Scabon'[PBR] | EGxp EPfP LRHS LSou |
| § | 'Butterfly Blue' | CMHG EBee ECGP ECtt ELon EPPr EPfP LBMP LRHS LSRN LSou MAsh MBri MTis NBPC NDov NLar SCoo SMrm SPer SPoG SWvt WAul WBrk WCAu WCot WFar WRHF WWEG |
| | ***caucasica*** | CMac EPfP GKev LAst LEdu NBlu WFar WHoo |
| | - var. ***alba*** | CBcs CBot CKno EPfP NGBl NPnk WFar WHoo |
| | - 'Blauer Atlas' **new** | EBee |
| | - 'Blausiegel' | CSam EBee ECtt IPot LBMP MCot MRav NBre NDov SMrm SPet SPoG WFar |
| | - 'Clive Greaves' ♀H4 | CHar EBee ECha ECtt ELan EPfP MBri MPkF MRav SRms SWvt WFar WHrl |
| | - 'Deep Waters' | CSpe EBee LRHS WPtf |
| | - 'Fama' | CWib EShb NBir NGBl NLar SMrm SPlb SRms WFar WWEG XLum |
| | - 'Goldingensis' | MHer NBre NGdn NPri WHil WPer |
| | - House's hybrids | CSBt NGdn SRms |
| | - 'Isaac House' | ELon NLar XLum |
| | - 'Kompliment' | GMac NBre NLar SMrm WWEG |
| | - 'Lavender Blue' | NBPC WFar |
| | - 'Miss Willmott' ♀H4 | CMMP CSam EBee ECha ECtt EHoe ELan EPfP EShb LBMP LHop LRHS MBri MCot MHer MLHP MRav NCGa SPoG SWvt WCAu WFar WGwG WHrl WMnd WWEG |
| | - 'Moerheim Blue' | EBee |
| | - Perfecta Series | CSpr CWib EBee LRHS MMHG NGdn NLar SBfd SPoG SWat WBor |
| | - - 'Perfecta Alba' | CAby CBar COlW CWCL CWib EBee ECtt GMaP GMac LAst LRHS MSpe MWat NChi NLar NOrc NPri SBfd SMrm SPad SPer SPoG STes SWat WPtf WWEG XLum |
| | - - 'Perfecta Blue' | CAby CBar MSpe XLum |
| | - - 'Perfecta Lilac Blue' | CWib EPfP GMaP GMac SBfd SPer STes WWEG |
| | - 'Stäfa' | CMMP EBee ECha EShb EWTr LBMP LRHS MBri MCot MRav NCGa NEgg NLar SUsu WFar WMnd |
| | - 'Thorp's Variegated' (v) **new** | WCot |
| | 'Chile Black' | see *S. atropurpurea* 'Chile Black' |
| | 'Chile Pepper' | see *S. atropurpurea* 'Chilli Pepper' |
| | 'Chile Sauce' | see *S. atropurpurea* 'Chilli Sauce' |
| | 'Chile Spice' | MBri |
| | ***cinerea*** | SPhx |
| § | ***columbaria*** | CHab EBee EWil LRHS MLLN MMuc MPet NBre NEgg NLan NMir NWCA SMrm WHer WJek WSFF WWEG |
| * | - ***alpina*** | WAbe |
| | - 'Misty Butterflies' | CCVN CFee ECtt EDAr EPfP EShb EWll LBMP LHop LSou NBPC NEgg NGdn NLar SBfd SMrm SPad STes WBor WFar WWEG |
| | - 'Nana' | CCse CMea EBee EShb LRHS NBir NGdn NLar NMen [illegible] [illegible] WFar WHrl XLum |
| | - 'Nana Pink' **new** | LRHS |
| § | - subsp. ***ochroleuca*** | CBot CKno CSpe ECha EShb GBBs GCal GLin LEdu LRHS MCot MLLN MRav MSpe NBir NLar SMad SMrm SPhx SPoG SRms WCAu WFar WPGP |
| | - - MESE 344 | EBee |
| | - - 'Moon Dance' | CMea EBee EDAr EPPr EShb GCal LBMP LLHF LRHS MSpe NCGa NLar NPri SBfd WHoo |
| | - 'Pincushion Blue' | EWll |
| | - 'Pincushion Pink' | EWTr NGdn WFar WWEG |
| | - pink-flowered **new** | LRHS |
| | ***cretica*** | CSpe XSen |
| | ***drakensbergensis*** | EBee EKen EWes GAbr LRHS MTPN SLon WCot WHrl WPtf |
| | ***farinosa*** | CBot CDes ECtt MMuc SAga SEND SGar WFar WSHC |
| | ***gigantea*** | see *Cephalaria gigantea* |
| | ***graminifolia*** | ECho GKev MDKP NBir NMen SBch SRms WWEG XLum |
| | - JM 990 | EBee |
| | - ***rosea*** | EWes |
| | 'Helen Dillon' | EBee ECtt EWes LSou WWEG |
| | 'Irish Perpetual Flowering' | see *S.* 'Butterfly Blue' |
| | ***japonica*** var. ***acutiloba*** | SPhx |
| | - var. ***alpina*** | CEnt CPrp EBee EPfP GKev MMuc NGdn SBfd SEND SPet SPhx WHoo WNew WTin XLum |
| | - - 'Blue Star' | NBre NCGa |
| | - 'Ritz Blue' | EPfP |
| | ***lachnophylla*** | GCal SPhx |
| | - 'Blue Horizon' | NDov WHil |
| | 'Little Emily' | ELon LSou SAga SUsu |
| | ***lucida*** | EAEE EBee ECho ECtt EPfP LRHS MRav WHrl WPGP WPer XLum |
| | 'Midnight' | CMea |
| | 'Miss Havisham' | ECtt EWes WPGP |
| | ***montana*** (Bieb.) DC. | see *Knautia tatarica* |
| | ***montana*** Mill. | see *Knautia arvensis* |
| | ***ochroleuca*** | see *S. columbaria* subsp. *ochroleuca* |
| | ***parnassi*** | see *Pterocephalus perennis* |
| | 'Peggotty' | ECtt |
| | 'Perpetual Flowering' | see *S.* 'Butterfly Blue' |
| | Pink Buttons = 'Walminipink' | CFir EBee LRHS LSou |
| | 'Pink Diamonds' **new** | MBri |
| | 'Pink Mist'[PBR] | EBee ECtt EPfP EWll LRHS MAsh MBri MPkF NBir NLar SCoo SMrm SPer SPoG SRms WCAu |
| | ***pterocephala*** | see *Pterocephalus perennis* |
| | ***rhodopensis*** | EBee |
| | 'Rosie's Pink' | ECtt |
| | ***rumelica*** | see *Knautia macedonica* |
| | 'Satchmo' | see *S. atropurpurea* 'Chile Black' |
| | ***speciosa*** 'Maharajah' | NLar |
| | ***succisa*** | see *Succisa pratensis* |
| | ***tatarica*** | see *Cephalaria gigantea* |

| | |
|---|---|
| ***tenuis*** | SPhx |
| ***triandra*** | EBee LHop |
| 'Ultra Violet' | NDov NLar |
| 'Vivid Violet' | CAbP ECtt LSou MNrw MTis NDov NLar SHar SMrm WBor WCot WCra |

## *Scabiosa* × *Cephalaria* (*Caprifoliaceae*)

| | |
|---|---|
| ***S. cinerea* × *C. alpina*** | LRHS |

## *Scadoxus* ✿ (*Amaryllidaceae*)

| | |
|---|---|
| ***multiflorus*** | CCCN ECho LAma |
| § - subsp. ***katherinae*** ♀H1 | CPne ECho WCot |
| § - subsp. ***multiflorus*** ♀H1 | WCot |
| ***natalensis*** | see *S. puniceus* |
| § ***puniceus*** | CLak WCot |

## *Scaevola* (*Goodeniaceae*)

| | |
|---|---|
| ***aemula*** 'Blue Fan'PBR | see *S. aemula* 'Blue Wonder' |
| § - 'Blue Wonder'PBR | NPer SWvt |
| - Diamond = 'Wesscaedia' | LSou |
| - 'Purple Fan' new | LAst |
| - Top Pot White = 'Wesscaetowhi'PBR new | LSou |
| - 'Zig Zag'PBR | CCCN LAst |
| Blauer Facher = 'Saphira'PBR | CCCN LHop |
| 'Brillant'PBR | LSou |
| ***crassifolia*** | SPlb |
| 'Mini Blue' | CCCN |
| 'Topaz Pink' | LHop LSou |

## *Schefflera* (*Araliaceae*)

| | |
|---|---|
| sp. new | WPGP |
| ***alpina*** B&SWJ 11827 | WCru |
| - HWJ 936 | WCru |
| - B&SWJ 8247 | WCru |
| ***arboricola*** ♀H1 | CHEx SEND XBlo |
| - 'Gold Capella' ♀H1 | SEND XBlo |
| - 'Kalahari' | XBlo |
| ***brevipedicellata*** HWJ 870 | WCru |
| - KWJ 12224 | WCru |
| § ***chapana*** B&SWJ 11848 | WCru |
| - HWJ 983 | WCru |
| ***delavayi*** | CHEx |
| ***digitata*** | CTrC |
| ***elegantissima*** ♀H1 | EShb |
| ***enneaphylla*** B&SWJ 11727 | WCru |
| - HWJ 1018 | WCru |
| ***fantsipanensis*** B&SWJ 11666 | WCru |
| - B&SWJ 11671 | WCru |
| ***fengii*** | GLin |
| ***gracilis*** HWJ 622 | WCru |
| - HWJ 878 | WCru |
| ***hoi*** B&SWJ 11747 | WCru |
| ***kornasii*** B&SWJ 11830 | WCru |
| - HWJ 918 | WCru |
| ***lenticellata*** B&SWJ 9762 | WCru |
| ***macrophylla*** B&SWJ 8210 | WCru |
| - B&SWJ 9788 | WCru |
| ***microphylla*** B&SWJ 3872 | WCru |
| aff. ***myriocarpa*** B&SWJ 11828 new | WCru |
| ***rhododendrifolia*** | CHEx |
| - GWJ 9375 | WCru |
| ***taiwaniana*** | CHEx |
| - B&SWJ 3575 | WCru |
| - B&SWJ 7096 | WCru |
| - RWJ 10000 | WCru |
| - RWJ 10016 | WCru |
| ***vietnamensis*** | see *S. chapana* |

## *Schima* (*Theaceae*)

| | |
|---|---|
| ***wallichii*** | CPLG |
| - subsp. ***noronhae*** var. ***superba*** | CCCN CPLG EPfP |

## *Schinus* (*Anacardiaceae*)

| | |
|---|---|
| ***latifolius*** new | CBcs |
| ***lentiscifolius*** new | SPlb |
| ***molle*** | SBrd SPlb |
| ***polygamus*** | CBcs SPlb |

## *Schisandra* (*Schisandraceae*)

| | |
|---|---|
| ***arisanensis*** B&SWJ 3050 | WCru |
| aff. ***bicolor*** BWJ 8151 | WCru |
| ***chinensis*** | CAgr CArn GPoy LEdu MSwo |
| - B&SWJ 4204 | WCru |
| - SDR 3980 | GKev |
| ***grandiflora*** | CDoC ELan EPfP LRHS MBlu NLar SCoo SKHP SPer WGwG |
| - B&SWJ 2245 | WCru |
| - 'Jamu' (m) | WCru |
| - 'Lahlu' (f/F) | WCru |
| ***grandiflora* × *rubriflora*** | WCru |
| ***henryi*** subsp. ***yunnanensis*** B&SWJ 6546 | WCru |
| aff. ***neglecta*** BWJ 7739 | WCru |
| ***nigra*** | see *S. repanda* |
| aff. ***plena*** HWJ 664 new | WCru |
| ***propinqua*** | CBot CMac CSPN LEdu MBlu NLar |
| subsp. ***sinensis*** | WSHC |
| - - BWJ 8148 | WCru |
| § ***repanda*** B&SWJ 5897 | WCru |
| - B&SWJ 11455 | WCru |
| ***rubriflora*** | CBcs CHEx CSPN CTri CWSG EPfP IDee LRHS MBlu MGos SKHP SLon SSpi |
| - (f) | ELan WSHC |
| - (m) | NHol |
| - BWJ 7557 | WCru |
| ***sphenanthera*** | ELan NLar WSHC |

## *Schivereckia* (*Brassicaceae*)

| | |
|---|---|
| ***doerfleri*** | MWat |

## *Schizachyrium* (*Poaceae*)

| | |
|---|---|
| § ***scoparium*** | CKno EBee EHoe EPPr GCal LBMP LRHS MWhi NSti SPhx SUsu WCot XLum |
| - 'Blaze' new | EPPr |
| - 'Cairo' | EBee |
| - 'Prairie Blues' | CKno EBee EPPr EShb GQue LRHS SMea SMrm SPhx WCot |
| - 'The Blues' | EPPr |

## *Schizocarphus* (*Asparagaceae*)

| | |
|---|---|
| ***nervosus*** | ECho WCot |

## *Schizocodon* see *Shortia*

## *Schizopetalon* (*Brassicaceae*)

| | |
|---|---|
| ***walkeri*** | CSpe |

## *Schizophragma* (*Hydrangeaceae*)

| | |
|---|---|
| ***corylifolium*** | NLar |
| - BWJ 8150 | WCru |

| | |
|---|---|
| aff. ***elliptifolium*** WWJ 11905 | WCru |
| ***hydrangeoides*** | CBcs CDoC CDul EBee ELan EPfP GKin LRHS MBlu MGos NPri SGol SLim SLon SPer SPoG SWvt WDin |
| - B&SWJ 5409 | WCru |
| - B&SWJ 5732 | WCru |
| - B&SWJ 5954 | WCru |
| - B&SWJ 6119 from Yakushima, Japan | WCru |
| - B&SWJ 8505 from Ulleungdo, Korea | WCru |
| - B&SWJ 8522 from Ulleungdo, Korea | WCru |
| - 'Brookside Littleleaf' | see *Hydrangea anomala* subsp. *petiolaris* var. *cordifolia* 'Brookside Littleleaf' |
| - 'Cheju's Early' | WCru |
| - 'Iwa Garami' | NLar |
| - 'Moonlight' | Widely available |
| * - f. ***quelpartensis*** B&SWJ 8771 | WCru |
| - 'Roseum' ♀H4 | CDoC CDul CMHG CMil CSPN EBee ELan EPfP EWes GKin IArd LRHS MBlu MBri MGos NCGa NLar SGol SKHP SLim SPer SPoG SSpi SWvt WCru WFar WKif WPGP |
| ***integrifolium*** ♀H4 | CBcs CDul CMac ELan EPfP LRHS NLar SKHP SSpi WKif WPGP WSHC |
| - var. ***fauriei*** | NLar WSHC |
| - - B&SWJ 1701 | WCru |
| - - B&SWJ 7052 | WCru |
| - - CWJ 12433 | WCru |

## *Schizostachyum* (*Poaceae*)

| | |
|---|---|
| § ***funghomii*** | EPla MMoz MMuc SEND |

## *Schizostylis* ✿ (*Iridaceae*)

| | |
|---|---|
| § ***coccinea*** | Widely available |
| - from Giants Castle | CTca |
| - f. ***alba*** | Widely available |
| - 'Ballyrogan Giant' | CFir CTca CYeo ECtt IBlr MAvo NCot NHol WHer WPGP WSHC WWEG |
| - 'Big Moma' | CPrp CYeo GMac MAvo |
| - 'Brick Red' | MAvo |
| - 'Cardinal' | NHol WFar WMoo |
| - 'Cindy Towe' | CYeo MAvo |
| - 'Countesse de Vere' | EBee GMac NCot |
| - early-flowering | CPrp NCot |
| - 'Elburton Glow' | CPrp CYeo GMac NLar WFar WHoo |
| - 'Fenland Daybreak' | Widely available |
| - 'Gigantea' | see *S. coccinea* 'Major' |
| - 'Good White' | CYeo MAvo NBir NCGa SUsu WCot |
| - 'Grandiflora' | see *S. coccinea* 'Major' |
| - 'Hilary Gould' | CPrp MAvo NCGa WFar WHal |
| - 'Hint of Pink' | MAvo MDKP |
| - 'Jack Frost' | EBee ECtt MAvo NCGa WMoo WWEG |
| - 'Jennifer' ♀H4 | CBro CElw CTca CTri CYeo EBee ELon EPfP EShb GAbr LRHS LSou MAsh MAvo MMuc MRav NCGa NCot NWad SApp SBfd SMrm SRms SUsu SWvt WFar WMoo WOld WWEG XLum |
| - late-flowering | NCot |
| - 'Maiden's Blush' | CPrp CYeo ECtt LRHS LSou MAvo MCot MDKP MWea NCot NHol NLar SBfd SPet WFar |
| § - 'Major' ♀H4 | Widely available |
| * - 'Marietta' | CYeo NCot |
| - 'Mollie Gould' | CPrp CTca CYeo EAEE EBee EBla ECtt EKen ELon EShb GCra LBMP LHop LSou MAvo MHer MMHG NBre NCGa NCot NHol NLar SCoo SPoG SRms WFar WHil WOld WTin WWEG |
| - 'Mrs Hegarty' | Widely available |
| - 'November Cheer' | CMac CPrp CSpr CTca CYeo IBlr NBir NCot NLar WFar WWEG XLum |
| - 'Oregon Sunset' | CPrp EBee GMac MDKP |
| - 'Pallida' | CMil CPom CSam CYeo ECha ECtt ELan MLHP MMuc MRav MWea NBir NLar WFar |
| - 'Pink Marg' | CPrp MAvo NCot NLar |
| - 'Professor Barnard' | CCCN CFee CHar CPrp CSpe CTca CYeo EBee ECho ECtt ELon EPfP EPri EShb GAbr MAvo MBNS MSpe NBir NCot NEgg SApp SRot WFar WMoo WOld WPtf WWEG |
| - 'Red Dragon' | CYeo ECtt GAbr LLHF NCGa NCot NHol WFar WHoo |
| - 'Salmon Charm' | ECtt GBee GBin LRHS NCGa WFar WMoo |
| - salmon-flowered | LSou NCot |
| - 'Salome' | GMac NCot |
| - 'Silver Pink' | IBlr |
| - 'Snow Maiden' | CElw ECtt GAbr GGar GKev MAvo |
| - 'Strawberry' | CPrp EBee NCot |
| § - 'Sunrise' ♀H4 | Widely available |
| - 'Sunset' | see *S. coccinea* 'Sunrise' |
| - 'Tambara' | CCse CPou CPrp CSam EBee GAbr LHop MAvo MWea NLar SApp SMrm WAbb WFar XLum |
| - 'The Bride' | CTri |
| - 'Viscountess Byng' | CBcs CBro CTca CTri CWCL CYeo EBee ELon EPau IBlr LRHS NBir NCot NLar SMrm SPav SPer STre WFar WPer WWEG |
| § - 'Wilfred H. Bryant' | Widely available |
| - 'Zeal Salmon' | CBro CFee CFir CPou CPrp CYeo ECha GAbr GMac MAvo NBir NCGa NCot NHol NLar SApp WFar |
| 'Pink Princess' | see *S. coccinea* 'Wilfred H. Bryant' |

## *Schoenoplectus* (*Cyperaceae*)

| | |
|---|---|
| § ***lacustris*** | CWat MMuc MSKA SEND WPnP |
| - subsp. ***tabernaemontani*** 'Albescens' (v) | CBen CKno CWat LPBA MNrw MSKA MWts SWat WHal |
| - - 'Zebrinus' (v) | CBen CBot CKno CWat ELan EPfP LPBA MMuc MNrw MSKA MWts NPla SPlb SWat WFar WHal WMAq |

## *Schoenoxiphium* (*Cyperaceae*)

| | |
|---|---|
| 'Golden Caterpillars' | WBox |

## *Schoenus* (*Cyperaceae*)

| | |
|---|---|
| ***pauciflorus*** | CWCL EHoe EWes LLWG NOak WMoo |

## *Sciadopitys* (*Sciadopityaceae*)

| | |
|---|---|
| ***verticillata*** ♀H4 | CBcs CDoC CDoy CDul CKen CSBt EHul EPfP ERom GKin IDee LRHS |

| | |
|---|---|
| | MBlu MBri MGos MMuc NHol NWea SBfd SCoo SLim SSpi SWvt WDin WEve WFar WHar |
| I - 'Compacta' | LRHS |
| - 'Firework' | CKen |
| - 'Globe' | CKen |
| - 'Gold Star' | CKen |
| - 'Goldammer' | NLar |
| - 'Golden Rush' | CKen NLar WEve |
| - 'Goldmahne' | CKen |
| - 'Grüne Kugel' | CKen NLar |
| - 'Jeddeloh Compact' | CKen |
| - 'Kugelblitz' | WEve |
| - 'Kupferschirm' | CKen |
| - 'Mecki' | CKen MBri MDev WEve |
| - 'Megaschirm' | CKen |
| - 'Ossorio Gold' | CKen WEve |
| - 'Picola' | CKen NLar |
| - 'Pygmy' | CKen |
| - 'Richie's Cushion' | CKen WEve |
| - 'Shorty' | CKen |
| - 'Speerspitze' | CKen |
| - 'Star Wars' | CKen |
| - 'Starburst' | CKen |
| - 'Sternschnuppe' | CKen MDev NLar WEve |
| - 'Wintergreen' | CKen |

## *Scilla* (*Asparagaceae*)

| | |
|---|---|
| ***adlamii*** | see *Ledebouria cooperi* |
| × ***allenii*** | see × *Chionoscilla allenii* |
| ***amethystina*** | see *S. litardierei* |
| ***amoena*** | ECho WCot |
| ***aristidis*** from Algeria | ECho |
| ***autumnalis*** | CAvo CDes CPom ECho EPot EWil GKev LAma NRya WShi WThu |
| - JCA 0.872.602 | WCot |
| ***bifolia*** ♀H4 | CAvo CBro CFFs CPom CTca ECho EPot GKev LAma LLWP SDeJ SPhx WShi |
| - RS 156/83 | ECho |
| - 'Alba' | ECho EPot SPhx |
| - 'Norman Stevens' | SCnR |
| - 'Rosea' | ECho EPot GKev LAma LLWP MWat SDeJ |
| ***bithynica*** ♀H4 | WShi |
| ***campanulata*** | see *Hyacinthoides hispanica* |
| ***caucasica*** | LWst |
| ***chinensis*** | see *S. scilloides* |
| ***cilicica*** | ECho SPhx |
| ***greilhuberi*** | ECho EPot LLHF WAbe WCot |
| ***haemorrhoidalis*** MS 923 | WCot |
| ***hohenackeri*** | SPhx WThu |
| - BSBE 811 | CDes WCot |
| § ***hughii*** | CDes ECho |
| ***hyacinthoides*** | ECho WCot |
| ***ingridiae*** | ECho |
| - var. ***taurica*** | ECho |
| ***italica*** | see *Hyacinthoides italica* |
| ***japonica*** | see *S. scilloides* |
| ***latifolia*** from Morocco | ECho |
| ***libanotica*** | see *Puschkinia scilloides* var. *libanotica* |
| ***liliohyacinthus*** | CBro CRow ECho IBlr MMHG WSHC WShi |
| ***lingulata*** | ECho LLHF NMen WCot |
| - S&F 253 | CDes |
| - var. ***ciliolata*** | CBro CPBP CPom ECho EPot |
| - var. ***lingulata*** | ECho WCot |
| § ***litardierei*** ♀H4 | CMea CTca ECho EPPr EPot LAma MBri NMen SBch SDeJ SEND SPhx WShi |
| ***lutea*** hort. | see *Ledebouria socialis* |
| ***madeirensis*** | CLak WCot |
| ***mauritanica*** | ECho |
| ***melaina*** | EPot WCot |
| - VVTA.118 **new** | LWst |
| ***mesopotamica*** **new** | LWst |
| ***messeniaca*** | CPom |
| - MS 38 from Greece | WCot |
| ***mischtschenkoana*** ♀H4 | CAvo CBro CHid ECho EPot IFro LAma MBri |
| § - 'Tubergeniana' ♀H4 | CMea ECho GKev SPhx WCot |
| - 'Zwanenburg' | ECho |
| ***monophyllos*** | ECho |
| ***natalensis*** | see *Merwilla plumbea* |
| ***non-scripta*** | see *Hyacinthoides non-scripta* |
| ***nutans*** | see *Hyacinthoides non-scripta* |
| ***obtusifolia*** | ECho |
| ***persica*** ♀H4 | CDes ECho SPhx WCot |
| ***peruviana*** | Widely available |
| - S&L 285 | WCot |
| - SB&L 20/1 | WCot |
| - 'Alba' | CBro CDes CFwr CPrp CTca ECho GKev WCot WHil XLum |
| * - var. ***ciliata*** | WCot |
| - var. ***elegans*** | CDes |
| - 'Hughii' | see *S. hughii* |
| - var. ***ifniensis*** | WCot |
| - var. ***venusta*** | CDes |
| - - S&L 311/2 | WCot |
| ***pratensis*** | see *S. litardierei* |
| ***puschkinioides*** | ECho |
| ***reverchonii*** | ECho |
| - from Spain | WCot |
| ***rosenii*** | ECho |
| § ***scilloides*** | ECho GKev SCnR |
| - B&SWJ 8812 | WCru |
| ***siberica*** ♀H4 | CAby CAvo CBro CFFs CTca ECho EPfP GAbr GKev LAma MLLN MMuc MWat SBch SMrm SPer SPhx WShi |
| - 'Alba' | CTca ECho EPfP EPot GKev LAma SBch SMrm WShi |
| - 'Boreas' **new** | LWst |
| - 'Spring Beauty' | CCse CMea ECGP ECho EPot GKev LAma MBri SDeJ SPhx SRms |
| 'Tubergeniana' | see *S. mischtschenkoana* 'Tubergeniana' |
| ***verna*** | CDes ECho EWil WCot WShi WThu |
| ***vicentina*** | see *Hyacinthoides vicentina* |
| ***violacea*** | see *Ledebouria socialis* |

## *Scirpoides* (*Cyperaceae*)

| | |
|---|---|
| § ***holoschoenus*** | CRWN |

## *Scirpus* (*Cyperaceae*)

| | |
|---|---|
| ***cernuus*** | see *Isolepis cernua* |
| ***holoschoenus*** | see *Scirpoides holoschoenus* |
| ***lacustris*** | see *Schoenoplectus lacustris* |
| - 'Spiralis' | see *Juncus effusus* f. *spiralis* |
| ***maritimus*** | see *Bolboschoenus maritimus* |

## *Scleranthus* (*Caryophyllaceae*)

| | |
|---|---|
| ***biflorus*** | CTrC ECho EDAr EWes LEdu MAsh NWCA SPlb WPer XLum |
| ***singuliflorus*** | WPat |

| | |
|---|---|
| ***uniflorus*** | CTrC ECho EShb SMad SPlb XLum |

## *Sclerochiton* (*Acanthaceae*)

| | |
|---|---|
| ***harveyanus*** | EShb GFai |

## *Scoliopus* (*Liliaceae*)

| | |
|---|---|
| ***bigelovii*** | CAby LWoo [illegible] WHal |
| ***hallii*** | EBee GEdr LEdu LWst NMen WCru |

## *Scolopendrium* see *Asplenium*

## *Scopolia* (*Solanaceae*)

| | |
|---|---|
| ***carniolica*** | CArn CAvo CFir EBee ELan EWld GKev GPoy LEdu MPhe NChi NLar NSti SPhx SPlb WAul WCru WFar WPGP WSHC XLum |
| - from Poland | LEdu |
| - from Slovenia | WCot |
| § - var. ***brevifolia*** | EPPr EWld GBin LEdu SPhx WTin |
| - - WM 9811 | MPhe |
| - subsp. ***hladnikiana*** | see *S. carniolica* var. *brevifolia* |
| - 'Zwanenburg' | CAvo EPPr EPot EWes LEdu NLar SPhx XLum |
| ***lurida*** | see *Anisodus luridus* |
| ***stramoniifolia*** | WAle |

## *Scorzonera* (*Asteraceae*)

| | |
|---|---|
| ***hispanica*** | SVic |
| ***suberosa*** subsp. ***cariensis*** | CPBP |

## *Scrophularia* (*Scrophulariaceae*)

| | |
|---|---|
| ***aquatica*** | see *S. auriculata* |
| § ***auriculata*** | CHab EWil LPBA MHer NMir NPer WHer |
| § - 'Variegata' (v) | CBcs EBee ECha EHoe ELan EPfP EShb GCal LLWG LPBA LRHS MAvo MHer NBid NEgg NSti SBfd SPer SPoG WFar WSHC |
| ***buergeriana*** 'Lemon and Lime' misapplied | see *Teucrium viscidum* 'Lemon and Lime' |
| - 'Lemon and Lime' (v) | NEgg |
| ***calliantha*** | MDKP |
| ***grandiflora*** | CPom NBre SAga WCot WFar |
| ***nodosa*** | CArn CRWN EBee GPoy NMir WHer WHfH |
| - ***variegata*** | see *S. auriculata* 'Variegata' |
| ***scopolii*** | EBee |

## *Scutellaria* ✿ (*Lamiaceae*)

| | |
|---|---|
| ***albida*** | WOut |
| § ***alpina*** | CPBP ECho GJos NWCA SPlb SRms SRot WGor WPer |
| - 'Arcobaleno' | LLHF NLar |
| - 'Greencourt' | WPat |
| - 'Moonbeam' | GEdr LRHS NLar |
| ***altissima*** | ECha ELan ELon GKev LRHS MMuc NBro SBfd SEND SGar SPlb WAle WOut WPtf XSen |
| 'Amazing Grace' | EWes |
| ***baicalensis*** | CArn EBee EWld GJos GPoy MAvo SMrm WPtf |
| ***barbata*** | CArn |
| ***canescens*** | see *S. incana* |
| ***diffusa*** | GLam |
| ***galericulata*** | CHab CWan GPoy MHer |
| ***hastata*** | see *S. hastifolia* |
| § ***hastifolia*** | CTri ECtt |
| § ***incana*** | CPom EBee ECGP ELan ELon EPPr GBee GMaP LHop LPla LSou MWea SUsu WCot |
| ***indica*** | EWld |
| - var. ***japonica*** | see *S. indica* var. *parvifolia* |
| § - var. ***parvifolia*** | CPBP EBee ECho EWes GEdr GJos LRHS NWCA SRot |
| - - 'Alba' | CPBP ECho LLHF NWCA |
| ***lateriflora*** | CArn GPoy LRHS NMun WJek |
| ***maekawae*** | EBee WPGP |
| - B&SWJ 557a | WCru |
| 'Mood Indigo' **new** | EPPr LRHS |
| ***novae-zelandiae*** | ECou |
| ***orientalis*** | CMea EBee ECtt GCal WAbe |
| - subsp. ***bicolor*** | ECtt NWCA |
| - subsp. ***pinnatifida*** | NWCA XSen |
| ***pontica*** | CPBP EBee EDAr SBch SMrm WFoF |
| ***scordiifolia*** | CMea CSam EBee ECha ECho EDAr LRHS MAsh NRya NWCA SBHP SBch SRms WFar WHal WHoo WTin |
| - 'Seoul Sapphire' | CSpe EWes GAbr LEdu LRHS LSou WPtf |
| ***sevanensis*** | EBee LHop WCot |
| 'Sherbert Lemon' | CMea MWea SBfd SRot |
| ***suffrutescens*** 'Texas Rose' | CMea CPBP CSpe EBee LLHF LRHS MAsh MWea SBch SBfd SRot WNew |
| ***supina*** | see *S. alpina* |
| ***tournefortii*** | ECtt LLWP |

## seakale see *Crambe maritima*

## *Sebaea* (*Gentianaceae*)

| | |
|---|---|
| ***rehmanii*** | SPlb |
| ***thomasii*** | GEdr WAbe |

## *Securigera* (*Papilionaceae*)

| | |
|---|---|
| § ***varia*** | CArn EPfP LHop MMuc NLar NPri SEND SRms XLum |

## *Sedastrum* see *Sedum*

## *Sedum* ✿ (*Crassulaceae*)

| | |
|---|---|
| 'Abbey Dore' | EBee ELan EPfP GCal LPla LRHS LSou MBri NBPC NCGa SBfd SRkn WAbb WAul WCAu WPGP |
| ***acre*** | CTri ECho EPfP GPoy LEdu LRHS MAsh MHer MNHC NBlu NMir SEND SPlb XLum |
| - 'Aureum' | ECho EDAr EHoe EPfP LAst LRHS MAsh NBlu NLar NPri NRya SPer SPoG WFar WNew WPat XLum |
| - 'Elegans' | ECtt |
| - 'Golden Queen' | ECho LRHS MSCN SPlb SPoG |
| - 'Helvetica' | WCot |
| - 'Minus' | ECho EDAr |
| § - subsp. ***neglectum*** var. ***majus*** | CChe EPfP NLar |
| ***adolphi*** | EPfP |
| ***aizoon*** | ECho GCal LAst NBre SIde SPlb WFar XLum |
| - 'Aurantiacum' | see *S. aizoon* 'Euphorbioides' |
| § - 'Euphorbioides' | ECha ECtt ELan MHer MMuc MRav NLar SEND SGar SHar SPer SPlb WFar WTin |
| ***albescens*** | see *S. forsterianum* f. *purpureum* |
| ***alboroseum*** | see *S. erythrostictum* |
| § ***album*** | ECho LRHS MMuc NBro NMir SEND XLum |

| | |
|---|---|
| - 'Coral Carpet' | ECho ECtt EDAr EPfP GJos GKev LRHS MAsh MRav MWat NRya SFgr SPoG WCot WFar XLum |
| - subsp. ***gypsicola*** | see *S. gypsicola* |
| - subsp. ***teretifolium*** var. ***micranthum*** 'Chloroticum' | XLum |
| § - - var. ***murale*** | CTri STre XLum |
| ***alpestre*** | XLum |
| ***altissimum*** | see *S. sediforme* |
| * ***altum*** | NBre WFar |
| § ***amplexicaule*** subsp. ***tenuifolium*** | GGar |
| ***anacampseros*** | NHol SEND SUsu XLum |
| ***athoum*** | see *S. album* |
| ***atlanticum*** | see *S. dasyphyllum* subsp. *dasyphyllum* var. *mesatlanticum* |
| 'Autumn Charm' | see *S.* (Herbstfreude Group) 'Lajos' |
| Autumn Joy | see *S.* 'Herbstfreude' |
| ***beauverdii*** HWJ 824 **new** | WCru |
| 'Bertram Anderson' ♀H4 | Widely available |
| ***beyrichianum*** misapplied | see *S. glaucophyllum* |
| ***bithynicum*** 'Aureum' | see *S. hispanicum* var. *minus* 'Aureum' |
| 'Black Beauty' | LRHS |
| 'Blade Runner' | EBee LRHS LSou MBri |
| ***brevifolium*** | NWCA |
| ***burrito*** | EShb |
| 'Carl' | CKno CPrp EAEE EBee EBla ECha ECrN ECtt EPfP EShb GBin GMaP LHop LRHS LSRN MCot MRav NBro NDov NOrc NSti SAga SMrm SRGP WCot WHoo WMnd WMoo WWEG XLum |
| ***caucasicum*** | WAbb WCot |
| ***cauticola*** ♀H4 | CSpe ECho EDAr GCal GEdr GLam MAvo MBrN MHer MRav NBre SRms SRot WAbe XLum |
| - from Lida | ECho |
| - 'Coca-Cola' | CBct CCVN CMac CWGN EAEE ECtt EHoe GJos LAst LBMP LRHS MAsh MCot NDov NPri SBfd SPhx SPoG SWvt WBor WFar WNew |
| - 'Lidakense' ♀H4 | CMea CSpe CWCL ECha ECho ECtt LRHS MAsh MBri MLHP MSCN NHol NSla SBch SPlb SRot WCot WFar WHil XLum |
| - 'Purpurine' | ECho GCal |
| - 'Robustum' | see *S.* 'Ruby Glow' |
| ***chrysicaulum*** **new** | EPot |
| 'Cloud Walker'$^{PBR}$ | CAbP EBee WCot |
| ***compressum*** | see *S. palmeri* subsp. *palmeri* tetraploid |
| ***confusum*** Hemsl. | SChr SEND WFar WHoo |
| ***crassipes*** | see *Rhodiola wallichiana* |
| ***crassularia*** | see *Crassula setulosa* 'Milfordiae' |
| 'Crazy Ruffles' | EBee ECtt EWTr WCot |
| ***cryptomerioides*** B&SWJ 054 | WCru |
| 'Dark Jack' | EBee MAvo NGdn SMrm |
| ***dasyphyllum*** | ECho EDAr NRya SPlb SRms STre |
| § - subsp. ***dasyphyllum*** var. ***mesatlanticum*** | GKev NBir |
| - ***mucronatis*** | see *S. dasyphyllum* subsp. *dasyphyllum* var. *mesatlanticum* |
| ***debile*** | WAbe |
| 'Diamond Edge' (v) | EBee ECtt WWEG |
| ***divergens*** | XLum |
| ***douglasii*** | see *S. stenopetalum* 'Douglasii' |
| ***drymarioides*** | LRHS NBre |
| 'Dudley Field' | MHer |
| 'Eleanor Fisher' | see *S. telephium* subsp. *ruprechtii* |
| ***ellacombeanum*** | see *S. kamtschaticum* var. *ellacombeanum* |
| 'Elworthy Rose' | CElw |
| § ***erythrostictum*** | CBot CWan LRHS WAbb XLum |
| - 'Frosty Morn' (v) | Widely available |
| § - 'Mediovariegatum' (v) | EAEE EBee ELan EShb LRHS MHer MNrw MRav NLar NPnk SBfd SBrd SPad SWvt WFar WMnd WMoo WWEG XLum |
| 'Evening Cloud' | ECha |
| ***ewersii*** | ECho ECtt EDAr GKev MAsh MMuc NBro NLar NSla SPhx SPlb XLum |
| - CC 5288 | EWld |
| - var. ***homophyllum*** 'Rosenteppich' | LBuc LRHS MBrN SWvt WMoo |
| ***fabaria*** | see *S. telephium* subsp. *fabaria* |
| ***farinosum*** | GGar |
| ***fastigiatum*** | see *Rhodiola fastigiata* |
| ***forsterianum*** subsp. ***elegans*** | SPlb XLum |
| § - f. ***purpureum*** | NRya |
| 'Frosted Fire' **new** | LSou |
| ***frutescens*** | STre |
| ***furfuraceum*** | NMen WAbe |
| Garnet Brocade = 'Garbro'$^{PBR}$ | CCVN ECtt WMoo |
| § ***glaucophyllum*** | WFar XLum |
| 'Gold Mound' | EPfP LAst LRHS MAsh NLar SSvw |
| 'Green Expectations' | ECtt GBin MRav MWat NBre |
| § ***gypsicola*** | EBee |
| (Herbstfreude Group) 'Autumn Fire' | EBee MAsh |
| - 'Beka' (v) | LSou |
| - 'Elsie's Gold' (v) | LRHS MAsh NLar |
| § - 'Herbstfreude' ♀H4 | Widely available |
| - 'Jaws'$^{PBR}$ | CKno EBee ECtt IKil LSou WCot |
| § - 'Lajos' (v) | EBee LSou MAsh |
| - 'Mini Joy' | LRHS |
| ***heterodontum*** | see *Rhodiola heterodonta* |
| ***hidakanum*** | ECtt EHoe EPot GMaP NBro NHol NMen NWad WHoo WTin |
| ***himalense*** misapplied | see *Rhodiola* 'Keston' |
| ***hispanicum*** | ECho EDAr NBre SPlb |
| - ***glaucum*** | see *S. hispanicum* var. *minus* |
| § - var. ***minus*** | ECho ECtt MMuc SEND SPlb |
| § - - 'Aureum' | ECho |
| ***humifusum*** | NWCA WThu |
| § ***hybridum*** | XLum |
| - 'Czar's Gold' | NGdn |
| 'Indian Chief' | see *S.* (Herbstfreude Group) 'Herbstfreude' |
| ***integrifolium*** | see *Rhodiola integrifolia* |
| ***ishidae*** | see *Rhodiola ishidae* |
| 'James Windsor' **new** | CRDP |
| 'José Aubergine'$^{PBR}$ | CPrp EBee ECtt GBin IPot LRHS MBri MCot NCGa NLar SBfd WWEG |
| 'Joyce Henderson' | EBee ECtt GQue LHop MCot MRav NLar SPer SRGP WBrk WCot WMoo WTin WWEG |
| ***kamtschaticum*** ♀H4 | ECho GAuc GJos WFar |
| - B&SWJ 10870 | WCru |
| § - var. ***ellacombeanum*** ♀H4 | MMuc NMen SEND WCot XLum |
| - - B&SWJ 8853 | WCru |
| § - var. ***floriferum*** 'Weihenstephaner Gold' | CEnt CTri ECho ECtt EDAr EPfP GAbr GEdr GGar GMaP MAsh |

| | | |
|---|---|---|
| | | MHer MMuc MRav MWat NBir NMen SPlb SPoG SRms WAbe WFar XLum |
| | - var. ***kamtschaticum*** 'Variegatum' (v) 🏆$^{H4}$ | CMea ECho ECtt EDAr EHoe LBMP LRHS MAsh MHer MMuc MWat NPri SPoG SRms SRot SWvt XLum |
| | ***lanceolatum*** | NBre |
| | ***lineare*** | LAst |
| | - 'Variegatum' (v) | XLum |
| | 'Little Gem' | see × *Cremnosedum* 'Little Gem' |
| § | ***lydium*** | CTri ECho MAsh MHer NBlu SFgr SPlb |
| | - 'Aureum' | see *S. hispanicum* var. *minus* 'Aureum' |
| | - 'Bronze Queen' | see *S. lydium* |
| | ***makinoi*** 'Ōgon' | EBee |
| I | 'Marchants Best Red' 🏆$^{H4}$ | SPhx SUsu |
| | 'Matrona' 🏆$^{H4}$ | Widely available |
| | ***maweanum*** | see *S. acre* subsp. *neglectum* var. *majus* |
| | ***middendorffianum*** | ECho MAsh MBrN MHer MWat NMen SEND SRms SRot WFar XLum |
| | 'Moonglow' | ECtt NMen |
| | ***moranense*** | MMuc SEND XLum |
| | ***morganianum*** 🏆$^{H1}$ | EBak MSCN STre |
| | ***morrisonense*** B&SWJ 7078 | WCru |
| | 'Mr Goodbud'$^{PBR}$ 🏆$^{H4}$ | CPrp EBee ECtt GBin LRHS MTis NDov SBfd WCot WWEG |
| | 'Munstead Red' | CAby CMea COlW CPrp CWCL EBee EBla ECha ECtt EPfP GBin LRHS MRav MWat NLar SBfd SGar SMrm SPer SPhx WFar WKif WMnd WMoo |
| | ***murale*** | see *S. album* subsp. *teretifolium* var. *murale* |
| | ***muscoideum*** **new** | EPot |
| | ***nevii*** misapplied | see *S. glaucophyllum* |
| | ***nevii*** ambig. | SPlb |
| | ***nicaeense*** | see *S. sediforme* |
| | ***niveum*** | NMen |
| | 'Novem'$^{PBR}$ **new** | NCGa |
| | ***obcordatum*** | NMen |
| | ***obtusatum*** misapplied | see *S. oreganum* |
| § | ***obtusatum*** A. Gray | NBro NSla STre WFar WPnn |
| | - subsp. ***boreale*** NNS 01-123 | NWCA |
| | ***obtusifolium*** | MAsh |
| | - var. ***listoniae*** **new** | EDAr |
| | ***ochroleucum*** | MMuc NBre SEND |
| | ***oppositifolium*** | see *S. spurium* 'Album' |
| § | ***oreganum*** | ECha ECho EDAr GAbr GGar GKev GMaP MHer MLLN MSCN MWat NMen SPlb SRms SRot STre XLum |
| | - 'Procumbens' | see *S. oreganum* subsp. *tenue* |
| § | - subsp. ***tenue*** | LEdu NRya NWad WAbe WPat |
| § | ***oregonense*** | ECho LRHS NMen |
| | ***oxypetalum*** | STre |
| | ***pachyclados*** | see *Rhodiola pachyclados* |
| | ***pachyphyllum*** | EPfP WNew |
| | ***palmeri*** | CHEx LSou MRav NBir SChr SSvw STre XLum |
| § | - subsp. ***palmeri*** tetraploid | SEND |
| | 'Parish Plum' **new** | SBch |
| | 'Pewter' | ECho |
| | ***pilosum*** | NMen |
| | 'Pink Dove' **new** | SBch |
| | 'Pinky' **new** | WHil |
| § | ***pluricaule*** | ECho LRHS NSla SPlb SRms |
| | ***populifolium*** | ECha GCal GJos MHer NLar SPhx STre WPer XLum |
| | ***praealtum*** | SChr SEND STre WCot |
| | ***pulchellum*** | SPlb |
| | ***purdyi*** | see *S. spathulifolium* subsp. *purdyi* |
| | 'Red Cauli' 🏆$^{H4}$ | CKno CSpe EBee ECha EPPr GBin IPot LHop LRHS LSou MAvo MBri MCot MLLN MNFA NCGa NDov NLar NPro SDix SPhx SSvw SUsu WCot WFar WHil WKif |
| | ***reflexum*** L. | see *S. rupestre* L. |
| | ***reptans*** | ECho |
| | ***rhodiola*** | see *Rhodiola rosea* |
| | ***rosea*** | see *Rhodiola rosea* |
| | ***rubroglaucum*** misapplied | see *S. oregonense* |
| | ***rubroglaucum*** Praeger | see *S. obtusatum* A. Gray |
| | × ***rubrotinctum*** | CHEx SChr |
| | - 'Aurora' | SChr |
| § | 'Ruby Glow' 🏆$^{H4}$ | Widely available |
| | 'Ruby Glow' variegated (v) | WPer |
| § | ***rupestre*** L. | ECho GJos MBNS MMuc MWat SEND SPlb SPoG WFar XLum |
| | - 'Angelina' | EBee EPPr EWes GLam LRHS MAsh MAvo MGos MHer NBir NDov NPri NPro NWad SBrd SPoG SRGP WCot XLum |
| | - 'Monstrosum Cristatum' | NBir SMad XLum |
| | ***ruprechtii*** | see *S. telephium* subsp. *ruprechtii* |
| | 'Samuel Oliphant' (v) | WCot |
| | ***sarcocaule*** hort. | see *Crassula sarcocaulis* |
| | ***sarmentosum*** | ECho XLum |
| § | ***sediforme*** | CArn EDAr GAbr LRHS |
| | - B&F MA 25 | WCot |
| | - 'Marrakesh' | MSCN |
| | - ***nicaeense*** | see *S. sediforme* |
| | ***selskianum*** | GJos NBre SBch WFar XLum |
| | - 'Goldilocks' **new** | GJos |
| | ***sempervivoides*** | ECho |
| | ***sexangulare*** | ECho EDAr EPot GGar MAsh MHer MMuc NRya SEND SFgr SPlb SRms STre WFar XLum |
| | ***sibiricum*** | see *S. hybridum* |
| | ***sieboldii*** | ECho |
| | - 'Dragon' **new** | LRHS |
| | - 'Mediovariegatum' (v) 🏆$^{H2-3}$ | CHEx COlW ECho MHer NSla SPlb WFar XLum |
| | 'Silvermoon' | ECtt |
| | ***spathulifolium*** | CTri ECha ECho EPot MDKP |
| | - 'Aureum' | ECho ECtt MWat WAbe |
| | - 'Cape Blanco' 🏆$^{H4}$ | Widely available |
| § | - subsp. ***purdyi*** | WAbe |
| | - 'Purpureum' 🏆$^{H4}$ | Widely available |
| | - subsp. ***yosemitense*** 'Red Raver' | CPBP |
| | ***spectabile*** 🏆$^{H4}$ | CArn CChe CHEx CHab CPrp CTri EBee ELan EPfP GJos GMaP LRHS MCot MHer MRav NGdn SBfd SGar SPlb SRms STre WBor WBrk WFar WSFF WTin WWEG |
| | - 'Album' | CHEx |
| | - Brilliant Group | CBar CHab LBMP LRHS WCAu |
| | - - 'Brilliant' 🏆$^{H4}$ | CBcs CKno CSBt CTri EBee ECha ECtt ELan EPfP LAst LRHS MAsh MBri MGos MMuc MRav NGdn NOrc SBfd SEND SMad SPer SPoG SWvt WFar WMoo WWEG |

| | | |
|---|---|---|
| | - - 'Carmen' | EBee LRHS XLum |
| | - - 'Hot Stuff' | WCot |
| | - - 'Lisa' | GBin MTPN NDov NLar |
| | - - 'Meteor' | CPrp EBee LPla MWat NLar SMrm WPer WWEG |
| | - - 'Neon' | EBee NCGa NDov |
| | - - 'Pink Fairy' | WHil |
| | - - 'Rosenteller' | EBee NBre NCGa WFar |
| § | - - 'Septemberglut' | EBee NBre WCot XLum |
| | - - 'Steven Ward' | EBee EWes SRGP |
| | - 'Humile' **new** | XLum |
| | - 'Iceberg' | Widely available |
| * | - 'Mini' | ELan MRav |
| | - 'Pink Chablis'[PBR] (v) | EBee NLar WCot |
| | - September Glow | see *S. spectabile* (Brilliant Group) 'Septemberglut' |
| | - 'Stardust' | CKno CPrp CTri EBee GKev GMaP LRHS MHer MRav NCGa NLar NVic SPer SPet WFar WGor WWEG XLum |
| | - 'Variegatum' | see *S. erythrostictum* 'Mediovariegatum' |
| | ***spinosum*** | see *Orostachys spinosa* |
| | ***spurium*** | CHEx ECho GAbr GJos MMuc NPro SEND SGar SRms STre XSen |
| § | - 'Album' | NRya XLum |
| | - 'Atropurpureum' | ECha ECho WMoo XLum |
| | - 'Coccineum' | ECho GJos MMuc MNHC SEND |
| | - Dragon's Blood | see *S. spurium* 'Schorbuser Blut' |
| | - 'Erdblut' | NMen |
| | - 'Fuldaglut' | CTri ECho EHoe EPfP GMaP GQue IPot LRHS MNrw NRya SMrm WFar WMoo WNew WPer WPnn |
| | - 'Green Mantle' | EBee ECha ECho EPfP |
| | - Purple Carpet | see *S. spurium* 'Purpurteppich' |
| | - 'Purpureum' | SRms |
| § | - 'Purpurteppich' | EBee ECho ECtt GJos MRav NBro NHol NLar NWad SRms |
| | - 'Roseum' | EWll SRms |
| | - 'Ruby Mantle' | EWll GKev MSCN NBro SBch SPoG SWvt WMoo XLum |
| § | - 'Schorbuser Blut' ♀H4 | CMea EBee ECho ECtt EPau EPfP GJos GKev MAsh MCot MLHP MWat NBir NRya NSla NVic SPlb SRGP SRms WFar WHoo WTin XLum |
| I | - 'Splendens Roseum' | XLum |
| | - 'Summer Glory' | NLar |
| § | - 'Tricolor' (v) | CTri EBee ECha ECho EHoe GEdr GJos GKev MAsh MHer MLHP MRav MSCN NBlu NHol NRya SPlb SPoG STre WFar WMoo XLum |
| | - 'Variegatum' | see *S. spurium* 'Tricolor' |
| | - 'Voodoo' | CEnt ECtt EPfP EWes GEdr MAsh MHer MSCN NBro NGdn WFar XLum |
| | ***stefco*** | XLum |
| | ***stenopetalum*** | SPlb |
| § | - 'Douglasii' | MHer SRms |
| | 'Stewed Rhubarb Mountain' | CAby CPrp EAEE EBee EBla ECha ECtt EPfP LHop LRHS MBNS MCot MNFA MRav NBro NCGa NLar NOrc SBfd SPur WCAu WFar WMoo WWEG |
| | ***stoloniferum*** | ECho |
| | ***stribrnyi*** | see *S. urvillei* Stribrnyi Group |
| | 'Sunset Cloud' | CHEx CMHG EBee ECtt EWes GCal IPot LPla MRav NBre |
| | ***takesimense*** | XLum |
| | - B&SWJ 8518 | WCru |
| | ***telephium*** | CArn NBir SRms XLum |
| § | - Atropurpureum Group ♀H4 | COlW EBee ELan EPfP MRav SWvt WCot WWEG |
| | - - 'African Pearl' | ECtt LRHS WCFE WCot WWEG |
| | - - 'Arthur Branch' | CPrp GBin LRHS WWEG |
| I | - - 'Atropurpureum Nanum' | WWEG |
| | - - 'Bon Bon' | CPrp EBee LRHS MBNS NLar SGar SPoG WPtf |
| | - - 'Chocolate' | CBcs EBee ECtt EPPr LRHS MAvo NLar |
| | - - 'Dark Knight' **new** | LRHS |
| | - - 'El Cid' | EBee EWes |
| | - - 'Hester' | EBee WWEG |
| | - - 'Karfunkelstein' ♀H4 | EBee ECha EPPr GBin MAvo MTis NDov SPhx SUsu WCot |
| | - - 'Leonore Zuuntz' | EBee NBre |
| | - - 'Lynda et Rodney' | EWes WCot |
| | - - 'Lynda Windsor' | EBee ECtt EPfP GAbr GQue NLar NPnk SRGP SWvt WFar |
| | - - 'Möhrchen' | EBee GBin GMaP LRHS MRav NGdn NLar NPnk SBfd SPoG WFar WMnd WMoo |
| | - - 'Picolette' | EBee LRHS LSou MSCN NCGa SPoG |
| | - - 'Postman's Pride'[PBR] | CKno CWGN EBee ECtt EPfP GQue LPla LRHS MTis MWat NGdn SUsu WCot |
| § | - - 'Purple Emperor' ♀H4 | Widely available |
| | - - 'Ringmore Ruby' | WCot WPGP WWEG |
| | - - 'Xenox'[PBR] ♀H4 | CWGN EBee ECtt EKen EPPr EPfP ETod EWll GBin IPot LRHS MAsh MBNS MCot NLar SBfd SHar SPoG WCot WHil WPGP WWEG |
| | - 'Bronco'[PBR] | NCGa |
| | - Emperor's Waves Group | NGdn |
| § | - subsp. ***fabaria*** | MRav SMrm WAbb WCot WFar WWEG |
| | - - var. ***borderei*** | CElw LPla SBch SPhx SUsu |
| | - 'Jennifer' | WCot |
| | - subsp. ***maximum*** | CBot |
| | - - 'Atropurpureum' | see *S. telephium* Atropurpureum Group |
| | - - 'Gooseberry Fool' | CAby CMea COlW CPrp EBee ECGP ECtt EPfP GMaP SBch SPhx SPur WFar WWEG |
| | - 'Roseum' | WWEG |
| § | - subsp. ***ruprechtii*** | CPrp EAEE ECha ECtt EPPr EPfP GAuc GMaP LRHS LSou MCot MNFA MRav NSti SPer SPet SPhx WFar WGwG WMoo WPer |
| | - - 'Citrus Twist' | EBee EBla ECtt LRHS MRav NPnk WPtf |
| | - - 'Hab Gray' | CSpe EBee ECtt ETod EWes GBin GQue LRHS MAvo MTis NBPC NLar SAga SUsu WCot |
| | - - 'Pink Dome' | ECha |
| | - 'Strawberries and Cream' | Widely available |
| | - subsp. ***telephium*** | GCra |
| | - 'Variegatum' (v) | LRHS MDKP |
| | ***tenuifolium*** | see *S. amplexicaule* subsp. *tenuifolium* |
| | - subsp. ***ibericum*** | see *S. amplexicaule* subsp. *tenuifolium* |
| | ***ternatum*** | WFar |
| | ***tetractinum*** | LRHS |
| | - 'Coral Reef' **new** | LRHS |
| | ***trollii*** | see *Rhodiola trollii* |
| | ***urvillei*** Sartorianum Group | MHer XLum |
| § | - Stribrnyi Group | XLum |
| | ***ussuriense*** | EBee ECha EPfP GCal LRHS NBir SBfd SUsu |

- 'Chuwangsan' EWld WCru
- 'Turkish Delight' EWll
'Veluwse Wakel' GBin
'Vera Jameson' ♀H4 Widely available
***viviparum*** B&SWJ 8662 WCru
'Wallaceum' NBlu
'Washfield Purple' see *S. telephium* 'Purple Emperor'
'Weihenstephaner Gold' see *S. kamtschaticum* var. *floriferum* 'Weihenstephaner Gold'
***weinbergii*** see *Graptopetalum paraguayense*
'Winky' **new** LSou MAsh
***yezoense*** see *S. pluricaule*
'Zebra' LRHS

## *Seemannia* see *Gloxinia*

## *Selaginella* (*Selaginellaceae*)

***braunii*** CLAP WCot
***erythropus*** CBty LRHS
var. ***sanguinea***
***kraussiana*** ♀H1 CLAP EDAr EShb GGar WRic
- 'Aurea' CBty CCCN LRHS SMad WRic
- 'Brownii' ♀H1 CBty CCCN ISha LRHS
- 'Gold Tips' CBty CCCN ISha LRHS
***lepidophylla*** SVic
***moellendorfii*** CBty ISha LRHS WRic
***tamariscina*** WAbe
***uncinata*** ♀H1 CBty CLAP ISha LRHS WRic

## *Selago* (*Scrophulariaceae*)

***galpinii*** CPBP
***thunbergii*** LHop

## *Selinum* (*Apiaceae*)

***carvifolium*** EBee EWil LRHS WWEG
***tenuifolium*** see *S. wallichianum*
§ ***wallichianum*** CAby CDes CSam CSpe ELan EPri EShb EWTr GCal GCra IPot LBMP LEdu LRHS MWat NBPC NCGa NDov NLar SPer SPhx SUsu WCAu WFar WHil WPtf WSHC WWEG
- EMAK 886 EBee GPoy SDix
- HWJK 2224 WCru
- HWJK 2347 WCru

## *Selliera* (*Goodeniaceae*)

***radicans*** ECou EDAr GAbr GBin GGar

## *Semele* (*Asparagaceae*)

***androgyna*** CHEx CRHN

## *Semiaquilegia* (*Ranunculaceae*)

§ ***adoxoides*** WCot
'Early Dwarf' EDif
§ ***ecalcarata*** CAby CBot CDes CPom EBee ECho GCal GGar GJos GKev MNrw NGdn SBch SRms SSvw WCru WFar WHal WPGP WTou
- Australian **new** CDes SBch
* - f. ***bicolor*** WCru WFar
- 'Flore Pleno' (d) WTou
- 'Snowbell' WCru
***simulatrix*** see *S. ecalcarata*
'Sugar Plum Fairy' EPfP LRHS SPoG

## *Semiarundinaria* (*Poaceae*)

from Korea EPla
§ ***fastuosa*** ♀H4 CBcs CDoC CEnt CHEx CPMA EAmu ENBC EPfP EPla LMaj LPal MMoz MMuc MWht SArc SEND SPlb WJun
- var. ***viridis*** CEnt EPla LPJP MWht SBig WCru WJun
***kagamiana*** CDoC ENBC EPla MMoz MMuc MWhi MWht SBig SEND WJun
§ ***lubrica*** MWht
***makinoi*** EAmu EPla MWht SLPl WJun
***nitida*** see *Fargesia nitida*
§ ***okuboi*** CEnt ENBC EPla LPal MMoz MWht WJun
***villosa*** see *S. okuboi*
***yamadorii*** EPla MMoz MWht WJun
- 'Brimscombe' EPla
***yashadake*** CEnt EPla WJun
- 'Gimmei' EPla
- f. ***kimmei*** CDoC CEnt EPla LRHS MGos MMoz MMuc MWht NLar SBig SEND WDyG WFar WJun WMoo WPGP
I - - 'Inversa' CEnt

## *Semnanthe* see *Erepsia*

## *Sempervivella* see *Rosularia*

## *Sempervivum* ✿ (*Crassulaceae*)

sp. SArc
McB 368 GLam
from Andorra ESem
from Sierra Nova ESem
'Aaroundina' **new** CWil
'Abba' EDAr NMen WHal WPer
'Adelaar' CWil NMen
'Adelmoed' CWil NMen SFgr
'Ageet' **new** CWil
'Aglow' ESem MHom NMen
'Aladdin' CWil ESem GEdr MSCN NMen SRms
'Alaric' **new** NMen
'Albernelli' SFgr
'Alchimist' ESem NMen XLum
'Alcithoë' ESem
'Aldo Moro' CWil ECha EDAr ESem GAbr LBee LRHS MHom NMen SFgr WIvy XLum
'Alice' ESem MSCN
'Alidae' ESem
***allionii*** see *Jovibarba allionii*
'Alluring' ESem GAbr NMen
'Alpha' ESem LBee LRHS MTis NMen SFgr SRms STre WHal WPer WTin XLum
***altum*** CWil ESem LRHS MHom MTis NMen SPlb XLum
'Amanda' CWil ECha EDAr ESem MBrN MTis NMen SRms WHoo WPer WTin
'Ambergreen' ESem NMen
***andreanum*** see *S. tectorum* var. *alpinum*
'Apache' Payne see *Jovibarba heuffelii* 'Apache'
'Apache' Haberer ESem NMen
'Apollo' SFgr XLum
'Apple Blossom' CMea ECha ESem NMen
***arachnoideum*** ♀H4 Widely available
- from Cascade Piste 7 ESem
- from the Abruzzi, Italy ESem
- 'Ararat' SDys
- 'Boria' ESem
- var. ***bryoides*** CWil ESem LRHS NMen WAbe WIvy WPer
- 'Cebennense' ESem GKev

| | |
|---|---|
| - 'Clärchen' | EPot ESem MSCN NMen NSla SFgr WAbe |
| - cristate | CWil |
| * - ***densum*** | EDAr MTis NMen WAbe WFar |
| - subsp. ***doellianum*** | see *S. arachnoideum* subsp. *tomentosum* var. *glabrescens* |
| - form No 1 | ECho |
| - 'Laggeri' | see *S. arachnoideum* subsp. *tomentosum* (C.B. Lehm. & Schnittsp.) Schinz & Thell. |
| - 'Opitz' | NMen WPer |
| - red | NMen |
| - 'Red Papaver' | NMen |
| - 'Red Wings' | ECha NMen SRms XLum |
| - 'Rubrum' | CHEx GMaP LRHS SPlb XLum |
| - 'Sultan' | ESem |
| - subsp. ***tomentosum*** misapplied | see *S.* × *barbulatum* 'Hookeri' |
| § - subsp. ***tomentosum*** (C.B. Lehm & Schnittsp.) Schinz & Thell. ♀H4 | CHEx CWil EPot ESem LRHS MSCN NMen NPer SFgr SPlb SRms WAbe WGor WPer |
| - - GDJ 92.04 | CWil |
| § - - var. ***glabrescens*** | NMen SDys WPat |
| - - 'Minus' | NMen |
| § - - 'Stansfieldii' | ESem GAbr LRHS NMen STre WHal |
| - 'Transsylvanicum' | ESem |
| § - 'White Christmas' | CWil MHer NMen |
| ***arachnoideum* × *calcareum*** | CWil NMen WIvy WTin |
| ***arachnoideum* × *montanum*** | see *S.* × *barbulatum* |
| ***arachnoideum* × *nevadense*** | CWil SDys |
| ***arachnoideum* × *pittonii*** | CWil MTis NMen WAbe |
| ***arenarium*** | see *Jovibarba arenaria* |
| 'Arlet' | EDAr |
| ***armenum*** | ESem NMen |
| - var. ***insigne*** | ESem |
| 'Arondina' | CWil NMen |
| 'Aross' | CMea ESem GAbr NMen |
| 'Arrowheads Red' | NMen |
| 'Artist' | CWil ESem NMen SFgr |
| ***arvernense*** | see *S. tectorum* |
| 'Ashes of Roses' | EPot ESem MHom NMen WAbe WGor WPer XLum |
| 'Asteroid' | CWil ESem NMen |
| 'Astrid' | CWil |
| ***atlanticum*** | ESem MHom NMen NSla SRot |
| - from Atlas Mountains, Morocco | CWil ESem |
| - from Oukaïmeden, Morocco | CWil ESem GAbr NMen WTin |
| - 'Edward Balls' | CWil ESem NMen SDys SFgr |
| 'Atlantis' ambig. | ESem |
| 'Atropurpureum' ambig. | CHEx CWil EDAr GEdr MAsh MBrN NMen SRms WGor WPer |
| 'Aureum' | see *Greenovia aurea* |
| 'Averil' | CWil NMen |
| 'Aymon Correvon' | ESem NMen |
| 'Baby Skrocki' **new** | CWil |
| ***balcanicum*** | CWil EDAr ESem NMen WIvy XLum |
| ***ballsii*** | LRHS NMen |
| - from Kambeecho, Greece | MHom |
| - from Smólikas, Greece | CWil ESem MHom NMen |
| - from Tschumba Petzi, Greece | CWil ESem MHom SDys XLum |
| 'Banderi' | ESem NMen |
| 'Banjo' | ESem NMen |
| 'Banyan' | ESem LRHS NMen |
| 'Barbarosa' | CWil ESem |
| § × ***barbulatum*** | CWil ESem GAbr LBee LRHS NMen SDys SFgr WPer |
| § - 'Hookeri' | CTri CWil EPot ESem MSCN NLar NMen SFgr WAbe WPer |
| 'Bascour Zilver' | CMea CWil ECha ESem LBee LRHS MSCN NMen WHal |
| 'Beaute' | ESem NMen |
| 'Bedazzled' | ESem NMen |
| 'Bedivere' | CPBP CWil LBee LRHS NMen SRms |
| 'Bedivere Crested' | NMen |
| * 'Bedley Hi' | ESem MHom |
| 'Bella Donna' | ESem MHom NMen WPer |
| 'Bella Meade' | CWil EDAr ESem NMen SFgr SRms WPer |
| 'Bellotts Pourpre' | CWil |
| 'Benny Hill' | CWil ESem |
| 'Bernstein' | CWil EDAr EPot ESem MHer NMen SFgr WHal XLum |
| 'Beta' | ESem MHom NMen WAbe WPer WTin XLum |
| 'Bethany' | CMea CWil ESem NMen WHal |
| 'Bicolor' ambig. | EPfP |
| 'Big Mal' | NMen |
| 'Big Red' **new** | NMen |
| 'Big Slipper' | ESem NMen |
| 'Binstead' | ESem |
| 'Birchmaier' | NMen SFgr |
| 'Black Beauty' | EPot |
| 'Black Cap' | NMen |
| 'Black Knight' | LRHS MHer SPlb SRms WHal |
| 'Black Mini' | CWil EPot ESem GAbr GKev MDKP NBir NMen SRms WAbe |
| 'Black Mountain' | CHEx CWil ESem GKev LBee LRHS NMen |
| 'Black Prince' | ECha ESem NMen |
| 'Black Velvet' | ESem NMen WIvy WPer |
| 'Bladon' | WPer |
| 'Blood of Winter' **new** | WGor |
| 'Blood Sucker' | ESem WGor |
| 'Blood Tip' | CHEx CMea CWil ECha ESem GAbr GCra GKev LAst LRHS MAsh MHer MSCN NHol NMen NRya SBch SEND SPlb SPoG SRms WFar WGor WHal WHoo WPer |
| 'Blue Boy' | CWil ECha EPPr EPot ESem GAbr GLam LBee LRHS MSCN NMen SFgr SRms WPer |
| 'Blue Moon' | ESem NMen |
| 'Blue Time' | ESem GEdr SFgr WHoo WTin XLum |
| 'Blush' | EDAr ESem |
| 'Boissieri' | see *S. tectorum* subsp. *tectorum* 'Boissieri' |
| 'Bold Chick' | ESem NMen |
| 'Bombardier' | EDAr |
| 'Booth's Red' | CHEx NMen WGor |
| 'Boreale' | see *Jovibarba hirta* subsp. *borealis* |
| ***borisii*** | see *S. ciliosum* var. *borisii* |
| ***borissovae*** | CWil ESem MHom NMen SDys |
| 'Boromir' | CWil EDAr ESem NMen XLum |
| 'Boule de Neige' | GEdr NMen NRya |
| 'Bowles's Variety' | NMen WPer |
| 'Braune Maus' | ESem SFgr |
| ***brevipilum*** from Turkey | ESem |
| 'Bright Eyes' | ESem |
| 'Britta' | ESem SDys |
| 'Brock' | CWil ECha ESem LRHS MHer MHom NMen WPer |
| 'Bronco' ♀H4 | CDes CHEx CWil ECho ESem GAbr LBee LRHS MHom NMen NRya |

| | |
|---|---|
| | SRms WCot WFar WHfH WPGP XLum |
| 'Bronze Beauty' | EDAr |
| 'Bronze Pastel' | CWil ECha EDAr ESem MHom NMen NSla SEND SFgr SRms SRot WGor WTin |
| 'Brown Owl' | CWil ECho ESem NMen SRms WFar |
| 'Brownii' | ESem GAbr NMen WPer WTin |
| 'Brunette' | ECho GAbr |
| 'Burgundy' | ECha ESem |
| 'Burgundy Velvet' | ESem NMen |
| 'Burnatii' | see *S. montanum* subsp. *burnatii* |
| 'Burning Desire' | WGor |
| 'Burnished Bronze' | ESem NMen |
| 'Butterbur' | ESem |
| 'Butterfly' | ESem NMen |
| 'Café' | CWil MSCN NMen SFgr SRms WIvy WPer |
| × ***calcaratum*** | EDAr SRms |
| ***calcareum*** | CMea CWil EWll GKev LRHS MAsh MMuc NBro NEgg NMen NWCA SEND SPlb SPoG SRms SRot WFar WHoo WPer XLum |
| - GDJ 92.15 from Petite Ceüse, France | CWil |
| - GDJ 92.16 from Petite Ceüse, France | CWil |
| - from Alps, France | CWil ESem NMen |
| - from Calde la Vanoise, France | CWil NMen |
| - from Ceüze, France | CWil ESem WIvy |
| - from Cleizé, France | see *S. calcareum* 'Limelight' |
| - from Col Bayard, France | CWil ESem GAbr NMen |
| - from Colle St Michel, France | CWil ESem NMen SFgr |
| - from Gorges supérieures du Cians, France | CWil ESem NMen |
| - from Mont Ventoux, France | CWil ESem |
| - from Petite Ceüse, France | ESem SRot |
| - from Queyras, France | CWil ESem NMen |
| - from Route d'Annôt, France | CWil ESem NMen |
| - from Triora, Italy | CWil ESem NMen |
| - 'Benz' | ESem SDys |
| - 'Extra' ♀H4 | CHEx CWil ESem GAbr GEdr MSCN NMen SFgr SRot |
| - 'Greenii' | CWil ESem GKev LRHS MMuc NMen SEND SPlb |
| § - 'Grigg's Surprise' | CWil ESem MHer NMen NWCA SPlb WFar |
| - 'Guillaumes' ♀H4 | CWil ESem NMen SFgr SRot WHoo |
| § - 'Limelight' | CMea CWil EDAr LRHS NMen WHal WIvy WPer WTin |
| - 'Monstrosum' | see *S. calcareum* 'Grigg's Surprise' |
| - 'Mrs Giuseppi' | CWil ECho ESem ETod GAbr GLam LBee LRHS NMen SFgr SRms STre WAbe WFar WPer XLum |
| - 'Pink Pearl' | CWil MSCN NMen SDys SFgr WIvy WTin XLum |
| - 'Sir William Lawrence' ♀H4 | CMea CPBP CWil ECho EDAr ESem NMen SFgr WAbe WHal WHoo WIvy WPer WThu WTin XLum |
| 'Caliph's Hat' | NMen |
| * ***calopticum* × *nevadense*** | WTin |
| 'Cameo' | see *Jovibarba heuffelii* var. *glabra* 'Cameo' |
| 'Canada Kate' | CWil ESem NMen WPer |
| 'Cancer' | ESem XLum |
| 'Candy Floss' | CWil NMen WGor |
| ***cantabricum*** | CWil ESem MMuc NMen SEND WThu XLum |
| - from Cue Vas de Sol | ESem |
| - from Cuengas Piedras | ESem |
| - from Cuevas del Sil, Spain | CWil |
| - from Navafria, Spain | CWil NMen WTin |
| - from Peña Prieta, Spain | NMen |
| - from Piedrafita, Spain | ESem |
| - from Riaño, Spain | CWil ESem GAbr |
| - from San Glorio, Spain | CWil ESem GAbr NMen |
| - from Tioveo | ESem NMen XLum |
| - from Tizneros, Spain | CWil |
| - from Valvarnera, Spain | ESem NMen |
| - subsp. ***cantabricum*** GDJ 93.13 from Peña de Llesba, Spain | CWil |
| - - from Leitariegos, Spain | CWil GAbr MHom NMen |
| - - from Pico del Lobo, Spain | CWil |
| - subsp. ***guadarramense*** | see *S. vicentei* subsp. *paui* |
| - - from Pico del Lobo, Spain, No 1 | SRot |
| - - from Pico del Lobo, Spain, No 2 | ESem |
| - - from Valvanera, Spain, No 1 | CWil NMen |
| - subsp. ***urbionense*** | CWil GEdr |
| - - from El Gatón, Spain | CWil |
| - - from Picos de Urbión, Spain | CWil ESem NMen |
| ***cantabricum* × *montanum*** subsp. ***stiriacum*** | WTin |
| ***cantabricum* × *montanum*** subsp. ***stiriacum*** 'Lloyd Praeger' | CWil |
| 'Caramel' | ESem NMen |
| * × ***carlsii*** | ESem |
| 'Carluke' | NMen |
| 'Carmen' | ESem GAbr NMen SFgr |
| 'Carneum' | ESem NMen |
| 'Carnival' | ESem NMen WPer |
| ***caucasicum*** | CWil ESem GEdr MHom NMen XLum |
| 'Cavo Doro' | CWil NMen SFgr |
| 'Celon' | ESem NMen |
| 'Centennial' | ESem NMen |
| 'Cerluke' | ESem |
| ***charadzeae*** | CWil ESem LBee LRHS NMen XLum |
| 'Charolensis' | ESem |
| 'Chartbury' | EDAr |
| 'Cherry Frost' | ECho NMen NRya SFgr STre WAbe XLum |
| 'Cherry Glow' | see *Jovibarba heuffelii* 'Cherry Glow' |
| 'Cherry Tart' | ESem |
| 'Chilli Pepper' | CYeo |
| 'Chivalry' | ESem NMen |
| 'Chocolate' | ESem NMen WAbe WPer |
| § × ***christii*** | ESem NMen |
| 'Christmas Time' | ESem NMen SFgr |
| ***chrysanthum*** | ESem |
| ***ciliosum*** ♀H4 | CMea CPBP CWil ECho ESem NMen NRya |
| - from Alí Butús, Bulgaria | SDys |
| - from Pestani | ESem |
| § - var. ***borisii*** | EPfP ESem GCal GKev NMen NRya WAbe WHal WOut |
| - var. ***ciliosum* × *ciliosum*** var. ***borisii*** | CTri NMen |
| - var. ***galicicum*** 'Mali Hat' | CPBP NMen WPer |
| ***ciliosum* × *grandiflorum*** | CWil ESem NMen |
| ***ciliosum* × *marmoreum*** | ESem NMen |

|  |  |
|---|---|
| ***ciliosum* × *tectorum*** | WTin |
| 'Cindy' | ESem SRms |
| 'Circlet' | CWil ESem NMen |
| 'Clara Noyes' | ESem NMen WFar WPer |
| 'Clare' | ESem MHer NMen |
| 'Claudine' | ESem |
| 'Clemanum' | ESem |
| 'Cleveland Morgan' | ECha ESem MHom NBro NMen XLum |
| 'Climax' ambig. | ECho EPfP ESem LRHS MHom NMen WFar |
| 'Clisette' | ESem |
| 'Cobweb Capers' | ESem MHom MTis NMen |
| 'Cobweb Centres' | ESem NMen |
| 'Cochise' | ESem |
| 'Collage' | ESem WPer |
| 'Collecteur Anchisi' | ESem SDys SFgr |
| 'Commander Hay' ♀H4 | CHEx EDAr EPfP ETod EWes GCra MHom MSCN NDov NMen NPer SRGP SRms STre WHal WIvy WJek WPer XLum |
| 'Comte de Congae' | ESem MTis NMen |
| 'Concorde' | LRHS |
| 'Congo' | ESem NMen SFgr XLum |
| 'Conran' | NMen |
| 'Corio' | ESem |
| 'Cornstone' | ECha ESem |
| 'Corona' | CWil ESem NMen SFgr SRms WPer |
| 'Coronet' | ESem |
| 'Corsair' | CWil ECha EPPr ESem GEdr GKev MBrN NMen SEND SFgr WGor WIvy WPer WTin |
| 'Cotopaxi' new | CWil |
| 'Cranberry' | ESem NMen |
| 'Cresta' | ESem |
| 'Crimson King' | SFgr |
| 'Crimson Velvet' | CHEx CMea ESem LBee LRHS NMen SFgr WPer XLum |
| 'Crimson Webb' | ESem |
| § 'Crispyn' ♀H4 | CWil EPot ESem LBee LRHS MHer MHom MSCN NMen SFgr WPer |
| 'Croky' | ESem |
| 'Croton' | ESem NMen WPer |
| 'Cupream' | CWil ESem NMen SRms WPer |
| 'Dakota' | CWil EDAr ESem NMen SFgr |
| 'Dallas' | CWil NMen SRms |
| 'Damask' | CWil LBee LRHS NMen SFgr WPer |
| 'Dame Arsac' | ESem |
| 'Dancer' | ESem |
| 'Dancer's Veil' | ESem |
| 'Darjeeling' | CWil NMen |
| 'Dark Beauty' | CMea CWil ECha ESem LRHS MSCN NMen WAbe WCot WGor WHal WPer |
| 'Dark Cloud' | CWil ESem GAbr LBee LRHS NMen WHoo WIvy WPer XLum |
| 'Dark Point' | CWil ESem MHom NMen SFgr |
| 'Dark Velvet' | CMea NMen |
| 'Darkie' | CWil ESem SFgr WPer |
| ***davisii*** | ECha NMen |
| 'De Kardijk' | NMen |
| 'Deep Fire' | CWil ESem NMen SRms WAbe WIvy WTin |
| × ***degenianum*** | ESem GAbr NMen SFgr WPer |
| 'Delta' ♀H4 | MHom NMen WHoo WTin |
| ***densum*** | see *S. tectorum* |
| 'Devon Glow' | MSCN |
| 'Devon Jewel' | WGor |
| 'Diamant' | ESem |
| 'Diane' | CWil ESem SFgr |
| 'Director Jacobs' | CWil EDAr ESem NMen SEND SFgr WPer WTin |
| 'Direktor General' new | GEdr |
| 'Disco Dancer' | ESem |
| ***dolomiticum*** | ESem NMen XLum |
| ***dolomiticum* × *montanum*** | ESem NBro NMen SFgr WTin |
| 'Donarrose' | ESem SFgr |
| 'Downland Queen' | CWil ESem NMen |
| 'Dragoness' | ESem NMen |
| 'Duke of Windsor' | NMen SFgr |
| 'Dunscar Hybrid' | ESem |
| 'Dunstan Seedling' | ESem |
| 'Dusky' | ESem |
| 'Dyke' | CTri CWil EDAr ESem GAbr NMen SFgr WHal |
| ***dzhavachischvilii*** | ESem NMen XLum |
| 'Edge of Night' | CWil NMen SRms |
| 'Educator Wollaert' new | NMen |
| 'Eefje' | CWil ESem NMen |
| 'El Greco' | ESem NMen |
| 'El Toro' | ECha ESem MHom NMen |
| 'Elgar' | NMen WPer |
| 'Elizabeth' | WPer |
| 'Elvis' | CWil GAbr MHom NMen SFgr |
| 'Emerald Giant' | CWil ESem SFgr SRms WPer WTin |
| 'Emerson's Giant' | CWil ESem NMen |
| 'Eminent' | ESem |
| 'Emma Jane' | ESem |
| 'Emmchen' | CWil NMen |
| 'Engle's' | CMea CTri ECha ESem GKev LRHS MHer MTis NMen SEND SRms WHal WPer |
| 'Engle's 13-2' | ESem NBro NMen |
| 'Engle's Rubrum' | CPBP EPot LBee NMen |
| ***erythraeum*** | CMea ESem LRHS MHom NMen SPlb WAbe WHal |
| - from Pirin, Bulgaria | NMen |
| - from Rila, Bulgaria | NMen |
| - 'Red Velvet' | NMen |
| 'Excalibur' | ESem NMen WIvy |
| 'Exhibita' | CWil EPPr ESem NMen SDys SRms |
| 'Exorna' | CWil ECha EDAr ESem MHom NMen SFgr WIvy WPer |
| 'Fair Lady' | CWil ESem GKev MHom MTis NMen |
| 'Fairy' | EPot |
| 'Fame' | ESem WGor |
| 'Fat Jack' | CWil NMen |
| × ***fauconnettii*** | CWil EDAr ESem NMen SFgr |
| - 'Thompsonii' | CWil ESem NMen |
| 'Feldmaier' | ESem GAbr NMen |
| 'Fernwood' new | ESem |
| 'Festival' | EDAr ESem NMen |
| 'Fiery Furness' | ESem NMen |
| 'Fiesta' ambig. | WHal |
| ***fimbriatum*** | see *S.* × *barbulatum* |
| 'Finerpointe' | ESem NMen |
| 'Fire Glint' | CWil ESem GEdr NMen SRms WIvy |
| 'Firebird' | ESem NMen SFgr |
| 'Firefly' | ESem |
| 'Firgrove Silver' new | SFgr |
| 'First Try' | ESem |
| ***flagelliforme*** | ESem XLum |
| 'Flaming Heart' | CWil EDAr ESem MAsh MBrN NMen WGor WPer |
| 'Flamingo' | ECha ESem NMen |
| 'Flanders Passion' | ECha LBee LRHS NMen SRms WPer |
| 'Flasher' | ESem NMen WPer |
| 'Fluweel' | NMen |

| |  |  |
|---|---|---|
| | 'Forden' | CHEx MSCN SFgr WGor |
| | 'Ford's Amiability' | ESem SDys |
| | 'Ford's Giant' | XLum |
| | 'Ford's Shadows' | SDys |
| | 'Ford's Spring' | CWil ESem NMen WIvy WPer |
| | 'Freckles' | NMen |
| | 'Freeland' | WPer |
| | 'Frigidum' | ESem |
| | 'Frolic' | ESem |
| | 'Fronika' | CWil NMen |
| | 'Frosty' | CWil ESem NMen SFgr SRms |
| | 'Fuego' ♀H4 | CWil ESem MHom NMen SFgr |
| | 'Fuji' | ESem NMen |
| | × ***funckii*** | CHEx CWil EDAr ESem MAsh MBrN NMen SDys WPer WTin XLum |
| | 'Furryness' | ESem NMen |
| | 'Fusilier' new | NMen |
| | 'Fuzzy Wuzzy' | EDAr ESem MTis NMen |
| | 'Galahad' | NMen |
| | 'Gallivarda' ♀H4 | CWil ESem MSCN NMen |
| | 'Gambol' | ESem |
| | 'Gamma' | CHEx CWil ESem LBee LRHS NMen SRms WTin |
| | 'Garnet' | ECho ESem WGor WIvy WPer |
| | 'Gay Jester' | CTri CWil ESem NMen SFgr WHoo WTin |
| | 'Gazelle' | ESem NMen WIvy WPer XLum |
| | 'Genevione' | CWil ESem NMen |
| | 'Georgette' | CWil ECha ESem NMen WPer XLum |
| | 'Gilosum' | EDAr |
| | 'Ginger' | ESem |
| | 'Ginnie's Delight' | CWil NMen |
| | 'Gipsy' | NMen |
| | ***giuseppii*** ♀H4 | GKev LBee MHer NMen WPer |
| | - from Coriscao, Spain | LRHS |
| | - GDJ 93.04 from Cumbre de Cebolleda | CWil |
| | - GDJ 93.17 from Coriscao, Spain | CWil |
| | - from Peña Espigüete, Spain | CWil ESem NMen SDys |
| | - from Peña Prieta, Spain | CWil NMen |
| | 'Gizmo' | CWil ESem NMen SFgr |
| | 'Gleam' | ESem |
| | 'Gloriosum' ambig. | EDAr ESem MSCN SFgr WPer |
| | 'Glowing Embers' | CWil ESem MHom NMen WHal WPer XLum |
| | 'Godaert' | SEND XLum |
| | 'Goldie' | ESem NMen |
| | 'Gollum' | NMen |
| | 'Goya' | ESem |
| | 'Graceum' | ESem |
| | 'Grammens' | ESem |
| | 'Granada' | EDAr ESem NMen |
| | 'Granat' | ESem LRHS MHer NMen SRms WPer XLum |
| | 'Granby' | CWil ECho LBee LRHS NMen SDys |
| | ***grandiflorum*** | CWil ESem NMen WPer WThu XLum |
| | - from Valpine | ESem NMen |
| | - 'Fasciatum' | ESem NMen |
| | - 'Keston' | ESem |
| | ***grandiflorum* × *montanum*** | see *S.* × *christii* |
| | 'Grannie's Favourite' | NMen |
| | 'Grape Idol' | CWil ESem NMen |
| | 'Grapetone' | ESem MHom NMen SDys WHal |
| | 'Graupurpur' | CWil XLum |
| | 'Green Apple' | CWil GAbr MHom NMen SDys |

| |  |  |
|---|---|---|
| | 'Green Dragon' | ESem LRHS MSCN NMen WOut |
| | 'Green Gables' | EDAr ESem WPer |
| | 'Green Giant' | ESem |
| | 'Green Ice' | CWil |
| | 'Greenwich Time' | EDAr ESem NMen |
| * | ***greigii*** | EPot |
| | 'Grenadier' | ESem |
| | 'Grey Dawn' | ESem LRHS MHom MTis NMen XLum |
| | 'Grey Ghost' | ESem NMen WIvy WPer |
| | 'Grey Green' | CWil |
| | 'Grey Lady' | CElw CMea CWil ESem NMen |
| | 'Grey Owl' | LRHS NMen |
| | 'Grey Velvet' | CWil |
| | 'Greyfriars' | CMea EDAr EPot ESem LBee LRHS MTis NMen SFgr WGor WPer |
| | 'Greyolla' | CWil ESem WPer |
| | 'Grünrand' | ESem |
| | 'Grünschnabel' | XLum |
| | × ***guiseppe*** | ESem LRHS SEND |
| | 'Gulle Dame' | CWil ESem MHom NMen SFgr |
| | 'Hades' | ESem |
| | 'Halemaumau' | CWil ESem |
| I | 'Hall's Hybrid' | CWil ESem GAbr MSCN NBro NMen SRms STre |
| | 'Hall's Seedling' | NMen |
| | 'Happy' | CWil ESem NMen SFgr SRms WGor WIvy WPer WThu |
| | 'Hart' | CWil NMen SRms WTin |
| | 'Haullauer's Seedling' | NMen |
| | 'Havana' | ESem NMen |
| | 'Hayling' | ESem LRHS NMen SRms WPer XLum |
| | 'Heigham Red' | CWil EPPr ESem LBee LRHS NMen WPer |
| | 'Heike' | CWil |
| | 'Helen' | EDAr |
| | 'Heliotroop' | ESem NMen SDys SRot |
| | ***helveticum*** | see *S. montanum* |
| | 'Hester' | CHEx CWil ECho ESem MAsh MBrN NBro NMen SRms WFar |
| | 'Hey-hey' | EPot ESem LBee LRHS MAsh MBrN NDov NMen SPlb SRms WPer XLum |
| | 'Hidde' | CWil ESem NMen SFgr WPer |
| | 'Hidde's Roosje' | ESem NMen |
| | 'Hirsutum' | see *Jovibarba allionii* |
| | ***hirtum*** | see *Jovibarba hirta* |
| | 'Hispidulum' | ESem |
| | 'Hookeri' | see *S.* × *barbulatum* 'Hookeri' |
| | 'Hopi' | CWil NMen SRms |
| | 'Hortulanus Smit' | NMen XLum |
| | 'Hot Peppermint' | ESem |
| | 'Hullabaloo' | EDAr ESem NMen SFgr |
| | 'Hurricane' | CWil ESem MTis NMen WIvy WPer |
| | 'Icicle' | CHEx CMea ESem LRHS MSCN NBro NHol NMen SRms WAbe WGor WOut |
| | ***imbricatum*** | see *S.* × *barbulatum* |
| | 'Imperial' | CWil MHom |
| | 'Inge' | see *Jovibarba heuffelii* 'Inge' |
| | ***ingwersenii*** | ESem MHom NMen XLum |
| | ***ingwersenii* × *pumilum*** | CWil ESem |
| | ***ingwersenii* × *pumilum*** from Spain | NMen |
| | 'Iophon' | LBee LRHS |
| | ***iranicum*** | NMen |
| | 'Irazu' | CWil ESem GAbr GLam LRHS MSCN NMen SDys SFgr SRms WPer |

| | |
|---|---|
| 'Irene' | ESem SFgr |
| 'Isaac Dyson' | SDys SRot |
| 'Isabelle' **new** | CWil |
| ***italicum*** | ESem MHom NMen XLum |
| 'Itchen' | ESem NMen |
| 'Ivonne' **new** | CWil |
| 'Iwo' | CHEx ESem NMen SFgr |
| 'Jack Frost' | CWil NBro NMen SFgr XLum |
| 'Jacquette' | CWil ESem NMen |
| 'Jadestern' **new** | CWil |
| 'Jamie's Pride' | WGor |
| 'Jane' | ESem |
| 'Jasper' | ESem |
| 'Jaspis' | ESem |
| 'Jelly Bean' | CWil ESem NMen SFgr |
| 'Jet Stream' 🏆H4 | CWil ESem LRHS MHom NMen SDys SPlb WGor |
| 'Jewel Case' | CWil ESem LRHS NMen SRms |
| I 'John Hobbs seedling No. 2' | ESem NMen |
| 'John T.' | ESem NMen |
| 'Jolly Green Giant' | ESem MHom NMen |
| 'Jubilee' | CMea CWil ECho EDAr ELan EPot ESem GEdr GKev MAsh MHer NMen SRms STre WGor WPer XLum |
| 'Jubilee Tricolor' | ESem NHol NMen SFgr WAbe |
| * 'Julia' | ESem |
| 'Jungle Fires' | CMea CWil EPot ESem NMen SDys SRms WHoo |
| 'Jungle Shadows' | EDAr ESem NMen XLum |
| 'Jupiter' | GKev XLum |
| 'Justine's Choice' | CWil NMen SRms |
| 'Kalinda' | ESem MHom NMen |
| 'Kappa' | CTri CWil ESem NBro NMen SDys SRot WPer |
| 'Katmai' | CWil ESem |
| 'Kaya' **new** | CWil |
| 'Kelly Jo' | CWil ESem NBro NMen WFar WTin |
| 'Kelut' | ESem NMen |
| 'Kermit' | ESem MHom NMen |
| 'Kia' | CWil |
| 'Kiara' **new** | CWil |
| 'Kibo' | ESem NMen WIvy |
| 'Kimble' | ESem NMen WPer |
| 'Kimono' | ESem |
| ***kindingeri*** | CWil ESem MHom NMen NWCA XLum |
| 'King George' | CTri CWil ECha ESem GKev LBee LRHS NMen SFgr SRms STre WGor WHal WHoo WPer WTin XLum |
| 'King Lear' | ESem NMen |
| 'Kip' | CMea ECha NMen WIvy WPer |
| 'Koko Flanel' | CWil ESem NMen SFgr |
| 'Korspel Glory' | NMen |
| 'Korspelsegietje' | CWil ESem GAbr |
| ***kosaninii*** | ESem NMen SFgr WPer WTin |
| - from Koprivnik, Slovenia | MSCN NMen SDys WAbe XLum |
| * - from Visitor | CWil |
| 'Krakeling' | NMen |
| 'Kramer's Purpur' | NMen |
| 'Kramer's Spinrad' | CHEx CMea CPBP CWil ECha EPPr EPot ESem GAbr LBee LRHS NMen NWCA SDys SFgr SPlb STre WHoo WIvy WTin |
| 'Krater' | CWil ESem NMen |
| 'Kubi' | ESem |
| 'Lady Kelly' | ESem NMen WIvy |
| 'L'Arte' | ESem |
| 'Launcelot' | ECha ESem WPer |
| 'Laura Lee' | ESem NMen SEND |

| | |
|---|---|
| 'Lavender and Old Lace' | CHEx CWil ESem GAbr LRHS MSCN NMen SFgr SPlb WNew WPer |
| 'Laysan' | CWil |
| Le Clair's hybrid No 4 | NMen |
| 'Lemon and Lime' | ESem |
| 'Lennik's Glory' | see *S.* 'Crispyn' |
| 'Lennik's Glory No.2' | ESem |
| 'Lennik's Time' | ESem |
| 'Lentezon' | ESem |
| 'Leocadia's Nephew' | ESem NMen |
| 'Leon Smits' | CWil ESem |
| 'Les Yielding' | ESem |
| ***leucanthum*** **new** | XLum |
| 'Lilac Time' 🏆H4 | CMea CWil EPPr ESem LRHS MBrN MHer MSCN NMen SFgr SPlb SRms WHal WIvy WOut WPer XLum |
| 'Lime Frost' | ESem |
| 'Lion King' | CWil ESem MSCN |
| 'Lipari' | CElw ECha EPot ESem NMen SRms XLum |
| 'Lipstick' | ESem NMen |
| 'Little Bo Bo' | ESem |
| 'Little Flirt' | MSCN |
| 'Lively Bug' | CWil EDAr ESem GEdr LBee LRHS MSCN NMen SDys SEND WGor WPer |
| 'Lloyd Praeger' | see *S. montanum* subsp. *stiriacum* 'Lloyd Praeger' |
| 'Long Shanks' | MSCN |
| 'Lonzo' | CWil SRms |
| 'Lynn's Choice' | CWil GAbr NMen SFgr WHal WIvy WPer |
| ***macedonicum*** | ESem GLam NMen WTin XLum |
| - from Ljuboten, Macedonia/Kosovo | CWil ESem NMen |
| 'Madeleine' | CWil ESem |
| 'Magic Spell' | CWil ESem NMen |
| 'Magical' | CWil NMen |
| 'Magnificum' | CWil ESem NMen WGor |
| 'Mahogany' | CHEx CTri CWil ECho EDAr ESem GKev LBee LRHS MAsh MHer NHol NMen NWCA SFgr SRms STre WGor WHal WIvy WNew XLum |
| 'Maigret' | CWil NMen WPer |
| 'Majestic' | CWil ESem LBee LRHS NMen |
| 'Major White' | CHEx |
| 'Malby's Hybrid' | see *S.* 'Reginald Malby' |
| 'Marella' | ESem WPer |
| 'Maria Laach' | CWil ESem MMuc NMen |
| 'Marijntje' | CWil ESem NMen WPer |
| 'Marjorie Newton' | CWil ESem NMen WPer |
| 'Marmalade' | ESem |
| § ***marmoreum*** | ECho EPot LBee LRHS MAsh NMen SRms STre WFar WHal WPer |
| - from Kanzan Gorge, Bulgaria | ESem NMen |
| - from Monte Tirone, Italy | LRHS SDys |
| - from Okol, Albania | ESem NMen |
| - 'Brunneifolium' | CWil ESem GAbr GCal LBee LRHS NMen WIvy WPer XLum |
| - 'Bruno' | STre |
| - subsp. ***marmoreum*** var. ***dinaricum*** | ESem MHer NMen |
| - - - from Karawanken | ESem |
| § - - 'Rubrifolium' | XLum |
| 'Martin' | ESem |
| 'Mate' | ESem NMen |
| 'Maubi' | CHEx |
| 'Mauna Kea' | NMen WPer |

'Mauvine' NMen XLum
'Mayfair' EDAr
'Mayfair Imp' NMen
'Maytime' ESem
'Medallion' ESem SFgr
'Mcissc' ECho
'Melanie' CWil ESem MBrN NMen WIvy
'Memorial Merit' ESem
'Mercury' CWil ESem GAbr LRHS NBro NMen SRms
'Merlin' ESem MSCN
'Metallicum' ESem
'Midas' CWil ECha ESem LRHS NMen SFgr
'Milá' CWil
'Mini Frost' CWil NMen WPer
'Minuet' NMen
'Missouri Rose' NMen
'Mixed Spice' CWil
'Moerkerk's Merit' CWil ESem GAbr MTis NMen XLum
'Mohair' NMen
'Mondstein' CWil ESem GKev SRms WIvy WPer
'Monique' WPer
'Monseigneur Desmet' ESem
'Montage' CWil
§ ***montanum*** ESem NMen WPer
- from Arbizion CWil
- from Gavarnie, France ESem
- from Ljuboten, Macedonia/Kosovo ESem
- from Monte Tirone, Italy LBee
- from Monte Tonale, Italy CWil
- from Windachtal, Germany CWil NMen
§ - subsp. ***burnatii*** CWil ESem MHom NMen WIvy
- 'Caesar' MSCN
- subsp. ***carpaticum*** CWil XLum
- - 'Cmiral's Yellow' ESem MSCN SFgr WAbe WIvy
* - Fragell form SFgr
- subsp. ***montanum*** CWil
- 'Rubrum' see *S.* 'Red Mountain'
- subsp. ***stiriacum*** CWil ESem NMen SFgr
- - from Mauterndorf, Austria ESem NMen
- - from Puerto de San Francisco, USA ESem
§ - - 'Lloyd Praeger' CWil ESem LBee LRHS NMen SDys SFgr WIvy WPer
***montanum* × *tectorum*** CWil
var. ***boutignyanum*** GDJ 94.15
'Moondrops' CWil
'More Honey' CWil NMen SFgr SRms
'Morning Glow' NMen WGor WHal WPer
'Mount Hood' ESem ETod LRHS NMen SRms WHal
'Mount Usher' **new** NMen
'Mrs Elliott' ESem NMen
'Mulberry Wine' CWil ESem LBee LRHS NMen WGor WHoo
'Mystic' CWil ESem MBrN NMen WPer
'Neon' CWil NMen
***nevadense*** CWil EPot NMen SFgr SRms
- GDJ 96A-07 from Calar de Santa Barbara, Spain CWil
- from Puerto de San Francisco CWil ESem
- 'Hirtellum' CWil NMen
'Nico' CWil NMen SRms
'Night Raven' CMea MTis NMen WIvy WPer
'Nigrum' see *S. tectorum* 'Nigrum'
'Niobe' ESem SFgr WHal
'Noellie' **new** CWil
'Noir' CWil EDAr ESem MSCN NBro NMen WAbe WGor
'Norbert' CWil EDAr SRms WIvy WPer XLum
'Norne' ESem
'Nouveau Pastel' CMea CWil ESem NMen WHal WPer XLum
'Octet' CWil NMen
***octopodes*** NBir SIde XLum
var. ***apetalum*** CWil ESem GAbr MBrN NMen SRms WIvy
'Oddity' CPBP ECha ESem ETod MBrN MHer NMen WHal WPer
'Ohio Burgundy' ECha ESem LRHS NMen WAbe WPer WTin
'Old Copper' ESem
'Old Rose' NMen
'Olivette' ECha ESem NMen WPer WTin XLum
'Omega' NMen WPer
'Ornatum' EPot ESem MHer MHom NMen SRms WAbe WHal WIvy WPer
***ossetiense*** CWil EDAr ESem GAbr GKev NMen XLum
'Othello' ♀H4 CDes CTri EPfP GCra NBir NMen STre WPGP WPer WTin XLum
'Ottelein' CWil
'Pacific Feather Power' NMen
'Pacific Hep' CWil
'Pacific Opal' **new** CWil
'Pacific Purple Shadows' CWil
'Packardian' CWil ESem NMen SFgr WIvy
'Painted Lady' CWil ESem NMen
'Palissander' EDAr ESem GAbr NMen SFgr WPer XLum
'Pam Wain' MHom NMen
'Panola Fire' WFar
'Passionata' CWil ESem NMen SFgr
'Pastel' CWil ESem NMen
***patens*** see *Jovibarba heuffelii*
'Patrician' CWil ESem LBee LRHS SRms
'Peggy' CWil ESem NMen WGor
'Pekinese' CWil EDAr EPot ESem GEdr LRHS MBrN NBro NMen SRms WGor WOut WPer XLum
'Peterson's Ornatum' SDys
'Petsy' ESem NMen SRms
'Pilatus' ECha EWes SRms WFar WPer
'Pine Cone' **new** WGor
'Pink Astrid' CWil ESem
'Pink Button' CWil
'Pink Cloud' CWil LRHS NMen SRms
'Pink Dawn' ESem
'Pink Delight' ESem MSCN
'Pink Flamingoes' NMen
'Pink Lemonade' CWil ESem MHom
'Pink Mist' NMen WPer
'Pink Puff' CWil ESem MHom NMen SRms
'Pippin' CWil ESem NMen SRms WPer
'Piran' CWil
***pittonii*** ♀H4 CMea CWil EPot ESem GAbr NMen WHal XLum
'Pixie' CPBP CWil ESem NMen SFgr WIvy WPer
'Plum Frosting' MSCN WGor
'Plumb Rose' CWil ESem NMen WIvy WPer
'Pluto' CWil ESem LBee LRHS NMen XLum
'Poke Eat' ESem NMen
'Polaris' CWil ESem MHom
'Poldark' ESem
'Pompeon' ESem
'Ponderosa' CWil
'Pottsii' CWil ESem

| |  |  |
|---|---|---|
| I | 'Powellii' | ESem |
| | 'Precious' | ESem |
| | 'President Arsac' | NMen XLum |
| | 'Procton' | ESem |
| | 'Proud Zelda' | CWil EDAr ESem GAbr MTis NMen |
| | 'Průhonice' | CWil NMen SRms WFar |
| | 'Pseudo-ornatum' | LBee LRHS SRms |
| | 'Pumaros' | NMen SDys |
| | ***pumilum*** | CWil LRHS NMen |
| | - from Adyl-Su, Chechnya, Russia, No 1 | CWil |
| | - from Armkhi | ESem SDys |
| | - from El'brus, Russia, No 1 | CWil ESem |
| | - from Techensis | CWil NMen |
| | - 'Sopa' | CWil ESem NMen |
| | 'Purdy' | MHom MSCN NMen WAbe |
| | 'Purdy's 50-6' | CWil ESem GAbr NMen |
| | 'Purdy's 70-40' | ESem |
| | 'Purple Beauty' | EPot ESem GLam NMen |
| | 'Purple King' | CMea MHom MTis NMen SDys |
| | 'Purple Passion' | ESem NMen |
| | 'Purple Queen' | CWil EDAr ESem LRHS NMen |
| | 'Pygmalion' | CWil ESem |
| | 'Queen Amalia' | see *S. reginae-amaliae* |
| | 'Quintessence' | CWil SFgr SRms |
| | 'Racey' | ESem NMen |
| | 'Ragtime' | ESem |
| | 'Ramses' | ESem SDys |
| | 'Raspberry Ice' | CMea LBee LRHS MSCN NBro NMen WPer |
| | 'Rauer Kulm' | CWil ESem NMen |
| * | 'Rauheit' | WFar |
| | 'Rauhreif' | ESem WFar XLum |
| | 'Red Ace' | CWil ECha GEdr MLLN NBro NDov NMen SFgr SRms WFar WPer |
| | 'Red Beam' | CWil ESem MSCN NMen |
| | 'Red Chief' | GKev |
| | 'Red Chips' | EDAr MHom |
| | 'Red Delta' | CDes CWil NBir NMen SFgr WCot WPGP |
| | 'Red Devil' | CMea CWil ECha ESem LRHS NMen SFgr SPlb WHoo WPer WTin |
| | 'Red Giant' | ESem NMen |
| | 'Red Lion' | CWil GEdr NMen SFgr |
| | 'Red Lynn' | CWil ESem |
| § | 'Red Mountain' | CWil ESem LBee LRHS SRms |
| | 'Red Pink' | CWil |
| | 'Red Robin' | EDAr ESem GMaP NMen |
| | 'Red Rum' | WPer |
| | 'Red Shadows' | LBee LRHS NMen WPer WTin |
| | 'Red Spider' | CWil EPot ESem MHom NBro NMen |
| | 'Red Summer' | ESem |
| | 'Regal' | ESem NMen |
| | 'Regina' | NMen |
| | ***reginae*** | see *S. reginae-amaliae* |
| § | ***reginae-amaliae*** | CWil EPot ESem NMen XLum |
| | - from Kambeecho, Greece, No 1 | ESem |
| | - from Kambeecho, Greece, No 2 | NMen SDys |
| | - from Mavri Petri, Greece | CWil ESem SDys |
| | - from Sarpun, Turkey | CWil ESem NMen SDys WTin |
| | - from Vardusa, Serbia | CWil ESem SDys |
| § | 'Reginald Malby' | CTri ECho ESem GMaP LRHS NMen SFgr SRms WIvy |
| | 'Reinhard' ♀H4 | CMea CWil CYeo ECha EDAr EPot ESem GEdr LRHS MAsh MBrN MHer NMen NRya SPlb SRms WFar WHal WHoo WIvy WOut WPer |
| | 'Remus' | CWil ECha ELan ESem NMen SDys SFgr SRms WGor |
| | 'Rex' | NMen |
| | 'Rhöne' | CWil ESem LBee LRHS |
| | 'Rich 'n' Fruity' | MSCN |
| | 'Risque' | CWil ESem LBee LRHS NMen WPer |
| | 'Rita Jane' | CWil ECha ESem MHom NMen SFgr WTin |
| | 'Robin' | LBee LRHS NBro NMen SRms WTin |
| | 'Ronny' | CWil ESem |
| | 'Roosemaryn' | EDAr ESem NMen |
| | 'Rose Queen' | ESem |
| | × ***roseum*** | ESem |
| | 'Rosie' | CMea CPBP CWil EPot GAbr GEdr GMaP LBee LRHS MAsh MSCN NMen SEND SRms WHal WHoo WPer WTin |
| | 'Rotkopf' ♀H4 | CWil ESem MSCN NMen SFgr SRms XLum |
| | 'Rotmantel' | NMen SDys WTin |
| | 'Rotsandsteinriese' | ESem |
| | 'Rotund' | CWil ESem GEdr MSCN |
| | 'Rouge' | ESem NMen |
| | 'Royal Mail' | ESem |
| | 'Royal Opera' | CWil EDAr ESem NMen |
| | 'Royal Ruby' | ECha ESem LBee MSCN NMen SRms WIvy WOut |
| | 'Royale' | SFgr |
| | 'Rubellum' | CWil ESem |
| | 'Rubellum Mahogany' | SFgr |
| | 'Rubikon Improved' | ESem NMen |
| | 'Rubin' | CMea CTri ECha EPfP GGar GKev MAsh MSCN NBir NBlu NEgg NMen NPri NWCA SPoG SRms WAbe WHoo WNew WOut WPer XLum |
| | 'Rubra Ash' | CWil ESem NMen WAbe WTin |
| | 'Rubra Ray' | CWil EDAr ESem SRms |
| | 'Rubrifolium' | see *S. marmoreum* subsp. *marmoreum* 'Rubrifolium' |
| * | 'Ruby Glow' | EDAr |
| | 'Ruby Heart' | EDAr |
| | 'Russian River' | CMea WHoo WTin |
| | 'Rusty' | CWil ESem SFgr |
| | ***ruthenicum*** | ESem LRHS MHom NRya |
| | - 'Regis-Fernandii' | ECho XLum |
| | 'Safara' | CWil ESem |
| | 'Saffron' | NMen |
| | 'Saga' | ESem MHom |
| | 'Sanford's Hybrid' | NMen |
| | 'Santis' | ESem |
| | 'Sarah' | EDAr ESem NMen |
| | 'Sarotte' | CWil NMen |
| | 'Sassy Frass' | ESem NMen |
| | 'Saturn' | ESem NMen |
| | ***schlehanii*** | see *S. marmoreum* |
| | ***schnittspahnii*** | ESem XLum |
| | 'Seminole' | CWil ESem NMen |
| | 'Serendipity' | EDAr |
| | 'Shadri' | ESem |
| | 'Sha-Na' | CWil |
| | 'Sharon's Pencil' | CWil ESem NMen |
| | 'Sheila' | GAbr |
| | 'Shirley Moore' | CWil EDAr ESem NMen SFgr WTin |
| | 'Shirley's Joy' | ESem NMen WTin XLum |
| | 'Sideshow' | CWil ESem NMen |
| | 'Sigi' | ESem |
| | 'Sigma' | ESem NMen |

| | | |
|---|---|---|
| | 'Silberkarneol' misapplied | see *S.* 'Silver Jubilee' |
| | 'Silberspitz' | CWil LRHS MHer MHom NBro NMen SPlb WPer |
| | 'Silver Cup' | CWil ESem NMen SFgr WIvy |
| § | 'Silver Jubilee' | CMea CWil ECha EDAr ESem LRHS NBro NRya SPlb SRms WGor XLum |
| | 'Silver Queen' | CWil ESem SFgr |
| | 'Silver Shadow' | MSCN WGor |
| | 'Silver Spring' | ESem NMen |
| | 'Silver Thaw' | CWil ECha EDAr NMen SFgr |
| | 'Silverine' | CWil EDAr NMen |
| | 'Silvertone' | CWil ESem NMen |
| | 'Simonkaianum' | see *Jovibarba hirta* |
| | 'Sioux' | CPBP CWil ESem GAbr LBee LRHS MBrN NMen WFar WHal WIvy WPer WTin |
| | 'Skrocki's Bronze' | ESem GAbr LRHS NMen WPer |
| | 'Slabber's Seedling' | CWil NMen |
| | 'Small Wonder' | CWil |
| | 'Smaragd' | CWil ECha ESem LBee LRHS NMen WFar XLum |
| | 'Smokey Jet' | ESem NMen SFgr |
| | 'Smokey Quartz' new | WGor |
| | 'Snowberger' | CWil EPot ESem MSCN NMen SFgr SRms WGor WHal WPer |
| | 'Soarte' | ESem |
| | ***soboliferum*** | see *Jovibarba sobolifera* |
| | 'Soothsayer' | CWil NMen |
| | ***sosnowskyi*** | CWil NMen |
| | 'Spanish Dancer' | NMen |
| | 'Speciosum' | ESem |
| | 'Spherette' | CWil EDAr MBrN MSCN NMen WAbe WPer |
| | 'Spider's Lair' ♀H4 | EDAr MHom |
| | 'Spinellii' | WThu WTin |
| | 'Spiver's Velvet' | NMen |
| | 'Springmist' | CWil EPot ESem LRHS MAsh MTis NBlu NMen SFgr SRms WGor WPer WTin |
| | 'Sprite' | CWil GEdr MLLN MTis NMen SDys WOut WTin |
| | 'Squib' | CWil ESem MSCN |
| | ***stansfieldii*** | see *S. arachnoideum* subsp. *tomentosum* 'Stansfieldii' |
| | 'Starburst' | CWil NMen |
| | 'Starion' | CWil |
| | 'Starshine' | MHer NMen SFgr |
| | 'State Fair' | CWil EDAr NMen WIvy WPer |
| * | ***stoloniferum*** | GAbr |
| | 'Strawberry Fields' | ESem |
| | 'Strawberry Sundae' new | ESem NMen |
| | 'Strider' | CWil WTin |
| | 'Stuffed Olive' | CWil SDys SRot |
| I | 'Subanum' | ESem |
| | 'Sugary' new | ESem |
| | 'Sun Waves' | CWil ESem NMen SDys SFgr |
| | 'Sunkist' | NMen |
| | 'Sunray Desire' new | WGor |
| | 'Sunray Magic' | WGor |
| | 'Sunrise' | ESem |
| | 'Super Dome' | CWil NMen |
| | 'Superama' | ESem |
| | 'Supernova' | ESem |
| | 'Syston Flame' | CWil NMen |
| | 'Tamberlane' | EDAr |
| | 'Tarita' | CWil NMen |
| § | ***tectorum*** ♀H4 | CArn CHby CTri ECho EDAr ELan EPfP GPoy LBee LRHS MHer MNHC NBlu NMen SBfd SIde SPlb STre WFar WJek XLum |
| | - from Eporn | CWil NMen |
| § | - var. ***alpinum*** | CWil ESem LRHS MHom NBro NMen |
| | - var. ***andreanum*** | CWil XLum |
| | - 'Atropurpureum' | ECho ELan NMen WTin |
| | - 'Atroviolaceum' | EDAr ESem NLar NMen WTar WIvy WTin XLum |
| * | - 'Aureum' | SFgr |
| | - var. ***boutignyanum*** GDJ 94.02 from Sant Joan de Caselles, Andorra | CWil |
| | - - GDJ 94.03 from Sant Joan de Caselles, Andorra | CWil |
| | - - GDJ 94.04 from Route de Tuixén, Spain | CWil |
| | - - from Route de Tuixén, Spain | ESem |
| | - var. ***calcareum*** | ECho |
| | - subsp. ***cantalicum*** | SRms |
| § | - 'Nigrum' | ESem LBee LRHS MHer NBro NMen SDys SRms WGor WTin |
| | - 'Red Flush' | CWil EDAr EPPr MBrN NMen SDys SFgr WFar WPer |
| | - 'Royanum' ♀H4 | ESem GAbr MSCN |
| * | - subsp. ***sanguineum*** | EDAr |
| | - 'Sunset' | CMea EDAr ESem NMen SDys SFgr WHal |
| | - subsp. ***tectorum*** | ESem GEdr |
| § | - - 'Boissieri' | CWil NMen SRms WIvy |
| | - - 'Triste' | CHEx CWil LBee LRHS NMen SRms WAbe WFar XLum |
| | - 'Tokajense' | ESem |
| | - 'Violaceum' | MHom SRms STre WAbe WGor |
| | ***tectorum* × *zeleborii*** | WTin |
| | 'Tederheid' | ESem |
| | 'Telfan' | NMen |
| | 'Terracotta Baby' | CWil ESem NMen SFgr |
| | 'Thayne' | NMen |
| | 'The Platters' | CWil NMen |
| | 'The Rocket' | CWil NMen |
| | × ***thompsonianum*** | CWil NMen SFgr |
| | 'Thunder' | CWil ESem NMen |
| | 'Tiffany' | WPer |
| | 'Tiger Bay' | NMen |
| | 'Tina' | WPer |
| | 'Tip Top' | CWil ESem GEdr NMen SFgr |
| | 'Titania' | CWil NBro NMen WHal WTin |
| | 'Tombago' | ESem |
| | 'Topaz' | CWil ECha ESem LBee LRHS NMen SFgr SRms XLum |
| | 'Tordeur's Memory' | CWil ESem GEdr LBee LRHS MSCN NMen SEND |
| | 'Tracy Sue' | EDAr XLum |
| | 'Trail Walker' | CWil ESem LBee LRHS NMen SRms |
| | ***transcaucasicum*** | CWil XLum |
| | 'Tree Beard' | CWil NMen |
| | 'Trine' new | CWil |
| | 'Tristesse' ♀H4 | CWil EDAr NMen SFgr WGor |
| | 'Truva' | CWil ESem NMen SFgr |
| | 'Twilight Blues' | CWil ESem LRHS NMen SFgr |
| | 'Undine' | CWil ESem NMen SFgr |
| | 'Unicorn' | ESem |
| | 'Utopian' | ESem |
| | × ***vaccarii*** | CWil NMen XLum |
| | 'Vanbaelen' | CWil NMen SDys |
| | 'Vanessa' | CWil |
| | 'Veuchelen' | CWil ESem |
| | ***vicentei*** | ESem MHom NMen WFar WTin |
| | - from Gaton | ESem LBee LRHS NMen |

| | | |
|---|---|---|
| § | - subsp. ***paui*** | NMen NSla |
| | 'Victorian' | ESem |
| | 'Video' | CWil ESem MHom NMen SFgr |
| | 'Vignola' **new** | CWil |
| | 'Viking' | NMen |
| | 'Violet Queen' | ESem NMen |
| | 'Virgil' | CWil EDAr ESem GAbr MBrN MSCN MTis NMen SDys WAbe WCot WGor WPer WTin |
| I | 'Virginius' | CWil GAbr |
| | 'Vulcano' | ESem NMen |
| | 'Waldalina' **new** | CWil |
| | 'Warners Pink' | MDKP |
| | 'Warrior' | EDAr |
| | 'Watermelon Rind' | ESem MTis NMen |
| | ***webbianum*** | see *S. arachnoideum* subsp. *tomentosum* (C.B. Lehm. & Schnittsp.) Schinz & Thell. |
| | 'Webby Flame' | CWil NMen |
| | 'Webby Ola' | NMen |
| | 'Webbyola' **new** | ESem |
| | 'Wega' | NMen |
| | 'Weirdo' | CWil ESem NMen |
| | 'Wendy' | ESem NMen |
| | 'Westerlin' | CWil ECha ESem NMen |
| | 'White Christmas' | see *S. arachnoideum* 'White Christmas' |
| | 'White Eyes' | NMen |
| | 'White Ladies' **new** | ESem |
| | 'Whitening' | EDAr NMen |
| | × ***widderi*** | NMen |
| I | 'Woolcott's Variety' | CWil ECho ESem MDKP MSCN NBir NMen WFar WPer WTin |
| | ***wulfenii*** | CWil NMen |
| * | - ***roseum*** | EDAr |
| | 'Xaviera' | CWil ESem NMen |
| | 'Yanisha' **new** | CWil |
| | 'Yarnton' **new** | ESem |
| | 'Yvette' **new** | CWil |
| | 'Zackenkrone' **new** | NMen |
| | 'Zaza' | CWil ESem NMen |
| | ***zeleborii*** | ESem SDys WHal |
| | 'Zenith' | CWil EDAr ESem GAbr NMen SFgr SRms |
| | 'Zenobia' | ESem MHom |
| | 'Zenocrate' | NMen WHal |
| | 'Zepherin' | CWil ESem MSCN NMen |
| | 'Zeppelin No 3' | NMen |
| | 'Zilver Moon' | CWil ESem NMen |
| | 'Zilver Snowflake' **new** | CWil |
| | 'Zilver Suzanna' | CWil |
| | 'Zilverprinsesje' **new** | CWil |
| | 'Zircon' | EDAr ESem NMen |
| | 'Zone' | CHEx ESem MTis NMen |
| | 'Zorba' | GLam NMen |
| | 'Zulu' | ECha NMen SFgr |

## *Senecio* (*Asteraceae*)

| | | |
|---|---|---|
| § | ***articulatus*** | EShb SGar STre |
| | ***bidwillii*** | see *Brachyglottis bidwillii* |
| | ***buchananii*** | see *Brachyglottis buchananii* |
| | ***candicans*** misapplied | see *S. cineraria* |
| | ***chrysanthemoides*** | see *Euryops chrysanthemoides* |
| § | ***cineraria*** | SEND |
| | - 'Silver Dust' ♀H3 | EPfP |
| | - 'White Diamond' | ECha |
| * | ***coccinilifera*** | SBch |
| | ***compactus*** | see *Brachyglottis compacta* |
| | ***confusus*** | see *Pseudogynoxys chenopodioides* |
| | ***crassissimus*** | EShb |
| | ***doria*** | EShb LRHS WFar WHrl |
| | ***ficoides*** **new** | EShb |
| | ***formosoides*** B&SWJ 10736 | WCru |
| | ***formosus*** B&SWJ 10700 | WCru |
| | - B&SWJ 10746 | WCru |
| | ***gerberifolius*** B&SWJ 10357 | WCru |
| | - B&SWJ 10361 | WCru |
| | ***glastifolius*** | LRHS |
| | ***grandifolius*** | see *Telanthophora grandifolia* |
| | 'Gregynog Gold' | see *Ligularia* 'Gregynog Gold' |
| | ***greyi*** misapplied | see *Brachyglottis* (Dunedin Group) 'Sunshine' |
| | ***greyi*** Hook. | see *Brachyglottis greyi* (Hook. f.) B. Nord. |
| | ***heritieri*** DC. | see *Pericallis lanata* (L'Hér.) B. Nord. |
| | ***hoffmannii*** | EShb |
| | ***integrifolius*** subsp. ***capitatus*** | SPlb |
| | ***kleiniiformis*** | EShb |
| | ***laxifolius*** hort. | see *Brachyglottis* (Dunedin Group) 'Sunshine' |
| | ***leucostachys*** | see *S. viravira* |
| | ***macroglossus*** | CHll CSpe EShb WFar |
| | - 'Variegatus' (v) ♀H1 | EShb |
| | ***maritimus*** | see *S. cineraria* |
| | ***mikanioides*** | see *Delairea odorata* |
| | ***monroi*** | see *Brachyglottis monroi* |
| | ***petasitis*** | CBcs CHEx CTrC SDix |
| | ***polyodon*** | CCCN CDes CSpe CSpr EBla EDAr EPPr EShb EWll GAbr GBin GMac LBMP MNrw MWea NDov NGdn NLar SPhx WCAu WHil WMoo WOut WPGP WSHC WWEG |
| | - S&SH 29 | EBee NCGa |
| | - subsp. ***subglaber*** | EWes |
| | - - McB 2919 | GLam |
| | ***przewalskii*** | see *Ligularia przewalskii* |
| | ***pulcher*** | CDTJ CDes CGHE CSam LEdu MNrw SHar SMrm SUsu WAbb WCot WPGP |
| | ***reinholdii*** | see *Brachyglottis rotundifolia* |
| | ***rowleyanus*** | EBak STre |
| | ***scandens*** | CBre CCCN CPLG EShb MNrw WPGP |
| | ***scaposus*** | WCot |
| | ***seminiveus*** | EBee |
| § | ***serpens*** | CDoC EShb SEND STre |
| § | ***smithii*** | ELan GBee NBid WCot WCru WFar WWEG |
| | ***spedenii*** | see *Brachyglottis spedenii* |
| | ***squalidus*** | WHer |
| | 'Sunshine' | see *Brachyglottis* (Dunedin Group) 'Sunshine' |
| | ***talinoides*** subsp. ***cylindricus*** 'Himalaya' | EShb |
| | ***tanguticus*** | see *Sinacalia tangutica* |
| § | ***viravira*** ♀H3-4 | CMea EPfP MCot SDix SMad SPer WSHC |

## *Senna* (*Caesalpiniaceae*)

| | | |
|---|---|---|
| | ***alata*** B&SWJ 9772 | WCru |
| | ***alexandrina*** | CCCN EBee EShb LRHS WPGP |
| § | ***corymbosa*** | CBcs CBot CCCN CHEx CRHN CTri EAmu SBrd SMrm |
| | × ***floribunda*** | LRHS |
| | ***hebecarpa*** | LRHS SBrt SPhx |

§ ***marilandica*** CArn EBee ELan EWes WHil
***multiglandulosa*** new CBcs
***retusa*** CHEx
***septemtrionalis*** CCCN EBee LRHS

## *Sequoia* (*Cupressaceae*)

***sempervirens*** ♀H4 CBcs CDoC CDul CLnd CMCN CMac CMen ECrN EHul EPfP ERom EWTr GKin LMaj LRHS MMuc NMun NWea SArc SEND SGol SLim SPoG STre WDin WEve WMou
- 'Adpressa' CDoC CDul CTho EHul EPfP EPla LRHS MAsh MBri MGos NWea SCoo SLim WFar
- 'Cantab' CDoC SLim WMou
- 'Henderson Blue' SLim
- 'Prostrata' CDoC GGar LRHS MMuc SLim WFar
- 'Simpson's Silver' SLim

## *Sequoiadendron* (*Cupressaceae*)

***giganteum*** ♀H4 Widely available
- 'Bajojeka' NLar
- 'Barabits Requiem' LRHS MBlu NLar SLim SMad
- 'Blauer Eichzwerg' NLar SLim
- 'Blue Iceberg' CKen
- 'Bultinck Yellow' MBlu NLar SMad
- 'Cannibal' NLar
- 'Curly Green' NLar
- 'French Beauty' NLar
- 'Glaucum' CDoC CDul CTho LRHS MBlu MBri NLar SLim SPoG
* - 'Glaucum Compactum' MBlu
- 'Greenpeace' MBlu NLar
- 'Little Stan' CKen NLar
- 'Pendulum' CDoC CDul CKen MBlu MGos NLar SLim SMad SWvt WEve
- 'Philip Curtis' NLar
- 'Pierie' NLar
- 'Pirat' NLar
- 'Powdered Blue' LRHS NLar SLim
- 'Variegatum' (v) MGos
- 'Von Martin' NLar

## *Serapias* (*Orchidaceae*)

***lingua*** SCnR

## *Serenoa* (*Arecaceae*)

***repens*** EAmu LPal

## *Seriphidium* (*Asteraceae*)

***caerulescens* var. *gallicum*** CEls
§ ***canum*** CEls MHer
§ ***ferganense*** CEls
§ ***fragrans*** CEls
§ ***maritimum*** CArn GGar ILis MHer
- var. ***maritimum*** CEls
§ ***nutans*** CEls MCot MRav
§ ***tridentatum*** CArn
- subsp. ***tridentatum*** CEls
***tripartitum* var. *rupicola*** CEls
§ ***vallesiacum*** ♀H4 CEls

## *Serissa* (*Rubiaceae*)

***foetida*** see *S. japonica*
§ ***japonica*** STre
- ***rosea*** STre
- 'Variegata' (v) STre

## *Serratula* (*Asteraceae*)

***coronata*** EBee LRHS
- subsp. ***insularis*** f. ***alba*** GAbr
§ ***seoanei*** CKno CMea CPom EBee ECha EDAr EWTr LHop LPla LRHS MHer MLHP MMuc MNrw MRav MWat SBch SDix SPhx SRms SUsu WCot WFar WPGP WPat WTin
***shawii*** see *S. seoanei*
***tinctoria*** CArn NLar NMir SPhx WOut
- subsp. ***macrocephala*** EBee
***wolffii*** EBee

## *Serruria* (*Proteaceae*)

***florida*** SPlb
***phylicoides*** new SPlb

## *Sesamum* (*Pedaliaceae*)

***indicum*** CArn

## *Sesbania* (*Papilionaceae*)

***punicea*** CCCN CSpe MOWG

## *Seseli* (*Apiaceae*)

***elatum*** CSpe
***gummiferum*** CArn CBot CHid CSam CSpe NLar SDix SEND SKHP SPhx SPur WPtf
***hippomarathrum*** EBee SPhx WCot WHrl WPGP
§ ***libanotis*** CSam CSpe LEdu LPla NDov NLar SAga SDix SPhx
***montanum*** CSpe LHop WPGP

## *Sesleria* (*Poaceae*)

§ ***argentea*** EHoe
***autumnalis*** CKno EBee LEdu LPla SPhx
***caerulea*** CBod CKno CSam EBee EHoe ELan EPfP GQue LEdu LTen MBrN MWhi SPoG WPtf
- 'Malvern Mop' EBee WHrl WPGP WWEG
* ***candida*** EPPr
***cylindrica*** see *S. argentea*
***glauca*** EHoe NLar NOak SBfd
'Greenlee' new CKno
***heufleriana*** CBod CWCL EBee EHoe EPPr EPla MLLN NLar SMea SPlb WCot WWEG
***insularis*** EBee EPPr EShb
'Morning Dew' EBee GCal
***nitida*** CKno EBee EHoe LEdu MBrN MMoz SApp SPhx WCot WPGP
***rigida*** EHoe
***sadleriana*** EBee EPPr EWes

## *Setaria* (*Poaceae*)

***macrostachya*** ♀H3 CKno LLWP NDov SBch SPhx
***palmifolia*** CHEx CHII CKno WCot WDyG
- BWJ 8132 WCru
***viridis*** CSpe WCot WTin

## *Setcreasea* see *Tradescantia*

## shaddock see *Citrus maxima*

## Sharon fruit see *Diospyros kaki*

## *Shepherdia* (*Elaeagnaceae*)

***argentea*** CBcs NLar

## *Shibataea* (*Poaceae*)

| | |
|---|---|
| ***chinensis*** | CBcs |
| ***kumasaca*** | CAbb CBcs CDoC CEnt CHEx ENBC EPfP EPla GCal IBal LEdu LPal LRHS MBrN MCCP MMoz MWht SBig SGol SLPl WDyG WJun WPGP |
| – 'Aureostriata' | EPla |
| ***lancifolia*** | EPla WJun |

## *Shortia* (*Diapensiaceae*)

| | |
|---|---|
| ***galacifolia*** | IBlr |
| ***soldanelloides*** | IBlr |
| – var. ***ilicifolia*** | IBlr |
| – var. ***magna*** | IBlr |
| ***uniflora*** | IBlr NHar |
| – var. ***orbicularis*** 'Grandiflora' | IBlr |

## *Sibbaldia* (*Rosaceae*)

| | |
|---|---|
| ***procumbens*** | GAuc |

## *Sibbaldiopsis* (*Rosaceae*)

| | |
|---|---|
| ***tridentata*** 'Lemon Mac' | CYeo NHar |
| – 'Nuuk' | GJos MAvo |

## *Sibthorpia* (*Plantaginaceae*)

| | |
|---|---|
| ***europaea*** | CGHE CHEx CPLG |

## *Sida* (*Malvaceae*)

| | |
|---|---|
| ***hermaphrodita*** | EBee |

## *Sidalcea* (*Malvaceae*)

| | |
|---|---|
| 'Brilliant' | CBcs EBee EPfP LAst LRHS MDKP MDev MNrw MSCN NBPC NBir NPri SHar SPer SPoG WMoo WWEG |
| ***campestris*** from Oregon, USA | EPPr |
| ***candida*** | CPrp CSam EBee ECtt ELan EPfP GCra GGar GMaP LAst LEdu LHop LRHS MBNS MCot MLLN MMuc MRav MTis NEgg NGdn NLar NSti SEND SMrm SPer STes WCAu WCot |
| – 'Bianca' | CBot EBee EPfP LRHS MSCN NBPC NGBl NLar NPri WFar WHal WMoo WPer WWEG |
| 'Candy Girl' | EBee GMac MDev |
| 'Croftway Red' | CFir EBee ELan EPfP GCra LRHS MAvo MCot MLLN NBro NGdn NHol NWad SAga SMrm SPer SPet SWvt WFar |
| ***cusickii*** | WOut |
| 'Elsie Heugh' ♀H4 | Widely available |
| ***hendersonii*** | EBee |
| ***hickmanii*** subsp. ***anomala*** | EBee |
| ***hirtipes*** | EBee |
| 'Interlaken' | LRHS |
| 'Little Princess'PBR | CElw CFir EBee EPfP EWes LBuc LRHS LSou MAsh NCGa NDov NGdn NLar SPoG WFar |
| 'Loveliness' | CMMP EBee ECtt ELan EShb GGar LHop LSou MAvo MRav NBro NCGa NGdn NHol NLar NWad SAga |
| ***malviflora*** | SRms |
| – 'Alba' | WFar |
| 'Monarch' | MDKP WFar |
| 'Moorland Rose Coronet' | WMoo |
| 'Mr Lindbergh' | EBee EPfP MAvo SAga WFar |
| 'Mrs Borrodaile' | CMac CPrp EBee MRav NBro NGdn NPro SMrm WFar WMoo WWEG |
| 'Mrs Galloway' | WFar |
| 'Mrs T. Alderson' | EBee WFar WMoo |
| 'My Love' | NDov SMrm |
| 'Oberon' | EBee MRav WFar |
| ***oregana*** (Nutt. ex Torr. & A. Gray) A. Gray | NBid NGdn |
| – subsp. ***spicata*** | WFar WMoo |
| 'Party Girl' | Widely available |
| 'Präriebrand' | SMrm |
| 'Purpetta' | COIW EBee LRHS NGBl NGdn NLar NPro SBfd STes WPer |
| ***reptans*** | CDes EBee |
| 'Reverend Page Roberts' | MAvo MRav WCot WFar WWEG |
| 'Rosaly' | EBee ELon IFoB LBMP LRHS NGdn NLar STes WFar WGor WHal |
| 'Rosanna' | EBee GMaP LRHS NGdn NLar SBfd WHal WPer WPtf |
| 'Rose Bud' | CElw CPrp EBee MAvo |
| 'Rose Queen' | EBee ECha LHop MAvo MCot MRav NBro NHol SPer SRms WFar |
| 'Rosy Gem' | ECtt NBre WFar |
| Stark's hybrids | LRHS SRms |
| 'Sussex Beauty' | CPrp CSam EBee GMac MArl MAvo MCot MLHP MLLN MRav NCGa NDov NEgg NGdn SMrm SPer WAul WFar WMoo WOut |
| 'William Smith' ♀H4 | CPrp CSam EBee ECha ECtt EPfP EWes LRHS LSRN MLLN MMuc MRav MWat NBir NCGa NChi NGdn NLar NOrc SEND SPer WFar WMoo WWEG |
| 'Wine Red' | CFir CMHG EBee EShb LRHS LSou MAvo MCot MDKP MTis NEgg NGdn SMrm SPoG SWvt WCAu WFar WWEG WWFP |

## *Sideritis* (*Lamiaceae*)

| | |
|---|---|
| ***clandestina*** | XSen |
| ***cypria*** | XSen |
| ***hyssopifolia*** | EBee |
| ***perfoliata*** new | XSen |
| ***phlomoides*** | XSen |
| ***phrygia*** new | XSen |
| ***scardica*** | XSen |
| ***syriaca*** | CArn NBre XSen |
| ***taurica*** new | XSen |

## *Sieversia* (*Rosaceae*)

| | |
|---|---|
| § ***pentapetala*** | GEdr WAbe |
| ***reptans*** | see *Geum reptans* |

## *Silaum* (*Apiaceae*)

| | |
|---|---|
| ***silaus*** | NMir |

## *Silene* (*Caryophyllaceae*)

| | |
|---|---|
| RBS | EPPr |
| from Uzbekistan | GCal |
| ***acaulis*** | ECho EDAr GJos MAsh MMuc NLar NMen SRms WAbe |
| § – subsp. ***acaulis*** | ECho SPlb SRms |
| – 'Alba' | ECho EDAr EWes GLam NLan NLar NMen WAbe WPat WThu |
| – 'Blush' | NMen NSla WAbe |
| § – subsp. ***bryoides*** | GLam NLar |
| – 'Correvoniana' | NLar |
| – subsp. ***elongata*** | see *S. acaulis* subsp. *acaulis* |

| |  |  |
|---|---|---|
| | - subsp. ***exscapa*** | see *S. acaulis* subsp. *bryoides* |
| | - 'Frances' | CYeo GLam GMaP NHar NMen NRya NSla NWCA WAbe |
| | - 'Francis Copeland' | ECho NMen |
| | - 'Helen's Double' (d) | ECho EDAr EPot GJos |
| | 'Mount Snowdon' | ECho ECtt EDAr ELan EPfP EPot EWes GGar GLam GMaP LBee MAsh MMuc NLar NMen NRya NWCA SPlb SPoG SRms SRot WHoo WPat |
| | - 'Pedunculata' | see *S. acaulis* subsp. *acaulis* |
| | - 'Select' **new** | GLam |
| | ***alba*** | see *S. latifolia* subsp. *alba* |
| § | ***alpestris*** | NLar SBch SRms SRot WFar WMoo WThu |
| | - 'Flore Pleno' (d) ♀H4 | CMea EWes LBee LRHS NSla SBch WAbe WPat |
| | ***araratica*** | WAbe |
| | ***argaea*** | WAbe |
| | × ***arkwrightii*** | see *Lychnis* × *arkwrightii* |
| | ***armeria*** | WHer |
| | - 'Electra' | CSpe |
| | ***asterias*** | GCal GCra MNrw NBre SBrt WWFP |
| | - MESE 429 | GBin |
| | ***atropurpurea*** | see *Lychnis viscaria* subsp. *atropurpurea* |
| | ***caroliniana*** subsp. ***wherryi*** | GAuc NGdn WFar |
| § | ***compacta*** | NLar |
| | 'Confetti' | EDif NChi |
| | 'Country Comet' **new** | NChi |
| § | ***davidii*** | CPBP GKev |
| | ***delavayi*** | LRHS |
| § | ***dioica*** | CArn CHab CRWN EWil LEdu MHer MNHC NLan NLar NMir NVic SGar SPoG SWat WMoo WSFF WShi |
| | - 'Clifford Moor' (v) | ECtt MSCN NSti SCoo |
| | - 'Compacta' | see *S. dioica* 'Minikin' |
| | - 'Firefly'[PBR] (d) | ECtt LBMP LSou MWea SHar SPoG |
| § | - 'Flore Pleno' (d) | GCra MRav NBid NBro NChi NGdn SMrm SSvw WFar WHoo WTin |
| | - 'Inane' | CDes EBee WBor WPGP WRHF WWFP |
| | - 'Innocence' | NChi |
| | - f. ***lactea*** | MHer |
| § | - 'Minikin' | ECha MSCN NGdn WTin |
| | - 'Purple Prince' | NChi WMoo |
| | - 'Richmond' (d) | EBee NBre |
| | - 'Rosea Plena' (d) | CBre |
| | - 'Rubra Plena' | see *S. dioica* 'Flore Pleno' |
| | - 'Thelma Kay' (d/v) | CFee ECtt EWes NBre NGdn WMoo WWFP |
| | - 'Underdine' | EBee EWes |
| | - 'Valley High' (v) | EBee ECtt EWes MMuc SPoG WHer WHil |
| | ***elisabethae*** | ECtt EPot EWld NBlu WCot |
| § | ***fimbriata*** | CFir CSpe EBee ELan EPPr EPyc EShb LPla LRHS MCot MMHG MNFA MRav NSti SBri SGar SMrm WAbb WCot WMoo WPGP WPtf WRHF WSHC WTin |
| | ***gigantea*** | EBee |
| | ***hookeri*** Ingramii Group | GKev WAbe |
| | ***kantzeensis*** | see *S. davidii* |
| | ***keiskei*** var. ***minor*** | ECho EWes LRHS WAbe |
| | ***laciniata*** 'Jack Flash' | GJos MWea WHrl |
| | ***latifolia*** | CArn CHab EWil MMuc NMir SEND WPtf |
| § | - subsp. ***alba*** | MNHC SEND |
| | ***maritima*** | see *S. uniflora* |
| | ***maroccana*** | CRWN |
| | ***multifida*** | see *S. fimbriata* |
| | ***noctiflora*** | CHab |
| | ***nutans*** | CArn SRms WHer WSFF |
| | ***orientalis*** | see *S. compacta* |
| | ***parishii*** var. ***latifolia*** NNS 03-556 | NWCA |
| | ***petersonii*** NNS 06-534 | NWCA |
| | ***pusilla*** | CPBP GLam NLar NMen |
| | ***quadridentata*** | see *S. alpestris* |
| | ***regia*** | NBre SPhx |
| | ***rubra*** | see *S. dioica* |
| | ***saxifraga*** | NLar |
| | ***schafta*** ♀H4 | CTri ECha ECho ECtt EPfP GGar GKev MAsh MMuc NBid NBlu NWCA SRms WFar WHoo WNew WPer XLum |
| | - SDR 6026 | GKev |
| | - SDR 6174 | GKev |
| | - 'Abbotswood' | see *Lychnis* × *walkeri* 'Abbotswood Rose' |
| | - 'Persian Carpet' | SBch WRHF |
| | - 'Robusta' | LRHS NDov |
| | - 'Shell Pink' | ECha EPot EWes GJos LBee LRHS NBid NDov WHoo |
| | ***sibirica*** **new** | LRHS |
| | ***sieboldii*** | see *Lychnis coronata* var. *sieboldii* |
| | ***thessalonica*** | LRHS |
| § | ***uniflora*** | CHab ECho ECtt EPfP GGar MMuc MSCN NBro SBch SEND SPlb SRms SRot WFar WMoo XLum |
| | - 'Alba Plena' | see *S. uniflora* 'Robin Whitebreast' |
| I | - 'Compacta' | ECho WMoo |
| § | - 'Druett's Variegated' (v) | CMea CTri ECha ECho ECtt EDAr ELon EPfP EPot EWes GJos LRHS MAsh MHer NBid NBlu NMen NPri NWCA SPet SPlb SPoG SRms WFar WPat XLum |
| | - 'Flore Pleno' | see *S. uniflora* 'Robin Whitebreast' |
| § | - 'Robin Whitebreast' (d) | CMea ECha ECho ECtt EPfP GCal NBPC NBid NBro SRms SRot SUsu WMoo WSHC |
| | - 'Rosea' | EBee ECtt EPfP GGar MMuc SEND SPlb SRot SUsu WFar WPer |
| | - 'Variegata' | see *S. uniflora* 'Druett's Variegated' |
| | - Weisskehlchen | see *S. uniflora* 'Robin Whitebreast' |
| | - 'White Bells' | CTri ECtt MAsh WKif WSHC |
| § | ***vulgaris*** | CArn CHab CRWN ELau EWil LEdu MHer MNHC NLan NMir |
| | - subsp. ***maritima*** | see *S. uniflora* |
| | ***wallichiana*** | see *S. vulgaris* |
| | 'Wisley Pink' | ECtt |
| | ***yunnanensis*** | SPhx WSHC |
| § | ***zawadskii*** | LRHS MDKP SWal WTin |

## *Siler* (*Umbelliferae*)

|  |  |
|---|---|
| ***montanum*** | see *Laserpitium siler* |

## *Silphium* (*Asteraceae*)

|  |  |
|---|---|
| ***integrifolium*** | NBre SAga SMad SPhx WCot WOld XLum |
| ***laciniatum*** | CArn CWCL EBee NBre NLar SMad SMrm SPhx WCot XLum |
| ***perfoliatum*** ♀H4 | CArn EBee ELon GPoy NBre NDov NLar SMrm SPhx SUsu WCot WFar WOld WWEG XLum |
| - var. ***connatum*** | SPhx |
| ***radula*** | EBee |
| ***terebinthinaceum*** | EPPr SPhx WCot XLum |
| ***trifoliatum*** | WCot |

## *Silybum* (Asteraceae)

**marianum** CArn EGHP ELan EPfP GAbr GPoy LRHS MNHC SIde SPav WFar WHer WHfH WOut WTou
- 'Adriana' SPav

## *Simmondsia* (Simmondsiaceae)

**chinensis** CArn EOHP

## *Sinacalia* (Asteraceae)

§ **tangutica** CSam ECha GGar MLLN NBid NBro NLar SDix WAbb WCot WFar

## *Sinarundinaria* (Poaceae)

**anceps** see *Yushania anceps*
**jaunsarensis** see *Yushania anceps*
**maling** see *Yushania maling*
**murielae** see *Fargesia murielae*
**nitida** see *Fargesia nitida*

## *Sinningia* (Gesneriaceae)

sp. EABi
* **caerulea** WDib
**canescens** ♀H1 WDib
§ **cardinalis** CSpe EBak WDib
- 'Innocent' WDib
**conspicua** WDib
**nivalis** WDib
**tuberosa** MCot
**tubiflora** CSpe SUsu WKif XLum

## *Sinobambusa* (Poaceae)

§ **intermedia** EPla
* **orthotropa** EPla
**rubroligula** EPla
**tootsik** EPla WJun
§ - 'Albostriata' (v) EPla LPJP WJun
- 'Variegata' see *S. tootsik* 'Albostriata'

## × *Sinocalycalycanthus* (Calycanthaceae)

**raulstonii** 'Hartlage Wine' CPMA EPfP GKin LRHS MBlu MBri NLar SPoG SSpi
'Venus' EPfP LRHS MBlu SSpi

## *Sinocalycanthus* (Calycanthaceae)

**chinensis** CArn CBcs CHII CMCN CMac CPMA EBee ELan EPfP GKin LRHS MBlu MPkF NLar WSHC

## *Sinofranchetia* (Lardizabalaceae)

**chinensis** CBcs WCru

## *Sinojackia* (Styracaceae)

**xylocarpa** CBcs NLar WFar

## *Sinopodophyllum* (Berberidaceae)

§ **hexandrum** CArn CBct CBro CRow EBla ECho GAbr GBBs GCra GPoy LAma LRHS MBri MCot MNrw MRav NBid NBir NChi NMen SKHP SPhx WCot WFar WPnP
§ - var. **chinense** CLAP CRow EBee EBla ECho GCal GEdr GKev IBlr LEdu LRHS LWst WCru
- - BWJ 7908 WCru
- - SDR 4409 CPLG
- - SDR 5936 GKev
- 'Chinese White' CPLG WCot
- var. **emodi** 'Majus' CFir CLAP EBee SMad WHal

## *Sinowilsonia* (Hamamelidaceae)

**henryi** NLar

## *Siphocranion* (Lamiaceae)

§ **macranthum** CDes EWes WPGP

## *Sison* (Apiaceae)

**amomum** CBre

## *Sisymbrium* (Brassicaceae)

§ **luteum** WHil

## *Sisyrinchium* ✿ (Iridaceae)

× **anceps** see *S. angustifolium*
§ **angustifolium** CMHG ECha LPBA MCot NBir NChi NLar SChF SPlb SRms WBrk WPer
- f. **album** MCot NChi NLar
§ **arenarium** CPBP MAvo SPet
**atlanticum** EDAr NBro
**bellum** hort. see *S. idahoense* var. *bellum*
**bermudiana** see *S. angustifolium*
- 'Album' see *S. graminoides* 'Album'
'Biscutella' CBod CEnt CKno CTri EBee ECho ECtt EPfP GLam GMaP LEdu LHop LRHS NMen NRya SAga SPad SPlb SPoG SWvt WFar WHal WHoo WKif WNew
'Blue France' EPot
'Blue Ice' CMea CPBP CWCL EDAr GEdr LRHS MAvo MCot WAbe WMoo WPat WPer
**boreale** see *S. californicum*
**brachypus** see *S. californicum* Brachypus Group
'Californian Skies' CAby CBro CElw CKno CPLG CSpe CTri CYeo EBee ECha ECho ECtt GCra GMaP LHop LRHS MAsh MAvo MNrw MWhi NBir NMen NSla SMrm SPhx SWvt WFar WKif WMoo WPat
§ **californicum** CBen ECho EHon EPfP LLWG LPBA LRHS NBro WFar WMAq WNew WPer XLum
§ - Brachypus Group CMac ECho EDAr EPfP GAbr LRHS MAsh MMuc MWat NBir NBlu NLar SGar SPlb SPoG SWvt WMoo
* **capsicum** CPLG
**coeruleum** see *Gelasine coerulea*
**commutatum** SGar
**convolutum** GGar NDov
- B&SWJ 9117 WCru
**cuspidatum** see *S. arenarium*
'Deep Seas' MAvo SUsu WWFP
**depauperatum** MNrw
'Devon Skies' CHid CTca CWCL CYeo ECho LRHS MDKP MNrw MTis MWea NMen SBch SWvt WAbe WFar
**douglasii** see *Olsynium douglasii*
'Dragon's Eye' CKno CMea CYeo EWes MAvo MBrN MHer MTis NRya NWCA SMrm SSvw WPer
'E.K. Balls' Widely available
**filifolium** see *Olsynium filifolium*
**graminoides** IFoB NBro
§ - 'Album' NBro
**grandiflorum** see *Olsynium douglasii*
'Hemswell Sky' EHoe GAbr NRya
'Iceberg' CElw EDAr EShb MWat SBch SSvw

| | | |
|---|---|---|
| | ***idahoense*** | CYeo ECha ECtt EDAr GAbr GEdr GLam LSou MHer NRya SPlb SRms |
| § | - var. ***bellum*** | CKno ECho EPfP IFro SGar SPet SRms WMoo WNew WPat XLum |
| | - - pale-flowered | CKno NDov SSvw |
| | - - 'Rocky Point' | CElw CSpe EBee EWes GJos LRHS MAvo SBod SDoC WFar WHoo WPat |
| | - var. ***macounii*** | EBee GEdr NSla SPlb WFar |
| § | - - 'Album' ♀H4 | CAby CMea CYeo ECho GAbr GKev GLam MWat SPet SPlb WAbe WFar WPat |
| | ***iridifolium*** | see *S. micranthum* |
| | ***junceum*** | see *Olsynium junceum* |
| | ***littorale*** | CPLG NLar |
| | ***macrocarpon*** misapplied | see *S. macrocarpum* |
| | ***macrocarpon*** ♀H2-3 | CPBP MNrw NMen |
| § | ***macrocarpum*** | CFee ECho EDAr MDKP WPer |
| | 'Marion' | CElw CMea CPBP EDAr MAvo MBrN NDov NLar SBch SMrm SPet WPer |
| | 'May Snow' | see *S. idahoense* var. *macounii* 'Album' |
| § | ***micranthum*** | ECho |
| | ***montanum* × *nudicaule*** | CFee ECho GAbr MNrw NRya NSla SRot |
| | 'Mrs Spivey' | ECtt MHer NBir |
| | 'North Star' | see *S.* 'Pole Star' |
| | ***palmifolium*** | CBod CDes CTrC GAbr LEdu MAvo MDKP MHer MNrw MWea SBch SGar SMad SPoG WCot WSHC XLum |
| | ***patagonicum*** | CPLG EDAr |
| § | 'Pole Star' | CFee CSpe WFar WPer |
| | 'Quaint and Queer' | COIW CPLG CWCL ECha ECtt EHoe EShb MBrN MLHP MNFA MNrw NBir NBro NChi SWvt WMnd WPer WSHC |
| | 'Raspberry' | CMea EBee |
| | 'Sapphire' | CPrp CYeo ECtt GJos LRHS MTis NPri SPoG WFar WGrn WMoo |
| | 'Sisland Blue' | EWes |
| § | ***striatum*** | Widely available |
| § | - 'Aunt May' (v) | Widely available |
| | - 'Variegatum' | see *S. striatum* 'Aunt May' |
| | aff. ***unispathaceum*** B&SWJ 10683 | WCru |

## *Sium* (*Apiaceae*)

| | |
|---|---|
| ***sisarum*** | ELau GPoy MHer |

## *Skimmia* ✿ (*Rutaceae*)

| | | |
|---|---|---|
| | ***anquetilia*** | CMac |
| | - (f) new | WCru |
| | - (m) new | WCru |
| | ***arborescens*** B&SWJ 11799 | WCru |
| | - subsp. ***nitida*** B&SWJ 8239 | WCru |
| | ***arisanensis*** B&SWJ 7114 | WCru |
| | - CWJ 12417 | WCru |
| | black-fruited B&SWJ 8259 from northern Vietnam (f/m) | WCru |
| | × ***confusa*** | WFar |
| | - 'Kew Green' (m) ♀H4 | Widely available |
| | ***japonica*** | CDul CMHG CMac CWib GQui MGos NPla SBrd SReu SSta WDin WFar |
| | - (f) | CDoy CMac CTri ELan EPfP GGal SRms |
| | - (m) | GGal |
| | - B&SWJ 5053 | WCru |
| | - - (f) | WCru |
| | - - (m) | WCru |
| | - 'Alba' | see *S. japonica* 'Wakehurst White' |
| | - 'Bowles's Dwarf Female' (f) | CDoC CMHG EBee ELan EPfP MBri MGos MRav MWht NHol SLim SLon |
| | - 'Bowles's Dwarf Male' (m) | CMHG MGos MRav MWht NHol SLim |
| | - 'Bronze Knight' (m) | CMac EQua MBri MRav NHol SLim WFar |
| | - 'Cecilia Brown' (f) | WFar |
| | - 'Chameleon' | CDul MBri NHol |
| | - compact (f) | GGal |
| | - 'Dad's Red Dragon' | MBri NHol |
| | - 'Emerald King' (m) | MAsh MBri WFar |
| N | - 'Foremanii' | see *S. japonica* 'Veitchii' |
| § | - 'Fragrans' (m) ♀H4 | CDoC CMac CSBt CTri CWSG CWib ECrN EPfP IVic LRHS LSRN MAsh MBri MGos MRav NHol NLar NPri NWea SBfd SBrd SLim SPer SPoG SWvt WFar WGob WGwG |
| | - 'Fragrant Cloud' | see *S. japonica* 'Fragrans' |
| | - 'Fragrantissima' (m) | WFar |
| | - 'Fructu Albo' | see *S. japonica* 'Wakehurst White' |
| | - 'Godrie's Dwarf' (m) | EPfP LRHS NLar WFar |
| | - var. ***intermedia*** f. ***repens*** | WFar |
| | - - - B&SWJ 5560 | WCru |
| | - - - B&SWJ 11165 | WCru |
| | - 'Keessen' (f) | WFar |
| | - 'Kew White' (f) | CAbP CDoC CWib EBee ELan EPfP EQua IArd LRHS MAsh MBri MGos NHol NPal NWad SLim SLon SPer SRms SWvt WCFE WCot WDin WFar |
| | - Luwian = 'Wanto' | NHol WCFE WFar |
| | - 'Magic Marlot'PBR (v) | EGxp EPfP LRHS MAsh MGos NLar SPoG |
| | - 'Marlot' (m) | EPfP LRHS MAsh NLar SPoG |
| | - 'Nymans' (f) ♀H4 | CDoC CEnd CSam EBee ELan EPfP LRHS MAsh MBri MRav SBfd SBrd SLim SPer SPoG SReu SRms SSpi SSta WFar WGob |
| | - 'Obovata' (f) | EPla |
| | - 'Pigmy' (f) | CPLG |
| | - 'Red Dragon' (f) | CMac |
| | - 'Red Princess' (f) | MAsh WFar |
| * | - 'Red Riding Hood' | MAsh NHol SLon |
| | - 'Redruth' (f) | CBcs CDoC CMac CSBt CSam ELon EQua LRHS MAsh MGos MWat NHol NLar SEND SSta WFar |
| § | - subsp. ***reevesiana*** | CBcs CDoC CDul CMHG CMac CSBt CTri CWSG CWib EBee EPfP GQui IVic LRHS MBri MGos MRav MSwo NHol NLar SBfd SPoG SSpi SWvt WDin WFar |
| | - - B&SWJ 3763 | MAsh WCru |
| | - - var. ***reevesiana*** | SPer |
| | - - - B&SWJ 3544 | WCru |
| § | - Rogersii Group | CMac CTri |
| | - - 'George Gardner' | LRHS |
| | - - 'Nana Mascula' (m) | CTri |
| | - - 'Snow Dwarf' (m) | WFar |
| | - 'Rubella' (m) ♀H4 | Widely available |
| | - 'Rubinetta' (m) | EPfP IArd LSRN MAsh MGos NHol SLim WFar |
| | - 'Ruby Dome' (m) | MBri NHol WFar |
| | - 'Ruby King' (m) | CDoC CSBt EQua IArd LSRN MAsh NHol NLar |

| | | |
|---|---|---|
| | – 'Scarlet Dwarf' (f) | MBri NHol |
| | – 'Snow White'PBR | EGxp |
| | – 'Tansley Gem' (f) | LRHS MAsh MBri MWht SPoG SSta WFar |
| | – 'Thelma King' | WFar |
| | – 'Thereza'PBR (m) new | LBuc |
| § | – 'Veitchii' (f) | CBar CBcs CDoy CDul CMac CSBt CTri EBee ELan EPfP IArd LRHS LSRN LTen MAsh MBri MGos MMuc MRav MWat NHol NLar SBrd SEND SLim SPoG SWvt WDin |
| § | – 'Wakehurst White' (f) | CBcs CMHG CMac CSBt CTri ELan EPfP LRHS MBri MRav SLim SLon SReu WFar |
| | – 'Winifred Crook' (f) | EBee MBri WFar |
| | – 'Wisley Female' (f) | CTri NHol WFar |
| | ***laureola*** | CDoC CPLG CSam EBee MRav SGar SRms WFar WSHC |
| | – GWJ 9364 | WCru |
| | – subsp. ***laureola*** HWJK 2095 | WCru |
| | – subsp. ***multinervia*** GWJ 9374 | WCru |
| | 'Olympic Fire' new | CWSG |
| | 'Olympic Flame' | EWTr IArd LRHS MAsh MBlu MGos SPoG WFar |
| | ***reevesiana*** | see *S. japonica* subsp. *reevesiana* |
| | ***rogersii*** | see *S. japonica* Rogersii Group |

## *Smilacina* see *Maianthemum*

## *Smilax* (*Smilacaceae*)

| | |
|---|---|
| sp. | WBor |
| B&SWJ 6628 from Thailand | WCru |
| from Thailand | LEdu |
| ***aspera*** | CArn CMac EShb EWld LEdu WCru WPGP |
| ***china*** B&SWJ 4427 | WCru |
| ***discotis*** | CBcs SEND |
| ***glaucophylla*** B&SWJ 2971 | WCru |
| ***nipponica*** B&SWJ 4331 | WCru |
| ***rotundifolia*** | LEdu |
| ***sieboldii*** | LEdu MRav |
| – B&SWJ 744 | WCru |

## *Smithiantha* (*Gesneriaceae*)

| | | |
|---|---|---|
| | 'Extra Sassy' | EABi EShb |
| | 'Little One' | EOHP WDib |
| | 'Multiflora' | EABi WDib |
| | 'Santa Clara' | EABi |
| I | 'Temple Bells' | EABi |

## *Smyrnium* (*Apiaceae*)

| | |
|---|---|
| ***olusatrum*** | CArn CHab CSev CSpe MHer MNHC SIde STre SWat WHer WSFF |
| ***perfoliatum*** | CHid CSpe EBee ELan ELon EWes NBir SDix SMrm WCot WFar WHal WSHC |
| ***rotundifolium*** | CArn LEdu WCot |

## *Solandra* (*Solanaceae*)

| | | |
|---|---|---|
| | ***grandiflora*** misapplied | see *S. maxima* |
| | ***hartwegii*** | see *S. maxima* |
| § | ***maxima*** | CCCN CHII EShb |

## *Solanum* (*Solanaceae*)

| | | |
|---|---|---|
| | ***atropurpureum*** | CDTJ CSpe |
| | ***aviculare*** G.Forst. | LRHS |
| | ***betaceum*** (F) | CCCN EShb SVic |
| | ***capsicastrum*** new | SPlb |
| | ***conchifolium*** hort. | see *S. linearifolium* |
| | ***crispum*** | NBir SGar WDin |
| | – 'Autumnale' | see *S. crispum* 'Glasnevin' |
| | – 'Elizabeth Jane Dunn' (v) | WCot WSHC |
| § | – 'Glasnevin' ♀H3 | Widely available |
| | ***dulcamara*** | CArn GPoy WHfH |
| | – var. ***album*** | EHoe LSRN |
| | – 'Variegatum' (v) | CMac CWan EHoe EPfP MAsh WFar |
| | ***hispidum*** | CHEx |
| | ***jasminoides*** | see *S. laxum* |
| | ***laciniatum*** | CArn CCCN CDTJ CHEx CPLG CSev CSpe EShb EWes GGal GGar MCot SBfd SBig SBst SEND SGar SPav SPlb WKif WWlt |
| § | ***laxum*** | EBee EShb GGal LRHS MSwo SPer SPoG SRms SWvt WDin WSHC |
| | – 'Album' ♀H3 | Widely available |
| | – 'Album Variegatum' (v) | CWib ELan LRHS WSHC |
| * | – 'Aureovariegatum' (v) | CMac EBee EShb LBMP MAsh MGos NEgg SLim SPlb |
| | – 'Coldham' | EShb GCal SMad |
| | – 'Creche ar Pape' | ECha |
| § | ***linearifolium*** | CSpe LBMP SKHP WCot WPGP |
| | ***muricatum*** (F) | CCCN CHII EShb SPlb |
| | ***pseudocapsicum*** 'Thurino' | EPfP |
| | – variegated (v) | WCot |
| | ***pyracanthum*** | CDTJ SMad |
| | ***quitoense*** (F) | CDTJ SBig |
| | ***rantonnetii*** | see *Lycianthes rantonnetii* |
| | ***seaforthianum*** | MOWG |
| | ***sisymbriifolium*** | WWlt |
| | aff. ***stenophyllum*** B&SWJ 10744 | WCru |
| | ***wendlandii*** | CHII |

## *Solaria* (*Alliaceae*)

| | |
|---|---|
| sp. | GCal |

## *Soldanella* (*Primulaceae*)

| | | |
|---|---|---|
| | ***alpicola*** new | GJos |
| | ***alpina*** | CMea EBee ECho GCra GKev NMen SRms WAbe |
| I | – 'Alba' | ECho GEdr NSla WAbe |
| | ***carpatica*** | ECho GKev LLHF NSla WAbe |
| | – 'Alba' | MDKP NHar NSla WAbe |
| | – hybrid | NMen |
| | ***carpatica* × *pusilla*** | CPBP ECho NHar NMen NRya NWad WAbe |
| | ***carpatica* × *villosa*** | ECho LEdu MDKP |
| | ***cyanaster*** | ECho GEdr GJos GKev NLBP NMen NRya WAbe |
| | ***dimoniei*** | CFee ECho GEdr GKev ITim NMen NWCA WAbe |
| | ***hungarica*** | ECho WAbe |
| | ***minima*** | ECho GJos GKev NMen |
| | – SDR 5481 | GKev |
| | ***montana*** | ECho EDAr GEdr GJos LLHF MDun NLar NMen SBch |
| | ***pindicola*** | ECho EPot EWes NMen NWCA WAbe WFar |
| | ***pusilla*** | GKev ITim |
| | 'Spring Symphony' | GEdr |
| | 'Sudden Spring' | GEdr WAbe |
| | ***villosa*** | CAby CDes EBee ECho GAbr GEdr GGar GKev ITim LEdu NRya NWad SBch WFar WPtf WSHC WThu |

## *Soleirolia* (*Urticaceae*)

| | | |
|---|---|---|
| | ***soleirolii*** | CHEx CTri EPot LPBA MCCP MWhi SMad SPer STre SVic SWvt WHer XLum |
| | – 'Argentea' | see *S. soloirolii* 'Variegata' |
| § | – 'Aurea' | CTca CTri EPot STre SVic SWvt |
| | – 'Golden Queen' | see *S. soleirolii* 'Aurea' |
| | – 'Silver Queen' | see *S. soleirolii* 'Variegata' |
| § | – 'Variegata' (v) | LPBA SVic WHer |

## *Solenomelus* (*Iridaceae*)

| | | |
|---|---|---|
| | ***chilensis*** | see *S. pedunculatus* |
| § | ***pedunculatus*** | CFee |

## *Solenopsis* (*Campanulaceae*)

| | | |
|---|---|---|
| | ***axillaris*** | see *Isotoma axillaris* |

## *Solenostemon* ✿ (*Lamiaceae*)

| | | |
|---|---|---|
| | 'Autumn Rainbow' | WDib |
| | 'Beauty' (v) | WDib |
| | 'Black Dragon' | LSou |
| | 'Black Heart' | WDib |
| | 'Black Prince' | WDib |
| | 'Brilliant' (v) | WDib |
| | 'Bronze Pagoda' | WDib |
| | 'Buttercup' | WDib |
| | 'Chamaeleon' (v) | WDib |
| | 'City of Sunderland' | WDib |
| | 'Combat' (v) | WDib |
| | 'Crimson Ruffles' (v) ♀H1 | WDib |
| | 'Dazzler' (v) | WDib |
| | 'Display' | WDib |
| | 'Durham Gala' | WDib |
| | 'Firelight' | WDib |
| | 'Freckles' (v) | WDib |
| | 'Illumination' | WDib |
| | 'Inky Fingers' (v) | WDib |
| | 'Juliet Quartermain' | WDib |
| | 'Kentish Fire' (v) | WDib |
| | 'Kiwi Fern' (v) | WDib |
| | 'Lemon Chiffon' | WDib |
| | 'Lord Falmouth' ♀H1 | WDib |
| | 'Mrs Pilkington' (v) | WDib |
| | 'Muriel Pedley' (v) | WDib |
| | 'Paisley Shawl' (v) ♀H1 | WDib |
| | 'Palisandra' | CSpe |
| | 'Peter Wonder' (v) | WDib |
| | 'Picturatus' (v) ♀H1 | WDib |
| | 'Pineapple Beauty' (v) ♀H1 | WDib |
| | 'Pineapplette' ♀H1 | WDib |
| | 'Pink Chaos' | WDib |
| | 'Red Angel' | WDib |
| | 'Red Velvet' | WDib |
| | 'Rose Blush' (v) | WDib |
| | 'Roy Pedley' | WDib |
| | 'Royal Scot' (v) ♀H1 | WDib |
| | 'Salmon Plumes' (v) | WDib |
| | 'Saturn' | LAst NPri WDib |
| | ***scutellarioides*** Henna = 'Balcenna' PBR <u>**new**</u> | NPri |
| | 'The Flume' | WDib |
| | ***thyrsoideus*** | see *Plectranthus thyrsoideus* |
| | 'Timotei' | WDib |
| | 'Walter Turner' (v) ♀H1 | WDib |
| | 'Winsome' (v) | WDib |
| | 'Winter Sun' (v) | WDib |
| | 'Wisley Flame' | WDib |
| | 'Wisley Tapestry' (v) ♀H1 | WDib |

## *Solidago* (*Asteraceae*)

| | | |
|---|---|---|
| | Babygold | see *S.* 'Goldkind' |
| | ***brachystachys*** | see *S. cutleri* |
| | ***caesia*** | EWes NBir WOld WTin |
| | ***canadensis*** | CTri EBee ELan MLLN MMuc NBre SEND SPlb WFar WHer XLum |
| | – var. ***salebrosa*** | LRHS |
| | – var. ***scabra*** | MAvo WOld WTin |
| | 'Citronella' | ECtt EWll GQue NBPC |
| | 'Cloth of Gold' | CMac EBee ECtt EPfP LRHS NPro SWvt WMnd |
| § | 'Crown of Rays' | CPrp ECtt ELon EPfP LRHS MRav WFar WMnd WWEG |
| § | ***cutleri*** | EBee ECho ELan GEdr MWat NLar SPlb SRms WFar WPat |
| I | – ***nana*** | ECho EWes |
| | 'Ducky' | EBee NBPC |
| | 'Early Bird' | NLar WFar |
| | 'Featherbush' | LRHS |
| § | ***flexicaulis*** | GMaP XLum |
| | – 'Variegata' (v) | CWan EBee ECtt ELan GMaP NLar WFar WHer WPer WWEG XLum |
| | 'Gardone' ♀H4 | WFar |
| | ***gigantea*** | WFar WPer |
| | ***glomerata*** | EBee EShb NBre NLar SMrm WPer |
| | Golden Baby | see *S.* 'Goldkind' |
| § | 'Golden Dwarf' | COlW CWCL SPoG WPtf WWEG XLum |
| | 'Golden Falls' | LRHS |
| | 'Golden Fleece' | see *S. sphacelata* 'Golden Fleece' |
| | Golden Gate = 'Dansolgold' | LRHS |
| | 'Golden Rays' | see *S.* 'Goldstrahl' |
| | 'Golden Thumb' | see *S.* 'Queenie' |
| | 'Golden Wings' | CBre MWat |
| | 'Goldenmosa' ♀H4 | CAby CMac CSBt EBee ECtt EPfP EWes GMaP LRHS MRav SPer SSvw WCot WFar |
| | 'Goldilocks' | NPri SRms |
| § | 'Goldkind' | CAby CMMP CSBt CTri EBee ECtt EPfP EShb GAbr LRHS MCot MMuc MSCN MWhi NBPC NEgg NOrc SBfd SEND SWvt WBrk WFar WWEG |
| § | 'Goldstrahl' | LRHS WFar |
| | Goldzwerg | see *S.* 'Golden Dwarf' |
| | 'Harvest Gold' | CAby CElw CHVG |
| | ***hybrida*** | see *S.* × ***luteus*** |
| | ***latifolia*** | see *S. flexicaulis* |
| | 'Laurin' | EBee LRHS NLar XLum |
| | 'Ledsham' | EBee ECtt EWll LEdu LRHS MCot NBre SPoG WMnd |
| | 'Leraft' | EBee |
| | 'Linner Gold' | NBre |
| | 'Little Lemon' | GCal NBPC |
| § | × ***luteus*** | EBee NBPC SRms WFar WHil XLum |
| | – 'Lemore' ♀H4 | CMea CPrp EBee ELan EPfP GMaP GMac GQue LAst LHop LRHS LSou MWat NCGa NPri NSti SMrm SPer SPhx WCot WFar WWEG XLum |
| | ***ohioensis*** | XLum |
| § | ***ptarmicoides*** | CSam EBee EBla LBMP WPer XLum |
| | – 'Mago' | EBee |
| § | 'Queenie' | ECha LRHS MHer MLHP NBre NVic SRms WWEG |
| | ***riddellii*** | EBee LRHS |
| | ***rigida*** | LRHS NBre SMrm WCot |
| | ***roanensis*** | NBre |

***rugosa*** ECha MBNS MMuc NBre SPhx WCot
- 'Fireworks' CBre CHVG CMHG COIW CPrp CSam EBee ECtt ELon EPPr GCal GQue MAvo MNFA NBPC NCGa NLar SPhx SUsu WBrk WCot WFar WHoo WOld WTin WWEG WWlt XLum
***sciaphila*** NBre
***sempervirens*** WCot WFar WOld
- 'Goldene Wellen' EBee
'Septembergold' CSam
***shortii*** EBee
***simplex*** subsp. ***simplex*** var. ***nana*** NWCA
'Sonnenschein' NBre
***speciosa*** LRHS NBre SPhx
- var. ***jejunifolia*** new LRHS
***spectabilis*** var. ***confinis*** EBee
§ ***sphacelata*** 'Golden Fleece' CBcs EBee NBre WFar WMnd WWEG
Strahlenkrone see *S.* 'Crown of Rays'
'Summer Sunshine' WWEG
'Super' CAby CPrp WCot
Sweety = 'Barseven'PBR LRHS
'Tom Thumb' CMac MRav NBir SRms
***uliginosa*** EShb XLum
***ulmifolia*** EBee
***virgaurea*** CArn EBee GPoy MHer MNHC NLar WHer
- subsp. ***alpestris*** var. ***minutissima*** CMea NBre WPat
- var. ***cambrica*** see *S. virgaurea* subsp. *minuta*
§ - subsp. ***minuta*** GBin
§ - 'Variegata' (v) CBre EHoe NPro
***vulgaris*** 'Variegata' see *S. virgaurea* 'Variegata'
'Yellow Springs' GJos
'Yellowstone' LRHS

## × *Solidaster* see *Solidago*

***hybridus*** see *Solidago* × *luteus*

## *Sollya* (*Pittosporaceae*)

***fusiformis*** see *S. heterophylla*
§ ***heterophylla*** ♀H1 Widely available
- 'Alba' CBcs CCCN EBee ELan EPfP LRHS MCot SLim SLon SPer SRms SWvt WSHC
- mauve-flowered ECou
- 'Pink Charmer' EBee ELan LRHS SLon
- pink-flowered CCCN CHGN CHll CSPN LBMP LRHS SEND SLim SPad SWvt

## *Sonchus* (*Asteraceae*)

***fruticosus*** CHEx GGar
***giganteus*** CHll
***pinnatus*** SPlb

## *Sophora* (*Papilionaceae*)

§ ***davidii*** CBcs CGHE CPLG CWGN CWib EBee EBtc EPfP LRHS MBlu MGos MMuc MOWG MWea SEND SPoG SSpi WPGP WSHC
***flavescens*** SBrt
***fulvida*** ECou
***howinsula*** ECou IRar
***japonica*** see *Styphnolobium japonicum*
§ 'Little Baby' CAbP CWib EBee ELan EPPr EPfP IVic LAst LBuc LRHS LSRN MGos SPoG SPtl SWvt WGrn
***longicarinata*** ECou
***macrocarpa*** CBcs
***microphylla*** CHEx CTri EBee ECou EPfP LHop LRHS SEND WPGP
***molloyi*** ECou
- 'Dragon's Gold' CBcs EBee ECou ELan EPfP LRHS MAsh SCoo SPoG SSpi SSta WDin
- 'Early Gold' WPGP
***prostrata*** misapplied see *S.* 'Little Baby'
***prostrata*** ambig. CBcs CGHE LRHS SEND WThu
***prostrata*** Buch. CBot CMac ECou
Sun King = 'Hilsop'PBR ♀H4 CBcs CCVT CWGN EBee ELan EPfP EWes IVic LRHS LSRN MGos MWea NCGa NLar NPri SBfd SCoo SLim SLon SPoG SPtl SWvt
***tetraptera*** ♀H3 CAbP CDul CFee CMac CTsd EBee ECou EPfP GGal LRHS NGBo SEND SRms WBor WPGP
***viciifolia*** see *S. davidii*

## *Sorbaria* (*Rosaceae*)

***aitchisonii*** see *S. tomentosa* var. *angustifolia*
***arborea*** see *S. kirilowii*
aff. ***assurgens*** BWJ 8185 WCru
§ ***kirilowii*** CMac CPLG MRav NLar SMad WDyG WOut
- AC 3433 MSnd
***sorbifolia*** CAbP CBcs CCVT EBee ECrN GAuc MLHP MMuc NLar NPro SEND SPer SPlb SPoG WDin WFar
- 'Sem'PBR Widely available
- var. ***stellipila*** SLPl
- - B&SWJ 776 WCru
§ ***tomentosa*** var. ***angustifolia*** ♀H4 CBcs CDul CTri CWan EBee ELan EPfP GAuc LRHS MMuc MRav NBid NPro SEND SLon SPer WFar WHer

## × *Sorbopyrus* (*Rosaceae*)

***auricularis*** MCoo
- 'Shipova' (F) CAgr

## *Sorbus* ✿ (*Rosaceae*)

sp. CMen
MF 96072 GKev
***adamii*** new CMCN
***alnifolia*** CLnd CMCN CPMA EPfP MBlu SLPl
- B&SWJ 8461 WCru
- B&SWJ 10948 WCru
- 'Red Bird' EPfP MBlu
***americana*** CLnd NWea
***anglica*** CDul CNat
***apiculata*** CLD 310 GAuc
'Apricot' CEnd
'Apricot Lady' GBin
'Apricot Queen' CLnd EBee ECrN LAst MMuc NEgg SGol WFar
***aria*** CCVT CDul CHab CLnd CSBt CTri ECrN GAuc LBuc MGos MMuc MSnd NWea SEND SEWo SGol WDin WMou
- 'Aurea' CLnd EBee MGos WFar
- 'Chrysophylla' CDul CSBt EBee ECrN NWea SPer SPoG
- 'Decaisneana' see *S. aria* 'Majestica'
- 'Lutescens' ♀H4 Widely available
- 'Magnifica' CDoC ECrN ELan LMaj NEgg SCoo SEWo WDin WJas
§ - 'Majestica' ♀H4 CCVT CDoC CDul CLnd CMac EBee ECrN LHop MAsh NWea SCoo SPer WHar WJas

| | |
|---|---|
| - 'Mitchellii' | see *S. thibetica* 'John Mitchell' |
| ***arnoldiana*** 'Golden Wonder' | see *S.* 'Lombarts Golden Wonder' |
| ***aronioides*** misapplied | see *S. caloneura* |
| § ***aucuparia*** | Widely available |
| - 'Aspleniifolia' | CBcs CCVT CDul CMCN CMac CDoC CWSG EBee ECrN GBin LAst LRHS MGos MRav MWat NPCo NWea SBfd SLim SPer SPoG WDin WFar WJas |
| § - 'Beissneri' | CAgr CDul GBin MGos NLar NPCo NWea SCoo SLon SPoG WHCr |
| - Cardinal Royal = 'Michred' | CCVT CDoC EBee ECrN GQui LRHS MMuc NEgg SBfd SCoo SEND SEWo SLon WJas |
| - 'Dirkenii' | GBin MAsh SGol WDin WJas |
| § - var. ***edulis*** (F) | CBcs CDul CLnd CTho EBee ECrN LBuc LMaj MCoo MGos SCoo WDin |
| - - 'Rossica' misapplied | see *S. aucuparia* var. *edulis* 'Rossica Major' |
| § - - 'Rossica Major' | CDul ECrN GQui SCoo SEWo WFar |
| § - 'Fastigiata' | CEnd CLnd CMac CTri ECrN EPfP GKin LAst LMaj MBlu MGos NPCo WDin WFar |
| - var. ***heteromorpha*** | GAuc |
| - 'Hilling's Spire' | CTho |
| - ***pluripinnata*** | see *S. scalaris* Koehne |
| - var. ***rossica*** Koehne | see *S. aucuparia* var. *edulis* |
| - 'Sheerwater Seedling' ♀H4 | CBcs CCVT CDoC CDul CMCN CSBt EBee ECrN ELan EPfP GKin LAst LHop LMaj MGos MMuc MRav MSwo NPri SBfd SEND SEWo SGol SLim SPer WDin WFar |
| - var. ***xanthocarpa*** ♀H4 | ECrN EPfP LMaj WDin |
| Autumn Spire = 'Flanrock' | CDoC CLnd CWSG EBee LRHS MAsh MBri MGos NLar SBfd SCoo SLim SLon SPoG SWvt WHCr WHar |
| ***bakonyensis*** **new** | IGor |
| 'Bellona' | WPat |
| ***brevipetiolata*** B&SWJ 11771 | WCru |
| ***bristoliensis*** | GAuc |
| 'Burka' | see *Aronia* × *Sorbus*, 'Burka' |
| § ***caloneura*** | EPfP MBlu SSpi WPat |
| 'Carpet of Gold' | CLnd |
| ***cashmiriana*** Hedl. ♀H4 | Widely available |
| ***chamaemespilus*** | GAuc |
| 'Chamois Glow' | MAsh WJas |
| 'Chinese Lace' | Widely available |
| § ***commixta*** | CBcs CDul CEnd CLnd CMCN CSto CTho EBee ECrN GAuc LAst MBlu MGos MMuc MSwo NLar SEND SGol SLim SPer WDin WJas |
| - B&SWJ 10839 | WCru |
| - B&SWJ 11043 | WCru |
| - 'Embley' ♀H4 | CBcs CCVT CDul CMCN CMac CSBt CTho CTri EBee ECrN ELan EPfP LHop MBlu MGos MMuc MRav NEgg NPCo NWea SEND SGol SPer SPoG WDin WFar |
| - Olympic Flame = 'Dodong' | IArd IDee LRHS MAsh MBlu MBri NLar SCoo SEWo SLim WHar |
| - 'Ravensbill' | EBee EPfP LRHS NLar SCoo WHCr WHar WMou |
| - var. ***rufoferruginea*** | GQui |
| - - B&SWJ 11486 | WCru |
| - var. ***sachalinensis*** B&SWJ 8496 | WCru |
| - - B&SWJ 8515 | WCru |
| ***conradinae*** misapplied | see *S. pohuashanensis* (Hance) Hedlund |
| ***conradinae*** Koehne | see *S. esserteauana* |
| 'Copper Kettle' | EBee EPfP MAsh MBri MWat NLar SCoo SPoG WHCr WHar |
| 'Coral Beauty' | CDul CLnd |
| ***corymbifera*** WWJ 11[illegible] | WCru |
| 'Covert Gold' | CEnd |
| ***croceocarpa*** | CDul |
| 'Croft Coral' | LRHS MAsh NPal |
| ***cuspidata*** | see *S. vestita* |
| * ***decora*** 'Grootendorst' | CDul |
| - var. ***nana*** | see *S. aucuparia* 'Fastigiata' |
| ***devoniensis*** | CDul CNat CTho |
| - 'Devon Beauty' | CAgr |
| ***discolor*** misapplied | see *S. commixta* |
| ***discolor*** (Maxim.) Maxim. | CLnd EBee GAuc LAst MBlu NWea SEND WJas |
| - MF 96172 | MAsh |
| ***domestica*** | CDul EPfP MMuc NWea SEND SLPl WDin |
| - 'Maliformis' | see *S. domestica* f. *pomifera* |
| § - f. ***pomifera*** | CLnd |
| § - f. ***pyrifera*** | CLnd |
| - 'Pyriformis' | see *S. domestica* f. *pyrifera* |
| - 'Rosie' | CAgr |
| 'Eastern Promise' | EBee ECrN EPfP GBin MAsh MBlu MBri MWat NLar NWea SCoo SLim WDin WHCr WJas WMou |
| § ***eburnea*** Harry Smith 12799 | GQui |
| ***eminens*** | CDul CNat |
| ***epidendron*** WWJ 11930 | WCru |
| § ***esserteauana*** | CTho EPfP WPat |
| 'Fastigiata' | see *S. aucuparia* 'Fastigiata', *S.* × *thuringiaca* 'Fastigiata' |
| ***folgneri*** | CEnd CPMA |
| - 'Emiel' | EPfP MBlu MBri |
| - 'Lemon Drop' | CDul CEnd CLnd CPMA EPfP MAsh NLar SCoo SMad |
| § ***foliolosa*** | CLnd NWea |
| ***forrestii*** | CBcs CMCN EPfP LRHS SEND SLPl |
| * ***fortunei*** | CLnd |
| § ***frutescens*** | CEnd CLnd EPfP NWea |
| ***fruticosa*** Crantz | CSto GAuc GKev NSla |
| - 'Koehneana' | see *S. koehneana* C.K. Schneid. |
| 'Ghose' | CEnd CLnd EBee MBri SCoo SPer |
| ***glabrescens*** | CSto |
| ***glabriuscula*** | GKev |
| ***glomerulata*** | LLHF |
| 'Golden Wonder' | see *S.* 'Lombarts Golden Wonder' |
| ***gonggashanica*** | EPfP |
| * ***gorrodini*** | CLnd |
| § ***graeca*** | GAuc |
| ***granulosa*** HWJ 1041 | WCru |
| ***harrowiana*** | WPat |
| ***hazslinszkyana*** **new** | IGor |
| ***hedlundii*** | CPLG EBee EBtc GBin MGos NLar NWea SKHP WPGP |
| ***hemsleyi*** | CDul CLnd CPLG WPGP |
| - 'John Bond' | EBee MAsh NLar NPal SPoG |
| × ***hostii*** | MRav |
| ***hupehensis*** C.K. Schneid. ♀H4 | CBcs CDul CEnd CLnd CMCN CMac CTho CTri EBee EPfP EWTr LHop MMuc NWea SBfd SEND SGol SLPl SPer WDin WFar WHar WJas WMou WPat |
| - MF 96170 | EPfP |
| - 'November Pink' | see *S. hupehensis* 'Pink Pagoda' |
| § - var. ***obtusa*** ♀H4 | CCVT CDoC CDul CLnd EPfP GCal NEgg NPCo WDin |

| |  |  |
|---|---|---|
| § | – 'Pink Pagoda' | CDoC CDul CLnd ECrN EPfP EWTr IArd LRHS LSRN MAsh MBlu MGos MMuc MRav MWat NLar NPri NWea SBfd SCoo SEND SEWo SLim SLon SPer SPoG WBor WDin WFar WHCr |
| | – 'Rosea' | see *S. hupehensis* var. *obtusa* |
| | × ***hybrida*** misapplied | see *S.* × *thuringiaca* |
| | × ***hybrida*** L. | ECrN |
| | – 'Gibbsii' ♀$^{H4}$ | CDoC CLnd EBee ELan EPfP GAuc SPoG SPur WHar |
| | ***insignis*** | EPfP WPGP WPat |
| | ***intermedia*** | CBcs CCVT CDul CLnd CSBt CTho CTri CWib EBee ECrN MGos NWea SEND SGol WDin WHar WMou |
| | – 'Brouwers' | ELan LMaj WMou |
| | ***japonica*** B&SWJ 10813 | WCru |
| | – B&SWJ 11048 | WCru |
| | 'Joseph Rock' | Widely available |
| § | × ***kewensis*** | CDul CLnd NWea SPlb |
| | 'Kirsten Pink' | CLnd CWib EBee ECrN SPer WFar |
| | ***koehneana*** misapplied | see *S. frutescens* |
| § | ***koehneana*** C.K. Schneid. ♀$^{H4}$ | CBcs EBee EWTr GQui IDee NMen NWea WTin |
| | aff. ***koehneana*** C.K. Schneid. | see *S. eburnea* |
| | aff. ***koehneana*** ambig. | NBlu |
| | ***lanata*** misapplied | see *S. vestita* |
| | ***lancastriensis*** | CDul CNat |
| | ***latifolia*** | CLnd WDin |
| | – 'Henk Vink' | CCVT LMaj |
| | 'Leonard Messel' | MAsh MBri SCoo WHCr |
| | 'Leonard Springer' | ECrN EPfP |
| | ***leptophylla*** | CDul |
| | ***ligustrifolia*** HWJ 984 | WCru |
| | – WWJ 12004 | WCru |
| | 'Likjornaja' | EPfP |
| § | 'Lombarts Golden Wonder' | CBcs CDul CLnd MMuc NWea SEND SGol WJas |
| | 'Maidenblush' | SGol |
| | ***matsumurana*** misapplied | see *S. commixta* |
| | ***megalocarpa*** | CDoC CDul CPMA EPfP SKHP SSpi WPGP WPat |
| | ***meliosmifolia*** B&SWJ 11709 | WCru |
| | ***microphylla*** | CMCN |
| | – GWJ 9252 | WCru |
| | ***monbeigii*** (Card.) Yü | GAuc GKev |
| | ***moravica*** 'Laciniata' | see *S. aucuparia* 'Beissneri' |
| § | ***munda*** | CMCN GBin |
| | aff. ***ovalis*** H 1948 | EBee |
| | 'Pearly King' | CBcs CTho MAsh WJas |
| § | 'Pink Pearl' | CDul |
| | 'Pink Veil' | NLar |
| | 'Pink-Ness' | MBlu NLar SCoo SPoG |
| | ***pogonopetala*** Koehne | GAuc |
| | ***pohuashanensis*** misapplied | see *S.* × *kewensis* |
| § | ***pohuashanensis*** (Hance) Hedlund | WPat |
| | ***porrigentiformis*** | CDul |
| | ***poteriifolia*** | GAuc GKev NHar WPat |
| | ***prattii*** misapplied | see *S. munda* |
| | ***prattii*** Koehne | EBee GKev MBri MMuc |
| | – var. ***subarachnoidea*** | see *S. munda* |
| | ***pseudovilmorinii*** | CDul GBin LRHS MBri |
| | – CLD 1437 | GAuc |
| | – MF 93044 | SSpi |
| | ***randaiensis*** | CSto GKev GQui SPlb |
| | – B&SWJ 3202 | EPfP SSpi WCru |
| | 'Red Tip' | CDul EWTr MWat |
| | ***reducta*** ♀$^{H4}$ | CBcs CEnd GAbr GAuc GBee GBin GEdr GKev GQui MBlu MMuc NHar NHol NSla SPer WDin WFar WPat |
| | ***reflexipetala*** misapplied | see *S. commixta* |
| | ***rehderiana*** misapplied | see *S. aucuparia* |
| | ***rehderiana*** Koehne | CDul CLnd |
| | ***rosea*** | GAbr GKev |
| | – 'Rosiness' | CLnd EBee EPfP MBri SCoo SLim |
| | 'Rowancroft Coral Pink' | CDul |
| | ***sambucifolia*** | GAuc SKHP |
| | ***sargentiana*** ♀$^{H4}$ | CCVT CDul CEnd CLnd CMCN CTho CTri EBee ECrN ELan EPfP GQui LAst MBlu MBri MGos MRav MSwo NLar NWea SLim SPer SPoG WDin WHCr WJas WMou |
| | ***scalaris*** ambig. | GAuc IDee MAsh MGos NWea WMou |
| § | ***scalaris*** Koehne | CBcs CCVT CDul CEnd CTho CTri EBee EPfP MBlu MGos SBfd SCoo SPer SPoG WDin WJas |
| | 'Schouten' | ECrN MGos |
| | ***scopulina*** misapplied | see *S. aucuparia* 'Fastigiata' |
| | ***simonkaiana*** | GAuc IGor |
| | ***subulata*** HWJ 925 | WCru |
| | – KWJ 12272 | WCru |
| | 'Sunshine' | CCVT CDoC CDul LTen MAsh MBri MGos MMuc NLar SEND WJas |
| § | ***thibetica*** 'John Mitchell' ♀$^{H4}$ | CAgr CDul CEnd CLnd CMCN CWib EBee EBtc ECrN EPfP MAsh MBlu MBri MGos MRav SLim SPer SPoG WFar WMou |
| | aff. ***thibetica*** BWJ 7757a | WCru |
| | ***thomsonii*** GWJ 9363 | WCru |
| § | × ***thuringiaca*** | GAuc |
| § | – 'Fastigiata' | CBcs CCVT CDul CLnd CMac CSBt EPfP MAsh MGos MMuc NEgg SCoo SEND WDin WJas |
| | ***tianschanica*** | GAuc |
| | ***torminalis*** | CAlb CCVT CDul CHab CLnd CMac CTho CTri EBee ECrN ELan EPfP MBlu MBri MGos MMuc MRav MSnd NLar NWea SCoo SEND SEWo SLPl SPer SPoG WFar WHar WMou |
| | ***umbellata*** var. ***cretica*** | see *S. graeca* |
| | ***ursina*** | see *S. foliolosa* |
| | × ***vagensis*** | CLnd WMou |
| § | ***vestita*** | CLnd CTho EPfP MBlu |
| | ***vexans*** | CDul GBin |
| | ***vilmorinii*** ♀$^{H4}$ | Widely available |
| | – 'Robusta' | see *S.* 'Pink Pearl' |
| | aff. ***vilmorinii*** | GKin |
| | ***wardii*** | CBcs CDul CLnd CTho EPfP MBlu |
| | 'White Swan' | ECrN NLar |
| | 'White Wax' | CDul EBee EPfP LAst MGos SGol SPer SPoG WDin WPat |
| | 'Wilfrid Fox' | CLnd EBee SLPl |
| | ***wilmottiana*** | CDul |
| | ***wilsoniana*** | CLnd GQui |
| | 'Wisley Gold' | CWSG EBee LRHS MAsh MGos SCoo SLim SPoG WHCr WMou |

## *Sorghastrum* (*Poaceae*)

| |  |  |
|---|---|---|
| | ***avenaceum*** | see *S. nutans* |
| § | ***nutans*** | CKno CRWN CWCL LEdu SMad SPhx |

- 'Indian Steel' CMHG EBee ECha GQue SDix WWEG XLum

## sorrel, common see *Rumex acetosa*

## sorrel, French see *Rumex scutatus*

## *Souliea* see *Actaea*

## *Sparaxis* (*Iridaceae*)

***auriculata*** 'Vanrhynsdorp' ECho
***bulbifera*** ECho
***fragrans*** 'Napier' ECho
***grandiflora*** subsp. ***acutiloba*** ECho
- subsp. ***fimbriata*** ECho
- subsp. ***grandiflora*** CGrW ECho WCot
- subsp. ***violacea*** 'Botriver' ECho
hybrids LAma
***meterlekampiae*** 'Piekenierskloof' ECho
- 'Rawsonville' ECho
***parviflora*** ECho
'Red Reflex' ECho
***tricolor*** ECho SDeJ
***variegata*** (v) ECho
***villosa*** ECho

## *Sparganium* (*Sparganiaceae*)

§ ***erectum*** CRow CWat EHon LPBA NMir NPer SWat WMAq WSFF
***ramosum*** see *S. erectum*

## *Sparrmannia* (*Malvaceae*)

***africana*** ♀H1 CBcs CHEx CHll EAmu EShb LRHS MBri SEND SPav SVen
- 'Flore Pleno' (d) **new** CBcs

## *Spathipappus* see *Tanacetum*

## *Spartina* (*Poaceae*)

'Dafken' EBee
***patens*** EPPr
***pectinata*** CHar SGol XLum
- 'Aureomarginata' (v) Widely available

## *Spartium* (*Papilionaceae*)

***junceum*** ♀H4 CArn CBcs CDoC CDul CEnd CTri ECrN ELan ELon EMil EPfP GCal LAst MGos MMuc MSCN MWat NSti SBfd SDix SEND SGar SPer SPoG SRms WDin XSen
- 'Brockhill Compact' CDoC IVic LRHS

## *Spartocytisus* see *Cytisus*

## *Spathantheum* (*Araceae*)

***orbignyanum*** WCot

## *Spathodea* (*Bignoniaceae*)

***campanulata*** SPlb

## spearmint see *Mentha spicata*

## *Speirantha* (*Asparagaceae*)

§ ***convallarioides*** CDes CGHE CLAP CPom EBee ECho ELon EPPr EPfP LEdu MNrw WCot WCru WPGP
***gardenii*** see *S. convallarioides*

## *Sphacele* see *Lepechinia*

## *Sphaeralcea* (*Malvaceae*)

***ambigua*** SPlb
'Childerley' CSpe LHop MCot SAga SMrm SPoG WCot
***coccinea*** SPlb WCot
***fendleri*** CBot CHll
- subsp. ***venusta*** LHop
'Hopleys Lavender' CSBt EBee LAst LHop LSou SAga SWvt
'Hyde Hall' ELan
***incana*** CSpe LHop LSou SAga WCot
***malviflora*** CDTJ
***miniata*** CCCN CHll SAga SMrm
***munroana*** CBot CDTJ CPom CSev ECGP ELan SAga SRkn WSHC
- pale pink-flowered ECtt
* - 'Shell Pink' CSpe ECGP
'Newleaze Coral' CSBt CWGN EBee ECtt EWld LBMP LHop LSou MAsh SAga SPad SPoG SRkn SUsu SWvt WCot
'Newleaze Pink' LHop SAga SRkn
***obtusiloba*** SAga
***remota*** CPLG EBee SPlb WBox
***rivularis*** EBee WBox
***umbellata*** see *Phymosia umbellata*

## *Sphaeromeria* (*Asteraceae*)

§ ***capitata*** CPBP NWCA

## *Spigelia* (*Loganiaceae*)

***marilandica*** EBee SKHP
- 'Red Feather' **new** NDov NLar
- 'White Feather' **new** WHil
- 'Wisley Jester' CSpr SBrt SChF SCoo SKHP

## *Spilanthes* (*Asteraceae*)

***acmella*** misapplied see *Acmella oleracea*
***oleracea*** see *Acmella oleracea*

## *Spiloxene* (*Hypoxidaceae*)

***canaliculata*** 'Kamiesberg' ECho
***capensis*** 'Somerset West' ECho
***minuta*** 'Nay' ECho
***serrata*** 'Saldanha' ECho

## *Spiraea* (*Rosaceae*)

SDR 6047 GKev
'Abigail' CDoC
***albiflora*** see *S. japonica* var. *albiflora*
***arborea*** see *Sorbaria kirilowii*
§ 'Arguta' ♀H4 Widely available
× ***arguta*** 'Bridal Wreath' see *S.* 'Arguta'
***bella*** SLon WTin
***betulifolia*** GKin MRav WDin
- var. ***aemiliana*** CBot EBee ECtt MMuc SBrd SLPl WFar
- 'Tor' EPPr
× ***billardii*** misapplied see *S.* × *pseudosalicifolia*
× ***bumalda*** 'Wulfenii' see *S. japonica* 'Walluf'
***callosa*** 'Alba' see *S. japonica* var. *albiflora*
***canescens*** CPLG GKin
- AC 1354 MSnd
§ ***cantoniensis*** SLon
'Flore Pleno' (d)
- 'Lanceata' see *S. cantoniensis* 'Flore Pleno'

| | | |
|---|---|---|
| | × ***cinerea*** 'Grefsheim' 🏆[H4] | CDoC CSBt EBee MBri MGos SEND SGol SLim SPer SPlb WDin |
| | ***crispifolia*** | see *S. japonica* 'Bullata' |
| | ***douglasii*** | CMac GAuc |
| | ***formosana*** B&SWJ 1597 | CPLG WCru |
| § | × ***foxii*** | SLPl |
| | ***fritschiana*** | CMac SLPl SLon |
| | ***hayatana*** | SLon |
| | - RWJ 10014 | WCru |
| | ***hendersonii*** | see *Petrophytum hendersonii* |
| | ***japonica*** | WFar |
| § | - var. ***albiflora*** | CBcs CDul CMac CSBt CTri CWib ELan ELon EPfP LRHS MAsh MGos MMuc MRav MSwo MWat NEgg NPri NWad SBfd SEND SGol SLim SPad SPer SRms SWvt WDin WFar WMoo |
| | - 'Alpina' | see *S. japonica* 'Nana' |
| | - 'Alpine Gold' | GBin NPro |
| | - 'Anthony Waterer' (v) | Widely available |
| | - 'Barkby Gold' | MGos |
| | - 'Blenheim' | SRms |
| § | - 'Bullata' | CFee CMac EPot GEdr NLar NWCA SRms WAbe |
| | - 'Candlelight' 🏆[H4] | CSBt EBee EPfP GKin LAst LRHS MAsh MBri MGos NCGa NEgg NHol NLar SCoo SGol SLim SPer SPoG SWvt WMoo |
| | - 'Crispa' | EPfP NPro WFar WGrn WMoo |
| | - 'Dart's Red' 🏆[H4] | GKin IVic WFar |
| | - 'Firelight' | Widely available |
| § | - 'Genpei' | CMac SGol SPer |
| | - 'Gold Mound' | CBar CMac CPLG CWSG CWib EBee EHoe ELan EPfP LBMP LRHS MAsh MGos MMuc MRav MSwo NHol NLar SCoo SEND SLim SPer SPlb SRms WDin WFar WHar |
| | - Golden Princess = 'Lisp'[PBR] 🏆[H4] | CMac CTri EPfP LBuc LRHS MAsh MGos NEgg NPri SCoo SGol SRms SSta WCFE WDin WFar WMoo |
| | - 'Goldflame' | Widely available |
| | - 'Jacobsen's Goldflame' | IVic |
| | - 'Little Princess' | CBar CBcs CDul CMac CWSG CWib EBee ECrN EShb LRHS MAsh MRav MSwo NHol NWea SBfd SCoo SGol SLim SPer SRGP SRms SSta STre SWvt WDin WFar WHar WMoo |
| § | - 'Macrophylla' | WGrn WPat |
| | - Magic Carpet = 'Walbuma'[PBR] (v) 🏆[H4] | EBee EPfP LBuc LRHS MAsh MMuc NLar SCoo SEND SPoG |
| | - 'Magnifica' | see *S. japonica* 'Macrophylla' |
| § | - 'Nana' 🏆[H4] | CMac CSBt ECho GEdr MAsh MRav SRms |
| | - 'Nyewoods' | see *S. japonica* 'Nana' |
| | - 'Shiburi' | see *S. japonica* var. *albiflora* |
| N | - 'Shirobana' misapplied | see *S. japonica* 'Genpei' |
| N | - 'Shirobana' | see *S. japonica* var. *albiflora* |
| | - 'Snow Cap' | CWib |
| § | - 'Walluf' | CMac CTri CWib |
| | - 'White Cloud' | ELan |
| | - 'White Gold'[PBR] | CSBt ELan EPfP LAst LRHS LSqu MAsh MBri NHol NPro NWad SBrd SCoo SLim SPer SPoG SWvt WHar WMoo |
| | ***latifolia*** | MMuc SEND |
| | 'Margaritae' | SPer SWvt |
| | ***micrantha*** | CPLG |
| | ***nipponica*** | CBcs |
| | - 'Halward's Silver' | MRav NPro SLPl |
| § | - 'Snowmound' 🏆[H4] | Widely available |
| | - var. ***tosaensis*** misapplied | see *S. nipponica* 'Snowmound' |
| | - var. ***tosaensis*** (Yatabe) Makino | LHop |
| | ***palmata*** 'Elegans' | see *Filipendula purpurea* 'Elegans' |
| | ***prunifolia*** (d) | CMac ECrN ELan LRHS MBlu MRav SPer SPoG WCFE WDin WGrn WPat |
| | × ***pseudosalicifolia*** 'Triumphans' | MMuc SEND |
| | ***salicifolia*** | MMuc WFar |
| | 'Summersnow' | SLPl |
| | 'Superba' | see *S.* × *foxii* |
| | ***tarokoensis*** | GAuc |
| | ***thunbergii*** 🏆[H4] | CDul CTri CWib EBee ECrN EPfP MMuc MRav NWea SBfd SCoo SEND SGol SLim SRms WDin |
| | - 'Aurea' | MAsh |
| | - 'Fujino Pink' | WDin |
| | - 'Golden Times' | LRHS SPoG |
| | - 'Mellow Yellow' | see *S. thunbergii* 'Ōgon' |
| | - 'Mount Fuji' | CMac CWib EHoe MMuc MRav NPro WFar |
| § | - 'Ōgon' | WFar |
| | ***ulmaria*** | see *Filipendula ulmaria* |
| | × ***vanhouttei*** | CBcs CDul CTri EBee EPfP MMuc MRav MSwo SEND SLim SPer SRms WDin WFar |
| | - 'Gold Fountain' | CWSG EShb GBin NHol SCoo SPoG WFar WRHF |
| | - 'Pink Ice' (v) | CDoC CWib EBee EHoe EPfP LAst LBMP LRHS MAsh MGos MMuc MRav SBfd SBrd SPer SPlb SPoG SWvt WDin WFar |
| | ***veitchii*** | MRav |
| | ***venusta*** 'Magnifica' | see *Filipendula rubra* 'Venusta' |

## *Spiranthes* (*Orchidaceae*)

| | | |
|---|---|---|
| | ***cernua*** | NGdn |
| | - var. ***odorata*** | LSou |
| | - - 'Chadd's Ford' | Widely available |
| | ***spiralis*** | NLAp WHer |

## *Spodiopogon* (*Poaceae*)

| | | |
|---|---|---|
| | ***sibiricus*** | CKno EBee EHoe EPPr LEdu SMad |

## *Sporobolus* (*Poaceae*)

| | | |
|---|---|---|
| | ***airoides*** | CKno EBee EHoe EPPr EShb GCal MWea SMad WHrl |
| | ***heterolepis*** | CKno EBee EHoe EShb GCal NDov SMad SMea SPhx |
| | - 'Cloud' | GBin |
| I | - 'Wisconsin Strain' | EPPr |
| | ***wrightii*** | EBee EPPr MWhi SPhx |

## *Sprekelia* (*Amaryllidaceae*)

| | | |
|---|---|---|
| | ***formosissima*** | CFir CSpe ECho LAma LEdu SPav |

## *Stachys* ✿ (*Lamiaceae*)

| | | |
|---|---|---|
| | ***aethiopica*** 'Danielle' | see *S. thunbergii* 'Danielle' |
| § | ***affinis*** | CArn CFir GPoy LEdu SVic |
| | ***albens*** | EBla IFro XSen |
| | ***albotomentosa*** | CMea EBla MDKP WCot WWlt |
| | ***balcanica*** | CDes EBee GKev |
| | - MESE | WPGP |
| | ***betonica*** | see *S. officinalis* |
| § | ***byzantina*** | Widely available |
| § | - 'Big Ears' | Widely available |
| § | - 'Cotton Boll' | COlW EBee ECha GCal SBch WFar WWEG XLum |

| |  |  |
|---|---|---|
| | - 'Countess Helen von Stein' | see *S. byzantina* 'Big Ears' |
| | - gold-leaved | see *S. byzantina* 'Primrose Heron' |
| | - large-leaved | see *S. byzantina* 'Big Ears' |
| | - 'Limelight' | WCot XLum |
| § | - 'Primrose Heron' | EBee ECha GBee GKev LRHS MRav MSpe NBid NLar NOrc NSti SMrm [illegible] WFar XLum |
| | - 'Sheila McQueen' | see *S. byzantina* 'Cotton Boll' |
| | - 'Silky Fleece' | EBee ECha EPfP EShb EWTr LRHS NBre SBfd WWEG XSen |
| | - 'Silver Carpet' | CBar CBcs COlW EBee ECha EHoe EPfP EWTr GMaP LAst LRHS LSRN MCot MRav NOrc NSti SPer SRms SWat SWvt WCAu WCot WFar WHoo WMnd WWEG XLum |
| § | - 'Striped Phantom' (v) | EBla |
| | - 'Variegata' | see *S. byzantina* 'Striped Phantom' |
| | ***chamissonis*** | EBee |
| | var. ***cooleyae*** | |
| | ***citrina*** | CMea GCal XSen |
| | ***coccinea*** | ECtt MCot SBch SPav WMoo |
| | ***cretica*** | XSen |
| | - subsp. ***salviifolia*** | XSen |
| | ***densiflora*** | see *S. monieri* (Gouan) P.W. Ball |
| § | ***discolor*** | CMea EBee IKil MDKP NLar |
| | ***germanica*** | EBee NBre SEND |
| | - subsp. ***bithynica*** | SMrm |
| | ***glutinosa*** | MDKP XSen |
| | ***grandiflora*** | see *S. macrantha* |
| | ***heraclea*** | LRHS |
| | 'Hidalgo' | CSpe SAga |
| | ***lanata*** | see *S. byzantina* |
| | ***lavandulifolia*** | WAbe XSen |
| § | ***macrantha*** | CAby CHar CKno CMac COlW CTri EBee ECha GKev LEdu LRHS LSRN MCot MLHP MMuc MWat NBir NOrc NSti SGar SPhx SRms STes SWat WCot WFar WTin WWEG |
| * | - 'Alba' | EBee ECha |
| | - 'Hummelo' | see *S. officinalis* 'Hummelo' |
| | - 'Morning Blush' **new** | WPer |
| * | - 'Nivea' | CSam ELan MMHG NBir |
| | - 'Robusta' ♀H4 | CDes ELan GCal LRHS MMuc NBro NGdn SMrm WCot WWEG |
| | - 'Rosea' | CElw CMHG EBee ELan GBee GMaP LLWP LRHS MArl MLHP SPlb SWat WCFE WPer |
| | - 'Superba' | CPrp CSpe EBee EBla ECtt EPfP GCra GKev GMaP LAst LBMP LEdu LRHS MAvo MMHG MRav MWhi NBPC NEgg SPer SWvt WBor WCot WFar WMnd WMoo WPtf XLum |
| | - 'Violacea' | EBee LRHS MAvo MBrN NChi WCot |
| | ***mexicana*** misapplied | see *S. thunbergii* |
| | ***monieri*** misapplied | see *S. officinalis* |
| | ***monieri*** ambig. | CAbP CMMP EBee EShb GKev LBMP MSCN NLar NSti |
| | - white-flowered | CSpe GKev |
| § | ***monieri*** (Gouan) P.W. Ball | CEnt GBin LEdu LRHS |
| * | - 'Rosea' | EBee LEdu NBre NDov NLar |
| | ***nivea*** | see *S. discolor* |
| | ***obliqua*** | NBre |
| § | ***officinalis*** | CArn CCVN CEnt CHab CPrp CRWN CSev CWan EBee EWil GPoy LEdu MCot MHer MMuc MNHC NLan NMir WCot WHer WHfH WJek |
| | - SDR 3554 | GKev |
| | - 'Alba' | CArn CPrp EBee LEdu MMuc NBro STes WCAu WFar WTin |
| | - dwarf | LRHS |
| | - dwarf, white-flowered | GCal |
| § | - 'Hummelo' | CPrp CSam EBee ECtt ELon EPPr EPfP GAbr GQue IKil LHop LPla LRHS LSou MDKP MLLN MRav NBPC NDov NLar SAga SMrm SPhx SUsu WCAu WFar WPtf WWEG [illegible] |
| | - mauve-flowered | WTin |
| | - 'Rosea' | CCVN CMea GCal GQue NBro STes WFar WSHC WTin WWEG |
| | - 'Rosea Superba' | EBee ECha MDKP MLLN NBre WCAu WCot WFar |
| | - 'Saharan Pink' | CMHG EBee EPfP LRHS LSou MHer MMuc WOut WWEG |
| | - 'Spitzenberg' | SUsu |
| | - 'Wisley White' | EBee GQue LRHS NPri WCot |
| | ***olympica*** | see *S. byzantina* |
| | ***ossetica*** | CDes EBee |
| | ***palustris*** | CArn CHab LLWG LPBA MMuc NLan NLar NMir SEND |
| | - from Islay, Hebrides | SEND |
| | ***recta*** | CEnt NLar WCAu |
| | ***scardica*** MESE 362 | MDKP |
| | ***setifera*** | EBla NBre |
| | ***spicata*** | see *S. macrantha* |
| | ***stricta*** | LRHS |
| | - 'Alba' **new** | LRHS |
| | ***swainsonii*** | XSen |
| | ***sylvatica*** | CArn CHab NLan NMir WHer WSFF |
| | - 'Huskers' (v) | NBre |
| | ***thirkei*** | XSen |
| § | ***thunbergii*** | CDes CSam EShb LEdu MBrN MDKP MSpe MWhi SBch SPhx SUsu WCot WOut WPGP |
| § | - 'Danielle' | CSam EBee ECtt LHop LIMB LRHS LSRN MHer NBre SRkn WMoo |
| | ***tuberifera*** | see *S. affinis* |

## *Stachyurus* (*Stachyuraceae*)

| |  |  |
|---|---|---|
| | B&SWJ 11508 from Yakushima Island, Japan | WCru |
| | ***chinensis*** | CBcs CMCN CPMA CTri CWib IArd MGos NLar SMad SPoG |
| | - 'Celina' | CPMA GKin LRHS MBlu NLar |
| | - 'Goldbeater' | NLar |
| | - 'Joy Forever' (v) | CBcs CDoC CDul CEnd CMCN CMac EBee EMil EPfP IArd IVic LLHF LRHS LSRN MBri MGos NLar SKHP SLim SPoG SSpi SSta SWvt |
| | - 'Senna' **new** | LRHS |
| | ***himalaicus*** | NLar |
| | - HWJCM 009 | WCru |
| | - HWJK 2035 | WCru |
| | aff. ***himalaicus*** HWJK 2052 | WCru |
| | 'Magpie' (v) | CPMA EPfP MBri NLar SAga WCru |
| | ***praecox*** ♀H4 | Widely available |
| | - B&SWJ 8898 | WCru |
| | - B&SWJ 10899 | WCru |
| | - var. ***leucotrichus*** | CPMA NLar |
| | - var. ***matsuzakii*** | CPMA NLar |
| | - - B&SWJ 2817 | WCru |
| | - - B&SWJ 11229 | WCru |
| | - - 'Issai' **new** | SSta |
| | - 'Oriental Sun' **new** | MBri |
| | - 'Petra' | CPMA |
| | ***retusus*** | CPLG NLar |
| | 'Rubriflorus' | CPMA ELan EPfP LRHS MAsh MBri NLar SChF WFar WPGP |
| | ***salicifolius*** | CBcs CGHE CPLG CPMA IDee MBri NLar SKHP SSpi WPGP WPat |

| | |
|---|---|
| ***sigeyosii*** | SBrd |
| - B&SWJ 6915 | WCru |
| - CWJ 12420 | WCru |
| - RWJ 10094 | WCru |
| aff. ***szechuanensis*** | CPLG |
| - - BWJ 8153 | WCru |
| ***yunnanensis*** | CPMA NLar SSpi WSHC |

## *Stanleya* (*Brassicaceae*)

| | |
|---|---|
| ***pinnata*** | SBrt |

## *Stapelia* (*Apocynaceae*)

| | |
|---|---|
| ***arenosa*** new | LToo |
| ***divaricata*** new | LToo |
| ***gettliffei*** | LToo |
| ***glanduliflora*** new | LToo |
| ***leendertziae*** | LToo |
| ***marmoratum*** | see *Orbea variegata* |
| ***variegata*** | see *Orbea variegata* |

## *Staphylea* ✿ (*Staphyleaceae*)

| | |
|---|---|
| ***bolanderi*** | CBcs |
| ***bumalda*** | CPMA NLar |
| - B&SWJ 11053 | WCru |
| ***colchica*** | CBcs CDul CHll CMCN CPMA EBtc ELan EPfP EWTr EWes LRHS MGos MMHG NPal SMad SPer WDin WKif WPat WSHC |
| ***holocarpa*** | CPMA EPfP MRav WFar |
| - 'Innocence' | CDul NLar |
| N - var. ***rosea*** | CPMA EPfP SMad |
| N - 'Rosea' | CBcs CPMA MBlu NLar SSpi |
| ***pinnata*** | CAgr CPMA EBtc EPfP IVic NLar SEND SMad |
| ***trifolia*** | CBcs CPMA NEgg |

## *Statice* see *Limonium*

## *Stauntonia* (*Lardizabalaceae*)

| | |
|---|---|
| B&SWJ 8223 | WCru |
| aff. ***chinensis*** DJHV 06175 | WCru |
| ***hexaphylla*** | CBcs CDoC CHEx CHll CSam CTri CWGN EBee EPfP LRHS MAsh NLar SAdn SKHP SPer SPoG SSpi SSta WSHC |
| - B&SWJ 4858 | WCru |
| ***leucantha*** KWJ 12218 | WCru |
| ***obovatifoliola*** B&SWJ 3685 | WCru |
| - CWJ 12353 | WCru |
| ***purpurea*** | NLar |
| - B&SWJ 3690 | WCru |
| ***yaoshanensis*** B&SWJ 8223 | WCru |
| - HWJ 1024 | WCru |

## *Stegnogramma* (*Thelypteridaceae*)

| | |
|---|---|
| ***pozoi*** | EFer |

## *Stellaria* (*Caryophyllaceae*)

| | |
|---|---|
| ***graminea*** | CHab |
| ***holostea*** | CArn CHab CRWN MNHC NBir NMir WShi |

## *Stemmacantha* (*Asteraceae*)

| | |
|---|---|
| ***carthamoides*** | CArn |
| § ***centaureoides*** | ECGP ECha EPPr GAbr GCal GQue LPla NBid SPhx SUsu |

## *Stenanthium* (*Melanthiaceae*)

| | |
|---|---|
| ***gramineum*** | EWes |
| ***robustum*** | WPGP |

## *Stenochlaena* (*Blechnaceae*)

| | |
|---|---|
| ***tenuifolia*** | WRic |

## *Stenomesson* (*Amaryllidaceae*)

| | |
|---|---|
| § ***miniatum*** | WCot |
| ***pearcei*** | ECho WCot |
| ***variegatum*** | WCot |
| - yellow-flowered | WCot |

## *Stenotaphrum* (*Poaceae*)

| | |
|---|---|
| ***secundatum*** | EShb |
| - 'Variegatum' (v) ♀H1 | EShb LSou |

## *Stephanandra* (*Rosaceae*)

| | |
|---|---|
| ***chinensis*** | SLon |
| ***incisa*** | CBcs CPLG |
| § - 'Crispa' | CDoC CDul CMac CTri EBee ELan EPfP EShb EWTr GKin LAst LHop LTen MBlu MRav NEgg NHol NLar SPer WCFE WDin WFar WMoo |
| - 'Dart's Horizon' | SLPl |
| - 'Prostrata' | see *S. incisa* 'Crispa' |
| ***tanakae*** | CBcs CDoC CDul CMac CPLG CTri EBee ELan EPfP EWTr LAst MBlu MRav NEgg SLPl SLon SPer WDin WFar |

## *Stephania* (*Menispermaceae*)

| | |
|---|---|
| ***longa*** KWJ 12163 | WCru |
| ***rotunda*** B&SWJ 2396 | WCru |
| ***sinica*** BWJ 8094 | WCru |
| aff. ***tetrandra*** WWJ 11896 | WCru |

## *Stephanotis* (*Apocynaceae*)

| | |
|---|---|
| ***floribunda*** ♀H1 | CBcs CCCN EBak MBri MOWG |

## *Sterculia* (*Malvaceae*)

| | |
|---|---|
| ***rupestris*** | see *Brachychiton rupestris* |

## *Sternbergia* (*Amaryllidaceae*)

| | |
|---|---|
| 'Autumn Gold' | ECho LAma |
| ***candida*** | CBro |
| ***fischeriana*** | CBro GKev |
| ***greuteriana*** | EPot LWst |
| ***lutea*** | CBro CPBP ECha ECho EPot ERCP EWes LAma LRHS NWCA SChF SDeJ SDix SPhx WTin |
| - Angustifolia Group | CBro CDes CMea WCot |
| ***sicula*** | CBro ECho EPot GKev NRya |
| - from Dodona, Greece | LWst |
| - 'Arcadian Sun' | ECho GKev LWst |
| - var. ***graeca*** | ECho |
| - - from Crete | ECho |
| - 'John Marr' | WThu |

## *Stevia* (*Asteraceae*)

| | |
|---|---|
| ***rebaudiana*** | CArn EOHP GPoy MDKP WCot WJek |

## *Stewartia* ✿ (*Theaceae*)

| | |
|---|---|
| ***gemmata*** | see *S. sinensis* |
| 'Korean Splendor' | see *S. pseudocamellia* Koreana Group |
| ***koreana*** | see *S. pseudocamellia* Koreana Group |
| ***malacodendron*** ♀H4 | EPfP SSpi |
| ***monadelpha*** | CMen LLHF MPkF NLar SSpi |
| ***ovata*** | SSpi |

| | |
|---|---|
| ***pseudocamellia*** ♀H4 | Widely available |
| – B&SWJ 11044 from North Japan new | WCru |
| § – Koreana Group ♀H4 | CDul CEnd CMCN EPfP GAuc LRHS NLar SSpi WDin WFar |
| – 'Ogisu' | NLar |
| ***pteropetiolata*** B&SWJ 11726 | WCru |
| – WWJ 11939 | WCru |
| ***rostrata*** | CBcs CPMA ELan EPfP IArd IDee MBlu MPkF NLar SSpi WCru |
| ***serrata*** | CMen CPMA MPkF |
| § ***sinensis*** ♀H4 | CBcs CPMA EPfP LRHS MBlu NLar NMun SSpi |

## *Stigmaphyllon* (*Malpighiaceae*)

| | |
|---|---|
| ***ciliatum*** | CCCN |
| ***littorale*** | CCCN |

## *Stipa* (*Poaceae*)

| | |
|---|---|
| F&M 248 | WPGP |
| ***arundinacea*** | see *Anemanthele lessoniana* |
| ***barbata*** | CAby CKno CSpe ECha EPPr EWes SApp SPer SPhx SUsu WKif |
| * ***boysterica*** | CFee |
| ***brachytricha*** | see *Calamagrostis brachytricha* |
| § ***calamagrostis*** | Widely available |
| – 'Algau' | GBin WCot |
| – 'Lemperg' | EPPr NDov |
| ***canescens*** | SPhx |
| ***capillata*** | EBee EPPr GCal MWhi |
| – 'Brautschleier' | CWib SWal WNew WPtf |
| * – 'Lace Veil' | MLLN |
| ***comata*** | EBee MSnd |
| ***elegantissima*** | CKno EHoe SHDw |
| ***extremiorientalis*** | CKno ECha EPPr MRav SMad |
| * ***gerardi*** | SApp |
| ***gigantea*** ♀H4 | Widely available |
| – 'Gold Fontaene' | CDes CElw CFir CKno EBee EPPr EWes LRHS MAvo MMoz MNrw NDov SBch SMad SPhx SUsu WCot WMoo WPGP WWEG |
| – 'Pixie' | NWsh SApp SPhx |
| ***grandis*** | CKno ECha EPPr GBin WMoo WPer |
| ***ichu*** | CKno MAvo SDix |
| – F&M 32 | WPGP |
| ***joannis*** | GCal |
| ***lasiagrostis*** | see *S. calamagrostis* |
| ***lessingiana*** | CPLG EBee EHoe EHul EPPr LRHS NCGa SBfd SEND WMoo |
| ***neomexicana*** | SPhx |
| ***offneri*** | EBee EPPr EWes LRHS SSvw |
| ***pennata*** | CKno CSpe EBee EPPr LRHS SBfd |
| § ***poeppigiana*** | GCal |
| ***pontica*** | SPhx |
| ***pseudoichu*** | MAvo WBox WCot |
| – RCB/Arg Y-1 | EBee ECGP ELon NCGa |
| ***pulcherrima*** | EBee EPPr GAbr GCal LBMP LRHS |
| – subsp. ***pulcherrima*** | SPhx |
| – 'Windfeder' | CFir |
| ***ramosissima*** | CKno |
| ***robusta*** | EBee EPPr SPhx |
| ***splendens*** misapplied | see *S. calamagrostis* |
| ***splendens*** Trin. | WFoF |
| ***stenophylla*** | see *S. tirsa* |
| ***tenacissima*** | EBee EHul LSRN SUsu WDin |
| ***tenuifolia*** misapplied | see *S. tenuissima* |
| ***tenuifolia*** Steud. | CHar CMea EBee EHul EPfP LRHS MBri MRav NBir NBro NOak NSti WHal WMoo XLum XSen |
| § ***tenuissima*** | Widely available |
| – 'Wind Whispers' | CSpe GBin MLLN NCGa SBfd |
| § ***tirsa*** | EPPr SPhx |
| ***turkestanica*** | EBee SBfd SUsu SWal SWat |
| ***ucrainica*** | EPPr |
| ***verticillata*** | CKno |

## *Stokesia* ✿ (*Asteraceae*)

| | |
|---|---|
| 'Color Wheel' new | IPot |
| ***cyanea*** | see *S. laevis* |
| § ***laevis*** | CPrp EBee ECGP ECha EPfP EWTr LRHS MMuc NBPC NLar SEND SMrm SPet SPlb WCAu WFar WHrl WMoo WPGP WPer WWEG XLum |
| – 'Alba' | CCVN CMMP COIW EBee ECha ELan EPfP EPri LEdu LRHS MRav NPnk SPer SPhx STes |
| – 'Blue Star' | CBcs COIW CSam CWGN EBee ELan ELon EPfP GBin LAst LBMP LEdu LRHS MBri MRav NHol NPnk NPri SAga SBfd SPad SPer SPhx SRot SWvt WHoo WMnd WMoo WSHC |
| – 'Klaus Jelitto' | CFwr EBee IPot LBuc LEdu LRHS SBrd SHar SPoG |
| – 'Mary Gregory' | Widely available |
| – mixed | CPou MLLN |
| – 'Omega Skyrocket' | CPou EBee GBin NHol NLar SMrm WFar WWEG |
| – 'Peach Melba' | EBee ECtt NCGa NLar WMoo |
| – 'Peachie's Pick' | NLar |
| – 'Purple Parasols' | Widely available |
| – 'Silver Moon' | CAbP COIW EAEE EBee ECtt EPfP EShb IPot LAst LRHS MTPN NBir NHol SMrm SPoG STes WAul WFar WWEG |
| § – 'Träumerei' | CWGN EAEE EBee EPfP GGar LAst LRHS NHol NLar SBfd SMrm SPet SPoG WMnd WMoo WPer WWEG |
| – 'White Star' | see *S. laevis* 'Träumerei' |

## *Stranvaesia* see *Photinia*

## × *Stranvinia* see *Photinia*

## *Stratiotes* (*Hydrocharitaceae*)

| | |
|---|---|
| ***aloides*** | CBen CWat EHon EWil LPBA MWts NPer SVic SWat WMAq WPnP |

## strawberry see *Fragaria*

## *Strelitzia* (*Strelitziaceae*)

| | |
|---|---|
| ***alba*** | CCCN EAmu NPla |
| ***juncea*** | XBlo |
| ***nicolai*** | CAbb CDTJ EAmu LPal NPer SPlb XBlo |
| ***reginae*** ♀H1 | CAbb CBcs ELan EShb LPal LRHS MREP NPal NPer NPla SArc SBig SChr SEND SPlb SRms XBlo |
| – 'Kirstenbosch Gold' | XBlo |

## *Streptocarpella* see *Streptocarpus*

## *Streptocarpus* ✿ (*Gesneriaceae*)

| | |
|---|---|
| 'Albatross' ♀H1 | WDib |
| 'Alice' | WDib |
| 'Alissa' | WDib |
| 'Amanda' Dibley ♀H1 | WDib |
| 'Amanda'[PBR] Fleischle (Marleen Series) | WDib |

| | |
|---|---|
| 'Anne' | CSpe WDib |
| 'Athena' | WDib |
| 'Awena' | WDib |
| ***baudertii*** | WDib |
| 'Beryl' | WDib |
| 'Bethan' ♀H1 | WDib |
| 'Bianca' **new** | WDib |
| 'Black Gardenia' | WDib |
| 'Black Panther' | EShb WDib |
| 'Blue Bird' | SBrm |
| 'Blue Gem' | WDib |
| 'Blue Heaven' | SBrm |
| 'Blue Moon' | WDib |
| 'Blue Nymph' | WDib |
| § 'Blue Upstart' | SBrm |
| 'Blushing Bride' (d) | WDib |
| * 'Boysenberry Delight' | WDib |
| 'Branwen' | WDib |
| 'Brimstone' | SBrm |
| 'Bristol's Black Bird' | WDib |
| 'Bristol's Very Best' | WDib |
| 'Buttons' | SBrm |
| ***caeruleus*** | WDib |
| 'Caitlin' | WDib |
| ***candidus*** | WDib |
| 'Carol' | WDib |
| 'Carolyn Ann' | SBrm |
| 'Carys' ♀H1 | WDib |
| 'Catrin' ♀H1 | WDib |
| ***caulescens*** | WDib |
| – var. ***pallescens*** | EOHP WDib |
| 'Charlotte' | EShb SBrm WDib |
| 'Chloe' | WDib |
| 'Chorus Line' ♀H1 | WDib |
| 'Christine' | SBrm |
| 'Clouds' | CSpe |
| 'Concord Blue' | WDib |
| 'Constant Nymph' | WDib |
| 'Copper Knob' | SBrm |
| 'Coral Flair' | WDib |
| 'Crystal Beauty' | WDib |
| 'Crystal Blush' | WDib |
| 'Crystal Charm' | WDib |
| 'Crystal Dawn' | WDib |
| 'Crystal Ice' PBR ♀H1 | WDib |
| 'Crystal Snow' | WDib |
| 'Crystal Wonder' | WDib |
| ***cyaneus*** | WDib |
| – subsp. ***polackii*** | WDib |
| 'Cynthia' ♀H1 | WDib |
| 'Dainty Lady' | SBrm |
| 'Daphne' ♀H1 | WDib |
| 'Dark Eyes Mary' | SBrm |
| 'Denim' **new** | WDib |
| ***denticulatus*** | WDib |
| 'Diana' | WDib |
| 'Dinas' | WDib |
| 'Dreamtime' | SBrm |
| ***dunnii*** | WDib |
| 'Elegance' | SBrm |
| 'Elizabeth' | SBrm |
| 'Ella' | SBrm |
| 'Ella Mae' | SBrm |
| 'Ellie' | WDib |
| 'Elsi' | WDib |
| 'Emily' | WDib |
| 'Emma' | WDib |
| 'Falling Stars' ♀H1 | CSpe WDib |
| 'Festival Wales' | WDib |
| 'Fiona' | WDib |
| ***floribundus*** hort. | WDib |
| 'Frances' | SBrm |
| 'Franken Alison' | SBrm |
| 'Franken Jenny' | SBrm |
| 'Franken Kelly' | SBrm |
| 'Franken Misty Blue' | SBrm |
| 'Franken Texas Sunset' | SBrm |
| 'Frosty Diamond' | WDib |
| ***gardenii*** | WDib |
| 'Gillian' | SBrm |
| ***glandulosissimus*** ♀H1 | EOHP WDib |
| 'Gloria' ♀H1 | CSpe WDib |
| 'Gower Daybreak' | SBrm |
| 'Gower Garnet' | SBrm |
| 'Gower Midnight' | SBrm |
| 'Gwen' | WDib |
| 'Hannah' | WDib |
| 'Hannah Ellis' | SBrm |
| 'Happy Snappy' ♀H1 | WDib |
| 'Harlequin Blue' **new** | WDib |
| 'Harriet' **new** | WDib |
| 'Heidi' ♀H1 | WDib |
| 'Helen' ♀H1 | WDib |
| 'Hope' | WDib |
| 'Huge White' | CSpe |
| 'Ida' | SBrm |
| 'Inky Fingers' | SBrm |
| 'Iona' | WDib |
| 'Izzy' | SBrm |
| 'Jacquie' | WDib |
| 'Jane Elizabeth' | SBrm |
| 'Jennifer' ♀H1 | WDib |
| 'Jessica' | WDib |
| 'Joanna' | WDib |
| ***johannis*** | WDib |
| 'Josie' | SBrm |
| 'Judith' | SBrm |
| 'Karen' | WDib |
| 'Katie' | WDib |
| ***kentaniensis*** | WDib |
| 'Kerry's Gold' | SBrm |
| 'Kim' ♀H1 | CSpe EShb WDib |
| ***kirkii*** | WDib |
| 'Kisie' | SBrm |
| 'Lady Lavender' | SBrm |
| 'Largesse' | SBrm |
| 'Laura' ♀H1 | WDib |
| 'Leyla' PBR | WDib |
| 'Little Gem' | CSpe |
| 'Louise' | WDib |
| 'Lucy' **new** | WDib |
| 'Lynne' | WDib |
| 'Maassen's White' ♀H1 | WDib |
| 'Magpie' | SBrm |
| 'Mandy' | WDib |
| 'Margaret' Gavin Brown | WDib |
| 'Marie' | WDib |
| 'Mary' | SBrm |
| 'Megan' | WDib |
| 'Melanie' Dibley ♀H1 | WDib |
| ***meyeri*** | WDib |
| 'Midnight Flame' | EShb WDib |
| 'Mini Nymph' | CSpe WDib |
| 'Misty Pink' | SBrm |
| 'Modbury Lady' | SBrm |
| ***modestus*** | WDib |
| 'Molly' | SBrm |
| 'Monica's Magic' | SBrm |
| 'Moonlight' | WDib |
| 'Myfanwy' **new** | WDib |

'Neptune' WDib
'Nerys' WDib
'Nia' CSpe WDib
'Nicola' WDib
'Olga' WDib
'Olwen' WDib
'Padarn' WDib
'Pale Rider' SBrm
'Party Doll' WDib
'Patricia' SBrm
'Paula' ♀H1 WDib
***pentherianus*** WDib
'Pink Fondant' CSpe
'Pink Leyla'PBR WDib
'Pink Souffle' WDib
***polyanthus*** WDib
  subsp. ***dracomontanus***
***primulifolius*** WDib
– subsp. ***formosus*** WDib
'Princesse' (Marleen Series) WDib
***prolixus*** WDib
'Raspberry Dream' SBrm
***rexii*** WDib
'Rhiannon' WDib
'Rosebud' WDib
'Rosemary' (d) WDib
(Roulette Series) WDib
  'Roulette Azur'
– 'Roulette Cherry' WDib
'Rubina' **new** WDib
'Ruby' ♀H1 WDib
'Ruby Anniversary' SBrm
'Ruffles' SBrm
'Sally' WDib
'Sandra' WDib
'Sarah' WDib
***saxorum*** ♀H1 CCCN EOHP EShb LSou SRms WDib WFar
– compact CCCN EOHP WDib
'Scarlett' **new** WDib
'Seren'PBR WDib
'Shannon' SBrm
'Sian' WDib
***silvaticus*** WDib
'Snow White' ♀H1 WDib
'Something Special' WDib
'Sophie' WDib
'Southshore' WDib
'Spider' SBrm
'Spirit'PBR WDib
'Stacey' SBrm
'Stella' ♀H1 WDib
'Stephanie' CSpe WDib
***stomandrus*** WDib
'Strawberry Fondant' SBrm
'Susan' ♀H1 WDib
'Swaybelle' SBrm
'Targa' (Marleen Series) WDib
'Tatan Blue' SBrm
'Terracotta' SBrm
'Texas Hot Chili' WDib
'Texas Sunrise' SBrm
***thompsonii*** WDib
'Tina' ♀H1 WDib
'Tracey' WDib
'Upstart' see *S.* 'Blue Upstart'
***vandeleurii*** **new** WDib
'Vanessa' SBrm
***variabilis*** WDib
'Velvet Underground' SBrm
'Vera' SBrm
'Violet Lace' CSpe
'Watermelon Wine' WDib
***wendlandii*** WDib
'Wendy' WDib
'White Wings' SBrm
'Wiesmoor Red' WDib
'Winifred' WDib

## *Streptopus* (*Liliaceae*)

***amplexifolius*** EBee ECho MNrw WCru
***roseus*** EBee ECho
***streptopoides*** EBee LRHS

## *Streptosolen* (*Solanaceae*)

***jamesonii*** ♀H1 CHll EBak ELan EShb SAga

## *Strobilanthes* (*Acanthaceae*)

sp. WBor
CC 4071 CPLG
CC 4573 CPLG
***anisophylla*** EShb WCot
***atropurpurea*** misapplied see *S. attenuata*
***atropurpurea*** Nees see *S. wallichii*
§ ***attenuata*** CBot CFir EBee ECGP ECha ECtt ELan EPfP GCal GCra LHop LRHS MCot MLLN MRav NCGa NChi NDov NSti SGar WCAu WCru WFar WMoo WPer WWlt XLum
– 'Aquarella' NDov
– 'Blue Carpet' NDov
– subsp. ***nepalensis*** CHll CLAP MWhi
***dyeriana*** ♀H1 CAbP EAmu EBak ECtt ELan EShb WCot WHil
***flexicaulis*** EBee WPGP
– B&SWJ 354 WCru
***gossypina*** EShb
aff. ***inflata*** B&SWJ 7754 WCru
***nutans*** CDes CLAP CPou EBee NSti
***pendula*** **new** WBor
aff. ***pentstemonoides*** WCru
  HWJK 2019
***rankanensis*** CDes CFir CLAP EBee EPPr NDov SDys WHil XLum
– B&SWJ 1771 WCru
***violacea*** CPrp EShb EWTr LHop WPer
§ ***wallichii*** CDes CLAP CMac CSam EBee EWes EWld LLWP NSti SUsu WCot WCru WFar WMoo WOld WSHC WWEG
'Wollerton' WWlt

## *Stromanthe* (*Marantaceae*)

***sanguinea*** 'Triostar'PBR (v) XBlo

## *Strongylodon* (*Papilionaceae*)

***macrobotrys*** MOWG

## *Strophanthus* (*Apocynaceae*)

***speciosus*** CCCN CHll EShb

## *Strumaria* (*Amaryllidaceae*)

***aestivalis*** ECho
***chaplinii*** ECho
***karooica*** 'Komsberg' ECho
***leipoldtii*** 'Vanrhynsdorp' ECho
***massoniella*** 'Reitfontein' ECho
***salteri*** 'Nardouwsberg' ECho
***truncata*** ECho
– 'Garies' ECho

## *Struthiopteris* (*Blechnaceae*)

| | |
|---|---|
| ***niponica*** | see *Blechnum niponicum* |

## *Stuartia* see *Stewartia*

## *Stylidium* (*Stylidiaceae*)

| | |
|---|---|
| ***adnatum*** new | ECou MOWG |
| ***graminifolium*** | SPlb |
| - 'Little Sapphire' | LEdu NOak SRot |
| - 'Tiny Trina' | LRHS NOak |

## *Stylophorum* (*Papaveraceae*)

| | |
|---|---|
| ***diphyllum*** | CPBP CPou EBee EWld GEdr MRav WCru WFar WPnP |
| ***lasiocarpum*** | CPLG CPom CSpe CSpr EWes EWld IGor NBid SGar WCru |

## *Styphelia* (*Epacridaceae*)

| | |
|---|---|
| ***colensoi*** | see *Leucopogon colensoi* |

## *Styphnolobium* (*Leguminosae*)

| | | |
|---|---|---|
| § | ***japonicum*** ♀H4 | CAbP CDul CHab CWib EPfP LMaj MGos MMuc SPlb WDin |
| | - 'Pendulum' | CDul ELan LMaj MBlu |

## *Styrax* (*Styracaceae*)

| | | |
|---|---|---|
| | ***americanus*** | GAuc NLar |
| | ***formosanus*** | CGHE EBee |
| | - var. ***formosanus*** | CPLG EPfP WPGP WPat |
| | - - B&SWJ 3803 | WCru |
| | - - B&SWJ 6786 | WCru |
| | - var. ***hayatiana*** B&SWJ 6823 | WCru |
| | ***hemsleyanus*** ♀H4 | CAbP CBcs CPLG CTho EPfP GBin IArd IDee MBlu MMuc NLar SPer SSpi WFar |
| | ***hookeri*** | CPLG |
| | ***japonicus*** ♀H4 | Widely available |
| | - B&SWJ 4405 | WCru |
| | - B&SWJ 8770 | WCru |
| | - (Benibana Group) 'Pink Chimes' | CBcs CEnd CMac CPLG CPMA ELan EPfP GKin IVic MBlu NLar SCoo SSpi |
| | - 'Carillon' | CPMA MBlu |
| I | - 'Compactus' | SSpi |
| | - 'Fargesii' | CBcs CDoC CDul CPLG CPMA CTho EPfP GBin SCoo SKHP SSpi |
| | - 'Pendulus' | CBcs NLar |
| | - 'Purple Dress' | CPMA MBlu NLar |
| | - 'Snowfall' new | CPMA |
| | - 'Sohuksan' | CPMA MBlu NLar SSpi |
| | ***obassia*** ♀H4 | CBcs CDul CMCN CTho EPfP GBin IDee LRHS MBlu MBri NLar SSpi |
| | - B&SWJ 6023 | WCru |
| | - B&SWJ 10890 | WCru |
| | ***odoratissimus*** | CPLG |
| | ***officinalis*** | CBcs |
| | ***suberifolius*** WWJ 11868 | WCru |
| * | ***taiwanensis*** | SKHP |
| * | ***triloba*** new | CPLG |
| | ***wilsonii*** | CPLG |

## *Succisa* (*Caprifoliaceae*)

| | | |
|---|---|---|
| § | ***pratensis*** | CArn CHab CMac CRDP EBee EPri EWil LEdu LLWG LRHS MHer MNHC MWea NLan NLar NMen NWCA SBch SPhx SUsu WHer WHoo WPtf WSFF WTin XLum |
| | - 'Alba' | EWes MDKP |
| | - 'Buttermilk' | CRDP |
| | - 'Cassop' | GEdr NRya |
| | - 'Derby Purple' | CSpe WPtf |
| | - 'Peddar's Pink' | EWes LEdu SPhx |

## *Succisella* (*Caprifoliaceae*)

| | |
|---|---|
| ***inflexa*** | MSpe SPhx |
| - 'Frosted Pearls' | CMHG CSpr EBee EDif LLWP MWat WHil |

## *Sullivantia* (*Saxifragaceae*)

| | |
|---|---|
| ***sullivantii*** dwarf new | WThu |

## sunberry see *Rubus* 'Sunberry'

## *Sutera* (*Scrophulariaceae*)

| | | |
|---|---|---|
| | (Abunda Series) Abunda Colossal Sky Blue = 'Balabolav' | NPri |
| | - Abunda Colossal White = 'Balabowite'PBR | NPri |
| | Cabana Trailing White = 'Sutcatrwhi'PBR (Cabana Series) | WGor |
| | (Cinderella Series) 'Cinderella Lavender' | NPri |
| | - 'Cinderella Salmon Eye' new | LAst |
| | (Copia Series) Copia Dark Pink = 'Dancop19'PBR | NPri |
| | - Copia Double White (d) | LAst LSou |
| | - Copia Gulliver Lavender = 'Dangul16'PBR | LSou |
| | - Copia Gulliver White = 'Dangul14'PBR | LSou |
| | ***cordata*** 'Blizzard' | LSou |
| | - 'Olympic Gold' (v) | SCoo |
| | - 'Pink Domino' | SPet |
| § | - 'Snowflake' | LAst NBlu NPer SCoo SPet SPoG |
| | Great Purple = 'Dancop21'PBR (Scopia Series) | LSou |
| | Gulliver Lilac = 'Dancop24'PBR (Scopia Series) | LSou |
| | ***microphylla*** | CPBP |
| | ***neglecta*** | SPlb WPGP |
| | Scopia Golden Leaves = 'Dancopgoleav' (Scopia Series) | NPri |
| | 'Secrets Blue Delight' new | LSou |
| | 'Secrets Central Pink' new | LSou |
| | 'Secrets Silver Sky' new | LSou |

## *Sutherlandia* ✿ (*Papilionaceae*)

| | |
|---|---|
| ***frutescens*** | CArn CBod CSpe GDun SPlb WJek |
| - fine-leaved new | GDun |
| ***montana*** | CSpe SBrt |

## *Swainsona* (*Papilionaceae*)

| | |
|---|---|
| ***galegifolia*** | CHII |
| - 'Albiflora' | MOWG WWlt |

## sweet cicely see *Myrrhis odorata*

## *Syagrus* (*Arecaceae*)

| | | |
|---|---|---|
| | ***botryophora*** | XBlo |
| § | ***romanzoffiana*** | CBrP EAmu LPal XBlo |
| | - 'Santa Caterina' new | EAmu |
| | ***weddeliana*** | see *Lytocaryum weddellianum* |

## × *Sycoparrotia* (*Hamamelidaceae*)

| | | |
|---|---|---|
| | ***semidecidua*** | CPMA MBlu NLar SLPl |
| | – 'Purple Haze' | CPMA NLar |

## *Sycopsis* (*Hamamelidaceae*)

| | | |
|---|---|---|
| | ***sinensis*** | CAbP CBcs CMCN CPLG CWib EBee EMil EPfP LHop LRHS NLar SKHP SPoG SSpi WDin WFar WPGP WSHC |

## *Symphoricarpos* (*Caprifoliaceae*)

| | | |
|---|---|---|
| | ***albus*** | CDul ECrN MSwo NWea WDin |
| | – 'Constance Spry' | SRms |
| § | – var. ***laevigatus*** | EPfP LBuc |
| § | – 'Taff's White' (v) | WMoo |
| | – 'Variegatus' | see *S. albus* 'Taff's White' |
| | × ***chenaultii*** 'Hancock' | CBar CMac ECrN ELan EPfP MGos MMuc MRav MSwo NPro SGol SLim SPer STre WDin |
| | × ***doorenbosii*** 'Magic Berry' | MRav SGol |
| | – Magical Candy = 'Kolmcan' **new** | EPfP |
| | – Magical Galaxy = 'Kolmgala' **new** | EPfP |
| | – 'Mother of Pearl' | ELan EPfP MGos MMuc MRav NWea SPer |
| | – 'White Hedge' | CSBt EBee ELan LBuc MMuc SPer SPlb |
| | ***guatemalensis*** B&SWJ 1016 | WCru |
| | ***orbiculatus*** | SLon |
| | – 'Albovariegatus' | see *S. orbiculatus* 'Taff's Silver Edge' |
| | – 'Argenteovariegatus' | see *S. orbiculatus* 'Taff's Silver Edge' |
| | – 'Bowles's Golden Variegated' | see *S. orbiculatus* 'Foliis Variegatis' |
| § | – 'Foliis Variegatis' (v) | CMac CTri EHoe ELan EPfP MGos MRav SGol SPer WDin WSHC |
| § | – 'Taff's Silver Edge' (v) | EHoe SGol |
| | – 'Variegatus' | see *S. orbiculatus* 'Foliis Variegatis' |
| | ***rivularis*** | see *S. albus* var. *laevigatus* |

## *Symphyandra* see *Campanula*

| | | |
|---|---|---|
| | ***asiatica*** | see *Hanabusaya asiatica* |

## *Symphyotrichum* see *Aster*

## *Symphytum* (*Boraginaceae*)

| | | |
|---|---|---|
| | ***asperum*** | CSev ECha ELan MRav NLar WMoo |
| * | ***azureum*** | EBee ELan LTen NLar WCAu WFar WMnd |
| | 'Belsay Gold' | NBir SDix |
| | ***caucasicum*** ♀H4 | CElw CMHG EBee ECha GPoy GQue IFro LEdu SBch SEND SIde SSvw WHer WHil WMoo WOut XLum |
| | – 'Norwich Sky' | CKno CPLG EWld |
| | ***cordatum*** | EBee EPPr LEdu MNrw SKHP |
| | 'Denford Variegated' (v) | NBid |
| § | 'Goldsmith' (v) | Widely available |
| | ***grandiflorum*** | CArn CMac CTri CWan EBee GPoy LEdu WGwG |
| * | – 'Sky-blue-pink' | IFro |
| | 'Grandiflorum' variegated (v) | LRHS |
| | 'Hidcote Blue' | CBre CPrp CTri EBee ECha ECtt EPfP EPla ILis LBMP LRHS MMuc NBro NEgg NHol NOrc SBfd SEND SLPl SPer SPoG WCAu WCru WMnd WMoo WOut WPtf WWEG |
| § | 'Hidcote Pink' | CPom CWCL EBee ECha ECtt EPla LBMP LRHS MMuc NBir NEgg SBch SEND SLPl SPer SPoG WCAu WFar WMnd WMoo [illegible] |
| | 'Hidcote Variegated' (v) | CMac |
| | ***ibericum*** | CArn CSam EBee ECha EPfP EPla GMaP GPoy LRHS MLHP MMuc NBlu NSti SEND SGar SRms WJek WMoo WOut |
| | – 'All Gold' | ECha ECtt MHer MNrw WMoo |
| | – 'Blaueglocken' | CSev EBee ECha LPla WMoo |
| | – dwarf | IFro WMoo |
| | – 'Gold in Spring' | NLar WFar |
| | – 'Jubilee' | see *S.* 'Goldsmith' |
| | – 'Lilacinum' | LRHS WHer |
| | – 'Variegatum' | see *S.* 'Goldsmith' |
| | – 'Wisley Blue' | CBcs CHab CPrp EBee EPfP NLar WFar WMnd WMoo WWEG |
| | 'Lambrook Sunrise' | CMac LEdu LRHS MBri NBro WCot WFar WMoo WWEG |
| | 'Langthorns Pink' | CPom ELan GCal |
| | 'Mereworth' | see *S.* × *uplandicum* 'Mereworth' |
| | ***officinale*** | CArn CHab CSev CWan EBee EGHP GJos GPoy MHer MNHC MNrw NPer NPri SBfd SIde SPoG SRms WHer WHfH WJek |
| * | – blue | SEND |
| | – 'Bohemicum' | ECho |
| | – var. ***ochroleucum*** | WHer |
| | ***orientale*** | CPom GCal MLLN |
| | ***peregrinum*** | see *S.* × *uplandicum* |
| | 'Roseum' | see *S.* 'Hidcote Pink' |
| | 'Rubrum' | CDes CEnt EAEE EBee ELan EPfP EWes GBin GCra LBMP LEdu LRHS MHer NBro NOrc SPer WBor WCAu WFar WGwG WPGP XLum |
| | 'Sera Howys' **new** | WOut |
| | 'Snape Cottage' **new** | CMea |
| | ***tuberosum*** | CArn CBre CElw CEnt CPom CSam EPPr GPoy LEdu MHer MMuc SEND WBor WCot WFar WHer |
| § | × ***uplandicum*** | CSev CTri EBee ELan GCra GPoy SIde SVic WJek |
| | – 'Axminster Gold' (v) | CDes CEnt CMea EWes SUsu WCot |
| | – 'Bocking 14' | CAgr CEnt CHby CPbn CPrp EOHP EWhm GAbr SIde WJAW WSFF XLum |
| | – 'Droitwich' (v) | WCot |
| § | – 'Mereworth' (v) | CBct LRHS MMuc SEND |
| | – 'Moorland Heather' | MAvo WMoo |
| | – purple-flowered | MMuc SEND |
| | – 'Variegatum' (v) ♀H4 | CBot ECtt ELan EPfP EWes LRHS MBri NBir NGdn SDix WCot WFar WMoo |

## *Symplocarpus* (*Araceae*)

| | | |
|---|---|---|
| | ***foetidus*** | CDes WCot |
| | ***nipponicus*** | WCru |
| | ***renifolius*** | WCru |

## *Symplocos* (*Symplocaceae*)

| | | |
|---|---|---|
| | ***paniculata*** | see *S. sawafutagi* |
| § | ***sawafutagi*** | CBcs EPfP NLar WCFE WPGP WPat |

## *Syneilesis* (*Asteraceae*)

| | | |
|---|---|---|
| | ***aconitifolia*** | CLAP GEdr WCot |
| | – B&SWJ 879 | WCru |

***palmata*** CLAP GEdr LEdu WCot
- B&SWJ 1003 WCru
- B&SWJ 11226 WCru
***subglabrata*** B&SWJ 298 LEdu WCru
aff. ***tagawae*** B&SWJ 11191 WCru

## *Syngonium* (*Araceae*)

***podophyllum*** ♀H1 XBlo

## *Synnotia* see *Sparaxis*

## *Synthyris* (*Plantaginaceae*)

***laciniata*** GKev
***missurica*** CDes CLAP GKev
- var. ***missurica*** GKev
NNS 07-502 new
- var. ***stellata*** CBod CLAP EAEE EBee EWes GCal LEdu LRHS MMHG SPoG WAul WFar WGwG WHal WPGP WWEG
***pinnatifida*** NBir
***reniformis*** CLAP WPGP WWEG

## *Syringa* ✿ (*Oleaceae*)

***afghanica*** misapplied see *S. protolaciniata*
***afghanica*** C.K. Schneid. IDee IVic
'Alexander's Pink' WGob
× ***chinensis*** 'Persian Lilac' WDin WFar WGob
- 'Saugeana' EBee NLar SLPl SPer
***emodi*** CBot
- 'Aurea' NLar
- 'Aureovariegata' see *S. emodi* 'Elegantissima'
§ - 'Elegantissima' (v) CBcs CDoC CEnd CMac CWGN EBee EPfP GQui LLHF LRHS MAsh NEgg SKHP SPoG SSpi WDin
- 'Variegata' (v) LRHS WPat
'Hagny' WGob
× ***hyacinthiflora*** 'Clarke's Giant' NLar
- 'Esther Staley' ♀H4 EPfP MRav SKHP
- 'Pocahontas' NLar
Josée = 'Morjos 060f' CDoC EPfP EQua LBMP MAsh NLar SPoG SWvt WFar WGob WPat
× ***josiflexa*** CPLG
- 'Agnes Smith' LAst MMuc NLar WGob WSHC
- 'Anna Amhoff' GBin NLar
- 'Bellicent' ♀H4 CEnd CLnd CMac EBee ELan EPfP LAst LRHS MAsh MMuc MRav NLar NSti SKHP SPer SPlb SPoG SRms SWvt WCFE WDin WGob WPat
- 'James MacFarlane' NLar WGob
- 'Lynette' EPla NPro
- 'Redwine' NLar SKHP
§ - 'Royalty' LRHS LTen NLar SKHP WGob
***josikaea*** CMCN CSBt NLar SCoo SPer WGob
'Kim' MRav
***komarowii*** NLar
§ - subsp. ***reflexa*** CDul EPfP EWTr LLHF MGos SLon WDin WFar WGob
§ × ***laciniata*** Mill. CBot CPMA EBee EGxp ELan EPfP LRHS MGos MMuc MRav MWea NLar SPer SPoG SSpi WCFE WGor WPGP WSHC
§ ***meyeri*** 'Palibin' ♀H4 Widely available
'Minuet' CBcs NLar SKHP WGob
'Miss Canada' NLar WGob
***oblata*** CMCN
***palibiniana*** see *S. meyeri* 'Palibin'
***patula*** misapplied see *S. meyeri* 'Palibin'
***patula*** (Palibin) Nakai see *S. pubescens* subsp. *patula*
***pekinensis*** see *S. reticulata* subsp. *pekinensis*
× ***persica*** ♀H4 CPLG CPMA CTri EPfP EWTr IDee MGos MRav NLar NPal SLon SPer
- 'Alba' ♀H4 CBot CPMA GQui LTen MAsh MRav WFar WPat WSHC
- var. ***laciniata*** see *S.* × *laciniata* Mill.
***pinnatifolia*** CBcs CBot IArd NLar
× ***prestoniae*** 'Coral' WFar
- 'Desdemona' LRHS MMuc SKHP SSta
- 'Donald Wyman' WGob
- 'Elinor' ♀H4 CMHG EPfP MRav NSti SKHP
- 'Nocturne' WFar WGob
- 'Royalty' see *S.* × *josiflexa* 'Royalty'
§ ***protolaciniata*** LBMP MAsh MGos NLar SKHP WFar
- 'Kabul' EPfP NLar
***pubescens*** SBrd WGob
subsp. ***julianae*** 'George Eastman'
- subsp. ***microphylla*** 'Superba' ♀H4 Widely available
§ - subsp. ***patula*** CMac ECho LRHS MMuc MRav NWea SEND WFar
- - 'Miss Kim' ♀H4 CDoC CMac CSBt CWSG EBee ELan IArd LAst LRHS LSRN MAsh MBri MGos MRav MSwo NEgg NHol NLar SCoo SKHP SLim SPoG SSta WBor WDin WFar WGob WPat
'Red Pixie' CHll CMac CWGN ELon LBuc LRHS MAsh MBri MGos MMHG NLar SCoo SKHP WGob
***reflexa*** see *S. komarowii* subsp. *reflexa*
***reticulata*** MBlu WDin
- 'Ivory Silk' CWSG EPfP LLHF LRHS NLar SKHP WGob
§ - subsp. ***pekinensis*** CBot CMCN GBin
- - Beijing Gold = 'Zhang Zhiiming' IArd
- - China Snow = 'Morton' SKHP
- - 'Yellow Fragrance' NLar
× ***swegiflexa*** CDul CPLG NLar
***sweginzowii*** GKin SPer WFar
- 'Superba' WMoo
***tomentella*** LRHS MBri NWea SRms
***velutina*** see *S. pubescens* subsp. *patula*
***villosa*** SPlb WDin WGob
***vulgaris*** EPfP LBuc NWea
- 'Albert F. Holden' WGob
§ - 'Andenken an Ludwig Späth' ♀H4 Widely available
- 'Aurea' EQua LBuc MGos MRav NPro WFar
- Beauty of Moscow see *S. vulgaris* 'Krasavitsa Moskvy'
- 'Belle de Nancy' (d) CCCN CDul CMac CWib EBee ELan ELon LAst MAsh MMuc MRav NEgg SEND SGol SWvt WDin WGob
- 'Charles Joly' (d) ♀H4 Widely available
- 'Congo' LSRN MRav WGob
- 'Decaisne' SPer
- 'Edward J. Gardner' (d) ELon SEND
- 'Etna' new WGob
- 'Firmament' ♀H4 ELan EPfP MRav NEgg SEND WGob
- 'Hope' see *S. vulgaris* 'Nadezhda'
- 'Katherine Havemeyer' (d) ♀H4 Widely available
§ - 'Krasavitsa Moskvy' (d) EPfP EWes IArd LRHS NLar WGob
- 'Lee Jewett Walker' SSta
- 'Madame Florent Stepman' CMac NLar WGob
- 'Madame Lemoine' (d) ♀H4 Widely available
- 'Masséna' MRav SPer
- 'Maud Notcutt' EWes

| | |
|---|---|
| – 'Michel Buchner' (d) | CBcs CDul CWib ELan LAst MGos MRav NBlu NLar SBfd SBrd SCoo SLim SPer WBor WGob |
| – 'Miss Ellen Willmott' (d) | IArd MRav NLar |
| – 'Mrs Edward Harding' (d) ♀H4 | EPfP LAst LBuc MRav NBlu NLar NWea SBrd SCoo SPer WGob |
| § – 'Nadezhda' (d) | WGob |
| – 'Olivier de Serres' (d) | NLar |
| – 'Paul Deschanel' (d) | NLar |
| – 'Président Grévy' (d) | CBar CDoC CLnd CMac EMil LRHS SLim SPer WGob |
| – 'Primrose' | CBcs CBot CCCN CDul CMac CWib EBee ELan ELon EPfP GBin IArd LRHS MAsh MBri MGos MMuc MRav MSnd NEgg NLar SCoo SEND SKHP SPer WDin WFar WGob |
| – 'Prince Wolkonsky' (d) | EBee EMil EPfP LSRN LTen WFar WGob |
| – 'Princesse Sturdza' | EMil |
| – 'Sensation' | CBcs CDoC CMac CSBt CWSG EBee ELon EPfP GAbr IArd LAst LRHS LSRN LSou MAsh MGos MMuc MRav MSwo NEgg NLar NWea SBrd SCoo SEND SKHP SLim SPer SPoG WGob |
| – 'Souvenir de Louis Spaeth' | see *S. vulgaris* 'Andenken an Ludwig Späth' |
| – 'Ukraina' **new** | WGob |
| – variegated (v) | EWes |
| – variegated double (d/v) | WCot |
| – 'Vestale' ♀H4 | EWes MRav |
| – 'Viviand-Morel' (d) | CMac LLHF NEgg SKHP WGob |
| – 'William Robinson' (d) **new** | SPer |
| ***wolfii*** | CArn EBtc |
| ***yunnanensis*** | CPLG LLHF |
| – 'Prophecy' | WGob |

## *Syringodea* (*Iridaceae*)

| | |
|---|---|
| ***longituba*** 'Perdekraal' | ECho |

## *Syzygium* (*Myrtaceae*)

| | |
|---|---|
| ***australe*** | ERom EShb IDee SArc |
| ***jambos*** | EShb |
| ***paniculatum*** | CPLG EShb IDee |

# T

## *Tabernaemontana* (*Apocynaceae*)

| | |
|---|---|
| ***coronaria*** | see *T. divaricata* |
| § ***divaricata*** | CCCN MOWG |

## *Tacca* (*Taccaceae*)

| | |
|---|---|
| ***chantrieri*** | CCCN EAmu EGxp |
| ***integrifolia*** | EAmu |

## *Tacitus* see *Graptopetalum*

## *Tagetes* (*Asteraceae*)

| | |
|---|---|
| 'Cinnabar' **new** | SDix |
| ***electa*** 'Vanilla' **new** | LAst |
| ***lemmonii*** | SBfd SDix SHDw SMad WJek |
| 'Lemon Gem' | WJek |
| ***lucida*** | CArn EOHP LEdu WJek |

## *Talbotia* (*Velloziaceae*)

| | |
|---|---|
| § ***elegans*** | CSpe WCot WFar |

## *Talinum* (*Portulacaceae*)

| | |
|---|---|
| ***okanoganense*** | CCCN NWCA |
| ***paniculatum*** | CCCN |
| 'Zoe' | CPBP |

## tamarillo see *Solanum betaceum*

## tamarind see *Tamarindus indica*

## *Tamarindus* (*Caesalpiniaceae*)

| | |
|---|---|
| ***indica*** (F) | SPlb |

## *Tamarix* (*Tamaricaceae*)

| | |
|---|---|
| ***chinensis*** | CSBt |
| ***gallica*** | CMen CSBt MGos SArc SEND WSHC |
| ***hampeana*** | SEND |
| § ***parviflora*** | CMac EPfP IVic LRHS MGos SPoG |
| ***pentandra*** | see *T. ramosissima* |
| § ***ramosissima*** | CCCN CMac CTri ECrN ELan EPfP MBrN MWhi SEWo SLim SLon SRms WDin WSHC |
| – 'Pink Cascade' | CBcs CCCN CDul CSBt EBee ELon EPfP GCal LRHS MBlu MBri MGos MMuc MREP MRav NEgg SBfd SBod SEND SGol SPer SPoG SWvt WDin |
| – 'Rosea' | CBcs |
| § – 'Rubra' ♀H4 | CDoC CWSG EBee EPfP IVic MGos NLar SLon SPer WDin |
| – 'Summer Glow' | see *T. ramosissima* 'Rubra' |
| ***tetrandra*** ♀H4 | Widely available |
| – 'Africance' | ERom |
| – var. ***purpurea*** | see *T. parviflora* |

## *Tamus* (*Dioscoreaceae*)

| | |
|---|---|
| ***communis*** | CArn |

## *Tanacetum* ✿ (*Asteraceae*)

| | |
|---|---|
| CC 6343 | GKev |
| § ***argenteum*** | ECho MRav SIde |
| – subsp. ***canum*** | ECho EWes LRHS MAsh SLon |
| § ***balsamita*** | CArn CPrp EBee ELan ELau GPoy LEdu MHer MNHC WHfH WJek WTin XLum XSen |
| § – subsp. ***balsamita*** | GPoy SIde |
| § – subsp. ***balsamitoides*** | CBod CHby CPrp MHer WJek |
| – var. ***tanacetoides*** | see *T. balsamita* subsp. *balsamita* |
| – ***tomentosum*** | see *T. balsamita* subsp. *balsamitoides* |
| ***capitatum*** | see *Sphaeromeria capitata* |
| § ***cinerariifolium*** | CArn CPrp CWan GPoy MNHC WJek |
| § ***coccineum*** | NBPC SPoG WFar |
| – 'Aphrodite' (d) | NEgg |
| – 'Beauty of Stapleford' | NEgg |
| – 'Bees' Pink Delight' | ECtt EWll NEgg |
| – 'Brenda' | EPfP MRav |
| – 'Duro' | LRHS |
| – 'Eileen May Robinson' ♀H4 | EBee ECtt EPfP LRHS LSRN NGdn |
| – 'Evenglow' | ECtt EPfP |
| – 'H.M. Pike' | ECtt |
| – 'James Kelway' ♀H4 | ECtt ELan EPfP MRav NBir |
| – 'King Size' | SGar WFar |
| – Robinson's giant-flowered | LRHS SRms |
| – Robinson's pink-flowered | CCse EBee ELan EPfP EWll GMaP LRHS NBre SBfd WWEG XLum |
| – Robinson's red-flowered | CSBt EBee EPfP GMaP LRHS MLHP NBPC NVic SBfd SPlb SPur SWvt WWEG XLum |

- Robinson's rose-flowered SBfd
- Robinson's, mixed SBfd
- 'Scarlet Glow' EWll
- 'Snow Cloud' ECtt ELan NBre WWEG
- 'Vanessa' ECtt LRHS MNrw

§ ***corymbosum*** GCal
- 'Festtafel' LPla

***densum*** ECho EDAr NBlu WCFE
- subsp. ***amani*** EBee ECha ECho ECre GMaP LRHS MAsh MHer MWat NWCA XSen
- subsp. ***sivasicum*** new XSen

§ ***haradjanii*** ECho ECtt ELan SBch WHer WKif

***huronense*** EBee

***macrophyllum*** misapplied see *Achillea grandifolia* Friv.

§ ***macrophyllum*** (Waldst. & Kit.) Sch.Bip. CPrp ECtt EPPr LPla SPhx
- 'Cream Klenza' WCot

***niveum*** ECha SBrt WCot
- 'Jackpot' CWib EBee EPfP EWes LRHS SSvw SWvt

§ ***parthenium*** CArn CHab CHby CPbn CWan ELau EWil GPoy MHer MNHC NPer SBfd SIde SRms SVic WHer WJek XLum
- 'Aureum' CHid CPbn CPrp CRow CWan ECha EGHP ELan ELau EWes GPoy MBri MHer MLHP MNHC MSCN NBlu SBfd SPer SPlb SRms SWvt WCot WFar WHer WJek WMoo XLum
- 'Cartwheels' SUsu
- double white-flowered (d) NPer SRms
- 'Golden Ball' EPfP
- 'Golden Moss' XLum
- 'Plenum' (d) SBch

§ - 'Rowallane' (d) ELan MMuc SEND WCot
- 'Sissinghurst White' see *T. parthenium* 'Rowallane'
- 'Snowball' (d) EPfP
- 'White Bobbles' LRHS

***poteriifolium*** EBee LRHS

§ ***ptarmiciflorum*** ♀H3-4 WCot
- 'Silver Feather' MNHC WJek

***tatsiense*** GKev

* ***tommansii*** LRHS

***vulgare*** CArn CHab CHby CMac CSev ECtt ELau EWil GPoy MHer MNHC SBfd SEND SIde SVic WJek WMoo WSFF XSen
- 'All Gold' CSev SMad
- var. ***crispum*** CHby CPrp CWan EBee ELau MHer MRav SBfd SIde SMad WFar WJek
- 'Golden Fleece' CWGN ECtt EWes LRHS LSou NSti SPer SUsu WCot
- 'Isla Gold' (v) CHVG EBee ECtt EWes GMaP LHop LPla MHer MMuc MRav NBre SEND SMrm WAbb WCAu WCot WFar WJek WMoo
- 'Silver Lace' (v) CBre EBee EGHP EWes MLLN NBid WFar WHer WJek WMoo

## *Tanakaea* (*Saxifragaceae*)

***radicans*** WCru

## tangelo see *Citrus* × *tangelo*

## tangerine see *Citrus reticulata*

## tangor see *Citrus* × *nobilis* Tangor Group

## *Taraxacum* (*Asteraceae*)

***albidum*** GLin

***faeroense*** EPPr WCot

***officinale*** agg. CArn CHab
- 'Nettleton' CNat

***rubrifolium*** CSpe EPPr

## tarragon see *Artemisia dracunculus*

## *Tasmannia* see *Drimys*

## *Taxodium* (*Cupressaceae*)

***ascendens*** 'Nutans' see *T. distichum* var. *imbricarium* 'Nutans'

***distichum*** ♀H4 Widely available
- 'Cascade Falls' PBR LRHS MBlu MBri MGos NLar NPri SLim
- 'Cave Hill' SLim
- 'Falling Waters' CBcs LRHS SGol SKHP
- 'Hursley Park' NLar SLim
- var. ***imbricarium*** CMCN EPfP LRHS

§ - - 'Nutans' ♀H4 CAlb CBcs CEnd EPfP IArd LRHS MBlu NLar SCoo SGol SLim SMad
- 'Little Leaf' NLar SLim
- 'Minaret' IArd MBlu

* - 'Pendulum' IArd IDee
- 'Peve Minaret' CDoC CMen LRHS MBri MGos NLar SGol SKHP SLim SPoG
- 'Peve Yellow' MBlu NLar
- 'Schloss Herten' LRHS NLar SLim
- 'Secrest' CBcs LRHS MBlu NLar SLim
- Shawnee Brave = 'Mickelson' MBlu

***mucronatum*** CDoC CPLG
- NJM 09.037 WPGP

## *Taxus* ✿ (*Taxaceae*)

***baccata*** ♀H4 Widely available
- 'Adpressa Aurea' (v) CKen GKin
- 'Adpressa Variegata' (m/v) ♀H4 CDoC
- 'Aldenham Gold' CKen
- 'Amersfoort' CDoC GKin LRHS NHol NLar SCoo SLim
- 'Argentea Minor' see *T. baccata* 'Dwarf White'
- Aurea Group CDul NHol SRms STre

I - 'Aureomarginata' (v) CBcs ECho MAsh NEgg SWvt
- 'Autumn Shades' CBcs NLar
- 'Bridget's Gold' CKen
- 'Compacta' EPla
- 'Corleys Coppertip' CKen ECho EPot LRHS MRav NHol NLar SCoo SEND SLim WEve WFar
- 'Cristata' CKen NLar
- 'David' IArd MBri NLar WEve
- 'Dovastoniana' (f) ♀H4 CMac NLar NWea WMou
- 'Dovastonii Aurea' (m/v) ♀H4 CBcs EPfP EPla GKin MBlu MBri MGos NEgg NLar NPCo NWea SCoo SGol SLim WCFE WDin WFar
- 'Drinkstone Gold' (v) ECho

§ - 'Dwarf White' (v) WGor
- 'Elegantissima' (f/v) CTho ECho ECrN EHul EPfP LRHS NPCo SCoo WFar
- 'Erecta' (f) EHul

§ - 'Fastigiata' (f) ♀H4 Widely available
- Fastigiata Aurea Group CLnd CWib ECho EPfP GKev IArd LBuc LMaj MAsh MGos NHol NPri SGol SRms STre WFar WHar
- 'Fastigiata Aureomarginata' (m/v) ♀H4 CDoC CDul CMac CSBt CTri EHul EPfP LBee LRHS MBri MGos NWea SAga SBfd SCoo SLim SLon SPer SPoG SWvt WCFE WDin WEve

| | | |
|---|---|---|
| | - 'Fastigiata Robusta' (f) | CDoC CSBt ECho EPfP EPla LRHS MBri NHol NLar NPCo SCoo SLim SPoG WEve WFar |
| | - 'Goud Elsje' | CKen MBri NLar |
| | - 'Grayswood Hill' | NLar |
| | - 'Green Column' | CKen |
| | - 'Green Diamond' | CKen NLar |
| | - 'Green Rocket' | CDul NLar |
| | - 'Hibernica' | see *T. baccata* 'Fastigiata' |
| | - 'Icicle' | CBcs EPla LRHS MAsh MGos NHol NLar NWad SLim WEve |
| | - 'Itsy Bitsy' | CKen |
| | - 'Ivory Tower' | CBcs CDoC CKen ELan MGos NEgg NHol NLar NPCo NWad SLim SPoG WEve WFar WGor |
| | - 'Klitzeklein' | CKen |
| | - 'Litfass' | NLar |
| | - 'Lutea' (f) | SLim |
| | - 'Nutans' | CDoC CKen |
| | - 'Pendula' | MRav |
| | - 'Prostrata' | CMac WFar |
| | - 'Pygmaea' | CKen WEve |
| | - 'Repandens' (f) $\Upsilon^{H4}$ | EHul IArd NWea WCFE WDin WFar |
| I | - 'Repens Aurea' (v) $\Upsilon^{H4}$ | CDoC CDul CKen CMac ECho EHul EPfP MGos NEgg SCoo WEve WFar |
| | - 'Rushmore' | MBri |
| | - 'Semperaurea' (m) $\Upsilon^{H4}$ | CBcs CDoC CMac ECho EHul EPla LBuc LTen MAsh MBri MGos NHol NWea SCoo SGol SLim SPoG WDin WFar |
| | - 'Silver Spire' (v) | CKen MDKP |
| | - 'Standishii' (f) $\Upsilon^{H4}$ | Widely available |
| | - 'Stove Pipe' | CKen |
| | - 'Summergold' (v) | ECho EHul ELan EPfP EPla LRHS MAsh MBri MGos MRav NBir NEgg NHol NLar SCoo SLim WDin WEve WFar |
| | - 'White Icicle' | MGos WGor |
| | ***brevifolia*** | NHol NLar |
| | ***cuspidata*** | CMen |
| | - 'Aurescens' (v) | CKen EPla SRms |
| | - 'Minuet' | CKen |
| | - 'Robusta' | EHul |
| | - 'Silver Queen' | SLim |
| | - 'Straight Hedge' | EMil LRHS SLim |
| | × ***media*** 'Brownii' | LBuc |
| | - 'Hicksii' (f) $\Upsilon^{H4}$ | CDul LBuc LMaj LRHS MGos NLar NWea SCoo SGol SLim WFar |
| | - 'Hillii' | LBMP LBuc LTen |
| | - 'Lodi' | LBee |
| | - 'Nixe' | SLim |

## Tayberry see *Rubus* Tayberry Group

## *Tecoma* (*Bignoniaceae*)

| | |
|---|---|
| × ***alata*** | MOWG |
| ***capensis*** $\Upsilon^{H1}$ | CHII MOWG MREP SVen |
| - 'Aurea' | EShb MOWG |
| - 'Coccinea' | EShb |
| - 'Lutea' | EShb |
| 'Orange Glow' | MOWG |
| ***ricasoliana*** | see *Podranea ricasoliana* |
| ***stans*** | MOWG |

## *Tecomanthe* (*Bignoniaceae*)

| | |
|---|---|
| ***speciosa*** | ECou MOWG |

## *Tecomaria* see *Tecoma*

## *Tecophilaea* (*Tecophilaeaceae*)

| | | |
|---|---|---|
| | ***cyanocrocus*** $\Upsilon^{H2}$ | CAvo CBro ECho LAma LLHF LRHS NMin WCot |
| | - 'Leichtlinii' $\Upsilon^{H2}$ | CBro ECho EPot LAma LLHF LRHS NMin SCnR |
| | - 'Purpurea' | see *T. cyanocrocus* 'Violacea' |
| | - Storm Cloud Group | CBro ECho LLHF |
| § | - 'Violacea' | CAvo CBro ECho EPot LLHF LRHS NMin |
| | ***violiflora*** | ECho LAma |

## *Tectaria* (*Tectariaceae*)

| | |
|---|---|
| ***gemmifera*** | WRic |

## *Telanthophora* (*Asteraceae*)

| | | |
|---|---|---|
| § | ***grandifolia*** | CHEx |

## *Telekia* (*Asteraceae*)

| | | |
|---|---|---|
| § | ***speciosa*** | CFir CMac COIW CSam CSpe EBee ELan EPPr EPfP GAbr LRHS MCCP MLLN MMuc NBro NChi NLar SDix SEND SLPl SPlb WBrk WCFE WFar WHer WHoo WMoo WWEG |

## *Telesonix* see *Boykinia*

## *Teline* see *Genista*

## *Tellima* (*Saxifragaceae*)

| | | |
|---|---|---|
| | ***grandiflora*** | Widely available |
| | - 'Bob's Choice' | WCot |
| | - 'Delphine' (v) | EBee EPPr WCot XLum |
| | - 'Forest Frost' | CBct CMac EBee LAst LRHS NBre NDov NLar NOrc WCot WGwG WMoo WWEG |
| | - Odorata Group | CBre ECha MRav WCot WMoo |
| | - 'Purpurea' | see *T. grandiflora* Rubra Group |
| | - 'Purpurteppich' | CHVG EBee ECha EHoe EPPr LRHS MRav NDov NVic WCot WMnd WMoo WPtf WWEG |
| § | - Rubra Group | Widely available |
| | - 'Silver Select' | EPPr |

## *Telopea* (*Proteaceae*)

| | |
|---|---|
| 'Dawn Fire' | CTrC |
| ***oreades*** | GGal SPlb |
| ***speciosissima*** | CCCN CTrC MOWG SPlb |
| - 'Red Embers' | CTrC |
| ***truncata*** | CCCN GGal SPlb WCru |

## *Templetonia* (*Papilionaceae*)

| | |
|---|---|
| ***retusa*** | ECou |

## *Temu* see *Blepharocalyx*

## *Tephrosia* (*Papilionaceae*)

| | |
|---|---|
| ***virginiana*** | SBrt |

## *Tetracentron* (*Trochodendraceae*)

| | |
|---|---|
| ***sinense*** | CBcs EPfP IArd NLar |

## *Tetradenia* (*Lamiaceae*)

| | |
|---|---|
| ***riparia*** | EOHP |

## *Tetradium* (*Rutaceae*)

| | | |
|---|---|---|
| § | ***daniellii*** | CBcs CCVT CMCN EPfP IArd IDee SSpi WPGP |
| * | - ***henryi*** | NLar |

| | |
|---|---|
| § - Hupehense Group | CMCN CTho GBin MBri MSnd NLar WDin |
| ***glabrifolium*** B&SWJ 6882 | WCru |
| - CWJ 12364 | WCru |
| ***ruticarpum*** | WPGP |
| - B&SWJ 3541 | WCru |
| * ***velutinum*** | NLar |

## *Tetraglochin* (*Rosaceae*)

| | |
|---|---|
| ***alata*** new | WAle |

## *Tetragonia* (*Aizoaceae*)

| | |
|---|---|
| ***tetragonoides*** | CArn |

## *Tetragonolobus* see *Lotus*

## *Tetraneuris* (*Asteraceae*)

| | |
|---|---|
| § ***grandiflora*** NNS 08-210 | GKev |
| ***scaposa*** | EPot |

## *Tetrapanax* (*Araliaceae*)

| | |
|---|---|
| § ***papyrifer*** ♀H2-3 | CBrP CChe CDTJ CHEx CHGN ESwi IDee MBri NLar SArc SBig SBst SPad SVen XBlo |
| - B&SWJ 7135 | WCru |
| - 'Di-Sue-Shan' | WCru |
| - 'Empress' | WCru |
| - 'Rex' | CAbb CBcs CDTJ CGHE CHEx CHid CPLG CSpe CTrC CWGN EAmu EExo EGFP ELon ESwi ETod ITim LRHS NGBo NLar SDix SKHP SMad SPoG WBox WCot WCru WGrn WHer WPGP |
| - 'Steroidal Giant' | CDTJ SBig SKHP |

## *Tetrapathaea* see *Passiflora*

## *Tetrastigma* (*Vitaceae*)

| | |
|---|---|
| ***obtectum*** | CCCN CTsd EBee ECre EWes EWld |
| ***voinierianum*** ♀H1 | EShb WCot |

## *Tetratheca* (*Elaeocarpaceae*)

| | |
|---|---|
| 'Bicentennial Belle' | LRHS |
| ***ciliata*** var. ***alba*** | MOWG |
| ***thymifolia*** pink-flowered | MOWG |

## *Teucridium* (*Lamiaceae*)

| | |
|---|---|
| ***parvifolium*** | ECou |

## *Teucrium* (*Lamiaceae*)

| | |
|---|---|
| * ***ackermannii*** | CMea ECho LBee NMen NWCA SBch WAbe WHoo WPat WTin XSen |
| ***arduinoi*** | SEND XSen |
| ***aroanium*** | ECho EPot GEdr MWat XSen |
| ***asiaticum*** | XSen |
| ***botrys*** | MHer |
| ***canadense*** | WWEG XSen |
| ***chamaedrys*** misapplied | see *T.* × *lucidrys* |
| ***chamaedrys*** L. | CPom CPrp CWan CWib EGHP ELon GMaP GPoy LEdu LRHS LSRN MNHC MSwo NWad SBfd SEND SLim SPlb SRms STre SVen WBrk WHfH WJek WWEG XSen |
| - 'Nanum' | ECho WPat |
| ***divaricatum*** | XSen |
| - NS 614 | NWCA |
| ***dunense*** | XSen |
| ***flavum*** | CArn EDAr EPPr NBre WJek XSen |
| ***fruticans*** | Widely available |
| - 'Azureum' ♀H3 | CAlb CBcs CBot CMMP COIW CWSG EBee ELan EPfP LAst LRHS LSRN MGos MRav SBfd SBrt SEND SPer SPoG SPtl WCFE WKif XSen |
| - 'Compactum' | CChe CDoC ELan ELon LAst LRHS LSRN MCCP MGos SLon SPer SPoG WCFE WPGP |
| - 'Drysdale' | CDoC CSBt LRHS |
| ***gnaphalodes*** | XSen |
| ***hircanicum*** | Widely available |
| - 'Flowtime' new | EBee |
| - 'Paradise Delight' | EBee ECtt EKen NBPC NLar NPnk WBor |
| - 'Purple Tails' | CChe COIW CPrp CSpe CWib EPfP LSou MDev MNHC NBPC NBir SMad SPad SWal WPer WWEG |
| § × ***lucidrys*** | CArn CChe CMea CSev CWan EBee ECha EGHP ELan EPfP LAst LRHS MGos MHer MMuc MNHC MRav NBlu SGar SIde SPer SPoG WCFE WHoo WJek XSen |
| ***lucidum*** | GCal |
| ***marum*** | CArn CMea CTri EGHP NMen WJek XSen |
| ***massiliense*** misapplied | see *T.* × *lucidrys* |
| ***massiliense*** L. | EBee XSen |
| ***montanum*** | WJek XSen |
| ***musimonum*** | EPot |
| ***nivale*** | EBee |
| ***orientale*** | XSen |
| ***polium*** | MWat WJek WPat WThu XSen |
| - subsp. ***aureum*** | XSen |
| ***pyrenaicum*** | CMea CPBP CPom EPot EWes GEdr NWCA SBch WPat XSen |
| - subsp. ***guarense*** new | XSen |
| ***scordium*** | CNat |
| ***scorodonia*** | CArn CHab CRWN GPoy MCot MHer MNHC NLar NMir WHer WJek XSen |
| - 'Binsted Gold' | EBee MMoz NSti |
| - 'Crispum' | LBMP LEdu LRHS MHer MMuc NBro NLar SBch SEND SPer WBox WGrn WGwG WJek WKif WMnd WMoo WPer |
| - 'Crispum Marginatum' (v) | CBot COIW EBee ECGP ECha EHoe EPPr EPfP ILis LSou MNrw MRav NSti WFar WTin WWEG |
| - 'Spring Morn' | EBee |
| - 'Winterdown' (v) | EBee MSCN NPro SBch |
| ***subspinosum*** | ECho GEdr LBee LLHF LRHS MWat NMen WHoo WPat WThu XSen |
| § ***viscidum*** 'Lemon and Lime' (v) | EBee LSou |
| ***webbianum*** | ECho XSen |
| 'Winterdown' | LEdu |

## *Thalia* (*Marantaceae*)

| | |
|---|---|
| ***dealbata*** | CBen CHEx CTrC EAmu LLWG LPBA MSKA MWts NLar SBig SDix SLon WMAq |

## *Thalictrum* (*Ranunculaceae*)

| | |
|---|---|
| CC 4576 | CPLG |
| SDR 5944 | GKev |
| from Afghanistan | see *T. isopyroides* |
| ***actaeifolium*** | CLAP CWib GMac MDKP |
| - B&SWJ 4664 | WCru |
| - B&SWJ 6310 | WCru |
| - var. ***brevistylum*** B&SWJ 8819 | WCru |

| |  |  |
|---|---|---|
| | - - 'Twinkling Star' | EBee |
| | - 'Perfume Star' | NLar WCot |
| | ***adiantifolium*** | see *T. minus* 'Adiantifolium' |
| | ***alpinum*** | EDAr EPPr XLum |
| | ***angustifolium*** | see *T. lucidum* |
| | 'Anne'PBR | IPot NDov NLar |
| | ***aquilegiifolium*** | Widely available |
| | - var. ***album*** | CBot CMea CSpe EBee ECha ELan EPfP GCra LAst LHop LRHS MMuc NBid SEND SKHP SPhx SWvt WCAu WMnd WPer WTcb WWEG |
| * | - 'Hybridum' | WFar WMoo WPer |
| | - 'Purpureum' | CPom CSev LBMP LRHS NLar WHoo |
| | - var. ***sibiricum*** B&SWJ 11007 | WCru |
| | - 'Small Thundercloud' | GCal |
| | - 'Thundercloud' ♀H4 | CAby CBct CCVN CFir CMHG CPLG CTca EBee ECtt ELon EPfP EWTr LHop LRHS MAvo MBri MCot MDKP MDun MTis NBPC NEgg NLar NSti SKHP SMrm SPer WBor WCot WWEG |
| | ***baicalense*** | CPom |
| | 'Black Stockings' | CKno CMac CPLG EBee ECtt EShb GBin IPot LRHS LSou NCGa NDov NLar NPnk SKHP SPoG WHil |
| | ***chelidonii*** | GMaP GMac LRHS |
| | - HWJK 2216 | WCru |
| | ***clavatum*** | CAby CLAP WPGP |
| | ***contortum*** | SDys |
| | ***coreanum*** | see *T. ichangense* |
| | ***cultratum*** | CDes WPGP |
| | - HWJCM 367 | NLar |
| | ***dasycarpum*** | EBee GMac MDKP NBre NLar WCot WFar WPnP |
| § | ***delavayi*** ♀H4 | Widely available |
| | - BWJ 7903 | WCru |
| | - var. ***acuminatum*** BWJ 7535 | WCru |
| | - - BWJ 7971 | WCru |
| | - 'Album' | Widely available |
| | - 'Ankum' | EBee |
| | - var. ***decorum*** | CDes CElw CLAP CPom CWCL EPPr GEdr GMac MCot NCGa NPnk WCot WCru WPGP WSHC |
| | - - BWJ 7770 | WCru |
| | - aff. var. ***decorum*** | CAby CPLG GQue |
| | - 'Gold Laced' | NLar |
| | - 'Hewitt's Double' (d) ♀H4 | Widely available |
| | - var. ***mucronatum*** | WCru |
| | - - DJHC 473 | WCru |
| | - purple-stemmed BWJ 7748 | WCru |
| | ***diffusiflorum*** | CLAP GMac WCru WSHC |
| | ***dipterocarpum*** misapplied | see *T. delavayi* |
| | ***dipterocarpum*** Franch. | CMac EBee LRHS WMnd XLum |
| | - ACE 4.878.280 | CMil |
| | 'Elin' | Widely available |
| | ***fendleri*** | GBin |
| | - NNS 06-547 | WCot |
| | ***filamentosum*** | EBee EPPr GMac |
| | - B&SWJ 777 | WCru |
| | - B&SWJ 4145 | WCru |
| | - var. ***yakusimense*** B&SWJ 6094 | WCru |
| | ***finetii*** | CLAP |
| | aff. ***finetii*** DJHC 473 | CLAP |
| | ***flavum*** | CHab CMac CWan ECtt EHon LRHS NBro NMir SMrm SPhx SWat WShi WWEG |
| | - 'Chollerton' | see *T. isopyroides* |
| § | - subsp. ***glaucum*** ♀H4 | Widely available |
| | - - dwarf | CDes WPGP |
| | - - 'True Blue' | NDov |
| | - 'Illuminator' | CDes CTri EBee ELon EPfP LRHS MArl MHer MRav SBfd SMad SMrm SPoG WCAu WCot WFar WPnP |
| | ***flexuosum*** | see *T. minus* subsp. *minus* |
| | ***foetidum*** | NBre |
| | - BWJ 7558 | WCru |
| | ***grandiflorum*** | WCot |
| | ***honanense*** | EBee MAvo MLLN SKHP |
| | - BWJ 7962 | WCru |
| | - 'Marble Leaf' **new** | SKHP |
| § | ***ichangense*** | LRHS WSHC |
| | - B&SWJ 8203 | WCru |
| * | - var. ***minus*** | WCru |
| | - - 'Chinese Chintz' | WCru |
| | - 'Purple Marble' | CWGN MCot MTis NCGa WCot |
| § | ***isopyroides*** | CFir CPom EAEE EBee GBin GCal GKev LRHS MCot MLLN MMuc MNFA MRav NChi NGdn NLar NMen NPnk WCot WKif WTin |
| | ***javanicum*** | LEdu |
| | - B&SWJ 9506 | WCru |
| | - var. ***puberulum*** B&SWJ 6770 | WCru |
| | ***johnstonii*** B&SWJ 9127 | WCru |
| | ***kiusianum*** | Widely available |
| | - Kew form | WSHC |
| | ***koreanum*** | see *T. ichangense* |
| § | ***lucidum*** | CElw CPLG EBee ECtt ELan EShb GBin GCal LRHS MMuc MTis NBPC NBre NLar NSti SGar SKHP SPhx WCot WFar WTcb |
| | ***minus*** | CArn EBee ECGP ELan LRHS MLLN MMuc NBre SEND |
| § | - 'Adiantifolium' | CMac EBee GBin MRav NBre NGdn NLar SHar SRms WFar WPer XLum |
| | - var. ***hypoleucum*** B&SWJ 8634 | WCru |
| | - subsp. ***kemense*** | EBee |
| § | - subsp. ***minus*** | NBre |
| | - subsp. ***saxatile*** | WPer |
| | - var. ***sipellatum*** B&SWJ 5051 | WCru |
| | ***morisonii*** | LRHS NBid |
| | ***omeiense*** | WPGP |
| | - BWJ 8049 | WCru |
| | ***orientale*** | EWes |
| | ***osmundifolium*** | WCru |
| | ***petaloideum*** | ECha EPPr EWTr GCal MDKP NLar WCot WTcb |
| | ***platycarpum*** B&SWJ 2261 | WCru |
| | ***polygamum*** | see *T. pubescens* Pursh |
| | ***przewalskii*** | WCru |
| § | ***pubescens*** Pursh | ECha GAuc GMaP LRHS NBre NCGa NDov SUsu WCot |
| | ***punctatum*** | CLAP |
| | - B&SWJ 1272 | WCru |
| | ***ramosum*** BWJ 8126 | WCru |
| | ***reniforme*** | CFir GMac IGor WCot |
| | - B&SWJ 2610 | WCru |
| | - GWJ 9311 | WCru |
| | - HWJK 2403 | WCru |
| | ***reticulatum*** | WCru |
| | - BWJ 7407 | WCru |

***rochebrunianum*** Widely available
***rubescens*** B&SWJ 10006 WCru
* ***rugosum*** LRHS
***sachalinense*** SWal WPGP WTcb
- RBS 0279 EBee EKen
***shensiense*** CPLG GEdr
***simplex*** var. ***brevipes*** B&SWJ 4794 WCru
***speciosissimum*** see *T. flavum* subsp. *glaucum*
* ***sphaerostachyum*** CElw GMac MNrw MWhi NBre SMrm WHal
'Splendide' CPLG CSpe ECtt ELon EPfP IPot MNrw MTis NBPC NDov NLar SUsu WCot WHil
***squarrosum*** EBee LRHS WPGP WTcb
***tenuisubulatum*** BWJ 7929 WCru
***tuberosum*** CElw CMea CRDP LLHF NDov SHar SUsu WPGP WPat
***tubiferum*** B&SWJ 10999 WCru
***uchiyamae*** CDes GBin LRHS WCot WPGP WTcb
***urbainii*** GEdr
***yunnanense*** WCru

## *Thamnocalamus* (*Poaceae*)

***aristatus*** EPfP EPla WDyG WPGP
***crassinodus*** EPla SBig
- dwarf EPla
- 'Gosainkund' CEnt EPla MWht
- 'Kew Beauty' CAbb CDTJ CDoC CEnt EPfP EPla MBrN MMoz MWht NPal SBig WCot WDyG WJun WPGP
- 'Lang Tang' CEnt EPla MMoz MWht WJun WPGP
- 'Merlyn' CDoC CEnt EPfP EPla MMoz MWht WJun WPGP
***falconeri*** see *Himalayacalamus falconeri*
***funghomii*** see *Schizostachyum funghomii*
***khasianus*** see *Drepanostachyum khasianum*
***maling*** see *Yushania maling*
***spathaceus*** misapplied see *Fargesia murielae*
§ ***spathiflorus*** CEnt EPla WJun
- subsp. ***nepalensis*** EPla MMoz MMuc MWht SBig WPGP
§ ***tessellatus*** EPla MMuc MWht SEND WDyG WJun

## *Thamnochortus* (*Restionaceae*)

***bachmannii*** CCtw
***cinereus*** CCtw CTrC
***fruticosus*** new CCtw
***insignis*** CCtw CSpe SPlb
***lucens*** CCtw SPlb
***pellucidus*** CCtw
***platypteris*** new CCtw
***pluristachyus*** new CCtw
***rigidus*** CCCN CCtw
***spicigerus*** CCtw CTrC

## *Thapsia* (*Apiaceae*)

***decipiens*** see *Melanoselinum decipiens*
***villosa*** CArn

## *Thea* see *Camellia*

## *Thelypteris* (*Thelypteridaceae*)

***erubescens*** WRic
***kunthii*** ISha WRic
***limbosperma*** see *Oreopteris limbosperma*
***ovata*** var. ***lindheimeri*** new ISha
***palustris*** CKel CRWN EBee LPBA NLar NVic SRms WFib WPnP WRic XLum
***phegopteris*** see *Phegopteris connectilis*

## *Themeda* (*Poaceae*)

***japonica*** EPPr

## *Thermopsis* (*Papilionaceae*)

***caroliniana*** see *T. villosa*
***chinensis*** EBee WHil
***fabacea*** see *T. lupinoides*
***lanceolata*** CMea CTri EBee EPfP EWTr GBin LRHS NBPC NPri NSti SAga SHar SMrm SPhx WAul WFar WHil WHrl WKif
§ ***lupinoides*** ECha LRHS MHer NBre
***mollis*** CPLG NBid
***montana*** see *T. rhombifolia* var. *montana*
§ ***rhombifolia*** var. ***montana*** CMHG CWCL EAEE EBee ELan ELon EPfP GAbr GCra GMaP LBMP LHop LRHS MSCN MWat NBir NBre NCGa NLar NOrc NSti NWad SPer SPoG WAbb WBor WHil WPer WWEG
§ ***villosa*** CAbP CPom CWCL EBee ELon EPPr LRHS MRav NBre NDov NGdn NLar SGar WCot WHil WHoo

## *Therorhodion* see *Rhododendron*

## *Thevetia* (*Apocynaceae*)

***neriifolia*** CCCN

## *Thladiantha* (*Cucurbitaceae*)

***dubia*** GCra SDix WCot

## *Thlaspi* (*Brassicaceae*)

sp. new NGdn
***biebersteinii*** see *Pachyphragma macrophyllum*

## *Thryptomene* (*Myrtaceae*)

***baeckeacea*** CCCN
***saxicola*** ECou LRHS

## *Thuja* ✿ (*Cupressaceae*)

'Extra Gold' see *T. plicata* 'Irish Gold'
'Green Giant' LRHS SLim
§ ***koraiensis*** CDoC IDee SCoo
***occidentalis*** NWea SEND
- 'Amber Glow' CDoC CKen CSBt ECho EPla LRHS MGos NHol NLar NWad SCoo SLim SPoG WBor WEve
- 'Aureospicata' EHul
- 'Bateman Broom' CKen
- 'Beaufort' (v) CKen EHul
- 'Brabant' CDul LMaj LRHS NLar NWea SCoo SLim WMou
- 'Brobecks Tower' CDoC CKen ECho LRHS NLar SLim
- 'Caespitosa' CKen WEve WGor
- 'Cristata Aurea' CKen
- 'Danica' ♀H4 CMac ECho EHul GKin MMuc NWea SBrd SCoo SEND SLim SRms WBor WCFE WEve WFar
- 'Degroot's Spire' CKen LRHS NLar SLim
- 'Dicksonii' EHul
- 'Douglasii Aurea' (v) CKen
- Emerald see *T. occidentalis* 'Smaragd'
- 'Ericoides' CDoC EHul MGos SRms
- 'Europa Gold' CDoC EHul MGos NLar SGol SLim

- 'Filiformis' CKen
I - 'Globosa Variegata' (v) CKen
- 'Gold Drop' CKen
- 'Golden Globe' CDoC EHul LRHS MGos SCoo SLim WDin
- 'Golden Minaret' EHul
- 'Golden Tuffet' CDoC ECho EHul GKin LRHS MBri MGos MPkF SCoo SLim SPer WGor
- 'Hetz Midget' CKen ECho EHul GKin LAst LRHS NHol NLar NWad SCoo SLim SPlb WDin WFar
- 'Holmstrup' ♀H4 CDoC CMac CTri CWib EHul NBlu SCoo SGol SLim SPoG SRms WDin WEve WFar
- 'Holmstrup's Yellow' EHul LRHS SLim SPoG
- 'Hoveyi' CTri EHul
- 'Linesville' CKen
- 'Little Champion' EHul NLar
- 'Little Gem' EHul MGos NHol NLar SRms WDin
- 'Lutea Nana' ♀H4 EHul WCFE
- 'Malonyana' NLar
- 'Malonyana Holub' SLim
- 'Marrisen's Sulphur' CDoC EHul
- 'Meineke's Zwerg' (v) CKen NLar
- 'Miky' CKen
- 'Mr Bowling Ball' CDoC LRHS NLar SCoo SLim SPoG
- 'Ohlendorffii' CDoC CKen EHul
- 'Pumila Sudworth' NLar
I - 'Pygmaea' CKen
- 'Pyramidalis Aurea' MGos WEve
- 'Pyramidalis Compacta' EHul NWea WGor
- 'Recurva Nana' EHul NWad
- 'Rheingold' ♀H4 Widely available
§ - 'Smaragd' ♀H4 CDoC CDul CSBt CWib ECho ECrN EHul EPfP LAst LBuc LRHS MAsh MGos NLar NWea SBfd SBrd SCoo SGol SLim SPer SPoG SWvt WCFE WEve WFar WMou
* - 'Smaragd Variegated' (v) CKen
- 'Smokey' CKen
- 'Southport' CKen WEve
- 'Spaethii' EHul
- 'Spiralis' EHul NLar WCFE
§ - 'Stolwijk' (v) ECho EHul MGos
- 'Sunkist' CKen CMac CTri CWib ECho EHul EPla LAst MGos NEgg SCoo SGol SLim SPoG WFar
- 'Teddy' CDoC ECho EHul LBee LRHS NHol NWad SCoo SLim SPoG WFar WGor
- 'Tiny Tim' CDoC CMac CWib EHul MGos NHol SGol WEve WFar WGor
- 'Trompenburg' CDoC EHul NLar
- 'Wansdyke Silver' (v) CMac EHul SCoo SLim SPoG
- 'Wareana' CMac
- 'Wareana Aurea' see *T. occidentalis* 'Wareana Lutescens'
§ - 'Wareana Lutescens' CWib EHul MGos NHol
- 'Waterfield' **new** NWad
- 'Yellow Ribbon' CKen CSBt EHul LRHS NLar SCoo SGol SLim SPoG WBor WEve WFar WHar

***orientalis*** see *Platycladus orientalis*
- 'Lemon 'n' Lime' (v) **new** LRHS
- 'Miller's Gold' see *Platycladus orientalis* 'Aurea Nana'

***plicata*** CCVT CDoy CDul CMac CSBt CTho EHul EPfP MGos NWea SLim SPer WDin WMou
- 'Atrovirens' ♀H4 CDul CTri LBee LBuc LMaj LRHS LTen MAsh MBri MGos MMuc SBfd SCoo SEND SEWo SGol SLim SRms WDin WEve WHar WMou
* - 'Atrovirens Aurea' WEve
- 'Aurea' ♀H4 EHul LRHS MAsh SLim SPoG SRms
- 'Brooks Gold' CKen
- 'Can-can' (v) ECho MAsh NLar SCoo
I - 'Cole's Variety' CDul CWib MGos
- 'Collyer's Gold' CDul EHul NLar SRms WEve
- 'Copper Kettle' CKen ECho EHul GKin LRHS NLar SCoo SLim WEve WGor
- 'Cuprea' CKen EHul
- 'Doone Valley' CKen EHul WFar
- 'Excelsa' CDul LMaj
- 'Fastigiata' ♀H4 CDul CMac
- 'Gelderland' ECho EHul LRHS LTen NEgg NLar SCoo SLim WFar
- Goldy = '4ever'PBR CDoC ECho MBri SPoG
- 'Gracilis Aurea' EHul
- 'Hillieri' CDoC CDul
§ - 'Irish Gold' (v) ♀H4 CDul CMac
- 'Martin' **new** CPMA
- 'Rogersii' CDoC CKen CMac ECho EHul EPfP MAsh MGos NHol SCoo SPoG SRms WFar
- 'Semperaurescens' (v) CMac
- 'Stolwijk's Gold' see *T. occidentalis* 'Stolwijk'
- 'Stoneham Gold' ♀H4 CDoC CMac EHul GKin LRHS MAsh MGos MMuc NPCo SPer SRms WEve
- 'Sunshine' CKen
- Verigold = 'Courtapli' CCVT MMuc SEND
- 'Whipcord' CBcs ECho EHul EPfP LRHS MPkF NLar SCoo SLim SPer SPoG WEve
* - 'Windsor Gold' EHul
- 'Winter Pink' (v) CKen
- 'Zebrina' (v) CBcs CDoC CDul CMac CTri CWib ECho EHul ELan EPfP LRHS MAsh MGos MMuc NEgg NLar NPri NWea SCoo SEND SLim SPer SPoG SWvt WDin WEve WFar WHar

***plicata* × *standishii*** CDul

## *Thujopsis* (*Cupressaceae*)

***dolabrata*** ♀H4 CBcs CDul EHul GKin MMuc NEgg NLar NWea WDin WEve WFar
- 'Aurea' (v) CDoC CKen EHul LRHS MGos NLar SCoo SLim WEve
- 'Laetevirens' see *T. dolabrata* 'Nana'
- 'Melbourne Gold' NLar WEve
§ - 'Nana' CDoC CKen CMac EHul LRHS MGos NLar SCoo SLim SRms STre WEve WFar
- 'Variegata' (v) CFee CMac EHul GKin LRHS MGos NLar NMun SCoo SLim SPoG WDin WEve WFar

***koraiensis*** (Nakai) hort. see *Thuja koraiensis*

## *Thunbergia* (*Acanthaceae*)

***alata*** EPfP SPoG
- 'African Sunset' CSpe
- 'Lemon' LSou
- 'Lemon Queen' **new** CHll
- 'Orange Beauty' LSou WBor

* ***arborea*** CCCN
***battiscombeii*** CCCN CSpe EShb LRHS MOWG
***coccinea*** CCCN
***erecta*** CCCN MOWG
***fragrans*** GWJ 9441 WCru
***grandiflora*** ♀H1 CCCN CHll ELan EShb MOWG
- 'Alba' CCCN CHll

***gregorii*** ♀H1+3 CCCN CHll EShb MOWG
– 'Mango' SPoG
'Moonglow' CCCN
***mysorensis*** ♀H1 CCCN MOWG SVen
***natalensis*** CCCN EShb
'Orange Wonder' CCCN

## thyme, caraway see *Thymus herba-barona*

## thyme, garden see *Thymus vulgaris*

## thyme, wild see *Thymus serpyllum*

## *Thymus* ✿ (*Lamiaceae*)

from Albania CArn
from Turkey EWes LLWP SBfd SHDw
§ 'Alan Bloom' LLWP
'Anderson's Gold' see *T. pulegioides* 'Bertram Anderson'
***azoricus*** see *T. caespititius*
'Bressingham' CArn CMea CPrp CTri CWan ECtt EDAr EGHP ELau LBee LLWP LRHS MHer MMuc MNHC NPri NSla SBfd SEND SPlb SRms SWal WFar WJek WPat WPer WWEG
'Brigantes' LLWP
'Caborn Fragrant Cloud' LLWP
'Caborn Grey Lady' LLWP
'Caborn Lilac Gem' LLWP SBfd SHDw
'Caborn Pink Beauty' **new** LLWP
'Caborn Pink Carpet' LLWP
'Caborn Rosanne' LLWP
'Caborn Wine and Roses' LLWP
§ ***caespititius*** CArn EDAr ELau GMaP GPoy MHer NMen NRya SBfd SPlb SRot WAbe WPer WWEG
***caespitosus*** CTri
***camphoratus*** CArn EGHP ELau EWes MHer MNHC NMen NSla SBfd SPhx WJek WWEG
– 'A Touch of Frost' SBfd SHDw
– 'Derry' CSpe
***capitatus*** CArn
***carnosus*** misapplied see *T. vulgaris* 'Erectus'
***carnosus*** Boiss. STre XSen
'Carol Ann' (v) ELau EWes LLWP MNHC WWEG
'Caroline' SBfd SHDw
***ciliatus*** LLWP WPer XSen
***cilicicus*** misapplied see *T. caespititius*
***cilicicus*** ambig. MNHC NMen WJek WWEG
***cilicicus*** Boiss. & Bail. CPBP EWes WAbe
***citriodorus*** misapplied see *T.* 'Culinary Lemon'
– 'Variegatus' see *T.* 'Golden King'
***citriodorus*** ambig. GKev WCFE XLum
***citriodorus*** (Pers.) Schreb. 'Archer's Gold' see *T. pulegioides* 'Archer's Gold'
– 'Aureus' see *T. pulegioides* 'Aureus'
– 'Bertram Anderson' see *T. pulegioides* 'Bertram Anderson'
– 'Silver Posie' see *T.* 'Silver Posie'
'Coccineus' see *T.* Coccineus Group
Coccineus Group ♀H4 CArn CPrp CTri ECha ECtt EGHP ELan ELau GMaP LBMP LLWP LRHS MBri MHer MMuc MNHC NPri NRya NSla SEND SPer SPoG SRms SRot WAbe WHoo WJek WPat
– 'Atropurpureus' Schleipfer see *T.* (Coccineus Group) 'Purple Beauty'
– 'Bethany' LLWP SGar
§ – 'Purple Beauty' EPot LLWP MHer SBfd SHDw WWEG
§ – 'Purpurteppich' LLWP
§ – 'Red Elf' MHer NMen SBfd WJek WWEG
'Coccineus Major' CMea CWan EDAr LRHS MHer MNHC SIde WJek
***comosus*** misapplied SBfd SHDw WJek WPer
'Cow Green' SBfd
'Creeping Lemon' misapplied see *T. pulegioides* 'Kurt'
'Creeping Orange' LEdu
§ 'Culinary Lemon' CArn CHby CWan EDAr EGHP ELau GPoy LLWP MBrN MHer MNHC MWat NPri SBfd WJek WPer
'Dark Eyes' SBfd SHDw
'Dartmoor' LLWP SBfd SHDw WJek WWEG
'Desboro' see *T. serpyllum* 'Desborough'
***doerfleri*** ECha LLWP XSen
'Doone Valley' (v) Widely available
***drucei*** see *T. polytrichus* subsp. *britannicus*
'E.B. Anderson' see *T. pulegioides* 'Bertram Anderson'
'Eastgrove Pink' LLWP SBfd SHDw
'Emma's Pink' LLWP
***erectus*** see *T. vulgaris* 'Erectus'
'Fragrantissimus' CArn CEnt CMea CWan EGHP ELau EWhm GGar GPoy LLWP MHer MNHC MWat NPri SIde SPlb SWal WFar WJek WOut WPer XSen
§ 'Golden King' (v) CWan ECha EDAr EGHP ELan LHop LLWP LSRN MAsh NBlu MBri MHer WWEG
'Golden Lemon' misapplied see *T. pulegioides* 'Aureus'
'Golden Lemon' (v) LLWP WJek
'Golden Queen' (v) EDAr EGHP GGar MHer MWat NBlu NPri SBfd SPet SRms WFar
'Gratian' LLWP SBfd SHDw
'Hadrian' LLWP
§ 'Hartington Silver' (v) ECha ECho ECtt EPot EWes GKev LBMP LHop LRHS MAsh MHer NRya NSla SPlb SPoG WFar WHoo WJek WPer WWEG
***herba-barona*** CArn CMea CPrp CTri CWan ECha EDAr EGHP ELau GPoy LEdu LLWP MHer MMuc MNHC MWat SEND SIde SRms STre WJek WPer WWEG
– ***citrata*** see *T. herba-barona* 'Lemon-scented'
§ – 'Lemon-scented' ECha GPoy LLWP MHer SBfd SHDw SIde WJek
'Highdown' ECtt SBfd SHDw
'Highdown Adur' SBfd SHDw
'Highdown Lemon' SBfd SHDw
'Highdown Red' SBfd SHDw
'Highdown Stretham' SBfd SHDw
'Highland Cream' see *T.* 'Hartington Silver'
***hirsutus*** NBir
§ 'Iden' WJek WWEG
'Jekka' WJek WWEG
§ 'Jürgens Rosenteppich' LLWP SBfd
'Kurt' see *T. pulegioides* 'Kurt'
'Lantanii' see *T.* 'Jürgens Rosenteppich'
***lanuginosus*** see *T. serpyllum* L.
'Lavender Sea' EWes LLWP
'Lemon Beauty' **new** LLWP
'Lemon Caraway' see *T. herba-barona* 'Lemon-scented'
'Lemon Curd' CPrp ELau LLWP MNHC NHol SBfd SHDw SIde SPlb SPoG WFar WJek WWEG

| |  |  |
|---|---|---|
| | 'Lemon Sorbet' | SBfd SHDw |
| | 'Lemon Supreme' | LLWP |
| * | 'Lemon Variegated' (v) | EDAr ELau EPfP EWhm MNHC SPer SPoG WWEG |
| | ***leucotrichus*** | XSen |
| | 'Lilac Time' | ECtt EGHP EWes LLWP MHer SBfd SHDw SIde SPlb WJek WPer WWEG |
| | 'Lindisfarne' **new** | LLWP |
| | ***longicaulis*** | CArn ECha ELau LLWP MHer WJek |
| | 'Marjorie' | LLWP |
| | ***marschallianus*** | see *T. pannonicus* |
| § | 'Massa' | LLWP SBfd SHDw WWEG |
| | ***mastichina*** | CArn WPer XSen |
| | - 'Didi' | MHer |
| | ***membranaceus*** | CPBP |
| | ***micans*** | see *T. caespititius* |
| | ***minus*** | see *Calamintha nepeta* |
| | ***montanus*** Waldst. & Kit. | see *T. pulegioides* |
| | 'Mountain Select' | LLWP SBfd SHDw |
| | ***neiceffii*** | CMea ECha ELau LLWP SBch WWEG XSen |
| § | 'Nettleton Pink Carpet' | LLWP WPer |
| | 'New Hall' | SBfd |
| § | Orange Spice = 'Tm95' | LLWP SBfd SHDw SPoG WWEG |
| | ***pallasianus*** | ELau SBfd SHDw |
| § | ***pannonicus*** | LLWP MHer WPer |
| | 'Peter Davis' | EGHP LHop LRHS LSRN MAsh MHer NBir NSla SBfd SIde SPoG XSen |
| § | 'Pinewood' | LLWP MHer SIde XSen |
| | 'Pink Ripple' | CBod CMea ECtt ELau EPot EWes LLWP MHer SBch SBfd SHDw SIde WHal WHoo WJek WPer WWEG |
| | ***polytrichus*** misapplied | see *T. praecox* |
| | ***polytrichus*** A. Kern. ex Borbás | EWil |
| § | - subsp. ***britannicus*** | CArn CHab GPoy MNHC SBfd SHDw SPlb WJek WPer WWEG |
| | - - 'Minor' | see *T.* 'Nettleton Pink Carpet' |
| | - - 'Nettleton Pink Carpet' | see *T.* 'Nettleton Pink Carpet' |
| | - - 'Thomas's White' | see *T.* 'Thomas's White' |
| | 'Porlock' | CMea CPrp CTri CWan EGHP ELau EPfP GMaP GPoy LLWP MAsh MHer MNHC SIde SRms WHoo WJek WPer WWEG |
| § | ***praecox*** | GJos MHer NLan NMir |
| | - 'Albiflorus' | EPot |
| | - subsp. ***arcticus*** | see *T. polytrichus* subsp. *britannicus* |
| | - - 'Albus' | see *T.* 'Thomas's White' |
| | ***pseudolanuginosus*** | see *T. serpyllum* L. |
| § | ***pulegioides*** | CArn CBod CHby ELau GGar GPoy LLWP MBri MHer MNHC SBch SBfd SHDw SIde WJek WPer |
| § | - 'Archer's Gold' | Widely available |
| § | - 'Aureus' ♀H4 | EPot GGar GMaP LLWP MAsh MBri MHer NBlu SBfd SPer SPlb STre WFar WHoo WJek |
| § | - 'Bertram Anderson' ♀H4 | CMea CSam ECha ECtt EGHP ELau EPfP GMaP LAst LLWP MAsh MHer NBir NPri NRya NVic SBfd SIde SPer SPoG SRGP SRms WAbe WFar WHoo WJek WWEG |
| | - 'Foxley' (v) | CBod CWan EGHP EHoe ELau EPfP EWhm LLWP MHer MNHC NHol NPri SBfd SHDw SIde SPlb SPoG WJek WWEG |

| |  |  |
|---|---|---|
| § | - 'Goldentime' | LLWP SWal |
| | - 'Hans' **new** | LLWP |
| § | - 'Kurt' | LLWP ELau MHer SBfd SHDw WJek WNew WWEG |
| | - 'Sir John Lawes' | LLWP MHer SBfd SHDw |
| | - 'Tabor' | EGHP EWhm GMaP MNHC SBfd SHDw |
| | 'Rainbow Falls' (v) | EPfP LLWP MNHC NHol SBfd SHDw SIde WWEG |
| | 'Rasta' (v) | ECtt LLWP MHer |
| § | 'Red Glow' | LLWP |
| | 'Redstart' | ECha ELau EPot LBee LLWP MHer NBlu SBch SBfd SHDw SIde WJek WWEG |
| | ***richardii*** subsp. ***nitidus*** misapplied | see *T. vulgaris* 'Suditin' |
| | - - 'Compactus Albus' | see *T. vulgaris* 'Snow White' |
| | 'Rosa Ceeping' | LLWP SBfd SHDw |
| | 'Rosalicht' | see *T.* 'Rosedrift' |
| | 'Rosalind' | SBfd SHDw |
| § | 'Rosedrift' | LLWP SBfd SHDw |
| § | 'Rosemary's Early Red' | LLWP |
| | ***rotundifolius*** misapplied | see *T. vulgaris* 'Elsbeth' |
| | 'Ruby Glow' | CEnt ECtt ELau EPot EWes MHer SBfd SHDw WFar WWEG |
| | ***serpyllum*** misapplied | see *T.* 'Rosemary's Early Red' |
| | ***serpyllum*** ambig. | SIde SPet XLum |
| § | ***serpyllum*** L. | CArn CTri CWan ECha EDAr EPot GJos GMaP LLWP MBNS MBri MHer MLHP MMuc MNHC NBir SEND SPlb SRms WHoo WJek WPer WWEG |
| | - var. ***albus*** | CPrp ECha EGHP ELau GLam GMaP GPoy LAst LLWP LRHS MNHC NPri SIde SPer SRms WAbe WHoo WJek WWEG |
| | - 'Albus Variegatus' | see *T.* 'Hartington Silver' |
| N | - 'Annie Hall' | CPrp CWan EDAr ELau EPfP EPot GGar LLWP LRHS MAsh MHer NPri SBfd SIde STre WCFE WJek WPer |
| | - 'Atropurpureus' Schleipfer | see *T.* (Coccineus Group) 'Purple Beauty' |
| | - ***coccineus*** 'Minor' misapplied | see *T.* Coccineus Group |
| | - - 'Minor' Bloom | see *T.* 'Alan Bloom' |
| | - 'Conwy Rose' | CPBP LLWP WAbe |
| § | - 'Desborough' | ECtt LLWP MHer WWEG |
| N | - 'East Lodge' | LLWP MNHC |
| | - 'Elfin' | ECho EWes LBee MBri SBfd SPlb WWEG |
| N | - 'Fulney Red' | EWes |
| | - 'Goldstream' (v) | CMea CPrp EGHP ELau EPfP LHop LLWP LRHS MBri MHer NBlu SPlb SRms WJek WPer |
| | - 'Iden' | see *T.* 'Iden' |
| | - 'Minimalist' | see *T. serpyllum* 'Minor' |
| | - 'Minimus' | see *T. serpyllum* 'Minor' |
| § | - 'Minor' | Widely available |
| | - 'Minus' | see *T. serpyllum* 'Minor' |
| | - 'Petite' | EWes LLWP |
| N | - 'Pink Chintz' ♀H4 | CMea ECha ECtt EDAr EGHP ELau EPfP EPot GPoy LLWP LRHS MAsh MBri MHer MNHC NBlu NPri SBfd SPer SPlb SPoG WHoo WJek WPer WWEG |
| | - 'Posh Pinky' | EPot LLWP NMen |
| | - 'Purple Beauty' | see *T.* (Coccineus Group) 'Purple Beauty' |
| | - 'Purpurteppich' | see *T.* (Coccineus Group) 'Purpurteppich' |

| | | |
|---|---|---|
| | - 'Pygmaeus' | LLWP |
| | - 'Red Carpet' | ECtt NHol |
| | - 'Red Elf' | see *T.* (Coccineus Group) 'Red Elf' |
| | - 'Red Glow' | see *T.* 'Red Glow' |
| | - 'Roger's Snowdrift' | LLWP |
| N | - 'Roseus' | SIde |
| N | - 'Russetings' | CPrp CYeo ECtt EGHP ELau EPfP EPot LLWP MAsh MHer MNHC SBch SBfd SIde SPoG SRms WFar WHoo WJek WNew WWEG |
| N | - 'September' | LLWP MHer |
| N | - 'Snowdrift' | CArn CMea CWan ECtt ELau EPfP EPot LLWP MHer MNHC MWat NMen NRya SBch SIde SPlb WCFE WFar WJek WPat WPer WWEG |
| | - subsp. ***tanaensis*** | CArn |
| | - 'Variegatus' | see *T.* 'Hartington Silver' |
| | - 'Vey' | CPBP EPot EWes GLam GMaP LLWP LRHS MHer SBfd SHDw WJek WWEG |
| | ***sibthorpii*** | CArn |
| | 'Silver Posie' | Widely available |
| | 'Silver Queen' (v) ♀$^{H4}$ | CBcs CMea CSam CWan ECha EDAr EGHP ELan EPfP GGar GKev GMaP LAst LLWP MHer MNHC NBlu SBfd SPlb WFar WJek WNew WWEG |
| | 'Snowdonia Idris' | LLWP |
| | 'Snowdonia Ifor' | LLWP |
| | 'Snowdonia Iorwerth' | LLWP |
| | 'Snowdonia Isolde' | LLWP |
| | 'Snowdonia Lass' | LLWP SBfd |
| | 'Snowdonia Pedr' | LLWP |
| | 'Snowdonia Pink Gem' | LLWP |
| | 'Snowdonia Pryderi' | LLWP |
| | 'Snowdonia Pwyll' | LLWP |
| | 'Snowdonia Rhiannon' | LLWP |
| | 'Snowdonia Rowena' | LLWP |
| | 'Snowman' | SBfd |
| | 'Spicy Orange' | see *T.* Orange Spice |
| § | 'Thomas's White' ♀$^{H4}$ | CTri |
| | ***valesiacus*** | see *T.* 'Massa' |
| § | ***vulgaris*** | Widely available |
| | - 'Aranjuez' **new** | LLWP |
| | - 'Aureus' hort. | see *T. pulegioides* 'Goldentime' |
| | - 'Château Queribus' **new** | LLWP |
| * | - 'Compactus' | CSam GPoy LLWP MNHC MRav WJek |
| | - 'Deutsche Auslese' | see *T. vulgaris* |
| | - 'Diamantis' | LLWP |
| | - 'Dorcas White' | LLWP MHer WPer |
| § | - 'Elsbeth' | ELau LLWP MHer SBfd SHDw |
| | - 'English Winter' | SIde |
| § | - 'Erectus' | MHer WPer |
| | - French | see *T. vulgaris* |
| | - French, summer | SIde |
| | - 'Golden Pins' | MHer |
| | - 'Lemon Queen' | ELau |
| | - 'Lucy' | LLWP MHer MNHC |
| | - 'Pinewood' | see *T.* 'Pinewood' |
| § | - 'Snow White' | ELau EWes LLWP SBfd SHDw WJek |
| § | - 'Suditin' | STre |
| | 'Widecombe' (v) | LLWP MHer SBfd SHDw |
| | ***zygis*** | CArn |

# *Tiarella* (*Saxifragaceae*)

| | | |
|---|---|---|
| | 'Appalachian Trail' **new** | MPnt |
| | 'Black Snowflake'$^{PBR}$ | EBee |
| | 'Black Velvet'$^{PBR}$ | EBee MLLN SHeu WFar |
| | 'Braveheart' | EBee WWEG |
| | 'Cascade Creeper' **new** | MPnt |
| | ***collina*** | see *T. wherryi* |
| | ***cordifolia*** ♀$^{H4}$ | Widely available |
| | - 'Glossy' | CBct |
| | - 'Milk Chocolate' **new** | MMoz |
| | - 'Oakleaf' | EBee MLLN NBre NBro |
| | - 'Rosalie' | see × *Heucherella alba* 'Rosalie' |
| | - 'Running Tapestry' | EBee |
| | - 'Slick Rock' | EPPr |
| | 'Crow Feather'$^{PBR}$ | EBee SHeu |
| | 'Cygnet'$^{PBR}$ | CBct CLAP EBee ECtt LHop LRHS SHeu SPer SPoG SRot WFar |
| | 'Dunvegan' | EBee WPnP |
| | 'Elizabeth Oliver' | CLAP |
| | 'Freckles' | LRHS MRav |
| | 'Happy Trails' **new** | MPnt SHeu |
| | 'Hidden Carpet' | CHid |
| | 'Inkblot' | EBee ELan LRHS MPnt NBro SHeu WFar WMoo |
| | 'Iron Butterfly'$^{PBR}$ (v) | CBct CLAP CMac CWCL EBee ECtt EPfP GBin GMaP LAst LHop LRHS LSRN MNrw MRav NBro NCGa SMrm SPer SPoG SRot STes WFar WPGP WWEG |
| | 'Jeepers Creepers'$^{PBR}$ | EBee MAsh MPnt NWad SHar SHeu |
| * | 'Laciniate Runner' | CLAP |
| | 'Martha Oliver' | CLAP EBee NBre SBch WPGP |
| | 'Mint Chocolate'$^{PBR}$ | CChe CLAP CYeo EAEE EBee ECha ECtt EHoe ELan EPfP GMaP LRHS LSou MLLN MNrw MRav MWhi NBir NGdn NLar SPer SPur SWvt WFar WPGP WWEG |
| | Morning Star = 'Tntia042'$^{PBR}$ | CHid EWll LAst LBMP LRHS MBri MPnt SHeu SRkn SRot WFar |
| | 'Mystic Mist' (v) | EBee ECtt LSou MAsh MPnt NLar NWad SHeu SPoG |
| | 'Neon Lights'$^{PBR}$ | CSpe EBee ECGP EWes MPnt NBPC NBir NPnk SHeu SWvt |
| § | 'Ninja'$^{PBR}$ | CHid EBee ECha ECtt ELan GMaP LAst LRHS MRav NBir NLar NSti SPer SWvt WCot WFar |
| | 'Pink Bouquet' | CAbP CLAP CMac CSpe CWGN EAEE EBee ECha ECtt GJos LBMP LRHS MBri MLLN NBro NDov NHol SBch WCot WFar WMoo |
| | 'Pink Brushes'$^{PBR}$ | CLAP WPnP |
| | 'Pink Skyrocket'$^{PBR}$ | CAbP CLAP CMil CWGN CYeo EBee ECtt LLHF LRHS LSRN MAvo MPnt NBir NGdn NHol NPnk NWad SHar SHeu SMrm SPer WBor WCot WCra WGor |
| | 'Pinwheel' | LRHS MRav NBre |
| | 'Pirate's Patch'$^{PBR}$ | LLHF NHol SHeu |
| | ***polyphylla*** | EBee ELan NBre NLar SBch SWal WFar |
| | - 'Baoxing Pink' | CLAP WCru |
| | - 'Filigran' | EBee EPfP NHol NLar |
| | - 'Moorgrün' | GCal LRHS |
| | - pink-flowered | CLAP GBin |
| | 'Running Tiger' | WWEG |
| | 'Sea Foam' | NHol NPnk SHeu |
| | 'Simsalabim' | EBee |
| | 'Skeleton Key' | EBee LRHS |
| | 'Skid's Variegated' (v) | EBee ECtt LRHS MNrw NSti SHeu SWvt WCot |
| | 'Skyrocket' | ECtt |
| | 'Spanish Cross'$^{PBR}$ | NHol SHeu |
| | 'Spring Symphony'$^{PBR}$ | CLAP EBee ECtt EShb GBin LBMP LRHS LSou MBri MLLN NCGa NHol NLar NPer NPnk SBfd WFar WHoo |
| | Starburst = 'Tntia041'$^{PBR}$ | SHeu |

| | |
|---|---|
| 'Starfish' | NBPC |
| 'Sugar and Spice'PBR | EBee MBrN MPnt NHol NPnk NWad SHeu SPoG |
| 'Tiger Stripe' | EBee EPfP LRHS MPnt MRav NBro NPnk WFar |
| 'Timbuktu' | MPnt SHeu |
| ***trifoliata*** | MRav WFar |
| - var. ***unifoliata*** | WWEG |
| 'Viking Ship'PBR | see × *Heucherella* 'Viking Ship' |
| § ***wherryi*** ♀H4 | CBcs COIW CWCL EBee ECtt ELan ELon EPfP GMaP LAst LBMP LRHS NBir NBro NDov NOrc NPri SBch SPer SPlb SRot SWvt WFar WPer WPnP WWEG XLum |
| - 'Bronze Beauty' | CLAP IGor MRav SBch WFar WPGP |
| - 'Green Velvet' | ECha |
| - 'Heronswood Mist' (v) | CAbP CBct CFir EBee ECtt MMoz SHeu SPer SWvt WCot |
| - 'Montrose' | WPGP |

## *Tibouchina* (*Melastomataceae*)

| | |
|---|---|
| ***grandifolia*** | CCCN |
| ***granulosa*** | MOWG WCot |
| ***heteromalla*** | CCCN CRHN |
| 'Jules' | MOWG |
| * ***laxa*** 'Skylab' | MOWG |
| ***organensis*** | CCCN CHII CMac MOWG SHeu WCot WPGP |
| ***paratropica*** | CRHN CSpe |
| - RCB/Arg X-4 | WCot |
| ***semidecandra*** hort. | see *T. urvilleana* |
| § ***urvilleana*** ♀H1 | CBcs CCCN CDoC CEnd CHEx CKno CRHN CSBt CTri CTsd EBak ECre ELan EPfP LRHS MCot MMuc MOWG NCGa NPri SBrd SEND SPer SPoG SRkn SRms WCot |
| - 'Compacta' | CCCN LRHS |
| - 'Edwardsii' | LSou SAdn SMrm SUsu WCot |
| - 'Nana' | CDoC |
| - 'Rich Blue Sun' | CSpe LRHS |
| - variegated (v) | CCCN LSou SUsu WCot |

## *Tigridia* ✿ (*Iridaceae*)

| | |
|---|---|
| ***lutea*** | ECho |
| ***orthantha*** 'Red-Hot Tiger' | WCru |
| ***pavonia*** | CBro CPLG CSpr ECho EDif EWld EWII LAma MBri |
| - 'Alba' | EDif |
| - 'Alba Immaculata' **new** | CSpe EDif |
| - 'Aurea' | MDev |
| - 'Canariensis' | CTca |
| - 'Lilacea' | ECho MDev |
| - 'Speciosa' | CTca |

## *Tilia* ✿ (*Malvaceae*)

| | |
|---|---|
| ***americana*** | CMCN |
| - 'Dentata' | CDul |
| - 'Nova' | CDoC |
| ***amurensis*** | CMCN |
| ***argentea*** | see *T. tomentosa* |
| ***begoniifolia*** | see *T. dasystyla* |
| ***chenmoui*** | CMCN EPfP MBlu WPGP |
| ***chinensis*** | CMCN NPCo WPGP |
| ***chingiana*** | CDul CMCN SBir SLon |
| ***cordata*** ♀H4 | CBcs CCVT CDul CHab CLnd CMac CSBt CTho CTri EBee ECrN ELan EPfP LBuc LMaj MAsh MMuc MSwo NWea SBfd SCoo SEND SEWo SPer STre WDin WMou |
| § - 'Böhlje' | CDul SLPl |
| - 'Dainty Leaf' | CDul |
| - 'Erecta' | see *T. cordata* 'Böhlje' |
| - 'Greenspire' ♀H4 | CCVT CDoC CDul CLnd CWib EBee ECrN LMaj LTen SBfd SEWo |
| - 'Len Parvin' | WPGP |
| - 'Lico' | LMaj |
| - 'Roelvo' | CDul |
| - 'Swedish Upright' | CDul CTho |
| - 'Winter Orange' | CDul CEnd EBee ECrN EPfP LRHS MBlu MBri NPCo SBfd SBir SCoo SEWo |
| § ***dasystyla*** | CMCN |
| - subsp. ***caucasica*** | WPGP |
| × ***euchlora*** ♀H4 | CBcs CCVT CDul CLnd CMCN EBee ECrN EPfP LMaj NWea SBfd SEWo SPer WDin WFar |
| § × ***europaea*** | CDul CLnd CRWN ELan EWTr MMuc SEND |
| - 'Koningslinde' | CDul |
| - 'Pallida' | CDul CLnd CTho LMaj LTen MBlu NWea |
| - 'Wratislaviensis' ♀H4 | CDoC CDul CLnd EPfP MAsh MBlu NWea |
| § 'Harold Hillier' | MBlu |
| ***henryana*** | CDoC CDul CEnd CLnd CMCN CTho CWib EBee ECrN ELan EMil EPfP IArd IDee LRHS MBlu MBri MMuc MREP NWea SBir SCoo WDin WPGP |
| - 'Arnold Select' **new** | WMou |
| § ***heterophylla*** | CMCN MBlu WPGP |
| - var. ***michauxii*** | CLnd |
| 'Hillieri' | see *T.* 'Harold Hillier' |
| ***insularis*** misapplied | see *T. japonica* 'Ernest Wilson' |
| ***intonsa*** | CMCN |
| ***japonica*** | CDul CMCN WPGP |
| § - 'Ernest Wilson' | CMCN MBlu |
| ***kiusiana*** | CMCN MBlu MBri WMou WPGP |
| ***mandshurica*** | CMCN WPGP |
| ***maximowicziana*** | WPGP |
| ***mexicana*** | EBee WPGP |
| ***miqueliana*** | CMCN |
| 'Moltkei' | CMCN EBee WPGP |
| ***mongolica*** | CDoC CDul CLnd CMCN EBee EPfP MBlu MMuc SCoo WMou WPGP |
| ***monticola*** | see *T. heterophylla* |
| ***oliveri*** | CDul CMCN MBlu NWea SBir WMou WPGP |
| 'Petiolaris' ♀H4 | CCVT CDoC CDul CEnd CLnd CMCN EBee ECrN ELan EPfP MBlu MSwo NWea SEND SPer WDin WMou |
| ***platyphyllos*** | CCVT CDul CHab CLnd CMCN CSBt CTho CTri EBee ECrN EMil EPfP EWTr LAst LBuc MMuc NWea SBfd SCoo SEND SPer WDin WMou |
| - 'Aurea' | CDul CTho ECrN MBlu |
| - 'Corallina' | see *T. platyphyllos* 'Rubra' |
| - 'Erecta' | see *T. platyphyllos* 'Fastigiata' |
| § - 'Fastigiata' | CDul ECrN SLPl |
| - 'Laciniata' | CDul CMCN CTho LMaj MBlu |
| § - 'Rubra' ♀H4 | CCVT CDoC CDul CLnd CTho EPfP LBuc MGos NWea SEWo WDin WFar |
| - 'Tortuosa' | MBlu WMou |
| § ***tomentosa*** | CDul CLnd CMCN ELan EMil LMaj MMuc NWea SCoo WDin WMou |
| - 'Brabant' ♀H4 | CDoC CDul EPfP LMaj WFar |
| ***tuan*** | CMCN WPGP |
| × ***vulgaris*** | see *T.* × *europaea* |

## *Tilingia* (*Apiaceae*)

| | |
|---|---|
| ***ajanensis*** B&SWJ 11202 | WCru |

## *Tillaea* see *Crassula*

## *Tillandsia* (*Bromeliaceae*)

| | |
|---|---|
| sp. **new** | XBlo |
| ***aeranthos*** | SChr |
| ***usneoides*** | SHmp |

## *Tinantia* (*Commelinaceae*)

| | |
|---|---|
| ***pringlei*** | LEdu SBrt SDys WHil WPGP |
| - AIM 77 | EBee WCot |
| - variegated (v) **new** | WCot |

## *Titanopsis* (*Aizoaceae*)

| | |
|---|---|
| ***calcarea*** ♀$^{H1}$ | CCCN EPfP |

## *Tithonia* (*Asteraceae*)

| | |
|---|---|
| ***rotundifolia*** | CSpe |
| - 'Torch' | CSpe SMrm |

## *Todea* (*Osmundaceae*)

| | |
|---|---|
| ***barbara*** | WRic |

## *Tofieldia* (*Tofieldiaceae*)

| | |
|---|---|
| ***coccinea*** | GCal WCru |

## *Tolmiea* (*Saxifragaceae*)

| | |
|---|---|
| ***menziesii*** | CMac EWld MCot SPer SWal XLum |
| - 'Goldsplash' | see *T. menziesii* 'Taff's Gold' |
| - 'Maculata' | see *T. menziesii* 'Taff's Gold' |
| § - 'Taff's Gold' (v) ♀$^{H4}$ | CWan EHoe EOHP EShb GMaP NBid NVic SPlb WHoo WTin XLum |
| - 'Variegata' | see *T. menziesii* 'Taff's Gold' |

## *Tolpis* (*Asteraceae*)

| | |
|---|---|
| ***barbata*** | CSpe |

## *Tonestus* (*Asteraceae*)

| | |
|---|---|
| § ***lyallii*** | WPer |

## *Toona* (*Meliaceae*)

| | |
|---|---|
| § ***sinensis*** | CArn CBcs CDul CEnd CGHE CTho CWib ELan EMil EPfP MMuc SEND WFar WPGP |
| - 'Flamingo' (v) | EPfP ESwi GKin LRHS MGos NLar SPoG SSta WCot |

## *Torenia* (*Linderniaceae*)

| | |
|---|---|
| (Moon Series) Blue Moon = 'Dantmoon' | LAst |
| - Purple Moon = 'Dantopur'$^{PBR}$ | LAst LSou |
| - White Moon = 'Dantorwhite'$^{PBR}$ | LAst |
| - Yellow Moon = 'Danmoon20'$^{PBR}$ | LAst |
| Summer Wave Series | CCCN SCoo |

## *Torilis* (*Apiaceae*)

| | |
|---|---|
| ***japonica*** | CBre CHab |

## *Torreya* (*Taxaceae*)

| | |
|---|---|
| ***jackii*** | EGFP |

## *Townsendia* (*Asteraceae*)

| | |
|---|---|
| ***alpigena*** | GKev |
| § - var. ***alpigena*** | CPBP GKev |
| ***formosa*** | ECho |
| ***incana*** | EPot WAbe |
| ***jonesii*** | EPot |
| ***leptotes*** | CPBP |
| ***montana*** | see *T. alpigena* var. *alpigena* |
| ***parryi*** | GKev |
| § ***rothrockii*** | EPot NMen |
| ***spathulata*** | CPBP |
| ***wilcoxiana*** misapplied | see *T. rothrockii* |

## *Toxicodendron* (*Anacardiaceae*)

| | |
|---|---|
| ***vernicifluum*** | see *Rhus verniciflua* |

## *Trachelium* (*Campanulaceae*)

| | |
|---|---|
| § ***asperuloides*** | WAbe |
| ***caeruleum*** ♀$^{H1}$ | SGar |
| - 'Black Knight' | CSpe |
| ***jacquinii*** subsp. ***rumelianum*** | NWCA WPat |

## *Trachelospermum* ✿ (*Apocynaceae*)

| | |
|---|---|
| from Nanking, China | EShb |
| § ***asiaticum*** ♀$^{H2-3}$ | Widely available |
| - B&SWJ 4814 | WCru |
| - 'Golden Memories' | CPLG CWGN EBee ELan EPfP LRHS LSRN LSqu MGos SKHP SLon SPoG SSpi SSta SWvt WCot WPat |
| - 'Goshiki' (v) | EShb WPat |
| - var. ***intermedium*** | NPal WPGP |
| - - B&SWJ 8733 | WCru |
| * - 'Kiejiu Chirimen' | SKHP |
| - 'Kulu Chirimen' | WCot |
| - 'Nagaba' (v) | SKHP |
| - 'Ōgon-nishiki' (v) | LRHS SKHP |
| - 'Pink Showers' **new** | SKHP |
| - 'Shirofu Chirimen' (v) | SKHP |
| - 'Theta' | SKHP WCot WPGP WPat |
| 'Chameleon' | EBee EGxp NPal SKHP |
| ***jasminoides*** ♀$^{H3-4}$ | Widely available |
| - B&SWJ 5117 | WCru |
| - 'Big White Star' | EPfP |
| § - 'Japonicum' | CRHN CSPN LRHS SLon SPer WSHC |
| - 'Major' | CSPN EBee ELan SEND SSpi |
| * - 'Oblanceolatum' | GCal |
| - 'Star of Toscana' **new** | EPfP |
| - 'Tricolor' (v) | CBcs LAst LRHS SGol SLim SWvt WCot |
| - 'Variegatum' (v) ♀$^{H3-4}$ | Widely available |
| - 'Waterwheel' | EBee ELan LRHS SKHP SSpi WPGP WSHC |
| - 'Wilsonii' | CBot CMac CPLG CSPN CSam EBee ELan EPfP GCal LHop LRHS LSRN MCCP NLar SEND SKHP SLim SPer SPoG SWvt WCot WCru WHar WPGP WPat |
| ***majus*** misapplied | see *T. jasminoides* 'Japonicum' |
| ***majus*** Nakai | see *T. asiaticum* |

## *Trachycarpus* (*Arecaceae*)

| | |
|---|---|
| sp. | EAmu |
| from Manipur | EAmu SChr |
| § ***fortunei*** ♀$^{H3-4}$ | Widely available |
| ***fortunei*** × ***wagnerianus*** **new** | WPGP |
| ***latisectus*** | CBrP EAmu LPJP LPal SBig |
| ***martianus*** | CDTJ CTrC EAmu LPJP LPal SBig SChr |
| ***nanus*** | CDTJ LPal |
| 'Nova' | EAmu |

| | |
|---|---|
| ***oreophilus*** | LPal |
| ***princeps*** | CBrP LPal |
| ***takil*** | CBrP CDTJ EAmu EPla LPal NPal |
| ***wagnerianus*** | CBrP CDTJ CGHE CHid CPHo CPLG CTrC EAmu EPla ETod LPJP LPal NPal NPla SBig SChr SMad WPGP |

## *Trachymene* (*Araliaceae*)

| | |
|---|---|
| ***coerulea*** | CSpe |

## *Trachyspermum* (*Apiaceae*)

| | |
|---|---|
| ***ammi*** | CArn |

## *Trachystemon* (*Boraginaceae*)

| | |
|---|---|
| ***orientalis*** | CBre CHEx CMac CPLG CSev EBee ECha ELan EPfP IKil LEdu LHop MAvo MCot MRav NBid NLar SBch SBig SBrd SKHP WBrk WCot WCru WDyG WFar WHer WMoo WPnP |

## *Tradescantia* ✿ (*Commelinaceae*)

| | | |
|---|---|---|
| | ***albiflora*** | see *T. fluminensis* |
| | × ***andersoniana*** | see *T.* Andersoniana Group |
| § | Andersoniana Group | CSpr CWib SPet SWal WHil WPer |
| | - 'Baby Doll' | XLum |
| | - 'Bilberry Ice' | Widely available |
| | - 'Blanca' | WWEG |
| | - 'Blue and Gold' | CBcs COIW EBee ECtt ELon EPPr EPfP LAst LHop LRHS MRav NLar NSti WCot WFar WWEG |
| | - 'Blue Stone' | CCse CMea CSBt EBee ECha ECtt MAvo MRav NPri SRms WFar WHoo WTin XLum |
| | - 'Bridal Veil' | CHll |
| | - 'Caerulea Plena' | see *T. virginiana* 'Caerulea Plena' |
| | - Carmine Glow | see *T.* (Andersoniana Group) 'Karminglut' |
| | - 'Charlotte' | CTca EBee ECha ECtt LRHS LSRN MAvo MCot NBre NBro NGdn NLar SBfd SRGP WCAu WMnd WWEG |
| | - 'Chedglow' | WWEG |
| | - 'Concord Grape' | Widely available |
| | - 'Danielle' | EPfP |
| | - 'Domaine de Courson' | EBee ECtt XLum |
| | - 'In the Navy' | NBre NLar |
| | - 'Innocence' | CMHG CSBt CTri EBee ECha ECtt ELan EPfP GCra GJos GMaP LAst LHop LRHS MLLN MMuc NBPC NBir NCGa NGdn NPnk NPri NSti SBfd SEND SPer STes WFar WMnd XLum |
| | - 'Iris Prichard' | CPrp CTca EBee ELan EPfP GCra GLog GMaP LAst NBre NCGa NLar SRGP WBor WFar |
| | - 'Isis' ♀H4 | CPrp CTri EBee ECGP ECtt ELan EPfP GCra LBMP LRHS MMuc MRav NBir NCGa NGdn NOrc SBfd SBrd SEND SPer WKif WMnd WNew WTin |
| | - 'J.C.Weguelin' ♀H4 | EBee EPfP NBir NBre NMRc NPnk SRms WCAu WMnd WWEG XLum |
| § | - 'Karminglut' | EBee ECtt ELan EPfP GLog GMaP NBir NGdn NPnk NVic WHoo WWEG XLum |
| | - 'Leonora' | EBee EPfP LRHS MMuc NLar SEND XLum |
| | - 'Little Doll' | CWCL ECtt EPfP GLog LAst LRHS MDKP MGos MNFA NBro NLar NPri WFar WWEG XLum |
| | - 'Little White Doll' | CPrp CWCL EBee ECtt LAst LRHS MDKP MNFA NBre NLar WFar WWEG |
| | - 'Mariella' | EBee |
| | - 'Mrs Loewer' | MAvo |
| | - 'Osprey' ♀H4 | CTri EBee ECha ECtt ELan EPfP GCal LBMP LRHS MAvo MLHP MRav MWhi NBPC NBro NGdn NLar NPri NSti NVic SPer SPoG SRms WBor WCAu WFar WHoo WKif WWEG XLum |
| | - 'Pauline' | EBee ECtt ELon EPla LAst MRav NBir NLar WFar WHoo WTin WWEG XLum |
| | - 'Perinne's Pink' | CWCL EBee EPfP LRHS MDev NBPC NLar NPnk NSti SUsu WCAu |
| | - 'Pink Chablis'PBR | CWCL ECtt MAvo NBro NLar |
| | - 'Purewell Giant' | CMac CTri EBee GBee GLog LHop LRHS NBro NLar SPer WGor WKif WMnd |
| | - 'Purple Dome' | EBee ECtt EPla GMaP LAst LRHS MAvo MCot MMuc MRav NBir NBro NCGa NGdn SBfd SEND SPoG STes WMnd WTin WWEG |
| | - 'Red Grape' | CTca EBee ECtt EWll LRHS MLLN MWhi NPro NSti WWEG |
| | - 'Rosi' | EBee |
| | - 'Rubra' | CPrp CSpr EBee NOrc SRms XLum |
| | - 'Satin Doll'PBR | CBcs EBee ECtt EPfP |
| | - 'Sunshine Charm' **new** | NLar |
| | - 'Sweet Kate' | CBct CMac CWCL EBee ECtt LRHS LSRN MBNS NBPC NBro SPoG SRGP XLum |
| | - 'Sylvana' | EBee LRHS SApp |
| | - 'Temptation' | ECtt |
| | - 'Valour' | CSBt EBee WFar |
| | - 'Zwanenburg Blue' | EBee ECha ECtt ELan GBee GLog LAst LRHS MLHP NCGa NPnk SPlb WMnd WWEG XLum |
| | 'Angel Eyes' | ECtt MDKP |
| | 'Baerbel' | SPad |
| | ***canaliculata*** | see *T. ohiensis* |
| § | ***fluminensis*** | SChr |
| | - 'Albovittata' | EShb |
| § | - 'Aurea' ♀H1 | EShb |
| | - 'Maiden's Blush' (v) | CSpe EShb SGar SRms WFoF |
| | - 'Quicksilver' (v) ♀H1 | EShb |
| | - 'Variegata' | see *T. fluminensis* 'Aurea' |
| | 'Gold Mound' **new** | WRHF |
| § | ***ohiensis*** | CFee LPBA MAvo |
| | ***pallida*** 'Kartuz Giant' | EShb WCot |
| § | - 'Purpurea' ♀H2-3 | EOHP EShb |
| | ***pendula*** | see *T. zebrina* |
| | 'Purple Sabre' | CBcs LAst SMrm |
| | ***purpurea*** | see *T. pallida* 'Purpurea' |
| | ***sillamontana*** ♀H1 | EShb |
| | ***spathacea*** | EShb |
| | ***tricolor*** | see *T. zebrina* |
| | ***virginiana*** | MWhi SGar |
| | - 'Alba' | CMac GCal WPer |
| * | - 'Brevicaulis' | ECha ECtt LRHS NBre NBro WWEG |
| § | - 'Caerulea Plena' (d) | CMHG EBee ELan EPfP EPla MRav NBPC SPer SRms STes WFar WTin WWEG |
| | - 'Rubra' | SPlb |
| § | ***zebrina*** ♀H1 | EShb |
| | - ***pendula*** | see *T. zebrina* |
| | - 'Purpusii' ♀H1 | SRms |

## *Tragopogon* (*Asteraceae*)

| | |
|---|---|
| ***crocifolius*** | CCVN CSpe SPhx WCot |
| ***porrifolius*** | GCal ILis MCot SVic |
| ***pratensis*** | CArn NMir |

## *Trapa* (*LythraceaeA*)

| | |
|---|---|
| ***natans*** | CBen |

## *Trautvetteria* (*Ranunculaceae*)

| | |
|---|---|
| ***carolinensis*** | CLAP GEdr WCru |
| var. ***japonica*** | |
| - - B&SWJ 10861 | WCru |
| - var. ***occidentalis*** | EBee GEdr WCru |

## *Trichopetalum* (*Asparagaceae*)

| | |
|---|---|
| § ***plumosum*** | CBro |

## *Trichostema* (*Lamiaceae*)

| | |
|---|---|
| ***dichotomum*** RCB RL 15 | WCot |

## *Tricuspidaria* see *Crinodendron*

## *Tricyrtis* ✿ (*Liliaceae*)

| | |
|---|---|
| B&SWJ 3229 from Taiwan | WCru WFar |
| from Taiwan | EBla |
| 'Adbane' | CAby CBct CChe CLAP EBee ELan EPPr EWes GKev IKil LRHS MMoz NGdn SMrm WFar WGwG WWEG |
| ***affinis*** | GAbr GGar |
| - B&SWJ 2804 | CLAP WCru |
| - B&SWJ 5645 | EBla WCru |
| - B&SWJ 6182 | WCru |
| - B&SWJ 11169 | WCru |
| - B&SWJ 11442 | WCru |
| - 'Early Bird' | EBla WCru WFar |
| - 'Sansyoku' | GEdr |
| 'Amanagowa' | CLAP |
| ***bakeri*** | see *T. latifolia* |
| 'Blue Wonder' | LRHS LSou MSCN NLar NPro SPer SPet |
| ***dilatata*** | see *T. macropoda* |
| 'Empress' | CBct COIW CPLG EBee EBla ECha ELon EPfP EWTr EWes IBal LAst LEdu LSou MAvo MTis NBPC NEgg NHol SPet SRkn WFar WWEG |
| ***flava*** | EBee LRHS WCru WFar |
| ***formosana*** ♀H4 | Widely available |
| - B&SWJ 306 | CLAP EBla MNrw WFar |
| - B&SWJ 355 | EBla WCru WFar |
| - B&SWJ 3073 | EBla WCru WFar |
| - B&SWJ 3616 | CPLG EBla WCru WFar |
| - B&SWJ 3635 | CLAP |
| - B&SWJ 3712 | EBla WCru WFar |
| - B&SWJ 6705 | CLAP |
| - B&SWJ 6741 | WCru WFar |
| - B&SWJ 6970 | EBla WCru WFar |
| - B&SWJ 7071 | WFar |
| - B&SWJ 7084 | WFar |
| - RWJ 10109 | EBla WCru |
| - 'Dark Beauty' | CDes CLAP CPLG CWCL EBee ECtt EWTr MBri MLLN MNrw MWat NBPC NPri SMrm SPad SPur SUsu WFar WPGP WWEG |
| - dark-flowered | NCGa WFar |
| - 'Emperor' (v) | EBee |
| - 'Gilt Edge' (v) | Widely available |
| - f. ***glandosa*** | WFar |
| - - B&SWJ 7084 | WCru |
| - aff. f. ***glandosa*** 'Blu-Shing Toad' | EBla WCru WFar |
| - var. ***grandiflora*** 'W-Ho-ping Toad' | EBla WCru WFar |
| - 'Kestrel' (v) **new** | WCot |
| - pale-flowered | CBct WFar WWEG |
| - 'Purple Beauty' | EBee GKev LSou MDKP MNrw MPkF NPnk |
| - 'Samurai' (v) | CLAP CWCL EPPr EWes NPnk WFar |
| - 'Shelley's' | CBct CLAP NBro SMrm WFar WWEG |
| - 'Small Wonder' | EBla WCru WFar |
| - 'Spotted Toad' | EBla LEdu WCru |
| § - Stolonifera Group | CAvo CBcs CBro CMMP CMac EBee ELan EPfP GGar LEdu LRHS MCot MWat NGdn NHol SDix WFar WMnd |
| - - B&SWJ 7046 | WCru WFar |
| - 'Taiwan Toad' | CPLG WFar |
| - 'Taroko Toad' | EBla WCru |
| - 'Tiny Toad' | WCru WFar |
| - 'Variegata' (v) | CBct CBro LEdu MMHG NBir WCru WFar |
| - 'Velvet Toad' | EBla WCru WFar |
| 'Golden Leopard' | EPfP LSou NCGa NMyG SPer |
| 'Harlequin' | LEdu WFar WWEG |
| § ***hirta*** | CAby CBcs CDes CHid CMac CPrp CTri CWCL EBee ECho EPfP GGar GKev ITim LRHS MCot MMuc NBro NGdn NHol SEND SGar SPav SPet SPlb SWal SWvt WFar WWEG |
| - B&SWJ 5971 | WCru |
| - B&SWJ 11182 | WCru |
| - B&SWJ 11227 | WCru |
| - 'Alba' | CMac WFar |
| - 'Albomarginata' (v) | CMac CPrp EAEE EBee EPPr EPfP GCra LRHS MAvo NEgg NHol NLar NSti SWvt WFar WPGP |
| - 'Golden Gleam' | LRHS WCot WFar |
| - 'Makinoi Gold' | WFar |
| - var. ***masamunei*** | EBla WCru |
| - 'Matsukaze' | CLAP CPLG CPom EWes MAvo SUsu WFar |
| - 'Miyazaki' | CFir CLAP CMac ECtt EPfP EWTr IFoB LRHS MAvo MCot MHer MNrw MPkF MTis NCGa NLar WFar WWEG |
| - 'Taiwan Atrianne' | EAEE EBee ECtt LRHS MDKP MNrw MRav NBro NCGa NEgg NHol WFar |
| - 'Variegata' (v) | CBct CTri ELon EWes GCra MTis WCot WFar WHrl WWEG |
| N Hototogisu | CBct CBro CLAP CPLG CPom EAEE EBee EBla ECtt ELan ELon EWTr LHop LRHS MCot NBir NEgg NHol NLar NMyG SMrm SPav WFar WHil WMnd WWEG |
| 'Imperial Banner' (v) **new** | EBee |
| ***ishiiana*** | CDes CLAP EBla MMoz SUsu WCot WCru WFar WPGP WSHC |
| - var. ***surugensis*** | EBla LEdu WCru WFar |
| 'Ivory Queen' | WFar |
| ***japonica*** | see *T. hirta* |
| 'Kohaku' | CBct CLAP EBla ELan EPPr EWes GKev NPro WFar WPGP WWEG |
| ***lasiocarpa*** | CLAP EBee LEdu MAvo |
| - B&SWJ 3635 | CAby CLAP CPLG EBla WCru WFar |
| - B&SWJ 6861 | EBla WCru WFar |
| - B&SWJ 7013 | CBct EBla WCru |
| - B&SWJ 7103 | WCru WFar |

| | | |
|---|---|---|
| | - 'Royal Toad' | WCru |
| § | ***latifolia*** | ELan GGar GLog GMaP LEdu LRHS NGdn NLar WCru WFar WWEG |
| | - B&SWJ 10996 from Japan | EBla WCru |
| | - from Japan | WFar |
| | - 'Yellow Sunrise' | CBct EBee ECtt EPPr MCot |
| | 'Lemon Lime' (v) | CBct CBro MDKP NPro WFar WWEG |
| | 'Lightning Strike' (v) | CBct EBee ECtt EWes LEdu LSou MDKP NBPC NHol NMyG NPnk WCot WFar |
| | 'Lilac Towers' | CBct ELan MAvo WCru WFar WWEG |
| | ***macrantha*** | GLog WCru WSHC |
| § | - subsp. ***macranthopsis*** | CBct CLAP CPLG EBla EPot GEdr MDKP WCot WCru WFar |
| | - - 'Juro' (d) | EBla WCru |
| | ***macranthopsis*** | see *T. macrantha* subsp. *macranthopsis* |
| N | ***macropoda*** | CBct EBee EBla ELan EPfP GAbr GLog GMaP LEdu LRHS MAvo NGdn NWCA SMad WFar WMnd WWEG |
| | - B&SWJ 1271 | EBla WCru WFar |
| | - B&SWJ 5013 | WCru WFar |
| | - B&SWJ 5556 | WCru |
| | - B&SWJ 5847 from Japan | WCru WFar |
| | - B&SWJ 6209 | WCru WFar |
| | - B&SWJ 8700 | WCru WFar |
| | - B&SWJ 8829 from Korea | WCru WFar |
| | - from Yungi Temple, China | CLAP EBla EPPr MDKP NCGa WFar |
| | - 'Tricolor' | CDes WCot |
| | ***maculata*** HWJCM 470 | WCru |
| | - HWJK 2010 | WCru WFar |
| | - HWJK 2411 | WCru WFar |
| | 'Moonlight Treasure'PBR | CLAP CPLG EBee NHol WCot |
| | ***nana*** | WCru |
| | - B&SWJ 11399 | WCru |
| | - 'Karasuba' | GEdr |
| | - 'Raven's Back' | WCru |
| | ***ohsumiensis*** | CBct CDes CLAP CPom EBla ECha GEdr LEdu LRHS MDKP SUsu WCru WFar WPGP |
| | ***perfoliata*** | CLAP EBla LEdu WCru WFar |
| | - 'Spring Shine' (v) | WCru WFar |
| | ***pilosa*** new | GKev |
| | Pink Freckles = 'Innotripf'PBR | LRHS LSou MTis SPoG |
| | 'Raspberry Mousse' | CDes CLAP EBee EKen IFoB IPot LHop LSou MAvo MBNS NMyG NSti WPGP |
| | ***setouchiensis*** | EBla WCru WFar |
| | 'Shimone' | CHid CLAP CPLG CPom ECha ELan NCGa WFar |
| | 'Sinonome' | EBee MAvo MPkF |
| | ***stolonifera*** | see *T. formosana* Stolonifera Group |
| | ***suzukii*** RWJ 10111 | EBla WCru WFar |
| | 'Taipei Silk'PBR | EBee EKen GAbr IFoB LSou NCGa NLar SBfd |
| | 'Tojen' | Widely available |
| | 'Tresahor White' | WFar |
| | 'Variegata' (*affinis* hybrid) (v) | WFar WWEG |
| | 'Washfields' | WFar WPGP |
| | 'White Towers' | CAby CBct CBro CHid CLAP CPLG CWCL EAEE EBee EBla ECha EPPr EPfP IFoB LRHS MAvo MRav MTis NCGa NEgg NHol NLar NPnk NSti SBfd SPer SRms WAul WFar WWEG |

## *Trientalis* (*Primulaceae*)

| | |
|---|---|
| ***europaea*** f. ***rosea*** | WHil |

## *Trifolium* (*Papilionaceae*)

| | | |
|---|---|---|
| | ***angustifolium*** | CArn |
| | ***incarnatum*** | CSpe MHer |
| | ***medium*** | EWil |
| | ***ochroleucon*** | CElw CHab EBee EPPr EWil GMaP LBMP LRHS MAvo MCot MMuc MSCN NSti SBch SSvw SWal WAul WCAu WFar WMoo WPer WWEG |
| | ***pannonicum*** | CCVN CMea GCal MNrw SUsu WFar WTin |
| | ***pratense*** | CHab EWil MHer NMir WSFF |
| | - 'Dolly North' | see *T. pratense* 'Susan Smith' |
| | - 'Ice Cool' | see *T. repens* 'Green Ice' |
| | - 'Purple Heart' | LRHS |
| § | - 'Susan Smith' (v) | CBre CCCN EBee EGHP EPfP EWes GCal MNrw NSti WFar WHer |
| | ***repens*** | EWil SVic WSFF |
| | - 'Dragon's Blood' | CDes CMea LEdu LLWG NPro SMrm SPoG WFar WPGP |
| | - 'Gold Net' | see *T. pratense* 'Susan Smith' |
| § | - 'Green Ice' | CBre EAEE EBee ECGP LLWG LRHS NSti WFar WHal |
| | - 'Harlequin' (v) | EBee MHer WCot WFar WMoo WOut WPer |
| | - 'Hullavington' new | CNat |
| | - 'Purpurascens' | CArn CBre CEnt EAEE EPfP GGar ILis LLWG LRHS MBNS MHer NEgg NSti SPoG WNew |
| § | - 'Purpurascens Quadrifolium' | CMea CWan EBee ECha EHoe EPau EWes GAbr MCot NEgg NMir NPer NPri SPer SPlb WFar WHer |
| | - 'Saint Patrick' | CNat |
| | - 'Tetraphyllum Purpureum' | see *T. repens* 'Purpurascens Quadrifolium' |
| | - 'Wheatfen' | CRow EBee EHoe NDov NPer |
| | - 'William' | CDes ECGP LEdu NDov SPur WCot WFar WOut |
| | ***rubens*** | Widely available |
| | - 'Drama' | MNrw SUsu |
| | - 'Peach Pink' | CElw CSpe EBee EPPr EShb LHop MAvo MLLN MMHG SBch SPhx SSvw SUsu WCot |
| | - 'Red Feathers' | CSpr EPPr LRHS MWat MWea SMrm WPer WWEG |
| | ***trichocephalum*** new | EPPr |

## *Triglochin* (*Juncaginaceae*)

| | |
|---|---|
| ***maritimum*** | CRWN |
| ***palustre*** | CRWN |

## *Trigonella* (*Papilionaceae*)

| | |
|---|---|
| ***foenum-graecum*** | CArn SIde |

## *Trillidium* see *Trillium*

## *Trillium* ✿ (*Melanthiaceae*)

| | |
|---|---|
| ***albidum*** | CWCL ECho EPot GGar GKev GMaP LLHF LRHS LWst MNrw NMen SKHP SSpi SUsu WCot WCru WHal |
| ***angustipetalum*** | WCru |
| ***apetalon*** | GEdr LWst |
| ***camschatcense*** | CPLG GEdr LAma WCru |
| - from Japan | LWst |

| | |
|---|---|
| § ***catesbyi*** | CLAP CPLG CWCL EBee ECho EPot GEdr GGar GKev LAma LLHF LWst MLLN MNrw NHol |
| ***cernuum*** | CLAP ECho GCra LRHS WCru WSHC |
| ***chloropetalum*** | CBro GBBs SSpi WFar WPGP |
| - var. ***chloropetalum*** × ***parviflorum*** | SKHP |
| § - var. ***giganteum*** ♀H4 | CLAP CPLG GEdr GKev LWst NMen NSla SPhx SSpi WCru WOld |
| - var. ***rubrum*** | see *T. chloropetalum* var. *giganteum* |
| - white-flowered | ECha |
| ***cuneatum*** | Widely available |
| - 'Ghost' **new** | SKHP |
| - 'Moonshine' **new** | SKHP |
| ***decipiens*** | LWst |
| ***decumbens*** | LWst SKHP |
| ***discolor*** | LWst SKHP |
| ***erectum*** ♀H4 | Widely available |
| - f. ***albiflorum*** | CFir CLAP CWCL EBee ECho GEdr GGar LAma LWst MLLN MNrw NHol NMen NMyG SKHP SSpi WCru |
| - 'Beige' | GKev |
| - f. ***luteum*** | CBct LWst SKHP |
| ***erectum*** × ***flexipes*** | CLAP ECho GEdr GGar LWst MNrw NBir NMen SKHP SSpi |
| ***flexipes*** | CLAP EBee ECho GAuc GEdr GKev LAma LWst MNrw NMen SKHP SSpi WCru |
| - erect | GAbr LWst MNrw NMen |
| I - 'Harvington Selection' | LRHS LWst MBri SKHP |
| ***foetidissimum*** | LWst SKHP |
| ***govanianum*** | EBee LWst |
| ***gracile*** **new** | LWst |
| ***grandiflorum*** ♀H4 | Widely available |
| - 'Kath's Dwarf' | GEdr |
| - f. ***polymerum*** | CLAP ECho LRHS LWst SCnR SKHP |
| 'Flore Pleno' (d) | WCra |
| - - 'Snowbunting' (d) | EWes LWst MMHG NHar WThu |
| - 'Quicksilver' | SKHP |
| - f. ***roseum*** | LWst WCra |
| ***kurabayashii*** | CAby CBct CFir CPLG ECho LRHS LWst MNrw SChF SKHP SSpi SUsu WCru WHal WPGP |
| ***lancifolium*** | LWst |
| ***ludovicianum*** | LWst |
| ***luteum*** ♀H4 | Widely available |
| ***maculatum*** | LWst |
| ***nivale*** | LWst NHar |
| ***ovatum*** | CLAP NMen SSpi |
| - f. ***hibbersonii*** | GCra NMen |
| - 'Roy Elliott' | CPLG MNrw NMen |
| ***parviflorum*** | ECho GEdr SKHP |
| ***pusillum*** | CLAP CPLG EBee ECho ELan EPot GBBs GEdr GKev LWst NHol NMen |
| * - var. ***alabamicum*** | SKHP |
| - var. ***virginianum*** | CLAP LAma |
| ***recurvatum*** | CBcs ECho EPot GAbr GBBs GEdr GKev LAma LWst NHol NMen NPnk SKHP WCru WFar WPnP |
| ***reliquum*** | LWst |
| ***rivale*** ♀H3 | CBro CElw CLAP CPLG ECho EPot GBBs ITim LLHF LWst NMen WFar WThu |
| - NNS 04-460 | WCot |
| - NNS 04-461 | NWCA WCot |
| - pink-flowered | GEdr NMen |
| - 'Purple Heart' | CLAP GEdr |
| ***rugelii*** | CBro CLAP EBee ECho EWes GAbr GMaP LWst MNrw NMen SKHP SSpi WCru |
| - Askival hybrids | EBee ECho GKev LWst MNrw NMen SKHP SSpi |
| - 'Orchard Pink' | LWst MNrw |
| ***rugelii*** × ***vaseyi*** | EWes LWst MNrw NMen SKHP SSpi |
| ***sessile*** | CPLG EBee ECho GBBs GKev LAma LRHS LWst MAvo NBPC NBir NMen NPnk SKHP SMrm WCot WFar WKif WPnP WSHC WShi |
| - 'Rubrum' | see *T. chloropetalum* var. *giganteum* |
| ***simile*** | CBro CLAP ECho GAbr LLHF LRHS LWst MNrw SKHP SSpi |
| ***smallii*** | LWst WCru |
| ***stamineum*** | ECho GEdr LWst WCot |
| ***stylosum*** | see *T. catesbyi* |
| ***sulcatum*** | CBro CLAP CPLG CWCL EBee ECho GAbr GEdr GMaP LRHS LWst MBri MNrw NMen SKHP SSpi WCot WCru WFar |
| - cream-flowered **new** | LWst |
| ***taiwanense*** B&SWJ 3411 | WCru |
| ***texanum*** | SKHP |
| ***tschonoskii*** | ECho GEdr LAma NMen |
| ***underwoodii*** | LWst |
| ***undulatum*** | EBee ECho GEdr LAma LWst MNrw NHol WCru |
| ***vaseyi*** | CBro CLAP ECho EWes GAbr GBBs GEdr GKev LAma LRHS LWst MNrw NMen SKHP SSpi WCru |
| - horizontal inflorescence | LWst MNrw |
| ***viride*** | EBla GBBs WFar WPnP |
| ***viridescens*** | EBee ECho GEdr LAma LWst WFar |

## *Triosteum* (*Caprifoliaceae*)

| | |
|---|---|
| ***erythrocarpum*** | EBee |
| ***himalayanum*** | EBee GCal GKev GLam WSHC |
| - BWJ 7907 | CLAP WCru |
| ***pinnatifidum*** | CLAP CPom EBee GCal GLam |
| - SDR 6014 | GKev |

## *Tripsacum* (*Poaceae*)

| | |
|---|---|
| ***dactyloides*** | EPPr |

## *Tripterospermum* (*Gentianaceae*)

| | |
|---|---|
| B&SWJ 11297 from Malaysia | WCru |
| * aff. ***chevalieri*** B&SWJ 8359 | WCru |
| ***cordifolium*** B&SWJ 081 | WCru |
| ***distylum*** B&SWJ 11491 | WCru |
| ***fasciculatum*** B&SWJ 7197 | WCru |
| - B&SWJ 11297 | WCru |
| ***hirticalyx*** | WCru |
| B&SWJ 11725 **new** | |
| - B&SWJ 11786 | WCru |
| ***japonicum*** | GEdr LLHF WCot |
| - B&SWJ 8920 | WCru |
| - B&SWJ 10876 | WCru |
| ***lanceolatum*** B&SWJ 085 | WCru |
| - RWJ 9918 | WCru |
| ***taiwanense*** B&SWJ 1205 | WCru |
| - RWJ 10115 | WCru |
| ***volubile*** B&SWJ 11774 **new** | WCru |

## *Tripterygium* (*Celastraceae*)

| | |
|---|---|
| ***regelii*** | NLar |
| - B&SWJ 5453 | WCru |
| - B&SWJ 10921 | WCru |
| ***wilfordii*** WWJ 12009 | WCru |

## *Tristagma* (*Alliaceae*)

| | |
|---|---|
| ***nivale*** f. ***nivale*** F&W 10284 | WCot |

## *Triteleia* (*Asparagaceae*)

| | |
|---|---|
| 4U | CAvo CMea EBee ECho |
| ***bridgesii*** | CAvo CBro ECho |
| – NNS 00-731 | WCot |
| ***californica*** | see *Brodiaea californica* |
| § 'Corrina' | CAvo CBro CFFs EBee ECho EPot |
| ***dudleyi*** new | WCot |
| ***grandiflora*** | ECho WCot |
| ***hendersonii*** | WCot |
| ***hyacinthina*** | EBee ECho GKev WCot |
| ***ixioides*** | ECho |
| – subsp. ***anilina*** NNS 95-537 new | WCot |
| – 'Splendens' | EBee ECho NMen |
| – 'Starlight' | CAvo CBro CFFs CTri EBee ECho EPot ERCP GKev SDeJ SMrm SPer |
| § ***laxa*** | ECho |
| – NNS 00-742 | WCot |
| – NNS 00-743 | WCot |
| – NNS 98-541 | WCot |
| – 'Allure' | CAvo EBee ECho GKev |
| § – 'Koningin Fabiola' | CBro CMea CSpe CTri EBee ECho EPfP EPot GKev IPot LAma LRHS MLHP MNrw NBir SDeJ SEND SPer WCot |
| – Queen Fabiola | see *T. laxa* 'Koningin Fabiola' |
| ***lilacina*** | ECho |
| § ***peduncularis*** | CAvo EBee ECho GLam WCot |
| 'Royal Blue' | CMea EPot ERCP WCot |
| 'Rudy' | CAvo CBro CFFs CHid CMea EBee ECho ERCP |
| × ***tubergenii*** | ECho |
| ***uniflora*** | see *Ipheion uniflorum* |

## *Trithrinax* (*Arecaceae*)

| | |
|---|---|
| ***brasiliensis*** | EAmu LPJP LPal SBig |
| ***campestris*** | CBrP EAmu LMaj LPal SBig |

## *Tritoma* see *Kniphofia*

## *Tritonia* (*Iridaceae*)

| | |
|---|---|
| ***crocata*** ♀H2-3 | CPou ECho |
| – 'Baby Doll' | CPrp CYeo EBee LEdu WHil |
| – 'Pink Sensation' | CDes CSpe EBee ECho WHil |
| – 'Plymouth Pastel' | CDes |
| – 'Prince of Orange' | CDes CPou |
| – 'Princess Beatrix' | CDes |
| – 'Riversdale' | ECho |
| – 'Serendipity' | CDes CPrp EBee EPri |
| – 'Tangerine' | CDes CPBP |
| ***deusta*** | CDes |
| § ***disticha*** | Widely available |
| subsp. ***rubrolucens*** | |
| – – short, red-pink-flowered new | CDes |
| – – tall, clear pink-flowered | CDes CTca |
| ***flabellifolia*** | ECho |
| ***florentiae*** 'Tanqua Karoo' | ECho |
| ***hyalina*** | CPou |
| ***karooica*** 'Middlepos' | ECho |
| ***laxifolia*** | CPrp CTca EBee ECho EPot LEdu |
| ***lineata*** | CAby CDes CFee CPou CTca EBee ECho WPGP |
| – 'Parvifolia' | EBee |
| ***pallida*** | ECho SPlb |
| ***rosea*** | see *T. disticha* subsp. *rubrolucens* |
| ***securigera*** | CDes ECho LEdu |
| ***squalida*** | ECho EPri |

## *Trochocarpa* (*Ericaceae*)

| | |
|---|---|
| ***clarkei*** | WThu |
| ***gunnii*** | WThu |
| ***thymifolia*** | WAbe WThu |
| – white-flowered | WThu |

## *Trochodendron* (*Trochodendraceae*)

| | |
|---|---|
| ***aralioides*** | Widely available |
| – B&SWJ 1651 from Taiwan | WCru |
| – CWJ 12357 from Taiwan | WCru |
| – RWJ 9845 from Taiwan | WCru |

## *Trollius* (*Ranunculaceae*)

| | |
|---|---|
| ACE 1187 | CPLG GEdr |
| SDR 4816 | GKev |
| ***acaulis*** | ECho EWes GKev NMen WFar WPat |
| ***asiaticus*** | EBee GKev WFar |
| § ***chinensis*** | ECha GCal SWat |
| – 'Golden Queen' ♀H4 | Widely available |
| × ***cultorum*** 'Alabaster' | Widely available |
| – 'Baudirektor Linne' | ECtt MRav NGdn WFar |
| – Bressingham hybrids | WFar |
| – 'Byrne's Giant' | EBee ECtt GBin WFar |
| – 'Canary Bird' | ELan EPfP GCal NGdn SRms |
| – 'Cheddar' | CWCL EBee EBla ECtt ELon EPPr EPfP EWTr GCal GMac LSou MBNS MBri MMHG MRav NBPC NBro NEgg NLar NOrc NPnk NPri NPro SKHP SPoG WBor WFar WWEG |
| – 'Commander-in-Chief' | CDes EBee SMad WFar |
| – 'Earliest of All' | CSam EBee EKen MBri NGdn SPer WFar WWEG |
| – 'Empire Day' | MBri |
| – 'Etna' | EBee SHar WFar WPnP WWEG |
| § – 'Feuertroll' | CMea EBee ECha ECtt GGar LBMP LRHS MBri MRav MSCN NBPC NEgg NGdn NPro SUsu WCra WFar |
| – Fireglobe | see *T.* × *cultorum* 'Feuertroll' |
| – 'Golden Cup' | NBir NGdn |
| – 'Golden Monarch' | WFar |
| – 'Goliath' | EWes WFar |
| – 'Helios' | CSam LRHS |
| – 'Lemon Queen' | CWat EBee ECtt EPfP GBin GKev GMaP LPBA LRHS MBri MNFA MRav NBPC NLar NPnk SPer SWat WFar WHil |
| – 'Maigold' | MAvo |
| – 'Meteor' | WFar |
| – new hybrids | WFar |
| – 'Orange Crest' | EBee ECtt GCal GMac LSou WFar WHal WWEG |
| – 'Orange Globe' | EBee NBPC SMrm WFar |
| – 'Orange Glow' | LLWG SMad |
| – 'Orange Princess' ♀H4 | CElw CWat EBee EPfP GMaP LLWG MCCP NBro NLar SPer SRms |
| – 'Orange Queen' | SWvt |
| – 'Prichard's Giant' | CMHG EBee EBla ECtt ELan NBro NEgg NGdn NLBP WFar WWEG |
| § – 'Superbus' ♀H4 | CWCL EBee ELan EPfP GMaP NGdn SPer WFar |
| – 'T. Smith' | NBro WFar WWEG |
| – 'Taleggio' | LEdu |
| – 'Yellow Beauty' | WFar |
| ***europaeus*** | CBot COIW CRWN CWCL EBee ECha GCal GGar LAst LEdu LHop MLHP MMuc MRav NGdn NHol |

| | |
|---|---|
| | NMir SBfd SBrt SPet SRot SWat WAul WFar WHoo WTin WWEG |
| - SDR 5441 | GKev |
| - SDR 5473 | GKev SEND |
| - 'Lemon Supreme' **new** | EDAr |
| - 'Superbus' | see *T.* × *cultorum* 'Superbus' |
| ***hondoensis*** | EBee GCal LLHF LRHS NLar NPro |
| ***ircuticus*** | EBee GKev |
| ***laxus*** | EWes |
| - 'Albiflorus' | CPLG NWCA |
| ***ledebourii*** misapplied | see *T. chinensis* |
| ***pumilus*** | CAby ECha ECho ELan EPPr EPfP GCal GGar LRHS NLar NSla NWCA SBfd SEND SPer WAbe WFar WPer |
| - ACE 1818 | CPLG EBee GCal |
| - 'Wargrave' | ECho |
| ***ranunculoides*** | GKev |
| ***riederianus*** | LRHS |
| ***stenopetalus*** | CDes EWes MBri MNrw MRav WFar |
| ***vaginatus*** | GKev |
| ***yunnanensis*** | EBee GKev WFar |
| - orange-flowered | CPLG GKev |

## *Tropaeolum* ✿ (*Tropaeolaceae*)

| | |
|---|---|
| ***azureum*** | CCCN EPot |
| ***beuthii*** | WCot |
| ***brachyceras*** | CCCN ECho EPot GGar WCot |
| ***ciliatum*** ♀H1 | CAvo CCCN CFir CGHE CSpr ECho ELan GCal NBid NLar WCot WCru WFar WHer WPGP |
| ***hookerianum*** subsp. ***austropurpureum*** | CGHE |
| ***incisum*** | CCCN CWCL |
| ***majus*** | SVic |
| - Alaska Series (v) ♀H3 | CPrp MNHC SEND SIde WJek |
| - 'Apricot Twist' | GBee |
| - 'Crimson Beauty' | CSpe |
| § - 'Darjeeling Double' (d) ♀H4 | GBee GCal WCot |
| - 'Darjeeling Gold' | see *T. majus* 'Darjeeling Double' |
| - 'Empress of India' | CPrp MNHC NBlu WJek |
| - 'Hermine Grashoff' (d) ♀H2-3 | CSpe GBee GCal NPer |
| - 'Margaret Long' (d) | CSpe GCal WCot |
| * - 'Peaches and Cream' | WJek |
| - 'Red Wonder' | CCCN CSpe EPfP LSou |
| - 'Ruffled Apricot' | CSpe |
| - 'Sunset Pink' | CPrp |
| - Tom Thumb mixed | MNHC WJek |
| ***pentaphyllum*** | CAvo CSpe EBee ECho ELan EWes GCal GGar LLHF WCot WPGP |
| ***peregrinum*** | CSpe ECho SBfd |
| ***polyphyllum*** | CCCN CWCL EBee ECho EPfP EPot NBir SCnR WAbe WPGP |
| ***sessilifolium*** | EBee ECho |
| ***speciosum*** ♀H4 | Widely available |
| ***tricolor*** ♀H1 | CAvo CCCN EBee ECho ELan GCal GGar WBor |
| ***tuberosum*** | CEnd ECho GPoy |
| - var. ***lineamaculatum*** 'Ken Aslet' ♀H3 | CBro CCCN CSpe ECha ECho ELan EOHP EPfP EPot GGar IFro LAma LHop LRHS SPer WFar |

## *Trymalium* (*Rhamnaceae*)

| | |
|---|---|
| ***ledifolium*** | CTrC |

## *Tsuga* ✿ (*Pinaceae*)

| | |
|---|---|
| ***canadensis*** | CDul EHul EPfP NWea WDin WEve |
| - 'Abbott's Dwarf' | CDoC CKen MGos NHol |
| § - 'Abbott's Pygmy' | CKen |
| - 'Albospica' (v) | WFar |
| - 'Arnold Gold Weeper' | CKen |
| - 'Aurea' (v) | NHol NLar WEve |
| - 'Bacon Cristate' | CKen |
| - 'Beehive' | WGor |
| - 'Betty Rose' (v) | CKen |
| - 'Birkett's White' | CKen |
| - 'Brandley' | CKen |
| § - 'Branklyn' | CKen |
| - 'Cappy's Choice' | CKen |
| - 'Cinnamonea' | CKen |
| - 'Coffin' | CKen |
| - 'Cole's Prostrate' | CKen MAsh NHol NLar SLim |
| - 'Creamey' (v) | CKen |
| - 'Curley' | CKen |
| - 'Curtis Ideal' | CKen |
| - 'Dr Hornbeck' | see *T. canadensis* 'Hornbeck' |
| - 'Essex' | NHol NWad |
| * - 'Everitt's Dense Leaf' | CKen |
| - 'Everitt's Golden' | CKen |
| - 'Fantana' | LRHS MAsh NHol NLar SCoo SLim WEve |
| - 'Gentsch White' (v) | MGos NLar |
| - 'Gracilis' | WThu |
| - 'Hedgehog' | CDoC NLar |
| § - 'Hornbeck' | CKen |
| - 'Horsford' | CKen NLar NWad |
| - 'Horstmann' No 1 | CKen |
| - 'Hussii' | CKen NHol NLar |
| - 'Jacqueline Verkade' | CKen NLar |
| - 'Jeddeloh' ♀H4 | CDoC CMac EPla EPot LRHS MAsh MGos NEgg NHol SCoo SGol SLim SPoG WDin WEve |
| - 'Jervis' | CKen NHol NLar NWad |
| - 'Julianne' | CKen |
| - 'Kingsville Spreader' | CKen |
| - 'Little Joe' | CKen |
| - 'Little Snow' | CKen |
| I - 'Lutea' | CKen |
| - 'Many Cones' | CKen |
| - 'Minima' | CKen |
| - 'Minuta' | CDoC CKen MGos NLar NWad WGor |
| - 'Moon Frost' | MAsh NLar |
| - 'Nana' | WDin |
| - 'Palomino' | CKen NLar |
| - 'Pendula' ♀H4 | CKen EPfP LRHS MAsh SLim WDin WEve WFar |
| - 'Pincushion' | CKen |
| - 'Prostrata' | see *T. canadensis* 'Branklyn' |
| - 'Pygmaea' | see *T. canadensis* 'Abbott's Pygmy' |
| - 'Rugg's Washington Dwarf' | CKen |
| - 'Snowflake' | CKen MGos |
| - 'Stewart's Gem' | CKen |
| - 'Verkade Petite' | CKen |
| - 'Verkade Recurved' | CKen NLar |
| - 'Vermeulen's Wintergold' **new** | NLar |
| - 'Von Helms' Dwarf' | CKen |
| - 'Warnham' | CKen MAsh |
| ***caroliniana*** 'La Bar Weeping' | CKen NLar |
| ***chinensis*** | CKen |
| - var. ***chinensis*** | NMun |
| ***diversifolia*** 'Gotelli' | CKen |
| ***dumosa*** | CKen |
| ***heterophylla*** ♀H4 | CBcs CCVT CDul CLnd EPfP LBuc NWea SGol SMad SPer STre WDin WEve |
| - 'Iron Springs' | CKen |

|  |  |
|---|---|
| – 'Laursen's Column' | CKen |
| – 'Thorsens Weeping' | CKen |
| ***menziesii*** | see *Pseudotsuga menziesii* |
| ***mertensiana*** | NWea |
| – 'Blue Star' | CKen MAsh |
| 'Elizabeth' | CKen |
| – 'Glauca' | CKen |
| I – 'Glauca Nana' | CKen |
| I – 'Horstmann' | CKen |
| – 'Quartz Mountain' | CKen |
| ***sieboldii*** 'Baldwin' | CKen |
| – 'Green Ball' | CKen |
| – 'Honeywell Estate' | CKen |
| – 'Nana' | CKen |

## *Tuberaria* (*Cistaceae*)

|  |  |
|---|---|
| ***lignosa*** | WAbe |

## *Tulbaghia* ✿ (*Alliaceae*)

|  |  |
|---|---|
| ***acutiloba*** | CPen CTca LEdu MHom NHoy WTul |
| 'African Moon' | NHoy |
| ***alliacea*** | CAvo CBro EBla ECho EShb MHom NHoy NWCA WCot WHil |
| ***alliacea* × *violacea*** | ECho |
| * ***allioides*** new | CBro |
| 'Bob Brown' | CDes WTul |
| 'Brenda' new | NWCA |
| 'Bright Eyes' | NHoy |
| ***capensis*** | CPou NBir NHoy WCot WTul |
| ***capensis* × *violacea*** CGV 1970 | WTul |
| 'Cariad' | WTul |
| ***cepacea* × *natalensis*** | NWCA |
| ***cernua*** CD&R 199 | CDes WTul |
| – hybrid | EPri NHoy WTul |
| ***cernua* × *violacea*** | WTul |
| 'Charlotte' new | NWCA |
| § ***coddii*** | EBee MHom NHoy WCot WTul |
| ***coddii* × *violacea*** | NHoy WTul |
| ***cominsii*** | CPLG EPri NWCA SBch WTul |
| – 'Harry Hay's Pink' | NHoy |
| ***cominsii* × *violacea*** | CAvo CPLG CTca EBee MHom NHoy WTul |
| – × – soft pink-flowered | WTul |
| 'Cosmic' | CPen CPou EPri LEdu NHoy WTul |
| 'Crystal' | NHoy |
| 'Dreaming Spires' | NHoy |
| ***dregeana*** | NHoy WCot |
| 'Elaine Ann' | NHoy |
| 'Enigma' | NHoy |
| 'Fairy Snow' | WTul |
| 'Fairy Star' | CDes CTca EBee EShb LEdu NHoy WCot WPGP WTul |
| ***fragrans*** | see *T. simmleri* |
| – 'Alba' | ELan EPot EWTr |
| ***galpinii*** | CPen NHoy NWCA WTul |
| 'Grey Dawn' | NHoy |
| 'Hazel' | CPen CPou CYeo NHoy WTul |
| 'Janet' | NHoy |
| 'John May's Special' | CAby CDes CKno EBee EShb LEdu MHom NHoy NWCA SUsu WCot WHil WPGP WTul |
| ***leucantha*** | CDes CTca EBee MHom NHoy NWCA WPGP WTul |
| – H&B 11996 | CDes WTul |
| – from Sentinel Peak, South Africa | WTul |
| 'Lilian' | WTul |
| 'Maggie May' new | NWCA |
| ***maritima*** | see *T. violacea* var. *maritima* |
| Marwood seedling | EBee MHom MTPN NHoy |
| ***montana*** | CDes EBee MHer NHoy NWCA WCot WPGP WTul |
| ***natalensis*** | CBro CPou CPrp ECho LEdu NHoy WHoo |
| – B&V 421 | CDes EBee |
| – – clone 1 white-flowered | NHoy WTul |
| – – clone 2 pink-flowered | NHoy WHil WTul |
| – CD&R 84 | NHoy WTul |
| – pink-flowered | CTca ECho MHom NHoy WTul |
| – white-flowered | CTca |
| ***natalensis* × *verdoorniae*** | WTul |
| – × – VOS 1966 | WTul |
| ***natalensis* × *violacea*** | NHoy NWCA WTul |
| ***poetica*** | see *T. coddii* |
| 'Premier' | NHoy |
| 'Purple Eyes' | WTul |
| 'Rainbow' | NHoy |
| 'Sally' new | NWCA |
| § ***simmleri*** | CPou CYeo EBee ECho EPot EPri EShb EWes GKev LAma LEdu NHoy WTul |
| – 'Cheryl Renshaw' | WTul |
| – pink-flowered | CPen CTca WPGP |
| – 'Snow Queen' | CPrp |
| – 'White Queen' new | CYeo |
| – white-flowered | CPen CPou CPrp CTca NHoy WTul |
| 'Snowball' | NHoy |
| 'Suzanne' | NHoy |
| ***verdoorniae*** | NHoy NWCA WHil |
| ***violacea*** | Widely available |
| – from RBGE | MHom NHoy |
| * – 'Alba' | EBee EPPr EPri GCal MCot MHer NHoy NMRc SWat WFar WHoo WTin |
| – 'Dissect White' | NHoy WTul |
| I – 'Fine Form' | CKno NHoy WKif |
| * – ***grandiflora*** | CAvo |
| – 'John Rider' | NHoy NWCA WTul |
| – 'Lowan' | NWCA WTul |
| * – var. ***maritima*** | CPMA CPen CYeo EDif EShb LEdu MHom NHoy NWCA SMrm WCot WTul |
| – var. ***obtusa*** | NHoy WTul |
| – 'Pallida' | CAvo CBro CCse CDes CPou CTca ECho LEdu NHoy NWCA WPGP WTul |
| – 'Pearl' | CPou NHoy WTul |
| – 'Peppermint Garlic' | CDes CTca WPGP WTul |
| – var. ***robustior*** | CPou CTca EBla EWes NHoy WTul |
| – 'Seren' | WTul |
| § – 'Silver Lace' (v) | Widely available |
| – 'Variegata' | see *T. violacea* 'Silver Lace' |
| – var. ***violacea*** | NHoy WTul |
| – 'White Goddess' | CPou WTul |
| – 'White Star' | EBee |
| ***violacea* × *violacea* var. *maritima*** | WTul |
| white-flowered new | WHil |

## *Tulipa* ✿ (*Liliaceae*)

|  |  |
|---|---|
| 'Abba' (2) | SDeJ |
| 'Absalon' (9) | GKev LAma |
| 'Abu Hassan' (3) | CAvo CFFs CMea ERCP LAma MBri SBch SDeJ SPhx |
| ***acuminata*** (15) | CAvo CBro CFFs CHid CTca ECho ERCP LAma MMHG NMin SDeJ SPhx |

| |  |  |
|---|---|---|
| | 'Ad Rem' (4) | MBri |
| | 'Addis' (14) ♀$^{H4}$ | LAma |
| | 'African Queen' (3) | LAma |
| | ***aitchisonii*** | see *T. clusiana* |
| | 'Aladdin' (6) | LAma SDeJ |
| | 'Aladdin's Record' (6) | CAvo CBro CFFs |
| | ***albertii*** (15) | ECho LAma NMin |
| | 'Aleppo' (7) | SDeJ |
| | 'Alfred Cortot' (12) ♀$^{H4}$ | LAma SDeJ |
| | 'Allegretto' (11) | MBri |
| | ***altaica*** (15) ♀$^{H4}$ | ECho EPot LAma |
| | ***amabilis*** | see *T. hoogiana* |
| | 'American Eagle' (7) | SDeJ |
| | 'Analita' (13) | LAma NMin |
| | 'Ancilla' (12) ♀$^{H4}$ | CAvo CBro CFFs LAma |
| | 'Angélique' (11) ♀$^{H4}$ | CAvo CFFs CTca EPfP ERCP GKev LAma MCot NBir SPer SPhx |
| | 'Annie Schilder' (3) | ERCP |
| | 'Antoinette'$^{PBR}$ (5) | LAma SPer |
| | 'Apeldoorn' (4) | EGxp GKev LAma MBri SDeJ SPer |
| | 'Apeldoorn's Elite' (4) ♀$^{H4}$ | LAma MBri SDeJ |
| | 'Apricot Beauty' (1) ♀$^{H4}$ | CHid CTca ERCP LAma MBri NBir SDeJ SPer SPhx |
| | 'Apricot Emperor' (13) **new** | MCot |
| | 'Apricot Impression'$^{PBR}$ (4) | LAma |
| | 'Apricot Jewel' | see *T. linifolia* (Batalinii Group) 'Apricot Jewel' |
| | 'Apricot Parrot' (10) ♀$^{H4}$ | CAvo CFFs LAma MBri MCot SPer |
| | 'Arabian Mystery' (3) | CAvo CFFs ERCP LAma SDeJ SPhx |
| | 'Artist' (8) ♀$^{H4}$ | ERCP LAma |
| | 'Attila' (3) | CAvo CFFs LAma SPhx |
| | ***aucheriana*** (15) ♀$^{H4}$ | CBro ECho EPot LAma LLHF NMin |
| | ***australis*** (15) | ECho |
| | ***aximensis*** (15) | ECho LAma NMin |
| | 'Bacchus' (7) | LAma |
| | ***bakeri*** | see *T. saxatilis* Bakeri Group |
| | 'Ballade' (6) ♀$^{H4}$ | CAvo CFFs ERCP LAma MCot |
| | 'Ballerina' (6) ♀$^{H4}$ | CAvo CBro CFFs CMea CTca ECho EPfP ERCP IFro LAma MBri MCot SPer SPhx |
| | 'Banja Luka' (4) | SDeJ |
| | 'Barbados' (7) | LAma |
| | 'Barcelona' (3) ♀$^{H4}$ | ERCP |
| | 'Bastogne Parrot'$^{PBR}$ (10) | LAma |
| | ***batalinii*** | see *T. linifolia* Batalinii Group |
| | 'Beau Monde' (3) ♀$^{H4}$ | SDeJ |
| | 'Beauty of Apeldoorn' (4) | LAma MBri |
| | 'Belicia' (2) | LAma |
| | 'Bellflower' (7) | LAma |
| | 'Bellona' (3) | SDeJ |
| | 'Berlioz' (12) | SDeJ |
| | ***biebersteiniana*** (15) | ECho NMin |
| § | ***biflora*** (15) | CAvo CBro CTca ECho EPot GKev LAma SDeJ SPhx WShi |
| | ***bifloriformis*** (15) | ECho |
| I | - 'Maxima' (15) | ECho NMin SPhx |
| | - 'Starlight' (15) ♀$^{H4}$ | ECho NMin SPhx |
| | 'Big Chief' (4) ♀$^{H4}$ | LAma |
| | 'Black Hero' (11) | CAvo CFFs EPfP ERCP LAma MCot SPer |
| | 'Black Jewel' (7) | ERCP LAma SDeJ |
| | 'Black Parrot' (10) ♀$^{H4}$ | CAvo CBro CFFs CHid EPfP ERCP LAma MBri SDeJ SPer SPhx |
| | 'Black Stallion' (11) | LAma |
| | 'Black Swan' (5) | SDeJ |
| | 'Bleu Aimable' (5) | CAvo CFFs ERCP MCot SDeJ |
| | 'Blue Diamond' (11) | CAvo CFFs ERCP SPer |
| | 'Blue Heron' (7) ♀$^{H4}$ | CAvo CFFs ERCP LAma MCot SDeJ |
| | 'Blue Parrot' (10) | CAvo CFFs EPfP ERCP LAma SDeJ |
| | 'Blue Ribbon' (3) | CAvo CFFs |
| | Blueberry Ripple | see *T.* 'Zurel' |
| | 'Blushing Beauty' (5) | SDeJ |
| | 'Blushing Bride' (5) | SDeJ |
| | 'Blushing Lady' (5) | MCot |
| | 'Boutade' (14) | NPer |
| | 'Bridesmaid' (5) | LAma |
| | 'Burgundy' (6) | CAvo CTca ERCP LAma SPhx |
| | 'Burgundy Lace' (7) | LAma SDeJ |
| | 'Burning Heart' (4) | SDeJ |
| | 'Café Noir' (5) | ERCP LAma |
| | 'Cairo'$^{PBR}$ | ERCP |
| | 'Calgary' (3) ♀$^{H4}$ | EPfP LAma |
| | 'Candela' (13) ♀$^{H4}$ | LAma SDeJ |
| | 'Candy Club' (5) | LAma |
| | 'Candy Prince'$^{PBR}$ (1) | EPfP |
| | 'Canova' (7) | SDeJ |
| | 'Cantata' (13) | CBro LAma |
| | 'Cape Cod' (14) | LAma |
| | 'Cardinal Mindszenty' (2) | ERCP MCot SDeJ |
| | ***carinata*** (15) | ECho NMin |
| | 'Carlton' (2) | MCot |
| | 'Carnaval de Nice' (11/v) ♀$^{H4}$ | CAvo CBro CFFs CTca ERCP LAma MBri SDeJ SPer |
| | 'Cassini' (3) | LAma SDeJ |
| § | ***celsiana*** (15) | ECho LAma |
| | 'China Lady' (14) ♀$^{H4}$ | SDeJ |
| | 'China Pink' (6) ♀$^{H4}$ | CAvo CBro CFFs CTca EPfP ERCP LAma MBri MCot SPhx |
| | 'China Town' (8) ♀$^{H4}$ | ERCP LAma MBri SDeJ |
| | 'Christmas Dream' (1) | SDeJ |
| | 'Christmas Marvel' (1) | LAma |
| | ***chrysantha*** Boiss. ex Baker | see *T. montana* |
| | 'City of Vancouver' (5) **new** | EPfP |
| | 'Claudia' (6) | EPfP SPer |
| | 'Cloud Nine' (5) | ECho |
| § | ***clusiana*** (15) | CBro ECho ERCP LAma LWst MSSP NMin SPhx WHer |
| | - var. ***chrysantha*** (15) ♀$^{H4}$ | CAvo CFFs ECho LAma SBch SPhx WHoo WShi |
| | - - 'Tubergen's Gem' (15) | ECho EPot GKev LAma MBri SPhx |
| | - 'Cynthia' (15) ♀$^{H4}$ | CTca ECho EPot ERCP GKev LAma MSSP NMin SDeJ SPhx |
| | - 'Sheila' (15) | ECho NMin SPhx |
| § | - var. ***stellata*** (15) | ECho |
| | 'Columbine' (5) | ECho LAma |
| | 'Concerto' (13) | CBro MBri NPer SDeJ SPhx |
| | 'Corona' (12) | ECho SDeJ |
| | 'Cortina' (9) | SDeJ |
| | 'Couleur Cardinal' (3) | CBro ERCP LAma SDeJ SPhx |
| | ***cretica*** (15) | ECho EPot LAma LWst NMin |
| | 'Crispion Dark' (7) **new** | ERCP |
| | 'Cum Laude' (5) | LAma |
| | 'Cummins' (7) | CAvo CFFs ERCP |
| | 'Curly Sue' (7) | CAvo CFFs ERCP LAma SPer |
| | 'Czaar Peter' (14) ♀$^{H4}$ | CAvo CFFs EPfP MBri NPer |
| | 'Dance' (13) | SDeJ |
| | 'Dancing Show' (8) | LAma |
| | ***dasystemon*** (15) | ECho EPot LAma SPhx |
| | ***dasystemonoides*** (15) | ECho |
| | 'Davenport' (7) | ERCP |
| | 'David Teniers' (2) | ERCP |
| | 'Daydream' (4) ♀$^{H4}$ | EGxp SPer |
| | 'Daytona' (7) **new** | CAvo |
| | 'Deirdre' (8) | ERCP |
| | ***didieri*** misapplied | see *T. passeriniana* |
| | 'Doll's Minuet' (8) | ERCP LAma SPer |
| | 'Don Quichotte' (3) ♀$^{H4}$ | MBri SDeJ |
| | 'Donna Bella' (14) ♀$^{H4}$ | EPfP SDeJ |
| | 'Dordogne' (5) ♀$^{H4}$ | SDeJ |
| | 'Double Price' (2) | ERCP |

|  |  |
|---|---|
| 'Douglas Bader' (5) | CAvo CFFs |
| 'Dreamboat' (14) | MBri |
| 'Dreaming Maid' (3) | EGxp LAma |
| 'Dreamland' (5) ♀H4 | MBri |
| 'Duc van Tol Max Cramoisie' (1) | LAma |
| 'Duc van Tol Primrose' (1) | LAma |
| 'Duc van Tol Red and Yellow' (1) | GKev WHer |
| 'Duc van Tol Rose' (1) | LAma |
| 'Duc van Tol Salmon' (1) | LAma |
| 'Duc van Tol Violet' (1) | LAma |
| 'Duc van Tol White' (1) | LAma |
| 'Early Harvest' (12) ♀H4 | CAvo CFFs SDeJ |
| 'Easter Surprise' (14) ♀H4 | MBri SDeJ |
| ***eichleri*** | see *T. undulatifolia* |
| 'Electra' (5) | LAma MBri |
| 'Elegans Alba' (6) | LAma |
| 'Elegant Lady' (6) | CAvo CBro CFFs EPfP LAma MCot SPer |
| 'Esperanto' (8/v) ♀H4 | LAma SDeJ |
| 'Estella Rijnveld' (10) | EGxp ERCP LAma MBri |
| 'Esther' (5) | ERCP |
| 'Eternal Flame' (2) | LAma |
| 'Exotic Emperor' | LAma |
| 'Fancy Frills' (7) ♀H4 | ERCP LAma SDeJ |
| 'Fantasy' (10) ♀H4 | LAma |
| 'Fashion' (12) | EPfP |
| ***ferganica*** (15) | ECho LAma NMin |
| 'Fidelio' (3) ♀H4 | SDeJ |
| 'Fire Queen' (3) ♀H4 | ERCP LAma |
| 'Flair' (1) | LAma SDeJ |
| 'Flaming Parrot' (10) | CAvo CFFs ERCP GKev LAma MBri |
| 'Flaming Purissima' (13) | CAvo CFFs SDeJ |
| 'Flaming Springgreen' (8) | CAvo CFFs ERCP LAma |
| 'Florosa' (8) | ERCP SDeJ |
| 'Foxtrot'PBR (2) | ERCP |
| 'Françoise' (3) | SDeJ |
| 'Fringed Family' (7) | SDeJ |
| 'Fritz Kreisler' (12) | LAma |
| 'Fulgens' (6) | LAma |
| 'Für Elise' (14) | SDeJ |
| 'Garden Party' (3) ♀H4 | LAma SDeJ |
| 'Gavota' (3) | CAvo CBro CFFs EGxp EPfP LAma MCot SDeJ SPer |
| 'Gemma' (10) | LAma |
| 'Generaal de Wet' (1) | LAma MBri SDeJ SPhx |
| 'Georgette' (5) | LAma MBri |
| 'Gerbrand Kieft' (11) ♀H4 | ERCP |
| 'Giuseppe Verdi' (12) | LAma MBri |
| 'Glück' (12) ♀H4 | ECho |
| 'Golden Apeldoorn' (4) | LAma MBri SDeJ |
| 'Golden Artist' (8) | EPfP LAma |
| 'Golden Emperor' (13) | LAma SPer |
| 'Golden Melody' (3) | MCot |
| 'Golden Oxford' (4) | LAma |
| 'Golden Parade' (4) | LAma |
| 'Gordon Cooper' (4) | SDeJ |
| 'Goudstuk' (12) | LAma |
| 'Green Eyes' (8) | SDeJ |
| 'Green River' (8) | SDeJ |
| 'Green Wave' (10) | ERCP LAma SDeJ |
| ***grengiolensis*** (15) | ECho LAma |
| 'Groenland' (8) | CAvo CBro CFFs LAma MBri MCot SPer |
| 'Gudoshnik' (4) | LAma |
| ***hageri*** (15) | ECho LAma MBri |
| - 'Red Cup' (13) | NMin |
| - 'Splendens' (15) | ECho EPot LAma SPhx WHoo |
| 'Hamilton' (7) ♀H4 | LAma SPhx |
| 'Happy Family' (3) | LAma |
| 'Happy Generation' (3) | LAma MBri |
| 'Happy Hour' (7) | ERCP |
| 'Havran' (3) | CAvo CFFs ERCP LAma |
| 'Heart's Delight' (12) | CBro ECho LAma MBri SDeJ SPhx |
| 'Hemisphere' (3) | EPfP ERCP LAma SPer |
| 'Hermitage' (3) | ERCP LAma |
| ***heweri*** (15) | ECho LAma NMin |
| 'Holland Bouquet' (3) | LAma |
| 'Holland Chic' (6) | LAma |
| 'Hollands Glorie' (4) ♀H4 | SDeJ |
| 'Hollywood' (8) | LAma |
| 'Honeymoon' (7) | LAma |
| 'Honky Tonk' (15) ♀H4 | CAvo CFFs ECho GKev NMin |
| § ***hoogiana*** (15) | ECho |
| 'Hotpants' (3) | LAma |
| § ***humilis*** (15) | CBro ECho GKev LAma MBri WShi |
| - 'China Carol' (15) | ECGP ECho |
| - 'Eastern Spice' (15) | ECho LAma NMin |
| - 'Eastern Star' (15) | ECho GKev LAma MBri NMin SPhx |
| - 'Helene' (15) **new** | GKev |
| § - 'Lilliput' (15) | CBro CMea ECho EPot GKev LAma LRHS NMin SPhx |
| - 'Magenta Queen' (15) | ECho |
| - 'Odalisque' (15) | ECho EPot ERCP GGar GKev LAma NMin SPhx |
| - 'Pegasus' (15) | NMin |
| - 'Persian Pearl' (15) | CAvo CFFs ECho EPfP EPot ERCP GKev LAma MBri NMin SDeJ SMrm SPer |
| § - var. ***pulchella*** | SPhx |
| - - Albocaerulea Oculata Group (15) | CPou CTca ECho EPot ERCP GKev LAma LLHF LWst NMin SPhx |
| § - Violacea Group (15) | CAvo CFFs CMea ECho LAma MBri |
| - - black base (15) | CBro ECho EPot ERCP GKev MBri NMin SBch |
| - - yellow base (15) | ECho EPot GKev LAma |
| - 'Zephyr' (15) | NMin |
| 'Humming Bird' (8) | LAma |
| 'Ile de France' (5) | ERCP LAma SDeJ SPer |
| ***iliensis*** (15) | ECho EPot NMin |
| 'India' (3) | ERCP |
| 'Indian Summer' (3) | MCot |
| ***ingens*** (15) | ECho LAma NMin SPhx |
| 'Insulinde' (9) | LAma |
| 'Inzell' (3) | EPfP LAma |
| 'Ivory Floradale' (4) ♀H4 | LAma SDeJ |
| 'Jackpot' (3) | ERCP |
| 'Jacqueline' (6) | MCot |
| 'Jan Reus' (3) | CAvo CFFs ERCP SPhx |
| 'Jazz' (6) | ERCP |
| 'Jewel of Spring' (4) ♀H4 | LAma |
| 'Joffre' (1) | MBri |
| 'Johann Strauss' (12) | ECho LAma MBri |
| 'Juan' (13) ♀H4 | MBri |
| ***julia*** (15) | ECho NMin |
| ***karabaghensis*** (15) **new** | LWst |
| 'Karel Doorman' (10) | LAma |
| ***kaufmanniana*** (12) | ECho EPot |
| § 'Kees Nelis' (3) | MBri |
| 'Keizerskroon' (1) ♀H4 | LAma SDeJ |
| 'Kingsblood' (5) ♀H4 | SDeJ |
| ***kolpakowskiana*** (15) ♀H4 | ECho EPfP EPot ERCP LAma MBri NMin SBch WShi |
| ***kurdica*** (15) | ECho LAma LWst SPhx |
| - purple-flowered (15) | ECho LWst |
| - red-flowered (15) | LWst |
| 'Lac van Rijn' (1) | GKev LAma |
| * 'Lady Diana' (14) | MBri |

| |  |  |
|---|---|---|
| | 'Lady Jane' (15) ♀H4 | CAvo CBro CFFs ECho EPfP ERCP MSSP NMin SPer SPhx WShi |
| | ***lanata*** (15) | ECho NMin |
| | 'Latvian Gold' (15) | ECho NMin |
| | 'Leen van der Mark' (3) | LAma MBri |
| | 'Libretto Parrot' (10) | LAma SDeJ |
| | 'Lighting Sun' (4) | LAma |
| | 'Lilac Perfection' (11) | CTca ERCP MBri |
| | 'Lilac Wonder' | see *T. saxatilis* (Bakeri Group) 'Lilac Wonder' |
| | 'Lilliput' | see *T. humilis* 'Lilliput' |
| | ***linifolia*** (15) ♀H4 | CAvo CBro CFFs ECho EPfP EPot ERCP GKev LAma MBri NMin SPhx WShi |
| § | - Batalinii Group (15) ♀H4 | ECho LAma MBri SPhx |
| § | - - 'Apricot Jewel' (15) | CBro ECho EPot ERCP GKev |
| | - - 'Bright Gem' (15) ♀H4 | CBro ECho EPot GKev LAma MBri SBch SPer SPhx |
| | - - 'Bronze Charm' (15) | CAvo CFFs CMea ECGP ECho EPot LAma MBri NMin SDeJ SPhx |
| | - - 'Red Gem' (15) | ECho GKev LAma SPhx |
| | - - 'Red Hunter' (15) ♀H4 | ECho ERCP SPer |
| | - - 'Red Jewel' (15) | ECho |
| | - - 'Yellow Jewel' (15) | ECho GKev LAma SPhx |
| § | - Maximowiczii Group (15) | ECho EPot LAma |
| | 'Lipgloss' (3) | LAma |
| | 'Little Beauty' (15) ♀H4 | CAvo CBro CFFs CMea CSam ECho EPfP GGar GKev LAma MBri SBch SDeJ SGar SPhx WHoo |
| | 'Little Princess' (15) ♀H4 | CAvo CBro CFFs CMea CSam CTca ECho EPfP ERCP GGar GKev LAma SPhx |
| | 'Lovely Surprise' (14) | SDeJ |
| | 'Lucky Strike' (3) | MBri |
| § | 'Lustige Witwe' (3) | SDeJ |
| | 'Mabel' (9) | LAma |
| § | 'Madame Lefeber' (13) | MBri SPhx |
| | 'Magier' (5) | MBri |
| | 'Maja' (7) | CAvo CFFs MBri MCot |
| | 'March of Time' (14) | MBri |
| | 'Mariette' (6) | CBro LAma MBri |
| | 'Marilyn' (6) | ERCP LAma |
| | ***marjolletii*** (15) | CAvo CBro ECho LAma NMin SPhx |
| | 'Maroon' | ERCP |
| | 'Mary Ann' (14) | LAma |
| | 'Matchpoint' (7/d) | ERCP |
| | 'Maureen' (5) ♀H4 | EGxp ERCP LAma |
| | ***mauritiana*** (15) | ECho |
| | - 'Cindy' (15) | ECho NMin SPhx |
| | ***maximowiczii*** | see *T. linifolia* Maximowiczii Group |
| | 'Maytime' (6) | CAvo CFFs ERCP LAma MBri MCot |
| | 'Maywonder' (11) ♀H4 | MBri MCot |
| | 'Menton' (5) ♀H4 | ERCP LAma |
| | Merry Widow | see *T.* 'Lustige Witwe' |
| | 'Mickey Mouse' (1) | MBri |
| | 'Miskodeed' (14) | SDeJ |
| | 'Miss Holland' (3) | MBri |
| | 'Mona Lisa' (6) | LAma SDeJ |
| § | ***montana*** (15) | CTca ECho EPot LAma NMin SPhx |
| | - yellow-flowered | ECho LAma NMin SPhx |
| | 'Monte Carlo' (2) ♀H4 | LAma MBri |
| | 'Montreux' (2) | ECho LAma |
| | 'Mount Tacoma' (11) | CAvo CBro CFFs EPfP ERCP LAma MBri SPer SPhx |
| | 'Mr Van der Hoef' (2) | LAma MBri SDeJ |
| | 'Muriel' (10) | ERCP |
| | 'Negrita' (3) | EGxp ERCP LAma MBri SDeJ SPer |
| | ***neustruevae*** (15) | CBro ECho EPot NMin SPhx |
| | 'New Design' (3/v) | ERCP LAma MBri |
| | 'Nightrider' (8) | CAvo MCot |
| | 'Ollioules' (4) ♀H4 | SDeJ |
| | 'Olympic Flame' (4) ♀H4 | SDeJ |
| | 'Orange Bouquet' (3) ♀H4 | LAma MBri |
| | 'Orange Elite' (14) | MBri |
| | 'Orange Emperor' (13) ♀H4 | CAvo CFFs LAma MBri SDeJ SPer SPhx |
| | 'Orange Favourite' (10) | ERCP LAma |
| | 'Orange Princess' (11) ♀H4 | CTca ERCP SDeJ |
| | 'Orange Sun' | see *T.* 'Oranjezon' |
| | 'Orange Triumph' (11) | MBri |
| | 'Oranje Nassau' (2) ♀H4 | LAma MBri |
| § | 'Oranjezon' (4) ♀H4 | ERCP |
| | 'Oratorio' (14) ♀H4 | MBri SDeJ |
| | 'Oriental Beauty' (14) ♀H4 | EPfP |
| | ***orithyioides*** | ECho NMin |
| | ***orphanidea*** (15) | ECho LAma NMin SCnR |
| | - 'Flava' (15) | ECho EPot ERCP LAma SPhx |
| § | - Whittallii Group (15) ♀H4 | CAvo CFFs ECho EPot ERCP GKev LAma MMHG NMin SPhx |
| | ***ostrowskiana*** (15) | ECho LAma NMin |
| | 'Oxford' (4) ♀H4 | LAma |
| | 'Oxford's Elite' (4) | LAma |
| | 'Page Polka' (3) | MBri SDeJ |
| | 'Palestrina' (3) | EPfP |
| | 'Pandour' (14) | MBri |
| | 'Papillon' (9) | LAma |
| | 'Parade' (4) ♀H4 | MBri |
| § | ***passeriniana*** (15) | ECho |
| | 'Passionale' (3) | EGxp EPfP SDeJ |
| | ***patens*** | ECho |
| | 'Paul Scherer' (3) | ERCP |
| | 'Peach Blossom' (2) | ERCP LAma MBri SDeJ SPer |
| * | 'Peaches and Cream' | SPer |
| | 'Peppermintstick' (15) ♀H4 | CAvo CFFs CTca ERCP NMin SPhx |
| | 'Perestroyka' (5) | MBri |
| | 'Perfecta' (10) new | GKev |
| | ***persica*** | see *T. celsiana* |
| | 'Philippe de Comines' (5) | LAma |
| | 'Piccolo' (15) | LAma |
| | 'Picture' (5) ♀H4 | ERCP LAma |
| | 'Pieter de Leur' (6) | EPfP LAma MBri SPer |
| | 'Pimpernel' (8/v) | LAma SDeJ |
| | 'Pink Diamond' (5) | EPfP ERCP SPer |
| | 'Pink Dwarf' (12) | SDeJ |
| | 'Pink Impression' (4) ♀H4 | LAma MBri SDeJ SPer |
| | 'Pinocchio' (14) | MBri SDeJ |
| | 'Plaisir' (14) ♀H4 | LAma MBri |
| | ***platystigma*** (15) | ECho LAma NMin |
| | ***polychroma*** | see *T. biflora* |
| | ***praestans*** (15) | ECho LAma SPer WShi |
| | - 'Fusilier' (15) ♀H4 | CBro ECho EPfP EPot LAma MBri NBir SDeJ SPhx |
| | - 'Unicum' (15/v) | ECho ERCP LAma MBri NMin SDeJ |
| | - 'Van Tubergen's Variety' (15) | ECho LAma SGar |
| | - 'Zwanenburg Variety' (15) | ECho |
| | 'Princeps' (13) | LAma MBri SDeJ |
| | 'Princess Unique' PBR (11) | LAma |
| | 'Princesse Charmante' (14) ♀H4 | MBri |
| | 'Prinses Irene' (3) ♀H4 | CAvo CBro CFFs CMea CTca EGxp EPfP ERCP LAma MBri NBir SDeJ SPhx |
| | 'Prinses Margriet' (3) new | ERCP |
| | 'Professor Röntgen' (10) | ERCP LAma SDeJ |
| | ***pulchella*** | see *T. humilis* var. *pulchella* |
| | - ***humilis*** | see *T. humilis* |
| § | 'Purissima' (13) ♀H4 | CAvo CBro CFFs EPfP LAma MBri SDeJ SPer SPhx |
| | 'Purple Bouquet' (3) | LAma |
| | 'Purple Prince' (5) | LAma SDeJ |
| | 'Quebec' (14) | SDeJ |

|  |  |
|---|---|
| 'Queen of Marvel' (2) | SDeJ |
| 'Queen of Night' (5) | CAvo CBro CFFs CMea CTca EGxp EPfP ERCP GKev LAma MBri SPer SPhx WPtf |
| 'Queen of Sheba' (6) ΨH4 | LAma |
| 'Quest' (3) | LAma |
| 'Recreado' (5) | CAvo CFFs ERCP SPhx |
| 'Red Emperor' | see *T.* 'Madame Lefeber' |
| 'Red Georgette' (5) ΨH4 | LAma MBri NBir |
| 'Red Princess' (11) **new** | ERCP |
| 'Red Riding Hood' (14) ΨH4 | CAvo CBro CFFs EGxp EPfP GKev LAma MBri NBir SDeJ SPer SPhx |
| 'Red Shine' (6) ΨH4 | CAvo CBro CFFs LAma MBri |
| 'Red Springgreen' (8) | LAma |
| 'Red Wing' (7) ΨH4 | SDeJ |
| Rembrandt mix (9) | MBri |
| 'Renown Unique' (11) | LAma |
| ***rhodopea*** | see *T. urumoffii* |
| 'Ringo' | see *T.* 'Kees Nelis' |
| 'Rococo' (10) | CBro ERCP MBri SDeJ |
| 'Ronaldo' (3) | EPfP ERCP LAma |
| 'Rosy Dream' (13) | SDeJ |
| 'Royal Virgin' (3) | CAvo |
| 'Salut' (13) | MCot |
| 'Sapporro' (6) | ERCP LAma |
| ***saracenica*** | ECho |
| ***saxatilis*** (15) | CBro ECho EPfP GKev LAma MBri MCot SDeJ WShi |
| § - Bakeri Group (15) | CPou ECho |
| § - - 'Lilac Wonder' (15) ΨH4 | CAvo CBro CFFs ECho EPot ERCP GKev LAma MBri SPhx |
| 'Scarlet Baby' (12) | EPfP MBri |
| 'Schoonoord' (2) | LAma MBri |
| ***schrenkii*** (15) | CMea ECho ERCP LAma NMin SBch |
| 'Shakespeare' (12) | CBro ECho LAma SDeJ |
| 'Shirley' (3) | CAvo CFFs EPfP ERCP LAma MBri MCot SDeJ SPer |
| 'Shirley Dream' (3) | EGxp |
| 'Showwinner' (12) ΨH4 | CAvo CBro CFFs LAma MBri |
| 'Silverstream' (4) | LAma |
| 'Snow Parrot' (10) | ERCP SPhx |
| ***sogdiana*** (15) | ECho LAma NMin |
| 'Sorbet' (5) ΨH4 | LAma |
| ***sosnowskyi*** (15) | ECho |
| ***sprengeri*** (15) ΨH4 | CAvo CBro CDes CFFs CLAP CMea CRDP CTca ECGP ECha ECho EPot ERCP LAma SCnR SDix WHal WIvy WShi |
| - Trotter's form (15) | WCot |
| 'Spring Green' (8) ΨH4 | CAvo CBro CFFs EGxp EPfP ERCP GKev LAma MBri MMHG SDeJ SPer SPhx |
| 'Spryng' (3) ΨH4 | SDeJ |
| 'Starfighter' (7) | SDeJ |
| ***stellata*** | see *T. clusiana* var. *stellata* |
| 'Stockholm' (2) ΨH4 | LAma |
| 'Stresa' (12) ΨH4 | CBro LAma |
| ***subpraestans*** (15) | ECho LAma |
| 'Super Parrot' (10) | CHid LAma |
| 'Swan Wings' (7) | ERCP LAma SDeJ SPer SPhx |
| 'Sweet Harmony' (5) ΨH4 | MBri |
| 'Sweetheart' (13) | CBro MBri SDeJ SPer |
| ***sylvestris*** (15) | CAby CAvo CBro CTca ECho EPfP EPot ERCP EWil LAma MBri NBir NMin SDeJ SPhx WCot WHer WShi |
| ***systola*** (15) | ECho NMin |
| ***tarda*** (15) ΨH4 | CAvo CBro CFFs ECho EPfP ERCP GGar GKev LAma LRHS LSou MBri SDeJ SPhx |
| 'Temple of Beauty' (5) ΨH4 | SPhx |
| 'Tequila Sun' (3) | LAma |
| ***tetraphylla*** (15) | ECho LAma NMin |
| 'Texas Flame' (10) | MBri SDeJ |
| 'Texas Gold' (10) | CHid LAma |
| 'The First' (12) | CAvo CFFs |
| 'The Lizard' (9) | LAma |
| 'Theeroos' (11) | LAma |
| 'Tinka' (15) ΨH4 | ECho LSou NMin SPhx |
| 'Toronto' (14) ΨH4 | CTca LAma LSou MBri SDeJ |
| 'Toulon' (13) ΨH4 | MBri |
| 'Très Chic' (6) | CTca SPhx |
| 'Trinket' (14) ΨH4 | LAma |
| 'Triumphator' (2) | EGxp |
| ***tschimganica*** (15) | ECho LAma LWst SPhx |
| ***tubergeniana*** (15) | ECho |
| - 'Keukenhof' (15) | ECho |
| ***turkestanica*** (15) ΨH4 | CBro CTca ECho EPfP EPot ERCP GKev LAma MBri SBch SDeJ SPhx WHoo |
| 'Turkish Delight' (14) | NPer |
| 'Typhoon' (3) | LAma |
| 'Uncle Tom' (11) | EGxp ERCP LAma MBri |
| § ***undulatifolia*** (15) | ECho LAma SPhx |
| - 'Clare Benedict' (15) | ECho NMin |
| - 'Excelsa' (15) | ECho NMin |
| 'Union Jack' (5) ΨH4 | LAma SPhx |
| 'United States' (14) | NPer |
| ***urumiensis*** (15) ΨH4 | CBro ECho EPot GKev LAma MBri NMin SBch SPhx |
| § ***urumoffii*** (15) | ECho LAma |
| 'Valentine' (3) ΨH4 | SDeJ |
| 'Valery Gergiev' (7) | ERCP |
| 'Van der Neer' (1) | SDeJ |
| 'Velvet Lily' (6) | NMin |
| 'Verona' (2) | SDeJ SPhx |
| ***violacea*** | see *T. humilis* Violacea Group |
| 'Violet Bird' (8) | ERCP SDeJ |
| 'Virichic' (8) | ERCP MCot |
| ***vvedenskyi*** (15) | ECho EPot GKev SPhx |
| - 'Bernadette' (15) **new** | SBch |
| - 'Tangerine Beauty' (15) ΨH4 | ECho GKev MBri SBch |
| 'Warbler' (7) | SDeJ |
| * 'Water Lily' | ECho SPer |
| 'Weber's Parrot' (10) | ERCP MBri |
| 'Weisse Berliner' (3) | CBro LAma |
| 'West Point' (6) ΨH4 | CAvo CBro CFFs CTca ERCP LAma MBri SPhx |
| 'White Dream' (3) | CAvo CFFs EPfP LAma MBri SDeJ |
| 'White Elegance' (6) | SPer |
| 'White Emperor' | see *T.* 'Purissima' |
| 'White Parrot' (10) | CAvo CFFs ERCP LAma SDeJ SPhx |
| 'White Triumphator' (6) ΨH4 | CAvo CBro CFFs CMea ERCP GKev LAma NBir SPhx |
| ***whittallii*** | see *T. orphanidea* Whittallii Group |
| 'Wildhof' (3) ΨH4 | ERCP |
| 'Willemsoord' (2) | LAma MBri SDeJ |
| 'William of Orange' | SDeJ |
| ***wilsoniana*** | see *T. montana* |
| 'Yellow Crown' (3) | LAma |
| 'Yellow Emperor' (5) | MBri |
| 'Yellow Flight' (3) | LAma SDeJ |
| 'Yellow Purissima' (13) ΨH4 | EPfP |
| 'Yellow Springgreen' (8) | ERCP |
| 'Yokohama' (3) | LAma SDeJ |
| 'Zampa' (14) ΨH4 | MBri |
| 'Zombie' (13) | LAma |
| 'Zomerschoon' (5) | LAma |
| § 'Zurel' (3) | CAvo CFFs EPfP ERCP LAma SPer |

**tummelberry** see *Rubus* 'Tummelberry'

## *Tunica* see *Petrorhagia*

## *Tupistra* (*Asparagaceae*)

| | |
|---|---|
| ***aurantiaca*** | GEdr |
| - B&SWJ 2267 | WCot WCru |
| - B&SWJ 2401 | WCru |
| ***chinensis*** 'Eco China Ruffles' | WCot |
| ***fimbriata*** | WCot |
| ***grandistigma*** | WCot |
| ***urotepala*** HWJ 562 **new** | WCru |
| ***wattii*** B&SWJ 8297 | WCru |

## *Tussilago* (*Asteraceae*)

| | |
|---|---|
| ***farfara*** | CArn GPoy MHer NMir WHer WHfH WSFF |

## *Tutcheria* (*Theaceae*)

| | |
|---|---|
| § ***spectabilis*** | EPfP |

## *Tweedia* (*Apocynaceae*)

| | |
|---|---|
| § ***caerulea*** ♀H2 | CBcs CCCN CDTJ CHll CSpe EShb SGar SPad SPer SWal WSFF |

## *Typha* (*Typhaceae*)

| | |
|---|---|
| ***angustifolia*** | CBen CKno CRow CWat EHon LLWG LPBA MMuc MSKA NLar NPer SLPl SPlb SWal SWat WFar WPnP |
| ***latifolia*** | CBen CRow CWat EHon LPBA MSKA NBir NLar NPer SVic SWat WFar WHer WMAq WPnP |
| - 'Variegata' (v) | CKno CRow ELan LLWG LPBA MSKA MWts NLar NPla WCot WMAq |
| § ***laxmannii*** | CBen CRow EHon LLWG LPBA MSKA NLar WPnP |
| ***minima*** | CBen CFir CRow CWat EHoe EHon ELan EPfP LPBA MSKA MWts NLar NPer SCoo SWat WFar WMAq WPnP |
| ***shuttleworthii*** | CRow LLWG |
| ***stenophylla*** | see *T. laxmannii* |

## *Typhonium* (*Araceae*)

| | |
|---|---|
| ***alpinum*** | EBee WCot |
| ***giganteum*** | SKHP WCot |
| ***kunmingense*** var. ***kunmingense*** | CDes |
| ***venosum*** | SBst |

## *Typhonodorum* (*Araceae*)

| | |
|---|---|
| ***lindleyanum*** | XBlo |

# U

## *Uapaca* (*Phyllanthaceae*)

| | |
|---|---|
| ***kirkiana*** (F) **new** | XBlo |

**ugli** see *Citrus* × *tangelo* 'Ugli'

## *Ugni* (*Myrtaceae*)

| | |
|---|---|
| § ***molinae*** | Widely available |
| - 'Flambeau' | CAgr CBcs CBod CMac EBee ELan EPfP EShb IVic LBMP LEdu LRHS MAsh MGos NLar SBfd SPoG SWvt |
| - 'Variegata' (v) | LEdu WJek |

## *Ulex* (*Papilionaceae*)

| | |
|---|---|
| ***europaeus*** | CAlb CArn CBcs CCVT CDoC CDul CHab CMac CRWN CTri ECrN ELan EPfP LBuc MCoo MGos MMuc NEgg NWea SCoo SEND SEWo SPer WDin WHar |
| - 'Aureus' | NLar |
| § - 'Flore Pleno' (d) ♀H4 | CAlb CBcs CDoC CDul CMac CSBt CTri ELan EPfP GAbr GCal GGar IArd LAst MBlu MGos MMuc NLar NWea SEND SPer WFar |
| - 'Plenus' | see *U. europaeus* 'Flore Pleno' |
| ***gallii*** | NLar WDin |
| - 'Mizen Head' | ELan GCal GGar MWhi SLon |

## *Ulmus* ✿ (*Ulmaceae*)

| | |
|---|---|
| ***americana*** 'Princeton' | CKno SGol |
| 'Beijing Gold' **new** | NLar |
| ***crassifolia*** | EGFP |
| 'Dodoens' | IArd MGos SCoo |
| § ***glabra*** | CRWN ECrN NWea SCoo WDin |
| - 'Camperdownii' | CMac EBee ECrN ELan LAst WMou |
| - 'Exoniensis' | CTho |
| - 'Gittisham' | CTho |
| - 'Horizontalis' | see *U. glabra* 'Pendula' |
| - 'Lutescens' | CEnd CTho CTri NPri NWea SCoo SEWo |
| § - 'Pendula' | CMac |
| × ***hollandica*** **new** | EGFP |
| § - 'Dampieri Aurea' | CBot CDul EBee ELan ELon EPfP LBuc LRHS MAsh MBlu MGos MRav NLar SPer SPoG WDin WPat |
| - 'Jacqueline Hillier' | CDul CMac CSpe ECho ELan LAst LMaj MGos MMuc MRav NLar SEND SGol WCFE WDin WFar WPat |
| - 'Lobel' | CCVT CDul MGos |
| - 'Wredei' | see *U.* × *hollandica* 'Dampieri Aurea' |
| ***laevis*** | ECrN |
| Lutèce = 'Nanguen' | CDoC SGol |
| ***minor*** | CDul |
| - subsp. ***angustifolia*** **new** | EGFP |
| - 'Dampieri Aurea' | see *U.* × *hollandica* 'Dampieri Aurea' |
| - 'Variegata' (v) | EBee |
| ***montana*** | see *U. glabra* |
| 'Morton Glossy' | CDul |
| ***parvifolia*** | CMCN CMen STre WPGP |
| - Everclear = 'Bsnupf' **new** | SGol |
| - 'Frosty' (v) | ECho |
| - 'Geisha' (v) | ECho ELan MAsh MGos MRav WPat |
| § - 'Hokkaido' | CMen EPot EWes GEdr LLHF WAbe WPat WThu |
| - 'Pygmaea' | see *U. parvifolia* 'Hokkaido' |
| - 'Yatsubusa' | ECho EWes LLHF MRav NLar STre WPat |
| ***procera*** | ECrN LBuc MCoo MGos WDin WSFF |
| - 'Argenteovariegata' (v) | MGos |
| ***pumila*** | EBee |
| ***rubra*** | CArn |
| 'Sapporo Autumn Gold' | CCVT EBee LBuc LMaj MRav SGol WCFE WDin |
| ***serotina*** | EGFP |
| Vada = 'Wanoux' **new** | SGol |

## *Umbellularia* (*Lauraceae*)
***californica*** CArn CMCN EPfP IArd IDee SSpi

## *Umbilicus* (*Crassulaceae*)
***rupestris*** CArn CRWN EWII SChr WHer WShi

## *Uncinia* (*Cyperaceae*)
from Chile GCal
* ***cyparissias*** from Chile NBir
***divaricata*** ECou
***egmontiana*** CHid EBee EBla EHoe EPfP LBMP LRHS WFoF WGrn WMnd WMoo WWEG
N ***rubra*** Widely available
– 'Everflame' **new** CKno LRHS SPoG
***uncinata*** CBcs CMMP ECha NHol SDix
* ***– rubra*** CFir CKno COIW CTri CWCL ELon IFro LAst LBMP LRHS MAsh MMHG MNrw SBfd SLim SMrm SPad SUsu SWvt

## *Uniola* (*Poaceae*)
***latifolia*** see *Chasmanthium latifolium*
***paniculata*** SApp

## *Urceolina* (*Amaryllidaceae*)
***miniata*** see *Stenomesson miniatum*
***peruviana*** see *Stenomesson miniatum*

## *Urginea* (*Asparagaceae*)
***capitata*** 'Sentinel Peak' ECho
***fugax*** EBee
***macrocentra*** ECho
***maritima*** CArn ECho LAma WCot
***ollivieri*** ECho
***undulata*** ECho

## *Urospermum* (*Asteraceae*)
***dalechampii*** CSam ECha LRHS MMHG SGar SUsu

## *Ursinia* (*Asteraceae*)
***alpina*** CPBP
***montana*** NWCA

## *Urtica* (*Urticaceae*)
***dioica*** 'Chedglow 2' (v) CNat
– 'Dog Trap Lane' CNat
– OGG mutant CNat
– 'Winter Yellow' CNat

## *Utricularia* (*Lentibulariaceae*)
sp. EECP
***alpina*** CSWC SHmp
***australis*** EFEx
***biloba*** CHew
***bisquamata*** CSWC SHmp
– 'Betty's Bay' CHew
***blancheti*** CSWC
***calycifida*** SHmp
***dichotoma*** CHew CSWC EFEx
***exoleta*** R. Brown see *U. gibba*
§ ***gibba*** EFEx
***heterosepala*** CHew
***intermedia*** EFEx
***lateriflora*** CHew EFEx
***livida*** CHew CSWC EECP EFEx SHmp
***longifolia*** CSWC SHmp
***macrorhiza*** CSWC
***menziesii*** EFEx
***microcalyx*** CHew SHmp
***monanthos*** CHew EFEx
***nephrophylla*** CHew SHmp
***novae-zelandiae*** CHew
***ochroleuca*** EFEx
***paulinae*** CHew
***praelonga*** CHew CSWC SHmp
***prehensilis*** CHew
***pubescens*** CSWC
***reniformis*** EFEx SHmp
***– nana*** EFEx
***sandersonii*** CHew CSWC EECP SHmp
– blue-flowered CSWC EECP
***simplex*** CHew
***subulata*** EFEx
***tricolor*** CHew CSWC SHmp
***uniflora*** CHew
***vulgaris*** EFEx
***warburgii*** CHew
***welwitschii*** CHew

## *Uvularia* (*Colchicaceae*)
§ ***caroliniana*** ECho
***disporum*** ECho
***grandiflora*** ♀H4 Widely available
– dwarf ECho
– gold-leaved CAby LWSt MAvo
– 'Lynda Windsor' CRDP SKHP
– orange flowered SKHP
– var. ***pallida*** CAby CAvo CBct CLAP CPom EBee ECha ECho EPPr EPfP EPot GCal GEdr IBlr LEdu LRHS LWSt MRav NCGa NHar NPnk SPhx SUsu WAbe WCru WFar WPnP
– 'Susie Lewis' WCru
***grandiflora × perfoliata*** ECho NBir WWEG
***perfoliata*** CAby CBct CLAP CPLG EBee ECha ECho EPPr EPfP EPla EPot EWTr GGar IBlr LEdu MRav NBir NPnk SPhx WAbe WCru WPnP
– tall EPPr
***pudica*** see *U. caroliniana*
***sessilifolia*** CBct CLAP CPLG CRDP EBee ECho EPot GEdr IBlr LEdu LRHS NMen SSvw WCru
– 'Cobblewood Gold' (v) EBla WCru

## *Vaccinium* ✿ (*Ericaceae*)
sp. LSRN
***angustifolium*** var. ***laevifolium*** GLin
***arctostaphylos*** NLar SWvt
'Berkeley' (F) CAgr CCCN CTrh CWib GKin LBuc LSRN MAsh MBlu NPla SDea SPoG WHar
'Bluecrop' (F) Widely available
'Bluejay' (F) CWib LAst LRHS MAsh SCoo SLon WHar
'Blueray' (F) CWib GKin GPri
'Brigitta' (F) CTrh ECrN EMil GTwe LRHS NPla SPoG
***chaetothrix*** **new** WThu
'Chandler' (F) CAgr CMac CTrh ERea GKin GPri LSRN SBfd SKee SPer

| | |
|---|---|
| ***consanguineum*** B&SWJ 10486 | WCru |
| ***corymbosum*** (F) ♀H4 | CBcs MGos MNHC SBfd SCoo SReu SSta WDin |
| - 'Blauweiss-goldtraube' (F) | CSBt CWSG CWib ERea GKin LRHS LSRN MAsh MGos NLar SDea SPoG SVic WFar WGwG WHar |
| - 'Blue Duke' (F) | LSRN |
| - 'Bluegold' (F) | CTrh EMil LRHS SPer |
| - 'Bluetta' (F) | CAgr CTri CWib GPri GTwe LRHS MGos SCoo SPoG WFar |
| - 'Coville' (F) | CWib NLar |
| - 'Darrow' (F) | CAgr CTrh GTwe LBuc |
| - 'Dixie' (F) | CSBt MSCN NPla WGwG |
| - 'Duke' (F) ♀H4 | CTrh CWib ELan EPfP GPri LRHS MAsh MGos NPla SDea |
| - 'Elizabeth' (F) | GPri |
| - 'Elliott' (F) | LSRN SBfd |
| - 'Grover' (F) | LRHS NLar |
| - 'Hannah's Choice' (F) | GPri |
| - 'Hardyblue' (F) | CAgr |
| - 'Ivanhoe' (F) | GKin |
| - 'Jersey' (F) | CAgr CWib EPfP LAst LRHS MAsh MCoo MGos MMuc NLar SCoo SDea SEND SPer SVic |
| - 'Nelson' (F) | GPri LRHS SCoo |
| - 'Nui' (F) | EPom LSRN |
| - 'Patriot' (F) | CAgr CSBt CTrh CWib ECrN GKin GPri GTwe LBuc LRHS MAsh MBri MGos MPkF MRav NPla SBfd SCoo SDea SPoG WGwG |
| - 'Reka' (F) | CAgr |
| - 'Sierra' (F) | GPri |
| - 'Spartan' (F) ♀H4 | CTrh CWib GTwe LRHS LSRN MAsh MGos SBfd SCoo SKee SPer |
| - 'Stanley' (F) | ELan LRHS MAsh |
| - 'Toro' (F) | EMil GPri GTwe LBuc LRHS MAsh MGos |
| - 'Weymouth' (F) | SDea |
| ***crassifolium*** | LRHS MAsh SPoG |
| subsp. ***sempervirens*** 'Well's Delight' (F) | |
| ***cylindraceum*** ♀H4 | EPfP MAsh NLar WFar WPat |
| ***delavayi*** | LRHS MAsh NHar NMen WAbe WFar WPat WThu |
| ***dunalianum*** | MMuc |
| - var. ***caudatifolium*** B&SWJ 1716 | WCru |
| - var. ***megaphyllum*** HWJ 515 | WCru |
| 'Earliblue' (F) | CAgr CSBt GKin LRHS MBri MGos SDea WFar |
| ***floribundum*** | CBcs CDoC CMHG LRHS MAsh NLar SSpi |
| ***glaucoalbum*** ♀H3-4 | CAbP CDoC CMac EPfP LRHS MAsh MRav SMad SPer SPoG SSpi WPat |
| 'Goldtraube 71' | LRHS NPla |
| * ***grandiflorum*** | ECho |
| ***griffithianum*** | SSta |
| 'Groover' | LSRN |
| 'Herbert' (F) | CAgr CMac CTrh ECrN EPom GTwe LBuc MGos |
| ***macrocarpon*** (F) | CArn ECho ELan GLam GTwe LRHS MAsh MMuc NHar NWCA SDea SRms |
| - 'Centennial' (F) | NHar |
| - 'CN' (F) | CAgr NLar |
| - 'Early Black' (F) | EGxp EPom GKin LBuc |
| - 'Franklin' (F) | CAgr |
| - 'Hamilton' | GEdr LLHF NMen WThu |
| - 'Howes' (F) | NHar |
| - 'Langlois' (F) | NLar |
| - 'Olson's Honkers' (F) | CAgr NLar |
| - 'Pilgrim' (F) | CAgr CMac GKin LEdu MAsh NHar WHar |
| 'Misty' (F) | CAgr |
| ***moupinense*** | CDoC GLam LRHS MAsh NMen WAbe WPat WThu |
| - 'Variegatum' (v) | LLHF |
| ***myrtillus*** | CAgr GPoy NLar NWea SVic WSFF |
| 'Northland' (F) | CSBt CWib GTwe LRHS MAsh MBri NLar NPla SCoo SDea SPoG |
| ***nummularia*** | EBee ECho GEdr LRHS MMuc NHar NMen SSpi WAbe WPat WThu |
| - McB 1108 | GLam |
| ***ovalifolium*** | GAuc |
| ***ovatum*** | CBcs CMHG CMac CTsd WThu |
| - 'Thundercloud' | CAbP LRHS MAsh |
| § ***oxycoccos*** (F) | CAgr CArn GPoy MCoo MGos NHar WThu |
| 'Ozarkblue' (F) | EPom GTwe LSRN SPer |
| ***padifolium*** | WPGP |
| ***pallidum*** | IBlr |
| ***palustre*** | see *V. oxycoccos* |
| ***retusum*** | IRar |
| 'Rubel' (F) | LRHS |
| 'Sunrise' (F) | GTwe |
| 'Sunshine Blue' (F) | CAgr ECrN EPom LBuc LRHS SDea SKee |
| 'Tophat' (F) | CCCN MPkF |
| ***vitis-idaea*** | EPfP EWes GGar GPoy LRHS MGos NBlu NWea SVic WFar |
| - 'Autumn Beauty' | NLar |
| - 'Compactum' | EWes LLHF LSou |
| - 'Ida' **new** | LBuc |
| - Koralle Group ♀H4 | CAgr EPfP GKin MBri MCoo NLar NWad SPoG |
| - subsp. ***minus*** | GEdr GPri MAsh NLar NMen WAbe WThu |
| - 'Red Pearl' | CSBt EPfP LRHS MAsh MGos NLar |
| * - 'Variegatum' (v) | EWes |

## *Vagaria* (*Amaryllidaceae*)

| | |
|---|---|
| ***ollivieri*** | ECho |

## *Valeriana* (*Caprifoliaceae*)

| | |
|---|---|
| 'Alba' | see *Centranthus ruber* 'Albus' |
| ***alliariifolia*** | EBee GCal NBro WCot |
| - 'Sirene' **new** | EBee |
| ***celtica*** | GPoy |
| 'Coccinea' | see *Centranthus ruber* |
| ***coreana*** | CFee |
| ***dioica*** | CHab |
| ***jatamansi*** | GPoy |
| ***montana*** | NBro NRya SRms SWat |
| ***officinalis*** | Widely available |
| - subsp. ***sambucifolia*** | CFee EPPr GCal MNrw MSpe SHar WOut |
| ***phu*** 'Aurea' | CArn CBod CBot CHby CMac EBee ECha EHoe ELan EPfP GKin LRHS MBri MCot MLHP MRav NBid NBir NBro NEgg NSti NWad SMrm SPer SPhx SRms WCAu WCot WFar WMoo |
| ***pyrenaica*** | ECha EPPr GCal LPla LRHS MMHG MMuc MNrw SEND SPhx WCot WMoo |
| ***saxatilis*** | NLar NRya |
| ***supina*** | CPBP GLam NWCA |

| | |
|---|---|
| ***wallrothii*** | EBee MAvo WCot |

## *Valerianella* (*Caprifoliaceae*)

| | |
|---|---|
| § ***locusta*** | GPoy SVic |
| ***olitoria*** | see *V. locusta* |

## *Vallea* (*Elaeocarpaceae*)

| | |
|---|---|
| ***stipularis*** | CHll CTsd IGor ILis |

## *Vallota* see *Cyrtanthus*

## *Vancouveria* (*Berberidaceae*)

| | |
|---|---|
| ***chrysantha*** | CFir CLAP CMil CPLG CPom ECha EPPr LEdu MRav NLar NRya NWCA SKHP SMad WCru WMoo WPGP WPtf |
| ***hexandra*** | CBct CFir CGHE CLAP CMac CPLG ECha EPPr EPfP EPla GEdr LEdu NRya NSti NWCA SKHP SPhx WCru WMoo WPGP WWEG |
| ***planipetala*** | CLAP WCru |

## *Vania* see *Thlaspi*

## veitchberry see *Rubus* 'Veitchberry'

## *Velleia* (*Goodeniaceae*)

| | |
|---|---|
| ***paradoxa*** | ECou |

## *Vellozia* (*Velloziaceae*)

| | |
|---|---|
| ***elegans*** | see *Talbotia elegans* |

## *Veltheimia* ✿ (*Asparagaceae*)

| | |
|---|---|
| § ***bracteata*** ♀H1 | CCse CHll CLak CPou EBak ECho ECre IBlr LToo NPal WCot |
| ***viridifolia*** Jacq. | see *V. bracteata* |

## × *Venidioarctotis* see *Arctotis*

## *Venidium* see *Arctotis*

## *Veratrum* ✿ (*Melanthiaceae*)

| | |
|---|---|
| ***album*** ♀H4 | CBct CPne EBee ECha ECho GCal GPoy LEdu MNrw MRav NBid WCru WFar |
| - var. ***flavum*** | CAby GCal MNrw SPhx WCru |
| - subsp. ***lobelianum*** | GCal |
| - 'Lorna's Green' | GCal |
| - var. ***oxysepalum*** | LWst WCru |
| ***californicum*** | CAby CHGN ECha GCal MNrw NBid WCot |
| - compact | MNrw |
| ***dolichopetalum*** B&SWJ 4195 | WCru |
| ***formosanum*** | EWld MNrw |
| - B&SWJ 1575 | GEdr WCru |
| - RWJ 9806 | WCru |
| ***grandiflorum*** B&SWJ 4416 | WCru |
| ***longebracteatum*** | WCru |
| ***maackii*** | GEdr WCot |
| - var. ***japonicum*** | WCru |
| - var. ***maackii*** B&SWJ 5831 | WCru |
| - var. ***parviflorum*** | GCal |
| ***nigrum*** ♀H4 | CBct CBot CFir EBee GCal GMaP IKil MAvo MLHP MNrw MRav NBPC NBid NBir NCGa NLar SMad SPhx SPlb WBor WCot WCru WFar WPnP |
| - B&SWJ 4450 from South Korea | WCru |
| ***schindleri*** | LWst |
| - B&SWJ 4068 | WCru |
| ***stamineum*** | LWst WCru |
| ***viride*** | CBct ECha EWes GCal MNrw |

## *Verbascum* (*Scrophulariaceae*)

| | |
|---|---|
| ***adzharicum*** | WHoo |
| 'Annie May' | EBee LSRN NOrc |
| 'Apricot Sunset' | EBee SPhx |
| 'Arctic Summer' | see *V. bombyciferum* 'Polarsommer' |
| ***arcturus*** | CFee |
| 'Aurora' | SJoh SPhx |
| 'Aztec Gold' | EBee SJoh |
| * ***bakerianum*** | EBla ECtt |
| 'Bill Bishop' | ECho |
| ***blattaria*** | NBPC NBir SPav SSvw SWat WFar WHer WWEG |
| - f. ***albiflorum*** | CSpe EBee EWTr IFro LLWP NDov SGar SPlb SWal WHer WMoo WTin |
| - yellow-flowered | SPav SWat |
| 'Blushing Bride'^PBR | LLHF |
| ***boerhavii*** | WHil |
| § ***bombyciferum*** | CBre CSev ECha GMaP NBPC NCGa NGBl |
| * - 'Arctic Snow' | SPav SPoG |
| § - 'Polarsommer' | CSpe EBee EPfP MBri NBir NBlu NVic SPer SPet SWat WWEG |
| - 'Silver Lining' | NLar NPer |
| 'Broussa' | see *V. bombyciferum* |
| 'Buttercup' | EBee ECtt LRHS WFar |
| 'Caribbean Crush' | CBcs CHab CMac EBee ECtt ELan EPfP EWll LRHS NBPC NLar SBfd SMrm SPer WWEG |
| ***chaixii*** | CSam ECha ECtt MLLN MMHG NBir WFar WMoo XLum |
| - 'Album' ♀H4 | Widely available |
| - 'Blackberry Crush' | MDKP |
| - 'Helene Bowles' | CHar |
| - 'Sixteen Candles' | CBod CSpr ECtt GJos GQue LRHS MBNS NChi NLar WHil WPtf |
| - 'Wedding Candles' | CBod GMac LRHS NGdn NLar SMrm WHil |
| ***chaixii*** × 'Wendy's Choice' | MDKP |
| 'Charlotte' | SJoh |
| 'Cherokee' | SJoh SUsu |
| 'Cherry Helen'^PBR | EBee ECtt LRHS LSRN MBri NEgg NGdn NLar NPnk SBfd SPer WWEG |
| 'Claire' | SJoh |
| 'Clementine' | LPla SJoh SPhx |
| 'Coneyhill Yellow' | ECtt EPPr |
| (Cotswold Group) 'Cotswold Beauty' ♀H4 | CSam EAEE EBee ECtt EPfP GMac LRHS MRav MWat NGdn SPer WCAu WMnd |
| - 'Cotswold Gem' | ECtt |
| - 'Cotswold Queen' | CBcs CHab CMMP EAEE EBee ECtt ELan EPPr EPfP LRHS MDKP MRav MWat NGdn SPer SPet SWvt WCAu WMnd WWEG |
| - 'Gainsborough' ♀H4 | Widely available |
| - 'Mont Blanc' | EAEE EBee GMaP LRHS SWat |
| - 'Pink Domino' ♀H4 | CBcs CBot CSam EBee ECtt ELan EPPr EPfP GMaP LRHS MLHP MRav MWat NGdn SBrd SPer SPet SWvt WFar WMnd WWEG WWFP |
| - 'Royal Highland' | EBee ECtt ELan EPfP NGdn NLar SWvt WFar |
| - 'White Domino' | EBee ECtt SPer |
| 'Cotswold King' | see *V. creticum* |
| § ***creticum*** | CSpe IKil SGar SPav WCot |
| 'Dark Eyes'^PBR **new** | MTis |

| | |
|---|---|
| § ***densiflorum*** | CArn EBee SPer |
| – BSSS 232 | WCru |
| 'Dijon' | ECtt EWes |
| ***dumulosum*** ♀H2-3 | EPot GCal WAbe |
| 'Eleanor's Blush' | LBuc |
| 'Elektra' | SJoh |
| 'Ellenbank Jewel' | GMac |
| ***epixanthinum*** ♀ | CSpe LRHS |
| 'Flower of Scotland'PBR | ECtt |
| 'Golden Wings' ♀H2-3 | ECtt ITim NMen WAbe |
| Harptree smokey hybrids | CHar |
| 'Helen Johnson' | CBcs CHab CMMP CWCL EAEE EBee ECtt EPfP GMaP LHop LRHS LSRN MGos MRav NBPC NLar NPnk NPri SBfd SCoo SPer SRkn SWvt WCAu WFar WWEG |
| 'Hiawatha' | SJoh SPhx |
| 'High Noon' | MTis SJoh |
| × ***hybridum*** 'Banana Custard' | EBee LRHS MNHC NGBl |
| – 'Copper Rose' | EPfP MBri |
| – 'Snow Maiden' | CTri EPfP MHer WCAu |
| – 'Wega' | NLar WCAu |
| 'Hyde Hall Sunrise' | EPfP LBuc SPoG |
| 'Innocence' | MDKP |
| 'Jackie' | CBcs CHar COIW EBee ECtt ELan LRHS LSRN MBri NGdn SCoo SPer SPoG WFar WHil WWEG |
| 'Jackie in Pink' | EWes LBuc LRHS MDev NGdn WFar |
| 'Jackie in Yellow'PBR | LLHF MDev NGdn |
| 'Jester' **new** | EBee |
| 'Jolly Eyes' | EBee ECtt MBri NPnk |
| 'June Johnson' | EAEE EBee ECtt LRHS SHar |
| 'Kalypso' | SJoh SPhx |
| 'Klondike' | SJoh |
| 'Lavender Lass' | ECtt |
| 'Letitia' ♀H3 | CBcs CMea EBee ECho ECtt ELan EWes GCal ITim LRHS NMen NWCA SRot SWvt WAbe WKif WPat |
| ***longifolium*** | WFar |
| – var. ***pannosum*** | see *V. olympicum* |
| ***lychnitis*** | CArn SPhx WKif WMoo |
| 'Megan's Mauve' | EAEE EBee ECtt LRHS SWvt |
| 'Merlin'PBR | EAEE ECtt LRHS LSRN LSou MBNS MCot MLLN MTis MWat NCGa SJoh SPoG |
| 'Monster' | CDes EBee |
| 'Moonlight' | ECtt |
| 'Moonshadow' | SJoh SPhx |
| 'Mystery Blonde' | SJoh SPhx |
| ***nigrum*** | CArn CHab EBee EGHP EPfP NGdn NLar WMnd WMoo |
| – var. ***album*** | EGHP NChi NGdn NLar WMoo |
| 'Norfolk Dawn' | EBee ECtt EPfP SPhx |
| § ***olympicum*** | EBee ELan EPfP GJos LRHS MAvo MBNS MWat NGBl SDix SEND WCAu WCot WWEG |
| 'Pandora' | LBuc LRHS |
| 'Patricia' | EBee SPhx |
| 'Petra' | LPla SJoh SPhx |
| ***phoeniceum*** | ELan EPfP GJos GLam LRHS NBro SBfd SGar SPlb SPoG SWal WMoo XLum |
| * – 'Album' | XLum |
| – 'Antique Rose' | WHrl |
| – 'Flush of White' | CBot EAEE ECtt EPPr EPfP GQue IFro NGBl NGdn NLar NPnk SPav SSvw WMoo WWEG XLum |
| – hybrids | CBot CTri GMaP NBlu NEgg NGdn SRms SWat WFar WPer WWEG |
| – 'Rosetta' | CBod CMea EPfP LRHS NGBl NGdn WCAu WHil |
| – 'Violetta' | CCVN CMea ECtt EPPr EPfP EWll LAst LBMP MLHP NEgg NGBl NGdn NSti NVic SPav SPer STes WCAu WCFE WCot WCra WFar WHrl WMoo WPtf XLum |
| 'Phoenix' | CTsd EBee |
| 'Pink Glow' | GMac |
| 'Pink Ice' | MDKP |
| 'Pink Kisses' | EBee LLHF LRHS LSRN NBPC |
| 'Pink Petticoats' | LBuc LRHS SBfd SBrd SPoG |
| (Pixie Series) 'Pixie Apricot' | ECtt WHlf |
| – 'Pixie Blue' | EBee ECtt WHlf |
| – 'Pixie White | ECtt WHlf |
| 'Plum Smokey'PBR | EBee ECtt LLHF LRHS SBfd WWEG |
| 'Primrose Cottage' | MBri NGdn |
| 'Primrose Path' | ECtt EPfP LRHS NPnk SBfd SRot |
| 'Purple Prince' | ECtt |
| ***pyramidatum*** | SPhx |
| 'Raspberry Ripple' | CMac EBee ECtt ELan LBMP LLHF |
| ***roripifolium*** | SSvw |
| 'Rosie' | NGdn SPoG |
| 'Sierra Sunset' | ECtt EPfP MTis NPnk |
| 'South Country' | SJoh |
| 'Southern Charm' | ECtt EPfP EWll GJos GMaP LRHS MBri MHer NChi NLBP NPnk SPoG STes WFar WHil WPtf WWEG |
| 'Spica' | GMac NLar |
| ***spicatum*** | CBot |
| 'Sugar Plum'PBR | CHar EBee ECtt EWll LLHF MTis WWEG |
| 'Summer Sorbet' | EBee ECtt ELan EPfP LRHS NSti SPoG |
| Sunset shades | GJos |
| ***thapsiforme*** | see *V. densiflorum* |
| ***thapsus*** | CHab GPoy MHer MNHC MSCN NMir SEND |
| 'Tropic Blush' | SJoh |
| 'Tropic Dawn' | SJoh |
| 'Tropic Moon' | SJoh |
| 'Tropic Rose' | SJoh |
| 'Tropic Spice' | SJoh |
| 'Tropic Sun' ♀H4 | SJoh |
| 'Twilight' | LBuc LRHS WHlf |
| 'Valerie Grace' | SPhx |
| 'Vernale' | CBot |
| ***wiedemannianum*** | CSpr |

## *Verbena* (*Verbenaceae*)

| | |
|---|---|
| (Aztec Series) Aztec Cherry Red = 'Balazcherd'PBR (G) | NPri |
| – Aztec Coral = 'Balazcoral'PBR (G) | NPri |
| – Aztec Dark Pink Magic = 'Balazdapima' (G) | NPri |
| – Aztec Pearl = 'Balazpearl'PBR (G) | SCoo |
| – Aztec Plum Magic = 'Balazplum'PBR (G) | NPri |
| – Aztec Red = 'Balazred' (G) | SCoo |
| – Aztec Silver Magic = 'Balazsilma'PBR (G) ♀H3 | MWea NPri SCoo |
| – Aztec White = 'Balazwhit' (G) | LRHS |
| 'Betty Lee' (G) | ECtt |
| 'Blue Prince' (G) | CSpe SUsu |
| § ***bonariensis*** ♀H3-4 | Widely available |

***brasiliensis*** misapplied — see *V. bonariensis*
***canadensis*** 'Perfecta' (G) — CSpe
'Candy Carousel' (G) — SPet
***chamaedrifolia*** — see *V. peruviana*
§ 'Claret' (G) ♀H3 — CMac CSev CSpe EBee ECtt ELan ELon EPfP LRHS LSRN LSou MCot MGos MTis MWea SAga SBfd SCoo SPet SPhx SUsu WWEG
***corymbosa*** — CAby CEnt CHid CHII CMMP CWCL EBee ECGP ECha EPPr LRHS MDKP MMuc MSpe NLar SAga SBfd SPer WPer WPtf WWEG
- 'Gravetye' — CPrp EBee WFar
'Diamond Merci' (G) — WHoo
Donalena Twinkle Pink (Donalena Series) **new** — NPri
'Edith Eddleman' (G) — CWGN EBee EPfP LRHS LSqH MWea
'Fiesta' (G) — LRHS
'Hammerstein Pink' — EBee EPfP LRHS
***hastata*** — CHar CSpe EBee ECtt EPfP LEdu LRHS MCot MNrw NDov NSti SGar SMrm SPhx SPlb SWat SWvt WBor WFar WMnd WMoo WPer WSHC
* - 'Alba' — EBee EPfP GCal MCot MDKP MNrw NBPC NLar SMrm WMoo WWFP
- 'Blue Spires' — EPfP IPot WWEG
- f. ***rosea*** — CElw CHar CMea CSpe EBee EHoe ELan EPfP LRHS MDKP MLHP MNrw MRav MSCN NBPC NBid NDov SBfd SMrm SPer SPhx SUsu SWat WCAu WFar WMoo WSHC WWEG
- - 'Pink Spires' — ECtt EKen EPfP LBMP LHop SPad WWEG
- 'White Spires' — CMea EPfP WWEG
'Homestead Purple' (G) — CBar CChe CMac COIW CPrp CSev CWCL EAEE EBee ECtt EPfP LRHS LSRN MCot MGos NDov SAga SBfd SBrd SMrm SPer SPet SUsu SWvt WWEG
'Jenny's Wine' — see *V.* 'Claret'
'La France' (G) — CHGN EBee ECha ECtt EPfP LRHS LSou MWea SAga SDix SMrm SPhx SUsu WHoo WMnd WSHC WWEG
'Lavender Spires' — SPhx
'Lois' Ruby' — see *V.* 'Claret'
***macdougalii*** — LHop MDKP SPhx
***officinalis*** — CArn CRWN CWan GPoy MHer MNHC SIde WHer WJek WPer
***patagonica*** — see *V. bonariensis*
§ ***peruviana*** (G) — EBee ELan EPfP LBMP LRHS SChF SRms XLum
'Pink Bouquet' — see *V.* 'Silver Anne'
'Pink Parasol' **new** — SBrd
'Pink Parfait' (G) — EPfP GKev LAst SAga SBfd
(Quartz Series) 'Quartz Red Polka Dot' — SAga SBfd SBrd
- 'Quartz Waterfall' mixed **new** — LAst
'Red Cascade' — SPet
§ ***rigida*** ♀H3 — Widely available
- f. ***lilacina*** — LSRN NLar
- - 'Lilac Haze' — CBod CMac EPfP LRHS NSti SBrd SPoG SRkn
- - 'Polaris' — CHar CPrp EBee ELon EPfP EShb EWTr IPot LBMP LHop LRHS MAvo MMuc MNrw MRav NDov NWad SHar SMrm SPet SPhx SPoG SUsu WSHC

Seabrook's Lavender = 'Sealav' — CBar CSev CWCL EPPr EPfP LRHS LSRN LSqH MNrw MTis MWea SBfd SHar SPer SWvt WSHC
***serpyllifolia*** — see *Junellia micrantha*
§ 'Silver Anne' (G) ♀H3 — MCot SAga SMrm SUsu
§ 'Sissinghurst' (G) ♀H2-3 — ECtt SAga SBfd SMrm SRms
'Sissinghurst Pink' — SPet
'Strawberry Kiss' **new** — MTis
***stricta*** — LRHS MDKP NLar SPhx
'Summer Breeze' (G) **new** — LRHS
(Superbena Series) — NPri
Superbena Bushy Merlot = 'Usbena5002'PBR (G)
- Superbena Ruby Red = 'Usbena5122'PBR (G) ♀H3 — SBfd
(Tapien Series) Tapien Pink Parfait (G) **new** — LSou
- Tapien Pink = 'Sunver'PBR (G) — LAst
- Tapien Red (G) **new** — LSou
- Tapien Salmon = 'Suntapiro'PBR (G) ♀H3 — LAst LSou WGor
- Tapien Sky Blue = 'Suntapilabu'PBR (G) ♀H3 — LSou
- Tapien Violet = 'Sunvop'PBR (G) — LAst LHop LSou WGor
- Tapien White = 'Suntapipurew'PBR (G) — LAst
(Temari Series) Temari Blue = 'Sunmariribu'PBR (G) — LAst LSou
- Temari Burgundy = 'Sunmariwaba'PBR (G) — LAst LSou
- Temari Coral Pink = 'Sunmariripi'PBR (G) — LAst LSou
- Temari Neon Red [3] = 'Sunmarineopi'PBR (G) ♀H — LAst
- Temari Vanilla = 'Sunmarivani'PBR (G) — LAst LSou
'Tenerife' — see *V.* 'Sissinghurst'
***tenuisecta*** (G) — NLar
(Vegas Series) 'Vegas Appleblossom' (G) — WGor
- 'Vegas Purple' (G) — LSou WGor
- 'Vegas Scarlet' (G) — LSou
***venosa*** — see *V. rigida*
'White Cascade' — SPet

## *Verbesina* (Asteraceae)

***alternifolia*** — CArn
- 'Goldstrahl' — EPPr WPer
***helianthoides*** — CSpr

## *Vernicia* (Euphorbiaceae)

***fordii*** — SPlb

## *Vernonia* (Asteraceae)

§ ***arkansana*** — CHGN ECha EPPr EWes EWhm IPot LRHS MMuc NDov NLar SDix SMad SPhx WBor WWEG XLum
- 'Betty Blindeman' — EBee
- 'Mammuth' — CDes EBee ECtt EWes LEdu LHop SMrm SPhx WPGP
***crinita*** — see *V. arkansana*
***fasciculata*** — EBee EShb EWes LPla MRav NLar SMrm WCot

| | |
|---|---|
| ***gigantea*** | CSpr EBee EWes MMuc MNrw NLar SBHP SMad WHrl |
| ***missurica*** | EBee |
| ***noveboracensis*** | EBee EWhm LRHS NLar SGar SMad SMrm WPer WRHF XLum |
| - 'Albiflora' | EPPr EWes |

## *Veronica* (Plantaginaceae)

| | |
|---|---|
| ***allionii*** | GKev |
| ***amethystina*** | see *V. spuria* L. |
| ***anagallis-aquatica*** | LLWG |
| 'Anna' PBR | NDov |
| ***armena*** | ECho EWes MDKP MHer MWat NMen SBch SRot WFar WPat XSen |
| 'Atomic Blue' **new** | LSou MAsh |
| 'Atomic Lavender' **new** | MAsh |
| 'Atomic Lilac' **new** | LSou MAsh WHlf |
| 'Atomic Pink' **new** | LSou MAsh MBri |
| 'Atomic Violet' **new** | MAsh MBri |
| § ***austriaca*** | NBre NChi WFar WMoo XLum |
| - var. ***dubia*** | see *V. prostrata* |
| - 'Ionian Skies' | CPBP CTri EBee ECha ECtt EPPr EWes LBee LRHS MMuc NEgg SEND SMrm SPer WFar WKif WPat WPer WSHC WWEG |
| - 'Jacqueline' | NBre |
| § - subsp. ***teucrium*** | CArn CSam CTri EBee ECho SRms WFar WKif WPer |
| - - 'Crater Lake Blue' 🏆H4 | EBee ECtt ELan EPfP EShb LEdu LHop LRHS MCot MNFA MRav NBre NGdn NVic SMrm SPhx SPlb SRms WCot WFar WMnd WPer WSHC |
| - - 'Kapitän' | ECha LRHS MNrw NGdn NPro WFar WPer |
| - - 'Knallblau' | SMrm SSvw WFar |
| - - 'Royal Blue' 🏆H4 | CCVN EBee EPfP EShb GMaP LRHS MWhi NCGa NSti SBch SBfd SRms WFar WKif WMnd XLum XSen |
| 'Baby Doll' PBR | LRHS LSou MBNS MBri NLar WCra |
| ***bachofenii*** | WTin |
| ***beccabunga*** | CArn CBen CHab CWat EHon EWil GPoy LPBA MSKA MWts NMir NPer SWat WHer WMAq WPnP WSFF XLum |
| 'Bergen's Blue' | CMac NLar SHar |
| Blue Bouquet | see *V. longifolia* 'Blaubündel' |
| 'Blue Indigo' | ELan LAst MNrw NBre NGdn |
| 'Blue Spire' | SWat WPer |
| ***bombycina*** | ECho WAbe |
| - subsp. ***bolkardaghensis*** | WAbe |
| ***caespitosa*** | CPBP |
| - subsp. ***caespitosa*** | NMen WAbe |
| ***candida*** | see *V. spicata* subsp. *incana* |
| × ***cantiana*** 'Kentish Pink' | WCFE WDyG WFar WMoo WPer WWEG |
| ***caucasica*** | MWat XSen |
| ***chamaedrys*** | ECho EWil NMir XLum |
| § - 'Miffy Brute' (v) | NBir |
| - 'Pam' (v) | ECtt |
| - 'Variegata' | see *V. chamaedrys* 'Miffy Brute' |
| 'Christy' | EPfP LBuc LRHS SPoG |
| ***cinerea*** 🏆H4 | GMaP MLHP SAga SBch SBrt WHoo WSHC XSen |
| ***dabneyi*** | CDes EBee WPGP |
| 'Dark Martje' | GBin |
| 'Darwin's Blue' PBR | GAbr NLar NOrc WHrl |
| 'Ellen Mae' | CElw ECtt EWes WCAu WMnd |
| 'Eveline' PBR | EBee ECtt EPfP MBri NDov NLar WCot |
| ***exaltata*** (D) | LRHS NChi SMrm WCot WPer |
| 'Fairytale' PBR | CCVN CWGN EPPr EPfP LRHS LSou MAsh MBNS MBri MDev MLLN MWea NSti WGrn |
| 'Fantasy' | MTis NDov SSvw |
| ***filiformis*** | XLum |
| - 'Fairyland' (v) | EWes |
| 'First Love' **new** | LSou MAsh |
| ***formosa*** | see *Parahebe formosa* |
| § ***fruticans*** | ECho GJos NMen |
| ***fruticulosa*** | LLHF |
| ***gentianoides*** 🏆H4 | Widely available |
| - 'Alba' | CMea GCal LRHS NBre NChi NSti |
| - 'Barbara Sherwood' | EKen GBin GMac LRHS NBre NGdn WWEG |
| - 'Blue Streak' | EWll LRHS WRHF |
| - 'Lilacina' | EBee LRHS |
| - 'Nana' | EBee EPfP |
| - 'Pallida' | CSpr EBee EPfP GAbr MBrN MMuc MRav SEND SPlb WBor WFar WWEG |
| - 'Robusta' | EBee ECtt LRHS NCGa NEgg NGdn SMrm WMnd |
| - 'Tissington White' | Widely available |
| - 'Variegata' (v) | EBee ECha ECtt ELan EPfP GCra GMaP LAst MHer MRav MSCN NBir NEgg NPnk NPri SBfd SPer SWat WAle WFar WMnd WWEG |
| ***gigantea*** | MMuc |
| 'Giles van Hees' | WCot |
| ***grandis*** | EBee GAbr IFro LEdu MDKP MMuc MWhi NChi NLar SBfd SEND WFar WHrl WMoo WPtf |
| × ***guthrieana*** | CAbP NMen SRms WFar |
| ***hendersonii*** | see *V. subsessilis hendersonii* |
| ***incana*** | see *V. spicata* subsp. *incana* |
| * - 'Candidissima' | GCal |
| 'Ink' **new** | MAvo |
| 'Inspiration' | CCse NBre NDov SMrm |
| 'Inspire Blue' | LBMP LBuc LSou |
| 'Inspire Pink' | LBMP LBuc LSou |
| ***kellereri*** | see *V. spicata* |
| ***kiusiana*** | CMHG IFro LPla LRHS MWhi NBPC NLar SAga SPhx WHrl |
| * - var. ***maxima*** | WPtf |
| ***kotschyana*** | GLam XSen |
| ***liwanensis*** | ECho NMen |
| - Mac&W 5936 | EPot MDKP |
| ***longifolia*** | CHar CMac CMea CSBt ECha ELan GCra LRHS MLHP NBPC NSti NVic WFar WMoo XLum |
| - 'Alba' | EBee ELan LBMP MMuc MWat NLar SEND STes WMoo |
| - 'Blaubart' **new** | XLum |
| § - 'Blaubündel' | CCse EBee NGdn |
| - 'Blauer Sommer' | EAEE EPfP LBMP MCot NDov NEgg NGdn SPoG |
| § - 'Blauriesin' | CCVN CTri EBee ECtt EPfP GMaP LRHS MWea NBre NSti SPer SSvw |
| - Blue Giantess | see *V. longifolia* 'Blauriesin' |
| - 'Blue John' | EBee GMac NBre NSti WCot |
| - blue-flowered | MWat |
| - 'Charming Pink' | LRHS |
| - 'Fascination' | ECtt LAst NGdn NPro |
| - 'Foerster's Blue' | see *V. longifolia* 'Blauriesin' |
| - 'Joseph's Coat' (v) | MLLN NBre |
| - 'Lila Karina' | EBee WPer |
| - 'Lilac Fantasy' | ECtt GQue MBri NSti |
| - 'Oxford Blue' | CBar EGxp LRHS NBlu WHoo |
| - 'Pacific Ocean' PBR | ECtt |

| |  |  |
|---|---|---|
| | - 'Pink Eveline'PBR **new** | NDov |
| | - pink-flowered | EShb STes |
| | - 'Rose Tone' | GJos MWea NLar WHrl WMoo |
| | - 'Rosea' | SBfd WPer |
| | - 'Schneeriesin' | CPrp EAEE EBee ECha EPfP GMaP LEdu MRav NBir NLar SPer |
| | ***lyallii*** | see *Parahebe lyallii* |
| | ***macrostachya*** | SKHP |
| | 'Martje' | SMrm XLum |
| | 'Mini Spires Blue' | EPfP LRHS MGos |
| | ***montana*** 'Corinne Tremaine' (v) | NBir NLar SRms WHer |
| | ***officinalis*** | CArn EWil XLum |
| | ***oltensis*** | CPBP ECho EDAr EPot EWes GJos LLHF MHer NMen WAbe WPat |
| | ***orchidea*** | GEdr LRHS SRms |
| | ***orientalis*** | NMen |
| | subsp. ***orientalis*** | |
| | ***ornata*** | WOld WPer |
| | ***pectinata*** 'Rosea' | ECho ECtt EWes XSen |
| | ***peduncularis*** 'Oxford Blue' | see *V. umbrosa* 'Georgia Blue' |
| | ***perfoliata*** | see *Parahebe perfoliata* |
| | ***petraea*** 'Madame Mercier' | SMrm XLum |
| | 'Pink Damask' | CHar CSpe CWCL EBee ECtt ELan ELon EPfP GMaP LRHS MCot MRav MWat NEgg NGdn NLar NSti SMrm SPhx WFar WHoo WMnd WTin WWEG |
| | ***porphyriana*** | EBee LRHS MMuc MWea |
| | ***prenja*** | see *V. austriaca* |
| § | ***prostrata*** ♀H4 | CMea CSam CTri ECho ECtt EPfP GJos GKev LAst LBee LRHS MAsh MLHP NEgg NHar SRms WBor WFar WHoo WMoo WNew XLum |
| | - 'Alba' | MLHP MWat WFar |
| | - 'Aztec Gold'PBR | CMac MSCN NLar NPro |
| § | - 'Blauspiegel' | CPBP LRHS SMrm |
| | - 'Blue Ice' | SMrm |
| | - Blue Mirror | see *V. prostrata* 'Blauspiegel' |
| | - 'Blue Sheen' | ECho ECtt GEdr LRHS NBir WAbe WFar WPer |
| | - 'Goldwell' | EPPr |
| | - 'Lilac Time' | CSpr ECho GEdr GKev GMaP LHop LRHS MTis NBir NLar SRms WRHF |
| | - 'Loddon Blue' | ECho SRms |
| | - 'Miss Willmott' | see *V. prostrata* 'Warley Blue' |
| | - 'Mrs Holt' | ECho ECtt GEdr LHop LRHS NBir NMen SRms WAbe WBrk WFar WHoo WPat |
| | - 'Nana' | ECho ECtt EPot EWes MWat NMen WAbe |
| | - 'Nestor' | CTri ECtt NGdn |
| | - 'Rosea' | ECho MWat WPer |
| | - 'Shirley Holt' | NBir |
| | - 'Spode Blue' ♀H4 | CBar CMac CMea ECho ECtt GAbr GMaP LHop LRHS MTis NWCA SPoG SRms WFar |
| | - 'Trehane' | EBee ECho ECtt EDAr EPfP LEdu LHop LRHS MAsh MHer MWat NEgg NRya SPlb SPoG SRms WFar WNew |
| § | - 'Warley Blue' | ECho |
| * | ***pseudolysimachion*** | WMoo |
| | 'Purpleicious' | CWGN EPfP LRHS LSou MBri SMrm WCAu |
| | ***repens*** | ECho EPfP GJos NBlu NPro SPlb |
| | - 'Sunshine' **new** | LRHS |
| | 'Rosalinde' | CBot NGdn WPer |
| | 'Royal Pink' | CPrp LAst NLar NSti |
| | ***rupestris*** | see *V. prostrata* |
| | ***saturejoides*** | CPBP GLam SRms |
| | ***saxatilis*** | see *V. fruticans* |
| | ***schmidtiana*** 'Nana' | GKev |
| | ***selleri*** | see *V. wormskjoldii* |
| | 'Shirley Blue' ♀H4 | CPrp CWib EBee ELan EPfP GAbr LSRN MCot MHer MMuc MWat SPer SPhx SRms WCFE WPer WWEG |
| § | ***spicata*** | CSam EBee ELan EPfP GJos LEdu LRHS MDun NBid NBlu NPnk SRms WBrk WCAu WFar WMoo WPer |
| | - 'Alba' | EBee GJos LRHS MRav MWat NLar WPer WTin WWEG |
| | - 'Barcarolle' | EBee ELan EPfP MAvo |
| § | - 'Blaufuchs' | ECtt |
| | - 'Blue Bouquet' | LRHS NBre NLar NPri |
| | - Blue Fox | see *V. spicata* 'Blaufuchs' |
| § | - 'Erika' | CPrp EBee ECha ECtt EPfP IPot LSou MNrw MSCN MWat NBid NBir NBre NGdn |
| § | - 'Glory'PBR | CPrp EBee ECtt EPfP LRHS LSou MDev MGos NBre NEgg SBrd SMrm SPad SPer SPoG WCot WCra WHil WWEG |
| | - 'Heidekind' | CCVN CWCL EBee ECho ECtt EDAr ELan EPfP GKev LAst LHop MLHP MWat NBir NGdn NWCA SBfd SMrm SPoG SRms SRot SWat WFar WHoo WPer WTin XLum |
| | - subsp. ***hybrida*** | WCot WHer |
| § | - 'Icicle' | EBee MAvo NBre SSvw WCAu WHlf |
| § | - subsp. ***incana*** | CMea CWan EBee ECho EHoe ELan EPfP GJos LRHS MMuc SBfd SEND SPlb SRms SWat WCFE WFar WMoo WPer WTin WWEG XSen |
| | - - 'Nana' | ECha MLHP NBir SRms |
| | - - 'Silbersee' | MLHP WHil |
| | - - 'Silver Carpet' | CPrp EBee ECtt LAst LHop MRav NBre SPer WGwG WMnd |
| | - - 'Wendy' | EWes GCal LPla |
| | - 'Minuet' | LRHS |
| | - 'Nana Blauteppich' | CPBP EPfP LRHS NBre NLar NWCA |
| | - 'Pink Goblin' | GQue NBre WPer |
| | - 'Pink Panther'PBR | EBee LSou MDev |
| | - Red Fox | see *V. spicata* 'Rotfuchs' |
| | - 'Romiley Purple' | EBee NBre SPer WWEG |
| | - 'Rosalind' | NLar |
| | - ***rosea*** | see *V. spicata* 'Erika' |
| | - 'Rosenrot' | ECho |
| § | - 'Rotfuchs' | CBcs CPrp EBee ECtt EHoe ELan ELon EPfP LAst LSou MCot MLLN MMuc MRav NBPC NBir NChi NGdn NOrc SBfd SBrd SMrm SPer SPoG SRms WCFE WFar WPer WSHC WWEG |
| | - 'Royal Candles'PBR | see *V. spicata* 'Glory' |
| | - 'Sightseeing' | CSpr CWib GJos NBir NBre SRms WFar |
| | - subsp. ***spicata*** 'Nana' | XSen |
| | - 'Total Eclipse'PBR **new** | LSou |
| | - 'Twilight'PBR | EPfP MBri |
| | - 'Ulster Blue Dwarf' | EPfP GAbr LSou MAsh MAvo MBri MLLN NGdn WPtf |
| | - ***variegata*** (v) | NBir |
| § | ***spuria*** L. | MMuc SEND WPer |
| | ***stelleri*** | see *V. wormskjoldii* |
| | ***subsessilis*** | WPer |
| | - 'Blaue Pyramide' | NBre WPtf |
| * | - ***hendersonii*** | NBre |

| | |
|---|---|
| ***sumilensis*** | LRHS |
| 'Sunny Border Blue' | EBee EPfP NBre NLar SPoG WFar |
| ***tauricola*** | XSen |
| ***telephiifolia*** | ECtt EWes MDKP NMen NWCA |
| ***teucrium*** | see *V. austriaca* subsp. *teucrium* |
| ***thessalica*** | EPot GLam |
| ***thymoides*** subsp. ***pseudocinerea*** | NWCA |
| § ***umbrosa*** 'Georgia Blue' | Widely available |
| ***virginica*** | see *Veronicastrum virginicum* |
| 'Waterperry Blue' | WFar WPer |
| ***wherryi*** | WPer |
| 'White Icicle' | see *V. spicata* 'Icicle' |
| 'White Jolanda' | ECtt MSCN NSti |
| 'White Spire' | CBot |
| ***whitleyi*** | MMuc SEND |
| § ***wormskjoldii*** | EBee ECho ECtt EDAr MBrN NLar NWCA SBch SRms |
| - 'Alba' | MLHP WPer |

## *Veronicastrum* (*Plantaginaceae*)

| | |
|---|---|
| 'Adoration' | NDov SPhx |
| ***brunonianum*** | CDes GCal |
| ***japonicum*** var. ***australe*** B&SWJ 11009 | WCru |
| ***latifolium*** | CDes GCal WCot |
| - BWJ 8158 | WCru WSHC |
| ***sibiricum*** | EBee ECha EShb GCal GQue LRHS MMuc NBid NBre WAul WCAu WMoo XLum |
| - BWJ 6352 | LEdu NLar WCru |
| - 'Red Arrows' | NDov NLar SPhx |
| - var. ***yezoense*** | MDKP WBox |
| - - RBS 0290 | NPro |
| ***villosulum*** | CDes CPom EWes NBid NBro SMrm WCru WSHC |
| § ***virginicum*** | CArn CEnt CKno EBee ECtt GCra GPoy LRHS MBrN MLHP MMuc NBir SRms WMoo WPer WWEG XLum |
| - 'Alboroseum' | WTin |
| - 'Album' | Widely available |
| - 'Apollo' | CBre EBee EBla ECtt EPPr EPfP EWTr EWll GAbr GMaP LPla LRHS LSou MAvo MBri MCot MLLN NBro NDov NLar NOrc NSti SMrm SPhx WAul WCAu WHrl WWEG |
| - 'Diane' | EBee GMaP NBre NDov SPhx SUsu WCAu |
| - 'Erica' | CCVN EBee ECtt EKen EPPr EPfP GBin GMac GQue IKil IPot LRHS LSou MBri MNrw NBPC NCGa NDov NPnk NSti SUsu WAul WBor WCAu WCot WWEG |
| - 'Fascination' | Widely available |
| - var. ***incarnatum*** | see *V. virginicum* f. *roseum* |
| - 'Lavendelturm' | CAby CDes CSam EBee ECha ECtt EPPr GMaP IPot LHop LRHS MCot NCGa NDov NLar NSti SMrm SPer SPhx WAul WCot WWEG |
| - light blue-flowered | MMuc SEND |
| - 'Pointed Finger' | CAby GCal GMaP LEdu NBre NLar SMrm SPhx SUsu |
| § - f. ***roseum*** | CAby EBee EBla ECha ELan GMaP LRHS MRav NBPC NBro NDov SPer SPhx SUsu WBor WCot WFar WKif WMoo XLum |
| - - 'Pink Glow' | Widely available |
| - 'Spring Dew' | CBre EBee ECtt EPfP LPla NBid NBro NPro WMnd |
| - 'Temptation' | EBee EWll GBin GMaP IPot LPla NBre NBro NPro SUsu WTin |
| 'White Jolan' | ECtt |

## *Verschaffeltia* (*Arecaceae*)

| | |
|---|---|
| ***splendida*** | XBlo |

## *Vestia* (*Solanaceae*)

| | |
|---|---|
| § ***foetida*** ♀H1 | CBcs CCCN CPLG CPom CTsd CWib EBee ELan ELon EMil EPfP GKev IDee LRHS MNrw NLar SBig SBrt SEND SGar SPoG WAle WGob WHil WSHC |
| ***lycioides*** | see *V. foetida* |

## *Viburnum* ✿ (*Adoxaceae*)

| | |
|---|---|
| B&SWJ 10290 from Mexico | WCru |
| ***acerifolium*** | GAuc LLHF WFar WPat |
| ***alnifolium*** | see *V. lantanoides* |
| ***annamensis*** B&SWJ 8302 | WCru |
| ***atrocyaneum*** | CDul CGHE CPLG CPMA EBee MBlu NLar NWad SKHP SPoG WFar WPat |
| - B&SWJ 7272 | WCru |
| - HIRD 113 | WPGP |
| § ***awabuki*** | CHEx CPLG EBee EPfP LRHS MBlu MGos NLar SEND SLim SMad SSpi WPGP WPat |
| - B&SWJ 8404 | WCru |
| - B&SWJ 11374 from Wabuka, Japan | WCru |
| § - 'Emerald Lustre' | CDoC CHEx WPGP WPat |
| ***betulifolium*** | CAbP CBcs CPLG CPMA EBee EPfP EQua GAuc GKin NLar SMad WFar |
| - 'Hohuanshan' | WCru |
| ***bitchiuense*** | CPMA NLar |
| × ***bodnantense*** | CBot CMac CTri EBee LMaj SAga WHar |
| - 'Charles Lamont' ♀H4 | Widely available |
| - 'Dawn' ♀H4 | Widely available |
| - 'Deben' ♀H4 | EPfP EQua MMHG NLar SPer WDin WFar WPat |
| ***bracteatum*** | NLar |
| ***buddlejifolium*** | CMac EBee EPfP EWes MMuc SKHP WCru WFar WPGP |
| × ***burkwoodii*** | Widely available |
| - 'Anika' | NLar |
| - 'Anne Russell' ♀H4 | Widely available |
| - 'Chenaultii' | MRav WDin |
| - 'Compact Beauty' | CPMA EPfP WPat |
| - 'Conoy' | CPMA CSpe LEdu MWat WPat |
| - 'Fulbrook' ♀H4 | CAbP EPfP LEdu LRHS MAsh MGos NLar WDin WFar WPat |
| - 'Mohawk' | CAbP CDoC CEnd CPMA EBee ELan EPfP LEdu LRHS MAsh MBri NHol NLar SAga SCoo SKHP SPoG SWvt WFar WPat |
| - 'Park Farm Hybrid' ♀H4 | CAbP CDoC CMac CPLG CPMA CSam CTri CWib EBee ECrN ELan ELon EPfP LAst LBMP LEdu LRHS MAsh MBri MRav MSwo NLar NSti SBrd SLPl SPer SPoG SRms WFar WPat |
| ***calvum*** | CPLG |
| × ***carlcephalum*** ♀H4 | Widely available |
| - 'Cayuga' | LEdu MAsh NLar WPat |
| * - 'Variegatum' (v) | CPMA |
| ***carlesii*** | CBcs CMac CTri CWib GKin LSRN MBlu MGos MRav MSwo SCoo SEWo SGol SLim SPer |

| | |
|---|---|
| - B&SWJ 8838 | WCru |
| - 'Aurora' ♀H4 | Widely available |
| - 'Charis' | CPMA CSBt LRHS NLar |
| - 'Compactum' | CPMA NHol |
| - 'Diana' | CDoC CEnd CMHG CMac CPMA EPfP LRHS LSRN MAsh MBlu MRav NLar SBrd SPer SPoG SSta WCFE WPat |
| - 'Marlou' | CPMA LEdu NLar WPat |
| ***cassinoides*** | EPfP GBin WFar WPat |
| - 'Bullatum' | EPfP |
| - 'Sear Charm' | WPat |
| 'Chesapeake' | CDul CPMA EWes MMuc SEND WDin |
| ***chingii*** | CGHE CPMA SLon WCru WPGP WPat |
| 'Chippewa' | CPMA |
| ***cinnamomifolium*** ♀H3 | CAbP CBcs CDoy CHEx CMac CPLG EPfP LRHS MAsh MBri MMuc SArc SCoo SEND SLPl SLon SPer SPoG SSpi WFar WPGP |
| ***cotinifolium*** | CPLG NLar |
| - CC4541 | CPLG NLar |
| ***cylindricum*** | CBot CGHE EBee EPfP EWTr GAuc LHop LRHS NLar SKHP WCru WPGP |
| - B&SWJ 6479 from Thailand | WCru |
| - B&SWJ 7239 | WCru WPGP |
| - B&SWJ 9719 from Vietnam | WCru |
| - BWJ 7778 from China | WCru |
| - HWJCM 434 from Nepal | WCru |
| ***dasyanthum*** | EPfP GAuc NLar |
| ***davidii*** ♀H4 | Widely available |
| - (f) | CBcs CBot CDoC CMac CSBt ELan EPfP EWTr LAst MAsh MGos SBrd SPer SPoG SRms WPat |
| - (m) | CBcs CBot CDoC CMac CSBt ELan EPfP MGos MRav SBrd SPoG SRms WPat |
| - 'Angustifolium' | EQua LTen WFar |
| ***dentatum*** | GAuc WPat |
| - Autumn Jazz | see *V. dentatum* 'Ralph Senior' |
| - Blue Muffin = 'Christom' | WPat |
| - Chicago Lustre | see *V. dentatum* 'Synnestvedt' |
| - 'Morton' | IArd |
| § - 'Ralph Senior' | NLar |
| § - 'Synnestvedt' | NLar |
| - 'White and Blue' | NLar |
| ***dilatatum*** B&SWJ 4456 | WCru |
| - B&SWJ 5844 | WCru |
| - B&SWJ 8734 | WCru |
| - B&SWJ 10894 | WCru |
| - 'Erie' | EPfP |
| - 'Inneke' | NLar |
| - 'Iroquois' | EPfP |
| - 'Michael Dodge' | EPfP MBri NLar |
| - 'Sealing Wax' | NLar |
| ***edule*** | GAuc |
| ***erosum*** B&SWJ 3585 | WCru |
| - B&SWJ 8735 | WCru |
| - B&SWJ 8893 | WCru |
| - B&SWJ 10880 | WCru |
| ***erubescens*** | CAbP CPMA IArd NLar WFar |
| - B&SWJ 8281 | WCru |
| - 'Foster' | NLar |
| - var. ***gracilipes*** | CPMA EPfP IArd WPat |
| - - HWJK 2163 | WCru |
| - 'Ward van Teylingen' | EPfP NLar |
| 'Eskimo' | CAbP CBcs CMac CPMA CSBt CWSG EBee EPfP LRHS LSRN MAsh MBNS MGos MRav SKHP SLim SPoG SSta SWvt WDin WFar |
| § ***farreri*** ♀H4 | CBcs CDoC CDoy CDul CSBt CTri CWib EBee ECtt ELan EPfP GGal LBuc LRHS LSRN MGos MRav MSwo NHol NLar SBrd SCoo SGol SPer SPoG SWvt WDin WFar WHar |
| - 'Album' | see *V. farreri* 'Candidissimum' |
| § - 'Candidissimum' | CBot CDul CMac CPLG EBee ELan EPfP IArd LHop LRHS MAsh MRav NLar SGol SPer SPoG |
| - 'December Dwarf' | CPMA NLar |
| - 'Farrer's Pink' | CAbP CPLG CPMA NLar |
| - 'Fioretta' | NLar |
| - 'Nanum' | CMac CPMA EBee EPfP LRHS MAsh MBrN MRav MWat NLar SKHP WFar WPat |
| ***foetens*** | see *V. grandiflorum* f. *foetens* |
| ***foetidum*** var. ***ceanothoides*** | NLar |
| - var. ***rectangulatum*** B&SWJ 1888 | WCru |
| - - B&SWJ 3451 | WCru |
| ***fragrans*** Bunge | see *V. farreri* |
| 'Fragrant Cloud' | ECrN |
| ***furcatum*** ♀H4 | EPfP GKin IArd NLar SKHP WPat |
| - B&SWJ 5939 | WCru |
| × ***globosum*** 'Jermyns Globe' | CAbP CCVT CDoC CMHG CMac EBee EPfP LAst MRav NLar SBrd SEND SLon SPoG WDin WFar |
| ***grandiflorum*** | CPMA EPfP NLar WDin |
| - 'De Oirsprong' **new** | NLar |
| § - f. ***foetens*** | CPMA EPfP NLar |
| - - GWJ 9227 | WCru |
| - 'Snow White' | CPMA |
| ***harryanum*** | CAbP CDoy EPfP MBNS MOWG NLar WCru WFar WSHC |
| ***henryi*** | CAbP CPMA EPfP IArd IDee NLar SBrt WDin WPat |
| × ***hillieri*** | CHGN MWhi WFar |
| - 'Winton' ♀H4 | CAbP CDoC CMac CPMA CWib EBee EPfP LHop LRHS LSRN LTen MBri MOWG NLar NPal SKHP SLon SPoG SSpi SVen WDin WFar WPGP |
| ***hupehense*** | GAuc |
| 'Huron' | EPfP |
| ***ichangense*** | CPMA NLar |
| ***japonicum*** | CMac CPLG EBee EPfP LRHS NLar SLon WFar WPGP |
| - B&SWJ 5968 | WCru |
| × ***juddii*** ♀H4 | Widely available |
| ***kansuense*** **new** | CPLG |
| ***koreanum*** B&SWJ 4231 | WCru |
| ***lantana*** | CCVT CDul CHab CLnd CRWN CTri CWib ECrN EShb GAuc LAst LBuc MAsh NLar NWea SEND SEWo SPer SVic WDin WFar WMou |
| - 'Aureum' | CMHG ECtt EHoe EPfP MAsh MBlu NLar |
| - var. ***discolor*** | NLar |
| - 'Mohican' | EBee NLar |
| - 'Variefolium' (v) | CPMA |
| § ***lantanoides*** | EPfP NLar SSpi |
| 'Le Bois Marquis' **new** | EPfP SBfd |
| ***lentago*** | CAbP CMac NLar |
| ***lobophyllum*** | EPfP NLar |
| ***luzonicum*** B&SWJ 3930 | WCru |
| * - var. ***floribundum*** B&SWJ 8281 | WCru |

| |  |  |
|---|---|---|
| | - var. ***oblongum*** B&SWJ 3549 | WCru |
| | ***macrocephalum*** | CPMA IArd SLon WDin |
| | ***mariesii*** | see *V. plicatum* f. *tomentosum* 'Mariesii' |
| | ***mullaha*** GWJ 9388 | WCru |
| | ***nervosum*** B&SWJ 2251a | WCru |
| | ***nudum*** | ECrN EPfP IArd IVic NLar |
| | - 'Pink Beauty' | CGHE CPMA EBee LRHS LSRN MMHG NLar WFar WPGP WPat |
| | - 'Winterthur' | CPMA NLar |
| | ***odoratissimum*** misapplied | see *V. awabuki* |
| | ***odoratissimum*** Ker Gawl. RWJ 10046 | WCru |
| | - 'Emerald Lustre' | see *V. awabuki* 'Emerald Lustre' |
| | aff. ***odoratissimum*** B&SWJ 3913 from the Philippines | WCru |
| | - 'Arboricolum' | WCru |
| | 'Oneida' | NLar WDin |
| | ***opulus*** | Widely available |
| | - var. ***americanum*** 'Bailey's Compact' | MAsh WPat |
| | - - 'Phillips' | CAgr |
| | - - 'Wentworth' | CAgr |
| | - 'Apricot' | NLar |
| | - 'Aureum' | CChe CMac CSam CWib EBee ECtt EHoe ELan EPfP LAst MAsh MGos MMuc MRav NEgg NHol NLar NMyG SPer WDin WFar WMoo |
| | - var. ***calvescens*** B&SWJ 10544 | WCru |
| | - 'Compactum' ΥH4 | Widely available |
| N | - 'Fructu Luteo' | SGol |
| * | - 'Harvest Gold' | EBee SCoo SLim SPoG |
| | - 'Nanum' | CAbP CBcs CMea EBee ELan ELon EPfP EPla EShb LAst MRav NHol NLar NMen WDin WFar WPat |
| | - 'Notcutt's Variety' ΥH4 | EPfP MGos SRms WPat |
| | - 'Park Harvest' | CDul EBee EPfP LRHS NLar SKHP SLPl WPat |
| § | - 'Roseum' ΥH4 | Widely available |
| | - 'Sterile' | see *V. opulus* 'Roseum' |
| * | - 'Sterile Compactum' | LAst SWvt |
| N | - 'Xanthocarpum' ΥH4 | Widely available |
| | ***parvifolium*** | NLar |
| | - B&SWJ 4009 | WCru |
| | ***pichinchense*** B&SWJ 10660 | WCru |
| N | ***plicatum*** | CTri CWib GAuc NLar WDin |
| | - 'Janny' | WPat |
| | - 'Mary Milton' | CPMA NLar |
| | - 'Nanum' | see *V. plicatum* f. *tomentosum* 'Nanum Semperflorens' |
| | - 'Pink Sensation' | CPMA GBin NCGa |
| | - f. ***plicatum*** 'Grandiflorum' | CAbP CDoC EPfP NLar WMoo |
| | - 'Popcorn' | CAbP CMac CPLG CPMA EPfP LEdu LRHS LSRN MAsh MRav SLim SPoG SSta WPat |
| | - 'Rosace' | EPfP MBlu NLar SSpi WPat |
| | - 'Shoshoni' | MBri NLar |
| | - f. ***tomentosum*** | EGxp EPfP EWTr WDin |
| | - - 'Cascade' | EBee EWTr LRHS MMHG NEgg NLar SSpi |
| | - - 'Dart's Red Robin' | ECtt LLHF NLar WPat |
| | - - 'Elizabeth Bullivant' | LLHF LRHS |
| | - - 'Igloo' | NLar |
| | - - 'Lanarth' | Widely available |
| § | - - 'Mariesii' ΥH4 | Widely available |
| | - - 'Molly Schroeder' | CPMA NLar |
| § | - - 'Nanum Semperflorens' | CAlb CDoC CMac ECtt EPla IArd LBMP MAsh MGos NLar SBfd SLPl SPoG WFar WPat WSHC |
| | - - Newport = 'Newzam' | CDoC NLar |
| | - - 'Pink Beauty' ΥH4 | Widely available |
| | - - 'Rotundifolium' | LRHS MAsh MRav NLar WPat |
| | - - 'Rowallane' | EPfP MAsh MBri WPat |
| | - - 'Saint Keverne' | GKin |
| | - - 'Shasta' | CDoC CMCN EPfP MBri NLar SKHP WDin WFar |
| | - - 'Summer Snowflake' | CDoC CEnd CWGN CWSG EBee ECrN EPfP LRHS MAsh MSwo NLar SKHP SLim SPer SPoG WDin WFar |
| | - Triumph = 'Trizam' | NLar |
| | - 'Watanabe' | see *V. plicatum* f. *tomentosum* 'Nanum Semperflorens' |
| | 'Pragense' ΥH4 | CAbP CBcs CDul CMCN EBee EPfP EQua LRHS MGos NHol SEND SLon SPer WDin WFar WPat |
| | ***propinquum*** | CAbP NLar WFar |
| | - B&SWJ 4009 | WCru |
| | ***prunifolium*** | NLar SGol WCru |
| | - 'Mrs Henry's Large' | CPMA |
| | ***punctatum*** B&SWJ 9532 | WCru |
| * | 'Regenteum' | CWib |
| | × ***rhytidophylloides*** | WFar |
| | - 'Alleghany' | NLar |
| | - Dart's Duke = 'Interduke' | SBrd SLPl WPat |
| | - 'Willowwood' | EBee LRHS MAsh NLar WPat |
| | ***rhytidophyllum*** | CBcs CDoy CDul CHEx CMac CTri EBee ECrN EPfP LHop LRHS LTen MGos MMuc MSwo NEgg SEND SGol SPer SRms WCFE WDin WFar WMoo WSFF |
| | - 'Aldenham' | GCal LSRN |
| | - 'Crathes Castle' | NLar |
| | - 'Roseum' | CBot CPLG SLPl SWvt |
| | - 'Variegatum' (v) | CPMA NLar WPat |
| | - 'Wisley Pink' | LRHS MAsh SSpi |
| | 'Royal Guard' | LLHF NLar |
| | ***sambucinum*** HWJ 838 **new** | WCru |
| | ***sargentii*** | GAuc |
| | - B&SWJ 8695 | WCru |
| | - f. ***flavum*** | NLar |
| | - 'Onondaga' ΥH4 | Widely available |
| | - 'Susquehanna' | EPfP NLar |
| | ***semperflorens*** | see *V. plicatum* f. *tomentosum* 'Nanum Semperflorens' |
| § | ***setigerum*** | EPfP GAuc IArd NLar SLPl WPat |
| | - 'Aurantiacum' | EPfP NLar |
| | ***sieboldii*** | GAuc |
| | - B&SWJ 2837 | WCru |
| | - 'Seneca' | EPfP NLar |
| | ***subalpinum*** | NLar |
| | ***taiwanianum*** B&SWJ 3009 | WCru |
| | ***ternatum*** | EPfP |
| | ***theiferum*** | see *V. setigerum* |
| | ***tinus*** | Widely available |
| | - 'Bewley's Variegated' (v) | CBcs EBee MRav SPer |
| I | - 'Compactum' | SWvt |
| | - 'Eve Price' ΥH4 | Widely available |
| | - 'French White' ΥH4 | CDoC CDul CMac EBee ELan ELon EPfP LRHS MGos MRav SBfd SCoo SLim SPoG SWvt WFar |
| | - 'Gwenllian' ΥH4 | Widely available |
| | - 'Israel' | EBee MBNS NLar SPer WFar |
| | - 'Little Bognor' | NLar |

| | |
|---|---|
| - 'Lucidum' | CBcs CPMA NLar WCFE WDin WFar |
| - 'Lucidum Variegatum' (v) | CMac CPMA SLim |
| * - 'Macrophyllum' | EBee EPfP LRHS NLar SPoG SWvt WFar |
| - 'Pink Prelude' | EPla |
| - 'Purpureum' | CBar CSBt EBee ECrN EHoe ELon EPfP EPla LRHS MAsh MGos MSwo NEgg SBfd SCoo SGol SLPl SLim SPer SPoG WDin WFar WMoo WPat |
| - Spirit = 'Anvi'PBR | CAbP CSBt EBee LRHS LSou MAsh NLar SBfd SCoo SPoG |
| - 'Spring Bouquet' | LBMP MAsh NHol NLar |
| - 'Variegatum' (v) | CBot CDul CMac CTri CWib EBee EHoe ELan ELon EPfP LAst LBMP LRHS MAsh MGos NEgg NLar NWad SBfd SGol SLim SPlb SPoG SWvt WDin WFar WPat |
| ***tomentosum*** | see *V. plicatum* |
| ***triphyllum*** B&SWJ 5784 **new** | WCru |
| ***urceolatum*** B&SWJ 6988 | WCru |
| ***utile*** | WFar WPat WThu |
| aff. ***venustum*** B&SWJ 10477 | WCru |
| ***wrightii*** | EPfP MRav NLar |
| - B&SWJ 8780 | WCru |
| - 'Hessei' | WPat |
| - var. ***stipellatum*** B&SWJ 5784 | WCru |
| - - B&SWJ 5844 | WCru |
| - - B&SWJ 5856 | WCru |

# *Vicia* (*Papilionaceae*)

| | |
|---|---|
| ***americana*** | EBee |
| ***cracca*** | CHab NLan NMir WSFF |
| ***oroboides*** | LRHS |
| ***sativa*** | CHab |
| ***sylvatica*** | CPom EWes |
| ***unijuga*** | CPom |

# *Vigna* (*Papilionaceae*)

| | |
|---|---|
| § ***caracalla*** | CCCN |

# *Viguiera* (*Asteraceae*)

| | |
|---|---|
| ***multiflora*** | EBee |

# *Villaresia* see *Citronella*

# *Villarsia* (*Menyanthaceae*)

| | |
|---|---|
| ***bennettii*** | see *Nymphoides peltata* 'Bennettii' |

# *Vinca* (*Apocynaceae*)

| | |
|---|---|
| ***balcanica*** | ILis XLum |
| ***difformis*** ♀H3-4 | CAlb CHar COlW CPom CTri CWan EBee ECha LLWP LRHS MGos SBri SDix WHer XLum |
| * - 'Alba' | CPom SBch |
| - Greystone form | CPLG EPPr EPfP LHop NHol NLar SEND WGwG WRHF |
| - 'Jenny Pym' | CAlb CBod COlW CPLG CPom CYeo EBee EPPr EPla EWTr EWes GGar LHop MBNS SBch SEND SMad SPoG WFar WOut WRHF |
| - 'Ruby Baker' | LRHS NChi WHrl |
| - 'Snowmound' | CAlb COlW CWan EBee LRHS MRav SPoG |
| 'Hidcote Purple' | see *V. major* var. *oxyloba* |
| ***major*** | CAlb CBcs CDul CMac CSBt CWib EBee ELan EPfP EShb GPoy LBuc LRHS MGos MSwo NPri NWea SBfd SGol SLim SPer SRms WDin WFar WGwG WMoo XLum |
| - 'Alba' | CMac CWib |
| - 'Elegantissima' | see *V. major* 'Variegata' |
| - 'Expoflora' (v) | NLar |
| - var. ***hirsuta*** hort. | see *V. major* var. *oxyloba* |
| § - subsp. ***hirsuta*** (Boiss.) Stearn | CMac XLum |
| 'Jason Hill' | CAlb |
| § - 'Maculata' (v) | CAlb CDoC COlW CSBt EHoe EShb LRHS LSou MGos MRav MSwo NBPC NPri SBfd SEND SLim SPer SPoG SWvt WFar WMoo |
| § - var. ***oxyloba*** | CMac COlW CPLG CTri ECha ECtt ELan EPla EPri LHop MLLN MRav MWat SPoG SRms WFar WHer |
| - var. ***pubescens*** | see *V. major* subsp. *hirsuta* (Boiss.) Stearn |
| - 'Reticulata' (v) | ELan |
| - 'Surrey Marble' | see *V. major* 'Maculata' |
| § - 'Variegata' (v) ♀H4 | Widely available |
| - Westwood form | CFee |
| - 'Wojo's Jem' (v) | CAlb CDoC CMac EBee EWes LBuc LRHS LSRN MBri MGos NPri SCoo SLim SWvt WCot |
| ***minor*** | CAlb CBar CBcs CDoC CDul CMac CSBt ECrN ELan EPfP GAbr GKin GPoy LAst LRHS MAsh MGos NPri NWea SBfd SLim SVic WDin WFar XLum |
| - f. ***alba*** ♀H4 | CAlb CBcs CBot CDoC CMac COlW EBee ECha EPPr EPfP LRHS LSRN MAsh MGos NEgg NLar NPri SBfd SPer STre WCAu WCFE WCot WFar WPtf XLum |
| § - - 'Alba Variegata' (v) | CPLG EHoe GGar LSRN MGos NHol NPro SPer SRms STre WCot WFar WHoo |
| - - 'Gertrude Jekyll' ♀H4 | CAlb CDoC CPLG CSBt CYeo EBee ELan EPfP EWTr GAbr IKil ILis LRHS LSRN LTen MAvo MBri MGos MRav MWat NPri SCoo SEND SLim SPer SPoG WBor WDin WMoo |
| - 'Alba Aureovariegata' | see *V. minor* f. *alba* 'Alba Variegata' |
| § - 'Argenteovariegata' (v) ♀H4 | Widely available |
| § - 'Atropurpurea' ♀H4 | Widely available |
| - 'Aurea' | SPoG WFar |
| § - 'Aureovariegata' (v) | CBcs CBot CMac GAbr MGos MRav NHol SBfd SGol SLim SPer SPlb WFar |
| - 'Azurea' | CHid |
| § - 'Azurea Flore Pleno' (d) ♀H4 | Widely available |
| * - 'Blue and Gold' | EAEE ECGP EPPr LRHS NBre |
| - 'Blue Drift' | EWes MSwo |
| - 'Bowles's Purple' **new** | WBor |
| - 'Bowles's Blue' | see *V. minor* 'La Grave' |
| - 'Bowles's Variety' | see *V. minor* 'La Grave' |
| - 'Burgundy' | CFee SRms |
| - 'Caerulea Plena' | see *V. minor* 'Azurea Flore Pleno' |
| - 'Dartington Star' | see *V. major* var. *oxyloba* |
| - 'Double Burgundy' | see *V. minor* 'Multiplex' |
| - Green Carpet | see *V. minor* 'Grüner Teppich' |
| § - 'Grüner Teppich' | WFar |
| - 'Hawaii' **new** | ELon |
| - 'Illumination' (v) | Widely available |
| § - 'La Grave' ♀H4 | Widely available |
| § - 'Multiplex' (d) | CAlb CYeo EBee ECtt EPPr LBuc NChi SLim SRms WHrl WOut |

| | | |
|---|---|---|
| | - 'Purpurea' | see *V. minor* 'Atropurpurea' |
| | - 'Ralph Shugert' | CPLG EBee ELon EPPr EPfP EWes LRHS LSRN LSqu MAsh NLar SBfd SCoo SGol SPoG |
| | - 'Rubra' | see *V. minor* 'Atropurpurea' |
| | - 'Sabinka' | CHid EPPr |
| | - 'Silver Service' (d/v) | CFee CHid CWan MRav WCot |
| | - 'Variegata' | see *V. minor* 'Argenteovariegata' |
| | - 'Variegata Aurea' | see *V. minor* 'Aureovariegata' |
| | - 'White Gold' | EBee NPro |
| | ***sardoa*** | CAlb COIW EPPr EWes |

## *Vincetoxicum* (*Apocynaceae*)

| | | |
|---|---|---|
| | ***forrestii*** | CPLG |
| § | ***hirundinaria*** | EBee EPPr GPoy LEdu |
| | - CC 6289 | EWld |
| | ***nigrum*** | CArn EBee GCal NChi NMyG SBrt WCot |
| | - I am a Tiny Star = 'Zotista' | MGos |
| | ***officinale*** | see *V. hirundinaria* |
| | ***scandens*** | CRHN |

## *Viola* ✿ (*Violaceae*)

| | | |
|---|---|---|
| | 'Admiration' (Va) | WBou |
| | ***adunca*** | CMea NWCA |
| | - var. ***minor*** | see *V. labradorica* ambig. |
| § | ***alba*** | EWes NMen |
| | 'Alethia' (Va) | GMac WBou |
| | 'Alice' (Vt) | CGro |
| | 'Alice Kate' | CAby WBou |
| | 'Alice Witter' (Vt) | CGro ECha NChi |
| * | 'Alison' (Va) | WBou |
| | 'Amelia' (Va) | WBou |
| I | 'Amethyst' (Vt) | CGro |
| I | 'Annie' (Vt) | CGro LLHF |
| | 'Aprikosenfarbe' (C) **new** | LRHS |
| | 'Ardross Gem' (Va) | ECho ECtt GMac WBou |
| | ***arenaria*** | see *V. rupestris* |
| | 'Arkwright's Ruby' (Va) | SRms |
| | ***arvensis*** | CHab |
| | 'Ashvale Blue' (PVt) | CGro |
| | 'Aspasia' (Va) ♀H4 | CAby GMac WBou |
| | 'Avril Lawson' (Va) | GQue SHar WBou |
| | 'Baby Blue' | NBlu |
| | 'Baby Franjo' | NVic |
| | 'Baby Lucia' (Va) | NVic SRms |
| | 'Barbara' (Va) | WBou |
| | 'Baroness de Rothschild' misapplied | see *V.* 'Baronne Alice de Rothschild' |
| | 'Baroness de Rothschild' ambig. (Vt) | CGro |
| § | 'Baronne Alice de Rothschild' (Vt) | GMaP NLar WCot |
| | 'Beatrice' (Vtta) | WBou |
| | 'Becky Groves' (Vt) | CGro |
| § | 'Belmont Blue' (C) | CAby CEnt CSam CTri EBee ELon EWes GCal GMaP GMac IFro LHop LRHS MCot MHer MMuc MRav MSCN NBir NCGa NDov SBch SMrm SPer SRkn SRms WBou WCot WFar |
| § | ***bertolonii*** | WBou |
| | 'Beshlie' (Va) ♀H4 | ECtt WBou |
| | ***biflora*** | CMHG |
| | 'Blue Butterfly' (C) | CAby GMac |
| | 'Blue Horns' (C) | ELon |
| | 'Blue Moon' (C) | WBou |
| | 'Blue Moonlight' (C) | CElw GMac LRHS MMuc |
| | 'Blue Tit' (Va) | ECtt |
| | 'Boughton Blue' | see *V.* 'Belmont Blue' |
| | 'Bournemouth Gem' (Vt) | CGro |
| § | 'Bowles's Black' (T) | CSpe EGHP EPfP GCal LBMP LEdu MAsh NBro NVic SRms WJek |
| | 'Boy Blue' (Vtta) | ECtt |
| | ***brevistipulata*** **new** | LWst |
| | 'Bruneau' (dVt) | CBre CYeo ECtt EWll NLar SMrm WCot |
| * | 'Bryony' (Vtta) | WBou |
| | 'Bullion' (Va) | WBou |
| | 'Burncoose Yellow' | WBou |
| | 'Buttercup' (Vtta) | COIW ECtt GMac LSRN NEgg NSla SPoG WBou |
| | 'Butterpat' (C) | GMac |
| | 'Buxton Blue' (Va) | WBou |
| | 'Candy' (Vt) | CGro |
| | ***canina*** | NBro NMir |
| | 'Carol' (Vt) | CGro |
| | 'Carol Loxton' (Vt) | CGro |
| | 'Charles Groves' ambig. | ELon |
| | 'Charlotte' | EDAr WBou WJek |
| | 'Chloe' (Vtta) | CGro |
| | 'Christie's Wedding' (Vt) | CGro |
| | 'Clementina' (Va) ♀H4 | MRav WBou |
| | 'Cleo' (Va) | WBou |
| | 'Clive Farrell' (Vt) | CGro |
| | 'Clive Groves' (Vt) | CGro ELon |
| | 'Coeur d'Alsace' (Vt) | CPBP ECtt GMaP NLar WHal XLum |
| | 'Colette' (Va) | WBou |
| | 'Colombine' (Vt) | CGro MAsh |
| | 'Columbine' (Va) | CAby EBee ECtt EPfP GMaP GMac LRHS MHer NBir NBlu NDov NEgg SAga SPer SPoG WBou WCot WFar WJek WNew |
| | 'Comte de Chambord' (dVt) | WFar |
| | 'Connigar' | CSam |
| § | 'Conte di Brazza' (dPVt) | NLar SHar WFar |
| | 'Cordelia' (Va) | WFar |
| | 'Cordelia' (Vt) | ECtt |
| | ***cornuta*** ♀H4 | CElw CMea ECho GGar MLHP MWat NBir NBro NChi NWCA SBch SRms WBou WFar WHoo WTou |
| | - Alba Group ♀H4 | Widely available |
| | - 'Alba Minor' | CAby CEnt ECho EPfP EWes GCal GMac IGor NBro NSla WFar |
| | - blue-flowered | ECho MHer MLHP WFar WMoo |
| | - 'Brimstone' | GMac |
| | - 'Cleopatra' (C) | GAbr GMac |
| | - 'Gypsy Moth' (C) | CAby GMac |
| | - 'Icy But Spicy' | EBee NDov SMrm WBou WCot |
| | - Lilacina Group (C) | ECha MRav SWat WFar WMnd WPtf |
| | - 'Maiden's Blush' | CAby GMac |
| | - 'Minor' ♀H4 | CSam GMac NBro NSla WBou |
| | - 'Netta Statham' | CAby NDov WBou |
| | - 'Pale Apollo' (C) | GMac |
| | - Purpurea Group | ECha GCal SBch WMnd |
| | - 'Rosea' | ECha |
| | - 'Spider' | GMac |
| | - 'Ulla' | SBfd |
| | - 'Victoria's Blush' (C) | CElw CSpe ECtt ELon EWTr GMaP GMac MCot MMuc NBir NDov SUsu WBou |
| | - 'Violacea' | GMac |
| | ***corsica*** | CMea CSpe NChi SBch |
| | 'Crepuscle' (Vt) | CGro |
| § | ***cucullata*** ♀H4 | ECho SRms WFar |
| § | - 'Alba' (Vt) | CBro ECho LLWP NBir SRms |
| | - ***rosea*** | EWes |
| * | - 'Striata Alba' | NBro |
| | 'Czar' | see *V.* 'The Czar' |

| | | |
|---|---|---|
| | 'Daisy Smith' (Va) | WBou |
| | 'Dancing Geisha' (Vt) | EPfP |
| | 'Danielle Molly' | WBou |
| | 'Dawn' (Vtta) | CMea EBee ECtt GMaP MAsh NEgg NSla SBch SPer SPoG WBou |
| | 'Delicia' (Vtta) | NDov WBou |
| | 'Delphine' (Va) | NChi |
| | 'Desdemona' (Va) | GMac WBou |
| | 'Devon Cream' (Va) | GMac WBou |
| | 'Diana Groves' (Vt) | CGro |
| | 'Dick o' the Hills' (Vt) | CGro |
| | ***dissecta*** | WCot |
| | 'Donau' (Vt) | CGro EBee WCot |
| | 'Doreen' (Vt) | CGro |
| | 'Duchesse de Parme' (dPVt) | CGro IFro NWCA SRms |
| | 'D'Udine' (dPVt) | ECtt MTis WCot |
| | 'Dusk' | WBou |
| | 'E.A. Bowles' | see *V.* 'Bowles's Black' |
| | 'Eastgrove Blue Scented' (C) | GMac WBou WOut WPtf |
| | 'Eastgrove Ice Blue' (C) | WBou |
| | 'Elaine Quin' | EBee ECtt MCot NBlu NDov NEgg NPri SPoG WBou WKif |
| § | ***elatior*** | EBee EPPr EWTr MNrw WHil WPer WPtf WSHC |
| | 'Elizabeth' (Va) | ECtt WBou |
| | 'Elizabeth Lee' | WCot |
| | 'Elliot Adam' (Va) | WBou |
| | 'Emperor Blue Vein' | EBee EPfP |
| | 'Emperor Magenta Red' | GJos LSou |
| | ***erecta*** | see *V. elatior* |
| | 'Eris' (Va) | WBou |
| | 'Etain' (Va) | COlW EBee ECho ECtt ELan EPfP EWes GMaP LRHS MAsh MTis NDov NEgg NPri SMrm SPoG SUsu WBou |
| | 'Fabiola' (Vtta) | GMac NBir |
| | 'Famecheck Apricot' | CPom |
| * | 'Fantasy' | WBou |
| | 'Ferndale' (Vt) | CGro |
| | 'Fiona' (Va) | CAby GMac MCot NChi WBou |
| | 'Fiona Lawrenson' (Va) | WBou |
| | ***flettii*** | WAbe |
| | 'Florence' (Va) | WBou |
| | 'Foxbrook Cream' (C) | WBou |
| | 'Freckles' | see *V. sororia* 'Freckles' |
| | Friolina Orange Cascadiz = 'Sunviobare' (Friolina Series) **new** | NPri |
| | ***glabella*** | SBch |
| | 'Gladys Findlay' (Va) | WBou |
| * | 'Glenda' | WBou |
| | 'Glenholme' | GMac |
| | 'Gloire de Verdun' (PVt) | CGro NWCA |
| | 'Governor Herrick' (Vt) | CGro ECtt NLar WCot WHer |
| § | ***gracilis*** | NBir WFar |
| | - 'Lutea' | CSam |
| | - 'Major' | WBou |
| | 'Green Goddess'PBR | WFar |
| | 'Grey Owl' (Va) | WBou |
| | 'Grovemount Blue' (C) | CElw CMea |
| § | ***grypoceras*** var. ***exilis*** | EBee NWCA |
| | - - 'Sylettas' | GGar NBPC |
| | 'Gustav Wermig' (C) | WBou |
| | 'Haslemere' | see *V.* 'Nellie Britton' |
| * | 'Heaselands' | SMrm |
| § | ***hederacea*** | EBee ECou GQui IFoB SRms WFar |
| | 'Helen' (Va) | ECtt |
| § | 'Helen Mount' (T) | LBMP |
| | 'Helena' (Va) | WBou |
| | 'Hespera' (Va) | WBou |
| | ***heterophylla*** subsp. ***epirota*** | see *V. bertolonii* |
| * | 'Hetty Gatenby' | WBou |
| | ***hirsutula*** | EBla |
| I | - 'Alba' | EBla |
| I | - 'Purpurea' | EBla |
| | 'Hudsons Blue' | CElw |
| | 'Huntercombe Purple' (Va) ♀H4 | ECho LHop LRHS MCot NBir SRms WBou WHal WKif |
| | 'Iden Gem' (Va) | NDov WBou |
| | 'Inverurie Beauty' (Va) ♀H4 | GMaP GMac NDov WBou WKif |
| | 'Irish Elegance' | see *V.* 'Sulfurea' |
| | 'Irish Molly' (Va) | CBot CSpe EBee ECho ECtt ELan EPfP GGar GMac LRHS MAsh MHer MTis NDov NEgg NPri NSla SPer SPoG SRms WBor WBou WFar |
| | 'Isabel' | NDov WBou |
| | 'Isabella' (Vt) | CGro |
| | 'Ivory Queen' (Va) | GMac MRav WBou |
| | 'Jack Sampson' (Vt) | CGro |
| | 'Jackanapes' (Va) ♀H4 | CMea EBee ECho ECtt ELan EPfP LRHS MAsh NEgg NPri SPer SPoG SRms WBou WFar |
| | 'Jane Mott' (Va) | GMac |
| | 'Janet' (Va) | EBee ECtt LSRN NBlu NPri SPer SPoG |
| | ***japonica*** | GGar |
| | 'Jeannie Bellew' (Va) | SRms WBou WFar |
| | 'Jennifer Andrews' (Va) | WBou |
| | 'Joanna' (Va) | WBou |
| | 'John Raddenbury' (Vt) | GMaP |
| | 'Johnny Jump Up' | see *V.* 'Helen Mount' |
| | ***jooi*** | CPBP EPfP GKev MWea NBir NMen SPhx SRms WPat WPtf |
| | 'Josie' (Va) | WBou |
| | 'Joyce Gray' (Va) | WBou |
| | 'Judy Goring' (Va) | GMac |
| | 'Julia' (Va) | WBou |
| | 'Julian' (Va) | CAby GMac LRHS SRms WBou |
| | 'Juno' (Va) | GMac |
| | 'Katerina' (Va) | WBou |
| | 'Kerry Girl' (Vt) | CGro |
| | 'Kim' | CGro |
| | 'Kitten' | CAby GAbr WBou |
| | 'Kitty White' (Va) | GMac |
| § | 'Königin Charlotte' (Vt) | CGro COlW EPfP GMac LBMP LRHS MCot MHer NEgg NWCA SBfd WCot WFar WMoo |
| | ***koreana*** | see *V. grypoceras* var. *exilis* |
| N | ***labradorica*** misapplied | see *V. riviniana* Purpurea Group |
| N | - ***purpurea*** | see *V. riviniana* Purpurea Group |
| § | ***labradorica*** ambig. | CHar GQui LRHS MAsh MCot MRav NBlu NPri SMrm WCAu WFar |
| | 'Lady Hume Campbell' (PVt) | CGro |
| | 'Lady Jane' (Vt) | CGro |
| | 'Lady Saville' | see *V.* 'Sissinghurst' |
| | 'Lavender Lady' (Vt) | CGro |
| | 'Lees Peachy Pink' (Vt) | CGro |
| | 'Letitia' (Va) | EBee MCot SRms WBou WFar |
| | 'Lianne' (Vt) | CGro LLHF WCot |
| | 'Lindsay' | WBou |
| | 'Lisa Tanner' (Va) | WBou |
| | 'Little David' (Vtta) ♀H4 | CSam CTri ECtt GMac MCot NDov SRms WBou |
| | 'Lord Plunket' (Va) | WBou |
| | 'Lorna Cawthorne' (C) | CAby WBou |
| | 'Lorna Moakes' (Va) | SAga |
| | 'Louisa' (Va) | GMac WBou |
| § | ***lutea*** | WBou |

| |  |  |
|---|---|---|
| | - subsp. ***elegans*** | see *V. lutea* |
| | 'Lutea Splendens' (C) new | LRHS |
| | 'Luxonne' (Vt) | CGro |
| | 'Lydia Groves' (Vt) | WCot |
| | 'Madame Armandine Pagès' (Vt) | CGro |
| | 'Magenta Maid' (Va) | LRHS |
| | 'Maggie Mott' (Va) ϒH4 | ECho ECtt GMac LHop MAsh MCot WBou WFar WWFP |
| | 'Magic' | WBou |
| | ***mandshurica*** | NWCA |
| | - 'Fuji Dawn' (v) | EBee SPad WCot |
| | - f. ***hasegawae*** | EPPr |
| | 'Margaret' (Va) | WBou |
| | 'Marie-Louise' (dPVt) | CGro ECtt NLar SHar |
| I | 'Mars' | CAbP ECtt GBin LSRN LSou MSCN WFar |
| | 'Mars' (Va) | EBee ECtt SMrm WHer |
| | 'Martin' (Va) ϒH4 | CAby COlW EBee ECha GMaP GMac LHop LSRN MAsh MHer NDov SPer SPoG WBou WFar |
| | 'Mary Mouse' | NDov WBou |
| | 'Mauve Haze' (Va) | WBou |
| | 'Mauve Radiance' (Va) | ECtt GMac WBou |
| | 'May Mott' (Va) | GMac WBou |
| | 'Mayfly' (Va) | WBou |
| | 'Melinda' (Vtta) | WBou |
| | 'Melting Moments' (Va) | NEgg |
| | 'Mercury' (Va) | WBou |
| | 'Milkmaid' (Va) | CAby EBee ELon NBir NBlu |
| | 'Miss Brookes' (Va) | WBou |
| | 'Misty Guy' (Vtta) | CAby WBou |
| | 'Molly Sanderson' (Va) ϒH4 | CAby COlW CSpe EBee ECha ECho ECtt ELan EPfP GGar LAst LHop LRHS MAsh MHer MMuc MRav NEgg NPri SPer SPlb SPoG WBou WFar WNew |
| | 'Moonlight' (Va) ϒH4 | ECho ELan LHop LRHS MHer MMuc WBou |
| | 'Moonraker' | GMaP NBir |
| | 'Morwenna' (Va) | ECtt MCot WBou WKif |
| | 'Mrs Lancaster' (Va) | CAby EBee GMaP GMac LHop LSRN NBir NPri NSla SPoG SRms WBou |
| | 'Mrs Pinehurst' (Vt) | CGro GMaP |
| | 'Mrs R. Barton' (Vt) | CGro SHar |
| | 'Mulberry' (Vt) | CGro |
| | 'Myfawnny' (Va) | CAby CMea ECho ECtt ELan EWes GMac LRHS MCot NDov SRms WBou WFar |
| | 'Neapolitan' | see *V.* 'Pallida Plena' |
| § | 'Nellie Britton' (Va) ϒH4 | ECho ECtt SRms |
| | 'Netta Statham' | see *V.* 'Belmont Blue' |
| | 'Nora' | NDov WBou |
| | 'Norah Church' (Vt) | CGro |
| | 'Norah Leigh' (Va) | EOHP WBou |
| | ***obliqua*** | see *V. cucullata* |
| | ***odorata*** (Vt) | CArn CBcs CBod CGro CHab CRWN EBee EPfP EWil GPoy MRav NMir NPri SIde SPer SRms SVic WJek |
| | - 'Alba' (Vt) | CPom CWan EBee ECho ELan EPfP MHer NPri SEND SRms WMoo |
| | - 'Alba Plena' (dVt) | CDes LSou |
| | - 'Albiflora' | CEnt |
| | - apricot-flowered | see *V.* 'Sulfurea' |
| | - 'Dawnie' (Vt) | CGro |
| | - var. ***dumetorum*** | see *V. alba* |
| | - 'Elsmeer' | WCot |
| | - 'Katy' | CPom ELon SBch |
| | - 'King of Violets' (dVt) | CBre EBee ECtt EWll LRHS LSou MTis NEgg SHar SPer WCot WFar |
| | - 'Melanie' | WCot |
| | - 'Perky' (Vt) | CGro |
| | - pink-flowered | see *V. odorata* Rosea Group |
| | - 'Port Breedy' (Vt) | CGro |
| | - 'Red Devil' | WCot WFar |
| | - ***rosea*** | see *V. odorata* Rosea Group |
| § | - Rosea Group (Vt) | CDes CEnt CPom EBee EWll GMac IFoB LRHS LSou MRav MTis NEgg SEND SIde SMrm SPer WCot WCra |
| | - 'Souvenier de Jules Josse' (Vt) | CGro |
| * | - subsp. ***subcarnea*** (Vt) | SEND |
| | - 'Sulphurea' | see *V.* 'Sulfurea' |
| | - 'Vin d'André Thorp' | ECtt NBPC WCot |
| I | - 'Violett Charm' | WCot |
| | - 'Weimar' | GBin |
| | - 'Wismar' | WCot |
| | 'Opéra' (Vt) | CGro LLHF |
| | 'Orchid Pink' (Vt) | CGro EBee GMaP |
| § | 'Pallida Plena' (dPVt) | CGro |
| | ***palustris*** | CRWN EWil LLWG WHer WSFF WShi |
| | 'Pamela Zambra' (Vt) | GMaP SHar WSHC |
| | ***papilionacea*** | see *V. sororia* |
| | 'Parchment' (Vt) | CGro |
| | 'Parme de Toulouse' (dPVt) | CGro XLum |
| | 'Pasha' (Va) | GMac |
| | 'Pat Creasy' (Va) | NDov WBou |
| | 'Pat Kavanagh' (C) | GAbr NDov WBou |
| | 'Patience' | WBou |
| | 'Pearl Rose' | ELon |
| | ***pedata*** | CBro EBee WAbe WHil |
| | - 'Bicolor' | WAbe |
| | ***pedatifida*** | IFoB |
| | ***pensylvanica*** | see *V. pubescens* var. *eriocarpa* |
| | 'Perle Rose' (Vt) | CGro |
| | 'Petra' (Vtta) | CAby GMac |
| | 'Phyl Dove' (Vt) | WCot |
| | 'Pickering Blue' (Va) | WBou |
| | 'Primrose Dame' (Va) | MHer WBou WCot |
| | 'Primrose Pixie' (Va) | WBou |
| | 'Prince Henry' (T) | MNHC |
| | 'Prince John' (T) | MNHC |
| | 'Princess Mab' (Vtta) | WBou |
| | 'Princess of Prussia' (Vt) | WCot |
| | 'Princess of Wales' | see *V.* 'Princesse de Galles' |
| § | 'Princesse de Galles' (Vt) | CTri |
| | 'Pritchard's Russian' (Vt) | CGro |
| | 'Prolific' (Vt) | CGro |
| § | ***pubescens*** var. ***eriocarpa*** | SRms WCot |
| | 'Purple Emperor' | SBfd |
| | 'Purple Wings' (Va) | WBou |
| | 'Putty' | ECou |
| | Queen Charlotte | see *V.* 'Königin Charlotte' |
| | 'Queen Victoria' | see *V.* 'Victoria Regina' |
| | 'Raven' | CAby GMac WBou |
| | 'Rebecca' (Vtta) | CAby CSam EBee ECho ECtt ELan EPfP GMaP GMac LRHS LSRN MAsh MCot MHer MTis NBir NBlu NCGa NChi NDov NEgg NPri SPer SPoG SRms WBou WFar |
| | 'Red Charm' (Vt) | EAEE EBee MWat |
| | 'Red Giant' (Vt) | EAEE EBla MRav NEgg |
| | 'Red Lion' (Vt) | CGro |
| | 'Red Queen' (Vt) | CGro |
| | ***reichei*** | CRWN |
| | 'Reine des Blanches' (dVt) | CBre EBee ECtt ELon LLWP LPla LRHS MTis NBPC NEgg NGdn NLar SMrm SPer WCot |

| | | |
|---|---|---|
| | ***reniforme*** | see *V. hederacea* |
| | ***riviniana*** | CArn CRWN EWil MHer MMuc WHer WSFF WShi |
| | - dark pink-flowered | MMuc |
| | - 'Ed's Variegated' (v) | EPPr WCot |
| § | - Purpurea Group | Widely available |
| | - white-flowered | EBee EWes MMuc |
| | 'Roscastle Black' | CMea EBee GMaP GMac LRHS MTis NDov SBfd SMrm WBou WCot WPtf |
| | 'Rosine' (Vt) | MAsh |
| | 'Royal Elk' (Vt) | CGro |
| | 'Rubin' (C) | LRHS |
| | 'Rubra' (Vt) | WPtf |
| § | ***rupestris*** | CTri CWan |
| * | - ***rosea*** | CEnt CPom EBee EPfP IFro LLWP MHer NWCA STre WHer WPtf |
| | 'Saint Helena' (Vt) | WCot |
| | ***schariensis*** | EWes |
| | ***selkirkii*** | GAuc NWCA WThu |
| | ***septentrionalis*** | see *V. sororia* |
| | 'Serena' (Va) | WBou |
| | 'Sherbet Dip' | WBou |
| | 'Sidborough Poppet' | CPBP CRDP EWes |
| | 'Silver Samurai' **new** | MPnt |
| § | 'Sissinghurst' (Va) | MHer NBir |
| | 'Sisters' (Vt) | CGro |
| | 'Smugglers' Moon' | CAby WBou |
| | 'Sophie' (Vtta) | WBou |
| § | ***sororia*** | EAEE EBee ECho EPPr MLHP MNrw NBir NBro WPtf |
| * | - 'Albiflora' ♀H4 | CHid EBee ECho EPPr EPfP EWll GGar LEdu MRav NWCA SPhx WCFE WFar WHil WJek XLum |
| | - 'Dark Freckles' | EBee ECho LHop SPhx XLum |
| § | - 'Freckles' | Widely available |
| | - 'Priceana' | EAEE EBee ECha EPri EPyc EWTr LEdu LRHS NBir NChi SMrm WCot |
| | - 'Speckles' (v) | EBla |
| | - 'Sweet Emma' **new** | SPhx |
| * | 'Spencer's Cottage' | WBou |
| | 'Staffordshire Blue' | NDov |
| | 'Steyning' (Va) | WBou |
| | ***stojanowii*** | CSpe ECho MAsh |
| § | 'Sulfurea' (Vt) | CEnt CPBP CPMA EBee LBMP LLWP MMHG NRya NWCA WCot WFar WPer |
| | 'Sulphurea' lemon-flowered (Vt) | CGro |
| | 'Sultan' (Vt) | CGro |
| | 'Susan Chilcott' (Vt) | CGro |
| | 'Susanne Lucas' (Vt) | CGro |
| | 'Susie' (Va) | WBou |
| | 'Swanley White' | see *V.* 'Conte di Brazza' |
| | 'Sybil' (SP) | WBou |
| | ***sylvatica*** **new** | CRDP |
| § | 'The Czar' (Vt) | CBre CGro WCot |
| | 'Tiger Eyes' (Va) | MAsh MTis SPoG |
| | 'Tom Tit' (Va) | ECtt WBou |
| | 'Tony Venison' (C/v) | CAby LEdu NBlu NEgg SPoG WBou WFar WHer WWFP |
| | ***tricolor*** | CHab CPrp ECho EGHP EPfP EWil GPoy MHer MNHC SIde WJek |
| | 'Vanessa' (Va) | GMac |
| | ***velutina*** | see *V. gracilis* |
| | ***verecunda*** | WSHC |
| | - B&SWJ 604a | CLAP WCru |
| § | - var. ***yakusimana*** | CRDP WThu |
| | 'Victoria Cawthorne' (C) | CAby CElw GMac MCot MHer NDov WBou |
| § | 'Victoria Regina' (Vt) | EPfP |
| | 'Virginia' (Va) | WBou |
| | 'Vita' (Va) | GMac SRms WBou |
| | 'White Ladies' | see *V. cucullata* 'Alba' |
| | 'White Pearl' (Va) | NDov SPhx WBou |
| | 'White Perfection' (C) | SPer |
| | 'White Superior' | LRHS |
| | 'William' (Va) | NDov |
| | 'Winifred Jones' (Va) | WBou |
| | 'Winifred Wargent' (Va) | NBlu |
| | 'Winona Cawthorne' (C) | GMac NDov |
| | 'Wisley White' | EBee EWes LPla WFar |
| | 'Woodlands Cream' (Va) | MHer WBou |
| | 'Woodlands Lilac' (Va) | WBou |
| | ***yakusimana*** | see *V. verecunda* var. *yakusimana* |
| | 'Yellow Prince' | LRHS |
| | 'Zara' (Va) | WBou |
| | 'Zoe' (Vtta) | ECtt EPfP NEgg NPri SMrm SPoG WBou WFar |

## *Viscaria* (*Caryophyllaceae*)

| | | |
|---|---|---|
| | ***vulgaris*** | see *Lychnis viscaria* |

## *Viscum* (*Santalaceae*)

| | | |
|---|---|---|
| | ***cruciatum*** B&F MA 24 **new** | WCot |

## *Vitaliana* (*Primulaceae*)

| | | |
|---|---|---|
| § | ***primuliflora*** | ECho GKev NMen NRya NSla |
| | - subsp. ***chionantha*** | WAbe |
| | - subsp. ***cinerea*** | GKev |
| | - subsp. ***praetutiana*** | CPBP NMen WAbe WPat WThu |
| | - subsp. ***tridentata*** | NMen |

## *Vitex* (*Lamiaceae*)

| | | |
|---|---|---|
| | ***agnus-castus*** | CArn CBcs CHll CWSG EBee EGFP EOHP EPri EShb GPoy LEdu LRHS LSou MCCP SBfd SEND SLon SPer WDin WFar WSHC XSen |
| | - 'Alba' | CDul CWib EPfP LTen |
| | - var. ***latifolia*** | CAlb CWib ELan ELon EPfP LRHS LSRN MGos MHer SBfd SPoG WPGP |
| I | - 'Rosea' | NLar XSen |
| | - 'Silver Spire' | CDul ELan LRHS SPoG WPGP WSHC |
| | ***chinensis*** | see *V. negundo* var. *heterophylla* |
| | ***incisa*** | see *V. negundo* var. *heterophylla* |
| | ***negundo*** | CArn EOHP |
| § | - var. ***heterophylla*** | EWes XSen |

## *Vitis* ✿ (*Vitaceae*)

| | | |
|---|---|---|
| | 'Abundante' (F) | WSuV |
| | 'Alden' (O/B) | WSuV |
| | 'Alnwick Seedling' (B/G) | ERea |
| | 'Amandin' (G/W) | WSuV |
| | ***amurensis*** | CAlb EBee EPfP NLar |
| | - B&SWJ 4138 | WCru |
| | - B&SWJ 4299 | WCru |
| | 'Atlantis' (O/W) | WSuV |
| § | 'Aurore' (W) | CAgr WSuV |
| | 'Baco Noir' (O/B) | CAgr ERea GTwe SDea WSuV |
| | ***betulifolia*** | EPfP |
| | 'Bianca' (O/W) | MCoo WSuV |
| | 'Birstaller Muscat' (W) | WSuV |
| | Black Hamburgh | see *V. vinifera* 'Schiava Grossa' |
| * | 'Black Strawberry' (B) | CAgr SDea WSuV |
| | 'Blanc Seedless' (W/S) **new** | SDea |
| § | 'Boskoop Glory' (O/B) ♀H4 | CMac LBuc MCoo NBlu NLar NPal SCoo SDea WSuV |
| | 'Brant' (O/B) ♀H4 | Widely available |
| | 'Brilliant' (B) | WSuV |

| |  |  |
|---|---|---|
| | 'Buffalo' (B) | WSuV |
| | ***californica*** (F) | NLar |
| | 'Canadice' (O/R/S) | SDea WSuV |
| | 'Cascade' | see *V.* Seibel 13053 |
| | Castel 19637 (B) | WSuV |
| | 'Chambourcin' (B) | WSuV |
| | ***coignetiae*** ♀H4 | Widely available |
| | - B&SWJ 4550 from Korea | WCru |
| | - B&SWJ 4744 | WCru |
| | - B&SWJ 8553 from Korea | WCru |
| | - B&SWJ 10882 from Japan | WCru |
| | - B&SWJ 10908 from Japan | WCru |
| | - Claret Cloak = 'Frovit'PBR | EBee ELan EPfP LRHS LSRN MAsh MRav NLar SCoo SPer SSpi WPGP WPat |
| | - cut-leaved | CMac |
| | - var. ***glabrescens*** B&SWJ 8537 | WCru |
| | - Sunningdale form | WGrn |
| | 'Dalkauer' (W) | WSuV |
| I | 'Diamond' (B) | WSuV |
| | 'Duchess of Buccleuch' (G/W) | ERea |
| | 'Dutch Black' (O/B) | WSuV |
| | 'Edwards No 1' (O/W) | WSuV |
| | 'Eger Csillaga' (O/W) | WSuV |
| | 'Einset' (B/S) | WSuV |
| | ***ficifolia*** | see *V. thunbergii* |
| | ***flexuosa*** B&SWJ 5568 | WCru |
| | - var. ***choii*** B&SWJ 4101 | WCru |
| § | 'Fragola' (O/R) | CAgr CMac CTri EBee ECha EPfP GTwe LRHS MAsh MRav NLar SDea SLim SPer SRms WSuV |
| | 'Gagarin Blue' (O/B) | CAgr EPom GTwe SDea WSuV |
| | 'Glenora' (F/B/S) | CAgr WSuV |
| | 'Hecker' (O/W) | WSuV |
| | ***henryana*** | see *Parthenocissus henryana* |
| | 'Himrod' (O/W/S) | CCCN ERea GTwe MGos NPal SDea WSuV |
| | 'Horizon' (O/W) | WSuV |
| | ***inconstans*** | see *Parthenocissus tricuspidata* |
| | 'Interlaken' (O/W/S) | CAgr ERea WSuV |
| | 'Johanniter' (W) | WSuV |
| | 'Kempsey Black' (O/B) | CAgr WSuV |
| | 'Kozmapalme Muscatoly' (O/W) | WSuV |
| | 'Kuibishevski' (O/R) | WSuV |
| | Landot 244 (O/B) | WSuV |
| | Landot 3217 (O/B) | WSuV |
| | 'L'Arcadie Blanche' (W) | WSuV |
| | 'Léon Millot' (O/G/B) | CAgr CSBt LSRN SDea WSuV |
| | 'Lucy Kuhlman' (B) | WSuV |
| | 'Maréchal Foch' (O/B) | EGxp WSuV |
| | 'Maréchal Joffre' (O/R) | CAgr GTwe WSuV |
| | 'Mars' (O/B/S) | WSuV |
| | 'Merzling' (O/W) | WSuV |
| | 'Munson R.W.' (O/R) | WSuV |
| | 'Muscat Bleu' (O/B) | CCCN EPom LRHS NLar SLim SPoG WSuV |
| | 'Nero'PBR | CAgr ERea |
| | 'New York Muscat' (O/B) ♀H4 | ERea WSuV |
| | 'New York Seedless' (O/W/S) | WSuV |
| | 'Niagara' (O/W) | WSuV |
| | 'Niederother Monschrebe' (O/R) | WSuV |
| | Oberlin 595 (O/B) | WSuV |
| | 'Orion' (O/W) | LRHS MAsh WSuV |
| | 'Paletina' (O/W) | WSuV |
| | parsley-leaved | see *V. vinifera* 'Ciotat' |
| | ***parvifolia*** | WPat |
| | - B&SWJ 1946 | WCru |
| | 'Perdin' (O/W) | WSuV |
| | 'Phönix' (O/W) | CAgr CCCN GTwe LRHS MAsh MBri MGos NLar NPla SKee SLim SPoG SVic WSuV |
| | ***piasezkii*** | WCru |
| * | 'Pink Strawberry' (O) | WSuV |
| | 'Pirovano 14' (O/B) | GTwe SDea WSuV |
| § | 'Plantet' (O/B) | WSuV |
| | 'Poloske Muscat' (W) | CCCN EPom GTwe WSuV |
| | ***purpurea*** 'Spetchley Park' (O/B) | CAgr WSuV |
| | ***quinquefolia*** | see *Parthenocissus quinquefolia* |
| | 'Ramdas' (O/W) | WSuV |
| | Ravat 51 (O/W) | WSuV |
| | 'Rayon d'Or' (O/W) | WSuV |
| | 'Regent'PBR (O/B) | CAgr CCCN CWSG EPom GTwe LRHS MBri MCoo MGos NLar SKee SLim SPoG WSuV |
| | 'Reliance' (O/R/S) | CAgr ERea WSuV |
| | 'Rembrant' (R) | CAgr NPal WSuV |
| | ***riparia*** | CArn NLar |
| | 'Romulus' (O/G/W/S) | WSuV |
| | 'Rondo' (O/B) | CAgr SVic WSuV |
| | 'Saturn' (O/R/S) | CAgr WSuV |
| | 'Schuyler' (O/B) | CAgr WSuV |
| | Seibel (F) | GTwe SDea |
| | Seibel 5279 | see *V.* 'Aurore' |
| | Seibel 5409 (W) | WSuV |
| | Seibel 5455 | see *V.* 'Plantet' |
| | Seibel 7053 | WSuV |
| | Seibel 9549 | WSuV |
| § | Seibel 13053 (O/B) | CMac LRHS MAsh MMuc SDea SEND WSuV |
| | Seibel 138315 (R) | WSuV |
| | 'Seneca' (W) | WSuV |
| | 'Serena' (O/W) | WSuV |
| § | 'Seyval Blanc' (O/W) | CAgr GTwe MMuc SDea SEND SVic WSuV |
| | Seyve Villard 12.375 | see *V.* 'Villard Blanc' |
| | Seyve Villard 20.473 (F) | MAsh NPer |
| | Seyve Villard 5276 | see *V.* 'Seyval Blanc' |
| | Seyve Villard ambig. | LRHS NPer |
| | 'Sirius' (B) | WSuV |
| | 'Solaris' (O/W) | WSuV |
| | 'Stauffer' (O/W) | WSuV |
| | 'Suffolk Seedless' (B/S) | ERea WSuV |
| | 'Tereshkova' (O/B) | CAgr ERea SDea WSuV |
| | 'Thornton' (O/S) | WSuV |
| § | ***thunbergii*** B&SWJ 4702 | WCru |
| | 'Triomphe d'Alsace' (O/B) | CAgr CSBt NPer SDea WSuV |
| | 'Trollinger' | see *V. vinifera* 'Schiava Grossa' |
| | 'Vanessa' (O/R/S) | SDea WSuV |
| § | 'Villard Blanc' (O/W) | WSuV |
| | ***vinifera*** | EAmu LTen MGos MREP |
| | - EM 323158B | WSuV |
| | - 'Abouriou' (O/B) | WSuV |
| | - 'Acolon' (O/B) | WSuV |
| | - 'Adelheidtraube' (O/W) | WSuV |
| | - 'Albalonga' (W) | WSuV |
| § | - 'Alicante' (G/B) | CBcs CMac EGxp GTwe NPal SDea WSuV |
| | - 'Apiifolia' | see *V. vinifera* 'Ciotat' |
| | - 'Augusta Louise' (O/W) | WSuV |
| | - 'Auxerrois' (O/W) | WSuV |
| | - 'Bacchus' (O/W) | CAgr LRHS MBri NLar SDea SLim SVic WSuV |
| | - 'Baresana' (G/W) | EGxp NPla WSuV |

| |  |  |
|---|---|---|
| | - 'Beauty' | CAgr |
| | - 'Black Alicante' | see *V. vinifera* 'Alicante' |
| | - 'Black Frontignan' (G/O/B) | WSuV |
| | - Black Hamburgh | see *V. vinifera* 'Schiava Grossa' |
| | - 'Black Monukka' (G/B/S) | ERea WSuV |
| | - 'Black Prince' (G/B) | CAgr WSuV |
| | - 'Blue Portuguese' | see *V. vinifera* 'Portugieser' |
| § | - 'Bouvier' (W) | WSuV |
| | - 'Bouviertraube' | see *V. vinifera* 'Bouvier' |
| | - 'Buckland Sweetwater' (G/W) | CDul GTwe LRHS SDea SLim WSuV |
| | - 'Cabernet Sauvignon' (O/B) | LRHS MAsh MGos NPer SDea WSuV |
| | - 'Canon Hall Muscat' (G/W) | ERea |
| | - 'Cardinal' (O/R) | LRHS WSuV |
| | - 'Carla' (O/R) | WSuV |
| | - 'Centennial' (O/N/S) | WSuV |
| | - 'Chardonnay' (O/W) | CAgr CCCN LRHS LSRN MAsh NPer SDea SPer SVic WSuV |
| § | - 'Chasselas' (G/O/W) | LRHS MAsh SDea WSuV |
| | - 'Chasselas Blanc' (O/W) | SVic |
| | - 'Chasselas de Fontainebleau' (F) | CCCN LRHS |
| | - 'Chasselas de Tramontaner' (F) | ECrN LRHS |
| | - 'Chasselas d'Or' | see *V. vinifera* 'Chasselas' |
| | - 'Chasselas Rosé' (G/R) | CAgr SVic WSuV |
| | - 'Chasselas Rosé Royal' (O/R) | CCCN |
| | - 'Chasselas Vibert' (G/W) | WSuV |
| | - 'Chenin Blanc' (O/W) | WSuV |
| § | - 'Ciotat' (F) | ERea EShb IDee MRav SDea WSuV |
| | - 'Cot Précoce de Tours' (O/B) | WSuV |
| | - 'Crimson Seedless' (R/S) | ERea LRHS WSuV |
| | - 'Csabyongye' (O/W) | WSuV |
| | - 'Dattier de Beyrouth' (G/W) | WSuV |
| | - 'Dattier Saint Vallier' (O/W) | SVic WSuV |
| | - 'Dolcetto' (O/B) | WSuV |
| | - 'Dornfelder' (O/R) | CCCN CSut NLar SLim SPoG WSuV |
| | - 'Dunkelfelder' (O/R) | WSuV |
| | - 'Early Van der Laan' (F) | CMac |
| | - 'Ehrenfelser' (O/W) | WSuV |
| | - 'Elbling' (O/W) | WSuV |
| | - 'Exalta' (G/W/S) | CCCN WSuV |
| | - 'Excelsior' (W) | WSuV |
| | - 'Faber' (O/W) | WSuV |
| | - 'Fiesta' (W/S) | WSuV |
| | - 'Findling' (W) | WSuV |
| | - 'Flame' | CAgr |
| | - 'Flame Red' (O/D) | CCCN EPom |
| | - 'Flame Seedless' (G/O/R/S) | SPoG WSuV |
| | - 'Forta' (O/W) | WSuV |
| | - 'Foster's Seedling' (G/W) | GTwe SDea SVic WSuV |
| | - 'Freisamer' (O/W) | WSuV |
| | - 'Frühburgunder' (O/B) | WSuV |
| | - 'Gamay Hâtif des Vosges' | WSuV |
| | - 'Gamay Noir' (O/B) | WSuV |
| | - Gamay Teinturier Group (O/B) | WSuV |
| | - 'Gewürztraminer' (O/R) | LRHS MAsh SDea WSuV |
| | - 'Glory of Boskoop' | see *V.* 'Boskoop Glory' |
| | - 'Golden Chasselas' | see *V. vinifera* 'Chasselas' |
| | - 'Golden Queen' (G/W) | ERea |
| | - 'Goldriesling' (O/W) | WSuV |

| |  |  |
|---|---|---|
| | - 'Gros Colmar' (G/B) | WSuV |
| | - 'Grüner Veltliner' (O/W) | WSuV |
| | - 'Gutenborner' (O/W) | WSuV |
| | - 'Helfensteiner' (O/R) | WSuV |
| | - 'Huxelrebe' (O/W) | WSuV |
| | - 'Incana' (O/B) | ELon GCal MRav WCFE WCot WHil |
| | - 'Italia' (O/W) | LRHS NPla |
| | - 'Juliaumsrebe' (O/W) | WSuV |
| | - 'Kanzler' (O/W) | WSuV |
| | - 'Kerner' (O/W) | WSuV |
| | - 'Kernling' (F) | WSuV |
| | - 'King's Ruby' (F/S) | ERea WSuV |
| | - 'Lakemont' (O/W/S) | CAgr CCCN CMac EPfP GTwe LRHS MBri MGos NLar NPla SDea SKee SLim SPoG WSuV |
| | - 'Lival' (O/B) | WSuV |
| | - 'Madeleine Angevine' (O/W) | CAgr GTwe LRHS LSRN MAsh NPer SDea SVic WSuV |
| | - 'Madeleine Celine' (B) | WSuV |
| | - 'Madeleine Royale' (G/W) | WSuV |
| | - 'Madeleine Silvaner' (O/W) | CSBt GTwe LRHS MAsh NPer SDea SPer WSuV |
| | - 'Madresfield Court' (G/B) | GTwe SLim WSuV |
| | - 'Merlot' (G/B) | LRHS SDea WSuV |
| § | - 'Meunier' (B) | WSuV |
| | - 'Mireille' (F) | GTwe SDea WSuV |
| | - 'Morio Muscat' (O/W) | WSuV |
| § | - 'Müller-Thurgau' (O/W) | GTwe LRHS LSRN MAsh MGos NPri SDea SPer SVic WSuV |
| | - 'Muscat Blanc à Petits Grains' (O/W) | SWvt WSuV |
| | - 'Muscat Champion' (G/R) | ERea |
| | - 'Muscat de Lierval' (O/B) | WSuV |
| | - 'Muscat de Saumur' (O/W) | WSuV |
| | - 'Muscat Hamburg' (G/B) | ECrN ERea LHop LRHS LSRN MAsh MGos SDea SWvt WSuV |
| | - 'Muscat of Alexandria' (G/W) | CBcs CCCN CMac ERea LRHS MAsh MRav NPal SDea SLim SVic |
| | - 'Muscat Ottonel' (O/W) | WSuV |
| | - 'Muscat Saint Laurent' (W) | WSuV |
| | - 'Nebbiolo' (O/B) | WSuV |
| | - 'No 69' (W) | WSuV |
| | - 'Noblessa' (W) | WSuV |
| | - 'Noir Hâtif de Marseille' (O/B) | WSuV |
| | - 'Olive Blanche' (O/W) | WSuV |
| | - 'Oliver Irsay' (O/W) | WSuV |
| | - 'Optima' (O/W) | WSuV |
| | - 'Ora' (O/W/S) | WSuV |
| | - 'Ortega' (O/W) | CCCN WSuV |
| | - 'Perle' (O/W) | WSuV |
| | - 'Perle de Czaba' (G/O/W) | WSuV |
| | - 'Perlette' (O/W/S) | CCCN CSut EPom ERea LRHS NPri WSuV |
| | - 'Petit Rouge' (R) | WSuV |
| | - 'Pinot Blanc' (O/W) | CCCN LRHS MAsh SVic WSuV |
| | - 'Pinot Gris' (O/B) | SDea WSuV |
| | - 'Pinot Noir' (O/B) | CCCN SVic WSuV |
| § | - 'Portugieser' (O/B) | WSuV |
| | - 'Précoce de Bousquet' (O/W) | WSuV |
| | - 'Précoce de Malingre' (O/W) | CAgr SDea |
| | - 'Prima' (O/B) | WSuV |
| | - 'Primavis Frontignan' (G/W) | WSuV |
| | - 'Purpurea' (O/B) ♀H4 | Widely available |
| | - 'Queen of Esther' (B) | GTwe MBri NLar SKee SLim WSuV |

- 'Regner' (O/W) WSuV
- 'Reichensteiner' (O/G/W) CAgr SDea WSuV
- 'Riesling' (O/W) CCCN LRHS MAsh SVic WSuV
- Riesling-Silvaner see *V. vinifera* 'Müller-Thurgau'
- 'Rish Baba' ERea
- 'Rotberger' (O/G/B) WSuV
- 'Royal Muscadine' (G/O/W) SPoG WSuV
- 'Saint Laurent' (G/O/W) SVic WSuV
- 'Sauvignon Blanc' (O/W) CCCN LRHS WSuV
- 'Scheurebe' (O/W) WSuV
§ - 'Schiava Grossa' (G/B/D) CCCN CMac CTri ELan EPfP EPom ERea GTwe LRHS LSRN MAsh MBri MRav NPer NPla NPri SBfd SDea SLim SPer SPoG SVic SWvt WDin WFar WMoo WSuV
- 'Schönburger' (O/W) SDea SVic WSuV
- 'Schwarzriesling' see *V. vinifera* 'Meunier'
- 'Sémillon' LRHS LSRN MAsh
- 'Senator' (O/W) WSuV
- 'Septimer' (O/W) WSuV
- 'Shiraz' (B) WSuV
- 'Siegerrebe' (O/W/D) CAgr GTwe LRHS MAsh NPer SDea SVic WSuV
- 'Silvaner' (O/W) WSuV
- 'Spetchley Red' WCot WCru WPGP WPat
- strawberry grape see *V.* 'Fragola'
§ - 'Sultana' (W/S) CAgr CCCN GTwe SDea WSuV
- 'Theresa' LRHS MBri NLar SKee SLim SPoG WSuV
- 'Thompson Seedless' see *V. vinifera* 'Sultana'
* - 'Triomphe' (O/B) SVic
- 'Triomphrebe' (W) WSuV
- 'Vroegeivan der Laan' CCVT NLar
- 'Wrotham Pinot' (O/B) ERea SDea WSuV
- 'Würzer' (O/W) WSuV
- 'Zweigeltrebe' (O/B) WSuV
* 'White Strawberry' (O/W) WSuV
'Zalagyöngye' (W) CAgr ERea WSuV

## *Vriesea* (*Bromeliaceae*)

***imperialis*** **new** EAmu
***splendens*** ♀H1 XBlo

# W

## *Wachendorfia* (*Haemodoraceae*)

***brachyandra*** GCal
***thyrsiflora*** CAbb CDes CFir CHEx CPLG CPne CTsd EShb IGor LEdu WCFE WPGP

## *Wahlenbergia* (*Campanulaceae*)

sp. ECou
***albomarginata*** ECho EWTr NWCA
- 'Blue Mist' ECho
***ceracea*** GKev
***congesta*** ECho GKev
***gloriosa*** ECou MOWG WAbe WFar
***gracilenta*** GKev
***hederacea*** GGar
***pumilio*** see *Edraianthus pumilio*
***rivularis*** GKev LLHF
- 'Snow-cap' GKev SBfd
***serpyllifolia*** see *Edraianthus serpyllifolius*
***stricta*** ECou
***undulata*** 'Melton Bluebird' GJos

## *Waldsteinia* (*Rosaceae*)

***fragarioides*** GKev
***geoides*** EBee EPfP LAst LRHS NBre NPro SPer WMoo WWEG XLum
***ternata*** Widely available
§ - 'Mozaick' (v) EBee EWes NBir NBre NPro
- 'Variegata' see *W. ternata* 'Mozaick'

## walnut, black see *Juglans nigra*

## walnut, common see *Juglans regia*

## *Wallichia* (*Arecaceae*)

***densiflora*** LPal
***disticha*** LPal

## *Wasabia* (*Brassicaceae*)

***wasabi*** CArn GPoy LEdu

## *Washingtonia* (*Arecaceae*)

'Filibusta' EAmu
***filifera*** ♀H1 CAbb CCCN CDoC CPHo EAmu ETod LPal LRHS SArc SBig SEND SPlb
***robusta*** CBcs EAmu LPal LRHS SBst SChr SPlb

## *Watsonia* (*Iridaceae*)

***aletroides*** CCtw CDes CTca EBee ECho GCal WCot WPGP
***amatolae*** IBlr
***angusta*** CDes CGHE CPLG CPne CPrp CTca EBee IBlr ITim WPGP
- JCA 3.950.409 WCot
'Apricot Queen' **new** GGar
***ardernei*** see *W. borbonica* subsp. *ardernei* (Sander) Goldblatt 'Arderne's White'
***beatricis*** see *W. pillansii*
I 'Best Red' WCot
§ ***borbonica*** CCtw CPne CPou CPrp GGal
- subsp. ***ardernei*** misapplied see *W. borbonica* subsp. *ardernei* 'Arderne's White'
§ - subsp. ***ardernei*** (Sander) Goldblatt 'Arderne's White' CAby CBre CDes CFir CGHE CPLG CPrp CTca EBee ECho GGar IBlr LRHS WCot WPGP
- subsp. ***borbonica*** CDes EBee IBlr WPGP
- 'Paarl' ECho
***brevifolia*** see *W. laccata*
brick red-flowered CDes WPGP
***coccinea*** Baker see *W. spectabilis*
***coccinea*** Herb. ex Baker WCot
- 'Somerset West' ECho
***densiflora*** CPou IBlr WCot
***distans*** EBee
***fourcadei*** CPne
***fulgens*** CPne LEdu
***galpinii*** CFir
- lavender-flowered IBlr
- pink-flowered EBee IBlr
***galpinii*** × ***knysnana*** IBlr
§ ***humilis*** CDes CPou EBee GCal LEdu SKHP
***knysnana*** CDes EBee IBlr WCot WPGP
§ ***laccata*** CDes CFir CPne CPrp EBee WCot WPGP
***latifolia*** IBlr
***lepida*** EBee ECho IBlr
× ***longifolia*** JCA 03.952.850 WCot

| | |
|---|---|
| ***marginata*** | CPou CPrp EBee ECho GGar WCot WPGP |
| - ***alba*** | SKHP |
| ***meriania*** | ERCP GGal GMac IBlr WCot WPtf |
| - var. ***bulbillifera*** | CGHE CPne CPrp CTca EBee ECho GAbr GCra GGal GGar IBlr SMrm WSHC |
| * 'Mount Congreve' | CTca |
| 'Peachy Pink Orphan' | CDes EBee WPGP |
| § ***pillansii*** | CAbb CCtw CGHE CHEx CPLG CPne CPou CPrp CTca CYeo EBee IBal IBlr NCGa SMrm SPoG WFar WMnd |
| - JCA 3.593.609 | WCot |
| - 'Cathcart' | ECho |
| - hybrid | SAga WHil |
| - peach-flowered | CPLG |
| - pink-flowered | CAby CPLG CPrp IVic |
| - red-flowered | CPLG GBin IVic |
| - soft pink-flowered **new** | EPri |
| pink-flowered | CDes EBee |
| ***pulchra*** | EBee |
| ***pyramidata*** | see *W. borbonica* |
| ***roseoalba*** | see *W. humilis* |
| ***schlechteri*** | EBee |
| § ***spectabilis*** | CPne |
| 'Stanford Scarlet' | CAby CDes CFir CPLG CPne CPou CPrp CSpr ELon GGar GMac IBlr SChF SChr SUsu WPGP WSHC |
| ***stenosiphon*** | EBee IBlr |
| ***strubeniae*** | IBlr |
| ***tabularis*** | CCtw |
| ***transvaalensis*** | EBee |
| 'Tresco Dwarf Pink' | CDes CFir CPLG CPrp CTca CYeo EBee IBlr LEdu WCot WPGP |
| Tresco hybrids | CAbb CHll CPLG CPne GGal LTen SAga SRkn WCFE |
| ***vanderspuyae*** | CCtw CPLG CPne CPrp IBlr WCot |
| 'White Dazzler' | SApp |
| ***wilmaniae*** | CPLG CPne CPou CPrp IBlr |
| - JCA 3.955200 | SKHP |
| - 'Ice Angel' | SKHP |
| ***zeyheri*** | EBee WHil |

## *Wattakaka* see *Dregea*

## *Weigela* ✿ (*Caprifoliaceae*)

| | |
|---|---|
| CC 1231 | CPLG |
| 'Abel Carrière' | CMac CTri EBee ECtt EPfP EWes GKin MGos NWea WCFE WFar |
| 'Avalanche' misapplied | see *W.* 'Candida' |
| 'Avalanche' Lemoine | see *W. praecox* 'Avalanche' |
| 'Avant Garde' **new** | WPat |
| Black and White = 'Courtacad1' **new** | SBfd |
| 'Boskoop Glory' | GQui SPer |
| § Briant Rubidor = 'Olympiade' (v) | CDoC CMac EBee ECtt EHoe EPfP LAst LRHS MAsh MDun MGos MMuc MNHC MRav NEgg NLar NVic SGol SLim SPer SPlb SPoG SWal WFar |
| 'Bristol Ruby' | Widely available |
| § 'Candida' | CTri ELan EWes MRav NLar SPer |
| Cappuccino = 'Verweig 2'^PBR | LBuc MBlu NBro NEgg NLar SPoG WRHF |
| Carnaval = 'Courtalor'^PBR | CBar CBcs CWib EBee EQua LRHS NLar |
| 'Conquête' | SLon |
| ***coraeensis*** | CHll MAsh MBlu MMHG SBrd SBrt WCot WPat |
| - 'Alba' | CHll SPer |
| ***decora*** | GQui |
| - B&SWJ 10834 | WCru |
| 'Eva Rathke' | GKin NBir NLar NWea |
| 'Evita' | GKin WFar |
| ***floribunda*** B&SWJ 10831 | WCru |
| ***florida*** | CDul CMac EPfP MGos |
| - B&SWJ 8439 | WCru |
| - f. ***alba*** | CBcs WFar |
| * - 'Albovariegata' (v) | CPLG |
| - 'Bicolor' | CMac ELan |
| - 'Bristol Snowflake' | CDul CMac EBee EPfP MBlu MHer MMuc MSwo NBir NLar SLon |
| - 'Foliis Purpureis' ♀H4 | Widely available |
| - 'Milk and Honey' | GKin LRHS MBri |
| - Minor Black = 'Verweig 3'^PBR | CWSG EPfP EWTr LBuc LRHS MBri MPkF NBro NHol NLar STes WMoo |
| - Monet = 'Verweig'^PBR (v) | Widely available |
| - Moulin Rouge = 'Brigela'^PBR | CBcs CDoC CSBt ELon EPfP LBuc LRHS MBri MGos SLim |
| - 'Pink Princess' | EBee LRHS MSwo SBrd |
| - Rubigold | see *W.* Briant Rubidor |
| - 'Samabor' | WFar |
| - 'Sunny Princess' | EQua NMun |
| - 'Suzanne' (v) | NPro |
| - 'Tango' | CPMA LRHS MAsh NPro |
| 'Florida Variegata' (v) ♀H4 | Widely available |
| ***florida*** 'Versicolor' | CMHG CMac CPLG CWib GQui SLon SMrm WFar WGor |
| - Wine and Roses = 'Alexandra' | CAbP CBcs CDoC CPLG CSBt CWSG EHoe ELan EMil EPfP EShb GKin LAst LRHS LSRN LSqu MAsh MBri MGos MRav MWat NBro NEgg NLar SBfd SPoG SRGP SWvt WFar WGrn |
| 'Gold Rush' | NLar |
| 'Golden Candy' | NPro |
| 'Gustave Malet' | CMCN GQui |
| ***hortensis*** | CPLG |
| 'Hulsdonk' **new** | CWSG |
| ***japonica*** 'Dart's Colourdream' | ECtt EHoe ELon EWes LAst MMuc SEND SLim |
| 'Jean's Gold' | ELan MBlu MGos MRav |
| 'Kosteriana Variegata' (v) | CSBt EBee EPfP GGar LRHS MAsh MMuc NEgg SBfd SEND SLon WFar |
| 'Looymansii Aurea' | CDul CMHG CPLG CTri EBee ELan EPfP LAst NLar SGol SPer WDin WFar WHar |
| Lucifer = 'Courtared'^PBR | CDoC |
| ***maximowiczii*** | CPLG GQui |
| § ***middendorffiana*** | Widely available |
| 'Minuet' | EBee EPfP LRHS MGos MRav MSwo NPro SLPl |
| 'Mont Blanc' | CBot MAsh MMHG |
| Nain Rouge = 'Courtanin'^PBR | CBcs CTri LRHS MBri |
| 'Nana Variegata' (v) | CPLG ECrN ELon EPfP EPla LRHS MBri SBfd SLPl WGwG |
| Naomi Campbell = 'Bokrashine'^PBR | GBin GKin MMHG MWea NEgg NHol NLar WFar WHar WMoo |
| 'Newport Red' | EBee GKin MBNS MWat NWea WFar |
| Pink Poppet = 'Plangen'^PBR | CAbP CSBt EBee EKen EMil EPfP GKin LAst LBMP LRHS LSRN MAsh NLar SBfd SCoo SLim SPoG SWvt |
| ***praecox*** | ECrN |
| - B&SWJ 8705 | WCru |

§ – 'Avalanche' ECtt SGar
'Praecox Variegata' (v) ♀H4 CMac CTri ELan EPfP LAst LRHS MAsh MDun MRav NBir SBfd SDix SPer SPoG SRms WCFE WCru WFar WPat
'Red Prince' ♀H4 EBee ECrN ELan LBuc LRHS MGos MSwo NEgg NLar SBrd SGol SLim SPoG
Rubidor see *W.* Briant Rubidor
Rubigold see *W.* Briant Rubidor
'Ruby Anniversary' LBuc SLon
'Ruby Queen'PBR CMac EPfP
Ruby Wedding **new** LSRN
'Rumba' CMac EWTr MRav NPro
***sessilifolia*** see *Diervilla sessilifolia*
'Snowflake' ECrN ECtt EWTr NPro SRms WDin WFar
'Stelzneri' MMuc
***subsessilis*** B&SWJ 1056 WCru
– B&SWJ 4206 WCru
'Victoria' CDul CMac CWib EBee ECrN EHoe ELan EPfP LBMP LRHS MGos MSwo NBir NWad SBfd SGol SPer WFar WGor WHar WMoo

## *Weinmannia* (*Cunoniaceae*)

***racemosa*** IDee
– 'Kamahi' CTrC
***trichosperma*** CBcs IArd IDee SArc SSpi

## *Weldenia* (*Commelinaceae*)

***candida*** EBla ECho IBlr LLHF MSCN NHar NMen WAbe

## *Westringia* (*Lamiaceae*)

***angustifolia*** ECou
***brevifolia*** ECou
– var. ***raleighii*** ECou
§ ***fruticosa*** ♀H1 CBcs CCCN CTsd ECou EShb SVen WJek
– 'Smokie' (v) CCCN CTsd ECou MOWG
– 'Variegata' (v) SVen WJek
***longifolia*** CCCN ECou
***rosmariniformis*** see *W. fruticosa*
'Wynyabbie Gem' CAbb LRHS SEND SVen

## whitecurrant see *Ribes rubrum* (W)

## *Whiteheadia* (*Asparagaceae*)

***bifolia*** 'Nardonwsberg' ECho

## *Widdringtonia* (*Cupressaceae*)

***schwarzii*** CDoC

## *Wigandia* (*Boraginaceae*)

***caracasana*** CHll

## *Wikstroemia* (*Thymelaeaceae*)

***gemmata*** LRHS SSta

## wineberry see *Rubus phoenicolasius*

## *Wisteria* ✿ (*Papilionaceae*)

§ ***brachybotrys*** CCVT SBrd SLau
§ – Murasaki-kapitan CEnd CTri CWGN EPfP LRHS SKHP
– 'Okayama' EPfP SKHP
– 'Pink Chiffon' EPfP LRHS MAsh SKHP
– 'Shiro-beni' CTri MGos MMuc SEND
§ – 'Shiro-kapitan' CBcs CEnd CSPN CTri CWGN EBee EBtc EPfP LRHS LSRN MAsh MBri MGos MRav NHol SKHP SLau SLim SPer WPGP WPat WSHC
* – 'White Silk' CBcs EPfP LRHS LSRN MAsh MGos NPla SLon WGwG
§ 'Burford' CEnd CSPN CWGN EPfP GBin LRHS LSRN MAsh MBri MWat NHol SCoo SKHP SLau SLim WHar WPGP
'Caroline' CBcs CCCN CDoC CHab CSPN CSam CWGN EBee EPfP EWTr LRHS LSRN MAsh MGos MRav NEgg NPCo SBrd SLau SPer SPoG SRms SSpi WPGP WSHC
***floribunda*** CBcs CCVT CRHN CWib ELan EPfP GGal MMuc NPCo SEWo SGol WDin WFar
§ – 'Alba' ♀H4 Widely available
– 'Black Dragon' see *W. floribunda* 'Yae-kokuryū'
– 'Burford' see *W.* 'Burford'
* – 'Cascade' CBcs LRHS MBri NEgg
§ – 'Domino' CBcs CCVT CMac CTri CWGN ELon EPfP IArd LHop LRHS LSRN MAsh MGos MRav NHol SBfd SCoo SEND SKHP SLau SLim SPer SSta WFar
– 'Fragrantissima' see *W. sinensis* 'Jako'
– 'Geisha' CBcs CEnd SKHP
– 'Harlequin' CBcs CSPN EBee ECrN ELon GCal LRHS MAsh NPCo NPla SBfd SEND SKHP WFar
– 'Hocker Edge' SLau
– 'Hon-beni' see *W. floribunda* 'Rosea'
– 'Honey Bee Pink' see *W. floribunda* 'Rosea'
– 'Honko' see *W. floribunda* 'Rosea'
– 'Issai' LSRN MSwo SGol
– 'Issai Perfect' LRHS LSRN NLar SCoo SLon
– 'Jakohn-fuji' see *W. sinensis* 'Jako'
§ – 'Kuchi-beni' CBcs CCVT CEnd CSPN EBee ELan GBin LRHS LSRN MAsh MBri MGos NEgg NHol NLar NPCo SEND SKHP SLau SPer SRms
– 'Lawrence' CBcs CCVT CEnd CSPN CWGN MBri NLar SBrd SKHP SLau SLim
– 'Lipstick' see *W. floribunda* 'Kuchi-beni'
– 'Longissima' see *W. floribunda* 'Multijuga'
– 'Longissima Alba' see *W. floribunda* 'Alba'
– 'Macrobotrys' see *W. floribunda* 'Multijuga'
– 'Magenta' LRHS NPla
§ – 'Multijuga' ♀H4 Widely available
– Murasaki-naga see *W. floribunda* 'Purple Patches'
– 'Nana Richin's Purple' CEnd SLau
– 'Peaches and Cream' see *W. floribunda* 'Kuchi-beni'
– 'Pink Ice' see *W. floribunda* 'Rosea'
§ – 'Purple Patches' NPri
– Reindeer see *W. sinensis* 'Jako'
§ – 'Rosea' ♀H4 Widely available
– 'Royal Purple' CEnd LRHS MBri SPoG WFar WGor
– 'Russelliana' CBcs EBee GBin LTen NLar
– 'Shiro-naga' see *W. floribunda* 'Alba'
– 'Shiro-nagi' see *W. floribunda* 'Alba'
– 'Shiro-noda' see *W. floribunda* 'Alba'
– 'Snow Showers' see *W. floribunda* 'Alba'
– 'Variegata' (v) CWGN
N – 'Violacea Plena' (d) CBcs CDoC CMac ECrN EPfP EQua LTen NLar NPri SKHP SPer SWvt WDin WFar
N – 'Yae-kokuryū' (d) Widely available
× ***formosa*** CEnd SLau SLim
– 'Black Dragon' see *W. floribunda* 'Yae-kokuryū'
– 'Domino' see *W. floribunda* 'Domino'
– 'Issai' Wada pro parte see *W. floribunda* 'Domino'

- 'Kokuryū' see *W. floribunda* 'Yae-kokuryū'
- 'Yae-kokuryū' see *W. floribunda* 'Yae-kokuryū'

***frutescens*** EBee SLim WFar
- 'Amethyst Falls'PBR CEnd CWGN IArd LRHS LSRN MGos NPri SCoo SLon SPoG WMoo

Kapitan-fuji see *W. brachybotrys*
'Lavender Lace' EBee ECrN LRHS LSRN MAsh NEgg NLar SLau WFar
***macrostachya*** 'Blue Moon' LRHS WHar
***multijuga*** 'Alba' see *W. floribunda* 'Alba'
'Showa-beni' CEnd CWGN EPfP LHop MGos SCoo SEND SKHP SLau SLim WPGP
***sinensis*** 𝕐H4 Widely available
- 'Alba' 𝕐H4 CBcs CDoC CDul CMen CWib EBee ECrN ELan EPfP LAst LRHS LSRN MAsh MGos MNHC MWat NEgg NPla SEND SLau SLim SPoG WDin WFar
- 'Amethyst' CBcs CEnd CHab CSPN CWCL EBee EPfP EShb LRHS LSRN LTen MAsh MBri MGos MRav MWat NPla NSti SBrd SKHP SLau SLim SPer WPat
- 'Blue Sapphire' CBcs CHab CSPN CWGN EBee LSRN NEgg NPCo NSti SLau SRms

* - 'Caerulea' GAuc
- 'Consequa' see *W. sinensis* 'Prolific'
- 'Cooke's Special' CWGN

§ - 'Jako' CEnd EBee EWTr
- 'Oosthoek's Variety' see *W. sinensis* 'Prolific'

I - 'Pink Ice' EWTr NEgg NPCo
- 'Prematura' see *W. floribunda* 'Domino'
- 'Prematura Alba' see *W. brachybotrys* 'Shiro-kapitan'

§ - 'Prolific' Widely available
- 'Rosea' LSRN SPur SWvt
- 'Shiro-capital' see *W. brachybotrys* 'Shiro-kapitan'

'Tiverton' CBcs EBee NPla WGwG
***venusta*** see *W. brachybotrys* 'Shiro-kapitan'
- 'Alba' see *W. brachybotrys* 'Shiro-kapitan'
- var. ***violacea*** misapplied see *W. brachybotrys* Murasaki-kapitan

## *Withania* (*Solanaceae*)

***somnifera*** CArn GPoy

## *Wittsteinia* (*Alseuosmiaceae*)

***vacciniacea*** WCru

## *Wodyetia* (*Arecaceae*)

***bifurcata*** EAmu LPal XBlo

## *Wollemia* (*Araucariaceae*)

***nobilis*** CDTJ CDoC CTho EAmu EPfP ESwi LRHS MGos WBor WEve WMou

## *Woodsia* (*Woodsiaceae*)

***obtusa*** CBty CDTJ CKel CLAP CWCL EBee EFer EMil LRHS NBro NLar NMyG SBfd SGol SPoG SRot WPnP WRic WWEG
***polystichoides*** 𝕐H4 GQui SRms

## *Woodwardia* (*Blechnaceae*)

from Emei Shan, China CLAP
***areolata*** SKHP WRic
***fimbriata*** Widely available
***orientalis*** CBty ESwi LRHS WFib WRic
- var. ***formosana*** WRic
- - B&SWJ 6865 CLAP WCru

***radicans*** 𝕐H3 CBcs CHEx CHid CLAP EWes EWld GQui SArc WFib WRic
***unigemmata*** CHEx CLAP EFer EWes EWld SArc SKHP WFib WHal WRic
***virginica*** CBty CLAP ISha WRic

## Worcesterberry see *Ribes* 'Worcesterberry'

## *Wulfenia* (*Plantaginaceae*)

***baldaccii*** new GKev
***carinthiaca*** EBee ECho GAbr GEdr GKev NBir NLar NWad SBHP WPer XLum
× ***schwarzii*** CDes EBee LEdu WPGP

## *Wurmbea* (*Colchicaceae*)

***pusilla*** 'Sentinel Peak' ECho
***recurva*** ECho
***spicata*** 'Rawsonville' ECho

# X

## *Xanthium* (*Asteraceae*)

***sibiricum*** CArn

## *Xanthoceras* (*Sapindaceae*)

***sorbifolium*** 𝕐H3-4 CAgr CArn CBcs CBot CMCN CWib ECrN ELan EPfP MBlu NLar SMad SPoG SSpi WBor WDin WPat

## *Xanthocyparis* (*Cupressaceae*)

***nootkatensis*** 'Aurea' WDin
- 'Aureovariegata' (v) EHul
- 'Compacta' CTri
- 'Glauca' NWea
- 'Gracilis' EHul
- 'Green Arrow' CKen LRHS NLar SCoo SLim WHar
- 'Jubilee' LRHS NPCo SCoo SLim WHar
- 'Kanada' NLar
- 'Lutea' CTri NWea
- 'Nordkroken' NLar
- 'Pendula' 𝕐H4 CDoC CDul CKen ELan EPfP EPla GKin LMaj LRHS MAsh MBlu MBri MGos MMuc NEgg NPCo NWea WCFE WDin WEve WFar
- 'Strict Weeper' CKen NLar SLim

## *Xanthorhiza* (*Ranunculaceae*)

***simplicissima*** CArn CBcs CGHE CRow EPfP GCal IVic LEdu MBri NLar SDys SSpi WPGP

## *Xanthorrhoea* (*Xanthorrhoeaceae*)

***australis*** SPlb
***fulva*** SPlb
***glauca*** CCCN CDTJ EAmu
***johnsonii*** SPlb
***macronema*** new SPlb
***media*** new SPlb
***preisii*** CDTJ SPlb
***quadrangulata*** new SPlb
***resinosa*** new SPlb
***semiplana*** new SPlb
- subsp. ***tateana*** new SPlb

## *Xanthosoma* (*Araceae*)

***sagittifolium*** CDTJ
***violaceum*** CDTJ EAmu

## *Xerochrysum* (*Asteraceae*)

| | | |
|---|---|---|
| § | ***bracteatum*** 'Coco' | CMHG CSpe WWlt |
| § | - 'Dargan Hill Monarch' | CHll CSpe MAJR SRms WWlt |
| § | - 'Skynet' | WWlt |
| | - 'Wollerton' | WWlt |
| | 'Sundaze Flame' | CWCL |

## *Xeronema* (*Xeronemataceae*)

| | | |
|---|---|---|
| | ***callistemon*** | CBcs CBrP CTrC |

## *Xerophyllum* (*Melanthiaceae*)

| | | |
|---|---|---|
| | ***tenax*** | GCal GGar NMen |

## *Xylotheca* (*Achariaceae*)

| | | |
|---|---|---|
| | ***kraussiana*** new | SPlb |

## Youngberry see *Rubus* 'Youngberry'

## *Ypsilandra* (*Melanthiaceae*)

| | | |
|---|---|---|
| | ***cavaleriei*** | CPLG EBee GEdr WCot |
| | ***thibetica*** | CDes CFir CGHE CPLG CPrp CSpe EBee EBla EPfP GEdr LAma LEdu LLHF LRHS NLar SChF SMad WCot WCru WPGP |

## *Yucca* ✿ (*Asparagaceae*)

| | | |
|---|---|---|
| | SDR 3701 | GKev |
| | ***aloifolia*** | CAbb CCCN CDoC CHEx EAmu ETod MGos MREP SArc SBfd SBig SChr SEND SPlb |
| § | - f. ***marginata*** (v) | EAmu LPal MREP SArc SBig |
| | - 'Purpurea' | SPlb |
| | - 'Tricolor' (v) | MREP |
| | - 'Variegata' | see *Y. aloifolia* f. *marginata* |
| | ***angustifolia*** | see *Y. glauca* |
| | ***baccata*** | CCCN CTrC EAmu ETod SPlb |
| | - NNS 99-510 | WCot |
| | ***carnerosana*** | CTrC EAmu |
| § | ***elata*** | CCCN CTrC EAmu WPGP |
| § | ***elephantipes*** 🏆$^{H1}$ | CDTJ EAmu SBfd SEND |
| | - 'Jewel' (v) | EAmu MMuc SEND |
| | - 'Puck' (v) | SEND |
| | - variegated (v) new | SEND |
| | ***faxoniana*** | EAmu SPlb |
| | ***filamentosa*** 🏆$^{H4}$ | Widely available |
| | - 'Antwerp' | GCal |
| | - 'Bright Edge' (v) 🏆$^{H3}$ | Widely available |
| | - 'Color Guard' (v) | CTrC LAst MBri NLar SChr WCot WFar |
| | - 'Garland's Gold' (v) | CBcs CCCN CDoC MAsh MGos SBig WFar |
| | - 'Variegata' (v) 🏆$^{H3}$ | CBcs MGos SRms WDin WFar |
| | ***filifera*** | EAmu ETod SPlb |
| | ***flaccida*** | MMuc SDix |
| | - 'Golden Sword' (v) 🏆$^{H3}$ | CBcs CDoC CMac CTrC EBee EHoe ELan EPfP GMaP LAst LRHS LSRN MAsh MCCP MGos MSCN MSwo NBlu NLar NPla SBfd SGol SLim SPer SPoG SWvt WCot WPat |
| | - 'Ivory' 🏆$^{H3-4}$ | CBcs CDoC CEnd EBee ECtt ELan ELon EPfP GCal GMaP LRHS LSRN MBlu MBri MGos MRav NLar SBfd SLPl SPer SRms STre WMoo |
| | × ***floribunda*** | SArc |
| § | ***glauca*** | EPfP GLin LEdu LRHS MBri |
| * | - var. ***radiosa*** | CTrC |
| | ***gloriosa*** 🏆$^{H4}$ | CBcs CDoC CHEx CMac CTri EAmu EPla LRHS MGos MREP NPla SArc SBfd SEND SPer SPlb SPoG SWvt WBrk |
| | - 'Aureovariegata' | see *Y. gloriosa* 'Variegata' |
| | - 'Bright Star' new | LRHS |
| § | - 'Variegata' (v) 🏆$^{H4}$ | Widely available |
| | ***guatemalensis*** | see *Y. elephantipes* |
| | ***linearifolia*** new | EAmu |
| | ***linearis*** | see *Y. thompsoniana* |
| | 'Nobilis' | CHEx SDix |
| | ***pallida*** | WPGP |
| | ***radiosa*** | see *Y. elata* |
| | ***recurvifolia*** 🏆$^{H4}$ | CHEx EAmu EPfP GCal MGos SArc SBfd |
| | - Banana Split = 'Monvil' (v) new | LRHS |
| | - 'Gold Stream' (v) | WCot |
| | ***rigida*** | CBrP CDTJ EAmu WPGP |
| | ***rostrata*** | CBrP CCCN CDTJ CTrC EAmu ETod LPal MREP SChr SPlb WCot |
| | - 'Sapphire Skies' new | WCot |
| | ***schidigera*** | EAmu |
| | - NNS 03-597 | WCot |
| | ***schottii*** | CTrC WCot |
| § | ***thompsoniana*** | CDTJ CTrC EAmu LPal |
| | - blue-leaved | EAmu |
| | ***torreyi*** | CTrC EAmu SChr |
| | ***treculeana*** | EAmu |
| | 'Vittorio Emanuele II' | SMad |
| | ***whipplei*** | CBcs CBrP CCCN CDoC EBee ELan IGor LRHS NPal SBig SEND SPoG WCot WPGP |
| | - NNS 01-412 | WCot |
| | - NNS 05-696 | WCot |
| | - subsp. ***caespitosa*** | WPGP |
| | - subsp. ***intermedia*** NNS 01-413 | WCot |
| | - subsp. ***whipplei*** NNS 05-701 | WCot |

## *Yushania* (*Poaceae*)

| | | |
|---|---|---|
| | KR 7698 new | MWht |
| § | ***anceps*** | CBcs CDoC CEnt CHEx CPLG ENBC EPfP EPla GBin MGos MMoz MMuc MWht SBig SEND WDyG WFar WMoo |
| | - 'Pitt White' | CEnt CPLG EPla MWht WJun WPGP |
| | - 'Pitt White Rejuvenated' | EPla WPGP |
| | ***brevipaniculata*** | EPla WJun |
| | ***chungii*** | CEnt CPLG EPla MWht WJun WPGP |
| * | ***equatus*** | WJun |
| | ***maculata*** | CEnt CPLG EPla MMoz MWht SBig WDyG WJun |
| § | ***maling*** | CPLG EPfP EPla MMoz WJun |
| | Yunnan 5 | CPLG EPla WPGP |

# Z

## *Zaluzianskya* (*Scrophulariaceae*)

| | | |
|---|---|---|
| | JCA 15665 | NMen WAbe |
| | ***capensis*** | GKev |
| | 'Katherine' | SRot |
| | ***microsiphon*** | SPlb |

'Orange Eye' ELon NMen NSla
***ovata*** CPBP CSpe EDAr EPfP EPot EWld GKev MSCN NSla NWCA SAga SPet SPlb SPoG
- 'Star Balsam' **new** EBee
***pulvinata*** SPlb
'Semonkong' GCal SUsu SWvt

## *Zamia* (*Zamiaceae*)

***furfuracea*** CBrP
***muricata*** LPal
***skinneri*** LPal

## *Zamioculcas* (*Araceae*)

***zamiifolia*** CCCN

## *Zantedeschia* (*Araceae*)

§ ***aethiopica*** ♀H3 Widely available
- 'Apple Court Babe' CAby CElw CRow ELon GCal MAvo MNrw SMrm WDyG
- 'Childsiana' LRHS SApp
- 'Crowborough' ♀H3 Widely available
- 'Gigantea' CHEx
- 'Glow' CBct CMac CPLG ECtt LRHS LSou MAvo MRav NCGa NGdn WGwG
- 'Green Goddess' ♀H3 Widely available
- 'Little Gem' SMad WFar
- 'Luzon Lovely' WCru
- 'Marshmallow' CBct EAEE ECtt ELan EPfP GGar LRHS NCGa NGdn SPet WFar
- 'Mr Martin' CBct CCCN CHid CMac CTrC EBee ECtt ELon LRHS MNrw NCGa SBfd SBig SMad SWvt WCot
- 'Pershore Fantasia' (v) CBct CPLG EBee MSKA WCot WFar WWEG
- pink-flowered CHEx
- 'Snow White' LRHS
- 'Whipped Cream' MDKP
- 'White Gnome' WCot WFar
- 'White Mischief' EBee
- 'White Sail' CBct CPrp EBee ECtt GCal ITim LRHS MRav NGdn SWat WFar WGwG
***albomaculata*** CSpr CTca EPfP LAma SPlb
'Anneke' CCCN EPfP
'Apricot Glow' CHll
'Ascari'PBR **new** CCCN
'Black Eyed Beauty' LAma
'Black Magic' CCCN CMac EPfP LRHS
'Black Pearl' LAma
'Black Star' see *Z.* 'Edge of Night'
'Cameo' CCCN LAma
(Captain Series) 'Captain Chelsea'PBR LAma
- 'Captain Eskimo'PBR SPoG
- 'Captain Palermo'PBR LAma
- 'Captain Romance'PBR **new** SPoG
- 'Captain Safari'PBR **new** SPoG
- 'Captain Samos' LAma
- 'Captain Tendens'PBR LAma SPoG
'Crystal Blue' **new** LRHS
'Crystal Blush' LAma
§ 'Edge of Night' CCCN ERCP
***elliottiana*** ♀H1 CBcs CFir CHEx CSpe CTri LAma
'Flame' CCCN CSpr EPfP LBMP LRHS SPad WGwG
'Flavo Gold' **new** LRHS
'Harvest Moon' LAma
'Helen O'Connor' CPLG
'Kiwi Blush' CBro CCCN CFir CHEx CPLG CPrp CSpe EAEE EBee ECtt ELan ELon EPfP EWll LPBA LRHS MAvo NGdn NPal SApp SBfd SEND SKHP SPad SPer SPet SRkn SWat WFar WGwG
'Lime Lady' CBct ECha
'Mango' EPfP LAma
'Mozart' CCCN
'Picasso'PBR CCCN ERCP SPad SPoG
'Pink Mist' CBct LAma SWal
'Pink Persuasion' LAma
'Purple Sensation' EPfP
'Red Sox'PBR CCCN
***rehmannii*** ♀H1 LAma NLar SRms
'Schwarzwalder'PBR EGxp
'Silver Lining' LAma
'White Giant' WPGP
'White Pixie' CAby EPfP

## *Zanthorhiza* see *Xanthorhiza*

## *Zanthoxylum* (*Rutaceae*)

***acanthopodium*** GWJ 9287 WCru
***ailanthoides*** B&SWJ 11115 from Japan WCru
- B&SWJ 11394 from Japan WCru
- f. ***inermis*** RWJ 10048 WCru
***americanum*** ELan LEdu
***armatum*** CAgr
- HWJK 2178 WCru
***bungeanum*** HWJK 2131 WCru
***fauriei*** B&SWJ 11080 WCru
aff. ***fauriei*** B&SWJ 11371 WCru
- B&SWJ 11523 WCru
* ***giraldii*** GAuc
***laetum*** WWJ 11678 WCru
- WWJ 11914 WCru
***myriacanthum*** B&SWJ 11844 WCru
***oxyphyllum*** HWJK 2199 WCru
***piperitum*** CAgr CBcs GPoy SEND SPoG
- B&SWJ 8543 WCru
- B&SWJ 11377 WCru
- B&SWJ 11433 WCru
- purple-leaved WPGP
***schinifolium*** CAgr LEdu
- B&SWJ 8593 WCru
- B&SWJ 11080 WCru
- B&SWJ 11391 WCru
***simulans*** CAgr CArn CBcs CPLG GBin IGor IVic LEdu MBlu NLar

## *Zauschneria* (*Onagraceae*)

§ ***californica*** CHll CSam CTri EBee ECho EDAr EPfP MBrN SLon SWat SWvt WHrl WOut WPnn XLum
§ - subsp. ***cana*** ECha SWat
- - 'Sir Cedric Morris' EPfP LRHS
§ - 'Dublin' ♀H3 CBcs EBee ECha ECho EPfP EPot GGar LHop LRHS MHer MMuc MSCN MWat NSla NWCA SAga SEND SPer SPlb SPoG SRkn SUsu SWvt WFar WHoo WKif WNew WPat WSHC XLum
- 'Ed Carman' EBee ECtt ELon LRHS LSou SEND XLum
§ - subsp. ***garrettii*** ECho GAbr NWCA SDys SWat
- 'Glasnevin' see *Z. californica* 'Dublin'
- subsp. ***latifolia*** 'Sally Walker' EWes

§ - subsp. ***mexicana*** MHer SRms
- 'Olbrich Silver' EBee ECha ECtt EShb EWes LRHS SUsu WFar WKif WPat XLum
- 'Sierra Salmon' WPat
- 'Solidarity Pink' ECha LHop NWCA WPat
- 'Western Hills' ♀H4 CFir CSpe CTri ECha ECho ECtt EPfP LHop LRHS LSou MMuc MRav NWCA SAga SEND SPhx SWvt WHoo WPat XLum

***cana villosa*** see *Z. californica* subsp. *mexicana*
I 'Pumilio' NMen NSla WAbe
§ ***septentrionalis*** WAbe

## *Zea* (*Poaceae*)

***mays*** 'Quadricolor' (v) SBfd

## *Zebrina* see *Tradescantia*

## *Zelkova* ✿ (*Ulmaceae*)

***carpinifolia*** CDul CLnd CMCN CMen CTho SPlb WDin
'Kiwi Sunset' CDul CEnd EBee MAsh NWea
***schneideriana*** CMCN CMen EGFP
***serrata*** ♀H4 CBcs CCVT CDul CLnd CMCN CMen CTho EBee ECrN ELan EPfP LMaj MMuc NMun NWea SBir SCoo SEND SGol SPer STre WDin WFar
- B&SWJ 8491 from Korea WCru
- 'Goblin' CPMA NLar WPat
- 'Green Vase' LMaj MBlu
- 'Musashino' **new** SGol
- 'Ogon' **new** SGol
- 'Variegata' (v) CMac CPMA MBlu NLar SGol
- 'Yatsubusa' STre

***sinica*** CMCN CMen
× ***verschaffeltii*** MBlu

## *Zenobia* (*Ericaceae*)

***pulverulenta*** CAbP CBcs CDoC CMac CSBt ELan EPfP IDee IVic LRHS MAsh MBlu MGos NLar SLon SPer SReu SSpi SSta WAbe WDin WFar WPat WSHC
- 'Blue Sky' CAbP CBcs CMCN EPfP GKin LRHS MAsh MBlu MBri MGos NLar SPoG SSpi SSta
- f. ***nitida*** CMac NLar
- 'Raspberry Ripple' GKin MBri NLar SSta
- 'Viridis' NLar

## *Zephyranthes* ✿ (*Amaryllidaceae*)

***atamasca*** SKHP
***candida*** CAvo CBro CFFs CPBP CSpe CYeo EBee ECho EPot EShb ITim LAma LRHS SDix SMrm WHil
***citrina*** CPLG EBee ECho EPot LAma WCot
***drummondii*** ECho WCot
***flavissima*** CDes CPBP ECho WCot WHil
'Grandjax' WCot
'La Buffa Rose' WCot
***lindleyana*** WCot
***mexicana*** EBee
***minima*** ECho LLHF
***robusta*** see *Habranthus robustus*
***rosea*** EBee EPot

## *Zigadenus* (*Melanthiaceae*)

***elegans*** ECGP ECha EPri EWll GBee GCal NWCA SMad SUsu WCot WHil WSHC WTin
***fremontii*** WCot
***nuttallii*** CRDP EBee ECho MDKP WCot
***venenosus*** NNS 03-605 WCot
***volcanicus*** B&SWJ 9110 WCru

## *Zingiber* ✿ (*Zingiberaceae*)

***mioga*** CMac EBee GPoy LEdu SChr SPlb SWal WPGP
- 'Crûg's Zing' LEdu WCru
- 'Dancing Crane' (v) CMac IFro

***officinale*** CTsd
***zerumbet*** 'Darceyi' (v) EBee

## *Zinnia* (*Asteraceae*)

'Red Spider' CSpe

## *Zizia* (*Apiaceae*)

***aptera*** LRHS SPhx
***aurea*** SDix SPhx WSHC WTin

## *Ziziphus* (*Rhamnaceae*)

§ ***jujuba*** (F) CAgr CBcs
- 'Lang' (F) CAgr
- 'Li' (F) CAgr
- var. ***spinosa*** CArn

***sativa*** see *Z. jujuba*

# BIBLIOGRAPHY

This is by no means exhaustive but lists some of the more useful works used in the preparation of the *RHS Plant Finder*. The websites of raisers of new plants (not listed here) are also an invaluable source of information.

## GENERAL


Allan, H.H., et al. 2000. *Flora of New Zealand.* Wellington. (5 vols). http://floraseries.landcareresearch.co.nz/pages/Book.aspx?fileName=Flora%201.xml

Ball Colegrave. 2007. Plant Catalogue 2008. West Adderbury, Oxon: Ball Colegrave.

Ball Colegrave. 2007. Seed Catalogue 2008. West Adderbury, Oxon: Ball Colegrave.

Bean, W.J. 1988. *Trees and Shrubs Hardy in the British Isles.* (8th ed. edited by Sir George Taylor & D.L. Clarke & Supp. ed. D.L. Clarke). London: John Murray.

Beckett, K. (ed.). 1994. *Alpine Garden Society Encyclopaedia of Alpines.* Pershore, Worcs.: Alpine Garden Society.

Boufford, D.E., et al. (eds). 2003. *Flora of Taiwan Checklist.* A checklist of the vascular plants of Taiwan. Taipei, Taiwan: NTU. http://tai2.ntu.edu.tw

Bramwell, D. & Bramwell, Z.I. 2001. *Wild Flowers of the Canary Islands.* (2nd ed.). Madrid: Editorial Rueda, S.L.

Brickell, C. (ed.). 2008. *The Royal Horticultural Society A-Z Encyclopedia of Garden Plants.* (3rd ed.) London: Dorling Kindersley.

Brickell, C.D. et al (eds.). 2009. *International Code of Nomenclature for Cultivated Plants* (8th ed.). ISHS.

Brummitt, R.K. (comp.). 1992. *Vascular Plant Families and Genera.* Kew: Royal Botanic Gardens. http://data.kew.org

Castroviejo, S. et al. (eds). *Flora Iberica.* 1987-2007. (Vols 1-8,, 10, 14, 15, 21). Madrid: Real Jardín Botánico, C.S.I.C.

Cave, Y. & Paddison, V. 1999. *The Gardener's Encyclopaedia of New Zealand Native Plants.* Auckland: Godwit.

Cooke, I. 1998. *The Plantfinder's Guide to Tender Perennials.* Newton Abbot, Devon: David & Charles.

Cronquist, A., Holmgren, A.H., Holmgren, N.H., Reveal, J.L. & Holmgren, P.H. et al. (eds). *Intermountain Flora: Vascular Plants of the Intermountain West, USA.* (1986-97). (Vols 1, 3-6). New York: New York Botanical Garden.

Davis, P.H., Mill, R.R. & Tan, K. (eds). 1965-88. *Flora of Turkey and the East Aegean Island.* (Vols 1-10). Edinburgh University Press.

Goldblatt, P. & Manning, J. 2000. *Cape Plants. A Conspectus of the Cape Flora of South Africa.* South Africa/USA: National Botanical Institute of South Africa/Missouri Botanical Garden.

Greuter, W., Brummitt, R.K., Farr, E., Kilian, N., Kirk, P.M. & Silva, P.C. (comps). 1993. *NCU-3.*

Grierson, A.J.C., Long, D.G. & Noltie, H.J. et al. (eds). 2001. *Flora of Bhutan.* Edinburgh: Royal Botanic Garden.

Grimshaw, J. & Bayton, R. 2009. *New Trees. Recent Introductions to Cultivation.* RBG Kew: Kew Publishing.

Güner, A., Özhatay, N., Ekîm, T., Baser, K.H.C. & Hedge, I.C. 2000. *Flora of Turkey and the East Aegean Islands.* Supp. 2. Vol. 11. Edinburgh: Edinburgh University Press.

Hickman, J.C. (ed.). 1993. *The Jepson Manual. Higher Plants of California.* Berkeley & Los Angeles: University of California Press. Jan 2010. http://ucjeps.berkeley.edu/interchange.html

Hillier, J. & Coombes, A. (eds). 2002. *The Hillier Manual of Trees & Shrubs.* (7th ed.). Newton Abbot, Devon: David & Charles.

Hirose, Y. & Yokoi, M. 1998. *Variegated Plants in Colour.* Iwakuni, Japan: Varie Nine.

Hirose, Y. & Yokoi, M. 2001. *Variegated Plants in Colour.* Vol. 2. Iwakuni, Japan: Varie Nine.

Hoffman, M. (ed.). 2005. *List of Woody Plants. International Standard ENA 2005-2010.* Netherlands: Applied Plant Research.

Huxley, A., Griffiths, M. & Levy, M. (eds). 1992. *The New RHS Dictionary of Gardening.* London: Macmillan.

Iwatsuki, K., et al. 1995. *Flora of Japan.* Vols I-IIIb. Tokyo, Japan: Kodansha Ltd.

Jelitto, L. & Schacht, W.R., Simon, H. 2002. *Die Freiland-Schmuchstauden.* Germany: Verlag Eugen Ulmer.

Krüssmann, G. & Epp, M.E. (trans.). 1986. *Manual of Cultivated Broad-leaved Trees and Shrubs.* London: Batsford (3 vols).

Leslie, A.C. (trans.). *New Cultivars of Herbaceous Perennial Plants 1985-1990.* Hardy Plant Society.

Mabberley, D.J. 2008. *Mabberley's Plant Book. A Portable Dictionary of Plants, their Classification and Uses.* (3rd ed.). Cambridge: Cambridge University Press.

McNeill, J. et al. (eds). 2006. *International Code of Botanical Nomenclature (Vienna Code).* Ruggell, Liechtenstein: A.R.G. Gantner Verlag. Jan 2010. http://ibot.sav.sk.

Metcalf, L.J. 1987. *The Cultivation of New Zealand Trees and Shrubs.* Auckland: Reed Methuen.

Nelson, E.C. 2000. *A Heritage of Beauty: The Garden Plants of Ireland: An Illustrated Encyclopaedia.* Dublin: Irish Garden Plant Society.

Ohwi, J. 1965. *Flora of Japan.* Washington DC: Smithsonian Institution.

Phillips, R. & Rix, M. 1997. *Conservatory and Indoor Plants.* London: Macmillan. (2 vols).

Platt, K. (comp.). 2002. *The Seed Search.* (5th ed.). Sheffield: Karen Platt.

Press, J.R. & Short, M.J. (eds). 1994. *Flora of Madeira.* London: Natural History Museum/ HMSO.

Rehder, A. 1940. *Manual of Cultivated Trees and Shrubs Hardy in North America.* (2nd ed.). New York: Macmillan.

Rice, G. (ed.), 2006. *Encyclopedia of Perennials.* London: Dorling Kindersley.

Stace, C. 1997. *New Flora of the British Isles.* (2nd ed.). Cambridge: Cambridge University Press.

Stearn, W.T. 1992. *Botanical Latin.* (4th ed.). Newton Abbot, Devon: David & Charles.

Stearn, W.T. 1996. *Stearn's Dictionary of Plant Names for Gardeners.* London: Cassell.

Thomas, G.S. 1990. *Perennial Garden Plants. A Modern Florilegium.* (3rd ed.). London: Dent.

Trehane, P. (comp.). 1989. *Index Hortensis. Vol. 1: Perennials.* Wimborne: Quarterjack

Tutin, T.G., et al. (ed.). 1993. *Flora Europaea. Vol. 1. Psilotaceae to Platanaceae.* (2nd ed.). Cambridge University Press.

Tutin, T.G., et al. 1964. *Flora Europaea.* Cambridge University Press. Vols 1-5. http://rbg-web2.rbge.org.uk

Walter, K.S. & Gillett, H.J. (eds). 1998. *1997 IUCN Red List of Threatened Plants.* Gland, Switzerland and Cambridge, UK: IUCN.

Walters, S.M. & Cullen, J. et al. (eds). 2000. *The European Garden Flora.* Cambridge: Cambridge University Press. (6 vols).

## General Periodicals

*Dendroflora*

*New, Rare and Unusual Plants.*

The Hardy Plant Society. *The Hardy Plant.*

The Hardy Plant Society. *The Sport.*

Internationale Stauden-Union. *ISU Yearbook.*

Royal Horticultural Society. *Hanburyana.*

Royal Horticultural Society. *The Garden.*

Royal Horticultural Society. *The Plantsman.*

Royal Horticultural Society. *The New Plantsman.*

Royal Horticultural Society. *The Plantsman* (new series).

## General Websites

Annotated Checklist of the Flowering Plants of Nepal. Jan 2010 www.efloras.org/flora_page-aspx?_id=110

Australian Cultivar Registration Authority. Jan 2010. www.anbg.gov.au/acra

Australian Plant Breeders Rights – Database Search. Jan 2010. http://pbr.ipaustralia.optus.com.au

Australian Plant Names Index. Australian National Botanic Gardens (comp.). Jan 2010. www.anbg.gov.au/apni/index.html

Bolivia Checklist. Jan 2010. www.efloras.org/flora_page.aspx?flora_id=40

Botanical Expedition in Myanmar Checklist. Jan 2010. http://botany.si-edu/myanmar/checklistNames.cfm

Brand, H. UConn Plant Database of Trees Shrubs and Vines. Jan 2010. www.hort.uconn.edu

Canadian Ornamental Plant Foundation. Jan 2010. www.copf.org

Canadian Plant Breeders Rights Office: Canadian Food Inspection Agency. Jan 2010. www.inspection.gc.ca

Catálogo de las Plantas Vasculares de las República Argentina. Jan 2010. www.darwin.edu.ar/Publicaciones/catalogoVaseII/CatalogoVaseII.asp

Catalogue of the Vascular Plants of Madagascar. Jan 2010. www.effloras.org/flora_page.aspx?flora_id+12

Darwin Checklist of Moroccan Vascular Plants. Jan 2010. www.herbarium.rdg.ac.uk/

DEFRA Plant Varieties and Seeds Gazette. Jan 2010. www.defra.gov.uk

Flora Himalaya Database. Jan 2010. www.leca.univ-savoie.fr

Flora Mesoamericana Internet Version (W3FM). Jan 2010. Missouri Botanical Garden. www.mobot.org/MOBOT/FM/intro.html

Flora of Australia Online. Jan 2010. Australian Biological Resources Study. www.environment.gov.au/biodiversity/abrs/online-resources/flora/index.html

Flora of Chile. Jan 2010. www.efloras.org/flora_page.aspx?flora_id=60

Flora of China Checklist. Jan 2010. http://flora.huh.harvard.edu/china

Flora of Pakistan. Jan 2010. www.efloras.org/flora_page.aspd?flora_id=5

Flora of North America Website. Jan 2010. Morin, N.R., et al. www.efloras.org-page.aspx/flora_id=1

GRIN (Germplasm Resources Information Network) Taxonomy. Jan 2010. www.ars-grin.gov

Hatch, D. New Ornamentals Society Database. Jan 2010. http://members.tripod.com/~Hatch_L/nos.html

International Plant Names Index. Jan 2010. www.ipni.org

International Plant Names Index: Author Query. Jan 2010. www.ipni.org/ipni

IOPI Provisional Global Plant Checklist. Jan 2010. www.bgbm.fu-berlin.de/iopi/gpl/query.asp

Manaaki Whenua: Landcare Research in New Zealand Plants Database Jan 2010. http://nzflora.landcareresearch.co.nz

Manual de plantas de Costa Rica. Jan 2010. www.mobot.org/manual.plantas

Plants Database. USDA, NRCS. Jan 2010. http://plants.usda.gov

Plants of Southern Africa: an Online Checklist. Jan 2010. http://posa.sanbi.org

New Zealand Plant Variety Rights Office www.iponz.govt.nz/cms/pvr

SKUD Database for Cultivated and Utilized Plants. Jan 2010. http://skud.ngb.se

Synonymized Checklist of the Vascular Flora of the United States, Puerto Rico and the Virgin Isles. BIOTA of North America Program. Jan 2010. www.bonap.org

Tropicos. Jan 2010. www.tropicos.org

US Patent Full-Text Database. US Patent and Trademark Office, (comp.). Jan 2010. www.uspto.gov/patft

World Checklist of Selected Families. Jan 2010. apps.kew.org/wcsp

## GENERA AND OTHER PLANT GROUPINGS

***Acer***

Gregory, P. & Angus, H. 2008. *World Checklist of Maple Cultivar Names.* Forestry Commission National Arboreta.

Harris, J.G.S. 2000. *The Gardener's Guide to Growing Maples.* Newton Abbot, Devon: David & Charles.

Van Gelderen, C.J. & Van Gelderen, D.M. 1999. *Maples for Gardens.* A Color Encyclopedia. Portland, Oregon: Timber Press.

Vertrees, J.D. 2001. *Japanese Maples.* Momiji and Kaede. (3rd ed.). Portland, Oregon: Timber Press.

***Actaea***

Compton, J.A., Culham, A. & Jury, S.L. 1998. Reclassification of *Actaea* to Include *Cimicifuga* and *Souliea* (*Ranunculaceae*). *Taxon* 47:593-634.

***Adiantum***

Goudey, C.J. 1985. *Maidenhair Ferns in Cultivation.* Melbourne: Lothian.

***Agapanthus***

Snoeijer, W. 2004. *Agapanthus. A Revision of the Genus.* Portland, Oregon: Timber Press.

***Agavaceae***

Irish, M. & Irish, G. 2000. *Agaves, Yuccas and Related Plants.* A Gardener's Guide. Portland, Oregon: Timber Press.

***Aizoaceae***

Burgoyne, P. et al. 1998. *Mesembs of the World. Illustrated Guide to a Remarkable Succulent Group.* South Africa: Briza Publications.

***Allium***

Davies, D. 1992. *Alliums. The Ornamental Onions.* London: Batsford

Gregory, M., et al. 1998. *Nomenclator Alliorum.* Kew: Royal Botanic Gardens.

Mathew, B. 1996. *A Review of Allium Section Allium.* Kew: Royal Botanic Gardens.

***Androsace***

Smith, G. & Lowe, D. 1997. *The Genus Androsace.* Pershore, Worcs.: Alpine Garden Society.

***Anemone,*** Japanese

McKendrick, M. 1990. Autumn Flowering Anemones. *The Plantsman* 12(3):140-151.

McKendrick, M. 1998. Japanese Anemones. *The Garden* (RHS) 123(9):628-633.

***Anthemis***

Leslie, A. 1997. Focus on Plants: *Anthemis tinctoria. The Garden* (RHS) 122(8):552-555.

***Apiaceae***

Pimenov, M.G. & Leonov, M.V. 1993. *The Genera of the Umbelliferae.* Kew: Royal Botanic Gardens.

***Aquilegia***

Munz, P.A. 1946. *Aquilegia:* the Cultivated and Wild Columbines. *Gentes Herb.* 7(1):1-150.

***Araceae***

Govaerts, R. & Frodin, D.G. 2002. *World Checklist and Bibliography of Araceae (and Acoraceae).* Kew:Royal Botanic Gardens

***Araliaceae***

Govaerts, R. & Frodin, D.G. 2002. *World Checklist and Bibliography of Araliaceae.* Kew: Royal Botanic Gardens

***Arecaceae*** (***Palmae,*** palms)

Craft, P. & Riffle, R.L. 2003. *Encyclopedia of Cultivated Palms.* Portland, Oregon: Timber Press.

Uhl, N.W. & Dransfield, J. 1987. *Genera Palmarum.* A Classification of Palms Based on the Work of Harold E. Moore Jr. Lawrence, Kansas: Allen Press.

***Argyranthemum***

Humphries, C.J. 1976. A Revision of the Macaronesian Genus *Argyranthemum. Bull. Brit. Mus. (Nat. Hist.) Bot.* 5(4):145-240.

***Arisaema***

Gusman, G. & Gusman, L. 2002. *The Genus Arisaema: A Monograph for Botanists and Nature Lovers.* Ruggell, Leichtenstein: A.R. Gantner Verlag Kommanditgesellschaft.

Pradhan, U.C. 1997. *Himalayan Cobra Lilies* (Arisaema). Their Botany and Culture. (2nd ed.). Kalimpong, West Bengal, India: Primulaceae Books.

***Arum***

Bown, D. 2000. *Plants of the Arum Family.* (2nd ed.). Portland, Oregon: Timber Press.

Boyce, P. 1993. *The Genus Arum.* London: HMSO.

***Asclepiadaceae***

Eggli, U. (ed.). 2002. *Illustrated Handbook of Succulent Plants: Asclepiadaceae.* Heidelberg, Germany: Springer-Verlag.

***Aster***

Picton, P. 1999. *The Gardener's Guide to Growing Asters.* Newton Abbot: David & Charles.

***Asteraceae***

Bremer, K. et al. 1994. *Asteraceae: Cladistics and Classification.* Portland, Oregon: Timber Press.

Cubey, J. & Grant, M. 2004. *Perennial Yellow Daisies: RHS Bulletin No 6.* Wisley, Surrey: RHS. www.rhs.org.uk/Plants/RHS-Publications/Plant-bulletins

***Astilbe***

Noblett, H. 2001. *Astilbe.* A Guide to the Identification of Cultivars and Common Species. Cumbria: Henry Noblett.

***Aubrieta***

1975. *International Registration Authority Checklist.* Weihenstephan, Germany: (Unpublished).

**Bamboos**

Ohrnberger, D. 1999. *The Bamboos of the World.* Amsterdam: Elsevier.

***Begonia***

American Begonia Society Astro Branch Begonia Data Base. Jan 2010. http://absastro.tripod.com

American Begonia Society Registered Begonias. Jan 2010. http://www.begonias.org

Ingles, J. 1990. *American Begonia Society Listing of Begonia Cultivars.* Revised Edition Buxton Checklist. American Begonia Society.

Tebbitt, M.C. 2005. *Begonias: Cultivation, Identification and Natural History.* Portland, Oregon: Timber Press.

Thompson, M.L. & Thompson, E.J. 1981. *Begonias.* The Complete Reference Guide. New York: Times Books.

***Berberidaceae***

Stearn, W.T. & Shaw, J.M.H. 2002. *The Genus Epimedium and Other Herbaceous Berberidaceae including the Genus Podophyllum.* Kew: Royal Botanic Gardens.

***Betula***

Ashburner, K. & Schilling. T. 1985. *Betula utilis* and its Varieties. *The Plantsman* 7(2):116-125.

Ashburner, K.B. 1980. *Betula* – a Survey. *The Plantsman* 2(1):31-53.

Hunt, D. (ed.). 1993. *Betula: Proceedings of the IDS Betula Symposium 1992.* Richmond, Surrey: International Dendrology Society.

***Boraginaceae***

Bennett, M. 2003. *Pulmonarias and the Borage Family.* London: Batsford.

***Bougainvillea***

Gillis, W.T. 1976. Bougainvilleas of Cultivation (*Nyctaginaceae*). *Baileya* 20(1):34-41.

Iredell, J. 1990. *The Bougainvillea Grower's Handbook.* Brookvale, Australia: Simon & Schuster.

Iredell, J. 1994. *Growing Bougainvilleas.* London: Cassell.

MacDaniels, L.H. 1981. A Study of Cultivars in *Bougainvillea* (*Nyctaginaceae*). *Baileya* 21(2):77-100.

Singh, B., Panwar, R.S., Voleti, S.R., Sharma, V.K. & Thakur, S. 1999. *The New International Bougainvillea Check List.* (2nd ed.). New Delhi: Indian Agricultural Research Institute.

***Bromeliaceae***

Beadle, D.A. 1991. *A Preliminary Listing of all the Known Cultivar and Grex Names for the Bromeliaceae.* Corpus Christi, Texas: Bromeliad Society.

Bromeliad Cultivar Registry Online Databases. Bromeliad Society International. Jan 2010. www.bsi.org

***Brugmansia***

Wreggitt, L. et al. (comp.). Jan 2010.. *Register of Brugmansia Cultivars and Checklist of Names in Use.* American Brugmansia and Datura Society. www.abads.org

***Buddleja***

Stuart, D.D. 2006. *Buddlejas: Royal Horticultural Society Collector Guide.* Portland, Oregon: Timber Press.

**Bulbs**

Leeds, R. 2000. *The Plantfinder's Guide to Early Bulbs.* Newton Abbot, Devon: David & Charles.

KAVB Online registration pages. Jan 2010. http://kavb.back2p.soft-orange.com

***Buxus***

Batdorf, L.R. 1995. *Boxwood Handbook. A Practical Guide to Knowing and Growing Boxwood.* Boyce, VA, USA: The American Boxwood Society. Jan 2010. www.boxwoodsociety.org

***Cactaceae***

Hunt, D. et al. 2006. *New Cactus Lexicon.* (2 vols.) Sherborne, Dorset: DH Books.

***Camellia***

Trujillo, D. J. (ed.). 2002. *Camellia Nomenclature.* (24th revd ed.). Southern California Camellia Society.

Savige, T.J. (comp.). 1993. *The International Camellia Register.* The International Camellia Society. (2 vols).

Savige, T.J. (comp.). 1997. *The International Camellia Register.* Supp. to vols 1 and 2. The International Camellia Society.

***Campanula***

Lewis, P. & Lynch, M. 1998. *Campanulas.* A Gardeners Guide. (2nd ed.). London: Batsford.

Lewis, P 2002. *Campanulas in the Garden.* Pershore, Worcs.: Hardy Plant Society.

***Campanulaceae***

Lammers, T.G. 2007. *World Checklist and Bibliography of Campanulaceae.* Kew Publishing.

***Canna***

Cooke, I. 2001. *The Gardener's Guide to Growing Cannas.* Newton Abbot, Devon: David & Charles.

Gray, J. & Grant, M. 2003. Canna: RHS Bulletin No 3. Wisley, Surrey: RHS. www.rhs.org.uk/Plants/RHS-Publications/Plant_bulletins

Hayward, K. Jan 2010. www.hartcanna.com

**Carnivorous Plants**

Schlauer, J. (comp.). Jan 2010. Carnivorous Plant Database. www.omnisterra.com

***Ceanothus***

Fross, D. & D. Wilken. 2006. *Ceanothus.* Portland, Oregon: Timber Press.

***Cercidiphyllum***

Dosmann, M.S. 1999. Katsura: a Review of *Cercidiphyllum* in Cultivation and in the Wild. *The New Plantsman* 6(1):52-62.

Dosmann, M., Andrews, S., Del Tredici, P. & Li, J. 2003. Classification and Nomenclature of Weeping Katsuras. *The Plantsman* 2(1):21-27.

***Chaenomeles***

Weber, C. 1963. Cultivars in the Genus *Chaenomeles*. *Arnoldia (Jamaica Plain)* 23(3):17-75.

***Chrysanthemum***

Brummitt, D. 1997. *Chrysanthemum* Once Again. *The Garden* (RHS) 122(9):662-663.

Gosling, S.G. (ed.). 1964. *British National Register of Chrysanthemums.* Whetstone, London: National Chrysanthemum Society.

National Chrysanthemum Society. 2000. *British National Register of Names of Chrysanthemums Amalgamated Edition 1964-1999.* Tamworth, Staffordshire: The National Chrysanthemum Society.

National Chrysanthemum Society UK Cultivar Database. Jan 2010. www.nationalchrysanthemumsociety.org.uk

***Cistus***

Demoly, J.-P. 2005. The identity of *Cistus* 'Grayswood Pink' and related plants. *The Plantsman* 4(2):76-80.

Page, R.G. Feb 2007. Cistus and Halimium Website. www.cistuspage.org.uk

***Citrus***

Davies, F.S. & Albrigo, L.G. 1994. *Citrus.* Wallingford, Oxon: Cab International.

Page, M. 2008. *Growing Citrus.* London: Timber Press

Saunt, J. 1990. *Citrus Varieties of the World.* An Illustrated Guide. Norwich: Sinclair

***Clematis***

Clematis on the Web. Jan 2008. www.clematis.hull.ac.uk

Grey-Wilson, C. 2000. *Clematis: the Genus.* London: Batsford

HelpMeFind Clematis. Nov 2006. www.helpmefind.com/clematis

Johnson, M. 2001. *The Genus Clematis.* Södertälje, Sweden: Magnus Johnsons Plantskola AB & Bengt Sundström.

Matthews, V. (comp.). 2002. *The International Clematis Register and Checklist 2002.* London: RHS.

Supps 1 (2004), 2 (2006) & 3 (2009). www.rhs.org.uk/Plants/RHS-Publications/Plant-registers

Toomey, M. & Leeds, E. 2001. *An Illustrated Encyclopedia of Clematis.* Portland, Oregon: Timber Press.

**Conifers**

den Ouden, P. & Boom, B.K. 1965. *Manual of Cultivated Conifers.* The Hague: Martinus Nijhof.

Eckenwalder, J.E. 2009. *Conifers of the World.* China:Timber Press

Farjon, A. 1998. *World Checklist and Bibliography of Conifers.* Kew: Royal Botanic Gardens.

Krüssmann, G. & Epp, M.E. (trans.). 1985. *Manual of Cultivated Conifers.* London: Batsford.

Lewis, J. & Leslie, A.C. 1987. *The International Conifer Register. Pt 1. Abies* to *Austrotaxus.* London: RHS.

Lewis, J. & Leslie, A.C. 1989. *The International Conifer Register. Pt 2. Belis* to *Pherosphaera,* excluding the Cypresses. London: RHS.

Lewis, J. & Leslie, A.C. 1992. *The International Conifer Register. Pt 3. The Cypresses.* London: RHS.

Lewis, J. & Leslie, A.C. 1998. *The International Conifer Register. Pt 4. Juniperus.* London: RHS.

Welch, H.J. 1979. *Manual of Dwarf Conifers.* New York: Theophrastus.

Welch, H.J. 1991. *The Conifer Manual.* Vol. 1. Dordrecht, Netherlands: Kluwer Academic Publishers.

Welch, H.J. 1993. *The World Checklist of Conifers.* Bromyard, Herefordshire: Landsman's Bookshops Ltd.

***Cornus***

Cappiello, P. & Shadow, D. 2005. *Dogwoods.* Portland, Oregon: Timber Press.

Howard, R.A. 1961. Registration Lists of Cultivar Names in *Cornus L. Arnoldia (Jamaica Plain)* 21(2):9-18.

***Corydalis***

Lidén, M. & Zetterlund, H. 1997. *Corydalis. A Gardener's Guide and a Monograph of the Tuberous Species.* Pershore, Worcs.: Alpine Garden Society Publications Ltd.

***Corylus***

Crawford, M. 1995. *Hazelnuts: Production and Culture.* Dartington, Devon: Agroforestry Research Trust.

***Cotoneaster***

Fryer, J. & Hylmö, B. 1998. Seven New Species of *Cotoneaster* in Cultivation. *The New Plantsman* 5(3):132-144.

Fryer, J. & Hylmö, B. 2001. Captivating Cotoneasters. *The New Plantsman* 8(4):227-238.

Fryer, J. & Hylmö, B. 2009. *Cotoneasters. A Comprehensive Guide to Shrubs for Flowers, Fruit and Foliage.* Portland, Oregon: Timber Press.

***Crassulaceae***

Rowley, G. 2003. *Crassula: A Grower's Guide.* Venegono superiore, Italy: Cactus & Co.

Eggli, U. (ed.) 2003. *Illustrated Handbook of Succulent Plants.* Springer.

***Crocosmia***

Goldblatt, P., Manning, J.C. & Dunlop, G. 2004. *Crocosmia and Chasmanthe.* Portland, Oregon: Timber Press.

***Crocus***

Jacobsen, N., van Scheepen, J. & Ørgaard, M. 1997. The *Crocus chrysanthus – biflorus* Cultivars. *The New Plantsman* 4(1):6-38.

Mathew, B. 1982. *The Crocus. A Review of the Genus Crocus (Iridaceae).* London: Batsford.

Mathew, B. 2002. *Crocus* Up-date. *The Plantsman* 1(1):44-56.

***Cyclamen***

Clennett, C. Jan 2010. Register of Cultivar Names. www.cyclamen.org

Grey-Wilson, C. 2003. *Cyclamen. A Guide for Gardeners, Horticulturists & Botanists.* London: Batsford.

Grey-Wilson, C. 2002 Sprenger's Alpine Cyclamen. *The Plantsman* 1(3):173-177.

***Cypripedium***

Cribb, P. 1997. *The Genus Cypripedium.* Portland, Oregon: Timber Press.

***Dahlia***

American Dahlia Society website. Jan 2010. www.dahlia.org

Bates, D. Dahlia Plant Finder 2007. Jan 2010. www.dahliaworld.co.uk

National Dahlia Society. 2005. *Classified Directory and Judging Rules.* (28th ed.) Aldershot, Hants: National Dahlia Society.

RHS & Hedge, R. (comps). 1969. *Tentative Classified List and International Register of Dahlia Names 1969.* (& Supps 1-13). London: RHS. Supps 13-20. 2002-09. http://www.rhs.org.uk/learning Winchester Growers Ltd English National Dahlia Collection website. Jan 2010. www.national-dahlia-collection.co.uk

***Daphne***

Brickell, C.D. & Mathew, B. 1976. *Daphne. The Genus in the Wild and in Cultivation.* Woking, Surrey: Alpine Garden Society.

Grey-Wilson, C. (ed.). 2001. *The Smaller Daphnes. The Proceedings of 'Daphne 2000', a Conference held at the Royal Horticultural Society.* Pershore, Worcs.: Alpine Garden Society.

White, R. 2006. *Daphnes: A Practical Guide for Gardeners.* Portland, Oregon: Timber Press.

***Delphinium***

1949. *A Tentative Check-list of Delphinium Names.* London: RHS.

1970. *A Tentative Check-list of Delphinium Names.* Addendum to the 1949 tentative check-list of *Delphinium* names. London: RHS.

Bassett, D. & Wesley, W. 2004. *Delphinium: RHS Bulletin No 5.* Wisley, Surrey: RHS. www.rhs.org.uk/plants/documents/delph04.pdf

Leslie, A.C. 1996. *The International Delphinium Register Cumulative Supp. 1970-1995.* London: RHS.

Leslie, A.C. 1996-2005. The International Delphinium Register Supp. 1994-99. *The Delphinium Society Year Book 1996-2005.* London: RHS.

***Dianthus***

Galbally, J. & Galbally, E. 1997. *Carnations and Pinks for Garden and Greenhouse.* Portland, Oregon: Timber Press.

Leslie, A.C. *The International Dianthus Register.* 1983-2002. (2nd ed. & Supps 1-19). London: RHS.

Supps 19-25. 2002-08. http://www.rhs.org.uk/Plants/RHS-Publications/Plant-registers

***Dierama***

Hilliard, O.M. & Burtt, B.L. 1991. *Dierama. The Harebells of Africa.* Johannesburg; London: Acorn Books.

***Dionysia***

Grey-Wilson, C. 1989. *The Genus Dionysia.* Woking, Surrey: Alpine Garden Society.

***Douglasia***

Mitchell, B. 1999. Celebrating the Bicentenary of David Douglas: a Review of *Douglasia* in Cultivation. *The New Plantsman* 6(2):101-108.

***Dracaena***

Bos, J.J., Graven, P., Hetterscheid, W.L.A. & van de Wege, J.J. 1992. Wild and cultivated *Dracaena fragrans. Edinburgh J. Bot.* 49(3):311-331.

***Echeveria***

Schulz, L. & Kapitany, A. *Echeveria Cultivars.* Teesdale, Australia: Schulz Publishing.

***Episcia***

Dates, J.D. 1993. *The Gesneriad Register 1993.* Check List of Names with Descriptions of Cultivated Plants in the Genera *Episcia* & *Alsobia.* Galesburg, Illinois: American Gloxinia & Gesneriad Society, Inc.

***Erica*** (see also Heathers)

Baker, H.A. & Oliver, E.G.H. 1967. *Heathers in Southern Africa.* Cape Town: Purnell.

Schumann, D., Kirsten, G. & Oliver, E.G.H. 1992. *Ericas of South Africa.* Vlaeberg, South Africa: Fernwood Press.

***Erodium***

Clifton, R. 1994. *Geranium Family Species Checklist. Pt 1 Erodium.* (4th ed.). The Geraniaceae Group.

Leslie, A.C. 1980. The Hybrid of *Erodium corsicum* with *Erodium reichardii. The Plantsman* 2:117-126.

Toomey, N., Cubey, J. & Culham, A. 2002. *Erodium × variabile. The Plantsman* 1(3): 166-172

Victor, D.X. (comp.). 2000. *Erodium: Register of Cultivar Names.* The Geraniaceae Group.

***Erythronium***

Mathew, B. 1992. A Taxonomic and Horticultural Review of *Erythronium* L. (*Liliaceae*). *J. Linn. Soc., Bot.* 109:453-471.

Mathew, B. 1998. The Genus *Erythronium. Bull. Alpine Gard. Soc. Gr. Brit.* 66(3):308-321.

***Eupatorium*** sensu lato

Hind, D.J.N. 2006. Splitting *Eupatorium. The Plantsman* (n.s.) 5(2):185-189.

***Euonymus***

Brown, N. 1996. Notes on Cultivated Species of *Euonymus. The New Plantsman* 3(4):238-243.

Lancaster, C.R. 1981. An Account of *Euonymus* in Cultivation and its Availability in Commerce. *The Plantsman* 3(3):133-166.

Lancaster, C.R. 1982. *Euonymus* in Cultivation – Addendum. *The Plantsman* 4:61-64, 253-254.

***Euphorbia***

Govaerts, R., Frodin, D.G. & Radcliffe-Smith, A. 2000. *World Checklist and Bibliography of Euphorbiaceae.* Kew: Royal Botanic Gardens.

Turner, R. 1995. *Euphorbias. A Gardeners Guide.* London: Batsford.

Witton, D. 2000. *Euphorbias.* Pershore, Worcs.: Hardy Plant Society.

***Fagales***

Gocaerts, R. & Frodin, D.G. 1998. *World Checklist and Bibliography of Fagales.* RBG Kew.

***Fagus***

Dönig, G. 1994. *Die Park-und Gartenformen der Rotbuche Fagus sylvatica L.* Erlangen, Germany: Verlag Gartenbild Heinz Hansmann.

Wyman, D. 1964. Registration List of Cultivar Names of *Fagus* L. *J. Arnold Arbor.* 24(1):1-8.

***Fascicularia***

Nelson, E.C. & Zizka, G. 1997. *Fascicularia* (*Bromeliaceae*): Which Species are Cultivated and Naturalized in Northwestern Europe. *The New Plantsman* 4(4):232-239.

Nelson, E.C., Zizka, G., Horres, R. & Weising, K. 1999. Revision of the Genus *Fascicularia* Mez (*Bromeliaceae*). *Botanical Journal of the Linnean Society* 129(4):315-332.

**Ferns**

Checklist of World Ferns. Jan 2010. http://homepages.caverock.net.nz/nbj/fern

Johns, R.J. 1996. *Index Filicum.* Supplementum Sextum pro annis 1976-1990. Kew:Royal Botanic Gardens.

Johns, R.J. 1997. *Index Filicum.* Supplementum Septimum pro annis 1991-1995. Kew:Royal Botanic Gardens.

Jones, D.L. 1987. *Encyclopaedia of Ferns.* Melbourne, Australia: Lothian.

Kaye, R. 1968. *Hardy Ferns.* London: Faber & Faber

Rickard, M.H. 2000. *The Plantfinder's Guide to Garden Ferns.* Newton Abbot, Devon: David & Charles.

Rush, R. 1984. *A Guide to Hardy Ferns.* London: British Pteridological Society.

***Forsythia***

INRA Forsythia website. Jan 2010. www.angers.inra.fr/forsy

***Fritillaria***

Clark, T. & Grey-Wilson, C. 2003. Crown Imperials. *The Plantsman* 2(1):33-47.

Mathew, B., et al. 2000. *Fritillaria* Issue. *Bot. Mag.* 17(3):145-185.

Pratt, K. & Jefferson-Brown, M. 1997. *The Gardener's Guide to Growing Fritillaries.* Newton Abbot: David & Charles.

Turrill, W.B. & Sealy, J.R. 1980. *Studies in the Genus Fritillaria (Liliaceae).* Hooker's Icones Plantarum Vol. 39 (1 & 2). Kew: Royal Botanic Gardens.

**Fruit**

Brogdale Horticultural Trust National Fruit Collection. Jan 2010. www.nationalfruitcollection.org.uk

Bowling, B.L. 2000. *The Berry Grower's Companion.* Portland, Oregon: Timber Press.

Hogg, R. 1884. *The Fruit Manual.* (5th ed.). London: Journal of Horticulture Office.

***Fuchsia***

American Fuchsia Society Registration Database. Jan 2010. www.americanfuchsiasociety.org

Bartlett, G. 1996. *Fuchsias – A Colour Guide.* Marlborough, Wilts: Crowood Press.

Boullemier, Leo.B. (comp.). 1991. *The Checklist of Species, Hybrids and Cultivars of the Genus Fuchsia.* London, New York, Sydney: Blandford Press.

Boullemier, Leo.B. (comp.). 1995. *Addendum No 1 to the 1991 Checklist of Species, Hybrids and Cultivars of the Genus Fuchsia.* Dyfed, Wales: The British Fuchsia Society.

Goulding, E. 1995. *Fuchsias: The Complete Guide.* London: Batsford.

Johns, E.A. 1997. *Fuchsias of the 19th and Early 20th Century.* An Historical Checklist of Fuchsia Species & Cultivars, pre-1939. Kidderminster, Worcs.: British Fuchsia Society

Jones, L. & Miller, D.M. 2005. *Hardy Fuchsias: RHS Bulletin No 12.* Wisley, Surrey: RHS. www.rhs.org.uk/Plants/RHS-Publications/Plant_bulletins

Stevens, R. Jan 2010. Find That Fuchsia. www.findthatfuchsia.info

***Galanthus***

Bishop, M., Davis, A. & Grimshaw, J. 2001. *Snowdrops. A monograph of cultivated Galanthus.* Maidenhead: Griffin Press.

Davis, A.P., Mathew, B. (ed.) & King, C. (ill.). 1999. *The Genus Galanthus. A Botanical Magazine Monograph.* Oregon: Timber Press.

***Gentiana***

Bartlett, M. 1975. *Gentians.* Dorset: Blandford Press.

Halda, J.J. 1996. *The Genus Gentiana.* Dobré, Czech Republic: Sen.

Ho T.N. & Liu S. 2001. *Worldwide Monograph of Gentiana.* Beijing: Science Press.

***Geranium***

Armitage, J. 2005. *Hardy Geraniums – Stage 1: RHS Bulletin No 10.* Wisley, Surrey: RHS. www.rhs.org.uk/Plants/RHS-Publications/Plant_bulletins

Armitage, J. 2006. *Hardy Geraniums – Stage 2: RHS Bulletin No 14.* Wisley, Surrey: RHS. www.rhs.org.uk/Plants/RHS-Publications/Plant_bulletins

Armitage, J. 2007. *Hardy Geraniums – Stage 3: RHS Bulletin No 18.* Wisley, Surrey: RHS.

www.rhs.org.uk/Plants/RHS-Publications/Plant_bulletins

Bath, T. & Jones, J. 1994. *The Gardener's Guide to Growing Hardy Geraniums.* Newton Abbot, Devon: David & Charles.

Bendtsen, B.H. 2005. *Gardening with Hardy Geraniums.* Portland, Oregon: Timber Press.

Clifton, R.T.F. 1995. *Geranium Family Species Check List Pt 2.* Geranium. (4th ed. issue 2). Dover: The Geraniaceae Group.

Jones, J., et al. 2001. *Hardy Geraniums for the Garden.* (3rd ed.). Pershore, Worcs.: Hardy Plant Society.

Victor, D.X. 2004. *Register of Geranium Cultivar Names.* (2nd ed.). The Geraniaceae Group.

Yeo, P.F. 2002. *Hardy Geraniums.* (3rd ed.). Kent: Croom Helm.

***Gesneriaceae***

The Gesneriad Society. Listing of registered gesneriads. Jan 2010. www.aggs.gesneriadsociety.org

Dates, J.D. 1986-1990. *The Gesneriad Register 1986-1987 & 1990.* Galesburg, Illinois: American Gloxinia & Gesneriad Society, Inc.

***Gladiolus***

British Gladiolus Society List of Cultivars Classified for Show Purposes 1994. Mayfield, Derbyshire: British Gladiolus Society.

1997-1998. British Gladiolus Society List of European, New Zealand & North American Cultivars Classified for Exhibition Purposes 1997 & 1998. Mayfield, Derbyshire: British Gladiolus Society.

Goldblatt, P. & Manning, J. 1998. *Gladiolus in Southern Africa.* Vlaeberg, South Africa: Fernwood Press.

Goldblatt, P. 1996. *Gladiolus in Tropical Africa.* Systematics Biology and Evolution. Oregon: Timber Press.

Lewis, G.J., Obermeyer, A.A. & Barnard, T.T. 1972. A Revision of the South African Species of *Gladiolus. J. S. African Bot.* (Supp. Vol. 10)

***Gleditsia***

Santamour, F.S. & McArdle, A.J. 1983. Checklist of Cultivars of Honeylocust (*Gleditsia triacanthos* L.). *J. Arboric.* 9:271-276.

***Grevillea***

Olde, P. & Marriott, N. 1995. *The Grevillea Book.* (3). Kenthurst, NSW: Kangaroo Press.

***Haemanthus***

Snijman, D. 1984. A Revision of the Genus *Haemanthus. J. S. African Bot.* (Supp. Vol. 12).

***Hamamelis***

Lane, C. 2005. *Witch Hazels.* Portland, Oregon: Timber Press.

**Heathers**

Nelson, E.C. Aug 2007. International Cultivar Registration Authority for Heathers. www.heathersociety.org.uk

***Hebe***

Chalk, D. 1988. *Hebes and Parahebes.* Bromley, Kent: Christopher Helm (Publishers) Ltd.

Hutchins, G. 1997. *Hebes: Here and There.* A Monograph on the Genus *Hebe.* Caversham, Berks: Hutchins & Davies.

Metcalf, L.J. 2001. *International Register of Hebe Cultivars.* Canterbury, New Zealand: Royal New Zealand Institute of Horticulture (Inc.).

Metcalf, L.J. 2006. *Hebes: A Guide to Species, Hybrids and Allied Genera.* Portland, Oregon: Timber Press.

***Hedera***

Jury, S. et al. 2006. *Hedera algeriensis*, a Fine Species of Ivy. *Sibbaldia* 4: 93-108.

McAllister, H. 1988. Canary and Algerian Ivies. *The Plantsman* 10(1):27-29.

McAllister, H.A. & Rutherford, A. 1990. *Hedera helix and H. hibernica* in the British Isles. *Watsonia* 18:7-15.

Rose, P.Q. 1996. *The Gardener's Guide to Growing Ivies.* Newton Abbot, Devon: David & Charles.

Rutherford, A., McAllister, H. & Mill, R.R. 1993. New Ivies from the Mediterranean Area and Macaronesia. *The Plantsman* 15(2):115-128.

***Heliconia***

Berry, F. & Kress, W.J. 1991. *Heliconia.* An Identification Guide. Washington: Smithsonian Institution Press.

***Helleborus***

Burrell, C.C. & Tyler, J.K. 2006. *Hellebores: A Comprehensive Guide.* Portland, Oregon: Timber Press.

Mathew, B. 1989. *Hellebores.* Woking: Alpine Garden Society.

Rice, G. & Strangman, E. 1993. *The Gardener's Guide to Growing Hellebores.* Newton Abbot, Devon: David & Charles.

***Hemerocallis***

Baxter, G.J. (comp.). American Daylily Society Registry of Daylily Cultivars. Jan 2010. www.daylilies.org

**Herbs**

Phillips, R. & Foy, N. 1990. *Herbs.* London: Pan Books Ltd.

***Heuchera and × Heucherella***

Heims, D. & Ware, G. 2005. *Heucheras and Heucherellas: Coral Bells and Foamy Bells.* Portland, Oregon: Timber Press.

***Hibiscus***

Noble, C. Apr 2007. Australian Hibiscus Society Database Register. www.australianhibiscus.com/

***Hosta***

Hosta Library. Aug 2006. www.hostalibrary.org

Grenfell, D. & Shadrack, M. 2004. *The Color Encyclopedia of Hostas.* Portland, Oregon: Timber Press.

Schmid, W.G. 1991. *The Genus Hosta.* London: Batsford.

***Hyacinthaceae***

Dashwood, M. & Mathew, B. 2006. *Hyacinthaceae – little blue bulbs: RHS Bulletin No 11.* Wisley, Surrey: RHS. www.rhs.org.uk/Plants/RHS-Publications/Plant_bulletins

Mathew, B. 2005. *Hardy Hyacinthaceae* Pt 1: *Muscari. The Plantsman* 4(1):40-53.

Mathew, B. 2005. *Hardy Hyacinthaceae* Pt 2: *Scilla, Chionodoxa* and × *Chinoscilla. The Plantsman* 4(2):110-121.

***Hydrangea***

Dirr, M.A. 2004. *Hydrangeas for American Gardens.* Portland, Oregon: Timber Press.

Haworth-Booth, M. 1975. *The Hydrangeas.* London: Garden Book Club.
Van Gelderen, C.J. & Van Gelderen, D.M. 2004. *Encyclopedia of Hydrangeas.* Portland, Oregon: Timber Press.
***Hypericum***
Lancaster, R. & Robson, N. 1997. Focus on Plants: Bowls of Beauty. *The Garden* (RHS) 122(8):566-571.
***Ilex***
Bailes, C. 2006. *Hollies for Gardeners.* Portland, Oregon: Timber Press.
Dudley, T.R. & Eisenbeiss, G.K. 1973 & 1992. *International Checklist of Cultivated Ilex.* Pt 1 *Ilex opaca* (1973), Pt 2 *Ilex crenata* (1992). Washington DC: United States Dept of Agriculture.
Galle, F.C. 1997. *Hollies: the Genus Ilex.* Portland, Oregon: Timber Press.
***Impatiens***
Morgan, R.J. 2007. *Impatiens: The Vibrant World of Busy Lizzies, Balsams and Touch-me-nots.* Portland, Oregon: Timber Press.
***Iris***
Austin, C. 2005. *Irises: A Gardener's Encyclopedia.* Oregon:Timber Press.
Hoog, M.H. 1980. Bulbous Irises . *The Plantsman* 2(3):141-64.
Keppel, K. (ed.) 2001. *Iris Check List of Registered Cultivar Names 1990-1999.* Hannibal, New York: the American Iris Society.
Mathew, B. 1981. *The Iris.* London: Batsford.
Mathew, B. 1993. The Spuria Irises. *The Plantsman* 15(1):14-25.
Service, N. 1990. *Iris unguicularis. The Plantsman* 12(1):1-9.
Stebbings, G. 1997. *The Gardener's Guide to Growing Iris.* Newton Abbot: David & Charles.
The Species Group of the British Iris Society, (ed.). 1997. *A Guide to Species Irises.* Their Identification and Cultivation. Cambridge: Cambridge University Press.
***Jovibarba*** see under ***Sempervivum***
***Kalmia***
Jaynes, R.A. 1997. *Kalmia. Mountain Laurel and Related Species.* Portland, Oregon: Timber Press.
***Kniphofia***
Grant-Downton, R. 1997. Notes on *Kniphofia thomsonii* in Cultivation and in the Wild. *The New Plantsman* 4(3):148-156.
Taylor, J. 1985. *Kniphofia* – a Survey. *The Plantsman* 7(3):129-160.
***Kohleria***
Dates, J.D. (ed.) & Batcheller, F.N. (comp.). 1985. *The Gesneriad Register 1985. Check List of Names with Descriptions of Cultivated Plants in the Genus Kohleria.* Lincoln Acres, California: American Gloxinia and Gesneriad Society, Inc.
***Lachenalia***
Duncan, G.D. 1988. *The Lachenalia Hand Book.* Kirstenbosch, South Africa: National Botanic Gardens.
***Lantana***
Howard, R.A. 1969. A Check List of Names Used in the Genus *Lantana. Arnoldia.* 29(11):73-109.
***Lathyrus***
Norton, S. 1996. *Lathyrus. Cousins of Sweet Pea.* Surrey: NCCPG.
***Lavandula***
Upson, T. & Andrews, S. 2004. *The Genus Lavandula.* Kew: Royal Botanic Garden.
**Legumes**
ILDIS. International Legume Database and Information Service. Jan 2010. Version 10.01. www.ildis.org/LegumeWeb
***Leptospermum***
Check List of *Leptospermum* Cultivars. 1963. *J. Roy. New Zealand Inst. Hort.* 5(5):224-30.
Dawson, M. 1997. A History of *Leptospermum scoparium* in Cultivation – Discoveries from the Wild. *The New Plantsman* 4(1):51-59.
Dawson, M. 1997. A History of *Leptospermum scoparium* in Cultivation – Garden Selections. *The New Plantsman* 4(2):67-78.
***Lewisia***
Davidson, B.L.R. 2000. *Lewisias.* Portland, Oregon: Timber Press.
Elliott, R. 1978. *Lewisias.* Woking: Alpine Garden Society.
Mathew, B. 1989. *The Genus Lewisia.* Bromley, Kent: Christopher Helm.
***Liliaceae*** sensu lato
Mathew, B. 1989. Splitting the *Liliaceae. The Plantsman* 11(2):89-105.
***Lilium***
Leslie, A.C. *The International Lily Register 1982-2002.* (4th ed. & 1st supp.). London: RHS.
1st supp. 2008. www.rhs.org.uk/Plants/RHS-Publications/Plant_bulletins
Online Lily Register. Jan 2010. www.lilyregister.com
***Lonicera***
Blahník, Z. 2006. *Lonicera* Cultivar Names: The First World List. *Acta Pruhoniciana* 81:59-64.
***Magnolia***
Callaway, D.J. Sep 2001. Magnolia Cultivar Checklist. www.magnoliasociety.org
Frodin, D.G. & Govaerts, R. 1996. *World Checklist and Bibliography of Magnoliaceae.* Kew: Royal Botanic Garden.
***Maianthemum***
Cubey, J.J. 2005 *The Incorporation of Smilacina within Maianthemum. The Plantsman* N.S.4(4).
***Malus***
Crawford, M. 1994. *Directory of Apple Cultivars.* Devon: Agroforestry Research Trust.
Fiala, J.L. 1994. *Flowering Crabapples.* The genus *Malus.* Portland, Oregon: Timber Press.

Rouèche, A. Oct 2007. Les Crets Fruits et Pomologie. www.pomologie.com

Smith, M.W.G. 1971. *National Apple Register of the United Kingdom*. London: MAFF

Spiers, V. 1996. *Burcombes, Queenies and Colloggetts.* St Dominic, Cornwall: West Brendon.

***Meconopsis***

Grey-Wilson, C. 1992. A Survey of the Genus *Meconopsis* in Cultivation. *The Plantsman* 14(1): 1-33.

Grey-Wilson, C. 2002. The True Identity of *Meconopsis napaulensis. Bot. Mag.* 23(2):176-209.

Meconopsis Group website. Jan 2010. www.meconopsis.org

Stevens, E. & Brickell, C. 2001. Problems with the Big Perennial Poppies. *The New Plantsman* 8(1):48-61.

Stevens, E. 2001. Further Observations on the Big Perennial Blue Poppies. *The New Plantsman* 8(2):105-111.

***Miscanthus***

Jones, L. 2004. Miscanthus: RHS Bulletin No 7. Wisley, Surrey: RHS. www.rhs.org.uk/Plants/RHS-Publications/Plant_bulletins

***Moraea***

Goldblatt, P. 1986. *The Moraeas of Southern Africa.* Kirstenbosch, South Africa: National Botanic Gardens.

***Musa***

Banana and Plantain Section of Biodiversity International 2001. http://bananas.bioversityinternational.org

INIBAP *Musa* Germplasm Information System. Jan 2010. www.crop-diversity.org/banana

***Narcissus***

Blanchard, J.W. 1990. *Narcissus – A Guide to Wild Daffodils.* Woking, Surrey: Alpine Garden Society.

Kington, S. (comp.). 2008. The International Daffodil Register and Classified List 2008 (4th ed. & Supps 1-2, 2007-2009). London: RHS. http://apps.rhs.org.uk/horticulturaldatabase/daffodilregister.asp

***Nematanthus***

Arnold, P. 1978. *The Gesneriad Register 1978.* Check List of *Nematanthus.* American Gloxinia and Gesneriad Society, Inc.

***Nerium***

Pagen, F.J.J. 1987. *Oleanders. Nerium L. and the Oleander Cultivars.* Wageningen, The Netherlands: Agricultural University Wageningen.

***Nymphaea***

Knotts, K. & Knotts, B. Victoria Adventure Website. Checklist of Waterlily Cultivars. Jan 2010. www.victoria-adventure.org

***Orchidaceae***

Shaw, J.M.H. Jan 2010. The International Orchid Register. http://apps.rhs.org.uk/horticulturaldatabase/orchidregister.asp

***Origanum***

Paton, A. 1994. Three Membranous-bracted Species of *Origanum. Kew Mag.* 11(3):109-117.

White, S. 1998. *Origanum. The Herb Marjoram and its Relatives.* Surrey: NCCPG.

***Paeonia***

HelpMeFind Peonies. Jan 2010. www.helpmefind.com/peony/index.php

Jakubowski, R. American Peony Society Peony Checklist. www.americanpeonysociety.org

Jakubowski, R. 2008. *Peonies 1997-2007. Registered Peony Cultivars, with a Checklist of Peony Names, References and Originators.* Missouri: American Peony Society.

Osti, G.L. 1999. *The Book of Tree Peonies.* Turin: Umberto Allemandi.

Wang, L., et al. 1998. *Chinese Tree Peony.* Beijing: China Forestry Publishing House.

***Papaver***

Grey-Wilson, C. 1998. Oriental Glories. *The Garden* (RHS) 123(5):320-325.

***Papaveraceae***

Grey-Wilson, C. 2000. *Poppies. The Poppy Family in the Wild and in Cultivation.* London: Batsford.

Tebbitt, M. Liden, M. Zetterlund, H. 2008. *Bleeding Hearts, Corydalis and their Relatives.* Portland, Oregon: Timber Press

***Passiflora***

King, L.A. Jan 2008. Passiflora online passion flower cultivar register. www.passionflow.co.uk

***Pelargonium***

Abbott, P.G. 1994. *A Guide to Scented Geraniaceae.* Angmering, West Sussex: Hill Publicity Services.

Anon. 1978. *A Checklist and Register of Pelargonium Cultivar Names.* Pt 1 A-B. Australian Pelargonium Society.

Anon. 1985. *A Checklist and Register of Pelargonium Cultivar Names.* Pt 2: C-F. Australian Pelargonium Society.

Bagust, H. 1988. *Miniature and Dwarf Geraniums.* London: Christopher Helm.

Clifford, D. 1958. *Pelargoniums.* London: Blandford Press.

Clifton, R. 1999. *Geranium Family Species Checklist, Pt 4: Pelargonium.* The Geraniaceae Group.

Complete Copy of the Spalding Pelargonium Checklist. (Unpublished). USA.

Key, H. 2000. *1001 Pelargoniums.* London: Batsford.

Miller, D. 1996. *Pelargonium.* A Gardener's Guide to the Species and Cultivars and Hybrids. London: Batsford.

Pelargonium Palette: The Geranium and Pelargonium Society of Sydney Incorporated. Varieties – Alphabetical List. Jan 2010. www.elj.com/geranium

Van der Walt, J.J.A., et al. 1977. *Pelargoniums of South Africa.* (1-3). Kirstenbosch, South Africa: National Botanic Gardens.

***Penstemon***
Lindgren, D.T. & Davenport, B. 1992. List and description of named cultivars in the genus *Penstemon* (1992). University of Nebraska.
Nold, R. 1999. *Penstemons*. Portland, Oregon: Timber Press.
Way, D. & James, P. 1998. *The Gardener's Guide to Growing Penstemons.* Newton Abbott, Devon: David & Charles.
Way, D. 2006. *Penstemons.* Pershore, Worcs.: Hardy Plant Society.
***Phlomis***
Mann Taylor, J. 1998. *Phlomis: The Neglected Genus.* Wisley: NCCPG.
***Phlox***
Harmer, J. & Elliott, J. 2001. *Phlox.* Pershore, Worcs.: Hardy Plant Society.
Stebbings, G. 1999. Simply Charming. *The Garden* (RHS) 124(7):518-521.
Wherry, E.T. 1955. *The Genus Phlox.* Philadelphia, Pennsylvania: Morris Arboretum.
***Phormium***
Heenan, P.B. 1991. *Checklist of Phormium Cultivars.* Royal New Zealand Institute of Horticulture.
McBride-Whitehead, V. 1998. Phormiums of the Future. *The Garden* (RHS) 123(1):42-45.
***Pieris***
Bond, J. 1982. *Pieris* – a Survey. *The Plantsman* 4(2):65-75.
Wagenknecht, B.L. 1961. Registration Lists of Cultivar Names in the Genus *Pieris* D. Don. *Arnoldia (Jamaica Plain)* 21(8):47-50.
***Pittosporum***
Miller, D.M. 2006. RHS Plant Assessments: *Pittosporum tenuifolium* hybrids & cultivars. www.rhs.org.uk/Plants/RHS-Publications/Plant-bulletins
***Plectranthus***
Addink, Wouter. Jan 2010. Coleus Finder. http://coleusfinder.org
Miller, D. & Morgan, N. 2000. Focus on Plants: A New Leaf. *The Garden* (RHS) 125(11):842-845.
Shaw, J.M.H. 1999. Notes on the Identity of Swedish Ivy and Other Cultivated *Plectranthus. The New Plantsman* 6(2):71-74.
Van Jaarsveld, E.J. 2006. *South African Plectranthus.* Vlaeberg, South Africa: Fernwood Press.
***Pleione***
Cribb, P. & Butterfield, I. 1999. *The Genus Pleione.* (2nd ed.). Kew: Royal Botanic Gardens.
Shaw, J.M.H. (comp.). Oct 2002. Provisional List of *Pleione* Cultivars. RHS.
***Poaceae* (*Gramineae*, grasses)**
Clayton, W.D., Harman, K.T. & Williamson, H. Jan 2010. GrassBase – The Online World Grass Flora. www.kew.org/data/grasses-syn
Clayton, W.D. & Renvoize, S.A. 1986. *Genera Graminum.* Grasses of the World. London: HMSO.
Darke, R. 2007. *Encyclopedia of Grasses for Livable Landscapes.* Portland, Oregon: Timber Press.
Govaerts, R. & Simpson, D.A. 2007 *World Checklist of Cyperaceae: Sedges.* Richmond, Surrey: RBG Kew
Grounds, R. 1998. *The Plantfinder's Guide to Ornamental Grasses.* Newton Abott, Devon: David & Charles.
Wood, T. 2002. *Garden Grasses, Rushes and Sedges.* (3rd ed.). Abingdon, Oxon: John Wood.
***Polemonium***
Nichol-Brown, D. 2000. *Polemonium.* Wisley: NCCPG.
***Potentilla***
Davidson, C.G., Enns, R.J. & Gobin, S. 1994. *A Checklist of Potentilla fruticosa: the Shrubby Potentillas.* Morden, Manitoba: Agriculture & Agri-Food Canada Research Centre. Data also on Plant Finder Reference Library professional version CD-ROM 1999/2000.
Miller, D.M. 2002. *Shrubby Potentilla: RHS Bulletin No 1.* Wisley, Surrey: RHS. www.rhs.org.uk/Plants/RHS-Publications/Plant-bulletins
***Primula***
Richards, J. 2002 (2nd ed.). *Primula.* London: Batsford.
***Primula allionii***
Archdale, B. & Richards, D. 1997. *Primula allionii Forms and Hybrids.* National Auricula & Primula Society, Midland & West Section.
***Primula auricula*** hort.
Baker, G. *Double Auriculas.* National Auricula & Primula Society, Midland & West Section.
Baker, G. & Ward, P. 1995. *Auriculas.* London: Batsford.
Gust, A. 2009. *The Auricula History, Cultivation and Varieties.* China: Garden Art Press
Hawkes, A. 1995. Striped Auriculas. National Auricula & Primula Society, Midland & West Section.
Nicholle, G. 1996. *Border Auriculas.* National Auricula & Primula Society, Midland & West Section.
Robinson, M.A. 2000. *Auriculas for Everyone.* How to Grow and Show Perfect Plants. Lewes, Sussex: Guild of Master Craftsmen Publications.
Telford, D. 1993. *Alpine Auriculas.* National Auricula & Primula Society, Midland & West Section.
Ward, P. 1991. *Show Auriculas.* National Auricula & Primula Society, Midland & West Section.
***Proteaceae***
International *Proteaceae* Register. July 2002. (7th ed.).
Rebelo, T. 1995. *Proteas.* A Field Guide to the Proteas of Southern Africa. Vlaeberg: Fernwood Press/National Botanical Institute.
***Prunus***
Crawford, M. 1996. *Plums.* Dartington, Devon: Agroforestry Research Trust.
Crawford, M. 1997. *Cherries: Production and Culture.* Dartington, Devon: Agroforestry Research Trust.

Jacobsen, A.L. 1992. *Purpleleaf Plums.* Portland, Oregon: Timber Press.

Jefferson, R.M. & Wain, K.K. 1984. *The Nomenclature of Cultivated Flowering Cherries (Prunus).* The Sato-Zakura Group. Washington DC: USDA.

Kuitert, W. 1999. *Japanese Flowering Cherries.* Portland, Oregon: Timber Press.

***Pulmonaria***

Bennett, M. 2003. *Pulmonarias and the borage family.* London: B.T. Batsford.

Hewitt, J. 1994. *Pulmonarias.* Pershore, Worcs.: Hardy Plant Society.

Hewitt, J. 1999. Well Spotted. *The Garden* (RHS) 124(2):98-103.

***Pyracantha***

Egolf, D.R. & Andrick, A.O. 1995. *A Checklist of Pyracantha Cultivars.* Washington DC: Agricultural Research Service.

***Pyrus***

Crawford, M. 1996. *Directory of Pear Cultivars.* Totnes, Devon: Agroforestry Research Institute.

Smith, M.W.G. 1976. *Catalogue of the British Pear.* Faversham, Kent: MAFF.

***Quercus***

Miller, H.A. & Lamb, S.H. 1985. *Oaks of North America.* Happy Camp, California: Naturegraph Publishers.

Mitchell, A. 1994. The Lucombe Oaks. *The Plantsman* 15(4):216-224.

***Rhododendron***

Argent, G., Fairweather, C. & Walter, K. 1996. *Accepted Names in Rhododendron section Vireya.* Edinburgh: Royal Botanic Garden.

Argent, G., Bond, J., Chamberlain, D., Cox, P. & Hardy, A. 1997. *The Rhododendron Handbook 1998.* Rhododendron Species in Cultivation. London: RHS.

Chamberlain, D.F. & Rae, S.J. 1990. A Revision of *Rhododendron* IV. Subgenus *Tsutsusi. Edinburgh J. Bot.* 47(2).

Chamberlain, D.F. 1982. A Revision of *Rhododendron* II. Subgenus *Hymenanthes. Notes Roy. Bot. Gard. Edinburgh* 39(2).

Chamberlain, D., Hyam, R., Argent, G., Fairweather, G. & Walter, K.S. 1996. *The Genus Rhododendron.* Edinburgh:Royal Botanic Garden.

Cullen, J. 1980. A Revision of *Rhododendron* I. Subgenus *Rhododendron* sections *Rhododendron* and *Pogonanthum. Notes Roy. Bot. Gard. Edinburgh* 39(1).

Davidian, H.H. 1982-1992 *The Rhododendron Species* (Vols 1-4). London: Batsford.

Galle, F.C. 1985. *Azaleas.* Portland, Oregon: Timber Press.

Leslie, A. C. (comp.). 1980. *The Rhododendron Handbook 1980.* London: RHS.

Leslie, A.C. (comp.) 2004. *The International Rhododendron Register and Checklist* (2nd ed. & supps. 1-5). London: RHS Supp. 1-5, 2006-2008. www.rhs.org.uk/Plants/RHS-Publications/Plant-registers

Tamura, T. (ed.). 1989. *Azaleas in Kurume.* Kurume, Japan: International Azalea Festival '89.

***Ribes***

Crawford, M. 1997. *Currants and Gooseberries: Production and Culture.* Dartington, Devon: Agroforestry Research Trust.

***Rosa***

Beales, P., Cairns, T., et al. 1998. *Botanica's Rose: The Encyclopedia of Roses.* Hoo, Kent: Grange Books.

Cairns, T. (ed.). 2000. *Modern Roses XI. The World Encyclopedia of Roses.* London: Academic Press.

Dickerson, B.C. 1999. *The Old Rose Advisor.* Portland, Oregon: Timber Press.

Haw, S.G. 1996. Notes on Some Chinese and Himalayan Rose Species of Section *Pimpinellifoliae. The New Plantsman* 3(3):143-146.

HelpMeFind Roses. Jan 2010. www.helpmefind.com

McCann, S. 1985. *Miniature Roses.* Newton Abbot, Devon: David & Charles.

Quest-Ritson, C. 2003. *Climbing Roses of the World.* Portland, Oregon: Timber Press.

Quest-Ritson, C. & Quest-Ritson, B. 2003. *The Royal Horticultural Society Encyclopedia of Roses: The Definitive A-Z Guide.* London: Dorling Kindersley.

Thomas, G.S. 1995. *The Graham Stuart Thomas Rose Book.* London: John Murray.

Verrier, S. 1996. *Rosa Gallica.* Balmain, Australia: Florilegium.

***Roscoea***

Cowley, J. 2007. *The Genus Roscoea.* Kew Publishing.

***Rosularia***

Eggli, U. 1988. A Monographic Study of the Genus *Rosularia. Bradleya* (Supp.) 6:1-118.

***Saintpaulia***

Goodship, G. 1987. *Saintpaulia Variety List* (Supp.). Slough, Bucks: Saintpaulia & Houseplant Society.

Moore, H.E. 1957. *African Violets, Gloxinias and Their Relatives.* A Guide to the Cultivated Gesneriads. New York: Macmillan.

***Salix***

Newsholme, C. 1992. *Willows.* The Genus *Salix.* London: Batsford.

Stott, K.G. 1971 *Willows for Amenity, Windbreaks and Other Uses.* Checklist of the Long Ashton Collection of Willows, with Notes on their Suitability for Various Purposes. Long Ashton Research Station: University of Bristol.

***Salvia***

Clebsch, B. 2003. *A Book of Salvias.* (2nd ed.). Portland, Oregon: Timber Press.

Compton, J. 1994. Mexican Salvias in Cultivation. *The Plantsman* 15(4):193-215.

Middleton, R. *Robin's Salvias.* Jan 2010. www.robinssalvias.com

***Saxifraga***

Bland, B. 2000. *Silver Saxifrages.* Pershore, Worcs.: Alpine Garden Society.

Dashwood, M. & Bland, B. 2005. Silver Saxifrages: RHS Bulletin No 9. Wisley, Surrey: RHS. www.rhs.org.uk/Plants/RHS-Publications/Plant-bulletins

McGregor, M. Jan 2010. Saxbase. Saxifrage Society. www.saxifraga.org

McGregor, M. 1995. *Saxifrages: The Complete Cultivars & Hybrids: International Register of Saxifrages*. (2nd ed.). Driffield, E. Yorks: Saxifrage Society.

Webb, D.A. & Gornall, R.J. 1989. *Saxifrages of Europe*. Bromley, Kent: Christopher Helm.

***Sedum***

Evans, R.L. 1983. *Handbook of Cultivated Sedums*. Motcombe, Dorset: Ivory Head Press.

Lord, T. 2006. *Sedum* up for assessment. *The Plantsman* 5(4):244-252.

Stephenson, R. 1994. *Sedum*. The Cultivated Stonecrops. Portland, Oregon: Timber Press.

***Sempervivum***

Diehm, H. Jan 2010. www.semperhorst.de

Miklánek, M. 2002. *The List of Cultivars: Sempervivum and Jovibarba v. 7.01*. Piešt'any, Slovakia: M. Miklánek (private distribution).

Miklánek, M. 2000. *List of Cultivars: Sempervivum and Jovibarba* v. 15.1. http://miklanek.tripod.com

***Sinningia***

Dates, J.D. 1988. *The Gesneriad Register 1988. Check List of Names with Descriptions of Cultivated Plants in the Genus Sinningia*. Galesburg, Illinois: American Gloxinia and Gesneriad Society, Inc.

***Solenostemon***

Pedley, W.K. & Pedley, R. 1974. *Coleus – A Guide to Cultivation and Identification*. Edinburgh: Bartholemew.

***Sorbus***

McAllister, H. 2005. *The Genus Sorbus: Mountain Ash and Other Rowans*. Kew: Royal Botanical Gardens.

Snyers d'Attenhoven, C. 1999. *Sorbus* Lombarts hybrids *Belgische Dendrologie*: 76-81. Belgium.

Wright, D. 1981. Sorbus – a Gardener's Evaluation. *The Plantsman* 3(2):65-98.

***Spiraea***

Miller, D.M. 2003. *Spiraea japonica with coloured leaves: RHS Bulletin No 4*. Wisley, Surrey: Royal Horticultural Society. www.rhs.org.uk/Plants/RHS-Publications/Plant-bulletins

***Streptocarpus***

Arnold, P. 1979. *The Gesneriad Register 1979: Check List of Streptocarpus*. Binghamton, New York: American Gloxinia & Gesneriad.

Dibleys Nurseries Online Catalogue. Jan 2010. www.dibleys.com.

**Succulents**

Eggli, U. (ed.) 2002. *Illustrated Handbook of Succulent Plants*. Heidelberg, Germany: Springer-Verlag.

Eggli, U. & Taylor, N. 1994. *List of Names of Succulent Plants other than Cacti Published 1950-92*. Kew: Royal Botanic Gardens.

Grantham, K. & Klaassen, P. 1999. *The Plantfinder's Guide to Cacti and Other Succulents*. Newton Abbot, Devon: David & Charles.

Jacobsen, H. 1973. *Lexicon of Succulent Plants*. London: Blandford.

***Syringa***

Vrugtman, F. 2000. *International Register of Cultivar Names in the Genus Syringa L. (Oleaceae)*. (Contribution No 91). Hamilton, Canada: Royal Botanic Gardens.

***Thymus***

Easter, M. 2009. *International* Thymus *Register and Checklist*. UK: Owl Publications.

***Tiliaceae***

Wild, H. 1984. *Flora of Southern Africa 21 (1: Tiliaceae)*. Pretoria: Botanical Research Institute, Dept of Agriculture.

***Tillandsia***

Kiff, L.F. 1991. *A Distributional Checklist of the Genus Tillandsia*. Encino, California: Botanical Diversions.

***Trillium***

Case, F.W.J. & Case, R.B. 1997. *Trilliums*. Portland, Oregon: Timber Press.

Jacobs, D.L. & Jacobs, R.L. 1997. *American Treasures*. Trilliums in Woodland Garden. Decatur, Georgia: Eco-Gardens.

***Tulipa***

KAVB Online registration pages. http://kavb.back2p.soft-orange.com

***Ulmus***

Green, P.S. 1964. Registratration of Cultivar Names in *Ulmus*. *Arnoldia (Jamaica Plain)* 24:41-80.

***Vaccinium***

Trehane, J. 2004. *Blueberries, Cranberries and Other Vacciniums*. Portland, Oregon: Timber Press.

**Vegetables**

Official Journal of the European Communities. Oct 2007. Common catalogue of varieties of agricultural plant species: consolidated version. http://ec.europa.eu/food

***Viburnum***

Dirr, M.A. 2007. *Viburnums: Flowering Shrubs for Every Season*. Portland, Oregon: Timber Press.

***Viola***

Coombes, R.E. 2003. *Violets*. (2nd ed.). London: Batsford.

Fuller, R. 1990. *Pansies, Violas & Violettas*. The Complete Guide. Marlborough: The Crowood Press.

Perfect, E.J. 1996. *Armand Millet and his Violets*. High Wycombe: Park Farm Press.

Robinson, P.M. & Snocken, J. 2003. Checklist of the Cultivated Forms of the Genus Viola including the Register of Cultivars. American Violet Society. http://americanvioletsociety.org

Zambra, G.L. 1950. *Violets for Garden and Market*. (2nd ed.). London: Collingridge.

***Vitis***

Pearkes, G. 1989. *Vine Growing in Britain.* London: Dent.

Robinson, J. 1989. *Vines, Grapes and Wines.* London: Mitchell Beazley.

***Watsonia***

Goldblatt, P. 1989. *The Genus Watsonia.* A Systematic Monograph. South Africa: National Botanic Gardens.

***Weigela***

Howard, R.A. 1965. A Checklist of Cultivar Names in *Weigela. Arnoldia (Jamaica Plain)* 25:49-69.

***Wisteria***

Valder, P. 1995. *Wisterias.* A Comprehensive Guide. Balmain, Australia: Florilegium.

***Yucca***

Smith, C. 2004. *Yuccas: Giants among the Lilies.* NCCPG.

***Zauschneria***

Raven, P.H. 1977. Generic and Sectional Delimitation in *Onagraceae,* Tribe *Epilobieae. Ann. Missouri Bot. Gard.* 63(2):326-340.

Robinson, A. 2000. Focus on Plants: Piping Hot (*Zauschneria* Cultivars). *The Garden* (RHS) 125(9):698-699.

***Zingiberaceae***

Branney, T.M.E. 2005. *Hardy Gingers. Including Hedychium, Roscoea and Zingiber.* Cambridge: Timber Press.

# International Plant Finders

## New Zealand

Gaddum, Meg (Comp.) *New Zealand Plant Finder* (2010). Lists over 47,200 plants and seeds and where to buy them. The largest list of plant names taken from New Zealand nursery catalogues, with data from over 180 New Zealand nurseries. Available online only at www.plantfinder.co.nz.

## United Kingdom

Pawsey, Angela (ed.) 28th Edition 2010-2011, *Find That Rose!* (May 2010). Lists over 3,600 cultivars available in the U.K, together with basic type, colour and fragrance, including all forms of standard roses. New cultivars are highlighted and cross-referenced, where applicable, to alternative selling names. Gives full details of around 50 growers/outlets many offering mail order for both bare-root and containerised plants. Also includes useful information on how to find a rose with a particular Christian name or to celebrate a special event; on charity roses and where to see roses in bloom. To order a copy send payment of £3.75 made out to *Find That Rose!* to 303 Mile End Road, Colchester, Essex CO4 5EA. If you require further information, including the price of a CD-ROM version, please send an sae to the same address. Visit the website on www.findthatrose.net

Pawsey, Angela *What's In A Name.* (Sep 2008). Listing the origin of the names of over 500 rose varieties, this is a companion booklet to *Find That Rose!* The simple 40 page booklet includes many roses linked with charities. Packed with interesting stories, this gives the background to how and why many roses get their name. To order send payment of £1.90 made out to *Find That Rose* to Angela Pawsey, 303 Mile End Road, Colchester CO4 5EA.

# NURSERIES

THE FOLLOWING NURSERIES BETWEEN THEM STOCK AN UNRIVALLED CHOICE OF PLANTS. BEFORE MAKING A VISIT, PLEASE REMEMBER TO CHECK WITH THE NURSERY THAT THE PLANT YOU SEEK IS CURRENTLY AVAILABLE.

# Nursery Codes and Symbols

The first letter of each nursery code represents the area of the country in which the nursery is situated.

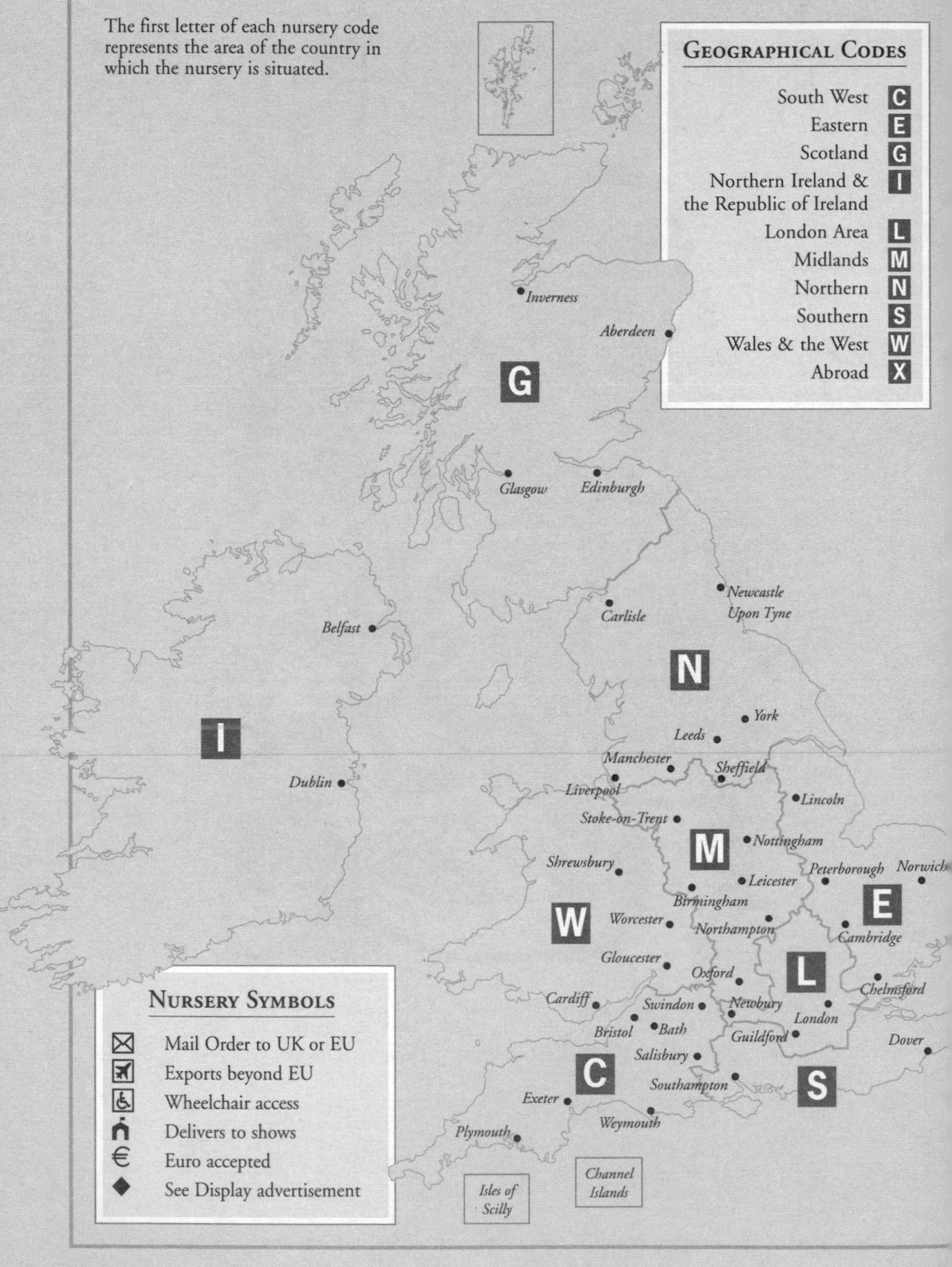


## Geographical Codes

| | |
|---|---|
| South West | C |
| Eastern | E |
| Scotland | G |
| Northern Ireland & the Republic of Ireland | I |
| London Area | L |
| Midlands | M |
| Northern | N |
| Southern | S |
| Wales & the West | W |
| Abroad | X |

## Nursery Symbols

- ☒ Mail Order to UK or EU
- Exports beyond EU
- Wheelchair access
- Delivers to shows
- € Euro accepted
- ◆ See Display advertisement

# USING THE THREE NURSERY LISTINGS

Your main reference from the Plant Directory is the Nursery Details by Code listing, which includes all relevant information for each nursery in order of nursery code. The Nursery Index by Name is an alphabetical list for those who know a nursery's name but not its code and wish to check its details in the main list. The Specialist Nurseries index is to aid those searching for a particular plant group.

## 1 NURSERY DETAILS BY CODE

Once you have found your plant in the Plant Directory, turn to this list to find out the name, address, opening times and other details of the nurseries whose codes accompany the plant.

KEY
- ⊠ Mail order to UK or EU
- Exports beyond EU
- Wheelchair access
- Delivers to shows
- € Euro accepted
- ◆ See Display advertisement

**WHil** **HILLVIEW HARDY PLANTS** ⊠ € ◆
(off B4176) Worfield, Nr Bridgnorth,
Shropshire, WV15 5NT
Ⓣ (01746) 716454
Ⓜ 07974 391608
Ⓕ (01746) 716454
Ⓔ hillview@themutual.net
Ⓦ www.hillviewhardyplants.com
**Contact:** Ingrid, John & Sarah Millington
**Opening Times:** 0900-1700 Mon-Sat Mar-mid Oct. At other times, please phone first.
**Min Mail Order UK:** £15.00 + p&p
**Min Mail Order EU:** £15.00 + p&p
**Cat. Cost:** 4 × 2nd class.
**Credit Cards:** All major credit/debit cards
**Specialities:** Choice herbaceous perennials incl. *Acanthus* & *Acanthaceae*, *Albuca*, *Aquilegia*, auricula, *Primula*, *Canna*, *Crocosmia*, *Eucomis*, *Ixia*, South African bulbs. Nat. Collections of *Acanthus* & *Albuca*.
**Notes:** Also sells wholesale.
**Map Ref:** W, B4 **OS Grid Ref:** SO772969

*A geographical code is followed by three letters reflecting the nursery's name*

*Refer to the box at the base of each right-hand page for a key to the symbols*

*Other information about the nursery*

*A brief summary of the plants available*

*The map letter is followed by the map square in which the nursery is located*

*The Ordnance Survey national grid reference for use with OS maps*

## 2 NURSERY INDEX BY NAME

If you seek a particular nursery, look it up in this alphabetical index. Note its code and turn to the Nursery Details by Code list for full information.

| | |
|---|---|
| High Garden Nurseries | CHGN |
| Highdown Nursery | SHDw |
| Hill House Nursery & Gardens | CHll |
| Hillview Hardy Plants | WHil |
| Himalayan Garden Co., The | NHim |
| Hoecroft Plants | EHoe |
| Holden Clough Nursery Ltd. | NHol |
| Home Plants | SHom |

## 3 SPECIALIST NURSERIES

A list of 32 categories under which nurseries have classified themselves if they exclusively, or predominantly, supply this range of plants.

### DROUGHT-TOLERANT

ECHA, EGLN, EHOE, ETOD, LIMB, LLWP, LPAL, MBPG, NFIR, NHOY, NMRC, SALL, SDOW, SEND, SJOH, SMEA, SPHX, SUSU, SVEN, WFIB, WHIL, WPNN, XLUM, XSEN

# How to Use the Nursery Listings

The details given for each nursery have been compiled from information supplied to us in answer to a questionnaire. In some cases, because of constraints of space, the entries have been slightly abbreviated.

**Nurseries are not charged for their entries and inclusion in no way implies a value judgement.**

## Nursery Details by Code (*page 836*)

Each nursery is allocated a code, for example GPoy. The first letter of each code indicates the main area of the country in which the nursery is situated. In this example, G=Scotland. The remaining three letters reflect the nursery's name, in this case Poyntzfield Herb Nursery.

In this main listing the nurseries are given in alphabetical order of codes for quick reference from the Plant Directory. All of the nurseries' details, such as address, opening times, mail order service etc., will be found here.

## Opening Times

Although opening times have been published as submitted and where applicable, **it is always advisable, especially if travelling a long distance, to check with the nursery first**. The initials NGS indicate that the nursery is open under the National Gardens Scheme.

## Mail Order ⊠

Many nurseries provide a mail order service. **This is, however, often restricted to certain times of the year or to particular genera**. Please check the **Notes** section of each nursery's entry for any restrictions or special conditions.

In some cases, the mail order service extends to all members of the European Union. Where this is offered, the minimum charge to the EU will be noted in the Nursery entry.

Where **'No minimum charge'** (**Nmc**) is shown, please note that to send even one plant may involve the nursery in substantial postage and packing costs. Some nurseries may not be prepared to send tender or bulky plants.

Where a nursery offers a **mail order only** service, this will be noted under **Opening Times** in the nursery entry. Many nurseries also offer an online mail order facility.

## Export ✈

Export refers to mail order beyond the European Union. Nurseries that are prepared to consider exporting are indicated. However, there is usually a substantial minimum charge and, in addition, all the costs of Phytosanitary Certificates and Customs have to be met by the purchaser.

## Catalogue Cost

Some nurseries offer their catalogue free, or for a few stamps, but a large (at least A5) stamped addressed envelope is always appreciated as well. Overseas customers should use an equivalent number of International Reply Coupons (IRCs) in place of stamps.

Increasingly, nurseries are finding it more cost effective to produce catalogues on the Internet rather than printing them.

## Wheelchair Access ♿

Nurseries are asked to indicate if their premises are suitable for wheelchair users. Where only partial access is indicated, this is noted in the **Notes** field and the nursery is not marked with the symbol.

The assessment of ease-of-access is entirely the responsibility of the individual nursery.

## Specialities

Nurseries list here the plants or genera that they supply and any National Collections of plants they may hold. Please note that some nurseries may charge an entry fee to visit a National Collection. Always enquire before visiting.

Nurseries will also note here if they only have small quantities of individual plants available for sale or if they will propagate to order.

## Notes

In this section, you will find notes on any restrictions to mail order or export; on limited wheelchair access; or the nursery site address, if this differs from the office address; together with any other non-horticultural information.

## Delivery to Shows ⛺

Many nurseries will deliver pre-ordered plants to flower shows for collection by customers. These are indicated by a marquee symbol. Contact the nursery for details of shows they attend.

## Payment in Euros €

A number of UK nurseries have indicated that they will accept payment in Euros. You should, however, check with the nursery concerned before making such a payment, as some will only accept cash and some only cheques, whilst others will expect the purchaser to pay bank charges.

## Maps

If you wish to visit any of the nurseries you can find its approximate location on the relevant map (following p.945), unless the nursery has requested this is not shown. Nurseries are also encouraged to provide their Ordnance Survey national grid reference for use with OS publications such as the Land Ranger series.

## Nursery Index by Name

For convenience, an alphabetical index of nurseries is included (*page 936*). This gives the names of all nurseries listed in the book in alphabetical order of nursery name together with their code.

## Specialist Nurseries (*page 942*)

This list of nurseries is intended to help those with an interest in finding specialist categories of plant. Nurseries have been asked to classify themselves under one or more headings where this represents the type of plant they *predominantly* or *exclusively* have in stock. For example, if you wish to find a nursery specialising in ornamental grasses, look up 'Grasses' in the listing where you will find a list of nursery codes. Then turn to the Nursery Details by Code, for details of the nurseries.

Please note that not all nurseries shown here will have plants listed in the Plant Directory. This may be their choice or because the *RHS Plant Finder* does not list seeds or annuals and only terrestrial orchids and hardy cacti. For space reasons, it is rare to find a nursery's full catalogue listed in the Plant Directory.

**In all cases, please ensure you ring to confirm the range available before embarking on a journey to the nursery.**

The specialist plant groups listed in this edition are:

Acid-loving
Alpines/rock
Aquatics
Bamboos
British wild flowers
Bulbous plants
Cacti & succulents
Carnivorous
Chalk-loving
Climbers
Coastal
Conifers
Conservatory
Drought-tolerant
Ferns
Fruit
Grasses
Hedging
Herbs
Marginal/bog
Orchids
Organic
Ornamental trees
Palms
Peat-free
Period plants
Propagate to order
Roses
Seed
Specimen-sized
Topiary
Tropical

Perennials and shrubs have been omitted as these are considered to be too general and serviced by a great proportion of the nurseries.

## Deleted Nurseries

Every year some nurseries ask to be removed from the book. This may be a temporary measure because they are moving, or it may be permanent due to closure, sale, retirement, or a change in the way in which they trade. Occasionally, nurseries are unable to meet the closing date and will re-enter the book in the following edition. Some nurseries simply do not reply and, as we have no current information on them, they are deleted.

*Please, never use an old edition*

# Nursery Details by Code

Please note that all these nurseries are listed in alphabetical order by their code. All nurseries are listed in alphabetical order by their name in the **Nursery Index by Name** on page 936.

## South West

**CAbb** **Abbotsbury Sub-Tropical Gardens** ⊠ ♿
Abbotsbury, Nr Weymouth, Dorset, DT3 4LA
Ⓣ (01305) 871344
Ⓕ (01305) 871344
Ⓔ info@abbotsburygardens.co.uk
Ⓦ www.abbotsburyplantsales.co.uk
**Contact:** David Sutton
**Opening Times:** 1000-1800 daily, mid Mar-1st Nov. 1000-1500, Nov-mid Mar.
**Min Mail Order UK:** Nmc
**Cat. Cost:** £2.00 + A4 sae
**Credit Cards:** Access, Visa, MasterCard, Switch
**Specialities:** Less common & tender shrubs incl. palms, tree ferns, bamboos & plants from Australia, New Zealand & S. Africa.

**CAbP** **Abbey Plants** ⊠ ♿
Chaffeymoor, Bourton, Gillingham, Dorset, SP8 5BY
Ⓣ (01747) 840841
**Contact:** K Potts
**Opening Times:** 1000-1300 & 1400-1700 Wed-Sat Mar-Nov. Dec-Feb by appt.
**Min Mail Order UK:** Nmc
**Cat. Cost:** 2 × 2nd class.
**Credit Cards:** None
**Specialities:** Flowering trees & shrubs.
**Map Ref:** C, B4 **OS Grid Ref:** ST762304

**CAby** **The Abbey Nursery** ♿
Forde Abbey, Chard, Somerset, TA20 4LU
Ⓣ (01460) 220088
Ⓕ (01460) 220088
Ⓔ TheAbbeyNursery@btconnect.com
**Contact:** Peter Sims
**Opening Times:** 1000-1700 7 days, 1st Mar-31st Oct. Please phone first to check opening times in Mar.
**Cat. Cost:** None issued.
**Credit Cards:** All major credit/debit cards
**Specialities:** Hardy herbaceous perennials.
**Map Ref:** C, C4 **OS Grid Ref:** ST359052

**CAgr** **Agroforestry Research Trust** ⊠
46 Hunters Moon, Dartington, Totnes, Devon, TQ9 6JT
Ⓕ (01803) 840776
Ⓔ mail@agroforestry.co.uk
Ⓦ www.agroforestry.co.uk
**Contact:** Martin Crawford
**Opening Times:** Not open. Mail order only.
**Min Mail Order UK:** Nmc
**Min Mail Order EU:** Nmc
**Cat. Cost:** 4 × 1st class.
**Credit Cards:** All major credit/debit cards
**Specialities:** Top & soft fruit, nut trees including *Castanea*, *Corylus*, *Juglans*, *Pinus*. Also seeds. Some plants in small quantities only.

**CAlb** **Albion Plants** ⊠ €
Roborough, Winkleigh, Devon, EX19 8TD
Ⓣ (01805) 603502
Ⓕ 08000 112024
Ⓔ huggons@albion-plants.co.uk
Ⓦ www.albion-plants.co.uk
**Contact:** Neil & Brenda Huggons
**Opening Times:** Mail order only. Open by appt. for wholesale quantities only.
**Min Mail Order UK:** Nmc
**Cat. Cost:** Available by email on request.
**Credit Cards:** All major credit/debit cards
**Specialities:** *Vinca*, *Cornus*, *Viburnum*, *Ceanothus*. Specimen-sized shrubs & container-grown trees.
**Notes:** Also sells wholesale.

**CAni** **Anita Allen** ⊠
Shapcott Barton Estate, East Knowstone, South Molton, Devon, EX36 4EE
Ⓣ (01398) 341664

Ⓕ (01398) 341664
**Contact:** Anita Allen
**Opening Times:** By appt. only. Garden open under NGS.
**Min Mail Order UK:** Nmc
Cat. Cost: 5 × 1st class & state which catalogue: Shasta daisies or *Buddleja*.
**Credit Cards:** None
**Specialities:** Nat. Collections of *Leucanthemum × superbum* & *Buddleja davidii* & hybrids, 70+ cvs. 80+ accurately named Shasta daisies, a few in very short supply. Also many hardy perennials.
**Map Ref:** C, B3 **OS Grid Ref:** SS846235

**CArn** **ARNE HERBS** ⊠ € ♿
Limeburn Nurseries, Limeburn Hill, Chew Magna, Bristol, BS40 8QW
Ⓣ (01275) 333399
Ⓔ anthony@arneherbs.co.uk
Ⓦ www.arneherbs.co.uk
**Contact:** A Lyman-Dixon & Jenny Thomas
**Opening Times:** 1000-1600 most weekdays by prior telephone appt. only.
**Min Mail Order UK:** Nmc
**Min Mail Order EU:** Nmc
**Cat. Cost:** Detailed illustrated catalogue online or A4 sae for free non-descriptive plantlist.
**Credit Cards:** None
**Specialities:** Herbs, some very rare. North American, Mediterranean & UK wild flowers. Also plants for reseach, conservation projects & historical recreations.
**Notes:** Also sells wholesale.
**Map Ref:** C, A5 **OS Grid Ref:** ST563638

**CAvo** **AVON BULBS** ⊠ 
Burnt House Farm, Mid-Lambrook, South Petherton, Somerset, TA13 5HE
Ⓣ (01460) 242177
Ⓕ (01460) 249025
Ⓔ info@avonbulbs.co.uk
Ⓦ www.avonbulbs.co.uk
**Contact:** C Ireland-Jones
**Opening Times:** Mail order only. Open Thu, Fri, Sat, mid-Sep-end Oct & mid Feb-end Mar for collection of pre-booked orders.
**Min Mail Order UK:** £10.00 + p&p
**Min Mail Order EU:** £20.00 + p&p
**Cat. Cost:** 4 × 2nd class.
**Credit Cards:** Visa, Access, Switch, MasterCard
**Specialities:** Some special snowdrops are only available in small quantities.

**CBar** **BARTERS PLANT CENTRE & NURSERY** ♿
Chapmanslade, Westbury, Wiltshire, BA13 4AL
Ⓣ (01373) 832694
Ⓕ (01373) 832677
Ⓔ plantcentre@barters.co.uk
Ⓦ www.barters.co.uk
**Contact:** Giles Hall
**Opening Times:** 0900-1700 Mon-Thu, 0900-1730 Fri & Sat, summer. 0900-1630 Mon-Thu, 0900-1700 Fri & Sat, winter. 1030-1630 Sun.
**Cat. Cost:** None issued.
**Credit Cards:** All, except American Express
**Specialities:** Wide range of shrubs. Ground cover, container trees, ferns, half-hardy perennials, grasses, herbaceous & climbers. Hedging, fruit trees, old fashioned roses & bare-root stock.
**Notes:** Also sells wholesale.

**CBcs** **BURNCOOSE NURSERIES** ⊠ ✈  ♿
Gwennap, Redruth, Cornwall, TR16 6BJ
Ⓣ (01209) 860316
Ⓕ (01209) 860011
Ⓔ burncoose@eclipse.co.uk
Ⓦ www.burncoose.co.uk
**Contact:** C H Williams
**Opening Times:** 0830-1700 Mon-Sat & 1100-1700 Sun.
**Min Mail Order UK:** Nmc
**Min Mail Order EU:** Individual quotations for EU sales.
**Cat. Cost:** Free
**Credit Cards:** Visa, Access, Switch, MasterCard
**Specialities:** Extensive range of over 3500 ornamental trees & shrubs and herbaceous. Rare & unusual *Magnolia*, *Rhododendron*. Conservatory plants. 30 acre garden.
**Notes:** Also sells wholesale.
**Map Ref:** C, D1 **OS Grid Ref:** SW742395

**CBct** **BARRACOTT PLANTS** ⊠  € ♿
Old Orchard, Calstock Road, Gunnislake, Cornwall, PL18 9AA
Ⓣ (01822) 832234
Ⓜ 07811 207186
Ⓔ geoffandthelma@barracott.eclipse.co.uk
Ⓦ www.barracottplants.co.uk
**Contact:** Geoff & Thelma Turner
**Opening Times:** 0900-1700 Thu & Fri, Mar-end Sep. Other times by appt.
**Min Mail Order UK:** Nmc
**Cat. Cost:** Large 1st class.
**Credit Cards:** None
**Specialities:** Herbaceous plants: shade-loving, foliage & form. *Acanthus*, *Aspidistra*,

KEY
⊠ Mail order to UK or EU  Delivers to shows
✈ Exports beyond EU € Euro accepted
♿ Accessible by wheelchair ◆ See Display advertisement

C

*Astrantia, Bergenia, Convallaria, Disporum, Liriope, Maianthemum, Polygonatum, Roscoea, Trillium, Tricyrtis* & *Uvularia*.
**Notes:** Also sells wholesale.
**Map Ref:** C, C3 **OS Grid Ref:** SX436702

**CBen** **Bennetts Water Gardens** ⊠ ♿
B3157 Chickerell Link Road, Weymouth, Dorset, DT3 4AF
Ⓣ (01305) 785150
Ⓔ info@waterlily.co.uk
Ⓦ www.waterlily.co.uk
**Contact:** James Bennett
**Opening Times:** 1000-1700 Mar-Oct. Closed Sat.
**Min Mail Order UK:** Nmc
**Min Mail Order EU:** Nmc
**Cat. Cost:** Sae for price list
**Credit Cards:** Visa, Access, MasterCard, Switch
**Specialities:** Aquatic plants. Nat. Collection of *Nymphaea*.
**Notes:** Mail order Apr-Sep only. Loose plants only by mail order. Potted plants available at nursery.
**Map Ref:** C, C5 **OS Grid Ref:** SY651797

**CBgR** **Beggar's Roost Plants** ⊠ €
Lilstock, Bridgwater, Somerset, TA5 1SU
Ⓣ (01278) 741519
Ⓔ ro@beggarsroostplants.co.uk
Ⓦ www.beggarsroostplants.co.uk
**Contact:** Rosemary FitzGerald
**Opening Times:** Closed in 2010 now mail order only.
**Min Mail Order UK:** £10.00
**Min Mail Order EU:** Nmc
**Cat. Cost:** 3 × large 2nd class.
**Credit Cards:** None
**Specialities:** *Hemerocallis* (incl. heritage) grown in British conditions. *Galanthus* (incl. West Country variants).
**Notes:** Mail order for specialities: *Crocosmia, Hemerocallis, Galanthus, Dahlia* (tubers), hardy *Nerine* (bulbs). Ask for lists.
**Map Ref:** C, B4 **OS Grid Ref:** ST168450

**CBod** **Bodmin Plant and Herb Nursery** ♿
Laveddon Mill, Laninval Hill, Bodmin, Cornwall, PL30 5JU
Ⓣ (01208) 72837
Ⓕ (01208) 76491
Ⓔ bodminnursery@aol.com
Ⓦ www.bodminnursery.co.uk
**Contact:** Mark Lawlor
**Opening Times:** 0900-1700 Mon-Sat Nov-Mar, 0900-1800 Mon-Sat Apr-Oct. 1000-1600 Sun.
**Credit Cards:** All major credit/debit cards
**Specialities:** Herbs, herbaceous & grasses, hardy geraniums & coastal plants. Interesting shrubs, fruit & ornamental trees.
**Map Ref:** C, C2 **OS Grid Ref:** SX053659

**CBot** **The Botanic Nursery** ⊠ ń € ♿
Atworth, Nr Melksham, Wiltshire, SN12 8NU
Ⓜ 07850 328756
Ⓕ (01225) 700953
Ⓔ botanicnursery@botanicguru.co.uk
Ⓦ www.botanicguru.co.uk
**Contact:** T. Baker
**Opening Times:** 1000-1700 Tue-Sat, Mar-Nov. Please avoid lunch time if possible.
**Min Mail Order UK:** £11.00 for 24hr carriage service. At cost for Royal Mail.
**Cat. Cost:** £1.00 in stamps.
**Credit Cards:** MasterCard, Visa
**Specialities:** Nursery propagates from large range of lime-tolerant plants in varying quantities, all peat free. Nat. Collection of *Digitalis*.
**Notes:** If travelling, please phone first to confirm specific plant availability. Partially accessible for wheelchairs.
**Map Ref:** C, A5

**CBre** **Bregover Plants** ⊠ ń
Hillbrooke, Middlewood, North Hill, Nr Launceston, Cornwall, PL15 7NN
Ⓣ (01566) 782661
**Contact:** Jennifer Bousfield
**Opening Times:** 1100-1700 Wed, Mar-mid Oct and by appt.
**Min Mail Order UK:** Nmc
**Min Mail Order EU:** Nmc
**Cat. Cost:** 3 × 1st class.
**Credit Cards:** None
**Specialities:** Unusual hardy perennials grown in small garden nursery. Available in small quantities only.
**Notes:** Mail order Oct-Mar only.
**Map Ref:** C, C2 **OS Grid Ref:** SX273752

**CBro** **Broadleigh Gardens** ⊠ ń € ♿
Bishops Hull, Taunton, Somerset, TA4 1AE
Ⓣ (01823) 286231
Ⓕ (01823) 323646
Ⓔ info@broadleighbulbs.co.uk
Ⓦ www.broadleighbulbs.co.uk
**Contact:** Lady Skelmersdale
**Opening Times:** 0900-1600 Mon-Fri for viewing only (charity donation). Orders collected if notice given.
**Min Mail Order UK:** Nmc
**Min Mail Order EU:** Nmc
**Cat. Cost:** 2 × 1st class.

**Credit Cards:** All major credit/debit cards
**Specialities:** Jan catalogue: bulbs in growth (*Galanthus, Cyclamen* etc.) & herbaceous woodland plants (trilliums, hellebores etc). Extensive list of *Agapanthus*. June catalogue: dwarf & unusual bulbs, *Iris* (DB & PC). Nat. Collection of Alec Grey hybrid daffodils.
**Notes:** Euro payment accepted as cash only.
**Map Ref:** C, B4 **OS Grid Ref:** ST195251

CBrP **BROOKLANDS PLANTS** ⊠
25 Treves Road, Dorchester, Dorset, DT1 2HE
Ⓣ (01305) 265846
Ⓔ cycads@btinternet.com
**Contact:** Ian Watt
**Opening Times:** By appt. only for collection of plants.
**Min Mail Order UK:** £25.00 + p&p
**Min Mail Order EU:** £25.00 + p&p
**Cat. Cost:** 2 × 2nd class.
**Credit Cards:** None
**Specialities:** Cycad nursery specialising in the more cold-tolerant species of *Encephalartos, Dioon, Macrozamia* & *Cycas*. Also specialist in cold-tolerant palms as well as plants from New Zealand. Some species available in small quantities only.
**Map Ref:** C, C5 **OS Grid Ref:** SY682897

CBty **BENTLEY PLANTS** ⊠ ⌂ € ♿
1 Bentley Wood Cottages, West Tytherley, Salisbury, Wiltshire, SP5 1QB
Ⓣ (01794) 340775
Ⓕ (01794) 340775
Ⓔ john@bentleyplants.fsnet.co.uk
Ⓦ www.bentleyplants.co.uk
**Contact:** John Wilson
**Opening Times:** By appt. only.
**Min Mail Order UK:** Nmc
**Credit Cards:** All major credit/debit cards
**Specialities:** Grows 90 varieties of ferns, a large range of shrubs, incl. more than 20 varieties of *Pittosporum*, bamboos & Japanese maples.
**Notes:** Mail order Oct-Mar.
**Map Ref:** C, B6 **OS Grid Ref:** SU258306

CBur **BURNHAM NURSERIES** ⊠ ✈ ⌂ € ♿
Forches Cross, Newton Abbot, Devon, TQ12 6PZ
Ⓣ (01626) 352233
Ⓕ (01626) 362167
Ⓔ mail@orchids.uk.com
Ⓦ www.orchids.uk.com
**Contact:** Any member of staff
**Opening Times:** 1000-1600 Mon-Sun.
**Min Mail Order UK:** Nmc
**Min Mail Order EU:** £100.00 + p&p
**Cat. Cost:** A4 sae + 48p stamp.
**Credit Cards:** Visa, American Express, MasterCard, Maestro
**Specialities:** All types of orchid except British native types.
**Notes:** Please ask for details on export beyond EU.
**Map Ref:** C, C4 **OS Grid Ref:** SX841732

CCAT **CIDER APPLE TREES** ⊠ €
Kerian, Corkscrew Lane, Woolston, Nr North Cadbury, Somerset, BA22 7BP
Ⓣ (01963) 441101
Ⓦ www.ciderappletrees.co.uk
**Contact:** Mr J Dennis
**Opening Times:** By appt. only.
**Min Mail Order UK:** £9.50
**Min Mail Order EU:** £9.50
**Cat. Cost:** Free.
**Credit Cards:** None
**Specialities:** *Malus* (speciality standard trees).
**Notes:** Also sells wholesale.
**Map Ref:** C, B5

CCCN **CROSS COMMON NURSERY** ⊠ ◆
The Lizard, Helston, Cornwall, TR12 7PD
Ⓣ (01326) 290722/290668
Ⓔ info@crosscommonnursery.co.uk
Ⓦ www.crosscommonnursery.co.uk
**Contact:** Kevin Bosustow
**Opening Times:** 1000-1700 7 days, Apr, May & Jun. Reduced hours Jul-Sep, please phone for opening times.
**Min Mail Order UK:** Nmc
**Cat. Cost:** Online only.
**Credit Cards:** All major credit/debit cards
**Specialities:** Tropical/sub-tropical, coastal plants & conservatory plants. Wide range of grapevines and citrus trees. Some plants available in small quantities only.
**Map Ref:** C, D1 **OS Grid Ref:** SW704116

CCha **CHAPEL FARM HOUSE NURSERY** € ♿
Halwill Junction, Beaworthy, Devon, EX21 5UF
Ⓣ (01409) 221594
Ⓕ (01409) 221594
**Contact:** Robin or Toshie Hull
**Opening Times:** 1000-1600 Tue-Sat, 1000-1600 Sun & B/hol Mons.
**Cat. Cost:** None issued.
**Credit Cards:** None

KEY
⊠ Mail order to UK or EU ⌂ Delivers to shows
✈ Exports beyond EU € Euro accepted
♿ Accessible by wheelchair ◆ See Display advertisement

C

**Specialities:** Plants from Japan. Also herbaceous. Japanese garden design service offered.
**Map Ref:** C, C3

**CChe** **CHERRY TREE NURSERY** ♿
(Sheltered Work Opportunities)
off New Road Roundabout, Northbourne, Bournemouth, Dorset, BH10 7DA
Ⓣ (01202) 593537 (01202) 590840
Ⓕ (01202) 590626
**Contact:** Stephen Jailler
**Opening Times:** 0830-1530 Mon-Fri, 0900-1500 Sat, Apr-Sep & 0900-1300 Sat, Oct-Mar.
**Cat. Cost:** A4 sae + 66p stamps.
**Credit Cards:** All, except American Express
**Specialities:** Hardy shrubs, perennials, climbers, grasses.
**Notes:** Debit cards accepted. Also sells wholesale.

**CClc** **CLASSIC GARDENER** € ♿
Pound Barn, West Kington, Nr Chippenham, Wiltshire, SN14 7JQ
Ⓣ (01249) 783880
Ⓔ info@classicgardener.co.uk
Ⓦ www.classicgardener.co.uk
**Contact:** Philip Stockitt
**Opening Times:** 1000-1700 Tue, Thu & Sat or by prior appt. only.
**Cat. Cost:** Online only.
**Credit Cards:** MasterCard, Visa
**Specialities:** Topiary.
**Notes:** Also sells wholesale.
**Map Ref:** C, A5

**CCse** **CHASE PLANTS (FORMERLY MEADOWS NURSERY)** ⊠ ⌂
Hookswood Cottage, Farnham, Blandford Forum, Dorset, DT11 8DQ
Ⓣ (01725) 516394
Ⓔ sales@chaseplants.co.uk
**Contact:** Sue Lees & Eddie Wheatley
**Opening Times:** By appt. only.
**Min Mail Order UK:** £10.00
**Credit Cards:** None
**Specialities:** Hardy perennials, shrubs & some conservatory plants.

**CCtw** **CHURCHTOWN NURSERIES** ⊠ ⌂ ♿
Gulval, Penzance, Cornwall, TR18 3BE
Ⓣ (01736) 362626
Ⓕ (01736) 363411
Ⓔ littlemanchris@hotmail.co.uk
Ⓦ www.kelnanplants.com
**Contact:** Chris or Fay Osborne
**Opening Times:** 1000-1700 Apr-Sep, 1000-1600 Oct-Mar or by appt.
**Min Mail Order UK:** Nmc
**Cat. Cost:** 1st class sae for list.
**Credit Cards:** None
**Specialities:** Good, ever-increasing, range of shrubs, herbaceous & tender perennials. *Restio*.
**Map Ref:** C, D1 **OS Grid Ref:** SW486317

**CCVN** **CULM VIEW NURSERY** ⊠ ⌂
Waterloo Farm, Clayhidon, Devon, EX15 3TN
Ⓣ (01823) 680698
Ⓔ plants@culmviewnursery.co.uk
Ⓦ www.culmviewnursery.co.uk
**Contact:** Brian & Alison Jacobs
**Opening Times:** By appt. only for collection.
**Min Mail Order UK:** Nmc
**Min Mail Order EU:** Nmc
**Credit Cards:** Paypal
**Specialities:** Hebaceous perennials grown in peat-free compost.
**Notes:** Mail order seed only.

**CCVT** **CHEW VALLEY TREES** ⊠ ♿
Winford Road, Chew Magna, Bristol, BS40 8HJ
Ⓣ (01275) 333752
Ⓕ (01275) 333746
Ⓔ info@chewvalleytrees.co.uk
Ⓦ www.chewvalleytrees.co.uk
**Contact:** J Scarth
**Opening Times:** 0800-1700 Mon-Fri all year. 0900-1600 Sat. Closed Sat, Sun & B/hols Jul & Aug.
**Min Mail Order UK:** Nmc
**Cat. Cost:** Free.
**Credit Cards:** All major credit/debit cards
**Specialities:** Native British & ornamental trees, shrubs, fruit trees & hedging.
**Notes:** Also sells wholesale.
**Map Ref:** C, A5 **OS Grid Ref:** ST558635

**CDes** **DESIRABLE PLANTS** ⊠ ⌂
(Office) Pentamar, Crosspark, Totnes, Devon, TQ9 5BQ
Ⓣ (01803) 864489 evenings
Ⓔ sutton.totnes@lineone.net
Ⓦ www.desirableplants.com
**Contact:** Dr J J & Mrs S A Sutton
**Opening Times:** Not open. Mail order only.
**Min Mail Order UK:** £15.00
**Cat. Cost:** 6 × 2nd class.
**Credit Cards:** None
**Specialities:** Eclectic range of choice & interesting herbaceous perennials & bulbs by mail order.
**Notes:** Nursery not at this address.

**CDob** **SAMUEL DOBIE & SON** ⊠
Long Road, Paignton, Devon,
TQ4 7SX
Ⓣ 0844 701 7623
Ⓕ 0844 701 7624
Ⓦ www.dobies.co.uk
**Contact:** Customer Services
**Opening Times:** Not open. Mail order only. Phone line open 0830-1700 Mon-Fri (office). Also answerphone.
**Min Mail Order UK:** Nmc
**Cat. Cost:** Free.
**Credit Cards:** Visa, MasterCard, Switch, Delta
**Specialities:** Wide selection of popular flower & vegetable seeds. Also includes young plants, summer-flowering bulbs & garden sundries.
**Notes:** Mail order to UK & Rep. of Ireland only.

**CDoC** **DUCHY OF CORNWALL** ⊠ ◆
Cott Road, Lostwithiel, Cornwall,
PL22 0HW
Ⓣ (01208) 872668
Ⓕ (01208) 872835
Ⓔ sales@duchyofcornwallnursery.co.uk
Ⓦ www.duchyofcornwallnursery.co.uk
**Contact:** Jim Stephens
**Opening Times:** 0900-1700 Mon-Sat, 1000-1700 Sun & B/hols.
**Min Mail Order UK:** £10.00
**Cat. Cost:** None issued.
**Credit Cards:** All major credit/debit cards
**Specialities:** *Camellia*, *Fuchsia*, conifers & *Magnolia*. Also a huge range of garden plants incl. trees, shrubs, roses, perennials, fruit & conservatory plants.
**Notes:** Nursery partially accessible to wheelchair users.
**Map Ref:** C, C2 **OS Grid Ref:** SX112614

**CDoy** **CARADOC DOY** ⊠ €
PO Box 28, Exeter, Devon, EX3 0WY
Ⓣ (01392) 877225
Ⓕ (01392) 877225
Ⓔ info@caradocdoy.co.uk
Ⓦ www.caradocdoy.co.uk
**Contact:** Caradoc Doy
**Opening Times:** 1000-1700, 7 days.
**Min Mail Order UK:** Nmc
**Cat. Cost:** 6 × 2nd class.
**Credit Cards:** All major credit/debit cards
**Specialities:** Olive trees. Plants introduced by the Veitch Nurseries. Some varieties only available in small quantities.
**Notes:** Nursery located at Busy Lizzie's Craft & Plant Shop, Newton Poppleford, EX10 0DE
**Map Ref:** C, C4 **OS Grid Ref:** SY065895

**CDTJ** **DESERT TO JUNGLE** ⊠ ⛺ ♿
Henlade Garden Nursery, Lower Henlade, Taunton, Somerset, TA3 5NB
Ⓣ (01823) 443701
Ⓕ (01458) 250521
Ⓔ plants@deserttojungle.com
Ⓦ www.deserttojungle.com
**Contact:** Rob Gudge, Dave Root
**Opening Times:** 1000-1700 Mon-Sun, 1st Mar-31st Oct. Thu, Fri & Sat only Nov-Feb, or phone first.
**Min Mail Order UK:** Nmc
**Credit Cards:** All major credit/debit cards
**Specialities:** Exotic-looking plants giving a desert or jungle effect in the garden. Incl. *Canna*, aroids, succulents, tree ferns & bamboos.
**Notes:** Nursery shares drive with Mount Somerset Hotel. Also sells wholesale.
**Map Ref:** C, B4 **OS Grid Ref:** ST273232

**CDul** **DULFORD NURSERIES** ⊠ ♿
Cullompton, Devon, EX15 2DG
Ⓣ (01884) 266361
Ⓕ (01884) 266663
Ⓔ dulford.nurseries@virgin.net
Ⓦ www.dulford-nurseries.co.uk
**Contact:** Paul Rawlings
**Opening Times:** 0730-1630 Mon-Fri.
**Min Mail Order UK:** Nmc
**Min Mail Order EU:** Nmc
**Cat. Cost:** Free.
**Credit Cards:** All major credit/debit cards
**Specialities:** Native, ornamental & unusual trees & shrubs incl. oaks, maples, beech, birch, chestnut, ash, lime, *Sorbus* & pines.
**Notes:** Also sells wholesale.
**Map Ref:** C, C4 **OS Grid Ref:** SY062062

**CEls** **ELSWORTH HERBS** ⊠ ♿
Farthingwood, Broadway,
Sidmouth, Devon,
EX10 8HS
Ⓣ (01395) 578689
Ⓔ john.twibell@btinternet.com
**Contact:** Drs J D & J M Twibell
**Opening Times:** By appt. only.
**Min Mail Order UK:** £10.00
**Cat. Cost:** 3 × 1st class or email.
**Credit Cards:** None
**Specialities:** Nat. Collections of *Artemisia* (incl. *Seriphidium*) & *Nerium oleander*. Wide range of *Artemisia* & *Seriphidium*, *Nerium oleander*. Stock available in small

KEY
⊠ Mail order to UK or EU ⛺ Delivers to shows
✈ Exports beyond EU € Euro accepted
♿ Accessible by wheelchair ◆ See Display advertisement

C

quantities only. Orders may require propagation from Collection material, for which we are the primary reference source.
**Notes:** Partially accessible for wheelchairs.
**Map Ref:** C, C4 **OS Grid Ref:** SY119881

**CElw** **ELWORTHY COTTAGE PLANTS** ♿
Elworthy Cottage, Elworthy, Nr Lydeard St Lawrence, Taunton, Somerset, TA4 3PX
Ⓣ (01984) 656427
Ⓔ mike@elworthy-cottage.co.uk
Ⓦ www.elworthy-cottage.co.uk
**Contact:** Mrs J M Spiller
**Opening Times:** 1000-1600 Thu & Fri, late Mar-end Jun. Thu only Jul & Aug. Also by appt. Feb-Nov.
**Cat. Cost:** 3 × 2nd class.
**Credit Cards:** None
**Specialities:** *Clematis* & unusual herbaceous plants esp. hardy *Geranium*, *Geum*, grasses, *Crocosmia*, *Pulmonaria*, *Astrantia*, *Viola* & *Galanthus*. Some varieties only available in small quantities.
**Notes:** Nursery on B3188, 5 miles north of Wiveliscombe, in centre of Elworthy village.
**Map Ref:** C, B4 **OS Grid Ref:** ST084349

**CEnd** **ENDSLEIGH GARDENS** ⊠ ♿ ◆
Milton Abbot, Tavistock, Devon, PL19 0PG
Ⓣ (01822) 870235
Ⓕ (01822) 870513
Ⓔ info@endsleigh-gardens.com
Ⓦ www.endsleigh-gardens.com
**Contact:** Michael Taylor
**Opening Times:** 0800-1700 Mon-Sat. 1000-1700 Sun.
**Min Mail Order UK:** Nmc
**Cat. Cost:** 2 × 1st class.
**Credit Cards:** Visa, Access, Switch, MasterCard
**Specialities:** Choice & unusual trees & shrubs incl. *Acer* & *Cornus* cvs. Old apples & cherries. *Wisteria*. Grafting service.
**Map Ref:** C, C3

**CEnt** **ENTWOOD FARM PLANTS**
Harcombe, Lyme Regis, Dorset, DT7 3RN
Ⓣ (01297) 444034
**Contact:** Jenny & Ivan Harding
**Opening Times:** Please phone for details.
**Credit Cards:** None
**Specialities:** Bamboo specialists, plus interesting selection of grasses, shrubs & perennials. Some stock in small quantities.
**Map Ref:** C, C4 **OS Grid Ref:** SY335953

**CFee** **FEEBERS HARDY PLANTS** ⊠ € ♿ ◆
1 Feeber Cottage, Westwood, Broadclyst, Nr Exeter, Devon, EX5 3DQ
Ⓣ (01404) 822118
Ⓔ Feebers@onetel.com
**Contact:** Mrs E Squires
**Opening Times:** Open at any reasonable time by prior telephone arrangement.
**Min Mail Order UK:** Nmc
**Min Mail Order EU:** Nmc
**Cat. Cost:** Sae + 36p stamp.
**Credit Cards:** None
**Specialities:** Plants for wet clay soils, alpines & hardy perennials incl. those raised by Amos Perry. Small quantities of plants held unless grown from seed.
**Notes:** Mail order limited. Nursery accessible for wheelchairs in dry weather only.
**Map Ref:** C, C4

**CFFs** **FLORAL FIREWORKS** ⊠
Burnt House Farm, Mid Lambrook, South Petherton, Somerset, TA13 5HE
Ⓣ (01460) 249060
Ⓕ (01460) 249025
Ⓔ info@floralfireworks.co.uk
Ⓦ www.floralfireworks.co.uk
**Contact:** Carol Atkins
**Opening Times:** Not open. Mail order only. Orders can be collected by prior arrangement.
**Min Mail Order UK:** £10.00 + p&p
**Min Mail Order EU:** £20.00 + p&p
**Cat. Cost:** 4 × 2nd class.
**Credit Cards:** All major credit/debit cards
**Specialities:** Bulbs.

**CFir** **FIR TREE FARM NURSERY** ⊠ € ♿
Tresahor, Constantine, Falmouth, Cornwall, TR11 5PL
Ⓣ (01326) 340593
Ⓔ plants@cornwallgardens.com
Ⓦ www.cornwallgardens.com
**Contact:** Sorcha Hitchcox
**Opening Times:** 1000-1700 Tue-Sat (closed Mon) & 1100-1600 Sun, Feb, July, Sep & Oct. By appt. Aug & Nov-Jan.
**Min Mail Order UK:** £25.00 + p&p
**Min Mail Order EU:** £40.00 + p&p
**Cat. Cost:** 6 × 1st class.
**Credit Cards:** Visa, Access, Delta, Switch
**Specialities:** Over 4000 varieties of cottage garden & rare perennials with many specialities. Also 80 varieties of *Clematis*. Some rare varieties available in small quantities only.
**Map Ref:** C, D1

**CFwr** **THE FLOWER BOWER** ⊠
Woodlands, Shurton, Stogursey,
Nr Bridgwater, Somerset, TA5 1QE
Ⓣ (01278) 732134
Ⓔ theflowerbower@yahoo.co.uk
Ⓦ www.theflowerbower.co.uk
**Contact:** Sheila Tucker
**Opening Times:** By appt. only.
**Min Mail Order UK:** Nmc
**Min Mail Order EU:** Nmc
**Cat. Cost:** 2 × 1st class.
**Credit Cards:** None
**Specialities:** *Hemerocallis*, esp. newer varieties & spiders. *Epiphyllum* 500+ varieties
**Notes:** Daylilies can also be pre-ordered for Autumn delivery. Newer & rarer varieties mostly available in small quantities.
**Map Ref:** C, B4 **OS Grid Ref:** ST203442

**CGHE** **GARDEN HOUSE ENTERPRISES** ⊠ ♿
The Garden House, Buckland Monachorum, Yelverton, Devon, PL20 7LQ
Ⓣ (01822) 854769
Ⓕ (01822) 855358
Ⓔ office@thegardenhouse.org.uk
Ⓦ www.thegardenhouse.org.uk
**Contact:** Jo Selman
**Opening Times:** 1030-1700 7 days 1st Mar-31st Oct.
**Min Mail Order UK:** Nmc
**Min Mail Order EU:** Nmc
**Cat. Cost:** None issued.
**Credit Cards:** All major credit/debit cards
**Specialities:** Choice woodland plants & dieramas.
**Map Ref:** C, C3 **OS Grid Ref:** SX496683

**CGro** **C W GROVES & SON LTD** ⊠ ♿
West Bay Road, Bridport, Dorset, DT6 4BA
Ⓣ (01308) 422654
Ⓕ (01308) 420888
Ⓔ garden@grovesnurseries.co.uk
Ⓦ www.grovesnurseries.co.uk
**Contact:** Clive Groves
**Opening Times:** 0830-1700 Mon-Sat, 1030-1630 Sun.
**Min Mail Order UK:** Nmc
**Min Mail Order EU:** £15.00 + p&p
**Cat. Cost:** 2 × 1st class.
**Credit Cards:** Visa, Switch, MasterCard
**Specialities:** Nursery & garden centre specialising in Parma & hardy *Viola*. Nat. Collection of *Viola odorata* cvs & Parma Violets. Also roses.
**Notes:** Mainly violets by mail order. Main display at nursery in Feb, Mar & Apr. Roses when dormant (Nov-Mar).
**Map Ref:** C, C5 **OS Grid Ref:** SY466918

**CGrW** **THE GREAT WESTERN GLADIOLUS NURSERY** ⊠ € ♿
17 Valley View, Clutton, Bristol, BS39 5SN
Ⓣ (01761) 452036
Ⓕ (01761) 452036
Ⓔ clutton.glads@btinternet.com
Ⓦ www.greatwesterngladiolus.co.uk
**Contact:** G F & J C Hazell
**Opening Times:** Mail order only. Open by appt. only.
**Min Mail Order UK:** Nmc
**Min Mail Order EU:** Nmc
**Cat. Cost:** 4 × 1st class (2 catalogues).
**Credit Cards:** None
**Specialities:** *Gladiolus* species & hybrids, corms & seeds. Other South African bulbous plants.
**Notes:** Also sells wholesale.

**CHab** **HABITAT AID LTD.** ⊠ ⛫
The Old Rectory, Lamyatt, Somerset, BA4 6NH
Ⓣ (01749) 812775
Ⓜ 07973 776613
Ⓕ (01749) 812971
Ⓔ info@habitataid.co.uk
Ⓦ www.habitataid.co.uk
**Contact:** Nick Mann
**Opening Times:** Not open. Mail order only.
**Min Mail Order UK:** £50.00, incl. p&p.
**Cat. Cost:** None issued.
**Credit Cards:** All major credit/debit cards
**Specialities:** British trees, plants and seeds. Local provenance seed mixes in small quantities only. Cottage garden perennials. Non-native trees for bees. Historic herbs.
**Notes:** Also sells wholesale.

**CHar** **WEST HARPTREE NURSERY** ⊠ ⛫ €
Bristol Road, West Harptree, Bath, Somerset, BS40 6HG
Ⓣ (01761) 221989
Ⓜ 07745 442385
Ⓔ bryn@harptreenursery.co.uk
Ⓦ www.harptreenursery.co.uk
**Contact:** Bryn Bowles
**Opening Times:** From 1000 Mon-Sun 7 days.
**Min Mail Order UK:** Nmc
**Min Mail Order EU:** Nmc
**Cat. Cost:** Large sae for free names list.
**Credit Cards:** MasterCard, Visa, Maestro, Paypal
**Specialities:** Unusual herbaceous perennials &

KEY
⊠ Mail order to UK or EU ⛫ Delivers to shows
✈ Exports beyond EU € Euro accepted
♿ Accessible by wheelchair ◆ See Display advertisement

C

shrubs. Bulbs & grasses. Many AGM plants.
**Notes:** Also sells wholesale.
**Map Ref:** C, B5

**CHby** **THE HERBARY** ⊠ ✈ €
161 Chapel Street, Horningsham, Warminster, Wiltshire, BA12 7LU
Ⓣ (01985) 844442
Ⓔ info@beansandherbs.co.uk
Ⓦ www.beansandherbs.co.uk
**Contact:** Pippa Rosen
**Opening Times:** May-Sep strictly by appt. only.
**Min Mail Order UK:** Nmc
**Min Mail Order EU:** Nmc
**Cat. Cost:** 4 × 1st class or online.
**Credit Cards:** None
**Specialities:** Culinary, medicinal & aromatic herbs organically grown in small quantities.
**Notes:** Mail order all year for organic vegetable seed & large variety of organic bean & herb seed. Also sells wholesale.
**Map Ref:** C, B5 **OS Grid Ref:** ST812414

**CHew** **HEWITT-COOPER CARNIVOROUS PLANTS** ⊠ ♠ € ♿
The Homestead, Glastonbury Road, West Pennard, Somerset, BA6 8NN
Ⓣ (01458) 832844
Ⓕ (01458) 832712
Ⓔ sales@hccarnivorousplants.co.uk
Ⓦ www.hccarnivorousplants.co.uk
**Contact:** Nigel Hewitt-Cooper
**Opening Times:** By appt.
**Min Mail Order UK:** £10.00 + p&p
**Min Mail Order EU:** £30.00
**Cat. Cost:** 1 × 1st class/1× IRC.
**Credit Cards:** All major credit/debit cards
**Specialities:** Carnivorous plants.
**Notes:** Mail order May-Nov.

**CHEx** **HARDY EXOTICS** ⊠ ♿
Gilly Lane, Whitecross, Penzance, Cornwall, TR20 8BZ
Ⓣ (01736) 740660
Ⓕ (01736) 741101
Ⓔ contact@hardyexotics.co.uk
Ⓦ www.hardyexotics.co.uk
**Contact:** C Shilton/J Smith
**Opening Times:** 1000-1700 7 days Apr-Oct, 1000-1700 Mon-Sat Nov-Feb. Please phone first in winter months if travelling a long way.
**Min Mail Order UK:** £25 carriage.
**Cat. Cost:** 4 × 1st class (no cheques).
**Credit Cards:** All major credit/debit cards
**Specialities:** Largest selection in the UK of trees, shrubs & herbaceous plants for tropical & desert effects. Hardy & half-hardy plants for gardens, patios & conservatories. Mature plants & plantings to inspire.
**Map Ref:** C, D1 **OS Grid Ref:** SW524345

**CHGN** **HIGH GARDEN NURSERIES** ♿
Chiverstone Lane, Kenton, Exeter, Devon, EX6 8NJ
Ⓣ (01626) 899106
Ⓔ highgarden@highgarden.co.uk
Ⓦ www.highgarden.co.uk
**Contact:** Chris Britton
**Opening Times:** 0900-1700 Tue-Fri
**Cat. Cost:** None issued.
**Credit Cards:** None
**Specialities:** Quality shrubs, trees & perennials, some unusual & different.
**Map Ref:** C, C4 **OS Grid Ref:** SX957836

**CHid** **HIDDEN VALLEY NURSERY** ♠ € ♿
Umberleigh, Devon, EX37 9BU
Ⓣ (01769) 560567
Ⓜ 07899 788789
Ⓔ plalindley@itsosbroadband.co.uk
**Contact:** Linda & Peter Lindley
**Opening Times:** Daylight hours but please phone first.
**Cat. Cost:** None issued.
**Credit Cards:** None
**Specialities:** Hardy perennials esp. shade lovers & Chatham Islands forget-me-nots (*Myosotidium hortensia*.)
**Map Ref:** C, B3 **OS Grid Ref:** SS567205

**CHll** **HILL HOUSE NURSERY & GARDENS** ⊠ € ♿
Landscove, Nr Ashburton, Devon, TQ13 7LY
Ⓣ (01803) 762273
Ⓕ (01803) 158218
Ⓔ info@hillhousenursery.com
Ⓦ www.hillhousenursery.co.uk
**Contact:** Raymond, Sacha & Matthew Hubbard
**Opening Times:** 1100-1700 7 days, all year. Open all B/hols incl. Easter Sun. Closed 24th Dec-7th Jan. Tearoom open 1st Mar-30th Sep.
**Min Mail Order UK:** Nmc
**Cat. Cost:** None issued.
**Credit Cards:** Delta, MasterCard, Switch, Visa
**Specialities:** 3000+ varieties of plants, most propagated on premises, many rare or unusual. The garden, open to the public, was laid out by Edward Hyams. Pioneers of glasshouse pest control by beneficial insects.
**Map Ref:** C, C3 **OS Grid Ref:** SX774664

**CHVG** **HIDDEN VALLEY GARDENS** € ♿
Treesmill, Nr Par, Cornwall, PL24 2TU
Ⓣ (01208) 873225
Ⓔ hiddenvalleygardens@yahoo.co.uk

Ⓦ www.hiddenvalleygardens.co.uk
**Contact:** Mrs P Howard
**Opening Times:** 1000-1800 Thu-Mon (closed Tue & Wed), 20th Mar-15th Oct. Please phone for directions. Garden open as nursery.
**Cat. Cost:** None issued.
**Credit Cards:** None
**Specialities:** Cottage garden plants, *Crocosmia* & many perennials which can be seen growing in the garden. Some stock available in small quantities.
**Notes:** Display garden.
**Map Ref:** C, D2 **OS Grid Ref:** SX094567

CIri **The Iris Garden** ⊠ € ♿
Yard House, Pilsdon, Bridport, Dorset, DT6 5PA
Ⓣ (01308) 868797
Ⓔ the_iris_garden@yahoo.com
Ⓦ www.theirisgarden.co.uk
**Contact:** Clive Russell
**Opening Times:** Show garden open by appt. only. Please email or phone for details.
**Min Mail Order UK:** £15.00 + p&p
**Min Mail Order EU:** £25.00 + p&p
**Cat. Cost:** 6 × 1st class.
**Credit Cards:** All major credit/debit cards
**Specialities:** Modern bearded & beardless *Iris* from breeders in UK, USA, France, Italy & Australia. Nat. Collection of Space Age *Iris*.
**Notes:** Orders for bearded iris & sibiricas must be received by end Jun & by end Aug for spurias & ensatas.
**Map Ref:** C, C5 **OS Grid Ref:** SY421988

CJas **Jasmine Cottage Gardens**
26 Channel Road, Walton St Mary, Clevedon, Somerset, BS21 7BY
Ⓣ (01275) 871850
Ⓔ margaret@bologrew.demon.co.uk
Ⓦ www.bologrew.pwp.blueyonder.co.uk
**Contact:** Mr & Mrs M Redgrave
**Opening Times:** May to Aug, daily by appt. Garden open at the same times.
**Cat. Cost:** None issued.
**Credit Cards:** None
**Specialities:** *Rhodochiton*, *Lophospermum*, *Maurandya*, *Dicentra macrocapnos*, *Salvia*, *Isotoma*, half-hardy geraniums.
**Map Ref:** C, A4 **OS Grid Ref:** ST405725

CKel **Kelways Ltd** ⊠ ✈ ⛺ € ♿
Langport, Somerset, TA10 9EZ
Ⓣ (01458) 250521
Ⓕ (01458) 253351
Ⓔ sales@kelways.co.uk
Ⓦ www.kelways.co.uk
**Contact:** Dave Root
**Opening Times:** 0900-1700 Mon-Fri, 0900-1700 Sat, 1000-1600 Sun.
**Min Mail Order UK:** £4.00 + p&p
**Min Mail Order EU:** £8.00 + p&p
**Cat. Cost:** Online only.
**Credit Cards:** All major credit/debit cards
**Specialities:** *Paeonia*, *Iris*, *Hemerocallis* & herbaceous perennials. Nat. Collection of *Paeonia lactiflora*. Wide range of trees, shrubs & herbaceous. Hardy ferns & tree ferns.
**Notes:** Also sells wholesale.
**Map Ref:** C, B5 **OS Grid Ref:** ST434273

CKen **Kenwith Nursery (Gordon Haddow)** ⊠ ✈ € ♿
Blinsham, Nr Torrington, Beaford, Winkleigh, Devon, EX19 8NT
Ⓣ (01805) 603274
Ⓕ (01805) 603663
Ⓔ conifers@kenwith63.freeserve.co.uk
Ⓦ www.kenwithnursery.co.uk
**Contact:** Gordon Haddow
**Opening Times:** 1000-1630 Tue-Sat all year. Closed all B/hols.
**Min Mail Order UK:** £15.00 + p&p
**Min Mail Order EU:** £50.00 + p&p
**Cat. Cost:** 3 × 1st class.
**Credit Cards:** Visa, MasterCard
**Specialities:** All conifer genera. Grafting a speciality. Many new introductions to UK. Nat. Collection of Dwarf Conifers.
**Map Ref:** C, B3 **OS Grid Ref:** SS518160

CKno **Knoll Gardens** ⊠ ⛺ ♿
Hampreston, Nr Wimborne, Dorset, BH21 7ND
Ⓣ (01202) 873931
Ⓕ (01202) 870842
Ⓔ enquiries@knollgardens.co.uk
Ⓦ www.knollgardens.co.uk
**Contact:** N R Lucas
**Opening Times:** 1000-1700 Tue-Sun, May-Oct. 1000-1600 Wed-Sat, Nov-Apr. Closed 19th Dec 2010 reopens 2nd Feb 2011. Open B/hol Mons.
**Min Mail Order UK:** Nmc
**Min Mail Order EU:** Nmc
**Cat. Cost:** Online only.
**Credit Cards:** Visa, MasterCard
**Specialities:** Grasses (main specialism). Select perennials. Nat. Collections of *Pennisetum*,

C

*Phygelius* & deciduous *Ceanothus*. Sole UK supplier of *Ulmus americana* 'Princeton'.
**Notes:** Also sells wholesale.
**Map Ref:** C, C6

**CLak** **LAKKA BULBS** ⊠
(Office) 127 Mill Street, Torrington, North Devon, EX38 8AW
Ⓣ (01805) 625071
Ⓔ lakkabulbs@tesco.net
**Contact:** Jonathan Hutchinson
**Opening Times:** Not open. Mail order only.
**Min Mail Order UK:** Nmc
**Min Mail Order EU:** Nmc
**Cat. Cost:** None issued.
**Credit Cards:** None
**Specialities:** Nat. Collections of *Urginea*, *Veltheimia* & *Scadoxus*. Other South African bulbs of families *Amaryllidaceae* & *Hyacinthaceae*. All available in small quantities only.

**CLAP** **LONG ACRE PLANTS** ⊠ ♿
South Marsh, Charlton Musgrove, Nr Wincanton, Somerset, BA9 8EX
Ⓣ (01963) 32802
Ⓕ (01963) 32802
Ⓔ info@plantsforshade.co.uk
Ⓦ www.plantsforshade.co.uk
**Contact:** Nigel & Michelle Rowland
**Opening Times:** 1000-1300 & 1400-1700 Thu & Fri only, Feb-Jun, Sep & Oct.
**Min Mail Order UK:** £20.00 + p&p
**Cat. Cost:** 3 × 1st class.
**Credit Cards:** MasterCard, Visa, Maestro, American Express, JCB
**Specialities:** Ferns, woodland bulbs & perennials. Marginal/bog plants.
**Notes:** Some plants available in small numbers only and only seasonally available.
**Map Ref:** C, B5

**CLnd** **LANDFORD TREES** €
Landford Lodge, Landford, Salisbury, Wiltshire, SP5 2EH
Ⓣ (01794) 390808
Ⓕ (01794) 390037
Ⓔ trees@landfordtrees.co.uk
Ⓦ www.landfordtrees.co.uk
**Contact:** C D Pilkington
**Opening Times:** 0800-1700 Mon-Fri.
**Cat. Cost:** Free.
**Credit Cards:** All, except American Express
**Specialities:** Deciduous ornamental trees.
**Map Ref:** C, B6 **OS Grid Ref:** SU247201

**CLng** **LONGCOMBE NURSERY AND GARDEN CENTRE** ⊠ ♿
Longcombe, Totnes, Devon, TQ9 6PL
Ⓣ 0844 335 6915
Ⓔ info@simplyclematis.co.uk
Ⓦ www.simplyclematis.co.uk
**Contact:** Linda Clarke
**Opening Times:** 0900-1700 Mon-Sat, 1000-1600 Sun.
**Min Mail Order UK:** Nmc
**Cat. Cost:** Online only.
**Credit Cards:** All major credit/debit cards
**Specialities:** *Clematis*.
**Notes:** Also sells wholesale.
**Map Ref:** C, C3 **OS Grid Ref:** SX834601

**CLoc** **C S LOCKYER (FUCHSIAS)** ⊠ ☒ € ◆
Lansbury, 70 Henfield Road, Coalpit Heath, Bristol, BS36 2UZ
Ⓣ (01454) 772219
Ⓕ (01454) 772219
Ⓔ sales@lockyerfuchsias.co.uk
Ⓦ www.lockyerfuchsias.co.uk
**Contact:** C S Lockyer
**Opening Times:** 1000-1300, 1430-1700 most days, please ring.
**Min Mail Order UK:** 6 plants + p&p
**Min Mail Order EU:** £12.00 + p&p
**Cat. Cost:** 4 × 1st class.
**Credit Cards:** All major credit/debit cards
**Specialities:** *Fuchsia*.
**Notes:** Many open days & coach parties. Partial wheelchair access. Also sells wholesale.
**Map Ref:** C, A5

**CMac** **MAC PENNYS NURSERIES** ⊠
154 Burley Road, Bransgore, Christchurch, Dorset, BH23 8DB
Ⓣ (01425) 672348
Ⓕ (01425) 673917
Ⓔ office@macpennys.co.uk
Ⓦ www.macpennys.co.uk
**Contact:** T & V Lowndes & S Lowndes
**Opening Times:** 0900-1700 Mon-Sat, 1000-1700 Sun. Closed Xmas-New Year.
**Min Mail Order UK:** Nmc
**Cat. Cost:** A4 sae with 4 × 1st class.
**Credit Cards:** All major credit/debit cards
**Specialities:** General. Plants available in small quantities only.
**Notes:** Mail order available Sep-Mar, UK only. Nursery partially accessible for wheelchairs. Also sells wholesale.
**Map Ref:** C, C6

**CMCN** **MALLET COURT NURSERY** ⊠ ☒ € ♿
Curry Mallet, Taunton, Somerset, TA3 6SY
Ⓣ (01823) 481493

Ⓕ (01823) 481493
Ⓔ malletcourtnursery@btinternet.com
Ⓦ www.malletcourt.co.uk
**Contact:** J G S & P M E Harris F.L.S.
**Opening Times:** 0930-1700 Mon-Fri summer, 0930-1600 winter. Sat & Sun by appt.
**Min Mail Order UK:** Nmc
**Min Mail Order EU:** Nmc
**Cat. Cost:** £1.50
**Credit Cards:** All major credit/debit cards
**Specialities:** Maples, oaks, *Magnolia*, hollies & other rare and unusual plants including those from China & South Korea.
**Notes:** Mail order Oct-Mar only. Also sells wholesale.
**Map Ref:** C, B4

**CMea** THE MEAD NURSERY ♿
Brokerswood, Nr Westbury, Wiltshire, BA13 4EG
Ⓣ (01373) 859990
Ⓦ www.themeadnursery.co.uk
**Contact:** Steve & Emma Lewis-Dale
**Opening Times:** 0900-1700 Wed-Sat & B/hols, 1200-1700 Sun, 1st Feb-10th Oct. Closed Easter Sun.
**Cat. Cost:** 5 × 1st class.
**Credit Cards:** All major credit/debit cards
**Specialities:** Perennials, alpines, pot-grown bulbs and grasses.
**Map Ref:** C, B5 **OS Grid Ref:** ST833517

**CMen** MENDIP BONSAI STUDIO ✉ ♿
Byways, Back Lane, Downside, Shepton Mallet, Somerset, BA4 4JR
Ⓣ (01749) 344274
Ⓜ 07711 205806
Ⓔ jr.trott@ukonline.co.uk
Ⓦ www.mendipbonsai.co.uk
**Contact:** John Trott
**Opening Times:** Private nursery. Visits by appt. only.
**Min Mail Order UK:** Nmc
**Cat. Cost:** Large sae for plant & workshop lists
**Credit Cards:** All major credit/debit cards
**Specialities:** Bonsai, Potensai, accent plants & garden stock. Acers, conifers, incl. many *Pinus thunbergii* species. Many plants available in small numbers only. Young trees for garden or bonsai culture.
**Notes:** Education classes, lectures, demonstrations & club talks on bonsai. Stockist of most bonsai sundries. Mail orders will be normally despatched late Sep/early Oct. Ltd wheelchair access.
**Map Ref:** C, B5

**CMHG** MARWOOD HILL GARDENS ♿
Marwood, Barnstaple, Devon, EX31 4EB
Ⓣ (01271) 342528
Ⓕ (01271) 342528
Ⓔ info@marwoodhillgarden.co.uk
Ⓦ www.marwoodhillgarden.co.uk
**Contact:** Malcolm Pharoah
**Opening Times:** 1100-1630, 7 days. Closed Nov-Feb.
**Cat. Cost:** 3 × 1st class.
**Credit Cards:** Visa, Delta, MasterCard, Switch, Solo
**Specialities:** Large range of unusual trees & shrubs. *Eucalyptus*, alpines, *Camellia*, *Astilbe*, bog plants & perennials. Nat. Collections of *Astilbe*, *Tulbaghia* & *Iris ensata*.
**Map Ref:** C, B3 **OS Grid Ref:** SS545375

**CMil** MILL COTTAGE PLANTS ✉ ♿
Henley Mill, Henley Lane, Wookey, Somerset, BA5 1AW
Ⓣ (01749) 676966
Ⓜ 07851 698759
Ⓔ millcottageplants@googlemail.com
Ⓦ www.millcottageplants.co.uk
**Contact:** Sally Gregson
**Opening Times:** By appt. only. Phone for directions.
**Min Mail Order UK:** Nmc
**Min Mail Order EU:** £25.00 + p&p
**Cat. Cost:** 4 × 1st class.
**Credit Cards:** All major credit/debit cards
**Specialities:** Rare *Hydrangea serrata* cvs, *H. aspera* cvs, shade-loving perennials incl. *Epimedium*, ferns & damp-loving plants.
**Map Ref:** C, B5

**CMMP** M & M PLANTS ♿
Lloret. Chittlehamholt, Umberleigh, Devon, EX37 9PD
Ⓣ (01769) 540448
Ⓕ (01769) 540448
Ⓔ mmplants@mail.com
**Contact:** Mr M Thorne
**Opening Times:** 0930-1700 Tue-Sat, Apr-Oct & 1000-1600 Tue-Fri, Nov-Mar. Sat by appt. in Aug.
**Cat. Cost:** 3 × 1st class.
**Credit Cards:** None
**Specialities:** Perennials. We also carry a good range of alpines, shrubs, trees & roses.
**Map Ref:** C, B3

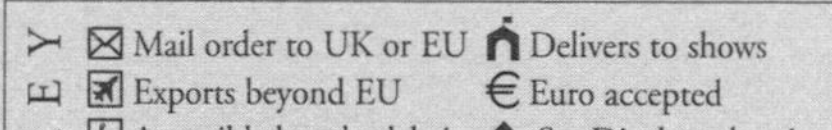

C

**CNat** **NATURAL SELECTION** ⊠ €
1 Station Cottages, Hullavington,
Chippenham, Wiltshire, SN14 6ET
Ⓣ (01666) 837369
Ⓜ 07800 583999
Ⓔ martin@worldmutation.demon.co.uk
Ⓦ www.worldmutation.demon.co.uk
**Contact:** Martin Barber
**Opening Times:** Please phone first.
**Min Mail Order UK:** £9.00 + p&p
**Cat. Cost:** 2 × 2nd class.
**Credit Cards:** None
**Specialities:** Unusual British natives & others. Also seed. Only available in small quantities.
**Map Ref:** C, A5

**COIW** **THE OLD WITHY GARDEN NURSERY** ⊠
Grange Fruit Farm, Gweek, Helston,
Cornwall, TR12 6BE
Ⓣ (01326) 221171
Ⓔ sales@theoldwithygardennursery.co.uk
Ⓦ www.theoldwithygardennursery.co.uk
**Contact:** Sheila Chandler or Nick Chandler
**Opening Times:** 0930-1700 7 days, Feb-end Oct. 1000-1600 Tue-Fri, Nov.
**Min Mail Order UK:** £15.00
**Cat. Cost:** 4 × 1st class.
**Credit Cards:** Maestro, MasterCard, Visa, Delta
**Specialities:** Cottage garden plants, perennials, some biennials & grasses. Some varieties in small quantities only.
**Notes:** Partially accessible for wheelchairs (gravel paths). Also sells wholesale.
**Map Ref:** C, D1 **OS Grid Ref:** SW688255

**CPar** **PARKS PERENNIALS** ⌂
242 Wallisdown Road, Wallisdown,
Bournemouth, Dorset, BH10 4HZ
Ⓣ (01202) 524464
Ⓔ parks.perennials@ntlworld.com
**Contact:** S. Parks
**Opening Times:** Apr-Oct most days, please phone first.
**Cat. Cost:** None issued.
**Credit Cards:** None
**Specialities:** Hardy herbaceous perennials.
**Map Ref:** C, C6

**CPbn** **PENBORN GOAT FARM** ⊠ ♿
Penborn, Bounds Cross, Holsworthy, Devon,
EX22 6LH
Ⓣ (01288) 381569
Ⓔ penborngoats@btinternet.com
Ⓦ www.penborngoats.com
**Contact:** P R Oldfield
**Opening Times:** By appt. only.
**Min Mail Order UK:** £10.00
**Min Mail Order EU:** £10.00
**Cat. Cost:** Online.
**Credit Cards:** None
**Specialities:** *Mentha*, *Melissa*. Available in small quantities only.
**Map Ref:** C, C2 **OS Grid Ref:** SS290021

**CPBP** **PARHAM BUNGALOW PLANTS** ⊠ ⌂ €
Parham Lane, Market Lavington, Devizes,
Wiltshire, SN10 4QA
Ⓣ (01380) 812605
Ⓔ jjs@pbplants.freeserve.co.uk
**Contact:** Mrs D E Sample
**Opening Times:** Please ring first.
**Min Mail Order UK:** Nmc
**Min Mail Order EU:** Nmc
**Cat. Cost:** Sae.
**Credit Cards:** None
**Specialities:** Alpines.
**Map Ref:** C, B6

**CPen** **PENNARD PLANTS** ⊠ ✈ ⌂ €
3 The Gardens, East Pennard, Shepton Mallet,
Somerset, BA4 6TU
Ⓣ (01749) 860039
Ⓕ 07043 017270
Ⓔ sales@pennardplants.com
Ⓦ www.pennardplants.com
**Contact:** Chris Smith
**Opening Times:** By appt. only.
**Min Mail Order UK:** Nmc
**Min Mail Order EU:** Nmc
**Cat. Cost:** 3 × 1st class.
**Credit Cards:** All major credit/debit cards
**Specialities:** *Agapanthus*, *Dierama* & *Gladioli* species. Nerines (*bowdenii* hybrids).
**Notes:** Nursery at The Walled Garden at East Pennard.
**Map Ref:** C, B5

**CPhi** **ALAN PHIPPS CACTI** ⊠ ⌂ €
62 Samuel White Road, Hanham, Bristol,
BS15 3LX
Ⓣ (0117) 9607591
Ⓦ www.cactus-mall.com/alan-phipps/index.html
**Contact:** A Phipps
**Opening Times:** 1000-1700 but prior phone call essential to ensure a greeting.
**Min Mail Order UK:** £5.00 + p&p
**Min Mail Order EU:** £20.00 + p&p
**Cat. Cost:** Sae or 2 × IRC (EC only).
**Credit Cards:** None
**Specialities:** *Mammillaria*, *Astrophytum* & *Ariocarpus*. Species & varieties will change with times. Ample quantities exist in spring. Limited range of *Agave*.
**Notes:** Euro accepted as cash only. Specimen-size plants not available by mail order.
**Map Ref:** C, A5 **OS Grid Ref:** ST644717

CPHo **The Palm House** ✉
8 North Street, Ottery St Mary, Devon, EX11 1DR
Ⓣ (01404) 815450
Ⓜ 07815 673397
Ⓔ george@thepalmhouse.co.uk
Ⓦ www.thepalmhouse.co.uk
**Contact:** George Gregory
**Opening Times:** Mail order only. Open by appt. only.
**Min Mail Order UK:** £15.00
**Min Mail Order EU:** £10.00
**Cat. Cost:** 2 × 1st class.
**Credit Cards:** All major credit/debit cards
**Specialities:** Palms.
**Notes:** Also sells wholesale.
**Map Ref:** C, C4 **OS Grid Ref:** SY098955

CPLG **Exclusive Plants (incorporating Pine Lodge Gardens & Nursery)** ✉ ♿
Pine Lodge Gardens, Holmbush, St Austell, Cornwall, PL25 3RQ
Ⓣ (01726) 77960
Ⓜ 07775 811385
Ⓕ (01726) 77960
Ⓔ pbonavia3@aol.com
Ⓦ www.exclusiveplants.co.uk
**Contact:** Paul Bonavia
**Opening Times:** 1000-1700 7 days all year, except 24th/25th/26th Dec.
**Min Mail Order UK:** Nmc
**Cat. Cost:** 3 × 2nd class.
**Credit Cards:** All major credit/debit cards
**Specialities:** Rare & unusual shrubs & herbaceous, some from seed collected on plant expeditions each year. Nat. Collection of *Grevillea*.
**Map Ref:** C, D2 **OS Grid Ref:** SX045527

CPMA **P M A Plant Specialities** ✉ €
Junker's Nursery Ltd., Lower Mead, West Hatch, Taunton, Somerset, TA3 5RN
Ⓣ (01823) 480774
Ⓔ karan@junker.co.uk
Ⓦ www.junker.co.uk
**Contact:** Karan or Nick Junker
**Opening Times:** Strictly by appt. only.
**Min Mail Order UK:** Nmc
**Min Mail Order EU:** Nmc
**Cat. Cost:** 6 × 2nd class or 5 × 1st class.
**Credit Cards:** None
**Specialities:** Choice & unusual shrubs incl. grafted *Acer palmatum*, *Cornus*, *Magnolia* & a wide range of *Daphne*. Small quantities only of some hard to propagate plants, esp. daphnes. Reserve orders accepted. Planted areas showing how the plants look growing in "real world" conditions. We propagate & grow all our own plants with an increasing number grown naturally in open ground as well as in pots.
**Notes:** Partial wheelchair access. Nursery will be relocating, so please ring or check website before visiting.
**Map Ref:** C, B4 **OS Grid Ref:** ST280203

CPne **Pine Cottage Plants** ✉ ✈ ⛺ €
Pine Cottage, Fourways, Eggesford, Chulmleigh, Devon, EX18 7QZ
Ⓣ (01769) 580076
Ⓜ 07718 505053
Ⓔ sales@pcplants.co.uk
Ⓦ www.pcplants.co.uk
**Contact:** Dick Fulcher
Opening Times: Special open weeks for *Agapanthus*, 1000-1500 daily 14th Jul-5th Sep excl. Sun. Other times by appt. only.
**Min Mail Order UK:** £20.00 + p&p
**Min Mail Order EU:** £50.00 + p&p
**Cat. Cost:** 4 × 1st class.
**Credit Cards:** Maestro, MasterCard, Visa
**Specialities:** Nat. Collection of *Agapanthus*. 200+ cvs available.
**Notes:** Mail order *Agapanthus* from Sep-Jun. Also sells wholesale.
**Map Ref:** C, B3 **OS Grid Ref:** SS683099

CPom **Pomeroy Plants**
Tower House, Pomeroy Lane, Wingfield, Trowbridge, Wiltshire, BA14 9LJ
Ⓣ (01225) 769551
Ⓜ 07895 096564
Ⓔ drsimonyoung@yahoo.co.uk
**Contact:** Simon Young
**Opening Times:** Mar-Nov. Please phone first.
**Cat. Cost:** 2 × 1st class.
**Credit Cards:** None
**Specialities:** Hardy, mainly species, herbaceous perennials. Many unusual and often small numbers. Specialities *Allium*, *Salvia* & shade-lovers, esp. *Epimedium*.
**Map Ref:** C, B5 **OS Grid Ref:** ST817569

CPou **Pounsley Plants** ✉ € ♿
Pounsley Combe, Spriddlestone, Brixton, Plymouth, Devon, PL9 0DW
Ⓣ (01752) 402873
Ⓜ 07770 758501
Ⓕ (01752) 402873
Ⓔ pou599@aol.com

KEY
✉ Mail order to UK or EU ⛺ Delivers to shows
✈ Exports beyond EU € Euro accepted
♿ Accessible by wheelchair ◆ See Display advertisement

C

Ⓦ www.pounsleyplants.com
**Contact:** Mrs Jane Hollow
**Opening Times:** Normally 1000-1700 Mon-Sat but please phone first.
**Min Mail Order UK:** £10.00 + p&p
**Min Mail Order EU:** £20.00 + p&p
**Cat. Cost:** 2 × 1st class.
**Credit Cards:** None
**Specialities:** Unusual herbaceous perennials, cottage plants & *Clematis*. Comprehensive range of Old Roses. Large selection of South African monocots.
**Notes:** Mail order Nov-Feb only. Also sells wholesale.
**Map Ref:** C, D3 **OS Grid Ref:** SX521538

**CPrp** PROPERPLANTS.COM ⊠ ✈ ♿
Penknight, Edgcumbe Road, Lostwithiel, Cornwall, PL22 0JD
Ⓣ (01208) 872291
Ⓔ info@ProperPlants.com
Ⓦ www.ProperPlants.com
**Contact:** Sarah Wilks
**Opening Times:** 1000-1800 or dusk if earlier, Tue & B/hols mid-Mar to end-Sep & by appt.
**Min Mail Order UK:** Nmc
**Min Mail Order EU:** Nmc
**Cat. Cost:** 4 × 1st class.
**Credit Cards:** All major credit/debit cards
**Specialities:** Wide range of unusual & easy herbaceous perennials, esp. of South African origin. Ferns & grasses. Less common herbs.
**Notes:** Partially accessible for wheelchair users.
**Map Ref:** C, C2 **OS Grid Ref:** SX093596

**CPSs** PLANTS FOR THE SENSES ⊠
Corner Cottage, North Street, Dolton, Winkleigh, Devon, EX19 8QQ
Ⓣ (01805) 804467
Ⓔ michaelross@freenetname.co.uk
**Contact:** Michael Ross
**Opening Times:** Not open. Mail order only.
**Min Mail Order UK:** Nmc
**Cat. Cost:** 1 × 1st class.
**Credit Cards:** None
**Specialities:** Some emphasis on scented plants. Some stock in small quantities only.

**CQua** QUALITY DAFFODILS ⊠ ✈ € ◆
14 Roscarrack Close, Falmouth, Cornwall, TR11 4PJ
Ⓣ (01326) 317959
Ⓜ 07989 243450
Ⓕ (01326) 317959
Ⓔ rascamp@daffodils.uk.com
Ⓦ www.qualitydaffodils.com
**Contact:** R A Scamp
**Opening Times:** Not open. Mail order only. Viewing by appt. only.
**Min Mail Order UK:** Nmc
**Min Mail Order EU:** Nmc
**Cat. Cost:** 3 × 1st class.
**Credit Cards:** All major credit/debit cards
**Specialities:** *Narcissus* hybrids & species. Some stocks are less than 100 bulbs.
**Notes:** Also sells wholesale.
**Map Ref:** C, D1

**CRDP** R D PLANTS ♿
Homelea Farm, Chard Road, Tytherleigh, Axminster, East Devon, EX13 7BG
Ⓣ (01460) 220206
Ⓕ (01460) 220206
**Contact:** Rodney Davey & Lynda Windsor
**Opening Times:** 1000-1600 most days, 1st Mar-30th Jun. Open 1st Feb for hellebores.
**Cat. Cost:** None issued.
**Credit Cards:** None
**Specialities:** Double & anemone-centred hellebores. Choice plants for moist shade. Established garden-worthy plants in flower for most situations.
**Map Ref:** C, C4 **OS Grid Ref:** ST3203

**CRea** REALLY WILD FLOWERS ⊠
H V Horticulture Ltd, Spring Mead, Bedchester, Shaftesbury, Dorset, SP7 0JU
Ⓣ (01747) 811778
Ⓕ 0844 443 2503
Ⓔ info@reallywildflowers.co.uk
Ⓦ www.reallywildflowers.co.uk
**Contact:** Grahame Dixie
**Opening Times:** Not open. Mail order only.
**Min Mail Order UK:** £40.00 + p&p
**Cat. Cost:** 3 × 1st class.
**Credit Cards:** All major credit/debit cards
**Specialities:** Native wild flowers for grasslands, woodlands & wetlands. Seeds & bulbs. Hedge plants & trees. Advisory & soil analysis services.
**Notes:** Credit card payment accepted for online orders only. Also sells wholesale.

**CRHN** ROSELAND HOUSE NURSERY ⊠ ♿
Chacewater, Truro, Cornwall, TR4 8QB
Ⓣ (01872) 560451
Ⓔ clematis@roselandhouse.co.uk
Ⓦ www.roselandhouse.co.uk
**Contact:** C R Pridham
**Opening Times:** 1300-1700 Tue & Wed, Apr-Sep. Other times by appt.
**Min Mail Order UK:** Nmc
**Min Mail Order EU:** Nmc
**Cat. Cost:** Online only.
**Credit Cards:** All major credit/debit cards
**Specialities:** Climbing & conservatory plants.

C

Nat. Collections of *Clematis viticella* & *Lapageria rosea*. Named *Lapageria* in short supply but occasionally available.
**Notes:** Garden open to the public. Credit cards accepted from mail order customers only.
**Map Ref:** C, D1 **OS Grid Ref:** SW752445

CRow **Rowden Gardens** ⊠ ✈ ♿
Brentor, Nr Tavistock, Devon, PL19 0NG
Ⓣ (01822) 810275
Ⓔ rowdengardens1@btinternet.com
Ⓦ www.rowdengardens.com
**Contact:** John R L Carter
**Opening Times:** By appt only.
**Min Mail Order UK:** Nmc
**Min Mail Order EU:** Nmc
**Cat. Cost:** 6 × 1st class.
**Credit Cards:** None
**Specialities:** Aquatics, damp loving & associated plants incl. rare & unusual varieties. Nat. Collections of *Caltha* & Water *Iris*. Some stock available in small quantities only.
**Notes:** Also sells wholesale.
**Map Ref:** C, C3

CRWN **The Really Wild Nursery** ⊠ ✈ €
19 Hoopers Way, Torrington, Devon, EX38 7NS
Ⓣ (01805) 624739
Ⓕ (01805) 624739
Ⓔ thereallywildnursery@yahoo.co.uk
Ⓦ www.thereallywildnursery.co.uk
**Contact:** Kathryn Moore
**Opening Times:** Not open. Mail order only.
**Min Mail Order UK:** £10.00 + p&p
**Min Mail Order EU:** £20.00 + p&p
**Cat. Cost:** 3 × 1st class.
**Credit Cards:** Paypal
**Specialities:** Wildflowers, bulbs & seeds.
**Notes:** Mail order all year round, grown to order (plants in pots or plugs). Also sells wholesale.

CSam **Sampford Shrubs** ⊠ € ♿
Sampford Peverell, Tiverton, Devon, EX16 7EN
Ⓣ (01884) 821164
Ⓔ via website
Ⓦ www.samshrub.co.uk
**Contact:** M Hughes-Jones & S Proud
**Opening Times:** 0900-1700 Tue-Sat, Mar-Oct.
**Cat. Cost:** A5 sae.
**Credit Cards:** All major credit/debit cards
**Specialities:** Large displays of *Pulmonaria* & *Crocosmia*. Nat. Collection of *Helenium*.
Plants suitable for naturalistic schemes.
**Notes:** Mail order only via dedicated e-commerce website. Despatched Oct-Mar.
**Map Ref:** C, B4 **OS Grid Ref:** ST043153

CSBt **St Bridget Nurseries Ltd** ⊠ ♠ ♿
Old Rydon Lane, Exeter, Devon, EX2 7JY
Ⓣ (01392) 873672
Ⓕ (01392) 876710
Ⓔ info@stbridgetnurseries.co.uk
Ⓦ www.stbridgetnurseries.co.uk
**Contact:** Garden Centre Plant Advice
**Opening Times:** 0900-1700 Mon-Sat, 1030-1630 Sun. Closed Xmas Day, Boxing Day, New Year's Day & Easter Sunday.
**Min Mail Order UK:** Nmc
**Cat. Cost:** Free.
**Credit Cards:** All major credit/debit cards
**Specialities:** Large general nursery, with two garden centres.
**Notes:** Mail order available between Nov & Mar.
**Map Ref:** C, C4 **OS Grid Ref:** SX955905

CSev **Lower Severalls Nursery** ⊠ ♿
Crewkerne, Somerset, TA18 7NX
Ⓣ (01460) 73234
Ⓜ 07769 273829
Ⓔ mary@lowerseveralls.co.uk
Ⓦ www.lowerseveralls.co.uk
**Contact:** Mary R Pring
**Opening Times:** 1000-1700 Tue, Wed, Fri, Sat, Mar-end Sep. Closed Aug.
**Min Mail Order UK:** £20.00
**Cat. Cost:** 4 × 1st class.
**Credit Cards:** None
**Specialities:** Herbs, herbaceous.
**Notes:** Mail order perennials only.
**Map Ref:** C, B5 **OS Grid Ref:** ST457111

CSil **Silver Dale Nurseries** €
Shute Lane, Combe Martin, Devon, EX34 0HT
Ⓣ (01271) 882539
Ⓔ silverdale.nurseries@virgin.net
**Contact:** Roger Gilbert
**Opening Times:** 1000-1700 7 days. Closed Nov-Jan.
**Cat. Cost:** 4 × 1st class.
**Credit Cards:** Visa, MasterCard, EuroCard
**Specialities:** Nat. Collection of *Fuchsia*. Hardy fuchsias (cultivars and species).
**Map Ref:** C, B3

KEY
⊠ Mail order to UK or EU ♠ Delivers to shows
✈ Exports beyond EU € Euro accepted
♿ Accessible by wheelchair ◆ See Display advertisement

C

**CSna** **SNAPE COTTAGE** ⊠
Chaffeymoor, Bourton, Dorset, SP8 5BZ
Ⓣ (01747) 840330 (evenings only).
Ⓔ ianandangela@snapecottagegarden.co.uk
Ⓦ www.snapestakes.com
**Contact:** Mrs Angela Whinfield
**Opening Times:** 1030-1700 last 2 Suns in Feb; 1400-1700 last Sat & Sun in month Mar-Aug incl.
**Min Mail Order UK:** Nmc
**Cat. Cost:** Sae.
**Credit Cards:** None
**Specialities:** 'Old' forms of many popular garden plants. Plantsman's garden open same time as nursery. Stock available in small quantities. Snape Stakes plant supports.
**Notes:** Mail order *Galanthus* only. List issued in Feb.
**Map Ref:** C, B5 **OS Grid Ref:** ST762303

**CSpe** **SPECIAL PLANTS** ⊠ ń €
Hill Farm Barn, Greenways Lane, Cold Ashton, Chippenham, Wiltshire, SN14 8LA
Ⓣ (01225) 891686
Ⓔ derry@specialplants.net
Ⓦ www.specialplants.net
**Contact:** Derry Watkins
**Opening Times:** 1000-1700 7 days Mar-Oct. Other times please ring first to check.
**Min Mail Order UK:** £10.00 + p&p
**Cat. Cost:** 4 × 1st class (A5 sae only for seed list).
**Credit Cards:** All major credit/debit cards
**Specialities:** Tender perennials, *Pelargonium*, *Salvia*, *Streptocarpus*, hardy geraniums, *Anemone*, *Erysimum*, *Papaver*, *Viola* & grasses. Many varieties prop. in small numbers only.
**Notes:** Mail order Sep-Mar only.
**Map Ref:** C, A5 **OS Grid Ref:** ST749726

**CSPN** **SHERSTON PARVA NURSERY** ⊠ ✈ ń €
♿
Malmesbury Road, Sherston, Wiltshire, SN16 0NX
Ⓣ (01666) 840348
Ⓜ 07887 814843
Ⓔ sherstonparva@aol.com
Ⓦ www.sherstonparva.com
**Contact:** Martin Rea
**Opening Times:** 1000-1700 7 days 1st Feb-31th Dec. Closed Jan.
**Min Mail Order UK:** Nmc
**Min Mail Order EU:** Nmc
**Cat. Cost:** Free.
**Credit Cards:** MasterCard, Delta, Visa, Switch
**Specialities:** *Clematis*, wall shrubs & climbers.
**Map Ref:** C, A5

**CSpr** **SPRINGFIELD PLANTS**
Springfield, Woolsery, Bideford, Devon, EX39 5PZ
Ⓣ (01237) 431162
Ⓔ asta.munro@tiscali.co.uk
**Contact:** Asta Munro
**Opening Times:** 1000-1600 Apr-Sep incl. Closed Mon. Other times please ring first.
**Cat. Cost:** List only, free by email.
**Credit Cards:** None
**Specialities:** Hardy perennials for wide variety of situations & plants with interesting foliage. Small quantities only. Hardy geraniums.
**Map Ref:** C, B2 **OS Grid Ref:** SS347206

**CSto** **STONE LANE GARDENS** ⊠
Stone Farm, Chagford, Devon, TQ13 8JU
Ⓣ (01647) 231311
Ⓔ orders@mythicgarden.eclipse.co.uk
Ⓦ www.stonelanegardens.com
**Contact:** Paul Bartlett
**Opening Times:** 0900-1700 Mon-Fri. Collection at w/ends possible. Please phone first if travelling a long distance.
**Min Mail Order UK:** Nmc
**Min Mail Order EU:** Nmc
**Cat. Cost:** 6 × 1st class for colour catalogue with photos.
**Credit Cards:** None
**Specialities:** Comprehensive selection of wild origin *Betula* & *Alnus*, both bare-root & in pots. Choice selection of specially grafted cvs. Nat. Collection of Birch & Alder.
**Notes:** Arboretum open all year with summer sculpture exhibition (charges apply). Planting service available in West Country, details on request. Also sells wholesale.
**Map Ref:** C, C3 **OS Grid Ref:** SX708908

**CSut** **SUTTONS SEEDS** ⊠
Woodview Road, Paignton, Devon, TQ4 7NG
Ⓣ 0844 922 2899
Ⓕ 0844 922 2265
Ⓦ www.suttons.co.uk
**Contact:** Customer Services
**Opening Times:** (Office) 0830-1700 Mon-Fri. Also answerphone.
**Min Mail Order UK:** Nmc
**Min Mail Order EU:** £5.00
**Cat. Cost:** Free.
**Credit Cards:** Visa, MasterCard, Switch, Delta
**Specialities:** Over 1,000 varieties of flower & vegetable seed, bulbs, plants & sundries.

**CSWC** **SOUTH WEST CARNIVOROUS PLANTS**
⊠ ✈
Blackwater Nursery, Blackwater Road, Culmstock, Cullompton, Devon, EX15 3HG

Ⓣ (01823) 681669
Ⓕ 0870 705 3083
Ⓔ flytraps@littleshopofhorrors.co.uk
Ⓦ www.littleshopofhorrors.co.uk
**Contact:** Jenny Pearce & Alistair Pearce
**Opening Times:** By appt.
**Min Mail Order UK:** Nmc
**Min Mail Order EU:** Nmc
**Cat. Cost:** 2 × 2nd class.
**Credit Cards:** All major credit/debit cards
**Specialities:** *Cephalotus*, *Nepenthes*, *Dionea*, *Drosera*, *Darlingtonia*, *Sarracenia*, *Pinguicula* & *Utricularia*. Specialists in hardy carnivorous plants & *Dionea muscipula* cvs.
**Map Ref:** C, B4

**CTca** **TRECANNA NURSERY** ⊠ ✈ ⛺
Rose Farm, Latchley, Nr Gunnislake, Cornwall, PL18 9AX
Ⓣ (01822) 834680
Ⓜ 07785 242148
Ⓔ mark@trecanna.com
Ⓦ www.trecanna.com
**Contact:** Mark Wash
**Opening Times:** 1000-1700 Wed-Sat, Mar-Nov incl.
**Min Mail Order UK:** £20
**Min Mail Order EU:** £40
**Cat. Cost:** £1.00
**Credit Cards:** All major credit/debit cards
**Specialities:** Hardy South African plants. Good collections of *Crocosmia*, *Eucomis*, *Kniphofia*, *Watsonia*, *Crinum*, *Albuca*, nerines, *Zantedeschia*, *Lachenalia* & *Moraea*. Wide range of dry bulbs from around the globe.
**Notes:** Talks to garden societies. Tours of the nursery. Partial wheelchair access.
**Map Ref:** C, C3 **OS Grid Ref:** SX247733

**CTgr** **TREGREHAN GARDEN** ⊠ ♿
Tregrehan Garden Cottages & Nursery, Par, Cornwall, PL24 2SJ
Ⓣ (01726) 812438
Ⓕ (01726) 814389
Ⓔ info@tregrehan.org
Ⓦ www.tregrehan.org
**Contact:** Tom Hudson
**Opening Times:** 1030-1700 Wed-Fri, also Sun & B/hol Mons, mid-Mar-end May. 1300-1630 Wed only, Jun-Aug. Other times by appt.
**Credit Cards:** None
**Specialities:** *Camellia*, *Rhododendron*, *Nothofagus*, *Myosotidium*, tender trees & shrubs.
**Notes:** Also sells *Camellia* cuttings & large plants wholesale.
**Map Ref:** C, D2 **OS Grid Ref:** SX0553

**CTho** **THORNHAYES NURSERY** ⊠ €
St Andrews Wood, Dulford, Cullompton, Devon, EX15 2DF
Ⓣ (01884) 266746
Ⓕ (01884) 266739
Ⓔ trees@thornhayes-nursery.co.uk
Ⓦ www.thornhayes-nursery.co.uk
**Contact:** K D Croucher
**Opening Times:** 0800-1600 Mon-Fri. 0930-1400 Sat (Sep-Apr).
**Min Mail Order UK:** £100
**Min Mail Order EU:** £100
**Credit Cards:** All major credit/debit cards
**Specialities:** A broad range of forms of ornamental, amenity & fruit trees incl. West Country apple varieties.
**Notes:** Limited wheelchair access. Also sells wholesale.
**Map Ref:** C, C4

**CTrC** **TREVENA CROSS NURSERIES** ⊠ € ♿
Breage, Helston, Cornwall, TR13 9PY
Ⓣ (01736) 763880
Ⓕ (01736) 762828
Ⓔ sales@trevenacross.co.uk
Ⓦ www.trevenacross.co.uk
**Contact:** John Eddy
**Opening Times:** 0900-1700 Mon-Sat, 1030-1630 Sun.
**Min Mail Order UK:** Nmc
**Cat. Cost:** Online only.
**Credit Cards:** Access, Visa, Switch
**Specialities:** South African, Australian & New Zealand plants, incl. *Aloe*, *Protea*, tree ferns, palms, *Restio*, hardy succulents & wide range of other exotics.
**Map Ref:** C, D1 **OS Grid Ref:** SW614284

**CTrh** **TREHANE CAMELLIA NURSERY** ⊠ ⛺ ♿
J Trehane & Sons Ltd, Stapehill Road, Hampreston, Wimborne, Dorset, BH21 7ND
Ⓣ (01202) 873490
Ⓕ (01202) 873490
Ⓔ camellias@trehanenursery.co.uk
Ⓦ www.trehanenursery.co.uk
**Contact:** Lorraine or Jeanette
**Opening Times:** 0830-1630 Mon-Fri all year (excl. Xmas & New Year). 1000-1600 Sat-Sun in spring & by special appt.
**Min Mail Order UK:** Nmc
**Cat. Cost:** £1.50 cat./book.
**Credit Cards:** All major credit/debit cards
**Specialities:** Extensive range of *Camellia*

KEY
⊠ Mail order to UK or EU — ⛺ Delivers to shows
✈ Exports beyond EU — € Euro accepted
♿ Accessible by wheelchair — ◆ See Display advertisement

species, cultivars & hybrids. Many new introductions. Evergreen azaleas, *Pieris*, *Magnolia* & blueberries.
**Notes:** Also sells wholesale.
**Map Ref:** C, C6 **OS Grid Ref:** SU059000

**CTri** **TRISCOMBE NURSERIES** ⊠ ♿ ◆
West Bagborough, Nr Taunton, Somerset, TA4 3HG
Ⓣ (01984) 618267
Ⓔ triscombe.nurseries2000@virgin.net
Ⓦ www.triscombenurseries.co.uk
**Contact:** S Parkman
**Opening Times:** 0900-1730 Mon-Sat. 1400-1730 Sun & B/hols.
**Min Mail Order UK:** Nmc
**Cat. Cost:** 1 × 1st class.
**Credit Cards:** None
**Specialities:** Trees, shrubs, roses, fruit, *Clematis*, herbaceous & rock plants.
**Map Ref:** C, B4

**CTsd** **TRESEDERS** ⊠ ♿
Wallcottage Nursery, Lockengate, St. Austell, Cornwall, PL26 8RU
Ⓣ (01208) 832234
Ⓔ Treseders@btconnect.com
Ⓦ www.treseders.co.uk
**Contact:** James Treseder
**Opening Times:** 0900-1700 Mon-Sat, 1000-1600 Sun.
**Min Mail Order UK:** Nmc
**Cat. Cost:** Plant list available on request.
**Credit Cards:** All major credit/debit cards
**Specialities:** A wide range of choice & unusual plants grown in peat-free compost. Establishing the Nat. Collection of *Prostanthera*.
**Notes:** Also sells wholesale.
**Map Ref:** C, C2 **OS Grid Ref:** SX034620

**CTuc** **EDWIN TUCKER & SONS** ⊠
Brewery Meadow, Stonepark, Ashburton, Newton Abbot, Devon, TQ13 7DG
Ⓣ (01364) 652233
Ⓕ (01364) 654211
Ⓔ seeds@edwintucker.com
Ⓦ www.edwintucker.com
**Contact:** Geoff Penton
**Opening Times:** 0800-1700 Mon-Fri, 0800-1600 Sat.
**Min Mail Order UK:** Nmc
**Min Mail Order EU:** Nmc
**Cat. Cost:** Free.
**Credit Cards:** All major credit/debit cards
**Specialities:** Nearly 120 varieties of seed potatoes, incl. 50 organic varieties. Wide range of vegetables, flowers, green manures & sprouting seeds in packets. None treated. Nearly 200 varieties of organically produced seeds.
**Notes:** Also sells wholesale.

**CTyn** **TYNINGS CLIMBERS (NATIONAL COLLECTION OF PASSIFLORA & JASMINUM)** ⊠ ⌂ €
109 Clevedon Road, Tickenham, North Somerset, BS21 6RE
Ⓣ (01275) 810712
Ⓜ 07812 134849
Ⓕ (01275) 852439
Ⓔ tynings.climbers@yahoo.co.uk
Ⓦ www.tyningsclimbers.co.uk
**Contact:** Jane Lindsay or Toni O'Connor
**Opening Times:** By appt. only.
**Min Mail Order UK:** £18.00
**Min Mail Order EU:** £25.00
**Cat. Cost:** 4 × 1st class.
**Specialities:** Nat. Collections of *Passiflora* & *Jasminum*. Certain species & cvs only propagated on request, please phone for more information.
**Notes:** Also sells wholesale.
**Map Ref:** C, A5

**CUpf** **UP FROM EARTH HERB NURSERY** ⊠ ⌂
Poplar Farm Herb Nursery, Burtle, Bridgwater, Somerset, TA7 8NB
Ⓣ (01278) 723567
Ⓔ upfromearth@googlemail.com
Ⓦ www.upfromearth.co.uk
**Contact:** Peter Masters
**Opening Times:** By appt. only. For visits please phone between 0900-1700.
**Min Mail Order UK:** Nmc
**Cat. Cost:** Free.
**Credit Cards:** Paypal
**Specialities:** Herbs. Available in large & small quantities.
**Notes:** Also sells wholesale.

**CWan** **WANBOROUGH HERB NURSERY** ⌂
Callas Hill, Wanborough, Swindon, Wiltshire, SN4 0DQ
Ⓣ (01793) 790327 (answering machine)
Ⓔ wanboroughnursery@btinternet.com
Ⓦ www.wanboroughherbnursery.moonfruit.com
**Contact:** Peter Biggs
**Opening Times:** 1000-1700 Fri-Mon, Mar-Oct. Other times by appt. only.
**Cat. Cost:** £1.00
**Credit Cards:** None
**Specialities:** Herbs, herbaceous, esp. culinary. Available in small quantities only.
**Notes:** Nursery located on Callas Hill between Wanborough & Fox Hill.
**Map Ref:** C, A6 **OS Grid Ref:** SU217828

**C**Wat **The Water Garden** ⊠ ♿
Hinton Parva, Swindon, Wiltshire, SN4 0DH
Ⓣ (01793) 790558
Ⓕ (01793) 791298
Ⓔ mike@thewatergarden.co.uk
Ⓦ www.thewatergarden.co.uk
**Contact:** Mike & Anne Newman
**Opening Times:** 1000-1700 Wed-Sun.
**Min Mail Order UK:** £10.00 + p&p
**Cat. Cost:** 4 × 1st class.
**Credit Cards:** Visa, Access, Switch
**Specialities:** Water lilies, marginal & moisture plants, oxygenators & alpines.
**Notes:** Also sells wholesale.
**Map Ref:** C, A6

**C**WCL **Westcountry Nurseries** ⊠ ♿
Donkey Meadow, Woolsery, Devon, EX39 5QH
Ⓣ (01237) 431111
Ⓕ (01237) 431111
Ⓔ info@westcountry-nurseries.co.uk
Ⓦ www.westcountry-nurseries.co.uk
**Contact:** Sarah Conibear
**Opening Times:** 1000-1700 Mar-Jul.
**Min Mail Order UK:** £10.00
**Cat. Cost:** 2 × 1st class + A5 sae for full colour cat.
**Credit Cards:** All major credit/debit cards
**Specialities:** *Lupinus*, *Lewisia*, *Hellebore*, *Clematis*, cyclamen, acers, lavender, select perennials, grasses, ferns & climbers. Nat. Collection of Lupins.
**Map Ref:** C, B2 **OS Grid Ref:** SS351219

**C**WGN **Walled Garden Nursery** ⊠ ♿
Brinkworth House, Brinkworth, Nr Malmesbury, Wiltshire, SN15 5DF
Ⓣ (01666) 826637
Ⓔ f.wescott@btinternet.com
Ⓦ www.clematis-nursery.co.uk
**Contact:** Fraser Wescott
**Opening Times:** 1000-1700, 7 days Mar-Oct. 1000-dusk, Mon-Fri Nov & Feb. Closed Dec & Jan.
**Credit Cards:** All major credit/debit cards
**Specialities:** *Clematis* & climbers, with a selection of unusual perennials & shrubs.
**Map Ref:** C, A6 **OS Grid Ref:** SU002849

**C**Wib **Wibble Farm Nurseries** ✈ ♿
Wibble Farm, West Quantoxhead, Nr Taunton, Somerset, TA4 4DD
Ⓣ (01984) 632303
Ⓕ (01984) 633168
Ⓔ sales@wibblefarmnurseries.co.uk
Ⓦ www.wibblefarmnurseries.co.uk
**Contact:** Mrs M L Francis
**Opening Times:** 0800-1700 Mon-Fri, 1000-1600 Sat. 1400-1600 Sun (open Sun Mar-Sep only). All year incl. some B/hols.
**Min Mail Order UK:** Nmc
**Min Mail Order EU:** Nmc
**Cat. Cost:** 3 × 1st class.
**Credit Cards:** All major credit/debit cards
**Specialities:** Growers of a wide range of hardy plants, many rare & unusual. Display gardens.
**Notes:** Also sells wholesale.
**Map Ref:** C, B4

**C**Wil **Fernwood Nursery** ⊠ ✈ € ♿
Peters Marland, Torrington, Devon, EX38 8QG
Ⓣ (01805) 601446
Ⓔ hw@fernwood-nursery.co.uk
Ⓦ www.fernwood-nursery.co.uk
**Contact:** Howard Wills & Sally Wills
**Opening Times:** Any time by appt. Please phone or email first.
**Min Mail Order UK:** Nmc
**Min Mail Order EU:** Nmc
**Cat. Cost:** Sae for list.
**Credit Cards:** Paypal
**Specialities:** Nat. Collection of *Sempervivum*, *Jovibarba*, *Rosularia* & *Phormium*.
**Notes:** Mail order for *Sempervivum*, *Jovibarba* & *Rosularia* only. 5 miles from RHS Rosemoor.
**Map Ref:** C, C3 **OS Grid Ref:** SS479133

**C**WiW **Windrush Willow** ⊠ ✈
Higher Barn, Sidmouth Road, Aylesbeare, Exeter, Devon, EX5 2JJ
Ⓣ (01395) 233669
Ⓕ (01395) 233669
Ⓔ windrushw@aol.com
Ⓦ www.windrushwillow.com
**Contact:** Richard Kerwood
**Opening Times:** Mail order only. Open by appt.
**Min Mail Order UK:** Nmc
**Min Mail Order EU:** Nmc
**Cat. Cost:** 2 × 1st class.
**Credit Cards:** None
**Specialities:** *Salix*. Unrooted cuttings available Dec-Mar.
**Notes:** Also sells wholesale.

**C**Won **The Wonder Tree** ⊠
35 Beaconsfield Road, Knowle, Bristol, BS4 2JE
Ⓣ 0117 908 9057
Ⓜ 07989 333507
Ⓔ Kevin@wondertree.co.uk

KEY
⊠ Mail order to UK or EU — Delivers to shows
✈ Exports beyond EU — € Euro accepted
♿ Accessible by wheelchair — ◆ See Display advertisement

Ⓦ www.wondertree.co.uk
**Contact:** Kevin Lindegaard
**Opening Times:** Not open. Mail order only.
**Min Mail Order UK:** Nmc
**Cat. Cost:** Online only.
**Credit Cards:** All major credit/debit cards
**Specialities:** *Salix*.
**Notes:** Also sells wholesale.
**Map Ref:** C, A5

**CWri** **Nigel Wright Rhododendrons** ♿
The Old Glebe, Eggesford, Chulmleigh, Devon, EX18 7QU
Ⓣ (01769) 580632
Ⓔ wrightrhodos@aol.com
Ⓦ www.wrightrhodos.com
**Contact:** Nigel Wright
**Opening Times:** By appt. only. 7 days.
**Cat. Cost:** 2 × 1st class.
**Credit Cards:** None
**Specialities:** *Rhododendron* & deciduous azaleas. 200 varieties field grown, root-balled, some potted. For collection only. Specialist grower. Free advice & planting plans.
**Notes:** Also sells wholesale.
**Map Ref:** C, B3 **OS Grid Ref:** SS684106

**CWSG** **West Somerset Garden Centre** ✉ ♿
Mart Road, Minehead, Somerset, TA24 5BJ
Ⓣ (01643) 703812
Ⓕ (01643) 706476
Ⓔ wsgc@btconnect.com
Ⓦ www.westsomersetgardencentre.co.uk
**Contact:** Ms J K Shoulders
**Opening Times:** 0800-1700 Mon-Sat, 1000-1600 Sun.
**Min Mail Order UK:** Nmc
**Cat. Cost:** None issued.
**Credit Cards:** Visa, Solo, Maestro, MasterCard
**Specialities:** Wide general range. *Ceanothus*.
**Map Ref:** C, B4

**CWVF** **White Veil Fuchsias** ✉ ♿
Verwood Road, Three Legged Cross, Wimborne, Dorset, BH21 6RP
Ⓣ (01202) 813998
**Contact:** A. C. Holloway
**Opening Times:** 0900-1300 & 1400-1700 Mon-Sat, 1000-1300 & 1400-1600 Sun, Jan-Aug. Closed Sat & Sun, Sep-Dec.
**Min Mail Order UK:** 8 plants of your choice.
**Cat. Cost:** 4 × 1st class.
**Credit Cards:** None
**Specialities:** Fuchsias. Small plants grown from Jan-Apr. Available in small quantities only.

**CYeo** **South Yeo Nursery** ✉ ⌂
Poughill, Crediton, Devon, EX17 4LF
Ⓣ (01363) 866740
Ⓜ 07971 412132
Ⓕ (01363) 866740
Ⓔ davidross@eclecticplants.co.uk
Ⓦ www.eclecticplants.co.uk
**Contact:** David & Penny Ross
**Opening Times:** Open most days but please phone in advance to check & get directions.
**Min Mail Order UK:** Nmc
**Min Mail Order EU:** Nmc
**Cat. Cost:** 6 × 1st class
**Credit Cards:** Paypal
**Specialities:** Small, family-run nursery specialising in South African & other plants. *Schizostylis, Agapanthus, Dierama, Crocosmia* & *Rhodohypoxis*. Also unusual alpines & other perennials.
**Notes:** Nursery located in Grade II* listed traditional Devon courtyard.
**Map Ref:** C, C3 **OS Grid Ref:** SS865085

## Eastern

**EABi** **Alison Bilverstone** ✉ €
22 Kings Street, Swaffham, Norfolk, PE37 7BU
Ⓣ (01760) 725026
Ⓔ a.bilverstone@tiscali.co.uk
**Contact:** Alison Bilverstone
**Opening Times:** Not open. Mail order only.
**Min Mail Order UK:** Nmc
**Min Mail Order EU:** Nmc
**Cat. Cost:** A4 sae.
**Credit Cards:** None
**Specialities:** *Achemene, Kohleria* & *Smithiantha* rhizomes, available Dec to mid-Apr. Stocked in small quantities.

**EACa** **Alpine Campanulas (Bellflower Nursery)** ✉ ⌂
Langham Hall Walled Garden, Langham, Nr Bury St Edmunds, Suffolk, IP31 3EE
Ⓜ 07879 644958
Ⓔ campanulas@btinternet.com
Ⓦ www.alpinecampanulas.co.uk
**Contact:** Sue Wooster
**Opening Times:** 1000-1600 Thu & Fri, Mar-Oct. Other times by appt.
**Min Mail Order UK:** £10.00
**Cat. Cost:** Sae or online.
**Specialities:** *Campanula*. Nat. Collection of Alpine Campanulas. Most stock in small numbers only.
**Notes:** Nursery at the Walled Garden, Langham Hall, Nr Bury St Edmunds, Suffolk. Groups welcome by appt.
**Map Ref:** E, C3 **OS Grid Ref:** TL978691

EAEE **AEE: A Lover of Plants** ⊠
38 Church Close, Roydon, Diss, Norfolk, IP22 5RQ
Ⓣ (01379) 651230
Ⓕ (01379) 651230
Ⓔ aeesales@fsmail.net
Ⓦ www.aeesupplyingplantlovers.com
**Contact:** Anne Etheridge
**Opening Times:** Plant stall 1000-1600 Wed-Sun, Mar-Sep at Roydon White Hart Garden, Roydon, Norfolk (off A1066).
**Min Mail Order UK:** Nmc
**Min Mail Order EU:** Nmc
**Cat. Cost:** 3 × 1st class.
**Credit Cards:** Paypal
**Specialities:** Perennials & grasses plus a few enticing alpines & shrubs. Alpines & shrubs available in small quantities only.
**Notes:** Talks available. Plants may be reserved for collection with a £5.00 deposit. Wheelchair access at plant sales site. Plants delivered free within 10 miles of Roydon.

EAmu **Amulree Exotics** ⊠ ♠ ♿
The Turnpike, Norwich Road (B1113), Fundenhall, Norwich, Norfolk, NR16 1EL
Ⓣ (01508) 488101
Ⓔ SDG@exotica.fsbusiness.co.uk
Ⓦ www.turn-it-tropical.co.uk
**Contact:** S Gridley
**Opening Times:** 0930-1730 7 days spring-autumn, 1000-1630 7 days autumn-spring.
**Min Mail Order UK:** Nmc
**Min Mail Order EU:** Nmc
**Cat. Cost:** 2 × 1st class.
**Credit Cards:** Visa, MasterCard, Electron, Solo, Switch
**Specialities:** Hardy & half-hardy plants for home, garden & conservatory. Palms, bamboos, bananas, tree ferns, cannas, gingers, cacti, succulents & much more.
**Notes:** Also sells wholesale.
**Map Ref:** E, B3 **OS Grid Ref:** DX123740

EBak **B & H M Baker** ♿
Bourne Brook Nurseries, Greenstead Green, Halstead, Essex, CO9 1RB
Ⓣ (01787) 476369
**Contact:** Clive Baker
**Opening Times:** 0800-1630 Mon-Fri, 0900-1200 & 1400-1630 Sat & Sun, Mar-30th Jun.
**Cat. Cost:** 2 × 1st class + 33p.
**Credit Cards:** All major credit/debit cards
**Specialities:** *Fuchsia* & conservatory plants.
**Notes:** Also sells wholesale.
**Map Ref:** E, C2

EBar **Barcham Trees** €
Eye Hill Drove, Ely, Cambridgeshire, CB7 5XF
Ⓣ (01565) 777636
Ⓕ 05603 113026
Ⓔ andrew@barchamtrees.co.uk
Ⓦ www.barcham.co.uk
**Contact:** Andrew Dunkley
**Opening Times:** 0900-1700 Mon-Fri. Visits to the nursery by appt. only.
**Cat. Cost:** Free.
**Credit Cards:** All major credit/debit cards
**Specialities:** Containerised trees.
**Notes:** Also sells wholesale. E-commerce site: www.barchamon-line.co.uk.
**Map Ref:** E, C2

EBee **Beeches Nursery** ⊠ ♿
Village Centre, Ashdon, Saffron Walden, Essex, CB10 2HB
Ⓣ (01799) 584362
Ⓕ (01799) 584421
Ⓔ sales@beechesnursery.co.uk
Ⓦ www.beechesnursery.co.uk
**Contact:** Alan Bidwell/Kevin Marsh
**Opening Times:** 0830-1700 Mon-Sat, 1000-1700 Sun & B/hols.
**Min Mail Order UK:** £12.00
**Min Mail Order EU:** £20.00
**Cat. Cost:** 6 × 2nd class for herbaceous list.
**Credit Cards:** Visa, Access, MasterCard, Switch
**Specialities:** Herbaceous specialists & extensive range of other garden plants. Rarieties available in ltd. numbers only.
**Notes:** Plants dispatched Oct-Feb only. Orders accepted throughout the year. No trees by mail order.
**Map Ref:** E, C2 **OS Grid Ref:** TL586420

EBla **Blacksmiths Cottage Nursery** ⊠ ♠ ♿
Langmere Road, Langmere, Dickleburgh, Nr Diss, Norfolk, IP21 4QA
Ⓣ (01379) 741136
Ⓔ Blackcottnursery@aol.com
Ⓦ www.blackcottnursery.co.uk
**Contact:** Ben, Sarah or Jill Potterton
**Opening Times:** 1000-1700 Thu-Sun & B/hol Mon, Mar-Oct.
**Min Mail Order UK:** Nmc
**Cat. Cost:** Online only.
**Credit Cards:** All major credit/debit cards

KEY
⊠ Mail order to UK or EU ♠ Delivers to shows
✈ Exports beyond EU € Euro accepted
♿ Accessible by wheelchair ◆ See Display advertisement

E

**Specialities:** Over 2000 species grown. Large selection of shade plants esp. *Anemone nemorosa* & *Poygonatum*, also large collection of *Geranium*, *Astrantia* & *Sanguisorba*.
**Notes:** Coffee Shop & toilets. Barn garden & bird collection. Group visits by appt.
**Map Ref:** E, C3 **OS Grid Ref:** TM192821

**EBls** **PETER BEALES ROSES** ⊠ ✈ ♿
London Road, Attleborough, Norfolk, NR17 1AY
Ⓣ (01953) 454707 or 0845 4810277
Ⓕ (01953) 456845
Ⓔ info@peterbealesroses.co.uk
Ⓦ www.classicroses.co.uk
**Contact:** Simon or Tina
**Opening Times:** 0900-1700 Mon-Sat, 1000-1600 Sun & B/hols.
**Min Mail Order UK:** Nmc
**Min Mail Order EU:** Nmc
**Cat. Cost:** Free to UK. Outside UK £5.00.
**Credit Cards:** All, except American Express
**Specialities:** Old fashioned roses & classic roses. Nat. Collection of Species Roses. Some stock available in small quantities only. Other plants on site.
**Notes:** Shop & bistro.
**Map Ref:** E, C3 **OS Grid Ref:** TM026929

**EBtc** **BOTANICA** ⊠
Chantry Farm, Campsea Ashe, Wickham Market, Suffolk, IP13 0PZ
Ⓣ (01728) 747113
Ⓕ (01728) 747725
Ⓔ info@botanica.org.uk
Ⓦ www.botanica.org.uk
**Contact:** Daniel Everett
**Opening Times:** 1000-1700 6 days summer, 1000-1600 7 days winter.
**Min Mail Order UK:** £15 + p&p
**Cat. Cost:** None issued.
**Credit Cards:** None
**Specialities:** Range of rare & unusual hardy plants.
**Notes:** Also sells wholesale.
**Map Ref:** E, C3 **OS Grid Ref:** 632824/255500

**ECGP** **CAMBRIDGE GARDEN PLANTS** ♿
The Lodge, Clayhithe Road, Horningsea, Cambridgeshire, CB25 9JD
Ⓣ (01223) 861370
Ⓔ kit@cambridgegardenplants.co.uk
**Contact:** Kit Buchdahl
**Opening Times:** 1100-1730 Thu-Sun mid Mar-31st Oct. Other times by appt.
**Cat. Cost:** 4 × 1st class.
**Credit Cards:** None
**Specialities:** Hardy perennials incl. wide range of *Geranium*, *Allium*, *Euphorbia*, *Cyclamen*, *Digitalis*. Also old roses.
**Map Ref:** E, C2 **OS Grid Ref:** TL497637

**ECha** **THE BETH CHATTO GARDENS LTD** ⊠ ♿
Elmstead Market, Colchester, Essex, CO7 7DB
Ⓣ (01206) 822007
Ⓕ (01206) 825933
Ⓔ info@bethchatto.fsnet.co.uk
Ⓦ www.bethchatto.co.uk
**Contact:** Beth Chatto
**Opening Times:** 0900-1700 Mon-Sat, 1000-1700 Sun, 1st Mar-31st Oct. 0900-1600 Mon-Sat, 1000-1600 Sun, 1st Nov to end Feb.
**Min Mail Order UK:** £20.00
**Min Mail Order EU:** Ask for details
**Cat. Cost:** Free plant list.
**Credit Cards:** Visa, MasterCard, Maestro
**Specialities:** Predominantly herbaceous. Many unusual for special situations.
**Map Ref:** E, D3 **OS Grid Ref:** TM069238

**ECho** **CHOICE LANDSCAPES** ⊠ ✈ ⌂ ♿
Priory Farm, 101 Salts Road, West Walton, Wisbech, Cambridgeshire, PE14 7EF
Ⓣ (01945) 585051
Ⓕ (01945) 580053
Ⓔ info@choicelandscapes.org
Ⓦ www.choicelandscapes.org
**Contact:** Michael Agg & Jillian Agg
**Opening Times:** 1000-1300 & 1400-1730 Tue-Sat, 9th Feb-30th Oct 2010. Not open on show dates, please phone. Other times by appt.
**Min Mail Order UK:** Nmc
**Min Mail Order EU:** £10.00 + p&p
**Cat. Cost:** 6 × 1st class or 6 IRC
**Credit Cards:** Maestro, Visa, MasterCard, Solo
**Specialities:** Dwarf conifers, alpines, acers, rhododendrons, bulbs, pines, lilies & South African bulbs & seed.
**Map Ref:** E, B1

**ECnt** **CANTS OF COLCHESTER** ⊠ ✈ ♿
Nayland Road, Mile End, Colchester, Essex, CO4 5EB
Ⓣ (01206) 844008
Ⓕ (01206) 855371
Ⓔ finder@cantsroses.co.uk
Ⓦ www.cantsroses.co.uk
**Contact:** Angela Pawsey
**Opening Times:** 0900-1300, 1400-1630 Mon-Fri. Sat varied, please phone first. Sun closed.

**Min Mail Order UK:** Nmc
**Min Mail Order EU:** Nmc
**Cat. Cost:** Free
**Credit Cards:** Visa, MasterCard, Delta, Solo, Switch
**Specialities:** Roses. Unstaffed rose field can be viewed dawn-dusk every day from end Jun-end Sep.
**Notes:** Bare-root mail order end Oct-end Mar, containers Apr-Aug. Partial wheelchair access.
**Map Ref:** E, C3

**ECou** **COUNTY PARK NURSERY**
Essex Gardens, Hornchurch, Essex, RM11 3BU
Ⓣ (01708) 445205
Ⓦ www.countyparknursery.co.uk
**Contact:** G Hutchins
**Opening Times:** 1000-1700 Mon-Sat excl. Wed, 1000-1700 Sun Mar-Oct. Nov-Feb by appt. only.
**Cat. Cost:** Online only.
**Credit Cards:** None
**Specialities:** Alpines & rare and unusual plants from New Zealand, Tasmania & the Falklands. Many plants in small quantities only.
**Map Ref:** E, D2

**ECre** **CREAKE PLANT CENTRE** ♿
Nursery View, Leicester Road, South Creake, Fakenham, Norfolk, NR21 9PW
Ⓣ (01328) 823018
Ⓜ 07760 762499
Ⓔ trevor-harrison@btinternet.com
**Contact:** Mr T Harrison
**Opening Times:** 1000-1300 & 1400-1730 7 days excl. Xmas.
**Cat. Cost:** None issued
**Credit Cards:** All major credit/debit cards
**Specialities:** Unusual shrubs, herbaceous, conservatory plants, old roses. Hellebores.
**Map Ref:** E, B1 **OS Grid Ref:** TF864353

**ECrN** **CROWN NURSERY** ⊠ ♿
High Street, Ufford, Suffolk, IP13 6EL
Ⓣ (01394) 460755
Ⓕ (01394) 460142
Ⓔ enquiries@crown-nursery.co.uk
Ⓦ www.crown-nursery.co.uk
**Contact:** Jill Proctor
**Opening Times:** 0900-1700 (1600 in winter) Mon-Sat.
**Min Mail Order UK:** Nmc
**Cat. Cost:** 2 × 1st class.
**Credit Cards:** All major credit/debit cards
**Specialities:** Mature & semi-mature native, ornamental & fruit trees. Heritage fruit varieties.
**Notes:** Mail order for small/young stock only. Also sells wholesale.
**Map Ref:** E, C3 **OS Grid Ref:** TM292528

**ECtt** **COTTAGE NURSERIES** ⊠ ♿
Thoresthorpe, Alford, Lincolnshire, LN13 0HX
Ⓣ (01507) 466968
Ⓕ (01507) 463409
Ⓔ bill@cottagenurseries.net
Ⓦ www.cottagenurseries.net
**Contact:** W H Denbigh
**Opening Times:** 0900-1700 7 days 1st Mar-31st Oct, 1000-1600 w/ends only Nov-Feb.
**Min Mail Order UK:** Nmc
**Cat. Cost:** 3 × 1st class.
**Credit Cards:** Visa, MasterCard, Maestro
**Specialities:** Hardy perennials. Wide general range.
**Map Ref:** E, A2 **OS Grid Ref:** TF423716

**EDAr** **D'ARCY & EVEREST** ⊠ € ♿
(Office) PO Box 78, St Ives, Huntingdon, Cambridgeshire, PE27 6ZA
Ⓣ (01480) 497672 answerphone
Ⓜ 07715 374440
Ⓕ (01480) 466042
Ⓔ angela@darcyeverest.co.uk
Ⓦ www.darcyeverest.co.uk
**Contact:** Angela Whiting, Richard Oliver
**Opening Times:** Wed-Fri, Mar-Sep, except show dates. Winter by appt. Coach parties welcome by appt.
**Min Mail Order UK:** £15.00 + p&p
**Min Mail Order EU:** £30.00 + p&p
**Cat. Cost:** 6 × 1st class.
**Credit Cards:** None
**Specialities:** Alpines & sempervivums.
**Notes:** Nursery is at Pidley Sheep Lane (B1040), Pidley, Huntingdon, Cambs.
**Map Ref:** E, C2 **OS Grid Ref:** TL533276

**EDif** **DIFFERENT PLANTS** ♿
The Mellis Stud, Gate Farm, Cranley Green, Eye, Suffolk, IP23 7NX
Ⓣ (01379) 870291
Ⓔ rickwtrs@talktalk.net
**Contact:** Fleur Waters
**Opening Times:** Sat-Thu by appt. only, closed Fri. Plant stall Eye market Fri 0900-1200.
**Cat. Cost:** 4 × 1st class.
**Credit Cards:** None
**Specialities:** *Mimulus aurantiacus* & hybrids,

KEY
⊠ Mail order to UK or EU — Delivers to shows
Exports beyond EU — € Euro accepted
♿ Accessible by wheelchair — ◆ See Display advertisement

half-hardy bulbous/cormous perennials incl. *Cypella, Tigridia* & *Anomatheca laxa*. Bulbs may be available in small quantities only.
**Map Ref:** E, C3

E

**EECP** **Essex Carnivorous Plants** ⊠ 
12 Strangman Avenue, Thundersley, Essex, SS7 1RB
Ⓣ (01702) 551467
Ⓔ Mark@essexcarnivorousplants.com
Ⓦ www.essexcarnivorousplants.com
**Contact:** Mark Haslett
**Opening Times:** By appt. only.
**Min Mail Order UK:** Nmc
**Min Mail Order EU:** Nmc
**Cat. Cost:** 2 × 1st class or online.
**Credit Cards:** None
**Specialities:** Good range of carnivorous plants. *Sarracenia, Drosera*. Nat. Collection of *Dionaea* forms & cvs. Some stock available in small quantities only. Nat. Collection of *Sarracenia* (hybrids & ssp.).
**Notes:** Also sells wholesale.
**Map Ref:** E, D2 **OS Grid Ref:** TQ797875

**EExo** **The Exotic Garden Company** ⊠ 
Saxmundham Road, Aldeburgh, Suffolk, IP15 5JD
Ⓣ (01728) 454456
Ⓦ http:\\stores.ebay.uk/exoticgardencompany
**Contact:** Matthew Couchy
**Opening Times:** 1000-1700 Mon-Sat, 1000-1600 Sun, Mar-Oct. 1000-dusk Nov-Dec. Closed Jan-Feb.
**Min Mail Order UK:** Nmc
**Min Mail Order EU:** Nmc
**Cat. Cost:** None issued.
**Credit Cards:** All major credit/debit cards
**Specialities:** Less common hardy & half-hardy exotic & unusual plants. Tree ferns, olives, shrubs & perennials.
**Map Ref:** E, C3

**EFer** **The Fern Nursery** ⊠ 
Grimsby Road, Binbrook, Lincolnshire, LN8 6DH
Ⓣ (01472) 398092
Ⓔ richard@timm984.fsnet.co.uk
Ⓦ www.fernnursery.co.uk
**Contact:** R N Timm
**Opening Times:** 0900-1700 Fri, Sat & Sun Apr-Oct or by appt.
**Min Mail Order UK:** Nmc
**Min Mail Order EU:** Nmc
**Cat. Cost:** 2 × 1st class.
**Credit Cards:** None
**Specialities:** Ferns. Display garden.
**Notes:** Only plants listed in the mail order part of the catalogue will be sent mail order. Also sells wholesale.
**Map Ref:** E, A1 **OS Grid Ref:** TF212942

**EFEx** **Flora Exotica** ⊠ €
Pasadena, South-Green, Fingringhoe, Colchester, Essex, CO5 7DR
Ⓣ (01206) 729414
Ⓜ 07972 068679
**Contact:** J Beddoes
**Opening Times:** Not open. Mail order only.
**Min Mail Order UK:** Nmc
**Min Mail Order EU:** Nmc
**Cat. Cost:** 4 × 1st class.
**Credit Cards:** None
**Specialities:** Exotica flora incl. orchids.

**EFly** **The Fly Trap Plants** ⊠  €
Cooke Road, Berghapton, Norwich, Norfolk, NR15 1BA
Ⓣ (01508) 480348
Ⓜ 07852 334413
Ⓔ sales@tftplants.co.uk
Ⓦ tftplants.co.uk
**Contact:** Pauline Steward
**Opening Times:** By appt. only.
**Min Mail Order UK:** Nmc
**Cat. Cost:** 1 × 1st class sae
**Credit Cards:** None
**Specialities:** All kinds of carnivorous plants, such as *Sarracenia, Drosera, Pinquicula*, to the *Utricularia* aquatic plants.

**EFtx** **Fernatix** ⊠  € 
Stoke Ash, Suffolk, IP23 7EN
Ⓣ (01379) 678197
Ⓕ (01379) 678197
Ⓔ mail@fernatix.co.uk
Ⓦ www.fernatix.co.uk
**Contact:** Steven Fletcher & Kerry Robinson
**Opening Times:** By appt. only.
**Min Mail Order UK:** £15.00
**Cat. Cost:** 8 × 1st or 9 × 2nd class for cat.
**Credit Cards:** All, except American Express
**Specialities:** Ferns, hardy & greenhouse species & cultivars. Some available in small quantities only. Mainly hardy ferns.
**Notes:** Delivers to shows, except Chelsea. 10 days notice required.
**Map Ref:** C, C3

**EGFP** **Grange Farm Plants** ⊠ 
Grange Farm, 38 Fishergate Road, Sutton St James, Spalding, Lincolnshire, PE12 0EZ
Ⓣ (01945) 440240
Ⓜ 07742 138760
Ⓕ (01945) 440355
Ⓔ ellis.family@tinyonline.co.uk

**Contact:** M C Ellis
**Opening Times:** Mail order only. Open by appt. only.
**Min Mail Order UK:** Nmc
**Min Mail Order EU:** Nmc
**Cat. Cost:** 1 × 1st class.
**Credit Cards:** None
**Specialities:** Rare trees & shrubs, esp. *Juglans*, *Fraxinus*. Some species available in small quantities only.
**Map Ref:** E, B2 **OS Grid Ref:** TF382186

EGHP **Green Garden Herbs** ⊠ ♠ ♿
Beech House, 82 Leiston Road, Aldeburgh, Suffolk, IP15 5PS
Ⓣ (01728) 452597
Ⓜ 07949 906290
Ⓔ info@greengardenherbs.co.uk
Ⓦ www.greengardenherbs.co.uk
**Contact:** Sarah Clark
**Opening Times:** 1000-1700 mid-Feb to end Sep. Other times by appt.
**Min Mail Order UK:** £15
**Min Mail Order EU:** £15
**Cat. Cost:** Online only. Plant list free with sae.
**Specialities:** Herbs, aromatic, culinary, medicinal & ornamental, incl. *Salvia*, *Echinacea*, *Monarda*, *Thymus* & wide selection of *Lavandula*. Plants & seed available.
**Notes:** Credit cards accepted at nursery only. Plants & seeds for sale at Bridge Nurseries, Dunwich, Suffolk. Also available at shows & plant fairs. Not available from Aldeburgh address except by mail order.
**Map Ref:** E, C3

EGln **Glenhirst Cactus Nursery** ⊠ €
Station Road, Swineshead, Nr Boston, Lincolnshire, PE20 3NX
Ⓣ (01205) 820314
Ⓕ (01205) 820614
Ⓔ info@cacti4u.co.uk
Ⓦ www.cacti4u.co.uk
**Contact:** N C & S A Bell
**Opening Times:** Visitors welcome, but by telephone appt. only.
**Min Mail Order UK:** £5.00
**Min Mail Order EU:** €15.00
**Cat. Cost:** 2 × 1st class.
**Credit Cards:** Maestro, Visa, MasterCard, Switch
**Specialities:** Extensive range of cacti & succulent plants, incl. orchid cacti.
**Notes:** Will accept payment in euros online only.
**Map Ref:** E, B1 **OS Grid Ref:** TF245408

EGol **Goldbrook Plants** ⊠ ✈
Hoxne, Eye, Suffolk, IP21 5AN
Ⓣ (01379) 668770
Ⓕ (01379) 668770
**Contact:** Sandra Bond
**Opening Times:** 1000-1700, Thu-Sun Apr-Sep, or by appt. Other times by appt.
**Min Mail Order UK:** £15.00 + p&p
**Min Mail Order EU:** £100.00 + p&p
**Cat. Cost:** 3 × 1st class.
**Credit Cards:** None
**Specialities:** Very large range of *Hosta*, esp. miniature & small varieties. *Hemerocallis*. Some small hostas available in ltd quantities. Larger hostas & *Hemerocallis* being phased out.
**Notes:** Also sells wholesale.
**Map Ref:** E, C3

EGxp **Gardening Express** ⊠ ◆
Mashbury Road, Chignal St James, Chelmsford, Essex, CM1 4UA
Ⓣ 08000 336161
Ⓔ Bonnett@GardeningExpress.co.uk
Ⓦ www.GardeningExpress.co.uk
**Contact:** Chris Bonnett
**Opening Times:** Not open. Mail order only.
**Min Mail Order UK:** Nmc
**Cat. Cost:** Online only.
**Credit Cards:** All major credit/debit cards
**Specialities:** 4-acre site growing wide range of perenials and shrubs.
**Notes:** Also sells wholesale.

EHoe **Hoecroft Plants** ⊠ € ♿
Severals Grange, Holt Road, Wood Norton, Dereham, Norfolk, NR20 5BL
Ⓣ (01362) 684206
Ⓔ hoecroft@hotmail.co.uk
Ⓦ www.hoecroft.co.uk
**Contact:** Jane Lister
**Opening Times:** 1000-1600 Thu-Sun, 1st Apr-31st Oct or by appt.
**Min Mail Order UK:** Nmc
**Min Mail Order EU:** Nmc
**Cat. Cost:** 5 × 2nd class.
**Credit Cards:** None
**Specialities:** An extensive range of coloured & variegated-leaved shrubs & herbaceous perennials. 260 ornamental grasses. Free entry to display gardens.
**Notes:** Nursery 2 miles north of Guist on B1110.
**Map Ref:** E, B3 **OS Grid Ref:** TG008289

KEY
⊠ Mail order to UK or EU — ♠ Delivers to shows
✈ Exports beyond EU — € Euro accepted
♿ Accessible by wheelchair — ◆ See Display advertisement

**EHon** **HONEYSOME AQUATIC NURSERY** ⊠
The Row, Sutton, Nr Ely, Cambridgeshire, CB6 2PB
Ⓣ (01353) 778889
Ⓕ (01353) 777291
Ⓔ info@honeysomeaquaticnursery.co.uk
Ⓦ www.honeysomeaquaticnursery.co.uk
**Contact:** Mrs L S Bond
**Opening Times:** At all times by appt. only.
**Min Mail Order UK:** Nmc
**Cat. Cost:** 2 × 1st class.
**Credit Cards:** None
**Specialities:** Hardy aquatic, bog & marginal.
**Notes:** Also sells wholesale.
**Map Ref:** E, C2

**EHul** **HULL FARM** ⊠ ♿
Spring Valley Lane, Ardleigh, Colchester, Essex, CO7 7SA
Ⓣ (01206) 230045
Ⓜ 07900 298366
Ⓕ (01206) 230820
Ⓔ conifers.hullfarm@tiscali.co.uk
Ⓦ www.fryersfarmshop.co.uk
**Contact:** Jack Fryer
**Opening Times:** 1000-1300 & 1400-1600 Mon-Fri. Closed B/hol.
**Min Mail Order UK:** £50.00 + p&p
**Cat. Cost:** 5 × 2nd class.
**Credit Cards:** MasterCard, Visa
**Specialities:** Conifers, grasses.
**Notes:** Also sells wholesale.
**Map Ref:** E, C3 **OS Grid Ref:** GR043274

**EIri** **IRISESONLINE** ⊠
Slade Cottage, Petts Lane, Little Walden, Essex, CB10 1XH
Ⓣ (01799) 526294
Ⓕ (01799) 526294
Ⓔ sales@irisesonline.co.uk
Ⓦ www.irisesonline.co.uk
**Contact:** Clare Kneen
**Opening Times:** By appt. only.
**Min Mail Order UK:** Nmc
**Cat. Cost:** 3 × 1st class or online.
**Credit Cards:** None
**Specialities:** *Iris*. Small family-run nursery. Some varieties available in small quantities only.
**Map Ref:** E, C2 **OS Grid Ref:** TL546416

**EJBD** **JOHN BOWERS DAYLILIES** ⊠
Whispering Trees Nursery, Wimbotsham, Kings Lynn, Norfolk, PE34 8QB
Ⓣ (01366) 386286
Ⓔ info@johnbowersdaylilies.co.uk
Ⓦ www.johnbowersdaylilies.co.uk
**Contact:** John Bowers
**Opening Times:** Mail order only. Open by arrangement.
**Min Mail Order UK:** Nmc
**Min Mail Order EU:** Nmc
**Cat. Cost:** £2.00
**Credit Cards:** All major credit/debit cards
**Specialities:** Daylilies (*Hemerocallis*).
**Notes:** Open to the public to view the daylilies when in bloom. Also sells wholesale.

**EJRN** **JOHN RAY NURSERY** € ♿
36 Station Road, Braintree, Essex, CM7 3QJ
Ⓜ 07826 162406
Ⓕ (01376) 322858
Ⓔ johnraynursery@talktalk.net
**Contact:** Brian James
**Opening Times:** 0900-1730 Sat, 1030-1630 Sun & B/Hol.
**Cat. Cost:** None issued.
**Credit Cards:** None
**Specialities:** *Pittosporum*.

**EJWh** **JILL WHITE** ⊠ ♿
78 Hurst Green, Brightlingsea, Essex, CO7 OEH
Ⓣ (01206) 303547
**Contact:** Jill White
**Opening Times:** By appt. only.
**Min Mail Order UK:** Nmc
**Min Mail Order EU:** Nmc
**Cat. Cost:** Sae.
**Credit Cards:** None
**Specialities:** *Cyclamen* species esp. *Cyclamen parviflorum. Cyclamen elegans*. Also seed.
**Notes:** Also sells wholesale.
**Map Ref:** E, D3 **OS Grid Ref:** TM088171

**EKen** **KENWICK FARMHOUSE NURSERIES** ⊠ ♿
Kenwick Road, Louth, Lincolnshire, LN11 8NW
Ⓣ (01507) 606469
Ⓕ (01507) 606469
Ⓔ info@kenwicknursery.co.uk
Ⓦ www.kenwicknursery.co.uk
**Contact:** Janet Elmhirst
**Opening Times:** 0930-1700 (dusk in winter) Tue-Sat, closed Mon except B/hol. 1000-1600 Sun. Closed Jan.
**Min Mail Order UK:** £12.00
**Credit Cards:** All, except American Express
**Specialities:** Hardy plants, grown in small quantities.
**Notes:** Mail order only if stock is available.
**Map Ref:** E, A2 **OS Grid Ref:** TF342853

**ELan** **LANGTHORNS PLANTERY** ⊠ ♿
High Cross Lane West, Little Canfield, Dunmow, Essex, CM6 1TD
Ⓣ (01371) 872611
Ⓕ 0871 661 4093
Ⓔ info@langthorns.com
Ⓦ www.langthorns.com
**Contact:** E Cannon
**Opening Times:** 1000-1700 or dusk (if earlier) 7 days excl. Xmas fortnight.
**Min Mail Order UK:** £15.00
**Cat. Cost:** £1.50
**Credit Cards:** Visa, Access, Switch, MasterCard, Delta
**Specialities:** Wide general range with many unusual plants.
**Notes:** Mail order anything under 5ft tall. Mail order not available during spring & summer months.
**Map Ref:** E, D2 **OS Grid Ref:** TL592204

**ELar** **LARKSPUR NURSERY** ⊠
Fourways, Dog Drove South, Holbeach Drove, Spalding, Lincolnshire, PE12 0SD
Ⓣ (01406) 330830
Ⓔ info@larkspur-nursery.co.uk
Ⓦ www.larkspur-nursery.co.uk
**Contact:** Ashley Ramsbottom
**Opening Times:** Mail order only. Open by prior arrangement. See website for details of nursery Open Days in Jun.
**Min Mail Order UK:** Nmc
**Min Mail Order EU:** Nmc
**Cat. Cost:** 2 × 1st class.
**Credit Cards:** None
**Specialities:** Delphiniums & *Abutilon.* Some varieties in small quantities. Order early to avoid disappointment. Also seed for sale.
**Notes:** Plants despatched from June in 7 or 8cm pots. See website for details.

**ELau** **LAUREL FARM HERBS** ⊠ ♿
Main Road (A12), Kelsale, Saxmundham, Suffolk, IP13 2RG
Ⓣ (01728) 668223
Ⓔ laurelfarmherbs@aol.com
Ⓦ www.laurelfarmherbs.co.uk
**Contact:** Chris Seagon
**Opening Times:** Please phone or check website for opening hours as times can vary.
**Min Mail Order UK:** 6 plants + p&p
**Min Mail Order EU:** 12 plants
**Cat. Cost:** Online only.
**Credit Cards:** Visa, MasterCard, Switch, Delta
**Specialities:** Herbs esp. rosemary, thyme, mint & sage.
**Notes:** Mail orders accepted by email, phone or post. Nursery may be moving in 2010, check website for details. Also sells wholesale.
**Map Ref:** E, C3

**ELon** **LONG HOUSE PLANTS** ♿
The Long House, Church Road, Noak Hill, Romford, Essex, RM4 1LD
Ⓣ (01708) 371719
Ⓕ (01708) 346649
Ⓔ tim@longhouse-plants.co.uk
Ⓦ www.longhouse-plants.co.uk
**Contact:** Tim Carter
**Opening Times:** 1000-1700 Fri, Sat & B/hols, 1000-1600 Sun, beginning Mar-end Sep, or by appt.
**Cat. Cost:** None issued.
**Credit Cards:** All major credit/debit cards
**Specialities:** Interesting range of choice shrubs, grasses & herbaceous perennials. Many unusual varieties.
**Map Ref:** E, D2 **OS Grid Ref:** TQ554194

**EMal** **MARSHALL'S MALMAISONS** ⊠ ♿
Hullwood Barn, Shelley, Ipswich, Suffolk, IP7 5RE
Ⓣ (01473) 822400
Ⓜ 07768 454875
Ⓔ jim@malmaisons.plus.com
**Contact:** J M Marshall/Sarah Cook
**Opening Times:** By appt. only.
**Min Mail Order UK:** £24.00 incl. p&p
**Min Mail Order EU:** £35.00 incl. p&p
**Cat. Cost:** 1st class sae.
**Credit Cards:** None
**Specialities:** Nat. Collections of Malmaison Carnations & Cedric Morris Irises. *Iris* stock only available in small quantities.
**Notes:** Also sells wholesale.
**Map Ref:** E, C3 **OS Grid Ref:** TM006394

**EMic** **MICKFIELD HOSTAS** ⊠ € ♿
The Poplars, Mickfield, Stowmarket, Suffolk, IP14 5LH
Ⓣ (01449) 711576
Ⓕ (01449) 711576
Ⓔ mickfieldhostas@btconnect.com
Ⓦ www.mickfieldhostas.co.uk
**Contact:** Mr & Mrs R L C Milton
**Opening Times:** For specified dates see catalogue or website.
**Min Mail Order UK:** Nmc
**Min Mail Order EU:** Nmc
**Cat. Cost:** 4 × 1st class.
**Credit Cards:** All, except American Express

KEY
⊠ Mail order to UK or EU — Delivers to shows
Exports beyond EU — € Euro accepted
♿ Accessible by wheelchair — ◆ See Display advertisement

E

**Specialities:** Holders of Nat. Collection of *Hosta* containing around 2000 varieties. See website for details of cvs held & latest availability. Will split parent plants for customers if practical. Also operates a waiting list for rarities.
**Map Ref:** E, C3 **OS Grid Ref:** TM136619

**EMil** **Mill Race Garden Centre** ⊠ ♿
New Road, Aldham, Colchester, Essex, CO6 3QT
Ⓣ (01206) 242521
Ⓕ (01206) 242073
Ⓔ avril.hall@millracegardencentre.co.uk
Ⓦ www.millracegardencentre.co.uk
**Contact:** Annette Bayliss
**Opening Times:** 0900-1730 7 days.
**Min Mail Order UK:** £15.00
**Credit Cards:** All major credit/debit cards
**Specialities:** Stock available in small quantities only.
**Notes:** Trees & large shrubs not sent by mail order.
**Map Ref:** E, C2 **OS Grid Ref:** TL918268

**ENBC** **Norfolk Bamboo Company** ⊠
Vine Cottage, The Drift, Ingoldisthorpe, King's Lynn, Norfolk, PE31 6NW
Ⓣ (01485) 543935
Ⓜ 07970 310880
Ⓕ (01485) 543314
Ⓔ Lewdyer@hotmail.com
Ⓦ www.norfolkbamboo.co.uk
**Contact:** Lewis Dyer
**Opening Times:** 1000-1700 Fri, Apr-Sep, or by appt.
**Min Mail Order UK:** £10.00 + p&p
**Cat. Cost:** 1 × 1st class sae for price list.
**Credit Cards:** None
**Specialities:** Bamboos.
**Map Ref:** E, B2 **OS Grid Ref:** TF684334

**EOHP** **Old Hall Plants** ⊠
1 The Old Hall, Barsham, Beccles, Suffolk, NR34 8HB
Ⓣ (01502) 717475
Ⓔ info@oldhallplants.co.uk
Ⓦ www.oldhallplants.co.uk
**Contact:** Janet Elliott
**Opening Times:** By appt. only. Please phone first.
**Min Mail Order UK:** Nmc
**Min Mail Order EU:** Nmc
**Cat. Cost:** 4 × 1st class.
**Credit Cards:** Paypal
**Specialities:** A variety of rare herbs, house plants, *Plectranthus*. Some plants available in small quantities.
**Notes:** Partial wheelchair access. Paypal accepted for overseas orders only.
**Map Ref:** E, C3 **OS Grid Ref:** TM395904

**EPau** **Paugers Plants** ♿
Bury Road, Depden, Bury St Edmunds, Suffolk, IP29 4BU
Ⓣ (01284) 850527
Ⓜ 07906 618603
Ⓔ geraldine.arnold@btinternet.com
**Contact:** Geraldine Arnold
**Opening Times:** 0900-1730 Wed-Sat, 1000-1700 Sun & B/hols, 1st Mar-30th Nov.
**Cat. Cost:** None issued.
**Credit Cards:** None
**Specialities:** Hardy shrubs & perennials in large or small quantities.
**Notes:** Also sells wholesale.
**Map Ref:** E, C2 **OS Grid Ref:** TL783568

**EPfP** **The Place for Plants** ⊠ ⌂ € ♿
East Bergholt Place, East Bergholt, Suffolk, CO7 6UP
Ⓣ (01206) 299224
Ⓕ (01206) 299229
Ⓔ sales@placeforplants.co.uk
Ⓦ www.placeforplants.co.uk
**Contact:** Rupert & Sara Eley
**Opening Times:** 1000-1700 (or dusk if earlier) 7 days. Closed Easter Sun. Garden open Mar-Oct.
**Min Mail Order UK:** Nmc
**Cat. Cost:** 2 × 1st class.
**Credit Cards:** All major credit/debit cards
**Specialities:** Wide range of specialist & popular plants. Nat. Collection of Deciduous *Euonymus*. 20 acre mature garden with free access to RHS members during season.
**Notes:** Mail order from Sep-Feb only.
**Map Ref:** E, C3

**EPGN** **Park Green Nurseries** ⊠ ☒ ⌂
Wetheringsett, Stowmarket, Suffolk, IP14 5QH
Ⓣ (01728) 860139
Ⓜ 07909 531143
Ⓕ (01728) 861277
Ⓔ nurseries@parkgreen.co.uk
Ⓦ www.parkgreen.co.uk
**Contact:** Richard & Mary Ford
**Opening Times:** 1000-1600 Mon-Sat, 1 Mar-30 Sep.
**Min Mail Order UK:** £3.00
**Min Mail Order EU:** £5.00
**Cat. Cost:** 4 × 1st class.
**Credit Cards:** Visa, MasterCard, Delta, Maestro
**Specialities:** *Hosta*, ornamental grasses, ferns & other herbaceous.

**Notes:** Mail order *Hosta* only.
**Map Ref:** E, C3 **OS Grid Ref:** TM136644

**EPla** **P W Plants** ⊠ ⌂ ♿
Sunnyside, Heath Road, Kenninghall, Norfolk, NR16 2DS
Ⓣ (01953) 888212
Ⓔ pw@hardybamboo.com
Ⓦ www.hardybamboo.com
**Contact:** Paul Whittaker
**Opening Times:** Every Fri & last Sat in every month, plus all Sats Apr-Sep.
**Min Mail Order UK:** Nmc
**Min Mail Order EU:** Nmc
**Cat. Cost:** Online only.
**Credit Cards:** All major credit/debit cards
**Specialities:** Bamboos, grasses, choice shrubs & perennials.
**Map Ref:** E, C3 **OS Grid Ref:** TM036846

**EPom** **Pomona Fruits Ltd** ⊠
Pomona House, 12 Third Avenue, Walton-on-the-Naze, Essex, CO14 8JU
Ⓣ 0845 676 0607
Ⓜ 07735 234286
Ⓕ 0845 676 0608
Ⓔ Info@PomonaFruits.co.uk
Ⓦ www.PomonaFruits.co.uk
**Contact:** Ming Yang/Claire Higgins
**Opening Times:** Not open. Mail order only.
**Min Mail Order UK:** Nmc
**Cat. Cost:** Free.
**Credit Cards:** All major credit/debit cards
**Specialities:** Fruit stock.
**Map Ref:** E, D3

**EPot** **Pottertons Nursery** ⊠ ✈ ⌂ € ♿
Moortown Road, Nettleton, Caistor, Lincolnshire, LN7 6HX
Ⓣ (01472) 851714
Ⓕ (01472) 852580
Ⓔ sales@pottertons.co.uk
Ⓦ www.pottertons.co.uk
**Contact:** Robert Potterton
**Opening Times:** 0900-1600 Tue-Sun. Closed Mon except B/hols. By appt. only Nov, Dec & Jan.
**Min Mail Order UK:** Nmc
**Min Mail Order EU:** Nmc
**Cat. Cost:** £2.00 in stamps
**Credit Cards:** Maestro, MasterCard, Visa
**Specialities:** Alpines, dwarf bulbs & woodland plants. Hardy orchids & *Pleione*.
**Notes:** External talks nationally & internationally to garden clubs & societies. Group nursery tours by arrangement.
**Map Ref:** E, A1 **OS Grid Ref:** TA091001

**EPPr** **The Plantsman's Preference** ⊠ ⌂ ♿
(Office) Lynwood, Hopton Road, Garboldisham, Diss, Norfolk, IP22 2QN
Ⓣ (01953) 681439 (office)
Ⓜ 07799 855559 (nursery)
Ⓔ tim@plantpref.co.uk
Ⓦ www.plantpref.co.uk
**Contact:** Tim Fuller
**Opening Times:** 0930-1700 Fri, Sat & Sun Mar-Oct. Other times by appt.
**Min Mail Order UK:** £15.00
**Min Mail Order EU:** £30.00
**Cat. Cost:** Online only.
**Credit Cards:** All major credit/debit cards
**Specialities:** Hardy geraniums & ornamental grasses. Unusual & interesting perennials incl. shade/woodland. Some choice shrubs esp. *Caprifoliaceae*. Nat. Collection of *Molinia*.
**Notes:** Nursery is on Church Road, South Lopham, Diss, IP22 2LW.
**Map Ref:** E, C3 **OS Grid Ref:** TM041819

**EPri** **Priory Plants** ⊠ ⌂
1 Covey Cottages, Hintlesham, Nr Ipswich, Suffolk, IP8 3NY
Ⓣ (01473) 652656
Ⓕ (01473) 652656
Ⓔ sue.mann3@btinternet.com
Ⓦ www.prioryplants.co.uk
**Contact:** Sue Mann
**Opening Times:** By appt. only. Please ring first to avoid disappointment.
**Min Mail Order UK:** £15.00 + p&p
**Min Mail Order EU:** £25.00
**Cat. Cost:** 3 × 1st class
**Credit Cards:** None
**Specialities:** Cottage garden perennials, as well as increasing range of South African plants. *Agapanthus*, *Astrantia*, *Geum*, Siberian *Iris*, *Tulbaghia* & *Watsonia*.
**Notes:** Sells at plant fairs & agricultural shows.
**Map Ref:** E, C3 **OS Grid Ref:** TM070448

**EPts** **Potash Nursery** ⊠ ⌂ ♿
Cow Green, Bacton, Stowmarket, Suffolk, IP14 4HJ
Ⓣ (01449) 781671
Ⓔ enquiries@potashnursery.co.uk
Ⓦ www.potashnursery.co.uk
**Contact:** M W Clare
**Opening Times:** Pre-ordered plants can be collected by appt. only.

KEY
⊠ Mail order to UK or EU ⌂ Delivers to shows
✈ Exports beyond EU € Euro accepted
♿ Accessible by wheelchair ◆ See Display advertisement

E

**Min Mail Order UK:** £12.90
**Cat. Cost:** 4 × 1st class.
**Credit Cards:** Visa, Delta, MasterCard
**Specialities:** *Fuchsia*.
**Map Ref:** E, C3 **OS Grid Ref:** TM0565NE

**EPyc** **PENNYCROSS PLANTS** ⊠ 🏠
Earith Road, Colne, Huntingdon, Cambridgeshire, PE28 3NL
Ⓣ (01487) 841520
Ⓔ salvias@pennycrossplants.co.uk
Ⓦ www.pennycrossplants.co.uk
**Contact:** Janet M Buist
**Opening Times:** 1000-1600 Mon-Fri, 1st Mar-31st Oct by appt.
**Min Mail Order UK:** Nmc
Cat. Cost: 1 × 2nd class for *Salvia* list only.
**Credit Cards:** None
**Specialities:** Hardy perennials. Salvias. Some plants available in ltd. quantities only. Will propagate salvias to order.
**Notes:** Mail order for young *Salvia* plants only.
**Map Ref:** E, C2 **OS Grid Ref:** TL378759

**EQua** **QUAYMOUNT NURSERY** ⊠ ♿
The Row, Wereham, Kings Lynn, Norfolk, PE33 9AY
Ⓣ (01366) 500691
Ⓕ (01366) 500611
Ⓔ info@quaymountplants.co.uk
Ⓦ www.quaymountplants.co.uk
**Contact:** Paul Markwell
**Opening Times:** 0900-1700 (or dusk if earlier) Mon-Fri, 1000-1600 Sat & Sun. Closed Sun Dec & Jan.
**Min Mail Order UK:** Nmc
**Cat. Cost:** 2 ×1st class.
**Credit Cards:** All major credit/debit cards
**Specialities:** Wide range of specialist & popular plants. *Hydrangea*.
**Notes:** Specimen plants collection only. Also sells wholesale.
**Map Ref:** E, B2 **OS Grid Ref:** TF679006

**ERCP** **ROSE COTTAGE PLANTS** ⊠ 🏠
Bay Tree Farm, Epping Green, Essex, CM16 6PU
Ⓣ (01992) 573775
Ⓕ (01992) 561198
Ⓔ anne@rosecottageplants.co.uk
Ⓦ www.rosecottageplants.co.uk
**Contact:** Anne & Jack Barnard
**Opening Times:** By appt. & for special events (see website for details).
**Min Mail Order UK:** Nmc
**Min Mail Order EU:** £20.00
**Cat. Cost:** Online only.
**Credit Cards:** All major credit/debit cards
**Specialities:** Bulbs.
**Notes:** Mail order, bulbs only (catalogue available online).
**Map Ref:** E, B1 **OS Grid Ref:** TL435053

**ERea** **READS NURSERY** ⊠ ✈ ♿
Hales Hall, Loddon, Norfolk, NR14 6QW
Ⓣ (01508) 548395
Ⓕ (01508) 548040
Ⓔ plants@readsnursery.co.uk
Ⓦ www.readsnursery.co.uk
**Contact:** Stephen Read
**Opening Times:** 1000-1630, or dusk if earlier, Wed-Sat.
**Min Mail Order UK:** Nmc
**Min Mail Order EU:** £25.00
**Cat. Cost:** Free.
**Credit Cards:** All major credit/debit cards
**Specialities:** Fruit trees, scented conservatory plants. Nat. Collections. of *Citrus* & figs.
**Notes:** Mostly accessible by wheelchair (some gravel paths).
**Map Ref:** E, C3 **OS Grid Ref:** TM369960

**ERhR** **RHODES & ROCKLIFFE** ⊠ ✈ €
2 Nursery Road, Nazeing, Essex, EN9 2JE
Ⓣ (01992) 451598 (office hours)
Ⓕ (01992) 440673
Ⓔ RRBegonias@aol.com
**Contact:** David Rhodes or John Rockliffe
**Opening Times:** By appt. only.
**Min Mail Order UK:** £3.00 + p&p
**Min Mail Order EU:** £5.00 + p&p
**Cat. Cost:** 2 × 1st class.
**Credit Cards:** None
**Specialities:** *Begonia* species & hybrids. Nat. Collection of *Begonia*. Plants propagated to order.
**Notes:** Mail order Apr-Sep only.
**Map Ref:** E, D2

**ERom** **THE ROMANTIC GARDEN** ⊠ ✈ € ♿ ◆
Swannington, Norwich, Norfolk, NR9 5NW
Ⓣ (01603) 261488
Ⓕ (01603) 864231
Ⓔ enquiries@romantic-garden-nursery.co.uk
Ⓦ www.romantic-garden-nursery.co.uk
**Contact:** John Powles/John Carrick
**Opening Times:** 1000-1700 Wed, Fri & Sat all year, plus B/hol Mons.
**Min Mail Order UK:** £5.00 + p&p
**Min Mail Order EU:** £30.00 + p&p
**Cat. Cost:** 6 × 1st class.
**Credit Cards:** All major credit/debit cards
**Specialities:** Conservatory. *Buxus* topiary,

ornamental standards, large specimens. Hedging. Topiary
**Notes:** Also sells wholesale.
**Map Ref:** E, B3

**ESem** **Semps by Post** ⊠
28 Mill Road, Newbourne, Woodbridge, Suffolk, IP12 4NP
Ⓣ (01473) 736440
Ⓔ Tricia@sempsbypost.co.uk
Ⓦ www.sempsbypost.co.uk
**Contact:** Tricia Newell
**Opening Times:** Not open.
**Min Mail Order UK:** Nmc
**Min Mail Order EU:** Nmc
**Cat. Cost:** Online only.
**Credit Cards:** Paypal
**Specialities:** *Sempervivum*. Some stock available in small quantities.

**ESgl** **Seagate Irises** ⊠ ✈ € ♿
A17 Long Sutton By-Pass, Long Sutton, Lincolnshire, PE12 9RX
Ⓣ (01406) 365138
Ⓜ 07887 856389
Ⓕ (01406) 365447
Ⓔ sales@irises.co.uk
Ⓦ www.irises.co.uk
**Contact:** Julian Browse or Wendy Browse
**Opening Times:** 1000-1700 daily Apr-mid Sep. Please phone for appt. mid-Jul to Mar.
**Min Mail Order UK:** Nmc
**Min Mail Order EU:** Nmc. Carriage at cost.
**Cat. Cost:** £3.50 or €8.00.
**Credit Cards:** Maestro, Visa, MasterCard
**Specialities:** Different types of *Iris*, bearded, beardless & species hybrids with about 1000 varieties in all, both historic & modern. Nat. Collection of Historic Tall Bearded Irises (pre-1964). Some only available in small quantities. Many container-grown available to callers.
**Map Ref:** E, B1 **OS Grid Ref:** TF437218

**EShb** **Shrubland Park Nurseries** ⊠ ♠
Coddenham, Ipswich, Suffolk, IP6 9QJ
Ⓣ (01473) 833187
Ⓜ 07890 527744
Ⓔ gill@shrublandparknurseries.co.uk
Ⓦ www.shrublandparknurseries.co.uk
**Contact:** Gill & Catherine Stitt
**Opening Times:** 1000-1600 Fri, Sat & Sun, Easter-30th Sep 2010.For other times please ring first or visit website.
**Min Mail Order UK:** Nmc
**Min Mail Order EU:** £30.00
**Cat. Cost:** 6 × 1st class or free by email.
**Credit Cards:** All major credit/debit cards, Nochex, Paypal
**Specialities:** Conservatory plants, succulents, hardy perennials, climbers, shrubs, ferns & grasses.
**Notes:** For directions phone or see website. nearest postcode for SatNav IP6 0PG. Partial wheelchair access.
**Map Ref:** E, C3 **OS Grid Ref:** TM128524

**ESty** **Style Roses** ⊠ ♠ ♿
10 Meridian Walk, Holbeach, Spalding, Lincolnshire, PE12 7NR
Ⓣ (01406) 424089
Ⓜ 07932 044093 or 07780 860415
Ⓕ (01406) 424089
Ⓔ styleroses@aol.com
Ⓦ www.styleroses.co.uk
**Contact:** Chris Styles, Margaret Styles
**Opening Times:** Vary. Please phone before visiting to avoid disappointment.
**Min Mail Order UK:** Nmc
**Min Mail Order EU:** Nmc
**Cat. Cost:** Free.
**Credit Cards:** All major credit/debit cards
**Specialities:** Standard & bush roses.
**Notes:** Export to EU during bare-root season Nov-Mar. Other countries subject to plant health requirements. Carriage & export certificates where required charged at cost. Also sells wholesale.
**Map Ref:** E, B1

**ESul** **Brian & Pearl Sulman** ⊠ ♠ ♿
54 Kingsway, Mildenhall, Bury St Edmunds, Suffolk, IP28 7HR
Ⓣ (01638) 712297
Ⓕ (01638) 712297
Ⓔ enquiries@sulmanspelargoniums.co.uk
Ⓦ www.sulmanspelargoniums.co.uk
**Contact:** Pearl Sulman
**Opening Times:** Mail order only. Not open, except for Open Days 5th/6th Jun 2010.
**Min Mail Order UK:** £25.00
**Cat. Cost:** 4 × 1st class.
**Credit Cards:** Visa, MasterCard
**Specialities:** *Pelargonium*. Some varieties only available in small quantities.
**Map Ref:** E, C2 **OS Grid Ref:** TL715747

**ESwi** **Swines Meadow Farm Nursery** ⊠ ♠ € ♿ ◆
47 Towngate East, Market Deeping, Peterborough, PE6 8LQ
Ⓣ 01778 343340
Ⓜ 07811 847933

KEY
⊠ Mail order to UK or EU ♠ Delivers to shows
✈ Exports beyond EU € Euro accepted
♿ Accessible by wheelchair ◆ See Display advertisement

E

Ⓔ info@swinesmeadowgardencentre.co.uk
Ⓦ www.swinesmeadowgardencentre.co.uk
**Contact:** Colin Ward
**Opening Times:** 0900-1700 Mon-Sat, 1000-1600 Sun (summer); 0900-1600 Mon-Sat, 1000-1600 Sun (winter).
**Min Mail Order UK:** £10.00
**Credit Cards:** All, except American Express
**Specialities:** Hardy exotics, tree ferns, bamboos & phormiums. Wollemi pine stockist. Many specialities available in small quantities only.
**Map Ref:** E, B1 **OS Grid Ref:** TF150113

**ETho** **Thorncroft Clematis Nursery** ⊠ ✈ ⌂ ♿
The Lings, Reymerston, Norwich, Norfolk, NR9 4QG
Ⓣ (01953) 850407
Ⓕ (01953) 851788
Ⓔ sales@thorncroftclematis.co.uk
Ⓦ www.thorncroftclematis.co.uk
**Contact:** Ruth P Gooch
**Opening Times:** 1000-1600 Tue-Sat all year, closed Sun & Mon. Open B/hol Mon.
**Min Mail Order UK:** Nmc
**Min Mail Order EU:** Nmc
**Cat. Cost:** 6 × 2nd class.
**Credit Cards:** All major credit/debit cards
**Specialities:** *Clematis.*
**Notes:** Does not export to USA, Canada or Australia.
**Map Ref:** E, B3 **OS Grid Ref:** TG039062

**ETMg** **Thompson & Morgan Young Plants Ltd** ⊠
Poplar Lane, Ipswich, Suffolk, IP8 3BU
Ⓣ 0844 573 2020
Ⓕ (01787) 882252 or (01473) 680199
Ⓔ ccare@thompson-morgan.com
Ⓦ www.thompson-morgan.com
**Contact:** Customer Care
**Opening Times:** Mail order only. Not open except for Open Weekend. Call centre open Mon-Fri 0800-1800, Sat & Sun 0900-1800.
**Min Mail Order UK:** Nmc
**Cat. Cost:** Free
**Credit Cards:** Visa, MasterCard

**ETod** **Todd's Botanics** ⊠ ⌂ €
West Street, Coggeshall, Colchester, Essex, CO6 1NT
Ⓣ (01376) 561212
Ⓜ 07970 643711
Ⓕ (01376) 561212
Ⓔ info@toddsbotanics.co.uk
Ⓦ www.toddsbotanics.co.uk
**Contact:** Mark Macdonald
**Opening Times:** 0900-1700 (or dusk) Thu-Sun. 1100-1600 Sun & B/hols. Open by appt. Mon-Wed. Open by appt. only in Jan.
**Min Mail Order UK:** Nmc
**Min Mail Order EU:** Nmc
**Cat. Cost:** 2 × 1st class.
**Credit Cards:** All major credit/debit cards
**Specialities:** Hardy exotics, herbaceous. Bamboos, palms, ferns, grasses, *Canna* & *Hedychium*. Olives, incl. named varieties.
**Notes:** Not all plants available mail order, contact nursery for details. Nursery partially accessible for wheelchairs. Also sells wholesale.
**Map Ref:** E, D2 **OS Grid Ref:** TL843224

**EWes** **West Acre Gardens** ⌂ ♿
West Acre, King's Lynn, Norfolk, PE32 1UJ
Ⓣ (01760) 755562
**Contact:** J J Tuite
**Opening Times:** 1000-1700 7 days 1st Feb-30th Nov. Other times by appt.
**Cat. Cost:** None issued.
**Credit Cards:** Visa, MasterCard, Delta, Switch
**Specialities:** Very wide selection of herbaceous & other garden plants incl. *Rhodohypoxis* & *Primula auricula*.
**Map Ref:** E, B1 **OS Grid Ref:** TF792182

**EWhm** **Waltham Herbs** ⌂
Willow Vale Nursery, North Kelsey Road, Caistor, Lincolnshire, LN7 6SF
Ⓣ (01472) 859481
Ⓜ 07949 883091
Ⓕ (01472) 859481
Ⓔ angelasach2@aol.com
Ⓦ www.waltham-herbs.co.uk
**Contact:** Angela Sach and Steve Penney
**Opening Times:** By appt. only.
**Specialities:** Herbs, lavenders and perennials, also some shrubs. Peat-free and pesticide-free.
**Notes:** Also sells wholesale.
**Map Ref:** E, A1

**EWil** **Wild Flower Shop** ⊠ ♿
Bridge Farm Barns, Monks Eleigh, Claydon, Ipswich, Suffolk, IP7 7AY
Ⓜ 07590 895590 or 07889 006231
Ⓔ kathy@wildflowershop.co.uk
Ⓦ www.wildflowershop.co.uk
**Contact:** Kathy Kalafat
**Opening Times:** 0930-1700 Mon-Sat, 1100-1700 Sun.
**Min Mail Order UK:** Nmc
**Cat. Cost:** £1.00 or free online.
**Credit Cards:** MasterCard, Visa, Delta, Maestro
**Specialities:** British wild flower plants, plugs,

bulbs & seeds. Native pond & water plants. From cultivated stock not taken from the wild. Available in small quantities.
**Map Ref:** E, C3 **OS Grid Ref:** TL972476

EWld **Woodlands**
Peppin Lane, Fotherby, Louth, Lincolnshire, LN11 0UW
Ⓣ (01507) 603586
Ⓜ 07866 161864
Ⓔ annbobarmstrong@uwclub.net
Ⓦ www.woodlandsplants.co.uk
**Contact:** Ann Armstrong
**Opening Times:** Flexible, but please phone or email to avoid disappointment.
**Cat. Cost:** None issued.
**Credit Cards:** None
**Specialities:** Small but interesting range of unusual plants, esp. woodland and *Salvia*, all grown on the nursery in limited quantity.
**Notes:** Mature garden, art gallery & refreshments.
**Map Ref:** E, A2 **OS Grid Ref:** TF322918

EWll **The Walled Garden** ♿ ◆
Park Road, Benhall, Saxmundham, Suffolk, IP17 1JB
Ⓣ (01728) 602510
Ⓕ (01728) 602510
Ⓔ jim@thewalledgarden.co.uk
Ⓦ www.thewalledgarden.co.uk
**Contact:** Jim Mountain
**Opening Times:** 0930-1700 Tue-Sun Mar-Nov, 0930-dusk Tue-Sat mid Nov-mid Feb.
**Cat. Cost:** 2 × 1st class.
**Credit Cards:** All major credit/debit cards
**Specialities:** Tender & hardy perennials. For current information see website.
**Map Ref:** E, C3 **OS Grid Ref:** TM371613

EWoo **Woottens Plants** ⊠ ♿
Wenhaston, Blackheath, Halesworth, Suffolk, IP19 9HD
Ⓣ (01502) 478258
Ⓕ (01502) 478888
Ⓔ sales@woottensplants.co.uk
Ⓦ www.woottensplants.co.uk
**Contact:** M Loftus
**Opening Times:** 0930-1700 7 days.
**Min Mail Order UK:** Nmc
**Min Mail Order EU:** Nmc
**Cat. Cost:** Online only.
**Credit Cards:** Access, Visa, American Express, Switch
**Specialities:** *Pelargonium*, *Hemerocallis*, *Primula auricula* & *Iris*. Grasses.
**Notes:** Also sells wholesale.
**Map Ref:** E, C3 **OS Grid Ref:** TM42714375

EWTr **Walnut Tree Garden Nursery** ⊠
Flymoor Lane, Rocklands, Attleborough, Norfolk, NR17 1BP
Ⓣ (01953) 488163
Ⓔ info@wtgn.co.uk
Ⓦ www.wtgn.co.uk
**Contact:** Jim Paine & Clare Billington
**Opening Times:** 0900-1800 Tue-Sun Feb-Nov & B/hols.
**Min Mail Order UK:** Nmc
**Cat. Cost:** 4 × 1st class.
**Credit Cards:** All major credit/debit cards
**Map Ref:** E, B1 **OS Grid Ref:** TL978973

## Scotland

GAbr **Abriachan Nurseries** ⊠ ♿
Loch Ness Side, Inverness, Inverness-shire, IV3 8LA
Ⓣ (01463) 861232
Ⓔ info@lochnessgarden.com
Ⓦ www.lochnessgarden.com
**Contact:** Mr & Mrs D Davidson
**Opening Times:** 0900-1900 daily (dusk if earlier) Feb-Nov.
**Min Mail Order UK:** Nmc
**Cat. Cost:** 4 × 1st class.
**Credit Cards:** All major credit/debit cards
**Specialities:** Herbaceous perennials, old-fashioned *Primula*, *Helianthemum*, hardy geraniums, *Sempervivum* & *Primula auricula*.
**Notes:** Wheelchair access to nursery only.
**Map Ref:** G, B2 **OS Grid Ref:** NH571347

GAgs **Angusplants** ⊠ ♿
3 Balfour Cottages, Menmuir, By Brechin, Angus, DD9 7RN
Ⓣ (01356) 660280
Ⓔ alison@angusplants.co.uk
Ⓦ www.angusplants.co.uk
**Contact:** Dr Alison S. Goldie & Mark A. Hutson
**Opening Times:** By appt. only. Please phone first. Light refreshments provided.
**Min Mail Order UK:** Nmc
**Cat. Cost:** 4 × 1st class
**Credit Cards:** None
**Specialities:** Predominantly *Primula auricula*, although other *Primula* species are offered. A few available in small quantities only.
**Notes:** Mail order available all year.
**Map Ref:** G, B3 **OS Grid Ref:** NO528643

KEY
⊠ Mail order to UK or EU — Delivers to shows
Exports beyond EU — € Euro accepted
♿ Accessible by wheelchair — ◆ See Display advertisement

G

G

**GAuc** **AUCHGOURISH BOTANIC GARDEN** ⊠ € ♿
Street of Kincardine, by Boat of Garten, Inverness-shire, PH24 3BY
Ⓣ (01479) 831464
Ⓜ 07746 122775
Ⓔ info@auchgourishbotanicgarden.org
Ⓦ www.thebotanicalnursery.com
**Contact:** Iain Brodie of Falsyde
**Opening Times:** 1000-1700 Mon-Fri, closed Sat, 1100-1700 Sun, 1st Apr-31st Oct.
**Min Mail Order UK:** £25.00 + £5.00 p&p
**Min Mail Order EU:** £35.00 + p&p at cost
**Cat. Cost:** Online only.
**Credit Cards:** All major credit/debit cards
**Specialities:** Botanical species. *Betulaceae*, *Rosaceae*, *Ericaceae*, *Iridaceae*, *Liliaceae* & *Primulaceae*. Nursery is at Auchgourish Botanic Gardens, Boat of Garten. Auchgourish Botanic Gardens are open 1st Apr-31st Oct.
**Notes:** Mail order despatch Sep-Apr incl. subject to weather. No despatch May-Aug but plants can be uplifted any time by prior arrangement. Credit cards accepted online only. Will deliver to Gardening Scotland show.
**Map Ref:** G, B2 **OS Grid Ref:** NH955194

**GBBs** **BORDER BELLES** ⊠ ♿
Old Branxton Cottages, Innerwick, Nr Dunbar, East Lothian, EH42 1QT
Ⓣ (01368) 840325
Ⓔ mail@borderbelles.com
Ⓦ www.borderbelles.com
**Contact:** Gillian Moynihan
**Opening Times:** 1000-1700 Sat, Mar-Sep.
**Min Mail Order UK:** Nmc
**Min Mail Order EU:** On request
**Cat. Cost:** Online only.
**Credit Cards:** All major credit/debit cards
**Specialities:** Hardy perennials & woodland plants.
**Notes:** Also sells wholesale.

**GBee** **BEECHES COTTAGE NURSERY** ♿
High Boreland, Lesmahagow, South Lanarkshire, ML11 9PY
Ⓣ (01555) 893369
Ⓜ 07930 343131
**Contact:** Margaret Harrison, Steve Harrison
**Opening Times:** 1000-1630 Wed-Sat, Mar-Oct. Other times by appt.
**Cat. Cost:** None issued.
**Credit Cards:** None
**Specialities:** Traditional & unusual hardy & half-hardy cottage garden perennials. Some plants available in small quantities only.
**Notes:** Wheelchair access to nursery only. Also sells wholesale.
**Map Ref:** G, C2 **OS Grid Ref:** NS837403

**GBin** **BINNY PLANTS** ⊠ € ♿
West Lodge, Binny Estate, Ecclesmachen Road, Nr Broxbourn, West Lothian, EH52 6NL
Ⓣ (01506) 858931
Ⓕ (01506) 858155
Ⓔ binnyplants@aol.com
Ⓦ www.binnyplants.co.uk
**Contact:** Billy Carruthers
**Opening Times:** 1000-1700 7 days. Closed mid-Dec to mid-Jan.
**Min Mail Order UK:** £25.00
**Min Mail Order EU:** £25.00
**Cat. Cost:** £2.50 refundable on ordering.
**Credit Cards:** Visa, MasterCard, EuroCard, Maestro
**Specialities:** Perennials incl. *Astilbe*, *Geranium*, *Hosta*, *Paeonia* & *Iris*. Plus large selection of grasses & ferns.
**Notes:** Mail order Sep-Apr only. Also sells wholesale.
**Map Ref:** G, C3

**GCai** **CAIRNSMORE NURSERY** ⊠ ♿
Chapmanton Road, Castle Douglas, Kirkcudbrightshire, DG7 2NU
Ⓣ (01556) 504819
Ⓜ 07980 176458
Ⓔ cairnsmorenursery@hotmail.com
Ⓦ www.cairnsmorenursery.co.uk
**Contact:** Valerie Smith
**Opening Times:** By appt. only.
**Min Mail Order UK:** Nmc
**Cat. Cost:** 4 × 1st class.
**Credit Cards:** None
**Specialities:** *Heuchera*.
**Map Ref:** G, D2 **OS Grid Ref:** NX756637

**GCal** **CALLY GARDENS** ⊠ ♿
Gatehouse of Fleet, Castle Douglas, Kirkcudbrightshire, DG7 2DJ
Ⓣ (01557) 815029 recorded information only.
Ⓔ info@callygardens.co.uk
Ⓦ www.callygardens.co.uk
**Contact:** Michael Wickenden
**Opening Times:** 1000-1730 Sat-Sun, 1400-1730 Tue-Fri. Easter Sat-last Sun in Sept.
**Min Mail Order UK:** £15.00 + p&p
**Cat. Cost:** 3 × 1st class.
**Credit Cards:** None
**Specialities:** Unusual perennials & grasses. Some rare shrubs, climbers & conservatory plants. 3500 varieties growing in an 2.7 acre walled garden built in the 1760s.

**Notes:** Also sells wholesale.
**Map Ref:** G, D2 **OS Grid Ref:** NX604549

GCoc **James Cocker & Sons** ⊠ ♿
Whitemyres, Lang Stracht, Aberdeen, Aberdeenshire, AB15 6XH
Ⓣ (01224) 313261
Ⓕ (01224) 312531
Ⓔ sales@roses.uk.com
Ⓦ www.roses.uk.com
**Contact:** Alec Cocker
**Opening Times:** 0900-1700 Mon-Fri.
**Min Mail Order UK:** Nmc
**Min Mail Order EU:** £6.25 + p&p
**Cat. Cost:** Free
**Credit Cards:** Visa, MasterCard, Delta, Maestro
**Specialities:** Roses.
**Notes:** Also sells wholesale.
**Map Ref:** G, B3

GCra **Craigieburn Garden** ♿
Craigieburn House, by Moffat, Dumfriesshire, DG10 9LF
Ⓣ (01683) 221250
Ⓕ (01683) 221250
Ⓔ ajmw1@aol.com
Ⓦ www.craigieburngarden.com
**Contact:** Janet & Andrew Wheatcroft
**Opening Times:** 1030-1800 daily, Easter-31st Oct. Other times by appt.
**Specialities:** *Meconopsis* plants for damp gardens, herbaceous perennials.
**Map Ref:** G, D3

GCro **Croft 16 Daffodils** ⊠
16 Midtown of Inverasdale, Poolewe, Achnasheen, Ross-shire, IV22 2LW
Ⓣ (01445) 781717
Ⓔ sales@croft16daffodils.co.uk
Ⓦ www.croft16daffodils.co.uk
**Contact:** Kate & Duncan Donald
**Opening Times:** By appt. only. Please phone or email first.
**Min Mail Order UK:** Nmc
**Min Mail Order EU:** Nmc
**Cat. Cost:** Online only.
**Credit Cards:** Paypal
**Specialities:** Daffodils bred pre-1930.
**Map Ref:** G, A1 **OS Grid Ref:** NG822851

GDun **Dunskey Gardens & Maze** ♿
Portpatrick, Stranraer, Wigtownshire, DG9 8TJ
Ⓣ (01776) 810905
Ⓜ 07899 092070
Ⓕ (01776) 810581
Ⓔ gabygardeners@btinternet.com
Ⓦ www.dunskey.com
**Contact:** Gabrielle Reynolds
**Opening Times:** 1000-1600 w/ends only Feb, 1000-1700 daily Easter-Oct.
**Credit Cards:** All major credit/debit cards
**Specialities:** Broad range, propagated from the gardens, incl. bulbs, tender perennials, herbaceous, trees and shrubs. Available in small quantities only. Provisional Nat. Collections of *Clianthus* & *Sutherlandia*.
**Notes:** Dunskey Estate Walled Garden & Maze open to the public. Sells at local plant shows.
**Map Ref:** G, D2 **OS Grid Ref:** NX004560

GEdr **Edrom Nurseries** ⊠ ♿
Coldingham, Eyemouth, Berwickshire, TD14 5TZ
Ⓣ (01890) 771386
Ⓕ (01890) 71387
Ⓔ info@edromnurseries.co.uk
Ⓦ www.edromnurseries.co.uk
**Contact:** Mr Terry Hunt
**Opening Times:** 0900-1700 Thu-Tue (closed Wed), 1st Mar-30th Sep. Other times by appt.
**Min Mail Order UK:** Nmc
**Min Mail Order EU:** £20.00
**Cat. Cost:** 4 × 2nd class. More plants listed online than in printed catalogue.
**Credit Cards:** All major credit/debit cards
**Specialities:** *Trillium*, *Arisaema*, *Primula*, *Gentiana*, *Meconopsis*, *Cypripedium*, *Fritillaria*, hardy orchids.
**Map Ref:** G, C3 **OS Grid Ref:** NT873663

GFai **Fairholm Plants** ⊠ €
Fairholm, Larkhall, Lanarkshire, ML9 2UQ
Ⓣ (01698) 881671
Ⓕ (01698) 888135
Ⓔ fairholm.plants@stevenson-hamilton.co.uk
**Contact:** Mrs J M Hamilton
**Opening Times:** Apr-Oct by appt.
**Min Mail Order UK:** Nmc
**Cat. Cost:** 1 × 2nd class for descriptive list.
**Credit Cards:** None
**Specialities:** *Abutilon* & unusual half-hardy perennials esp. South African. Nat. Collection of *Abutilon* cvs. Plants available in small quantities only.
**Notes:** Mail order for young/small plants.
**Map Ref:** G, C2 **OS Grid Ref:** NS754515

KEY
⊠ Mail order to UK or EU — Delivers to shows
Exports beyond EU — € Euro accepted
♿ Accessible by wheelchair — ◆ See Display advertisement

G

**GGal** **GALLOWAY PLANTS** ⊠ ♿
Claymoddie, Whithorn, Newton Stewart, Dumfries & Galloway, DG8 8LX
Ⓣ (01988) 500422
Ⓔ gallowayplants@aol.com
Ⓦ www.gallowayplants.co.uk
**Contact:** Robin & Mary Nicholson
**Opening Times:** 1400-1700 Fri, Sat & Sun, 2nd Apr-12th Sep 2010, other times by prior appt.
**Min Mail Order UK:** £50.00 + p&p
**Cat. Cost:** 2 × 1st class.
**Credit Cards:** None
**Specialities:** Southern hemisphere *Hydrangea*. Available in small quantities only.
**Notes:** Also sells wholesale.
**Map Ref:** G, D2 **OS Grid Ref:** NX450377

**GGar** **GARDEN COTTAGE NURSERY** ⊠ ♿
Tournaig, Poolewe, Achnasheen, Ross-shire, IV22 2LH
Ⓣ (01445) 781777
Ⓔ ben@gcnursery.co.uk
Ⓦ www.gcnursery.co.uk
**Contact:** Ben Rushbrooke
**Opening Times:** 1000-1800 Mon-Sat mid Mar-mid Oct or by appt.
**Min Mail Order UK:** Nmc
**Cat. Cost:** Free.
**Credit Cards:** Visa, Switch, MasterCard
**Specialities:** A wide range of plants esp. those from the southern hemisphere & plants for bog & coastal gardens.
**Map Ref:** G, A2 **OS Grid Ref:** NG878835

**GJos** **JO'S GARDEN ENTERPRISE** ♿
Easter Balmungle Farm, Eathie Road, by Rosemarkie, Ross-shire, IV10 8SL
Ⓣ (01381) 621006
Ⓔ anne.chance@ukonline.co.uk
**Contact:** Joanna Chance
**Opening Times:** 1000 to dusk, 7 days.
**Cat. Cost:** None
**Credit Cards:** None
**Specialities:** Alpines & herbaceous perennials. Selection of native wild flowers.
**Map Ref:** G, B2 **OS Grid Ref:** NH600742

**GKev** **KEVOCK GARDEN PLANTS** ⊠ ✈ €
16 Kevock Road, Lasswade, Midlothian, EH18 1HT
Ⓣ 0131 454 0660
Ⓜ 07811 321585
Ⓕ 0131 454 0660
Ⓔ info@kevockgarden.co.uk
Ⓦ www.kevockgarden.co.uk
**Contact:** Stella Rankin
**Opening Times:** Not open. Mail order & plant stalls only.
**Min Mail Order UK:** £20.00
**Min Mail Order EU:** £20.00
**Cat. Cost:** 4 × 1st class.
**Credit Cards:** Visa, MasterCard, Switch
**Specialities:** Chinese & Himalayan plants. *Androsace*, *Daphne*, *Paeonia*, *Primula*, *Meconopsis*, *Iris*, woodland plants, alpines, rock, marginal, bog.
**Notes:** Also sells wholesale.

**GKin** **KINLOCHLAICH GARDEN PLANT CENTRE** ♿
Appin, Argyll, PA38 4BB
Ⓣ (01631) 730342
Ⓜ 07881 525754
Ⓕ (01631) 730482
Ⓔ fiona@kinlochlaich.plus.com
Ⓦ www.kinlochlaichgardencentre.co.uk
**Contact:** Fiona Hutchison
**Opening Times:** 0900-1730, 7 days, Mar-Oct. (Winter) 0900-until dusk, Mon-Sat.
**Cat. Cost:** None issued
**Credit Cards:** All major credit/debit cards
**Specialities:** Hardy shrubs, trees, azaleas, perennials. Also Gulf Stream plants such as *Tropaeolum*, *Embothrium*, *Eucryphia*, *Drymis* & more. Good selection of hardy seaside plants.
**Notes:** Does not offer mail order but will post where possible.

**GLam** **LAMBERTON NURSERY** ⊠ ✈ €
No. 3, Lamberton, Berwickshire, TD15 1XB
Ⓣ (01289) 308515
Ⓕ (01289) 308515
Ⓔ Ron@LambertonNursery.co.uk
Ⓦ www.lambertonnursery.co.uk
**Contact:** Ron McBeath
**Opening Times:** 1000-1700 Sun, Mon & Tue, 1st Apr-30th Sep.
**Min Mail Order UK:** Nmc
**Min Mail Order EU:** Nmc
**Cat. Cost:** 4 × 1st class.
**Credit Cards:** Visa, MasterCard
**Specialities:** *Primula*, *Campanula*, *Rhododendron*, *Gentiana* & *Dianthus*. Many in small quantities only.
**Notes:** Partially accessible for wheelchairs.
**Map Ref:** G, C3 **OS Grid Ref:** NT969574

**GLin** **LINN BOTANIC GARDENS** € ♿
Cove, Helensburgh, Dunbartonshire, G84 0NR
Ⓣ (01436) 842084
Ⓔ jamie@linnbotanicgardens.org.uk
Ⓦ www.linnbotanicgardens.org.uk
**Contact:** Jamie Taggart
**Opening Times:** 1100-1700, 7 days.

**Cat. Cost:** 4 × 1st class or by email.
**Credit Cards:** None
**Specialities:** Small plant sales area offering diverse range of plants.
**Notes:** Botanic Gardens open (charges apply). Wheelchair access to plant sales area but not gardens.
**Map Ref:** G, C2 **OS Grid Ref:** NS223827

GLog **LOGIE STEADING PLANTS** ♿
Forres, Moray, IV36 2QN
Ⓣ (01309) 611222 or 611278
Ⓕ (01309) 611300
Ⓔ panny@logie.co.uk
Ⓦ www.logie.co.uk
**Contact:** Mrs Panny Laing
**Opening Times:** 1030-1700 hours, 7 days, April-end Oct.
**Credit Cards:** All major credit/debit cards
**Specialities:** Unusual hardy plants, grown in Scotland for Scottish gardens. Large range of hardy geraniums & marginal plants.
**Notes:** Logie House Garden open every day. Café, farm shop, gallery, second-hand books, antiques, river walk.
**Map Ref:** G, B2 **OS Grid Ref:** NJ006504

GMac **ELIZABETH MACGREGOR** ⊠ ♿
Ellenbank, Tongland Road, Kirkcudbright, Dumfries & Galloway, DG6 4UU
Ⓣ (01557) 330620
Ⓕ (01557) 330620
Ⓔ elizabeth.violas@btinternet.com
Ⓦ www.elizabethmacgregornursery.co.uk
**Contact:** Elizabeth MacGregor
**Opening Times:** 1000-1700 Mon, Fri & Sat May-Sep, or please phone.
**Min Mail Order UK:** 6 plants + p&p
**Min Mail Order EU:** £50.00 + p&p
**Cat. Cost:** 4 × 1st class or 5 × 2nd class
**Credit Cards:** All major credit/debit cards
**Specialities:** Violets, violas & violettas, old and new varieties. *Campanula*, *Geranium*, *Eryngium*, *Penstemon*, *Aster*, *Primula*, *Iris* & other unusual herbaceous.
**Notes:** Half-acre walled garden.
**Map Ref:** G, D2 **OS Grid Ref:** NX692525

GMaP **MACPLANTS** ⊠ 🚚
Berrybank Nursery, 5 Boggs Holdings, Pencaitland, East Lothian, EH34 5BA
Ⓣ (01875) 341179
Ⓕ (01875) 340842
Ⓔ sales@macplants.co.uk
Ⓦ www.macplants.co.uk
**Contact:** Gavin McNaughton
**Opening Times:** 1030-1700, 7 days, Mar-end Sep.
**Min Mail Order UK:** Nmc
**Min Mail Order EU:** Nmc
**Cat. Cost:** 4 × 2nd class.
**Credit Cards:** MasterCard, Switch, Visa
**Specialities:** Herbaceous perennials, alpines, hardy ferns, violas & grasses.
**Notes:** Nursery partially accessible to wheelchairs. Also sells wholesale.
**Map Ref:** G, C3 **OS Grid Ref:** NT447703

GPoy **POYNTZFIELD HERB NURSERY** ⊠ ✈ ♿
Nr Balblair, Black Isle, Dingwall, Ross-shire, IV7 8LX
Ⓣ (01381) 610352
Ⓕ (01381) 610352
Ⓔ info@poyntzfieldherbs.co.uk
Ⓦ www.poyntzfieldherbs.co.uk
**Contact:** Duncan Ross
**Opening Times:** 1300-1700 Mon-Sat 1st Mar-30th Sep, 1300-1700 Sun May-Aug.
**Min Mail Order UK:** £10.00 + p&p
**Min Mail Order EU:** £10.00 + p&p
**Cat. Cost:** 4 × 1st class.
**Credit Cards:** All major credit/debit cards
**Specialities:** Over 400 popular, unusual & rare herbs esp. medicinal. Also seeds.
**Notes:** Phone between 1200-1300 & 1800-1900 Mon-Sat only.
**Map Ref:** G, B2 **OS Grid Ref:** NH711642

GPri **PRIVICK MILL NURSERY** ⊠ ♿
Privick Mill Road, Annbank, Ayr, KA6 5JA
Ⓣ (01292) 521003
Ⓔ jackie@privickmillnursery.co.uk
Ⓦ www.privickmillnursery.co.uk
**Contact:** Jackie Jess
**Opening Times:** By appt. only for collection of plants.
**Min Mail Order UK:** Nmc
**Cat. Cost:** Free.
**Credit Cards:** None
**Specialities:** Soft fruit bushes. Blueberries. Black raspberries. *Rubus* hybrids. Available in small quantities only. All plants organically grown but not certified by Soil Assoc.
**Map Ref:** G, D2 **OS Grid Ref:** NS405224

GQue **QUERCUS GARDEN PLANTS** ♿
Rankeilour Gardens, Rankeilour Estate, Springfield, Fife, KY15 5RE
Ⓣ (01337) 810444
Ⓕ (01337) 810444
Ⓔ colin@quercus.uk.net

KEY
⊠ Mail order to UK or EU | 🚚 Delivers to shows
✈ Exports beyond EU | € Euro accepted
♿ Accessible by wheelchair | ◆ See Display advertisement

Ⓦ www.quercus.uk.net
**Contact:** Colin McBeath
**Opening Times:** 1000-1700 Thu-Sun, 1st w/end Apr-mid Oct. By appt. only, Nov-Feb. 1000-1400 Sat only, Mar.
**Cat. Cost:** 4 × 1st class.
**Credit Cards:** All major credit/debit cards
**Specialities:** Easy & unusual plants for contemporary Scottish gardens.
**Notes:** Delivery service available on large orders at nursery's discretion. Also sells wholesale.
**Map Ref:** G, C3 **OS Grid Ref:** NO330118

**GQui** **QUINISH GARDEN NURSERY** ⊠
Dervaig, Isle of Mull, Argyll,
PA75 6QL
Ⓣ (01688) 400344
Ⓕ (01688) 400344
Ⓔ quinishplants@aol.com
Ⓦ www.Q-gardens.org
**Contact:** Nicholas Reed
**Opening Times:** By appt. only.
**Min Mail Order UK:** Nmc
**Min Mail Order EU:** Nmc
**Cat. Cost:** 2 × 1st class.
**Credit Cards:** None
**Specialities:** Choice garden shrubs & conservatory plants.
**Map Ref:** G, C1

**GSec** **THE SECRET GARDEN** ⊠
10 Pilmuir Road West, Forres, Moray,
IV36 2HL
Ⓣ (01309) 674634
Ⓔ fixandig@aol.com
**Contact:** Mrs L. Dingwall
**Opening Times:** Mail order only. Open by appt. only.
**Min Mail Order UK:** Nmc
**Min Mail Order EU:** Nmc
**Cat. Cost:** 84p
**Credit Cards:** None
**Specialities:** *Hosta.*

**GTwe** **J TWEEDIE FRUIT TREES** ⊠
Maryfield Road Nursery, Nr Terregles,
Dumfriesshire, DG2 9TH
Ⓣ (01387) 720880
**Contact:** John Tweedie
**Opening Times:** Please ring for times. Collections by appt.
**Min Mail Order UK:** Nmc
**Cat. Cost:** Sae
**Credit Cards:** None
**Specialities:** Fruit trees & bushes. A wide range of old & new varieties.
**Map Ref:** G, D2

## N. IRELAND & REPUBLIC

**IArd** **ARDCARNE GARDEN CENTRE** € ♿
Ardcarne, Boyle, Co. Roscommon, Ireland
Ⓣ 00 353 (0)7196 67091
Ⓕ 00 353 (0)7196 67341
Ⓔ ardcarne@indigo.ie
Ⓦ www.ardcarnegc.com
**Contact:** James Wickham, Mary Frances Dwyer, Kirsty Ainge
**Opening Times:** 0900-1800 Mon-Sat, 1300-1800 Sun & B/hols.
**Credit Cards:** Access, Visa, American Express
**Specialities:** Native & unusual trees, fruit trees, perennials, roses, plants for coastal areas, specimen plants & semi-mature trees. Wide general range.
**Map Ref:** I, B1

**IBal** **BALI-HAI MAIL ORDER NURSERY** ⊠ ✈ €
42 Largy Road, Carnlough, Ballymena,
Co. Antrim, N. Ireland, BT44 0EZ
Ⓣ 028 2888 5289
Ⓕ 028 2888 5289
Ⓔ balihainursery@btinternet.com
Ⓦ www.mailorderplants4me.com
**Contact:** Mrs M E Scroggy
**Opening Times:** Mon-Sat by appt. only.
**Min Mail Order UK:** Nmc
**Min Mail Order EU:** Nmc
**Cat. Cost:** £3.00 cheque, made payable to Mrs M.E. Scroggy.
**Credit Cards:** All major credit/debit cards
**Specialities:** *Hosta*, *Rhodohypoxis* & other perennials. Tree ferns.
**Notes:** Exports beyond EU restricted to bare root perennials, no grasses. Also sells wholesale.
**Map Ref:** I, A3 **OS Grid Ref:** D287184

**IBlr** **BALLYROGAN NURSERIES** ⊠ € ♿
The Grange, Ballyrogan, Newtownards,
Co. Down, N. Ireland,
BT23 4SD
Ⓣ 028 9181 0451 (evenings)
Ⓔ gary.dunlop@btinternet.com
**Contact:** Gary Dunlop
**Opening Times:** Only open by appt.
**Min Mail Order UK:** £10.00 + p&p
**Min Mail Order EU:** £20.00 + p&p
**Cat. Cost:** 2 × 1st class.
**Credit Cards:** None
**Specialities:** Choice herbaceous. *Agapanthus*, *Celmisia*, *Crocosmia*, *Rodgersia*, *Iris*, *Dierama*, *Erythronium* & *Roscoea*.
**Notes:** Also sells wholesale.
**Map Ref:** I, B3

IGor

IGor

ICro **Crocknafeola Nursery** €
Killybegs, Co. Donegal,
Ireland
Ⓣ 00 353 (0)74 97 51018
Ⓕ 00 353 (0)74 97 51095
Ⓔ crocknafeola@hotmail.com
**Contact:** Fionn McKenna
**Opening Times:** 0900-1800 Mon, Tue, Thu-Sat, closed Wed. 1200-1800 Sun.
**Cat. Cost:** None issued
**Credit Cards:** None
**Specialities:** Bedding plants, herbaceous perennials, rhododendrons, plants for containers, roses, plus shrubs & hedging for coastal areas.
**Notes:** Also sells wholesale.
**Map Ref:** I, D2

IDee **Deelish Garden Centre** ⊠ €
Skibbereen, Co. Cork,
Ireland
Ⓣ 00 353 (0)28 21374
Ⓕ 00 353 (0)28 21374
Ⓔ deel@eircom.net
Ⓦ www.deelish.ie
**Contact:** Bill & Rain Chase
**Opening Times:** 1000-1800 Mon-Sat, 1400-1800 Sun.
**Min Mail Order EU:** €50 (Ireland only).
**Cat. Cost:** Sae
**Credit Cards:** Visa, Access
**Specialities:** Unusual plants for the mild coastal climate of Ireland. Conservatory plants. Sole Irish agents for Chase Organic Seeds.
**Notes:** No mail order outside Ireland.
**Map Ref:** I, D1

IDic **Dickson Nurseries Ltd** ⊠ ✈
Milecross Road, Newtownards, Co. Down,
N. Ireland, BT23 4SS
Ⓣ 028 9181 2206
Ⓕ 028 9181 3366
Ⓔ mail@dickson-roses.co.uk
Ⓦ www.dickson-roses.co.uk
**Contact:** Colin Dickson
**Opening Times:** 0800-1230 & 1300-1700 Mon-Thu. 0800-1230 Fri. Closes at 1600 Mon-Thu Dec-Jan.
**Min Mail Order UK:** Nmc
**Min Mail Order EU:** £25.00 + p&p
**Cat. Cost:** Free
**Credit Cards:** None
**Specialities:** Roses esp. modern Dickson varieties. Most varieties are available in small quantities only.
**Notes:** Also sells wholesale.
**Map Ref:** I, B3

IFoB **Field of Blooms** ⊠ € ♿
Ballymackey, Lisnamoe, Nenagh,
Co. Tipperary, Ireland
Ⓣ 00 353 (0)67 29974
Ⓜ 08764 06044
Ⓔ guy2002@eircom.net
Ⓦ www.fieldofblooms.ie
**Contact:** Guy de Schrijver
**Opening Times:** Strictly by appt.
**Min Mail Order UK:** Nmc
**Min Mail Order EU:** Nmc
**Cat. Cost:** Free.
**Credit Cards:** None
**Specialities:** Hellebores, herbaceous, hardy perennials, ornamental grasses & woodland plants.
**Map Ref:** I, C2

IFro **Frogswell Nursery** €
Cloonconlan, Straide, Foxford, Co. Mayo,
Ireland
Ⓣ 00 353 (0)94 903 1420
Ⓜ 00 353 8621 06166
Ⓔ frogswell@gmail.com
Ⓦ www.frogswell.net
**Contact:** Celia Graebner
**Opening Times:** Feb-Oct by appt. Please phone first. Also Garden Open Days & workshops; see website for details.
**Cat. Cost:** Online list for 2010.
**Credit Cards:** None
**Specialities:** A small nursery specialising in shade & woodland plants incl. hybrid hellebores & hardy geraniums, plus unusual perennials for the Irish climate, all raised on site & without chemical inputs. Some in very small quantities.
**Notes:** Garden visits by arrangement. See website for location map.

IGor **Gortkelly Castle Nursery & Arboretum** ⊠ €
Upperchurch, Thurles, Co. Tipperary,
Ireland
Ⓣ 00 353 (0)504 54441
**Contact:** Clare Beumer
**Opening Times:** Mail order only. Not open to the public.
**Min Mail Order UK:** Nmc
**Min Mail Order EU:** Nmc
**Cat. Cost:** 5 × 1st class (UK), 5 × 55c (Rep. of Ireland).
**Credit Cards:** None

KEY
⊠ Mail order to UK or EU | Delivers to shows
✈ Exports beyond EU | € Euro accepted
♿ Accessible by wheelchair | ◆ See Display advertisement

**Specialities:** Choice perennials. Cultivars of Irish origin. Rare trees & shrubs in small sizes.
**Map Ref:** I, C2

IKil **Kilmurry Nursery** ⊠ € ♿
Gorey, Co. Wexford,
Ireland
Ⓣ 00 353 (0)53 948 0223
Ⓜ 353 (0)8681 80623
Ⓕ 00 353 (0)53 948 0223
Ⓔ info@kilmurrynursery.com
Ⓦ www.kilmurrynursery.com
**Contact:** Paul & Orla Woods
**Opening Times:** 0900-1700 Mon-Fri, Mar-Sep. Wintertime by appt.
**Min Mail Order UK:** Nmc
**Min Mail Order EU:** Nmc
**Cat. Cost:** 3 × 1st class.
**Credit Cards:** None
**Specialities:** Herbaceous perennials and grasses.
**Notes:** Also sells wholesale.
**Map Ref:** I, C3 **OS Grid Ref:** 3C

ILis **Lisdoonan Herbs** ⊠ € ♿
98 Belfast Road, Saintfield, Co. Down,
N. Ireland, BT24 7HF
Ⓣ 028 9081 3624
Ⓔ b.pilcher@lisdoonanherbs.co.uk
Ⓦ www.lisdoonanherbs.co.uk
**Contact:** Barbara Pilcher
**Opening Times:** Please phone for appt.
**Min Mail Order UK:** Nmc
**Min Mail Order EU:** Nmc
**Cat. Cost:** Online only.
**Credit Cards:** None
**Specialities:** Aromatics, herbs, kitchen garden plants, period plants, some native species. Freshly cut herbs & salads. Some stock available in limited quantities only. All peat-free.
**Map Ref:** I, B3 **OS Grid Ref:** J390624

IPen **Peninsula Primulas** ⊠ ♠ €
72 Ballyeasborough Road,
Kircubbin, Co. Down, N. Ireland,
BT22 1AD
Ⓣ 028 4277 2193
Ⓔ Peninsula.primulas@btinternet.com
Ⓦ www.primulasandauriculas.com
**Contact:** Philip Bankhead
**Opening Times:** Mail order only. Not open.
**Min Mail Order UK:** Nmc
**Min Mail Order EU:** Nmc
**Cat. Cost:** Free
**Credit Cards:** Paypal
**Specialities:** Extensive selection of *Primula* species, plus auriculas.

IPot **The Potting Shed** ⊠ ♠ € ♿
Bolinaspick, Camolin, Enniscorthy,
Co. Wexford, Ireland
Ⓣ 00 353 (0)5393 83629
Ⓕ 00 353 (0)5393 83629
Ⓔ sricher@iol.ie
Ⓦ www.camolinpottingshed.com
**Contact:** Susan Carrick
**Opening Times:** 1300-1800, Thu-Sat (incl.), Mar-Sep 2010. Other times by appt.
**Min Mail Order UK:** Nmc
**Min Mail Order EU:** Nmc
**Cat. Cost:** 3 × 1st class.
**Credit Cards:** MasterCard, Visa
**Specialities:** Herbaceous & ornamental grasses.
**Map Ref:** I, C3

IPPN **Perennial Plants Nursery** ⊠ ♠ €
Nr Ballymaloe, Barnabrow,
Midleton, Co. Cork,
Ireland
Ⓣ 00 353 (0)21 465 2122
Ⓔ perennialplants@eircom.net
Ⓦ www.perennialplants.biz
**Contact:** Sandy McCarthy
**Opening Times:** Please ring for times.
**Min Mail Order UK:** Nmc
**Min Mail Order EU:** Nmc
**Cat. Cost:** None issued.
**Credit Cards:** None
**Specialities:** Many unusual herbaceous, ornamental grasses, tender perennials. Some available in small quantities only.
**Notes:** Will accept payment in sterling.
**Map Ref:** I, D2 **OS Grid Ref:** W9568

IRar **Rare Plants** ⊠ €
Kinsealy Cottage, Kinsealy Lane,
Malahide, Co. Dublin,
Ireland
Ⓔ info@rareplants.ie
Ⓦ www.rareplants.ie
**Contact:** Brian Murphy, Christopher Heavey
**Opening Times:** Not open to the public.
**Min Mail Order UK:** Nmc
**Min Mail Order EU:** Nmc
**Cat. Cost:** Online only.
**Credit Cards:** All major credit/debit cards
**Specialities:** Propagates & raises a range of rare & unusual plants incl. trees, shrubs, herbaceous & alpine. Specialises in difficult to obtain & slightly tender plants. All propagated from superior clones. Only available in small quantities.
**Notes:** P&p costs on request. Also sells wholesale.
**Map Ref:** I, C3 **OS Grid Ref:** 0 220 462

IRhd **Ringhaddy Daffodils** ⊠ ✈ €
Ringhaddy Road, Killinchy,
Newtownards, Co. Down, N. Ireland,
BT23 6TU
Ⓣ 028 9754 1007
Ⓜ 07762 337534
Ⓔ info@ringhaddy-daffodils.com
Ⓦ www.ringhaddy-daffodils.com
**Contact:** Nial Watson
**Opening Times:** Mail order only. Not open.
**Min Mail Order UK:** £20.00 + p&p
**Min Mail Order EU:** £50.00 + p&p
**Cat. Cost:** £2.50 redeemable on order.
**Credit Cards:** Paypal
**Specialities:** New daffodil varieties for exhibitors and hybridisers. Small stock of some varieties.

ISha **Shady Plants** ⊠ ⌂ € ♿
Coolbooa, Clashmore, Youghal, Co. Cork, Ireland
Ⓣ 024 96735
Ⓜ 08605 42171
Ⓔ mike@shadyplants.ie
Ⓦ www.shadyplants.net
**Contact:** Mike Keep
**Opening Times:** By appt. only Mar-May, Jul-Oct.
**Min Mail Order UK:** Nmc
**Min Mail Order EU:** Nmc
**Cat. Cost:** €3.00
**Credit Cards:** Paypal
**Specialities:** Specialist fern nursery based near the south coast of Ireland.
**Map Ref:** I, D2 **OS Grid Ref:** 613,585

ISsi **Seaside Nursery** ⊠ € ♿
Claddaghduff, Co. Galway,
Ireland
Ⓣ 00 353 (0)95 44687
Ⓜ 00 353 (0)86 3391555
Ⓕ 00 353 (0)95 44761
Ⓔ Tom@seasidenursery.biz
Ⓦ www.seasidenursery.biz
**Contact:** Tom Dyck
**Opening Times:** 1000-1300 & 1400-1800 Mon-Sat, 1400-1800 Sun. Closed Sun 1st Oct-31st Mar.
**Min Mail Order UK:** Nmc
**Min Mail Order EU:** Nmc
**Cat. Cost:** €3.50
**Credit Cards:** Visa, MasterCard
**Specialities:** Plants & hedging suitable for seaside locations. Rare plants originating from Australia & New Zealand esp. *Phormium*, *Astelia*.
**Notes:** Also sells wholesale.
**Map Ref:** I, B1

ITim **Timpany Nurseries & Gardens** ⊠ ⌂ ♿
77 Magheratimpany Road, Ballynahinch,
Co. Down, N. Ireland, BT24 8PA
Ⓣ 028 9756 2812
Ⓕ 028 9756 2812
Ⓔ s.tindall@btconnect.com
Ⓦ www.timpanynurseries.com
**Contact:** Susan Tindall
**Opening Times:** 1000-1730 Tue-Sat, Sun by appt.
**Min Mail Order UK:** Nmc
**Min Mail Order EU:** £30.00 + p&p
**Cat. Cost:** £2.00
**Credit Cards:** Visa, MasterCard
**Specialities:** *Celmisia*, *Androsace*, *Primula*, *Saxifraga*, *Dianthus*, *Meconopsis*, *Cassiope*, *Rhodohypoxis*, *Cyclamen* & *Primula auricula*.
**Notes:** Also sells wholesale.
**Map Ref:** I, B3

IVic **Victoria's Nursery & Garden** €
Upper Kells, Kells, Cahirceveen, Co Kerry, Ireland
Ⓣ 00 353 (0)66 947 7605
Ⓜ 00 353 879 111465
Ⓔ kellshouse@eircom.net
**Contact:** Victoria Vogel
**Opening Times:** 1000-1700 Wed-Sun all year except Xmas. Closed Mon & Tue, except B/hols & by arrangement.
**Cat. Cost:** None issued.
**Credit Cards:** None
**Specialities:** *Rhododendron*, azaleas, *Acer*, treeferns, seaside & woodland plants, South African & Mediterranean bulbs, *Saxifraga fortunei* forms.
**Notes:** Drive along Ring of Kerry, at Kells follow signs to Kells Bay Garden towards Kells Beach, nursery to left after little bridge.
**Map Ref:** I, D1

## London Area

LAma **Jacques Amand International** ⊠ ✈ ⌂ € ♿
The Nurseries,145 Clamp Hill, Stanmore,
Middlesex, HA7 3JS
Ⓣ (020) 8420 7110
Ⓕ (020) 8954 6784
Ⓔ bulbs@jacquesamand.co.uk
Ⓦ www.jacquesamand.com
**Contact:** John Amand & Stuart Chapman

KEY
⊠ Mail order to UK or EU ⌂ Delivers to shows
✈ Exports beyond EU € Euro accepted
♿ Accessible by wheelchair ◆ See Display advertisement

**Opening Times:** 0900-1700 Mon-Fri, 1000-1400 Sat.
**Min Mail Order UK:** Nmc
**Min Mail Order EU:** Nmc
**Cat. Cost:** 1 × 1st class.
**Credit Cards:** All major credit/debit cards
**Specialities:** Rare and unusual species bulbs esp. *Arisaema*, *Trillium*, *Fritillaria*, tulips.
**Notes:** Also sells wholesale.
**Map Ref:** L, B3

L

LAst **Asterby & Chalkcroft Nursery** ⊠ ♿
The Ridgeway, Blunham, Bedfordshire, MK44 3PH
Ⓣ (01767) 640148
Ⓔ sales@asterbyplants.co.uk
Ⓦ www.asterbyplants.co.uk
**Contact:** Simon & Eva Aldridge
**Opening Times:** 1000-1700 7 days. Closed Xmas & Jan.
**Credit Cards:** Visa, MasterCard, Maestro
**Specialities:** Hardy shrubs, herbaceous & trees.
**Notes:** Please ring for mail order information.
**Map Ref:** L, A3 **OS Grid Ref:** TL151497

LAyl **Aylett Nurseries Ltd** ♿ ◆
North Orbital Road, St Albans, Hertfordshire, AL2 1DH
Ⓣ (01727) 822255
Ⓕ (01727) 823024
Ⓔ info@aylettnurseries.co.uk
Ⓦ www.aylettnurseries.co.uk
**Contact:** Roger S Aylett
**Opening Times:** 0830-1730 Mon-Fri, 0830-1700 Sat, 1030-1630 Sun.
**Cat. Cost:** Free.
**Credit Cards:** All major credit/debit cards
**Specialities:** *Dahlia*. 2-acre trial ground adjacent to garden centre.
**Map Ref:** L, B3 **OS Grid Ref:** TL169049

LBee **Beechcroft Nursery** ♿
127 Reigate Road, Ewell, Surrey, KT17 3DE
Ⓣ 0208 393 4265
Ⓕ 0208 393 4265
**Contact:** C Kimber
**Opening Times:** 1000-1600 Mon-Sat, 1000-1400 Sun and B/hols. Closed Xmas-New Year week.
**Cat. Cost:** None issued.
**Credit Cards:** All major credit/debit cards
**Specialities:** Conifers & alpines.
**Notes:** Also sells wholesale.
**Map Ref:** L, C3

LBMP **Blooming Marvellous Plants** ⌂
Korketts Farm, Aylesbury Road, Shipton, Winslow, Buckinghamshire, MK18 3JL
Ⓣ (01296) 714714
Ⓜ 07963 747305
Ⓔ alex@bmplants.co.uk
Ⓦ www.bmplants.co.uk
**Contact:** Alexia Ballance
**Opening Times:** 0900-1700 Tue-Sat & 1000-1600 Sun, 1st Feb-31st Oct. Closed Mons. By appt. only Nov-Jan.
**Cat. Cost:** £1.00 in stamps.
**Credit Cards:** All major credit/debit cards
**Specialities:** A mixture of unusual and familiar perennials, shrubs, grasses, ferns & bedding plants, most in more generous sizes than usually found in nurseries.
**Notes:** Located on the A413 just outside Winslow (heading in the Aylesbury direction). Partial wheelchair access.
**Map Ref:** L, A2 **OS Grid Ref:** SP777271

LBuc **Buckingham Nurseries** ⊠ € ♿ ◆
14 Tingewick Road, Buckingham, MK18 4AE
Ⓣ (01280) 822133
Ⓕ (01280) 815491
Ⓔ enquiries@buckingham-nurseries.co.uk
Ⓦ www.buckingham-nurseries.co.uk
**Contact:** R J & P L Brown
**Opening Times:** 0830-1730 (1800 in summer) Mon-Sat, 1030-1630 Sun.
**Min Mail Order UK:** Nmc
**Min Mail Order EU:** Nmc
**Cat. Cost:** Free.
**Credit Cards:** Visa, MasterCard, Switch
**Specialities:** Bare rooted and container grown hedging. Trees, shrubs, herbaceous perennials, alpines, grasses & ferns.
**Map Ref:** L, A2 **OS Grid Ref:** SP675333

LCla **Clay Lane Nursery** ⊠ ⌂
3 Clay Lane, South Nutfield, Nr Redhill, Surrey, RH1 4EG
Ⓣ (01737) 823307
Ⓔ claylane.nursery@btinternet.com
Ⓦ www.claylane-fuchsias.co.uk
**Contact:** K W Belton
**Opening Times:** Variable opening times. Please phone before travelling.
**Min Mail Order UK:** £7.00
**Cat. Cost:** 3 × 2nd class.
**Credit Cards:** None
**Specialities:** *Fuchsia*. Many varieties in small quantities only.
**Notes:** Mail order by telephone pre-arangement only.
**Map Ref:** L, C4

LCtg **Cottage Garden Nursery** ◆
Barnet Road, Arkley, Barnet,
Hertfordshire,
EN5 3JX
Ⓣ (020) 8441 8829
Ⓕ (020) 8531 3178
Ⓔ nurseryinfo@cottagegardennursery-barnet.co.uk
Ⓦ www.cottagegardennursery-barnet.co.uk
**Contact:** David and Wendy Spicer
**Opening Times:** 0930-1700 Tue-Sat Mar-Oct, 0930-1600 Tue-Sat Nov-Feb, 1000-1600 Sun & B/hol Mon all year.
**Cat. Cost:** None issued.
**Credit Cards:** All major credit/debit cards
**Specialities:** General range of hardy shrubs, trees, fruit trees & bushes, perennials. Architectural & exotics, *Fuchsia*, seasonal bedding, patio plants.
**Map Ref:** L, B3 **OS Grid Ref:** TQ226958

LDea **Derek Lloyd Dean** ⊠ ✈ ⛟
8 Lynwood Close, South Harrow,
Middlesex, HA2 9PR
Ⓣ 0208 864 0899
Ⓔ lloyddeancbtinternet.com
Ⓦ www.dereklloyddean.com
**Contact:** Derek Lloyd Dean
**Opening Times:** Not open. Mail order only.
**Min Mail Order UK:** £2.50 + p&p
**Min Mail Order EU:** £2.50 + p&p
**Cat. Cost:** 2 × 1st class.
**Credit Cards:** None
**Specialities:** Regal, angel & scented leaf *Pelargonium*. Nat. Collection of Angel *Pelargonium*.

LEdu **Edulis** ⊠ ⛟ € ♿
(office) 1 Flowers Piece,
Ashampstead, Reading, Berkshire,
RG8 8SG
Ⓣ (01635) 578113
Ⓜ 07802 812781
Ⓔ edulis.nursery@virgin.net
Ⓦ www.edulis.co.uk
**Contact:** Paul Barney
**Opening Times:** By appt. only.
**Min Mail Order UK:** £10.00 + p&p
**Min Mail Order EU:** £50.00 + p&p
**Cat. Cost:** 4 × 1st class.
**Credit Cards:** None
**Specialities:** Unusual edibles, architectural plants, permaculture plants.
**Notes:** Nursery is at Bere Court Farm, Tidmarsh Lane, Pangbourne, RG8 8HT. Also sells wholesale.
**Map Ref:** L, B2 **OS Grid Ref:** SU615747

LHel **Herts Hellebores** ⊠ €
Green Lane Farm, Levens Green,
Nr Ware, Hertfordshire,
SG11 1HD
Ⓣ (01920) 438458
Ⓔ lorna@herts-hellebore.co.uk
Ⓦ www.herts-hellebore.co.uk
**Contact:** Lorna Jones
**Opening Times:** 1000-1600 Wed & Sat only, 30th Jan-31st Mar 2010. Other times Jan-Apr by appt. only. Check with nursery for 2011 opening times.
**Min Mail Order UK:** £18
**Min Mail Order EU:** £18
**Cat. Cost:** Free.
**Credit Cards:** All major credit/debit cards
**Specialities:** Hellebore hybrids. Specialising in developments of double & anemone centred hybrids. Seed-raised plants offered by colour. Some available in small quantities only.
**Map Ref:** L, A4 **OS Grid Ref:** TL357224

LHop **Hopleys Plants Ltd** ⊠ ⛟ ♿ ◆
High Street, Much Hadham, Hertfordshire,
SG10 6BU
Ⓣ (01279) 842509
Ⓕ (01279) 843784
Ⓔ plants@hopleys.co.uk
Ⓦ www.hopleys.co.uk
**Contact:** Mr Aubrey Barker
**Opening Times:** 0900-1700 Mon & Wed-Sat, 1400-1700 Sun. Closed Jan-Feb except by appt.
**Min Mail Order UK:** Nmc
**Cat. Cost:** 5 × 1st class.
**Credit Cards:** Visa, Access, Switch
**Specialities:** Wide range of hardy & half-hardy shrubs & perennials.
**Map Ref:** L, A4 **OS Grid Ref:** TL428196

LIMB **I.M.B. Plants** ⊠
2 Ashdown Close, Giffard Park,
Milton Keynes, Buckinghamshire,
MK14 5PX
Ⓣ (01908) 618911
Ⓔ imbrazier@btinternet.com
**Contact:** Ian Brazier
**Opening Times:** Not open. Mail order only.
**Min Mail Order UK:** Nmc
**Credit Cards:** None
**Specialities:** *Helianthemum*. All plants propagated in small quantities. Will propagate to order.

KEY
⊠ Mail order to UK or EU ⛟ Delivers to shows
✈ Exports beyond EU € Euro accepted
♿ Accessible by wheelchair ◆ See Display advertisement

L

L

**LLHF** **LITTLE HEATH FARM (UK) (FORMERLY TWO JAYS ALPINES)** ⌂
Little Heath Lane, Potten End, Berkhamsted, Hertfordshire, HP4 2RY
Ⓣ (01442) 864951
Ⓔ lhfnursery@gmail.com
Ⓦ www.littleheathfarmnursery.co.uk
**Contact:** John Spokes
**Opening Times:** 1000-1700 or dusk if earlier, 7 days.
**Cat. Cost:** Online only.
**Credit Cards:** Visa, MasterCard
**Specialities:** Large range of alpines, herbaceous, shrubs, many available in small quantities only.
**Map Ref:** L, B3

**LLWG** **LILIES WATER GARDENS** ⊠ ⌂ ♿
Broad Lane, Newdigate, Surrey, RH5 5AT
Ⓣ (01306) 631064
Ⓜ 07801 166244
Ⓕ (01306) 631693
Ⓔ mail@lilieswatergardens.co.uk
Ⓦ www.lilieswatergardens.co.uk
**Contact:** Simon Harman
**Opening Times:** 0900-1700 Tue-Sat, Mar-Aug. By appt. only Sep-Feb.
**Min Mail Order UK:** Nmc but flat rate £10.00 delivery charge.
**Cat. Cost:** Online only.
**Credit Cards:** All major credit/debit cards
**Specialities:** Waterlilies, moist perennials, bog-garden plants, primulas, marginal plants. Ferns, alpines & oxygenating plants. Pond, aquatic, water-garden, floating, stream, deep-water & waterfall plants. Rushes & grasses.
**Map Ref:** L, C3

**LLWP** **L W PLANTS** ⊠ ⌂
23 Wroxham Way, Harpenden, Hertfordshire, AL5 4PP
Ⓣ (01582) 768467
Ⓔ lwplants@waitrose.com
Ⓦ www.thymus.co.uk
**Contact:** Mrs Margaret Easter
**Opening Times:** 1000-1700 most days, but please phone first.
**Min Mail Order UK:** Nmc
**Cat. Cost:** A5 sae + 5 × 2nd class (loose).
**Credit Cards:** None
**Specialities:** Plants from a plantsman's garden, esp. *Geranium*, grasses, *Penstemon* & *Thymus*. Some available in small quantities only. Nat. Collections of *Thymus* (Scientific), *Hyssopus* & *Satureja*. *Thymus* ICRA (provisional). *Thymus* propagated to order.
**Notes:** Mail order *Thymus* only.
**Map Ref:** L, B3 **OS Grid Ref:** TL141153

**LMaj** **MAJESTIC TREES** ⌂ €
Chequers Meadow, Chequers Hill, Flamstead, St Albans, Hertfordshire, AL3 8ET
Ⓣ (01582) 843881
Ⓕ (01582) 843882
Ⓔ info@majesticgroup.co.uk
Ⓦ www.majestictrees.co.uk
**Contact:** Andrew Austin
**Opening Times:** 0830-1700 Mon-Fri. 1000-1600 (1700 Mar-Oct) Sat. Closed Sun, B/hols & Xmas/New Year.
**Cat. Cost:** 6 × 1st class.
**Credit Cards:** MasterCard, Visa, Switch, Maestro
**Specialities:** Semi-mature & mature containerised trees grown in airpot from 50 ltr to 5000 ltr.
**Notes:** Partial wheelchair access. Also sells wholesale.
**Map Ref:** L, B3 **OS Grid Ref:** TL08140815

**LMil** **MILLAIS NURSERIES** ⊠ ♿
Crosswater Farm, Crosswater Lane, Churt, Surrey, GU10 2JN
Ⓣ (01252) 792698
Ⓕ (01252) 792526
Ⓔ sales@rhododendrons.co.uk
Ⓦ www.rhododendrons.co.uk
**Contact:** David Millais
**Opening Times:** 1000-1700 Mon-Fri all year. Sat in spring & autumn. Daily in May.
**Min Mail Order UK:** Nmc
**Min Mail Order EU:** Nmc
**Cat. Cost:** Free list on request or Online.
**Credit Cards:** All major credit/debit cards
**Specialities:** Rhododendrons, azaleas, magnolias, camellias & acers.
**Notes:** Mail order all year. Also sells wholesale.
**Map Ref:** L, C3 **OS Grid Ref:** SU856397

**LMor** **MOREHAVENS** ⊠ ♿
Sandpit Hill, Buckland Common, Tring, Hertfordshire, HP23 6NG
Ⓣ (01494) 758642
Ⓔ morehavens@hotmail.co.uk
Ⓦ www.camomilelawns.co.uk
**Contact:** B Farmer
**Opening Times:** Mail order only. Open only for collection.
**Min Mail Order UK:** £14.00
**Min Mail Order EU:** £14.00 + p&p
**Cat. Cost:** Free.
**Credit Cards:** None
**Specialities:** *Camomile* 'Treneague' and dwarf variety.
**Notes:** Also sells wholesale.

LPal **The Palm Centre** ⊠ ✈ ⌂ € ♿
Ham Central Nursery, opposite Riverside Drive, Ham Street, Ham, Richmond, Surrey, TW10 7HA
Ⓣ (020) 8255 6191
Ⓕ (020) 8255 6192
Ⓔ mail@palmcentre.co.uk
Ⓦ palmcentre.co.uk
**Contact:** Martin Gibbons
**Opening Times:** 0900-1700 (dusk in winter) 7 days. Admin & Order Dept. 0900-1700 Mon-Fri.
**Min Mail Order UK:** £10.00 + p&p
**Min Mail Order EU:** £10.00 + p&p
**Cat. Cost:** Free.
**Credit Cards:** Visa, MasterCard, Switch
**Specialities:** Palms & cycads, exotic & sub-tropical, hardy, half-hardy & tropical. Seedlings to mature trees. Also bamboos, tree ferns & many other exotics. *Trachycarpus*.
**Notes:** Also sells wholesale.
**Map Ref:** L, B3

LPBA **Paul Bromfield – Aquatics** ⊠ ✈ € ♿
Maydencroft Lane, Gosmore, Hitchin, Hertfordshire, SG4 7QD
Ⓣ (01462) 457399
Ⓜ 07969 358857
Ⓕ (01462) 422652
Ⓔ info@bromfieldaquatics.co.uk
Ⓦ www.bromfieldaquatics.co.uk
**Contact:** Debbie Edwards
**Opening Times:** Mail order only. Order online at website. Office open 1000-1700 Mon-Sat, Feb-Oct. Visitors please ring for appt.
**Min Mail Order UK:** Nmc
**Min Mail Order EU:** £100.00 incl.
**Cat. Cost:** Online only.
**Credit Cards:** Visa, MasterCard, Delta, JCB, Switch
**Specialities:** Water lilies, marginals & bog.
**Notes:** Also sells wholesale.

LPen **Penstemons by Colour** ⊠
Peterley Manor, Peterley, Prestwood, Great Missenden, Buckinghamshire, HP16 0HH
Ⓣ (01494) 866420
Ⓕ (01494) 866420
Ⓔ debra@peterleymanor.co.uk
**Contact:** Debra Hughes
**Opening Times:** Any time by appt.
**Min Mail Order UK:** £10.00
**Cat. Cost:** Free
**Credit Cards:** None
**Specialities:** *Penstemon*.
**Map Ref:** L, B3 **OS Grid Ref:** SU880994

LPJP **PJ's Palms and Exotics** ⊠ €
41 Salcombe Road, Ashford, Middlesex, TW15 3BS
Ⓣ (01784) 250181
Ⓜ 07905 742649
**Contact:** Peter Jenkins
**Opening Times:** Mail order only 1st Mar-30th Nov. Visits by arrangement.
**Min Mail Order UK:** Nmc
**Min Mail Order EU:** Nmc
**Cat. Cost:** 2 × 1st clas.
**Credit Cards:** None
**Specialities:** Palms, bananas & other exotic foliage plants, hardy & half-hardy. *Trachycarpus wagnerianus* seeds available. Plants available in small quantities.
**Notes:** Also sells wholesale.
**Map Ref:** L, B3

LPla **The Plant Specialist**
7 Whitefield Lane, Great Missenden, Buckinghamshire, HP16 0BH
Ⓣ (01494) 866650
Ⓕ (01494) 866650
Ⓔ enquire@theplantspecialist.co.uk
Ⓦ www.theplantspecialist.co.uk
**Contact:** Sean Walter
**Opening Times:** 1000-1700 Wed-Sat, 1000-1600 Sun, Apr-Oct.
**Cat. Cost:** None issued.
**Credit Cards:** All major credit/debit cards
**Specialities:** Herbaceous perennials, grasses, half-hardy perennials, bulbs.
**Notes:** Ltd. wheelchair access.

LRHS **Wisley Plant Centre (RHS)** ♿ ◆
RHS Garden, Wisley, Woking, Surrey, GU23 6QB
Ⓣ (01483) 211113 or 0845 060 9800
Ⓕ (01483) 212372
Ⓔ wisleyplantcentre@rhs.org.uk
Ⓦ www.rhs.org.uk/wisleyplantcentre
**Contact:** Plant Centre Staff
**Opening Times:** 0930-1700 Mon-Sat, Oct-Feb. 0930-1800 Mon-Sat, Mar-Sep. 1100-1700 Sun all year, browsing from 1030.
**Cat. Cost:** Online only.
**Credit Cards:** All major credit/debit cards
**Specialities:** Over 10,000 plants, many rare or unusual, reflecting the range of the RHS flagship garden at Wisley. Plants subject to seasonal availability. For plants not in stock, we operate a reservation service by phone & in person.

KEY
⊠ Mail order to UK or EU · ⌂ Delivers to shows
✈ Exports beyond EU · € Euro accepted
♿ Accessible by wheelchair · ◆ See Display advertisement

**Notes:** Programme of free plant events throughout the year. Please ring or check website for details.
**Map Ref:** L, C3

LSee **SEEDS BY SIZE** ⊠ ☒ €
45 Crouchfield, Boxmoor, Hemel Hempstead, Hertfordshire, HP1 1PA
Ⓣ (01442) 251458
Ⓔ john-robert-size@seeds-by-size.co.uk
Ⓦ www.seeds-by-size.co.uk
**Contact:** John Robert Size
**Opening Times:** Not open. Mail order only.
**Min Mail Order UK:** Nmc
**Min Mail Order EU:** Nmc
**Cat. Cost:** Online only.
**Credit Cards:** Paypal
**Specialities:** Seeds. Over 20,000 varieties of flower, vegetable & herb seeds, including sweet peas, pansies, petunias, *Impatiens*, marigolds, ornamental grasses, cabbages, tomatoes, cauliflowers, herbs & onions. Oriental vegetables, hot peppers & sweet peppers in 226 specialities plus other lists.
**Notes:** Euros only accepted as cash payments. Also sells wholesale.

LShp **SQUIRE'S GARDEN CENTRE, SHEPPERTON** ♿
Halliford Road, Upper Halliford, Shepperton, Middlesex, TW17 8RU
Ⓣ (01932) 784121
Ⓕ (01932) 780569
Ⓔ shepp.plants@squiresgardencentres.co.uk
Ⓦ www.squiresgardencentres.co.uk
**Contact:** Plant Area Manager
**Opening Times:** 0900-1800 Mon-Sat, 1030-1630 Sun.
**Cat. Cost:** None issued.
**Credit Cards:** All major credit/debit cards
**Specialities:** Roses.
**Notes:** Other garden centres in Middlesex & Surrey.

LSou **SOUTHON PLANTS** ⊠ ♿
Mutton Hill, Dormansland, Lingfield, Surrey, RH7 6NP
Ⓣ (01342) 870150
Ⓔ info@southonplants.com
Ⓦ www.southonplants.com
**Contact:** Mr Southon
**Opening Times:** 0900-1730 Feb-Oct. For Nov, Dec & Jan please phone first.
**Min Mail Order UK:** Nmc
**Cat. Cost:** Online only.
**Credit Cards:** All major credit/debit cards
**Specialities:** New & unusual hardy & tender perennials, specialising in *Agapanthus* (over 30 varieties), *Coreopsis*, *Euphorbia* & *Heuchera* (over 40 varieties).
**Notes:** Mail order. Please phone/email for details.
**Map Ref:** L, C4

LSqH **SQUIRE'S GARDEN CENTRE, WEST HORSLEY** ♿
Epsom Road, West Horsley, Leatherhead, Surrey, KT24 6AR
Ⓣ (01483) 282911
Ⓕ (01483) 281380
Ⓔ hors.plants.squiresgardencentres.co.uk
Ⓦ www.squiresgardencentres.co.uk
**Contact:** Plant Area Manager
**Opening Times:** 0900-1800 Mon-Sat, 1030-1630 Sun.
**Cat. Cost:** None issued.
**Credit Cards:** All major credit/debit cards
**Specialities:** Herbaceous.
**Notes:** Other garden centres in Middlesex & Surrey.

LSqu **SQUIRE'S GARDEN CENTRE, TWICKENHAM** ♿
Sixth Cross Road, Twickenham, Middlesex, TW2 5PA
Ⓣ 0208 977 9241
Ⓕ 0208 943 4024
Ⓔ twic.plants@squiresgardencentres.co.uk
Ⓦ www.squiresgardencentres.co.uk
**Contact:** Plant Area Manager
**Opening Times:** 0900-1800 Mon-Sat, 1030-1630 Sun.
**Credit Cards:** All major credit/debit cards
**Specialities:** *Clematis*.
**Notes:** Other garden centres in Middlesex & Surrey.

LSRN **SPRING REACH NURSERY** ⊠ ♿
Long Reach, Ockham, Guildford, Surrey, GU23 6PG
Ⓣ (01483) 284769
Ⓜ 07884 432666
Ⓕ (01483) 284769
Ⓔ info@springreachnursery.co.uk
Ⓦ www.springreachnursery.co.uk
**Contact:** Nick & Lissa Hourhan
**Opening Times:** 7 days. 1000-1700 Mon-Sat, 1030-1630 Sun. Open B/hols.
**Min Mail Order UK:** Nmc
**Min Mail Order EU:** Nmc
**Credit Cards:** All major credit/debit cards
**Specialities:** Shrubs, evergreen climbers, *Clematis*, perennials, roses, grasses, ferns, bamboos, trees, hedging, soft fruit & top fruit. Plants for chalk & clay. Deer & rabbit proof plants. Specimen & acid-loving plants.

**Notes:** Please ring for mail order details. Also sells wholesale.
**Map Ref:** L, C3

LStr **Henry Street Nursery** ⊠ ♿
Swallowfield Road, Arborfield,
Reading, Berkshire,
RG2 9JY
Ⓣ (0118) 9761223
Ⓕ (0118) 9761417
Ⓔ info@henrystreet.co.uk
Ⓦ www.henrystreet.co.uk
**Contact:** Mr M C Goold
**Opening Times:** 0900-1730 Mon-Sat, 1030-1630 Sun.
**Min Mail Order UK:** Nmc
**Min Mail Order EU:** Nmc
**Cat. Cost:** Free
**Credit Cards:** Visa, Access, Switch
**Specialities:** Roses.
**Notes:** Also sells wholesale.
**Map Ref:** L, C3

LTen **Tendercare Nurseries Ltd** ♿
Southlands Road, Denham, Middlesex,
UB9 4HD
Ⓣ (01895) 835544
Ⓕ (01895) 835036
Ⓔ sales@tendercare.co.uk
Ⓦ www.tendercare.co.uk
**Contact:** Saija Haivala-Kendrick
**Opening Times:** 0900-1700 Mon-Sat.
**Credit Cards:** All major credit/debit cards
**Specialities:** Mature trees, shrubs, hedging, climbers & herbaceous plants.
**Notes:** Also sells wholesale.
**Map Ref:** L, B3

LToo **Toobees Exotics** ⊠ €
20 Inglewood, St Johns, Woking, Surrey,
GU21 3HX
Ⓣ (01483) 722600
Ⓜ 07836 334011
Ⓕ (01483) 751995
Ⓔ bbpotter@woking.plus.com
Ⓦ www.toobees-exotics.com
**Contact:** Bob Potter
**Opening Times:** Not open. Mail order & online shop only. Visits by appt. only.
**Min Mail Order UK:** Nmc
**Min Mail Order EU:** Nmc
**Cat. Cost:** Sae
**Credit Cards:** All major credit/debit cards
**Specialities:** South African & Madagascan succulents, many rare & unusual species, *Euphorbia* & *Pachypodium*. Stock varies constantly.
**Notes:** Credit cards accepted online only.

LWst **Westonbirt Plants** ⊠ €
17 Stanley Road, Carshalton, Surrey,
SM5 4LE
Ⓜ 07788 676079
Ⓔ office@westonbirtplants.co.uk
Ⓦ www.westonbirtplants.co.uk
**Contact:** Tony Dickerson
**Opening Times:** Not open. Mail order & shows only.
**Min Mail Order UK:** Nmc
**Min Mail Order EU:** Nmc
**Cat. Cost:** 3 × 1st class.
**Credit Cards:** All major credit/debit cards
**Specialities:** Bulbs & woodland plants incl. *Anemonella*, *Arisaema*, *Colchicum*, *Corydalis*, *Erythronium*, *Fritillaria*, *Iris* (Juno & Oncocyclus), *Lilium*, *Paeonia*, *Roscoea*, *Trillium* & hardy orchids (*Calanthe*, *Cypripedium* & *Epipactis*). Many rare plants in ltd. numbers. Japanese woodland plants.

LYaf **Yaffles** ⊠ ♿
Harvest Hill, Bourne End, Buckinghamshire,
SL8 5JJ
Ⓣ (01628) 525455
**Contact:** I Butterfield
**Opening Times:** 0900-1300 & 1400-1700. Please phone beforehand in case we are attending shows.
**Min Mail Order UK:** Nmc
**Min Mail Order EU:** £30.00 + p&p
**Cat. Cost:** 2 × 2nd class.
**Credit Cards:** None
**Specialities:** Nat. Collection of *Pleione*. Scientific Award 1999. *Dahlia* for collection only.
**Notes:** Only *Pleione* by mail order.

## Midlands

MAga **Agave Nursery** ⊠ €
97 Nottingham Road, Somercotes,
Derbyshire, DE55 4JH
Ⓜ 01773 605843 or 07814 787555 or 07791 627358
Ⓔ jon@agavenursery.wanadoo.co.uk
Ⓦ www.agave-nursery.co.uk
**Contact:** Jon & Sue Dudek
**Opening Times:** Mail order only. Open by appt. only.
**Min Mail Order UK:** Nmc
**Min Mail Order EU:** Nmc
**Cat. Cost:** Free

KEY
⊠ Mail order to UK or EU — Delivers to shows
Exports beyond EU — € Euro accepted
♿ Accessible by wheelchair — ◆ See Display advertisement

M

**Credit Cards:** None
**Specialities:** *Agave, Furcraea* & *Manfreda.*
**Map Ref:** M, B2

**MAJR** **A J Robinson** ⊠
Sycamore Farm, Foston, Derbyshire, DE65 5PW
Ⓣ (01283) 815635
Ⓔ argyspot@aol.com
**Contact:** A J Robinson
**Opening Times:** By appt. for collection of plants only.
**Min Mail Order UK:** £14.00
**Cat. Cost:** 2 × 1st class for list.
**Credit Cards:** None
**Specialities:** Extensive collection of tender perennials. Salvias. Nat. Collection of *Argyranthemum.*
**Notes:** Mail order argyranthemums only.
**Map Ref:** M, B2

**MArl** **Arley Hall Nursery** ♿
Arley Hall Nursery, Northwich, Cheshire, CW9 6NA
Ⓣ (01565) 777479 or 777231
Ⓕ (01565) 777465
Ⓦ www.arleyhallandgardens.com
**Contact:** Jane Foster
**Opening Times:** 1100-1730 Tue-Sun 22nd Mar-end Sep. Also B/hol Mons.
**Cat. Cost:** 4 × 1st class.
**Credit Cards:** All major credit/debit cards
**Specialities:** Wide range of herbaceous incl. many unusual varieties, some in small quantities. Wide range of unusual pelargoniums.
**Notes:** Nursery is beside car park at Arley Hall Gardens.
**Map Ref:** M, A1 **OS Grid Ref:** SJ673808

**MAsh** **Ashwood Nurseries Ltd** ⊠ ♿
Ashwood Lower Lane, Ashwood, Kingswinford, West Midlands, DY6 0AE
Ⓣ (01384) 401996
Ⓕ (01384) 401108
Ⓔ mailorder@ashwoodnurseries.com
Ⓦ www.ashwoodnurseries.com
**Contact:** Karrina Gilbert & Rachel Kendall
**Opening Times:** 0900-1700 Mon-Sat & 0930-1700 Sun excl. Xmas & Boxing Day.
**Min Mail Order UK:** Nmc
**Min Mail Order EU:** Nmc
**Cat. Cost:** 6 × 1st class.
**Credit Cards:** All major credit/debit cards
**Specialities:** Large range of hardy plants, shrubs & dwarf conifers. Roses, alpines & herbaceous plants. Also specialises in *Auricula, Cyclamen, Galanthus,* hellebores, *Hepatica, Hydrangea* & *Salvia.* Nat. Collection of *Lewisia.*
**Notes:** Tea room overlooking display garden. Ample parking. Regular events. Groups by appt. to visit private garden.
**Map Ref:** M, C2 **OS Grid Ref:** SO865879

**MAus** **David Austin Roses Ltd** ⊠ ✈ € ♿ ◆
Bowling Green Lane, Albrighton, Wolverhampton, West Midlands, WV7 3HB
Ⓣ (01902) 376300
Ⓕ (01902) 375177
Ⓔ retail@davidaustinroses.co.uk
Ⓦ www.davidaustinroses.com
**Contact:** Customer Services Dept
**Opening Times:** 0900-1700, 7 days.
**Min Mail Order UK:** Nmc
**Min Mail Order EU:** Nmc
**Cat. Cost:** Free.
**Credit Cards:** Switch, Visa, MasterCard, Maestro, Access
**Specialities:** Roses. Nat. Collection of English Roses.
**Notes:** Also sells wholesale.
**Map Ref:** M, B2 **OS Grid Ref:** SJ798042

**MAvo** **Avondale Nursery** 🏠 ♿
(Office) 3 Avondale Road, Earlsdon, Coventry, Warwickshire, CV5 6DZ
Ⓣ (024) 766 73662
Ⓜ 07979 093096
Ⓕ (024) 766 73662
Ⓔ enquiries@avondalenursery.co.uk
Ⓦ www.avondalenursery.co.uk
**Contact:** Brian Ellis
**Opening Times:** 1000-1230, 1400-1700 Mon-Fri, 1000-1700 Sat, 1030-1630 Sun, Mar-Sep. Other times by appt.
**Cat. Cost:** 4 × 1st class.
**Credit Cards:** All major credit/debit cards
**Specialities:** Rare & unusual perennials esp. *Aster, Eryngium, Leucanthemum, Geum, Crocosmia, Sanguisorba* & grasses. Display garden open. Groups welcome.
**Notes:** Nursery is at Russell's Nursery, Mill Hill, Baginton, Nr Coventry, CV8 3AG.
**Map Ref:** M, C2 **OS Grid Ref:** SP339751

**MBlu** **Bluebell Arboretum & Nursery** ⊠ 🏠 ♿
Annwell Lane, Smisby, Nr Ashby de la Zouch, Derbyshire, LE65 2TA
Ⓣ (01530) 413700
Ⓕ (01530) 417600
Ⓔ sales@bluebellnursery.com
Ⓦ www.bluebellnursery.com
**Contact:** Robert & Suzette Vernon
**Opening Times:** 0900-1700 Mon-Sat &

1030-1630 Sun Mar-Oct, 0900-1600 Mon-Sat (not Sun) Nov-Feb. Closed 24th Dec-1st Jan incl. & Easter Sun.
**Min Mail Order UK:** £9.50
**Min Mail Order EU:** Nmc
**Cat. Cost:** £1.50 + 3 × 1st class.
**Credit Cards:** Visa, Access, Switch, MasterCard
**Specialities:** Uncommon trees & shrubs. Woody climbers. Display garden & arboretum.
**Map Ref:** M, B1 **OS Grid Ref:** SK344187

**MBNS** **BARNSDALE GARDENS** ⊠ ♦
Exton Avenue, Exton, Oakham, Rutland, LE15 8AH
Ⓣ (01572) 813200
Ⓕ (01572) 813346
Ⓔ info@barnsdalegardens.co.uk
Ⓦ www.barnsdalegardens.co.uk
**Contact:** Nick Hamilton
**Opening Times:** 0900-1700 Mar-May & Sep-Oct, 0900-1900 Jun-Aug, 1000-1600 Nov-Feb, 7 days. Closed 24th & 25th Dec.
**Min Mail Order UK:** Nmc
**Min Mail Order EU:** Nmc
**Cat. Cost:** Online only.
**Credit Cards:** All major credit/debit cards
**Specialities:** Wide range of choice & unusual garden plants. Over 160 varieties of *Penstemon*, over 250 varieties of *Hemerocallis*.
**Notes:** Mail order from website or by telephone ordering only.
**Map Ref:** M, B3 **OS Grid Ref:** SK912108

**MBPg** **BARNFIELD PELARGONIUMS** ⊠
Barnfield, off Wilnecote Lane, Belgrave, Tamworth, Staffordshire, B77 2LF
Ⓣ (01827) 250123
Ⓕ (01827) 250123
Ⓔ brianandjenniewhite@hotmail.com
**Contact:** Jennie & Brian White
**Opening Times:** Open by appt. only.
**Min Mail Order UK:** £6.00
**Min Mail Order EU:** £10.00
**Cat. Cost:** 4 × 2nd class.
**Credit Cards:** None
**Specialities:** Over 200 varieties of scented leaf pelargoniums.

**MBri** **BRIDGEMERE NURSERIES** €
Bridgemere, Nr Nantwich, Cheshire, CW5 7QB
Ⓣ (01270) 521100
Ⓕ (01270) 520215
Ⓔ customer.service@bridgemere.co.uk
Ⓦ www.bridgemere.co.uk
**Contact:** Keith Atkey, Roger Pierce
**Opening Times:** 0900-1800 7 days. Closed 25th & 26th Dec.
**Cat. Cost:** None issued.
**Credit Cards:** Visa, Access, MasterCard, Switch
**Specialities:** Huge range outdoor & indoor plants, many rare & unusual. Specimen shrubs.
**Map Ref:** M, B1 **OS Grid Ref:** SJ727435

**MBrN** **BRIDGE NURSERY** €
Tomlow Road, Napton-on-the-Hill, Nr Rugby, Warwickshire, CV47 8HX
Ⓣ (01926) 812737
Ⓔ pemartino@tiscali.co.uk
Ⓦ www.Bridge-Nursery.co.uk
**Contact:** Christine Dakin & Philip Martino
**Opening Times:** 1000-1600 Mon-Sun 1st Feb-mid Dec. Other times by appt.
**Cat. Cost:** Online only.
**Credit Cards:** All major credit/debit cards
**Specialities:** Ornamental grasses, sedges & bamboos. Also range of shrubs & perennials. Display garden.
**Notes:** Also sells wholesale.
**Map Ref:** M, C2 **OS Grid Ref:** SP463625

**MCCP** **COLLECTORS CORNER PLANTS** ⊠
33 Rugby Road, Clifton-upon-Dunsmore, Rugby, Warwickshire, CV23 0DE
Ⓣ (01788) 571881
**Contact:** Pat Neesam
**Opening Times:** By appt. only.
**Min Mail Order UK:** £20.00
**Cat. Cost:** 6 × 1st class.
**Credit Cards:** None
**Specialities:** General range of choice herbaceous perennials, grasses, shrubs, palms, ferns & bamboos.
**Map Ref:** M, C3

**MCms** **CHRYSANTHEMUMS DIRECT** ⊠
Holmes Chapel Road, Over Peover, Knutsford, Cheshire, WA16 9RA
Ⓣ 0800 046 7443
Ⓜ 07977 312 593
Ⓕ (01565) 722740
Ⓔ sales@chrysanthemumsdirect.co.uk
Ⓦ www.chrysanthemumsdirect.co.uk
**Contact:** Martyn Flint
**Opening Times:** Not open. Mail order only.
**Min Mail Order UK:** Nmc
**Min Mail Order EU:** Nmc

KEY
⊠ Mail order to UK or EU — Delivers to shows
Exports beyond EU — € Euro accepted
Accessible by wheelchair — ♦ See Display advertisement

M

**Cat. Cost:** 2 × 1st class.
**Credit Cards:** All major credit/debit cards
**Specialities:** Chrysanthemums. Young plants grown to order. Delivery within 14 days.

MCoo **Cool Temperate** ⊠ ✈

(office) 45 Stamford Street, Awsworth, Nottinghamshire, NG16 2QL
Ⓣ (0115) 916 2673
Ⓕ (0115) 916 2673
Ⓔ phil.corbett@cooltemperate.co.uk
Ⓦ www.cooltemperate.co.uk
**Contact:** Phil Corbett
**Opening Times:** 0900-1700, 7 days. Please ring/write first.
**Min Mail Order UK:** Nmc
**Min Mail Order EU:** Nmc
**Cat. Cost:** 3 × 1st class.
**Credit Cards:** None
**Specialities:** Tree fruit, soft fruit, nitrogen-fixers, hedging, own-root fruit trees. Many species available in small quantities only.
**Notes:** Nursery at Trinity Farm, Awsworth Lane, Cossall, Notts. Also sells wholesale.
**Map Ref:** M, B2 **OS Grid Ref:** SK482435

M

MCot **Coton Manor Garden** ♿

Guilsborough, Northampton, Northamptonshire, NN6 8RQ
Ⓣ (01604) 740219
Ⓕ (01604) 740838
Ⓔ nursery@cotonmanor.co.uk
Ⓦ www.cotonmanor.co.uk
**Contact:** Caroline Tait
**Opening Times:** 1200-1730 Tue-Sat, 1st April (or Easter if earlier) to 30th Sep. Also Sun Apr, May & B/hol w/ends. Other times in working hours by appt.
**Cat. Cost:** None issued.
**Credit Cards:** All major credit/debit cards
**Specialities:** Wide-range of herbaceous perennials (3000+ varieties), some available in small quantities only. Also tender perennials & selected shrubs.
**Notes:** Garden open. Tea rooms. Garden School. Partial wheelchair access.
**Map Ref:** M, C3 **OS Grid Ref:** SP675715

MCri **Crin Gardens** ⊠ €

79 Partons Road, Kings Heath, Birmingham, B14 6TD
Ⓣ 0121 443 3815
Ⓜ 07504 907553
Ⓕ 0121 443 3815
Ⓔ cringardens@tiscali.co.uk
Ⓦ www.cringardens.co.uk
**Contact:** M Milinkovic
**Opening Times:** Not open. Mail order only.
**Min Mail Order UK:** Nmc
**Min Mail Order EU:** Nmc
**Cat. Cost:** 2 × 1st class + 1× 2nd.
**Credit Cards:** None
**Specialities:** Lilies. Limited stock available on first come, first served basis.

MDev **Devon Croft Nursery** ⊠ ♿

81 Farndon Road, Newark, Nottinghamshire, NG24 4SQ
Ⓣ (01636) 704013
Ⓜ 07930 318813
Ⓔ susan@devoncroftnursery.co.uk
Ⓦ www.devoncroftnursery.co.uk
**Contact:** Susan Richardson
**Opening Times:** Wed-Sun mid-Feb to late Dec. 7 days Easter-end Jun. W/ends only Aug.
**Min Mail Order UK:** Nmc
**Cat. Cost:** Online only.
**Credit Cards:** All major credit/debit cards
**Specialities:** Wide range of *Bamboo* & hostas, many specimen-sized plants. Hardy herbaceous perennials. Some plants in small quantities.
**Map Ref:** M, B3 **OS Grid Ref:** SK786528

MDKP **D K Plants** ⌂

(Office) 19 Harbourne Road, Cheadle, Stoke on Trent, Staffordshire, ST10 1JU
Ⓣ Office: (01538) 754460
Ⓜ Nursery: 07779 545015
Ⓔ davidknoxc@aol.com
**Contact:** Dave Knox
**Opening Times:** 0900-2000 (or dusk if earlier) Mon-Tue & Thu-Fri. Other times by appt.
**Cat. Cost:** 4 × 1st class A4 sae plus 44p 1st or 37p 2nd class.
**Credit Cards:** None
**Specialities:** Unusual hardy alpines & perennials. All grown on the nursery.
**Notes:** Nursery is at new roundabout across from Queen's Arms pub, Freehay Crossroads, Freehay, Cheadle, ST10 1TR.
**Map Ref:** M, B1

MDun **Dunge Valley Rhododendron Gardens** € ♿

Windgather Rocks, Kettleshulme, High Peak, Cheshire, SK23 7RF
Ⓣ (01663) 733787
Ⓕ (01663) 733787
Ⓔ david@dungevalley.co.uk
Ⓦ www.dungevalley.co.uk
**Contact:** David Ketley
**Opening Times:** 1030-1700 Thu-Sun Mar-Jun. Open B/hols. Otherwise by appt.
**Cat. Cost:** Online only.

**Credit Cards:** All major credit/debit cards
**Specialities:** *Rhododendron* species & hybrids. Azaleas, acers, *Meconopsis*, shrubs & perennials, some rare & wild collected. Some terrestrial orchids.
**Notes:** Also sells wholesale.
**Map Ref:** M, A2 **OS Grid Ref:** SJ989777

**MFie** **FIELD HOUSE NURSERY** ⊠ ☗ € ♿
Leake Road, Gotham, Nottinghamshire, NG11 0JN
Ⓣ (01159) 830278
Ⓜ 07504 125209
Ⓔ auricula@btinternet.com
**Contact:** Valerie A Woolley & Bob Taylor
**Opening Times:** 0900-1600 Fri-Wed or by appt.
**Min Mail Order UK:** 4 plants.
**Min Mail Order EU:** £30.00
**Cat. Cost:** 4 × 1st class or 4 × IRC.
**Credit Cards:** Visa, MasterCard, Electron, Maestro, Solo
**Specialities:** *Primula auricula* & seed, *Astrantia*, herbaceous perennials. Nat. Collections of *Primula auricula* (Shows & Alpines) & *Astrantia*.
**Notes:** Mail order for *Astrantia*, *Auricula*, small *Primula*, & seeds.

**MGbk** **GOSBROOK PELARGONIUMS** ⊠
30 Damson Trees, Shrivenham, Oxfordshire, SN6 8BB
Ⓣ (01793) 783329
Ⓜ 07921 089908
Ⓔ enquiries@gosbrookpelargoniums.com
Ⓦ www.gosbrookpelargoniums.com
**Contact:** David Taylor
**Opening Times:** Please ring for appt.
**Min Mail Order UK:** £20.00
**Min Mail Order EU:** £20.00
**Cat. Cost:** 3 × 1st class
**Specialities:** *Pelargonium*.
**Notes:** Credit cards accepted online only.
**Map Ref:** M, D2 **OS Grid Ref:** SU233889

**MGos** **GOSCOTE NURSERIES LTD** ♿ ◆
Syston Road, Cossington, Leicestershire, LE7 4UZ
Ⓣ (01509) 812121
Ⓕ (01509) 814231
Ⓔ sales@goscote.co.uk
Ⓦ www.goscote.co.uk
**Contact:** James Toone
**Opening Times:** 7 days, year round, apart from between Xmas & New Year.
**Cat. Cost:** Online only.
**Credit Cards:** Visa, Access, MasterCard, Delta, Switch
**Specialities:** Japanese maples, rhododendrons & azaleas, *Magnolia*, *Camellia*, *Pieris* & other *Ericaceae*. Ornamental trees & shrubs, conifers, fruit, heathers, alpines, roses, *Clematis* & unusual climbers. Show Garden to visit.
**Notes:** Design & landscaping service available. Also sells wholesale.
**Map Ref:** M, B3 **OS Grid Ref:** SK602130

**MHer** **THE HERB NURSERY** ♿
Thistleton, Oakham, Rutland, LE15 7RE
Ⓣ (01572) 767658
Ⓔ herbnursery@southwitham.net
Ⓦ www.herbnursery.co.uk
**Contact:** Peter Bench
**Opening Times:** 0900-1800 (or dusk) 7 days excl. Xmas-New Year.
**Cat. Cost:** A5 sae.
**Credit Cards:** None
**Specialities:** Herbs, wild flowers, cottage garden plants, scented-leaf pelargoniums. Esp. *Thymus*, *Mentha*, *Lavandula*.
**Map Ref:** M, B3

**MHom** **HOMESTEAD PLANTS** ⊠
The Homestead, Normanton, Bottesford, Nottingham, NG13 0EP
Ⓣ (01949) 842745
Ⓦ www.homesteadplants.co.uk
**Contact:** Mrs S Palmer
**Opening Times:** By appt.
**Min Mail Order UK:** Nmc
**Cat. Cost:** 2 × 2nd class.
**Credit Cards:** None
**Specialities:** Unusual hardy & half-hardy perennials, esp. *Paeonia* species. *Hosta*, *Jovibarba*, *Salvia*, *Sempervivum* & Heliotrope. Drought-tolerant asters. Most available only in small quantities. Nat. Collection of *Heliotropium* cultivars.
**Map Ref:** M, B3 **OS Grid Ref:** SK812407

**MJac** **JACKSON'S NURSERIES**
Clifton Campville, Nr Tamworth, Staffordshire, B79 0AP
Ⓣ (01827) 373307
**Contact:** N Jackson
**Opening Times:** 0900-1800 Mon Wed-Sat, 1000-1700 Sun.
**Cat. Cost:** 2 × 1st class.
**Credit Cards:** None
**Specialities:** *Fuchsia*.

KEY
⊠ Mail order to UK or EU ☗ Delivers to shows
✈ Exports beyond EU € Euro accepted
♿ Accessible by wheelchair ◆ See Display advertisement

M

**Notes:** Also sells wholesale.
**Map Ref:** M, B1

**MLea** **Lea Rhododendron Gardens Ltd** ✉ ✈ ♿
Lea, Matlock, Derbyshire, DE4 5GH
Ⓣ (01629) 534380/534260
Ⓕ (01629) 534260
Ⓦ www.leagarden.co.uk
**Contact:** Peter Tye
**Opening Times:** 1000-1730 7 days 20 Mar-30 Jun. Out of season by appt.
**Min Mail Order UK:** £15.00 + p&p
**Min Mail Order EU:** £15.00 + p&p
**Cat. Cost:** 30p + sae.
**Credit Cards:** All major credit/debit cards
**Specialities:** Rhododendrons & azaleas.
**Map Ref:** M, B1 **OS Grid Ref:** SK324571

**MLHP** **Longstone Hardy Plant Nursery** ♿
(office) Stancil House, Barn Furlong, Great Longstone, Nr Bakewell, Derbyshire, DE45 1TR
Ⓣ (01629) 640136
Ⓜ 07762 083674
Ⓔ lucyinlongstone@hotmail.com
Ⓦ www.longstonehardyplants.co.uk
**Contact:** Lucy Wright
**Opening Times:** 1300-1700 Tue-Sat & B/hols, 1st Apr-30th Sep. 1300-1700 Sat, Mar-Oct. Other times by appt.
**Credit Cards:** None
**Specialities:** Specialist peat-free nursery displaying all our own hardy perennials, ornamental grasses, herbs & shrubs, incl. many unusual varieties. Some stock available in small quantities only. Can propagate to order.
**Notes:** Nursery in Station Road 150 yds on right after turning onto it at the village green. Postcode DE45 1TS.
**Map Ref:** M, A2 **OS Grid Ref:** SK198717

**MLLN** **Lodge Lane Nursery** ✉ ♿
Lodge Lane, Dutton, Nr Warrington, Cheshire, WA4 4HP
Ⓣ (01928) 713718
Ⓕ (01928) 713718
Ⓔ info@lodgelane.co.uk
Ⓦ www.lodgelane.co.uk
**Contact:** Sue Beesley
**Opening Times:** 1000-1700 Wed-Sun & B/hols, mid Mar-mid Sep. By appt. outside these dates.
**Min Mail Order UK:** £10.00
**Cat. Cost:** By email or online.
**Credit Cards:** All major credit/debit cards
**Specialities:** Unusual perennials & shrubs incl. *Achillea, Astrantia, Campanula, Digitalis, Penstemon, Geranium, Heuchera, Kniphofia, Nepeta, Papaver, Salvia* & ornamental grasses.
**Map Ref:** M, A1 **OS Grid Ref:** SJ586779

**MLod** **Lodge Farm Plants & Wildflowers** ✉ € ♿
Case Lane, Fiveways, Hatton, Warwickshire, CV35 7JD
Ⓣ (01926) 484649
Ⓜ 07977 631368
Ⓕ (01926) 484649
Ⓔ lodgefarmplants@btinternet.com
Ⓦ www.lodgefarmplants.com
**Contact:** Janet Cook & Nick Cook
**Opening Times:** Open 7 days all year, except Xmas Day & Boxing Day.
**Min Mail Order UK:** Nmc
**Cat. Cost:** Online only.
**Credit Cards:** None
**Specialities:** Wildflower plants. Vegetable plants, soft fruit. Native trees & hedging. Wildflower seeds. Fruit trees, espalier, fan, stepovers & cordons.
**Notes:** Also sells wholesale.
**Map Ref:** M, C2 **OS Grid Ref:** SP223700

**MMHG** **Morton Nurseries Ltd** ✉ ♿
Morton Hall, Ranby, Retford, Nottinghamshire, DN22 8HW
Ⓣ (01777) 702530
Ⓜ 07940 434398
Ⓔ enquiries@morton-nurseries.com
Ⓦ www.morton-nurseries.co.uk
**Contact:** Gill McMaster
**Opening Times:** By appt.only
**Min Mail Order UK:** £5.00 + p&p
**Cat. Cost:** 3 × 1st class.
**Credit Cards:** None
**Specialities:** Shrubs & perennials.
**Map Ref:** M, A3

**MMoz** **Mozart House Nursery Garden**
84 Central Avenue, Wigston, Leicestershire, LE18 2AA
Ⓣ (0116) 288 9548
**Contact:** Des Martin
**Opening Times:** 1000-1300 last Sat of the month, Mar to Sep 2010. Other times by appt.
**Cat. Cost:** Phone for list.
**Credit Cards:** None
**Specialities:** Bamboos, ornamental grasses, rushes & sedges, ferns. Expanding range of shade & woodland plants. Some stock available in small quantities.
**Map Ref:** M, C3

M

MMuc **Mucklestone Nurseries** ⊠ ♿ ◆
Rock Lane, Mucklestone,
Nr Market Drayton, Shropshire,
TF9 4DN
Ⓜ 07985 425829
Ⓔ info@botanyplants.co.uk
Ⓦ www.botanyplants.co.uk
**Contact:** Brian Watkins
**Opening Times:** 0900-1700 Thu-Sun, Mar-Oct. Other times by appt.
**Min Mail Order UK:** Nmc
**Cat. Cost:** Online only.
**Specialities:** Trees, shrubs, grasses & perennials for acid & damp soils of the north & west UK.
**Notes:** For mail order contact William Friend 07714 241668. Any plants on website or listed under nursery code SEND can be collected from Mucklestone Nurseries.
**Map Ref:** M, B2 **OS Grid Ref:** SJ728373

MNFA **The Nursery Further Afield** ⊠ ♿
Evenley Road, Mixbury,
Nr Brackley, Northamptonshire,
NN13 5YR
Ⓣ (01280) 848808
Ⓔ sinclair@nurseryfurtherafield.co.uk
**Contact:** Gerald & Mary Sinclair
**Opening Times:** 1000-1700 Wed-Sat, Apr-mid Sep. Other times by appt.
**Min Mail Order UK:** £15.00
**Cat. Cost:** 3 × 1st class.
**Credit Cards:** None
**Specialities:** Worthwhile hardy perennials, many unusual. Large selection of *Geranium* & *Hemerocallis*. Nat. Collection of *Hemerocallis* on display 1400-1700 14th-18th Jul 2010.
**Notes:** Mail order for *Hemerocallis* only.
**Map Ref:** M, C3 **OS Grid Ref:** SP608344

MNHC **The National Herb Centre** ⊠ ♿
Banbury Road, Warmington, Nr Banbury,
Oxfordshire, OX17 1DF
Ⓣ (01295) 690999
Ⓕ (01295) 690034
Ⓦ www.herbcentre.co.uk
**Contact:** Plant Centre Staff
**Opening Times:** 0900-1730 Mon-Sat, 1030-1700 Sun.
**Min Mail Order UK:** Nmc
**Credit Cards:** All major credit/debit cards
**Specialities:** Herbs, culinary & medicinal. Extensive selection of rosemary, thyme & lavender, in particular.
**Notes:** Carriage charge of £9.00 up to 15kg, higher for heavier parcels. Next day delivery. UK mainland only. Signature required.
**Map Ref:** M, C2 **OS Grid Ref:** SP413471

MNrw **Norwell Nurseries** ⊠ ⛫ ♿ ◆
Woodhouse Road, Norwell, Newark,
Nottinghamshire, NG23 6JX
Ⓣ (01636) 636337
Ⓔ wardha@aol.com
Ⓦ www.norwellnurseries.co.uk
**Contact:** Dr Andrew Ward
**Opening Times:** 1000-1700 Mon, Wed-Fri & Sun (Wed-Mon May & Jun). By appt. Aug & 20th Oct-1st Mar.
**Min Mail Order UK:** £15.00 + p&p
**Min Mail Order EU:** £40.00
**Cat. Cost:** 3 × 1st class or online.
**Credit Cards:** None
**Specialities:** A large collection of unusual & choice herbaceous perennials & alpines esp., hardy geraniums, *Geum*, pond & bog plants, cottage garden plants, *Hemerocallis*, grasses, hardy chrysanthemums & woodland plants. One acre garden open.
**Notes:** Also sells wholesale.
**Map Ref:** M, B3 **OS Grid Ref:** SK767616

MOld **Old Hall Nursery** ♿
Winkhill, Leek, Staffordshire, ST13 7PN
Ⓣ (01538) 308257
Ⓜ 07866 175881
Ⓔ oldhallnursery@hotmail.co.uk
**Contact:** Sandra Henshall
**Opening Times:** 1000-1600, 7 days.
**Cat. Cost:** Not available.
**Credit Cards:** None
**Specialities:** Large selection of herbaceous, herbs & alpines. Also shrubs, climbers & fruit trees. All hardy.
**Map Ref:** M, B2 **OS Grid Ref:** SK051521

MOWG **The Old Walled Garden** ⊠ ⛫ ♿
Honeybourne Road, Pebworth, Stratford upon-Avon, Warwickshire, CV37 8XP
Ⓣ (01789) 720788
Ⓕ (01789) 721162
Ⓔ Heather@oldwalledgarden.com
Ⓦ www.oldwalledgarden.com
**Contact:** Heather Angrave
**Opening Times:** 0900-1700 Mon-Sat, 1st Mar-31st Aug. 0900-1600 Mon-Fri, 1st Sep-1st Mar. 1030-1600 Sat & Sun, 6th Mar-25th Jul. Closed last 2 weeks of Dec -1st week Jan, Easter Sun & Aug B/hol Mon.
**Min Mail Order UK:** Nmc
**Cat. Cost:** 2 × 1st class
**Credit Cards:** Switch, MasterCard, Visa

KEY
⊠ Mail order to UK or EU ⛫ Delivers to shows
✈ Exports beyond EU € Euro accepted
♿ Accessible by wheelchair ◆ See Display advertisement

M

**Specialities:** Many rare & unusual shrubs. Wide range of conservatory plants esp. Australian. Nat. Collection of *Callistemon*.
**Map Ref:** M, C2 **OS Grid Ref:** SP133458

**MPet** **PETER GRAYSON (SWEET PEA SEEDSMAN)** ⊠ ⊠
34 Glenthorne Close, Brampton, Chesterfield, Derbyshire, S40 3AR
Ⓣ (01246) 278503
Ⓕ (01246) 278503
**Contact:** Peter Grayson
**Opening Times:** Not open. Mail order only.
**Min Mail Order UK:** Nmc
**Min Mail Order EU:** Nmc
**Cat. Cost:** C5 sae, 1 × 2nd class.
**Credit Cards:** None
**Specialities:** *Lathyrus* species & cvs. Large collection of old-fashioned sweet peas & over 100 Spencer sweet peas incl. own cultivars and collection of old-fashioned cottage garden annuals & perennials.
**Notes:** Mail order for seeds only. Also sells wholesale.

**MPhe** **PHEDAR NURSERY** ⊠ ⊠ €
42 Bunkers Hill, Romiley, Stockport, Cheshire, SK6 3DS
Ⓣ (0161) 430 3772
Ⓕ (0161) 430 3772
Ⓔ mclewin@phedar.com
Ⓦ www.phedar.com
**Contact:** Will McLewin
**Opening Times:** Frequent but irregular. Please phone to arrange appt.
**Min Mail Order UK:** Nmc
**Min Mail Order EU:** Nmc
**Cat. Cost:** 2 × A5 envelopes or address labels + 4 × 1st class.
**Credit Cards:** All major credit/debit cards
**Specialities:** *Helleborus*, *Paeonia*. Limited stock of some rare items.
**Notes:** Non-EU exports subject to destination & on an ad hoc basis only. Please contact nursery for details. Credit cards accepted for online orders only. Also sells wholesale.
**Map Ref:** M, A2 **OS Grid Ref:** SJ936897

**MPkF** **PACKHORSE FARM NURSERY** ⌂ ♿
Sandyford House, Lant Lane, Tansley, Matlock, Derbyshire, DE4 5FW
Ⓣ (01629) 57206
Ⓜ 07974 095752
Ⓕ (01629) 57206
**Contact:** Hilton W Haynes
**Opening Times:** 1000-1700 Tue & Wed, 1st Mar-31st Oct. Any other time by appt. only.
**Cat. Cost:** 2 × 1st class for plant list.
**Credit Cards:** None
**Specialities:** *Acer*, rare stock is limited in supply. Other more unusual hardy shrubs, trees & conifers.
**Map Ref:** M, B2 **OS Grid Ref:** SK322617

**MPnt** **PLANTAGOGO.COM** ⊠ ⌂ ♿
Jubilee Cottage Nursery, Snape Lane, Englesea Brook, Crewe, Cheshire, CW2 5QN
Ⓣ (01270) 820335
Ⓜ 07713 518271
Ⓔ foxy@plantagogo.freeserve.co.uk
Ⓦ www.plantagogo.com
**Contact:** Vicky & Richard Fox
**Opening Times:** By appt. only. Also Open Days 16th & 17th Oct 2010.
**Min Mail Order UK:** £7.95 single payment.
**Min Mail Order EU:** Price on application or see website.
**Cat. Cost:** 4 × 1st class.
**Credit Cards:** All major credit/debit cards
**Specialities:** *Heuchera*, *Tiarella*, Nat. Collections of *Heuchera* & *Heucherella*. Perennials. Will propagate to order.
**Map Ref:** M, B1 **OS Grid Ref:** SJ750516

**MRav** **RAVENSTHORPE NURSERY** ⊠ ♿
6 East Haddon Road, Ravensthorpe, Northamptonshire, NN6 8ES
Ⓣ (01604) 770548
Ⓕ (01604) 770548
Ⓔ ravensthorpenursery@hotmail.com
**Contact:** Jean & Richard Wiseman
**Opening Times:** 1000-1800 (dusk if earlier) Tue-Sun. Also B/hol Mons.
**Min Mail Order UK:** Nmc
**Min Mail Order EU:** Nmc
**Cat. Cost:** None issued.
**Credit Cards:** Visa, MasterCard
**Specialities:** Over 3000 different trees, shrubs & perennials with many unusual varieties.
**Notes:** Search & delivery service for large orders, winter months only.
**Map Ref:** M, C3 **OS Grid Ref:** SP665699

**MREP** **RARE AND EXOTIC PLANTS AT WOODSHOOT NURSERIES** ⊠ ♿
King's Bromley, Burton-upon-Trent, Staffordshire, DE13 7HN
Ⓣ (01543) 472233
Ⓜ 07802 737676
Ⓕ (01543) 472115
Ⓔ sales@rareandexoticplants.com
Ⓦ www.rareandexoticplants.com
**Contact:** Richard Flint
**Opening Times:** 0900-1700, 7 days.
**Min Mail Order UK:** £20.00 + p&p
**Cat. Cost:** 1 × 1st class.

**Credit Cards:** All major credit/debit cards
**Specialities:** *Acacia, Agave, Arbutus, Bamboo, Citrus, Cordyline, Dicksonia, Phormium, Pittosporum*, palms, olives, *Yucca*, topiary & specimens.
**Notes:** Also sells wholesale.
**Map Ref:** M, B2 **OS Grid Ref:** SK127164

MSCN **Stonyford Cottage Nursery** ⊠ ♿
Stonyford Lane, Cuddington, Northwich, Cheshire, CW8 2TF
Ⓣ (01606) 888970/888128 (answerphone)
Ⓜ 07714 205177
Ⓔ stonyfordcottage@yahoo.co.uk
Ⓦ www.stonyfordcottagenursery.co.uk
**Contact:** Andrew Overland
**Opening Times:** 1000-1700 Tue-Sun & B/hol Mons 1st Feb-31st Oct.
**Min Mail Order UK:** Nmc
**Min Mail Order EU:** Nmc
**Cat. Cost:** Not available this year
**Credit Cards:** All major credit/debit cards
**Specialities:** Wide range of herbaceous perennials, *Iris*, hardy *Geranium*, moisture-loving & bog plants. *Sempervivum, Paeonia*, Candelabra *Primula*.
**Notes:** Also sells wholesale.
**Map Ref:** M, A1 **OS Grid Ref:** SJ580710

MSKA **Sweet Knowle Aquatics** ⊠ ♿
Wimpstone-Ilmington Road, Stratford-upon-Avon, Warwickshire, CV37 8NR
Ⓣ (01789) 450036
Ⓕ (01789) 450036
Ⓔ sweetknowleaquatics@hotmail.com
Ⓦ www.sweetknowleaquatics.co.uk
**Contact:** Zoe Harding
**Opening Times:** 0930-1700 Sun-Fri, closed Sat. Open B/hols.
**Min Mail Order UK:** Nmc
**Min Mail Order EU:** Nmc
**Cat. Cost:** By email only.
**Credit Cards:** All major credit/debit cards
**Specialities:** Aquatics. Hardy & tropical water lilies, marginals & oxygenators.
**Notes:** 2-acre display garden open to the public (no charge).
**Map Ref:** M, C2 **OS Grid Ref:** SP207480

MSnd **Sound Garden Rhododendrons** ⊠ ⌂
(Office) 184 Crow Lane East, Newton-le-Willows, Merseyside, WA12 9UA
Ⓣ (01925) 229100
Ⓜ 07931 340836
Ⓔ info@soundgardendesign.com
Ⓦ www.s-g-d-uk.com
**Contact:** Tim Atkinson
**Opening Times:** By appt. only.
**Min Mail Order UK:** £50.00
**Min Mail Order EU:** £100.00
**Cat. Cost:** 2 × 1st class
**Credit Cards:** None
**Specialities:** Species & rare *Rhododendron*. Hardy hybrid rhododendrons, azaleas, primulas.
**Notes:** Nursery at Middledale Farm, Dale Road, Marple, Cheshire SK6 6NL.
**Map Ref:** N, B1 **OS Grid Ref:** SJ948901

MSpe **SpecialPerennials.com** ⊠ ⌂ ♿
Yew Tree House, Hall Lane, Hankelow, Crewe, Cheshire, CW3 0JB
Ⓣ (01270) 811443
Ⓜ 07716 990695
Ⓔ plants@specialperennials.com
Ⓦ www.specialperennials.com
**Contact:** Janet & Martin Blow
Opening Times: See website for details. Nat. Collection of *Helenium* Open Days 14th/15th Aug.
**Min Mail Order UK:** Nmc
**Cat. Cost:** 2 × 1st class or online.
**Credit Cards:** Paypal
**Specialities:** Herbaceous perennials. Nat. Collection of *Helenium* (100+ varieties for sale). Nat. Collection of *Centaurea* applied for (50+ varieties). Also *Geum*, border *Phlox, Hemerocallis, Monada* & *Persciaria*. Some plants, esp. *Hemerocallis*, available in small quantities only.
**Notes:** All plants grown in garden nursery. Garden open for NGS. Talks given. Group visits to garden & nursery welcomed. Special study events. See website or send sae for details.
**Map Ref:** M, B1 **OS Grid Ref:** SJ699452

MSSP **S & S Perennials** ⊠
24 Main Street, Normanton Le Heath, Leicestershire, LE67 2TB
Ⓣ (01530) 262250
**Contact:** Shirley Pierce
**Opening Times:** Afternoons only, otherwise please phone.
**Min Mail Order UK:** Nmc
**Cat. Cost:** 2 × 1st class.
**Credit Cards:** None
**Specialities:** *Erythronium, Fritillaria*, dwarf *Narcissus* & *Anemone*. Stock available in small quantities only.
**Map Ref:** M, B1

KEY
⊠ Mail order to UK or EU ⌂ Delivers to shows
✈ Exports beyond EU € Euro accepted
♿ Accessible by wheelchair ◆ See Display advertisement

**MSwo** **Swallows Nursery** ⊠ ♿
Mixbury, Brackley, Northamptonshire, NN13 5RR
Ⓣ (01280) 847721
Ⓕ (01280) 848611
Ⓔ enq@swallowsnursery.co.uk
Ⓦ www.swallowsnursery.co.uk
**Contact:** Chris Swallow
**Opening Times:** 0900-1300 & 1400-1700 (earlier in winter) Mon-Fri, 0900-1300 Sat.
**Min Mail Order UK:** £15.00
**Cat. Cost:** 3 × 1st class (plus phone number).
**Credit Cards:** All major credit/debit cards
**Specialities:** Growing a wide range, particularly shrubs, climbers, trees & roses.
**Notes:** No mail order for trees unless part of larger order. Nursery transport used where possible, esp. for trees. Also sells wholesale.
**Map Ref:** M, C3 **OS Grid Ref:** SP607336

M

**MTis** **Tissington Nursery** ⊠ ⌂ ♿
The Old Kitchen Gardens, Tissington, Asbourne, Derbyshire, DE6 1RA
Ⓣ (01335) 390650
Ⓜ 07929 720284
Ⓔ info@tissington-nursery.co.uk
Ⓦ www.tissington-nursery.co.uk
**Contact:** Mairi Longdon
**Opening Times:** 1000-1700 daily, 3rd Mar-end Oct.
**Min Mail Order UK:** Nmc
**Cat. Cost:** 4 × 1st class.
**Credit Cards:** All major credit/debit cards
**Specialities:** Choice & unusual perennials esp. *Achillea*, *Geranium*, *Geum*, *Helenium*, *Heuchera*, *Penstemon*, *Sempervivum* & grasses.
**Map Ref:** M, B1 **OS Grid Ref:** SK176521

**MTPN** **Smart Plants** ⊠ ♿
Sandy Hill Lane, off Overstone Road, Moulton, Northampton, NN3 7JB
Ⓣ (01604) 454106
Ⓜ 07519 339508
**Contact:** Stuart Smart
**Opening Times:** 1000-1500 Thu & Fri, 1000-1700 Sat. Other times by appt.
**Min Mail Order UK:** Nmc
**Cat. Cost:** 3 × 1st class
**Credit Cards:** None
**Specialities:** Wide range of herbaceous, alpines, shrubs, grasses, hardy *Geranium*. Some plants available in small quantities only.

**MWat** **Waterperry Gardens Ltd** ⊠ ♿
Waterperry, Nr Wheatley, Oxfordshire, OX33 1JZ
Ⓣ (01844) 339226/254
Ⓕ (01844) 339883
Ⓔ management@waterperrygardens.co.uk
Ⓦ www.waterperrygardens.co.uk
**Contact:** Mr R Jacobs
**Opening Times:** 1000-1730 summer. 1000-1700 winter.
**Min Mail Order UK:** £30.00
**Cat. Cost:** Online only.
**Credit Cards:** All major credit/debit cards
**Specialities:** General, large range of herbaceous esp. *Aster*, also Nat. Collection of *Saxifraga* (subsect. *Kabschia* & *Engleria*).
**Map Ref:** M, D3 **OS Grid Ref:** SP630064

**MWea** **Wear's Nursery** ♿
(Office) 84 Wantage Road, Wallingford, Oxfordshire, OX10 0LY
Ⓣ 07790 425284
**Contact:** David Wear
**Opening Times:** 1000-1700 Mon-Sat, Feb-Oct. 1000-1600 Mon-Sat, Nov-Jan, please phone first as may be closed on some days in winter. 1000-1600 Sun, Mar-Jun.
**Cat. Cost:** None issued.
**Credit Cards:** None
**Specialities:** Unusual herbaceous varieties & shrubs. Large selection of *Geranium*. Some plants only available in small numbers.
**Notes:** Nursery sited at High Road, Brightwell-cum-Sotwell, Wallingford.
**Map Ref:** M, D3 **OS Grid Ref:** SU590910

**MWhi** **Whitehill Farm Nursery** ⊠ € ♿
Whitehill Farm, Burford, Oxfordshire, OX18 4DT
Ⓣ (01993) 823218
Ⓕ (01993) 822894
Ⓔ a.youngson@virgin.net
Ⓦ www.whitehillfarmnursery.co.uk
**Contact:** P J M Youngson
**Opening Times:** 0900-1800 (or dusk if earlier) 7 days, Feb-Nov.
**Min Mail Order UK:** £5.00 + p&p
**Min Mail Order EU:** £5.00 + p&p
**Cat. Cost:** 4 × 1st class.
**Credit Cards:** All major credit/debit cards
**Specialities:** Grasses & bamboos, less common shrubs & perennials. Some available in small quantities only.
**Notes:** £1.00 of catalogue cost refunded on 1st order.
**Map Ref:** M, D2 **OS Grid Ref:** SP268113

**MWht** **Whitelea Nursery** ⊠ ♿
Whitelea Lane, Tansley, Matlock, Derbyshire, DE4 5FL
Ⓣ (01629) 55010
Ⓔ sales@uk-bamboos.co.uk
Ⓦ www.uk-bamboos.co.uk
**Contact:** David Wilson

**Opening Times:** By appt.
**Min Mail Order UK:** Nmc
**Cat. Cost:** Online only. Price list available 2 × 1st class.
**Credit Cards:** None
**Specialities:** Bamboos. Substantial quantities of 45 cvs & species of bamboo, remainder stocked in small numbers only. Ltd stocks of grasses, trees & shrubs.
**Notes:** Mail order limited by carrier restrictions, please contact nursery or see website for details. Also sells wholesale.
**Map Ref:** M, B1 **OS Grid Ref:** SK325603

**MWts** **WATERSIDE NURSERY** ✉ ⌂
Sharnford, Leicestershire, LE10 3QD
Ⓣ (01455) 273730
Ⓜ 07931 557082
Ⓔ linda@watersidenursery.co.uk
Ⓦ www.watersidenursery.co.uk
**Contact:** Linda Smith
**Opening Times:** By appt. only.
**Min Mail Order UK:** Nmc
**Cat. Cost:** Online only.
**Credit Cards:** All major credit/debit cards
**Specialities:** Aquatics, marginal pond plants, miniature water lilies, waterlilies, bog garden plants & moisture-loving plants.

## NORTHERN

**NBid** **BIDE-A-WEE COTTAGE GARDENS** ✉ ♿
Stanton, Netherwitton, Morpeth, Northumberland, NE65 8PR
Ⓣ (01670) 772238
Ⓕ (01670) 772238
Ⓔ info@bideawee.co.uk
Ⓦ www.bideawee.co.uk
**Contact:** Mark Robson
**Opening Times:** 1330-1700 Sat & Wed, 24th Apr-28th Aug 2010. Group visits at other times, except Sun.
**Min Mail Order UK:** £20.00
**Cat. Cost:** Online only.
**Credit Cards:** All major credit/debit cards
**Specialities:** Unusual herbaceous perennials, *Agapanthus*, *Primula*, ferns, grasses. Nat. Collection of *Centaurea*.
**Map Ref:** N, B2 **OS Grid Ref:** NZ132900

**NBir** **BIRKHEADS SECRET GARDENS & NURSERY** ✉ ♿
Nr Hedley Hall Woods, Sunniside, Gateshead, Tyne & Wear, NE16 5EL
Ⓣ (01207) 232262
Ⓜ 07778 447920
Ⓕ (01207) 232262
Ⓔ birkheadsnursery@gmail.com
Ⓦ www.birkheadssecretgardens.co.uk
**Contact:** Mrs Christine Liddle
**Opening Times:** 1000-1700 daily (except Mon) Mar-Oct. Groups by appt.
**Min Mail Order UK:** £12
**Cat. Cost:** None issued.
**Credit Cards:** All major credit/debit cards
**Specialities:** Hardy herbaceous perennials, grasses, bulbs & herbs. *Allium*, *Digitalis*, *Euphorbia*, *Galanthus* & *Geranium*. Max. 30 of any plant propagated each year.
**Notes:** Mail order Nov-Feb only. Orders taken all year for winter deliveries.
**Map Ref:** N, B2 **OS Grid Ref:** NZ220569

**NBlu** **BLUNDELL'S NURSERIES** ♿
68 Southport New Road, Tarleton, Preston, Lancashire, PR4 6HY
Ⓣ (01772) 815442
Ⓕ (01772) 613917
Ⓔ jerplusjeff@aol.com
**Contact:** Any member of staff
**Opening Times:** 0905-1700 daily. Closed around Xmas/New Year.
**Cat. Cost:** None issued.
**Credit Cards:** All major credit/debit cards
**Specialities:** Trees, shrubs, incl. topiary & large specimens, conifers. Perennials, alpines, ferns, heathers, herbs, hanging basket/bedding/conservatory plants, hedging, roses.
**Notes:** Also sells wholesale.
**Map Ref:** N, D1

**NBPC** **THE BARN PLANT CENTRE & GIFT SHOP** ♿
The Square, Scorton, Preston, Lancashire, PR3 1AU
Ⓣ (01524) 793533
Ⓕ (01524) 793533
Ⓔ sales@plantsandgifts.co.uk
Ⓦ www.plantsandgifts.co.uk
**Contact:** Neil Anderton
**Opening Times:** 0900-1700 Mon-Sat, 1000-1800 Sun.
**Credit Cards:** All major credit/debit cards
**Specialities:** 800 varieties of perennials.
**Notes:** Large gift shop & coffee bar.
**Map Ref:** N, C1 **OS Grid Ref:** GR501487

**NBre** **BREEZY KNEES NURSERIES** ♿
Common Lane, Warthill, York, YO19 5XS
Ⓣ (01904) 488800
Ⓦ www.breezyknees.co.uk

KEY
✉ Mail order to UK or EU — ⌂ Delivers to shows
✈ Exports beyond EU — € Euro accepted
♿ Accessible by wheelchair — ◆ See Display advertisement

N

**Contact:** Any member of staff
**Opening Times:** 1000-1700 7 days (open 1100 Sun), 1st Apr-15th Sep.
**Credit Cards:** All major credit/debit cards
**Specialities:** Very wide range of perennials. All can be viewed in 14-acre landscaped garden (open 24th May-15th Sep).
**Map Ref:** N, C3 **OS Grid Ref:** SE675565

NBro **Brownthwaite Hardy Plants** ⊠ ♠ ♿
Fell Yeat, Casterton, Kirkby Lonsdale, Lancashire, LA6 2JW
Ⓣ (01524) 271340 (after 1800).
Ⓦ www.hardyplantsofcumbria.co.uk
**Contact:** Chris Benson
**Opening Times:** 1000-1700, 1st Apr-30th Sep.
**Min Mail Order UK:** Nmc
Cat. Cost: 3 × 1st class for *Hydrangea* catalogue. Sae for auricula list.
**Credit Cards:** None
**Specialities:** Herbaceous perennials incl. *Geranium, Hosta,* also *Tiarella, Heucherella* & *Primula auricula.* Mail order for *Hydrangea.* Nat. Collection of *Ligularia.*
**Notes:** Follow brown signs from A65 between Kirkby Lonsdale & Cowan Bridge.
**Map Ref:** N, C1 **OS Grid Ref:** SD632794

NCGa **Caths Garden Plants** ⊠ ♠ ♿
The Walled Garden, Heaves Hotel, Heaves, Levens, Cumbria, LA8 8EF
Ⓣ (01539) 561126
Ⓕ (01539) 561126
Ⓔ cath@cathsgardenplants.fsbusiness.co.uk
Ⓦ www.cathsgardenplants.co.uk
**Contact:** Bob Sanderson
**Opening Times:** 1030-1630 Mon-Fri all year, except Xmas & New Year weeks. 1030-1700 Sat & Sun, Mar-Oct.
**Min Mail Order UK:** £15.00 + p&p
**Min Mail Order EU:** £25.00
**Cat. Cost:** Online only.
**Credit Cards:** All major credit/debit cards
**Specialities:** Wide variety of perennials, incl. uncommon varieties & selections of grasses, ferns, shrubs & climbing plants.
**Notes:** On A590 follow signs for Heaves (not in Levens village).
**Map Ref:** N, C1 **OS Grid Ref:** SD497867

NChi **Chipchase Castle Nursery** ⊠ ♠ ♿
Chipchase Castle, Wark, Hexham, Northumberland, NE48 3NT
Ⓣ (01434) 230083
Ⓜ 07881 630398
Ⓔ info@chipchaseplants.co.uk
Ⓦ www.chipchaseplants.co.uk
**Contact:** Joyce Hunt & Alison Jones
**Opening Times:** 1000-1700 Thu-Sun & B/hol Mons Easter (or 1st Apr)-end Aug.
**Min Mail Order UK:** Nmc
**Min Mail Order EU:** Nmc
**Cat. Cost:** A5 sae for list
**Credit Cards:** All major credit/debit cards
**Specialities:** Unusual herbaceous esp. *Eryngium, Geum, Geranium,* & *Penstemon.* Some plants only available in small quantities.
**Notes:** Suitable for accompanied wheelchair users.
**Map Ref:** N, B2 **OS Grid Ref:** NY880758

NChl **Chiltern Seeds** ⊠ ⊠ €
Bortree Stile, Ulverston, Cumbria, LA12 7PB
Ⓣ (01229) 581137 (24 hrs)
Ⓕ (01229) 584549
Ⓔ info@chilternseeds.co.uk
Ⓦ www.chilternseeds.co.uk
**Opening Times:** Mail order only. Normal office hours, Mon-Fri.
**Min Mail Order UK:** Nmc
**Min Mail Order EU:** Nmc
**Cat. Cost:** 3 × 2nd class.
**Credit Cards:** All major credit/debit cards
**Specialities:** Over 4,500 items of all kinds – wild flowers, trees, shrubs, cacti, annuals, houseplants, vegetables & herbs.

NChu **Churchtown Carnivores** ⊠ € ♿
8 Sandheys Drive, Churchtown, Southport, Merseyside, PR9 9PQ
Ⓣ (01704) 228175
Ⓜ 07928 567431
Ⓔ churchtowncarnivores@yahoo.co.uk
Ⓦ www.churchtowncarnivores.co.uk
**Contact:** Alan Leyland
**Opening Times:** By appt. only.
**Min Mail Order UK:** £10.00
**Min Mail Order EU:** £10.00
**Cat. Cost:** Online only.
**Credit Cards:** None
**Specialities:** Carnivorous plants. *Sarracenia, Dionaea muscipula* & forms, *Darlingtonia, Drosera.*
**Map Ref:** N, D1 **OS Grid Ref:** SD355183

NCot **Cottage Garden Plants** ⊠ €
1 Sycamore Close, Whitehaven, Cumbria, CA28 6LE
Ⓣ (01946) 695831
Ⓔ expressplants@aol.com
Ⓦ www.cottagegardenplants.com
**Contact:** Mrs J Purkiss
**Opening Times:** Open by appt. only for

collecting orders & viewing garden. Consult local press & radio for charity openings.
**Min Mail Order UK:** Nmc
**Min Mail Order EU:** Nmc
**Cat. Cost:** 4 × 1st class sae.
**Credit Cards:** Paypal
**Specialities:** Hardy perennials incl. *Crocosmia*, *Galanthus*, *Geranium*, *Primula*, *Schizostylis* & bog plants. Small quantities only. Nat. Collection of *Geranium phaeum* Group. Viewing by appt. & on specified Open Days (check local press & radio).
**Map Ref:** N, C1

NCro **Croston Cactus** ⊠ € ♿
43 Southport Road, Eccleston, Chorley, Lancashire, PR7 6ET
Ⓣ (01257) 452555
Ⓕ (01257) 452555
Ⓔ sales@croston-cactus.co.uk
Ⓦ www.croston-cactus.co.uk
**Contact:** John Henshaw
**Opening Times:** 0930-1700 by appt. only.
**Min Mail Order UK:** £5.00 + p&p
**Min Mail Order EU:** £10.00 + p&p
**Cat. Cost:** 2 × 1st class or 2 × IRCs.
**Credit Cards:** All major credit/debit cards
**Specialities:** Mexican cacti, *Echeveria* hybrids & some bromeliads & *Tillandsia*. Some items held in small quantities only. See catalogue.
**Notes:** Credit card payment accepted for online orders only.
**Map Ref:** N, D1 **OS Grid Ref:** SD522186

NDav **Dave Parkinson Plants** ⊠ ⛟
4 West Bank, Carlton, Goole, East Yorkshire, DN14 9PZ
Ⓣ (01405) 860693
Ⓜ 07773 564945
Ⓕ (01405) 860693
Ⓦ www.daveparkinsonplants.co.uk
**Contact:** Mary Parkinson
**Opening Times:** Not open. Mail order only.
**Min Mail Order UK:** £12 +p&p
**Credit Cards:** None
**Specialities:** Hardy orchids. Terrestrial South African *Disa* orchids, species & hybrids.

NDov **Dove Cottage Nursery & Garden** ⊠ ♿
Shibden Hall Road, Halifax, West Yorkshire, HX3 9XA
Ⓣ (01422) 203553
Ⓔ info@dovecottagenursery.co.uk
Ⓦ www.dovecottagenursery.co.uk
**Contact:** Stephen & Kim Rogers
**Opening Times:** 1000-1700 Tue-Sun & B/hols Mar-Dec or by appt. at other times.
**Min Mail Order UK:** £20.00
**Min Mail Order EU:** £20.00
**Cat. Cost:** 6 × 2nd class.
**Credit Cards:** All major credit/debit cards
**Specialities:** Herbaceous perennials & selected grasses, many displayed in adjoining naturalistic garden.
**Map Ref:** N, D2 **OS Grid Ref:** SE115256

NDro **Drointon Nurseries** ⊠ ✈ ⛟
Plaster Pitts, Norton Conyers, Ripon, North Yorkshire, HG4 5EF
Ⓣ (01765) 641849
Ⓜ 07909 971529
Ⓕ (01765) 640888
Ⓔ info@auricula-plants.co.uk
Ⓦ www.auricula-plants.co.uk
**Contact:** Robin & Annabel Graham
**Opening Times:** Open days in spring, otherwise by appt. only.
**Min Mail Order UK:** Nmc
**Min Mail Order EU:** Nmc
**Cat. Cost:** 4 × 1st class.
**Credit Cards:** All major credit/debit cards
**Specialities:** *Primula auricula*. More than 800 cvs of show, alpine, double & border auriculas. Ltd stocks of any one cultivar. Nat. Collection of *Primula auricula* (borders).
**Map Ref:** N, C2 **OS Grid Ref:** SE315753

NEgg **Eggleston Hall Gardens** € ♿
Eggleston, Barnard Castle, Co. Durham, DL12 0AG
Ⓣ (01833) 650115
Ⓕ (01833) 650971
Ⓔ mbhock@btinternet.com
Ⓦ www.plantsmanscorner.co.uk
**Contact:** Malcolm Hockham
**Opening Times:** 1000-1700 7 days. Closed Xmas Day, Boxing Day & New Year's Day only.
**Cat. Cost:** Online only.
**Credit Cards:** All major credit/debit cards
**Notes:** Collection from nursery only.

NEqu **Equatorial Plant Co.** ⊠ ✈ ⛟ €
7 Gray Lane, Barñard Castle, Co. Durham, DL12 8PD
Ⓣ (01833) 690519
Ⓕ (01833) 690519
Ⓔ equatorialplants@teesdaleonline.co.uk
Ⓦ www.equatorialplants.com
**Contact:** Dr Richard Warren

KEY
⊠ Mail order to UK or EU ⛟ Delivers to shows
✈ Exports beyond EU € Euro accepted
♿ Accessible by wheelchair ◆ See Display advertisement

**Opening Times:** By appt. only.
**Min Mail Order UK:** Nmc
**Min Mail Order EU:** Nmc
**Cat. Cost:** Free.
**Credit Cards:** Visa, Access
**Specialities:** Laboratory-raised orchids only.
**Notes:** Also sells wholesale.

**NExo** **EXOTIC UNUSUAL.CO.UK** ⊠ ✈
8 Hoskers Nook, Westhoughton, Bolton, Lancashire, BL5 2RS
Ⓣ (01942) 790027
Ⓔ info@exoticunusual.co.uk
Ⓦ www.exoticunusual.co.uk
**Contact:** Lou Davies
**Opening Times:** Not Open. Mail order only.
**Min Mail Order UK:** £15.00
**Cat. Cost:** Online only.
**Credit Cards:** All major credit/debit cards
**Specialities:** Rare, exotic & unusual plants, particularly *Cestrum*, chillies & ornamental grasses. Some plants in small quantities only.

N

**NFir** **FIR TREES PELARGONIUM NURSERY** ⊠ ♿
Stokesley, Middlesbrough, Cleveland, TS9 5LD
Ⓣ (01642) 713066
Ⓕ (01642) 713066
Ⓔ mark@firtreespelargoniums.co.uk
Ⓦ www.firtreespelargoniums.co.uk
**Contact:** Helen Bainbridge
**Opening Times:** 1000-1600 7 days 1st Apr-31st Aug, 1000-1600 Mon-Fri 1st Sep-31st Mar.
**Min Mail Order UK:** £3.75 + p&p
**Cat. Cost:** 4 × 1st class or £1.00 coin.
**Credit Cards:** All major credit/debit cards
**Specialities:** All types of *Pelargonium* – fancy leaf, regal, decorative regal, oriental regal, angel, miniature, zonal, ivy leaf, stellar, scented, dwarf, unique, golden stellar & species. Also dieramas.
**Map Ref:** N, C2

**NGBl** **GARDEN BLOOMS** ⊠ ♿
Fieldgate, Mill Field Road, Fishlake, Doncaster, Yorkshire, DN7 5GH
Ⓣ 0845 5440964
Ⓔ info@gardenblooms.co.uk
Ⓦ www.gardenblooms.co.uk
**Contact:** Liz Webster
**Opening Times:** Thu-Sun, Mar-Sep. Please check website for exact dates.
**Min Mail Order UK:** Nmc
**Cat. Cost:** A5 sae or online.
**Credit Cards:** None
**Specialities:** Hardy & tender perennials & ornamental grasses. Available in small quantities only.
**Notes:** Credit cards accepted online only.
**Map Ref:** N, D2 **OS Grid Ref:** SE659148

**NGBo** **GARDENERS BOUTIQUE (FORMERLY PLANTS OF SPECIAL INTEREST)** ⊠ ♿
4 High Street, Braithwell, Nr Rotherham, South Yorkshire, S66 7AL
Ⓣ (01709) 790642
Ⓕ (01709) 790342
Ⓦ www.gardenersboutique.co.uk
**Contact:** Leisha Dunstan
**Opening Times:** 1000-1700 Tue-Sun, Jan-Dec. Closed Mons.
**Cat. Cost:** None issued.
**Credit Cards:** Switch, Visa, MasterCard, Maestro
**Specialities:** Wide range of herbaceous perennials, trees & shrubs.
**Notes:** Gift shop. Restaurant. RHS Gold Medal, garden design.
**Map Ref:** N, D2

**NGdn** **GARDEN HOUSE NURSERY** ♿
The Square, Dalston, Carlisle, Cumbria, CA5 7LL
Ⓣ (01228) 710297
Ⓔ stephickso@hotmail.co.uk
Ⓦ www.gardenhousenursery.co.uk
**Contact:** Stephen Hickson
**Opening Times:** 0900-1700 7 days Mar-Oct.
**Cat. Cost:** Plant list online only.
**Credit Cards:** None
**Specialities:** *Geranium*, *Hosta*, *Hemerocallis*, *Iris*, grasses & bamboos.
**Notes:** Also sells wholesale.
**Map Ref:** N, B1 **OS Grid Ref:** NY369503

**NHal** **HALLS OF HEDDON** ⊠ ✈
West Heddon Nurseries, Heddon-on-the-Wall, Northumberland, NE15 0JS
Ⓣ (01661) 852445
Ⓕ (01661) 852398
Ⓔ enquiry@hallsofheddon.co.uk
Ⓦ www.hallsofheddon.co.uk
**Contact:** David Hall
**Opening Times:** 0900-1700 Mon-Sat 1000-1700 Sun.
**Min Mail Order UK:** £10.00
**Min Mail Order EU:** £25.00
**Cat. Cost:** 3 × 2nd class
**Credit Cards:** MasterCard, Visa, Switch, Delta
**Specialities:** *Chrysanthemum* & *Dahlia*.
**Notes:** Also sells wholesale.
**Map Ref:** N, B2 **OS Grid Ref:** NZ122679

**NHar** **HARTSIDE NURSERY GARDEN** ✉ ⛺
Nr Alston, Cumbria, CA9 3BL
Ⓣ (01434) 381372
Ⓕ (01434) 381372
Ⓔ enquiries@plantswithaltitude.co.uk
Ⓦ www.plantswithaltitude.co.uk
**Contact:** S L & N Huntley
**Opening Times:** 1130-1630 Mon-Fri, 1230-1600 Sat, Sun & B/hols, mid Mar-31st Oct. All other times & winter by appt. Times may vary during show season, so please phone before travelling.
**Min Mail Order UK:** Nmc
**Min Mail Order EU:** £50.00 + p&p
**Cat. Cost:** 4 × 1st class or 3 × IRC
**Credit Cards:** All major credit/debit cards
**Specialities:** Alpines grown at altitude of 1100 feet in Pennines. *Primula*, ferns, *Gentian* & *Meconopsis*.
**Map Ref:** N, B1 **OS Grid Ref:** NY708447

**NHaw** **THE HAWTHORNES NURSERY** ✉ ♿
Marsh Road, Hesketh Bank, Nr Preston, Lancashire, PR4 6XT
Ⓣ (01772) 812379
Ⓔ richardhaw@talktalk.net
Ⓦ www.hawthornes-nursery.co.uk
**Contact:** Irene & Richard Hodson
**Opening Times:** 0900-1800 7 days 1st Mar-30th Jun, Thu-Sun July-Oct. Gardens open for NGS.
**Min Mail Order UK:** £10.00
**Cat. Cost:** None issued.
**Credit Cards:** None
**Specialities:** *Clematis*, honeysuckle, choice selection of shrub & climbing roses, extensive range of perennials, mostly on display in the garden. Nat. Collection of *Clematis viticella*.
**Map Ref:** N, D1

**NHer** **HERTERTON HOUSE GARDEN NURSERY**
Hartington, Cambo, Morpeth, Northumberland, NE61 4BN
Ⓣ (01670) 774278
**Contact:** Mrs M Lawley & Mr Frank Lawley
**Opening Times:** 1330-1730 Mon, Wed, Fri-Sun 1st Apr-end Sep. (Earlier or later in the year weather permitting.)
**Cat. Cost:** None issued.
**Credit Cards:** None
**Specialities:** Country garden flowers.
**Map Ref:** N, B2 **OS Grid Ref:** NZ022880

**NHim** **THE HIMALAYAN GARDEN CO.** ✉ € ♿
The Hutts, Grewelthorpe, Ripon, Yorkshire, HG4 3DA
Ⓣ (01765) 658009
Ⓕ (01765) 658912
Ⓔ info@himalayangarden.com
Ⓦ www.himalayangarden.com
**Contact:** Peter Roberts
**Opening Times:** 1000-1600, Tue-Sun & B/hol Mon, mid Apr-mid Jun. During the rest of the year by appt. only.
**Min Mail Order UK:** £10.00 to £15.00
**Min Mail Order EU:** £50.00
**Cat. Cost:** Free.
**Credit Cards:** All major credit/debit cards
**Specialities:** Rare and unusual species & hybrid rhododendrons, azaleas, magnolias & *Cornus*, as well as other Himalayan plants.
**Notes:** Limited wheelchair access. Also sells wholesale.
**Map Ref:** N, C2 **OS Grid Ref:** SE218769

N

**NHol** **HOLDEN CLOUGH NURSERY LTD.** ✉ ✈ ⛺ ♿
Holden, Bolton-by-Bowland, Clitheroe, Lancashire, BB7 4PF
Ⓣ (01200) 447615
Ⓔ info@holdencloughnursery.co.uk
Ⓦ www.holdencloughnursery.co.uk
**Contact:** John Foley
**Opening Times:** 0900-1630 Mon-Fri Mar-Oct & B/hol Mons, 0900-1630 Sat all year. Nov-Feb by appt. only.
**Min Mail Order UK:** Nmc
**Min Mail Order EU:** Nmc
**Cat. Cost:** Free
**Credit Cards:** All major credit/debit cards
**Specialities:** Large general list incl. perennials, esp. *Crocosmia*, *Astilbe* & *Hosta*, shrubs, dwarf conifers, alpines, heathers, grasses & ferns.
**Notes:** Seasonal mail order on some items. Also sells wholesale.
**Map Ref:** N, C2 **OS Grid Ref:** SD773496

**NHoy** **HOYLAND PLANT CENTRE** ✉ ✈ ⛺ € ♿
54 Greenside Lane, Hoyland, Barnsley, Yorkshire, S74 9PZ
Ⓣ (01226) 744466
Ⓜ 07717 182169
Ⓕ (01226) 744466
Ⓔ stevenhickman@btconnect.com
Ⓦ www.somethingforthegarden.co.uk
**Contact:** Steven Hickman
**Opening Times:** All year round by appt. only.
**Min Mail Order UK:** Nmc
**Min Mail Order EU:** Nmc
**Cat. Cost:** 4 × 1st class.

KEY
✉ Mail order to UK or EU ⛺ Delivers to shows
✈ Exports beyond EU € Euro accepted
♿ Accessible by wheelchair ◆ See Display advertisement

**Credit Cards:** All major credit/debit cards
**Specialities:** *Agapanthus* (400+ cvs) & *Tulbaghia* (80+ cvs). Some available in small quantities only. Nat. Collections of *Agapanthus* & *Tulbaghia* (Provisional).
**Notes:** Daily practical workshops available, ring for details. Also sells wholesale.
**Map Ref:** N, D2 **OS Grid Ref:** SE372010

**NLan** **Landlife Wildflowers Ltd** ⊠ ♿
National Wildflower Centre, Court Hey Park, Liverpool, L16 3NA
Ⓣ (0151) 737 1819
Ⓕ (0151) 737 1820
Ⓔ gill@landlife.org.uk
Ⓦ www.wildflower.org.uk
**Contact:** Gillian Watson
**Opening Times:** 1000-1700, 7 days, 1st Mar-31st Aug.
**Min Mail Order UK:** £30.00 plants, no min. for seeds.
**Cat. Cost:** Free.
**Credit Cards:** Visa, Delta, Access, Switch, Solo
**Specialities:** Wild herbaceous plants & seeds.
**Notes:** Cafe & shop. Visitor centre, admission charge. Also sells wholesale.
**Map Ref:** N, D1

**NLAp** **Laneside Hardy Orchid Nursery** ⊠ ⌂ € ♿
74 Croston Road, Garstang, Preston, Lancashire, PR3 1HR
Ⓣ (01995) 605537
Ⓜ 07946 659661
Ⓔ jcrhutch@aol.com
Ⓦ www.lanesidehardyorchids.com
**Contact:** Jeff Hutchings
**Opening Times:** Please contact nursery for general & special opening days. Orders can be taken at Shows. Shows list on website.
**Min Mail Order UK:** £35.00
**Min Mail Order EU:** £50.00
**Cat. Cost:** Sae.
**Credit Cards:** All major credit/debit cards
**Specialities:** 100+ species of hardy terrestrial orchids plus composts & cultivation notes.
**Notes:** Mail order for orchids only during the winter. Lists updated every month. Also hardy orchid composts & pumice from the nursery or from shows if ordered.
**Map Ref:** N, D1

**NLar** **Larch Cottage Nurseries** ⊠ € ♿ ◆
Melkinthorpe, Penrith, Cumbria, CA10 2DR
Ⓣ (01931) 712404
Ⓕ (01931) 712727
Ⓔ plants@larchcottage.co.uk
Ⓦ www.larchcottage.co.uk
**Contact:** Peter Stott & Joanne McCullock
**Opening Times:** Daily from 1000-1730 (or dusk in winter), all year round.
**Min Mail Order UK:** Nmc
**Min Mail Order EU:** Nmc
**Cat. Cost:** £7.00
**Credit Cards:** All major credit/debit cards
**Specialities:** Comprehensive plant collection in unique garden setting. Rare & unusual plants; particularly shrubs, trees, perennials, dwarf conifers & Japanese maples. *Acer, Hamamelis, Magnolia* & *Cornus kousa* cvs. Old-fashioned roses, bamboo & alpines.
**Notes:** Terraced restaurant & art gallery.
**Map Ref:** N, C1 **OS Grid Ref:** NY315602

**NLBP** **L.B. Plants** ⊠ ⌂ ♿
Whitworth Hall Country Park, Spennymoor, Co. Durham, DH16 7QX
Ⓜ 079321 59204 or 077478 95096
Ⓔ enquiries@lbplants.co.uk
Ⓦ www.lbplants.co.uk
**Contact:** Howard Leslie & Sharon Bartle
**Opening Times:** 1000-1800 (or sunset in winter), 7 days.
**Min Mail Order UK:** Nmc
**Cat. Cost:** 3 × 1st class.
**Credit Cards:** None
**Specialities:** Hardy herbaceous & shrubby perennials, incl. lesser known and harder to find plants.
**Notes:** Also sells wholesale.
**Map Ref:** N, B2

**NLLv** **Leeds Lavender** ⊠ ♿
at Greenscapes Nursery, Brandon Crescent, Shadwell, Leeds, LS17 9JH
Ⓣ (0113) 2892922
Ⓜ 07778 839706
Ⓔ ruth@rdorrington.freeserve.co.uk
Ⓦ www.greenscapesnursery.co.uk
**Contact:** Ruth Dorrington
**Opening Times:** 1000-1700, Mon-Sun, Feb-Nov. 1200-1600 Mon-Sun, Nov/Dec/Jan.
**Min Mail Order UK:** Nmc
**Cat. Cost:** 2 × 1st class.
**Credit Cards:** None
**Specialities:** *Lavandula.* Limited numbers of particular varieties available at certain times, esp. at end of summer.
**Notes:** Wheelchair access difficult in some areas. Plug plants only by mail order.
**Map Ref:** N, D2

**NMen** **Mendle Nursery** ⊠ ⌂ ♿
Holme, Scunthorpe, North Lincolnshire, DN16 3RF
Ⓣ (01724) 850864

Ⓔ annearnshaw@lineone.net
Ⓦ www.mendlenursery.com
**Contact:** Mrs A Earnshaw
**Opening Times:** 1000-1600 Tue-Sun.
**Min Mail Order UK:** Nmc
**Min Mail Order EU:** Nmc
**Cat. Cost:** 3 × 1st class.
**Credit Cards:** All major credit/debit cards
**Specialities:** Many unusual alpines esp. *Saxifraga* & *Sempervivum*.
**Map Ref:** N, D3 **OS Grid Ref:** SE925070

NMil **Millthorpe Nursery**
(Office) 74 Meadowhead, Sheffield, Yorkshire, S8 7UE
Ⓣ 0114 258 4007
Ⓜ 07899 963939
Ⓦ www.millthorpenursery.co.uk
**Contact:** John & Anne Dawson
**Opening Times:** 0900-1630 Tue-Sat, 1000-1630 Sun. Closed Mon, except B/hols. Open by appt. only in Jan & Feb.
**Credit Cards:** None
**Specialities:** Good range of shrubs, herbaceous, ferns, grasses & edibles.
**Notes:** Nursery at Millthorpe Lane, Millthorpe, near Holmesfield, Derbyshire S18 7SA.
**Map Ref:** N, D2 **OS Grid Ref:** SK321767

NMin **Miniature Bulbs & Wildflower Bulbs** ⊠ ⛫ €
The Warren Estate, 9 Greengate Drive, Knaresborough, North Yorkshire, HG5 9EN
Ⓣ (01423) 542819
Ⓕ (01423) 542819
Ⓦ www.miniaturebulbs.co.uk
**Contact:** Ivor Fox
**Opening Times:** Not open. Mail order only.
**Min Mail Order UK:** £10.00
**Min Mail Order EU:** £15.00
**Cat. Cost:** 2 × 1st class.
**Credit Cards:** All major credit/debit cards
**Specialities:** Rare & unusual miniature & wildflower bulbs, incl. *Narcissus, Tulipa, Iris, Crocus, Fritillaria* & others. Spring bulb list sent out in April. Some stock in small quantities.

NMir **Mires Beck Nursery** ⊠ ♿
Low Mill Lane, North Cave, Brough, East Riding, Yorkshire, HU15 2NR
Ⓣ (01430) 421543
Ⓕ (01430) 421543
Ⓔ admin@miresbeck.co.uk
Ⓦ www.miresbeck.co.uk
**Contact:** Judy Burrow & Martin Rowland
**Opening Times:** 1000-1600 Mon-Sat 1st Mar-30th Sep. 1000-1500 Mon-Fri 1st Oct-30th Nov & by appt.
**Min Mail Order UK:** Nmc
**Min Mail Order EU:** Nmc
**Cat. Cost:** 3 × 1st class.
**Credit Cards:** None
**Specialities:** Wildflower plants of Yorkshire provenance.
**Notes:** Mail order for wildflower plants, plugs & seeds only. Also sells wholesale.
**Map Ref:** N, D3 **OS Grid Ref:** SE889316

NMRc **Millrace Nursery** ♿
84 Selby Road, Garforth, Leeds, LS25 1LP
Ⓣ (0113) 286 9233
Ⓕ (0113) 286 9908
Ⓔ carol@millrace-plants.co.uk
Ⓦ www.millrace-plants.co.uk
**Contact:** C Carthy
**Opening Times:** 1000-1700 Tue, Thu & Sat & by appt.
**Cat. Cost:** 4 × 1st class.
**Credit Cards:** None
**Specialities:** Unusual perennials, especially drought-resistant, incl. hardy geraniums, alliums, campanulas, penstemnons, potentillas & veronicas. Some plants in small quantities only.
**Map Ref:** N, D2

NMun **Muncaster Castle** ⊠ ♿
Ravenglass, Cumbria, CA18 1RQ
Ⓣ (01229) 717614
Ⓕ (01229) 717010
Ⓔ info@muncasterplantcentre.co.uk
Ⓦ www.muncasterplantcentre.co.uk
**Contact:** Jason Haine
**Opening Times:** 1030-1700, 7 days, 10th Feb-5th Nov. Other times by appt.
**Min Mail Order UK:** Nmc
**Cat. Cost:** 2 × 1st class.
**Credit Cards:** All major credit/debit cards
**Specialities:** Hardy plants. *Rhododendron, Camellia, Magnolia*. Some rarer varieties may be in limited supply.
**Notes:** Mail order mainly Oct-Apr.
**Map Ref:** N, C1 **OS Grid Ref:** SD103964

NMyG **Mary Green** ⊠ ⛫ ♿
The Walled Garden, Hornby, Lancaster, Lancashire, LA2 8LD
Ⓣ (01524) 221989
Ⓜ 07778 910348

KEY
⊠ Mail order to UK or EU ⛫ Delivers to shows
✈ Exports beyond EU € Euro accepted
♿ Accessible by wheelchair ◆ See Display advertisement

N

Ⓕ (01524) 221989
Ⓔ Marygreenplants@aol.com
**Contact:** Mary Green
**Opening Times:** By appt. only.
**Min Mail Order UK:** £10.00
**Cat. Cost:** 4 × 1st class.
**Credit Cards:** None
**Specialities:** Hostas, astilbes, ferns & other shade-loving perennials.
**Map Ref:** N, C1 **OS Grid Ref:** SD588688

**NNor** **NORCROFT NURSERIES** ⊠ ♿
Roadends, Intack, Southwaite, Carlisle, Cumbria, CA4 0LH
Ⓣ (01697) 473933
Ⓔ stellagbell@btinternet.com
**Contact:** Keith Bell
**Opening Times:** Every afternoon excl. Mon (open B/hol), Mar-Oct, or ring for appt.
**Min Mail Order UK:** Nmc
**Cat. Cost:** 2 × 2nd class
**Credit Cards:** None
**Specialities:** Hardy herbaceous, *Dianthus, Aquilegia*, hostas, *Lilium*, *Papaver*.
**Map Ref:** N, B1 **OS Grid Ref:** NY474433

N

**NOaD** **OAK DENE NURSERIES** ⊠ ⌂
10 Back Lane West, Royston, Barnsley, South Yorkshire, S71 4SB
Ⓣ (01226) 722253
**Contact:** J Foster or G Foster
**Opening Times:** 0900-1800 1st Apr-30th Sep, 1000-1600 1st Oct-31st Mar. (Closed 1230-1330.)
**Min Mail Order UK:** Phone for details.
**Min Mail Order EU:** Phone for details.
Cat. Cost: 1 × 2nd class for *Lithops* list.
**Credit Cards:** None
**Specialities:** Cacti, succulents (*Lithops*) & South African bulbs.
**Notes:** Also sells wholesale.
**Map Ref:** N, D2

**NOak** **OAK TREE NURSERY** ⊠ ♿
Mill Lane, Barlow, Selby, North Yorkshire, YO8 8EY
Ⓣ (01757) 618409
Ⓔ gill@oaktreenursery.plus.com
Ⓦ www.oaktreenursery.com
**Contact:** Gill Plowes
**Opening Times:** By appt. only.
**Min Mail Order UK:** £10.00 + p&p
**Min Mail Order EU:** Nmc
**Cat. Cost:** 4 × 1st class.
**Credit Cards:** None
**Specialities:** Ornamental grasses & grass-like plants.
**Notes:** Will export seeds only beyond the EU.

**NOrc** **ORCHARD HOUSE NURSERY**
Orchard House, Wormald Green, Nr Harrogate, North Yorkshire, HG3 3NQ
Ⓣ (01765) 677541
Ⓕ (01765) 677541
**Contact:** Mr B M Corner
**Opening Times:** 0800-1630 Mon-Fri. Closed B/hols.
**Cat. Cost:** 4 × 1st class.
**Credit Cards:** None
**Specialities:** Herbaceous perennials, ferns, grasses, bog plants & unusual cottage garden plants.
**Notes:** Also sells wholesale.
**Map Ref:** N, C2

**NPal** **THE PALM FARM** ⊠ € ♿
Thornton Hall Gardens, Station Road, Thornton Curtis, Nr Ulceby, Humberside, DN39 6XF
Ⓣ (01469) 531232
Ⓕ (01469) 531232 (please phone first)
Ⓔ bill@thepalmfarm.co.uk
Ⓦ www.thepalmfarm.co.uk
**Contact:** W W Spink
**Opening Times:** 1400-1700 7 days. Please phone first in winter.
**Min Mail Order UK:** £11.00 + p&p
**Cat. Cost:** 1 × 2nd class.
**Credit Cards:** None
**Specialities:** Hardy & half-hardy palms, unusual trees, shrubs & conservatory plants. Some plants available only in small quantities.
**Notes:** Euro payment accepted only if purchaser pays bank commission. Mail order only if small enough to go by post (min. charge £12.50 p&p) or large enough to go by Palletline (min. charge £39.00 p&p). Also sells wholesale.
**Map Ref:** N, D3 **OS Grid Ref:** TA100183

**NPCo** **PLANTSMAN'S CORNER**
Sunniside, Barningham, Richmond, Yorkshire, DL11 7DW
Ⓜ 07707 694310
Ⓔ plantsmanscorner@btinternet.com
Ⓦ www.plantsmanscorner.co.uk
**Contact:** Malcolm Hockham
**Opening Times:** Not yet fully open. Visits by appt. only. Plant orders can be collected by prior arrangement or from Eggleston Hall Gardens (see nursery NEgg for opening hours). Please contact nursery for details.
**Credit Cards:** All major credit/debit cards
**Specialities:** *Cornus*, *Ilex*, & Japanese maples. Variable stock levels.

NPer **Perry's Plants** € ♿
The River Garden, Sleights, Whitby, North Yorkshire, YO21 1RR
Ⓣ (01947) 810329
Ⓜ 07879 498623
Ⓔ sharon.perry@virgin.net
Ⓦ www.perrysplants.co.uk
**Contact:** Pat & Richard Perry
**Opening Times:** 1000-1700 mid-March to Oct.
**Cat. Cost:** Large (A4) sae.
**Credit Cards:** None
**Specialities:** *Lavatera*, *Malva*, *Erysimum*, *Euphorbia*, *Anthemis*, *Osteospermum* & *Hebe*. Uncommon hardy & container plants & aquatic plants.
**Map Ref:** N, C3 **OS Grid Ref:** NZ869082

NPla **The Plant Directory (formerly Scawsby Hall Nurseries)** ✉
Barnsley Road, Scawsby, Doncaster, South Yorkshire, DN5 7UB
Ⓣ (01302) 783434
Ⓔ mail@the-plant-directory.com
Ⓦ www.the-plant-directory.com
**Contact:** David Lawson
**Opening Times:** Not open. Mail order only.
**Min Mail Order UK:** Nmc
**Cat. Cost:** None issued
**Credit Cards:** Maestro, Visa, MasterCard, Solo, Paypal
**Specialities:** A wide range of herbaceous perennials, hardy trees, shrubs & indoor plants. Some indoor & aquatic plants in small quantities only.

NPnk **Primrose Bank** ✉ ⌂ ♿
Redroofs, Dauby Lane, Kexby, Yorkshire, YO41 5LH
Ⓣ (01759) 380220
Ⓜ 07774 944447
Ⓔ sue.goodwill@yahoo.co.uk
Ⓦ www.primrosebank.co.uk
**Contact:** Sue Goodwill
**Opening Times:** 1000-1700, Thu-Sun, 1st Apr-30th Jun. Every day in Dec. By appt. only at other times.
**Min Mail Order UK:** Nmc
**Cat. Cost:** 4 × 1st class
**Credit Cards:** All major credit/debit cards
**Specialities:** Unusual hardy perennials, woodland garden & shade-tolerant plants. *Astrantia*, *Echinacea* & *Heuchera*.
**Map Ref:** N, C3 **OS Grid Ref:** SE695508

NPri **Primrose Cottage Nursery** ♿
Ringway Road, Moss Nook, Wythenshawe, Manchester, M22 5WF
Ⓣ (0161) 437 1557
Ⓔ info@primrosecottagenursery.co.uk
Ⓦ www.primrosecottagenursery.co.uk
**Contact:** Caroline Dumville
**Opening Times:** 0830-1730 Mon-Sat, 0930-1730 Sun (summer). 0830-1700 Mon Sat, 0930-1700 Sun (winter).
**Cat. Cost:** 1 × 80p stamp or by email.
**Credit Cards:** All major credit/debit cards
**Specialities:** Hardy herbaceous perennials, alpines, herbs, roses, patio & hanging basket plants. Shrubs, ornamental trees, fruit trees, soft fruit bushes & vegetable plants.
**Notes:** Coffee shop open daily.
**Map Ref:** N, D2

NPro **ProudPlants** ⌂ ♿
East of Eden Nurseries, Ainstable, Carlisle, Cumbria, CA4 9QN
Ⓣ (01768) 896604
Ⓜ 07788 142969
Ⓔ rogereastofeden@hotmail.com
**Contact:** Roger Proud
**Opening Times:** By appt. only, Mar-Oct.
**Cat. Cost:** None issued
**Credit Cards:** None
**Specialities:** Interesting & unusual shrubs, perennials & alpines, esp. astilbes and geums.
**Map Ref:** N, B1 **OS Grid Ref:** NY467504

NRib **Ribblesdale Nurseries** ♿
Newsham Hall Lane, Woodplumpton, Preston, Lancashire, PR4 0AS
Ⓣ (01772) 863081
Ⓕ (01772) 861884
Ⓔ philsd@btinternet.com
Ⓦ www.ribblesdalenurseries.co.uk
**Contact:** Mr & Mrs Dunnett
**Opening Times:** 0900-1800 Mon-Sat, Apr-Sep. 0900-1700 Mon-Sat, Oct-Mar. 1030 1630 Sun.
**Credit Cards:** Visa, MasterCard, Delta, Switch
**Specialities:** Trees, shrubs & perennials. Conifers, hedging, alpines, fruit, climbers, herbs, aquatics, ferns & wildflowers.

NRob **W Robinson & Sons Ltd** ✉ ✈ € ♿
Sunny Bank, Forton, Nr Preston, Lancashire, PR3 0BN
Ⓣ (01524) 791210
Ⓕ (01524) 791933
Ⓔ info@mammothonion.co.uk
Ⓦ www.mammothonion.co.uk

KEY
✉ Mail order to UK or EU ⌂ Delivers to shows
✈ Exports beyond EU € Euro accepted
♿ Accessible by wheelchair ◆ See Display advertisement

N

**Contact:** Miss Robinson
**Opening Times:** 0900-1600 7 days Mar-Jun, 0800-1700 Mon-Fri Jul-Feb.
**Min Mail Order UK:** Nmc
**Min Mail Order EU:** Nmc
**Cat. Cost:** Free.
**Credit Cards:** Visa, Access, American Express, Switch
**Specialities:** Mammoth vegetable seed. Onions, leeks, tomatoes & beans. Range of vegetable plants in the spring.
**Notes:** Also sells wholesale.

**NRya** **RYAL NURSERY**
East Farm Cottage, Ryal, Northumberland, NE20 0SA
Ⓣ (01661) 886562
Ⓔ alpines@ryal.freeserve.co.uk
**Contact:** R F Hadden
**Opening Times:** 1000-1600 Sun Mar-Jul & other times by appt.
**Cat. Cost:** Sae.
**Credit Cards:** None
**Specialities:** Alpine & woodland plants. Mainly available in small quantities only. Nat. Collection of *Primula marginata*.
**Notes:** Also sells wholesale.
**Map Ref:** N, B2 **OS Grid Ref:** NZ015744

**NSla** **SLACK TOP NURSERIES** €
Hebden Bridge, West Yorkshire, HX7 7HA
Ⓣ (01422) 845348
Ⓔ enquiries@slacktopnurseries.co.uk
Ⓦ www.slacktopnurseries.co.uk
**Contact:** Michael Mitchell
**Opening Times:** 1000-1700 Fri-Sun 1st Mar-30th Sep & B/hols. Other times by appt.
**Min Mail Order UK:** £30.00
**Cat. Cost:** 2 × 1st class A5 sae or online.
**Credit Cards:** None
**Specialities:** Alpine & rockery plants incl. *Celmisia semi-cordata, Saxifraga, Hepatica* & native primrose.
**Notes:** Some areas of garden inaccessible for wheelchairs. Talks given to gardening clubs & other groups by appt.
**Map Ref:** N, D2 **OS Grid Ref:** SD977286

**NSti** **STILLINGFLEET LODGE NURSERIES**
Stewart Lane, Stillingfleet, North Yorkshire, YO19 6HP
Ⓣ (01904) 728506
Ⓕ (01904) 728506
Ⓔ vanessa.cook@stillingfleetlodgenurseries.co.uk
Ⓦ www.stillingfleetlodgenurseries.co.uk
**Contact:** Vanessa Cook
**Opening Times:** 1300-1700 Wed & Fri 3rd Apr-30th Sep. 1300-1700, 1st & 3rd Sat & Sun in each month.
**Cat. Cost:** Online only.
**Credit Cards:** None
**Specialities:** Foliage & unusual perennials. Hardy geraniums, *Pulmonaria*, variegated plants & grasses, interesting climbers.

**NSum** **SUMMERDALE GARDEN NURSERY**
Summerdale House, Cow Brow, Lupton, Carnforth, Lancashire, LA6 1PE
Ⓣ (01539) 567210
Ⓔ summerdalenursery@btinternet.com
Ⓦ www.summerdalegardenplants.co.uk
**Contact:** Gail Sheals
**Opening Times:** 0930-1630 Thu, Fri & Sat, 1st Feb-31st Oct. Other times by appt. only.
**Cat. Cost:** 4 × 1st class.
**Credit Cards:** All major credit/debit cards
**Specialities:** Wide variety of pernnials, large collection of *Primula*. Many moist and shade-loving plants incl. *Meconopsis* & hellebores.
**Map Ref:** N, C1 **OS Grid Ref:** SD545819

**NTay** **TAYLORS CLEMATIS NURSERY**
Sutton Road, Sutton, Nr Askern, Doncaster, South Yorkshire, DN6 9JZ
Ⓣ (01302) 700716
Ⓕ (01302) 708415
Ⓔ info@taylorsclematis.co.uk
Ⓦ www.taylorsclematis.co.uk
**Contact:** Chris & Suzy Cocks
**Opening Times:** Open by appt. only. Please ring for details.
**Min Mail Order UK:** Nmc
**Min Mail Order EU:** Nmc
**Cat. Cost:** 4 × 2nd class.
**Credit Cards:** All major credit/debit cards
**Specialities:** *Clematis* (over 300 varieties).
**Map Ref:** N, D2 **OS Grid Ref:** SE552121

**NVic** **THE VICARAGE GARDEN**
Carrington, Manchester, M31 4AG
Ⓣ (0161) 775 2750
Ⓕ (0161) 775 2750
Ⓔ info@vicaragebotanicalgardens.co.uk
Ⓦ www.vicaragebotanicalgardens.co.uk
**Contact:** Daniel Alexander
**Opening Times:** 0900-1700 Mon-Sat, closed Thu. 1000-1630 Sun all year.
**Min Mail Order UK:** £9.00
**Cat. Cost:** Online only.
**Credit Cards:** All, except American Express
**Specialities:** Herbaceous, alpines, grasses, ferns.
**Notes:** Free admission to 5-acre garden with coffee shop & mini zoo.
**Map Ref:** N, D2 **OS Grid Ref:** SJ729926

NWad **Waddow Lodge Garden** ✉ ♿
Clitheroe Road, Waddington,
Clitheroe, Lancashire,
BB7 3HQ
Ⓣ (01200) 429145
Ⓔ peterfoleyhen@hotmail.co.uk
Ⓦ www.gardentalks.co.uk
**Contact:** Peter Foley
**Opening Times:** By appt. only all year.
**Min Mail Order UK:** Nmc
**Min Mail Order EU:** nmc
**Cat. Cost:** Online only.
**Credit Cards:** Visa, MasterCard, Delta
**Specialities:** A developing plantsman's garden with a wide ranging interesting plant collection.
**Notes:** Open for group visits by appt., incl. evenings.
**Map Ref:** N, C1 **OS Grid Ref:** SD732434

NWCA **White Cottage Alpines** ✉ ♿
Sunnyside Nurseries, Hornsea Road,
Sigglesthorne, East Yorkshire,
HU11 5QL
Ⓣ (01964) 542692
Ⓜ 07792 761662
Ⓔ plants@whitecottagealpines.co.uk
Ⓦ www.whitecottagealpines.co.uk
**Contact:** Sally E Cummins
**Opening Times:** By appt. only for collection of plants. Please phone first.
**Min Mail Order UK:** Nmc
**Min Mail Order EU:** £15.00 + p&p by card only.
**Cat. Cost:** 4 × 1st class.
**Credit Cards:** Visa, MasterCard, Switch
**Specialities:** Alpines & rock garden plants. Range of American alpines, dwarf willows & an increasing range of South African alpines incl. *Tulbaghia*.
**Notes:** Euro payments by card only.
**Map Ref:** N, C3

NWea **Weasdale Nurseries Ltd.** ✉
Newbiggin-on-Lune, Kirkby Stephen,
Cumbria, CA17 4LX
Ⓣ (01539) 623246
Ⓕ (01539) 623277
Ⓔ sales@weasdale.com
Ⓦ www.weasdale.com
**Contact:** Andrew Forsyth
**Opening Times:** 0830-1730 Mon-Fri. Closed w/ends, B/hols, Xmas through to the New Year.
**Min Mail Order UK:** Nmc
**Min Mail Order EU:** Nmc
**Cat. Cost:** Free of charge in UK or £2.00 to EU.
**Credit Cards:** All major credit/debit cards
**Specialities:** Hardy forest trees, hedging, broadleaved & conifers. Specimen trees & shrubs grown at 850 feet (260 metre) elevation.
**Notes:** Mail order a speciality. Mail order Nov-Apr only. Also sells wholesale to VAT registered customers.
**Map Ref:** N, C1 **OS Grid Ref:** NY690039

NWit **D S Witton** ✉
26 Casson Drive, Harthill, Sheffield,
Yorkshire, S26 7WA
Ⓣ (01909) 771366
Ⓕ (01909) 771366
Ⓔ donshardyeuphorbias@btopenworld.com
Ⓦ www.euphorbias.co.uk
**Contact:** Don Witton
**Opening Times:** By appt. only. Open Day, 1300-1600, Sun 9th May 2010.
**Min Mail Order UK:** Nmc
**Cat. Cost:** 1 × 1st class + sae.
**Credit Cards:** None
**Specialities:** Nat. Collection of Hardy *Euphorbia*. Over 130 varieties.
**Notes:** Mail order plants, Oct-Feb. Mail order seed Oct-June.
**Map Ref:** N, D2 **OS Grid Ref:** SK494812

NWsh **Westshores Nurseries** ✉
82 West Street, Winterton, Lincolnshire,
DN15 9QF
Ⓣ (01724) 733940
Ⓔ westshnur@aol.com
Ⓦ www.westshores.co.uk
**Contact:** Gail & John Summerfield
**Opening Times:** 1st Mar-31st Oct by appt. only.
**Min Mail Order UK:** £15.00
**Credit Cards:** All major credit/debit cards
**Specialities:** Ornamental grasses.
**Map Ref:** N, D3 **OS Grid Ref:** SE927187

NWyk **Wykeham Mature Plants** ✉ €
The Walled Garden, Wykeham Abbey,
Scarborough, N. Yorkshire, YO13 9QS
Ⓣ (01723) 862406
Ⓕ (01723) 865643
Ⓔ m.howe@wykeham.co.uk
Ⓦ www.wykehammatureplants.co.uk
**Contact:** Martin Howe
**Opening Times:** 0930-1630 Mon-Sat, 1030-1500 Sun, Mar May & Nov. Closed throughout Xmas.

KEY
✉ Mail order to UK or EU — Delivers to shows
Exports beyond EU — € Euro accepted
♿ Accessible by wheelchair — ◆ See Display advertisement

N

**Min Mail Order UK:** Nmc
**Cat. Cost:** None issued.
**Credit Cards:** All, except American Express
**Specialities:** Trees, shrubs, hedging as mature plants for instant effect.
**Notes:** Large stock only. Delivery by pallet or large haulage wagon, heavy stock. Also sells wholesale.
**Map Ref:** N, C3 **OS Grid Ref:** SE959818

## SOUTHERN

**SAdn** **ASHDOWN FOREST GARDEN CENTRE & NURSERY** ♿
Duddleswell, Ashdown Forest, Nr Uckfield, East Sussex, TN22 3JP
Ⓣ (01825) 712300
Ⓦ www.ashdownforestgardencentre.co.uk
**Contact:** Gill Tolton
**Opening Times:** 0900-1700 winter, 0900-1800 summer.
**Credit Cards:** All major credit/debit cards
**Specialities:** Ornamental grasses, *Lapageria*, *Lavandula*, fuchsias, conservatory climbers, unusual shrubs. Allotment suppliers.
**Notes:** Also sells wholesale.
**Map Ref:** S, C4 **OS Grid Ref:** TQ468283

**SAga** **AGAR'S NURSERY (FORMERLY BLUEBELL COTTAGE)** € ♿
Agars Lane, Hordle, Lymington, Hampshire, SO41 0FL
Ⓜ 07508 848010
**Contact:** Diana Tombs
**Opening Times:** 1000-1700 (closed Thu), Mar-Sep. Open most days but please phone first.
**Specialities:** *Penstemon* & *Salvia*. Also wide range of hardy plants incl. hardy & tender shrubs, climbers & herbaceous. Many plants not listed may be available.
**Map Ref:** S, D2 **OS Grid Ref:** SZ275960

**SAll** **ALLWOODS** ⊠ ♿
London Road, Hassocks, West Sussex, BN6 9NB
Ⓣ (01273) 844229
Ⓔ info@allwoods.net
Ⓦ www.allwoods.net
**Contact:** David & Emma James
**Opening Times:** Office: 0900-1630 Mon-Fri. Answer machine all other times. Nursery: 1st Mar-30th Jun 7 days.
**Min Mail Order UK:** Nmc
**Min Mail Order EU:** Nmc
**Cat. Cost:** 2 × 1st class.
**Credit Cards:** Access, Visa, MasterCard, Switch, Maestro
**Specialities:** *Dianthus* incl. hardy border carnations, pinks, perpetual flowering carnations, Malmaisons & *D. allwoodii*, some available as seed. Certain lavender varieties. Penstemons.
**Notes:** All listed varieties available as plugs but choice varies depending on time of year. Please phone before travelling to avoid disappointment.
**Map Ref:** S, D4 **OS Grid Ref:** TQ303170

**SApp** **APPLE COURT** ⊠ € ♿
Hordle Lane, Hordle, Lymington, Hampshire, S041 0HU
Ⓣ (01590) 642130
Ⓕ (01590) 644220
Ⓔ applecourt@btinternet.com
Ⓦ www.applecourt.com
**Contact:** Angela & Charles Meads
**Opening Times:** 1000-1700 Fri, Sat, Sun & B/hol 1st Mar-31st Oct. Closed Nov-Feb.
**Min Mail Order UK:** Nmc
**Min Mail Order EU:** Nmc
**Cat. Cost:** 4 × 1st class.
**Credit Cards:** All major credit/debit cards
**Specialities:** *Hemerocallis*, *Hosta*, grasses & ferns.
**Map Ref:** S, D2 **OS Grid Ref:** SZ270941

**SArc** **ARCHITECTURAL PLANTS** ⊠ € ♿
Cooks Farm, Nuthurst, Horsham, West Sussex, RH13 6LH
Ⓣ (01403) 891772
Ⓕ (01403) 891056
Ⓔ enquiries@architecturalplants.com
Ⓦ www.architecturalplants.com
**Contact:** Sarah Chandler
**Opening Times:** 0900-1700 Mon-Sat, closed Sun.
**Min Mail Order UK:** Nmc
**Min Mail Order EU:** Nmc, restricted by delivery costs & conditions.
**Cat. Cost:** Free
**Credit Cards:** All major credit/debit cards
**Specialities:** Architectural plants & hardy exotics & rare broadleaved trees, bamboos, spiky plants, ferns & climbers.
**Notes:** Ltd selection of plants suitable for mail order, please ask. Also sells wholesale.

**SBch** **BIRCHWOOD PLANTS** ⌂ ♿
(Office) 10 Westering, Romsey, Hampshire, SO51 7LY
Ⓣ (01794) 502192 or (02380) 814345
Ⓔ info@birchwoodplants.co.uk
Ⓦ www.birchwoodplants.co.uk
**Contact:** Lesley Baker
**Opening Times:** Open on 2nd & 4th Fri & Sat in Mar & Apr, & every Fri-Sat in May

(incl. 30th Apr) 2010. Also open B/hol Mon 31st May. Plants can be collected by arrangement from nursery or from NCCPG sale at Longstock, Hants on 3rd May or HPS sale at Chandlers Ford on12th Jun. Further dates in Sep will be posted on website.
**Cat. Cost:** Online only.
**Credit Cards:** None
**Specialities:** Wide range of plants, mainly herbaceous, many unusual. Large range of Mottisfont herbaceous plants. Good selection of hardy geraniums, salvias & *Dianthus*. Scented plants & those to attract bees & butterflies. Drought-tolerant plants & some alpines. Some stock available in small quantities only.
**Notes:** Nursery at Silverwood House, Gardener's Lane, Nr Romsey, SO51 6AD. Mostly accessible for wheelchairs.
**Map Ref:** S, D2 **OS Grid Ref:** SU333190

SBfd **BIRCHFIELD NURSERY** ⊠ ♿
Kidders Lane, Henfield, West Sussex, BN5 9AB
Ⓣ (01273) 494058/491392
Ⓕ (01273) 493696
Ⓔ sales@birchfieldnursery.com
Ⓦ www.birchfieldnursery.com
**Contact:** Clive Parker or Joanne Peate
**Opening Times:** 0830-1700 Mon-Fri, 0930-1630 Sat & Sun, all year except Xmas/New Year period. For winter hours please phone first. Please phone before visiting to ensure plant availability & to check opening hours.
**Min Mail Order UK:** Nmc
**Cat. Cost:** Online only.
**Credit Cards:** All, except American Express
**Specialities:** Very wide general range of plants incl. many unusual & new varieties, plus fruit, young veg. plants & seasonal bedding. Some plants (esp. *Canna*) available in small quantities only.
**Notes:** Also sells wholesale.
**Map Ref:** S, D3 **OS Grid Ref:** TQ213178

SBHP **BLEAK HILL PLANTS** ♿
Braemoor, Bleak Hill, Harbridge, Ringwood, Hampshire, BH24 3PX
Ⓣ (01425) 652983
Ⓔ tracy@bleakhillplants.co.uk
**Contact:** Tracy Netherway
**Opening Times:** 0900-1800, Mon, Tue, Fri, Sat & 1000-1600 Sun, Mar-Oct. Closed Wed & Thu.
**Cat. Cost:** 2 × 1st class.
**Credit Cards:** None
**Specialities:** Hardy & half-hardy herbaceous perennials. Stock available in small quantities.
**Map Ref:** S, D1 **OS Grid Ref:** SU132111

SBig **BIG PLANT NURSERY** ⊠ ♿ ◆
Hole Street, Ashington, West Sussex, RH20 3DE
Ⓣ (01903) 891466
Ⓜ 07957 262845
Ⓕ (01903) 892829
Ⓔ info@bigplantnursery.co.uk
Ⓦ www.bigplantnursery.co.uk
**Contact:** Bruce Jordan
**Opening Times:** 0900-1700 Mon-Sat, 1000-1600 Sun & B/hols.
**Min Mail Order UK:** Please phone for further info.
**Cat. Cost:** A5 sae with 2 × 1st class.
**Credit Cards:** All major credit/debit cards
**Specialities:** Bamboos, hardy exotics & palms, *Ginkgo*, *Betula*.
**Notes:** Also sells wholesale.
**Map Ref:** S, D3 **OS Grid Ref:** TQ132153

S

SBir **BIRCHFLEET NURSERIES** ◆
Greenfields Close, Nyewood, Petersfield, Hampshire, GU31 5JQ
Ⓣ (01730) 821636
Ⓕ (01730) 821636
Ⓔ gammoak@aol.com
Ⓦ www.birchfleetnurseries.co.uk
**Contact:** John & Daphne Gammon
**Opening Times:** By appt. only. Please phone.
**Cat. Cost:** 2 × 1st class.
**Credit Cards:** None
**Specialities:** Oaks. Beech. *Carpinus*. Nat. Collection of *Liquidambar*.
**Notes:** Nursery accessible for wheelchairs in dry weather. Also sells wholesale.
**Map Ref:** S, C3

SBod **BODIAM NURSERY**
Bodiam, Robertsbridge, East Sussex, TN32 5RA
Ⓣ (01580) 830811
Ⓜ 07971 419302
Ⓔ enquiries@bodiamnursery.co.uk
Ⓦ www.bodiamnursery.co.uk
**Contact:** Jill Kaye
**Opening Times:** 1000-1600 Tue-Sun (closed Mon). Closed Jan.
**Cat. Cost:** None issued.
**Credit Cards:** All major credit/debit cards
**Specialities:** *Acer*, herbaceous perennials & grasses.

KEY
⊠ Mail order to UK or EU — Delivers to shows
Exports beyond EU — € Euro accepted
♿ Accessible by wheelchair — ◆ See Display advertisement

**SBrd** **BROADVIEW GARDEN CENTRE** ♿
Hadlow College, Hadlow, Tonbridge, Kent, TN11 0AL
Ⓣ (01732) 853211
Ⓕ (01732) 851169
Ⓔ broadviewgardens.co.uk
**Contact:** Denise Lowe
**Opening Times:** 0900-1700 Mon-Sat, 1000-1600 Sun. Closed Easter Sun & Xmas Day to New Year's Day.
**Cat. Cost:** None issued.
**Credit Cards:** All major credit/debit cards
**Specialities:** Many plants produced at own nursery & available in small quantities. Please ring to check availability before travelling. 8-acre garden, holding Nat. Collection of *Helleborus*, open free of charge 7 days a week.
**Notes:** Tearoom open 1000-1600. Also sells wholesale.
**Map Ref:** S, C4 **OS Grid Ref:** TQ627497

S

**SBri** **BRICKWALL COTTAGE NURSERY** ⊠ ♿
1 Brickwall Cottages, Frittenden, Cranbrook, Kent, TN17 2DH
Ⓣ (01580) 852425
Ⓜ 07714 529946
Ⓔ sue.martin@talktalk.net
**Contact:** Sue Martin
**Opening Times:** By appt. only.
**Min Mail Order UK:** Nmc
**Min Mail Order EU:** Nmc
**Credit Cards:** None
**Specialities:** Hardy perennials. Stock available in small quantities only. Nat. Collection of *Geum*.
**Map Ref:** S, C5 **OS Grid Ref:** TQ815410

**SBrk** **BROOKFIELD PLANTS** ⊠ ñ
Bigelle, Sandyhurst Lane, Ashford, Kent, TN25 4NX
Ⓣ (01233) 624934
Ⓜ 07944 213891
Ⓔ paulharris34@btinternet.com
Ⓦ www.brookfieldplants.com
**Contact:** Paul Harris
**Opening Times:** Visitors by appt. only.
**Min Mail Order UK:** Nmc
**Cat. Cost:** £1.00
**Credit Cards:** None
**Specialities:** *Hemerocallis* & *Hosta*.
**Notes:** Sells at shows.

**SBrm** **BRAMBLY HEDGE** ⊠
Mill Lane, Sway, Hampshire, SO41 8LN
Ⓣ (01590) 683570
**Contact:** Kim Williams
**Opening Times:** By appt. only.
**Min Mail Order UK:** Nmc
**Cat. Cost:** Sae for descriptive list.
**Credit Cards:** None
**Specialities:** Nat. Collection of *Streptocarpus*. Available in small quantities only.
**Notes:** Mail order Mar-Aug, small quantities only available.

**SBrt** **BRIGHTON PLANTS** ⊠ € ♿
3 Badger Copse, Henfield, Sussex, BN5 9HE
Ⓣ (01273) 491583
Ⓔ peganum1@yahoo.co.uk
Ⓦ http://brightonplants.blogspot.com
**Contact:** Steve Law
**Opening Times:** By appt. only.
**Min Mail Order UK:** Nmc
**Cat. Cost:** 2 × 1st class.
**Credit Cards:** None
**Specialities:** Hardy herbaceous and woody plants. Available in small quantities only.
**Map Ref:** S, D3 **OS Grid Ref:** TQ213167

**SBst** **BEAST PLANTS**
24 Arundel Road, Boyatt Wood, Eastleigh, Hampshire, SO50 4PQ
Ⓣ 02380 485307
Ⓜ 07887 997263
Ⓔ beastplants@tiscali.co.uk
**Contact:** Toni & Steve Newell
**Opening Times:** By appt. only.
**Cat. Cost:** Free.
**Credit Cards:** None
**Specialities:** Exotic, sub-tropical & unusual plants.

**SCac** **CACTI & SUCCULENTS** ⊠
Hammerfield, Crockham Hill, Edenbridge, Kent, TN8 6RR
Ⓣ (01732) 866295
**Contact:** Geoff Southon
**Opening Times:** Flexible. Please phone first.
**Min Mail Order UK:** Nmc
**Cat. Cost:** None issued.
**Credit Cards:** None
**Specialities:** *Echeveria* & related genera & hybrids. *Agave*, haworthias, aloes, gasterias & crassulas. A large range of aeoniums, both species & hybrids. A large range of plants available in small quantities.

**SCam** **CAMELLIA GROVE NURSERY** ⊠ ⊠ ñ € ♿
Market Garden, Lower Beeding, West Sussex, RH13 6PP
Ⓣ (01403) 891412
Ⓔ sales@camellia-grove.com
Ⓦ www.camellia-grove.com
**Contact:** Chris Loder
**Opening Times:** 1000-1600 Mon-Sat, please

phone first so we can give try to give you our undivided attention.
**Min Mail Order UK:** Nmc
**Min Mail Order EU:** Nmc
**Cat. Cost:** 2 × 1st class.
**Credit Cards:** All, except American Express
**Specialities:** Camellias & azaleas. Also rhododendrons & hydrangeas. Some in very ltd. quantities only.
**Notes:** Also sells wholesale.
**Map Ref:** S, C3 **OS Grid Ref:** TQ221255

SChF **CHARLESHURST FARM NURSERY** ⊠ € 
Loxwood Road, Plaistow, Billingshurst, West Sussex, RH14 0NY
Ⓣ (01403) 752273
Ⓜ 07736 522788
Ⓔ Charleshurstfarm@aol.com
Ⓦ www.charleshurstplants.co.uk
**Contact:** Clive Mellor
**Opening Times:** Normally 0900-1730 Fri, Sat, Sun, Feb-Oct, but please ring first before travelling.
**Min Mail Order UK:** Nmc
**Min Mail Order EU:** Nmc
**Cat. Cost:** 2 × 1st class.
**Credit Cards:** All major credit/debit cards
**Specialities:** Shrubs including some more unusual species. Good range of daphnes & Japanese maples.
**Map Ref:** S, C3 **OS Grid Ref:** TQ015308

SChr **JOHN CHURCHER** ⊠
47 Grove Avenue, Portchester, Fareham, Hampshire, PO16 9EZ
Ⓣ (023) 9232 6740
Ⓜ 07917 350928
Ⓔ churchers.47@tiscali.co.uk
**Contact:** John Churcher
**Opening Times:** By appt. only. Please phone or email.
**Min Mail Order UK:** Nmc
**Min Mail Order EU:** Nmc
**Cat. Cost:** None issued.
**Credit Cards:** None
**Specialities:** Hardy exotics for the Mediterranean-style garden, incl. palms, tree ferns, *Musa*, hedychiums, cycads, *Agave*, *Aloe*, *Opuntia* & echiums. Stock available in small quantities only.
**Map Ref:** S, D2 **OS Grid Ref:** SU614047

SCmr **CROMAR NURSERY** ⊠
39 Livesey Street, North Pole, Wateringbury, Maidstone, Kent, ME18 5BQ
Ⓣ (01622) 812380
Ⓔ CromarNursery@aol.com
Ⓦ www.cromarnursery.co.uk
**Contact:** Debra & Martin Cronk
**Opening Times:** 0930-1700 daily except Wed. Winter opening 0930-1630 Thu, Fri, Sat, Sun.
**Min Mail Order UK:** Nmc
**Min Mail Order EU:** Nmc
**Cat. Cost:** 2 × 1st class.
**Credit Cards:** All major credit/debit cards
**Specialities:** Ornamental & fruit trees.
**Map Ref:** S, C4 **OS Grid Ref:** TQ697547

SCnR **COLIN ROBERTS** ⊠
Tragumna, Morgay Wood Lane, Three Oaks, Guestling, East Sussex, TN35 4NF
Ⓜ 07933 060905
**Contact:** Colin Roberts
**Opening Times:** Not open. Mail order only.
**Min Mail Order UK:** £20.00
**Cat. Cost:** 2 × 1st class.
**Credit Cards:** None
**Specialities:** Dwarf bulbs & woodland plants incl. many rare & unusual, in small numbers.

SCog **COGHURST CAMELLIAS** ⊠ €
Ivy House Lane, Near Three Oaks, Hastings, East Sussex, TN35 4NP
Ⓣ (01424) 756228
Ⓔ rotherview@btinternet.com
Ⓦ www.rotherview.com
**Contact:** R Bates & W Bates
**Opening Times:** 0930-1600 7 days.
**Min Mail Order UK:** Nmc
**Min Mail Order EU:** Nmc
**Cat. Cost:** 6 × 1st class.
**Credit Cards:** All major credit/debit cards
**Specialities:** *Camellia*.
**Notes:** Nursery is on the same site as Rotherview Nursery. Also sells wholesale.
**Map Ref:** S, D5

SCoo **COOLING'S NURSERIES LTD**
Rushmore Hill, Knockholt, Sevenoaks, Kent, TN14 7NN
Ⓣ (01959) 532269
Ⓕ (01959) 534092
Ⓔ Plantfinder@coolings.co.uk
Ⓦ www.coolings.co.uk
**Contact:** Mark Reeve or Toby Davies
**Opening Times:** 0900-1700 Mon-Sat & 1000-1630 Sun.
**Cat. Cost:** None issued
**Credit Cards:** All, except American Express

KEY
⊠ Mail order to UK or EU — Delivers to shows
Exports beyond EU — € Euro accepted
Accessible by wheelchair — ◆ See Display advertisement

S

**Specialities:** Large range of perennials, conifers & bedding plants. Many unusual shrubs & trees. Third generation family business.
**Notes:** Display garden. Coffee shop.
**Map Ref:** S, C4 **OS Grid Ref:** TK477610

**SCrf** **Crofters Nurseries** € ♿
Church Hill, Charing Heath, Near Ashford, Kent, TN27 0BU
Ⓣ (01233) 712798
Ⓕ (01233) 712798
Ⓔ croftersnursery@yahoo.co.uk
**Contact:** John & Sue Webb
**Opening Times:** 1000-1700. Closed Sun-Tue. Please check first.
**Cat. Cost:** 3 × 1st class.
**Credit Cards:** None
**Specialities:** Fruit, ornamental trees. Old apple varieties. Small number of *Prunus serrula* with grafted ornamental heads.
**Map Ref:** S, C5 **OS Grid Ref:** TQ923493

**SDay** **A La Carte Daylilies** ⊠ €
Little Hermitage, St Catherine's Down, Nr Ventnor, Isle of Wight, PO38 2PD
Ⓣ (01983) 730512
Ⓔ andy@alacartedaylilies.co.uk
Ⓦ www.alacartedaylilies.co.uk
**Contact:** Jan & Andy Wyers
**Opening Times:** Mail order only. Open by appt. only. Difficult to find on an unmade private road.
**Min Mail Order UK:** Nmc
**Min Mail Order EU:** Nmc
**Cat. Cost:** 3 × 1st class.
**Credit Cards:** None
**Specialities:** *Hemerocallis*. Nat. Collections of Miniature & Small Flowered *Hemerocallis* & Large Flowered *Hemerocallis* (post-1960 award-winning cultivars).
**Map Ref:** S, D2 **OS Grid Ref:** SZ499787

**SDea** **Deacon's Nursery** ⊠ ✈ € ◆
Moor View, Godshill, Isle of Wight, PO38 3HW
Ⓣ (01983) 840750 (24 hrs) or (01983) 522243
Ⓕ (01983) 523575
Ⓔ info@deaconsnurseryfruits.co.uk
Ⓦ www.deaconsnurseryfruits.co.uk
**Contact:** G D & B H W Deacon
**Opening Times:** 0800-1600 Mon-Fri May-Sep, 0800-1700 Mon-Fri 0800-1200 Sat Oct-Apr.
**Min Mail Order UK:** Nmc
**Min Mail Order EU:** Nmc
**Cat. Cost:** Free.
**Credit Cards:** All major credit/debit cards
**Specialities:** Over 300 varieties of apple, old & new, pears, plums, gages, damsons, cherries. Modern soft fruit, grapes, hops, nuts & family trees.
**Notes:** Also sells wholesale.
**Map Ref:** S, D2

**SDeJ** **P. De Jager & Sons Ltd** ⊠ ✈ ♿ ◆
The Old Forge, Chartway Street, East Sutton, Maidstone, Kent, ME17 3DW
Ⓣ (01622) 840229
Ⓕ (01622) 844073
Ⓔ flowerbulbs@dejager.co.uk
Ⓦ www.dejager.co.uk
**Contact:** George Clowes
**Opening Times:** Mail order only. Orders taken from 0900-1700 Mon-Fri
**Min Mail Order UK:** Nmc
**Min Mail Order EU:** Nmc
**Cat. Cost:** Free
**Credit Cards:** All major credit/debit cards
**Specialities:** Complete range of all flower bulbs.
**Notes:** Also sells wholesale.

**SDix** **Great Dixter Nurseries** ⊠
Northiam, Rye, East Sussex, TN31 6PH
Ⓣ (01797) 253107
Ⓕ (01797) 252879
Ⓔ nursery@greatdixter.co.uk
Ⓦ www.greatdixter.co.uk
**Contact:** K Leighton
**Opening Times:** 0900-1700 Mon-Fri, 0900-1230 Sat all year. Also 1400-1700 Sat, Sun & B/hols Apr-Oct.
**Min Mail Order UK:** Nmc
**Min Mail Order EU:** Nmc
**Cat. Cost:** 5 × 1st class.
**Credit Cards:** All major credit/debit cards
**Specialities:** *Clematis*, shrubs and plants. Gardens open.
**Notes:** Plants dispatched Sep-Mar only. Partially accessible for wheelchairs.

**SDow** **Downderry Nursery** ⊠ ✈ € ♿
Pillar Box Lane, Hadlow, Nr Tonbridge, Kent, TN11 9SW
Ⓣ (01732) 810081
Ⓕ (01732) 811398
Ⓔ info@downderry-nursery.co.uk
Ⓦ www.downderry-nursery.co.uk
**Contact:** Dr Simon Charlesworth
**Opening Times:** 1000-1700 Tue-Sun 1st May-31st Oct & B/hols. Other times by appt.
**Min Mail Order UK:** Nmc
**Min Mail Order EU:** Nmc
**Cat. Cost:** 3 × 1st class.

**Credit Cards:** Delta, MasterCard, Maestro, Visa
**Specialities:** Nat. Collections of *Lavandula* and *Rosmarinus*.
**Map Ref:** S, C4 **OS Grid Ref:** TQ625521

SDys **Dysons Nurseries** ♿
Great Comp Garden, Platt, Sevenoaks, Kent, TN15 8QS
Ⓣ (01732) 885094
Ⓜ 07887 997663
Ⓔ dysonsnurseries@aol.com
Ⓦ www.greatcompgarden.co.uk
**Contact:** William T Dyson
**Opening Times:** 1100-1700 7 days 1st Apr-31st Oct. Other times by appt.
**Cat. Cost:** None issued.
**Credit Cards:** All major credit/debit cards
**Specialities:** Salvias & an eclectic range of choice and uncommon plants.
**Map Ref:** S, C4

SEND **East Northdown Farm Nursery** ☒ € ♿ ◆
Margate, Kent, CT9 3TS
Ⓣ (01843) 862060
Ⓜ 07714 241668
Ⓔ friend.northdown@btinternet.com
Ⓦ www.botanyplants.co.uk
**Contact:** Louise & William Friend
**Opening Times:** 0900-1700 Mon-Sat, 1000-1700 Sun all year. Closed Sun in Oct, Nov & Jan. Closed Xmas for 2 weeks.
**Min Mail Order UK:** Nmc
**Cat. Cost:** Online only.
**Credit Cards:** Visa, Switch, MasterCard
**Specialities:** Chalk & coast-loving plants.
**Notes:** Plants from nursery MMuc available for collection to order.
**Map Ref:** S, B6 **OS Grid Ref:** TR383702

SEWo **English Woodlands** ☒ ♿
Burrow Nursery, Herrings Lane, Cross-in-Hand, Heathfield, East Sussex, TN21 0UG
Ⓣ (01435) 862992
Ⓕ (01435) 867742
Ⓔ sales@englishwoodlands.com
Ⓦ www.englishwoodlands.com
**Contact:** Joanne Carter
**Opening Times:** 0800-1700 Mon-Fri. 0800-1630 Sat. Closed Sun & B/hols.
**Min Mail Order UK:** £25.00
**Cat. Cost:** Free.
**Credit Cards:** All, except American Express
**Specialities:** Trees, shrubs, hedging.
**Notes:** Also sells wholesale.
**Map Ref:** S, C4 **OS Grid Ref:** TQ567222

SFai **Fairweather's Garden Centre** ☒ ✈ € ♿
High Street, Beaulieu, Hampshire, SO42 7YB
Ⓣ (01590) 612307
Ⓕ (01590) 612519
Ⓔ info@fairweathers.co.uk
Ⓦ www.fairweathers.co.uk
**Contact:** Sue Greaves
**Opening Times:** 0930-1700 7 days.
**Min Mail Order UK:** Nmc
**Min Mail Order EU:** Nmc
**Cat. Cost:** None issued.
**Credit Cards:** Visa, MasterCard
**Specialities:** *Agapanthus*, *Heuchera* & *Lavandula*.
**Notes:** Also sells wholesale.
**Map Ref:** S, D2

SFam **Family Trees** ☒ ♿
Sandy Lane, Shedfield, Hampshire, SO32 2HQ
Ⓣ (01329) 834812
Ⓦ www.familytreesnursery.co.uk
**Contact:** Philip House
**Opening Times:** 0930-1230 Tue, Wed, Fri & Sat mid-Oct-end Apr (closed 20th Dec-10th Jan).
**Min Mail Order UK:** £10.00
**Cat. Cost:** Free
**Credit Cards:** None
**Specialities:** Fruit & ornamental trees. Trained fruit tree specialists: standards, espaliers, cordons. Other trees, old-fashioned & climbing roses, evergreens. Trees, except evergreens, sold bare-rooted.

SFgr **Firgrove Plants** ☒
24 Wykeham Field, Wickham, Fareham, Hampshire, PO17 5AB
Ⓣ (01329) 835206 after 1900 hours.
Ⓔ jenny@firgroveplants.demon.co.uk
Ⓦ www.firgroveplants.demon.co.uk
**Contact:** Jenny MacKinnon
**Opening Times:** Not open. Mail order only.
**Min Mail Order UK:** £7.00
**Cat. Cost:** Sae.
**Credit Cards:** None
**Specialities:** Wide range of houseleeks & smaller range of other alpines in small quantities.
**Notes:** Houseleeks by mail order Apr-mid Oct.

KEY
☒ Mail order to UK or EU · Delivers to shows
✈ Exports beyond EU · € Euro accepted
♿ Accessible by wheelchair · ◆ See Display advertisement

S

**SGar** **Garden Plants** ⊠
Windy Ridge, Victory Road, St Margarets-at-Cliffe, Dover, Kent, CT15 6HF
Ⓣ (01304) 853225
Ⓔ GardenPlants@GardenPlants-nursery.co.uk
Ⓦ www.GardenPlants-nursery.co.uk
**Contact:** Teresa Ryder & David Ryder
**Opening Times:** 1000-1730 summer, 1000-1700 winter. Closed Tue.
**Min Mail Order UK:** Nmc
**Cat. Cost:** 2 × 1st class + A5 sae.
**Credit Cards:** Visa, MasterCard
**Specialities:** Unusual perennials, *Penstemon* & *Salvia.*
**Notes:** Plantsman's garden open to view. Map essential for first visit.
**Map Ref:** S, C6 **OS Grid Ref:** TR358464

**SGol** **Golden Hill Nurseries** ⊠ € ♿
Lordsfield, Goudhurst Road, Marden, Kent, TN12 9LT
Ⓣ (01622) 833218
Ⓜ 07826 523655
Ⓕ (01622) 832528
Ⓔ enquiries@goldenhillplants.com
Ⓦ www.goldenhillplants.com
**Contact:** Roger Butler
**Opening Times:** 0900-1700 Mon-Sat, 1st Mar-31st Oct. 0900-1600 Mon-Sat, 1st Nov-28th Feb. 1100-1600 Suns from 3rd Sun in Feb until Xmas.
**Min Mail Order UK:** Nmc
**Cat. Cost:** Online only.
**Credit Cards:** All major credit/debit cards
**Specialities:** Specimen plants, shrubs, grasses, bamboos, Japanese maples, conifers & trees.
**Notes:** Also sells wholesale.

**SHar** **Hardy's Cottage Garden Plants** ⊠ ♿
Priory Lane Nursery, Freefolk Priors, Whitchurch, Hampshire, RG28 7NJ
Ⓣ (01256) 896533
Ⓕ (01256) 896572
Ⓔ info@hardys-plants.co.uk
Ⓦ www.hardys-plants.co.uk
**Contact:** Rosemary Hardy
**Opening Times:** 1000-1700 7 days, 1st Mar-30th Sep. 1000-1600 Mon-Fri, 1st Oct-31st Oct, 1000-1500 Mon-Fri, 1st Nov-28th Feb. Closed 23rd Dec-4th Jan 2010.
**Min Mail Order UK:** Nmc
**Cat. Cost:** 10 × 1st class.
**Credit Cards:** Visa, Access, Electron, Switch, Solo
**Specialities:** Wide range of herbaceous perennials incl. *Achillea*, *Alstroemeria*, *Geranium*, *Hemerocallis*, *Heuchera*, *Paeonia*, *Penstemon* & *Salvia.*
**Notes:** Accepts HTA Gift Tokens. Offers trade discount.
**Map Ref:** S, C2

**SHDw** **Highdown Nursery** ⊠ € ♿
New Hall Lane, Small Dole, Nr Henfield, West Sussex, BN5 9YH
Ⓣ (01273) 492976
Ⓜ 07900 956456
Ⓕ (01273) 492976
Ⓔ highdown.herbs@btopenworld.com
Ⓦ www.highdownnursery.com
**Contact:** A G & J H Shearing
**Opening Times:** 0900-1700 7 days.
**Min Mail Order UK:** £10.00 + p&p
**Min Mail Order EU:** £10.00 + p&p
**Cat. Cost:** 3 × 1st class.
**Credit Cards:** None
**Specialities:** Herbs. Grasses.
**Notes:** Partial wheelchair access. Also sells wholesale.
**Map Ref:** S, D3 **OS Grid Ref:** TV214134

**SHea** **Heaselands Garden Nursery** ⊠ €
The Old Lodge, Isaacs Lane, Haywards Heath, West Sussex, RH16 4SA
Ⓣ (01444) 458084
Ⓜ 07743 939490
Ⓕ (01444) 458084
Ⓔ headgardener@heaselandsnursery.co.uk
Ⓦ www.heaselandsnursery.co.uk
**Contact:** Stephen Harding
**Opening Times:** 0800-1700, Mon-Fri, but please phone first. W/ends by appt. only.
**Min Mail Order UK:** Nmc
**Min Mail Order EU:** Nmc
**Cat. Cost:** Online only. Monthly availability lists.
**Credit Cards:** None
**Specialities:** *Rhododendron* hybrids and deciduous azaleas, home-produced from cuttings. Some varieties in small quantities. Nat. Collection of Mollis Azaleas & Knaphill/Exbury Azaleas.
**Notes:** Also sells wholesale.
**Map Ref:** S, C4 **OS Grid Ref:** TQ314230

**SHeS** **The Heather Society (Plant Ordering Service)** ⊠ €
78 Woodland Way, West Wickham, Kent, BR4 9LR
Ⓣ 020 8777 5161
Ⓜ 07905 825818
Ⓔ allisonfitzearle@yahoo.co.uk
Ⓦ www.plant-orderingservice.co.uk
**Contact:** Allison Fitz-Earle
**Opening Times:** Not open. Mail order only.

**Min Mail Order UK:** Nmc
**Min Mail Order EU:** Nmc
**Cat. Cost:** Free.
**Credit Cards:** None
**Specialities:** Heathers.
**Notes:** Mail order plants available year round. Also sells wholesale.

SHeu **Heucheraholics (formerly Jooles Plants)** ⊠ ♠ ♿
(Office) The Paddock, Pilley Street, Pilley, Lymington, Hampshire, SO41 5QP
Ⓣ (01590) 670581
Ⓜ 07973 291062
Ⓔ jooles.heucheraholics@googlemail.com
Ⓦ www.heucheraholics.co.uk
**Contact:** Julie Burton
**Opening Times:** By appt. only. Please phone first.
**Min Mail Order UK:** Nmc
**Credit Cards:** All major credit/debit cards
**Specialities:** Heucheras, heucherellas & tiarellas. Other foliage plants. Some varieties only available in small quantities.
**Notes:** Nursery is located at Spring Hill Nurseries, Shirley Holms Road, Lymington, SO41 8NG.
**Map Ref:** S, D2 **OS Grid Ref:** SZ310934

SHmp **Hampshire Carnivorous Plants** ⊠ ✈ ♠ €
Ya-Mayla, Allington Lane, West End, Southampton, Hampshire, SO30 3HQ
Ⓣ (023) 8047 3314
Ⓜ 07703 258296
Ⓕ (023) 80473314
Ⓔ matthew@msoper.freeserve.co.uk
Ⓦ www.hantsflytrap.com
**Contact:** Matthew Soper
**Opening Times:** Mail order only. Open by appt. only.
**Min Mail Order UK:** Nmc
**Min Mail Order EU:** £50.00 + p&p
**Credit Cards:** All major credit/debit cards
**Specialities:** Carnivorous plants esp. *Nepenthes, Heliamphora, Sarracenia Pinguicula* & *Utricularia*.
**Notes:** Also sells wholesale.

SHom **Home Plants**
52 Dorman Ave North, Aylesham, Canterbury, Kent, CT3 3BW
Ⓣ (01304) 841746
Ⓔ homeplants@tiscali.co.uk
**Contact:** Stuart & Sue Roycroft
**Opening Times:** By appt. only, please phone first.
**Cat. Cost:** Sae for list.
**Credit Cards:** None
**Specialities:** *Phygelius* & unusual South African hardy plants. Limited stock, please phone first.

SHyH **Hydrangea Haven** ⊠ ✈ ♠ € ♿
Market Garden, Lower Beeding, West Sussex, RH13 6PP
Ⓣ (01403) 891412
Ⓔ sales@hydrangea-haven.com
Ⓦ www.hydrangea-haven.com
**Contact:** Chris Loder
**Opening Times:** 1000-1600 Mon-Sat, please phone first, so we can give you our undivided attention.
**Min Mail Order UK:** Nmc
**Min Mail Order EU:** Nmc
**Cat. Cost:** 2 × 1st class.
**Credit Cards:** All, except American Express
**Specialities:** *Hydrangea*. Some available in very ltd. quantities only.
**Notes:** Also sells wholesale.
**Map Ref:** S, C3 **OS Grid Ref:** TQ221255

SIde **Iden Croft Herbs** ⊠ ♿
Frittenden Road, Staplehurst, Kent, TN12 0DH
Ⓣ (01580) 891432
Ⓕ (01580) 892416
Ⓔ idencroftherbs@yahoo.co.uk
Ⓦ www.uk-herbs.com
**Contact:** Tracey Connors-Parry
**Opening Times:** 0900-1700 Mon-Sat & 1100-1700 Sun & B/hols, Mar-Sep. Closed Oct-Feb.
**Min Mail Order UK:** £10.00
**Min Mail Order EU:** £25.00
**Cat. Cost:** 4 × 1st class.
**Credit Cards:** All major credit/debit cards
**Specialities:** Herbs, aromatic & wildflower plants & plants for bees & butterflies. Nat. Collections of *Mentha, Nepeta* & *Origanum*.
**Notes:** Wheelchairs available at nursery.
**Map Ref:** S, C5

SIri **Iris of Sissinghurst** ⊠ ♠ € ◆
Roughlands Farm, Goudhurst Road, Marden, Kent, TN12 9NH
Ⓣ (01622) 831511
Ⓔ orders@irisofsissinghurst.com
Ⓦ www.irisofsissinghurst.com
**Contact:** Sue Marshall

KEY
⊠ Mail order to UK or EU ♠ Delivers to shows
✈ Exports beyond EU € Euro accepted
♿ Accessible by wheelchair ◆ See Display advertisement

S

**Opening Times:** Contact nursery or see website for opening times.
**Min Mail Order UK:** Nmc
**Min Mail Order EU:** Nmc
**Cat. Cost:** 2 × 1st class.
**Credit Cards:** None
**Specialities:** *Iris*, short, intermediate & tall bearded, *ensata*, *sibirica* & many species.
**Map Ref:** S, C4 **OS Grid Ref:** TQ735437

**SJoh** **Vic Johnstone and Claire Wilson** €
43 Winchester Street, Whitchurch, Hampshire, RG28 7AJ
Ⓣ (01256) 893144
**Contact:** Vic Johnstone, Claire Wilson
**Opening Times:** By appt. Please telephone first.
**Cat. Cost:** 2 × 1st class.
**Credit Cards:** None
**Specialities:** Former Nat. Collection of *Verbascum*. Stock available in small quantities.
**Map Ref:** S, C2 **OS Grid Ref:** SU463478

S

**SKee** **Keepers Nursery** ⊠
Gallants Court, Gallants Lane, East Farleigh, Maidstone, Kent, ME15 0LE
Ⓣ (01622) 726465
Ⓕ 0870 705 2145
Ⓔ info@keepers-nursery.co.uk
Ⓦ www.keepers-nursery.co.uk
**Contact:** Hamid Habibi
**Opening Times:** Only on a limited number of Open Days & for collection of trees & plants by arrangement.
**Min Mail Order UK:** Nmc
**Cat. Cost:** Online only.
**Credit Cards:** Visa, MasterCard, Switch, Maestro
**Specialities:** A very large range of fruit trees incl. old & rare varieties as well as modern varieties. Soft fruit plants & nut trees.
**Map Ref:** S, C4

**SKen** **Kent Street Nurseries** ⊠
Kent Street (A21), Sedlescombe, Battle, East Sussex, TN33 0SF
Ⓣ (01424) 751134
Ⓔ peter@1066-countryplants.co.uk
Ⓦ www.1066-countryplants.co.uk
**Contact:** P Stapley
**Opening Times:** 0900-1700 Mon-Sat, 1030-1600 Sun.
**Min Mail Order UK:** £12.00
**Cat. Cost:** 2 × 1st class.
**Credit Cards:** All major credit/debit cards
**Specialities:** *Pelargonium*, bedding & perennials.
**Notes:** Mail order *Pelargonium* list only. Credit cards not accepted for mail order. Nursery partially accessible for wheelchair users.

**SKHP** **Kevin Hughes Plants** ⊠ ✈ € ♿
(Office) 89 Ladysmith, East Gomeldon, Salisbury, Wiltshire, SP4 6LE
Ⓣ (01722) 782504
Ⓜ 07720 718671
Ⓕ (01772) 782504
Ⓔ info@kevinsplants.co.uk
Ⓦ www.kevinsplants.co.uk
**Contact:** Kevin Hughes
**Opening Times:** 1000-1700 Wed-Sun, 1st Feb-31st Oct. Other times by appt. only.
**Min Mail Order UK:** £10.00
**Min Mail Order EU:** £20.00
**Cat. Cost:** 3 × 1st class
**Credit Cards:** All, except American Express
**Specialities:** Less common & new hardy garden plants with a particular emphasis on *Magnolia*, *Trillium*, climbers, *Philadelphus*, *Viburnum* & *Syringa*. We try to select plants that are garden-worthy & attract wildlife. Many plants are slow to propagate & will always be in short supply. None are from wild-dug sources.
**Notes:** Nursery at Heale Garden, Middle Woodford, Salisbury, SP4 5NT.
**Map Ref:** S, C1 **OS Grid Ref:** SU125363

**SLau** **The Laurels Nursery** ⊠ €
Benenden, Cranbrook, Kent, TN17 4JU
Ⓣ (01580) 240463
Ⓕ (01580) 240463
Ⓦ www.thelaurelsnursery.co.uk
**Contact:** Peter or Sylvia Kellett
**Opening Times:** 0800-1600 Mon-Fri, 0900-1200 Sat, Sun by appt. only.
**Min Mail Order UK:** £27.00
**Cat. Cost:** Free.
**Credit Cards:** None
**Specialities:** Open ground & container ornamental trees, shrubs & climbers especially birch, beech & *Wisteria*.
**Notes:** Mail order of small *Wisteria* only. Also sells wholesale.
**Map Ref:** S, C5 **OS Grid Ref:** TQ815313

**SLay** **Layham Garden Centre & Nursery** ⊠ ♿
Lower Road, Staple, Nr Canterbury, Kent, CT3 1LH
Ⓣ (01304) 813267
Ⓕ (01304) 814007
Ⓔ info@layhamgardencentre.co.uk
Ⓦ www.layhamgardencentre.co.uk

**Contact:** Ellen Wessel
**Opening Times:** 0900-1700 7 days.
**Min Mail Order UK:** Nmc
**Min Mail Order EU:** £25.00 + p&p
**Cat. Cost:** Free.
**Credit Cards:** Visa, MasterCard, Maestro
**Specialities:** Roses, herbaceous, shrubs, trees & hedging plants.
**Notes:** Also sells wholesale.
**Map Ref:** S, C6 **OS Grid Ref:** TR276567

SLBF **Little Brook Fuchsias** ♿
Ash Green Lane West, Ash Green,
Nr Aldershot, Hampshire, GU12 6HL
Ⓣ (01252) 329731
Ⓔ carol.gubler@ntlbusiness.com
Ⓦ www.littlebrookfuchsias.co.uk
**Contact:** Carol Gubler
**Opening Times:** 1000-1700 Wed-Sun 1st Jan-4th Jul.
**Cat. Cost:** 50p + sae.
**Credit Cards:** All major credit/debit cards
**Specialities:** Fuchsias, old & new.
**Notes:** Nursery located off White Lane in Ash Green.
**Map Ref:** S, C3

SLdr **Loder Plants** ✉ ✈ ⌂ € ♿
Market Garden, Lower Beeding, West Sussex, RH13 6PP
Ⓣ (01403) 891412
Ⓔ sales@rhododendrons.com
Ⓦ www.rhododendrons.com
**Contact:** Chris Loder
**Opening Times:** 1000-1600 Mon-Sat, please ring first so we can try to give you our undivided attention.
**Min Mail Order UK:** Nmc
**Min Mail Order EU:** Nmc
**Cat. Cost:** 2 × 1st class.
**Credit Cards:** All, except American Express
**Specialities:** Rhododendrons & azaleas in all sizes. Some in very ltd. quantities only.
**Notes:** Also sells wholesale.
**Map Ref:** S, C3 **OS Grid Ref:** TQ221255

SLim **Lime Cross Nursery** ✉ ♿ ◆
Herstmonceux, Hailsham, East Sussex, BN27 4RS
Ⓣ (01323) 833229
Ⓕ (01323) 833944
Ⓔ info@limecross.co.uk
Ⓦ www.limecross.co.uk
**Contact:** Jonathan Tate, Anita Green
**Opening Times:** 0830-1700 Mon-Sat & 1000-1600 Sun.
**Min Mail Order UK:** Nmc
**Min Mail Order EU:** £50.00
**Cat. Cost:** Free of charge.
**Credit Cards:** All major credit/debit cards
**Specialities:** Conifers, trees & shrubs, climbers.
**Notes:** Also sells wholesale.
**Map Ref:** S, D4 **OS Grid Ref:** TQ642125

SLon **Longstock Park Nursery** ✉ € ♿
Longstock, Stockbridge, Hampshire, SO20 6EH
Ⓣ (01264) 810894
Ⓕ (01264) 810924
Ⓔ longstocknursery@leckfordestate.co.uk
Ⓦ www.longstocknursery.co.uk
**Contact:** Peter Moore
**Opening Times:** 0830-1630 Mon-Sat all year excl. Xmas & New Year, & 1100-1700 Sun Mar-Oct, 1000-1600 Sun, Nov-Feb.
**Min Mail Order UK:** Nmc
Cat. Cost: 2 × 1st class or email for lists of *Buddleja*, *Penstemon*, roses & fruit
**Credit Cards:** All major credit/debit cards
**Specialities:** A wide range, over 2000 varieties, of trees, shrubs, perennials, climbers, aquatics & ferns. Nat. Collections of *Buddleja* & *Clematis viticella*.
**Notes:** Mail order for *Buddleja* only.
**Map Ref:** S, C2 **OS Grid Ref:** SO365389

SLPl **Landscape Plants** ✉ ✈ ♿
Cattamount, Grafty Green, Maidstone, Kent, ME17 2AP
Ⓣ (01622) 850245
Ⓕ (01622) 858063
Ⓔ landscapeplants@aol.com
**Contact:** Tom La Dell
**Opening Times:** 0800-1600 Mon-Fri, by appt. only.
**Min Mail Order UK:** £100.00 + p&p
**Min Mail Order EU:** £200.00 + p&p
**Cat. Cost:** 2 × 1st class.
**Credit Cards:** None
**Specialities:** Garden & landscape shrubs & perennials.
**Notes:** Also sells wholesale.
**Map Ref:** S, C5 **OS Grid Ref:** TQ772468

SMad **Madrona Nursery** ✉ ⌂ € ♿
Pluckley Road, Bethersden, Kent, TN26 3DD
Ⓣ (01233) 820100
Ⓕ (01233) 820091
Ⓔ madrona@fsmail.net
Ⓦ www.madrona.co.uk

KEY
✉ Mail order to UK or EU ⌂ Delivers to shows
✈ Exports beyond EU € Euro accepted
♿ Accessible by wheelchair ◆ See Display advertisement

S

**Contact:** Liam MacKenzie
**Opening Times:** 1000-1700 Sat-Tue 13th Mar-2nd Nov. Closed 7th-17th Aug 2010.
**Min Mail Order UK:** Nmc
**Cat. Cost:** Free
**Credit Cards:** All major credit/debit cards
**Specialities:** Unusual shrubs, conifers & perennials. Eryngiums, *Pseudopanax*.
**Map Ref:** S, C5 **OS Grid Ref:** TQ918419

**SMDP** **MARCUS DANCER PLANTS** ⊠ ♠
Kilcreggan, Alderholt Road, Sandleheath, Fordingbridge, Hampshire, SP6 1PT
Ⓣ (01425) 652747
Ⓜ 07709 922730
Ⓔ marcus.dancer@btopenworld.com
Ⓦ clematisplants.co.uk
**Contact:** Marcus Dancer
**Opening Times:** By appointment only.
**Min Mail Order UK:** Nmc
**Cat. Cost:** 3 × 1st class.
**Credit Cards:** None
**Specialities:** Wide range of *Clematis*, smaller range of *Daphne*. Some varieties available in small quantities only.
**Map Ref:** S, D1

**SMea** **MEADOWGATE NURSERY** ⊠ ♠
Street End Lane, Sidlesham, Chichester, West Sussex, PO20 7RG
Ⓣ (01243) 641997
Ⓜ 07736 523262
Ⓔ meadowgatenursery@tiscali.co.uk
Ⓦ www.meadowgatenursery.co.uk
**Contact:** David Allen
**Opening Times:** 1000-1700 Sat-Wed.
**Min Mail Order UK:** Nmc
**Credit Cards:** All major credit/debit cards
**Specialities:** Ornamental grasses and complimentary perennials.

**SMrm** **MERRIMENTS GARDENS** ♿
Hawkhurst Road, Hurst Green, East Sussex, TN19 7RA
Ⓣ (01580) 860666
Ⓕ (01580) 860324
Ⓔ info@merriments.co.uk
Ⓦ www.merriments.co.uk
**Contact:** Taryn Murrells
**Opening Times:** 0900-1730 Mon-Sat, 1030-1730 Sun (or dusk in winter).
**Cat. Cost:** Online only.
**Credit Cards:** Visa, Access, American Express
**Specialities:** Extensive range of unusual perennials, tender perennials, grasses & annuals. Also large selection of roses & seasonal shrubs. 4-acre show garden.
**Map Ref:** S, C4

**SMrs** **MRS MITCHELL'S KITCHEN & GARDEN** ♠ €
2 Warren Farm Cottages, The Warren, West Tytherley, Salisbury, Wiltshire, SP5 1LU
Ⓣ (01980) 863101
Ⓔ julianm05@aol.com
Ⓦ www.mrsmitchellskitchenandgarden.co.uk
**Contact:** Louise Mitchell
**Opening Times:** Open by appt. only on Fri or some Sat.
**Cat. Cost:** Online only.
**Credit Cards:** None
**Specialities:** Family-run nursery stocking less usual cottage garden plants, esp. hardy geraniums, oriental poppies, *Phlox* Michaelmas daisies & *Chrysanthemum*. Some items in small quantities. Grown in peat-free compost.
**Notes:** Despite postal designation, nursery is in Hampshire. Accessible, but difficult, for wheelchairs because of deep gravel. Sells mostly at plant shows & Hampshire Farmers' Markets. See website for details of shows & markets attended.
**Map Ref:** S, C2 **OS Grid Ref:** SU261333

**SPad** **PADDOCK PLANTS** ⊠ ♠
The Paddock, Upper Toothill Road, Rownhams, Southampton, Hampshire, SO16 8AL
Ⓣ (023) 8073 9912
Ⓜ 07763 386717
Ⓔ rob@paddockplants.co.uk
Ⓦ www.paddockplants.co.uk
**Contact:** Robert Courtney
**Opening Times:** By appt. only. Please telephone in advance.
**Min Mail Order UK:** Nmc
**Cat. Cost:** Free.
**Credit Cards:** None
**Specialities:** Family-run nursery offering interesting range of perennials, grasses, ferns & shrubs, incl. some more unusual varieties. Some varieties grown in small quantities.
**Notes:** Online descriptive catalogue & ordering. Local delivery by our own transport.
**Map Ref:** S, D2 **OS Grid Ref:** SU383177

**SPav** **PAVILION PLANTS** ⊠
18 Pavilion Road, Worthing, West Sussex, BN14 7EF
Ⓣ (01903) 821338
Ⓔ rewrew18@hotmail.com
**Contact:** Andrew Muggeridge
**Opening Times:** Mail order only. Please phone for details.
**Min Mail Order UK:** Nmc
**Cat. Cost:** 4 × 1st class.

**Credit Cards:** None
**Specialities:** Perennials and bulbs. *Digitalis*.
**Notes:** Also sells wholesale.
**Map Ref:** S, D3

SPer **Perryhill Nurseries Ltd** ✉ ♿
Edenbridge Road, Hartfield, East Sussex, TN7 4JP
Ⓣ (01892) 770377
Ⓕ (01892) 770929
Ⓔ sales@perryhillnurseries.co.uk
Ⓦ www.perryhillnurseries.co.uk
**Contact:** P J Chapman
**Opening Times:** 0900-1700 7 days 1st Mar-31st Oct. 0900-1630 1st Nov-28th Feb.
**Min Mail Order UK:** Nmc
**Cat. Cost:** Online only.
**Credit Cards:** Maestro, Visa, Access, MasterCard
**Specialities:** Wide range of trees, shrubs, conifers, *Rhododendron* etc. Over 1300 herbaceous varieties, over 500 rose varieties. Unusual & rare plants may be available in small quantities.
**Notes:** Mail order despatch depends on size & weight of plants.
**Map Ref:** S, C4 **OS Grid Ref:** TQ480375

SPet **Pettet's Nursery** ♿
Poison Cross, Eastry, Sandwich, Kent, CT13 0EA
Ⓣ (01304) 613869
Ⓜ 07961 998354
Ⓕ (01304) 613869
Ⓔ terry@pettetsnursery.fsnet.co.uk
Ⓦ www.pettetsnursery.co.uk
**Contact:** T & E H P Pettet
**Opening Times:** 0900-1700 daily Mar-Jun. 1000-1600 Jul-Oct weekdays only.
**Credit Cards:** None
**Specialities:** *Clematis*, herbaceous perennials, pelargoniums, fuchsias.
**Map Ref:** S, C6

SPhx **Phoenix Perennial Plants** ♿
Paice Lane, Medstead, Alton, Hampshire, GU34 5PR
Ⓣ (01420) 560695
Ⓕ (01420) 563640
Ⓔ marina@phoenixperennialplants.co.uk
Ⓦ www.phoenixperennialplants.co.uk
**Contact:** Marina Christopher
**Opening Times:** 2010: 1100-1700 Fri & Sat 19th Mar-23rd Oct. 2011: 1100-1600 Fri & Sat 11th/12th Feb, 25th/26th Feb, 11th/12th Mar. 1100-1700 Fri & Sat 25th Mar-22nd Oct. Other times by appt. only.
**Cat. Cost:** 4 × 1st class.
**Credit Cards:** All major credit/debit cards
**Specialities:** Perennials, many uncommon. *Achillea*, *Eryngium*, hardy chrysanthemums, *Monarda*, *Phlox*, *Sanguisorba*, *Thalictrum*, *Verbascum*, centaureas, bulbs, prairie plants, grasses esp. *Molinia* & late-flowering perennials.
**Notes:** Co-located with Select Seeds SSss. Also sells wholesale.
**Map Ref:** S, C2 **OS Grid Ref:** SU657362

SPin **John and Lynsey's Plants** ♿
2 Hillside Cottages, Trampers Lane, North Boarhunt, Fareham, Hampshire, PO17 6DA
Ⓣ (01329) 832786
**Contact:** Mrs Lynsey Pink
**Opening Times:** By appt. only. Open under NGS.
**Cat. Cost:** None issued.
**Credit Cards:** None
**Specialities:** Mainly *Salvia* with a wide range of other unusual perennials. Stock available in small quantities only, we will be happy to try & propagate to order. Nat. Collection of *Salvia* species.
**Map Ref:** S, D2 **OS Grid Ref:** SU603109

SPlb **Plantbase** ✉ € ♿
Sleepers Stile Road, Cousley Wood, Wadhurst, East Sussex, TN5 6QX
Ⓣ (01892) 785599
Ⓜ 07967 601064
Ⓔ graham@plantbase.freeserve.co.uk
Ⓦ www.plantbase.co.uk
**Contact:** Graham Blunt
**Opening Times:** 1000-1700, 7 days all year (appt. advisable).
**Min Mail Order UK:** Nmc
**Min Mail Order EU:** Nmc
**Cat. Cost:** Online only.
**Credit Cards:** All major credit/debit cards
**Specialities:** Wide range of alpines, perennials, shrubs, climbers, waterside plants, herbs, Australasian, South African & South American plants in particular.
**Map Ref:** S, C5

SPoG **The Potted Garden Nursery** ♿
Ashford Road, Bearsted, Maidstone, Kent, ME14 4NH
Ⓣ (01622) 737801
Ⓦ www.thepottedgarden.co.uk

KEY
✉ Mail order to UK or EU — Delivers to shows
Exports beyond EU — € Euro accepted
♿ Accessible by wheelchair — ◆ See Display advertisement

S

**Contact:** Any staff member
**Opening Times:** 0900-1730 (dusk in winter) 7 days. Xmas/New Year period opening times on website or answerphone.
**Credit Cards:** All major credit/debit cards
**Notes:** Mail order not available.
**Map Ref:** S, C5 **OS Grid Ref:** TQ810550

SPol **Pollie's Perennials and Daylily Nursery** ⊠ € ♿
Lodore, Mount Pleasant Lane, Sway, Lymington, Hampshire, SO41 8LS
Ⓣ (01590) 682577
Ⓕ (01590) 682577
Ⓔ terry@maasz.fsnet.co.uk
Ⓦ www.polliesdaylilies.co.uk
**Contact:** Pollie Maasz
**Opening Times:** 1000-1730 w/ends & 1400-1730 Mon-Fri during the daylily season, late-May to mid-Aug. Other times by appt. only.
**Min Mail Order UK:** Nmc
**Min Mail Order EU:** £20.00
**Cat. Cost:** 2 × 1st class.
**Credit Cards:** None
**Specialities:** *Hemerocallis*, also less commonly available hardy perennials. Stock available in small quantities only. Nat. Collection of Spider & Unusual Form *Hemerocallis*. 1400+ different cvs can be viewed, mid Jun-mid Sep.
**Notes:** Mail order, daylilies only.
**Map Ref:** S, D2

SPop **Pops Plants** ⊠ ⊠ ♿ €
Pops Cottage, Barford Lane, Downton, Salisbury, Wiltshire, SP5 3PZ
Ⓣ (01725) 511421
Ⓔ mail@popsplants.com
Ⓦ www.popsplants.com
**Contact:** Gill Dawson
**Opening Times:** By appt. only.
**Min Mail Order UK:** 5 plants.
**Min Mail Order EU:** 5 plants.
**Cat. Cost:** £2.00
**Credit Cards:** None
**Specialities:** *Primula auricula*. Some varieties in ltd. numbers. Nat. Collection of Show, Alpine, Double & Striped Auriculas.
**Notes:** Credit cards accepted online only. Min. mail order outside EU, 10 plants.

SPPs **POGS Penstemons** ⊠ €
78 Woodland Way, West Wickham, Kent, BR4 9LR
Ⓣ 020 8777 5161
Ⓜ 07905 825818
Ⓔ alipog2004@yahoo.co.uk
Ⓦ www.pogspenstemons.co.uk
**Contact:** Allison Fitz-Earle
**Opening Times:** Not open. Mail order only.
**Min Mail Order UK:** Nmc
**Min Mail Order EU:** Nmc
**Cat. Cost:** Free.
**Credit Cards:** None
**Specialities:** Penstemons.
**Notes:** Mail order plants available all year. Also sells wholesale.

SPtl **Petals for Plants** ♿
Burwash Road, Broad Oak, Heathfield, East Sussex, TN21 8XG
Ⓣ (01435) 884111
Ⓔ pauleast@petalsforplants.co.uk
Ⓦ www.petalsforplants.co.uk
**Contact:** Paul East
**Opening Times:** 0900-1730 Mon-Sat, 1015-1630 Sun (summer). 0900-1700 Mon-Sat, 1015-1630 Sun (winter).
**Credit Cards:** All, except American Express
**Specialities:** Roses, shrubs, fruit trees, conifers & hellebores.
**Map Ref:** S, C4 **OS Grid Ref:** TQ6021

SPur **Pure Plants**
Blackboys Nursery, Blackboys, Uckfield, East Sussex, TN22 5LS
Ⓣ (01825) 890858
Ⓕ (01825) 890878
Ⓔ info@pureplants.com
Ⓦ www.pureplants.com
**Contact:** Brian Fidler
**Opening Times:** 0900-1700 Tue-Sat. Closed Sun & Mon except B/hol Mon 0900-1700.
**Cat. Cost:** 2 × 1st class.
**Credit Cards:** All major credit/debit cards
**Specialities:** Trees, shrubs, herbaceous, grasses & ferns. Many unusual varieties offered.
**Map Ref:** S, C4 **OS Grid Ref:** TQ515206

SReu **G Reuthe Ltd** ⊠
Crown Point Nursery, Sevenoaks Road, Ightham, Nr Sevenoaks, Kent, TN15 0HB
Ⓣ (01732) 810694
Ⓜ (01732) 865614
Ⓕ (01732) 862166
Ⓔ reuthe@hotmail.co.uk
**Contact:** C & P Tomlin
**Opening Times:** 0900-1600 Thu-Sat. Closed Jan, Jul & Aug.
**Min Mail Order UK:** £30.00 + p&p
**Min Mail Order EU:** £500.00
**Cat. Cost:** £2.50
**Credit Cards:** Visa, Access
**Specialities:** Rhododendrons & azaleas, trees, shrubs & climbers.
**Notes:** Mail order certain plants only to EU.
**Map Ref:** S, C4

S

**SRGP** **Rosie's Garden Plants** ⊠ ☒ ⛫
Fieldview Cottage, Pratling Street, Aylesford, Kent, ME20 7DG
Ⓣ (01622) 715777
Ⓜ 07740 696277
Ⓕ (01622) 715777
Ⓔ jcaviolet@aol.com
Ⓦ www.rosiesgardenplants.biz
**Contact:** J C Aviolet
**Opening Times:** Not open. Mail order only.
**Min Mail Order UK:** Nmc
**Min Mail Order EU:** Nmc
**Cat. Cost:** Online only.
**Credit Cards:** Visa, MasterCard, Switch
**Specialities:** Hardy *Geranium*, *Buddleja* & *Aster*. 'Named' herbaceous & shrubs. Roses.
**Notes:** Check web or catalogue for dates of shows, talks & Farmers Markets.

**SRiF** **Riverside Fuchsias** ⊠ ☒ ⛫ € ♿
Gravel Road, Sutton-at-Hone, Dartford, Kent, DA4 9HQ
Ⓣ (01322) 863891
Ⓕ (01322) 863891
Ⓔ riverside_fuchsias@btopenworld.com
Ⓦ www.riversidefuchsias.pwp.blueyonder.co.uk
**Contact:** George & Nellie Puddefoot
**Opening Times:** 0900-1700, Tue, Wed, Fri, Sat & Sun.
**Min Mail Order UK:** £1.50 per plant, 10 plants min. order (incl. p&p).
**Min Mail Order EU:** €20.00.
**Cat. Cost:** 3 × 1st class. Addendum available Mar.
**Credit Cards:** All major credit/debit cards
**Specialities:** *Fuchsia*. Nat. Collection holder.
**Notes:** Specimen-sized plants available May-end Jul.
**Map Ref:** S, B4

**SRiv** **River Garden Nurseries** ⊠ €
Troutbeck, Otford, Sevenoaks, Kent, TN14 5PH
Ⓣ (01959) 525588
Ⓕ (01959) 525810
Ⓔ box@river-garden.co.uk
Ⓦ www.river-garden.co.uk
**Contact:** Jenny Alban Davies
**Opening Times:** By appt. only.
**Min Mail Order UK:** £10.00 + p&p
**Min Mail Order EU:** £50.00 + p&p
**Cat. Cost:** 2 × 1st class.
**Credit Cards:** All major credit/debit cards
**Specialities:** *Buxus* species, cultivars & *Buxus* hedging. *Buxus* topiary.
**Notes:** Also sells wholesale.
**Map Ref:** S, C4 **OS Grid Ref:** TQ523593

**SRkn** **Rapkyns Nursery** ⊠ ⛫ ♿
Street End Lane, Broad Oak, Heathfield, East Sussex, TN21 8UB
Ⓣ (01825) 830065
Ⓜ 07771 916933
Ⓕ (01825) 830065
Ⓔ rapkyns@homecall.co.uk
Ⓦ www.rapkynsnursery.co.uk
**Contact:** Steven & Fiona Moore
**Opening Times:** 1000-1700 Tue, Thu & Fri, Mar-Oct incl.
**Min Mail Order UK:** Nmc
**Min Mail Order EU:** Nmc
**Cat. Cost:** 2 × 1st class.
**Credit Cards:** None
**Specialities:** Unusual shrubs, perennials & climbers. Asters, Campanulas, *Ceanothus*, geraniums, lavenders, *Clematis*, penstemons & grasses. New collections of *Phormium*, *Phygelius*, *Crocosmia*, *Anemone*, *Heuchera*, *Heucherella*, *Echinacea*, *Phlox*, *Coreopsis*, *Helleborus* & *Kniphofia*. Extensive range of salvias.
**Notes:** Nursery next door to Scotsford Farm, TN21 8UB. Mail order Sep-Apr incl. Also sells wholesale.
**Map Ref:** S, C4 **OS Grid Ref:** TQ604248

**SRms** **Rumsey Gardens** ⊠ ♿ ◆
117 Drift Road, Clanfield, Waterlooville, Hampshire, PO8 0PD
Ⓣ (023) 9259 3367
Ⓔ info@rumsey-gardens.co.uk
Ⓦ www.rumsey-gardens.co.uk
**Contact:** Mrs M A Giles
**Opening Times:** 0900-1700 Mon-Sat & 1000-1600 Sun & B/hols. Closed Sun Nov-Feb.
**Min Mail Order UK:** £15.00
**Cat. Cost:** Online only.
**Credit Cards:** Visa, MasterCard, Switch
**Specialities:** Wide general range. Herbaceous, alpines, heathers & ferns. Nat. & International Collection of *Cotoneaster*.
**Map Ref:** S, D2

**SRot** **Rotherview Nursery** ⊠ ⛫ € ♿
Ivy House Lane, Three Oaks, Hastings, East Sussex, TN35 4NP
Ⓣ (01424) 756228
Ⓔ rotherview@btinternet.com
Ⓦ www.rotherview.com

KEY
⊠ Mail order to UK or EU ⛫ Delivers to shows
☒ Exports beyond EU € Euro accepted
♿ Accessible by wheelchair ◆ See Display advertisement

**Contact:** Ray & Wendy Bates
**Opening Times:** 1000-1700 Mar-Oct, 1000-1530 Nov-Feb, 7 days.
**Min Mail Order UK:** Nmc
**Min Mail Order EU:** Nmc
**Cat. Cost:** 6 × 1st class.
**Credit Cards:** All major credit/debit cards
**Specialities:** Alpines.
**Notes:** Nursery is on same site as Coghurst Camellias. Also sells wholesale.
**Map Ref:** S, D5

**SSea** **Seale Nurseries**
Seale Lane, Seale,
Farnham, Surrey,
GU10 1LD
Ⓣ (01252) 782410
Ⓦ www.sealenurseries.co.uk
**Contact:** David & Catherine May
**Opening Times:** 1000-1600 Tue-Sat incl. Other times by appt. Closed 25th Dec-mid Jan.
**Cat. Cost:** None issued.
**Credit Cards:** Visa, Switch, Access, Delta
**Specialities:** Roses & *Pelargonium*. Some varieties in short supply, please phone first.
**Map Ref:** S, C3 **OS Grid Ref:** SU887477

**SSpi** **Spinners Garden**
School Lane, Boldre, Lymington, Hampshire, SO41 5QE
Ⓣ (01590) 675488
Ⓜ 07545 432090
Ⓔ info@spinnersgarden.co.uk
Ⓦ www.spinnersgarden.co.uk
**Contact:** Andrew Roberts
**Opening Times:** 1000-1700 Mon-Sat, Mar-Oct. By appt. only Nov, Dec, Jan & Feb.
**Cat. Cost:** Sae for plant list.
**Credit Cards:** All major credit/debit cards
**Specialities:** Less common trees & shrubs esp. *Acer*, *Magnolia*, species & lace-cap *Hydrangea*. Bog & woodland plants.

**SSPN** **Spring Park Nursery** €
78 Woodland Way, West Wickham, Kent, BR4 9LR
Ⓣ 020 8777 5161
Ⓔ julianfitzearle@aol.com
Ⓦ www.springparknursery.co.uk
**Contact:** Julian Fitz-Earle
**Opening Times:** Not open. Mail order only.
**Min Mail Order UK:** Nmc
**Min Mail Order EU:** Nmc
**Cat. Cost:** Free.
**Credit Cards:** None
**Specialities:** Heathers.
**Notes:** Mail order plants available all year.

**SSrw** **Scarecrow Plants**
Five Oaks Cottage, West Burton,
Nr Pulborough, West Sussex, RH20 1HD
Ⓣ (01798) 831286
Ⓜ 07939 272443
Ⓔ jestjsck@tiscali.co.uk
Ⓦ www.wildflowersandwatercolours.co.uk
**Contact:** Jean Jackman
**Opening Times:** By prior telephone or email appt. only.
**Cat. Cost:** None issued.
**Credit Cards:** None
**Specialities:** Plants to attract wildlife, especially English native wildflowers. Also shade plants, umbellifers & plants with green flowers. Garden open for NGS. All plants grown in small quantities.

**SSss** **Select Seeds**
Paice Lane, Medstead, Nr Alton, Hampshire, GU34 5PR
Ⓣ (01420) 560695
Ⓕ (01420) 563640
Ⓔ marina@phoenixperennialplants.co.uk
**Contact:** Marina Christopher
**Opening Times:** Not open. Mail order only.
**Min Mail Order UK:** £10.00
**Cat. Cost:** 3 × 1st class.
**Credit Cards:** All major credit/debit cards
**Specialities:** Seeds. *Aconitum*, *Eryngium*, *Thalictrum*, *Sanguisorba* & *Angelica*.
**Notes:** Only sells seed by mail order. Credit cards not accepted by phone. Co-located with Phoenix Perennial Plants SPhx.
**Map Ref:** S, C2 **OS Grid Ref:** SU657362

**SSta** **Starborough Nursery**
Starborough Road, Marsh Green,
Edenbridge, Kent,
TN8 5RB
Ⓣ (01732) 865614
Ⓕ (01732) 862166
Ⓔ starborough@hotmail.co.uk
**Contact:** C & P Tomlin
**Opening Times:** 0900-1600 Thu, Fri & Sat. Closed Jan, Jul & Aug.
**Min Mail Order UK:** £30.00 + p&p
**Cat. Cost:** £2.50
**Credit Cards:** Visa, Access
**Specialities:** Rare and unusual shrubs esp. *Daphne*, *Acer*, *Cercis*, rhododendrons & azaleas, *Magnolia* & *Nyssa*.
**Notes:** Certain plants only to EU.

**SSth** **Southease Plants**
Corner Cottage, Southease, Nr Lewes,
East Sussex, BN7 3HX
Ⓣ (01273) 513681

Ⓜ 07791 856206
Ⓕ (01273) 513681
**Contact:** Adrian Orchard
**Opening Times:** 1100-1700 Wed-Sat, 1400-1700 Sun & by appt.
**Cat. Cost:** None issued.
**Credit Cards:** None
**Specialities:** A small nursery concentrating on *Helleborus* hybrids, grown on the nursery from seed collected from selected plants. Small quantities only.
**Map Ref:** S, D4 **OS Grid Ref:** TQ422052

SSvw **Southview Nurseries** ⊠ ⌂ ♿
Chequers Lane, Eversley Cross,
Hook, Hampshire,
RG27 0NT
Ⓣ (0118) 9732206
Ⓔ Mark@Trenear.freeserve.co.uk
Ⓦ www.southviewnurseries.co.uk
**Contact:** Mark & Elaine Trenear
**Opening Times:** 1000-1600 Thu, Fri & Sat, Apr-Jun, except 17th-30th Jun when closed.
**Min Mail Order UK:** Nmc
**Cat. Cost:** Free
**Credit Cards:** None
**Specialities:** Unusual hardy plants, specialising in old-fashioned pinks & period plants. Nat. Collection of Old Pinks. Pinks collection open in June. Please ring for details.
**Notes:** Orders by prior arrangement only. Gives talks to garden societies & groups.
**Map Ref:** S, C3 **OS Grid Ref:** SU795612

STas **Tasteful Plants** € ♿
Macknade, Selling Road,
Faversham, Kent,
ME13 8XF
Ⓣ (01795) 534795
Ⓔ info@tastefulplants.co.uk
Ⓦ www.tastefulplants.co.uk
**Contact:** William Denne
**Opening Times:** 1000-1700 Wed-Sun.
**Credit Cards:** All major credit/debit cards
**Specialities:** Herbs and hostas.
**Notes:** Also sells wholesale.
**Map Ref:** S, C5 **OS Grid Ref:** TR023602

STes **Test Valley Nursery** ⊠ ⌂
Stockbridge Road, Timsbury, Romsey,
Hampshire, SO51 0NG
Ⓣ (01794) 368881
Ⓔ julia@testvalleynursery.co.uk
Ⓦ www.testvalleynursery.co.uk
**Contact:** Julia Benn
**Opening Times:** By appt. only.
**Min Mail Order UK:** Nmc
**Cat. Cost:** 3 × 1st class.
**Specialities:** Large range of herbaceous perennials, incl. unusual & new varieties. Some varieties available in small quantities only. Phone first to avoid disappointment.
**Map Ref:** S, C2

STil **Tile Barn Nursery** ⊠ ✈ ⌂ €
Standen Street, Iden Green, Benenden, Kent,
TN17 4LB
Ⓣ (01580) 240221
Ⓕ (01580) 240221
Ⓔ tilebarn.nursery@virgin.net
Ⓦ www.tilebarn-cyclamen.co.uk
**Contact:** Peter Moore
**Opening Times:** 0900-1700 Wed-Sat.
**Min Mail Order UK:** £10.00 + p&p
**Min Mail Order EU:** £25.00 + p&p
**Cat. Cost:** Sae
**Credit Cards:** None
**Specialities:** *Cyclamen* species.
**Notes:** Also sells wholesale.
**Map Ref:** S, C5 **OS Grid Ref:** TQ805301

STre **Peter Trenear** ⊠ ♿
Chantreyland, Chequers Lane, Eversley Cross,
Hampshire, RG27 0NX
Ⓣ (0118) 9732300
Ⓔ petertrenear@fsmail.net
Ⓦ www.trenear.co.uk
**Contact:** Peter Trenear
**Opening Times:** 0900-1630 Mon-Sat.
**Min Mail Order UK:** £7.00 + p&p
**Cat. Cost:** 1 × 1st class.
**Credit Cards:** Paypal
**Specialities:** Trees, shrubs, conifers, bonsai & succulents.
**Map Ref:** S, C3 **OS Grid Ref:** SU795612

STrG **Terrace Gardener** ⊠ €
8 Foxbush, Hildenborough, Kent, TN11 9HT
Ⓣ (01732) 832762
Ⓔ johan@terracegardener.com
Ⓦ www.terracegardener.co.uk
**Contact:** Mr J Hall
**Opening Times:** Not open. Mail order only, incl. online & by phone. Telephone orders 0800-1700 Mon-Fri.
**Min Mail Order UK:** Nmc
**Cat. Cost:** Free
**Credit Cards:** All major credit/debit cards
**Specialities:** Mediterranean trees & plants. Container gardening. Architectural & hardy exotics.

KEY
⊠ Mail order to UK or EU ⌂ Delivers to shows
✈ Exports beyond EU € Euro accepted
♿ Accessible by wheelchair ◆ See Display advertisement

**SUsu** **USUAL & UNUSUAL PLANTS** ⌂ €
Onslow House, Magham Down,
Hailsham, East Sussex,
BN27 1PL
Ⓣ (01323) 840967
Ⓔ jennie@uuplants.co.uk
Ⓦ www.uuplants.co.uk
**Contact:** Jennie Maillard
**Opening Times:** 0930-1730 Wed-Sat, 17th Mar-16th Oct. Other times can be arranged but strictly by appt. only.
**Cat. Cost:** £2.00 + sae or online.
**Credit Cards:** None
**Specialities:** Small quantities of a wide variety of unusual garden-worthy perennials esp. *Agapanthus*, *Echinacea*, *Erysimum*, *Euphorbia*, *Geum*, hardy *Geranium*, *Salvia*, *Sanguisorba*, *Sedum*, *Thalictrum* & grasses.
**Map Ref:** S, D4 **OS Grid Ref:** TQ607113

S

**SVen** **VENTNOR BOTANIC GARDEN** ⊠ ♿
Undercliff Drive, Ventnor,
Isle of Wight,
PO38 1UL
Ⓣ (01983) 855397
Ⓕ (01983) 856756
Ⓔ susan.everson@iow.gov.uk
Ⓦ botanic.co.uk
**Contact:** Sue Everson
**Opening Times:** 1000-1700 7 days, Mar-Oct.
**Min Mail Order UK:** Nmc
**Min Mail Order EU:** Nmc
**Cat. Cost:** None issued
**Credit Cards:** All, except American Express
**Specialities:** Coastal, drought-tolerant, Mediterranean & southern hemisphere plants. Some of the more unusual plants may only be available in small numbers.
**Map Ref:** S, D2 **OS Grid Ref:** SZ548768

**SVic** **VICTORIANA NURSERY GARDENS** ⊠ ♿
Challock, Ashford, Kent,
TN25 4DG
Ⓣ (01233) 740529
Ⓕ 0203 292 1529
Ⓔ For email, use contact form on website.
Ⓦ www.victoriananursery.co.uk
**Contact:** Serena Shirley
**Opening Times:** 0930-1630 (or dusk if sooner) Mon-Fri. 1030-1530 (or dusk if sooner) Sat.
**Min Mail Order UK:** £1.95
**Cat. Cost:** Free by post or online.
**Credit Cards:** All major credit/debit cards
**Specialities:** Heritage & unusual vegetable plants, seeds, fruit trees & bushes. Also 600+ varieties of *Fuchsia*.
**Notes:** Also sells wholesale.
**Map Ref:** S, C5 **OS Grid Ref:** TR018501

**SWal** **WALLACE PLANTS** ⌂
Lewes Road Nursery,
Lewes Road (B2124), Laughton,
East Sussex,
BN8 6BN
Ⓣ (01323) 811729
Ⓔ plants@wallace-plants.co.uk
Ⓦ www.wallace-plants.co.uk
**Contact:** Simon Wallace
**Opening Times:** 1000-1800, Mar-Sep, 1000-1600 Oct-Feb. 7 days, incl. B/hols.
**Cat. Cost:** 2 × 1st class for availability list.
**Credit Cards:** None
**Specialities:** Ornamental grasses, hebes, herbaceous/perennials, shrubs, salvias, penstemons, herbs, cacti & choice, rare & unusual plants.
**Map Ref:** S, D4 **OS Grid Ref:** TQ513126

**SWat** **WATER MEADOW NURSERY** ⊠ ✈ ⌂ ♿
Cheriton, Nr Alresford,
Hampshire,
SO24 0QB
Ⓣ (01962) 771895
Ⓕ (01962) 771119
Ⓔ plantaholic@onetel.com
Ⓦ www.plantaholic.co.uk
**Contact:** Mrs Sandy Worth
**Opening Times:** 1000-1700 Wed-Sat, Mar-Jul. 1000-1700 or dusk Fri & Sat, Aug-Oct.
**Min Mail Order UK:** £10.00 + p&p
**Min Mail Order EU:** £50.00 + p&p
**Cat. Cost:** Full catalogue online only. 2 × 1st class for individual plant lists.
**Credit Cards:** All major credit/debit cards
**Specialities:** Water lilies, extensive water garden plants, unusual herbaceous perennials, aromatic herbs & wildflowers. New Super Poppy Range. Nat. Collection of *Papaver orientale* group & *Papaver* Super Poppy Series.
**Notes:** Mail order by 24 or 48 hour courier service only. Also sells wholesale.
**Map Ref:** S, C2

**SWCr** **WYCH CROSS NURSERIES** ♿
Wych Cross, Forest Row, East Sussex,
RH18 5JW
Ⓣ (01342) 822705
Ⓕ (01342) 828246
Ⓔ roses@wychcross.co.uk
Ⓦ www.wychcross.co.uk
**Contact:** J Paisley
**Opening Times:** 0900-1730 Mon-Sat.
**Cat. Cost:** Free
**Credit Cards:** All major credit/debit cards
**Specialities:** Roses.
**Map Ref:** S, C4 **OS Grid Ref:** TQ420320

SWhi **John Hall Plants Ltd** ✉ ✈ ⛺ € ♿
Whitehall Nursery, Red Lane
(Off Churt Road), Headley Down,
Hampshire, GU35 8SR
Ⓣ (01428) 715505
Ⓜ 07714 344327
Ⓔ info@johnhallplants.com
Ⓦ www.johnhallplants.com
**Contact:** John Hall
**Opening Times:** 0900-1630 Mon-Fri, 0900-1300 Sat, by appt. only.
**Min Mail Order UK:** Nmc
**Min Mail Order EU:** Nmc
**Cat. Cost:** By email only.
**Credit Cards:** None
**Specialities:** *Erica* and *Calluna*.
**Notes:** Also sells wholesale.
**Map Ref:** S, C3 **OS Grid Ref:** SU837371

SWvt **Wolverton Plants Ltd** € ♿ ◆
Wolverton Common,
Tadley, Hampshire,
RG26 5RU
Ⓣ (01635) 298453
Ⓕ (01635) 299075
Ⓔ Julian@wolvertonplants.co.uk
Ⓦ www.wolvertonplants.co.uk
**Contact:** Julian Jones
**Opening Times:** 0900-1800 (or dusk Nov-Feb), 7 days. Closed Xmas/New Year.
**Cat. Cost:** Online only.
**Credit Cards:** All major credit/debit cards
**Specialities:** Wide range of herbaceous perennials & shrubs grown on a commercial scale for the public.
**Notes:** Horticultural club visits welcome by prior arrangement. Also sells wholesale.
**Map Ref:** S, C2 **OS Grid Ref:** SU555589

## Wales and the West

WAbb **Abbey Dore Court Garden** € ♿
Abbey Dore Court, Abbey Dore,
Herefordshire, HR2 0AD
Ⓣ (01981) 240419
Ⓕ (01981) 240419
Ⓦ www.abbeydorecourt.co.uk
**Contact:** Mrs C Ward
**Opening Times:** Garden & nursery open Apr-Sep any day. A prior phone call is essential if coming any distance.
**Cat. Cost:** None issued
**Credit Cards:** None
**Specialities:** Mainly hardy perennials, many unusual, which may be seen growing in the garden. *Astrantia*, *Crocosmia*, *Helleborus*, *Paeonia*, *Pulmonaria* & *Sedum*.
**Map Ref:** W, C4 **OS Grid Ref:** SO388308

WAbe **Aberconwy Nursery** ⛺
Graig, Glan Conwy, Colwyn Bay, Conwy,
LL28 5TL
Ⓣ (01492) 580875
**Contact:** Dr & Mrs K G Lever
**Opening Times:** 1000-1700 Tue-Sun Mar-Sep incl.
**Cat. Cost:** 2 × 2nd class.
**Credit Cards:** Visa, MasterCard
**Specialities:** Alpines, including specialist varieties, esp. gentians, dionysias, dwarf *Dianthus*, *Primula*, *Saxifraga* & dwarf ericaceous plants. Some choice shrubs & woodland plants incl. smaller ferns.
**Map Ref:** W, A3 **OS Grid Ref:** SH799744

WAle **Alerce & Roble Nursery** ✉
(Office) The Dame School, Castle Street,
Wigmore, Herefordshire, HR6 9UA
Ⓜ 07966 580812
Ⓔ alerceandroble@googlemail.com
**Contact:** Mark Paviour
**Opening Times:** Not open. Mail order only at present.
**Min Mail Order UK:** Nmc
**Cat. Cost:** Email for plant list.
**Credit Cards:** None
**Specialities:** A developing range of southern hemisphere plants with emphasis on Chilean species as well as plants for 'Mediterranean' gardens. Some plants available in small quantities only.
**Notes:** Nursery at separate site.

WAul **Aulden Farm** ✉
Aulden, Leominster, Herefordshire, HR6 0JT
Ⓣ (01568) 720129
Ⓔ pf@auldenfarm.co.uk
Ⓦ www.auldenfarm.co.uk
**Contact:** Alun & Jill Whitehead
**Opening Times:** 1000-1700 Tue & Thu Apr-Aug. Thu only in Sep. Other times by appt. Please phone.
**Min Mail Order UK:** Nmc
**Min Mail Order EU:** £20.00
**Cat. Cost:** 2 × 1st class.
**Credit Cards:** Paypal
**Specialities:** Hardy herbaceous perennials, with a special interest in *Hemerocallis* & *Iris*. Nat. Collection of Siberian *Iris*.
**Notes:** Mail order available for small quantities. Garden & nursery open for NGS, see website for details.
**Map Ref:** W, C4 **OS Grid Ref:** SO462548

KEY
✉ Mail order to UK or EU ⛺ Delivers to shows
✈ Exports beyond EU € Euro accepted
♿ Accessible by wheelchair ◆ See Display advertisement

W

**WBor** **BORDERVALE PLANTS** ⊠ ⌂ ♿
Nantyderi, Sandy Lane, Ystradowen, Cowbridge, Vale of Glamorgan, CF71 7SX
Ⓣ (01446) 774036
Ⓔ lonytwod@googlemail.com
Ⓦ www.bordervale.co.uk
**Contact:** Claire E Jenkins
**Opening Times:** 1000-1700 Fri-Sun & B/hols Mar-early Oct. Other times please phone.
**Min Mail Order UK:** £20.00 + p&p
**Cat. Cost:** 3 × 1st class.
**Credit Cards:** None
**Specialities:** Unusual herbaceous perennials, trees & shrubs, as well as cottage garden plants, many displayed in the 2-acre garden.
**Notes:** Mail order available for most items, subject to size & season. Garden open May-Sep when nursery open. Also open for NGS. See website for details.
**Map Ref:** W, D3 **OS Grid Ref:** ST022776

**WBou** **BOUTS COTTAGE NURSERIES** ⊠ ⌂ ♿
Bouts Lane, Inkberrow, Worcestershire, WR7 4HP
Ⓣ (01386) 792923
Ⓦ www.boutsviolas.co.uk
**Contact:** M & S Roberts
**Opening Times:** Strictly by appt. only.
**Min Mail Order UK:** Nmc
**Min Mail Order EU:** Nmc
**Cat. Cost:** 1st class sae.
**Credit Cards:** None
**Specialities:** *Viola.*

**WBox** **BOX COURT PLANTS & GARDENS** ⊠
(Office) 1 Anthony's Cross, Newent, Gloucestershire, GL18 1JQ
Ⓣ (01531) 828289
Ⓜ 07771 559429
Ⓔ info@boxcourt.co.uk
Ⓦ www.boxcourt.co.uk
**Contact:** Paul Hervey-Brookes & Sean Hervey-Brookes
**Opening Times:** 1100-1700, 7 days, 10th Jan-4th Nov.
**Min Mail Order UK:** Nmc
**Min Mail Order EU:** Nmc
**Cat. Cost:** Online only.
**Credit Cards:** None
**Specialities:** Herbaceous plants.
**Notes:** Nursery at Painswick Rococo Gardens, Painswick, Glos, GL6 6TH.
**Map Ref:** W, C4 **OS Grid Ref:** SO863105

**WBrk** **BROCKAMIN PLANTS** ⌂ ♿
Brockamin, Old Hills, Callow End, Worcestershire, WR2 4TQ
Ⓣ (01905) 830370
Ⓔ dickstonebrockamin@tinyworld.co.uk
**Contact:** Margaret Stone
**Opening Times:** By appt. only.
**Cat. Cost:** Free.
**Credit Cards:** None
**Specialities:** Nat. Collections of *Aster novae-angliae, Erigeron* cvs, *Geranium sanguineum, G. macrorrhizum* & *G.* × *cantabrigiense.* Plants available in small quantities only.
**Map Ref:** W, C5 **OS Grid Ref:** SO830488

**WBuc** **BUCKNELL NURSERIES** ⊠
Bucknell, Shropshire, SY7 0EL
Ⓣ (01547) 530606
Ⓕ (01547) 530699
Ⓔ nickcoull@yahoo.co.uk
**Contact:** A N Coull
**Opening Times:** 0800-1700 Mon-Fri & 1000-1300 Sat.
**Min Mail Order UK:** Nmc
**Cat. Cost:** Free
**Credit Cards:** None
**Specialities:** Bare-rooted hedging conifers & forest trees.
**Notes:** Also sells wholesale.

**WCAu** **CLAIRE AUSTIN HARDY PLANTS** ⊠ ♿
Edgebolton, Shawbury, Shrewsbury, Shropshire, SY4 4EL
Ⓣ (01939) 251173
Ⓕ (01939) 251311
Ⓔ enquiries@claireaustin-hardyplants.co.uk
Ⓦ www.claireaustin-hardyplants.co.uk
**Contact:** Claire Austin
**Opening Times:** 0900-1700 Mon-Sat, 1000-1600 Sun, Apr-end Jun. Open by appt. at other times of the year.
**Min Mail Order UK:** Nmc
**Min Mail Order EU:** Nmc
**Cat. Cost:** UK £3.50, Europe €7.00
**Credit Cards:** MasterCard, Visa, Switch
**Specialities:** *Paeonia, Iris, Hemerocallis* & hardy plants. Nat. Collections of Bearded *Iris* & Hybrid Herbaceous *Paeonia.*
**Map Ref:** W, B4

**WCFE** **CHARLES F ELLIS** ⊠ €
Oak Piece Nurseries, Stanton, Nr Broadway, Worcestershire, WR12 7NQ
Ⓣ (01386) 584077
Ⓕ (01386) 584491
Ⓔ ellisplants@cooptel.net
Ⓦ www.ellisplants.co.uk
**Contact:** Charles Ellis
**Opening Times:** 1000-1600 7 days 1st Apr-30th Sep. Other times by appt.
**Min Mail Order UK:** Nmc
**Cat. Cost:** None issued.
**Credit Cards:** None

**Specialities:** Wide range of shrubs, conifers & climbers, some of them unusual.
**Map Ref:** W, C5

WChG **Chennels Gate Gardens & Nursery** ♿
Eardisley, Herefordshire, HR3 6LT
Ⓣ (01544) 327288
**Contact:** Mark Dawson
**Opening Times:** 1000-1700 7 days Mar-Oct.
**Cat. Cost:** None issued.
**Credit Cards:** None
**Specialities:** Interesting & unusual cottage garden plants, grasses & shrubs.
**Map Ref:** W, C4

WCot **Cotswold Garden Flowers** ✉ € 
Sands Lane, Badsey, Evesham, Worcestershire, WR11 7EZ
Ⓣ Nursery: (01386) 833849 or Mail Order: (01386) 422829
Ⓜ 07812 833849
Ⓕ nursery (01386) 49844
Ⓔ info@cgf.net
Ⓦ www.cgf.net
**Contact:** Bob Brown
**Opening Times:** 0900-1730 Mon-Fri, 1000-1730 Sat & Sun, Mar-Sep. 0900-1630 Mon-Fri, w/ends by appt. only, Oct-Feb.
**Min Mail Order UK:** Nmc
**Min Mail Order EU:** Nmc
**Cat. Cost:** £1.50 or 6 × 1st class.
**Credit Cards:** MasterCard, Access, Visa, Switch
**Specialities:** A very wide range of easy & unusual perennials.
**Notes:** Ltd wheelchair access. Also sells wholesale.
**Map Ref:** W, C5 **OS Grid Ref:** SP077426

WCra **Cranesbill Nursery** ✉ ♿
White Cottage, Earls Common Road, Stock Green, Redditch, Worcestershire, B96 6SZ
Ⓣ (01386) 792414
Ⓕ (01386) 792280
Ⓔ cranesbilluk@aol.com
Ⓦ www.cranesbillnursery.com
**Contact:** Mrs J Bates
**Opening Times:** Not open. Mail order only. Visitors, incl. groups, are welcome but by prior appt. only.
**Min Mail Order UK:** Nmc
**Min Mail Order EU:** Nmc
**Cat. Cost:** 4 × 1st class
**Credit Cards:** MasterCard, Visa, Maestro, Delta
**Specialities:** Hardy geraniums & other herbaceous plants.
**Map Ref:** W, C5 **OS Grid Ref:** 975585

WCre **Crescent Plants** ✉ ♿
Stoney Cross, Marden, Hereford, Herefordshire, HR1 3EW
Ⓣ (01432) 880262
Ⓕ (01432) 880262
Ⓔ june@auriculas.co.uk
Ⓦ www.auriculas.co.uk
**Contact:** June Poole
**Opening Times:** Open by appt. only. Essential to phone first.
**Min Mail Order UK:** Nmc
**Min Mail Order EU:** Nmc
**Cat. Cost:** Free
**Credit Cards:** Paypal
**Specialities:** Named varieties of *Primula auricula* incl. show, alpine, double, striped & border types.
**Notes:** Payment by Paypal via website, cheque with order or invoice. Orders dispatched post free.
**Map Ref:** W, C4 **OS Grid Ref:** SO525477

WCru **Crûg Farm Plants** ✉ ♿
Griffith's Crossing, Caernarfon, Gwynedd, LL55 1TU
Ⓣ (01248) 670232
Ⓔ info@crug-farm.co.uk
Ⓦ www.mailorder.crug-farm.co.uk
**Contact:** B and S Wynn-Jones
**Opening Times:** 1000-1700 Thu-Sun 2nd Sat Mar to last Sun Jun plus B/hols, then Thu-Sat until 1st Sat in Oct. Or by appt.
**Min Mail Order UK:** Nmc
**Min Mail Order EU:** Nmc
**Cat. Cost:** 5 × 2nd class or free online download.
**Credit Cards:** All major credit/debit cards
**Specialities:** Unusual & rare inc. trees, shrubs, herbaceous & bulbous, mostly self-collected new introductions from the Far East & the Americas. Rare woody & climbers esp. *Acer, Araliaceae, Carpinus, Hydrangeaceae* & *Magnolia* with many other extraordinary introductions. Shade plants esp. *Convallariaceae, Liliaceae, Ranunculaceae* & *Saxifragaceae*. Many supplied bare rooted. Nat. Collections of *Coriaria, Paris* & *Polygonatum*.
**Notes:** Delivery by overnight carrier for UK & Ireland. Courier for rest of EU.
**Map Ref:** W, A2 **OS Grid Ref:** SH509652

KEY
✉ Mail order to UK or EU — Delivers to shows
Exports beyond EU — € Euro accepted
♿ Accessible by wheelchair — ◆ See Display advertisement

**WDib** **Dibley's Nurseries** ⊠ ⌂ € ♿ ◆
Llanelidan, Ruthin, Denbighshire, LL15 2LG
Ⓣ (01978) 790677
Ⓕ (01978) 790668
Ⓔ sales@dibleys.com
Ⓦ www.dibleys.com
**Contact:** R Dibley
**Opening Times:** 1000-1700 7 days, Apr-Aug. 1000-1700 Mon-Fri, Mar, Sep & Oct.
**Min Mail Order UK:** Nmc
**Min Mail Order EU:** Nmc
**Cat. Cost:** Free
**Credit Cards:** Visa, Access, Switch, Electron, Solo
**Specialities:** *Streptocarpus*, *Columnea*, *Solenostemon*, *Saintpaulia* & other gesneriads & *Begonia*. Nat. Collection of *Streptocarpus*.
**Notes:** Also sells wholesale.
**Map Ref:** W, A3

**WDin** **Dingle Nurseries** ⊠ ♿ ◆
Welshpool, Powys, SY21 9JD
Ⓣ (01938) 555145
Ⓕ (01938) 555778
Ⓔ info@dinglenurseryandgarden.co.uk
Ⓦ www.dinglenurseryandgarden.co.uk
**Contact:** Jill Rock
**Opening Times:** 0900-1700, 7 days.
**Min Mail Order UK:** £15.00
**Cat. Cost:** Free plant list.
**Credit Cards:** MasterCard, Switch, EuroCard, Delta, Visa
**Specialities:** Largest range of trees & shrubs in Wales. Wide seasonal selection of garden plants incl. roses, herbaceous perennials, conifers & bare-rooted forestry, hedging & fruit. All sizes incl. many mature specimens.
**Notes:** Mail order for bare-rooted hedging only. Also sells wholesale.
**Map Ref:** W, B4 **OS Grid Ref:** SJ196082

**WDyG** **Dyffryn Gwyddno Nursery** ⌂
Dyffryn Farm, Lampeter Velfrey, Narberth, Pembrokeshire, SA67 8UN
Ⓣ (01834) 861684
Ⓔ sally.polson@virgin.net
Ⓦ www.pembrokeshireplants.co.uk
**Contact:** Mrs S L Polson
**Opening Times:** By appt. only.
**Credit Cards:** None
**Specialities:** Eclectic, yet wide-ranging, from tender salvias & grasses to bog. Bamboos. Peat-free & principled. Plants available in small quantities only.
**Notes:** Bamboo collection open by appt. in aid of NGS. Also sells wholesale.
**Map Ref:** W, D2 **OS Grid Ref:** SR138148

**WEve** **Evergreen Conifer Centre** ⊠ ♿ ◆
Tenbury Road, Rock, Nr Kidderminster, Worcestershire, DY14 9RB
Ⓣ (01299) 266581
Ⓕ (01299) 266755
Ⓔ brian@evergreen-conifers.co.uk
Ⓦ www.evergreen-conifers.co.uk
**Contact:** Brian Warrington
**Opening Times:** 0900-1630 Tue-Sat (closed Sun & Mon). Please phone before travelling some distance.
**Min Mail Order UK:** Nmc
**Cat. Cost:** 4 × 1st class.
**Credit Cards:** All major credit/debit cards
**Specialities:** Acers. Dwarf, ornamental, rare & specimen conifers. Hedging conifers. Ornamental trees & heathers.
**Notes:** Mail order for dwarf conifers only.
**Map Ref:** W, C4 **OS Grid Ref:** SO731737

**WFar** **Farmyard Nurseries** ⊠ ⊠ ♿ ◆
Dol Llan Road, Llandysul, Carmarthenshire, SA44 4RL
Ⓣ (01559) 363389
Ⓕ (01559) 362200
Ⓔ richard@farmyardnurseries.co.uk
Ⓦ www.farmyardnurseries.co.uk
**Contact:** Richard Bramley
**Opening Times:** 1000-1700 7 days excl. Xmas, Boxing & New Year's Day.
**Min Mail Order UK:** Nmc
**Min Mail Order EU:** Nmc
**Cat. Cost:** 4 × 1st class.
**Credit Cards:** Visa, Switch, MasterCard
**Specialities:** Excellent general range esp. *Helleborus*, *Hosta*, *Tricyrtis* & *Schizostylis*, plus shrubs, trees, climbers, alpines & esp. herbaceous. Nat. Collection of *Tricyrtis*.
**Notes:** Also sells wholesale.
**Map Ref:** W, C2 **OS Grid Ref:** SN421406

**WFib** **Fibrex Nurseries Ltd** ⊠ ⊠ ⌂ ♿
Honeybourne Road, Pebworth, Stratford-on-Avon, Warwickshire, CV37 8XP
Ⓣ (01789) 720788
Ⓕ (01789) 721162
Ⓔ sales@fibrex.co.uk
Ⓦ www.fibrex.co.uk
**Contact:** U Key-Davis & R L Godard-Key
**Opening Times:** 0900-1700 Mon-Fri, 1st Mar-31st Aug. 0900-1600 Mon-Fri, 1st Sep-28th Feb. 1030-1600 Sat & Sun, 6th Mar-25th Jul. Closed last 2 weeks Dec & 1st week Jan. Closed Easter Sun & Aug B/hol Mon.
**Min Mail Order UK:** £10.00 + p&p
**Min Mail Order EU:** £20.00 + p&p
**Cat. Cost:** 2 × 1st class.
**Credit Cards:** Switch, MasterCard, Visa, Maestro

**Specialities:** *Hedera*, ferns, *Pelargonium*. Nat. Collections of *Pelargonium* & *Hedera*. Plant collections subject to time of year, please check by phone.
**Notes:** Also sells wholesale.
**Map Ref:** W, C5 **OS Grid Ref:** SP133458

**WFoF** **FLOWERS OF THE FIELD** €
Field Farm, Weobley, Herefordshire, HR4 8QJ
Ⓣ (01544) 318262
Ⓜ 07966 790090
Ⓕ (01544) 318262
Ⓔ info@flowersofthefield.co.uk
Ⓦ www.flowersofthefield.co.uk
**Contact:** Kathy Davies
**Opening Times:** 0900-1900 7 days.
**Cat. Cost:** Online only.
**Credit Cards:** None
**Specialities:** Traditional & unusual perennials, grasses, shrubs, trees & herbs. Many varieties of flowers for cutting incl. Oriental lilies, freesias, *Ranunculus* & dahlias.
**Notes:** Nursery partially accessible for wheelchairs. Also sells wholesale.
**Map Ref:** W, C4 **OS Grid Ref:** SO406506

**WGob** **THE GOBBETT NURSERY** ⊠
Farlow, Kidderminster, Worcestershire, DY14 8TD
Ⓣ (01746) 718647
Ⓕ (01746) 718647
Ⓔ christine.link@lineone.net
Ⓦ www.thegobbettnursery.co.uk
**Contact:** C H Link
**Opening Times:** 1030-1700, Mon-Sat.
**Min Mail Order UK:** £10.00
**Min Mail Order EU:** £50.00
**Cat. Cost:** 3 × 1st class.
**Credit Cards:** None
**Specialities:** *Syringa*, *Magnolia*, *Camellia* & *Cornus*. Some varieties available in small quantities only.
**Map Ref:** W, B4 **OS Grid Ref:** SO648811

**WGor** **GORDON'S NURSERY** ⊠ ♠ ♿
1 Cefnpennar Cottages, Cefnpennar, Mountain Ash, Mid-Glamorgan, CF45 4EE
Ⓣ (01443) 474593
Ⓕ (01443) 475835
Ⓔ sales@gordonsnursery.co.uk
Ⓦ www.gordonsnursery.co.uk
**Contact:** D A Gordon
**Opening Times:** 1000-1800 7 days Mar-Jun. 1000-1700 7 days Jul-Oct. 1100-1600 weekends only Nov & Feb. Closed Dec-Jan.
**Min Mail Order UK:** Nmc
**Cat. Cost:** 3 × 1st class.
**Credit Cards:** All major credit/debit cards
**Specialities:** Shrubs, perennials, alpines & dwarf conifers. Some plants available in small quantities only.
**Notes:** Mail order only available in some cases, please check for conditions in catalogue.
**Map Ref:** W, D3 **OS Grid Ref:** SO037012

**WGrn** **GREEN'S LEAVES** ⊠ ♠ ♿
36 Ford House Road, Newent, Gloucestershire, GL18 1LQ
Ⓣ (01531) 820154
Ⓜ 07890 413036
Ⓔ r.paul.green@hotmail.co.uk
**Contact:** Paul Green
**Opening Times:** By appt. only, w/ends preferred.
**Min Mail Order UK:** £10.00 + p&p
**Cat. Cost:** 4 × 2nd class.
**Credit Cards:** None
**Specialities:** Ornamental grasses, sedges & phormiums. Increasing range of rare & choice shrubs, also some perennials.
**Notes:** Also sells wholesale.
**Map Ref:** W, C4 **OS Grid Ref:** SO732273

**WGwG** **GWYNFOR GROWERS** ⊠ ♠ ♿
Gwynfor, Pontgarreg, Llangranog, Llandysul, Ceredigion, SA44 6AU
Ⓣ (01239) 654151
Ⓔ info@gwynfor.co.uk
Ⓦ www.gwynfor.co.uk
**Contact:** Steve & Angie Hipkin
**Opening Times:** 1000 to 2000 or sunset if earlier, Wed, Thu & Sun, all year round.
**Min Mail Order UK:** Nmc
**Cat. Cost:** PDF list available by email.
**Credit Cards:** Paypal
**Specialities:** Classic & contemporary plants to intrigue & delight plantsmen & garden designers alike. Heritage Welsh fruit trees. Some plants available in small quantities only. Rarities propagated to order.
**Notes:** Plants also available at Aberystwyth & farmers' markets & Ceredigion Growers' Assoc. plant fairs.
**Map Ref:** W, C2 **OS Grid Ref:** SN331536

**WHal** **HALL FARM NURSERY** ⊠ ♠ € ♿
Vicarage Lane, Kinnerley, Nr Oswestry, Shropshire, SY10 8DH
Ⓣ (01691) 682135
Ⓕ (01691) 682135
Ⓔ info@hallfarmnursery.co.uk

KEY
⊠ Mail order to UK or EU ♠ Delivers to shows
✈ Exports beyond EU € Euro accepted
♿ Accessible by wheelchair ◆ See Display advertisement

W

Ⓦ www.hallfarmnursery.co.uk
**Contact:** Christine & Nick Ffoulkes-Jones
**Opening Times:** 1000-1700 Tue-Sat 1st Mar-31st Oct 2010.
**Min Mail Order UK:** £20.00
**Cat. Cost:** Online only.
**Credit Cards:** Visa, MasterCard, Electron, Maestro
**Specialities:** Unusual herbaceous plants, grasses, bog plants & pool marginals, late-flowering perennials, foliage plants.
**Notes:** Nursery partially accessible for wheelchairs.
**Map Ref:** W, B4 **OS Grid Ref:** SJ333209

**WHar** **Harley Nursery** ⊠ ♿
Harley, Shrewsbury, Shropshire, SY5 6LN
Ⓣ (01952) 510241
Ⓕ (01952) 510570
Ⓔ plants@harleynursery.co.uk
Ⓦ www.harleynursery.co.uk
**Contact:** Nick Murphy
**Opening Times:** 0900-1730 Mon & Thu-Sat (closed Tue & Wed), 1000-1600 Sun & B/hols. Winter hours 0830-1630 Mon & Thu-Sat (closed Tue & Wed), 1000-1600 Sun & B/hols.
**Min Mail Order UK:** Nmc
**Cat. Cost:** 2 × 1st class.
**Credit Cards:** All major credit/debit cards
**Specialities:** Wide range of ornamental & fruit trees & fruit bushes. Own grown shrubs, climbers, wide range of hedging plants. Top fruit propagated to order.
**Map Ref:** W, B4

W

**WHCr** **Hergest Croft Gardens**
Kington, Herefordshire, HR5 3EG
Ⓣ (01544) 230160
Ⓜ 07968 435627
Ⓕ (01544) 232031
Ⓔ gardens@hergest.co.uk
Ⓦ www.hergest.co.uk
**Contact:** Stephen Lloyd
**Opening Times:** 1200-1730 7 days, Apr-Oct.
**Cat. Cost:** None issued
**Credit Cards:** All major credit/debit cards
**Specialities:** *Acer*, *Betula* & unusual woody plants.
**Notes:** Limited wheelchair access.

**WHer** **The Herb Garden & Historical Plant Nursery** ⊠
Ty Capel Pensarn, Pentre Berw, Anglesey, Gwynedd, LL60 6LG
Ⓣ (01248) 422208 or (01545) 580893
Ⓜ 07751 583958
Ⓕ (01248) 422208
Ⓦ www.HistoricalPlants.co.uk
**Contact:** Corinne & David Tremaine-Stevenson
**Opening Times:** By appt. only.
**Min Mail Order UK:** £15.00 + p&p
**Min Mail Order EU:** £50.00 + p&p sterling only.
**Cat. Cost:** Online only.
**Credit Cards:** None
**Specialities:** Rarer herbs, rare natives & wild flowers; rare & unusual & historical perennials & old roses.
**Map Ref:** W, A2

**WHfH** **Herbs for Healing** ⊠ ♿
(Office) Rose Cottage, London Road, Poulton, Cirencester, Gloucestershire, GL7 5JG
Ⓣ (01285) 851457
Ⓜ 07773 687493
Ⓔ herbs@herbsforhealing.net
Ⓦ www.herbsforhealing.net
**Contact:** Davina Wynne-Jones
**Opening Times:** 1000-1500 Wed, plus Fri afternoons.
**Min Mail Order UK:** Nmc
**Credit Cards:** Paypal
**Specialities:** Medicinal & some culinary herbs. Display garden.
**Notes:** Courses and workshops on use of herbs. Sells at local farmers markets. Nursery in Clapton's Lane, Barnsley, Nr Cirencester, behind Barnsley House Hotel. See web for directions.
**Map Ref:** W, D5 **OS Grid Ref:** SP048177

**WHil** **Hillview Hardy Plants** ⊠ ✈ ⌂ € ♿ ◆
(off B4176) Worfield, Nr Bridgnorth, Shropshire, WV15 5NT
Ⓣ (01746) 716454
Ⓜ 07974 391608
Ⓕ (01746) 716454
Ⓔ hillview@themutual.net
Ⓦ www.hillviewhardyplants.com
**Contact:** Ingrid, John & Sarah Millington
**Opening Times:** 0900-1700 Mon-Sat Mar-mid Oct. At other times, please phone first.
**Min Mail Order UK:** £15.00 + p&p
**Min Mail Order EU:** £15.00 + p&p
**Cat. Cost:** 4 × 2nd class.
**Credit Cards:** All major credit/debit cards
**Specialities:** Choice herbaceous perennials incl. *Acanthus* & *Acanthaceae*, *Albuca*, *Aquilegia*, auricula, *Primula*, *Canna*, *Crocosmia*, *Eucomis*, *Ixia*, South African bulbs. Nat. Collections of *Acanthus* & *Albuca*.
**Notes:** Also sells wholesale.
**Map Ref:** W, B4 **OS Grid Ref:** SO772969

WHlf **Hayloft Plants** ⊠
Manor Farm, Pensham, Pershore, Worcestershire, WR10 3HB
Ⓣ (01386) 554440 or (01386) 562999
Ⓕ (01386) 553833
Ⓔ info@hayloftplants.co.uk
Ⓦ www.hayloftplants.co.uk
**Contact:** Yvonne Walker
**Opening Times:** Not open. Mail order only.
**Min Mail Order UK:** Nmc
**Min Mail Order EU:** Nmc
**Cat. Cost:** Free.
**Credit Cards:** All major credit/debit cards

WHoo **Hoo House Nursery** € ♿ ◆
Hoo House, Gloucester Road, Tewkesbury, Gloucestershire, GL20 7DA
Ⓣ (01684) 293389
Ⓕ (01684) 293389
Ⓔ nursery@hoohouse.co.uk
Ⓦ www.hoohouse.co.uk
**Contact:** Robin & Julie Ritchie
**Opening Times:** 1000-1700 Mon-Sat, 1100-1700 Sun.
**Cat. Cost:** 3 × 1st class.
**Credit Cards:** All major credit/debit cards
**Specialities:** Wide range of herbaceous & alpines incl. *Aster*, *Cyclamen*, *Geranium*, *Penstemon* & many later-flowering varieties. Nat. Collections of *Platycodon* & *Gentiana asclepiadea* cvs.
**Notes:** Also sells wholesale.
**Map Ref:** W, C5 **OS Grid Ref:** SO893293

WHrl **Harrells Hardy Plants** ⊠
(Office) 15 Coxlea Close, Evesham, Worcestershire, WR11 4JS
Ⓣ (01386) 443077
Ⓜ 07799 577120 or 07733 446606
Ⓔ mail@harrellshardyplants.co.uk
Ⓦ www.harrellshardyplants.co.uk
**Contact:** Liz Nicklin & Kate Phillips
**Opening Times:** 1000-1200 Sun Mar-Nov. Other times by appt. Please phone.
**Min Mail Order UK:** Nmc
**Cat. Cost:** 4 × 2nd class.
**Credit Cards:** None
**Specialities:** Display gardens showcase wide range of hardy perennials, esp. *Hemerocallis* & grasses.
**Notes:** Nursery located off Rudge Rd, Evesham. Please phone for directions or see catalogue. Partial wheelchair access. Mail order Nov-Mar only.
**Map Ref:** W, C5 **OS Grid Ref:** SP033443

WIvy **Ivycroft Plants** ⊠ € ♿
Upper Ivington, Leominster, Herefordshire, HR6 0JN
Ⓣ (01568) 720344
Ⓔ ivycroft@homecall.co.uk
Ⓦ www.ivycroft.freeserve.co.uk
**Contact:** Roger Norman
**Opening Times:** 0900-1600 Thu, Feb & Apr-Sep. Other times by appt., please phone.
**Min Mail Order UK:** Nmc
**Min Mail Order EU:** Nmc
**Cat. Cost:** Sae for specialist lists.
**Credit Cards:** None
**Specialities:** *Cyclamen*, *Galanthus*, *Salix*, alpines, herbaceous & ferns.
**Notes:** Mail order for *Galanthus* & *Salix* only.
**Map Ref:** W, C4 **OS Grid Ref:** SO464562

WJas **Paul Jasper Trees** ⊠
(Office) The Lighthouse, Bridge Street, Leominster, Herefordshire, HR6 8DX
Ⓕ (01568) 616499 for orders.
Ⓔ enquiries@jaspertrees.co.uk
Ⓦ www.jaspertrees.co.uk
**Contact:** Paul Jasper
**Opening Times:** Not open. Mail order only.
**Min Mail Order UK:** £40.00 + p&p
**Cat. Cost:** Online only.
**Credit Cards:** None
**Specialities:** Full range of fruit & ornamental trees. Over 100 modern and traditional fruit tree varieties plus 100 ornamental tree varieties, all direct from the grower. Many unusual varieties of *Malus domestica* & *Prunus*.
**Notes:** Regular catalogue updates & notes on website. Also sells wholesale.
**Map Ref:** W, C4 **OS Grid Ref:** 495595

WJAW **J A Wood** ⊠
6 Stanley Street, Beaumaris, Anglesey, LL58 8ET
Ⓣ (01248) 810661
Ⓔ zallen5@btinternet.com
Ⓦ www.allenstudio6.com
**Contact:** Allen Wood
**Opening Times:** Not open. Mail order only.
**Min Mail Order UK:** Nmc
**Cat. Cost:** None issued.
**Credit Cards:** None
**Specialities:** Lawn camomile and comfrey.

WJek **Jekka's Herb Farm** ⊠ ⌂ ♿
Rose Cottage, Shellards Lane, Alveston, Bristol, South Gloucestershire, BS35 3SY
Ⓣ (01454) 418878
Ⓕ (01454) 424907
Ⓔ sales@jekkasherbfarm.com

| KEY | | |
|---|---|---|
| | ⊠ Mail order to UK or EU | ⌂ Delivers to shows |
| | ✈ Exports beyond EU | € Euro accepted |
| | ♿ Accessible by wheelchair | ◆ See Display advertisement |

W

Ⓦ www.jekkasherbfarm.com
**Contact:** Jekka McVicar
**Opening Times:** 4 times a year. Please check website for dates.
**Min Mail Order UK:** £15 plants
**Min Mail Order EU:** Seeds only to the EU.
**Cat. Cost:** 4 × 1st class.
**Credit Cards:** Visa, MasterCard, Delta, Maestro
**Specialities:** Culinary, medicinal, aromatic, decorative herbs. Soil Association licensed G5869.
**Map Ref:** W, D4

**WJPR** **JPR Environmental** ⊠
(Office) Unit 2, Breadstone Business Centre, Breadstone, Berkeley, Gloucestershire, GL13 9HF
Ⓣ (01453) 811537
Ⓕ (01453) 810646
Ⓔ enquiries@jprenvironmental.co.uk
Ⓦ www.jprwillow.co.uk
**Contact:** John Robinthwaite
**Opening Times:** 0900-1700.
**Min Mail Order UK:** £6.00
**Credit Cards:** All, except American Express
**Specialities:** *Salix.*
**Notes:** Also sells wholesale.
**Map Ref:** W, D4 **OS Grid Ref:** SO712009

**WJun** **Jungle Giants** ⊠ ✈ € ♿
Ferney, Onibury, Craven Arms, Shropshire, SY7 9BJ
Ⓣ (01584) 856200
Ⓕ (01584) 856663
Ⓔ bamboo@junglegiants.co.uk
Ⓦ www.junglegiants.co.uk
**Contact:** Michael Brisbane
**Opening Times:** 7 days. By appt. only please.
**Min Mail Order UK:** £25.00 + p&p
**Min Mail Order EU:** £100.00 + p&p
**Cat. Cost:** Online only.
**Credit Cards:** Access, MasterCard, Visa
**Specialities:** Bamboos.
**Notes:** Also sells wholesale.
**Map Ref:** W, C4 **OS Grid Ref:** SO430779

**WKif** **Kiftsgate Court Gardens** ♿
Kiftsgate Court, Chipping Camden, Gloucestershire, GL55 6LN
Ⓣ (01386) 438777
Ⓕ (01386) 438777
Ⓔ anne@kiftsgate.co.uk
Ⓦ www.kiftsgate.co.uk
**Contact:** Mrs J Chambers
**Opening Times:** 1200-1800 Sat-Wed, May, Jun & Jul. 1400-1800 Sat-Wed, Aug. 1400-1800 Sun, Mon & Wed, Apr & Sep.
**Cat. Cost:** None issued
**Credit Cards:** All, except American Express
**Specialities:** Small range of unusual plants.
**Map Ref:** W, C5 **OS Grid Ref:** SP170430

**WLav** **The Lavender Garden** ⊠ ⌂ €
Ashcroft Nurseries, Nr Ozleworth, Kingscote, Tetbury, Gloucestershire, GL8 8YF
Ⓣ (01453) 860356 or 549286
Ⓜ 07837 582943
Ⓔ Andrew007Bullock@aol.com
Ⓦ www.TheLavenderG.co.uk
**Contact:** Andrew Bullock
**Opening Times:** 1100-1700 Sat & Sun. Weekdays variable, please phone. 1st Nov-1st Mar by appt. only.
**Min Mail Order UK:** £20.00 + p&p
**Min Mail Order EU:** £20.00 + p&p
**Cat. Cost:** 2 × 1st class.
**Credit Cards:** All major credit/debit cards
**Specialities:** *Lavandula*, *Buddleja*, plants to attract butterflies. Herbs, wildflowers. Nat. Collection of *Buddleja.*
**Notes:** Also sells wholesale.
**Map Ref:** W, D5 **OS Grid Ref:** ST798948

**WLHH** **Lawton Hall Herbs**
Lawton Hall, Eardisland, Herefordshire, HR6 9AX
Ⓣ (01568) 709215
Ⓔ herbs@lawtonhall.co.uk
Ⓦ www.LawtonHall.co.uk
**Contact:** Alexandra Fox
**Opening Times:** 1030-1730 Tue-Sat. For other times please check first.
**Cat. Cost:** Available by email only.
**Credit Cards:** None
**Specialities:** Herbs, culinary, aromatic & medicinal. Herb & wild flower seeds.
**Notes:** Herb gardens & shop.
**Map Ref:** W, C4 **OS Grid Ref:** SO445595

**WMAq** **Merebrook Water Plants** ⊠
Kingfisher Barn, Merebrook Farm, Hanley Swan, Worcestershire, WR8 0DX
Ⓣ (01684) 310950
Ⓜ 07876 777066
Ⓔ enquiries@pondplants.co.uk
Ⓦ www.pondplants.co.uk
**Contact:** Roger Kings & Biddi Kings
**Opening Times:** Not open. Mail order only.
**Min Mail Order UK:** Nmc
**Min Mail Order EU:** £25.00
**Cat. Cost:** Online only.
**Credit Cards:** All major credit/debit cards
**Specialities:** *Nymphaea*, Louisiana irises & other aquatic plants. International Waterlily & Water Gardening Soc. accredited collection.

**W**Mnd **MYND HARDY PLANTS** ♿
Delbury Hall Estate, Diddlebury, Craven Arms, Shropshire, SY7 9DH
Ⓣ (01584) 841222
Ⓔ myndhardyplants@aol.com
Ⓦ www.myndplants.co.uk
**Contact:** Mark Zenick
**Opening Times:** 1300-1700 Wed-Fri, 1000-1700 Sat, 1st Apr-Sep. 1300-1700 B/hol Mons. Other times phone for appt.
**Cat. Cost:** 4 × 2nd class.
**Credit Cards:** All major credit/debit cards
**Specialities:** Herbaceous plants, specialising in American bred, British grown, *Hemerocallis*. Home to New Hope Garden's *Hemerocallis* plants.
**Notes:** Also sells wholesale.
**Map Ref:** W, B4 **OS Grid Ref:** SO510852

**W**Moo **MOORLAND COTTAGE PLANTS** ⊠ ♿
Rhyd-y-Groes, Brynberian, Crymych, Pembrokeshire, SA41 3TT
Ⓣ (01239) 891363
Ⓔ jenny@moorlandcottageplants.co.uk
Ⓦ www.moorlandcottageplants.co.uk
**Contact:** Jennifer Matthews
**Opening Times:** 1030-1730 daily excl. Wed 1st Mar-30th Sep.
**Min Mail Order UK:** See cat. for details.
**Cat. Cost:** 4 × 1st class.
**Credit Cards:** None
**Specialities:** Traditional & unusual hardy perennials. Many garden-worthy rarities. Cottage garden plants, ferns & many shade plants, moisture lovers, ornamental grasses & bamboos, colourful ground cover.
**Notes:** Display garden open for NGS from mid-May.
**Map Ref:** W, C2 **OS Grid Ref:** SN091343

**W**Mou **MOUNT PLEASANT TREES**
Rockhampton, Berkeley, Gloucestershire, GL13 9DU
Ⓣ (01454) 260348
Ⓔ info@mountpleasanttrees.com
Ⓦ www.mountpleasanttrees.com
**Contact:** Tom Locke & Elizabeth Murphy
**Opening Times:** By appt. only.
**Cat. Cost:** Free.
**Credit Cards:** All major credit/debit cards
**Specialities:** Wide range of trees for forestry, hedging, woodlands & gardens esp. *Populus*, *Salix*, *Tilia* & *Quercus*.
**Notes:** Also sells wholesale.
**Map Ref:** W, D4 **OS Grid Ref:** ST654929

**W**New **NEWBRIDGE NURSERY** ⊠ ♿
Crundale, Haverfordwest, Pembrokeshire, SA62 4EJ
Ⓣ (01437) 731678
Ⓕ (01437) 731678
Ⓔ newbridgenursery@ukonline.co.uk
Ⓦ www.newbridgeplantcentre.co.uk
**Contact:** Phil & Jane Davies
**Opening Times:** 1000-1730 daily throughout year.
**Min Mail Order UK:** Nmc
**Cat. Cost:** 2 × 1st class.
**Credit Cards:** All major credit/debit cards
**Specialities:** Wide range of herbaceous perennials & alpines from the common to the more unusual. Also a selection of coastal & acid-loving shrubs.
**Notes:** Credit cards not accepted for mail order. Plants also sold at Haverfordwest Farmers Market.
**Map Ref:** W, D2 **OS Grid Ref:** SM991196

**W**NHG **NEW HOPE GARDENS** ⊠ ♿
The Old Chapel, Cefn Einion, Nr Bishops Castle, Shropshire, SY9 5LF
Ⓣ Office: (01588) 630750 or Nursery: (01584) 841222
Ⓔ Newhopegardensmz@aol.com
Ⓦ www.newhopegardens.com
**Contact:** Mark Zenick
**Opening Times:** 1300-1700 Wed-Fri, 1000-1700 Sat, Apr-Sep. 1300-1700 B/hol Mons during season. Other times phone nursery for appt.
**Min Mail Order UK:** Nmc
**Cat. Cost:** Online only. Plant list on request.
**Credit Cards:** All major credit/debit cards
**Specialities:** American bred, British grown, *Hemerocallis*. Ships bare-rooted plants.
**Map Ref:** W, B4

**W**Old **OLD COURT NURSERIES** ⊠ € ♿
Colwall, Nr Malvern, Worcestershire, WR13 6QE
Ⓣ (01684) 540416
Ⓔ paulpicton@btinternet.com
Ⓦ www.autumnasters.co.uk
**Contact:** Paul, Meriel or Helen Picton
**Opening Times:** 1430-1700 Fri-Sun, May-Aug. 1300-1700 7 days, 1st week Sep-2nd week Oct. Also by appt. May to Oct.
**Min Mail Order UK:** Nmc
**Min Mail Order EU:** Nmc
**Cat. Cost:** 1 × 1st class.
**Credit Cards:** None

KEY
⊠ Mail order to UK or EU — Delivers to shows
✈ Exports beyond EU — € Euro accepted
♿ Accessible by wheelchair — ◆ See Display advertisement

**Specialities:** Nat. Collection of Michaelmas Daisies. Herbaceous perennials.
**Notes:** Mail order for *Aster* only.
**Map Ref:** W, C4 **OS Grid Ref:** SO759430

**WOut** **OUT OF THE COMMON WAY** ⊠ € 
(Office) Penhyddgan, Boduan, Pwllheli, Gwynedd, LL53 8YH
Ⓣ Office: (01758) 721577 or Nursery: (01407) 720431
Ⓔ ziggymen22@tesco.net
**Contact:** Joanna Davidson (nursery) Margaret Mason (office & mail order)
**Opening Times:** By arrangement.
**Min Mail Order UK:** Nmc
**Min Mail Order EU:** Nmc
**Cat. Cost:** A5 sae letter rate postage. Next catalogue autumn 2010.
**Credit Cards:** None
**Specialities:** *Labiates*, esp. *Nepeta* & *Salvia*. *Aster*, *Geranium* & *Crocosmia*. Native plants. Some plants propagated in small quantities only. Will propagate salvias to order.
**Notes:** Nursery is at Pandy Treban, Bryngwran, Anglesey. Partially accessible for wheelchairs.
**Map Ref:** W, A2 **OS Grid Ref:** SH370778

W

**WPat** **CHRIS PATTISON** ⊠ € ♿
Brookend, Pendock, Gloucestershire, GL19 3PL
Ⓣ (01531) 650480
Ⓕ (01531) 650480
Ⓔ cp@chris-pattison.co.uk
Ⓦ www.chris-pattison.co.uk
**Contact:** Chris Pattison
**Opening Times:** 0900-1700 Mon-Fri. W/ends by appt. only.
**Min Mail Order UK:** £10.00 +p&p
**Cat. Cost:** 3 × 1st class.
**Credit Cards:** None
**Specialities:** Choice rare shrubs & alpines. Grafted stock esp. Japanese maples & liquidambars. Wide range of *Viburnum* & dwarf/miniature trees & shrubs.
**Notes:** Mail order Nov-Feb only. Also sells wholesale.
**Map Ref:** W, C5 **OS Grid Ref:** SO781327

**WPer** **PERHILL NURSERIES** ⊠ € ♿
Worcester Road, Great Witley, Worcestershire, WR6 6JT
Ⓣ (01299) 896329
Ⓕ (01299) 896990
Ⓔ perhillp@btconnect.com
Ⓦ www.perhillplants.co.uk
**Contact:** Duncan Straw
**Opening Times:** 0900-1700 most weekdays but please phone first if travelling any distance. Closed weekends.
**Min Mail Order UK:** Nmc
**Min Mail Order EU:** £10.00
**Cat. Cost:** 6 × 2nd class.
**Credit Cards:** All major credit/debit cards
**Specialities:** 2000+ varieties of rare, unusual alpines & herbaceous perennials incl. *Penstemon*, *Campanula*, *Salvia*, *Thymus*, herbs, *Veronica*.
**Notes:** Coach parties welcome. Also sells wholesale.
**Map Ref:** W, C4 **OS Grid Ref:** SO763656

**WPGP** **PAN-GLOBAL PLANTS** ♿
The Walled Garden, Frampton Court, Frampton-on-Severn, Gloucestershire, GL2 7EX
Ⓣ (01452) 741641
Ⓜ 07801 275138
Ⓔ info@panglobalplants.com
Ⓦ www.panglobalplants.com
**Contact:** Nick Macer
**Opening Times:** 1100-1700 Wed-Sun 1st Feb-31st Oct. Also B/hols. Closed 2nd Sun in Sep. Winter months by appt., please phone first.
**Cat. Cost:** 6 × 1st class.
**Credit Cards:** Maestro, MasterCard, Visa, Solo, Delta
**Specialities:** A plantsman's nursery offering a very wide selection of rare & desirable trees, shrubs, herbaceous, bamboos, exotics, climbers, ferns etc. Specialities incl. *Magnolia*, *Hydrangea*, *Bamboo* & *Agavaceae*.
**Map Ref:** W, D5 **OS Grid Ref:** SO750080

**WPnn** **THE PERENNIAL NURSERY** ⊠
Rhosygilwen, Llanrhian Road, St Davids, Pembrokeshire, SA62 6DB
Ⓣ (01437) 721954
Ⓦ www.droughttolerantplants.co.uk
**Contact:** Mrs Philipa Symons
**Opening Times:** 1030-1630 Mar-Oct. Closed Sun & Mon.
**Min Mail Order UK:** Nmc
**Min Mail Order EU:** Nmc
**Cat. Cost:** Online only.
**Credit Cards:** Paypal
**Specialities:** *Rosmarinus*, *Lampranthus*, wind & drought-tolerant plants.
**Notes:** Also sells wholesale.
**Map Ref:** W, C1 **OS Grid Ref:** SM775292

**WPnP** **PENLAN PERENNIALS** ⊠ ☒ € ♿
Penlan Farm, Penrhiw-pâl, Llandysul, Ceredigion, SA44 5QH
Ⓣ (01239) 711102

Ⓜ 07857 675312
Ⓕ (01239) 851244
Ⓔ rcain@penlanperennials.co.uk
Ⓦ www.penlanperennials.co.uk
**Contact:** Richard Cain
**Opening Times:** Mail order only. Open by appt. only.
**Min Mail Order UK:** Nmc
**Min Mail Order EU:** Nmc
**Cat. Cost:** Online, or sae for CD-ROM.
**Credit Cards:** All major credit/debit cards
**Specialities:** Aquatic, marginal & bog plants. Shade-loving & woodland perennials, ferns, grasses & hardy geraniums, all grown peat-free.
**Notes:** Mail order all year, next day delivery. Secure web ordering online.
**Map Ref:** W, C2 **OS Grid Ref:** SN344457

WPtf **PANTYFOD GARDEN NURSERY** ⊠
Llandewi Brefi, Tregaron, Ceredigion, SY25 6PE
Ⓣ (01570) 493564
Ⓔ sales@pantyfodgarden.co.uk
Ⓦ www.pantyfodgarden.co.uk
**Contact:** Susan Rowe
**Opening Times:** Mail order only. Not open, except by prior arrangement.
**Min Mail Order UK:** Nmc
**Cat. Cost:** Online only.
**Credit Cards:** Paypal
**Specialities:** Unusual hardy perennials, hardy geraniums, black plants, woodland plants, plants for moist soil, all grown largely peat-free. Many plants available in small quantities. Stock changes throughout the year. See website for regular updates or phone/email for availability.
**Map Ref:** W, C3 **OS Grid Ref:** SN654540

WRHF **RED HOUSE FARM** ♿
Flying Horse Lane, Bradley Green, Nr Redditch, Worcestershire, B96 6QT
Ⓣ (01527) 821269
Ⓕ (01527) 821674
Ⓦ www.redhousefarmgardenandnursery.co.uk
**Contact:** Mrs Maureen Weaver
**Opening Times:** 0900-1700 Mon-Sat all year. 1000-1700 Sun & B/hols.
**Cat. Cost:** 2 × 1st class.
**Credit Cards:** None
**Specialities:** Cottage garden perennials.
**Map Ref:** W, C5 **OS Grid Ref:** SO986623

WRic **WORLD OF FERNS (RICKARDS FERNS LTD)** ⊠ ✈ €
Carreg y Fedwen, Lôn Rallt, Pentir, Bangor, Gwynedd, LL57 4RP
Ⓣ (01248) 600385
Ⓜ 07875 093352
Ⓕ (01248) 600385
Ⓔ info@world-of-ferns.co.uk
Ⓦ www.world-of-ferns.co.uk
**Contact:** Ben Kettle
**Opening Times:** Open by appt. only.
**Min Mail Order UK:** £30.00 + p&p
**Min Mail Order EU:** £50.00 + p&p
**Cat. Cost:** 5 × 1st class or 6 × 2nd class or online.
**Credit Cards:** All major credit/debit cards
**Specialities:** Ferns, incl. tree ferns.
**Notes:** When visiting, please use Lôn Rallt, Pentir, Bangor as address and not our postcode. Also sells wholesale.
**Map Ref:** W, A3 **OS Grid Ref:** SH592669

WRou **ROUALEYN NURSERIES** ⊠ ♙ ♿
Trefriw, Conwy, LL27 0SX
Ⓣ (01492) 640548
Ⓔ roualeynnursery@btinternet.com
Ⓦ www.roualeynfuchsias.co.uk
**Contact:** Doug Jones
**Opening Times:** 1000-1700 weekdays 1st Mar-31st Aug, 1000-1600 Sat, Sun & B/hols.
**Min Mail Order UK:** £15.00
**Cat. Cost:** 2 × 1st class.
**Credit Cards:** All major credit/debit cards
**Specialities:** Fuchsias, incl. species.
**Notes:** Orders may be collected from any of the flower shows listed in current catalogue.
**Map Ref:** W, A3 **OS Grid Ref:** SH632778

WSFF **SAITH FFYNNON WILDLIFE PLANTS** ⊠ € ♿
Whitford, Holywell, Flintshire, CH8 9EQ
Ⓣ (01352) 711198
Ⓕ (01352) 716777
Ⓔ jan@7wells.org
Ⓦ www.7wells.co.uk
**Contact:** Jan Miller
**Opening Times:** By appt. only.
**Min Mail Order UK:** Nmc
**Min Mail Order EU:** Nmc
**Cat. Cost:** 2 × 1st class (list only) or full catalogue online.
**Credit Cards:** All major credit/debit cards
**Specialities:** Plants and seeds to attract butterflies and moths. Natural dye plants. Nat. Collection of *Eupatorium*. Stock available in small quantities unless ordered well in advance.

**Notes:** Percentage of profits go to Butterfly Conservation. Credit cards accepted via website only. Also sells wholesale.

**WSHC** **Stone House Cottage Nurseries** ♿
Stone, Nr Kidderminster, Worcestershire, DY10 4BG
Ⓣ (01562) 69902
Ⓔ louisa@shcn.co.uk
Ⓦ www.shcn.co.uk
**Contact:** L N Arbuthnott
**Opening Times:** 1000-1700 Wed-Sat. By appt. only mid Sep-mid Mar.
**Cat. Cost:** Sae
**Credit Cards:** None
**Specialities:** Small general range esp. wall shrubs, climbers & unusual plants.
**Map Ref:** W, C5 **OS Grid Ref:** SO863750

**WShi** **Shipton Bulbs** ✉ € 
Y Felin, Henllan Amgoed, Whitland, Carmarthenshire, SA34 0SL
Ⓣ (01994) 240125
Ⓕ (01994) 241180
Ⓔ bluebell@zoo.co.uk
Ⓦ www.bluebellbulbs.co.uk
**Contact:** John Shipton & Aelfwyn Shipton
**Opening Times:** By appt. only.
**Min Mail Order UK:** Nmc
**Min Mail Order EU:** Nmc
**Cat. Cost:** Sae.
**Credit Cards:** All major credit/debit cards
**Specialities:** Native British bulbs, & bulbs & plants for naturalising.
**Map Ref:** W, D2 **OS Grid Ref:** SN188207

**WSSs** **Shropshire Sarracenias** ✉ € ♿
5 Field Close, Malinslee, Telford, Shropshire, TF4 2EH
Ⓣ (01952) 501598
Ⓔ mike@carnivorousplants.uk.com
Ⓦ www.carnivorousplants.uk.com
**Contact:** Mike King
**Opening Times:** By appt. only.
**Min Mail Order UK:** Nmc
**Min Mail Order EU:** Nmc
**Cat. Cost:** 2 × 1st class.
**Credit Cards:** Paypal
**Specialities:** *Sarracenia. Dionaea muscipula* & forms. Some stock available in small quantities only. Nat. Collections of *Sarracenia* & *Dionaea*.
**Map Ref:** W, B4 **OS Grid Ref:** SJ689085

**WSuV** **Sunnybank Vine Nursery (National Vine Collection)** ✉
Cwm Barn, King Street, Ewyas Harold, Rowlestone, Herefordshire, HR2 OEE
Ⓣ (01981) 240256
Ⓔ Sarah@sunnybankvines.co.uk
Ⓦ www.sunnybankvines.co.uk
**Contact:** Sarah Bell
**Opening Times:** Not open. Mail order only.
**Min Mail Order UK:** £10.00 incl. p&p
**Min Mail Order EU:** £15.00 incl. p&p
**Cat. Cost:** Online only.
**Credit Cards:** None
**Specialities:** Vines. Nat. Collection of *Vitis vinifera* (hardy, incl. dessert & wine). 70 varieties available as rooted plants, the entire Collection usually available as bare wood cuttings for own propagation.
**Notes:** EU sales by arrangement.

**WTan** **Tan-y-Llyn Nurseries** ✉
Meifod, Powys, SY22 6YB
Ⓣ (01938) 500370
Ⓔ info@tanyllyn-nursery.co.uk
Ⓦ www.tanyllyn-nursery.co.uk
**Contact:** Callum Johnston
**Opening Times:** 1000-1700 Tue-Sat, Mar-Jun. Other times by appt.
**Min Mail Order UK:** Nmc
**Cat. Cost:** 2 × 1st class or online.
**Credit Cards:** None
**Specialities:** Herbs, alpines, perennials.
**Map Ref:** W, B3 **OS Grid Ref:** SJ167125

**WTcb** **T-Cubed Plants** ✉ ♿
Wall End Nursery, Wall End Farm, Stoke Prior, Herefordshire, HR6 0ND
Ⓣ (01568) 760152
Ⓔ t3plants@aol.com
Ⓦ www.t3plants.co.uk
**Contact:** Eric Turner & Leila Jackson
**Opening Times:** 1000-1500 Mon-Sat, Apr-Oct. Other times by appt.
**Min Mail Order UK:** Nmc
**Min Mail Order EU:** Nmc
**Cat. Cost:** 3 × 1st class.
**Specialities:** *Abutilon*, *Salvia*, *Rudbeckia*, *Sanguisorba*, *Persicaria* & *Thalictrum*. Many shown by genus in display beds.
**Notes:** Open for group visits & talks. Evening visits for horticultural groups by prior arrangement. See website for special events.
**Map Ref:** W, C4 **OS Grid Ref:** SO524566

**WThu** **Thuya Alpine Nursery** ✉
Glebelands, Hartpury, Gloucestershire, GL19 3BW
Ⓣ (01452) 700548
**Contact:** S W Bond
**Opening Times:** 1000-dusk Sat & Bank hol. 1100-dusk Sun, Weekdays appt. advised.
**Min Mail Order UK:** £4.00 + p&p

**Min Mail Order EU:** £10.00 + p&p
**Cat. Cost:** 4 × 2nd class.
**Credit Cards:** None
**Specialities:** Wide and changing range including rarities, available in smallish numbers.
**Notes:** Partially accessible for wheelchair users. Will deliver plants to AGS shows.
**Map Ref:** W, C5

WTin **Tinpenny Plants** ⊠
Smithfield Cottage, The Green, Bishops Norton, Gloucestershire, GL2 9LP
Ⓣ (01452) 731013
Ⓔ elaine@lime.ws
Ⓦ www.tinpenny.plus.com
**Contact:** Elaine Horton
**Opening Times:** By appt. all year round. Email for details.
**Cat. Cost:** None issued.
**Credit Cards:** None
**Specialities:** Wide range of hardy garden-worthy plants esp. *Helleborus*, *Iris* & *Sempervivum*. Small nursery will propagate to order rare plants from own stock. Small quantities only of some plants.

WTou **Touchwood Plants** ⊠ ✈
4 Clyne Valley Cottages, Killay, Swansea, West Glamorgan, SA2 7DU
Ⓣ (01792) 522443
Ⓔ Carrie.Thomas@ntlworld.com
Ⓦ www.touchwoodplants.co.uk
**Contact:** Carrie Thomas
**Opening Times:** Most reasonable days/times. Please phone first.
**Min Mail Order UK:** Nmc
**Min Mail Order EU:** Nmc
**Cat. Cost:** 2 × 1st class.
**Credit Cards:** All major credit/debit cards
**Specialities:** Seeds & plants. Nat. Collection of *Aquilegia vulgaris* cvs & hybrids. Plant stocks held in small quantities. Main stock is seed. Garden & *Aquilegia* Collection open.
**Notes:** Plants sent bare-rooted at relevant times of the year. Beyond the UK only seeds exported. Credit cards accepted online only.
**Map Ref:** W, D3 **OS Grid Ref:** SS600924

WTul **National Collection of Tulbaghia** ⊠
Llety Moel, Rhos-y-Garth, Llanilar, Nr Aberystwyth, Ceredigion, SY23 4SG
Ⓣ (01974) 241505
Ⓜ 07891 333656
Ⓔ liz.powney@btinternet.com
Ⓦ www.tulbaghia.com
**Contact:** Elizabeth Powney
**Opening Times:** Open by appt. only.
**Min Mail Order UK:** Nmc
**Cat. Cost:** None issued.
**Credit Cards:** None
**Specialities:** Nat. Collection of *Tulbaghia*. Plants sold to support the Collection. Available in small quantities only.

WViv **Viv Marsh Postal Plants** ⊠
Walford Heath, Shrewsbury, Shropshire, SY4 2HT
Ⓣ (01939) 291475
Ⓔ mail@postalplants.co.uk
Ⓦ www.postalplants.co.uk
**Contact:** Mr Viv Marsh
**Opening Times:** Selected w/ends in spring & autumn. Please phone for details. Other times by appt. only.
**Min Mail Order UK:** £30.00 plant value
**Min Mail Order EU:** £30.00 plant value
**Cat. Cost:** 5 × 1st class or online.
**Credit Cards:** All major credit/debit cards
**Specialities:** Specialists in *Alstroemeria*, *Iris* & *Lathyrus*.
**Notes:** Wheelchair access with assistance. No disabled toilet.
**Map Ref:** W, B4 **OS Grid Ref:** SJ446198

WWau **Waun Nurseries** ⊠ ⌂
Rhydlewis, Llandysul, Ceredigion, SA44 5PS
Ⓣ (01239) 851359
Ⓔ damson@dsl.pipex.com
Ⓦ www.waunnurseries.co.uk
**Contact:** A Matthews
**Opening Times:** 1000-1600 Thu & Fri. Other times by appt. only
**Min Mail Order UK:** Nmc
**Cat. Cost:** Online only.
**Credit Cards:** All major credit/debit cards
**Specialities:** *Prunus laurocerasus*, *Photinia* & *Eucalyptus*. Some stock available in small quantities only.
**Notes:** Mail order for plants up to max. size 2 ltr pots only. Also sells wholesale.
**Map Ref:** W, C2

WWct **Walcot Organic Nursery** ⊠
Lower Walcot Farm, Walcot Lane, Drakes Broughton, Pershore, Worcestershire, WR10 2AL
Ⓣ (01905) 841587
Ⓜ 07780 547983
Ⓕ (01905) 841587

KEY
⊠ Mail order to UK or EU ⌂ Delivers to shows
✈ Exports beyond EU € Euro accepted
♿ Accessible by wheelchair ◆ See Display advertisement

W

Ⓔ enquiries@walcotnursery.co.uk
Ⓦ www.walcotnursery.co.uk
**Contact:** Kevin O'Neill
**Opening Times:** 0800-1700 Mon-Fri. 1000-1300 Sat. Nov-Mar only.
**Min Mail Order UK:** £12.00
**Min Mail Order EU:** By quotation.
**Cat. Cost:** 1 × 2nd class.
**Credit Cards:** All major credit/debit cards
**Specialities:** Organic fruit trees. Apples, plums, pears, cherries, quinces etc on different rootstocks.
**Notes:** Also sells wholesale.
**Map Ref:** W, C5 **OS Grid Ref:** 944482

**WWEG** **World's End Garden Nursery** ⊠ ◆
Moseley Road, Hallow, Worcester, Worcestershire, WR2 6NJ
Ⓣ (01905) 640977
Ⓕ (01905) 641373
Ⓔ info@worldsendgarden.co.uk
Ⓦ www.worldsendgarden.co.uk
**Contact:** Kristina & Robin Pearce
**Opening Times:** Open by appt. only.
**Min Mail Order UK:** £20.00
**Cat. Cost:** Online only.
**Credit Cards:** All major credit/debit cards
**Specialities:** Wide range of herbaceous perennials, hardy ferns & ornamental grasses. Especially *Hosta*, *Geum*, *Leucantheum*, *Helenium*.
**Notes:** Also sells wholesale.
**Map Ref:** W, C5 **OS Grid Ref:** SO815597

**WWFP** **Whitehall Farmhouse Plants** ⊠ 
Sevenhampton, Cheltenham, Gloucestershire, GL54 5TL
Ⓣ (01242) 820772
Ⓜ 07711 021034
Ⓕ (01242) 821226
Ⓔ info@wfplants.co.uk
Ⓦ www.wfplants.co.uk
**Contact:** Victoria Logue
**Opening Times:** By appt. only.
**Min Mail Order UK:** Nmc
**Cat. Cost:** 2 × 1st class.
**Credit Cards:** None
**Specialities:** A small nursery producing a range of interesting & easy hardy perennials for the garden. Some plants held in small quantities only.
**Map Ref:** W, C5 **OS Grid Ref:** SP018229

**WWFS** **Welsh Fruit Stocks** ⊠
Bryngwyn, Kington, Herefordshire, HR5 3QZ
Ⓣ (01497) 851209
Ⓔ sian@welshfruitstocks.co.uk
Ⓦ www.welshfruitstocks.co.uk
**Contact:** Sîan Fromant
**Opening Times:** By prior appt. only. Mail order only.
**Min Mail Order UK:** Nmc
**Cat. Cost:** Sae.
**Credit Cards:** All major credit/debit cards
**Specialities:** Soft fruit.
**Notes:** Credit cards accepted for online orders only. Also sells wholesale.

**WWHy** **Welsh Holly** ⊠ € 
Llyn-y-gors, Tenby Road, St Clears, Carmarthenshire, SA33 4JP
Ⓣ (01994) 231789
Ⓕ (01994) 231789
Ⓔ info@welsh-holly.co.uk
Ⓦ www.welsh-holly.co.uk
**Contact:** Philip Lanc
**Opening Times:** By appt. only.
**Min Mail Order UK:** Nmc
**Min Mail Order EU:** Nmc
**Cat. Cost:** 2 × 1st class.
**Credit Cards:** None
**Specialities:** Hollies. Limited stock of less common plants.
**Notes:** Also sells wholesale.

**WWlt** **Wollerton Old Hall Garden** 
Wollerton, Market Drayton, Shropshire, TF9 3NA
Ⓣ (01630) 685760
Ⓕ (01630) 685583
Ⓔ info@wollertonoldhallgarden.com
Ⓦ www.wollertonoldhallgarden.com
**Contact:** Mr John Jenkins
**Opening Times:** 1200-1700 Fri, Sun & B/hols Easter-end Sep.
**Cat. Cost:** None issued
**Credit Cards:** All, except American Express
**Specialities:** Perennials, hardy & half-hardy.
**Map Ref:** W, B4 **OS Grid Ref:** SJ624296

## Abroad

**XBlo** **Table Bay View Nursery** ⊠ €
(Office) 60 Molteno Road, Oranjezicht, Cape Town 8001, South Africa
Ⓣ (27) 21 683 5108
Ⓕ (27) 21 683 5108
Ⓔ info@tablebayviewnursery.co.za
**Contact:** Terence Bloch
**Opening Times:** Mail order only. No personal callers.
**Min Mail Order UK:** £15.00 + p&p
**Min Mail Order EU:** £15.00
**Cat. Cost:** £3.40 (postal order)
**Credit Cards:** None
**Specialities:** Tropical & sub-tropical

ornamental & fruiting plants. Self-harvested seed, predominently from our own inventory of mother stock plants.
**Notes:** Due to high local bank charges, cannot accept foreign bank cheques, only undated postal orders.

XDel **PÉPINIÈRE DELPHWOOD** ⊠ ✈ ⌂ € ♿
La Forêterie, 16500 Manot, Charante, France
Ⓣ (33) 5 4571 4451
Ⓜ (33) 61085 1187
Ⓕ (33) 5 4571 4451
Ⓔ delphwood@orange.fr
Ⓦ www.juste-plantes-rustique.eu
**Contact:** Robert Justice-Leeson
**Opening Times:** 1200-1900, 7 days.
**Min Mail Order UK:** Nmc
**Min Mail Order EU:** Nmc
**Credit Cards:** Paypal
**Specialities:** Hardy *Hibiscus.*
**Notes:** Garden open to the public. Mail order autumn-spring.

XEll **ELLEBORE** ⊠ ✈ ⌂ €
La Chamotière, 61 360 Saint-Jouin-de-Blavon, France
Ⓣ (33) 2 3383 3772
Ⓜ (33) 6802 28674
Ⓕ (33) 2 3383 3773
Ⓔ pepiniere.ellebore@orange.fr
Ⓦ www.pepiniere-ellebore.fr
**Contact:** Nadine Albouy & Christian Geoffroy
**Opening Times:** 1000-1800 Wed-Sat, mid-Feb to late Jun & Sep-Dec. 1500-1800 Thu, Fri & Sat, Jul, Aug & Jan to mid-Feb.
**Min Mail Order UK:** Nmc
**Min Mail Order EU:** Nmc
**Cat. Cost:** Free.
**Credit Cards:** All major credit/debit cards
**Specialities:** *Helleborus.* Bulbs. *Clematis.*
**Notes:** Also sells wholesale.

XFro **FROSCH EXCLUSIVE PERENNIALS** ⊠ ✈ €
Ziegelstadelweg 5, D-83623 Dietramszell-Lochen, Germany
Ⓣ (49) 172 8422050
Ⓕ (49) 8027 9049975
Ⓔ info@cypripedium.de
Ⓦ www.cypripedium.de
**Contact:** Michael Weinert
**Opening Times:** Not open. Mail order only. Orders taken between 0700-2200 hours.
**Min Mail Order UK:** £350.00 + p&p
**Min Mail Order EU:** £350.00 + p&p
**Cat. Cost:** Online only.
**Credit Cards:** None
**Specialities:** *Cypripedium* hybrids. Hardy orchids.
**Notes:** Also sells wholesale.

XLum **LUMEN PLANTES VIVACES** ⊠ ✈ ⌂ €
Les Coutets, 24100 Creysse-Bergerac, Occitania, France
Ⓣ (33) 5 5357 6215
Ⓕ (33) 5 5358 5488
Ⓔ lumenviva@aol.com
Ⓦ www.lumen.fr
**Contact:** Michel Lumen
**Opening Times:** 0900-1200 & 1300-1630 Mon-Thu, 0900-1200 & 1300-1530 Fri. Closed Sat, Sun & B/hols. 0900-1200 & 1300-1830 Mon-Sat, Mar-Jun.
**Min Mail Order UK:** Nmc
**Min Mail Order EU:** Nmc
**Cat. Cost:** Online only.
**Credit Cards:** Visa, MasterCard
**Specialities:** Hardy perennials. French Nat. Collection of *Miscanthus.*
**Notes:** Also sells wholesale.

XSen **LES SENTEURS DU QUERCY** ⊠ € ♿
Mas de Fraysse, Escamps, Lot 46230, France
Ⓣ (33) 5652 10167
Ⓔ melie.fred@aliceadsl.fr
Ⓦ www.senteursduquercy.com
**Contact:** Frédéric Prévot
**Opening Times:** 1400-1800 spring & summer (excl. Aug). Other times, incl. Aug by appt.
**Min Mail Order UK:** Nmc
**Min Mail Order EU:** Nmc
**Cat. Cost:** €5.00
**Specialities:** *Salvia, Iris, Phlomis* and drought tolerant plants. French Nat. Coll. of *Salvia* species.

W

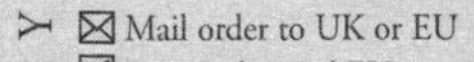

KEY
⊠ Mail order to UK or EU ⌂ Delivers to shows
✈ Exports beyond EU € Euro accepted
♿ Accessible by wheelchair ◆ See Display advertisement

# Nursery Index by Name

Nurseries that are included in the *RHS Plant Finder* for the first time this year (or have been reintroduced) are marked in **bold type**. Full details of the nurseries will be found in **Nursery Details by Code** on page 836. For a key to the geographical codes, see the start of **Nurseries**.

**Layham Garden Centre & Nursery** **SLay**
Lea Rhododendron Gardens Ltd MLea
Leeds Lavender NLLv
Lilies Water Gardens LLWG
Lime Cross Nursery SLim
Linn Botanic Gardens GLin
Lisdoonan Herbs ILis
Little Brook Fuchsias SLBF
Little Heath Farm (UK) (formerly Two Jays Alpines) LLHF
C S Lockyer (Fuchsias) CLoc
Loder Plants SLdr
Lodge Farm Plants & Wildflowers MLod
Lodge Lane Nursery MLLN
Logie Steading Plants GLog
Long Acre Plants CLAP
Long House Plants ELon
Longcombe Nursery and Garden Centre CLng
Longstock Park Nursery SLon
Longstone Hardy Plant Nursery MLHP
Lower Severalls Nursery CSev
**Lumen Plantes Vivaces** **XLum**
M & M Plants CMMP
Mac Pennys Nurseries CMac
MacGregor, Elizabeth GMac
Macplants GMaP
Madrona Nursery SMad
Majestic Trees LMaj
Mallet Court Nursery CMCN
Marcus Dancer Plants SMDP
Marshall's Malmaisons EMal
Marwood Hill Gardens CMHG
Mead Nursery, The CMea
Meadowgate Nursery SMea
Mendip Bonsai Studio CMen
Mendle Nursery NMen
Merebrook Water Plants WMAq
Merriments Gardens SMrm
Mickfield Hostas EMic
Mill Cottage Plants CMil
Mill Race Garden Centre EMil
Millais Nurseries LMil
Millrace Nursery NMRc
Millthorpe Nursery NMil
Miniature Bulbs & Wildflower Bulbs NMin
Mires Beck Nursery NMir
Mrs Mitchell's Kitchen & Garden SMrs
Moorland Cottage Plants WMoo
Morehavens LMor
Morton Nurseries Ltd MMHG
Mount Pleasant Trees WMou
Mozart House Nursery Garden MMoz
Mucklestone Nurseries MMuc
Muncaster Castle NMun
Mynd Hardy Plants WMnd
**National Collection of Tulbaghia** **WTul**
National Herb Centre, The MNHC
Natural Selection CNat
New Hope Gardens WNHG
Newbridge Nursery WNew
Nigel Wright Rhododendrons CWri
Norcroft Nurseries NNor
Norfolk Bamboo Company ENBC
Norwell Nurseries MNrw
Nursery Further Afield, The MNFA
Oak Dene Nurseries NOaD
Oak Tree Nursery NOak
Old Court Nurseries WOld
Old Hall Nursery MOld
Old Hall Plants EOHP
Old Walled Garden, The MOWG
Old Withy Garden Nursery, The COlW
**Orchard House Nursery** **NOrc**
Out of the Common Way WOut
PJ's Palms and Exotics LPJP
P M A Plant Specialities CPMA
P W Plants EPla
Packhorse Farm Nursery MPkF
Paddock Plants SPad
Palm Centre, The LPal
Palm Farm, The NPal
Palm House, The CPHo
Pan-Global Plants WPGP
Pantyfod Garden Nursery WPtf
Parham Bungalow Plants CPBP
Park Green Nurseries EPGN
Parks Perennials CPar
Pattison, Chris WPat
Paugers Plants EPau
Paul Jasper Trees WJas
Pavilion Plants SPav
Penborn Goat Farm CPbn
Peninsula Primulas IPen
Penlan Perennials WPnP
Pennard Plants CPen
Pennycross Plants EPyc
Penstemons by Colour LPen
**Pépinière Delphwood** **XDel**
Perennial Nursery, The WPnn
Perennial Plants Nursery IPPN
Perhill Nurseries WPer
Perry's Plants NPer
Perryhill Nurseries Ltd SPer
**Petals for Plants** **SPtl**
Peter Beales Roses EBls
Peter Grayson (Sweet Pea Seedsman) MPet
Pettet's Nursery SPet
Phedar Nursery MPhe
Phoenix Perennial Plants SPhx
Pine Cottage Plants CPne
Place for Plants, The EPfP
Plant Directory, The (formerly Scawsby Hall Nurseries) NPla
Plant Specialist, The LPla
Plantagogo.com MPnt
Plantbase SPlb

Tile Barn Nursery STil
Timpany Nurseries & Gardens ITim
Tinpenny Plants WTin
Tissington Nursery MTis
Todd's Botanics ETod
Toobees Exotics LToo
Touchwood Plants WTou
Trecanna Nursery CTca
Tregrehan Garden CTgr
Trehane Camellia Nursery CTrh
Trenear, Peter STre
Treseders CTsd
Trevena Cross Nurseries CTrC
Triscombe Nurseries CTri
Tweedie, J. Fruit Trees GTwe
**Tynings Climbers (National Collection of Passiflora & Jasminum) CTyn**
**Up From Earth Herb Nursery CUpf**
Usual & Unusual Plants SUsu
**Ventnor Botanic Garden SVen**
Vicarage Garden, The NVic
Victoria's Nursery & Garden IVic
Victoriana Nursery Gardens SVic
Viv Marsh Postal Plants WViv
**Waddow Lodge Garden NWad**
Walcot Organic Nursery WWct
Wallace Plants SWal
Walled Garden, The EWll
Walled Garden Nursery CWGN
Walnut Tree Garden Nursery EWTr
**Waltham Herbs EWhm**
Wanborough Herb Nursery CWan
Water Garden, The CWat
Water Meadow Nursery SWat
Waterperry Gardens Ltd MWat
Waterside Nursery MWts
**Waun Nurseries WWau**
Wear's Nursery MWea
Weasdale Nurseries Ltd. NWea
**Welsh Fruit Stocks WWFS**
Welsh Holly WWHy
West Acre Gardens EWes
West Harptree Nursery CHar
West Somerset Garden Centre CWSG
Westcountry Nurseries CWCL
Westonbirt Plants LWst
Westshores Nurseries NWsh
White Cottage Alpines NWCA
White, Jill EJWh
White Veil Fuchsias CWVF
Whitehall Farmhouse Plants WWFP
Whitehill Farm Nursery MWhi
Whitelea Nursery MWht
Wibble Farm Nurseries CWib
**Wild Flower Shop EWil**
Windrush Willow CWiW
Wisley Plant Centre (RHS) LRHS
Witton, D S NWit
Wollerton Old Hall Garden WWlt
Wolverton Plants Ltd SWvt
Wonder Tree, The CWon
**Wood, J A WJAW**
Woodlands EWld
Woottens Plants EWoo
World of Ferns (Rickards Ferns Ltd) WRic
World's End Garden Nursery WWEG
Wych Cross Nurseries SWCr
Wykeham Mature Plants NWyk
Yaffles LYaf

# Specialist Nurseries

Nurseries have classified themselves under the following headings where they *exclusively* or *predominantly* supply this range of plants. Plant groups are set out in alphabetical order. Refer to **Nursery Details by Code** on page 836 for details of the nurseries whose codes are listed under the plant group which interests you. See page 833 for a fuller explanation.

## Acid-loving Plants

CBcs, CMac, CMen, CTrh, CWCL, CWri, EFly, GAuc, GGar, GLam, IBlr, IPen, ITim, IVic, LMil, MFie, MGos, MLea, MMuc, MSnd, NHar, NHim, NLar, NMun, SCam, SCog, SFai, SLdr, SReu, SRot, SWhi, WAbe, WRic, WThu

## Alpine/Rock Plants

CEls, CWat, CWil, EBur, ECho, EDAr, EHoe, EPot, GAgs, GEdr, GKev, GLam, IBal, IPen, ITim, LIMB, LWst, NHar, NMen, NMin, NRya, NSla, NWad, NWCA, SCog, SPop, SRot, WAbe, WCre, WGor, WHoo, WPrP, WThu

## Aquatic Plants

CBen, CRow, CWat, EHon, LLWG, LPBA, MSKA, MWts, SWat, WMAq, WPnP

## Bamboos

CAgr, CDTJ, CEnt, CPHo, ENBC, EPla, GBin, GLin, LPal, MBrN, MDev, MMoz, MMuc, MWhi, MWht, NGdn, NPal, WDyG, WJun, WPGP

## British Wild Flowers

CArn, CHab, COld, CRea, EWil, GPoy, MHer, MLod, NBir, NLan, NLAp, NMin, NMir, SSrw, SWat, WHer, WHfH, WJek, WLav, WSFF, WShi

## Bulbous Plants

CAvo, CBro, CFFs, CGrW, CLak, CPne, CQua, CRea, CTca, CWCL, ECho, EPot, ERCP, LAma, LWst, MCri, MSSP, NHoy, NMin, SDeJ, SPhx, STil, WPrP, WShi, XEll

## Cactus and Succulents

CFwr, CPhi, CTrC, EAmu, EGln, EShb, ETod, LToo, NCro, NOaD, SCac, SChr, WPGP

## Carnivorous Plants

CHew, CSWC, EECP, EFEx, EFly, NChu, SHmp, WSSs

## Chalk-loving Plants

CBot, CSev, CSpe, LSRN, SAll, SEND, SGar, SHar, SJoh, SKHP, SMrs, SSss, SUsu, XEll

## Climbers

CFir, CLng, CRHN, CSPN, CTri, CTyn, CWGN, EBls, ELan, ETho, LSRN, MBlu, MCri, MGos, MOWG, NBea, NSti, NTay, SKHP, SLau, WCru, WFib, WSHC, XEll

## Coastal Plants

CBod, CCCN, CPne, CTrC, GGar, IBal, ISsi, IVic, MOWG, NHoy, SBod, SChr, SEND, SGar, SMea, SVen, WPnn, WWau, XDel

## Conifers

CKen, CMac, CMen, ECho, EHul, EPla, MBlu, MPkF, NLar, NWyk, SLim, WEve, WGor, WMou, WThu

## Conservatory Plants

CBcs, CBrP, CCCN, CEls, CFwr, CLak, CRHN, CSpe, CTyn, EBak, EGln, EOHP, ERea, EShb, ESul, IFro, LToo, MBPg, MOWG, MREP, NExo, NFir, WTcb, XBlo

## Drought-tolerant Plants

CBot, CKno, CPne, ECGP, ECha, EGln, EHoe, ETod, LIMB, LLWP, LPal, MBPg, NFir, NHoy, NMRc, SAll, SDow, SEND, SJoh, SMea, SPhx, SUsu, SVen, WFib, WHil, WPnn, XLum, XSen

## Ferns

CBty, CDTJ, CLAP, EFer, EFtx, ELan, GBin, GLin, IBal, ISha, LLWG, MMoz, NHar, NMyG, SApp, SCog, SRot, WAbe, WFib, WMoo, WPnP, WRic, WWEG

## Fruit

CAgr, CCAT, CTho, CTri, ECrN, EPom, ERea, GPri, GTwe, LBuc, LEdu, MCoo, MLod, SCmr, SCrf, SDea, SEWo, SFam, SKee, SVic, WHar, WJas, WWct

## Grasses

CBod, CKno, CWCL, EHoe, EPla, EPPr, GBin, GCal, IFoB, LEdu, LLWP, MBrN, MLLN, MMoz, MNrw, MWhi, NBea, NExo, NGdn, NMRc, NOak, NWsh, SApp, SHDw, SMea, SPhx, SSss, SUsu, SWal, WGrn, WHal, WMoo, WPrP, WWEG, XLum

## Hedging

CCVT, CSil, CTho, CTrC, CTri, ECrN, EHul, ERom, ISsi, LBuc, NWyk, SDow, SEWo, SLay, SVic, WBuc, WEve, WHar, WLav, WMou, WWau

## Herbs

CArn, CBod, CHby, COld, CPbn, CSev, CUpf, CWan, ELau, EOHP, EWhm, GPoy, ILis, LEdu, LLWP, LMor, MHer, MLod, NBir, NLLv, SDow, EGHP, SHDw, STas, SVic, SWat, WHfH, WJAW, WJek, WLav, WLHH

## Marginal/Bog Plants

CLAP, CMHG, CWat, EECP, EFly, EHon, EWil, GKev, GLam, IPen, IVic, LLWG, MMuc, MSKA, MWts, NBir, NCot, NHim, NMRc, NWad, WHal, WMAq, WMoo, WPnP, WSFF, WShi, XDel

## Orchids

CBur, CLAP, EFEx, GEdr, LWst, LYaf, NDav, NEqu, NLAp, WHer, XFro

## Organic

CBgR, CHby, COld, CTuc, CWon, EPla, GAuc, GPoy, ILis, LEdu, LLWP, MLLN, MLod, NHoy, SHmp, SPav, SPol, SRiF, SSrw, STas, WGwG, WJAW, WJek, WPnP, WSFF, WShi, WWct, WWFS, XEll

## Ornamental trees

CBcs, CBty, CCVT, CDul, CEnd, CMac, CMen, CPMA, CSto, CTho, CTri, CWon, ECrN, EGFP, ELan, ERom, GAuc, LBuc, LMaj, LMil, MBlu, MGos, MPkF, NBea, NHim, NLar, NPal, NWyk, SBir, SCrf, SEWo, SKHP, SLau, SLay, SLim, WBuc, WCru, WEve, WHar, WHCr, WJas, WMou, WPGP, XLum

## Palms

CDTJ, CPHo, EAmu, ETod, LPal, LPJP, MREP, NPal, SChr

## Peat Free

CBgR, CBot, CCse, CCVN, CDoy, CElw, CHby, CLAP, CMea, CPHo, CPom, CRHN, CSam, CSev, CTca, CTho, CTsd, CWon, EBla, EBtc, ECrN, ELau, EMal, EPts, ERea, EWhm, IBlr, ILis, LEdu, LLWP, MBNS, MCri, MLHP, MLLN, MLod, MMoz, MWhi, NBid, NLan, NWCA, SAll, SBch, SBrt, SMrs, SPav, SRiF, STes, WCAu, WCru, WDyG, WGwG, WHoo, WJek, WPnP, WPrP, WSFF, WShi, WTcb, WWct, XEll

## Period Plants

CArn, CSev, CSil, EBls, ESgI, ILis, MPet, SAll, SPop, WHer, WWau

## Propagate to Order

CArn, CBot, CCCN, CCse, CEls, CElw, CFir, CLAP, CMac, CMen, CPbn, CPne, CSev, CTsd, CWon, EBls, ECho, ECrN, EECP, EHoe, EPla, EPri, ERea, ERhR, EShb, ESul, EWhm, GKev, GQue, IFro, ILis, IPPN, IRar, LBMP, LEdu, LIMB, LLWP, LMil, MBrN, MDev, MLHP, MMoz, MNrw, MPnt, MRav, NChi, NCot, NHoy, NLLv, NRya, NWCA, SAga, SBch, SCam, SCrf, SDea, SFam, SGar, SHDw, SHmp, SHyH, SLau, SLdr, SPin, SPol, SRiF, SSea, SSrw, STes, SUsu, SVen, SWat, WCru, WFib, WGwG, WHer, WHil, WJek, WLav, WPat, WPnP, WPrP, WRic, WSFF, WSSs, WTin, WWct, XBlo, XLum

## Roses

CGro, CPou, EBls, ECnt, ESty, GCoc, IDic, LShp, LSRN, LStr, MAus, SFam, SLay, SRGP, SSea, SWCr

## Seed

CBot, CDob, CHby, CKno, CRea, CSpe, CSut, CTuc, EWil, GAuc, GPoy, LSee, MFie, MPet, NChl, NEqu, NLan, NRob, EGHP, SSss, WHil, WJek, WSFF, WTou, XBlo

## Specimen-sized Plants

CBty, CClc, CCVT, CPhi, CPMA, CPne, CSWC, CWon, EAmu, EBtc, ECrN, EECP, EHoe, ELau, EPla, EQua, ERea, ERom, EShb, ETod, GAuc, LEdu, LMaj, LMil, MDev, MGos, MLea, MPhe, MREP, MWht, NCro, NGBo, NHim, NHoy, NLAp, NWyk, SBig, SCam, SCrf, SEWo, SFai, SGol, SHDw, SHmp, SHyH, SLdr, SMea, SReu, SRiv, SSta, SWat, WCru, WEve, WHer, WJek, WJun, WPat, WRic, XBlo

## Topiary

CClc, ERom, MREP, SRiv

## Tropical

CCCN, CFir, CFwr, EAmu, EShb, ISsi, LToo, MREP, NExo, SBst, WCru, WHil, WRic, XBlo

# RHS Plant Trials Bulletins

The Trials Bulletins give the results and findings of RHS Trials. The detailed descriptions and images of the plants that have been given the Award of Garden Merit are included, as well as updates on nomenclature, cultivation details and a table comparing the different characteristics of the entries in the trial.

*Begonia* Rex Cultorum Group
*Canna*
*Clematis alpina* and *C. macropetala*
*Dahlia*
Daisies (yellow perennial)
*Delphinium*
*Fuchsia*, hardy
*Geranium*, hardy (Stage 1)
*Geranium*, hardy (Stage 2)
*Geranium*, hardy (Stage 3)
*Hyacinthaceae* (little blue bulbs)
*Hydrangea paniculata*
*Iris*, bearded
*Lavandula*, hardy
*Miscanthus*
Peppers, chilli
Peppers, sweet
Potatoes, salad
*Potentilla*, shrubby
*Rhododendron yakushimanum* and hybrids
Runner Beans
*Saxifraga*, silver
*Sedum*, herbaceous

**If you would like a copy of any of these, please contact:**
The Trials Office, RHS Garden Wisley, Woking, Surrey GU23 6QB. Please enclose an A4 SAE and a cheque for £2.00 per copy (as a donation towards costs) made out to the Royal Horticultural Society.

In addition to the above there are four bulletins that are only available on the RHS Website: *Caryopteris, Perovskia, Pittosporum* and *Spiraea japonica*.
To view and download any of these RHS Plant Trials Bulletins online, please visit:
**www.rhs.org.uk/plants/RHS-publications/Plant-bulletins**

# INDEX MAP

The maps on the following pages show the approximate location of the nurseries whose details are listed in this directory.

KEY

CHEx Details of nurseries with letter codes in boxes are given in the Nursery Details by Code Index starting on page 836.

1
2
3
C
MAP ONE
SOUTH WEST
A
B
C
D
Llanelli
M4
Neath
Swansea
CSil
Ilfracombe
Combe Martin
CMHG
Barnstaple
CSpr
Bideford
CMMP
CHid
CWCL
CKen
CWri
A377
Bude
CWil
A39
CCha
CPbn
Okehampton
CSto
Launceston
CBre
CEnd
CRow
Tavistock
Newton A
Wadebridge
CBct
CTca
CGHE
CHll
CBod
Bodmin
Liskeard
CTsd
CDoC
Newquay
CPrp
Plymouth
A38
CPLG
A30
CHVG
St Austell
CTGr
CPou
CRHN
Truro
St Ives
Redruth
CHEx
Camborne
CBcS
CTrC
CCtw
Falmouth
Helston
Penzance
COIW
CFir
CQua
CCCN
1
2
3

4
5
6
A
B
C
D
Stroud
Cirencester
Pontypool
Cwmbran
Newport
CARDIFF
Bristol
Clevedon
Weston Super Mare
Swindon
Chippenham
Marlborough
Calne
Newbury
Bath
Melksham
Trowbridge
Devizes
Burnham on Sea
Williton
Wells
Frome
Warminster
Andover
Bridgwater
Glastonbury
Salisbury
Wincanton
Shaftesbury
Taunton
Wellington
Yeovil
Chard
Southampton
Ringwood
Blandford Forum
Honiton
Lymington
Winborne Minster
Bridport
Lyme Regis
Dorchester
Poole
Bournemouth
Weymouth
Exmouth
M5
M4
M3
A36
A303
A354
A35
CSPN
CWGN
CLoc
CNat
CWat
CWan
CPhi
CClc
CJas
CSpe
CTyn
CWon
CBot
CArn
CCVT
CHar
CPom
CPBP
CMea
CFwr
CMil
CMen
CWib
CHby
CBgR
CTri
CSna
CElw
CPen
CAbP
CBty
CBro
CKel
CLAP
CDTJ
CCAT
CSam
CMCN
CLnd
CPMA
CSWC
CSev
CDul
CRDP
CKno
CTrh
CAby
CIri
CMac
CFee
CEnt
CPHo
CBrP
CPar
CGro
CDoy
CEls
CBen

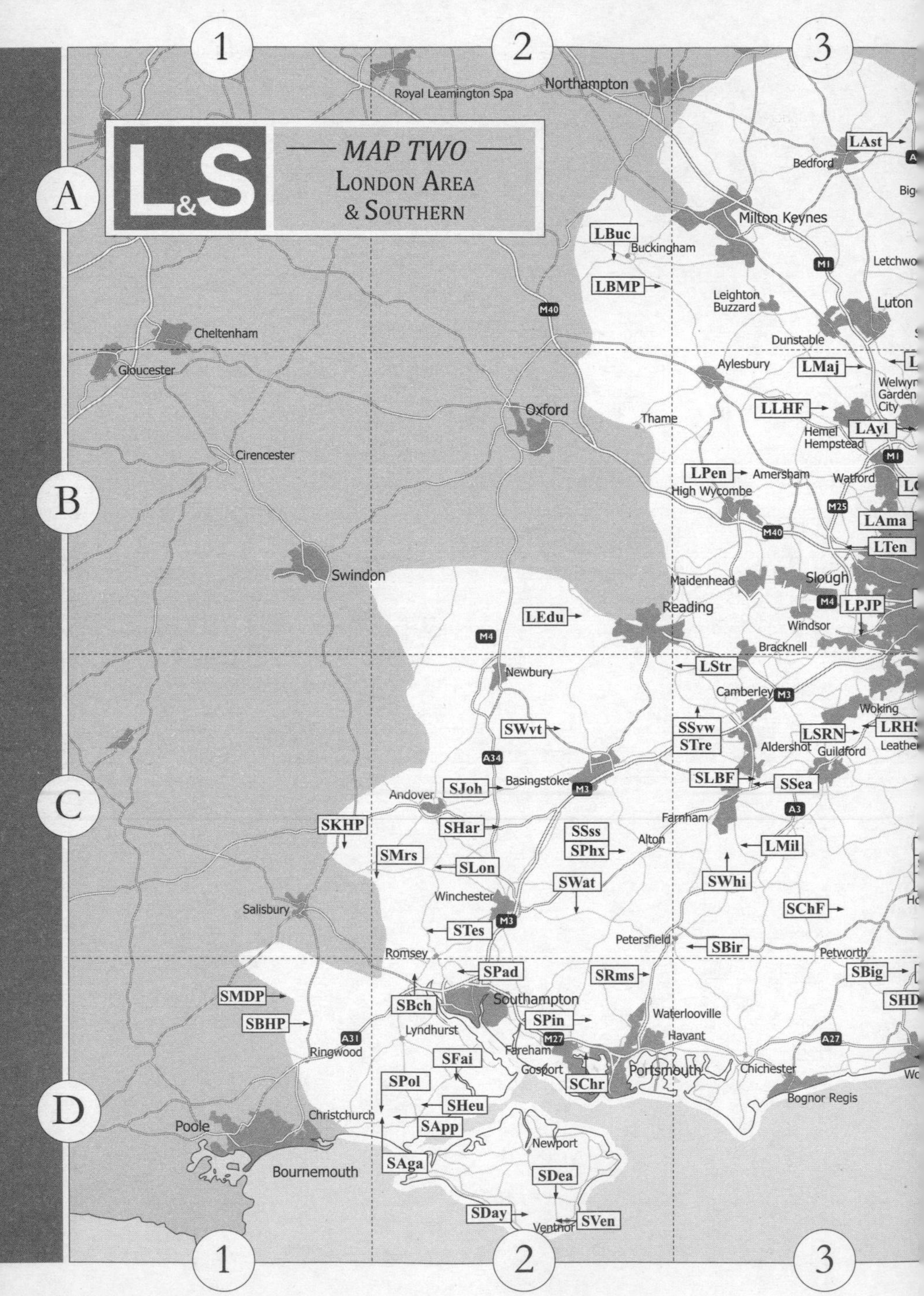

L&S
MAP TWO
London Area & Southern
1
2
3
A
B
C
D
Northampton
Royal Leamington Spa
LAst
Bedford
Milton Keynes
LBuc
Buckingham
LBMP
M1
Leighton Buzzard
Luton
Dunstable
M40
Cheltenham
Gloucester
Aylesbury
LMaj
Oxford
Thame
LLHF
LAyl
Hemel Hempstead
Cirencester
LPen
Amersham
High Wycombe
Watford
M25
LAma
LTen
Swindon
Maidenhead
Slough
M4
LPJP
Reading
Windsor
LEdu
Bracknell
LStr
Newbury
Camberley
M3
Woking
SWvt
SSvw
STre
LSRN
LRHS
Aldershot
Guildford
A34
Basingstoke
SLBF
SSea
SJoh
Andover
A3
Farnham
SKHP
SHar
SSss
SPhx
Alton
LMil
SMrs
SLon
SWat
SWhi
Winchester
SChF
Salisbury
STes
Petersfield
SBir
Romsey
Petworth
SPad
SRms
SBig
SMDP
SBch
Southampton
SHD
SBHP
SPin
Waterlooville
Lyndhurst
A31
M27
Havant
A27
Ringwood
Fareham
SFai
Gosport
SChr
Portsmouth
Chichester
SPol
SHeu
Bognor Regis
Christchurch
Poole
SApp
Newport
SAga
Bournemouth
SDea
SDay
SVen
Ventnor

4
5
6
A
B
C
D
Bury St E
Cambridge
Ipswich
Hel
A10
LHop
Bishops Stortford
Braintree
Colchester
Clacton on Sea
Chelmsford
Harlow
A10
M11
M25
Billericay
Brentwood
Rayleigh
Basildon
Southend on Sea
Canvey Island
DON
Grays
M25
Sheerness
SEND
Margate
Gravesend
Gillingham
Herne Bay
SRiF
Chatham
STas
Ramsgate
M25
SRiv
SDys
SCmr
Sittingbourne
Maidstone
M20
M2
Canterbury
Sandwich
SCoo
M26
SPoG
SVic
SPet
SReu
SLPI
SCrf
SLay
SBrd
SPlb
SKee
A2
LSou
Tonbridge
SMad
SGar
SDow
SIde
Ashford
SPer
SBri
Dover
M20
Tunbridge Wells
SIri
STil
Folkestone
SLau
SMrm
SAdn
SWCr
SRkn
SEWo
Hurst Green
Haywards Heath
Maresfield
SPtl
SPur
SAll
SWal
SLim
Hastings
Lewes
Hailsham
SUsu
SCog
SRot
Bexhill
SSth
Eastbourne

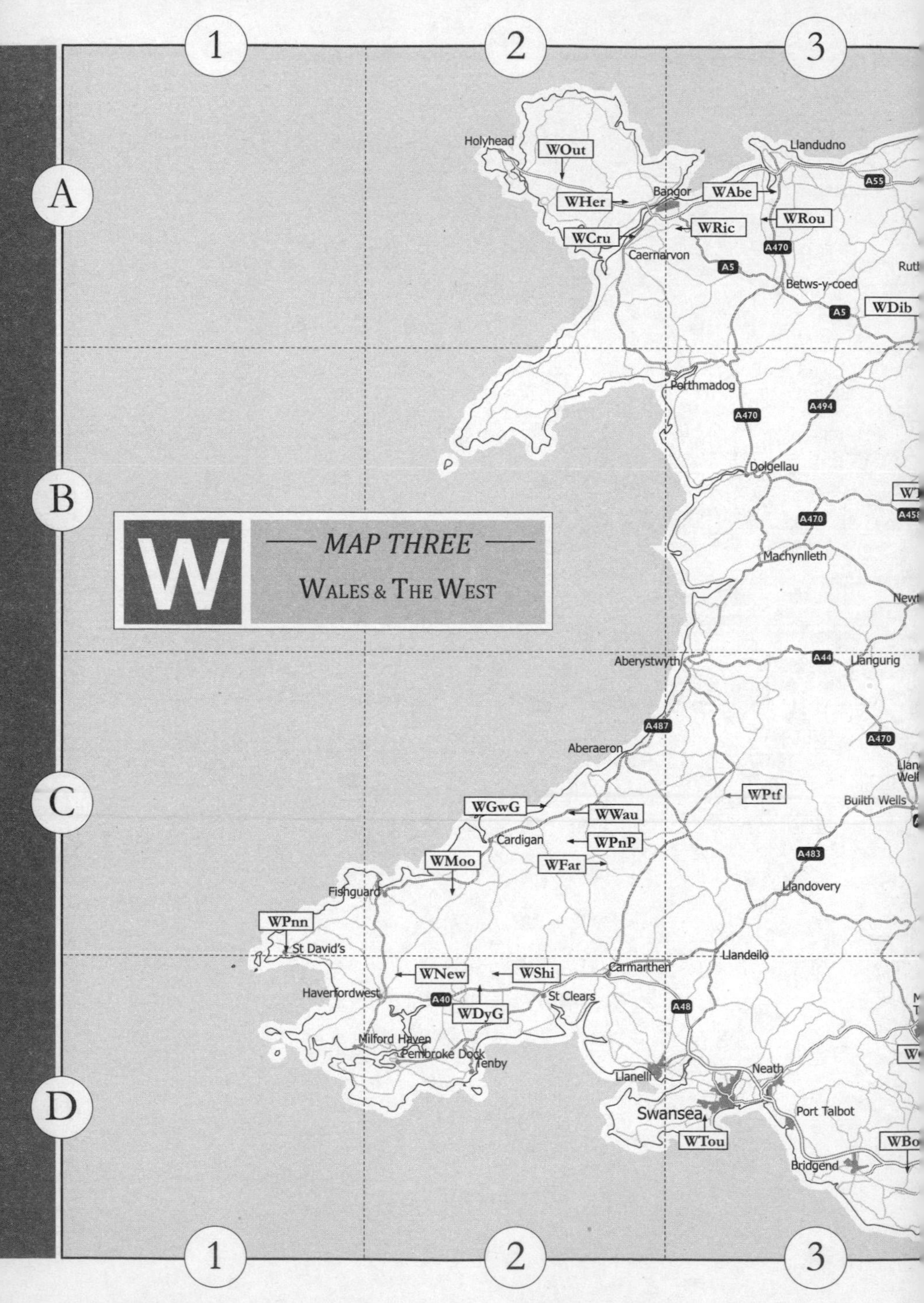
1
2
3
A
B
C
D
W
MAP THREE
Wales & The West
Holyhead
WOut
WHer
Bangor
WAbe
Llandudno
A55
WRou
WRic
WCru
Caernarvon
A470
A5
Betws-y-coed
WDib
Porthmadog
A470
A494
Dolgellau
A470
Machynlleth
Aberystwyth
A44
Llangurig
A487
Aberaeron
A470
WPtf
Builth Wells
WGwG
WWau
Cardigan
WPnP
WFar
WMoo
A483
Llandovery
Fishguard
WPnn
St David's
Llandeilo
WNew
WShi
Carmarthen
Haverfordwest
A40
St Clears
WDyG
A48
Milford Haven
Pembroke Dock
Tenby
Llanelli
Neath
Swansea
Port Talbot
WTou
WBo
Bridgend

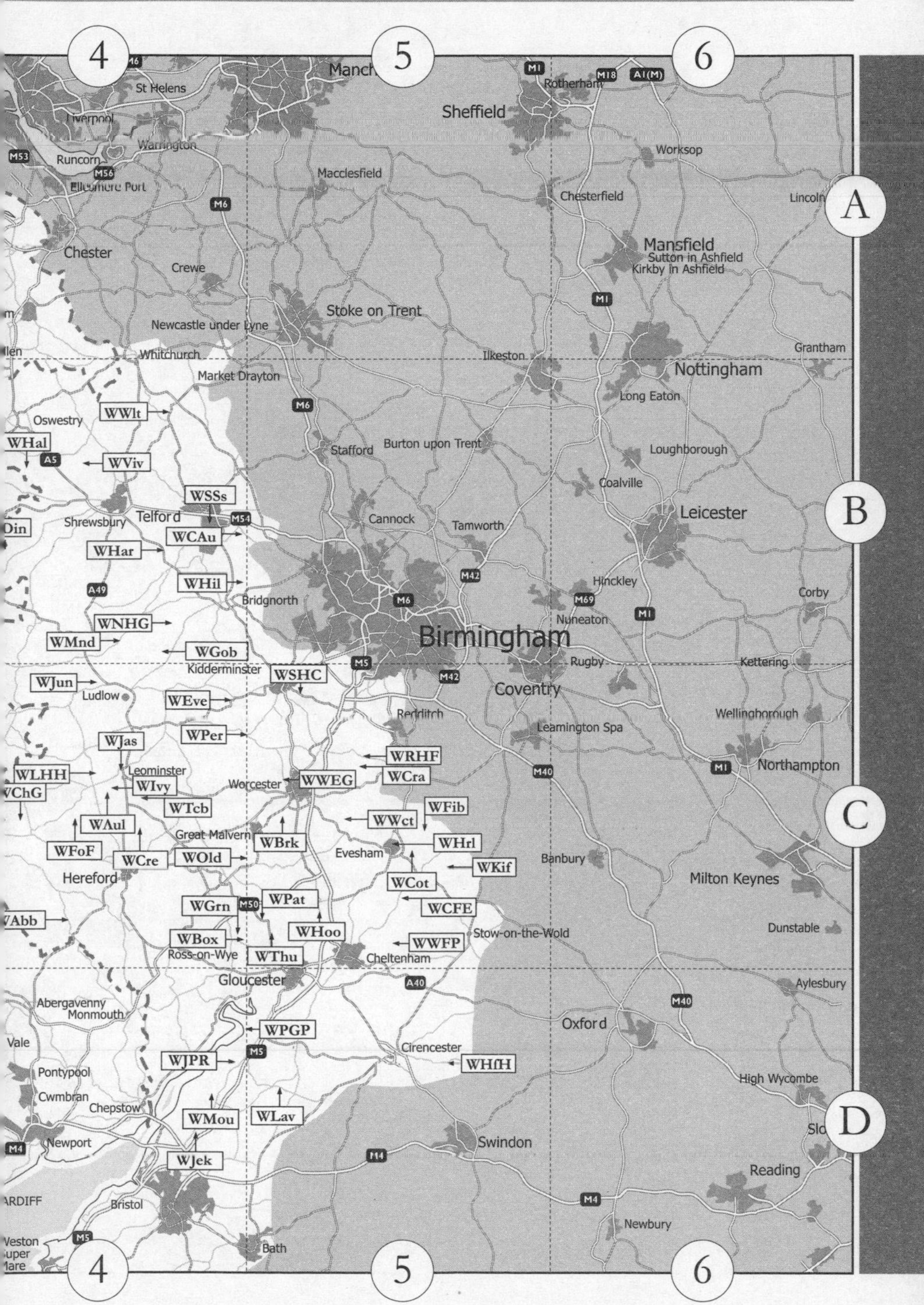

4
5
6
A
B
C
D
Manch
St Helens
Liverpool
Warrington
Runcorn
Ellesmere Port
Chester
Crewe
Macclesfield
Sheffield
Rotherham
Worksop
Chesterfield
Lincoln
Mansfield
Sutton in Ashfield
Kirkby in Ashfield
Stoke on Trent
Newcastle under Lyne
Whitchurch
Market Drayton
Ilkeston
Nottingham
Long Eaton
Grantham
Oswestry
Stafford
Burton upon Trent
Loughborough
Coalville
Leicester
Shrewsbury
Telford
Cannock
Tamworth
Hinckley
Bridgnorth
Nuneaton
Corby
Birmingham
Kidderminster
Rugby
Kettering
Coventry
Ludlow
Redditch
Wellingborough
Leamington Spa
Leominster
Worcester
Northampton
Great Malvern
Evesham
Banbury
Hereford
Milton Keynes
Stow-on-the-Wold
Dunstable
Ross-on-Wye
Cheltenham
Gloucester
Aylesbury
Abergavenny
Monmouth
Oxford
Cirencester
Vale
Pontypool
Cwmbran
Chepstow
High Wycombe
Newport
Swindon
Reading
ARDIFF
Bristol
Newbury
Weston
super
Mare
Bath
WWlt
WHal
WViv
WSSs
Din
WCAu
WHar
WHil
WNHG
WMnd
WGob
WSHC
WJun
WEve
WPer
WJas
WRHF
WCra
WLHH
WWEG
WIvy
WChG
WTcb
WFib
WWct
WAul
WBrk
WHrl
WFoF
WCre
WOld
WKif
WCot
WCFE
WGrn
WPat
WAbb
WHoo
WBox
WWFP
WThu
WPGP
WJPR
WHfH
WMou
WLav
WJek
M6
M53
M56
M1
M18
A1(M)
A5
M54
A49
M42
M69
M5
M40
M50
A40
M4

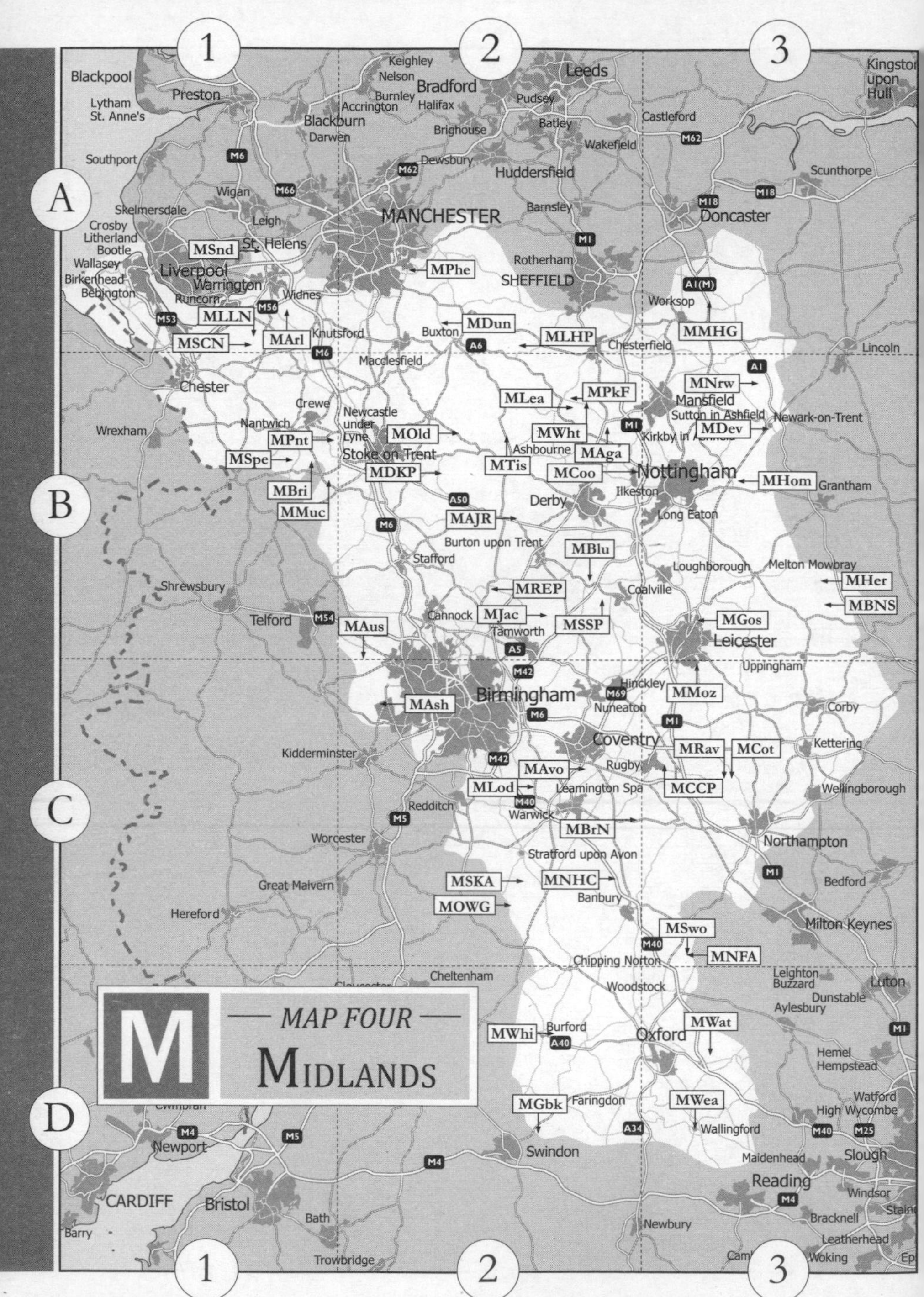

1
2
3
A
B
C
D
MAP FOUR
M
MIDLANDS
Blackpool
Lytham St. Anne's
Preston
Southport
Wigan
Skelmersdale
Crosby
Litherland
Bootle
Wallasey
Birkenhead
Bebington
Liverpool
Warrington
Runcorn
Widnes
St. Helens
Leigh
Blackburn
Darwen
Accrington
Burnley
Nelson
Keighley
Bradford
Halifax
Brighouse
Dewsbury
Huddersfield
Leeds
Pudsey
Batley
Wakefield
Castleford
Kingston upon Hull
Scunthorpe
Doncaster
Barnsley
MANCHESTER
Rotherham
SHEFFIELD
Worksop
Chesterfield
Lincoln
Buxton
Knutsford
Macclesfield
Chester
Crewe
Nantwich
Wrexham
Newcastle under Lyne
Stoke on Trent
Ashbourne
Mansfield
Sutton in Ashfield
Kirkby in Ashfield
Newark-on-Trent
Nottingham
Ilkeston
Derby
Long Eaton
Grantham
Burton upon Trent
Stafford
Loughborough
Melton Mowbray
Coalville
Shrewsbury
Telford
Cannock
Tamworth
Leicester
Uppingham
Hinckley
Nuneaton
Birmingham
Corby
Coventry
Kettering
Kidderminster
Rugby
Leamington Spa
Wellingborough
Redditch
Warwick
Worcester
Stratford upon Avon
Northampton
Great Malvern
Bedford
Hereford
Banbury
Milton Keynes
Chipping Norton
Leighton Buzzard
Cheltenham
Woodstock
Luton
Dunstable
Aylesbury
Burford
Oxford
Hemel Hempstead
Faringdon
Watford
High Wycombe
Wallingford
Newport
Swindon
Maidenhead
Slough
Reading
Windsor
CARDIFF
Bristol
Bath
Barry
Trowbridge
Newbury
Bracknell
Leatherhead
Woking
M6
M66
M62
M61
M18
M1
A1(M)
M56
M53
A6
A1
A50
M54
A5
M42
M69
M5
M40
M4
A40
A34
M25
MSnd
MPhe
MLLN
MArl
MSCN
MDun
MLHP
MMHG
MNrw
MLea
MPkF
MDev
MWht
MAga
MPnt
MOld
MSpe
MDKP
MTis
MCoo
MHom
MBri
MMuc
MAJR
MBlu
MHer
MBNS
MREP
MJac
MSSP
MGos
MAus
MMoz
MAsh
MRav
MCot
MAvo
MLod
MCCP
MBrN
MSKA
MNHC
MOWG
MSwo
MNFA
MWhi
MWat
MGbk
MWea

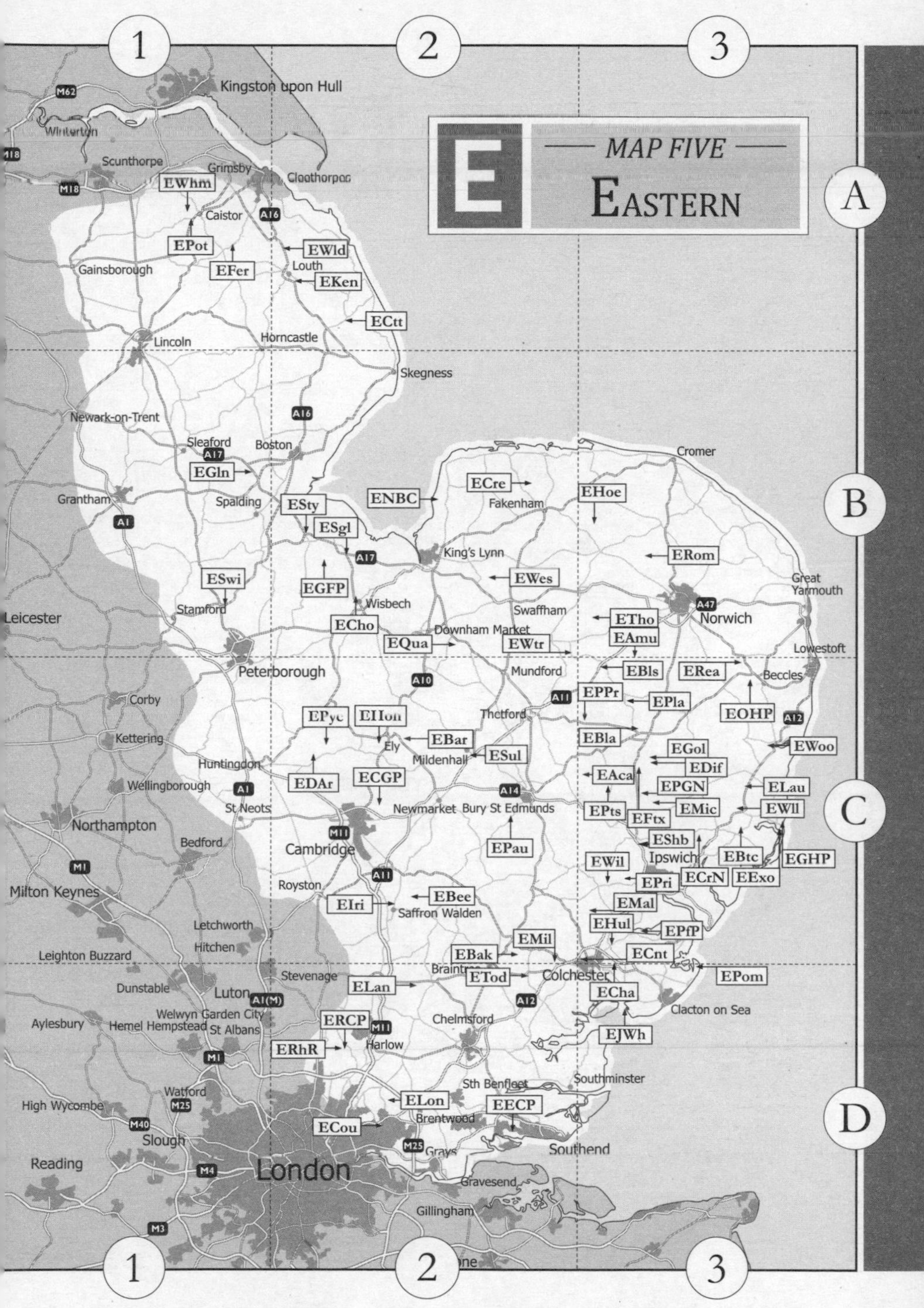
MAP FIVE
E
EASTERN
1
2
3
A
B
C
D
Kingston upon Hull
Winterton
Scunthorpe
Grimsby
Cleethorpes
EWhm
Caistor
EPot
EWld
Louth
EKen
EFer
Gainsborough
ECtt
Lincoln
Horncastle
Skegness
Newark-on-Trent
Sleaford
Boston
EGln
Grantham
Spalding
ESty
ESgl
ENBC
ECre
Fakenham
EHoe
Cromer
King's Lynn
ERom
ESwi
EGFP
EWes
Great Yarmouth
Stamford
Wisbech
Swaffham
ETho
Norwich
Leicester
ECho
Downham Market
EAmu
EQua
EWtr
Lowestoft
Peterborough
Mundford
EBls
ERea
Beccles
EPPr
EPla
Corby
EPyc
EHon
Thetford
EOHP
Kettering
EBar
EBla
EGol
EWoo
Ely
ESul
Mildenhall
EDif
Huntingdon
EACa
ELau
Wellingborough
EDAr
ECGP
EPGN
St Neots
Newmarket
Bury St Edmunds
EPts
EFtx
EMic
EWll
Northampton
EShb
Bedford
Cambridge
EPau
Ipswich
EBtc
EGHP
EWil
ECrN
EExo
Royston
EPri
Milton Keynes
EIri
EBee
EMal
Saffron Walden
Letchworth
EHul
EPfP
Hitchen
EMil
Leighton Buzzard
EBak
ECnt
Braintree
ETod
Colchester
EPom
Stevenage
ELan
Dunstable
Luton
ECha
Welwyn Garden City
Clacton on Sea
Aylesbury
Hemel Hempstead
St Albans
ERCP
Chelmsford
EJWh
ERhR
Harlow
Southminster
Watford
Sth Benfleet
High Wycombe
ELon
EECP
Brentwood
ECou
Slough
Grays
Southend
Reading
London
Gravesend
Gillingham
M62
M18
A16
A17
A1
A47
A10
A11
A12
A14
M11
M1
A1(M)
M25
M40
M4
M3

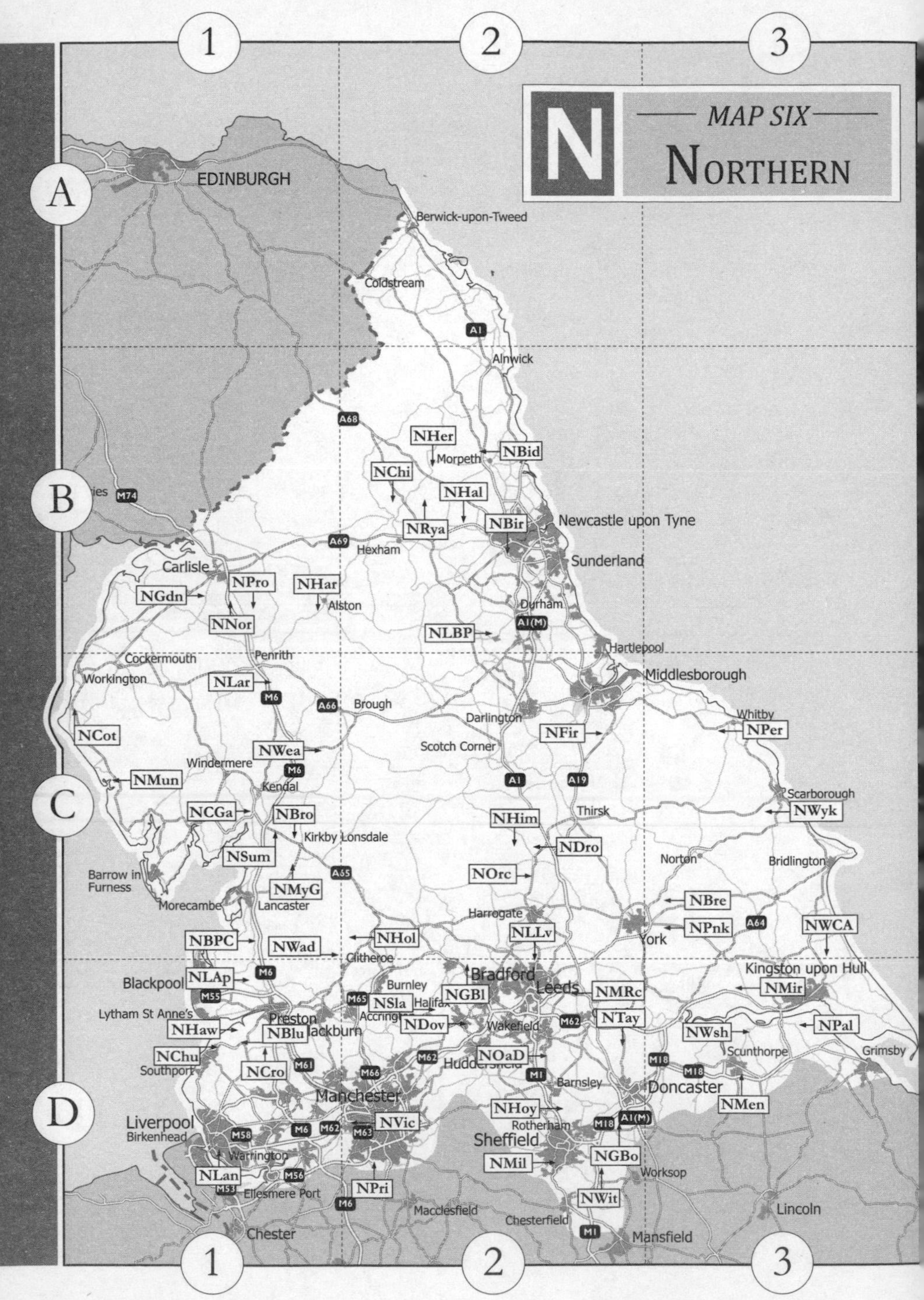

N
MAP SIX
NORTHERN
1
2
3
A
B
C
D
EDINBURGH
Berwick-upon-Tweed
Coldstream
A1
Alnwick
A68
NHer
NBid
Morpeth
NChi
NHal
M74
NRya
NBir
Newcastle upon Tyne
A69
Hexham
Sunderland
Carlisle
NPro
NHar
NGdn
Alston
NNor
Durham
A1(M)
NLBP
Hartlepool
Penrith
Cockermouth
Middlesborough
Workington
NLar
M6
A66
Brough
Whitby
Darlington
NCot
NFir
NPer
Scotch Corner
NWea
Windermere
M6
NMun
Kendal
A1
A19
Scarborough
NCGa
NBro
Thirsk
NWyk
NHim
Kirkby Lonsdale
NDro
NSum
Norton
Bridlington
Barrow in Furness
A65
NOrc
NMyG
Morecambe
Lancaster
NBre
Harrogate
NBPC
NHol
NLLv
NPnk
A64
NWCA
NWad
York
Clitheroe
Kingston upon Hull
M6
Blackpool
NLAp
Bradford
Burnley
Leeds
NMRc
M55
M65
NSla
Halifax
NGBl
NMir
Lytham St Anne's
Preston
NTay
NHaw
NBlu
NDov
Wakefield
M62
NWsh
NPal
Grimsby
NChu
Scunthorpe
NOaD
M62
M18
Southport
NCro
M61
M66
M18
Huddersfield
M1
Barnsley
Doncaster
Manchester
NMen
Liverpool
NHoy
Birkenhead
NVic
Rotherham
M18
A1(M)
M58
M6
M62
M63
Sheffield
Warrington
NMil
NGBo
NLan
M56
Worksop
NPri
M53
Ellesmere Port
NWit
M6
Macclesfield
Chesterfield
Lincoln
Chester
M1
Mansfield
1
2
3

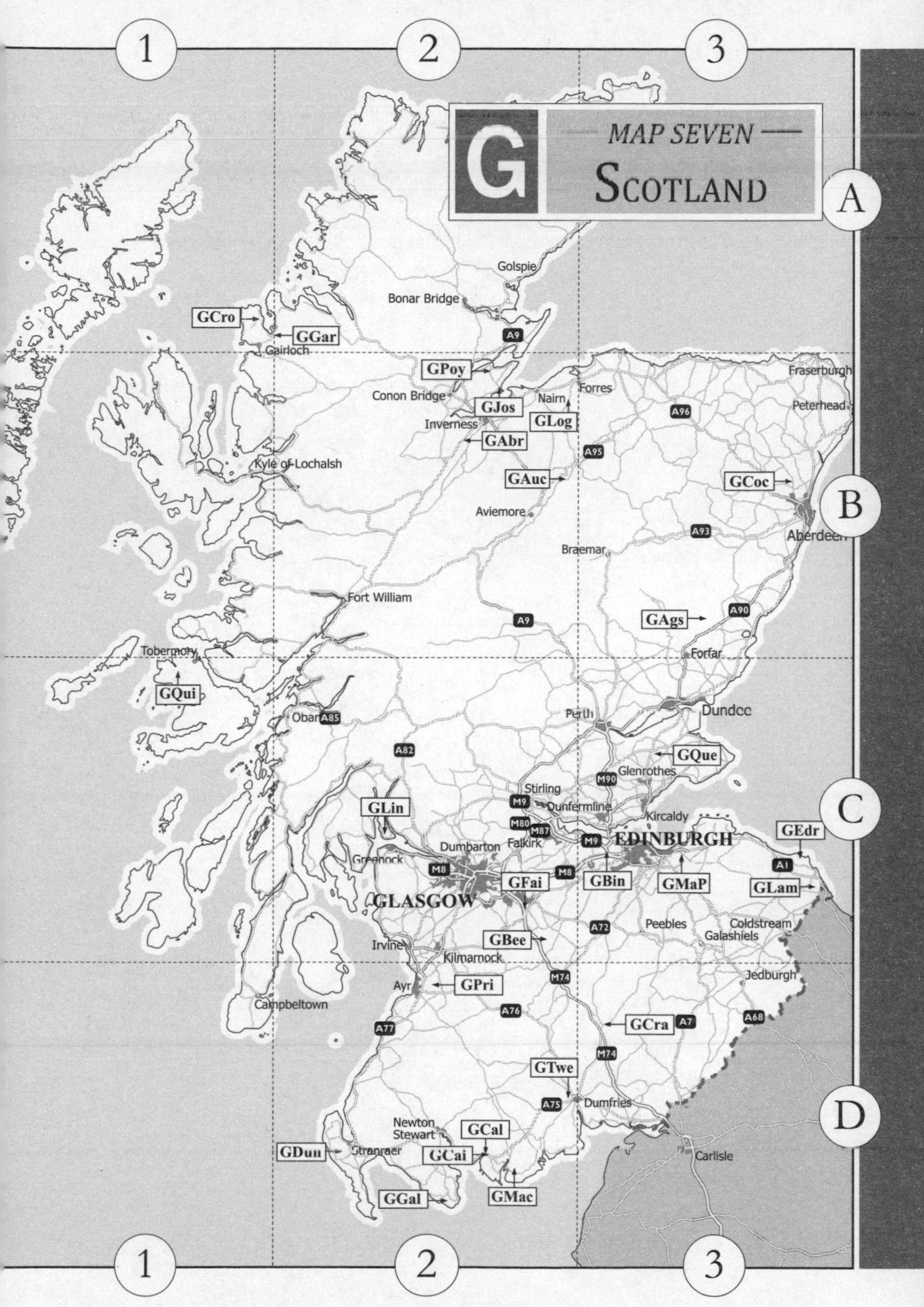
MAP SEVEN —
G
SCOTLAND
1
2
3
A
B
C
D
Golspie
Bonar Bridge
GCro
GGar
A9
Gairloch
GPoy
Conon Bridge
GJos
Nairn
Forres
Fraserburgh
Peterhead
A96
Inverness
GLog
GAbr
Kyle of Lochalsh
A95
GAuc
GCoc
Aviemore
Aberdeen
A93
Braemar
Fort William
A9
GAgs
A90
Tobermory
Forfar
GQui
Oban
A85
Perth
Dundee
A82
GQue
Glenrothes
M90
Stirling
M9
Dunfermline
GLin
M80
M87
Kircaldy
GEdr
Dumbarton
Falkirk
M9
EDINBURGH
Greenock
M8
A1
GFai
M8
GBin
GMaP
GLam
GLASGOW
Peebles
Coldstream
Galashiels
GBee
A72
Irvine
Kilmarnock
Jedburgh
Ayr
GPri
M74
Campbeltown
A76
GCra
A7
A68
A77
M74
GTwe
A75
Dumfries
Newton Stewart
GCal
GDun
Stranraer
GCai
Carlisle
GGal
GMac

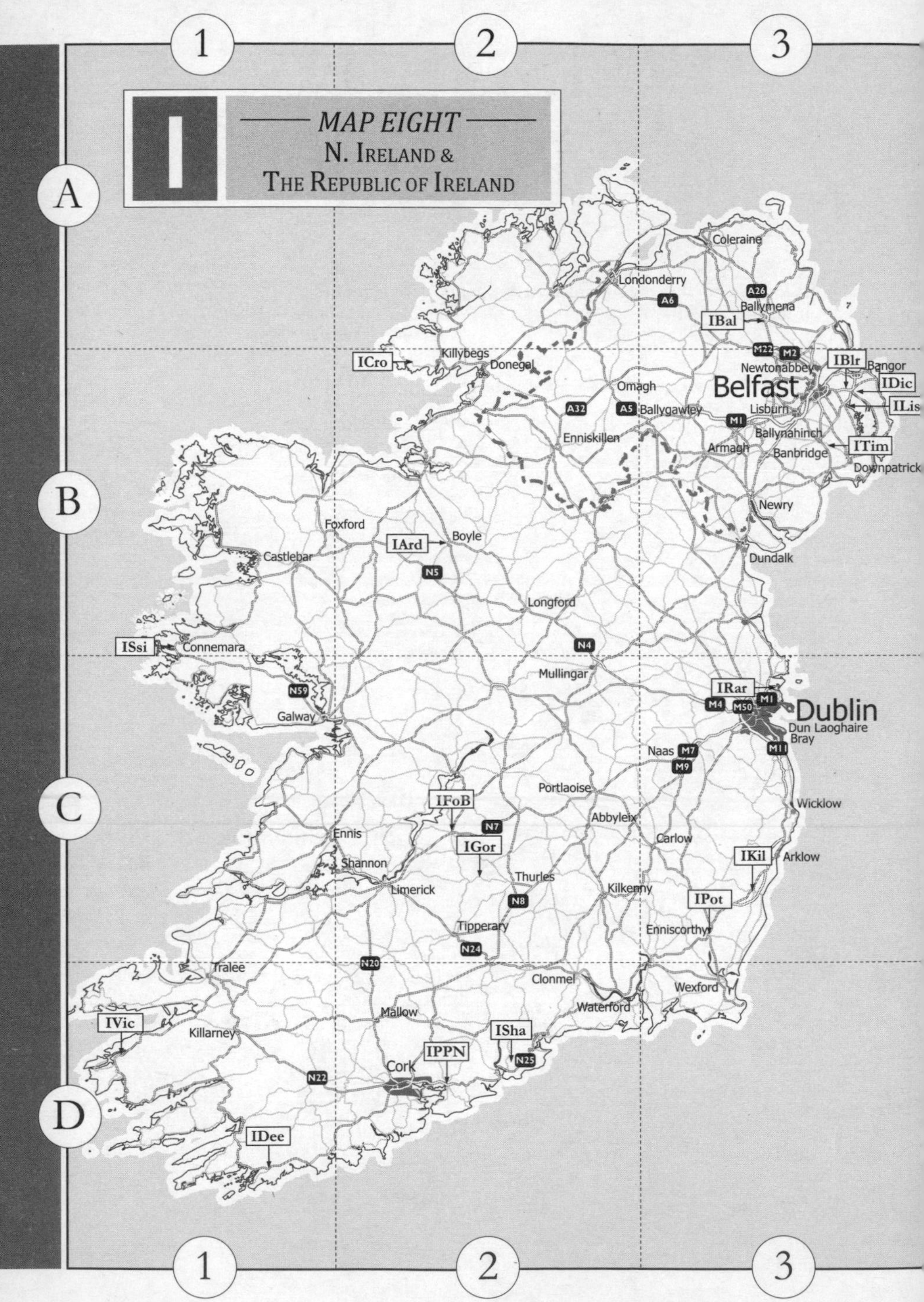

1
2
3
A
B
C
D
I
MAP EIGHT
N. Ireland &
The Republic of Ireland
Coleraine
Londonderry
A6
A26
Ballymena
IBal
M22
M2
IBlr
Bangor
Newtonabbey
IDic
ICro
Killybegs
Donegal
Omagh
Belfast
ILis
A32
A5
Ballygawley
Lisburn
M1
Enniskillen
Ballynahinch
Armagh
Banbridge
ITim
Downpatrick
Newry
Foxford
IArd
Boyle
Castlebar
Dundalk
N5
Longford
ISsi
Connemara
N4
Mullingar
IRar
M1
M4
M50
Dublin
N59
Galway
Dun Laoghaire
Bray
M11
Naas
M7
M9
Portlaoise
IFoB
Wicklow
N7
Abbyleix
Ennis
IGor
Carlow
IKil
Arklow
Shannon
Thurles
Limerick
Kilkenny
IPot
N8
Tipperary
Enniscorthy
N24
N20
Tralee
Clonmel
Wexford
Waterford
IVic
Mallow
ISha
Killarney
IPPN
N25
Cork
N22
IDee

# RHS Show Awards 2009

*RHS Plant Finder* nurseries that were awarded RHS medals at four major RHS Shows in 2009.

## London Gold

Ashwood Nurseries Ltd
Avon Bulbs

## London Silver-Gilt

Jacques Amand International
Broadleigh Gardens
Crûg Farm Plants
Fibrex Nurseries Ltd
Trehane Camellia Nursery
World of Ferns (Rickards Ferns Ltd)

## London Silver

The Botanic Nursery
Burncoose Nurseries
The Old Walled Garden
Brian & Pearl Sulman

## London Bronze

Hardy's Cottage Garden Plants
Long Acre Plants

## Chelsea Gold

Jacques Amand International
Avon Bulbs
Peter Beales Roses
Burncoose Nurseries
Burnham Nurseries
Chrysanthemums Direct
Dibley's Nurseries
Hampshire Carnivorous Plants
Hardy's Cottage Garden Plants
Hewitt-Cooper Carnivorous Plants
Jekka's Herb Farm
Knoll Gardens
Millais Nurseries
Plantagogo.com
Rhodes & Rockcliffe
Roualeyn Nurseries
Brian & Pearl Sulman
Thorncroft Clematis Nursery

## Chelsea Silver-Gilt

David Austin Roses Ltd
Broadleigh Gardens
Churchtown Nurseries
Culm View Nursery
Downderry Nursery
Heucheraholics (formerly Jooles Plants)
Hoyland Plant Centre
Mendip Bonsai Studio
Oak Tree Nursery
Pennard Plants (**Lindley Silver-Gilt**)
Potash Nursery
Tendercare Nurseries Ltd
Westcountry Nurseries

## Chelsea Silver

Barnsdale Gardens
Big Plant Nursery
The Botanic Nursery
D'Arcy & Everest
Fibrex Nurseries Ltd (two awards)
Hartside Nursery Garden
Kelways Ltd.
The Old Walled Garden
Primrose Bank
W Robinson & Sons Ltd (**Knightian Silver**)
Tynings Climbers

## Chelsea Bronze

Todd's Botanics

## Hampton Court Gold

David Austin Roses Ltd
Avon Bulbs
Chrysanthemums Direct
Churchtown Nurseries
Desert to Jungle
Dibley's Nurseries (two awards)

Downderry Nursery
Fernatix
Fernwood Nursery
Fir Trees Pelargonium Nursery
Goldbrook Plants
Hampshire Carnivorous Plants
Hardy's Cottage Garden Plants
Hewitt-Cooper Carnivorous Plants
Hopleys Plants Ltd
C S Lockyer (Fuchsias)
Mallet Court Nursery
Mendip Bonsai Studio
Dave Parkinson Plants
Pine Cottage Plants
Plantagogo.com
Potash Nursery
Rotherview Nursery
Roualeyn Nurseries
Brian & Pearl Sulman
Taylors Clematis Nursery

## HAMPTON COURT SILVER-GILT

Jacques Amand International
David Austin Roses Ltd (**Festival of Roses Silver-Gilt**)
Peter Beales Roses (**Festival of Roses Silver-Gilt**)
Big Plant Nursery
Burncoose Nurseries
Culm View Nursery
Derek Lloyd Dean
Fibrex Nurseries Ltd (two awards)
Heucheraholics (as Solva Plants)
Hoyland Plant Centre
Oak Tree Nursery
P W Plants
The Palm Centre
Primrose Bank
Seale Nurseries (**Festival of Roses Silver-Gilt**)
South West Carnivorous Plants
Styles Roses (**Festival of Roses Silver-Gilt**)
Todd's Botanics
Tynings Climbers
Waterside Nursery

## HAMPTON COURT SILVER

Amulree Exotics
The Botanic Nursery
Burnham Nurseries
Mickfield Hostas
The Old Walled Garden
Pennard Plants
Squires Garden Centres
Trecanna Nursery
Trevena Cross Nurseries

## TATTON GOLD

Cath's Garden Plants
Chrysanthemums Direct
Churchtown Nurseries
Dibley's Nurseries (two awards)
Fernatix
Fernwood Nursery
Fibrex Nurseries Ltd
Fir Trees Pelargonium Nursery
Mary Green
Hampshire Carnivorous Plants
Elizabeth MacGregor
Mendip Bonsai Studio
Packhorse Farm Nursery
Dave Parkinson Plants
Plantagogo.com
Potash Nursery
W Robinson & Sons Ltd
Roualeyn Nurseries
Brian & Pearl Sulman
Taylors Clematis Nursery
Tynings Climbers
Waterside Nursery

## TATTON SILVER-GILT

Big Plant Nursery
Broadleigh Gardens
Culm View Nursery
Desert to Jungle
Green Garden Herbs
Hall Farm Nursery
Hardy's Cottage Garden Plants
Hartside Nursery Garden
Heucheraholics (as Solva Plants)
Oak Tree Nursery
Pennard Plants
Primrose Bank
Slack Top Alpines

## TATTON SILVER

Jacques Amand International
Peter Beales Roses
The Botanic Nursery
Brownthwaite Hardy Plants
Hoyland Plant Centre
Mickfield Hostas
Trecanna Nursery
White Cottage Alpines

## TATTON BRONZE

Barnsdale Gardens
Cairnsmore Nursery
Hillview Hardy Plants

*Geranium* 'Rozanne'

OVER 2500 DIFFERENT CHOICE AND UNUSUAL HERBACEOUS PERENNIALS & ALPINES

**NORWELL NURSERIES AND GARDENS**

HARDY GERANIUMS & CHRYSANTHEMUMS, GEUMS, HEMEROCALLIS, GRASSES, WOODLAND & COTTAGE GARDEN PLANTS

**www.norwellnurseries.co.uk**

**Tel: 01636 636337**

**Norwell Nurseries, Woodhouse Road, Norwell, Newark, Notts NG23 6JX**

# UNUSUAL HOUSEPLANTS

Streptocarpus, Saintpaulias, Columneas, Begonias, Chiritas, Gesneriads, Achimenes and Solenostemons (Coleus)

See us at all the major flower shows or visit our nurseries. We despatch mail order and we also supply over 200 Garden Centres throughout Britain.

We hold the National Collection of Streptocarpus.

FOR FREE COLOUR CATALOGUE PLEASE TELEPHONE OR WRITE TO:

LLANELIDAN, RUTHIN, NORTH WALES, LL15 2LG

Tel Number 01978 790677 Fax Number 01978 790668

Web page: www.dibleys.com Email: sales@dibleys.com

**RUMSEY GARDENS**

*Est Over 30 years*

*TRADITIONAL NURSERY & PLANT CENTRE*

117 Drift Road, Clanfield
Waterlooville, Hants PO8 0PD

Telephone 02392 593367

**www.rumsey-gardens.co.uk**

*SPECIALIST GROWERS OF:*

Trees & Shrubs, Fruit Trees & Bushes, Herbaceous & Alpine Plants, Hardy Ferns, Conifers, Climbers & Twiners, Shrub Roses, Old Fashioned and Modern.

*FIVE ACRES OF PLANTS ON DISPLAY MANY UNUSUAL VARIETIES, including THE NATIONAL & INTERNATIONAL COLLECTION OF COTONEASTERS*

*Nursery Shop, Seeds & Sundries*

*SRMS*

**GARDENS & NURSERIES**

**Comprehensive Plant Range**

especially for coast and dry/chalk soils

**For details go to**

**www.botanyplants.co.uk**

**Margate, Kent. CT9 3TS. Tel: 01843 862060**

on B2052 (George Hill Rd) between Cliftonville and Kingsgate.

**Comprehensive Plant Range**

especially for acid and moist soils

**For details go to:**

**www.botanyplants.co.uk**

**Nr. Market Drayton, Shropshire. TF9 4DN**

**Tel. Brian Watkins 07985 425829**

Near Loggerheads off the A53, 5 miles from Bridgemere

Liquidambars Carpinus
Fugus Acers

*Birchfleet Nurseries*

Greenfields Close, Nyewood, Petersfield GU31 5JQ
**BY APPOINTMENT ONLY**
01730 821636
www.birchfleetnurseries.co.uk

**Hoo House Nursery**

Gloucester Road, Tewkesbury,
Gloucestershire, GL20 7DA.

Tel/Fax 01684 293389
www.hoohouse.co.uk

Open 10-5pm Mon-Sat, 11-5pm Sun
Perennials & Alpines grown peat-free
Prices reasonable, Advice free.

**IRIS OF SISSINGHURST**

Irises - Bearded, Sibiricas and many Species.

**Roughlands Farm, Marden, Kent TN12 9NH**
**tel: 01622 831511**

**email: orders@irisofsissinghurst.com**
**www.irisofsissinghurst.com**

A miscellany of plants - reflective of our interests and of plants that will grow (even thrive) in wet clay; our 3/4 acre garden is open to visitors.

FEEBERS HARDY PLANTS
(PROP: MRS E. SQUIRES)
1 FEEBERS COTTAGE, WESTWOOD
BROADCLYST, DEVON EX5 3DQ
**Telephone: 01404 822118**
Anytime by prior appointment.
Limited mail order.

From B3181 Dog Village, Broadclyst, take Whimple Road for 1.25m; take left turn (signed Westwood) continue further 1.25m; Nursery on right entering Westwood.

**BIG TREES**

SPECIMEN DECIDUOUS TREES

Visit our beautiful nursery on the slope of the Sussex Downs and choose your own from a wide range from 6-60cm girth.

Our trees are grown at 3 metre spacing in open ground, and carefully pruned to develop full and well shaped crowns. Wide range of Crabapples available.

**MOUNT HARRY TREES**
**Offham, Lewes, Sussex, BN7 3QW**
**Tel: 01273 474 456**
**mountharry@googlemail.com**

**EVERGREEN CONIFER CENTRE**

Extensive collection of miniature, dwarf, slow growing and unusual conifers.
Mature conifers and hedging conifers.

**CLOSED ON SUNDAY & MONDAY**

For further details including mail order
**Tel: 01299 266581**
**Email: brian@evergreen-conifers.co.uk**
**Web Site: evergreen-conifers.co.uk**
**Tenbury Road, Rock, Kidderminster, Worcs DY14 9RB**

**C.S. LOCKYER**
(Fuchsias)

Established over 50 years - 46 years Chelsea Exhibitor
Colour mail order catalogue 4 x 1st class stamps
*All Fuchsia lovers welcome inc. Clubs & Parties*
**Please ring to avoid disappointment**
*Many Talks and Demonstrations,*
*Video or DVD £14.99 p&p £1.50*
*Fuchsias The Easy Way*
*Fuchsias Advanced Techniques*
See Cloc Nursery code
**C.S. Lockyer (Fuchsias) "Lansbury"**
**70 Henfield Road, Coalpit Heath,**
**Bristol BS36 2UZ - Tel/Fax: 01454 772219**
Web Site: www.lockyerfuchsias.co.uk
Email: sales@lockyerfuchsias.co.uk

# INDEX OF ADVERTISERS

# *The* HARDY PLANT SOCIETY

*Explores, encourages and conserves all that is best in gardens*

## Membership Application 2010

**Annual Subscription**

- Subscriptions are renewable annually on 1 January.
- Subscriptions of members joining after 1 October are valid until the end of the following year.
- Overseas members are requested to pay in pounds sterling by International Money Order or by Visa/Master Card. An optional charge of £10.00 is made for airmail postage outside Europe of all literature, if preferred.

Please use BLOCK CAPITALS and send this form with your payment to the Administrator or alternatively you can telephone the Administrator with details of your Visa or Master card.

Please tick the type of membership required and if airmail postage option required:

☐ Single £17.00 per year (one member)

☐ Joint £19.00 per year (two members at the same address)

☐ Airmail postage £10.00 per year (optional for members outside Europe only)

NAME(S) ............................................................ / ............................................................

ADDRESS ............................................................................................................................

.................................................................................................. POSTCODE ..............................

TELEPHONE ........................................................ MOBILE ........................................................

EMAIL ..................................................................................................................................

**Payment Option 1:** I enclose ◯ cheque* ◯ postal order* payable to **The Hardy Plant Society**

for £..................... in pounds sterling ONLY please. *(* indicate cheque or postal order as appropriate)*

*(Please also write your address on reverse of cheque/postal order)*

**Payment Option 2:** Please debit my Visa/Master Card (only) by the sum of £....................

CARD NUMBER ☐☐☐☐ ☐☐☐☐ ☐☐☐☐ ☐☐☐☐

EXPIRY DATE ☐☐ / ☐☐ SECURITY CODE *(last three digits)* ☐☐☐

*(MM)* *(YY)*

Name as printed on card ..........................................................................................

Signature ............................................................ Date ............................................

Send this completed form (or a photocopy) with payment to:

**The Administrator, Pam Adams, The Hardy Plant Society, Little Orchard, Great Comberton, Pershore, WR10 3DP**

**Tel: 01386 710 317 Email: admin@hardy-plant.org.uk**

**The Hardy Plant Society is a Registered Charity, number 208080** RHS PF/2010

# THE NATIONAL PLANT COLLECTIONS®

## Plant Heritage

Patron: HRH The Prince of Wales

### The Lost Garden of Britain

**We have a long history of gardening, plant collecting and breeding in the British Isles so our gardens contain an amazing diversity of plants. Due to the imperatives of marketing and fashion, the desire for 'new' varieties and the practicalities of bulk cultivation, many plants unique to British gardens have been lost. This diversity is important as a genetic resource for the future and as a cultural link to the past.**

### What is Plant Heritage?

The mission of Plant Heritage is to conserve, document and make available this resource for the benefit of horticulture, education and science. The main conservation vehicle is the National Plant Collection® scheme where individuals or organisations undertake to preserve a group of related plants in trust for the future. Our 40 local groups across Britain support the administration of the scheme, the collection holders and propagate rare plants; working to promote the conservation of cultivated plants.

### Who are the National Plant Collection® Holders?

Collection holders come from every sector of horticulture, amateur and professional. Almost half of the existing 660 National Collections are in private ownership and include allotments, back gardens and large estates. 121 collections are found in nurseries, which range from large commercial concerns to the small specialist grower. 57 local authorities are involved in the scheme, including Sir Harold Hillier Gardens & Arboretum (Hampshire County Council) and Leeds City Council. Universities, agricultural colleges, schools, arboreta and botanic gardens all add to the diversity, and there are also a number of collections on properties belonging to English Heritage, The National Trust and The National Trust for Scotland.

*Please see Membership Application Form*

### What do Collection Holders do?

Collection holders subscribe to the scheme's ideals and stringent regulations. As well as protecting the living plants in their chosen group, they also work on areas including education, scientific research and nomenclature, with the common aim of conserving cultivated plants.

### How can you Help Plant Heritage?

You can play your part in supporting plant conservation by becoming a member of Plant Heritage. Regular journals will keep you informed of how your support is helping to save our plant biodiversity. Through your local group you can play a more active role in plant conservation working with collection holders, attending talks, plant sales, local horticultural shows and nursery visits.

### How to Join:

**Please contact**
**Membership**
**Plant Heritage**
**12 Home Farm, Loseley Park**
**Guildford**
**Surrey**
**GU3 1HS**

**Tel: (01483) 447540**
**Fax: (01483) 458933**
**E-mail: membership@plantheritage.org.uk**
**Website: www.plantheritage.com**

***'Plant Heritage seeks to conserve, document, promote and make available Britain and Ireland's rich biodiversity of garden plants for the benefit of everyone through horticulture, education and science'***

## Your support ensures the future of endangered plants through the guardianship of the National Plant Collections.

We invite you to choose your own level of subscription (minimum £25) from the following range of options.

☐ £25 ☐ £30 ☐ £50 ☐ £125 (Friend)

e complete in CAPITALS

_____ Forename ____________

ame ____________

me Telephone ____________

____________

Address ____________

____________

____________ Postcode ____________

Where did you get this leaflet? ____________

ake cheques yable to NCCPG d send to the dress below.

you wish to y by credit card ease call us on **483 447 540**

*giftaid it*

Gift Aid Declaration:

**Are you a UK taxpayer?**

**If you are, we can claim 28% from the government on your subscription at no extra cost to you.**

I would like the National Council for the Conservation of Plants & Gardens to reclaim the tax on any membership subscription or donation that I make/ have made in the previous six tax years and all subscriptions and donations I make in the future, until I notify you otherwise. I have paid an amount of UK income tax or capital gains tax equal to any tax reclaimed. (Remember that if you receive a company pension, income tax may well be paid at source.)

Gift Aid Signature

Date

## by Direct Debit and receive 15 months membership for the price of 12

(offer closes 30th September 2010)

### ruction to your Bank or Building Society to pay by Direct Debit

and full postal address of your Bank or Building Society

Manager | Bank/Building Society

ss

Postcode

s) of Account Holder(s)

r Building Society Account Number

Sort Code

Originators Identification Number

DIRECT Debit

| 9 | 7 | 4 | 2 | 1 | 2 |
|---|---|---|---|---|---|

Reference Number (Office use only)

### Instruction to your Bank or Building Society

Please pay The National Council for the Conservation of Plants & Gardens direct debits from the account detailed in this instruction, subject to the safeguards assured by the Direct Debit Guarantee. I understand that this instruction may remain with the NCCPG and if so, details will be passed electronically to my Bank/Building Society.

Signature(s)

Date

Protection Act: Records for each member are kept at NCCPG National Office and by local Group Officers. Under no circumstances are membership records used for purposes other than those connected to the legitimate activities of The National Council for the Conservation of Plants & Gardens.

**Please return your form with payment to**: Plant Heritage, 12 Home Farm, Loseley Park, Guildford, GU3 1HS.

**Tel: 01483 447 540 Email: membership@plantheritage.org.uk www.plantheritage.com**

Plant Heritage is the working name of the National Council for the Conservation of Plants & Gardens.
Company Limited by Guarantee. Registered in Cardiff 2222953. Registered Charity Number 1004009.